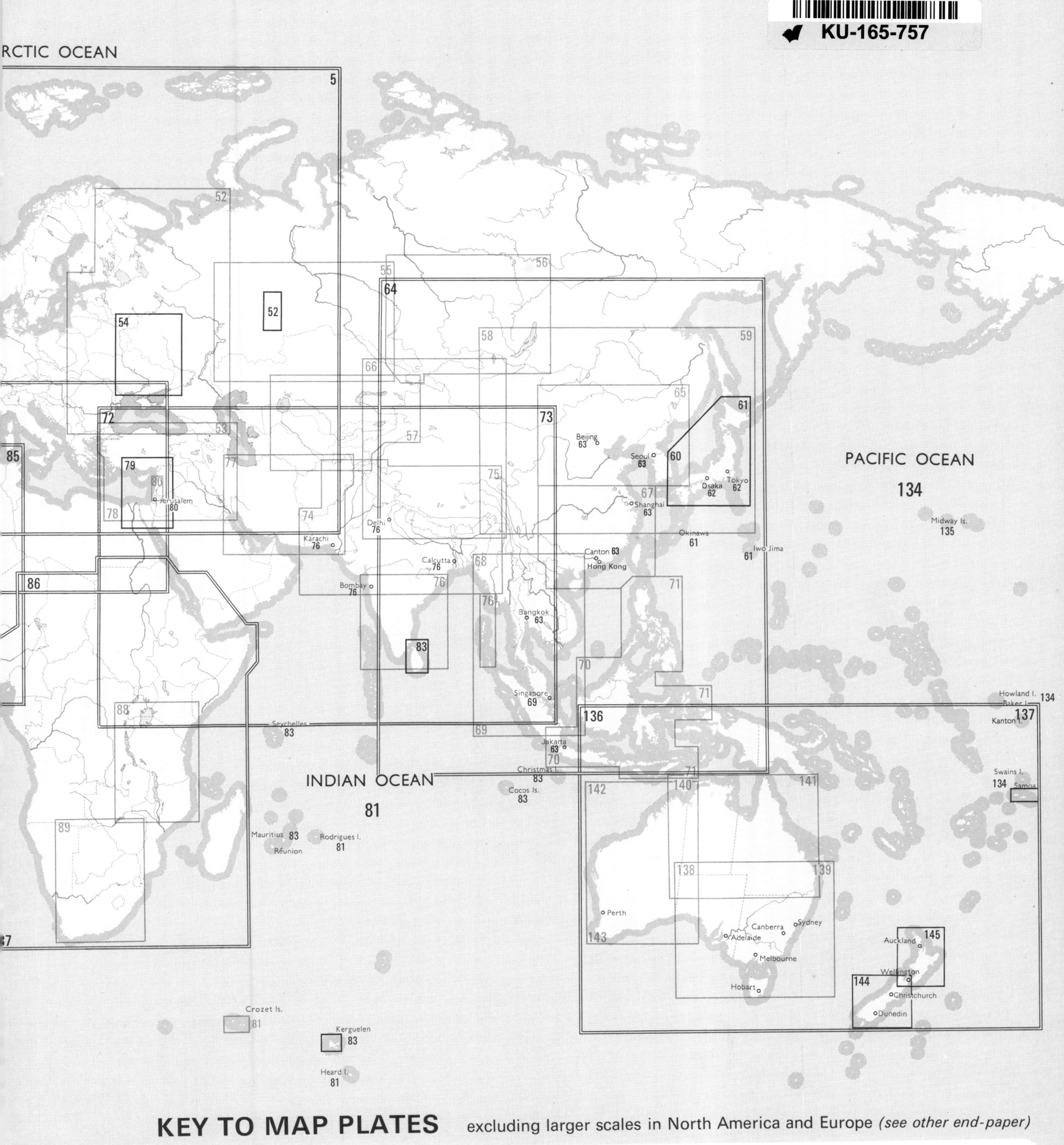

ARCTIC OCEAN

PACIFIC OCEAN
134

INDIAN OCEAN
81

KEY TO MAP PLATES excluding larger scales in North America and Europe *(see other end-paper)*

114 1:12 000 000 and smaller	**83** 1:3 000 000
116 1:6 000 000 and smaller	**80** 1:1 000 000 and larger

Inset maps of islands, cities, etc. are named

Introductory Section

4-6	States and territories of the world
7	Metropolitan areas
8/9	Geographical Comparisons
10/23	Physical Earth
24/25	Star Charts
26/27	Universe
28/29	Solar System
30/31	Space flight
32/33	Earth structure
34/35	Dynamic Earth
36/37	Climate
38/39	Vegetation and Minerals
40/41	Energy
42/43	Food and Population
44	Map projections

General Maps

2/3	World - Political
50/51	Russian Federation
82	Africa
91	The Americas
146	Antarctica
147	Arctic Ocean

THE TIMES
ATLAS
OF THE
WORLD

CONCISE EDITION

BCA

LONDON · NEW YORK · SYDNEY · TORONTO

This edition published 1992
by BCA by arrangement with
Times Books
A Division of HarperCollins*Publishers*
77–85 Fulham Palace Road
Hammersmith
London W6 8JB

First Edition 1972
Reprinted with revisions 1973, 1974
Second Edition 1975
Reprinted 1976, 1978
Third Edition 1978
Reprinted with revisions 1979
Fourth Edition 1980
Reprinted with revisions 1982
Reprinted 1984
Fifth Edition 1986
Reprinted with revisions 1987, 1988,
1989, 1990, 1991
Sixth Edition 1992

Copyright © Times Books and
Bartholomew 1992

Maps prepared and printed by
Bartholomew, Edinburgh

Physical Earth Maps by
Duncan Mackay

Geographical Consultants
Mr H.A.G. Lewis OBE
Mr P.J.M. Geelan

Index processed and typeset by
Stibo Datagrafik, Århus,
Denmark

Index printed by
Scotprint, Musselburgh,
Scotland

Books bound by
Sigloch, Künzelsau,
Germany

CN 5759

FOREWORD

This new edition of *The Times Concise Atlas of the World* will, it is hoped, find as much favour with those who acquire a copy for the first time as it has with those familiar with the earlier editions.

Every effort has been made to ensure that the maps are as up-to-date as possible. The index of names has, in consequence, been augmented. It now contains some 100,000 entries but it still does not contain all the names which appear on the maps. The reader may, however, rest assured that the names of all important inhabited places and physical features are included together with the page number, country name and grid reference.

Great attention has been paid to the spelling of geographical names, a matter of great complexity due to the multiplicity of the World's languages, the diverse forms of writing or the absence of any writing system whatsoever. For want of a standard way of spelling names a variety of spellings has been used over the centuries establishing in each of the major languages of the world its own conventional way of spelling which differs greatly from the name found locally. In this atlas the name taken is always the name used by the official administering body. Where necessary that name has been converted into the Roman alphabet by systems which follow English language usage. Those systems accord with the transcription and transliteration systems accepted for official use in the United States and the United Kingdom. For added reference the English language conventional names have been added parenthetically e.g. Roma (Rome), Moskva (Moscow).

Names like maps often invoke political protestations. The status of areas, the international boundaries and the names associated with them as shown in this edition are those which reflect the situation pertaining on the ground at the time of publication: where boundaries are the subject of international dispute this portrayal will not win the approval of the contending parties but, in the view of the publishers, the function of an atlas is to show facts and not to adjudicate between the rights and wrongs of political issues.

In the introductory section is a list of countries of the World. It shows a world re-cast in a mould unforeseen and unforeseeable at the end of the Second World War. Yet the changes in the political scene are small in comparison with the way science has altered the pattern of life. No century in the world's history has witnessed changes so fundamental and widespread. Of more significance than the magnitude of the change is its rate, now such that any reliable prediction of the future beyond a decade or two cannot be made.

The trend is vividly demonstrated in the diagram showing the demand for energy but it is no less apparent under other subject headings.

Unabated growth of that kind cannot continue indefinitely. The maps which make up the body of the atlas show the physical and political world of to-day. How the same maps will look in the future depends on the size of the world's population; the pattern of settlement; the spread of industry; the availability of food, minerals and sources of energy; the world's vegetation, atmosphere and climate all of which are in risk of catastrophic change.

To sustain ever increasing numbers of people requires constant stock-taking of natural resources. Remote-sensing, a product of the space age, is now beginning to reveal its eventual capacity for the kind of global monitoring required.

The space age has barely dawned yet it has already stretched the confines of our world to include the solar system and embrace more and more of the universe.

Our atlas, therefore, includes the Earth we live on, the solar system and the universe beyond. May it bring pleasure and interest to all who use it.

CONTENTS

STATES AND TERRITORIES OF THE WORLD

State/Territory	Capital or main town	Sq. km	(Sq. miles)	Population	Date
A					
Afghanistan	Kābul	652,225	(251,773)	16,433,000	1991
Albania	Tiranë (Tirana)	28,750	(11,100)	3,250,000	1990
Algeria	El-Djezaïr (Algiers)	2,381,745	(919,355)	24,960,000	1990
American Samoa	Pago Pago	197	(76)	39,000	1990
Andorra	Andorra la Vella	465	(180)	52,000	1990
Angola	Luanda	1,246,700	(481,225)	10,020,000	1990
Anguilla	The Valley	91	(35)	7,019	1989
Antigua and Barbuda	St. John's	442	(171)	85,000	1990
Argentina	Buenos Aires	2,777,815	(1,072,240)	32,610,000*	1991
Armenia	Yerevan	30,000	(11,580)	3,300,000	1990
Aruba	Oranjestad	193	(75)	62,500	1988
Ascension	Georgetown	88	(34)	1,007	1988
Australia	Canberra	7,682,300	(2,965,370)	17,086,197	1990
Australian Capital Territory	Canberra	2,432	(939)	284,985	1990
New South Wales	Sydney	801,430	(309,350)	5,827,373	1990
Northern Territory	Darwin	1,346,200	(519,635)	157,304	1990
Queensland	Brisbane	1,727,000	(666,620)	2,906,838	1990
South Australia	Adelaide	984,380	(79,970)	1,439,157	1990
Tasmania	Hobart	68,330	(26,375)	456,663	1990
Victoria	Melbourne	227,600	(87,855)	4,379,981	1990
Western Australia	Perth	2,525.500	(974,845)	1,633,896	1990
Austria	Wien (Vienna)	83,855	(32,370)	7,761,700	1990
Azerbaijan	Baku	87,000	(33,580)	7,100,000	1990
Azores	Ponta Delgada	2,335	(901)	253,600	1988
B					
Bahamas	Nassau	13,865	(5,350)	254,685*	1990
Bahrain	Al Manāmah (Manama)	661	(255)	503,000	1990
Bangladesh	Dhaka	144,000	(55,585)	109,291,000	1990
Barbados	Bridgetown	430	(166)	257,082*	1990
Belgium	Bruxelles/(Brussels)	30,520	(11,780)	9,845,000	1990
Belize	Belmopan	22,965	(8,865)	188,000	1990
Belorussia	Minsk	208,000	(80,290)	10,200,000	1990
Benin	Porto Novo	112,620	(43,470)	4,736,000	1990
Bermuda	Hamilton	54	(21)	61,000	1990
Bhutan	Thimphu	46,620	(17,995)	1,517,000	1990
Bolivia	La Paz	1,098,575	(424,050)	7,400,000	1990
Bosnia-Herzegovina	Sarajevo	51,130	(19,735)	4,795,000	1990
Botswana	Gaborone	575,000	(221,950)	1,291,000	1990
Brazil	Brasília	8,511,965	(3,285,620)	153,322,000	1991
Brunei	Bandar Seri Begawan	5,765	(2,225)	266,000	1990
Bulgaria	Sofiya (Sofia)	110,910	(42,810)	9,011,000	1990
Burkina	Ouagadougou	274,122	(105,811)	9,001,000	1990
Burma	Rangoon	678,030	(261,720)	39,300,000	1990
Burundi	Bujumbura	27,835	(10,745)	5,458,000	1990
C					
Cambodia	Phnom Penh	181,000	(69,865)	8,700,000	1991
Cameroon	Yaoundé	475,500	(183,545)	11,834,000	1990
Canada	Ottawa	9,922,385	(3,830,840)	26,800,000	1991
Canary Islands	Las Palmas (on Gran Canaria) and Santa Cruz (on Tenerife)	7,275	(2,810)	1,589,403	1990
Cape Verde	Praia	4,035	(1,560)	370,000	1990
Cayman Islands	George Town	259	(100)	27,000	1990
Central African Republic	Bangui	624,975	(241,240)	3,039,000	1990
Chad	Ndjamena	1,284,000	(495,625)	5,679,000	1990
Channel Islands	St Helier (on Jersey) St Peter Port (on Guernsey)	194	(75)	140,711	1989
Chile	Santiago	751,625	(290,125)	13,386,000	1991
China	Beijing (Peking)	9,597,000	(3,704,440)	1,088,870,000	1989
Colombia	Bogotá	1,138,915	(439,620)	32,987,000	1990
Comoros	Moroni	1,860	(718)	551,000	1990
Congo	Brazzaville	342,000	(132,010)	2,271,000	1990
Croatia	Zagreb	56,540	(21,825)	4,726,000	1990
Cuba	Habana (Havana)	114,525	(44,205)	10,617,000	1990
Cyprus	Nicosia	9,250	(3,570)	707,000	1990
Czechoslovakia	Praha (Prague)	127,870	(49,360)	15,678,000	1991
D					
Denmark	København (Copenhagen)	43,075	(16,625)	5,140,000	1990
Djibouti	Djibouti	23,000	(8,800)	409,000	1990
Dominica	Roseau	751	(290)	81,200	1988
Dominican Republic	Santo Domingo	48,440	(18,700)	7,170,000	1990
E					
Ecuador	Quito	461,475	(178,130)	10,782,000	1990
Egypt	Cairo	1,000,250	(386,095)	57,000,000	1991
El Salvador	San Salvador	21,395	(8,260)	5,252,000	1990
Equatorial Guinea	Malabo	28,050	(10,825)	348,000	1990
Estonia	Tallinn	45,100	(17,413)	1,583,000	1991
Ethiopia	Ādīs Ābeba (Addis Ababa)	1,023,050	(394,895)	50,774,000	1990
F					
Faeroes	Tórshavn	1,399	(540)	47,663	1988
Falkland Islands	Port Stanley	12,175	(4,700)	2,000	1990
Fiji	Suva	18,330	(7,075)	765,000	1990
Finland	Helsinki	337,030	(130,095)	4,986,000	1990
France	Paris	543,965	(209,970)	56,556,000*	1990
French Guiana	Cayenne	91,000	(35,125)	93,540	1989
French Polynesia	Papeete	3,940	(1,520)	188,814*	1988
G					
Gabon	Libreville	267,665	(103,320)	1,172,000	1990
Gambia, The	Banjul	10,690	(4,125)	861,000	1990
Georgia	Tbilisi	69,700	(26,905)	5,400,000	1990
Germany	Berlin	356,840	(137,740)	78,500,000	1990
Baden-Württemberg	Stuttgart	35,730	(13,790)	9,400,000	1990
Bayern (Bavaria)	München (Munich)	70,545	(27,230)	11,000,000	1990
Berlin		883	(341)	3,400,000	1990
Brandenburg	Potsdam	29,059	(11,220)	2,700,000	1990
Bremen		404	(156)	700,000	1990
Hamburg		755	(291)	1,600,000	1990
Hessen	Wiesbaden	21,115	(8,150)	5,600,000	1990
Mecklenburg-Vorpommern	Schwerin	23,838	(9,204)	2,100,000	1990
Niedersachsen	Hannover	47,425	(18,305)	7,200,000	1990
Nordrhein-Westfalen	Dusseldorf	34,070	(13,150)	16,900,000	1990
Rheinland-Pfalz	Mainz	19,840	(7,660)	3,700,000	1990
Saarland	Saarbrücken	2,575	(994)	1,100,000	1990
Sachsen (Saxony)	Dresden	18,337	(7,080)	4,900,000	1990
Sachsen-Anhalt	Halle	20,445	(7,894)	3,000,000	1990
Schleswig-Holstein	Kiel	15,710	(6,065)	2,600,000	1990
Thüringen	Erfurt	16,251	(6,275)	2,500,000	1990
Ghana	Accra	238,305	(91,985)	15,028,000	1990
Gibraltar		6.5	(2.5)	30,689	1989
Greece	Athínai (Athens)	131,985	(50,954)	10,269,074*	1991
Greenland	Godthåb (Nuuk)	2,175,600	(839,780)	55,558	1990
Grenada	St George's	345	(133)	110,000	1989
Guadeloupe	Basse-Terre	1,780	(687)	344,000	1990
Guam	Agaña	450	(174)	132,726	1990
Guatemala	Guatemala	108,890	(42,030)	9,197,000	1990
Guinea	Conakry	245,855	(94,900)	5,756,000	1990
Guinea-Bissau	Bissau	36,125	(13,945)	965,000	1990
Guyana	Georgetown	214,970	(82,980)	990,000	1989

BOLD TYPE INDICATES INDEPENDENT STATE

ITALIC TYPE INDICATES DEPENDENT TERRITORIES AND STATES

* INDICATES THAT THE POPULATION FIGURE RELATES TO A CENSUS

State/Territory	Capital or main town	Sq. km	(Sq. miles)	Population	Date
H					
Haiti	Port-au-Prince	27,750	(10,710)	6,486,000	1990
Honduras	Tegucigalpa	112,085	(43,265)	5,105,000	1990
Hong Kong		1,062	(410)	5,448,000	1990
Hungary	Budapest	93,030	(35,910)	10,344,000	1991
I					
Iceland	Reykjavík	102,820	(39,690)	255,000	1990
India	New Delhi	3,166,830	(1,222,395)	843,930,861*	1991
Indonesia	Jakarta	1,919,445	(740,905)	179,321,641*	1990
Iran	Tehrān	1,648,000	(636,130)	58,031,000	1991
Iraq	Baghdad	438,445	(169,240)	18,920,000	1990
Ireland, Republic of (Eire)	Dublin (Baile Átha Cliath)	68,895	(26,595)	3,523,000	1991
Israel	Jerusalem	20,770	(8,015)	4,822,000	1990
Italy	Roma (Rome)	301,245	(116,280)	57,690,000	1990
Ivory Coast	Yamoussoukro	322,465	(124,470)	11,998,000	1990
J					
Jamaica	Kingston	11,425	(4,410)	2,420,000	1990
Japan	Tōkyō	396,700	(142,705)	123,612,000	1990
Jordan	Amman	90,650	(35,000)	3,170,000	1989
K					
Kazakhstan	Alma-Ata	2,717,300	(1,048,880)	16,700,000	1990
Kenya	Nairobi	582,645	(224,900)	24,032,000	1990
Kiribati	Bairiki	684	(264)	66,000	1990
Korea, North	Pyŏngyang	122,310	(47,210)	21,773,000	1990
Korea, South	Sŏul (Seoul)	98,445	(38,000)	43,302,000	1991
Kuwait	Al Kuwayṭ (Kuwait)	24,280	(9,370)	2,600,000	1991
Kyrgyzstan	Bishkek	198,500	(76,620)	4,400,000	1990
L					
Laos	Viangchan (Vientiane)	236,725	(91,375)	4,139,000	1990
Latvia	Rīga	63,700	(24,590)	2,686,000	1991
Lebanon	Beyrouth (Beirut)	10,400	(4,015)	3,200,000	1991
Lesotho	Maseru	30,345	(11,715)	1,774,000	1990
Liberia	Monrovia	111,370	(42,990)	2,607,000	1990
Libya	Ṭarābulus (Tripoli)	1,759,540	(679,180)	4,545,000	1990
Liechtenstein	Vaduz	160	(62)	29,000	1990
Lithuania	Vilnius	65,200	(25,165)	3,739,000	1991
Luxembourg	Luxembourg	2,585	(998)	384,000	1991
M					
Macao	Macao	17	(7)	479,000	1990
Madagascar	Antananarivo	594,180	(229,345)	11,197,000	1990
Madeira	Funchal	796	(307)	273,200	1988
Malawi	Lilongwe	94,080	(36,315)	8,556,000	1991
Malaysia	Kuala Lumpur	332,965	(128,525)	17,861,000	1990
Peninsular Malaysia	Kuala Lumpur	131,585	(50,790)	14,005,000	1988
Sabah	Kota Kinabalu	76,115	(29,380)	1,600,000	1988
Sarawak	Kuching	124,965	(48,235)	1,400,000	1988
Maldives	Malé	298	(115)	214,139	1990
Mali	Bamako	1,240,140	(478,695)	8,156,000	1990
Malta	Valletta	316	(122)	356,000	1990
Man, Isle of	Douglas	588	(227)	64,000	1990
Marshall Islands	Majuro	181	(69)	40,609	1988
Martinique	Fort-de-France	1,079	(417)	359,000	1990
Mauritania	Nouakchott	1,030,700	(397,850)	2,025,000	1990
Mauritius	Port Louis	1,865	(720)	1,075,000	1990
Mexico	Mexico City	1,972,545	(761,400)	81,140,952*	1990
Micronesia	Kolonia	702	(271)	109,000	1990
Moldavia	Kishinev	33,700	(13,010)	4,400,000	1990
Monaco	Monaco	1.6	(0.6)	29,876	1990
Mongolia	Ulaanbaatar (Ulan Bator)	1,565,000	(604,090)	2,095,000	1989

State/Territory	Capital or main town	Sq. km	(Sq. miles)	Population	Date
Montserrat	Plymouth	104	(40)	13,000	1990
Morocco (inc. W. Sahara)	Rabat	710,850	(274,460)	25,061,000	1990
Mozambique	Maputo	784,755	(302,915)	15,656,000	1990
N					
Namibia	Windhoek	824,295	(318,180)	1,781,000	1990
Nauru	Yaren	21	(8)	10,000	1990
Nepal	Kathmandu	141,415	(54,585)	18,916,000	1990
Netherlands	Amsterdam (seat of government: The Hague)	41,160	(15,891)	15,019,000	1991
Netherlands Antilles	Willemstad	800	(308)	192,866	1988
New Caledonia	Nouméa	19,105	(7,375)	144,051*	1989
New Zealand	Wellington	265,150	(102,350)	3,390,000	1990
Nicaragua	Managua	148,000	(57,130)	3,871,000	1990
Niger	Niamey	1,186,410	(457,955)	7,732,000	1989
Nigeria	Lagos (seat of government: Abuja)	923,850	(356,605)	108,542,000	1990
Northern Mariana Islands	Saipan	471	(182)	20,591	1988
Norway	Oslo	323,895	(125,025)	4,242,000	1990
O					
Oman	Masqaṭ (Muscat)	271,950	(104,970)	2,000,000	1990
P					
Pakistan	Islamabad	803,940	(310,320)	112,050,000	1990
Palau	Koror	365	(141)	14,106	1988
Panama	Panama	78,515	(30,305)	2,446,000	1991
Papua New Guinea	Port Moresby	462,840	(178,655)	3,699,000	1990
Paraguay	Asunción	406,750	(157,005)	4,277,000	1990
Peru	Lima	1,285,215	(496,095)	22,332,000	1990
Philippines	Manila	300,000	(115,800)	62,868,000	1991
Pitcairn Island	Adamstown	42	(16.2)	59	1990
Poland	Warszawa (Warsaw)	312,685	(120,695)	38,180,000	1990
Portugal	Lisboa (Lisbon)	91,630	(35,370)	10,525,000	1990
Puerto Rico	San Juan	8,960	(3,460)	3,599,000	1990
Q					
Qatar	Ad Dawḥah (Doha)	11,435	(4,415)	368,000	1990
R					
Réunion	Saint-Denis	2,510	(969)	596,000	1990
Romania	Bucureşti (Bucharest)	237,500	(91,675)	23,193,000	1991
Russian Federation	Moskva (Moscow)	17,078,005	(6,592,110)	148,100,000	1990
Rwanda	Kigali	26,330	(10,165)	7,181,000	1990
S					
St Kitts – Nevis	Basseterre	261	(101)	44,000	1990
St Helena	Jamestown	122	(47)	5,564	1988
St Lucia	Castries	616	(238)	146,600	1988
St Pierre and Miquelon	St Pierre	241	(93)	6,392*	1990
St Vincent	Kingstown	389	(150)	113,950	1987
San Marino	San Marino	61	(24)	24,000	1990
São Tomé and Príncipe	São Tomé	964	(372)	115,600	1988
Saudi Arabia	Ar Riyāḍ (Riyadh)	2,400,900	(926,745)	10,500,000	1991
Senegal	Dakar	196,720	(75,935)	7,327,000	1990
Seychelles	Victoria	404	(156)	67,000	1990
Sierra Leone	Freetown	72,325	(27,920)	4,151,000	1990

State/Territory	Capital or main town	Sq. km	(Sq. miles)	Population	Date
Singapore	Singapore	616	(238)	3,002,800*	1990
Slovenia	Ljubljana	20,250	(7,815)	1,924,000	1990
Solomon Islands	Honiara	29,790	(11,500)	321,000	1990
Somalia	Muqdisho (Mogadishu)	630,000	(243,180)	7,497,000	1990
South Africa	Pretoria (administrative) Cape Town (legislative)	1,184,825	(457,345)	35,282,000	1990
Cape Province		656,640	(253,465)	4,901,261	1986
Natal		86,965	(33,570)	2,145,018	1985
Orange Free State		127,990	(49,405)	1,863,327	1987
Transvaal		268,915	(103,800)	7,532,179	1985
Spain	Madrid	504,880	(194,885)	38,991,000	1990
Sri Lanka	Colombo	65,610	(25,325)	16,993,000	1990
Sudan	Khartoum	2,505,815	(967,245)	25,204,000	1990
Surinam	Paramaribo	163,820	(63,235)	422,000	1990
Svalbard	Longyearbyen	62,000	(23,930)	3,942	1986
Swaziland	Mbabane	17,365	(6,705)	768,000	1990
Sweden	Stockholm	449,790	(173,620)	8,618,000	1991
Switzerland	Bern	41,285	(15,935)	6,712,000	1990
Syria	Dimashq (Damascus)	185,680	(71,675)	12,116,000	1990

T

State/Territory	Capital or main town	Sq. km	(Sq. miles)	Population	Date
Taiwan	T'ai-pei (Taipei)	35,990	(13,890)	19,700,000	1987
Tajikistan	Dushanbe	143,100	(55,235)	5,200,000	1990
Tanzania	Dodoma	939,760	(362,750)	25,635,000	1990
Thailand	Krung Thep (Bangkok)	514,000	(198,405)	54,532,000*	1990
Togo	Lomé	56,785	(21,920)	3,531,000	1990
Tonga	Nuku'alofa	699	(270)	95,000	1990
Trinidad and Tobago	Port of Spain	5,130	(1,980)	1,234,388*	1990
Tristan da Cunha		201	(78)	306	1988
Tunisia	Tunis	164,150	(63,360)	8,180,000	1990
Turkey	Ankara	779,450	(300,870)	58,687,000	1990
Turkmenistan	Ashkhabad	488,100	(188,405)	3,600,000	1990
Turks and Caicos Islands	Cockburn Town	430	(166)	11,696	1990
Tuvalu	Funafuti	24.6	(9.5)	10,000	1990

U

State/Territory	Capital or main town	Sq. km	(Sq. miles)	Population	Date
Uganda	Kampala	236,580	(91,320)	16,582,674*	1991
Ukraine	Kiev	603,700	(233,030)	51,800,000	1990
United Arab Emirates (U.A.E.)	Abu Dhabi	75,150	(29,010)	1,600,000	1988
United Kingdom of Great Britain and Northern Ireland (U.K.)	London	244,755	(94,475)	55,514,500*	1991
England	London	130,360	(50,320)	46,170,300*	1991
Northern Ireland	Belfast	14,150	(5,460)	1,589,000	1990
Scotland	Edinburgh	78,750	(30,400)	4,957,000*	1991
Wales	Cardiff	20,760	(8,015)	2,798,200*	1991
United States of America (U.S.A.)	Washington D.C.	9,363,130	(3,614,170)	248,709,873*	1990
Alabama	Montgomery	131,485	(50,755)	3,984,000*	1990
Alaska	Juneau	1,478,450	(570,680)	546,000*	1990
Arizona	Phoenix	293,985	(113,480)	3,619,000*	1990
Arkansas	Little Rock	134,880	(52,065)	2,337,000*	1990
California	Sacramento	404,815	(156,260)	29,279,000*	1990
Colorado	Denver	268,310	(103,570)	3,272,000*	1990
Connecticut	Hartford	12,620	(4,870)	3,227,000*	1990
Delaware	Dover	5,005	(1,930)	658,000*	1990
District of Columbia	Washington	163	(63)	575,000*	1990
Florida	Tallahassee	140,255	(54,140)	12,775,000*	1990
Georgia	Atlanta	150,365	(58,040)	6,387,000*	1990
Hawaii	Honolulu	16,640	(6,425)	1,095,000*	1990
Idaho	Boise	213,455	(82,390)	1,004,000*	1990

State/Territory	Capital or main town	Sq. km	(Sq. miles)	Population	Date
Illinois	Springfield	144,120	(55,630)	11,325,000*	1990
Indiana	Indianapolis	93,065	(35,925)	5,499,000*	1990
Iowa	Des Moines	144,950	(55,950)	2,767,000*	1990
Kansas	Topeka	211,805	(81,755)	2,467,000*	1990
Kentucky	Frankfort	102,740	(39,660)	3,665,000*	1990
Louisiana	Baton Rouge	115,310	(44,510)	4,181,000*	1990
Maine	Augusta	80,275	(30,985)	1,218,000*	1990
Maryland	Annapolis	25,480	(9,835)	4,733,000*	1990
Massachusetts	Boston	20,265	(7,820)	5,928,000*	1990
Michigan	Lansing	147,510	(56,940)	9,179,000*	1990
Minnesota	St Paul	206,030	(79,530)	4,359,000*	1990
Mississippi	Jackson	122,335	(47,220)	2,535,000*	1990
Missouri	Jefferson City	178,565	(68,925)	5,079,000*	1990
Montana	Helena	376,555	(145,350)	794,000*	1990
Nebraska	Lincoln	198,505	(76,625)	1,573,000*	1990
Nevada	Carson City	284,625	(109,865)	1,193,000*	1990
New Hampshire	Concord	23,290	(8,990)	1,103,000*	1990
New Jersey	Trenton	19,340	(7,465)	7,617,000*	1990
New Mexico	Sante Fe	314,255	(121,300)	1,490,000*	1990
New York	Albany	122,705	(47,365)	17,627,000*	1990
North Carolina	Raleigh	126,505	(48,830)	6,553,000*	1990
North Dakota	Bismarck	179,485	(69,280)	634,000*	1990
Ohio	Columbus	106,200	(40,995)	10,778,000*	1990
Oklahoma	Oklahoma City	177,815	(68,635)	3,124,000*	1990
Oregon	Salem	249,115	(96,160)	2,828,000*	1990
Pennsylvania	Harrisburg	116,260	(44,875)	11,764,000*	1990
Rhode Island	Providence	2,730	(1,055)	989,000*	1990
South Carolina	Columbia	78,225	(30,195)	3,272,000*	1990
South Dakota	Pierre	196,715	(75,930)	693,000*	1990
Tennessee	Nashville	106,590	(41,145)	4,822,000*	1990
Texas	Austin	678,620	(261,950)	16,825,000*	1990
Utah	Salt Lake City	212,570	(82,050)	1,711,000*	1990
Vermont	Montpelier	24,015	(9,270)	560,000*	1990
Virginia	Richmond	102,835	(39,695)	6,128,000*	1990
Washington	Olympia	172,265	(66,495)	4,827,000*	1990
West Virginia	Charleston	62,470	(24,115)	1,783,000*	1990
Wisconsin	Madison	140,965	(54,415)	4,870,000*	1990
Wyoming	Cheyenne	251,200	(96,965)	450,000*	1990
Uruguay	Montevideo	186,925	(72,155)	3,094,000	1990
Uzbekistan	Tashkent	447,400	(172,695)	20,300,000	1990

V

State/Territory	Capital or main town	Sq. km	(Sq. miles)	Population	Date
Vanuatu	Port Vila	14,765	(5,700)	147,000	1990
Vatican City	Vatican City	0.44	(0.17)	766	1988
Venezuela	Caracas	912,045	(352,050)	19,735,000	1990
Vietnam	Hanoi	329,566	(127,246)	66,200,000	1990
Virgin Islands (U.K.)	Road Town	153	(59)	13,000	1990
Virgin Islands (U.S.A.)	Charlotte Amalie	345	(133)	117,000	1990

W

State/Territory	Capital or main town	Sq. km	(Sq. miles)	Population	Date
Wallis and Futuna Islands	Mata-Utu	255	(98)	15,400	1988
Western Sahara		252,120	(97,345)	179,000	1990
Western Samoa	Apia	2,840	(1,095)	170,000	1990

Y

State/Territory	Capital or main town	Sq. km	(Sq. miles)	Population	Date
Yemen	San'ā	477,530	(184,325)	12,000,000	1990
Yugoslavia	Beograd (Belgrade)	127,885	(49,383)	12,453,000	1991
Macedonia	Skopje	25,715	(9,925)	2,193,000	1990
Montenegro	Podgorica	13,810	(5,330)	664,000	1990
Serbia	Beograd (Belgrade)	88,360	(34,105)	9,815,000	1990

Z

State/Territory	Capital or main town	Sq. km	(Sq. miles)	Population	Date
Zaire	Kinshasa	2,345,410	(905,330)	35,562,000	1990
Zambia	Lusaka	752,615	(290,510)	7,818,447*	1990
Zimbabwe	Harare	390,310	(150,660)	9,369,000	1990

METROPOLITAN AREAS

A metropolitan area is a continuous built-up area containing a number of cities and towns. The total combined population is given either as an estimate or from census returns.

Metropolitan areas with populations greater than 7 million.

Country	Metropolitan area	Population
Mexico	MEXICO CITY	18,748,000
Brazil	SÃO PAULO	17,112,712
USA	NEW YORK	16,198,000
Egypt	CAIRO	15,000,000
China	SHANGHAI	13,341,896
Argentina	BUENOS AIRES	12,604,018
India	BOMBAY	12,571,720
Japan	TOKYO	11,935,700
Brazil	RIO DE JANEIRO	11,205,567
South Korea	SEOUL	10,979,000
India	CALCUTTA	10,916,272
USA	LOS ANGELES	10,845,000
China	BEIJING	10,819,407
Indonesia	JAKARTA	9,253,000
France	PARIS	9,060,000
Russian Fed.	MOSCOW	9,000,000
China	TIANJIN	8,785,402
UK	LONDON	8,620,333
Japan	OSAKA-KOBE	8,520,000
India	DELHI	8,375,188
Philippines	MANILA – QUEZON CITY	7,832,000
Pakistan	KARACHI	7,702,000

Country	Metropolitan area	population
Afghanistan	Kābul	2,000,000
Algeria	Algiers	3,033,000
Angola	Luanda	1,717,000
Argentina	Buenos Aires	12,604,018
	Córdoba	1,136,000
	Rosario	1,084,000
Armenia	Yerevan	1,300,000
Australia	Adelaide	1,050,000
	Brisbane	1,302,000
	Canberra	310,000
	Melbourne	3,081,000
	Perth	1,193,000
	Sydney	3,657,000
Austria	Vienna	1,531,000
Azerbaijan	Baku	1,780,000
Bangladesh	Chittagong	2,289,000
	Dhākā	6,646,000
Belgium	Antwerp	473,082
	Brussels	970,501
Belorussia	Minsk	1,637,000
Brazil	Belem	1,418,061
	Belo Horizonte	3,615,234
	Brasília	1,803,478
	Curitiba	1,966,426
	Pôrto Alegre	2,906,472
	Recife	2,814,795
	Rio de Janeiro	11,205,567
	Salvador	2,424,878
	São Paulo	17,112,712
Bulgaria	Sofia	1,190,000
Burma	Rangoon	3,295,000
Canada	Montreal	3,084,100
	Ottawa	885,300
	Quebec	622,000
	Toronto	3,822,400
	Vancouver	1,586,600
	Winnipeg	648,500
Chile	Santiago	4,734,000
China	Anshan	2,517,080
	Baotou	1,257,000
	Beijing (Peking)	10,819,407
	Changchun	2,214,000
	Changsha	1,362,000
	Chengdu	3,004,000
	Chongqing	3,151,000
	Dalian	2,543,000

Country	Metropolitan area	population
	Fushun	1,420,000
	Fuzhou	1,361,000
	Guangzhou (Canton)	3,671,000
	Guiyang	1,587,000
	Hangzhou	1,412,000
	Harbin	2,966,000
	Huainan	1,519,420
	Jilin	1,327,000
	Jinan	2,415,000
	Kunming	1,718,000
	Lanzhou	1,566,000
	Luoyang	1,227,000
	Nanchang	1,415,000
	Nanjing	2,265,000
	Qingdao	2,010,000
	Qiqihar	1,460,000
	Shanghai	13,341,896
	Shenyang	4,763,000
	Shijiazhuang	1,352,000
	Taiyuan	2,199,000
	Tangshan	1,590,000
	Tianjin	8,785,402
	Wuhan	3,921,000
	Xian	2,859,000
	Zhengzhou	1,759,000
	Zibo	2,400,000
Colombia	Barranquilla	1,019,000
	Bogotá	4,851,000
	Cali	1,555,000
	Medellín	1,585,000
Croatia	Zagreb	1,174,512
Cuba	Havana	2,099,000
Czechoslovakia	Prague	1,294,000
Denmark	Copenhagen	1,337,114
Dominican Republic	Santo Domingo	2,203,000
Ecuador	Guayaquil	1,764,170
	Quito	1,281,849
Egypt	Alexandria	3,684,000
	Cairo	15,000,000
	El Giza	1,670,800
Estonia	Tallinn	482,000
Ethiopia	Addis Ababa	1,891,000
France	Marseilles	1,087,000
	Paris	9,060,000
Georgia	Tbilisi	1,264,000
Germany	Berlin	3,400,000
	Bonn	280,000
	Bremen	700,000
	Cologne	934,000
	Dresden	501,000
	Duisburg	525,000
	Düsseldorf	567,000
	Essen – Dortmund	2,745,700
	Frankfurt	624,000
	Hamburg	1,600,000
	Hanover	497,000
	Leipzig	530,000
	Munich	1,631,000
	Nuremberg	477,000
	Stuttgart	560,000
Greece	Athens	3,097,000
Guatemala	Guatemala City	2,000,000
Haiti	Port-au-Prince	1,031,000
Hong Kong	Hong Kong	5,448,000
Hungary	Budapest	2,115,000
India	Ahmadabad	3,279,655
	Bangalore	4,086,548
	Bombay	12,571,720
	Calcutta	10,916,272
	Delhi	8,375,188
	Hyderabad	4,280,261
	Jaipur	1,514,425
	Kanpur	2,111,284
	Lucknow	1,642,134
	Madras	5,361,468
	Nagpur	1,661,409
	Pune	2,485,014
Indonesia	Bandung	2,535,000
	Jakarta	9,253,000
	Medan	1,850,000
	Semarang	1,224,000

Country	Metropolitan area	population
	Surabaya	2,383,000
Iran	Isfahan	1,484,000
	Mashhad	1,882,000
	Tehran	6,773,000
Iraq	Baghdad	4,044,000
Ireland, (Rep. of)	Dublin	926,000
Israel	Jerusalem	508,000
	Tel Aviv	1,029,700
Italy	Milan	1,449,403
	Naples	1,204,149
	Rome	3,051,000
	Turin	1,002,863
Ivory Coast	Abidjan	2,168,000
Japan	Fukuoka	1,169,000
	Hiroshima	1,049,000
	Kawasaki	1,128,000
	Kitakyushu	1,030,000
	Kyoto	1,460,000
	Nagoya	2,160,000
	Osaka-Kobe	8,520,000
	Sapporo	1,670,000
	Tōkyō	11,935,700
	Yokohama	3,220,000
Jordan	Amman	1,025,000
Kazakhstan	Alma-Ata	1,151,300
Kenya	Nairobi	1,503,000
Korea, North	Pyŏngyang	2,230,000
Korea, South	Inchon	1,739,000
	Pusan	3,875,000
	Seoul	10,979,000
	Taegu	2,518,000
Kuwait	Kuwait	200,000
Latvia	Rīga	915,000
Lebanon	Beirut	1,500,000
Libya	Tripoli	2,062,000
Lithuania	Vilnius	582,000
Malaysia	Kuala Lumpur	1,711,000
Mexico	Guadalajara	2,846,720
	Mexico City	18,748,000
	Monterrey	2,521,697
	Puebla de Zaragoza	1,267,000
Morocco	Casablanca	3,213,000
	Rabat	1,068,000
Netherlands	Amsterdam	1,062,000
	The Hague	683,631
	Rotterdam	1,037,000
New Zealand	Auckland	864,700
	Christchurch	303,400
	Wellington	325,700
Nicaragua	Managua	1,012,000
Nigeria	Abuja	523,900
	Lagos	4,100,000
Norway	Oslo	458,364
Pakistan	Faisalabad	1,507,000
	Islamabad	537,000
	Karachi	7,702,000
	Lahore	4,092,000
	Rawalpindi	1,099,000
Peru	Lima	6,404,500
Philippines	Manila – Quezon City	7,832,000
Poland	Warsaw	1,655,100
Portugal	Lisbon	1,603,000
	Oporto	1,314,794
Puerto Rico	San Juan	1,390,000
Romania	Bucharest	2,194,000
Russian Federation	Chelyabinsk	1,143,000
	Kazan	1,094,000
	Moscow	9,000,000
	Nizhniy Novgorod (formerly Gorkiy)	1,438,000
	Novosibirsk	1,436,000
	Omsk	1,148,000
	Perm	1,091,000
	Rostov-on-Don	1,020,000
	Samara (formerly Kuybyshev)	1,257,000
	St Petersburg (formerly Leningrad)	5,035,000
	Ufa	1,083,000
	Volgograd	999,000

Country	Metropolitan area	population
	Yekaterinburg (formerly Sverdlovsk)	1,367,000
Saudi Arabia	Jeddah	1,800,000
	Riyadh	1,500,000
Senegal	Dakar	1,492,000
Singapore	Singapore	2,723,000
South Africa	Cape Town	2,310,000
	Durban	1,057,000
	Johannesburg	1,714,000
Spain	Barcelona	1,677,699
	Madrid	2,991,223
Sri Lanka	Colombo	616,000
Sudan	Khartoum	1,947,000
Sweden	Stockholm	1,662,000
Switzerland	Geneva	373,000
Syria	Aleppo	2,501,000
	Damascus	2,651,000
Taiwan	Kaohsiung	1,512,000
	Taipei	2,961,000
Tanzania	Dar-es-Salaam	1,657,000
Thailand	Bangkok	5,832,843
Tunisia	Tunis	1,636,000
Turkey	Ankara	3,022,236
	Istanbul	6,665,000
	Izmir	2,665,105
UK	Birmingham	2,207,800
	Glasgow	872,900
	Leeds	1,461,000
	Liverpool	1,227,700
	London	8,620,333
	Manchester	2,445,000
Ukraine	Dnepropetrovsk	1,179,000
	Donetsk	1,110,000
	Kharkov	1,611,000
	Kiev	2,624,000
	Odessa	1,115,000
Uruguay	Montevideo	1,197,000
USA	Atlanta	2,737,000
	Baltimore	2,342,000
	Boston	2,845,000
	Buffalo	959,000
	Chicago	6,216,000
	Cincinnati	1,449,000
	Cleveland	1,845,000
	Columbus	1,344,000
	Dallas – Fort Worth	3,766,000
	Denver	1,640,000
	Detroit	4,352,000
	Houston	3,247,000
	Indianapolis	1,237,000
	Kansas City	1,575,000
	Los Angeles	10,845,000
	Miami	1,814,000
	Milwaukee	1,398,000
	Minneapolis – St Paul	2,388,000
	New Orleans	1,307,000
	New York	16,198,000
	Oklahoma City	964,000
	Philadelphia	4,920,000
	Phoenix	2,030,000
	Pittsburg	2,094,000
	Portland	1,188,000
	Rochester	980,000
	Sacramento	1,385,000
	San Antonio	1,323,000
	San Diego	2,370,000
	San Francisco	5,028,000
	Seattle	1,862,000
	St Louis	2,467,000
	Tampa – St Petersburg	1,995,000
	Washington DC	3,734,000
Uzbekistan	Tashkent	2,100,000
Venezuela	Caracas	4,092,000
	Maracaibo	1,365,308
	Valencia	1,227,472
Vietnam	Haiphong	1,397,000
	Hanoi	1,088,862
	Ho Chi Minh (Saigon)	3,237,000
Yugoslavia	Belgrade	1,575,000
Zaire	Kinshasa	3,505,000

GEOGRAPHICAL COMPARISONS

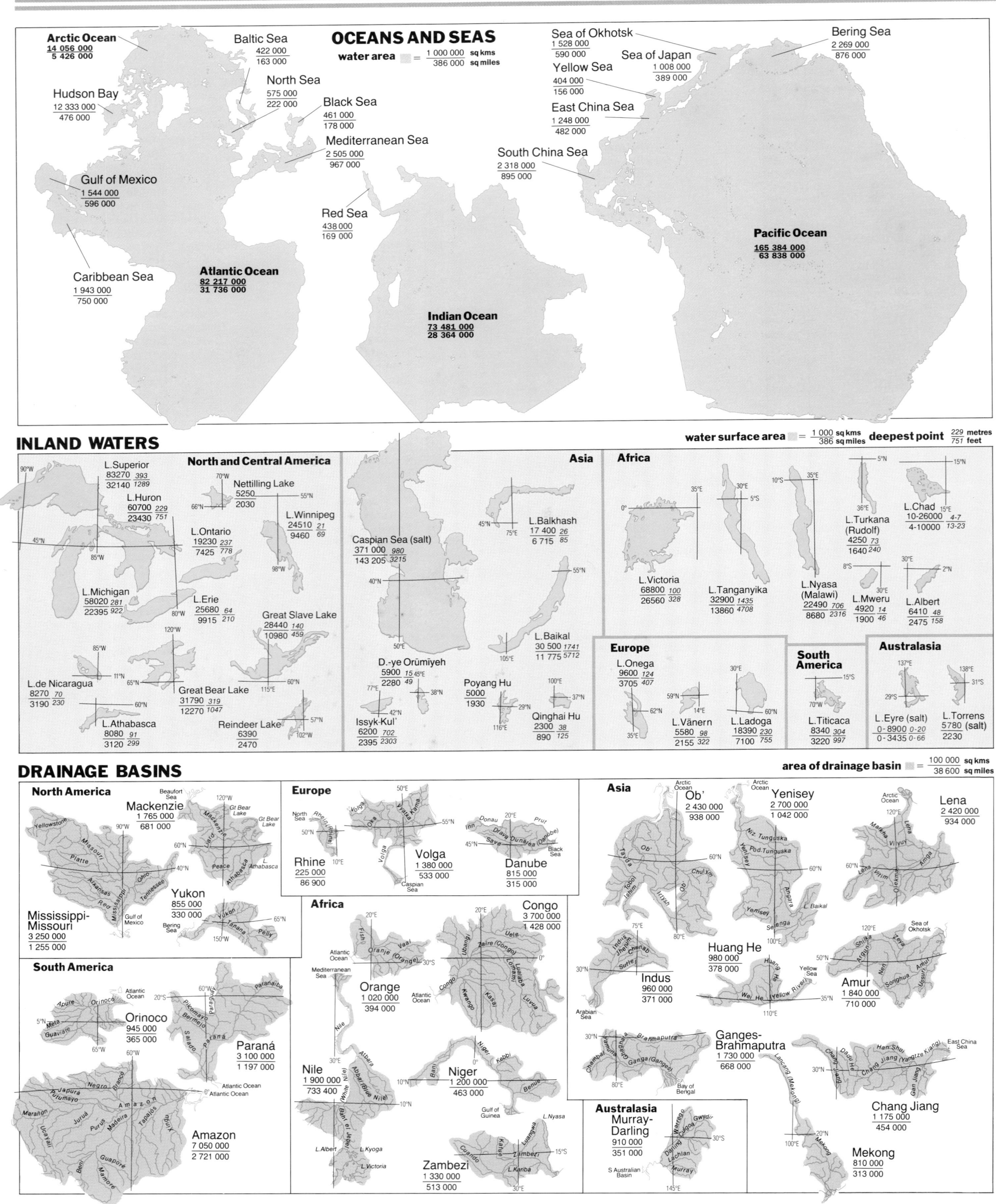

MOUNTAIN HEIGHTS

Mountain	Metres	Feet	Location
Everest (Qomolangma Feng)	8,848	29,028	China-Nepal
K2 (Godwin Austen) (Qogir Feng)	8,611	28,250	Kashmir-China
Kangchenjunga	8,586	28,170	India-Nepal
Makalu	8,463	27,766	China-Nepal
Cho Oyu	8,201	26,906	China-Nepal
Dhaulagiri	8,167	26,795	Nepal
Manaslu	8,163	26,781	Nepal
Nanga Parbat	8,125	26,657	Kashmir
Annapurna	8,091	26,545	Nepal
Gasherbrum	8,068	26,470	Kashmir
Xixabangma Feng (Gosainthan)	8,012	26,286	Tibet, China
Distaghil Sar	7,885	25,869	Kashmir
Masherbrum	7,821	25,659	Kashmir
Nanda Devi	7,816	25,643	India
Kamet	7,756	25,446	India
Namjagbarwa Feng (Namcha Barwa)	7,756	25,446	Tibet, China
Gurla Mandhata	7,728	25,354	Tibet, China
Muztag	7,723	25,338	East Sinkiang, Tibet
Kongur Shan (Kungur)	7,719	25,325	China
Tirich Mir	7,690	25,230	Pakistan
Gongga Shan	7,556	24,790	Sichuan, China
Pik Kommunizma	7,495	24,590	Tajikistan
Pik Pobedy (Tomur Feng)	7,439	24,406	Kyrgyzstan-China
Aconcagua	6,960	22,834	Argentina
Ojos del Salado	6,880	22,572	Argentina-Chile
Bonete	6,872	22,546	Argentina
Huascarán	6,768	22,205	Peru
Sajama	6,542	21,463	Bolivia
Illampu	6,485	21,276	Bolivia
Chimborazo	6,310	20,702	Ecuador
McKinley	6,194	20,320	Alaska, U.S.A.
Logan	5,951	19,524	Yukon, Canada
Cotopaxi	5,896	19,344	Ecuador
Kilimanjaro	5,895	19,340	Tanzania
Citlaltépetl (Orizaba)	5,699	18,697	Mexico
Damávand	5,671	18,605	Iran
El'brus	5,642	18,510	Caucasus, Russian Federation
Kenya (Kirinyaga)	5,200	17,058	Kenya
Vinson Massif	5,140	16,860	Antarctica
Ararat (Büyük Ağri Daği)	5,123	16,808	Turkey
Jaya (Carstensz)	5,030	16,503	New Guinea, Indonesia
Mont Blanc	4,808	15,774	France-Italy
Ras Dashen	4,620	15,157	Ethiopia
Meru	4,565	14,979	Tanzania
Dom (Mischabel group)	4,545	14,910	Switzerland
Kirkpatrick	4,528	14,855	Antarctica
Karisimbi	4,507	14,786	Rwanda-Zaire
Matterhorn	4,478	14,690	Italy-Switzerland
Whitney	4,418	14,495	U.S.A.
Elbert	4,398	14,431	U.S.A.
Rainier	4,392	14,410	U.S.A.
Elgon	4,321	14,178	Kenya-Uganda
Mauna Kea	4,205	13,796	Hawaii, U.S.A.
Toubkal	4,165	13,664	Morocco
Cameroon (Caméroun)	4,095	13,435	Cameroon
Kinabalu	4,094	13,431	Sabah, Malaysia
Eiger	3,975	13,041	Switzerland
Erebus	3,794	12,447	Antarctica
Fuji	3,776	12,388	Japan
Cook	3,764	12,349	New Zealand
Teide	3,718	12,198	Canary Is.
Mulhacén	3,482	11,424	Spain
Etna	3,323	10,902	Sicily, Italy
Kosciusko	2,230	7,316	Australia

The mountains listed here are a selection from every continent rather than a strict numerical ordering.

RIVER LENGTHS

River	Kms	Miles	Location
Nile	6,695	4,160	Africa
Amazon	6,515	4,050	South America
Yangtze (Chang Jiang)	6,380	3,965	Asia
Mississippi-Missouri	6,019	3,740	U.S.A.
Ob'-Irtysh	5,570	3,460	Russian Federation-Kazakhstan
Yenisei	5,550	3,450	Russian Federation
Yellow River (Huang He)	5,464	3,395	China
Congo (Zaire)	4,667	2,900	Africa
Paraná	4,500	2,800	South America
Mekong	4,425	2,750	Asia
Amur	4,416	2,744	Russian Federation-China
Lena	4,400	2,730	Russian Federation
Mackenzie	4,250	2,640	Canada
Niger	4,030	2,505	Africa
Missouri	3,969	2,266	U.S.A.
Mississippi	3,779	2,348	U.S.A.
Murray-Darling	3,750	2,330	Australia
Volga	3,688	2,290	Russian Federation
Madeira	3,200	1,990	Brazil
Yukon	3,185	1,980	Canada-Alaska
Indus	3,180	1,975	Pakistan
Syrdar'ya	3,078	1,913	Kazakhstan
Salween	3,060	1,901	Asia
St Lawrence	3,058	1,900	Canada
São Francisco	2,900	1,800	Brazil
Rio Grande	2,870	1,785	U.S.A.-Mexico
Danube	2,850	1,770	Europe
Brahmaputra	2,840	1,765	India-Tibet
Euphrates	2,815	1,750	Iraq-Syria-Turkey
Pará-Tocantins	2,750	1,710	Brazil
Zambezi	2,650	1,650	Africa
Amudar'ya	2,620	1,630	Uzbekistan-Turkmenistan
Paraguay	2,600	1,615	South America
Nelson-Saskatchewan	2,570	1,600	Canada
Ural	2,534	1,575	Russian Federation-Kazakhstan
Ganges (Ganga)	2,510	1,560	India
Orinoco	2,500	1,555	Venezuela
Shabeelle	2,490	1,550	Somalia-Ethiopia
Arkansas	2,348	1,459	U.S.A.
Colorado	2,333	1,450	U.S.A.
Dnieper (Dnepr)	2,285	1,420	Ukraine-Belorussia
Irrawaddy	2,150	1,335	Burma
Don	1,870	1,162	Russian Federation
Orange	1,860	1,155	Africa
Rhine	1,320	820	Europe
Elbe	1,159	720	Germany-Czechoslovakia
Vistula (Wisła)	1,014	630	Poland
Loire	1,012	629	France
Tagus (Tejo)	1,006	625	Portugal-Spain

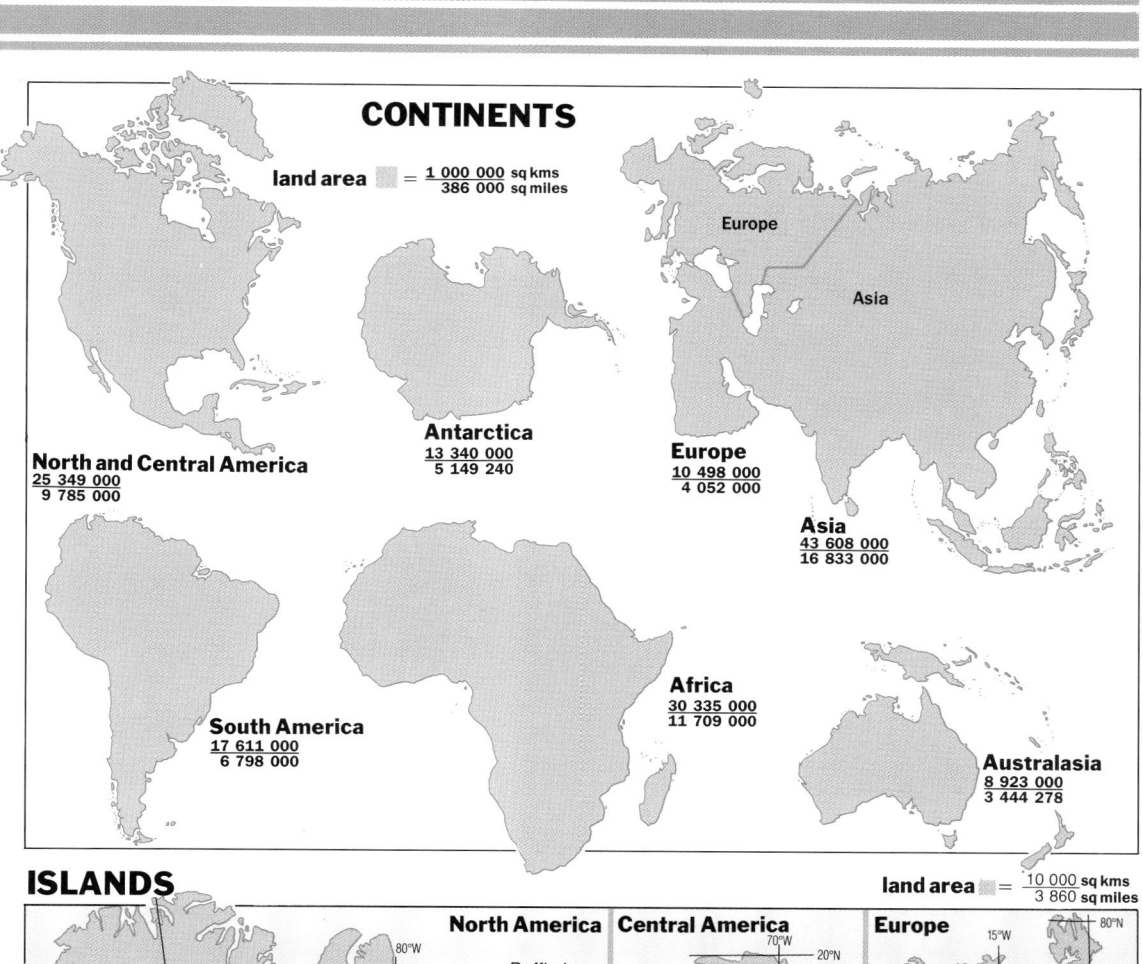

CONTINENTS

land area ▢ = 1 000 000 sq kms / 386 000 sq miles

North and Central America
25 349 000
9 785 000

Antarctica
13 340 000
5 149 240

Europe
10 498 000
4 052 000

Asia
43 608 000
16 833 000

South America
17 611 000
6 798 000

Africa
30 335 000
11 709 000

Australasia
8 923 000
3 444 278

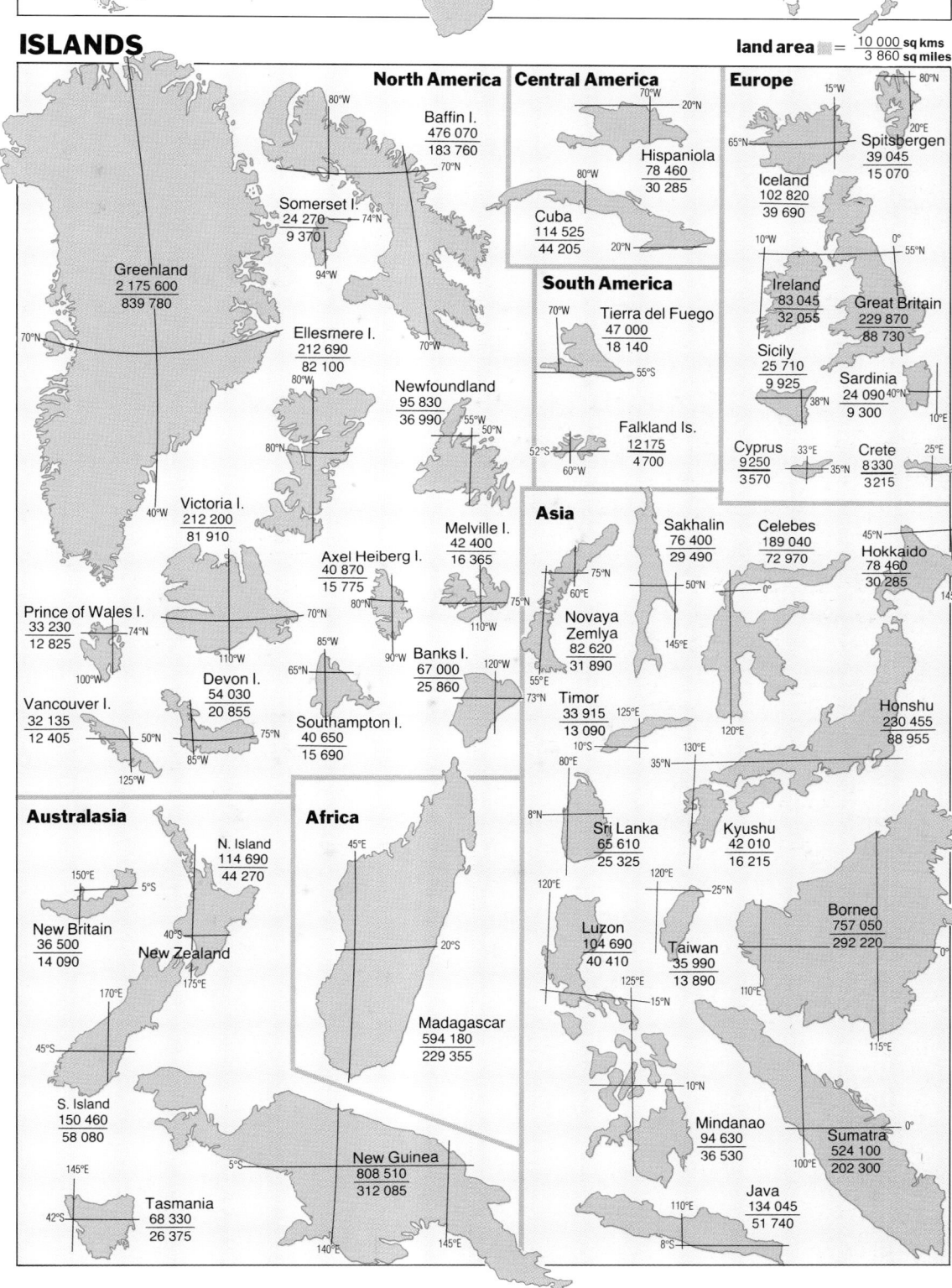

ISLANDS

land area = 10 000 sq kms / 3 860 sq miles

North America
Greenland 2 175 600 / 839 780
Baffin I. 476 070 / 183 760
Somerset I. 24 270 / 9 370
Ellesmere I. 212 690 / 82 100
Newfoundland 95 830 / 36 990
Victoria I. 212 200 / 81 910
Melville I. 42 400 / 16 365
Axel Heiberg I. 40 870 / 15 775
Banks I. 67 000 / 25 860
Prince of Wales I. 33 230 / 12 825
Devon I. 54 030 / 20 855
Vancouver I. 32 135 / 12 405
Southampton I. 40 650 / 15 690

Central America
Hispaniola 78 460 / 30 285
Cuba 114 525 / 44 205

South America
Tierra del Fuego 47 000 / 18 140
Falkland Is. 12 175 / 4 700

Europe
Spitsbergen 39 045 / 15 070
Iceland 102 820 / 39 690
Ireland 83 045 / 32 055
Great Britain 229 870 / 88 730
Sicily 25 710 / 9 925
Sardinia 24 090 / 9 300
Cyprus 9 250 / 3 570
Crete 8 330 / 3 215

Asia
Sakhalin 76 400 / 29 490
Celebes 189 040 / 72 970
Hokkaido 78 460 / 30 285
Novaya Zemlya 82 620 / 31 890
Honshu 230 455 / 88 955
Timor 33 915 / 13 090
Sri Lanka 65 610 / 25 325
Kyushu 42 010 / 16 215
Luzon 104 690 / 40 410
Taiwan 35 990 / 13 890
Borneo 757 050 / 292 220
Mindanao 94 630 / 36 530
Sumatra 524 100 / 202 300
Java 134 045 / 51 740

Australasia
N. Island 114 690 / 44 270
New Britain 36 500 / 14 090
New Zealand
S. Island 150 460 / 58 080
Tasmania 68 330 / 26 375

Africa
Madagascar 594 180 / 229 355
New Guinea 808 510 / 312 085

Honshu

Sakhalin

Hokkaido

Sea of Okhotsk

Kolyma

Novosibirskiye
Ostrova

ARCTIC

OCEAN

Kuril Islands

Kamchatka

Anadyr

Ostrov
Vrangelya

Chukchi

Chukotskiy
Poluostrov

Sea

Bering

Bering Strait

Point Barrow

Aleutian Islands

Sea

Beaufort

Sea

Brooks Range

Ba
Island

Yukon

Alaska Range
Mount
McKinley

Mackenzie Mountains

Aleutian Range

Mackenzie

Great
Bear
Lake

Kodiak Island

Gulf
of
Alaska

Coast Mountains

NORTH

R O C K Y

Gr
Slave

Midway Islands

Peace

Athabasca

Queen
Charlotte
Islands

PACIFIC

Vancouver
Island

Fraser

M o u n t a i n

Mount Rainier
Mount St Helens

Columbia

Cascade Range

Snake

OCEAN

Coast Ranges

Sierra Nevada

Great Salt
Lake

Hawaiian

Islands

Mount
Whitney

Colorado

Gulf of California

Sierra Madre Occi

Lower California

Yenisey
Ob'
Urals
Novaya Zemlya
Severnaya Zemlya
North Cape
SCANDINAVIA
Black Sea
Limit of permanent pack ice
Svalbard
Norwegian Sea
NORTH POLE
North Sea
Mediterranean Sea
Jan Mayen
Greenland
Denmark Strait
Iceland
BRITISH ISLES
Bay of Biscay
Ellesmere Island
Queen Elizabeth Islands
NORTH AFRICA
Parry Islands
Baffin Bay
Davis Strait
Victoria Island
Baffin Island
Cape Farewell
Madeira
NORTH
Canary Islands
Foxe Basin
Southampton Island
Hudson Strait
Cape Chidley
Labrador Sea
Azores
Hudson Bay
Labrador
Lake Athabasca
Churchill
Reindeer Lake
Southern Indian Lake
La Grande Rivière
Laurentian Highlands
Newfoundland
Cape Race
James Bay
Rupert
ATLANTIC
Saskatchewan
Lake Winnipeg
Nova Scotia
Lake Manitoba
Lake of the Woods
Lake Superior
St Lawrence
Cape Cod
Lake Huron
Lake Ontario
Lake Michigan
Missouri
Mississippi
Lake Erie
Appalachian Mountains
Great Plains
Platte
Ohio
Bermuda
OCEAN
Cape Hatteras
Ozark Plateaus
Tennessee
Savannah
Arkansas
Red River
Florida
Bahamas
West Indies
Rio Grande
Gulf of Mexico
Sierra Madre Oriental
Caribbean Sea
Orinoco
Yucatan

Colo[rado]

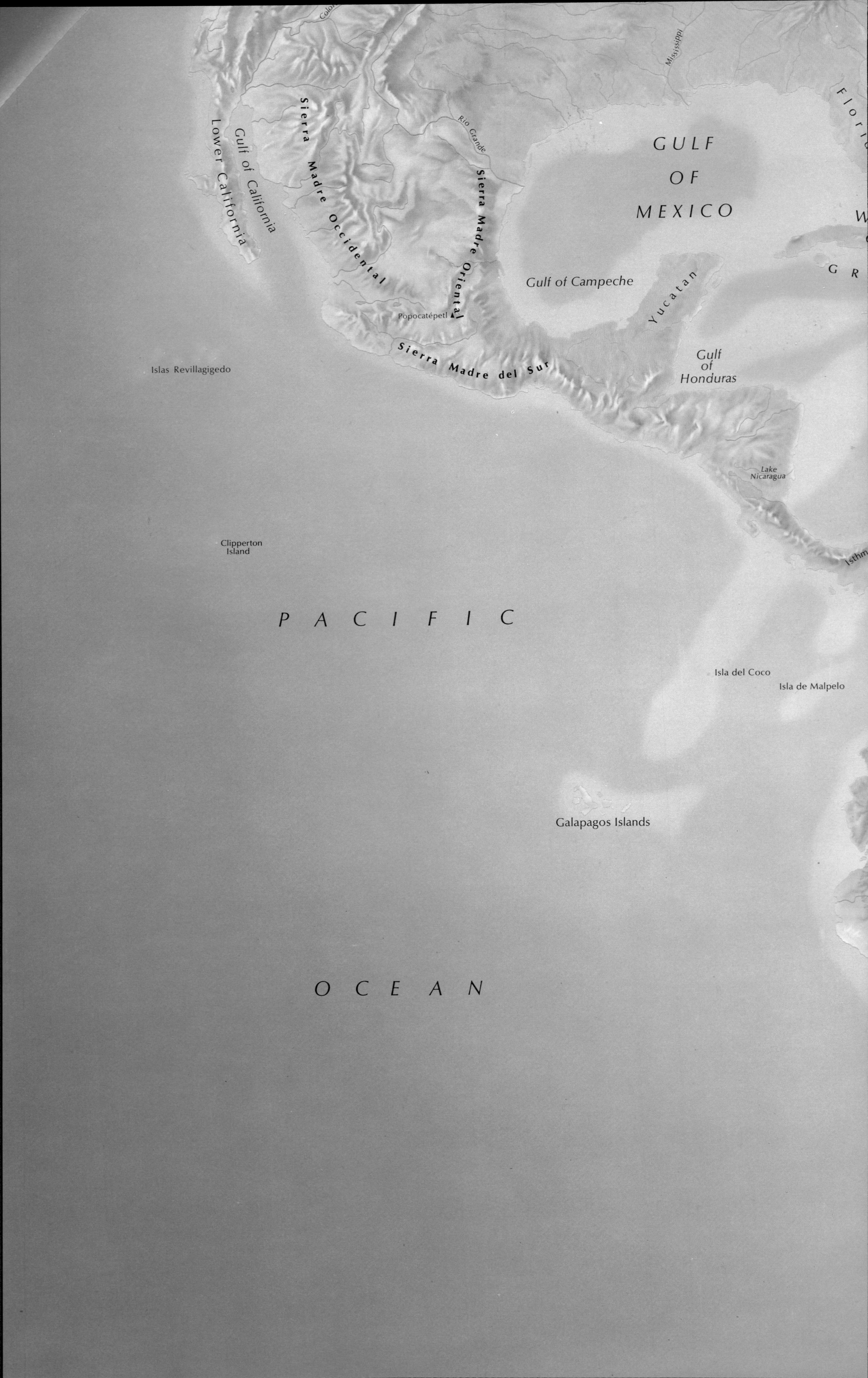

Mississippi

Rio Grande

Sierra Madre Occidental

Gulf of California

Lower California

Sierra Madre Oriental

Flori[da]

GULF

OF

MEXICO

W

G R

Gulf of Campeche

Yucatan

Popocatépetl

Sierra Madre del Sur

Gulf
of
Honduras

Islas Revillagigedo

Lake
Nicaragua

Clipperton
Island

Isthm[us]

P A C I F I C

Isla del Coco

Isla de Malpelo

Galapagos Islands

O C E A N

NORTH

ATLANTIC

OCEAN

BAHAMAS

WEST INDIES

Bermuda

Cuba

Jamaica

Hispaniola

Puerto
Rico

Greater ANTILLES

CARIBBEAN

SEA

LESSER ANTILLES

Gulf
of
Darien

Panama

Trinidad

Lake
Maracaibo

Orinoco

L L A N O S

Cordillera Occidental

Cauca

Magdalena

Cordillera Oriental

Guiana

Roraima ▲

Highlands

Mouths
of the
Amazon

Branco

Cordillera

▲Cotopaxi

Chimborazo

Negro

Japurá

Amazon

Putumayo

Amazon

Marañón

Juruá

Tapajós

Xingu

Tocantins

A
N
D
E
S

Ucayali

Purus

Madeira

▲Huascarán

Madre de Dios

Araguaia

Parnaíba

São Francisco

MATO

GROSSO

Lake
Titicaca

▲Ancohuma

Brazilian Highlands

Lake
Poopó

Salar
de
Uyuni

GRAN CHACO

Paraguay

Paraná

Atacama Desert

Pilcomayo

Galapagos Islands

San Félix · San Ambrosio

Aconcagua ▲

Juan Fernández

Lake Titicaca

Salar de Uyuni

Lake Poopó

Gran Chaco

Pilcomayo

Paraguay

Bermejo

Salado

Parana

Uruguay

Plate

Colorado

Negro

Pampas

A N D E S

Z

Chico

Chubut

Deseado

Patagonia

Falkland Islands

Tierra del Fuego

Cape Horn

Drake Passage

Elephant Island

South Shetland Islands

S O U T H

Sala y Gomez

Easter Island

P A C I F I C

Ducie Island

Henderson Island

Pitcairn Island

Graham Land

Palmer Land

ANTARCTIC PENINSULA

Peter I Island

Bellingshausen Sea

O C E A N

Ellsworth Land

Rapa

S O U T H E R N

A N

Marie Byrd Land

Ross Ice Shelf

Ross Sea

Mount Erebus ▲

Scott Island

Chatham Islands

Bounty Islands

Antipodes

New Zealand

Balleny Islands

Campbell Island

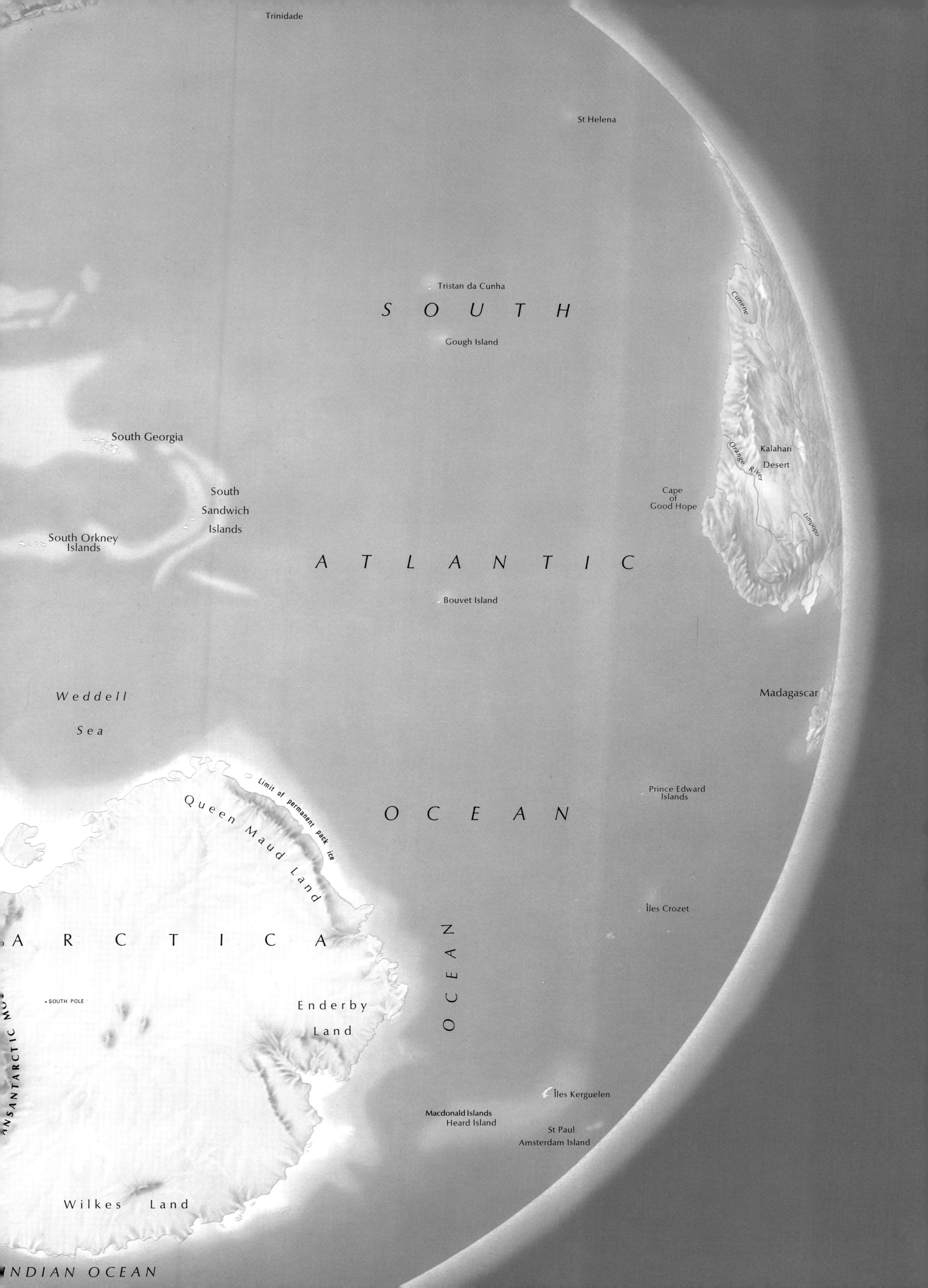

Trinidade

St Helena

Tristan da Cunha

S O U T H

Gough Island

Cumene

South Georgia

South
Sandwich
Islands

Kalahari
Desert

Orange River

South Orkney
Islands

A T L A N T I C

Cape
of
Good Hope

Limpopo

Bouvet Island

Weddell

Madagascar

Sea

O C E A N

Prince Edward
Islands

Limit of permanent pack ice

Queen Maud Land

O C E A N

ARCTICA

Îles Crozet

• SOUTH POLE

Enderby
Land

O C E A N

ANSANTARCTIC MO

Îles Kerguelen

Macdonald Islands
Heard Island

St Paul
Amsterdam Island

Wilkes   Land

NDIAN OCEAN

NORTH

ATLANTIC

OCEAN

Azores

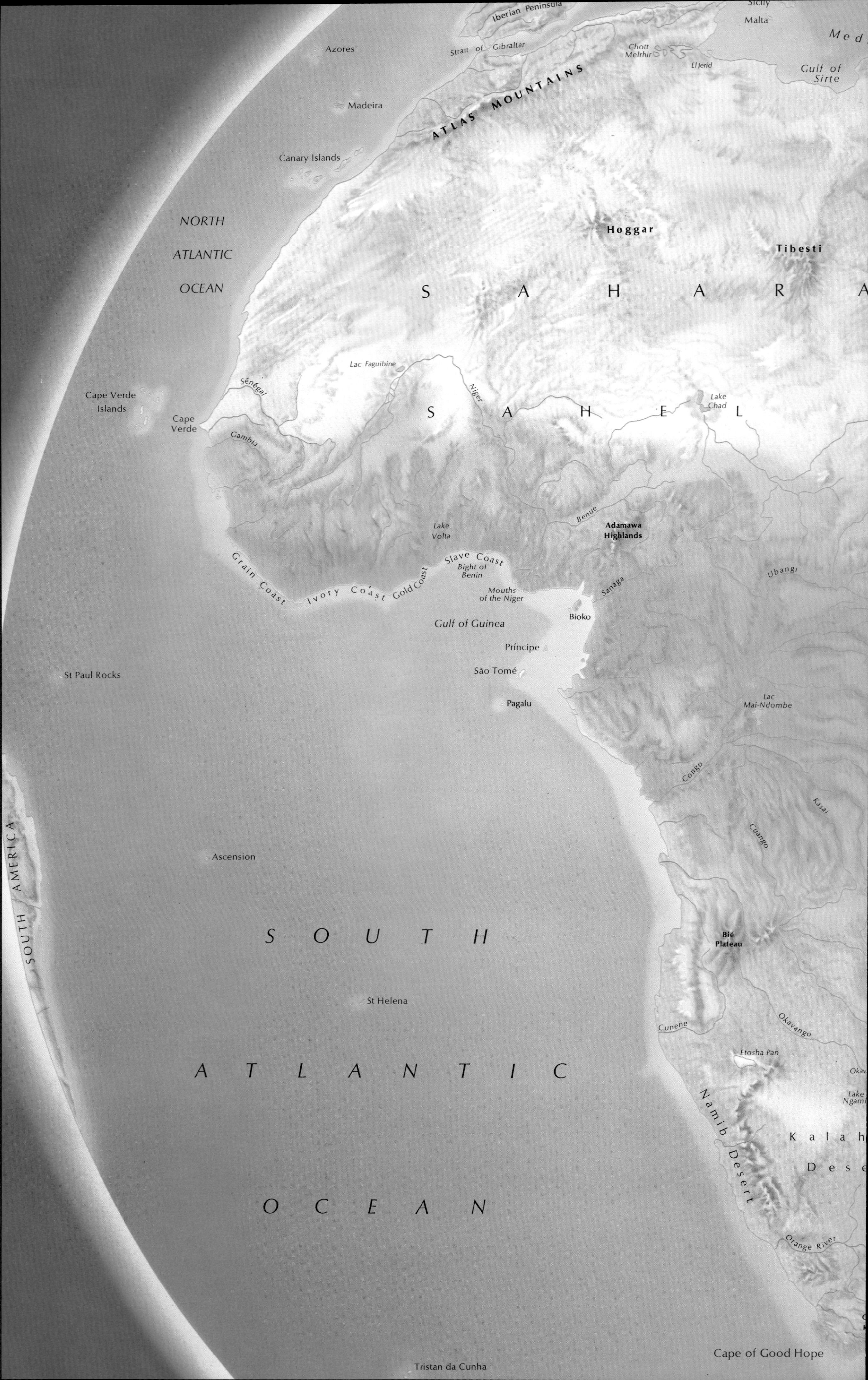

Iberian Peninsula

Madeira

Strait of Gibraltar

Sicily

Malta

Med

Gulf of
Sirte

Chott
Melrhir

El Jerid

Canary Islands

ATLAS MOUNTAINS

Hoggar

Tibesti

S   A   H   A   R   A

Cape Verde
Islands

Sénégal

Lac Faguibine

Niger

S   A   H   E   L

Lake
Chad

Cape
Verde

Gambia

Grain Coast

Ivory Coast

Gold Coast

Lake
Volta

Slave Coast
Bight of
Benin

Benue

Adamawa
Highlands

Ubangi

Mouths
of the Niger

Gulf of Guinea

Bioko

Sanaga

St Paul Rocks

Príncipe

São Tomé

Pagalu

Lac
Mai-Ndombe

Congo

Kasai

Cuango

Ascension

SOUTH AMERICA

SOUTH

Bié
Plateau

St Helena

ATLANTIC

Okavango

Cunene

Etosha Pan

Okav

Lake
Ngami

OCEAN

Namib Desert

Kalah

Dese

Orange River

Cape of Good Hope

Tristan da Cunha

16

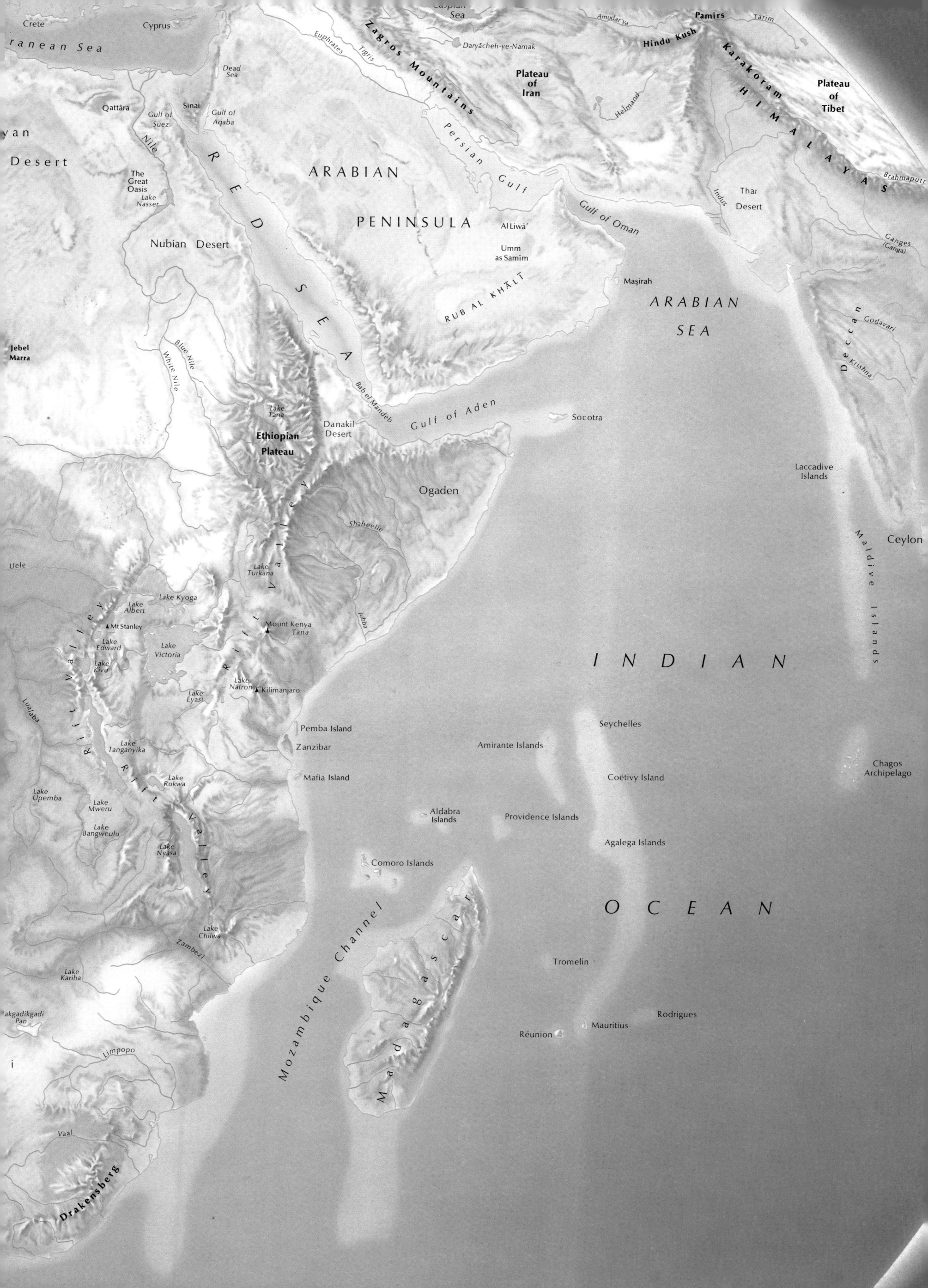

Crete
Cyprus
ranean Sea

Zagros Mountains

Caspian Sea

Amudar'ya
Pamirs
Tārim

Daryācheh-ye-Namak

Hindu Kush

Karakoram

Plateau
of
Tibet

Euphrates
Tigris

Plateau
of
Iran

HIMALAYAS

Brahmaputr

Dead
Sea

Sinai

Gulf of
Aqaba

ARABIAN

Helmand

Indus

Thar
Desert

Qattâra

Gulf of
Suez

Ganges
(Ganga)

yan

Nile

Desert

The
Great
Oasis

Lake
Nasser

PENINSULA

Persian Gulf

Al Liwā'

Gulf of Oman

Nubian Desert

Umm
as Samim

Maşirah

ARABIAN

Deccan

Godavari

SEA

RED

SEA

Jebel
Marra

Blue Nile

White Nile

RUB AL KHĀLĪ

Krishna

Lake
Tana

Ethiopian
Plateau

Bab el Mandeb

Danakil
Desert

Gulf of Aden

Socotra

Laccadive
Islands

Ceylon

Uele

Rift

Ogaden

Shabeelle

Lake
Turkana

Lake
Kyoga

Lake
Albert

▲ Mt Stanley

Lake
Edward

Lake
Kivu

Lake
Victoria

Jubba

Mount Kenya
Tana
▲

INDIAN

Maldive
Islands

Valley

Lake
Eyasi

Lake
Natron

▲ Kilimanjaro

Pemba Island

Seychelles

Chagos
Archipelago

Luluaba

Rift

Lake
Tanganyika

Zanzibar

Amirante Islands

Lake
Upemba

Lake
Rukwa

Mafia Island

Coëtivy Island

Lake
Mweru

Lake
Bangweulu

Valley

Lake
Nyasa

Aldabra
Islands

Providence Islands

Agalega Islands

Rift

Comoro Islands

OCEAN

Lake
Chilwa

Zambezi

Mozambique Channel

Madagascar

Lake
Kariba

akgadikgadi
Pan

Limpopo

Tromelin

i

Rodrigues

Réunion

Mauritius

Vaal

Drakensberg

NORTH P

ARCTIC

Ellesmere Island

Greenland
Sea

Hudson Bay

Baffin Island

Davis Strait

G r e e n l a n d

Greenland

Jan Mayen

LABRADOR

Denmark Strait

Norwegian

Cape Farewell

Iceland

Sea

Faeroe Islands

N O R T H

S
C
A
N
D

Vänern

British
Isles

Grampians

North

Vättern

Sea

A T L A N T I C

Irish Sea

Elbe

Severn

Thames

Rhine

N O

English Channel

Seine

Loire

Bay
of
Biscay

Massif
Central

Rhône

A L P S

Po

Adria

O C E A N

Mt. Blanc

Apennin

Azores

Cantabrian Mts

P y r e n e e s

Caronne

Ebro

Corsica

Tagus

Balearic Islands

Sardinia

Guadalquivir

M E D I T E R

Strait of Gibraltar

Madeira

Sicily

Malta

R

A T L A S   M O U N T A I N S

Chott Melrhir

El Jerid

Canary Islands

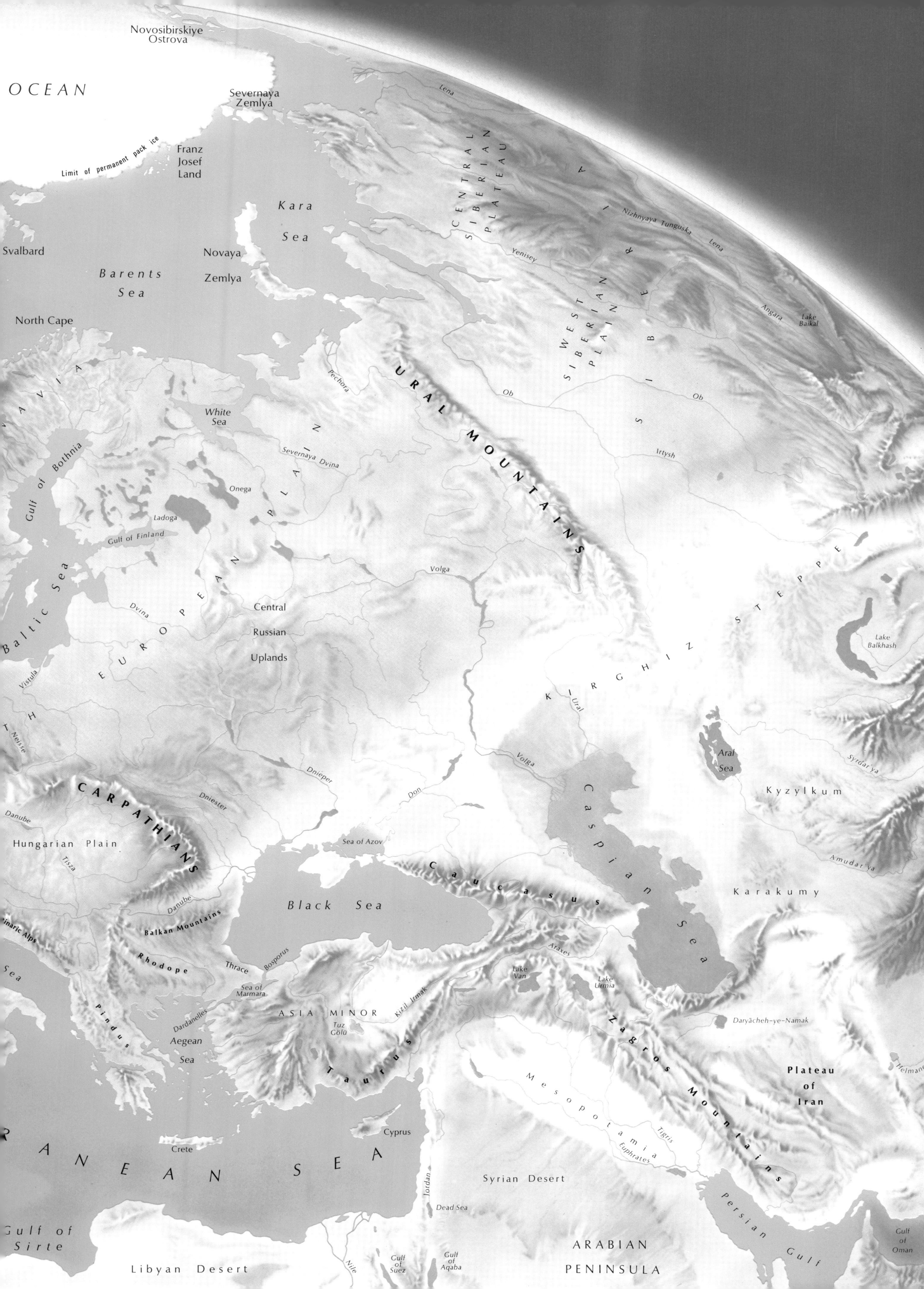

OCEAN

Novosibirskiye
Ostrova

Severnaya
Zemlya

Franz
Josef
Land

Limit of permanent pack ice

Svalbard

Barents
Sea

Kara
Sea

Novaya
Zemlya

North Cape

CENTRAL SIBERIAN PLATEAU

Lena

Nizhnyaya Tunguska

Lena

Yenisey

Angara

Lake
Baikal

S
I
B
E
R
I
A

WEST SIBERIAN PLAIN

Pechora

URAL MOUNTAINS

Ob

Ob

Irtysh

White
Sea

Severnaya Dvina

Onega

Gulf of Bothnia

Ladoga

Gulf of Finland

Baltic Sea

Dvina

Vistula

Neisse

EUROPEAN PLAIN

Volga

Central
Russian
Uplands

KIRGHIZ STEPPE

Lake
Balkhash

Ural

Volga

Aral
Sea

Kyzylkum

Syrdar'ya

CARPATHIANS

Dnieper

Dniester

Don

Sea of Azov

Caspian Sea

Amudar'ya

Danube

Hungarian Plain

Tisza

Karakumy

Danube

Balkan Mountains

Black Sea

Caucasus

Dinaric Alps

Rhodope

Thrace

Bosporus

Araxes

Lake
Van

Lake
Urmia

Daryācheh-ye-Namak

Pindus

Sea

Sea of
Marmara

Dardanelles

Aegean
Sea

ASIA MINOR

Kizil Irmak

Tuz
Gölü

Taurus

Zagros Mountains

Plateau
of
Iran

Helmand

Crete

Cyprus

Mesopotamia

Tigris

Euphrates

R A N E A N   S E A

Jordan

Syrian Desert

Dead Sea

Persian
Gulf

Gulf of
Sirte

Libyan Desert

Nile

Gulf
of
Suez

Gulf
of
Aqaba

ARABIAN
PENINSULA

Gulf
of
Oman

Barents Sea

Scandinavia

Kheta

White
Sea

Baltic Sea

Peshora

Lake
Ladoga

Lake
Onega

C E N T R A L

S I B E R I A N

NORTH EUROPEAN PLAIN

Ob

W E S T

Nizhnyaya Tunguska

P L A T E A U

Dnieper

Ural Mountains

S I B E R I A N

Yenisey

Tobol

S I B

Volga

Angara

Ural

Ishim

P L A I N

Don

Ozero
Tengiz

Ob

Volga

Black
Sea

K i r g h i z

Caucusus

Irtysh

Hövsgöl Nuur

Lake
Baikal

Caspian Sea

S t e p p e

Selenga

Aral
Sea

Ozero
Zaysan

A L T A I

Syrdar'ya

M O N G O

Kyzylkum

Ozero Alakol'

Lake
Balkhash

G O B I

Ebinur Hu

Karakumy

Amudar'ya

Ili

D z u n g a r i a

Issyk Kul

Bosten Hu

Turfan
Depression

Tien Shan

Tarim

Plateau
of
Iran

Pik Kommunizma

Yellow River
(Huang He)

Lop Nur

Pamirs

Takla Makan

Hindu Kush

Altun Shan

Karakoram

K2

Qaidam Pendi

Kunlun Shan

Qinghai
Hu

Helmand

H

Yangtze Kiang
(Chang Jiang)

Yellow River
(Huang He)

Qin Ling

I

Plateau

Chenab

M

of

Indus

Sutlej

A

Tibet

Red
Basin

Indo-Gangetic

L

Salween

Yangtze Kiang
(Chang Jiang)

Thar
Desert

A

Brahmaputra

Mekong

Y

Plain

Everest

A

Kangchenjunga

Nan Ling

Ganges
(Ganga)

Narmada

Khasi Hills

Naga Hills

Arabian

Mahanadi

Mouths
of the
Ganges

Red River
(Song Hong)

Sea

Arakan

Gulf
of
Tongking

Western Ghats

Deccan

Godavari

Irrawaddy

Hainan

Krishna

Eastern Ghats

B a y

Salween

o f

Laccadive
Islands

Cauvery

B e n g a l

Chao Phraya

Mekong

I N D O C H I N A

Palk Strait

Andaman Islands

A n d a m a n

Maldive Islands

Ceylon

S e a

Gulf
of
Thailand

Kra Isthmus

Nicobar
Islands

Malay Peninsula

Strait of Malacca

INDIAN   OCEAN

Sumatra

Laptev Sea

Novosibirskiye Ostrova

Bering Strait

Alaska

Yana

Indigirka

Kolyma

Anadyr

Nunivak Island

Verkhoyanskiy Khrebet

Lena

Vilyuy

S I B E R I A

Aldan

Kht. Dzhungdzhur

Kamchatka

Bering Sea

Aleutian Islands

Komandorskiye Ostrova

Sea of Okhotsk

Yablonovyy Khrebet

Shilka

Greater Khingan Range

Kerulen

Hulun Nur

MONGOLIA

Manchuria

Songhua

Amur

Ussuri

Oz. Khanka

Sikhote Alin

Sakhalin

Tatarskiy Proliv

Kuril Islands

Hokkaido

Changbai Shan

Korea

Sea of Japan

Honshu

NORTH

PACIFIC

Midway Islands

Bo Hai

Yellow River (Huang He)

Great Plain of China

Yellow Sea

Korea Strait

Shikoku

Kyushu

Yangtze Kiang (Chang Jiang)

Dongting Hu

Poyang Hu

East China Sea

Bonin Islands

OCEAN

Taiwan Strait

Ryukyu Islands

Volcano Islands

Taiwan

M a r i a n a s

Marshall Islands

South

China

Sea

PHILIPPINES

Paracel Islands

Luzon

Guam

Kiribati

Mindoro

Samar

Panay

Caroline Islands

Palawan

Negros

Mindanao

Spratly Islands

Sulu Sea

Celebes Sea

Borneo

Admiralty Islands

New Ireland

South
China
Sea

Malay Peninsula

Strait of Malacca

Sumatra

Borneo

Celebes
Sea

Celebes

Makassar Strait

Moluccas

Java
Sea

Banda
Sea

Arafura
Sea

E

Java

Bali

Timor

Timor
Sea

A

S

T

I

N

D

I

E

S

Christmas Island

Cocos (Keeling) Islands

Arnhem Land

Victoria

Barkly

Kimberley
Plateau

Fitzroy

Tanami
Desert

Great
Sandy
Desert

Ashburton

Macdonnell Ranges

Si
D

Gascoyne

Gibson
Desert

Lake
Amadeus

Finke

I N D I A N

Great Victoria Desert

Lake
Barlee

Lake
Moore

Nullarbor Plain

Lake
Gardner

Great Australian Bight

O C E A N

S O U T H E R N

St Paul

Kerguelen

Heard Island
Macdonald Islands

A N T A R C T I C A

oline Islands Pohnpei MICRONESIA Marshall Islands

TH PACIFIC OCEAN SOUTH

M E L Admiralty Islands Nauru

New Guinea A Bismarck New Ireland Banaba

Sea N Kiribati

New Britain Bougainville E S Tokelau Islands

Torres Strait Solomon Islands I PACIFIC Tuvalu

Great Cape York Peninsula Coral S Santa Cruz Islands

Gulf of arpentaria Barrier Vanuatu Samoan Islands

ableland Sea Fiji Tahiti Society Islands

Georgina Flinders Reef A Tonga

on t Diamantina Great Dividing Range New Caledonia OCEAN

Lake Eyre Cooper Creek Norfolk Island

Lake Torrens Barwon Lord Howe Island Kermadec Islands

Murray Darling Lachlan

Murrumbidgee

Mount Kosciusko Murray Australian Alps Tasman

Bass Strait Sea New Zealand Cook Strait

Tasmania Chatham Islands

OCEAN Bounty Islands

Auckland Islands Antipodes Islands

Campbell Island

Macquarie Island

STAR CHARTS

NORTHERN SKY

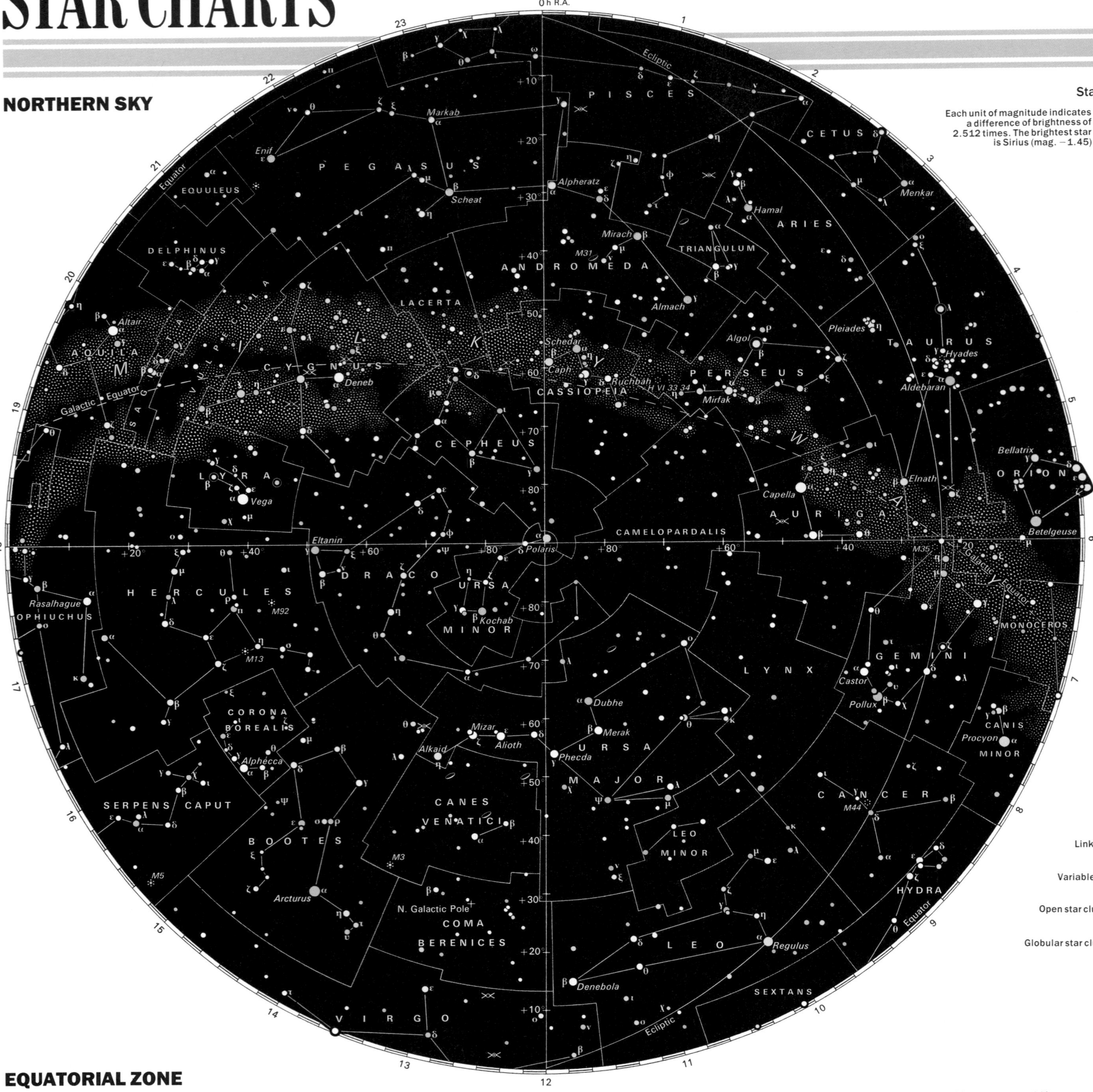

0 h R.A.
PISCES
CETUS
PEGASUS
Markab
Enif
Scheat
Alpheratz
EQUULEUS
DELPHINUS
ANDROMEDA
M31
Mirach
TRIANGULUM
ARIES
Hamal
Menkar
Almach
LACERTA
Altair
AQUILA
SAGITTA
CYGNUS
Deneb
Galactic Equator
Schedar
Caph
CASSIOPEIA
Ruchbah
H VI 33 34
PERSEUS
Mirfak
Algol
Pleiades
TAURUS
Hyades
Aldebaran
CEPHEUS
LYRA
Vega
Capella
AURIGA
Elnath
Bellatrix
ORION
Betelgeuse
CAMELOPARDALIS
Eltanin
DRACO
Polaris
URSA MINOR
Kochab
M35
MONOCEROS
HERCULES
M92
M13
Rasalhague
OPHIUCHUS
LYNX
GEMINI
Castor
Pollux
CANIS MINOR
Procyon
Dubhe
Merak
Phecda
URSA MAJOR
Mizar
Alioth
Alkaid
CORONA BOREALIS
Alphecca
SERPENS CAPUT
CANES VENATICI
CANCER
M44
LEO MINOR
BOOTES
M3
M5
Arcturus
N. Galactic Pole
COMA BERENICES
HYDRA
Equator
LEO
Regulus
Denebola
SEXTANS
VIRGO
Ecliptic
Star Magnitude
Each unit of magnitude indicates a difference of brightness of 2.512 times. The brightest star is Sirius (mag. −1.45)
0
1
2
3
4
5
Link Line
Variable star
Open star cluster
Globular star cluster

EQUATORIAL ZONE

1 h
0 h
23 h
22 h
21 h
20 h
19 h
18 h
17 h
16 h
15 h
14 h
13 h
+30°
+15°
0°
−15°
−30°
Declination
Right Ascension
ANDROMEDA
Alpheratz
Scheat
CYGNUS
LYRA
CORONA BOREALIS
Alphecca
CANES VENATICI
N. Galactic Pole
COMA BERENICES
PEGASUS
VULPECULA
SAGITTA
HERCULES
BOOTES
Arcturus
Markab
DELPHINUS
Enif
Altair
Rasalhague
SERPENS CAPUT
PISCES
Spring Equinox
Mar 15
EQUULEUS
Equator
AQUILA
OPHIUCHUS
VIRGO
Oct 16
Spica
AQUARIUS
SCUTUM SOBIESKI
SERPENS CAUDA
LIBRA
CETUS
Feb 12
Winter Solstice
Dec 15
Nov 15
Zubenelgenubi
Sabik
CORVUS
Diphda
CAPRICORNUS
Jan 13
Ecliptic
S. Galactic Pole
PISCIS AUSTRINUS
Fomalhaut
SAGITTARIUS
Nunki
Antares
HYDRA
SCULPTOR
MICROSCOPIUM
Kaus Australis
SCORPIUS
LUPUS
CENTAURUS

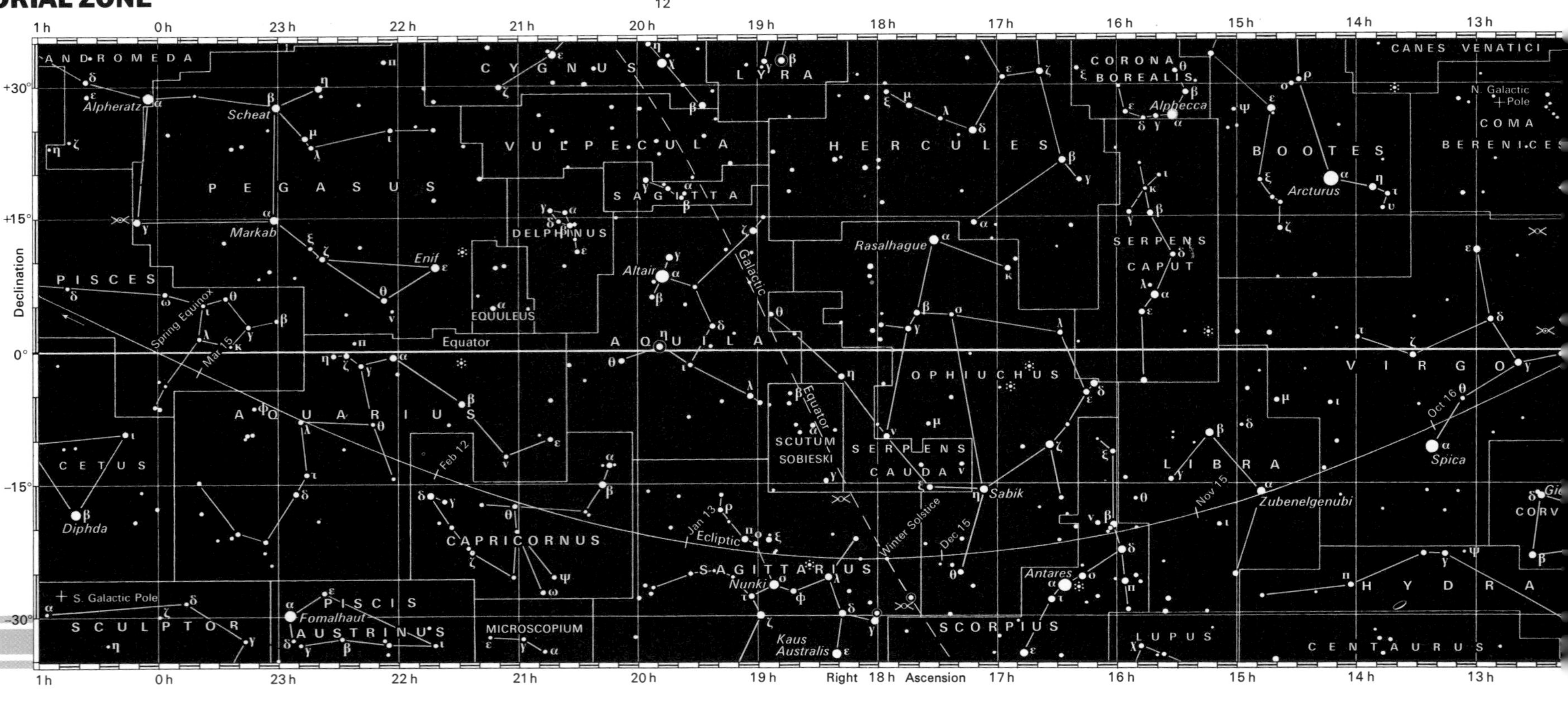

Star Colours and Spectral Types

	*Temp in 000°C	
O-B		50.0–25.0
A		11.0
F		7.5
G		6.0
K		5.0
M		3.5

The surface temperature of a star is indicated both by its colour and its spectrum

Galaxy
Quasar
Radio source
Constellation boundary

0 h R.A.

PISCES
AQUARIUS
CETUS
Diphda
SCULPTOR
S. Galactic Pole
Fomalhaut
PISCIS AUSTRINUS
FORNAX
PHOENIX
Ankaa
GRUS
Al Na'ir
CAPRICORNUS
MICROSCOPIUM
ERIDANUS
Acamar
Achernar
TUCANA
INDUS
AQUILA
HOROLOGIUM
Nubecula Minor
Peacock
SAGITTARIUS
CAELUM
RETICULUM
HYDRUS
PAVO
TELESCOPIUM
CORONA AUSTRINA
Nunki
M22
SCUTUM SOBIESKI
Rigel
ORION
Alnilam
LEPUS
COLUMBA
PICTOR
DORADO
MENSA
OCTANS
APUS
ARA
Kaus Australis
SERPENS CAUDA
Canopus
Nubecula Major
VOLANS
CHAMAELEON
Atria
TRIANGULUM AUSTRALE
Shaula
Direction of centre of the Galaxy
Galactic Nucleus
Sabik
CANIS MAJOR
Sirius
M41
Adhara
Avior
Miaplacidus
CARINA
MUSCA
CIRCINUS
NORMA
SCORPIUS
OPHIUCHUS
Antares
MONOCEROS
Galactic Equator
PUPPIS
Suhail
VELA
Acrux
CRUX
Becrux
Gacrux
Rigil Kent
Hadar
LUPUS
PYXIS
ANTLIA
CENTAURUS
Menkent
LIBRA
HYDRA
Alphard
HYDRA
Zubenelgenubi
SEXTANS
CRATER
CORVUS
Gienah
Spica
VIRGO
LEO
Ecliptic

© John Bartholomew & Son Ltd. Edinburgh

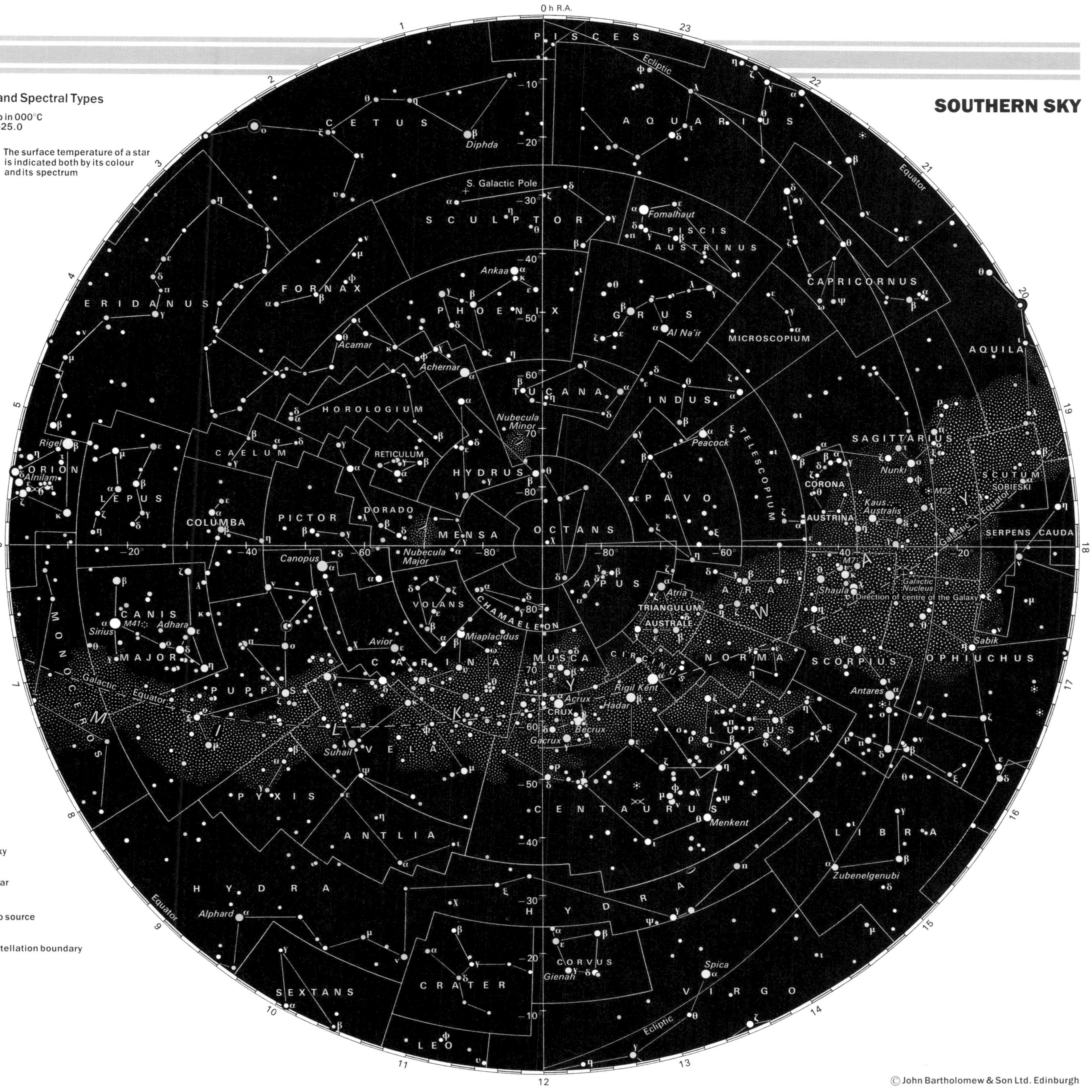

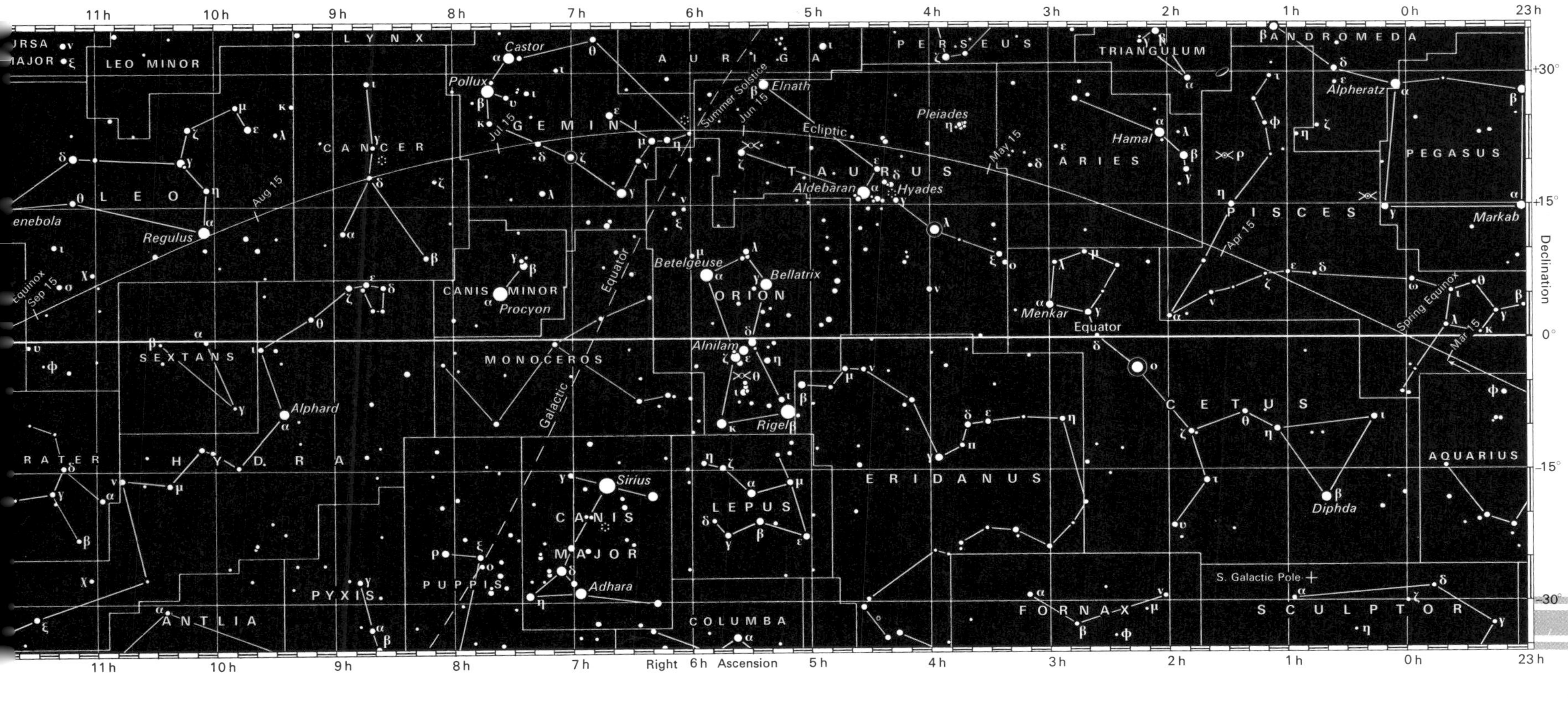

URSA MAJOR
LEO MINOR
LYNX
Castor
Pollux
AURIGA
PERSEUS
TRIANGULUM
ANDROMEDA
CANCER
GEMINI
Elnath
Pleiades
Hamal
ARIES
Alpheratz
PEGASUS
LEO
Regulus
Denebola
Summer Solstice
Ecliptic
TAURUS
Aldebaran
Hyades
PISCES
Markab
CANIS MINOR
Procyon
Betelgeuse
Bellatrix
ORION
Menkar
CETUS
Equator
SEXTANS
Alnilam
MONOCEROS
Galactic
Rigel
Spring Equinox
HYDRA
Alphard
CRATER
CANIS MAJOR
Sirius
LEPUS
ERIDANUS
AQUARIUS
Diphda
PYXIS
PUPPIS
Adhara
COLUMBA
FORNAX
SCULPTOR
S. Galactic Pole
ANTLIA
Right Ascension

UNIVERSE

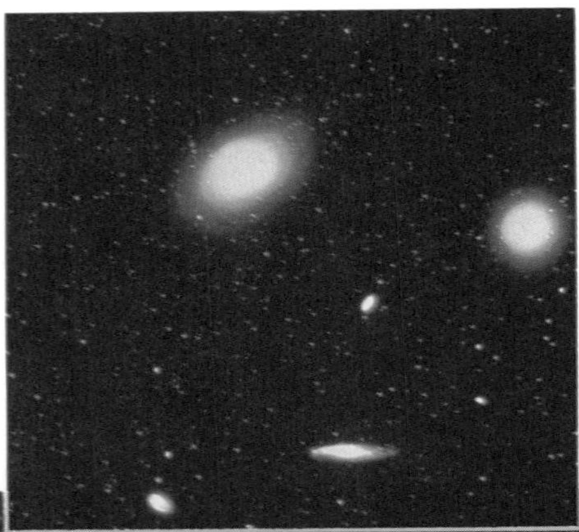

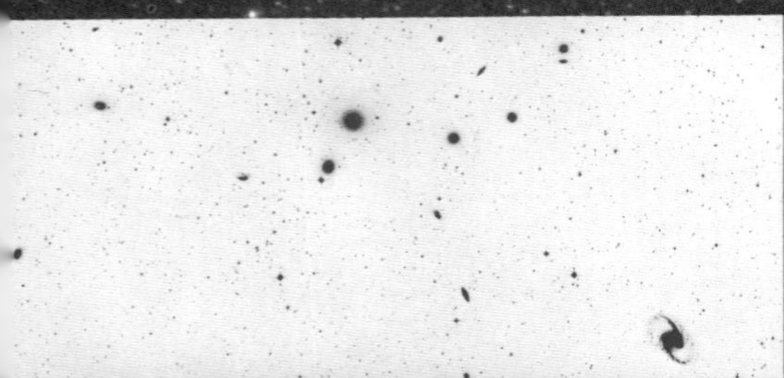

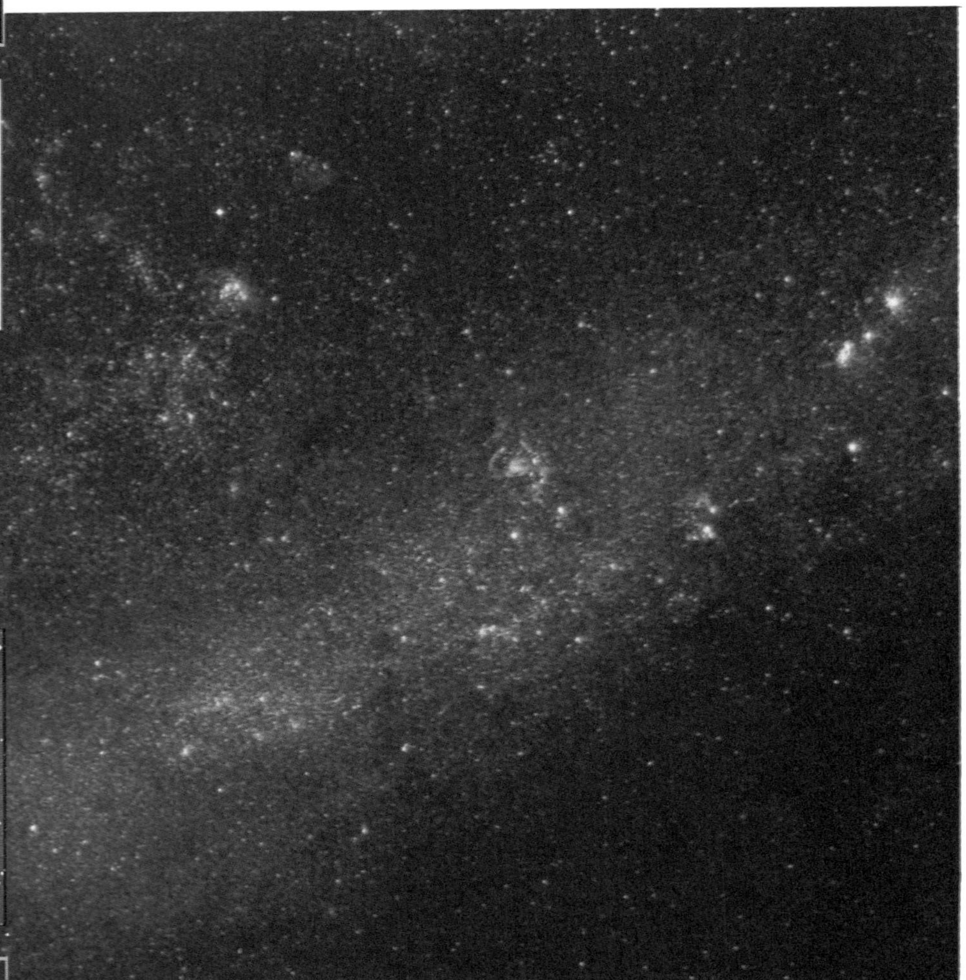

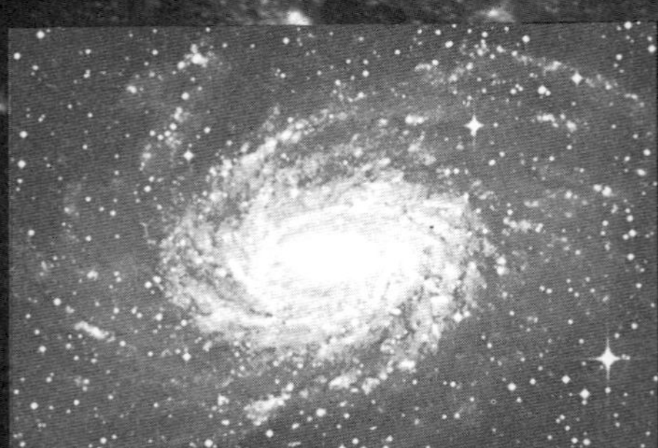

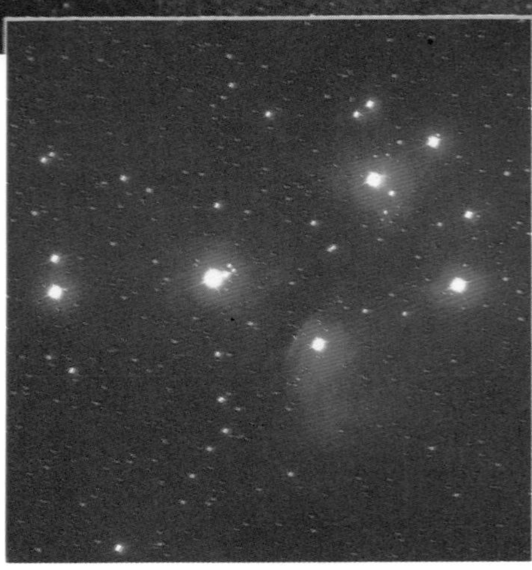

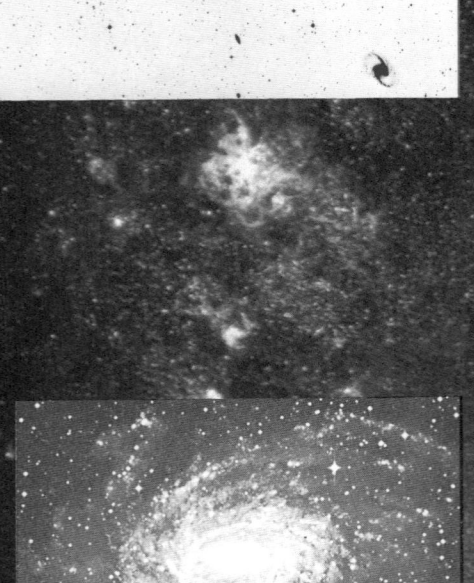

ORIGIN AND STRUCTURE OF THE UNIVERSE

Most astronomers believe that the Universe was created some ten to twenty thousand million years ago in an event often called the big bang or primordial fireball. The subsequent evolution of the universe can be described mathematically but the very early stages in particular are difficult to imagine.

The very high temperature mix of particles and radiation, the products of the big bang, expanded and cooled quickly allowing hydrogen and helium atoms to form and gravitate together to form huge clouds of gas. Turbulence within these contracting clouds caused them to fragment into rotating galaxy-sized clouds. Within these primitive galaxies smaller gas clouds condensed into clusters of stars, populating the galaxies much as we see them today. Most of these galaxies still belong to clusters, some containing thousands of members. There are probably several thousand million galaxies within the universe to the farthest distance so far observed.

Due to light travelling through space at a finite speed we see distant objects as they were when the light left them and in looking deep into space we also look far back in time. Over the past 40 years, larger optical telescopes, radio telescopes, space-borne instruments and computers have allowed astronomers to study the universe over a much wider range of the electromagnetic spectrum, much of it inaccessible from the Earth's surface.

Some galaxies are powerful emitters of radio waves and quasars, probably the nuclei of early galaxies, were first discovered by radio methods and later identified with optical objects: they appear so compact that they were mistaken for stars in our own galaxy. Many show very large 'red shifts' interpreted as velocities of recession which would make them amongst the most distant objects known. If all quasars are distant objects, it means that either our part of the universe is different from the rest or that they only occurred early on in the history of the universe. However, a few very experienced astronomers still believe they are nearer objects and that their red shifts have another origin. Perhaps the most difficult problem to be faced is that of finding reliable confirmation of estimates for the distances of the more distant galaxies and quasars.

In intergalactic space the more distant the object, the faster it seems to be receding from us. This is the expanding universe and the Hubble constant relates speed and distance. Already we believe we see objects receding at speeds approaching that of light or more then four-fifths of the way back to the big bang. However, the study of the universe even closer to its origin will be increasingly difficult and the moment of the big bang itself will be forever inaccessible to observation but the predicted isotropic background radiation from soon after this event has been observed.

Astronomy moves forward by theories to account for observations and further observations to test these theories. Two generally accepted simplifying principles were that our part of the universe is typical of the whole and that the same physical laws we apply to the present can also be applied to the past. The second principle is difficult to test back beyond the age of the Earth.

It is becoming more difficult to say what is a typical part of the universe now that surveys have confirmed a picture of the clustering of clusters of galaxies, which seem to be concentrated on a very large scale into 'walls' or surfaces with large intervening voids, likened to the surfaces of bubbles. Did these galaxies condense from this early distribution of gas or have these structures formed from existing galaxies? The formation of galaxies was probably largely completed within the first five billion years after the big bang when the universe was smaller, so the more distant galaxies or clusters of galaxies should be more closely packed as we look back into the past. This would be easier to test if galaxies were randomly distributed in space as was once thought and not concentrated in superclusters.

The average density of matter in the universe is thought to determine its future evolution, whether it will continue to grow larger, slow to a halt or eventually begin to contract. A current problem is that all the matter so far discovered in the universe in galaxies, interstellar dust and gas, stars and other forms appears to be insufficient to account for the behaviour of the universe as we find it. Some astronomers believe that as much as nine-tenths of the total matter in the universe remains to be discovered. It could be in the form of intergalactic matter, faint or dead stars or black holes, or hard to detect atomic particles such as neutrinos.

Black holes have been postulated to explain the origin of intense but small energy sources. If they exist they are so dense that not even light can escape from them so they can only be studied from the effects they have on nearby matter and radiation. Their strong gravitational fields draw in dust, gas, stars and perhaps even galaxies and the enormous amounts of energy released as this matter falls together and heats up produces light, heat and radio waves. As they become more massive their sphere of influence grows larger. Quasars may be the observable effects of the largest of black holes of the early universe, producing more light than a whole galaxy and very strong radiation at radio wavelengths. At the other end of the scale uncountable small or even microscopic black holes have been proposed to account for some extra mass. Knowledge of the nature, form and whereabouts of this 'missing mass' is of urgent importance.

Main picture The Large Magellanic Cloud (Nebecula Major), at 160,000 light years, is our nearest neighbour galaxy. The bright object (left centre) is the 30 Doradus or 'Tarantula' nebula near which SN1987A appeared.

Top Some of the thousands of elliptical and spiral galaxies in the Virgo cluster.

Top centre The Fornax cluster forms a small part of the Southern Supercluster of galaxies.

Bottom centre The spiral galaxy NGC 6744. Our galaxy is similar but being in a spiral arm ourselves, we see our stars concentrated into a bright band, the Milky Way.

Bottom The Pleiades (the 'seven sisters' of mythology) is a conspicuous star cluster in Taurus. Formed 80 million years ago, this cluster is 400 light years away.

Below In February 1987 a supernova (SN1987A) was discovered in the Large Magellanic Cloud being visible to the naked eye despite the LMC's great distance. The false-colour image by the Hubble Space Telescope in August 1990 shows expanding debris surrounding the exploding star as a red blob in the centre of the yellow ring of gas (1.3 light years across). This gas, expelled from the star thousands of years earlier, is being made to shine by radiation from the supernova explosion. The two blue stars to the left and right are not associated with the supernova.

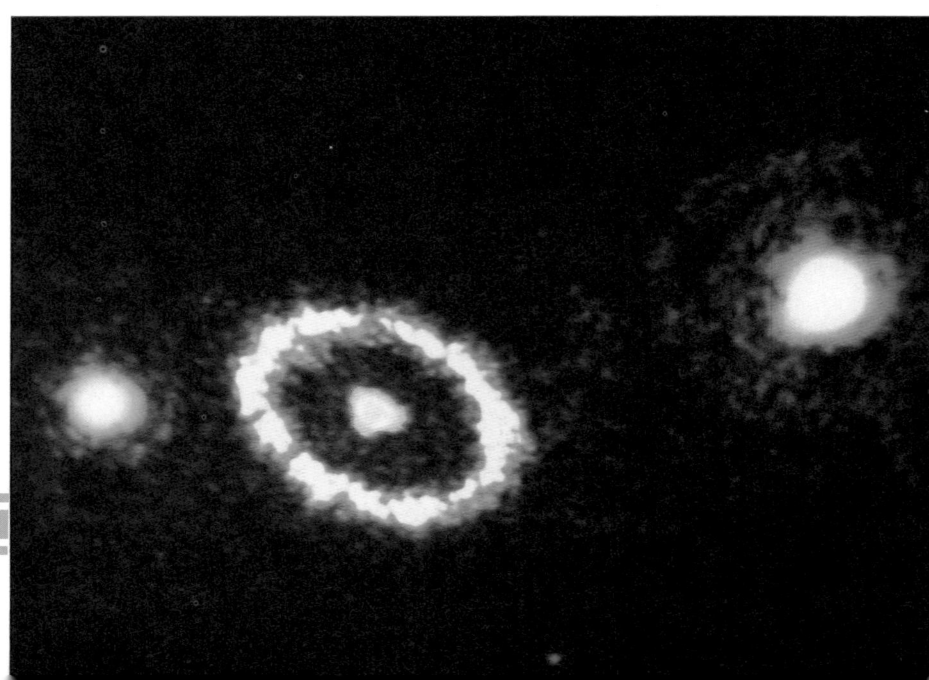

GALAXIES AND STARS

Galaxies take many forms from the giant globular galaxies, through ellipticals, spirals, barred spirals to irregular forms. This was once thought to be an evolutionary sequence but is now believed to reflect the speed with which star formation proceeded, the ellipticals turning their gas into stars before there was time for some of it to flatten into a disc where star formation could continue to form spiral arms.

The Virgo cluster is 75 million light years away and contains thousands of galaxies. On its fringes is the Local Group which contains our Milky Way system (the Galaxy), two other large spiral galaxies, the Magellanic Clouds and about twenty-five other smaller galaxies. These all lie within a distance of 5 million light years and form a gravitationally-bound group. In these galaxies astronomers can recognise many individual bright stars and nebulae while only exceptionally bright objects such as supernovae are visible in more distant galaxies.

Our Galaxy is a spiral, some hundred thousand light years across containing one or two hundred thousand million stars. At its centre in the direction of the great star clouds in Sagittarius is a massive core which may be like a supercluster of stars, almost a small galaxy in itself, and some astronomers believe, a black hole. The centre of the Galaxy is hidden by dust clouds from optical telescopes but these are largely transparent to some infrared and radio waves.

Like other similar galaxies it has two populations of stars. Population II stars form a more globular distribution and were formed first from hydrogen and helium. Population I stars lie mostly in the plane of the spiral arms and formed later from the flattened gas clouds and contain some heavier elements produced inside the first generation stars which were later expelled into space by exploding stars called supernovae. The Sun condensed from this contaminated gas and dust, and some of the matter left over from the birth of the Sun became the solar system. Without these heavier elements created inside stars there could be no Earth and no life as we know it. Elliptical galaxies contain mainly Population II stars.

Stars are still forming inside clouds of dust and gas such as the Horsehead Nebula in Orion. As the globules of gas contract they heat up until nuclear reactions start in their cores, turning hydrogen into helium. The outflow of radiation blows away remaining dust and gas to reveal a new star cluster. The stars are moving round the galactic centre, along with everything else in the Galaxy, and in time the stars in the cluster will disperse. The spiral arms are the areas of a galaxy where star formation is continuing and are mainly defined by a relatively small number of very bright hot stars. The bulk of the faint stars which greatly predominate are more uniformly spread throughout the galaxy.

The most massive stars use up their main source of energy quickly and fade within a

few million years while a star such as the Sun, a yellow dwarf star, has been in much the same state for five thousand million years and will continue for as long again before major changes take place. When it can no longer convert hydrogen into helium it will start to convert helium to heavier elements swelling to become a red giant, enveloping the Earth and inner planets. However, these reactions can only proceed so far and as less heat is produced the Sun will shrink to become a very dense hot white dwarf about the size of the Earth, later cooling and fading to obscurity. Stars more than 1.4 times the mass of the Sun are unstable in the white-dwarf stage and collapse into even smaller bodies only a few kilometres across called neutron stars.

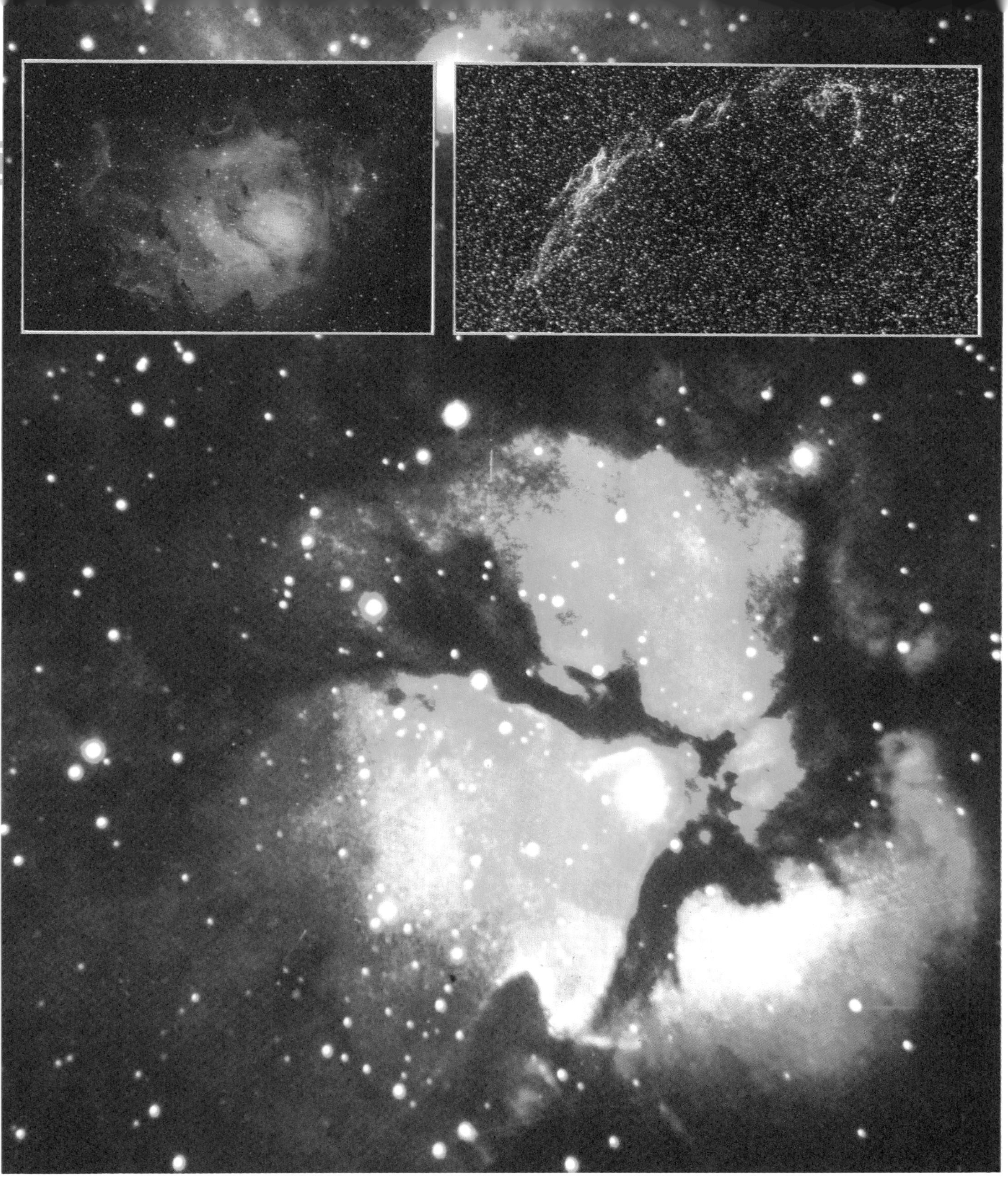

Above The Trifid Nebula is an example of a vast cloud of gas and dust. Globules of cold gas develop and condense and form new stars.
Below left The Hubble Space Telescope was released from the Shuttle Discovery in 1991. At 540 km above the Earth, objects can now be observed unhindered by the atmosphere.

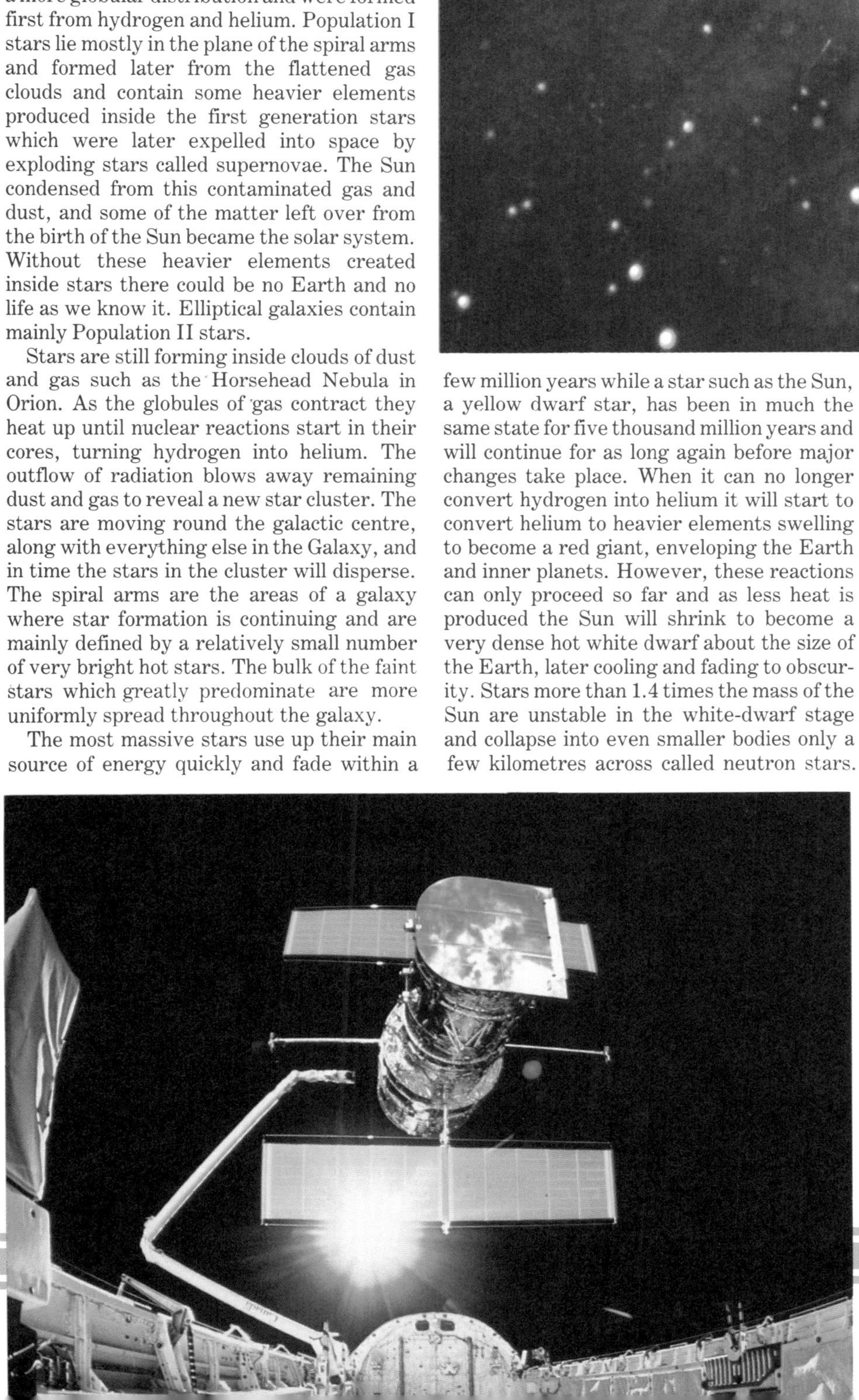

Some collapse towards this stage so rapidly that the sudden generation of radiation blows off the outer layers of the star in a supernova explosion, for a few weeks giving off as much light as a whole galaxy of stars. Indeed supernovae are regularly observed in distant galaxies and can outshine the combined light of billions of more ordinary stars.

Early sky surveys revealed that many stars have companions; they appear double. Some were just chance alignments, but in many cases the stars are revolving around each other. The spectrograph reveals binary stars too close together to be seen directly. Stars show a wide variation in their colour, which is a measure of surface temperature, ranging from hot blue stars like Rigel through cooler yellow stars like Capella and the Sun to cool red stars like Betelgeuse. The spectrograph also tells astronomers about stars' composition.

Double stars give us stars' masses which range from about 50 times to one tenth that of the Sun while their diameters range from 2000 times the Sun to a hundredth or less. Stars differ in intrinsic brightness from 50,000 times (Deneb, Rigel) to only one-

Top left The Lagoon Nebula in the constellation of Sagittarius consists of a cloud of hydrogen and dust. The brightest region includes the new star Herschel 36, less than 10 000 years old.
Top right The Veil Nebula in Cygnus is the remnant of a supernova. The dust will eventually break up into small cold clouds.

thousandth that of the Sun. Many stars vary in brightness, the more violent changes occurring in novae and in supernovae where the collapse in seconds of a complete star can make it appear as bright as a whole galaxy.

Astronomers' means of studying the universe have widened dramatically over the past fifty years. Parts of the energy spectrum inaccessible from the ground can be studied from artificial satellites, from gamma rays, X-rays, ultra violet to some infrared wavelengths while infrared telescopes and radio telescopes are operated on the ground. New detectors, much more sensitive than photographic film, are now commonplace, and computer-controlled optics are making it possible to build eight- and ten-metre aperture optical telescopes. Radio telescopes on different continents can be linked together to give an equivalent aperture of thousands of kilometres, allowing very fine structure to be studied that even the best optical telescopes are unable to resolve. The Hubble Space Telescope, despite its problems, shows much finer detail than telescopes on the surface of the Earth. New facilities to detect neutrinos and gravity waves are planned.

SOLAR SYSTEM

Current theory suggests that the solar system condensed from a primitive solar nebula of gas and dust during an interval of a few tens of millions of years about 4600 million years ago. Gravity caused this nebula to contract, drawing most of its mass into the proto-sun at the centre. Turbulence gave the original cloud a tendency to rotate, and as it contracted conservation of angular momentum caused the proto-sun to spin faster and faster, forcing the remainder of the cloud into a disc shape.

The centre of the cloud heated up as it compressed, and so eventually became hot enough for the Sun to begin to shine, through nuclear energy released at its core. Meanwhile the surrounding disc cooled, allowing material to condense into solid form. Particles stuck together as they col-

lided and progressively larger bodies were built up. These swept up most of the debris to form the planets, which orbit the Sun close to the plane of the now vanished disc. The first materials to condense were the least volatile refractory compounds such as oxides of iron, nickel and aluminium. Decreasing temperature allowed rocky silicate material to appear followed by more volatile compounds such as water and methane. Thus composition of the planets progressed from less refractory cores to more volatile outer layers.

The planets nearest to the Sun are dense with metallic cores mantled by rocky silicate materials; planets further from the Sun accreted and retained large volumes of volatiles and are thus much more massive. They may have cores of rock and ice, surround-

ed by solid or liquid hydrogen enveloped in thick gassy atmospheres. These Gas Giants are accompanied by captured rocky and icy satellites which are mostly too small to have accreted and held atmospheres.

The subsequent evolution of the solar system was dominated by continuing chemical segregation within the planets and surface bombardment by waning numbers of smaller bodies. This bombardment was over by 3–4000 million years ago, although minor impacts still occur. Traces of these events remain on the surfaces of those bodies which have insufficient internal heat to drive any kind of resurfacing process.

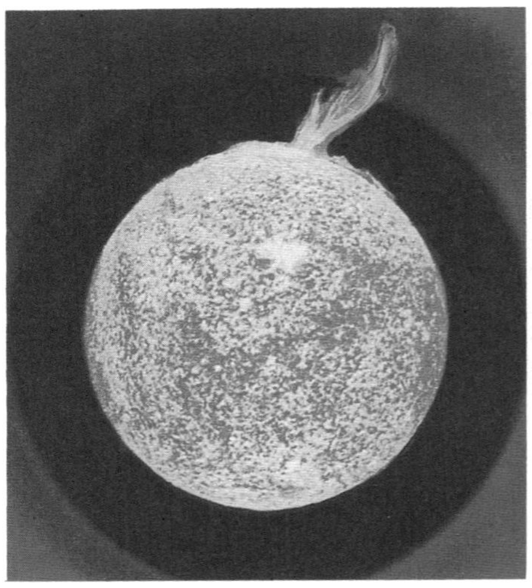

Right An ultra-violet image of the Sun from Skylab in 1973. A spectacular eruption of gas rises for half a million kilometres, channelled by the Sun's magnetic field.

	SUN	MERCURY	VENUS	EARTH	(MOON)	MARS	JUPITER	SATURN	URANUS	NEPTUNE	PLUTO
Mass (Earth=1)	333 400	0.055	0.815	1 (5.97 10^{24}kg)	0.012	0.107	317.8	95.2	14.5	17.2	0.003
Volume (Earth=1)	1 306 000	0.06	0.88	1	0.020	0.150	1 323	752	64	54	0.007
Density (water=1)	1.41	5.43	5.24	5.52	3.34	3.94	1.33	0.70	1.30	1.64	2.0
Equatorial diameter (km)	1 392 000	4878	12 104	12 756	3 476	6 794	142 800	120 000	52 000	48 400	2 302
Polar flattening	0	0	0	0.003	0	0.005	0.065	0.108	0.060	0.021	0
'Surface' gravity (Earth=1)	27.9	0.37	0.88	1	0.16	0.38	2.69	1.19	0.93	1.22	0.05
Number of satellites greater than 100 km diameter	—	0	0	1	—	0	7	13	7	6	1
Total number of satellites	—	0	0	1	—	2	16	17	15	8	1
Period of rotation (in Earth days)	25.38	58.65	−243 (retrograde)	23hr 56m 4 secs	27.32	1.03	0.414	0.426	−0.74 (retrograde)	0.67	−6.39 (retrograde)
Length of year (in Earth days and years)	—	88 days	224.7 days	365.26 days	—	687 days	11.86 years	29.46 years	84.01 years	164.8 years	247.7 years
Distance from Sun (max) Mkm	—	69.7	109	152.1	—	249.1	815.7	1 507	3 004	4 537	7 375
Distance from Sun (min) Mkm	—	45.9	107.4	147.1	—	206.7	740.9	1 347	2 735	4 456	4 425
Distance from Sun (mean) Mkm	—	57.9	108.9	149.6	—	227.9	778.3	1 427	2 870	4 497	5 900
Mean orbital velocity km/sec	—	47.9	35.0	29.8	—	24.1	13.1	9.6	6.8	5.4	4.7
Inclination of equator to orbit plane	7.25°	0.0°	177.3°	23.45°	6.68°	25.19°	3.12°	26.73°	97.86°	29.56°	122°
Inclination of orbit to ecliptic	—	7.01°	3.39°	0°	5.15°	1.85°	1.30°	2.48°	0.77°	1.77°	17.13°

	Mean Distance from Planet (1 000km)	Orbital Period (days) R=retrograde	Diameter (km)*
Mars			
Phobos	9.38	0.319	28x22x18
Deimos	23.46	1.262	16x12x12
Jupiter			
Metis	128.00	0.295	(40)
Adrastrea	129.00	0.297	(24x16)
Amalthea	181.30	0.498	(270x150)
Thebe	221.90	0.675	(100)
Io	421.60	1.769	3 630
Europa	670.90	3.551	3 138
Ganymede	1 070.00	7.155	5 262
Callisto	1 880.00	16.689	4 800
Leda	11 094.00	238.700	(15)
Himalia	11 480.00	250.600	(180)
Lysithea	11 720.00	259.200	(40)
Elara	11 737.00	259.700	(80)
Ananke	21 200.00	631R	(30)
Carme	22 600.00	692R	(45)
Pasiphae	23 500.00	735R	(70)
Sinope	23 700.00	758R	(40)
Saturn			
Atlas	137.70	0.602	40x30
Prometheus	139.50	0.613	140x80
Pandora	141.70	0.629	110x70
Epimetheus	151.40	0.694	140x100
Janus	151.50	0.695	220x160
Mimas	185.50	0.942	392
Enceladus	238.00	1.370	500
Tethys	294.70	1.888	1 060
Telesto	294.70	1.888	(24)
Calypso	294.70	1.888	30x20
Dione	377.40	2.737	1 120
Helene	377.40	2.737	36x30
Rhea	527.00	4.518	1 530
Titan	1 221.80	15.945	5 150
Hyperion	1 481.10	21.277	350x200
Iapetus	3 561.30	79.331	1 440
Phoebe	12 952.00	550.480R	220
Uranus			
Cordelia	49.75	0.335	(30)
Ophelia	53.76	0.376	(30)
Bianca	59.16	0.435	(50)
Cressida	61.77	0.464	(70)
Desdemona	62.66	0.475	(60)
Juliet	64.36	0.493	(80)
Portia	66.09	0.513	(110)
Rosalind	69.92	0.588	(60)
Belinda	75.26	0.624	(70)
Puck	85.89	0.762	150
Miranda	129.40	1.414	470
Ariel	191.20	2.520	1 160
Umbriel	266.00	4.144	1 170
Titania	435.90	8.706	1 580
Oberon	582.60	13.463	1 520
Neptune			
Naiad	48.20	0.296	(50)
Thalassa	50.00	0.312	(80)
Despina	52.50	0.333	(180)
Galatea	62.00	0.429	(150)
Larissa	73.60	0.554	(190)
Proteus	117.60	1.121	(400)
Triton	354.80	5.877	2 700
Nereid	5 513.40	360.160	(340)
Pluto			
Charon	19.64	6.387	1 190

*Many satellites are not spherical in shape, in which case two or three axes are quoted. Dimensions given in brackets are uncertain by at least ten per cent.

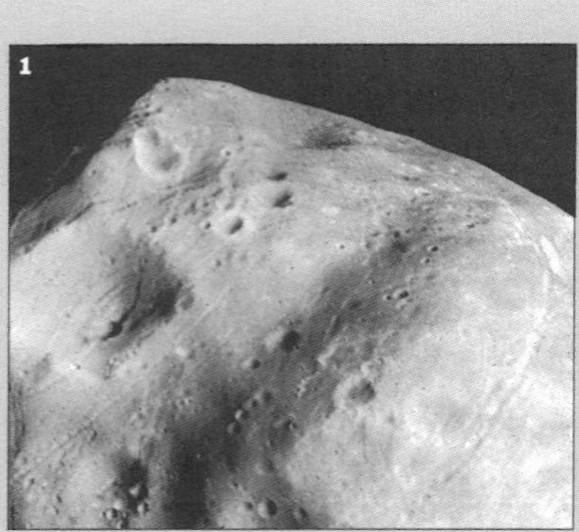

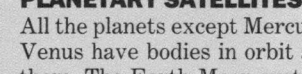

PLANETARY SATELLITES

All the planets except Mercury and Venus have bodies in orbit around them. The Earth-Moon system can be described as a double planet, whereas Mars' two satellites appear to be captured asteroids. The Gas Giants have a greater number of satellites ranging from bodies of less than 100 km across to larger moons of around 1000 km in diameter with rocky cores and usually icy crusts. Some of the more interesting bodies are illustrated here: the table on the left gives the full list.

1 Deimos is the smaller, outer irregular-shaped moon of Mars. The surface is covered by about 10 metres of loose rock.
2 The dark background material of **Ganymede** shows a high density of impact craters. The lighter network of grooves may have been formed by movements of the ice crust.
3 Callisto is among the most cratered in the Solar System with a surface at least 4 billion years old.
4 This Voyager 1 image of **Io** shows a plume of vaporized sulphur rising for 300 km above the first known active extraterrestrial volcano, Pele.
5 Titan is Saturn's largest moon and holds an extremely dense

atmosphere of nitrogen and methane above a surface of rock and ice.
6 Enceladus has experienced recent geological activity which has modified the cratered landscape.
7 The surface of **Mimas** is heavily cratered and shows no sign of geological activity.
8 This Voyager 2 mosaic of **Miranda** shows a variety of geological features.
9 Much of **Ariel**'s surface is pitted with craters 5 to 10 kms across and criss-crossed by valleys.
10 Titania displays many impact scars and also evidence of geological activity.

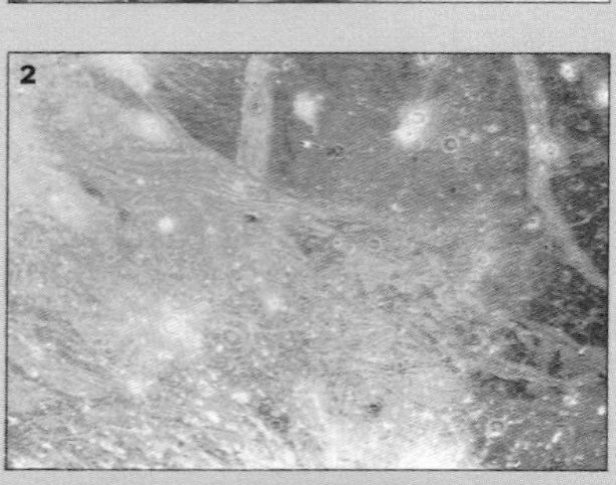

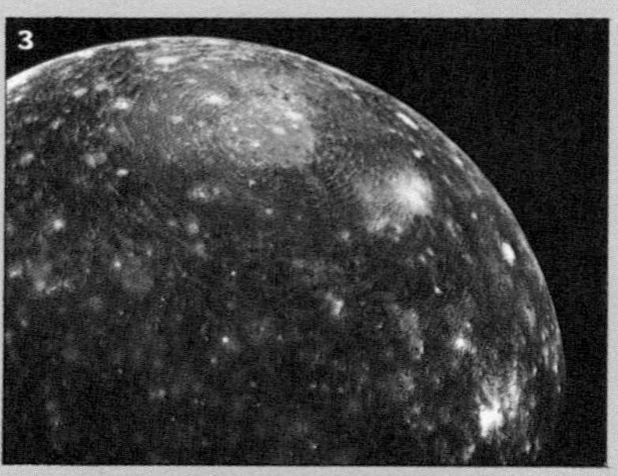

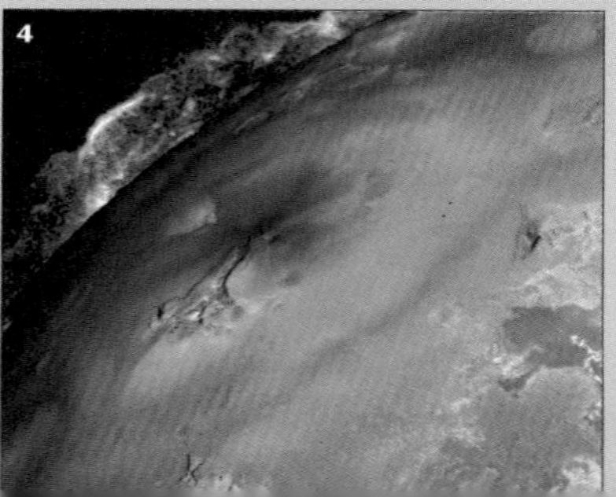

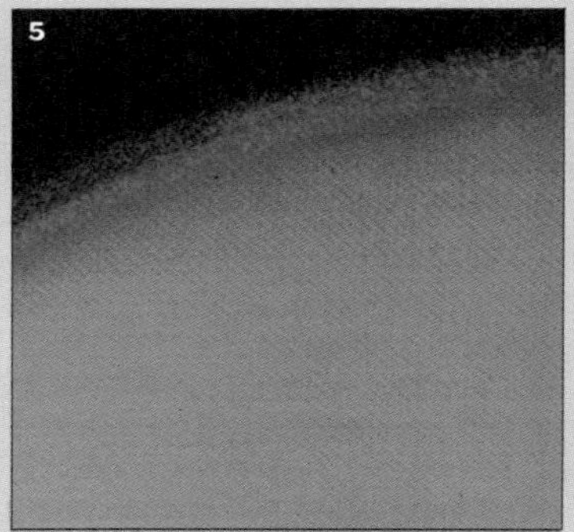

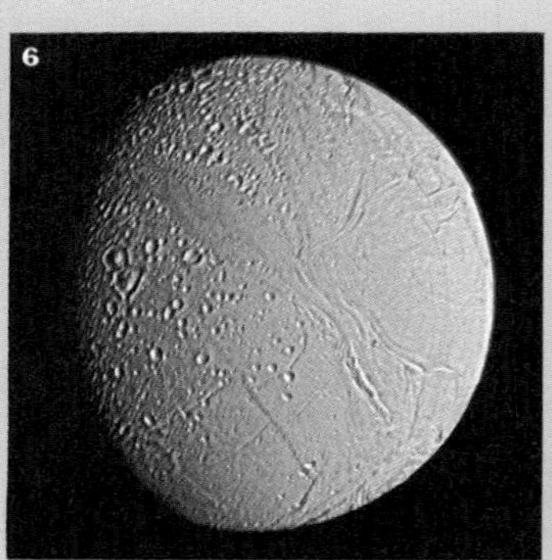

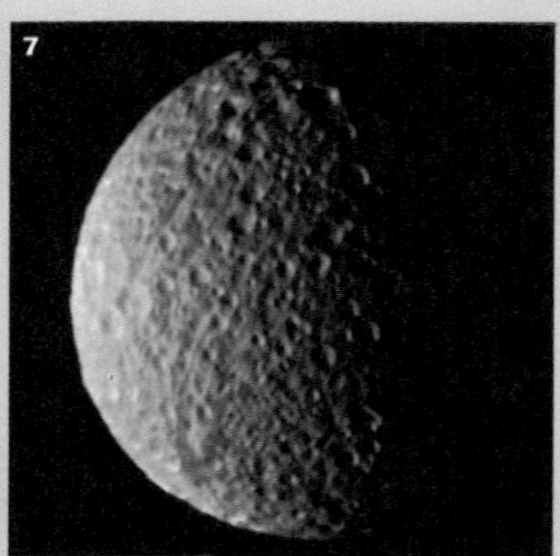

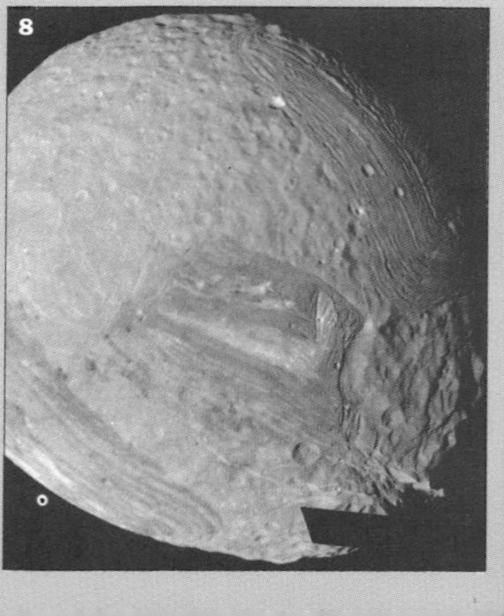

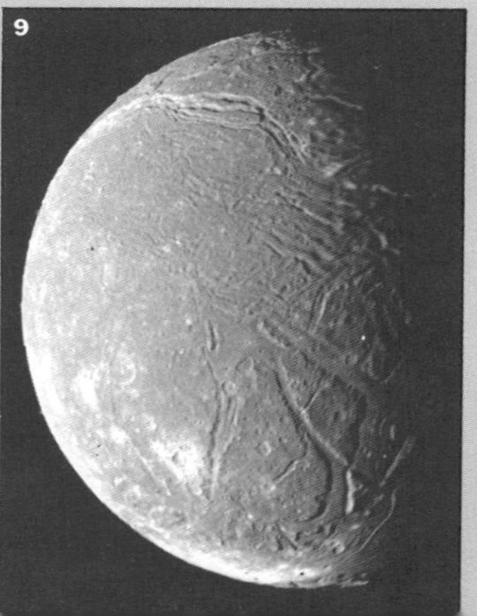

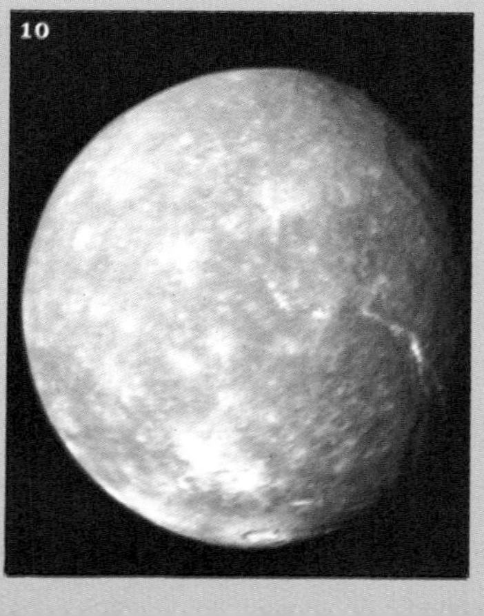

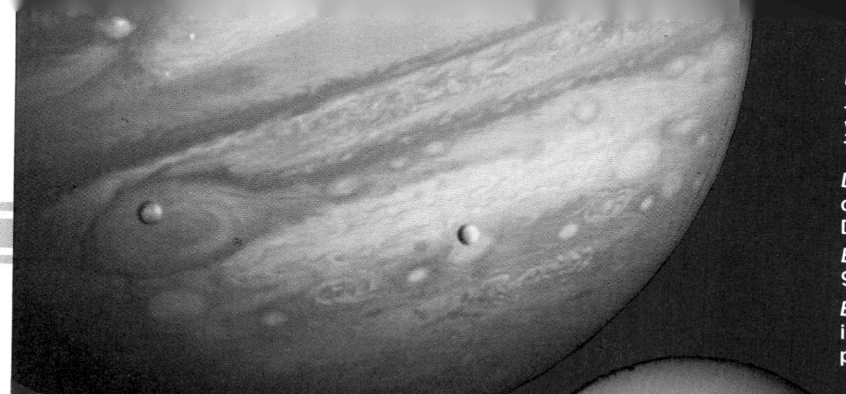

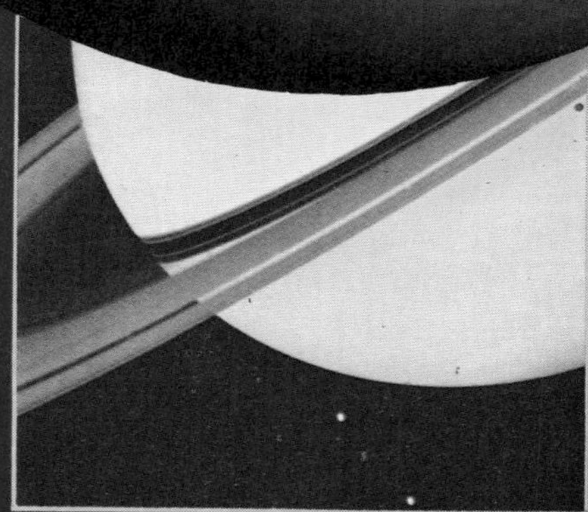

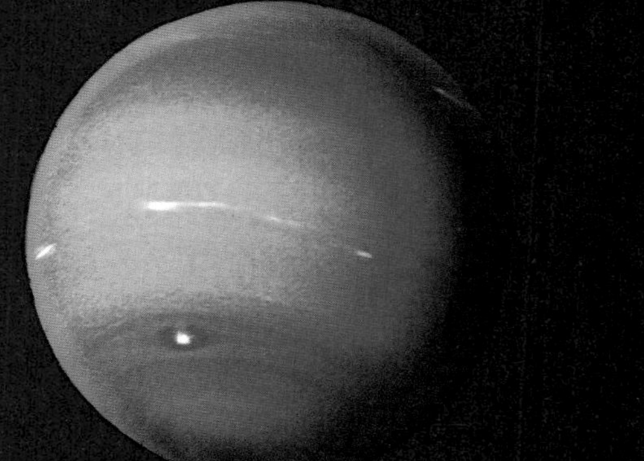

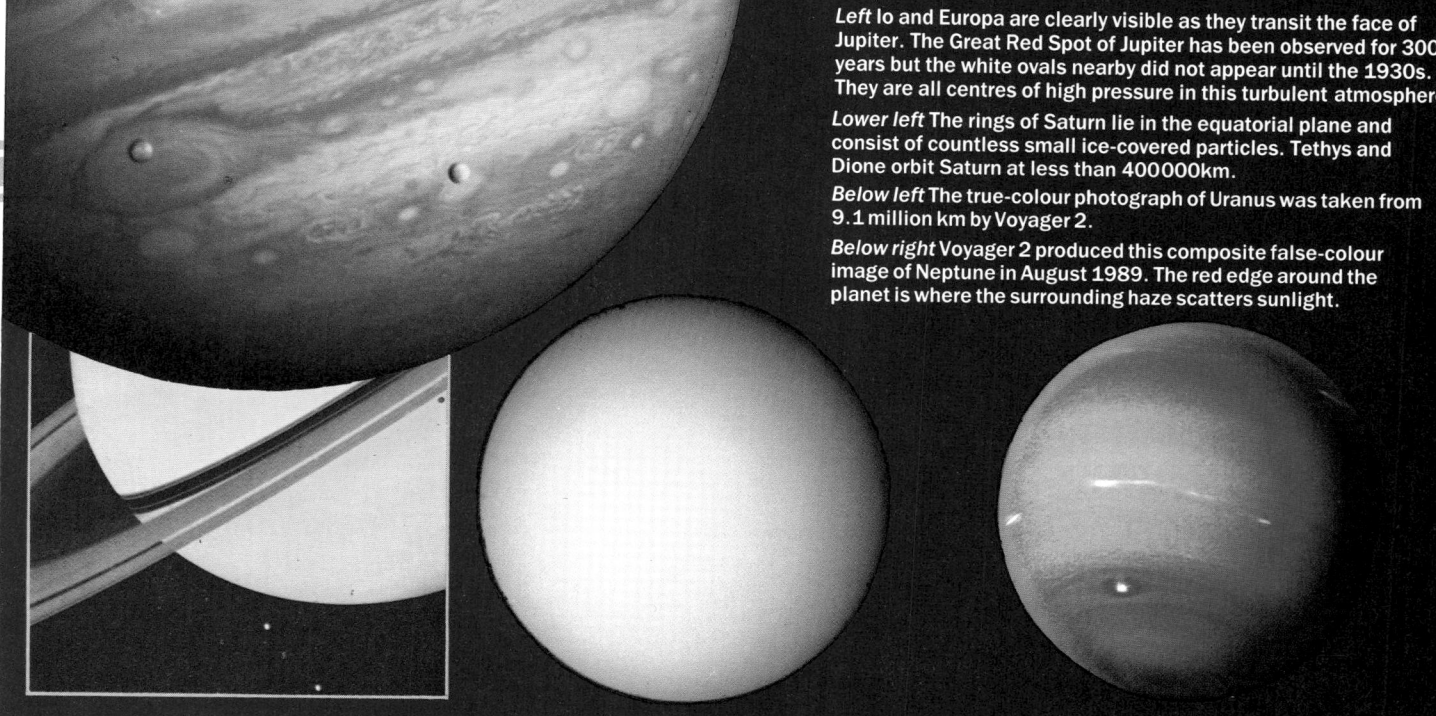

Left Io and Europa are clearly visible as they transit the face of Jupiter. The Great Red Spot of Jupiter has been observed for 300 years but the white ovals nearby did not appear until the 1930s. They are all centres of high pressure in this turbulent atmosphere.

Lower left The rings of Saturn lie in the equatorial plane and consist of countless small ice-covered particles. Tethys and Dione orbit Saturn at less than 400000km.

Below left The true-colour photograph of Uranus was taken from 9.1 million km by Voyager 2.

Below right Voyager 2 produced this composite false-colour image of Neptune in August 1989. The red edge around the planet is where the surrounding haze scatters sunlight.

GAS GIANTS

Jupiter has at least 16 satellites and a debris ring system about 50000km above the cloud tops. The outer atmosphere is all that can be directly observed of the planet itself. It is mostly hydrogen with lesser amounts of helium, ammonia, methane, water vapour and more exotic compounds. Jupiter's rapid rotation causes it to be flattened towards the poles. This rotation and heat flow convection from the interior cause complex weather patterns. Liquid droplets and solid particles of ammonia and other compounds, cause the clouds to be opaque. Where cloud systems interact vast storms can occur in the form of vortices. Some last only a few days, but the most persistent of these, the Great Red Spot, has been present since it was first detected in the 17th century.

The internal structure of Jupiter can be deduced. At about 1000km below the cloud tops hydrogen and helium may liquify to form a 10000km layer. Convection currents in this region generate the planet's intense magnetic field. The denser core, about 4% of the planet's mass, is mostly of rock and ice, with a little iron near the centre.

Saturn is the least dense of the planets. It has a stormy atmosphere situated above a 30000km layer of liquid molecular hydrogen and helium distorted by the planet's rotation. Below is a thin shell of liquid metallic hydrogen wrapped around a rock and ice core containing 25% of Saturn's mass.

The rings of Saturn are thought to be mostly made of icy debris, from 10m down to a few microns in size, derived from the break-up of a satellite. The rings are less than 1km thick but extend from above the cloud layer out to about 170000km from the centre. The rings are divided by gaps swept clear by complex gravitational interaction.

Uranus was little known until Voyager 2 flew by it in January 1986. It has a cloud cover even more featureless than either Jupiter or Saturn, and consists mostly of hydrogen. Unique among the planets, its axis is tilted almost into the plane of its orbit, with the south pole presently facing towards the Sun. Voyager 2 discovered ten more satellites and provided detailed images of the planet's eleven rings of icy debris.

Neptune provided a number of surprises when Voyager 2 flew by, on 24 August 1989, passing within 5,000 km of the planet's north pole. The planet rotates in 16 hours 3 minutes, one hour faster than was believed to be the rate. Six new satellites were discovered, all irregular in shape and with impact craters, little changed since soon after their formation. Neptune has four rings. The magnetic axis is inclined 50° to the axis of rotation and displaced 10,000 km from the centre. Neptune's atmosphere, a mixture of hydrogen, helium and methane, exhibits great turbulence. There is a great dark spot at 22°S latitude and a smaller dark spot nearer the south pole. Triton was found to be smaller than previous estimates.

Pluto, usually the most distant planet, is temporarily within the orbit of Neptune. The atmosphere is thought to be composed mostly of methane.

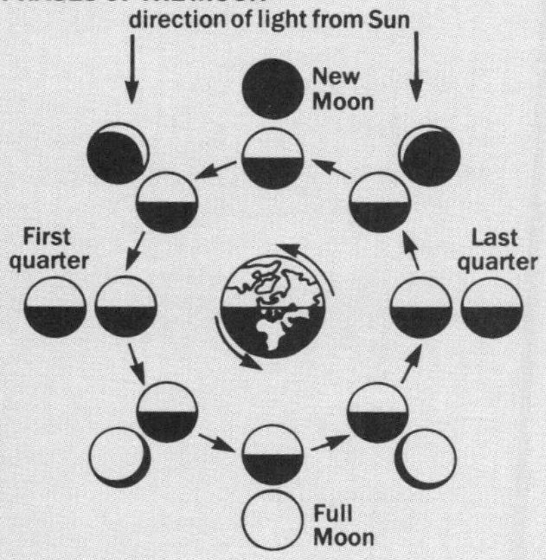

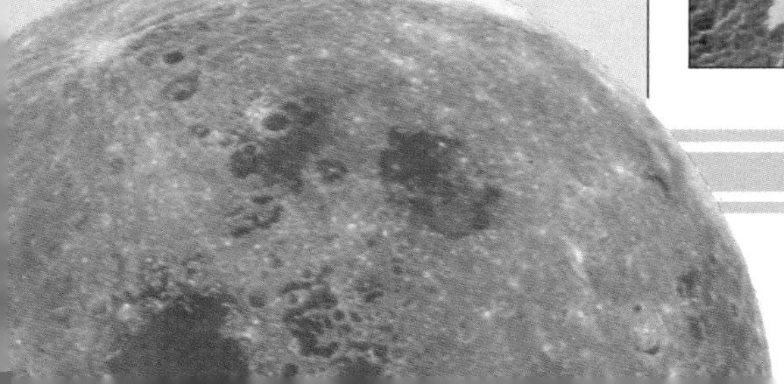

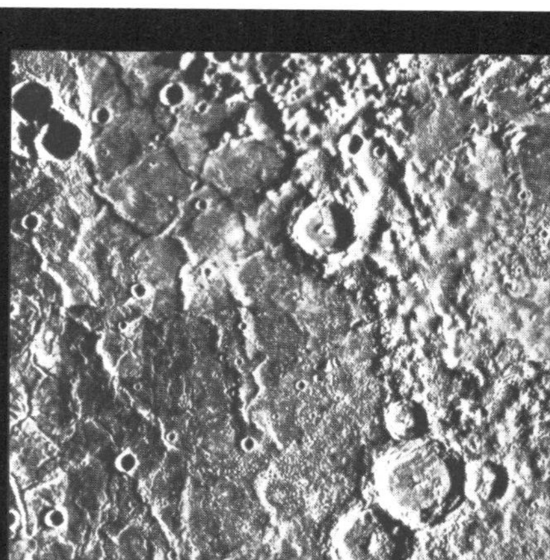

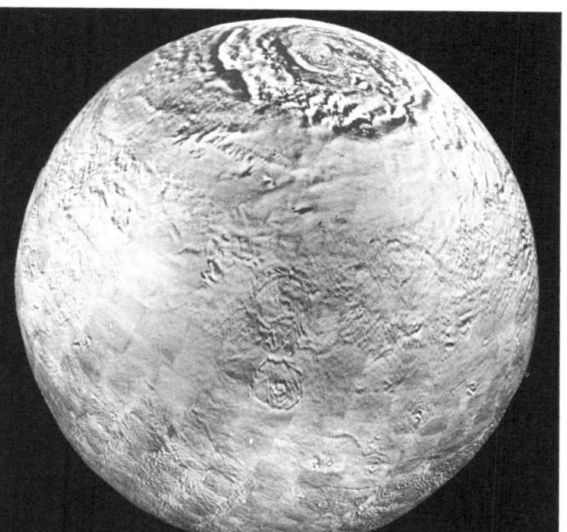

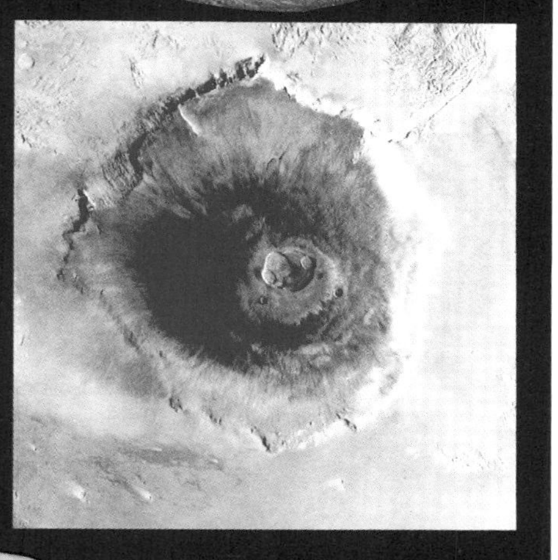

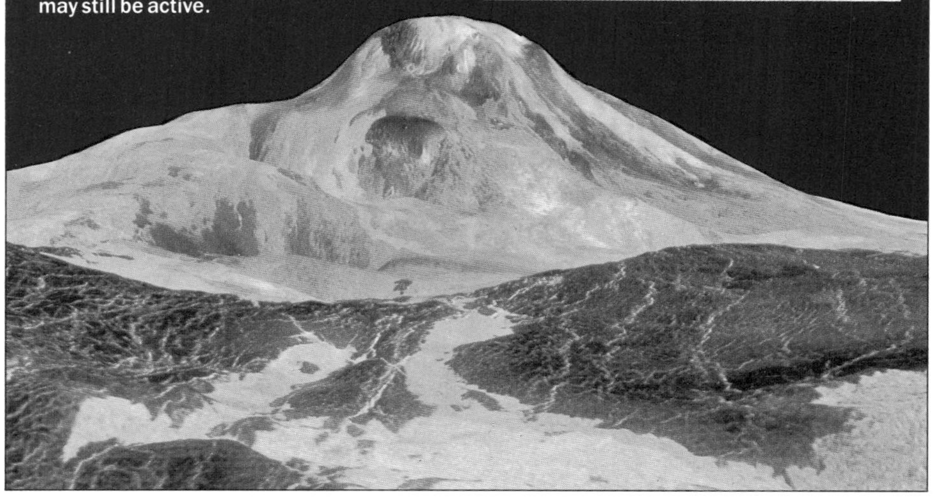

EARTHLIKE PLANETS

Mercury is the nearest planet to the Sun, spinning three times for every two orbits around the Sun. It has an exceptionally large metallic core which may be responsible for Mercury's weak magnetic field. Mercury is an airless world subject to vast extremes of temperature, from –180°C at night to 430°C near the middle of its long day.

The Mariner 10 spacecraft probe during the mid-1970s, revealed the surface to be dominated by heavily cratered areas dating from the early meteorite bombardment of the inner solar system. As the bombardment was tailing off Mercury's radius contracted by between 1 and 2km, forming compressional features (lobate scarps) which may have been caused by a change in the core from liquid to solid.

Venus has a dense atmosphere of 96% carbon dioxide mixed with nitrogen, oxygen, sulphur dioxide and water vapour which hides the surface under permanent cloud and maintains a mean surface temperature of about 480°C. The planet's slow rotation means that weather systems are driven mostly by solar heat, rather than by spin. As a result, beyond 10 kilometres above the surface, westerly winds of up to 100 m/sec cause a bulk rotation of the atmosphere in about four days.

Russian spacecraft have landed and sent back pictures of the surface. Imaging radar has been used to map most of the planet from orbiting spacecraft. The most recent survey by the Magellan probe began in 1990 and resolves features as small as 150m across. Mountains, valleys, impact craters and many other features have been mapped and 3-dimensional simulations generated by computer from the Magellan data.

Mars has a thin atmosphere of about 95% carbon dioxide mixed with other minor constituents. The polar caps consist of semi-permanent water ice and ephemeral solid carbon dioxide. Day and night surface temperatures vary between about –120°C and –20°C. Mars has two small satellites, each less than about 25km across, probably captured asteroids.

A variety of landscapes has been identified, including ancient heavily cratered terrains and plains which may consist of lava flows. There are several large volcanoes; the best preserved of these, Olympus Mons, rises 26km above the surface and is 550km across at its base.

Mars shows evidence of erosional processes. The effect of winds is seen in the degraded form of the older craters and the deposition of sand dunes. Dust storms frequently obscure the surface. The large channels, such as the 5000km long Valles Marineris, may have been cut by flowing water. Water is abundant in the polar caps and may be widespread held in as permafrost below the surface.

LUNAR DATA

Earth/Moon Mass Ratio	M_e/M_m 81.3015
Density (mean)	3.34g/cm³
Synodic Month (new Moon to new Moon)	29.530 588d
Sidereal Month (fixed star to fixed star)	27.321661 days
Inclination of Lunar orbit to ecliptic	5°8'43"
Inclination of equator to ecliptic	1°40'32"
Distance from Moon to Earth (mean)	384 400 km (238 860 mi)
Optical libration	longitude ± 7.6° latitude ± 6.7°
Magnitude (mean of full Moon)	−12.7
Temperature	−153°C to + 134°C (−244°F to +273°F)
Escape velocity	2.38 km/sec (1.48 mi/sec)
Diameter of Moon	3 476 km (2 160mi)
Surface gravity	162.2 cm/sec²

PHASES OF THE MOON

direction of light from Sun

New Moon

First quarter

Last quarter

Full Moon

Above The Moon passes through a cycle of passes from New Moon to Full Moon.
Below An Apollo 16 photograph of the Moon.

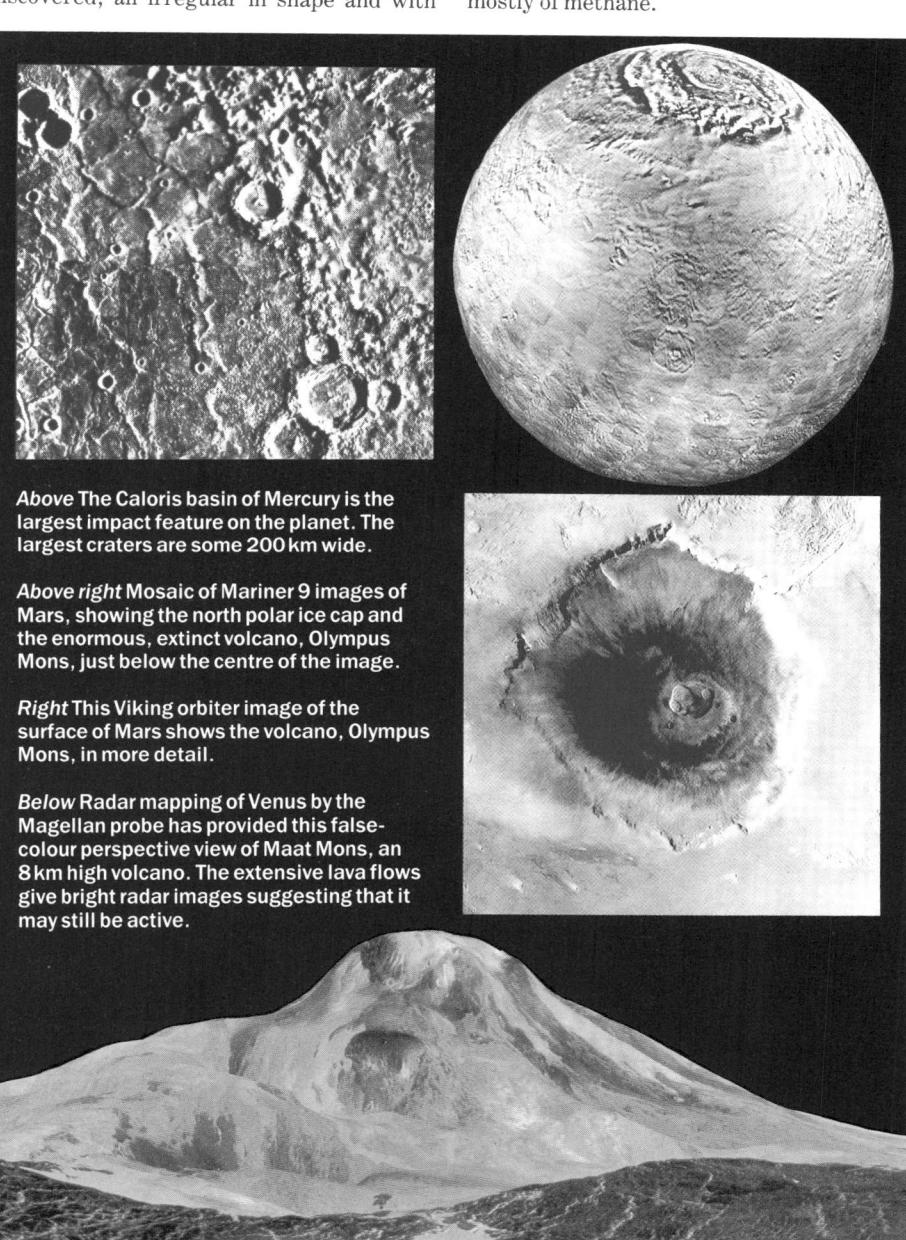

Above The Caloris basin of Mercury is the largest impact feature on the planet. The largest craters are some 200 km wide.

Above right Mosaic of Mariner 9 images of Mars, showing the north polar ice cap and the enormous, extinct volcano, Olympus Mons, just below the centre of the image.

Right This Viking orbiter image of the surface of Mars shows the volcano, Olympus Mons, in more detail.

Below Radar mapping of Venus by the Magellan probe has provided this false-colour perspective view of Maat Mons, an 8 km high volcano. The extensive lava flows give bright radar images suggesting that it may still be active.

SPACE FLIGHT

Possibly no other field of human endeavour has excited the imaginations of so many people over the past thirty-five years as the exploration of space. There are many difficulties involved in leaving the Earth. A large amount of energy is needed to lift a worthwhile payload 200km or more but it will fall back to the Earth's surface unless it is also given a velocity parallel to the ground of 29,000km per hour. To put a satellite into a higher orbit, or accelerate a spacecraft away from the Earth to the Moon or another planet, requires even greater energy and larger rockets for the same payload. Expendable rocket boosters are used which are jetisoned in stages as their fuel becomes exhausted.

On 4 October 1957 the USSR launched the first artificial satellite, Sputnik 1. The first American satellite, Explorer 1, followed within four months and discovered the Van Allen radiation belt about the Earth. The Russian lead in what developed into a space race was maintained by the first pictures of the far side of the Moon (Luna 3, 1959) and the first manned spaceflight (Yuri Gagarin, 1961), whereas the Americans at the same time were developing specialist satellites such as TIROS 1 (the first weather satellite), Transit 1B (the first navigation satellite) and Echo 1 (the first communications satellite), all launched in 1960.

During the 1960s and 1970s the nearby planets began to be investigated by flybys, orbiting probes and hard (crash) and soft landings, the Russians being more successful with Venus and the Americans with Mars. The surface of the Moon was studied by the US Ranger craft (1964/65) which resolved detail to a metre or so just before impact, the seven soft-landing Surveyors (1966/68) which surveyed potential manned landing sites and five Lunar Orbiters (1966/67) which provided what is still the only

detailed survey of most of the lunar surface. Meanwhile the one-man Mercury and two-man Gemini flights of up to 14 days continued during which the techniques required for travel to the Moon were developed. On 20 July 1969 the first manned landing was made using the Saturn V rocket (US astronauts Armstrong, Aldrin and Collins, Apollo XI).

The Russian manned programme continued with longer flights in Earth orbit and the launch of their first Salyut space stations (from 1971) while their lunar program continued with robot exploration and the return of small samples to Earth.

The American probe Pioneer 10 (1972) was the first to cross the asteroid belt: both Pioneer 10 and 11 were, by 1992, well beyond the farthest planets and still being tracked. Skylab provided a useful working area in orbit (1973/74). A large part of Mercury was mapped by Mariner 10 (1973/

Top Right The Hubble Space Telescope still attached to the Remote Manipulator Arm (lower right) of the Space Shuttle Discovery during deployment in 1990.

Above ESA's Ariane launch vehicle, developed and built in France, being prepared for flight at Kourou, French Guiana.

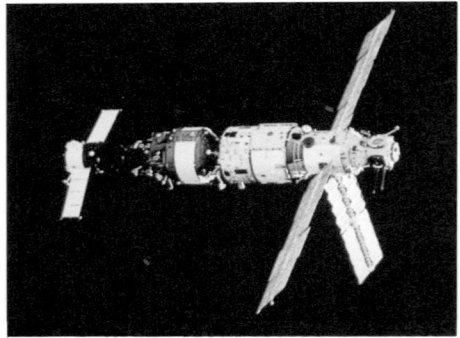

Left The first modules of the Mir space-station were launched into Earth orbit by the former USSR in 1986. It has been inhabited continuously by relays of cosmonauts.

74), a survey that has not yet been repeated. The USSR started its long series of Venera spacecraft to Venus (from 1975) using orbiters and probes which descended to send back the first pictures of the surface and the US Viking 1 and 2 mapped Mars in great detail from orbit and their landers sampled the surface material, made tests for signs of life and recorded the weather (1976/77).

The US Voyagers 1 and 2 were launched in 1977 with Voyager 2 visiting Jupiter (1979), Saturn (1981), Uranus (1986) and Neptune (1989), sending back detailed images of all these planets and many of their satellites and discovering many new satellites and rings around Neptune. IRAS (1983) mapped the whole sky in the infra-red discovering many new objects: so much data was sent back in its few months operation that much is still not analysed. Other satellites observed gamma-rays, x-rays and the ultra-violet region of the spectrum while another large group of satellites looked towards the Earth to study the weather, the sea, land utilisation and many other aspects of the Earth's environment, many of which have commercial and military applications while both the USA and USSR have made much use of reconnaissance or spy satellites. The Soviet Mir space station which was launched in 1986 has been inhabited continuously by relays of cosmonauts, some of whom were in orbit for a year, some new modules having been added.

The UK launched only one small satellite

before abandoning its own launch programme to join what is now the European Space Agency (ESA) which has used the Ariane rocket (developed and built in France from 1965) to launch both commercial satellites and space probes. China, Japan and India also now have their own launch capability and many nations use or participate in space projects of various kinds, especially in the fields of communications, weather and Earth resources.

The American ICE probe passed through the tail of comet Giacobini-Zinner in 1985 and two Japanese, two Soviet and the ESA Giotto made observations of Halley's comet in 1986, Giotto giving us the first close look at a comet's nucleus. Giotto is being reactivated to observe comet Grigg-Skjellerup in 1992. The Magellan orbiter commenced detailed radar mapping of Venus in 1989 and the Hubble Space Telescope was launched in 1990 by the Space Shuttle and despite problems with the optics is making observations of a quality impossible from the ground. Meanwhile, the spacecraft Galileo (1989) sent back the first-ever close-up picture of an asteroid, Gaspra (1991) on its way to Jupiter (1995). Ulysses (1990) which will pass over the Sun's poles (1994/95) will be swung out of the plane of the Earth's orbit by a close approach to Jupiter in 1992. Japan sent a small spacecraft carrying a tiny probe which was put into orbit around the Moon (1990). The Compton Gamma Ray Observatory was launched in 1991.

WEATHER SATELLITES

The impact of space flight on meteorology is becoming more obvious now that satellite pictures are routinely used as illustrations on TV weather forecasts. However, weather monitoring was among the major military and civil aims of the early space programme. Weather satellites can operate on a global basis, observing phenomena distant from meteorological observatories, such as over the ocean or unfriendly territory.

The most famous series of weather satellites, TIROS (Television and Infra-Red Observation Satellite), began with TIROS 1 in 1960 and continues, in advanced form, today. TIROS satellites are placed in non-synchronous orbits inclined to the equator to give close-up repeat coverage of middle and lower latitudes. Other satellites in higher,

Right Weather satellites placed in geo-stationary orbits provide coverage over much of a hemisphere. However, to remain stationary relative to the ground they must be located over the equator, leading to severe foreshortening near the polar regions, as this Meteosat image shows.

geosynchronous orbits provide effectively continuous low resolution coverage of almost complete hemispheres. A good example is the European Space Agency's Meteosats situated above 0°N, 0°W which have produced half-hourly images in the visible, water vapour infra-red and thermal infra-red bands since late 1977. The higher latitudes and polar regions, foreshortened by Meteosats, are best covered by weather satellites in lower, high inclination orbits.

Such satellites can detect and monitor hurricane formation and movement, allowing advance warning which has saved countless lives and minimised damage to property. More routinely, cloud patterns, water vapour content and vertical temperature profiles within the atmosphere and ground surface temperature are determined, which permit accurate forecasts a week in advance. Satellite observations are also essential for global investigation of the radiative properties of the Earth's surface and atmosphere so that we understand the dynamics of our climate much more fully than before the space age.

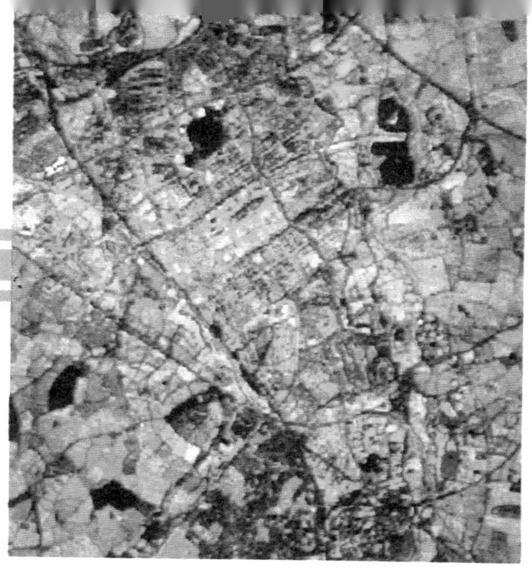

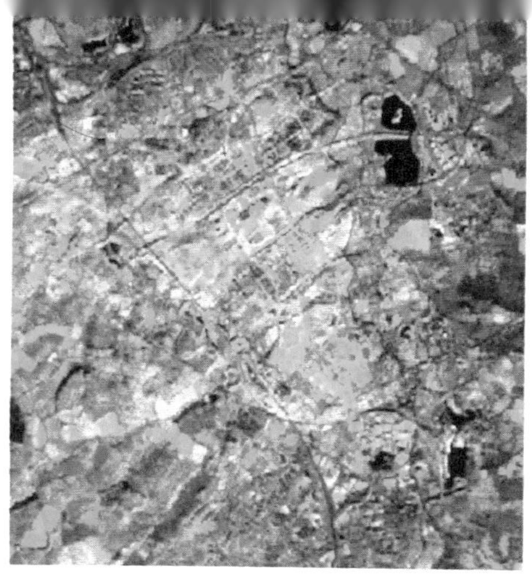

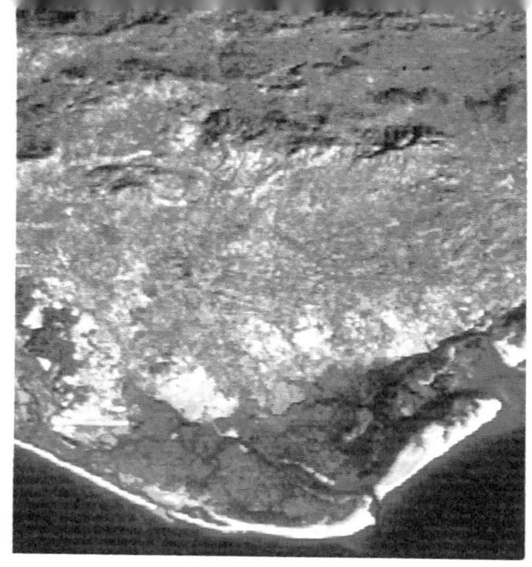

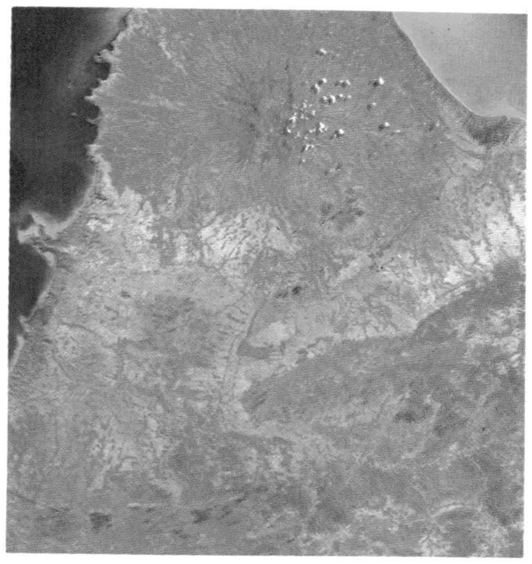

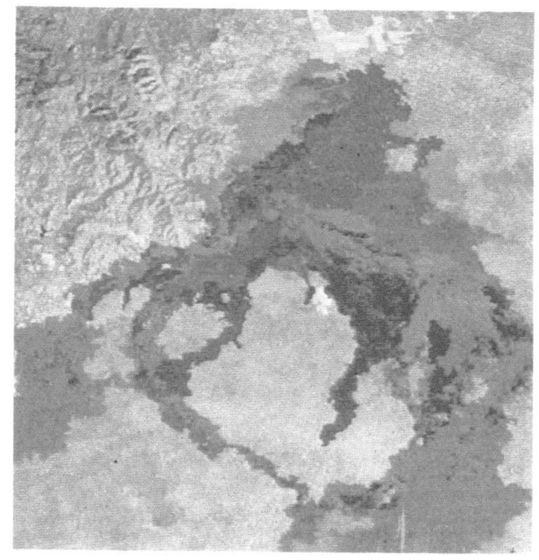

REMOTE SENSING

From orbit a camera or other imaging system is ideally placed to record and monitor large areas of the Earth on a regular basis. Photography is still useful in that it can provide a high resolution record, but it is restricted to visible and near infrared wavelengths and requires return of the film to Earth. Images recorded in digital form, not restricted to the photographic region of the spectrum, can be transmitted to a ground receiving station while the satellite continues in orbit. Computerised image processing techniques can reveal hidden structures within the data.

Digital images are recorded using electronic sensors. Usually the forward motion of the satellite is used to build up a picture line by line. The data within each line is broken into a string of numbers, each representing the brightness of one spot (or pixel) on the ground. This digital data may be transmitted in real time (direct to a ground receiving station or via a relay satellite), or recorded on board to be transmitted later as the satellite passes within range of a ground receiving station.

In order to cover most of the globe, remote sensing satellites are usually placed in polar orbits, highly inclined to the equator, which pass over a wide latitude range. Most are put in sun-synchronous orbit arranged so that the Earth rotates beneath them at a rate sufficient to keep the satellites over points at approximately the same local time throughout their north-south passage. The orbit then takes them from north to north on the nightside of the Earth before beginning another north-south passage further west at the same local time.

The most widely used satellite remote sensing data is that from multispectral scanners carried by the Landsat programme, begun in 1972. Initially known as ERTS (Earth Resources Technology Satellites),

Above left The false colour Landsat Thematic Mapper image of Milton Keynes, England, depicts built-up areas as blue, water black and vegetation red. The same image *above centre* has been computer enhanced to reveal recent landscape changes. Colour has been used to show areas of the same spectral characteristics.
Above right Landsat Multispectral Scanner false colour image of the south coast of Portugal near Faro. The airport runway shows as a bright line by the lagoon in the lower left-hand corner.
Left Another multi-spectral Landsat image showing Gunung Muryo (1602m) and Tanjung (Cape) Bugel on the island of Java. This area is shown on page 70—N9.
Right Landsat Multispectral Scanner false colour image of Craters of the Moon in Idaho, U.S.A. There is little vegetation except in and near the mountainous area in the north-west.

the first three in the series were placed in near polar sun-synchronous orbits at an altitiude of about 920km and overpassing the ground at about 09.30 local time. Complete global coverage, in four visible and near infrared bands with a pixel size of 80 m across, was achieved every 18 days. The succeeding generation of Landsats has a wider choice of spectral bands, a pixel size of 30m and a global repeat every 16 days at an altitude of about 700km. Landsat has enabled the observation of large-scale features in the Earth's crust, such as major folds and fault patterns, that from the surface (or an aircraft), cannot be seen in their entirety and often were not previously recognised, which has been used as an aid to hydrocarbon and mineral exploration. Some mineral occurrences are also highlighted by anomalous reflectance spectra which can be picked out especially well by the new sensors. The frequency repeat of Landsat coverage enables the monitoring of crops as they mature or are stricken by drought or disease, and the recording of major floods and forest fires. Changes in land use over the years since the programme began can be seen readily, without the expense of a large on-the-ground survey operation.

Nowadays we take live intercontinental television broadcasts for granted: these have been made possible only by the use of communication satellites. Civil communications satellites are the biggest group after military satellites, and nearly half are in geosynchronous orbits. A single satellite can handle thousands of telephone and several television channels.

The large number of satellites interfere with some observations from the ground but the problem in space is potentially much more serious with thousands of items of space junk in orbit. These range from spent booster rockets to flecks of paint, which have damaged Space Shuttle windows. Even these very small items travelling at a high relative speed are potentially lethal to astronauts working outside. Although items more than a few centimetres across are regularly tracked by radar, the smaller pieces are effectively lost.

THE FUTURE

From a purely scientific point of view spaceflight could have a very bright future, extensions of known technology being sufficient for the manned exploration of the Moon and even Mars and further unmanned exploration of the universe. However, there has been a decline in public interest in space and with future projects requiring more resources, a difficulty in raising the necessary funds. In the USA projects such as the CRAF (Comet Rendezvous Asteroid Flyby) have been delayed repeatedly and the proposed Freedom space station was pronounced too ambitious but looks set to continue in redesigned form. With the present uncertainties concerning the states of the former USSR, the future scope of their space programme must be in doubt. Their space shuttle Buran has flown only twice, unmanned (to 1991), and the Mir space station is reported to need considerable repair and updating before 1994. Several designs for Mir 2 are under discussion. There is a Mars mission scheduled for 1994 and there has been open discussion of a manned expedition to Mars before 2010.

Other future missions include the US Mars Observer flight (1992) to map the surface for one Martian year, the ESA ISO (Infra-red Space Observatory) for launch in 1993 and the Cassini/Huygens Saturn NASA/ESA project for launch in 1995 with Saturn arrival in 2004 with touchdown on Titan the same year. Japan plans to launch Lunar-A to the Moon in 1996. ESA's space laboratory, Columbus, could be launched in 1998 and there are possible US Pluto Flyby and Neptune Orbiter missions in 2001-3.

Nearer to home is a trend to commercialisation of space ventures making it more expensive for developing countries and research institutes to afford to purchase data. Along with increasing emphasis on commercialisation comes a difficult period for space law. Despite United Nations treaties declaring outer space not subject to claims of sovereignty, many equatorial nations are claiming ownership of the geostationary orbit locations above. Problems loom also over the worldwide dissemination of increasingly high resolution imagery, because poor nations are disadvantaged compared with richer neighbours and foreign investors lacking the technology and expertise to process and interpret this information about their own resources. Similar unrest is developing over the direct broadcasting of television from satellites into territories whose governments wish to exercise political or moral censorship.

There are over a thousand satellites in Earth orbit, of which over a third are used for military purposes: these include surveillance, early warning and specialist communication satellites. Nuclear weapons are banned from space by treaty, but both superpowers have developed sophisticated anti-satellite weapons, such as hunter-killer satellites, which threaten the fragile security afforded by mutual surveillance by intelligence satellites.

Other satellite multispectral instruments are designed to monitor the oceans. For instance, the Nimbus 7 coastal-zone colour scanner (pixel size about 1km) is sensitive in narrow spectral bands responsive to changes in chlorophyll concentration for mapping phytoplankton distribution and a thermal infrared channel which can show temperture variations and ocean surface currents.

Imaging by radar can be processed to give a picture resembling a black and white photograph. This had been used over land to map tropical regions which are permanently cloud covered, to see through very dry sand deserts to the rocky structures beneath, and over the sea to determine roughness and wave patterns. Canada plans to launch such a satellite (Radarsat) to monitor sea-ice in Arctic waters. ERS-1, the ESA remote sensing satellite designed to study oceans, coastal regions and climates, was launched in 1991.

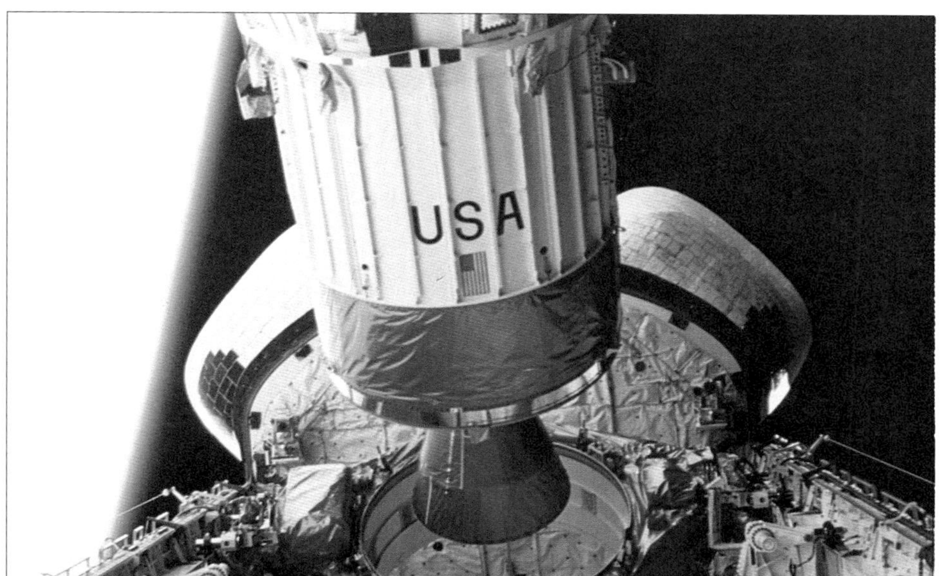

Right The Jupiter probe Galileo is taking a gravity-assisted route to Jupiter with close approaches to Venus (1990) and Earth (1990 and 1992). In 1995 a probe will be released to descend through Jupiter's atmosphere while the main spacecraft orbits the planet. In October 1991 Galileo passed only 1600km from asteroid Gaspra.

EARTH STRUCTURE

Internally the earth may be divided broadly into crust, mantle and core.

The crust is a thin shell constituting only 0.2% of the mass of the Earth. The continental crust varies in thickness from 20 to 90km and is less dense than ocean crust. Two-thirds of the continents are overlain by sedimentary rocks of average thickness less than 2km but attaining 20km. Ocean crust is on average 7km thick. It is composed of igneous rocks, basalts and gabbros.

Crust and mantle are separated by the Mohorovičić Discontinuity (Moho). The mantle differs from the crust. It is largely igneous. The upper mantle extends to 350km. There is a low velocity zone between 50km and 150km indicating a partial melting. The lower mantle has a more uniform composition. A sharp discontinuity defines the meeting of mantle and core. The inability of the outer core to transmit seismic waves suggests it is liquid. It is probably of metallic iron with other elements – sulphur, silicon, oxygen, potassium and hydrogen have all been suggested. The inner core is solid and probably of nickel-iron.

Temperature at the core-mantle boundary is about 3700°C and 4000°–4500°C in the inner core.

Evolution of the lithosphere, hydrosphere and atmosphere has been strongly influenced by the biosphere – the sphere of living things. The ancestral atmosphere lacked free oxygen. Plant life added oxygen to the atmosphere and transferred carbon dioxide to the crustal rocks and the hydrosphere. The composition of air at 79% nitrogen and 20% oxygen remains stable by the same mechanism.

Solar energy is distributed around the Earth by the atmosphere. Most of the weather and climate processes occur in the troposphere. The atmosphere also shields the Earth. Ozone which exists to the extent of 2 parts per million is at its maximum at 30km. It is the only gas which absorbs ultra-violet radiation. Water-vapour and CO_2 keep out infra-red radiation.

Above 80km nitrogen and oxygen cannot retain their molecular form. They tend to separate into atoms which become ionized (an ion is an atom lacking one or more of its electrons).

The ionosphere is a zone of ionized belts which reflect radio waves back to earth. These electrification belts change their position dependent on light and darkness and external factors.

Beyond the ionosphere, the magnetosphere extends to outer space. Ionized particles form a plasma (a fourth state of matter i.e. other than solid, liquid, gas) constrained by the Earth's magnetic field.

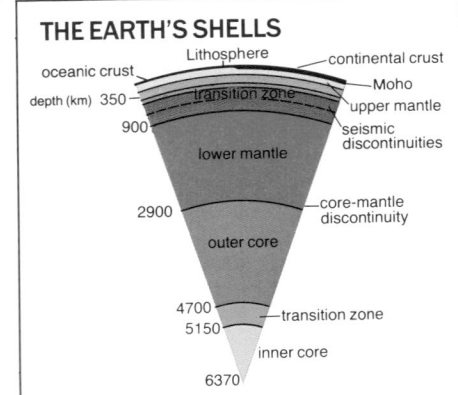

THE EARTH'S SHELLS

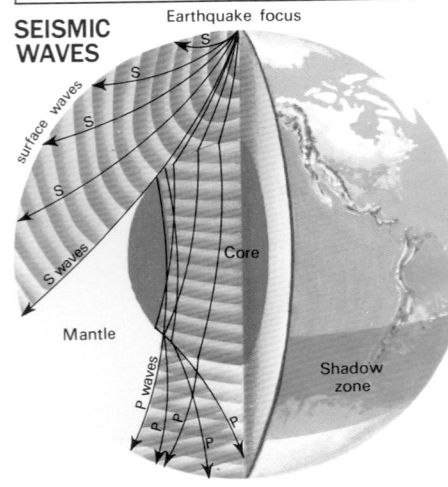

SEISMIC WAVES

Earthquake focus

Above In an earthquake the shock generates vibrations, or seismic waves, which radiate in all directions from the focus. Surface waves travel close to the surface of the Earth. They cause most motion in the ground and, therefore, most damage to structures.

Other waves known as body waves pass through the body of the Earth. They are of two kinds. Primary (P) waves are compressional waves. They are able to travel through solids and fluids and cause the particles of the Earth to vibrate in the direction of travel of the wave. Secondary (S) waves are transverse, or shear, waves. They can only pass through solids. They travel at about half the velocity of 'P' waves and they vibrate at right angles to the path travelled by the wave.

Both types of wave obey normal rules of reflection and refraction. Their velocities depend on the nature of the medium through which they pass. Where the physical or chemical properties of the Earth change, the velocity and path of the waves are changed too. From the way the waves travel the nature of the internal layers of the Earth is revealed. By the same means the fluid nature of the outer core is confirmed. Because of the different paths followed by the two types of waves, there is a 'shadow zone' at 105° to 142° from the earthquake focus where waves of both kinds fail to reach the surface.

EARTH'S GRAVITY AND MAGNETIC FIELDS

The Earth is spheroidal in form because it is a rotating body. Were it not so it would take the form of a sphere. The shape is determined by the mass of the Earth and its rate of rotation. Centrifugal force acting outwards reduces the pull of gravity acting inwards so that gravity at the equator is less than at the poles. In theory gravity would be expected to vary progressively from the equator to the poles. In fact, it does not. Uneven distribution of matter within the Earth distorts the shape taken up by the mean sea-level surface (the geoid). In consequence a plumb-line or spirit-level may depart from the assumed vertical or horizontal. Moreover, the orbits of artificial satellites are perturbed by the irregularity of the Earth's gravity.

MAGNETISM

Like gravity, magnetism is strongest at the poles and weakest at the equator. The magnetic field of the Earth resembles that of a bar magnet displaced slightly from the geographical poles. It was long believed that the core being made of iron acted as a magnet but the temperatures prevailing there would destroy such magnetism. Today the belief is that electric currents generated in the semi-molten outer core are responsible for the magnetic field. The magnetic poles are not coincident with the geographical poles. Were a bar magnet substituted for the Earth's field it would not pass through the centre of the Earth but through a point in the plane of the equator about 1200km from the centre in the direction of Indonesia. The bar itself would be inclined at about 12° to the Earth's axis. The magnetic poles change their position from year to year so maps of magnetic declination used for navigation need to be updated annually.

Magnetism is expressed scientifically in three components, intensity, declination (departure from true north), and dip (the inclination in the vertical plane).

When molten rocks cool and solidify materials which are magnetic acquire the alignment of the Earth's local magnetic field at the time they solidified. The magnetism becomes frozen in the rocks. From this historic record the geographical position of the rocks at the time can be estimated from the magnetic alignments within the rocks. From such rock it was discovered that the Earth's magnetic poles had experienced a number of reversals the north pole becoming the south and vice-versa. A system of classification of the field allowed the ages of the various parts of the ocean floor to be deduced thus providing the evidence for sea-floor spreading and plate tectonics.

THE MAGNETOSPHERE

A stream of ionized gas, or plasma, the solar wind pours out from the Sun. Travelling at 1000km/sec its encounter with the Earth's magnetic field creates a bow shock wave. The magnetopause, the effective limit of the magnetic field, is pushed back to within 10 Earth radii measured in the direction of the Sun. It is stretched out in a long tail on the opposite side of the Earth. Between the bow-wave and magnetopause is the magnetosheath a region of charged particles producing fluctuations in the magnetic field. On the inner side of the magnetopause is a transition zone where charged particles react with the magnetic field and the magnetosheath. From this zone particles enter the internal magnetic field by the magnetic poles to produce aurorae. Particles trapped by the Earth's magnetism are deflected at the polar cusps and become trapped to form the Van Allen belts at about 5 Earth radii measured from the magnetic equator.

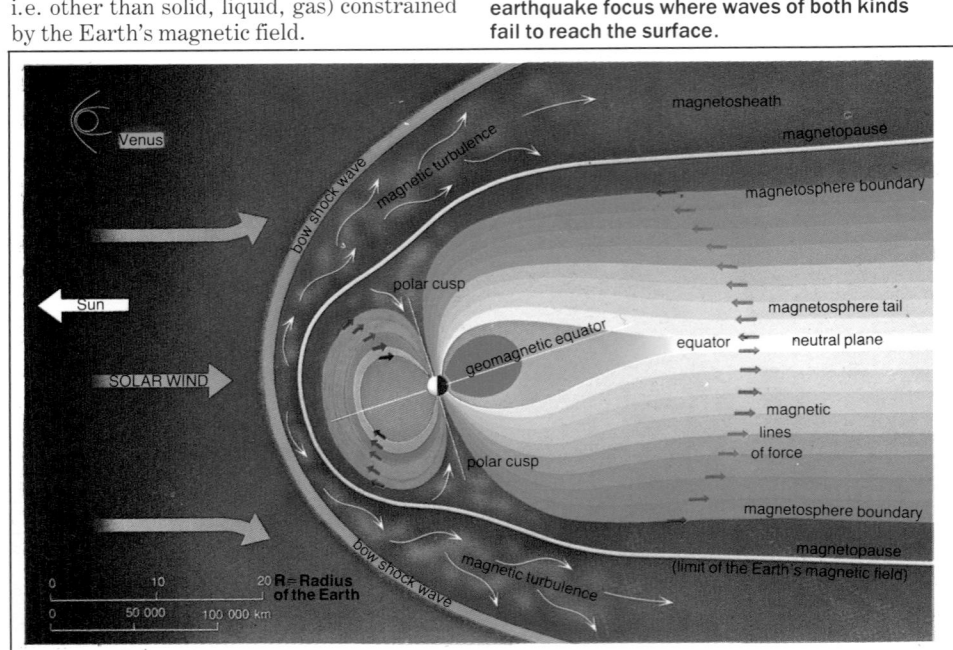

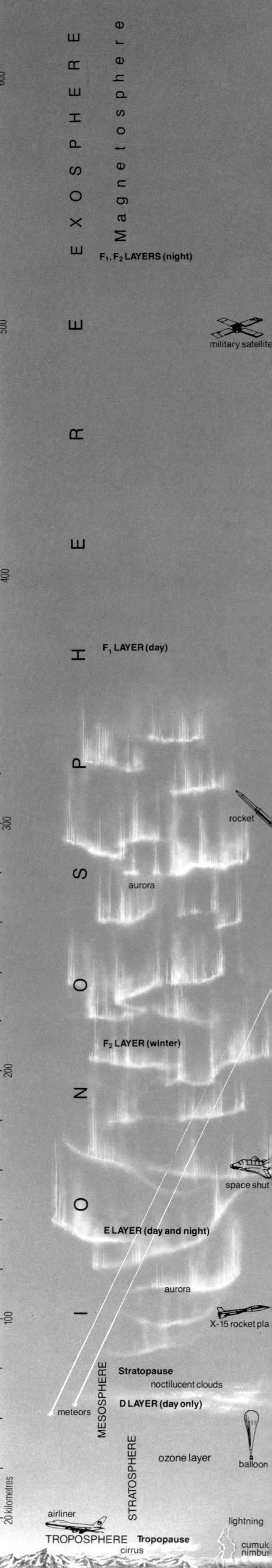

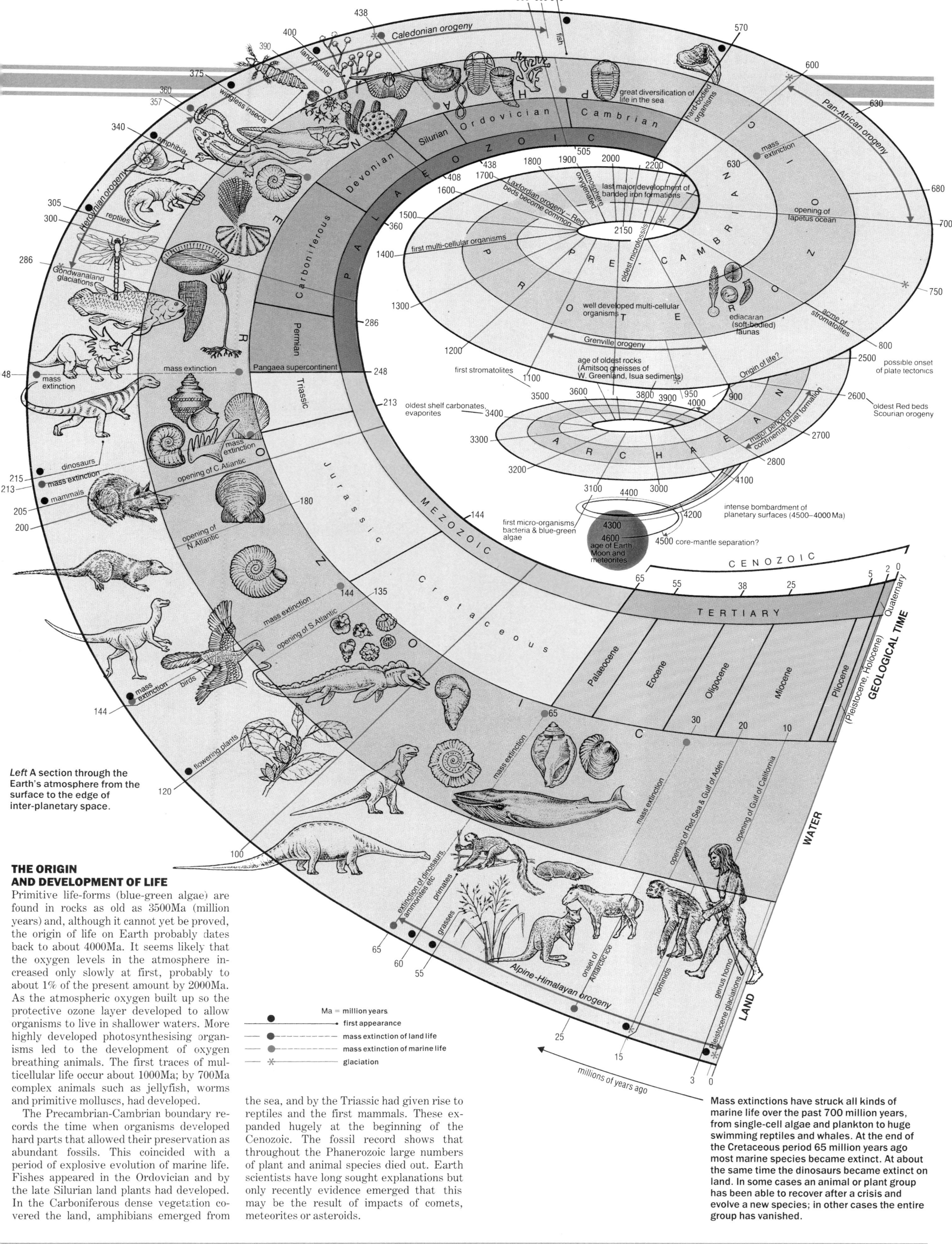

500 505 510
438
400
390
Caledonian orogeny
land plants
375
360
357
340
wingless insects
amphibia
Acadian orogeny
305
300
reptiles
286
Gondwanaland
glaciations
48
mass
extinction
215
213
205
200
dinosaurs
mass extinction
mammals

570
600
630
680
700
750
mass
extinction
great diversification of
life in the sea
Pan-African orogeny
opening of
Iapetus ocean

PALAEOZOIC
Silurian
Ordovician
Cambrian
Devonian
Carboniferous
Permian
Triassic

PRE-CAMBRIAN
PROTEROZOIC

408
438
2000
1900
2200
1800
1700
1600
1500
1400
1300
1200
1100
360
2150

Laxfordian orogeny – Red
beds become common
atmosphere
oxygenated
last major development of
banded iron formations
oldest microfossils

first multi-cellular organisms

well developed multi-cellular
organisms
Grenville orogeny
age of oldest rocks
(Amitsoq gneisses of
W. Greenland, Isua sediments)
first stromatolites
oldest shelf carbonates,
evaporites

ediacaran
(soft-bodied)
faunas
acme of
stromatolites
800
2500
possible onset
of plate tectonics
2600
oldest Red beds
Scourian orogeny
2700
2800
Origin of life?
900
950
3400
3300
3200
3500
3600
3800
3900
4000
4100

ARCHAEAN
630

3100
4400
3000
4200
intense bombardment of
planetary surfaces (4500–4000 Ma)
first micro-organisms
bacteria & blue-green
algae
4300
4600
age of Earth
Moon and
meteorites
4500 core-mantle separation?

286
Pangaea supercontinent
248
213
mass
extinction
opening of C. Atlantic
opening of
N. Atlantic

MEZOZOIC
Jurassic
Cretaceous

180
144
144
135
mass extinction
opening of S. Atlantic

CENOZOIC
65
55
38
25
5 2 0

TERTIARY
GEOLOGICAL TIME

Palaeocene
Eocene
Oligocene
Miocene
Pliocene
Quaternary
(Pleistocene, Holocene)

mass
extinction
birds
144
flowering plants
120
100

30
20
10
65
mass extinction

mass extinction
opening of Red Sea & Gulf of Aden
opening of Gulf of California

WATER
LAND

extinction of dinosaurs,
ammonites etc
primates
grasses
65
60
55
onset of
Antarctica
hominids
genus homo
Alpine-Himalayan orogeny
Pleistocene glaciations
25
15
3
0
millions of years ago

25

Left A section through the
Earth's atmosphere from the
surface to the edge of
inter-planetary space.

**THE ORIGIN
AND DEVELOPMENT OF LIFE**

Primitive life-forms (blue-green algae) are
found in rocks as old as 3500Ma (million
years) and, although it cannot yet be proved,
the origin of life on Earth probably dates
back to about 4000Ma. It seems likely that
the oxygen levels in the atmosphere increased only slowly at first, probably to
about 1% of the present amount by 2000Ma.
As the atmospheric oxygen built up so the
protective ozone layer developed to allow
organisms to live in shallower waters. More
highly developed photosynthesising organisms led to the development of oxygen
breathing animals. The first traces of mul-
ticellular life occur about 1000Ma; by 700Ma
complex animals such as jellyfish, worms
and primitive molluscs, had developed.

The Precambrian-Cambrian boundary re-
cords the time when organisms developed
hard parts that allowed their preservation as
abundant fossils. This coincided with a
period of explosive evolution of marine life.
Fishes appeared in the Ordovician and by
the late Silurian land plants had developed.
In the Carboniferous dense vegetation covered the land, amphibians emerged from

Ma = million years
first appearance
mass extinction of land life
mass extinction of marine life
glaciation

the sea, and by the Triassic had given rise to
reptiles and the first mammals. These expanded hugely at the beginning of the
Cenozoic. The fossil record shows that
throughout the Phanerozoic large numbers
of plant and animal species died out. Earth
scientists have long sought explanations but
only recently evidence emerged that this
may be the result of impacts of comets,
meteorites or asteroids.

Mass extinctions have struck all kinds of
marine life over the past 700 million years,
from single-cell algae and plankton to huge
swimming reptiles and whales. At the end of
the Cretaceous period 65 million years ago
most marine species became extinct. At about
the same time the dinosaurs became extinct on
land. In some cases an animal or plant group
has been able to recover after a crisis and
evolve a new species; in other cases the entire
group has vanished.

Map 1
50 million years ago

Map 2
100 million years ago

Map 3
150 million years ago

Map 4
200 million years ago

PLATE TECTONICS

Tectonics means the act of building. As applied to geology, the word, which comes from Greek, refers to study of the processes which produce faults, joints, folds and cleavage or cause magma to rise to the surface as the Earth's crust reacts to forces from below. Plate tectonics attribute such tectonic effects to the movement of the parts of the lithosphere. The lithosphere is defined as the rigid outer layer of the Earth consisting of the crust and the part of the upper mantle immediately below. Together they form a rigid layer which is split into a number of plates all in motion, like rafts, carrying the continents and the oceans with them to drift apart, to collide, to unite or sub-divide in a process of destruction and renewal. There are six major plates and a number of minor ones diverging, converging or sliding past each other at varying rates.

The plates are able to move because the rigid lithosphere rests on a less rigid asthenosphere a zone where the mantle is hotter and less resistant. Temperature increases at the rate of 20°C to 40°C with each km of depth in the outer parts of the Earth.

At mid-ocean ridges, a continuous chain some 40 000km in length running through all the oceans, new crust is created. Magma (hot molten rock) rises to flow out of the rift and solidify as pillow lavas or gabbros without reaching the crustal surface. The intrusion of new material forces the rift sides to move outwards and they are pushed further apart as still more magma injects itself into the rift. The rifts are regions of low seismic activity with a high heat flow.

Evidence of sea-floor spreading is provided by the magnetism locked into the rocks at the time they solidified. Evidence is also provided by the ocean sediments which become increasingly thicker outwards from the rift indicating a longer period of time for their deposition and consequently a greater age of the ocean floor on which they lie.

At mid-ocean ridges the plate margins are divergent (or extensional), new crust is formed and the boundary is said to be constructive. Where two plates meet the margins are convergent (or compressional) and are destructive. One plate slides under the other the plate margin descending at a steep angle, sometimes to a depth of 700km, into the asthenosphere, until melting occurs. Lighter material rises to attach itself to the underside of the continents. Continental plates containing much lighter material float over the ocean plates. Where the ocean plate is subducted, the subduction zone is marked by an ocean trench. Island areas are also formed in the oceans and young folded mountain ranges at the edge of a continent.

At some plate boundaries crust is neither created nor destroyed: the plates slide past each other at transform faults. The margins are translational and by type, conservative.

From study of all the oceans it can be said that the ocean floors are less than 200M years old. The Pacific plate contains only ocean crust. The other major plates consist of both continental and ocean crust. A fairly authoritative account can be given of the way the continents have drifted, divided and collided over the past 200M years. A very incomplete picture can be drawn of the course of events in the preceding 400M years and only a sketchy picture before that.

RELATIVE MOTIONS OF TECTONIC PLATES

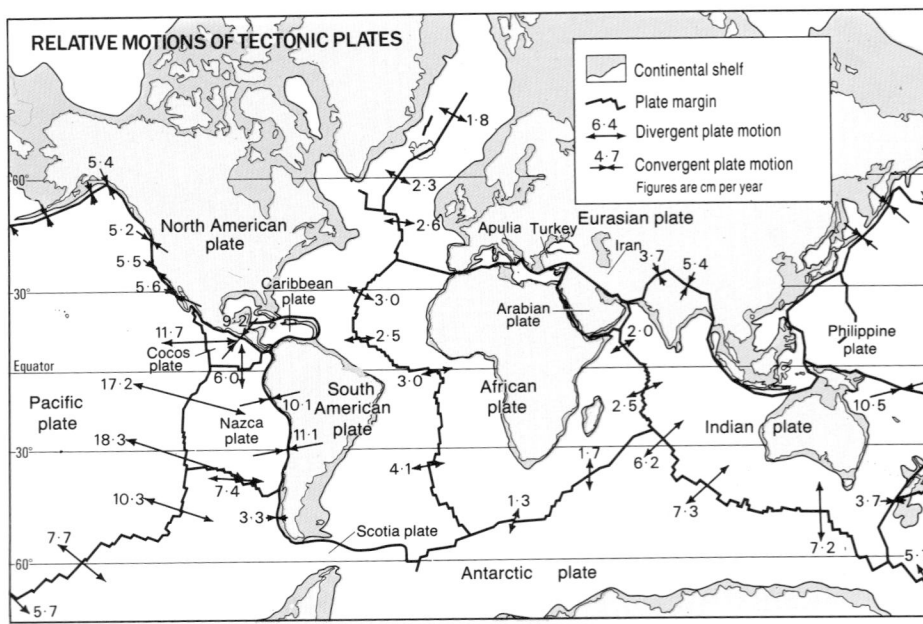

PLATE TECTONIC CYCLE

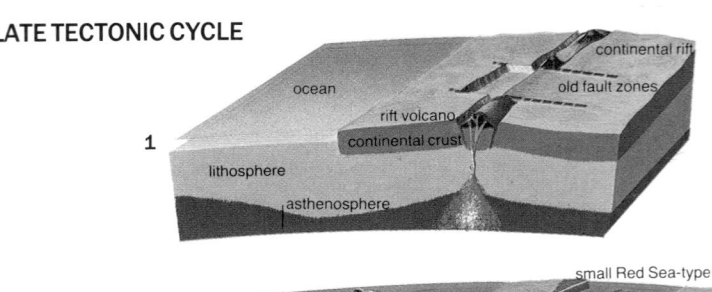

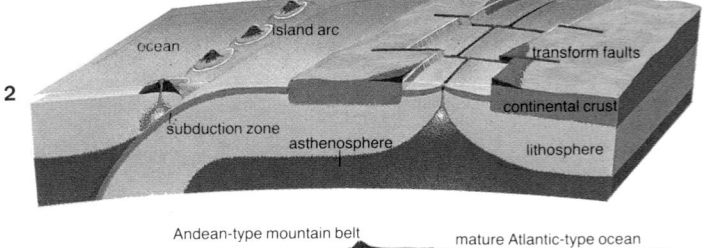

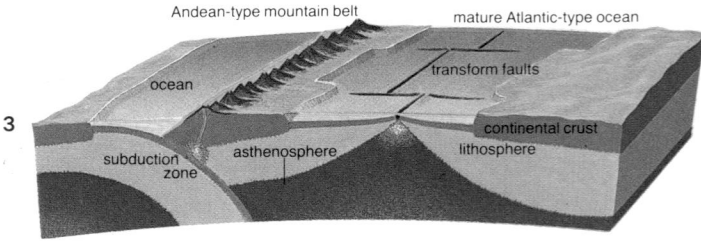

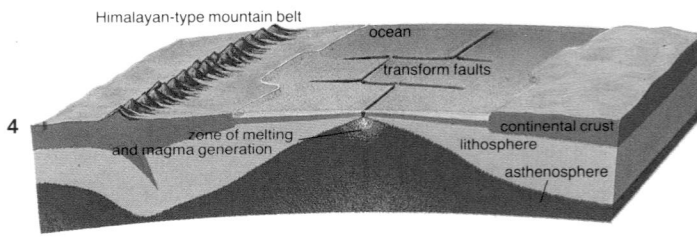

Above When continental lithosphere is subjected to tensional forces, it can become so attenuated that fault zones develop and crustal rocks subside. Hot magma rises from the asthenosphere to fill the space and that increases the heat flow through the lithosphere. Partial melting of mantle material ensues in the process of basaltic volcanism at a mid-ocean ridge. A rift develops in the continent and the two sides of the rift are forced further apart. Separation may be arrested after a while as in the case of the Rio Grande of south-west USA and the rift valley of East Africa. Should the process not be arrested, the rift will lengthen until the continent is split into two diverging plates.

1 Continental rifting in part following old faults in the continental basement.
2 Continental break-up with the formation of new oceanic crust in a small Red Sea-type ocean basin. Transform faults follow continental fractures.
3 A large mature Atlantic-type ocean basin has now formed on the site of the former continent. The subduction zone changes in direction (flips) to dip beneath the continent, forming a cordillera-type mountain belt.
4 Where continental collision occurs one continent partly underthrusts the other producing a Himalayan-type mountain belt underlain by thick continental crust (75-90km).

MAJOR TECTONIC FEATURES

Right Particular features are associated with different types of mineral deposits: continental rifts with tin and fluorine, mid-ocean ridges with marine metallic sulphides, island arcs and cordilleran-type mountains with a variety of metallic deposits.

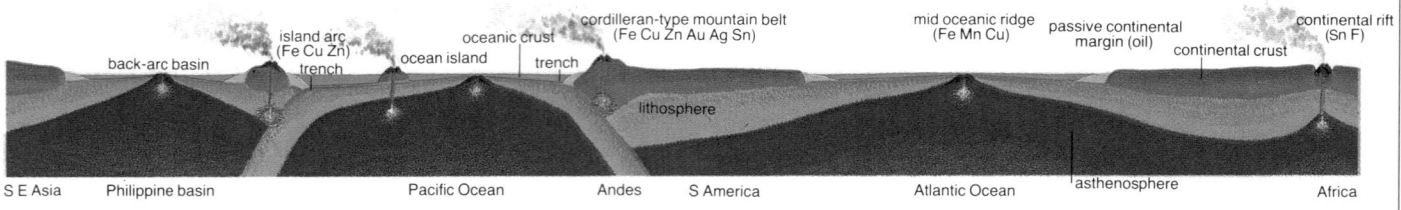

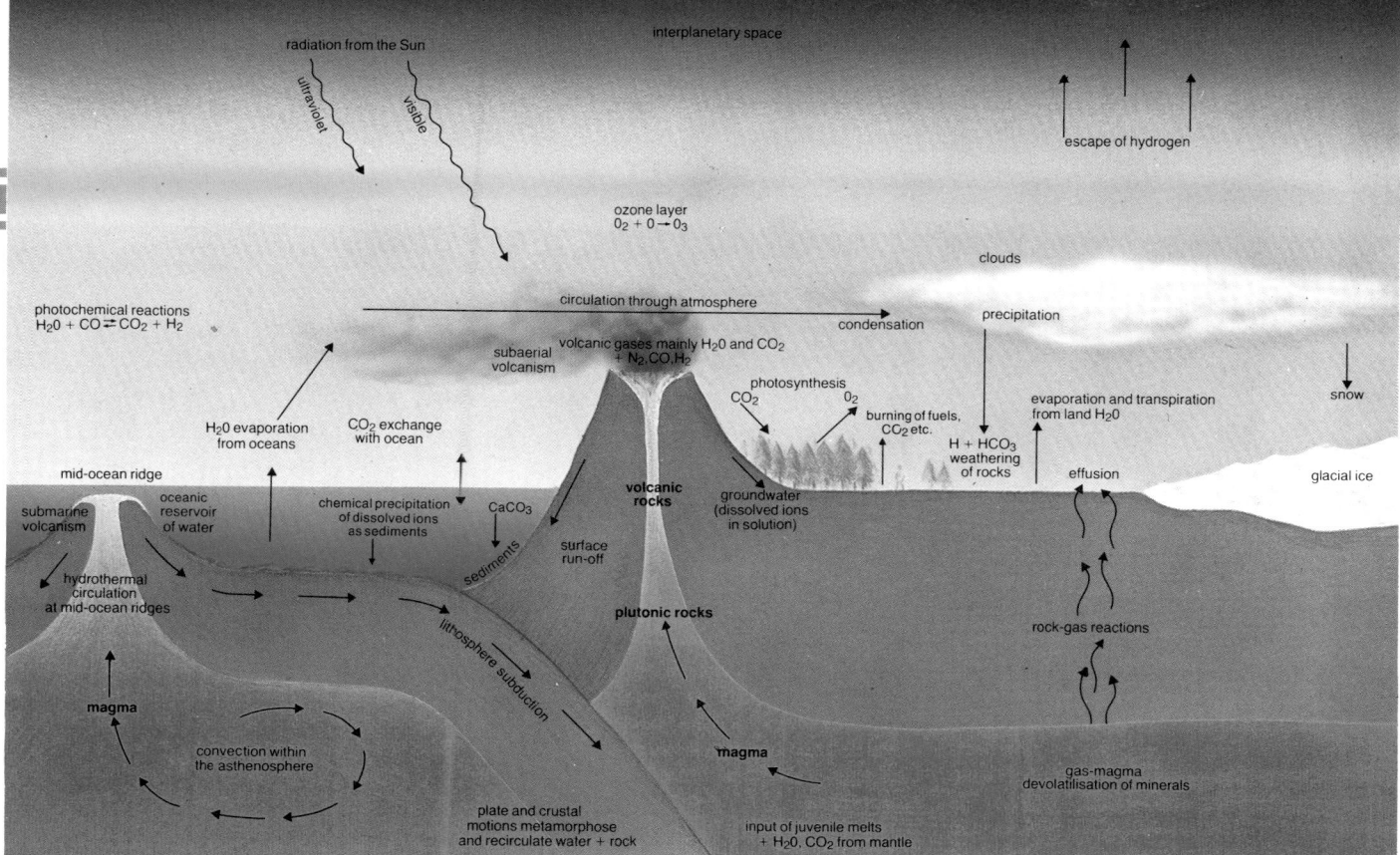

ROCK AND HYDROLOGICAL CYCLES

Left In the most familiar cycle rain falls onto the land, drains to the sea, evaporates, condenses into cloud and is precipitated onto the land again. Water is also released and recirculated as a result of plate movements and volcanic activity. In the rock cycle rocks are weathered and eroded, forming sediments which are in turn compacted into rocks that are eventually exposed and then weathered again. Man's industrial activity has modified the atmosphere by increasing the amount of CO_2 and adding other gases that may affect the vital ozone layer that shields the Earth from the Sun's ultra-violet rays. In the oceans, CO_2 and calcium are converted into calcium carbonate which forms sedimentary rocks which are re-cycled by the action of plate tectonics. In the atmosphere, CO_2, dust and water-vapour absorb infra-red energy and re-radiate it both to space and the atmosphere. If the level of CO_2 is increased, less of the Earth's own heat escapes to space, more is returned to the atmosphere and the Earth becomes warmer.

SURFACE PROCESSES

The lithosphere, the outermost layer of the Earth; the hydrosphere of salt and fresh water and the atmosphere composed of gases are all closely connected. There is a constant transfer of material from one to the other. The air in the atmosphere does not remain motionless. Convection and other influences impart complex patterns of motion in which matter is conveyed from one area to another. Atmospheric water vapour deposited on the lithosphere as water containing dissolved gases, reacts physically and chemically with surface rocks.

Variation in temperature, particularly frost, precipitation and winds cause a gradual fragmentation of surface rocks and physical decay in the process called weathering. Vegetation also plays its part in the alteration of surface rocks, by adding organic matter to weathered rocks to create soils and by resisting erosion. Water, however, is the major factor since it also acts as a transport medium.

Rivers transport enormous quantities of material varying from large boulders to particles of sand or clay carried in suspension. Where rivers overflow their banks, sand, gravel and clays are deposited in the flood plains to produce fertile valleys. On reaching the ocean or a lake the carrying capacity of the current is dissipated and material carried in suspension is deposited to form a delta.

Slumping of ocean floor material or earthquakes can put large quantities of fine sediments into suspension as a turbid layer which erodes the continental slope, thereby gathering more material all of which is deposited on the continental rise or the floor of the abyssal plain as "turbidites".

VOLCANOES

Almost all the world's active volcanoes, numbering 500–600 are located at convergent plate boundaries. Those are the volcanoes which give spectacular demonstrations of volcanic activity. Yet far greater volcanic activity continues unnoticed and without cessation at mid-ocean ridges where magma from the upper mantle is quietly being extruded on to the ocean floor to create new crustal material. The basalts erupted there are derived more or less directly from material of the mantle. Similar lavas are seen in the Columbia plateau, U.S.A. and the Deccan, India.

Chemical composition of magmas and the amount of gas they contain are important factors in determining the nature of a volcanic eruption. Gas-charged basalts produce cinder cones. Mount Etna in Italy has numerous such cinder cones. Violent eruptions usually occur when large clouds of lava come into contact with water to produce fine-grained ash. The name Surtseyan is given to this type after the volcanic island which appeared off Iceland in 1963. Andesites are more viscous. When charged with gas they erupt with explosive violence. Volcanoes like Fujiyama, Vesuvius and most of the other renowned volcanoes with steep sides are of this type.

Nuées ardentes (burning clouds) are extremely destructive. They are produced by rhyolitic magmas which erupt explosively sending molten lava fragments and gas at great speed down the mountain sides.

In spite of the destructiveness of many volcanoes people still live in their vicinity because of the fertile volcanic soils. Geothermal energy in regions of volcanic activity is another source of attraction.

EARTHQUAKES

Earthquakes are the manifestation of a slippage at a geological fault. The majority occur at tectonic plate boundaries. The interior of a plate tends to be stable and less subject to earthquakes. When plates slide past each other strain energy is suddenly released. Even though the amount of movement is very small the energy released is colossal. It is transferred in shock waves.

Most earthquakes originate at not very great depths – 5km or so. At the San Andreas fault earthquakes originate at about 20km depth. Over 70% of all foci are at depths of less than 70km. Some, however, may be as deep as 700km. The precise cause of those very deep earthquakes is not known. The point from which the earthquake is generated is the focus and the point on the surface immediately above the focus is the epicentre. Plotting the foci of deep earthquakes at convergent plate boundaries allows the path of the subducted plate to be traced.

Two types of scale are used to define the magnitude of earthquakes. In the logarithmic Richter Scale each unit is ten times the intensity of the next lower on the scale. The intensity is recorded by seismographs. There is no upper limit but the greatest magnitude yet recorded is 8·9.

The Modified Mercalli Earthquake Intensity Scale is in common use. It is based on the observed effects of an earthquake. At the lowest end the numeral I means the shock is felt by only a few people under special circumstances. A shock felt generally, with minor breakages indoors is classed as V. General alarm is equivalent to VIII and 'Panic' with varying categories of total destruction are graded IX to XII.

EXTERNAL INFLUENCES

Every day over a million tons of extra-terrestrial material falls on the Earth. Most of this material is ultra-fine cosmic dust. Only a small proportion of the incoming material actually reaches the surface of the Earth. Most is burned up by friction with the atmosphere where it vaporises after being heated to incandescence when it may be seen as so-called shooting stars.

Meteors come both sporadically and in showers. They are part of the solar system and rotate round the Sun. When the Earth comes in contact with them a meteor display occurs.

Occasionally a larger body survives passage through the atmosphere and strikes the ground. One very large meteorite fell in Arizona about 25,000 years ago. Meteor Crater is the result. Another devastating impact occurred in 1908 when an object struck the Tunguska area of Siberia, devastating an area of several kilometres radius in which all the trees were felled.

Tektites are curious objects. They are small and glassy and are found lying on the surface in several places – Australia, South-East Asia, Ivory Coast and Czechoslovakia. Terrestrial and extra-terrestrial origins have been ascribed to them. They have the appearance of melted rocks formed as the result of meteorite impact but no local evidence of such impact has been detected at any of the sites.

It seems inevitable that a comet or an asteroid will, in the course of time, collide with the Earth. Both comets and asteroids pass within the Earth's orbit. A collision will occur if the Earth happens to be located in that part of its orbit when one or the other crosses it.

Left When the Earth's crust bends under compression, folds develop. The simplest of these is a monocline, a one-sided fold, although downfolds (synclines) and upfolds (anticlines) are more usual. Increasing pressure steepens the side facing the pressure until one side is pushed under the other, to form a recumbent fold. Finally it may break along its axis, one limb being thrust over the other. Mountain chains often demonstrate intense folding between converging plates.

Faults occur when the Earth's crust breaks, often causing earthquakes. When tension stretches the crust normal faulting occurs and the rocks on one side of the fault-plane override those on the other.

A horst is a block of the crust thrust up between faults; the reverse is a graben or rift valley. Repeated horst and graben forms give basin and range topography as in Nevada, USA.

The upward movement of a plug of salt, some thousands of feet in depth, may force up strata and the surface layers to form a salt dome, often associated with oil and gas.

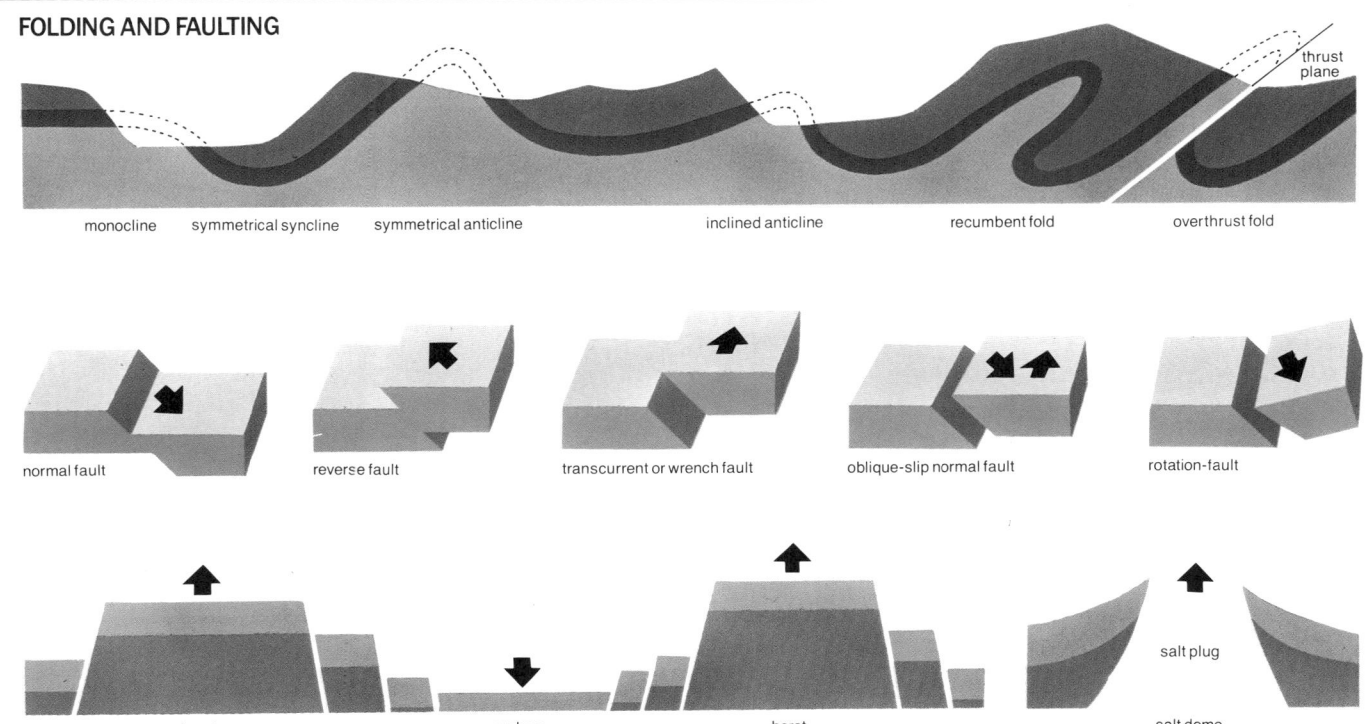

FOLDING AND FAULTING

monocline   symmetrical syncline   symmetrical anticline   inclined anticline   recumbent fold   overthrust fold

normal fault   reverse fault   transcurrent or wrench fault   oblique-slip normal fault   rotation-fault

horst   graben   horst   salt plug   salt dome

CLIMATE

Climate is generally said to be the average weather conditions observed over a long period. The factors which determine climate are temperature and rainfall.

Although heated slightly by the passage of the Sun's rays the atmosphere is warmed by the re-radiation of solar heat energy stored in the oceans and continents. Air which contains as much water vapour as possible (i.e. the air is saturated) is said to have a relative humidity of 100 and half-saturated air, 50. Air at a temperature of 32°C (90°F) can hold more than nine times as much water vapour as air at 0°C (32°F). For this reason polar regions have low precipitation.

Near the equator where the north-east and south-east trade winds meet is a zone known as the Inter-tropical Convergence Zone. Here warm, water-laden air rises to some 12-15km in altitude, its high content of water-vapour visible as cumulonimbus clouds. On cooling with altitude rain falls. This low-pressure doldrum zone of light winds has daily afternoon rains.

The two tropics are zones of descending air and, therefore, high atmospheric pressure and low rainfall. On the other hand, the

arctic and antarctic circles are low pressure zones and between them and the tropics the winds are 'anti-trade' i.e. blowing from the SW and NW respectively in the northern and southern hemispheres. This is the zone of the 'westerlies' in which weather is determined by depressions (low-pressure centres) and anti-cyclones (high pressure centres), the first rain-bearing, the second dry. In the polar regions the winds tend to be easterly. The poles themselves are high-pressure areas.

But for the rotation of the Earth, winds would blow south or north from high-pressure zones at the poles and tropics towards the polar circles and equator. Rotation and centrifugal force impart a west or east motion. The system of pressure belts moves from 6° to 10° north or south following the seasonal movements of the Sun.

Continents and oceans also influence the global pattern especially in the northern hemisphere where most land lies. The interiors of N. America and Eurasia become

very hot in summer and very cold in winter causing air to flow respectively from and to the oceans. Monsoons are an expression of this seasonal reversal of direction.

Tropical cyclones (typhoons and hurricanes and many local names) are highly destructive systems. They occur in a belt between 5° and 30° latitude, the majority in the northern hemisphere. They can be 800km in diameter, rotating clockwise in the southern hemisphere and counter-clockwise in the northern. Wind speeds above Force

MEAN TEMPERATURE JANUARY
1:210 000 000

MEAN TEMPERATURE JULY
1:210 000 000

ANNUAL RAINFALL DISTRIBUTION AND OCEAN CURRENTS
1:110 000 000

Prevailing surface wind

−40 −30 −20 −10 0 10 20 30 40 50 60 70 80 90 °F
−40 −30 −20 −10 0 10 20 30 °C

Warm current | Cold current
Sea weed | Coral reef

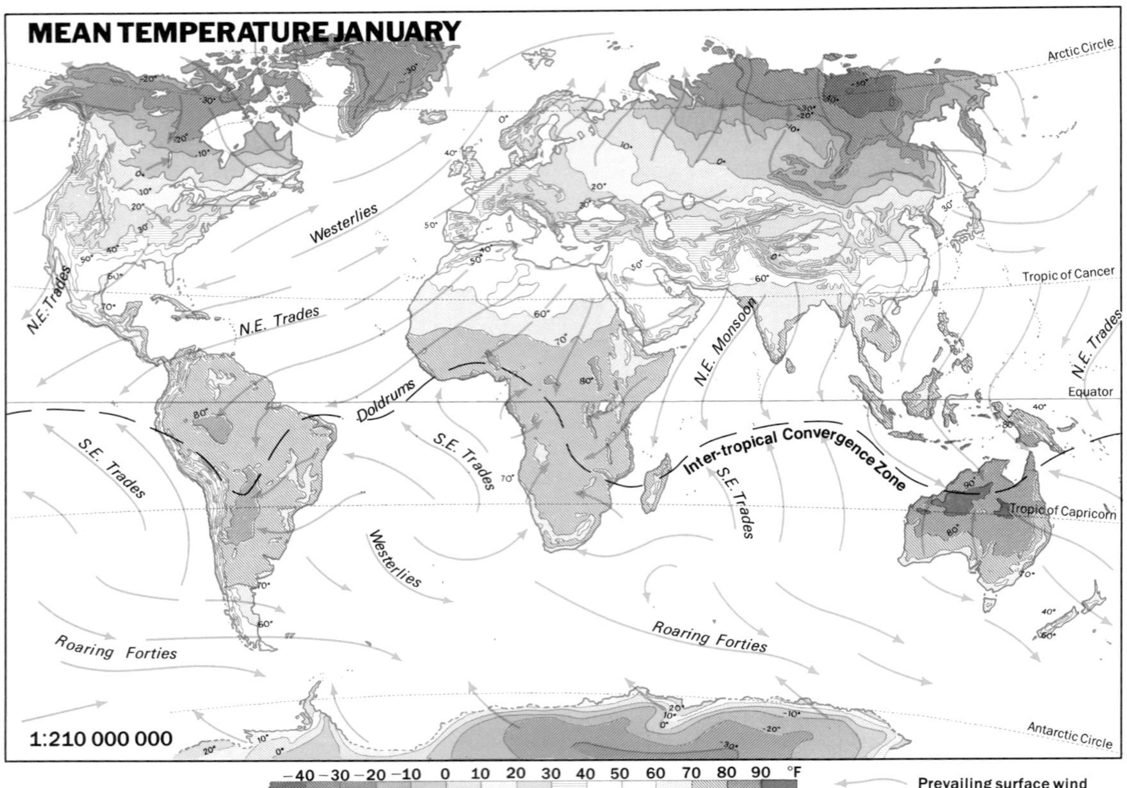

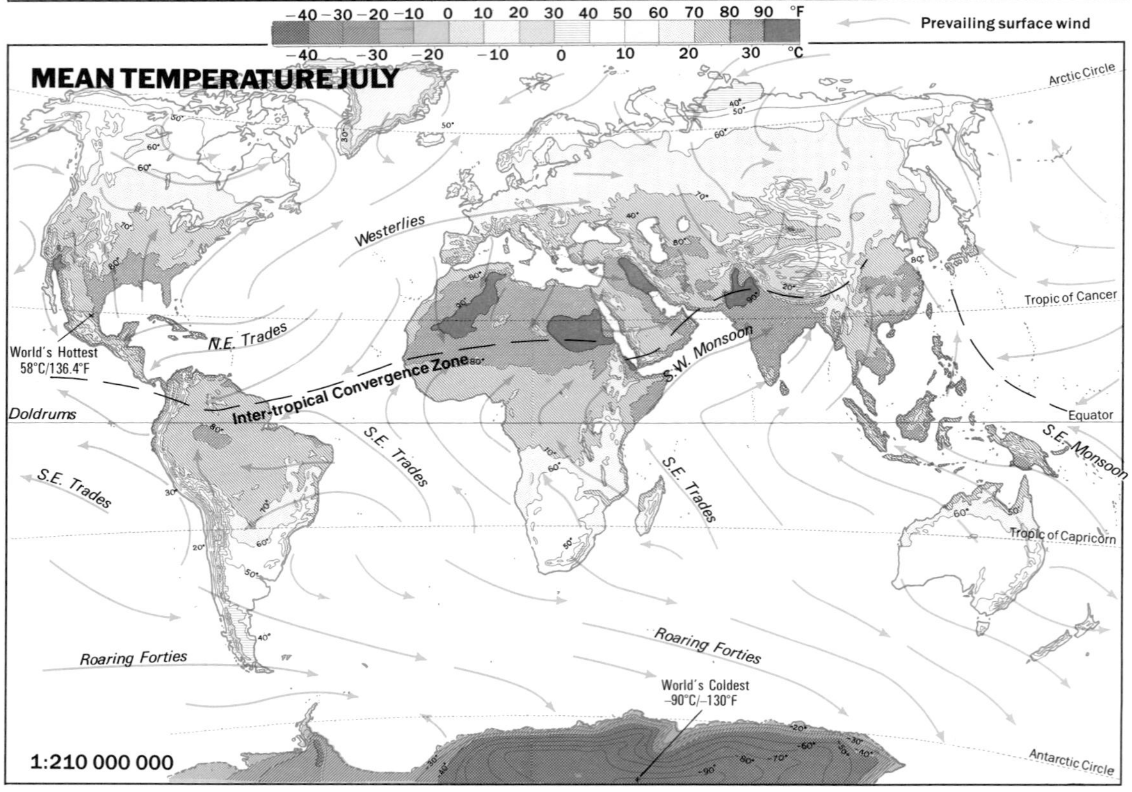

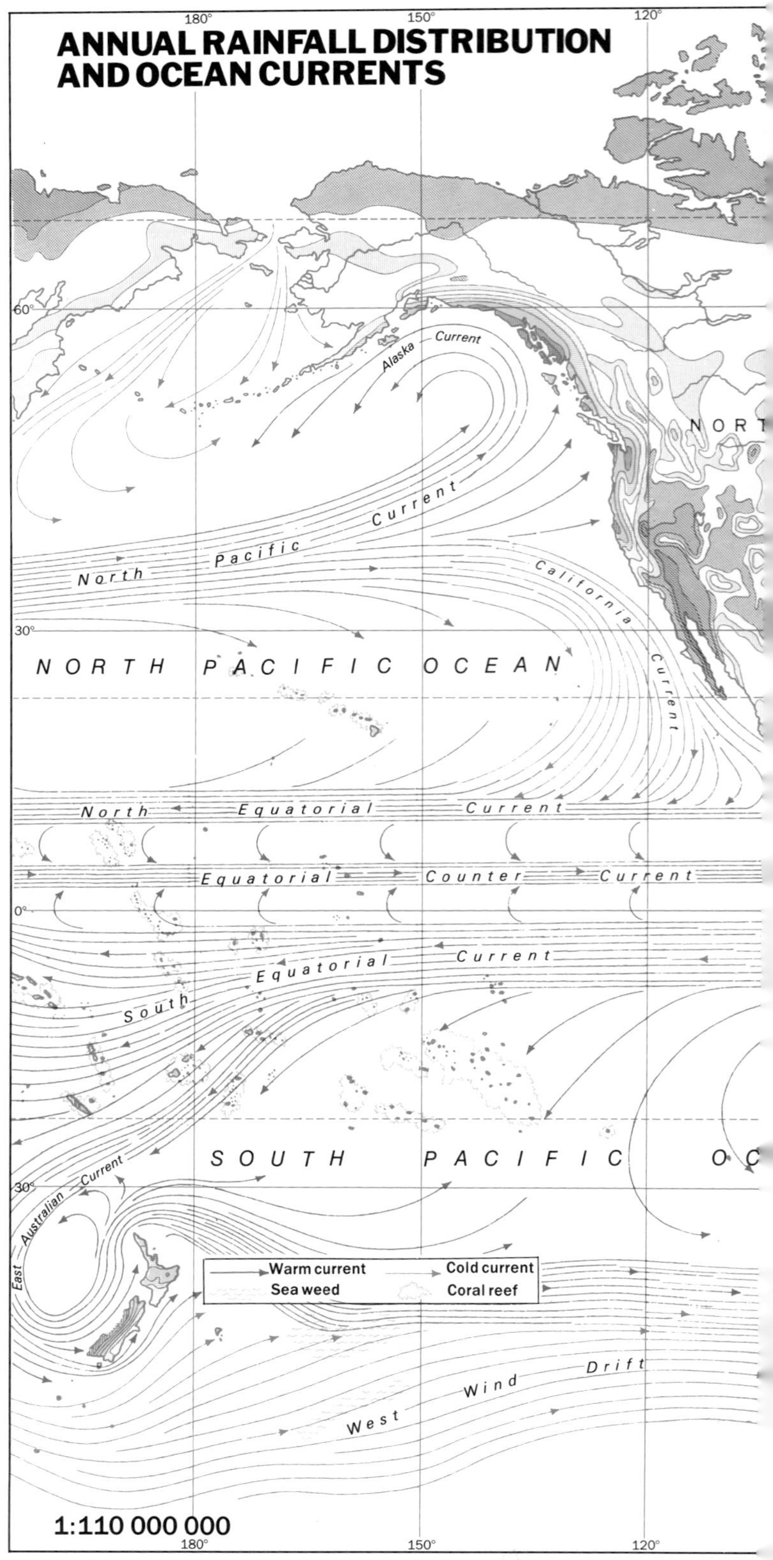

<table>
<tr><td>84</td><td>97</td><td>104</td></tr>
<tr><td>12.0</td><td>over 16.0</td><td>over 16.0</td></tr>
<tr><td>**10**</td><td>**11**</td><td>**12**</td></tr>
<tr><td>Trees uprooted considerable damage.</td><td>Major destruction.</td><td>Disastrous destruction</td></tr>
</table>

Left In 1805, the British admiral, Francis Beaufort, devised a sequence of numbers to indicate the force of winds at sea. Associated effects at sea and on land were added later to show that 'white horses' occasional at Force 3 became widespread at Force 6, that waves became higher and longer, that spray and foam increased with turbulence until visibility was affected. Wind speeds were added later still. More scientific methods exist but the scale is easily assimilable and the Beaufort number with temperature; pressure; precipitation; visibility and outlook together provide a concise weather summary.

12, seas rising to 16–17m and torrential rain cause the destruction.

Far from destructive are the Chinook of N. America and the Föhn winds of the Alps. Air, depleted of moisture, is warmed in its descent of the rain-shadow side of high mountain ranges.

Tsunamis, destructive ocean waves, are not the result of weather but of submarine seismic activity. A wave of no more than 1m but travelling at 650km/hr can rise to 16m or more on impact with the shore.

Right Waterspouts are sea tornadoes, short-lived phenomena lasting from one minute to half-an-hour. A rapidly gyrating vortex descends from a cumulus or cumulonimbus cloud whipping the sea and sucking up a column of water from 1m to 300m diameter which travels with the cloud but with the base moving at a different speed. High velocity peripheral winds, the disturbed sea-surface and descent of water inflict the damage. It should be noted that the African tornado, also highly destructive, is actually a violent squall.

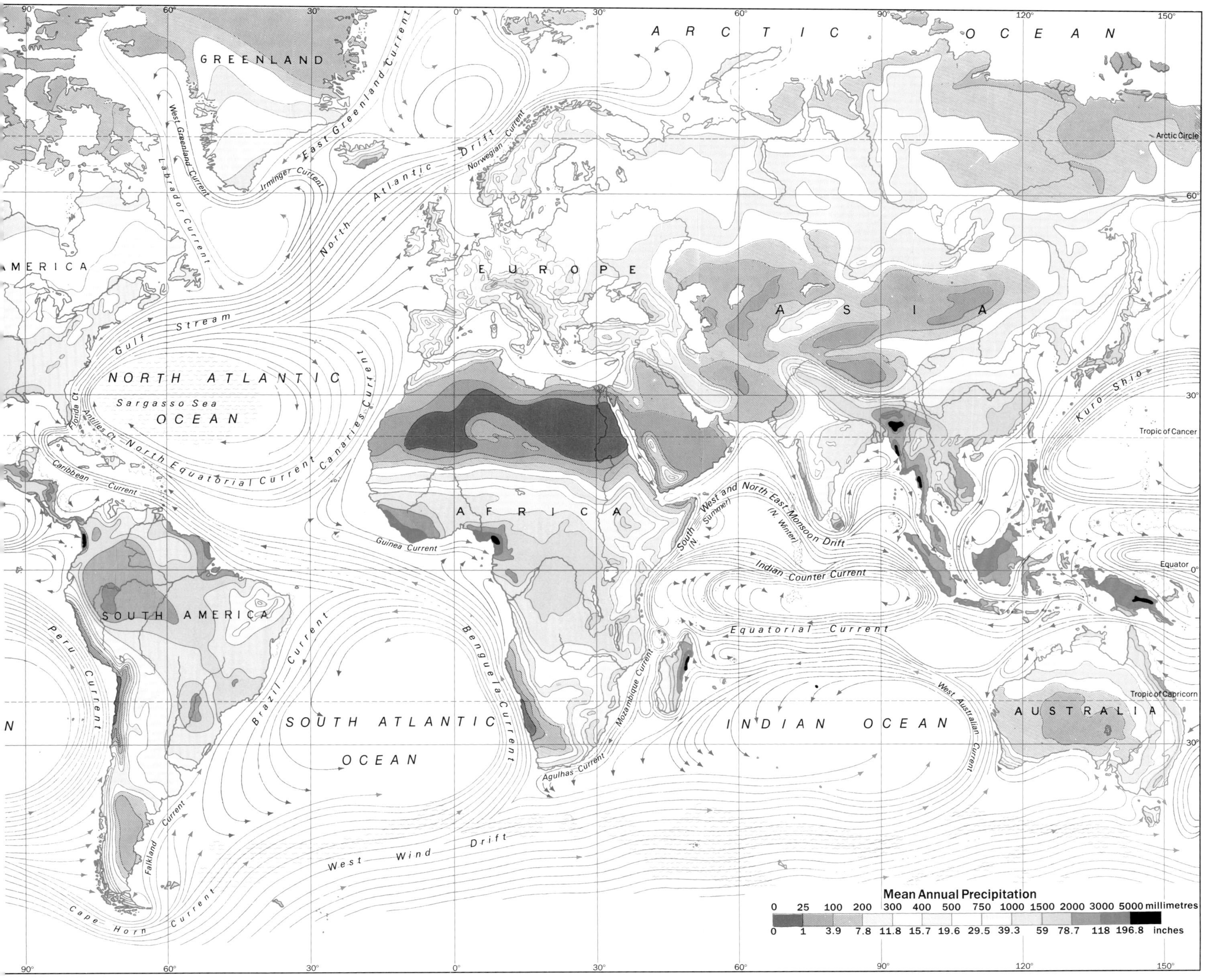

Mean Annual Precipitation

0	25	100	200	300	400	500	750	1000	1500	2000	3000	5000 millimetres
0	1	3.9	7.8	11.8	15.7	19.6	29.5	39.3	59	78.7	118	196.8 inches

VEGETATION

In a world so subordinated to human beings, it is salutory to be reminded that the atmosphere itself and fertile soils which support agriculture are the creations of plant life. Yet there is far less general concern for the preservation of plants threatened with extinction than there is over endangered animal species.

Perhaps the most remarkable feature of plant life is its almost complete ubiquity. Unless inhibited by ice, plants establish themselves wherever conditions allow and once established encourage the formation or collection of soil and the means to generate their species. The type of plant is determined primarily by climate and soil. Soil is composed of solid, liquid and gas, the solid part being the primary parent rock with secondary rock material changed through moisture and chemical reaction. Humus, decayed vegetable matter, is both solid and liquid. The gas is air.

Russian research first linked soil type to climate, so Russian terms are used for soils. Vegetation zones broadly match soil classes. Thus in the tundra, low temperature and a permanently frozen sub-soil retard organic decay. Thaw in the peaty surface produces swamps. Trees and shrubs are sparse and stunted. South of the tundra is the boreal forest (taiga) of coniferous trees, largely evergreen with some deciduous trees. Their resinous leaves protect against extreme cold and limit transpiration. Soils are podzols, a name applied to whitish-grey sandy soils in which leaching has taken place, a process by which water percolates downwards carrying organic and other matter in solution. These soils are acid. The coniferous vegetation does not produce a rich humus when it decays. Because Siberian rivers flow north the lower reaches are still frozen when the upper reaches thaw. Floods then ensue.

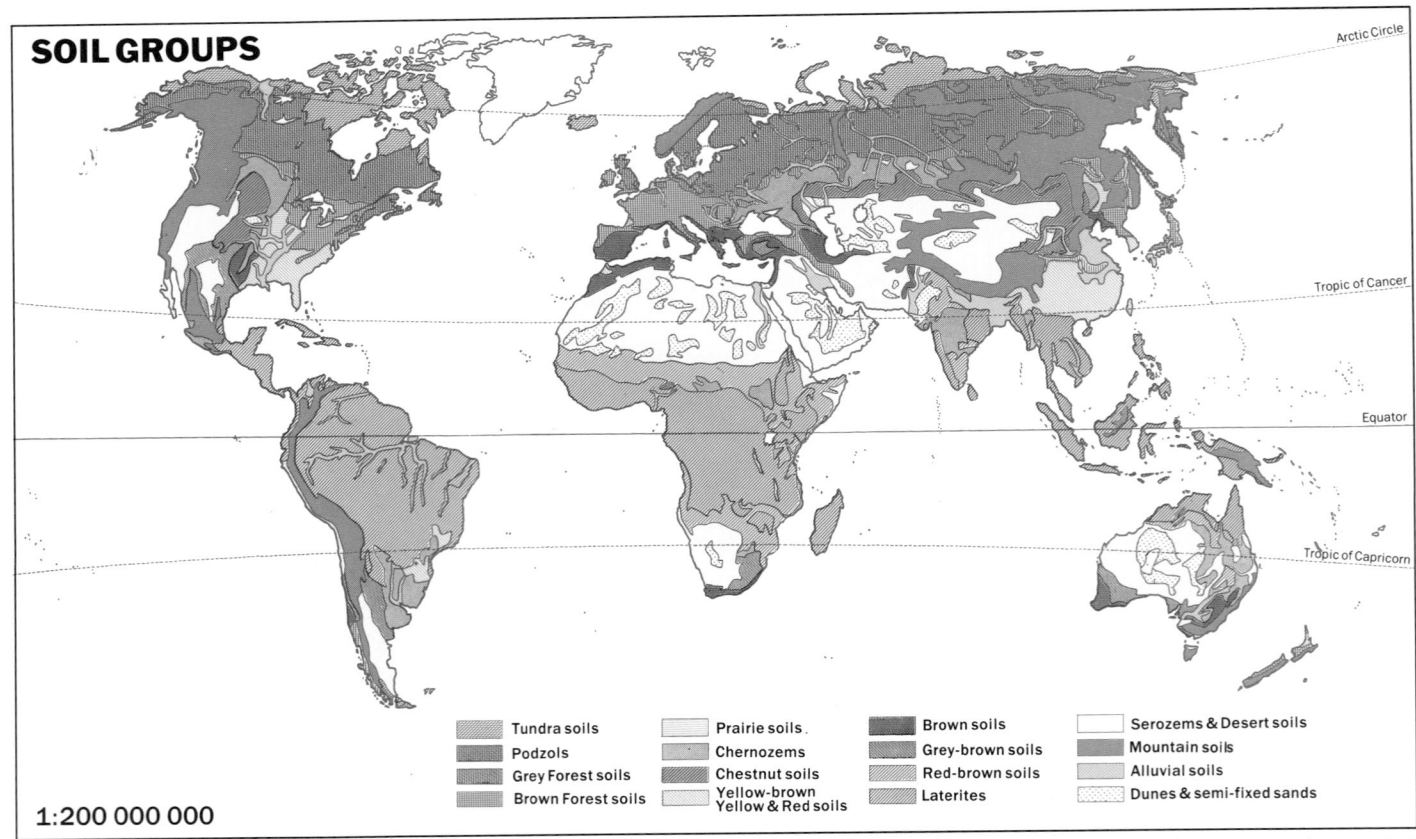

SOIL GROUPS

1:200 000 000

Tundra soils	Prairie soils	Brown soils	Serozems & Desert soils
Podzols	Chernozems	Grey-brown soils	Mountain soils
Grey Forest soils	Chestnut soils	Red-brown soils	Alluvial soils
Brown Forest soils	Yellow-brown Yellow & Red soils	Laterites	Dunes & semi-fixed sands

Trees of the taiga are, therefore, less healthy than those of N. America.

South of the taiga the mixed coniferous and deciduous temperate forests merge into a zone of deciduous forests where trees have a resting period in winter and summers are dry enough and warm enough to allow humus to form. Further south again are the chernozems, fine-grained loams rich in humus hence their name 'black-earth'. This is the zone of the naturally occurring wooded grassy steppes. The soils are of various kinds but they are very like the loess of northern China where the cohesive properties of the soil allow it to form vertical faces. These fertile soils which are found in Europe, Asia and N. & S. America have all been given over to agriculture.

South again are the rather less fertile chestnut soils of the true steppes. Next follow red and grey soils of the semi-desert and desert steppes.

Beyond the hot deserts are the tropical grasslands and finally at the equator the rain forests (selva) where very tall evergreen trees form a dense forest, denser in S. America than in Africa or Asia. The resting period in which the trees shed their leaves occurs at various times throughout the year.

More than two fifths of all living things on earth are found in the rain forests and there is a tremendous variety of trees and other forms of life in even a small area of forest.

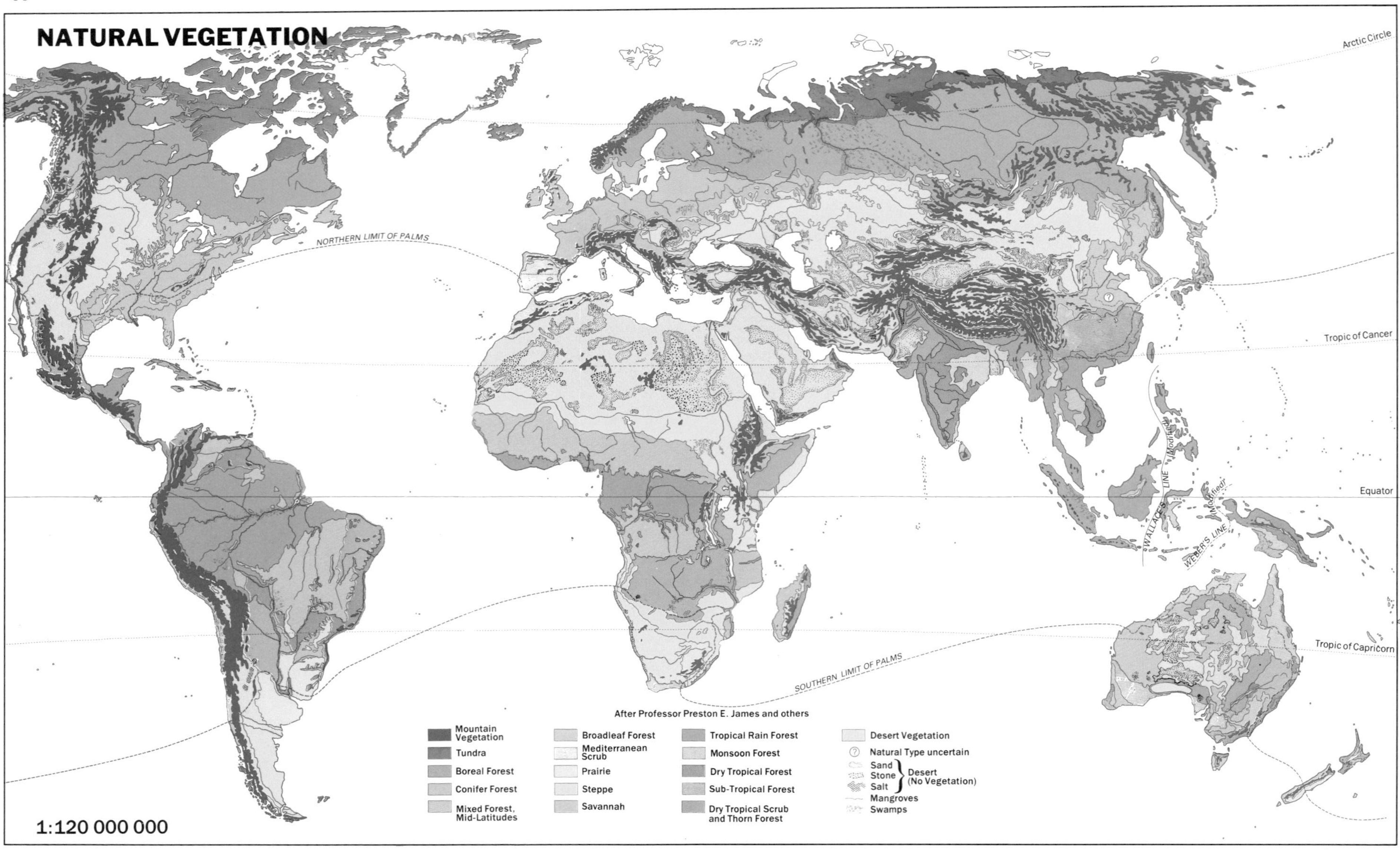

NATURAL VEGETATION

NORTHERN LIMIT OF PALMS

SOUTHERN LIMIT OF PALMS

After Professor Preston E. James and others

1:120 000 000

Mountain Vegetation	Broadleaf Forest	Tropical Rain Forest	Desert Vegetation
Tundra	Mediterranean Scrub	Monsoon Forest	Natural Type uncertain
Boreal Forest	Prairie	Dry Tropical Forest	Sand / Stone / Salt } Desert (No Vegetation)
Conifer Forest	Steppe	Sub-Tropical Forest	Mangroves
Mixed Forest, Mid-Latitudes	Savannah	Dry Tropical Scrub and Thorn Forest	Swamps

MINERALS

Rare metals

Uranium, the best known and most important of the rare metals owes the expansion of its production to the development of nuclear power and related industries. North America is the largest producer but there are significant deposits in Australia, South Africa, Niger and France. Niobium, a metal used in alloys and toolmaking is mined mainly in Brazil, Canada and Russian Federation, while Tantalum, a corrosion resistant metal valuable to the electronic and chemical industries is found in N. America and Nigeria.

Precious metals

Over and above their more glamorous associations, gold, platinum and silver have a wide range of applications within industry including electronics, chemicals and photography. South Africa dominates the western world's production of gold and platinum,

Above Manganese nodules form gradually over millions of years around a foreign body. Although they occur over 20% of the ocean floor, only in limited areas are they of economic importance.

accounting for over 30% of total output (the major platinum mines are located in Bophuthatswana). Russian Federation, also a substantial producer of platinum is the other major gold producing country while smaller amounts are found in North America and several other localities worldwide. Silver production is less dominated by any one country and is mined throughout the Americas, Central Asia and Australia.

Chemical and Fertilizer minerals

This grouping embraces a variety of minerals occurring in a range of forms and requiring very different recovery techniques. Their usage is widespread in chemical processes throughout industry, apatite, potash and phosphate rock being especially

important in the manufacture of fertilizers. Phosphate rock is exploited widely, though the main volume of production is from U.S.A., Russian Federation and Morocco. The former U.S.S.R., North America, Germany and France are the leading suppliers of potash. Sources of borax, fluorite and sulphur occur throughout N. America, Europe and western Asia, with U.S.A. a leading producer of all three.

Other Industrial minerals

Asbestos, well-known as a fibrous insulating material; it is produced in Central Asia, North America, Canada, Southern Africa, China and Italy. China clay, a fine white clay used in the paper, ceramic and cosmetic industries is found in China, Europe and U.S.A.

Magnesite, a magnesium ore comes particularly from Central Asia, Europe and China for use in the production of refractories and chemicals.

Mica, used as an electrical insulator, is principally produced in U.S.A. and in smaller quantities throughout Europe and Asia.

Talc, a soft greasy mineral is used as a lubricant and in paper manufacture, paint and cosmetics. Production is mainly from U.S.A., Russian Federation and Europe.

Light metals

Aluminium is extracted from bauxite, an ore occurring in feldspars and other silicates which readily breaks down in tropical conditions. It is therefore often found as a surface crust in tropical areas. Principal producers are Australia, Guinea and Jamaica with smaller but substantial amounts from S.E. Europe, Central Asia and the northern regions of South America. Titanium is a heat resistant metal used in high grade steel alloys largely in the aircraft and aerospace industries. The two main ores, rutile and ilmenite,

are widespread and plentiful; the main sources include Brazil, Canada and Norway.

Iron

Iron is the second most abundant metallic element in the Earth's crust after aluminium. Rarely found as a free metal it exists in ores of varying constitutions which are smelted to produce metallic iron. Further processing produces steel and combination with other metals makes special steels and alloys. Iron ore is mined in many locations but the principal producing areas are Ukraine, Russian Federation, Australia, Brazil and U.S.A. followed by Canada, China and India. Many other countries produce smaller but nonetheless substantial tonnages.

Ferro-alloy metals

These metals are variously mined in many locations throughout the world but, taken collectively, the most important producing areas are the former U.S.S.R., South Africa and Canada followed by U.S.A. and China. All of these metals offer specific qualities and properties for the manufacture of a variety of special steels and alloys. Nickel and chromium, for example, are necessary for the production of high quality stainless steel whilst vanadium and tungsten help produce very hard steels.

Base metals

Generally mined as ores and compounds the free metal is released after smelting. Antimony, copper, tin and zinc are important in the making of alloys but each has individual uses related to its specific properties. Copper, lead, tin and zinc for example, are corrosion resistant under certain conditions, and the liquidity of mercury has obvious uses. Often found together or in combination with other metals, they are distributed widely over the earth's surface and there are many significant producing countries.

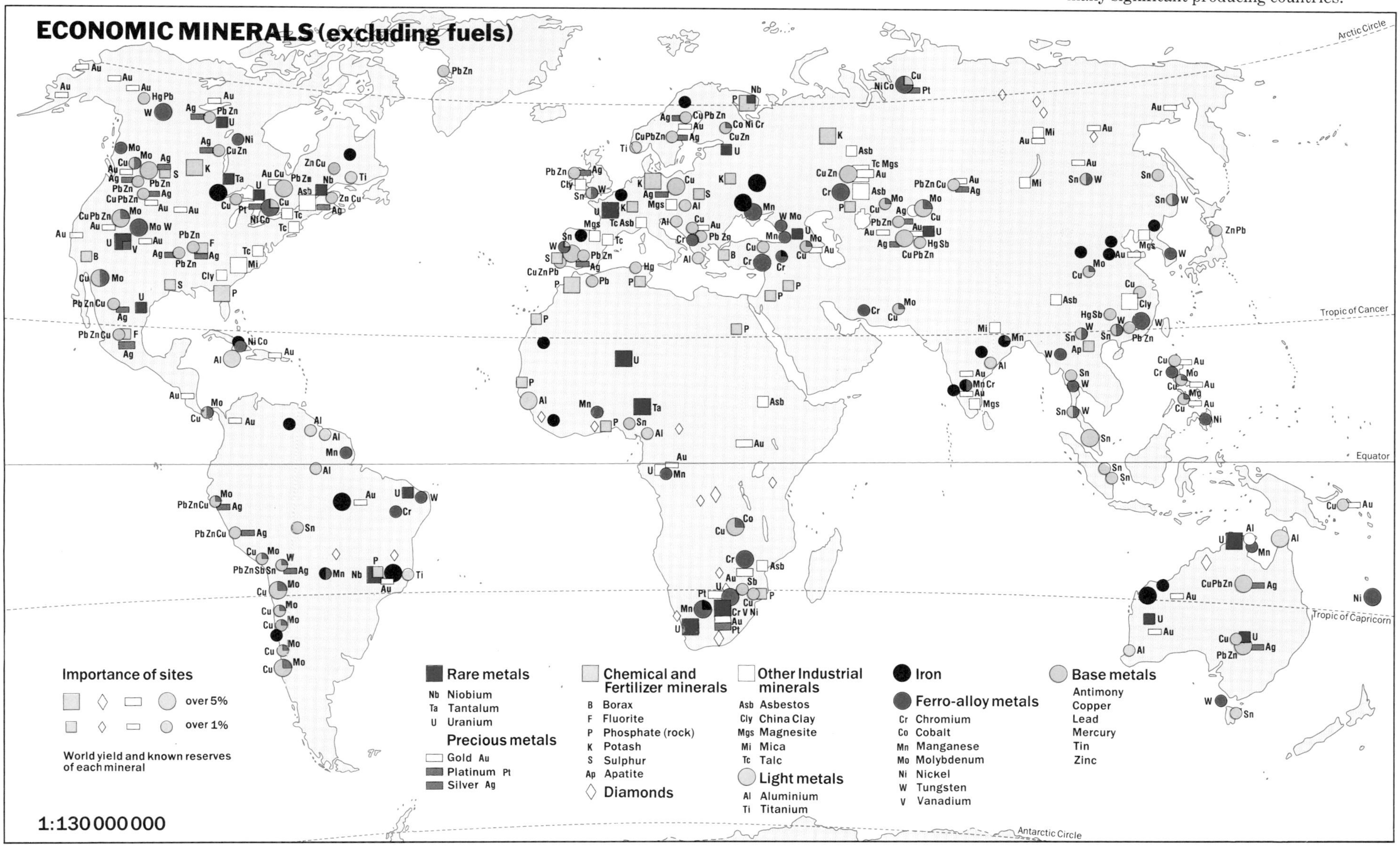

ECONOMIC MINERALS (excluding fuels)

1:130 000 000

Importance of sites

over 5%

over 1%

World yield and known reserves of each mineral

Rare metals
Nb Niobium
Ta Tantalum
U Uranium

Precious metals
Gold Au
Platinum Pt
Silver Ag

Chemical and Fertilizer minerals
B Borax
F Fluorite
P Phosphate (rock)
K Potash
S Sulphur
Ap Apatite
◇ Diamonds

Other Industrial minerals
Asb Asbestos
Cly China Clay
Mgs Magnesite
Mi Mica
Tc Talc

Light metals
Al Aluminium
Ti Titanium

Iron

Ferro-alloy metals
Cr Chromium
Co Cobalt
Mn Manganese
Mo Molybdenum
Ni Nickel
W Tungsten
V Vanadium

Base metals
Antimony
Copper
Lead
Mercury
Tin
Zinc

ENERGY

Taken together, the maps and diagrams though concerned with energy, give in graphic form, a summary of two centuries of economic growth.

Coal powered the industrial revolution and replaced wood as the primary source for industrial and domestic heat.

From the end of World War I another economic transformation began. Oil which had been used since remotest times to provide light and heat began to achieve major industrial importance. The last coal-fired ships vanished from the seas and with them the coal-bunkering stations disposed around the world. On land the internal-combustion engine replaced the horse; oil-fired electricity generation began to challenge coal-fired plants.

The end of World War II marked the start of unparalleled economic growth. Between 1950 and 1990 world energy demand increased four-fold, the steepest rise occurring between 1960 and 1970. In this period coal lost its pre-eminence as a source of energy. An oil industry developed to produce a variety of fuels and lubricants. It contained a large petro-chemical element.

Eighty per cent of this stupendous industrial expansion was based in North America (particularly the U.S.A.), Europe, the former U.S.S.R. and Japan. Oil and gas were the sources of the additional energy required for the expansion and the Middle East was the source of half the oil consumed.

The oil producing and exporting nations (OPEC) decided to raise the price of oil in 1973 thus bringing to an end the era of low-price energy. Revolution in Iran and the outbreak of war between Iraq and Iran caused a further escalation in price in 1979. Oil was then 17 times dearer than in 1972. Demand fell. The continued search for alternative sources was intensified. Rate of production fell below rate of discovery once more. Middle East share of world oil production fell from 50% to 27% by 1990. However, the Middle East still possesses over 50% of proved reserves.

Off-shore technology in exploration and exploitation have created a new oil technology. Operations in Alaska and Siberia have taxed the ingenuity of the oil-industry in combating severe climatic conditions.

Oil and gas reserves are constantly reviewed as new discoveries are made but the life of both is relatively short. Coal reserves are probably adequate for the next 250 years. In the coming decades the use of oil will increasingly be restricted to areas like transport where no alternative exists. Coal will once more be in the ascendancy. Coal gas which has been virtually replaced by natural gas may once more be used. Extraction of oil from coal may also be practised. Other sources of oil and gas are bituminous shales and tar sands.

Among the possible alternative energy sources are those in which the energy expended is renewed. Wind-generation and tidal power are two such examples. Although they may well be economically operated the installation costs are prodigious.

Nuclear energy alone promises to be capable of meeting future demands. Early promises of this form of generation providing abundant and cheap energy were not fulfilled. Fears that the supply of uranium would run out have been dispelled by enrichment techniques which yield 50 to 60 times the output. Strong opposition from those concerned for the environment has been the principle reason why the nuclear industry has been retarded. The accident at Three-Mile Island in the United States in 1979 had a profound effect on public opinion which was reinforced by the Chernobyl' disaster in the Ukraine in April 1986.

Still further options remain. All nuclear energy at the moment is based on nuclear fission. If nuclear fusion can be harnessed then an unlimited supply of energy could be provided by the oceans. The process would be the same as that by which the Sun creates its energy. Geothermal power is practical and feasible. Another source is the transformation of the Sun's light into electricity by photovoltaique techniques. Alternatively, solar energy can be converted into micro-waves by satellite. Such methods are for the next century, not this.

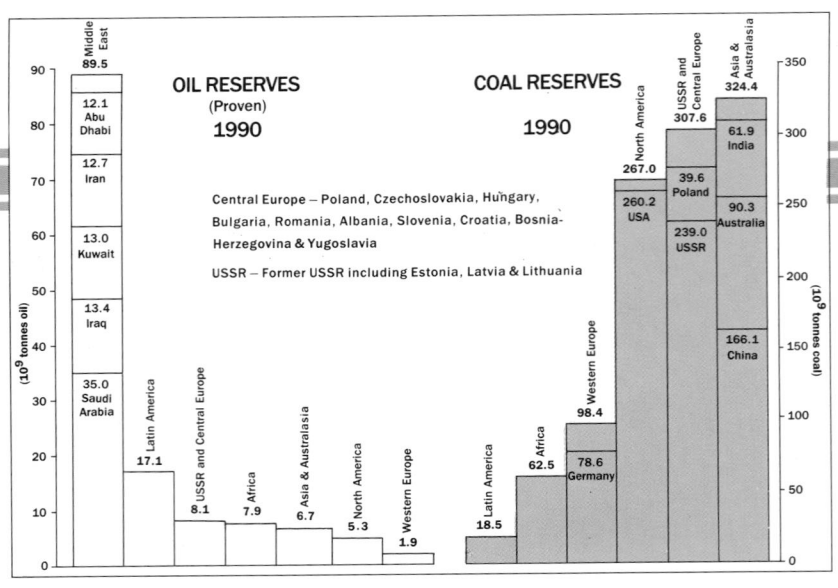

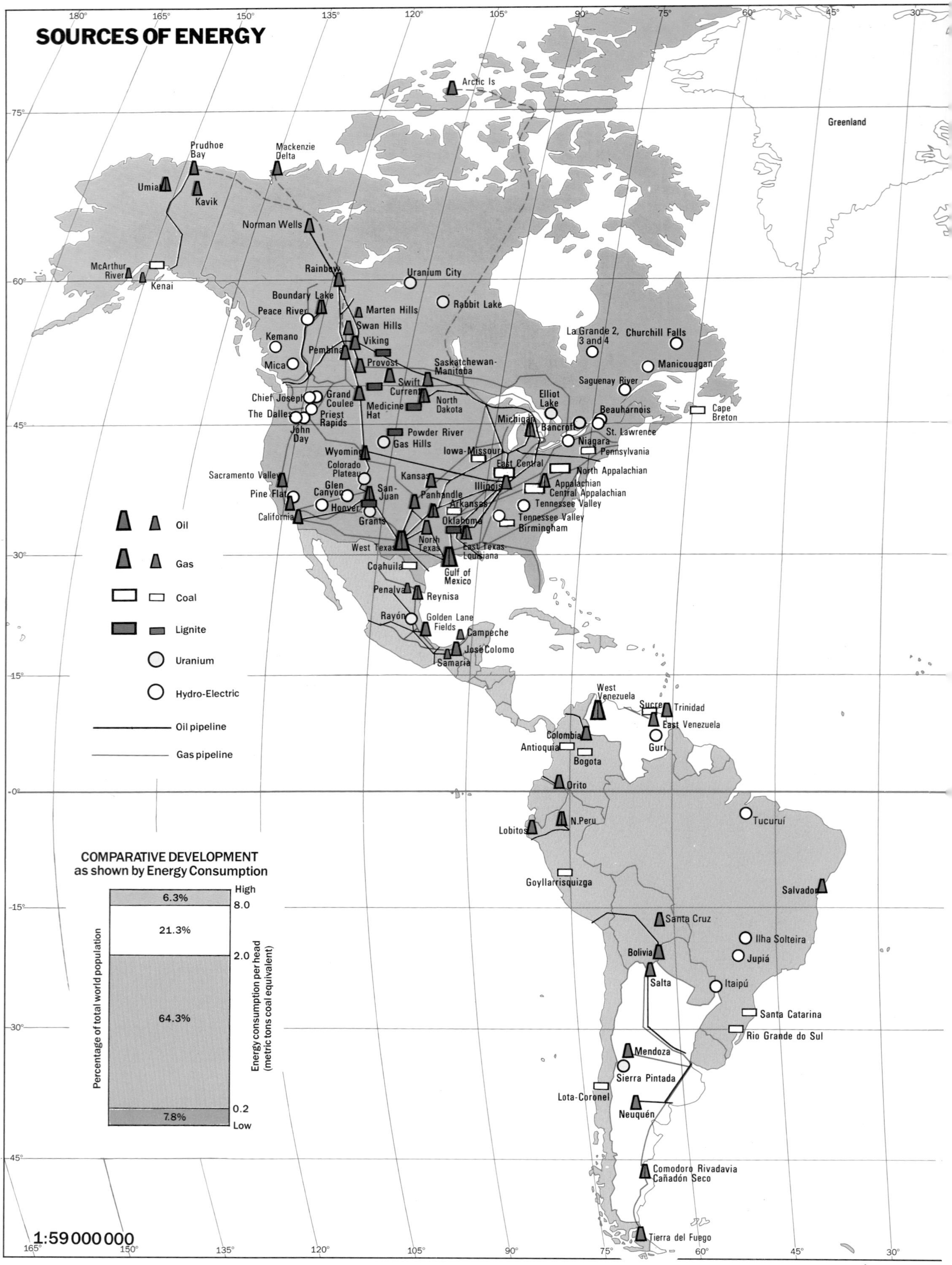

OIL RESERVES (Proven) 1990

COAL RESERVES 1990

Central Europe — Poland, Czechoslovakia, Hungary, Bulgaria, Romania, Albania, Slovenia, Croatia, Bosnia-Herzegovina & Yugoslavia

USSR — Former USSR including Estonia, Latvia & Lithuania

SOURCES OF ENERGY

Oil
Gas
Coal
Lignite
Uranium
Hydro-Electric
Oil pipeline
Gas pipeline

COMPARATIVE DEVELOPMENT
as shown by Energy Consumption

High 8.0

6.3%
21.3%
64.3%
7.8%

Percentage of total world population

Energy consumption per head (metric tons coal equivalent)

2.0

0.2
Low

1:59 000 000

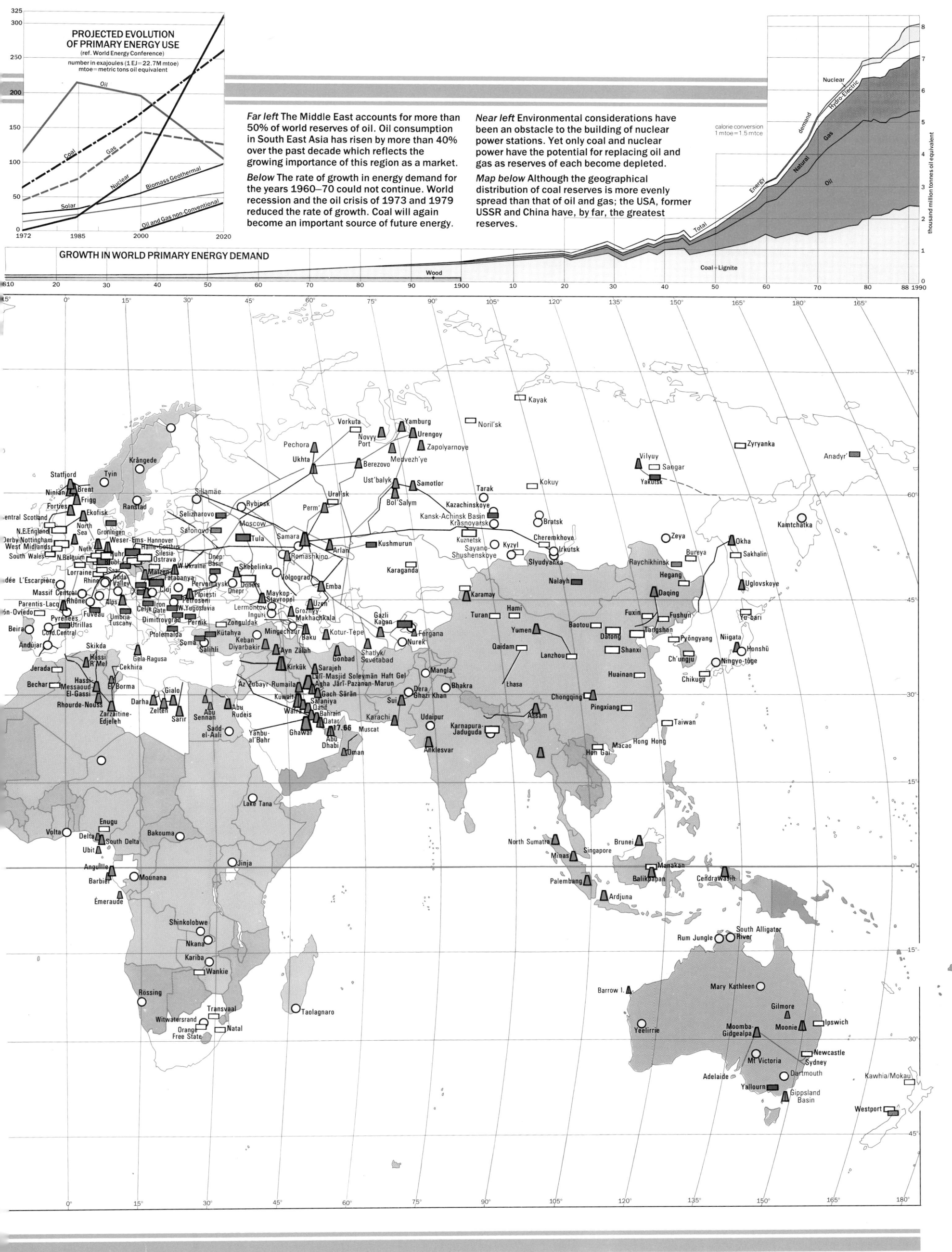

PROJECTED EVOLUTION
OF PRIMARY ENERGY USE
(ref. World Energy Conference)

number in exajoules (1 EJ = 22.7M mtoe)
mtoe = metric tons oil equivalent

Oil
Coal
Gas
Nuclear
Biomass Geothermal
Solar
Oil and Gas non-Conventional

Far left The Middle East accounts for more than 50% of world reserves of oil. Oil consumption in South East Asia has risen by more than 40% over the past decade which reflects the growing importance of this region as a market.

Below The rate of growth in energy demand for the years 1960–70 could not continue. World recession and the oil crisis of 1973 and 1979 reduced the rate of growth. Coal will again become an important source of future energy.

Near left Environmental considerations have been an obstacle to the building of nuclear power stations. Yet only coal and nuclear power have the potential for replacing oil and gas as reserves of each become depleted.

Map below Although the geographical distribution of coal reserves is more evenly spread than that of oil and gas; the USA, former USSR and China have, by far, the greatest reserves.

calorie conversion
1 mtoe = 1.5 mtce

GROWTH IN WORLD PRIMARY ENERGY DEMAND

Wood

Coal + Lignite

Nuclear
Hydro-Electric
Gas
Natural
Oil
Energy demand
Total

thousand million tonnes oil equivalent

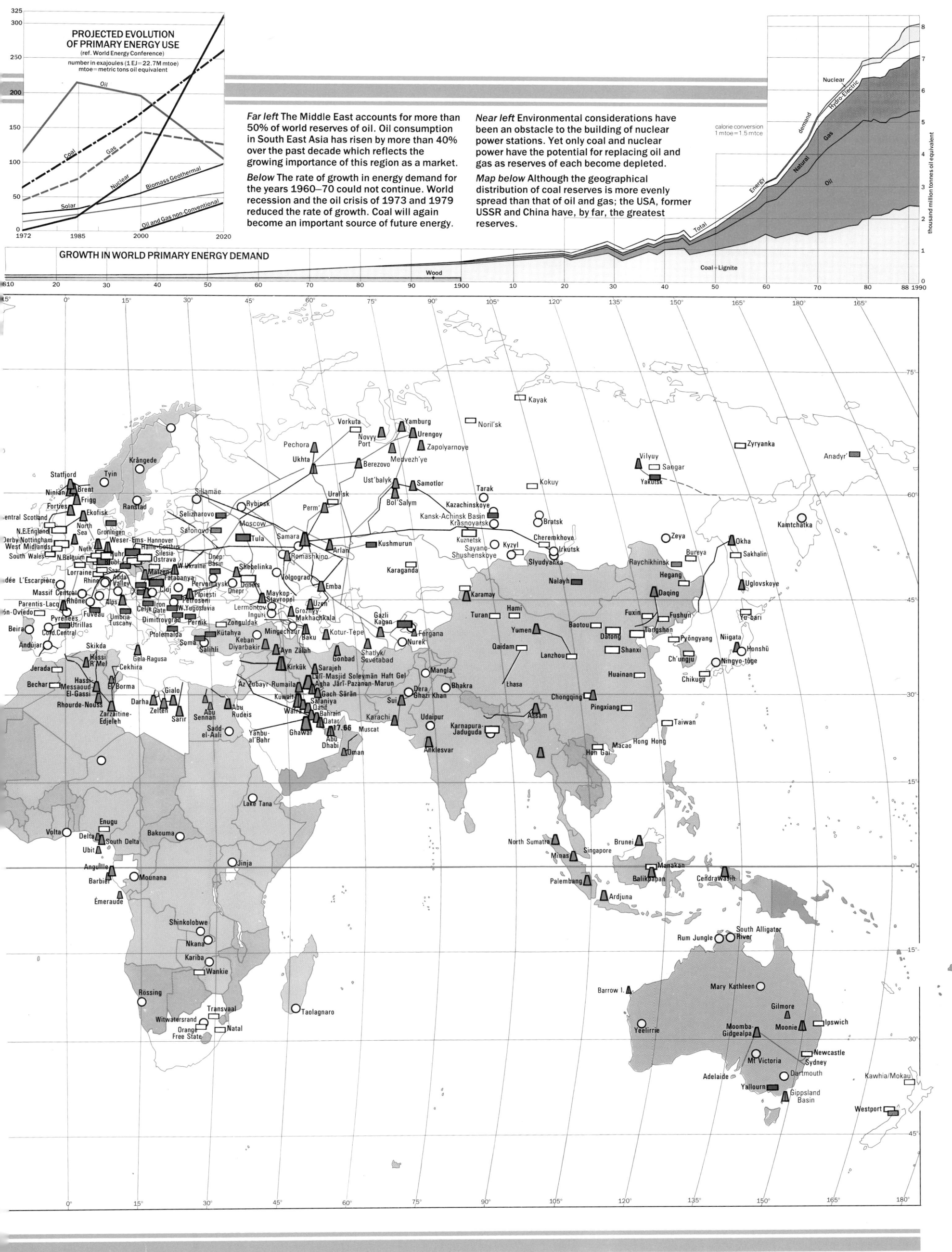

41

FOOD

With a world population which has doubled in the half-century between 1925 and 1975, it is a source of wonderment that more people are not starving. Especially since a further increase of 25% in the number of mouths to feed occurred in the decade up to 1985. It is still more remarkable when it is remembered that only about 11% of the Earth's land surface is under cultivation and that includes areas of non-food products like rubber. The credit for this achievement must be given to the development of artificial fertilizers; the conditioning of plants to alien climates; the development of high-yield seeds and new strains and generally improved agricultural technology. There is no great reserve of land ready to be brought into crop production. The outlook for the future is of a world in which the poorest areas have the highest population growth and the greatest difficulty in producing sufficient food. Matters of immediate concern are the current rate of soil erosion through the felling of trees, over-cropping, and the loss of fertility of world soils through unwise use of artificial fertilizers. Animal manure and vegetable waste are frequently used as fuel. Cash crops are planted where food crops are needed. Even if organic matter were returned to the soil and all the land were devoted to food crops, the required yields would not necessarily be achieved. In many of the poorest areas improved seeds and fertilizers would still be required. Food provision is not therefore, simply a matter of agricultural technology and distribution. Political and social factors are also involved.

From the land now under cultivation 98% of all food is produced. The other 2% comes from the sea. Unless, through some miracle of laboratory science, protein can be artificially created in sufficient quantities, the sea

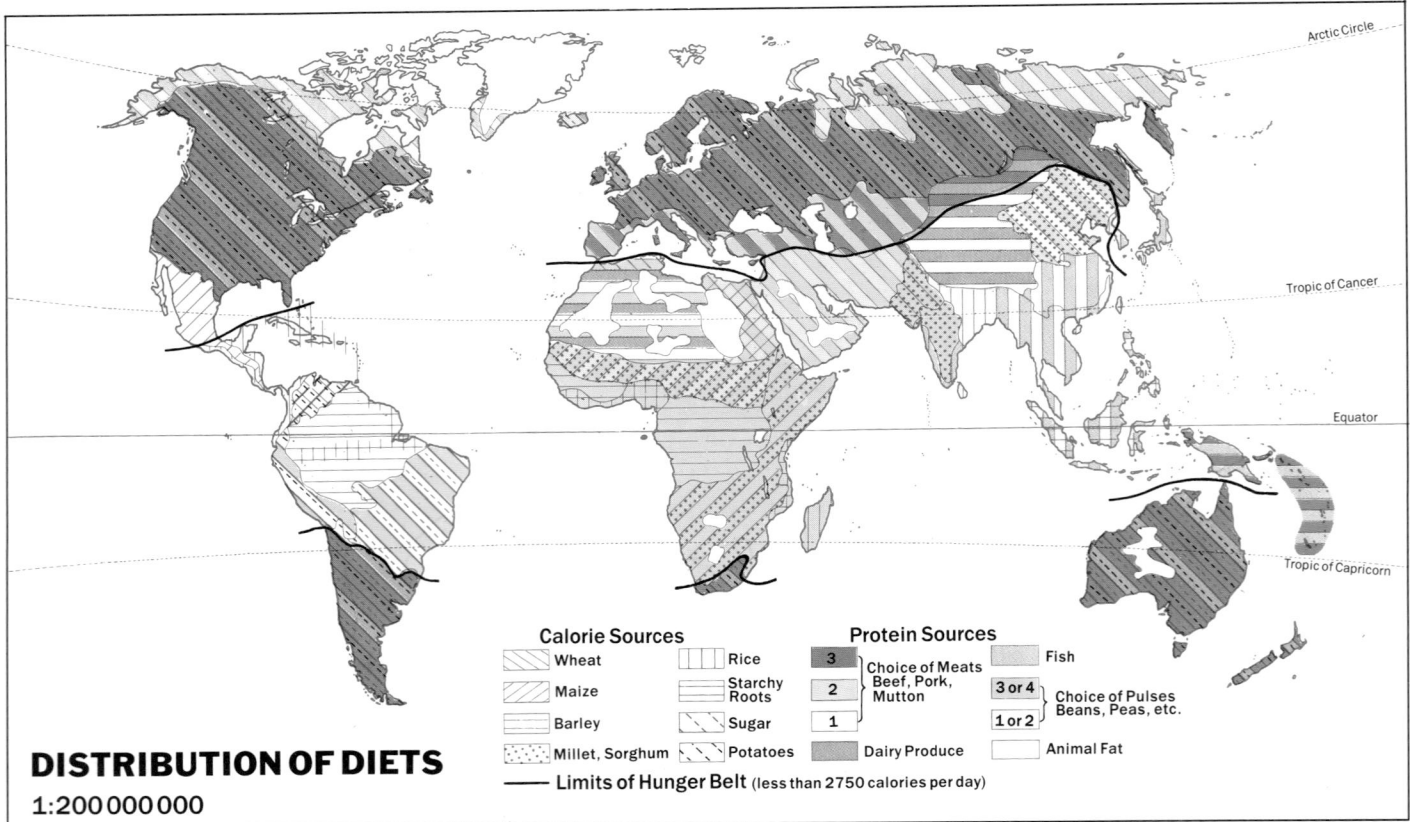

DISTRIBUTION OF DIETS
1:200 000 000

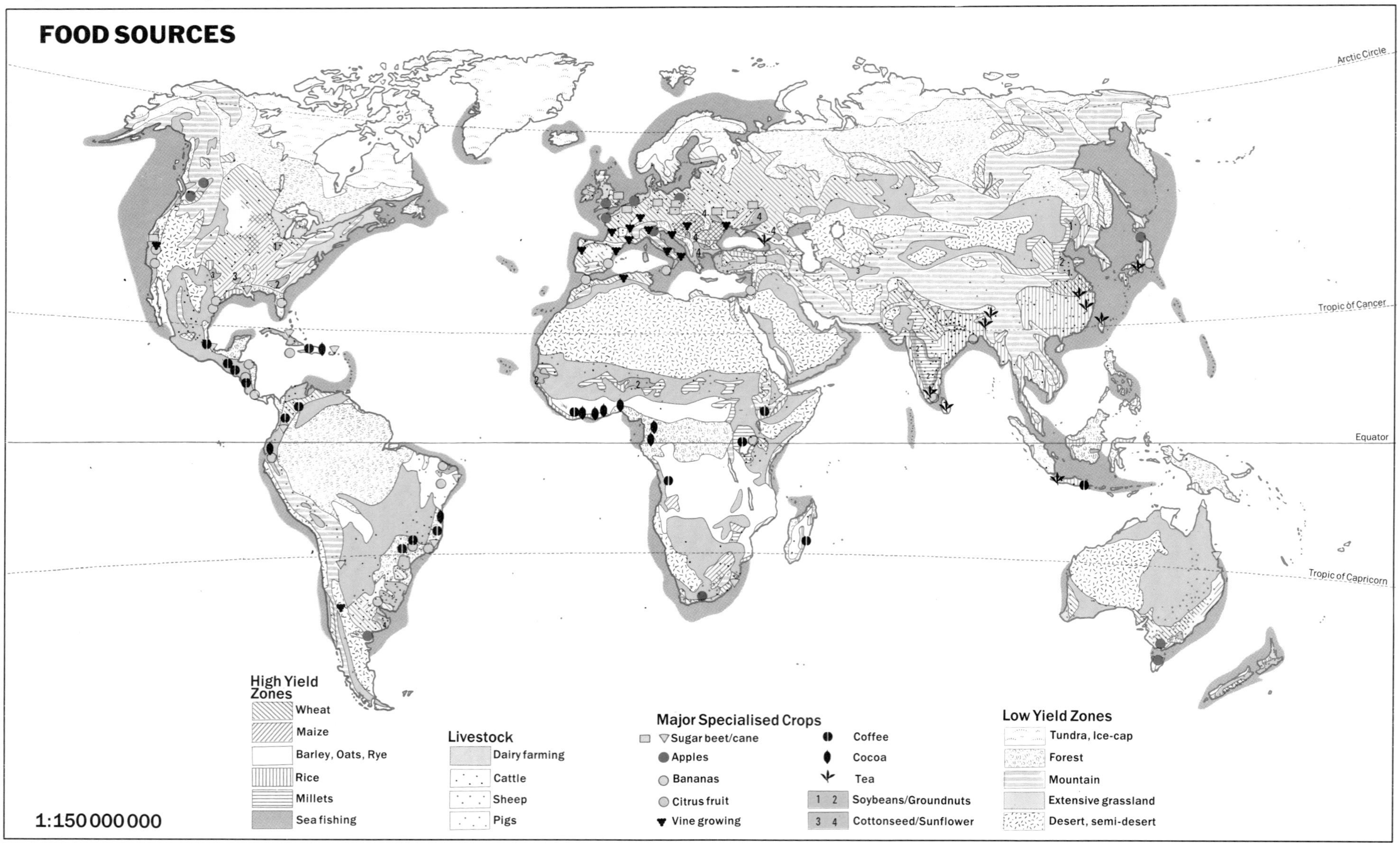

Calorie Sources
Wheat · Maize · Barley · Millet, Sorghum · Rice · Starchy Roots · Sugar · Potatoes

Protein Sources
3 Choice of Meats Beef, Pork, Mutton · 2 · 1 · Dairy Produce · Fish · 3 or 4 Choice of Pulses Beans, Peas, etc. · 1 or 2 · Animal Fat

— Limits of Hunger Belt (less than 2750 calories per day)

is the only major source available in the immediate future for supplementing the food potential of the land. Fish-farming, practised in East Asia for four thousand years, has been taken up in several parts of the world but it has been restricted to certain types of fish and shell-fish. The land, however, remains the main source of food and future yields depend on soil conservation and recovery; the development of new strains; conservation of food plants now

under threat of extinction; elimination of pests and diseases; improved animal husbandry; investigating new sources of vegetable protein and synthetic food production.

Nutritional standards vary from nation to nation as do diets. North America, Western Europe, Australia and New Zealand are the great meat-eaters; East Asia consumes more fish and less meat but much of the world is dependent on cereal crops, beans and pulses. In overall calorie terms the

best-fed nations take in on average, daily, almost three times the average of the worst-fed. Comparing the daily calorie intake of average low-calorie groups of countries with Canada, the United States, Argentina, Western Europe, Australia, and New Zealand there is a gap of more than 1300 calories. Reducing this disparity must depend on improved local food production provided at the same time the present high rate of population growth can be abated.

FOOD SOURCES

High Yield Zones
Wheat · Maize · Barley, Oats, Rye · Rice · Millets · Sea fishing

1:150 000 000

Livestock
Dairy farming · Cattle · Sheep · Pigs

Major Specialised Crops
▽ Sugar beet/cane · Apples · Bananas · Citrus fruit · ▼ Vine growing · Coffee · Cocoa · ↓ Tea · 1 2 Soybeans/Groundnuts · 3 4 Cottonseed/Sunflower

Low Yield Zones
Tundra, Ice-cap · Forest · Mountain · Extensive grassland · Desert, semi-desert

In the view of many people, proliferation of the human race is, in itself and its environmental consequences, a threat to the future of all life on this planet. The twentieth century promises to close with 3.6 times as many people as there were at the beginning. Fortunately, the high rate of annual increase (1.99%) of the period up to 1975 has been reduced, and consequently, there will be almost 1.5 billion fewer people at the end of the century than was at one time anticipated. Assuming that the present growth (1.67%) continues, there will be 6.1 billion people by AD2000.

For any country a growth rate in excess of 2% can spell disaster: 2% means a doubling of population in 35 years, 2.5% gives a doubling in 28 years and a growth of 3.5% doubles in only 20 years. Rate of growth is dependent on the number of live births, infant mortality and the death rate. The increase in numbers has been largely the result of reduction in infant mortality and the death rate in adults. People are living longer and a reduction in the number of live births may well be counter-balanced by prolonged life.

There is a kind of north-south divide, if one excludes Australia and New Zealand, with the technologically developed world approaching zero growth while the rest of the world continues to increase, in some areas at an alarming rate. In Africa, many countries have a growth rate of more than 3% in spite of shorter life expectancy and higher infant mortality (114 per 1000 compared with 16 for Europe and 12 for North America). The Middle Eastern countries although sparsely populated are now seeing increases of well over 4%

Today, Albania alone in Europe has a rate of growth in excess of 2%. The United Kingdom, Italy, Sweden, Denmark, Austria, Belgium and Bulgaria have achieved a growth

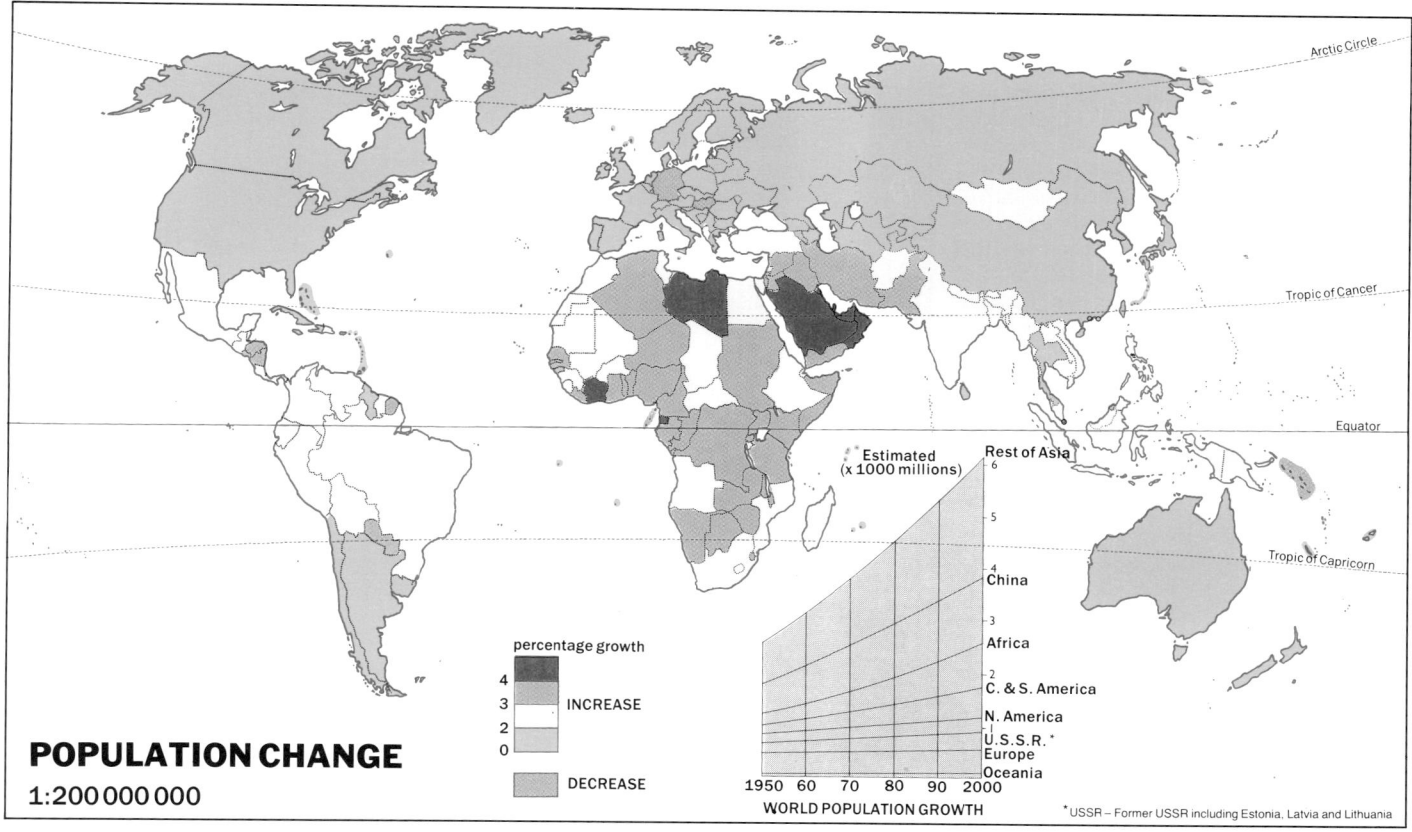

POPULATION CHANGE
1:200 000 000

percentage growth

4
3
2
0 — INCREASE

DECREASE

Estimated (x 1000 millions)

Rest of Asia
China
Africa
C. & S. America
N. America
U.S.S.R.*
Europe
Oceania

1950 60 70 80 90 2000
WORLD POPULATION GROWTH

*USSR – Former USSR including Estonia, Latvia and Lithuania

rate of less than 0.2%, with Germany and Hungary now experiencing negative growth. Japan and the former U.S.S.R. have achieved a rate below 1%.

China's policy of population control has brought the growth rate down to 1.3% not far removed from U.S.A. and Canada (both 1.0%) the highest of the northern nations. India, likewise has, by its birth control policy, slowed its rate of growth yet at present rates the combined populations of China and

India will exceed 2½ billion by the end of the century at which time the population of Asia will have equalled or surpassed the total world population of 1975.

In Central and South America a high average birth-rate by country is accompanied by a general lowering of the death-rate which for most of the area is about the same as that of Canada and U.S.A., Europe, the former U.S.S.R., Japan, China, Australia and New Zealand all of which are either 10 or less per

1000 compared with 10 to 20 for Africa and Southern Asia (except Malaysia, Thailand and Philippines). Life expectancy is lowest in parts of Africa and Asia – below 40 years compared with over 70 for almost all the developed world.

Increased longevity, reduced infant mortality and a high birth rate will inevitably change the numbers of young and old who live as dependents. Providing for them is a great challenge for the next few generations.

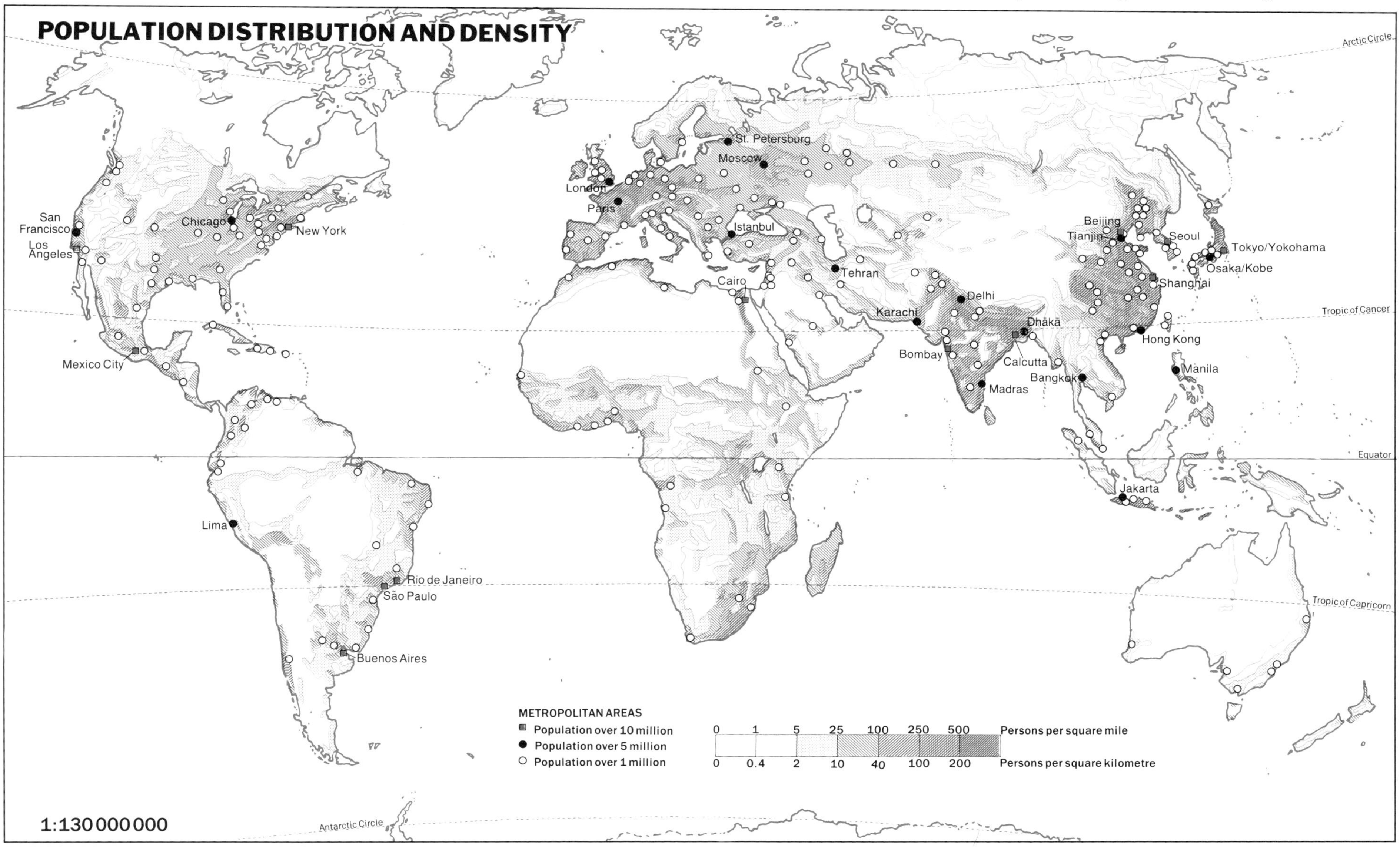

POPULATION DISTRIBUTION AND DENSITY

San Francisco
Los Angeles
Chicago
New York
Mexico City
Lima
Rio de Janeiro
São Paulo
Buenos Aires

St. Petersburg
Moscow
London
Paris
Istanbul
Cairo
Tehran
Karachi
Delhi
Bombay
Dhaka
Calcutta
Madras
Bangkok

Beijing
Tianjin
Seoul
Shanghai
Osaka/Kobe
Tokyo/Yokohama
Hong Kong
Manila

Jakarta

METROPOLITAN AREAS

■ Population over 10 million
● Population over 5 million
○ Population over 1 million

0   1   5   25   100   250   500   Persons per square mile
0   0.4   2   10   40   100   200   Persons per square kilometre

1:130 000 000

MAP PROJECTIONS

Map projection is the means by which the imaginary lines of latitude and longitude (the graticule) on a three-dimensional globe are transferred to two-dimensional paper. This transfer cannot be made without error of some kind. Most map projections are no more than a mathematical arrangement of the lines of latitude and longitude to try to achieve a specified result but their underlying principles are firmly based on the concept of perspective projection from a view-point, or light-source onto a plane, a cone or a cylinder tangent to (touching) the globe or secant to (cutting) it.

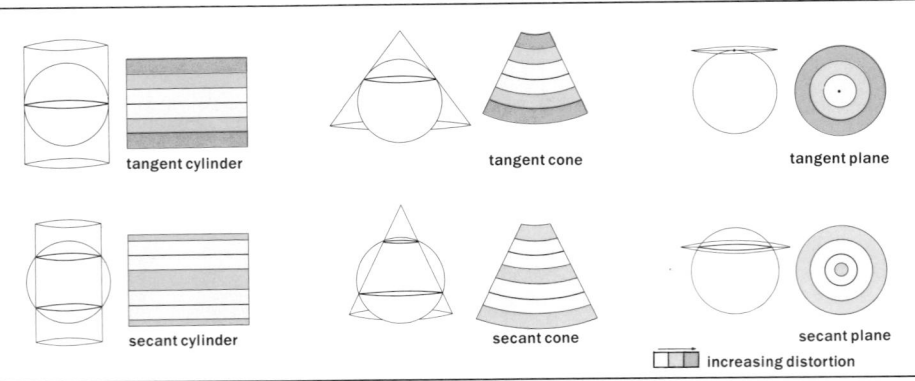

tangent cylinder   tangent cone   tangent plane

secant cylinder   secant cone   secant plane

increasing distortion

The cylinder and the cone can be opened to form a plane and, therefore, serve for projection of the graticule. Either may be tangent, with one standard parallel, or be secant, with two in order to reduce scale-errors overall. Projections may preserve shape (be *conformal*) or area (when they are called *equal-area*) or preserve distance from a central point (be *equidistant*). No two of those properties can exist in a single projection. A projection may dispense with all three in favour of another property e.g. minimum scale-error. It may just aim at good general shape for land, ocean or a region.

MAPS OF THE HEMISPHERE

Orthographic projection gives the view as seen from an infinite distance. It is most used for the visible face of the Moon. Other azimuthal projections are best explained by their polar case. In the *stereographic* the projection is from one pole on to a plane tangent at the other. Meridians and parallels plot as circles, arcs of circles or straight lines. In the *equidistant*, the straight, radiating meridians are true to scale. The parallels are equally-spaced concentric circles. Distances are correct along a meridian (but not in other directions). In *Lambert's Equal-Area*, the parallels are so spaced that the area enclosed by two meridians and any two parallels is in true proportion to the corresponding area on the globe.

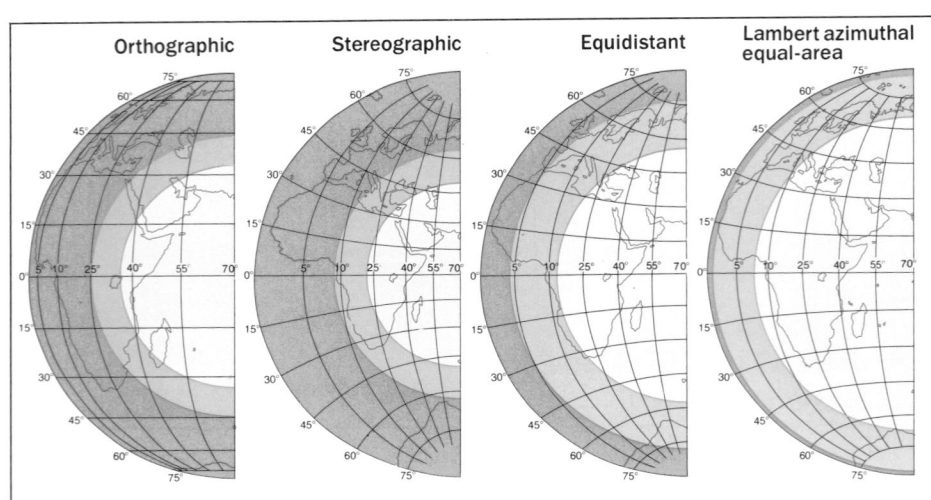

Orthographic   Stereographic   Equidistant   Lambert azimuthal equal-area

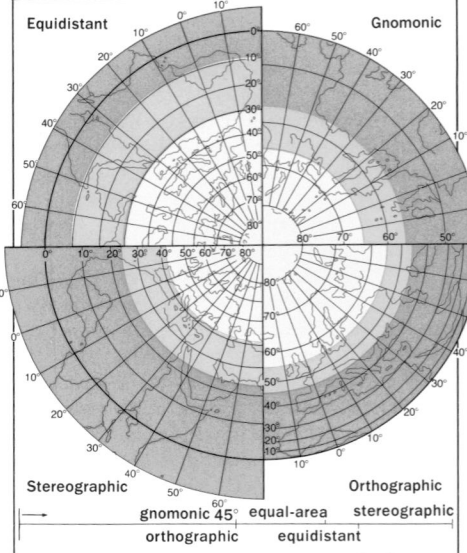

Equidistant   Gnomonic

Stereographic   Orthographic

gnomonic   equal-area   stereographic
orthographic   equidistant

The bar scale shows the comparative lengths of half-meridians (90°) in four projections. To these, Lambert's Equal-Area has been added.

POLAR PROJECTIONS

The *gnomonic* is the projection (view) from the centre of the Earth. The limit plotted here is 45° from the tangent point (the pole). This gives a circle equal in radius to 90° (the equator) on the *orthographic* projection. The other two projections are plotted on this same equator. They are, therefore, not to scale but they show the way the parallels are equally spaced in the *equidistant*; are increasingly spaced in the *stereographic* and become very crowded near the equator in the *orthographic* projection.

REGIONAL MAPS

In the *conic with one standard parallel*, the parallel of tangency is made true to scale. Others are concentric circles drawn from the apex of the cone, usually at their correct spacing. Scale errors are reduced with *two standard parallels* of true length and spacing. Neither projection is conformal or equal-area but they can be made so. The conformal version of both has been widely used in topographic maps and aeronautical charts. *Bonne*, a modified conic with one standard parallel is equal-area. The central meridian and all parallels are correctly subdivided. The standard parallel is true to scale. Other parallels are arcs of circles concentric with it. Meridians are curved lines where they are straight in the other two.

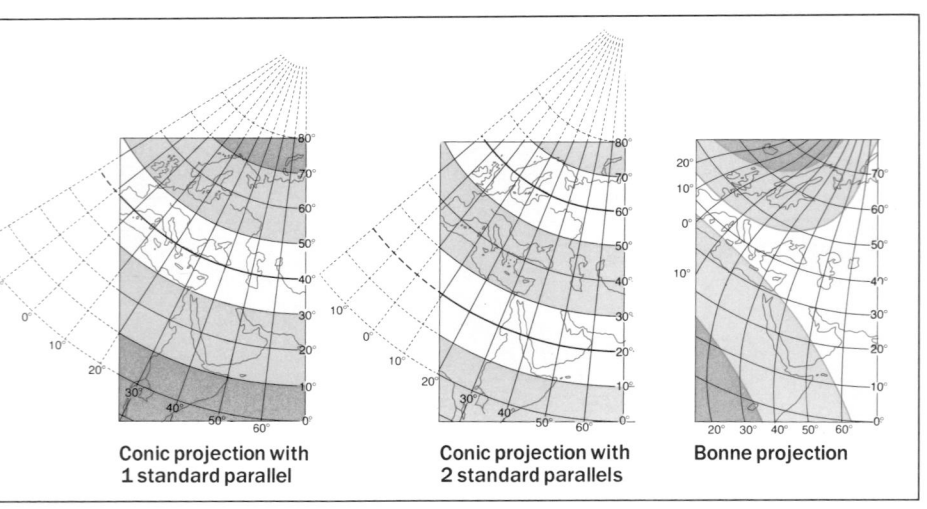

Conic projection with 1 standard parallel   Conic projection with 2 standard parallels   Bonne projection

WORLD MAPS

Mercator is conformal (scale at any point is the same in all directions). Lines of constant bearing (loxodromes or rhumb lines) plot as straight lines, hence its importance to navigators. *Gall's* projection, a kind of stereographic is neither conformal nor equal-area. A cylinder is secant at 45°N and S. Projection is from a point on the equator diametrically opposite. *"The Times"* projection has Gall's parallels but the meridians are modified from the sinusoidal and considerably less curved. In the *sinusoidal* projection, the central meridian is perpendicular to the equator and half its length. Parallels are straight, equally spaced and equally subdivided. Meridians drawn through the subdivisions are sine curves. In *Mollweide*, the central meridian cuts the equator and all parallels at right angles. All are subdivided equally. Meridians 90° east and west of centre form a circle equal in area to a hemisphere. From that equation the spacing of the parallels can be calculated. *Hammer's* projection, derived from Lambert's equal-area, has the equator doubled in length. All three projections are equal-area. *Winkel Tripel* is the mean of Hammer and Plate Carrée. It is not equal-area. *Plate Carrée*, the simplest projection (not shown here) is a system of squares based on the equator.

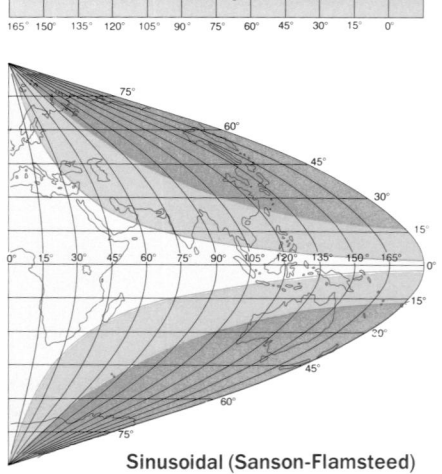

Mercator

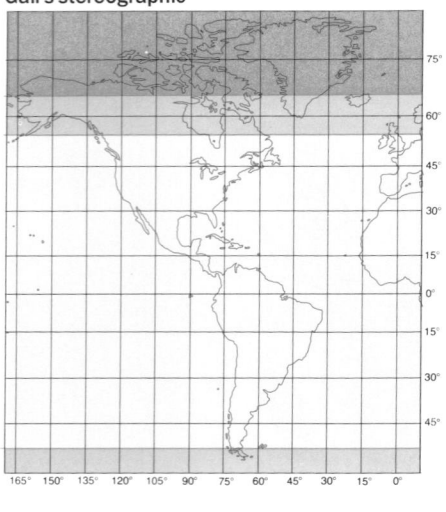

Gall's stereographic

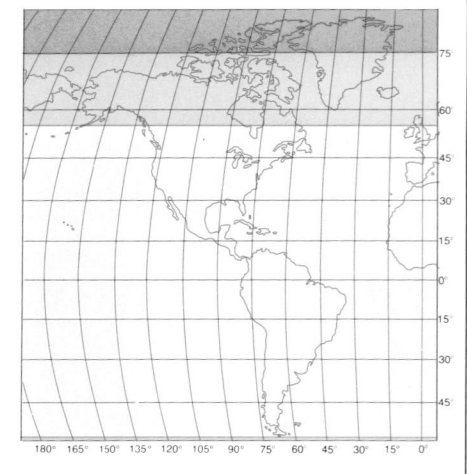

Bartholomew's 'The Times'

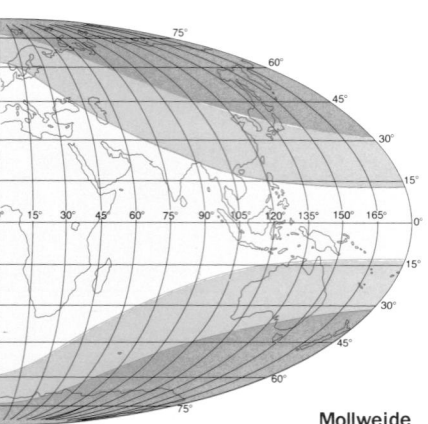

Sinusoidal (Sanson-Flamsteed)

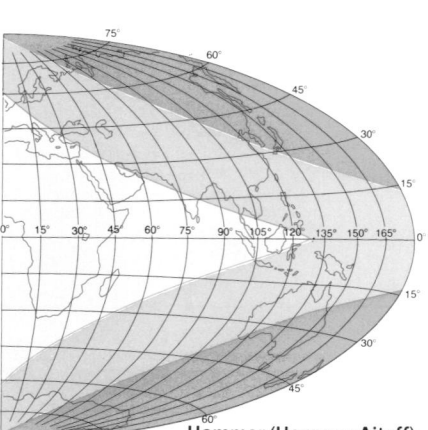

Mollweide   Hammer (Hammer-Aitoff)

BOUNDARIES

- International
- International, Undefined or Alignment Uncertain
- Limits of Sovereignty across Water Areas
- Autonomous, Federal State
- Main Administrative
- Other Administrative
- Offshore Administrative
- Armistice, Cease-Fire Line
- Demilitarised Zone
- National Park
- Reserve, Reservation

LAKE TYPES

- Fresh-water
- Reservoir
- Seasonal Fresh
- Seasonal Brackish
- Salt-lake, Lagoon
- Perennial Salt-lake
- Seasonal Salt-lake
- Saline Mud-flat
- Salt-flat

OTHER FEATURES

- River, Stream
- Seasonal Watercourses
- Seasonal Flood-plain
- Undefined Course of River
- Pass; Gorges
- Waterfalls, Rapids
- Dam, Barrage
- Escarpments
- Flood Dyke
- Limits of Ice-shelf
- Reefs
- Rocks
- Spot Depth
- Lighthouse
- Lightship; Beacon
- Waterhole, Well
- Active Volcano
- Summit, Peak
- Oil Wells
- Oil or Natural Gas Pipeline
- Mine
- Site of Battle
- Historic Site
- Historic Ruin
- Ancient Walls
- Mosque, Sheikh's Tomb
- Cathedral, Monastery, Church
- International or Main Airport
- Airport, Airfield

CITY MAPS

- State Boundary
- County, Department Boundary
- City Limits
- Borough, District Boundary
- Main Railways
- Other Railways
- Projected Railways
- Underground Railway
- Special Highway
- Main Road
- Secondary Road
- Other Road, Street
- Track
- Road Tunnel
- Bridge; Flyover
- Seaway
- Canals
- Drainage Canal
- Waterfalls, Rapids
- Historic Walls
- Airports
- Racecourses
- Stadium
- Cemetery; Churches
- Woodland, Park
- Built-up Area

COMMUNICATIONS

- Main Railways
- Other Railway
- Light Railway
- Projected Railways
- Railway Tunnels
- Road Tunnel
- Special Highway
- Main Road
- Other Road
- Tracks
- Car Ferries
- Rail Ferries
- Navigable Canals
- Projected or Disused Canal
- Drainage or Irrigation Canal
- Canal Tunnel
- Tunnel Aqueduct

LANDSCAPE FEATURES

- Ice-field and Glaciers
- Ice-cap, Ice-sheet
- Lava-fields
- Lava-fields
- Sand Desert, Dunes
- Saline Marsh, Salt Desert
- Marsh, Swamp
- Swamp, Flood-area
- Mangrove Swamp
- Tidal Area
- Atoll

STYLES OF LETTERING

Sample	Meaning
TOGO	Country Name
ALBERTA	Administrative Divisions - Major
KENT CHER	Administrative Divisions - Other
PARIS Bern	National Capitals
Omsk Denver Kraków	Administrative Centres
GANDER Gatwick	Airports
MOAB	Historic Region
DECCAN SINAI Mato Grosso	Physical Regions
ATLAS Nile Mt Blanc Thames	Physical Features
BASIN Ridge	Ocean Bottom Features
MASAI	Tribal Name

PRINCIPAL MAP ABBREVIATIONS

A.	1. Alp, Alpen, Alpi. 2. Alt
Abb^{e}	Abbaye
A.C.T.	Australian Capital Territory
Aig.	Aiguille
Akr.	Ákra, Akrotírion
Anch.	Anchorage
A.O.	Avtonomnaya Oblast'
App^{no}	Appennino
Aqued.	Aqueduct
Ar.	Arroyo
Arch.	Archipel, Archipelago, Archipiélago
Arr.	Arrecife
Ay.	Ayía, Áyioi, Áyion, Áyios
B.	1. Baai, Bahía, Baía, Baie, Baja, Bay, Bucht, Bukhta, Bukt. 2. Bad. 3. Ban. 4. Barazh, Barrage, Barragem. 5. Bayou. 6. Bir. 7. Bonto. 8. Bulu
B^{c}	Banc
B^{ca}	Boca
Bel.	Belgium, Belgian
Bg.	Berg
Bge	Barrage
Bgt.	Bight, Bugt
B^{i}	Bani, Beni
B^{j}	Burj
B^{k}	Bank
Bk.	Buku
B^{n}	Basin
Bol.	Bol'shoy, -oye, -aya, -iye
Bos.	Bosanski
Br.	1. Branch. 2. Bredning. 3. Bridge, Brücke. 4. Britain, British. 5. Burun
Bt.	Bukit
Bü.	Büyük
Bukh.	Bukhta
C.	1. Cabo, Cap, Cape. 2. Česká, -é, -ý. 3. Col.
Ç	Çay
Cab^{o}	Cabeço
Cach.	Cachoeira, -o
Can.	1. Canal. 2. Canale. 3. Canavese. 4. Cañon, Canyon
Cas.	Castle
Cat.	1. Cataract. 2. Catena
Cath.	Cathedral
C^{d}	Ciudad
Červ.	Červená, -é
Ch.	1. Chapel, Chapelle, Church. 2. Chaung. 3. Chott.
Chan.	Channel
Ch^{au}	Château
Ch^{e}	Chaine
Ch^{lle}	Chapelle
C^{ma}	Cima
C^{no}	Corno
C^{o}	Cerro
$Const^{n}$	Construction
Cord.	Cordillera
Cr.	Creek
Cuch.	Cuchilla
Cuc^{ru}	Cuccuru
Cy.	City
Czo.	Cozzo
D.	1. Da, Dag, Dagh, Dağı, Dağları. 2 Danau. 3. Darreh. 4 Daryācheh
-d.	-dake
D.C.	District of Columbia
Den.	Denmark
Dists.	Districts
Div.	Division
Dj.	Djebel
Dns.	Downs
Dz.	Dzong
E.	East
Eil.	Eiland, Eilanden
Escarp.	Escarpment
Est.	Estación
E^{tg}	Étang
F.	Firth
F.D.	Federal District
Fj.	1. Fjell. 2. Fjord, Fjörður
F^{k}	Fork
Fl.	Fleuve
Fr.	France, French
Ft.	Fort
F^{te}	Fonte
Fy.	Ferry
-g	-gawa
G.	1. Gebel. 2. Ghedir. 3. Göl, Gölü, Gōl. 4. Golfe, Golfo, Gulf. 5. Gompa. 6. Gora, Gory. 7. Guba, 8. Gunung
G^{a}	Gara
G^{d}	Grand
G^{de}	Grande
Geb.	Gebergte, Gebirge
$Geog^{l}$	Geographical
Gez.	Gezira
Ghub.	Ghubba
Gl.	1. Gamle, Gammel. 2.Glacier
Gp.	Group
Gr.	1. Graben. 2. Gross, -e, Grande
G^{r}	Gasr
Gr^{tes}	Grottes
Gt.	Great, Groot, -e
H.	1. Hawr. 2. Hill. 3. Hoch. 4. Hora, Hory
Halv.	Halvøy
Har.	Harbour
H^{d}	Head
H.E.P.	Hydro-Electric Power
H^{g}	Hegység
H^{gts}	Heights
H^{i}	Hasi, Hasy
Hist.	Historic
H^{n}	Horn
Hosp.	1. Hospice, Hospiz. 2. Hospital
Ht.	Haut
Hte.	Haute
H^{ter}	Hinter
H^{y}	Highway
I.	Île, Ilha, Insel, Isla, Island, Isle, Isola, Isole
IJ.	IJssel
im.	imeni
In.	1. Inder, Indre, Inner, Inre. 2. Inlet
IND.	India
Inf.	Inferior, -e, Inférieure
Int.	International
I^{s}	Îles, Ilhas, Islands, Islas, Isles
ISR.	Israel
Isth.	Isthmus
J.	1. Jabal, Jebel, Jibāl. 2. Järvi, Jaure, Jazira, Jezero, Jezioro. 3. Jökull
Jap.	Japan, Japanese
Jct.	Junction
K.	1. Kaap, Kap, Kapp. 2. Kaikyō. 3. Kato. 4. Kerang, Kering. 5. Kiang. 6. Kirke. 7. Ko. 8. Koh, Kūh, Kūhha. 9. Kólpos. 10. Kopf. 11. Kuala. 12. Kyst
Kan.	Kanal, Kanaal
Kap.	Kapelle
Kep.	Kepulauan
Kg.	Kampong, Kompong, Kong
Kh.	1. Khawr. 2. Khirbet, Khīābān, -e. 3. Khowr
Khr.	Khrebet
Kl.	1. Kechil. 2. Klein, -e
Kör.	Körfez, -i
Kr.	Kangar
Kü.	Küçük
L.	1. Lac, Lago, Lagôa, Lake, Liman, Limni, Liqen, Loch, Lough. 2. Lam
Lag.	Lagoon, Laguna, -e
L^{d}	Land
Ldg.	Landing
Lit.	Little
Ll.	Lille
M.	1. Mae, Me. 2. Meer. 3. Muang. 4. Muntil. 5. Muong. 6. Mys. 7. Monte
m	metre/s
Mal.	Malyy, -aya, -oye
Mem.	Memorial
Mex.	Mexico, Mexican
M^{f}	Massif
M^{gna}	Montagna
M^{gne}	Montagne
Mkt.	Markt
Mon.	Monasterio, Monastery
Mont.	Monument
Mt.	Mont, Mount, Mountain
Mte.	Monte
M^{tes}	Montes
Mti.	Monti, Munţi
Mts.	Monts, Mountains
N.	1. Nam. 2. Neu, Ny. 3. Nevado, Nudo. 4. Noord, Nord, Nörre, Nørre, North. 5. Nos
N^{a}	Nuestra
Nat.	National
N.D.	Notre Dame
N^{dr}	Neder, Nieder
N.E.	North East
Neth.	Netherlands
Nizh.	Nizhne, -neye, -niy, -nyaya
Nizm.	Nizmennost
N.O.	Noord Oost, Nord Ost
Nor.	Norway, Norwegian
N^{os}	Nudos
Nov.	Novyy, -aya, -iye, -oye
N^{r}	Nether
N.W.	North West
N.Z.	New Zealand
O.	1. Old. 2. Oost, Ost. 3. Ostrov
Ö.	1. Östre. 2. Öy
Ø.	1. Østre. 2. Øy
Ob.	Ober
O^{de}	Oude
O^{et}	Oguilet
Ogl.	Oglat
O.L.V.	Onze Lieve Vrouw
Or.	Óri, Óros
Orm.	Ormos
Os(t)	Ostrova
Ot.	Olet
Öv.	Över, Övre
O^{va}	Ostrov, -a
Oz.	Ozero
P.	1. Pass. 2. Pic, Pico, Piz. 3. Pulau. 4. Pou
Pal.	Palace, Palacio, Palais
Pass.	Passage
Peg.	Pegunungan
Pen.	Peninsula, Penisola
Per.	Pereval
Ph.	Phum
Phn.	Phnom
P^{gio}	Poggio
Pk.	1. Park. 2. Peak, Pik
Pkwy.	Parkway
Pl.	1. Planina, Planinski. 2. Plei
P^{la}	Playa
Plat.	Plateau
Plosk.	Ploskogor'ye
P^{no}	Pantano
P^{nte}	Pointe
Pol.	Poluostrov
Por.	Porog
Port.	Portugal, Portuguese
P^{ov}	Poluostrov
P.P.	Pulau-pulau
Pr.	1. Proliv. 2. Przylądek. 3. Prince
$Prom^{y}$	Promontory
Prop.	Proposed
PROT.	Protectorate
PROV.	Provincial
Psa	Presa
P^{so}	Passo
Pt.	1. Point. 2. Pont
P^{t}	1. Petit. 2. Point. 3. Pont
P^{ta}	1. Ponta, Punta. 2. Puerta
P^{te}	1. Pointe. 2. Ponte, Puente
P^{to}	1. Porto, Puerto. 2. Ponto, Punto
P^{zo}	Pizzo
Q.	Qala, Qara, Qarn
R.	1. Reka, Río, River, Rivière, Rud, Rzeka. 2. Ria
Ra.	Range
Rap.	Rapids
R^{ca}	Rocca
R^{d}	Road
REC.	Recreation
Res.	Reservoir
Resp.	Respublika
R^{f}	Reef
R^{ge}	Ridge
Rib^{a}	Ribeira
Rly.	Railway
Rom.	Romania, Romanian
R^{te}	Route
Rus. Fed.	Russian Federation
S.	1. Salar, Salina. 2. San. 3. Saw. 4. See. 5. Seto. 6. Sjö. 7. Sör, South, Syd. 8. Sung. 9. sur. 10. Sebjet
S^{a}	Serra, Sierra
Sab.	Sabkhat
Sc.	Scoglio
S^{d}	Sound, Sund
S.E.	South East
Seb.	Sebjet, Sebkhat, Sebkra
Sev.	Sever, -naya, -nyy
S^{gno}	Stagno
Sh.	1. Sh'aīb. 2. Sharif. 3. Shatt. 4. Shima. 5. Shankou
S^{i}	Sidi
S^{knoll}	Seaknoll
S^{kt}	Sankt
Sl.	Slieve
S^{mt}	Seamount
Snr^{a}	Senhora
Snr^{o}	Senhoro
Sp.	1. Spain, Spanish. 2. Spitze
S^{pk}	Seapeak
Spr.	Spring
S^{r}	Sönder, Sønder
Sr.	Sredniy, -nyaya
S^{t}	Saint, Sint, Staryy
St.	1. State. 2. Stor, Store. 3. Stung
Sta	Santa
Sta.	Station
Stby.	Staby, Statsjonsby
S^{te}	Sainte
Ste.	Store
Sten.	Stenón, Stenós
S^{to}	Santo
Str.	Strait
S^{tu}	Stuvina
Sv.	Svaty, Sveti
S.W.	South West
T.	1. Tal. 2. Tal, Tall, Tell. 3. Tepe, Tepesi
Talsp.	Talsperre
Tel.	Teluk
Terr.	Terrace
$Terr^{y}$	Territory
Tg.	Tanjung
Thwy.	Throughway, Thruway
Tk.	Teluk
T^{mt}	Tablemount
T^{o}	Tando
Tpk.	Turnpike
Tr.	Trench, Trough
T^{re}	Torre
Tun.	Tunnel
U	Uad
U.A.E.	United Arab Emirates
Ug.	Udjung
U.K.	United Kingdom
Unt.	Unter
Up^{r}	Upper
U.S.A.	United States of America
V.	1. Val, Valle. 2. Väster, Vest, Vester. 3. Vatn. 4. Ville. 5. Vorder. 6. Volcán
V^{a}	Vila
Vdkhr.	Vodokhranilishche
Vel.	Velikiy, -aya, -iye
Ven.	Venezuela, Venezuelan
Verkh.	Verkhniy, -neye, -ne, -nyaya
Vn.	Volcán
Vol.	Volcán, Volcano, Vulkán
Vost.	Vostochnyy
Vozv.	Vozvyshennost'
W.	1. Wadi. 2. Wald. 3. Wan. 4. Water. 5. Well. 6. West
W^{r}	Wester
-y	-yama
Y^{t}	Ytre, Ytter, Ytri
Yuzh.	Yuzhnaya, -no, -nyy
Z.	Zaliv
Zal.	Zaliv
Zap.	Zapadnyy, -aya, -o, -oye
Zem.	Zemlya

Population Key

Capitals | Cities & Towns
- ■ ● over 3 mill.
- ■ ● over 1 mill.
- □ ○ under 1 mill.

Communications
— Roads
— Railways
Main Shipping Routes
Other Shipping Routes

Limits of Pack-ice
Permanent Pack-ice
Average Winter Limit

BARTHOLOMEWS "THE TIMES" PROJECTION

Independence gained since 1939
from former sovereign powers:

Year of Independence
60 = 1960:

UK	France	Neths.	Portugal
Belgium	Italy	Spain	S. Africa
Denmark	Japan	USA	Yug.

Territory ceded or annexed since 1939
Territory annexed by the former USSR between 1939 and 1945
— Boundary adjustments
• Transfers of territory
Independent before 1939
Dependent territory
Area of the former USSR

E/G5251

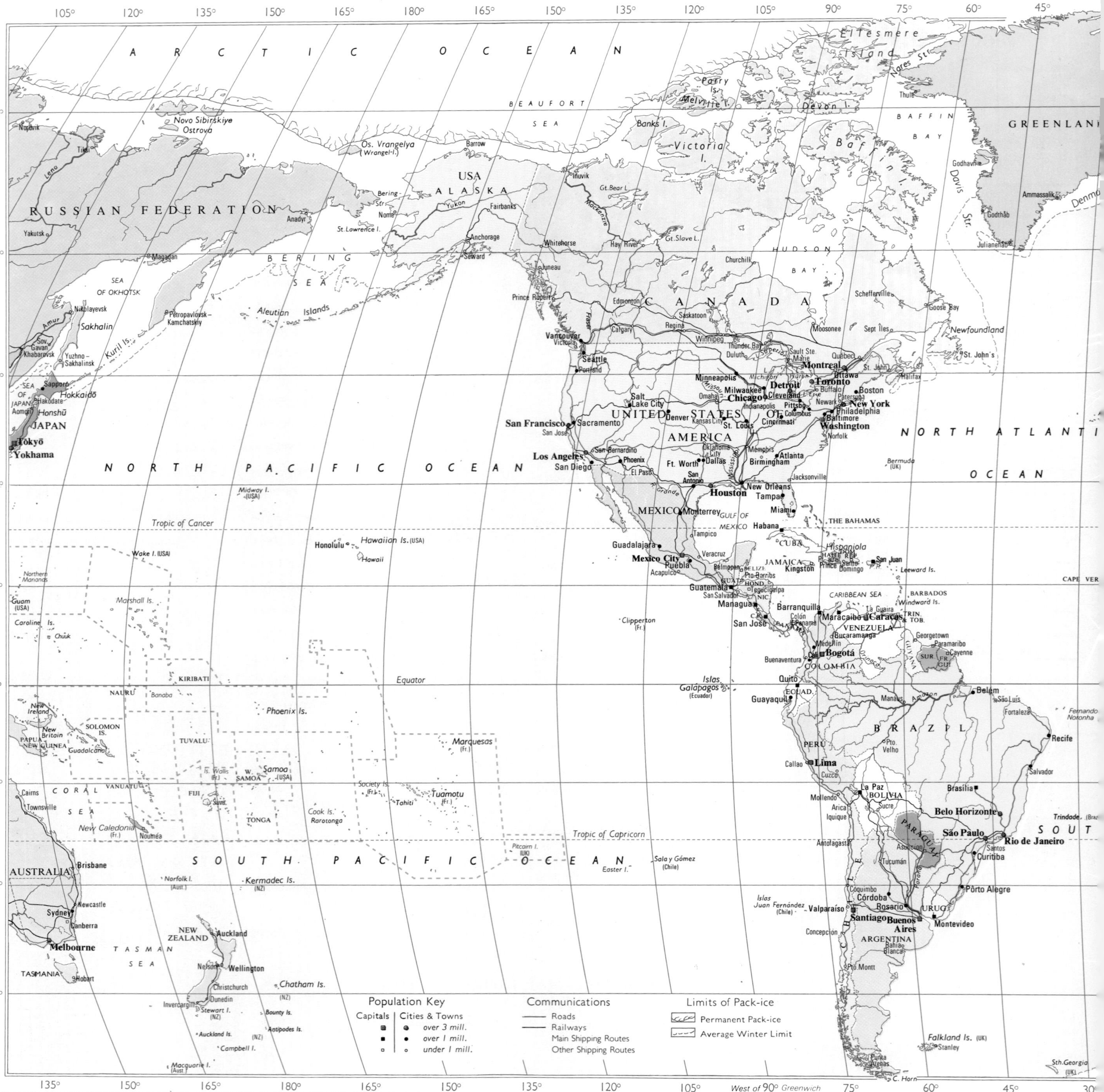

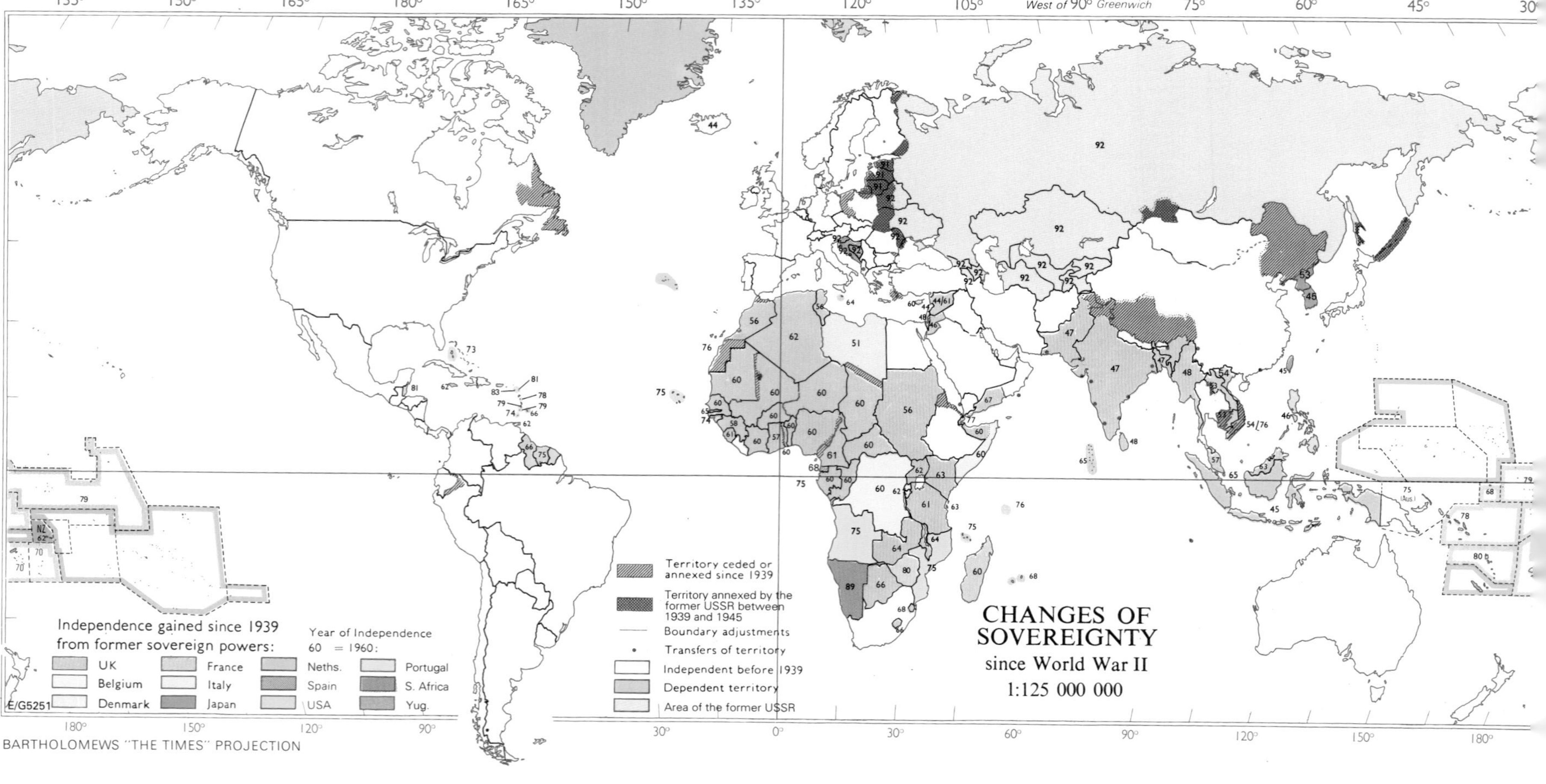

CHANGES OF SOVEREIGNTY
since World War II
1:125 000 000

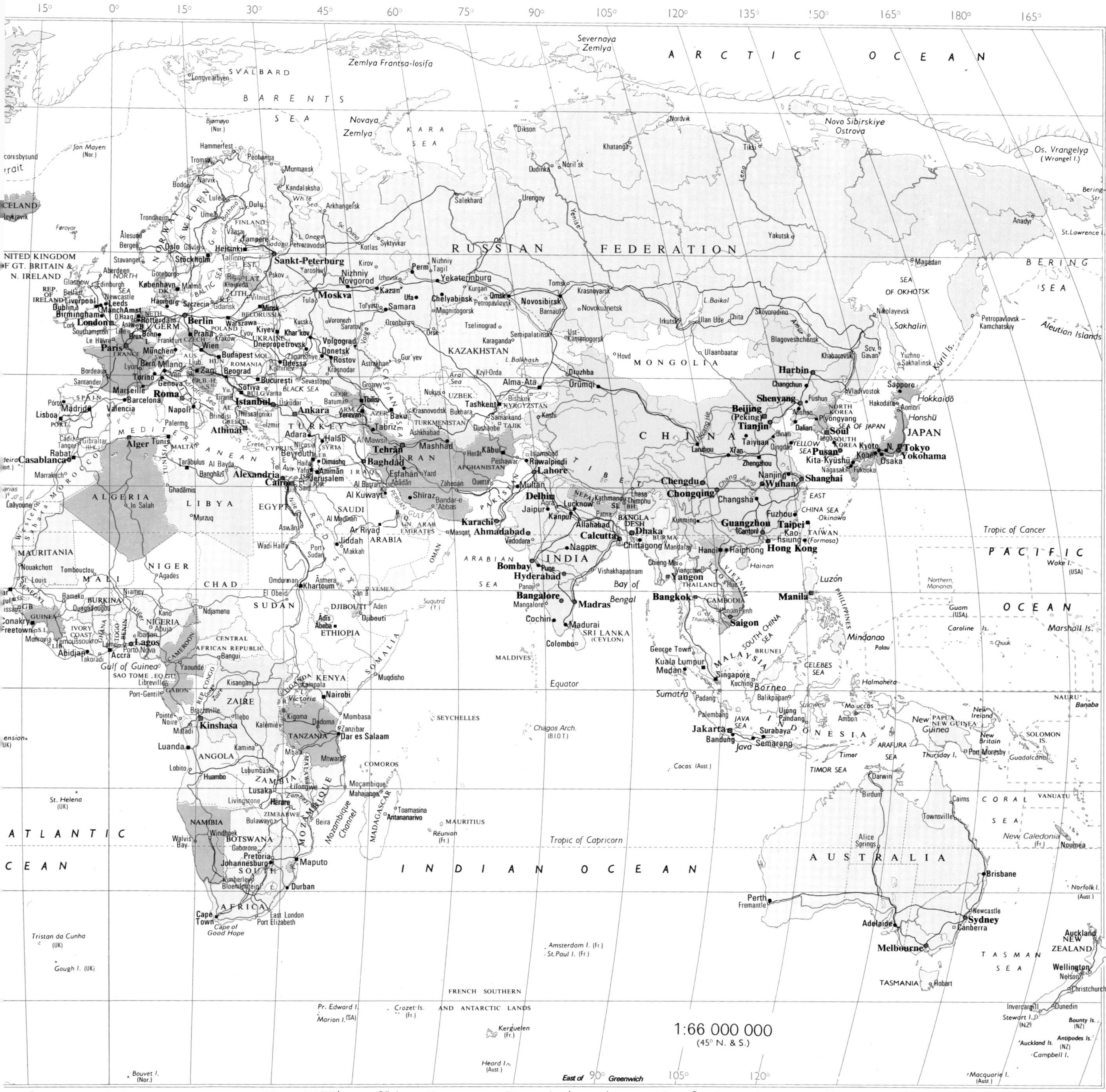

ARCTIC OCEAN
Severnaya Zemlya
Zemlya Frantsa-Iosifa
SVALBARD
BARENTS SEA
Novaya Zemlya
KARA SEA
Novo Sibirskiye Ostrova
Os. Vrangelya (Wrangel I.)
RUSSIAN FEDERATION
SEA OF OKHOTSK
BERING SEA
Aleutian Islands
Sakhalin
KAZAKHSTAN
MONGOLIA
CHINA
JAPAN
SEA OF JAPAN
YELLOW SEA
EAST CHINA SEA
TAIWAN (Formosa)
Tropic of Cancer
PACIFIC OCEAN
Wake I. (USA)
Northern Marianas
Guam (USA)
Caroline Is.
Marshall Is.
PHILIPPINES
SOUTH CHINA SEA
CELEBES SEA
MALAYSIA
INDONESIA
NAURU
Banaba
SOLOMON IS.
PAPUA NEW GUINEA
New Guinea
ARAFURA SEA
TIMOR SEA
CORAL SEA
VANUATU
New Caledonia (Fr.)
Nouméa
AUSTRALIA
Norfolk I. (Aust.)
TASMAN SEA
NEW ZEALAND
TASMANIA
Tropic of Capricorn
INDIAN OCEAN
Chagos Arch. (B.I.O.T.)
SEYCHELLES
MALDIVES
MAURITIUS
Réunion (Fr.)
Cocos (Aust.)
Amsterdam I. (Fr.)
St. Paul I. (Fr.)
FRENCH SOUTHERN AND ANTARCTIC LANDS
Kerguelen (Fr.)
Heard I. (Aust.)
Pr. Edward I.
Marion I. (SA)
Crozet Is. (Fr.)
Bouvet I. (Nor.)
Macquarie I. (Aust.)
Auckland Is. (NZ)
Campbell I.
Antipodes Is. (NZ)
Bounty Is. (NZ)
Stewart I. (NZ)
Equator
ATLANTIC OCEAN
St. Helena (UK)
Tristan da Cunha (UK)
Gough I. (UK)
Jan Mayen (Nor.)
ICELAND
UNITED KINGDOM OF GT. BRITAIN & N. IRELAND
REP. OF IRELAND
NORTH SEA
NORWAY
SWEDEN
FINLAND
FRANCE
SPAIN
PORT.
ITALY
GERM.
POLAND
UKRAINE
BELORUSSIA
ROMANIA
BULGARIA
GREECE
TURKEY
BLACK SEA
CASPIAN SEA
MEDITERRANEAN SEA
CYPRUS
SYRIA
IRAQ
IRAN
AFGHANISTAN
PAKISTAN
INDIA
NEPAL
BHUTAN
BANGLADESH
BURMA
THAILAND
CAMBODIA
VIETNAM
LAOS
SRI LANKA (CEYLON)
Bay of Bengal
ARABIAN SEA
SAUDI ARABIA
U.A.E.
OMAN
YEMEN
EGYPT
LIBYA
ALGERIA
MOROCCO
TUNISIA
MAURITANIA
MALI
NIGER
CHAD
SUDAN
ETHIOPIA
SOMALIA
KENYA
TANZANIA
ZAIRE
ANGOLA
ZAMBIA
NAMIBIA
BOTSWANA
ZIMBABWE
MOZAMBIQUE
MADAGASCAR
SOUTH AFRICA
NIGERIA
CAMEROON
GABON
CENTRAL AFRICAN REPUBLIC
BURKINA
GUINEA
IVORY COAST
GHANA
TOGO
BENIN
COMOROS
Gulf of Guinea
Mozambique Channel
Cape of Good Hope
London
Paris
Berlin
Roma
Madrid
Moskva
Sankt-Peterburg
Istanbul
Ankara
Cairo
Alexandria
Baghdad
Tehrān
Karachi
Delhi
Bombay
Calcutta
Madras
Bangalore
Hyderabad
Dhaka
Yangon
Bangkok
Saigon
Hong Kong
Manila
Beijing (Peking)
Shanghai
Wuhan
Tianjin
Shenyang
Harbin
Guangzhou (Canton)
Chongqing
Chengdu
Soul
Tokyo
Yokohama
Osaka
Jakarta
Singapore
Kuala Lumpur
Sydney
Melbourne
Brisbane
Adelaide
Perth
Auckland
Wellington
Christchurch
Lagos
Kinshasa
Nairobi
Dar es Salaam
Johannesburg
Cape Town
Durban
Maputo
Alger
Casablanca
Khartoum
Addis Abeba
Tashkent
Alma-Ata
Novosibirsk
Yekaterinburg
1:66 000 000
(45° N. & S.)
Meridian of 0° Greenwich
East of 90° Greenwich

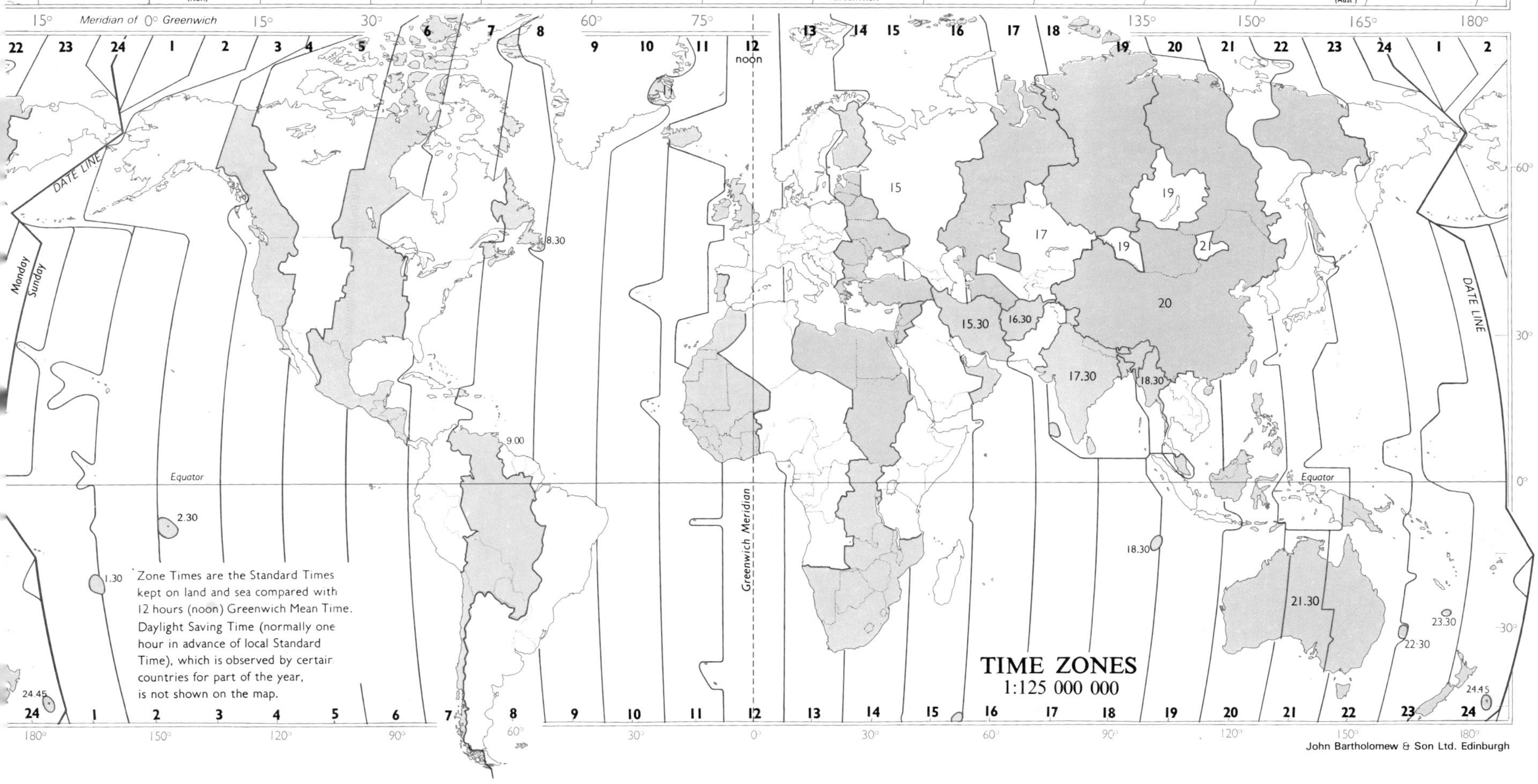

DATE LINE
Monday
Sunday
Greenwich Meridian
Equator
Zone Times are the Standard Times kept on land and sea compared with 12 hours (noon) Greenwich Mean Time. Daylight Saving Time (normally one hour in advance of local Standard Time), which is observed by certain countries for part of the year, is not shown on the map.
TIME ZONES
1:125 000 000
12 noon
15.30
16.30
17.30
18.30
21.30
23.30
22.30
8.30
9.00
2.30
1.30
24.45

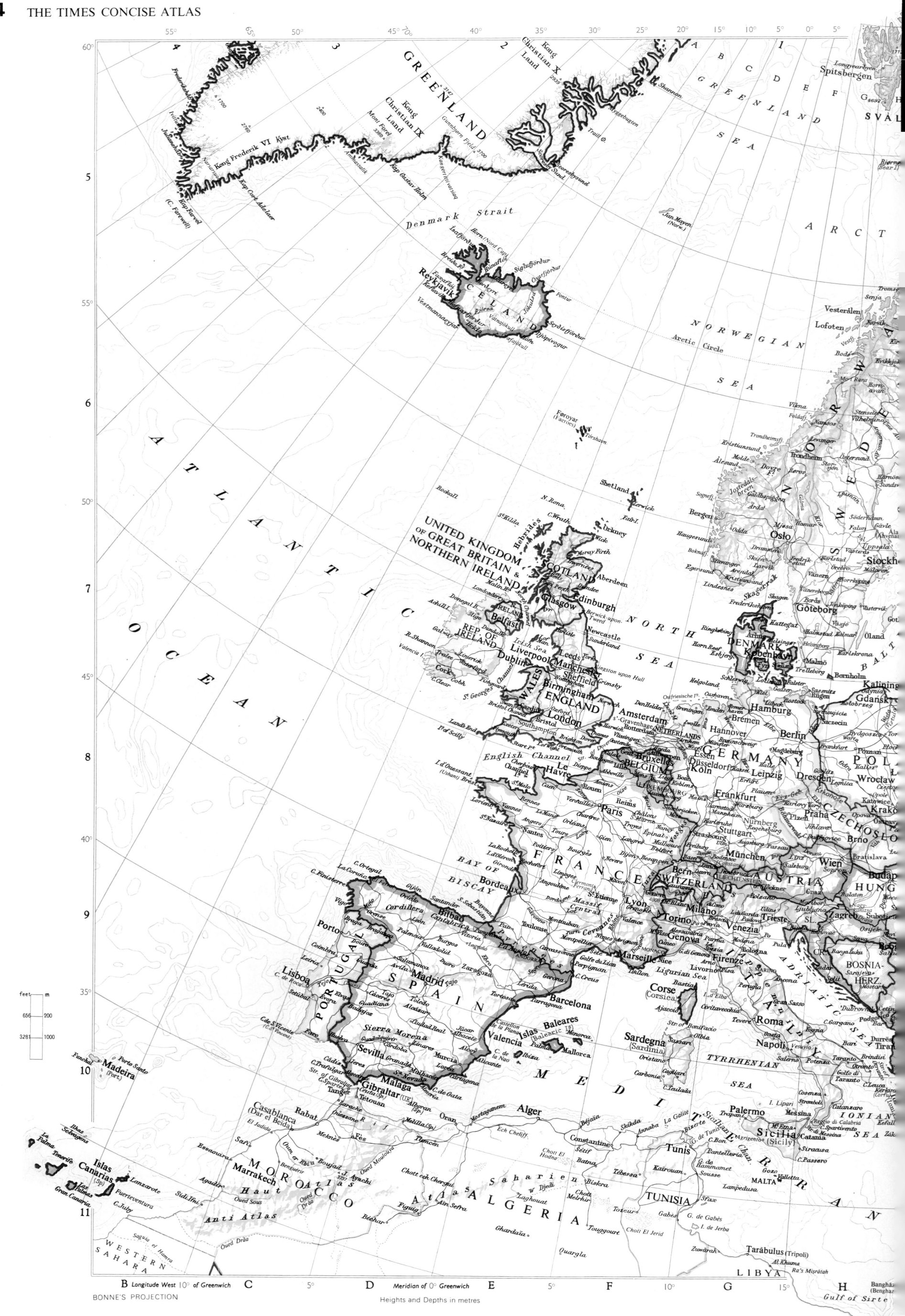
GREENLAND
Kong Christian X Land
Kong Christian IX Land
Kong Frederik VI Kyst
Kap Farvel (C. Farewell)
GREENLAND SEA
Spitsbergen
Jan Mayen (Norw.)
Denmark Strait
ICELAND
Reykjavík
ARCTIC
Arctic Circle
NORWEGIAN SEA
Lofoten
Vesterålen
Føroyar (Faeroes)
Tórshavn
Rockall
Shetland
Orkney
ATLANTIC OCEAN
UNITED KINGDOM OF GREAT BRITAIN & NORTHERN IRELAND
SCOTLAND
Aberdeen
Edinburgh
Glasgow
Belfast
N. IRELAND
REP. OF IRELAND
Dublin
Cork
Liverpool
Manchester
Leeds
Sheffield
Newcastle
Birmingham
WALES
ENGLAND
Bristol
London
Southampton
Irish Sea
NORTH SEA
Bergen
Oslo
Stavanger
Göteborg
Trondheim
Skagerrak
Kattegat
DENMARK
København
Malmö
Stockholm
Uppsala
Öland
Amsterdam
NETHERLANDS
Rotterdam
BELGIUM
Bruxelles
Hamburg
Bremen
Hannover
Berlin
Gdańsk
Szczecin
GERMANY
Essen
Düsseldorf
Köln
Leipzig
Dresden
Wrocław
Frankfurt
Praha
Brno
Nürnberg
Stuttgart
München
Wien
Bratislava
AUSTRIA
HUNG
Budap
English Channel
Le Havre
Channel Is.
Paris
FRANCE
Reims
Nantes
Bordeaux
Lyon
Marseille
Toulouse
Nice
MONACO
BAY OF BISCAY
SWITZERLAND
Bern
LIECHTENSTEIN
Milano
Torino
Genova
Venezia
Trieste
Zagreb
Bologna
Firenze
ITALY
Roma
Napoli
ADRIATIC SEA
BOSNIA-HERZ.
Corse (Corsica)
Sardegna (Sardinia)
TYRRHENIAN SEA
Palermo
Sicilia (Sicily)
MALTA
IONIAN SEA
Ligurian Sea
SPAIN
PORTUGAL
Porto
Lisboa
Madrid
Bilbao
Zaragoza
Barcelona
Valencia
Islas Baleares (Balearic Is.)
Mallorca
Sevilla
Málaga
Gibraltar (U.K.)
Sierra Morena
MEDITERRANEAN SEA
Madeira (Port.)
Islas Canarias (Sp.)
Tanger
Rabat
Casablanca (Dar el Beida)
Marrakech
MOROCCO
Fès
Alger
Oran
ALGERIA
Tunis
TUNISIA
Tarābulus (Tripoli)
LIBYA
WESTERN SAHARA
Anti Atlas
Haut Atlas
Gulf of Sirte
Longitude West 10° of Greenwich
Meridian of 0° Greenwich
BONNE'S PROJECTION
Heights and Depths in metres

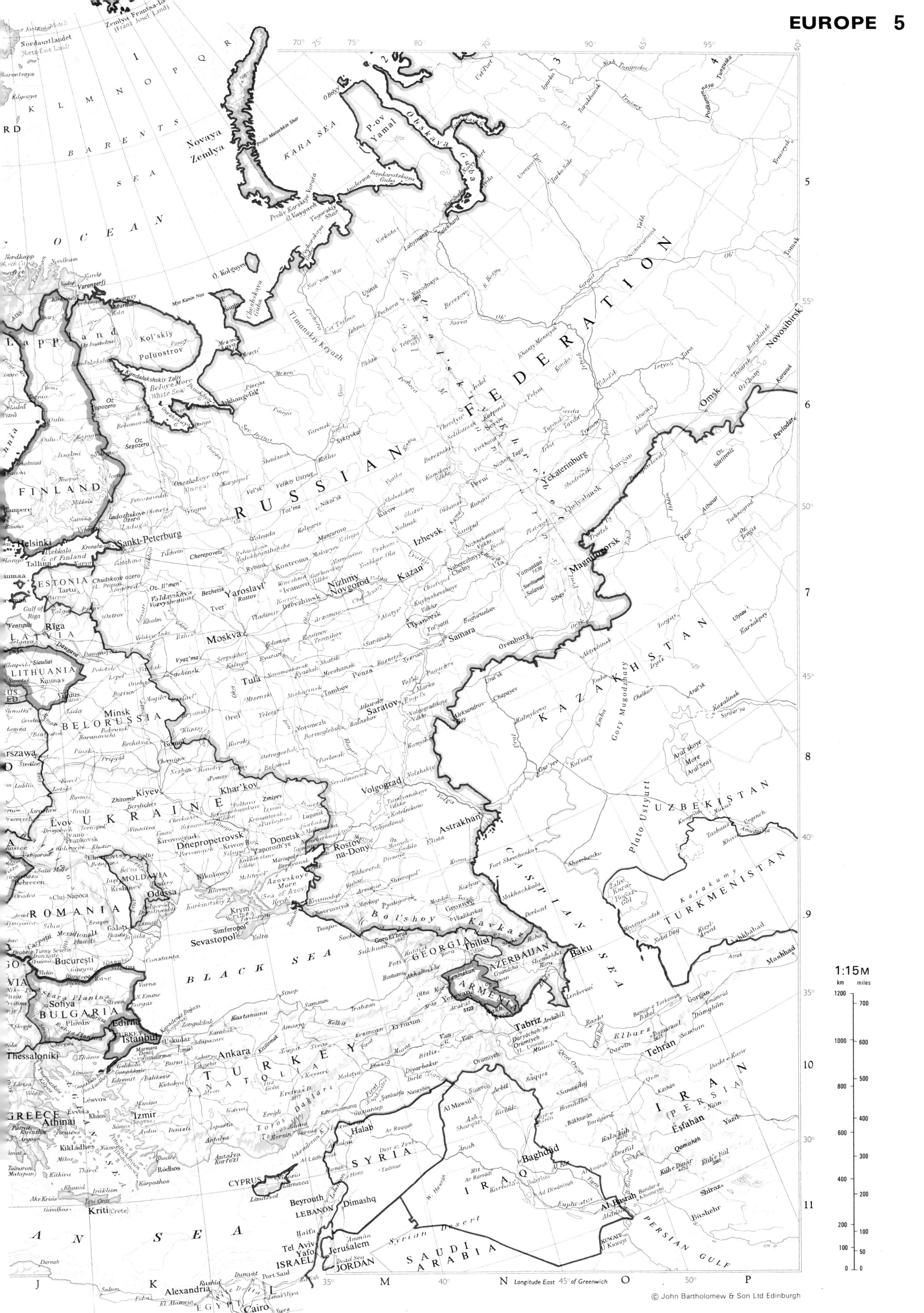

1:15M

© John Bartholomew & Son Ltd Edinburgh

RUSSIAN FEDERATION
KAZAKHSTAN
UZBEKISTAN
TURKMENISTAN
FINLAND
ESTONIA
LATVIA
LITHUANIA
BELORUSSIA
UKRAINE
MOLDAVIA
ROMANIA
BULGARIA
GREECE
TURKEY
GEORGIA
AZERBAIJAN
ARMENIA
SYRIA
IRAQ
IRAN (PERSIA)
LEBANON
ISRAEL
JORDAN
SAUDI ARABIA
KUWAIT
CYPRUS
EGYPT
BARENTS SEA
OCEAN
KARA SEA
BLACK SEA
CASPIAN SEA
Aral'skoye More (Aral Sea)
PERSIAN GULF
Novaya Zemlya
P-ov Yamal
Obskaya Guba
Kol'skiy Poluostrov
Beloye More (White Sea)
Ural'skiy Khrebet
Bol'shoy Kavkaz
Karakumy
Plato Ustyurt
Gory Mugodzhary
Elburz
Syrian Desert
Sankt-Peterburg
Helsinki
Tallinn
Riga
Kaunas
Minsk
Moskva
Yaroslavl'
Nizhniy Novgorod
Kazan'
Izhevsk
Perm'
Yekaterinburg
Chelyabinsk
Magnitogorsk
Ufa
Samara
Saratov
Volgograd
Astrakhan'
Orenburg
Omsk
Novosibirsk
Pavlodar
Kiyev
Khar'kov
Dnepropetrovsk
Donetsk
Odessa
Lvov
Rostov na-Donu
Tbilisi
Baku
Yerevan
Tula
Tambov
Penza
Ul'yanovsk
Tol'yatti
Syktyvkar
Arkhangel'sk
Murmansk
Vorkuta
Salekhard
Bucureşti
Sofiya
Edirne
Istanbul
Ankara
Izmir
Athinai
Thessaloniki
Halab
Dimashq
Beyrouth
Baghdad
Tabriz
Tehrān
Eşfahān
Al Başrah
Jerusalem
Tel Aviv-Yafo
Alexandria
Cairo
Kriti (Crete)
Simferopol'
Sevastopol
Longitude East 45° of Greenwich

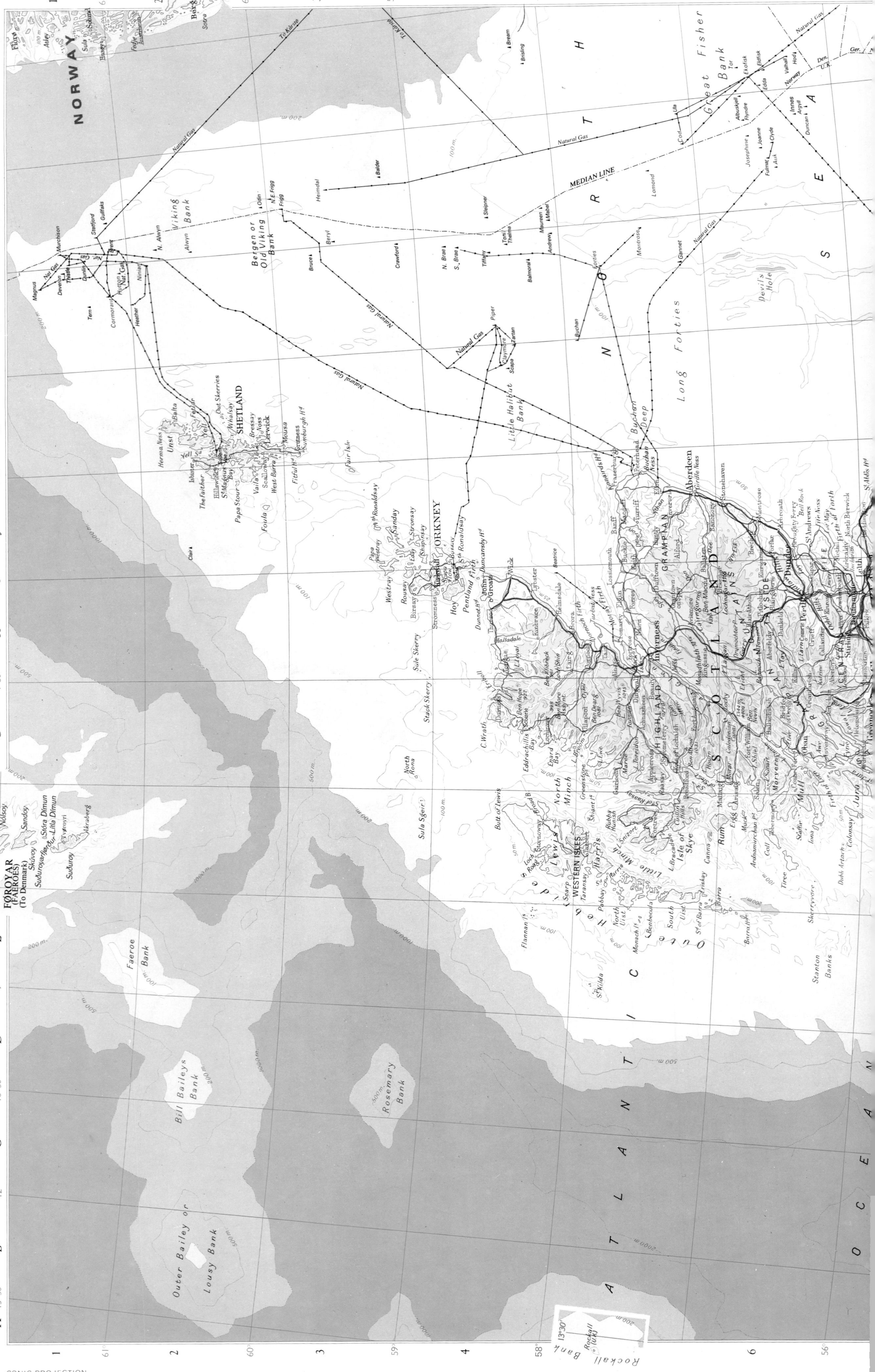

NORWAY

Bergen

FØROYAR
(FAEROES)
(To Denmark)

SHETLAND

ORKNEY

SCOTLAND

HIGHLANDS

GRAMPIAN MOUNTAINS

Aberdeen
Inverness
Wick
Thurso

WESTERN ISLES

Isle of Lewis
North Uist
South Uist
Barra
Isle of Skye
Mull
Jura

Outer Bailey or Lousy Bank

Bill Baileys Bank

Rosemary Bank

Faeroe Bank

Viking Bank

Bergen or Old Viking Bank

Little Halibut Bank

Long Forties

Great Fisher Bank

Devil's Hole

Buchan Deep

Natural Gas

MEDIAN LINE

NORTH SEA

ATLANTIC OCEAN

Rockall Bank
Rockall (UK)

Sula Sgeir
North Rona
Stack Skerry
Sule Skerry

Fair Isle
Foula
Fitful Hd.
Sumburgh Hd.

Pentland Firth
John o'Groats
Duncansby Hd.

Stanton Banks

St. Kilda
Flannan Is.

CONIC PROJECTION

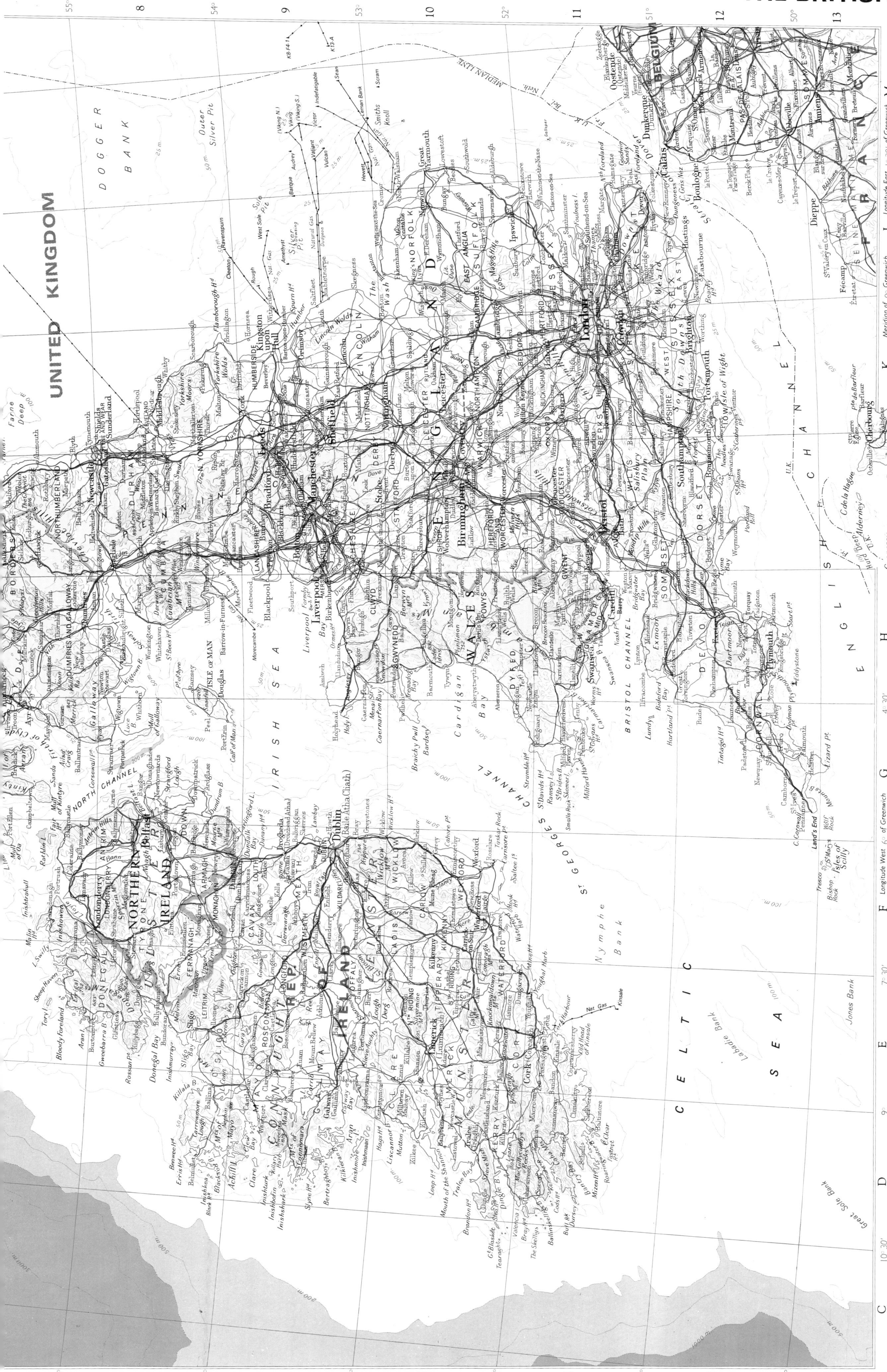

UNITED KINGDOM

DOGGER BANK

NORTH SEA

IRISH SEA

ENGLAND

WALES

REP. OF IRELAND

NORTHERN IRELAND

ULSTER

CONNAUGHT

LEINSTER

MUNSTER

ISLE OF MAN

CELTIC SEA

ENGLISH CHANNEL

ST GEORGE'S CHANNEL

BRISTOL CHANNEL

NORTH CHANNEL

CHANNEL ISLANDS

BELGIUM

FRANCE

London
Dublin (Baile Átha Cliath)
Belfast
Manchester
Liverpool
Birmingham
Sheffield
Leeds
Bradford
Newcastle
Sunderland
Middlesbrough
Kingston upon Hull
Nottingham
Leicester
Derby
Stoke
Cardiff
Swansea
Bristol
Plymouth
Southampton
Portsmouth
Brighton
Dover
Calais
Dunkerque
Ostende
Dieppe
Cherbourg
Guernsey Sark
Jersey
Alderney
Isle of Wight
Land's End
Lizard Pt

Heights and Depths in Metres

1:3 M

Meridian of 0° Greenwich

Longitude West 6° of Greenwich
Longitude East 1° 30' of Greenwich

© John Bartholomew & Son Ltd Edinburgh

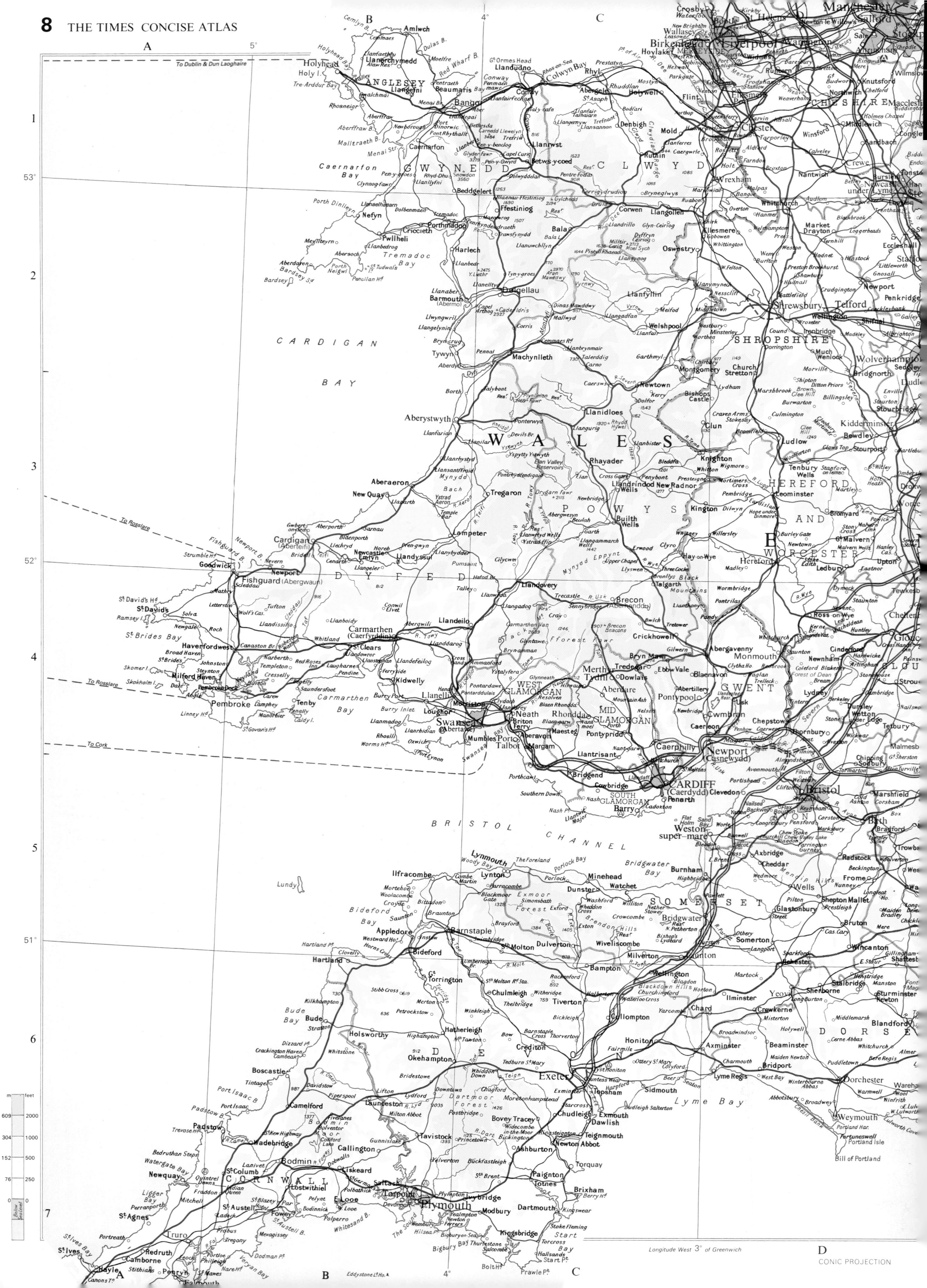
A
B
C
D
1
2
3
4
5
6
7
53°
52°
51°
5°
4°
To Dublin & Dun Laoghaire
To Rosslare
To Cork
WALES
GWYNEDD
CLWYD
POWYS
DYFED
WEST GLAMORGAN
MID GLAMORGAN
SOUTH GLAMORGAN
GWENT
SHROPSHIRE
HEREFORD AND WORCESTER
CHESHIRE
MERSEYSIDE
SOMERSET
DEVON
CORNWALL
DORSET
ANGLESEY
CARDIGAN BAY
BRISTOL CHANNEL
Carmarthen Bay
Lyme Bay
Tremadoc Bay
St Brides Bay
Bideford Bay
Bude Bay
Lundy
Holyhead
Bangor
Caernarfon
Llandudno
Colwyn Bay
Rhyl
Conwy
Denbigh
Mold
Wrexham
Llangollen
Bala
Ffestiniog
Porthmadog
Pwllheli
Barmouth
Dolgellau
Machynlleth
Aberystwyth
Llanidloes
Newtown
Welshpool
Rhayader
Aberaeron
New Quay
Cardigan
Fishguard
St David's
Haverfordwest
Milford Haven
Pembroke
Tenby
Carmarthen
Llandeilo
Llandovery
Lampeter
Tregaron
Builth Wells
Brecon
Abergavenny
Monmouth
Merthyr Tydfil
Swansea
Neath
Port Talbot
Bridgend
Llanelli
Pontypridd
Caerphilly
Newport
CARDIFF
Barry
Chester
Liverpool
Birkenhead
St Helens
Manchester
Crewe
Shrewsbury
Telford
Wolverhampton
Kidderminster
Ludlow
Leominster
Hereford
Ross on Wye
Chepstow
Bristol
Bath
Weston super-mare
Minehead
Taunton
Bridgwater
Wells
Yeovil
Ilfracombe
Barnstaple
Bideford
Tiverton
Exeter
Exmouth
Torquay
Paignton
Dartmouth
Plymouth
Tavistock
Launceston
Bodmin
Newquay
St Austell
Truro
Falmouth
Penzance
Bude
Okehampton
Honiton
Sidmouth
Lyme Regis
Bridport
Dorchester
Weymouth
Bill of Portland
m
feet
609
2000
304
1000
152
500
76
250
0
0
Below Sea Level
Longitude West 3° of Greenwich
CONIC PROJECTION

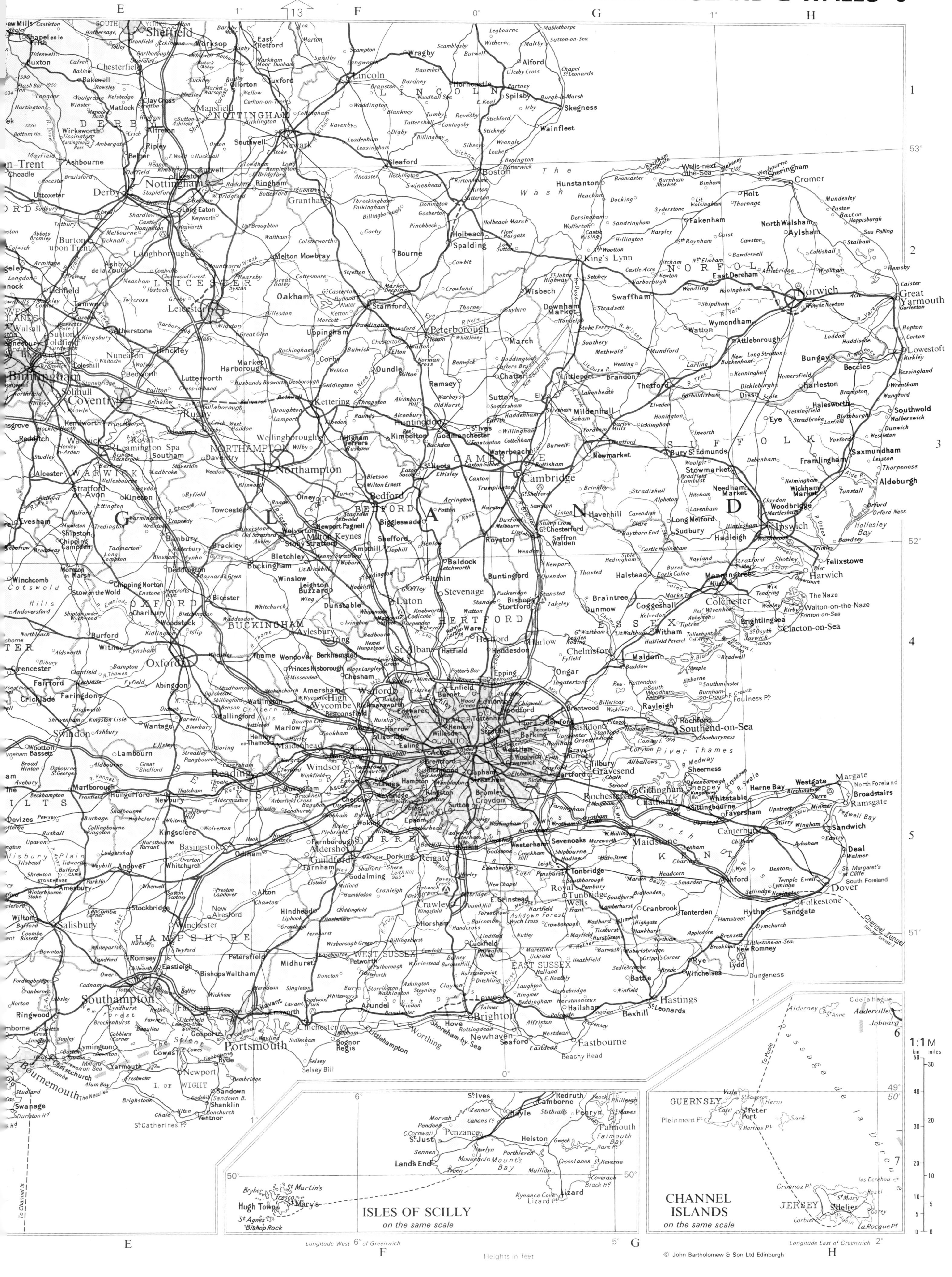

ISLES OF SCILLY
on the same scale

CHANNEL ISLANDS
on the same scale

GUERNSEY

JERSEY

1:1 M

Longitude West 6° of Greenwich

Longitude East of Greenwich 2°

Heights in feet

© John Bartholomew & Son Ltd Edinburgh

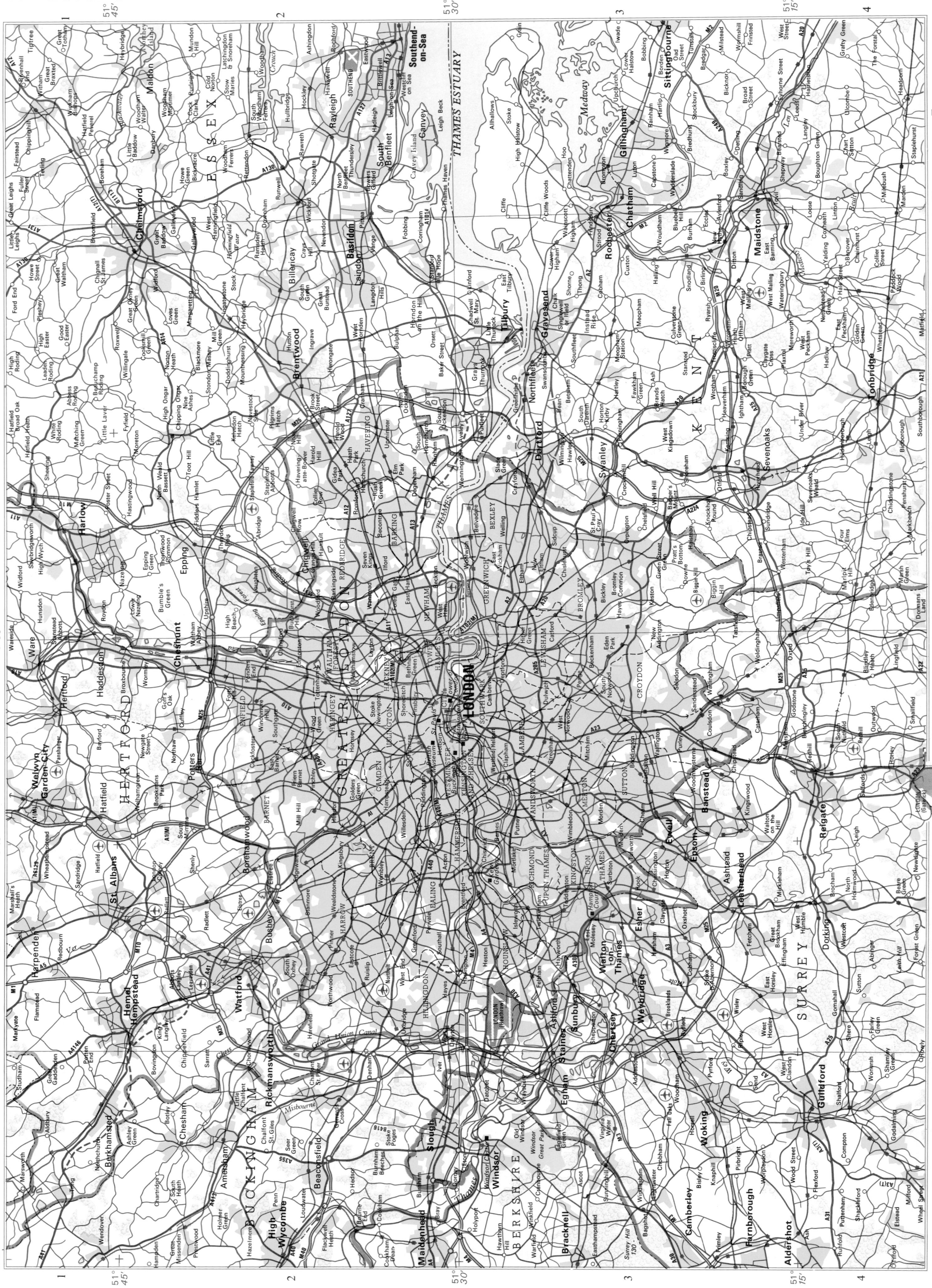

THAMES ESTUARY

GREATER LONDON

LONDON

ESSEX

HERTFORD

BUCKINGHAM

BERKSHIRE

SURREY

KENT

© Times Books Ltd

1:300 000

0   5   10   15 km

0   5   10 miles

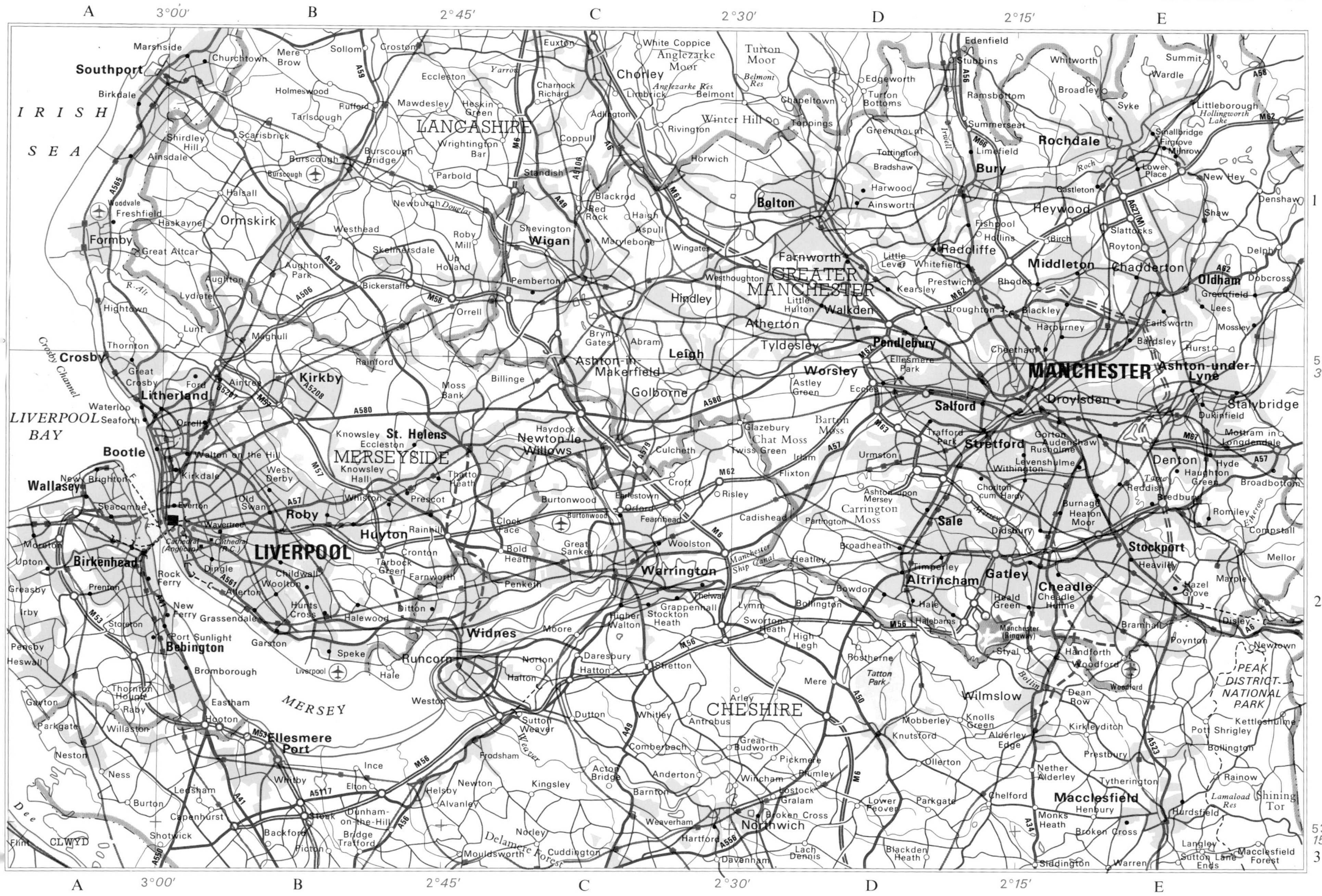

WEST MIDLANDS

1:300000

© Times Books Ltd

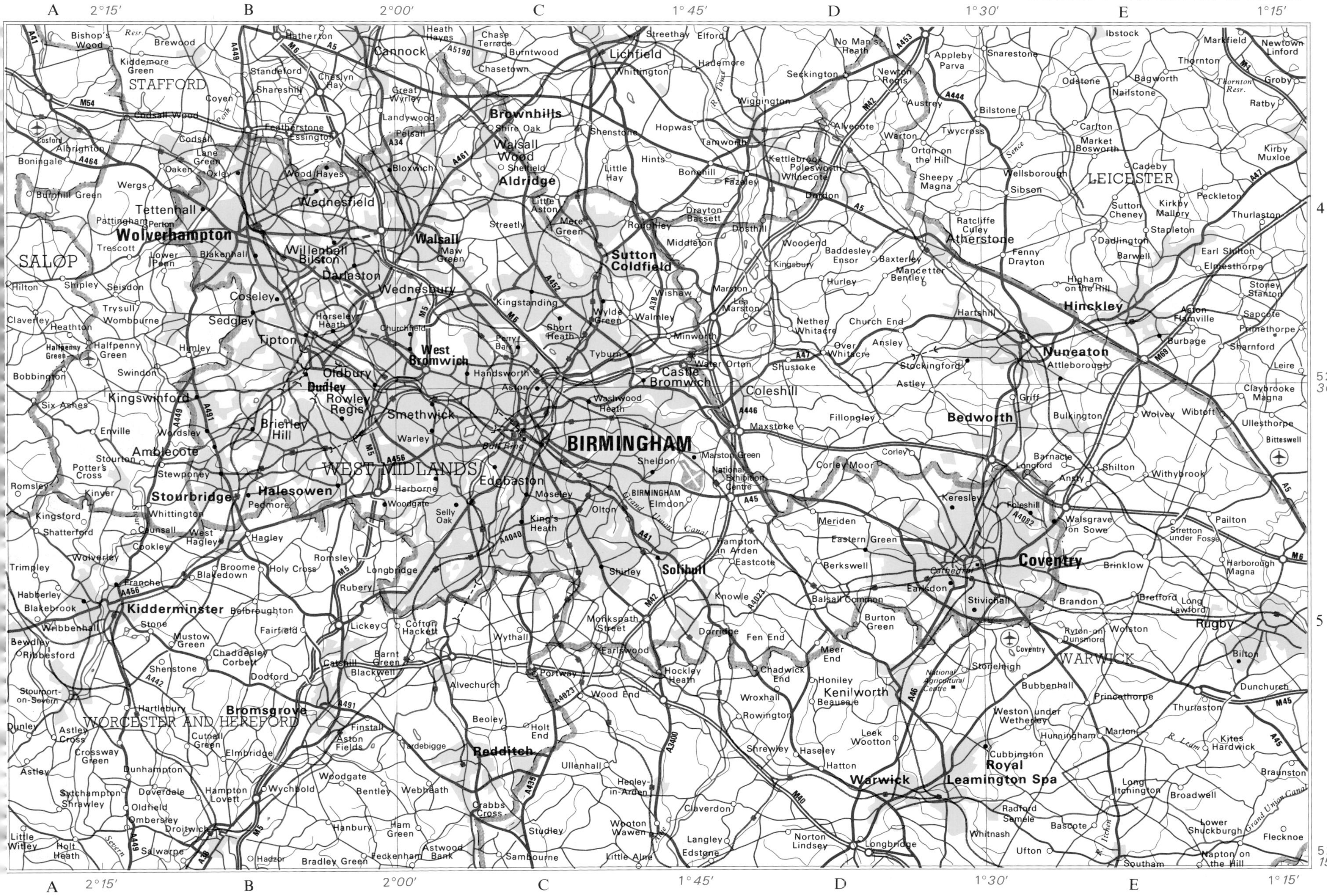

IRISH SEA
LIVERPOOL BAY
Southport
Formby
Ormskirk
Crosby
Litherland
Bootle
Wallasey
Birkenhead
LIVERPOOL
Kirkby
St. Helens
MERSEYSIDE
Huyton
Widnes
Runcorn
Bebington
Ellesmere Port
MERSEY
LANCASHIRE
Wigan
Chorley
Bolton
Bury
Rochdale
Heywood
Middleton
Oldham
Leigh
Atherton
Hindley
Tyldesley
Walkden
Farnworth
Radcliffe
GREATER MANCHESTER
MANCHESTER
Salford
Stretford
Sale
Altrincham
Stockport
Cheadle
Gatley
Ashton-under-Lyne
Stalybridge
Denton
Droylsden
Warrington
Newton-le-Willows
Golborne
Ashton-in-Makerfield
CHESHIRE
Northwich
Wilmslow
Macclesfield
PEAK DISTRICT NATIONAL PARK
CLWYD
Pendlebury
Worsley
STAFFORD
SALOP
Cannock
Lichfield
Brownhills
Aldridge
Walsall
Wolverhampton
Wednesfield
Willenhall
Bilston
Darlaston
Wednesbury
Tipton
Sedgley
Coseley
Oldbury
Dudley
Rowley Regis
West Bromwich
Smethwick
Brierley Hill
Stourbridge
Halesowen
Sutton Coldfield
BIRMINGHAM
Tamworth
Atherstone
Nuneaton
Hinckley
Bedworth
Coventry
LEICESTER
Rugby
WARWICK
Kidderminster
Bromsgrove
WORCESTER AND HEREFORD
Redditch
Solihull
Kenilworth
Warwick
Royal Leamington Spa
Castle Bromwich
Coleshill
Edgbaston

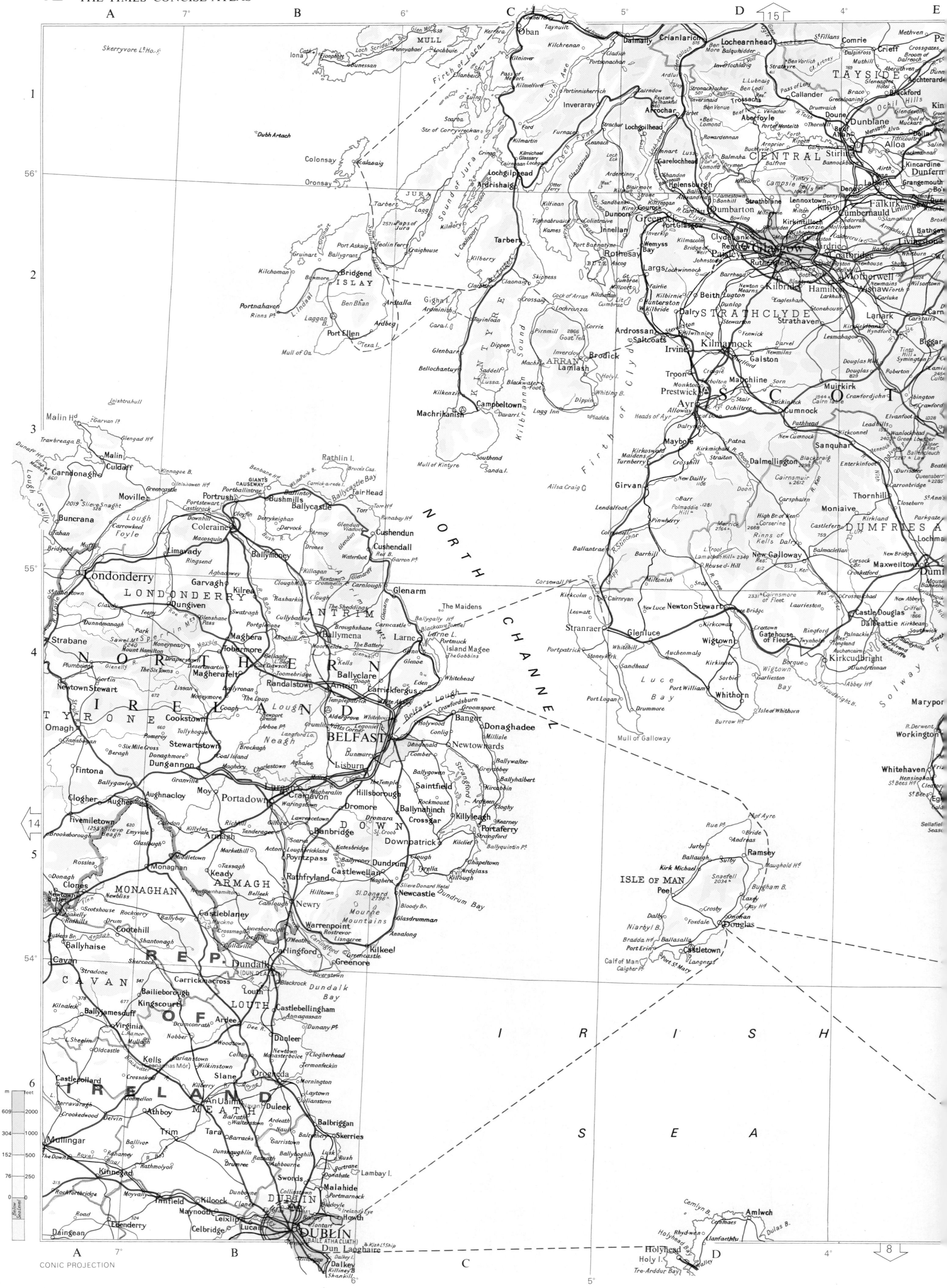

MULL

Oban

TAYSICE

CENTRAL

Glasgow

STRATHCLYDE

Belfast

NORTHERN IRELAND

LONDONDERRY

ANTRIM

TYRONE

DOWN

ARMAGH

MONAGHAN

CAVAN

LOUTH

MEATH

REP. OF IRELAND

DUBLIN
(BAILE ÁTHA CLIATH)

ISLE OF MAN

Douglas

NORTH CHANNEL

IRISH SEA

DUMFRIES

Londonderry

Omagh

Cookstown

Dungannon

Armagh

Monaghan

Dundalk

Drogheda

Mullingar

Kells

Trim

Conic Projection

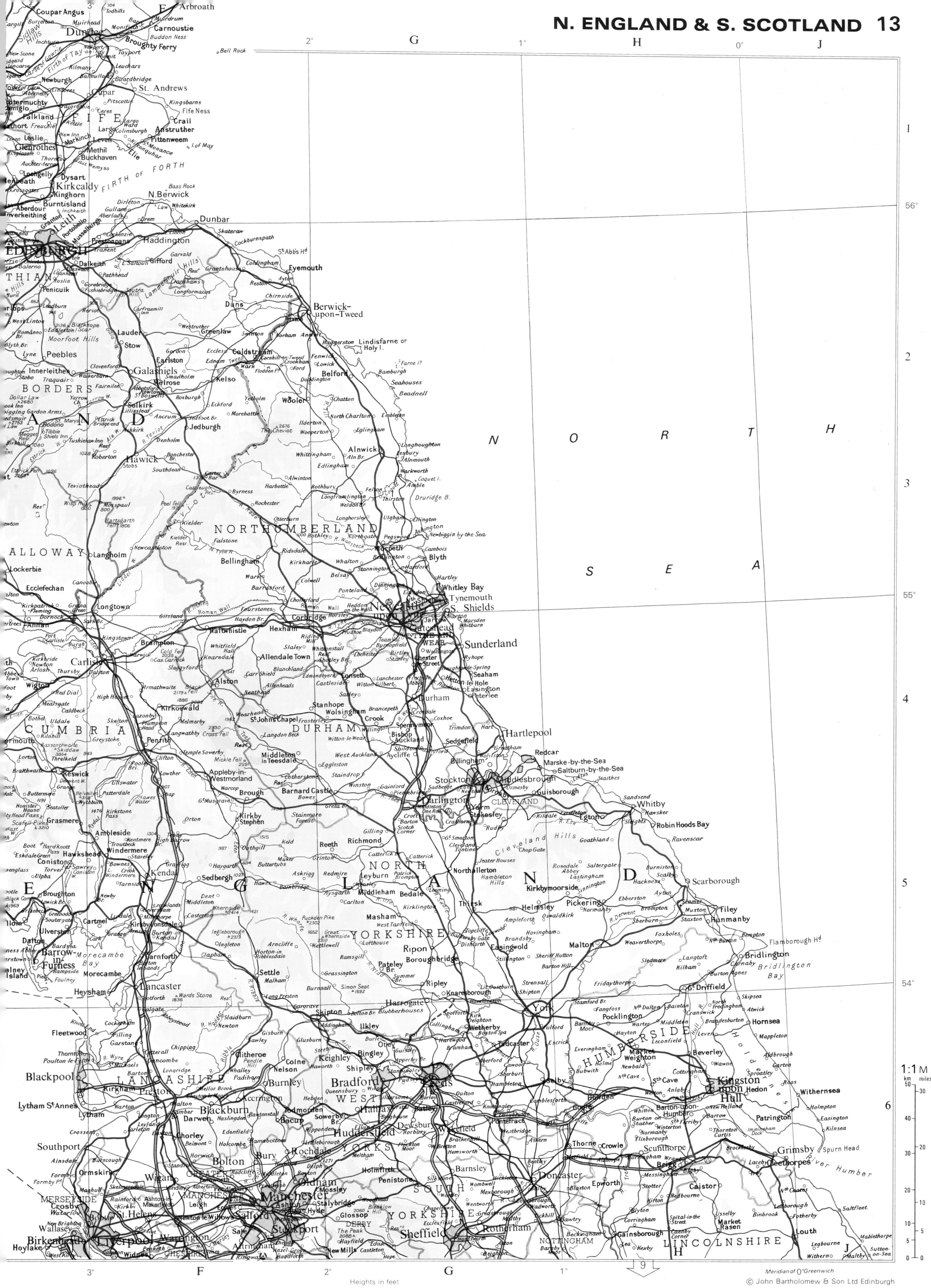
NORTH SEA
NORTHUMBERLAND
CUMBRIA
DURHAM
NORTH YORKSHIRE
CLEVELAND
TYNE AND WEAR
LANCASHIRE
HUMBERSIDE
WEST YORKS
SOUTH YORKSHIRE
GREATER MANCHESTER
MERSEYSIDE
LINCOLNSHIRE
NOTTINGHAM
DERBY
CHESHIRE
BORDERS
FIFE
EDINBURGH
Newcastle upon Tyne
Sunderland
Middlesbrough
Leeds
Bradford
Manchester
Liverpool
Sheffield
Kingston upon Hull
York
Carlisle
FIRTH OF FORTH
Morecambe Bay
River Humber
Bridlington Bay
1:1M
km
miles
Meridian of 0° Greenwich
Heights in feet
9

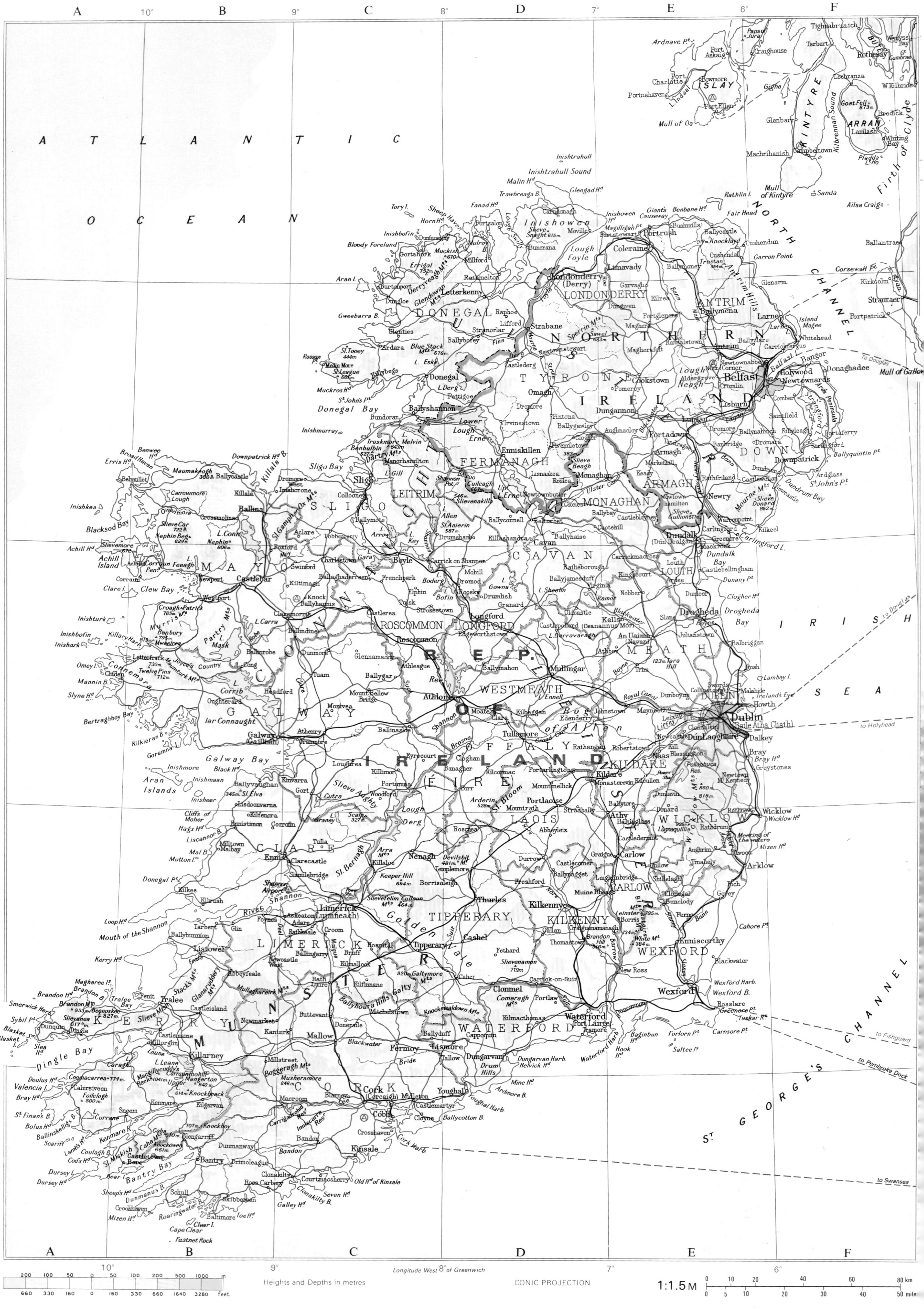

A   B   C   D   E   F

ATLANTIC OCEAN

IRISH SEA

NORTH CHANNEL

ST GEORGE'S CHANNEL

NORTHERN IRELAND

REP. OF IRELAND (ÉIRE)

Provinces / regions: ULSTER, CONNACHT, LEINSTER, MUNSTER

Counties: DONEGAL, LONDONDERRY, ANTRIM, TYRONE, FERMANAGH, DOWN, ARMAGH, MONAGHAN, CAVAN, LEITRIM, SLIGO, MAYO, ROSCOMMON, LONGFORD, WESTMEATH, MEATH, LOUTH, GALWAY, OFFALY, KILDARE, DUBLIN, WICKLOW, CLARE, LAOIS, TIPPERARY, CARLOW, KILKENNY, WEXFORD, LIMERICK, KERRY, CORK, WATERFORD

Major towns: Londonderry (Derry), Coleraine, Belfast, Lisburn, Newry, Dundalk, Sligo, Ballina, Castlebar, Westport, Galway (Gaillimh), Athlone, Mullingar, Drogheda, Dublin (Baile Átha Cliath), Dún Laoghaire, Bray, Ennis, Limerick (Luimneach), Tralee, Killarney, Cork (Corcaigh), Cobh, Waterford (Port Láirge), Wexford, Kilkenny, Carlow, Wicklow, Arklow, Enniskillen, Omagh, Armagh, Monaghan, Cavan, Longford, Roscommon, Tuam, Clonmel, Cashel, Thurles, Nenagh, Mallow, Bantry

Scotland (inset): ISLAY, KINTYRE, ARRAN, Firth of Clyde, Campbeltown, Brodick

Scale 1:1.5 M

Longitude West 8° of Greenwich

CONIC PROJECTION

Heights and Depths in metres

200 100 50 0 50 100 200 500 1000 m
660 330 160 0 160 330 660 1640 3280 feet

0 10 20 40 60 80 km
0 5 10 20 30 40 50 mile

to Holyhead   to Douglas   to Fishguard   to Pembroke Dock   to Swansea

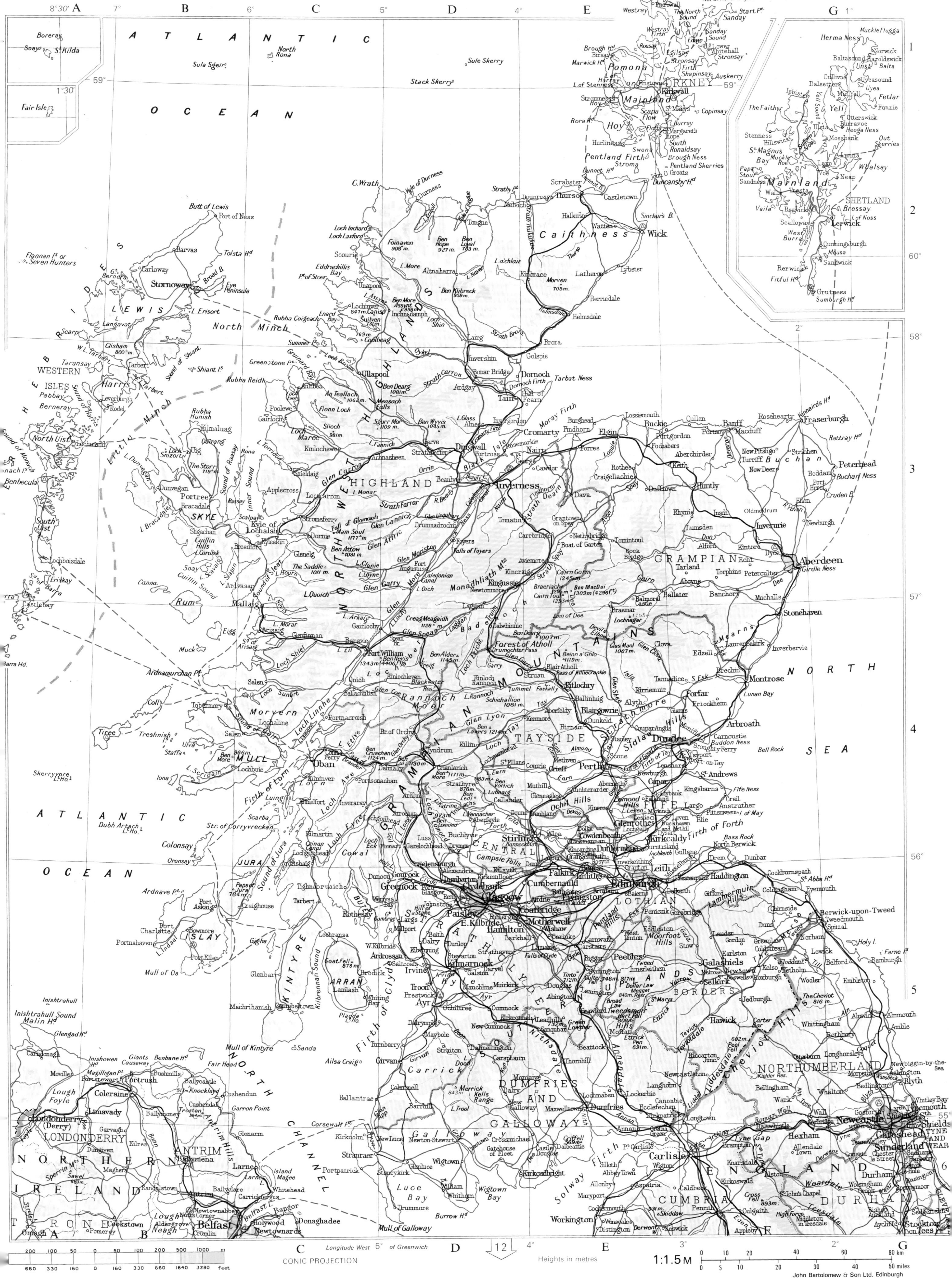
ATLANTIC OCEAN
St Kilda
Fair Isle
North Rona
Sula Sgeir
Sule Skerry
Stack Skerry
ORKNEY
Mainland
Hoy
Kirkwall
Stromness
Pentland Firth
Westray
Sanday
Stronsay
South Ronaldsay
Duncansby Hd
SHETLAND
Mainland
Yell
Unst
Lerwick
Sumburgh Hd
Muckle Flugga
Caithness
Thurso
Wick
Helmsdale
C. Wrath
Butt of Lewis
Stornoway
LEWIS
Harris
North Minch
Little Minch
OUTER HEBRIDES
WESTERN ISLES
North Uist
Benbecula
South Uist
Barra
SKYE
Portree
Kyle of Lochalsh
Rum
Eigg
Muck
Canna
Coll
Tiree
MULL
Iona
Colonsay
JURA
ISLAY
Oban
Fort William
Mallaig
Ullapool
Inverness
HIGHLAND
NORTH WEST HIGHLANDS
GRAMPIAN MOUNTAINS
Ben Nevis
Monadhliath Mts
Cairn Gorm
Ben MacDui
Moray Firth
Dornoch
Tain
Elgin
Banff
Fraserburgh
Peterhead
Aberdeen
GRAMPIAN
Stonehaven
Montrose
NORTH SEA
Arbroath
Dundee
Perth
TAYSIDE
Pitlochry
Firth of Tay
St Andrews
FIFE
Kirkcaldy
Dunfermline
Firth of Forth
Stirling
CENTRAL
Falkirk
Edinburgh
LOTHIAN
Leith
Dunbar
Glasgow
Greenock
Paisley
Motherwell
Hamilton
Kilmarnock
Ayr
Irvine
ARRAN
KINTYRE
Mull of Kintyre
Firth of Clyde
STRATHCLYDE
SOUTHERN UPLANDS
Peebles
Galashiels
BORDERS
Jedburgh
Hawick
Berwick-upon-Tweed
Cheviot Hills
DUMFRIES AND GALLOWAY
Dumfries
Stranraer
Wigtown
Kirkcudbright
Solway Firth
NORTH CHANNEL
Carlisle
CUMBRIA
Workington
ENGLAND
NORTHUMBERLAND
Newcastle
Sunderland
Durham
NORTHERN IRELAND
Londonderry
Coleraine
ANTRIM
Ballymena
Larne
Belfast
Lough Neagh
TYRONE
Omagh
Cookstown
Malin Hd
Lough Foyle
CONIC PROJECTION
Longitude West of Greenwich
Heights in metres
1:1.5M
John Bartholomew & Son Ltd. Edinburgh

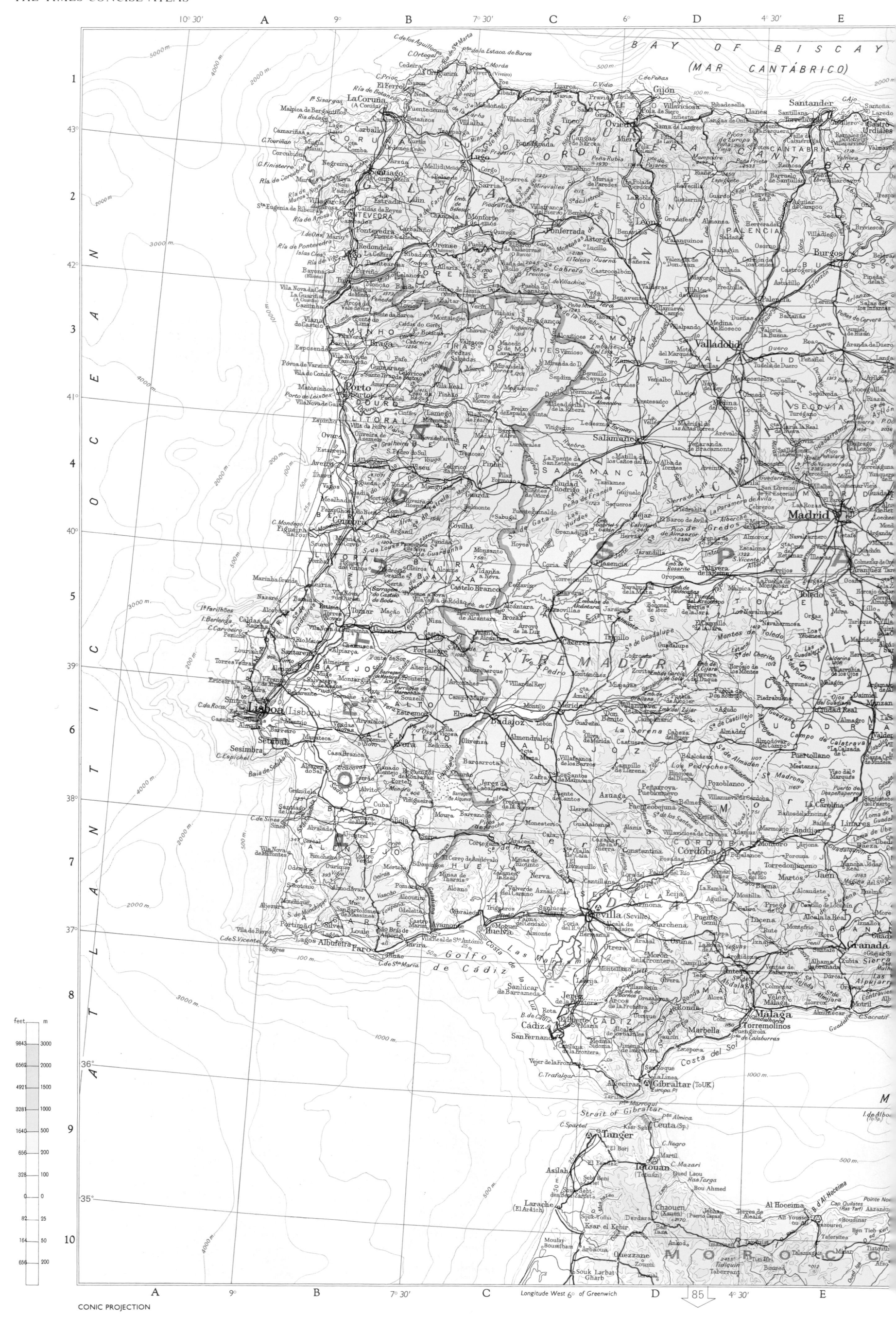
BAY OF BISCAY
(MAR CANTÁBRICO)
ATLANTIC OCEAN
Golfo de Cádiz
Strait of Gibraltar
Costa del Sol
GALICIA
ASTURIAS
CORDILLERA CANTÁBRICA
LEÓN
ZAMORA
VALLADOLID
SALAMANCA
ÁVILA
SEGOVIA
MADRID
TOLEDO
CÁCERES
EXTREMADURA
BADAJOZ
CIUDAD REAL
CÓRDOBA
SEVILLA
HUELVA
CÁDIZ
MÁLAGA
GRANADA
JAÉN
ANDALUCÍA
PORTUGAL
SPAIN
MOROCCO
MINHO
DOURO LITORAL
BEIRA ALTA
BEIRA BAIXA
ALTO ALENTEJO
BAIXO ALENTEJO
ALGARVE
La Coruña
Santiago de Compostela
Lugo
Oviedo
Gijón
Santander
Burgos
León
Orense
Pontevedra
Vigo
Braga
Porto
Coimbra
Viseu
Guarda
Bragança
Valladolid
Zamora
Salamanca
Ávila
Segovia
Madrid (Madrid)
Toledo
Aranjuez
Talavera de la Reina
Plasencia
Cáceres
Mérida
Badajoz
Elvas
Évora
Setúbal
Lisboa (Lisbon)
Santarém
Leiria
Castelo Branco
Portalegre
Beja
Faro
Huelva
Sevilla (Seville)
Córdoba
Jaén
Granada
Málaga
Torremolinos
Marbella
Jerez
Cádiz
San Fernando
Algeciras
Gibraltar (To UK)
Ceuta (Sp.)
Tanger
Tetouan (Tétuán)
Larache (El Araïch)
Ksar el Kebir
Chaouen (Xauen)
Al Hoceima
C. Finisterre
C. Ortegal
C. de S. Vicente
C. Espichel
C. da Roca
C. Trafalgar
Linares
Puertollano
Daimiel
Ciudad Real
Almadén
Mérida
Huelva
Ayamonte
Lagos
Albufeira
Portimão
Sines
Sesimbra
Nazaré
Figueira da Foz
Aveiro
Ovar
Espinho
Matosinhos
Viana do Castelo
Ferrol
Betanzos
Tuy
Ponferrada
Astorga
Benavente
Palencia
Medina del Campo
Tordesillas
Toro
Ciudad Rodrigo
Béjar
Trujillo
Coria
Almendralejo
Zafra
Llerena
Écija
Carmona
Osuna
Antequera
Ronda
Arcos de la Frontera
Vejer de la Frontera
Tarifa
10° 30′
9°
7° 30′
6°
4° 30′
43°
42°
41°
40°
39°
38°
37°
36°
35°
A
B
C
D
E
1
2
3
4
5
6
7
8
9
10
Longitude West 6° of Greenwich
feet
m
9843
3000
6562
2000
4921
1500
3281
1000
1640
500
656
200
328
100
0
0
82
25
164
50
656
200
5000 m.
4000 m.
3000 m.
2000 m.
1000 m.
500 m.
200 m.
100 m.

85

CONIC PROJECTION

MADRID
1:60 000

1:3 M

© John Bartholomew & Son Ltd Edinburgh

1:3M

CONIC PROJECTION

Longitude West 1° 30' of Greenwich   Meridian of 0° Greenwich

Heights and Depths in metres

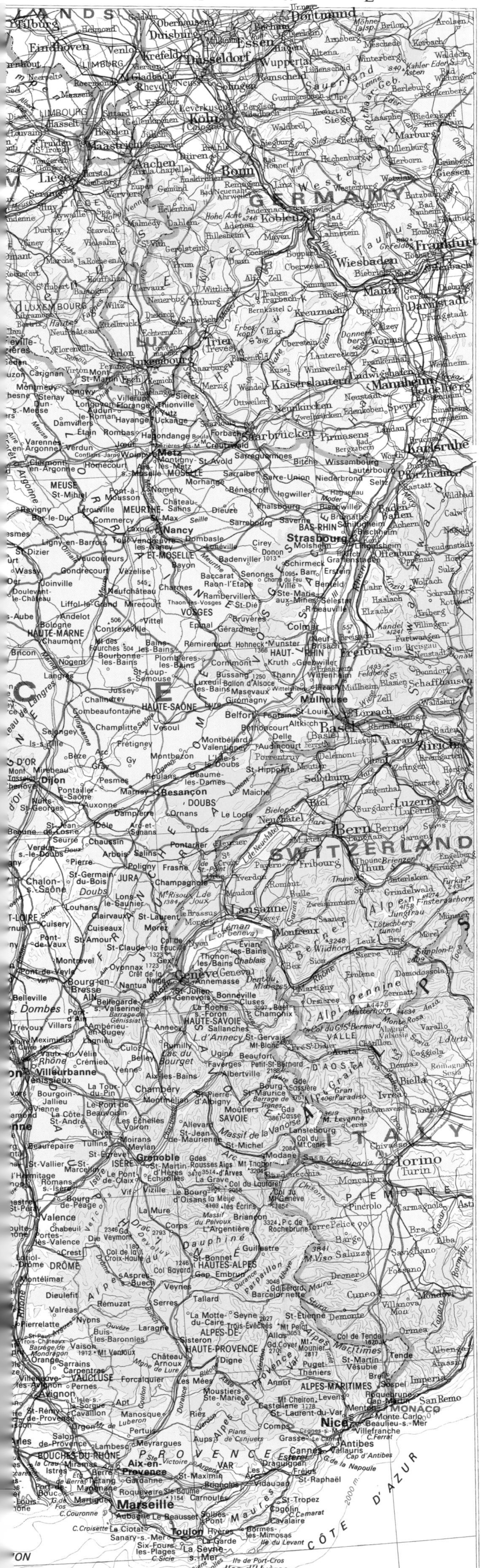

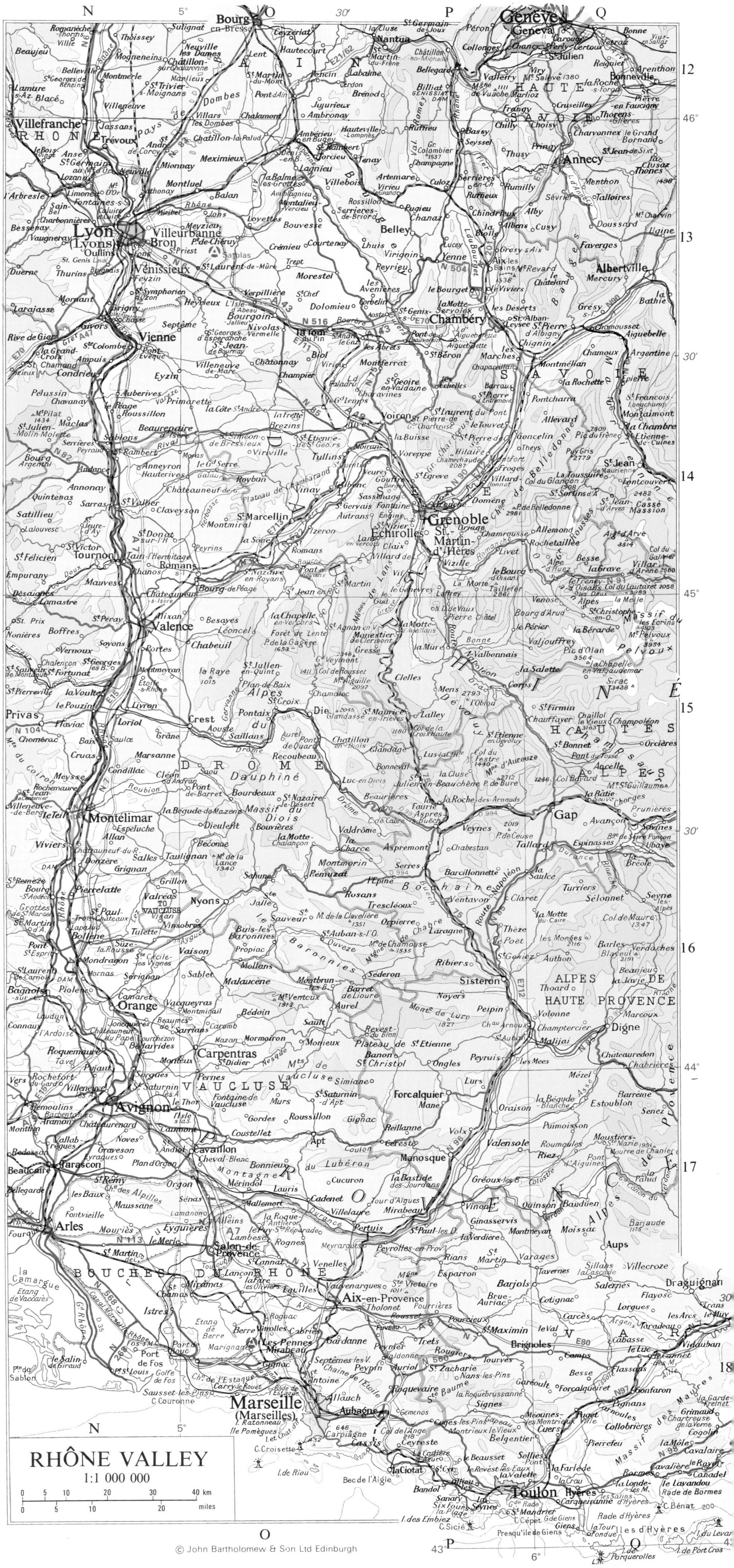

RHÔNE VALLEY

1:1 000 000

0 5 10   20   40 km
0 5 10   20 miles

Longitude East 6° of Greenwich

GERMANY

SWITZERLAND

ITALY

MEDITERRANEAN SEA

CÔTE D'AZUR

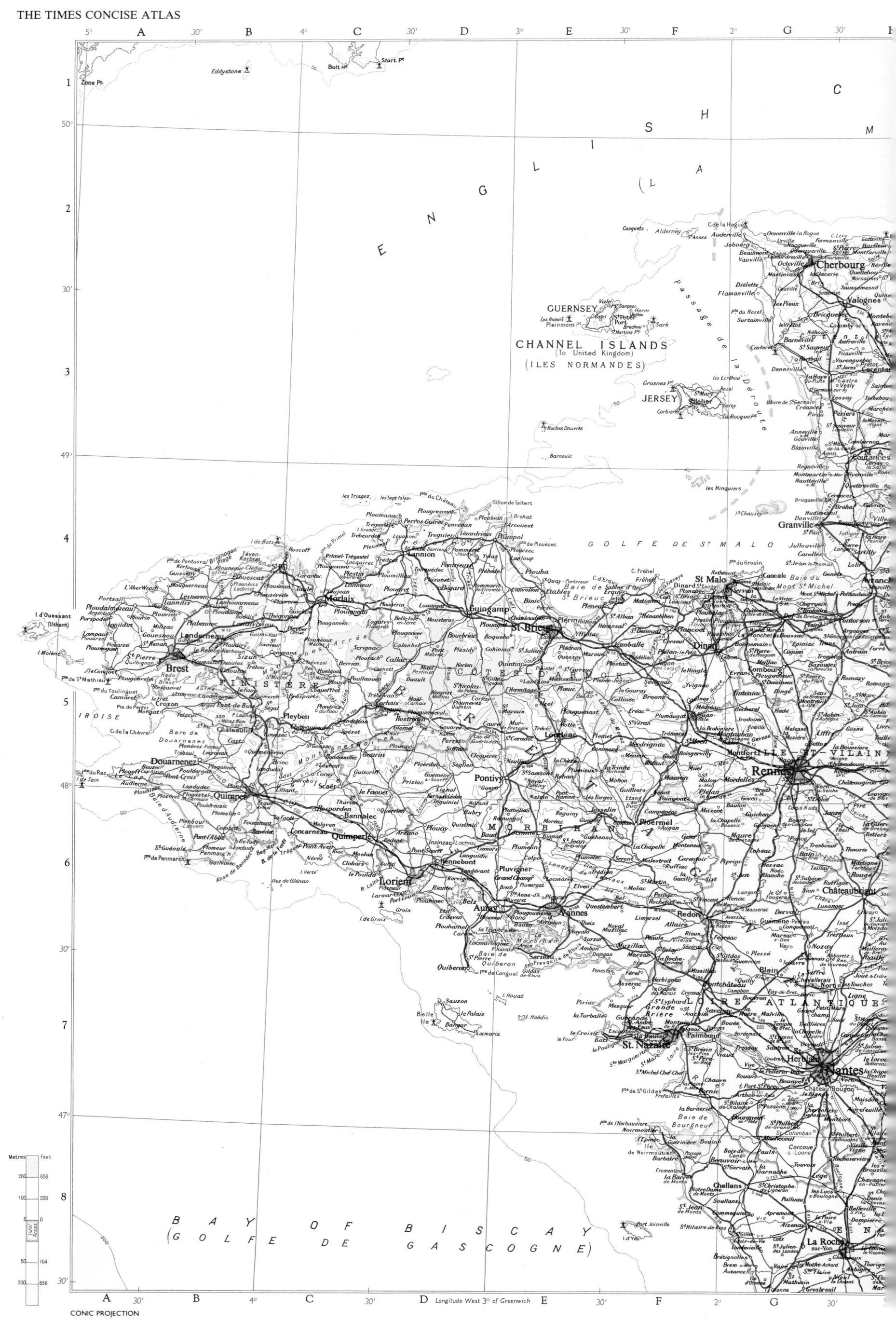
ENGLISH CHANNEL
(LA MANCHE)
CHANNEL ISLANDS
(To United Kingdom)
(ILES NORMANDES)
GUERNSEY
JERSEY
Alderney
Sark
Passage de la Déroute
GOLFE DE ST MALO
BAY OF BISCAY
(GOLFE DE GASCOGNE)
IROISE
Baie de Douarnenez
Baie d'Audierne
I. d'Ouessant (Ushant)
Belle Ile
Quiberon
I. de Groix
Iles de Glénan
Ile de Noirmoutier
I. d'Yeu
FINISTÈRE
CÔTES-D'ARMOR
MORBIHAN
ILLE-ET-VILAINE
LOIRE-ATLANTIQUE
BRETAGNE
Cherbourg
Valognes
Granville
St Malo
Dinan
Rennes
Brest
Morlaix
Lannion
Guingamp
St Brieuc
Quimper
Douarnenez
Pontivy
Lorient
Vannes
Auray
Redon
St Nazaire
Nantes
La Roche-sur-Yon
Challans
Châteaubriant
Metres
Feet
200
656
100
328
0
Tidal Areas
50
164
200
656
Longitude West 3° of Greenwich

CONIC PROJECTION

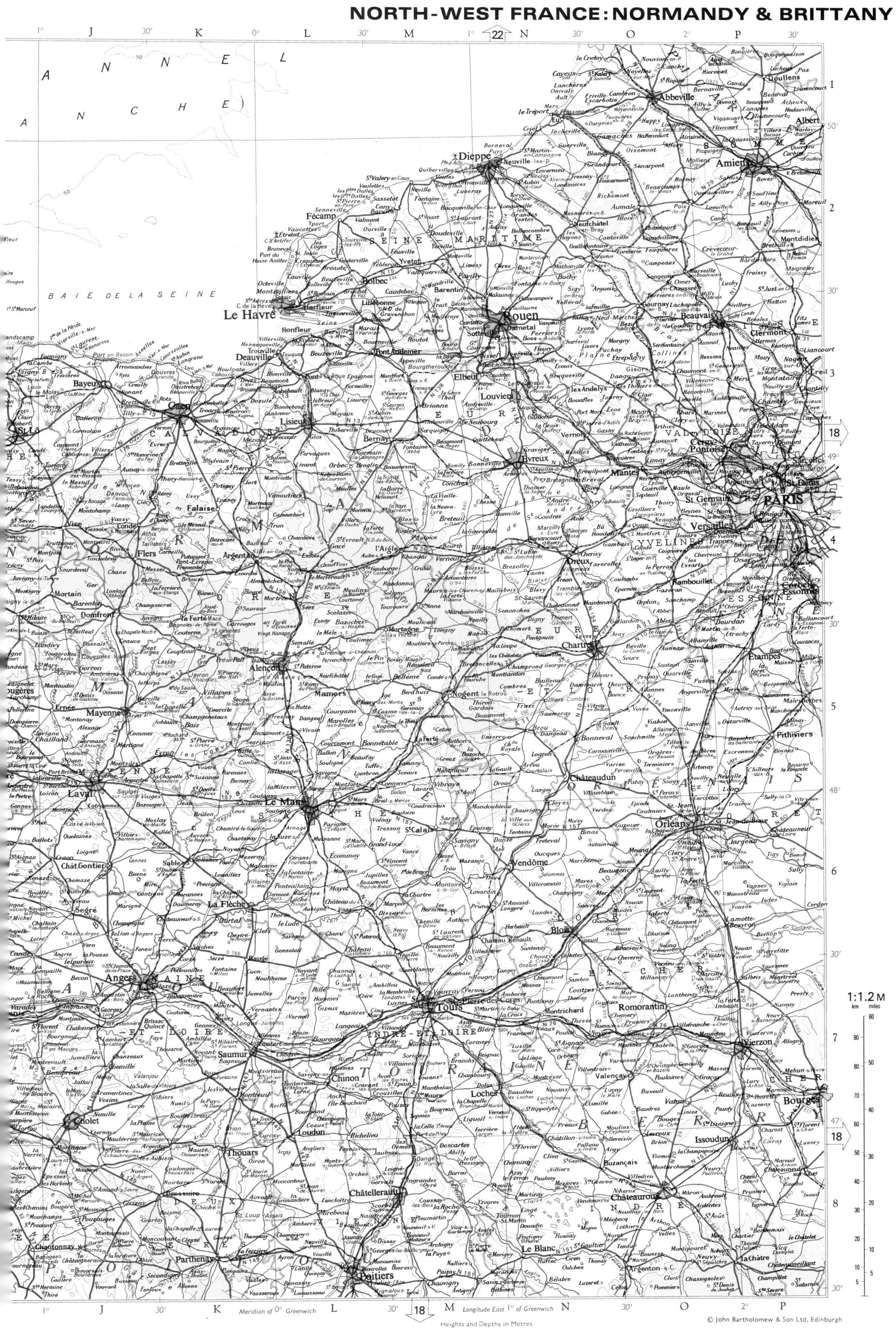

1:1.2 M

Meridian of 0° Greenwich

Longitude East 1° of Greenwich

Heights and Depths in Metres

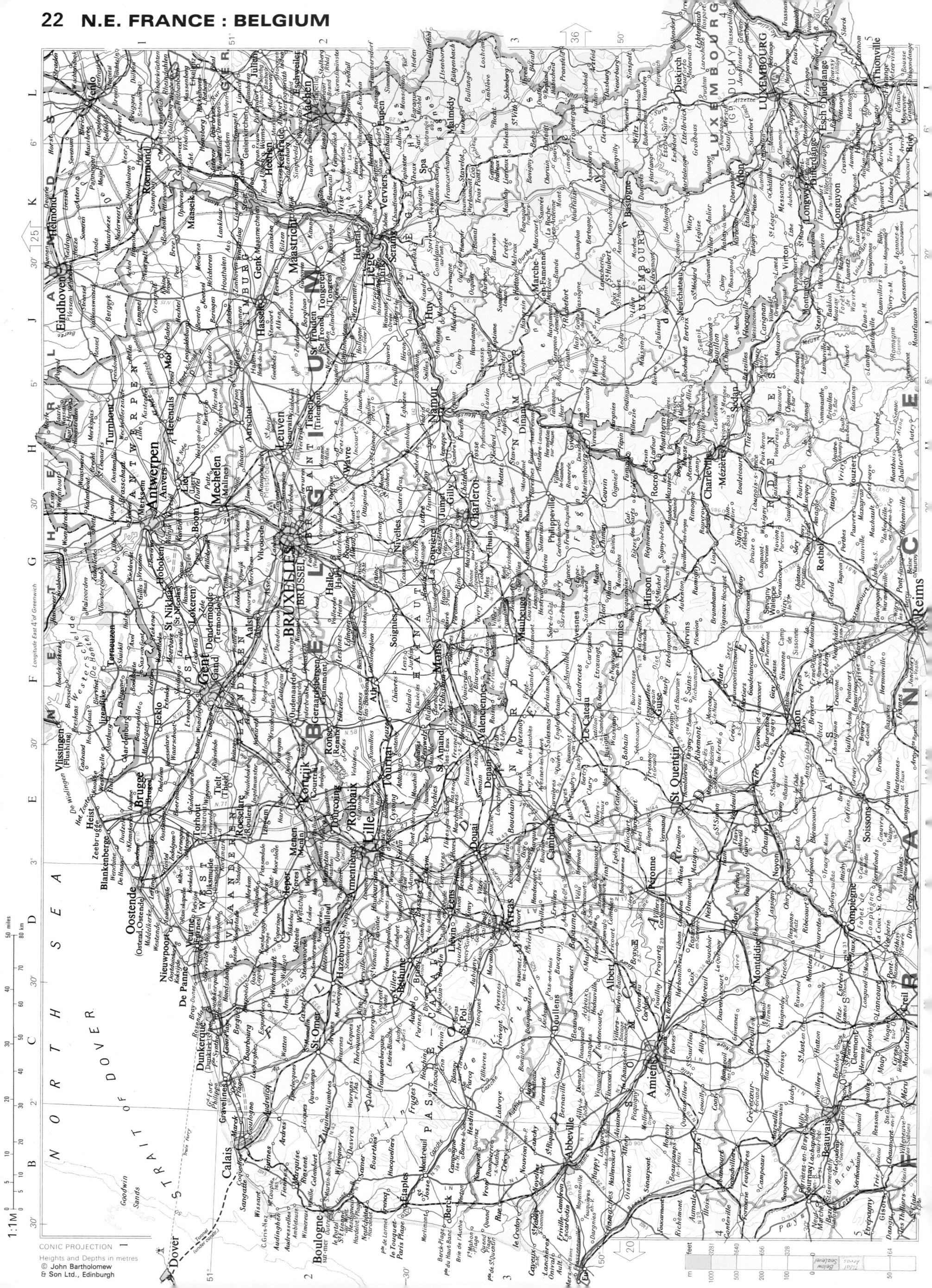
CONIC PROJECTION
Heights and Depths in metres
© John Bartholomew & Son Ltd., Edinburgh
1:1M
NORTH SEA
STRAIT OF DOVER
BELGIUM
FRANCE
LUXEMBOURG

PARIS
Versailles
Melun
Meaux
Rambouillet
Mantes-la-Jolie
St-Germain-en-Laye
Corbeil-Essonnes
Pontoise
Orly
AEROPORT CHARLES DE GAULLE
SEINE-ET-MARNE
YVELINES
ESSONNE
VAL D'OISE
EURE ET LOIR
SEINE
MARNE

0 5 10 15 km
0 5 10 miles

1:300 000

BRUSSELS

Map: Amsterdam / The Hague (top) and Brussels (bottom)

NORTH SEA

NOORDHOLLAND

ZUID-HOLLAND

UTRECHT

MARKERWAARD

ZUIDELIJK FLEVOLAND

GOOIMEER

IJMEER

AMSTERDAM
Amstelveen
Haarlem
Heemstede
Zaandam
Ijmuiden
Hilversum
Bussum
Naarden
Huizen
Weesp
Leiden
Oegstgeest
Wassenaar
Katwijk aan Zee
Noordwijk aan Zee
Voorschoten
Scheveningen
DEN HAAG
's-Gravenhage
The Hague
Voorburg
Rijswijk
Zoetermeer
Waddinxveen
Alphen aan den Rijn
Woerden
Utrecht
De Bilt

OOST VLAANDEREN

BRABANT

HAINAUT

Gent / Gand
Genthrugge
Sint-Amandsberg
Lokeren
Zele
Dendermonde
Aalst
Ninove
Oudenaarde
Ronse
ANTWERPEN
Mechelen
Willebroek
Boom
Niel
Temse
Lier
Duffel
Kontich
BRUXELLES / BRUSSEL
Vilvoorde
Halle
Waterloo
Wavre

© Times Books Ltd

1 : 300 000

© Times Books Ltd

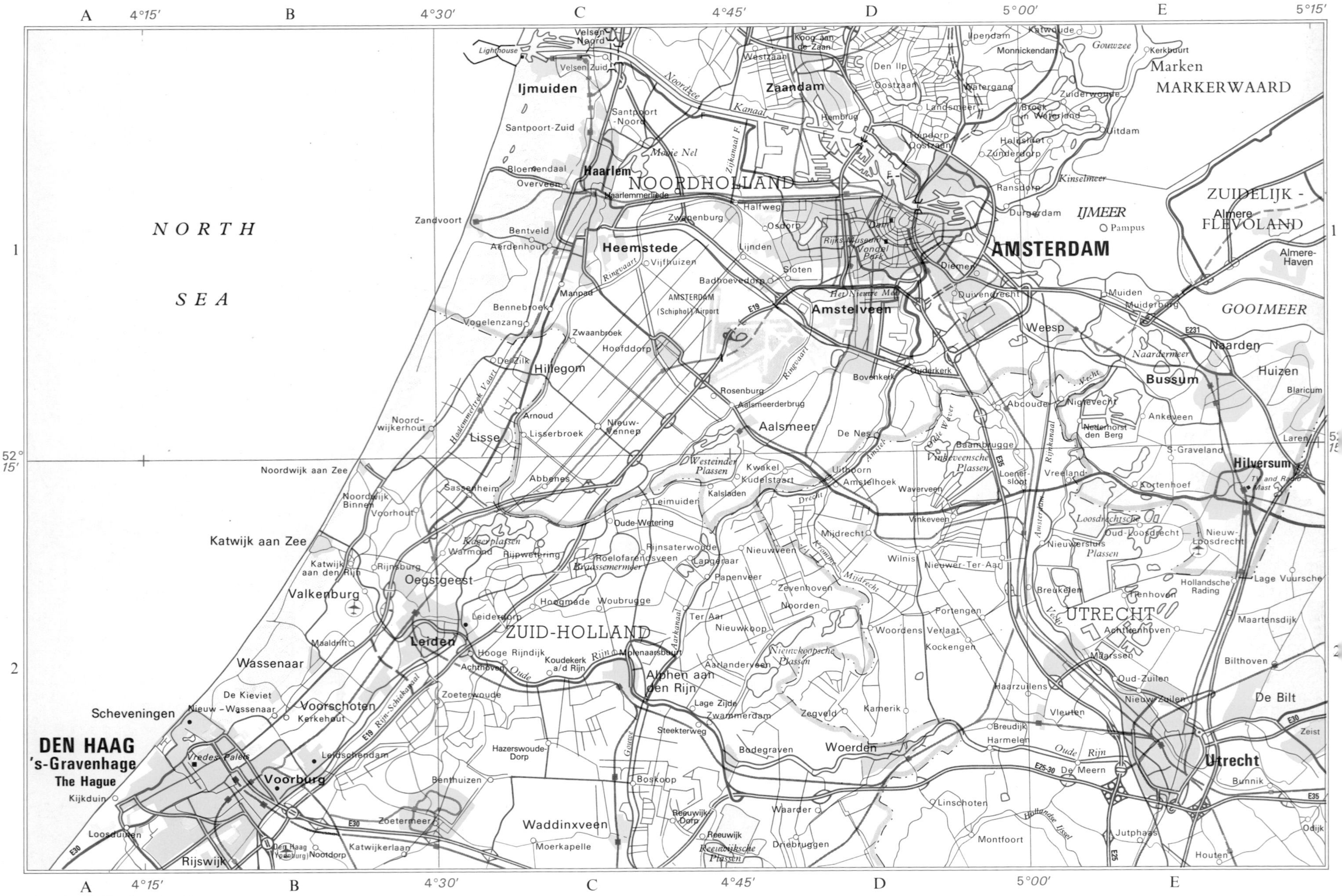

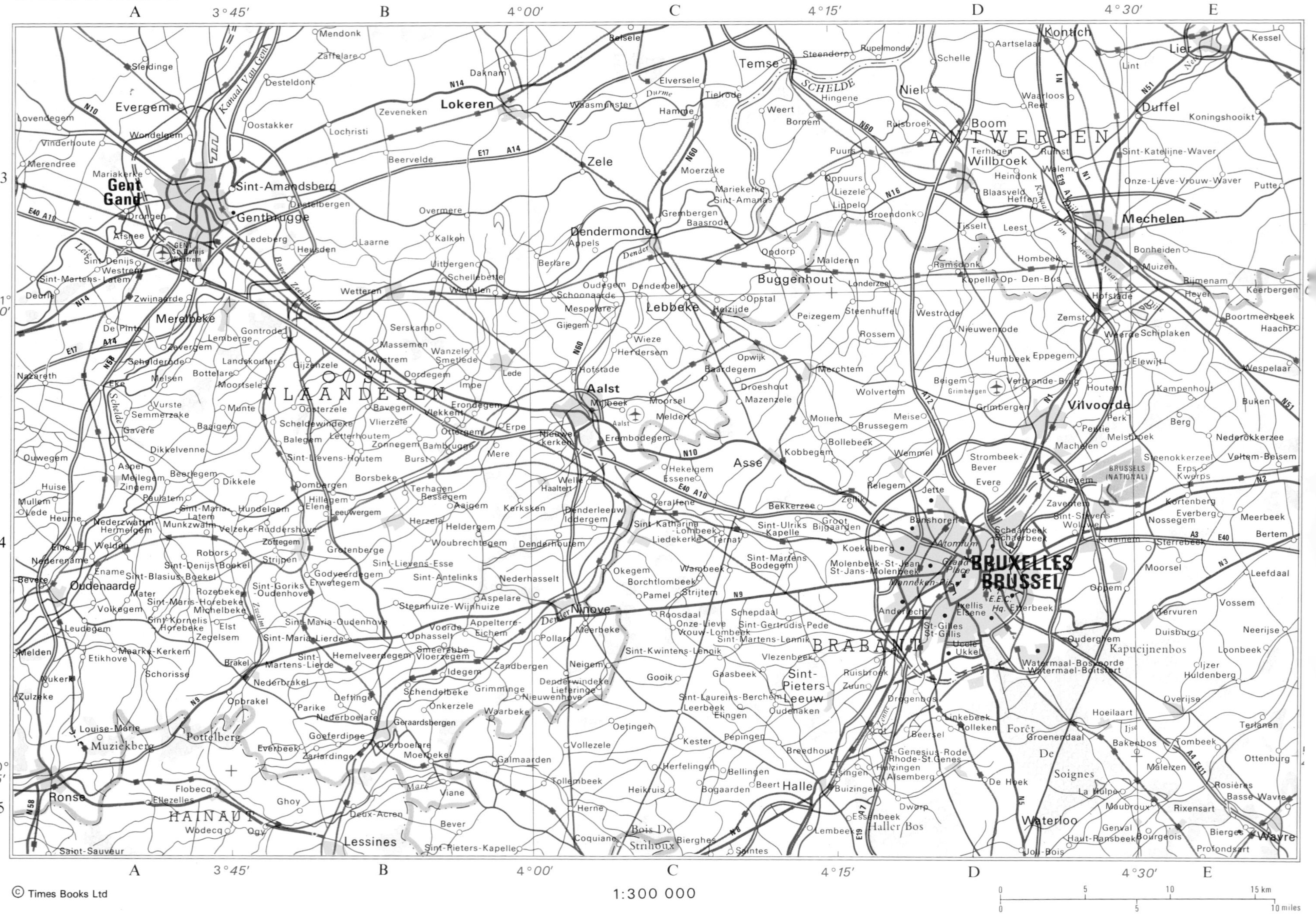

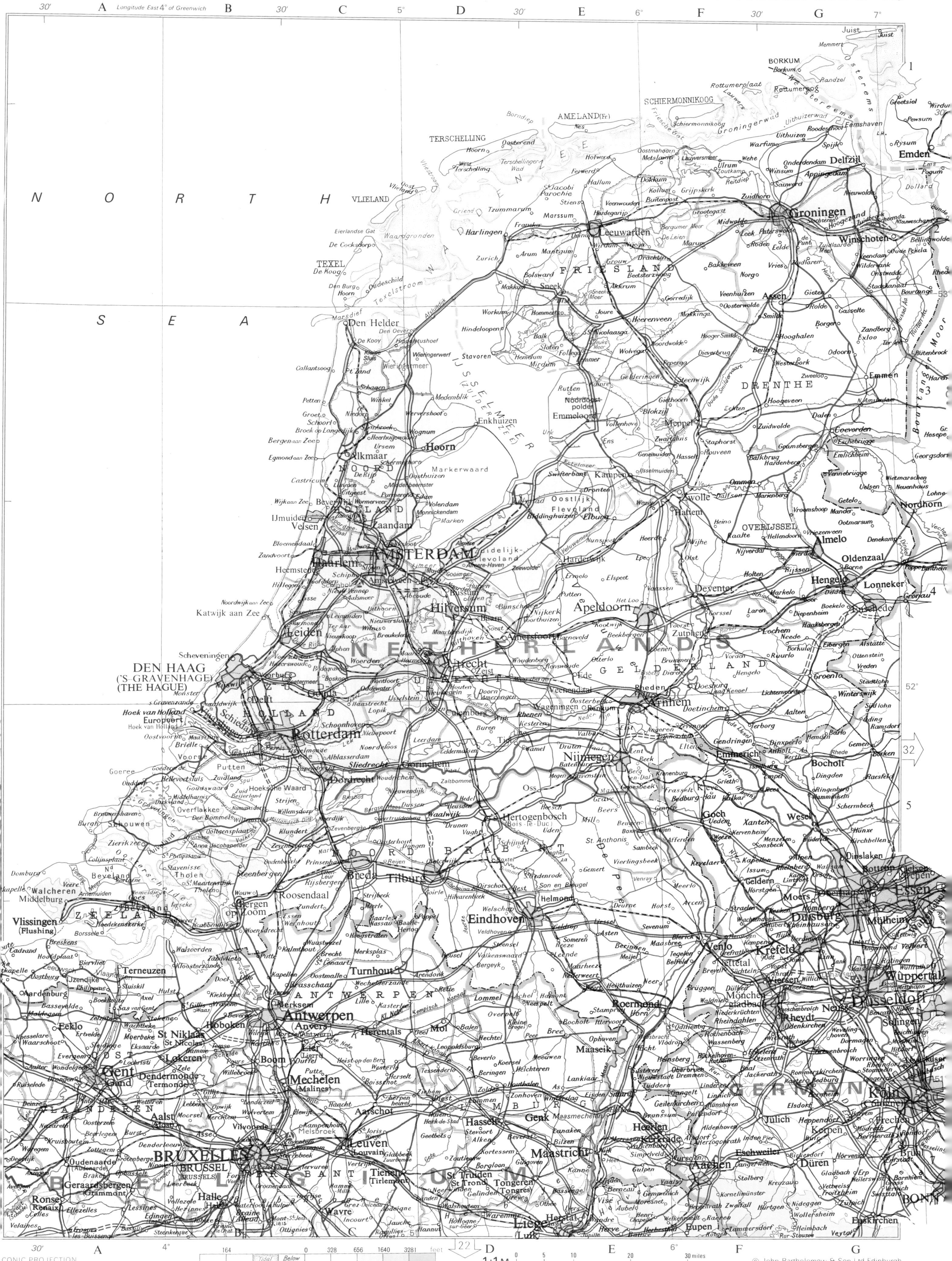

Longitude East 4° of Greenwich

NORTH SEA

NETHERLANDS

GERMANY

BELGIUM

FRIESLAND
DRENTHE
OVERIJSSEL
GELDERLAND
NOORD HOLLAND
ZUID HOLLAND
ZEELAND
NOORD BRABANT
LIMBURG

Groningen
Leeuwarden
Winschoten
Emden
Delfzijl
Assen
Emmen
Meppel
Zwolle
Almelo
Hengelo
Oldenzaal
Lonneker
Enschede
Deventer
Apeldoorn
Zutphen
Den Helder
Alkmaar
Hoorn
Enkhuizen
Haarlem
AMSTERDAM
Zaandam
IJmuiden
Velsen
Hilversum
Amersfoort
Arnhem
Nijmegen
Leiden
Utrecht
Ede
DEN HAAG ('S-GRAVENHAGE) (THE HAGUE)
Scheveningen
Delft
Gouda
Rotterdam
Schiedam
Dordrecht
Gorinchem
Hertogenbosch (Bois-le-Duc)
Tilburg
Breda
Roosendaal
Bergen op Zoom
Eindhoven
Helmond
Venlo
Roermond
Middelburg
Vlissingen (Flushing)
Terneuzen
Maastricht
Heerlen
Kerkrade

Hoek van Holland
Europoort
Katwijk aan Zee
Zandvoort

BELGIUM
Antwerpen (Anvers)
Gent (Gand)
BRUXELLES (BRUSSEL) (BRUSSELS)
Mechelen (Malines)
Leuven (Louvain)
Turnhout
Hasselt
Genk
Sint Niklaas
Lier (Lierre)
Aalst
Dendermonde (Termonde)
Oudenaarde (Audenarde)
Ronse (Renaix)
Liège (Luik)

GERMANY
Essen
Duisburg
Mülheim
Wuppertal
Düsseldorf
Neuss
Krefeld
Mönchengladbach
Köln
Aachen
Düren
Wesel
Bocholt
Nordhorn
Kleve
Emmerich
Goch
Geldern
Kempen

CONIC PROJECTION

1:1 M

© John Bartholomew & Son Ltd Edinburgh

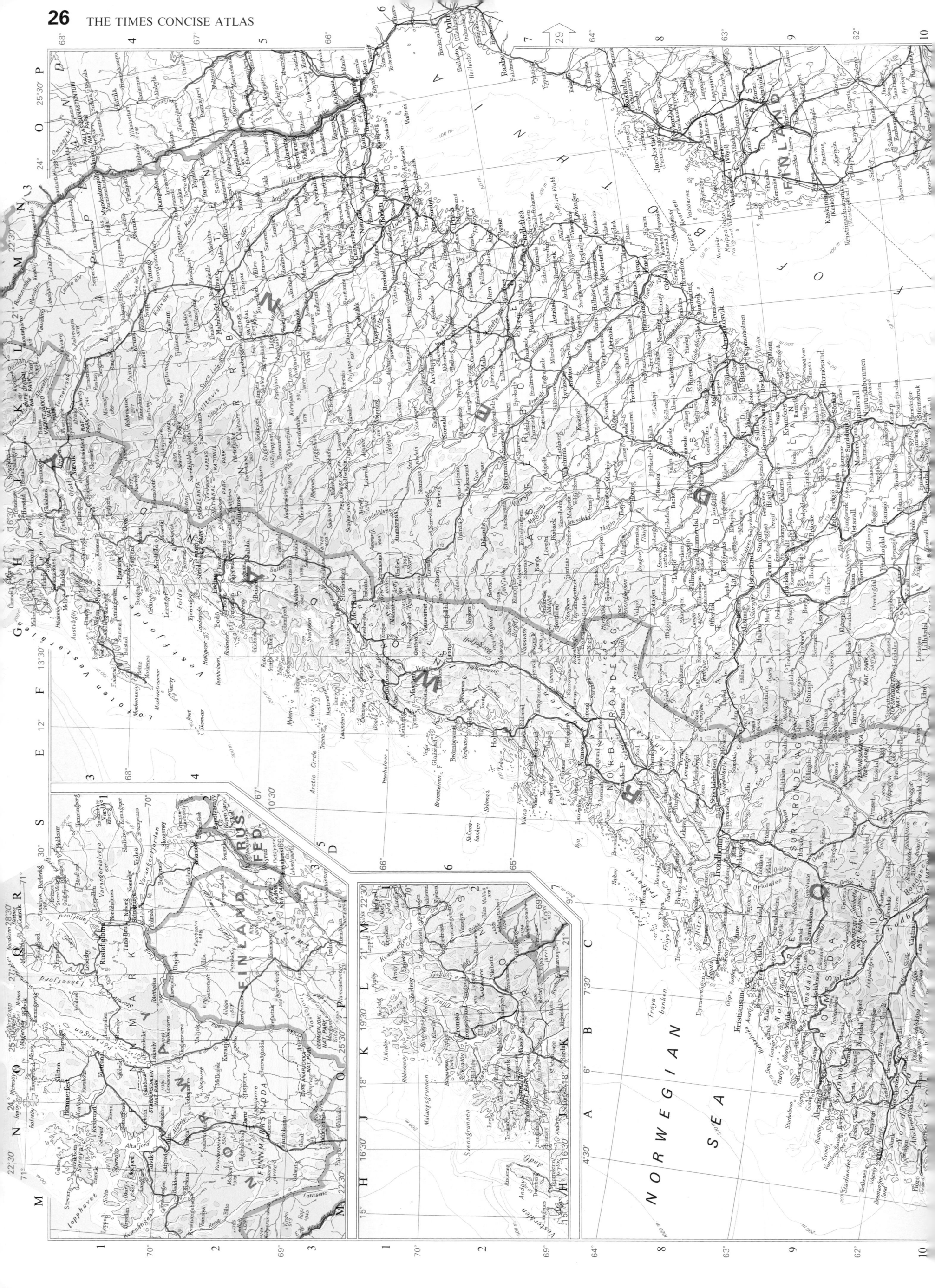
NORWEGIAN SEA
FINLAND
RUS. FED.
Arctic Circle
Trondheim
Narvik
Bodø
Kristiansund
Ålesund
Tromsø
Hammerfest
Umeå
Luleå
Oulu
Vaasa
Östersund
Härnösand
Sundsvall

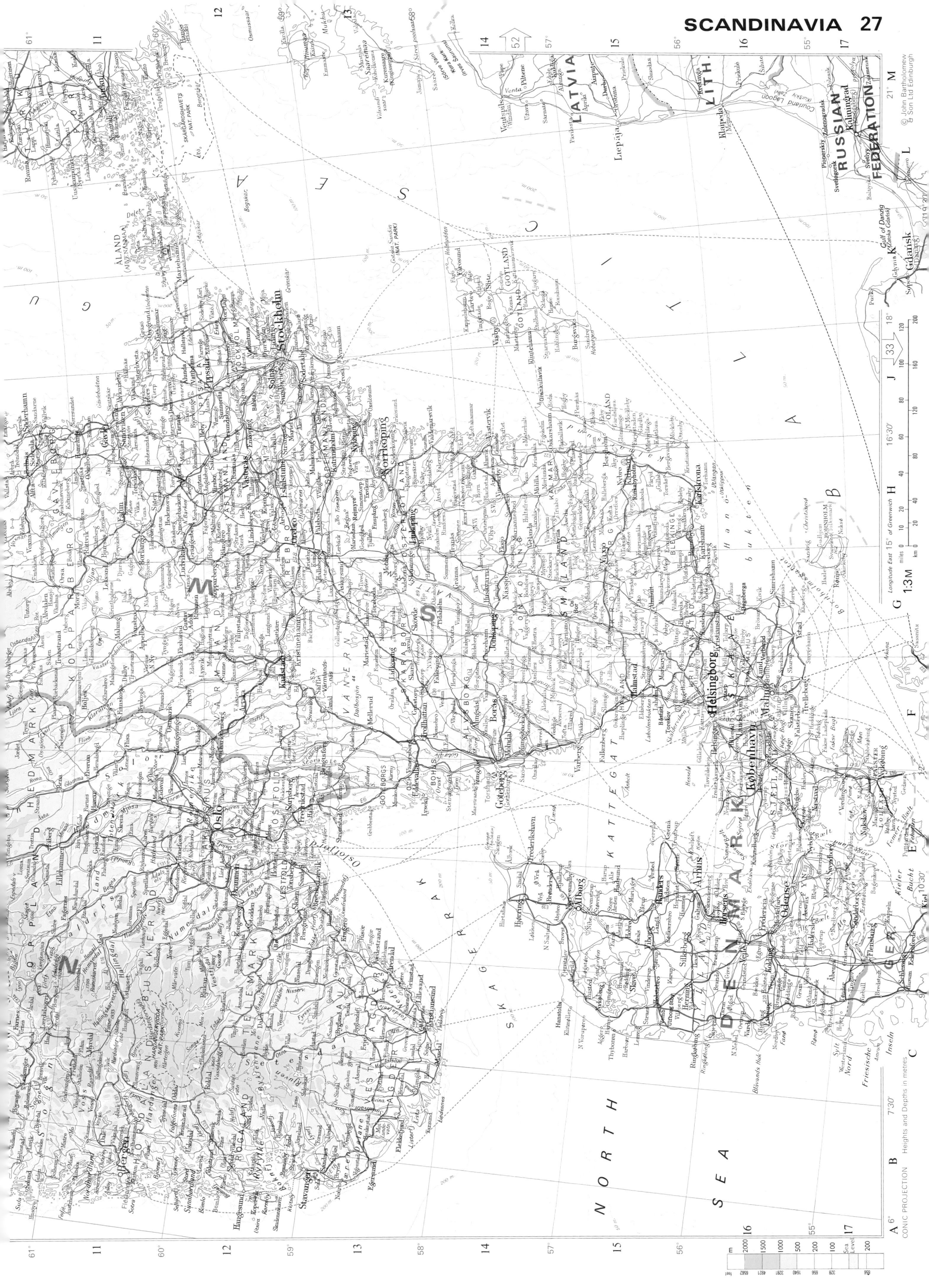
LATVIA
LITH.
RUSSIAN FEDERATION
DENMARK
NORTH SEA
SKAGERRAK
KATTEGAT
GOTLAND
ÖLAND
BORNHOLM
ÅLAND
Stockholm
Oslo
Göteborg
København
Malmö
Helsingborg
Bergen
Stavanger
Kristiansand
Ålborg
Århus
Odense
Norrköping
Linköping
Jönköping
Örebro
Västerås
Uppsala
Gävle
Karlstad
Kalmar
Karlskrona
Gdańsk
Kaliningrad
Klaipėda
Liepāja
Ventspils
Visby
Flensburg
Kiel
Longitude East 15° of Greenwich
1:3M
CONIC PROJECTION
Heights and Depths in metres
© John Bartholomew & Son Ltd Edinburgh

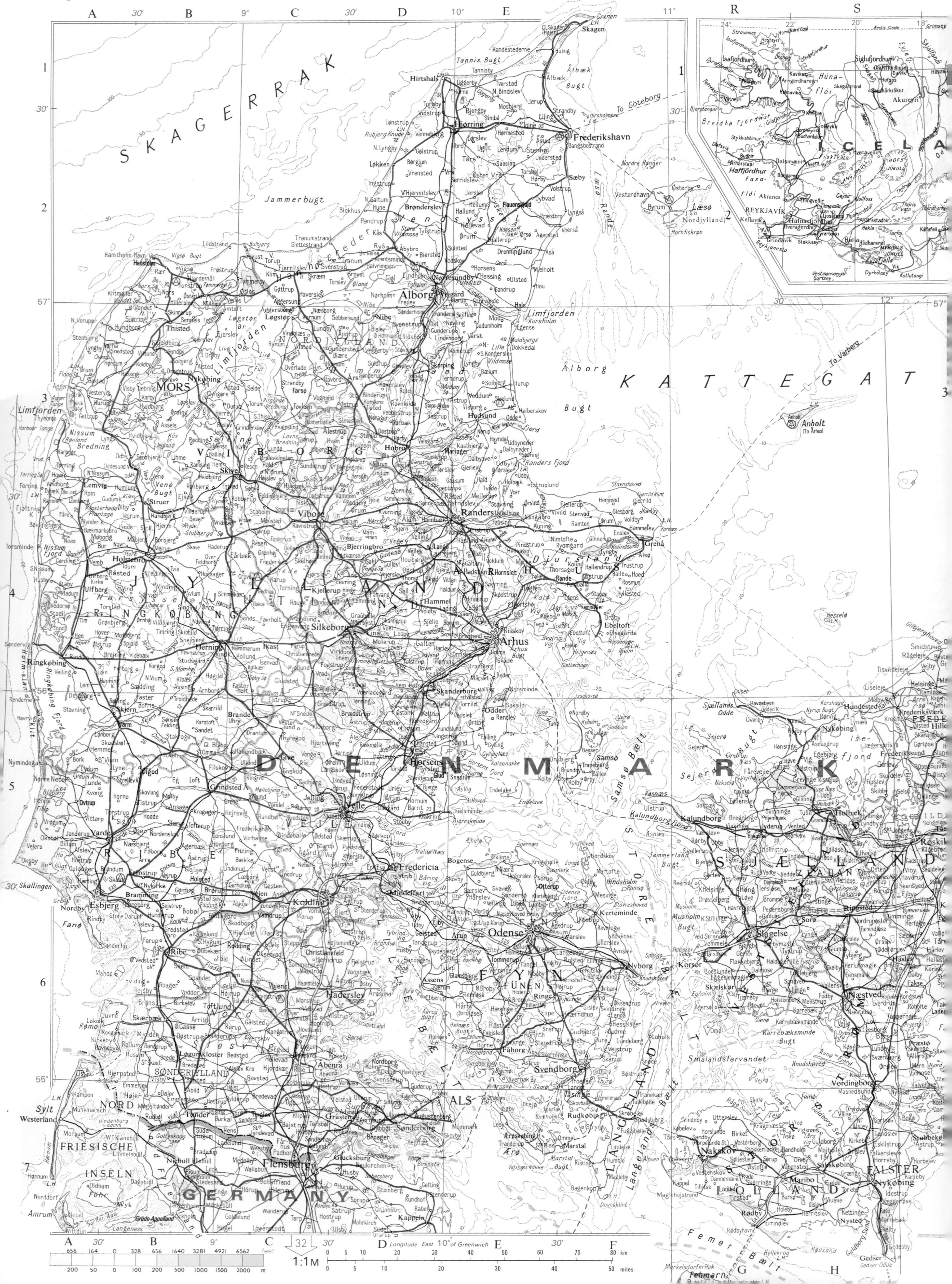
SKAGERRAK
KATTEGAT
Jammerbugt
Skagen
Grenen
Hirtshals
Hjørring
Frederikshavn
To Göteborg
Læsø
Løkken
Brønderslev
Vendsyssel
Sæby
Nørresundby
Alborg
Limfjorden
Hanstholm
Thisted
MORS
Nykøbing
NORDJYLLAND
Himmerland
Hobro
Mariager
Randers
VIBORG
Viborg
Skive
Struer
Lemvig
Holstebro
Herning
RINGKØBING
Ringkøbing
Skjern
Silkeborg
Århus
Grenå
Djursland
Ebeltoft
Anholt
To Varberg
Ålborg Bugt
Skanderborg
Horsens
Odder
Samsø
DENMARK
Vejle
VEJLE
Varde
RIBE
Ribe
Esbjerg
Fanø
Kolding
Fredericia
Middelfart
Odense
FYN
(FÜNEN)
Nyborg
Svendborg
Fåborg
Assens
Haderslev
Åbenrå
SØNDERJYLLAND
Tønder
Rømø
Sylt
Westerland
NORDFRIESISCHE INSELN
Flensburg
GERMANY
ALS
Sønderborg
Ærø
Langeland
Rudkøbing
Kalundborg
Holbæk
Roskilde
SJÆLLAND
(ZEALAND)
Slagelse
Korsør
Sorø
Ringsted
Næstved
Vordingborg
LOLLAND
Nakskov
Maribo
Rødby
FALSTER
Nykøbing
Femer Bælt
Fehmarn
STORE BÆLT
LILLE BÆLT
Samsø Bælt
Smålandsfarvandet
Helsingør
Hundested
ICELAND
REYKJAVÍK
Akureyri
Húnaflói
Faxaflói
Hafnarfjördhur
Longitude East 10° of Greenwich
1:1M
32

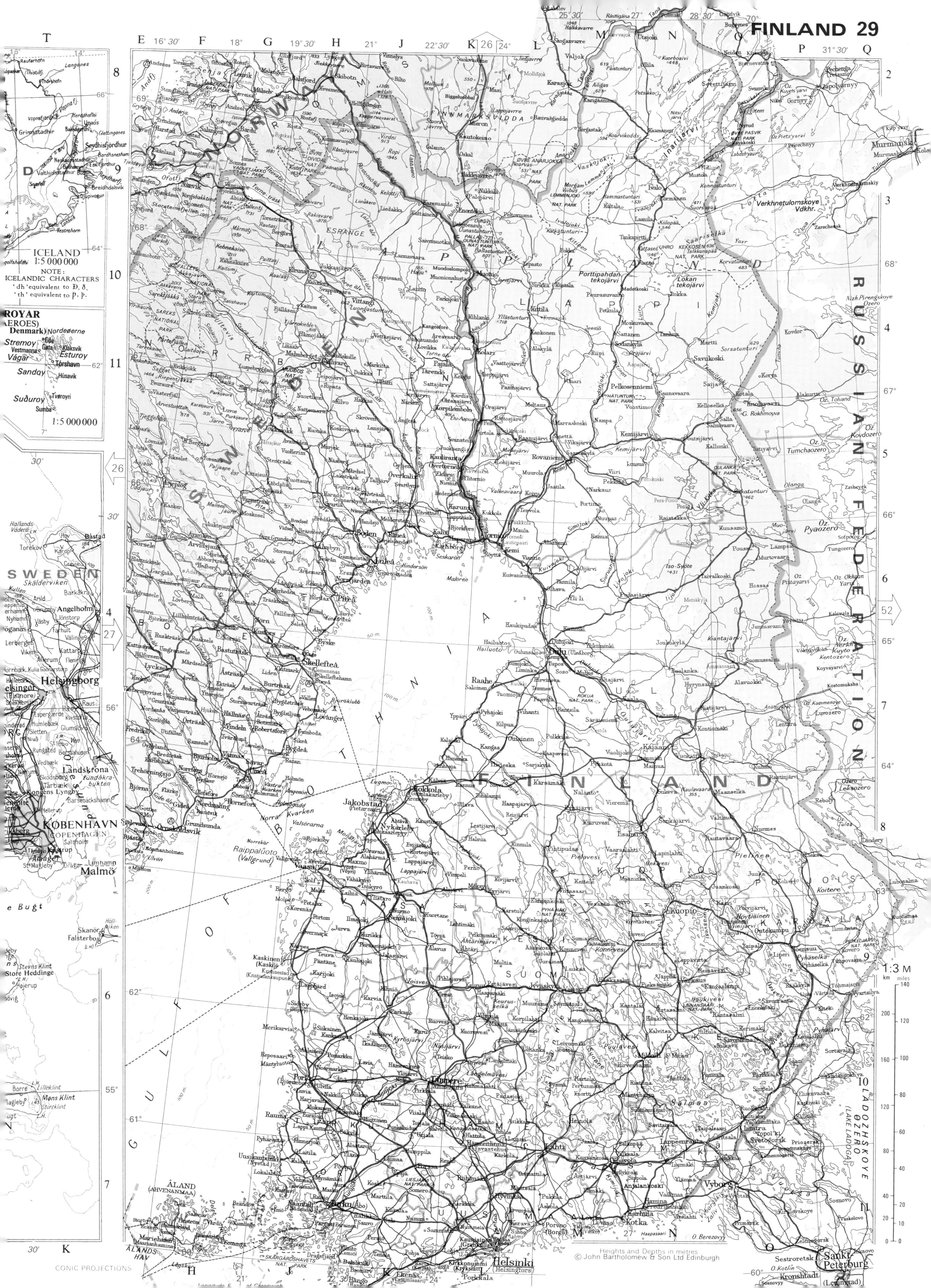
FINLAND
SWEDEN
NORWAY
RUSSIAN FEDERATION
GULF OF BOTHNIA
ICELAND
1:5 000 000
NOTE:
ICELANDIC CHARACTERS
'dh' equivalent to Ð, ð,
'th' equivalent to Þ, þ.
(FAEROES)
(Denmark)
1:5 000 000
Helsinki
(Helsingfors)
Tampere
Turku (Åbo)
Oulu (Uleåborg)
Vaasa
Kuopio
Jyväskylä
Rovaniemi
Pori
Lahti
Kotka
Vyborg
Sankt Peterburg
(Leningrad)
Murmansk
Narvik
Kiruna
Luleå
Umeå
Skellefteå
Piteå
Boden
Haparanda
Tornio
Kemi
Kokkola
Jakobstad
(Pietarsaari)
Helsingborg
Malmö
KØBENHAVN
(COPENHAGEN)
Landskrona
ÅLAND
(AHVENANMAA)
Mariehamn
Saimaa
Pielinen
LADOZHSKOYE OZERO
(LAKE LADOGA)
1:3 M
km
miles
Heights and Depths in metres
© John Bartholomew & Son Ltd Edinburgh
CONIC PROJECTIONS

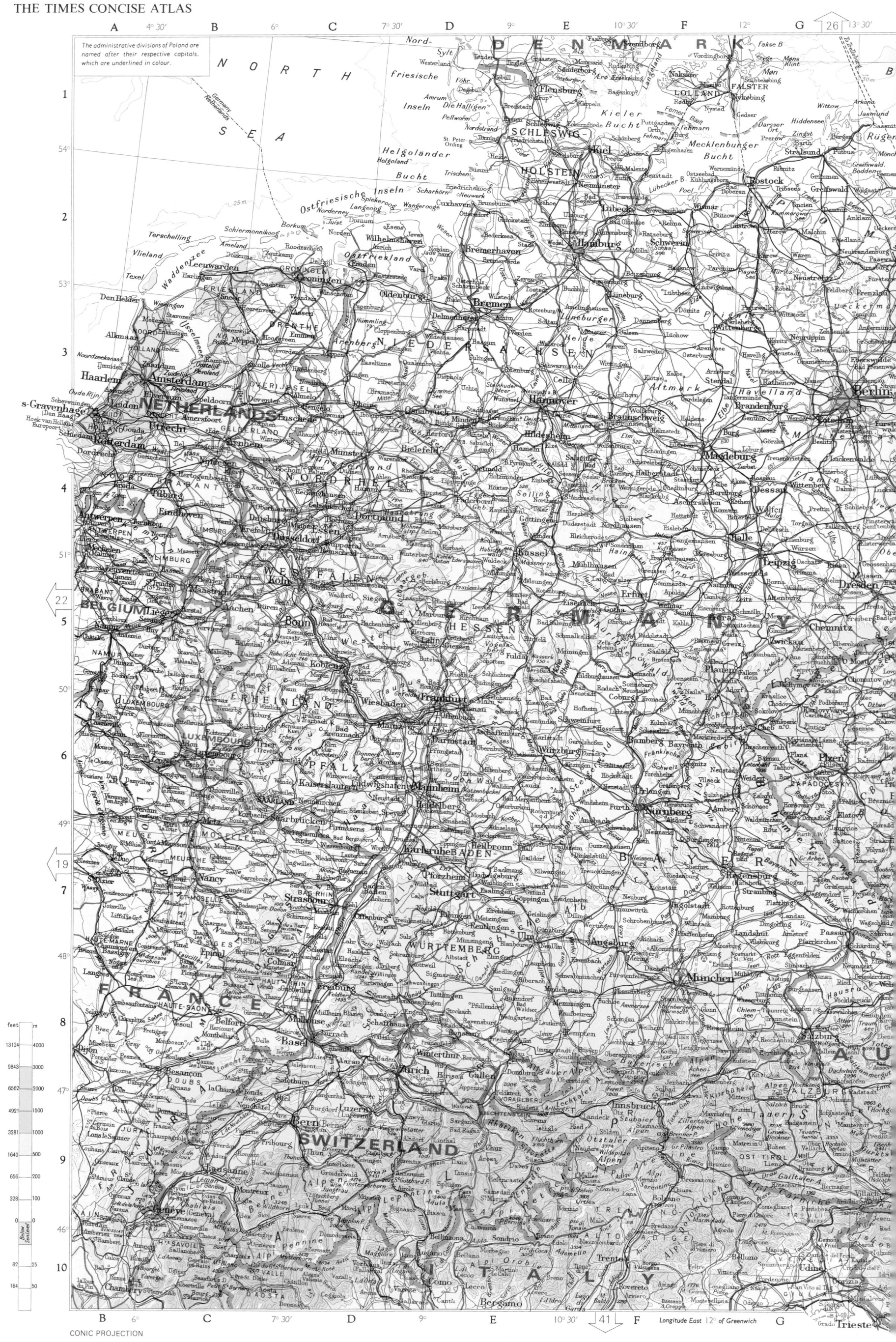
The administrative divisions of Poland are named after their respective capitals, which are underlined in colour.
NORTH SEA
DENMARK
NETHERLANDS
BELGIUM
LUXEMBOURG
GERMANY
FRANCE
SWITZERLAND
ITALY
AUSTRIA
NIEDERSACHSEN
SCHLESWIG-HOLSTEIN
NORDRHEIN-WESTFALEN
HESSEN
RHEINLAND-PFALZ
SAARLAND
BADEN-WÜRTTEMBERG
BAYERN
Amsterdam
Rotterdam
Hamburg
Bremen
Hannover
Berlin
Leipzig
Dresden
Frankfurt
München
Stuttgart
Nürnberg
Köln
Bonn
Düsseldorf
Zürich
Bern
Genève
Innsbruck
Salzburg
Trieste
feet
m
13124 4000
9843 3000
6562 2000
4921 1500
3281 1000
1640 500
656 200
328 100
0 0
Below Sea Level
82 25
164 50
Longitude East 12° of Greenwich

CONIC PROJECTION

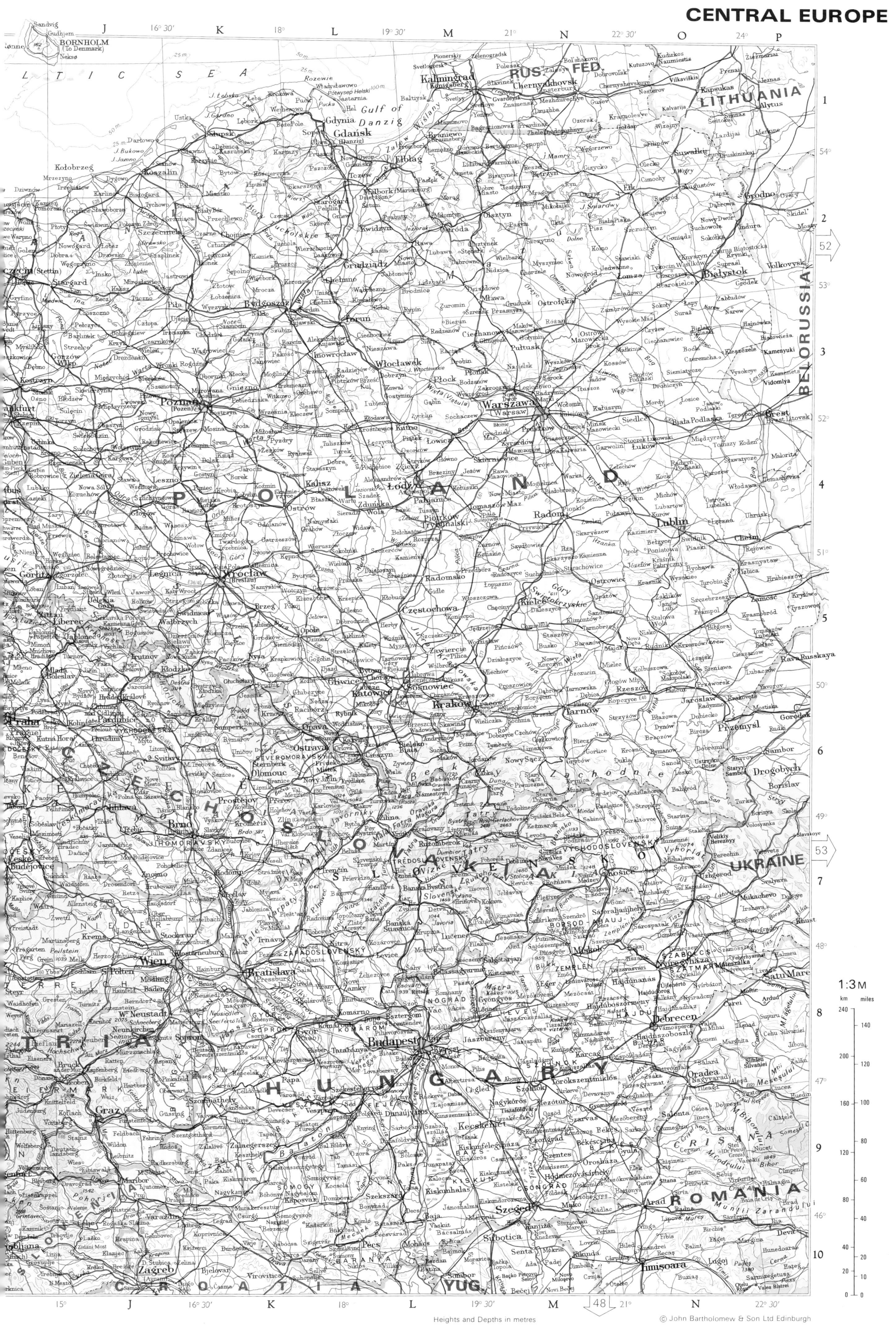
POLAND
CZECHOSLOVAKIA
HUNGARY
LITHUANIA
BELORUSSIA
UKRAINE
ROMANIA
RUS. FED.
SLOVENIA
CROATIA
YUG.
BALTIC SEA
Gulf of Danzig
Warszawa
Kraków
Wrocław
Poznań
Gdańsk
Łódź
Lublin
Białystok
Budapest
Bratislava
Wien
Praha
Debrecen
Kaliningrad
Brest
Košice
1:3M
Heights and Depths in metres

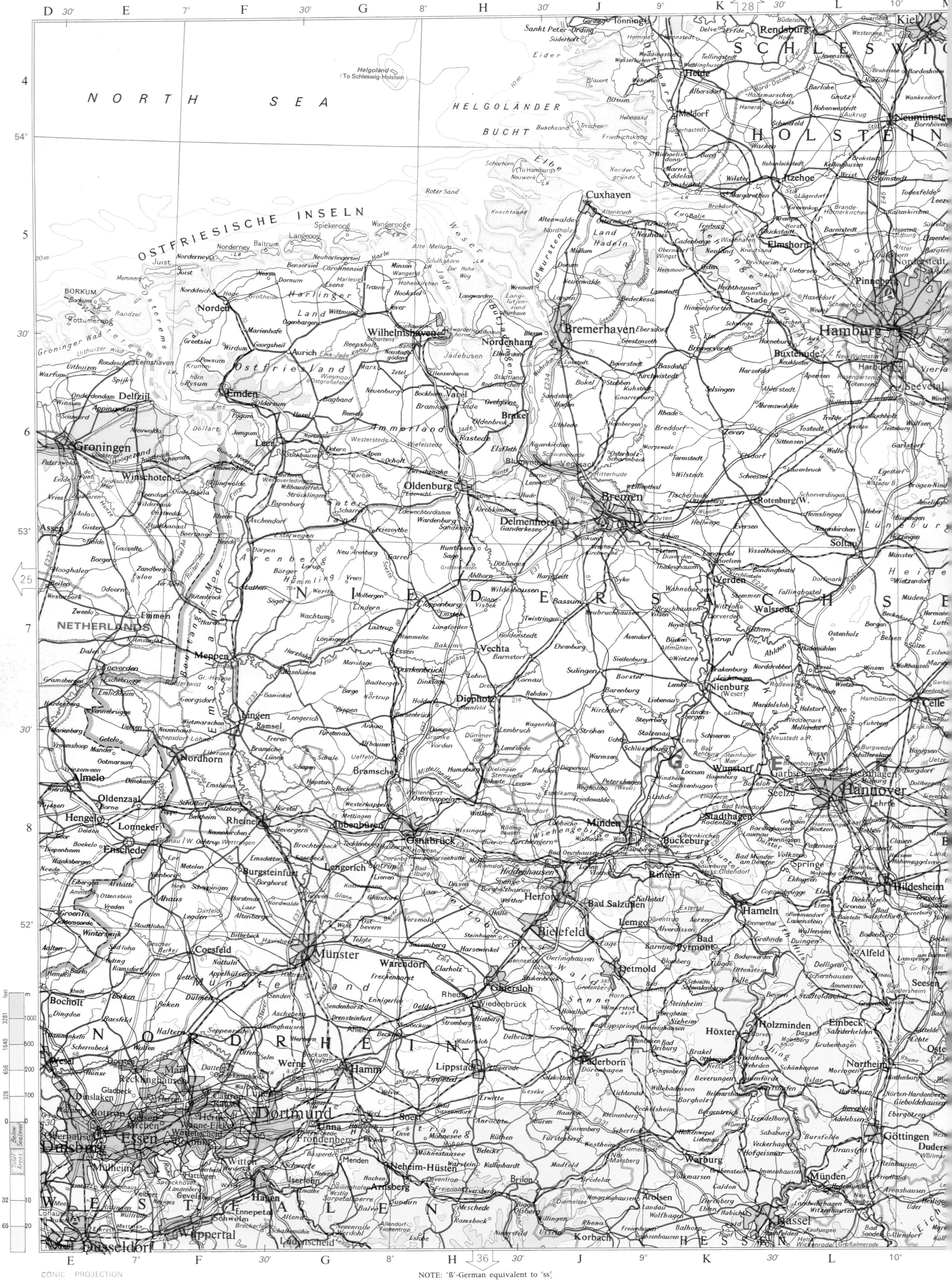

NORTH SEA

HELGOLÄNDER BUCHT

OSTFRIESISCHE INSELN

OSTFRIESLAND

NETHERLANDS

NIEDERSACHSEN

SCHLESWIG HOLSTEIN

NORDRHEIN

WESTFALEN

HESSEN

Hamburg
Bremen
Bremerhaven
Cuxhaven
Wilhelmshaven
Nordenham
Oldenburg
Groningen
Emden
Norden
Delmenhorst
Osnabrück
Münster
Dortmund
Essen
Duisburg
Düsseldorf
Wuppertal
Hannover
Hildesheim
Bielefeld
Paderborn
Göttingen
Kassel
Neumünster
Pinneberg

CONIC PROJECTION

NOTE: 'ß'-German equivalent to 'ss'.

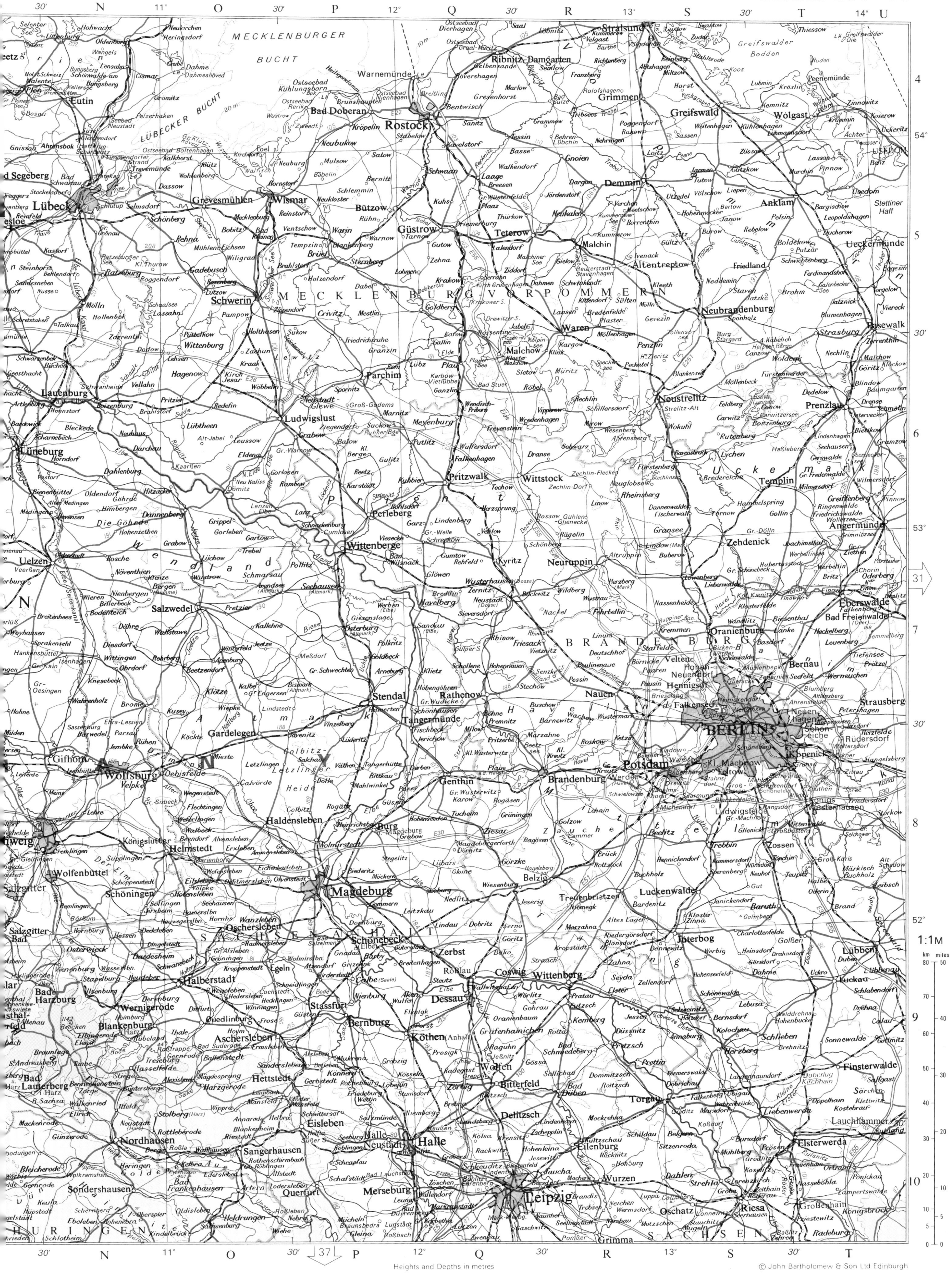

MECKLENBURGER BUCHT

LÜBECKER BUCHT

MECKLENBURG-VORPOMMERN

Lübeck
Schwerin
Rostock
Warnemünde
Bad Doberan
Wismar
Grevesmühlen
Güstrow
Teterow
Demmin
Anklam
Greifswald
Wolgast
Stralsund
Ribnitz-Damgarten
Grimmen
Waren
Malchow
Parchim
Ludwigslust
Neustrelitz
Prenzlau
Pasewalk
Neubrandenburg
Lüneburg
Lauenburg
Uelzen
Salzwedel
Wittenberge
Perleberg
Pritzwalk
Wittstock
Neuruppin
Zehdenick
Angermünde
Eberswalde
Bad Freienwalde
Templin
Oranienburg
Bernau
Stendal
Gardelegen
Rathenow
Nauen
Tangermünde
Wolfsburg
Gifhorn
Helmstedt
Haldensleben
Burg
Genthin
Brandenburg
Potsdam
BERLIN
BRANDENBURG
Magdeburg
Oschersleben
Schönebeck
Zerbst
Wittenberg
Dessau
Luckenwalde
Jüterbog
Lübben
Wolfenbüttel
Schöningen
Halberstadt
Wernigerode
Blankenburg
Quedlinburg
Aschersleben
Bernburg
Köthen
Bitterfeld
Wolfen
Herzberg
Finsterwalde
Nordhausen
Sangerhausen
Eisleben
Halle
Merseburg
Delitzsch
Torgau
Elsterwerda
SACHSEN-ANHALT
THÜRINGEN
SACHSEN
Leipzig
Riesa
Querfurt

Heights and Depths in metres

© John Bartholomew & Son Ltd Edinburgh

1:1M

km miles

HAMBURG

Coordinates (top): A 9°30' B 9°45' C 10°00' D 10°15' E 10°30' F

Side: 53°45', 53°30'

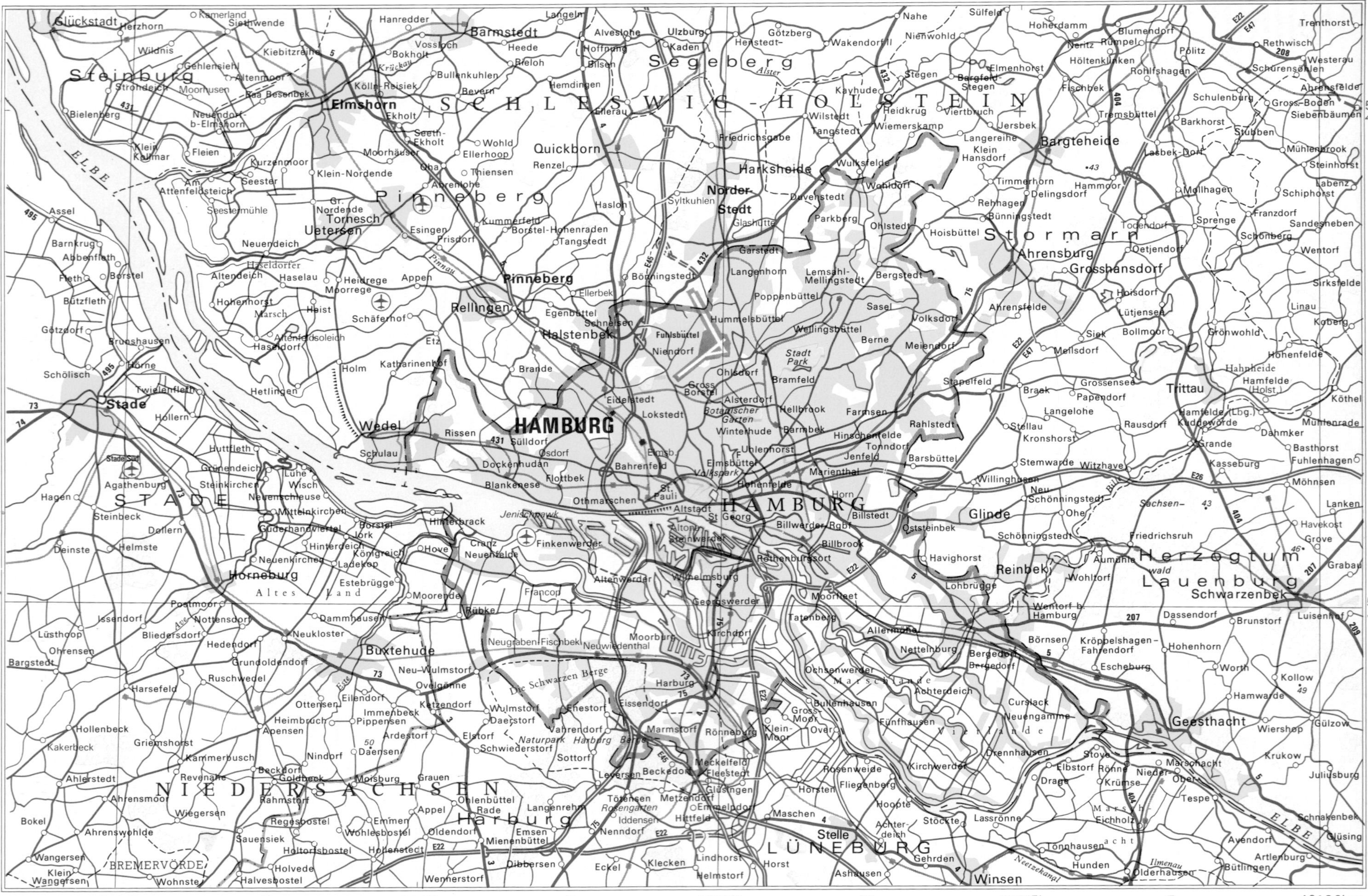

SCHLESWIG-HOLSTEIN · Steinburg · Segeberg · Pinneberg · Stormarn · STADE · NIEDERSACHSEN · Harburg · LÜNEBURG · Herzogtum Lauenburg

Major places: Glückstadt, Elmshorn, Quickborn, Norderstedt, Ahrensburg, Grosshansdorf, Pinneberg, Rellingen, Halstenbek, Wedel, **HAMBURG**, Stade, Buxtehude, Horneburg, Reinbek, Schwarzenbek, Trittau, Geesthacht, Harburg, Winsen, Bargteheide

Coordinates (bottom): A 9°30' B 9°45' C 10°00' D 10°15' E 10°30' F

BERLIN

Coordinates (top): A 13°00' B 13°15' C 13°30' D 13°45' E

Side: 52°30'

BRANDENBURG

Major places: Nauen, Velten, Hennigsdorf, Falkensee, Spandau, Charlottenburg, Wilmersdorf, Steglitz, Zehlendorf, Potsdam, Werder, Teltow, **BERLIN** Mitte, Wedding, Prenzlauer Berg, Tiergarten, Schöneberg, Kreuzberg, Friedrichshain, Tempelhof, Neukölln, Britz, Buckow, Marienfelde, Lichtenrade, Pankow, Weissensee, Reinickendorf, Wittenau, Tegel, Niederschönhausen, Hohenschönhausen, Marzahn, Köpenick, Friedrichshagen, Johannisthal, Oberschöneweide, Niederschöneweide, Karlshorst, Mahlsdorf, Biesdorf, Friedrichsfelde, Bernau, Werneuchen, Strausberg, Atlandsberg, Schöneiche, Königs Wusterhausen, Zeuthen, Ludwigsfelde

Coordinates (bottom): A 13°00' B 13°15' C 13°30' D 13°45' E

1:300 000

0 5 10 15 km

0 5 10 mile

© Times Books Ltd

DÜSSELDORF
ESSEN
Dortmund
Wuppertal
Duisburg
Krefeld
Oberhausen
Bochum
Gelsenkirchen
Mülheim
Neuss
Recklinghausen
Bottrop
Herne
Wanne-Eickel
Castrop
Rauxel
Wattenscheid
Witten
Hagen
Hamm
Lünen
Waltrop
Datteln
Marl
Dorsten
Wesel
Dinslaken
Voerde
Homberg
Rheinhausen
Moers
Kamp-Lintfort
Ratingen
Mettmann
Velbert
Heiligenhaus
Langenfeld
Opladen
Hilden
Solingen
Remscheid
Hückeswagen
Wermelskirchen
Radevormwald
Schwelm
Gevelsberg
Ennepetal
Herdecke
Wetter
Herbede
Hattingen
Sprockhövel
Menden
Hemer
Iserlohn
Letmathe
Hohenlimburg
Lüdenscheid
Kierspe
Meinerzhagen
Heessen
Bergkamen
Werne
Herringen
Kamen
Unna
Schwerte
Rheinberg
Neukirchen
Büderich
Meerbusch
Mönchengladbach
Rheydt
Grevenbroich
Dormagen
Erkrath
Kaarst
Willich
Viersen

ENNEPE-RUHR-KREIS
MÄRKISCHER KREIS
OBERBERGISCHER KREIS
RHEINISCH-BERGISCHER KREIS
KÖLN
WESEL
DÜSSELDORF
MÜNSTER
ARNSBERG
DUISBURG
DIE HAARD

RHEIN
RUHR
WUPPER
LIPPE

51°30'
51°15'
6°30'
6°45'
7°00'
7°15'
7°30'
7°45'

1   2   3
A B C D E F G

5   10   15 km
5   10 miles

1:300 000

© Times Books Ltd

NORDRHEIN

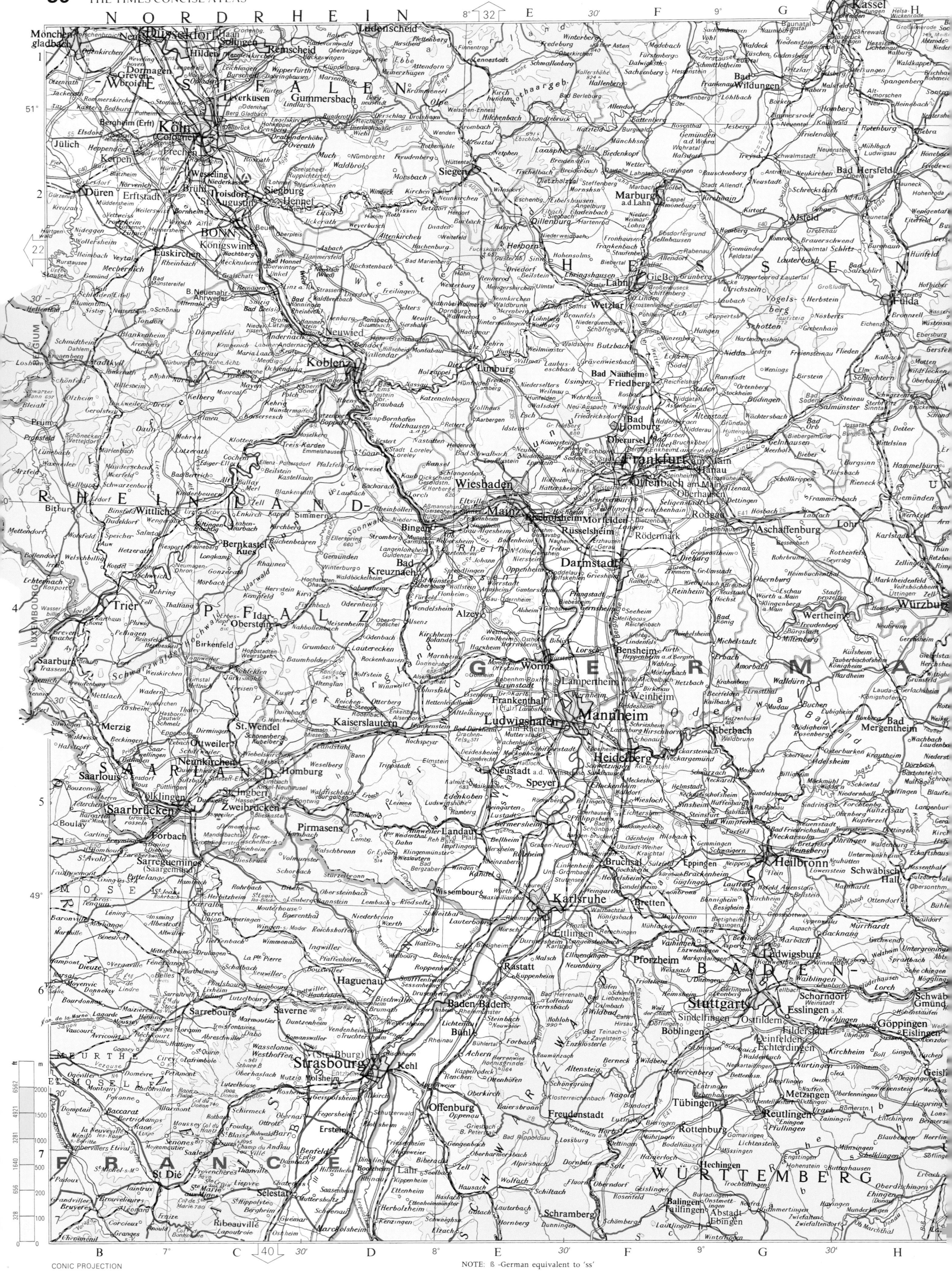

NORDRHEIN-WESTFALEN

Mönchengladbach • Neuss • Düsseldorf • Solingen • Remscheid • Lüdenscheid
Dormagen • Leverkusen • Hilden • Gummersbach
Köln (Cologne) • Frechen • Brühl
Bergheim (Erft) • Kerpen
Jülich • Düren • Erftstadt • Troisdorf • Siegburg • St. Augustin • Hennef • Siegen
Euskirchen • BONN • Königswinter
Marburg a.d. Lahn • Alsfeld • Bad Hersfeld

HESSEN

Neuwied • Koblenz • Limburg • Bad Nauheim • Friedberg • Bad Homburg • Oberursel
Wetzlar • Gießen • Fulda
Frankfurt am Main • Hanau • Offenbach am Main
Wiesbaden • Mainz • Rüsselsheim • Darmstadt • Aschaffenburg

RHEINLAND-PFALZ

Bitburg • Wittlich • Bernkastel-Kues • Bingen • Bad Kreuznach • Alzey • Worms
Trier • Idar-Oberstein • Birkenfeld
Würzburg • Wertheim

GERMANY

Lampertheim • Weinheim • Mannheim • Ludwigshafen
Frankenthal • Heidelberg • Eberbach
Saarburg • Merzig
Kaiserslautern • Neustadt a.d. Weinstrasse • Speyer • Heilbronn

SAARLAND

St. Wendel • Ottweiler • Neunkirchen • Homburg
Saarlouis • Völklingen • St. Ingbert • Zweibrücken • Pirmasens • Landau
Saarbrücken • Germersheim
Forbach • Sarreguemines (Saargemünd) • Karlsruhe • Bretten

BADEN-WÜRTTEMBERG

Rastatt • Pforzheim • Ludwigsburg
Baden-Baden • Stuttgart • Esslingen a.N. • Göppingen • Eislingen
Offenburg • Sindelfingen • Böblingen • Ostfildern • Leinfelden-Echterdingen
Tübingen • Reutlingen • Metzingen
Freudenstadt • Rottenburg • Hechingen
Balingen • Ebingen

FRANCE

Sarrebourg • Saverne • Haguenau • Strasbourg (Straßburg) • Kehl
St. Dié • Sélestat • Ribeauvillé

MOSELLE

LUXEMBOURG

BELGIUM

NOTE: ß -German equivalent to 'ss'

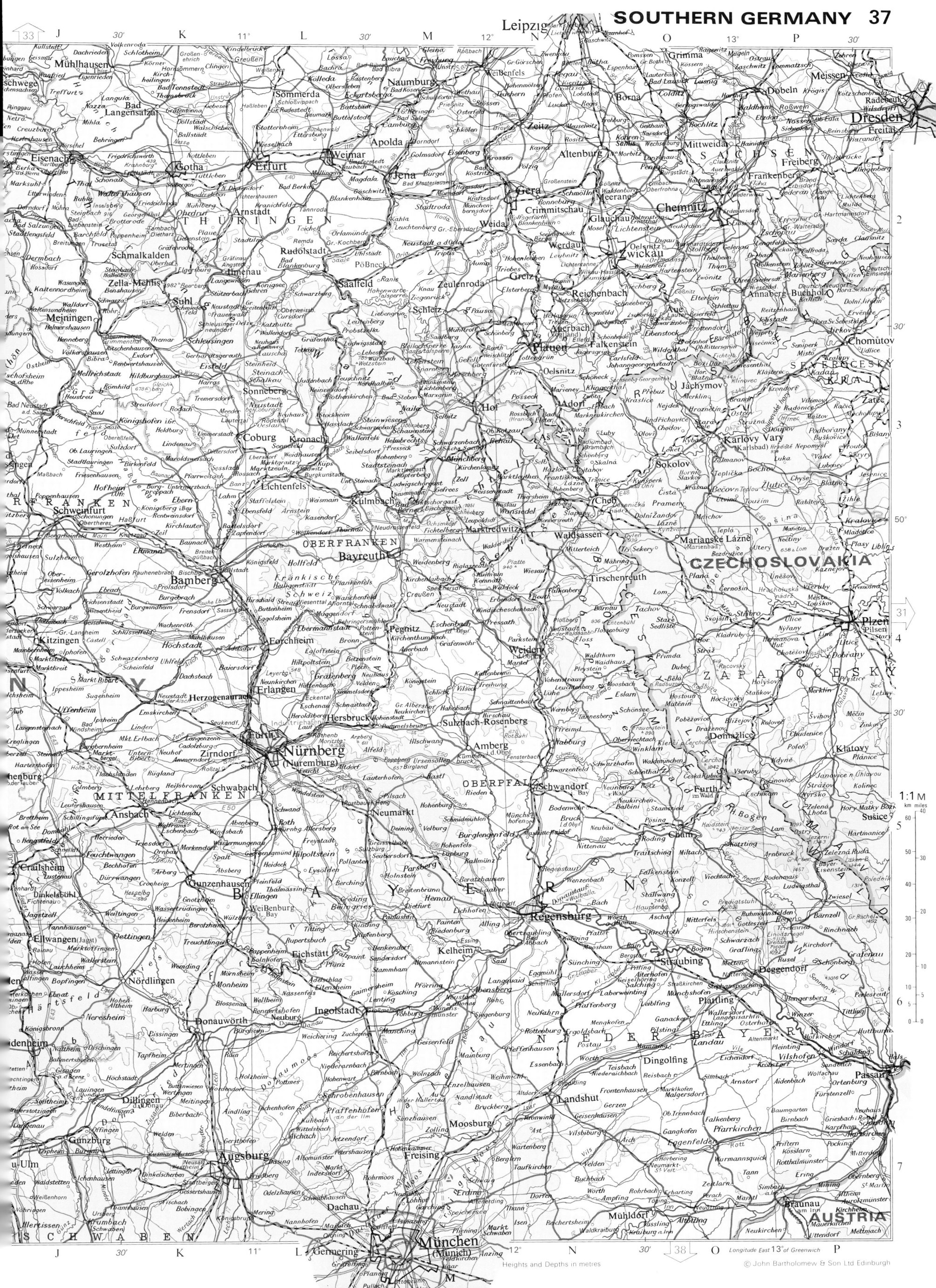

Heights and Depths in metres

Longitude East 13° of Greenwich

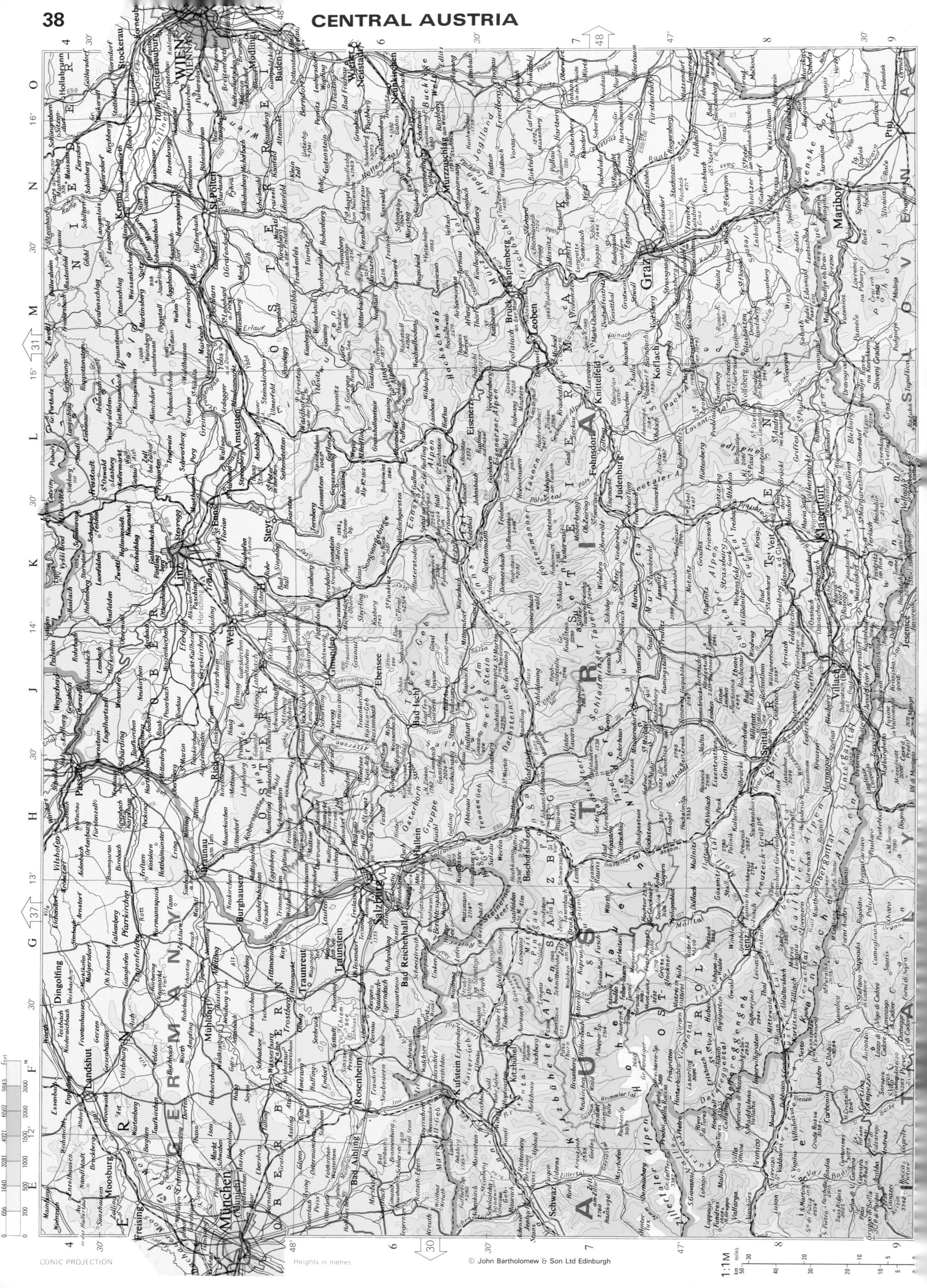

CONIC PROJECTION

Heights in metres

© John Bartholomew & Son Ltd Edinburgh

1:1 M

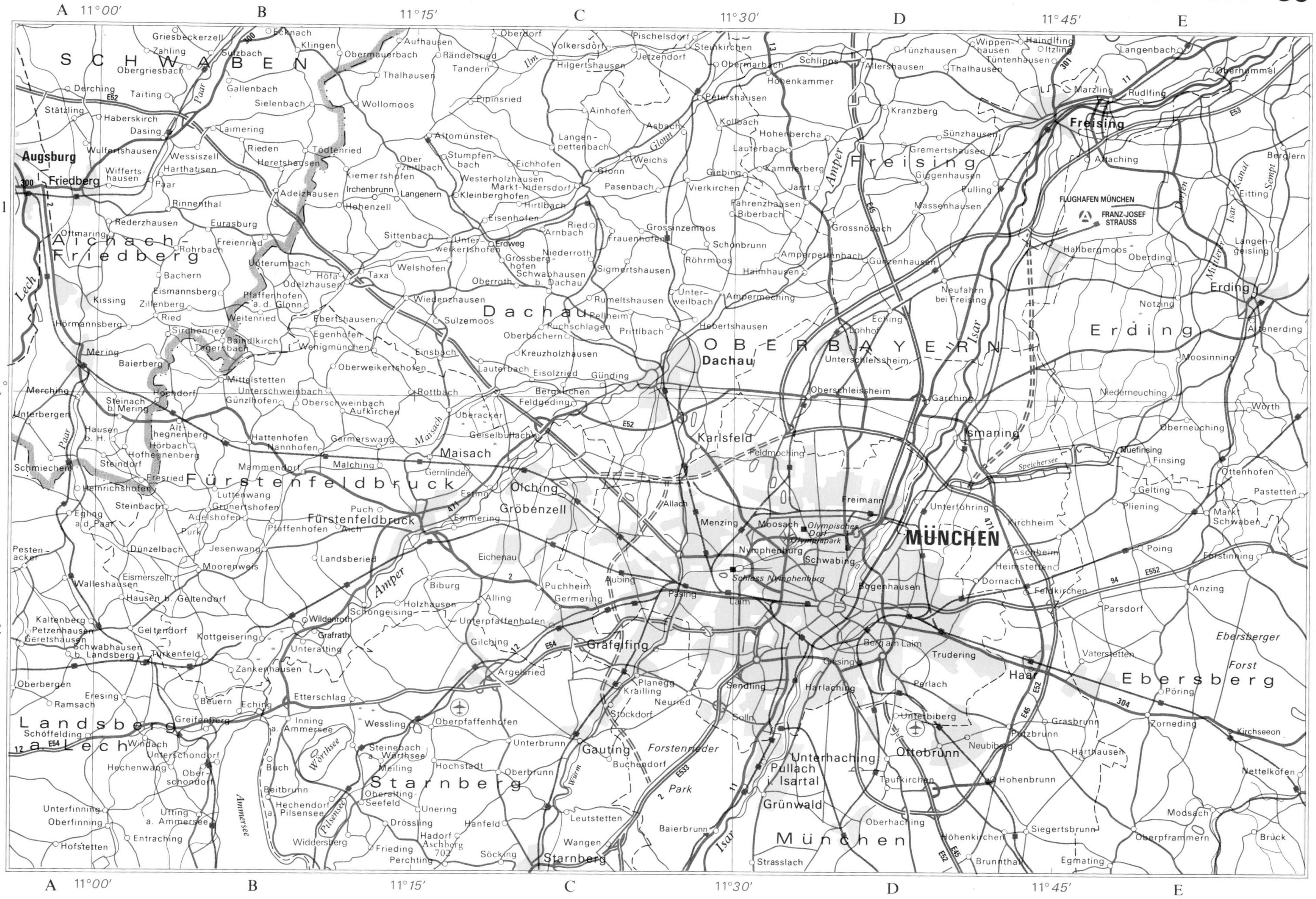

A 11°00' B 11°15' C 11°30' D 11°45' E

SCHWABEN

Augsburg
Friedberg

Aichach-Friedberg

Landsberg a. Lech

Fürstenfeldbruck

Dachau
Dachau

OBERBAYERN

Karlsfeld

MÜNCHEN

Freising

Freising

FLUGHAFEN MÜNCHEN
FRANZ-JOSEF STRAUSS

Erding

Erding

Starnberg

Grafelfing
Gauting

München

Grünwald
Pullach i. Isartal
Unterhaching
Ottobrunn

Haar

Ebersberg
Ebersberger Forst

48°15'

A 11°00' B 11°15' C 11°30' D 11°45' E

MILAN

A 8°45' B 9°00' C 9°15' D 9°30' E

Como

Gallarate

Varese

Busto Arsizio

Legnano

Saronno

Seregno
Monza

Meda
Desio
Lissone

Parabiago

Cinisello Balsamo

Sesto San Giovanni
Cologno Monzese
Cusano Milanino

Rho

LOMBARDIA

Milano

MILANO

Novara

PIEMONTE

TICINO

Abbiategrasso

Corsico

Vigevano

Pavia

Melegnano

Lodi

Cremona

45°30'

45°15'

A 8°45' B 9°00' C 9°15' D 9°30' E

1:300 000

0 5 10 15 km
0 5 10 miles

© Times Books Ltd

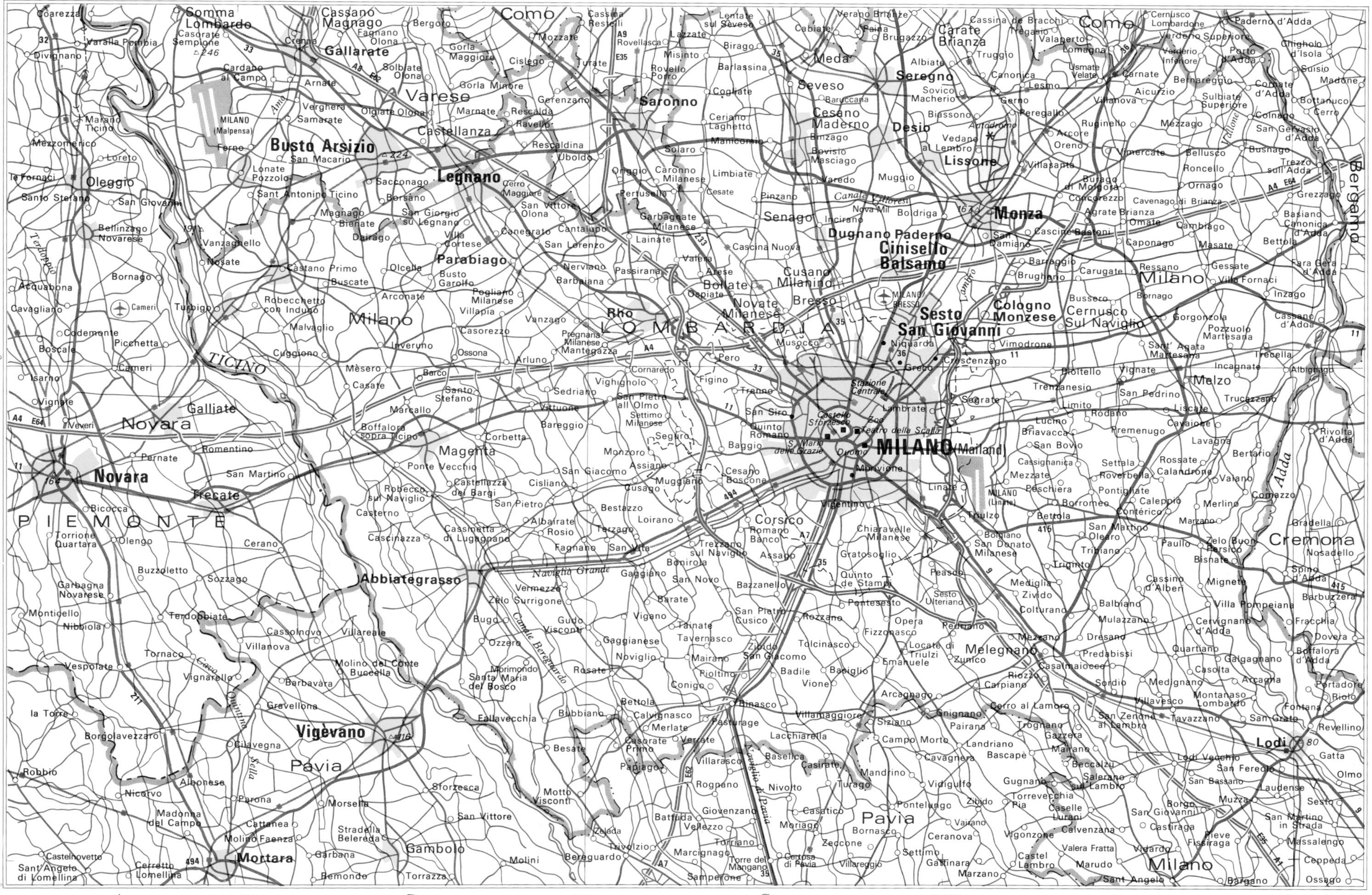

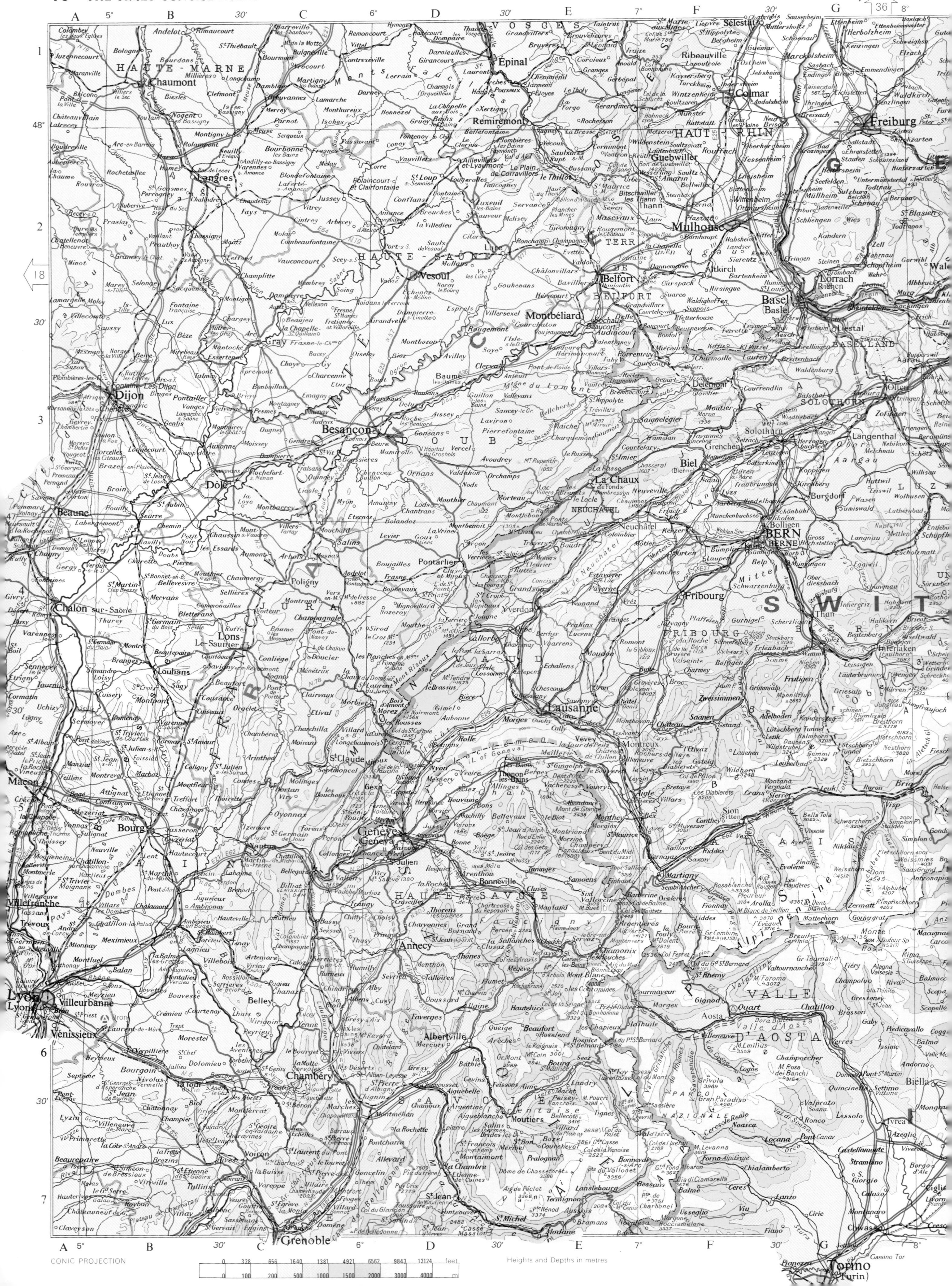

HAUTE-MARNE

Chaumont

Langres

Épinal

Remiremont

Colmar

HAUT-RHIN

Freiburg

Mulhouse

Belfort

TERR.

BELFORT

Montbéliard

Vesoul

HAUTE-SAÔNE

Dijon

Besançon

DOUBS

Dôle

Beaune

Basel (Basle)

BASELLAND

SOLOTHURN

Delémont

La Chaux de Fonds

Le Locle

NEUCHÂTEL

Neuchâtel

BERN

Berne

Biel

Solothurn

Chalon-sur-Saône

Lons-le-Saunier

JURA

Poligny

Pontarlier

Fribourg

FRIBOURG

SWITZ

Lausanne

VAUD

Mâcon

Bourg

AIN

Genève (Geneva)

L. of Geneva

Vevey

Montreux

Aigle

Sion

VALAIS

Lyon

Villeurbanne

Vénissieux

Villefranche

Trévoux

HAUTE-SAVOIE

Annecy

Chamonix

Mont Blanc

Courmayeur

Aosta

VALLE D'AOSTA

Chambéry

SAVOIE

Albertville

ISÈRE

Grenoble

Torino (Turin)

CONIC PROJECTION

Heights and Depths in metres

| | 328 | 656 | 1640 | 3281 | 4921 | 6562 | 9843 | 13124 | feet |
| 0 | 100 | 200 | 500 | 1000 | 1500 | 2000 | 3000 | 4000 | m |

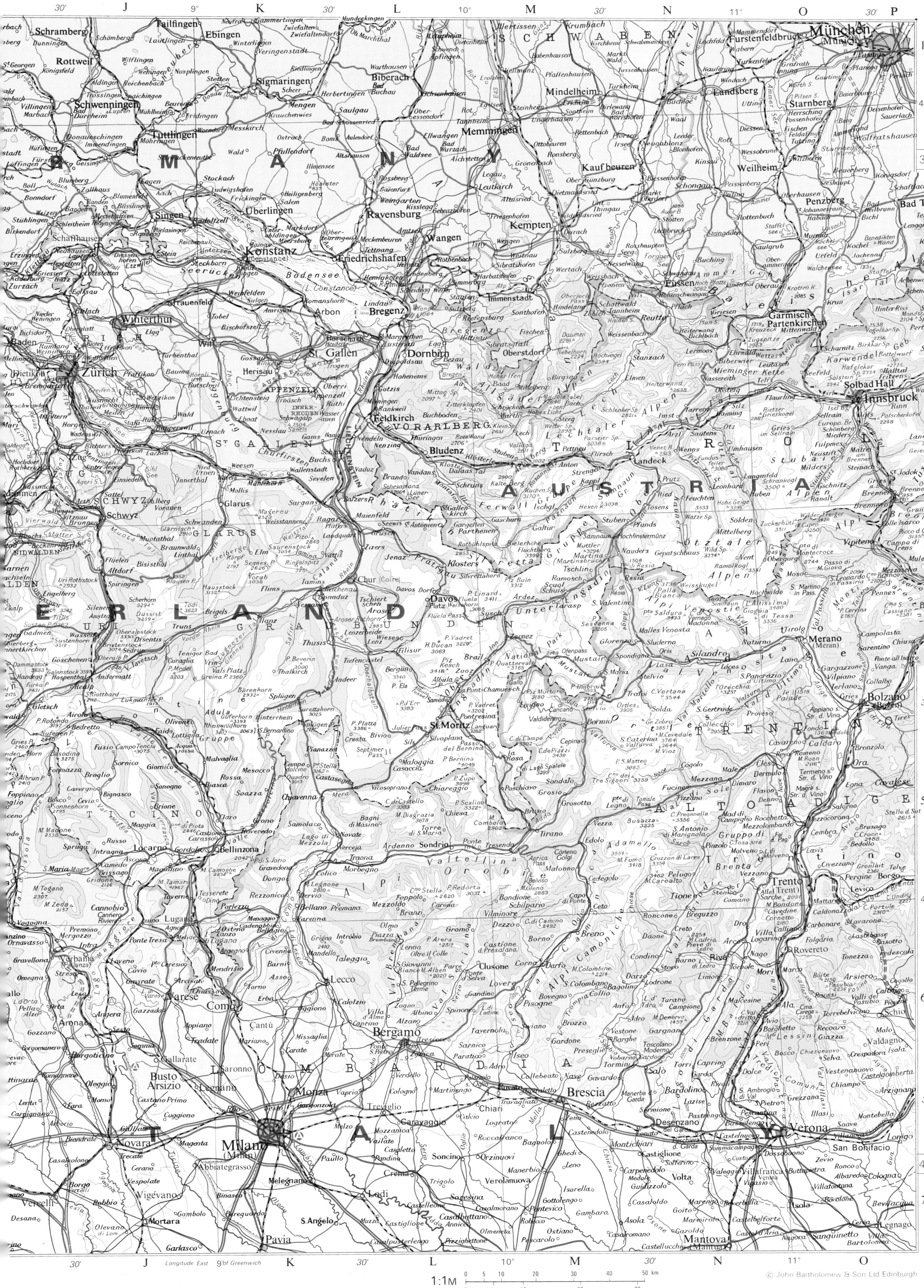

1:1M

Longitude East 9 of Greenwich

© John Bartholomew & Son Ltd Edinburgh

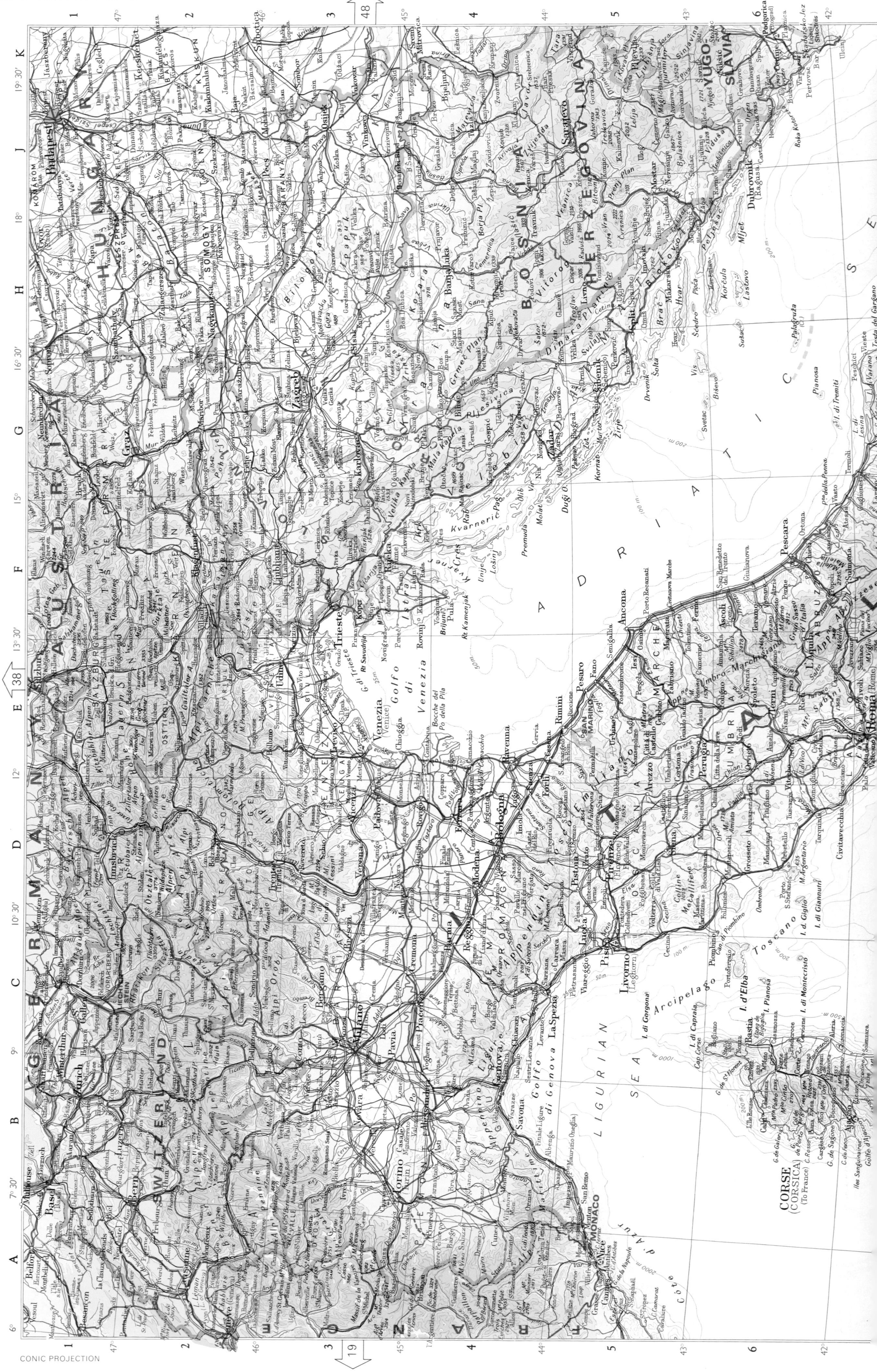
48
38
19
AUSTRIA
HUNGARY
SWITZERLAND
ITALIA
YUGOSLAVIA
BOSNIA
HERZEGOVINA
CORSE (CORSICA) (To France)
MONACO
SAN MARINO
ADRIATIC SEA
LIGURIAN SEA
Budapest
Zagreb
Ljubljana
Trieste
Venezia (Venice)
Milano
Torino (Turin)
Genova
Bologna
Firenze (Florence)
Ancona
Pescara
Sarajevo
Mostar
Split
Dubrovnik
Graz
Innsbruck
Bern
Basel
Zürich
Nice
Livorno
Pisa
La Spezia
Roma (Rome)

CONIC PROJECTION

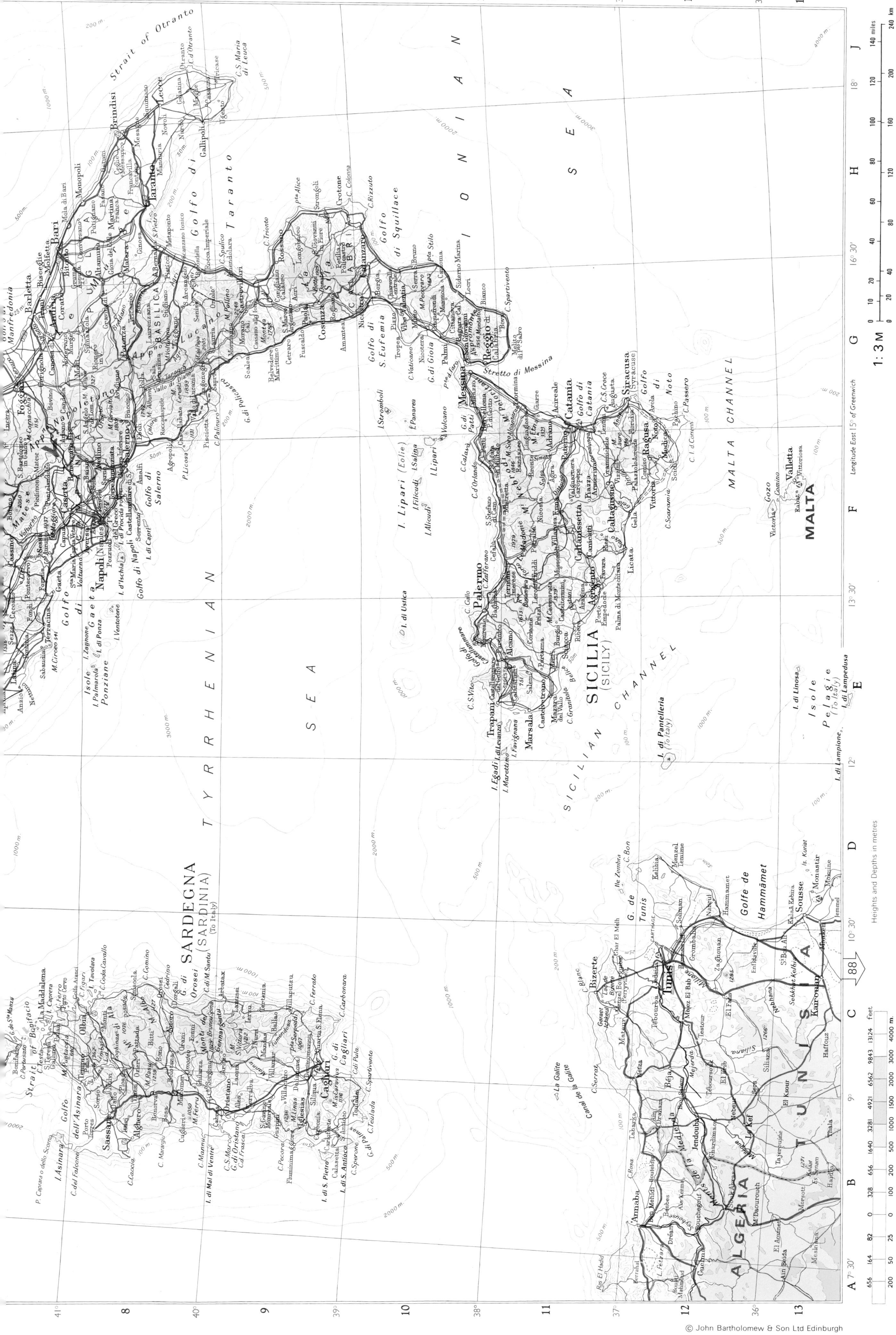

Strait of Otranto

IONIAN SEA

TYRRHENIAN SEA

SICILIAN CHANNEL

MALTA CHANNEL

SARDEGNA (SARDINIA) (To Italy)

SICILIA (SICILY)

MALTA

TUNISIA

ALGERIA

Brindisi
Lecce
Taranto
Golfo di Taranto
Bari
Barletta
Manfredonia
Foggia
Napoli (Naples)
Golfo di Salerno
Golfo di Gaeta
BASILICATA
PUGLIA
CALABRIA
Golfo di Squillace
Crotone
C. Rizzuto
C. Colonna
Catanzaro
Reggio di Calabria
Messina
Stretto di Messina
Catania
Golfo di Catania
Siracusa (Syracuse)
Golfo di Noto
C. Passero
Palermo
Trapani
Marsala
Agrigento
Caltanissetta
Caltagirone
Ragusa
Gela
I. Lipari (Eolie)
I. di Ustica
G. di Salerno
I. d'Ischia
I. di Capri
I. di Ponza
Isole Ponziane
Cagliari
Golfo di Cagliari
Oristano
G. di Oristano
Sassari
Alghero
Olbia
G. di Orosei
Strait of Bonifacio
La Maddalena
Golfo dell'Asinara

Isole Pelagie (To Italy)
I. di Pantelleria (To Italy)
I. di Lampedusa
I. di Linosa
I. di Lampione

Tunis
Bizerte
Sousse
Kairouan
Golfe de Hammamet
G. de Tunis
C. Bon
Monastir
Kebili

Longitude East 15° of Greenwich

1:3 M

Heights and Depths in metres

© John Bartholomew & Son Ltd Edinburgh

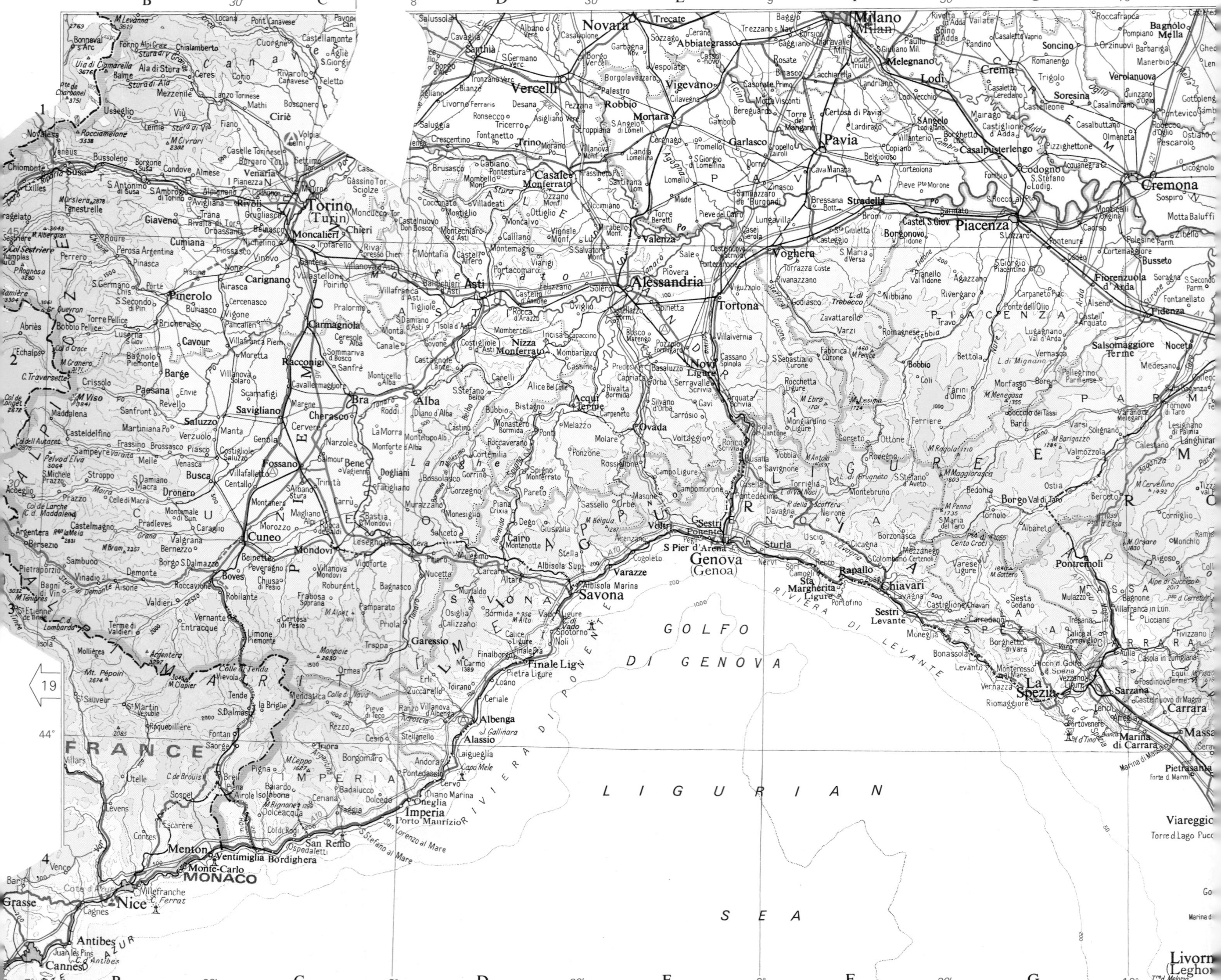

FRANCE
LIGURIAN SEA
GOLFO DI GENOVA
RIVIERA DI PONENTE
RIVIERA DI LEVANTE
Torino (Turin)
Milano (Milan)
Genova (Genoa)
Alessandria
Asti
Cuneo
Savona
Imperia
Alessandria
Pavia
Piacenza
Cremona
La Spezia
Nice
Monaco
San Remo
19

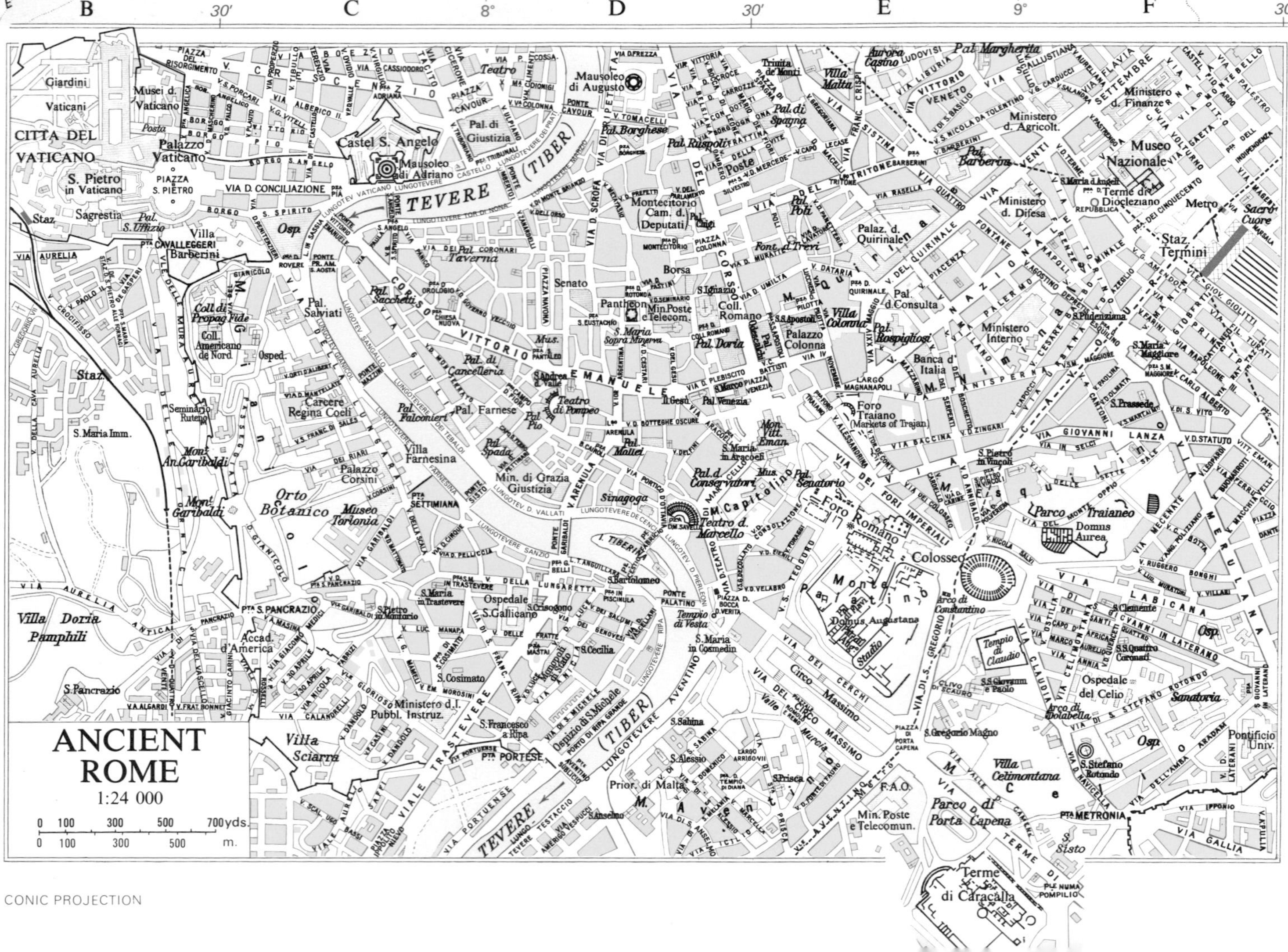

ANCIENT ROME
1:24 000
CITTA DEL VATICANO
TEVERE (TIBER)
Colosseo
Foro Romano
Castel S. Angelo

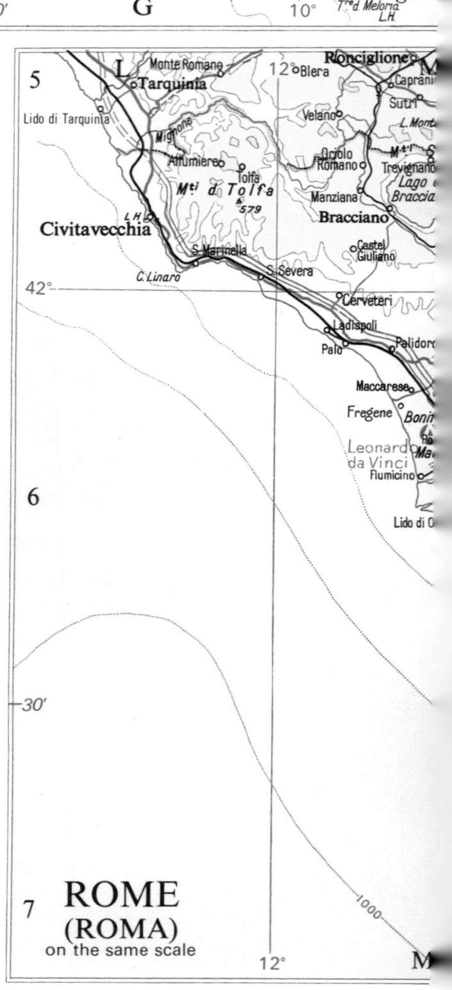

ROME (ROMA)
on the same scale
Civitavecchia
Tarquinia
Bracciano

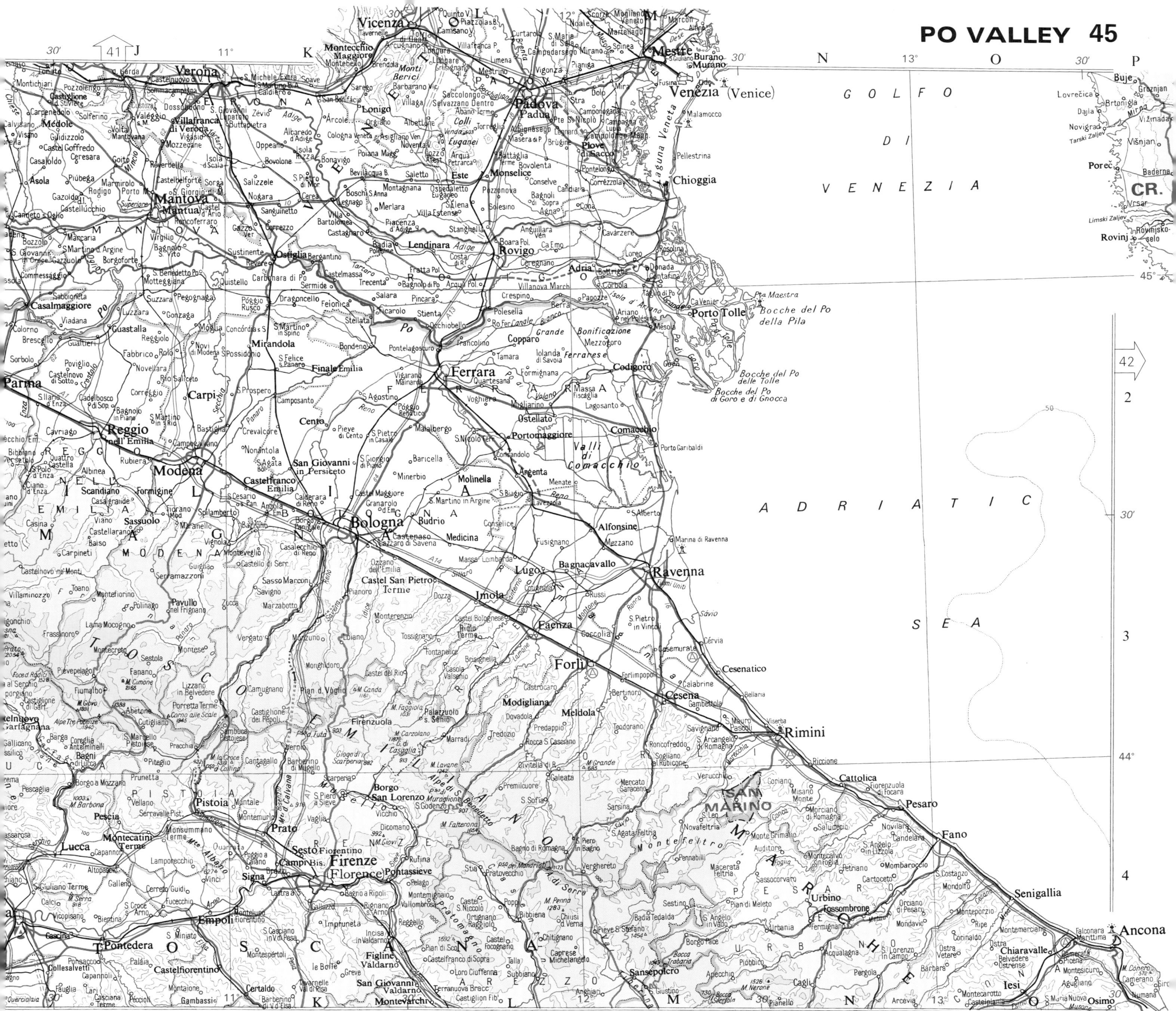

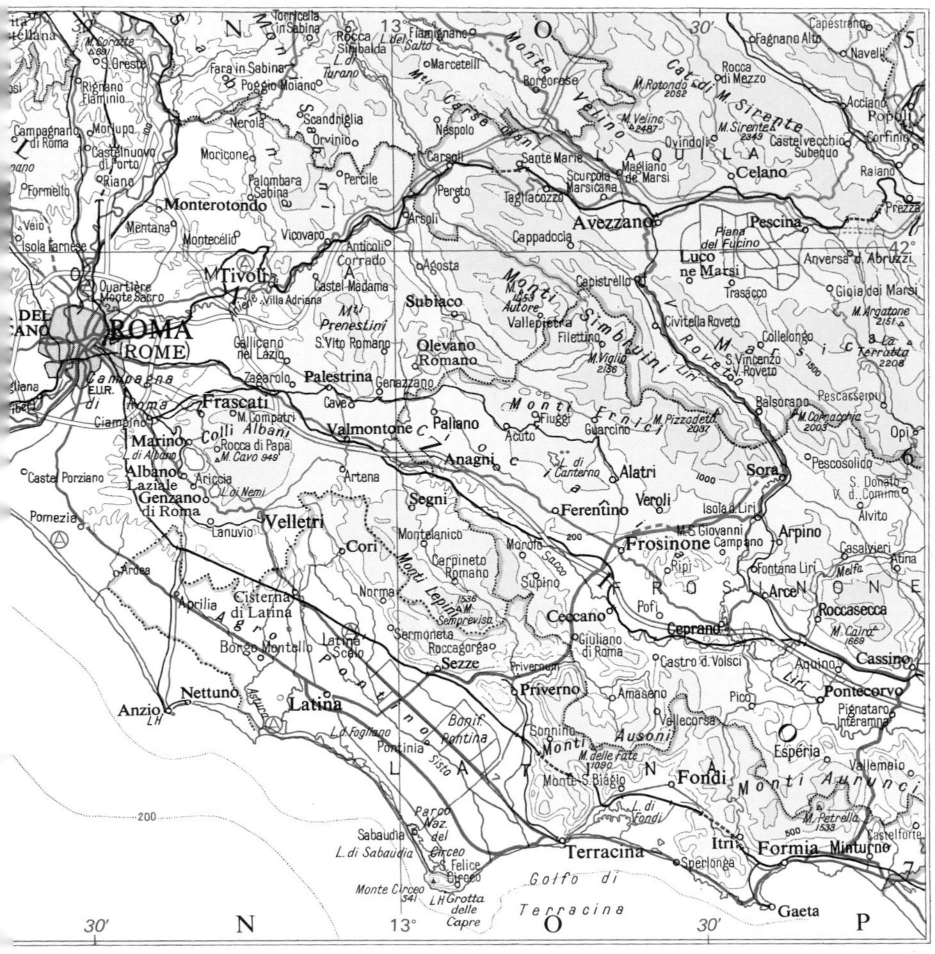

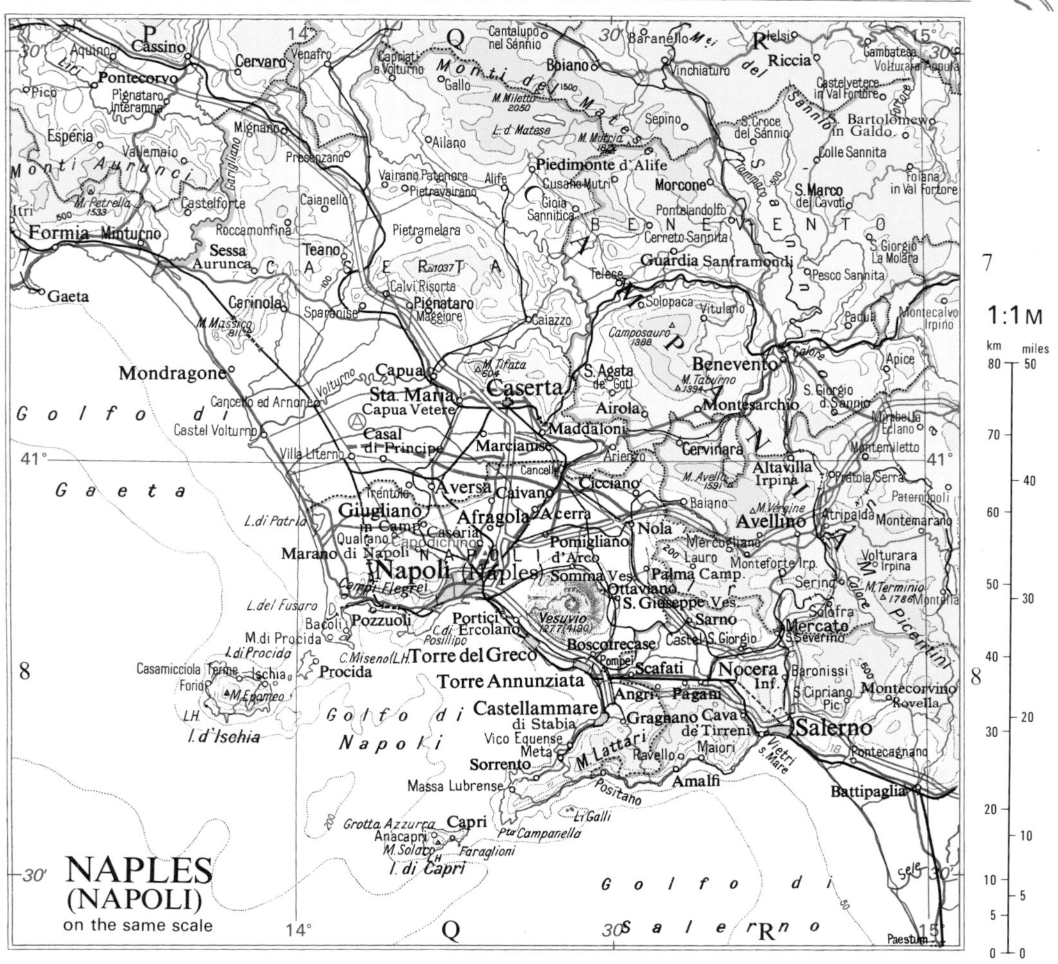

NAPLES
(NAPOLI)
on the same scale

1:1M

Heights and Depths in metres

© John Bartholomew & Son Ltd Edinburgh

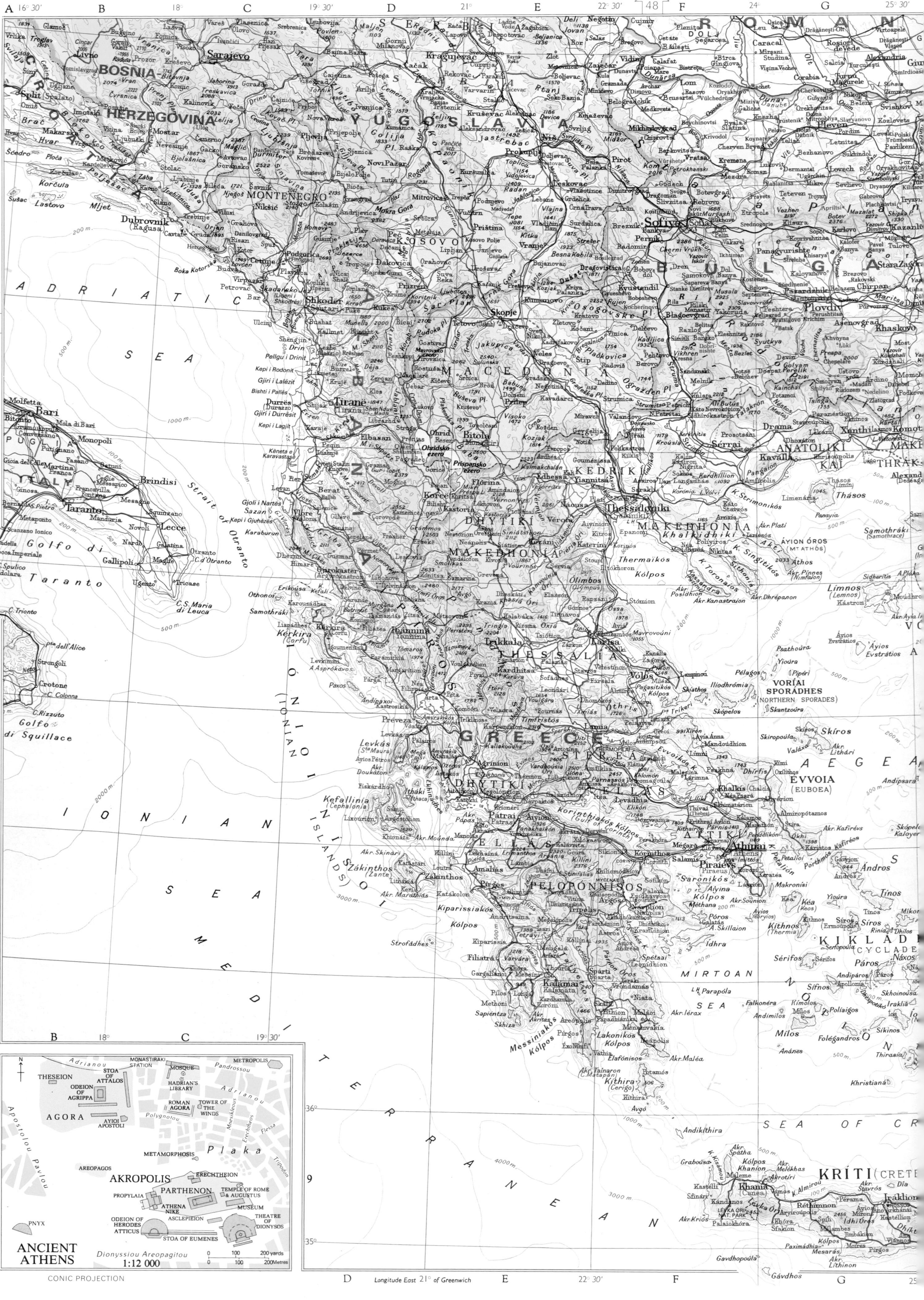

ANCIENT ATHENS
Dionyssiou Areopagitou
1:12 000

CONIC PROJECTION

Longitude East 21° of Greenwich

1 : 3 M

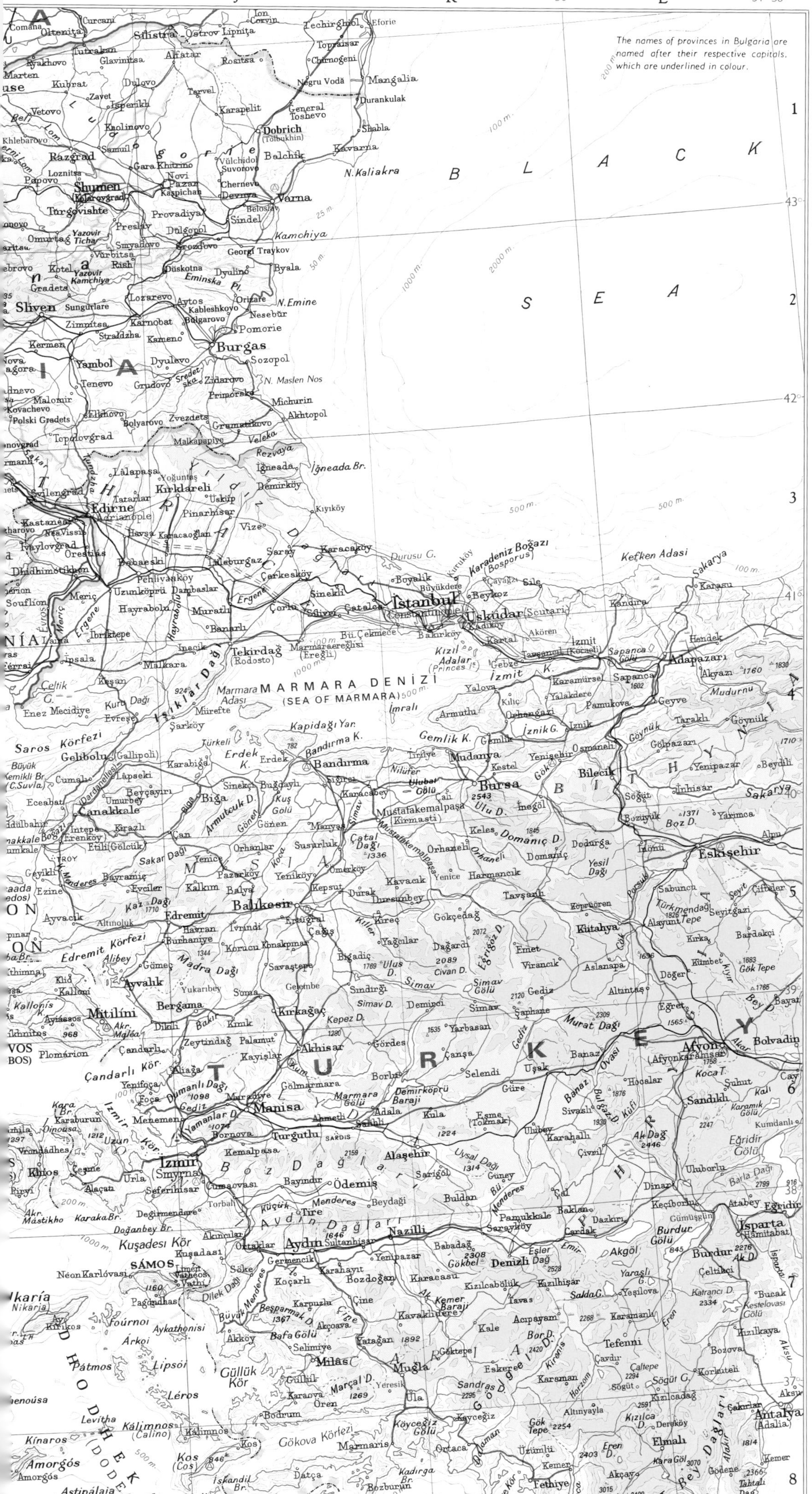

The names of provinces in Bulgaria are named after their respective capitals, which are underlined in colour.

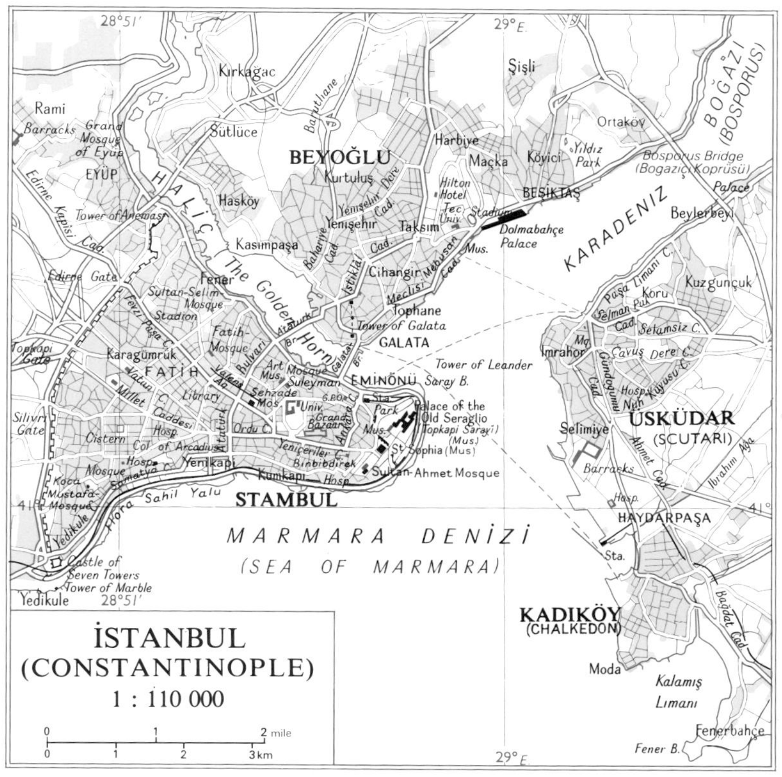

İSTANBUL
(CONSTANTINOPLE)
1 : 110 000

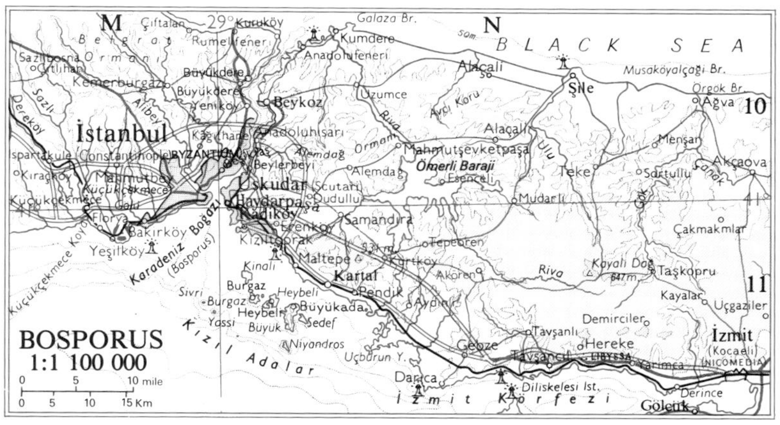

BOSPORUS
1:1 100 000

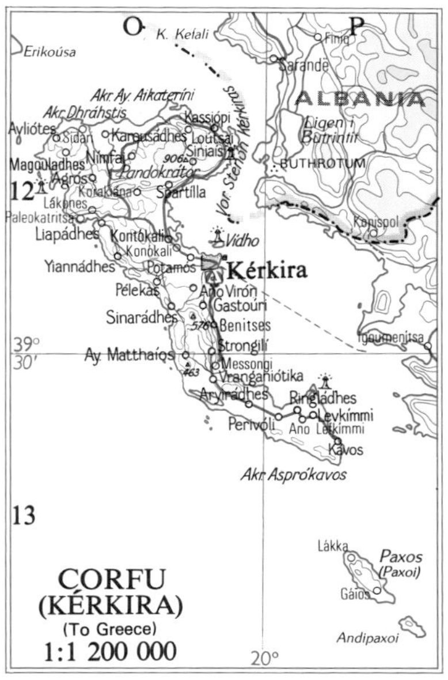

CORFU
(KÉRKIRA)
(To Greece)
1:1 200 000

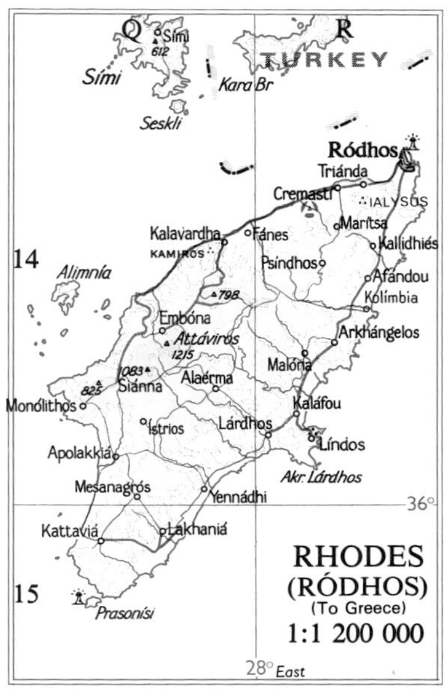

RHODES
(RÓDHOS)
(To Greece)
1:1 200 000

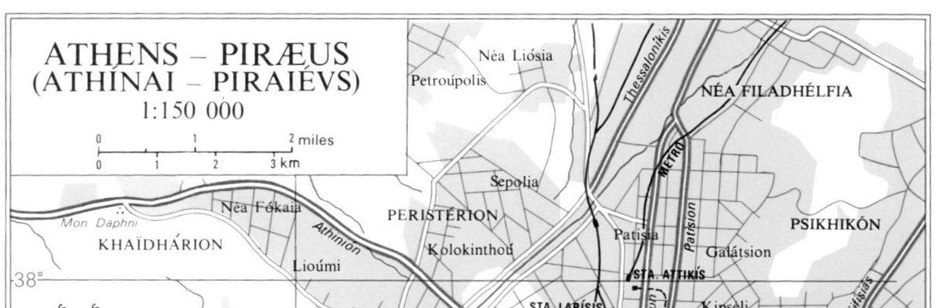

ATHENS – PIRÆUS
(ATHÍNAI – PIRAIÉVS)
1:150 000

© John Bartholomew & Son Ltd Edinburgh

Heights and Depths in metres

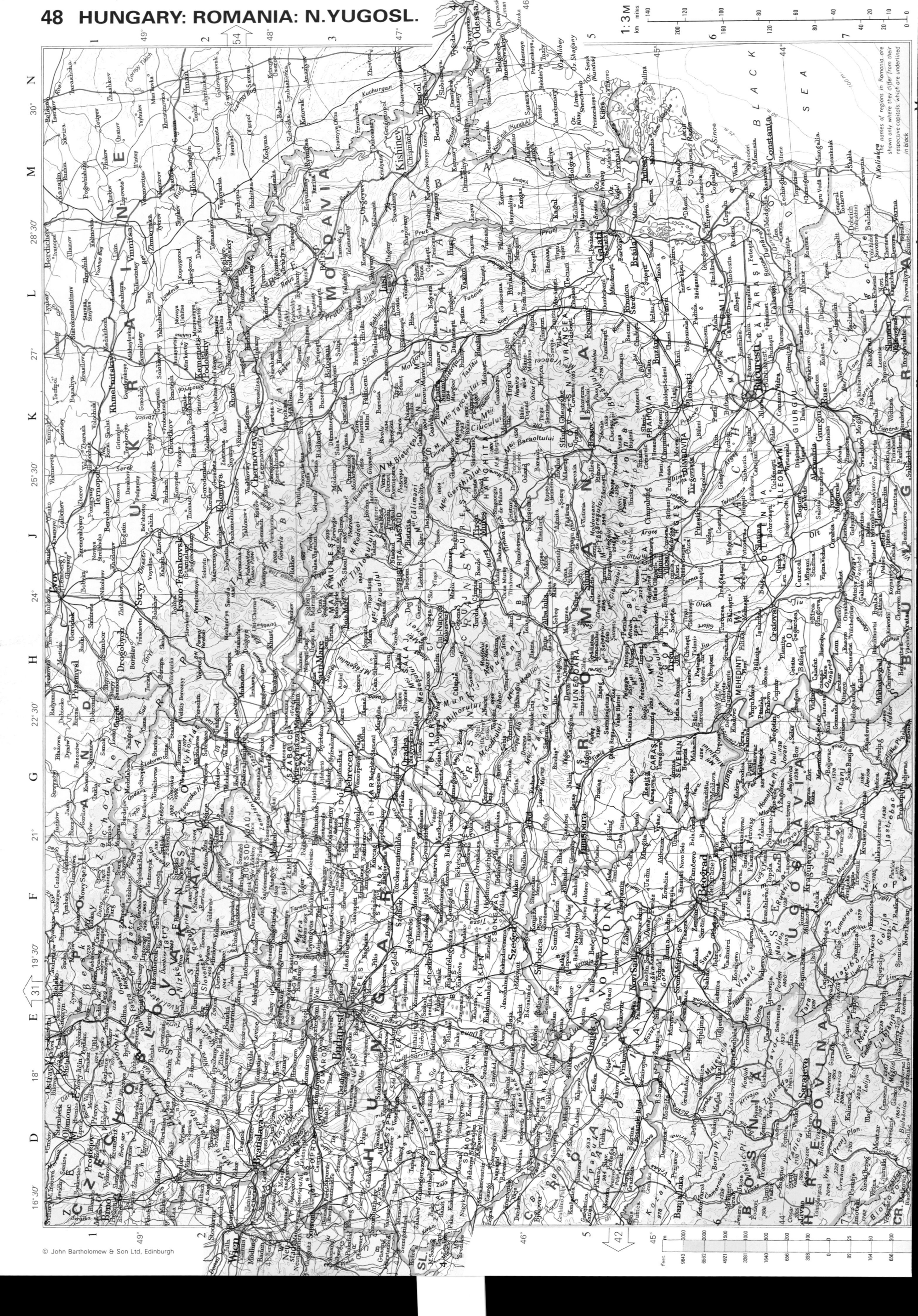
1:3M
km
miles
The names of regions in Romania are shown only where they differ from their respective capitals, which are underlined in black
BLACK SEA
HUNGARY
ROMANIA
YUGOSLAVIA
MOLDAVIA
Budapest
Beograd
Bucureşti
Wien
Bratislava
Debrecen
Szeged
Kishinev
Odessa
Constanţa
Sarajevo

MOSCOW

1:300 000

© Times Books Ltd

A
F
29°45′
30°15′
30°30′
30°45′
60° 00′
59° 45′
2
Sestroretsk
Ozero Sestroretskiy Razliv
Levashovo
Sovkhoz
Shuvalovo
Pargolovo
Novo-Pargolovskaya Koloniya
Kamenka
Aleksandrovskaya
Gorskaya
Kaupilovo
Lisiy Nos
Dubki
Ol'gino
Ostrov Kotlin
Kronshtadt
approximate alignment
Kolomyagi
Udel'naya
Lesnoy
Grazhdanka
Ruchi
Bugry
Lavriki
Novoye Devyatkino
Murino
Medvezhiy Stan
Babino
Uglovo
Ozero Bol'shoye
Romanovka
Settlement 3
Settlement 4
Settlement 16
Settlement 6
Irinovka
Vsevolozhsk
Kovalevo
Rybatskaya
Smol'naya
Rzhevka
Kal'tino
Krasnaya Gorka
Sel'tsy
Orovo
Kamenka
Tsentral'nyy
Dunay
Staraya Derevnya
Ostrov Krestovskiy
Polustrovo
Grazhdanka
Porokhovyye
Imeni Maya Pervaya
Khirvosti
Kolbino
Kostushi
Kiretskoye Pole
GULF OF FINLAND
Ostrov Vasil'yevskiy
Fortress
Hermitage
Winter Palace
St Isaac's Cathedral
SANKT - PETERBURG
Zanevka
Yanino
Pavlovo
Kirkino
Berezovka
Nizhniy Poselok
Yablonovka
Stantsiya Yanino
Staraya
Stantsiya Zanevskiy Post
Bol'shoye Aro
Tavry
Virki
Chernaya Rechka
Kudrovo
Novo-Sergiyevka
Razmitelevo
Myaglovo
Ozerki
Yeksolovo
Lomonosov
Malaya Izhora
Krasnaya Sloboda
Langerevo
Martyshkino
Prosveshcheniye
Venki
Soykino
Karasta
Kukushkino
Dachi Novyye Mesta
Petrodvorets
Poeziya
Znamenka
Znamenskaya
Sashino
Kostino
Nizino
Sanino
Ol'gino
Strel'na
Nizhnyaya Koloniya
Mar'ino
Lenina
Srednyaya
Ul'yanka
Avtovo
Kobrinskoye
Utkina Zavod
Aleksandrovskoye
Novosaratovka
Ust'-Slavyanka
Khaboye
Novaya Pustosh'
Maloye Manushkino
Bol'shoye Manushkino
Samarka
Chernaya Rechka
Dubrovka
Pervyy Gorodok
Peski
Bol'shoy Simonogont
Mishino
Nemetskaya
Novopol'ye
Sosnovaya
Polyana
Staropanovo
LENINGRAD AIRPORT
Malyy Simonogont
Vzigonty
Volodarskiy
Ligovskiy Kanal
Novosel'ye
Gorelovo
Kiskino
Kamenka
Petro Slavyanka
Shushary
Imeni Marti
Ust'-Izhora
Izhora
Otsino
Imeni Sverdlova
Oranzhereyka
Ostrovki
Mustolovo
Pavlovo
Petrushino
Tsnigri
Otradnoye
NEVA
Petrovskoye
Boloto Porzolovskoye
Krasnaya Baltika
Porozhki
Pavkulya
Nastolovo
Razbegayevo
Ryumki
Niukazi
Konstantinovka
Peski
Pulkovo
Metallostroy
Kokhmino
Pontonnyy
Sapernyy
Novaya
Maslovo
Pella
Gory
Oliki
Kuttuzi
Annino
Veneryazi
Slobodka Pavlovskaya
Verkhneye
Moskovskaya
Kolpino
Ivanovskoye
Vil'povitsy
Isayevo-Malkunova
Yelagino
Khaboni
Kameryazi
Krasnoye Selo
Bol'shoye Vittolovo
Aleksandrovskaya
Bol'shaya
Slavyanka
Pokrovskoye
Mikhaylovskaya
Lipitsy
Kempelevo
Solozi
Khannolovo
Kuz'minka
Mokkolovo
Kolpinskaya
Tarforazrabotki
Il'ino
Glyadino
Yal'gelevo
Mikhaylovka
Nikolayevka
Mykkalovo
Rod
Pushkin
Novo Vesti
Pereroz
Voskresenskoye
Zakhozh'ye
Pervyy Ul'yanovskiy
Dyatlitsy
Sokuli
Ropsha
Malyye Gorki
Russko-Vysotskoye
Telezi
Mozharskiy
Lagola
Nagornoye
Payular
Varlisolovo
Kurgelovo
Soboleva
Sofiya
Tyarlevo
Putrolovo
Yam Izhora
Mishkino
Ul'yanovskiy
Volosovo
Vyselki
Nikozemyagi
Bol'shiye Gorki
Aropakkozi
Khyuttelya
Raskolovo
Karvala
Pelgola
Kovrovo
Pendolovo
Pushkin
Pavlovsk
Voyskorovo
Toskobstshchina
Krasnyy Bor
Porkuzi
Novaya Derevnya
Nikol'skoye
Vtoroy Ul'yanovskiy
Pustyn'ka
Novyy Bor
Glukhovo
Kelozi
Kipen'
Pellya
Rattalya
Nizhnyaya
Novaya Tikhvinka
Kargankyulya
Zaytsevo
Komolovo
Gukkalovo
Pyazelevo
Myza
Kordelevo
Fedorovskoye
Raykolovo
Kozlovka
Ul'yanovka
Cheremykino
E20
Trudovik
Volkovitsy
Muldiya
Yuvayzi
Skvoritsy
Istinka
Taytsy
Antropshino
Chernaya Rechka
Gertovo
E95
Voyskorovka
A
37°15′
37°30′
37°45′
38°00′
38°15′
55° 45′
4
5
Andreyevka
Zhilino
Kryukovo
Goretovka
Bakeyevo
Kamenka
Kutuzovo
Yelino
E95
Dubrovka
Nazar'yevo
Isakovo
Novokirillovka
Dzhunkovka
Sheremet'yevskiy
SHEREMET'YEVO AIRPORT
Khaz'ma
Ivakino
Gorki
Pavel'tsevo
Povedniki
Terpigorevo
Pirogovskoye Vodokhranilishche
Afanasovo
Sorokino
Korgashino
Mamontovka
Zvyagino
Ivanteyevka
Tarasovka
Baybaki
Neberezhnoye
Neberezhnaya
Fryazino
Chizhovo
Novogrebnevo
Mishnevo
Bokovo
Mizinovo
Gromkovo
Ruzino
Ligachevo
Firsanovka
Savrasovo
Skhodnya
Cherkizovo
Mel'kisarovo
Gribki
Krasnaya Volga
Boltino
Vysokovo
Komarovka
Gorki
Potapovo
Ulitkino
Toporkovo
Brekhovo
Ladushkino
Mtsyri
Podolino
Morshchikino
Vashutino
Kolovo
Vinogradovo
Severnyy
Dolgoprudnyy
Belyaninovo
Khovrino
Mytishchi
Pervomayskiy
Bol'shevo
Kaliningrad
Shchelkovo
Mal'tsevo
Amerevo
Kozhino
Rayki
Avdot'ino
Pyatkovo
Khovanskoye
Dedovo
Obshchestvennik
Uskovo
Gnilushi
Zabolot'ye
Veshki
Borodino
Volkovo
Yadreyevo
Kostino
Valentinovka
Zhegalovo
Khotovo
Sverdlovskiy
Nadovrazhino
Shemetkovo
Yurlovo
Ivanovskoye
Mashkino
Il'insky
Pushkinskoye
Tayninskoye
Serkovo
Aniskino
Mityanino
Selivanikha
Turovo
Bol'shakovo
Fedorovka
Korostovo
Novaya Luzha
Khimki
Busino
Liandzovo
Bibirevo
Druzhba
Oboldino
Ledovo
Shchelkovo
Lenino
Talitsa
Talitsy
Kozino
Saburovo
Kurkino
Andreyevanovo
Korovino
Beskudnikovo
Vatutino
Suponevo
Osevevskaya
Proletarskiy
Zhelyabino
Mar'ino
Znamenskoye
Dudino
Aleshkino
Degunino
Slobodka
Babushkin
Medvezh'i Ozera
Bol'shiye Zherebtsy
Dedovsk
Nakhabino
Putilkovo
Petrovo
Novo-Khovrino
Medvedkovo
Krasnyy Severyanin
Staroye Ledovo
Kishkino
Novo-Nikol'skoye
Pekhra-Pokrovskaya
M O S K V A
Monaseyevo
Monino
Losino-Petrovskiy
Zelenkovo
Penyagino
Spas
Tushino
Rostokino
Abramtsevo
Lukino
Shevelkino
Chudinki
Monino
Lobanovo
Anikeyevka
Pushkinskoye
Opalikha
Nikol'skiy
Krasnogorsk
Gol'yanovo
Shchitnikovo
Nikol'skoye
Pavlovskaya Sloboda
Peshkovo
Gorenosovo
Myakinino
Strogino
Bogorodskoye
Kaloshino
Nikolayevka
Novoye
Mikhalevo
Staraya Kupavna
Nikol'skoye
Uryupino
Veledinkovo
Voronki
Troitse-Lykovo
Central
Izmaylovo
Gorenki
Balashikha
Leonovo
Bezmenkovo
Kutuzovo
Ivanovskoy
Pozdnyakovo
Zakharkovo
Khoroshevo
Vishnyaki
Biserevo
Timoshino
Stepanovskoye
Glukhovo
Rublevo
Ivanovskoye
Saltykovka
Ozero Bisserovskoye
Narkommfiota
Kudinovo
617
Dimitrovskoye
Buzlanovo
Il'inskoye
Tatarovo
Nizhniye Mnevniki
Bolshoi Theatre
Leshkye Polyany
Fedurnovo
Chernoye
463
Cherepkovo
Fili
Red Square
Kremlin
MOSKVA
Reutov
Kupavna
Belaya
Petrovo-Dal'neye
Kargashino
Plyushchevo
Savvino
Gribanovo
Znamenskoye
Barvikha
Romashkovo
Perovo
Serebryanka
Zheleznodorozhnyy
Dyatlovka
Ubory
Dubtsy
Usovo
Vavkova
Davydkovo
Vladychino
Fenino
Sobolikha
Gorki
Zhukovka
Vtoryye
Mikhaylovskoye
Kuskovo
Temnikovo
Purshevo
Elektrougli
Borki
Buzayevo
Podushkino
Novoivanovskoye
Matveyevskoye
Karacharovo
Kozhukhovo
Kosino
Bol'shoye Sarevevo
692
Kuntsevo
GOROD MOSKVA
Vykhino
Mikhel'son
Novyy Milet
Poltevo
Isakovo
Salosovo
Marfino
Amin'yevo
Vorob'yevo
Novokuz'minki
Zhulebino
Motyakovo
Rusavkino Popovshchina
Mar'ino Pervoye
Tagan'kovo
Mamonovo
666
Ochakovo
Cheryomushki
Nagatino
Marusino
Kopninc
Dar'ino
Lapino
Skolkovo
Bakovka
Meshcherskiy
Kolomenskoye
Lyublino
Lyubertsy
Polushkino
Strokino
Aksenovo
Semenkovo
Dubki
Odintsovo
Gubkino
Troparevo
Semenovskoye
Volkhonka
Sadovniki
Kraskovo
Ustinovka
Perkhushkovo
Yudino
Akulovo
Vnukovo
Belyayevo
Kur'yanovo
Batyunino
Belyye Dachi
Tomilino
Vyalki
479
Zhavoronki
Borodki
Peredelkino
Chebotv
Solntsevo
Sotorovo
Deveylovo
D'yakovo
Brateyevo
Chagino
Kotel'niki
Udel'noye
Lesnoy Gorodok
Orlovo
Rumyantsevo
820
Kon'kovo
Shaydrovo
Borisovo
Dzerzhinskiy
Chasovnya
Vtoroye
Malakhovka
Kripan
Shchedrino
Osorgino
Rasskazovka
Lenino
Tsaritsyno
Gremyachevo
Zhilino
Mikhnevo
Zhukovskiy
Likino
Solmonovo
Pykhtino
Uzkoye
Drozdovo
Kishino
Oktyabr'skiy
Pekhorka
Mikhevo
Bykovo
Il'inskoe
Zaytsevo
Lapshinka
Kartmazovo
Tëplyy Stan
Krasnyy Mayak
Orekhovo
Besedy
Bolyatino
Udel'naya
Kratovo
Mit'kino
Kokoshkino
Shel'butovo
Bol'shoye Golubino
Yasenevo
Mil'kovo
Novoye Brekhovo
Postnikovo
VNUKOVO AIRPORT
M O S K V A
Vyrubki
Biryulevo
Mamonovo
Sloboda
Ostrovtsy
Pekhorka
MOSKVA
Kreksino
Sanino
Davydkovo
Nikolo-Khovanskoye
Novyye Bittsy
Kartino
Lytkarino
Ramenskoye
Shatapovo
Annino
Valuyevo
Verkhneye
Baturino
Prudishche
Vlasovo
Golenishchevo
Prokshino
Kachalovo
Bittsy
Aparinki
Misailovo
Molokovo
Verkhneye Myachkovo
Kulakovo
Bol'shoye Pokrovskoye
Zimenki
Mikhaylovskoye
Bulatnikovo
Chulkovo
Ramenskoye
Pervomayskiy
Sokolovo
Filimonki
Letovo
Sosenki
Zhabkino
Maloye Tabolovo
Aprelevka
Marfino
Akin'shino
Khanino
Gavrikovo
Butovo
Rastorguyevo
Zhukovo
Andreyevskoye
610
E95
5 10 15 km
5 10 miles

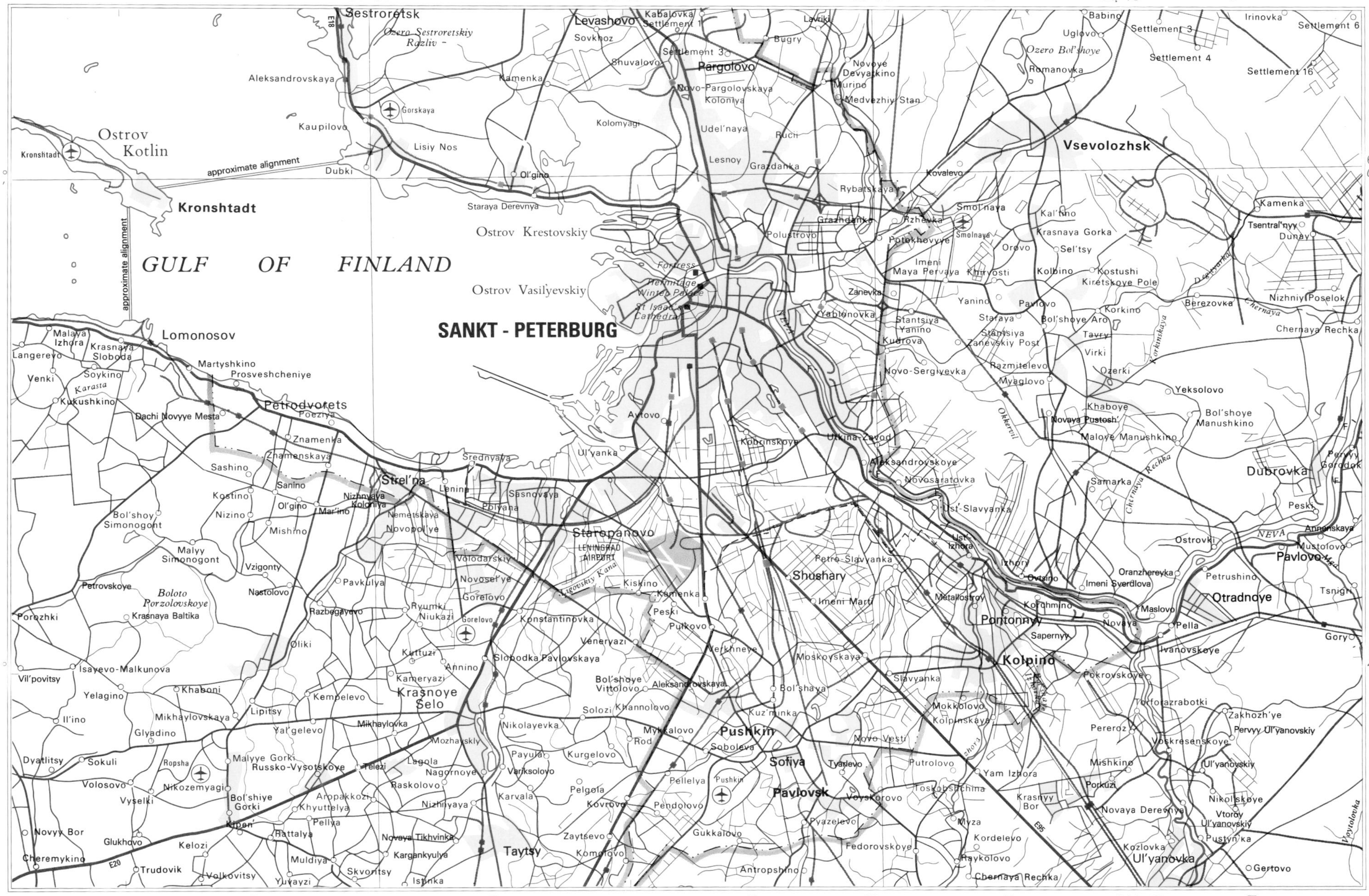

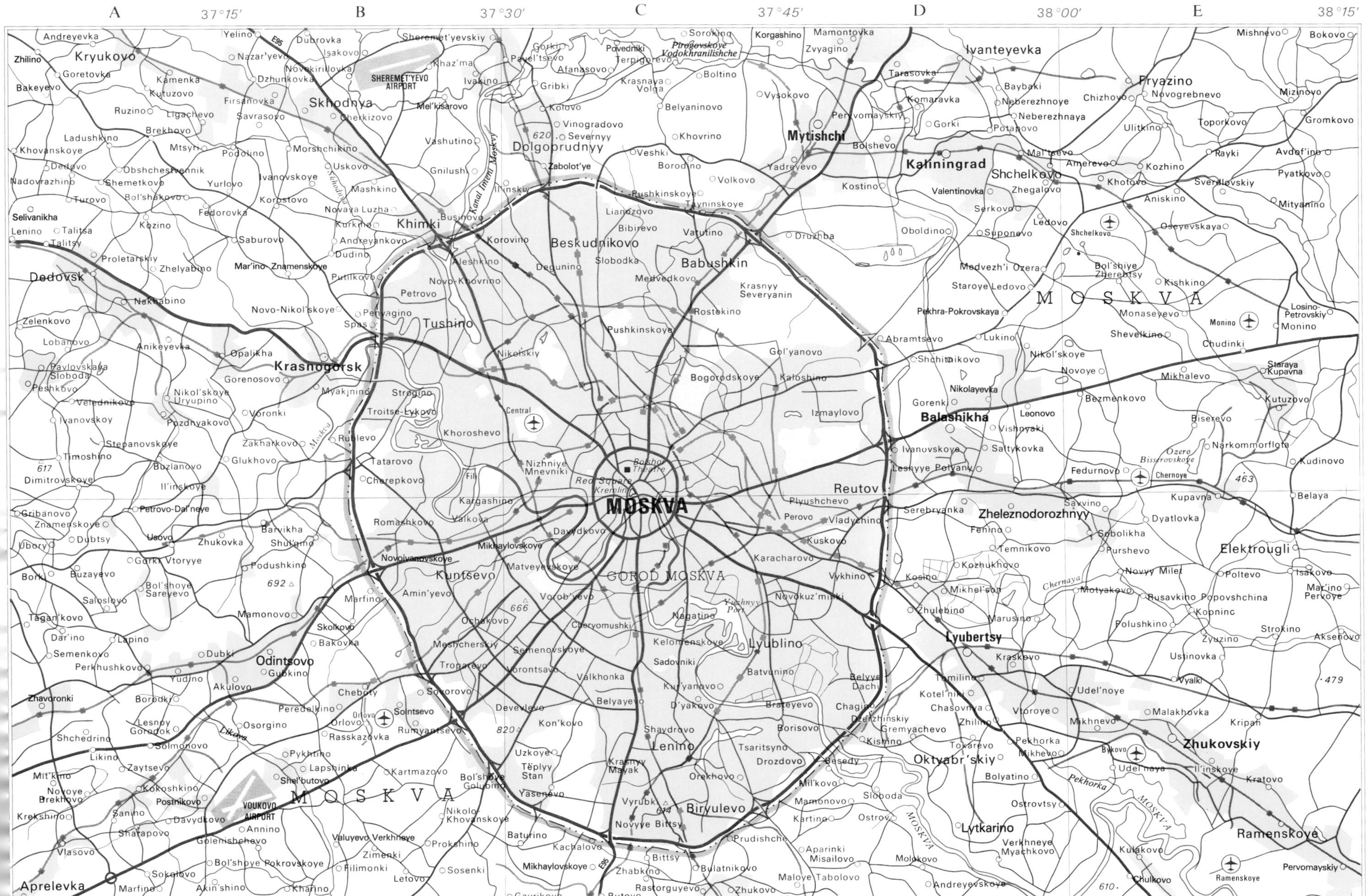

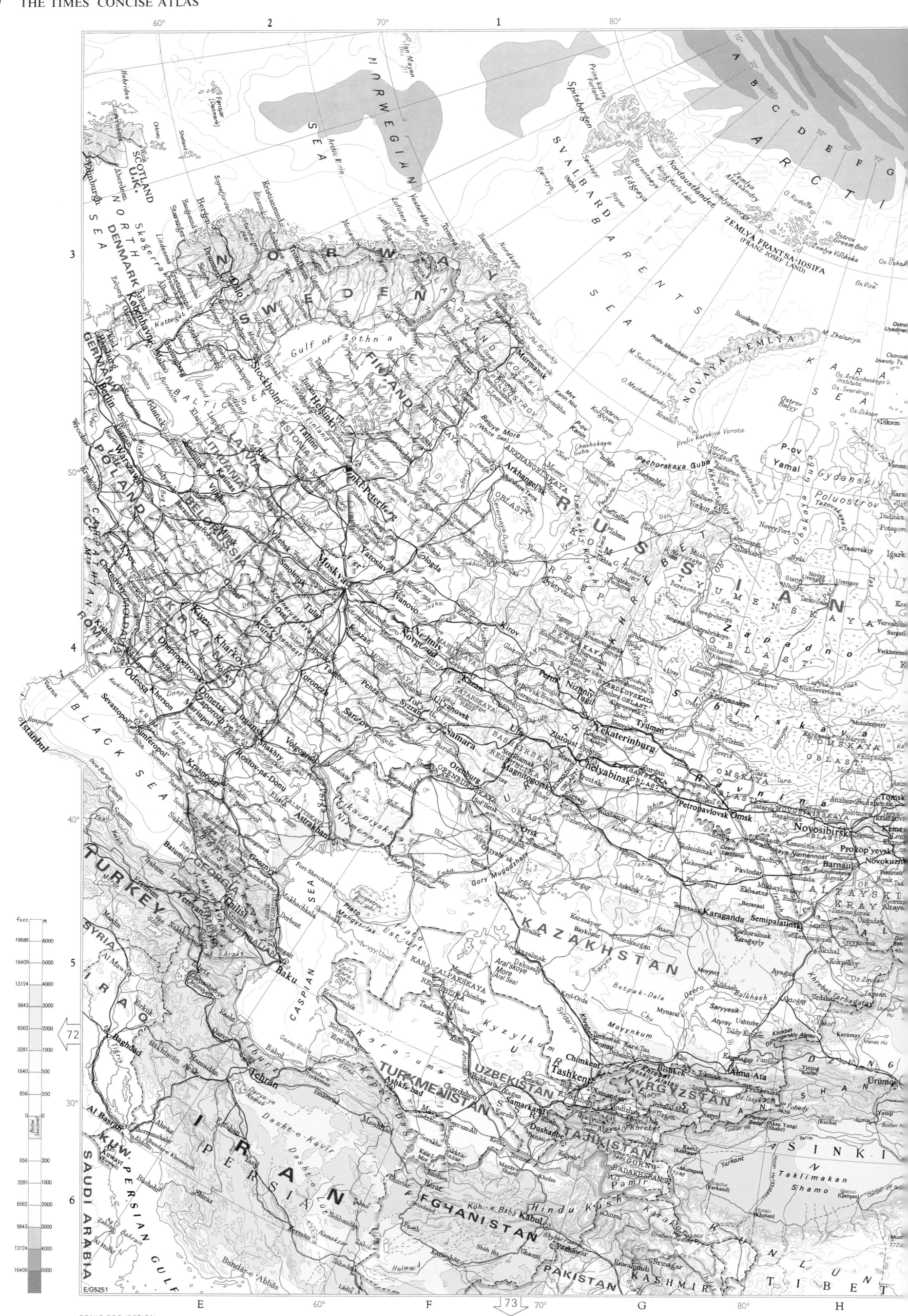
NORWEGIAN SEA
BARENTS SEA
KARA SEA
NORTH SEA
BALTIC SEA
BLACK SEA
CASPIAN SEA
PERSIAN GULF
Gulf of Bothnia
Gulf of Finland
SVALBARD (NOR.)
Spitsbergen
ZEMLYA FRANTSA-IOSIFA (FRANZ JOSEF LAND)
NOVAYA ZEMLYA
NORWAY
SWEDEN
FINLAND
DENMARK
U.K.
SCOTLAND
GERMANY
POLAND
LITHUANIA
LATVIA
ESTONIA
BELORUSSIA
UKRAINE
MOLDOVA
ROMANIA
TURKEY
GEORGIA
ARMENIA
AZERBAIJAN
SYRIA
IRAQ
IRAN
PERSIA
KUWAIT
SAUDI ARABIA
AFGHANISTAN
PAKISTAN
KASHMIR
TURKMENISTAN
UZBEKISTAN
KYRGYZSTAN
TAJIKISTAN
KAZAKHSTAN
RUSSIAN FEDERATION
TIBET
Moskva
Sankt-Peterburg
Stockholm
Helsinki
Oslo
København
Berlin
Warszawa
Minsk
Kiyev
Kharkov
Odessa
Volgograd
Astrakhan'
Samara
Kazan'
Perm'
Yekaterinburg
Chelyabinsk
Omsk
Novosibirsk
Tyumen'
Arkhangel'sk
Murmansk
Baku
Tbilisi
Tehrān
Baghdad
Tashkent
Alma-Ata
Bishkek
Dushanbe
Kabul
Aral'skoye More (Aral Sea)
Karaganda
Semipalatinsk
Barnaul
Tomsk
Ürümqi
Taklimakan Shamo
Hindu Kush
Pamir
feet
m
19686
6000
16409
5000
13124
4000
9843
3000
6562
2000
3281
1000
1640
500
656
200
0
Below Sea Level
72
73
E/G5251
60°
70°
80°
E
F
G
H
1
2
3
4
5
6

CONIC PROJECTION

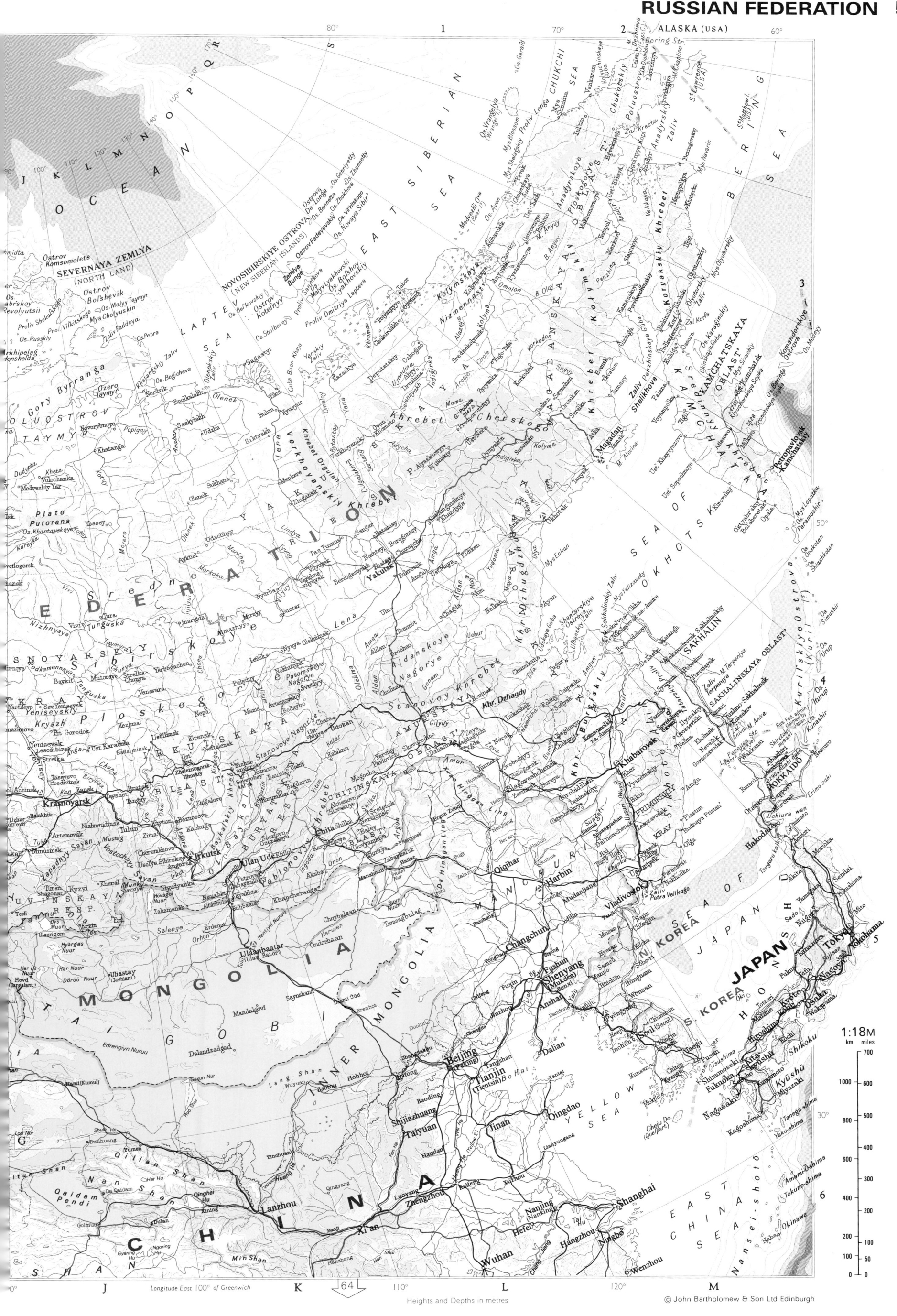

ALASKA (USA)

ARCTIC OCEAN

SEVERNAYA ZEMLYA
(NORTH LAND)

EAST SIBERIAN SEA

CHUKCHI SEA

BERING SEA

NOVOSIBIRSKIYE OSTROVA
(NEW SIBERIAN ISLANDS)

LAPTEV SEA

MAGADANSKAYA OBLAST'

KAMCHATSKAYA OBLAST'

Petropavlovsk-Kamchatskiy

SEA OF OKHOTSK

Plato Putorana

Yakutsk

SAKHALIN

SAKHALINSKAYA OBLAST'
Yuzhno-Sakhalinsk

Kurilskiye Ostrova (Kuril Is)

KRASNOYARSKIY KRAY

Stanovoy Khrebet

Khr. Dzhagdy

Krasnoyarsk

IRKUTSKAYA OBLAST'

Khabarovsk

HOKKAIDO

CHITINSKAYA OBLAST'

AMURSKAYA OBLAST'

Chita

PRIMORSKIY KRAY

Hakodate

Irkutsk

BURYATS

Ulan Ude

Vladivostok

SEA OF JAPAN

Harbin

Qiqihar

Changchun

MANCHURIA

N. KOREA

JAPAN

HONSHŪ

Ulaanbaatar
(Ulan Bator)

MONGOLIA

Fushun
Shenyang (Mukden)
Benxi
Anshan

S. KOREA

Seoul (Soul)

Tokyo
Yokohama
Nagoya
Ōsaka
Kyōto

GOBI

INNER MONGOLIA

Beijing (Peking)

Tianjin (Tientsin)

Bo Hai

Dalian

YELLOW SEA

1:18M
km miles

SHIKOKU
KYŪSHŪ

Baoding

Shijiazhuang

Jinan

Qingdao

Taiyuan

Handan

Lanzhou

Zhengzhou

Xi'an

Luoyang

Nanjing (Nanking)

Shanghai

Hefei

Hangzhou

Ningbo

EAST CHINA SEA

Wuhan

CHINA

Nanseishotō

INDUSTRIAL URALS
Central Area
1:3 000 000
RUSSIAN FEDERATION
FINLAND
ESTONIA
LATVIA
LITHUANIA
MURMANSKAYA OBLAST'
BELOYE MORE (WHITE SEA)
MOSKVA
Sankt-Peterburg
Helsinki
Yekaterinburg
Chelyabinsk

1:6M
CONIC PROJECTION
BLACK SEA
CHERNOYE MORE
KARA DENIZ
CASPIAN SEA
SEA OF AZOV
AZOVSKOYE MORE
KAZAKHSTAN
UKRAINE
BELORUSSIA
POLAND
ROMANIA
BULGARIA
TURKEY
GEORGIA
AZERBAIJAN
KALMYTSKAYA RESPUBLIKA
Volgograd
Astrakhan
Rostov-na-Donu
Donetsk
Kharkov
Kiyev (Kiev)
Odessa
Simferopol
Sevastopol
Krasnodar
Stavropol
Groznyy
Makhachkala
Tbilisi
Batumi
Trabzon
Samsun
Sinop
İstanbul (Constantinople)
Bucureşti (Bucharest)
Varna
Kishinev
Minsk
Warszawa
Voronezh
Saratov
Samara
Tula
Orel
Kursk
Smolensk
Gomel
Longitude East 35° of Greenwich

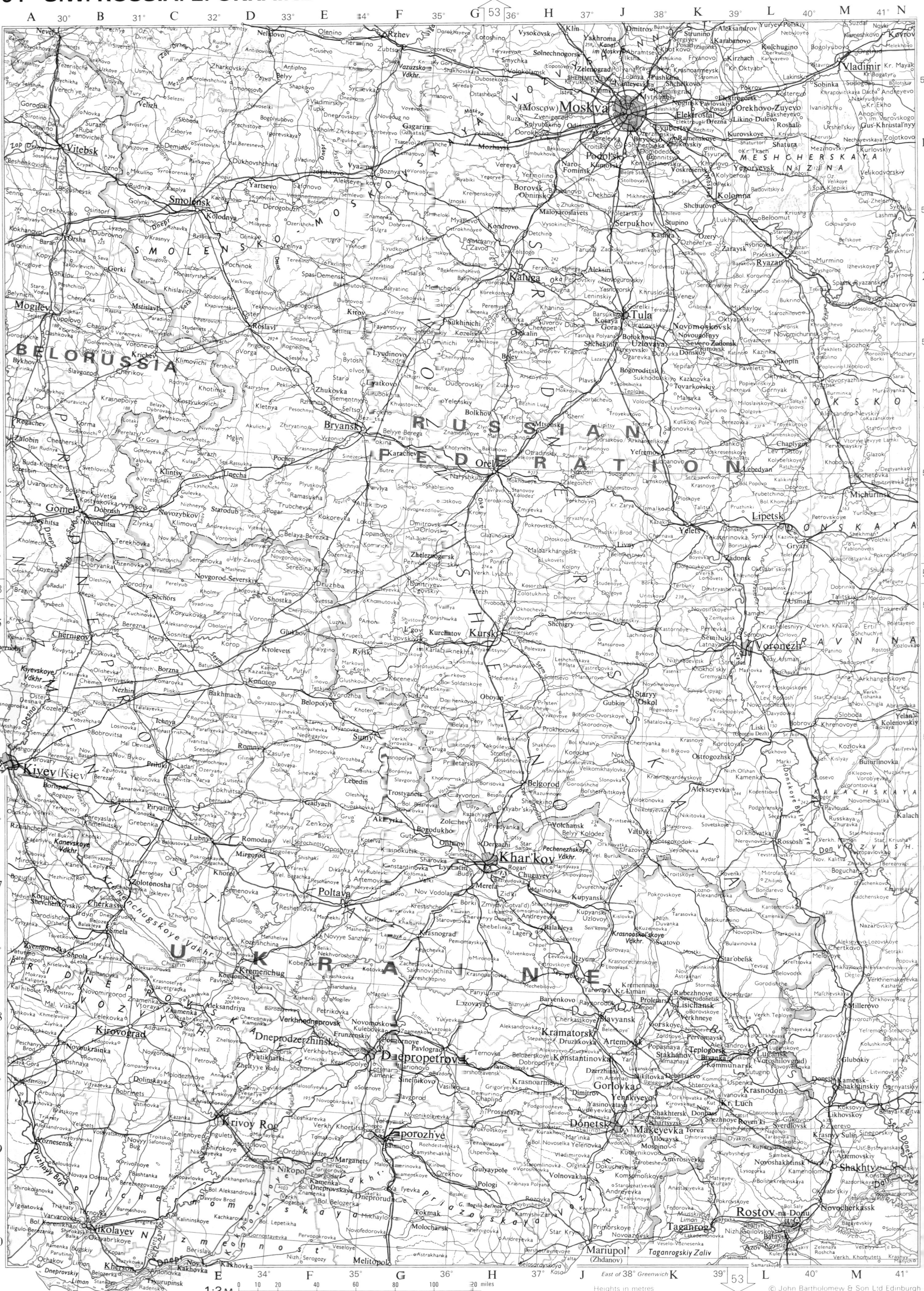

BELORUSSIA

RUSSIAN FEDERATION

UKRAINE

SMOLENSKO

Moskva (Moscow)

Vitebsk · Smolensk · Mogilev · Bryansk · Orel · Kursk · Voronezh · Lipetsk · Tula · Kaluga · Ryazan · Michurinsk

Gomel · Chernigov · Kiyev (Kiev) · Sumy · Belgorod · Kharkov · Poltava

Kremenchugskoye Vdkhr. · Cherkassy · Kirovograd · Krivoy Rog · Dnepropetrovsk · Zaporozhye · Donetsk · Makeyevka · Lugansk

Nikolayev · Kherson · Melitopol · Mariupol' (Zhdanov) · Taganrog · Rostov-na-Donu · Novocherkassk · Shakhty

MESHCHERSKAYA NIZINA · OKSKO-DONSKAYA RAVNINA · PRIDNEPROVSKAYA NIZMENNOST'

CONIC PROJECTION

1:3 M

Heights in metres

© John Bartholomew & Son Ltd Edinburgh

East of 38° Greenwich

0 10 20 40 60 80 miles
0 20 40 80 120 160 200 km

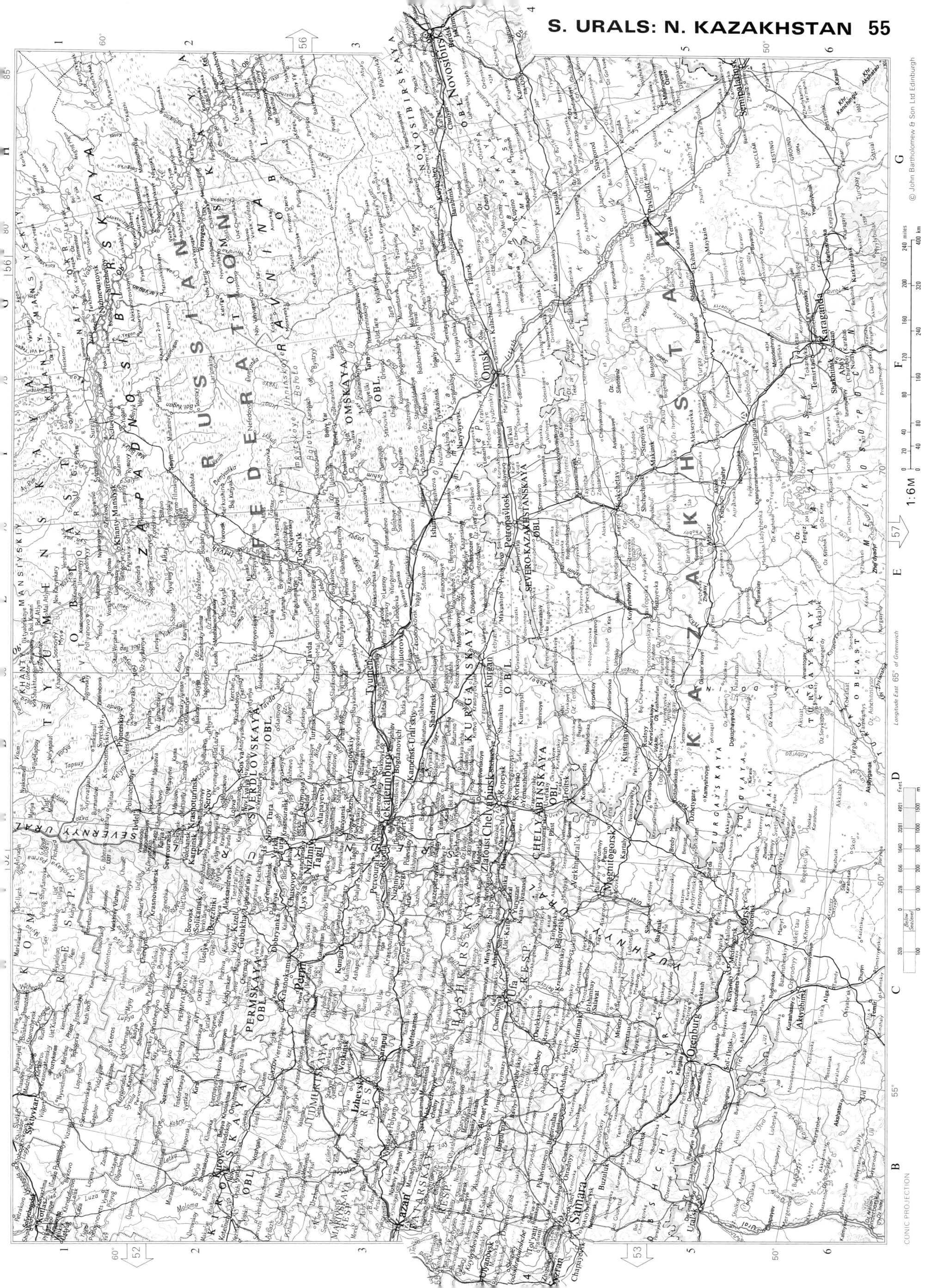

1 : 6 M

CONIC PROJECTION

Longitude East 65° of Greenwich

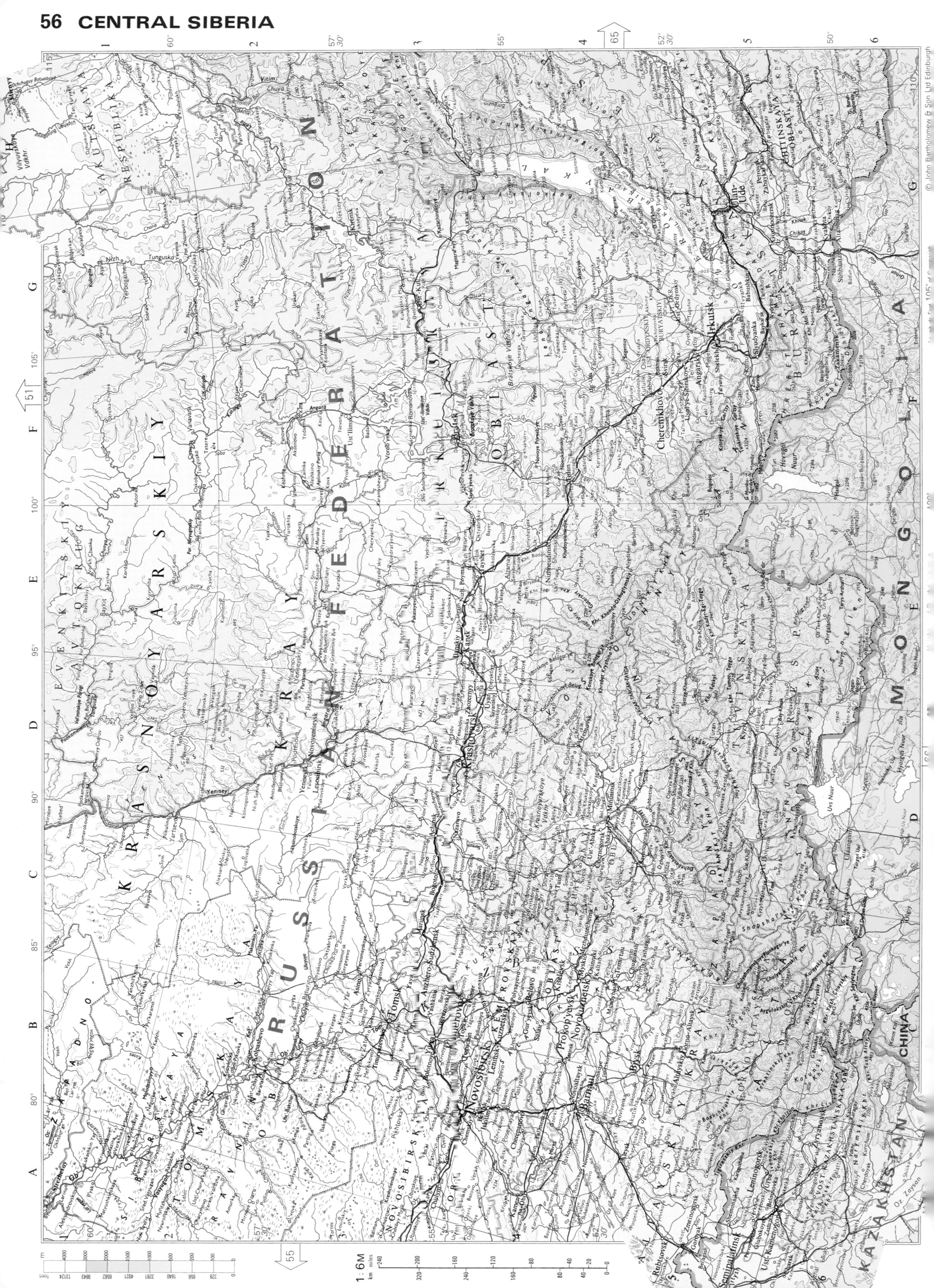
RUSSIAN FEDERATION
KRASNOYARSKIY KRAY
IRKUTSKAYA OBLAST'
MONGOLIA
CHINA
KAZAKHSTAN
Novosibirsk
Krasnoyarsk
Irkutsk
Tomsk
Barnaul
Ulan-Ude
1:6M
© John Bartholomew & Son Ltd Edinburgh

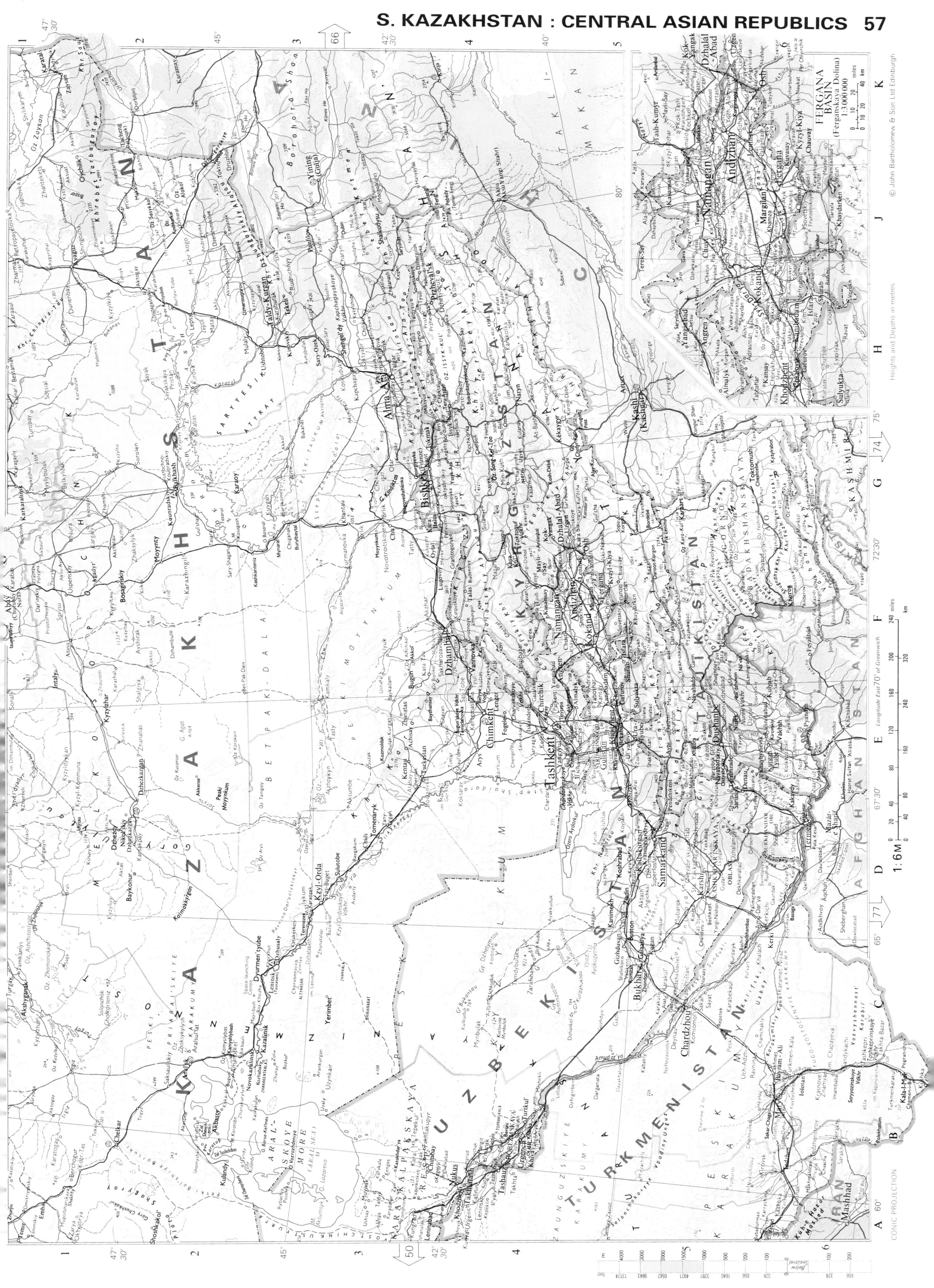

FERGANA
BASIN
(Fergamskaya Dolina)
1:3000000

© John Bartholomew & Son Ltd Edinburgh

Heights and Depths in metres

CONIC PROJECTION

1:6M

Longitude East 70° of Greenwich

RUSSIAN

MONGOLIA

ULAANBAATAR (ULAN BATOR)

Irkutsk

Ulan-Ude

Chita

Manzho

GOBI

XINJIANG UYGUR ZIZHIQU

NEI MONGOLIA (INNER MONGOLIA)

Hohhot (Huhehot)

Baotou

Zhangjiakou (Kalgan)

BEIJING (PEKING)

Datong

Tangshan

Tianjin (Tients)

HEBEI

Taiyuan

SHANXI

Baoding

Shijiazhuang

QINGHAI (TSINGHAI)

Xining

Lanzhou

NINGXIA

Yinchuan (Ning-hsia)

SHAANXI

Yan'an

Handan

Anyang

Jinan

SHANDONG

Xinxiang

Kaifeng

Zhengzhou

HENAN

Xuzhou

Luoyang

Xi'an

Baoji

Qin Ling

Nanyang

Hanzhong

Chengdu

SICHUAN

Nanchong

Wanxian

Chongqing (Chungking)

Wuhan

Hanyang

ANHUI

Nanjing (Nanking)

Hefei

Wuhu

INDIA

BURMA

ALBERS CONIC PROJECTION

FEDERATION
AMURSKAYA
OBLAST'
KHABAROVSKIY KRAY
YEVREYSKAYA (Jewish) A.O.
PRIMORSKIY KRAY
OKHOTSKOYE MORE (SEA OF OKHOTSK)
SAKHALIN
HOKKAIDŌ
HONSHU
SHIKOKU
KYŪSHŪ
JAPAN
SEA OF JAPAN
PACIFIC OCEAN
NORTH KOREA
SOUTH KOREA
YELLOW SEA (HUANG HAI)
EAST CHINA SEA
Korea Bay
Korea Strait
Tatarskiy Proliv
La Perouse Str. (Sōya-kaikyō)
Tsugaru-kaikyō
Proliv Friza
Zaliv Terpeniya
Zaliv Aniva
Zaliv Petra Velikogo
Liaodong Wan
Shandong Bandao
Da Hinggan Ling
Xiao Hinggan Ling
Changbai Shan
Okha
Tynda
Skovorodino
Mogocha
Blagoveshchensk
Belogorsk
Svobodnyy
Shimanovsk
Komsomol'sk-na-Amure
Khabarovsk
Birobidzhan
Sovetskaya Gavan'
Vanino
Aleksandrovsk-Sakhalinskiy
Poronaysk
Makarov
Yuzhno-Sakhalinsk
Korsakov
Vladivostok
Nakhodka
Ussuriysk
Lesozavodsk
Hailar
Qiqihar (Tsitsihar)
Harbin
Jiamusi
Mudanjiang
Jilin
Changchun
Siping
Shenyang (Mukden)
Fushun
Anshan
Benxi
Jinzhou
Dandong
Dalian (Lüda) (Dairen)
Lüshun (Port Arthur)
Qinhuangdao
Yantai (Chefoo)
Weihai
Qingdao (Tsingtao)
Nantong
Wuxi
Suzhou (Soochow)
Shanghai
Hangzhou (Hangchow)
Ningbo (Ningpo)
Zhoushan Qundao
Ch'ŏngjin
Hamhŭng
Hŭngnam
P'YŎNGYANG
Wŏnsan
Kaesŏng
SOUL (SEOUL)
Inch'ŏn
Taejŏn
Taegu
Kwangju
Pusan
Masan
Mokp'o
Cheju-do
Ullung do
Tok-to (Take-shima) (Liancourt Rocks)
Oki
Sado
Asahikawa
Sapporo
Kushiro
Muroran
Hakodate
Aomori
Hachinohe
Morioka
Akita
Sendai
Yamagata
Niigata
Toyama
Kanazawa
Nagano
Maebashi
Utsunomiya
Mito
TŌKYŌ
Yokohama
Yokosuka
Kawasaki
Fuji-san 3776
Shizuoka
Hamamatsu
Nagoya
Gifu
Kyōto
Kōbe
Ōsaka
Sakai
Wakayama
Himeji
Okayama
Hiroshima
Tokushima
Takamatsu
Matsuyama
Kōchi
Shimonoseki
Kita-Kyūshū
Fukuoka
Kurume
Nagasaki
Kumamoto
Kuju-san 1788
Ōita
Miyazaki
Kagoshima
Tanega-shima
Yaku-shima
Ōsumi-shoto
Tokara-retto
O.Iturup
O. Kunashir
Shikotan
Habomai-Shoto
Rus. Fed. admin. claimed by Japan
Ramapo Deep 10374
Ogasawara-shoto (Bonin Is.)
Chichi-jima
Muko-jima
Hachijō-jima
Miyake-jima
Sumisu-jima
120° 125° 130° 135° 140° 145° 150°
30° 35° 40° 45° 50°

Continuation on the same scale
SEA OF OKHOTSK
SEA OF JAPAN
HOKKAIDŌ
Sapporo
Asahikawa
Hakodate
Kushiro
Obihiro
Otaru
Muroran
Abashiri
Nemuro
Shiretoko misaki
Rus. Fed. admin. claimed by Japan
Sōya-misaki
Rebun-tō
Rishiri-tō
Okushiri-tō
Erimo-misaki
Uchiura wan (Volcano Bay)
Tsugaru kaikyō
Aomori
Mutsu-wan
SOUTH KOREA
Taegu
Pusan
Masan
Chinju
Kŏje-do
KOREA STRAIT
Nishi-suidō (Chōsen-kaikyō)
Higashi-suidō
Tsushima
Iki
Oki
Dōzen
Dōgo
Matsue
Tottori
Okayama
Himeji
Kōbe
Hiroshima
Fukuyama
Kurashiki
Takamatsu
Tokushima
Matsuyama
Kōchi
Uwajima
Muroto-zaki
Ashizuri-misaki
Kita Kyūshū
Shimonoseki
Yamaguchi
Fukuoka
Saga
Sasebo
Nagasaki
Kumamoto
Ōita
Beppu
Nobeoka
Miyazaki
Kagoshima
Sendai
Sata-misaki
Gotō-rettō
Suō-nada
Iyo-nada
Hiuchi-nada
Harima-nada
Tosa-wan
Kii-suidō
Bungo-suidō
Genkai-nada
CONIC PROJECTION
feet m
9843 3000
6562 2000
4921 1500
3281 1000
1640 500
656 200
328 100
0 0
656 200
6562 2000
13124 4000
26248 8000

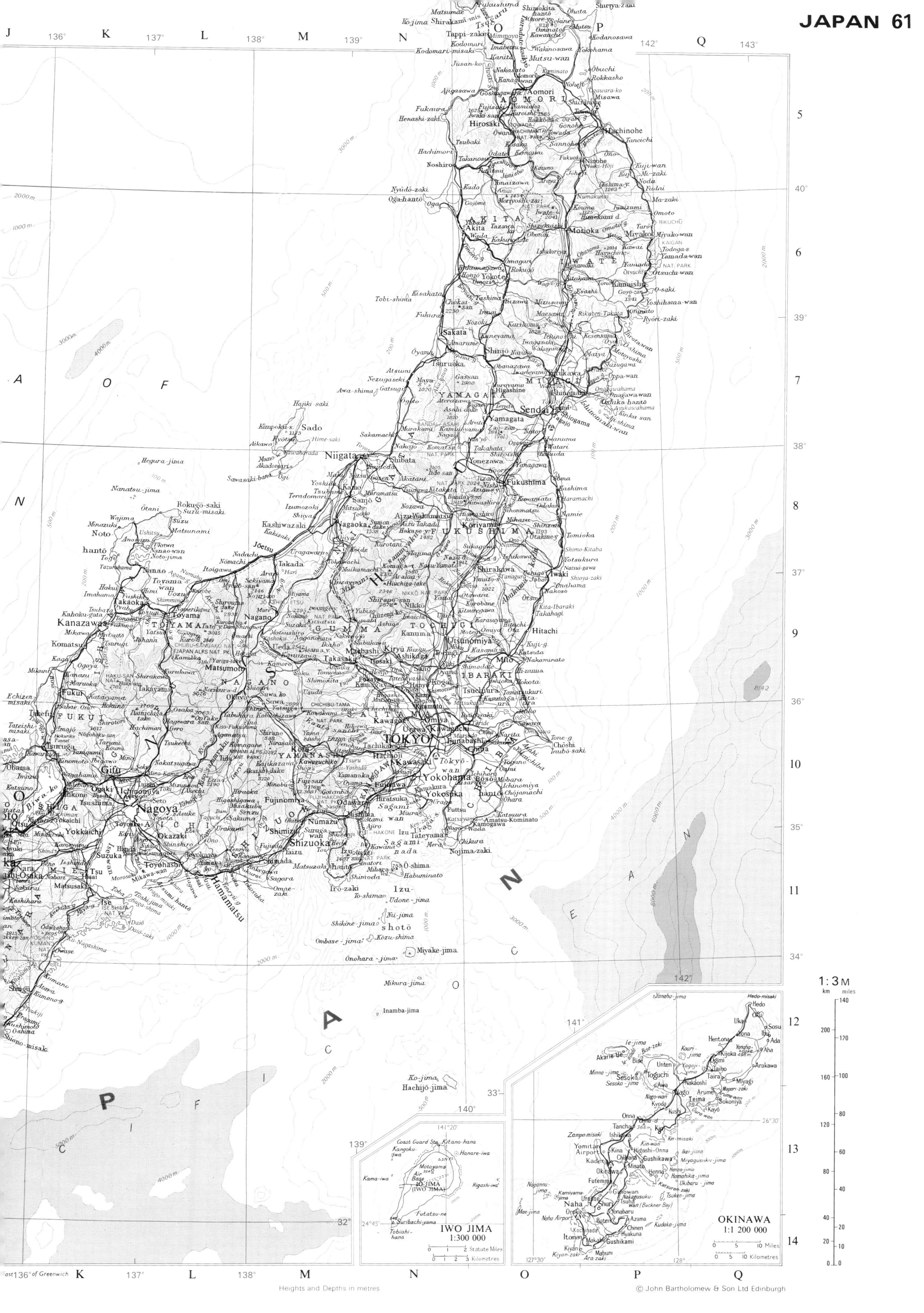

1 : 3 M

IWO JIMA
1:300 000

OKINAWA
1:1 200 000

Heights and Depths in metres

© John Bartholomew & Son Ltd Edinburgh

TOKYO

SAITAMA-KEN
TŌKYŌ-TO
CHIBA-KEN
KANAGAWA-KEN
TŌKYŌ-WAN
TŌKYŌ
YOKOHAMA
Kawasaki
Chiba
Funabashi
Ichikawa
Matsudo
Kawaguchi
Warabi
Sōka
Urawa
Shinjuku
Shibuya
Setagaya
Meguro
Shinagawa
Minato
Chūō
Chiyoda
Taitō
Sumida
Kōtō
Edogawa
Katsushika
Adachi
Arakawa
Kita
Itabashi
Nerima
Toshima
Nakano
Suginami
Musashino
Mitaka
Chōfu
Fuchū
Koganei
Kokubunji
Tachikawa
Akishima
Hino
Hachiōji
Machida
Sagamihara
Yamato
Zama
Atsugi
Ebina
Tokorozawa
Iruma
Kiyose
Higashi-Murayama
Musashi-Murayama
Tanashi
Kodaira
Kunitachi
Komae
Tama
Asaka
Shiki
Niiza
Toda
Hatogaya
Yashio
Misato
Urayasu
Narashino
Yachiyo
Kamagaya
Ichihara
Nishi
Naka
Totsuka
Hodogaya
Isogo
TOKYO INTERNATIONAL AIRPORT HANEDA
Road Tunnel under const.
A B C D
1 2 3
139°30′ 139°45′ 140°00′
35° 45′
35° 30′

OSAKA

HYŌGO-KEN
ŌSAKA-FU
KYŌTO-FU
NARA-KEN
SHIGA-KEN
ŌSAKA-WAN
ŌSAKA
KŌBE
KYŌTO
Sakai
Nishinomiya
Amagasaki
Ashiya
Itami
Toyonaka
Ikeda
Kawanishi
Takarazuka
Suita
Settsu
Ibaraki
Takatsuki
Hirakata
Neyagawa
Moriguchi
Kadoma
Daitō
Higashi-Ōsaka
Yao
Kashiwara
Fujiidera
Matsubara
Habikino
Katano
Shijōnawate
Uji
Jōyō
Nagaoka
Mukō
Yawata
Kizu
Nara
Yamato-Kōriyama
Ikaruga
Sanda
Arima
Nagata
Suma
Hyōgo
OSAKA INTERNATIONAL AIRPORT
See Inset
A B C D
4 5
135°15′ 135°30′ 135°45′
34° 45′

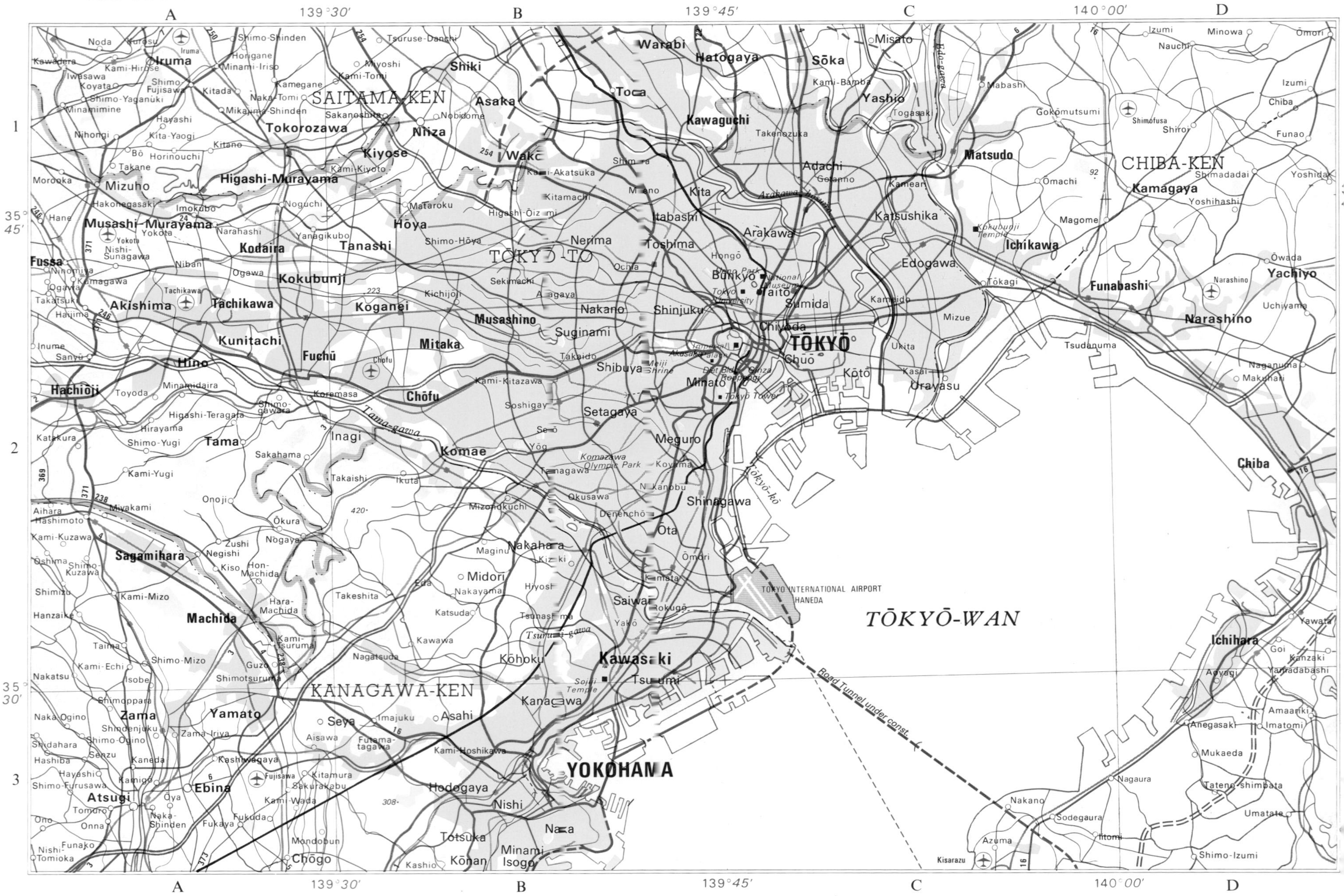

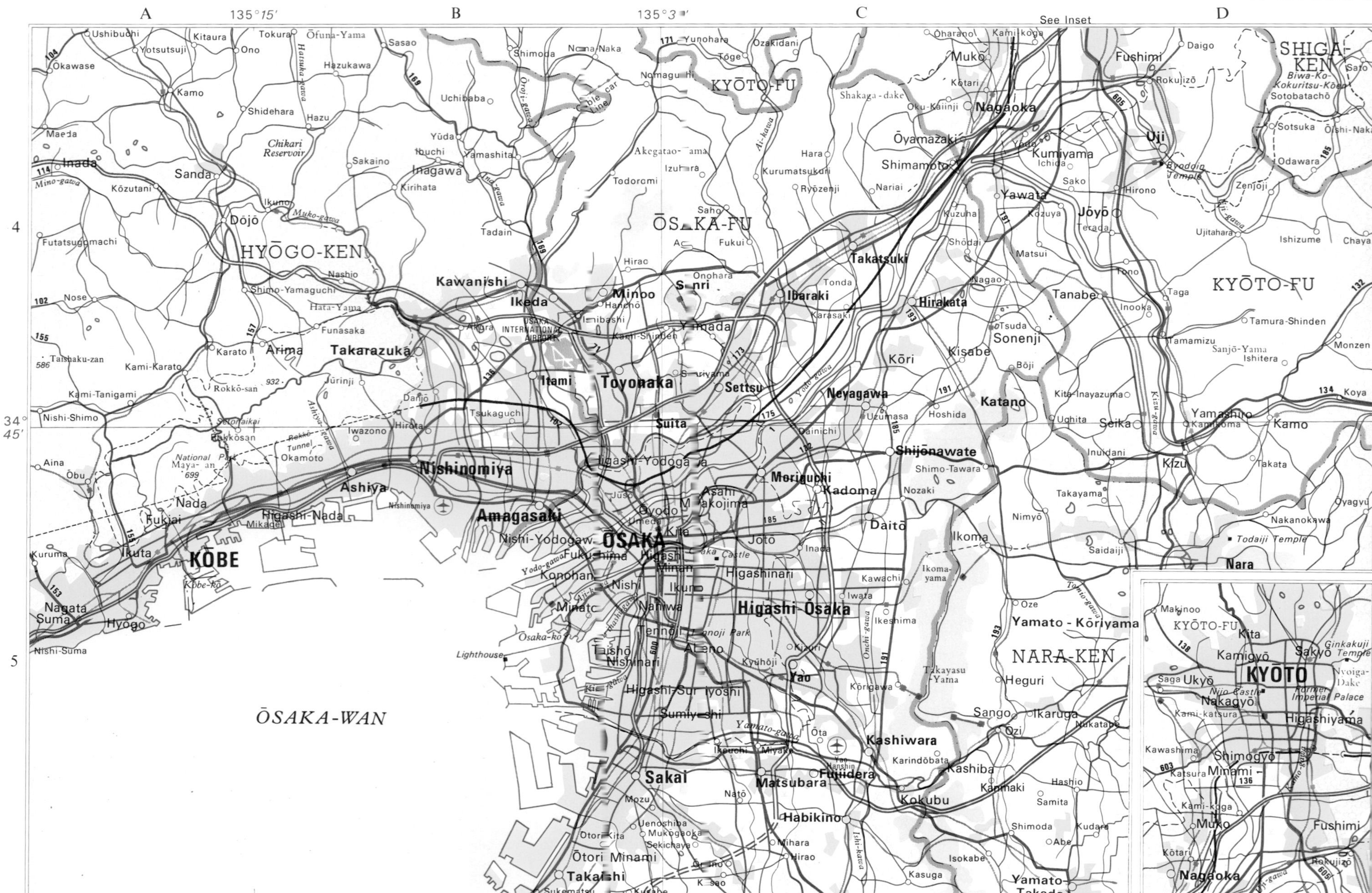

1:300 000

0 5 10 15 km
0 5 10 miles

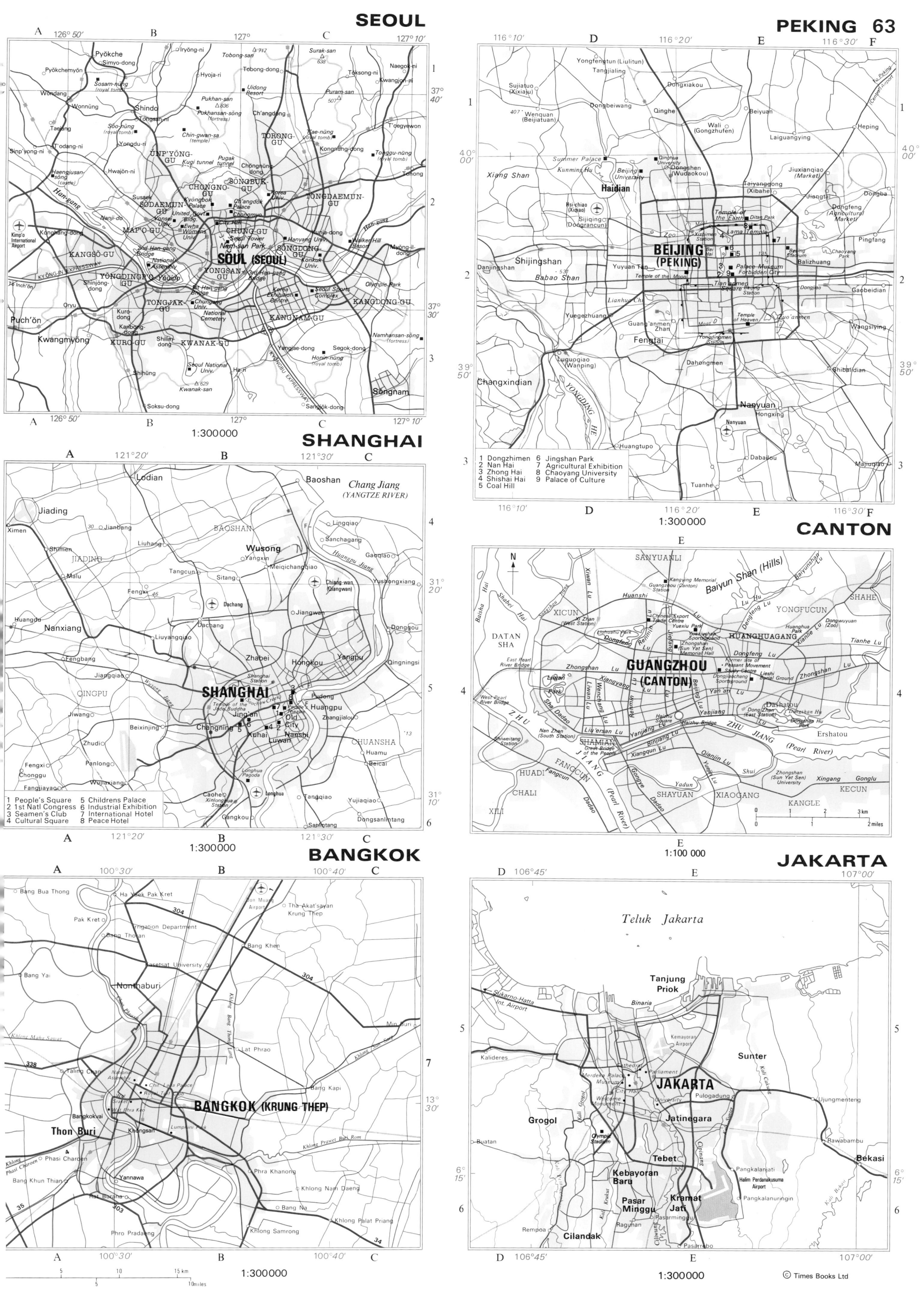

SEOUL

1:300000

PEKING 63

1 Dongzhimen
2 Nan Hai
3 Zhong Hai
4 Shishai Hai
5 Coal Hill
6 Jingshan Park
7 Agricultural Exhibition
8 Chaoyang University
9 Palace of Culture

1:300000

SHANGHAI

1 People's Square
2 1st Nat'l Congress
3 Seamen's Club
4 Cultural Square
5 Childrens Palace
6 Industrial Exhibition
7 International Hotel
8 Peace Hotel

1:300000

CANTON

1:100 000

BANGKOK

1:300000

JAKARTA

1:300000

© Times Books Ltd

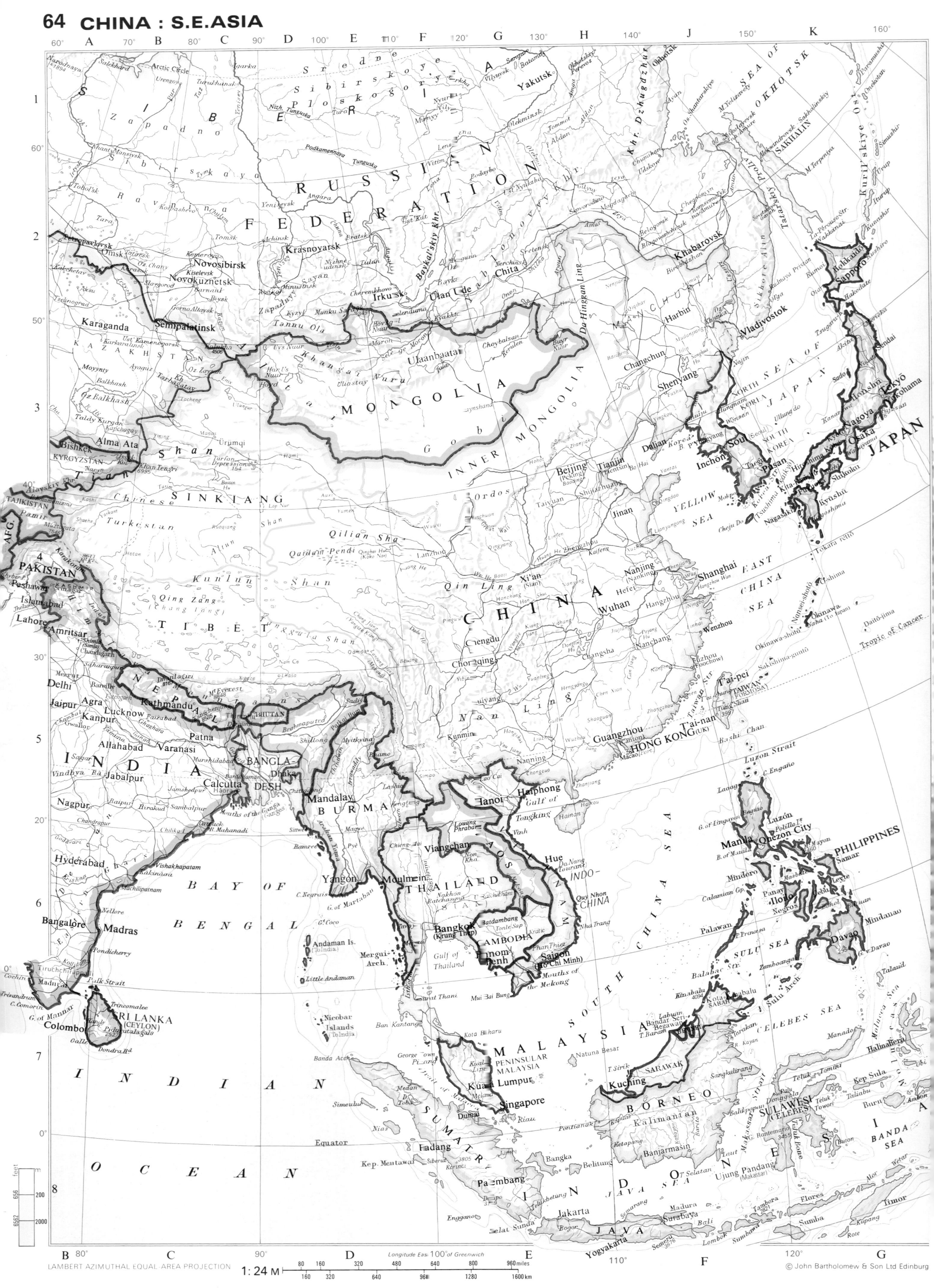

© John Bartholomew & Son Ltd Edinburgh

RUSSIAN FEDERATION
MONGOLIA
CHINA
SINKIANG
TIBET
INNER MONGOLIA
MANCHURIA
KAZAKHSTAN
KYRGYZSTAN
TAJIKISTAN
AFG.
PAKISTAN
KASHMIR
INDIA
NEPAL
BHUTAN
BANGLA-DESH
BURMA
THAILAND
LAOS
CAMBODIA
VIETNAM
MALAYSIA
PENINSULAR MALAYSIA
SINGAPORE
INDONESIA
PHILIPPINES
NORTH KOREA
SOUTH KOREA
JAPAN
TAIWAN (FORMOSA)
HONG KONG (UK)
SRI LANKA (CEYLON)
SEA OF OKHOTSK
SEA OF JAPAN
YELLOW SEA
EAST CHINA SEA
SOUTH CHINA SEA
BAY OF BENGAL
INDIAN OCEAN
CELEBES SEA
SULU SEA
JAVA SEA
BANDA SEA
Gulf of Tongking
Gulf of Thailand
Luzon Strait
Tropic of Cancer
Equator
Arctic Circle
BORNEO
SUMATRA
JAVA
SULAWESI (CELEBES)
SAKHALIN
Hokkaido
Honshu
Kyushu
Shikoku
Novosibirsk
Krasnoyarsk
Omsk
Irkutsk
Chita
Khabarovsk
Vladivostok
Yakutsk
Ulaanbaatar
Harbin
Changchun
Shenyang
Beijing (Peking)
Tianjin
Dalian
Jinan
Nanjing (Nanking)
Shanghai
Wuhan
Chengdu
Chongqing
Xi'an (Sian)
Lanzhou
Guangzhou (Canton)
Ürümqi
Hong Kong
Macao
Tokyo
Yokohama
Osaka
Nagoya
Sendai
Sapporo
Seoul
Pusan
Inchon
P'yongyang
T'ai-pei
T'ai-nan
Manila
Quezon City
Davao
Hanoi
Haiphong
Saigon (Ho Chi Minh)
Phnom Penh
Bangkok (Krung Thep)
Viangchan
Yangon
Mandalay
Dhaka
Calcutta
Delhi
Kathmandu
Lahore
Islamabad
Peshawar
Amritsar
Bishkek
Alma Ata
Karaganda
Semipalatinsk
Hyderabad
Madras
Bangalore
Colombo
Kuala Lumpur
Jakarta
Surabaya
Palembang
Padang
Medan
Kuching
Ujung Pandang (Makassar)
Banjarmasin
LAMBERT AZIMUTHAL EQUAL AREA PROJECTION
1:24 M
Longitude East 100° of Greenwich

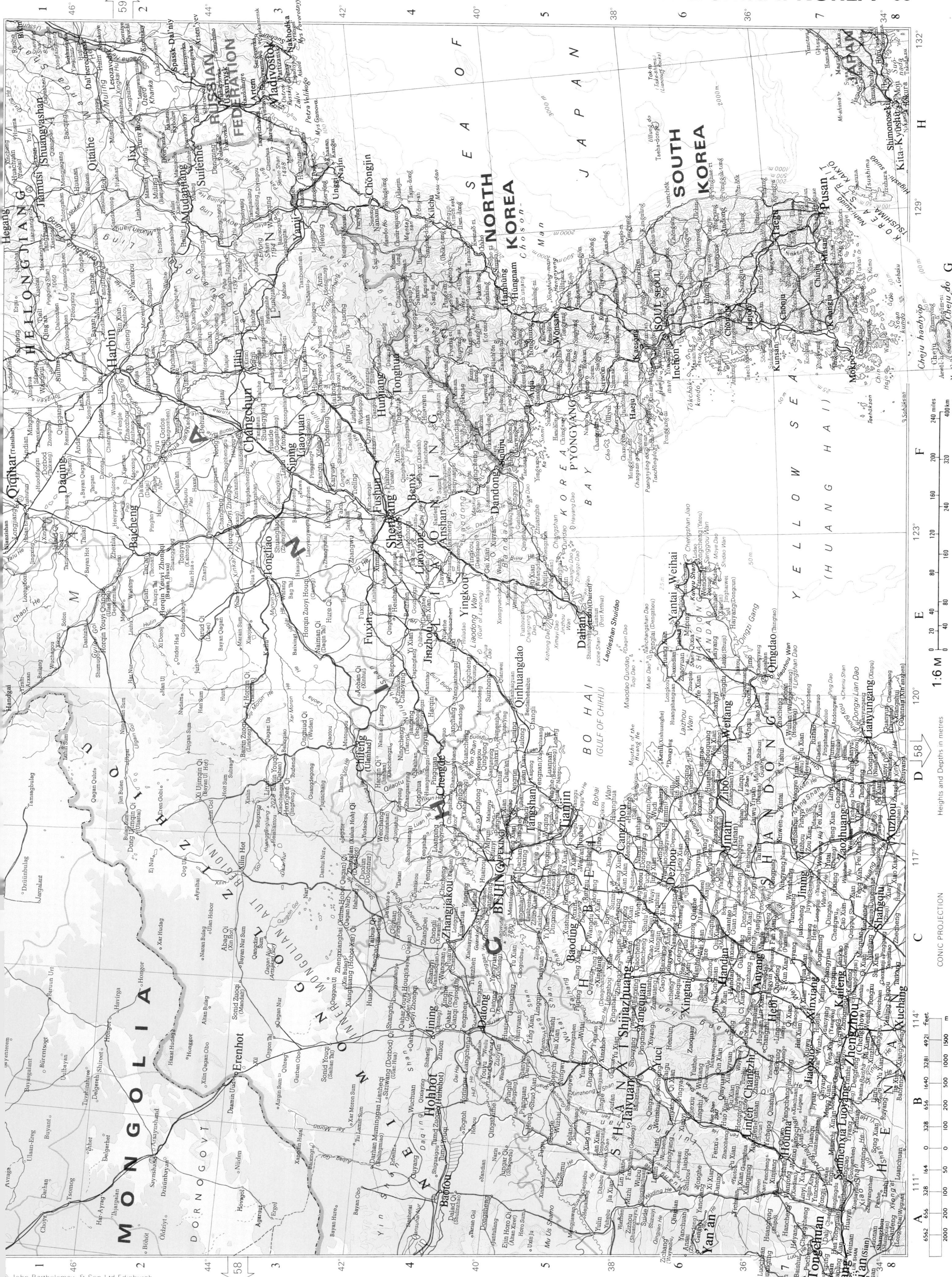

MONGOLIA

RUSSIAN FEDERATION

HEILONGJIANG

JILIN

LIAONING

NEI MONGOL (INNER MONGOLIA) AUT. REGION

SHANXI

HEBEI

SHANDONG

NORTH KOREA

SOUTH KOREA

JAPAN

SEA OF JAPAN

YELLOW SEA (HUANG HAI)

BO HAI (GULF OF CHIHLI)

KOREA BAY

KOREA STRAIT

Harbin
Changchun
Jilin
Siping
Liaoyuan
Tongliao
Shenyang
Fushun
Benxi
Anshan
Dandong
Jinzhou
Fuxin
Chaoyang
Chifeng (Ulanhad)
Chengde
Beijing
Tianjin
Tangshan
Baoding
Shijiazhuang
Taiyuan
Yangquan
Handan
Anyang
Xinxiang
Zhengzhou
Kaifeng
Jinan
Zibo
Weifang
Qingdao
Yantai
Weihai
Dalian (Dairen)
Yingkou
Qinhuangdao
Datong
Hohhot (Huhehot)
Jining
Baotou
Qiqihar
Daqing
Baicheng
Lianyungang
Xuzhou

PYONGYANG
Hamhung
Hungnam
Wonsan
Haeju
SEOUL (Soul)
Inchon
Taejon
Taegu
Pusan
Kwangju
Mokpo
Cheju

Vladivostok
Ussuriysk
Nakhodka

1:6 M

CONIC PROJECTION

Heights and Depths in metres

© John Bartholomew & Son Ltd Edinburgh
© Times Books Ltd

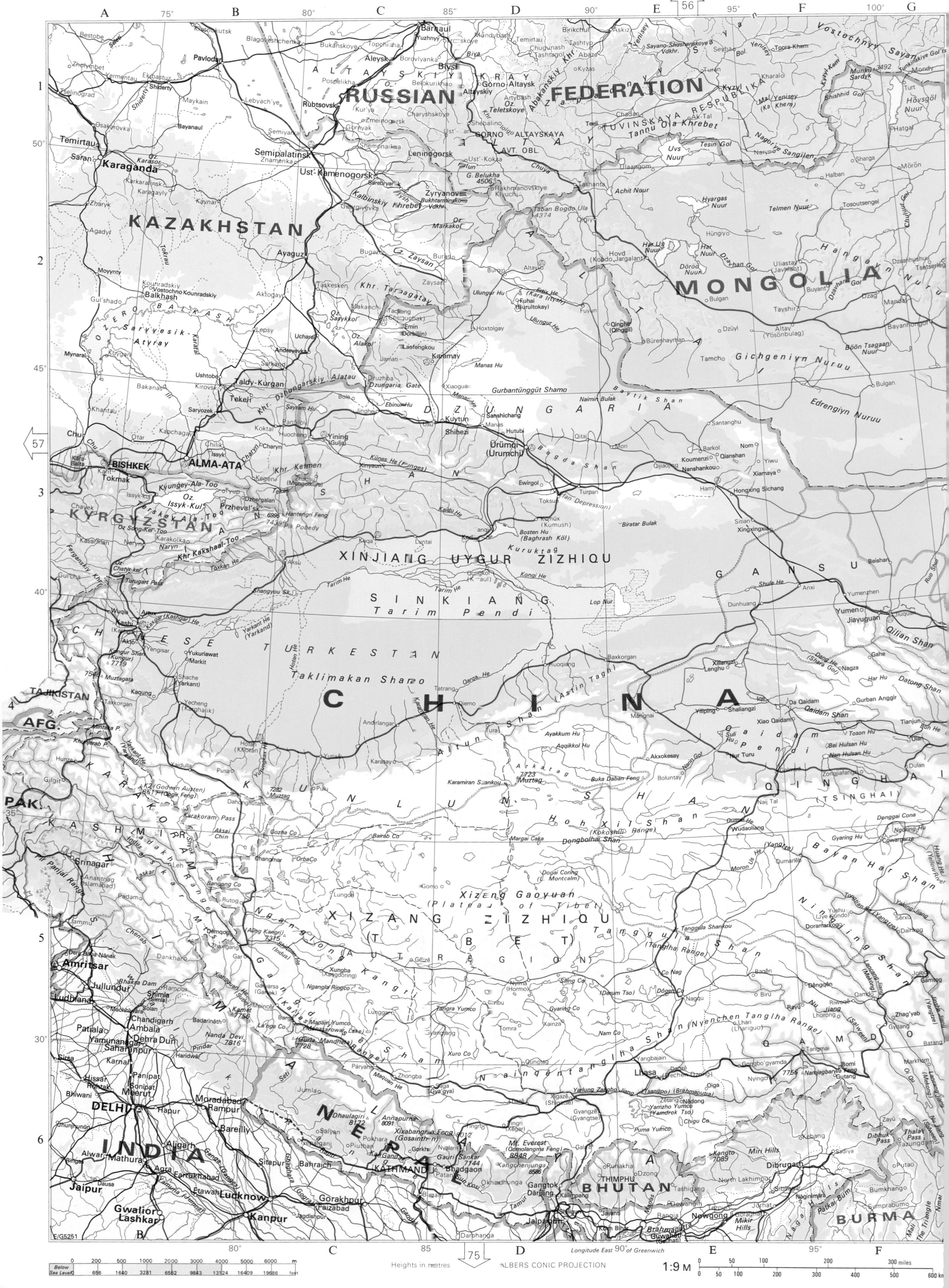
A
B
C
D
E
F
G
75°
80°
85°
90°
95°
100°
56
57
75
RUSSIAN FEDERATION
KAZAKHSTAN
MONGOLIA
KYRGYZSTAN
TAJIKISTAN
AFG.
PAK.
INDIA
NEPAL
BHUTAN
BURMA
CHINA
XINJIANG UYGUR ZIZHIQU
SINKIANG
Tarim Pendi
TURKESTAN
Taklimakan Shamo
DZUNGARIA
Gurbantünggüt Shamo
TIAN SHAN
KUNLUN SHAN
KARAKORAM
KASHMIR
XIZANG ZIZHIQU
(TIBET AUTONOMOUS REGION)
Xizang Gaoyuan
(Plateau of Tibet)
QINGHAI
(TSINGHAI)
GANSU
QAMDO
Qaidam Pendi
Hoh Xil Shan
Tanggula Shan
(Tanglha Range)
Nyainqentanglha Shan
Gangdisê Shan
ALTAYSKIY KRAY
GORNO ALTAYSKAYA AVT. OBL.
TUVINSKAYA RESPUBLIKA
Tannu Ola Khrebet
Barnaul
Biysk
Rubtsovsk
Semipalatinsk
Ust'-Kamenogorsk
Leninogorsk
Pavlodar
Karaganda
Temirtau
Balkhash
Ozero Balkhash
Ayaguz
Taldy-Kurgan
Alma-Ata
Bishkek
Tokmak
Oz. Issyk-Kul'
Przheval'sk
Pik Pobedy 7439
Khan Tengri Feng 6995
Ürümqi (Urumchi)
Turpan
Turpan Depression
Hami
Karamay
Yining (Gulja)
Shihezi
Korla
Bosten Hu
Aksu
Kuqa
Kashi (Kashgar)
Shache (Yarkant)
Yecheng (Karghalik)
Hotan (Khotan)
Qiemo
Ruoqiang
Lop Nur
Dunhuang
Yumen
Jiayuguan
Qilian Shan
Golmud
Muztagata 7546
Kongur Shan (Kungur) 7719
K2 (Godwin Austen) 8611
Muztag 7723
Srinagar
Jammu
Leh
Amritsar
Jullundur
Ludhiana
Shimla
Chandigarh
Ambala
Patiala
Dehra Dun
Saharanpur
Meerut
Delhi
Moradabad
Bareilly
Aligarh
Agra
Mathura
Jaipur
Gwalior Lashkar
Kanpur
Lucknow
Gorakhpur
Kathmandu
Mt. Everest (Qomolangma Feng) 8848
Kangchenjunga 8586
Dhaulagiri 8172
Annapurna 8091
Nanda Devi 7816
Kamet 7756
Gurla Mandhata 7728
Lhasa
Xigazê (Shigatse)
Gyangzê (Gyangtse)
Yarlung Zangbo Jiang (Tsangpo) (Brahmaputra)
Namjagbarwa Feng 7756
Thimphu
Gangtok
Darjiling
Dibrugarh
Jiayuguan
Hovd
Uliastay
Altay
Hangayn Nuruu
Uvs Nuur
Hyargas Nuur
Heights in metres
ALBERS CONIC PROJECTION
Longitude East 90° of Greenwich
1:9 M
300 miles
600 km
E/G5251

HONG KONG
1:300,000

SOUTH CHINA SEA

TAIWAN
(FORMOSA)

ANHUI

ZHEJIANG

Shanghai

Hangzhou

FUJIAN

JIANGXI

HUBEI

HUNAN

GUANGDONG

Guangzhou

MACAO

HONG KONG (U.K.)

GUIZHOU

GUANGXI

Nanning

HAINAN

Haikou

SICHUAN

Chengdu

Chongqing

YUNNAN

Kunming

VIETNAM

HANOI

LAOS

GULF OF TONGKING

Heights and Depths in metres

CONIC PROJECTION

1:6M

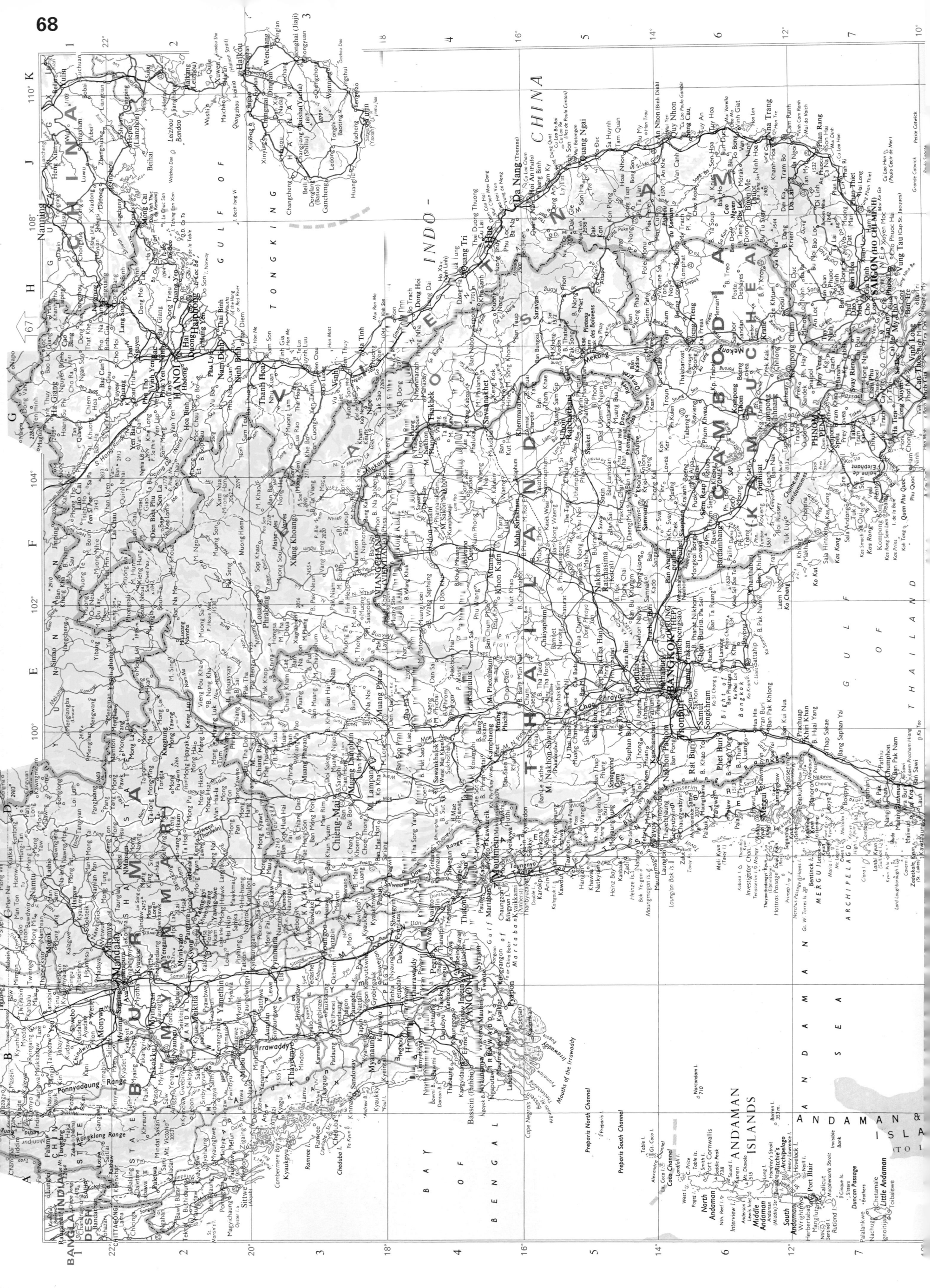
CHINA
INDO-CHINA
GULF OF TONGKING
HAINAN
THAILAND
ANDAMAN ISLANDS
ANDAMAN SEA
BAY OF BENGAL
GULF OF THAILAND
HANOI
Haiphong
Nanning
Haikou
Da Nang
Hue
SAIGON (HO CHI MINH)
Vung Tau
BANGKOK (KRUNG THEP)
Thonburi
Chieng Mai
Vientiane
Luang Phrabang
Mandalay
RANGOON
Moulmein
Bassein
Pegu
Port Blair
Mergui
Mergui Archipelago
North Andaman
Middle Andaman
South Andaman
Little Andaman
Mouths of the Irrawaddy
Gulf of Martaban
Mekong
Tonle Sap
Plateau des Bolovens
Bight of Bangkok
Phnom Penh
Chittagong
Sittwe (Akyab)
Ramree I.
Cheduba I.
Preparis North Channel
Preparis South Channel
Coco Channel
Ten Degree Channel
67

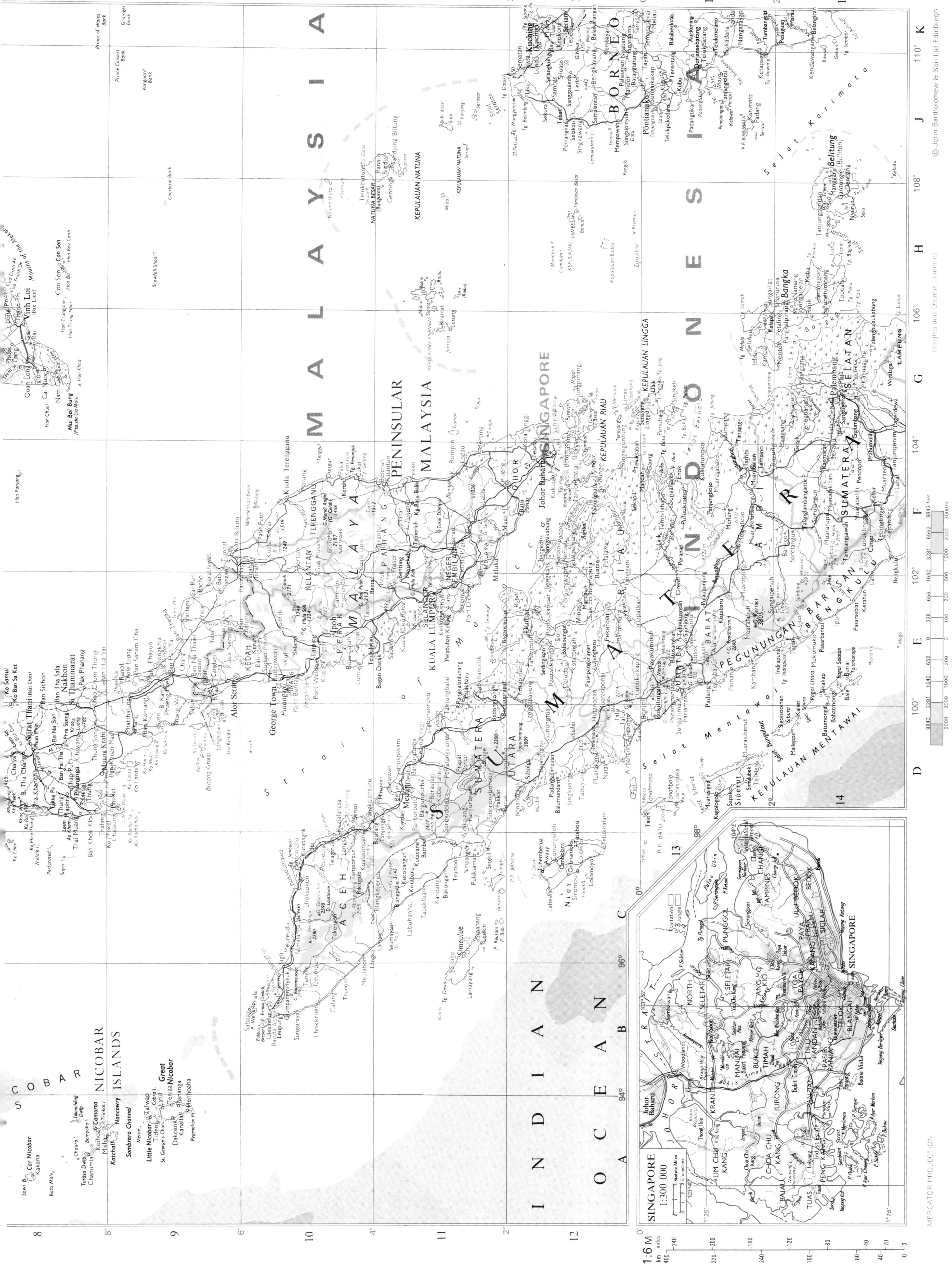

© John Bartholomew & Son Ltd Edinburgh

MERCATOR PROJECTION

1:6 M

SINGAPORE
1:300 000

Heights and Depths in metres

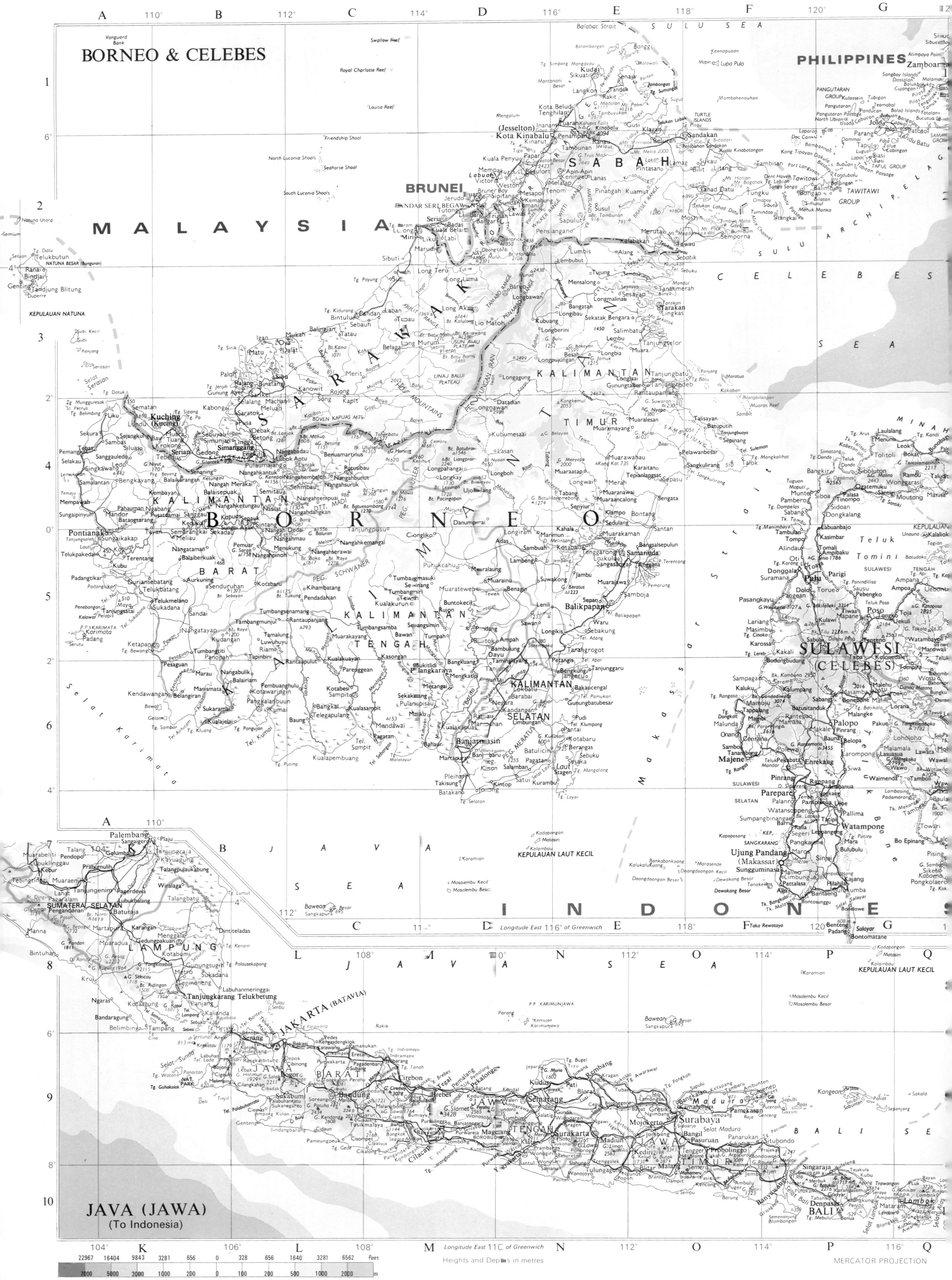

BORNEO & CELEBES

PHILIPPINES

MALAYSIA

BRUNEI

SULU SEA

SABAH

Kota Kinabalu
(Jesselton)

Sandakan

SARAWAK

Kuching (Kuching)

Simanggang

BORNEO

KALIMANTAN
BARAT

Pontianak

KALIMANTAN
TENGAH

KALIMANTAN
TIMUR

Samarinda

Balikpapan

KALIMANTAN
SELATAN

Banjarmasin

CELEBES SEA

SULAWESI
(CELEBES)

SULAWESI
TENGAH

Palu

Poso

SULAWESI
SELATAN

Parepare

Ujung Pandang
(Makassar)

Teluk
Tomini

JAVA SEA

KEPULAUAN LAUT KECIL

KEPULAUAN NATUNA

SUMATERA
SELATAN

Palembang

LAMPUNG

JAKARTA (BATAVIA)

JAWA
BARAT

Bandung

Bogor

JAWA
TENGAH

Semarang

Surakarta

JAWA
TIMUR

Surabaya

Madura

BALI

Denpasar

JAVA (JAWA)
(To Indonesia)

INDONESIA

Longitude East 116° of Greenwich

Longitude East 110° of Greenwich

Heights and Depths in metres

MERCATOR PROJECTION

Feet
22967 16404 9843 3281 656 0 328 656 1640 3281 6562
7000 5000 3000 1000 200 0 100 200 500 1000 2000

NORTH MOLUCCAS
(To Indonesia)

HALMAHERA
(JAILOLO GILOLO)

Halmahera Sea

KEPULAUAN OBI

LUZON

PHILIPPINES

MANILA

MINDORO

PANAY

NEGROS

SAMAR

CEBU

BOHOL

PALAWAN

Puerto Princesa

SULU SEA

MINDANAO

Moro Gulf

Davao

Zamboanga

SABAH

SULU ARCHIPELAGO

Longitude East 124° of Greenwich

SA PENINSULA

Manado

SULAWESI TENGGARA

BUTON

KEPULAUAN BANGGAI

KEPULAUAN SULA

TUKANGBESI

Equator

FLORES SEA

KEPULAUAN SABALANA

NUSA TENGGARA BARAT

SUMBAWA

KEPULAUAN BARAT DAYA

WETAR

TIMOR TIMUR

ALOR

KEPULAUAN LETI

KEPULAUAN SERMATA

BABAR

FLORES

KOMODO

SUMBA

NUSA TENGGARA TIMUR

SAWU SEA

TIMOR

TIMOR SEA

LESSER SUNDA IS.
(To Indonesia)

John Bartholomew & Son Ltd

Longitude East 126° of Greenwich

Equatorial Scale 1:6 M

0 40 80 120 160 200 240 280 miles
0 80 160 240 320 400 km

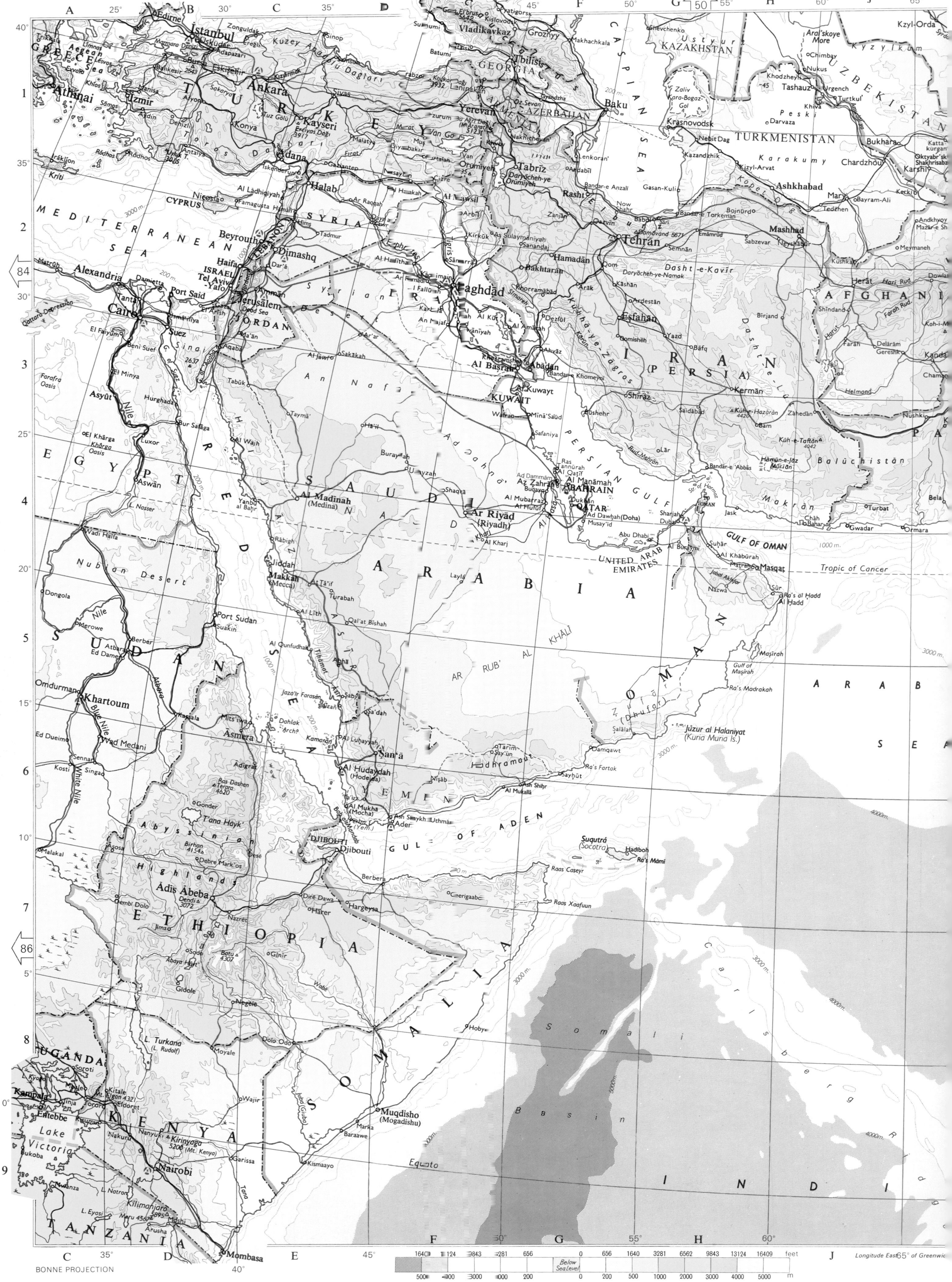

MEDITERRANEAN SEA
TURKEY
İstanbul
Ankara
İzmir
Adana
Konya
Kayseri
Athinai
GREECE
Kriti
Ródhos
CYPRUS
Nicosia
SYRIA
Halab
Dimashq
Beyrouth
LEBANON
ISRAEL
Haifa
Tel Aviv-Yafo
Jerusalem
JORDAN
'Amman
Alexandria
Port Said
Cairo
Suez
EGYPT
Asyût
Luxor
Aswân
L. Nasser
Wadi Halfa
Nubian Desert
Port Sudan
SUDAN
Khartoum
Omdurman
Kassala
Wad Medani
Blue Nile
White Nile
Nile
Asmera
Red Sea
GEORGIA
Tbilisi
ARMENIA
Yerevan
AZERBAIJAN
Baku
CASPIAN SEA
KAZAKHSTAN
UZBEKISTAN
TURKMENISTAN
Ashkhabad
Krasnovodsk
Bukhara
Mashhad
Tehrān
Tabrīz
IRAN (PERSIA)
Esfahān
Shīrāz
Kermān
AFGHANISTAN
Herāt
IRAQ
Baghdād
Al Basrah
Ābādān
KUWAIT
Al Kuwayt
PERSIAN GULF
BAHRAIN
Al Manāmah
QATAR
Ad Dawhah (Doha)
UNITED ARAB EMIRATES
Abu Dhabi
Dubai
GULF OF OMAN
Masqat
OMAN
Tropic of Cancer
SAUDI ARABIA
Ar Riyāḑ (Riyadh)
Al Madīnah (Medina)
Makkah (Mecca)
Jiddah
An Nafūd
AR RUB' AL KHĀLĪ
YEMEN
Şan'ā'
Al Ḩudaydah (Hodeida)
'Adan
GULF OF ADEN
DJIBOUTI
Djibouti
Suqutrā (Socotra)
ETHIOPIA
Ādīs Ābeba
Abyssinian Highlands
T'ana Hāyk'
SOMALIA
Muqdisho (Mogadishu)
Kismaayo
KENYA
Nairobi
Mombasa
UGANDA
Kampala
Lake Victoria
TANZANIA
Kilimanjaro 5895
L. Turkana (L. Rudolf)
ARABIAN SEA
Somali Basin
Carlsberg Ridge
INDIAN OCEAN
Equator
BONNE PROJECTION
Longitude East 65° of Greenwich

KAZAKHSTAN
Moynkum
Dzhambul
Alma-Ata
Bishkek
KYRGYZSTAN
Tashkent
TAJIKISTAN
Dushanbe
Samarkand
Kabul
Peshawar
Islamabad
KASHMIR
Srinagar
Rawalpindi
Lahore
Amritsar
PAKISTAN
Multan
Delhi
Meerut
Bikaner
Jaipur
Agra
Lucknow
Kanpur
Varanasi
Allahabad
Patna
Jodhpur
Ajmer
Kota
Udaipur
Ahmadabad
Vadodara
Indore
Jabalpur
Bhopal
Nagpur
INDIA
Surat
Bombay
Pune
Hyderabad
Bangalore
Madras
Mysore
Calicut
Cochin
Trivandrum
Madurai
Colombo
Kandy
SRI LANKA (CEYLON)

SINKIANG (XINJIANG)
Taklimakan Shamo
Kashi (Kashgar)
Hotan
TIBET (XIZANG)
Qing Zang (Chang Tang)
Lhasa
Mt. Everest 8848
Kathmandu
NEPAL
BHUTAN
HIMALAYA
Darjeeling
Shillong
BANGLADESH
Dhaka
Calcutta
BURMA
Mandalay
Yangon
Moulmein
THAILAND
Bangkok (Krung Thep)
CAMBODIA
VIETNAM
Hanoi
Chengdu
Chongqing (Chungking)
CHINA
Kunming
Xi'an (Sian)
Lanzhou
Urumqi

BAY OF BENGAL
ANDAMAN ISLANDS (To India)
North Andaman
Middle Andaman
South Andaman
Port Blair
Little Andaman
NICOBAR ISLANDS (To India)
Car Nicobar
Little Nicobar
Great Nicobar

LACCADIVE ISLANDS (To India)
Amindivi
Minicoy I.
MALDIVES
Male

INDIAN OCEAN
GULF OF THAILAND

PEN. MALAYSIA
Kuala Lumpur
George Town
Medan

1:15 M

Heights and Depths in metres

© John Bartholomew & Son Ltd Edinburgh

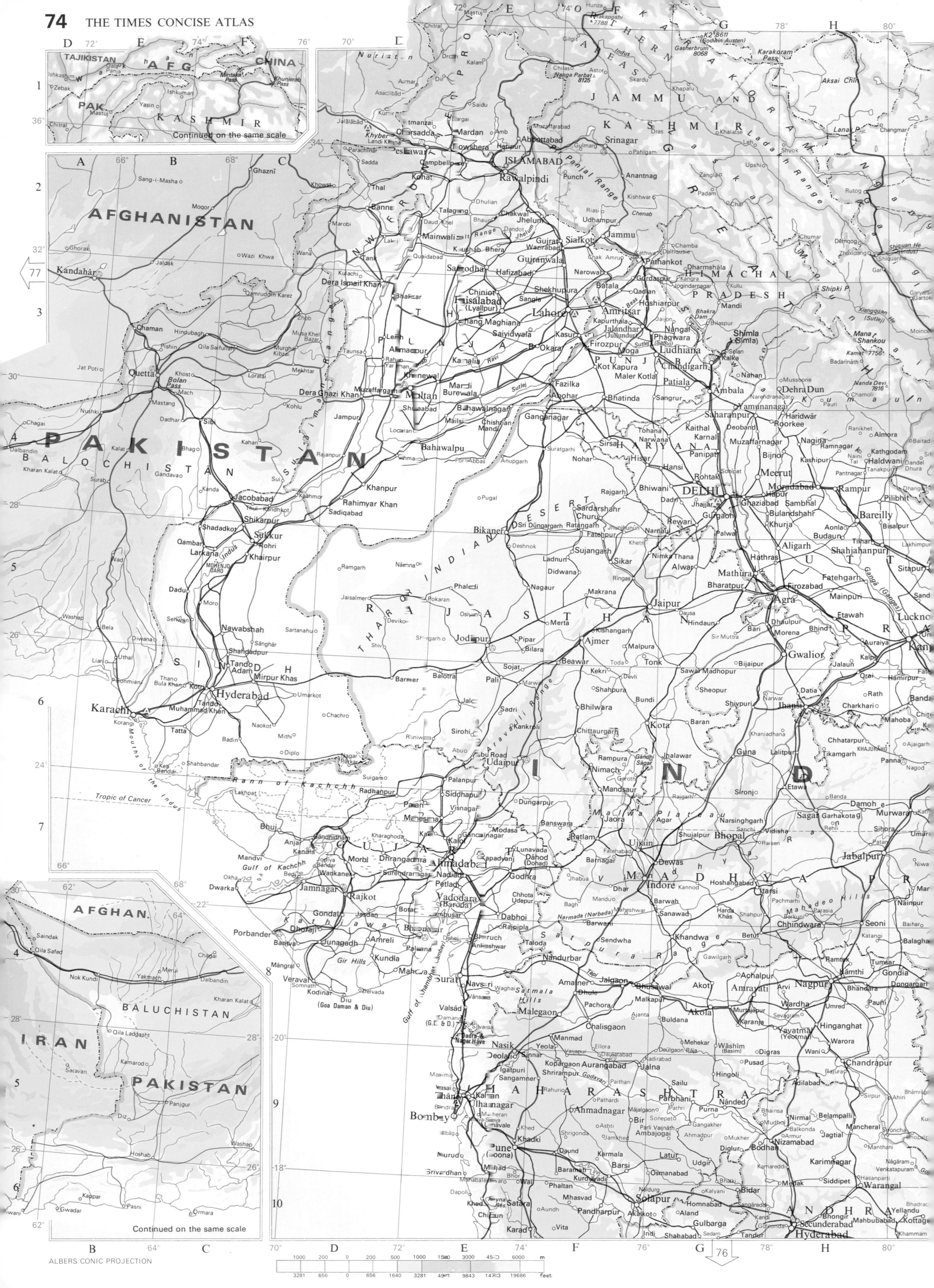
TAJIKISTAN
AFG
CHINA
PAK
KASHMIR
Continued on the same scale
AFGHANISTAN
PAKISTAN
BALOCHISTAN
SIND
PUNJAB
JAMMU AND KASHMIR
HIMACHAL PRADESH
HARYANA
RAJASTHAN
GUJARAT
MADHYA PRADESH
MAHARASHTRA
ANDHRA
UTTAR PRADESH
INDIA
THAR OR INDIAN DESERT
KARAKORAM
Kumaun Himalaya
Satpura Range
Aravalli Range
Malwa Plateau
Rann of Kachchh
Gulf of Kachchh
Gulf of Khambhat
Tropic of Cancer
Mouths of the Indus
ISLAMABAD
Rawalpindi
Peshawar
Kabul
Srinagar
Jammu
Lahore
Amritsar
Faisalabad (Lyallpur)
Multan
Quetta
Kandahār
Chaman
Sukkur
Hyderabad
Karachi
Jacobabad
Bahawalpur
Ludhiana
Chandigarh
Shimla (Simla)
DELHI
Meerut
Agra
Gwalior
Jaipur
Ajmer
Jodhpur
Bikaner
Udaipur
Kota
Ahmadabad
Vadodara (Baroda)
Rajkot
Jamnagar
Bhavnagar
Surat
Bombay
Pune (Poona)
Nasik
Aurangabad
Ahmadnagar
Solapur
Indore
Bhopal
Ujjain
Jabalpur
Nagpur
Amravati
Akola
Chandrapur
Nizamabad
Warangal
Secunderabad
Hyderabad
Bareilly
Moradabad
Aligarh
Mathura
Jhansi
Saharanpur
Dehra Dun
Ambala
Patiala
K2 8611 (Godwin Austen)
Nanga Parbat 8125
Rakaposhi 7788
Nanda Devi 7816
Kamet 7756
Khyber Pass
Bolan Pass
Karakoram Pass
AFGHAN.
BALUCHISTAN
IRAN
PAKISTAN
Continued on the same scale
Diu (Goa Daman & Diu)
Dadra & Nagar Have
ALBERS CONIC PROJECTION
1000 200 0 200 500 1000 1500 3000 4500 6000 m
3281 656 0 656 1640 3281 4921 9843 14763 19686 feet
77
76

Heights and Depths in metres

1:6 M

longitude East 82 of Greenwich

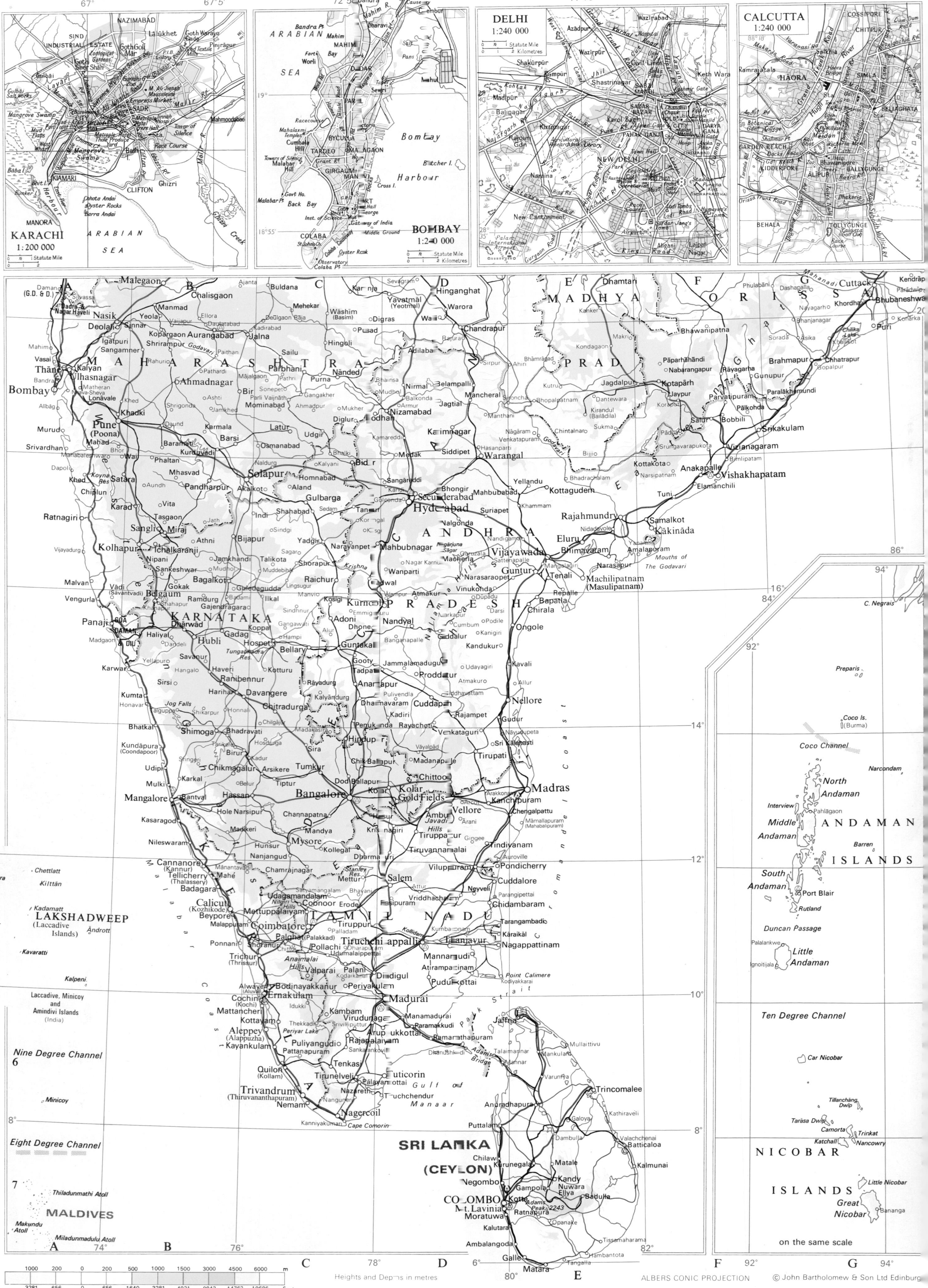

Inset maps

KARACHI 1:200 000

BOMBAY 1:240 000

DELHI 1:240 000
NEW DELHI

CALCUTTA 1:240 000
HAORA

ARABIAN SEA

1:6 M
miles km
200 — 320
160 — 240
120 — 160
80 — 80
40 — 40
0 — 0

Main map

MAHARASHTRA

MADHYA PRADESH

ORISSA

Bombay
Pune (Poona)
Nasik
Malegaon
Ahmadnagar
Solapur
Satara
Kolhapur
Ratnagiri

Cuttack
Bhubaneshwar
Brahmapur
Chhatrapur
Puri

Hyderabad
Secunderabad
Warangal
Nizamabad
Karimnagar

ANDHRA PRADESH

Vijayawada
Guntur
Vishakhapatam
Vizianagaram
Srikakulam
Rajahmundry
Kakinada
Machilipatnam (Masulipatnam)
Eluru
Nellore
Ongole
Kurnool
Nandyal
Cuddapah
Tirupati
Anantapur

KARNATAKA

Bangalore
Mangalore
Mysore
Hubli
Dharwad
Belgaum
Bellary
Shimoga
Chitradurga
Tumkur
Bijapur
Gulbarga
Raichur
Panaji GOA

Madras
Vellore
Kanchipuram
Salem
Coimbatore
Tiruchchirappalli
Thanjavur
Madurai
Nagappattinam
Pondicherry
Cuddalore
Chidambaram
Tirunelveli
Tuticorin
Nagercoil
Cape Comorin

TAMIL NADU

Calicut (Kozhikode)
Cochin (Kochi)
Ernakulam
Alleppey (Alappuzha)
Quilon (Kollam)
Trivandrum (Thiruvananthapuram)
Trichur (Thrissur)
Kottayam

LAKSHADWEEP (Laccadive Islands)
Minicoy
Kavaratti
Andrott

Laccadive, Minicoy and Amindivi Islands (India)

Nine Degree Channel
Eight Degree Channel
Ten Degree Channel

MALDIVES
Thiladunmathi Atoll
Miladunmadulu Atoll
Makunudu Atoll

SRI LANKA (CEYLON)
COLOMBO
Mt. Lavinia
Kandy
Nuwara Eliya
Galle
Matara
Jaffna
Trincomalee
Batticaloa
Anuradhapura
Negombo
Ratnapura
Adam's Bridge

ANDAMAN ISLANDS
North Andaman
Middle Andaman
South Andaman
Port Blair
Little Andaman
Duncan Passage

NICOBAR ISLANDS
Car Nicobar
Little Nicobar
Great Nicobar

Arabian Sea
Bay of Bengal
Gulf of Mannar
Palk Strait

Heights and Depths in metres

1000 200 0 200 500 1000 2000 3000 4000 6000 m
3281 656 0 656 1640 3281 4921 9843 14763 19686 feet

ALBERS CONIC PROJECTION

© John Bartholomew & Son Ltd Edinburgh

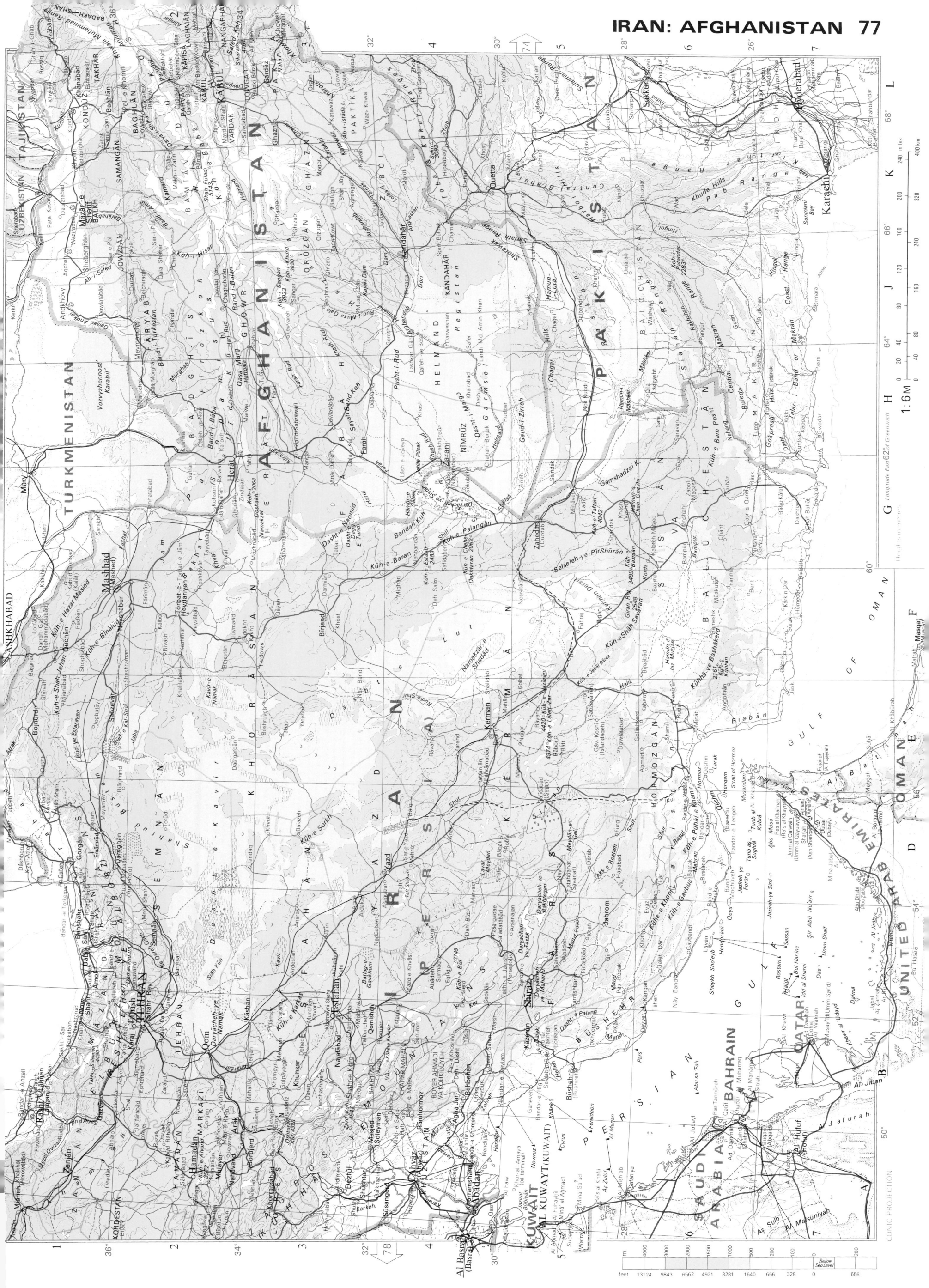
AFGHANISTAN
IRAN
PAKISTAN
TURKMENISTAN
UZBEKISTAN
TAJIKISTAN
KUWAIT
BAHRAIN
QATAR
SAUDI ARABIA
UNITED ARAB EMIRATES
OMAN
PERSIAN GULF
GULF OF OMAN
TEHRAN
Mashhad
Herat
Kandahar
Quetta
Karachi
Hyderabad
Sukkur
Kerman
Yazd
Esfahan
Shiraz
Zahedan
Bushehr
Masqat
Mary
ASHKHABAD
Dasht-e Lut
1:6M
CONIC PROJECTION

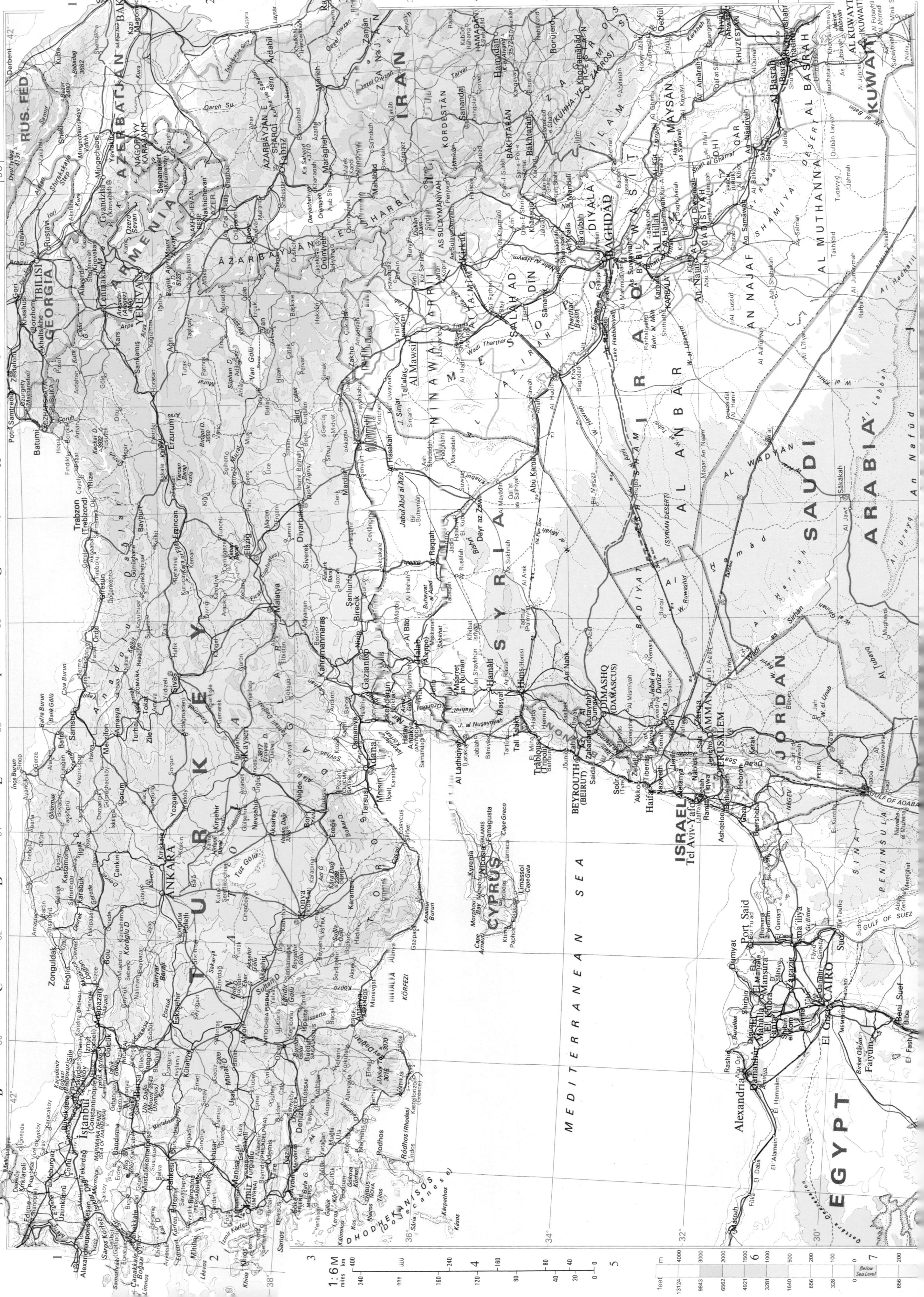
TURKEY
SYRIA
IRAQ
JORDAN
SAUDI ARABIA
EGYPT
ISRAEL
CYPRUS
IRAN
ARMENIA
AZERBAIJAN
GEORGIA
RUS. FED.
KUWAIT
MEDITERRANEAN SEA
ANKARA
İstanbul
İzmir
Adana
Konya
BAGHDĀD
DIMASHQ (DAMASCUS)
'AMMĀN
JERUSALEM
BEYROUTH (BEIRUT)
CAIRO
Alexandria
Port Said
Tel Aviv-Yafo
Halab (Aleppo)
Al Mawsil
TBILISI
YEREVAN
BAKI
Tabrīz
Nicosia
Limassol
1:6M
Below Sea Level

TURKEY

CYPRUS

MEDITERRANEAN SEA

LEBANON

SYRIA

ISRAEL

JORDAN

EGYPT

SAUDI ARABIA

SINAI

Antalya Körfezi

Gaziantep
Adana
Tarsus
Mersin
İskenderun
Halab (Aleppo)
Al Bāb
Hatay (Antakya) (Antioch)
Idlib
Al Ladhiqiyah (Latakia)
Jablah
Baniyās
Hamāh
Tartūs
Ḥims (Homs)
Tall Kalakh
Trâblous (Tripoli)
Batroun
Bcharré
Baalbek
Hermel
Jbail (Biblos)
Jounié
BEYROUTH (BEIRUT)
Zahlé
An Nabk
Yabrūd
Damour
Saida (Sidon)
Az Zabadāni
DIMASHQ (DAMASCUS, ESH SHEM, DAMAS)
Jayrūd
Soûr (Tyre)
Qunayṭirah
Nahariya
(Acre) Akko
Haifa
Tiberias
Zefat (Safad)
Darʿā
Nazareth
Aṣ Suwaydāʾ
Hadera
Jenin
Ajlūn
Irbid
Netanya
Tulkarm
Mafraq
Herzliyya
Nablus
Tel Aviv
Yafo
Petah Tiqwa
Salt
Zarqa
Ramallah
ʿAMMAN
Rishon le Ziyyon
Rehovot
Jericho
Ashdod
JERUSALEM (EL QUDS ESH SHERIF)
Mādaba
Ashqelon
Bethlehem
Gaza
Hebron
Khān Yūnis
Rafah
Beersheba
Karak
El ʿArish
Ṭafila
Port Said
Dumyât (Damietta)
El Manṣûra
Alexandria (El Iskandarîya)
Tanta
El Qantara
Ismaʿîliya
Maʿān
Zagazig
Benha
Suez
Port Taufîq
CAIRO (EL QÂHIRA)
El Gîza
Helwan
Beni Suef
El Fayûm
Aqaba

Gebel Katherîna

MEDITERRANEAN

CEASE FIRE LINES 1974

Badiet esh Sham

(Syrian Desert)

Heights and Depths in metres
© John Bartholomew & Son Ltd Edinburgh

CONIC PROJECTION

1:3 M

Longitude East of Greenwich

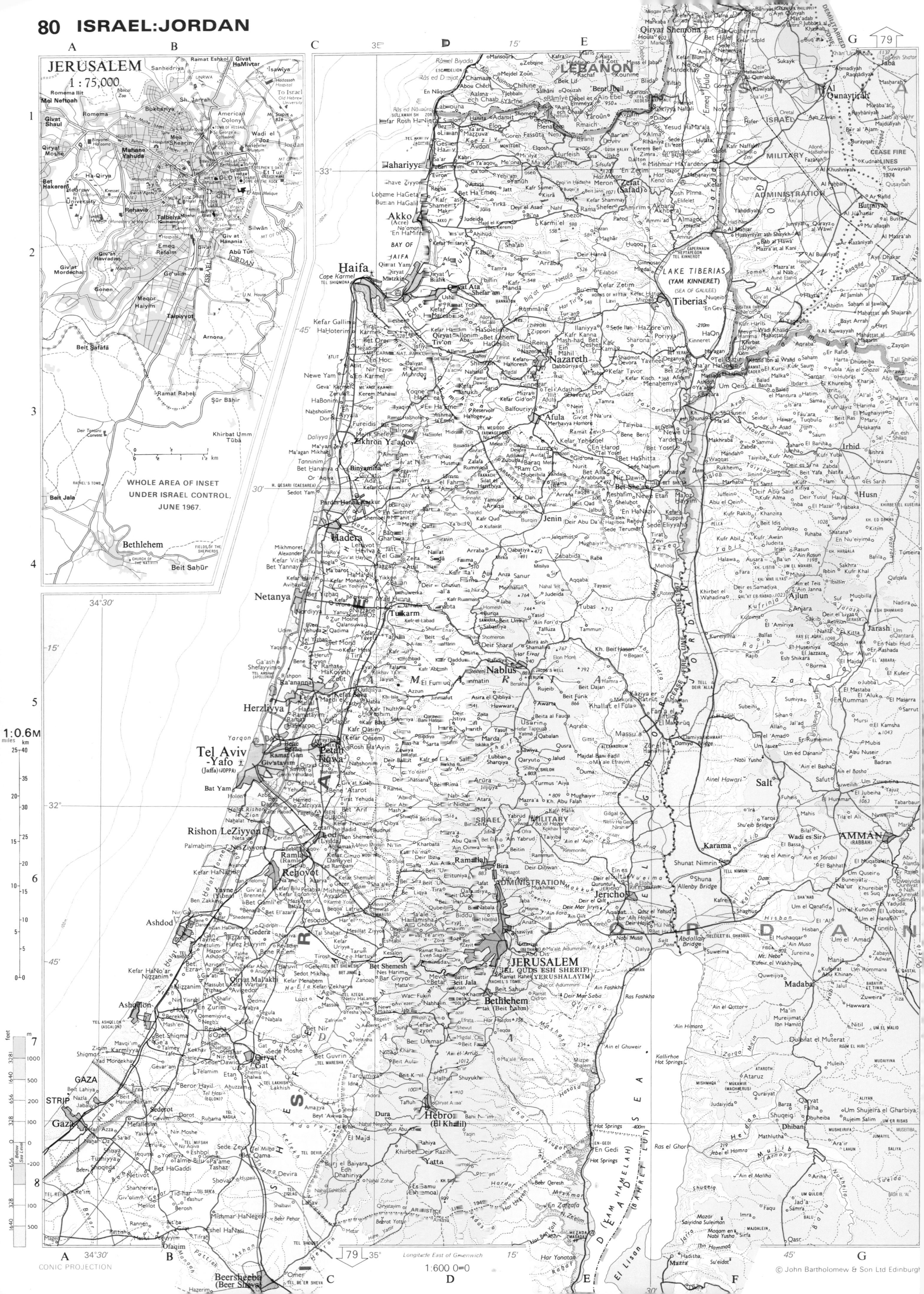
JERUSALEM
1 : 75,000
WHOLE AREA OF INSET UNDER ISRAEL CONTROL, JUNE 1967.
Bethlehem
1:0.6M
LEBANON
SYRIA
ISRAEL
JORDAN
LAKE TIBERIAS (YAM KINNERET) (SEA OF GALILEE)
BAY OF HAIFA
Haifa
Akko (Acre)
Nazareth
Tiberias
Zefat (Safad)
Qiryat Shemona
Al Qunaytirah
Irbid
Ajlun
Jarash
Hadera
Netanya
Herzliyya
Tel Aviv-Yafo (Jaffa) (JOPPA)
Bat Yam
Rishon LeZiyyon
Rehovot
Ramla (Ramle)
Lod (Lydda)
Petah Tiqwa
Ashdod
Ashqelon
GAZA STRIP
Gaza
Qiryat Gat
Beersheba (Beer Sheva)
Jenin
Nablus
Tulkarm
Afula
Ramallah
Jericho
JERUSALEM (EL QUDS ESH SHERIF) (YERUSHALAYIM)
Bethlehem (Beit Lahm)
Hebron (El Khalil)
Salt
AMMAN (RABBAH)
Madaba
Dhiban
DEAD SEA
ISRAEL MILITARY ADMINISTRATION
CEASE FIRE LINE
CONIC PROJECTION
Longitude East of Greenwich
1:600 000
© John Bartholomew & Son Ltd Edinburgh

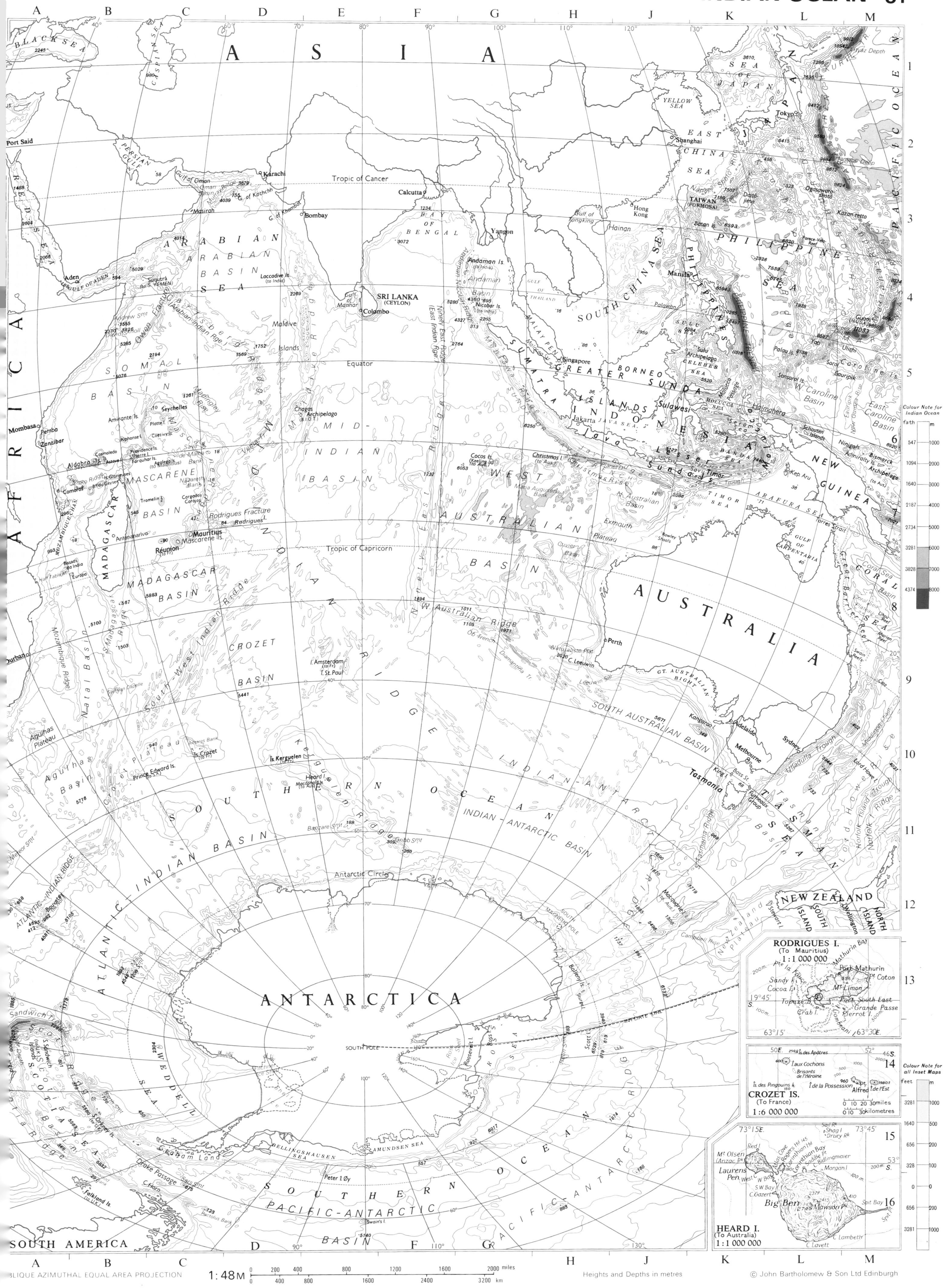
ASIA
AFRICA
AUSTRALIA
ANTARCTICA
SOUTH AMERICA
NEW ZEALAND
NEW GUINEA
MADAGASCAR
ARABIAN SEA
BAY OF BENGAL
SOUTH CHINA SEA
EAST CHINA SEA
SEA OF JAPAN
YELLOW SEA
PHILIPPINE SEA
TASMAN SEA
CORAL SEA
ARAFURA SEA
TIMOR SEA
WEDDELL SEA
ROSS SEA
SCOTIA SEA
BELLINGSHAUSEN SEA
AMUNDSEN SEA
BLACK SEA
CASPIAN SEA
RED SEA
PERSIAN GULF
GULF OF ADEN
SOUTHERN OCEAN
PACIFIC OCEAN
ARABIAN BASIN
SOMALI BASIN
MASCARENE BASIN
MADAGASCAR BASIN
CROZET BASIN
MID-INDIAN BASIN
WEST AUSTRALIAN BASIN
SOUTH AUSTRALIAN BASIN
INDIAN-ANTARCTIC BASIN
ATLANTIC-INDIAN BASIN
PACIFIC-ANTARCTIC BASIN
MID-INDIAN RIDGE
SOUTH-WEST INDIAN RIDGE
INDIAN-ANTARCTIC RIDGE
PACIFIC-ANTARCTIC RIDGE
ATLANTIC-INDIAN RIDGE
Ninety East Ridge
Kerguelen Ridge
Tropic of Cancer
Equator
Tropic of Capricorn
Antarctic Circle
SOUTH POLE
INDONESIA
GREATER SUNDA ISLANDS
PHILIPPINES
JAPAN
Port Said
Aden
Karachi
Bombay
Calcutta
Yangon
Colombo
SRI LANKA (CEYLON)
Mombasa
Zanzibar
Durban
Singapore
Jakarta
Manila
Hong Kong
Shanghai
Tokyo
Perth
Adelaide
Melbourne
Sydney
Tasmania
Wellington
Seychelles
Mauritius
Réunion
Kerguelen Is.
Heard I.
Crozet Is.
Prince Edward Is.
I. Amsterdam
I. St. Paul
Cocos Is.
Christmas I.
Andaman Is.
Nicobar Is.
Maldive Islands
Laccadive Is.
Chagos Archipelago
Graham Land
Drake Passage
Falkland Is.
Peter I Øy
RODRIGUES I.
(To Mauritius)
1:1 000 000
Port Mathurin
Port South East
CROZET IS.
(To France)
1:6 000 000
Î. de la Possession
Île de l'Est
HEARD I.
(To Australia)
1:1 000 000
Big Ben
Laurens Pen
Colour Note for Indian Ocean
Colour Note for all Inset Maps
OBLIQUE AZIMUTHAL EQUAL AREA PROJECTION
1:48M
miles
km
Heights and Depths in metres
© John Bartholomew & Son Ltd Edinburgh

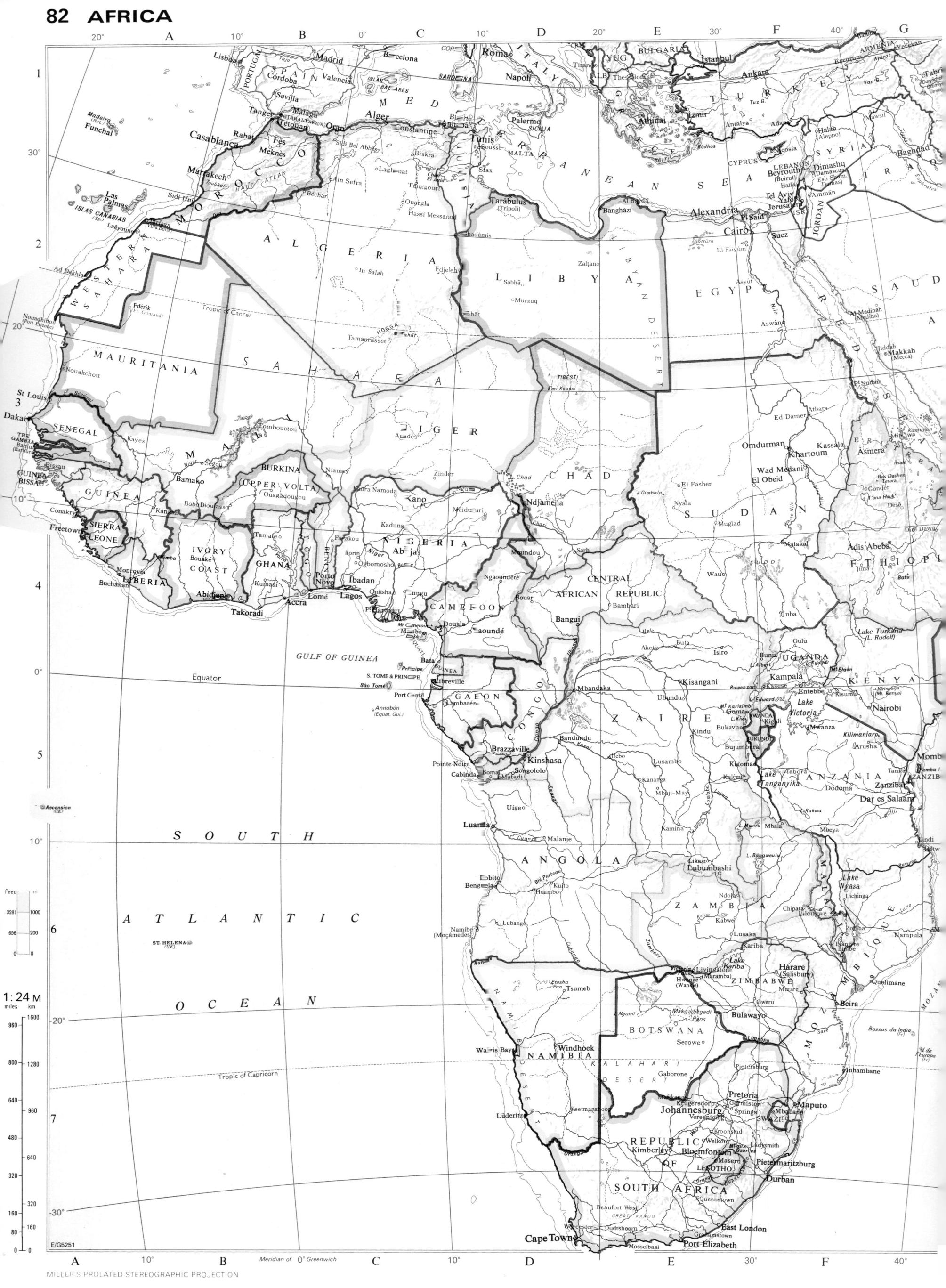
MEDITERRANEAN SEA
GULF OF GUINEA
SOUTH ATLANTIC OCEAN
Equator
Tropic of Cancer
Tropic of Capricorn
Meridian of 0° Greenwich
SAHARA
LIBYAN DESERT
NAMIB DESERT
KALAHARI DESERT
MOROCCO
WESTERN SAHARA
ALGERIA
LIBYA
EGYPT
MAURITANIA
MALI
NIGER
CHAD
SUDAN
ETHIOPIA
SENEGAL
THE GAMBIA
GUINEA BISSAU
GUINEA
SIERRA LEONE
LIBERIA
IVORY COAST
GHANA
TOGO
BENIN
BURKINA (UPPER VOLTA)
NIGERIA
CAMEROON
CENTRAL AFRICAN REPUBLIC
GABON
CONGO
ZAIRE
UGANDA
KENYA
RWANDA
BURUNDI
TANZANIA
ANGOLA
ZAMBIA
MALAWI
MOZAMBIQUE
ZIMBABWE
BOTSWANA
NAMIBIA
SWAZI
LESOTHO
REPUBLIC OF SOUTH AFRICA
SPAIN
PORTUGAL
ITALY
GREECE
TURKEY
CYPRUS
LEBANON
SYRIA
JORDAN
ISRAEL
BULGARIA
Lisboa
Madrid
Barcelona
Roma
Napoli
Istanbul
Ankara
Athinai
Izmir
Rabat
Casablanca
Fès
Marrakech
Alger
Oran
Tunis
Tarabulus (Tripoli)
Banghazi
Alexandria
Cairo
Port Said
Suez
Aswân
Beyrouth (Beirut)
Dimashq (Damascus)
Tel Aviv Yafo
Jerusalem
Baghdad
Makkah (Mecca)
Al Madinah (Medina)
Las Palmas
ISLAS CANARIAS
Madeira
Funchal
Laayoune
Ad Dakhla
Nouadhibou (Port Étienne)
Nouakchott
St Louis
Dakar
Banjul
Bissau
Conakry
Freetown
Monrovia
Bamako
Tombouctou
Ouagadougou
Niamey
Abidjan
Accra
Lomé
Porto Novo
Lagos
Ibadan
Abuja
Kano
Ndjamena
Douala
Yaoundé
Bangui
Libreville
Brazzaville
Kinshasa
Khartoum
Omdurman
Asmera
Adis Abeba
Kampala
Nairobi
Mombasa
Zanzibar
Dar es Salaam
Dodoma
Kigali
Bujumbura
Kisangani
Lake Victoria
Lake Tanganyika
Lake Nyasa
Lake Kariba
Luanda
Lobito
Benguela
Huambo
Lusaka
Lubumbashi
Lilongwe
Harare (Salisbury)
Bulawayo
Beira
Maputo
Mbabane
Windhoek
Walvis Bay
Lüderitz
Gaborone
Pretoria
Johannesburg
Bloemfontein
Maseru
Kimberley
Durban
Pietermaritzburg
East London
Port Elizabeth
Cape Town
Mosselbaai
ST. HELENA (U.K.)
Ascension (U.K.)
S. TOME & PRINCIPE
Annobón (Equat. Gui.)
Kilimanjaro
TIBESTI
Emi Koussi
1: 24 M
E/G5251
MILLER'S PROLATED STEREOGRAPHIC PROJECTION

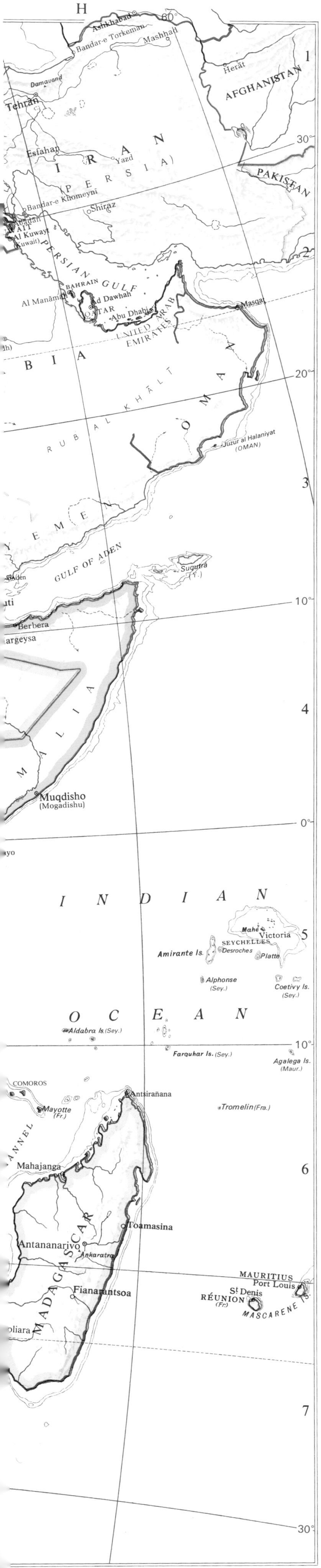

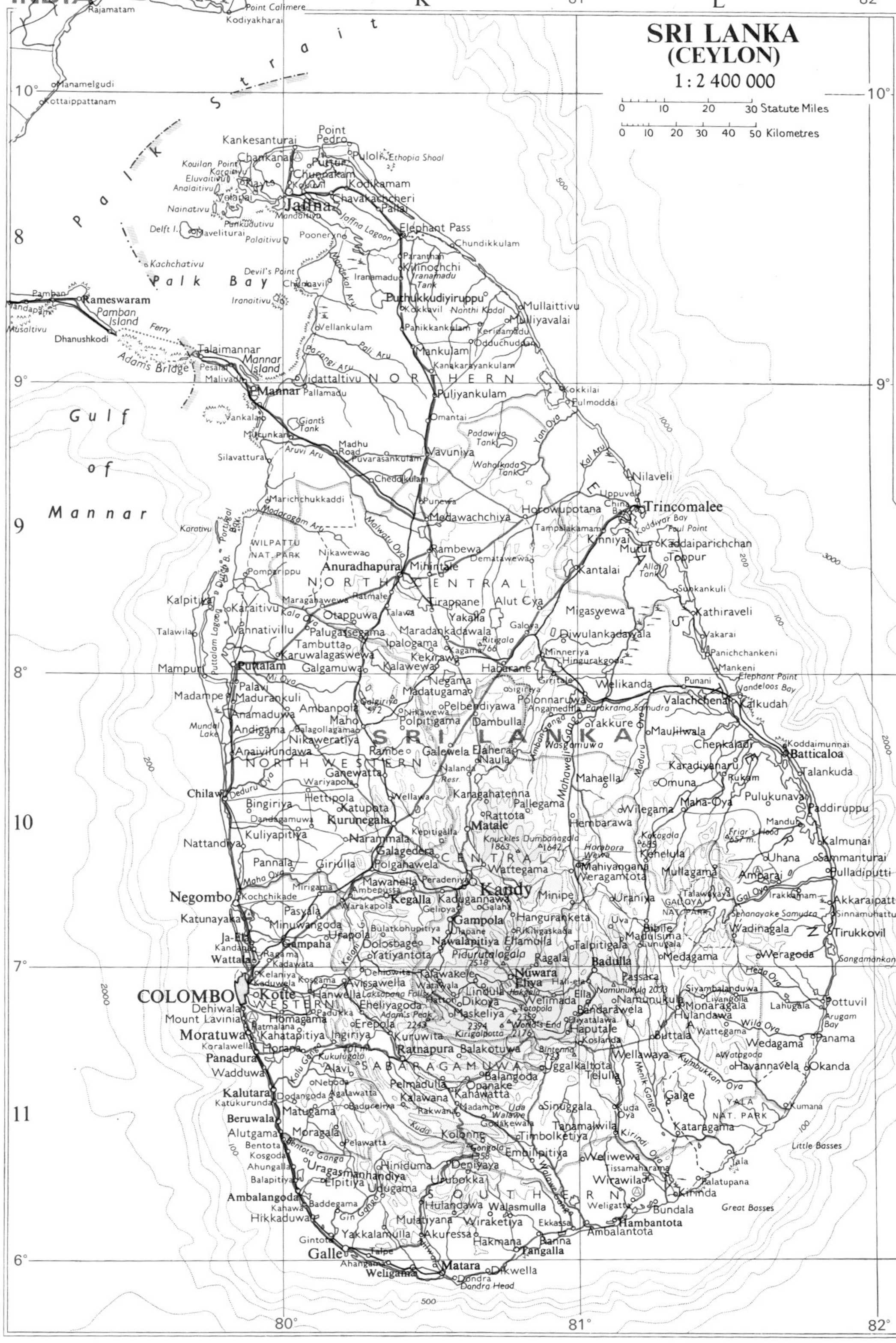

SRI LANKA
(CEYLON)
1 : 2 400 000
0 10 20 30 Statute Miles
0 10 20 30 40 50 Kilometres
LAMBERT CONFORMAL
CONIC PROJECTION
Palk Strait
Palk Bay
Gulf of Mannar
Jaffna
Trincomalee
Anuradhapura
Kandy
COLOMBO
Negombo
Galle
Matara
Batticaloa
Hambantota
COCOS IS.
(KEELING IS.)
(To Australia)
1 : 1 000 000
CHRISTMAS I.
(To Australia)
1 : 1 000 000
SEYCHELLES
1 : 3 000 000
MAHÉ
1 : 1 000 000
MAURITIUS
1 : 1 000 000
10 Statute Miles
20 Kilometres
Port Louis
RÉUNION
(To France)
1 : 1 000 000
St Denis
KERGUELEN
(To France)
1 : 3 000 000
20 Statute Miles
40 Kilometres
INDIAN OCEAN
AFGHANISTAN
IRAN (PERSIA)
PAKISTAN
OMAN
GULF OF ADEN
Muqdisho (Mogadishu)
MADAGASCAR
Antananarivo
Longitude East 50° of Greenwich

Heights in metres

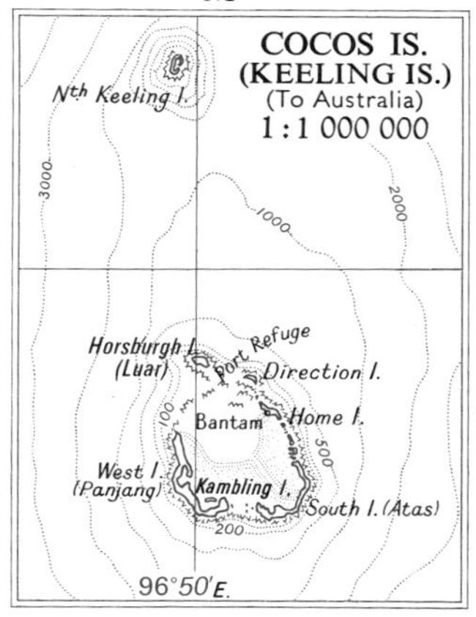

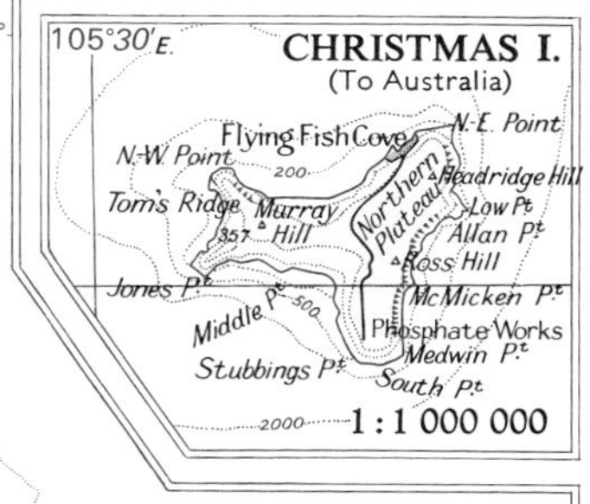

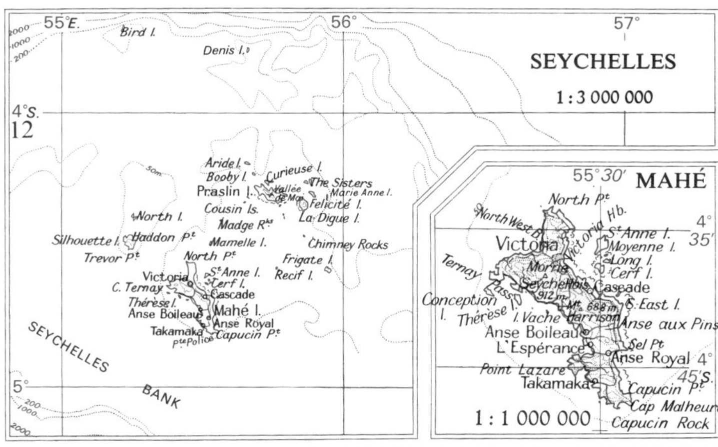

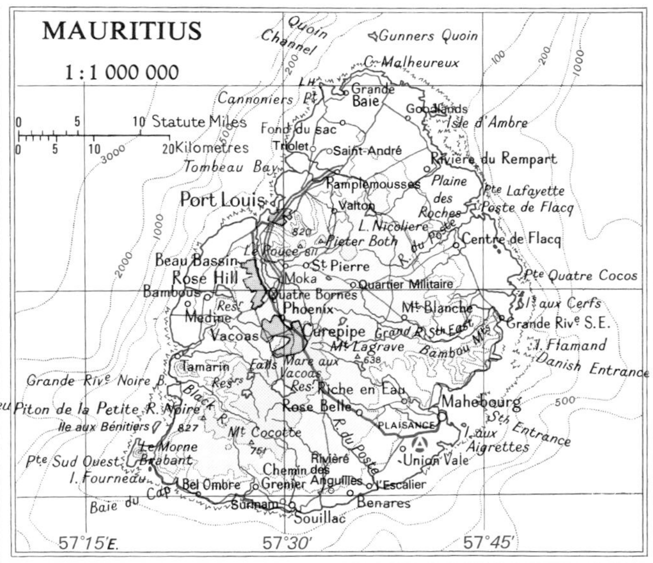

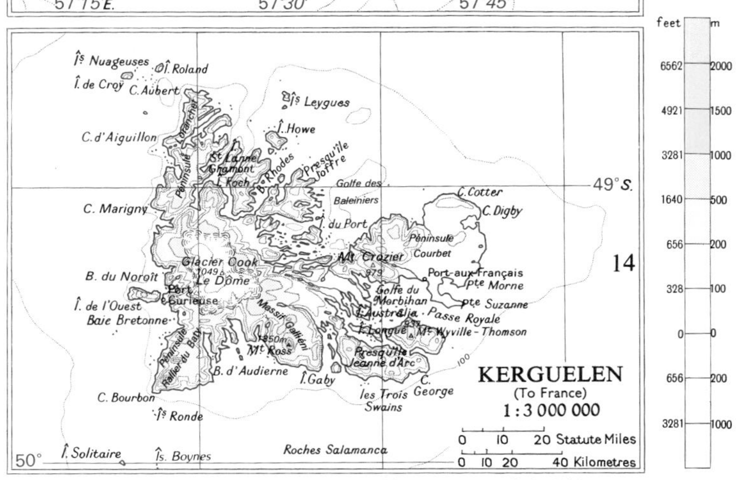

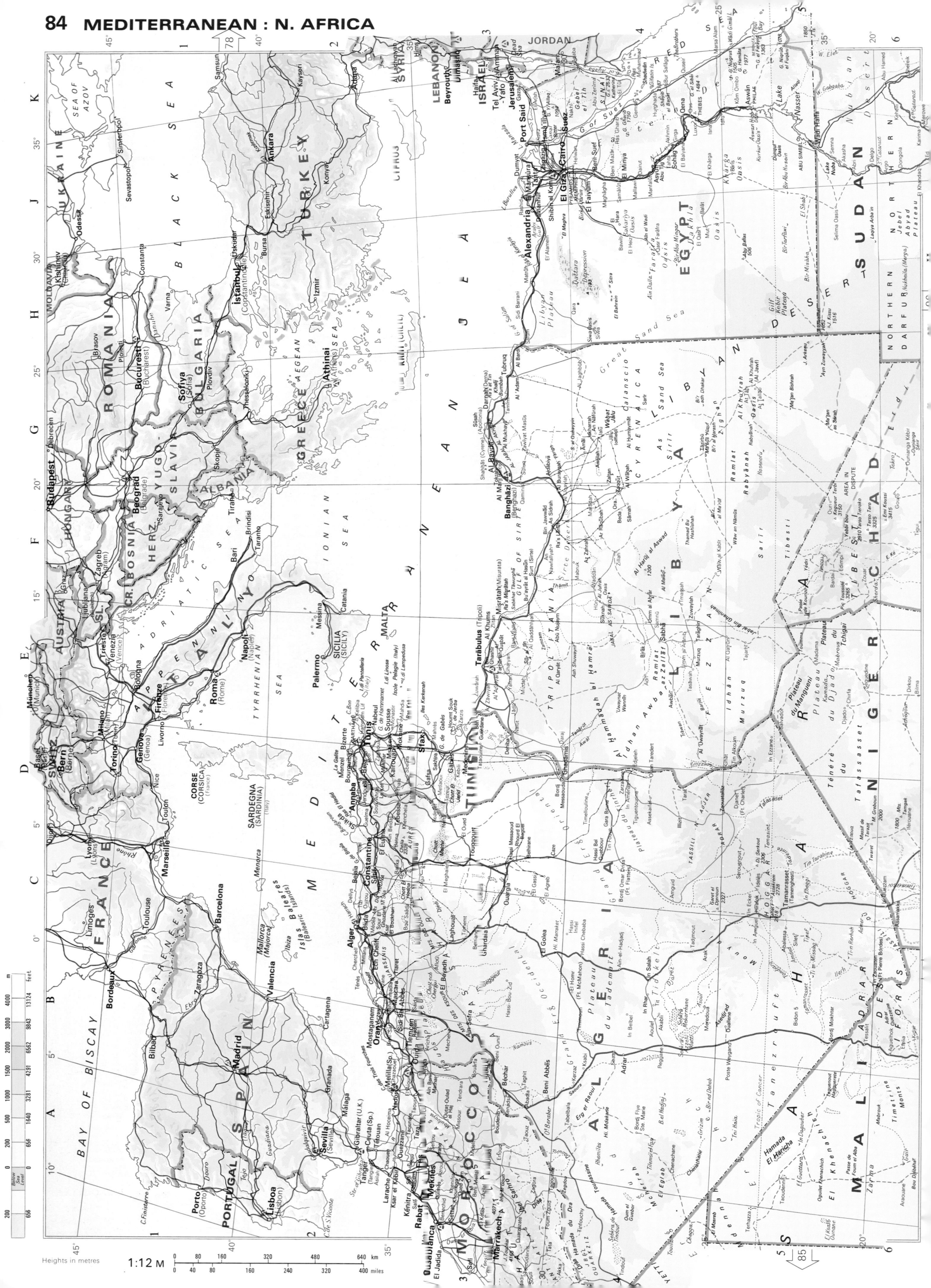

Heights in metres

1:12 M

0   80   160   320   480   640 km
0   40 80   160   240   320   400 miles

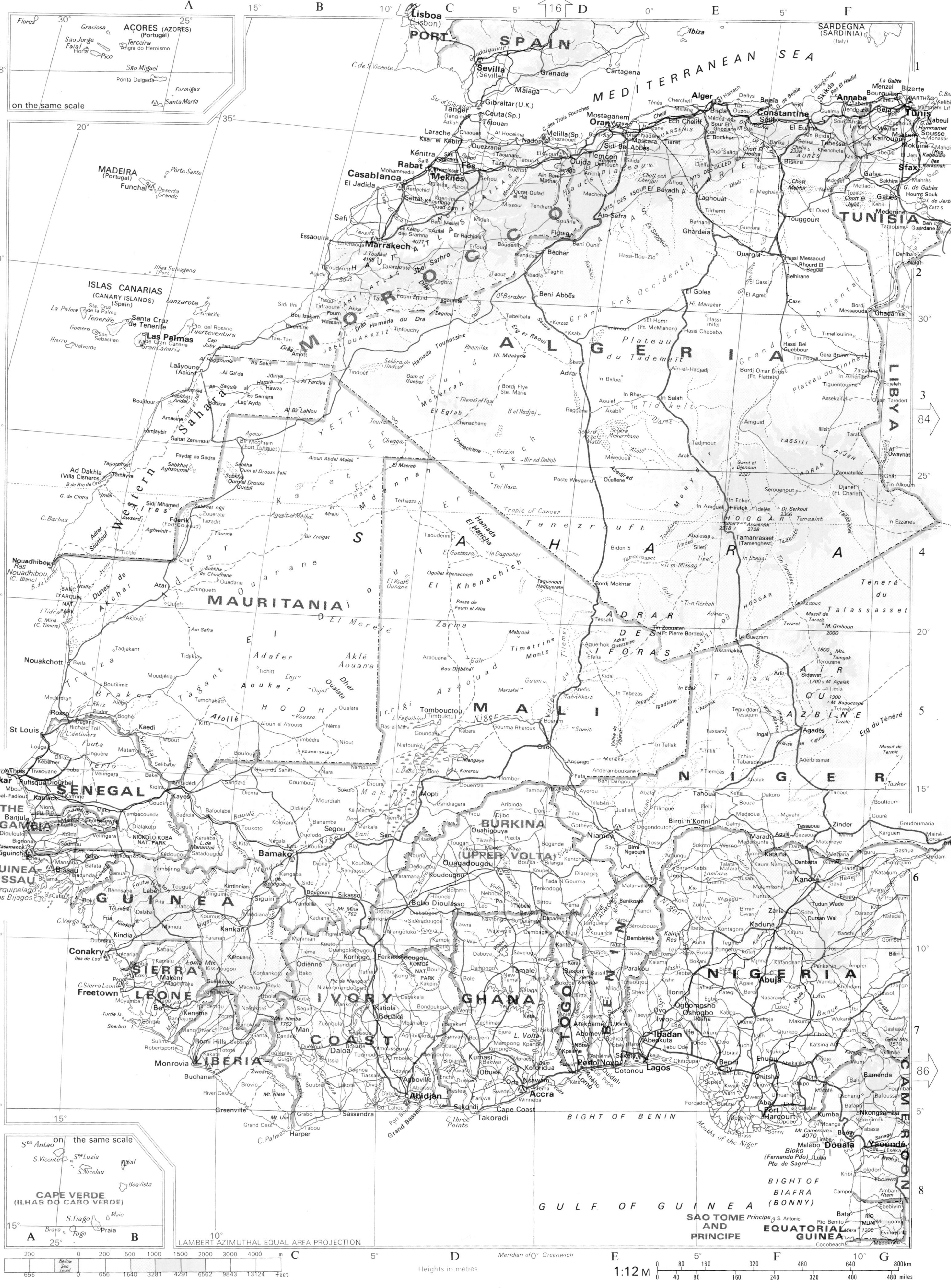

ACORES (AZORES)
(Portugal)
on the same scale

Flores · Graciosa · Terceira · Angra do Heroismo · São Jorge · Faial · Horta · Pico · São Miguel · Ponta Delgada · Formigas · Santa Maria

MADEIRA (Portugal) · Porto Santo · Funchal · Deserta Grande · Ilhas Selvagens (Port.)

ISLAS CANARIAS (CANARY ISLANDS) (Spain)
Lanzarote · La Palma · Sta. Cruz de la Palma · Tenerife · Santa Cruz de Tenerife · Gomera · San Sebastian · Hierro · Valverde · Gran Canaria · Las Palmas · Pto. del Rosario · Fuerteventura

CAPE VERDE (ILHAS DO CABO VERDE)
on the same scale
Sto Antão · S. Vicente · S. Nicolau · S. Luzia · Sal · Boa Vista · Maio · Brava · Fogo · S. Tiago · Praia

PORTUGAL · Lisboa (Lisbon) · SPAIN · Sevilla (Seville) · Granada · Málaga · Cartagena · Ibiza · Gibraltar (U.K.) · Tánger (Tangier) · Ceuta (Sp.) · Tétouan · Melilla (Sp.) · Oran

MEDITERRANEAN SEA

SARDEGNA (SARDINIA) (Italy)

Alger · Constantine · Annaba · Tunis · TUNISIA · Sfax · Gabès

MOROCCO · Rabat · Casablanca · Meknès · Marrakech · Safi · Essaouira · Agadir

ALGERIA

WESTERN SAHARA · Laâyoune (Aaiún) · Ad Dakhla (Villa Cisneros) · Nouadhibou

MAURITANIA · Nouakchott · Atar · Akjoujt

S A H A R A · Tropic of Cancer · Tombouctou (Timbuktu)

M A L I · Bamako · Gao

SENEGAL · Dakar · St Louis · Thiès

THE GAMBIA · Banjul

GUINEA-BISSAU · Bissau

GUINEA · Conakry · Labé · Kankan

SIERRA LEONE · Freetown · Makeni

LIBERIA · Monrovia · Buchanan · Greenville · Harper

IVORY COAST · Abidjan · Bouaké · Daloa · Man

GHANA · Accra · Kumasi · Sekondi · Cape Coast · Takoradi

BURKINA (UPPER VOLTA) · Ouagadougou · Bobo Dioulasso · Koudougou

TOGO · Lomé

BENIN · Porto Novo · Cotonou

NIGER · Niamey · Agadès · Zinder · Maradi

NIGERIA · Abuja · Lagos · Ibadan · Ibadan · Abeokuta · Benin · Port Harcourt · Onitsha · Kano · Kaduna · Zaria

LIBYA

CAMEROON · Yaoundé · Douala · Nkongsamba

EQUATORIAL GUINEA · Malabo · Bioko (Fernando Pdo) · SAO TOME AND PRINCIPE

BIGHT OF BENIN · BIGHT OF BIAFRA (BONNY) · GULF OF GUINEA · Mouths of the Niger

LAMBERT AZIMUTHAL EQUAL AREA PROJECTION
Meridian of 0° Greenwich
Heights in metres
1:12 M

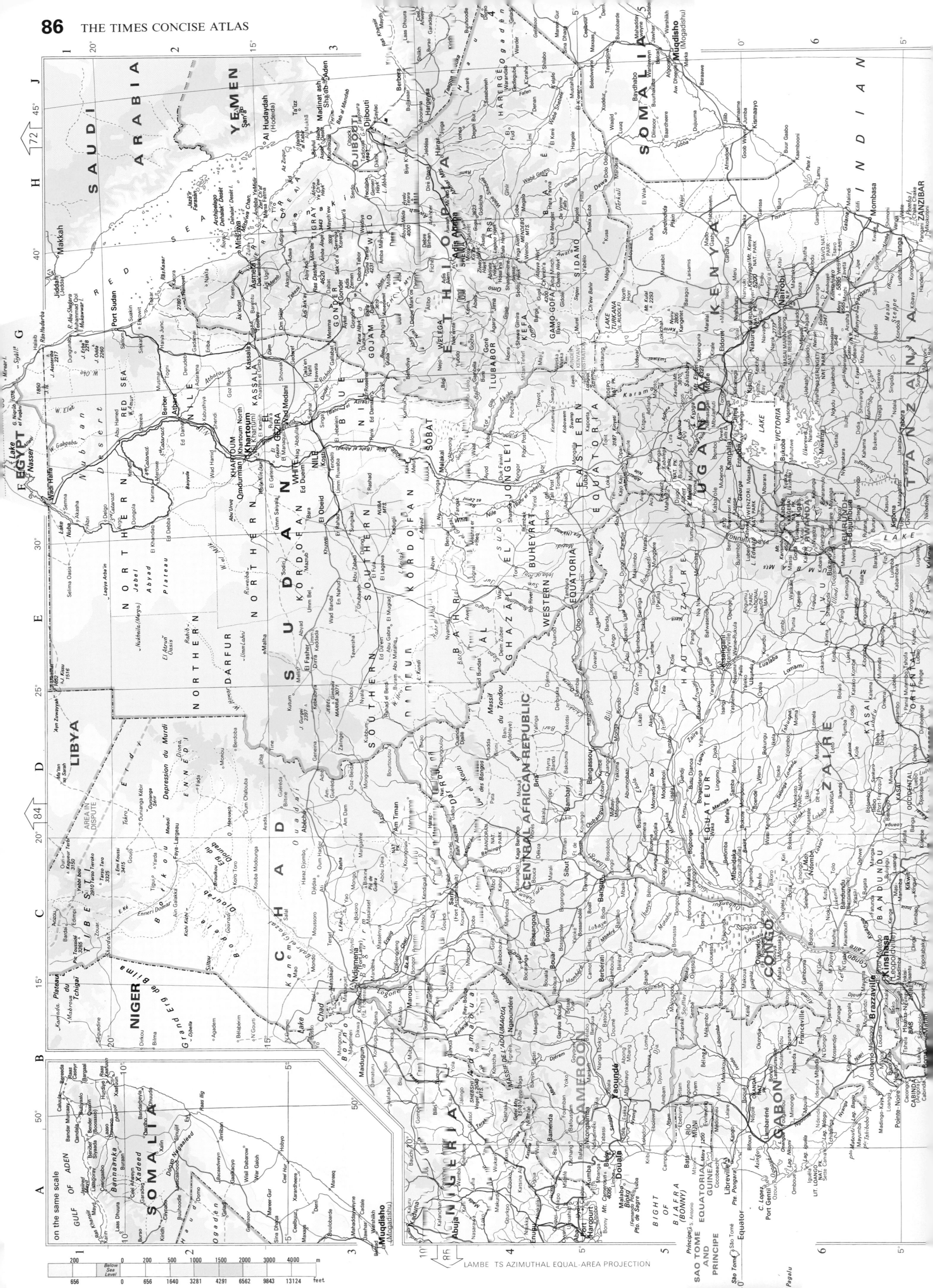
SAUDI ARABIA
YEMEN
RED SEA
EGYPT
LIBYA
SUDAN
CHAD
NIGER
NIGERIA
CAMEROON
CENTRAL AFRICAN REPUBLIC
ETHIOPIA
DJIBOUTI
SOMALIA
KENYA
UGANDA
ZAIRE
CONGO
GABON
on the same scale
200 0 200 500 1000 1500 2000 3000 4000 m
Below Sea Level
656 0 656 1640 3281 4291 6562 9843 13124 feet
LAMBE TS AZIMUTHAL EQUAL-AREA PROJECTION

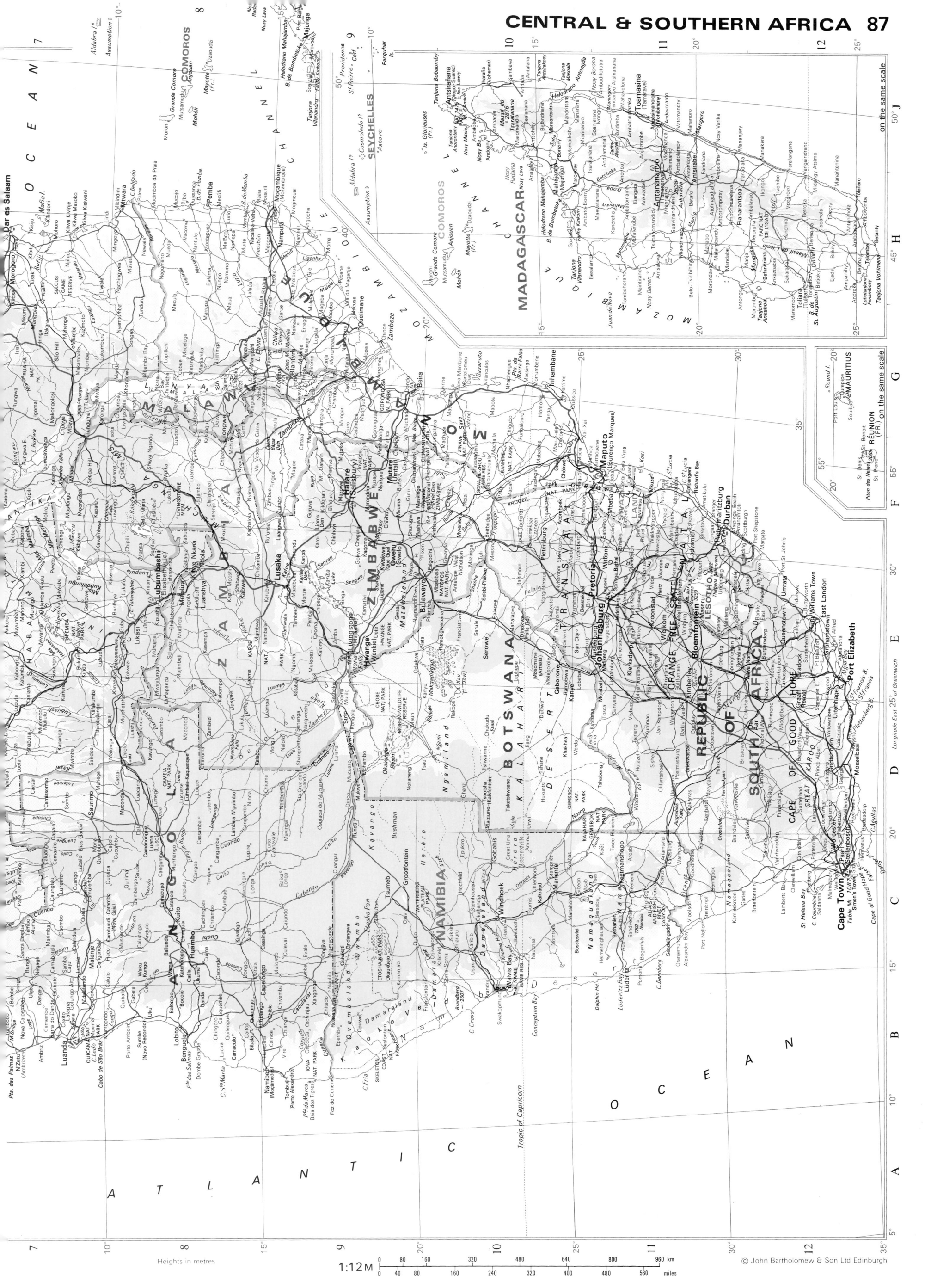

Heights in metres

1:12 M

0	80	160	240	320	400	480	560	640	720	800	880	960 km

| 0 | 40 | 80 | 120 | 160 | 200 | 240 | 280 | 320 | 360 | 400 | 440 | 480 | 520 | 560 miles |

© John Bartholomew & Son Ltd Edinburgh

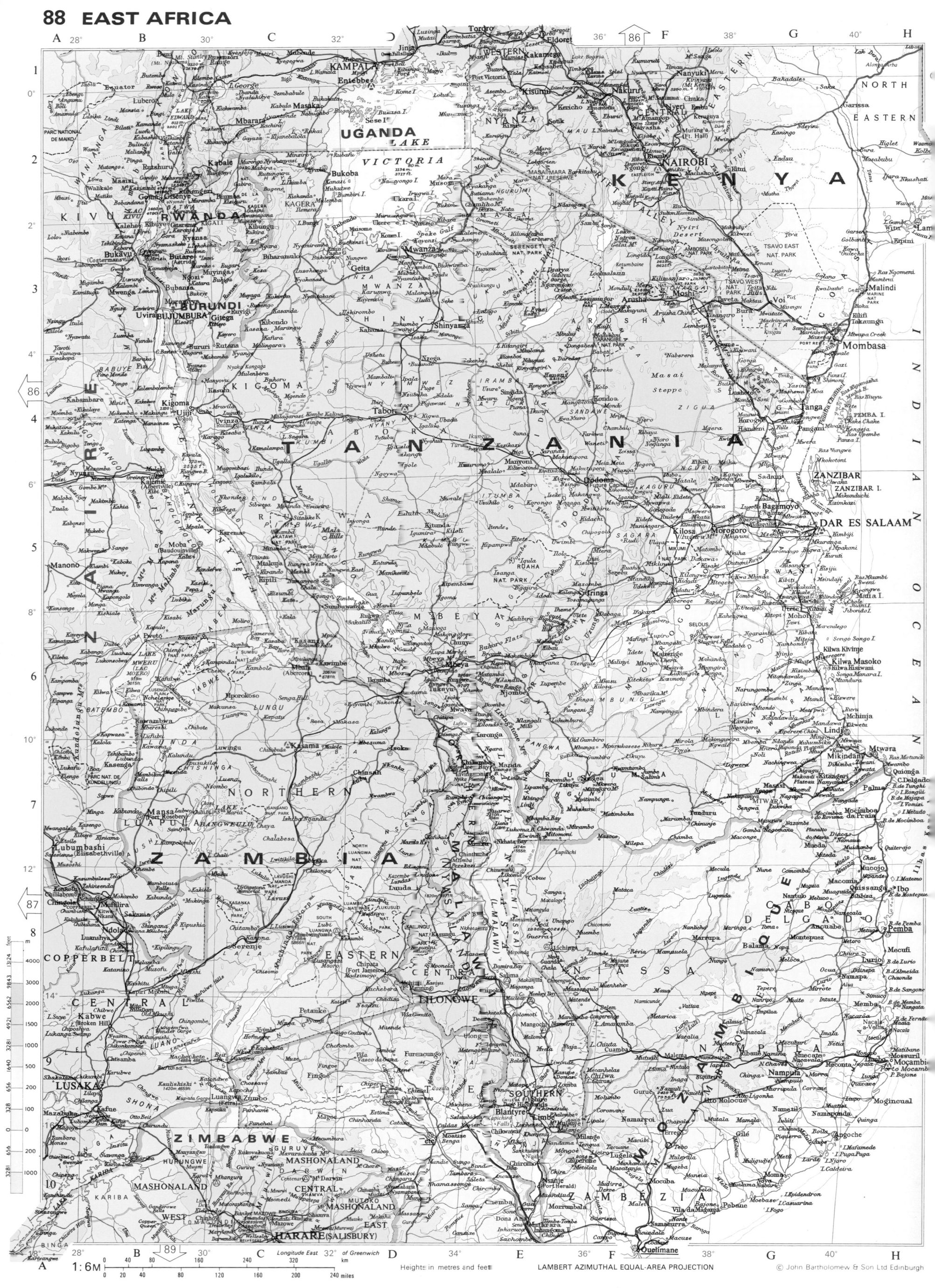

1 : 6 M

LAMBERT AZIMUTHAL EQUAL-AREA PROJECTION

Heights in metres and feet

© John Bartholomew & Son Ltd Edinburgh

WITWATERSRAND inset

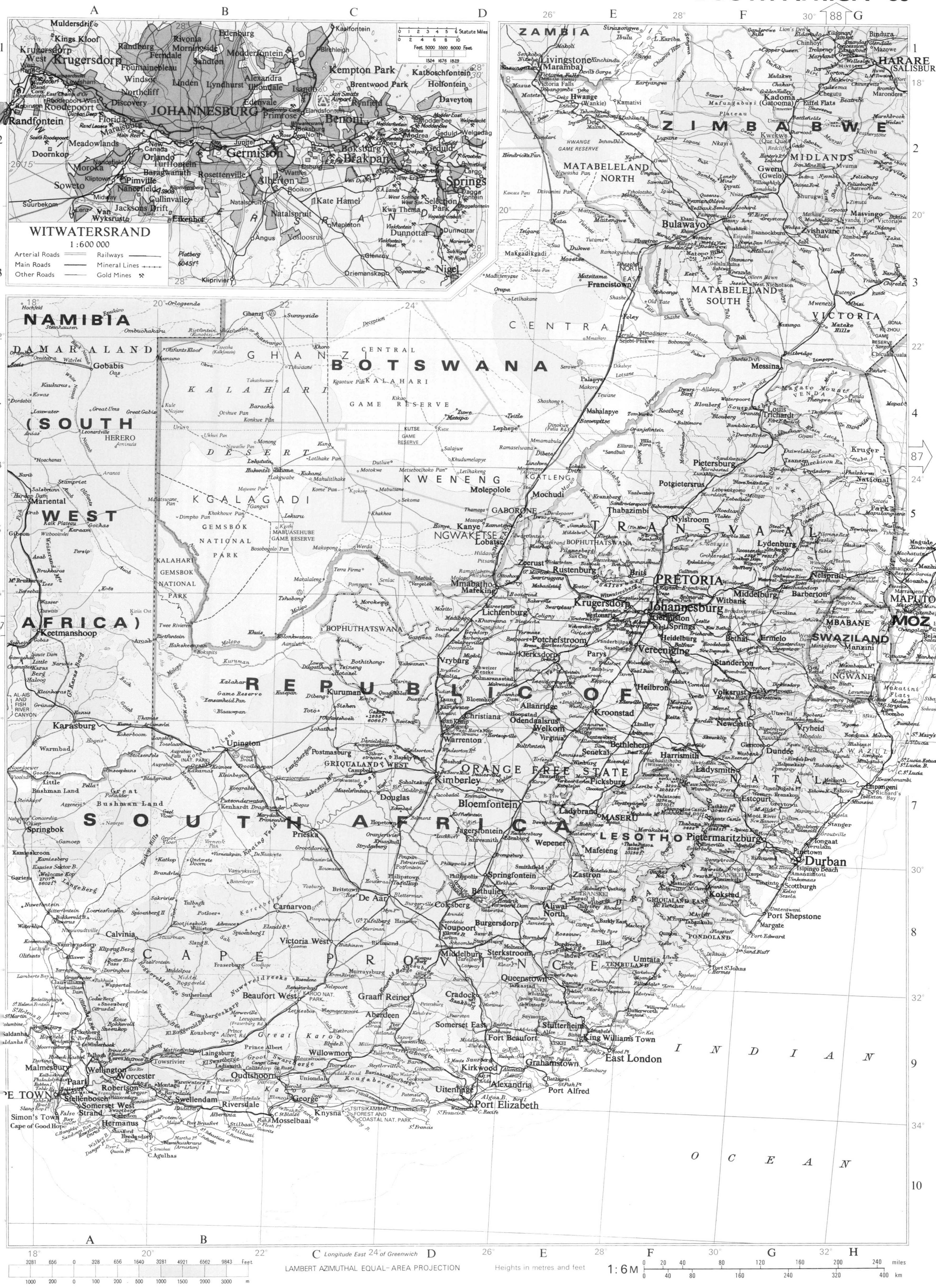

WITWATERSRAND
1:600 000

Arterial Roads
Main Roads
Other Roads
Railways
Mineral Lines
Gold Mines

JOHANNESBURG
Krugersdorp
Randfontein
Roodepoort
Germiston
Benoni
Brakpan
Springs
Boksburg
Alberton
Soweto
Kempton Park
Nigel

Statute Miles
Feet 5000 3500 6000 Feet
1524 1676 1829

Main map

ZAMBIA
ZIMBABWE
HARARE (SALISBURY)
Bulawayo
Victoria Falls
Hwange (Wankie)
MATABELELAND NORTH
MATABELELAND SOUTH
MIDLANDS
Gweru (Gwelo)
Masvingo
Messina

NAMIBIA
DAMARALAND
SOUTH WEST AFRICA
HERERO
Gobabis
Keetmanshoop
Karasburg
Mariental
Springbok

BOTSWANA
CENTRAL
GHANZI
KALAHARI
KALAHARI GEMSBOK NATIONAL PARK
GEMSBOK NATIONAL PARK
KGALAGADI
CENTRAL KALAHARI GAME RESERVE
KWENENG
GABORONE
KGATLENG
NGWAKETSE
Kanye
Lobatse
Francistown
Makgadikgadi

REPUBLIC OF SOUTH AFRICA
TRANSVAAL
PRETORIA
JOHANNESBURG
Krugersdorp
Germiston
Witbank
Rustenburg
Nelspruit
Lichtenburg
Klerksdorp
Potchefstroom
Vereeniging
BOPHUTHATSWANA
Mafeking
Mmabatho
Zeerust
Vryburg
Kuruman
Upington
GRIQUALAND WEST
Kimberley
ORANGE FREE STATE
Bloemfontein
Welkom
Kroonstad
Bethlehem
Harrismith
Ladybrand
LESOTHO
MASERU
CAPE PROVINCE
De Aar
Beaufort West
Graaff Reinet
Victoria West
Carnarvon
Calvinia
Cradock
Queenstown
Grahamstown
Port Elizabeth
Uitenhage
East London
King William's Town
TRANSKEI
Umtata
CISKEI
Oudtshoorn
George
Mossel Bay
Knysna
Worcester
Paarl
Stellenbosch
CAPE TOWN
Cape of Good Hope
C. Agulhas

NATAL
KWAZULU
Durban
Pietermaritzburg
Ladysmith
Newcastle
Dundee
Port Shepstone
Margate
Kokstad
PONDOLAND
TEMBULAND

SWAZILAND
MBABANE
Manzini
NGWANE

MOZ.
MAPUTO

INDIAN OCEAN

LAMBERT AZIMUTHAL EQUAL-AREA PROJECTION
Longitude East of Greenwich
Heights in metres and feet
1:6 M

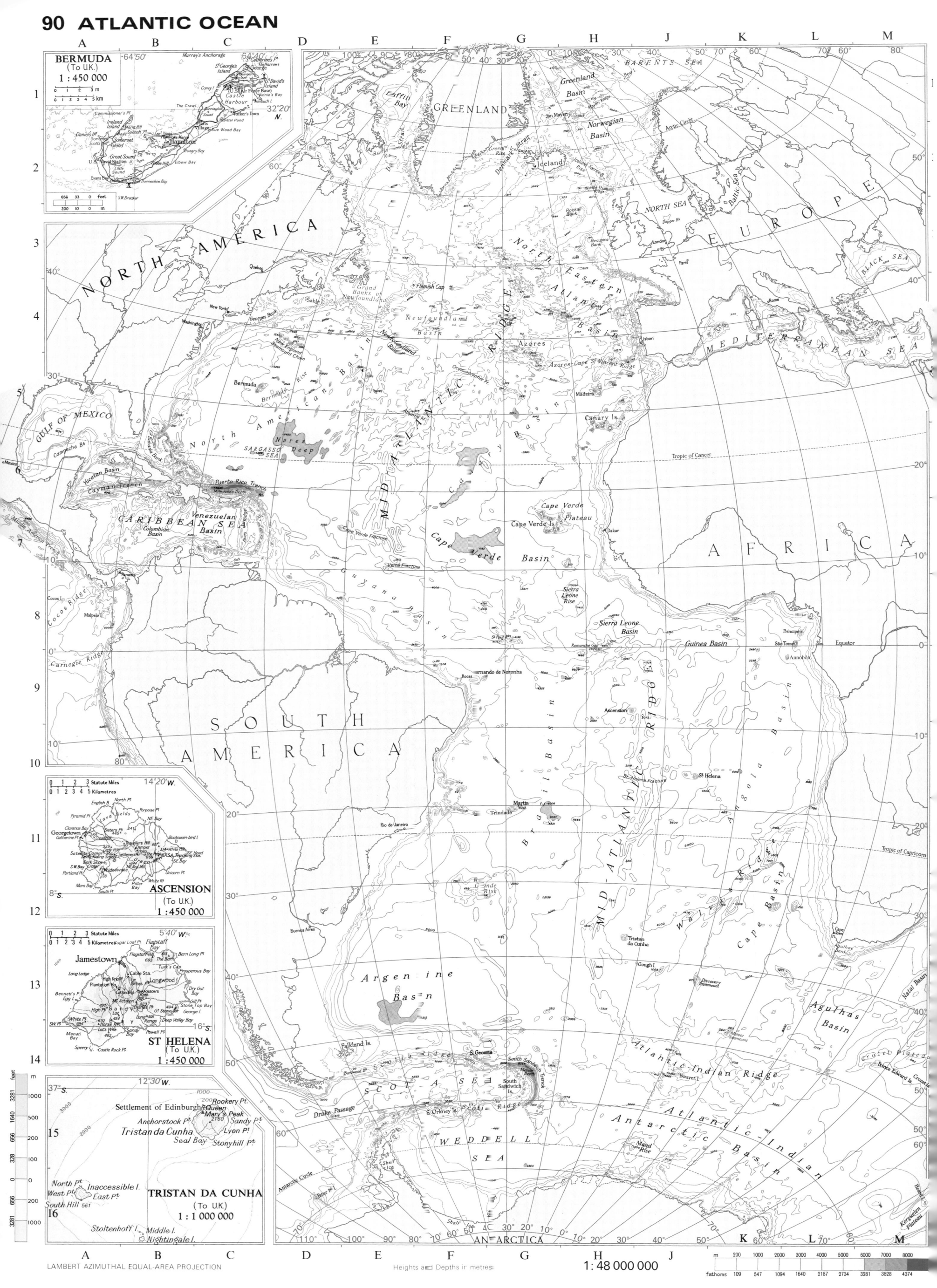

BERMUDA
(To U.K.)
1 : 450 000

ASCENSION
(To U.K.)
1 : 450 000

ST HELENA
(To U.K.)
1 : 450 000

TRISTAN DA CUNHA
(To U.K.)
1 : 1 000 000

NORTH AMERICA

SOUTH AMERICA

GREENLAND

EUROPE

AFRICA

ANTARCTICA

GULF OF MEXICO

CARIBBEAN SEA

SARGASSO SEA

MID ATLANTIC RIDGE

MEDITERRANEAN SEA

BLACK SEA

NORTH SEA

BARENTS SEA

WEDDELL SEA

SCOTIA SEA

DRAKE PASSAGE

LAMBERT AZIMUTHAL EQUAL-AREA PROJECTION

Heights and Depths in metres

1 : 48 000 000

m	200	1000	2000	3000	4000	5000	6000	7000	8000
fathoms	109	547	1094	1640	2187	2734	3281	3828	4374

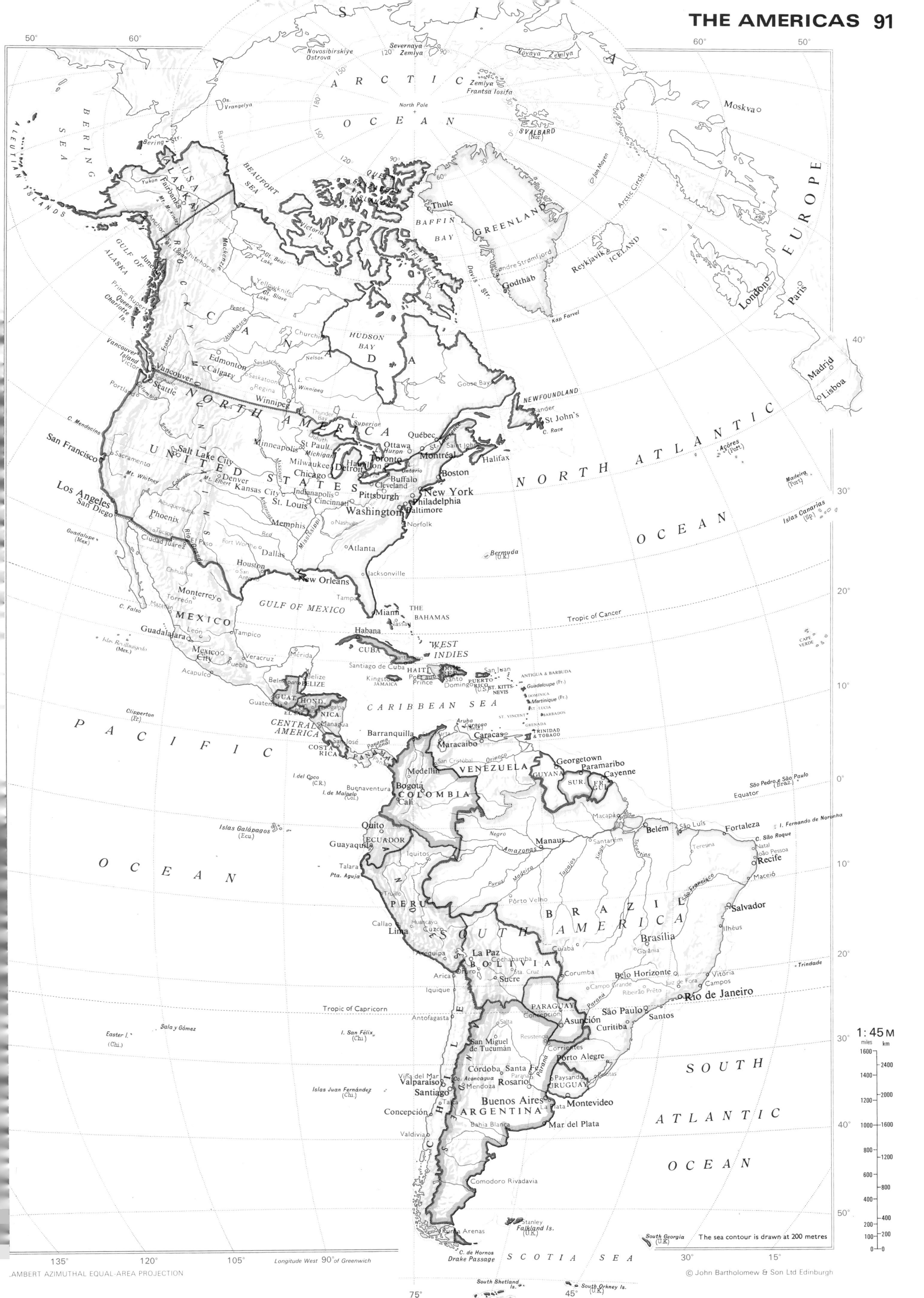

LAMBERT AZIMUTHAL EQUAL-AREA PROJECTION

1:45 M

The sea contour is drawn at 200 metres

Projection by courtesy of the
National Geographic Society, Washington, D.C.

© John Bartholomew & Son Ltd Edinburgh

ATLANTIC OCEAN

BERMUDA (To U.K.)
Hamilton

THE BAHAMAS
Nassau

Tropic of Cancer

1:12.5M

HABANA (HAVANA)
CUBA
JAMAICA
Kingston

HISPANIOLA
HAITI
DOMINICAN REPUBLIC
Santo Domingo
Port au Prince

PUERTO RICO (To U.S.A.)
San Juan

WEST INDIES

GREATER ANTILLES

LEEWARD ISLANDS

WINDWARD ISLANDS

LESSER ANTILLES

CARIBBEAN SEA

ST. LUCIA
BARBADOS
ST. VINCENT
GRENADA
DOMINICA
MARTINIQUE (Fr)

TRINIDAD TOBAGO
Port of Spain
San Fernando

NETHERLANDS ANTILLES

VENEZUELA
Caracas
Maracay

HONDURAS
Tegucigalpa
NIC.
BELIZE

Heights in feet   Depths in metres

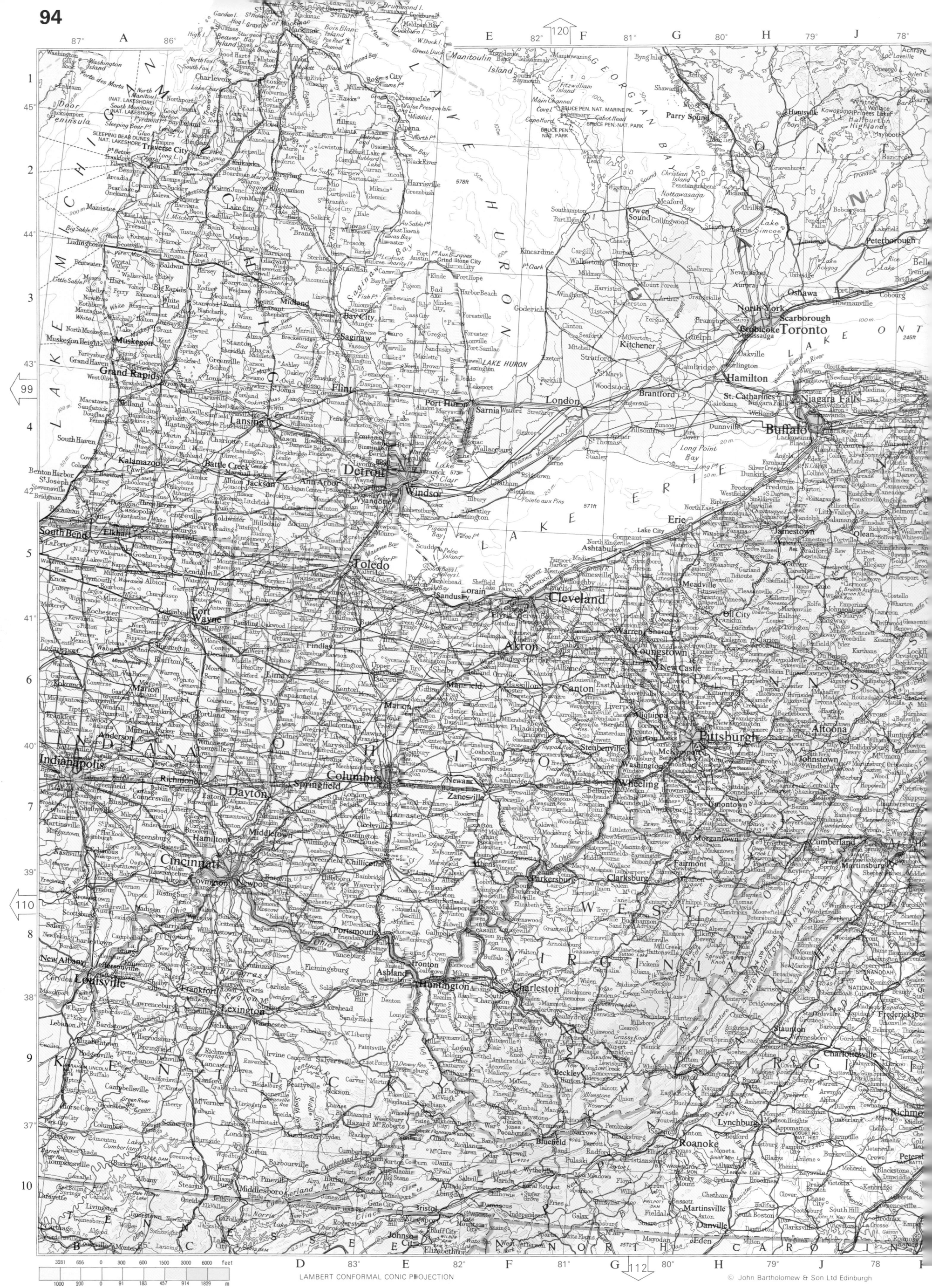

LAMBERT CONFORMAL CONIC PROJECTION

© John Bartholomew & Son Ltd Edinburgh

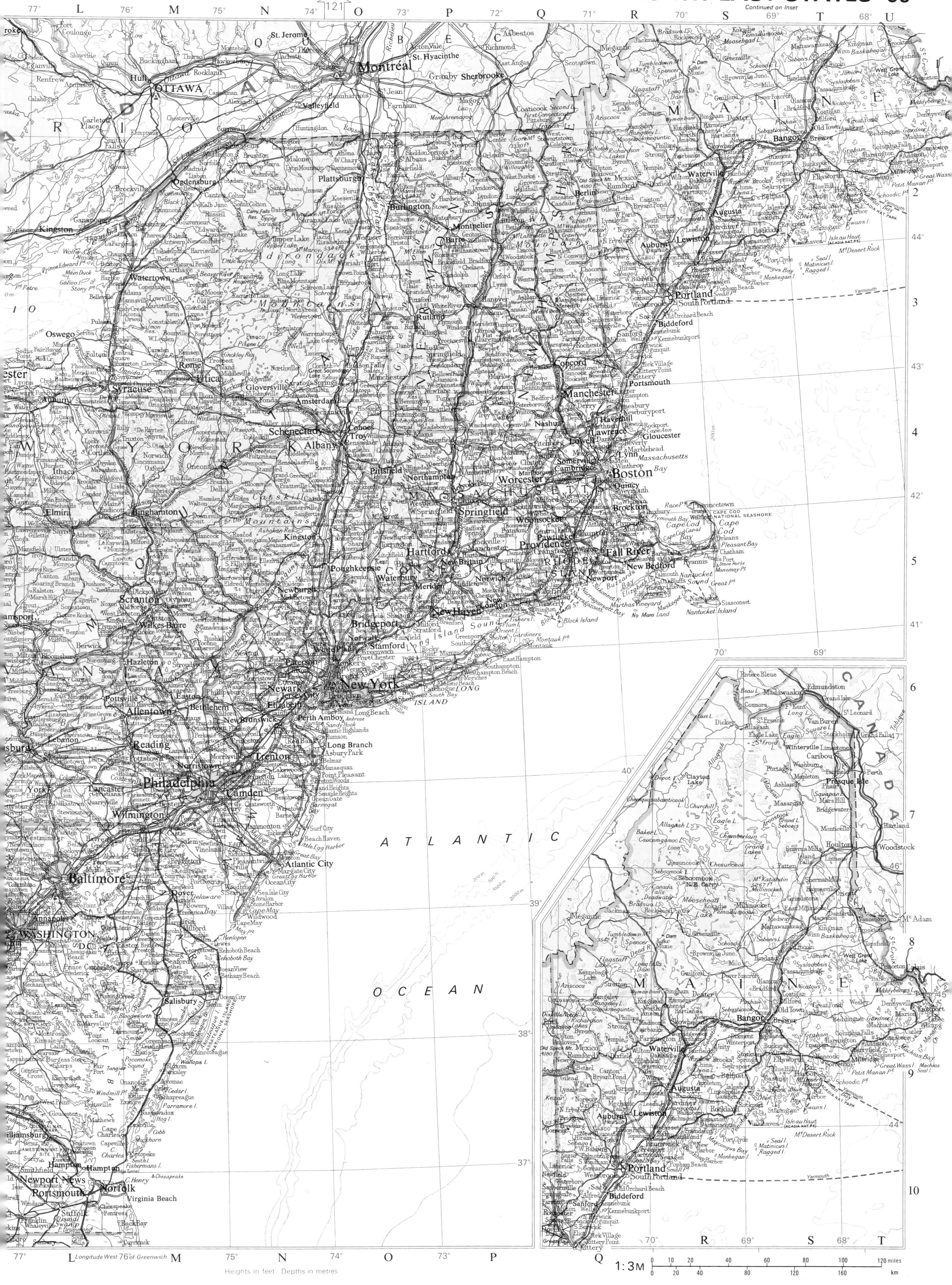
121
Continued on Inset
CANADA
QUEBEC
ONTARIO
MAINE
VERMONT
NEW HAMPSHIRE
NEW YORK
MASSACHUSETTS
CONNECTICUT
RHODE ISLAND
NEW JERSEY
DELAWARE
MARYLAND
PENNSYLVANIA
ATLANTIC
OCEAN
Montréal
OTTAWA
Kingston
Sherbrooke
Syracuse
Utica
Rome
Schenectady
Albany
Troy
Binghamton
Scranton
Wilkes-Barre
Allentown
Reading
Philadelphia
Camden
Trenton
Wilmington
Baltimore
WASHINGTON D.C.
Annapolis
Norfolk
Portsmouth
Newport News
Hampton
Virginia Beach
Salisbury
Dover
Atlantic City
New York
Newark
Jersey City
Paterson
Elizabeth
Perth Amboy
Bridgeport
New Haven
Stamford
Hartford
New Britain
Waterbury
Springfield
Worcester
Providence
Pawtucket
Fall River
New Bedford
Boston
Cambridge
Lynn
Lawrence
Lowell
Manchester
Concord
Portsmouth
Portland
South Portland
Biddeford
Lewiston
Auburn
Augusta
Waterville
Bangor
Burlington
Montpelier
Plattsburgh
Adirondack Mts.
Catskill Mountains
White Mountains
Green Mountains
Long Island Sound
Cape Cod
Nantucket Island
Martha's Vineyard
Block Island
Chesapeake Bay
Delaware Bay
Cape May
Presque Isle
Caribou
Houlton
Millinocket
Mt Katahdin
Moosehead Lake
1:3M
Heights in feet Depths in metres
Longitude West 76° of Greenwich
miles
km

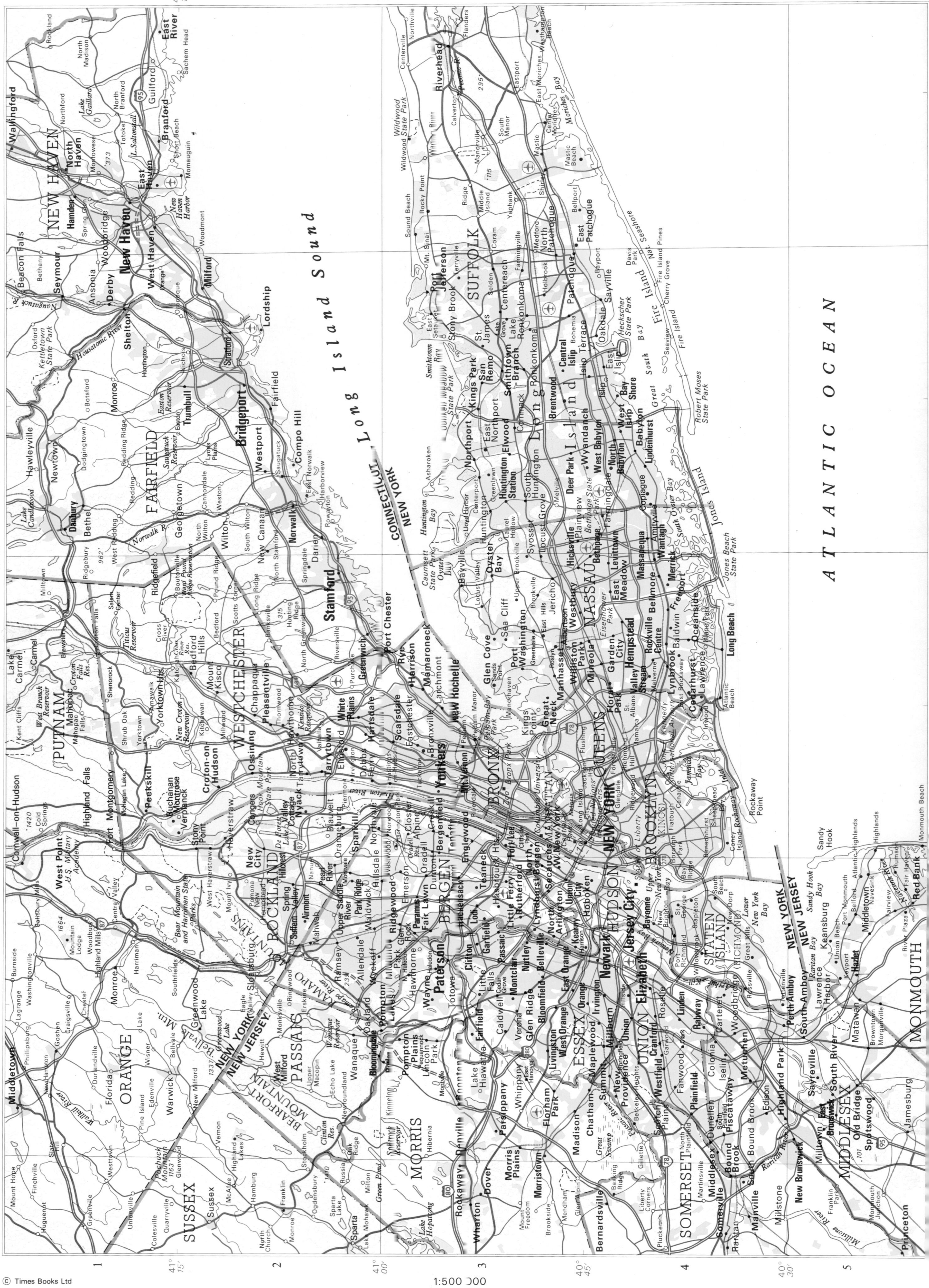

Long Island Sound

ATLANTIC OCEAN

CONNECTICUT
NEW YORK

NEW JERSEY
NEW YORK

NEW HAVEN
New Haven
West Haven
Hamden
Derby
Ansonia
Seymour
Beacon Falls
Shelton
Milford

FAIRFIELD
Bridgeport
Westport
Trumbull
Fairfield
Danbury
Bethel
Newtown
Monroe
Ridgefield
Norwalk
Stamford
Compo Hill

PUTNAM
Carmel
Lake Carmel
Mahopac
Brewster

WESTCHESTER
White Plains
Yonkers
Ossining
Peekskill
Croton-on-Hudson
Mount Kisco
Pleasantville
Scarsdale
Harrison
Rye
Port Chester
Greenwich
New Rochelle
Mamaroneck
Eastchester
Mount Vernon
Tarrytown

ROCKLAND
New City
Nyack
Spring Valley
Suffern
Nanuet
Haverstraw
Stony Point

ORANGE
Middletown
Warwick
Monroe
Goshen
Chester
West Point
Cornwall-on-Hudson
Highland Falls

SUSSEX
Sussex

PASSAIC
Paterson
Clifton
Passaic
Wayne
Pompton Lakes

BERGEN
Hackensack
Englewood
Teaneck
Ridgewood
Fort Lee
Paramus
Garfield

MORRIS
Morristown
Dover
Madison
Parsippany
Chatham

ESSEX
Newark
East Orange
Montclair
Bloomfield
Livingston
West Orange
Maplewood
Belleville
Nutley
Irvington

HUDSON
Jersey City
Bayonne
Hoboken

UNION
Elizabeth
Plainfield
Summit
Cranford
Westfield
Rahway
Linden
Roselle

SOMERSET
Somerville
Bound Brook
Bernardsville

MIDDLESEX
New Brunswick
Perth Amboy
South Amboy
Woodbridge
Metuchen
Edison
Highland Park
Carteret
Sayreville
Spotswood

MONMOUTH
Red Bank
Keansburg
Matawan
Hazlet
Middletown
Sandy Hook
Highlands

SUFFOLK
Riverhead
Patchogue
Islip
Bay Shore
Brentwood
Smithtown
Northport
Huntington
Babylon
Deer Park
West Islip
Central Islip
Sayville
Oakdale
Kings Park
Commack
Ronkonkoma
Medford

NASSAU
Hempstead
Hicksville
Levittown
Mineola
Freeport
Garden City
Massapequa
Westbury
Merrick
Oyster Bay
Glen Cove
Port Washington
Great Neck
Baldwin
Oceanside
Long Beach
Valley Stream
Lynbrook
Rockville Centre
Bethpage
Wantagh
Plainview
Syosset
Farmingdale
Amityville
Copiague
Manhasset
Floral Park
East Meadow

BRONX
MANHATTAN
NEW YORK
QUEENS
BROOKLYN (KINGS)
STATEN ISLAND (RICHMOND)

Hudson River
Housatonic River
Naugatuck R.
Raritan River
Passaic River
Ramapo River

RAMAPO MOUNTAINS
BEARFORT MOUNTAIN

Bear Mountain and Harriman State Parks
Wildwood State Park
Heckscher State Park
Robert Moses State Park
Jones Beach State Park
Fire Island Nat. Seashore

Jamaica Bay
Raritan Bay
Lower New York Bay
Upper New York Bay
Sandy Hook Bay
Huntington Bay
Oyster Bay
Great South Bay
Moriches Bay
Peconic Bay

1:500 000

PHILADELPHIA

A
75°15'
B
75°00'
C
1
2
3
4
40° 15'
40° 00'
39° 45'
Green Lane
Souderton
New Britain
Doylestown
Pineville
Hatfield
Chalfont
BUCKS
Harleysville
Schwenksville
Wrightstown
Dolington
Lansdale
Montgomeryville
Jacksonville
Yardley
Skippack
North Wales
Warminster
Richboro
Newtown
MONTGOMERY
Holland
Hatboro
Southampton
Langhorne
Trooper
Center Square
Ambler
Fort Washington
Willow Grove
Feasterville
Levittown
Audubon
Norristown
Abington
Valley Forge State Park
Bridgeport
Glenside
Croydon
Bristol
King of Prussia
Conshohocken
Jenkintown
Cornwells Hts.
CHESTER
Elkins Park
Burlington
Berwyn
Wayne
Fairmount Park
Germantown
Riverside
Paoli
Bryn Mawr
Schuylkill River
Olney
Willingboro
Ardmore
Frankford
Palmyra
Cinnaminson
Newton Square
Havertown
Delaware River
BURLINGTON
Ridley Creek State Park
Broomall
Upper Darby
Zoo
PHILADELPHIA
Moorestown
DELAWARE
Drexel Hill
Pennsauken
Maple Shade
Springfield
Lansdowne
Camden
Merchantville
Clifton Heights
Yeadon
Lima
Collingdale
Darby
Collingswood
Cherry Hill
Media
Sharon Hill
Swarthmore
Gloucester City
Haddonfield
Medford
Norwood
Glenolden
Philadelphia International Airport
Audubon
Ridley Park
Prospect Park
Naval Shipyard
Haddon Hts.
Marlton
Village Green
Brookhaven
National Park
Magnolia
Ashland
Chester
PENNSYLVANIA
NEW JERSEY
Paulsboro
Woodbury
Deptford
Runnemede
Gibbsboro
Boothwyn
Stratford
Lindenwold
Gibbstown
Woodbury Hts.
West Berlin
Berlin
Claymont
Bridgeport
Mantua
Wenonah
Blackwood
Pine Hill
Sewell
Swedesboro
Mullica Hill
CAMDEN
Penns Grove
Pitman
GLOUCESTER
Glassboro
Williamstown
Woodstown
Clayton
SALEM
Pole Tavern
Franklinville
A
75°15'
B
75°00'
C

BOSTON

D
71°15'
E
71°00'
F
1
2
3
42° 30'
42° 15'
42° 00'
Methuen
Lawrence
Georgetown
Rowley
NEW HAMPSHIRE
MASSACHUSETTS
Georgetown Rowley State Forest
ESSEX
Ipswich
Dracutt
Merrimack
Willowdale State Forest
Andover
Boxford State Forest
Lowell
Boston Hill
Palmer State Park
West Chelmsford
Shawsheen River
Harold Parker State Forest
South Hamilton
Wenham
Chelmsford Center
North Reading
Robins Hill
N. Billerica
Danvers
Billerica
Silver Lake
Beverly
Wilmington
Lynnfield
Littleton Common
Nutting Lake
Reading
Peabody
Carlisle
Pinehurst
Salem
Bakers I.
Concord River
Burlington
North Woburn
Wakefield
South Lynnfield
South Peabody
Marblehead
Acton
Bedford
Woburn
Stoneham
Lynn Woods Reservation
Lynn
Swampscott
Concord
Melrose
Saugus
West Concord
Lexington
Winchester
Nahant Bay
Minute Man Natural History Park
Malden
Maynard
Lincoln
Arlington
Medford
Revere
Nahant
MIDDLESEX
Belmont
Somerville
Everett
Massachusetts Bay
Sudbury
Waltham
Harvard University
Chelsea
Winthrop
Weston
Cambridge
Boston Bay
Logan International Airport
South Sudbury
Wayland
Watertown
Newton
Brookline
BOSTON
Boston Harbor
Cochituate
Roxbury
Wellesley
Newton Center
Point Allerton
Allerton
Framingham
Natick
Arnold Arboretum
SUFFOLK
Quincy Bay
Nantasket Beach
Needham
Milton
Quincy
North Weymouth
Hingham
Underground Aqueduct
Dover
Charles R.
Dedham
Sherborn
Islington
Braintree
Weymouth
Whitney Woods Reservation
Blue Hills Reservation
Holliston
Harding
Westwood
Medfield
Norwood
North Randolph
NORFOLK
Millis
Randolph
South Weymouth
Norwell
369 Noon Hill
East Walpole
Canton
Holbrook
Medway
Walpole
North Abington
Avon
Rockland
Hanover
Sharon
Stoughton
Abington
Franklin
Brockton
PLYMOUTH
Wrentham
North Easton
Whitman
Foxboro
Bryantville
Mansfield
East Bridgewater
MASS.
R.I.
BRISTOL
D
71°15'
E
71°00'
F

WASHINGTON

77°15'
G
77°00'
H
5
6
7
39° 15'
39° 00'
38° 45'
Etchison
Glenelg
Ellicott City
Baltimore
Clarksburg
Dayton
Elioak
Halethorpe
Columbia
Goshen
Laytonsville
Triadelphia Reservoir
HOWARD
Elkridge
Neelsville
MONTGOMERY
Highland
Clarksville
Stony Run
Germantown
Brookeville
Simpsonville
Friendship International Airport
Gaithersburg
Fulton
Jessup
Ashton
Redland
Olney
Ednor
Rocky Gorge Reservoir
Severn
Rock Creek
Spencerville
ANNE ARUNDEL
Darnestown
Norbeck
Burtonsville
Laurel
Hunting Hill
Odenton
Rockville
Travilah
Glenmont
Meadowood
Patuxent River
Potomac River
Wheaton
Beltsville
Randolph Hills
White Oak
Great Falls of the Potomac
Potomac
Kensington
Bowie
Woodside
Silver Spring
College Park
Greenbelt
Greenbelt Park
Springfield
Cabin John
Bethesda
Chevy Chase
Langley Park
Glenn Dale
Takoma Park
Seabrook
Collington
FAIRFAX
Glen Echo
Riverdale
Lanham
Spring Hill
McLean
Mt. Rainier
Hyattsville
Rock Creek Park
Bladensburg
Glenarden
Cheverly
Mitchellville
Tysons' Corner
Pimmit Hills
D.C.
Zoo
Brightseat
Vienna
Franklin Park
Georgetown
WASHINGTON
Fairmount Hts.
White House
The Capitol
Oakton
Falls Church
Arlington
Seat Pleasant
Largo
Arlington Nat. Cemetery
Capitol Hts.
Hall
Merrifield
Pentagon
Anacostia
Ritchie
Masonville
Suitland
District Hts
Fairfax
Baileys Crossroads
Congress Hts.
Forestville
Annandale
Lincolnia
Forest Hts.
Hillcrest Hts
Morningside
Meadows
Upper Marlboro
Alexandria
Fairfax Station
North Springfield
Temple Hills
Camp Springs
Burke
Phelps Corner
Springfield
Belle Haven
PRINCE GEORGES
Donovans Corner
West Springfield
Groveton
Clinton
Gum Springs
Tippett
Silesia
Piscataway Creek
North Keys
Lorton
Pohick
Accotink
Mt. Vernon
Piscataway
Brandywine
Nottingham
Marshall Hall
Accokeek
Agnewville
Potomac
Woodbridge
Baden
Berry
VIRGINIA
MARYLAND
Bryans Road
Waldorf
Malcolm
Pomonkey
CHARLES
Indian Head
Potomac Hts.
Mason Springs
White Plains
Dumfries
Pomfret
Bryantown
Triangle
Rison
Eagle Harbor
77°15'
G
77°00'
H
76°45'

BALTIMORE

J
76°45'
K
76°30'
L
4
5
6
7
39° 30'
39° 15'
39° 00'
Greenmount
Pretty Boy Reservoir
Shawsville
Madonna
Hampstead
Whitehouse
Hereford
Jarrettsville
Forest Hill
HARFORD
Churchville
BALTIMORE
Manor
Fowblesburg
Butler
Bel Air
Phoenix
Jacksonville
Benson
Finksburg
Shawan
Baldwin
Winters Run
Cockeysville
Long Green
Abingdon
Glyndon
Reisterstown
Fork
Loch Raven Reservoir
Kingsville
Liberty Reservoir
Cronhardt
Lutherville
Timonium
Gunpowder Falls
Edgewood
Owings Mills
Perry Hall
Joppatowne
Garrison
Ruxton
Towson
Carney
Harrisonville
Pikesville
Parkville
White Marsh
Bush River
Randallstown
Stoneleigh
Fullerton
Harewood Park
Chase
CITY OF BALTIMORE
Overlea
Middle River
Granite
Rockdale
Lochearn
Johns Hopkins University
Golden Ring
Bowleys Quarters
Patapsco State Park
Woodlawn
Druid Hill Park
Rosedale
Washington Monument
Essex
Middle River
Poples Island
Belmont
BALTIMORE
Catonsville
Fort McHenry Nat. Mon.
Ellicott City
Arbutus
Dundalk
Hart Island
Elioak
Patapsco R.
Lansdowne
Edgemere
Back River
Columbia
Halethorpe
Curtis Bay
HOWARD
Elkridge
Sparrows Point
Fort Howard
Stony Run
Linthicum Hts.
Patapsco River
Simpsonville
Orchard Beach
Friendship International Airport
Glen Burnie
Fort Smallwood
Rivera Beach
Jessup
Severn
Green Haven
Pinehurst
Chesapeake Bay
Laurel
ANNE ARUNDEL
Jacobsville
Pasadena
Odenton
Millersville
Severna Park
Herald Harbor
Magothy River
Patuxent River
Severn River
Beltsville
Crownsville
Love Point
Arnold
Skidmore
Kent Island
Greenbelt
Bowie
Springfield
Glenn Dale
Parole
Annapolis
CHESAPEAKE BAY BRIDGE
Stevensville
Chester
Lanham
Seabrook
Collington
Rutland
Eastport
PRINCE GEORGES
Riva
Normans
Cheverly
Davidsonville
Woodland Beach
Brightseat
Mitchellville
Arundel on the Bay
J
76°45'
K
76°30'
L
76°15'
km
miles
25
20
15
10
5
0

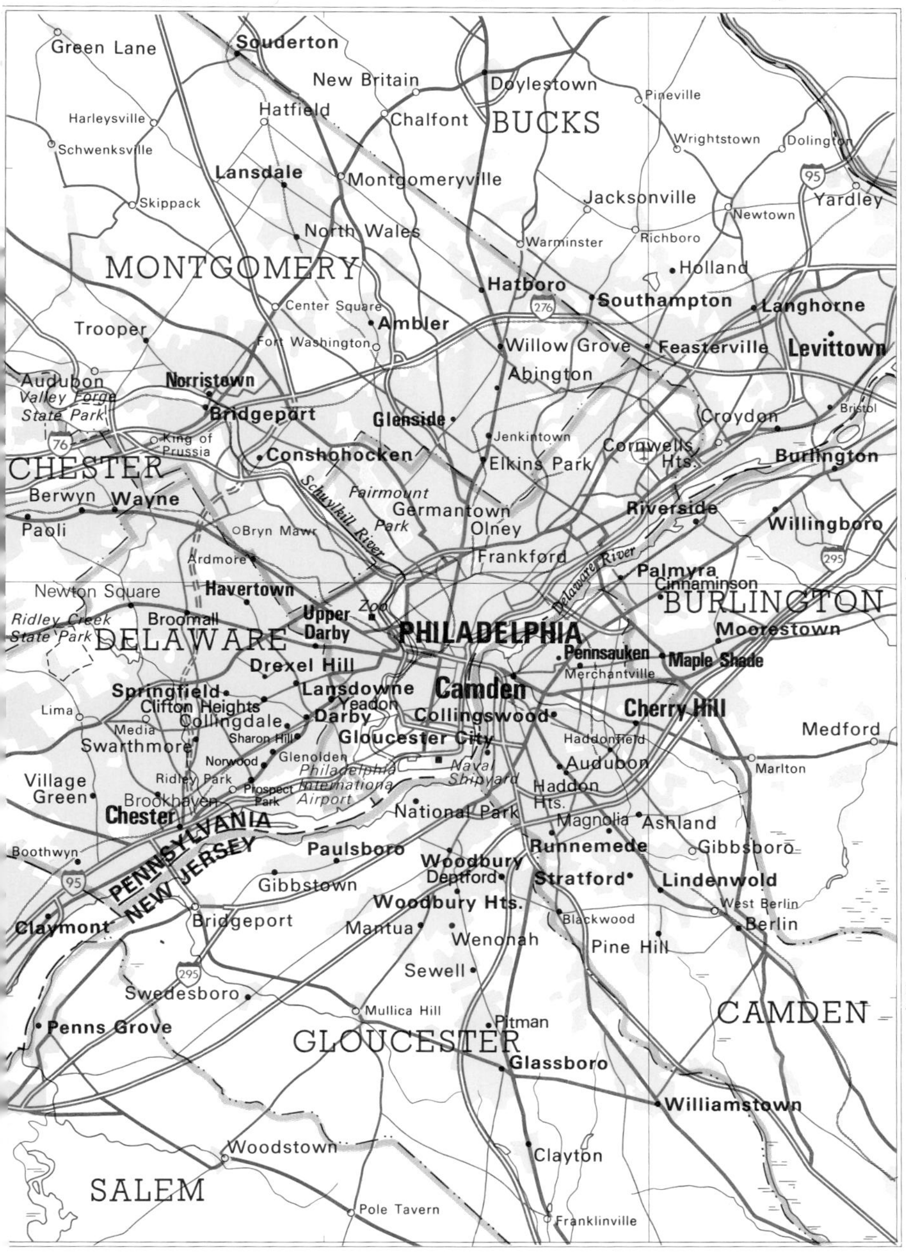

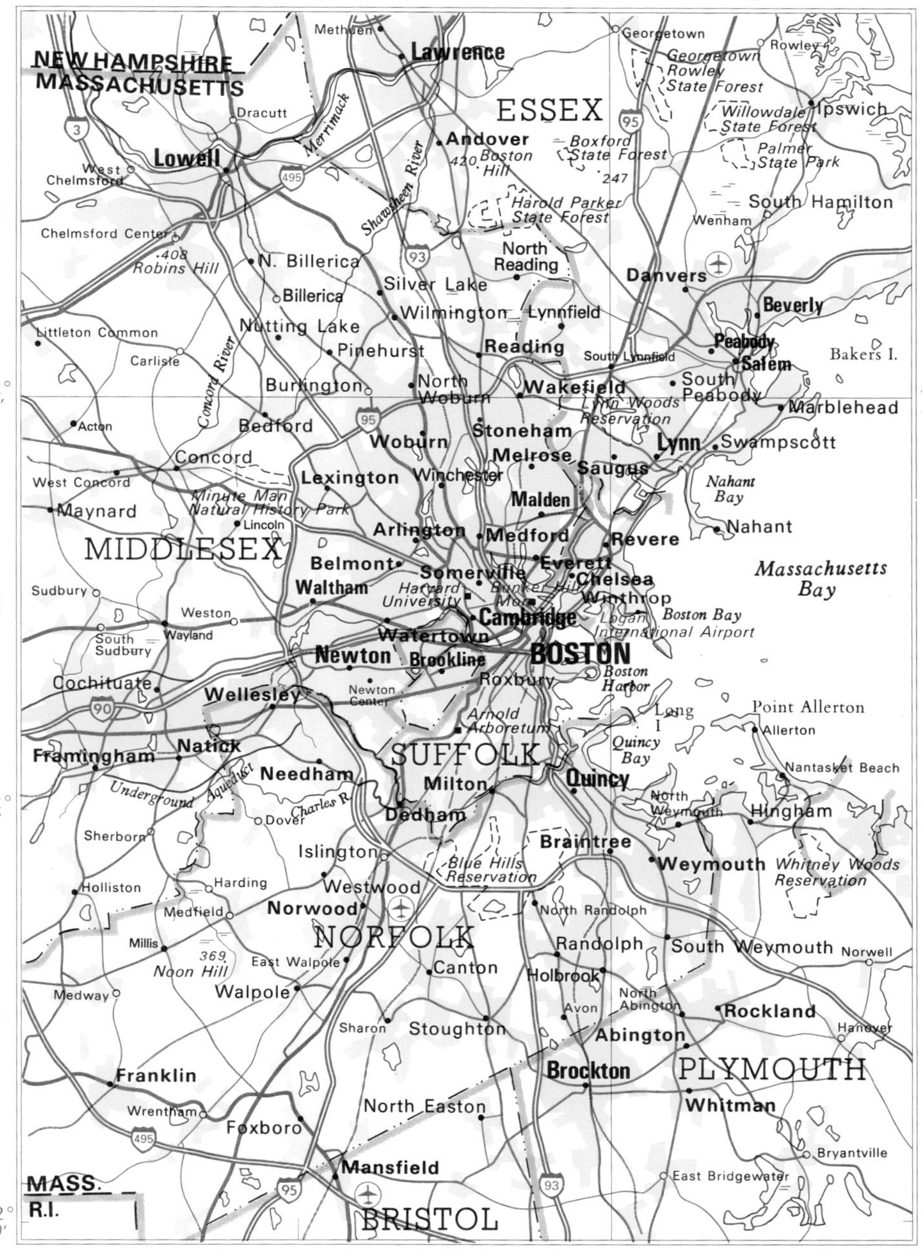

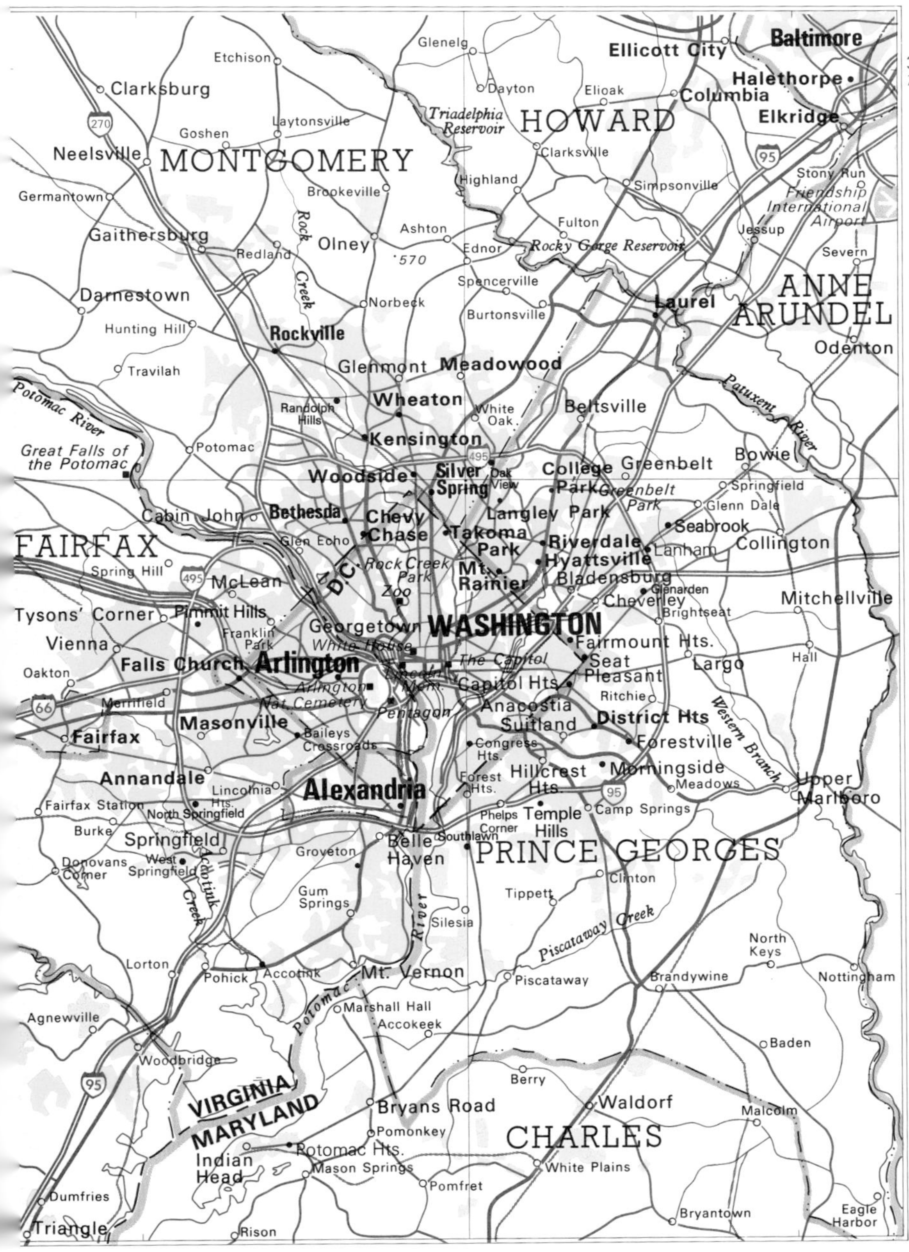

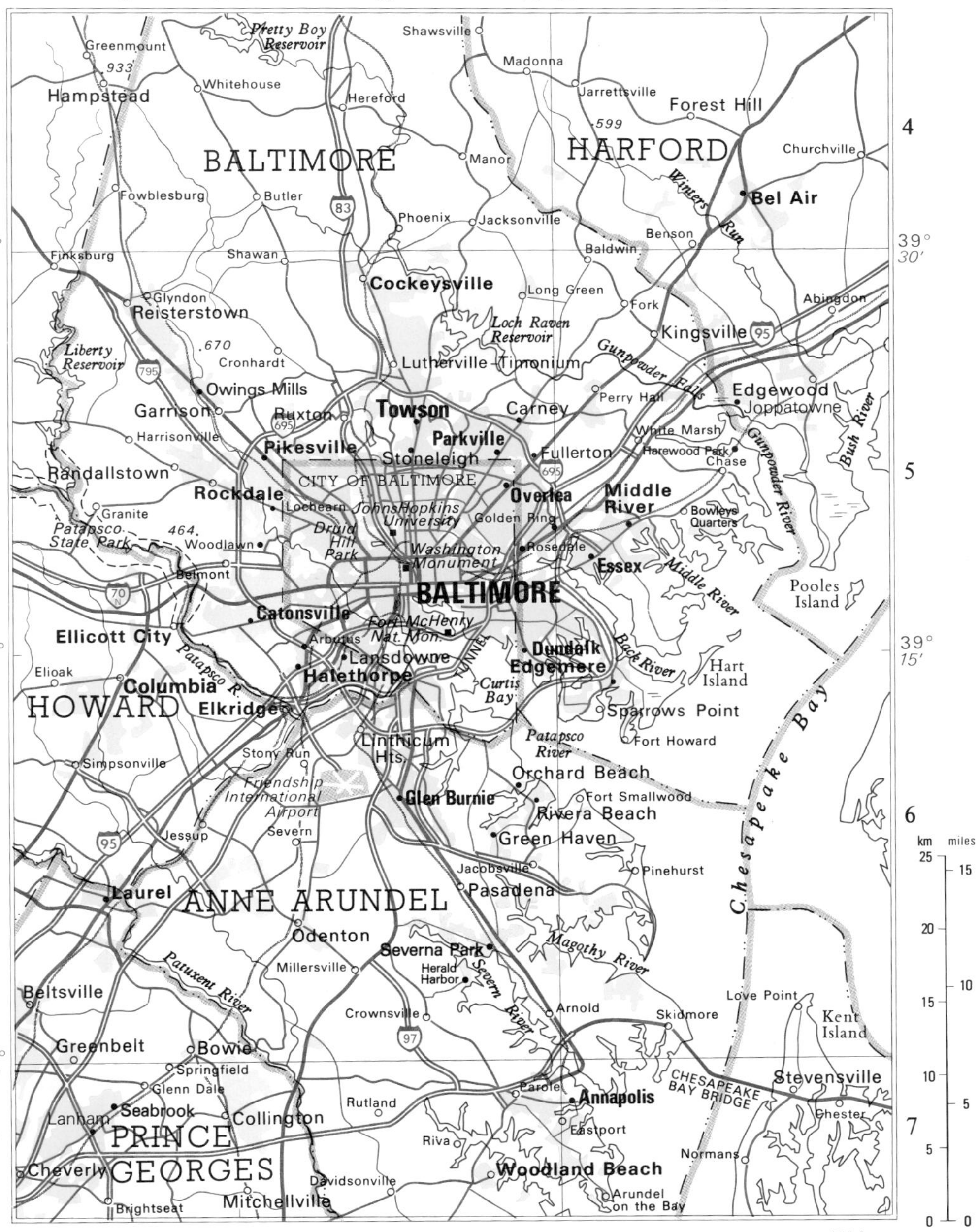

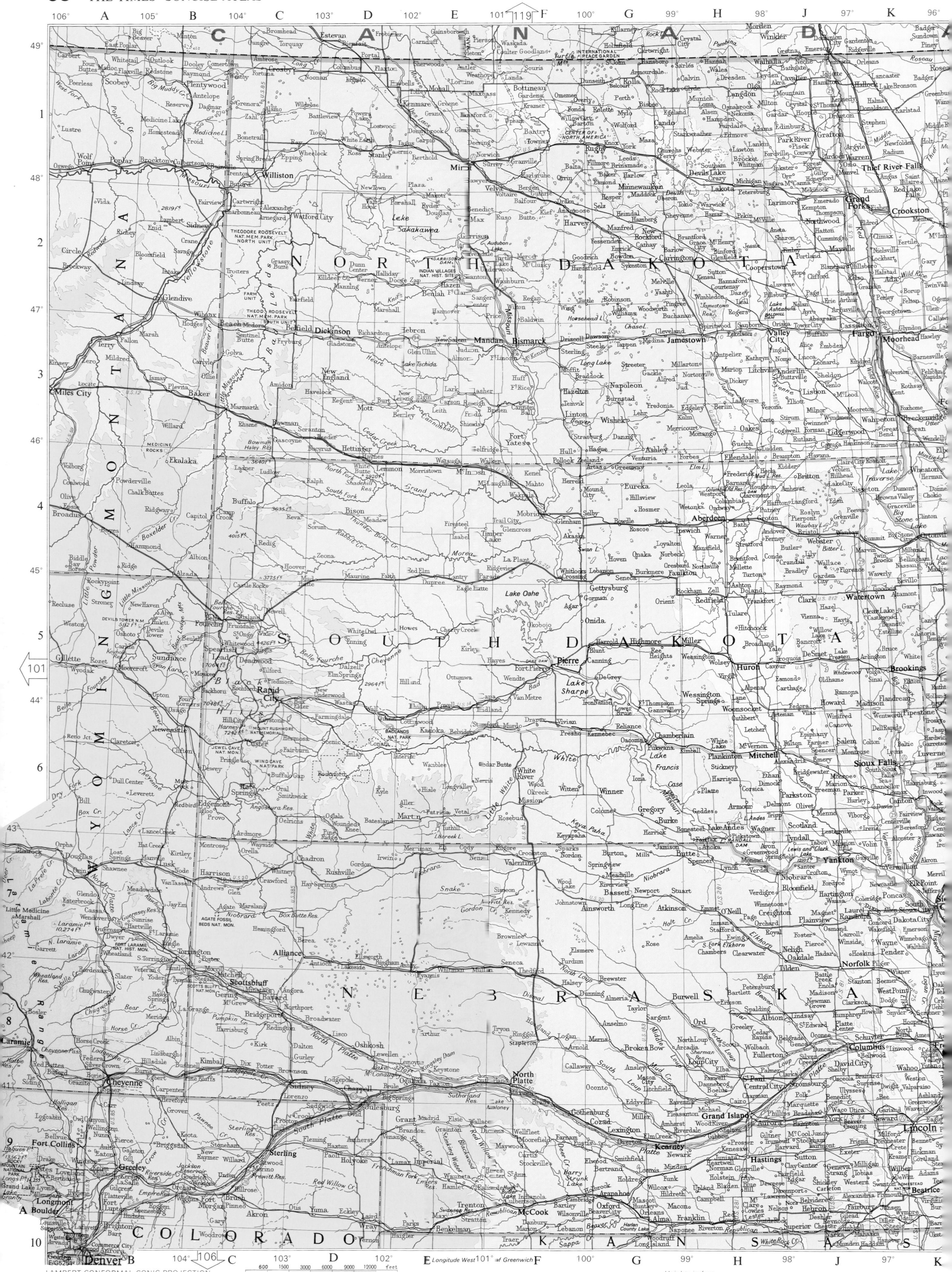
CANADA
NORTH DAKOTA
SOUTH DAKOTA
NEBRASKA
MONTANA
WYOMING
COLORADO
KANSAS
Lake Sakakawea
Lake Oahe
Bismarck
Pierre
Fargo
Grand Forks
Minot
Rapid City
Cheyenne
Lincoln
Denver
Sioux Falls
Aberdeen
Jamestown
Dickinson
Williston
Miles City
Scottsbluff
North Platte
Grand Island
Kearney
Norfolk
Yankton
Huron
Watertown
Mitchell
Valentine
Alliance
Sidney
Greeley
Fort Collins
Laramie
Moorhead
Brookings
Columbus
Hastings
Mandan
Glendive
Spearfish
Lead
Deadwood
Sturgis
McCook
Longitude West 101° of Greenwich
119
101
106
Heights in feet

LAMBERT CONFORMAL CONIC PROJECTION

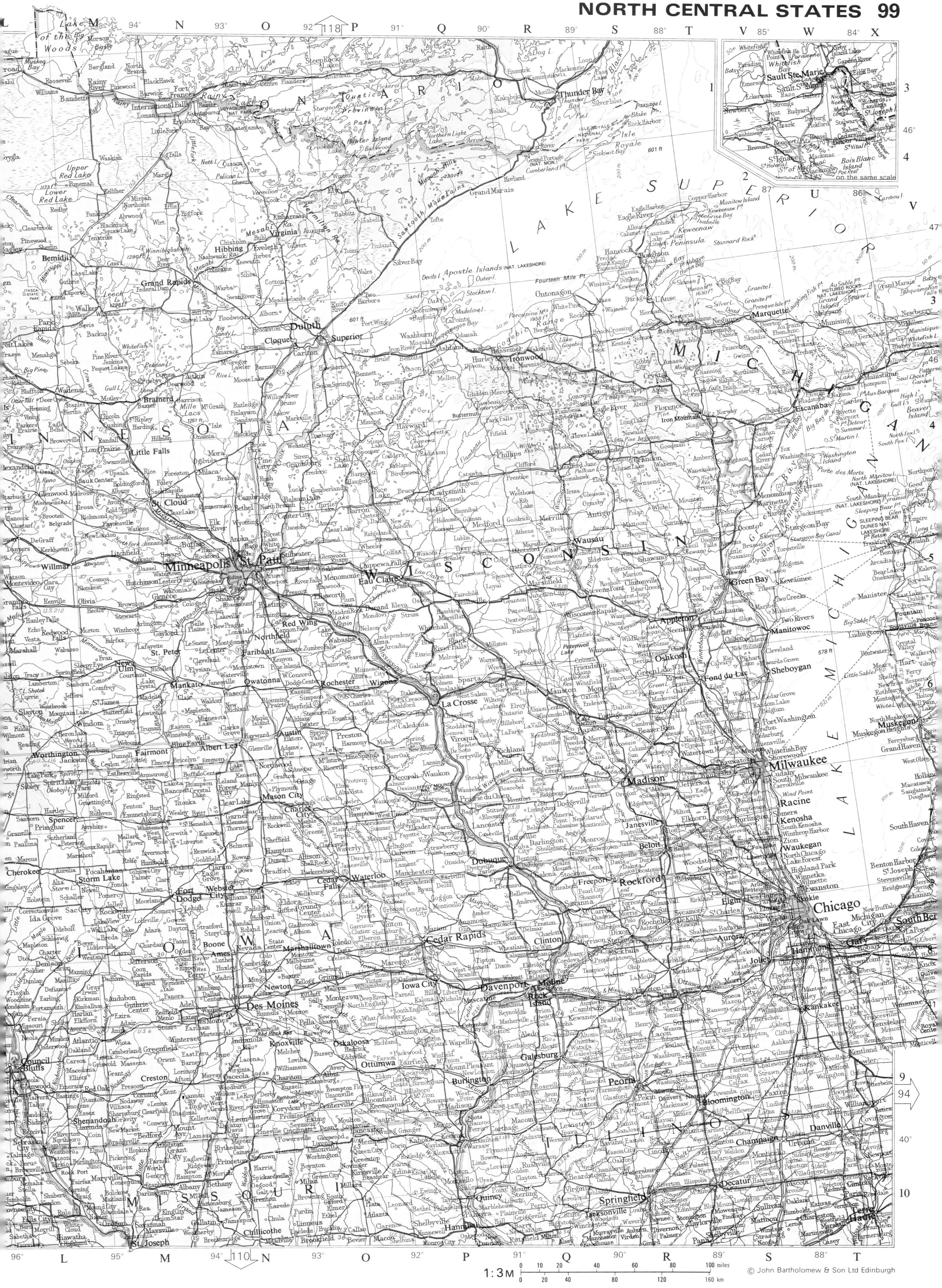
LAKE SUPERIOR
LAKE MICHIGAN
ONTARIO
MINNESOTA
WISCONSIN
MICHIGAN
IOWA
ILLINOIS
MISSOURI
Quetico Provincial Park
Isle Royale
Apostle Islands (NAT. LAKESHORE)
Thunder Bay
Duluth
Superior
Minneapolis
St Paul
St Cloud
Rochester
Winona
La Crosse
Eau Claire
Wausau
Green Bay
Appleton
Oshkosh
Sheboygan
Manitowoc
Milwaukee
Racine
Kenosha
Waukegan
Madison
Rockford
Chicago
Evanston
Skokie
Hammond
Gary
South Bend
Joliet
Aurora
Elgin
Kankakee
Peoria
Bloomington
Champaign
Danville
Decatur
Springfield
Galesburg
Moline
Rock Island
Davenport
Clinton
Dubuque
Cedar Rapids
Iowa City
Waterloo
Des Moines
Ames
Fort Dodge
Mason City
Council Bluffs
Ottumwa
Burlington
Quincy
Hannibal
St Joseph
Sault Ste Marie
Marquette
Escanaba
Muskegon
Grand Haven
Benton Harbor
Terre Haute
Mankato
Owatonna
Albert Lea
Austin
Brainerd
Bemidji
Hibbing
Grand Rapids
International Falls
Little Falls
Worthington
Spencer
Storm Lake
Shenandoah
Chillicothe
1 : 3M
© John Bartholomew & Son Ltd Edinburgh

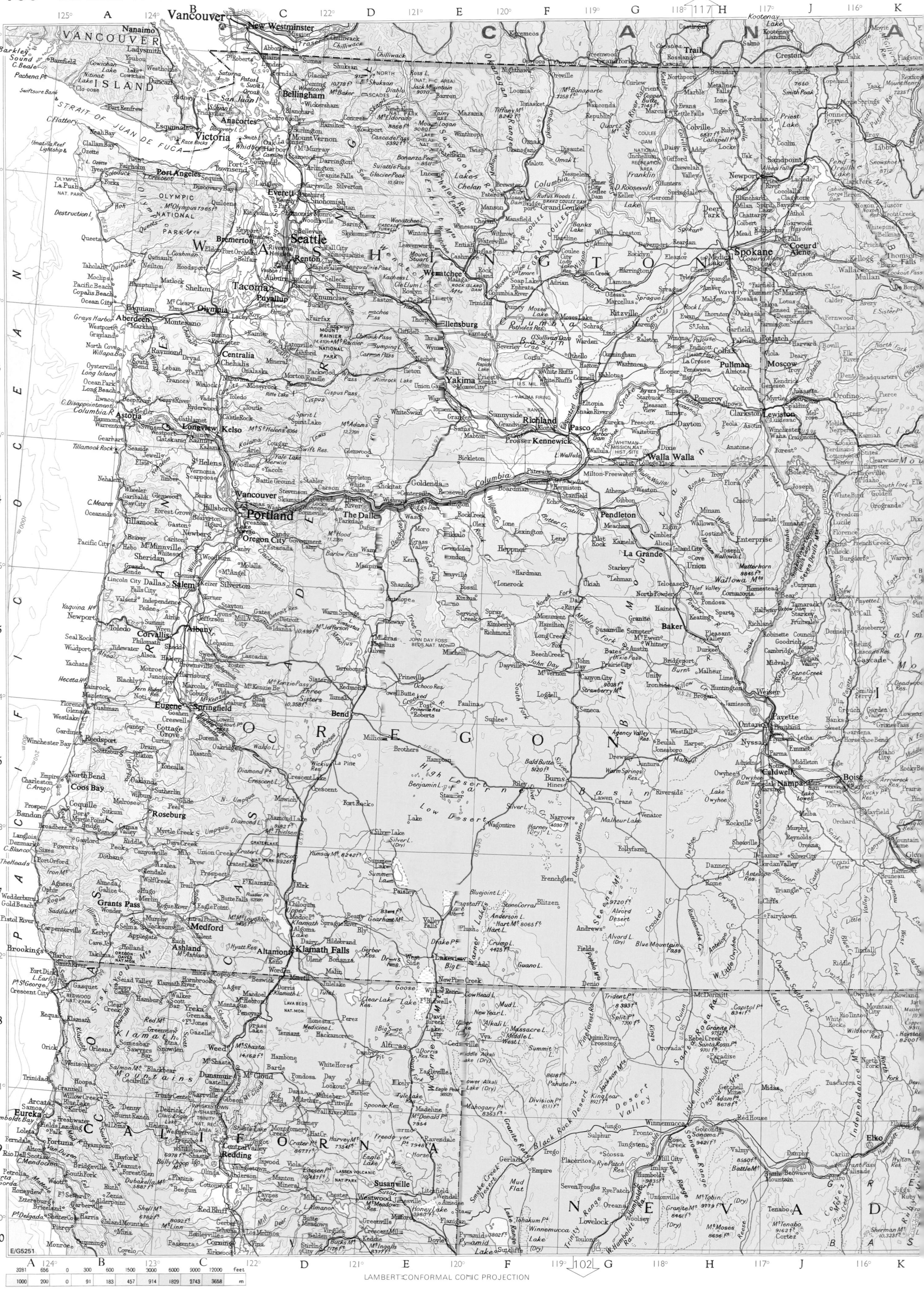
CANADA
WASHINGTON
OREGON
IDAHO
CALIFORNIA
NEVADA
PACIFIC OCEAN
VANCOUVER ISLAND
STRAIT OF JUAN DE FUCA
Vancouver
Victoria
Nanaimo
New Westminster
Bellingham
Everett
Seattle
Tacoma
Olympia
Aberdeen
Bremerton
Port Angeles
Wenatchee
Ellensburg
Yakima
Richland
Kennewick
Pasco
Walla Walla
Spokane
Coeur d'Alene
Pullman
Moscow
Lewiston
Clarkston
Longview
Kelso
Astoria
Vancouver
Portland
Oregon City
The Dalles
Pendleton
La Grande
Baker
Salem
Albany
Corvallis
Eugene
Springfield
Bend
Roseburg
Coos Bay
North Bend
Grants Pass
Medford
Ashland
Klamath Falls
Altamont
Lakeview
Burns
Ontario
Payette
Weiser
Caldwell
Nampa
Boise
Eureka
Arcata
Fortuna
Redding
Susanville
Yreka
Weed
Dunsmuir
Alturas
Winnemucca
Lovelock
Elko
Columbia
Snake
Cascade Range
Olympic Mts
Blue Mountains
Wallowa Mts
Klamath Mountains
Black Rock Desert
Mt Rainier 14,410 ft
Mt St Helens
Mt Hood 11,235 ft
Mt Shasta 14,162 ft
Crater Lake
Mt Adams 12,276 ft
Lassen Peak
E/G5251
LAMBERT CONFORMAL CONIC PROJECTION
feet
m
117
102

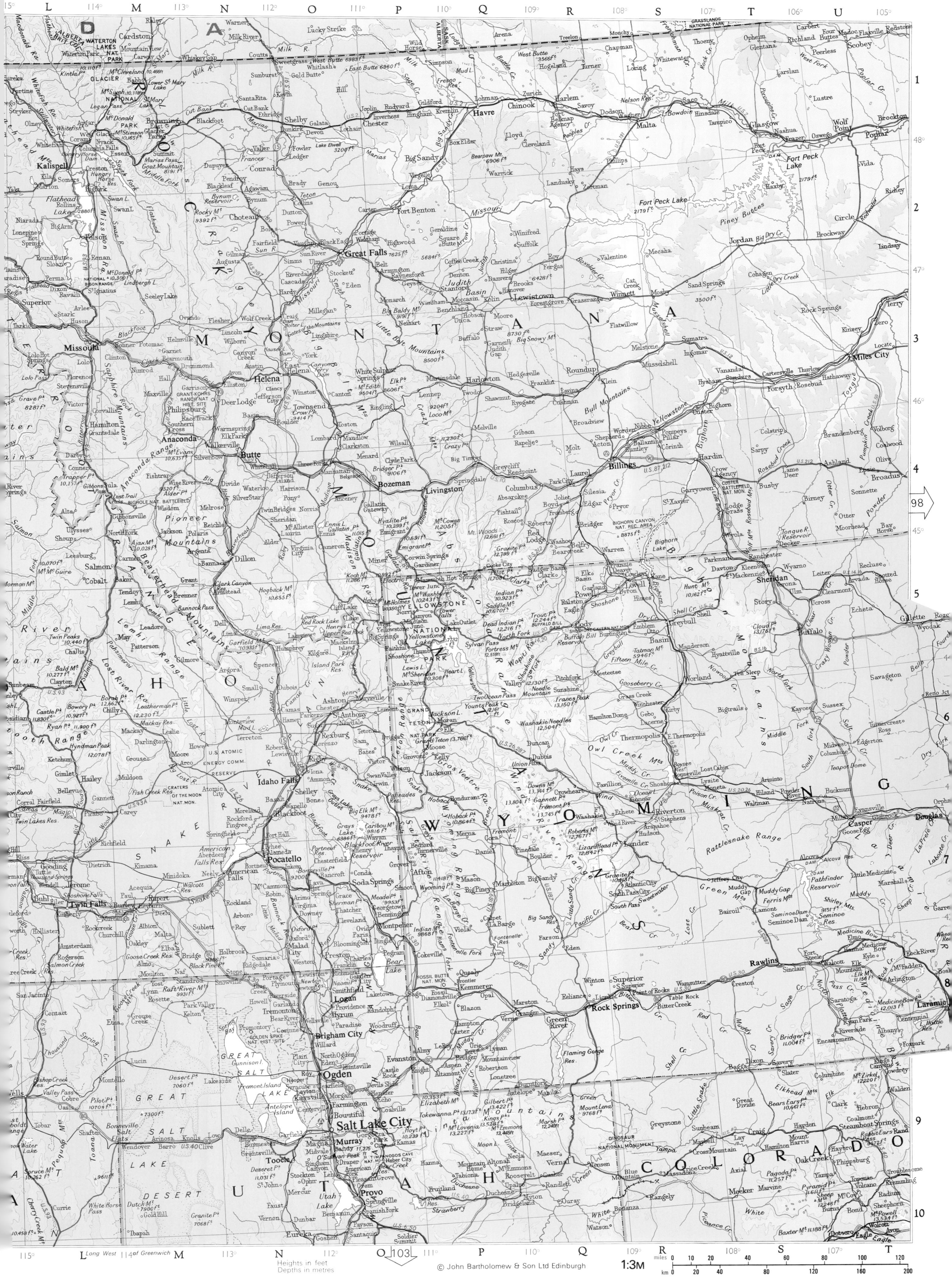

MONTANA

IDAHO

WYOMING

UTAH

COLORADO

Helena

Great Falls

Missoula

Kalispell

Butte

Bozeman

Billings

Miles City

Havre

Sheridan

Idaho Falls

Pocatello

Twin Falls

Salt Lake City

Ogden

Provo

Logan

Brigham City

Rock Springs

Rawlins

Casper

Laramie

GREAT SALT LAKE

GREAT SALT LAKE DESERT

YELLOWSTONE NATIONAL PARK

GRAND TETON NAT. PARK

GLACIER NATIONAL PARK

Fort Peck Lake

Heights in feet
Depths in metres

© John Bartholomew & Son Ltd Edinburgh

1:3M

miles
km

OAHU
(HONOLULU COUNTY)

1:1M

HAWAIIAN ISLANDS
(To U.S.A.)

1:9 000 000

also on page 135

LAMBERT CONFORMAL CONIC PROJECTION

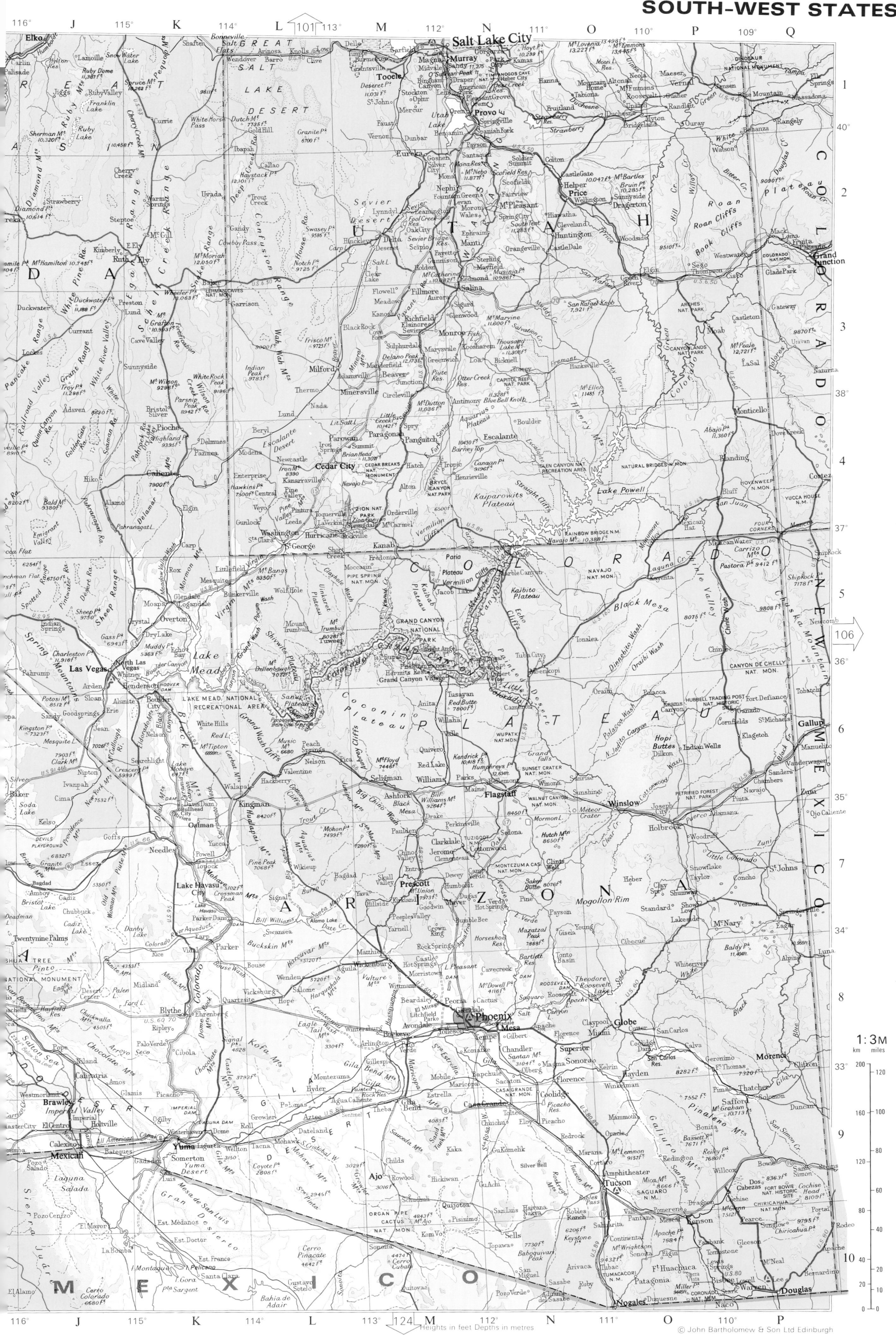
101
106
124
UTAH
NEVADA
ARIZONA
COLORADO
NEW MEXICO
MEXICO
COLORADO PLATEAU
GREAT SALT LAKE DESERT
Salt Lake City
Murray
Tooele
Provo
Eureka
Nephi
Price
Helper
Delta
Fillmore
Richfield
Salina
Milford
Beaver
Cedar City
Parowan
Panguitch
St. George
Kanab
Moab
Green River
Grand Junction
Monticello
Blanding
Lake Powell
Ely
Pioche
Caliente
Las Vegas
North Las Vegas
Henderson
Boulder City
Lake Mead
Kingman
Needles
Lake Havasu City
Parker
Blythe
Yuma
Brawley
El Centro
Calexico
Mexicali
Salton Sea
Imperial Valley
Flagstaff
Williams
Prescott
Winslow
Holbrook
Gallup
Tuba City
Grand Canyon Village
GRAND CANYON NATIONAL PARK
Sedona
Phoenix
Mesa
Tempe
Chandler
Glendale
Wickenburg
Globe
Miami
Superior
Florence
Coolidge
Casa Grande
Gila Bend
Ajo
Tucson
Nogales
Benson
Bisbee
Douglas
Safford
Morenci
Mogollon Rim
Black Mesa
Hopi Buttes
Lake Mead National Recreational Area
Gran Desierto
1:3M
km miles
Heights in feet Depths in metres
© John Bartholomew & Son Ltd Edinburgh

104 SAN FRANCISCO

122°45' A 122°30' B 122°15' C 122°00' D 121°45' E 121°30' F

Kent Lake
McNears Beach
San Anselmo San Pablo Bay
Ross San Rafael San Pablo El Sobran 80
Kentfield Concord
MARIN RICHMOND- Richmond Pleasant Hill Antioch
Larkspur SAN RAFAEL San Pablo Res. Cowell Oakley
Mt. Tamalpais BRIDGE Richmond Briones Re. Clayton Sand Hill Knightsen
2571 San Corte Madera Ridge Chabt CONTRA Brentwood
Mt. Tamalpais Mill Quentin El Cerrito Charl Lee Tilden 680 Walnut Creek State Game
State Park Valley Albany Regional Orinda Refuge COSTA
Stinson Muir Woods University of California Park Village Mt. Diablo Middle River
Beach Nat. Monument Angel Island Berkeley Orinda afayette State Park 3849 Byron
Belvedere State Park Lafayette Reservoir Alamo Black Hills Union Island
Sausalito Tiburon Piedmont CALDECOTT Danville SAN
GOLDEN GATE BRIDGE Alcatraz I. TUNNEL Moraga JOAQUIN
Treasure Oakland San Ramon
Golden Gate Island Redwood 680 Old River
SAN FRANCISCO Regional Upper Tracy
37° Park San Leandro San Ramon Village 580
45' Golden Gate Park Univ. of San Francisco Reservoir Carbona
Sunset Mission Alameda Dublin Livermore
Lake Mt. Davidson San Oakland Delta Mendota
Merced 929 Leandro International Lake Chabot Pleasanton Canal
Daly City Naval Shipyard Airport Castro 580
Brisbane San Francisco Bay Valley ALAMEDA
South San Francisco San Hayward
37° Pacifica Lorenzo Sanol
30' San Bruno 280 San SAN Mt. Ed n Union City Niles
Shelter Cove Francisco Hetch Hetchy Aqueduct DIABLO
Point San Pedro International Millbrae Fremont (Underground)
PACIFIC Pedro Airport MATEO Newark Irvington Mission
Valley San Andreas Burlingame Hillsborough B IDGE San Jose Alameda Cr. 3817 RANGE
Lake San Mateo Foster City Alameda Cr. Dam
OCEAN Montara San Francisco State Fish and Game Refuge Monument STANISLAUS
Moss Beach El Granada Belmont Warm Peak Calaveras
Crystal San Springs 2594 Reservoir
Pillar Point Half SAN Springs Carlos Milpitas Black Mountain
37° Moon Bay MATEO Res. Redwood City Alviso 3951
Woodside Menlo Pal Alto DIABLO
Half Moon Bay Park Milpitas
Stanford Mountain Agnew
San Gregorio University Vi w Berryessa
Portola Los Alum Rock Mt. Hamilton
3 Valley Altos SANTA CLARA 4261
Tunitas Blac Sunnyvale
Redwood Mountain Santa Clara Lick
Terrace 275 San Jose Observatory
La Honda Stevens Cr. Cupertino Evergreen
SANTA CRUZ MTS Reservoir Campbell

122°45' A 122°30' B 122°15' C 122°00' D 121°45' E 121°30' F

LOS ANGELES

118°45' G 118°30' H 113°15' J 118°00' K 117°45' L 117°30'

Santa Susana ANGE ES NATIONAL 8020 FOREST
Van Norman Lakes Sa Gabriel Mountains Mt. San Antonio
4 318 Sylmar 10,064
Simi Valley San Fernando San Gabriel Peak
34° Chatsworth Northridge Sunland 6161 Cogswell SAN
15' Chatsworth Sepulveda La Crescenta Reservoir
Reservoir Canoga Park Sun Valley LOS Montrose San Gabriel Mt. Wilson BERNARDINO
VENTURA Winnetka San Verdugo La Canada Observatory Reservoir
Tarzana Fernando North ANGELES San Gabriel
Woodland Valley Hollywood Burbank Rose La Canada Morris Azusa
Hills Sherman Glendale Bowl Sierra Madre Reservoir Glendora
Santa Monica Mts Encino Oaks Griffith Park Pasadena Monrovia Duarte San Dimas
Hollywood Eagle Rock South San Arcadia Puddingstone Etiwanda
Saddle Peak Bowl Pasadena Marino Temple City Reservoir
2805 West Beverly Hills Hollywood Arroyo Alhambra Baldwin Covina La Verne Claremont
Hollywood Dodgers Seco San Rosemead Park Upland Rancho Cucamonga
Topanga University Sta. Park Gabriel South West Pomona
Beach of California El ian East Los Angeles Monterey San Gabriel El Monte Covina Ontario
Malibu Pacific LOS ANGELES Park Commerce La Puente North Whittier
Palisades Culver City Boyle Montebello Hts. Chino
Santa Monica Heights Pico Rivera Puente Hills Diamond Los
Maywood Hacienda La Habra Bar Serranos
Venice Florence Huntington Park Whittier Hts. Heights
Marina Inglewood Bell Gardens South Whittier La Habra Chino Hills
del Rey West Gate La Mirada Heights
34° Los Angeles Lennox South Downey South Prado Flood
00' Santa International Hawthorne Gate Lynwood Whittier La Habra Control Basin Norco
Monica Airport Willow ydale Paramount Norwalk Brea Yorba Linda
Bay El Segundo Lawndale Brook Compton Bellflower La Mirada Prado Dam
Hermosa Manhattan Gardena Dor ngtez Buena RIVERSIDE Corona Home
PACIFIC Beach Beach ills Nort Artesia Park Fullerton Gardens
Santa Cerritos La Palma SANTA
Redondo Lakewood Anaheim ANA Pedley
OCEAN Monica Beach Torrance Carson Cypress Arlanza
Bay Los Disneyland Village
Palos Verdes Alamitos Stanton SANTA
Estates Signal Hill Rossmoor Garden Orange ANA
Palos Verdes Pt. Lomita Wilmington Grove Cowan Heights MTS
Rancho San Pedro Santa Ana Santiago
Palos Verdes Long Westminster Tustin Res. 4007
Marineland Beach Seal Lemon Heights CLEVELAND
of the Pacific San Pedro Bay Beach Sunset NATIONAL
Point Sa Pedro Bay Sunset Beach Bay FOREST
Fermin Passenger Ferry 405 Fountain Santiago
Santa Catalina Island Valley ORANGE Peak 5687
San Pedro Channel Huntington Beach Como
Costa Mesa Irvine
Newport Beach 5

118°45' G 118°30' H 118° J 118°00' K 117°45' L 117°30'

km miles
25 15
20
10
5
0

© Times Books Ltd 1:5 000 000

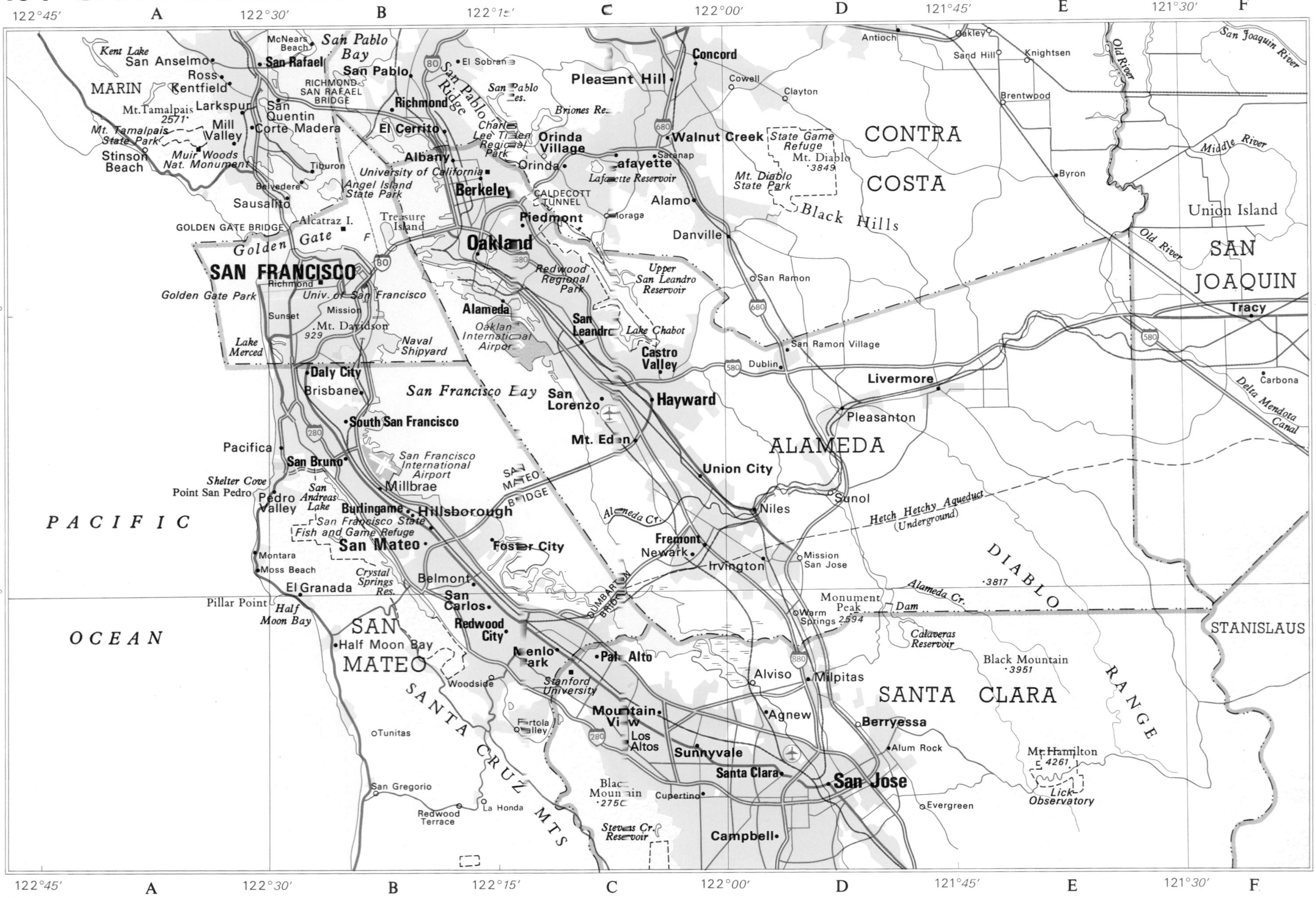

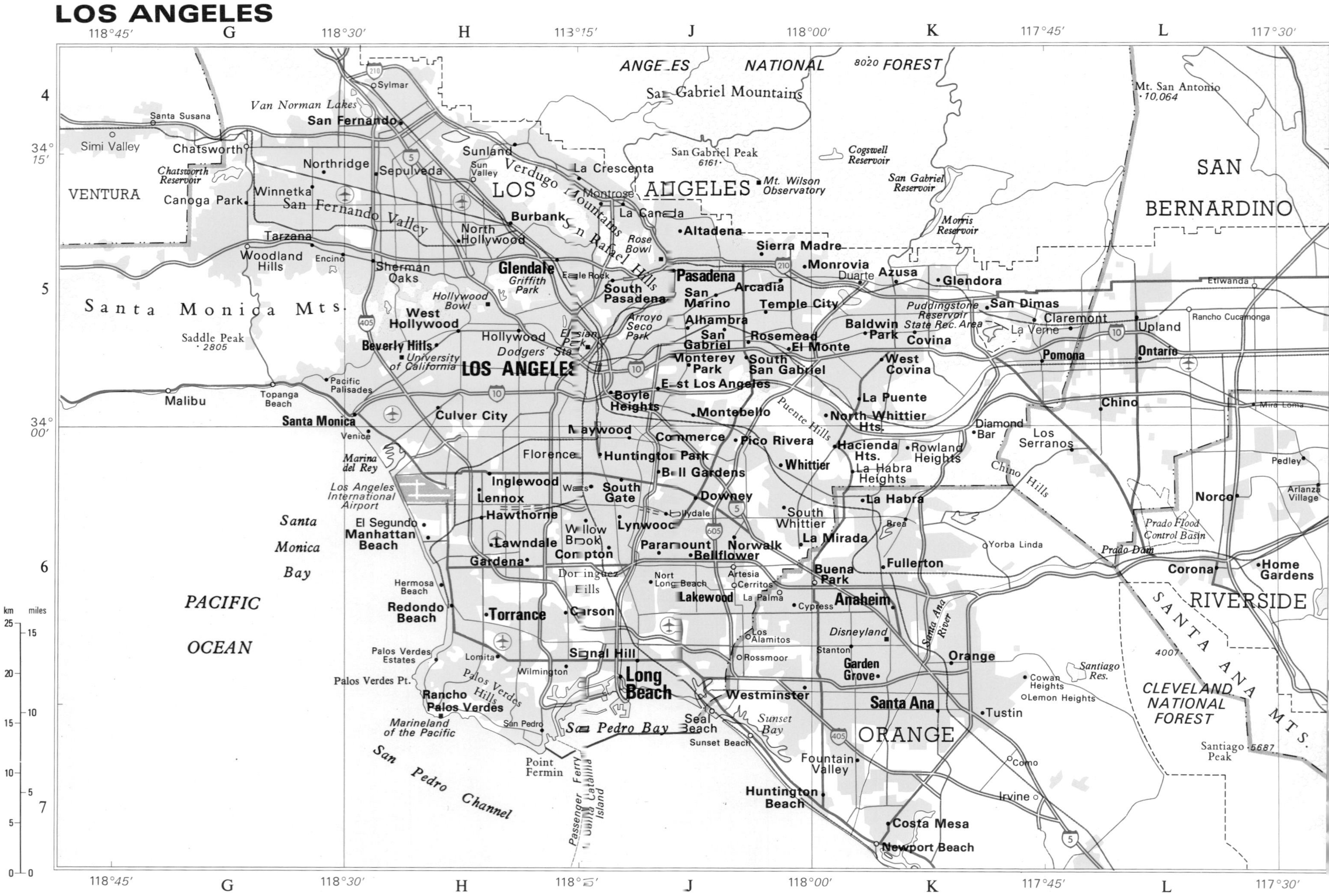

88°15′
A
88°00′
B
87°45′
C
87°30′
D
87°15′
E
87°00′
LAKE
COOK
DU PAGE
KANE
KENDALL
WILL
Algonquin
Cuba
Barrington
Buffalo Grove
Deerfield
Highland Park
Spring Lake Reserve
Wheeling
Glencoe
Carpentersville
Inverness
Palatine
Northbrook
Winnetka
Kenilworth
Sutton
Prospect Hts.
Arlington Hts.
Wilmette
Rolling Meadows
Mt. Prospect
Elgin
Glenview
Hoffman Estates
Busse Forest
Des Plaines
Morton Grove
Skokie
Evanston
Schaumburg
Niles
S. Elgin
Elk Grove Village
Park Ridge
Lincolnwood
Bartlett
Des Plaines River
Hanover Park
Keeneyville
O'Hare International Airport
Roselle
Itasca
Bensenville
Harwood Hts.
Lincoln Park
Valley View
Fox River
Wayne
Bloomingdale
Wood Dale
Belmont Harbor
St. Charles
Addison
Franklin Park
Elmwood Park
LAKE MICHIGAN
Geneva
Villa Park
Elmhurst
Melrose Park
Oak Park
CHICAGO
W.Chicago
Lombard
Glen Ellyn
Bell Wood
Maywood
Art Institute
Chicago Harbor
Batavia
Wheaton
Broadview
Berwyn
Forest Park
Brookfield Zoo
Cicero
North Aurora
Warrenhurst
Warrenville
Morton Arboretum
Riverside
Stickney
La Grange
Brookfield
Lisle
Hinsdale
ILLINOIS
MICHIGAN
Downers Grove
Jackson Park
Museum of Science and Industry
Naperville
Summit
University of Chicago
Aurora
Bridgeview
South Chicago
INDIANA
Barbers Corner
Willow Springs
Oak Lawn
Evergreen Park
Argonne Forest
Calumet Harbor
Michigan City
Oswego
Hastings
Sag Bridge
Worth
Merrionette Park
Lake Calumet
Whiting
Lemont
Palos Park
Palos Hts.
Calumet Park
Beverly Shores
Normantown
Riverdale
Wolf Lake
East Chicago
Dune Acres
Tremont
Romeoville
Blue Island
Goodings Grove
Orland Park
Midlothian
Harvey
Dolton
Burnham
Calumet City
Ogden Dunes
Plainfield
Du Page River
Oak Forest
Hammond
Chesterton
Lockport
Markham
S. Holland
Gary
Crest Hill
Tinley Park
Lansing
Lake Station
Otis
Homewood
Black Oak
Munster
Highland
New Chicago
Portage
Woodville
Marley
Mokena
Flossmoor
Liverpool
Shorewood
Joliet
Ridgewood
Glen Park
Hobart
PORTER
Westville
Rockdale
Ingalls Park
New Lenox
Lincoln Estates
Chicago Hts.
Griffith
Lake George
Wheeler
Coburg
Lottaville
Matteson
S. Chicago Heights
Schererville
Merrillville
Sedley
Birds
Frankfort
Park Forest
Independence Hill
Valparaiso
42° 00′
41° 45′
41° 30′
1
2
3

ST. LOUIS

F
90°30′
G
90°15′
H
90°00′
Pere Marquette State Park
Grafton
Fosterburg
Brussels
Godfrey
Melville
MADISON
Centerville
Mississippi River
Portage des Sioux
ILLINOIS
MISSOURI
Alton
Midway
Bethalto
Orchard Farm
Black Walnut
East Alton
Gard
Peruque
West Alton
Wood River
Kampville
Fort Bellefontaine
Roxana
Boschertown
ST. CHARLES
Missouri River
Edwardsville
St. Peters
Spanish Lake
St.Charles
Florissant
Hazelwood
Larimore
Lewis and Clark State Memorial
Harvester
Bridgeton
Robertson
Ferguson
Bellefontaine Neighbors
Mitchell
Berkeley
Maryland Hts.
St. Ann
Jennings
Pontoon Beach
Overland
Breckenridge Hills
Granite City
Pagedale
Madison
Horseshoe Lake
Olivette
University City
Venice
Collinsville
Creve Coeur
Clayton
Bellefontaine
Forest Park
ST. LOUIS
Ladue
Washington University
Washington Park
Caseyville
Clarkson Valley
Richmond Hts.
East St.Louis
Des Peres
Rock Hill
Jefferson Nat. Expansion Mem.
French Village
Ballwin
Manchester
Glendale
Maplewood
Brentwood
Frank Holten State Park
Fairview Hts.
Kirkwood
Webster Groves
Alorton
Cahokia
Centerville
Valley Park
Crestwood
Affton
E. Carondelet
Belleville
Sappington
Lemay
Times Beach
Dupo
ST. CLAIR
Murphy
Mehlville
Oakville
High Ridge
Paulina Hills
Millstadt
Byrnes Mill
Arnold
Columbia
Maxville
House Springs
Seckman
Smithton
JEFFERSON
Ottoville
Antonia
MONROE
Floraville
Sand Ridge
Barnhart
Fountain
Waterloo
Foster Pond
Hecker
Belew Creek
Valmeyer
Harrisonville
Burksville
Madonnaville
38° 45′
38° 30′
4
5
6

ATLANTA

J
84°30′
K
84°15′
L
Allatoona Reservoir
CHEROKEE
Arnold Mill
FORSYTH
Big Creek
Woodstock
Crabapple
Acworth
Noonday
Sweat Mountain 1688
Alpharetta
Blackwells
Big Creek
Kennesaw
Roswell
Warsaw
Due West
Kennesaw Mtn. National Battlefield Park
Marietta
Mt. Bethel
GWINNETT
Dunwoody
Fair Oaks
Sandy Springs
Norcross
Macland
COBB
Chamblee
Doraville
Smyrna
North Atlanta
Lilburn
Powder Springs
Vinings
Brookhaven
Oakdale
Clarkdale
Harryat
Oak Grove
Tucker
Austell
Mableton
Buckhead
Stone Mountain Park
Cooks
Emory University
Clarkston
Stone Mountain
Emory
Scottdale
Decatur
ATLANTA
Avondale Estates
Grove Park
DOUGLAS
Chattahoochee River
State Capitol
Glen Haven
Redan
Cascade Heights
Lakewood Heights
DE KALB
Lithonia
Panthersville
Constitution
East Point
Snapfinger
Hapeville
Henrico
College Park
Panola
Klondike
Conley
Red Oak
Hartsfield Atlanta Airport
Forest Park
Camp Smyrna
FULTON
ROCKDALE
Union City
Morrow
Lake-City
Fairburn
CLAYTON
Whitehouse
Stockbridge
Jonesboro
Palmetto
Flint River
HENRY
FAYETTE
Stop
Hastings
Fayetteville
McDonough
34° 00′
33° 45′
33° 30′
km
miles
4
5
6
7

1:500 000

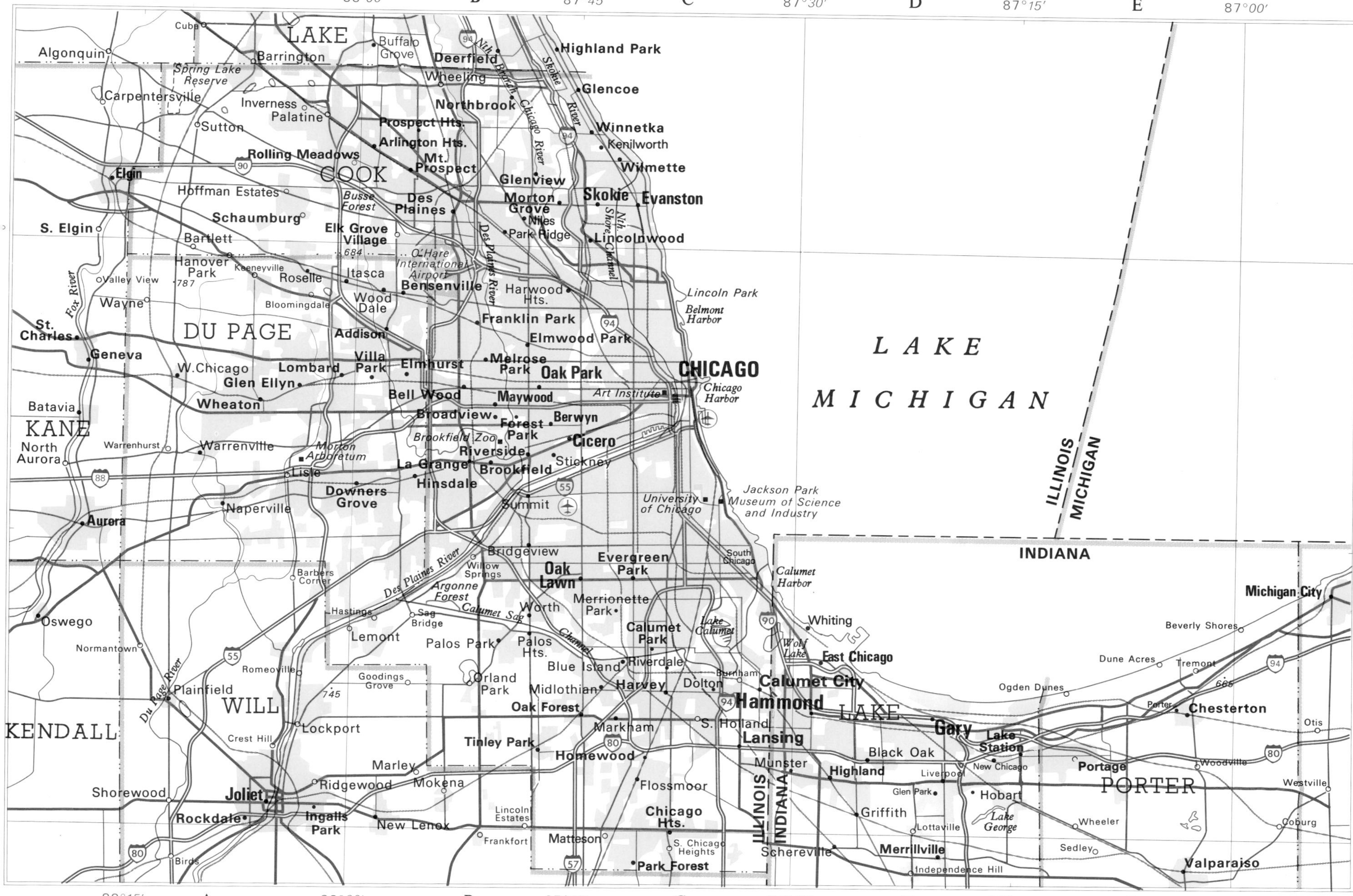

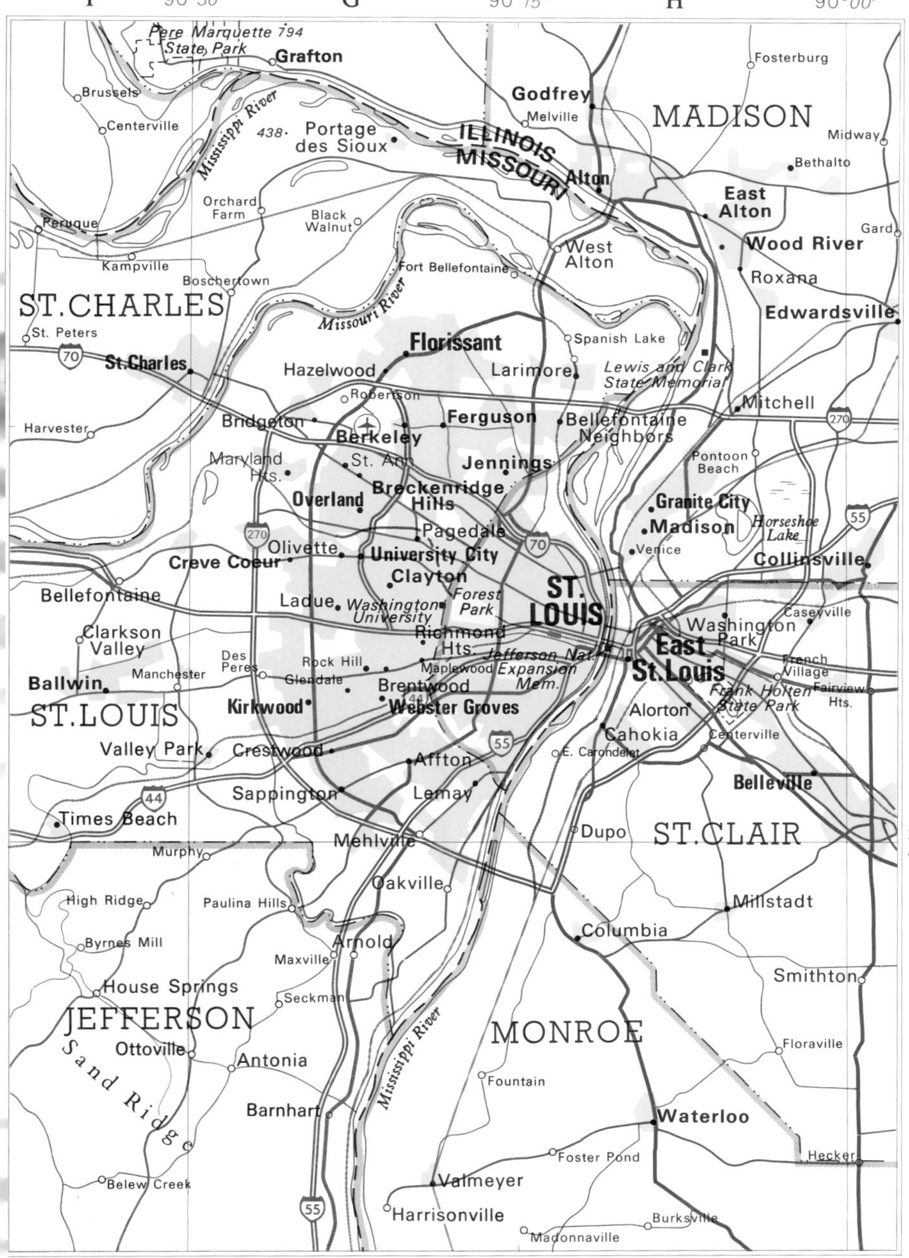

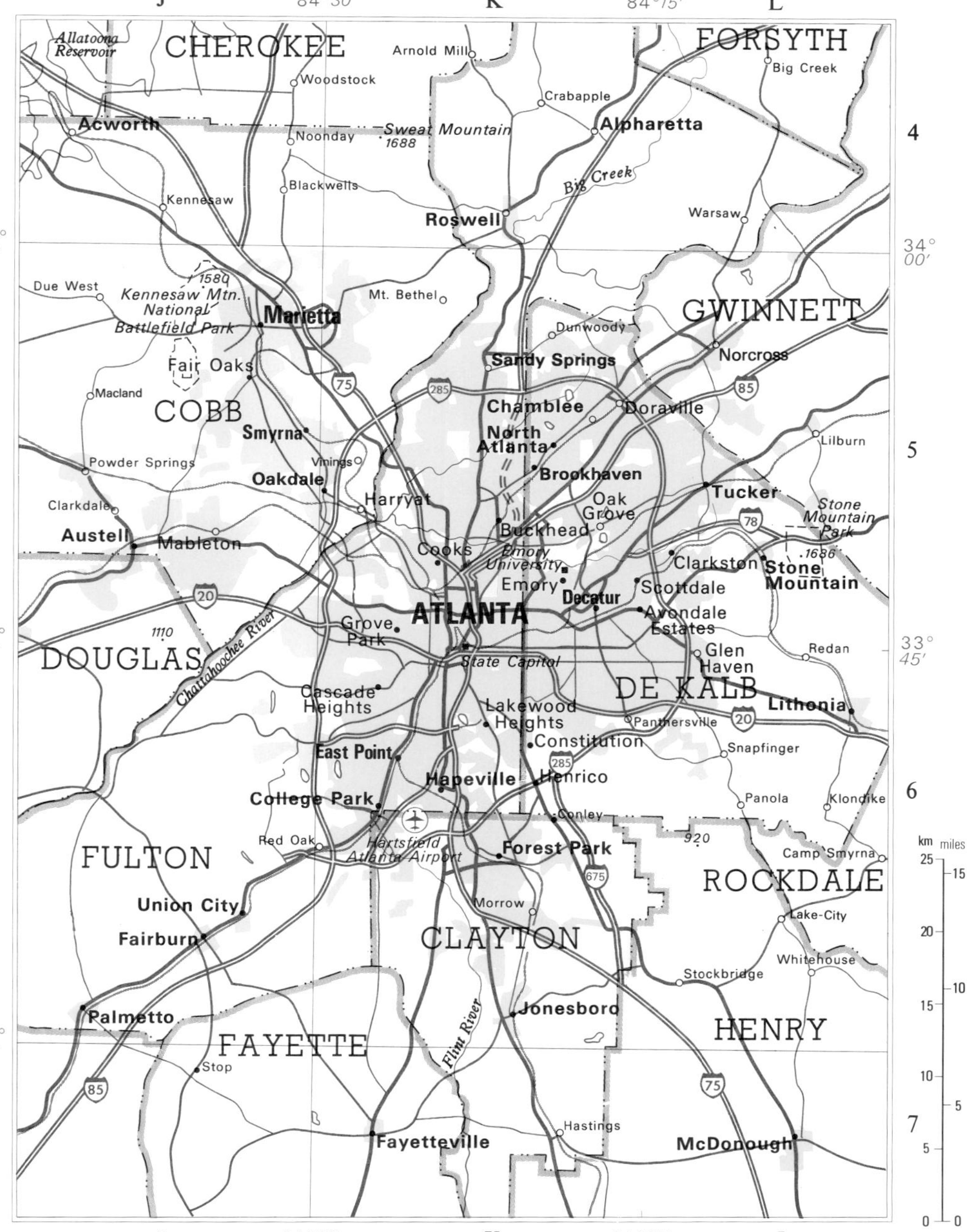

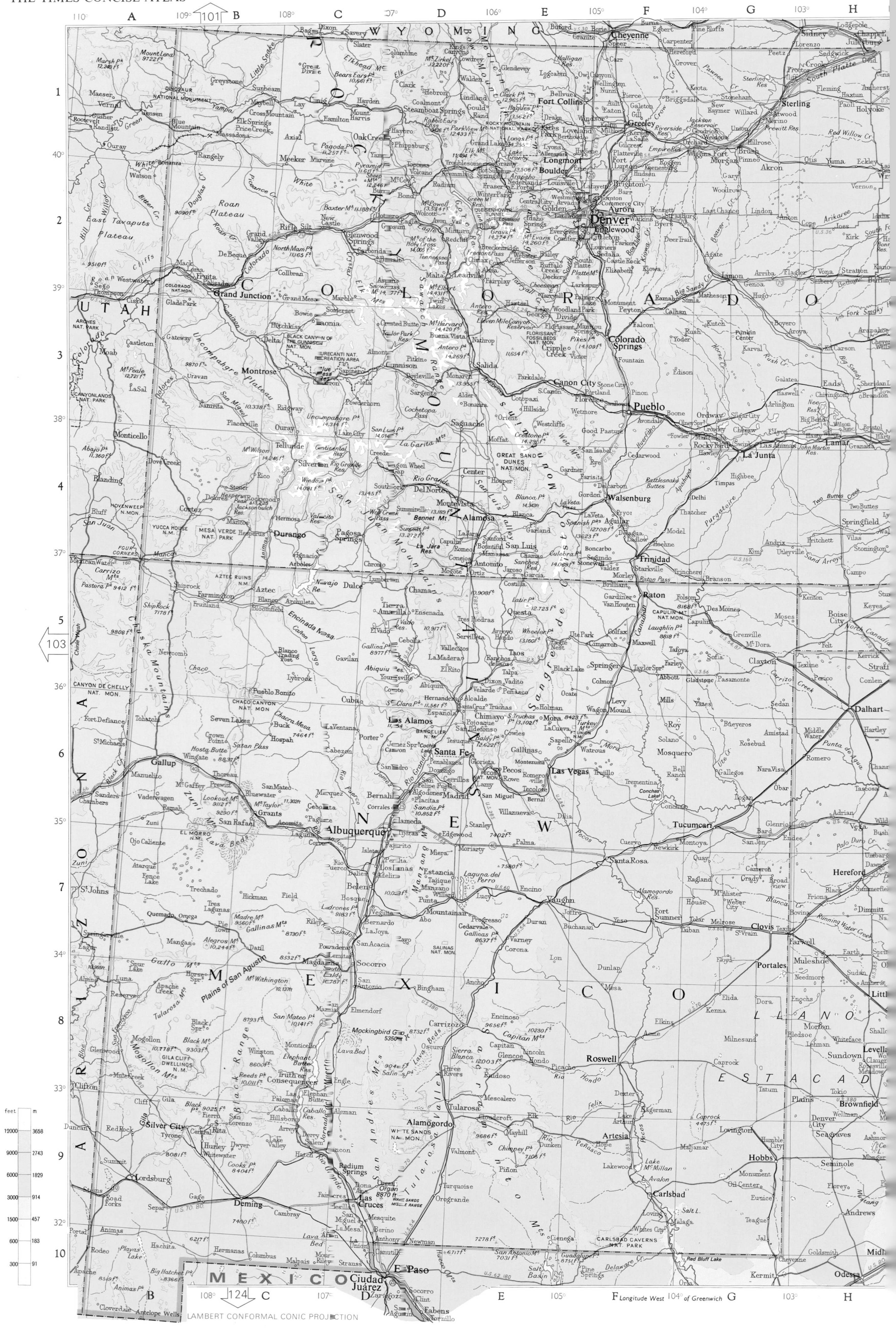

WYOMING

UTAH

COLORADO

ARIZONA

NEW MEXICO

MEXICO

Denver
Boulder
Longmont
Fort Collins
Greeley
Cheyenne
Sterling
Colorado Springs
Pueblo
Canon City
La Junta
Lamar
Grand Junction
Montrose
Durango
Trinidad
Raton
Albuquerque
Santa Fe
Las Vegas
Tucumcari
Gallup
Grants
Socorro
Roswell
Clovis
Portales
Hobbs
Carlsbad
Las Cruces
El Paso
Ciudad Juárez
Alamogordo
Silver City
Lordsburg
Deming

feet	m
12000	3658
9000	2743
6000	1829
3000	914
1500	457
600	183
300	91

Longitude West of Greenwich

LAMBERT CONFORMAL CONIC PROJECTION

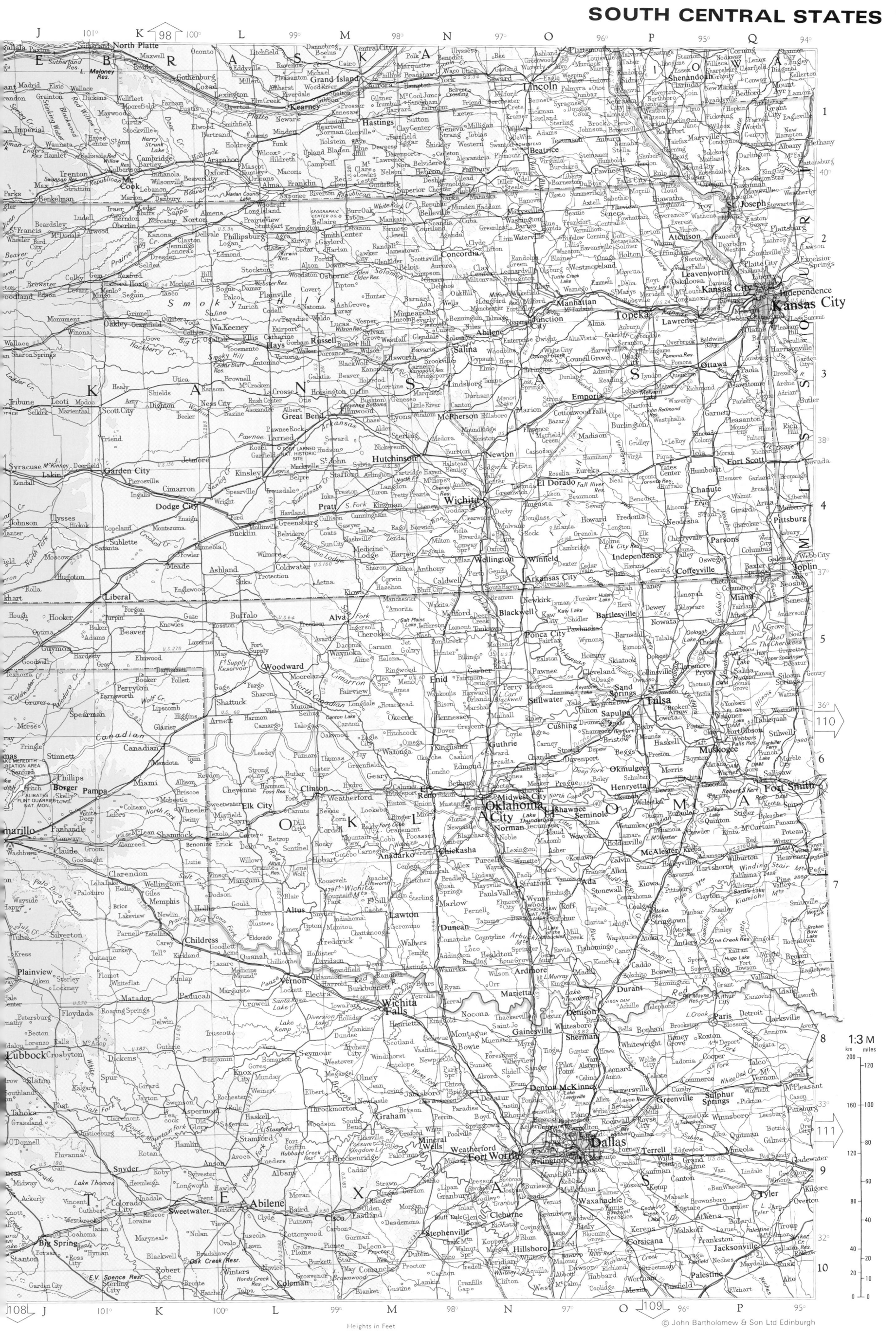

1:3 M
km miles

© John Bartholomew & Son Ltd Edinburgh

Heights in Feet

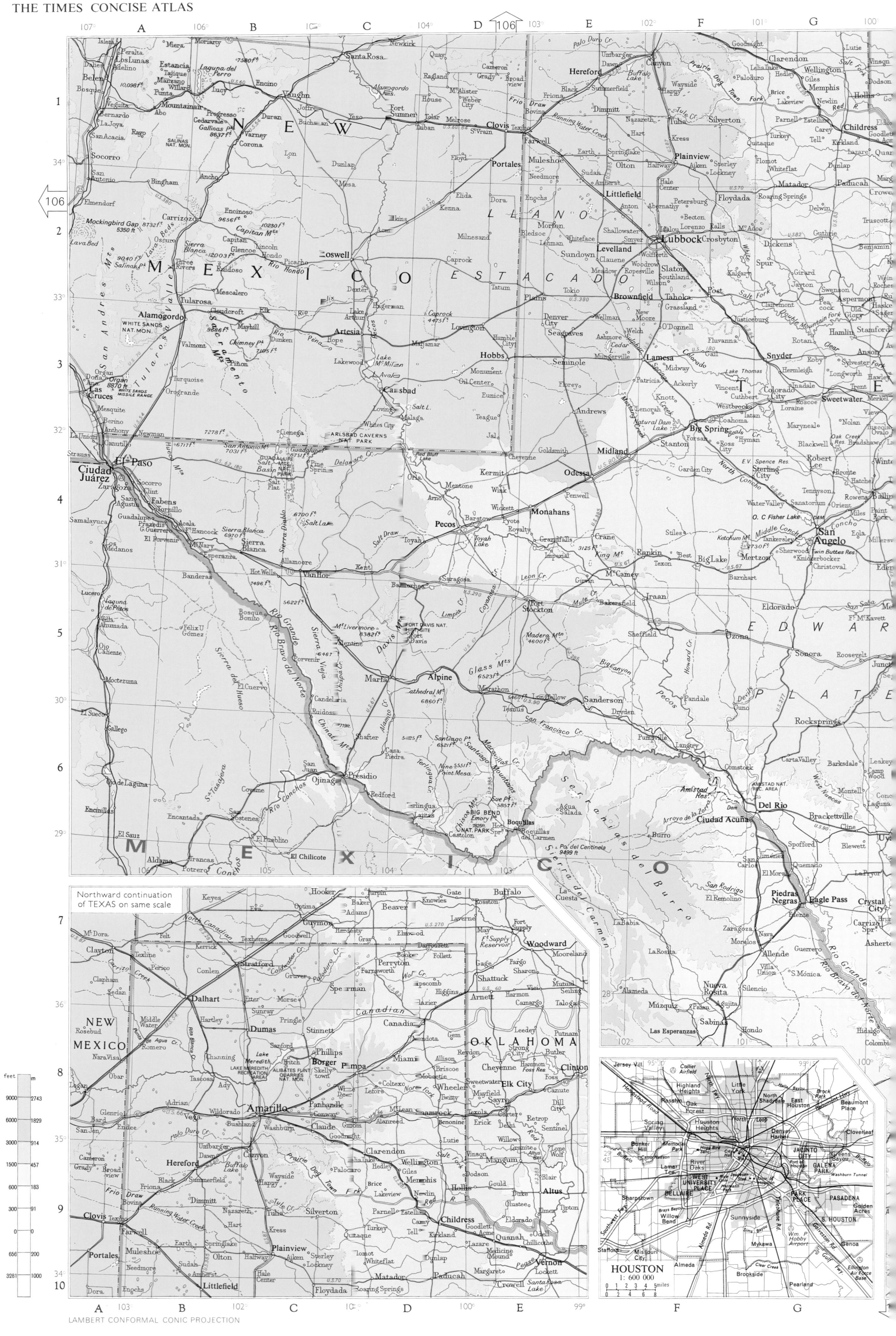

NEW MEXICO
LLANO ESTACADO
TEXAS
MEXICO
EDWARDS PLATEAU
Sierra del Burro
Sierra del Carmen
OKLAHOMA
Northward continuation of TEXAS on same scale
HOUSTON
1: 600 000
Socorro
Carrizozo
Alamogordo
Las Cruces
El Paso
Ciudad Juárez
Roswell
Artesia
Carlsbad
Hobbs
Clovis
Portales
Lubbock
Plainview
Midland
Odessa
Big Spring
San Angelo
Pecos
Alpine
Marfa
Presidio
Ojinaga
Fort Stockton
Del Rio
Ciudad Acuña
Piedras Negras
Eagle Pass
Amarillo
Dalhart
Borger
Pampa
Childress
Vernon
Altus
Woodward
Guymon
Hereford
WHITE SANDS NAT. MON.
CARLSBAD CAVERNS NAT. PARK
BIG BEND NAT. PARK
Rio Grande
Pecos
LAMBERT CONFORMAL CONIC PROJECTION

FORT WORTH-DALLAS
1:720 000

1:3M

Longitude West 99 of Greenwich

Heights in feet
Depths in metres

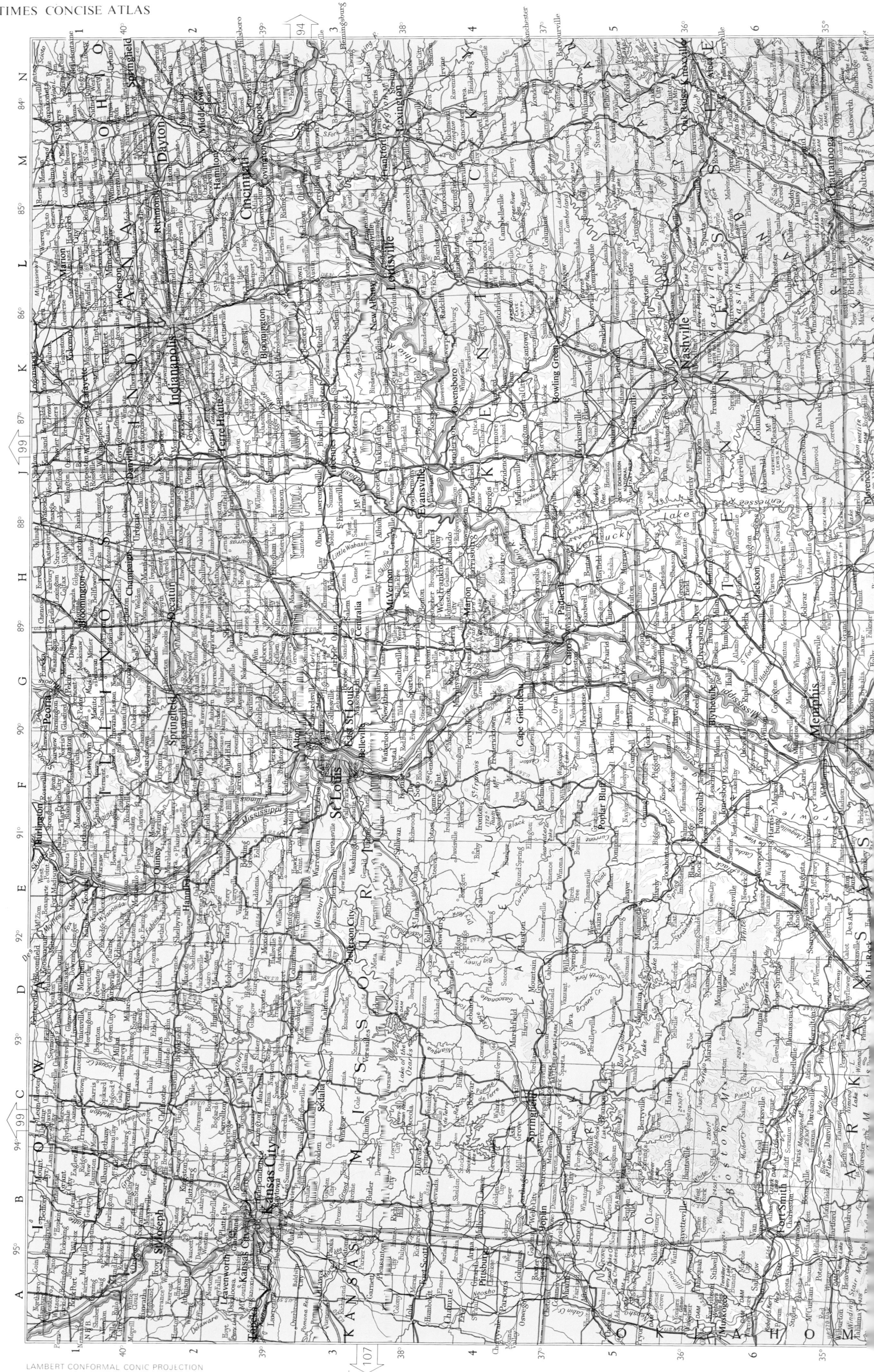
OHIO
INDIANA
ILLINOIS
KENTUCKY
MISSOURI
TENNESSEE
ARKANSAS
KANSAS
OKLAHOMA
IOWA
Cincinnati
Dayton
Indianapolis
Louisville
Lexington
Nashville
Knoxville
Chattanooga
Evansville
St Louis
East St Louis
Memphis
Kansas City
Springfield
Peoria
Decatur
94
99
107

LAMBERT CONFORMAL CONIC PROJECTION

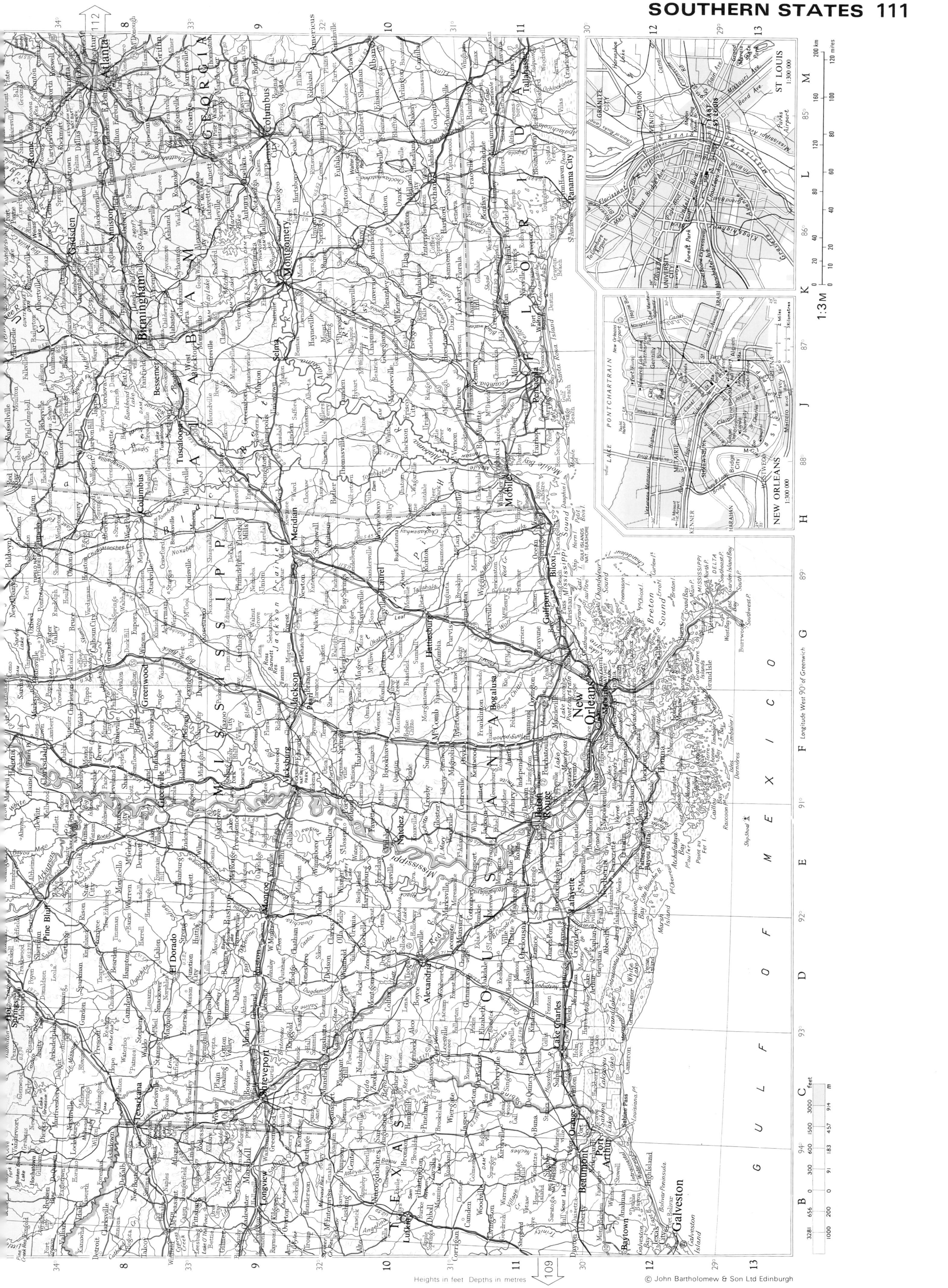

GEORGIA

ALABAMA

MISSISSIPPI

LOUISIANA

TEXAS

FLORIDA

GULF OF MEXICO

Atlanta
Rome
Birmingham
Gadsden
Anniston
Tuscaloosa
Columbus
Montgomery
Selma
Meridian
Mobile
Pensacola
Panama City
Tallahassee
Biloxi
Gulfport
Jackson
Vicksburg
Natchez
Hattiesburg
Laurel
Greenwood
Clarksdale
Greenville
Baton Rouge
New Orleans
Lafayette
Lake Charles
Alexandria
Monroe
Shreveport
Longview
Nacogdoches
Beaumont
Port Arthur
Orange
Galveston
Baytown
Pine Bluff
El Dorado
Texarkana

ST LOUIS
1:3 M
GRANITE CITY
VENICE
E. St Louis
UNIVERSITY CITY
Forest Park
Parks Airport

NEW ORLEANS
1:300 000
LAKE PONTCHARTRAIN
METAIRIE
KENNER
HARAHAN
GRETNA
ARABI
MISSISSIPPI DELTA

200 km
120 miles

Heights in feet Depths in metres

© John Bartholomew & Son Ltd Edinburgh

feet   m
3000   914
1500   457
600   183
300   91
0   0
656   200
1000   328

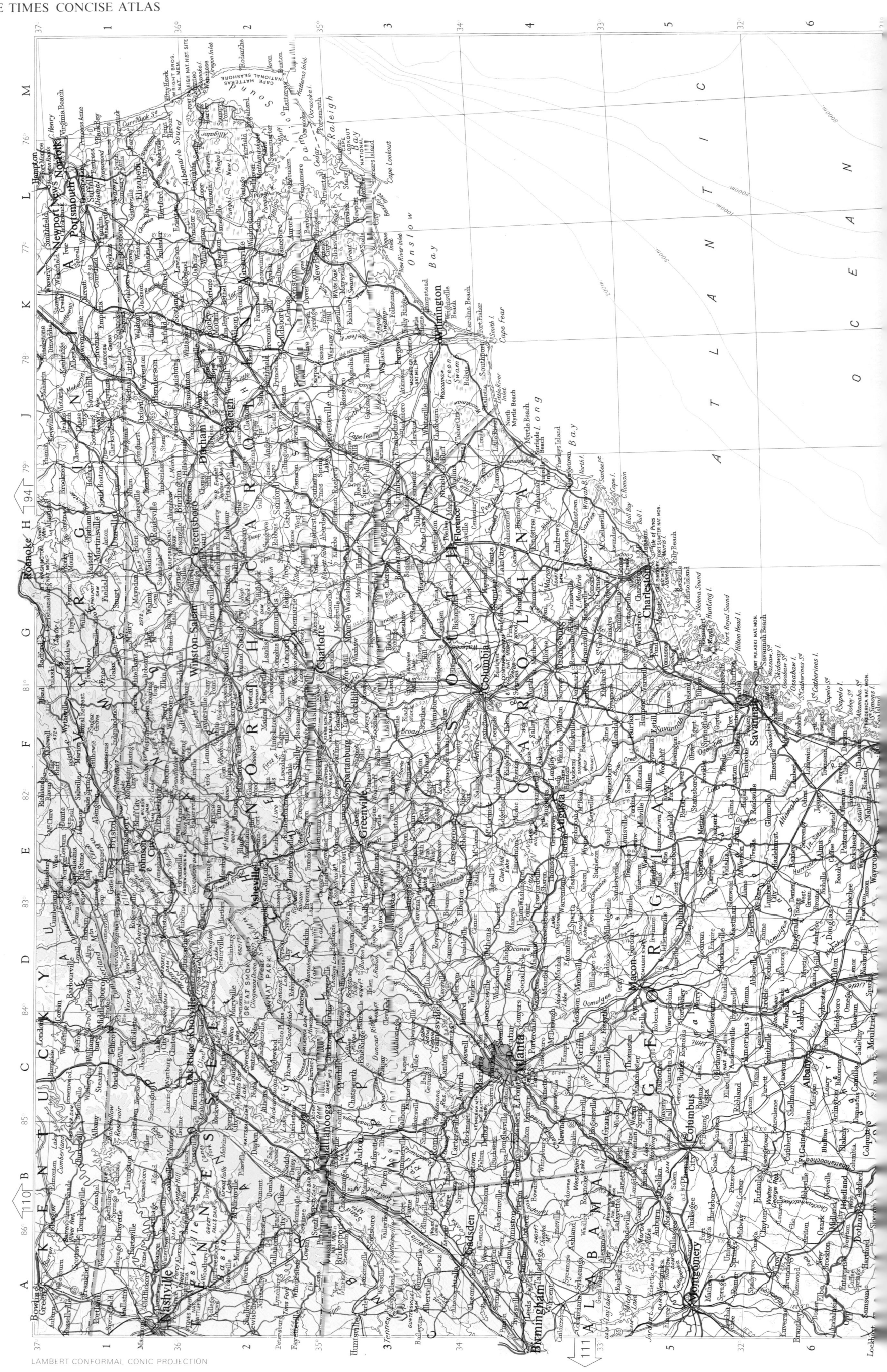
ATLANTIC OCEAN
KENTUCKY
VIRGINIA
TENNESSEE
NORTH CAROLINA
SOUTH CAROLINA
GEORGIA
ALABAMA
Onslow Bay
Long Bay
Nashville
Knoxville
Chattanooga
Asheville
Charlotte
Winston-Salem
Greensboro
Durham
Raleigh
Wilmington
Norfolk
Portsmouth
Newport News
Roanoke
Columbia
Charleston
Florence
Greenville
Spartanburg
Augusta
Savannah
Macon
Atlanta
Columbus
Montgomery
Birmingham
Gadsden
Albany

94
110
111

LAMBERT CONFORMAL CONIC PROJECTION

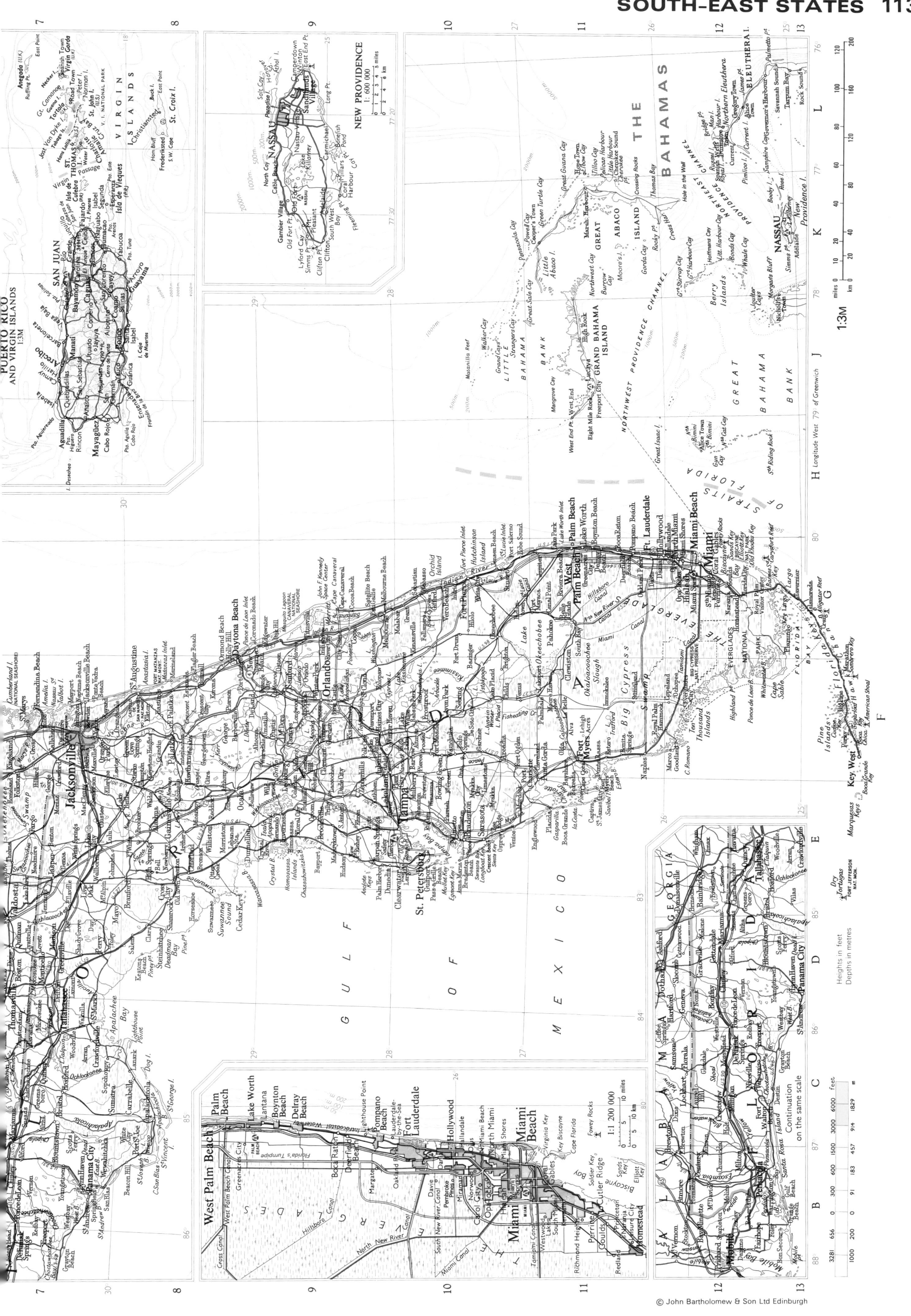
PUERTO RICO AND VIRGIN ISLANDS
1:3M
NEW PROVIDENCE
1: 600 000
NASSAU
THE BAHAMAS
GREAT BAHAMA ISLAND
GREAT ABACO ISLAND
ELEUTHERA I.
NORTHWEST PROVIDENCE CHANNEL
STRAITS OF FLORIDA
GULF OF MEXICO
FLORIDA
GEORGIA
ALABAMA
Jacksonville
Tallahassee
Tampa
St. Petersburg
Orlando
Daytona Beach
Miami
Miami Beach
Ft. Lauderdale
West Palm Beach
Key West
Panama City
Pensacola
Mobile
1:3M
Longitude West of Greenwich
1:1 200 000
Heights in feet
Depths in metres
Continuation on the same scale

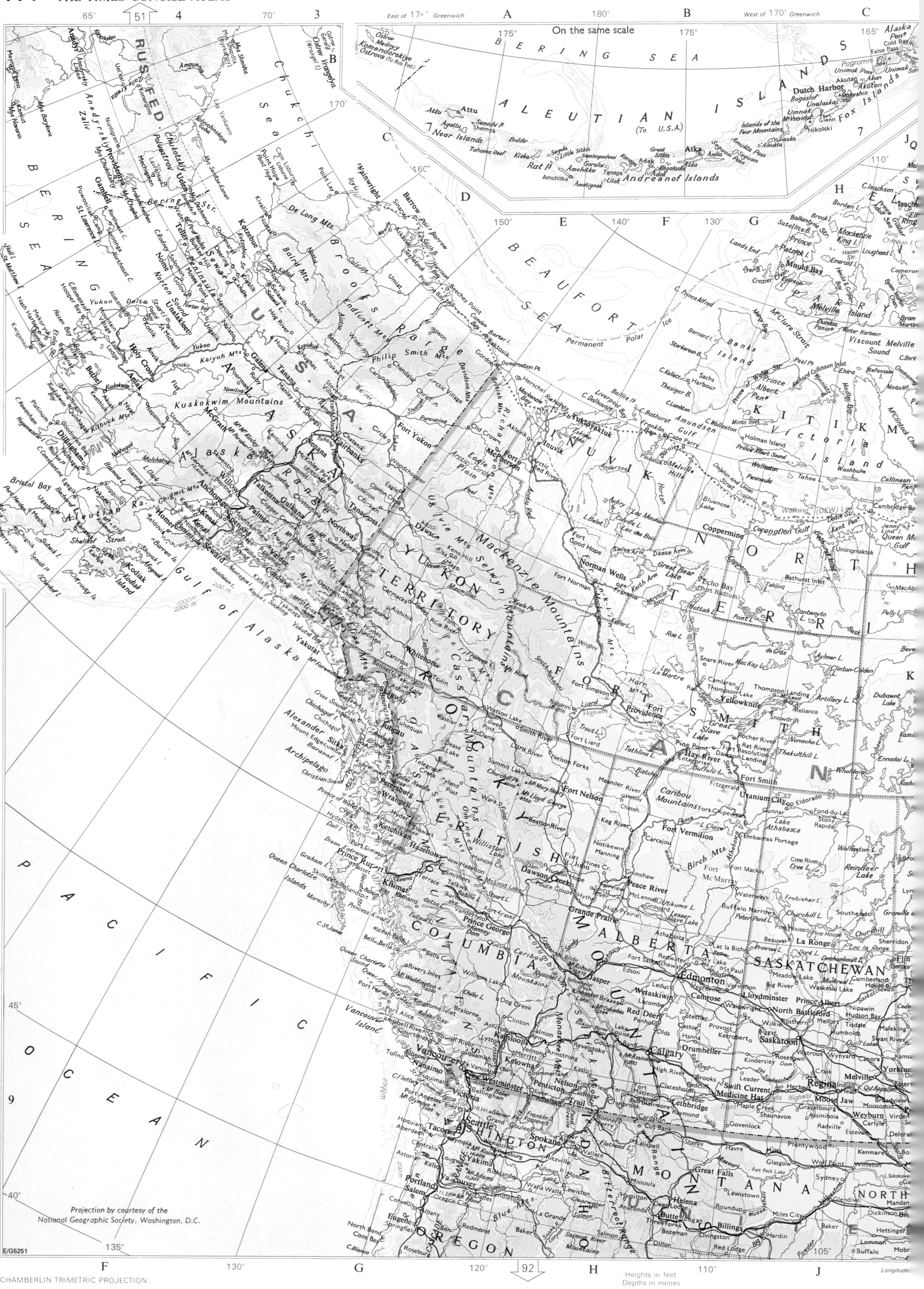

On the same scale

Projection by courtesy of the
National Geographic Society, Washington, D.C.

E/G5251

Heights in feet
Depths in metres

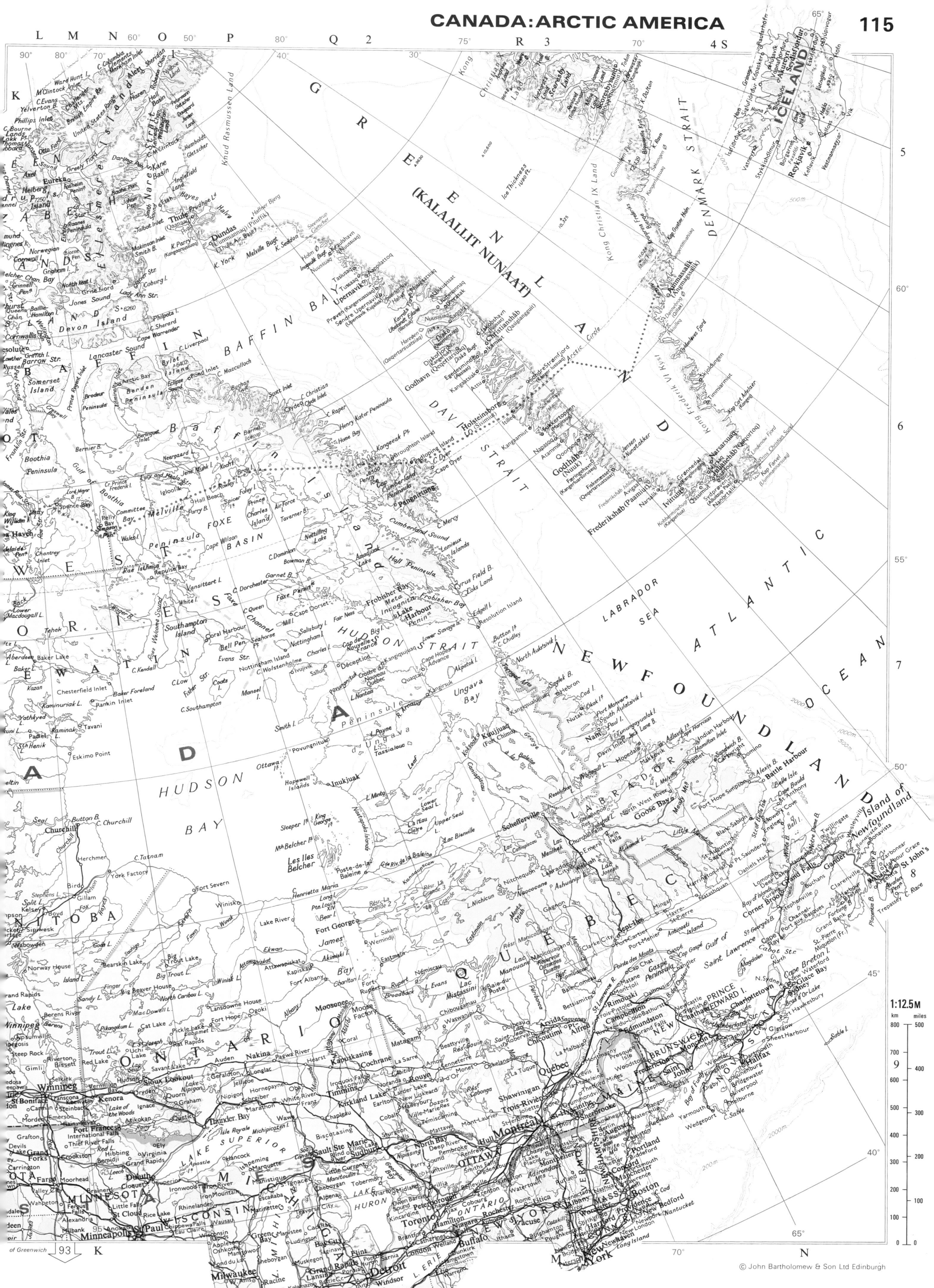

© John Bartholomew & Son Ltd Edinburgh

GREENLAND
(KALAALLIT NUNAAT)
ICELAND
BAFFIN BAY
DAVIS STRAIT
DENMARK STRAIT
LABRADOR SEA
ATLANTIC OCEAN
HUDSON BAY
HUDSON STRAIT
FOXE BASIN
Ungava Bay
Baffin Island
Ellesmere Island
Devon Island
Somerset Island
Southampton Island
NEWFOUNDLAND
Island of Newfoundland
LABRADOR
QUEBEC
ONTARIO
MANITOBA
NEW BRUNSWICK
NOVA SCOTIA
PRINCE EDWARD I.
MAINE
MINNESOTA
WISCONSIN
MICHIGAN
NEW YORK
LAKE SUPERIOR
LAKE HURON
L. ERIE
Gulf of Saint Lawrence
Reykjavik
Thule
Godthåb (Nuuk)
Frobisher Bay
Churchill
Schefferville
Québec
Montreal
OTTAWA
Toronto
Winnipeg
Halifax
St John's
Boston
Detroit
Minneapolis
1:12.5M
km
miles
of Greenwich
93

ARCTIC OCEAN

CHUKCHI SEA

BEAUFORT SEA

BROOKS RANGE

ENDICOTT MOUNTAINS

De Long Mountains

Baird Mountains

NOATAK NATIONAL PRESERVE

GATES OF THE ARCTIC NATIONAL PARK AND PRESERVE

ARCTIC NATIONAL WILDLIFE REFUGE

British Mountains

BROOKS RANGE

CANADA

CHUKOTSKIY POLUOSTROV

RUSS. FED.

BERING STRAIT

Point Barrow
Barrow
Wainwright
Point Lay
Icy Cape
Point Hope (Tigara)
C. Lisburne
Cape Krusenstern
Kivalina
Noatak
Kotzebue
Kotzebue Sound
Kobuk
Noorvik
Selawik
Wiseman
Bettles
Prudhoe Bay
Deadhorse
Umiat
Anaktuvuk Pass
Atigun Pass
Fort Yukon
Venetie
Arctic Village
Old Crow
Chalkyitsik

Shishmaref
Wales
Diomede Is.
Little Diomede
Big Diomede
Teller
Nome
SEWARD PENINSULA
Candle
Buckland
Koyuk
Unalakleet
St. Michael
Stebbins

ST. LAWRENCE I.
Gambell
Savoonga

NORTON SOUND

YUKON DELTA
Alakanuk
Mountain Village
St. Marys
Marshall
Holy Cross
Russian Mission
Kalskag
Aniak
McGrath
Tanana
College
Fairbanks
Nenana
DENALI NATIONAL PARK AND PRESERVE
Mt. McKinley
DENALI
Mt. Foraker
Healy
Big Delta
Delta Junction
Tok
Northway
Eagle
Circle
Central

Hooper Bay
Chevak
NUNIVAK I.
Bethel
Kwethluk
Kwigillingok

KUSKOKWIM BAY
KUSKOKWIM MOUNTAINS

Dillingham
BRISTOL BAY
Aleknagik
Togiak

ALASKA RANGE

WRANGELL MOUNTAINS
Mt. Blackburn

Anchorage
Palmer
Wasilla
Willow
Spenard
Whittier
Cordova
Valdez
KENAI PENINSULA
Kenai
Soldotna
Seldovia
Homer
Seward

GULF OF ALASKA

Kodiak
KODIAK ISLAND
Larsen Bay
Old Harbor

Chignik
ALASKA PENINSULA
Port Heiden (Meshik)
Port Moller

Pribilof Is.
St. Paul I.
St. George I.

St. Matthew I.

U.S.A.
ALASKA

Arctic Circle

PROVIDENIYA

UNIMAK I.
Dutch Harbor
UNALASKA I.
Fort Randall
False Pass
Cold Bay

SHUMAGIN ISLANDS

Dutch Harbor
UMNAK I.
UNALASKA I.
Akutan
FOX ISLANDS
Islands of the Four Mountains
ATKA I.
AMLIA I.

ALEUTIAN ISLANDS
NEAR ISLANDS
ATTU I.
Attu
Agattu I.
KISKA I.
Kiska
AMCHITKA I.
RAT ISLANDS
Amchitka Pass
TANAGA I.
KANAGA I.
ADAK I.
Adak
ANDREANOF ISLANDS

CONIC PROJECTION

Heights in feet
Depths in metres

1 : 6M

0 40 80 120 160 200 240 miles

0 100 200 300 400 km

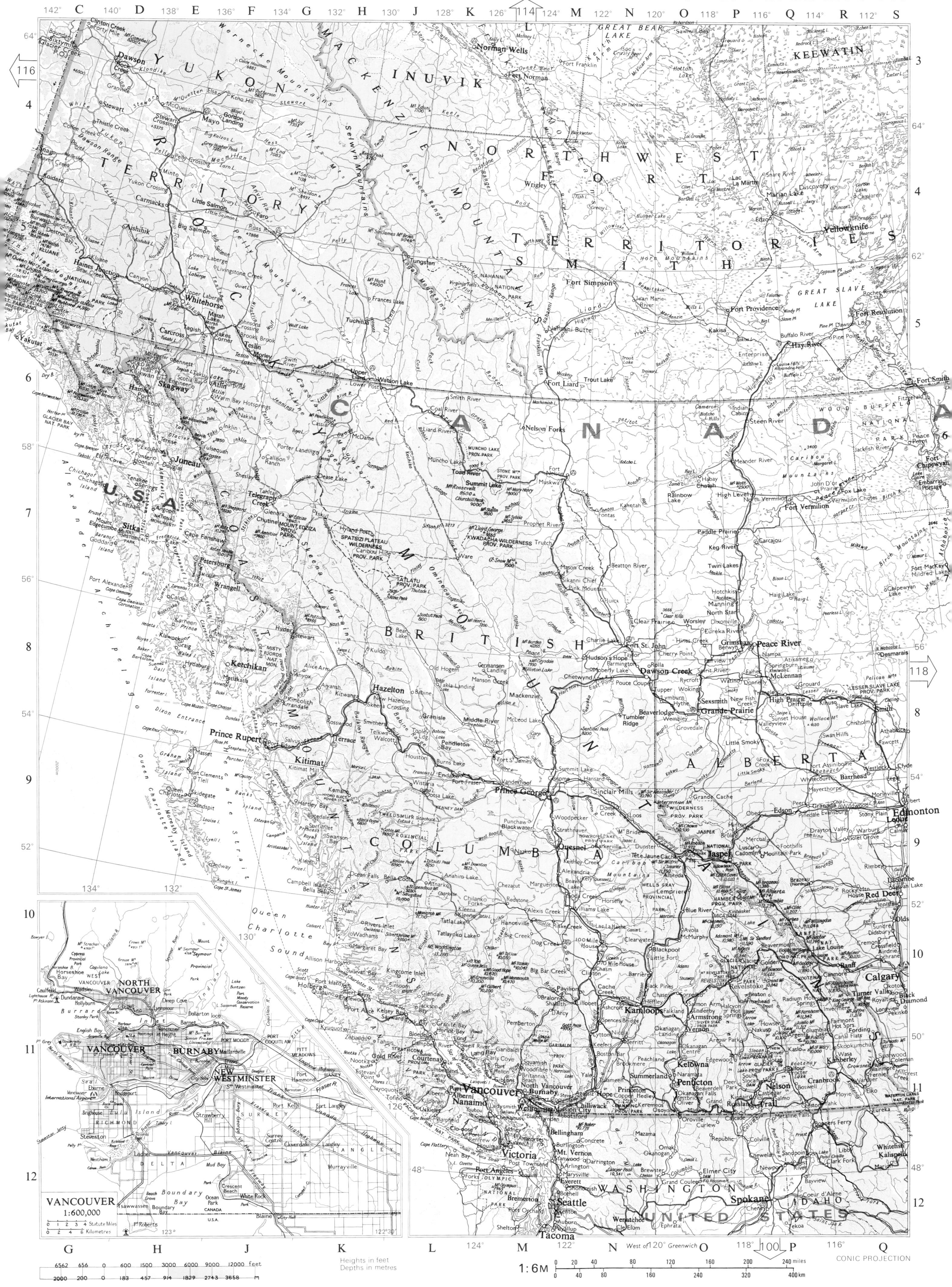

YUKON TERRITORY

NORTHWEST TERRITORIES

KEEWATIN

BRITISH COLUMBIA

ALBERTA

CANADA

U.S.A.

WASHINGTON

IDAHO

UNITED STATES

COAST MOUNTAINS

MACKENZIE MOUNTAINS

ROCKY MOUNTAINS

GREAT BEAR LAKE

GREAT SLAVE LAKE

Queen Charlotte Islands

Queen Charlotte Sound

Dixon Entrance

Alexander Archipelago

Selected place names:
Dawson, Mayo, Whitehorse, Carcross, Skagway, Juneau, Sitka, Ketchikan, Prince Rupert, Kitimat, Terrace, Hazelton, Prince George, Quesnel, Williams Lake, Kamloops, Vancouver, Victoria, Nanaimo, Kelowna, Penticton, Nelson, Trail, Cranbrook, Calgary, Banff, Lake Louise, Jasper, Edmonton, Red Deer, Grande Prairie, Peace River, Dawson Creek, Fort St. John, Norman Wells, Yellowknife, Fort Smith, Fort Chipewyan, Fort Vermilion, High Level, Hay River, Fort Resolution, Fort Providence, Fort Simpson, Watson Lake, Norman Wells, Seattle, Tacoma, Spokane, Bellingham

NORTH VANCOUVER, WEST VANCOUVER, VANCOUVER, BURNABY, NEW WESTMINSTER, RICHMOND, DELTA

Heights in feet
Depths in metres

1:6M

CONIC PROJECTION

6562 656 0 600 1500 3000 6000 9000 12000 feet
2000 200 0 183 457 914 1829 2743 3658 m

0 40 80 120 160 200 240 miles
0 40 80 120 160 240 320 400 km

West of 20° Greenwich

WINNIPEG
1:300 000
KILDONAN
ST. JAMES
TRANSCONA
ST. BONIFACE
Brooklands
Tuxedo
Charleswood
ST. CHARLES
Fort Whyte
ST. VITAL
Continuation on the same scale
Winnipeg
St. Boniface
Steinbach
Kenora
Keewatin
Dryden
Rainy River
Fort Frances
International Falls
Baudette
Warroad
Roseau
ONTA
ALBERTA
SASKA
Peace River
McLennan
High Prairie
Lesser Slave Lake
SWAN HILLS
Swan Hills
Athabasca
Lac la Biche
Whitecourt
Barrhead
Westlock
St. Paul
Edmonton
Vegreville
Camrose
Wetaskiwin
Ponoka
Lacombe
Red Deer
Stettler
Wainwright
Lloydminster
North Battleford
Battleford
Meadow Lake
Ile-a-la-Crosse
Saskatoon
Biggar
Kindersley
Rosetown
Drumheller
Olds
Calgary
Banff
Canmore
Brooks
Medicine Hat
Swift Current
Maple Creek
Lethbridge
Fort Macleod
Claresholm
High River
Okotoks
Cardston
Taber
CYPRESS HILLS
ROCKY MOUNTAINS
BRITISH COLUMBIA
Fernie
CANADA
U.S.A.
Sweetgrass
Coutts
BOUNDARY PLATEAU
GRASSLANDS NATIONAL PARK
117
101
115
CONIC PROJECTION
Longitude West
feet m
9000 2743
6000 1829
3000 914
1500 457
600 183
0 0

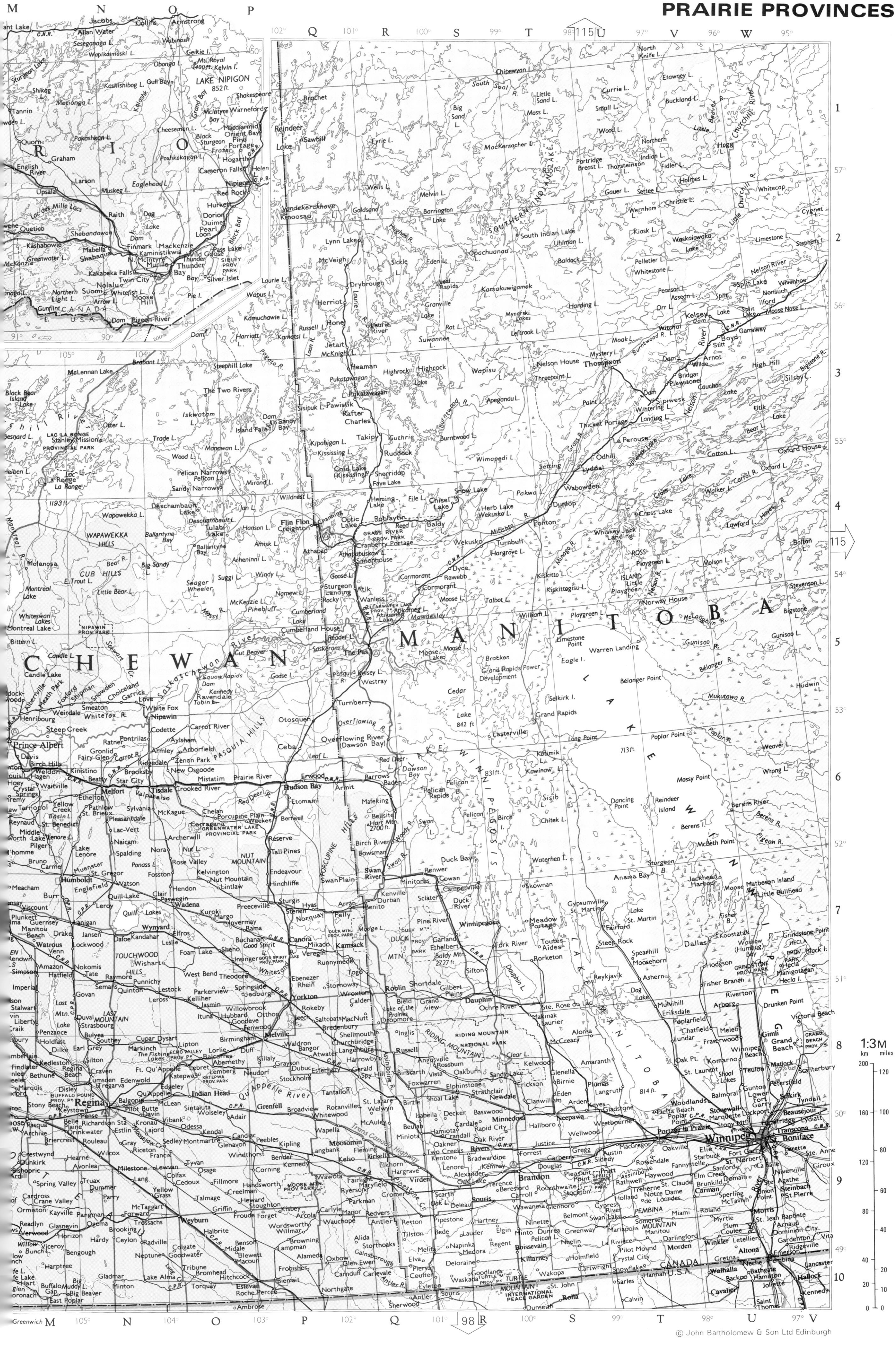

MANITOBA

SASKATCHEWAN (CHEWAN)

LAKE NIPIGON 852 ft.

LAKE WINNIPEG

LAKE WINNIPEGOSIS

LAKE MANITOBA

Prince Albert

Regina

Winnipeg

Brandon

Thompson

Flin Flon

The Pas

Melville

Yorkton

Dauphin

Weyburn

RIDING MOUNTAIN NATIONAL PARK

GRASS RIVER PROV. PARK

Trans Canada Highway

1:3 M

© John Bartholomew & Son Ltd Edinburgh

LAKE SUPERIOR
LAKE NIPIGON
LAKE MICHIGAN
LAKE HURON
LAKE ERIE
GEORGIAN BAY
ONTARIO
MICHIGAN
CANADA
U.S.A.
Isle Royale NATIONAL PARK
Thunder Bay
Nipigon
Geraldton
Hearst
Kapuskasing
Moosonee
Moose Factory
Cochrane
Timmins
South Porcupine
Chapleau
Wawa
Sault Ste. Marie
Sudbury
Marquette
Escanaba
Manistique
Mackinaw City
Cheboygan
Petoskey
Alpena
Gaylord
Grayling
Bay City
Saginaw
Flint
Lansing
Detroit
Windsor
Port Huron
Sarnia
London
Stratford
Kitchener
Guelph
Owen Sound
Goderich
Chatham
St. Thomas
Drummond I.
North Channel
Manitoulin Island
Saginaw Bay
Thunder Bay
OTTAWA
1:240 000
HULL
VANIER
TORONTO
1:300 000
NORTH YORK
EAST YORK
SCARBOROUGH
ETOBICOKE
LAKE ONTARIO
Feet
Metres
3000
914
1500
457
600
183
300
91
0
0
Longitude West 81° of Greenwich
99
115
94

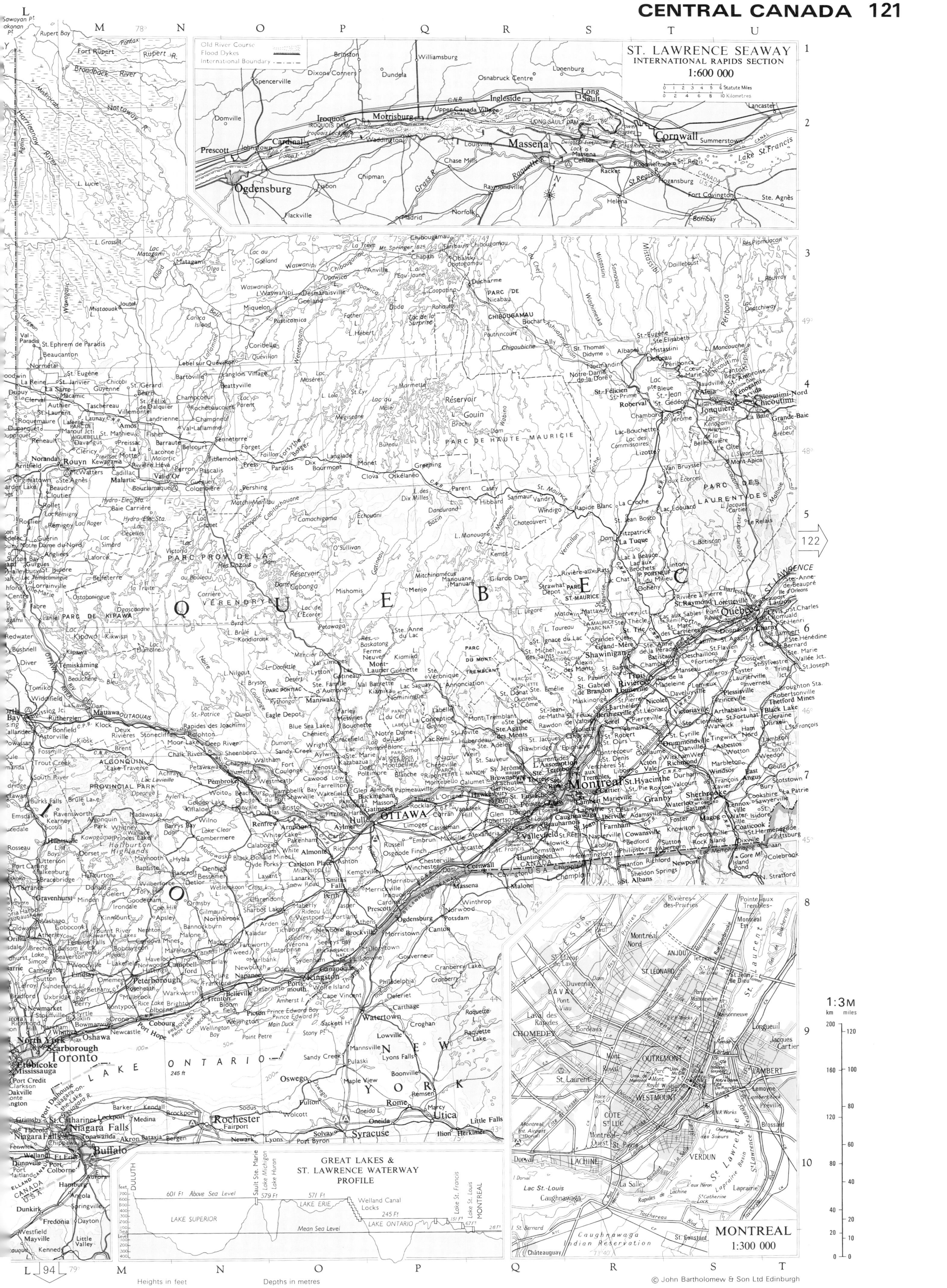

ST. LAWRENCE SEAWAY
INTERNATIONAL RAPIDS SECTION
1:600 000

Statute Miles
Kilometres

Old River Course
Flood Dykes
International Boundary

GREAT LAKES & ST. LAWRENCE WATERWAY PROFILE

601 Ft Above Sea Level
579 Ft
571 Ft
LAKE SUPERIOR
Sault Ste. Marie
Lake Michigan
Lake Huron
LAKE ERIE
Welland Canal Locks
245 Ft
Mean Sea Level
LAKE ONTARIO
Lake St. Francis
Montreal
St. Lambert

MONTREAL
1:300 000

1:3M
km miles

Heights in feet   Depths in metres

© John Bartholomew & Son Ltd Edinburgh

QUEBEC

ONTARIO

NEW YORK

LAKE ONTARIO

Montreal
Ottawa
Québec
Toronto
Buffalo
Niagara Falls
Rochester
Syracuse
Utica
Kingston
Peterborough
Shawinigan
Trois Rivières
Sherbrooke
Cornwall
Massena
Ogdensburg
Prescott
Chicoutimi
Jonquière
Alma

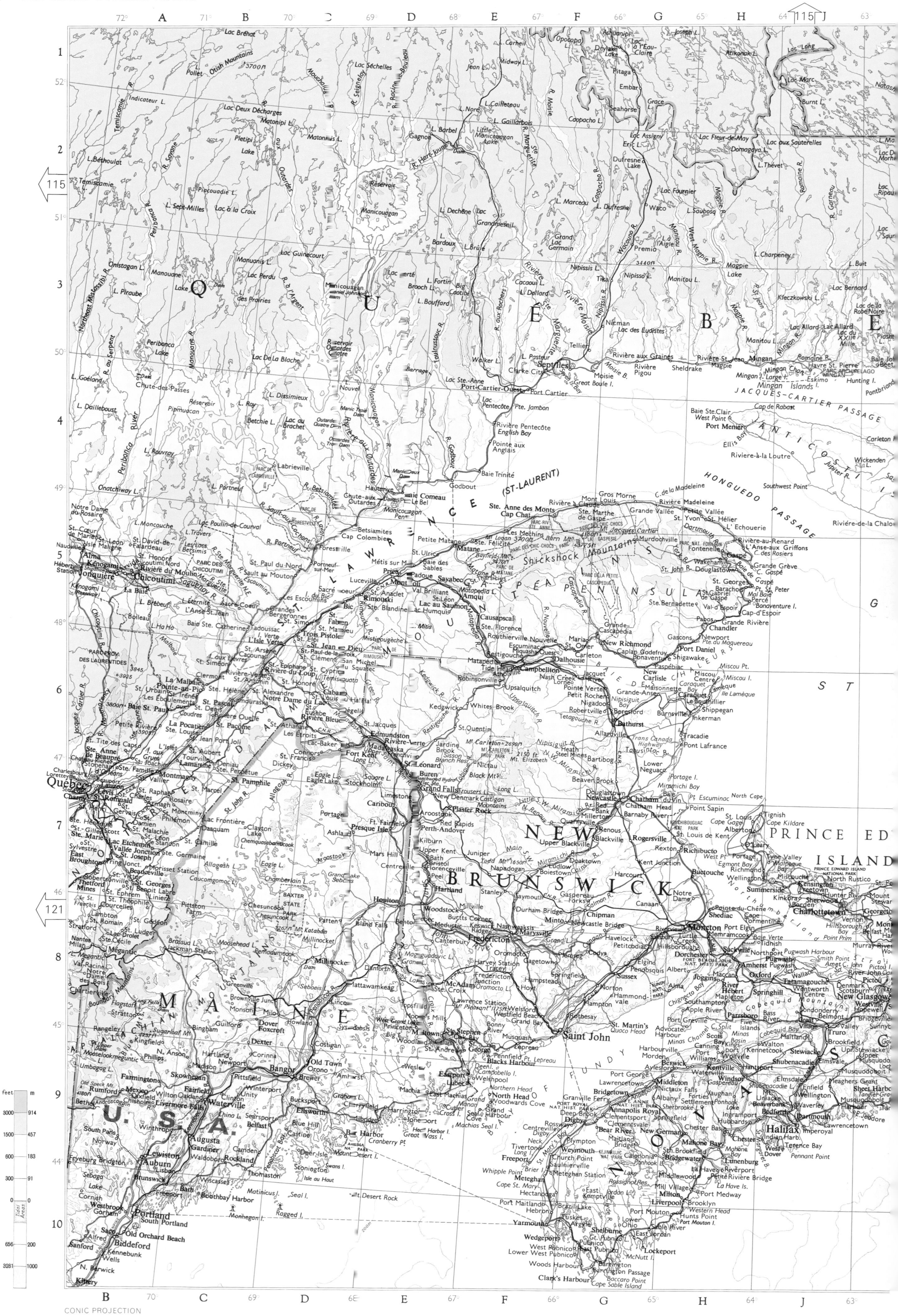
115
121
QUÉBEC
NEW BRUNSWICK
PRINCE EDWARD ISLAND
MAINE
U.S.A.
GASPÉ PENINSULA
ST. LAWRENCE (ST-LAURENT)
ANTICOSTI
HONGUEDO PASSAGE
JACQUES-CARTIER PASSAGE
BAY OF FUNDY
Shickshock Mountains
Québec
Chicoutimi
Jonquière
Alma
Septîles
Baie Comeau
Rimouski
Matane
Gaspé
Campbellton
Dalhousie
Bathurst
Chatham
Newcastle
Moncton
Fredericton
Saint John
Charlottetown
Summerside
Truro
Halifax
Dartmouth
Yarmouth
Digby
Bangor
Augusta
Portland
Lewiston
Auburn
Waterville
Presque Isle
Houlton
Edmundston
Rivière du Loup
Montmagny
Sherbrooke
feet
m
3000
914
1500
457
600
183
300
91
0
0
656
200
3281
1000

QUEBEC
1:120 000

Statute Miles

Kilometres

1:3 M

km miles

ARIZONA

NEW MEXICO

U N I T E D   S T A T E S

T E X A S

San Diego
Tijuana
Ensenada
Mexicali
Yuma
El Centro
Tucson
Nogales
Douglas
Ciudad Juárez
El Paso
Las Cruces
Deming
Lordsburg
Carlsbad
Hobbs
Lamesa
Big Spring
Midland
Odessa
Pecos
Marfa
Stockton

BAJA CALIFORNIA

SONORA

CHIHUAHUA

COAHUILA

Hermosillo
Guaymas
Empalme
Ciudad Obregón
Navojoa
Huatabampo
Los Mochis
Culiacán
Chihuahua
Cuauhtémoc
Delicias
Ciudad Camargo
Hidalgo del Parral
Santa Bárbara
San Francisco del Oro

BAJA CALIFORNIA SUR

La Paz
S. José del Cabo
S. Lucas

Mazatlán
Rosario
Durango

DURANGO

ZACATECAS

Tropic of Cancer

P A C I F I C

M E X I C O

Tuxpan
Tepic
Zacatecas
Aguascalientes
Jerez
Fresnillo
Lagos de Moreno
León
Silao
Irapuato
Guadalajara
Salamanca

Manzanillo
Colima
Tecomán

JALISCO

MICHOACÁN

feet   m
13124   4000
9843   3000
6562   2000
3281   1000
1640   500
656   200
0
Below Sea Level
656   200
6562   2000

MEXICO CITY

NAUCALPAN DE JUÁREZ
AZCAPOTZALCO
VILLA GUSTAVO A. MADERO
JUAN GONZÁLEZ ROMERO
TACUBA
LOMAS CHAPULTEPEC
Bosque de Chapultepec
Aeropuerto Internacional
IZTACALCO
MIXCOAC
COYOACÁN
IZTAPALAPA
Ciudad Universitaria
VILLA OBREGÓN
TLALPAN
Estadio Azteca

1:250 000
0 1 2 3 4 5 km

PANAMA CANAL
1:900 000

CARIBBEAN SEA
Colón
Cristóbal
Gatún
Gatun Lake
Madden L.
Gamboa
Balboa
PANAMÁ
Río Abajo

PACIFIC OCEAN

Statute Miles
0 2 4 6 8 10
Kilometres
0 2 4 6 8 10 12 14 16
feet 164 65 0 328 656 1640 feet
m 50 20 0 100 200 500 m

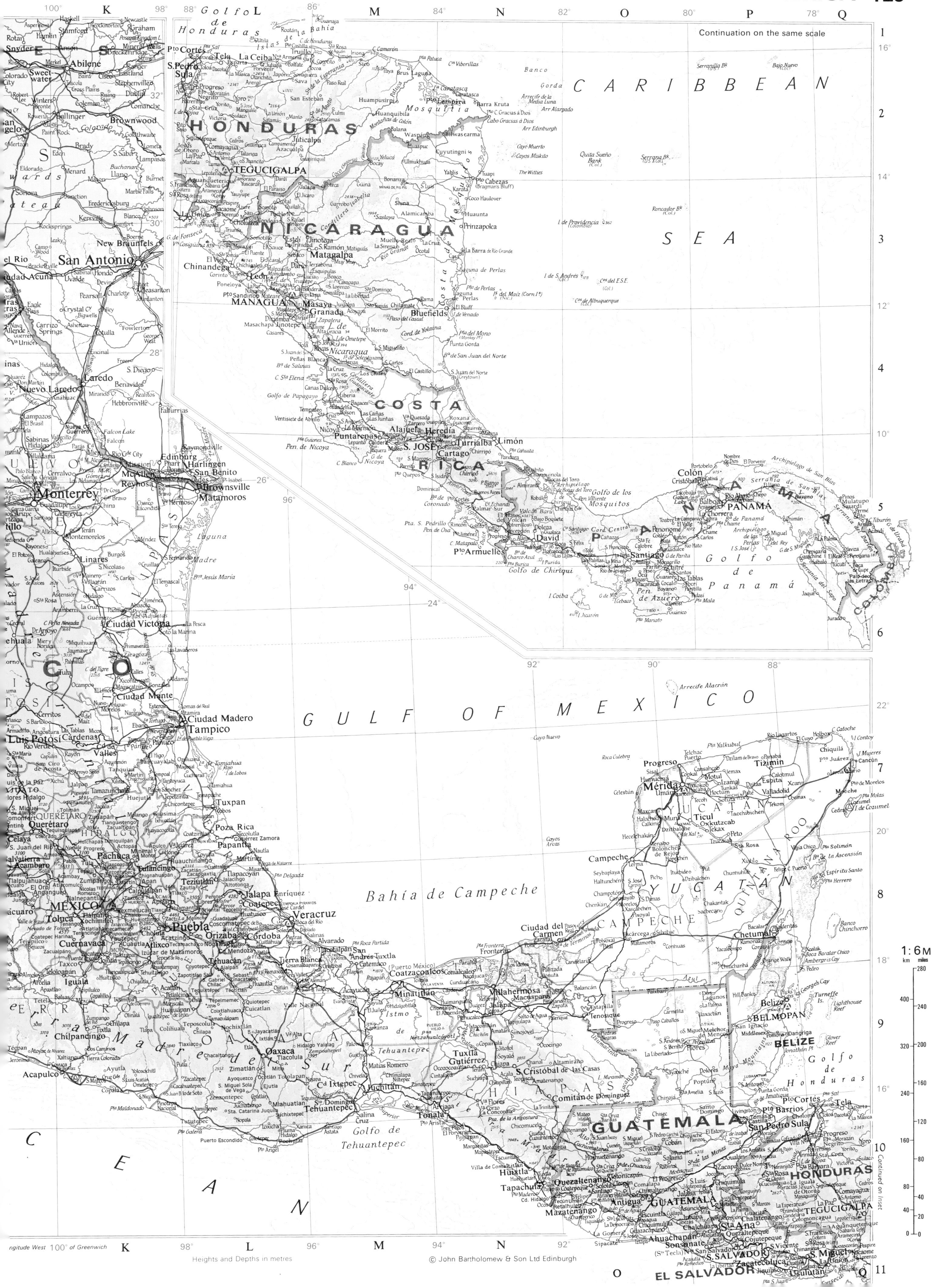

Continuation on the same scale

C A R I B B E A N

S E A

HONDURAS

TEGUCIGALPA

NICARAGUA

Estelí Jinotega Matagalpa

Chinandega León

MANAGUA Masaya Granada

Bluefields

COSTA RICA

Puntarenas Alajuela Heredia

S. JOSÉ Cartago Turrialba Limón

Liberia

PANAMÁ

David Santiago PANAMÁ Colón

Balboa Cristóbal

Golfo de Chiriquí

Golfo de Panamá

Pen. de Azuero

Pto Armuelles

San Antonio

Nuevo Laredo Laredo

Monterrey

Reynosa Matamoros

Brownsville

Linares

Ciudad Victoria

G U L F   O F   M E X I C O

Tampico Ciudad Madero

Bahía de Campeche

Veracruz Boca del Río

Poza Rica Papantla

Tuxpan

Pachuca

MÉXICO Puebla Orizaba Córdoba

Toluca Cuernavaca

Coatzacoalcos Minatitlán

Villahermosa Macuspana

Ciudad del Carmen

Campeche

CAMPECHE

YUCATÁN

Mérida Progreso Motul Tizimín Valladolid

Ticul

QUINTANA ROO

Chetumal

Cancún

I. de Cozumel

Acapulco

Chilpancingo

Iguala Taxco

Oaxaca

Tuxtla Gutiérrez

Tehuantepec Juchitán Salina Cruz

Golfo de Tehuantepec

CHIAPAS

S. Cristóbal de las Casas

Comitán de Domínguez

Tapachula Tonalá Arriaga

GUATEMALA

Quezaltenango Mazatenango

Antigua GUATEMALA

BELIZE

Belize BELMOPAN

Golfo de Honduras

San Pedro Sula Pto Barrios

TEGUCIGALPA

EL SALVADOR

S. SALVADOR Sta Ana S. Miguel

O C E A N

Scale 1 : 6 M

km miles

CURAÇAO
1:1 500 000
ARUBA
1:1 500 000
BONAIRE
1:1.5m
Oranjestad
Sint Nicolaas
Willemstad
Kralendijk
FLORIDA
U.S.A.
Palm Beach
Ft. Lauderdale
Miami
Miami Beach
Key West
Straits of Florida
GRAND BAHAMA
GREAT ABACO
ELEUTHERA
NEW PROVIDENCE
Nassau
ANDROS
GREAT EXUMA
THE BAHAMAS
SAN SALVADOR
LONG I.
ACKLINS I.
Tropic of Cancer
HABANA
Matanzas
Pinar del Rio
Cienfuegos
Santa Clara
Sancti Spíritus
Camagüey
Holguín
Bayamo
Santiago de Cuba
Guantánamo
CUBA
Isla de la Juventud
Yucatan Channel
MEXICO
Cancún
Cozumel
Little Cayman
Cayman Brac
Grand Cayman
CAYMAN TRENCH
Montego Bay
KINGSTON
JAMAICA
Pedro Bank
Swan Is
Islas de la Bahía
La Ceiba
HONDURAS
NICARAGUA
León
MANAGUA
Masaya
Granada
Lago de Nicaragua
Bluefields
COSTA RICA
SAN JOSE
Puntarenas
Limón
PANAMA
Colón
Barranquilla
Santa Marta
Cartagena
COLOMBIA
CARIBBEAN SEA
GREAT BAHAMA BANK
PACIFIC OCEAN
Golfo de Panamá
CONIC PROJECTION
Longitude West 74° of Greenwich
113
125
128

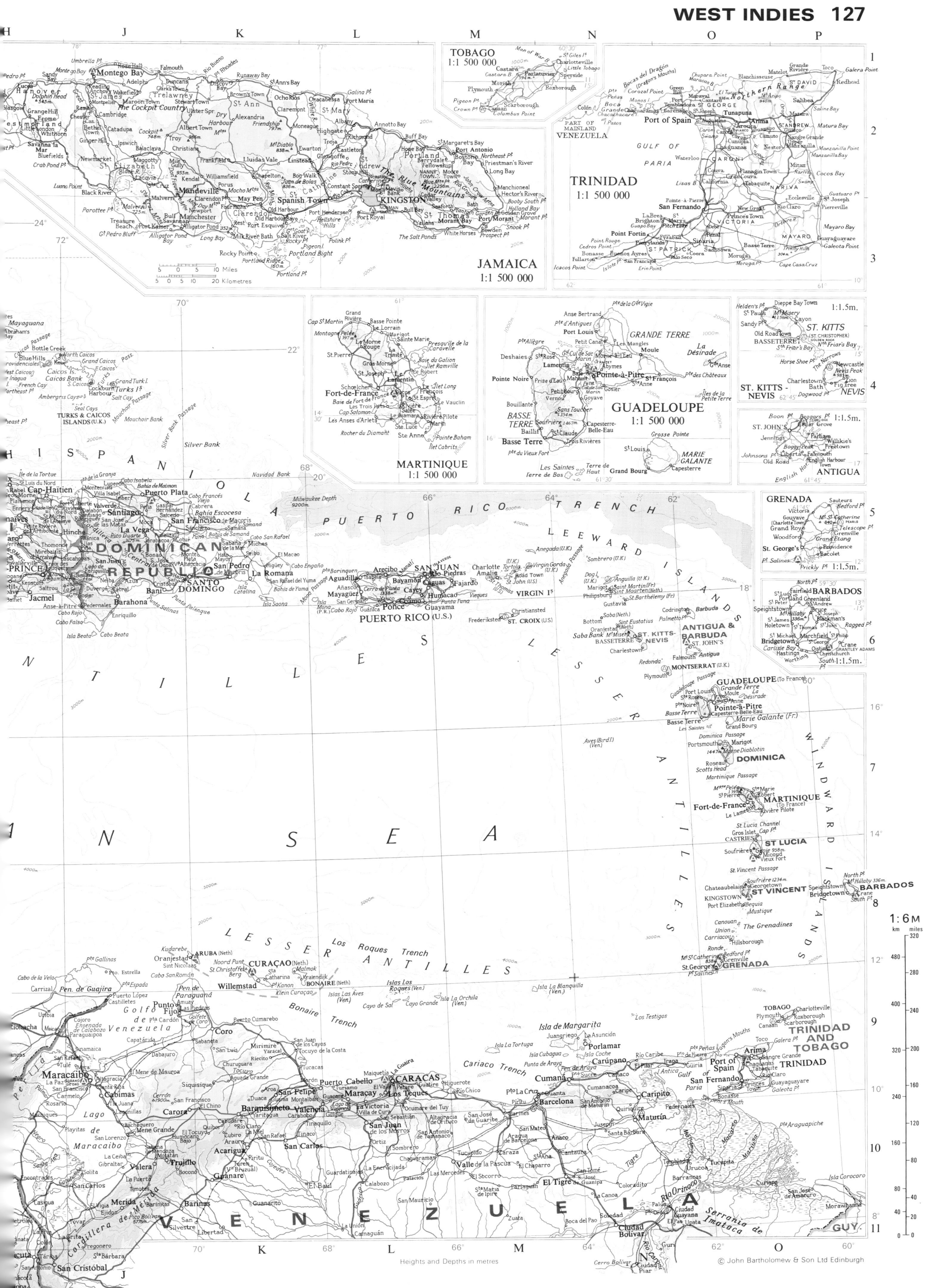
TOBAGO
1:1 500 000
JAMAICA
1:1 500 000
TRINIDAD
1:1 500 000
MARTINIQUE
1:1 500 000
GUADELOUPE
1:1 500 000
ST. KITTS - NEVIS
1:1.5m.
ANTIGUA
1:1.5m.
GRENADA
1:1.5m.
BARBADOS
1:1.5m.
Montego Bay
Kingston
Spanish Town
Port of Spain
San Fernando
Fort-de-France
Pointe-à-Pitre
Basse Terre
Cap-Haïtien
DOMINICAN REPUBLIC
SANTO DOMINGO
Santiago
SAN JUAN
PUERTO RICO (U.S.)
Ponce
Mayagüez
PUERTO RICO TRENCH
LEEWARD ISLANDS
VIRGIN Is
ANTIGUA & BARBUDA
ST. KITTS-NEVIS
DOMINICA
MARTINIQUE
ST LUCIA
ST VINCENT
BARBADOS
GRENADA
WINDWARD ISLANDS
LESSER ANTILLES
ARUBA (Neth)
CURAÇAO (Neth)
BONAIRE (Neth)
Willemstad
Isla de Margarita
TRINIDAD AND TOBAGO
Maracaibo
Lago de Maracaibo
Golfo de Venezuela
CARACAS
Valencia
Maracay
Barquisimeto
Barcelona
Cumaná
Maturín
Ciudad Bolívar
Ciudad Guayana
VENEZUELA
GUY.
Río Orinoco
1:6 M

Heights and Depths in metres

NICARAGUA

COSTA RICA

PANAMA

COLOMBIA

VENEZUELA

GUYANA

ECUADOR

PERU

BRASIL

BOLIVIA

CHILE

ARG.

SOUTH PACIFIC OCEAN

Bogotá

Caracas

Medellín

Cali

Quito

Guayaquil

Lima

Callao

La Paz

Cochabamba

Sucre

Potosí

Oruro

Arequipa

Antofagasta

GALAPAGOS ISLANDS
(ARCHIPIÉLAGO DE COLÓN)
(To Ecuador)

Culpepper
Wenman
Pinta (Abingdon)
Marchena (Bindloe)
Genovesa (Tower)
San Salvador (James I.)
Fernandina (Narborough)
Isla Isabela (Albemarle I.)
Santa Cruz (Indefatigable I.)
San Cristóbal (Chatham I.)
Santa María (Charles I.)
Española (Hood I.)

On the same scale

LAMBERT AZIMUTHAL EQUAL AREA PROJECTION

Heights in metres

m
10000
6000
5000
4000
3000
2000
1000
500
200
0
Below Sea Level
200

Longitude West 50° of Greenwich
NORTH ATLANTIC OCEAN
Equator
SURINAME
FRENCH GUIANA
Paramaribo
Cayenne
Macapá
AMAPÁ
Belém
São Luís
Teresina
Fortaleza (Ceará)
Natal
João Pessoa
Recife (Pernambuco)
Maceió
Aracaju
Salvador (Bahia)
Brasília
Goiânia
Belo Horizonte
Vitória
Rio de Janeiro
São Paulo
Santos
Cuiabá
Campo Grande
Santarém
MARANHÃO
PIAUÍ
CEARÁ
BAHIA
TOCANTINS
MATO GROSSO
MATO GROSSO DO SUL
MINAS GERAIS
ESPÍRITO SANTO
SÃO PAULO
PARANÁ
GOIÁS
Planalto de Mato Grosso
Amazonas
Fernando de Noronha (To Brazil)
I. Martin Vaz
I. Trindade (To Brazil)
1:12 M

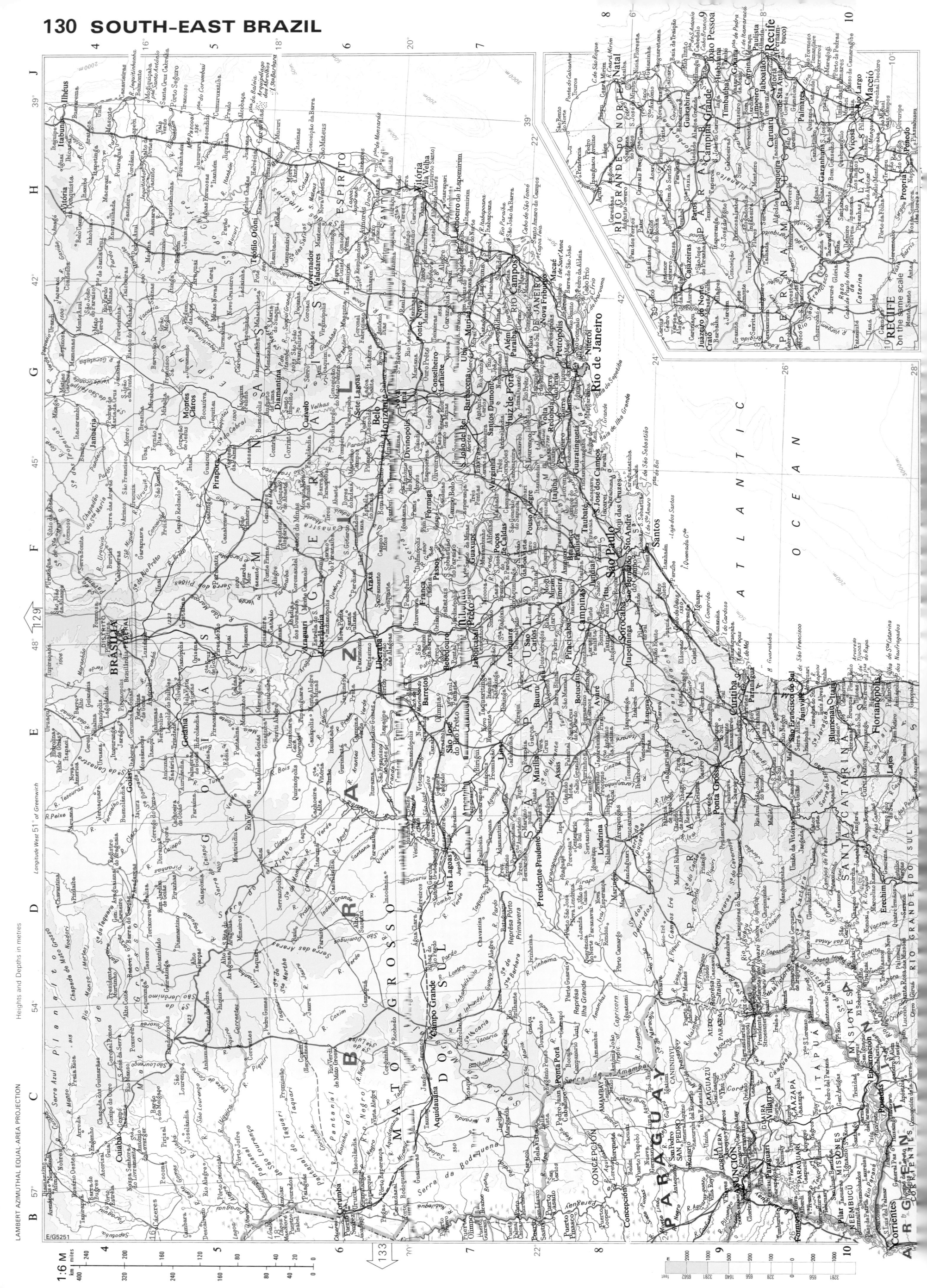

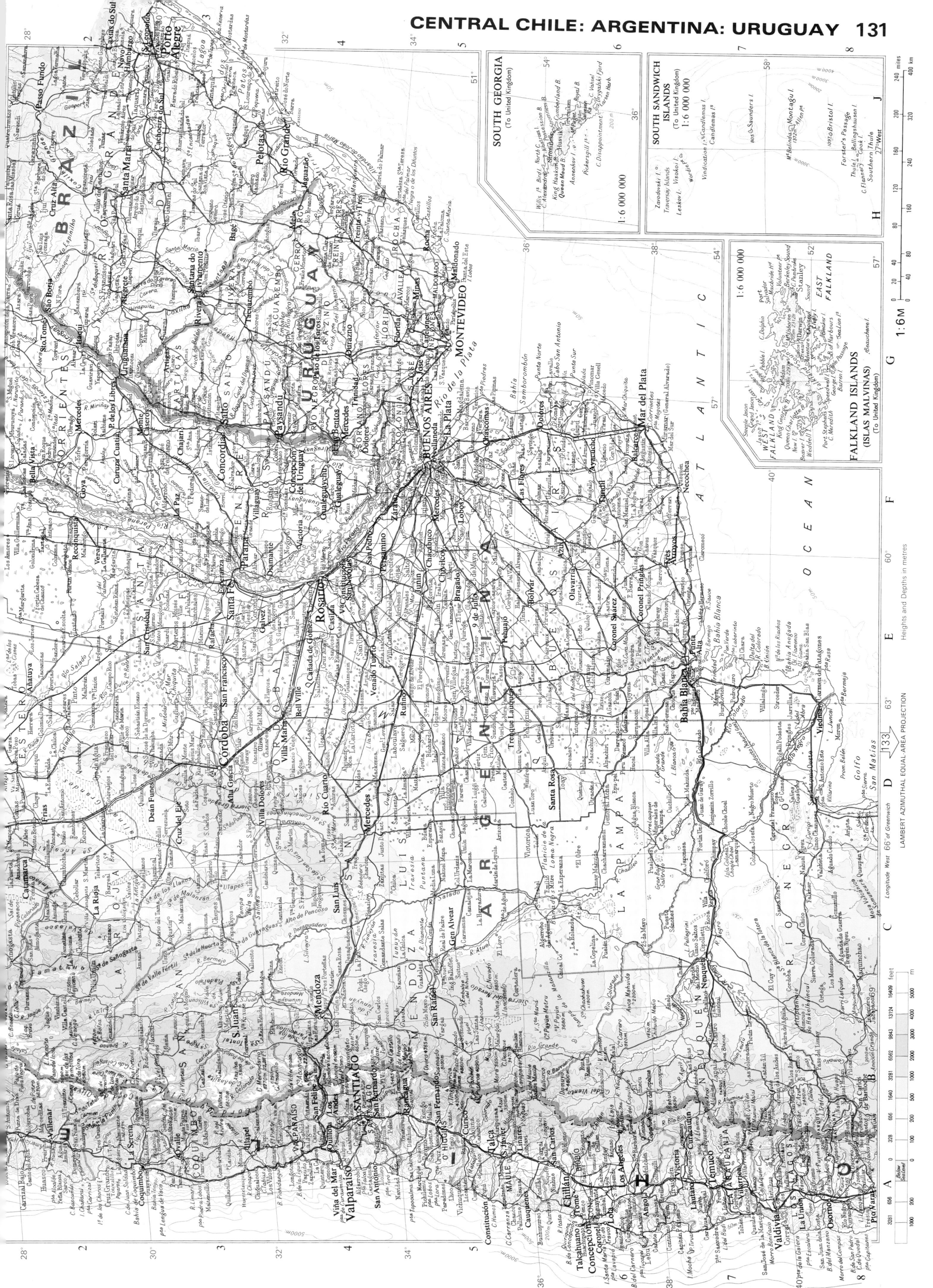

SOUTH GEORGIA
(To United Kingdom)
1:6 000 000

SOUTH SANDWICH
ISLANDS
(To United Kingdom)
1:6 000 000

FALKLAND ISLANDS
(ISLAS MALVINAS)
(To United Kingdom)
1:6 000 000

1:6M

BRAZIL

URUGUAY

ARGENTINA

MONTEVIDEO

BUENOS AIRES

SANTIAGO

ATLANTIC OCEAN

LAMBERT AZIMUTHAL EQUAL-AREA PROJECTION

Heights and Depths in metres

RIO DE JANEIRO

A 43°30' E 43°15' C 43°00' D

RIO DE JANEIRO

Teófilo Cunha
Aliezur
Caramujos
Rio d'Ouro
Cachoeiras
São Bernardino
DUQUE DE CAXIAS
MAGÉ
Suruí
Magé
Sernambitiba
Magé-Mirim
Olaria
Piedade
São Francisco do Croará
Maramba
ITABORAÍ

Amaral
Aiva
Figueira
Cava
Campos Elyseos
Ipiranga
Guia de Pacobaiba
Guaxindiba
Itambi

Carlos Sampaio
Santa Rita
Ambaí
Miguel Couto
Itaipu
Núcleo Colonial São Bento
Iguaçu
BAIA DE
Lighthouse
RIO DE JANEIRO
Queimados
Aostin
Andrade Araujo
Anéia Branca
Tramacho
GUANABARA
Ponta Grossa
Ilha do Boqueirão
Ilha de Paquetá
Luz Inborn
Morro do Itaúna 281
DE
Morro Agudo
Nova Iguaçu
Praia
Belforc Roxo
Coel o da Rocha
Duque de Caxias
ILHA DO GOVERNADOR
Galeão
Cocotá
Ilha D'Agua
Lighthouse
Ponta da Rabeira
Ilha dos Tavares
Lighthouse
São Gonçalo
Pacheco
Sacramentos
S. Isabel
GONÇALO

NOVA IGUAÇU
Rocha Sobrinho
Mesquita
Lago tinho Pôrto
São João de Meriti
Nilópolis
São Mateus
Olinda
Guadalup
Vila Pedro
BALEÃO
Penha
Olaria
Ilha Santa Cruz
Sete Pontes
Neves
Baldeador
Maria Paula
Vila Progresso
Rio d'Ouro
Cala das Mocas
Inoa

Serra de Madureira
Morro do Capim
Melado 438
De doro
Ramos
Bonsucesso
Serra da Misericórdia
Cidade Universitária
Ponte Costa e Silva
Triboba
Badu
Canto de Rio
JANEIRO

Marapicu
Rocha Miranda
Bastos
Madureira
Pavuna
Benfica
Caju
RIO DE JANEIRO
Museu
Santos
Dumont
Centro
Morro Boa Vista 217
Niterói
Varzeas das Mocas

Santissimo
Timbo
Realengo
Campo dos Afonsos
Cascadura
Meier
Eng Novo
Cristovão
Gamboa
Ponta da Armação
Lighthouse
Ponta do Catalão
NITERÓI
Engenho do Mato

Bangu
Padre Miguel
Praça Sêca
Encantado
Pra dade
Catumbi
A R Comprido
Campista
Lapa
Ponta do Fora
Piratininga
Lago de Piratininga
MARICÁ

GUANABARA
Campo Grande
Boca do Mato
Vila Isabel
Andraí
Fab das Chitas
Palacio
Glória
Catete
Enseada de Jurujuba
Piratininga

Inhoaiba
Cosmos
Pechincha
Tijuca
Laranjeiras
Urca
Pão de Açúcar (Sugar Loaf)
Canto do Pontes
Lago de Itaipu

Pedra Branca 1025
Taquara
Jacarepag
Floresta da Tijuca
Pico da Tijuca 1022
Serra da Carioca
Bogafogo
Lagoa Rodrigo de Freitas
Ilha do Veado
Ilha da Mãe
Itaipu

Serra da Pedra Branca
Morro de Santa Bárbara 851
Baixada de Jacarepagua
Gávea
Niemeyer
Leblon
Ipanema
Copacabana
Ilha do Pai
Ponta de Itacoatiara

Vargem Grande
Lagoa de Jacarepaguá
125
Morro Amorim
Pedra da Gávea 845
São Conrado
Ilha das Palmas

Ilha da Bom Jardim
365
Morro de Guaratiba
Lago de Marapendi
Praia dos Bandeirantes
Pontal do Mariscó
Ilha da Alfavaca
Ilha das Palmas
Lighthouse
Ilha Comprida
Ilha Rasa
Lighthouse

Baía de Sepetibá
Ponta da Praia Funda
Pontal de Sernambitiba
Ilha Pontuda
Ilha Redonda

Ilha Rasa da Guaratiba

ATLANTIC OCEAN

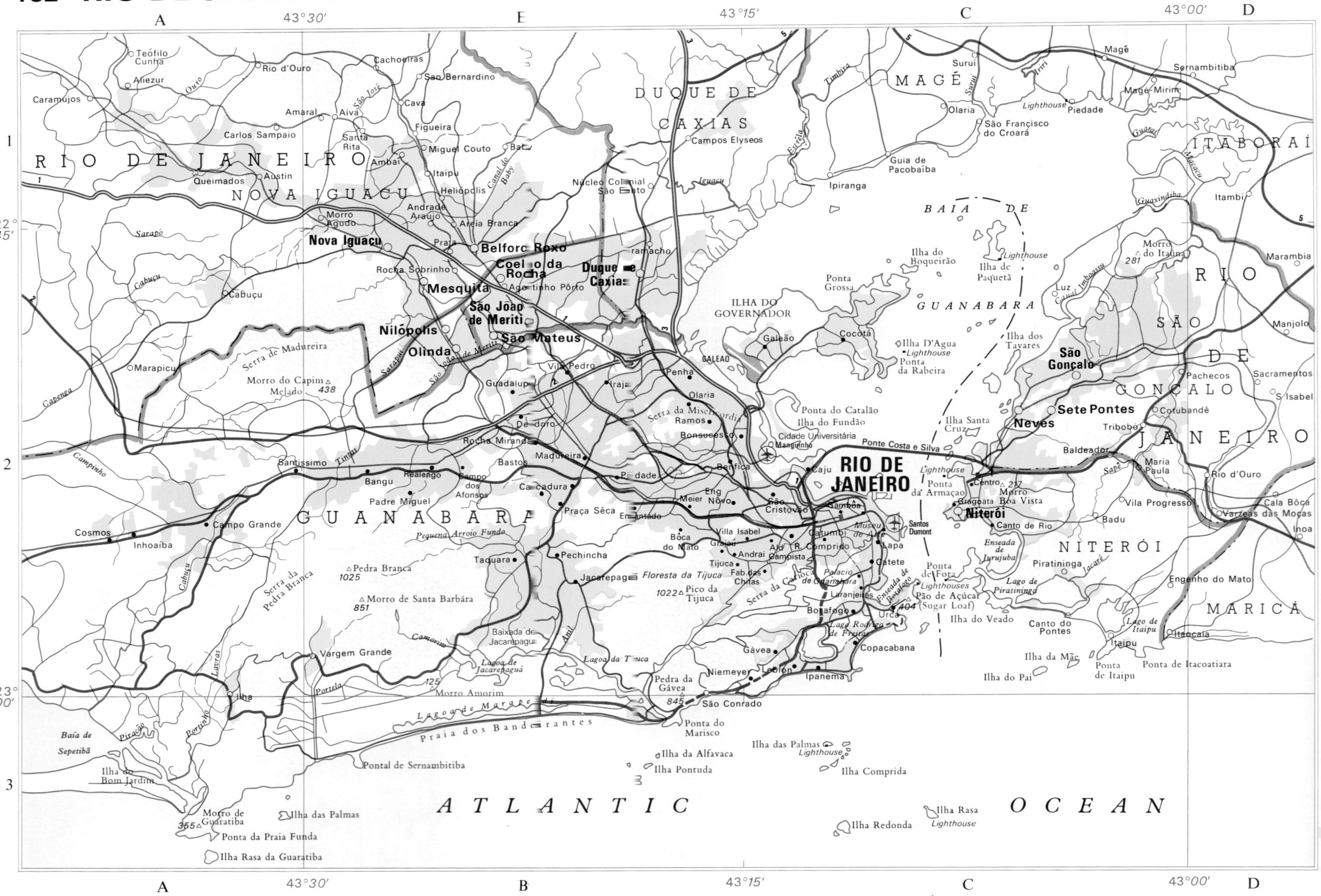

A 43°30' B 43°15' C 43°00' D

BUENOS AIRES

A 58°45' B 58°30' C 58°15' D

ESCOBAR
Benavidez
Gatin
TIGRE
Tigre
San Fernando

Villa Rosa
Garin
General Pacheco
Victoria
Beccar

Pilar
PILAR
Del Viso
El Talar
SAN FERNANDO
San Isidro
Juan Anchorena
RÍO DE

Tortuguitas
Don Torcuato
Don Torcuato
SAN ISIDRO
Martinez

Presidente Derqui
Manzone
Toro
Piñero
GENERAL
Los Polvorines
Don Torcuato
Olivos
Vicente López
LA PLATA

Villa de Mayo
SARMIENTO
Boulogne
Villa Adelina
VICENTE LÓPEZ
Florida

José C Paz
General Sarmiento
Muñiz
Villa José L
Suárez
Munro
Saavedra
Aeroparque

General Rodriguez
Bella Vista
GENERAL SAN MARTÍN
Villa Ballester
Belgrano
Hipodromo Argentino
Núñez
Nuñez

Francisco Alvarez
Los Berros
General San Martín
General Urquiza

BUENOS
TRES DE FEBRERO
Villa Lynch
Palermo
BUENOS AIRES

GENERAL RODRIGUEZ
MORENO
Hurlingham
El Palomar
Caseros
Villa Bosch
Villa Sáenz Peña
Once
DISTRITO
Plaza Nacional de Mayo
Boca

General Rodriguez
El Palomar
MORON
Villa Santos Lugares
Villa Real
Versailles
Caballito
FEDERAL
Constitución
Barracas

Moreno
Paso del Rey
Castelar
Morón
Ramos Mejia
Nueva Chicago
Nueva Pompeya
Avellaneda
Avellaneda

Merlo
Ituzaingó
Maria J. Ha
San Justo
Villa Madero
Parque Almirante Guillermo Brown
Valentin Alsina
Gerli
Villa Dominico

San Antonio de Pádua
Tablada
Tapiales
Aldo Bonzi
Villa Diamante
Lanús
Wilde
Don Bosco
Bernal

MERLO
Libertad
Rafael Castillo
Isidro Casanova
Ciudad General Belgrano
Florito
Remedios de Escalada
QUILMES
Quilmes

AIRES
Mariano Acosta
Pontevedra
MATANZA
San Justo
Laferrere
MATANZA
Ingeniero Budge
Monte Chingolo
Berazategui
BERAZATEGUI

MARCOS PAZ
González Catan
Lomas de Zamora
LOMAS DE ZAMORA
Santa Catalina
Temperley
Rafael Calzada
Gobernador Monteverde
Villa Giambruno

Marcos Paz
ESTEBAN ECHEVERRIA
Monte Grande
Llavallol
Almirante Brown
ALMIRANTE BROWN
Florencio Varela
FLORENCIO VARELA

EZEIZA
Esteban Echeverría
Burzaco
Ranelagh
Ezpeleta

A 58°45' B 58°30' C 58°15' D

1:3 000 000

E/G5251   © Times Books Ltd

0 5 10 15 km
0 5 miles

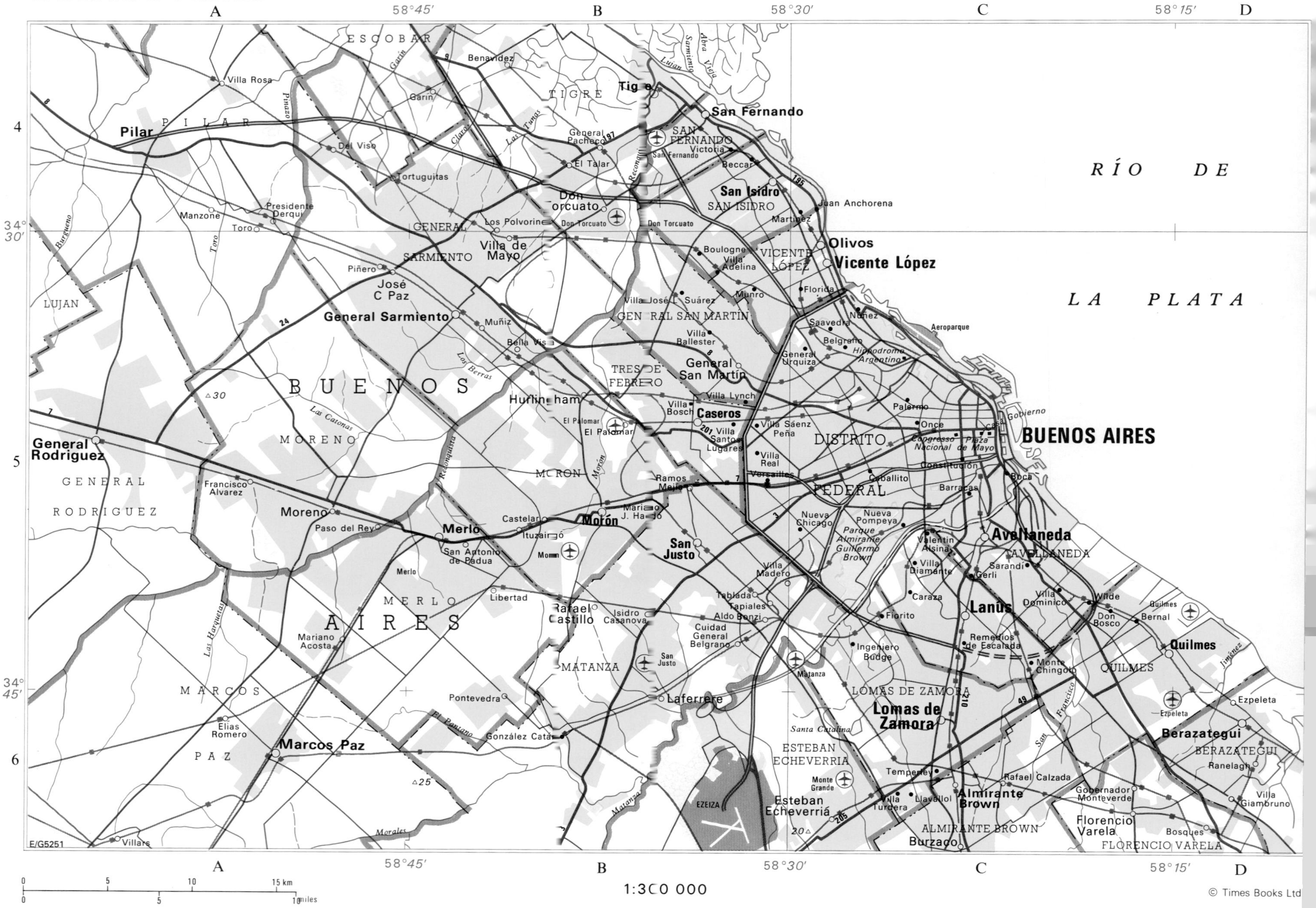

SOUTH PACIFIC OCEAN
SOUTH ATLANTIC OCEAN
ARGENTINA
CHILE
BOLIVIA
PARAGUAY
BRAZIL
URUGUAY
FALKLAND ISLANDS
(ISLAS MALVINAS)
(To U.K.)
West Falkland
East Falkland
Tropic of Capricorn
Buenos Aires
Montevideo
Santiago
Valparaíso
Asunción
Córdoba
Rosario
Mendoza
Porto Alegre
São Paulo
Curitiba
Mar del Plata
Bahía Blanca
Antofagasta
Tierra del Fuego
Golfo San Matías
Golfo San Jorge
Islas Juan Fernández
(To Chile)
Alejandro Selkirk
(Mas Afuera)
Robinson Crusoe
(Mas Atierra)
Sta Clara
San Félix
San Ambrosio
(To Chile)
South Georgia
(To U.K.)
Shag Rocks
(To U.K.)
Clerke Rocks
on the same scale
on the same scale
on the same scale
LAMBERT AZIMUTHAL EQUAL AREA PROJECTION
Heights in metres
1:12 M
feet
656 0 656 1640 3281 6562 9843 13123 16404 19685
Below Sea Level
200 0 200 500 1000 2000 3000 4000 5000 6000 m
miles 0 40 80 160 240 320 400 480
km 0 80 160 320 480 640 800

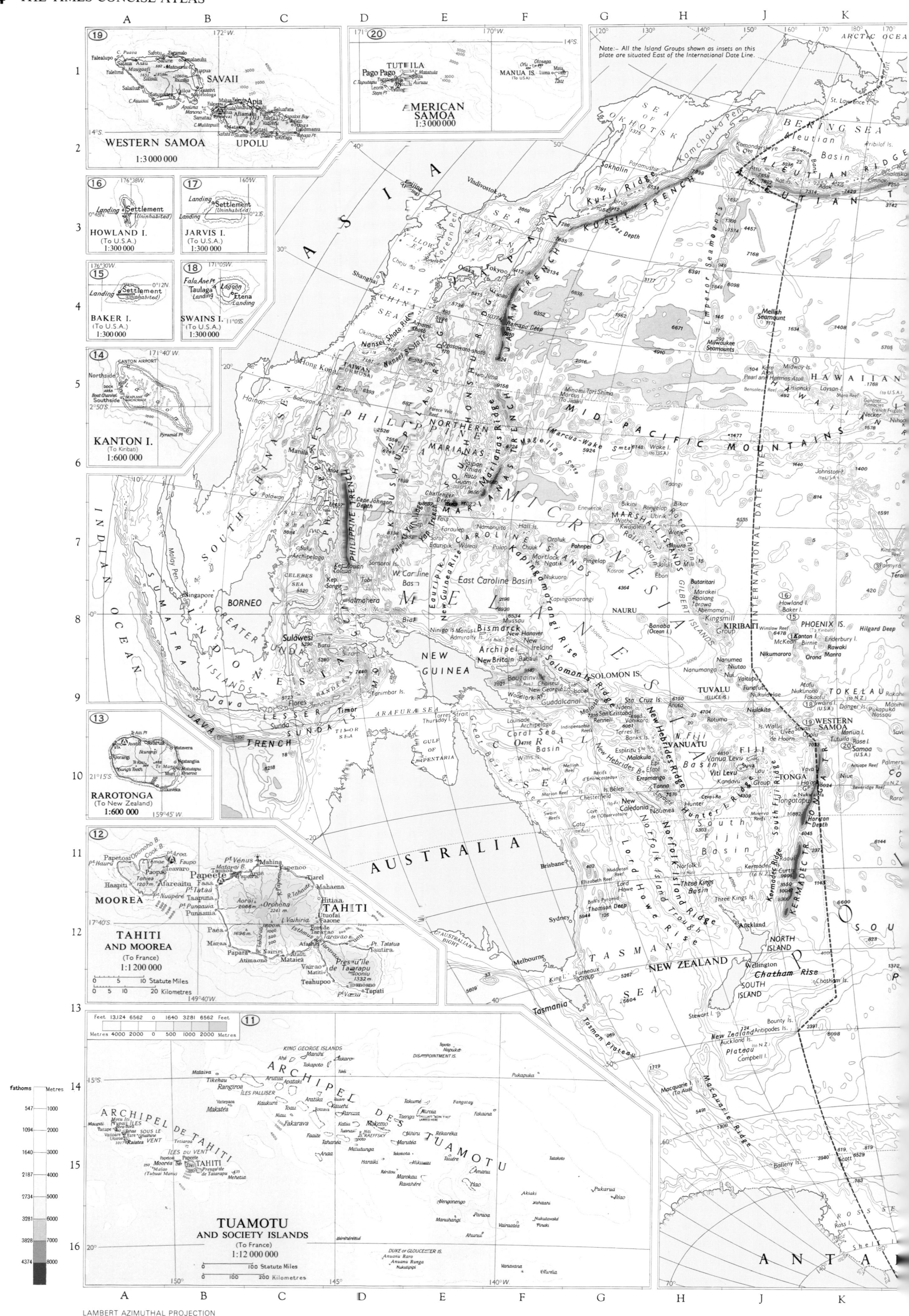
WESTERN SAMOA
1:3 000 000
SAVAII
UPOLU
Apia
AMERICAN SAMOA
1:3 000 000
TUTUILA
Pago Pago
MANUA IS. (To U.S.A.)
HOWLAND I.
(To U.S.A.)
1:300 000
JARVIS I.
(To U.S.A.)
1:300 000
BAKER I.
(To U.S.A.)
1:300 000
SWAINS I.
(To U.S.A.)
1:300 000
KANTON I.
(To Kiribati)
1:600 000
RAROTONGA
(To New Zealand)
1:600 000
TAHITI AND MOOREA
(To France)
1:1 200 000
Statute Miles
Kilometres
MOOREA
TAHITI
Papeete
TUAMOTU AND SOCIETY ISLANDS
(To France)
1:12 000 000
ARCHIPEL DES TUAMOTU
ARCHIPEL DE TAHITI
Note:- All the Island Groups shown as insets on this plate are situated East of the International Date Line.
ASIA
SEA OF OKHOTSK
BERING SEA
ALEUTIAN RIDGE
ALEUTIAN TRENCH
Aleutian Basin
Kamchatka Pen.
Kuril Ridge
KURIL TRENCH
SEA OF JAPAN
JAPAN TRENCH
EAST CHINA SEA
SOUTH CHINA SEA
PHILIPPINE SEA
PHILIPPINE TRENCH
NORTHERN MARIANAS
Marianas Ridge
MARIANAS TRENCH
Emperor Seamounts
HAWAIIAN RIDGE
MID-PACIFIC MOUNTAINS
MICRONESIA
MARSHALL ISLANDS
CAROLINE ISLANDS
East Caroline Basin
MELANESIA
NAURU
KIRIBATI
PHOENIX IS.
TUVALU
TOKELAU
SOLOMON IS.
VANUATU
FIJI
TONGA
WESTERN SAMOA
NEW GUINEA
Bismarck Archipel
BORNEO
Sulawesi
INDONESIA
JAVA TRENCH
SUNDA
INDIAN OCEAN
ARAFURA SEA
Coral Sea Basin
CORAL SEA
AUSTRALIA
South Fiji Basin
TONGA TRENCH
KERMADEC TRENCH
TASMAN SEA
Lord Howe Rise
Norfolk Island Ridge
NEW ZEALAND
NORTH ISLAND
SOUTH ISLAND
Chatham Rise
Tasmania
Campbell Plateau
Macquarie Ridge
INTERNATIONAL DATE LINE
ANTARCTICA
fathoms
Metres
Feet

LAMBERT AZIMUTHAL PROJECTION

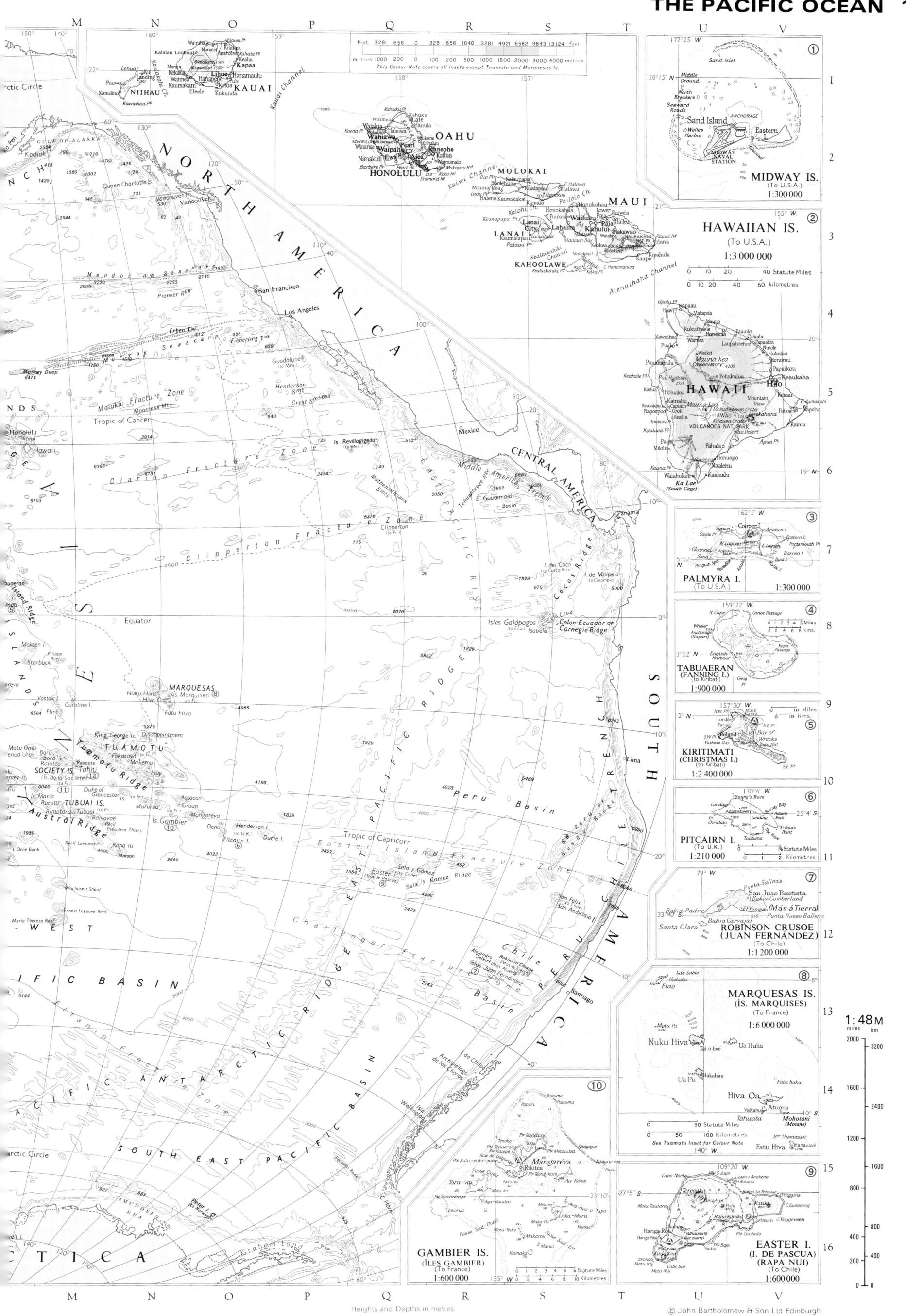

Heights and Depths in metres

© John Bartholomew & Son Ltd Edinburgh

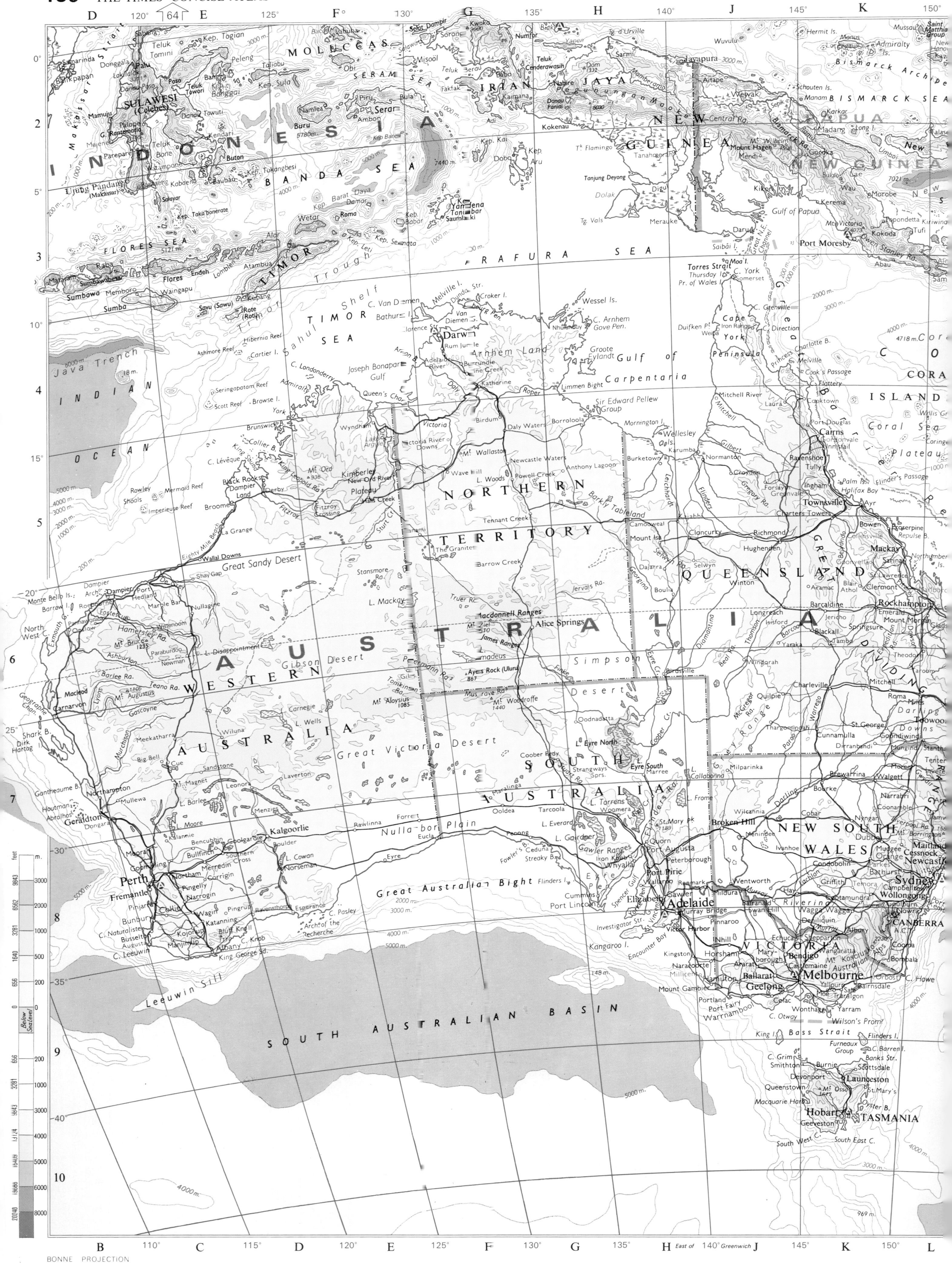

D 120° 64 E 125° F° 130° G 135° H 140° J 145° K 150°

MOLUCCAS

SERAM SEA

INDONESIA

SULAWESI (Celebes)

BANDA SEA

FLORES SEA

IRIAN JAYA

Jayapura

NEW GUINEA

PAPUA

NEW GUINEA

BISMARCK SEA

Bismarck Archipelago

Admiralty Is.

Port Moresby

Gulf of Papua

Torres Strait

Thursday I.
Pr. of Wales I.

ARAFURA SEA

TIMOR SEA

Timor Trough

Flores

Sumbawa

Sumba

INDIAN

OCEAN

Java Trench

Darwin

Arnhem Land

Gulf of Carpentaria

Groote Eylandt

Cape York Peninsula

Cairns

Coral Sea

CORAL SEA ISLAND

Coral Sea Plateau

Townsville

NORTHERN TERRITORY

Tennant Creek

Great Sandy Desert

Broome

Port Hedland

Marble Bar

Kimberley Plateau

QUEENSLAND

Mount Isa

Cloncurry

Hughenden

Winton

Longreach

Barcaldine

Rockhampton

AUSTRALIA

Alice Springs

Macdonnell Ranges

Ayers Rock (Uluru)

Simpson Desert

Gibson Desert

WESTERN AUSTRALIA

Great Victoria Desert

SOUTH AUSTRALIA

Charleville

Roma

Darling Downs

Toowoomba

NEW SOUTH WALES

Carnarvon

Meekatharra

Wiluna

Laverton

Kalgoorlie

Coober Pedy

L. Eyre North

Broken Hill

Bourke

Nullarbor Plain

Great Australian Bight

Eucla

L. Torrens

L. Gairdner

Port Augusta

Whyalla

Port Pirie

Port Lincoln

Wilcannia

Cobar

Dubbo

Newcastle

Geraldton

Perth

Fremantle

Bunbury

Albany

Esperance

Norseman

Adelaide

Murray Bridge

Mildura

Wagga Wagga

Sydney

Wollongong

CANBERRA A.C.T.

VICTORIA

Bendigo

Ballarat

Geelong

Melbourne

Horsham

Mount Gambier

Portland

Warrnambool

Bass Strait

King I.

Flinders I.

TASMANIA

Launceston

Hobart

SOUTH AUSTRALIAN BASIN

Leeuwin Sill

East of 140° Greenwich

BONNE PROJECTION

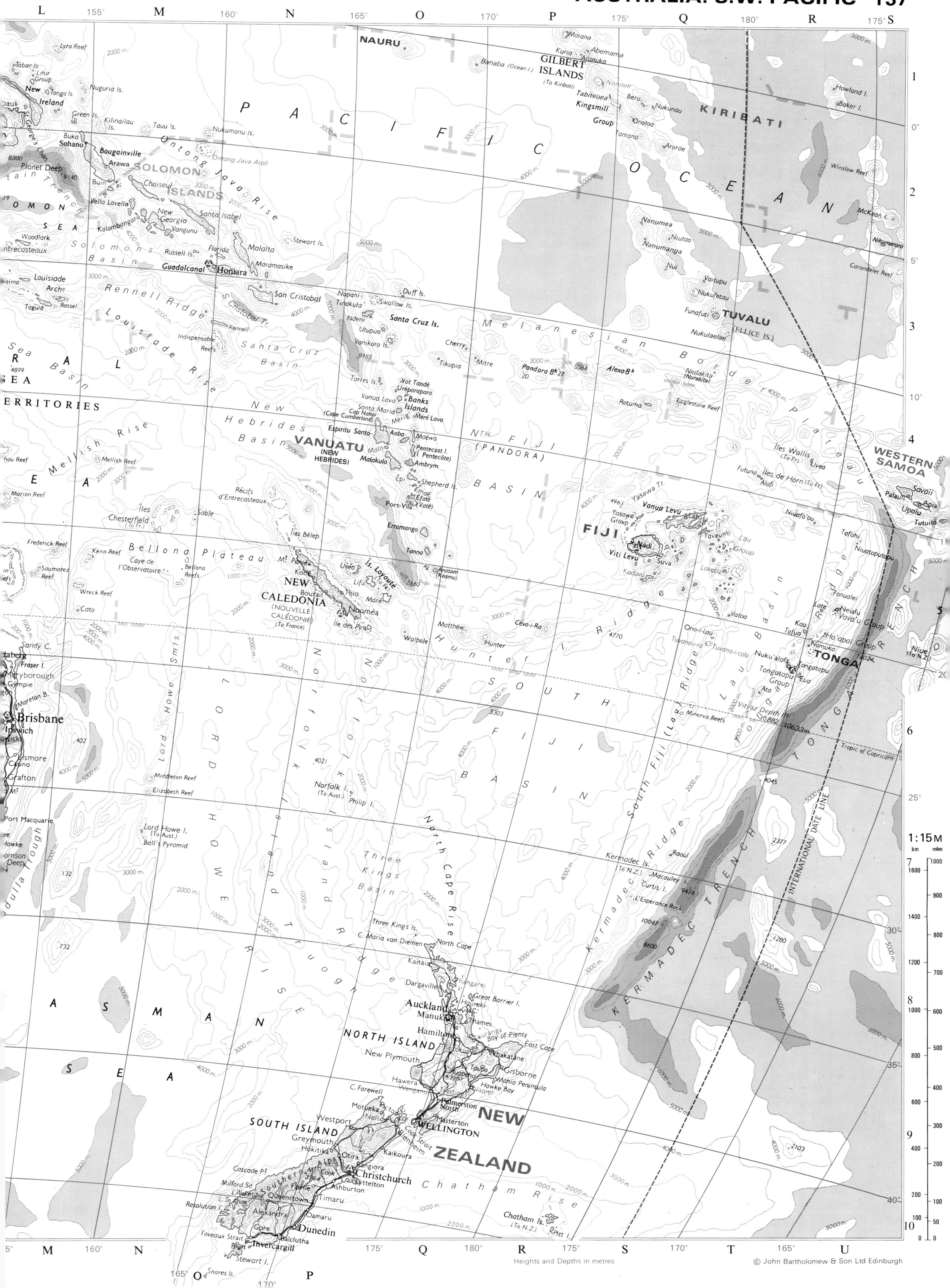

PACIFIC OCEAN

NAURU

GILBERT ISLANDS
(To Kiribati)

KIRIBATI

Kingsmill Group

SOLOMON ISLANDS

Bougainville
Arawa
Buka
Sohano
Buin
New Georgia
Vella Lavella
Kolombangara
Vangunu
Santa Isabel
Florida
Malaita
Maramasike
Guadalcanal
Honiara
San Cristobal

New Ireland
Tabar Is.
Lihir Group
Nuguria Is.
Tanga Is.
Green Is.
Kilinailau Is.
Tauu Is.
Nukumanu Is.
Ontong Java Atoll

Ontong Java Rise
Rennell Ridge
Louisiade Rise

SOLOMON SEA
Woodlark
D'entrecasteaux
Louisiade Archy.
Tagula
Rossel

Solomons Basin

CORAL SEA
Mellish Rise
Mellish Reef
Marion Reef
Frederick Reef
Saumarez Reef
Wreck Reef
Cato
Kenn Reef

Santa Cruz Is.
Duff Is.
Swallow Is.
Ndeni
Utupua
Vanikoro
Tikopia
Cherry
Mitre
Torres Is.

Banks Islands
Vot Tandé
Ureparapara
Vanua Lava
Santa Maria
Merig
Meré Lava
Espiritu Santo
Aoba
Maéwo
Pentecost I. (I. Pentecôte)
Malo
Malakula
Ambrym
Épi
Émaé
Shepherd Is.
Éfaté
Vaté
Port-Vila
Erromango
Tanna
Anatom (Keamu)

VANUATU
(NEW HEBRIDES)

New Hebrides Basin

NTH. FIJI (PANDORA) BASIN

Melanesian Border Plateau

TUVALU (ELLICE IS.)
Funafuti
Nanumea
Niutao
Nanumanga
Nui
Vaitupu
Nukufetau
Nukulaelae
Rotuma

WESTERN SAMOA
Savaii
Apia
Upolu
Tutuila
Tafahi
Niuatoputapu

Îles Wallis
Uvea
Futuna
Îles de Horn (To Fr.)
Alofi

FIJI
Vanua Levu
Yasawa Group
Taveuni
Viti Levu
Nadi
Suva
Kadavu
Vatoa
Lau Group
Lakeba

NEW CALEDONIA
(NOUVELLE CALÉDONIE)
(To France)
Nouméa
Bourail
Koné
Mt. Panié
Île des Pins

Récifs d'Entrecasteaux
Îles Bélep
Îles Loyauté
Uvéa
Lifu
Thio
Maré

Bellona Plateau
Chesterfield Reefs
Îles Chesterfield (To Fr.)
Caye de l'Observatoire

Matthew
Hunter
Walpole
Céva-i-Ra
Ono-i-Lau
Tuvana-i-ra
Tuvana-i-colo

SOUTH FIJI BASIN

Norfolk Ridge
Norfolk I. (To Aust.)
Philip I.

Lord Howe Rise
Lord Howe I. (To Aust.)
Ball's Pyramid
Middleton Reef
Elizabeth Reef

TONGA
Nuku'alofa
Tongatapu Group
Tongatapu
Eua
Ata
Minerva Reefs
Ha'apai Group
Nomuka
Kao
Tofua
Namuka
Neiafu
Vava'u Group
Fonualei
Niue (To N.Z.)

Vityaz Depth

TASMAN SEA

Brisbane
Ipswich
Lismore
Casino
Grafton
Port Macquarie
Maryborough
Gympie
Moreton B.
Fraser I.

Three Kings Basin
Three Kings Is.
C. Maria van Diemen
North Cape
Kaitaia
Kaikohe
Kerikeri
Whangarei
Dargaville
Great Barrier I.
Hauraki
Auckland
Manukau
Hamilton
Thames
Bay of Plenty
Tauranga
East Cape
New Plymouth
Whakatane
Taupo
Gisborne
Rotorua
Mahia Peninsula
Hawera
Wanganui
Napier
Hawke Bay
C. Farewell
Motueka
Nelson
Palmerston North
Masterton
WELLINGTON
Cook Strait
Blenheim

NORTH ISLAND

SOUTH ISLAND

NEW ZEALAND

Westport
Greymouth
Hokitika
Otira
Kaikoura
Rangiora
Christchurch
Lyttelton
Ashburton
Timaru
Oamaru
Cascade Pt.
Milford Sd.
Mt. Cook
Wanaka
Queenstown
Alexandra
Gore
Dunedin
Balclutha
Invercargill
Bluff
Foveaux Strait
Stewart I.
Snares Is.

Southern Alps

Chatham Rise
Chatham Is. (To N.Z.)
Pitt I.

North Cape Rise

Norfolk Island Trough

Kermadec Ridge
Kermadec Is. (To N.Z.)
Raoul
Macauley I.
Curtis I.
L'Esperance Rock

KERMADEC TRENCH

TONGA TRENCH

Lau (Lau) Ridge
Lau Basin

INTERNATIONAL DATE LINE

Tropic of Capricorn

1:15 M

Heights and Depths in metres

© John Bartholomew & Son Ltd Edinburgh

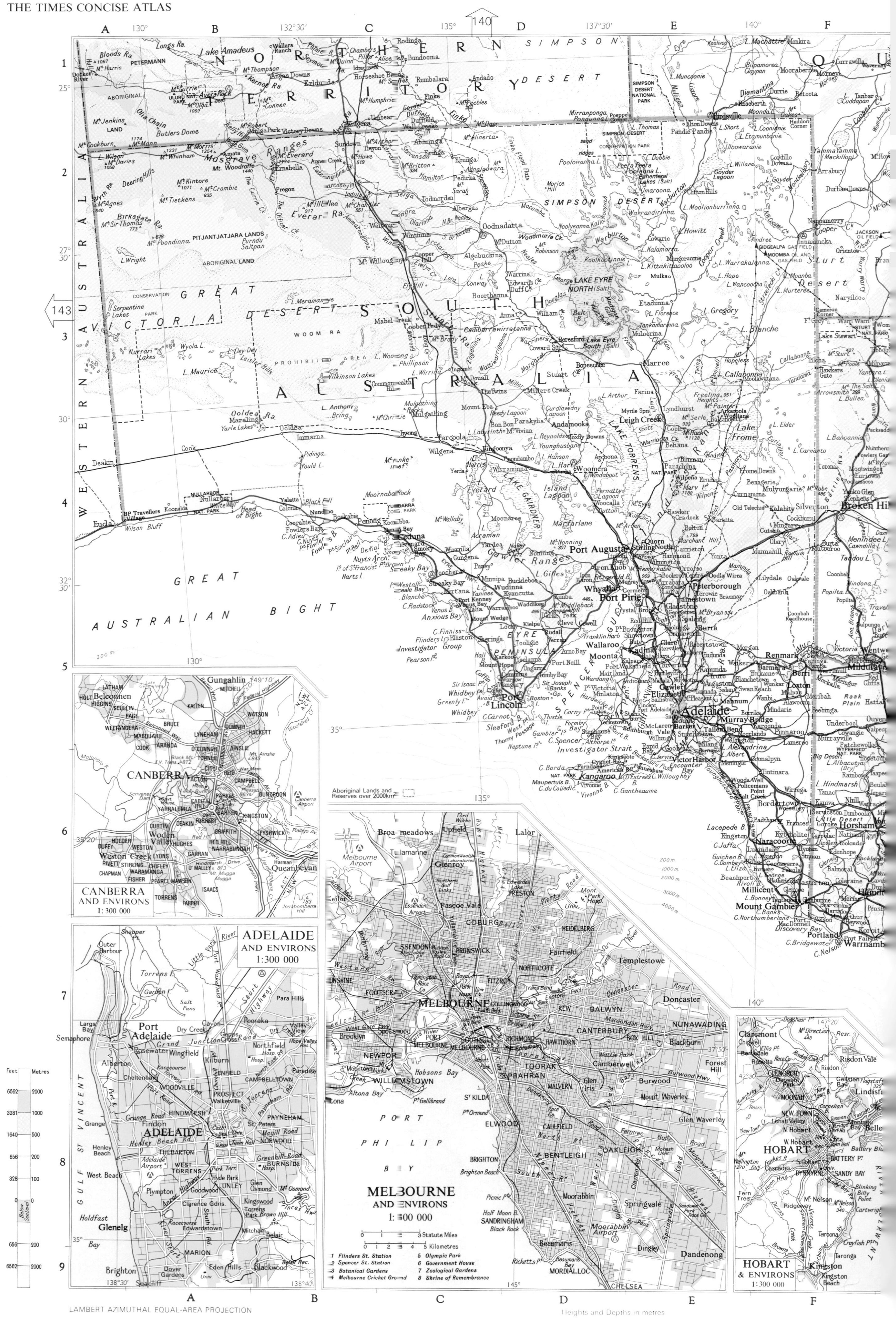
140
143
NORTHERN TERRITORY
SIMPSON DESERT
QUEENSLAND
WESTERN AUSTRALIA
SOUTH AUSTRALIA
GREAT VICTORIA DESERT
GREAT AUSTRALIAN BIGHT
Sturt Desert
LAKE EYRE NORTH (Salt)
Lake Eyre South (Salt)
LAKE TORRENS
LAKE GAIRDNER
Lake Frome
Gawler Ranges
Musgrave Ranges
EYRE PENINSULA
SPENCER GULF
GULF ST. VINCENT
Investigator Strait
Kangaroo I.
Encounter Bay
Oodnadatta
Coober Pedy
Port Augusta
Whyalla
Port Pirie
Port Lincoln
Ceduna
Adelaide
Murray Bridge
Victor Harbor
Mount Gambier
Broken Hill
Mildura
Horsham
Aboriginal Lands and Reserves over 2000km²
CANBERRA AND ENVIRONS 1: 300 000
CANBERRA
Queanbeyan
ADELAIDE AND ENVIRONS 1:300 000
ADELAIDE
Port Adelaide
Glenelg
MELBOURNE AND ENVIRONS 1: 300 000
MELBOURNE
PORT PHILLIP BAY
3 Statute Miles
5 Kilometres
1 Flinders St. Station
2 Spencer St. Station
3 Botanical Gardens
4 Melbourne Cricket Ground
5 Olympic Park
6 Government House
7 Zoological Gardens
8 Shrine of Remembrance
HOBART & ENVIRONS 1:300 000
HOBART
Feet Metres
6562 2000
3281 1000
1640 500
656 200
328 100
0 0
Below Sea Level
656 200
6562 2000

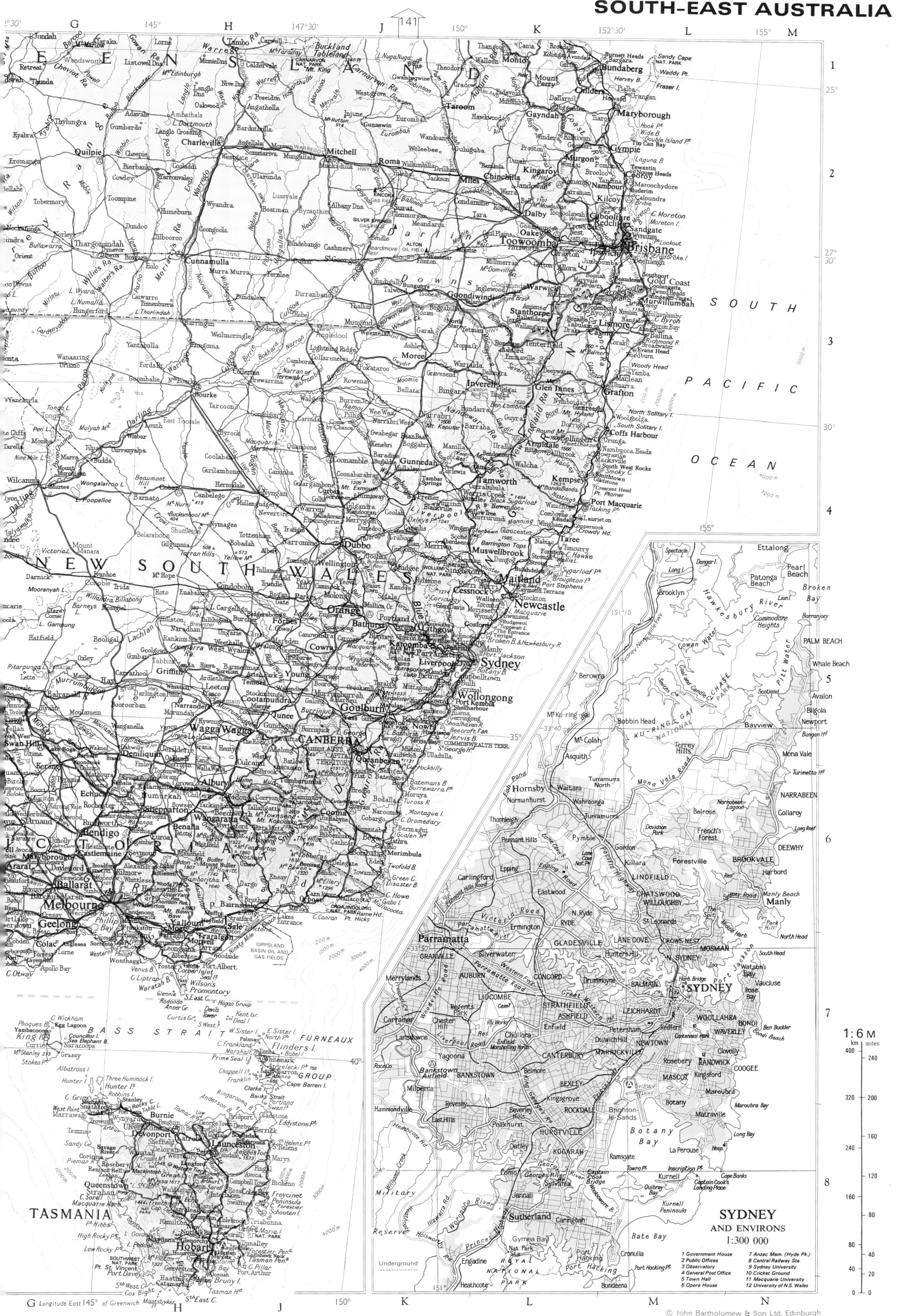

SYDNEY
AND ENVIRONS
1:300 000

1 Government House
2 Public Offices
3 Observatory
4 General Post Office
5 Town Hall
6 Opera House
7 Anzac Mem. (Hyde Pk.)
8 Central Railway Sta.
9 Sydney University
10 Cricket Ground
11 Macquarie University
12 University of N.S.W.

1:6 M

© John Bartholomew & Son Ltd. Edinburgh

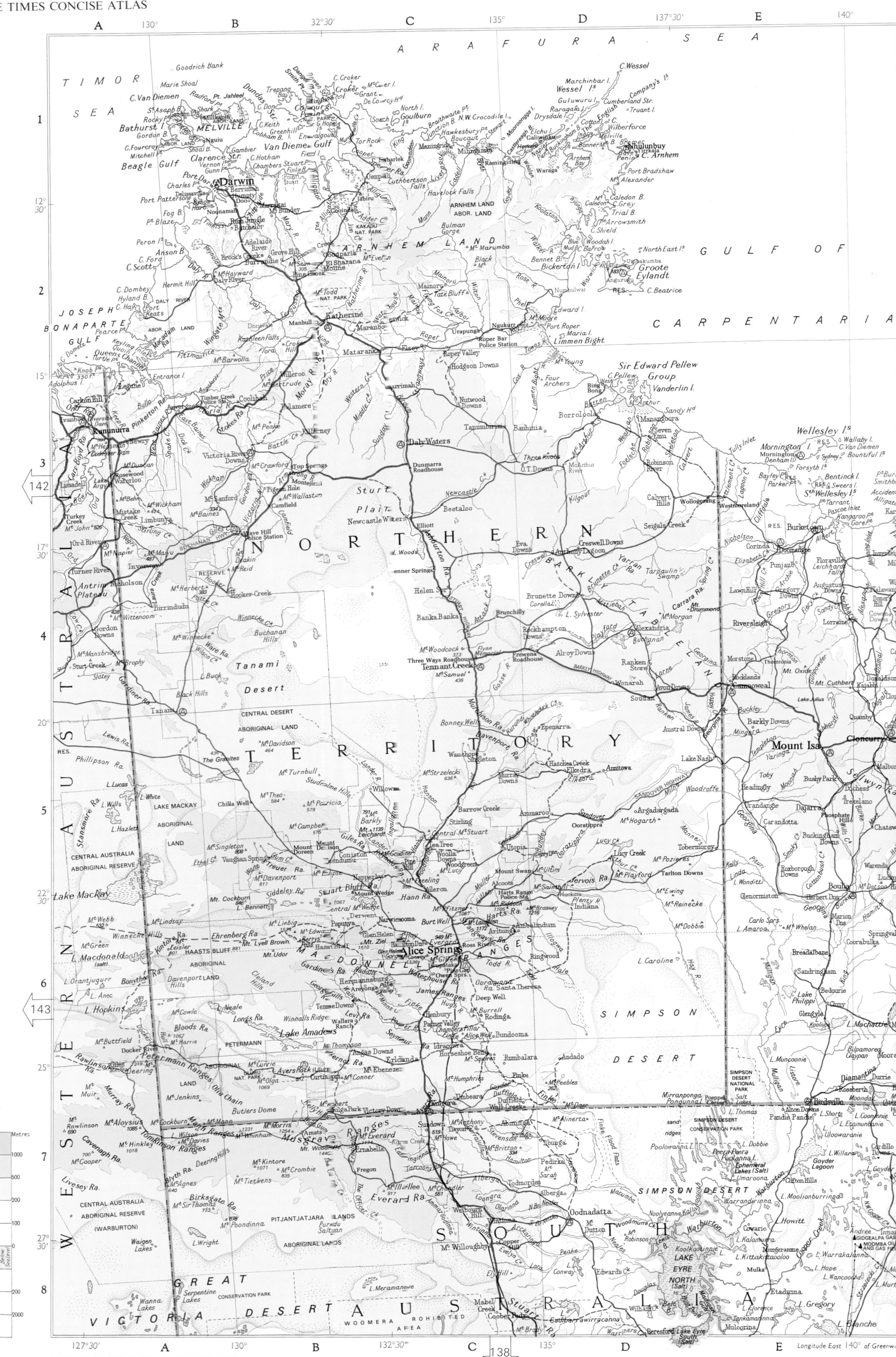
ARAFURA SEA
TIMOR SEA
GULF OF CARPENTARIA
JOSEPH BONAPARTE GULF
NORTHERN TERRITORY
WESTERN AUSTRALIA
SOUTH AUSTRALIA
ARNHEM LAND
Tanami Desert
SIMPSON DESERT
GREAT VICTORIA DESERT
BARKLY TABLELAND
Sturt Plain
MACDONNELL RANGES
Musgrave Ranges
Petermann Ranges
Darwin
Katherine
Daly Waters
Tennant Creek
Alice Springs
Mount Isa
Cloncurry
Camooweal
Burketown
Birdsville
Oodnadatta
Kununurra
Nhulunbuy
Groote Eylandt
Melville I.
Bathurst I.
Wessel Is
Sir Edward Pellew Group
Wellesley Is
Lake Mackay
Lake Amadeus
LAKE EYRE NORTH (Salt)
Lake Eyre South (Salt)
Ayers Rock (Uluru)
Mt Olga
SIMPSON DESERT NATIONAL PARK
KAKADU NAT. PARK
CENTRAL AUSTRALIA ABORIGINAL RESERVE
WOOMERA PROHIBITED AREA
142
143
138
Feet
Metres
3281 1000
1640 500
656 200
328 100
0 0
Below Sea Level
656 200
6562 2000
Longitude East 140° of Greenwich

LAMBERT AZIMUTHAL EQUAL-AREA PROJECTION

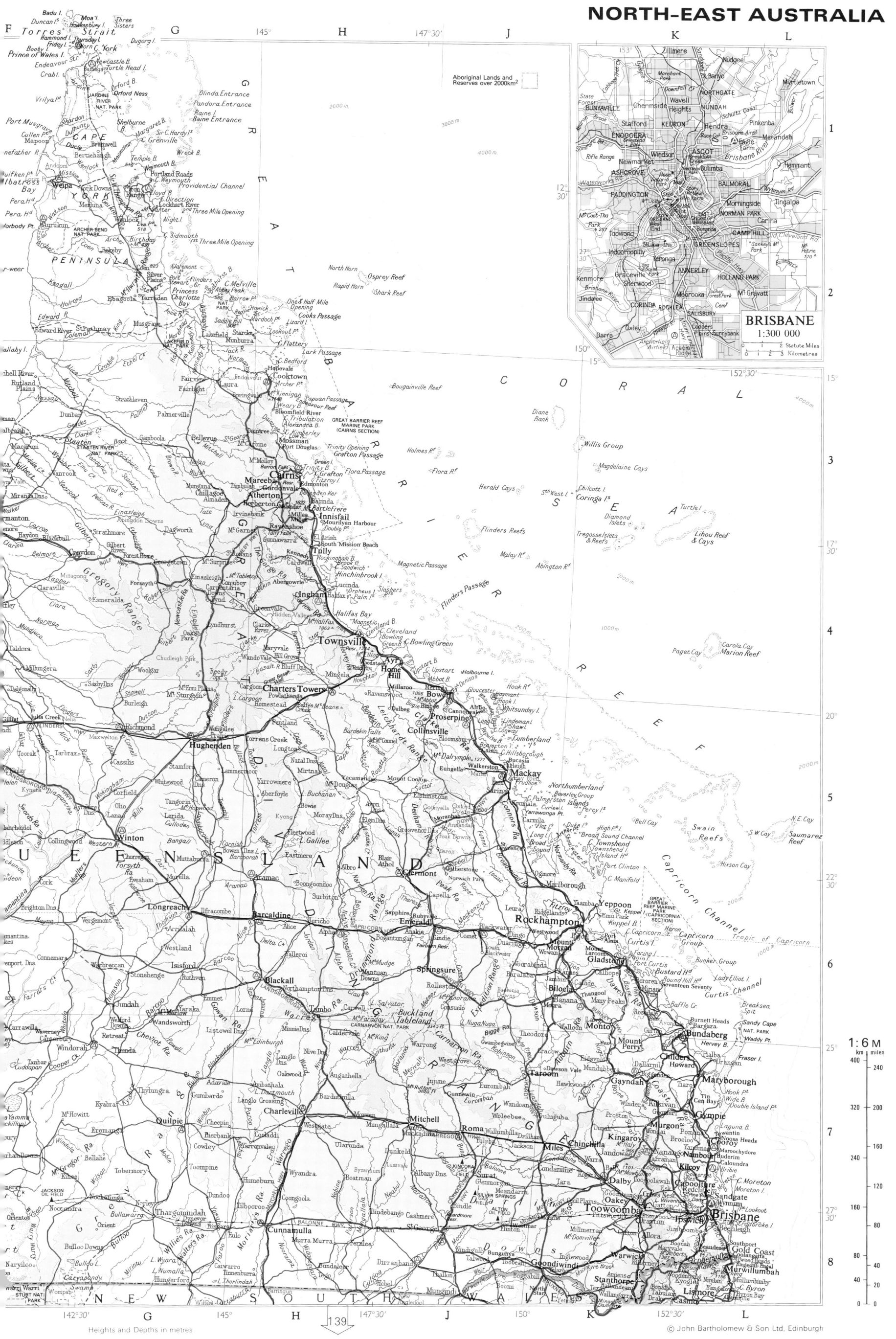

BRISBANE
1:300 000

1:6 M

© John Bartholomew & Son Ltd. Edinburgh

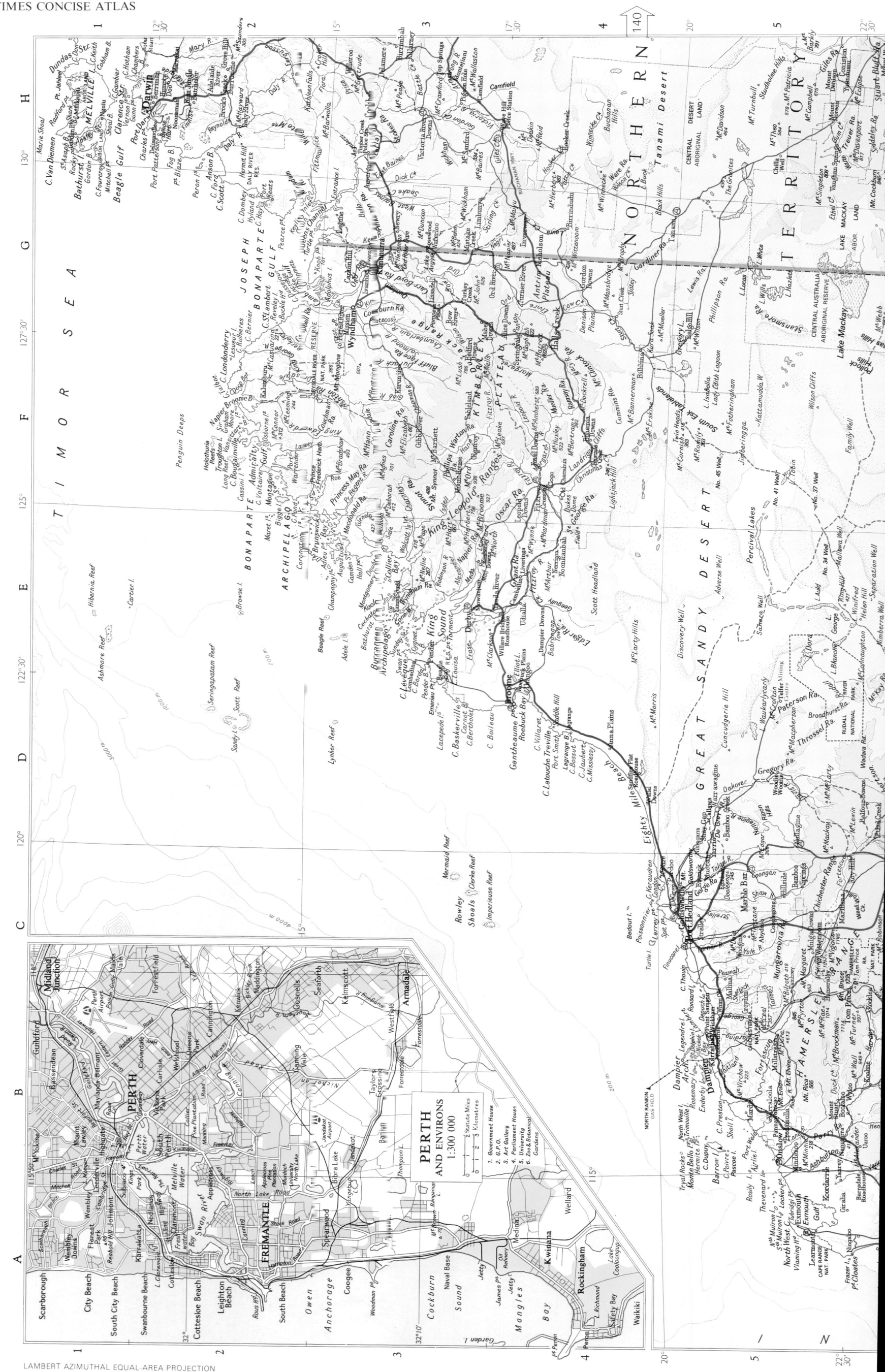

LAMBERT AZIMUTHAL EQUAL-AREA PROJECTION

PERTH
AND ENVIRONS
1:300 000

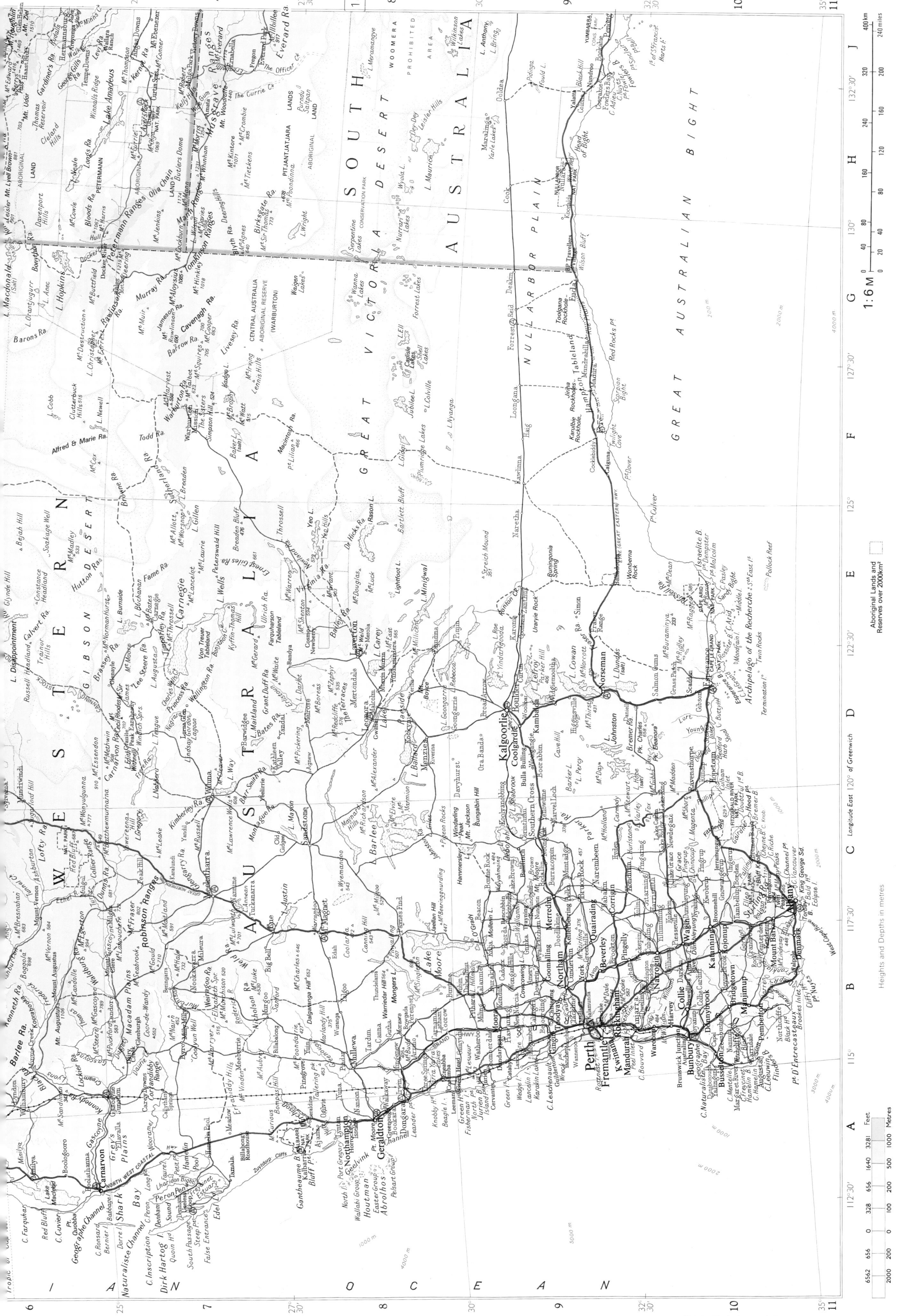

WESTERN AUSTRALIA

SOUTH AUSTRALIA

GREAT VICTORIA DESERT

GIBSON DESERT

GREAT AUSTRALIAN BIGHT

NULLARBOR PLAIN

INDIAN OCEAN

Perth
Fremantle
Kalgoorlie
Coolgardie
Norseman
Geraldton
Carnarvon
Albany
Bunbury
Northampton

1:6 M

Heights and Depths in metres

Aboriginal Lands and Reserves over 2000km²

Longitude East 120° of Greenwich

© John Bartholomew & Son Ltd, Edinburgh

CHRISTCHURCH
AND ENVIRONS
1:300 000

DUNEDIN
AND ENVIRONS
1:300 000

SOUTH ISLAND

TASMAN SEA

PACIFIC OCEAN

CLUTHA/CENTRAL OTAGO

SOUTHLAND

STEWART ISLAND

FOVEAUX STRAIT

NELSON BAYS

MARLBOROUGH

CANTERBURY

AORANGI

COASTAL/NORTH OTAGO

WEST COAST

CONIC PROJECTION

Longitude East 170° of Greenwich

© John Bartholomew & Son Ltd Edinburgh

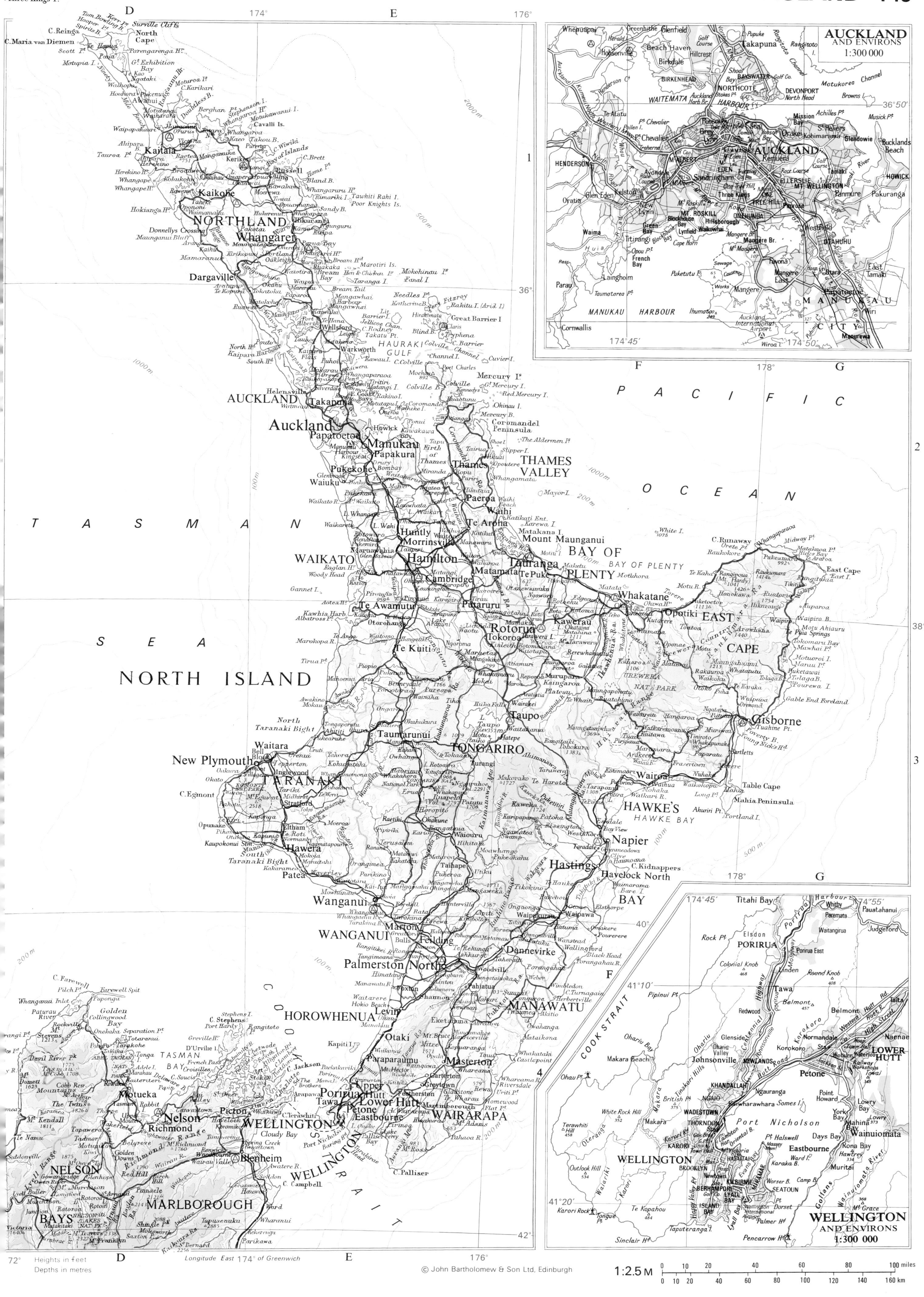

AUCKLAND
AND ENVIRONS
1:300 000

PACIFIC

OCEAN

TASMAN

SEA

NORTH ISLAND

NORTHLAND

AUCKLAND

WAIKATO

THAMES
VALLEY

BAY OF

PLENTY

BAY OF PLENTY

EAST
CAPE

TARANAKI

TONGARIRO

HAWKE'S

HAWKE BAY

MANAWATU

WANGANUI

HOROWHENUA

WAIRARAPA

WELLINGTON

NELSON

MARLBOROUGH

BAYS

PORIRUA

COOK STRAIT

LOWER
HUTT

WELLINGTON
AND ENVIRONS
1:300 000

Heights in feet
Depths in metres

Longitude East 174° of Greenwich

© John Bartholomew & Son Ltd, Edinburgh

1:2.5 M

0 10 20 40 60 80 100 miles
0 10 20 40 60 80 100 120 140 160 km

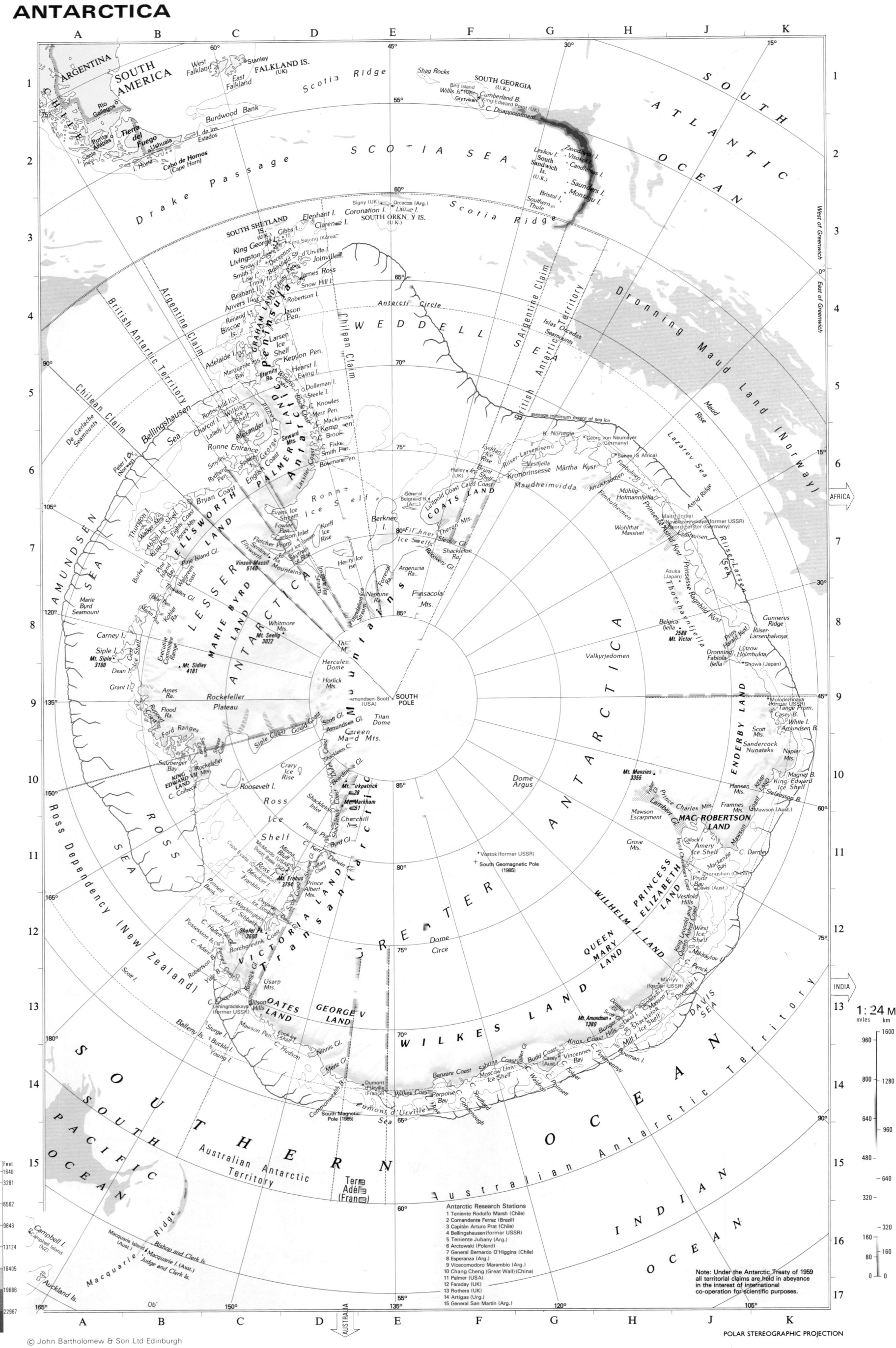

1 : 24 M

Metres	Feet
500	1640
1000	3281
2000	6562
3000	9843
4000	13124
5000	16405
6000	19686
7000	22967

Antarctic Research Stations
1 Teniente Rodolfo Marsh (Chile)
2 Comandante Ferraz (Brazil)
3 Capitán Arturo Prat (Chile)
4 Bellingshausen (former USSR)
5 Teniente Jubany (Arg.)
6 Arctowski (Poland)
7 General Bernardo O'Higgins (Chile)
8 Esperanza (Arg.)
9 Vicecomodoro Marambio (Arg.)
10 Chang Cheng (Great Wall) (China)
11 Palmer (USA)
12 Faraday (UK)
13 Rothera (UK)
14 Artigas (Urg.)
15 General San Martín (Arg.)

Note: Under the Antarctic Treaty of 1959
all territorial claims are held in abeyance
in the interest of international
co-operation for scientific purposes.

POLAR STEREOGRAPHIC PROJECTION

© John Bartholomew & Son Ltd Edinburgh

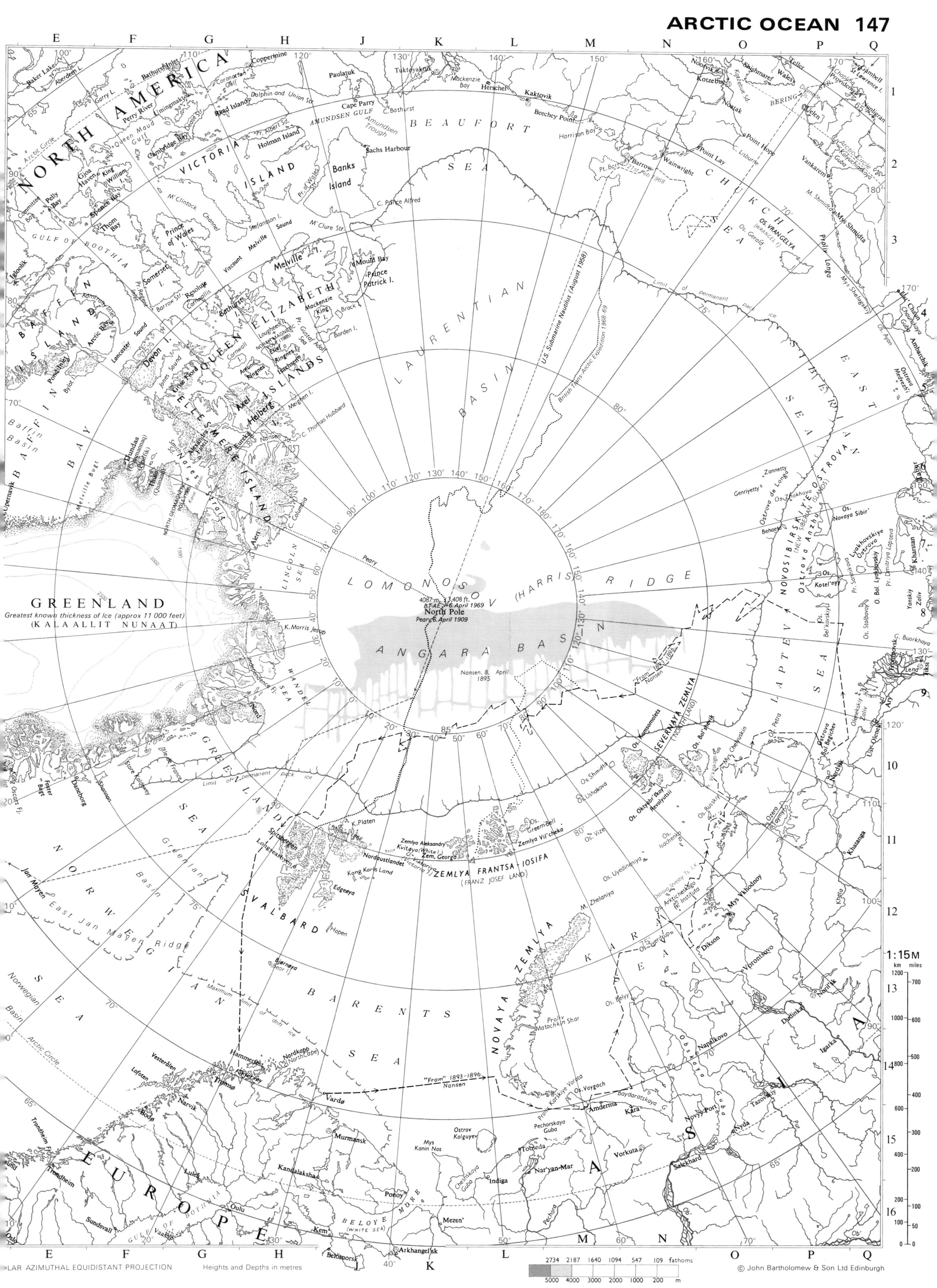

GLOSSARY

Language Abbreviations

The entries in this short glossary have been restricted to the less widely-known geographical terms. It also omits terms which are visually similar eg. banc, banco, bank.

Afr	Afrikaans	*Kor*	Korean
Alb	Albanian	*Lao*	Laotian
Ar	Arabic	*Lap*	Lappish
Ben	Bengali	*Lat*	Latvian
Ber	Berber	*Mal*	Malay
Bul	Bulgarian	*Mlg*	Malagasy
Bur	Burmese	*Mon*	Mongolian
Cam	Cambodian	*Nor*	Norwegian
Ch	Chinese	*Per*	Persian
Cz	Czech	*Pol*	Polish
Dan	Danish	*Por*	Portuguese
Dut	Dutch	*Rom*	Romanian
Est	Estonian	*Rus*	Russian
Fae	Faeroese	*Sca*	Scandinavian
Fin	Finnish	*S-C*	Serbo-Croat
Fr	French	*Sla*	Slavonic
Gae	Gaelic	*Som*	Somali
Ger	German	*Sp*	Spanish
Gr	Greek	*Swe*	Swedish
Heb	Hebrew	*Th*	Thai (Siamese)
Hin	Hindi	*Tib*	Tibetan
Hun	Hungarian	*Tu*	Turkish
Ice	Icelandic	*Ur*	Urdu
Ind	Indonesian	*Vt*	Vietnamese
It	Italian	*Wel*	Welsh
Jpn	Japanese		

Name	Language	Meaning
A, –å, –á	*Sca, Ice*	stream
Adasi	*Tu*	island
Adrar	*Ber*	mountains
Aiguille	*Fr*	peak, needle
Ain, 'Aīn, 'Ayn	*Ar*	spring, well
Akrotírion	*Gr*	cape, point
Ala–	*Fin*	lower
Alt–a, –o	*It, Por, Sp*	upper
Ao	*Ch, Th*	bay
Arro-io, yo	*Por, Sp*	watercourse
Au	*Cam*	river
Aust–	*Nor*	east(ern)
Ayía, Ayios	*Gr*	saint
Ba	*Vt*	mountain
Bāb	*Ar*	strait
Bādiyah, Badiet	*Ar*	desert
Baelt	*Dan*	strait
Bahía	*Sp*	bay
Bahr, Baḥrah	*Ar*	sea, channel
Baixo	*Por*	lower
Baj–a, –o	*Sp*	lower
Ban	*Cam, Lao, Th*	village
–bana	*Jpn*	point, cape
Bandao	*Ch*	peninsula
Bandar	*Ar, Mal, Per,*	port, harbour
Bas, –se	*Fr*	lower
Batin, Batn	*Ar*	depression
Be'er(ot)	*Heb*	well(s)
Bei	*Ch*	north(ern)
Bereg	*Rus*	bank, shore
–berg, Berg(e)	*Sca, Ger*	mountain(s)
Bid	*Ar*	waterhole
Bir, Bîr, B'ir	*Ar*	well
Birk–at, –et	*Ar*	well, pool
–bjerg	*Dan*	hill
Boca	*Por, Sp*	mouth
Bocche	*It*	mouths, estuary
Boğazi	*Tu*	strait
Bol'sh–e, –aya, –oy	*Rus*	big
Bonom	*Vt*	mountain
–botn, –botten	*Nor, Swe*	valley floor
Bouche	*Fr*	mouth, estuary
–bre(en)	*Nor*	glacier
Bredning	*Dan*	bay
Bucht	*Ger*	bay
Bugt	*Dan*	bay
Bukhta	*Rus*	bay
Bukt(en)	*Nor, Swe*	bay
Bur–un, –nu	*Tu*	point, cape
Cabo	*Por, Sp*	cape, highland
Caka	*Tib*	salt lake
cañad–a, –ón	*Sp*	ravine, gorge
Canon	*Sp*	canyon
Cap, Capo	*Fr, It*	cape, headland
Cerro	*Sp*	hill, peak
Chaco	*Sp*	jungle region
Chaine, Chaîne	*Fr*	mountain chain
Chiang	*Th*	town
Chott	*Ar*	salt lake, marsh
Cima, Cime	*It, Sp, Fr*	summit
Citta	*It*	town, city
Ciudad	*Sp*	town, city
Co	*Tib*	lake
Col	*Fr*	high pass
Cordillera	*Sp*	mountain chain
Corn–e, –o	*Fr, It*	peak
Côte	*Fr*	coast, slope
Cu Lao	*Vt*	island
Cua	*Vt*	estuary inlet
Cun	*Ch*	village
Da	*Vt*	river
Da	*Ch*	big
Dag–i	*Tu*	mountain
Dagh	*Per*	mountain
Daglar–i	*Tu*	mountains
–dal, –ur	*Sca, Ice, Afr*	valley
–dalur	*Ice*	valley
Dao	*Ch*	island
Darreh	*Per*	valley
Daryachech	*Per*	lake
Dasht	*Per, Ur*	desert
Denizi	*Tu*	sea
–diep	*Dut*	channel
Djebel, Djibal	*Ar*	mountain
–djup	*Ice*	fjord
Do, –do	*Vt, Kor*	island
Dolina	*Rus*	valley
Dong	*Ch*	east(ern)
Dorf, –dorf	*Ger, Afr*	village
–dwip	*Hin*	island
Eiland(en)	*Afr, Dut*	island(s)
–elv(a)	*Nor*	river
Embalse	*Sp*	reservoir
Embouchure	*Fr*	estuary
'Emeq	*Heb*	plain
Erg	*Ar*	desert with dunes
Eski	*Tu*	old
Espigao	*Por*	upland
Estero	*Sp*	inlet, estuary; swamp
Estrecho	*Sp*	strait
Estreito	*Por*	strait
Etang	*Fr*	lake, lagoon
–ye(jar)	*Ice*	island(s)
Ezers	*Lat*	lake
Fels	*Ger*	rock
Feng	*Ch*	peak
Fiume	*It*	river
–fjall, fjell	*Swe, Nor*	mountain
–fjord(en)	*Dan, Nor*	fjord; lagoon
–fjordhur	*Ice*	fjord
–floi	*Ice*	bay
Foce, Foci	*It*	river-mouth
–fonn	*Nor*	glacier
Fuente	*Sp*	source, well
Gang	*Ch*	harbour
–gata	*Jpn*	inlet, lagoon
–gawa	*Jpn*	river
Gebel	*Ar*	mountain
Gebirge	*Ger*	mountains
Geziret	*Ar*	island
Gipfel	*Ger*	peak
Gji	*Alb*	inlet, bay
Gletscher	*Ger*	glacier
Gobi	*Mon*	desert
Gol	*Mon*	river
Göl(u)	*Tu*	lake
Gonglu	*Ch*	highway
Gor–a, –y	*Rus, (Sla)*	mountain(s)
–got	*Kor*	point, cape
Greben'	*Rus*	ridge
Gryada	*Rus*	ridge
Guan	*Ch*	pass
Guba	*Rus*	bay
–gunto	*Jpn*	island, group
Gunung	*Ind, Mal*	mountain
–haehyop	*Kor*	strait
Haff	*Ger*	bay
Hai	*Ch*	sea
Halbinsel	*Ger*	peninsula
halvoya	*Nor*	peninsula
Ham(m)ad–a	*Ar*	plateau
Hamakhtesh	*Heb*	depression
Hassi	*Ar*	well
–haug	*Nor*	hill
–havn	*Dan, Fae, Nor*	harbour
He	*Ch*	river
–hede, hei	*Dan, Nor*	heath
–hegyseg	*Hun*	mountains
Heide	*Ger*	heath, moor
Hka	*Bur*	river
–ho	*Nor*	peak
Hon	*Vt*	island
Hory	*Cz*	mountains
Hot	*Mon*	town
Hu	*Ch*	lake
Ia	*Vt*	stream, river
imeni	*Rus*	in the name of
Ipsoma	*Gr*	high ground
Irhzer	*Ber*	watercourse
Irmak	*Tu*	large river
'Irq	*Ar*	sand dunes
Iso–	*Fin*	big
Jabal	*Ar*	mountain
–jarv, –i	*Est, Fin*	lake
–jaure, javrre	*Lap*	lake
Jazīrah	*Ar*	island
Jezioro	*Pol*	lake
Jiang	*Ch*	river
–jima	*Jpn*	island
–jok–i, –ka	*Fin, Lap*	river
–jokull	*Ice*	glacier
–kai	*Jpn*	bay, inlet, sea
–kaikyo	*Jpn*	strait
Kamen'	*Rus*	stone
–kawa	*Jpn*	river
Kefar	*Heb*	village
Kenet	*Alb*	inlet
Kep	*Alb*	point, cape
Kepulauan	*Ind*	archipelago, islands
Khalig, Khalij	*Ar*	bay, gulf
Khawr	*Ar*	inlet
Khersonisos	*Gr*	peninsula
Khrebet	*Rus*	mountain range
Klit	*Dan*	dunes
Klong	*Th*	canal, creek
–ko	*Jpn*	lake, inlet
Ko	*Th*	island
Kofel, Koge(e)l	*Ger*	dome-shaped hill
Kolpos	*Gr*	gulf
Kopf	*Ger*	hill
Körfezi(i)	*Tu*	bay, gulf
Kosa	*Rus*	spit of land
Kray	*Rus*	region
Kryazh	*Rus*	ridge
Kuh(ha)	*Per*	mountains(s)
Kum	*Rus*	sandy desert
–kundo	*Kor*	island group
Laem	*Th*	point
Lago	*It, Por, Sp*	lake
laht	*Est*	bay
Lam	*Th*	stream
Lande	*Ger*	sandy moor, heath
Laut	*Ind*	sea
Lednik	*Rus*	glacier
Les	*Cz, Rus*	woods, forest
les, lez	*Fr*	near, beside
Lieh-tao	*Ch*	group of islands
Liman	*Rus*	bay, gulf
Liman–i	*Tu*	harbour, port
Limni	*Gr*	lake, lagoon
Ling	*Ch*	mountain range
Llano	*Sp*	plain, prairie
Llyn	*Wel*	lake
Lohatanjona	*Mlg*	point
Loma	*Sp*	hill
Lu	*Ch*	street, road
Madinat	*Ar*	town, city
Mae Nam	*Th*	river
Mal	*Alb*	mountain(s)
Mal–a, –o, –yy	*Sla*	small
Male	*Cz*	small
Marsa, Mersa	*Ar*	anchorage, inlet
Masabb	*Ar*	canal, estuary
Mega, Magal–a, –o	*Gr*	big
Mesto	*Sla*	place, town
Mikr–i, on	*Gr*	small
Mina'	*Ar*	port, harbour
Moni	*Gr*	monastery
More	*Rus*	sea
Muntii	*Rom*	mountains
Mynydd	*Wel*	mountain
–myr	*Nor, Swe*	moor, swamp
Mys	*Rus*	cape
na	*Sla*	on
nad	*Sla*	above, over
Nafud	*Ar*	desert, dune
Nagor'ye	*Rus*	highland, uplands
Nagy–	*Hun*	big, great
Nahr	*Ar*	river
Nakhon	*Th*	town
Nam	*Bur, Th, Vt*	river
Nan	*Ch*	south(ern)
Ne–a, –on, –os	*Gr*	new
Nei	*Ch*	inner
–nes	*Ice, Nor*	point, cape
Ngoc	*Vt*	mountain, peak
–ni	*Kor*	village
Nizhn–eye, –iy	*Rus*	lower
Nizina	*Cz, Rus*	lowland
Nizmennost'	*Rus*	lowlands
Nos	*Bul, Rus*	ness, point
Nosy	*Mlg*	island
Nov–a, –o	*Sla*	new
Nuur	*Mon*	lake
Ny–	*Sca*	new
ø, øy	*Sca*	island
Okrug	*Rus*	district
–oog	*Ger*	island
Ormos	*Gr*	bay
Oros (Ori)	*Ger*	mountain(s)
Ostrov(a)	*Rus*	island(s)
Otok(i)	*S–C*	island(s)
Oued	*Ar*	dry river-bed
Ozero (Ozera)	*Rus*	lake(s)
pää	*Fin*	hill
Pal–a, –ai, –o, –io	*Gr*	old
Parbat	*Ur*	mountain
Pegunungan	*Ind*	mountain range
Pelabohan	*Mal*	harbour
Pellg	*Alb*	bay
Pendi	*Ch*	basin
Pereval	*Rus*	pass
Pertuis	*Fr*	opening, strait
Perv–o, –yy	*Rus*	first
Peski	*Rus*	sands, desert
Pingyuan	*Ch*	plain
Ploskogor'ye	*Rus*	plateau
Pod	*Sla*	under, sub–
Poluostrov	*Rus*	peninsula
Polwysep	*Pol*	peninsula
Porogi	*Rus*	rapids
Poselok	*Rus*	settlement
Pradesh	*Hin*	state
presqu'ile	*Fr*	peninsula
Pri	*Rus*	near, cis–
Proliv	*Rus*	strait
Protok–a	*Rus*	channel
pulau	*Ind, Mal*	island(s)
Puy	*Fr*	peak
Qi	*Ch*	admin. div.
Qiao	*Ch*	bridge
Qiryat	*Heb*	town
Qu	*Tib*	stream
Quan	*Ch*	spring
Qundao	*Ch*	archipelago
Rade	*Fr*	roadstead
rags	*Lat*	point, cape
Ramlat	*Ar*	sands
–rani	*Ice*	spur
Ra's	*Ar, Per*	point, cape
Ravnina	*Rus*	plain
Rayon	*Rus*	district
Represa	*Por*	dam
Reshteh	*Per*	mountain range
–retsugan	*Jpn*	chain of rocks
–retto	*Jpn*	chain of islands
–rev	*Nor*	reef, cliff
Ri	*Tib*	mountain
–ri	*Kor*	village
Rosh	*Heb*	point, cape
Rt	*S–C*	point, cape
Rubha	*Gae*	point, cape
Rud (khaneh)	*Per*	river
Rudohorie	*Cz*	mountains
–saar(i)	*Est, Fin*	island
Sabkhat	*Ar*	salt-flat
Saghir	*Ar*	small
sahra	*Ar*	plain
saḥrā, saḥārā	*Ar*	desert(s)
–saki, –misaki	*Jpn*	point, cape
San, –san	*Lao, Jpn, Kor*	mountain
Sebkra	*Ar*	salt-flat
Selat	*Ind*	strait, channel
Selatan	*Ind, Mal*	south(ern)
selka	*Fin*	ridge; open water
Selo	*Rus, S–C*	village
Selva	*Sp*	forest
–sen	*Jpn*	mountain
–seto	*Jpn*	strait, channel
Sever–o, –naya	*Rus*	north(ern)
Shamo	*Ch*	desert
Shan	*Ch*	mountain(s)
Shandi	*Ch*	mountainous area
Shang	*Ch*	upper
Shankou	*Ch*	pass
Shanmai	*Ch*	mountain range
Shatt	*Ar*	river (–mouth)
–shima	*Jpn*	island
–shoto	*Jpn*	group of islands
Shuiku	*Ch*	reservoir
–sjo	*Nor*	lake
So	*Dan, Nor*	lake
Song	*Vt*	river
Spitze	*Ger*	peak
Sredn–a, –e, –ayz	*Sla*	middle
Sredn–e, –eye, –iy, –yaya	*Rus*	middle
Star–a, –e	*Cz*	old
Star–a, –i	*S–C*	old
Star–aya, –oye, –yy, –yye	*Rus*	old
Step'	*Rus*	steppe
Stor–, Stora	*Swe*	big
–suido	*Jpn*	strait, channel
Sungai	*Ind, Mal*	river
–suo	*Fin*	swamp, marsh
Sveti	*S–C*	saint
Szenti–	*Hun*	saint
–take	*Jpn*	peak
Tanjong	*Ind, Mal*	cape, point
Tao	*Ch*	island
Tasek	*Mal*	lake
Tassili	*Ber*	plateau
Tau	*Rus*	mountain(s)
Tekojarvi	*Fin*	reservoir
Teluk	*Ind*	bay
Tengah	*Ind*	middle
Tepe–si	*Tu*	hill, peak
Thale	*Th*	lake
Timur	*Ind*	east(ern)
–tjakka	*Lap*	mountain
–to	*Jpn*	island
–tong	*Kor*	village
Tonle	*Cam*	lake
–udden	*Swe*	point, cape
Uj–	*Hun*	new
Ujung	*Ind*	point, cape
Urzyq	*Ar*	area of dunes
Ust'ye	*Rus*	estuary
Utara, Uttar	*Ind, Hin*	north(ern)
v	*Sla*	in
-vaara(t)	*Fin*	hill(s)
–vag	*Nor*	bay
–vann, Vatn	*Nor*	lake
–varos	*Hun*	town
–varre	*Nor*	mountain
Vast–er, –ra	*Swe*	western
Vaux	*Fr*	valleys
Velik–a, –o, –aya	*Sla*	big
Verkhn–e, –aya, –iy	*Rus*	upper
–vesi	*Fin*	water, lake
Vig–ik	*Dan, Nor*	bay
Vinh	*Vt*	bay
Vodokhranil-ishche	*Rus*	reservoir
Vorota	*Rus*	gate, strait
Vostochn –aya, –yy	*Rus*	eastern
Vozvyshennost'	*Rus*	uplands
Vpadina	*Rus*	depression
Vrch(y)	*Cz*	mountain(s)
Vung	*Vt*	bay, gulf
Vysok–aya, –o, –iy	*Rus*	high
Vyssh–aya, –e, –iy	*Rus*	higher
Wad	*Dut*	sand–flat
Wadi	*Ar*	watercourse
Wai	*Ch*	outer
Wan	*Ch*	bay
–wan	*Jpn*	bay
Wielk–a, –i, –o	*Pol*	big
Wysok–a, –i, –o	*Pol*	high
Xi	*Ch*	west; stream
Xia	*Ch*	lower; gorge
Xian	*Ch*	country
Xiao	*Ch*	small
Xu	*Ch*	islet
Yam	*Heb*	lake, sea
–yama	*Jpn*	mountain(s)
Ye	*Bur*	island
Yli–	*Fin*	upper
Yoma	*Bur*	mountain range
You	*Ch*	right
Yuzhn–o, –yy	*Rus*	southern
Za	*Rus*	behind, beyond
–zaki	*Jpn*	point, cape
Zalew, Zaliv	*Pol, Rus*	bay
–zan	*Jpn*	mountain
Zapadn–aya, –o	*Rus*	western
Zapovednik	*Rus*	reserve
Zemlya	*Rus*	land
–zhen	*Ch*	town
Zhong	*Ch*	middle
Zhou	*Ch*	islet
Zui	*Ch*	point, spit
Zuid	*Dut*	south
Zuidelijk	*Dut*	southern

INDEX

Abbreviations used in the Index

Afghan Afghanistan	**Czech** Czechoslovakia	**Hist site** Historic site	**N** North, Northern, New	**Pr** Prince	**Switz** Switzerland	
Afr Africa, African	**Den** Denmark	**I, isld** Island	**Nat Park** National Park	**Prefect** Prefecture	**Tenn** Tennessee	
Ala Alabama	**Dept** Department, Département	**Ind** Indian	**Neth, Nether, Neths** Netherlands	**Princ** Principality	**Terr** Territory	
Amer America, American	**Des** Desert	**Is, islds** Islands	**Nev** Nevada	**Prom** Promontory	**Tex** Texas	
Anc mon Ancient monument	**Dist** District	**Isld king** Island kingdom	**New Bruns** New Brunswick	**Prot** Protectorate	**Tribal dist** Tribal district	
Anc site Ancient site	**Div** Division	**Isth** Isthmus	**New Hamps** New Hampshire	**Prov** Province	**U.A.E.** United Arab Emirates	
Arch Archipel, archipelago, archipiélago	**Dom Rep** Dominican Republic	**Jct, junc, junct** Junction	**New Mex** New Mexico	**Pt, Pta, Pto** Point	**U.K.** United Kingdom	
Arg Argentina	**E** East, Eastern	**L** Lake	**Nfld** Newfoundland	**Qnsld** Queensland	**Union Terr** Union Territory	
Ariz Arizona	**Eng** England, English	**Lancs** Lancashire	**N Scotia** Nova Scotia	**R** Rio, river	**U.S.A.** United States of America	
Ark Arkansas	**Eq, Equat** Equatorial	**Lincs** Lincolnshire	**Notts** Nottinghamshire	**Ra** Range	**V** Valley	
Aust Australia	**Est** Estuary	**Lt Ho** Lighthouse	**N S W** New South Wales	**Rdg** Ridge	**Ven** Venezuela	
Aut Autonomous	**Fed** Federation	**Madhya Prad** Madhya Pradesh	**N W Terr** Northwest Territories	**Reg** Region	**Vict** Victoria	
B Bay	**Fj** Fjord	**Man** Manitoba	**N Y** New York	**Rep** Republic	**Virg** Virginia	
Berks Berkshire	**Fr** French	**Mass** Massachusetts	**Oc** Ocean	**Res** Reservoir	**Vol** Volcano	
Br British	**G** Gulf	**Med** Mediterranean	**Okla** Oklahoma	**Rus. Fed.** Russian Federation	**W** West, Western	
Br Col British Columbia	**Ger** Germany	**Mich** Michigan	**Old prov** Old province	**S** South, Southern	**Wash** Washington	
Bucks Buckinghamshire	**Gla** Glacier	**Minn** Minnesota	**Oxon** Oxford, Oxfordshire	**Sa** Serra, Sierra	**W I** West Indies	
C Cape	**Gloucs** Gloucestershire	**Miss** Mississippi	**Pac** Pacific	**Sask** Saskatchewan	**Wilts** Wiltshire	
Cal, Calif California	**Grp** Group	**Mon** Monument	**Pass** Passage	**Sd** Sound	**Wyo** Wyoming	
Can Canal	**Gt** Great	**Mont** Montana	**Pen** Peninsula	**Sk** Shuiku (reservoir)	**Yorks** Yorkshire	
Cat(s) Cataract(s)	**Hants** Hampshire	**Moz** Mozambique	**Penn** Pennsylvania	**Span** Spanish		
Cent Central	**Hbr** Harbour	**Mt, Mte** Mountain	**People's Rep** People's Republic	**Spr** Spring		
Chan Channel	**Hd** Head	**Mt ra** Mountain range	**Physical reg** Physical region	**St, Ste** Saint, Sainte		
Co County, Coast	**H.E.** Hydro Electric	**Mth(s)** Mouth(s)	**Pk** Peak	**Sta** Station		
Colo Colorado	**Herts** Hertfordshire	**Mts** Mountains	**Plat** Plateau	**Staffs** Staffordshire		
Conn Connecticut	**Hist reg** Historic region		**Port** Portugal, Portuguese	**Stat Area** Statistical Area		
				Str Strait		

Aa — Águilas

124 H8 **Aguililla de Iturbide** Mexico
58 D4 **Aguin Sum** China
133 D8 **Aguirre,B** Argentina
71 F5 **Aguisan** Philippines
128 D1 **Aguja,C.de la** *C* Colombia
128 B5 **Aguja, Pta** *pt* Peru
56 E3 **Agul** *R* Russian Federation
90 L13 **Agulhas Bank** Atlantic Oc
90 L13 **Agulhas Basin** Indian Oc
89 B10 **Agulhas,C** S Africa
130 G8 **Agulhas Negras** *pk* Brazil
81 A10 **Agulhas Plateau** Indian Oc
70 P10 **Agung, G** *mt* Bali Indonesia
80 C7 **'Agur** Israel
71 G6 **Agusan** *R* Mindanao Philippines
71 E5 **Agutaya** *isld* Philippines
47 N10 **Ağva** Turkey
61 Q12 **Aha** Okinawa
78 L2 **Ahar** Iran
79 H3 **Aḩaş, Jebel** *mts* Syria
144 C5 **Ahaura** New Zealand
32 F8 **Ahaus** Germany
145 F3 **Ahimanawa Range** New Zealand
145 D1 **Ahipara** New Zealand
76 E1 **Ahiri** India
79 C1 **Ahırlı** Turkey
145 E3 **Ahititi** New Zealand
116 G7 **Ahklun Mts** Alaska U.S.A.
29 J10 **Ahlainen** Finland
32 L7 **Ahlden** Germany
32 G9 **Ahlen** Germany
32 K6 **Ahlerstedt** Germany
32 H7 **Ahlhorn** Germany
74 E7 **Ahmadabad** India
77 E6 **Ahmadī** Iran
77 A5 **Aḩmadi, Al** Kuwait
80 G1 **Ahmadīyah** Syria
74 F9 **Ahmadnagar** India
74 G9 **Ahmadpur** India
74 D3 **Ahmadpur** Pakistan
74 D4 **Ahmadpur** Pakistan
86 H4 **Ahmar Mts** Ethiopia
47 J6 **Ahmetli** Turkey
124 E5 **Ahome** Mexico
37 L4 **Ahorntal** Germany
112 K1 **Ahoskie** North Carolina U.S.A.
Ah-pa *see* **Aba**
36 B3 **Ahr** *R* Germany
36 B3 **Ahrdorf** Germany
33 S6 **Ahrensberg** Germany
33 N4 **Ahrensbök** Germany
32 M5 **Ahrensburg** Germany
33 T7 **Ahrensfelde** Germany
32 K6 **Ahrenswohlde** Germany
Ahrweiler *see* **Bad Neuenahr-Ahrweiler**
32 H9 **Ahse** *R* Germany
29 L9 **Ähtäri** Finland
29 L9 **Ähtärinjärvi** *L* Finland
68 B4 **Ahtaung** Burma
29 K8 **Ähtävä** Finland
124 G7 **Ahuacatlán** Mexico
125 P11 **Ahuachapán** El Salvador
124 H7 **Ahualulco de Mercado** Mexico
145 F3 **Ahuriri Pt** New Zealand
144 B6 **Ahuriri R** New Zealand
27 G16 **Åhus** Sweden
77 A4 **Ahvāz** Iran
116 K8 **Aiaktalik I** Alaska U.S.A.
128 F4 **Aiapua,L** Brazil
128 E3 **Aiari** *R* Brazil
65 A3 **Aibag Gol** *R* China
60 Q2 **Aibetsu** Japan
38 J7 **Aich** *R* Austria
37 N7 **Aich** Germany
37 L7 **Aichach** Germany
61 L10 **Aichi** *prefect* Japan
116 Q2 **Aichilik** *R* Alaska U.S.A.
26 N3 **Aiddejavrre** Norway
37 P6 **Aidenbach** Germany
46 F6 **Aidhipsoú** Greece
80 G3 **Aidun** Jordan
102 S12 **Aiea** Hawaiian Is
40 E5 **Aigle** Switzerland
21 M4 **Aigle, l'** France
122 G2 **Aigle, L. à l'** Quebec Canada
18 H8 **Aigoual,Mt** France
18 E7 **Aigre** France
18 E6 **Aigrefeuille d'Aunis** France
20 H7 **Aigrefeuille-sur-Maine** France
19 Q14 **Aigu** France
19 Q13 **Aiguebelle** France
121 M4 **Aiguebelle, Parc de** Quebec Canada
18 H9 **Aigues-Mortes** France
40 E6 **Aiguille du Midi** *mt* France
19 Q14 **Aiguilles d'Arves** *mts* France
40 E6 **Aiguille Verte** *mt* France
18 F8 **Aiguillon** France
83 L13 **Aiguillon,C d'** Kerguelen Indian Oc
18 G6 **Aigurande** France
Aihui *see* **Heihe**
47 O12 **Aikateríni, Akra Ayios** *C* Greece
61 M7 **Aikawa** Japan
112 F4 **Aiken** South Carolina U.S.A.
45 Q7 **Ailano** Italy
140 C6 **Aileron** N Terr Australia
22 E5 **Ailette** *R* France
71 M9 **Aileu** Timor
29 M2 **Ailigas** *mt* Finland
19 Q18 **Aille** *R* France
40 D2 **Aillevillers-et-Lyaumont** France
21 P1 **Ailly-le-Haut-Clocher** France
21 M2 **Ailly, Pte, d'** France
21 P2 **Ailly-sur-Noye** France
120 J9 **Ailsa Craig** Ontario Canada
12 C3 **Ailsa Craig** *isld* Scotland
51 N3 **Aim** Russian Federation
71 L9 **Aimaro** Indonesia
71 K9 **Aimere** Indonesia
129 K7 **Aimores** Brazil
129 K7 **Aimores,Serra dos** *mts* Brazil
40 B5 **Ain** *dept* France
40 B6 **Ain** *R* France
52 B5 **Ainaži** Latvia
43 A13 **Aïn Beïda** Algeria
85 D2 **Aïn Beni Mathar** Morocco
21 O3 **Aincourt** France
84 H4 **'Ain Dalla** Egypt
37 K7 **Aindling** Germany
43 B12 **Aïn Draham** Tunisia
80 E1 **Aïn Ebel** Lebanon
80 G3 **Ain el Ghazal** Jordan
80 E7 **'Ain el Ghuweir** Jordan
85 E3 **Aïn-el-Hadjadj** Algeria
17 H10 **Ain el Hadjar** Algeria
84 H4 **Aîn el Wadi** Egypt
80 G3 **Ain esh Shilaq** Jordan
86 C2 **Aïn Galakka** Chad
68 B2 **Ainggyi** Burma
80 G4 **Ain Janna** Jordan
43 B12 **Aïn Kerma** Algeria
80 E6 **Ain Qilt** Jordan
17 H2 **Ainsa** Spain
85 B5 **Ain Safra** Mauritania
Ain Salah *see* **In Salah**
13 E6 **Ainsdale** England
85 D2 **Aïn Sefra** Algeria
123 L7 **Ainslie,L** C Breton I, Nova Scotia
79 C9 **'Ain Sukhna** Egypt
98 G7 **Ainsworth** Nebraska U.S.A.
17 H9 **Ain Tédèles** Algeria
17 G9 **Ain Témouchent** Algeria
Aïn Touta *see* **El Homr**
60 R2 **Aioi** Japan
60 H11 **Aioi** Japan
85 C4 **Aïoun Abdel Malek** Mauritania
85 C5 **Aïoun el Atrouss** Mauritania
128 E7 **Aiquile** Bolivia
69 H11 **Air** *isld* Indonesia
21 O2 **Airaines** France
128 F4 **Airao** Brazil
69 D12 **Airbangis** Sumatra
118 C7 **Airdrie** Alberta Canada
12 D2 **Airdrie** Scotland
22 C2 **Aire** France
17 K5 **Aire,I.del** Balearic Is
21 H3 **Airel** France
13 G6 **Aire,R** England
18 E9 **Airè sur L'Adour** France
115 M4 **Air Force I** Northwest Territories Canada
65 B3 **Airgin Sum** China
141 J5 **Airlie** Queensland Australia
100 B5 **Airlie** Oregon U.S.A.
142 B5 **Airlie I** W Australia Australia
45 R7 **Airola** Italy
85 F5 **Aïr ou Azbine** *mt reg* Niger
71 M8 **Airpanas** Indonesia
8 C1 **Air,Pt of** Wales
12 E1 **Airth** Scotland
21 K8 **Airvault** France
37 K4 **Aisch** *R* Germany
133 C7 **Aisén** *prov* Chile
117 E5 **Aishihik** Yukon Territory Canada
22 F5 **Aisne** *dept* France
22 H5 **Aisne** *R* France
40 D3 **Aissey** France
80 E1 **Aïta ech Chaab** Lebanon
136 J2 **Aitape** Papua New Guinea
80 E1 **Aitaroun** Lebanon
37 O6 **Aiterhofen** Germany
144 A7 **Aitken, Mt** New Zealand
99 N3 **Aitkin** Minnesota U.S.A.
46 E6 **Aitolikón** Greece
55 B4 **Aitova** Russian Federation
16 E9 **Aït Youssef ou Ali** Morocco
48 H4 **Aiud** Romania
18 E6 **Aix** *isld* France
18 G5 **Aix d'Angillon,les** France
19 O18 **Aix-en-Provence** France
18 F7 **Aixe-sur-Vienne** France
Aix-la-Chapelle *see* **Aachen**
117 J8 **Aiyansh** British Columbia Canada
79 B9 **'Aiyat,El** Egypt
46 F7 **Aíyina** *isld* Greece
46 F4 **Aiyínion** Greece
46 E6 **Aíyion** Greece
46 F7 **Áiyos Andréas** Greece
47 H9 **Áiyos Ioánnis, Akr** *C* Crete Greece
75 P7 **Aizawl** India
87 C10 **Aizeb** *R* Namibia
20 G8 **Aizenay** France
27 M15 **Aizpute** Latvia
61 N8 **Aizu-Takada** Japan
61 N8 **Aizu-Wakamatsu** Japan
78 L3 **Ajab Shir** Iran
18 L11 **Ajaccio** Corsica
74 J6 **Ajaigarh** India
128 D3 **Ajaju** *R* Colombia
80 G3 **'Ajamī** Syria
143 A8 **Ajana** W Australia Australia
121 M9 **Ajax** Ontario Canada
144 D5 **Ajax, Mt** New Zealand
101 M4 **Ajax Mt** Idaho/Montana U.S.A.
84 G3 **Ajdābiyā** Libya
42 F3 **Ajdovščina** Slovenia
61 O5 **Ajigasawa** Japan
61 N10 **Ajiro** Japan
61 P7 **Aji-shima** *isld* Japan
48 D3 **Ajka** Hungary
80 G4 **Ajlun** Jordan
77 D7 **'Ajmān** U.A.E.
74 F5 **Ajmer** India
103 M9 **Ajo** Arizona U.S.A.
16 E1 **Ajo,C** Spain
129 G3 **Ajoewa** Suriname
103 M9 **Ajo,Mt** Arizona U.S.A.
71 C2 **Aju** *isld* W Irian
128 E4 **Ajuana** *R* Brazil
125 J8 **Ajuchitlán** Mexico
71 F5 **Ajuy** Philippines
60 Q2 **Akabira** Japan
85 E3 **Akabli** Algeria
59 L1 **Akademii, Zaliv** *B* Russian Federation
71 M9 **Akadirunsikun** Indonesia
61 M8 **Akadomari** Japan
61 M10 **Akaishi-dake** *pk* Japan
74 G10 **Akalkot** India
60 S2 **Akan** Japan
79 D3 **Akanthou** Cyprus
60 G12 **Akaoka** Japan
47 L6 **Akar** *R* Turkey
61 P12 **Akarie-Ue** Okinawa
144 D5 **Akaroa** New Zealand
27 G15 **Åkarp, N** Sweden
78 H3 **Akarsu** Turkey
60 G10 **Akasaki** Japan
86 F1 **Akasha** Sudan
60 H11 **Akashi** Japan
29 K4 **Äkäsjoki** *R* Finland
29 K4 **Äkäsjokisuu** Finland
98 F4 **Akaska** South Dakota U.S.A.
61 N8 **Akatani** Japan
26 J4 **Akavare** *mt* Sweden
80 F2 **'Akbara** Israel
57 B2 **Akbasty** Kazakhstan
57 G1 **Akbaur** Kazakhstan
55 F5 **Akbeit** Kazakhstan
55 C5 **Akbulak** Russian Federation
78 F2 **Akçadağ** Turkey
78 G3 **Akçakale** Turkey
78 C1 **Akçakoca Dağları** *mts* Turkey
47 N10 **Akçaova** Turkey
47 K8 **Akçay** Turkey
85 A4 **Akchar,Dunes de l'** Mauritania
57 G1 **Akchatau** Kazakhstan
57 H3 **Akchi** Kazakhstan
47 J7 **Akçoava** Turkey
47 K6 **Ak Dağ** *mt* Turkey
78 E2 **Akdağmadeni** Turkey
56 D5 **Ak Dovurak** Russian Federation
61 L10 **Akechi** Japan
71 B2 **Akelamo** Halmahera Indonesia
9 F3 **Akeley** England
99 M2 **Akeley** Minnesota U.S.A.
27 B13 **Åkernes** Norway
27 K12 **Akersberga** Sweden
27 E12 **Akershus** *county* Norway
26 G8 **Åkersjön** Sweden
27 J12 **Akers-styckebruk** Sweden
71 B2 **Akeselaka** Halmahera Indonesia
57 B2 **Akespe** Kazakhstan
47 K7 **Akgöl** *L* Turkey
53 F12 **Akhalkalaki** Georgia
53 F12 **Akhaltsikhe** Georgia
57 E4 **Akhangaran** Uzbekistan
46 F6 **Akharnaí** Greece
80 F2 **'Akhbera** Israel
84 G3 **Akhḑar, Al Jabal al** *mts* Libya
79 G10 **Akhḑar, Wādī al** *watercourse* Saudi Arabia
46 E5 **Akhelóös** *R* Greece
116 K8 **Akhiok** Alaska U.S.A.
78 A2 **Akhisar** Turkey
84 J4 **Akhmim** Egypt
Akhna *see* **Athna**
79 H2 **Akhterīn** Syria
53 C12 **Akhtopol** Bulgaria
53 G9 **Akhtubinsk** Russian Federation
53 G12 **Akhty** Russian Federation
53 D8 **Akhtyrka** Ukraine
57 K6 **Akhunbabayev** Uzbekistan
60 G12 **Aki** Japan
116 G6 **Akiak** Alaska U.S.A.
52 H3 **Akim** Russian Federation
58 G1 **Akima** Russian Federation
115 L7 **Akimiski I** Northwest Territories Canada
53 E10 **Akimovka** Ukraine
60 F11 **Aki-nada** *sea* Japan
79 F2 **Akıncı Burun** *C* Turkey
47 J7 **Akıncılar** Turkey
27 G16 **Åkirkeby** Denmark
61 O6 **Akita** Japan
145 F4 **Akitio** New Zealand
56 G3 **Akitkan, Khrebet** *mts* Russian Federation
85 B5 **Akjoujt** Mauritania
80 G4 **'Akka** Jordan
85 C3 **Akka** Morocco
55 D6 **Akkabak** Kazakhstan
26 J4 **Akkajaure** *L* Sweden
116 B4 **Akkani** Russian Federation
55 D5 **Akkarga** Kazakhstan
57 E2 **Akkense** Kazakhstan
60 S2 **Akkeshi** Japan
80 D2 **'Akko** Israel
57 H2 **Akkol'** Kazakhstan
57 F3 **Akkol'** Kazakhstan
47 J7 **Akköy** Turkey
55 B6 **Akkozinskiy** Kazakhstan
25 E2 **Akkrum** Netherlands
53 G10 **Akkystau** Kazakhstan
46 F7 **Akladhókambos** Greece
114 F4 **Aklavik** Northwest Territories Canada
85 C5 **Aklé Aouana** *reg* Mauritania
52 B6 **Akmene** Lithuania
52 C6 **Akniste** Latvia
86 F4 **Akobo** *R* Ethiopia/Sudan
74 G8 **Akola** India
116 F6 **Akolmiut** Alaska U.S.A.
86 G2 **Āk'ordat** Ethiopia
47 N11 **Akören** Turkey
74 G8 **Akot** India
56 C5 **Ak-Oyuk, Gora** *mt* Russian Federation
115 N5 **Akpatok I** Northwest Territories Canada
79 D1 **Akpınar** Turkey
57 J4 **Akqi** China
98 J1 **Akra** North Dakota U.S.A.
79 G2 **Akrād, Jabal al** *mt* Syria
27 B12 **Åkrafjorden** *inlet* Norway
28 R9 **Akranes** Iceland
46 E6 **Akráta** Greece
46 E8 **Akrítas, Akra** *C* Greece
28 D6 **Åkrog Bugt** *B* Denmark
120 F4 **Akron** Ontario Canada
111 J9 **Akron** Alabama U.S.A.
98 C9 **Akron** Colorado U.S.A.
94 A5 **Akron** Indiana U.S.A.
98 K7 **Akron** Iowa U.S.A.
94 D3 **Akron** Michigan U.S.A.
94 J3 **Akron** New York U.S.A.
94 F5 **Akron** Ohio U.S.A.
95 L6 **Akron** Pennsylvania U.S.A.
46 G9 **Akrotíri** Crete Greece
79 D4 **Akrotiri B** Cyprus
74 H1 **Aksai Chin** *L* Kashmir
55 B4 **Aksakovo** Russian Federation
78 E2 **Aksaray** Turkey
57 H4 **Aksay** *R* Kyrgyzstan
78 C2 **Akşehir** Turkey
78 C2 **Akşehir Gölü** *L* Turkey
55 B4 **Aksenovo** Russian Federation
58 G1 **Aksenovo-Zilovskoye** Russian Federation
77 D5 **Aks-e Rostam** *R* Iran
51 L3 **Aksha** Russian Federation
55 B6 **Akshatau** Kazakhstan
57 J1 **Akshatau, Khrebet** Kazakhstan
57 C1 **Akshyganak** Kazakhstan
53 G12 **Akstata** Azerbaijan
66 C3 **Aksu** China
57 J2 **Aksu** *R* Kazakhstan
47 L7 **Aksu** *R* Turkey
47 L8 **Aksu** Turkey
55 D5 **Aksuat** Kazakhstan
52 H7 **Aksubayevo** Russian Federation
57 J4 **Aksu He** *R* China
86 G3 **Aksum** Ethiopia
57 E3 **Aksumbe** Kazakhstan
Aksu Yangi Shahr *see* **Aksu** China
52 H6 **Aktanysh** Russian Federation
57 D1 **Aktas** Kazakhstan
56 C5 **Aktash** Russian Federation
57 D5 **Aktash** Uzbekistan
55 D5 **Aktasty** Kazakhstan
55 F5 **Aktau** Kazakhstan
46 G4 **Akti** Greece
66 B4 **Akto** China
57 B1 **Aktogay** Kazakhstan
57 J2 **Aktogay** Kazakhstan
57 H5 **Aktu** China
57 A3 **Aktumsyk, Mys** *C* Uzbekistan
55 C5 **Aktyubinsk** Kazakhstan
53 D7 **Akulichi** Russian Federation
60 D13 **Akune** Japan
116 E9 **Akun I** Aleutian Is
85 F7 **Akure** Nigeria
28 S9 **Akureyri** Iceland
116 D9 **Akutan I** Aleutian I
116 D9 **Akutan Pass** Aleutian Is
56 B5 **Akutikha** Russian Federation
Akyab *see* **Sittwe**
55 C5 **Ak'yar** Russian Federation
79 F2 **Akyatan Göl** *L* Turkey
47 L4 **Akyazı** Turkey
56 B6 **Akzhal** Kazakhstan
57 L1 **Akzhar** Kazakhstan
57 E3 **Akzhaykin, Ozero** Kazakhstan
27 C11 **Ål** Norway
41 O6 **Ala** Italy
111 K8 **Alabama** *state* U.S.A.
111 J10 **Alabama R** Alabama U.S.A.
111 K8 **Alabaster** Alabama U.S.A.
94 D2 **Alabaster** Michigan U.S.A.
144 B6 **Alabaster, L** New Zealand
71 F3 **Alabat** *isld* Luzon Philippines
55 E4 **Alabota, Oz** *L* Kazakhstan
78 E1 **Alaca** Turkey
47 N10 **Alaçah** Turkey
47 N10 **Alaçali** Turkey
47 H6 **Alaçatı** Turkey
113 E8 **Alachua** Florida U.S.A.
16 D3 **Alaejos** Spain
47 Q14 **Alaérma** Rhodes Greece
86 G3 **Ālagē** *mt* Ethiopia
53 F11 **Alagir** Russian Federation
40 G6 **Alagna Valsesia** Italy
18 H7 **Alagnon** *R* France
130 J9 **Alagoa Grande** Brazil
130 H10 **Alagoas** *state* Brazil
129 L6 **Alagoinhas** Brazil
16 C4 **Alagón** *R* Spain
17 G3 **Alagón** Spain
71 G7 **Alah** Mindanao Philippines
69 E13 **Alahanpanjang** Sumatra
29 K8 **Alahärmä** Finland
87 C11 **Al-Ais and Fish River Canyon** *nat park* Namibia
79 F3 **Ālāja** Syria
29 K8 **Alajärvi** Finland
79 G3 **'Alā,Jebel al** *mts* Syria
125 M4 **Alajuela** Costa Rica
47 L8 **Alakır** *R* Turkey
57 K2 **Alakol', Ozero** *L* Kazakhstan
29 P5 **Alakurtti** Russian Federation
29 L4 **Alakylä** Finland
80 G3 **'Al'al** Jordan
135 T3 **Alalakeiki Channel** Hawaiian Is
128 F4 **Alalaú** *R* Brazil
119 P9 **Alameda** Saskatchewan Canada
124 H3 **Alameda** Mexico
102 B4 **Alameda** California U.S.A.
101 N7 **Alameda** Idaho U.S.A.
106 D6 **Alameda** New Mexico U.S.A.
71 D2 **Alaminos** Luzon Philippines
124 D3 **Alamito** Mexico
108 C6 **Alamito Creek** Texas U.S.A.
124 H4 **Alamitos, Sa. de los** *ra* Mexico
103 J9 **Alamo** *R* California U.S.A.
112 E5 **Alamo** Georgia U.S.A.
103 J4 **Alamo** Nevada U.S.A.
98 C1 **Alamo** North Dakota U.S.A.
110 G6 **Alamo** Tennessee U.S.A.
109 J9 **Alamo** Texas U.S.A.
106 E9 **Alamogordo** New Mexico U.S.A.
106 F7 **Alamogordo Res** New Mexico U.S.A.
103 L7 **Alamo Lake** *res* Arizona U.S.A.
43 C8 **Ala, Monti di** Sardinia
124 E4 **Alamos** Mexico
106 E4 **Alamosa** Colorado U.S.A.
124 F2 **Alamos de Peña** Mexico
76 D3 **Alampur** India
26 H7 **Alanäs** Sweden
29 H11 **Aland** *isld* Finland
33 P7 **Aland** *R* Germany
74 G10 **Aland** India
27 J12 **Aland** Sweden
26 J9 **Alandsbro** Sweden
29 H11 **Alands Hav** Finland/Sweden
70 E2 **Alang** Kalimantan
88 H1 **Alanga Bay** Kenya
70 E6 **Alangalang Tg** Kalimantan
69 G13 **Alangangtang** *isld* Sumatra
29 L6 **Alaniemi** Finland
108 D8 **Alanreed** Texas U.S.A.
87 H11 **Alaotra, Farihy** *L* Madagascar
112 D6 **Alapaha** *R* Georgia U.S.A.
55 D2 **Alapayevsk** Russian Federation
Alappuzha *see* **Aleppey**
80 G2 **Alaq** *R* Syria
79 F9 **Alāqān** Saudi Arabia
17 F5 **Alarcón, Embalse de** Spain
71 H9 **Alas** Indonesia
78 B2 **Alaşehir** Turkey
56 C5 **Alash** *R* Russian Federation
77 A4 **Al Ashār** Iran
116 **Alaska** *state* U.S.A.
116 O7 **Alaska,G.of** Alaska U.S.A.
135 L2 **Alaska Pen** Alaska U.S.A.
70 Q10 **Alas,Selat** Indonesia
44 D3 **Alassio** Italy
29 K11 **Alastaro** Finland
57 C5 **Alat** Uzbekistan
116 L3 **Alatna** Alaska U.S.A.
45 O6 **Alatri** Italy
52 G7 **Alatyr'** Russian Federation
17 F2 **Alava** *prov* Spain
78 K1 **Alaverdi** Armenia
29 O7 **Alavuokki** Finland
29 K9 **Alavus** Finland
138 F5 **Alawoona** South Australia Australia
8 B1 **Alaw Res** Wales
57 G4 **Alay-Ku** Kyrgyzstan
17 K5 **Alayor** Menorca
57 F5 **Alayskiy Khrebet** *mts* Tajikistan/Kyrgyzstan
47 L5 **Alayunt** Turkey
78 L1 **Alazan** *R* Azerbaijan/Georgia
109 K8 **Alazan Bay** Texas U.S.A.
53 G12 **Alazani** *R* Georgia
51 P2 **Alazeya** *R* Russian Federation
40 H2 **Alb** *R* Germany
44 D2 **Alba** Italy
48 H4 **Alba** *reg* Romania
94 C2 **Alba** Michigan U.S.A.
109 M3 **Alba** Texas U.S.A.
17 F5 **Albacete** Spain
17 F6 **Albacete** *prov* Spain
138 F6 **Albacutya,L** Victoria Australia
16 D4 **Alba de Tormes** Spain
28 E1 **Albæk** Denmark
28 E1 **Albæk Bugt** *B* Denmark
56 C5 **Albagan, Gora** *mt* Russian Federation
79 F3 **Al Bahlūlīyeh** Syria
17 G6 **Albaida** Spain
48 H4 **Alba Iulia** Romania
144 B6 **Alba, Mt** New Zealand
121 S4 **Albanel** Quebec Canada
46 D2 **Albania** *rep* S Europe
42 E7 **Albani,Colli** *hills* Italy
45 N6 **Albano** *L* Italy
45 N6 **Albano Laziale** Italy
45 J4 **Albano, Mte** Italy
143 C10 **Albany** W Australia Australia
127 L2 **Albany** Jamaica
111 M10 **Albany** Georgia U.S.A.
99 Q8 **Albany** Illinois U.S.A.
110 L1 **Albany** Indiana U.S.A.
110 L5 **Albany** Kentucky U.S.A.
111 F11 **Albany** Louisiana U.S.A.
110 B1 **Albany** Missouri U.S.A.
95 O4 **Albany** New York U.S.A.
94 E7 **Albany** Ohio U.S.A.
100 B5 **Albany** Oregon U.S.A.
109 H3 **Albany** Texas U.S.A.
95 P2 **Albany** Vermont U.S.A.
101 T8 **Albany** Wyoming U.S.A.
141 J7 **Albany Downs** Queensland Australia
133 D4 **Albardón** Argentina
45 K1 **Albaredo d'Adige** Italy
40 B6 **Albarine** *R* France
17 F4 **Albarracín, Sa. de** *mt* Spain
141 F2 **Albatross B** Queensland Australia
126 G6 **Albatross Bank** Caribbean
32 K9 **Albaxen** Germany
71 F4 **Albay Gulf** Luzon Philippines
40 H2 **Albbruck** Germany
112 G2 **Albemarle** North Carolina U.S.A.
112 L1 **Albemarle Sound** North Carolina U.S.A.
44 D3 **Albenga** Italy
100 J1 **Albeni Falls Dam** Idaho U.S.A.
16 E4 **Alberche** *R* Spain
130 B10 **Alberdi** Paraguay
18 G10 **Albères** *mts* France
138 D2 **Alberga** South Australia Australia
16 B4 **Albergaria a Valha** Portugal
17 G5 **Alberique** Spain
117 L11 **Alberni** British Columbia Canada
32 K4 **Albersdorf** Germany
140 E4 **Albert** *R* Queensland Australia
122 H8 **Albert** New Brunswick Canada
22 D3 **Albert** France
107 L3 **Albert** Kansas U.S.A.
114 H7 **Alberta** *prov* Canada
118 D5 **Alberta** Canada
111 J9 **Alberta** Alabama U.S.A.
94 K10 **Alberta** Virginia U.S.A.
117 P9 **Alberta,Mt** Alberta Canada
48 F3 **Albertirsa** Hungary
22 J1 **Albert Kanaal** Belgium
138 E6 **Albert, L** South Australia Australia
86 F5 **Albert, L** Uganda/Zaire
100 E7 **Albert, L** Oregon U.S.A.
86 F5 **Albert Nile** *R* Uganda
122 H7 **Alberton** Prince Edward I Canada
126 G3 **Albert Town** Long Cay Bahamas
127 K2 **Albert Town** Jamaica
144 B6 **Albert Town** New Zealand
Albertville *see* **Kalémié**
119 M5 **Albertville** Saskatchewan Canada
40 D6 **Albertville** France
48 L6 **Albeşti** Romania
36 B6 **Albestroff** France
45 L1 **Albettone** Italy
18 G9 **Albi** France
99 O8 **Albia** Iowa U.S.A.
45 L1 **Albignásego** Italy
98 B8 **Albin** Wyoming U.S.A.
129 H2 **Albina** Suriname
45 J2 **Albinea** Italy
102 A2 **Albion** California U.S.A.
101 M7 **Albion** Idaho U.S.A.
110 H3 **Albion** Illinois U.S.A.
94 B5 **Albion** Indiana U.S.A.
99 O7 **Albion** Iowa U.S.A.
94 C4 **Albion** Michigan U.S.A.
98 B4 **Albion** Montana U.S.A.
98 H8 **Albion** Nebraska U.S.A.
94 J3 **Albion** New York U.S.A.
110 A7 **Albion** Oklahoma U.S.A.
94 G5 **Albion** Pennsylvania U.S.A.
44 E3 **Albisola Marina** Italy
44 D3 **Albisola Superior** Italy
44 D3 **Albissola-Marina** Italy
25 C5 **Alblasserdam** Netherlands
17 H4 **Albocácer** Spain
27 J15 **Alböke** Sweden
43 C8 **Albo,M** Sardinia
17 G5 **Alboraya** Spain
Ålborg *co see* **Nordjylland** *co*
28 D2 **Ålborg** Denmark
99 O3 **Alborn** Minnesota U.S.A.
17 F7 **Albox** Spain
117 O9 **Albreda** British Columbia Canada
8 D2 **Albrighton** England
141 H6 **Albro** Queensland Australia
16 B7 **Albufeira** Portugal
17 G5 **Albufera** *L* Spain
41 L4 **Albula Pass** Switzerland
37 J1 **Albungen** Germany
16 E8 **Albuñol** Spain
130 B6 **Albuquerque** Brazil
106 D6 **Albuquerque** New Mexico U.S.A.
84 F3 **Al Burayqah** Libya
95 O2 **Alburg** Vermont U.S.A.
43 G8 **Alburno, Monte** Italy
16 C5 **Alburquerque** Spain
139 H6 **Albury** Victoria Australia
144 C6 **Albury** New Zealand
6 M6 **Albuskjell** *oil rig* North Sea
19 Q13 **Alby** France
26 H9 **Alby** Sweden
16 B6 **Alcacer do Sal** Portugal
17 H4 **Alcalá de Chisvert** Spain
16 D7 **Alcalá de Guadaira** Spain
17 G5 **Alcalá del Júcar** Spain
16 D8 **Alcalá de los Gazules** Spain
16 E7 **Alcala la Real** Spain
131 B2 **Alcalde, Pta** *C* Chile
43 E11 **Alcamo** Sicily
17 G3 **Alcanadre** *R* Spain
17 H4 **Alcanar** Spain
16 C3 **Alcañices** Spain
17 G3 **Alcañiz** Spain
16 C5 **Alcántara** Spain
16 C5 **Alcántara, Embalse de** *res* Spain
17 G7 **Alcantarilla** Spain
130 D5 **Alcantilado** Brazil
17 F6 **Alcaraz** Spain
17 F6 **Alcaraz, Sa. de** *mts* Spain
16 E7 **Alcaudete** Spain
16 E5 **Alcázar de San Juan** Spain
9 E3 **Alcester** England
98 K6 **Alcester** South Dakota U.S.A.
17 G5 **Alcira** Spain
111 C10 **Alco** Louisiana U.S.A.
112 D2 **Alcoa** Tennessee U.S.A.
129 L7 **Alcobaça** Brazil
16 B5 **Alcobaca** Portugal
17 F3 **Alcolea del Pinar** Spain
112 G4 **Alcolu** South Carolina U.S.A.
118 D5 **Alcomdale** Alberta Canada
118 L1 **Alcona** Ontario Canada
9 F3 **Alconbury Hill** England
140 C6 **Alcoota** N Terr Australia
17 G4 **Alcora** Spain
17 G4 **Alcorisa** Spain
101 T7 **Alcova** Wyoming U.S.A.
17 G6 **Alcoy** Spain
17 G3 **Alcubbiere, Sa. de** *mt* Spain
83 G5 **Aldabra Is** Seychelles Indian Oc
124 G3 **Aldama** Mexico
51 M3 **Aldan** Russian Federation
51 M3 **Aldanskoye Nagorye** Russian Federation
9 E5 **Aldbourne** England
13 H6 **Aldbrough** England
16 C3 **Aldeadávila de la Ribera** Spain
9 H3 **Aldeburgh** England
107 M3 **Alden** Kansas U.S.A.
94 B2 **Alden** Michigan U.S.A.
94 J4 **Alden** New York U.S.A.
25 F7 **Aldenhoven** Germany
9 H3 **Alde,R** England
106 D3 **Alder** Colorado U.S.A.
101 N4 **Alder** Montana U.S.A.
14 E2 **Aldergrove** N Ireland
100 C3 **Alder L** Washington U.S.A.
9 E5 **Aldermaston** England
145 F2 **Aldermen Is, The** New Zealand
20 F2 **Alderney** *isld* Channel Is
102 C6 **Alder Pk** California U.S.A.
101 M4 **Alder Pk** Montana U.S.A.
102 A1 **Alderpoint** California U.S.A.
9 F5 **Aldershot** England
28 D4 **Alderslyst** Denmark
118 F8 **Alderson** Alberta Canada
94 G9 **Alderson** West Virginia U.S.A.
118 D8 **Aldersyde** Alberta Canada
8 D1 **Aldford** England
9 E4 **Aldsworth** England
28 D5 **Åle** Denmark
99 Q8 **Aledo** Illinois U.S.A.
85 B5 **Aleg** Mauritania
130 B5 **Alegra** *R* Brazil
130 F6 **Alegre** Brazil
133 F3 **Alegrete** Brazil
106 B7 **Alegros Mt** New Mexico U.S.A.
133 A9 **Alejandro Selkirk** *isld* Juan Fernández Is Pacific Oc
116 H7 **Aleknagik** Alaska U.S.A.
54 E8 **Aleksandriya** Ukraine
54 M3 **Aleksandro-Nevskiy** Russian Federation
52 E6 **Aleksandrov** Russian Federation
48 G6 **Aleksandrovac** Serbia Yugoslavia
53 G8 **Aleksandrov Gay** Russian Federation
52 J5 **Aleksandrovsk** Russian Federation
58 G1 **Aleksandrovskiy Zavod** Russian Federation
53 F11 **Aleksandrovskoye** Russian Federation
59 M1 **Aleksandrovsk Sakhalinskiy** Russian Federation
31 L4 **Aleksandrów** Poland
31 L3 **Aleksandrów Kujawski** Poland
147 K11 **Aleksandry, Zemlya** Russian Federation
55 E4 **Alekseyevka** Kazakhstan
56 G2 **Alekseyevsk** Russian Federation
53 F8 **Alekseyevskaya** Russian Federation
54 F1 **Alekseyevskoye** Russian Federation
53 F8 **Aleksikovskiy** Russian Federation
54 J2 **Aleksin** Russian Federation
46 E1 **Aleksinac** Serbia Yugoslavia
27 F14 **Älekulla** Sweden
27 H15 **Ålem** Sweden
106 C9 **Aleman** New Mexico U.S.A.
133 D3 **Alemania** Argentina
47 N10 **Alemdağ** Turkey
47 N10 **Alemdağ Ormanı** *forest* Turkey
129 K8 **Alem Paraíba** Brazil
21 L5 **Alençon** France
21 L5 **Alençon, Campagne d'** *plain* France
129 H4 **Alenquer** Brazil
16 A5 **Alenquer** Portugal
102 V13 **Alenuihaha Chan** Hawaiian Is
76 C6 **Aleppey** India
Aleppo *see* **Halab**
115 N1 **Alert** Northwest Territories Canada
128 D6 **Alerta** Peru
117 K10 **Alert Bay** British Columbia Canada
18 H8 **Alès** France
43 B9 **Ales** Sardinia
48 G3 **Aleşd** Romania
52 G2 **Alëshki** Russian Federation
26 K3 **Alesjaure** *L* Sweden
44 D1 **Alessandria** *prov* Italy
44 E2 **Alessándria** Italy
Alessio *see* **Lezhë**
28 C3 **Ålestrup** Denmark
26 B9 **Ålesund** Norway
18 G10 **Alet** France
116 L10 **Aleutian Is** Alaska U.S.A.
116 H8 **Aleutian Ra** Alaska U.S.A.
107 N7 **Alex** Oklahoma U.S.A.
137 Q4 **Alexa Bank** Pacific Oc
21 J5 **Alexain** France
119 R9 **Alexander** Manitoba Canada
80 C4 **Alexander** Israel
107 L3 **Alexander** Kansas U.S.A.
98 C2 **Alexander** North Dakota U.S.A.
117 E7 **Alexander Archipelago** Alaska U.S.A.
87 C11 **Alexander B** S Africa
111 L9 **Alexander City** Alabama U.S.A.
146 C5 **Alexander Island** Antarctica
140 D2 **Alexander, Mt** N Terr Australia
142 B6 **Alexander, Mt** W Australia Australia
143 D8 **Alexander, Mt** W Australia Australia
140 F4 **Alexandra** *R* Queensland Australia
144 B6 **Alexandra** New Zealand
131 H6 **Alexandra,C** S Georgia
117 P5 **Alexandra Falls** Northwest Territories Canada
147 G6 **Alexandra Fiord** Northwest Territories Canada
140 D4 **Alexandria** N Terr Australia
117 M9 **Alexandria** British Columbia Canada
121 Q7 **Alexandria** Ontario Canada
79 A7 **Alexandria** Egypt
84 H3 **Alexandria** Egypt
127 K2 **Alexandria** Jamaica
46 G1 **Alexandria** Romania
89 E9 **Alexandria** S Africa
12 D2 **Alexandria** Scotland
110 L1 **Alexandria** Indiana U.S.A.
110 M3 **Alexandria** Kentucky U.S.A.
111 D10 **Alexandria** Louisiana U.S.A.
99 L4 **Alexandria** Minnesota U.S.A.
110 E1 **Alexandria** Missouri U.S.A.
98 J9 **Alexandria** Nebraska U.S.A.
98 J6 **Alexandria** South Dakota U.S.A.
110 K5 **Alexandria** Tennessee U.S.A.
95 K8 **Alexandria** Virginia U.S.A.
95 M2 **Alexandria Bay** New York U.S.A.
138 E6 **Alexandrina, L** South Australia Australia
144 C5 **Alexandrina, L** New Zealand
80 E5 **Alexandrium** Jordan
78 A1 **Alexandroúpolis** Greece
99 Q8 **Alexis** Illinois U.S.A.
115 O7 **Alexis B** Labrador, Nfld Canada
33 O9 **Alexisbad** Germany
117 M9 **Alexis Creek** British Columbia Canada
123 P1 **Alexis R** Labrador, Nfld Canada
118 B6 **Alexo** Alberta Canada
79 F5 **'Aley** Lebanon
56 B4 **Aley** *R* Russian Federation
56 B5 **Aleysk** Russian Federation
36 B3 **Alf** *R* Germany
36 C3 **Alf** Germany
17 G4 **Alfambra** *R* Spain
128 C4 **Alfaro** Ecuador
17 F2 **Alfaro** Spain
47 J1 **Alfatar** Bulgaria
32 L9 **Alfeld** Germany
37 M5 **Alfeld** Germany
130 F7 **Alfenas** Brazil
55 G4 **Alferovka** Russian Federation
32 G8 **Alfhausen** Germany
45 M3 **Alfonsine** Italy
9 G1 **Alford** England
15 F3 **Alford** Scotland
111 L11 **Alford** Florida U.S.A.
26 A10 **Ålfotbreen** *gla* Norway
95 R3 **Alfred** Maine U.S.A.
98 G3 **Alfred** North Dakota U.S.A.
143 F6 **Alfred and Marie Ra** W Australia Australia
130 H7 **Alfredo Chaves** Brazil
145 E4 **Alfredton** New Zealand
9 E1 **Alfreton** England
9 G6 **Alfriston** England
27 H10 **Alfta** Sweden
36 C2 **Alfter** Germany
55 C6 **Alga** Kazakhstan
27 A13 **Algård** Norway
133 D5 **Algarrobo del Aguila** Argentina
16 B7 **Algarve** *prov* Portugal
53 F7 **Algasovo** Russian Federation
57 F3 **Algatart** Kazakhstan
16 D8 **Algeciras** Spain
85 E1 **Alger** Algeria
94 C2 **Alger** Michigan U.S.A.
94 D6 **Alger** Ohio U.S.A.
84 B4 **Algeria** *rep* N Africa
43 B8 **Alghero** Sardinia
27 H14 **Älghult** Sweden
Algiers *see* **Alger**
111 J12 **Algiers** New Orleans, Louisiana U.S.A.
17 G5 **Alginet** Spain
89 D9 **Algoa B** S Africa
130 H10 **Algodões** Brazil
106 D6 **Algodones** New Mexico U.S.A.
16 E5 **Algodor** *R* Spain
120 H6 **Algoma** Ontario Canada
100 D7 **Algoma** Oregon U.S.A.
99 T5 **Algoma** Wisconsin U.S.A.
99 M6 **Algona** Iowa U.S.A.
121 M7 **Algonquin Park** Ontario Canada
110 L5 **Algood** Tennessee U.S.A.
22 L5 **Algrange** France
26 J7 **Älgsjön** Sweden
68 B5 **Alguada Reef** Burma
17 F2 **Alhama** *R* Spain
78 G5 **Al Ḩamād** *reg* Jordan/Saudi Arabia
17 F3 **Alhama de Aragón** Spain
16 E7 **Alhama de Granada** Spain
17 F7 **Alhama de Murcia** Spain
17 F8 **Alhamilla, Sa** *mt* Spain
84 E4 **Al Ḩammādah al Ḩamrā'** *plateau* Libya
78 G3 **Al Hīshah** Syria
16 E9 **Al Hoceima** Morocco
16 E9 **Al Hoceima, B d'** Morocco
86 H3 **Al Hudaydah** Yemen
79 E9 **Al Ḩumayḑah** Egypt
84 G4 **Al Ḩumaymāt** Libya
26 B10 **Ålhus** Norway
57 E6 **'Alīābād** Afghanistan
17 G4 **Aliaga** Spain
47 H6 **Aliağa** Turkey
46 E4 **Aliákmon** *R* Greece
71 N9 **Aliambata** Indonesia
74 F9 **Alībāg** India
74 E9 **Alibagh** India
47 M10 **Alibey** *R* Turkey
48 M5 **Alibey,Oz** *L* Ukraine
71 F4 **Alibijaban** Luzon Philippines
86 G4 **Ālībo** Ethiopia
48 F5 **Alibunar** Serbia Yugoslavia
46 F3 **Ali Butús** *mt* Greece
124 F5 **Alicama** Mexico
17 G6 **Alicante** *prov* Spain
17 G6 **Alicante** Spain
141 F3 **Alice** *R* Queensland Australia
141 H6 **Alice** Queensland Australia
98 J3 **Alice** North Dakota U.S.A.
109 J8 **Alice** Texas U.S.A.
117 J8 **Alice Arm** British Columbia Canada
142 G4 **Alice Downs** W Australia Australia
100 H4 **Alicel** Oregon U.S.A.
43 H9 **Alice,Pta** Italy
126 E6 **Alice Shoal** Caribbean
140 C6 **Alice Springs** N Terr Australia
113 H12 **Alice Town** Bahamas
126 E2 **Alice Town** Bimini Is Bahamas
111 H8 **Aliceville** Alabama U.S.A.
140 C6 **Alice Well** N Terr Australia
71 F7 **Alicia** Mindanao Philippines
110 E6 **Alicia** Arkansas U.S.A.
141 F5 **Alick** *R* Queensland Australia
43 F10 **Alicudi, I** Italy
119 Q9 **Alida** Saskatchewan Canada
45 Q7 **Alife** Italy
74 H5 **Aligarh** India
77 A3 **Alīgudarz** Iran
Alihe *see* **Oroqen Zizhiqi**
59 H1 **A-li-ho** China
77 L3 **Alī Kheyl** Afghanistan
52 G6 **Alikovo** Russian Federation
86 B6 **Alima** *R* Congo
125 M3 **Alimicamba** Nicaragua
47 U17 **Alimniá** *isld* Greece
71 F5 **Alimodian** Philippines
71 E7 **Alimpaya Pt** Mindanao Philippines
86 D4 **Alindao** Cent Afr Republic
70 F5 **Alindau** Sulawesi Indonesia
107 M5 **Aline** Oklahoma U.S.A.
138 D2 **Alinerta,Mt** South Australia Australia
77 L2 **Alingar** *R* Afghanistan
66 C5 **Aling Kangri** *mt* China
27 F14 **Alingsås** Sweden
94 G6 **Aliquippa** Pennsylvania U.S.A.
124 D2 **Alisos** *R* Mexico
46 F3 **Alistáti** Greece
116 K8 **Alitak B** Alaska U.S.A.
46 G6 **Alivérion** Greece
89 E8 **Aliwal North** S Africa
118 D6 **Alix** Alberta Canada
80 G7 **Aliyan** Jordan
Al Jawf *see* **Al Khufrah**
16 B7 **Aljezur** Portugal
80 G2 **Al Jukhadar** Syria
16 B7 **Aljustrel** Portugal
100 F8 **Alkali L** Nevada U.S.A.
22 J2 **Alken** Belgium
84 G5 **Al Khufrah** Libya
25 C3 **Alkmaar** Netherlands
95 R6 **Allagash** Maine U.S.A.
95 R7 **Allagash L** Maine U.S.A.
75 J6 **Allahabad** India
21 O5 **Allaines-Mervilliers** France
21 O5 **Allainville** France
20 F6 **Allaire** France
83 L9 **Allai Tank** *L* Sri Lanka
103 J9 **All American Can** California U.S.A.
108 C4 **Allamoore** Texas U.S.A.
118 L7 **Allan** Saskatchewan Canada
19 N16 **Allan** France
80 G2 **'Allan** *R* Syria
83 M9 **Allan Pt** Christmas I Indian Oc
89 E6 **Allanridge** S Africa
84 J5 **Allaqi,Radi** Egypt
121 N3 **Allard** *R* Quebec Canada
122 G6 **Allardville** New Brunswick Canada
16 B2 **Allariz** Spain
36 C7 **Allarmont** France
112 C3 **Allatoona Res** Georgia U.S.A.
22 H4 **Alle** Belgium
94 B4 **Allegan** Michigan U.S.A.
94 J4 **Allegany** New York U.S.A.
94 H5 **Allegheny** *R* Pennsylvania U.S.A.
94 E10 **Allegheny Mts** U.S.A.
94 H5 **Allegheny Res** Pennsylvania U.S.A.
127 M4 **Allègre, Pte** Guadeloupe W Indies
19 O17 **Alleins** France
111 F12 **Allemands** Louisiana U.S.A.
89 E7 **Allemanskraal Dam** *res* S Africa
19 Q14 **Allemont** France
71 G4 **Allen** Philippines
94 E9 **Allen** Kentucky U.S.A.
98 K7 **Allen** Nebraska U.S.A.
109 L1 **Allen** Oklahoma U.S.A.
98 E6 **Allen** South Dakota U.S.A.
109 L2 **Allen** Texas U.S.A.
14 D3 **Allen, Bog of** Ireland
112 F4 **Allendale** South Carolina U.S.A.
13 F4 **Allendale Town** England
125 J3 **Allende** Mexico
32 G10 **Allendorf** Germany
32 L10 **Allendorf** Germany
36 F1 **Allendorf** Germany
36 F2 **Allendorf** Germany
120 J8 **Allenford** Ontario Canada
13 F4 **Allenheads** England
119 M7 **Allen Hills** Saskatchewan Canada
14 C2 **Allen,L** Ireland
144 A7 **Allen, Mt** New Zealand
116 Q5 **Allen,Mt** Alaska U.S.A.
106 E1 **Allenspark** Colorado U.S.A.
31 J7 **Allensteig** Austria
95 Q3 **Allenstown** New Hampshire U.S.A.
110 J5 **Allensville** Kentucky U.S.A.
95 M6 **Allentown** Pennsylvania U.S.A.
33 M7 **Aller** *R* Germany
22 K3 **Allerborn** Luxembourg
36 E6 **Allerheiligen** Germany
37 L5 **Allersberg** Germany
28 J6 **Allerslev** Denmark
110 C1 **Allerton** Iowa U.S.A.
29 K4 **Allerum** Sweden
21 O2 **Allery** France
40 D7 **Allevard** France
127 K3 **Alley,The** Jamaica
109 L6 **Alleyton** Texas U.S.A.
41 M3 **Allgäuer Alpen** *mts* Austria/Germany
8 D1 **Allgreave** England
9 G5 **Allhallows** England
118 F6 **Alliance** Alberta Canada
98 D7 **Alliance** Nebraska U.S.A.
94 F6 **Alliance** Ohio U.S.A.
18 H6 **Allier** *R* France
18 H6 **Allier** *dept* France
145 E4 **Alligator Headland** New Zealand
127 J3 **Alligator Pond** Jamaica
112 L2 **Alligator R** North Carolina U.S.A.
140 C2 **Alligator R., E** N Terr Australia
113 G13 **Alligator Reef** Florida U.S.A.
28 D4 **Alling** Denmark
37 M6 **Alling** Germany
28 E4 **Alling Å** *R* Denmark
28 E4 **Allingåbro** Denmark
99 O7 **Allison** Iowa U.S.A.
117 K10 **Allison Harbour** British Columbia Canada
12 E1 **Alloa** Scotland
21 P7 **Allogny** France
13 E4 **Allonby** England
80 G1 **Alloné HaBashan** Syria
80 D2 **Allon HaGalil** Israel
80 D3 **Allonim** Israel
21 K8 **Allonne** Deux Sèvres France
21 P3 **Allonne** Oise France
21 O5 **Allonnes** Eure-et-Loir France
21 L7 **Allonnes** Maine-et-Loire France
80 D7 **Allon Shevut** Jordan
141 K8 **Allora** Queensland Australia
143 E7 **Allott, Mt** W Australia Australia
99 S2 **Allouez** Michigan U.S.A.
12 D3 **Alloway** Scotland
33 O10 **Allstedt** Germany
70 F7 **Allu** Sulawesi Indonesia
Alluitsup Paa *see* **Sydprøven**
121 N7 **Allumette I** Quebec Canada
121 R4 **Ally** Quebec Canada

Column 1

38 J6 Alm R Austria
38 G7 Alm Austria
122 H8 Alma New Brunswick Canada
121 T4 Alma Quebec Canada
110 B6 Alma Arkansas U.S.A.
106 D2 Alma Colorado U.S.A.
112 E6 Alma Georgia U.S.A.
107 O2 Alma Kansas U.S.A.
94 C3 Alma Michigan U.S.A.
110 C2 Alma Missouri U.S.A.
98 G9 Alma Nebraska U.S.A.
99 P5 Alma Wisconsin U.S.A.
57 H3 Alma-Ata Kazakhstan
16 A6 Almada Portugal
141 G3 Almaden Queensland Australia
16 D6 Almadén Spain
16 D6 Almadén, Sa. de mts Spain
80 F2 Almagor Israel
71 G5 Almagro isld Philippines
48 G6 Almajului Muntii mts Romania
84 F4 Al Malâqî well Libya
57 E4 Almalyk Uzbekistan
102 C1 Almanor, L California U.S.A.
17 G6 Almansa Spain
16 D2 Almansa Spain
117 K7 Alma Peak British Columbia Canada
17 F3 Almarza Spain
48 H3 Almaş R Romania
130 E4 Almas, R das Brazil
17 F3 Almazán Spain
57 E4 Almazar Uzbekistan
54 K8 Almaznaya Ukraine
56 H1 Almaznyy Russian Federation
27 H12 Almby Sweden
32 J9 Alme R Germany
27 H15 Almeboda Sweden
100 B7 Almeda Oregon U.S.A.
129 H4 Almeirim Brazil
16 B5 Almeirim Portugal
25 G4 Almelo Netherlands
107 L2 Almena Kansas U.S.A.
129 K7 Almenara Brazil
17 F7 Almenara, Sa. de mt Spain
17 F3 Almenar de Soria Spain
16 C3 Almendra, Embalse de res Spain
16 C6 Almendralejo Spain
21 L4 Almenêches France
55 D4 Al'menevo Russian Federation
8 D6 Almer England
25 D4 Almere Netherlands
25 D4 Almere-Haven Netherlands
17 F7 Almeria prov Spain
17 F8 Almeria Spain
98 G8 Almeria Nebraska U.S.A.
17 F8 Almeria,G. de Spain
52 H7 Al'met'yevsk Russian Federation
27 G15 Almhult Sweden
16 E8 Almijara, Sierra de mts Spain
28 C5 Almind Vejle Denmark
28 C4 Almind Viborg Denmark
130 E9 Almira Washington U.S.A.
130 E9 Almirante Tamandaré Brazil
46 G6 Almiropótamos Greece
46 F5 Almirós Greece
46 G9 Almiroú Kólpos G Crete Greece
101 M7 Almo Idaho U.S.A.
16 B7 Almodôvar Portugal
16 E6 Almodóvar del Campo Spain
17 F5 Almodóvar del Pinar Spain
133 D3 Almogasta Argentina
94 K4 Almond New York U.S.A.
99 R5 Almond Wisconsin U.S.A.
9 E4 Almond,R Scotland
8 D4 Almondsbury England
106 D3 Almont Colorado U.S.A.
94 D1 Almont Michigan U.S.A.
98 E3 Almont North Dakota U.S.A.
121 O7 Almonte Ontario Canada
17 B8 Almonte R Spain
74 H4 Almora India
16 E4 Almorox Spain
100 H3 Almota Washington U.S.A.
79 F9 Al Mudawwara Jordan
86 H3 Al Mukhâ Yemen
47 J7 Almudévar Spain
16 E8 Almuñécar Spain
27 H14 Almvik Sweden
101 P8 Almy Wyoming U.S.A.
111 E7 Almyra Arkansas U.S.A.
13 G3 Aln Br England
15 D3 Alnes Scotland
13 G3 Alnmouth England
26 J9 Alnö Sweden
13 G3 Alnwick England
137 R4 Alofi isld Îles de Horn Pacific Oc
94 C1 Aloha Michigan U.S.A.
68 B1 Alon Burma
139 H9 Alonnah Tasmania Australia
71 O6 Alonon Pt Philippines
119 T8 Alonsa Manitoba Canada
71 M9 Alor isld Indonesia
71 M8 Alor Setar Malaysia
71 M8 Alor,Kep isld Indonesia
71 L9 Alor,Selat Indonesia
69 E9 Alor Setar Malaysia
31 H7 Alosno Spain
Alost see Aalst
141 G7 Aloysius, Mt W Australia Australia
52 D2 Alozero Russian Federation
133 E5 Alpachiri Argentina
38 E7 Alpbach Austria
13 G6 Alpe d'Huez mt France
110 C5 Alpena Arkansas U.S.A.
94 D1 Alpena Michigan U.S.A.
98 H5 Alpena South Dakota U.S.A.
94 H8 Alpena West Virginia U.S.A.
94 D1 Alpena Spain
129 J5 Alpercatas, Serra das mts Brazil
19 K8 Alpes-de-Haute-Provence dept France
19 O15 Alpes du Dauphiné mts France
46 D2 Alpet mt Albania
47 K9 Alpet mt Italy
141 H6 Alpha Queensland Australia
99 Q8 Alpha Illinois U.S.A.
95 M6 Alpha New Jersey U.S.A.
94 J9 Alpha Virginia U.S.A.
25 C4 Alphen Netherlands
83 H5 Alphonse I Seychelles Indian Oc
16 B5 Alpiarça Portugal
44 B1 Alpignano Italy
103 P8 Alpine Arizona U.S.A.
108 B5 Alpine Texas U.S.A.
36 E7 Alpirsbach Germany
16 B7 Alportel,S Braz de Portugal
4 F7 Alps, The mt ra Europe
47 L5 Alpu Turkey
79 G3 Al Qadmûs Syria
79 G4 Alquines France
79 D4 Al Quşayr Syria
98 E3 Al Quşbat Libya
79 G5 Al Qutayfah Syria
123 L6 Alright I Madeleine, Is Quebec Canada
28 E5 Alrø isld Denmark
140 D4 Alroy Downs N Terr Australia
28 E5 Als Denmark
19 K4 Alsace prov France
118 H7 Alsask Saskatchewan Canada
17 F2 Alsasua Spain
25 F7 Alsdorf Germany
100 B5 Alsea Oregon U.S.A.
117 E6 Alsek R British Columbia Canada
98 H1 Alsen North Dakota U.S.A.
36 E4 Alsenz Germany
110 F2 Alsey Illinois U.S.A.
36 G2 Alsfeld Germany

Column 2

28 D6 Als Fjord inlet Denmark
36 E4 Alsheim Germany
26 J5 Alsjaur L Sweden
33 P9 Alsleben Germany
28 A5 Alslev Denmark
28 C6 Alslev Kro Denmark
28 F4 Also Denmark
32 E6 Alstahaug Norway
95 P3 Alstead New Hampshire U.S.A.
26 F6 Alsten isld Norway
32 M5 Alster R Germany
13 F4 Alston England
27 M15 Alsunga Latvia
26 N2 Alta Norway
101 L4 Alta Montana U.S.A.
26 N2 Altaelv R Norway
26 N1 Altafjord inlet Norway
131 D3 Alta Gracia Argentina
127 J9 Altagracia Venezuela
128 E2 Altagracia de Orituco Venezuela
109 L6 Altair Texas U.S.A.
128 E7 Altamachi Bolivia
112 E6 Altamaha R Georgia U.S.A.
133 E4 Altamelincué Argentina
129 H4 Altamira Brazil
125 N9 Altamira Mexico
102 C4 Altamont California U.S.A.
110 H2 Altamont Illinois U.S.A.
100 D7 Altamont Oregon U.S.A.
98 K5 Altamont South Dakota U.S.A.
110 L6 Altamont Tennessee U.S.A.
101 P8 Altamont Wyoming U.S.A.
144 B6 Alta, Mt New Zealand
43 H8 Altamura Italy
65 B2 Altan Bulag China
56 E6 Altanbulag Mongolia
124 D2 Altar Mexico
118 G7 Altario Alberta Canada
124 F5 Altata Mexico
44 F4 Altavilla Irpina Italy
94 D8 Alta Vista Iowa U.S.A.
107 O6 Alta Vista Kansas U.S.A.
94 H9 Altavista Virginia U.S.A.
58 C2 Altay Mongolia
56 C5 Altay China
56 C5 Altay R Russian Federation
56 C5 Altayskiy Russian Federation
56 B5 Altayskiy Kray terr Russian Federation
37 L5 Altdorf Germany
37 N6 Altdorf Niederbayern Germany
41 J4 Altdorf Switzerland
17 G6 Altea Spain
33 O6 Alte Elde R Germany
32 H5 Alte Mellum Germany
33 N8 Altenahr Germany
33 M9 Altenau Germany
32 J9 Altenbeken Germany
32 F8 Altenberge Germany
32 J5 Altenbruch Germany
37 N2 Altenburg Germany
37 M4 Altenburg Germany
36 C4 Altenglan Germany
33 N8 Altenhundem Germany
38 E1 Altenkirchen Germany
38 L6 Altenmarkt Ober Österreich Austria
28 E5 Altenmarkt Salzburg Austria
37 P6 Altenmarkt Germany
33 N6 Alten Medingen Germany
36 H6 Altenstadt Baden-Württemberg Germany
36 F3 Altenstadt Hessen Germany
36 F6 Altenriep Germany
33 S5 Altentreptow Germany
33 J2 Altenwalde Germany
16 B5 Alter do Chão Portugal
33 R8 Altes Lager Germany
26 K3 Altevatn L Norway
111 L11 Altha Florida U.S.A.
37 J2 Altheim Germany
111 E7 Altheimer Arkansas U.S.A.
40 D2 Althorne France
40 D3 Althorne France
94 E7 Althorpe England
138 D6 Althorpe Is South Australia Australia
139 G3 Altibouillin, L New South Wales Australia
45 M1 Altino Italy
47 H5 Altinoluk Turkey
47 L5 Altintas Turkey
47 K8 Altinyala Turkey
47 J4 Alt-Jabel Germany
19 K5 Altkirch France
33 T7 Altlandsberg Germany
36 E5 Altleiningen Germany
94 K4 Altmar New York U.S.A.
33 O7 Altmark reg Germany
36 H1 Altmorschen Germany
37 K5 Altmühl R Germany
32 K7 Altmühl Germany
15 D2 Altnaharra Scotland
9 F5 Alton England
102 A1 Alton California U.S.A.
110 F4 Alton Illinois U.S.A.
103 H3 Alton Utah U.S.A.
118 D1 Altona Manitoba Canada
110 G5 Altona Illinois U.S.A.
101 P9 Altona Utah U.S.A.
95 P3 Altona South Dakota U.S.A.
141 J8 Alton Oilfield Queensland Australia
111 K7 Altoona Alabama U.S.A.
111 K7 Altoona Florida U.S.A.
107 P4 Altoona Kansas U.S.A.
128 G8 Alto Paraguay dept Paraguay
130 C9 Alto Paraná R Paraguay
129 J5 Alto Parnaíba Brazil
129 H7 Altopascio Italy
129 H7 Alto Sucuriú Brazil
38 G5 Altötting Germany
130 C10 Alto Uruguai Brazil
126 A1 Alto Vista hill Aruba W Indies
13 F6 Altrincham England
33 R7 Altruppin Germany
85 G8 Alt-Schadow Germany
54 F4 Altukhovo Russian Federation
133 K10 Altun Köprü Iraq
70 N9 Altun Shan mts China
102 D1 Alturas California U.S.A.
107 L6 Altus Oklahoma U.S.A.
18 E8 Alturas Res Oklahoma U.S.A.
141 H7 Altusried Germany
32 J5 Altwilter France
53 G10 Altynay Kazakhstan
52 C6 Altynay Russian Federation
133 G5 Altyn-Khutsan, Ozero Russian Federation
52 C6 Alūksne Latvia
9 E6 Alum Bay England
116 J8 Aluminé Argentina
37 M5 Ålund Sweden
99 T4 Alunda Sweden
16 E1 Alunite Nevada U.S.A.
127 J4 Alupka Ukraine
76 C3 Alur India
54 K8 Alushta Ukraine
17 F4 Alustante Spain
83 J11 Alutgama Sri Lanka
83 K9 Alut Oya Sri Lanka

Column 3

Aluva see Alwaye
84 E4 Al 'Uwaynât Libya
16 B4 Alva R Portugal
12 E1 Alva Scotland
113 F11 Alva Kentucky U.S.A.
94 D10 Alva Oklahoma U.S.A.
107 M5 Alva Oklahoma U.S.A.
54 B5 Alva Wyoming U.S.A.
16 B7 Alvaiade Portugal
125 M8 Alvarado Mexico
109 K3 Alvarado Texas U.S.A.
128 F4 Alvaraes Brazil
26 E9 Alvdal Norway
27 G13 Älvdalen Sweden
118 L6 Alverca R Portugal
33 O8 Alvesdissen Germany
32 K8 Alverdissen Germany
117 D5 Alverstone Mt Alaska/Yukon Terr U.S.A./Canada
2 A11 Alversund Norway
27 G15 Alvesta Sweden
8 D4 Alveston England
27 G10 Ålvho Sweden
110 J1 Alvin Illinois U.S.A.
109 M6 Alvin Texas U.S.A.
51 S4 Alvin Wisconsin U.S.A.
45 P6 Alviti Italy
16 B6 Alvito Portugal
27 J11 Älvkarleby Sweden
98 K9 Alvo Nebraska U.S.A.
109 K2 Alvord Texas U.S.A.
100 G7 Alvord L Oregon U.S.A.
21 O8 Alvros Sweden
27 F14 Älvsborg reg Sweden
26 M6 Älvsbyn Sweden
27 F14 Alvsered Sweden
99 M2 Alwood Minnesota U.S.A.
78 H6 Al Wadyân reg Iraq/Saudi Arabia
84 G4 Al Wahah Libya
87 E12 Awal Nth S Africa
74 G5 Alwar India
76 C5 Alwaye India
13 F3 Alwinton England
94 O10 Al Wurî reg North Sea
71 K9 Alxa Zuoqi Arkansas U.S.A.
110 C7 Alyangula N Terr Australia
51 N2 Alyaskitovyy Russian Federation
55 E2 Alymka R Russian Federation
15 E4 Alyth Scotland
31 P1 Alytus Lithuania
38 G5 Alz R Germany
98 B4 Alzada Montana U.S.A.
36 G3 Alzenau Germany
32 L6 Alzette R Luxembourg
36 E4 Alzey Germany
128 F2 Amacuro Delta Venezuela
140 B6 Amadeus,L N Terr Australia
86 F4 Amadi Sudan
115 M4 Amadjuak L Northwest Territories Canada
60 J11 Amagasaki Japan
29 K5 Amager isld Denmark
60 D12 Amagi Japan
61 N11 Amagi-san mt Japan
22 G5 Amagne France
21 L4 Amain, Mt. d' France
116 F9 Amak I Alaska U.S.A.
60 D13 Amakusa-nada sea Japan
60 C13 Amakusa-Shimo-shima isld Japan
84 D4 Amâl Libya
27 F12 Åmål Sweden
76 F2 Amalapuram India
43 H8 Amalfi Italy
46 E7 Amaliás Greece
74 F8 Amalner India
129 G8 Amambaí Brazil
130 C8 Amambai, Serra de mts Brazil/Paraguay
128 C8 Amambaí Brazil
133 F2 Amambay dept Paraguay
129 G7 Amambay, Sa. de mts Brazil/Paraguay
128 F4 Amaná,L Brazil
40 D2 Amance France
40 D3 Amance France
94 K7 Amanda Ohio U.S.A.
42 E6 Amandola Italy
55 E6 Amangel'dy Kazakhstan
146 B9 Amankaragay Kazakhstan
94 F7 Amano-hashidate inlet Japan
43 G9 Amantea Italy
91 E5 Amaokanga Kazakhstan
87 F12 Amanzimtoti S Africa
129 H3 Amapá Brazil
129 H3 Amapá,Sa de mts Brazil/Paraguay
88 F9 Amaramba,L Mozambique
129 K5 Amarante Brazil
119 T8 Amaranth Manitoba Canada
68 C2 Amarapura Burma
102 H5 Amargosa Ra California U.S.A.
103 K6 Amarillo New Mexico U.S.A.
108 C8 Amarillo Texas U.S.A.
51 N4 Amaro Argentina
59 L2 Amaro,Cerro pk Argentina
75 J7 Amarkantak India
85 F3 Amaro Leite Brazil
59 K1 Amaro,L Queensland Australia
61 N7 Amarume Japan
80 B8 'Amasa Jordan
45 F2 Amaseno Italy
45 O7 Amaseno Italy
88 H1 Amassama Western Sahara
78 D1 Amasra Turkey
78 F1 Amasya Turkey
95 P4 Amata South Australia Australia
138 B2 Amata South Australia Australia
128 E4 Amataura Brazil
125 N9 Amatenango Mexico
87 F13 Amatikulu S Africa
124 H7 Amatitlán Mexico
125 L8 Amatlan Mexico
124 G7 Amatlan de Cañas Mexico
61 O10 Amatsu-Kominato Japan
22 J2 Amay Belgium
86 G3 Amazar R see Amazonas R Brazil
119 M7 Amazon Saskatchewan Canada
128 E4 Amazonas state Brazil
128 C4 Amazonas div Colombia
128 D5 Amazonas dept Peru
129 H4 Amazonas R S America
128 E5 Amazonas state Venezuela
129 J3 Amazon,Mouths of the Brazil

Column 4

22 K3 Amberloup Belgium
21 L8 Ambère France
18 H7 Ambert France
18 G9 Ambert France
85 B6 Ambidédi Mali
75 K7 Ambikapur India
71 E4 Ambil isld Philippines
21 K7 Ambillou France
21 L7 Amboulat Portugal
87 H10 Amboile Madagascar
117 H7 Ambition,Mt British Columbia Canada
21 P3 Amblainville France
13 G3 Ambleside England
116 J3 Ambler R Alaska U.S.A.
13 F5 Ambleside England
22 B2 Ambleteuse France
22 L3 Amblève Belgium
131 F2 Amboasary Madagascar
87 H12 Amboasary Madagascar
87 H10 Ambodifotatra Madagascar
87 H12 Ambohimahasoa Madagascar
21 N7 Amboise France
20 E6 Ambon France
136 F2 Ambon Moluccas Indonesia
87 H10 Ambon France
86 G6 Amboseli, L Kenya
87 H10 Ambositra Madagascar
21 L8 Ambovombe Madagascar
103 J7 Amboy California U.S.A.
70 D5 Amboy Illinois U.S.A.
95 N6 Amboy,S New Jersey U.S.A.
21 O8 Amboz Sweden
94 G6 Ambridge Pennsylvania U.S.A.
21 J5 Ambrières-les-Vallées France
87 B7 Ambriz Angola
19 O12 Ambronay France
12 D6 Ambrose Georgia U.S.A.
98 C1 Ambrose North Dakota U.S.A.
137 O5 Ambrym isld Vanuatu
71 E2 Ambuklao Dam Luzon Philippines
71 K9 Ambulombo Vol Indonesia
70 O10 Ambulu Java
70 O9 Ambunten Java
76 D4 Ambur India
141 J7 Amby Queensland Australia
80 D2 Åmdal Norway
27 C12 Åmdal Norway
86 D3 Am Dam Chad
98 C1 Amded watercourse Algeria
50 F2 Amderma Russian Federation
75 O2 Amdo China
86 G3 Amdadet mt Ethiopia
102 D1 Amedee California U.S.A.
25 E2 Ameland isld Netherlands
42 E6 Amelia Italy
98 H7 Amelia Nebraska U.S.A.
94 K9 Amelia Virginia U.S.A.
13 F7 Amelia I Florida U.S.A.
32 M6 Amelinghausen Germany
43 H9 Amendola Italy
81 E5 Ameng China
38 L5 Amer Spain
102 D2 American R California U.S.A.
86 B2 American Falls Idaho U.S.A.
101 N7 American Falls Idaho U.S.A.
127 J9 American Fork Utah U.S.A.
103 N1 American River South Australia Australia
138 E6 American Samoa Pacific Oc
134 E1 American Shoal lighthouse Florida U.S.A.
113 F13 American Shoal lighthouse Florida U.S.A.
112 C5 Americus Georgia U.S.A.
25 D4 Amerongen Netherlands
25 D4 Amersfoort Netherlands
147 J1 Amersham England
147 H13 Amery W Australia Australia
99 O4 Amery Wisconsin U.S.A.
146 J11 Amery Ice Shelf Antarctica
99 N7 Ames Iowa U.S.A.
98 K8 Ames Iowa U.S.A.
107 M5 Ames Oklahoma U.S.A.
118 E3 Amesbury Alberta Canada
9 E5 Amesbury England
95 R4 Amesbury Massachusetts U.S.A.
118 J1 Amesdale Ontario Canada
95 U1 Ames Range mts Antarctica
146 B9 Ames Range mts Antarctica
94 F7 Amesville Ohio U.S.A.
59 J1 Amethyst ool nth New South Wales Australia
122 J8 Amet Sound Nova Scotia Canada
55 C4 Amga Russian Federation
58 G2 Amgalang Bulag China
51 N4 Amga Russian Federation
59 L2 Amgu Russian Federation
59 K1 Am Guéréda Chad
59 F3 Amguid Algeria
59 K1 Amgun' R Russian Federation
86 G3 Amhara rep Ethiopia
101 N3 Amherst see Kyaikkami
122 H8 Amherst Nova Scotia Canada
100 H1 Amherst Colorado U.S.A.
95 T2 Amherst Maine U.S.A.
95 P4 Amherst Massachusetts U.S.A.
98 G8 Amherst Nebraska U.S.A.
95 P3 Amherst New Hampshire U.S.A.
94 G5 Amherst Ohio U.S.A.
98 J4 Amherst South Dakota U.S.A.
94 H9 Amherst Virginia U.S.A.
120 G10 Amherstburg Ontario Canada
94 G10 Amherstdale West Virginia U.S.A.
123 K6 Amherst I Madeleine Is, Quebec Canada
121 O8 Amherst I Ontario Canada
99 R5 Amherst Junction Wisconsin U.S.A.
142 F4 Amherst, Mt W Australia Australia
42 D6 Amiata,Monte Italy
98 C3 Amidon North Dakota U.S.A.
141 K8 Amiens Queensland Australia
21 P2 Amiens France
116 M2 Amij,Wadi Iraq
46 E4 Amindaion Greece
73 L6 Amindivi Is Lakshadweep Indian Oc
60 N10 Amino Japan
87 H12 Amino Madagascar
116 J8 Amino Madagascar
80 C4 Amintou Namibia
119 T7 Amiou Lebanon
80 F1 'Amir Israel
73 H8 Amirante Is Indian Oc
69 G11 Amisk Alberta Canada
61 L2 Amisk L Saskatchewan Canada
59 F2 Amisus Turkey
106 F6 Amistad New Mexico U.S.A.
108 G106 Amistad Nat. Recreation Area Texas U.S.A.
80 E7 Amîta Tunisia
111 H7 Amîte L Louisiana U.S.A.
111 H11 Amite River Louisiana U.S.A.
111 D7 Amity Arkansas U.S.A.
71 J7 Amity Pennsylvania U.S.A.
75 L5 Amlekhganj Nepal
27 C13 Åmli Norway
11 C6 Amlwch Wales
100 H2 Ammanford Wales
8 C4 Ammanford Wales
129 H4 'Ammân Jordan
79 F9 'Ammân Jordan
130 E3 Amman R Brazil
73 G5 Amme Denmark
37 M6 Ammerfjallet mt Norway
77 G3 Ammarnäs Sweden
28 F6 Ammarosa mt New Terr Australia
77 G3 Ammaroo N Terr Australia
30 D8 Ammassalik see Angmagssalik
28 E4 Ammeberg Sweden
28 C6 Ammelhede Denmark
19 O13 Ambérieu-en-Bugey France
120 J8 Amberley Ontario Canada
32 L9 Amberley New Zealand
144 D5 Amberley New Zealand

Column 5

41 N2 Ammer Gebirge mt Germany
32 G6 Ammerland Germany
41 O2 Ammerland Germany
116 R2 Ammerman Mt Yukon Territory Canada
37 K5 Ammerndorf Germany
41 O1 Ammer See L Germany
29 O7 Ännättijärvi L Finland
131 E2 Amná isd Israel
101 O6 Amnon Idaho U.S.A.
68 G5 Amnat Charoen Thailand
69 G8 Amne Machin see n'ŷnémaqên Shan
80 F2 Amnun Israel
101 O4 Amoney Montana U.S.A.
21 H7 Amoenis France
21 L7 Amche France
130 H1 Amoebeurg Germany
22 B2 Amorbach Germany
131 F2 Amores R Argentina
41 G6 Amorgós isld Greece
116 N6 Amorebieta Spain
94 B8 Amorita Oklahoma U.S.A.
111 H9 Amory Mississippi U.S.A.
121 J6 Amos Quebec Canada
85 F7 Amos California U.S.A.
127 J2 Åmose Å R Denmark
65 C5 Amoy see Xiamen
128 E7 Ampah Kalimantan
70 Q10 Ampana Sulawesi Indonesia
17 H4 Ampanihy Madagascar
9 F3 Ampara Brazil
87 G12 Ampara Brazil
130 E3 Ampasimanolotra Madagascar
128 D7 Ampato, Cord. de mts Peru
70 Q10 Ampenan Indonesia
37 N7 Amper R Germany
88 G8 Amperante Mozambique
103 O9 Amphitheater Arizona U.S.A.
70 G5 Ampibaku Sulawesi
85 F7 Ampier Nigeria
9 F3 Ampleforth England
128 D6 Ampoa Sulawesi Indonesia
107 N4 Ample L Kansas U.S.A.
133 D3 Ampoa Sulawesi Indonesia
26 O9 Ampuis Norway
21 J2 Ampurdán Spain
80 D2 'Amqa Israel
122 E5 Amqui Quebec Canada
74 G8 Amravati India
52 G5 Amreli India
77 L2 Amritsar India
81 J7 Åmsele Sweden
26 K7 Åmsele Sweden
79 H4 Am Stein mt Austria
76 G2 Amstelveen Netherlands
24 Amsterdam conurbation Netherlands
25 C7 Amsterdam Netherlands
113 C7 Amsterdam Georgia U.S.A.
101 L7 Amsterdam Idaho U.S.A.
95 N4 Amsterdam New York U.S.A.
94 G5 Amsterdam Ohio U.S.A.
22 J3 Amsterdam, I Indian Oc
38 L5 Amstetten Austria
85 E3 Amtervik, V Sweden
26 J2 Amtoft Denmark
36 C3 Amtzell Germany
41 L2 Amtzell Germany
26 L7 Amuay Venezuela
114 G4 Amudar'ya R Turkmenistan/Uzbekistan
147 H5 Amund Ringness I Northwest Territories Canada
100 Q9 Amundsen B Antarctica
146 D9 Amundsen Glacier Antarctica
139 H8 Amundsen Gulf Northwest Territories Canada
146 H13 Amundsen, Mt Antarctica
146 D9 Amundsen-Scott U.S.A. Base Antarctica
101 K6 Amundsen Sea Antarctica
146 A8 Amundsen Trough Arctic Oc
112 C5 Amungen L Sweden
70 D6 Amur R Russian Federation
59 L1 Amur R Russian Federation
59 L1 Amurang Sulawesi Indonesia
59 J4 Amurang Teluk W Sulawesi Indonesia
133 D3 Amur Plateau New Zealand
144 D5 Amuri Pass New Zealand
17 F1 Amurrio Spain
26 H2 Amursk Russian Federation
59 J1 Amurskaya Oblast' prov Russian Federation
78 B3 Anadalia,Sierra de mt Spain
83 J10 Anadigama Sri Lanka
21 L8 Anadikitra isld Greece
46 E6 Andamaloa Madagascar
46 G8 Andimilos isld Greece
45 J5 Andiparos isld Greece
47 P13 Andipaxi isld Greece
47 H7 Andirin Turkey
64 C4 Andirlangar China
77 G3 Andoany Madagascar
130 H4 Andolsheim France
52 E4 Andomadze Russian Federation
100 M4 Anda Branch R New South Wales Australia
130 H10 Anadolu Daglari mt Turkey
44 B8 Anadia Brazil
26 J3 Anadja isld Indonesia
16 E2 Anadolu Daglari mt Turkey
47 N10 Anadolufeneri Turkey
17 H2 Anadolulsari Turkey
51 R2 Anadyr Russian Federation
95 Q3 Anadyr' R Russian Federation
51 R2 Anadyr, Zaliv G Russian Federation
86 G3 Amhara rep Ethiopia

Column 6

78 D2 Anatolia reg Turkey
46 E3 Anatoliki Makedhonia Kai Thráki admin region Greece
137 O6 Anatom isld Vanuatu
100 H3 Anatone Washington U.S.A.
80 E6 'Anatot Jordan
126 E2 Andros isld Bahamas
131 E2 Andros isld Bahamas
95 R2 Androscogg R New Federation
116 Q9 Andropov see Rybinsk
116 Q9 Andropov see Rybinsk
52 L6 Andrott I Lakshadweep Indian Oc
74 A5 Androshevka Ukraine
53 C8 Andrushevka Ukraine
31 L6 Andrychów Poland
55 D2 Andryushino Russian Federation
26 K2 Andselv Norway
16 E6 Andújar Spain
87 C8 Andulo Angola
27 G14 Aneby Sweden
18 H8 Ance France
85 E5 Anecon Grande pk Argentina
85 E5 Anefis Mali
113 L7 Anegada isld Virgin Is
133 E6 Anegado, B Argentina
85 E7 Aného Togo
118 K7 Aneroid Saskatchewan Canada
21 N4 Anet France
21 N4 Anet France
67 E3 Anfu China
140 B3 Angalarri R N Terr Australia
133 C2 Angamos, Pta C Chile
125 J8 Angangueo Mexico
59 H2 Ang'angxi China
56 D2 Angara R Russian Federation
147 K8 Angara Basin Arctic Oc
56 F4 Angarsk Russian Federation
140 B7 Angas Downs N Terr Australia
142 G6 Angas R W Australia Australia
138 E5 Angaston South Australia Australia
71 E3 Angat Luzon Philippines
130 E8 Angatuba Brazil
9 E3 Angebo Sweden
26 H10 Angebo Sweden
124 C3 Angel de la Guarda isld Mexico
71 E3 Angeles Luzon Philippines
128 F2 Angel Falls waterfall Venezuela
27 F15 Ångelholm Sweden
94 J4 Angelica New York U.S.A.
111 B10 Angelina R Texas U.S.A.
9 E4 Angeln reg Germany
100 J2 Angels Camp California U.S.A.
27 H12 Angelsberg Sweden
102 D3 Angels Camp California U.S.A.
27 J7 Anger Austria
26 L10 Ängersjö Sweden
26 J8 Angerdmand Germany
26 N5 Ångesan R Sweden
18 F4 Ångeson isld Sweden
21 J7 Angers France
26 L10 Ångermanälven R Sweden
26 J8 Ångermünde Germany
21 J7 Angers France
26 J8 Angerville France
19 O5 Angerville France
70 L8 Angeson isld Sweden
70 E3 Anggana Kalimantan
70 O5 Anggowala, Bk mt Sulawesi Indonesia
44 B2 Anghiari Italy
112 J2 Angier North Carolina U.S.A.
115 K5 Angikuni L Northwest Territories Canada
8 A4 Angle Wales
144 A4 Angiem, Mt New Zealand
120 D4 Angler Ontario Canada
143 D7 Anglesea Victoria Australia
11 C5 Anglesey isld Wales
8 B1 Anglesey isld Wales
19 M8 Angles sur-l'Anglin France
18 D9 Anglet France
109 L6 Angleton Texas U.S.A.
21 L8 Angliers France
21 N8 Anglin R France
Angmagssalik see Ammassalik
88 G10 Angoche Mozambique
85 B6 Angohran Iran
131 A6 Angol Chile
87 B8 Angola rep Africa
92 B4 Angola New York U.S.A.
90 K11 Angola Basin Atlantic Oc
112 K3 Angola Swamp North Carolina U.S.A.
117 F7 Angoon Alaska U.S.A.
98 G3 Angora Nebraska U.S.A.
125 M6 Angostura Mexico
125 P8 Angostura Mexico
127 M3 Angostura, I Salto cataract Colombia
124 E2 Angostura, Presa de la res Mexico
125 N9 Angostura, Psa. de la res Mexico
106 E3 Angostura Reserve South Dakota U.S.A.
21 L8 Angoulême France
79 C6 Angoumois prov France
129 H7 Angra dos Reis Brazil
45 B2 Angri Italy
131 B2 Angrie France
130 E7 Angstedt-Gräfinau Germany
68 G4 Ang Thong Thailand
98 K1 Angus Minnesota U.S.A.
88 G10 Anguilla Manitoba Canada
127 M7 Anguilla isld Lesser Antilles
45 L1 Anguilla C Newfoundland Canada
123 N6 Anguille, C Newfoundland Canada
86 E6 Angul India
90 C5 Angumu Zaire
65 D4 Angun China
130 D2 Anguruage Northern Territory Australia
99 K1 Angus Minnesota U.S.A.

Column 7

46 E7 Andritsaina Greece
106 G4 Andrix Colorado U.S.A.
87 G12 Androka Madagascar
116 Q9 Andronica I Alaska U.S.A.
46 G7 Andropov see Rybinsk
95 R2 Androscogg R New
126 E2 Andros isld Bahamas
46 G7 Andros Greece
73 L6 Androth I Lakshadweep Indian Oc
74 A5 Andros Town North Carolina U.S.A.
126 F2 Andros Town Bahamas
53 L6 Andújar Spain
31 L6 Andulo Angola
55 D2 Andulo Angola
27 G14 Aneby Sweden
18 H8 Anecto France
85 E5 Anecon Grande pk Argentina
85 E5 Anefis Mali
113 L7 Anegada isld Virgin Is
133 E6 Anegado, B Argentina
85 E7 Aného Togo
118 K7 Aneroid Saskatchewan Canada
21 N4 Anet France
67 E3 Anfu China
140 B3 Angalarri R N Terr Australia
133 C2 Angamos, Pta C Chile
125 J8 Angangueo Mexico
59 H2 Ang'angxi China
59 N3 Angara R Russian Federation
45 M4 Angara Basin Arctic Oc
21 J7 Anger Austria
41 J6 Angera Italy
41 J6 Angera Italy
27 H12 Angelholm Sweden
94 J4 Angelica New York U.S.A.
88 G10 Angelina R Texas U.S.A.
77 E6 Angeln reg Germany
45 M4 Angels Camp California U.S.A.
54 F4 Angan Russian Federation
140 B7 Angas Downs N Terr
142 G6 Angas R W Australia
138 E5 Angaston South Australia
21 J7 Angat Luzon Philippines
130 E8 Angatuba Brazil
9 E3 Angebo Sweden
26 H10 Angebo Sweden
124 C3 Angel de la Guarda isld
85 E5 Angeles Luzon Philippines
128 E7 Ancona Peru
45 O4 Ancona Italy
113 B9 Ancon de Sardinas B.de Ecuador
118 F7 Ancud Saskatchewan Canada
128 E7 Anco Peru
116 N6 Ancud Chile
94 B8 Ancud Chile
101 K6 Andreyevskaya Russian Federation
95 U1 Anderson River Australia
146 D9 Anderson River Australia
101 K6 Anderson Ranch Res Idaho
112 C5 Andersonville Georgia U.S.A.
110 L2 Andersonville Indiana U.S.A.
27 G14 Anderstorp Sweden
144 A4 Andes, Cordillera de los mts S America
98 H1 Anderyevka Russian Federation
16 F3 Andevorranto Madagascar
21 M8 Andfjord inlet Norway
18 D9 Andfjord inlet Norway
76 D2 Andhra Pradesh prov India
83 J10 Andigama Sri Lanka
21 L8 Andikíthira isld Greece
46 G6 Andilamena Madagascar
46 G8 Andimilos isld Greece
45 J5 Andiparos isld Greece
47 P13 Andipaxi isld Greece
47 H7 Andirin Turkey
64 C4 Andirlangar China
77 G3 Andoany Madagascar
130 H4 Andolsheim France
52 E4 Andomadze Russian Federation
100 M4 Anda Branch R New South Wales Australia
130 H10 Andoom Queensland Australia
44 B8 Andorra princ Pyrenees
26 J3 Andorra la Vella Andorra
16 E2 Andouille France
47 N10 Andover England
17 H2 Andover Connecticut U.S.A.
98 H2 Andover Maine U.S.A.
127 M10 Andover New Hampshire U.S.A.
26 F9 Andover New Jersey U.S.A.
95 K5 Andover New York U.S.A.
94 G5 Andover Ohio U.S.A.
98 K4 Andover South Dakota U.S.A.
9 E4 Andoversford England
130 D7 Andradas Brazil
130 D7 Andradina Brazil
116 G4 Andreanof Is Aleutian Is U.S.A.
130 E3 Andreapol' Russian Federation
12 D5 Andreas I of Man U.K.
54 N1 Andreas,C Cyprus
99 S5 Andreba Madagascar
115 R3 Andrée Land Greenland
119 T7 Andrei lândia Brazil
31 M4 Andrespol Poland
55 E2 Andreyevka Russian Federation
54 G5 Andreyevka Russian Federation
54 K8 Andreyevo Russian Federation
106 A1 Andreyevo-Ivanovka Russian Federation
55 E2 Andreyevka, Oz, L Russian Federation
65 C5 Andreyevkovichi Russian Federation
103 H6 Andrijevica Montenegro Yugoslavia

Column 8

46 E7 Andritsaina Greece
106 G4 Andrix Colorado U.S.A.
87 G12 Androka Madagascar
116 Q9 Andronica I Alaska U.S.A.
46 G7 Andros Greece
126 E2 Andros isld Bahamas
73 L6 Androth I Lakshadweep Indian Oc
74 A5 Andrushevka Ukraine
53 C8 Andrushevka Ukraine
31 L6 Andrychów Poland
55 D2 Andryushino Russian Federation
26 K2 Andselv Norway
16 E6 Andújar Spain
87 C8 Andulo Angola
27 G14 Aneby Sweden
18 H8 Ance France
85 E5 Anecon Grande pk Argentina
85 E5 Anefis Mali
113 L7 Anegada isld Virgin Is
133 E6 Anegado, B Argentina
85 E7 Aného Togo
118 K7 Aneroid Saskatchewan Canada
21 N4 Anet France
67 E3 Anfu China
140 B3 Angalarri R N Terr Australia
133 C2 Angamos, Pta C Chile
125 J8 Angangueo Mexico
59 H2 Ang'angxi China
56 D2 Angara R Russian Federation
147 K8 Angara Basin Arctic Oc
56 F4 Angarsk Russian Federation
140 B7 Angas Downs N Terr Australia
142 G6 Angas R W Australia Australia
138 E5 Angaston South Australia Australia
71 E3 Angat Luzon Philippines
130 E8 Angatuba Brazil
9 E3 Angebo Sweden
26 H10 Angebo Sweden
124 C3 Angel de la Guarda isld Mexico
71 E3 Angeles Luzon Philippines
128 F2 Angel Falls waterfall Venezuela
27 F15 Ångelholm Sweden
94 J4 Angelica New York U.S.A.
111 B10 Angelina R Texas U.S.A.
9 E4 Angeln reg Germany
100 J2 Angels Camp California U.S.A.
102 D3 Angels Camp California U.S.A.
27 H12 Angelsberg Sweden
27 J7 Anger Austria
41 J6 Angera Italy
26 L10 Ängersjö Sweden
19 O5 Angerville France
26 N5 Ångesan R Sweden
70 L8 Angeson isld Sweden
21 J7 Angers France
26 L10 Ångermanälven R Sweden
26 J8 Ångermünde Germany
21 J7 Angers France
19 O5 Angerville France
70 E3 Anggana Kalimantan
70 O5 Anggowala, Bk mt Sulawesi Indonesia
44 B2 Anghiari Italy
112 J2 Angier North Carolina U.S.A.
115 K5 Angikuni L Northwest Territories Canada
8 A4 Angle Wales
144 A4 Angiem, Mt New Zealand
120 D4 Angler Ontario Canada
143 D7 Anglesea Victoria Australia
11 C5 Anglesey isld Wales
8 B1 Anglesey isld Wales
19 M8 Angles sur-l'Anglin France
18 D9 Anglet France
109 L6 Angleton Texas U.S.A.
21 L8 Angliers France
21 N8 Anglin R France
88 G10 Angoche Mozambique
85 B6 Angohran Iran
131 A6 Angol Chile
87 B8 Angola rep Africa
92 B4 Angola New York U.S.A.
90 K11 Angola Basin Atlantic Oc
112 K3 Angola Swamp North Carolina U.S.A.
117 F7 Angoon Alaska U.S.A.
98 G3 Angora Nebraska U.S.A.
125 M6 Angostura Mexico
125 P8 Angostura Mexico
127 M3 Angostura, I Salto cataract Colombia
124 E2 Angostura, Presa de la res Mexico
125 N9 Angostura, Psa. de la res Mexico
106 E3 Angostura Reserve South Dakota U.S.A.
21 L8 Angoulême France
79 C6 Angoumois prov France
129 H7 Angra dos Reis Brazil
45 B2 Angri Italy
131 B2 Angrie France
130 E7 Angstedt-Gräfinau Germany
68 G4 Ang Thong Thailand
99 K1 Angus Minnesota U.S.A.
88 G10 Anguilla Manitoba Canada
127 M7 Anguilla isld Lesser Antilles
123 N6 Anguille, C Newfoundland Canada
86 E6 Angul India
90 C5 Angumu Zaire
65 D4 Angun China
130 D2 Anguruage Northern Territory Australia
65 C5 Anhua prov China
65 C5 Anhui prov China
130 E4 Anhumas Brazil
130 F3 Anhwei see Anhui prov China
61 O15 Ani Japan
130 E10 Aniai Japan
116 H8 Aniakchak Nat Mon and Preserve Alaska U.S.A.
21 K4 Aniche France
116 H8 Anicuns Brazil
130 E4 Anidhros isld Greece
46 H8 Anié Togo
27 G14 Anie, Pic d' mt Spain/France
18 D9 Anie, Pic d' mt Spain/France
55 D5 Anikhovka Russian Federation
21 K8 Animas R Colorado U.S.A.
106 E5 Animas New Mexico U.S.A.
106 A5 Animas Pk New Mexico U.S.A.
48 G5 Anina Romania
103 H8 Anita Arizona U.S.A.
99 M8 Anita Iowa U.S.A.
71 G5 Anitaguipan Pt Philippines
130 E10 Anitápolis Brazil

152

Aniuk — Arrats

116 J2 Aniuk R Alaska U.S.A.
59 M2 Aniva, Zaliv B Russian Federation
99 R4 Aniwa Wisconsin U.S.A.
22 E4 Anizy-le-Château France
29 M11 Anjalankoski Finland
74 D7 Anjar India
80 G4 'Anjara Jordan
67 F1 Anji China
65 G2 Anjia China
Anjiang see Qianyang
Anjiangying see Luanping
61 L11 Anjō Japan
21 H7 Anjou reg France
87 G10 Anjouan isld Comoros
87 H11 Anjozorobe Madagascar
59 J4 Anjŭ N Korea
77 L2 Anjuman reg Afghanistan
87 G12 Ankaboa, Tanjona C Madagascar
58 E5 Ankang China
78 D2 Ankara Turkey
87 H11 Ankaratra mt Madagascar
27 H14 Ankarsrum Sweden
26 J6 Ankarsund Sweden
87 G12 Ankazoabo Madagascar
99 N8 Ankeny Iowa U.S.A.
68 J6 An Khe Vietnam
33 T5 Anklam Germany
74 E8 Ankleshwar India
86 G4 Ānkober Ethiopia
16 D10 Ankod Morocco
38 H7 Ankogel mt Austria
87 E7 Ankoro Zaire
52 E6 An'kovo Russian Federation
32 G7 Ankum Germany
13 H6 Anlaby England
67 E3 Anle China
22 K4 Anlier Belgium
68 H7 An Loc Vietnam
67 B4 Anlong China
68 G5 Anlong Veng Cambodia
58 F5 Anlu China
26 F8 Ånn Sweden
25 C3 Anna Netherlands
53 F8 Anna Russian Federation
110 G4 Anna Illinois U.S.A.
94 C6 Anna Ohio U.S.A.
109 L2 Anna Texas U.S.A.
85 F1 Annaba Algeria
38 H7 Annaberg Austria
37 P2 Annaberg-Buchholz Germany
79 G4 An Nabk Syria
33 S9 Annaburg Germany
84 G4 An Nāfūrah Libya
128 G3 Annai Guyana
25 B5 Anna Jacobapolder Netherlands
61 M9 Annaka Japan
94 K8 Anna, L Virginia U.S.A.
68 G3 Annam reg Vietnam
113 E10 Anna Maria Florida U.S.A.
13 E4 Annan Scotland
141 J5 Annandale Queensland Australia
15 E5 Annandale Scotland
99 M4 Annandale Minnesota U.S.A.
13 E3 Annan Water Scotland
133 C7 Anna Pink, B Chile
142 D4 Anna Plains W Australia Australia
95 L8 Annapolis Maryland U.S.A.
122 G9 Annapolis R Nova Scotia Canada
75 K4 Annapurna mt Nepal
94 D4 Ann Arbor Michigan U.S.A.
33 O9 Annarode Germany
78 L7 An Nāsirīyah Iraq
99 R8 Annawan Illinois U.S.A.
143 C7 Annean, L W Australia Australia
21 L3 Annebault France
19 Q13 Annecy France
40 D6 Annecy,L.d' France
131 H6 Annenkov Is S Georgia
141 K2 Annerley dist Brisbane, Qnsld Australia
117 H8 Annette I Alaska U.S.A.
20 G3 Anneville-sur-Mer France
19 N14 Anneyron France
68 J6 An Nhon Vietnam
141 G2 Annie R Queensland Australia
123 P5 Annieopsquotch Mts Newfoundland Canada
58 D6 Anning He R China
28 J5 Annisse Denmark
111 L8 Anniston Alabama U.S.A.
140 D5 Annitowa N Terr Australia
40 G5 Anniviers Val d' Switzerland
Annobón isld see Pagalu isld
90 L9 Annobón isld Equat Guinea
109 N2 Annona Texas U.S.A.
19 N14 Annonay France
127 L2 Annotto Bay Jamaica
22 D2 Annœulin France
36 D5 Annweiler Germany
46 G9 Áno Arkhánai Crete Greece
99 N4 Anoka Minnesota U.S.A.
98 H7 Anoka Nebraska U.S.A.
47 P13 Áno Lefkimmi Greece
54 M1 Anopino Russian Federation
22 G4 Anor France
87 H10 Anorontany, Tanjona C Madagascar
36 B7 Anould France
46 G9 Áno Viánnos Crete Greece
47 O12 Áno Virón Greece
68 J7 An Phuoc Vietnam
65 C5 Anping China
67 C6 Anpu China
67 C6 Anpu Gang B China
58 G5 Anqing China
65 D6 Anqiu China
25 F6 Anrath Germany
67 D3 Anren China
32 H9 Anröchte Germany
22 K2 Ans Belgium
28 B5 Ansager Denmark
65 A6 Ansai China
37 K5 Ansbach Germany
40 A6 Anse France
127 H5 Anse-à-Galets Haiti
127 J5 Anse-à-Pitre Haiti
122 H5 Anse-au-Griffon Quebec Canada
126 H5 Anse-à-Veau Haiti
127 N4 Anse Bertrand Guadeloupe W Indies
126 G5 Anse d'Hainault Haiti
98 G8 Anselmo Nebraska U.S.A.
22 H3 Anseremme Belgium
139 H7 Anser Gr islds Tasmania Australia
122 B5 Anse St.Jean,L' Quebec Canada
127 L4 Anses d'Arlets, Les Martinique W Indies
59 H3 Anshan China
67 B3 Anshun China
131 B3 Ansilta pk Argentina
131 B3 Ansilta, Cord. de ra Argentina
109 P3 Ansley Louisiana U.S.A.
98 G8 Ansley Nebraska U.S.A.
140 B2 Anson B N Terr Australia
85 E5 Ansongo Mali
94 C6 Ansonia Ohio U.S.A.
120 K4 Ansonville Ontario Canada
112 G2 Ansonville North Carolina U.S.A.
28 C6 Anst Denmark
94 F8 Ansted West Virginia U.S.A.
15 F4 Anstruther Scotland
128 D6 Anta Peru
Antakya see Hatay
78 C3 Antalya Turkey
87 H11 Antananarivo Madagascar
87 H11 Antanifotsy Madagascar
87 H12 Antanimora Madagascar
146 Antarctica
90 D16 Antarctic Circle
146 D6 Antarctic Pen Antarctica
81 C10 Antares Bank Indian Oc
130 H11 Antas Brazil
130 D10 Antas,R das Brazil
15 C3 An Teallach mt Scotland
118 J8 Antelope Saskatchewan Canada
98 B1 Antelope Montana U.S.A.
98 D3 Antelope North Dakota U.S.A.
109 J2 Antelope Texas U.S.A.
101 Q9 Antelope Utah U.S.A.
87 E10 Antelope Zimbabwe
100 H7 Antelope Cr Oregon U.S.A.
130 H9 Antenor Navarro Brazil
16 D7 Antequera Spain
130 B9 Antequera,Pto Paraguay
106 D3 Antero Pk Colorado U.S.A.
106 E3 Antero Res Colorado U.S.A.
38 F8 Anterselva di Mezzo Italy
107 N4 Anthony Kansas U.S.A.
106 D9 Anthony New Mexico U.S.A.
108 A3 Anthony New Mex/Tex U.S.A.
138 C4 Anthony, L South Australia Australia
140 D4 Anthony Lagoon N Terr Australia
138 C2 Anthony,Mt South Australia Australia
85 C3 Anti Atlas mts Morocco
44 B4 Antibes France
44 B4 Antibes,C.d' France
127 N9 Antica, I Venezuela
45 N5 Anticoli Corrado Italy
122 J4 Anticosti I Quebec Canada
21 L2 Antifer,C.d' France
21 M8 Antigny France
123 K8 Antigonish Nova Scotia Canada
125 O10 Antigua Guatemala
127 P4 Antigua isld Lesser Antilles
127 O6 Antigua and Barbuda islds West Indies
127 N4 Antigues Pte. d' Guadeloupe W Indies
118 B3 Antikameg Alberta Canada
133 C5 Antilhue Chile
126 G4 Antilla Cuba
103 N3 Antimony Utah U.S.A.
Antioch see Hatay
102 C3 Antioch California U.S.A.
99 S7 Antioch Illinois U.S.A.
98 D7 Antioch Nebraska U.S.A.
18 E6 Antioche, Pertuis d' B France
128 C2 Antioquia div Colombia
80 C5 Antipatris Israel
52 D6 Antipovo Russian Federation
128 C4 Antisana mt Ecuador
119 Q9 Antler Saskatchewan Canada
98 E1 Antler North Dakota U.S.A.
107 P7 Antlers Oklahoma U.S.A.
133 C2 Antofagasta Chile
133 D3 Antofagasta de la Sierra Argentina
133 D3 Antofalla vol Argentina
109 O1 Antoine Arkansas U.S.A.
22 E2 Antoing Belgium
44 F2 Antola,Monte Italy
106 G2 Anton Colorado U.S.A.
108 E2 Anton Texas U.S.A.
87 J11 Antongila, Helodrano B Madagascar
87 G12 Antongo Madagascar
130 E9 Antonina Brazil
107 L3 Antonino Kansas U.S.A.
48 K1 Antoniny Ukraine
129 K7 Antônio R Brazil
130 G7 Antônio Carlos Brazil
130 G6 Antônio Dias Brazil
Antonio Enes see Angoche
130 C8 Antônio João Brazil
106 D4 Antonito Colorado U.S.A.
54 D10 Antonovka Ukraine
47 H1 Antonovo Bulgaria
126 D3 Antón Recio Cuba
21 P4 Antony France
140 D4 Antony Lagoon N Terr Australia
20 H5 Antrain France
52 C4 Antrea Russian Federation
36 G5 Antrefftal Germany
14 E2 Antrim co N Ireland
14 E2 Antrim N Ireland
95 P3 Antrim New Hampshire U.S.A.
95 K5 Antrim Pennsylvania U.S.A.
14 E2 Antrim Hills N Ireland
142 G4 Antrim Plat W Australia Australia
87 G11 Antsalova Madagascar
52 D5 Antsiferovo Russian Federation
87 H11 Antsirabe Madagascar
87 J11 Antsirakosy, Tanjona C Madagascar
87 H10 Antsirañana Madagascar
52 C5 Antsla Estonia
87 H10 Antsohihy Madagascar
29 N10 Anttola Finland
65 G3 Antu China
Antwerp see Antwerpen
95 M2 Antwerp New York U.S.A.
94 C5 Antwerp Ohio U.S.A.
22 H1 Antwerpen Belgium
14 E3 An Uaimh Ireland
75 L8 Anugul India
116 F6 Anukslak L Alaska U.S.A.
26 K8 Anundsjö Sweden
74 E4 Anupgarh India
83 K9 Anuradhapura Sri Lanka
Anvers see Antwerpen
45 P6 Anversa degli Abruzzi Italy
146 C4 Anvers Island Antarctica
116 G5 Anvik Alaska U.S.A.
121 P3 Anvilla Quebec Canada
117 G4 Anvil Range Yukon Territory Canada
22 C3 Anvin France
58 C3 Anxi China
67 F4 Anxi China
67 A1 An Xian China
67 D2 Anxiang China
65 C5 Anxin China
138 C5 Anxious B South Australia Australia
58 F4 Anyang China
70 K9 Anyar Java
58 C5 A'nyêmaqên Shan mts China
65 B7 Anyi China
67 E2 Anyi China
67 D7 Anyou China
117 J8 Anyox British Columbia Canada
67 E4 Anyuan China
52 J3 An'yudin Russian Federation
67 B1 Anyue China
51 Q2 Anyuy R Russian Federation
42 B3 Anza R Italy
118 F2 Anzac Alberta Canada
17 G2 Anzánigo Spain
40 H6 Anzasca, Valle Italy
18 F10 Anzat France
65 B6 Anze China
22 E2 Anzegem Belgium
56 C3 Anzhero-Sudzhensk Russian Federation
147 P7 Anzhu Os isld Russian Federation
22 E3 Anzin France
38 E5 Anzing Germany
45 N7 Anzio Italy
128 F2 Anzoátegui state Venezuela
45 K2 Anzola dell'Emilia Italy
137 O5 Aoba isld Vanuatu
59 L5 Aoga-shima isld Japan
65 D3 Aohan Qi China
18 E10 Aoiz Spain
61 O5 Aomori Japan
60 N3 Aonae Japan
144 C6 Aorangi admin region New Zealand
145 E4 Aorangi Mts New Zealand
145 D4 Aorere R New Zealand
68 D7 Ao Sawi B Thailand
40 F6 Aosta Italy
145 E3 Aotea Harbour New Zealand
85 C5 Aouker reg Mauritania
85 E3 Aoulef Algeria
67 B3 Aoxi China
60 G10 Aoya Japan
86 C1 Aozou Chad
103 P10 Apache Arizona U.S.A.
109 J1 Apache Oklahoma U.S.A.
106 B8 Apache Creek New Mexico U.S.A.
103 N8 Apache Junct Arizona U.S.A.
103 O10 Apache Pk Arizona U.S.A.
113 C7 Apalachee B Florida U.S.A.
112 C2 Apalachia Dam North Carolina U.S.A.
113 C8 Apalachicola Florida U.S.A.
128 D3 Apaporis R Colombia
130 B8 Apa.R Brazil/Paraguay
130 D7 Aparecida do Taboado Brazil
144 B7 Aparima R New Zealand
71 E1 Aparri Luzon Philippines
70 E6 Apar, Teluk B Kalimantan
145 D2 Apata New Zealand
48 E5 Apatin Serbia Yugoslavia
52 D1 Apatity Russian Federation
124 H8 Apatzingán Mexico
116 C5 Apavawook C St Lawrence I, Alaska U.S.A.
52 C5 Ape Latvia
45 M4 Apecchio Italy
119 S3 Apeganau L Manitoba Canada
25 E4 Apeldoorn Netherlands
32 G6 Apen Germany
33 O7 Apenburg Germany
32 L6 Apensen Germany
128 E6 Apere R Bolivia
112 J2 Apex North Carolina U.S.A.
41 L1 Apfingen Germany
101 L1 Apgar Montana U.S.A.
80 C5 Aphek Israel
116 E6 Aphrewn R Alaska U.S.A.
86 E5 Api Zaire
134 C1 Apia Western Samoa
129 G5 Apiacás,Serra dos mts Brazil
130 E9 Apiaí Brazil
45 R7 Apice Italy
71 J9 Api,Gunung vol Indonesia
70 E2 Apin-Apin Sabah
130 B10 Apipe Grande isld Argentina
106 F4 Apishapa R Colorado U.S.A.
70 G5 Api,Tg C Sulawesi Indonesia
145 E3 Apiti New Zealand
125 K8 Apizaco Mexico
124 H5 Apizolaya Mexico
56 F2 Aplinskiy Porog falls Russian Federation
129 L5 Apodi R Brazil
71 E4 Apo East Pass Philippines
47 Q14 Apolakkiá Rhodes Greece
37 M1 Apolda Germany
Apollonia see Sūsah
46 G8 Apollonía Greece
128 E6 Apolo Bolivia
113 F9 Apopka Florida U.S.A.
113 F9 Apopka,L Florida U.S.A.
133 G1 Aporé R Brazil
129 H3 Aporema Brazil
99 Q2 Apostle Is Michigan U.S.A.
133 F3 Apostoles Argentina
54 E9 Apostolovo Ukraine
128 G3 Apoteri Guyana
71 E4 Apo West Pass Philippines
94 E10 Appalachia Virginia U.S.A.
94 F10 Appalachian Mts U.S.A.
27 G11 Äppelbo Sweden
32 F9 Appelhülsen Germany
44 D3 Appennino Ligure mt Italy
42 C4 Appennino Tosco-Emiliano mts Italy
42 E5 Appennino Umbro Marchigiano mts Italy
36 D6 Appenweier Germany
41 K3 Appenzell canton Switzerland
13 G6 Apperley Br England
21 M3 Appeville France
41 O5 Appiano sulla Strada del Vino Italy
25 G2 Appingedam Netherlands
109 N4 Appleby Texas U.S.A.
13 F4 Appleby-in-Westmorland England
142 A2 Applecross dist Perth, W Aust Australia
8 B5 Appledore Devon England
9 G5 Appledore Kent England
102 D3 Applegate California U.S.A.
100 B7 Applegate Oregon U.S.A.
122 H8 Apple River Nova Scotia Canada
109 N4 Apple Springs Texas U.S.A.
95 S2 Appleton Maine U.S.A.
100 D4 Appleton Washington U.S.A.
99 S5 Appleton Wisconsin U.S.A.
110 B3 Appleton City Missouri U.S.A.
94 J9 Appomattox Virginia U.S.A.
54 J1 Aprelevka Russian Federation
22 J5 Apremont France
20 G8 Apremont Vendée France
27 M15 Apriki Latvia
43 E7 Aprilia Italy
46 G2 Apriltsi Bulgaria
53 E11 Apsheronsk Russian Federation
138 F6 Apsley Victoria Australia
121 M8 Apsley Ontario Canada
140 B1 Apsley Str N Terr Australia
19 O17 Apt France
45 H3 Apuane Italy
135 V6 Apua Pt Hawaiian Is
130 D8 Apucarana Brazil
130 D8 Apucarana, Serra da mts Brazil
71 D6 Apurauan Philippines
128 E2 Apure state Venezuela
128 D6 Apurímac dept Peru
48 H4 Apuseni Muntii mt Romania
88 D6 Apwa Tanzania
79 F9 'Aqaba Jordan
84 J4 Aqaba,G.of Red Sea
77 J1 Aqchah Afghanistan
78 K2 Aq Chai Iran
77 D1 Āq Qal'eh Iran
66 D4 Aqqikkol Hu L China
80 G3 'Aqraba Jordan
103 L7 Aquarius Mts Arizona U.S.A.
103 N4 Aquarius Plat Utah U.S.A.
130 B8 Aquidabán,R Paraguay
130 C7 Aquidauana Brazil
130 C6 Aquidauana,R Brazil
124 G3 Aquiles Serdán Mexico
109 K4 Aquilla Texas U.S.A.
126 H5 Aquin Haiti
45 P7 Aquino Italy
75 L6 Ara India
17 G2 Ara R Spain
80 F3 Arab R Jordan
79 F3 'Arab al Mulk Syria
38 E8 Arabba Italy
112 D6 Arabi Georgia U.S.A.
111 K12 Arabi New Orleans, Louisiana U.S.A.
Arabian Gulf see Persian Gulf
123 N3 Arabian L Quebec Canada
84 H3 Arabs Gulf Egypt
78 D1 Araç Turkey
128 F3 Araçá R Brazil
129 L6 Aracaju Brazil
130 C9 Aracanguy, Mt de Paraguay
126 G9 Aracataca Colombia
129 L4 Aracati Brazil
130 E7 Araçatuba Brazil
16 C7 Aracena Spain
16 C7 Aracena, Sa. de mts Spain
130 G5 Araçuaí Brazil
48 G4 Arad Romania
86 D2 Arada Chad
56 D5 Aradanskiy Khrebet mts Russian Federation
81 L7 Arafura Sea Aust/New Guinea
129 H7 Aragarças Brazil
78 J1 Aragats mt Armenia
61 M9 Ara-gawa R Japan
100 A6 Arago,Cape Oregon U.S.A.
17 G2 Aragón R Spain
17 G4 Aragon reg Spain
43 F11 Aragona Sicily
17 F4 Aragoncillo mt Spain
128 E2 Aragua state Venezuela
129 J6 Araguaçu Brazil
128 F2 Aragua de Barcelona Venezuela
129 H3 Araguari R Brazil
129 J7 Araguari Brazil
133 H1 Araguari R Brazil
129 J5 Araguatins Brazil
53 F12 Aragvi R Georgia
144 C5 Arahura New Zealand
61 M8 Arai Japan
79 E8 Araif el Naqa mt Egypt
80 G8 Ara'ir Jordan
85 E3 Arak Algeria
77 A2 Arāk Iran
61 N8 Arakai-yama mt Japan
128 G2 Arakaka Guyana
78 G4 Arak, Al Syria
116 A4 Arakamchechen, Ostrov isld Russian Federation
68 A2 Arakan prov Burma
68 B2 Arakan Yoma ra Burma
46 F6 Arákhova Greece
46 D5 Árakhthos R Greece
76 D4 Arakkonam India
120 C2 Ara L Ontario Canada
57 B2 Aral'sk Kazakhstan
57 A3 Aral'skoye More sea Kazakhstan/Uzbekistan
55 B6 Aralsor, Oz L Kazakhstan
26 A9 Aram Norway
141 G6 Aramac R Queensland Australia
141 H6 Aramac Queensland Australia
125 K5 Aramberri Mexico
19 N17 Aramon France
43 C7 Aranci, G Sardinia
16 E3 Aranda de Duero Spain
17 F3 Aranda de Moncayo Spain
87 B10 Arandis Namibia
145 D1 Aranga New Zealand
128 E7 Arani Bolivia
76 D4 Arani India
14 C1 Aran I Ireland
16 E4 Aranjuez Spain
8 C2 Aran Mawddwy mt Wales
89 A5 Aranos Namibia
109 L7 Aransas B Texas U.S.A.
109 K8 Aransas Pass Texas U.S.A.
130 E6 Arantes,R Brazil
137 P1 Aranuka isld Kiribati
85 D5 Araouane Mali
106 E1 Arapaho mt Colorado U.S.A.
106 H3 Arapahoe Colorado U.S.A.
98 G9 Arapahoe Nebraska U.S.A.
101 R7 Arapahoe Wyoming U.S.A.
128 E7 Arapa,L Peru
145 E4 Arapawa I New Zealand
133 F4 Arapey Uruguay
131 G3 Arapey Grande R Uruguay
130 H10 Arapiraca Brazil
78 G2 Arapkir Turkey
130 D8 Arapongas Brazil
145 E3 Arapuni New Zealand
130 E10 Araquari Brazil
78 H6 Ar'ar Saudi Arabia
80 D4 Ar'Ara Israel
133 H3 Araranguá Brazil
129 J8 Araraquara Brazil
130 F8 Araras São Paulo Brazil
130 D6 Araras,Serra das Mato Grosso Brazil
130 D9 Araras, Serra das mts Paraná Brazil
139 G6 Ararat Victoria Australia
Ararat,Mt see Bügük Ağri
129 K4 Arari Brazil
75 M5 Araria India
130 G8 Araruama L.de Brazil
78 H6 Arar,Wadi Saudi Arabia
80 D5 Aras Jordan
78 J1 Aras R Turkey
17 G5 Aras de Alpuente Spain
126 A1 Arasji Aruba W Indies
145 D2 Aratapu New Zealand
145 F3 Aratiatia New Zealand
61 O7 Arato Japan
128 F5 Araua R Brazil
128 D2 Arauca Colombia
133 C5 Arauco Chile
127 K10 Araure Venezuela
80 E2 Arav Israel
74 E6 Aravalli Range India
137 M3 Arawa Bougainville I Papua New Guinea
144 B6 Arawata R New Zealand
129 J7 Araxá Brazil
128 F1 Araya,P.de Venezuela
61 P14 Ara-zaki C Okinawa
17 G3 Arba R Spain
86 G4 Arba Minch' Ethiopia
43 C9 Arbatax Sardinia
52 G5 Arbazh Russian Federation
40 C2 Arbecey France
37 K5 Arberg Germany
78 J4 Arbīl prov Iraq
27 H12 Arboga Sweden
27 H12 Arbogaån R Sweden
40 C4 Arbois France
41 K2 Arbon Switzerland
101 N7 Arbon Idaho U.S.A.
119 O5 Arborfield Saskatchewan Canada
9 F5 Arborfield Cross England
119 U8 Arborg Manitoba Canada
99 R4 Arbor Vitae Wisconsin U.S.A.
27 H10 Arbrå Sweden
13 F1 Arbroath Scotland
102 B2 Arbuckle California U.S.A.
113 F10 Arbuckle,L Florida U.S.A.
109 K1 Arbuckle Mts Oklahoma U.S.A.
107 O7 Arbuckles, Lake of the Oklahoma U.S.A.
110 F5 Arbyrd Missouri U.S.A.
19 J5 Arc France
19 O18 Arc R France
18 E8 Arcachon France
94 J4 Arcade New York U.S.A.
118 A3 Arcadia Alberta Canada
113 F10 Arcadia Florida U.S.A.
94 A6 Arcadia Indiana U.S.A.
107 Q4 Arcadia Kansas U.S.A.
111 D9 Arcadia Louisiana U.S.A.
99 U5 Arcadia Michigan U.S.A.
110 F4 Arcadia Missouri U.S.A.
98 G8 Arcadia Nebraska U.S.A.
94 D5 Arcadia Ohio U.S.A.
107 N6 Arcadia Oklahoma U.S.A.
99 P5 Arcadia Wisconsin U.S.A.
95 T2 Arcadia Nat. Park Maine U.S.A.
43 G8 Arcangelo,S Italy
94 C7 Arcanum Ohio U.S.A.
21 L8 Arçay France
102 G3 Arc Dome mt Nevada U.S.A.
45 P6 Arce Italy
125 J8 Arcelia Mexico
25 F6 Arcen Netherlands
45 N4 Arcévia Italy
46 F1 Archar Bulgaria
95 M5 Archbald Pennsylvania U.S.A.
94 C5 Archbold Ohio U.S.A.
112 H2 Archdale North Carolina U.S.A.
141 F2 Archer R Queensland Australia
113 E8 Archer Florida U.S.A.
141 F2 Archer Bend Nat. Park Queensland Australia
109 J2 Archer City Texas U.S.A.
141 K2 Archerfield Airfield Brisbane, Qnsld Australia
141 H3 Archer Pt Queensland Australia
119 O6 Archerwill Saskatchewan Canada
40 E1 Arches France
103 P3 Arches Nat. Park Utah U.S.A.
110 B3 Archie Missouri U.S.A.
21 M8 Archigny France
119 M8 Archive Saskatchewan Canada
106 C5 Archuleta New Mexico U.S.A.
18 H4 Arcis sur Aube France
138 C2 Arckaringa R South Australia Australia
101 M6 Arco Idaho U.S.A.
98 K5 Arco Minnesota U.S.A.
119 P9 Arcola Saskatchewan Canada
99 S10 Arcola Illinois U.S.A.
111 F8 Arcola Mississippi U.S.A.
45 K1 Árcole Italy
18 H6 Arconce R France
138 D4 Arcoona South Australia Australia
131 B7 Arco, Paso de Arg/Chile
130 F7 Arcos Brazil
16 D8 Arcos de la Frontera Spain
16 B3 Arcos de Vale de Vez Portugal
17 G3 Arcos,Sierra de mt Spain
76 D4 Arcot India
20 D4 Arcouest,l' France
130 H10 Arcoverde Brazil
19 J5 Arc-Senans France
147 F4 Arctic Bay Northwest Territories Canada
90 J2 Arctic Circle
116 D4 Arctic Lagoon Alaska U.S.A.
147 Arctic Ocean
114 F4 Arctic Red River Northwest Territories Canada
116 P2 Arctic Village Alaska U.S.A.
146 D3 Arctowski, Henryk Poland Base Antarctica
45 L1 Arcugnano Italy
22 E5 Arcy-Ste. Restitue France
44 G2 Arda R Italy
78 M2 Ardabīl Iran
38 L5 Ardagger Austria
78 J1 Ardahan Turkey
77 C3 Ardakan Esfahān Iran
77 B4 Ardal Iran
27 C10 Årdal Opland Norway
27 B12 Årdal Rogaland Norway
14 C2 Ardara Ireland
118 K7 Ardath Saskatchewan Canada
52 F6 Ardatov Russian Federation
120 K7 Ardbeg Ontario Canada
12 B2 Ardbeg Scotland
45 N6 Ardea Italy
18 H8 Ardèche dept France
14 E3 Ardee Ireland
119 S8 Arden Manitoba Canada
121 O8 Arden Ontario Canada
103 J5 Arden Nevada U.S.A.
138 E4 Arden Mt South Australia Australia
18 H3 Ardennes dept France
22 H4 Ardennes France
21 O8 Ardentes France
12 D1 Ardentinny Scotland
77 C3 Ardestān Iran
15 D3 Ardgay Scotland
14 F2 Ardglass N Ireland
46 E4 Ardhéa Greece
16 C6 Ardila,R Spain
119 M9 Ardill Saskatchewan Canada
124 H6 Ardilla, Cerro La pk Mexico
46 G3 Ardino Bulgaria
18 E10 Ardisa Spain
70 P9 Ardjasa Java
70 O9 Ardjuna,G mt Java
145 F3 Ardkeen New Zealand
118 D6 Ardley Alberta Canada
15 D4 Ardlui Scotland
12 C2 Ardminish Scotland
139 H6 Ardmona Victoria Australia
118 G4 Ardmore Alberta Canada
107 N7 Ardmore Oklahoma U.S.A.
98 C6 Ardmore South Dakota U.S.A.
110 K6 Ardmore Tennessee U.S.A.
14 D5 Ardmore B Ireland
15 B4 Ardnamurchan Pt Scotland
15 B5 Ardnave Pt Scotland
98 J1 Ardoch North Dakota U.S.A.
22 B2 Ardres France
12 C1 Ardrishaig Scotland
138 E5 Ardrossan South Australia Australia
118 D5 Ardrossan Alberta Canada
15 D5 Ardrossan Scotland
14 F2 Ards Pen N Ireland
12 B2 Ardtalla Scotland
48 H3 Ardud Romania
15 C3 Ardvasar Scotland
53 F7 Ardym Russian Federation
26 F8 Åre Sweden
26 N4 Areavaara Sweden
127 L5 Arecibo Puerto Rico
131 F5 Areco R Argentina
48 J5 Areful Romania
129 L4 Areia Branca Brazil
45 Q7 Areinzo Italy
118 K6 Arelee Saskatchewan Canada
27 E12 Aremark Norway
36 B3 Aremberg Germany
118 H9 Arena Saskatchewan Canada
71 E6 Arena Philippines
95 N4 Arena New York U.S.A.
133 C7 Arenales mt Chile
130 C4 Arenápolis Brazil
71 F4 Arena Pt Luzon Philippines
124 E6 Arena, Pta C Mexico
16 D4 Arenas de S.Pedro Spain
128 D8 Arenas,Pta C Chile
32 F7 Arenberg reg Germany
27 C13 Arendal Norway
22 J1 Arendonk Belgium
33 O7 Arendsee Germany
32 L10 Arenshausen Germany
19 Q12 Arenthon France
28 D2 Arentsminde Denmark
17 J3 Arenys de Mar Spain
46 E8 Areópolis Greece
128 D7 Arequipa Peru
129 H4 Arere Brazil
18 E8 Arés France
16 D3 Arévalo Spain
140 B6 Areyonga N Terr Australia
42 D5 Arezzo Italy
46 E7 Arfará Greece
17 F2 Arga R Spain
140 D5 Argadargada N Terr Australia
58 E2 Argalant Mongolia
16 E5 Argamasilla de Alba Spain
16 E4 Arganda Spain
16 B4 Arganil Portugal
71 F6 Argao Philippines
45 P6 Argatone, M mt Italy
55 D3 Argayash Russian Federation
55 D3 Argazi, Oz Russian Federation
18 H10 Argelès sur Mer France
41 L2 Argen R Germany
21 K3 Argences France
19 Q18 Argens R France
117 P10 Argenta British Columbia Canada
45 L2 Argenta Italy
101 N4 Argenta Montana U.S.A.
21 K4 Argentan France
42 D6 Argentario,Monte Italy
18 G7 Argentat France
44 B3 Argentera Mt Italy
21 P4 Argenteuil Seine-et-Oise France
123 S6 Argentia Newfoundland Canada
40 E6 Argentières France
44 C4 Argentina R Italy
131 D5 Argentina rep S America
146 E7 Argentina Range mts Antarctica
90 E13 Argentine Basin Atlantic Oc
133 C8 Argentino,L Argentina
20 A4 Argenton France
21 K7 Argenton R France
21 K8 Argenton-Château France
21 O8 Argenton-sur-Creuse France
122 C3 Argent,R à l' Quebec Canada
21 J5 Argentre France
21 H5 Argentré-du-Plessis France
18 G5 Argent sur Sauldre France
48 J5 Argeş R Romania
48 J5 Argeş reg Romania
48 J6 Argeşel R Romania
77 J4 Arghandab R Afghanistan
77 K4 Arghastan R Afghanistan
84 J6 Argo Sudan
20 B5 Argol France
46 F7 Argolikós Kólpos B Greece
107 N4 Argonia Kansas U.S.A.
22 J5 Argonne reg France
99 S4 Argonne Wisconsin U.S.A.
70 O9 Argopura G mt Java
101 N5 Argora Idaho U.S.A.
46 F7 Argos Greece
94 A5 Argos Indiana U.S.A.
46 E4 Árgos Orestikón Greece
20 H4 Argouges France
18 D10 Arguedas Spain
21 O2 Argueil France
20 F5 Arguenon R France
59 H1 Argun R China/Rus Fed
85 E6 Argungu Nigeria
146 G10 Argus, Dome ice dome Antarctica
102 G6 Argus Ra California U.S.A.
98 J2 Argusville North Dakota U.S.A.
21 N8 Argy France
122 G10 Argyle Nova Scotia Canada
112 E6 Argyle Georgia U.S.A.
94 E3 Argyle Michigan U.S.A.
98 K1 Argyle Minnesota U.S.A.
99 R7 Argyle Wisconsin U.S.A.
142 G3 Argyle, L W Australia Australia
Argyll co see Strathclyde and Highland regions
6 M6 Argyll oil rig North Sea
Argyrokastron see Gjirokastër
65 E3 Ar Horquin Qi China
28 E4 Århus Denmark
28 E4 Århus co Denmark
145 E3 Aria New Zealand
139 H5 Ariah Pk New South Wales Australia
60 D13 Ariake-kai G Japan
87 C11 Ariamsvlei Namibia
43 G7 Ariano Irpino Italy
45 M2 Ariano Nel Polésine Italy
128 D3 Ariari R Colombia
73 L8 Ari Atoll Maldives
85 D6 Aribinda Burkina
128 D7 Arica Chile
128 D4 Arica Colombia
45 N6 Ariccia Italy
123 M8 Arichat C Breton I, Nova Scotia
60 J11 Arida Japan
60 J11 Arida-gawa R Japan
85 B3 Aridal, Sabkhat salt lake Western Sahara
143 E10 Arid, C W Australia Australia
83 J12 Aride I Seychelles
Arid I see Rakitu I
18 G9 Ariège dept France
18 G10 Ariège R France
80 D5 Ari'el Jordan
100 C4 Ariel Washington U.S.A.
48 H4 Arieş R Romania
80 G8 Ariha Jordan
79 G3 Arīḩā Syria
106 H2 Arikaree R Colorado U.S.A.
60 C13 Arikawa Japan
29 K4 Arild Sweden
48 F7 Arilje Serbia Yugoslavia
128 F5 Arima Brazil
60 J11 Arima Japan
127 O2 Arima Trinidad
101 N7 Arimo Idaho U.S.A.
128 G3 Arinda Guyana
129 G6 Arinos R Brazil
129 J7 Arinos Brazil
101 M9 Arinosa Utah U.S.A.
99 L8 Arion Iowa U.S.A.
127 P1 Aripo, Mt Trinidad
128 D2 Ariporo R Colombia
128 F5 Aripuana R Brazil
128 F5 Ariquemes Brazil
130 D5 Ariranha R Brazil
15 C4 Arisaig Scotland
79 D7 'Arîsh, El Egypt
117 J9 Aristazabal I British Columbia Canada
133 D7 Aristizábal, C Argentina
111 L10 Ariton Alabama U.S.A.
43 C9 Aritzo Sardinia
103 N10 Arivaca Arizona U.S.A.
87 H11 Arivonimamo Madagascar
17 F3 Ariza Spain
18 F9 Arize R France
133 D5 Arizona Argentina
103 L7 Arizona state U.S.A.
124 D2 Arizpe Mexico
27 F12 Årjäng Sweden
26 J5 Arjeplog Sweden
128 D1 Arjona Colombia
16 E7 Arjona Spain
51 O2 Arka Russian Federation
110 F7 Arkabutla Res Mississippi U.S.A.
53 F8 Arkadak Russian Federation
109 O1 Arkadelphia Arkansas U.S.A.
55 E5 Arkalyk Kazakhstan
109 O1 Arkansas state U.S.A.
110 C6 Arkansas R Arkansas U.S.A.
111 E8 Arkansas City Arkansas U.S.A.
107 O4 Arkansas City Kansas U.S.A.
111 E7 Arkansas Post Nat. Mem Arkansas U.S.A.
84 G5 Arkanu Jebel mt Libya
138 E4 Arkaroola South Australia Australia
47 J9 Arkása Kárpathos I Greece
66 D4 Arkatag mts China
117 F5 Arkell,Mt Yukon Territory Canada
27 G15 Arkelstorp Sweden
47 V14 Arkhángelos Rhodes Greece
52 F3 Arkhangel'sk Russian Federation
53 F11 Arkhangel'skoye Russian Federation
59 K2 Arkhara Russian Federation
53 D7 Arkhipovka Russian Federation
53 D8 Arkino Russian Federation
14 E4 Arklow Ireland
47 H7 Árkoi isld Greece
120 J9 Arkona Ontario Canada
30 H1 Arkona Germany
27 J13 Arkösund Sweden
94 K4 Arkport New York U.S.A.
52 H6 Arkul' Russian Federation
95 N4 Arkville New York U.S.A.
27 J12 Ärla Sweden
18 H7 Arlanc France
16 E2 Arlanza R Spain
41 M3 Arlberg pass Austria
101 L2 Arlee Montana U.S.A.
19 N17 Arles Bouches du Rhône France
18 G10 Arles Pyrénées-Orientales France
22 E3 Arleux France
100 J5 Arling Idaho U.S.A.
8 D4 Arlingham England
103 M8 Arlington Arizona U.S.A.
102 G8 Arlington California U.S.A.
106 G3 Arlington Colorado U.S.A.
113 F7 Arlington Florida U.S.A.
112 C6 Arlington Georgia U.S.A.
99 P7 Arlington Iowa U.S.A.
107 M4 Arlington Kansas U.S.A.
110 G5 Arlington Kentucky U.S.A.
99 M5 Arlington Minnesota U.S.A.
98 K8 Arlington Nebraska U.S.A.
94 D6 Arlington Ohio U.S.A.
100 E4 Arlington Oregon U.S.A.
98 J5 Arlington South Dakota U.S.A.
110 G6 Arlington Tennessee U.S.A.
109 N9 Arlington Texas U.S.A.
95 O3 Arlington Vermont U.S.A.
95 K8 Arlington Virginia U.S.A.
117 M11 Arlington Washington U.S.A.
101 T8 Arlington Wyoming U.S.A.
99 S7 Arlington Heights Illinois U.S.A.
110 E4 Arlington Res Missouri U.S.A.
85 F5 Arlit Niger
22 K4 Arlon Belgium
140 C6 Arltunga N Terr Australia
107 Q4 Arma Kansas U.S.A.
118 E8 Armada Alberta Canada
143 B9 Armadale W Australia Australia
12 E2 Armadale Scotland
122 B7 Armagh Quebec Canada
14 E2 Armagh co N Ireland
14 E2 Armagh N Ireland
18 F9 Armagnac reg France
18 H5 Armançon R France
47 H9 Armathia isld Greece
13 F4 Armathwaite England
53 F10 Armavir Russian Federation
Armaynskaya S.S.R. see Armenia
128 C3 Armenia Colombia
78 K1 Armenia rep E Europe
48 G5 Armeniş Romania
22 D2 Armentières France
21 M4 Armentières Eure France
101 P2 Armington Montana U.S.A.
101 S6 Arminto Wyoming U.S.A.
119 Q6 Armit Saskatchewan Canada
9 E2 Armitage England
55 E3 Armizonskoye Russian Federation
119 N5 Armley Saskatchewan Canada
98 H6 Armour South Dakota U.S.A.
98 G1 Armourdale North Dakota U.S.A.
120 D3 Arms Ontario Canada
36 E4 Armsheim Germany
101 N5 Armstead Montana U.S.A.
140 B3 Armstrong R N Terr Australia
117 O10 Armstrong British Columbia Canada
99 T9 Armstrong Illinois U.S.A.
99 M6 Armstrong Iowa U.S.A.
110 D2 Armstrong Missouri U.S.A.
109 K9 Armstrong Texas U.S.A.
59 L2 Armu R Russian Federation
74 H9 Armur India
47 J4 Armutcuk Dağ mt Turkey
47 K4 Armutlu Turkey
53 D10 Armyansk Ukraine
28 B7 Arnå R Denmark
21 L6 Arnage France
46 F4 Arnaía Greece
28 R9 Arnarstapi Iceland
118 D1 Arnaud Manitoba Canada
115 M6 Arnaud,R Quebec Canada
79 C3 Arnauti, C Cyprus
18 J5 Arnay le Duc France
28 B4 Arnborg Denmark
37 P5 Arnbruck Germany
33 Q7 Arneburg Germany
18 D10 Arnedo Spain
98 C2 Arnegard North Dakota U.S.A.
22 C2 Arneke France
26 M6 Arnemark Sweden
25 A6 Arnemuiden Netherlands
27 E11 Årnes Norway
107 L5 Arnett Oklahoma U.S.A.
94 F9 Arnett West Virginia U.S.A.
28 R9 Arngerdhareyri Iceland
25 E5 Arnhem Netherlands
140 D1 Arnhem,C N Terr Australia
140 C2 Arnhem Land reg N Terr Australia
140 C2 Arnhem Land Aboriginal Land N Terr Australia
21 N4 Arnières France
45 H4 Arno R Italy
138 D5 Arno Bay South Australia Australia
102 D3 Arnold California U.S.A.
110 F3 Arnold Missouri U.S.A.
98 F8 Arnold Nebraska U.S.A.
94 H6 Arnold Pennsylvania U.S.A.
99 L6 Arnolds Park Iowa U.S.A.
38 J8 Arnoldstein Austria
21 P7 Arnon R France
119 V3 Arnot Manitoba Canada
26 L1 Arnöy Norway
16 B2 Arnoya R Spain
12 D1 Arnprior Scotland
32 G10 Arnsberg Germany
13 F5 Arnside England
37 K2 Arnstadt Germany
37 L3 Arnstein Germany
37 O6 Arnstorf Germany
121 L4 Arntfield Quebec Canada
28 B6 Arnum Denmark
128 F2 Aro R Venezuela
127 K9 Aroa Venezuela
87 C11 Aroab Namibia
46 E7 Aroánia mt Greece
124 H4 Arocha Mexico
130 C7 Aroeira Brazil
32 K10 Arolsen Germany
55 E3 Aromashevo Russian Federation
21 J5 Aron France
21 J5 Aron R Mayenne France
42 B3 Arona Italy
122 E7 Aroostook New Brunswick Canada
95 S7 Aroostook R Maine U.S.A.
116 E6 Aropuk L Alaska U.S.A.
137 Q2 Arorae isld Kiribati
71 F4 Aroroy Philippines
28 D6 Arøsund Denmark
127 O2 Arouca Trinidad
17 F9 Aroui, Mt Morocco
145 F3 Arowhana mt New Zealand
106 G3 Aroya Colorado U.S.A.
109 M3 Arp Texas U.S.A.
57 G4 Arpa Kyrgyzstan
18 G8 Arpajon France
21 P4 Arpajon France
48 J5 Arpasu de Jos Romania
55 D1 Arpavla Russian Federation
120 K4 Arpin Ontario Canada
45 P6 Arpino Italy
45 L1 Arquà Petrarca Italy
45 L1 Arquà Polesine Italy
21 N2 Arques R France
22 C2 Arques Pas-de-Calais France
21 N2 Arques-la-Bataille France
80 E2 'Arraba Israel
141 F7 Arrabury Queensland Australia
36 B6 Arracourt France
20 E6 Arradon France
131 D2 Arraga Argentina
16 C4 Arrago R Spain
129 J6 Arraias Brazil
16 B6 Arraiolos Portugal
14 C4 Arra Mts Ireland
119 Q7 Arran Saskatchewan Canada
15 C5 Arran isld Scotland
111 M11 Arran Florida U.S.A.
80 E4 'Arrana Jordan
117 H8 Arrandale British Columbia Canada
78 G4 Ar Raqqah Syria
84 F4 Ar Rāqūbah Libya
22 D3 Arras Pas-de-Calais France
79 G4 Ar Rastan Syria
18 F9 Arrats R France

Ref	Name
28 B5	Arre Denmark
18 F10	Arreau France
128 E3	Arrecifal Colombia
85 B3	Arrecife Canary Is
28 C9	Arrée,Mtgne.d' France
28 J5	Arrese L Denmark
106 C9	Arrey New Mexico U.S.A.
45 L4	Arrezzo reg Italy
38 J8	Arriach Austria
125 N9	Arriaga Mexico
106 C2	Arriba Colorado U.S.A.
141 G6	Arrilalah Queensland Australia
28 B6	Arrild Denmark
9 F3	Arrington England
143 B8	Arrino W Australia Australia
12 D1	Arrochar Scotland
133 G4	Arroio Grande Brazil
21 J3	Arromanches France
16 C5	Arronches Portugal
44 M6	Arrone R Italy
18 F9	Arros R France
21 N5	Arroux France
18 H6	Arroux R France
101 Q2	Arrow Cr Montana U.S.A.
117 P10	Arrowhead British Columbia Canada
119 Q2	Arrow L Ontario Canada
14 C2	Arrow,L Ireland
117 O10	Arrow Park British Columbia Canada
110 D2	Arrow Rock Missouri U.S.A.
100 K6	Arrowrock Res Idaho U.S.A.
138 F4	Arrowsmith Mt New South Wales Australia
144 C5	Arrowsmith, Mt New Zealand
140 D2	Arrowsmith Pt N Terr Australia
144 B6	Arrowtown New Zealand
118 D8	Arrow Wood Alberta Canada
16 C5	Arroyo de la Luz Spain
108 F6	Arroyo de la Zorra r Mexico
131 F6	Arroyo Grande R Argentina
102 D6	Arroyo Grande California U.S.A.
106 E5	Arroyo Hondo New Mexico U.S.A.
131 F4	Arroyo Negro R Uruguay
103 J8	Arroyo Seco R California U.S.A.
128 F6	Arroyos,L de Los Bolivia
130 B9	Arroyos-y-Esteros Paraguay
130 C4	Arruda Brazil
78 G4	Ar Ruşāfah Syria
79 H3	Ar Ruwaydah Syria
28 D3	Års Denmark
77 C5	Arsenjan Iran
118 J3	Arsenault L Saskatchewan Canada
117 Q3	Arseno L Northwest Territories Canada
59 K3	Arsen'yev Russian Federation
55 C3	Arshinka Russian Federation
86 G4	Ārsi prov Ethiopia
41 Q6	Arsiero Italy
76 C4	Arsikere India
52 G6	Arsk Russian Federation
26 J9	Årskogen Sweden
57 G4	Arslanbal Kyrgyzstan
45 O5	Arsoli Italy
19 K3	Ars-sur-Moselle France
27 J11	Årsunda Sweden
79 F2	Arsuz Turkey
22 D5	Arsy France
46 D5	Árta Greece
18 E4	Artá Majorca
80 D7	Artas Jordan
98 G4	Artas South Dakota U.S.A.
17 K5	Artá,Sierra de,Mt Majorca
124 H8	Arteaga Mexico
59 K3	Artem Russian Federation
19 P13	Artemare France
126 C3	Artemisa Cuba
51 J3	Artemovsk Russian Federation
54 G7	Artemovka Ukraine
56 D4	Artemovsk Russian Federation
53 F9	Artemovskiy Russian Federation
45 N6	Artena Italy
21 O5	Artenay France
33 O10	Artern Germany
17 H3	Artesa de Segre Spain
46 E5	Artesia see Mosonmag...
111 H8	Artesia Mississippi U.S.A.
98 J5	Artesian South Dakota U.S.A.
109 H7	Artesia Wells Texas U.S.A.
26 G6	Artfjället mt Sweden
121 T6	Artabaska Quebec Canada
18 E9	Arthez France
21 O3	Arthies France
21 O8	Arthon France
20 G7	Arthon-en-Retz France
139 H8	Arthur R Tasmania Australia
110 H2	Arthur R Illinois U.S.A.
98 E8	Arthur R Nebraska U.S.A.
98 J2	Arthur North Dakota U.S.A.
109 M2	Arthur City Texas U.S.A.
138 E4	Arthur,L South Australia Australia
139 H8	Arthur,L Tasmania Australia
142 E4	Arthur, Mt W Australia Australia
145 D4	Arthur New Zealand
141 K5	Arthur Pt Queensland Australia
143 B10	Arthur River W Australia Australia
144 C5	Arthur's Pass New Zealand
126 G2	Arthur's Town Cat I Bahamas
55 C3	Arti Russian Federation
146 G3	Artigas Uruguay Base Antarctica
133 F4	Artigas Uruguay
114 J5	Artillery L Northwest Territories Canada
29 M11	Artjärvi Finland
118 H6	Artland Saskatchewan Canada
33 M6	Artlenburg Germany
22 G3	Artois prov France
102 B2	Artois California U.S.A.
22 D3	Artois Collines d' France
46 E6	Artotina Turkey
78 F1	Artova Turkey
	Artsakan Nor see Qagan Nur L
48 M6	Artsiz Ukraine
66 B4	Artux China
129 A1	Aru Halmahera Indonesia
86 F5	Aru L Zaire
80 E8	Arudy France
80 E8	Arugot R Jordan
136 G3	Aru,Kep islds Moluccas Indonesia
25 D2	Arum Netherlands
128 H4	Arumã Brazil
61 Q12	Arume B Okinawa
75 Q4	Arunachal Pradesh prov India
9 G6	Arundel England
110 C4	Arundel New Zealand
9 F5	Arun,R England
28 D6	Arup Denmark
76 D6	Aruppukkottai India
80 D5	'Arūra Jordan
88 F3	Arusha Tanzania
136 C3	Arus,Tg C Sulawesi Indonesia
70 K5	Arut R Kalimantan
70 K5	Arut,Tg C Kalimantan
83 K9	Aruvi Aru R Sri Lanka
101 T5	Arvada Wyoming U.S.A.
101 T5	Arvada Colorado U.S.A.
58 D2	Arvayheer Mongolia
26 K5	Arve R France
26 K5	Arvestuottar mt Sweden

Ref	Name
74 H8	Arvi India
121 T4	Arvida Quebec Canada
26 K6	Arvidsjaur Sweden
27 F12	Arvika Sweden
102 F6	Arvin California U.S.A.
74 J9	Arvonia Virginia U.S.A.
65 E1	Arxan China
147 Q9	Ary Russian Federation
55 C3	Aryazh Russian Federation
47 O13	Aryirádhes Greece
46 G9	Aryiroúpolis Crete Greece
51 K5	Aryk-Balyk Kazakhstan
57 E4	Arys' R Kazakhstan
57 E4	Arys' Kazakhstan
57 D2	Arys,Ozero L Kazakhstan
20 E6	Arz R France
20 F6	Arzal, Barrage d' dam France
52 F6	Arzamas Russian Federation
20 D6	Arzano France
37 N3	Arzberg Germany
37 L5	Arzberg mt Germany
32 K8	Ärzen Germany
37 L5	Arzew Algeria
36 B3	Arzfeld Germany
53 F10	Arzgir Russian Federation
41 O6	Arzignano Italy
41 N3	Arzl Austria
20 E6	Arzon France
16 B2	Arzúa Spain
22 K1	As Syria/Lebanon
37 N3	Aš Czechoslovakia
8 N	Ås Norway
28 E2	Åsa Denmark
27 F14	Åsa Sweden
87 C11	Asab Namibia
74 D1	Asadābād Afghanistan
69 D11	Asadābād Iran
60 G10	Asahi R Japan
61 O10	Asahi Chiba Japan
60 Q2	Asahi-dake mt Japan
60 Q2	Asahi-dake mt Japan
60 Q2	Asahikawa Japan
86 H3	Āsala L Ethiopia
61 M9	Asama yama vol Japan
65 G6	Asan Man B S Korea
75 M7	Ansansol India
84 F5	Åsarna Sweden
84 K4	Asawanwah Libya
36 C2	Asbach Germany
71 C3	Asbakin W Irian
55 D3	Asbest Russian Federation
121 T7	Asbestos Quebec Canada
89 C7	Asbestos Mts S Africa
107 Q4	Asbury Missouri U.S.A.
110 B4	Asbury Park New Jersey U.S.A.
90 B12	Ascension isld Atlantic Oc
128 F7	Ascensión Bolivia
124 E2	Ascensión Chihuahua Mexico
126 A4	Ascension Curaçao W Indies
37 O6	Ascha Germany
38 L5	Ascheberg Germany
33 M4	Ascheberg Nordrhein-Westalen Germany
32 G9	Aschendorf Germany
32 F6	Aschères-le-Marché France
86 G4	Åsele Sweden
26 J7	Åsele Sweden
28 E8	Åsen Sweden
27 G10	Åsen Sweden
32 K7	Asendorf Germany
46 G3	Asenovgrad Bulgaria
27 B13	Åseral Norway
79 G5	Aşfar, Tall al mt Syria
22 G5	Asfeld-la-ville France
17 G4	Asfordby England
80 C8	Ash R Israel
52 J5	Ashan Russian Federation
55 C3	Ashap Russian Federation
9 E1	Ashbourne England
112 D6	Ashburn Georgia U.S.A.
142 B6	Ashburton R W Australia Australia
8 C6	Ashburton England
144 C5	Ashburton Ra N Terr Australia
140 C4	Ashburton Ra N Terr Australia

Ref	Name
60 R2	Ashoro Japan
80 B7	Ashqelon Israel
78 J4	Ash Sharqat Iraq
72 F6	Ash Shaykh' Uthmān Yemen
72 F6	Ash Shihr Yemen
84 E4	Ash Shuwayrif Libya
94 G5	Ashtabula,L Ohio U.S.A.
98 J2	Ashtabula,L North Dakota U.S.A.
74 F9	Ashti India
77 A4	Ashtián Iran
121 O7	Ashton Ontario Canada
101 O5	Ashton Idaho U.S.A.
99 R8	Ashton Illinois U.S.A.
94 B3	Ashton Michigan U.S.A.
98 H5	Ashton South Dakota U.S.A.
13 F6	Ashton-in-Makerfield England
142 F3	Ashton Ra W Australia Australia
13 F6	Ashton-under-Lyne England
115 N7	Ashuanipi,L Labrador, Nfld Canada
72 F6	Ashur Iraq
84 E4	Ashuriyah, Al Iraq
111 K8	Ashville Alabama U.S.A.
79 G3	'Āsi R Syria/Lebanon
42 D3	Asiago Italy
71 C2	Asia Pulau Pulau islds Indonesia
71 F4	Asid Gulf Philippines
124 H6	Asientos Mexico
45 K1	Asigliano Ven Italy
75 L9	Asika India
85 C1	Asilah Morocco
71 A1	Asimiro Halmahera Indonesia
43 B7	Asinara, Golfo dell' Sardinia
43 B7	Asinara, I Sardinia
56 C3	Asino Russian Federation
78 H2	Asiale Turkey
53 D10	Askaniya Nova Ukraine
80 D5	Askar R Jordan
71 M9	Askara isld Indonesia
86 F7	Askeaton Ireland
14 C4	Askeaton Adare Ireland
27 D12	Asker Norway
13 G6	Askern England
27 G13	Askersund Sweden
72 H1	Askīkale Iran
26 J7	Åskilje Sweden
112 K2	Askim Norway
55 C3	Askin North Carolina U.S.A.
58 G7	Askino Russian Federation
71 M9	Askira France
27 M11	Askola Finland
65 J3	Askol'd, O isld Russian Federation
28 C6	Askov Denmark
99 O3	Askov Minnesota U.S.A.
13 F5	Askrigg England
27 A10	Askvoll Norway
84 A3	Asl Egypt
79 E2	Aslanpaşa Turkey
79 E2	Aslankÿ Dere str Turkey
74 D1	Asmar Afghanistan
97 F3	Asmara see Āsmera
86 G2	Āsmera Ethiopia
29 K5	Äsnen Sweden
28 F5	Åsnæs pen Denmark
42 F6	Aso R Italy
21 J3	Asnelles France
27 E11	Åsnes Sweden
27 G15	Åsnen Sweden
129 G3	Asoenangka Brazil
45 J1	Asola Italy
28 S9	Asólfsstadhir Iceland
60 C11	Asó-wan B Japan
60 zan vol Japan	
36 G6	Aspach Germany
48 C3	Aspang Austria
110 K7	Aspås Sweden
27 J8	Aspås Sweden
17 G6	Aspe Spain
106 D3	Aspen Colorado U.S.A.
101 P8	Aspen Wyoming U.S.A.
118 D6	Aspen Beach Prov. Park Alberta Canada
21 P5	Asperg Germany
38 G5	Asperup Denmark
109 M3	Aspermont Texas U.S.A.
19 P16	Aspremont France
45 P13	Asprókavos, Akr C Greece
43 G10	Asprókavos, Akra C Greece
123 M7	Aspy B C Breton I, Nova Scotia Canada
118 K6	Asquith Saskatchewan Canada
79 H3	Aş Şa'an Syria
79 H2	Assad-Abad Afghanistan
74 D3	Aş Safirah Syria
21 K3	Assais-les-Jumeaux France
75 O5	Assam prov India
84 E2	Assamakka Niger
74 B2	Assateague I Maryland U.S.A.
22 G2	Asse Belgium
21 J2	Asse R France
119 V2	Assean L Manitoba Canada
118 L9	Assegai R Swaziland
85 F4	Assekaifaf Algeria
85 F4	Assekreme mt Algeria
32 K5	Assel Germany
21 K5	Asse le Boisne France
36 F3	Asselborn Luxembourg
32 G3	Assen Germany
25 F4	Assen Netherlands
28 C5	Assens Århus Denmark
28 F7	Assens Fyn Denmark
20 F7	Assérac France
32 K8	Assesse Belgium
122 J2	Assigny,L Quebec Canada
118 L9	Assiniboia Saskatchewan Canada
119 Q4	Assing Denmark
118 L9	Assiniboia Saskatchewan Canada
117 Q10	Assiniboine,Mt Br Col/Alberta Canada
115 N7	Assiniboine R Manitoba/Sask Canada
122 H1	Assini L Labrador, Nfld Canada
84 G4	As Sirr sands Libya
129 H8	Assis Brazil
73 H1	Assisi Italy
36 G3	Assmannshausen Germany
45 P6	Assna Italy
41 K6	Asso Italy
78 J4	As Sukhnah Syria
51 P2	Assumption L Seychelles
110 G2	Assumption Illinois U.S.A.
78 K5	As Suwayrih Iraq
116 J1	Assweiler Germany
123 N2	Astaffort France
17 F3	Astakidha isld Greece
46 F8	Astakós Greece
71 A3	Astaneh Iran
28 D4	Åsted Denmark
28 A3	Åsted Viborg Denmark
28 B5	Åsted Nordjylland Denmark
41 O4	Asten Netherlands
77 C1	Asterabad Iran
42 D2	Asti Italy
16 E1	Astillero Spain
	Astin Tagh mt ra see Altun Shan
47 H8	Astipálaia isld Greece
45 P6	Astley England
13 F6	Astley Mine Cheshire England
77 G2	Aston England
99 K2	Astor Kashmir
99 O3	Astorga Spain
103 K7	Astoria Illinois U.S.A.
94 B1	Astoria Oregon U.S.A.
98 M5	Astoria South Dakota U.S.A.
28 E4	Åstorp Sweden
121 T8	Astove isld Br Indian Oc Terr
53 G10	Astrakhan' Russian Federation

Ref	Name
55 E5	Astrakhanka Kazakhstan
26 L7	Åsträsk Sweden
146 J6	Astrid Ridge ridge Antarctica
46 F7	Astros Greece
28 E6	Ăstrup Fyn Denmark
28 B5	Åstrup Ribe Denmark
28 D6	Åstrup Sønderjylland Denmark
28 J7	Åstrup islð Storstrøm Denmark
28 D5	Åstrup Vejle Denmark
16 E2	Astudillo Spain
125 K8	Astura R Italy
16 C1	Asturias reg Spain
130 E7	Astwood England
28 E6	Åsum Denmark
127 H14	Asunción Paraguay
27 H14	Asunden L Sweden
75 L9	Asunden L Sweden
60 E11	Asuta R Japan
87 H12	Aswân Egypt
84 J5	Aswân High Dam Egypt
84 J5	Aswân Egypt
84 J4	Asyûţ Egypt
78 J4	Aşur Iraq
41 N3	Āsi R Iraq
20 E6	Aszod Hungary
111 K8	Āsi R Pacific Oc
79 G3	Atabay Kazakhstan
47 L7	Atabey Turkey
124 H7	Atotonilco el Alto Mexico
77 E1	Atrak R Iran
126 C2	Atrato R Colombia
42 F6	Atri Italy
45 R8	Atripalda Italy
56 G4	Atsikpak Russian Federation
61 N10	Atsugi Japan
61 N7	Atsumi Japan
61 N7	Atsumi-mantō pen Japan
140 C4	Attack Cr N Terr Australia
111 K7	Attala Mississippi U.S.A.
68 H5	Attapu Laos
47 U14	Attaviros mt Rhodes Greece
115 L7	Attawapiskat Ontario Canada
80 G1	Aţ Ţayḩah Syria
36 D1	Attendorn Germany
37 M6	Attersee Austria
110 J1	Attica Indiana U.S.A.
107 M4	Attica Kansas U.S.A.
94 J4	Attica Michigan U.S.A.
94 E5	Attica New York U.S.A.
22 E5	Attica Ohio U.S.A.
112 K1	Attichy France
22 H5	Attigny France
18 E6	Attignat France
94 H8	Attleboro Massachusetts U.S.A.
80 F7	Attu Greenland
110 A3	Attwood R Argentina
94 J4	Attica Michigan U.S.A.
22 H5	Attigny France
143 B6	Aube R France
107 P2	Atchison Kansas U.S.A.
116 J9	Atchueelinguk R Alaska
112 C4	Atchuelingk R Alaska
75 D5	Attur India
133 D5	Atuel R Argentina
131 C4	Atuel R Argentina
27 H13	Åtvidaberg Sweden
119 P8	Atwater Saskatchewan Canada
102 D4	Atwater California U.S.A.
99 M4	Atwater Minnesota U.S.A.
116 J3	Atwick England
106 J1	Atwood Colorado U.S.A.
110 H2	Atwood Illinois U.S.A.
107 J2	Atwood Kansas U.S.A.
94 F6	Atwood Res Ohio U.S.A.
53 G7	Atyashevo Russian Federation
55 D5	Atyrau Federation
38 N5	Atzenbrugg Austria
33 P9	Atzendorf Germany
36 D2	Au Rheinland-Pfalz Germany
128 E4	Auati-Paraná R Brazil
69 G11	Aubagne France
19 G8	Aubagne Belgium
29 K11	Aubange France
19 P18	Aubagne France
19 K11	Aube dept France
22 K4	Aube R France
21 J3	Aube dept France
22 K2	Aubel Belgium
21 J3	Aure R France
23 C8	Aure R France
109 J3	Aubenas France
22 G7	Aubenton France
80 C8	Aubépine R France
19 O16	Aubergenville France
19 N5	Auberive France
22 G3	Aubers France
41 M5	Aubertin France
122 K2	Aubette, L R France
18 E8	Aubigné France
22 D3	Aubigny Pas-de-Calais France
20 H8	Aubigny Vendée France
21 P3	Aubigny sur Nère France
21 Q5	Aubin France
22 G4	Aubrac, Mts d' France
107 N2	Aubrey L Northwest Territories Canada
110 C5	Aubrey, Mt W Australia Australia
112 L2	Aubry L Northwest Territories Canada
102 N3	Auburn Alabama U.S.A.
74 B4	Auburn R Queensland Australia
29 L6	Auburn California U.S.A.
112 J2	Auburn Illinois U.S.A.
141 K7	Auburn Indiana U.S.A.
107 P3	Auburn Kentucky U.S.A.
110 K5	Auburn Maine U.S.A.
94 B3	Auburn Michigan U.S.A.
99 R9	Auburn Nebraska U.S.A.
95 M1	Auburn New York U.S.A.
95 O2	Auburn Washington U.S.A.
141 K7	Auburn Ra Queensland Australia
112 D8	Auburndale Wisconsin

Ref	Name
90 J14	Atlantic-Indian Ridge S Atlantic Oc
128 D1	Atlántico div Colombia
94 D4	Atlantic Oc
90 E5	Atlantis Fracture Atlantic Oc
85 C2	Atlas Michigan U.S.A.
85 C2	Atlas, Haut mts Morocco
85 C2	Atlas, Moyen mts Morocco
118 G8	Atlas Saharien mts Algeria
117 G6	Atlee British Columbia Canada
80 C3	'Atlit Israel
125 K8	Atlixco Mexico
26 A10	Atløy island Norway
89 B7	Atløy isld Norway
94 D2	Atmore Alabama U.S.A.
37 K7	Atnarko British Columbia Canada
26 D10	Atnsjø L Norway
43 G11	Atoka Oklahoma U.S.A.
102 G6	Atoka California U.S.A.
101 N4	Atomic City Idaho U.S.A.
124 H7	Atotonilco el Alto Mexico
77 E1	Atrak R Iran
126 C2	Atrato R Colombia
42 F6	Atri Italy
56 G4	Atsikpak Russian Federation
94 H8	Atsugi Japan
130 H8	Atsumi Japan
130 H8	Atsumi-mantō pen Japan
31 O2	Augustow Poland
140 E4	Augustus Downs Queensland Australia
142 E3	Augustus Island W Australia Australia
143 B6	Augustus, Mt W Australia Australia
116 R6	Augusta,Mt Yukon Territory Canada
94 H8	Augusta Springs Virginia U.S.A.
43 E7	Augusta, L W Australia Australia
110 L7	Augustine L Alaska
130 G6	Augusto de Lima Brazil
130 H8	Augusto Severo Brazil
141 H7	Augathella Queensland Australia
14 E2	Aughnacloy N Ireland
14 E4	Aughrim Ireland
89 B7	Augrabies S Africa
89 B7	Augrabies Falls Orange R S Africa
94 D2	Au Gres Michigan U.S.A.
37 K7	Augsburg Germany
143 B10	Augusta W Australia Australia
43 G12	Augusta Sicily
110 E2	Augusta Arkansas U.S.A.
112 E4	Augusta Georgia U.S.A.
110 F1	Augusta Illinois U.S.A.
107 O4	Augusta Kansas U.S.A.
94 C8	Augusta Kentucky U.S.A.
94 B4	Augusta Michigan U.S.A.
101 N2	Augusta Montana U.S.A.
99 P5	Augusta Wisconsin U.S.A.

Ref	Name
36 G5	Auenstein Germany
37 N2	Auerbach Germany
37 N2	Auerbach Hessen Germany
37 O2	Auer Berg mt Germany
37 O2	Auerswalde Germany
111 E12	Au Far, Point Louisiana U.S.A.
21 N2	Auffay France
22 F4	Augan France
141 H7	Augathella Queensland Australia
14 E2	Aughnacloy N Ireland
14 E4	Aughrim Ireland
89 B7	Augrabies S Africa
89 B7	Augrabies Falls Orange R S Africa
94 D2	Au Gres Michigan U.S.A.
37 K7	Augsburg Germany
43 B10	Augusta W Australia Australia
26 J9	Aujon R France
110 E6	Auk oil rig North Sea
26 K6	Auktsjaur Sweden
112 K1	Aulander North Carolina U.S.A.
142 E3	Auld, L W Australia Australia
18 E6	Aulnay de Saintonge France
21 P5	Aulnay-la-Rivière France
20 B5	Aulne R France
118 H1	Aulneau Pen Ontario Canada
22 F3	Aulnoye France
106 F1	Ault Colorado U.S.A.
15 C3	Aultbea Scotland
54 F8	Auly Ukraine
37 M2	Auma R Germany
37 M2	Auma Germany
21 Q2	Aumale France
18 E6	Aumance R France
19 L12	Aumont France
19 O8	Aumont France
109 N2	Aumsville Oregon U.S.A.
40 C4	Auminzatau,Gory mt Uzbekistan
18 H8	Aumont Lozère France
33 M5	Aumühle Germany
21 J3	Aunay-sur-Odon France
21 J3	Aundh India
74 D10	Aundh India
21 L6	Aune R France
21 O5	Auneau France
21 P3	Auneuil France
28 B3	Aunglan Burma
68 B3	Aunglan Burma
18 E6	Aunis prov France
87 C11	Auob R Namibia
47 J5	Auponhia Moluccas Indonesia
133 F4	Auponhia Moluccas Indonesia
15 C5	Aur island Malaysia
29 K11	Aura R Finland
36 H4	Aurach Germany
26 J7	Auraia India
29 K11	Aurajoki R Finland
74 F9	Aurangabad India
16 D1	Auray France
27 B9	Aure Norway
21 J3	Aure R France
18 H5	Aurec-sur-Loire France
32 F6	Aurich Germany
130 E6	Aurilândia Brazil
18 G8	Aurillac France
19 P18	Auriol France
112 C4	Aurlandsvangen Norway
27 B11	Auron Norway
80 G2	Aurora R France
130 H7	Aurora Brazil
121 J2	Aurora Illinois U.S.A.
106 F2	Aurora Colorado U.S.A.
99 S8	Aurora Indiana U.S.A.
94 C6	Aurora Kansas U.S.A.
107 M2	Aurora Minnesota U.S.A.
110 D4	Aurora Missouri U.S.A.
99 N3	Aurora Nebraska U.S.A.
98 H9	Aurora North Carolina U.S.A.
112 L3	Aurora Utah U.S.A.
95 F1	Aurora Maine U.S.A.
74 D4	Auroville India
37 M2	Aursjøen L Norway
141 F2	Aurukun Queensland Australia
8 D4	Aust Austria
110 F3	Ausable R Michigan U.S.A.
110 F3	Ausable R New York U.S.A.
88 F7	Ausangate mt Peru
98 F1	Auskerry Scotland
15 F1	Ausonia Italy
45 N6	Ausonia Italy
33 N5	Ausser-Rhoden dist Switzerland
27 C13	Austad Norway
27 A9	Austad Agder Fylker Norway
119 T9	Austell Georgia U.S.A.
110 G3	Austerlitz see Slavkov
119 T9	Austin Indiana U.S.A.
99 N6	Austin Minnesota U.S.A.
102 F2	Austin Nevada U.S.A.
100 G5	Austin Pennsylvania U.S.A.
94 A8	Austin Texas U.S.A.
109 L5	Austin Texas U.S.A.
142 E5	Austin, L W Australia Australia
139 M4	Austral Downs N Terr Australia
140 E5	Austral Downs N Terr Australia
146 F15	Australian Antarctic Territory Antarctica
135 M11	Austral Ridge Pacific Oc
8 B5	Austråt Norway
27 A11	Austvägøy isld Norway
36 C2	Autenried Germany
36 C2	Autesiodorum see Auxerre
22 K5	Authe France
123 O2	Authie R Quebec Canada
22 C3	Authie R France
21 N6	Authon France
21 L4	Authon-du-Perche France
21 M4	Authon-la-Plaine France
45 O6	Autore, M mt Italy
99 U3	Au Train Michigan U.S.A.

Ref	Name
19 P14	Autrans France
21 P5	Autruy-sur-Juine France
21 J3	Autry France
140 B3	Auvergne N Terr Australia
18 H6	Auvergne prov France
21 K6	Auvers-le-Hamon France
21 P3	Auvers-sur-Oise France
21 N3	Auvezère R France
22 G4	Auvillers-les-Forges France
22 G4	Auxances R France
94 E2	Aux Barques, Pt Michigan U.S.A.
19 K8	Auxerre France
18 H5	Auxi-la-Château France
22 D3	Auxonne France
110 E2	Auvasse R Missouri U.S.A.
128 F2	Auyán Tepui mt Venezuela
115 M4	Auyuittuq Nat Park NW Terr Canada
20 G8	Auzance France
18 G6	Auzances France
34 Au Burma	
18 F6	Availles-Limouzine France
18 F6	Avalik R Alaska U.S.A.
18 H5	Avallon France
102 F8	Avalon California U.S.A.
111 F8	Avalon Mississippi U.S.A.
95 N7	Avalon New Jersey U.S.A.
123 T6	Avalon Pen Newfoundland Canada
131 F2	Avalos R Argentina
25 F3	Avalos Mexico
19 Q15	Avançon France
107 M5	Avard Oklahoma U.S.A.
129 J8	Avaré Brazil
57 H4	Avarskoye Koysu R Russian Federation
47 H4	Åvas Greece
116 F9	Avatanak I Aleutian Is
26 L5	Åvaträsk Sweden
26 K6	Åvaviken Sweden
102 H6	Avawatz Mts California U.S.A.
47 N10	Avci Koru forest Turkey
54 J8	Avdeyevka Ukraine
9 E5	Avebury England
16 D4	Aveinte Spain
129 G4	Aveiro Brazil
16 B4	Aveiro Portugal
16 B4	Aveiro Portugal
77 A4	Avej Iran
22 K2	Avelgem Belgium
94 G6	Avella Pennsylvania U.S.A.
133 F4	Avellaneda Argentina
45 R8	Avellino Italy
102 D6	Avenal California U.S.A.
40 A3	Avenches Switzerland
94 G5	Aver Massachusetts U.S.A.
28 B5	Avernak By ö Denmark
28 B8	Avernak ö Denmark
45 N6	Aversa Italy
100 K2	Avery Idaho U.S.A.
19 O8	Avery Texas U.S.A.
109 N2	Avery Texas U.S.A.
111 E12	Avery Island Louisiana U.S.A.
22 F3	Avesnes France
22 D3	Avesnes le Comte France
22 F3	Avesnes-sur-Helpe France
22 D3	Avesnes-les-Aubert France
27 H11	Avesta Sweden
18 G8	Aveyron R France
18 G8	Aveyron dept France
45 N6	Avezzano Italy
18 H8	Avgó Italy
47 H9	Avgó isld Greece
46 F8	Avgó Greece
100 K2	Avery Idaho U.S.A.
133 E3	Aviá Terai Argentina
144 C6	Aviemore, L New Zealand
15 P5	Aviemore Scotland
80 P7	Avigad Israel
19 N17	Avignon France
16 D1	Ávila prov Spain
16 D3	Ávila, Sa. de mts Spain
109 N3	Avinger Texas U.S.A.
16 D1	Avión Spain
95 F2	Avis Pennsylvania U.S.A.
16 B5	Aviz Portugal
28 B4	Avlum Denmark
28 B4	Avne Etan Syria
80 C2	Avne Etan Syria
28 H6	Avne Fjord inlet Denmark
139 G6	Avoca Victoria Australia
14 E3	Avoca Ireland
110 D4	Avoca New Zealand
94 C5	Avoca Michigan U.S.A.
110 C3	Avoca Iowa U.S.A.
94 E3	Avoca New York U.S.A.
108 H3	Avoca Texas U.S.A.
98 L5	Avoca South Dakota U.S.A.
14 E3	Avoca,Vale of Ireland
117 O10	Avola British Columbia Canada
43 G12	Avola Sicily
18 D4	Avon co Scotland
110 C2	Avon R Scotland
100 K4	Avon R Colorado U.S.A.
95 P5	Avon R Connecticut U.S.A.
94 B4	Avon Illinois U.S.A.
99 M4	Avon Minnesota U.S.A.
101 K4	Avon R Montana U.S.A.
95 N1	Avon New York U.S.A.
102 C2	Avon Ohio U.S.A.
138 D5	Avon South Dakota U.S.A.
9 E5	Avon R England
9 F6	Avon R England
103 M8	Avondale Arizona U.S.A.
106 F3	Avondale Colorado U.S.A.
110 B2	Avondale Missouri U.S.A.
140 D4	Avon Downs N Terr Australia
141 G7	Avon Downs Queensland Australia
112 E7	Avon Lake Ohio U.S.A.
119 M8	Avonlea Saskatchewan Canada
21 L7	Avon-les-Roches France
74 D6	Avonmore Pennsylvania U.S.A.
8 D4	Avonmouth England
143 B9	Avon Park W Australia Australia
143 B10	Avon, R W Australia Australia
9 E5	Avon, R England
22 D4	Avre R France
22 D4	Avre R France
21 L4	Avre R Eure France
31 B6	Avrig Romania
18 E5	Avrillé France
16 J3	Avtovac Bosnia-Herzegovina
8 D4	Awaday Indonesia
110 H1	Awaji-shima isld Japan
85 E4	Awakino New Zealand
145 E4	Awali watercourse Libya
84 G1	Awanui New Zealand
145 D1	Awanui New Zealand
86 H4	Awârë Ethiopia
144 B6	Awarua Pt New Zealand
86 H4	Awasa Ghana
86 G2	Āwash R Ethiopia
61 N7	Awa-shima isld Japan
66 E3	Awat China
86 G3	Āwat'a Ethiopia
145 E4	Awatere R New Zealand

Column 1

84 E4 Awbārī Libya
86 H5 Aw Dheegle Somalia
12 C1 Awe,L Scotland
112 H4 Awendaw South Carolina U.S.A.
84 A4 Awjilah Libya
70 G6 Awo R Sulawesi Indonesia
117 O4 Awry L Northwest Territories Canada
85 B4 Awserd Mauritania
116 J2 Awuna R Alaska U.S.A.
8 D5 Axbridge England
25 A6 Axel Netherlands
27 F14 Axelfors Sweden
147 H5 Axel Heiberg I Northwest Territories Canada
106 C1 Axial Colorado U.S.A.
128 C4 Axim Ghana
18 G10 Ax-les-Thermes France
8 D6 Axminster England
112 E6 Axson Georgia U.S.A.
107 O2 Axtell Kansas U.S.A.
27 G13 Axvall Sweden
18 H3 Ay France
20 H3 Ay R France
128 C4 Ayabaca Peru
60 J10 Ayabe Japan
78 D1 Ayagüz Turkey
133 F5 Ayacucho Argentina
128 D6 Ayacucho Peru
68 B1 Ayadaw Burma
57 K1 Ayaguz Kazakhstan
57 D4 Ayakkuduk Uzbekistan
66 D4 Ayakkum Hu L China
16 C7 Ayamonte Spain
78 E1 Ayancık Turkey
80 C6 Ayanot Israel
126 G10 Ayapel Colombia
128 D6 Ayaviri Peru
77 L1 Aybak Afghanistan
13 G4 Aycliffe England
54 L8 Aydabul' Kazakhstan
54 L8 Aydar R Ukraine
57 C4 Aydarkul', Ozero L Uzbekistan
112 K2 Ayden North Carolina U.S.A.
47 J1 Aydın Turkey
78 A3 Aydin Turkey
Aydıncık see Gilindire
47 J7 Aydın Dağlar mts Turkey
79 B1 Aydınkent Turkey
47 N11 Aydınlı Turkey
55 C5 Ayerlinskiy Russian Federation
86 H3 Ayelu Terara mt Ethiopia
40 G5 Ayer Switzerland
17 G2 Ayerbe Spain
100 G3 Ayers Washington U.S.A.
140 C7 Ayers Ra N Terr Australia
140 B7 Ayers Rock mt N Terr Australia
55 F3 Ayev R Russian Federation
19 C10 Aygues R France
56 C5 Aygulaksiy Khrebet mts Russian Federation
46 F5 Ayía Greece
46 F6 Ayía Ánna Greece
47 H5 Ayía Iríni Akra C Greece
47 H5 Ayiássos Greece
46 G4 Ayíon Óros reg Greece
46 F7 Ayíos oil Greece
46 G5 Áyios Evstrátios isld Greece
47 O12 Áyios Matthaíos Greece
46 G9 Áyios Miron Crete Greece
46 D6 Áyios Nikólaos Crete Greece
Áyios Pétros Greece
79 D3 Áyios Seryios Cyprus
79 E3 Áyios Theodhoros Cyprus
116 L2 Ayiyak R Alaska U.S.A.
47 H7 Aykathonisi isld Greece
86 G3 Aykel Ethiopia
54 H7 Ay Kirikos Greece
36 B4 Ayl Germany
121 N7 Aylen,L Ontario Canada
119 M8 Aylesbury Saskatchewan Canada
9 F4 Aylesbury England
144 D5 Aylesbury New Zealand
122 H8 Aylesford Nova Scotia Canada
9 H2 Aylesham England
117 D6 Aylesworth, Mt Br Col/Alaska Canada/U.S.A.
16 E3 Ayllón Spain
16 E3 Ayllón, Sa. de mts Spain
121 P7 Aylmer Quebec Canada
114 J5 Aylmer L Northwest Territories Canada
118 B7 Aylmer,Mt Alberta Canada
119 O5 Aylsham Saskatchewan Canada
9 H2 Aylsham England
121 O7 Aylwin Quebec Canada
17 F6 Ayna Spain
79 H4 'Ayn al Baydā' Syria
78 J3 'Ayn Diwār Syria
9 E3 Aynho England
112 H4 Aynor South Carolina U.S.A.
80 C1 'Ayn Zīwan Syria
84 G5 'Ayn Zuwayyah well Libya
147 Q4 Ayon,Ostrov isld Russian Federation
17 G5 Ayora Spain
85 E6 Ayorou Niger
55 G2 Aypolovo Russian Federation
Ayr cc see Strathclyde reg
141 H4 Ayr Queensland Australia
12 D3 Ayr Scotland
98 H9 Ayr R Nebraska U.S.A.
21 L8 Ayron France
99 M6 Ayrshire Iowa U.S.A.
141 G5 Ayrshire Downs Queensland Australia
55 F4 Aysarinskoye Kazakhstan
13 G5 Aysgarth England
86 H3 Aysha Ethiopia
57 F1 Ayshirak Kazakhstan
13 H5 Ayton N Yorks England
13 H5 Ayton Scotland
47 J2 Aytos Bulgaria
57 C4 Aytym Uzbekistan
61 P7 Ayukawahama Japan
65 C2 Ayulhai China
124 E5 Ayutla Mexico
78 A2 Ayvacık Turkey
47 N5 Ayvalık Turkey
22 K3 Aywaille Belgium
80 E1 Ayyelet Ha Shaḥar Israel
77 D1 Āzād Shahr Iran
100 A1 Azalea Oregon U.S.A.
61 P13 Azama Okinawa
Azamān, Qā' depression Saudi Arabia
75 K5 Azamgarh India
Azangulovo Russian Federation
55 D2 Azanka Russian Federation
22 J5 Azannes-et-Soumazannes France
77 A1 Āzārān Iran
78 K2 Āzārbāyjān-e Gharbī Iran
78 K2 Āzārbāyjān-e Sharqī Iran
85 G6 Azare Nigeria
Azatskoye, Oz L Russian Federation
21 N8 Azay-le-Ferron France
21 C1 Azay-le-Rideau France
21 M7 Azay-sur-Cher France
21 M7 Azay-sur-Thouet France
79 H2 'A'zāz Syria
Azbine reg Niger see Aïr ou Azbine
21 N6 Azé Loire France
40 G7 Azéglio Italy
78 L1 Azerbaijan rep E Europe
Azerbaydzhanskaya S.S.R. see Azerbaijan
19 N13 Azergues R France
27 F13 Azeyevo Russian Federation
55 G4 Azhbulat, Oz L Kazakhstan
65 C5 Azho-Tayga, Gora mt Russian Federation

Column 2

85 C2 Azilal Morocco
22 C3 Azincourt France
86 A6 Azingo, L Gabon
95 R1 Aziscos L Maine U.S.A.
84 E3 'Azīzīyan, Al Libya
16 C7 Aznalcóllar Spain
128 C4 Azogues Ecuador
52 G2 Azopol'ye Russian Federation
Azores islds see Açores
90 G5 Azores-Cape St Vincent Ridge Atlantic Oc
86 D3 Azoum R Chad
54 L9 Azov Russian Federation
Azov,Sea of see Azovskoye More
54 L9 Azovskiy Kanal Russian Federation
53 E10 Azovskoye More Rus Fed/Ukraine
17 F1 Azpeitia Spain
85 C2 Azrou Morocco
103 L9 Aztec Arizona U.S.A.
106 C5 Aztec New Mexico U.S.A.
106 B5 Aztec Ruins Nat.Mon New Mexico U.S.A.
127 J5 Azua Dominican Rep
16 D6 Azuaga Spain
17 G3 Azuara Spain
128 C4 Azuay prov Ecuador
60 C12 Azuch-Ō-shima isld Japan
17 F6 Azuer R Spain
124 E5 Azuero,Pen.de Panama
48 K5 Azuga Romania
133 F5 Azul Argentina
131 B5 Azul pk Chile
125 P9 Azul R Mexico
131 B8 Azul,Cerro pk Neuquén Argentina
130 E7 Azul Paulista, Mte Brazil
130 C4 Azul,Serra ms Mato Grosso Brazil
61 O8 Azuma-yama mt Japan
80 B8 Azza Israel
79 G5 Az Zabadānī Syria
84 F4 Az Zahrah Libya

B

71 L10 Baa Indonesia
41 M3 Baad Austria
74 F4 Baal R Kalimantan
25 F6 Baal Germany
79 G4 Baalbek Lebanon
86 H5 Baardheere Somalia
25 C6 Baarle-Hertog Belgium
25 C6 Baarle-Nassau Netherlands
25 D6 Baarn Netherlands
60 D14 Baba Japan
46 E4 Baba mt Macedonia Yugoslavia
47 H5 Baba Burun C Turkey
78 M3 Baba mt Azerbaijan
37 M3 Babadag Romania
36 D3 Babaeski Turkey
48 K5 Babadag Romania
28 F7 Babahoyo Ecuador
128 C4 Babak Philippines
71 G7 Babakin W Australia
143 C9 Bābā, Koh-i- mts Afghanistan
77 K2 Bab, Al Syria
81 A5 Bab al Mandab str Arabia/Djibouti
86 G6 Babanna Syria
45 P1 Baberna Croatia
33 U7 Babelthuap isld Pacific Oc
71 G10 Babenberg Germany
38 M8 Badderkenstedt Germany
26 M2 Badderen Norway
33 P4 Baabaru Tanzania
38 M8 Baberhausen Germany
102 E5 Babb Montana U.S.A.
116 J5 Babbage R Yukon Territory Canada
143 A6 Babbage I W Australia
99 P2 Babbitt Minnesota U.S.A.
99 Q5 Babcock Wisconsin U.S.A.
33 P5 Babelin Germany
88 C5 Babemba tribe Zaire
88 C7 Babemba tribe Zambia
36 F4 Babenhausen Hessen Germany
31 M6 Babia Góra mts Czech/Poland
124 E3 Babicora Mexico
124 E3 Babicora, L. de Mexico
78 K5 Bābil prov Iraq
141 H3 Babinda Queensland Australia
112 C6 Babine L British Columbia Canada
112 C6 Babine Ra British Columbia Canada
117 L8 Babine R British Columbia Canada
69 C11 Babi, Pulau isld Indonesia
74 E3 Babo W Irian
77 D1 Bābol Iran
77 D1 Bābol Sar Iran
103 N10 Baboquivari Pk Arizona U.S.A.
142 E4 Babrongan Tower mt W Australia
113 F10 Babson Park Florida U.S.A.
36 G5 Babstadt Germany
16 D9 Bab Taza Morocco
67 O1 Babu China
64 M4 Babuna mt Macedonia Yugoslavia
46 G5 Babushkin Russian Federation
56 G5 Babuyan islds Philippines
71 O6 Babuyan Ch Philippines
71 O6 Babuyan I Philippines
124 E4 Bacabache Mexico
124 F4 Bacabal Somalia
129 G5 Bacabal Brazil
129 H4 Bacaja R Brazil
71 A3 Bacanora Mexico
71 E1 Bacarra Philippines
18 K4 Bacau Vietnam
19 K4 Baccarat France
122 G10 Baccaro Pt Nova Scotia Canada
21 K5 Bacchiglione R Italy
68 H4 Baceno Italy
123 D7 Băceşti Romania
69 H8 Bac Giang Vietnam
68 H2 Bach Michigan U.S.A.
95 L10 Bach Long Vi isld Vietnam
69 E9 Bacho Thailand
37 L1 Bacho Germany
37 L3 Bachu China
35 N9 Backa reg Serbia Yugoslavia
27 G14 Bäckaby Sweden
36 E5 Backa Palanka Serbia Yugoslavia
33 R9 Backa Topola Serbia Yugoslavia

Column 3

48 F5 Bačko Petrovo Selo Serbia Yugoslavia
138 E6 Backstairs Pass South Australia Australia
26 H6 Bäckstrand Sweden
99 M3 Backus Minnesota U.S.A.
8 D5 Backwell England
71 E2 Bac Lieu see Vinh Loi
127 P5 Bacolet Grenada
71 F5 Bacolod Philippines
33 P7 Baco,mt Philippines
37 J5 Baco, mt Philippines
112 C6 Baconton Georgia U.S.A.
59 K1 Bacon,Sea of see Azov
21 C2 Bács-Kiskun co Hungary
H2 Bacton England
124 F5 Bacubirito Mexico
71 G7 Baculin Bay Mindanao
13 G6 Bacup England
129 J4 Bacuri,I de Brazil
16 E7 Bacurrup Spain (?)
98 B8 Bad R South Dakota U.S.A.
86 B4 Bada see Xilin
35 B6 Bada Barabil India
38 E6 Bad Abbach Germany
76 B5 Badagara India
38 E8 Bad Aibling Germany
109 K8 Badajós Brazil
147 L6 Baffin Bay Greenland/Canada
115 N3 Baffin Bay Greenland/Canada
16 C6 Badajoz Spain
16 C6 Badajoz, L Spain
77 L1 Badakhshān prov Afghanistan
17 J3 Badalona Spain
76 B3 Bādāmi India
75 M7 Bādāmpāhār India
56 E3 Bada, Khrebet m = Russian Federation
65 H3 Badaohe China
79 H2 Badaojiang see Huajiang
124 F5 Badariguato Mexico
72 D2 Badas Brunei
69 H12 Badas,Kep isld Indonesia
58 D3 Bad Aussee Austria
94 E3 Bad Axe Michigan U.S.A.
32 G7 Badbergen Germany
36 D5 Bad Bergzabern Germany
38 G5 Bad Berka Germany
36 E1 Bad Berleburg Germany
37 M3 Bad Berneck Germany
36 B3 Bad Bertrich Germany
37 M1 Bad Bibra Sachsen-Anhalt Germany
37 L2 Bad Blankenburg German
69 E11 Bad Bocklet Germany
142 A3 Bad Bramstedt Germany
123 M7 Baddeck C Breton Nova Scotia
58 F2 Baga Nuur Mongolia
44 H2 Baganza R Italy
55 D3 Bagaryak Russian Federation
48 J5 Bagband Germany
32 G6 Bagdad Mexico
103 L7 Bagdad Arizona U.S.A.
103 J7 Bagdad California U.S.A.
110 L3 Bagdad Kentucky U.S.A.
59 F1 Bagdarin Russian Federation
28 F7 Bagé Brazil
27 D7 Bagenkop Denmark
95 U1 Baggs Wyoming U.S.A.
14 C3 Baggy Pt Ireland
77 A4 Bāgh-e Malek Iran
75 N7 Bagherhat Bangladesh
22 K4 Bagheria Sicily
77 L1 Baghlān Afghanistan
75 K7 Baghlān prov Afghanistan
119 H6 Baglan Hd Ireland
69 H14 Bagnoa, Tanjong C Indonesia
99 L2 Badger Minnesota U.S.A.
99 P7 Badger Wisconsin U.S.A.
116 Q6 Badger Newfoundland Canada
102 E5 Badger California U.S.A.
98 K1 Badger Minnesota U.S.A.
101 Q5 Badger Basin Wyoming U.S.A.
77 H2 Bādghis Afghanistan
38 N8 Bad Godesberg Germany
30 H5 Bad Gottleuba Germany
32 M9 Bad Grund Germany
38 G6 Bad Hall Austria
21 K7 Bad Harzburg Germany
36 E6 Bad Herrenalb Germany
36 H2 Bad Hersfeld Germany
38 H7 Bad Hofgastein Austria
44 B3 Bad Homburg Germany
45 L1 Bad Honnef Germany
44 H3 Badia Polesine Ital
44 E4 Badia Tedalda Italy
32 H8 Bad Iburg Germany
79 H6 Badiet esh Sham desert Jordan/Syria
74 C6 Badin Pakistan
112 G2 Badin North Carolina U.S.A.
112 G2 Badin North Carolina U.S.A.
38 J6 Bad Ischl Austria
37 J3 Bad Kissingen Germany
38 J3 Bad Kleinen Germany
... Bad Klosterlausnitz Germany
37 M1 Bad Kösen Germany
9 F5 Bad Kreuznach Germany
98 B8 Bad Lands reg North Dakota U.S.A.
31 K1 Bad Langensalza Germany
33 P10 Bad Lauchstädt Germany
37 O1 Bad Lausik Germany
33 M9 Bad Lauterberg Germany
38 K8 Bad Leonhard Austria
37 K2 Bad Liebenstein Germany
36 F2 Bad Liebenzell Germany
36 F4 Bad Lippspringe Germany
126 F2 Bad Meinberg Germany
127 M4 Bad Mergentheim Germany
... Bad Münder am Deister Germany
84 H4 Bad Münster Germany
31 H4 Bad Muskau Germany
70 D6 Bad Nauheim Germany
74 D4 Bad Nenndorf Germany
79 B7 Bad Neuenahr Germany
... Bad Neuenahr-Ahrweiler Germany
88 E4 Bad Neustadt Germany
86 D3 Bad Oeynhausen Germany
125 L1 Bad Oldesloe Germany
124 D3 Badong China
133 D7 Badou Vietnam
85 C4 Bad Orb Germany
86 B4 Bad Peterstal Germany
86 B5 Bad Pyrmont Germany
86 G8 Bad Reichenhall Germany
69 H8 Bad Rippoldsau Germany
... Bad Saarow-Pieskow Germany
79 B7 Bad Salzdetfurth Germany
75 J5 Bad Salzuflen Germany
77 B6 Bad Schmiedeberg Germany
86 D5 Bad Schönborn Germany
86 E4 Bad Schwalbach Germany
86 E4 Bad Schwartau Germany
37 R9 Bad Segeberg Germany
33 P10 Bad Soden Germany
85 R2 Bad Steben Germany
33 R4 Bad Sülze Germany

Column 4

36 F6 Bad Teinach-Zavelstein Germany
37 K1 Bad Tennstedt Germany
141 F1 Badu I Queensland Australia
83 L10 Badulla Sri Lanka
36 F3 Bad Vilbel Germany
38 G7 Bad Voslau Austria
87 B9 Bad Waldsee Germany
128 F7 Bad Wildungen Germany
48 H3 Baia Mare Romania
95 P2 Bakersfield Vermont U.S.A.
9 E1 Bakewell England
86 C3 Bakhanin Iran
48 H3 Baia Sprie Romania
48 R8 Baiano Italy
37 D3 Bad Windsheim Germany
86 D4 Balboukoum Chad
86 D4 Baicaogou China
65 H3 Baicheng China
78 L4 Bākhtarān Iran
77 B3 Bakhtiarī va Chahār Maḥāll prov Iran
122 D4 Baie-Comeau Quebec Canada
29 T9 Bakkagerdhi Iceland
25 F2 Bakkeveen Netherlands
124 K7 Bakke Turkey
126 H5 Baie de Henne Haiti
122 E5 Baie de Sables Quebec Canada
123 P2 Baie-du-Milieu Quebec Canada
69 C11 Bakongan Sumatra
118 K6 Bakony mts Hungary
86 D4 Bakony Cent Afr Republic
85 C6 Bakoye R Guinea/Mali
54 L1 Baksheyevo Russian Federation
26 K6 Baktsjaure Sweden
78 M1 Baku Azerbaijan
71 K1 Bakubung Pt Mindanao
77 K1 Bakkhab R Afghanistan
57 G2 Bakkhash Kazakhstan
57 G2 Bakkhash, Ozero L Kazakhstan
74 H9 Balkonda India
15 C4 Ballachulish Scotland
143 E9 Balladonia W Australia
8 C2 Bala Wales
78 D2 Bālā Turkey
70 B4 Balabac Str Borneo/Philippines
21 P4 Balancourt-sur-Essonne France
141 K8 Ballandean Queensland Australia
26 J3 Ballangen Norway
101 R4 Ballantine Montana U.S.A.
15 C5 Ballantrae Scotland
119 O4 Ballantyne Bay Saskatchewan Canada
114 H2 Ballantyne Str Northwest Territories Canada
43 C9 Ballao Sardinia
139 G6 Ballarat Victoria Australia
102 L3 Ballarat California U.S.A.
143 D8 Ballard, L W Australia
84 F4 Ballas Jordan
15 E3 Ballater Scotland
12 D5 Ballaugh I of Man U.K.
28 F4 Balle Denmark
21 K6 Ballée France
28 F4 Ballen Denmark
133 C3 Ballena, Pta C Chile
134 C13 Balleny Islands Antarctica
21 J3 Balleroy France
29 K5 Ballerup Denmark
112 C3 Ball Ground Georgia U.S.A.
75 L6 Ballia India
14 C3 Ballina Ireland
14 C3 Ballina Ireland
14 D2 Ballinasloe Ireland
28 B3 Ballindine Ireland
14 C4 Ballingarry Ireland
108 H4 Ballinger Texas U.S.A.
14 C3 Ballinluig Scotland
14 B3 Ballinrobe Ireland
37 J6 Ballmertshofen Germany
118 B7 Ball,Mt Alberta Canada
12 D1 Balloch Scotland
20 D4 Ballon d'Alsace mt France
21 L6 Ballots France
21 H6 Ballstädt Germany
137 M8 Ball's Pyramid isld Pacific Oc
37 K1 Ballstädt Germany
95 O4 Ballston Spa New York U.S.A.
28 B6 Ballum Denmark
14 E2 Ballybay Ireland
14 D2 Ballybofey Ireland
14 D2 Ballybunion Ireland
14 E1 Ballycastle N Ireland
14 C3 Ballyclare N Ireland
14 D3 Ballyconnell Ireland
14 D3 Ballycotton B Ireland
14 D2 Ballyduff Ireland
12 D3 Ballygrant Scotland
14 D2 Ballyhaise Ireland
14 C3 Ballyhaunis Ireland
14 D3 Ballyhoura Hills Ireland
14 C3 Ballyjamesduff Ireland
14 C4 Ballymahon Ireland
14 E1 Ballymena N Ireland
14 E1 Ballymoney N Ireland
14 E1 Ballynahinch N Ireland
14 E1 Ballyquintin Pt N Ireland
14 D2 Ballyragget Ireland
14 C3 Ballyshannon Ireland
14 E1 Ballyvaughan Ireland
14 B3 Ballyvourney Ireland
14 D2 Balmaclellan Scotland
40 G5 Balmazújváros Hungary
42 D2 Balme Italy
40 C5 Balmhorn mt Switzerland
141 K1 Balmoral Victoria Australia
128 F6 Balmoral Manitoba Canada
144 D5 Balmoral New Zealand
144 D5 Balmoral oil rig North Sea
15 E3 Balmoral Castle Scotland
108 D6 Balmorhea Texas U.S.A.
13 H5 Balmullo Scotland
84 H4 Balochistān prov Pakistan
87 B8 Balombo Angola
114 E2 Balonne R Queensland Australia
70 G10 Balonne R Queensland Australia
95 P4 Baldwinville Massachusetts U.S.A.
74 E6 Balotra India
33 J6 Balow Germany
12 D4 Balquhidder Scotland
75 J8 Balrampur India
33 G3 Balsam L Wisconsin U.S.A.
121 J5 Balsam Lake Ontario Canada

Column 5

71 H6 Bahubulu isld Sulawesi Indonesia
77 G7 Bāhu Kalāt Iran
129 J4 Baía de Aramã Romania
48 H6 Baia de Criş Romania
125 P9 Bakersfield California U.S.A.
102 F6 Bakersfield California U.S.A.
112 E1 Bakersfield North Carolina U.S.A.
108 E5 Bakersfield Texas U.S.A.
48 H3 Baia Mare Romania
9 F2 Bakewell England
86 C3 Bakhardok Iran
48 H3 Baia Sprie Romania
87 B9 Baiano Italy
86 C4 Baibokoum Chad
86 C4 Baicaogou China
65 H3 Baicheng China
78 L4 Bākhtarān Iran
77 B3 Bakhtiarī va Chahār Maḥāll prov Iran
122 D4 Baie-Comeau Quebec Canada
29 T9 Bakkagerdhi Iceland
25 F2 Bakkeveen Netherlands
124 K7 Bakke Turkey
126 H5 Baie de Henne Haiti
122 E5 Baie de Sables Quebec Canada
123 P2 Baie-du-Milieu Quebec Canada
69 C11 Bakongan Sumatra
86 D4 Bakony mts Hungary
... Baie de Vin New Brunswick Canada
115 M7 Baie-du-Poste Quebec Canada
86 D4 Bakouma Cent Afr Republic
85 C6 Bakoye R Guinea/Mali
122 G6 Baie de Vin New Brunswick Canada
26 K6 Baksheyevo Russian Federation
78 M1 Baie Johan Beetz Quebec Canada
122 K3 Baie Johan Beetz Quebec
127 N4 Baie Mahault Guadeloupe W Indies
32 H7 Bakum Germany
69 G12 Bakung isld Indonesia
121 L7 Bala Ontario Canada
78 D2 Bālā Turkey
8 C2 Bala Wales
141 K8 Baie St.Catherine Quebec Canada
36 F7 Baiersbronn Germany
122 C5 Baie Ste.Catherine Quebec Canada
122 E4 Baie Ste.Ste.Marie Quebec Canada
122 B6 Baie St.Paul Quebec Canada
70 B4 Balabac Str Borneo/Philippines
14 C3 Balabalangan, Kep islds Indonesia
71 C7 Balabec isld Palawan Philippines
122 K3 Baie Trinité Quebec Canada
122 E4 Baie Verte New Brunswick Canada
123 Q4 Baie Verte Newfoundland Canada
71 H8 Balabalangan Pulau Pulau islds Indonesia
54 G2 Baifang China
48 G6 Baiguan see Shangyu
54 H1 Baïkal L see Baykal,Ozero L
74 J3 Baikunthpur India
17 H3 Baïkal L see Baykal,Ozero L
75 K7 Bāilādila see Kirandul
65 E1 Baïlādila see Kirandul
128 E6 Baile Átha see Dublin
80 F3 Balagansk Russian Federation
80 B4 Bāile Govora Romania
16 B3 Balaghat India
56 F4 Bāile Herculane Romania
48 G6 Bāilen Spain
74 H8 Balaguer Spain
17 H3 Bāile Oláneşti Romania
... Bāile Tuşnad Romania
70 B4 Balaïkarangan Kalimantan
111 K7 Bailey Colorado U.S.A.
70 B4 Balai Purugu Sumatra
112 J2 Bailey North Carolina U.S.A.
70 B6 Balairam Kalimantan
70 K8 Baileysepuac Kalimantan
111 K7 Baileyton Alabama U.S.A.
29 K5 Balak, Gunung Sumatra
70 K8 Baileyville Illinois U.S.A.
138 E5 Balaklava South Australia Australia
75 L6 Ballia India
48 G6 Bailieborough Ireland
54 H7 Balakleya Ukraine
14 D3 Balla Ireland
8 C2 Bailieul France
129 F2 Bailique, I France
87 D1 Balama Mozambique
21 K4 Bailleul Orne France
141 H2 Balambangan isld Malaysia
22 J2 Bailleul-la-Pin France
28 B3 Balbriggan Ireland
21 K5 Bailleul-Sire-Berthoult France
71 G4 Balanacan Luzon Philippines
28 A5 BalnHeights Germany
21 K4 Bailleval France
115 K2 Baillie Hamilton I Northwest Territories Canada
124 B3 Balcancán Mexico
114 G3 Baillie Is Northwest Territories Canada
75 K3 Balángir India
85 D7 Baillif Guadeloupe W Indies
70 B4 Balangala Java
127 M4 Baillif Guadeloupe W Indies
70 M9 Balapulang Java
72 D1 Balase R Sulawesi
77 H5 Bāilundo Angola
21 H6 Balassagyarmat Hungary
99 L2 Bagley Minnesota U.S.A.
84 E7 Balát Egypt
99 P7 Bagley Wisconsin U.S.A.
137 M8 Balaton L Hungary
111 M11 Bainbridge Georgia U.S.A.
48 E2 Balatonfüred Hungary
95 L6 Bainbridge New York U.S.A.
94 D7 Bainbridge Ohio U.S.A.
99 L5 Bain-de-Bretagne France
140 B3 Baines, Mt N Terr Australia
48 D4 Balatonszárszó Hungary
37 K1 Balázsfalva
122 H5 Baines Quebec Canada
95 O5 Ballston Spa New York U.S.A.
... Baini see Yuqing
19 K4 Bains-les-Bains France
28 B6 Ballum Denmark
98 B1 Bainville Montana U.S.A.
124 F10 Balboa Panama
141 H8 Baiona see Bayona Spain
14 E2 Ballybay Ireland
59 J2 Bairab Co L China
14 D2 Ballybofey Ireland
109 H3 Baird Texas U.S.A.
14 D2 Ballybunion Ireland
116 E3 Baird Inlet Alaska U.S.A.
144 D5 Baird New Zealand
138 F4 Balcarce Argentina
116 G3 Baird Mts Alaska U.S.A.
119 O8 Balcarres Saskatchewan Canada
65 D3 Bairin Youqi China
62 C3 Bairin Youqi China
133 F6 Balcarce Argentina
101 S7 Bairoil Wyoming U.S.A.
79 H7 Bār'ir, Wādī watercourse Jordan
47 J1 Balchik Bulgaria
139 H7 Bairnsdale Victoria Australia
109 O3 Balch Springs Texas U.S.A.
139 J7 Bairnsdale Victoria Australia
144 F7 Balclutha New Zealand
21 K5 Bais Ille-et-Vilaine France
9 F5 Balcombe England
15 B7 Bais Mayenne France
100 H6 Bald Eagle Mt Oregon U.S.A.
28 C7 Baisha China
94 K6 Bald Eagle Mt Pennsylvania U.S.A.
28 D7 Baisha China
67 E3 Baishan Shaiku res China
41 H3 Baldegg See L Switzerland
67 C8 Baishui Feng mt China
113 C11 Bald Hd W Australia Australia
65 A7 Baishui China
44 D2 Baldichieri d'Asti Italy
70 H3 Baishui Jiang R China
94 F9 Bald Knob West Virginia U.S.A.
22 D5 Baisieux France
13 G6 Baslow England
128 C4 Bait Peru
13 G6 Baldock England
95 J2 Baisioga Lithuania
102 J4 Baldo, Mt Italy
128 F4 Baitadi Nepal
70 H6 Baldwin Florida U.S.A.
69 P7 Bai Thuong Vietnam
110 L3 Baldwin Louisiana U.S.A.
86 A3 Baixing China
94 D3 Baldwin Michigan U.S.A.
86 C3 Baixing China
110 K3 Baldwin Kansas U.S.A.
86 E4 Baixo Alentejo prov Portugal
99 P5 Baldwin Wisconsin U.S.A.
130 B4 Baixo Guandu Brazil
98 B2 Baldwin North Dakota U.S.A.
87 B7 Baixo Longa Angola
144 D5 Baldwin Park California U.S.A.
65 C7 Baiyang Dian L China
70 D1 Baldwin Pen Alaska U.S.A.
65 C9 Baiyangping China
118 C6 Baldwin Saskatchewan Canada
72 F4 Baiyashi see Dong'an
13 J7 Baldwin North Dakota U.S.A.
58 D4 Baiyin Sudan
95 P4 Baldwinville Massachusetts U.S.A.
86 C3 Baiyu China
87 B8 Balombo Angola
65 A8 Baiyu Shan mts China
114 E2 Balonne R Queensland Australia
84 F4 Balzi Hungary
119 H7 Baldy Mt Manitoba Canada
48 D2 Baja Hungary
106 D3 Baldy Peak mt New Mexico U.S.A.
124 B3 Baja,Pta C Mexico
86 B4 Balé mt Ethiopia
74 E6 Balotra India
84 B3 Baja Blanca Argentina
33 J6 Balow Germany
71 K9 Bais, Islas de Indonesia
12 D4 Balquhidder Scotland
124 C3 Bahía Kino Mexico
17 J7 Baleares, Islas prov Spain
75 J8 Balrampur India
133 C3 Bahía Pargua Chile
48 E5 Balearic Islands see Baleares, Islas arch
33 G3 Balsam L Wisconsin U.S.A.
126 D2 Bahía Tortugas Mexico
128 C7 Balsas Brazil
121 J5 Balsam Lake Ontario Canada

Column 6

143 F7 Baker Lake W Australia Australia
115 K5 Baker Lake Northwest Territories Canada
100 D1 Baker,Mt Washington U.S.A.
125 P9 Bakers Belize
102 P6 Bakersfield California U.S.A.
112 E1 Bakersfield North Carolina U.S.A.
108 E5 Bakers Texas U.S.A.
95 P2 Bakersfield Vermont U.S.A.
9 E1 Bakewell England
86 C3 Bakhardok Iran
54 D11 Bakhmach Ukraine
54 D5 Bakhmut Ukraine
78 L4 Bākhtarān Iran
77 B3 Bakhtiarī va Chahār Maḥāll prov Iran
77 B3 Bakir R Turkey
47 M11 Bakır R Turkey
29 T9 Bakkagerdhi Iceland
25 F2 Bakkeveen Netherlands
124 K7 Bakke Turkey
86 D5 Bako Ethiopia
85 C6 Bako Ivory Coast
69 C11 Bakongan Sumatra
86 D4 Bakony mts Hungary
86 D4 Bakony Cent Afr Republic
85 C6 Bakoye R Guinea/Mali
54 L1 Baksheyevo Russian Federation
26 K6 Baktsjaure Sweden
78 M1 Baku Azerbaijan
71 K1 Bakubung Pt Mindanao
77 K1 Bakkhab R Afghanistan
57 G2 Bakkhash Kazakhstan
57 G2 Bakkhash, Ozero L Kazakhstan
32 H7 Bakum Germany
69 G12 Bakung isld Indonesia
121 L7 Bala Ontario Canada
78 D2 Bālā Turkey
8 C2 Bala Wales
70 B4 Balabac Str Borneo/Philippines
71 C7 Balabec isld Palawan Philippines
70 H8 Balabalangan, Kep islds Indonesia
141 K8 Balabalangan Pulau Pulau islds Indonesia
26 J3 Balabino Ukraine
128 C6 Bala,Cerros de mts Bolivia
127 J2 Balaclava Jamaica
48 E4 Balaclava California U.S.A.
48 H4 Baladeh Iran
102 L3 Balaghat India
80 F3 Balagansk Russian Federation
74 J3 Balaghat India
56 F4 Balagansk Russian Federation
74 H8 Balaguer Spain
74 B3 Balaikarangan Kalimantan
70 B4 Balaipurugu Sumatra
70 B6 Balairam Kalimantan
70 K8 Balaisepuac Kalimantan
29 K5 Balak, Gunung Sumatra
138 E5 Balaklava South Australia Australia
54 H7 Balakleya Ukraine
54 H7 Balakovo Russian Federation
8 C2 Balakovo Russian Federation
87 D1 Balama Mozambique
141 H2 Balambangan isld Malaysia
28 B3 Balbriggan Ireland
71 G4 Balanacan Luzon Philippines
28 A5 Balnin Germany
124 B3 Balcancán Mexico
75 K3 Balángir India
70 B4 Balangala Java
70 M9 Balapulang Java
72 D1 Balase R Sulawesi
21 H6 Balassagyarmat Hungary
84 E7 Balát Egypt
137 M8 Balaton L Hungary
48 E2 Balatonfüred Hungary
48 D4 Balatonszárszó Hungary
37 K1 Balázsfalva
95 O5 Ballston Spa New York U.S.A.
28 B6 Ballum Denmark
124 F10 Balboa Panama
14 E2 Ballybay Ireland
14 D2 Ballybofey Ireland
14 D2 Ballybunion Ireland
14 E1 Ballycastle N Ireland
133 F6 Balcarce Argentina
119 O8 Balcarres Saskatchewan Canada
14 D2 Ballyduff Ireland
47 J1 Balchik Bulgaria
109 O3 Balch Springs Texas U.S.A.
144 F7 Balclutha New Zealand
9 F5 Balcombe England
100 H6 Bald Eagle Mt Oregon U.S.A.
94 K6 Bald Eagle Mt Pennsylvania U.S.A.
41 H3 Baldegg See L Switzerland
113 C11 Bald Hd W Australia Australia
44 D2 Baldichieri d'Asti Italy
94 F9 Bald Knob West Virginia U.S.A.
13 G6 Baslow England
13 G6 Baldock England
102 J4 Baldo, Mt Italy
70 H6 Baldwin Florida U.S.A.
110 L3 Baldwin Louisiana U.S.A.
94 D3 Baldwin Michigan U.S.A.
110 K3 Baldwin Kansas U.S.A.
99 P5 Baldwin Wisconsin U.S.A.
98 B2 Baldwin North Dakota U.S.A.
144 D5 Baldwin Park California U.S.A.
70 D1 Baldwin Pen Alaska U.S.A.
118 C6 Baldwin Saskatchewan Canada
13 J7 Baldwin North Dakota U.S.A.
95 P4 Baldwinville Massachusetts U.S.A.
119 H7 Baldy Mt Manitoba Canada
106 D3 Baldy Peak mt New Mexico U.S.A.
86 B4 Balé mt Ethiopia
84 B3 Baja Blanca Argentina
12 D4 Balquhidder Scotland
17 J7 Baleares, Islas prov Spain
48 E5 Balearic Islands see Baleares, Islas arch
128 C7 Balsas Brazil

Column 7

119 N8 Balgonie Saskatchewan Canada
32 K10 Balhorn Germany
86 B4 Bali Cameroon
70 P10 Bali isld Indonesia
71 F6 Bali Philippines
69 D11 Balige Sumatra
31 N6 Baligród Poland
73 G4 Balihan
72 A1 Balikesir T Syria
86 C3 Bali Illi R Chad
70 G2 Balimbing Tawitaw isld Philippines
69 E10 Baling Malaysia
65 D3 Balingan Sarawak
65 D3 Balingiao China
48 G5 Balint Romania
70 P9 Bali, Selat Bali/Java
70 P10 Bali Selat Bali/Java
70 G2 Balingup Australia
120 D5 Baliza Brazil
130 D5 Baliza Brazil
32 K5 Balk Netherlands
48 G3 Bálkány Hungary
55 C4 Balkany Russian Federation
55 C4 Balkashino Kazakhstan
25 F3 Balkbrug Netherlands
77 K1 Balkh Afghanistan
57 G2 Balkhash Kazakhstan
57 G2 Balkhash Kazakhstan
74 H9 Balkonda India
15 C4 Ballachulish Scotland
143 E9 Balladonia W Australia
84 F4 Ballas Jordan
15 E3 Ballater Scotland
12 D5 Ballaugh I of Man U.K.
28 F4 Balle Denmark
28 F4 Ballen Denmark
133 C3 Ballena, Pta C Chile
134 C13 Balleny Islands Antarctica
29 K5 Ballerup Denmark
112 C3 Ball Ground Georgia U.S.A.
75 L6 Ballia India
14 C3 Ballina Ireland
14 C3 Ballinasloe Ireland
14 D2 Ballindine Ireland
14 C4 Ballingarry Ireland
108 H4 Ballinger Texas U.S.A.
14 C3 Ballinluig Scotland
14 B3 Ballinrobe Ireland
37 J6 Ballmertshofen Germany
118 B7 Ball,Mt Alberta Canada
12 D1 Balloch Scotland
20 D4 Ballon d'Alsace mt France
21 L6 Ballots France
21 H6 Ballstädt Germany
137 M8 Ball's Pyramid isld Pacific Oc
37 K1 Ballstädt Germany
95 O4 Ballston Spa New York U.S.A.
28 B6 Ballum Denmark
14 E2 Ballybay Ireland
14 D2 Ballybofey Ireland
14 D2 Ballybunion Ireland
14 E1 Ballycastle N Ireland
14 C3 Ballyclare N Ireland
14 D3 Ballyconnell Ireland
14 D3 Ballycotton B Ireland
14 D2 Ballyduff Ireland
12 D3 Ballygrant Scotland
14 D2 Ballyhaise Ireland
14 C3 Ballyhaunis Ireland
14 D3 Ballyhoura Hills Ireland
14 C3 Ballyjamesduff Ireland
14 C4 Ballymahon Ireland
14 E1 Ballymena N Ireland
14 E1 Ballymoney N Ireland
14 E1 Ballynahinch N Ireland
14 E1 Ballyquintin Pt N Ireland
14 D2 Ballyragget Ireland
14 C3 Ballyshannon Ireland
14 E1 Ballyvaughan Ireland
14 B3 Ballyvourney Ireland
14 D2 Balmaclellan Scotland
48 E2 Balmazújváros Hungary
42 D2 Balme Italy
40 C5 Balmhorn mt Switzerland
141 K1 Balmoral Victoria Australia
119 O4 Balmoral Manitoba Canada
144 D5 Balmoral New Zealand
144 D5 Balmoral oil rig North Sea
15 E3 Balmoral Castle Scotland
108 D6 Balmorhea Texas U.S.A.
13 H5 Balmullo Scotland
84 H4 Balochistān prov Pakistan
87 B8 Balombo Angola
114 E2 Balonne R Queensland Australia
74 E6 Balotra India
33 J6 Balow Germany
12 D4 Balquhidder Scotland
75 J8 Balrampur India
33 G3 Balsam L Wisconsin U.S.A.
121 J5 Balsam Lake Ontario Canada
129 G6 Balsas Brazil
124 H8 Balsas Mexico
25 K8 Balsas R Mexico
21 H6 Balsham England
79 B7 Balsjö Sweden
27 K8 Balsta Sweden
29 L4 Bålsta Sweden
20 G5 Balsthal Switzerland
54 C8 Balta Ukraine
98 C1 Balta North Dakota U.S.A.
132 E3 Baltar Argentina
16 C2 Baltar Spain
28 B3 Baltasar Brum Uruguay
54 C8 Bălţi Moldova
84 C3 Baltim Egypt
80 A7 Baltimore Ireland
88 E8 Baltimore S Africa
95 L7 Baltimore Maryland U.S.A.
94 D6 Baltimore conurbation Maryland U.S.A.
14 E4 Balfron Scotland
Baltit see Hunza
31 M1 Baltiysk Russian Federation
Baltrum see Baltruß (?)
80 G8 Balu Jordan

77 G6 **Balūchestān va Sīstān** Iran
Balūchistān *prov see* **Balochistān**
72 J3 **Balūchistān** *reg* Pakistan/ Iran
70 C3 **Balui** *R* Sarawak
71 E7 **Balukbaluk** *isld* Philippines
69 D12 **Balumundan** Sumatra
70 C5 **Baluran, Gunung** *mt* Kalimantan
75 N6 **Balurghat** India
71 G8 **Balut** *isld* Philippines
32 G10 **Balve** Germany
52 C6 **Balvi** Latvia
47 J5 **Balya** Turkey
84 J4 **Balyana,El** Egypt
56 H4 **Bal Yeravnoye, Oz** *L* Russian Federation
56 C4 **Balyksa** Russian Federation
56 E5 **Balyktyg Khem** *R* Russian Federation
118 C7 **Balzac** Alberta Canada
77 F5 **Bam** Iran
67 B4 **Bama** China
86 B3 **Bama** Nigeria
141 F1 **Bamaga** Queensland Australia
85 C6 **Bamako** Mali
128 C5 **Bambamarca** Peru
71 E3 **Bamban** Luzon Philippines
71 E2 **Bambang** Luzon Philippines
71 E8 **Bambannan** *isld* Philippines
86 D4 **Bambari** Cent Afr Republic
141 H4 **Bambaroo** Queensland Australia
13 F6 **Bamber Br** England
37 K4 **Bamberg** Germany
112 F4 **Bamberg** South Carolina U.S.A.
86 E5 **Bambesa** Zaire
86 E5 **Bambili** Zaire
86 C5 **Bambio** Cent Afr Republic
27 D13 **Bamble** Norway
142 D5 **Bamboo Creek** W Australia Australia
142 C5 **Bamboo Springs** W Australia Australia
83 M13 **Bambou Mts** Mauritius
130 F7 **Bambui** Brazil
70 D5 **Bambulung** Kalimantan
13 G2 **Bamburgh** England
86 B4 **Bamenda** Cameroon
117 L11 **Bamfield** British Columbia Canada
77 K2 **Bāmīān** Afghanistan
67 C4 **Bamian** China
65 F3 **Bamiancheng** China
Bamiantong *see* **Muling**
86 C4 **Bamingui** *R* Cent Afr Republic
86 C4 **Bamingui-Bangoran Nat. Park** Cent Afr Republic
68 G6 **Bam Nak** Cambodia
68 E5 **Bamnet Narong** Thailand
124 E5 **Bamoa** Mexico
69 A8 **Bampoka I** Nicobar Is
77 H6 **Bam Posht, Kūh-e** *mts* Iran
8 C6 **Bampton** England
9 E4 **Bampton** England
77 G6 **Bampūr** Iran
77 G6 **Bampur** *R* Iran
74 J9 **Bāmrāgad** India
68 H4 **Ba Na** Vietnam
137 O1 **Banaba** *isld* Pacific Oc
129 L5 **Banabuiu Açude** *res* Brazil
14 D3 **Banagher** Ireland
71 E4 **Banahao, Mt** Luzon Philippines
86 E5 **Banalia** Zaire
68 G7 **Banam** Cambodia
85 C6 **Banamba** Mali
124 D2 **Banámichi** Mexico
141 K6 **Banana** Queensland Australia
129 H6 **Bananal, Ilha do** Brazil
113 G9 **Banana R** Florida U.S.A.
130 J9 **Bananeiras** Brazil
76 G7 **Bananga** Nicobar Is
68 F6 **Ban Aranyaprathet** Thailand
47 J3 **Banarlı** Turkey
69 D8 **Ba Na San** Thailand
48 F6 **Banatsko Novo Selo** Serbia Yugoslavia
15 C4 **Banavie** Scotland
71 J8 **Banawaja** *isld* Indonesia
78 B2 **Banaz** Turkey
68 E4 **Ban Bang Mun Nak** Thailand
68 E4 **Ban Bang Rakam** Thailand
71 G6 **Banbayan Pt** Mindanao Philippines
69 E10 **Ban Betong** Thailand
68 J6 **Ban Bik** Vietnam
14 E2 **Banbridge** N Ireland
68 E5 **Ban Bua Chum** Thailand
68 F5 **Ban Bua Yai** Thailand
68 E5 **Ban Bu Khanum** Thailand
68 G5 **Ban Bungxai** Laos
68 H5 **Ban Bungxai** Laos
9 E3 **Banbury** England
71 C6 **Bancalan** Palawan Philippines
138 F4 **Bancannia, L** New South Wales Australia
85 A4 **Banc d'Arguin Nat. Park** Mauritania
68 D3 **Ban Chang Khoeng** Thailand
68 F4 **Ban Channabot** Thailand
68 D3 **Ban Chiang Dao** Thailand
15 F3 **Banchory** Scotland
68 E4 **Ban Chum Phae** Thailand
125 Q8 **Banco Chinchorro** *isld* Mexico
71 D7 **Bancoron** *isld* Philippines
121 N7 **Bancroft** Ontario Canada
101 O7 **Bancroft** Idaho U.S.A.
99 M6 **Bancroft** Iowa U.S.A.
98 J5 **Bancroft** South Dakota U.S.A.
48 J4 **Band** Romania
74 J6 **Banda** India
69 B10 **Banda Aceh** Sumatra
69 C11 **Bandahara, Gunung** *mt* Sumatra
61 N7 **Bandai-Asahi Nat.Pk** Japan
61 O8 **Bandai-san** *mt* Japan
85 B7 **Bandajuma** Sierra Leone
27 C12 **Bandak** *L* Norway
85 C7 **Bandama** *R* Ivory Coast
68 G5 **Ban Dan** Thailand
77 G4 **Bandan Kuh** *mt* Iran
Bandar *see* **Machilipatnam**
77 J2 **Bandar** Afghanistan
87 F9 **Bandar** Mozambique
75 J4 **Bandar** Nepal
70 K8 **Bandaragung** Sumatra
86 B2 **Bandarbeyla** Somalia
77 E6 **Bandar-e 'Abbās** Iran
77 A1 **Bandar-e Anzalī** Iran
77 B4 **Bandar-e Deylam** Iran
77 D6 **Bandar-e Khoemir** Iran
77 A4 **Bandar-e Khomeynī** Iran
77 D6 **Bandar-e Lengeh** Iran
77 A4 **Bandar-e Ma'shūr** Iran
77 B5 **Bandar-e Rīg** Iran
77 D1 **Bandar-e Torkeman** Iran
86 B1 **Bandar Murcaay** Somalia
70 D2 **Bandar Seri Begawan** Brunei
136 F3 **Banda Sea** Indonesia
88 E7 **Bandawe** Malawi
22 J3 **Bande** Belgium
16 B2 **Bande** Spain
129 K8 **Bandeira** *mt* Brazil
130 H7 **Bandeira** *mt* Brazil
130 E8 **Bandeirantes** Brazil
130 D8 **Bandeirantes, I. dos** Brazil
106 D6 **Bandelier Nat.Mon** New Mexico U.S.A.
77 D6 **Band-e Moghūyeh** Iran
109 H6 **Bandera** Texas U.S.A.
108 B4 **Banderas** Mexico
124 G7 **Banderas,B de** Mexico
28 G7 **Bandholm** Denmark
85 D6 **Bandiagara** Mali
77 K2 **Band-i-Amur** *R* Afghanistan
77 J2 **Band-i-Balan** *mts* Afghanistan
78 B1 **Bandırma** Turkey
47 J4 **Bandırma Körfezi** *G* Turkey
77 J2 **Band-i-Turkestan** *mts* Afghanistan
70 M9 **Bandjar** Java
70 D6 **Bandjarmasin** Kalimantan
70 M9 **Bandjarnegara** Java
19 P18 **Bandol** France
Ban Don *see* **Surat Thani**
14 C5 **Bandon** *R* Ireland
14 C5 **Bandon** Ireland
100 A6 **Bandon** Oregon U.S.A.
68 G4 **Ban Dong** Laos
68 F4 **Ban Don Khi** Thailand
74 E9 **Bandra** India
86 C6 **Bandundu** Zaire
70 L9 **Bandung** Java
69 F12 **Bandung** Sumatra
68 G4 **Ban Dupre** Laos
94 F9 **Bandy** Virginia U.S.A.
143 D7 **Bandya** W Australia Australia
48 L5 **Băneasa** Romania
78 K4 **Baneh** Iran
71 B2 **Banema** Halmahera Indonesia
17 G6 **Bañeras** Spain
126 G4 **Banes** Cuba
69 D8 **Ban Fai Tha** Thailand
Banff *co see* **Grampian** *reg*
118 B7 **Banff** Alberta Canada
15 F3 **Banff** Scotland
85 D6 **Banfora** Burkina
86 D7 **Banga** Zaire
71 F7 **Bangaan** Mindanao Philippines
71 G7 **Bangai Pt** Mindanao Philippines
71 E7 **Bangalao** *isld* Philippines
76 C4 **Bangalore** India
71 E2 **Bangar** Luzon Philippines
70 D2 **Bangar** Sarawak
70 E3 **Bangatan** Kalimantan
71 H7 **Bangbong** Sulawesi
27 H12 **Bångbro** Sweden
86 C5 **Bangé** Cameroon
110 E4 **Bangert** Missouri U.S.A.
70 C4 **Bang,G** *mt* Kalimantan
71 H6 **Banggai, Kep** *islds* Indonesia
71 C7 **Banggi** *isld* Sabah
84 F3 **Banghāzī** Libya
68 G4 **Bang Hieng** *R* Laos
70 O9 **Bangil** Java
69 G14 **Bangka** *isld* Indonesia
71 J4 **Bangka** Sulawesi Indonesia
70 C8 **Bangkal** Kalimantan
70 O9 **Bangkalan** Java
70 F7 **Bangkala, Teluk** *B* Sulawesi
69 C11 **Bangkaru** *isld* Sumatra
69 G14 **Bangka,Selat** *str* Sumatra
69 D12 **Bangkinang** Sumatra
70 G4 **Bangkir** Sulawesi Indonesia
69 F14 **Bangko** Sumatra
63 **Bangkok** *conurbation* Thailand
68 E6 **Bangkok,Bight of** Thailand
70 D6 **Bangkuang** Kalimantan
71 H5 **Bangkulu** Sulawesi Indonesia
71 H9 **Bangkulua** Sumbawa Indonesia
75 N6 **Bangladesh** *rep* S Asia
68 E6 **Bang Lamung** Thailand
68 J7 **Ba Ngoi** Vietnam
66 B5 **Bangong Co** *L* China
119 P8 **Bangor** Saskatchewan Canada
20 B7 **Bangor** France
14 F2 **Bangor** N Ireland
95 T2 **Bangor** Maine U.S.A.
94 A4 **Bangor** Michigan U.S.A.
95 M6 **Bangor** Pennsylvania U.S.A.
8 B1 **Bangor** Wales
86 C4 **Bangoran** *R* Cent Afr Republic
109 H4 **Bangs** Texas U.S.A.
70 E5 **Bangsalsepulun** Kalimantan
68 D7 **Bang Saphan Yai** Thailand
28 F2 **Bangsbostrand** Denmark
103 L5 **Bangs,Mt** Arizona U.S.A.
26 E7 **Bangsund** Norway
71 E2 **Bangued** Luzon Philippines
86 C5 **Bangui** Cent Afr Republic
71 E1 **Bangui** Luzon Philippines
69 D11 **Bangunpurba** Sumatra
88 B7 **Bangweulu, L** Zambia
68 F3 **Ban Hai** Laos
68 D4 **Ban Hat Sao** Thailand
69 E9 **Ban Hat Yai** Thailand
87 F10 **Banhine Nat. Park** Mozambique
68 F3 **Ban Hin Heup** Laos
68 J6 **Ban Ho** Vietnam
68 E2 **Ban Houayxay** Laos
68 F3 **Ban Huai Kho** Thailand
68 D7 **Ban Huai Yang** Thailand
86 D4 **Bani** Cent Afr Republic
127 J5 **Baní** Dominican Rep
85 C6 **Bani** *R* Mali
71 D2 **Bani** Luzon Philippines
116 L7 **Ban I** Alaska U.S.A.
85 E5 **Bani Bangou** Niger
127 J5 **Bánica** Dominican Rep
31 H2 **Banie** Poland
85 E6 **Banikoara** Benin
86 B6 **Banio, Lagune** *lagoon* Gabon
71 D3 **Bani Pt** Luzon Philippines
94 H10 **Banister** *R* Virginia U.S.A.
84 E3 **Banī Walīd** Libya
79 F3 **Baniyās** Syria
80 F1 **Bāniyās** Syria
48 E6 **Banja Koviljača** Bosnia-Herzegovina
42 H4 **Banja Luka** Bosnia-Herzegovina
70 D6 **Banjarbaru** Kalimantan
68 H6 **Ban Jeng Drom** Vietnam
85 A6 **Banjul** The Gambia
70 M9 **Banjumas** Java
142 B3 **Banjup** *dist* Perth, W Aust Australia
140 C4 **Banka Banka** N Terr Australia
68 G5 **Ban Kadian** Laos
68 E4 **Ban Kaeng** Thailand
69 E9 **Ban Kam Phaeng Phet** Thailand
69 D9 **Ban Kantang** Thailand
89 D9 **Bankberg** *mts* S Africa
12 E3 **Bankend** Scotland
68 H5 **Ban Keng Phao** Cambodia
68 F2 **Ban Keo Lom** Vietnam
68 E6 **Ban Khai** Thailand
68 F1 **Ban Khang Kha** Vietnam
68 D6 **Ban Khao Yoi** Thailand
111 J8 **Bankhead L** Alabama U.S.A.
68 E3 **Ban Khing** Laos
68 F6 **Ban Khlung** Thailand
69 D8 **Ban Khok Kloi** Thailand
69 D9 **Ban Khuan Mao** Thailand
68 F4 **Ban Khuk Muang** Thailand
68 E3 **Ban Khun Ban Hai** Thailand
68 F5 **Ban Khu Noi** Thailand
68 C3 **Ban Khun Yuam** Thailand
68 J6 **Ban Kniet** Vietnam
70 E7 **Bankobankoang** *isld* Indonesia
68 D4 **Ban Krai** Thailand
100 J5 **Banks** Idaho U.S.A.
110 F7 **Banks** Mississippi U.S.A.
100 B4 **Banks** Oregon U.S.A.
138 F7 **Banks,C** South Australia Australia
117 H9 **Banks I** British Columbia Canada
147 J2 **Banks I** Northwest Territories Canada
100 F2 **Banks L** Washington U.S.A.
144 D5 **Banks Peninsula** New Zealand
139 K7 **Bankstown Airfield** Sydney, New S Wales Australia
68 D6 **Ban Kui Nua** Thailand
75 M7 **Bankura** India
68 G4 **Ban Kut Hae** Thailand
46 F2 **Bankya** Bulgaria
68 F5 **Ban Lamduan** Thailand
71 F3 **Banla Pt** Philippines
68 D5 **Ban Le Kathe** Thailand
68 E5 **Ban Len** Thailand
68 C3 **Ban Mae La Luang** Thailand
68 D3 **Ban Mae Mo** Thailand
68 D4 **Ban Mae Ramat** Thailand
68 C3 **Ban Mae Sariang** Thailand
68 D4 **Ban Mae Sot** Thailand
68 D3 **Ban Mae Suai** Thailand
68 D3 **Ban Mae Thalop** Thailand
68 E5 **Ban Mi** Thailand
68 D3 **Ban Mong Pong** Thailand
68 E3 **Ban Muang** Thailand
68 F5 **Ban Muang Phon** Thailand
14 E4 **Bann** *R* Ireland
14 E2 **Bann** *R* N Ireland
71 E1 **Banna** Luzon Philippines
69 D8 **Ban Na** Thailand
68 F4 **Ban Na Baek** Thailand
68 H4 **Ban Nabo** Laos
101 N4 **Bannack** Montana U.S.A.
68 G4 **Ban Na Kae** Thailand
68 E3 **Ban Na Kon** Thailand
20 C6 **Bannalec** France
68 E2 **Ban Na Mo** Laos
68 E4 **Ban Nam Pong** Thailand
68 F1 **Ban Nam Sau** Vietnam
68 E3 **Ban Na Noi** Thailand
68 F3 **Ban Naphong** Laos
68 F3 **Ban Na Sabaeng** Thailand
69 E9 **Ban Na Thawi** Thailand
142 F4 **Bannerman, Mt** W Australia Australia
126 F2 **Bannerman Town** Eleuthera Bahamas
102 H8 **Banning** California U.S.A.
Banningville *see* **Bandundu**
40 H6 **Bannio** Italy
41 H6 **Bannio-Anzino** Italy
121 N8 **Bannockburn** Ontario Canada
144 B6 **Bannockburn** New Zealand
12 E1 **Bannockburn** Scotland
101 M5 **Bannock Pass** Idaho/ Montana U.S.A.
101 N7 **Bannock Ra** Idaho U.S.A.
68 C4 **Ban Noi** Thailand
68 E2 **Ban Nong Kha** Laos
68 F5 **Ban Nong Makha** Thailand
68 H5 **Ban Nong Met** Laos
68 F5 **Ban Nong Waeng** Thailand
74 D2 **Bannu** Pakistan
17 J2 **Bañolas** Spain
19 P16 **Banon** France
124 H6 **Bañón** Mexico
31 L7 **Bánovce** Czechoslovakia
Banow *see* **Andarāb**
68 F3 **Ban Pacpeup** Laos
68 D3 **Ban Pak Bong** Thailand
68 D7 **Ban Pak Chan** Thailand
68 D6 **Ban Pak Khlong** Thailand
68 E6 **Ban Pak Nam** Thailand
68 D7 **Ban Pak Nam** Thailand
68 E3 **Ban Pak Neun** Laos
68 F5 **Ban Pak Thong Chai** Thailand
68 E5 **Ban Phachi** Thailand
68 G4 **Ban Phaeng** Thailand
68 F5 **Ban Phai** Thailand
68 E6 **Ban Phanat Nikhom** Thailand
68 D6 **Ban Phattaya** Thailand
68 H5 **Ban Phon** Laos
68 G5 **Ban Phon Ngam** Thailand
68 D5 **Banphot Phisai** Thailand
68 D4 **Ban Phran Katai** Thailand
68 E4 **Ban Phrom Phirom** Thailand
68 F5 **Ban Phutthaisong** Thailand
Ban Pla Soi *see* **Chon Buri**
68 D6 **Ban Pong** Thailand
67 A3 **Banqiao** China
65 D7 **Banquan** China
68 D4 **Ban Saen To** Thailand
68 E2 **Ban Sai** Laos
68 F5 **Ban Sai** Thailand
68 D5 **Ban Sai Yok** Thailand
69 E9 **Ban Sanam Chai** Thailand
68 F5 **Ban Sangae** Thailand
68 D3 **Ban Saraphi Chae Hom** Thailand
68 E6 **Ban Sattahip** Thailand
68 D7 **Ban Sawi** Thailand
75 K5 **Bansi** India
69 E8 **Ban Sichon** Thailand
31 L7 **Banská Bystrica** Czechoslovakia
31 L7 **Banská Stiavnica** Czechoslovakia
46 F3 **Bansko** Bulgaria
68 D3 **Ban Sop Huai Hai** Thailand
68 D4 **Ban Sop Prap** Thailand
68 G3 **Ban Sot** Laos
68 D4 **Ban Sut Ta** Thailand
68 F5 **Ban Suwai** Thailand
74 F7 **Banswara** India
71 J9 **Banta** *isld* Sumbawa Indonesia
70 F7 **Bantaeng** Sulawesi Indonesia
68 E5 **Ban Ta Khli** Thailand
69 E13 **Bantal** Sumatra
83 M8 **Bantam** Cocos Is Indian Oc
68 F5 **Ban Tan** Thailand
68 F6 **Ban Ta Ruang** Thailand
68 H4 **Ban Taup** Laos
68 F3 **Ban Ta Viang** Laos
71 F5 **Bantayan** *isld* Philippines
32 L8 **Banteln** Germany
70 L9 **Banten** Java
69 D8 **Ban Tha Chang** Thailand
68 G5 **Ban Tham Khae** Thailand
68 D5 **Ban Thap Phung** Thailand
69 E8 **Ban Tha Sala** Thailand
68 D4 **Ban Tha Song Yang** Thailand
68 E5 **Ban Tha Tako** Thailand
68 H5 **Ban Thateng** Laos
68 G4 **Ban Tha Uthen** Thailand
69 E9 **Ban Thepha** Thailand
22 J5 **Bantheville** France
68 D6 **Ban Thung Luang** Thailand
71 F4 **Banton** *isld* Philippines
68 H6 **Ban Treo** Cambodia
14 B5 **Bantry** Ireland
98 F1 **Bantry** North Dakota U.S.A.
14 B5 **Bantry B** Ireland
70 N9 **Bantul** Java
74 D8 **Bantva** India
76 B4 **Bantval** India
68 F4 **Ban Waeng Noi** Thailand
68 E4 **Ban Wang Saphong** Thailand
68 G4 **Ban Wang Ta Mua** Thailand
8 D5 **Banwell** England
68 F4 **Ban Wiang Khuk** Thailand
46 G2 **Banya** Bulgaria
69 C11 **Banyak, Kep.** *isld* Indonesia
68 F4 **Ban Yang Talat** Thailand
68 D6 **Ban Yang Yong** Thailand
68 H6 **Ban Ya Soup** Vietnam
141 K1 **Banyo** *dist* Brisbane, Qnsld Australia
86 B4 **Banyo** Cameroon
Bañyoles *see* **Bañolas**
69 G14 **Banyuasin** *R* Sumatra
70 P10 **Banyuwangi** Java
37 L3 **Banz** Germany
146 E14 **Banzare Coast** Antarctica
81 E11 **Banzare Seamount** Southern Oc
67 B4 **Bao'an** China
67 E5 **Bao'an** China
Baocheng *see* **Taibus Qi**
58 F4 **Baode** China
65 D5 **Baodi** China
58 G4 **Baoding** China
65 B7 **Baofeng** China
67 A5 **Bao Ha** Vietnam
65 D4 **Bao He** *R* China
58 E5 **Baoji** China
67 C2 **Baojing** China
Baokang *see* **Horqin Zouyi Zhongqi**
67 D1 **Baokang** China
68 G1 **Bao Lac** Vietnam
65 F3 **Baolizhen** China
68 H7 **Bao Loc** Vietnam
65 J1 **Baoqing** China
67 G1 **Baoshan** China
68 J3 **Baoting** China
58 E3 **Baotou** China
85 C6 **Baoulé** *R* Mali
59 G5 **Baoying** China
Baoyou *see* **Ledong**
76 E3 **Bapatla** India
22 D3 **Bapaume** France
103 N8 **Bapchule** Arizona U.S.A.
121 M7 **Baptiste** Ontario Canada
80 D4 **Bāqa el Gharbiya** Israel
66 E5 **Baqên** China
79 F9 **Bāqir, J** *mt* Jordan
78 K5 **Ba'Qūbah** Iraq
80 F3 **Baqura** Jordan
22 H4 **Bar** *R* France
48 L1 **Bar** Ukraine
42 J6 **Bar** Montenegro Yugoslavia
86 F3 **Bara** Sudan
68 H7 **Ba Ra** Vietnam
86 H5 **Baraawe** Somalia
70 D6 **Barabai** Kalimantan
55 G3 **Barabinsk** Russian Federation
55 G4 **Barabinskaya Nizmennost'** *lowland* Russian Federation
99 R6 **Baraboo** Wisconsin U.S.A.
122 H5 **Barachois** Quebec Canada
126 G4 **Baracoa** Cuba
79 H3 **Baradah** Syria
99 S3 **Baraga** Michigan U.S.A.
48 L6 **Bărăganul** Romania
75 K8 **Baragarh** India
86 G5 **Baragoi** Kenya
75 N7 **Barahanager** India
127 J5 **Barahona** Dominican Rep
Barak *see* **Karkamiş**
57 F6 **Barak** Afghanistan
79 H2 **Barak** Turkey
88 B4 **Baraka** Zaire
77 L3 **Baraki Barak** Afghanistan
75 L8 **Barakot** India
55 E5 **Barakpay** Kazakhstan
141 K7 **Barakula** Queensland Australia
141 J6 **Baralaba** Queensland Australia
80 E1 **Bar'am** Israel
70 D3 **Baram** *R* Sarawak
128 G2 **Barama** *R* Guyana
74 F9 **Baramati** India
141 K7 **Barambah** *R* Queensland Australia
70 C2 **Baram,Tg** *C* Sarawak
54 B2 **Baran'** Belorussia
74 G6 **Baran** India
55 C2 **Baranchinskiy** Russian Federation
45 R6 **Baranello** Italy
86 E5 **Baranga** Zaire
21 P7 **Barangeon** *R* France
77 G4 **Baran, Kūh-e-** *mts* Iran
126 G9 **Baranoa** Colombia
117 F7 **Baranof I** Alaska U.S.A.
31 N5 **Baranów** Poland
48 E5 **Baranya** *co* Hungary
129 G6 **Barao de Capenema** Brazil
130 C5 **Barão de Melgaço** Mato Grosso Brazil
48 K4 **Baraolt** Romania
48 K4 **Baraoltului Munti** *mt* Romania
22 K3 **Baraque-le Fraiture** Belgium
22 L2 **Baraque Michel** Belgium
70 L9 **Barat** Java
70 B5 **Barat** Kalimantan
111 F12 **Barataria** Louisiana U.S.A.
111 G12 **Barataria B** Louisiana U.S.A.
71 N8 **Barat Daya, Kep** *islds* Philippines
71 L9 **Barati** Indonesia
138 E4 **Baratta** South Australia Australia
70 E5 **Baratus, Gunung** *mt* Kalimantan
75 M6 **Barauni** India
130 G7 **Barbacena** Minas Gerais Brazil
128 C3 **Barbacoas** Colombia
127 P6 **Barbados** Lesser Antilles
130 G9 **Barbalha** Brazil
45 O4 **Bárbara** Italy
120 C3 **Barbara L** Ontario Canada
45 L1 **Barbarano Vicentino** Italy
85 A4 **Barbas,C** Western Sahara
20 F8 **Barbâtre** France
122 D2 **Barbel,L** Quebec Canada
100 J6 **Barber** Idaho U.S.A.
45 K3 **Barberino di Mugello** Italy
45 K4 **Barberino di Val d'Elsa** Italy
102 R12 **Barbers Pt** Hawaiian Is
89 G5 **Barberton** S Africa
94 F5 **Barberton** Ohio U.S.A.
113 F8 **Barberville** Florida U.S.A.
18 E7 **Barbezieux** France
45 J4 **Barbona, M** *mt* Italy
128 D2 **Barbosa** Colombia
48 L5 **Barbosi** Romania
94 J8 **Barboursville** Virginia U.S.A.
110 N5 **Barbourville** Kentucky U.S.A.
127 O6 **Barbuda** *isld* Lesser Antilles
33 P9 **Barby** Germany
16 C4 **Barca d'Alva** Portugal
126 A2 **Barcadera** Aruba W Indies
126 A2 **Barcadera** Bonaire W Indies
141 H6 **Barcaldine** Queensland Australia
16 C6 **Barcarrota** Spain
17 J3 **Barcelona** *prov* Spain
17 J3 **Barcelona** Spain
127 M9 **Barcelona** Venezuela
128 F4 **Barcelos** Brazil
16 B3 **Barcelos** Portugal
37 J2 **Barchfeld** Germany
19 P16 **Barcillonnette** France
31 K3 **Barcin** Poland
112 L1 **Barco** North Carolina U.S.A.
141 G6 **Barcoo** *R* Queensland Australia
141 G6 **Barcoo Cr** Qnsld/S Aust Australia
141 H6 **Barcoorah, L** Queensland Australia
48 D5 **Barcs** Hungary
106 G6 **Bard** New Mexico U.S.A.
84 F5 **Bardaï** Chad
47 L5 **Bardakçi** Turkey
75 M7 **Barddhamān** India
31 N6 **Bardejov** Czechoslovakia
33 R8 **Bardenitz** Germany
84 G3 **Bardī, Al** Libya
139 J4 **Bardine** New South Wales Australia
9 F1 **Bardney** England
41 N6 **Bardolino** Italy
122 E2 **Bardoux,L** Quebec Canada
33 M6 **Bardowick** Germany
13 E5 **Bardsea** England
8 B2 **Bardsey** *isld* Wales
8 B2 **Bardsey Sd.** Wales
110 L4 **Bardstown** Kentucky U.S.A.
26 K3 **Bardu** Norway
26 K3 **Barduelv** *R* Norway
141 H7 **Barduthulla** Queensland Australia
110 G5 **Bardwell** Kentucky U.S.A.
109 L3 **Bardwell** Texas U.S.A.
145 F3 **Bare I** New Zealand
74 H4 **Bareilly** India
32 J7 **Barenburg** Germany
37 O3 **Bärenstein** Germany
21 M2 **Barentin** France
21 J4 **Barenton** France
22 F4 **Barenton-Bugny** France
50 B1 **Barentsöya** *isld* Spitzbergen
147 J13 **Barents Sea** Arctic Oc
86 G2 **Barentu** Ethiopia
70 D3 **Bareo** Sarawak
20 H2 **Barfleur** France
20 H2 **Barfleur, Pte. de** France
9 E3 **Barford** England
9 E5 **Barford** England
66 C5 **Barga** China
45 H3 **Barga** Italy
86 B1 **Bargaal** Somalia
141 K6 **Bargara** Queensland Australia
16 E5 **Bargas** Spain
86 G4 **Bargē** Ethiopia
44 B2 **Barge** Italy
123 Q2 **Barge B** Labrador, Nfld Canada
33 T5 **Bargischow** Germany
32 M5 **Bargteheide** Germany
56 H3 **Barguzin** *R* Russian Federation
56 G4 **Barguzinskiy Khrebet** *mts* Russian Federation
56 G4 **Barguzinskiy Zaliv** *G* Russian Federation
139 G6 **Barham** New South Wales Australia
95 T2 **Bar Harbor** Maine U.S.A.
75 L6 **Barhi** India
86 D4 **Bari** *R* Cent Afr Republic
74 G5 **Bari** India
43 H7 **Bari** Italy
128 E3 **Baria** *R* Venezuela
45 L2 **Baricella** Italy
44 G2 **Barigazzo Monte** Italy
85 F1 **Barika** Algeria
71 M9 **Barike** Indonesia
128 F2 **Barima,Pta** *C* Venezuela
127 J10 **Barinas** Venezuela
128 D2 **Barinas** Venezuela
110 D1 **Baring** Missouri U.S.A.
100 D2 **Baring** Washington U.S.A.
143 E10 **Baring, Mt** W Australia Australia
28 D5 **Båring Vig** *B* Denmark
127 J10 **Barinitas** Venezuela
75 M8 **Baripada** India
130 E8 **Bariri** Brazil
84 J5 **Bârîs** Egypt
22 E4 **Barisis** France
70 D5 **Barito** *R* Kalimantan
19 Q17 **Barjaude** *mt* France
19 P17 **Barjols** France
84 E4 **Barjūj** *watercourse* Libya
29 K4 **Barkåkra** Sweden
58 D5 **Barkam** China
27 H11 **Barken,N** *L* Sweden
94 J3 **Barker** New York U.S.A.
143 D9 **Barker L** W Australia Australia
117 N9 **Barkerville** British Columbia Canada
94 H5 **Barkeyville** Pennsylvania U.S.A.
9 G4 **Barking** England
120 H6 **Bark L** Ontario Canada
110 J5 **Barkley Res** Kentucky U.S.A.
100 A1 **Barkley Sound** British Columbia Canada
140 E5 **Barkly Downs** Queensland Australia
140 D4 **Barkly Highway** N Terr Australia
140 B5 **Barkly, Mt** N Terr Australia
140 D4 **Barkly Tableland** Qnsld/N Terr Australia
89 D7 **Barkly West** S Africa
66 E3 **Barkol** China
99 T4 **Bark River** Michigan U.S.A.
108 G6 **Barksdale** Texas U.S.A.
47 L6 **Barla Dağı** *mt* Turkey
9 E1 **Barlborough** England
19 J4 **Bar le Duc** France
143 C8 **Barlee** *L* W Australia Australia
143 B6 **Barlee Ra** W Australia Australia
8 C5 **Barle, R** England
19 Q16 **Barles** France
43 G7 **Barletta** Italy
22 D3 **Barlin** France
31 J3 **Barlinek** Poland
27 K14 **Barlingbo** *isld* Gotland Sweden
32 E9 **Barlo** Germany
32 L4 **Barlohe** Germany
98 G2 **Barlow** North Dakota U.S.A.
100 D4 **Barlow Pass** Oregon U.S.A.
13 H6 **Barmby Moor** England
139 H5 **Barmedman** New South Wales Australia
74 D6 **Barmer** India
138 F5 **Barmera** South Australia Australia
8 B2 **Barmouth** Wales
32 L5 **Barmstedt** Germany
122 G7 **Barnaby River** New Brunswick Canada
74 F7 **Barnagar** India
107 N2 **Barnard** Kansas U.S.A.
98 H4 **Barnard** South Dakota U.S.A.
13 G4 **Barnard Castle** England
117 E6 **Barnard,Mt** Br Col/Alaska Canada/U.S.A.
37 N4 **Bärnau** Germany
56 B4 **Barnaul** Russian Federation
56 B4 **Barnaulka** *R* Russian Federation
9 E1 **Barnby Moor** England
95 N7 **Barnegat** New Jersey U.S.A.
107 O2 **Barnes** Kansas U.S.A.
94 J6 **Barnesboro** Pennsylvania U.S.A.
115 M3 **Barnes Icecap** Northwest Territories Canada
113 G12 **Barnes Sd** Florida U.S.A.
98 K9 **Barneston** Nebraska U.S.A.
112 C4 **Barnesville** Georgia U.S.A.
98 K3 **Barnesville** Minnesota U.S.A.
9 F4 **Barnet** England
25 E4 **Barneveld** Netherlands
20 G3 **Barneville** France
33 R7 **Barnewitz** Germany
99 M8 **Barney** Iowa U.S.A.
103 N4 **Barney Top** *mt* Utah U.S.A.
108 F4 **Barnhart** Texas U.S.A.
33 T7 **Barnim** *reg* Germany
122 F5 **Barn Mtn** Quebec Canada
20 E3 **Barnouic** *isld* France
107 O5 **Barnsdall** Oklahoma U.S.A.
13 G6 **Barnsley** England
95 R5 **Barnstable** Massachusetts U.S.A.
8 B5 **Barnstaple** England
8 C6 **Barnstaple Cross** England
95 Q3 **Barnstead** New Hampshire U.S.A.
32 H7 **Barnstorf** Germany
32 K9 **Barntrup** Germany
99 O3 **Barnum** Minnesota U.S.A.
118 E9 **Barnwell** Alberta Canada
112 F4 **Barnwell** South Carolina U.S.A.
37 P6 **Bärnzell** Germany
86 F4 **Baro** *R* Ethiopia
85 F7 **Baro** Nigeria
Baroda *see* **Vadodara**
22 K5 **Baroncourt** France
45 R8 **Baronissi** Italy
19 O16 **Baronnies, Les** *reg* France
118 D9 **Barons** Alberta Canada
143 F6 **Baron's Ra** W Australia Australia
36 B6 **Baronville** France
87 D8 **Barotseland** *reg* Zambia
75 O5 **Barpeta** India
80 D4 **Barqay** Israel
7 L9 **Barque** *gas field* North Sea
99 U4 **Barques, Pt. Aux** Michigan U.S.A.
127 K9 **Barquisimeto** Venezuela
19 K4 **Barr** France
12 D3 **Barr** Scotland
98 B10 **Barr** Colorado U.S.A.
129 K6 **Barra** Brazil
15 A3 **Barra** *isld* Scotland
130 E8 **Barra Bonita** Brazil
130 G5 **Barracão** Brazil
128 G5 **Barracão do Barreto** Brazil
89 B10 **Barracouta,C** S Africa
129 K6 **Barra da Estiva** Brazil
142 A6 **Barradale Roadhouse** W Australia Australia
124 G8 **Barra de Navidad** Mexico
130 H8 **Barra de sã João** Brazil
130 B4 **Barra do Bugres** Brazil
129 J5 **Barra do Corda** Brazil
130 H6 **Barra do Cuieté** Brazil
87 B7 **Barra do Dande** Angola
130 D4 **Barra do Garças** Brazil
130 F6 **Barra do Paraopeba** Brazil
130 G8 **Barra do Pirai** Brazil
129 G5 **Barra do São Manuel** Brazil
87 G10 **Barra Falsa,Pta.da** Mozambique
16 B5 **Barragem de Maranhão** *res* Portugal
16 B5 **Barragem de Montargil Res** Portugal
16 B5 **Barragem do Castello do Bode** Portugal
138 E6 **Barrages** South Australia Australia
15 A4 **Barra Head** Scotland
129 K8 **Barra Mansa** Brazil
128 C4 **Barranca** Peru
128 D2 **Barrancabermeja** Colombia
131 F2 **Barrancas** *R* Corrientes Argentina
127 H9 **Barrancas** Colombia
127 N10 **Barrancas** Venezuela
131 B6 **Barrancas,R** Mendoza Argentina
130 B7 **Barranco Branco** Brazil
16 C6 **Barrancos** Portugal
133 F3 **Barranqueras** Argentina
126 G9 **Barranquilla** Colombia
13 F3 **Barrasford** England
121 N4 **Barraute** Quebec Canada
19 P14 **Barraux** France
17 F5 **Barrax** Spain
95 P4 **Barre** Massachusetts U.S.A.
95 P2 **Barre** Vermont U.S.A.
20 F8 **Barre-de-Monts, la** France
21 M4 **Barre-en-Ouche, la** France
129 K6 **Barreiras** Brazil
129 G4 **Barreirinha** Brazil
129 K4 **Barreirinhas** Brazil
130 D4 **Barreiro** *R* Brazil
16 A6 **Barreiro** Portugal
130 J10 **Barreiros** Brazil
110 K5 **Barren** *R* Kentucky U.S.A.
68 A6 **Barren I** Andaman Is
116 L7 **Barren Is** Alaska U.S.A.
110 K5 **Barren River Res** Kentucky U.S.A.
19 P16 **Barret de Lioure** France
129 J8 **Barretos** Brazil
102 H9 **Barrett L** California U.S.A.
142 F4 **Barrett, Mt** W Australia Australia
118 C4 **Barrhead** Alberta Canada
12 D2 **Barrhead** Scotland
15 D5 **Barrhill** Scotland
121 L8 **Barrie** Ontario Canada
120 H7 **Barrie I** Ontario Canada
145 E2 **Barrier, C** New Zealand
117 N10 **Barrière** British Columbia Canada
138 F4 **Barrier Range** New South Wales Australia
141 H8 **Barrington** New South Wales Australia
122 G10 **Barrington** Nova Scotia Canada
99 S7 **Barrington** Illinois U.S.A.
119 R1 **Barrington L** Manitoba Canada
139 K4 **Barrington Tops** New South Wales Australia
141 H8 **Barringun** New South Wales Australia
129 L6 **Barris** *R* Brazil
28 D5 **Barrit** Denmark
101 M9 **Barro** Utah U.S.A.
130 E4 **Barro Alto** Brazil
100 E1 **Barron** Washington U.S.A.
99 P4 **Barron** Wisconsin U.S.A.
99 P4 **Barronett** Wisconsin U.S.A.
141 H3 **Barron Falls** Queensland Australia
109 J8 **Barroso** Texas U.S.A.
124 J4 **Barroterán** Mexico
21 M8 **Barrou** France
133 E5 **Barrow** Argentina
14 E4 **Barrow** *R* Ireland
116 J1 **Barrow** Alaska U.S.A.
140 D2 **Barrow, C** N Terr Australia
140 C5 **Barrow Creek** N Terr Australia
142 B5 **Barrow I** W Australia Australia
13 E5 **Barrow-in-Furness** England
141 G2 **Barrow Pt** Queensland Australia
147 M2 **Barrow,Pt** Alaska U.S.A.
143 F7 **Barrow Ra** W Australia Australia
119 Q6 **Barrows** Manitoba Canada
115 K3 **Barrow Str** Northwest Territories Canada
143 D7 **Barr Smith Ra** W Australia Australia
70 F7 **Barru** Sulawesi
16 E2 **Barruelo de Santullán** Spain
13 F1 **Barry** Scotland
110 E2 **Barry** Illinois U.S.A.
8 C5 **Barry** Wales
121 N7 **Barrys Bay** Ontario Canada
94 B3 **Barryton** Michigan U.S.A.
144 C5 **Barrytown** New Zealand
95 N5 **Barryville** New York U.S.A.
28 H6 **Bårse** Denmark
29 K5 **Barsebäckshamn** Sweden
76 B1 **Barsi** India
32 K8 **Barsinghausen** Germany
28 D6 **Barsø** *isld* Denmark
32 G6 **Barssel** Germany
102 G7 **Barstow** California U.S.A.
108 D4 **Barstow** Texas U.S.A.
54 J2 **Barsuki** Russian Federation
19 J4 **Bar-sur-Aube** France
18 H4 **Bar-sur-Seine** France
80 D4 **Barta'a** Jordan
36 H5 **Bartenstein** Germany
116 Q1 **Barter I** Alaska U.S.A.
30 G1 **Barth** Germany
33 R4 **Barthe** *R* Germany
122 G6 **Bartibog** New Brunswick Canada
128 G2 **Bartica** Guyana
78 D1 **Bartin** Turkey
100 D8 **Bartle** California U.S.A.
141 H3 **Bartle Frere,Mt** Queensland Australia
103 O2 **Bartles,Mt** Utah U.S.A.
107 P5 **Bartlesville** Oklahoma U.S.A.
98 H8 **Bartlett** Nebraska U.S.A.
95 Q2 **Bartlett** New Hampshire U.S.A.
109 K5 **Bartlett** Texas U.S.A.
117 O4 **Bartlett L** Northwest Territories Canada
103 N8 **Bartlett Res** Arizona U.S.A.
145 F3 **Bartletts** New Zealand
123 P3 **Bartlett's Harbour** Newfoundland Canada
143 E8 **Bartlett Soak** *L* W Australia Australia
98 F9 **Bartley** Nebraska U.S.A.
117 G8 **Bartolome, C** Alaska U.S.A.
87 G10 **Bartolomeu Dias** Mozambique
13 F6 **Barton** England
71 D5 **Barton** Palawan Philippines
98 F1 **Barton** North Dakota U.S.A.
95 P2 **Barton** Vermont U.S.A.
94 D2 **Barton City** Michigan U.S.A.
9 G3 **Barton Mills** England
13 H6 **Barton-upon-Humber** England
31 M1 **Bartoszyce** Poland
121 N4 **Bartoville** Quebec Canada
33 S5 **Bartow** Germany
113 F10 **Bartow** Florida U.S.A.
112 E5 **Bartow** Georgia U.S.A.
126 G9 **Barú, I. de** Colombia
69 E12 **Barumun** *R* Sumatra
70 O10 **Barung** *isld* Java
56 G6 **Barun-Shabartuy, Gora** *mt* Russian Federation
69 D11 **Barus** Sumatra
33 S8 **Baruth** Germany
58 E2 **Baruunharaa** Mongolia
58 F2 **Baruun Urt** Mongolia
125 N5 **Barú, Volcán** Panama
15 B2 **Barvas** Scotland
22 J3 **Barvaux** Belgium
54 J8 **Barvenkovo** Ukraine
74 G7 **Barwah** India
74 F7 **Barwani** India
33 N7 **Barwedel** Germany
99 N1 **Barwick** Ontario Canada
113 D7 **Barwick** Georgia U.S.A.
143 D7 **Barwidgee** W Australia Australia
140 B2 **Barwolla, Mt** N Terr Australia
80 F7 **Barza** Jordan
57 D5 **Basaga** Turkmenistan
77 D6 **Basaidu** Iran
106 D2 **Basalt** Colorado U.S.A.
101 N6 **Basalt** Idaho U.S.A.
102 F3 **Basalt** Nevada U.S.A.
141 H4 **Basalt R** Queensland Australia
86 C5 **Basankusu** Zaire
48 L6 **Basarabi** Romania
57 G2 **Basaral, Ozero** *L* Kazakhstan
71 F6 **Basay** Negros Philippines
71 E8 **Basbas** Philippines
131 B2 **Bascuñán,C** Chile
32 K6 **Basdahl** Germany
33 S7 **Basdorf** Germany
22 F2 **Basècles** Belgium
40 G2 **Basel** Switzerland
40 G3 **Baselland** *canton* Switzerland
43 G8 **Basento** *R* Italy
48 K2 **Başeu** *R* Romania
71 G5 **Basey** Samar Philippines
77 F6 **Bashākerd, Kūhhā-ye** *mts* Iran
118 E6 **Bashaw** Alberta Canada
56 B5 **Bashchelakskiy Khrebet** *mts* Russian Federation
57 C5 **Bashir** Turkmenistan
56 C5 **Bashkaus** *R* Russian Federation
55 C3 **Bashkirskaya Respublika** Russian Federation
Bashkortostan *see* **Bashkirskaya Respublika**
71 F3 **Basiad Bay** Luzon Philippines
71 F7 **Basilan** *isld* Mindanao Philippines
71 F7 **Basilan Str** Mindanao Philippines
9 G4 **Basildon** England
111 D11 **Basile** Louisiana U.S.A.
43 G8 **Basilicata** *prov* Italy
Basim *see* **Wāshīm**
101 N3 **Basin** Montana U.S.A.
101 R5 **Basin** Wyoming U.S.A.
113 F10 **Basinger** Florida U.S.A.
9 E5 **Basingstoke** England
119 M6 **Basin L** Saskatchewan Canada
95 U1 **Baskahegan L** Maine U.S.A.
78 K2 **Başkale** Turkey
121 P6 **Baskatong, Rés** Quebec Canada
142 D3 **Baskerville, C** W Australia Australia
79 C2 **Başköy** Turkey
Basle *see* **Basel**
9 E1 **Baslow** England
26 G5 **Båsmoen** Norway
69 F13 **Baso** *isld* Sumatra
41 H5 **Basodino** *mt* Switzerland
86 D5 **Basoko** Zaire
86 D6 **Basongo** Zaire
126 A2 **Basora,Pt** Aruba W Indies
78 L6 **Basrah, Al** Iraq
78 L6 **Başrah, Al** *prov* Iraq
36 D6 **Bas Rhin** *dept* France
118 E8 **Bassano** Alberta Canada
42 D3 **Bassano del Grappa** Italy
85 E7 **Bassar** Togo
81 A8 **Bassas da India** *isld* Mozambique Chan
33 R5 **Basse** Germany
22 D3 **Bassée, la** France
68 B4 **Bassein** Burma
142 B1 **Bassendean** *dist* Perth, W Aust Australia
22 K2 **Bassenge** Belgium
13 E4 **Bassenthwaite** *L* England
127 L4 **Basse Pointe** Martinique W Indies
127 O3 **Basse Terre** Trinidad
127 M4 **Basse Terre** Guadeloupe W Indies
127 P4 **Basseterre** St Kitts W Indies
98 G7 **Bassett** Nebraska U.S.A.
103 O9 **Bassett Pk** Arizona U.S.A.
22 F1 **Bassevelde** Belgium
111 G10 **Bassfield** Mississippi U.S.A.
85 E7 **Bassila** Benin
22 F2 **Bassilly** Belgium
102 E4 **Bass Lake** California U.S.A.
33 T10 **Basslitz** Germany
122 J8 **Bass River** Nova Scotia Canada
15 F4 **Bass Rock** Scotland
139 H7 **Bass Strait** Tasmania Australia
32 J7 **Bassum** Germany
119 R8 **Basswood** Manitoba Canada
99 P1 **Basswood L** Ontario Canada
19 P13 **Bassy** France
27 F15 **Båstad** Sweden
77 D6 **Bastak** Iran
77 D1 **Bastam** Iran
18 M10 **Bastia** Corsica
45 J2 **Bastiglia** Italy
123 M2 **Bastille,L** Quebec Canada
22 K3 **Bastogne** Belgium
112 E4 **Bastonville** Georgia U.S.A.
111 E9 **Bastrop** Louisiana U.S.A.
109 K5 **Bastrop** Texas U.S.A.
26 L7 **Bastuträsk** Sweden
Basuo *see* **Dongfang**
69 F13 **Basu, Tanjong** *C* Sumatra
Basutoland *see* **Lesotho**
55 D2 **Bas'yanovskiy** Russian Federation
86 B7 **Bas Zaïre** *prov* Zaire
86 A5 **Bata** Equat Guinea
85 F8 **Bata** Mbini Equat Guinea
71 E3 **Bataan Penin** Luzon Philippines
126 C3 **Batabanó, G. de** Cuba
71 E1 **Batac** Luzon Philippines
71 G4 **Batag** *isld* Philippines
130 D7 **Bataguaçu** Brazil
46 G3 **Batak** Bulgaria
74 F3 **Batala** India
16 B5 **Batalha** Portugal
51 M2 **Batamay** Russian Federation
71 G4 **Batan** *isld* Philippines
58 C5 **Batang** China
70 M9 **Batang** Java
86 C4 **Batangafo** Cent Afr Republic
71 E4 **Batangas** Luzon Philippines
69 F13 **Batanghari** *R* Sumatra
71 C3 **Batangpele** Waigeo Indonesia
69 J12 **Batangtarang** Indonesia
69 D12 **Batangtoru** Sumatra
71 C3 **Batanta** *isld* W Irian
48 E4 **Bataszék** Hungary
130 F7 **Batatais** Brazil
Batavia *see* **Jakarta**
133 D4 **Batavia** Argentina
99 S8 **Batavia** Illinois U.S.A.
94 J3 **Batavia** New York U.S.A.
110 M2 **Batavia** Ohio U.S.A.
54 L9 **Bataysk** Russian Federation
71 E5 **Batbatan** Panay Philippines
120 F6 **Batchawana** Ontario Canada
140 B2 **Batchelor** N Terr Australia
68 F6 **Batdambang** Cambodia
69 B10 **Bateemeucica, Gunung** *mt* Sumatra
88 B6 **Batembo** Zaire
61 P13 **Baten** Okinawa
25 E5 **Batenburg** Netherlands
56 D4 **Batenevskiy Kryazh** *ridge* Russian Federation
103 J9 **Bateques** Mexico
101 O6 **Bates** Idaho U.S.A.

100 G5 Bates Oregon U.S.A.
112 F4 Batesburg South Carolina U.S.A.
98 D6 Batesland South Dakota U.S.A.
143 E7 Bates,Mt W Australia Australia
143 D7 Bates Ra W Australia Australia
110 E6 Batesville Arkansas U.S.A.
110 L2 Batesville Indiana U.S.A.
111 G7 Batesville Mississippi U.S.A.
109 H7 Batesville Texas U.S.A.
52 D5 Batetsky Russian Federation
122 E7 Bath New Brunswick Canada
8 D5 Bath England
127 M3 Bath Jamaica
11 H7 Bath Illinois U.S.A.
95 S3 Bath Maine U.S.A.
95 K4 Bath New York U.S.A.
112 L2 Bath North Carolina U.S.A.
112 F4 Bath South Carolina U.S.A.
98 H4 Bath South Dakota U.S.A.
127 P4 Bath Nevis W Indies
86 C3 Batha R Chad
68 G6 Batheay Cambodia
12 E2 Bathgate Scotland
98 J1 Bathgate North Dakota U.S.A.
139 J5 Bathurst New South Wales Australia
122 G6 Bathurst New Brunswick Canada
Bathurst The Gambia see Banjul
141 G2 Bathurst Bay Queensland Australia
114 G3 Bathurst,C Northwest Territories Canada
140 B1 Bathurst I N Terr Australia
115 K2 Bathurst I Northwest Territories Canada
114 J4 Bathurst Inlet Northwest Territories Canada
142 E3 Bathurst Is W Australia Australia
85 D7 Batié Burkina
70 E6 Batikala,Tg B Sulawesi Indonesia
48 E5 Batina Croatia
78 L7 Batin, Wadi al Iraq
69 E10 Bati Putih, Gunung mt Malaysia
121 S6 Batiscan Quebec Canada
121 T5 Batiscan,L Quebec Canada
77 G3 Batlag-e-Gavkhuni Iran
13 G6 Batley England
78 H3 Batman Turkey
85 F1 Batna Algeria
71 F4 Bato,L Luzon Philippines
111 E11 Baton Rouge Louisiana U.S.A.
86 B5 Batouri Cameroon
130 D4 Batovi Brazil
68 H7 Ba Tri Vietnam
42 H3 Batrina Croatia
79 F4 Batroûn Lebanon
26 R1 Båtsfjord Norway
80 D3 Bat Shelomo Israel
45 L1 Battáglia Terme Italy
140 D3 Batten R N Terr Australia
36 F1 Battenberg Germany
143 C6 Batthewmurrarna mt W Australia Australia
83 L10 Batticaloa Sri Lanka
22 K2 Battice Belgium
69 A8 Batti Malv isld Nicobar Is
45 R8 Battipáglia Italy
9 G6 Battle England
140 B3 Battle Cr N Terr Australia
100 J7 Battle Cr Idaho U.S.A.
101 Q1 Battle Cr Montana U.S.A.
98 J8 Battle Cr Nebraska U.S.A.
118 H9 Battle Creek Saskatchewan Canada
94 B4 Battle Creek Michigan U.S.A.
8 D2 Battlefield England
118 J6 Battleford Saskatchewan Canada
118 J5 Battlefords Prov.Park,The Saskatchewan Canada
100 C4 Battle Ground Washington U.S.A.
123 R1 Battle Harbour Labrador, Nfld Canada
102 G1 Battle Mt Nevada U.S.A.
118 F6 Battle R Alberta Canada
118 H6 Battle R Saskatchewan Canada
98 D1 Battleview North Dakota U.S.A.
48 G4 Battonya Hungary
118 J8 Battrum Saskatchewan Canada
70 D4 Batuajau, Bt mt Kalimantan
71 H8 Batuata isld Indonesia
70 D4 Batu Balik, Kampung Malaysia
69 H14 Batubetumbang Indonesia
70 D3 Batu Bora mt Sarawak
70 D4 Batubrok, Bt mt Kalimantan
70 G5 Batudaka Indonesia
70 C4 Batuesambang, Bukit mt Kalimantan
69 E10 Batu Gajah Malaysia
71 H5 Batuhitam,Tg C Sulawesi Indonesia
70 D4 Batuliangmebang, G mt Kalimantan
70 P10 Batukau, Bt mt Bali Indonesia
71 H9 Batulanteh Indonesia
70 D6 Batulilin Kalimantan
70 D3 Batu Mabun mt Sarawak
78 H1 Batumi Georgia
70 D14 Batumonga Indonesia
69 F12 Batu Pahat Malaysia
69 C13 Batu,Pulaupulau isld Indonesia
70 E4 Batuputih Kalimantan
70 N8 Baturaja Sumatra Indonesia
70 P10 Baturetno Java
52 D6 Baturino Russian Federation
129 L4 Baturité Brazil
69 H14 Baturusa Indonesia
69 E13 Batusangkar Sumatra
70 G5 Batusitandut Sulawesi
70 F3 Batu Tg B Malaysia
71 L10 Batutuah Indonesia
80 B5 Bat Yam Israel
20 F7 Batz France
71 H7 Baubau Sulawesi Indonesia
86 A3 Bauchi Nigeria
20 F8 Baud France
75 L8 Bauda India
128 C2 Baudo, Sa. de mts Colombia
21 O7 Baudres France
19 Q17 Bauduen France
21 K6 Baugé France
19 Q13 Bauges dist France
140 D3 Bauhinia N Terr Australia
140 J6 Bauhinia Downs Queensland Australia
71 N9 Baukau Timor
70 G7 Baula Sulawesi
123 R2 Bauld,C Newfoundland Canada
20 E8 Baule,la France
20 G6 Baulon France
41 J3 Bauma Switzerland
9 F1 Baumber England
19 K5 Baume-les-Dames France
37 T6 Baumgarten Germany
37 O7 Baumgarten Germany
70 G6 Bauna Sulawesi
37 K4 Baunach Germany
37 K3 Baunach R Germany
128 F6 Baures Bolivia
130 E8 Bauru Brazil

130 D6 Baús Brazil
52 B6 Bauska Latvia
31 H4 Bautzen Germany
109 P1 Bautzen Arkansas U.S.A.
Bavaria see Bayern
107 N3 Bavaria Kansas U.S.A.
22 F3 Bavay France
89 C9 Bavianskloofberge mts S Africa
124 E2 Bavispe Mexico
127 L5 Bayamón Puerto Rico
59 J2 Bayan China
55 S5 Bayanaul Kazakhstan
56 G4 Bayandu Russian Federation
Bayan Gol see Dengkou
58 S4 Bayan Har Shan China
58 D2 Bayanhongor Mongolia
65 E1 Bayan Hot China
65 A3 Bayan Hure China
Bayan Huru see Horqin Youyi Zhongqi
65 C3 Bayan Nur Sum China
58 E3 Bayan Obo China
126 E10 Bayano, L. Panama
Bayan Qagan see Qahar Youyi Houqi
65 F1 Bayan Qagan China
65 F2 Bayan Qagan China
113 F7 Bayard Florida U.S.A.
13 G2 Bayard England
98 C8 Bayard Nebraska U.S.A.
94 H7 Bayard West Virginia U.S.A.
19 Q15 Bayard, Col pass France
65 B1 Bayasgalant Mongolia
47 L6 Bayat Turkey
71 F6 Baybay Negros Philippines
71 G5 Baybay Leyte Philippines
112 L2 Bayboro North Carolina U.S.A.
123 U6 Bay Bulls Newfoundland Canada
78 H1 Bayburt Turkey
69 H8 Bay Canh, Hon isld Vietnam
94 D3 Bay City Michigan U.S.A.
100 B4 Bay City Oregon U.S.A.
109 J4 Bay City Texas U.S.A.
94 A3 Bay City Wisconsin U.S.A.
84 G3 Baydá,Al Libya
50 F2 Baydaratskaya Guba G Russian Federation
84 H5 Bay de Verde Newfoundland Canada
84 H5 Baydhabo Somalia
41 O2 Bayerische Alpen mt Germany
37 N5 Bayerischer Wald mts Germany
37 K6 Bayern admin Germany
21 J3 Bayeux France
99 Q3 Bayfield Wisconsin U.S.A.
123 O2 Bayfield I Quebec Canada
122 E5 Bayfield Mtn Quebec Canada
57 D3 Baygakum Kazakhstan
55 D4 Baygara Kazakhstan
98 A4 Bay Horse Montana U.S.A.
47 J6 Bayındır Turkey
20 K6 Baykal Russian Federation
119 V3 Baykal,L Russian Federation
101 Q7 Baykal,Ozero L Russian Federation
117 K7 Baykal'sk Russian Federation
94 A2 Bay Lake Michigan U.S.A.
98 B5 Bay Lodge Mts Wyoming U.S.A.
101 M3 Baykal'skiy Khrebet mts Russian Federation
56 D5 Bay-Khaak Russian Federation
55 C2 Bay-Khozha Kazakhstan
55 C3 Baykibashevo Russian Federation
57 E1 Baykonur Kazakhstan
71 E3 Bay, Laguna de Luzon Philippines
123 R6 Bayley Pt Queensland Australia
140 E3 Baymak Russian Federation
55 C4 Baymaklíya Moldavia
48 L4 Bay Minette Alabama U.S.A.
111 J11 Baynard's Green England
9 E4 Bayombong Luzon Philippines
71 E2 Bayon France
19 K4 Bayona Spain
16 B2 Bayou Bartholomew R Arkansas U.S.A.
111 F9 Bayou D'Arbonne Louisiana
111 D9 Bayou D'Arbonne L Louisiana U.S.A.
110 E6 Bayou de View R Arkansas
111 F12 Bayou La Batre Alabama
111 F12 Bayou Lafourche R Louisiana
111 F11 Bayou Macon R Louisiana
111 N17 Bayou Meto R Arkansas
111 F9 Bayou Pierre R Mississippi
111 E12 Bayou Vista Louisiana
128 B5 Bayovar Peru
113 E7 Bayport Florida U.S.A.
99 T5 Bayport Minnesota U.S.A.
21 L4 Bay Pt British Columbia
71 D5 Bay Pt Philippines
47 M4 Bayramiç Turkey
37 L5 Bayreuth Germany
123 T6 Bay Roberts Newfoundland Canada
58 T4 Baysa Russian Federation
111 G11 Bay St.Louis Mississippi
79 F5 Bayshore Florida U.S.A.
95 O6 Bay Shore Long I, New York
112 E1 Bay Springs Mississippi
56 E5 Bay-Soot Russian Federation
Baytag Bogdo see Baytik Shan
9 G3 Baythorn End England

66 E2 Baytik Shan mt ra China/Mongolia
109 N6 Baytown Texas U.S.A.
145 F3 Bay View New Zealand
117 P12 Bayview Idaho U.S.A.
18 H6 Bayville Maine/New Brunswick U.S.A./Canada
17 F7 Baza Spain
48 K1 Bazaliya Ukraine
22 N7 Bazancourt France
15 D3 Bazar China
107 O3 Bazar Kansas U.S.A.
53 G12 Bazardyuzu, Gora mt Azerbaijan/Rus Fed
21 M3 Bazarnye Mataki Russian Federation
22 G3 Bazeaumont Belgium
123 R4 Beaumont Newfoundland Canada
18 E8 Bazas France
21 L8 Bazeilles France
144 B6 Beaumont New Zealand
102 H8 Beaumont California U.S.A.
107 O4 Beaumont Kansas U.S.A.
21 H10 Beaumont Mississippi U.S.A.
111 B11 Beaumont Texas U.S.A.
18 F9 Beaumont de Lomagne France
18 F8 Beaumont de Périgord France
22 J4 Beaumont-en-Argonne France
22 E3 Beaumont-en-Cambrésis France
20 G2 Beaumont-Hague France
21 M6 Beaumont-la-Ronce France
21 M3 Beaumont-le-Roger France
21 M5 Beaumont-les-Autels France
21 L6 Beaumont-Pied-de-Bœuf France
21 L5 Beaumont-sur-Oise France
21 P3 Beaumont-sur-Sarthe France
8 A7 Beaune France
26 C6 Beaune la Rolande France
9 E3 Beauport Quebec Canada
98 G4 Beaupréau France
141 H7 Beauquesne France
21 O5 Beaurepaire d'Isère France
69 E11 Beaurepaire France
142 A4 Beaurieux France
70 B6 Beausejour Manitoba Canada
46 E1 Beauval France
139 H4 Beauval Saskatchewan Canada
21 P1 Beauvais France
118 K5 Beauvais Lake Prov. Park Alberta Canada
118 K8 Beauvoir-sur-Mer France
117 L5 Beaver Yukon Terr/Br Col
32 M7 Beaver Alaska U.S.A.
33 N3 Beaver Kansas U.S.A.
55 E4 Beaver R North Dakota U.S.A.
110 O3 Beaver Oklahoma U.S.A.
100 A4 Beaver Oregon U.S.A.
94 L6 Beaver Pennsylvania U.S.A.
103 L3 Beaver R Utah U.S.A.
33 O8 Beaver R Saskatchewan
141 L8 Beaverbank Nova Scotia
94 K5 Beaver Brook New Brunswick Canada
98 G9 Beaver City Nebraska U.S.A.
116 C4 Beaver Cr Alaska U.S.A.
106 Q2 Beaver Cr Colorado U.S.A.
101 N5 Beaver Cr Idaho U.S.A.
22 F2 Beaver Cr Kansas U.S.A.
79 F8 Beaver Cr Missouri U.S.A.
33 N4 Beaver Cr Montana U.S.A.
72 E9 Beaver Cr Montana U.S.A.
80 C8 Beaver Cr Wyoming U.S.A.
28 E5 Beaver Cr Wyoming U.S.A.
117 C4 Beaver Creek Yukon Territory Canada
25 D6 Beaver Crossing Nebraska U.S.A.
31 H3 Beaver Dam Kentucky U.S.A.
99 S6 Beaver Dam Wisconsin U.S.A.
140 C3 Beaverhead R Montana U.S.A.
144 G6 Beaverhead Mts Idaho/Montana U.S.A.
101 N4 Beaverhead R Montana
101 M4 Beaver Island Ontario U.S.A.
118 E5 Beaverhill L Alberta Canada
99 V4 Beaver I Michigan U.S.A.
123 N2 Beaver Island L Quebec Canada
94 F5 Beaver Lake Michigan U.S.A.
99 U3 Beaver L Michigan U.S.A.
117 N9 Beaver Lake British Columbia U.S.A.
110 O7 Beaver Lodge Alberta Canada
117 P10 Beavermouth British Columbia Canada
116 J5 Beaver Mts Alaska U.S.A.
118 F4 Beaver R Alberta Canada
117 H4 Beaver R Saskatchewan
114 B4 Beaver R.City Utah U.S.A.
110 C5 Beaver Res Arkansas U.S.A.
95 M3 Beaver R.Flow New York U.S.A.
121 L8 Beaverton Ontario Canada
94 C3 Beaverton Michigan U.S.A.
100 C4 Beaverton Oregon U.S.A.
95 K6 Beavertown Pennsylvania U.S.A.
75 F6 Beawar India
131 C8 Beazley Argentina
131 C4 Bedero, Salina Argentina
68 J8 Bebandana France
129 J8 Bebedouro Brazil
36 F2 Beberbrunn Austria
36 J7 Bebington England
63 A5 Běbra Mozambique
36 J7 Bebra Germany
19 J6 Becán Romania
37 C1 Becerreá Spain
126 C7 Becerro,Cayos reefs Caribbean
84 D7 Bechar Algeria
100 D7 Becharof National Alaska U.S.A.
116 J8 Bécharof L Alaska U.S.A.
19 J7 Béchar R Algeria
21 L4 Bechy France
36 B5 Becken Germany
36 J6 Beckingen Germany
94 F9 Beckley West Virginia U.S.A.
8 E3 Beckton England
116 J8 Beckville Texas U.S.A.
145 G4 Beclean Romania
30 J6 Becon-les-Granits France
20 G5 Bécon France
94 H7 Beauford Castle hist Scotland
19 Q16 Beaucourt France
36 H6 Beaudesert Queensland
32 M7 Beaudy England
70 D2 Beaufort France
94 F9 Beaufort Luxembourg
71 L4 Beaufort Sabah
21 H6 Beaufort West Australia
112 G1 Beaufort North Carolina
112 E4 Beaufort South Carolina
21 L4 Beaufort-en-Vallée France
147 E1 Beaufort I Antarctica
74 F5 Beaufort Sea Arctic O
21 M6 Beaufort West S Africa
87 P7 Beaugency France
145 G5 Beale England
18 H9 Beaulais Botswana

19 N16 Bedarrides France
36 B1 Bedburg Germany
8 B1 Beddgelert Wales
36 H8 Beddingham England
119 R9 Bede Manitoba Canada
20 G5 Bédée France
28 E4 Beder Denmark
32 J5 Bederkesa Germany
55 C3 Bedeyeva Polyana Russian Federation
57 E4 Bedkad Tajikistan
70 L9 Bekasi Java
48 F4 Békés co Hungary
110 K3 Bedford Indiana U.S.A.
99 M9 Bedford Iowa U.S.A.
94 B8 Bedford Kentucky U.S.A.
85 D7 Bedford Pennsylvania U.S.A.
87 F11 Bédira France
36 H7 Bedarra I Queensland Australia
143 D10 Bedford Harb W Australia
127 P5 Bedford Pt Grenada
70 D4 Bedford R England
69 H14 Bedding Indonesia
19 O16 Bédoin France
69 E11 Bedongkong Sumatra
119 U5 Bedourie Queensland Australia
117 L11 Bedout I W Australia
70 B6 Bedsted Denmark
9 E3 Bedworth England
36 E6 Bee Nebraska U.S.A.
98 G4 Beebe South Dakota U.S.A.
141 H7 Beechport Australia
100 F5 Beech Cr Oregon U.S.A.
54 M8 Beech Creek Kentucky
99 S3 Beecher Illinois U.S.A.
116 N1 Beecher Illinois U.S.A.
104 L4 Beech Fork R Kentucky
110 K2 Beech Grove Indiana U.S.A.
99 S3 Beechwood Michigan U.S.A.
139 H6 Beechworth Australia
118 K8 Beechy Saskatchewan Canada
17 O3 Beek Gelderland Netherlands
22 N4 Beek Noord-Brabant Neth
98 C1 Beekbergen Netherlands
107 K3 Beeler Kansas U.S.A.
94 B3 Beelitz Germany
52 D5 Beeltz Russian Federation
37 K2 Beerberg mt Germany
33 K2 Beeren Germany
32 F2 Beeringnurding, Mt W Australia Australia
79 F8 Beerlegem Belgium
33 R8 Beer Menuha Israel
109 K7 Beer Sheba Israel
98 P2 Beersel Belgium
124 H7 Be'er Pehar Israel
80 C8 Beers Netherlands
80 E5 Be'er Ora Israel
86 B2 Beelesar, Embalse de res Spain
54 M3 Beerze Netherlands
19 P18 Beeskow Germany
31 H3 Beeskow Germany
100 C7 Beestekraal S Africa
112 K7 Beeston England
140 C3 Beetaloo N Terr Australia
33 R8 Beetzendorf Germany
95 S2 Beetz G Germany
109 K7 Beeville Texas U.S.A.
87 H11 Befandriana Madagascar
86 F3 Befori Zaire
8 D4 Bega,R England
80 E5 Begelly Wales
80 B4 Beggars Pt Antigua W Indies
78 F6 Beggs Oklahoma U.S.A.
86 P4 Běgi Ethiopia
33 S10 Begichev, Ostrov isld Russian Federation
31 H3 Beeskow Germany
99 T6 Beg-Meil France
72 D11 Begna R Norway
19 N15 Begude-de-Mazenc, La France
86 B7 Behanan Iran
86 D4 Behbehan Germany
80 B4 Behh,R Iran
22 L3 Beho Belgium
37 T1 Behren-Lübchin Germany
37 L4 Behrensmühle Germany
59 J2 Běhshahr Iran
69 G7 Bei'an China
85 D7 Beichuan China
85 F3 Beida Saudi Arabia
116 J8 Beihai China
33 P8 Beihai Germany
67 B6 Bei Hulsan Hu China
63 A5 Bei Jiang R China
60 K8 Beila Mauritania
38 B3 Beilen Netherlands
18 G5 Bein China
37 O3 Beilngries Germany
54 B4 Beilrode Germany
37 J6 Beilstein Baden-Württemberg Germany
36 H7 Beilstein Hessen Germany
46 G13 Beinn Rhineland-Pfalz Germany
19 Q14 Beine-Nauroy France
44 H3 Beinasco Italy
36 E6 Beine France
36 E6 Beinheim France
98 A5 Beila Mauritania
78 F9 Beinwil Switzerland
80 F1 Beipan Jiang R China
59 J2 Beipiao China
121 N3 Beira Mozambique
84 B4 Beira Alta prov Portugal
80 D3 Beira Baixa prov Portugal
80 F4 Beira Litoral prov Portugal
79 E7 Beirut see Beyrouth
19 J6 Beith Scotland
36 E5 Beius Romania
67 B6 Beiyang China
110 E3 Beizhen China

65 D6 Beizhen China
16 B6 Beja Portugal
43 C12 Béja Tunisia
143 E6 Bejah Hill W Australia Australia
85 E1 Bejaïa Algeria
85 F1 Bejaïa, Golfe de G Algeria
16 A4 Béjar Spain
77 F2 Bejestán Iran
143 B9 Bejoording W Australia Australia
57 E4 Bekabad Tajikistan
70 L9 Bekasi Java
48 F4 Békés co Hungary
48 G4 Békéscsaba Hungary
85 D7 Bekwai Ghana
48 E5 Bela se Villach
74 B5 Bela Pakistan
80 F3 Béla R India
86 B4 Bélâbérim Niger
86 B4 Bélabo Cameroon
21 N8 Béla Crkva Serbia Yugoslavia
62 D3 Bela Pradesh India
143 D10 Bel-Air France
25 L7 Bel Air Maryland U.S.A.
70 D4 Belajan, G of Kalimantan
16 D2 Belaícazar Spain
74 J4 Belamballi India
37 O4 Bélá nad Radbuzou Czechoslovakia
71 J4 Bélanger Pt Manitoba
87 M9 Bélanger R Manitoba
71 J4 Belangiran Kalimantan
46 E1 Bela Palanka Serbia Yugoslavia
139 H4 Belaraboon New South Wales Australia
16 C3 Belarus see Belorussia
130 C8 Bela Vista Mozambique
130 D8 Bela Vista Paraguay
69 D11 Bela Vista de Goiás Brazil
54 G5 Belawan Sumatra
84 B4 Belaya Russian Federation
113 F8 Belaya Russian Federation
119 N12 Belaya-Kalitva Russian Federation
110 G3 Belaya Kholunitsa Russian Federation
107 N2 Belaya Tserkov' Ukraine
48 N1 Belbo R Italy
48 K2 Belçeşti Romania
115 K2 Belcher Chan Northwest Territories Canada
115 M6 Belcher, Les Iles Northwest Territories Canada
17 D2 Belchite Spain
14 D2 Belco Ireland
98 D1 Belcourt North Dakota U.S.A.
98 D1 Belden California U.S.A.
94 B4 Belding Michigan U.S.A.
52 D7 Belebey Russian Federation
86 J5 Beledweyne Somalia
129 J4 Belém de São Francisco Brazil
123 L6 Belém Colombia
21 H7 Belén Paraguay
131 A1 Belén,Nuevo Mexico U.S.A.
108 A1 Belén Cuchilla de mt Uruguay
114 H7 Belen del Refugio Mexico
127 N5 Belep,Îles New Caledonia
86 G3 Beles R Ethiopia
16 B2 Belesar, Embalse de res Spain
54 H3 Beleza Russian Federation
86 C5 Belêbé Cent Afr Republic
100 C2 Belfair Washington U.S.A.
100 C2 Belfast N Terr Australia
144 M6 Belfast New Zealand
102 C3 Belfast N Ireland
21 K4 Belfast Maine U.S.A.
95 P3 Belfast Vermont U.S.A.
58 T4 Belfield North Dakota U.S.A.
54 J16 Belfodiya Ethiopia
8 B4 Belford England
40 E2 Belfort, Terr De France
76 B3 Belfry Montana U.S.A.
81 L1 Belgaum India
132 P3 Belgern Germany
99 S10 Belgica Antarctica
105 S10 Belgicafjella ra Antarctica
94 F9 Belgium W Europe
22 F2 Belgorod Russian Federation
48 M7 Belgorod Dnestrovskiy
53 B2 Belgorodkaya Oblast' prov Russian Federation
38 M8 Belgrade see Beograd
101 Q1 Belgrade Montana U.S.A.
75 L9 Belgrano, Pto Argentina
55 R9 Belgrano, Pto forest Argentina
142 B1 Belgrove New Zealand
85 D7 Bel Guebbour, Hassi Algeria
94 F9 Behaven North Carolina U.S.A.
85 E7 Belhirane Algeria
21 N4 Belhomert France
43 E11 Belice R Sicily
53 Q12 Belidzhi Russian Federation
87 H11 Beli Lom R Bulgaria
70 B4 Beli Manastir Croatia
69 J12 Belimbing, Tanjong C Indonesia
18 E8 Belin France
86 A5 Belinga Gabon
94 H7 Belington West Virginia U.S.A.
69 G13 Belitung, I Indonesia
46 F3 Belitsa Bulgaria
125 P9 Belize Belize
125 P9 Belize Central America
130 H3 Bélize R China
36 H3 Belkovskiy Os isld Russian Federation

123 R6 Belle B Newfoundland Canada
36 B6 Belle Germany
33 P9 Bellben Germany
94 D6 Belle Center Ohio U.S.A.
40 E7 Belle France
19 P14 Belledonne, Pic de mt France
94 D6 Bellefontaine Ohio U.S.A.
94 K6 Bellefonte Pennsylvania U.S.A.
98 C5 Belle Fourche South Dakota U.S.A.
98 A5 Belle Fourche R Wyoming U.S.A.
18 G5 Bellegarde France
19 P12 Bellegarde France
18 G7 Bellegarde-en-Marche France
113 G11 Belle Glade Florida U.S.A.
40 E3 Bellehébert France
20 D7 Belle Ile France
123 R2 Belle Isle Newfoundland Canada
20 D4 Belle-Isle-en-Terre France
123 R2 Belle Isle Landing Belle Isle, Nfld
123 Q2 Belle Isle,Strait of Newfoundland Canada
21 M5 Belle Meade Tennessee U.S.A.
103 N6 Bellemont Arizona U.S.A.
21 N2 Bellencombre France
141 H3 Bellenden Ker ra Queensland Australia
22 E4 Belleoram Newfoundland Canada
119 M8 Belle Plaine Saskatchewan Canada
99 O8 Belle Plaine Iowa U.S.A.
107 N4 Belle Plaine Kansas U.S.A.
99 N5 Belle Plaine Minnesota U.S.A.
110 H3 Belle Rive Illinois U.S.A.
121 T4 Belle-Rivière,Lac de la Quebec Canada
40 E5 Bellevesvre France
80 B4 Belleville France
113 E8 Belleville Florida U.S.A.
121 L8 Belleville Ontario Canada
110 G3 Belleville Illinois U.S.A.
107 N2 Belleville Kansas U.S.A.
95 K5 Belleville New York U.S.A.
94 K6 Belleville Pennsylvania U.S.A.
94 F7 Belleville West Virginia U.S.A.
99 H8 Belleville sur Vie France
141 G3 Belleville Queensland Australia
118 C9 Bellevue Alberta Canada
101 L6 Bellevue Idaho U.S.A.
99 Q7 Bellevue Iowa U.S.A.
94 B4 Bellevue Michigan U.S.A.
94 E5 Bellevue Ohio U.S.A.
109 J2 Bellevue Texas U.S.A.
100 C3 Bellevue Washington U.S.A.
19 P13 Belley France
110 H1 Bellflower Illinois U.S.A.
110 H1 Bellflower Missouri U.S.A.
36 E5 Bellheim Germany
123 R3 Bell I. Newfoundland Canada
25 E4 Bellicourt France
21 H7 Belligne France
22 J8 Bellingham Minnesota U.S.A.
100 C1 Bellingham Washington U.S.A.
146 D3 Bellingshausen former U.S.S.R. Base Antarctica
146 B6 Bellingshausen Sea Antarctica
25 H2 Bellingwolde Netherlands
33 N5 Bellis Alberta Canada
36 F2 Bellmann Germany
137 M6 Bellona Plateau Coral Sea
102 C3 Bellota California U.S.A.
21 K4 Bellows Falls Vermont U.S.A.
95 P3 Bellows Falls Vermont U.S.A.
21 P3 Belloy-en-France France
115 L5 Bell Pen Northwest Territories Canada
138 C4 Bell,Pt South Australia
106 F6 Bell Ranch New Mexico
13 F1 Bell Rock Scotland
109 G6 Bells Tennessee U.S.A.
110 G6 Bells Texas U.S.A.
22 E2 Bellsite Manitoba Canada
24 E2 Belluno Italy
131 D4 Bell Ville Argentina
94 C6 Bellville Ohio U.S.A.
109 K4 Bellville Texas U.S.A.
109 K4 Belluwood Louisiana U.S.A.
94 H7 Bellwood Pennsylvania U.S.A.
118 D6 Belly R Alberta Canada
21 N6 Belmar New Jersey U.S.A.
130 H3 Belmez Spain
90 N7 Belmont Quebec Canada
142 B1 Belmont dist Perth, W Aust Australia
119 S9 Belmont Manitoba Canada
122 D5 Belmont Nova Scotia Canada
120 J10 Belmont Ontario Canada
102 H3 Belmont Nevada U.S.A.
95 P3 Belmont New Hampshire U.S.A.
95 K4 Belmont New York U.S.A.
112 G2 Belmont North Carolina U.S.A.
109 K6 Belmont Texas U.S.A.
94 K8 Belmont Virginia U.S.A.
99 S6 Belmont Wisconsin U.S.A.
129 M3 Belmonte Brazil
16 C3 Belmonte Portugal
17 F5 Belmonte Spain
125 P9 Belmopan Belize
141 F5 Belmore Queensland Australia
14 A2 Belmullet Ireland
130 H4 Belo Campo Brazil
63 A5 Belogorsk China
55 C4 Belogorsk Russian Federation
59 J1 Belogorsk Russian Federation
147 J16 Belogradchik Bulgaria
46 F1 Belo Horizonte Brazil
87 K7 Belo Jardim Brazil
48 M5 Beloeil Quebec Canada
48 H5 Belóeles'ye Russian Federation
130 H10 Beloie more Russian Federation
130 C4 Belomorsk Russian Federation
147 J16 Beloretsk Russian Federation
54 M6 Belorechensk Russian Federation
54 B3 Belorussia rep E Europe

12 E1 Braco Scotland
43 G8 Bradano R Italy
98 F3 Braddock North Dakota U.S.A.
94 H6 Braddock Pennsylvania U.S.A.
99 L9 Braddyville Iowa U.S.A.
113 E10 Bradenton Florida U.S.A.
113 E10 Bradenton Beach Florida U.S.A.
28 B7 Braderup Germany
121 L8 Bradford Ontario Canada
8 D5 Bradford England
13 G6 Bradford England
110 E6 Bradford Arkansas U.S.A.
99 R8 Bradford Illinois U.S.A.
99 N7 Bradford Iowa U.S.A.
95 T1 Bradford Maine U.S.A.
95 P3 Bradford New Hampshire U.S.A.
94 C6 Bradford Ohio U.S.A.
94 J5 Bradford Pennsylvania U.S.A.
95 Q5 Bradford Rhode I U.S.A.
94 B9 Bradfordsville Kentucky U.S.A.
111 C8 Bradley Arkansas U.S.A.
102 D6 Bradley California U.S.A.
99 T8 Bradley Illinois U.S.A.
107 N7 Bradley Oklahoma U.S.A.
110 D5 Bradleyville Missouri U.S.A.
94 D5 Bradner Ohio U.S.A.
123 P2 Bradore Bay Quebec Canada
123 P2 Bradore Hills Quebec Canada
140 B3 Bradshaw N Terr Australia
98 J9 Bradshaw Nebraska U.S.A.
142 F3 Bradshaw,Mt W Australia Australia
119 R9 Bradwardine Manitoba Canada
118 L7 Bradwell Saskatchewan Canada
9 G4 Bradwell England
98 F8 Brady Nebraska U.S.A.
109 H4 Brady Texas U.S.A.
117 E6 Brady Glacier Alaska U.S.A.
138 C3 Brady,Mt South Australia Australia
28 D5 Brædstrup Denmark
138 E5 Braemar South Australia Australia
15 E3 Braemar Scotland
15 E3 Braeriach mt Scotland
16 B3 Braga Portugal
131 E5 Bragado Argentina
129 J4 Bragança Brazil
16 C3 Bragança Portugal
130 F8 Bragança Paulista Brazil
112 E6 Braganza Georgia U.S.A.
110 G5 Bragg City Missouri U.S.A.
118 C7 Bragg Creek Prov. Park Alberta Canada
54 B5 Bragin Belorussia
99 N4 Braham Minnesota U.S.A.
33 N6 Brahlstorf Mecklenburg-Vorpommern Germany
75 O7 Brahmanbaria Bangladesh
75 L9 Brahmapur India
75 P5 Brahmaputra R S Asia
32 L4 Brahmsee L Germany
77 K5 Brahui,Cen reg Pakistan
99 S8 Braidwood Illinois U.S.A.
48 L5 Brăila Romania
9 E2 Brailsford England
98 J8 Brainard Nebraska U.S.A.
22 F5 Braine France
22 G2 Braine L'Alleud Belgium
22 G2 Braine-le Château Belgium
22 G2 Braine-le Comte Belgium
99 M3 Brainerd Minnesota U.S.A.
21 L7 Brain-sur-Allonnes France
9 G4 Braintree England
13 E4 Braithwaite England
111 G12 Braithwaite Louisiana U.S.A.
140 C1 Braithwaite Pt N Terr Australia
22 J2 Braives Belgium
89 F4 Brak R S Africa
32 H6 Brake Germany
22 F2 Brakel Belgium
32 K9 Brakel Germany
85 B5 Brakna reg Mauritania
57 D1 Brali Kazakhstan
117 M10 Bralorne British Columbia Canada
107 N5 Braman Oklahoma U.S.A.
Brambach see Radiumbad-Brambach
38 F7 Bramberg Austria
13 G6 Bramham England
32 H6 Bramloge Germany
28 B6 Bramming Denmark
44 B3 Bram,Monte Italy
26 J9 Brämö isld Sweden
9 H3 Brampton England
98 J3 Brampton North Dakota U.S.A.
141 J5 Brampton I Queensland Australia
32 G8 Bramsche Germany
141 G1 Bramwell Queensland Australia
94 F9 Bramwell West Virginia U.S.A.
9 G2 Brancaster England
13 G4 Brancepeth England
123 T7 Branch Newfoundland Canada
99 U6 Branch Michigan U.S.A.
95 K4 Branchport New York U.S.A.
112 G4 Branchville South Carolina U.S.A.
130 B7 Branco R Mato Grosso Brazil
128 F3 Branco R Roraima Brazil
130 J9 Branco,Cabo Brazil
131 B2 Branco,R Argentina
41 L3 Brand Austria
37 O3 Brand Czechoslovakia
87 B10 Brandberg mt Namibia
26 H9 Brändbo Sweden
28 C5 Brande Denmark
32 L5 Brande-Hörnerkirchen Germany
101 T4 Brandenberg Montana U.S.A.
33 R8 Brandenburg Germany
33 R7 Brandenburg land Germany
110 K4 Brandenburg Kentucky U.S.A.
37 P2 Brand-Erbisdorf Germany
28 C6 Branderup Denmark
13 H6 Brandesburton England
89 E7 Brandfort S Africa
33 R10 Brandis Germany
29 J11 Brändö Finland
119 S9 Brandon Manitoba Canada
9 G3 Brandon England
106 H3 Brandon Colorado U.S.A.
98 E9 Brandon Nebraska U.S.A.
95 O3 Brandon Vermont U.S.A.
99 S6 Brandon Wisconsin U.S.A.
14 A4 Brandon B Ireland
14 A4 Brandon Hd Ireland
14 E4 Brandon Hill mt Ireland
14 A4 Brandon Mt Ireland
95 N3 Brandreth New York U.S.A.
13 G5 Brandsby England
133 F5 Brandsen Argentina
28 D6 Brandsø isld Denmark
110 E5 Brandsville Missouri U.S.A.
98 K5 Brandt South Dakota U.S.A.
27 F11 Brandval Norway
87 D12 Brandvlei S Africa
94 K8 Brandy Virginia U.S.A.
95 L8 Brandywine Maryland U.S.A.
48 K6 Brăneşti Romania
95 P5 Branford Connecticut U.S.A.
113 E8 Branford Florida U.S.A.
27 L17 Braniewo Poland
31 M1 Braniewo Poland
31 M6 Branisko mts Czechoslovakia
18 E8 Branne France
102 A2 Branscomb California U.S.A.
146 C3 Bransfield Str Antarctica
106 G4 Branson Colorado U.S.A.
110 C5 Branson Missouri U.S.A.
9 F1 Branston England
118 D8 Brant Alberta Canada
70 O9 Brantas Java
70 O10 Brantas R Java
120 K9 Brantford Ontario Canada
98 H2 Brantford North Dakota U.S.A.
111 K10 Brantley Alabama U.S.A.
18 F7 Brantôme France
138 F7 Branxholme Victoria Australia
123 M8 Bras d'or L Nova Scotia Canada
99 O9 Brashear Missouri U.S.A.
128 E6 Brasiléia Brazil
129 J7 Brasília Brazil
129 G4 Brasilia Legal Brazil
52 C6 Braslav Belorussia
48 K5 Brasov Romania
20 C5 Brasparts France
85 F8 Brass Nigeria
22 G1 Brasschaat Belgium
140 C6 Brassey Mt N Terr Australia
143 D6 Brassey Ra W Australia Australia
70 E2 Brassey Ra mts Sabah
139 G5 Brassi New South Wales Australia
28 D4 Brassø L Denmark
95 R1 Brassua L Maine U.S.A.
48 H4 Bratca Romania
48 L5 Brates, L Romania
46 G1 Brateş, Lacul L Romania
31 K7 Bratislava Czechoslovakia
46 G3 Bratsigovo Bulgaria
56 F3 Bratsk Russian Federation
56 F3 Bratskoye Vodokhranilishche res Russian Federation
48 M2 Bratslav Ukraine
26 K7 Bratten Sweden
95 P4 Brattleboro Vermont U.S.A.
32 M8 Brau Germany
36 D3 Braubach Germany
36 G2 Brauerschwend Germany
38 H5 Braunau Austria
36 E3 Braunfels Germany
33 N9 Braunlage Germany
33 P10 Braunsbedra Germany
Braunsberg see Braniewo Poland
33 N8 Braunschweig Germany
8 B5 Braunton England
36 B2 Brauweiler Germany
131 D4 Brava, L. la Argentina
94 G7 Brave Pennsylvania U.S.A.
27 H13 Bråviken L Sweden
131 D2 Bravo,Sa mt Argentina
14 E3 Bray Ireland
22 D1 Bray-Dunes France
22 E5 Braye France
21 M6 Braye,R France
21 O3 Bray-et-Lû France
8 C5 Brayford England
14 A5 Bray Hd Ireland
115 M4 Bray I Northwest Territories Canada
110 C2 Braymer Missouri U.S.A.
18 H4 Bray sur Seine France
22 D4 Bray-sur-Somme France
118 A6 Brazeau Alberta Canada
118 B6 Brazeau Dam Alberta Canada
128 F6 Brazil rep S America
110 J2 Brazil Indiana U.S.A.
90 G11 Brazil Basin Atlantic Oc
109 M6 Brazoria Texas U.S.A.
109 L4 Brazos R Texas U.S.A.
86 C6 Brazzaville Congo
48 E6 Brčko Bosnia-Herzegovina
31 K2 Brda R Poland
48 D1 Brdo mt Czechoslovakia
140 E6 Breadalbane Queensland Australia
143 E7 Breaden Bluff hill W Australia Australia
143 F7 Breaden,L W Australia Australia
141 K1 Breakfast Creek dist Brisbane, Qnsld Australia
144 A6 Breaksea I New Zealand
144 B7 Breaksea Is New Zealand
141 L6 Breaksea Spit Queensland Australia
20 G5 Bréal-sous-Montfort France
8 D4 Bream England
6 N4 Bream oil rig North Sea
145 E1 Bream Bay New Zealand
27 F15 Breared Sweden
21 L2 Bréaute France
111 E11 Breaux Bridge Louisiana U.S.A.
48 K5 Breaza Romania
70 M9 Brebes Java
70 M9 Brebes,Tg C Java
121 U4 Brébeuf, L Quebec Canada
122 B5 Brébeuf,L Quebec Canada
21 H4 Brécey France
20 E6 Brech France
36 E3 Brechen Germany
121 L8 Brechin Ontario Canada
15 F4 Brechin Scotland
20 F3 Brechou isld Channel Is English Chan
22 H1 Brecht Belgium
106 D2 Breckenridge Colorado U.S.A.
98 K3 Breckenridge Minnesota U.S.A.
110 C2 Breckenridge Missouri U.S.A.
109 J3 Breckenridge Texas U.S.A.
133 C8 Brecknock, Pen Chile
31 K7 Břeclav Czechoslovakia
8 C4 Brecon Wales
8 C4 Brecon Beacons mts Wales
Breconshire co see Powys, Gwent, Mid Glamorgan counties
25 C5 Breda Netherlands
99 M7 Breda Iowa U.S.A.
26 M6 Bredåker Sweden
27 H15 Bredåkra Sweden
27 G14 Bredaryd Sweden
87 D12 Bredasdorp S Africa
33 Q7 Breddin Germany
32 K6 Breddorf Germany
28 B6 Brede Denmark
9 G6 Brede England
28 B6 Brede Å R Denmark
28 B6 Bredebro Denmark
32 J10 Bredelar Germany
22 E1 Bredene Belgium
33 R5 Bredenfelde Germany
119 P8 Bredenyur Saskatchewan Canada
33 S6 Bredereiche Germany
28 C7 Bredevad Denmark
26 L6 Bredsel Sweden
27 G12 Bredsjö Sweden
30 E1 Bredstedt Germany
28 C5 Bredsten Denmark
26 K8 Bredträsk Sweden
55 D4 Bredy Russian Federation
22 K1 Bree Belgium
89 A9 Breede R S Africa
110 G3 Breese Illinois U.S.A.
33 Q5 Breesen Germany
46 E3 Bregalnica R Macedonia Yugoslavia
41 H2 Brege R Germany
41 L2 Bregenz Austria
41 L3 Bregenzer Ache R Austria
41 L3 Bregenzer Wald mt Austria
28 G5 Bregninge Denmark
48 H6 Bregovo Bulgaria
20 G4 Bréhal France
20 E4 Bréhat isld France
122 B1 Bréhat, L Quebec Canada
33 Q9 Brehna Germany
33 T9 Brehnitz Germany
36 E2 Breidenbach Germany
28 R9 Breidhafjördhur B Iceland
29 T9 Breidhdalsvik Iceland
98 E3 Breien North Dakota U.S.A.
21 L5 Breil-sur-Mérize,le France
26 B10 Breim Norway
40 G1 Breisach Germany
37 M5 Breitenbrunn Germany
33 Q10 Breitenfeld Germany
37 K4 Breitengüssbach Germany
33 P9 Breitenhagen Germany
33 M7 Breitenhees Germany
37 O3 Breitenhof Germany
33 S6 Breiter Luzinsee L Germany
40 G5 Breithorn mt Switzerland
33 Q4 Breitling Germany
37 J2 Breitungen Germany
26 M1 Breivikbotn Norway
28 A4 Brejning Denmark
129 K4 Brejo Brazil
94 C3 Brekenridge Michigan U.S.A.
26 E9 Brekken Norway
26 D8 Brekstad Norway
26 A10 Bremangerlandet isld Norway
41 L6 Brembana, Val Italy
41 L6 Brembo R Italy
32 J6 Bremen Germany
112 B4 Bremen Georgia U.S.A.
94 A5 Bremen Indiana U.S.A.
94 E7 Bremen Ohio U.S.A.
140 D1 Bremer isld N Terr Australia
143 C10 Bremer Bay W Australia Australia
32 J5 Bremerhaven Germany
143 D10 Bremer Ra W Australia Australia
117 M12 Bremerton Washington U.S.A.
32 K6 Bremervörde Germany
41 H3 Bremgarten Switzerland
116 Q6 Bremner R Alaska U.S.A.
109 L4 Bremond Texas U.S.A.
26 E6 Bremsteinen lighthouse Norway
139 H3 Brenda New South Wales Australia
28 D6 Brenderup Denmark
45 K1 Brendola Italy
8 C5 Brendon Hills England
109 L5 Brenham Texas U.S.A.
21 N8 Brenne reg France
21 M6 Brenne R Indre-et-Loire France
41 O3 Brenner Austria
101 M5 Brenner Montana U.S.A.
41 O4 Brennero Italy
41 O3 Brenner Pass Austria/Italy
41 M6 Breno Italy
42 C3 Breno Italy
19 P12 Brénod France
36 C5 Brenschelbach Germany
121 M6 Brent Ontario Canada
6 M1 Brent oil rig North Sea
111 J9 Brent Alabama U.S.A.
42 D3 Brenta R Italy
41 N5 Brenta, Gruppa di mt Italy
9 F5 Brentford England
98 H4 Brentford South Dakota U.S.A.
123 T4 Brenton Rock Newfoundland Canada
9 G4 Brentwood England
102 C4 Brentwood California U.S.A.
37 J6 Brenz R Germany
9 G5 Brenzett England
89 G6 Brereton Park S Africa
45 J2 Brescello Italy
41 M6 Brescia Italy
25 A6 Breskens Netherlands
Breslau see Wrocław
21 O2 Bresle R France
21 P3 Bresles France
143 C6 Bresnahan,Mt W Australia Australia
41 P4 Bressanone Italy
40 B5 Bresse reg France
21 K8 Bressuire France
31 O3 Brest Belorussia
20 B5 Brest France
20 D5 Brest à Nantes, Canal de France
46 E1 Brestovac Serbia Yugoslavia
20 A5 Brest,Rade de B France
83 J14 Bretagne, Pnte de Réunion Indian Oc
21 N4 Bretagnolles France
48 K4 Breţcu Romania
18 G8 Bretenoux France
21 M4 Breteuil-sur-Iton France
21 P2 Breteuil-sur-Noye France
20 G8 Brétignolles-sur-Mer France
21 P4 Brétigny France
118 C5 Breton Alberta Canada
21 M5 Bretoncelles France
111 G12 Breton I Louisiana U.S.A.
18 E6 Breton, Pertuis d' B France
95 N6 Breton Woods New Jersey U.S.A.
38 K7 Bretstein Austria
145 E1 Brett, C New Zealand
36 F5 Bretten Germany
21 K3 Bretteville France
21 K3 Bretteville-l'Orgueilleuse France
37 J5 Brettheim Germany
36 G5 Bretzfeld Germany
36 G4 Breuberg Germany
69 B10 Breueh, Pulau isl Sumatra
21 L3 Breuil-en-Auge,le France
21 N4 Breuilpont France
25 D4 Breukelen Netherlands
40 C1 Breuvannes France
21 O4 Bréval France
112 E2 Brevard North Carolina U.S.A.
129 H4 Breves Brazil
27 D12 Brevik Norway
95 T2 Brewer Maine U.S.A.
95 L3 Brewerton New York U.S.A.
113 E10 Brewster Florida U.S.A.
107 J2 Brewster Kansas U.S.A.
98 G8 Brewster Nebraska U.S.A.
95 O5 Brewster New York U.S.A.
94 F6 Brewster Ohio U.S.A.
117 O11 Brewster Washington U.S.A.
115 R3 Brewster, Kap C Greenland
144 B6 Brewster, Mt New Zealand
111 J10 Brewton Alabama U.S.A.
25 F6 Breyell Germany
Brezhnev see Naberezhnyye Chelny
19 O14 Brezins France
46 F2 Breznik Bulgaria
48 F2 Brezno Czechoslovakia
38 M8 Brezno Slovenia
48 J5 Brezoi Romania
21 N4 Brezolles France
16 D2 Brezo, Sa. del mts Spain
46 G2 Brezovo Bulgaria
42 H3 Brezovo Polje mt Croatia
86 D4 Bria Cent Afr Republic
103 M4 Brian Head Utah U.S.A.
18 G5 Briare France
141 L7 Bribie I Queensland Australia
108 G1 Brice Texas U.S.A.
99 N6 Bricelyn Minnesota U.S.A.
48 L2 Brichany Moldavia
110 F7 Brickeys Arkansas U.S.A.
19 J4 Bricon France
123 M2* Briconnet,L Quebec Canada
20 G3 Bricquebec France
20 G4 Bricqueville-sur-Mer France
14 C4 Bride R Ireland
12 D5 Bride I of Man U.K.
8 B3 Bridell Wales
8 B6 Bridestowe England
119 U3 Bridgar Manitoba Canada
117 M10 Bridge R British Columbia Canada
101 M7 Bridge Idaho U.S.A.
112 D6 Bridgeboro Georgia U.S.A.
12 B2 Bridgend Islay Scotland
13 E1 Bridgend Tayside Scotland
8 C5 Bridgend Wales
12 E1 Bridge of Allan Scotland
12 D3 Bridge of Doon Scotland
12 D2 Bridge of Weir Scotland
110 L7 Bridgeport Alabama U.S.A.
102 E3 Bridgeport California U.S.A.
95 O5 Bridgeport Connecticut U.S.A.
107 N3 Bridgeport Kansas U.S.A.
98 C8 Bridgeport Nebraska U.S.A.
100 H5 Bridgeport Oregon U.S.A.
100 F2 Bridgeport Washington U.S.A.
109 K2 Bridgeport, L Texas U.S.A.
102 E3 Bridgeport Res California U.S.A.
113 L12 Bridge Pt Bahamas
101 R4 Bridger Montana U.S.A.
101 P4 Bridger Pk Montana U.S.A.
101 S8 Bridger Pk Wyoming U.S.A.
95 M7 Bridgeton New Jersey U.S.A.
112 K2 Bridgeton North Carolina U.S.A.
143 B10 Bridgetown W Australia Australia
127 P6 Bridgetown Barbados
122 G9 Bridgetown Nova Scotia Canada
122 K8 Bridgeville Nova Scotia Canada
100 B9 Bridgeville California U.S.A.
122 H9 Bridgewater Nova Scotia Canada
95 S7 Bridgewater Maine U.S.A.
95 R5 Bridgewater Massachusetts U.S.A.
98 J6 Bridgewater South Dakota U.S.A.
94 J8 Bridgewater Virginia U.S.A.
138 F7 Bridgewater,C Victoria Australia
94 A5 Bridgman Michigan U.S.A.
8 D2 Bridgnorth England
95 R2 Bridgton Maine U.S.A.
8 C5 Bridgwater England
13 H5 Bridlington England
139 H8 Bridport Tasmania Australia
8 D6 Bridport England
18 G4 Brie reg France
20 B5 Briec France
25 B5 Brielle Netherlands
112 F4 Brier Creek Georgia U.S.A.
119 M8 Briercrest Saskatchewan Canada
118 F4 Briereville Alberta Canada
122 F9 Brier I Nova Scotia Canada
22 H5 Brieulles-sur-Bar France
21 O4 Brieval France
22 K5 Briey France
40 G5 Brig Switzerland
41 H1 Brigarh R Germany
120 H10 Brigden Ontario Canada
13 H6 Brigg England
109 K5 Briggs Texas U.S.A.
98 B9 Briggsdale Colorado U.S.A.
101 N8 Brigham City Utah U.S.A.
13 G6 Brighouse England
9 E6 Brighstone England
103 M5 Bright Angel Pt Arizona U.S.A.
9 H4 Brightlingsea England
138 E6 Brighton South Australia Australia
121 N8 Brighton Ontario Canada
9 F6 Brighton England
98 B10 Brighton Colorado U.S.A.
113 F10 Brighton Florida U.S.A.
110 F2 Brighton Illinois U.S.A.
99 P8 Brighton Iowa U.S.A.
94 D4 Brighton Michigan U.S.A.
141 F6 Brighton Downs Queensland Australia
145 D4 Brightwater New Zealand
20 B4 Brignogan-Plage France
123 T6 Brigus Newfoundland Canada
17 F4 Brihuega Spain
42 F4 Brijuni isld Croatia
26 G4 Briksvoer isld Norway
130 C7 Brilhante,R Brazil
106 F5 Brilliant New Mexico U.S.A.
99 S5 Brillion Wisconsin U.S.A.
32 J10 Brilon Germany
99 R9 Brimfield Illinois U.S.A.
43 H8 Brindisi Italy
138 C4 Bring,L South Australia Australia
94 E6 Brinkhaven Ohio U.S.A.
9 G3 Brinkley England
110 E7 Brinkley Arkansas U.S.A.
9 E3 Brinklow England
53 E10 Brin'kovskaya Russian Federation
32 J6 Brinkum Germany
138 E5 Brinkworth South Australia Australia
21 P6 Brinon-sur-Sauldre France
98 G1 Brinsmade North Dakota U.S.A.
113 C7 Brinson Georgia U.S.A.
21 J6 Briollay France
21 O8 Brion Indre France
123 L6 Brion, I Madeleine Is, Quebec Canada
21 M3 Brionne France
21 K7 Brion-près-Thouet France
18 H7 Brioude France
21 K4 Briouze France
141 L8 Brisbane Queensland Australia
141 L7 Brisbane R Queensland Australia
108 D8 Briscoe Texas U.S.A.
45 L3 Brisighella Italy
6 N4 Brisling oil rig North Sea
21 K7 Brissac-Quincé France
41 J4 Bristenstock mt Switzerland
122 E7 Bristol New Brunswick Canada
121 O7 Bristol Quebec Canada
8 D5 Bristol England
106 H3 Bristol Colorado U.S.A.
95 P5 Bristol Connecticut U.S.A.
113 C7 Bristol Florida U.S.A.
112 E6 Bristol Georgia U.S.A.
94 B5 Bristol Indiana U.S.A.
95 Q3 Bristol New Hampshire U.S.A.
95 M6 Bristol Pennsylvania U.S.A.
95 Q5 Bristol Rhode I U.S.A.
98 J4 Bristol South Dakota U.S.A.
95 O2 Bristol Vermont U.S.A.
94 E10 Bristol Virginia/Tenn U.S.A.
116 G8 Bristol B Alaska U.S.A.
8 C5 Bristol Chan England/Wales
146 G3 Bristol I S Sandwich Is Atlantic Oc
103 J7 Bristol L California U.S.A.
103 J7 Bristol Mts California U.S.A.
103 K3 Bristol Silver Nevada U.S.A.
107 O6 Bristow Oklahoma U.S.A.
117 M11 Britannia Beach British Columbia Canada
146 A3 British Antarctic Terr Antarctica
117 K7 British Columbia prov Canada
115 L1 British Empire Ra Northwest Territories Canada
British Guiana see Guyana
British Honduras see Belize
81 E6 British Ind.Oc.Terr colony Indian Oc
116 Q2 British Mts Alaska/Yukon Terr U.S.A./Canada
British N. Borneo see Sabah
British Solomon Is see Solomon Is.
123 M7 Briton Cove C Breton I, Nova Scotia
8 C4 Briton Ferry Wales
87 E11 Brits S Africa
87 D12 Britstown S Africa
120 K7 Britt Ontario Canada
99 N6 Britt Iowa U.S.A.
27 G14 Brittatorp Sweden
107 N6 Britton Oklahoma U.S.A.
98 J4 Britton South Dakota U.S.A.
138 C2 Britton,Mt South Australia Australia
33 T7 Britz Germany
18 G7 Brive-la-Gaillarde France
16 E2 Briviesca Spain
20 G2 Brix France
38 F7 Brixental V Austria
8 C7 Brixham England
48 D1 Brno Czechoslovakia
27 F12 Bro Sweden
112 D3 Broad R Georgia U.S.A.
112 F3 Broad R South Carolina U.S.A.
118 J6 Broadacres Saskatchewan Canada
95 N3 Broadalbin New York U.S.A.
143 D9 Broad Arrow W Australia Australia
121 M1 Broadback R Quebec Canada
15 B2 Broad Bay Scotland
100 A6 Broadbent Oregon U.S.A.
109 N4 Broaddus Texas U.S.A.
15 C3 Broadford Scotland
14 B2 Broad Haven Ireland
8 A4 Broad Haven Wales
9 E5 Broad Hinton England
142 D5 Broadhurst Ra W Australia Australia
98 H5 Broadland South Dakota U.S.A.
15 E5 Broad Law Scotland
116 N5 Broad Pass Alaska U.S.A.
141 J5 Broad Sound Queensland Australia
141 K5 Broad Sound Chan Queensland Australia
141 J6 Broadsound Ra Queensland Australia
9 H5 Broadstairs England
98 A4 Broadus Montana U.S.A.
119 P8 Broadview Saskatchewan Canada
101 R3 Broadview Montana U.S.A.
108 A9 Broadview New Mexico U.S.A.
9 F6 Broadwater England
98 D8 Broadwater Nebraska U.S.A.
9 E3 Broadway England
8 D6 Broadwey England
8 D6 Broadwindsor England
145 D1 Broadwood New Zealand
126 C3 Broa, Ensenada de la B Cuba
28 D7 Broager Denmark
28 E6 Broby Denmark
27 G15 Broby Sweden
119 Q1 Brochet Manitoba Canada
122 C4 Brochet,L.au Quebec Canada
32 G8 Brochterbeck Germany
121 Q4 Brochu,L Quebec Canada
118 J7 Brock Saskatchewan Canada
99 L9 Brock Nebraska U.S.A.
32 L6 Brockel Germany
33 N9 Brocken mt Germany
9 E6 Brockenhurst England
118 D9 Brocket Alberta Canada
98 H1 Brocket North Dakota U.S.A.
114 H2 Brock I Northwest Territories Canada
13 H6 Brocklesby England
142 B5 Brockman,Mt W Australia Australia
94 K3 Brockport New York U.S.A.
98 G7 Brocksburg Nebraska U.S.A.
140 B2 Brock's Creek N Terr Australia
95 Q4 Brockton Massachusetts U.S.A.
98 B1 Brockton Montana U.S.A.
121 P8 Brockville Ontario Canada
98 A2 Brockway Montana U.S.A.
94 J5 Brockway Pennsylvania U.S.A.
110 J2 Brocton Illinois U.S.A.
94 H4 Brocton New York U.S.A.
48 F7 Brodarevo Serbia Yugoslavia
118 L7 Broderick Saskatchewan Canada
115 L3 Brodeur Pen Northwest Territories Canada
99 R7 Brodhead Wisconsin U.S.A.
48 G6 Brodica Serbia Yugoslavia
12 C2 Brodick Scotland
94 K10 Brodnax Virginia U.S.A.
31 L2 Brodnica Poland
55 D3 Brodokalmak Russian Federation
25 C3 Broek op Langedijk Netherlands
100 H5 Brogan Oregon U.S.A.
21 M3 Broglie France
20 F5 Brohinière,la France
36 C3 Brohl-Lützing Germany
33 T5 Brohm-Cosa Germany
33 M8 Broistedt Germany
31 N3 Brok Poland
99 R4 Brokaw Wisconsin U.S.A.
32 K5 Brokdorf Germany
107 P5 Broken Arrow Oklahoma U.S.A.
139 K5 Broken Bay New South Wales Australia
98 G8 Broken Bow Nebraska U.S.A.
107 Q7 Broken Bow Oklahoma U.S.A.
107 Q7 Broken Bow L Oklahoma U.S.A.
138 F4 Broken Hill New South Wales Australia
Broken Hill Zambia see Kabwe
129 G3 Brokopondomeer L Suriname
29 K12 Bromarv Finland
33 N7 Brome Germany
8 D3 Bromfield England
98 C1 Bromhead Saskatchewan Canada
9 G5 Bromley England
27 D11 Bromma Norway
28 G5 Bromme Denmark
70 O9 Bromo mt Java
13 H5 Brompton England
99 O9 Brompton Iowa U.S.A.
8 D3 Bromsgrove England
8 D3 Bromyard England
19 N13 Bron France
40 A6 Bron France
110 B4 Bronaugh Missouri U.S.A.
28 D2 Brønderslev Denmark
28 A5 Brøndum Denmark
8 C3 Bronllys Wales
37 L4 Bronn Germany
27 G15 Brönnestad Sweden
55 E2 Bronnikovo Russian Federation
26 F6 Brönnöysund Norway
36 H2 Bronnzell Germany
28 B6 Brøns Denmark
113 E8 Bronson Florida U.S.A.
94 B5 Bronson Michigan U.S.A.
109 N4 Bronson Texas U.S.A.
121 L9 Bronte Ontario Canada
43 F11 Bronte Sicily
108 G4 Bronte Texas U.S.A.
139 H8 Bronte Park Tasmania Australia
95 O6 Bronx New York U.S.A.
41 O5 Bronzolo Italy
122 E3 Brooch L Quebec Canada
99 T9 Brook Indiana U.S.A.
94 K8 Brooke Virginia U.S.A.
109 O4 Brookeland Texas U.S.A.
113 E8 Brooker Florida U.S.A.
71 C6 Brooke's Pt Palawan Philippines
122 J8 Brookfield Nova Scotia Canada
110 C2 Brookfield Missouri U.S.A.
111 F10 Brookhaven Mississippi U.S.A.
119 N9 Brooking Saskatchewan Canada
100 A7 Brookings Oregon U.S.A.
98 K5 Brookings South Dakota U.S.A.
141 H4 Brook Is.Lt.Ho Queensland Australia
9 G6 Brookland England
94 K5 Brookland Pennsylvania U.S.A.
112 F5 Brooklet Georgia U.S.A.
121 M9 Brooklin Ontario Canada
95 Q4 Brookline Massachusetts U.S.A.
110 K2 Brooklyn Indiana U.S.A.
99 O8 Brooklyn Iowa U.S.A.
94 C4 Brooklyn Michigan U.S.A.
111 G10 Brooklyn Mississippi U.S.A.
95 O6 Brooklyn New York U.S.A.
95 M5 Brooklyn Pennsylvania U.S.A.
117 N11 Brookmere British Columbia Canada
94 H10 Brookneal Virginia U.S.A.
99 N4 Brook Park Minnesota U.S.A.
110 H4 Brookport Illinois U.S.A.
118 F8 Brooks Alberta Canada
95 S2 Brooks Maine U.S.A.
101 Q2 Brooks Montana U.S.A.
117 G5 Brooks Brook Yukon Territory Canada
119 N5 Brooksby Saskatchewan Canada
146 D6 Brooks, Cape C Antarctica
109 M6 Brookshire Texas U.S.A.
116 D4 Brooks Mt Alaska U.S.A.
116 M5 Brooks,Mt Alaska U.S.A.
116 H2 Brooks Range Alaska U.S.A.
99 O3 Brookston Minnesota U.S.A.
109 M2 Brookston Texas U.S.A.
113 E9 Brooksville Florida U.S.A.
111 H8 Brooksville Mississippi U.S.A.
143 B9 Brookton W Australia Australia
95 U1 Brookton Maine U.S.A.
95 L4 Brooktondale New York U.S.A.
110 M2 Brookville Indiana U.S.A.
107 N3 Brookville Kansas U.S.A.
94 H5 Brookville Pennsylvania U.S.A.
111 J8 Brookwood Alabama U.S.A.
141 L7 Brooloo Queensland Australia
123 K4 Broom B Anticosti I, Quebec
142 D4 Broome W Australia Australia
143 C10 Broomehill W Australia Australia
142 F3 Broome, Mt W Australia Australia
20 F5 Broons France
99 L4 Brooten Minnesota U.S.A.
142 G4 Brophy,Mt W Australia Australia
143 F7 Brophy,Mt W Australia Australia
15 E2 Brora Scotland
28 B5 Brørup Denmark
27 G16 Brösarp Sweden
14 D3 Brosna R Ireland
48 K3 Brosteni Romania
68 A7 Brothers islds Andaman Is
100 E6 Brothers Oregon U.S.A.
145 E4 Brothers, The New Zealand
84 K4 Brothers,The islds Red Sea
37 J2 Brotterode Germany
21 N5 Brou France
13 F4 Brough England
15 E1 Brough Hd Orkney Scotland
15 F2 Brough Ness Scotland
9 F3 Broughton England
13 E5 Broughton Cumbria England
13 E2 Broughton Scotland
110 H4 Broughton Illinois U.S.A.
107 N2 Broughton Kansas U.S.A.
121 T6 Broughton Station Quebec Canada
15 F4 Broughty Ferry Scotland
86 C2 Broulkou Chad
36 B7 Brouvelieures France
25 A5 Brouwershaven Netherlands
20 H8 Brouzils,les France
40 E4 Brove R Switzerland
85 C7 Brovio Liberia
28 D2 Brovst Denmark
99 L3 Browerville Minnesota U.S.A.
71 C5 Brown Bank Palawan Philippines
94 E3 Brown City Michigan U.S.A.
107 L3 Brownell Kansas U.S.A.
143 E7 Browne Ra W Australia Australia
108 E2 Brownfield Texas U.S.A.
119 P9 Browning Saskatchewan Canada
110 C1 Browning Missouri U.S.A.
101 M1 Browning Montana U.S.A.
144 C5 Browning Pass New Zealand
143 C9 Brown,L W Australia Australia
119 M8 Brownlee Saskatchewan Canada
98 F7 Brownlee Nebraska U.S.A.
138 F3 Brown,Mt South Australia Australia
138 E4 Brown,Mt South Australia Australia
142 A3 Brown,Mt W Australia Australia
138 C4 Brown Pt South Australia Australia
141 G3 Brown R Queensland Australia
120 J3 Brownrigg Ontario Canada
144 B7 Browns New Zealand
110 J3 Browns Illinois U.S.A.
109 M3 Brownsboro Texas U.S.A.
121 Q7 Brownsburg Quebec Canada
110 K2 Brownsburg Indiana U.S.A.
126 E2 Browns Cay isld Bahamas
145 G1 Browns I New Zealand
98 C8 Brownson Nebraska U.S.A.
127 K2 Brown's Town Jamaica
94 A8 Brownstown Indiana U.S.A.
98 K4 Browns Valley Minnesota U.S.A.
110 L2 Brownsville Indiana U.S.A.
110 K4 Brownsville Kentucky U.S.A.
100 C5 Brownsville Oregon U.S.A.
94 H6 Brownsville Pennsylvania U.S.A.
110 G6 Brownsville Tennessee U.S.A.
109 K10 Brownsville Texas U.S.A.
99 M5 Brownton Minnesota U.S.A.
99 R7 Browntown Wisconsin U.S.A.
111 J8 Brownville Alabama U.S.A.
99 L9 Brownville Nebraska U.S.A.
95 M2 Brownville New York U.S.A.
95 S1 Brownville Junc Maine U.S.A.
109 J4 Brownwood, L Texas U.S.A.
142 E2 Browse I Australia
142 E2 Browse I Indian Oc
15 E5 Broxburn Scotland
112 E6 Broxton Georgia U.S.A.
16 C5 Brozas Spain
45 K4 Brozzi Italy
45 P1 Brtonigla Croatia
22 D3 Bruay France
22 F3 Bruay-sur-l'Escaut France
127 P6 Bruce Barbados
118 E5 Bruce Alberta Canada
145 E4 Bruce New Zealand
6 L3 Bruce oil rig North Sea
111 G7 Bruce Mississippi U.S.A.
99 P4 Bruce Wisconsin U.S.A.
144 B5 Bruce Bay New Zealand
99 R3 Bruce Crossing Michigan U.S.A.
120 J9 Brucefield Ontario Canada
142 C5 Bruce,Mt W Australia Australia
120 J7 Bruce Pen Ontario Canada
120 J7 Bruce Peninsula National Marine Park nat park Ontario Canada
120 J7 Bruce Peninsula National Park nat park Ontario Canada
143 C9 Bruce Rock W Australia Australia
110 H5 Bruceton Tennessee U.S.A.
109 K4 Bruceville Texas U.S.A.
19 K4 Bruche R France
32 K7 Bruchhausen-Vilsen Germany
36 F3 Bruchköbel Germany
36 F5 Bruchsal Germany
31 K7 Bruck Austria
33 R8 Brück Germany
37 L4 Bruck Bayern Germany
38 M7 Bruck-an-der-Mur Austria
37 M6 Bruckberg Germany
38 L8 Brückl Austria
21 K3 Brucourt France
19 P18 Brue-Auriac France
118 E5 Bruederheim Alberta Canada
33 P5 Brüel Germany
14 C4 Bruff Ireland
20 H7 Bruffière,la France
Bruges see Brugge
40 H3 Brugg Switzerland
22 E1 Brugge Belgium
36 D1 Brügge Germany
25 F6 Brüggen Germany
45 L1 Brùgine Italy
44 F2 Brugneto, L. di Italy
36 B2 Brühl Germany
94 H5 Bruin Pennsylvania U.S.A.
103 O2 Bruin Pt Utah U.S.A.
117 P9 Brûlé Alberta Canada
98 E8 Brule Nebraska U.S.A.
99 P3 Brule Wisconsin U.S.A.
121 N6 Brûlé, L Quebec Canada
121 M7 Brûlé Lake Ontario Canada
21 K6 Brûlon France
22 J4 Brûly Belgium
129 K6 Brumado Brazil
25 F4 Brummen Netherlands
140 C4 Brunchilly N Terr Australia
43 C8 Bruncu Spina mt Sardinia
108 H7 Brundage Texas U.S.A.
111 L10 Brundidge Alabama U.S.A.
100 K7 Bruneau Idaho U.S.A.
22 G4 Brunehamel France
70 D2 Brunei state Borneo
70 D2 Brunei B Brunei
Brunei Town see Bandar Seri Begawan
140 D4 Brunette Downs N Terr Australia
123 Q6 Brunette I Newfoundland Canada
21 L2 Bruneval France
26 G8 Brunflo Sweden
109 J8 Bruni Texas U.S.A.
42 D2 Brunico Italy
118 D1 Brunkild Manitoba Canada
Brünn see Brno
37 N2 Brunn Germany
29 K4 Brunnby Sweden
41 J3 Brunnen Switzerland
119 M6 Bruno Saskatchewan Canada
99 O3 Bruno Minnesota U.S.A.
32 K5 Brunsbüttelkoog Germany
32 L5 Brunshausen Germany
25 E7 Brunssum Netherlands
Brunswick see Braunschweig
112 F6 Brunswick Georgia U.S.A.
95 S3 Brunswick Maine U.S.A.
94 K7 Brunswick Maryland U.S.A.
94 F5 Brunswick Ohio U.S.A.
142 E3 Brunswick B W Australia Australia
143 B10 Brunswick Junction W Australia Australia
120 G3 Brunswick L Ontario Canada
133 C8 Brunswick, Pen. de Chile
31 K6 Bruntál Czechoslovakia
146 F6 Brunt Ice Shelf ice shelf Antarctica
139 H9 Bruny I Tasmania Australia
46 F1 Brusartsi Bulgaria
106 G1 Brush Colorado U.S.A.
95 N2 Brushton New York U.S.A.
112 F1 Brushy Mts North Carolina U.S.A.
130 E10 Brusque Brazil
Brussels see Bruxelles
120 J9 Brussels Ontario Canada
99 T5 Brussels Wisconsin U.S.A.
8 D5 Bruton England
22 G2 Bruxelles Belgium
24 Bruxelles conurbation Belgium
19 K4 Bruyères France
20 G5 Bruz France
128 E2 Bruzual Venezuela
22 F3 Bry France
94 C5 Bryan Ohio U.S.A.
109 L5 Bryan Texas U.S.A.
146 C6 Bryan Coast Antarctica
54 K8 Bryanka Ukraine
138 E5 Bryan,Mt South Australia Australia
53 G11 Bryansk Russian Federation
54 F3 Bryansk Russian Federation
53 D8 Bryanskaya Oblast' prov Russian Federation
109 P1 Bryant Arkansas U.S.A.
110 M1 Bryant Indiana U.S.A.
110 D5 Bryant Cr Missouri U.S.A.
95 R2 Bryant Pond Maine U.S.A.
22 C3 Bryas France
103 M4 Bryce Canyon Nat. Park Utah U.S.A.
144 B7 Brydone New Zealand
9 F7 Bryher isld Isles of Scilly England
8 C4 Bryn-amman Wales
8 B2 Bryn-crug Wales
8 C1 Bryneglwys Wales
26 M1 Brynilen Norway
8 C4 Bryn Mawr Wales
48 L2 Brynzeny Moldavia
28 C4 Bryrup Denmark
112 D2 Bryson City North Carolina U.S.A.
121 N6 Bryson,L Quebec Canada
48 G6 Brza Palanka Serbia Yugoslavia
31 K5 Brzeg Poland
31 L3 Brześć Kuj Poland
31 M6 Brzesko Poland
31 L6 Brzeszcze Poland
31 M4 Brzeziny Poland
31 L4 Brzeźnica Poland
31 N6 Brzozów Poland
21 O4 Bû France
88 E8 Bua R Malawi
71 H5 Buabuang Sulawesi
71 H7 Buagi Indonesia
21 J4 Buais France
69 D12 Buatan Sumatra
84 F3 Bu'ayrāt al Hasūn Libya
33 S7 Buberow Germany
89 F2 Bubi R Zimbabwe
77 A5 Būbiyān, Jazīrat isld Kuwait
20 D6 Bubry France
71 F7 Bubuan isld Mindanao Philippines
13 H6 Bubwith England
87 F10 Bubye R Zimbabwe
47 L7 Bucak Turkey
128 D2 Bucaramanga Colombia
71 G6 Bucas Grande Philippines
141 J5 Bucasia Queensland Australia
111 H10 Bucatunda Mississippi U.S.A.
142 E3 Buccaneer Arch W Australia Australia
43 G8 Buccino Italy
48 K3 Bucecea Romania
47 K3 Bü Çekmece Turkey
48 J1 Buchach Ukraine
6 L5 Buchan oil rig North Sea
15 F3 Buchan dist Scotland
140 D4 Buchanan R N Terr Australia

Buchanan — Cadiz
161

119 P7 **Buchanan** Saskatchewan Canada
85 B7 **Buchanan** Liberia
112 B4 **Buchanan** Georgia U.S.A.
99 U8 **Buchanan** Michigan U.S.A.
106 F7 **Buchanan** New Mexico U.S.A.
98 G2 **Buchanan** North Dakota U.S.A.
94 H9 **Buchanan** Virginia U.S.A.
109 J5 **Buchanan Dam** Texas U.S.A.
140 B4 **Buchanan Hills** N Terr Australia
141 H5 **Buchanan,L** Queensland Australia
143 E7 **Buchanan,L** W Australia Australia
109 J5 **Buchanan, L** Texas U.S.A.
115 M3 **Buchan Gulf** Northwest Territories Canada
15 G3 **Buchan Ness** Scotland
123 Q5 **Buchans** Newfoundland Canada
123 Q5 **Buchans Jnct** Newfoundland Canada
133 E4 **Buchardo** Argentina
Bucharest *see* **Bucureşti**
37 N7 **Buchbach** Germany
36 G4 **Buchen** Germany
36 C4 **Büchenbeuren** Germany
37 L1 **Buchenwald** Germany
32 L6 **Buchholz** Germany
33 R8 **Buchholz** Germany
41 N2 **Buching** Germany
41 N1 **Buchloe** Germany
15 D4 **Buchlyvie** Scotland
41 K3 **Buchs** Switzerland
21 N2 **Buchy** France
106 C6 **Buck** New Mexico U.S.A.
9 F3 **Buckden** England
32 K8 **Bückeburg** Germany
32 K7 **Bücken** Germany
103 M8 **Buckeye** Arizona U.S.A.
94 E7 **Buckeye Lake** Ohio U.S.A.
95 K7 **Buckeystown** Maryland U.S.A.
8 C7 **Buckfastleigh** England
94 G8 **Buckhannon** West Virginia U.S.A.
15 E4 **Buckhaven & Methil** Scotland
98 C5 **Buckhorn** Wyoming U.S.A.
15 E3 **Buckie** Scotland
121 P7 **Buckingham** Quebec Canada
9 E3 **Buckingham** England
94 J9 **Buckingham** Virginia U.S.A.
140 D1 **Buckingham B** N Terr Australia
140 E5 **Buckingham Downs** Queensland Australia
140 B4 **Buck,L** N Terr Australia
118 C5 **Buck L** Alberta Canada
116 G4 **Buckland** Alaska U.S.A.
119 V1 **Buckland L** Manitoba Canada
145 G1 **Bucklands Beach** New Zealand
141 J6 **Buckland Tableland** Queensland Australia
146 C13 **Buckle I** Antarctica
140 E5 **Buckley** *R* Queensland Australia
110 H1 **Buckley** Illinois U.S.A.
94 B2 **Buckley** Michigan U.S.A.
100 C2 **Buckley** Washington U.S.A.
38 O6 **Bucklige Welt** *reg* Austria
107 L4 **Bucklin** Kansas U.S.A.
110 D2 **Bucklin** Missouri U.S.A.
Buckner Bay *see* **Nakagusuku-wan**
102 C2 **Bucks** California U.S.A.
103 L7 **Buckskin Mts** Arizona U.S.A.
102 C2 **Bucks Mt** California U.S.A.
95 T2 **Bucksport** Maine U.S.A.
33 Q7 **Bückwitz** Germany
31 K6 **Bučovice** Czechoslovakia
86 B6 **Buco Zau** Angola
22 D3 **Bucquoy** France
122 H7 **Buctouche** New Brunswick Canada
48 K6 **Bucureşti** Romania
71 E7 **Bucutua** *isld* Philippines
22 F4 **Bucy-les-Pierrepont** France
98 D3 **Bucyrus** North Dakota U.S.A.
26 B9 **Bud** Norway
68 D7 **Buda** *isld* Burma
109 K5 **Buda** Texas U.S.A.
48 E3 **Budafok** Hungary
54 B4 **Buda-Koshelevo** Belorussia
68 B1 **Budalin** Burma
48 E3 **Budapest** Hungary
74 H4 **Budaun** India
9 E1 **Budby** England
146 G14 **Budd Coast** Antarctica
53 F10 **Buddenovsk** Russian Federation
143 B8 **Budd,Mt** W Australia Australia
15 F4 **Buddon Ness** Scotland
8 B6 **Bude** England
32 L4 **Büdelsdorf** Germany
32 G9 **Büderich** Germany
141 L7 **Buderim** Queensland Australia
22 K4 **Buderscheid** Luxembourg
48 K6 **Budeşti** Romania
139 K5 **Budgewoi** New South Wales Australia
28 S9 **Budhardalur** Iceland
29 T9 **Budhareyri** Iceland
28 R9 **Budhir** Iceland
29 T9 **Búdhir** Iceland
131 A7 **Budi,L.del** Chile
36 G3 **Büdingen** Germany
86 C5 **Budjala** Zaire
8 C6 **Budleigh Salterton** England
45 L2 **Budrio** Italy
70 F6 **Budungbudung** Sulawesi
42 J6 **Budva** Montenegro Yugoslavia
54 H7 **Budy** Ukraine
86 A5 **Buéa** Cameroon
19 P16 **Buech** *R* France
21 N4 **Buéil** France
102 D7 **Buellton** California U.S.A.
128 C3 **Buenaventura** Colombia
71 E4 **Buenavista** Philippines
71 G6 **Buenavista** Mindanao Philippines
106 D3 **Buena Vista** Colorado U.S.A.
112 C5 **Buena Vista** Georgia U.S.A.
94 H9 **Buena Vista** Virginia U.S.A.
126 E3 **Buenavista, B. de** Cuba
17 F4 **Buendía, Embalse de** Spain
Buene *R* *see* **Bojana**
131 A8 **Bueno** *R* Chile
130 E4 **Buenolândia** Brazil
129 K7 **Buenópolis** Brazil
131 E6 **Buenos Aires** *prov* Argentina
132 **Buenos Aires** *conurbation* Argentina
128 D4 **Buenos Aires** Colombia
133 C7 **Buenos Aires,L** Chile/Arg
127 N3 **Buenos Ayres** Trinidad
133 D7 **Buen Pasto** Argentina
133 D8 **Buen Tiempo,C** Argentina
130 H4 **Buerarema** Brazil
40 E5 **Buet,Mt** France
117 Q6 **Buffalo** *R* Alberta/N W Terr Canada
89 G6 **Buffalo** *R* S Africa
110 C5 **Buffalo** *R* Arkansas U.S.A.
107 P4 **Buffalo** Kansas U.S.A.
110 L4 **Buffalo** Kentucky U.S.A.
98 K3 **Buffalo** *R* Minnesota U.S.A.
99 N4 **Buffalo** Minnesota U.S.A.
110 C4 **Buffalo** Missouri U.S.A.
101 Q3 **Buffalo** Montana U.S.A.
94 J4 **Buffalo** New York U.S.A.
107 L5 **Buffalo** Oklahoma U.S.A.
112 F3 **Buffalo** South Carolina U.S.A.
98 C4 **Buffalo** South Dakota U.S.A.
110 J6 **Buffalo** *R* Tennessee U.S.A.
99 P5 **Buffalo** *R* Wisconsin U.S.A.
101 T5 **Buffalo** Wyoming U.S.A.
101 Q5 **Buffalo Bill Dam** Wyoming U.S.A.
101 Q5 **Buffalo Bill Res** Wyoming U.S.A.
99 N6 **Buffalo Center** Iowa U.S.A.
106 E2 **Buffalo Creek** Colorado U.S.A.
119 M9 **Buffalo Gap** Saskatchewan Canada
98 C6 **Buffalo Gap** South Dakota U.S.A.
118 E6 **Buffalo, L** Alberta Canada
117 Q5 **Buffalo L** Northwest Territories Canada
108 E1 **Buffalo L** Texas U.S.A.
139 H6 **Buffalo,Mt** Victoria Australia
118 J3 **Buffalo Narrows** Saskatchewan Canada
119 M8 **Buffalo Pound Prov Park** Saskatchewan Canada
127 L2 **Buff Bay** Jamaica
112 C3 **Buford** Georgia U.S.A.
98 C1 **Buford** North Dakota U.S.A.
98 A8 **Buford** Wyoming U.S.A.
48 K6 **Buftea** Romania
31 O4 **Bug** *R* Belorussia/Poland etc
128 C3 **Buga** Colombia
18 G10 **Bugarach, Pic de** *mt* France
58 G1 **Bugarikhta** Russian Federation
47 J4 **Buğdaylı** Turkey
70 N9 **Bugel,Tg** Java
40 B6 **Bugey** *dist* France
Buggs Island Lake *see* **John H. Kerr Res.** N Carolina/Virginia
88 D1 **Bugiri** Uganda
26 R2 **Bugöynes** Norway
54 C10 **Bugskiy Liman** *lagoon* Ukraine
71 C6 **Bugsuk** *isld* Palawan Philippines
59 H2 **Bugt** China
18 F8 **Bugue,Le** France
71 E1 **Buguey** Luzon Philippines
78 K2 **Bügük Ağri** *mt* Turkey
57 F3 **Bugun'** Kazakhstan
57 E3 **Bugun'skoye Vodokhranilishche** *res* Kazakhstan
78 G4 **Buhayrat al Asad** *L* Syria
87 F9 **Buhera** Zimbabwe
58 C4 **Buh He** *R* China
71 F4 **Buhi** Luzon Philippines
36 E6 **Bühl** Germany
101 L7 **Buhl** Idaho U.S.A.
99 O2 **Buhl** Minnesota U.S.A.
36 E6 **Bühlerhöhe** Germany
36 E6 **Bühlertal** Germany
36 H5 **Bühlertann** Germany
88 E6 **Buhoro Flats** Tanzania
48 K4 **Buhuşi** Romania
117 N7 **Buick** British Columbia Canada
25 C4 **Buiksloot** Netherlands
8 C3 **Builth Wells** Wales
137 M3 **Buin** Bougainville I Papua New Guinea
41 M4 **Buin,Piz** *mt* Switz/Austria
130 H10 **Buique** Brazil
36 B2 **Buir** Germany
22 B3 **Buire-le-Sec** France
22 F4 **Buironfosse** France
19 O16 **Buis-les-Baronnies** France
25 F2 **Buitenpost** Netherlands
67 B7 **Bui Thon** Vietnam
122 J2 **Buit,L** Quebec Canada
16 E7 **Bujalance** Spain
46 E2 **Bujanovac** Serbia Yugoslavia
17 G3 **Bujaraloz** Spain
42 F3 **Buje** Croatia
88 B3 **Bujumbura** Burundi
48 D3 **Bük** Hungary
137 L3 **Buka** *isld* Papua New Guinea
66 E4 **Buka Daban Feng** *mt* China
88 D2 **Bukakata** Uganda
87 E7 **Bukama** Zaire
88 D2 **Bukasa I** Uganda
88 B3 **Bukavu** Zaire
88 C2 **Bukene** Tanzania
88 B3 **Bukeye** Burundi
57 C5 **Bukhara** Uzbekistan
46 F2 **Bukhovo** Bulgaria
56 B6 **Bukhtarminskoye Vodokhranilishche** *res* Kazakhstan
70 C6 **Bukitlidi** Kalimantan
69 E13 **Bukittinggi** Sumatra
48 F2 **Bükk** *mt* Hungary
79 F8 **Bukka, J. el** *mt* Jordan
48 D4 **Bükkösd** Hungary
33 Q9 **Buko** Germany
88 C2 **Bukoba** Tanzania
48 J2 **Bukovina** *old prov* Romania/Ukraine
31 J1 **Bukowo,Jezioro** *L* Poland
136 G2 **Bula** Moluccas Indonesia
71 H4 **Bula anguki** Sulawesi
41 J2 **Bülach** Switzerland
56 H5 **Bulagansk** Russian Federation
65 D2 **Bulag Sum** China
139 K4 **Bulahdelah** New South Wales Australia
71 E4 **Bulalacao** Philippines
71 E5 **Bulalacao** Calamian Group Philippines
71 F4 **Bulan** Philippines
71 E7 **Bulan** *isld* Philippines
55 D3 **Bulanash** Russian Federation
55 C4 **Bulanavo** Russian Federation
89 F3 **Bulawayo** Zimbabwe
55 F3 **Bulayevo** Kazakhstan
28 C2 **Bulbjerg** *hill* Denmark
47 K6 **Buldan** Turkey
74 G8 **Buldana** India
77 H6 **Buleda** *reg* Pakistan
70 P10 **Buleleng** Bali Indonesia
89 G5 **Bulembu** Swaziland
9 E5 **Bulford** England
58 B2 **Bulgan** Mongolia
58 D2 **Bulgan** Mongolia
58 C3 **Bulgan** Mongolia
56 F5 **Bulgan** Mongolia
46 F2 **Bulgaria** *rep* E Europe
47 J2 **Bŭlgarovo** Bulgaria
47 K6 **Bulgaz Dağ** *mt* Turkey
40 C1 **Bulgnéville** France
77 C7 **Bul Hanine** *oil well* Persian Gulf
71 B2 **Buli** Halmahera Indonesia
71 C6 **Buliluyan,C** Palawan Philippines
141 K1 **Bulimba** *dist* Brisbane, Qnsld Australia
141 L2 **Bulimba Cr** Brisbane, Qnsld Australia
67 B4 **Buliu He** *R* China
117 K8 **Bulkley** *R* British Columbia Canada
143 D9 **Bulla Bulling** W Australia Australia
22 L3 **Bullange** Belgium
16 E5 **Bullaque** *R* Spain
109 M3 **Bullard** Texas U.S.A.
27 E13 **Bullaren S** *L* Sweden
17 F6 **Bullas** Spain
141 G8 **Bullawarra,L** Queensland Australia
86 H3 **Bullaxaar** Somalia
36 C3 **Bullay** Germany
127 L3 **Bull Bay** Jamaica
112 H5 **Bull Bay** South Carolina U.S.A.
40 F4 **Bulle** Switzerland
138 F4 **Bullea,L** New South Wales Australia
116 O1 **Bullen** Alaska U.S.A.
126 A1 **Bullen Baai** *B* Curaçao
139 H6 **Buller, Mt** Victoria Australia
145 D4 **Buller R** New Zealand
143 C9 **Bullfinch** W Australia Australia
103 K6 **Bullhead City** Nevada U.S.A.
112 H5 **Bull I** South Carolina U.S.A.
102 H7 **Bullion Mts** California U.S.A.
101 R3 **Bull Mts** Montana U.S.A.
141 G5 **Bullock** *R* Queensland Australia
141 G8 **Bulloo** *R* Queensland Australia
141 G8 **Bulloo Downs** Queensland Australia
141 F8 **Bulloo, L** Queensland Australia
133 F8 **Bull Pt** Falkland Is
118 B9 **Bull R** British Columbia Canada
145 E4 **Bulls** New Zealand
127 J3 **Bull Savannah** Jamaica
110 D5 **Bull Shoals Lake** Missouri U.S.A.
22 D3 **Bully** France
100 C9 **Bully Choop Mt** California U.S.A.
140 C2 **Bulman Gorge** N Terr Australia
139 G6 **Buloke,L** Victoria Australia
77 L2 **Bulola** Afghanistan
136 K3 **Bulolo** Papua New Guinea
138 F5 **Bulpunga** New South Wales Australia
87 E11 **Bultfontein** S Africa
71 G7 **Buluan** Mindanao Philippines
70 G7 **Bulubulu** Sulawesi
70 E3 **Bulu, G** *mt* Kalimantan
70 G7 **Bulukumba** Sulawesi
51 M1 **Bulun** Russian Federation
86 D7 **Bulungu** Zaire
71 G4 **Bulusan** Luzon Philippines
118 F6 **Bulwark** Alberta Canada
9 E2 **Bulwell** England
141 L1 **Bulwer I** Brisbane, Qnsld Australia
9 F2 **Bulwick** England
119 N8 **Bulyea** Saskatchewan Canada
86 D5 **Bumba** Zaire
84 G3 **Bumbah, Khalīj** Libya
48 H5 **Bumbeşti-Jiu** Romania
103 M7 **Bumble Bee** Arizona U.S.A.
70 G4 **Bumbulan** Sulawesi Indonesia
70 F2 **Bum-Bum** Sabah
70 M9 **Bumiaju** Java
66 F6 **Bumkhang** Burma
100 D3 **Bumping L** Washington U.S.A.
40 F4 **Bümpliz** Switzerland
75 O5 **Bumthang** Bhutan
109 O5 **Buna** Texas U.S.A.
71 G7 **Bunawan** Mindanao Philippines
143 B10 **Bunbury** W Australia Australia
110 B6 **Bunch** Oklahoma U.S.A.
14 E4 **Bunclody** Ireland
14 D1 **Buncrana** Ireland
141 K6 **Bundaberg** Queensland Australia
141 H8 **Bundaleer** Queensland Australia
32 F6 **Bunde** Germany
32 J8 **Bünde** Germany
140 D5 **Bundey** *R* N Terr Australia
74 F6 **Bundi** India
111 C11 **Bundick L** Louisiana U.S.A.
111 C11 **Bundicks Cr** Louisiana U.S.A.
140 C6 **Bundooma** N Terr Australia
14 C2 **Bundoran** Ireland
68 J6 **Bun Duc** Vietnam
12 B1 **Bunessan** Scotland
71 G7 **Bunga** *R* Mindanao Philippines
143 C9 **Bungalbin Hill** W Australia Australia
9 H3 **Bungay** England
68 E5 **Bung Boraphet** *L* Thailand
146 H13 **Bunger Hills** Antarctica
141 J7 **Bungil** *R* Queensland Australia
71 H6 **Bunginkela** *isld* Sulawesi Indonesia
68 F3 **Bung Kan** Thailand
70 G6 **Bungku** Sulawesi Indonesia
87 C7 **Bungo** Angola
60 G2 **Bungo-suidō** *str* Japan
141 J8 **Bungunya** Queensland Australia
Bunguran *see* **Natuna Besar**
Bunguran Utara, Kepulauan *see* **Natuna Besar**
86 B3 **Buni** Nigeria
86 F5 **Bunia** Zaire
143 E9 **Buningonia Spring** *spring* W Australia Australia
70 E3 **Bunju** *isld* Kalimantan
110 E4 **Bunker** Missouri U.S.A.
141 K6 **Bunker Grp** *islds* Gt Barrier Reef Aust
116 E4 **Bunker Hill** Alaska U.S.A.
110 G2 **Bunker Hill** Illinois U.S.A.
110 K1 **Bunker Hill** Indiana U.S.A.
107 M3 **Bunker Hill** Kansas U.S.A.
103 K5 **Bunkerville** Nevada U.S.A.
87 E8 **Bunkeya** Zaire
111 D11 **Bunkie** Louisiana U.S.A.
113 F8 **Bunnell** Florida U.S.A.
145 E4 **Bunnythorpe** New Zealand
70 G4 **Bunobagu** Sulawesi
68 H7 **Bu Noi** Vietnam
17 G5 **Buñol** Spain
25 D4 **Bunschoten** Netherlands
143 B8 **Buntine** W Australia Australia
9 F4 **Buntingford** England
70 D5 **Buntok** Kalimantan
70 D5 **Buntokecil** Kalimantan
141 K1 **Bunyaville** *dist* Brisbane, Qnsld Australia
68 E3 **Bun Yun** Thailand
51 L1 **Buolkalakh** Russian Federation
68 J6 **Buon Me Thuot** Vietnam
51 N1 **Buor-khaya, Guba** *G* Russian Federation
80 G1 **Buq'ātā** Syria
77 A7 **Buqayq** Saudi Arabia
28 A4 **Bur** Denmark
88 G3 **Bura** Kenya
86 A1 **Buraan** Somalia
71 L10 **Buraen** Timor Indonesia
Buraimi *see* **Buraymī, Al**
143 B9 **Burakin** W Australia Australia
86 E3 **Buram** Sudan
143 E10 **Buraminya,Mt** W Australia Australia
141 K2 **Buranda** *dist* Brisbane, Qnsld Australia
75 J3 **Burang** China
130 H5 **Buranhaém** Brazil
45 M1 **Burano** Italy
86 J4 **Burao** Somalia
111 G12 **Buras** Louisiana U.S.A.
71 G5 **Burauen** Leyte Philippines
72 E3 **Buraydah** Saudi Arabia
55 C3 **Burayevo** Russian Federation
79 G4 **Burayj, Al** Syria
77 D7 **Buraymī, Al** U.A.E.
80 G1 **Burayqah** Syria
36 E2 **Burbach** Germany
9 E5 **Burbage** England
102 F7 **Burbank** California U.S.A.
98 K9 **Burchard** Nebraska U.S.A.
139 H5 **Burcher** New South Wales Australia
99 N6 **Burchinal** Iowa U.S.A.
57 C5 **Burdalyk** Turkmenistan
141 H5 **Burdekin** *R* Queensland Australia
141 H5 **Burdekin Falls** Queensland Australia
117 M7 **Burden,Mt** British Columbia Canada
118 F9 **Burdett** Alberta Canada
95 L4 **Burdett** New York U.S.A.
48 K3 **Burdujeni** Romania
78 C3 **Burdur** Turkey
47 L7 **Burdur Gölü** *L* Turkey
90 E14 **Burdwood Bank** Atlantic Oc
86 G3 **Burē** Ethiopia
86 G4 **Burē** Ethiopia
26 M7 **Bureå** Sweden
121 P4 **Bureau, L** Quebec Canada
59 K1 **Bureinskiy, Khrebet** *mts* Russian Federation
32 J9 **Büren** Germany
25 D5 **Buren** Netherlands
58 B2 **Bürenhayrhan** Mongolia
65 B1 **Bürentsogt** Mongolia
59 K1 **Bureya** *R* Russian Federation
59 J2 **Bureya** Russian Federation
9 E4 **Burford** England
32 K5 **Burg** Germany
33 P8 **Burg** Germany
36 D5 **Burgalben** Germany
47 J2 **Burgas** Bulgaria
38 O7 **Burgau** Austria
37 J7 **Burgau** Germany
112 J3 **Burgaw** North Carolina U.S.A.
47 N11 **Burgaz** Turkey
47 N11 **Burgaz** *isld* Turkey
37 J5 **Burgbernheim** Germany
32 M8 **Burgdorf** Germany
40 G3 **Burgdorf** Switzerland
100 K4 **Burgdorf** Idaho U.S.A.
37 K4 **Burgebrach** Germany
37 M2 **Bürgel** Germany
48 C3 **Burgenland** *prov* Austria
123 P6 **Burgeo** Newfoundland Canada
87 E12 **Burgersdorp** S Africa
9 F6 **Burgess Hill** England
95 L9 **Burgess Store** Virginia U.S.A.
13 E4 **Burgh** England
25 A5 **Burgh** Netherlands
36 H2 **Burghaun** Germany
38 G5 **Burghausen** Germany
37 L6 **Burgheim** Germany
9 G1 **Burgh-le-Marsh** England
43 E11 **Burgio** Sicily
36 H3 **Burgjoss** Germany
37 L3 **Burgkunstadt** Germany
37 N5 **Burglengenfeld** Germany
16 E2 **Burgos** *prov* Spain
16 E2 **Burgos** Spain
37 K3 **Burgpreppach** Germany
36 H3 **Burgsinn** Germany
36 G4 **Bürgstadt** Germany
37 O2 **Burgstädt** Germany
33 S6 **Burg Stargard** Germany
32 F8 **Burgsteinfurt** Germany
27 K14 **Burgsvik** Sweden
17 G2 **Burguete** Spain
36 F2 **Burgwald** Germany
32 L7 **Burgwedel** Germany
37 K4 **Burgwindheim** Germany
47 H5 **Burhaniye** Turkey
32 H5 **Burhave** Germany
130 E8 **Buri** Brazil
69 E14 **Buriai** Indonesia
71 F4 **Burias** *isld* Philippines
71 F4 **Burias Pass** Luzon Philippines
123 R6 **Burin** Newfoundland Canada
68 F5 **Buriram** Thailand
130 E7 **Buritama** Brazil
128 G6 **Buriti** *R* Brazil
130 E6 **Buriti Alegre** Brazil
129 K5 **Buriti Bravo** Brazil
130 F4 **Buritis** Brazil
80 C8 **Burj el Baiyara** Jordan
79 G4 **Burj Sāfīta** Syria
28 C7 **Burkal** Denmark
109 J1 **Burkburnett** Texas U.S.A.
140 F5 **Burke** *R* Queensland Australia
140 E6 **Burke** *R* Queensland Australia
100 K2 **Burke** Idaho U.S.A.
98 G6 **Burke** South Dakota U.S.A.
109 N4 **Burke** Texas U.S.A.
117 K9 **Burke Chan** British Columbia Canada
146 B7 **Burke I** Antarctica
144 C6 **Burke Pass** New Zealand
110 L5 **Burkesville** Kentucky U.S.A.
140 E4 **Burketown** Queensland Australia
109 H4 **Burkett** Texas U.S.A.
94 J9 **Burkeville** Virginia U.S.A.
37 O2 **Burkhardtsdorf** Germany
85 D6 **Burkina** *rep* W Africa
98 G4 **Burkmere** South Dakota U.S.A.
121 L7 **Burk's Falls** Ontario Canada
55 G4 **Burla** Russian Federation
36 G7 **Burladingen** Germany
141 G5 **Burleigh** Queensland Australia
109 K3 **Burleson** Texas U.S.A.
13 G6 **Burley** England
101 M7 **Burley** Idaho U.S.A.
8 D3 **Burley Gate** England
55 D4 **Burli** Kazakhstan
55 B5 **Burlin** Kazakhstan
107 P3 **Burlingame** Kansas U.S.A.
123 Q4 **Burlington** Newfoundland Canada
121 L9 **Burlington** Ontario Canada
106 H2 **Burlington** Colorado U.S.A.
99 P9 **Burlington** Iowa U.S.A.
107 P3 **Burlington** Kansas U.S.A.
95 N6 **Burlington** New Jersey U.S.A.
112 H1 **Burlington** North Carolina U.S.A.
95 O2 **Burlington** Vermont U.S.A.
117 M11 **Burlington** Washington U.S.A.
101 R5 **Burlington** Wyoming U.S.A.
110 A1 **Burlington Junction** Missouri U.S.A.
8 D2 **Burlton** England
57 J2 **Burlyu-Tobe** Kazakhstan
80 G5 **Burma** Jordan
68 B2 **Burma** *rep* S E Asia
139 H6 **Burmah Forest** Victoria Australia
55 D1 **Burmantovo** Russian Federation
101 N9 **Burmester** Utah U.S.A.
118 C9 **Burmis** Alberta Canada
144 D5 **Burnbrae** New Zealand
109 J5 **Burnet** Texas U.S.A.
141 K7 **Burnett** *R* Queensland Australia
141 K6 **Burnett Heads** Queensland Australia
100 D9 **Burney** California U.S.A.
8 C5 **Burnham** England
144 D5 **Burnham** New Zealand
95 S2 **Burnham** Maine U.S.A.
94 K6 **Burnham** Pennsylvania U.S.A.
9 G2 **Burnham Deepdale** England
9 G2 **Burnham Market** England
9 G4 **Burnham-on-Crouch** Essex England
40 F2 **Burnhaupt** France
139 H8 **Burnie** Tasmania Australia
13 H5 **Burniston** England
13 F6 **Burnley** England
13 G4 **Burnopfield** England
57 F3 **Burnoye** Kazakhstan
101 T10 **Burns** Colorado U.S.A.
100 F6 **Burns** Oregon U.S.A.
98 B8 **Burns** Wyoming U.S.A.
13 G5 **Burnsall** England
110 M5 **Burnside** Kentucky U.S.A.
94 J6 **Burnside** Pennsylvania U.S.A.
143 E7 **Burnside,L** W Australia Australia
117 L8 **Burns Lake** British Columbia Canada
98 G3 **Burnstad** North Dakota U.S.A.
122 G6 **Burnsville** New Brunswick Canada
110 H7 **Burnsville** Mississippi U.S.A.
112 E2 **Burnsville** North Carolina U.S.A.
94 G8 **Burnsville** West Virginia U.S.A.
101 P8 **Burntfork** Wyoming U.S.A.
126 G3 **Burnt Ground** Long I Bahamas
13 E1 **Burntisland** Scotland
122 J1 **Burnt L** Labrador, Nfld Canada
116 Q3 **Burnt Paw** Alaska U.S.A.
100 H5 **Burnt R** Oregon U.S.A.
100 B9 **Burnt Ranch** California U.S.A.
121 M8 **Burnt River** Ontario Canada
119 R3 **Burntwood L** Manitoba Canada
33 S5 **Burow** Germany
66 D2 **Burqin** China
119 M6 **Burr** Saskatchewan Canada
138 E5 **Burra** South Australia Australia
143 C9 **Burracoppin** W Australia Australia
139 K5 **Burragorang L** New South Wales Australia
15 F2 **Burray** Scotland
46 D3 **Burrel** Albania
140 C6 **Burrell,Mt** N Terr Australia
13 E1 **Burrelton** Scotland
139 J5 **Burrendong Res.** New South Wales Australia
17 G5 **Burriana** Spain
13 H6 **Burringham** England
124 J3 **Burro** Mexico
108 F6 **Burro** Mexico
99 P6 **Burr Oak** Iowa U.S.A.
107 M2 **Burr Oak** Kansas U.S.A.
94 B5 **Burr Oak** Michigan U.S.A.
94 E7 **Burr Oak Res** Ohio U.S.A.
103 L7 **Burro Cr** Arizona U.S.A.
108 E6 **Burro, Serranias del** *mts* Mexico
113 K11 **Burrow Cay** Bahamas
140 F3 **Burrowes, Pt** Queensland Australia
15 D6 **Burrow Head** Scotland
107 N3 **Burrton** Kansas U.S.A.
140 B2 **Burrundie** N Terr Australia
133 E3 **Burruyacú** Argentina
111 G13 **Burrwood** Louisiana U.S.A.
8 B4 **Burry Port** Wales
78 B1 **Bursa** Turkey
84 J4 **Bur Safâga** Egypt
36 C1 **Burscheid** Germany
13 F6 **Burscough** England
32 L9 **Bursfelde** Germany
8 D1 **Burslem** England
28 G7 **Bursø** Denmark
22 F2 **Burst** Belgium
118 H8 **Burstall** Saskatchewan Canada
99 M6 **Burt** Iowa U.S.A.
98 D3 **Burt** North Dakota U.S.A.
138 F4 **Burta** New South Wales Australia
94 C1 **Burt L** Michigan U.S.A.
9 E6 **Burton** England
98 G7 **Burton** Nebraska U.S.A.
109 L5 **Burton** Texas U.S.A.
8 B4 **Burton** Wales
13 H5 **Burton Agnes** England
13 F5 **Burton-in-Kendal** England
112 D3 **Burton L** Georgia U.S.A.
14 C2 **Burtonport** Ireland
9 E2 **Burton upon Trent** England
26 L7 **Burträsk** Sweden
122 F7 **Burtts Corner** New Brunswick Canada
138 F5 **Burtundy** New South Wales Australia
140 C6 **Burt Well** N Terr Australia
136 F2 **Buru** *isld* Moluccas Indonesia
84 J3 **Burullus** *L* Egypt
Burultokay *see* **Fuhai**
88 B3 **Burundi** *rep* Cent Africa
88 B3 **Bururi** Burundi
85 F7 **Burutu** Nigeria
8 D3 **Burwarton** England
9 G6 **Burwash** England
9 G1 **Burwell** England
98 G8 **Burwell** Nebraska U.S.A.
33 S10 **Burxdorf** Germany
121 T7 **Bury** Quebec Canada
9 F6 **Bury** England
13 F6 **Bury** Greater Manchester England
56 F5 **Buryatskaya Respublika** Russian Federation
9 G3 **Bury St.Edmunds** England
43 E11 **Busambra, Rca** *mt* Sicily
71 F7 **Busan B** Mindanao Philippines
87 D7 **Busango** Zaire
118 D5 **Busby** Alberta Canada
101 T4 **Busby** Montana U.S.A.
44 B2 **Busca** Italy
33 R7 **Buschow** Germany
32 J4 **Buschsand** *isld* Germany
46 E3 **Buševa Planina** *mt* Macedonia Yugoslavia
46 D3 **Bushat** Albania
77 B5 **Būshehr** Iran
88 C2 **Bushenyi** Uganda
95 M5 **Bushkill** Pennsylvania U.S.A.
87 C9 **Bushland** *homeland* Namibia
108 B8 **Bushland** Texas U.S.A.
121 L6 **Bushnell** Ontario Canada
113 E9 **Bushnell** Florida U.S.A.
110 F1 **Bushnell** Illinois U.S.A.
98 C8 **Bushnell** Nebraska U.S.A.
107 M3 **Bushton** Kansas U.S.A.
140 E5 **Bushy Park** Queensland Australia
89 F1 **Busi** *R* Zimbabwe
88 E1 **Busia** Uganda
22 E3 **Busigny** France
86 D5 **Businga** Zaire
86 C6 **Busira** *R* Zaire
48 J1 **Busk** Ukraine
27 C11 **Buskerud** *reg* Norway
31 M5 **Busko** Poland
37 P3 **Buškovice** Czechoslovakia
55 D4 **Buskul'** Kazakhstan
71 B1 **Busobuso** Halmahera Indonesia
79 G6 **Buşrá ash Shām** Syria
19 K5 **Bussang** France
40 E2 **Bussang,Col.de** *pass* France
21 J8 **Busseau,le** France
143 B10 **Busselton** W Australia Australia
44 H2 **Busseto** Italy
99 O8 **Bussey** Iowa U.S.A.
41 N7 **Bussolengo** Italy
25 D4 **Bussum** Netherlands
77 D6 **Bustaneh** Iran
80 D2 **Bustan Ha Galil** Israel
141 K6 **Bustard Hd** Queensland Australia
48 K5 **Buşteni** Romania
42 B3 **Busto Arsizio** Italy
57 C4 **Buston** Uzbekistan
71 D4 **Busuanga** Philippines
86 D5 **Busu Djanoa** Zaire
32 J4 **Büsum** Germany
86 D5 **Buta** Zaire
131 G2 **Butai** *R* Brazil
70 O9 **Butak, G** *mt* Java
69 D9 **Butang Group** *isld* Thailand
133 D5 **Buta Ranquil** Argentina
88 B3 **Butare** Rwanda
71 F3 **Butaunan** *isld* Philippines
Bute *co* *see* **Strathclyde** *reg*
138 E5 **Bute** South Australia Australia
15 C5 **Bute** *isld* Scotland
117 J9 **Butedale** British Columbia Canada
117 L10 **Bute Inlet** British Columbia Canada
88 B1 **Butembo** Zaire
22 L3 **Bütgenbach** Belgium
Butha Qi *see* **Zalantun**
68 A2 **Buthidaung** Burma
47 P12 **Buthrotum** *hist site* Albania
86 F5 **Butiaba** Uganda
86 B1 **Butiyaalo** Somalia
32 H5 **Butjadingen** *reg* Germany
55 D3 **Butka** Russian Federation
68 B3 **Butle** *R* Burma
111 H9 **Butler** Alabama U.S.A.
112 C5 **Butler** Georgia U.S.A.
94 C5 **Butler** Indiana U.S.A.
110 M3 **Butler** Kentucky U.S.A.
110 B3 **Butler** Missouri U.S.A.
95 N6 **Butler** New Jersey U.S.A.
94 E6 **Butler** Ohio U.S.A.
107 L6 **Butler** Oklahoma U.S.A.
94 H6 **Butler** Pennsylvania U.S.A.
98 J4 **Butler** South Dakota U.S.A.
138 B2 **Butlers Dome** *mt* N Terr Australia
80 G2 **Butmiye** Syria
71 H7 **Buton** *isld* Sulawesi Indonesia
71 H7 **Buton, Selat** *str* Indonesia
46 D5 **Butrintit, Liqen i** *L* Albania
41 K3 **Bütschwil** Switzerland
45 K1 **Buttapietra** Italy
101 N4 **Butte** Montana U.S.A.
98 H7 **Butte** Nebraska U.S.A.
98 F2 **Butte** North Dakota U.S.A.
100 C7 **Butte Falls** Oregon U.S.A.
37 L1 **Buttelstedt** Germany
102 C1 **Butte Meadows** California U.S.A.
36 G7 **Buttenhausen** Germany
37 L4 **Buttenheim** Germany
37 K6 **Buttenwiesen** Germany
100 F4 **Butter Cr** Oregon U.S.A.
99 M6 **Butterfield** Minnesota U.S.A.
13 E5 **Buttermere** England
9 G2 **Butterwick** England
87 E12 **Butterworth** S Africa
14 C4 **Buttevant** Ireland
143 G6 **Buttfield, Mt** W Australia Australia
27 K14 **Buttle** Sweden
117 L11 **Buttle L** British Columbia Canada
15 B2 **Butt of Lewis** Scotland
115 K6 **Button B** Manitoba Canada
115 N5 **Button Is** Northwest Territories Canada
102 E6 **Buttonwillow** California U.S.A.
37 L1 **Buttstädt** Germany
98 J3 **Buttzville** North Dakota U.S.A.
71 G6 **Butuan** Mindanao Philippines
71 G6 **Butuan B** Mindanao Philippines
Butung *isld* *see* **Buton**
54 M6 **Buturlinovka** Russian Federation
68 H6 **Bu Tu Suay** Vietnam
36 F3 **Butzbach** Germany
33 P5 **Bützow** Germany
86 J4 **Buuhoodle** Somalia
86 J5 **Buulobarde** Somalia
86 H6 **Buur Gaabo** Somalia
84 H5 **Buurhakaba** Somalia
26 E9 **Buvika** Norway
79 E10 **Buwārah, J** *mt* Saudi Arabia
21 L8 **Buxerolles** France
21 O7 **Buxeuil** France
32 L6 **Buxtehude** Germany
9 E1 **Buxton** England
112 M2 **Buxton** North Carolina U.S.A.
19 J6 **Buxy** France
55 C3 **Buy** *R* Russian Federation
58 C2 **Buyant** Mongolia
65 A1 **Buyant** Mongolia
58 G2 **Buyr Nuur** *L* Mongolia
47 N11 **Büyük** *isld* Turkey
47 N11 **Büyükada** Turkey
47 N10 **Büyükdere** Turkey
47 H4 **Büyük Kemikli Br** *C* Turkey
47 J7 **Büyük Menderes** *R* Turkey
21 N8 **Buzançais** France
22 H5 **Buzancy** France
48 K5 **Buzău** *R* Romania
48 K5 **Buzău** Romania
48 K5 **Buzăului Muntii** *mt* Romania
55 B4 **Buzdyak** Russian Federation
60 E12 **Buzen** Japan
87 F9 **Buzi** Mozambique
48 G5 **Buziaş** Romania
55 C4 **Buzov'yazy** Russian Federation
95 R5 **Buzzards B** Massachusetts U.S.A.
8 C4 **Bwlch** Wales
27 H11 **By** Sweden
47 H1 **Byala** Bulgaria
46 F1 **Byala Slatina** Bulgaria
114 J2 **Byam Martin I** Northwest Territories Canada
109 K1 **Byars** Oklahoma U.S.A.
31 O4 **Bychawa** Poland
31 L4 **Byczyna** Poland
31 K2 **Bydgoszcz** Poland
Byelorussia *see* **Belorussia**
106 F2 **Byers** Colorado U.S.A.
109 J1 **Byers** Texas U.S.A.
94 F7 **Byesville** Ohio U.S.A.
9 E3 **Byfield** England
9 F5 **Byfleet** England
26 L7 **Bygdeå** Sweden
26 L7 **Bygdeträsk** Sweden
27 C10 **Bygdin** *L* Norway
26 L7 **Bygdsiljum** Sweden
28 D5 **Bygholm Å** *R* Denmark
27 C13 **Bygland** Norway
27 C13 **Byglandsfj** Norway
110 G7 **Byhalia** Mississippi U.S.A.
54 B3 **Bykhov** Belorussia
27 B12 **Bykle** Norway
27 B12 **Bykleheiane** Norway
59 M2 **Bykov** Russian Federation
28 C7 **Bylderup** Denmark
57 H1 **Bylkyldak** Kazakhstan
115 M3 **Bylot I** Northwest Territories Canada
140 F4 **Bynoe** *R* Queensland Australia
140 B2 **Bynoe Harbour** N Terr Australia
101 N2 **Bynum Res** Montana U.S.A.
111 F9 **Byram** Mississippi U.S.A.
146 D11 **Byrd Glacier** Antarctica
121 O5 **Byrd,L** Quebec Canada
13 F3 **Byrness** England
143 B7 **Byro** W Australia Australia
112 D5 **Byromville** Georgia U.S.A.
102 C4 **Byron** California U.S.A.
99 R7 **Byron** Illinois U.S.A.
95 R2 **Byron** Maine U.S.A.
101 R5 **Byron** Wyoming U.S.A.
139 L3 **Byron Bay** New South Wales Australia
51 J1 **Byrranga,Gory** *mt* Russian Federation
109 J2 **Byrson** Texas U.S.A.
28 F2 **Byrum** Denmark
26 M7 **Byske** Sweden
26 L6 **Byske älv** *R* Sweden
48 F1 **Bystra** *mt* Czechoslovakia
55 F2 **Bystryy** Russian Federation
31 K5 **Bystrzyca Kłodzka** Poland
51 N2 **Bytantay** *R* Russian Federation
31 L6 **Bytča** Czechoslovakia
31 L5 **Bytom** Poland
54 F3 **Bytosh** Russian Federation
31 K1 **Bytów** Poland
Byzantium *see* **İstanbul**
141 J7 **Byzantium** Queensland Australia
31 M3 **Bzura** *R* Poland

C

130 B9 **Caacupé** Paraguay
130 C9 **Caaguazú** *dept* Paraguay
133 F3 **Caaguazu** Paraguay
130 C9 **Caaguazú, Cord de** *mts* Paraguay
87 C8 **Caála** Angola
130 B10 **Caapucú** Paraguay
130 C8 **Caarapó** Brazil
130 F5 **Caatinga** Brazil
130 C10 **Caazapá** Paraguay
129 G7 **Cabacal** *R* Brazil
130 H9 **Cabaceiras** Brazil
126 E3 **Cabaiguán** Cuba
71 E3 **Cabalantian** Luzon Philippines
71 G5 **Cabalian** Leyte Philippines
106 C9 **Caballo** New Mexico U.S.A.
128 D4 **Caballococha** Peru
106 C9 **Caballo Res** New Mexico U.S.A.
124 G3 **Caballos Mesteños, Llano de los** Mexico
71 E3 **Cabanatuan** Luzon Philippines
122 D6 **Cabano** Quebec Canada
71 E2 **Cabarruyan** *isld* Luzon Philippines
19 Q18 **Cabasse** France
141 K1 **Cabbage Tree Cr** Brisbane, Qnsld Australia
16 B2 **Cabe** *R* Spain
130 F4 **Cabeceiras** Brazil
130 J9 **Cabedelo** Brazil
99 S8 **Cabery** Illinois U.S.A.
16 D6 **Cabeza del Buey** Spain
128 F7 **Cabezas** Bolivia
106 C6 **Cabezon** New Mexico U.S.A.
71 F6 **Cabilao** *isld* Philippines
127 J9 **Cabimas** Venezuela
107 P5 **Cabin Creek** Oklahoma U.S.A.
86 B7 **Cabinda** Angola
100 J1 **Cabinet Gorge Dam** Idaho U.S.A.
100 J1 **Cabinet Mts** Idaho U.S.A.
71 E8 **Cabingan** *isld* Philippines
99 P3 **Cable** Wisconsin U.S.A.
113 L9 **Cable Beach** New Providence I Bahamas
133 D7 **Cabo Blanco** Argentina
17 F8 **Cabo de Gata,Sierra del** Spain
88 G8 **Cabo Delgado** *dist* Mozambique
130 G8 **Cabo Frio** Brazil
121 O5 **Cabonga, Rés** Quebec Canada
110 D4 **Cabool** Missouri U.S.A.
141 L7 **Caboolture** Queensland Australia
88 D9 **Cabora Bassa Dam** Mozambique
133 D6 **Cabo Raso** Argentina
113 H7 **Cabo Rojo** Puerto Rico
110 E6 **Cabot** Arkansas U.S.A.
120 J7 **Cabot Head** *C* Ontario Canada
123 M6 **Cabot Str** Nfld/Nova Scotia Canada
21 K3 **Cabourg** France
85 A8 **Cabo Verde, Ilhas do** *islds* Atlantic Oc
71 E4 **Cabra** *isld* Philippines
16 E7 **Cabra del Santo Cristo** Spain
69 A9 **Cabra I** Nicobar Is
127 J5 **Cabral** Dominican Rep
130 G5 **Cabral,Serra do** *mts* Brazil
43 B9 **Cabras** Sardinia
19 P15 **Cabre, Col de** *pass* France
16 B3 **Cabreira** *mt* Portugal
17 J5 **Cabrera** *isld* Balearic Is
127 K5 **Cabrera** Dominican Rep
16 C2 **Cabrera** *R* Spain
126 F4 **Cabreras** *R* Cuba
16 C2 **Cabrera,Sierra** *mt* Spain
118 J8 **Cabri** Saskatchewan Canada
17 F5 **Cabriel** *R* Spain
19 O18 **Cabriès** France
102 G9 **Cabrillo Nat Mon** California U.S.A.
127 M4 **Cabrits, I** Martinique W Indies
130 G10 **Cabrobó** Brazil
128 E2 **Cabruta** Venezuela
71 E7 **Cabucan** *isld* Philippines
71 E2 **Cabugao** Luzon Philippines
71 E5 **Cabulauan** *isld* Philippines
124 E2 **Cabullona** Mexico
71 G8 **Caburan** Mindanao Philippines
128 E1 **Cabure** Venezuela
71 F1 **Cabutunan Pt** Luzon Philippines
133 G3 **Caçador** Brazil
46 D1 **Čačak** Serbia Yugoslavia
122 F3 **Cacaoui L** Quebec Canada
130 F8 **Cacapava** Brazil
133 G4 **Caçapava do Sul** Brazil
94 J7 **Cacapon** *R* West Virginia U.S.A.
68 H2 **Cac Ba** *isld* Vietnam
43 B8 **Caccia,C** Sardinia
133 G3 **Cacequi** Brazil
129 G7 **Cáceres** Brazil
130 B5 **Cáceres** Brazil
16 C5 **Cáceres** *prov* Spain
16 C5 **Cáceres** Spain
110 E6 **Cache** *R* Arkansas U.S.A.
110 G4 **Cache** *R* Illinois U.S.A.
107 M7 **Cache** Oklahoma U.S.A.
120 K6 **Cache Bay** Ontario Canada
102 B3 **Cache Cr** California U.S.A.
85 A6 **Cacheu** Guinea-Bissau
129 G5 **Cachimbo, Serra do** *mts* Brazil
133 D2 **Cachinal** Chile
87 C8 **Cachingues** Angola
129 L6 **Cachoeira** Brazil
130 E6 **Cachoeira Alta** Brazil
130 E5 **Cachoeira de Goiás** Brazil
131 H3 **Cachoeira do Sul** Brazil
130 F8 **Cachoeira Paulista** Brazil
130 H7 **Cachoeiro de Itapemirim** Brazil
102 E7 **Cachuma, L** California U.S.A.
16 E7 **Cacin** *R* Spain
42 H3 **Cačinci** Croatia
71 D5 **Cacnipa** *isld* Philippines
87 C8 **Cacolo** Angola
87 C8 **Caconda** Angola
86 B7 **Cacongo** Angola
122 C6 **Cacouna** Quebec Canada
103 M8 **Cactus** Arizona U.S.A.
109 H8 **Cactus** Texas U.S.A.
118 H6 **Cactus Lake** Saskatchewan Canada
102 H4 **Cactus Ra** Nevada U.S.A.
130 D6 **Caçu** Brazil
87 B9 **Caculavar** *R* Angola
129 K6 **Caculé** Brazil
130 D5 **Caçununga** Brazil
86 J5 **Cadale** Somalia
31 L6 **Čadca** Czechoslovakia
111 C7 **Caddo** *R* Arkansas U.S.A.
107 O7 **Caddo** Oklahoma U.S.A.
109 J3 **Caddo** Texas U.S.A.
111 B9 **Caddo L** Texas U.S.A.
109 L2 **Caddo Mills** Texas U.S.A.
45 J2 **Cadelbosco di Sopra** Italy
111 F12 **Cade,L.de** Louisiana U.S.A.
140 C1 **Cadell** *R* N Terr Australia
141 F5 **Cadell** *R* Queensland Australia
128 D6 **Cadena del Pantiacolla** Peru
32 K5 **Cadenberge** Germany
19 O17 **Cadenet** France
125 K5 **Cadereyta** Mexico
8 C2 **Cader Idris** *mt* Wales
112 H4 **Cades** South Carolina U.S.A.
138 D3 **Cadibarrawirracanna,L** South Australia Australia
19 P18 **Cadière-d'Azur** France
71 F3 **Cadig Mts** Philippines
121 M4 **Cadillac** Quebec Canada
118 K9 **Cadillac** Saskatchewan Canada
18 E8 **Cadillac** France
94 B2 **Cadillac** Michigan U.S.A.
18 G10 **Cadi, Sierra del** *mts* Spain
71 F5 **Cadiz** Negros Philippines
16 C8 **Cádiz** Spain
16 D8 **Cádiz** *prov* Spain
103 J7 **Cadiz** California U.S.A.

164 Cedar Bluff Res — Chehe

107 L3 **Cedar Bluff Res** Kansas U.S.A.
107 K2 **Cedar Bluffs** Kansas U.S.A.
98 K8 **Cedar Bluffs** Nebraska U.S.A.
103 M4 **Cedar Breaks Nat.Mon** Utah U.S.A.
99 T6 **Cedarburg** Wisconsin U.S.A.
98 E6 **Cedar Butte** South Dakota U.S.A.
110 D3 **Cedar City** Missouri U.S.A.
103 L4 **Cedar City** Utah U.S.A.
98 D3 **Cedar Cr** North Dakota U.S.A.
109 K5 **Cedar Creek** Texas U.S.A.
109 O9 **Cedar Crest** Texas U.S.A.
109 L3 **Cedar Cr. L** Texas U.S.A.
101 L7 **Cedar Cr.Res** Idaho U.S.A.
99 O7 **Cedar Falls** Iowa U.S.A.
94 F8 **Cedar Grove** West Virginia U.S.A.
99 T6 **Cedar Grove** Wisconsin U.S.A.
127 P4 **Cedar Grove** Antigua W Indies
112 L2 **Cedar I** North Carolina U.S.A.
95 M9 **Cedar I** Virginia U.S.A.
113 D8 **Cedar Key** Florida U.S.A.
119 R5 **Cedar L** Manitoba Canada
108 E3 **Cedar L** Texas U.S.A.
99 T8 **Cedar Lake** Indiana U.S.A.
109 M7 **Cedar Lane** Texas U.S.A.
102 G3 **Cedar Mts** Nevada U.S.A.
94 D5 **Cedar Pt** Ohio U.S.A.
99 P8 **Cedar Rapids** Iowa U.S.A.
98 H8 **Cedar Rapids** Nebraska U.S.A.
95 K5 **Cedar Run** Pennsylvania U.S.A.
120 H10 **Cedar Springs** Ontario Canada
94 B3 **Cedar Springs** Michigan U.S.A.
111 L7 **Cedartown** Georgia U.S.A.
107 O4 **Cedar Vale** Kansas U.S.A.
106 E7 **Cedarvale** New Mexico U.S.A.
127 L2 **Cedar Valley** Jamaica
100 E8 **Cedarville** California U.S.A.
95 M7 **Cedarville** New Jersey U.S.A.
110 N2 **Cedarville** Ohio U.S.A.
106 F4 **Cedarwood** Colorado U.S.A.
94 K8 **Cedon** Virginia U.S.A.
119 O9 **Cedoux** Saskatchewan Canada
43 C8 **Cedrino** *R* Sardinia
130 G9 **Cedro** Brazil
124 B3 **Cedros** *isld* Mexico
124 E4 **Cedros** Mexico
127 N3 **Cedros Pt** Trinidad
138 C4 **Ceduna** South Australia Australia
86 J4 **Ceel Afweyn** Somalia
86 A3 **Ceelbuur** Somalia
86 A2 **Ceel Hur** Somalia
86 A1 **Ceerigaabo** Somalia
43 F10 **Cefalù** Sicily
16 E3 **Cega** *R* Spain
48 F3 **Cegléd** Hungary
43 H8 **Ceglie Messapico** Italy
17 F6 **Cehegin** Spain
67 B4 **Ceheng** China
48 H3 **Cehu Silvaniei** Romania
48 G4 **Ceica** Romania
128 E3 **Cejal** Colombia
87 C8 **Cela** Angola
Celah, Gunung *see* **Mandi Angin, Gunung**
45 P5 **Celano** Italy
16 B2 **Celanova** Spain
125 J7 **Celaya** Mexico
Celebes *isld see* **Sulawesi**
70 G3 **Celebes Sea** Indonesia
109 L2 **Celeste** Texas U.S.A.
94 C6 **Celina** Ohio U.S.A.
94 B10 **Celina** Tennessee U.S.A.
109 L2 **Celina** Texas U.S.A.
17 G4 **Cella** Spain
48 D3 **Celldömölk** Hungary
32 M7 **Celle** Germany
22 E2 **Celles** Belgium
21 M7 **Celle-St.Avant,la** France
21 N6 **Cellettes** France
21 N8 **Celon** France
16 B3 **Celorico de Basto** Portugal
7 E12 **Celtic Sea** British Isles/France
47 L7 **Çeltikçi** Turkey
47 H4 **Çeltik Gölü** *L* Turkey
41 O5 **Cembra** Italy
107 M7 **Cement** Oklahoma U.S.A.
94 C4 **Cement City** Michigan U.S.A.
46 D1 **Čemerna Planina** *mt* Serbia Yugoslavia
42 H4 **Čemernica** *mt* Bosnia-Herzegovina
48 E7 **Čemerno** Bosnia-Herzegovina
8 B1 **Cemlyn B** Wales
8 B1 **Cemmaes** Wales
17 F6 **Cenajo, Embalse del** *res* Spain
8 B3 **Cenarth** Wales
136 H2 **Cenderawasih, Teluk** *B* W Irian
71 A3 **Cenga** Indonesia
44 G2 **Ceno** *R* Italy
133 C6 **Cenoa** *R* Argentina
86 C4 **Cent.Afr.Rep** Equat Africa
130 D8 **Centenario do Sul** Brazil
112 H3 **Centenary** South Carolina U.S.A.
101 T8 **Centennial** Wyoming U.S.A.
103 L8 **Centennial Wash** *R* Arizona U.S.A.
106 D4 **Center** Colorado U.S.A.
110 E2 **Center** Missouri U.S.A.
98 E2 **Center** North Dakota U.S.A.
111 B10 **Center** Texas U.S.A.
94 E6 **Centerburg** Ohio U.S.A.
99 O4 **Center City** Minnesota U.S.A.
95 L9 **Center Cross** Virginia U.S.A.
113 F9 **Center Hill** Florida U.S.A.
110 L5 **Center Hill L** Tennessee U.S.A.
95 P6 **Center Moriches** Long I, New York U.S.A.
95 Q3 **Center Ossipee** New Hampshire U.S.A.
109 H6 **Center Point** Texas U.S.A.
110 D1 **Centerville** Iowa U.S.A.
111 E12 **Centerville** Louisiana U.S.A.
94 H6 **Centerville** Pennsylvania U.S.A.
98 K6 **Centerville** South Dakota U.S.A.
110 J6 **Centerville** Tennessee U.S.A.
109 M4 **Centerville** Texas U.S.A.
101 O9 **Centerville** Utah U.S.A.
100 E4 **Centerville** Washington U.S.A.
108 E6 **Centinela, Picacho del** *pk* Mexico
124 H3 **Centinela, Pico del** *mt* Mexico
42 D4 **Cento** Italy
44 G3 **Cento Croci, Passo di** Italy
107 O7 **Centrahoma** Oklahoma U.S.A.
89 D3 **Central** *dist* Botswana
130 B9 **Central** *dept* Paraguay
15 D4 **Central** *reg* Scotland
116 P4 **Central** Alaska U.S.A.
106 B9 **Central** New Mexico U.S.A.
112 E3 **Central** South Carolina U.S.A.
103 L4 **Central** Utah U.S.A.
86 C4 **Central African Republic** Africa
118 L8 **Central Butt** Saskatchewan Canada
106 E2 **Central City** Colorado U.S.A.
99 P7 **Central City** Iowa U.S.A.
110 J4 **Central City** Kentucky U.S.A.
98 H8 **Central City** Nebraska U.S.A.
94 J6 **Central City** Pennsylvania U.S.A.
140 B5 **Central Desert Aboriginal Land** N Terr Australia
95 Q5 **Central Falls** Rhode I U.S.A.
110 G3 **Centralia** Illinois U.S.A.
107 O2 **Centralia** Kansas U.S.A.
110 D2 **Centralia** Missouri U.S.A.
100 C3 **Centralia** Washington U.S.A.
94 G8 **Centralia** West Virginia U.S.A.
94 B1 **Central Lake** Michigan U.S.A.
140 C5 **Central Mt. Stewart** N Terr Australia
100 C7 **Central Point** Oregon U.S.A.
136 J2 **Central Ra** Papua New Guinea
56 **Central Siberia**
95 L3 **Central Square** New York U.S.A.
102 B1 **Central Valley** California U.S.A.
111 L7 **Centre** Alabama U.S.A.
144 A7 **Centre I** New Zealand
122 E7 **Centreville** New Brunswick Canada
122 F9 **Centreville** Nova Scotia Canada
111 J9 **Centreville** Alabama U.S.A.
95 L7 **Centreville** Maryland U.S.A.
94 B5 **Centreville** Michigan U.S.A.
111 E10 **Centreville** Mississippi U.S.A.
111 J11 **Century** Florida U.S.A.
94 G7 **Century** West Virginia U.S.A.
67 B4 **Cenwanglao Shan** *mt* China
67 C5 **Cenxi** China
48 E7 **Čeotina** *R* Bosnia-Herzegovina/Yugoslavia
19 P18 **Cépet,C** France
Cephalonia *isld* Greece *see* **Kefallinia** *isld*
41 M5 **Cepina** Italy
44 C4 **Ceppo Monte** *mt* Italy
45 O6 **Ceprano** Italy
21 L6 **Cérans-Foulletourte** France
128 E2 **Cerbatana, Sa. de la** *mts* Venezuela
103 K6 **Cerbat Mts** Arizona U.S.A.
18 H10 **Cerbère, C** France
16 B7 **Cercal** Portugal
16 E4 **Cercedilla** Spain
37 O5 **Čerchov** *mt* Czechoslovakia
21 O6 **Cercottes** France
18 H6 **Cercy la Tour** France
18 G10 **Cerdaña** *dist* Spain
21 P6 **Cerdon** France
18 G8 **Cère** *R* France
45 K1 **Cerea** Italy
118 G7 **Cereal** Alberta Canada
45 L1 **Ceregnano** Italy
21 N7 **Ceré-la-Ronde** France
20 H4 **Cérences** France
130 E4 **Ceres** Brazil
40 F7 **Ceres** Italy
87 C12 **Ceres** S Africa
13 F1 **Ceres** Scotland
102 C4 **Ceres** California U.S.A.
45 J1 **Ceresara** Italy
40 F7 **Ceresole Reale** Italy
18 G10 **Céret** France
126 G10 **Cereté** Colombia
87 J9 **Cerf** *isld* Br Indian Oc Terr
83 J12 **Cerf I** Mahé I Indian Oc
121 P6 **Cerf. L du** Quebec Canada
22 G3 **Cerfontaine** Belgium
21 P3 **Cergy-Pontoise** France
44 D3 **Ceriale** Italy
43 G7 **Cerignola** Italy
Cerigo *isld* Greece *see* **Kíthira** *isld*
18 G6 **Cerilly** France
21 J3 **Cerisy-la Forêt** France
20 H3 **Cerisy-la-Salle** France
21 J8 **Cérizay** France
47 J3 **Çerkesköy** Turkey
42 F3 **Cerknica** Slovenia
48 G4 **Cermei** Romania
48 H5 **Cerna** *R* Romania
48 L5 **Cerna** Romania
48 L6 **Cernavodă** Romania
19 K5 **Cernay** France
8 D6 **Cerne Abbas** England
42 H3 **Cernik** Croatia
37 O4 **Černošín** Czechoslovakia
109 H9 **Cerralvo** Mexico
124 E5 **Cerralvo** *isld* Mexico
45 J4 **Cerreto Guidi** Italy
44 H3 **Cerreto, Passo di** Italy
45 R7 **Cerreto Sannita** Italy
8 C1 **Cerrigydrudion** Wales
46 D3 **Cerrik** Albania
106 D6 **Cerrillos** New Mexico U.S.A.
125 J6 **Cerritos** Mexico
130 E9 **Cêrro Azul** Brazil
128 C6 **Cerro de Pasco** Peru
127 L5 **Cerro de Punta** *pk* Puerto Rico
110 H2 **Cerro Gordo** Illinois U.S.A.
131 G4 **Cerro Largo** *dept* Uruguay
127 J9 **Cerrón** *mt* Venezuela
124 F4 **Cerro Prieto** Mexico
21 K7 **Cersay** France
45 K4 **Certaldo** Italy
143 B9 **Cervantes** W Australia Australia
43 G7 **Cervaro** *R* Italy
45 P7 **Cervaro** Italy
43 G8 **Cervati, M** *mt* Italy
44 H2 **Cervellino** *mt* Italy
17 H3 **Cervera** Spain
17 F2 **Cervera del Rio Alhama** Spain
16 D2 **Cervera de P** Spain
42 E4 **Cervia** Italy
43 G8 **Cervialto, M** *mt* Italy
45 R7 **Cervinara** Italy
41 H7 **Cervo** *R* Italy
44 D4 **Cervo** Italy
128 D2 **César** *div* Colombia
126 H10 **César,R** Colombia
42 E4 **Cesena** Italy
45 M3 **Cesenatico** Italy
52 C6 **Cēsis** Latvia
37 O5 **Česká Kubice** Czechoslovakia
31 H5 **Česká Lípa** Czechoslovakia
31 H7 **Ceské Budějovice** Czechoslovakia
31 H6 **Českézemé** *reg* Czechoslovakia
31 J6 **Českomoravská Vysočina** *mts* Czechoslovakia
31 H5 **Český Brod** Czechoslovakia
31 H7 **Český Krumlov** Czechoslovakia
37 O4 **Český les Sumava** *mts* Czechoslovakia
48 E1 **Český Těšin** Czechoslovakia
78 A2 **Çesme** Turkey
47 H6 **Çeşnie** Turkey
139 K5 **Cessnock** New South Wales Australia
48 H6 **Cetate** Romania
42 H5 **Cetina** *R* Croatia
42 J6 **Cetinje** Montenegro Yugoslavia
21 M5 **Ceton** France
43 G9 **Cetraro** Italy
19 P15 **Ceuse, Pic de** *mt* France
85 C1 **Ceuta** *Spanish exclave* Morocco
16 D9 **Ceuta** Spain
137 P6 **Ceva-i-Ra** *reef* Pacific Oc
41 N5 **Cevedale** *mt* Italy
18 H8 **Cevennes** *mts* France
78 G3 **Ceylânpınar** Turkey
Ceylon *rep see* **Sri Lanka** *rep*
119 N9 **Ceylon** Saskatchewan Canada
99 M6 **Ceylon** Minnesota U.S.A.
19 P18 **Ceyreste** France
57 B6 **Chaacha** Turkmenistan
19 P16 **Chabestan** France
19 O15 **Chabeuil** France
142 A6 **Chabjuwardoo B** W Australia Australia
18 H5 **Chablis** France
19 P16 **Chabre, Mt de** France
19 Q16 **Chabrières** France
21 O7 **Chabris** France
133 C1 **Chaca** Chile
131 E5 **Chacabuco** Argentina
127 N1 **Chacachacare** Trinidad
133 D2 **Chacance** Chile
133 C6 **Chacao, Canal de** Chile
133 D6 **Chacays, Sa. de los** *mts* Argentina
131 C6 **Chachahuen,Sa** *mt* Argentina
128 D7 **Chachani** *mt* Peru
128 C5 **Chachapoyas** Peru
68 E6 **Chachoengsao** Thailand
74 D6 **Chachro** Pakistan
133 E3 **Chaco** *prov* Argentina
128 F8 **Chaco** *dept* Paraguay
133 E3 **Chaco Austral** *reg* Argentina
133 E2 **Chaco Boreal** *reg* Paraguay
106 B5 **Chaco Canyon Nat. Mon** New Mexico U.S.A.
133 E2 **Chaco Central** *reg* Argentina
117 H8 **Chacon,C** Prince of Wales I, Alaska
129 G5 **Chacorão, Cachoeira do** *waterfall* Brazil
106 C6 **Chacra Mesa** *mt* New Mexico U.S.A.
86 C3 **Chad** *rep* Equat Africa
56 D5 **Chadan** Russian Federation
112 J3 **Chadbourn** North Carolina U.S.A.
131 C6 **Chadileo,R** Argentina
133 D5 **Chadileuvú** *R* Argentina
86 B3 **Chad,L** Equat Africa
56 F2 **Chadobets** *R* Russian Federation
98 D7 **Chadron** Nebraska U.S.A.
99 R7 **Chadwick** Illinois U.S.A.
48 M4 **Chadyr Lunga** Moldavia
110 G4 **Chaffee** Missouri U.S.A.
94 J4 **Chaffee** New York U.S.A.
74 A4 **Chagai** Pakistan
77 H5 **Chagai Hills** Pakistan
53 H8 **Chagan** *R* Kazakhstan/Rus Fed
51 N3 **Chagda** Russian Federation
8 C6 **Chagford** England
77 J2 **Chaghcharān** Afghanistan
55 E4 **Chaglinka** *R* Kazakhstan
40 A4 **Chagny** France
52 E5 **Chagoda** Russian Federation
52 E5 **Chagodoshcha** *R* Russian Federation
81 E6 **Chagos Arch** Indian Oc
94 F5 **Chagrin Falls** Ohio U.S.A.
127 O2 **Chaguanas** Trinidad
127 N1 **Chaguaramas** Trinidad
127 L10 **Chaguaramas** Venezuela
77 H4 **Chahah Burjak** Afghanistan
77 G7 **Chāh Bahār** Iran
77 G5 **Chah Ghevhī, Hāmún-e** *L* Iran
77 L1 **Chāh-i-Ghab** Afghanistan
78 K4 **Chah-I-Surkh** Iraq
68 E5 **Chai Badan** Thailand
75 L7 **Chāībāssa** India
Chaigoubu *see* **Huai'an**
21 J5 **Chailland** France
19 P14 **Chaine de Belledonne** *mts* France
85 E6 **Chaîne de l'Atakora** *mts* Benin
19 N17 **Chaine des Alpilles** *mts* France
18 H7 **Chaise Dieu, la** France
69 D8 **Chaiya** Thailand
68 E5 **Chaiyaphum** Thailand
20 H8 **Chaize-le-Vicomte,la** France
131 F3 **Chajari** Argentina
116 L6 **Chakachamna L** Alaska U.S.A.
74 F2 **Chak Amru** Pakistan
88 G4 **Chake Chake** Tanzania
77 H4 **Chakhānsūr** Afghanistan
74 E2 **Chakwal** Pakistan
128 D7 **Chala** Peru
87 F8 **Chalabesa** Zambia
40 C4 **Chalain,L.de** France
18 F7 **Chalais** France
59 H2 **Cha-lan-t'un** China
128 D7 **Chala,Pta** Peru
125 P10 **Chalatenango** Honduras
69 D9 **Chalaung** Thailand
124 H6 **Chalchihuites** Mexico
125 P11 **Chalchuapa** El Salvador
Chalcis *see* **Khalkis**
9 E6 **Chale** England
122 G6 **Chaleurs, Baie des** Quebec/New Brunswick Canada
128 D6 **Chalhuanca** Peru
133 C7 **Chalia** *R* Argentina
88 B7 **Chali,L** Zambia
19 J5 **Chalindrey** France
67 D3 **Chaling** China
74 F8 **Chalisgaon** India
9 G5 **Chalk** England
98 B4 **Chalk Buttes** Montana U.S.A.
109 K3 **Chalk Mountain** Texas U.S.A.
121 N6 **Chalk River** Ontario Canada
144 A7 **Chalky Inlet** New Zealand
116 Q3 **Chalkyitsik** Alaska U.S.A.
21 H6 **Challain-la-Potherie** France
20 G8 **Challans** France
133 D1 **Challapata** Bolivia
115 M1 **Challenger Mts** Northwest Territories Canada
22 H5 **Challerange** France
101 L5 **Challis** Idaho U.S.A.
52 E2 **Chal'mny Varre** Russian Federation
75 N7 **Chalna** Bangladesh
52 D4 **Chalna** Russian Federation
21 J7 **Chalonnes** France
18 H4 **Chalons-sur-Marne** France
19 J6 **Chalon-sur-Saône** France
65 J3 **Chaluhe** China
18 F7 **Châlus** France
57 B4 **Chalysh** Uzbekistan
37 O5 **Cham** *R* Germany
37 O5 **Cham** Germany
106 E4 **Chama** Colorado U.S.A.
106 D5 **Chama** New Mexico U.S.A.
74 B3 **Chaman** Pakistan
68 E6 **Chamao,Khao** *mt* Thailand
106 D5 **Chama, R** New Mexico U.S.A.
128 C5 **Chamaya** *R* Peru
74 G2 **Chamba** India
73 M3 **Chambal** *R* Madhya Prad/Rajasthan India
40 B7 **Chambaran, Plat. de** France
126 E3 **Chambas** Cuba
119 M8 **Chamberlain** Saskatchewan Canada
98 G6 **Chamberlain** South Dakota U.S.A.
95 R7 **Chamberlain L** Maine U.S.A.
142 G3 **Chamberlain R** W Australia Australia
116 P2 **Chamberlin,Mt** Alaska U.S.A.
103 P6 **Chambers** Arizona U.S.A.
98 H7 **Chambers** Nebraska U.S.A.
140 B1 **Chambers B** N Terr Australia
94 K7 **Chambersburg** Pennsylvania U.S.A.
99 T4 **Chambers I** Wisconsin U.S.A.
138 C1 **Chambers Pillar** *pk* N Terr Australia
19 P13 **Chambéry** France
88 C7 **Chambeshi** *R* Zambia
128 C4 **Chambira** *R* Peru
21 P3 **Chambly** France
21 L4 **Chambois** France
18 H7 **Chambon, le** Loire France
121 S4 **Chambord** Quebec Canada
21 O6 **Chambord** France
21 M7 **Chambourg-sur-Indre** France
66 E5 **Chamdo** *prov* China
124 G8 **Chamela** Mexico
77 B4 **Cham-e Zeydun** Iran
77 B3 **Chamgordan** Iran
133 D4 **Chamical** Argentina
106 D5 **Chamita** New Mexico U.S.A.
86 G4 **Chamo Hāyk'** *L* Ethiopia
110 E3 **Chamois** Missouri U.S.A.
74 H3 **Chamoli** India
40 E6 **Chamonix** France
19 P1 **Chamouse,Mt.de** France
75 K7 **Champa** India
89 F7 **Champagne Castle** *mt* Lesotho
40 C4 **Champagnole** France
142 E3 **Champagny Is** W Australia Australia
99 S9 **Champaign** Illinois U.S.A.
131 D3 **Champaqui** *pk* Argentina
68 G5 **Cham Pasak** Laos
121 N4 **Champcoeur** Quebec Canada
36 C7 **Champ du Feu** *mt* France
21 O8 **Champenoise,la** France
21 K5 **Champgeneteux** France
19 O1 **Champier** France
21 J6 **Champigné** France
21 N6 **Champigny** France
21 L8 **Champigny le Sec** France
21 L7 **Champigny-sur-Veude** France
21 P8 **Champillet** France
22 J3 **Champion** Belgium
118 D8 **Champion** Alberta Canada
99 T3 **Champion** Michigan U.S.A.
94 G5 **Champion Heights** Ohio U.S.A.
121 S6 **Champlain** Quebec Canada
95 O2 **Champlain** New York U.S.A.
121 R8 **Champlain** New York U.S.A.
95 O3 **Champlain Canal** New York U.S.A.
19 J5 **Champlitte** France
40 B2 **Champlitte** France
121 N4 **Champneuf** Quebec Canada
19 Q1 **Champoléon** France
40 G6 **Champorcher** Italy
21 N5 **Champrond** France
21 J4 **Champsecret** France
21 J7 **Champtocé** France
20 H7 **Champtoceaux** France
76 C5 **Chamrajnagar** India
19 P1 **Chamrousse** France
16 B5 **Chamusca** Portugal
69 E9 **Chana** Thailand
18 H8 **Chanac** France
131 B2 **Chañaral** *R* Chile
133 C3 **Chañaral** Chile
131 B2 **Chañaral, I** Chile
98 K6 **Chancellor** South Dakota U.S.A.
133 C5 **Chanco** Chile
21 M4 **Chandai** France
116 P2 **Chandalar** *R* Alaska U.S.A.
116 N3 **Chandalar** Alaska U.S.A.
111 G1 **Chandeleur Sound** Louisiana U.S.A.
122 H5 **Chandler** Quebec Canada
116 M2 **Chandler** *R* Alaska U.S.A.
103 N8 **Chandler** Arizona U.S.A.
107 O6 **Chandler** Oklahoma U.S.A.
109 M3 **Chandler** Texas U.S.A.
116 L2 **Chandler L** Alaska U.S.A.
138 C2 **Chandler,Mt** South Australia Australia
99 Q9 **Chandlerville** Illinois U.S.A.
128 D6 **Chandless** *R* Peru/Brazil
75 O7 **Chandpur** Bangladesh
74 H9 **Chandrapur** India
77 G6 **Chānf** Iran
Chang'an *see* **Rong'an**
65 A7 **Chang'an** China
87 F9 **Changara** Mozambique
65 G4 **Changbai** China
65 G4 **Changbai Shan** *mt ra* China
146 D3 **Chang Cheng** *China Base* Antarctica
68 J3 **Changcheng** China
67 B1 **Changchi** China
65 F3 **Changchun** China
65 F2 **Changchunling** China
67 F1 **Changdang Hu** *L* China
67 D2 **Changde** China
123 S4 **Change I** Newfoundland Canada
65 B7 **Changge** China
65 E5 **Changhai** China
58 F5 **Chang Hu** *L* China
67 F1 **Changhua** China
67 G4 **Chang-hua** Taiwan
67 C7 **Changhua Jiang** *R* China
67 C1 **Chang Jiang** *R* China
67 C7 **Changjiang** China
67 E2 **Chang Jiang** *R* Jiangxi China
65 G4 **Changjin Res** N Korea
68 F6 **Chang,Ko** *isld* Thailand
65 D6 **Changle** China
67 G2 **Changle** China
67 F4 **Changle** China
65 D5 **Changli** China
59 H3 **Changling** China
66 B5 **Changmar** China
67 A2 **Changning** China
67 D3 **Changning** China
65 C4 **Changping** China
Changpuzhen *see* **Suining**
65 C6 **Changqing** China
65 F5 **Changsan-got** *C* N Korea
67 D2 **Changsha** China
67 F2 **Changshan** China
65 E5 **Changshan Qundao** *islds* China
65 D4 **Changshanyu** China
67 B2 **Changshou** China
67 G1 **Changshu** China
67 B3 **Changshun** China
67 F4 **Changtai** China
65 G2 **Changting** China
67 E4 **Changting** China
65 F3 **Changtu** China
65 G2 **Changwu** China
67 F1 **Changxing** China
65 E5 **Changxing Dao** *isld* China
67 D1 **Changyang** China
65 D6 **Changyi** China
59 H4 **Changyon** N Korea
65 C7 **Changyuan** China
Changzhai *see* **Changshun**
65 B6 **Changzhi** China
67 G1 **Changzhou** Jiangsu China
67 E1 **Changzhuyuan** China
83 J8 **Chankanai** Sri Lanka
116 H8 **Chankluit I** Alaska U.S.A.
69 C8 **Chan,Ko** *isld* Thailand
21 L7 **Channay-sur-Lathan** France
145 E2 **Channel I** New Zealand
102 E8 **Channel Is** California U.S.A.
20 E3 **Channel Islands** English Chan
123 N6 **Channel-Port aux Basques** Newfoundland Canada
143 C10 **Channel Pt** W Australia Australia
126 F3 **Channel Rock** Bahamas
76 C4 **Channiapatna** India
119 P4 **Channing** *airfield* Manitoba Canada
99 S3 **Channing** Michigan U.S.A.
108 B8 **Channing** Texas U.S.A.
16 B2 **Chantada** Spain
21 K6 **Chantenay** Sarthe France
68 F6 **Chanthaburi** Thailand
21 P3 **Chantilly** France
21 H8 **Chantonnay** France
115 K4 **Chantrey Inlet** Northwest Territories Canada
21 J4 **Chanu** France
69 A8 **Chanumla** Nicobar Is
107 P4 **Chanute** Kansas U.S.A.
110 A4 **Chanute** Kansas U.S.A.
55 G3 **Chany** Russian Federation
21 J7 **Chanzeaux** France
17 G10 **Chanzy** Algeria
Chao'an *see* **Chaozhou**
65 C6 **Chaocheng** China
16 D9 **Chaoen** Morocco
58 G5 **Chao Hu** *L* China
128 C5 **Chao, I** Peru
68 E5 **Chao Phraya Ra** Thailand
65 E1 **Chaor He** *R* China
58 E5 **Chaotianyi** China
67 F1 **Chao Xian** China
Chaoyang *see* **Huinan**
59 K2 **Ch'ao-Yang** China
67 E5 **Chaoyang** Guangdong China
65 E4 **Chaoyang** Liaoning China
65 A7 **Chaoyi** China
67 E5 **Chaozhou** China
129 J5 **Chapada das Mangabeiras** *mts* Brazil
129 K6 **Chapada Diamantina** *mts* Brazil
129 K5 **Chapada do Araripe** *mts* Brazil
130 C4 **Chapada dos Guimarães** Brazil
129 K4 **Chapadinha** Brazil
121 Q3 **Chapais** Quebec Canada
124 H7 **Chapala,L.de** Mexico
129 K8 **Chaparao,Serra do** *mts* Brazil
53 H8 **Chapayev** Kazakhstan
57 C6 **Chapayeva, Imeni** Turkmenistan
53 G7 **Chapayevsk** Russian Federation
121 N7 **Chapeau** Quebec Canada
130 D10 **Chapecó** Brazil
130 D10 **Chapecózinho** *R* Brazil
9 E1 **Chapel en le Frith** England
112 H2 **Chapel Hill** North Carolina U.S.A.
110 K6 **Chapel Hill** Tennessee U.S.A.
21 K5 **Chapelle-au-Riboul,la** France
40 D1 **Chapelle-aux-Bois, La** France
20 H7 **Chapelle Basse Mer, la** France
21 M7 **Chapelle, Blanche-St. Martin, la** France
20 G6 **Chapelle-Bouexic,la** France
21 K6 **Chapelle d'Aligné, la** France
18 G5 **Chapelle d' Angillon,la** France
20 F7 **Chapelle-des-Marais,la** France
21 H6 **Chapelle-Glain,la** France
20 H7 **Chapelle-Heulin,la** France
22 J4 **Chapelle, la** France
20 F6 **Chapelle,La** Morbihan France
123 L3 **Chapelle,L. de la** Quebec Canada
21 K4 **Chapelle-Moche,la** France
21 J5 **Chapelle-Rainsouin,la** France
21 N5 **Chapelle Royale** France
21 K8 **Chapelle St. Laurent, la** France
21 O6 **Chapelle-st.Mesmin,la** France
20 G7 **Chapelle-sur-Erdre, La** France
9 G1 **Chapel St Leonards** England
127 K2 **Chapelton** Jamaica
13 G6 **Chapeltown** England
99 Q10 **Chapin** Illinois U.S.A.
110 F2 **Chapin** Illinois U.S.A.
120 G4 **Chapleau** *R* Ontario Canada
120 G5 **Chapleau** Ontario Canada
120 H4 **Chapleau-Nemecosenda Wild R. Prov. Pk** Ontario Canada
118 L8 **Chaplin** Saskatchewan Canada
147 P1 **Chaplina,Mys** *C* Russian Federation
54 H8 **Chaplino** Ukraine
54 L3 **Chaplygin** Russian Federation
111 K10 **Chapman** Alabama U.S.A.
107 N3 **Chapman** Kansas U.S.A.
101 R1 **Chapman** Montana U.S.A.
98 H8 **Chapman** Nebraska U.S.A.
117 O10 **Chapman,Mt** British Columbia Canada
142 F3 **Chapman R** W Australia Australia
109 K8 **Chapman Ranch** Texas U.S.A.
94 E9 **Chapmanville** West Virginia U.S.A.
52 E2 **Chapoma** Russian Federation
98 D8 **Chappell** Nebraska U.S.A.
109 L5 **Chappell Hill** Texas U.S.A.
139 J8 **Chappell Is** Tasmania Australia
95 L8 **Chaptico** Maryland U.S.A.
18 E7 **Chapus, le** France
120 K4 **Chaput** Ontario Canada
128 E7 **Chaqui** Bolivia
133 D1 **Chaqui** Bolivia
74 G2 **Char** Kashmir
85 B4 **Char** Mauritania
51 L3 **Chara** Russian Federation
133 E1 **Charagua** Bolivia
124 E4 **Charay** Mexico
98 C2 **Charbonneau** North Dakota U.S.A.
40 C3 **Charcenne** France
21 K5 **Charchigné** France
109 K7 **Charco** Texas U.S.A.
146 C5 **Charcot I** Antarctica
118 G3 **Chard** Alberta Canada
8 D6 **Chard** England
57 E4 **Chardara** Kazakhstan
57 E4 **Chardarinskoye Vdkhr** *res* Kazakhstan/Uzbekistan
94 F5 **Chardon** Ohio U.S.A.
126 G5 **Chardonnière** Haiti
57 C5 **Chardzhou** Turkmenistan
18 E7 **Charente** *R* France
18 E7 **Charente** *dept* France
18 E7 **Charente-Maritime** *dept* France
21 M3 **Charentonne** *R* France
18 G6 **Charenton-sur-Cher** France
86 C3 **Chari** *R* Chad
77 L2 **Chārīkār** Afghanistan
9 G5 **Charing** England
116 D2 **Chariot** Alaska U.S.A.
18 H5 **Charité, la** France
99 N8 **Chariton** Iowa U.S.A.
99 N9 **Chariton** *R* Iowa U.S.A.
110 D2 **Chariton** *R* Missouri U.S.A.
128 G2 **Charity** Guyana
52 H2 **Charkayuvom** Russian Federation
74 H6 **Charkhari** India
9 E4 **Charlbury** England
22 H3 **Charleroi** Belgium
94 H6 **Charleroi** Pennsylvania U.S.A.
119 Q3 **Charles** Manitoba Canada
121 T6 **Charlesbourg** Quebec Canada
95 M9 **Charles,C** Virginia U.S.A.
99 O6 **Charles City** Iowa U.S.A.
115 M5 **Charles I** Northwest Territories Canada
143 B8 **Charles,Mt** W Australia Australia
143 D10 **Charles Pk** W Australia Australia
140 B1 **Charles Pt** N Terr Australia
144 A6 **Charles Sd** New Zealand
144 C4 **Charleston** New Zealand
110 B6 **Charleston** Arkansas U.S.A.
99 S10 **Charleston** Illinois U.S.A.
111 F7 **Charleston** Mississippi U.S.A.
110 G5 **Charleston** Missouri U.S.A.
100 A6 **Charleston** Oregon U.S.A.
112 H5 **Charleston** South Carolina U.S.A.
112 C2 **Charleston** Tennessee U.S.A.
94 F8 **Charleston** West Virginia U.S.A.
103 J5 **Charleston Pk** Nevada U.S.A.
14 C3 **Charlestown** Ireland
94 B8 **Charlestown** Indiana U.S.A.
95 P3 **Charlestown** New Hampshire U.S.A.
94 K7 **Charles Town** West Virginia U.S.A.
127 P4 **Charlestown** Nevis W Indies
118 A1 **Charles Wood** Manitoba Canada
Charlet,Ft *see* **Djanet**
21 N3 **Charleval** France
141 H7 **Charleville** Queensland Australia
22 H4 **Charleville-Mézières** France
94 B1 **Charlevoix** Michigan U.S.A.
94 B1 **Charlevoix,L** Michigan U.S.A.
116 Q4 **Charley** *R* Alaska U.S.A.
117 N7 **Charlie Lake** British Columbia Canada
18 H6 **Charlieu** France
94 C4 **Charlotte** Michigan U.S.A.
112 G2 **Charlotte** North Carolina U.S.A.
109 J7 **Charlotte** Texas U.S.A.
127 M5 **Charlotte Amalie** Virgin Is
117 L9 **Charlotte L** British Columbia Canada
27 F12 **Charlottenberg** Sweden
33 S7 **Charlottenburg** Berlin
33 S9 **Charlottenfelde** Germany
94 J8 **Charlottesville** Virginia U.S.A.
122 J7 **Charlottetown** Prince Edward I Canada
Charlotte Town Grenada *see* **Gouyave**
127 N1 **Charlotteville** Tobago
139 G6 **Charlton** Victoria Australia
120 K5 **Charlton** Ontario Canada
115 M7 **Charlton I** Northwest Territories Canada
19 K4 **Charmes** France
40 F4 **Charmey** Switzerland
40 F3 **Chärmoille** Switzerland
8 D6 **Charmouth** England
21 M8 **Charnizay** France
142 F3 **Charnley,R** W Australia Australia
121 T6 **Charny** Quebec Canada
60 R2 **Charo-gawa** *R* Japan
18 H6 **Charolles** France
21 P8 **Charost** France
52 E4 **Charozero** Russian Federation
122 J2 **Charpeney,L** Quebec Canada
21 O3 **Chars** France
74 D1 **Charsadda** Pakistan
57 D5 **Charshanga** Turkmenistan
56 B6 **Charsk** Kazakhstan
99 L7 **Charter Oak** Iowa U.S.A.
141 H5 **Charters Towers** Queensland Australia
122 A8 **Chartierville** Quebec Canada
21 M6 **Chartre,la** France
21 N5 **Chartres** France
57 F4 **Charvakskoye Vdkhr.** Uzbekistan
19 Q13 **Charvin, Mt** France
19 Q13 **Charvonnex** France
56 B5 **Charysh** *R* Russian Federation
131 F5 **Chascomas** Argentina
117 O10 **Chase** British Columbia Canada
107 M3 **Chase** Kansas U.S.A.
99 P6 **Chaseburg** Wisconsin U.S.A.
94 J10 **Chase City** Virginia U.S.A.
98 G3 **Chase L** North Dakota U.S.A.
55 D3 **Chashi** Russian Federation
57 B5 **Chashkent** Turkmenistan
99 N5 **Chaska** Minnesota U.S.A.
144 B7 **Chaslands Mistake** New Zealand
117 N10 **Chasm** British Columbia Canada
52 D1 **Chasnachorr, Gora** *mt* Russian Federation
52 E3 **Chasovenskaya** Russian Federation
52 H4 **Chasovo** Russian Federation
54 J8 **Chasov Yar** Ukraine
113 E9 **Chassahowitzka B** Florida U.S.A.
99 S2 **Chassell** Michigan U.S.A.
18 F7 **Chasseneuil** France
18 H8 **Chassezac** *R* France
21 O8 **Chassignoles** France
21 K5 **Chassille** France
55 E3 **Chastoozer'ye** Russian Federation
52 H6 **Chastyye** Russian Federation
21 J8 **Châtaigneraie,la** France
116 O4 **Chatanika** Alaska U.S.A.
121 L10 **Chatauqua L** New York U.S.A.
127 O8 **Chateaubelair** St Vincent
20 G7 **Chateau Bougon** *airport* France
20 H5 **Châteaubourg** France
20 H6 **Châteaubriant** France
18 H5 **Château Chinon** France
19 O18 **Château d'If** *isld* France
18 E7 **Château d'Oléron, le** France
21 L6 **Château-du-Loir** France
21 N5 **Châteaudun** France
21 P4 **Châteaufort** France
95 N2 **Chateaugay** New York U.S.A.
20 H5 **Châteaugiron** France
21 J6 **Château-Gontier** France
21 L6 **Château-la-Vallière** France
20 B5 **Châteaulin** France
21 P8 **Châteaumeillant** France
19 N14 **Châteauneuf-de-Galaure** France
20 G4 **Châteauneuf-d'Ille-et-Vilaine** France
20 C5 **Châteauneuf-du-Faou** France
21 N4 **Châteauneuf-en-Thymerais** France
18 E7 **Châteauneuf-sur-Charente** France
21 P8 **Châteauneuf-sur-Cher** France
21 P6 **Châteauneuf-sur-Loire** France
21 J6 **Châteauneuf-sur-Sarthe** France
22 G4 **Château-Porcien** France
20 D4 **Château,Pte.du** France
19 Q16 **Châteauredon** France
19 N17 **Châteaurenard** France
21 M6 **Château-Renault** France
122 A7 **Chateau Richer** Quebec Canada
21 O8 **Châteauroux** Indre France
19 K4 **Château Salins** France
18 H3 **Château-Thierry** France
121 R5 **Chateauvert, L** Quebec Canada
127 O4 **Châteaux, Pte. des** Guadeloupe W Indies
117 O6 **Chateh** Alberta Canada
20 E4 **Châtelaudren** France
22 H3 **Châtelet** Belgium
21 P8 **Châtelet,le** France
21 N5 **Châtelets,les** France
18 H7 **Chatelguyon** France
40 A2 **Chatellenot** France
21 M8 **Châtellerault** France
36 C7 **Chatenois** France
99 O6 **Chatfield** Minnesota U.S.A.
122 G6 **Chatham** New Brunswick Canada
120 H10 **Chatham** Ontario Canada
9 G5 **Chatham** England
117 F7 **Chatham** Alaska U.S.A.
99 R10 **Chatham** Illinois U.S.A.
110 G2 **Chatham** Illinois U.S.A.
111 D9 **Chatham** Louisiana U.S.A.
95 S5 **Chatham** Massachusetts U.S.A.
95 O4 **Chatham** New York U.S.A.
94 H10 **Chatham** Virginia U.S.A.
137 R10 **Chatham Is** Pacific Oc
117 H8 **Chatham Sd** British Columbia Canada
133 C8 **Chatham Stokes** *mt* Chile
22 K4 **Châtillon** Belgium
40 G6 **Châtillon** Italy
18 G5 **Châtillon-Coligny** France
19 P12 **Châtillon de Michaille** France
21 H5 **Châtillon-en-Vendelais** France
19 O13 **Châtillon-la-Palud** France
21 N8 **Châtillon-sur-Indre** France
18 G5 **Châtillon-sur-Loire** France
57 F4 **Chatkal** *R* Kyrgyzstan
57 F4 **Chatkal'skiy Khr** *mts* Kyrgyzstan/Uzbekistan
111 H10 **Chatom** Alabama U.S.A.
75 L6 **Chatra** India
21 O8 **Châtre, la** France
140 F5 **Chatsworth** Queensland Australia
120 K8 **Chatsworth** Ontario Canada
112 C3 **Chatsworth** Georgia U.S.A.
110 H1 **Chatsworth** Illinois U.S.A.
95 N7 **Chatsworth** New Jersey U.S.A.
89 G2 **Chatsworth** Zimbabwe
111 L8 **Chattahoochee** *R* Alabama/Georgia
111 M11 **Chattahoochee** Florida U.S.A.
112 B2 **Chattanooga** Tennessee U.S.A.
100 H2 **Chattaroy** Washington U.S.A.
94 E9 **Chattaroy** West Virginia U.S.A.
9 G3 **Chatteris** England
144 B6 **Chatto Cr** New Zealand
13 G2 **Chatton** England
111 L7 **Chattooga** *R* Georgia/Alabama U.S.A.
112 D3 **Chattooga** *R* S Carolina/Georgia U.S.A.
112 D2 **Chatuge L** North Carolina U.S.A.
68 E5 **Chaturat** Thailand
57 H4 **Chatyr-Kël' Ozero** *L* Kyrgyzstan
20 H8 **Chauché** France
18 H8 **Chaudes-Aigues** France
22 K2 **Chaudfontaine** Belgium
Chau Doc *see* **Chau Phu**
21 J7 **Chaudron-en-Mauges** France
22 E5 **Chaudun** France
116 H6 **Chauekuktuli L** Alaska U.S.A.
19 Q15 **Chauffayer** France
68 B2 **Chauk** Burma
75 R5 **Chaukan Pass** Burma/India
22 D4 **Chaulnes** France
40 B4 **Chaumergy** France
40 D3 **Chaumont** *mt* France
19 J4 **Chaumont** Haute-Marne France
21 O3 **Chaumont-en-Vexin** France
22 G4 **Chaumont-Porcien** France
21 N7 **Chaumont-sur-Loire** France
21 O6 **Chaumont-sur-Tharonne** France
94 E7 **Chauncey** Ohio U.S.A.
68 D6 **Chaungwabyin** Burma
68 C4 **Chaungzon** Burma
51 Q2 **Chaunskaya Guba** *G* Russian Federation
22 E4 **Chauny** France
68 G7 **Chau Phu** Vietnam
69 A8 **Chaura I** Nicobar Is
20 G4 **Chausey Is** France
21 P2 **Chaussée-Tirancourt,la** France
19 J6 **Chaussin** France
54 B3 **Chausy** Belorussia
94 H4 **Chautauqua** New York U.S.A.
94 H4 **Chautauqua L** New York U.S.A.
57 F4 **Chauvay** Kyrgyzstan
20 G7 **Chauvé** France
21 N6 **Chauvigny** Loir-et-Cher France
21 M8 **Chauvigny** Vienne France
118 G6 **Chauvin** Alberta Canada
19 K5 **Chaux de Fonds, la** France
40 E3 **Chaux de Fonds, La** Switzerland
20 H8 **Chavagnes-en-Paillers** France
19 N14 **Chavanay** France
52 E2 **Chavan'ga** Russian Federation
130 D4 **Chavantina** Brazil
130 D7 **Chavantina** Brazil
16 C3 **Chaves** Portugal
94 D9 **Chavies** Kentucky U.S.A.
22 F5 **Chavignon** France
87 D8 **Chavuma** Zambia
69 D8 **Chawang** Thailand
9 F5 **Chawton** England
56 G2 **Chaya** *R* Russian Federation
88 C7 **Chaya, L** Zambia
57 E3 **Chayan** Kazakhstan
57 G4 **Chayek** Kyrgyzstan
52 H6 **Chaykovskiy** Russian Federation
78 K2 **Chāypareh** Iran
66 F6 **Ch'a-yü** China
21 J6 **Chazé-sur-Argos** France
52 H4 **Chazhegovo** Russian Federation
133 E4 **Chazon** Argentina
95 O2 **Chazy** New York U.S.A.
118 D7 **Cheadle** Alberta Canada
9 E2 **Cheadle** England
111 L8 **Cheaha Mt** Alabama U.S.A.
94 H7 **Cheat** *R* West Virginia U.S.A.
110 J5 **Cheatham L** Tennessee U.S.A.
37 N3 **Cheb** Czechoslovakia
55 D4 **Chebarkul'** Russian Federation
52 G6 **Cheboksary** Russian Federation
94 C1 **Cheboygan** Michigan U.S.A.
52 E5 **Chebsara** Russian Federation
53 G11 **Checheno-Ingushskaya Respublika** Russian Federation
54 B4 **Chechersk** Belorussia
31 M5 **Chęciny** Poland
107 P6 **Checotah** Oklahoma U.S.A.
21 P6 **Chécy** France
123 L8 **Chedabucto B** Nova Scotia Canada
8 D5 **Cheddar** England
83 K9 **Cheddikulam** Sri Lanka
68 A3 **Cheduba** *isld* Burma
68 A3 **Cheduba** Burma
68 A3 **Cheduba Str** Burma
118 G2 **Cheecham** Alberta Canada
120 J2 **Cheepash** *R* Ontario Canada
120 G1 **Cheepay** *R* Ontario Canada
141 G7 **Cheepie** Queensland Australia
119 O1 **Cheeseman L** Ontario Canada
106 E2 **Cheesman,L** Colorado U.S.A.
146 C13 **Cheetham,C** Antarctica
18 E6 **Chef-Boutonne** France
111 G11 **Chef Menteur** Louisiana U.S.A.
Chefoo *see* **Yantai**
116 E6 **Chefornak** Alaska U.S.A.
121 R3 **Chef,R.du** Quebec Canada
59 K1 **Chegdomyn** Russian Federation
85 C3 **Chegga** Mauritania
116 A3 **Chegitun** *R* Russian Federation
89 G2 **Chegutu** Zimbabwe
100 B3 **Chehalis** *R* Washington U.S.A.
100 C3 **Chehalis** Washington U.S.A.
67 B4 **Chehe** China

87 F8 **Cheif Serenje** Zambia
21 L7 **Cheillé** France
59 J5 **Cheju** S Korea
65 G8 **Cheju do** *isld* S Korea
65 G8 **Cheju haehyŏp** *str* S Korea
54 H2 **Chekalin** Russian Federation
52 H7 **Chekan** Russian Federation
54 J1 **Chekhov** Russian Federation
Chekiang *prov see* **Zhejiang**
55 G2 **Chekino** Russian Federation
51 N3 **Chekunda** Russian Federation
52 E3 **Chekuyevo** Russian Federation
119 O6 **Chelan** Saskatchewan Canada
100 F2 **Chelan** Washington U.S.A.
100 E1 **Chelan,L** Washington U.S.A.
100 E1 **Chelan Range** Washington U.S.A.
116 M5 **Chelatna L** Alaska U.S.A.
133 D5 **Chelforó** Argentina
85 F1 **Chelia** *mt* Algeria
85 E1 **Chélif** *R* Algeria
55 C3 **Chelkakovo** Russian Federation
57 A1 **Chelkar** Kazakhstan
31 O4 **Chełm** Poland
31 L2 **Chełmno** Poland
120 J6 **Chelmsford** Ontario Canada
9 G4 **Chelmsford** England
52 E3 **Chelmuzhi** Russian Federation
31 L2 **Chełmża** Poland
99 O8 **Chelsea** Iowa U.S.A.
94 C4 **Chelsea** Michigan U.S.A.
107 P5 **Chelsea** Oklahoma U.S.A.
95 P3 **Chelsea** Vermont U.S.A.
8 D4 **Cheltenham** England
20 H6 **Chelun** France
17 G5 **Chelva** Spain
55 D3 **Chelyabinsk** Russian Federation
55 D4 **Chelyabinskaya Oblast'** *prov* Russian Federation
94 F8 **Chelyan** West Virginia U.S.A.
56 C5 **Chelyush** Russian Federation
51 K1 **Chelyuskin,Mys** *C* Russian Federation
117 M11 **Chemainus** British Columbia Canada
100 C4 **Chemawa** Oregon U.S.A.
21 J6 **Chemaze** France
87 F9 **Chemba** Mozambique
57 B6 **Chemen-i-Bit** Turkmenistan
21 N7 **Chemery** France
22 H4 **Chémery-sur-Bar** France
21 J7 **Chemillé** France
21 M6 **Chemillé-sur-Dême** France
40 B4 **Chemin** France
21 K6 **Chemiré-le-Gaudin** France
37 O2 **Chemnitz** Germany
95 R7 **Chemquasabamticook L** Maine U.S.A.
56 B4 **Chemskiy** Russian Federation
95 K4 **Chemung** *R* New York U.S.A.
116 O4 **Chena** *R* Alaska U.S.A.
74 D3 **Chenab** *R* Pakistan
85 D3 **Chenachane** *watercourse* Algeria
85 D3 **Chenachane** Algeria
116 O4 **Chena Hot Springs** Alaska U.S.A.
95 M4 **Chenango** *R* New York U.S.A.
86 G4 **Ch'ench'a** Ethiopia
22 K2 **Chênée** Belgium
18 G6 **Chénérailles** France
121 P7 **Chénéville** Quebec Canada
107 N4 **Cheney** Kansas U.S.A.
100 H2 **Cheney** Washington U.S.A.
111 D10 **Cheneyville** Louisiana U.S.A.
76 E4 **Chengalpattu** India
65 C6 **Cheng'an** China
67 B4 **Chengbihe Shuiku** *res* China
67 C3 **Chengbu** China
65 A7 **Chengcheng** China
Chengchow *see* **Zhengzhou**
65 D4 **Chengde** China
67 E1 **Chengdong Hu** *L* China
67 A1 **Chengdu** China
67 A4 **Chenggong** China
67 E5 **Chenghai** China
67 A4 **Chengjiang** China
65 D5 **Chengkou** China
67 C1 **Chengkou** China
67 C7 **Chengmai** China
65 E6 **Chengshan Jiao** *pen* China
Chengtu *see* **Chengdu**
65 C7 **Chengwu** China
65 E6 **Chengyang** China
67 F2 **Chengyang** China
65 E5 **Chengzitan** China
121 O6 **Chenier** Quebec Canada
123 N2 **Chenil,L** Quebec Canada
36 B7 **Cheniménil** France
65 D7 **Cheniu Shan** *isld* China
65 D7 **Chenjiagang** China
65 C7 **Chenliu** China
110 H1 **Chenoa** Illinois U.S.A.
21 N7 **Chenonceaux** France
40 B3 **Chenôve** France
67 G1 **Chenqian Shan** *isld* China
21 L6 **Chenu** France
67 C2 **Chenxi** China
67 D4 **Chen Xian** China
Chenying *see* **Wannian**
68 J6 **Cheo Reo** Vietnam
67 F3 **Chepan** China
46 G3 **Chepelare** Bulgaria
128 C5 **Chepén** Peru
133 D4 **Chepes** Argentina
8 D4 **Chepstow** Wales
99 Q3 **Chequamegon B** Wisconsin U.S.A.
21 M7 **Cher** *R* France
22 K3 **Cherain** Belgium
44 C2 **Cherasco** Italy
106 G3 **Cheraw** Colorado U.S.A.
111 G10 **Cheraw** Mississippi U.S.A.
112 H3 **Cheraw** South Carolina U.S.A.
20 G2 **Cherbourg** France
85 E1 **Cherchell** Algeria
52 J4 **Cherdyn'** Russian Federation
20 G6 **Chère** *R* France
52 B2 **Cheremisskoye** Russian Federation
56 F4 **Cheremkhovo** Russian Federation
55 D3 **Cheremshanka** Russian Federation
55 D1 **Cheremukhovo** Russian Federation
56 D4 **Cheremushki** Russian Federation
56 B4 **Cherepanovo** Russian Federation
54 H2 **Cherepet'** Russian Federation
52 E5 **Cherepovets** Russian Federation
52 D5 **Chereptsovo** Russian Federation
118 C5 **Cherhill** Alberta Canada
54 C3 **Cherikov** Belorussia
21 N4 **Cherisy** France
54 J8 **Cherkasskoye** Ukraine
53 F11 **Cherkessk** Russian Federation
46 G1 **Cherkovitsa** Bulgaria
55 F4 **Cherlak** Russian Federation
52 J5 **Chermoz** Russian Federation
141 K1 **Chermside** *dist* Brisbane, Qnsld Australia
116 H9 **Chernabura I** Alaska U.S.A.
46 G3 **Chernatitsa** *hills* Bulgaria
55 D2 **Chernaya** *R* Russian Federation
52 H5 **Chernaya Kholunitsa** Russian Federation
48 J2 **Chernaya Tisa** *R* Ukraine
Chernenko *see* **Sharypovo**
47 J1 **Chernevo** Bulgaria
54 C5 **Chernigov** Ukraine
59 K3 **Chernigovka** Russian Federation
116 F9 **Cherni I** Alaska U.S.A.
55 C4 **Chernikovsk** Russian Federation
47 H1 **Cherni Lom** *R* Bulgaria
46 F2 **Cherni Vrŭkh** *mt* Bulgaria
53 D8 **Chernobyl'** Ukraine
56 D4 **Chernogorsk** Russian Federation
55 C2 **Chernoistochinsk** Russian Federation
55 G4 **Chernoretskoye** Kazakhstan
55 F4 **Chernousovka** Russian Federation
52 G6 **Chernovskoye** Russian Federation
48 K2 **Chernovtsy** Ukraine
55 E2 **Chernoye** Russian Federation
55 E3 **Chernoye, Oz** *L* Russian Federation
55 C3 **Chernushka** Russian Federation
52 G3 **Chernut'yevo** Russian Federation
31 N1 **Chernyakhovsk** Russian Federation
52 J2 **Chernysheva, Gryada** *ridge* Russian Federation
58 G1 **Chernyshevsk** Russian Federation
31 O1 **Chernyshevskoye** Russian Federation
53 G10 **Chernyye Zemli** Russian Federation
55 C5 **Chernyy Otrog** Russian Federation
53 G9 **Chernyy Yar** Russian Federation
110 J7 **Cherokee** Alabama U.S.A.
99 L7 **Cherokee** Iowa U.S.A.
107 Q4 **Cherokee** Kansas U.S.A.
107 M5 **Cherokee** Oklahoma U.S.A.
109 J5 **Cherokee** Texas U.S.A.
112 D1 **Cherokee Dam** Tennessee U.S.A.
94 D10 **Cherokee L** Tennessee U.S.A.
111 B9 **Cherokee,L** Texas U.S.A.
113 K11 **Cherokee Pt** Bahamas
110 B5 **Cherokees, L O'The** Oklahoma U.S.A.
126 F1 **Cherokee Sound** Great Abaco I Bahamas
55 E2 **Cherpiya** Russian Federation
75 O6 **Cherrapunji** India
20 G4 **Cherrueix** France
137 O4 **Cherry** *isld* Santa Cruz Is
103 K2 **Cherry Cr** Nevada U.S.A.
98 E5 **Cherry Cr** South Dakota U.S.A.
94 H4 **Cherry Creek** New York U.S.A.
103 K1 **Cherry Cr.Mt** Nevada U.S.A.
95 U2 **Cherryfield** Maine U.S.A.
117 O7 **Cherry Point** Alberta Canada
107 P4 **Cherryvale** Kansas U.S.A.
95 N4 **Cherry Valley** New York U.S.A.
112 F2 **Cherryville** North Carolina U.S.A.
56 G3 **Cherskogo,Gora** *mt* Russian Federation
51 O2 **Cherskogo,Khrebet** *mts* Russian Federation
17 H4 **Cherta** Spain
54 M7 **Chertkovo** Russian Federation
54 E1 **Chertolino** Russian Federation
9 F5 **Chertsey** England
144 C5 **Chertsey** New Zealand
52 F6 **Cherusti** Russian Federation
19 O13 **Cheruy,Pt.de** France
52 G4 **Cherva** Russian Federation
48 N3 **Chervonoz-namenka** Ukraine
9 E3 **Cherwell,R** England
94 C3 **Chesaning** Michigan U.S.A.
94 E8 **Chesapeake** Ohio U.S.A.
95 L10 **Chesapeake** Virginia U.S.A.
95 L8 **Chesapeake B** U.S.A.
95 L8 **Chesapeake Beach** Maryland U.S.A.
95 M7 **Chesapeake City** Maryland U.S.A.
9 F4 **Chesham** England
8 D1 **Cheshire** *co* England
95 O4 **Cheshire** Massachusetts U.S.A.
52 G2 **Chëshskaya Guba** *B* Russian Federation
57 G5 **Cheshtebe** Tajikistan
88 B6 **Chesi,L** Zambia
8 D6 **Chesil Bank** England
120 J8 **Chesley** Ontario Canada
55 D4 **Chesma** Russian Federation
112 F2 **Chesnee** South Carolina U.S.A.
22 H5 **Chesne, le** Ardennes France
21 M4 **Chesne,le** Eure France
122 H9 **Chester** Nova Scotia Canada
8 D1 **Chester** England
110 B6 **Chester** Arkansas U.S.A.
100 D9 **Chester** California U.S.A.
95 P5 **Chester** Connecticut U.S.A.
101 O5 **Chester** Idaho U.S.A.
110 G4 **Chester** Illinois U.S.A.
95 L7 **Chester** *R* Maryland U.S.A.
95 P4 **Chester** Massachusetts U.S.A.
101 P1 **Chester** Montana U.S.A.
98 J9 **Chester** Nebraska U.S.A.
95 M6 **Chester** Pennsylvania U.S.A.
112 F3 **Chester** South Carolina U.S.A.
109 N5 **Chester** Texas U.S.A.
95 P3 **Chester** Vermont U.S.A.
94 K9 **Chester** Virginia U.S.A.
122 H9 **Chester Basin** Nova Scotia Canada
9 E1 **Chesterfield** England
101 O7 **Chesterfield** Idaho U.S.A.
110 F2 **Chesterfield** Illinois U.S.A.
112 G3 **Chesterfield** South Carolina U.S.A.
94 K9 **Chesterfield** Virginia U.S.A.
137 M5 **Chesterfield, Îles** Coral Sea
115 K5 **Chesterfield Inlet** Northwest Territories Canada
94 F7 **Chesterhill** Ohio U.S.A.
9 F2 **Chesterton** England
99 T8 **Chesterton** Indiana U.S.A.
95 L7 **Chestertown** Maryland U.S.A.
95 O3 **Chestertown** New York U.S.A.
121 P7 **Chesterville** Ontario Canada
109 O3 **Chestnut** Louisiana U.S.A.
94 H6 **Chestnut Ridge** Pennsylvania U.S.A.
144 D5 **Chest Pk** New Zealand
95 R7 **Chesuncook L** Maine U.S.A.
95 M7 **Cheswold** Delaware U.S.A.
56 C3 **Chet'** *R* Russian Federation
68 A7 **Chetamale** Andaman Is
99 P4 **Chetek** Wisconsin U.S.A.
123 L7 **Cheticamp** C Breton I, Nova Scotia
73 L6 **Chetlat** *isld* Lakshadweep Indian Oc
107 P4 **Chetopa** Kansas U.S.A.
76 A5 **Chettlatt** *isld* Indian Oc
125 P8 **Chetumal** Mexico
145 E4 **Chetwode Is** New Zealand
117 N8 **Chetwynd** British Columbia Canada
116 E6 **Chevak** Alaska U.S.A.
19 O17 **Cheval-Blanc** France
20 G7 **Chevallerais, La** Loire-Atlantique France
21 O5 **Chevilly** France
118 L6 **Cheviot** Saskatchewan Canada
144 D5 **Cheviot** New Zealand
13 F3 **Cheviot Hills** England/Scotland
141 G7 **Cheviot Ra** Queensland Australia
21 K6 **Cheviré-le-Rouge** France
20 A5 **Chèvre, C. de la** France
111 E12 **Chevreuil, Point** Louisiana U.S.A.
21 P4 **Chevreuse** France
40 E7 **Chevril,L** France
20 G7 **Chevrolière, la** France
88 D9 **Chewa** Mozambique
86 G5 **Ch'ew Bahir** *L* Ethiopia
100 H1 **Chewelah** Washington U.S.A.
8 D5 **Chew valley L** England
107 L6 **Cheyenne** Oklahoma U.S.A.
98 D5 **Cheyenne** *R* South Dakota U.S.A.
108 D4 **Cheyenne** Texas U.S.A.
98 B8 **Cheyenne** Wyoming U.S.A.
107 M3 **Cheyenne Bottoms** Kansas U.S.A.
98 A8 **Cheyenne Pass** Wyoming U.S.A.
106 H3 **Cheyenne Wells** Colorado U.S.A.
18 H8 **Cheylard, le** France
143 C10 **Cheyne B** W Australia Australia
117 M9 **Chezacut** British Columbia Canada
21 P8 **Chezal-Benoît** France
20 E5 **Chèze,la** France
75 L6 **Chhapra** India
74 H6 **Chhatarpur** India
75 L9 **Chhatrapur** India
68 G6 **Chhlong** Cambodia
68 H6 **Chhlong** *R* Cambodia
74 F7 **Chhota Udepur** India
68 G7 **Chhuk** Cambodia
116 H9 **Chiachi I** Alaska U.S.A.
67 G5 **Chia-i** Taiwan
66 D5 **Chia-jen Ts'o** *L* China
40 F7 **Chialamberto** Italy
66 D5 **Chia-man-t'e-k'a-mu Hu** *L* China
87 B9 **Chiange** Angola
68 E2 **Chiang Saen** Thailand
42 E6 **Chiani** *R* Italy
125 N9 **Chiapa del Corzo** Mexico
45 O4 **Chiaravalle** Italy
43 G10 **Chiaravalle Centrale** Italy
41 L5 **Chiareggio** Italy
41 L6 **Chiari** Italy
125 K8 **Chiautla** Mexico
44 F3 **Chiavari** Italy
41 K5 **Chiavenna** Italy
61 O10 **Chiba** *prefect* Japan
61 O10 **Chiba** Japan
61 P13 **Chibana** Okinawa
87 B9 **Chibia** Angola
68 E5 **Chi Bon Dam** Thailand
121 P3 **Chibougamau** *R* Quebec Canada
121 Q3 **Chibougamau** Quebec Canada
121 R3 **Chibougamau,Parc de** Quebec Canada
88 B8 **Chibuluma** Zambia
60 G9 **Chiburi-shima** *isld* Japan
87 F10 **Chibuto** Mozambique
87 E8 **Chibwe** Zambia
99 T8 **Chicago** Illinois U.S.A.
105 **Chicago** *conurbation* Illinois U.S.A.
99 T8 **Chicago Heights** Illinois U.S.A.
122 F5 **Chic-Chocs,Parc des** Quebec Canada
117 E7 **Chichagof I** Alaska U.S.A.
85 C2 **Chichaoua** Morocco
21 K8 **Chiché** France
65 C4 **Chicheng** China
125 P7 **Chichén Itza** *ruins* Mexico
9 F6 **Chichester** England
142 C5 **Chichester Ra** W Australia Australia
142 B5 **Chichester Ra Nat Park** W Australia Australia
61 N10 **Chichibu** Japan
61 M9 **Chichibu Tama Nat. Park** Japan
56 C3 **Chichka-Yul** *R* Russian Federation
95 K9 **Chickahominy** *R* Virginia U.S.A.
112 B3 **Chickamauga** Georgia U.S.A.
112 B2 **Chickamauga Dam** Tennessee U.S.A.
111 H10 **Chickasawhay** *R* Mississippi U.S.A.
107 O7 **Chickasaw Nat. Recreation Area** Oklahoma U.S.A.
107 N6 **Chickasha** Oklahoma U.S.A.
116 R4 **Chicken** Alaska U.S.A.
8 D5 **Chicklade** England
16 C8 **Chiclana de la Frontera** Spain
128 C5 **Chiclayo** Peru
133 D6 **Chico** *R* Argentina
71 E2 **Chico** *R* Luzon Philippines
102 C2 **Chico** California U.S.A.
100 H4 **Chico** Oregon U.S.A.
109 K2 **Chico** Texas U.S.A.
133 D3 **Chicoana** Argentina
121 M4 **Chicobi,L** Quebec Canada
87 F10 **Chicomo** Mozambique
125 K7 **Chicontepec** Mexico
87 D7 **Chicopa** *R* Angola
95 P4 **Chicopee** Massachusetts U.S.A.
121 T4 **Chicoutimi** Quebec Canada
121 T5 **Chicoutimi** *R* Quebec Canada
122 B5 **Chicoutimi, Parc des** Quebec Canada
89 G4 **Chicualacuala** Mozambique
76 D5 **Chidambaram** India
9 F5 **Chiddingford** England
109 O2 **Chidester** Arkansas U.S.A.
115 N5 **Chidley,C** Quebec Canada
100 F1 **Chief Joseph Dam** Washington U.S.A.
113 E8 **Chiefland** Florida U.S.A.
120 J8 **Chiefs Pt** Ontario Canada
67 B5 **Chiem Hoa** Vietnam
87 E7 **Chiengi** Zambia
68 D3 **Chieng-Mai** Thailand
42 F5 **Chienti** *R* Italy
44 C1 **Chieri** Italy
22 K5 **Chiers** *R* France
41 L5 **Chiesa** Italy
41 M5 **Chiese** *R* Italy
42 F6 **Chieti** Italy
22 F2 **Chièvres** Belgium
130 H5 **Chifre,Serra do** *mts* Brazil
57 G2 **Chiganak** Kazakhstan
61 N10 **Chigasaki** Japan
116 J8 **Chiginigak Vol., Mt** Alaska U.S.A.
54 D7 **Chigirin** Ukraine
116 L6 **Chigmit Mts** Alaska U.S.A.
122 H8 **Chignecto B** Nova Scotia/New Bruns Canada
116 H8 **Chignik** Alaska U.S.A.
19 Q13 **Chignin** France
121 R3 **Chigoubiche, L** Quebec Canada
87 F10 **Chigubo** Mozambique
66 E6 **Chigu Co** *L* China
9 G4 **Chigwell** England
Chihli,G. of *see* **Bo Hai**
124 F3 **Chihuahua** Mexico
131 B7 **Chihuido Medio** *pk* Argentina
57 D3 **Chiili** Kazakhstan
67 C6 **Chikan** China
107 N5 **Chikaskia** *R* Okla/Kansas U.S.A.
76 C4 **Chik Ballapur** India
52 C6 **Chikhachevo** Russian Federation
60 O3 **Chikiu-misaki** *C* Japan
76 B4 **Chikmagalur** India
56 G5 **Chikoy** *R* Russian Federation
68 G6 **Chikreng** *R* Cambodia
60 D12 **Chikugo** *R* Japan
60 D12 **Chikugo** Japan
61 M9 **Chikuma** *R* Japan
116 H6 **Chikuminuk L** Alaska U.S.A.
61 N11 **Chikura** Japan
88 E10 **Chikwawa** Malawi
68 A2 **Chi-kyaw** Burma
117 L9 **Chilanko Forks** British Columbia Canada
74 F1 **Chilas** Kashmir
83 J10 **Chilaw** Sri Lanka
128 C6 **Chilca, Pta. de** *pt* Peru
102 D2 **Chilcoot** California U.S.A.
117 M10 **Chilcotin** *R* British Columbia Canada
141 K3 **Chilcott I** Gt Barrier Reef Aust
141 K7 **Childers** Queensland Australia
111 K8 **Childersburg** Alabama U.S.A.
108 G1 **Childress** Texas U.S.A.
103 M9 **Childs** Arizona U.S.A.
113 F10 **Childs** Florida U.S.A.
133 C6 **Chile** *rep* S America
128 C5 **Chilete** Peru
76 C3 **Chilgājūr** India
9 G5 **Chilham** England
110 C3 **Chilhowee** Missouri U.S.A.
94 F10 **Chilhowie** Virginia U.S.A.
116 K6 **Chilikadrotna** *R* Alaska U.S.A.
75 L9 **Chilika Lake** India
87 E8 **Chililabombwe** Zambia
89 G2 **Chilimanzi** Zimbabwe
59 H1 **Chi-liu Ho** *R* China
117 F6 **Chilkat** *R* Alaska U.S.A.
117 M10 **Chilko** *R* British Columbia Canada
141 G3 **Chillagoe** Queensland Australia
131 A6 **Chillán** Chile
140 B5 **Chilla Well** N Terr Australia
21 P5 **Chilleurs-aux-Bois** France
99 R9 **Chillicothe** Illinois U.S.A.
110 C2 **Chillicothe** Missouri U.S.A.
94 D7 **Chillicothe** Ohio U.S.A.
109 H1 **Chillicothe** Texas U.S.A.
139 G6 **Chillingollah** Victoria Australia
100 D1 **Chilliwack** British Columbia Canada
19 P13 **Chilly** France
101 M5 **Chilly** Idaho U.S.A.
116 J6 **Chilnuk Mts** Alaska U.S.A.
133 C6 **Chiloé** *prov* Chile
135 R14 **Chiloe, I. de** Chile
88 C8 **Chilonga** Zambia
87 F8 **Chilongazi** Zambia
100 D7 **Chiloquin** Oregon U.S.A.
125 K9 **Chilpancingo** Mexico
139 H6 **Chiltern** Victoria Australia
9 F4 **Chiltern Hills** England
99 S5 **Chilton** Wisconsin U.S.A.
88 E7 **Chilumba** Malawi
67 G4 **Chi-lung** Taiwan
88 F9 **Chilwa,L** Malawi
9 E6 **Chilworth** England
125 M9 **Chimalapa** Mexico
87 F9 **Chimanimani** Zimbabwe
87 F10 **Chimanimani Nat. Park** Zimbabwe
22 G3 **Chimay** Belgium
106 E6 **Chimayo** New Mexico U.S.A.
57 A3 **Chimbay** Uzbekistan
128 C4 **Chimborazo** *mt* Ecuador
128 C5 **Chimbote** Peru
88 C8 **Chimbwin-gombi** *mt* Zambia
55 E3 **Chimeyevo** Russian Federation
57 F4 **Chimion** Kyrgyzstan
48 M4 **Chimishliya** Moldavia
57 E4 **Chimkent** Kazakhstan
123 P4 **Chimney Cove** Newfoundland Canada
108 B3 **Chimney Peak** New Mexico U.S.A.
106 E9 **Chimney Pk** New Mexico U.S.A.
83 J12 **Chimney Rocks** Seychelles
87 F9 **Chimoio** Mozambique
118 E9 **Chin** Alberta Canada
65 F7 **Chin** *isld* S Korea
58 D4 **China** *rep* E Asia
95 S2 **China** Maine U.S.A.
68 C4 **China Bakir** *R* Burma
124 G5 **Chinacates** Mexico
112 G2 **China Grove** North Carolina U.S.A.
125 L3 **Chinandega** Nicaragua
102 F9 **China Pt** California U.S.A.
109 K4 **China Spring** Texas U.S.A.
108 C6 **Chinati Mts** Texas U.S.A.
57 E4 **Chinaz** Uzbekistan
120 J7 **Chin, Cape** Ontario Canada
128 C6 **Chincha Alta** Peru
117 O6 **Chinchaga** *R* Alberta Canada
128 C6 **Chincha, Is** Peru
141 K7 **Chinchilla** Queensland Australia
17 F6 **Chinchilla de Monte Aragón** Spain
128 C4 **Chinchipe** *R* Ecuador/Peru
16 E4 **Chinchón** Spain
95 M9 **Chincoteague** Virginia U.S.A.
95 M8 **Chincoteague B** Maryland U.S.A.
87 G9 **Chinde** Mozambique
73 P4 **Chindwin** *R* Burma
61 P14 **Chinen** Okinawa
88 E8 **Chinengue** Mozambique
66 B4 **Chinese Turkestan** *reg* Xinjiang Uygur Zizhiqu China
67 D1 **Ching-Chiang Res** China
Chinghai *prov see* **Qinghai** *prov*
55 B5 **Chingirlau** Kazakhstan
88 A8 **Chingola** Zambia
87 B8 **Chingoroi** Angola
87 C8 **Chinguai** Angola
73 P4 **Chin Hills** Burma
88 C10 **Chinhoyi** Zimbabwe
116 L8 **Chiniak,C** Alaska U.S.A.
Chining *see* **Jining**
74 E3 **Chiniot** Pakistan
124 E4 **Chinipas** Mexico
116 L7 **Chinitna B** Alaska U.S.A.
65 G7 **Chinju** S Korea
86 D4 **Chinko** *R* Cent Afr Republic
103 P5 **Chinle** Arizona U.S.A.
103 P5 **Chinle V** Arizona U.S.A.
103 P5 **Chinle Wash** Arizona U.S.A.
67 F4 **Chin-men** Taiwan
143 C10 **Chinocup, L** W Australia Australia
21 L7 **Chinon** France
118 G7 **Chinook** Alberta Canada
101 Q1 **Chinook** Montana U.S.A.
100 D3 **Chinook Pass** Washington U.S.A.
103 M7 **Chino Valley** Arizona U.S.A.
87 F8 **Chinsali** Zambia
88 D7 **Chinsali** Zambia
68 A1 **Chin State** Burma
75 P8 **Chin State** *prov* Burma
76 E1 **Chintalnar** India
88 E7 **Chintheche** Malawi
126 G10 **Chinú** Colombia
22 J4 **Chiny** Belgium
55 G3 **Chinyavino** Russian Federation
42 E3 **Chioggia** Italy
Chios *isld see* **Khíos** *isld*
88 D8 **Chipata** Zambia
87 E9 **Chipepo** Zambia
88 D9 **Chipera** Mozambique
88 E10 **Chiperone** *mt* Mozambique
119 T1 **Chipewyan,L** Manitoba Canada
117 R7 **Chipewyan Lake** Alberta Canada
87 E8 **Chipili** Zambia
65 C6 **Chiping** China
87 F10 **Chipinge** Zimbabwe
117 Q9 **Chip Lake** Alberta Canada
111 L11 **Chipley** Florida U.S.A.
111 M9 **Chipley** Georgia U.S.A.
74 E10 **Chiplun** India
122 G7 **Chipman** New Brunswick Canada
120 D3 **Chipman L** Ontario Canada
88 E8 **Chipoka** Malawi
111 L11 **Chipola** *R* Florida U.S.A.
88 A9 **Chiposhya, L** Zambia
68 G7 **Chi Pou** Cambodia
121 L9 **Chippawa** Ontario Canada
8 D5 **Chippenham** England
99 L4 **Chippewa** *R* Minnesota U.S.A.
99 P5 **Chippewa Falls** Wisconsin U.S.A.
99 P4 **Chippewa Lake** Wisconsin U.S.A.
13 F6 **Chipping** England
9 E3 **Chipping Campden** England
9 E4 **Chipping Norton** England
8 D4 **Chipping Sodbury** England
46 F1 **Chiprovtsi** Bulgaria
128 C6 **Chiquian** Peru
128 D2 **Chiquinquirá** Colombia
131 F6 **Chiquita, L. Mar** Buenos Aires Argentina
128 F7 **Chiquitos, Llanos de** Bolivia
128 B4 **Chira** *R* Peru
76 E3 **Chirala** India
87 F9 **Chiramba** Mozambique
128 C3 **Chirambirá, Pta** *pt* Colombia
77 J2 **Chiras** Afghanistan
57 E4 **Chirchik** Uzbekistan
87 F10 **Chiredzi** Zimbabwe
89 G3 **Chiredzi** *R* Zimbabwe
109 N4 **Chireno** Texas U.S.A.
111 B10 **Chireno** Texas U.S.A.
84 E5 **Chirfa** Niger
103 P9 **Chirica Hua Nat.Mon** Arizona U.S.A.
103 P10 **Chiricahua Pk** Arizona U.S.A.
126 H10 **Chiriguaná** Colombia
116 K9 **Chirikof I** Alaska U.S.A.
75 P8 **Chiringa** Bangladesh
125 N5 **Chiriqui,G.de** Panama
75 K7 **Chirmiri** India
47 J1 **Chirnogeni** Romania
13 F2 **Chirnside** Scotland
15 F5 **Chirnside** Borders Scotland
88 E10 **Chiromo** Malawi
46 G2 **Chirpan** Bulgaria
Chirua, L *see* **Chilwa, L**
87 E9 **Chirundu** Zimbabwe
22 D4 **Chiry-Ourscamps** France
88 B9 **Chisamba** Zambia
116 R5 **Chisana** Alaska U.S.A.
116 Q6 **Chisana Glacier** Alaska U.S.A.
44 B2 **Chisane** *R* Italy
119 R4 **Chisel Lake** Manitoba Canada
88 D6 **Chisenga** Malawi
55 C4 **Chishmy** Russian Federation
118 C4 **Chisholm** Alberta Canada
95 R2 **Chisholm** Maine U.S.A.
99 O2 **Chisholm** Minnesota U.S.A.
74 E4 **Chishtian Mandi** Pakistan
67 B2 **Chishui** China
67 F4 **Chishui** China
67 B3 **Chishui He** *R* China
88 B7 **Chisi** *isld* Zambia
Chisimaio *see* **Kismaayo**
87 F8 **Chisimba Falls** Zambia
Chişinău *see* **Kishinev**
48 G4 **Chişineu-Criş** Romania
108 D6 **Chisos Mts** Texas U.S.A.
108 C5 **Chispa Cr** Texas U.S.A.
116 P5 **Chistochina** Alaska U.S.A.
55 G4 **Chisto-ozernoye** Russian Federation
52 H6 **Chistopol** Russian Federation
55 E4 **Chistopol'ye** Kazakhstan
55 G4 **Chistovo** Russian Federation
55 F4 **Chistyakovskoye** Kazakhstan
88 E8 **Chisumulu** *isld* Mozambique
58 F1 **Chita** Russian Federation
87 B9 **Chitado** Angola
116 L4 **Chitanana** *R* Alaska U.S.A.
58 C5 **Chi-t'ang** China
61 K11 **Chita wan** *G* Japan
52 G4 **Chitayevo** Russian Federation
118 K5 **Chitek** Saskatchewan Canada
119 S6 **Chitek L** Manitoba Canada
87 C8 **Chitembo** Angola
45 L4 **Chitignano** Italy
116 P6 **Chitina** Alaska U.S.A.
116 Q6 **Chitina** *R* Alaska U.S.A.
56 G5 **Chitinskaya Oblast'** *prov* Russian Federation
60 P3 **Chitose** Japan
76 C3 **Chitradurga** India
74 J6 **Chitrakut** India
74 D1 **Chitral** Pakistan
125 O6 **Chitré** Panama
75 O7 **Chittagong** Bangladesh
75 M7 **Chittaranjan** India
74 F6 **Chittaurgarh** India
143 B9 **Chittering** W Australia Australia
76 D4 **Chittoor** India
76 C5 **Chittur** India
89 G1 **Chitungwiza** Zimbabwe
88 F8 **Chiulézi** *R* Mozambique
87 D9 **Chiume** Angola
42 D2 **Chiusa** Italy
42 D5 **Chiusi** Italy
45 L4 **Chiusi di Verna** Italy
87 G8 **Chiuta, L** Malawi
88 E9 **Chiuta,L** Mozambique
17 G5 **Chiva** Spain
40 G7 **Chivasso** Italy
124 C4 **Chivato,Pta** *C* Mexico
128 D7 **Chivay** Peru
87 B9 **Chivemba** Angola
89 G2 **Chivhu** Zimbabwe
131 E5 **Chivilcoy** Argentina
106 H3 **Chivington** Colorado U.S.A.
22 F4 **Chivy** France
67 D6 **Chixi** China
125 O10 **Chixoy** *R* Guatemala
89 E1 **Chizarira Hills** Zimbabwe
52 F2 **Chizha** Russian Federation
Chizhou *see* **Guichi**
60 H10 **Chizu** Japan
55 F4 **Chkalovo** Kazakhstan
57 H6 **Chkalovsk** Tajikistan
52 D2 **Chkalovskiy** Russian Federation
31 J5 **Chlumec nad Cidlinou** Czechoslovakia
31 M5 **Chmielnik** Poland
65 F5 **Cho** *isld* N Korea
65 G7 **Ch'o** *isld* S Korea
68 G5 **Choam Ksan** Cambodia
131 B3 **Choapo,R** Chile
87 D9 **Chobe Nat. Park** Botswana
9 F5 **Chobham** England
68 G2 **Cho Bo** Vietnam
31 J5 **Choceň** Czechoslovakia
121 O5 **Chochocouane** *R* Quebec Canada
67 B6 **Cho Chu** Vietnam
31 J4 **Chocianów** Poland
128 C2 **Chocó** *div* Colombia
103 K8 **Chocolate Mts** Arizona U.S.A.
103 J8 **Chocolate Mts** California U.S.A.
95 Q3 **Chocorua** New Hampshire U.S.A.
112 K2 **Chocowinity** North Carolina U.S.A.
107 N6 **Choctaw** Oklahoma U.S.A.
111 K11 **Choctawhatchee B** Florida U.S.A.
37 O3 **Chodov** Czechoslovakia
31 K3 **Chodzież** Poland
133 D5 **Choele Choel** Argentina
88 C9 **Chofombo** Mozambique
68 H7 **Cho Giua** Vietnam
119 N5 **Choiceland** Saskatchewan Canada
137 M3 **Choiseul** *isld* Solomon Is
133 F8 **Choiseul Sd** Falkland Is
19 Q12 **Choisy** France
22 D5 **Choisy-au-Bac** France
124 E4 **Choix** Mexico
31 H3 **Chojna** Poland
31 K2 **Chojnice** Poland
31 J4 **Chojnów** Poland
61 O6 **Chōkai-san** *mt* Japan
86 G3 **Ch'ok'ē Mts** Ethiopia
98 K4 **Chokio** Minnesota U.S.A.
57 G3 **Choknar** Kazakhstan
57 H4 **Choktal** Kyrgyzstan
51 O1 **Chokurdakh** Russian Federation
87 F10 **Chókwè** Mozambique
102 D6 **Cholame** California U.S.A.
102 D6 **Cholame Cr** California U.S.A.
133 C4 **Cholchagua** *prov* Chile
21 J7 **Cholet** France
13 F3 **Chollerford** England
68 H7 **Cho Lon** Vietnam
57 H4 **Cholpon** Kyrgyzstan
57 H4 **Cholpon-Ata** Kyrgyzstan
125 K8 **Cholula** Mexico
125 L3 **Choluleca** Honduras
87 E9 **Choma** Zambia
68 F7 **Chomna** Cambodia
68 G2 **Cho Moi** Vietnam
75 N5 **Chomo Lhari** *mt* Bhutan/China
68 D3 **Chom Thong** Thailand
37 P3 **Chomutov** Czechoslovakia
56 H1 **Chona** *R* Russian Federation
68 E6 **Chon Buri** Thailand
68 E4 **Chon Daen** Thailand
128 B4 **Chone** Ecuador
67 F3 **Chong'an** China
67 G1 **Chongde** China
65 H4 **Ch'ŏngjin** N Korea
65 F5 **Chŏngju** N Korea
65 G6 **Ch'ŏngju** S Korea
68 F6 **Chong Kal** Cambodia
65 C4 **Chongli** China
67 G1 **Chongming** China
67 G1 **Chongming Dao** *isld* China
67 A1 **Chongqing** China
67 B2 **Chongqing** China
67 E3 **Chongren** China
67 E4 **Chongshi** China
88 B9 **Chongwe** *R* Zambia
67 E2 **Chongyang** China
67 F3 **Chongyang Xi** *R* China
67 E4 **Chongyi** China
56 D5 **Chongyz-Tayga, Gora** *mt* Russian Federation
68 H1 **Chongzuo** China
65 G7 **Chŏnju** S Korea
133 C6 **Chonos,Arch.de los** *islds* Chile
125 N9 **Chontalpa** Mexico
68 H7 **Chon Thanh** Vietnam
75 M4 **Cho Oyu** *pk* China/Nepal
48 G2 **Chop** Ukraine
13 G5 **Chop Gate** England
68 H7 **Cho Phuoc Hai** Vietnam
130 D9 **Chopim, R** Brazil
130 D9 **Chopimzinho** Brazil
95 M8 **Choptank** *R* Maryland U.S.A.
56 F3 **Chora** *R* Russian Federation
68 G1 **Cho Ra** Vietnam
33 T7 **Chorin** Germany
16 E5 **Chorito, Sa. del** *mts* Spain
57 F5 **Chorku** Kyrgyzstan
13 F6 **Chorley** England
131 B2 **Choros** *R* Chile
131 B2 **Choros,I.de los** Chile
31 O2 **Choroszcz** Poland
141 G6 **Chorregon** Queensland Australia
128 C6 **Chorrillos** Peru
130 G10 **Chorrochó** Brazil
48 K1 **Chortkov** Ukraine
31 M2 **Chorzele** Poland
31 L5 **Chorzów** Poland
Chōsen-kaikyō *see* **Nishi-suido**
61 O10 **Chōshi** Japan
133 C5 **Chos Malal** Argentina
65 G5 **Choson-Man** *B* N Korea
31 J2 **Choszczno** Poland
128 C5 **Chota** Peru
75 K7 **Chota Nagpur** *reg* India
101 N2 **Choteau** Montana U.S.A.
107 P5 **Choteau** Oklahoma U.S.A.
31 J6 **Chotěbor** Czechoslovakia
37 P4 **Chotěšov** Czechoslovakia
85 E2 **Chott ech Chergui** *salt lake* Algeria
85 E1 **Chott El Hodna** *marsh* Algeria
85 F2 **Chott El Jerid** *salt flats* Tunisia
85 F2 **Chott Melrhir** *salt flats* Algeria
21 L7 **Chouzé-sur-Loire** France
21 N6 **Chouzy-sur-Cisse** France
112 L1 **Chowan** *R* North Carolina U.S.A.
102 D4 **Chowchilla** California U.S.A.
138 F5 **Chowilla Dam** South Australia Australia
117 O9 **Chown,Mt** Alberta Canada
58 F2 **Choybalsan** Mongolia
40 C3 **Choye** France
65 A1 **Choyr** Mongolia
31 K6 **Chřiby** *dist* Czechoslovakia
48 D1 **Chřiby** Czechoslovakia
109 L5 **Chriesman** Texas U.S.A.
99 T10 **Chrisman** Illinois U.S.A.
89 G6 **Chrissiesmeer** S Africa
144 D5 **Christabel, L** New Zealand
127 P6 **Christchurch** *parish* Barbados
9 E6 **Christchurch** England
144 B4 **Christchurch** New Zealand
116 P3 **Christian** Alaska U.S.A.
127 K2 **Christiana** Jamaica
89 D6 **Christiana** S Africa
95 L7 **Christiana** Pennsylvania U.S.A.
115 N3 **Christian,C** Northwest Territories Canada
120 K8 **Christian I** Ontario Canada
94 C6 **Christiansburg** Ohio U.S.A.
110 M1 **Christiansburg** Ohio U.S.A.
94 G9 **Christiansburg** Virginia U.S.A.
28 C6 **Christiansfeld** Denmark
115 O4 **Christianshåb** Greenland
28 C4 **Christianshede** Denmark
27 H16 **Christiansø** *isld* Denmark
127 M6 **Christiansted** Virgin Is
69 C8 **Christie I** Burma
119 V2 **Christie L** Manitoba Canada
101 Q2 **Christina** Montana U.S.A.
118 G3 **Christina,L** Alberta Canada
100 G1 **Christina L** British Columbia Canada
144 B6 **Christina, Mt** New Zealand
118 G2 **Christina R** Alberta Canada
109 J7 **Christine** Texas U.S.A.
142 F4 **Christmas Creek** W Australia Australia
Christmas I *see* **Kiritimati**
83 M9 **Christmas I** Indian Oc
120 H2 **Christopher Falls** Ontario Canada
143 G6 **Christopher, L** W Australia
108 G4 **Christoval** Texas U.S.A.
131 H3 **Christovão Pereira,Pte** Brazil
106 D4 **Chromo** Colorado U.S.A.
31 J6 **Chrudim** Czechoslovakia
31 L5 **Chrzanow** Poland
57 G3 **Chu** Kazakhstan
57 F3 **Chu** *R* Kazakhstan/Kyrgyzstan
125 O10 **Chuacús,Sa.de** *ra* Guatemala
67 F2 **Chuankeng** China
67 G1 **Chuansha** China
57 J1 **Chubartau** Kazakhstan
103 J7 **Chubbuck** California U.S.A.
61 L9 **Chubu-Sangaku Nat. Park** Japan
133 D6 **Chubut** *R* Argentina
133 D6 **Chubut** *prov* Argentina
Chuchow *see* **Zhuzhou**
103 J8 **Chuckwalla Mts** California U.S.A.
133 E4 **Chucul** Argentina
37 P5 **Chudenice** Czechoslovakia
55 D4 **Chudinovo** Russian Federation
8 C6 **Chudleigh** England
141 G4 **Chudleigh Park** Queensland Australia
120 K6 **Chudleigh River Valley** Ontario Canada
52 D5 **Chudovo** Russian Federation
Chudskoye, Ozero *see* **Peipus, L**
116 M7 **Chugach Is** Alaska U.S.A.
116 O6 **Chugach Mts** Alaska U.S.A.
60 F11 **Chūgoku sanchi** *mts* Japan
Chuguchak *see* **Tacheng**
56 C4 **Chugunash** Russian Federation
55 F3 **Chugunly** Russian Federation
54 H7 **Chuguyev** Ukraine
98 B8 **Chugwater** Wyoming U.S.A.
98 B8 **Chugwater Cr** Wyoming U.S.A.
103 N9 **Chuichu** Arizona U.S.A.
59 L1 **Chukchagirskoye, Oz** *L* Russian Federation
147 O3 **Chukchi Sea** Arctic Oc
52 F5 **Chukhloma** Russian Federation
52 F5 **Chukhlomskoye, Oz** *L* Russian Federation
116 A3 **Chukotskiy Poluostrov** Russian Federation
56 G2 **Chula** *R* Russian Federation
112 D6 **Chula** Georgia U.S.A.
99 N10 **Chula** Missouri U.S.A.
94 K9 **Chula** Virginia U.S.A.
57 E3 **Chulak-Kurgan** Kazakhstan
52 G3 **Chulasa** Russian Federation
102 G9 **Chula Vista** California U.S.A.
116 N5 **Chulitna** *R* Alaska U.S.A.
51 M3 **Chul'man** Russian Federation
8 C6 **Chulmleigh** England
128 B5 **Chulucanas** Peru
58 D2 **Chuluut Gol** *R* Mongolia
56 B3 **Chulym** Russian Federation
56 D3 **Chulym** *R* Russian Federation
56 C5 **Chulyshman** *R* Russian Federation
56 C5 **Chulyshmunskiy Khrebet** *mts* Russian Federation
74 H2 **Chumar** Kashmir
133 D3 **Chumbicha** Argentina
56 C6 **Chumek** Kazakhstan
47 H2 **Chumerna** *mt* Bulgaria
59 L1 **Chumikan** Russian Federation
68 D7 **Chumphon** Thailand
68 E5 **Chum Saeng** Thailand
111 J11 **Chumuckla** Florida U.S.A.
56 B4 **Chumysh** *R* Russian Federation
56 E2 **Chuna** *R* Russian Federation
67 F2 **Chun'an** China
65 G6 **Ch'unch'ŏn** S Korea
111 H11 **Chunchula** Alabama U.S.A.
75 N7 **Chunchura** India
Chungking *see* **Chongqing**
66 C6 **Chung-pa** China
68 K3 **Chung-yüan** China
65 H3 **Chunhua** China
56 E1 **Chunku** *R* Russian Federation
58 D6 **Chün-lien** China
67 C1 **Chunmuying** China
83 K8 **Chunnakam** Sri Lanka
56 E2 **Chunoyar** Russian Federation
56 E1 **Chunya** *R* Russian Federation
88 D6 **Chunya** Tanzania
59 J3 **Chunyang** China
69 G8 **Chuoi,Hon** *isld* Vietnam
52 D2 **Chupa** Russian Federation
127 O1 **Chupara Pt** Trinidad
128 D6 **Chuquibambilla** Peru
133 D2 **Chuquicamata** Chile
133 E2 **Chuquisaca** *dept* Bolivia
52 H6 **Chur** Russian Federation
41 L4 **Chur** Switzerland
52 J5 **Churaki** Russian Federation
51 N2 **Churapcha** Russian Federation
55 C3 **Churayevo** Russian Federation
119 Q8 **Churchbridge** Saskatchewan Canada
95 L8 **Church Creek** Maryland U.S.A.
94 E10 **Church Hill** Tennessee U.S.A.
115 N7 **Churchill** *R* Labrador, Nfld Canada
115 K6 **Churchill** Manitoba Canada
118 L3 **Churchill** *R* Saskatchewan Canada
8 D5 **Churchill** England
101 M7 **Churchill** Idaho U.S.A.
118 J2 **Churchill L** Saskatchewan Canada
95 R7 **Churchill L** Maine U.S.A.
146 D11 **Churchill Mts** Antarctica
117 L6 **Churchill Pk** British Columbia Canada
119 W1 **Churchill R** Manitoba Canada
8 C6 **Churchingford** England
111 D11 **Church Point** Louisiana U.S.A.
122 F9 **Church Pt** Nova Scotia Canada
98 G1 **Churchs Ferry** North Dakota U.S.A.
8 D2 **Church Stretton** England
94 K3 **Churchville** New York U.S.A.
94 H8 **Churchville** Virginia U.S.A.
99 M7 **Churdan** Iowa U.S.A.
56 D5 **Chureg-Tag,Gora** *mt* Russian Federation
41 K3 **Churfirsten** *mt* Switzerland
75 K6 **Churk** India
52 F3 **Churkino** Russian Federation
74 F4 **Churu** India
94 B5 **Churubusco** Indiana U.S.A.
128 E1 **Churuguara** Venezuela
52 F4 **Chushevitsy** Russian Federation
106 B5 **Chuska Mts** Ariz/New Mex U.S.A.
55 C2 **Chusovaya** *R* Russian Federation
55 C2 **Chusovoy** Russian Federation
52 J4 **Chusovskoy** Russian Federation
57 F4 **Chust** Uzbekistan
122 D4 **Chute-aux-Outardes** Quebec Canada
122 A4 **Chute-des-Passes** Quebec Canada
134 F7 **Chuuk Is** Caroline Is Pacific Oc
52 J4 **Chuval** Russian Federation
52 G6 **Chuvashskaya Respublika** Russian Federation
67 F1 **Chu Xian** China
61 N9 **Chūzenji-ko** *L* Japan
37 P3 **Chyše** Czechoslovakia
88 F3 **Chyulu Ra** Kenya
70 M9 **Ciamis** Java
45 N6 **Ciampino** Italy
70 L9 **Cianjur** Java
42 C4 **Ciano d'Enza** Italy
103 O7 **Cibecue** Arizona U.S.A.
70 L9 **Cibinong** Java
48 H5 **Cibinului,Munţii** *mts* Romania
103 K8 **Cibola** Arizona U.S.A.
70 L9 **Ci Buni** *R* Java
124 D2 **Cibuta** Mexico
42 F3 **Čičarija** *mt* Croatia

45 R8 **Cicciano** Italy
94 A6 **Cicero** Indiana U.S.A.
95 L3 **Cicero** New York U.S.A.
129 L6 **Cicero Dantas** Brazil
46 E1 **Čicevac** Serbia Yugoslavia
67 G1 **Cicheng** China
17 F2 **Cidacos** *R* Spain
70 L9 **Cidaun** Java
78 D1 **Cide** Turkey
31 J5 **Cidlina** *R* Czechoslovakia
31 M3 **Ciéchanow** Poland
31 N3 **Ciechanowiec** Poland
31 L3 **Ciechocinek** Poland
126 E4 **Ciego de Avila** Cuba
70 L9 **Ciemas** Java
128 D1 **Ciénaga** Colombia
126 G10 **Ciénaga de Oro** Colombia
126 G10 **Ciénaga Grande** *marshy lake* Colombia
106 E9 **Cienega** New Mexico U.S.A.
124 H5 **Ciénega del Carmen** Mexico
124 H5 **Cieneguilla** Mexico
124 D3 **Cieneguita** Mexico
126 D3 **Cienfuegos** Cuba
22 J3 **Ciergnon** Belgium
31 O5 **Cieszanow** Poland
31 L6 **Cieszyn** Poland
17 G6 **Cieza** Spain
31 M6 **Ciężkowice** Poland
47 M10 **Çiftalan** Turkey
47 L5 **Çifteler** Turkey
17 F4 **Cifuentes** Spain
70 K9 **Cigeulis** Java
40 H7 **Cigliano** Italy
17 F5 **Cigüela** *R* Spain
78 D2 **Cihanbeyli** Turkey
124 G8 **Cihuatlán** Mexico
16 D5 **Cijara, Embalse de** *res* Spain
70 M9 **Cikalong** Java
46 D4 **Çikës, Mal i** *mt* Albania
70 M9 **Cilacap** Java
70 L9 **Cilangkahan** Java
78 J1 **Cildir G** *L* Turkey
67 D2 **Cili** China
8 C3 **Cilycwm** Wales
103 J6 **Cima** California U.S.A.
70 L9 **Cimahi** Java
70 M9 **Ci Manuk** *R* Java
106 C3 **Cimarron** Colorado U.S.A.
107 K4 **Cimarron** Kansas U.S.A.
106 F5 **Cimarron** New Mexico U.S.A.
107 M5 **Cimarron** *R* Okla/Kansas U.S.A.
31 O2 **Cimochy** Poland
42 D4 **Cimone, M** *mt* Italy
48 H4 **Cîmpeni** Romania
48 H4 **Cîmpia Turzii** Romania
48 K5 **Cîmpina** Romania
48 J5 **Cîmpulung** Romania
48 K3 **Cîmpulung Moldovenesc** Romania
48 K4 **Cîmpuri** Romania
128 E2 **Cinaruco** *R* Venezuela
18 F10 **Cinca** *R* Spain
42 H5 **Cincar** *mt* Bosnia-Herzegovina
99 O9 **Cincinnati** Iowa U.S.A.
94 C7 **Cincinnati** Ohio U.S.A.
95 M4 **Cincinnatus** New York U.S.A.
126 E4 **Cinco-Balas, Cayo** *islds* Cuba
116 H8 **Cinder** *R* Alaska U.S.A.
8 D4 **Cinderford** England
48 K5 **Cîndeşti** Romania
48 H5 **Cîndrelu** *mt* Romania
47 J7 **Çine** *R* Turkey
47 J7 **Çine** Turkey
22 J3 **Ciney** Belgium
16 B3 **Cinfães** Portugal
70 F5 **Cinoko, Tanjong** *C* Sulawesi
21 L7 **Cinq Mars** France
68 A7 **Cinque I** Andaman Is
129 J5 **Cinta,Serra da** *mts* Brazil
85 A4 **Cintra, G.de** Western Sahara
45 O6 **Ciociaria** Italy
48 J6 **Ciolăneşti** Romania
70 M9 **Cipatuja** Java
67 E3 **Ciping** China
21 K5 **Ciral** France
17 G4 **Cirat** Spain
146 E12 **Circe, Dome** *ice dome* Antarctica
43 E7 **Circeo, M** *mt* Italy
43 E7 **Circeo, M** *lighthouse* Italy
116 P4 **Circle** Alaska U.S.A.
98 A2 **Circle** Montana U.S.A.
94 E7 **Circleville** Ohio U.S.A.
103 M3 **Circleville** Utah U.S.A.
70 M9 **Cirebon** Java
9 E4 **Cirencester** England
69 E13 **Cirenti** Sumatra
21 P3 **Cires-les-Mello** France
19 K4 **Cirey** France
36 B6 **Cirey-sur-Vezouse** France
44 C1 **Ciriè** Italy
18 E8 **Ciron** *R* France
21 N8 **Ciron** France
44 G3 **Cisa, Passo di** Italy
99 S9 **Cisco** Illinois U.S.A.
109 J3 **Cisco** Texas U.S.A.
103 P3 **Cisco** Utah U.S.A.
89 E9 **Ciskei** *homeland* S Africa
48 K5 **Cislău** Romania
33 N4 **Cismar** Germany
31 N6 **Cisna** Poland
48 J5 **Cisnadie** Romania
110 H3 **Cisne** Illinois U.S.A.
128 C2 **Cisneros** Colombia
133 C6 **Cisnes** *R* Chile
70 L9 **Cisompet** Java
100 D3 **Cispus** *R* Washington U.S.A.
100 D3 **Cispus Pass** Washington U.S.A.
21 N6 **Cisse** *R* France
37 O3 **Čistá** Czechoslovakia
109 K6 **Cistern** Texas U.S.A.
45 N6 **Cisterna di Latina** Italy
16 D2 **Cistierna** Spain
129 G3 **Citare** *R* Brazil
125 L8 **Citlaltépetl** Mexico
113 E8 **Citra** Florida U.S.A.
111 H10 **Citronelle** Alabama U.S.A.
87 C12 **Citrusdal** S Africa
42 D3 **Cittadella** Italy
42 E6 **Citta della Pieve** Italy
42 E5 **Città di Castello** Italy
43 G10 **Cittanova** Italy
142 A1 **City Beach** *dist* Perth, W Aust Australia
113 G9 **City Point** Florida U.S.A.
48 K5 **Ciucaşu** *mt* Romania
48 H4 **Ciucea** Romania
48 K4 **Ciucului Muntii** *mt* Romania
108 G6 **Ciudad Acuña** Mexico
125 J8 **Ciudad Altamirano** Mexico
128 F2 **Ciudad Bolívar** Venezuela
109 J9 **Ciudad Camargo** Mexico
124 G4 **Ciudad Camargo** Mexico
125 O8 **Ciudad del Carmen** Mexico
124 G3 **Ciudad Delicias** Mexico
17 K4 **Ciudadela** Spain
127 N10 **Ciudad Guayana** Venezuela
124 F3 **Ciudad Guerrero** Mexico
124 H8 **Ciudad Guzmán** Mexico
125 N10 **Ciudad Hidalgo** Mexico
106 D10 **Ciudad Juárez** Mexico
124 H5 **Ciudad Lerdo** Mexico
125 L6 **Ciudad Madero** Mexico
125 K6 **Ciudad Mante** Mexico
124 E4 **Ciudad Obregón** Mexico
128 F2 **Ciudad Piar** Venezuela
16 E6 **Ciudad Real** *prov* Spain
16 E6 **Ciudad Real** Spain
16 C4 **Ciudad Rodrigo** Spain
125 N10 **Ciudad Tecún Umán** Mexico
Ciudad Trujillo *see* **Santo Domingo** Dominican Rep
125 K6 **Ciudad Victoria** Mexico
48 G4 **Ciumeghiu** Romania
48 L5 **Ciuşlea** Romania
47 K5 **Civan Dağı** *mt* Turkey
42 E2 **Cividale del F** Italy
42 E6 **Civita Castellana** Italy
42 F5 **Civitanova Marche** Italy
44 L5 **Civitavecchia** *lighthouse* Italy
45 L3 **Civitella di Romagna** Italy
45 O6 **Civitella Roveto** Italy
44 B1 **Civrari Monte** Italy
18 F6 **Civray** France
21 P8 **Civray** Cher France
47 K6 **Çivril** Turkey
67 G1 **Cixi** China
65 C6 **Ci Xian** China
78 J3 **Cizre** Turkey
12 C2 **Clachan** Scotland
100 C4 **Clackamas** *R* Oregon U.S.A.
143 B9 **Clackline** W Australia Australia
Clackmannon *co see* **Central** *reg*
9 H4 **Clacton-on-Sea** England
12 C1 **Cladich** Scotland
107 M3 **Claflin** Kansas U.S.A.
100 J1 **Clagstone** Idaho U.S.A.
20 E6 **Claie,R** France
21 L8 **Clain** *R* France
119 N6 **Clair** Saskatchewan Canada
6 J2 **Clair** *oil rig* North Sea
68 G1 **Claire** *R* Vietnam
98 J4 **Claire City** South Dakota U.S.A.
117 R6 **Claire, L** Alberta Canada
108 G2 **Clairemont** Texas U.S.A.
94 H6 **Clairton** Pennsylvania U.S.A.
19 J6 **Clairvaux** France
21 N8 **Claise** *R* France
100 A1 **Clallam Bay** Washington U.S.A.
18 H5 **Clamecy** France
102 G2 **Clan Alpine Mts** Nevada U.S.A.
101 N3 **Clancy** Montana U.S.A.
144 C6 **Clandeboye** New Zealand
118 F5 **Clandonald** Alberta Canada
9 E4 **Clanfield** England
111 K9 **Clanton** Alabama U.S.A.
119 S8 **Clanwilliam** Manitoba Canada
87 C12 **Clanwilliam** S Africa
12 C2 **Claonaig** Scotland
9 F5 **Clapham** England
13 F5 **Clapham** N Yorks England
44 B3 **Clapier, Mt** France
141 F4 **Clara** *R* Queensland Australia
14 D3 **Clara** Ireland
113 D8 **Clara** Florida U.S.A.
99 L5 **Clara City** Minnesota U.S.A.
68 C7 **Clara I** Burma
141 F4 **Claraville** Queensland Australia
138 E5 **Clare** South Australia Australia
9 G3 **Clare** England
14 C3 **Clare** *R* Ireland
14 C4 **Clare** *co* Ireland
99 M7 **Clare** Iowa U.S.A.
94 C3 **Clare** Michigan U.S.A.
14 C4 **Clarecastle** Ireland
139 G5 **Clare Corner** New South Wales Australia
14 A3 **Clare I** Ireland
142 A2 **Claremont** *dist* Perth, W Aust Australia
127 K2 **Claremont** Jamaica
95 P3 **Claremont** New Hampshire U.S.A.
98 H4 **Claremont** South Dakota U.S.A.
141 G2 **Claremont Is** Gt Barrier Reef Australia
14 C3 **Claremorris** Ireland
139 L3 **Clarence** *R* New South Wales Australia
144 D5 **Clarence** New Zealand
99 P8 **Clarence** Iowa U.S.A.
99 O10 **Clarence** Missouri U.S.A.
110 D2 **Clarence Cannon Res** Missouri U.S.A.
146 D3 **Clarence I** South Shetland Is Antarctica
133 C8 **Clarence,I** Chile
140 B1 **Clarence Str** N Terr Australia
117 G8 **Clarence Str** Alaska U.S.A.
126 G3 **Clarence Town** Long I Bahamas
121 O8 **Clarendon** Ontario Canada
127 K3 **Clarendon** *parish* Jamaica
110 E7 **Clarendon** Arkansas U.S.A.
94 H5 **Clarendon** Pennsylvania U.S.A.
108 G1 **Clarendon** Texas U.S.A.
123 S5 **Clarenville** Newfoundland Canada
118 D8 **Claresholm** Alberta Canada
19 P16 **Claret** France
98 B6 **Clareton** Wyoming U.S.A.
32 H9 **Clarholz** Germany
141 F4 **Clarina** *R* Queensland Australia
99 L9 **Clarinda** Iowa U.S.A.
127 M10 **Clarines** Venezuela
94 H5 **Clarington** Pennsylvania U.S.A.
99 N7 **Clarion** Iowa U.S.A.
94 H5 **Clarion** *R* Pennsylvania U.S.A.
94 H5 **Clarion** Pennsylvania U.S.A.
126 H4 **Clarion Bank** Bahamas
145 E2 **Claris** New Zealand
107 O7 **Clarita** Oklahoma U.S.A.
102 H8 **Clark** *L* California U.S.A.
101 T9 **Clark** Colorado U.S.A.
110 D2 **Clark** Missouri U.S.A.
98 J5 **Clark** South Dakota U.S.A.
101 N4 **Clark Canyon Res** Montana U.S.A.
103 M7 **Clarkdale** Arizona U.S.A.
141 G4 **Clarke** *R* Queensland Australia
122 F3 **Clarke City** Quebec Canada
139 J8 **Clarke I** Tasmania Australia
118 K4 **Clarke L** Saskatchewan Canada
141 J5 **Clarke Ra** Queensland Australia
141 H4 **Clarke River** Queensland Australia
112 D3 **Clarkesville** Georgia U.S.A.
98 L5 **Clarkfield** Minnesota U.S.A.
100 J1 **Clark Fork** Idaho U.S.A.
117 Q12 **Clark Fork** *R* Idaho U.S.A.
112 E4 **Clark Hill Dam** Georgia U.S.A.
112 E4 **Clark Hill L** *res* Georgia U.S.A.
100 J2 **Clarkia** Idaho U.S.A.
116 K6 **Clark,L** Alaska U.S.A.
117 M3 **Clark,Mt** Northwest Territories Canada
103 J6 **Clark Mt** California U.S.A.
106 E1 **Clark Pk** Colorado U.S.A.
120 J8 **Clark Pt** Ontario Canada
111 D9 **Clarks** Louisiana U.S.A.
98 J8 **Clarks** Nebraska U.S.A.
101 Q5 **Clarks** *R* Wyoming U.S.A.
110 H6 **Clarksburg** Tennessee U.S.A.
94 G7 **Clarksburg** West Virginia U.S.A.
111 F7 **Clarksdale** Mississippi U.S.A.
99 N6 **Clarks Grove** Minnesota U.S.A.
122 G10 **Clark's Harbour** Nova Scotia Canada
110 K1 **Clarks Hill** Indiana U.S.A.
144 C6 **Clarks Junction** New Zealand
121 L9 **Clarkson** Ontario Canada
98 J8 **Clarkson** Nebraska U.S.A.
142 E4 **Clarkson, Mt** W Australia Australia
116 H7 **Clarks Point** Alaska U.S.A.
94 D4 **Clarkston** Michigan U.S.A.
101 O3 **Clarkston** Montana U.S.A.
100 H3 **Clarkston** Washington U.S.A.
127 K2 **Clark's Town** Jamaica
144 B7 **Clarksville** New Zealand
110 C6 **Clarksville** Arkansas U.S.A.
110 F2 **Clarksville** Illinois U.S.A.
99 O7 **Clarksville** Iowa U.S.A.
94 B4 **Clarksville** Michigan U.S.A.
110 J5 **Clarksville** Tennessee U.S.A.
109 M2 **Clarksville** Texas U.S.A.
94 J10 **Clarksville** Virginia U.S.A.
112 J3 **Clarkton** North Carolina U.S.A.
109 K8 **Clarkwood** Texas U.S.A.
100 E5 **Clarno** Oregon U.S.A.
129 H7 **Claro** *R* Brazil
22 E3 **Clary** France
141 H6 **Claude** *R* Queensland Australia
108 C8 **Claude** Texas U.S.A.
130 G7 **Cláudio** Brazil
32 M8 **Clauen** Germany
37 O2 **Claussnitz** Germany
33 M9 **Clausthal-Zellerfeld** Germany
71 E1 **Claveria** Luzon Philippines
118 L8 **Clavet** Saskatchewan Canada
19 N14 **Claveyson** France
112 F5 **Claxton** Georgia U.S.A.
102 C3 **Clay** California U.S.A.
110 J4 **Clay** Kentucky U.S.A.
109 L5 **Clay** Texas U.S.A.
94 F8 **Clay** West Virginia U.S.A.
107 N2 **Clay Center** Kansas U.S.A.
98 H9 **Clay Center** Nebraska U.S.A.
110 H3 **Clay City** Illinois U.S.A.
110 J2 **Clay City** Indiana U.S.A.
110 N4 **Clay City** Kentucky U.S.A.
9 E1 **Clay Cross** England
118 J9 **Claydon** Saskatchewan Canada
9 H3 **Claydon** England
18 H6 **Clayette, la** France
103 L5 **Clayhole Wash** *creek* Arizona U.S.A.
118 J1 **Clay L** Ontario Canada
6 K4 **Claymore** *oil rig* North Sea
107 P5 **Claymore** Oklahoma U.S.A.
117 L11 **Clayoquot** British Columbia Canada
103 O8 **Claypool** Arizona U.S.A.
103 O7 **Clay Springs** Arizona U.S.A.
94 G6 **Claysville** Pennsylvania U.S.A.
138 E3 **Clayton** *R* South Australia Australia
9 F6 **Clayton** England
111 L10 **Clayton** Alabama U.S.A.
112 D3 **Clayton** Georgia U.S.A.
101 L5 **Clayton** Idaho U.S.A.
99 Q9 **Clayton** Illinois U.S.A.
110 K2 **Clayton** Indiana U.S.A.
107 K2 **Clayton** Kansas U.S.A.
106 G5 **Clayton** New Mexico U.S.A.
95 L2 **Clayton** New York U.S.A.
112 J2 **Clayton** North Carolina U.S.A.
107 P7 **Clayton** Oklahoma U.S.A.
95 R7 **Clayton Lake** Maine U.S.A.
13 F6 **Clayton-le-Moors** England
94 G9 **Claytor Lake** Virginia U.S.A.
95 M4 **Clayville** New York U.S.A.
131 F4 **Clé** *R* Argentina
107 O7 **Clear Boggy Cr** Oklahoma U.S.A.
99 L2 **Clearbrook** Minnesota U.S.A.
144 C6 **Clearburn** New Zealand
14 B5 **Clear,C** Ireland
94 G8 **Clearco** West Virginia U.S.A.
103 O7 **Clear Cr** *R* Arizona U.S.A.
101 T5 **Clear Cr** Wyoming U.S.A.
100 B8 **Clear Creek** California U.S.A.
116 O7 **Cleare,C** Alaska U.S.A.
99 M9 **Clearfield** Iowa U.S.A.
94 J5 **Clearfield** Pennsylvania U.S.A.
101 N8 **Clearfield** Utah U.S.A.
108 G3 **Clear Fork** *R* Texas U.S.A.
117 O7 **Clear Hills** Alberta Canada
14 B5 **Clear I** Ireland
119 S8 **Clear L** Manitoba Canada
121 N7 **Clear, L** Ontario Canada
102 B2 **Clear L** California U.S.A.
99 N6 **Clear L** Iowa U.S.A.
109 P4 **Clear L** Louisiana U.S.A.
99 N4 **Clear L** Minnesota U.S.A.
98 K5 **Clear L** South Dakota U.S.A.
103 M2 **Clear L** Utah U.S.A.
99 O4 **Clear L** Wisconsin U.S.A.
100 D8 **Clear L. Res** California U.S.A.
101 T5 **Clearmont** Wyoming U.S.A.
117 O7 **Clear Prairie** Alberta Canada
117 N10 **Clearwater** British Columbia Canada
113 E10 **Clearwater** Florida U.S.A.
100 J3 **Clearwater** *R* Idaho U.S.A.
100 K3 **Clearwater** Idaho U.S.A.
107 N4 **Clearwater** Kansas U.S.A.
98 H7 **Clearwater** Nebraska U.S.A.
119 Q4 **Clearwater L. Prov. Park** Manitoba Canada
100 K3 **Clearwater Mts** Idaho U.S.A.
118 B6 **Clearwater R** Alberta Canada
110 F4 **Clearwater Res** Missouri U.S.A.
99 L2 **Clearwter** *R* Minnesota U.S.A.
143 D7 **Cleaver, Mt** W Australia Australia
107 O2 **Cleburne** Kansas U.S.A.
109 K3 **Cleburne** Texas U.S.A.
21 K4 **Clécy** France
8 B4 **Cleddau, R** Wales
20 B4 **Cléder** France
8 D3 **Clee Hill** England
100 D2 **Cle Elum L** Washington U.S.A.
13 H6 **Cleethorpes** England
7 L8 **Cleeton** *gas field* North Sea
118 H5 **Cleeves** Saskatchewan Canada
40 B1 **Clefmont** France
21 K6 **Clefs** France
109 J7 **Clegg** Texas U.S.A.
20 D5 **Cléguérec** France
140 B6 **Cleland Hills** N Terr Australia
22 K4 **Clemency** Luxembourg
102 C3 **Clements** California U.S.A.
115 N1 **Clements Markham Inlet** Northwest Territories Canada
122 G9 **Clementsport** Nova Scotia Canada
122 G9 **Clementsvale** Nova Scotia Canada
94 F8 **Clendenin** West Virginia U.S.A.
94 F6 **Clendening Res** Ohio U.S.A.
8 D3 **Cleobury Mortimer** England
71 D5 **Cleopatra Needle** *mt* Philippines
107 M5 **Cleo Springs** Oklahoma U.S.A.
21 L7 **Cléré** France
21 N2 **Clères** France
121 M4 **Cléricy** Quebec Canada
40 D2 **Clerjus, Le** France
142 C3 **Clerke Reef** Indian Oc
133 J9 **Clerke Rocks** S Georgia
141 J6 **Clermont** Queensland Australia
122 B6 **Clermont** Quebec Canada
21 P3 **Clermont** Oise France
113 F9 **Clermont** Florida U.S.A.
99 P6 **Clermont** Iowa U.S.A.
94 J5 **Clermont** Pennsylvania U.S.A.
21 K6 **Clermont-Créans** France
19 J3 **Clermont en Argonne** France
18 H7 **Clermont Ferrand** France
18 H9 **Clermont l'Herault** France
121 L4 **Clerval** Quebec Canada
40 D3 **Clerval** France
22 L3 **Clervaux** Luxembourg
21 O3 **Cléry-en-Vexin** France
21 O6 **Cléry-St. André** France
22 D4 **Cléry-sur-Somme** France
42 D2 **Cles** Italy
21 K8 **Clessé** France
138 D5 **Cleve** South Australia Australia
8 D5 **Clevedon** England
13 G4 **Cleveland** *co* England
110 D **Cleveland** Arkansas U.S.A.
113 F1 **Cleveland** Florida U.S.A.
112 D **Cleveland** Georgia U.S.A.
101 O **Cleveland** Idaho U.S.A.
99 N **Cleveland** Minnesota U.S.A.
111 F8 **Cleveland** Mississippi U.S.A.
101 Q **Cleveland** Montana U.S.A.
95 M **Cleveland** New York U.S.A.
112 G **Cleveland** North Carolina U.S.A.
98 G **Cleveland** North Dakota U.S.A.
94 F5 **Cleveland** Ohio U.S.A.
107 O **Cleveland** Oklahoma U.S.A.
112 E2 **Cleveland** South Carolina U.S.A.
112 C2 **Cleveland** Tennessee U.S.A.
109 M **Cleveland** Texas U.S.A.
103 O2 **Cleveland** Utah U.S.A.
99 T6 **Cleveland** Wisconsin U.S.A.
141 H4 **Cleveland, C** Queensland Australia
13 G4 **Cleveland Hills** England
130 D1 **Clevelândia** Brazil
101 M1 **Cleveland,Mt** Montana U.S.A.
113 G1 **Clewiston** Florida U.S.A.
9 H2 **Cley** England
14 A3 **Clifden** Ireland
144 A7 **Clifden** New Zealand
106 B9 **Cliff** New Mexico U.S.A.
100 D3 **Cliffdell** Washington U.S.A.
71 D5 **Cliff Head** Philippines
101 O5 **Cliff Lake** Montana U.S.A.
94 D3 **Clifford** Michigan U.S.A.
98 J2 **Clifford** North Dakota U.S.A.
94 H9 **Clifford** Virginia U.S.A.
99 Q4 **Clifford** Wisconsin U.S.A.
100 H7 **Cliffs** Idaho U.S.A.
112 F2 **Cliffside** North Carolina U.S.A.
141 K8 **Clifton** Queensland Australia
113 K9 **Clifton** New Providence I Bahamas
8 D5 **Clifton** England
103 P8 **Clifton** Arizona U.S.A.
99 T9 **Clifton** Illinois U.S.A.
107 N2 **Clifton** Kansas U.S.A.
95 N6 **Clifton** New Jersey U.S.A.
98 B6 **Clifton** Wyoming U.S.A.
94 H9 **Clifton Forge** Virginia U.S.A.
138 E2 **Clifton Hills** South Australia Australia
113 K9 **Clifton Pt** New Providence I Bahamas
118 J9 **Climax** Saskatchewan Canada
106 D2 **Climax** Colorado U.S.A.
111 M1 **Climax** Georgia U.S.A.
94 B4 **Climax** Michigan U.S.A.
98 K2 **Climax** Minnesota U.S.A.
112 C2 **Clinch** *R* Tennessee U.S.A.
94 E9 **Clinchco** Virginia U.S.A.
94 E1 **Clinch Mt** Tenn/Virg U.S.A.
94 E1 **Clinchport** Virginia U.S.A.
117 P9 **Cline, Mt** Alberta Canada
37 K1 **Clingen** Germany
112 D2 **Clingmans Dome** Tennessee U.S.A.
108 A4 **Clint** Texas U.S.A.
117 N1 **Clinton** British Columbia Canada
120 J9 **Clinton** Ontario Canada
144 B7 **Clinton** New Zealand
110 D6 **Clinton** Arkansas U.S.A.
95 P5 **Clinton** Connecticut U.S.A.
99 S9 **Clinton** Illinois U.S.A.
99 T10 **Clinton** Indiana U.S.A.
99 Q8 **Clinton** Iowa U.S.A.
110 H5 **Clinton** Kentucky U.S.A.
111 E11 **Clinton** Louisiana U.S.A.
95 S2 **Clinton** Maine U.S.A.
95 Q4 **Clinton** Massachusetts U.S.A.
94 D4 **Clinton** Michigan U.S.A.
98 K4 **Clinton** Minnesota U.S.A.
111 F9 **Clinton** Mississippi U.S.A.
110 C3 **Clinton** Missouri U.S.A.
101 M3 **Clinton** Montana U.S.A.
95 M3 **Clinton** New York U.S.A.
107 M6 **Clinton** Oklahoma U.S.A.
112 F3 **Clinton** South Carolina U.S.A.
112 C1 **Clinton** Tennessee U.S.A.
99 S7 **Clinton** Wisconsin U.S.A.
114 J5 **Clinton-Colden L** Northwest Territories Canada
114 E5 **Clinton Creek** Yukon Territory Canada
99 S5 **Clintonville** Wisconsin U.S.A.
103 N7 **Clints Well** Arizona U.S.A.
110 C1 **Clio** Iowa U.S.A.
94 D3 **Clio** Michigan U.S.A.
112 H3 **Clio** South Carolina U.S.A.
21 N8 **Clion** France
135 Q7 **Clipperton** *atoll* Pacific Oc
15 B3 **Clisham Mt** Lewis Scotland
20 H7 **Clisson** France
13 F6 **Clitheroe** England
118 D6 **Clive** Alberta Canada
145 F3 **Clive** New Zealand
101 M9 **Clive** Utah U.S.A.
117 O4 **Clive L** Northwest Territories Canada
118 J6 **Cloan** Saskatchewan Canada
14 D3 **Cloghan** Ireland
14 D2 **Clogher** N Ireland
14 E3 **Clogher Hd** Ireland
20 C6 **Clohars** France
140 F5 **Clonagh** Queensland Australia
14 C5 **Clonakilty** Ireland
14 C5 **Clonakilty B** Ireland
140 F4 **Cloncurry** *R* Queensland Australia
140 F5 **Cloncurry** Queensland Australia
14 E3 **Clondalkin** Ireland
14 E4 **Clonegal** Ireland
14 D2 **Clones** Ireland
59 J3 **Clŏngjin** N Korea
14 D4 **Clonmel** Ireland
99 L4 **Clontarf** Minnesota U.S.A.
117 L11 **Clo-oose** British Columbia Canada
9 F3 **Clophill** England
32 H7 **Cloppenburg** Germany
99 O3 **Cloquet** Minnesota U.S.A.
130 B9 **Clorinda** Argentina
12 E3 **Closeburn** Scotland
123 L3 **Cloudberry Pt** Quebec Canada
106 E9 **Cloudcroft** New Mexico U.S.A.
101 S5 **Cloud Pk** Wyoming U.S.A.
145 E4 **Cloudy Bay** New Zealand
116 J5 **Cloudy Mt** Alaska U.S.A.
121 L4 **Cloutier** Quebec Canada
20 H8 **Clouzeaux, les** France
121 P4 **Clova** Quebec Canada
15 E4 **Clova** Scotland
8 B5 **Clovelly** England
13 F2 **Clovenfords** Scotland
112 F2 **Clover** South Carolina U.S.A.
94 J10 **Clover** Virginia U.S.A.
102 A3 **Cloverdale** California U.S.A.
110 K2 **Cloverdale** Indiana U.S.A.
106 B10 **Cloverdale** New Mexico U.S.A.
110 K4 **Cloverport** Kentucky U.S.A.
106 G7 **Clovis** New Mexico U.S.A.
8 D3 **Clows Top** England
21 N6 **Cloyes** France
14 C5 **Cloyne** Ireland
21 O8 **Cluis** France
48 H4 **Cluj** *reg* Romania
48 H4 **Cluj-Napoca** Romania
8 C3 **Clun** England
139 G7 **Clunes** Victoria Australia
140 E6 **Cluny** Queensland Australia
118 E8 **Cluny** Alberta Canada
102 H1 **Cluro** Nevada U.S.A.
40 E5 **Cluses** France
41 L6 **Clusone** Italy
120 J3 **Clute** Ontario Canada
144 B6 **Clutha** *R* New Zealand
144 A6 **Clutha/Central Otago** *admin region* New Zealand
144 B7 **Clutha R** New Zealand
99 O7 **Clutier** Iowa U.S.A.
117 P3 **Clut L** Northwest Territories Canada
143 F6 **Clutterbuck Hills** W Australia Australia
8 C1 **Clwyd** *R* Wales
8 C1 **Clwyd** *co* Wales
113 D7 **Clyattville** Georgia U.S.A.
8 C4 **Clydach** Wales
118 D4 **Clyde** Alberta Canada
115 N3 **Clyde** Northwest Territories Canada
144 B6 **Clyde** New Zealand
6 M6 **Clyde** *oil rig* North Sea
107 N2 **Clyde** Kansas U.S.A.
95 L3 **Clyde** New York U.S.A.
98 H1 **Clyde** North Dakota U.S.A.
94 E5 **Clyde** Ohio U.S.A.
109 H3 **Clyde** Texas U.S.A.
12 D2 **Clydebank** Scotland
12 D3 **Clyde,Firth of** Scotland
121 O7 **Clyde Forks** Ontario Canada
101 P4 **Clyde Park** Montana U.S.A.
122 G10 **Clyde R** Nova Scotia Canada
12 D2 **Clyde,R** Scotland
144 B7 **Clydevale** New Zealand
99 S6 **Clyman** Wisconsin U.S.A.
94 H6 **Clymer** Pennsylvania U.S.A.
8 B1 **Clynnog-fawr** Wales
8 C3 **Clyro** Wales
8 C6 **Clyst Honiton** England
16 C4 **Coa** *R* Portugal
103 H8 **Coachella** California U.S.A.
123 M3 **Coacoachou L** Quebec Canada
108 F3 **Coahoma** Texas U.S.A.
124 H4 **Coahuila** *state* Mexico
117 K5 **Coal** *R* Br Col/Yukon Terr Canada
94 F8 **Coal** *R* West Virginia U.S.A.
99 S8 **Coal City** Illinois U.S.A.
124 H8 **Coalcomán de Matamoros** Mexico
116 Q4 **Coal Creek** Alaska U.S.A.
118 E9 **Coaldale** Alberta Canada
102 G3 **Coaldale** Nevada U.S.A.
144 C5 **Coalgate** New Zealand
107 O7 **Coalgate** Oklahoma U.S.A.
94 E8 **Coal Grove** Ohio U.S.A.
110 C6 **Coal Hill** Arkansas U.S.A.
144 A7 **Coal I** New Zealand
102 D5 **Coalinga** California U.S.A.
101 T9 **Coalmont** Colorado U.S.A.
94 J6 **Coalport** Pennsylvania U.S.A.
117 K6 **Coal River** British Columbia Canada
94 E7 **Coalton** Ohio U.S.A.
9 E2 **Coalville** England
101 O9 **Coalville** Utah U.S.A.
98 A4 **Coalwood** Montana U.S.A.
127 L5 **Coamo** Puerto Rico
128 F4 **Coari** Brazil
144 C6 **Coastal North Otago** *admin region* New Zealand
117 G7 **Coast Mts** British Columbia Canada
141 K7 **Coast Ra** Queensland Australia
141 K7 **Coast Ra** *mts* Queensland Australia
100 B9 **Coast Range** *mts* U.S.A.
102 A1 **Coast Rge** California U.S.A.
12 E2 **Coatbridge** Scotland
125 L8 **Coatepec** Mexico
95 M6 **Coatesville** Pennsylvania U.S.A.
121 T7 **Coaticook** Quebec Canada
107 M4 **Coats** Kansas U.S.A.
112 J2 **Coats** North Carolina U.S.A.
115 L5 **Coats I** Northwest Territories Canada
146 E7 **Coats Land** Antarctica
110 D1 **Coatsville** Iowa U.S.A.
125 M8 **Coatzacoalcos** Mexico
121 L5 **Cobalt** Ontario Canada
101 L4 **Cobalt** Idaho U.S.A.
125 O10 **Cobán** Guatemala
139 H4 **Cobar** New South Wales Australia
139 J6 **Cobargo** New South Wales Australia
99 Q7 **Cobb** Wisconsin U.S.A.
139 J6 **Cobberas,Mt** Victoria Australia
143 F6 **Cobb, L** W Australia Australia
9 E6 **Cobblers Corner** England
145 D4 **Cobb Res** New Zealand
139 G7 **Cobden** Victoria Australia
121 O7 **Cobden** Ontario Canada
110 G4 **Cobden** Illinois U.S.A.
122 J8 **Cobequid B** Nova Scotia Canada
122 J8 **Cobequid Mts** Nova Scotia Canada
14 C5 **Cóbh** Ireland
140 B1 **Cobham B** N Terr Australia
128 E6 **Cobija** Bolivia
95 N4 **Cobleskill** New York U.S.A.
121 M8 **Coboconk** Ontario Canada
121 M9 **Cobourg** Ontario Canada
140 B1 **Cobourg Pen** N Terr Australia
143 B6 **Cobra** W Australia Australia
139 H6 **Cobram** New South Wales Australia
101 L8 **Cobre** Nevada U.S.A.
127 L2 **Cobre, R** Jamaica
87 F8 **Cobue** Mozambique
37 K3 **Coburg** Germany
100 B5 **Coburg** Oregon U.S.A.
115 M2 **Coburg I** Northwest Territories Canada
16 D3 **Coca** Spain
128 D7 **Cocachacra** Peru
128 D6 **Cocamá** Peru
42 C2 **Coca, Pzo. di** Italy
45 M3 **Coccolia** Italy
17 G6 **Cocentaina** Spain
128 E7 **Cochabamba** Bolivia
128 C3 **Cocha, L** Colombia
127 N9 **Coche, I** Venezuela
106 D3 **Cochetopa Pass** Colorado U.S.A.
76 C6 **Cochin** India
68 G7 **Cochin** *reg* Vietnam
128 E8 **Cochinoca** Argentina
126 D3 **Cochinos, B. de** Cuba
103 P9 **Cochise** Arizona U.S.A.
103 P9 **Cochise Head** *mt* Arizona U.S.A.
106 D6 **Cochiti L** New Mexico U.S.A.
112 D5 **Cochran** Georgia U.S.A.
118 C7 **Cochrane** Alberta Canada
120 J3 **Cochrane** Ontario Canada
133 C7 **Cochrane, L** Chile/Arg
94 G5 **Cochranton** Pennsylvania U.S.A.
33 O9 **Cochstedt** Germany
142 E3 **Cockatoo I** W Australia Australia
15 E3 **Cock Bridge** Scotland
141 G3 **Cockburn** *R* Queensland Australia
138 F4 **Cockburn** South Australia Australia
133 C8 **Cockburn, Canal** *str* Chile
127 J4 **Cockburn Harbour** Turks & Caicos Is
120 G7 **Cockburn I** Ontario Canada
140 B6 **Cockburn, Mt** N Terr Australia
140 A7 **Cockburn, Mt** N Terr Australia
142 G3 **Cockburn Ra** W Australia Australia
142 A3 **Cockburn Sd** W Australia Australia
13 F2 **Cockburnspath** Scotland
126 G2 **Cockburn Town** San Salvador Bahamas
13 F2 **Cockenzie** Scotland
13 F6 **Cockerham** England
13 E4 **Cockermouth** England
95 L7 **Cockeysville** Maryland U.S.A.
143 F9 **Cocklebiddy** W Australia Australia
127 J2 **Cockpit** *pk* Jamaica
127 J2 **Cockpit Country, The** *reg* Jamaica
109 N9 **Cockrell Hill** Texas U.S.A.
15 F5 **Cocksburnpath** Scotland
89 D9 **Cockscomb** *mt* S Africa
129 J5 **Côco** *R* Brazil
125 M2 **Coco** *R* Honduras/Nicaragua
113 G9 **Cocoa** Florida U.S.A.
113 G9 **Cocoa Beach** Florida U.S.A.
126 E3 **Coco, Cayo** *isld* Cuba
111 F12 **Cocodrie** Louisiana U.S.A.
100 J1 **Cocolalla** Idaho U.S.A.
103 M6 **Coconino Plat** Arizona U.S.A.
139 H5 **Cocoparra Rge** New South Wales Australia
71 E5 **Cocoro** *isld* Philippines
127 P2 **Cocos B** Trinidad
81 G6 **Cocos I** Indian Oc
90 A8 **Cocos I** Pacific Oc
90 A8 **Cocos Ridge** Pacific Oc
83 L13 **Cocotte, Mt** Mauritius
124 H7 **Cocula** Mexico
6 M5 **Cod** *oil rig* North Sea
43 C8 **Coda Cavallo, C** Sardinia
48 L4 **Codăeşti** Romania
128 F4 **Codajas** Brazil
107 L2 **Codell** Kansas U.S.A.
118 L8 **Coderre** Saskatchewan Canada
119 N5 **Codette** Saskatchewan Canada
144 A7 **Codfish I** New Zealand
115 N6 **Cod I** Labrador, Nfld Canada
9 F4 **Codicote** England
42 E4 **Codigoro** Italy
48 J5 **Codlea** Romania
129 K4 **Codó** Brazil
44 G1 **Codogno** Italy
127 N6 **Codrington** Barbuda W Indies
123 N6 **Codroy** Newfoundland Canada
123 O5 **Codroy Pond** Newfoundland Canada
48 G4 **Codrului Muntii** *mts* Romania
122 G8 **Cody** New Brunswick Canada
98 E7 **Cody** Nebraska U.S.A.
101 Q5 **Cody** Wyoming U.S.A.
94 E10 **Coeburn** Virginia U.S.A.
121 N8 **Coe Hill** Ontario Canada
141 F2 **Coen** *R* Queensland Australia
141 G2 **Coen** Queensland Australia
32 F9 **Coesfeld** Germany
83 H5 **Coëtivy Is** Seychelles Indian Oc
100 J2 **Coeur d'Alene** Idaho U.S.A.
22 E5 **Coeuvres et Valsery** France
25 G3 **Coevorden** Netherlands
21 K5 **Coevrons, les** *mts* France
20 G8 **Coëx** France
112 E6 **Coffee** Georgia U.S.A.
117 D4 **Coffee Creek** Yukon Territory Canada
101 P2 **Coffee Creek** Montana U.S.A.
110 G2 **Coffeen** Illinois U.S.A.
111 L10 **Coffee Springs** Alabama U.S.A.
111 G8 **Coffeeville** Mississippi U.S.A.
107 P4 **Coffeyville** Kansas U.S.A.
138 D5 **Coffin B** South Australia Australia
123 L6 **Coffin I** Madeleine Is, Quebec Canada
139 L4 **Coffs Harbour** New South Wales Australia
17 G5 **Cofrentes** Spain
48 M6 **Cogealac** Romania
9 G4 **Coggeshall** England
42 B3 **Coggiola** Italy
99 P7 **Coggon** Iowa U.S.A.
43 B8 **Coghinas** *R* Sardinia
43 C8 **Coghinas, L.d** Sardinia
142 G4 **Coghlan, Mt** W Australia Australia
18 E7 **Cognac** France
40 F6 **Cogne, V.de** Italy
44 E3 **Cogoleto** Italy
16 E4 **Cogolludo** Spain
41 N5 **Cógolo** Italy
98 J3 **Cogswell** North Dakota U.S.A.
101 T2 **Cohagen** Montana U.S.A.
20 E5 **Cohiniac** France
94 K4 **Cohocton** New York U.S.A.
95 K4 **Cohocton** *R* New York U.S.A.
95 O4 **Cohoes** New York U.S.A.
139 G6 **Cohuna** Victoria Australia
112 C3 **Cohutta** Georgia U.S.A.
125 O6 **Coiba, I** Panama
133 C8 **Coig** *R* Argentina
21 O4 **Coignières** France
133 C7 **Coihaique** Chile
76 C5 **Coimbatore** India
129 G7 **Coimbra** Brazil
16 B4 **Coimbra** Portugal
16 D8 **Coin** Spain
110 A1 **Coin** Iowa U.S.A.
128 E7 **Coipasa, L** Bolivia
Coire *see* **Chur** Switzerland
19 N15 **Coiron, Mts du** France
128 E2 **Cojedes** *state* Venezuela
128 B3 **Cojimies** Ecuador
48 H4 **Cojocna** Romania
127 J9 **Cojoro** Venezuela
133 D7 **Cojudo Blanco** *mt* Argentina
47 N10 **Cok** *R* Turkey
99 M4 **Cokato** Minnesota U.S.A.
94 G6 **Cokeburg** Pennsylvania U.S.A.
101 P7 **Cokeville** Wyoming U.S.A.
26 O2 **Cokkarassa** *mt* Norway
139 G7 **Colac** Victoria Australia
144 A7 **Colac** New Zealand
131 B2 **Colanguil, Cerro de** *mt* Argentina
130 H6 **Colatina** Brazil
36 F2 **Cölbe** Germany
146 B10 **Colbeck, C** Antarctica
100 H2 **Colbert** Washington U.S.A.
33 P8 **Colbitz** Germany
33 P8 **Colbitz-Letzlinger Heide** Germany
121 N8 **Colborne** Ontario Canada
107 J2 **Colby** Kansas U.S.A.
99 Q5 **Colby** Wisconsin U.S.A.
128 D7 **Colca** *R* Peru
9 G4 **Colchester** England
95 P5 **Colchester** Connecticut U.S.A.
99 Q9 **Colchester** Illinois U.S.A.
8 D5 **Cold Ashton** England
116 F9 **Cold B** Alaska U.S.A.
44 B2 **Col de Longet** France
94 J4 **Colden** New York U.S.A.
13 F4 **Cold Fell** *mt* England
13 F2 **Coldingham** Scotland
37 O1 **Colditz** Germany
118 G4 **Cold L** Alberta Canada
119 Q3 **Cold L** Manitoba Canada
99 M4 **Cold Spring** Minnesota U.S.A.
109 M5 **Coldspring** Texas U.S.A.
13 F2 **Coldstream** Scotland
121 L8 **Coldwater** Ontario Canada
107 L4 **Coldwater** Kansas U.S.A.
94 C5 **Coldwater** Michigan U.S.A.
111 F7 **Coldwater** *R* Mississippi U.S.A.
110 M1 **Coldwater** Ohio U.S.A.
108 C7 **Coldwater Cr** Texas/Okla U.S.A.
120 D4 **Coldwell** Ontario Canada
139 H8 **Colebrook** Tasmania Australia
121 T8 **Colebrook** New Hampshire U.S.A.
110 C3 **Cole Camp** Missouri U.S.A.
116 Q2 **Coleen** *R* Alaska U.S.A.
8 D4 **Coleford** England
94 J5 **Colegrove** Pennsylvania U.S.A.
141 F2 **Coleman** *R* Queensland Australia
118 C9 **Coleman** Alberta Canada
113 E9 **Coleman** Florida U.S.A.
94 C3 **Coleman** Michigan U.S.A.
109 H4 **Coleman** Texas U.S.A.
22 B2 **Colembert** France
138 F6 **Coleraine** Victoria Australia
121 T7 **Coleraine** Quebec Canada
14 E1 **Coleraine** N Ireland
99 N2 **Coleraine** Minnesota U.S.A.
118 G9 **Coleridge** Alberta Canada
98 J7 **Coleridge** Nebraska U.S.A.
139 J8 **Coles B** Tasmania Australia
89 D8 **Colesberg** S Africa
8 E4 **Colesborne** England
9 E2 **Coleshill** England
128 D7 **Coles, Pta** *C* Peru
118 H7 **Coleville** Saskatchewan Canada
102 E3 **Coleville** California U.S.A.
119 O9 **Colfax** Saskatchewan Canada
102 D2 **Colfax** California U.S.A.
110 H1 **Colfax** Illinois U.S.A.
110 K1 **Colfax** Indiana U.S.A.
99 N8 **Colfax** Iowa U.S.A.
111 D10 **Colfax** Louisiana U.S.A.
106 F5 **Colfax** New Mexico U.S.A.
100 H3 **Colfax** Washington U.S.A.
99 P4 **Colfax** Wisconsin U.S.A.
119 O9 **Colgate** Saskatchewan Canada
133 D7 **Colhué Huapí, L** Argentina
131 B5 **Coliauco** Argentina
131 B7 **Colico, L** Chile
25 A5 **Colijnsplaat** Netherlands
124 H8 **Colima** Mexico
129 K5 **Colinas** Brazil
13 F1 **Colinsburgh** Scotland
118 D4 **Colinton** Alberta Canada
13 E2 **Colinton** Scotland
12 C2 **Colintraive** Scotland
15 B4 **Coll** *isld* Scotland
139 H4 **Collabah** New South Wales Australia
139 J3 **Collarenebri** New South Wales Australia
106 C2 **Collbran** Colorado U.S.A.
42 D5 **Colle di Val d'Elsa** Italy
89 F3 **Colleen Bawn** Zimbabwe
116 O4 **College** Alaska U.S.A.
110 M2 **College Corner** Indiana U.S.A.
110 K6 **College Grove** Tennessee U.S.A.
111 M8 **College Park** Georgia U.S.A.
95 L7 **College Park** Maryland U.S.A.
100 G3 **College Place** Washington U.S.A.
109 L5 **College Station** Texas U.S.A.
45 P6 **Collelongo** Italy
139 H3 **Collerina** New South Wales Australia
42 C5 **Collesalvetti** Italy
45 J4 **Collesalvetti** Italy
45 R7 **Colle Sannita** Italy
109 N9 **Colleyville** Texas U.S.A.
45 N6 **Colli Albani** Italy
139 J4 **Collie** New South Wales Australia
143 B10 **Collie** W Australia Australia
143 B10 **Collie Cardiff** W Australia Australia
142 E3 **Collier B** W Australia Australia
113 F12 **Collier City** Florida U.S.A.
143 C6 **Collier Ra** *mts* W Australia Australia
110 G6 **Collierville** Tennessee U.S.A.
8 B6 **Colliford L** England
12 E3 **Collin** Scotland
45 J3 **Collina, Passo di** Italy
20 E5 **Collinée** France
21 O3 **Collines-du-Vexin, Plaine et** France
9 E5 **Collingbourne Kingston** England
9 F1 **Collingham** England
13 G6 **Collingham** England
95 N7 **Collingswood** New Jersey U.S.A.
141 F5 **Collingwood** Queensland Australia
120 K8 **Collingwood** Ontario Canada
145 D4 **Collingwood** New Zealand
112 E5 **Collins** Georgia U.S.A.
111 G10 **Collins** Mississippi U.S.A.
110 C4 **Collins** Missouri U.S.A.
101 O2 **Collins** Montana U.S.A.
94 J4 **Collins** New York U.S.A.
114 J3 **Collinson Pen** Northwest Territories Canada
111 E9 **Collinston** Louisiana U.S.A.
14 E3 **Collinstown** Ireland
141 J5 **Collinsville** Queensland Australia
111 L7 **Collinsville** Alabama U.S.A.
110 G3 **Collinsville** Illinois U.S.A.
107 P5 **Collinsville** Oklahoma U.S.A.
110 J6 **Collinwood** Tennessee U.S.A.
41 M6 **Collio** Italy
120 J1 **Collis** Ontario Canada
37 Q1 **Cölln** Germany
19 Q18 **Collobrières** France
131 B8 **Collon Cura** *R* Argentina
14 C2 **Collooney** Ireland
107 K2 **Collyer** Kansas U.S.A.
40 F1 **Colmar** France
37 J5 **Colmberg** Germany
133 E3 **Colmena** Argentina
16 E8 **Colmenar** Spain
16 E4 **Colmenar de Oreja** Spain
16 E4 **Colmenar Vieja** Spain
109 N5 **Colmesneil** Texas U.S.A.
12 D3 **Colmonell** Scotland
21 J5 **Colmont** *R* France
106 F5 **Colmor** New Mexico U.S.A.
13 F6 **Colne** England
9 G4 **Colne, R** England
124 A2 **Colnett, C** Mexico
139 K5 **Colo** *R* New South Wales Australia
99 N7 **Colo** Iowa U.S.A.
41 O7 **Cologna** Italy
45 K1 **Cologna Veneta** Italy
Cologne *see* **Köln**
99 N5 **Cologne** Minnesota U.S.A.
94 A4 **Coloma** Michigan U.S.A.
99 R5 **Coloma** Wisconsin U.S.A.
21 K3 **Colombelles** France
40 A1 **Colombey les Deux Églises** France
129 J8 **Colombia** Brazil
108 H8 **Colombia** Mexico
128 C3 **Colombia** *rep* S America
90 B7 **Colombian Basin** Atlantic Oc
121 N4 **Colombiere** Quebec Canada
83 J11 **Colombo** Sri Lanka
20 G3 **Colomby** France
98 G6 **Colome** South Dakota U.S.A.
133 E4 **Colón** Argentina
126 D3 **Colón** Cuba
125 P5 **Colón** Panama
94 B5 **Colon** Michigan U.S.A.
138 B4 **Colona** South Australia Australia
126 G3 **Colonel Hill** Crooked I Bahamas
131 F5 **Colonia** Uruguay
133 D5 **Colonia Catriel** Argentina
131 D7 **Colonia Choele Choel** *isld* Argentina
133 F4 **Colonia del Sac** Uruguay
124 E2 **Colonia Díaz** Mexico
133 D7 **Colonia las Heras** Argentina
95 K8 **Colonial Beach** Virginia U.S.A.

94 K9 Colonial Heights Virginia U.S.A.
95 L9 Colonial Nat. Hist. Park Virginia U.S.A.
130 H4 Colônia, R Brazil
125 M2 Colón, Montañas de ra Honduras
43 H9 Colonna, C Italy
119 M7 Colonsay Saskatchewan Canada
15 B4 Colonsay isld Scotland
107 P3 Colony Kansas U.S.A.
131 D7 Colorada Grande, L Argentina
127 N10 Coloradito Venezuela
131 B5 Colorado R Chile
106 B2 Colorado state U.S.A.
103 L5 Colorado R Arizona U.S.A.
106 B2 Colorado R Colorado U.S.A.
109 J4 Colorado R Texas U.S.A.
103 J10 Colorado, Cerro pk Mexico
108 G3 Colorado City Texas U.S.A.
131 E7 Colorado, Delta del R Argentina
106 B2 Colorado Nat.Mon Colorado U.S.A.
103 N5 Colorado Plat Arizona U.S.A.
103 K7 Colorado R.Aqueduct California U.S.A.
106 F3 Colorado Springs Colorado U.S.A.
16 C4 Colorico da Beira Portugal
45 H2 Colorno Italy
19 Q17 Colostre R France
125 L10 Colotepec Mexico
124 H6 Colotlán Mexico
20 E6 Colpo France
120 K8 Colpoys B Ontario Canada
133 D1 Colquechaca Bolivia
111 M10 Colquitt Georgia U.S.A.
9 F2 Colsterworth England
101 T4 Colstrip Montana U.S.A.
108 D8 Coltexo Texas U.S.A.
9 H2 Coltishall England
102 G7 Colton California U.S.A.
95 L8 Colton Maryland U.S.A.
95 N2 Colton New York U.S.A.
98 K6 Colton South Dakota U.S.A.
103 O2 Colton Utah U.S.A.
100 H3 Colton Washington U.S.A.
117 O10 Columbia R British Columbia Canada
111 L10 Columbia Alabama U.S.A.
113 E7 Columbia Florida U.S.A.
110 F3 Columbia Illinois U.S.A.
94 B9 Columbia Kentucky U.S.A.
111 D9 Columbia Louisiana U.S.A.
95 L7 Columbia Maryland U.S.A.
111 G10 Columbia Mississippi U.S.A.
110 D3 Columbia Missouri U.S.A.
112 L2 Columbia North Carolina U.S.A.
95 L6 Columbia Pennsylvania U.S.A.
112 F3 Columbia South Carolina U.S.A.
98 H4 Columbia South Dakota U.S.A.
110 J6 Columbia Tennessee U.S.A.
94 J9 Columbia Virginia U.S.A.
100 E4 Columbia R Wash/Oregon U.S.A.
117 O11 Columbia R Wash/Br Col U.S.A./Canada
100 F2 Columbia Basin reg Washington U.S.A.
115 N1 Columbia, C Northwest Territories Canada
94 B5 Columbia City Indiana U.S.A.
95 L8 Columbia, Dist. of (D.C.) U.S.A.
101 L1 Columbia Falls Montana U.S.A.
116 O6 Columbia Glacier Alaska U.S.A.
117 Q10 Columbia Lake British Columbia Canada
117 P9 Columbia, Mt Br Col/Alberta Canada
114 G7 Columbia Mts British Columbia Canada
111 K8 Columbiana Alabama U.S.A.
94 G6 Columbiana Ohio U.S.A.
100 E2 Columbia River Washington U.S.A.
98 H4 Columbia Road Res South Dakota U.S.A.
95 O4 Columbiaville New York U.S.A.
106 D1 Columbine Colorado U.S.A.
101 T6 Columbine Wyoming U.S.A.
89 A9 Columbine, C S Africa
17 H5 Columbretes, I Spain
111 M9 Columbus Georgia U.S.A.
110 L2 Columbus Indiana U.S.A.
107 Q4 Columbus Kansas U.S.A.
111 H8 Columbus Mississippi U.S.A.
101 Q4 Columbus Montana U.S.A.
98 J8 Columbus Nebraska U.S.A.
106 C10 Columbus New Mexico U.S.A.
98 D1 Columbus North Dakota U.S.A.
94 D7 Columbus Ohio U.S.A.
109 L6 Columbus Texas U.S.A.
99 R6 Columbus Wisconsin U.S.A.
126 G3 Columbus Bank Bahamas
99 P8 Columbus City Iowa U.S.A.
126 G2 Columbus Mon San Salvador Bahamas
126 G2 Columbus Pt Cat I Bahamas
127 M2 Columbus Pt Tobago
102 B2 Colusa California U.S.A.
12 E4 Colvend Scotland
94 J6 Colver Pennsylvania U.S.A.
145 E2 Colville New Zealand
116 L2 Colville R Alaska U.S.A.
100 H1 Colville Washington U.S.A.
114 G4 Colville L Northwest Territories Canada
143 F8 Colville, Lake W Australia Australia
137 Q8 Colville Ridge sea feature Pacific Oc
13 F3 Colwell England
99 O6 Colwell Iowa U.S.A.
8 C1 Colwyn Bay Wales
8 C6 Colyford England
45 M2 Comacchio Italy
125 O10 Comalapa Guatemala
125 N8 Comalcalco Mexico
131 B8 Comallo R Argentina
48 K6 Comana Romania
107 N7 Comanche Oklahoma U.S.A.
109 J4 Comanche Texas U.S.A.
146 D3 Comandante Ferraz Brazil Base Antarctica
133 D7 Comandante Luis Piedrabuena Argentina
133 D4 Comandante Salas Argentina
48 K4 Comăneşti Romania
48 K5 Comarnic Romania
125 L2 Comayagua Honduras
16 B4 Comba Dão Portugal
112 G5 Combahee R South Carolina U.S.A.
133 C4 Combarbala Chile
40 C2 Combeaufontaine France
8 B5 Combe Martin England
120 H10 Comber Ontario Canada
14 F2 Comber N Ireland
121 N7 Combermere Ontario Canada
68 A3 Combermere B Burma
109 K9 Combes Texas U.S.A.
22 D3 Combles France
69 F12 Combol isld Indonesia
25 C6 Combourg France
139 L4 Comboyne New South Wales Australia
21 N5 Combres France
20 B6 Combrit France
94 D7 Combs Kentucky U.S.A.
131 D4 Comechingones, Sa. de ra Argentina
38 G8 Comeglians Italy
38 G8 Comelico Italy
130 E6 Comendador Gomes Brazil
111 L9 Comer Alabama U.S.A.
112 D3 Comer Georgia U.S.A.
14 D4 Comeragh Mts Ireland
130 H5 Comercinho Brazil
98 B1 Comertown Montana U.S.A.
141 J6 Comet R Queensland Australia
141 J6 Comet Queensland Australia
109 J6 Comfort Texas U.S.A.
99 M5 Comfrey Minnesota U.S.A.
75 O7 Comilla Bangladesh
22 E2 Comines France
43 F12 Comino isld Malta
43 C8 Comino, C Sardinia
94 C2 Comins Michigan U.S.A.
43 F12 Comiso Sicily
125 N9 Comitán de Dominguez Mexico
20 C5 Commana France
121 L7 Commanda Ontario Canada
18 G6 Commentry France
20 G8 Commequiers France
21 J5 Commer France
112 D3 Commerce Georgia U.S.A.
107 Q5 Commerce Oklahoma U.S.A.
109 M2 Commerce Texas U.S.A.
106 F2 Commerce City Colorado U.S.A.
19 J4 Commercy France
45 J1 Commessaggio Italy
121 S4 Commissaires, Lac des Quebec Canada
115 L4 Committee B Northwest Territories Canada
146 D14 Commonwealth B Antarctica
138 C3 Commonwealth Hill South Australia Australia
139 K6 Commonwealth Terr New South Wales Australia
41 K6 Como Italy
106 E2 Como Colorado U.S.A.
111 G7 Como Mississippi U.S.A.
133 D7 Comodoro Rivadavia Argentina
41 K5 Como, Lago di Italy
124 D4 Comondú Mexico
125 J7 Comonfort Mexico
76 C6 Comorin, C India
81 B7 Comoro Ridge Indian Oc
87 G10 Comoros islds, rep Indian Oc
118 G7 Compeer Alberta Canada
22 D5 Compiègne France
22 D5 Compiègne, Forêt de France
124 G7 Compostela Mexico
71 G7 Compostela Mindanao Philippines
130 F9 Comprida, I São Paulo Brazil
102 A2 Comptche California U.S.A.
102 F8 Compton California U.S.A.
99 R8 Compton Illinois U.S.A.
12 E1 Comrie Scotland
95 O3 Comstock New York U.S.A.
108 F6 Comstock Texas U.S.A.
45 O4 Cona Italy
66 E5 Co Nag L China
85 B7 Conakry Guinea
133 D6 Cona Niyeo Argentina
112 C3 Conasauga R Georgia U.S.A.
98 D6 Conata South Dakota U.S.A.
45 N4 Conca R Italy
108 H6 Concan Texas U.S.A.
20 C6 Concarneau France
130 H9 Conceição Paraiba Brazil
130 H6 Conceição da Barra Brazil
130 E6 Conceição das Alagoas Brazil
129 J5 Conceição do Araguaia Brazil
130 G6 Conceição do Mato Dentro Brazil
133 D3 Concepción Argentina
128 E6 Concepcion Beni Bolivia
128 F7 Concepcion Santa Cruz Bolivia
131 A6 Concepción Chile
124 C2 Concepcion R Mexico
133 F2 Concepción dept Paraguay
130 B8 Concepción Paraguay
131 A6 Concepción, B. del Chile
133 B8 Concepción, Can str Chile
130 C10 Concepción de la Sierra Argentina
124 J5 Concepción del Oro Mexico
131 F4 Concepción del Uruguay Argentina
128 F7 Concepción, L Bolivia
124 D4 Concepción, Pta C Mexico
99 M9 Conception Missouri U.S.A.
123 U6 Conception B Newfoundland Canada
87 B10 Conception B Namibia
123 T6 Conception Harb Newfoundland Canada
126 G3 Conception I Bahamas
83 K12 Conception I Mahé I Indian Oc
124 G6 Concha Mexico
130 E8 Conchas Brazil
106 F6 Conchas New Mexico U.S.A.
106 F6 Conchas Lake New Mexico U.S.A.
21 M4 Conches France
133 D2 Conchi Chile
124 G4 Concho Mexico
103 P7 Concho Arizona U.S.A.
107 N6 Concho Oklahoma U.S.A.
108 G4 Concho R Texas U.S.A.
108 B7 Conchos, Rio Mexico
102 B4 Concord California U.S.A.
111 M8 Concord Georgia U.S.A.
94 C4 Concord Michigan U.S.A.
98 K7 Concord Nebraska U.S.A.
95 Q3 Concord New Hampshire U.S.A.
112 G2 Concord North Carolina U.S.A.
95 Q2 Concord Vermont U.S.A.
131 F3 Concordia Argentina
130 D10 Concórdia Brazil
124 F6 Concordia Mexico
107 N2 Concordia Kansas U.S.A.
110 C3 Concordia Missouri U.S.A.
45 J2 Concordia sulla Secchia Italy
100 D1 Concrete Washington U.S.A.
68 G3 Con Cuong Vietnam
101 O7 Conda Idaho U.S.A.
141 K7 Condamine R Queensland Australia
141 K7 Condamine Queensland Australia
18 G7 Condat France
129 L6 Conde Brazil
98 H4 Conde South Dakota U.S.A.
88 E9 Condédzi R Mozambique
125 L3 Condega Nicaragua
21 M5 Condé-sur-Huîsne France
22 F3 Condé-sur-l'Escaut France
21 O4 Condé-sur-Noireau France
21 O4 Condé-sur-Vesgres France
21 H3 Condé-sur-Vire France
130 H4 Condeúba Brazil
139 H5 Condobolin New South Wales Australia
18 F9 Condom France
100 E4 Condon Oregon U.S.A.
142 C5 Condon Creek B W Australia Australia
128 C4 Condor, Cord. del mts Ecuador/Peru
12 D2 Condorrat Scotland
19 N14 Condrieu France
22 J3 Condroz Belgium
142 E3 Cone B W Australia Australia
111 K10 Conecuh R Alabama U.S.A.
42 E3 Conegliano Italy
17 J5 Conejera isld Balearic Is
106 D4 Conejos Colorado U.S.A.
94 H6 Conemaugh R Pennsylvania U.S.A.
45 O4 Cònero, M mt Italy
133 E6 Conesa Argentina
94 K4 Conesus L New York U.S.A.
99 P8 Conesville Iowa U.S.A.
94 F6 Conesville Ohio U.S.A.
123 Q4 Coney Arm Newfoundland Canada
90 C1 Coney I Bermuda
95 O6 Coney Island New York U.S.A.
40 D2 Conflans France
19 J3 Conflans-Jarny France
21 P4 Conflans-Ste. Honorine France
21 P2 Conflans-Ste. Honorine Villers-Bretonneux France
94 H7 Confluence Pennsylvania U.S.A.
18 F6 Confolens France
103 L2 Confusion Range Utah U.S.A.
130 B9 Confuso, R Paraguay
14 B3 Cong Ireland
112 G4 Congaree R South Carolina U.S.A.
112 G4 Congaree Swamp Nat. Mon South Carolina U.S.A.
67 D5 Conghua China
67 C4 Congjiang China
8 D1 Congleton England
86 C6 Congo rep W Africa
85 C6 Congo R West Africa
Congo (Brazzaville) rep see Congo rep
Congo (Kinshasa) rep see Zaïre rep
130 G7 Congonhas Brazil
8 D5 Congresbury England
118 L9 Congress Saskatchewan Canada
21 H6 Congrier France
68 J5 Cong Tum Vietnam
20 D7 Conguel, Pte. de France
133 C6 Cónico mt Chile/Arg
21 N5 Conie R France
106 E2 Conifer Colorado U.S.A.
9 F1 Coningsby England
13 G6 Conisbrough England
140 B5 Coniston N Terr Australia
120 K6 Coniston Ontario Canada
13 E5 Coniston England
141 G4 Conjuboy Queensland Australia
118 F3 Conklin Alberta Canada
108 B7 Conlen Texas U.S.A.
21 K5 Conlie France
40 C4 Conliège France
120 K4 Connaught Ontario Canada
14 B3 Connaught prov Ireland
142 E6 Connaughton, M W Australia Australia
19 N16 Connaux France
94 C5 Conneaut Ohio U.S.A.
94 G5 Conneautville Pennsylvania U.S.A.
95 P3 Connecticut R U.S.A.
95 O5 Connecticut state U.S.A.
15 C4 Connel Ferry Scotland
100 G3 Connell Washington U.S.A.
94 H6 Connellsville Pennsylvania U.S.A.
141 F6 Connemara Queensland Australia
14 B3 Connemara dist Ireland
101 L4 Conner Montana U.S.A.
138 B2 Conner, Mt N Terr Australia
140 B7 Conner, Mt N Terr Australia
21 M5 Connerre France
94 B7 Connersville Indiana U.S.A.
14 B2 Conn, L Ireland
142 F2 Connor, Mt W Australia Australia
122 D6 Connors New Brunswick Canada
141 J5 Connors Ra mts Queensland Australia
128 C4 Cononaco R Ecuador
112 F2 Conover North Carolina U.S.A.
99 R3 Conover Wisconsin U.S.A.
33 S6 Conow Germany
20 G6 Conquereuil France
118 K7 Conquest Saskatchewan Canada
20 A5 Conquet, le France
130 F6 Conquista Brazil
101 O1 Conrad Montana U.S.A.
139 J7 Conran, C Victoria Australia
99 Q4 Conrath Wisconsin U.S.A.
109 M5 Conroe Texas U.S.A.
109 M5 Conroe, L Texas U.S.A.
45 L2 Consandolo Italy
121 N9 Consecon Ontario Canada
130 G7 Conselheiro Lafaiete Brazil
45 L3 Conselice Italy
45 L1 Conselve Italy
22 J5 Consenvoye France
13 G4 Consett England
95 M6 Conshohocken Pennsylvania U.S.A.
22 H4 Cons-la-Grandville France
126 C4 Consolación del Sur Cuba
69 H8 Con Son isld Vietnam
69 H8 Con Son Vietnam
118 G6 Consort Alberta Canada
95 M3 Constableville New York U.S.A.
Constance see Konstanz
143 E6 Constance Headland hill W Australia Australia
Constance, L see Bodensee
128 F5 Constância dos Baetas Brazil
48 M6 Constanţa Romania
16 D7 Constantina Spain
85 F1 Constantine Algeria
94 B5 Constantine Michigan U.S.A.
116 H7 Constantine, C Alaska U.S.A.
117 C5 Constantine, Mt Yukon Territory Canada
Constantinople see Istanbul
127 N4 Constant, Morne hill Guadeloupe W Indies
127 L2 Constant Spring Jamaica
131 A5 Constitución Chile
141 J6 Consuelo Queensland Australia
118 H9 Consul Saskatchewan Canada
101 L8 Contact Nevada U.S.A.
130 G7 Contagalo Brazil
128 D5 Contamana Peru
128 F3 Contão Brazil
131 D4 Contara R Argentina
45 M1 Contarina Italy
129 K6 Contas R Brazil
21 O2 Conteville France
40 F5 Conthey Switzerland
21 J6 Contigné France
103 O10 Continental Arizona U.S.A.
94 C5 Continental Ohio U.S.A.
106 C4 Continental Res Colorado U.S.A.
95 Q3 Contoocook New Hampshire U.S.A.
125 Q7 Contoy, I Mexico
16 E8 Contraviesa, Sa mts Spain
121 R7 Contrecoeur Quebec Canada
133 C8 Contreras, I Chile
21 N7 Contres Loir-et-Cher France
22 H5 Contreuve France
40 C1 Contrexéville France
130 G6 Contria Brazil
118 F7 Control Alberta Canada
36 C5 Contwig Germany
114 J4 Contwoyto L Northwest Territories Canada
21 P2 Conty France
126 H10 Convención Colombia
43 H8 Conversano Italy
94 B6 Converse Indiana U.S.A.
111 C10 Converse Louisiana U.S.A.
94 C6 Convoy Ohio U.S.A.
110 D6 Conway Arkansas U.S.A.
99 M9 Conway Iowa U.S.A.
110 D4 Conway Missouri U.S.A.
95 Q3 Conway New Hampshire U.S.A.
112 K1 Conway North Carolina U.S.A.
98 J1 Conway North Dakota U.S.A.
112 H4 Conway South Carolina U.S.A.
8 C1 Conway B Wales
141 J5 Conway, C Queensland Australia
138 D3 Conway, L South Australia Australia
110 D5 Conway, L Arkansas U.S.A.
140 C6 Conway, Mt N Terr Australia
95 Q2 Conway, N New Hampshire U.S.A.
144 D5 Conway R New Zealand
107 N4 Conway Springs Kansas U.S.A.
8 B4 Conwil Elvet Wales
8 C1 Conwy Wales
8 C1 Conwy R Wales
112 C4 Conyers Georgia U.S.A.
22 K3 Coo Belgium
138 C3 Coober Pedy South Australia Australia
9 G6 Cooden England
142 A3 Coogee dist Perth, W Aust Australia
142 A3 Coogee L W Australia Australia
142 C5 Cooglegong W Australia Australia
141 J7 Coogoon R Queensland Australia
140 C2 Cooinda N Terr Australia
138 B4 Cook South Australia Australia
99 O2 Cook Minnesota U.S.A.
99 K9 Cook Nebraska U.S.A.
133 C9 Cook, B.de Chile
117 K10 Cook, C British Columbia Canada
101 Q4 Cooke City Montana U.S.A.
143 E9 Cooke, Mt W Australia Australia
94 E10 Cookeville Tennessee U.S.A.
9 F4 Cookham England
146 D13 Cook Ice Shelf Antarctica
118 D5 Cooking L Alberta Canada
116 L7 Cook Inlet Alaska U.S.A.
134 L10 Cook Is Pacific Oc
144 C5 Cook, Mt New Zealand
117 D5 Cook, Mt Alaska/Yukon Terr U.S.A./Canada
99 U4 Cooks Michigan U.S.A.
123 Q2 Cook's Hbr Newfoundland Canada
121 T7 Cookshire Quebec Canada
141 H2 Cook's Passage Queensland Australia
106 C9 Cooks Pk New Mexico U.S.A.
121 L8 Cookstown Ontario Canada
14 E2 Cookstown N Ireland
145 E4 Cook Strait New Zealand
141 H3 Cooktown Queensland Australia
141 H7 Cooladdi Queensland Australia
139 J4 Coolah New South Wales Australia
139 H5 Coolamon New South Wales Australia
139 L3 Coolangatta New South Wales Australia
141 L8 Coolangatta Queensland Australia
143 C8 Coolcalalaya hill W Australia Australia
142 A2 Coolbellup, L W Australia Australia
112 G2 Cooleemee North Carolina U.S.A.
143 D9 Coolgardie W Australia Australia
140 B3 Coolibah N Terr Australia
103 N9 Coolidge Arizona U.S.A.
112 D6 Coolidge Georgia U.S.A.
109 L4 Coolidge Texas U.S.A.
127 P4 Coolidge airport Antigua W Indies
103 O8 Coolidge Dam Arizona U.S.A.
143 B8 Coolimba W Australia Australia
100 J1 Coolin Idaho U.S.A.
141 K8 Coolmunda Dam Queensland Australia
142 A4 Cooloongup, L W Australia Australia
94 F7 Coolville Ohio U.S.A.
143 B7 Coolyun Well W Australia Australia
139 J6 Cooma New South Wales Australia
14 A5 Coomacarrea mt Ireland
9 E5 Coombe Bissett England
8 D4 Coombe Hill England
143 B9 Coomberdale W Australia Australia
139 J4 Coonabarabran New South Wales Australia
138 F6 Coonalpyn South Australia Australia
139 J4 Coonamble New South Wales Australia
143 E9 Coonana W Australia Australia
138 F6 Coonawarra South Australia Australia
138 F5 Coonbah Roadhouse New South Wales Australia
138 D4 Coondambo South Australia Australia
Coondapoor see Kundāpura
142 C5 Coongan, R W Australia Australia
141 H8 Coongoola Queensland Australia
138 C2 Coongra R South Australia Australia
138 F2 Cooninnie, L South Australia Australia
76 C5 Coonoor India
99 M8 Coon Rapids Iowa U.S.A.
99 N4 Coon Rapids Minnesota U.S.A.
140 C1 Cooper R N Terr Australia
129 G8 Cooper Paraguay
109 M2 Cooper Texas U.S.A.
141 F7 Cooper Cr Qnsld/S Aust Australia
141 F7 Cooper Creek R Queensland Australia
144 A6 Cooper I New Zealand
143 G7 Cooper, Mt W Australia Australia
139 L4 Coopernook New South Wales Australia
141 K2 Coopers Plains dist Brisbane, Qnsld Australia
113 K11 Cooper's Town Bahamas
126 F1 Coopers Town Great Abaco I Bahamas
95 M4 Cooperstown New York U.S.A.
98 H2 Cooperstown North Dakota U.S.A.
94 B3 Coopersville Michigan U.S.A.
127 O3 Coora Trinidad
138 B4 Coorabie South Australia Australia
140 F6 Coorabulka Queensland Australia
143 B7 Coor-de-Wandy mt W Australia Australia
138 E6 Coorong, The L South Australia Australia
143 B8 Coorow W Australia Australia
141 L7 Cooroy Queensland Australia
111 L7 Coosa R Alabama U.S.A.
112 C3 Coosawattee R Georgia U.S.A.
112 F5 Coosawhatchie R South Carolina U.S.A.
100 A6 Coos Bay Oregon U.S.A.
139 J5 Cootamundra New South Wales Australia
14 E2 Cootehill Ireland
141 H7 Cooyar Queensland Australia
131 B6 Copahué pk Chile
133 C5 Copahue mt Chile/Arg
100 A2 Copalis Beach Washington U.S.A.
109 K7 Copano B Texas U.S.A.
100 C8 Copco California U.S.A.
106 H2 Cope Colorado U.S.A.
128 F4 Copea, Paraná R Brazil
113 F12 Copeland Florida U.S.A.
100 J1 Copeland Idaho U.S.A.
107 K4 Copeland Kansas U.S.A.
94 B2 Copemish Michigan U.S.A.
Copenhagen see København
95 M3 Copenhagen New York U.S.A.
133 E5 Copetonas Argentina
139 K3 Copeton Res. New South Wales Australia
133 C3 Copiapó Chile
133 D3 Copiapo vol Chile
15 F2 Copinsay Scotland
138 E4 Copley South Australia Australia
128 D6 Coporaque Peru
45 L2 Copparo Italy
120 G3 Coppell Ontario Canada
109 N8 Coppell Texas U.S.A.
129 G2 Coppename R Suriname
32 L8 Coppenbrügge Germany
116 P5 Copper R Alaska U.S.A.
109 K4 Copperas Cove Texas U.S.A.
100 G1 Copper Butte mt Washington U.S.A.
116 P6 Copper Center Alaska U.S.A.
120 J6 Copper Cliff Ontario Canada
99 T2 Copper Hbr Michigan U.S.A.
138 C3 Copper Hill South Australia Australia
114 H4 Coppermine Northwest Territories Canada
120 F6 Coppermine Pt C Ontario Canada
117 N11 Copper Mt British Columbia Canada
100 K8 Copper Mt Nevada U.S.A.
117 Q5 Copp L Northwest Territories Canada
48 J4 Copşa Mică Romania
131 B6 Copulhue, Paso del Arg/Chile
75 L3 Coqên China
22 B2 Coquelles France
13 G3 Coquet I England
13 G3 Coquet, R England
Coquilhatville see Mbandaka
100 A6 Coquille Oregon U.S.A.
131 B2 Coquimbo Chile
101 P7 Cora Wyoming U.S.A.
46 G1 Corabia Romania
130 G5 Coração de Jesus Brazil
139 L3 Coraki New South Wales Australia
120 J2 Coral Ontario Canada
71 C6 Coral B Palawan Philippines
113 L9 Coral Harbour New Providence I Bahamas
115 L5 Coral Harbour Northwest Territories Canada
137 K4 Coral Sea Islands Terr Australasia
99 P8 Coralville Lake res Iowa U.S.A.
101 L1 Coram Montana U.S.A.
139 G7 Corangamite, L Victoria Australia
129 G3 Corantijn R Suriname
94 G6 Coraopolis Pennsylvania U.S.A.
43 G7 Corato Italy
20 C5 Coray France
21 P4 Corbeil-Essonnes France
19 P13 Corbelin France
22 F5 Corbény France
120 K8 Corbetton Ontario Canada
21 P2 Corbie France
20 F3 Corbière Channel Is
18 G10 Corbières reg France
18 H5 Corbigny France
94 C10 Corbin Kentucky U.S.A.
123 R7 Corbin Hd Newfoundland Canada
45 M1 Còrbola Italy
16 D7 Corbones R Spain
13 F4 Corbridge England
9 F2 Corby Lincs England
9 F2 Corby Northants England
Corcaigh see Cork
36 B7 Corcieux France
102 E5 Corcoran California U.S.A.
20 G8 Corcoué-sur-Logne France
133 C6 Corcovado mt Chile
133 C6 Corcovado, Golfo Chile
16 A2 Corcubion Spain
112 D6 Cordele Georgia U.S.A.
107 M6 Cordell Oklahoma U.S.A.
20 G7 Cordemais France
18 G8 Cordes France
129 J5 Cordilheiras, Serra das mts Brazil
16 D1 Cordillera Cantábrica mts Spain
128 C3 Cordillera Central mts Colombia
127 J5 Cordillera Central mts Dominican Rep
125 O5 Cordillera Central mts Panama
128 C5 Cordillera Central mts Peru
71 E2 Cordillera Central mts Luzon Philippines
127 J10 Cordillera de Mérida mts Venezuela
128 C3 Cordillera Occidental mts Colombia
128 D2 Cordillera Oriental mts Colombia
71 F5 Cordilleras Ra Panay Philippines
138 F2 Cordillo Downs South Australia Australia
130 G6 Cordisburgo Brazil
131 D3 Córdoba Argentina
131 D4 Córdoba prov Argentina
128 C2 Córdoba div Colombia
125 L8 Córdoba Mexico
16 D7 Córdoba prov Spain
16 D7 Córdoba Spain
131 D3 Córdoba, Sierra de ra Argentina
128 C6 Córdova Peru
111 J8 Cordova Alabama U.S.A.
116 P6 Cordova Alaska U.S.A.
99 Q8 Cordova Illinois U.S.A.
121 N8 Cordova Mines Ontario Canada
116 P6 Cordova Pk Alaska U.S.A.
45 J3 Coreglia Antelminelli Italy
140 F4 Corella R Queensland Australia
140 D4 Corella L N Terr Australia
141 G5 Corfield Queensland Australia
45 P5 Corfinio Italy
Corfu isld Greece see Kérkira isld
94 J4 Corfu New York U.S.A.
100 F3 Corfu Washington U.S.A.
16 C2 Corgo Spain
130 C6 Corguinho Brazil
45 N6 Cori Italy
16 C5 Coria Spain
16 C7 Coria del R Spain
45 N4 Coriano Italy
121 O3 Coribelle Quebec Canada
139 K5 Coricudgy mt New South Wales Australia
43 H9 Corigliano Calabro Italy
45 O4 Corinaldo Italy
141 K2 Corinda dist Brisbane, Qnsld Australia
140 E4 Corinda Queensland Australia
141 K3 Coringa Is Gt Barrier Reef Aust
141 K3 Coringa Is Coral Sea
139 H8 Corinna Tasmania Australia
101 N8 Corinne Utah U.S.A.
Corinth see Kórinthos
101 S4 Corinth Montana U.S.A.
95 O3 Corinth New York U.S.A.
Corinth, Gulf of see Korinthiakós Kólpos
143 C9 Corinthian W Australia Australia
130 G6 Corinto Brazil
130 C6 Corixinha, R Brazil
14 C5 Cork co Ireland
14 C5 Cork Ireland
20 D5 Corlay France
43 E11 Corleone Sicily
47 J3 Çorlu Turkey
123 P4 Cormack Newfoundland Canada
123 Q5 Cormack mt Newfoundland Canada
21 O5 Cormainville France
21 L3 Cormeilles France
21 M7 Cormery France
22 F5 Cormicy France
123 L2 Cormier, L Quebec Canada
21 J3 Cormolain France
119 R4 Cormorant Manitoba Canada
6 L1 Cormorant oil rig North Sea
123 L4 Cormorant Pt Anticosti I, Quebec
107 M6 Corn Oklahoma U.S.A.
41 M6 Corna Italy
45 P6 Cornacchia, Monte Italy
32 H7 Cornau Germany
21 K7 Corne France
112 D3 Cornelia Georgia U.S.A.
133 G2 Cornélio Procópio Brazil
99 S9 Cornell Illinois U.S.A.
99 P4 Cornell Wisconsin U.S.A.
123 P5 Corner Brook Newfoundland Canada
139 H7 Corner Inlet Victoria Australia
110 K6 Cornersville Tennessee U.S.A.
111 D9 Corney L Louisiana U.S.A.
103 P6 Cornfields Arizona U.S.A.
13 F2 Cornhill-on-Tweed England
20 H5 Cornille France
40 E2 Cornimont France
119 P9 Corning Saskatchewan Canada
110 F5 Corning Arkansas U.S.A.
99 M9 Corning Iowa U.S.A.
107 O2 Corning Kansas U.S.A.
99 L9 Corning Missouri U.S.A.
95 K4 Corning New York U.S.A.
94 F7 Corning Ohio U.S.A.
Corn Is see Maíz, Is. del
141 G5 Cornish R Queensland Australia
95 P3 Cornish Flat New Hampshire U.S.A.
142 F5 Cornish, Mt W Australia Australia
45 J3 Corno alle Scale mt Italy
42 F6 Corno, M mt Italy
20 B5 Cornouaille reg France
21 J6 Cornuaille, la France
100 H4 Cornucopia Oregon U.S.A.
99 P3 Cornucopia Wisconsin U.S.A.
18 H9 Cornus France
121 Q7 Cornwall Ontario Canada
8 B7 Cornwall co England
115 K2 Cornwallis I Northwest Territories Canada
138 D5 Corny Pt South Australia Australia
127 K9 Coro Venezuela
130 G6 Coroaci Brazil
129 K4 Coroatá Brazil
87 B9 Coroca R Angola
128 E7 Corocoro Bolivia
128 E7 Coroico Bolivia
130 F6 Coromandel Brazil
145 E2 Coromandel New Zealand
76 E5 Coromandel Coast India
145 E2 Coromandel Peninsula New Zealand
21 J7 Coron France
71 E4 Coron Philippines
138 F4 Corona New South Wales Australia
102 G8 Corona California U.S.A.
106 E7 Corona New Mexico U.S.A.
119 M9 Coronach Saskatchewan Canada
102 G9 Coronado California U.S.A.
71 F7 Coronado B Mindanao Philippines
125 N5 Coronado, B.de Costa Rica
113 G8 Coronado Beach Florida U.S.A.
103 O10 Coronado Nat. Mem Arizona U.S.A.
118 F6 Coronation Alberta Canada
114 H4 Coronation G Northwest Territories Canada
146 E3 Coronation I S Orkney Is Antarctica
142 E2 Coronation Is W Australia Australia
71 E5 Coron B Philippines
71 E5 Coron Delian isld Philippines
131 A6 Coronel Chile
133 E5 Coronel Dorrego Argentina
130 G6 Coronel Fabriciano Brazil
130 C9 Coronel Oviedo Paraguay
130 C4 Coronel Ponce Brazil
131 E6 Coronel Pringles Argentina
131 E6 Coronel Suárez Argentina
133 F5 Coronel Vidal Argentina
144 B6 Coronet Pk New Zealand
128 D7 Coropuna mt Peru
46 D4 Çorovodë Albania
139 H6 Corowa New South Wales Australia
126 G10 Corozal Colombia
127 O1 Corozal Pt Trinidad
20 G6 Corps-Nuds France
130 C10 Corpus Argentina
109 K8 Corpus Christi Texas U.S.A.
133 D1 Corque Bolivia
101 L6 Corral Idaho U.S.A.
16 E5 Corrales Almaguer Spain
124 G5 Corrales Mexico
16 D3 Corrales Spain
133 F4 Corrales Uruguay
126 D3 Corralillo Cuba
124 F2 Corralitos Mexico
143 B7 Corrandibby Ra mts W Australia Australia
14 B3 Corraun Ireland
14 B3 Corraun Pen Ireland
99 L7 Correctionville Iowa U.S.A.
71 E3 Corregidor Luzon Philippines
130 E5 Córrego do Ouro Brazil
129 J6 Corrente Brazil
130 D6 Corrente, R Goiás Brazil
43 F12 Correnti, C.I. de Sicily
129 K6 Correntina Brazil
106 C7 Correo New Mexico U.S.A.
18 G7 Corrèze dept France
18 G7 Corrèze R France
45 K1 Correzzo Italy
45 M1 Corrèzzola Italy
14 B3 Corrib, L Ireland
12 C2 Corrie Scotland
130 B10 Corrientes Argentina
131 F2 Corrientes prov Argentina
133 F3 Corrientes R Argentina
128 C4 Corrientes R Peru
133 F5 Corrientes, C Argentina
126 B4 Corrientes, C Cuba
124 G7 Corrientes, C Mexico
109 N5 Corrigan Texas U.S.A.
143 C9 Corrigin W Australia Australia
139 K5 Corrimal New South Wales Australia
13 H6 Corringham England
14 B4 Corrofin Ireland
94 H5 Corry Pennsylvania U.S.A.
139 J6 Corryong Victoria Australia
12 C1 Corryvreckan, Str.of Scotland
18 L11 Corse-du-Sud dept Corsica
20 F5 Corseul France
12 C3 Corsewall Pt Scotland
8 D5 Corsham England
18 L10 Corsica isld France
98 H6 Corsica South Dakota U.S.A.
109 L3 Corsicana Texas U.S.A.
12 E3 Corsock Br Scotland
8 D5 Corston England
13 E2 Corstorphine Scotland
115 P5 Cort Adelaer, Kap C Greenland
103 N9 Cortaro Arizona U.S.A.
16 C7 Cortegana Spain
130 J10 Cortês Brazil
106 B4 Cortez Colorado U.S.A.
102 H1 Cortez Nevada U.S.A.
38 F8 Cortina d'Ampezzo Italy
98 K9 Cortland Nebraska U.S.A.
95 L4 Cortland New York U.S.A.
95 G5 Cortland Ohio U.S.A.
9 H2 Corton England
42 D5 Cortona Italy
85 B6 Corubal R Guinea/Guinea-Bissau
16 B6 Coruche Portugal
78 H1 Çoruh R Turkey
15 B3 Coruisk, L Scotland
78 E1 Çorum Turkey
130 B6 Corumbá Brazil
130 E4 Corumbá de Goiás Brazil
130 E6 Corumbaiba Brazil
130 E5 Corumbá, R Brazil
130 H5 Corumbaú, Pta. do C Brazil
128 F6 Corumbiara R Brazil
128 F2 Corumo R Venezuela
16 B1 Coruña prov Spain
94 C4 Corunna Michigan U.S.A.
130 H11 Corurípe Brazil
101 L3 Corvallis Montana U.S.A.
100 B5 Corvallis Oregon U.S.A.
38 E8 Corvara in Badia Italy
32 K9 Corvey Germany
8 C2 Corwen Wales
107 M4 Corwin Kansas U.S.A.
116 E7 Corwin, C Alaska U.S.A.
101 P4 Corwin Springs Montana U.S.A.
94 A8 Corydon Indiana U.S.A.
110 K3 Corydon Indiana U.S.A.
99 N9 Corydon Iowa U.S.A.
110 J4 Corydon Kentucky U.S.A.
94 J5 Corydon Pennsylvania U.S.A.
9 G5 Coryton England
21 K6 Corzé France
Cos isld see Kos isld
124 F5 Cosalá Mexico
125 M8 Cosamaloapan Mexico
43 G9 Cosenza Italy
9 E6 Cosham England
94 F6 Coshocton Ohio U.S.A.
81 B6 Cosmoledo Is Indian Oc
143 E8 Cosmo Newberry W Australia Australia
99 M5 Cosmos Minnesota U.S.A.
18 G5 Cosne France
18 G6 Cosne-d'Allier France
102 G5 Coso Junction California U.S.A.
133 E4 Cosquín Argentina
21 J6 Cossé-le-Vivien France
21 O6 Cosson R France
109 K6 Cost Texas U.S.A.
17 G7 Costa Blanca reg Spain
17 K3 Costa Brava reg Spain
16 C7 Costa de la Luz reg Spain
17 F8 Costa del Sol Spain
45 L1 Costa di Rovigo Italy
113 E11 Costa, L la Florida U.S.A.
102 G8 Costa Mesa California U.S.A.
125 M4 Costa Rica rep Central America
124 C2 Costa Rica Mexico
123 K3 Costebelle, L Quebec Canada
94 J5 Costello Pennsylvania U.S.A.
Costermansville see Bukavu
48 J6 Costeşhi Romania
95 T1 Costigan Maine U.S.A.
106 E5 Costilla New Mexico U.S.A.
33 Q9 Coswig Germany
71 G7 Cotabato Mindanao Philippines
128 E8 Cotagaita Bolivia
128 D7 Cotahuasi Peru
102 B3 Cotati California U.S.A.
130 H6 Cotaxé, R Brazil
121 Q7 Côteau Station Quebec Canada
118 K7 Coteau, The Saskatchewan Canada
126 G5 Coteaux Haiti
111 E12 Cote Blanche B Louisiana U.S.A.
44 B4 Côte d'Azur France
19 J5 Côte d'Or dept France
19 J5 Côte d'Or France
20 G3 Cotentin pen France
18 C4 Côtes d'Armor dept France
141 J6 Cotherstone Queensland Australia
13 F4 Cotherstone England
19 Q18 Cotignac France
45 L3 Cotignola Italy
128 F3 Cotingo R Brazil
85 E7 Cotonou Benin
128 C4 Cotopaxi vol Ecuador
106 E3 Cotopaxi Colorado U.S.A.
9 E4 Cotswold Hills England
100 B6 Cottage Grove Oregon U.S.A.
112 G5 Cottageville South Carolina U.S.A.
94 F8 Cottageville West Virginia U.S.A.
31 H4 Cottbus Germany
123 T5 Cottel I Newfoundland Canada
9 G3 Cottenham England
110 D5 Cotter Arkansas U.S.A.
83 M14 Cotter, C Mauritius
142 A2 Cottesloe Beach dist Perth, W Aust Australia
9 F2 Cottesmore England
129 H3 Cottica Suriname
13 H6 Cottingham England
99 O2 Cotton Minnesota U.S.A.
140 E6 Cottonbush Cr Queensland Australia
111 J8 Cottondale Alabama U.S.A.
111 L11 Cottondale Florida U.S.A.
140 D1 Cotton I N Terr Australia
119 V3 Cotton L Manitoba Canada
110 E6 Cotton Plant Arkansas U.S.A.
111 D11 Cottonport Louisiana U.S.A.
109 O3 Cotton Valley Louisiana U.S.A.
111 L10 Cottonwood Alabama U.S.A.
103 N7 Cottonwood Arizona U.S.A.
100 C9 Cottonwood California U.S.A.
100 J3 Cottonwood Idaho U.S.A.
99 M5 Cottonwood R Minnesota U.S.A.
98 E6 Cottonwood South Dakota U.S.A.
109 H3 Cottonwood Texas U.S.A.
103 L6 Cottonwood Cliffs Arizona U.S.A.
107 O3 Cottonwood Falls Kansas U.S.A.
103 O6 Cottonwood Wash R Arizona U.S.A.
127 J5 Cotuí Dominican Rep
109 H7 Cotulla Texas U.S.A.

168

Coubre, Pointe de la — Czaplinek

18 E7 **Coubre, Pointe de la** *pt* France
142 F3 **Couchman Ra** W Australia Australia
22 E4 **Coucy-le-Château Auffrique** France
21 N7 **Couddes** France
22 C1 **Coudekerque-Branche** France
99 P4 **Couderay** Wisconsin U.S.A.
94 J5 **Coudersport** Pennsylvania U.S.A.
21 O3 **Coudray-St. Germer, le** France
21 M6 **Coudrecieux** France
21 N4 **Coudres** France
122 B6 **Coudres, I.aux** Quebec Canada
138 D6 **Coüedic, C.de** South Australia Australia
20 G7 **Couëron** France
21 J5 **Couesmes-Vaucé** France
20 H5 **Couesnon** *R* France
20 H7 **Couffé** France
100 C3 **Cougar** Washington U.S.A.
18 F6 **Couhé** France
14 A5 **Coulagh B** Ireland
21 L5 **Coulans** France
15 C2 **Coulbeag Mt** Scotland
100 F2 **Coulee City** Washington U.S.A.
100 G1 **Coulee Dam** Washington U.S.A.
100 G1 **Coulee Dam Nat. Recreation Area** Washington U.S.A.
21 L5 **Coulimer** France
146 C12 **Coulman I** Antarctica
21 O6 **Coulmiers** France
22 B2 **Coulogne** France
21 O4 **Coulombs** Eure France
121 O6 **Coulonge** *R* Quebec Canada
18 E6 **Coulonges-Sur-l'Autize** France
21 K8 **Coulonges Thouarsais** France
21 H4 **Coulouvray-Boisbenâtre** France
119 R9 **Coulter** Manitoba Canada
102 D4 **Coulterville** California U.S.A.
110 G3 **Coulterville** Illinois U.S.A.
116 F4 **Council** Alaska U.S.A.
100 J5 **Council** Idaho U.S.A.
99 L8 **Council Bluffs** Iowa U.S.A.
107 O3 **Council Grove** Kansas U.S.A.
8 D2 **Cound** England
107 N7 **Countyline** Oklahoma U.S.A.
15 E4 **Coupar Angus** Scotland
123 Q7 **Coupe, C** Langlade I Atlantic Oc
100 C1 **Coupeville** Washington U.S.A.
109 K5 **Coupland** Texas U.S.A.
22 B2 **Couple, Mt** France
21 K5 **Couptrain** France
117 S3 **Courageous L** Northwest Territories Canada
21 P5 **Courances** France
122 B8 **Courcelles** Quebec Canada
21 L5 **Courcemont** France
21 N6 **Cour Cheverny** France
21 K5 **Courcité** France
21 L5 **Courgains** France
27 M16 **Courland Lagoon** Lithuania/Rus Fed
21 J8 **Courlay** France
18 H7 **Courpière** France
22 D3 **Courrières** France
18 H9 **Coursan** France
21 K3 **Courseulles** France
18 H5 **Courson les Carrières** France
21 N5 **Courtalain** France
40 F3 **Courtelary** Switzerland
117 L11 **Courtenay** British Columbia Canada
98 H2 **Courtenay** North Dakota U.S.A.
18 G7 **Courtine, la** France
110 J7 **Courtland** Alabama U.S.A.
107 N2 **Courtland** Kansas U.S.A.
99 M5 **Courtland** Minnesota U.S.A.
95 K10 **Courtland** Virginia U.S.A.
14 C5 **Courtmacsherry** Ireland
109 L5 **Courtney** Texas U.S.A.
21 L4 **Courtomer** France
Courtrai *see* **Kortrijk**
22 H2 **Court Saint-Etienne** Belgium
118 L8 **Courval** Saskatchewan Canada
21 N5 **Courville** France
109 O3 **Coushatta** Louisiana U.S.A.
83 J12 **Cousin I** Seychelles
22 G3 **Cousolre** France
21 M8 **Coussay-les-Bois** France
19 O17 **Coustellet** France
87 D9 **Coutada do Mucusso** Angola
20 H3 **Coutances** France
21 K4 **Couterne** France
22 J2 **Couthuin** Belgium
18 E7 **Coutras** France
101 N1 **Coutts** Alberta Canada
21 K7 **Coutures** France
127 O2 **Couva** Trinidad
20 G2 **Couville** France
22 H3 **Couvin** Belgium
22 F4 **Couvron-et-Aumencourt** France
48 K5 **Covasna** Romania
48 K5 **Covasna** *reg* Romania
109 N1 **Cove** Arkansas U.S.A.
100 H4 **Cove** Oregon U.S.A.
112 K2 **Cove City** North Carolina U.S.A.
103 M3 **Cove Fort** Utah U.S.A.
100 B10 **Covelo** California U.S.A.
94 K7 **Cove Mt** Pennsylvania U.S.A.
126 G10 **Coveñas** Colombia
9 E3 **Coventry** England
95 L8 **Cove Point** Maryland U.S.A.
107 M2 **Covert** Kansas U.S.A.
94 A4 **Covert** Michigan U.S.A.
94 J9 **Covesville** Virginia U.S.A.
16 B4 **Covilhã** Portugal
116 K7 **Coville, L** Alaska U.S.A.
112 D4 **Covington** Georgia U.S.A.
99 T9 **Covington** Indiana U.S.A.
94 C7 **Covington** Kentucky U.S.A.
111 F11 **Covington** Louisiana U.S.A.
99 S3 **Covington** Michigan U.S.A.
94 C6 **Covington** Ohio U.S.A.
107 N5 **Covington** Oklahoma U.S.A.
110 G6 **Covington** Tennessee U.S.A.
109 K3 **Covington** Texas U.S.A.
94 G9 **Covington** Virginia U.S.A.
120 G5 **Cow** *R* Ontario Canada
15 C4 **Cowal** Scotland
139 J5 **Cowal, L** New South Wales Australia
119 R6 **Cowan** Manitoba Canada
110 K6 **Cowan** Tennessee U.S.A.
140 E4 **Cowan Downs** Queensland Australia
138 F6 **Cowangie** Victoria Australia
118 K4 **Cowan L** Saskatchewan Canada
143 D9 **Cowan, Lake** W Australia Australia
101 P4 **Cowan, Mt** Montana U.S.A.
121 S7 **Cowansville** Quebec Canada
138 D3 **Coward Springs** South Australia Australia
58 C5 **Cowargarzê** China
138 E2 **Cowarie** South Australia Australia
9 F2 **Cowbit** England
103 L2 **Cowboy Pass** Utah U.S.A.
8 C5 **Cowbridge** Wales
143 B9 **Cowcowing L** W Australia Australia
100 G2 **Cow Cr** Washington U.S.A.
110 H2 **Cowden** Illinois U.S.A.
13 E1 **Cowdenbeath** Scotland
101 T9 **Cowdrey** Colorado U.S.A.
138 D5 **Cowell** South Australia Australia
94 G8 **Cowen** West Virginia U.S.A.
139 H7 **Cowes** Victoria Australia
9 E6 **Cowes** England
107 P6 **Coweta** Oklahoma U.S.A.
9 F6 **Cowfold** England
123 P4 **Cow Head** Newfoundland Canada
100 E8 **Cow Head L** California U.S.A.
100 A1 **Cowichan, L** British Columbia Canada
140 A6 **Cowle, Mt** N Terr Australia
98 H9 **Cowles** Nebraska U.S.A.
106 E6 **Cowles** New Mexico U.S.A.
141 G7 **Cowley** Queensland Australia
118 D9 **Cowley** Alberta Canada
101 R5 **Cowley** Wyoming U.S.A.
100 C3 **Cowlitz** *R* Washington U.S.A.
100 D3 **Cowlitz Pass** Washington U.S.A.
94 H8 **Cowpasture** *R* Virginia U.S.A.
112 F2 **Cowpens** South Carolina U.S.A.
112 F2 **Cowpens Nat.Bat.Site** South Carolina U.S.A.
139 J5 **Cowra** New South Wales Australia
130 G4 **Coxa, R** Brazil
139 H9 **Cox Bight** Tasmania Australia
13 G4 **Coxhoe** England
130 C4 **Coxibó do Ouro** Brazil
130 C6 **Coxim** Brazil
123 O2 **Coxipi L** Quebec Canada
130 C4 **Coxipó da Ponté** Brazil
143 F6 **Cox,Mt** W Australia Australia
140 D3 **Cox R** N Terr Australia
95 O4 **Coxsackie** New York U.S.A.
75 O8 **Cox's Bazar** Bangladesh
123 P4 **Cox's Cove** Newfoundland Canada
108 B6 **Coyame** Mexico
108 D5 **Coyanosa Cr** Texas U.S.A.
21 P3 **Coye-la-Forêt** France
107 N6 **Coyle** Oklahoma U.S.A.
102 C4 **Coyote** California U.S.A.
102 H6 **Coyote L** California U.S.A.
102 F5 **Coyote Peak** California U.S.A.
103 L9 **Coyote Pk** Arizona U.S.A.
124 D5 **Coyote, Pta** *C* Mexico
124 F6 **Coyotitán** Mexico
98 G9 **Cozad** Nebraska U.S.A.
44 B2 **Cozie Alpi** *mt* Italy
124 C2 **Cozón, Cerro** *mt* Mexico
125 Q7 **Cozumel, I.de** Mexico
100 F3 **Crab Cr** Washington U.S.A.
141 F1 **Crab I** Queensland Australia
139 J4 **Craboon** New South Wales Australia
94 C9 **Crab Orchard** Kentucky U.S.A.
112 C2 **Crab Orchard** Tennessee U.S.A.
110 G4 **Crab Orchard L** Illinois U.S.A.
127 H2 **Crab Pond Pt** Jamaica
139 H7 **Crab Pt** Victoria Australia
8 B6 **Crackington Haven** England
8 D2 **Crackleybank** England
Cracow *see* **Kraków**
141 K7 **Cracow** Queensland Australia
139 H8 **Cradle, Mt** Tasmania Australia
138 E4 **Cradock** South Australia Australia
89 D9 **Cradock** S Africa
117 G8 **Craig** Alaska U.S.A.
101 S9 **Craig** Colorado U.S.A.
113 G13 **Craig** Florida U.S.A.
99 L9 **Craig** Missouri U.S.A.
101 O2 **Craig** Montana U.S.A.
98 K8 **Craig** Nebraska U.S.A.
15 E3 **Craigellachie** Scotland
13 E1 **Craigend** Scotland
15 C5 **Craighouse** Scotland
12 D2 **Craigie** Scotland
144 C5 **Craigieburn** New Zealand
100 J3 **Craigmont** Idaho U.S.A.
116 R6 **Craig, Mt** Alaska U.S.A.
118 E7 **Craigmyle** Alberta Canada
13 E1 **Craigrothie** Scotland
94 H8 **Craigsville** Virginia U.S.A.
14 D4 **Craiguenamanagh** Ireland
119 M7 **Craik** Saskatchewan Canada
13 F1 **Crail** Scotland
37 J5 **Crailsheim** Germany
48 H6 **Craiova** Romania
13 E2 **Cramond** Scotland
121 Q8 **Cranberry, L** New York U.S.A.
119 Q4 **Cranberry Portage** Manitoba Canada
9 E6 **Cranborne** England
143 C10 **Cranbrook** W Australia Australia
117 Q11 **Cranbrook** British Columbia Canada
9 G5 **Cranbrook** England
119 R8 **Crandall** Manitoba Canada
98 J4 **Crandall** South Dakota U.S.A.
109 L3 **Crandall** Texas U.S.A.
99 S4 **Crandon** Wisconsin U.S.A.
127 P6 **Crane** Barbados
110 C5 **Crane** Missouri U.S.A.
98 B2 **Crane** Montana U.S.A.
100 G6 **Crane** Oregon U.S.A.
108 E4 **Crane** Texas U.S.A.
100 J5 **Crane Cr.Res** Idaho U.S.A.
118 H8 **Crane L** Saskatchewan Canada
119 M9 **Crane Valley** Saskatchewan Canada
109 K4 **Cranfills Gap** Texas U.S.A.
9 F5 **Cranleigh** England
100 A8 **Crannell** California U.S.A.
13 F2 **Cranshaws** Scotland
95 Q5 **Cranston** Rhode I U.S.A.
13 H6 **Cranswick** England
21 J6 **Craon** France
22 F5 **Craonne** France
18 H7 **Craponne-sur-Arzon** France
98 H1 **Crary** North Dakota U.S.A.
146 D10 **Crary Ice Rise** *ice rise* Antarctica
48 H3 **Crasna** *R* Romania
48 L4 **Crasna** Romania
48 H3 **Crasnei, Muntii** *mt* Romania
100 C7 **Crater L** Oregon U.S.A.
100 C7 **Crater Lake Nat. Park** Oregon U.S.A.
100 D9 **Crater Peak** *mt* California U.S.A.
101 M6 **Craters of the Moon Nat.Mon** Idaho U.S.A.
43 G9 **Crati** *R* Italy
130 G9 **Crato** Brazil
21 L7 **Cravant-les Coteaux** Indre-et-Loire France
119 N8 **Craven** Saskatchewan Canada
130 F7 **Cravinhos** Brazil
128 D2 **Cravo Norte** *R* Colombia
6 L3 **Crawford** *oil rig* North Sea
12 E3 **Crawford** Scotland
112 D4 **Crawford** Georgia U.S.A.
111 H8 **Crawford** Mississippi U.S.A.
98 C7 **Crawford** Nebraska U.S.A.
109 K4 **Crawford** Texas U.S.A.
12 E3 **Crawfordjohn** Scotland
140 B3 **Crawford,Mt** N Terr Australia
95 Q2 **Crawford Notch** New Hampshire U.S.A.
71 D5 **Crawford Pt** Philippines
110 K1 **Crawfordsville** Indiana U.S.A.
111 M11 **Crawfordville** Florida U.S.A.
112 E4 **Crawfordville** Georgia U.S.A.
9 F5 **Crawley** England
8 C4 **Cray** Wales
9 G5 **Crayford** England
116 P4 **Crazy Mts** Alaska U.S.A.
101 P3 **Crazy Mts** Montana U.S.A.
101 P4 **Crazy Pk** Montana U.S.A.
101 T5 **Crazy Woman Cr** Wyoming U.S.A.
15 D4 **Creag Meagaidh** *mt* Scotland
143 B6 **Cream, R** W Australia Australia
20 G3 **Créances** France
118 L4 **Crean L** Saskatchewan Canada
40 A5 **Crêches** France
22 B3 **Crécy-en-Ponthieu** France
22 F4 **Crécy-sur-Serre** France
8 C6 **Crediton** England
12 D4 **Cree Bridge** Scotland
106 D4 **Creede** Colorado U.S.A.
112 J1 **Creedmoor** North Carolina U.S.A.
101 R9 **Creek** Colorado U.S.A.
94 H6 **Creekside** Pennsylvania U.S.A.
113 L9 **Creek Village** New Providence I Bahamas
114 J6 **Cree L** Saskatchewan Canada
124 F4 **Creel** Mexico
119 O9 **Creelman** Saskatchewan Canada
120 K8 **Creemore** Ontario Canada
12 D3 **Cree, R** Scotland
114 J6 **Cree River** Saskatchewan Canada
12 D4 **Creetown** Scotland
37 J5 **Creglingen** Germany
119 P4 **Creighton** Saskatchewan Canada
98 H7 **Creighton** Nebraska U.S.A.
120 J6 **Creighton Mine** Ontario Canada
21 P3 **Creil** France
44 G1 **Crema** Italy
47 R14 **Cremasti** Rhodes Greece
19 O13 **Crémieu** France
118 C7 **Cremona** Alberta Canada
44 G1 **Crémona** Italy
111 F7 **Crenshaw** Mississippi U.S.A.
18 E8 **Créon** France
48 F5 **Crepaja** Serbia Yugoslavia
129 G5 **Crepori** *R* Brazil
22 D5 **Crépy-en-Valois** France
120 K6 **Crerar** Ontario Canada
42 F4 **Cres** Croatia
98 G4 **Cresbard** South Dakota U.S.A.
107 N6 **Crescent** Oklahoma U.S.A.
113 G10 **Crescent Beach** Florida U.S.A.
112 J4 **Crescent Beach** South Carolina U.S.A.
100 A8 **Crescent City** California U.S.A.
139 K4 **Crescent Head** New South Wales Australia
113 F8 **Crescent L** Florida U.S.A.
100 D6 **Crescent L** Oregon U.S.A.
100 B1 **Crescent, L** Washington U.S.A.
100 E9 **Crescent Mills** California U.S.A.
103 J6 **Crescent Pk** Nevada U.S.A.
99 O6 **Cresco** Iowa U.S.A.
45 L2 **Crespino** Italy
8 B4 **Cresselly** Wales
109 K3 **Cresson** Texas U.S.A.
139 H8 **Cressy** Tasmania Australia
139 G7 **Cressy** Victoria Australia
19 O15 **Crest** France
94 E6 **Crestline** Ohio U.S.A.
100 J1 **Creston** British Columbia Canada
123 R6 **Creston** Newfoundland Canada
99 M8 **Creston** Iowa U.S.A.
101 L1 **Creston** Montana U.S.A.
100 G2 **Creston** Washington U.S.A.
101 S8 **Creston** Wyoming U.S.A.
106 E3 **Crestone Pk** Colorado U.S.A.
111 K11 **Crestview** Florida U.S.A.
110 J6 **Crestview** Tennessee U.S.A.
119 M8 **Crestwynd** Saskatchewan Canada
112 L2 **Creswell** North Carolina U.S.A.
100 B6 **Creswell** Oregon U.S.A.
115 K3 **Creswell B** Northwest Territories Canada
140 D4 **Creswell Downs** N Terr Australia
139 G7 **Creswick** Victoria Australia
19 J6 **Crêt de la Neige** *mt* France
Crete *isld see* **Kriti** *isld*
99 T8 **Crete** Illinois U.S.A.
98 K9 **Crete** Nebraska U.S.A.
98 H3 **Crete** North Dakota U.S.A.
46 G9 **Crete, Sea of** Greece
21 J3 **Creully** France
17 K2 **Creus, C** Spain
18 G6 **Creuse** *dept* France
21 N8 **Creuse** *R* France
37 M4 **Creussen** Germany
37 J1 **Creuzburg** Germany
45 K2 **Crevalcore** Italy
21 P2 **Crèvecoeur-le-Grand** France
21 L3 **Crêvecœur** France
17 G6 **Crevillente** Spain
41 H5 **Crevola** Italy
8 D1 **Crewe** England
94 J9 **Crewe** Virginia U.S.A.
8 D6 **Crewkerne** England
12 D1 **Crianlarich** Scotland
8 B2 **Criccieth** Wales
9 E1 **Crich** England
118 K9 **Crichton** Saskatchewan Canada
133 H3 **Criciuma** Brazil
9 E3 **Crick** England
8 C4 **Crickhowell** Wales
9 E4 **Cricklade** England
94 C6 **Cridersville** Ohio U.S.A.
12 E1 **Crieff** Scotland
21 N1 **Criel-sur-Mer** France
15 E6 **Criffell** *mt* Scotland
42 F3 **Crikvenica** Croatia
117 E6 **Crillon, Mt** Alaska U.S.A.
99 O1 **Crilly** Ontario Canada
Crimea *see* **Krymskaya Oblast'**
37 N2 **Crimmitschau** Germany
12 C1 **Crinan** Scotland
15 C4 **Crinan Canal** Scotland
106 E3 **Cripple Creek** Colorado U.S.A.
116 J5 **Cripple Landing** Alaska U.S.A.
9 G6 **Cripps's Corner** England
21 L2 **Criquetot-l'Esneval** France
48 G4 **Crişana** Romania
130 F5 **Cristalina** Brazil
129 H6 **Cristalino** *R* Brazil
38 F8 **Cristallo** *mt* Italy
126 H10 **Cristóbal Colón, Pico** *mt* Colombia
48 J4 **Cristuru Secuiesc** Romania
48 G4 **Crişul Alb** *R* Romania
48 G4 **Crişul Negru** *R* Romania
48 H4 **Crişul Repede** *R* Romania
94 C8 **Crittenden** Kentucky U.S.A.
33 P5 **Crivitz** Germany
99 S4 **Crivitz** Wisconsin U.S.A.
38 L9 **Črna** Slovenia
46 E3 **Crna** *R* Macedonia Yugoslavia
Crna Gora *see* **Montenegro**
46 E2 **Crna Gora** *mt* Macedonia/Serbia Yugoslavia
46 E2 **Crna Trava** Serbia Yugoslavia
46 D3 **Crni Drim** *R* Macedonia Yugoslavia
38 M9 **Črni-vrh** *mt* Slovenia
14 B3 **Croagh Patrick Mt** Ireland
139 J7 **Croajingolong Nat. Park** Victoria Australia
42 G4 **Croatia** *rep* S Europe
41 O5 **Croce, C** *mt* Italy
43 G1 **Croce, S., C** Sicily
110 D4 **Crocker** Missouri U.S.A.
70 D2 **Crocker Ra** Borneo
12 E3 **Crocketford** Scotland
109 M4 **Crockett** Texas U.S.A.
9 G5 **Crockham Hill** England
21 K4 **Crocy** France
38 F8 **Croda Rossa** *mt* Italy
110 J4 **Crofton** Kentucky U.S.A.
98 J7 **Crofton** Nebraska U.S.A.
142 D5 **Crofton,Mt** W Australia Australia
95 M3 **Croghan** New York U.S.A.
19 O1 **Croisette, C** France
20 E7 **Croisic,le** France
22 D3 **Croisilles** France
145 D4 **Croisilles Harbour** New Zealand
127 H5 **Croix des Bouquets** Haiti
19 P15 **Croix Haute, Col de la** *pass* France
21 H5 **Croixille,la** France
21 M7 **Croix,la** France
122 B2 **Croix, L.à la** Quebec Canada
122 E8 **Croix R** New Brunswick Canada
22 D5 **Croix-St.Ouen, la** France
21 N3 **Croix-st.Leufroy,la** France
120 K8 **Croker, Cape** Ontario Canada
140 B2 **Croker Hill** N Terr Australia
140 C1 **Croker I** N Terr Australia
15 D3 **Cromarty** Scotland
15 D3 **Cromarty Firth** Scotland
138 B2 **Crombie, Mt** South Australia Australia
119 Q9 **Cromer** Manitoba Canada
9 H2 **Cromer** England
144 B6 **Cromwell** New Zealand
99 O3 **Cromwell** Minnesota U.S.A.
144 C5 **Cronadun** New Zealand
37 K5 **Cronheim** Germany
13 F5 **Crook** Cumbria England
13 G4 **Crook** Durham England
98 D9 **Crook** Colorado U.S.A.
107 K4 **Crooked Cr** Kansas U.S.A.
100 G7 **Crooked Cr** Oregon U.S.A.
126 G3 **Crooked I** Bahamas
126 G3 **Crooked I.Passage** Bahamas
123 Q5 **Crooked L** Newfoundland Canada
113 F10 **Crooked L** Florida U.S.A.
117 M8 **Crooked R** British Columbia Canada
100 E5 **Crooked R** Oregon U.S.A.
119 O6 **Crooked River** Saskatchewan Canada
13 F2 **Crookham** England
14 B5 **Crookhaven** Ireland
109 M2 **Crook, L** Texas U.S.A.
13 F5 **Crooklands** England
12 E1 **Crook of Devon** Scotland
98 K2 **Crookston** Minnesota U.S.A.
98 F7 **Crookston** Nebraska U.S.A.
94 E7 **Crooksville** Ohio U.S.A.
139 J5 **Crookwell** New South Wales Australia
14 C4 **Croom** Ireland
113 E9 **Croom** Florida U.S.A.
139 K3 **Croppa Cr** New South Wales Australia
9 E3 **Cropredy** England
123 R2 **Croque** Newfoundland Canada
141 G3 **Crosbie** *R* Queensland Australia
99 N3 **Crosby** Minnesota U.S.A.
111 E10 **Crosby** Mississippi U.S.A.
98 C1 **Crosby** North Dakota U.S.A.
109 M6 **Crosby** Texas U.S.A.
108 F2 **Crosbyton** Texas U.S.A.
8 D5 **Cross** England
85 F7 **Cross** *R* Nigeria
20 F7 **Crossac** France
12 C2 **Crossaig** Scotland
87 B10 **Cross, C** Namibia
113 D8 **Cross City** Florida U.S.A.
111 E8 **Crossett** Arkansas U.S.A.
13 F4 **Cross Fell** England
118 C7 **Crossfield** Alberta Canada
13 E1 **Crossgates** Scotland
8 C3 **Cross Gates** Wales
8 B4 **Cross Hands** Wales
113 K12 **Cross Harbour** Bahamas
14 C5 **Crosshaven** Ireland
12 D3 **Crosshill** Scotland
112 F3 **Cross Hill** South Carolina U.S.A.
113 K11 **Crossing Rocks** Bahamas
121 O8 **Cross, L** Ontario Canada
111 C9 **Cross L** Louisiana U.S.A.
119 U4 **Cross Lake** Manitoba Canada
144 D5 **Crossley, Mt** New Zealand
118 D4 **Cross L. Prov. Park** Alberta Canada
12 B5 **Crossmaglen** N Ireland
103 K7 **Crossman Pk** Arizona U.S.A.
12 E4 **Crossmichael** Scotland
14 B2 **Crossmolina** Ireland
106 B1 **Cross Mountain** Colorado U.S.A.
109 H3 **Cross Plains** Texas U.S.A.
94 B1 **Cross Village** Michigan U.S.A.
110 L6 **Crossville** Tennessee U.S.A.
116 P5 **Crosswind L** Alaska U.S.A.
45 J2 **Crostolo** *R* Italy
94 E3 **Croswell** Michigan U.S.A.
110 L3 **Crothersville** Indiana U.S.A.
43 H9 **Crotone** Italy
21 O1 **Crotoy,le** France
37 O3 **Crottendorf** Germany
100 K5 **Crouch** Idaho U.S.A.
9 G4 **Crouch, R** England
22 E5 **Crouy** France
21 L7 **Crouzilles** France
101 S4 **Crow Agency** Montana U.S.A.
139 H4 **Crowal** *R* New South Wales Australia
9 G5 **Crowborough** England
8 C5 **Crowcombe** England
106 F1 **Crow Cr** Colorado U.S.A.
111 F7 **Crowder** Mississippi U.S.A.
107 P6 **Crowder** Oklahoma U.S.A.
118 F1 **Crowduck L.** Manitoba Canada
139 L4 **Crowdy Hd** New South Wales Australia
108 H2 **Crowell** Texas U.S.A.
139 G7 **Crowes** Victoria Australia
101 Q6 **Crowheart** Wyoming U.S.A.
139 H4 **Crowl** *R* New South Wales Australia
9 F2 **Crowland** England
13 H6 **Crowle** England
106 G3 **Crowley** Colorado U.S.A.
111 D11 **Crowley** Louisiana U.S.A.
102 F4 **Crowley, L** California U.S.A.
94 E8 **Crown City** Ohio U.S.A.
103 M7 **Crown King** Arizona U.S.A.
106 B6 **Crown Point** New Mexico U.S.A.
95 O3 **Crown Point** New York U.S.A.
115 L4 **Crown Prince Frederick I** Northwest Territories Canada
127 M2 **Crown Pt** Tobago
99 T8 **Crown Pt** Indiana U.S.A.
101 O3 **Crow Peak** Montana U.S.A.
141 K7 **Crow's Nest** Queensland Australia
118 C9 **Crowsnest Pass** Alberta/Br Col Canada
99 M3 **Crow Wing** *R* Minnesota U.S.A.
13 G4 **Croxdale** England
8 B5 **Croyde** England
141 F4 **Croydon** Queensland Australia
142 C5 **Croydon** W Australia Australia
9 F5 **Croydon** England
144 B7 **Croydon** New Zealand
83 L13 **Croy, Î de** Kerguelen Indian Oc
94 J8 **Crozet** Virginia U.S.A.
81 D9 **Crozet Basin** Indian Oc
81 C10 **Crozet, Îs** Indian Oc
81 B10 **Crozet Plateau** Indian Oc
114 G2 **Crozier Chan** Northwest Territories Canada
20 B5 **Crozon** France
19 N15 **Cruas** France
126 D3 **Cruces** Cuba
128 C2 **Cruces, Pta** *pt* Colombia
22 L4 **Cruchten** Luxembourg
94 H7 **Crucible** Pennsylvania U.S.A.
15 G3 **Cruden B** Scotland
8 D2 **Crudgington** England
8 D4 **Crudwell** England
111 F8 **Cruger** Mississippi U.S.A.
21 M4 **Crûlai** France
14 E2 **Crumlin** N Ireland
100 F7 **Crump L** Oregon U.S.A.
19 Q12 **Cruseilles** France
22 K5 **Crusnes** France
133 E4 **Cruz** Argentina
133 G3 **Cruz Alta** Brazil
131 D3 **Cruz del Eje** Argentina
130 G8 **Cruzeiro** Brazil
133 G2 **Cruzeiro do Oeste** Brazil
128 D5 **Cruzeiro do Sul** Brazil
133 C3 **Cruz Grande** Chile
128 C3 **Cruz, La** Colombia
18 G9 **Cruzy** France
117 M8 **Crysdale, Mt** British Columbia Canada
106 C2 **Crystal** *R* Colorado U.S.A.
103 K5 **Crystal** Nevada U.S.A.
98 J1 **Crystal** North Dakota U.S.A.
113 E9 **Crystal B** Florida U.S.A.
138 E5 **Crystal Brook** South Australia Australia
119 T9 **Crystal City** Manitoba Canada
108 H7 **Crystal City** Texas U.S.A.
99 S3 **Crystal Falls** Michigan U.S.A.
99 S7 **Crystal L** Illinois U.S.A.
99 U5 **Crystal L** Michigan U.S.A.
99 N6 **Crystal Lake** Iowa U.S.A.
113 E9 **Crystal River** Florida U.S.A.
119 M6 **Crystal Springs** Saskatchewan Canada
111 F9 **Crystal Springs** Mississippi U.S.A.
99 U6 **Crystal Valley** Michigan U.S.A.
48 F4 **Csanytelek** Hungary
48 E3 **Csepel Sziget** *R* Hungary
48 F4 **Csongrád** *co* Hungary
48 F4 **Csongrád** Hungary
48 D3 **Csorna** Hungary
48 F4 **Csorvas** Hungary
48 E3 **Csóványos** *mt* Hungary
48 D4 **Csurgó** Hungary
127 L9 **Cúa** Venezuela
88 F9 **Cuambo** Mozambique
87 D9 **Cuando** *R* Angola
87 C9 **Cuangar** Angola
87 C7 **Cuango** Angola
86 C7 **Cuango** Zaire
87 B7 **Cuanza** *R* Angola
67 A7 **Cua Rao** Vietnam
133 F4 **Cuareim** Brazil
131 F3 **Cuaro** *R* Uruguay
133 E4 **Cuarto** *R* Argentina
124 H4 **Cuatro Ciénegas de Carranza** Mexico
68 H4 **Cua Tung** Vietnam
124 F3 **Cuauhtémoc** Mexico
124 G8 **Cuautitlán** Mexico
125 K8 **Cuautla** Mexico
16 B6 **Cuba** Portugal
110 F1 **Cuba** Illinois U.S.A.
107 N2 **Cuba** Kansas U.S.A.
110 E3 **Cuba** Missouri U.S.A.
106 D5 **Cuba** New Mexico U.S.A.
94 J4 **Cuba** New York U.S.A.
126 D4 **Cuba** *rep* W Indies
103 M10 **Cubabi, Cerro** *pk* Mexico
99 Q7 **Cuba City** Wisconsin U.S.A.
127 M9 **Cubagua, I** Venezuela
143 B10 **Cuballing** W Australia Australia
87 C9 **Cubango** *R* Angola
130 F8 **Cubatão** Brazil
119 N4 **Cub Hills** Saskatchewan Canada
127 K10 **Cubiro** Venezuela
48 J6 **Cuca** Romania
133 C6 **Cucao, B.de** Chile
133 F4 **Cuchilla de Haedo** *hills* Uruguay
9 F5 **Cuckfield** England
9 E1 **Cuckney** England
94 K9 **Cuckoo** Virginia U.S.A.
87 C8 **Cucumbi** Angola
124 D2 **Cucurpe** Mexico
128 D2 **Cúcuta** Colombia
99 T7 **Cudahy** Wisconsin U.S.A.
76 D5 **Cuddalore** India
76 D3 **Cuddapah** India
141 F7 **Cuddapan,L** Queensland Australia
102 G6 **Cuddeback L** California U.S.A.
113 F13 **Cudjoe Key** *isld* Florida U.S.A.
119 M6 **Cudworth** Saskatchewan Canada
143 C7 **Cue** W Australia Australia
16 E3 **Cuéllar** Spain
128 C4 **Cuenca** Ecuador
71 E4 **Cuenca** Philippines
17 F4 **Cuenca** Spain
17 F5 **Cuenca** *prov* Spain
124 H5 **Cuencamé de Ceniceros** Mexico
17 F4 **Cuenca, Serrania de** *mts* Spain
125 K8 **Cuernavaca** Mexico
109 K6 **Cuero** Texas U.S.A.
19 Q18 **Cuers** France
106 F6 **Cuervo** New Mexico U.S.A.
102 D6 **Cuesta Pass** California U.S.A.
126 G4 **Cueto** Cuba
17 F7 **Cuevas del Almanzora** Spain
133 E2 **Cuevo** Bolivia
22 E5 **Cuffies** France
123 N2 **Cuff L** Quebec Canada
19 P18 **Cuges-les-Pins** France
48 H5 **Cugir** Romania
43 B8 **Cuglieri** Sardinia
20 G5 **Cuguen** France
130 C4 **Cuiabá** Brazil
14 D2 **Cuilcagh** *mt* N Ireland
15 B3 **Cuillin Hills** Scotland
87 C7 **Cuilo** *R* Angola
59 J2 **Cuiluan** China
87 C8 **Cuima** Angola
22 D2 **Cuinchy** France
36 B4 **Cuint** Germany
22 E5 **Cuise-la-Motte** France
130 H9 **Cuité** Brazil
130 H6 **Cuité, R** Brazil
87 C9 **Cuito** *R* Angola
87 C9 **Cuito Cuanavale** Angola
128 F4 **Cuiuni** *R* Brazil
110 E2 **Cuivre** *R* Missouri U.S.A.
71 E7 **Cujangan** *isld* Philippines
48 H6 **Cujmir** Romania
69 F10 **Cukai** Malaysia
78 J3 **Çukurca** Turkey
68 H4 **Cu Lai** Vietnam
18 G6 **Culan** France
68 J5 **Cu Lao Bo Bai** *isld* Vietnam
68 J5 **Cu Lao Cham** *isld* Vietnam
68 J7 **Cu Lao Hon** *isld* Vietnam
68 J5 **Cu Lao Re** *isld* Vietnam
71 F5 **Culasi** Panay Philippines
98 B1 **Culbertson** Montana U.S.A.
98 F9 **Culbertson** Nebraska U.S.A.
139 H6 **Culcairn** New South Wales Australia
22 G4 **Cul-des-Sarts** Belgium
106 E4 **Culebra Pk** Colorado U.S.A.
16 C3 **Culebra, Sa de la** *mts* Spain
25 D5 **Culemborg** Netherlands
87 C9 **Culevai** Angola
141 H8 **Culgoa** *R* N S W/Qnsld Australia
139 H3 **Culgoa, R** New S Wales/Queensland
124 F5 **Culiacán** Mexico
124 F5 **Culiacancito** Mexico
71 D5 **Culion** Philippines
129 H6 **Culiseu** *R* Brazil
17 F7 **Cúllar de Baza** Spain
139 J5 **Cullarin Rge** New South Wales Australia
15 F3 **Cullen** Scotland
17 G5 **Cullera** Spain
107 M4 **Cullison** Kansas U.S.A.
111 K7 **Cullman** Alabama U.S.A.
141 G5 **Culloden** *R* Queensland Australia
8 C6 **Cullompton** England
125 M2 **Culmi** Honduras
8 D3 **Culmington** England
19 P13 **Culoz** France
94 J8 **Culpeper** Virginia U.S.A.
128 A7 **Culpepper** *isld* Galapagos Is
15 E5 **Culter Fell** Scotland
129 H6 **Culuene** *R* Brazil
99 U8 **Culver** Indiana U.S.A.
107 N3 **Culver** Kansas U.S.A.
100 D5 **Culver** Oregon U.S.A.
144 D5 **Culverden** New Zealand
143 E10 **Culver,Pt** W Australia Australia
129 K4 **Cuma, B.de** Brazil
47 H4 **Cumalı** Turkey
128 F1 **Cumana** Venezuela
127 N9 **Cumanacoa** Venezuela
47 J6 **Cumaovası** Turkey
130 E6 **Cumari** Brazil
Cumberland *co see* **Cumbria**
117 L11 **Cumberland** British Columbia Canada
99 M8 **Cumberland** Iowa U.S.A.
94 D9 **Cumberland** Kentucky U.S.A.
94 J7 **Cumberland** Maryland U.S.A.
94 F7 **Cumberland** Ohio U.S.A.
110 J5 **Cumberland** *R* Tennessee U.S.A.
94 J9 **Cumberland** Virginia U.S.A.
99 O4 **Cumberland** Wisconsin U.S.A.
Cumberland, C *see* **Nahoï, C**
110 J5 **Cumberland City** Tennessee U.S.A.
94 D10 **Cumberland Gap** Tenn/Virg U.S.A.
119 P5 **Cumberland House** Saskatchewan Canada
113 F7 **Cumberland I** Georgia U.S.A.
141 J5 **Cumberland Is** Queensland Australia
119 P4 **Cumberland L** Saskatchewan Canada
94 B10 **Cumberland, L** Kentucky U.S.A.
110 L5 **Cumberland, L** Kentucky U.S.A.
94 D10 **Cumberland Mt** Tennessee U.S.A.
115 N4 **Cumberland Pen** Northwest Territories Canada
111 K7 **Cumberland Plateau** Alabama U.S.A.
99 R2 **Cumberland Pt** Michigan U.S.A.
94 D10 **Cumberland R** Kentucky U.S.A.
94 J7 **Cumberland Res** Pennsylvania U.S.A.
115 N4 **Cumberland Sound** Northwest Territories Canada
140 D1 **Cumberland Str** N Terr Australia
12 E2 **Cumbernauld** Scotland
139 J3 **Cumborah** New South Wales Australia
133 C7 **Cumbrera** *mt* Chile
13 E4 **Cumbria** *co* England
76 D3 **Cumbum** India
109 M2 **Cumby** Texas U.S.A.
44 B2 **Cumiana** Italy
129 G4 **Cumina** *R* Brazil
129 G3 **Cuminapanema** *R* Brazil
13 E4 **Cummertrees** Scotland
112 C3 **Cumming** Georgia U.S.A.
102 A2 **Cummings** California U.S.A.
98 J2 **Cummings** North Dakota U.S.A.
138 D5 **Cummins** South Australia Australia
142 F4 **Cummins Ra** W Australia Australia
139 J5 **Cumnock** New South Wales Australia
12 D3 **Cumnock** Scotland
124 E2 **Cumpas** Mexico
78 D3 **Çumra** Turkey
124 E3 **Cumuripa** Mexico
130 H5 **Cumuruxatiba** Brazil
127 O2 **Cumuto** Trinidad
126 E3 **Cunagua** Cuba
129 H3 **Cunani** Brazil
124 D6 **Cuñaño** Mexico
131 G3 **Cuñapiru** *R* Uruguay
133 C5 **Cunco** Chile
142 D5 **Cuncudgerie Hill** W Australia Australia
143 B9 **Cunderdin** W Australia Australia
128 D3 **Cundinamarca** *div* Colombia
87 B9 **Cunene** *R* Angola
44 C3 **Cúneo** Italy
138 C4 **Cungena** South Australia Australia
17 H6 **Cunillera** *isld* Balearic Is
18 H7 **Cunlhat** France
141 H8 **Cunnamulla** Queensland Australia
107 M4 **Cunningham** Kansas U.S.A.
100 G3 **Cunningham** Washington U.S.A.
127 O2 **Cunupia** Trinidad
21 K7 **Cuon** France
119 N8 **Cupar** Saskatchewan Canada
13 E1 **Cupar** Scotland
128 C2 **Cupica, G.de** Colombia
46 E1 **Čuprija** Serbia Yugoslavia
100 J4 **Cuprum** Idaho U.S.A.
124 D5 **Cupula, P** Mexico
71 B1 **Cur** Halmahera Indonesia
129 G7 **Curabá** *R* Brazil
129 L5 **Curaçá** Brazil
126 B1 **Curaçao** *isld* W Indies
131 B7 **Curacáutin** Chile
131 D7 **Curaco, R** Argentina
131 E6 **Cura Malal, Cerro** *pk* Argentina
133 C5 **Curanilahue** Chile
128 C4 **Curaray** *R* Peru/Ecuador
131 B4 **Curaumilla, Pta de** *C* Chile
48 K6 **Curcani** Romania
21 K7 **Curçay-sur-Dive** France
138 D4 **Curdlawidny Lagoon** South Australia Australia
9 E2 **Curdworth** England
18 H5 **Cure** *R* France
106 C3 **Curecanti Nat. Recreation Area** Colorado U.S.A.
83 M13 **Curepipe** Mauritius
133 C5 **Curepto** Chile
127 O10 **Curiapo** Venezuela
131 B5 **Curico** Chile
131 D8 **Curico, L** Argentina
128 E4 **Curicuriari** *R* Brazil
83 J12 **Curieuse I** Seychelles
130 J9 **Curimataú** *R* Brazil
143 A7 **Curious,Mt** W Australia Australia
128 D3 **Curiplaya** Colombia
133 H3 **Curitiba** Brazil
130 E10 **Curitibanos** Brazil
100 G1 **Curlew** Washington U.S.A.
141 J5 **Curlew I** Queensland Australia
139 K4 **Curlewis** New South Wales Australia
111 H12 **Curlew Is** Louisiana U.S.A.
116 F5 **Curlew L** Alaska U.S.A.
123 L3 **Curlew Pt** Quebec Canada
123 O5 **Curling** Newfoundland Canada
138 E4 **Curnamona** South Australia Australia
44 F2 **Curone** *R* Italy
139 K4 **Currabubula** New South Wales Australia
130 H9 **Currais Novas** Brazil
138 C2 **Curralulla** *R* South Australia Australia
121 Q7 **Curran** Ontario Canada
94 D2 **Curran** Michigan U.S.A.
103 J3 **Currant** Nevada U.S.A.
139 G4 **Curranyalpa** New South Wales Australia
141 F7 **Currawilla** Queensland Australia
126 F2 **Current** Eleuthera Bahamas
110 E4 **Current** *R* Missouri U.S.A.
113 L12 **Current I** Bahamas
139 G7 **Currie** Tasmania Australia
13 E2 **Currie** Scotland
99 L5 **Currie** Minnesota U.S.A.
103 K1 **Currie** Nevada U.S.A.
112 J3 **Currie** North Carolina U.S.A.
138 B2 **Currie Cr., The** South Australia Australia
119 U1 **Currie L** Manitoba Canada
140 B7 **Currie,Mt** N Terr Australia
112 L1 **Currituck** North Carolina U.S.A.
112 M1 **Currituck Sound** North Carolina U.S.A.
139 K6 **Currockbilly, Mt** New South Wales Australia
110 E2 **Curryville** Missouri U.S.A.
37 L2 **Cursdorf** Germany
45 L1 **Curtarolo** Italy
48 J5 **Curtea de Argeş** Romania
48 G4 **Curtici** Romania
143 D9 **Curtin** W Australia Australia
100 B6 **Curtin** Oregon U.S.A.
140 B7 **Curtin Springs** N Terr Australia
16 B1 **Curtis** Spain
111 C9 **Curtis** Louisiana U.S.A.
99 V3 **Curtis** Michigan U.S.A.
98 F9 **Curtis** Nebraska U.S.A.
141 L6 **Curtis Chan** Gt Barrier Reef Australia
139 H7 **Curtis Group** *islds* Tasmania Australia
141 K6 **Curtis I** Queensland Australia
137 R8 **Curtis I** Kermadec Is Pacific Oc
94 D2 **Curtisville** Michigan U.S.A.
129 G4 **Curuá** Brazil
129 H5 **Curuaés** *R* Brazil
129 H3 **Curuá, I** Brazil
129 G3 **Curuapanema** *R* Brazil
128 D5 **Curuçá** *R* Brazil
129 J4 **Curuca** Brazil
133 F2 **Curuguaty** Paraguay
69 F14 **Curup** Sumatra
129 J4 **Cururupu** Brazil
131 F2 **Curuzú Cuatiá** Argentina
129 K7 **Curvelo** Brazil
94 J6 **Curwensville** Pennsylvania U.S.A.
14 E1 **Cushendall** N Ireland
14 E1 **Cushendun** N Ireland
99 M3 **Cushing** Minnesota U.S.A.
107 O6 **Cushing** Oklahoma U.S.A.
111 B10 **Cushing** Texas U.S.A.
110 E6 **Cushman** Arkansas U.S.A.
101 Q3 **Cushman** Montana U.S.A.
100 A6 **Cushman** Oregon U.S.A.
100 B2 **Cushman, L** Washington U.S.A.
124 F3 **Cusihuiráchic** Mexico
45 H3 **Cusna, Mt** Italy
18 H6 **Cusset** France
112 C5 **Cusseta** Georgia U.S.A.
99 O1 **Cusson** Minnesota U.S.A.
144 D5 **Cust** New Zealand
101 S3 **Custer** Montana U.S.A.
98 C6 **Custer** South Dakota U.S.A.
101 S4 **Custer Battlefield Nat.Mon** Montana U.S.A.
107 M6 **Custer City** Oklahoma U.S.A.
45 J1 **Custoza** Italy
117 O8 **Cutbank** *R* Alberta Canada
101 N1 **Cut Bank** Montana U.S.A.
119 P5 **Cut Beaver L** Saskatchewan Canada
111 A8 **Cuthand Cr** Texas U.S.A.
112 C6 **Cuthbert** Georgia U.S.A.
98 H6 **Cuthbert** South Dakota U.S.A.
108 F3 **Cuthbert** Texas U.S.A.
140 E4 **Cuthbert, Mt** Queensland Australia
45 J3 **Cutigliano** Italy
118 H6 **Cut Knife** Saskatchewan Canada
120 H6 **Cutler** Ontario Canada
116 H3 **Cutler** *R* Alaska U.S.A.
102 E5 **Cutler** California U.S.A.
95 T9 **Cutler** Maine U.S.A.
14 C3 **Cutra, L** Ireland
22 E4 **Cuts** France
139 H3 **Cuttaburra** *R* New South Wales Australia
75 L8 **Cuttack** India
103 O8 **Cutter** Arizona U.S.A.
81 H7 **Cuvier Basin** Indian Oc
143 A6 **Cuvier,C** W Australia Australia
145 E2 **Cuvier I** New Zealand
87 C8 **Cuvo** *R* Angola
32 J5 **Cuxhaven** Germany
Cu Xu, I *see* **Quan Dao Co To**
94 F5 **Cuyahoga** *R* Ohio U.S.A.
94 F5 **Cuyahoga Falls** Ohio U.S.A.
102 E6 **Cuyama** *R* California U.S.A.
71 E3 **Cuyapo** Luzon Philippines
71 E5 **Cuyo** *isld* Philippines
71 E5 **Cuyo East Passage** Philippines
71 E5 **Cuyo West Passage** Philippines
99 N3 **Cuyuna** Minnesota U.S.A.
128 G2 **Cuyuni** *R* Guyana
125 N2 **Cuyu Tigni** Nicaragua
128 E8 **Cuzco** *mt* Bolivia
128 D6 **Cuzco** Peru
42 H5 **Čvrsnica** *mt* Bosnia-Herzegovina
8 C4 **Cwmbran** Wales
88 B3 **Cyangugu** Rwanda
31 H3 **Cybinka** Poland
Cyclades *islds see* **Kikládhes** *islds*
139 H9 **Cygnet** Tasmania Australia
119 W2 **Cygnet L** Manitoba Canada
138 D6 **Cygnet River** South Australia Australia
118 B5 **Cynthia** Alberta Canada
110 M3 **Cynthiana** Kentucky U.S.A.
110 G4 **Cypress** Illinois U.S.A.
111 C10 **Cypress** Louisiana U.S.A.
109 M6 **Cypress** Texas U.S.A.
111 A8 **Cypress Cr** Texas U.S.A.
109 N3 **Cypress Cr., Lit** Texas U.S.A.
118 H9 **Cypress Hills** Saskatchewan Canada
118 G9 **Cypress Hills Prov. Park** Alberta Canada
113 F9 **Cypress L** Florida U.S.A.
119 S9 **Cypress River** Manitoba Canada
79 D4 **Cyprus** *rep* Mediterranean Sea
84 G4 **Cyrenaica** *reg* Libya
Cyrene *see* **Shaḩḩāt**
77 A5 **Cyrus** *oil well* Persian Gulf
115 N5 **Cyrus Field B** Northwest Territories Canada
22 E2 **Cysoing** France
31 J2 **Czaplinek** Poland

170
Deir Abu Said — Djoum

80 F4 **Deir Abu Said** Jordan
80 F4 **Deir es Samadiya** Jordan
80 D5 **Deir Istiya** Jordan
80 E6 **Deir Mar Jiryis** Jordan
80 D4 **Deir Sharal** Jordan
32 K8 **Deister** *hills* Germany
48 H3 **Dej** Romania
46 D3 **Dêja** *mt* Albania
71 B2 **Dejailolo, Selat** *str* Indonesia
28 A5 **Dejbjerg** Denmark
27 F12 **Deje** Sweden
86 G3 **Dejen** Ethiopia
67 C2 **Dejiang** China
99 S8 **De Kalb** Illinois U.S.A.
111 H9 **De Kalb** Mississippi U.S.A.
109 N2 **De Kalb** Texas U.S.A.
95 M2 **De Kalb Junc** New York U.S.A.
59 M1 **De Kastri** Russian Federation
86 G2 **Dek'emhāre** Ethiopia
86 D6 **Dekese** Zaire
86 C4 **Dékoa** Cent Afr Republic
25 C2 **De Koog** Netherlands
111 G12 **Delacroix** Louisiana U.S.A.
106 F4 **Delagua** Colorado U.S.A.
100 J6 **Delamar** Idaho U.S.A.
103 K4 **Delamar Mts** Nevada U.S.A.
140 B3 **Delamere** N Terr Australia
113 F8 **De Land** Florida U.S.A.
102 E6 **Delano** California U.S.A.
103 M3 **Delano Peak** Utah U.S.A.
77 H3 **Delārām** Afghanistan
118 K4 **Delaronde L** Saskatchewan Canada
110 G1 **Delavan** Illinois U.S.A.
99 S7 **Delavan** Wisconsin U.S.A.
95 N5 **Delaware** *R* U.S.A.
95 M7 **Delaware** *state* U.S.A.
107 P2 **Delaware** *R* Kansas U.S.A.
94 D6 **Delaware** Ohio U.S.A.
107 P5 **Delaware** Oklahoma U.S.A.
145 D4 **Delaware B** New Zealand
95 M7 **Delaware B** U.S.A.
95 M7 **Delaware City** Delaware U.S.A.
108 C4 **Delaware Cr** Texas/New Mex U.S.A.
94 D6 **Delaware Res** Ohio U.S.A.
118 E9 **Del Bonita** Alberta Canada
32 J9 **Delbrück** Germany
118 D6 **Delburne** Alberta Canada
111 E12 **Delcambre** Louisiana U.S.A.
106 F4 **Delcarbon** Colorado U.S.A.
46 F3 **Delčevo** Macedonia Yugoslavia
87 E8 **Delcommune, L** Zaire
25 G4 **Delden** Netherlands
119 R9 **Deleau** Manitoba Canada
139 J6 **Delegate** New South Wales Australia
25 F2 **De Leien** Netherlands
40 F3 **Delémont** Switzerland
109 J3 **De Leon** Texas U.S.A.
29 H11 **Delet Teili** *chan* Finland
22 C2 **Delettes** France
102 B2 **Delevan** California U.S.A.
94 J4 **Delevan** New York U.S.A.
130 F7 **Delfinópolis** Brazil
25 B5 **Delfshaven** Netherlands
25 B4 **Delft** Netherlands
83 J8 **Delft** *isld* Sri Lanka
25 G2 **Delfzijl** Netherlands
100 A9 **Delgada, Pt** California U.S.A.
133 E6 **Delgada, Pta** Argentina
88 H7 **Delgado, C** Mozambique
86 F1 **Delgo** Sudan
120 K10 **Delhi** Ontario Canada
74 G4 **Delhi** India
99 P7 **Delhi** Iowa U.S.A.
111 E9 **Delhi** Louisiana U.S.A.
107 L6 **Delhi** Oklahoma U.S.A.
70 K9 **Deli** *isld* Java
118 E7 **Delia** Alberta Canada
107 P2 **Delia** Kansas U.S.A.
129 H3 **Delices** Fr Guiana
109 O1 **Delight** Arkansas U.S.A.
77 B3 **Delijan** Iran
46 E1 **Deli Jovan** *mt* Serbia Yugoslavia
58 C4 **Delingha** China
118 K7 **Delisle** Saskatchewan Canada
140 B2 **Delissaville** N Terr Australia
69 D11 **Delitua** Sumatra
33 Q9 **Delitzsch** Germany
110 F6 **Dell** Arkansas U.S.A.
101 N5 **Dell** Montana U.S.A.
36 C2 **Dellbrück** Germany
40 E2 **Delle** France
101 N9 **Delle** Utah U.S.A.
103 L5 **Dellenbaugh, Mt** Arizona U.S.A.
26 J10 **Dellen, N** *L* Sweden
32 L9 **Delligsen** Germany
100 B9 **Del Loma** California U.S.A.
98 K6 **Dell Rapids** South Dakota U.S.A.
107 L2 **Dellvale** Kansas U.S.A.
85 E1 **Dellys** Algeria
102 G9 **Del Mar** California U.S.A.
99 Q7 **Delmar** Iowa U.S.A.
95 M8 **Delmar** Maryland U.S.A.
118 J6 **Delmas** Saskatchewan Canada
32 J6 **Delmenhorst** Germany
130 H10 **Delmiro Gouveia** Brazil
98 H6 **Delmont** South Dakota U.S.A.
103 K4 **Delmues** Nevada U.S.A.
42 F3 **Delnice** Croatia
106 D4 **Del Norte** Colorado U.S.A.
116 F2 **De Long Mts** Alaska U.S.A.
139 H8 **Deloraine** Tasmania Australia
119 R9 **Deloraine** Manitoba Canada
13 F6 **Delph** England
46 E6 **Delphi** Greece
110 K1 **Delphi** Indiana U.S.A.
107 N2 **Delphos** Kansas U.S.A.
94 C6 **Delphos** Ohio U.S.A.
113 G11 **Delray Beach** Florida U.S.A.
124 D2 **Del Río** Mexico
108 G6 **Del Rio** Texas U.S.A.
26 J10 **Delsbo** Sweden
106 B3 **Delta** Colorado U.S.A.
110 G4 **Delta** Missouri U.S.A.
94 C5 **Delta** Ohio U.S.A.
95 L7 **Delta** Pennsylvania U.S.A.
103 M2 **Delta** Utah U.S.A.
119 T8 **Delta Beach** Manitoba Canada
141 F3 **Delta Downs** Queensland Australia
116 O4 **Delta Junction** Alaska U.S.A.
102 C4 **Delta Mendota Canal** California U.S.A.
95 M3 **Delta Res** New York U.S.A.
95 L9 **Deltaville** Virginia U.S.A.
94 B4 **Delton** Michigan U.S.A.
139 K3 **Delungra** New South Wales Australia
74 D8 **Delvada** India
109 K5 **Del Valle** Texas U.S.A.
32 K4 **Delve** Germany
46 D5 **Delvinákion** Greece
46 D5 **Delvinë** Albania
108 G2 **Delwin** Texas U.S.A.
48 J2 **Delyatin** Ukraine
55 B4 **Dema** *R* Russian Federation
118 K8 **Demaine** Saskatchewan Canada
70 N9 **Demak** Java
16 E2 **Demando, S. de la** *mts* Spain
116 R2 **Demarcation Pt** Alaska U.S.A.
86 D7 **Demba** Zaire
86 D4 **Dembia** Cent Afr Republic
86 F4 **Dembī Dolo** Ethiopia
48 G2 **Demecser** Hungary
22 J2 **Demer** *R* Belgium
Demerara *see* **Georgetown** Guyana
54 C1 **Demidov** Russian Federation
55 D3 **Demina** Russian Federation
106 C9 **Deming** New Mexico U.S.A.
100 C1 **Deming** Washington U.S.A.
128 F3 **Demini** *R* Brazil
79 B2 **Demirçat** Turkey
47 K5 **Demirci** Turkey
47 N11 **Demirciler** Turkey
47 J6 **Demirköprü Baraji** *L* Turkey
47 J3 **Demirköy** Turkey
33 S5 **Demmin** Germany
128 F5 **Democracia** Brazil
111 J9 **Demopolis** Alabama U.S.A.
68 C3 **Demoso** Burma
143 E10 **Dempster, Pt** W Australia Australia
74 H2 **Dêmqog** India
55 F2 **Dem'yanka** *R* Russian Federation
52 D5 **Demyansk** Russian Federation
55 E2 **Dem'yanskoye** Russian Federation
22 E3 **Denain** France
86 H3 **Denakil** *tribal dist* Ethiopia
116 O5 **Denali** Alaska U.S.A.
116 M5 **Denali Nat Park and Preserve** Alaska U.S.A.
86 H4 **Denan** Ethiopia
114 J7 **Denare Beach** Saskatchewan Canada
57 E5 **Denau** Uzbekistan
Denbigh *co see* **Clwyd and Gwynedd** *counties*
121 N7 **Denbigh** Ontario Canada
8 C1 **Denbigh** Wales
116 G4 **Denbigh, C** Alaska U.S.A.
25 B5 **Den Bommel** Netherlands
25 C2 **Den Burg** Netherlands
68 E4 **Den Chai** Thailand
69 J14 **Dendang** Indonesia
22 G2 **Dender** *R* Belgium
22 G2 **Denderleeuw** Belgium
22 G1 **Dendermonde** Belgium
25 D3 **Den Dever** Netherlands
86 G4 **Dendi** *mt* Ethiopia
118 K8 **Dendron** Saskatchewan Canada
25 H4 **Denekamp** Netherlands
55 C1 **Denezhkin Kamen', G** *mt* Russian Federation
65 B7 **Dengfeng** China
58 E3 **Dengkou** China
66 F5 **Dêngqên** China
58 F5 **Deng Xian** China
65 C4 **Dengyoufang** China
65 E6 **Dengzhou** China
24 A2 **Den Haag** *conurbation* Netherlands
143 A7 **Denham** W Australia Australia
9 F4 **Denham** England
140 E3 **Denham I** Queensland Australia
141 J5 **Denham Ra** Queensland Australia
143 A7 **Denham Sd** W Australia Australia
111 F11 **Denham Springs** Louisiana U.S.A.
25 C3 **Den Helder** Netherlands
118 K6 **Denholm** Saskatchewan Canada
13 F3 **Denholm** Scotland
17 G7 **Denia** Spain
138 C4 **Denial Bay** South Australia Australia
122 C6 **Deniau** Quebec Canada
139 G6 **Deniliquin** New South Wales Australia
100 G7 **Denio** Oregon U.S.A.
83 J12 **Denis I** Seychelles
99 L7 **Denison** Iowa U.S.A.
109 L2 **Denison** Texas U.S.A.
107 O8 **Denison Dam** Oklahoma U.S.A.
140 B5 **Denison, Mt** N Terr Australia
116 K7 **Denison, Mt** Alaska U.S.A.
142 G4 **Denison Plains** W Australia Australia
141 J4 **Denison Pt** Queensland Australia
52 J2 **Denisovka** Komi Respublika Russian Federation
83 K11 **Deniyaya** Sri Lanka
47 K7 **Denizli** Turkey
37 L6 **Denkendorf** Germany
139 K4 **Denman** New South Wales Australia
146 H13 **Denman Glacier** Antarctica
143 B10 **Denmark** W Australia Australia
122 J8 **Denmark** Nova Scotia Canada
28 **Denmark** *kingdom* N W Europe
100 A7 **Denmark** Oregon U.S.A.
112 F4 **Denmark** South Carolina U.S.A.
99 T5 **Denmark** Wisconsin U.S.A.
115 R4 **Denmark Str** Greenland/Iceland
20 G3 **Denneville** France
33 S9 **Dennewitz** Germany
94 F6 **Dennison** Ohio U.S.A.
95 R5 **Dennis Port** Massachusetts U.S.A.
144 C4 **Denniston** New Zealand
94 H10 **Denniston** Virginia U.S.A.
12 E1 **Denny** Scotland
100 B9 **Denny** California U.S.A.
12 E2 **Dennyloanhead** Scotland
95 U2 **Dennysville** Maine U.S.A.
70 P10 **Denpasar** Bali Indonesia
70 G6 **Densongi** Sulawesi
13 F5 **Dent** England
100 J3 **Dent** Idaho U.S.A.
48 G5 **Denta** Romania
40 G5 **Dent Blanche** *mt* Switzerland
40 E5 **Dent du Midi** *mt* Switzerland
9 H5 **Denton** England
112 E6 **Denton** Georgia U.S.A.
94 E8 **Denton** Kentucky U.S.A.
95 M8 **Denton** Maryland U.S.A.
109 K2 **Denton** Texas U.S.A.
137 L3 **D'Entrecasteaux Is** Papua New Guinea
106 E2 **Denver** Colorado U.S.A.
100 J4 **Denver** Idaho U.S.A.
94 A6 **Denver** Indiana U.S.A.
99 O7 **Denver** Iowa U.S.A.
95 L6 **Denver** Pennsylvania U.S.A.
108 E3 **Denver City** Texas U.S.A.
118 H6 **Denzil** Saskatchewan Canada
86 B4 **Déo** *R* Cameroon
74 G4 **Deoband** India
75 M6 **Deogarh** India
68 J4 **Deo Hai Van** Vietnam
74 E9 **Deolali** India
21 O8 **Déols** France
68 J6 **Deo Ma** Vietnam
22 D1 **De Panne** Belgium
25 E5 **De Peel** Netherlands
99 S5 **De Pere** Wisconsin U.S.A.
94 J4 **Depew** New York U.S.A.
107 O6 **Depew** Oklahoma U.S.A.
65 C6 **Deping** China
22 F2 **De Pinte** Belgium
70 L9 **Depok** Java
109 M2 **Deport** Texas U.S.A.
95 M4 **Deposit** New York U.S.A.
128 F3 **Depósito** Brazil
95 Q4 **Depot** New Hampshire U.S.A.
120 K7 **Depot Harbour** Ontario Canada
86 D2 **Depression du Murdi** Chad
9 E5 **Deptford** England
142 C5 **Depuch I** W Australia Australia
99 R8 **Depue** Illinois U.S.A.
25 G2 **De Punt** Netherlands
51 O2 **Deputatskiy** Russian Federation
58 C6 **Dêqên** China
67 G1 **Deqing** China
67 D5 **Deqing** China
111 B7 **De Queen** Arkansas U.S.A.
111 C11 **De Quincy** Louisiana U.S.A.
77 L5 **Dera Bugti** Pakistan
74 D3 **Dera Ghazi Khan** Pakistan
74 D3 **Dera Ismail Khan** Pakistan
46 D2 **Deravica** *mt* Serbia Yugoslavia
48 L1 **Derazhnya** Ukraine
33 Q8 **Derben** Germany
78 M1 **Derbent** Russian Federation
86 D4 **Derbisaka** Cent Afr Republic
139 J8 **Derby** Tasmania Australia
142 E3 **Derby** W Australia Australia
9 E2 **Derby** England
95 O5 **Derby** Connecticut U.S.A.
99 N9 **Derby** Iowa U.S.A.
107 N4 **Derby** Kansas U.S.A.
109 H7 **Derby** Texas U.S.A.
95 P2 **Derby Center** Vermont U.S.A.
9 E1 **Derbyshire** *co* England
16 D9 **Derdara** Morocco
48 G3 **Derecske** Hungary
47 K8 **Dereköy** Turkey
47 M10 **Dereköy** *R* Turkey
78 A1 **Derekoy** Turkey
33 N8 **Der Elm** *hills* Germany
33 N9 **Derenburg** Germany
52 D4 **Derevyanka** Russian Federation
14 D2 **Derg** *R* N Ireland
54 H6 **Dergachi** Ukraine
14 D2 **Derg, L** Ireland
32 H5 **Der Hohe Weg** *sandbank* Germany
111 C11 **De Ridder** Louisiana U.S.A.
25 C3 **De Rijp** Netherlands
139 G7 **Derinallum** Victoria Australia
47 N11 **Derince** Turkey
86 H5 **Derkali** Kenya
54 L8 **Derkul** *R* Rus Fed/Ukraine
46 G1 **Dermantsi** Bulgaria
37 J2 **Dermbach** Germany
111 E8 **Dermott** Arkansas U.S.A.
Derna *see* **Darnah**
87 C11 **Dernberg, C** Namibia
32 M8 **Derneburg** Germany
111 F12 **Dernieres, Is** Louisiana U.S.A.
138 C2 **De Rose Hill** South Australia Australia
20 G3 **Déroute,Pass de la** France
14 D3 **Derravaragh, L** Ireland
86 J5 **Derri** Somalia
Derry *see* **Londonderry**
95 Q4 **Derry** New Hampshire U.S.A.
106 C9 **Derry** New Mexico U.S.A.
94 H6 **Derry** Pennsylvania U.S.A.
140 D5 **Derry Downs** N Terr Australia
14 C2 **Derryveagh Mts** Ireland
36 D1 **Derschlag** Germany
9 G2 **Dersingham** England
86 G2 **Derudeb** Sudan
95 M4 **De Ruyter** New York U.S.A.
20 G6 **Derval** France
46 E6 **Dervéni** Greece
42 H4 **Derventa** Bosnia Herzegovina
140 B6 **Derwent** N Terr Australia
139 H8 **Derwent** *R* Tasmania Australia
118 F5 **Derwent** Alberta Canada
12 E4 **Derwent, R** England
13 E4 **Derwent Water** England
55 E5 **Derzhavinsk** Kazakhstan
133 D4 **Desaguadero** *R* Argentina
131 B5 **Desague, Cerro** *pk* Argentina
110 E7 **Des Arc** Arkansas U.S.A.
110 F4 **Des Arc** Missouri U.S.A.
102 G2 **Desatoya Mts** Nevada U.S.A.
9 F3 **Desborough** England
130 B5 **Descalvado** Mato Grosso Brazil
130 F7 **Descalvado** São Paulo Brazil
124 A1 **Descanso** Mexico
102 H9 **Descanso** California U.S.A.
21 M8 **Descartes** France
121 S6 **Deschaillons** Quebec Canada
100 E4 **Deschutes** *R* Oregon U.S.A.
109 J3 **Desdemona** Texas U.S.A.
86 G3 **Desē** Ethiopia
45 M1 **Dese** *R* Italy
133 P7 **Deseado** Argentina
41 N7 **Desenzano del Garda** Italy
103 M2 **Deseret** Utah U.S.A.
101 N9 **Deseret Pk** Utah U.S.A.
121 N8 **Deseronto** Ontario Canada
103 J8 **Desert Center** California U.S.A.
102 H8 **Desert Hot Springs** California U.S.A.
121 O6 **Desért, L** Quebec Canada
101 M8 **Desert Pk** Utah U.S.A.
103 J5 **Desert Ra** Nevada U.S.A.
100 G8 **Desert Valley** Nevada U.S.A.
103 N5 **Desert View** Arizona U.S.A.
127 M4 **Deshaies** Guadeloupe W Indies
67 A3 **Deshengpo** China
98 J9 **Deshler** Nebraska U.S.A.
94 D5 **Deshler** Ohio U.S.A.
74 E5 **Deshnok** India
77 H4 **Deshu** Afghanistan
124 B1 **Desierto de Altar** *desert* Mexico
17 H4 **Desierto de las Palmas** Spain
98 E1 **Des Lacs** *R* North Dakota U.S.A.
118 D3 **Desmarais** Alberta Canada
121 O3 **Desmaraisville** Quebec Canada
100 J2 **Desmet** Idaho U.S.A.
101 L3 **De Smet** Montana U.S.A.
98 J5 **De Smet** South Dakota U.S.A.
130 B10 **Desmochados** Paraguay
99 M7 **Des Moines** *R* Iowa U.S.A.
99 N8 **Des Moines** Iowa U.S.A.
99 L6 **Des Moines** *R* Minnesota U.S.A.
106 G5 **Des Moines** New Mexico U.S.A.
54 B6 **Desna** *R* Ukraine
54 E2 **Desnogorsk** Russian Federation
133 C8 **Desolación, I** Chile
71 G5 **Desolation Pt** Philippines
110 G4 **De Soto** Illinois U.S.A.
107 Q3 **De Soto** Kansas U.S.A.
110 F3 **De Soto** Missouri U.S.A.
99 P6 **De Soto** Wisconsin U.S.A.
113 F10 **De Soto City** Florida U.S.A.
16 E6 **Despeñaperros, Pto. de** Spain
99 T7 **Des Plaines** Illinois U.S.A.
48 G6 **Despotovac** Serbia Yugoslavia
83 H5 **Desroches** *isld* Seychelles
33 Q9 **Dessau** Germany
40 E3 **Dessoubre** *R* France
111 K11 **Destin** Florida U.S.A.
31 K5 **Deštná** *mt* Poland
138 E6 **D'Estrees, B** South Australia Australia
117 D5 **Destruction Bay** Yukon Territory Canada
100 A2 **Destruction I** Washington U.S.A.
143 G6 **Destruction,Mt** W Australia Australia
22 B2 **Desvres** France
48 G5 **Deta** Romania
87 E9 **Dete** Zimbabwe
32 G6 **Detern** Germany
121 N7 **Detlor** Ontario Canada
32 J9 **Detmold** Germany
94 D1 **Detour Passage** Michigan U.S.A.
99 U4 **Detour, Pt** Michigan U.S.A.
94 D1 **Detour Village** Michigan U.S.A.
94 D4 **Detroit** Michigan U.S.A.
109 M2 **Detroit** Texas U.S.A.
122 H4 **Détroit d'Honguedo** Quebec Canada
99 L3 **Detroit Lakes** Minnesota U.S.A.
94 D4 **Detroit R** Michigan U.S.A.
100 C5 **Detroit Res** Oregon U.S.A.
37 J4 **Dettelbach** Germany
36 G6 **Dettenhausen** Germany
36 H3 **Detter** Germany
36 F7 **Dettingen** Baden-Württemberg Germany
36 G3 **Dettingen** Bayern Germany
36 C6 **Dettwiller** France
68 G5 **Det Udom** Thailand
48 E2 **Detva** Czechoslovakia
74 G8 **Deūlgaon Rāja** India
25 E6 **Deurne** Netherlands
37 Q2 **Deutsch-Einsiedel** Germany
33 R7 **Deutschhof** Germany
48 D3 **Deutschkreutz** Austria
37 P2 **Deutsch-Neudorf** Germany
122 B2 **Deux Décharges, L** Quebec Canada
121 M6 **Deux Rivieres** Ontario Canada
18 E6 **Deux-Sèvres** *dept* France
48 H5 **Deva** Romania
16 D1 **Deva** *R* Spain
110 E7 **De Valls Bluff** Arkansas U.S.A.
48 F3 **Dévaványa** Hungary
47 L8 **Devecitaşi Adası** *isld* Turkey
48 D3 **Devecser** Hungary
78 E2 **Develi** Turkey
25 F4 **Deventer** Netherlands
112 D4 **Devereux** Georgia U.S.A.
86 H4 **De Verme Falls** Ethiopia
6 L1 **Deveron** *oil rig* North Sea
15 F3 **Deveron** *R* Scotland
46 E1 **Devica** *mt* Serbia Yugoslavia
74 D5 **Devikot** India
21 N3 **Deville** France
116 E3 **Devil Mt** Alaska U.S.A.
145 D4 **Devil River Pk** New Zealand
108 F5 **Devils** *R* Texas U.S.A.
14 D4 **Devilsbit Mt** Ireland
8 C3 **Devils Bridge** Wales
102 E6 **Devils Den** California U.S.A.
15 E4 **Devil's Elbow** Scotland
116 K5 **Devils Elbow** *V* Alaska U.S.A.
102 E3 **Devils Gate** California U.S.A.
89 E1 **Devil's Gorge** Zambia
6 L6 **Devil's Hole** North Sea
99 Q2 **Devils I** Michigan U.S.A.
110 H4 **Devil's Kitchen L** Illinois U.S.A.
98 H1 **Devils Lake** North Dakota U.S.A.
100 K8 **Devils L. Res** Nevada U.S.A.
117 G6 **Devils Paw** *mt* Br Col/Alaska Canada/U.S.A.
102 E4 **Devils Pk** California U.S.A.
103 J7 **Devils Playground** *desert* California U.S.A.
126 G2 **Devil's Point** Cat I Bahamas
102 E4 **Devils Postpile Nat.Mon** California U.S.A.
101 O8 **Devils Slide** Utah U.S.A.
139 H7 **Devils Tower** *isld* Tasmania Australia
98 B5 **Devils Tower** Wyoming U.S.A.
46 G3 **Devin** Bulgaria
109 J6 **Devine** Texas U.S.A.
80 C8 **Devira** Israel
9 E5 **Devizes** England
74 F6 **Devli** India
107 M7 **Devol** Oklahoma U.S.A.
46 D4 **Devoll** *R* Albania
118 D5 **Devon** Alberta Canada
120 G5 **Devon** Ontario Canada
8 C6 **Devon** *co* England
101 O1 **Devon** Montana U.S.A.
115 L2 **Devon I** Northwest Territories Canada
139 H8 **Devonport** Tasmania Australia
8 B7 **Devonport** England
80 E3 **Devora** Israel
78 D1 **Devrek** *R* Turkey
78 D1 **Devrez** *R* Turkey
89 G2 **Devuli** *R* Zimbabwe
52 H6 **Devyaternya** Russian Federation
52 E4 **Devyatiny** Russian Federation
55 E2 **Devyatkova** Russian Federation
70 F7 **Dewakang Besar** *isld* Indonesia
70 F7 **Dewakang Ketjil** *isld* Indonesia
107 P6 **Dewar** Oklahoma U.S.A.
118 H7 **Dewar Lake** Saskatchewan Canada
74 G7 **Dewas** India
69 B11 **Dewa, Tanjong** *C* Indonesia
118 G5 **Dewberry** Alberta Canada
98 H9 **Deweese** Nebraska U.S.A.
103 M7 **Dewey** Arizona U.S.A.
107 P5 **Dewey** Oklahoma U.S.A.
98 C6 **Dewey** South Dakota U.S.A.
94 E9 **Dewey Res** Kentucky U.S.A.
22 E1 **De Wielingen** Belgium/Neths
118 C8 **De Winton** Alberta Canada
111 E7 **De Witt** Arkansas U.S.A.
94 C4 **De Witt** Michigan U.S.A.
110 C2 **De Witt** Missouri U.S.A.
98 K9 **De Witt** Nebraska U.S.A.
95 L3 **De Witt** New York U.S.A.
13 G6 **Dewsbury** England
67 F2 **Dexing** China
111 D7 **Dexter** Arkansas U.S.A.
99 M8 **Dexter** Iowa U.S.A.
107 O4 **Dexter** Kansas U.S.A.
95 S1 **Dexter** Maine U.S.A.
94 D4 **Dexter** Michigan U.S.A.
99 O6 **Dexter** Minnesota U.S.A.
110 G5 **Dexter** Missouri U.S.A.
108 C2 **Dexter** New Mexico U.S.A.
95 L2 **Dexter** New York U.S.A.
109 L2 **Dexter** Texas U.S.A.
113 F8 **Dexter, L** Florida U.S.A.
99 Q5 **Dexterville** Wisconsin U.S.A.
138 B3 **Dey-Dey, L** South Australia Australia
22 L3 **Deyfeldt** Belgium
77 E3 **Deyhuk** Iran
57 C5 **Deynau** Turkmenistan
136 H3 **Deyong, Tanjung** *C* W Irian
77 B6 **Deyyer** Iran
117 E5 **Dezadeash L** Yukon Territory Canada
77 A3 **Dezfūl** Iran
77 B4 **Dez Gerd** Iran
65 C6 **Dezhou** China
41 M6 **Dezzo** Italy
46 E7 **Dháfni** Greece
79 G6 **Dhahab, Wādī adh** *watercourse* Syria
Dhahran *see* **Zahrān, Az**
75 O7 **Dhaka** Bangladesh
79 D3 **Dhali** Cyprus
75 J8 **Dhamtari** India
75 M7 **Dhanbad** India
74 J4 **Dhangarhi** Nepal
109 H6 **Dhanis** Texas U.S.A.
75 M5 **Dhankuta** Nepal
76 D6 **Dhanushkodi** India
74 F7 **Dhar** India
76 C5 **Dharapuram** India
75 K7 **Dharmajaygarh** India
76 D4 **Dharmapuri** India
76 C3 **Dharmavaram** India
74 G2 **Dharmshāla** India
86 A1 **Dharoor** *R* Somalia
85 C5 **Dhar Oualata** *plateau* Mauritania
76 B3 **Dhārwād** India
66 C6 **Dhaulagiri** *mt* Nepal
74 G5 **Dhaulpur** India
75 L8 **Dhenkanal** India
47 H7 **Dhenoúsa** *isld* Greece
46 D4 **Dhërmi** Albania
46 E5 **Dheskáti** Greece
46 G8 **Dhespotikó** *isld* Greece
40 A4 **Dheune** *R* France
80 G7 **Dhiban** Jordan
46 F7 **Dhídhimoi** Greece
47 H3 **Dhidhimótikhon** Greece
46 G9 **Dhíkti Ori** *mt* Crete Greece
46 G7 **Dhílos** *isld* Greece
46 E7 **Dhimitsána** Greece
78 L6 **Dhī Qar** *prov* Iraq
80 F8 **Dhira** Jordan
46 F6 **Dhírfis** *mt* Greece
47 H7 **Dhodhekánisos** *islds* Greece
74 G5 **Dholpur** India
46 E5 **Dhomokós** Greece
76 C3 **Dhone** India
74 D8 **Dhoraji** India
46 G3 **Dhoxáton** Greece
46 G7 **Dhragonísi** *isld* Greece
47 O12 **Dhráhstis, Akra** *C* Greece
74 D7 **Dhrangadhra** India
46 F5 **Dhrépanon, Ákr** *C* Greece
46 D5 **Dhrin** *R* Albania
75 N5 **Dhuburi** India
Dhufar *see* **Zufār**
21 O6 **Dhuison** France
74 F8 **Dhule** India
74 E2 **Dhulian** Pakistan
86 B2 **Dhuudo** Somalia
46 E6 **Dhytikí Ellas** *admin region* Greece
46 E4 **Dhytikí Makedhonía** *admin region* Greece
46 G9 **Día** *isld* Crete Greece
129 H2 **Diable, I.du** Fr Guiana
40 F5 **Diablerets** *mt* Switzerland
100 D1 **Diablo L** Washington U.S.A.
127 K2 **Diablo, Mt** Jamaica
108 C4 **Diablo, Sa** *mts* Texas U.S.A.
127 O7 **Diablotin, Morne** *hill* Dominica
99 M9 **Diagonal** Iowa U.S.A.
85 B6 **Dialakoto** Senegal
131 E4 **Diamante** Argentina
133 D4 **Diamante** *R* Argentina
141 F6 **Diamantina** *R* Queensland Australia
129 K7 **Diamantina** Brazil
130 G6 **Diamantina** Minas Gerais Brazil
141 F6 **Diamantina Lakes** Queensland Australia
129 G6 **Diamantino** Brazil
130 C4 **Diamantino** Mato Grosso Brazil
130 D5 **Diamantino** Mato Grosso Brazil
110 B5 **Diamond** Missouri U.S.A.
118 E9 **Diamond City** Alberta Canada
75 N7 **Diamond Harb** India
144 D5 **Diamond Harbour** New Zealand
102 S12 **Diamond Hd** Hawaiian Is
141 K3 **Diamond Islets** Gt Barrier Reef Australia
100 C6 **Diamond L** Oregon U.S.A.
103 J2 **Diamond Mts** Nevada U.S.A.
100 C6 **Diamond Peak** *mt* Oregon U.S.A.
103 J2 **Diamond Pk** Nevada U.S.A.
102 D3 **Diamond Springs** California U.S.A.
101 P8 **Diamondville** Wyoming U.S.A.
94 G8 **Diana** West Virginia U.S.A.
141 J3 **Diana Bank** Gt Barrier Reef Aust
28 G5 **Dianaland** Denmark
67 C6 **Dianbai** China
Dianbu *see* **Feidong**
67 A4 **Dian Chi** *L* China
67 B1 **Dianjiang** China
44 D4 **Diano Marina** Italy
129 J6 **Dianópolis** Brazil
65 H2 **Diaoling** China
85 E6 **Diapaga** Burkina
71 F2 **Diapitan B** Luzon Philippines
46 F4 **Diavata** Greece
68 A6 **Diavolo, Mt** Andaman Is
65 A5 **Dibabu** China
87 D7 **Dibaya** Zaire
86 D3 **Dibbis** Sudan
66 F6 **Dibhuk Pass** India/Burma
86 B4 **Dibi** Cameroon
109 N4 **Diboll** Texas U.S.A.
66 E6 **Dibrugarh** India
75 Q5 **Dibrugarh** India
71 E3 **Dicapanisan Pt** Luzon Philippines
Diciosănmârtin *see* **Tîrnăveni**
98 E9 **Dickens** Nebraska U.S.A.
108 G2 **Dickens** Texas U.S.A.
95 R6 **Dickey** Maine U.S.A.
98 H3 **Dickey** North Dakota U.S.A.
98 D3 **Dickinson** North Dakota U.S.A.
109 M6 **Dickinson** Texas U.S.A.
9 H3 **Dickleburgh** England
36 D3 **Dickscheid-Geroldstein** Germany
110 J5 **Dickson** Tennessee U.S.A.
95 M5 **Dickson City** Pennsylvania U.S.A.
78 H3 **Dicle** *R* Turkey
45 L4 **Dicomano** Italy
71 F1 **Didacas** *isld* Luzon Philippines
9 E4 **Didcot** England
85 C6 **Didiéni** Mali
109 L8 **Dido** Texas U.S.A.
118 C7 **Didsbury** Alberta Canada
74 F5 **Didwana** India
121 S4 **Didyme** Quebec Canada
19 O15 **Die** France
89 G5 **Die Berg** *mt* S Africa
36 B5 **Diebling** France
85 D6 **Diébougou** Burkina
36 F4 **Dieburg** Germany
118 K7 **Diefenbaker, L** Saskatchewan Canada
33 N6 **Die Göhrde** *reg* Germany
131 F3 **Diego Lamas** Uruguay
133 D9 **Diego Ramírez, Is** Chile
Diego Suarez *see* **Antsiranana**
30 D1 **Die Halligen** *inlet* Germany
32 L8 **Diekholzen** Germany
22 L4 **Diekirch** Luxembourg
20 G2 **Diélette** France
32 H8 **Dielingen** Germany
85 C6 **Diema** Mali
32 K9 **Diemel** *R* Germany
36 C6 **Diemeringen** France
68 F2 **Dien Bien Phu** Vietnam
68 G3 **Dien Chau** Vietnam
32 J8 **Diepenau** Germany
25 G4 **Diepenheim** Netherlands
32 H7 **Diepholz** Germany
21 N2 **Dieppe** France
127 P4 **Dieppe Bay Town** St Kitts W Indies
36 D2 **Dierdorf** Germany
25 F4 **Dieren** Netherlands
33 Q4 **Dierhagen** Germany
36 D2 **Dieringhausen** Germany
109 N1 **Dierks** Arkansas U.S.A.
65 F2 **Di'er Songhua Jiang** *R* China
33 N7 **Diesdorf** Germany
41 J2 **Diessenhofen** Switzerland
22 J2 **Diest** Belgium
110 H2 **Dieterich** Illinois U.S.A.
37 K3 **Dietersdorf** Germany
37 M5 **Dietfurt** Germany
41 H3 **Dietikon** Switzerland
101 L7 **Dietrich** Idaho U.S.A.
36 F3 **Dietzenbach** Germany
19 O15 **Dieulefit** France
19 K4 **Dieuze** France
25 F3 **Dieverbrug** Netherlands
36 B2 **Die Ville** *reg* Germany
36 E3 **Diez** Germany
65 D7 **Difang** China
22 K4 **Differdange** Luxembourg
67 F1 **Digang** China
75 Q5 **Digboi** India
122 G9 **Digby** Nova Scotia Canada
9 F1 **Digby** England
83 M14 **Digby, C** Kerguelen Indian Oc
122 F9 **Digby Neck** Nova Scotia Canada
107 K3 **Dighton** Kansas U.S.A.
95 Q5 **Dighton** Massachusetts U.S.A.
94 B2 **Dighton** Michigan U.S.A.
74 G9 **Diglur** India
19 Q16 **Digne** France
21 N4 **Digny** France
18 H6 **Digoin** France
71 F2 **Digollorin Pt** Luzon Philippines
71 G7 **Digos** Mindanao Philippines
74 G8 **Digras** India
136 H3 **Digul** *R* W Irian
86 H5 **Diinsoor** Somalia
71 E5 **Diit** *isld* Philippines
22 H2 **Dijle** *R* Belgium
19 J5 **Dijon** France
86 C4 **Dik** Chad
89 E4 **Dikabeye** Botswana
26 H6 **Dikanäs** Sweden
86 H3 **Dikhil** Djibouti
47 H5 **Dikili** Turkey
79 B7 **Dîkirnis** Egypt
22 D2 **Dikkebus** Belgium
67 F3 **Dikou** China
83 K11 **Dikoya** Sri Lanka
55 D2 **Dikoye, Oz** *L* Russian Federation
22 D1 **Diksmuide** Belgium
50 H1 **Dikson** Russian Federation
50 G1 **Dikson, Ostrov** *isld* Russian Federation
86 B3 **Dikwa** Nigeria
47 J7 **Dilek Dağ** *mt* Turkey
71 M9 **Dili** Timor Indonesia
106 E6 **Dilia** New Mexico U.S.A.
68 A6 **Diligent Str** Andaman Is
68 J7 **Di Linh** Vietnam
47 N11 **Diliskelesi Ist** *lighthouse* Turkey
119 M8 **Dilke** Saskatchewan Canada
103 O6 **Dilkon** Arizona U.S.A.
36 E2 **Dill** *R* Germany
118 G6 **Dillberry L. Prov Park** Alberta Canada
107 L6 **Dill City** Oklahoma U.S.A.
36 E2 **Dillenburg** Germany
98 K9 **Diller** Nebraska U.S.A.
109 H7 **Dilley** Texas U.S.A.
86 E3 **Dilling** Sudan
36 B5 **Dillingen** Germany
116 H7 **Dillingham** Alaska U.S.A.
118 H3 **Dillon** Saskatchewan Canada
106 D2 **Dillon** Colorado U.S.A.
101 N4 **Dillon** Montana U.S.A.
112 H3 **Dillon** South Carolina U.S.A.
144 D5 **Dillon Cone** *mt* New Zealand
94 E6 **Dillon Res** Ohio U.S.A.
95 K6 **Dillsburg** Pennsylvania U.S.A.
94 J9 **Dillwyn** Virginia U.S.A.
87 D8 **Dilolo** Zaire
75 P6 **Dimapur** India
124 F6 **Dimas** Mexico
79 G5 **Dimashq** Syria
86 D7 **Dimbelenge** Zaire
85 D7 **Dimbokro** Ivory Coast
138 F6 **Dimboola** Victoria Australia
48 J5 **Dîmbo Vița** *R* Romania
48 J6 **Dîmbovița** *reg* Romania
141 H3 **Dimbulah** Queensland Australia
54 J8 **Dimitrov** Ukraine
54 E8 **Dimitrova** Ukraine
47 H2 **Dimitrovgrad** Bulgaria
53 G7 **Dimitrovgrad** Russian Federation
46 F1 **Dimitrovgrad** Serbia Yugoslavia
46 G2 **Dimitrov, Yazovir G.** *res* Bulgaria
108 E1 **Dimmitt** Texas U.S.A.
98 H6 **Dimock** South Dakota U.S.A.
79 F7 **Dīmona** Israel
46 F1 **Dimovo** Bulgaria
71 G5 **Dinagat** *isld* Philippines
71 G5 **Dinagat Sound** Philippines
75 N6 **Dinajpur** Bangladesh
20 F5 **Dinan** France
22 H3 **Dinant** Belgium
47 L6 **Dinar** Turkey
42 G4 **Dinara Planina** *R* Bosnia-Herzegovina/Croatia
20 F4 **Dinard-St.Enogat** France
86 F3 **Dinder** *R* Sudan
76 C5 **Dindigul** India
109 K7 **Dinero** Texas U.S.A.
86 C7 **Dinga** Zaire
71 E3 **Dingalan B** Luzon Philippines
68 K3 **Ding'an** China
58 E4 **Dingbian** China
32 E9 **Dingden** Germany
20 G5 **Dingé** France
33 M10 **Dingelstädt** Germany
33 O9 **Dingelstedt** Germany
48 K3 **Dîngeni** Romania
75 M4 **Dinggyê** China
67 G1 **Dinghai** China
101 O7 **Dingle** Idaho U.S.A.
14 A4 **Dingle B** Ireland
67 E4 **Dingnan** China
141 J6 **Dingo** Queensland Australia
37 O6 **Dingolfing** Germany
71 E1 **Dingras** Luzon Philippines
65 C7 **Dingtao** China
85 B6 **Dinguiraye** Guinea
123 M7 **Dingwall** C Breton I, Nova Scotia
15 D3 **Dingwall** Scotland
58 D4 **Dingxi** China
65 C5 **Ding Xian** China
65 B5 **Dingxiang** China
65 C5 **Dingxing** China
65 E6 **Dingzi Gang** *B* China
69 H8 **Dinh An, Cua** *river mouth* Vietnam
67 B6 **Dinh Lap** Vietnam
25 H4 **Dinkel** *R* Netherlands
37 J5 **Dinkelsbühl** Germany
37 K7 **Dinkelscherben** Germany
32 H7 **Dinklage** Germany
103 O5 **Dinnebito Wash** *creek* Arizona U.S.A.
13 G3 **Dinnington** England
87 E10 **Dinokwe** Botswana
118 K1 **Dinorwic L** Ontario Canada
101 Q9 **Dinosaur Nat.Mon** Utah/Colo U.S.A.
78 J4 **Dīn, Şalāḩ ad** *prov* Iraq
32 E9 **Dinslaken** Germany
118 K7 **Dinsmore** Saskatchewan Canada
113 F7 **Dinsmore** Florida U.S.A.
70 K8 **Dintiteladas** *C* Sumatra
102 E5 **Dinuba** California U.S.A.
94 K9 **Dinwiddie** Virginia U.S.A.
25 F5 **Dinxperlo** Netherlands
27 G15 **Diö** Sweden
85 C6 **Dioila** Mali
116 C4 **Diomede Is** Bering Str
51 S2 **Diomida, Ostrova** *islds* Russian Federation
22 H3 **Dion** Belgium
86 D2 **Diona** Chad
130 D10 **Dionisio Cerqueira** Brazil
130 D5 **Diorama** Brazil
48 F2 **Diósgyör** Hungary
85 A6 **Diouloulou** Senegal
85 C6 **Dioura** Mali
85 A6 **Diourbel** Senegal
74 C6 **Diplo** Pakistan
71 F6 **Dipolog** Mindanao Philippines
22 L4 **Dippach** Luxembourg
12 C2 **Dippen** Scotland
12 C3 **Dippin** Scotland
144 B6 **Dipton** New Zealand
74 D1 **Dir** Pakistan
27 B13 **Dirdal** Norway
141 G2 **Direction,C** Queensland Australia
83 M8 **Direction I** Cocos Is Indian Oc
86 H4 **Dirē Dawa** Ethiopia
125 L4 **Diriamba** Nicaragua
87 D9 **Dirico** Angola
43 F11 **Dirillo** *R* Sicily
143 A7 **Dirk Hartog I** W Australia Australia
84 E6 **Dirkou** Niger
25 B5 **Dirksland** Netherlands
13 F1 **Dirleton** Scotland
36 C5 **Dirmingen** Germany
86 E3 **Dirra** Sudan
141 J8 **Dirranbandi** Queensland Australia
103 O3 **Dirty Devil** *R* Utah U.S.A.
102 T13 **Disappearing I** Hawaiian Is
131 H6 **Disappointment, C** S Georgia
100 A3 **Disappointment, C** Washington U.S.A.
135 N9 **Disappointment Is** Tuamotu Arch Pacific Oc
143 E6 **Disappointment,L** W Australia Australia
139 K6 **Disaster B** New South Wales Australia
100 F1 **Disautel** Washington U.S.A.
37 J6 **Dischingen** Germany
117 Q4 **Discovery** Northwest Territories Canada
138 F7 **Discovery B** S Aust/Vict Australia
127 K1 **Discovery Bay** Jamaica
100 C2 **Discovery Bay** Washington U.S.A.
100 C1 **Discovery I** Washington U.S.A.
90 J13 **Discovery Tablemount** S Atlantic Oc
142 E5 **Discovery Well** W Australia Australia
41 J4 **Disentis** Switzerland
13 G5 **Dishforth** England
116 J5 **Dishkakat** Alaska U.S.A.
116 J5 **Dishna** *R* Alaska U.S.A.
80 F1 **Dishon** *R* Israel
80 F1 **Dishon** Israel
115 O4 **Disko** *isld* Greenland
115 O4 **Diskofjord** Greenland
119 M8 **Disley** Saskatchewan Canada
140 F4 **Dismal** *R* Queensland Australia
98 F8 **Dismal** *R* Nebraska U.S.A.
95 L10 **Dismal Swamp** Virginia U.S.A.
52 C6 **Disna** Belorussia
22 K2 **Dison** Belgium
95 K9 **Disputanta** Virginia U.S.A.
121 T7 **Disraëli** Quebec Canada
9 H3 **Diss** England
21 L8 **Dissay** France
21 L6 **Dissay-sous-Courcillon** France
32 H8 **Dissen** Germany
122 C4 **Dissimieux, L** Quebec Canada
100 C6 **Disston** Oregon U.S.A.
79 A7 **Disûq** Egypt
9 F6 **Ditchling** England
33 O9 **Ditfurt** Germany
32 K4 **Dithmarschen** *reg* Germany
43 F11 **Dittaino** *R* Sicily
36 G6 **Ditzingen** Germany
74 D8 **Diu** India
71 G6 **Diuata Mts** Mindanao Philippines
21 K7 **Dive** *R* France
52 D5 **Divenskaya** Russian Federation
121 L6 **Diver** Ontario Canada
110 G2 **Divernon** Illinois U.S.A.
142 G3 **Diversion Dam** W Australia Australia
109 H2 **Diversion L** Texas U.S.A.
21 K3 **Dives** *R* France
21 K3 **Dives sur Mer** France
20 G2 **Divette** *R* France
26 L3 **Dividal** *R* Norway
106 E3 **Divide** Colorado U.S.A.
141 H6 **Dividing Range** Queensland Australia
71 F2 **Divilacan B** Luzon Philippines
87 F10 **Divinhe** Mozambique
130 G7 **Divinópolis** Brazil
22 C3 **Divion** France
100 F8 **Division Peak** *mt* Nevada U.S.A.
53 F10 **Divnoye** Russian Federation
85 C7 **Divo** Ivory Coast
78 G2 **Divriği** Turkey
74 B5 **Diwana** Pakistan
78 K6 **Dīwānīyah, Ad** Iraq
121 O4 **Dix** Quebec Canada
98 C8 **Dix** Nebraska U.S.A.
95 R2 **Dixfield** Maine U.S.A.
111 K8 **Dixiana** Alabama U.S.A.
111 K10 **Dixie** Alabama U.S.A.
113 D7 **Dixie** Georgia U.S.A.
100 K4 **Dixie** Idaho U.S.A.
100 G3 **Dixie** Washington U.S.A.
100 G5 **Dixie Pass** Oregon U.S.A.
102 F2 **Dixie Valley** Nevada U.S.A.
121 Q5 **Dix Milles, L.des** Quebec Canada
95 S2 **Dixmont** Maine U.S.A.
95 O2 **Dix Mt** New York U.S.A.
Dixmude *see* **Diksmuide**
102 C3 **Dixon** California U.S.A.
99 R8 **Dixon** Illinois U.S.A.
110 D4 **Dixon** Missouri U.S.A.
101 L2 **Dixon** Montana U.S.A.
98 K7 **Dixon** Nebraska U.S.A.
106 E5 **Dixon** New Mexico U.S.A.
101 S8 **Dixon** Wyoming U.S.A.
117 G8 **Dixon Entrance** *str* Br Col/Alaska Canada/U.S.A.
111 J9 **Dixons Mills** Alabama U.S.A.
117 P7 **Dixonville** Alberta Canada
94 H6 **Dixonville** Pennsylvania U.S.A.
67 A4 **Dixu** China
121 T7 **Dixville** Quebec Canada
78 K5 **Diyālá** *prov* Iraq
78 H3 **Diyarbakır** Turkey
65 H3 **Diyingou** China
74 B9 **Diz** Pakistan
77 H6 **Diz** Pakistan
67 C2 **Dizhuang** China
8 B6 **Dizzard Pt** England
86 B5 **Dja** *R* Cameroon
84 E5 **Djado** Niger
84 E5 **Djado, Pl.du** Niger
71 A2 **Djailolo** Halmahera Indonesia
Djailolo Gilolo *isld see* **Halmahera** *isld*
Djajapura *see* **Jayapura**
86 B6 **Djambala** Congo
69 F13 **Djambi** *prov* Sumatra
70 L9 **Djampang-Kulon** Java
85 F4 **Djanet** Algeria
70 E6 **Djangeru** Kalimantan
70 E3 **Djanlonong** Kalimantan
85 E3 **Djaret** *watercourse* Algeria
70 L9 **Djatinegara** Java
70 M9 **Djatiwangi** Java
86 B2 **Djbella** Niger
69 G13 **Djebus** Indonesia
86 C3 **Djédaa** Chad
85 E2 **Djedi** *watercourse* Algeria
85 E2 **Djelfa** Algeria
86 E4 **Djéma** Cent Afr Republic
70 F7 **Djeneponto** Sulawesi
Djerba, I de *see* **Jerba, I de**
86 B4 **Djérem** *R* Cameroon
Djezair, El *see* **Alger**
85 D6 **Djibasso** Burkina
85 D6 **Djibo** Burkina
86 H3 **Djibouti** Djibouti
86 H3 **Djibouti** *rep* N E Africa
86 D7 **Djokopunda** Zaire
86 D5 **Djolu** Zaire
70 D7 **Djorong** Kalimantan
86 B6 **Djoué** *R* Congo
85 C5 **Djouf, El** *reg* Mauritania/Mali
85 E7 **Djougou** Benin
86 B5 **Djoum** Cameroon

Djourab — Duifken Pt
171

86 C2 **Djourab** *dist* Chad
86 F5 **Djugu** Zaire
29 T9 **Djupivogur** Iceland
27 H11 **Djura** Sweden
27 K12 **Djursholm** Sweden
28 E4 **Djursland** *reg* Denmark
111 G10 **D'Lo** Mississippi U.S.A.
51 O1 **Dmitriya Lapteva, Proliv** *str* Russian Federation
55 G3 **Dmitriyevka** Russian Federation
54 G4 **Dmitriyev-L'govskiy** Russian Federation
54 J1 **Dmitrov** Russian Federation
54 D6 **Dmitrovka** Ukraine
54 G4 **Dmitrovsk-Orlovskiy** Russian Federation
54 B4 **Dnepr** *R* Belorussia/Rus Fed etc
54 F8 **Dneprodzerzhinsk** Ukraine
54 G8 **Dnepropetrovsk** Ukraine
54 F9 **Dneprorudnoye** Ukraine
53 C7 **Dneprovskaya Nizmennost** *lowland* Belorussia/Ukraine
54 C10 **Dneprovskiy Liman** *lagoon* Ukraine
53 C9 **Dnestr** *R* Europe
48 M4 **Dnestrovsk** Moldavia
48 N4 **Dnestrovskiy Liman** *lagoon* Ukraine
Dnieper *R see* **Dnepr** *R*
Dniester *R see* **Dnestr** *R*
52 C5 **Dno** Russian Federation
77 K2 **Doāb Mekh-i-Zarīn** Afghanistan
122 F7 **Doaktown** New Brunswick Canada
70 E7 **Doangdoangan Besar** *isld* Indonesia
70 E7 **Doangdoangan Ketjil** *isld* Indonesia
67 B6 **Doan Hung** Vietnam
86 C4 **Doba** Chad
33 Q5 **Dobbertin** Germany
138 E2 **Dobbie, L** South Australia Australia
140 E6 **Dobbie,Mt** N Terr Australia
109 M5 **Dobbin** Texas U.S.A.
31 M6 **Dobczyce** Poland
52 B6 **Dobele** Latvia
37 P1 **Döbeln** Germany
33 T9 **Doberlug Kirchhain** Germany
31 J3 **Dobiegniew** Poland
133 E5 **Doblas** Argentina
136 G3 **Dobo** Moluccas Indonesia
48 E6 **Doboj** Bosnia-Herzegovina
112 F6 **Doboy Sd** Georgia U.S.A.
31 J2 **Dobra** Poland
37 M3 **Döbraberg** *mt* Germany
37 P4 **Dobřany** Czechoslovakia
38 J8 **Dobratsch** *mt* Austria
31 M2 **Dobre Miasto** Poland
48 G4 **Dobresti** Romania
48 H6 **Dobreta-Turnu-Severin** Romania
38 J8 **Döbriach** Austria
47 J1 **Dobrich** Bulgaria
33 S9 **Döbrichau** Germany
46 F3 **Dobrinishte** Bulgaria
31 H6 **Dobřiš** Czechoslovakia
33 Q8 **Dobritz** Germany
31 L5 **Dobrodzień** Poland
31 O6 **Dobromil** Ukraine
54 J8 **Dobropol'ye** Ukraine
48 J6 **Dobroteşti** Romania
54 F2 **Dobroye** Russian Federation
54 C4 **Dobrush** Belorussia
54 C4 **Dobryanka** Ukraine
31 L3 **Dobrzyn** Poland
48 F2 **Dobšiná** Czechoslovakia
144 C5 **Dobson** New Zealand
144 B6 **Dobson** *R* New Zealand
112 G1 **Dobson** North Carolina U.S.A.
8 B7 **Dobwalls** England
127 N1 **Docas del Dragón** *chan* Trinidad/Ven
71 D7 **Doc Can** *isld* Sulu Arch Philippines
130 G6 **Doce, R** Brazil
143 G6 **Docker Cr** W Australia Australia
140 A6 **Docker River** N Terr Australia
9 G2 **Docking** England
26 H9 **Dockmyr** Sweden
142 F4 **Dockrell, Mt** W Australia Australia
26 K8 **Docksta** Sweden
36 B3 **Dockweiler** Germany
109 H10 **Doctor Cos** Mexico
143 E8 **Doctor Hicks Ra** W Australia Australia
Doctor Petru Groza *see* **Ştei**
121 P3 **Doda, L** Quebec Canada
76 C4 **Dod Ballapur** India
13 F2 **Doddington** England
109 O2 **Doddridge** Arkansas U.S.A.
118 E5 **Dodds** Alberta Canada
Dodecanese *islds see* **Dhodhekánisos** *islds*
98 K8 **Dodge** Nebraska U.S.A.
98 D2 **Dodge** North Dakota U.S.A.
99 O5 **Dodge Center** Minnesota U.S.A.
107 K4 **Dodge City** Kansas U.S.A.
99 Q7 **Dodgeville** Wisconsin U.S.A.
8 B7 **Dodman Pt** England
88 E5 **Dodoma** Tanzania
33 O6 **Dodow** Germany
118 J7 **Dodsland** Saskatchewan Canada
109 P3 **Dodson** Louisiana U.S.A.
101 R1 **Dodson** Montana U.S.A.
47 K5 **Dodurga** Turkey
22 G1 **Doel** Belgium
112 D6 **Doerun** Georgia U.S.A.
25 F4 **Doesburg** Netherlands
25 F5 **Doetinchem** Netherlands
71 J5 **Dofa** Indonesia
36 F6 **Doffingen** Germany
66 D5 **Dogai Coring** *L* China
47 H6 **Doğanbey Burun** *C* Turkey
78 G1 **Doğankent** Turkey
79 F2 **Doğankent** Turkey
117 M10 **Dog Creek** British Columbia Canada
66 E5 **Dogên Co** *L* China
47 L5 **Döğer** Turkey
7 M8 **Dogger Bank** North Sea
127 N5 **Dog I** Lesser Antilles
144 B7 **Dog I** New Zealand
113 C8 **Dog I** Florida U.S.A.
119 T7 **Dog L** Manitoba Canada
99 R1 **Dog L** Ontario Canada
44 C2 **Dogliani** Italy
38 H9 **Dogna** Italy
60 G9 **Dōgo** *isld* Japan
85 E6 **Dogondoutchi** Niger
60 G10 **Dōgo-yama** *mt* Japan
118 C7 **Dog Pound** Alberta Canada
126 E2 **Dog Rocks** Bahamas
78 K2 **Doğubayazit** Turkey
127 P4 **Dogwood Pt** Nevis W Indies
Doha *see* **Dawḥah, Ad**
Dohad *see* **Dāhod**
75 P7 **Dohazar** Bangladesh
121 S5 **Doheny** Quebec Canada
33 N4 **Döhnsdorf** Germany
71 A1 **Doi** Indonesia
68 D3 **Doi Saket** Thailand
22 H3 **Doische** Belgium
130 E8 **Dois Córregos** Brazil
46 F3 **Dojran** Macedonia Yugoslavia
46 F3 **Dojrawsko ezero** *L* Macedonia Yugoslavia
27 D11 **Dokka** Norway
26 M4 **Dokkas** Sweden
28 E3 **Dokkedal** Denmark
25 E2 **Dokkum** Netherlands
55 D5 **Dokuchayevka** Kazakhstan
54 J9 **Dokuchayevsk** Ukraine
136 H3 **Dolak** *isld* W Irian
98 H5 **Doland** South Dakota U.S.A.
121 S4 **Dolbeau** Quebec Canada
32 G9 **Dolberg** Germany
20 G4 **Dol-de Bretagne** France
19 J5 **Dôle** France
125 N5 **Dolega** Panama
42 G3 **Dolenjske Toplice** Slovenia
8 C3 **Dolfor** Wales
8 C2 **Dolgellau** Wales
95 N3 **Dolgeville** New York U.S.A.
116 G9 **Dolgoi I** Alaska U.S.A.
55 E3 **Dolgovskoye** Russian Federation
48 H2 **Dolgoye** Ukraine
43 C9 **Dolianova** Sardinia
48 H2 **Dolina** Ukraine
59 M2 **Dolinsk** Russian Federation
54 D8 **Dolinskaya** Ukraine
71 A3 **Dolit** Indonesia
46 F1 **Dolj** Romania
46 E1 **Doljevac** Serbia Yugoslavia
38 G8 **Döllach** Austria
12 E1 **Dollar** Scotland
118 J9 **Dollard** Saskatchewan Canada
122 F3 **Dollard, L** Quebec Canada
15 E5 **Dollar Law** *mt* Scotland
32 F6 **Dollart** *inlet* Germany/Neths
32 M8 **Dollbergen** Germany
33 P8 **Dolle** Germany
146 D5 **Dolleman I** Antarctica
28 C4 **Dollerup** Denmark
37 L6 **Dollnstein** Germany
21 M5 **Dollon** France
37 K1 **Döllstädt** Germany
46 G1 **Dolna Mitropbliya** Bulgaria
46 E3 **Dolneni** Macedonia Yugoslavia
46 G1 **Dolni Dŭbnik** Bulgaria
37 Q2 **Dolní Jiřetin** Czechoslovakia
31 J6 **Dolní Králòvice** Czechoslovakia
37 O3 **Dolní Žandov** Czechoslovakia
45 M1 **Dolo** Italy
70 F5 **Dolo** Sulawesi
19 P13 **Dolomieu** France
42 D2 **Dolomitiche, Alpi** Italy
Dolonnur *see* **Duolun**
86 H5 **Dolo Odo** Ethiopia
131 F6 **Dolores** Argentina
125 P9 **Dolores** Guatemala
17 G6 **Dolores** Spain
131 F4 **Dolores** Uruguay
106 B3 **Dolores** *R* Colorado U.S.A.
106 B4 **Dolores** Colorado U.S.A.
125 J7 **Dolores Hidalgo** Mexico
133 F8 **Dolphin, C** Falkland Is
127 H1 **Dolphin Hd** *hill* Jamaica
87 B11 **Dolphin Hd** Namibia
142 B5 **Dolphin I** W Australia Australia
13 E2 **Dolphinton** Scotland
114 H4 **Dolphin & Union Str** Northwest Territories Canada
38 G8 **Dölsach** Austria
31 K4 **Dolsk** Poland
68 G3 **Do Luong** Vietnam
21 M7 **Dolus-le-Sec** France
8 C1 **Dolwyddelan** Wales
136 H2 **Dom** *mt* W Irian
122 H2 **Domagaya L** Labrador, Nfld Canada
119 U9 **Domain** Manitoba Canada
47 K5 **Domaniç** Turkey
47 K5 **Domaniç Dağı** *mt* Turkey
21 P1 **Domart-en-Ponthieu** France
37 O5 **Domažlice** Czechoslovakia
55 C5 **Dombarovskiy** Russian Federation
26 D9 **Dombås** Norway
19 K4 **Dombasle** France
87 B8 **Dombe Grande** Angola
140 A2 **Dombey,C** N Terr Australia
48 E4 **Dombóvár** Hungary
48 G2 **Dombrád** Hungary
37 J5 **Dombühl** Germany
25 A5 **Domburg** Netherlands
103 K9 **Dome** Arizona U.S.A.
117 N9 **Dome Creek** British Columbia Canada
40 E7 **Dôme-de-Chasseforêt** France
103 K8 **Dome Rock Mts** Arizona U.S.A.
144 D5 **Domett** New Zealand
145 D4 **Domett, Mt** New Zealand
36 B6 **Domèvre** France
21 J4 **Domfront** France
106 D6 **Domingo** New Mexico U.S.A.
127 O7 **Dominica** *isld* Lesser Antilles
127 J5 **Dominican Rep** W Indies
123 M7 **Dominion** C Breton I, Nova Scotia
115 M4 **Dominion, C** Northwest Territories Canada
119 U9 **Dominion City** Manitoba Canada
123 L1 **Dominion L** Labrador, Nfld Canada
115 O7 **Domino** Labrador, Nfld Canada
33 O6 **Dömitz** Germany
21 H4 **Domjean** France
130 G6 **Dom Joaquim** Brazil
41 K4 **Domleschg** *R* Switzerland
18 F8 **Domme** France
25 D6 **Dommel** *R* Netherlands
33 R9 **Dommitzsch** Germany
86 A2 **Domo** Ethiopia
54 J1 **Domodedovo** Russian Federation
41 H5 **Domodossola** Italy
21 P3 **Domont** France
146 E14 **Domont d'Urville Sea** Antarctica
40 D1 **Dompaire** France
21 H5 **Dompierre-du-Chemin** France
22 B3 **Dompierre-sur-Authie** France
20 H8 **Dompierre-sur-Yon** France
36 B7 **Domptail** France
71 J9 **Dompu** Sumbawa Indonesia
119 M6 **Domremy** Saskatchewan Canada
26 K8 **Domsjö** Sweden
88 E9 **Domue** *pk* Mozambique
131 B6 **Domuyo** *pk* Argentina
141 K8 **Domville** *mt* Queensland Australia
141 K8 **Domville,Mt** Queensland Australia
46 F6 **Domvraína** Greece
42 F2 **Domžale** Slovenia
141 J5 **Don** *R* Queensland Australia
20 G6 **Don** *R* France
22 D2 **Don** France
124 E4 **Don** Mexico
54 L5 **Don** *R* Russian Federation
15 F3 **Don** *R* Scotland
106 D9 **Dona Ana** New Mexico U.S.A.
45 M1 **Donada** Italy
14 F2 **Donaghadee** N Ireland
139 G6 **Donald** Victoria Australia
121 M8 **Donald** Ontario Canada
118 E6 **Donalda** Alberta Canada
144 A6 **Donald, Mt** New Zealand
140 F4 **Donaldson** Queensland Australia
109 P1 **Donaldson** Arkansas U.S.A.
98 K1 **Donaldson** Minnesota U.S.A.
111 E11 **Donaldsonville** Louisiana U.S.A.
112 C6 **Donalsonville** Georgia U.S.A.
14 E3 **Donard** Ireland
124 G5 **Donato Guerra** Mexico
38 L5 **Donau** *R* Austria
37 L6 **Donau** *R* Germany
41 J2 **Donaueschingen** Germany
37 L6 **Donaumoos** *reg* Germany
37 K6 **Donauried** *reg* Germany
37 N5 **Donaustauf** Germany
37 K6 **Donauwörth** Germany
118 K7 **Donavon** Saskatchewan Canada
38 M7 **Donawitz** Austria
54 J8 **Donbass (Donetskiy Ugol'nyy Basseyn)** Ukraine
16 D6 **Don Benito** Spain
140 B1 **Don,C** N Terr Australia
13 G6 **Doncaster** England
95 K8 **Doncaster** Maryland U.S.A.
22 H4 **Donchery** France
22 K4 **Doncols** Luxembourg
87 B7 **Dondo** Angola
87 F9 **Dondo** Mozambique
71 E6 **Dondonay** *isld* Philippines
70 G4 **Dondo, Teluk** *B* Sulawesi
70 G4 **Dondo, Tg** *C* Sulawesi
73 N7 **Dondra Head** *C* Sri Lanka
48 L2 **Dondyushany** Moldavia
14 C2 **Donegal** Ireland
14 D2 **Donegal** *co* Ireland
14 C2 **Donegal Bay** *B* Ireland
14 B4 **Donegal Pt** Ireland
110 K5 **Donelson** Tennessee U.S.A.
14 C4 **Doneraile** Ireland
54 J8 **Donetsk** Ukraine
53 E9 **Donetskiy Kryazh** *mts* Rus Fed/Ukraine
127 J2 **Don Figuerero Mts** Jamaica
86 B4 **Donga** *R* Nigeria
59 K2 **Dong'an** China
67 D3 **Dong'an** China
68 J5 **Dong An** Vietnam
143 A8 **Dongara** W Australia
74 J8 **Dongargarh** India
66 D4 **Dongbolhai Shan** *mts* China
Dongchangshou *see* **Xinle**
Dongcun *see* **Haiyang**
68 H2 **Dong Dang** Vietnam
65 C6 **Dong'e** China
25 C5 **Dongen** Netherlands
20 F7 **Donges** France
68 J3 **Dongfang** China
65 J1 **Dongfanghong** China
65 F3 **Dongfeng** China
70 F5 **Donggala** Sulawesi
58 C4 **Donggi Cona** *L* China
67 D1 **Donggong** China
65 F4 **Donggou** China
67 E3 **Donggu** China
67 E5 **Dongguan** China
65 C6 **Dongguang** China
68 H4 **Dong Ha** Vietnam
65 D7 **Donghai** China
67 C6 **Donghai Dao** *isld* China
58 D3 **Dong He** *R* China
58 E4 **Dong He** *R* China
68 H4 **Dong Hoi** Vietnam
Donghuang *see* **Xishui** Guizhou
67 C4 **Dongjiang** China
65 H2 **Dongjingcheng** China
70 F6 **Dongkait, Tanjong** *C* Sulawesi
70 G4 **Dongkalang** Sulawesi
68 H1 **Dong Khe** Vietnam
67 C3 **Dongkou** China
67 B4 **Donglan** China
Dongliao *see* **Liaoyuan**
65 F3 **Dongliao He** *R* China
67 B5 **Dongling** China
67 E1 **Dongliu** China
65 C7 **Dongming** China
68 H7 **Dong Nai** *R* Vietnam
59 K2 **Dongning** China
87 C8 **Dongo** Angola
41 K5 **Dongo** Italy
86 C5 **Dongo** Zaire
84 J6 **Dongola** Sudan
86 C5 **Dongou** Congo
68 E4 **Dong Phraya Fai** *ra* Thailand
68 E5 **Dong Phraya Yen** Thailand
Dongping *see* **Anhua**
65 C7 **Dongping** China
65 C6 **Dongping Hu** *L* China
68 H7 **Dong Sai** Vietnam
67 F5 **Dongshan** China
67 F5 **Dongshan Dao** *isld* China
67 E6 **Dongsha Qundao** *isld* China
65 A5 **Dongsheng** China
67 B2 **Dongsheng** China
67 D2 **Dongting Hu** *L* China
67 G3 **Dongtou** China
67 B6 **Dong Trieu** Vietnam
65 D2 **Dong Ujimqin Qi** China
68 G1 **Dong Van** Vietnam
87 D8 **Dongwe** *R* Zambia
67 B2 **Dongxi** China
67 E2 **Dongxiang** China
65 D7 **Dongxi Lian Dao** *isld* China
65 G1 **Dongxing** China
67 B6 **Dongxing** China
67 G2 **Dongyang** China
65 D6 **Dongying** China
67 F1 **Dongzhi** China
109 L4 **Donie** Texas U.S.A.
9 F2 **Donington** England
110 F5 **Doniphan** Missouri U.S.A.
117 D4 **Donjek** *R* Yukon Territory Canada
48 G6 **Donji Milanovac** Serbia Yugoslavia
42 H4 **Donji Vakuf** Bosnia-Herzegovina
18 H6 **Donjon, le** France
99 S3 **Donken** Michigan U.S.A.
26 F5 **Dönna** *isld* Norway
109 J9 **Donna** Texas U.S.A.
121 T6 **Donnacona** Quebec Canada
42 B3 **Donnas** Italy
36 B6 **Donnelay** France
110 G2 **Donnellson** Illinois U.S.A.
117 P8 **Donnelly** Alberta Canada
100 J5 **Donnelly** Idaho U.S.A.
98 K4 **Donnelly** Minnesota U.S.A.
145 D1 **Donnelly's Crossing** New Zealand
102 D2 **Donner Pass** California U.S.A.
38 K7 **Donnersbach** Austria
38 K7 **Donnersbach Wald** Austria
36 D4 **Donnersberg** *mt* Germany
100 G6 **Donner und Blitzen** *R* Oregon U.S.A.
26 F5 **Dönnes** Norway
143 B10 **Donnybrook** W Australia Australia
98 E1 **Donnybrook** North Dakota U.S.A.
19 K4 **Donon** *mt* France
36 C7 **Donon, Col du** *pass* France
94 H6 **Donora** Pennsylvania U.S.A.
140 F4 **Donor's Hill** Queensland Australia
Donostia *see* **San Sebastian**
99 T9 **Donovan** Illinois U.S.A.
102 D4 **Don Pedro Res** California U.S.A.
13 G6 **Don, R** England
54 K3 **Donskoy** Russian Federation
54 L6 **Donskoye Belogorye** Russian Federation
28 B5 **Donslund** Denmark
68 C4 **Donthami** *R* Burma
20 G4 **Donville** France
36 H6 **Donzdorf** Germany
18 G7 **Donzenac** France
19 N16 **Donzère** France
18 H5 **Donzy** France
143 C9 **Doodlakine** W Australia Australia
109 H4 **Doole** Texas U.S.A.
142 C5 **Dooleena** *mt* W Australia Australia
98 B1 **Dooley** Montana U.S.A.
121 O6 **Doolittle, L** Quebec Canada
140 E4 **Doomadgee** Queensland Australia
116 M3 **Doonerak, Mt** Alaska U.S.A.
12 D3 **Doon, L** Scotland
12 D3 **Doon, R** Scotland
25 D4 **Doorn** Netherlands
99 T5 **Door Pen** Wisconsin U.S.A.
86 A2 **Dooxo Nugaaleed** *V* Somalia
44 B1 **Dora** Italy
111 J8 **Dora** Alabama U.S.A.
106 G8 **Dora** New Mexico U.S.A.
42 B3 **Dora Baltea** *R* Italy
124 G4 **Dorado** Mexico
142 E5 **Dora,L** W Australia Australia
66 F5 **Doramarkog** China
113 F9 **Dora, Mt** Florida U.S.A.
98 K3 **Doran** Minnesota U.S.A.
27 G15 **Dörarp** Sweden
18 F6 **Dorat, le** France
Dorbiljin *see* **Emin**
Dorbiljin *see* **Emin**
Dorbod *see* **Siziwang Qi**
65 F1 **Dorbod** China
122 H8 **Dorchester** New Brunswick Canada
8 D6 **Dorchester** England
9 E4 **Dorchester** England
98 J9 **Dorchester** Nebraska U.S.A.
99 Q4 **Dorchester** Wisconsin U.S.A.
115 M4 **Dorchester, C** Northwest Territories Canada
89 A4 **Dordabis** Namibia
18 F7 **Dordogne** *dept* France
18 E8 **Dordogne** *R* France
25 C5 **Dordrecht** Netherlands
18 H7 **Dore** *R* France
140 B5 **Doreen, Mt** N Terr Australia
118 K4 **Doré L** Saskatchewan Canada
18 G7 **Dore, Mont** *mt* France
100 C6 **Dorena** Oregon U.S.A.
32 H8 **Dörenberg** *mt* Germany
32 J9 **Dörenhagen** Germany
118 E6 **Dorenlee** Alberta Canada
32 J8 **Dörentrup** Germany
130 F6 **Dores do Indaiá** Brazil
37 N7 **Dorfen** Germany
32 L7 **Dorfmark** Germany
33 R6 **Dorf Zechlin** Germany
43 C8 **Dorgali** Sardinia
77 J4 **Dori** *R* Afghanistan
85 D6 **Dori** Burkina
75 K5 **Dorīghāt** India
89 A8 **Doring** *R* S Africa
118 J4 **Dorintosh** Saskatchewan Canada
120 B4 **Dorion** Ontario Canada
121 Q7 **Dorion** Quebec Canada
140 B2 **Dorisvale** N Terr Australia
9 F5 **Dorking** England
36 B1 **Dormagen** Germany
18 H3 **Dormans** France
19 N13 **D'Or, Mt** France
41 L3 **Dornbirn** Austria
36 E2 **Dornburg** Germany
37 M1 **Dorndorf** Germany
37 J2 **Dorndorf** Germany
48 K3 **Dorneşti** Romania
36 F7 **Dornhan** Germany
15 C3 **Dornie** Scotland
48 J3 **Dornişoara** Romania
33 Q8 **Dörnitz** Germany
15 D3 **Dornoch** Scotland
15 D3 **Dornoch Firth** Scotland
13 E4 **Dornock** Scotland
65 A2 **Dornogovĭ** *prov* Mongolia
36 F7 **Dornstetten** Germany
32 F5 **Dornum** Germany
48 E3 **Dorog** Hungary
54 E2 **Dorogobuzh** Russian Federation
52 F2 **Dorogorskoye** Russian Federation
48 K3 **Dorohoi** Romania
54 H1 **Dorokhovo** Russian Federation
26 H7 **Dorotea** Sweden
118 E7 **Dorothy** Alberta Canada
52 G5 **Dorovitsa** Russian Federation
32 F7 **Dörpen** Germany
107 M3 **Dorrance** Kansas U.S.A.
143 A7 **Dorre I** W Australia Australia
139 L4 **Dorrigo** New South Wales Australia
8 D2 **Dorrington** England
100 D8 **Dorris** California U.S.A.
100 E8 **Dorris Res** California U.S.A.
121 M7 **Dorset** Ontario Canada
8 D6 **Dorset** *co* England
94 G5 **Dorset** Ohio U.S.A.
95 O3 **Dorset** Vermont U.S.A.
32 E9 **Dorsten** Germany
32 G9 **Dortmund** Germany
32 J5 **Dorum** Germany
86 E5 **Doruma** Zaire
121 R7 **Dorval** Quebec Canada
36 H5 **Dörzbach** Germany
133 D6 **Dos Bahías, C** Argentina
125 P9 **Dos Bocas** Belize
103 P9 **Dos Cabezas** Arizona U.S.A.
77 G2 **Doshakh, Koh-I** *mt* Afghanistan
71 E4 **Dos Hermanas** *isld* Philippines
16 D7 **Dos Hermanas** Spain
68 H2 **Do Son** Vietnam
102 D5 **Dos Palos** California U.S.A.
46 G3 **Dospat** Bulgaria
121 T6 **Dosquet** Quebec Canada
102 A2 **Dos Rios** California U.S.A.
109 H5 **Doss** Texas U.S.A.
33 R6 **Dosse** *R* Germany
85 E6 **Dosso** Niger
45 J1 **Dossobuono** Italy
50 E4 **Dossor** Kazakhstan
28 D3 **Døstrup** Denmark
94 K9 **Doswell** Virginia U.S.A.
111 L10 **Dothan** Alabama U.S.A.
100 B7 **Dothan** Oregon U.S.A.
123 T4 **Doting Cove** Newfoundland Canada
116 P5 **Dot Lake** Alaska U.S.A.
32 H7 **Dötlingen** Germany
101 S10 **Dotsero** Colorado U.S.A.
36 H5 **Döttingen** Germany
21 N8 **Douadic** France
22 E3 **Douai** France
86 A5 **Douala** Cameroon
20 B5 **Douarnenez** France
20 B5 **Douarnenez, Baie de** France
109 N6 **Double Bayou** Texas U.S.A.
126 D3 **Double Headed Shot Cays** *islds* Bahamas
68 C5 **Double I** Burma
141 L7 **Double Island Pt** Queensland Australia
108 G2 **Double Mountain Fork** *R* Texas U.S.A.
102 F6 **Double Mt** California U.S.A.
116 L6 **Double Peak** Alaska U.S.A.
141 H4 **Double Pt** *C* Queensland Australia
111 J7 **Double Springs** Alabama U.S.A.
31 J6 **Doubrava** *R* Czechoslovakia
19 J6 **Doubs** *R* France
40 D3 **Doubs** *dept* France
40 F3 **Doubs** *R* Switzerland
142 E3 **Doubtful B** W Australia Australia
143 C10 **Doubtful Island B** W Australia Australia
144 A6 **Doubtful Sd** New Zealand
145 D1 **Doubtless B** New Zealand
40 C4 **Doucier** France
21 M2 **Doudeville** France
99 O9 **Douds** Iowa U.S.A.
21 K7 **Doué-la-Fontaine** Maine-et-Loire France
85 D6 **Douentza** Mali
144 A7 **Doughboy Bay** New Zealand
138 D3 **Douglas** *R* South Australia Australia
119 S9 **Douglas** Manitoba Canada
121 O7 **Douglas** Ontario Canada
89 C7 **Douglas** S Africa
12 E3 **Douglas** Scotland
12 D5 **Douglas** I of Man U.K.
117 F6 **Douglas** Alaska U.S.A.
103 P10 **Douglas** Arizona U.S.A.
112 E6 **Douglas** Georgia U.S.A.
99 U7 **Douglas** Michigan U.S.A.
98 K9 **Douglas** Nebraska U.S.A.
98 E2 **Douglas** North Dakota U.S.A.
100 E2 **Douglas** Washington U.S.A.
98 A7 **Douglas** Wyoming U.S.A.
117 J9 **Douglas Chan** British Columbia Canada
106 B2 **Douglas Cr** Colorado U.S.A.
112 D1 **Douglas Dam** Tennessee U.S.A.
94 C1 **Douglas L** Michigan U.S.A.
112 D2 **Douglas L** Tennessee U.S.A.
12 E2 **Douglas Mill** Scotland
143 E8 **Douglas,Mount** W Australia Australia
116 L7 **Douglas, Mt** Alaska U.S.A.
120 J8 **Douglas Pt** Ontario Canada
107 O4 **Douglass** Kansas U.S.A.
122 G6 **Douglastown** New Brunswick Canada
122 H5 **Douglastown** Quebec Canada
111 M8 **Douglasville** Georgia U.S.A.
22 F3 **Doui** Belgium
46 D6 **Doukáton,Akr** *C* Greece
19 J4 **Doulevant le Château** France
21 P1 **Doullens** France
20 H7 **Doulon** France
14 A5 **Doulus Hd** Ireland
86 B5 **Doumé** Cameroon
67 D5 **Doumen** China
67 A5 **Doumuge** China
12 D1 **Doune** Scotland
15 E2 **Dounreay** Scotland
85 C7 **Douobé** *R* Liberia
37 P3 **Doupov** Czechoslovakia
22 F3 **Dour** France
130 E6 **Dourada, Cachoeira** *rapids* Brazil
129 J6 **Dourada,Serra** *mts* Brazil
130 E5 **Dourada,Serra** *mts* Brazil
130 B6 **Dourados** Brazil
130 C8 **Dourados** Brazil
133 F2 **Dourados** *R* Brazil
130 D8 **Dourados,Serra dos** *mts* Brazil
21 P4 **Dourdan** France
18 G9 **Dourdou** *R* France
22 B3 **Douriez** France
16 C3 **Douro** *R* Portugal
16 B3 **Douro Litoral** *prov* Portugal
Doushi *see* **Gong'an**
19 Q13 **Doussard** France
20 H3 **Douve** *R* France
21 K3 **Douvres-la-Délivrande** France
19 N14 **Doux** *R* France
18 E9 **Douze** *R* France
22 J4 **Douzy** France
45 L3 **Dovadola** Italy
106 B4 **Dove Creek** Colorado U.S.A.
142 C5 **Dove,Mt** W Australia Australia
139 H9 **Dover** Tasmania Australia
28 D4 **Dover** Denmark
9 E1 **Dove,R** England
9 H5 **Dover** England
110 C6 **Dover** Arkansas U.S.A.
95 M7 **Dover** Delaware U.S.A.
113 E9 **Dover** Florida U.S.A.
112 F5 **Dover** Georgia U.S.A.
110 N3 **Dover** Kentucky U.S.A.
95 Q3 **Dover** New Hampshire U.S.A.
95 N6 **Dover** New Jersey U.S.A.
112 K2 **Dover** North Carolina U.S.A.
94 F6 **Dover** Ohio U.S.A.
107 N6 **Dover** Oklahoma U.S.A.
110 J5 **Dover** Tennessee U.S.A.
95 S1 **Dover Foxcroft** Maine U.S.A.
143 F10 **Dover,Pt** W Australia Australia
22 C1 **Dover,Str.of** France/England
38 J9 **Dovje** Slovenia
28 F7 **Dovnsklint** Denmark
26 D9 **Dovre** Norway
26 D9 **Dovrefjell** Norway
26 D9 **Dovrefjell Nat. Park** Norway
88 D8 **Dowa** Malawi
94 A5 **Dowagiac** Michigan U.S.A.
143 B9 **Dowerin** W Australia Australia
Dow, L. *see* **Xau, L.**
8 C4 **Dowlais** Wales
77 J1 **Dowlatābād** Afghanistan
77 H3 **Dowlatābād** Afghanistan
77 E5 **Dowlatābād** Iran
77 J2 **Dowlat Yār** Afghanistan
118 F7 **Dowling** Alberta Canada
14 F2 **Down** *co* N Ireland
99 T8 **Downers Grove** Illinois U.S.A.
102 F8 **Downey** California U.S.A.
101 N7 **Downey** Idaho U.S.A.
141 K1 **Downfall Cr** Brisbane, Qnsld Australia
9 G2 **Downham Market** England
102 D2 **Downieville** California U.S.A.
99 O9 **Downing** Missouri U.S.A.
95 M6 **Downingtown** Pennsylvania U.S.A.
14 F2 **Downpatrick** N Ireland
14 B2 **Downpatrick Hd** Ireland
107 M2 **Downs** Kansas U.S.A.
101 Q6 **Downs Mt** Wyoming U.S.A.
95 M4 **Downsville** New York U.S.A.
9 E5 **Downton** England
117 L9 **Downton,Mt** British Columbia Canada
8 B6 **Downtown** England
99 N7 **Dows** Iowa U.S.A.
77 L2 **Dowshī** Afghanistan
7 L9 **Dowsing Lightship** North Sea
69 C12 **Dowu, Tanjung** *C* Indonesia
102 D1 **Doyle** California U.S.A.
110 L6 **Doyle** Tennessee U.S.A.
144 D5 **Doyleston** New Zealand
95 M6 **Doylestown** Pennsylvania U.S.A.
106 D3 **Doyleville** Colorado U.S.A.
60 F9 **Dōzen** *islds* Japan
59 K4 **Dōzen Nishi Jima** *isld* Japan
111 K10 **Dozier** Alabama U.S.A.
121 N5 **Dozois, Rés** Quebec Canada
21 K3 **Dozulé** France
45 L3 **Dozza** Italy
85 C2 **Drâa** *R* Morocco/Algeria
36 C2 **Drabenderhöhe** Germany
28 F4 **Dråby** Denmark
19 P15 **Drac** *R* France
130 D7 **Dracena** Brazil
46 E3 **Dračevo** Macedonia Yugoslavia
36 E5 **Drachenfels** *mt* Germany
25 F2 **Drachten** Netherlands
95 Q4 **Dracut** Massachusetts U.S.A.
28 F6 **Dræby** Denmark
48 L6 **Dragalina** Romania
26 H7 **Dragan** *L* Sweden
48 J6 **Drăgăneşti-Olt** Romania
48 K6 **Drăgăneşti-Vlaşca** Romania
48 J6 **Drăgăşani** Romania
103 O2 **Dragerton** Utah U.S.A.
46 E3 **Dragoevo** Macedonia Yugoslavia
46 F2 **Dragoman** Bulgaria
45 K2 **Dragoncello** Italy
Dragon's Mouths *chan see* **Bocas del Dragon**
103 O9 **Dragoon** Arizona U.S.A.
29 K5 **Dragør** Denmark
46 F2 **Dragovistica** Bulgaria
29 J11 **Dragsfjärd** Finland
28 B3 **Dragstrup** Denmark
19 Q17 **Draguignan** France
33 T9 **Drahnsdorf** Germany
100 B6 **Drain** Oregon U.S.A.
22 G4 **Draize** France
139 K3 **Drake** New South Wales Australia
119 M7 **Drake** Saskatchewan Canada
103 M7 **Drake** Arizona U.S.A.
98 A9 **Drake** Colorado U.S.A.
98 F2 **Drake** North Dakota U.S.A.
32 K7 **Drakenburg** Germany
89 F8 **Drakensberg** *mts* S Africa
89 G5 **Drakensberg Garden** S Africa
146 B3 **Drake Passage** Antarctica
100 E7 **Drake Peak** *mt* Oregon U.S.A.
102 B4 **Drakes Bay** California U.S.A.
110 J4 **Drakesboro** Kentucky U.S.A.
94 J10 **Drakes Branch** Virginia U.S.A.
46 G3 **Dráma** Greece
27 D12 **Drammen** Norway
27 D12 **Dramsfj** *inlet* Norway
40 F5 **Drance** *R* Switzerland
48 L4 **Drânceni** Romania
27 D12 **Drangedal** Norway
40 E5 **Dranse** *R* France
33 R6 **Dranse** Germany
32 L9 **Dransfeld** Germany
28 C5 **Drantum** Denmark
112 H1 **Draper** North Carolina U.S.A.
98 F6 **Draper** South Dakota U.S.A.
101 O9 **Draper** Utah U.S.A.
117 D6 **Draper, Mt** Alaska U.S.A.
74 F1 **Dras** Kashmir
38 G8 **Drau** *R* Austria
38 N9 **Drava** *R* Slovenia
42 G2 **Dravograd** Slovenia
31 J2 **Drawa** *R* Poland
31 J2 **Drawsko** Poland
141 K8 **Drayton** Queensland Australia
98 J1 **Drayton** North Dakota U.S.A.
118 B5 **Drayton Val** Alberta Canada
37 O5 **Draženov** Czechoslovakia
43 B12 **Dréan** Algeria
37 P2 **Drebach** Germany
32 H7 **Drebber** Germany
48 E2 **Drégelypalánk** Hungary
33 M5 **Dreggers** Germany
36 F3 **Dreieichenhain** Germany
Dreihausen *see* **Ebsdorfergrund**
38 F7 **Dreiherrn-Spitze** *mt* Italy/Austria
36 B3 **Dreis** Germany
40 G1 **Dreisam** *R* Germany
37 P6 **Dreitannenriegel** *mt* Germany
28 E7 **Drejø** Denmark
13 F1 **Drem** Scotland
46 F2 **Dren** Bulgaria
33 T6 **Drense** Germany
32 G9 **Drensteinfurt** Germany
25 G3 **Drenthe** *prov* Netherlands
120 H10 **Dresden** Ontario Canada
37 Q1 **Dresden** Germany
107 K2 **Dresden** Kansas U.S.A.
98 H1 **Dresden** North Dakota U.S.A.
94 E6 **Dresden** Ohio U.S.A.
110 H5 **Dresden** Tennessee U.S.A.
52 C6 **Dretun'** Belorussia
21 N4 **Dreux** France
26 F10 **Drevsjö** Norway
111 F8 **Drew** Mississippi U.S.A.
100 C7 **Drew** Oregon U.S.A.
33 Q5 **Drewitzer See** *L* Germany
100 G6 **Drewsey** Oregon U.S.A.
100 E7 **Drews Res** Oregon U.S.A.
110 B3 **Drexel** Missouri U.S.A.
31 J3 **Drezdenko** Poland
52 E6 **Drezna** Russian Federation
54 K1 **Drezna** Russian Federation
36 E2 **Driedorf** Germany
113 D7 **Drifton** Florida U.S.A.
118 B3 **Driftpile** Alberta Canada
120 J3 **Driftwood** Ontario Canada
94 J5 **Driftwood** Pennsylvania U.S.A.
101 O6 **Driggs** Idaho U.S.A.
141 J7 **Drillham** Queensland Australia
46 D2 **Drim** *R* Serbia Yugoslavia
14 B5 **Drimoleague** Ireland
46 D2 **Drin** *R* Albania
48 E7 **Drina** *R* Bosnia-Herzegovina/Yugoslavia
32 K9 **Dringenberg** Germany
46 D3 **Drinit, Pellgu i** *B* Albania
46 D3 **Drin i zi** *R* Albania
119 M8 **Drinkwater** Saskatchewan Canada
109 J5 **Dripping Springs** Texas U.S.A.
109 K8 **Driscoll** Texas U.S.A.
52 C6 **Drissa** *R* Belorussia
26 D9 **Driva** *R* Norway
26 D9 **Drivstua** Norway
42 G5 **Drniš** Croatia
41 N6 **Dro** Italy
27 E12 **Dröbak** Norway
31 M3 **Drobin** Poland
55 F4 **Drobyshevo** Russian Federation
48 G4 **Drocea** *mt* Romania
32 K5 **Drochtersen** Germany
22 D3 **Drocourt** France
26 H3 **Drog** Norway
32 M6 **Drögen Nindorf** Germany
14 E3 **Drogheda** Ireland
14 E3 **Drogheda B** Ireland
48 H1 **Drogobych** Ukraine
31 O3 **Drohiczyn** Poland
8 D3 **Droitwich** England
48 L2 **Drokiya** Moldavia
36 D1 **Drolshagen** Germany
139 H7 **Dromana** Victoria Australia
14 F2 **Dromara** N Ireland
19 O15 **Drôme** *dept* France
21 J3 **Drome** *R* Calvados France
139 K6 **Dromedary,C** New South Wales Australia
33 O8 **Dromling** Germany
14 D3 **Dromod** Ireland
14 D2 **Dromore** N Ireland
14 C2 **Dromore West** Ireland
44 B3 **Dronero** Italy
9 E1 **Dronfield** England
22 F1 **Drongen** Belgium
18 F7 **Dronne** *R* France
146 J8 **Dronning Fabiolafjella** *ra* Antarctica
28 E2 **Dronninglund** Denmark
146 H4 **Dronning Maud Land** Antarctica
119 Q7 **Dropmore** Manitoba Canada
18 F8 **Dropt** *R* France
31 J7 **Drosendorf** Austria
74 D1 **Drosh** Pakistan
28 G6 **Drøsselbjerg** Denmark
21 N5 **Droué** France
120 E2 **Drowning** *R* Ontario Canada
37 N1 **Droyssig** Germany
21 L3 **Drucourt** France
118 J7 **Druid** Saskatchewan Canada
8 C2 **Druid** Wales
126 A1 **Druif** Aruba W Indies
36 C6 **Drulingen** France
118 E7 **Drumheller** Alberta Canada
14 D4 **Drum Hills** Ireland
14 D3 **Drumlish** Ireland
144 B7 **Drummond** New Zealand
101 M3 **Drummond** Montana U.S.A.
99 P3 **Drummond** Wisconsin U.S.A.
94 D1 **Drummond I** Michigan U.S.A.
95 L10 **Drummond,L** Virginia U.S.A.
140 D4 **Drummond,Mt** N Terr Australia
141 H6 **Drummond Ra** Queensland Australia
121 S7 **Drummondville** Quebec Canada
12 D4 **Drummore** Scotland
15 D3 **Drumnadrochit** Scotland
15 D4 **Drumochter Pass** Scotland
107 O6 **Drumright** Oklahoma U.S.A.
14 C2 **Drumshanbo** Ireland
12 D1 **Drumvaich** Scotland
25 D5 **Drunen** Netherlands
119 V8 **Drunken Point** *C* Manitoba Canada
13 G3 **Druridge B** England
145 E2 **Drury** New Zealand
117 F4 **Drury L** Yukon Territory Canada
36 D6 **Drusenheim** France
31 O1 **Druskininkai** Lithuania
25 E5 **Druten** Netherlands
52 C6 **Druya** Belorussia
54 E4 **Druzhba** Ukraine
51 O2 **Druzhina** Russian Federation
55 C3 **Druzhinino** Russian Federation
54 J8 **Druzhkovka** Ukraine
42 G4 **Drvar** Bosnia-Herzegovina
42 G5 **Drvenik** *isld* Croatia
100 B3 **Dryad** Washington U.S.A.
46 G2 **Dryanovo** Bulgaria
117 D6 **Dry B** Alaska U.S.A.
118 J1 **Dryberry L** Ontario Canada
119 Q2 **Drybrough** Manitoba Canada
101 R5 **Dry Cr** Wyoming U.S.A.
118 K1 **Dryden** Ontario Canada
94 D4 **Dryden** Michigan U.S.A.
95 L4 **Dryden** New York U.S.A.
108 E5 **Dryden** Texas U.S.A.
110 E4 **Dry Fork** *R* Missouri U.S.A.
98 A6 **Dry Fork** *R* Wyoming U.S.A.
146 J13 **Drygalski I.** Antarctica
146 C12 **Drygalski Ice Tongue** *ice tongue* Antarctica
8 C3 **Drygarn Fawr** *mt* Wales
127 K2 **Dry Harbour Mts** Jamaica
102 G2 **Dry L** Nevada U.S.A.
122 F1 **Drylake** Labrador, Nfld Canada
103 K5 **Dry Lake** Nevada U.S.A.
103 K4 **Dry Lake Valley** Nevada U.S.A.
12 D1 **Drymen** Scotland
111 D10 **Dry Prong** Louisiana U.S.A.
141 G4 **Dry R** Queensland Australia
140 D1 **Drysdale I** N Terr Australia
142 F2 **Drysdale River Nat Park** W Australia Australia
113 E13 **Dry Tortugas** *islds* Florida U.S.A.
85 G7 **Dschang** Cameroon
99 V5 **Dtblin** Michigan U.S.A.
86 D5 **Dua** *R* Zaire
127 K9 **Duaca** Venezuela
67 C4 **Du'an** China
Duancun *see* **Wuxiang**
95 N2 **Duane** New York U.S.A.
141 J6 **Duaringa** Queensland Australia
127 J5 **Duarte, Pico** *mt* Dominican Rep
130 E8 **Duartina** Brazil
130 D8 **Duas Onças,Ilha das** Brazil
20 D5 **Duault** France
109 P3 **Dubach** Louisiana U.S.A.
77 D7 **Dubai** U.A.E.
100 B9 **Dubakella Mt** California U.S.A.
114 J5 **Dubawnt** *R* Northwest Territories Canada
Dubayy *see* **Dubai**
139 J4 **Dubbo** New South Wales Australia
56 C1 **Dubches** *R* Russian Federation
37 O4 **Dubec** Czechoslovakia
33 T9 **Duben** Germany
55 C5 **Dubenskiy** Russian Federation
12 B1 **Dubh Artach** *isld* Scotland
48 G1 **Dubiecko** Poland
57 K3 **Dubin** Kazakhstan
124 F2 **Dublán** Mexico
120 J9 **Dublin** Ontario Canada
14 E3 **Dublin** *co* Ireland
14 E3 **Dublin** Ireland
112 E5 **Dublin** Georgia U.S.A.
94 B7 **Dublin** Indiana U.S.A.
111 F7 **Dublin** Mississippi U.S.A.
94 D6 **Dublin** Ohio U.S.A.
109 J3 **Dublin** Texas U.S.A.
52 E6 **Dubna** *R* Russian Federation
54 H2 **Dubna** Russian Federation
101 N5 **Dubois** Idaho U.S.A.
99 K9 **Du Bois** Nebraska U.S.A.
94 J5 **Du Bois** Pennsylvania U.S.A.
101 Q6 **Dubois** Wyoming U.S.A.
48 M3 **Dubossary** Moldavia
54 K3 **Dubovka** Russian Federation
85 B7 **Dubréka** Guinea
54 E3 **Dubrovka** Russian Federation
42 J6 **Dubrovnik** Croatia
54 B2 **Dubrovno** Belorussia
55 E2 **Dubrovnoye** Russian Federation
119 P8 **Dubuc** Saskatchewan Canada
99 Q7 **Dubuque** Iowa U.S.A.
52 G6 **Dub'yazy** Russian Federation
20 F6 **Duc,Etang au** *L* France
20 H4 **Ducey** France
67 E2 **Duchang** China
121 Q3 **Ducharme** Quebec Canada
30 H5 **Duchcov** Czechoslovakia
33 T5 **Ducherow** Germany
101 P9 **Duchesne** Utah U.S.A.
140 E5 **Duchess** Queensland Australia
118 F8 **Duchess** Alberta Canada
141 F1 **Ducie** *R* Queensland Australia
135 O11 **Ducie I** Pacific Oc
110 J6 **Duck** *R* Tennessee U.S.A.
119 R6 **Duck Bay** Manitoba Canada
111 G8 **Duck Hill** Mississippi U.S.A.
118 L6 **Duck Lake** Saskatchewan Canada
119 Q7 **Duck Mt** *ra* Manitoba Canada
119 R7 **Duck Mt. Prov. Park** Manitoba Canada
112 C2 **Ducktown** Tennessee U.S.A.
103 J3 **Duckwater** Nevada U.S.A.
103 J3 **Duckwater Pk** Nevada U.S.A.
21 M3 **Duclair** France
102 E6 **Ducor** California U.S.A.
127 L4 **Ducos** Martinique W Indies
9 F2 **Duddington** England
22 L5 **Dudelange** Luxembourg
36 B4 **Dudeldorf** Germany
32 M9 **Duderstadt** Germany
109 P3 **Dudgemona** *R* Louisiana U.S.A.
7 L9 **Dudgeon Lightship** North Sea
50 H2 **Dudinka** Russian Federation
8 D2 **Dudley** England
112 D5 **Dudley** Georgia U.S.A.
110 F5 **Dudley** Missouri U.S.A.
54 G3 **Dudorovskiy** Russian Federation
47 N10 **Dudullu** Turkey
36 C5 **Dudweiler** Germany
51 J1 **Dudypta** *R* Russian Federation
22 E1 **Dudzele** Belgium
85 C7 **Duékoué** Ivory Coast
16 D3 **Dueñas** Spain
16 C2 **Duerna** *R* Spain
17 F3 **Duero** *R* Spain
112 E3 **Due West** South Carolina U.S.A.
146 D10 **Dufek Coast** Antarctica
119 O8 **Duff** Saskatchewan Canada
22 H1 **Duffel** Belgium
138 C2 **Duffield** *R* N Terr Australia
140 C7 **Duffield** N Terr Australia
118 C5 **Duffield** Alberta Canada
137 O3 **Duff Is** Santa Cruz Is
15 E3 **Dufftown** Scotland
122 F2 **Dufresne,L** Quebec Canada
122 G2 **Dufresne Lake** Quebec Canada
100 D4 **Dufur** Oregon U.S.A.
140 F5 **Dugald** *R* Queensland Australia
103 N7 **Dugas** Arizona U.S.A.
111 D9 **Dugdemona** *R* Louisiana U.S.A.
110 J2 **Dugger** Indiana U.S.A.
42 F4 **Dugi O** Croatia
54 H2 **Dugna** Russian Federation
141 G1 **Dugong I** Gt Barrier Reef Aust
118 E6 **Duhamel** Alberta Canada
131 D2 **Duice, R** Argentina
128 E3 **Duida, Co** *mt* Venezuela
141 F2 **Duifken Pt** Queensland Australia

32 L8 **Duingen** Germany
32 E10 **Duisburg** Germany
25 A5 **Duiveland** Netherlands
67 C4 **Dujiang** China
86 H5 **Dujuuma** Somalia
46 E2 **Dukat** Serbia/Macedonia Yugoslavia
107 L7 **Duke** Oklahoma U.S.A.
117 H8 **Duke I** Alaska U.S.A.
141 K5 **Duke Is** Queensland Australia
135 N10 **Duke of Gloucester Is** Pacific Oc
142 F4 **Dukes Dome** *mt* W Australia Australia
86 F4 **Duk Faiwil** Sudan
77 B7 **Dukhān** Qatar
53 G8 **Dukhovnitskoye** Russian Federation
54 D1 **Dukhovshchina** Russian Federation
59 L1 **Duki** Russian Federation
31 N6 **Dukla** Poland
52 C6 **Dukstas** Lithuania
111 F12 **Dulac** Louisiana U.S.A.
58 C4 **Dulan** China
8 B1 **Dulas B** Wales
71 G7 **Dulawan** Mindanao Philippines
116 K4 **Dulbi** *R* Alaska U.S.A.
106 D5 **Dulce** New Mexico U.S.A.
80 G7 **Duleilat el Muterat** Jordan
51 N2 **Dulgalakh** *R* Russian Federation
47 J1 **Dŭlgopol** Bulgaria
141 F1 **Dulhunty** *R* Queensland Australia
70 D3 **Dulit Ra** Sarawak
67 C4 **Duliu Jiang** *R* China
71 G5 **Duljugan Pt** Leyte Philippines
25 F6 **Dülken** Germany
75 P6 **Dullabchara** India
98 B6 **Dull Center** Wyoming U.S.A.
32 F9 **Dülmen** Germany
67 A5 **Dulong** China
47 J1 **Dulovo** Bulgaria
99 O3 **Duluth** Minnesota U.S.A.
8 C5 **Dulverton** England
71 F6 **Dumaguete** Negros Philippines
69 E12 **Dumai** Sumatra
47 J6 **Dumanlı Dağı** *mt* Turkey
71 F7 **Dumanquilas B** Mindanao Philippines
71 D5 **Dumaran** *isld* Philippines
139 K3 **Dumaresq** *R* New S Wales/Queensland
111 E8 **Dumas** Arkansas U.S.A.
108 C8 **Dumas** Texas U.S.A.
79 G5 **Ḍumayr** Syria
79 G5 **Ḍumayr,Jebel** *mts* Syria
83 K10 **Dumbanagala** *mt* Sri Lanka
12 D2 **Dumbarton** Scotland
48 F2 **Ďumbier** *mt* Czechoslovakia
143 C10 **Dumbleyung** W Australia Australia
143 C10 **Dumbleyung, L** W Australia Australia
86 B3 **Dumboa** Nigeria
48 J4 **Dumbrăveni** Romania
48 L5 **Dumbrăveni** Romania
69 H12 **Dumdum** *isld* Indonesia
Dumfries *co see* **Dumfries and Galloway** *reg*
12 E3 **Dumfries** Scotland
15 D5 **Dumfries and Galloway** *reg* Scotland
54 G3 **Duminichi** Russian Federation
48 K5 **Dumitreşti** Romania
75 M6 **Dumka** India
119 N9 **Dummer** Saskatchewan Canada
32 H7 **Dümmersee** *L* Germany
71 J4 **Dumoga** Sulawesi
71 H4 **Dumoga Ketjil** Sulawesi
121 N6 **Dumoine, L** Quebec Canada
98 K4 **Dumont** Minnesota U.S.A.
146 E14 **Dumont d'Urville** *France Base* Antarctica
121 O6 **Dumont,L** Quebec Canada
36 B3 **Dümpelfeld** Germany
65 J1 **Dumune** China
79 B7 **Dumyât** Egypt
48 E4 **Duna** *R* Hungary
48 D3 **Dunaj** *R* Czechoslovakia
31 M6 **Dunajec** *R* Poland
14 E3 **Dunany Pt** Ireland
48 E4 **Dunapataj** Hungary
48 L6 **Dunărea** *R* Romania
48 E4 **Dunaújváros** Hungary
48 F5 **Dunav** *R* S Europe
46 F1 **Dunavtsi** Bulgaria
48 K2 **Dunayevtsy** Ukraine
144 C6 **Dunback** New Zealand
141 F3 **Dunbar** Queensland Australia
13 F1 **Dunbar** Scotland
107 P7 **Dunbar** Oklahoma U.S.A.
101 N9 **Dunbar** Utah U.S.A.
94 F8 **Dunbar** West Virginia U.S.A.
99 S4 **Dunbar** Wisconsin U.S.A.
Dunbarton *co see* **Strathclyde** *reg*
118 L7 **Dunblane** Saskatchewan Canada
12 E1 **Dunblane** Scotland
14 E3 **Dunboyne** Ireland
100 B1 **Duncan** British Columbia Canada
6 M6 **Duncan** *oil rig* North Sea
103 P9 **Duncan** Arizona U.S.A.
98 J8 **Duncan** Nebraska U.S.A.
107 N7 **Duncan** Oklahoma U.S.A.
101 Q6 **Duncan** Wyoming U.S.A.
141 F1 **Duncan Is** Queensland Australia
117 R4 **Duncan L** Northwest Territories Canada
140 A3 **Duncan, Mt** N Terr Australia
14 E4 **Duncannon** Ireland
95 K6 **Duncannon** Pennsylvania U.S.A.
68 A7 **Duncan Passage** Andaman Is
112 C3 **Duncan Ridge** Georgia U.S.A.
127 K1 **Duncans** Jamaica
15 E2 **Duncansby Hd** Scotland
126 G3 **Duncan Town** Bahamas
109 N10 **Duncanville** Texas U.S.A.
9 E3 **Dunchurch** England
13 F6 **Duncombe** England
9 F6 **Duncton** England
52 B6 **Dundaga** Latvia
120 K8 **Dundalk** Ontario Canada
14 E2 **Dundalk** Ireland
14 E3 **Dundalk B** Ireland
147 F6 **Dundas** Northwest Territories Canada
115 N2 **Dundas** Greenland
94 E7 **Dundas** Ohio U.S.A.
117 H8 **Dundas I** British Columbia Canada
143 D9 **Dundas L** W Australia Australia
140 B1 **Dundas Str** N Terr Australia
89 G7 **Dundee** S Africa
13 F1 **Dundee** Scotland
94 D5 **Dundee** Michigan U.S.A.
95 L4 **Dundee** New York U.S.A.
109 J2 **Dundee** Texas U.S.A.
26 G5 **Dunderlands-dal** *V* Norway
Dund Hot *see* **Zhenglan Qi**
141 G8 **Dundoo** Queensland Australia
12 E4 **Dundrennan** Scotland
14 F2 **Dundrum** N Ireland
14 F2 **Dundrum B** N Ireland
118 L7 **Dundurn** Saskatchewan Canada
144 C7 **Dunedin** New Zealand
113 E9 **Dunedin** Florida U.S.A.
139 J4 **Dunedoo** New South Wales Australia
57 J1 **Dunenbay** Kazakhstan
14 D1 **Dunfanaghy** Ireland
15 E4 **Dunfermline** Scotland
120 J9 **Dungannon** Ontario Canada
14 E2 **Dungannon** N Ireland
74 E7 **Dungarpur** India
14 D4 **Dungarvan** Ireland
14 D4 **Dungarvan Harb** Ireland
9 G6 **Dungeness** England
133 D8 **Dungeness,Pta** Arg/Chile
14 E2 **Dungiven** N Ireland
14 C2 **Dungloe** Ireland
139 K4 **Dungog** New South Wales Australia
86 E5 **Dungu** Zaire
69 F10 **Dungun** Malaysia
86 G1 **Dungunab** Sudan
142 G3 **Dunham** *R* W Australia Australia
9 F1 **Dunham** England
59 J3 **Dunhua** China
58 B3 **Dunhuang** China
141 J7 **Dunkeld** Queensland Australia
138 F6 **Dunkeld** Victoria Australia
15 E4 **Dunkeld** Scotland
106 E9 **Dunken** New Mexico U.S.A.
22 C1 **Dunkerque** France
Dunkirk *see* **Dunkerque**
119 M8 **Dunkirk** Saskatchewan Canada
110 L1 **Dunkirk** Indiana U.S.A.
101 O1 **Dunkirk** Montana U.S.A.
121 L10 **Dunkirk** New York U.S.A.
86 G3 **Dunkur** Ethiopia
85 D7 **Dunkwa** Ghana
14 E3 **Dún Laoghaire** Ireland
99 L8 **Dunlap** Iowa U.S.A.
107 O3 **Dunlap** Kansas U.S.A.
106 F7 **Dunlap** New Mexico U.S.A.
108 G1 **Dunlap** Texas U.S.A.
14 E3 **Dunlavin** Ireland
109 J6 **Dunlay** Texas U.S.A.
14 E3 **Dunleer** Ireland
18 G6 **Dun-le-Palestel** France
6 L1 **Dunlin** *oil rig* North Sea
119 T4 **Dunlop** Manitoba Canada
120 J9 **Dunlop** Ontario Canada
12 D2 **Dunlop** Scotland
14 B5 **Dunmanus B** Ireland
14 B5 **Dunmanway** Ireland
140 C3 **Dunmarra Roadhouse** N Terr Australia
14 C3 **Dunmore** Ireland
95 M5 **Dunmore** Pennsylvania U.S.A.
113 L12 **Dunmore Town** Bahamas
126 F2 **Dunmore Town** Eleuthera Bahamas
9 G4 **Dunmow** England
112 J2 **Dunn** North Carolina U.S.A.
98 D2 **Dunn Center** North Dakota U.S.A.
99 M6 **Dunnell** Minnesota U.S.A.
113 E8 **Dunnellon** Florida U.S.A.
15 E2 **Dunnet B** Scotland
15 E2 **Dunnet Hd** Scotland
12 E1 **Dunning** Scotland
98 F8 **Dunning** Nebraska U.S.A.
36 E7 **Dunningen** Germany
143 C6 **Dunns Ra** W Australia Australia
120 G6 **Dunn Valley** Ontario Canada
121 L10 **Dunnville** Ontario Canada
139 G6 **Dunolly** Victoria Australia
12 D2 **Dunoon** Scotland
100 J9 **Dunphy** Nevada U.S.A.
14 A4 **Dunquin** Ireland
84 J5 **Dunqul Oasis** Egypt
120 G4 **Dunrankin** Ontario Canada
119 S9 **Dunrea** Manitoba Canada
13 F2 **Duns** Scotland
144 D5 **Dunsandel** New Zealand
143 B10 **Dunsborough** W Australia Australia
98 G1 **Dunseith** North Dakota U.S.A.
100 C8 **Dunsmuir** California U.S.A.
9 F4 **Dunstable** England
144 B6 **Dunstan Mts** New Zealand
117 O9 **Dunster** British Columbia Canada
8 C5 **Dunster** England
31 K7 **Dun Streda** Czechoslovakia
18 G6 **Dun sur Auron** France
22 J5 **Dun-sur-Meuse** France
120 K8 **Duntroon** Ontario Canada
144 C6 **Duntroon** New Zealand
36 D6 **Duntzenheim** France
15 B3 **Dunvegan** Scotland
15 B3 **Dunvegan,L** Scotland
123 T6 **Dunville** Newfoundland Canada
9 H3 **Dunwich** England
58 G3 **Duolun** China
76 D3 **Dūpādu** India
67 D4 **Dupang Ling** *mts* China
121 L4 **Duparquet** Quebec Canada
69 J11 **Duperre I** Indonesia
94 B8 **Dupont** Indiana U.S.A.
95 M5 **Dupont** Pennsylvania U.S.A.
98 E4 **Dupree** South Dakota U.S.A.
121 L4 **Dupuy** Quebec Canada
142 B5 **Dupuy,C** W Australia Australia
101 N1 **Dupuyer** Montana U.S.A.
130 G8 **Duque de Caxias** Brazil
133 B8 **Duque de York,I** Chile
103 O10 **Duquesne** Arizona U.S.A.
94 H6 **Duquesne** Pennsylvania U.S.A.
110 G3 **Du Quoin** Illinois U.S.A.
80 D7 **Dura** Jordan
41 M2 **Durach** Germany
142 F3 **Durack,R** W Australia Australia
142 F3 **Durack Ra** W Australia Australia
78 E1 **Durağan** Turkey
141 K7 **Durah** Queensland Australia
47 J5 **Durak** Turkey
106 E7 **Duran** New Mexico U.S.A.
19 Q16 **Durance** *R* France
99 R7 **Durand** Illinois U.S.A.
94 D4 **Durand** Michigan U.S.A.
99 P5 **Durand** Wisconsin U.S.A.
124 G5 **Durango** Mexico
18 D9 **Durango** Spain
106 C4 **Durango** Colorado U.S.A.
47 J1 **Durankulak** Bulgaria
111 G8 **Durant** Mississippi U.S.A.
107 O8 **Durant** Oklahoma U.S.A.
16 E3 **Duratón** *R* Spain
131 G4 **Durazno** *dept* Uruguay
131 G4 **Durazno** Uruguay
Durazzo *see* **Durrës**
89 G7 **Durban** S Africa
56 C6 **Durbat-Daba, Pereval** *pass* Mongolia/Rus Fed
27 M15 **Durbe** Latvia
94 H8 **Durbin** West Virginia U.S.A.
22 J3 **Durbuy** Belgium
16 E8 **Dúrcal** Spain
36 B2 **Düren** Germany
75 J8 **Durg** India
75 M7 **Durgapur** India
120 K8 **Durham** Ontario Canada
121 S7 **Durham** Quebec Canada
13 G4 **Durham** *co* England
13 G4 **Durham** England
102 C2 **Durham** California U.S.A.
107 N3 **Durham** Kansas U.S.A.
95 R3 **Durham** New Hampshire U.S.A.
112 J2 **Durham** North Carolina U.S.A.
122 F7 **Durham Br** New Brunswick Canada
141 F7 **Durham Downs** Queensland Australia
12 E3 **Durisdeer** Scotland
100 H5 **Durkee** Oregon U.S.A.
36 E6 **Durlach** Germany
9 E6 **Durlston Hd** England
36 E6 **Durmersheim** Germany
42 J5 **Durmitor** *mt* Montenegro Yugoslavia
15 D2 **Durness** Scotland
38 N5 **Durnstein** Austria
123 L3 **Durocher,L** Quebec Canada
38 M6 **Durrenstein** *mt* Austria
46 C3 **Durrës** Albania
46 C3 **Durrësit, Gjiri i** *B* Albania
140 F7 **Durrie** Queensland Australia
14 D4 **Durrow** Ireland
37 J5 **Dürrwangen** Germany
14 A5 **Dursey Hd** Ireland
14 A5 **Dursey I** Ireland
8 D4 **Dursley** England
8 C5 **Durston** England
47 K5 **Dursunbey** Turkey
21 K6 **Durtal** France
Duru *see* **Wuchuan**
28 B3 **Durup** Denmark
47 K3 **Durusu Gölü** *L* Turkey
79 G6 **Durūz, Jabal ad** *mts* Syria
145 D4 **D'Urville I** New Zealand
77 J2 **Durzab** Afghanistan
120 D1 **Dusey** *R* Ontario Canada
57 A6 **Dushak** Turkmenistan
67 B4 **Dushan** China
57 E5 **Dushanbe** Tajikistan
65 C4 **Dushikou** China
95 L5 **Dushore** Pennsylvania U.S.A.
47 J2 **Dŭskotna** Bulgaria
144 A6 **Dusky Sd** New Zealand
32 E10 **Düsseldorf** Germany
25 C5 **Dussen** Netherlands
41 J4 **Düssist** *mt* Switzerland
33 R9 **Düssnitz** Germany
107 O6 **Dustin** Oklahoma U.S.A.
83 J9 **Dutch B** Sri Lanka
Dutch Guiana *see* **Surīname**
116 D10 **Dutch Harbor** Aleutian Is
101 M9 **Dutch Mt** Utah U.S.A.
89 C4 **Dutlwe** Botswana
52 J3 **Dutovo** Russian Federation
85 F6 **Dutsan Wai** Nigeria
141 G5 **Dutton** *R* Queensland Australia
120 J10 **Dutton** Ontario Canada
101 O2 **Dutton** Montana U.S.A.
138 D4 **Dutton,L** South Australia Australia
103 M3 **Dutton,Mt** Utah U.S.A.
119 N7 **Duval** Saskatchewan Canada
127 H5 **Duvalierville** Haiti
121 N6 **Duval,L** Quebec Canada
55 C3 **Duvan** Russian Federation
144 D5 **Duvauchelle** New Zealand
26 F8 **Duved** Sweden
127 J5 **Duvergé** Dominican Rep
52 D3 **Duvogero** Russian Federation
22 D5 **Duvy** France
95 R4 **Duxbury** Massachusetts U.S.A.
9 G3 **Duxford** England
67 B4 **Duyang Shan** *mt* China
68 C4 **Duyinzeik** Burma
67 B3 **Duyun** China
78 C1 **Düzce** Turkey
47 H1 **Dve Mogili** Bulgaria
26 H2 **Dverberg** Norway
52 F3 **Dvina, Severnaya** *R* Russian Federation
52 E2 **Dvinskaya Guba** *B* Russian Federation
54 C1 **Dvin'ye,Oz** *L* Russian Federation
31 K6 **Dvorec** Czechoslovakia
31 J5 **Dvůr Králové** Czechoslovakia
88 D8 **Dwangwa** *R* Malawi
143 B10 **Dwarda** W Australia Australia
74 C7 **Dwarka** India
89 E5 **Dwars Berg** *mts* S Africa
143 B10 **Dwellingup** W Australia Australia
99 S8 **Dwight** Illinois U.S.A.
107 O3 **Dwight** Kansas U.S.A.
98 J8 **Dwight** Nebraska U.S.A.
94 F9 **Dwight** Virginia U.S.A.
100 K3 **Dworshak Res.** Idaho U.S.A.
106 C9 **Dwyer** New Mexico U.S.A.
98 B7 **Dwyer** Wyoming U.S.A.
54 F3 **Dyat'kovo** Russia Federation
28 D7 **Dybbøl** Denmark
28 A3 **Dybe Kirke** Denmark
28 H6 **Dybsø Fjord** *inlet* Denmark
119 R4 **Dyce** Manitoba Canada
15 F3 **Dyce** Scotland
99 T5 **Dyckesville** Wisconsin U.S.A.
110 H5 **Dyer** Tennessee U.S.A.
114 G2 **Dyer B** Northwest Territories Canada
120 J7 **Dyer Bay** Ontario Canada
110 G5 **Dyersburg** Tennessee U.S.A.
99 P7 **Dyersville** Iowa U.S.A.
8 B3 **Dyfed** *co* Wales
8 B2 **Dyfi** *R* Wales
31 J1 **Dygowo** Poland
31 J7 **Dyje** *R* Czechoslovakia
53 F11 **Dykhtau** *mt* Georgia/Rus Fed
22 H2 **Dyle** *R* Belgium
9 G5 **Dymchurch** England
118 K1 **Dyment** Ontario Canada
8 D4 **Dymock** England
141 G8 **Dynevor Downs** Queensland Australia
31 N6 **Dynów** Poland
102 F4 **Dyor** Nevada U.S.A.
28 E6 **Dyreborg** Denmark
26 C8 **Dyrnesvågen** Norway
26 J2 **Dyröy** Norway
119 N8 **Dysart** Saskatchewan Canada
13 E1 **Dysart** Scotland
99 O7 **Dysart** Iowa U.S.A.
47 J2 **Dyulevo** Bulgaria
47 J2 **Dyulino** Bulgaria
78 L1 **Dyul'tydag** *mt* Russian Federation
57 C2 **Dyurmen'tyube** Kazakhstan
58 D2 **Dzaanhushuu** Mongolia
58 C2 **Dzag** Mongolia
58 F3 **Dzamīn Üüde** Mongolia
87 H10 **Dzaoudzi** Comoros
56 E6 **Dzargal Hid** Mongolia
58 C2 **Dzavhan Gol** *R* Mongolia
30 H5 **Džban** *mt* Czechoslovakia
54 J8 **Dzerzhinsk** Ukraine
57 K2 **Dzerzhinskoye** Kazakhstan
59 K1 **Dzhagdy,Khrebet** *mts* Russian Federation
56 D5 **Dzhakul', Gora** *mt* Russian Federation
57 G4 **Dzhalal-Abad** Kyrgyzstan
59 H1 **Dzhalinda** Russian Federation
55 B5 **Dzhambeyty** Kazakhstan
57 C4 **Dzhankel'dy** Uzbekistan
57 J2 **Dzhansugurov** Kazakhstan
56 D5 **Dzhebashskiy Khrebet** *mts* Russian Federation
46 G3 **Dzhebel** Bulgaria
57 J3 **Dzhergalan** Kyrgyzstan
55 D5 **Dzhetygara** Kazakhstan
57 C4 **Dzhetymtau, Gory** *mts* Uzbekistan
57 D1 **Dzhezdy** Kazakhstan
57 E1 **Dzhezkazgan** Kazakhstan
56 G5 **Dzhida** *R* Russian Federation
56 F5 **Dzhidinskiy,Khrebet** *mts* Mongolia/Rus Fed
57 B4 **Dzhigirbent** Turkmenistan
57 E4 **Dzhizak** Uzbekistan
56 D4 **Dzhoyskiy Khrebet** *mts* Russian Federation
57 D5 **Dzhuma** Uzbekistan
57 K2 **Dzhungarskiy Alatau Khrebet** *mts* Kazakhstan
48 L2 **Dzhurin** Ukraine
57 C2 **Dzhusaly** Kazakhstan
31 M2 **Działdowo** Poland
31 M5 **Działoszyce** Poland
31 L4 **Działoszyn** Poland
31 L2 **Dzierżgoń** Poland
31 K5 **Dzierżoniów** Poland
125 O7 **Dzitbalché** Mexico
31 H1 **Dziwnów** Poland
56 E5 **Dzöölon** Mongolia
52 B6 **Džūkste** Latvia
66 C3 **Dzungaria** *reg* China
66 C2 **Dzungarian Gate** *pass* China/Kazakhstan
58 E3 **Dzüünbayan** Mongolia
65 C1 **Dzüünbulag** Mongolia
58 B2 **Dzüyl** Mongolia

E

106 H3 **Eads** Colorado U.S.A.
103 P7 **Eagar** Arizona U.S.A.
101 T10 **Eagle** Colorado U.S.A.
100 J6 **Eagle** Idaho U.S.A.
110 M3 **Eagle** *R* Kentucky U.S.A.
98 K9 **Eagle** Nebraska U.S.A.
99 S7 **Eagle** Wisconsin U.S.A.
101 R5 **Eagle** Wyoming U.S.A.
98 E4 **Eagle Butte** South Dakota U.S.A.
107 M6 **Eagle City** Oklahoma U.S.A.
102 G6 **Eagle Crags** California U.S.A.
121 O6 **Eagle Depot** Quebec Canada
141 K1 **Eagle Farm** *dist* Brisbane, Qnsld Australia
99 N7 **Eagle Grove** Iowa U.S.A.
99 S2 **Eagle Harbor** Michigan U.S.A.
139 J9 **Eaglehawk Neck** Tasmania Australia
119 O1 **Eaglehead L** Ontario Canada
119 T5 **Eagle I** Manitoba Canada
118 J1 **Eagle L** Ontario Canada
100 E9 **Eagle L** California U.S.A.
95 S6 **Eagle L** Maine U.S.A.
95 R7 **Eagle L** Maine U.S.A.
113 F10 **Eagle Lake** Florida U.S.A.
109 L6 **Eagle Lake** Texas U.S.A.
103 J8 **Eagle Mts** California U.S.A.
106 E5 **Eagle Nest** New Mexico U.S.A.
108 G7 **Eagle Pass** Texas U.S.A.
100 E8 **Eagle Peak** *mt* California U.S.A.
114 F4 **Eagle Plain** Yukon Territory Canada
100 C7 **Eagle Point** Oregon U.S.A.
99 S2 **Eagle River** Michigan U.S.A.
99 R4 **Eagle River** Wisconsin U.S.A.
94 H9 **Eagle Rock** Virginia U.S.A.
12 D2 **Eaglesham** Scotland
137 Q4 **Eaglestone Reef** Pacific Oc
116 O4 **Eagle Summit** Alaska U.S.A.
103 L8 **Eagle Tail Mts** Arizona U.S.A.
109 N1 **Eagleton** Arkansas U.S.A.
107 Q7 **Eagletown** Oklahoma U.S.A.
100 E8 **Eagleville** California U.S.A.
71 L10 **Eahun** Roti Indonesia
61 O7 **Eai-gawa** *R* Japan
68 H6 **Ea Kan** *R* Vietnam
9 F4 **Ealing** England
144 C6 **Ealing** New Zealand
143 D7 **Earaheedy** W Australia Australia
8 D3 **Eardisland** England
117 L11 **Ear Lakes Cove** British Columbia Canada
110 F6 **Earle** Arkansas U.S.A.
99 M8 **Earlham** Iowa U.S.A.
102 E6 **Earlimart** California U.S.A.
99 L8 **Earling** Iowa U.S.A.
110 J4 **Earlington** Kentucky U.S.A.
100 A8 **Earl,L** California U.S.A.
144 A6 **Earl Mts** New Zealand
13 F2 **Earlston** Scotland
121 L5 **Earlton** Ontario Canada
99 S8 **Earlville** Illinois U.S.A.
99 P7 **Earlville** Iowa U.S.A.
13 E1 **Earn,Br.of** Scotland
117 F4 **Earn L** Yukon Territory Canada
12 D1 **Earn,L** Scotland
12 E1 **Earn,R** Scotland
144 B6 **Earnslaw, Mt** New Zealand
103 K7 **Earp** California U.S.A.
13 G3 **Earsdon** England
9 F6 **Easebourne** England
13 G4 **Easington** Durham England
13 J6 **Easington** Humberside England
13 G5 **Easingwold** England
112 E3 **Easley** South Carolina U.S.A.
110 F3 **East Alton** Illinois U.S.A.
121 T7 **East Angus** Quebec Canada
123 M7 **East B** C Breton I, Nova Scotia
113 B7 **East B** Florida U.S.A.
111 G12 **East B** Louisiana U.S.A.
111 B12 **East B** Texas U.S.A.
112 G1 **East Bend** North Carolina U.S.A.
95 L7 **East Berlin** Pennsylvania U.S.A.
109 L6 **East Bernard** Texas U.S.A.
9 G6 **Eastbourne** England
145 G4 **Eastbourne** New Zealand
94 H6 **East Brady** Pennsylvania U.S.A.
8 D5 **East Brent** England
111 J10 **East Brewton** Alabama U.S.A.
71 G6 **East Bucas** Philippines
101 O1 **East Butte** *mt* Montana U.S.A.
127 J4 **East Caicos** *isld* Turks & Caicos Is
145 G2 **East Cape** New Zealand
145 F3 **East Cape** *admin region* New Zealand
99 T8 **East Chicago** Indiana U.S.A.
64 G4 **East China Sea**
145 E2 **East Coast Bays** New Zealand
118 E7 **East Coulee** Alberta Canada
9 G6 **Eastdean** England
9 G2 **East Dereham** England
99 Q7 **East Dubuque** Illinois U.S.A.
103 K2 **East Ely** Nevada U.S.A.
118 J9 **Eastend** Saskatchewan Canada
143 A8 **Easter Grp** *islds* W Australia Australia
135 U16 **Easter I** Pacific Oc
141 F5 **Eastern Creek** Queensland Australia
84 J4 **Eastern Desert** Egypt
86 F4 **Eastern Equatoria** *prov* Sudan
76 C4 **Eastern Ghats** *mts* India
123 S5 **Eastern Meelpaeg** *L* Newfoundland Canada
119 S5 **Easterville** Manitoba Canada
122 E7 **East Florenceville** New Brunswick Canada
120 J3 **Eastford** Ontario Canada
99 Q9 **East Galesburg** Illinois U.S.A.
102 G2 **Eastgate** Nevada U.S.A.
East Germany *see* **Germany**
101 M1 **East Glacier Park** Montana U.S.A.
9 F5 **East Grinstead** England
8 D1 **Eastham** England
95 P6 **East Hampton** Long I, New York U.S.A.
95 P4 **Easthampton** Massachusetts U.S.A.
101 O3 **East Helena** Montana U.S.A.
9 G6 **East Hoathly** England
123 L6 **East I** Madeleine Is, Quebec Canada
9 E4 **East Ilsley** England
95 P4 **East Jaffrey** New Hampshire U.S.A.
147 E12 **East Jan Mayen Rdg** Norwegian Sea
122 J9 **East Jeddore** Nova Scotia Canada
122 G10 **East Jordan** Nova Scotia Canada
94 B1 **East Jordan** Michigan U.S.A.
9 G1 **East Keal** England
122 G9 **East Kemptville** Nova Scotia Canada
12 D2 **East Kilbride** Scotland
95 R6 **East L** Maine U.S.A.
99 U5 **East Lake** Michigan U.S.A.
109 J3 **Eastland** Texas U.S.A.
94 C4 **East Lansing** Michigan U.S.A.
9 E6 **Eastleigh** England
110 N1 **East Liberty** Ohio U.S.A.
13 F2 **East Linton** Scotland
94 G6 **East Liverpool** Ohio U.S.A.
89 E9 **East London** S Africa
East Lothian *co see* **Lothian** *reg*
94 E8 **East Lynn** West Virginia U.S.A.
115 M7 **Eastmain** Quebec Canada
112 D5 **Eastman** Georgia U.S.A.
141 H6 **Eastmere** Queensland Australia
143 E8 **East, Mt** W Australia Australia
8 D3 **Eastnor** England
99 R9 **Easton** Illinois U.S.A.
95 Q4 **Easton** Massachusetts U.S.A.
99 N6 **Easton** Minnesota U.S.A.
110 B2 **Easton** Missouri U.S.A.
95 M6 **Easton** Pennsylvania U.S.A.
100 D2 **Easton** Washington U.S.A.
112 G4 **Eastover** South Carolina U.S.A.
East Pakistan *see* **Bangladesh**
113 F8 **East Palatka** Florida U.S.A.
94 G6 **East Palestine** Ohio U.S.A.
102 B2 **East Park Res** California U.S.A.
99 N8 **East Peru** Iowa U.S.A.
117 N8 **East Pine** British Columbia Canada
123 L6 **East Point** Madeleine Is, Quebec Canada
121 L1 **East Point** Ontario Canada
123 L7 **East Point** Prince Edward I Canada
123 N10 **East Point** Sable I, Nova Scotia
111 M8 **East Point** Georgia U.S.A.
94 E9 **East Point** Kentucky U.S.A.
119 M9 **East Poplar** Saskatchewan Canada
106 E2 **East Portal** Colorado U.S.A.
110 G5 **East Prairie** Missouri U.S.A.
122 G10 **East Pubnico** Nova Scotia Canada
94 G9 **East Rainelle** West Virginia U.S.A.
100 H9 **East Range** Nevada U.S.A.
9 F1 **East Retford** England
9 H5 **Eastry** England
110 F3 **East St Louis** Illinois U.S.A.
147 P5 **East Siberian Sea** Arctic Oc
139 J7 **East Sister I** Tasmania Australia
100 K2 **East Sister Peak** *mt* Idaho U.S.A.
9 F1 **East Stoke** England
8 D5 **East Stour** England
9 G6 **East Sussex** *co* England
94 D2 **East Tawas** Michigan U.S.A.
139 H4 **East Toorale** New South Wales Australia
119 N4 **East Trout L** Saskatchewan Canada
99 S7 **East Troy** Wisconsin U.S.A.
103 N7 **East Verde** *R* Arizona U.S.A.
95 M9 **Eastville** Virginia U.S.A.
13 E1 **East Wemyss** Scotland
9 E1 **East Wood** England
138 C2 **Eateringinna Cr** South Australia Australia
98 B9 **Eaton** Colorado U.S.A.
110 L1 **Eaton** Indiana U.S.A.
110 M2 **Eaton** Ohio U.S.A.
118 H7 **Eatonia** Saskatchewan Canada
94 C4 **Eaton Rapids** Michigan U.S.A.
9 F3 **Eaton Socon** England
112 D4 **Eatonton** Georgia U.S.A.
100 C3 **Eatonville** Washington U.S.A.
17 F9 **Eau, C. de l'** Morocco
99 U7 **Eau Claire** Michigan U.S.A.
99 P5 **Eau Claire** *R* Wisconsin U.S.A.
99 P5 **Eau Claire** Wisconsin U.S.A.
122 G1 **Eau-Claire, L. à l'** Labrador, Nfld Canada
115 M6 **Eau Claire, L. à l'** Quebec Canada
113 G9 **Eau Gallie** Florida U.S.A.
121 Q3 **Eau-Jaune, L. a l'** Quebec Canada
21 N2 **Eaulne** *R* France
134 E7 **Eauripik - New Guinea Rise** Pacific Oc
18 F9 **Eauze** France
141 G2 **Ebagoola** Queensland Australia
125 K6 **Ebano** Mexico
36 D1 **Ebbe** *mts* Germany
13 H5 **Ebberston** England
28 D6 **Ebberup** Denmark
8 C4 **Ebbw Vale** Wales
86 B5 **Ebebiyin** Equat Guinea
33 N10 **Ebeleben** Germany
28 F4 **Ebeltoft** Denmark
28 F4 **Ebeltoft Vig** *B* Denmark
119 P7 **Ebenezer** Saskatchewan Canada
99 U3 **Eben Junction** Michigan U.S.A.
94 J6 **Ebensburg** Pennsylvania U.S.A.
38 J6 **Ebensee** Austria
37 K3 **Ebensfeld** Germany
36 G5 **Eberbach** Germany
78 C2 **Eber Gölü** Turkey
32 M9 **Ebergötzen** Germany
37 L4 **Ebermannstadt** Germany
37 K3 **Ebern** Germany
36 D4 **Ebernburg** Germany
110 M4 **E Bernstadt** Kentucky U.S.A.
36 H6 **Ebersbach** Germany
36 H3 **Ebersburg** Germany
37 L3 **Ebersdorf** Germany
36 F4 **Eberstadt** Germany
38 L8 **Eberstein** Austria
33 T7 **Eberswalde** Germany
60 P2 **Ebetsu** Japan
55 F4 **Ebeyty, Oz** *L* Russian Federation
67 A2 **Ebian** China
36 G7 **Ebingen** Germany
60 D13 **Ebino** Japan
66 C3 **Ebinur Hu** *L* China
79 G3 **Ebla** *anc site* Syria
37 J6 **Ebnat** Germany
41 K3 **Ebnat** Switzerland
86 D5 **Ebola** *R* Zaire
43 G8 **Eboli** Italy
86 B5 **Ebolowa** Cameroon
37 K4 **Ebrach** Germany
9 F2 **E Bridgford** England
44 F2 **Ebro** *mt* Italy
16 E2 **Ebro** *R* Spain
16 E2 **Ebro, Embalse del** *res* Spain
36 E2 **Ebschloh** *mt* Germany
36 F2 **Ebsdorfergrund** Germany
33 M6 **Ebstorf** Germany
22 G2 **Ecaussines** Belgium
13 E3 **Ecclefechan** Scotland
13 F2 **Eccles** Scotland
94 F9 **Eccles** West Virginia U.S.A.
13 G6 **Ecclesfield** England
8 D2 **Eccleshall** England
127 P2 **Ecclesville** Trinidad
47 H4 **Eceabat** Turkey
40 E4 **Echallens** Switzerland
21 L4 **Échauffour** France
85 E1 **Ech Cheliff** Algeria
67 E1 **Echeng** China
101 U5 **Echeta** Wyoming U.S.A.
19 P14 **Échirolles** France
61 J10 **Echizen-misaki** *C* Japan
99 L5 **Echo** Minnesota U.S.A.
100 F4 **Echo** Oregon U.S.A.
101 O9 **Echo** Utah U.S.A.
103 K5 **Echo B** Nevada U.S.A.
120 G6 **Echo Bay** Ontario Canada
103 N5 **Echo Cliffs** Arizona U.S.A.
139 H8 **Echo,L** Tasmania Australia
121 P5 **Échouani L** Quebec Canada
122 H4 **Echouerie, L'** Quebec Canada
119 O8 **Echo Valley Prov. Park** Saskatchewan Canada
25 E6 **Echt** Netherlands
15 F3 **Echt** Scotland
32 M9 **Echte** Germany
25 F3 **Echten** Netherlands
22 L4 **Echternach** Luxembourg
139 G6 **Echuca** Victoria Australia
36 F3 **Echzell** Germany
16 D7 **Écija** Spain
36 H5 **Eckartshausen** Germany
98 H3 **Eckelson** North Dakota U.S.A.
37 L4 **Eckental** Germany
30 E1 **Eckernförde** Germany
109 J5 **Eckert** Texas U.S.A.
13 F3 **Eckford** Scotland
8 D3 **Eckington** England
9 E1 **Eckington** England
12 C1 **Eck,L** Scotland
98 D9 **Eckley** Colorado U.S.A.
94 F9 **Eckman** West Virginia U.S.A.
118 C6 **Eckville** Alberta Canada
32 H5 **Eckwarderhörne** Germany
111 K9 **Eclectic** Alabama U.S.A.
143 C11 **Eclipse I** W Australia Australia
140 B5 **Eclipse, Mt** N Terr Australia
115 M3 **Eclipse Sound** Northwest Territories Canada
21 L6 **Écommoy** France
110 L2 **Economy** Indiana U.S.A.
121 O5 **Écorces,L.aux** Quebec Canada
21 O3 **Ecos** France
21 K4 **Écouché** France
21 N3 **Ecouis** France
21 L4 **Écouves, Forêt d'** France
22 J4 **Ecouviez** Belgium
22 C2 **Ecques** France
20 G3 **Ecréhou, les** English Chan
111 G7 **Ecru** Mississippi U.S.A.
128 C4 **Ecuador** *rep* S America
21 N7 **Écueillé** France
123 K9 **Ecum Secum** Nova Scotia Canada
86 H3 **Ēd** Ethiopia
143 B8 **Edah** W Australia Australia
118 J5 **Edam** Saskatchewan Canada
25 D3 **Edam** Netherlands
15 F1 **Eday** Scotland
118 E6 **Edberg** Alberta Canada
109 K9 **Edcouch** Texas U.S.A.
6 N6 **Edda** *oil rig* North Sea
86 E3 **Ed Da'ein** Sudan
86 F3 **Ed Damazin** Sudan
86 F2 **Ed Damer** Sudan
86 F2 **Ed Debba** Sudan
32 K5 **Eddelak** Germany
123 Q2 **Eddies Cove** Newfoundland Canada
13 E2 **Eddleston** Scotland
15 C2 **Eddrachillis B** Scotland
86 F3 **Ed Dueim** Sudan
100 K2 **Eddy** Montana U.S.A.
109 K4 **Eddy** Texas U.S.A.
8 B7 **Eddystone Lt. Ho** English Chan
139 J8 **Eddystone Pt** Tasmania Australia
99 O8 **Eddyville** Iowa U.S.A.
110 H4 **Eddyville** Kentucky U.S.A.
98 G8 **Eddyville** Nebraska U.S.A.
25 E4 **Ede** Netherlands
85 E7 **Ede** Nigeria
86 B5 **Edéa** Cameroon
27 G11 **Edebäck** Sweden
27 K11 **Edebo** Sweden
130 E5 **Edéia** Brazil
48 F2 **Edelény** Hungary
143 A7 **Edel Land** *pen* W Australia Australia
139 J6 **Eden** New South Wales Australia
119 S8 **Eden** Manitoba Canada
101 O2 **Eden** Montana U.S.A.
94 J4 **Eden** New York U.S.A.
94 H10 **Eden** North Carolina U.S.A.
112 H1 **Eden** North Carolina U.S.A.
98 J4 **Eden** South Dakota U.S.A.
108 H4 **Eden** Texas U.S.A.
101 O8 **Eden** Utah U.S.A.
99 S6 **Eden** Wisconsin U.S.A.
101 Q7 **Eden** Wyoming U.S.A.
9 G5 **Edenbridge** England
89 D7 **Edenburg** S Africa
144 B7 **Edendale** New Zealand
14 D3 **Edenderry** Ireland
13 F6 **Edenfield** England
138 F6 **Edenhope** Victoria Australia
120 J8 **Edenhurst** Ontario Canada
36 E5 **Edenkoben** Germany
119 R2 **Eden L** Manitoba Canada
9 G5 **Eden,R** England
71 N9 **Eden,Tg** *C* Indonesia
112 L1 **Edenton** North Carolina U.S.A.
94 C3 **Edenville** Michigan U.S.A.
119 N8 **Edenwold** Saskatchewan Canada
36 E1 **Eder** *R* Germany
36 G1 **Edermünde** Germany
33 O10 **Edersleben** Germany
36 F1 **Ederstausee** *res* Germany
36 G1 **Edertal** Germany
27 F13 **Edet, L** Sweden
32 G6 **Edewecht** Germany
32 G6 **Edewechterdamm** Germany
101 R4 **Edgar** Montana U.S.A.
98 J9 **Edgar** Nebraska U.S.A.
111 F11 **Edgard** Louisiana U.S.A.
142 D5 **Edgar, Mt** W Australia Australia
142 E4 **Edgar Ra** W Australia Australia
110 E4 **Edgar Springs** Missouri U.S.A.
95 R5 **Edgartown** Massachusetts U.S.A.
109 M9 **Edgecliff** Texas U.S.A.
145 F2 **Edgecumbe** New Zealand
112 F4 **Edgefield** South Carolina U.S.A.
119 O8 **Edgeley** Saskatchewan Canada
98 H3 **Edgeley** North Dakota U.S.A.
115 N5 **Edgell I** Northwest Territories Canada
110 D6 **Edgemont** Arkansas U.S.A.
98 C6 **Edgemont** South Dakota U.S.A.
50 B1 **Edgeöya** *isld* Spitzbergen
109 O5 **Edgerly** Louisiana U.S.A.
118 G6 **Edgerton** Alberta Canada
94 C5 **Edgerton** Ohio U.S.A.
99 R7 **Edgerton** Wisconsin U.S.A.
101 T6 **Edgerton** Wyoming U.S.A.
113 G9 **Edgewater** Florida U.S.A.
117 O11 **Edgewood** British Columbia Canada
110 H3 **Edgewood** Illinois U.S.A.
95 L7 **Edgewood** Maryland U.S.A.
106 D6 **Edgewood** New Mexico U.S.A.
109 M3 **Edgewood** Texas U.S.A.
9 F4 **Edgware** England
80 C8 **Edh Dhahiriya** Jordan
46 E4 **Édhessa** Greece
144 B6 **Edievale** New Zealand
36 C3 **Ediger-Eller** Germany
84 F5 **Edimpi** Chad
99 N5 **Edina** Minnesota U.S.A.
94 G5 **Edinboro** Pennsylvania U.S.A.
99 R10 **Edinburg** Illinois U.S.A.
111 G9 **Edinburg** Mississippi U.S.A.
98 J1 **Edinburg** North Dakota U.S.A.
109 J9 **Edinburg** Texas U.S.A.
94 J8 **Edinburg** Virginia U.S.A.
13 E2 **Edinburgh** Scotland
110 L2 **Edinburgh** Indiana U.S.A.
141 H7 **Edinburgh, Mt** Queensland Australia
22 F2 **Edingen** Belgium
47 H3 **Edirne** Turkey
102 F6 **Edison** California U.S.A.
106 F3 **Edison** Colorado U.S.A.
111 M10 **Edison** Georgia U.S.A.
112 G4 **Edisto** *R* South Carolina U.S.A.
112 G5 **Edisto Island** South Carolina U.S.A.
138 E6 **Edithburgh** South Australia Australia
117 P9 **Edith Cavell,Mt** Alberta Canada
101 O3 **Edith, Mt** Montana U.S.A.
143 D7 **Edith Withnell, L** W Australia Australia
85 F3 **Edjeleh** Algeria
143 D8 **Edjudina** W Australia Australia
13 G3 **Edlingham** England
38 O6 **Edlitz** Austria
95 M4 **Edmeston** New York U.S.A.
107 L2 **Edmond** Kansas U.S.A.
107 N6 **Edmond** Oklahoma U.S.A.
100 C2 **Edmonds** Washington U.S.A.
141 H3 **Edmonton** Queensland Australia
118 D5 **Edmonton** Alberta Canada
9 F4 **Edmonton** England
94 C3 **Edmore** Michigan U.S.A.
98 H1 **Edmore** North Dakota U.S.A.
122 D6 **Edmundston** New Brunswick Canada
109 L7 **Edna** Texas U.S.A.
13 F2 **Ednam** Scotland
27 J13 **Ed, O** Sweden
61 N10 **Edo-gawa** *R* Japan
27 M14 **Edole** Latvia
42 C2 **Edolo** Italy
26 C8 **Edoy** *isld* Norway
47 J5 **Edremit** Turkey
47 H5 **Edremit Körfezi** *B* Turkey
58 C3 **Edrengiyn Nuruu** *mt* Mongolia
109 K8 **Edroy** Texas U.S.A.
27 K12 **Edsbro** Sweden
27 H13 **Edsbruk** Sweden
27 H10 **Edsbyn** Sweden
26 J8 **Edsele** Sweden
58 D3 **Edsin Gol** China
117 P9 **Edson** Alberta Canada
107 J2 **Edson** Kansas U.S.A.
27 J14 **Ed, V** Sweden
118 E4 **Edwand** Alberta Canada
139 G6 **Edward** *R* New South Wales Australia
140 D2 **Edward I** N Terr Australia
120 B4 **Edward I** Ontario Canada
88 B2 **Edward, L** Zaire
140 B6 **Edward, Mt** N Terr Australia
141 F2 **Edward River** Queensland Australia
102 G7 **Edwards** California U.S.A.
99 Q8 **Edwards** *R* Illinois U.S.A.
111 F9 **Edwards** Mississippi U.S.A.
95 M2 **Edwards** New York U.S.A.
94 A5 **Edwardsburg** Michigan U.S.A.
138 D3 **Edwards Creek** South Australia Australia
144 B7 **Edwardson, C** New Zealand
144 A6 **Edwardson Sd** New Zealand
108 G5 **Edwards Plateau** Texas U.S.A.
110 G3 **Edwardsville** Illinois U.S.A.
15 F4 **Edzell** Scotland
117 H7 **Edziza, Mt** British Columbia Canada
22 F1 **Eeklo** Belgium
100 B9 **Eel** *R* California U.S.A.
94 B6 **Eel** *R* Indiana U.S.A.
25 G2 **Eelde** Netherlands
25 D4 **Eem** *R* Netherlands
25 D4 **Eem Meer** Netherlands
25 G2 **Eemshaven** Netherlands
89 B6 **Eenzamheid Pan** *salt lake* S Africa
22 E1 **Eernegem** Belgium
137 O5 **Éfaté** *isld* Vanuatu
38 K5 **Eferding** Austria
99 N2 **Effie** Minnesota U.S.A.
99 P6 **Effigy Mounds Nat. Mon.** Iowa U.S.A.
110 H2 **Effingham** Illinois U.S.A.
107 P2 **Effingham** Kansas U.S.A.
48 M6 **Eforie** Romania
80 D7 **Efrata** Jordan
71 B3 **Ef Torobi** *isld* W Irian
28 B5 **Eg** Denmark
28 E4 **Egå** Denmark
18 D10 **Ega** *R* Spain
43 E10 **Egadi, I** Sicily
133 F5 **Egaña** Argentina
103 K2 **Egan Range** Nevada U.S.A.
121 N7 **Eganville** Ontario Canada
85 F7 **Egbe** Nigeria
98 B8 **Egbert** Wyoming U.S.A.
28 H5 **Egebjerg** Denmark
115 O4 **Egedesminde** Greenland
116 J7 **Egegik B** Alaska U.S.A.
98 G1 **Egeland** North Dakota U.S.A.
33 O9 **Egeln** Germany
28 D7 **Egen** Denmark
28 F4 **Egens** Denmark
28 E3 **Egense** Denmark
37 J6 **Eger** *R* Germany
48 F3 **Eger** Hungary
28 D7 **Egernsund** Denmark
27 A13 **Egersund** Norway
143 C6 **Egerton, Mt** W Australia Australia
32 M6 **Egestorf** Germany
41 L3 **Egg** Austria
27 D11 **Eggedal** Norway
31 J7 **Eggenburg** Austria
37 O7 **Eggenfelden** Germany
33 U5 **Eggesin** Germany
28 G6 **Eggeslevmagle** Denmark
99 T4 **Egg Harbor** Wisconsin U.S.A.
95 N7 **Egg Harbor City** New Jersey U.S.A.
95 N7 **Egg Harbor, Gt** New Jersey U.S.A.
95 N7 **Egg Harbor, Little** New Jersey U.S.A.
116 G5 **Egg I** Alaska U.S.A.
139 G7 **Egg Lagoon** Tasmania Australia
13 G4 **Eggleston** England
37 N6 **Eggmühl** Germany
37 L4 **Eggolsheim** Germany
9 F5 **Egham** England
22 H2 **Eghezee** Belgium
28 G6 **Egholm** *isld* Denmark
28 D2 **Egholm** *isld* Nordjylland Denmark
15 F1 **Egilsay** Scotland
142 C5 **Eginbah** W Australia Australia
85 D3 **Eglab,El** *reg* Algeria
18 G7 **Egletons** France
36 G1 **Egling** Germany
13 G3 **Eglingham** England
144 B6 **Eglinton** *R* New Zealand
114 H2 **Eglinton I** Northwest Territories Canada
41 J2 **Eglisau** Switzerland
37 L4 **Egloffstein** Germany
25 C3 **Egmond aan Zee** Netherlands
122 H7 **Egmont B** Prince Edward I Canada
113 E10 **Egmont Key** *isld* Florida U.S.A.
145 E3 **Egmont, Mt** New Zealand
145 E3 **Egmont Village** New Zealand
28 J6 **Egøje** Denmark

118 D4 **Egremont** Alberta Canada
47 L6 **Eğret** Turkey
47 L7 **Eğridir** Turkey
78 C2 **Egridir Gölü** *L* Turkey
47 K5 **Eğrigöz Dağı** *mt* Turkey
13 H5 **Egton** England
28 C5 **Egtved** Denmark
71 E7 **Eguet Pt** Philippines
19 O17 **Eguilles** France
18 G6 **Éguzon** France
28 C6 **Egvad** Denmark
48 F3 **Egyek** Hungary
84 H4 **Egypt** *rep* Africa
112 F5 **Egypt** Georgia U.S.A.
111 H8 **Egypt** Mississippi U.S.A.
109 L6 **Egypt** Texas U.S.A.
79 F4 **Ehden** Lebanon
36 H7 **Ehingen** Germany
33 Q8 **Ehle** *R* Germany
32 K10 **Ehlen** Germany
36 F6 **Ehningen** Germany
33 N7 **Ehra-Lessien** Germany
113 E9 **Ehren** Florida U.S.A.
103 K8 **Ehrenberg** Arizona U.S.A.
140 B6 **Ehrenberg Ra** N Terr Australia
36 D3 **Ehrenbreitstein** Germany
32 J7 **Ehrenburg** Germany
37 O2 **Ehrenfriedersdorf** Germany
112 F4 **Ehrhardt** South Carolina U.S.A.
36 E2 **Ehringshausen** Germany
60 D14 **Ei** Japan
36 E2 **Eibach** Germany
36 E2 **Eibelshausen** Germany
37 J4 **Eibelstadt** Germany
37 O3 **Eibenstock** Germany
25 G4 **Eibergen** Netherlands
38 M8 **Eibiswald** Austria
33 O8 **Eichenbarleben** Germany
37 O6 **Eichendorf** Germany
37 M5 **Eichhofen** Germany
32 M10 **Eichsfeld** *mts* Germany
37 L6 **Eichstätt** Germany
40 G1 **Eichstetten** Germany
36 F5 **Eichtersheim** Germany
33 T8 **Eichwalde** Germany
36 H2 **Eichzell** Germany
32 M7 **Eicklingen** Germany
27 D12 **Eidanger** Norway
26 B9 **Eide** Norway
32 J4 **Eider** Germany
32 L4 **Eider** *R* Germany
6 F1 **Eiði** Faeroes
26 G3 **Eidsfjord** Norway
27 D12 **Eidsfoss** Norway
27 F11 **Eidskog** Norway
26 C9 **Eidsvåg** Norway
141 K7 **Eidsvold** Queensland Australia
27 E11 **Eidsvoll** Norway
25 C2 **Eierlandse Gat** Netherlands
36 B3 **Eifel** *mts* Germany
89 F2 **Eiffel Flats** Zimbabwe
37 J1 **Eigenrieden** Germany
40 G4 **Eiger** *mt* Switzerland
15 B4 **Eigg** *isld* Scotland
113 J11 **Eight Mile Rock** Bahamas
146 B7 **Eights Coast** Antarctica
142 D4 **Eighty Mile Beach** W Australia Australia
26 A10 **Eikefjord** Norway
27 D12 **Eikeren** *R* Norway
26 C9 **Eikesdalsvatn** *L* Norway
139 H6 **Eildon** Victoria Australia
33 R10 **Eilenburg** Germany
129 G3 **Eilerts de Haan Geb** *mts* Suriname
33 O8 **Eilsleben** Germany
32 L8 **Eime** Germany
33 M7 **Eimke** Germany
27 E11 **Eina** Norway
141 G4 **Einasleigh** Queensland Australia
32 L9 **Einbeck** Germany
25 D6 **Eindhoven** Netherlands
32 L4 **Einfeld** Germany
68 B4 **Einme** Burma
36 C5 **Einöd** Germany
37 P6 **Einödsriegel** *mt* Germany
Einsiedel *see* **Deutsch-Einsiedel**
79 F8 **Ein Yahav** Israel
Éire *rep see* **Ireland, Rep of**
120 G4 **Eire River** Ontario Canada
128 E5 **Eirunepe** Brazil
22 L4 **Eisch** *R* Luxembourg
22 K2 **Eisden** Belgium
25 E7 **Eisden** Netherlands
36 C4 **Eisen** Germany
37 J2 **Eisenach** Germany
36 E4 **Eisenberg** Germany
37 M2 **Eisenberg** Germany
38 L6 **Eisenerz** Austria
38 L7 **Eisenerzer-Alpen** *mts* Austria
106 E2 **Eisenhower Tunnel** Colorado U.S.A.
38 J8 **Eisenhut** *mt* Austria
31 H3 **Eisenhüttenstadt** Germany
38 L8 **Eisenkappel** Austria
48 D3 **Eisenstadt** Austria
38 J8 **Eisentratten** Austria
38 L5 **Eisenwurzen** *reg* Austria
36 D2 **Eiserfeld** Germany
37 K3 **Eisfeld** Germany
33 P9 **Eisleben** Germany
36 H6 **Eislingen** Germany
37 L6 **Eitensheim** Germany
36 H2 **Eiterfeld** Germany
36 C2 **Eitorf** Germany
17 G2 **Ejea de los Caballeros** Spain
87 G12 **Ejeda** Madagascar
28 D5 **Ejer Bavnehoj** *hill* Denmark
28 B3 **Ejerslev** Denmark
127 J10 **Ejido** Venezuela
65 A5 **Ejin Horo Qi** China
65 C2 **Ej Nur** China
28 B3 **Ejsing** Denmark
28 C5 **Ejstrup** Denmark
85 D7 **Ejura** Ghana
98 B4 **Ekalaka** Montana U.S.A.
27 J15 **Ekby** Sweden
22 F2 **Eke** Belgium
29 K12 **Ekenäs** Finland
22 G1 **Ekeren** Belgium
145 E4 **Eketahuna** New Zealand
26 N5 **Ekfors** Sweden
46 D6 **Ekhinádhes** *isld* Greece
46 G3 **Ekhínos** Greece
55 G5 **Ekibastuz** Kazakhstan
59 K1 **Ekimchan** Russian Federation
116 N6 **Eklutna** Alaska U.S.A.
6 N6 **Ekofisk** *oil rig* North Sea
27 J12 **Ekoln** *L* Sweden
22 F1 **Eksaarde** Belgium
27 G11 **Ekshärad** Sweden
27 G14 **Eksjö** Sweden
26 L7 **Ekträsk** Sweden
115 L7 **Ekwan** *R* Ontario Canada
116 J7 **Ekwok** Alaska U.S.A.
68 C3 **Ela** Burma
El Aaiún *see* **Laâyoune**
46 F8 **Elafónisos** *isld* Greece
111 F7 **Elaine** Arkansas U.S.A.
80 E5 **El 'Ajājira** Jordan
103 H10 **El Alamo** Mexico
75 K10 **Elamanchili** India
99 R5 **Eland** Wisconsin U.S.A.
89 E5 **Elands** *R* S Africa
89 C8 **Elands Berg** *mt* S Africa
8 C3 **Elan Valley Reservoirs** Wales
43 B13 **El Aouinet** Algeria
41 L4 **Ela, Piz** *mt* Switzerland
16 D7 **El Arahal** Spain
El Arâich *see* **Larache** Morocco
124 C4 **El Arco** Mexico
80 F5 **El Ardah** Jordan
141 H4 **El Arish** Queensland Australia
46 E5 **Elassón** Greece
79 E9 **Elat** Israel
46 F6 **Elátia** Greece
86 E2 **El Atrun Oasis** Sudan
80 D7 **El 'Azar** Jordan
78 G2 **Elâziğ** Turkey
111 K10 **Elba** Alabama U.S.A.
101 M7 **Elba** Idaho U.S.A.
98 H8 **Elba** Nebraska U.S.A.
94 J3 **Elba** New York U.S.A.
42 C6 **Elba, I.d'** Italy
126 H10 **El Banco** Colombia
16 D4 **El Barco de Avila** Spain
46 D3 **Elbasan** Albania
127 K10 **El Baúl** Venezuela
32 J5 **Elbe** *est* Germany
33 M6 **Elbe** *R* Germany
33 N5 **Elbe-Lübeck Kanal** Germany
79 G4 **El Beqa'a** *R* Lebanon
110 J3 **Elberfield** Indiana U.S.A.
32 F8 **Elbergen** Germany
99 O7 **Elberon** Iowa U.S.A.
109 J2 **Elbert** Texas U.S.A.
99 U5 **Elberta** Michigan U.S.A.
106 D2 **Elbert,Mt** Colorado U.S.A.
112 E3 **Elberton** Georgia U.S.A.
21 N3 **Elbeuf** France
33 N9 **Elbingerode** Germany
78 F2 **Elbistan** Turkey
31 L1 **Elblag** Poland
17 F6 **El Bonillo** Spain
124 H6 **El Bordo** Mexico
16 D9 **El Borj** Morocco
118 L7 **Elbow** Saskatchewan Canada
113 L11 **Elbow Cay** *isld* Bahamas
98 K4 **Elbow L** Minnesota U.S.A.
118 C8 **Elbow R** Alberta Canada
124 J6 **El Bozal** Mexico
53 F11 **El'brus** *mt* Russian Federation
86 E4 **El Buheyrat** *prov* Sudan
25 E4 **Elburg** Netherlands
16 E3 **El Burgo de Osma** Spain
100 K9 **Elburz** Nevada U.S.A.
77 B1 **Elburz Mountains** Iran
102 H9 **El Cajon** California U.S.A.
128 F2 **El Callao** Venezuela
16 D5 **El Campillo de la Jara** Spain
109 L6 **El Campo** Texas U.S.A.
102 H9 **El Capitan Res** California U.S.A.
128 C2 **El Carmen** Colombia
124 G5 **El Casco** Mexico
17 G3 **El Castellar** Spain
103 J9 **El Centro** California U.S.A.
128 F7 **El Cerro** Bolivia
16 C7 **El Cerro de Andévalo** Spain
124 F3 **El Charco** Mexico
17 G6 **Elche** Spain
17 F6 **Elche de la Sierra** Spain
125 N9 **El Chichón** *vol* Mexico
124 G3 **El Chilicote** Mexico
127 K9 **El Chino** Venezuela
99 R4 **Elcho** Wisconsin U.S.A.
140 D1 **Elcho I** N Terr Australia
133 E2 **El Chorro** Argentina
124 H5 **El Cobre** Mexico
128 D2 **El Cocuy** Colombia
126 C3 **El Cotorro** Cuba
126 G4 **El Cristo** Cuba
108 B5 **El Cuervo** Mexico
32 L8 **Eldagsen** Germany
124 C2 **El Dátil** Mexico
33 Q6 **Elde** *R* Germany
33 O6 **Eldena** Germany
138 F4 **Elder,L** South Australia Australia
99 R5 **Elderon** Wisconsin U.S.A.
6 N6 **Eldfisk** *oil rig* North Sea
126 A4 **El Díaz** Mexico
126 G10 **El Difícil** Colombia
33 M7 **Eldingen** Germany
124 G8 **El Divisadero** Mexico
128 C3 **El Diviso** Colombia
124 B2 **El Doctor** Mexico
99 O9 **Eldon** Iowa U.S.A.
110 D3 **Eldon** Missouri U.S.A.
100 B2 **Eldon** Washington U.S.A.
99 N7 **Eldora** Iowa U.S.A.
130 C10 **Eldorado** Argentina
130 E9 **Eldorado** Brazil
114 J6 **Eldorado** Saskatchewan Canada
124 F5 **Eldorado** Mexico
109 P2 **El Dorado** Arkansas U.S.A.
110 H4 **Eldorado** Illinois U.S.A.
107 O4 **El Dorado** Kansas U.S.A.
107 L7 **Eldorado** Oklahoma U.S.A.
108 G5 **Eldorado** Texas U.S.A.
128 F2 **El Dorado** Venezuela
89 G1 **Eldorado** Zimbabwe
100 D1 **Eldorado,Mt** Washington U.S.A.
103 K6 **Eldorado Mts** Nevada U.S.A.
110 B4 **El Dorado Springs** Missouri U.S.A.
88 E1 **Eldoret** Kenya
98 K2 **Eldred** Minnesota U.S.A.
95 N5 **Eldred** New York U.S.A.
94 J5 **Eldred** Pennsylvania U.S.A.
27 F15 **Eldsberga** Sweden
100 H2 **Eleanor** Washington U.S.A.
143 D10 **Eleanora Pk** W Australia Australia
102 E3 **Eleanor, L** California U.S.A.
89 E4 **Elebe** *mt* Botswana
109 J1 **Electra** Texas U.S.A.
101 P5 **Electric Pk** Mont/Wyoming U.S.A.
135 O1 **Eleele** Hawaiian Is
52 B6 **Eleja** Latvia
48 G4 **Elek** Hungary
54 K1 **Elektrogorsk** Russian Federation
54 K1 **Elektrostal'** Russian Federation
22 J2 **Elemalle** Belgium
47 H2 **Elena** Bulgaria
128 D4 **El Encanto** Colombia
33 N9 **Elend** Germany
106 C8 **Elephant Butte** New Mexico U.S.A.
106 C8 **Elephant Butte Res** New Mexico U.S.A.
68 G7 **Elephant, Chaine de l'** *mts* Cambodia
146 D3 **Elephant I** South Shetland Is Antarctica
83 K8 **Elephant Pass** Sri Lanka
116 G3 **Elephant Point** Alaska U.S.A.
46 F3 **Eleshnitsa** Bulgaria
128 E3 **El Esmeralda** Venezuela
128 C3 **El Espinal** Colombia
56 H4 **Elesun** Russian Federation
84 J5 **Elet, Wadi** *watercourse* Sudan
85 F1 **El Eulma** Algeria
113 L12 **Eleuthera I** Bahamas
99 P5 **Eleva** Wisconsin U.S.A.
106 E3 **Eleven Mile Canyon Res** Colorado U.S.A.
110 E5 **Eleven Point** *R* Missouri U.S.A.
46 F6 **Elevsís** Greece
22 H2 **Elewijt** Belgium
20 C5 **Elez** *R* France
80 G2 **El Fahham** Syria
43 C12 **El Fahs** Tunisia
86 E3 **El Fasher** Sudan
16 D9 **El Fendek** Morocco
16 B1 **El Ferrol** Spain
117 E6 **Elfin Cove** Alaska U.S.A.
119 O7 **Elfros** Saskatchewan Canada
86 H4 **El Fud** Ethiopia
124 E4 **El Fuerte** Mexico
86 E3 **El Fula** Sudan
80 D5 **El Fundug** Jordan
26 E9 **Elgå** Norway
26 E9 **Elgepiggen** *mt* Norway
37 K2 **Elgersburg** Germany
86 F3 **El Geteina** Sudan
86 F3 **El Gezira** *prov* Sudan
80 F5 **El Ghor** Jordan
119 R9 **Elgin** Manitoba Canada
122 G8 **Elgin** New Brunswick Canada
15 E3 **Elgin** Scotland
103 O10 **Elgin** Arizona U.S.A.
99 S7 **Elgin** Illinois U.S.A.
99 P7 **Elgin** Iowa U.S.A.
98 H8 **Elgin** Nebraska U.S.A.
103 K4 **Elgin** Nevada U.S.A.
98 E3 **Elgin** North Dakota U.S.A.
107 M7 **Elgin** Oklahoma U.S.A.
100 H4 **Elgin** Oregon U.S.A.
109 K5 **Elgin** Texas U.S.A.
103 O3 **Elgin** Utah U.S.A.
141 H5 **Elgin Downs** Queensland Australia
86 F5 **Elgon, Mt** Uganda
17 H2 **El Grado** Spain
124 G8 **El Grullo** Mexico
128 D3 **El Guamo** Colombia
84 H4 **El Harra** Egypt
86 F3 **El Hawata** Sudan
85 E3 **El Homr** Algeria
87 D7 **Elias Garcia** Angola
127 J5 **Elías Piña** Dominican Rep
109 J3 **Eliasville** Texas U.S.A.
108 D2 **Elida** New Mexico U.S.A.
119 U9 **Elie** Manitoba Canada
13 F1 **Elie** Scotland
46 F6 **Elikón** *mt* Greece
29 M11 **Elimäki** Finland
46 F2 **Elin Pelin** Bulgaria
95 R3 **Eliot** Maine U.S.A.
29 O10 **Elisenvaara** Russian Federation
129 K5 **Eliseu Martins** Brazil
80 E6 **Elisha'** Jordan
53 F10 **Elista** Russian Federation
106 F2 **Elizabeth** Colorado U.S.A.
99 Q7 **Elizabeth** Illinois U.S.A.
109 P5 **Elizabeth** Louisiana U.S.A.
95 N6 **Elizabeth** New Jersey U.S.A.
94 F7 **Elizabeth** West Virginia U.S.A.
112 L1 **Elizabeth City** North Carolina U.S.A.
95 R5 **Elizabeth Is** Massachusetts U.S.A.
142 F3 **Elizabeth, Mt** W Australia Australia
122 F6 **Elizabeth,Mt** New Brunswick Canada
101 P9 **Elizabeth Mt** Utah U.S.A.
137 M7 **Elizabeth Reef** Pacific Oc
143 B7 **Elizabeth Spring** W Australia Australia
94 E10 **Elizabethton** Tennessee U.S.A.
94 B7 **Elizabethtown** Indiana U.S.A.
94 B9 **Elizabethtown** Kentucky U.S.A.
95 O2 **Elizabethtown** New York U.S.A.
112 J3 **Elizabethtown** North Carolina U.S.A.
95 L6 **Elizabethtown** Pennsylvania U.S.A.
Elizabethville *see* **Lubumbashi**
95 L6 **Elizabethville** Pennsylvania U.S.A.
138 E6 **Eliza,L** South Australia Australia
18 D9 **Elizondo** Spain
124 G4 **El Jaralito** Mexico
86 F3 **El Jebelein** Sudan
126 E4 **El Jíbaro** Cuba
31 N2 **Ełk** Poland
102 A2 **Elk** California U.S.A.
110 B5 **Elk** *R* Missouri U.S.A.
108 B3 **Elk** New Mexico U.S.A.
95 M7 **Elk** *R* Penn/Maryland U.S.A.
110 K6 **Elk** *R* Tennessee U.S.A.
94 F8 **Elk** *R* West Virginia U.S.A.
101 P6 **Elk** Wyoming U.S.A.
99 P7 **Elkader** Iowa U.S.A.
86 F2 **El Kamlin** Sudan
101 R5 **Elk Basin** Wyoming U.S.A.
100 K4 **Elk City** Idaho U.S.A.
107 P4 **Elk City** Kansas U.S.A.
107 L6 **Elk City** Oklahoma U.S.A.
102 B2 **Elk Creek** California U.S.A.
140 D5 **Elkedra** N Terr Australia
43 B12 **El Kef** Tunisia
85 C2 **El Kelaâ des Srarhna** Morocco
86 H4 **Ēl Kerē** Ethiopia
102 C3 **Elk Grove** California U.S.A.
86 F2 **El Khandaq** Sudan
79 E7 **El Kharrûba** Egypt
94 B5 **Elkhart** Indiana U.S.A.
107 J4 **Elkhart** Kansas U.S.A.
109 M4 **Elkhart** Texas U.S.A.
99 T6 **Elkhart Lake** Wisconsin U.S.A.
101 S9 **Elkhead Mts** Colorado U.S.A.
119 Q9 **Elkhorn** Manitoba Canada
99 L8 **Elk Horn** Iowa U.S.A.
98 H7 **Elkhorn** *R* Nebraska U.S.A.
99 S7 **Elkhorn** Wisconsin U.S.A.
47 H2 **Elkhovo** Bulgaria
112 G1 **Elkin** North Carolina U.S.A.
118 E5 **Elk I. Nat. Park** Alberta Canada
108 C2 **Elkins** New Mexico U.S.A.
94 H8 **Elkins** West Virginia U.S.A.
94 B2 **Elk L** Michigan U.S.A.
120 K5 **Elk Lake** Ontario Canada
95 K4 **Elkland** Pennsylvania U.S.A.
110 K7 **Elkmont** Alabama U.S.A.
106 D1 **Elk Mt** Colorado U.S.A.
101 T8 **Elk Mt** Wyoming U.S.A.
100 K1 **Elko** British Columbia Canada
100 K9 **Elko** Nevada U.S.A.
101 P8 **Elkol** Wyoming U.S.A.
86 H4 **Ēl K'oran** Ethiopia
101 N3 **Elk Park** Montana U.S.A.
112 F1 **Elk Park** North Carolina U.S.A.
118 G5 **Elk Point** Alberta Canada
98 K7 **Elk Pt** South Dakota U.S.A.
118 C9 **Elk R** British Columbia Canada
99 N4 **Elk R** Minnesota U.S.A.
94 B2 **Elk Rapids** Michigan U.S.A.
43 C12 **El Krib** Tunisia
100 J3 **Elk River** Idaho U.S.A.
43 B13 **El Ksour** Tunisia
106 B1 **Elk Springs** Colorado U.S.A.
113 F8 **Elkton** Florida U.S.A.
110 J5 **Elkton** Kentucky U.S.A.
95 M7 **Elkton** Maryland U.S.A.
99 O6 **Elkton** Minnesota U.S.A.
100 B6 **Elkton** Oregon U.S.A.
98 K5 **Elkton** South Dakota U.S.A.
110 K6 **Elkton** Tennessee U.S.A.
94 J8 **Elkton** Virginia U.S.A.
79 E9 **El Kuntilla** Egypt
94 C10 **Elk Valley** Tennessee U.S.A.
110 G4 **Elkville** Illinois U.S.A.
79 G4 **El Laboue** Lebanon
86 E3 **El Lagowa** Sudan
83 K10 **Ellamulla** Sri Lanka
12 C1 **Ellanbeich** Scotland
13 G6 **Elland** England
143 A7 **Ellavalla** W Australia Australia
113 D7 **Ellaville** Florida U.S.A.
111 M9 **Ellaville** Georgia U.S.A.
20 D5 **Elle** *R* France
37 N3 **Ellefeld** Germany
114 J2 **Ellef Ringnes I** Northwest Territories Canada
143 C10 **Elleker** W Australia Australia
95 O2 **Ellenburg** New York U.S.A.
95 M8 **Ellendale** Delaware U.S.A.
111 F12 **Ellendale** Louisiana U.S.A.
98 H3 **Ellendale** North Dakota U.S.A.
103 O3 **Ellen,Mt** Utah U.S.A.
95 P2 **Ellen,Mt** Vermont U.S.A.
143 C10 **Ellen Pk** W Australia Australia
13 E4 **Ellen,R** England
100 E2 **Ellensburg** Washington U.S.A.
32 H6 **Ellenserdamm** Germany
113 E10 **Ellenton** Florida U.S.A.
95 N5 **Ellenville** New York U.S.A.
36 C3 **Ellenz-Poltersdorf** Germany
112 G2 **Eller** North Carolina U.S.A.
112 H2 **Ellerbe** North Carolina U.S.A.
113 E7 **Ellerbee** Florida U.S.A.
36 D4 **Ellerspring** *mt* Germany
144 B6 **Ellery, L** New Zealand
139 J6 **Ellery,Mt** Victoria Australia
8 D2 **Ellesmere** England
115 L2 **Ellesmere I** Northwest Territories Canada
144 D5 **Ellesmere, L** New Zealand
8 D1 **Ellesmere Port** England
110 K2 **Ellettsville** Indiana U.S.A.
22 F2 **Ellezelles** Belgium
20 C5 **Elliant** France
Ellice Is. *see* **Tuvalu** *islds state*
95 L7 **Ellicott City** Maryland U.S.A.
94 J4 **Ellicottville** New York U.S.A.
28 D3 **Ellidshøj** Denmark
112 C3 **Ellijay** Georgia U.S.A.
28 E2 **Elling** Denmark
28 F6 **Ellinge** Denmark
37 K5 **Ellingen** Germany
13 G3 **Ellington** England
110 F4 **Ellington** Missouri U.S.A.
107 M3 **Ellinwood** Kansas U.S.A.
89 E8 **Elliot** S Africa
95 L8 **Elliot** Maryland U.S.A.
112 G3 **Elliot** South Carolina U.S.A.
142 E4 **Elliot Lake** W Australia Australia
120 H6 **Elliot Lake** Ontario Canada
141 H4 **Elliot, Mt** Queensland Australia
140 C3 **Elliott** N Terr Australia
99 L8 **Elliott** Iowa U.S.A.
98 J3 **Elliott** North Dakota U.S.A.
113 G12 **Elliott Key** *isld* Florida U.S.A.
122 H4 **Ellis B** Quebec Canada
89 E4 **Ellisras** S Africa
138 C5 **Elliston** South Australia Australia
123 T5 **Elliston** Newfoundland Canada
101 N3 **Elliston** Montana U.S.A.
94 G9 **Elliston** Virginia U.S.A.
111 G10 **Ellisville** Mississippi U.S.A.
143 G8 **Ell, L** W Australia Australia
38 F6 **Ellmau** Austria
36 F6 **Ellmendingen** Germany
15 F3 **Ellon** Scotland
74 F8 **Ellora** India
112 G4 **Elloree** South Carolina U.S.A.
33 N9 **Ellrich** Germany
118 E4 **Ellscott** Alberta Canada
110 F5 **Ellsinore** Missouri U.S.A.
107 M3 **Ellsworth** Kansas U.S.A.
95 T2 **Ellsworth** Maine U.S.A.
99 L6 **Ellsworth** Minnesota U.S.A.
98 D7 **Ellsworth** Nebraska U.S.A.
99 O5 **Ellsworth** Wisconsin U.S.A.
109 J1 **Ellsworth,L** Oklahoma U.S.A.
146 B7 **Ellsworth Land** Antarctica
146 C7 **Ellsworth Mts** Antarctica
37 J6 **Ellwangen** Germany
94 G6 **Ellwood City** Pennsylvania U.S.A.
32 H6 **Ellwürden** Germany
32 K5 **Elm** Germany
41 K4 **Elm** Switzerland
99 O6 **Elma** Iowa U.S.A.
100 B2 **Elma** Washington U.S.A.
133 C6 **El Maitén** Argentina
47 K8 **Elmalı** Turkey
86 F3 **El Manaquil** Sudan
124 A2 **El Maneadero** Mexico
124 G5 **El Martinez** Mexico
109 L7 **Elmaton** Texas U.S.A.
103 J9 **El Mayor** Mexico
79 D7 **El Mazâr** Egypt
112 K2 **Elm City** North Carolina U.S.A.
98 G9 **Elm Cr** Nebraska U.S.A.
118 D1 **Elm Creek** Manitoba Canada
107 N6 **Elm Cr.Res.,E** Oklahoma U.S.A.
108 A2 **Elmendorf** New Mexico U.S.A.
127 J9 **El Mene de Mauroa** Venezuela
32 M5 **Elmenhorst** Germany
99 O10 **Elmer** Missouri U.S.A.
95 M7 **Elmer** New Jersey U.S.A.
109 H1 **Elmer** Oklahoma U.S.A.
100 G1 **Elmer City** Washington U.S.A.
43 B13 **El Meskiana** Algeria
99 T8 **Elmhurst** Illinois U.S.A.
79 F4 **El Mīna** Lebanon
123 K7 **Elmira** Prince Edward I Canada
102 C3 **Elmira** California U.S.A.
94 C1 **Elmira** Michigan U.S.A.
95 L4 **Elmira** New York U.S.A.
103 M8 **El Mirage** Arizona U.S.A.
98 H4 **Elm L** South Dakota U.S.A.
109 K4 **Elm Mott** Texas U.S.A.
107 N3 **Elmo** Kansas U.S.A.
99 L9 **Elmo** Missouri U.S.A.
101 T8 **Elmo** Wyoming U.S.A.
16 E4 **El Molar** Spain
108 G7 **El Moral** Mexico
139 G6 **Elmore** Victoria Australia
111 K9 **Elmore** Alabama U.S.A.
99 M6 **Elmore** Minnesota U.S.A.
94 D5 **Elmore** Ohio U.S.A.
109 K1 **Elmore City** Oklahoma U.S.A.
106 B6 **El Morro Nat.Mon** New Mexico U.S.A.
122 J9 **Elmsdale** Nova Scotia Canada
32 L5 **Elmshorn** Germany
98 D5 **Elm Springs** South Dakota U.S.A.
36 D5 **Elmstein** Germany
122 J8 **Elmsvale** Nova Scotia Canada
86 E3 **El Muglad** Sudan
120 J8 **Elmwood** Ontario Canada
110 G1 **Elmwood** Illinois U.S.A.
107 K5 **Elmwood** Oklahoma U.S.A.
99 O5 **Elmwood** Wisconsin U.S.A.
18 G10 **Elne** France
71 D5 **El Nido** Philippines
118 D7 **Elnora** Alberta Canada
110 J3 **Elnora** Indiana U.S.A.
86 F3 **El Obeid** Sudan
111 G12 **Eloi Bay** Louisiana U.S.A.
80 D1 **Elon** Israel
80 E5 **Elon Moré** Jordan
110 K6 **Elora** Tennessee U.S.A.
20 B5 **Elorn** *R* France
128 C4 **El Oro** *prov* Ecuador
125 J8 **El Oro** Mexico
124 F6 **Elota** Mexico
103 N9 **Eloy** Arizona U.S.A.
124 G5 **El Palmito** Mexico
128 F2 **El Pao** Venezuela
16 E4 **El Pardo** Spain
99 R9 **El Paso** Illinois U.S.A.
108 A4 **El Paso** Texas U.S.A.
131 B4 **El Peñón** *pk* Chile
14 C3 **Elphin** Ireland
141 J5 **Elphinstone** Queensland Australia
119 R8 **Elphinstone** Manitoba Canada
127 N9 **El Pilar** Venezuela
133 E2 **El Pintado** Argentina
83 K11 **Elpitiya** Sri Lanka
102 E4 **El Portal** California U.S.A.
128 C5 **El Portugues** Peru
108 B4 **El Porvenir** Mexico
16 D5 **El Puente del Arzobispo** Spain
16 C8 **El Puerto de Sta. Maria** Spain
80 D5 **Elqana** Jordan
80 E1 **El Qouzah** Lebanon
131 B2 **Elqui** *R* Chile
79 E8 **El Quşeima** Egypt
79 F9 **El Quweira** Jordan
124 G6 **El Regocijo** Mexico
108 F7 **El Remolino** Mexico
125 J6 **El Retorno** Mexico
116 N5 **Elridge Glacier** Alaska U.S.A.
106 D5 **El Rito** New Mexico U.S.A.
16 C7 **El Ronquillo** Spain
99 M4 **Elrosa** Minnesota U.S.A.
118 J7 **Elrose** Saskatchewan Canada
99 Q6 **Elroy** Wisconsin U.S.A.
124 H6 **El Rucio** Mexico
117 F4 **Elsa** Yukon Territory Canada
42 D5 **Elsa** *R* Italy
109 K9 **Elsa** Texas U.S.A.
124 G6 **El Salto** Mexico
125 P11 **El Salvador** *rep* Central America
71 G6 **El Salvador** Mindanao Philippines
120 H4 **Elsas** Ontario Canada
108 A6 **El Sauz** Mexico
109 J9 **El Sauz** Texas U.S.A.
25 E4 **Elsberg** *hill* Netherlands
110 F2 **Elsberry** Missouri U.S.A.
32 K6 **Elsdorf** Germany
32 H8 **Else** *R* Germany
22 L3 **Elsenborn** Belgium
36 F5 **Elsenz** *R* Germany
140 C2 **Elsey** N Terr Australia
26 G5 **Elsfjord** Norway
32 H6 **Elsfleth** Germany
98 E9 **Elsie** Nebraska U.S.A.
100 B4 **Elsie** Oregon U.S.A.
103 M3 **Elsinore** Utah U.S.A.
102 G8 **Elsinore L** California U.S.A.
25 E7 **Elsloo** Netherlands
98 F7 **Elsmere** Nebraska U.S.A.
107 P4 **Elsmore** Kansas U.S.A.
33 Q9 **Elsnigk** Germany
130 C10 **El Soberbio** Argentina
127 M10 **El Socorro** Venezuela
127 L10 **El Sombrero** Venezuela
116 K1 **Elson Lagoon** Alaska U.S.A.
25 E4 **Elspeet** Netherlands
25 E5 **Elst** Netherlands
9 F5 **Elstead** England
33 R9 **Elster** Germany
33 Q10 **Elster** *R* Germany
37 N2 **Elsterberg** Germany
33 T10 **Elsterwerda** Germany
145 F3 **Elsthorpe** New Zealand
9 F4 **Elstree** England
108 A6 **El Sueco** Mexico
124 G8 **El Tabaco** Mexico
16 C2 **El Teleno** *mt* Spain
25 F5 **Elten** Germany
37 O2 **Elterlein** Germany
9 G5 **Eltham** England
145 E3 **Eltham** New Zealand
79 E9 **El Thamad** Egypt
128 F2 **El Tigre** Venezuela
9 F3 **Eltisley** England
37 K4 **Eltmann** Germany
128 E2 **El Tocuyo** Venezuela
109 P5 **Elton** Louisiana U.S.A.
100 G3 **Eltopia** Washington U.S.A.
133 C3 **El toro** Chile
102 G8 **El Toro** California U.S.A.
133 C3 **El Tránsito** Chile
124 C2 **El Tren** Mexico
124 D6 **El Triunfo** Mexico
118 K1 **Eltrut L** Ontario Canada
127 O2 **El Tucuche** *mt* Trinidad
133 C8 **El Turbio** Argentina
36 E3 **Eltville** Germany
76 E2 **Eluru** India
119 Q9 **Elva** Manitoba Canada
52 C5 **Elva** Estonia
106 D5 **El Vado** New Mexico U.S.A.
128 C2 **El Valle** Colombia
127 L9 **El Valle** Venezuela
12 E3 **Elvanfoot** Scotland
79 E2 **Elvanlı** Turkey
27 E10 **Elvdal** Norway
26 N2 **Elvebakken** Norway
20 E6 **Elven** France
27 E11 **Elverum** Norway
125 L3 **El Viejo** Nicaragua
128 D2 **El Vigia** Venezuela
128 D5 **Elvira** Brazil
114 J3 **Elvira,C** Northwest Territories Canada
142 B5 **Elvire, Mt** W Australia Australia
143 C8 **Elvire, Mt** W Australia Australia
142 G4 **Elvire, R** W Australia Australia
44 D1 **Elvo** *R* Italy
133 C4 **El Volcán** Chile
86 H5 **El Wak** Kenya
101 O1 **Elwell, L** *res* Montana U.S.A.
99 S8 **Elwood** Illinois U.S.A.
94 B6 **Elwood** Indiana U.S.A.
110 B2 **Elwood** Missouri U.S.A.
98 G9 **Elwood** Nebraska U.S.A.
9 G3 **Ely** England
99 P8 **Ely** Iowa U.S.A.
99 P2 **Ely** Minnesota U.S.A.
103 K2 **Ely** Nevada U.S.A.
80 D3 **Elyaqim** Israel
138 C3 **Ely Hill** South Australia Australia
99 N5 **Elysian** Minnesota U.S.A.
36 E3 **Elz** Germany
40 H1 **Elz** *R* Germany
36 E7 **Elzach** Germany
124 G5 **El Zape** Mexico
32 L7 **Elze** Germany
27 G10 **Emådalen** Sweden
137 O5 **Émaé** *isld* Vanuatu
77 D1 **Emāmrūd** Iran
27 H14 **Emån** *R* Sweden
50 E4 **Emba** *R* Kazakhstan
57 A1 **Emba** Kazakhstan
122 G1 **Embar** Labrador, Nfld Canada
133 E2 **Embarcación** Argentina
110 H2 **Embarras** *R* Illinois U.S.A.
117 R6 **Embarras Portage** Alberta Canada
99 O2 **Embarrass** Minnesota U.S.A.
98 J3 **Embden** North Dakota U.S.A.
60 P1 **Embetsu** Japan
128 D5 **Embira** *R* Brazil
101 R5 **Emblem** Wyoming U.S.A.
13 G3 **Embleton** England
47 U14 **Embóna** Rhodes Greece
121 P7 **Embrun** Ontario Canada
88 F2 **Embu** Kenya
32 F6 **Emden** Germany
99 R9 **Emden** Illinois U.S.A.
67 A2 **Emei** China
67 A2 **Emei Shan** *mt* China
80 F1 **Emeq Ḩula** Israel
80 D2 **'Emeq Ẕevulun** Israel
98 J2 **Emerado** North Dakota U.S.A.
141 J6 **Emerald** Queensland Australia
114 H2 **Emerald I** Northwest Territories Canada
71 D5 **Emergency Pt** Philippines
142 E3 **Emeriau Pt** W Australia Australia
115 N7 **Emeril** Labrador, Nfld Canada
119 U9 **Emerson** Manitoba Canada
99 L8 **Emerson** Iowa U.S.A.
98 K7 **Emerson** Nebraska U.S.A.
98 J6 **Emery** South Dakota U.S.A.
47 K5 **Emet** Turkey
101 P4 **Emigrant** Montana U.S.A.
102 D2 **Emigrant Gap** California U.S.A.
100 J9 **Emigrant Pass** Nevada U.S.A.
101 P4 **Emigrant Pk** Montana U.S.A.
103 J4 **Emigrant Valley** Nevada U.S.A.
86 C2 **Emi Koussi** *mt* Chad
42 D4 **Emilia-Romagna** *prov* Italy
40 F6 **Emilius, M** Italy
57 L2 **Emin** China
66 C2 **Emin** China
47 J2 **Emine,N** Bulgaria
94 B8 **Eminence** Kentucky U.S.A.
110 E4 **Eminence** Missouri U.S.A.
47 J2 **Eminska Planina** *plateau* Bulgaria
47 K7 **Emir** *R* Turkey
78 C2 **Emirdag** Turkey
139 J7 **Emita** Flinders I, Tasmania Australia
94 H5 **Emlenton** Pennsylvania U.S.A.
32 E7 **Emlichheim** Germany
27 H15 **Emmaboda** Sweden
126 B1 **Emmastad** Curaçao
27 N13 **Emmaste** Estonia
95 M6 **Emmaus** Pennsylvania U.S.A.
139 K3 **Emmaville** New South Wales Australia
40 G4 **Emme** *R* Switzerland
118 L3 **Emmeline L** Saskatchewan Canada
25 E3 **Emmeloord** Netherlands
25 G3 **Emmen** Netherlands
41 H3 **Emmen** Switzerland
40 G4 **Emmen Tal** Switzerland
25 F5 **Emmerich** Germany
28 B7 **Emmerlev** Denmark
32 K8 **Emmern** Germany
38 M5 **Emmersdorf** Austria
28 B7 **Emmerske** Denmark
32 K9 **Emmerthal** Germany
32 K8 **Emmerthal** Germany
141 G6 **Emmet** Queensland Australia
100 J6 **Emmet** Idaho U.S.A.
98 H7 **Emmet** Nebraska U.S.A.
99 M6 **Emmetsburg** Iowa U.S.A.
107 O2 **Emmett** Kansas U.S.A.
76 C3 **Emmiganuru** India
95 K7 **Emmitsburg** Maryland U.S.A.
103 O1 **Emmons,Mt** Utah U.S.A.
99 N1 **Emo** Ontario Canada
48 F3 **Emöd** Hungary
109 M3 **Emory** Texas U.S.A.
108 D6 **Emory Pk** Texas U.S.A.
124 D4 **Empalme** Mexico
89 G7 **Empangeni** S Africa
32 K7 **Empede** Germany
133 F3 **Empedrado** Argentina
25 F5 **Empel** Germany
112 D5 **Empire** Georgia U.S.A.
99 U5 **Empire** Michigan U.S.A.
100 F9 **Empire** Nevada U.S.A.
100 A6 **Empire** Oregon U.S.A.
106 F1 **Empire Res** Colorado U.S.A.
42 D5 **Empoli** Italy
107 O3 **Emporia** Kansas U.S.A.
94 K10 **Emporia** Virginia U.S.A.
94 J5 **Emporium** Pennsylvania U.S.A.
118 G8 **Empress** Alberta Canada
22 J3 **Emptinne** Belgium
19 N14 **Empurany** France
98 G2 **Emrick** North Dakota U.S.A.
32 F6 **Ems** *R* Germany
32 F8 **Emsbüren** Germany
32 F9 **Emscher** *R* Germany
121 L7 **Emsdale** Ontario Canada
32 G8 **Emsdetten** Germany
32 G6 **Ems-Jade Kanal** Germany
37 K4 **Emskirchen** Germany
32 F7 **Emslage** Germany
36 G1 **Emstal** Germany
32 H7 **Emstek** Germany
9 F6 **Emsworth** England
65 G3 **Emu** China
141 F3 **Emu Ck** Queensland Australia
61 L10 **Ena** Japan
27 J10 **Enånger** Sweden
80 D4 **'Enav** Jordan
80 C3 **'En Ayyala** Israel
101 T8 **Encampment** Wyoming U.S.A.
17 H4 **Encanade** *mt* Spain
108 B6 **Encantada** Mexico
124 B2 **Encantada, Cerro de la** Mexico
131 H3 **Encantadas,Sa** *mts* Brazil
124 C4 **Encantado, Cerro** *mt* Mexico
71 E3 **Encanto,C** Luzon Philippines
124 H7 **Encarnación** Mexico
130 C10 **Encarnación** Paraguay
118 E8 **Enchant** Alberta Canada
85 D7 **Enchi** Ghana
106 C5 **Encinada Mesa** *tableland* New Mexico U.S.A.
109 H7 **Encinal** Texas U.S.A.
108 A6 **Encinillas** Mexico
102 G8 **Encinitas** California U.S.A.
108 B1 **Encino** New Mexico U.S.A.
108 B2 **Encinoso** New Mexico U.S.A.
128 D2 **Encontrados** Venezuela
138 E6 **Encounter B** South Australia Australia
133 G4 **Encruzilhada do Sul** Brazil
48 G2 **Encs** Hungary
117 L8 **Endako** British Columbia Canada
69 F11 **Endau** *R* Malaysia
69 F11 **Endau** Malaysia
71 K9 **Ende** *isld* Flores Indonesia
99 R6 **Endeavor** Wisconsin U.S.A.
141 H3 **Endeavour** Queensland Australia
119 P6 **Endeavour** Saskatchewan Canada
141 F1 **Endeavour Str** Queensland Australia
108 A8 **Endee** New Mexico U.S.A.
71 K9 **Endeh** Indonesia
28 E5 **Endelave** Denmark
134 K8 **Enderbury I** Phoenix Is Pacific Oc
117 O10 **Enderby** British Columbia Canada
142 B5 **Enderby I** W Australia Australia
146 J10 **Enderby Land** Antarctica
98 J3 **Enderlin** North Dakota U.S.A.
98 E9 **Enders Res** Nebraska U.S.A.
118 E7 **Endiang** Alberta Canada
95 L4 **Endicott** New York U.S.A.
100 H3 **Endicott** Washington U.S.A.
117 G7 **Endicott Arm** *pen* Alaska U.S.A.
116 L3 **Endicott Mts** Alaska U.S.A.
117 G4 **End,Mt** Yukon Territory Canada
8 D1 **Endon** England
80 E3 **'En Dor** Israel
140 C1 **Endyalgout I** N Terr Australia
128 D6 **Ene** *R* Peru
143 B8 **Eneabba** W Australia Australia
55 C5 **Energetik** Russian Federation
54 F9 **Energodar** Ukraine
134 G7 **Enewetak** *atoll* Marshall Is Pacific Oc
47 H4 **Enez** Turkey
78 A1 **Enez** Turkey
79 F4 **Enfe** Lebanon
43 C12 **Enfida** Tunisia
122 J9 **Enfield** Nova Scotia Canada
9 F4 **Enfield** England
110 H3 **Enfield** Illinois U.S.A.
95 P3 **Enfield** New Hampshire U.S.A.
112 K1 **Enfield** North Carolina U.S.A.
127 K5 **Engaño, C** Dominican Rep
71 E1 **Engaño,C** Luzon Philippines
60 R1 **Engaru** Japan
28 B7 **Enge** Germany
80 E8 **En Gedi** Israel
41 H4 **Engelberg** Switzerland
112 M2 **Engelhard** North Carolina U.S.A.
38 J5 **Engelhartszell** Austria
53 G8 **Engel's** Russian Federation
36 C2 **Engelskirchen** Germany
41 J2 **Engen** Germany
130 C4 **Engenho** Brazil
138 D3 **Engenina** *R* South Australia Australia
32 J8 **Enger** Germany
26 E10 **Engerdal** Norway
27 F10 **Engeren,L** Norway
36 D3 **Engers** Germany
28 C4 **Engesvang** Denmark
80 F2 **'En Gev** Israel
Enghien *see* **Edingen**
21 P4 **Enghien-les-Bains** France
117 F6 **Engineer** British Columbia Canada
22 J2 **Engis** Belgium
70 B4 **Engkilili** Sarawak
8 D3 **England** U.K.
111 E7 **England** Arkansas U.S.A.
106 C8 **Engle** New Mexico U.S.A.
123 Q3 **Englee** Newfoundland Canada
119 N6 **Englefield** Saskatchewan Canada
117 K10 **Englewood** British Columbia Canada
106 F2 **Englewood** Colorado U.S.A.
113 E11 **Englewood** Florida U.S.A.
107 L4 **Englewood** Kansas U.S.A.
112 C2 **Englewood** Tennessee U.S.A.
110 K3 **English** Indiana U.S.A.
122 E4 **English Bay** Quebec Canada
116 L7 **English Bay** Alaska U.S.A.
7 H13 **English Channel** England/France
146 C6 **English Coast** Antarctica
140 D1 **English Company's Is** N Terr Australia
127 P4 **English Harbour Town** Antigua W Indies
123 R6 **English Harbour W** Newfoundland Canada
119 N1 **English River** Ontario Canada
52 D2 **Engozero** Russian Federation
36 G7 **Engstingen** Germany
17 G6 **Énguera** Spain
52 B6 **Engure** Latvia
80 D3 **'En Ha'Emeq** Israel
80 D2 **'En HaMifraẕ** Israel
80 E3 **'En Ḩarod** Israel
79 F8 **'En Hazeva** Israel
80 C3 **'En Hod** Israel
98 B2 **Enid** Montana U.S.A.
107 N5 **Enid** Oklahoma U.S.A.
111 G7 **Enid L** Mississippi U.S.A.
142 B5 **Enid, Mt** W Australia Australia
118 A3 **Enilda** Alberta Canada
36 G7 **Eningen** Germany
60 P3 **Eniwa** Japan
60 P3 **Eniwa dake** *mt* Japan
85 C5 **Enji** Mauritania
80 C3 **'En Karmel** Israel
36 D5 **Enkenbach-Alsenborn** Germany
25 D3 **Enkhuizen** Netherlands
36 C4 **Enkirch** Germany
27 J12 **Enköping** Sweden
128 G8 **En Madrejón** Paraguay
114 J5 **Ennadai** Northwest Territories Canada
86 E3 **En Nahud** Sudan
86 D2 **Ennedi** *plateau* Chad
14 D3 **Ennell,L** Ireland
32 F10 **Ennepetal** Germany
127 H5 **Ennery** Haiti
139 H3 **Enngonia** New South Wales Australia
32 H9 **Ennigerloh** Germany
98 D5 **Enning** South Dakota U.S.A.
27 E13 **Enningdal** Norway
14 C4 **Ennis** Ireland
101 O4 **Ennis** Montana U.S.A.
109 L3 **Ennis** Texas U.S.A.
14 E4 **Enniscorthy** Ireland
14 D2 **Enniskillen** N Ireland
14 B4 **Ennistimon** Ireland
80 D1 **Enn Nâqoûra** Lebanon
38 K6 **Ennstaler Alpen** *mts* Austria
80 G4 **En Nu'eiyima** Jordan
29 P9 **Eno** Finland
108 E2 **Enochs** Texas U.S.A.
141 K1 **Enoggera** *dist* Brisbane, Qnsld Australia
69 F13 **Enok** Sumatra
98 J8 **Enola** Nebraska U.S.A.
29 O9 **Enonkoski** Finland
29 K3 **Enontekiö** Finland
112 F3 **Enoree** *R* South Carolina U.S.A.
112 F3 **Enoree** South Carolina U.S.A.
95 P2 **Enosburg Falls** Vermont U.S.A.
67 D5 **Enping** China
70 F6 **Enrekang** Sulawesi
71 E2 **Enrile** Luzon Philippines
127 J5 **Enriquillo, Lago de** Dominican Rep
25 E3 **Ens** Netherlands
139 J6 **Ensay** Victoria Australia
25 G4 **Enschede** Netherlands
36 B5 **Ensdorf** Germany
32 H10 **Ense** Germany
133 F4 **Ensenada** Argentina
124 A2 **Ensenada** Mexico
106 D5 **Ensenada** New Mexico U.S.A.
126 B3 **Ensenada de Guadiana** *B* Cuba
36 C5 **Ensheim** Germany
80 D4 **'En Shemer** Israel
67 C1 **Enshi** China
118 D8 **Ensign** Alberta Canada
107 K4 **Ensign** Kansas U.S.A.
99 U4 **Ensign** Michigan U.S.A.
19 K5 **Ensisheim** France
28 F4 **Enslev** Denmark
9 E4 **Enstone** England
86 F5 **Entebbe** Uganda
37 N4 **Entenbühl** *mt* Germany
12 E3 **Enterkinfoot** Scotland
117 P5 **Enterprise** Northwest Territories Canada
121 O8 **Enterprise** Ontario Canada
111 L10 **Enterprise** Alabama U.S.A.
107 N3 **Enterprise** Kansas U.S.A.
111 H9 **Enterprise** Mississippi U.S.A.
100 H4 **Enterprise** Oregon U.S.A.
103 L4 **Enterprise** Utah U.S.A.
71 D5 **Enterprise Pt** Philippines
100 E2 **Entiat Mts** Washington U.S.A.
70 C4 **Entimau, Bt** *mt* Sarawak
17 F8 **Entinas,Pta. De Las** Spain
133 D8 **Entrada,Pta** Argentina
18 H5 **Entrains** France
21 J6 **Entrammes** France
140 A3 **Entrance I** N Terr Australia
18 G8 **Entraygues** France
143 B10 **Entrecasteaux, Pt.d'** W Australia Australia
137 N5 **Entrecasteaux, Récifs D'** *reefs* New Caledonia
83 J14 **Entre-Deux** Réunion Indian Oc
123 L6 **Entré, I. d'** Madeleine Is, Quebec Canada
129 H5 **Entre Rios** Brazil
130 G7 **Entre Rios de Minas** Brazil
36 F6 **Entringen** Germany
103 M7 **Entro** Arizona U.S.A.
89 E2 **Entuba** Zimbabwe
118 C5 **Entwistle** Alberta Canada
85 F7 **Enugu** Nigeria
100 D2 **Enumclaw** Washington U.S.A.
21 N2 **Envermeu** France
27 H11 **Enviken** Sweden
8 D3 **Enville** England
128 D5 **Envira** Brazil
67 B1 **Enyang** China
48 E4 **Enying** Hungary
144 C5 **Enys, Mt** New Zealand
36 F6 **Enz** *R* Germany
45 H2 **Enza** *R* Italy
80 E8 **'En Ẕafẕafa** Israel
61 M10 **Enzan** Japan
37 M6 **Enzelhausen** Germany
36 E6 **Enzklösterle** Germany
80 B7 **En Ẕurim** Israel
36 F6 **Enzweihingen** Germany
111 D11 **Eola** Louisiana U.S.A.
110 E2 **Eolia** Missouri U.S.A.
21 L3 **Epaignes** France
45 P8 **Epameo, M** *mt* Italy

21 K4 Epaney France
46 F4 Epanomi Greece
32 F8 Epe Germany
25 E4 Epe Netherlands
133 E5 Epecuén,L Argentina
22 E3 Epéhy France
140 D5 Epenarra N Terr Australia
22 C2 Éperlecques France
18 H3 Épernay France
87 B9 Epernbe Namibia
21 O4 Épernon France
111 H9 Epes Alabama U.S.A.
21 J8 Epesses, les France
36 C7 Epfig France
138 E2 Ephemeral Lakes South Australia Australia
103 N2 Ephraim Utah U.S.A.
95 L6 Ephrata Pennsylvania U.S.A.
100 F2 Ephrata Washington U.S.A.
137 O5 Épi isld Vanuatu
88 G10 Epidendron isld Mozambique
46 F7 Epidhavros Greece
21 O6 Epieds France
17 G3 Épila Spain
19 K4 Epinal France
20 F8 Epine, l' Vendée France
20 G5 Epiniac France
98 J6 Epiphany South Dakota U.S.A.
79 C4 Episkopi Cyprus
21 O4 Epône France
36 B5 Eppelborn Germany
37 P2 Eppendorf Germany
22 F4 Eppes France
22 G3 Eppe-Sauvage France
9 G4 Epping England
95 Q3 Epping New Hampshire U.S.A.
98 C1 Epping North Dakota U.S.A.
36 F5 Eppingen Germany
36 E3 Eppstein Germany
98 A4 Epsie Montana U.S.A.
9 F5 Epsom England
21 M6 Epuisay France
87 C10 Epukiro Namibia
13 H6 Epworth England
99 Q7 Epworth Iowa U.S.A.
77 C4 Eqlīd Iran
110 H4 Equality Illinois U.S.A.
86 D5 Equateur prov Zaire
86 E4 Equatoria prov Sudan
73 L9 Equatorial Chan Maldives
85 F8 Equatorial Guinea rep W Africa
20 G2 Equeurdreville France
95 M5 Equmunk Pennsylvania U.S.A.
60 O4 Era Japan
86 E4 Era watercourse Sudan
141 H7 Erac R Queensland Australia
71 C6 Eran Palawan Philippines
71 C6 Eran Bay Palawan Philippines
111 D12 Erath Louisiana U.S.A.
78 F1 Erbaa Turkey
36 D5 Erbach R Germany
36 H7 Erbach Baden-Württemberg Germany
36 G4 Erbach Hessen Germany
86 G1 Erba, Jebel mt Sudan
37 N4 Erbendorf Germany
135 N4 Erben Tablemount Pacific Oc
36 C4 Erbes Kopf mt Germany
20 H6 Erbray France
22 D4 Ercheu France
78 J2 Erciş Turkey
78 E2 Erciyas Dag Turkey
45 Q8 Ercolana Italy
48 E3 Ercsi Hungary
48 E3 Erd Hungary
65 H2 Erdaohezi China
65 G3 Erdao Jiang R China
47 J4 Erdek Turkey
47 J4 Erdek Körfezi B Turkey
79 E2 Erdemli Turkey
56 F6 Erdenet Mongolia
20 D6 Erdeven France
86 D2 Erdi dist Chad
37 M7 Erding Germany
37 M7 Erdinger Moos marsh Germany
9 E2 Erdington England
37 P2 Erdmansdorf Germany
36 B3 Erdorf Germany
20 H6 Erdre R France
20 F5 Éréac France
128 F2 Erebato R Venezuela
146 D11 Erebus, Mt vol Ross I Antarctica
78 K6 Erech Iraq
130 D10 Erechim Brazil
58 G2 Ereentsav Mongolia
Ereğli see Marmaraereğlisi
78 C1 Ereğli Turkey
71 H7 Ereke Indonesia
47 L7 Eren R Turkey
47 K8 Eren Dağ mt Turkey
65 D2 Eren Gobi China
65 B3 Erenhot China
Erenköy see İntepe
47 N11 Erenköy Turkey
129 G4 Erepecu, L Brazil
16 D3 Eresma R Spain
47 H5 Eressós Greece
80 B7 Erez Israel
22 K3 Erezée Belgium
32 K4 Erfde Germany
89 E7 Erfenis Dam res S Africa
65 A4 Erfenzi China
85 D2 Erfoud Morocco
36 B2 Erft R Germany
36 B2 Erftstadt Germany
37 L2 Erfurt Germany
56 D4 Ergak-Targak-Tayga, Khrebet mts Russian Federation
78 G2 Ergani Turkey
85 D4 Erg Chech desert region Mali/Algeria
86 C2 Erg du Djourab dist Chad
65 A3 Ergel Mongolia
47 H3 Ergene R Turkey
85 D3 Erg er Raoui desert region Algeria
85 C3 Erg Iguid sand desert Algeria/Mauritania
55 E1 Erginskiy Sor, Oz L Russian Federation
52 C6 Ērgli Latvia
37 N6 Ergolding Germany
37 N6 Ergoldsbach Germany
65 G1 Ergu China
20 B6 Ergué-Armel France
86 C3 Erguig R Chad
Ergun He R see Argun R
59 H1 Ergun Youqi China
59 H1 Ergun Zuoqi China
37 O7 Erharting Germany
16 D2 Eria R Spain
86 G2 Eriba Sudan
16 A6 Ericeira Portugal
32 K7 Erichshagen Germany
107 L6 Erick Oklahoma U.S.A.
119 S8 Erickson Manitoba Canada
122 G2 Eric L Quebec Canada
99 N1 Ericsburg Minnesota U.S.A.
98 H8 Ericson Nebraska U.S.A.
98 A9 Erie Colorado U.S.A.
99 Q8 Erie Illinois U.S.A.
107 P4 Erie Kansas U.S.A.
94 D5 Erie Michigan U.S.A.
103 J6 Erie Nevada U.S.A.
98 J2 Erie North Dakota U.S.A.
94 G4 Erie Pennsylvania U.S.A.
120 J10 Erieau Ontario Canada
94 G4 Erie,L U.S.A./Canada
79 H1 Erikli Turkey
47 O12 Erikoúsa isld Greece
119 T8 Eriksdale Manitoba Canada
46 E7 Erímanthos mt Greece
60 R4 Erimo-misaki C Japan
22 C3 Erin France
37 P7 Ering Germany
27 H15 Eringsboda Sweden
127 N3 Erin Pt Trinidad
15 A3 Eriskay isld Scotland
9 G5 Erith England
46 F6 Erithraí Greece
Eritrea see Ertra
25 F6 Erkelenz Germany
27 K12 Erken Sweden
33 T8 Erkner Germany
86 G2 Erkowit Sudan
32 E10 Erkrath Germany
38 F6 Erl Austria
Erlangdiang see Dawu
37 L4 Erlangen Germany
94 C7 Erlanger Kentucky U.S.A.
38 M5 Erlauf R Austria
37 N3 Erlbach Germany
140 C7 Erldunda N Terr Australia
36 F3 Erlensee Germany
111 C8 Erling,L Arkansas U.S.A.
65 G3 Erlong Shan mt China
38 F8 Erlsbach Austria
25 E4 Ermelo Netherlands
89 F6 Ermelo S Africa
78 D3 Ermenek Turkey
79 D2 Ermenek R Turkey
71 M9 Ermera Indonesia
Ermoúpolis see Síros
33 O9 Ermsleben Germany
138 B2 Ernabella South Australia Australia
138 B2 Ernabella R South Australia Australia
76 C6 Ernakulam India
36 E1 Erndtebrück Germany
14 C2 Erne R Ireland
21 J5 Ernée France
21 J5 Ernée R France
14 D2 Erne,L.Lower N Ireland
14 D2 Erne,L.Upper N Ireland
143 E7 Ernest Giles Ra W Australia Australia
144 A7 Ernest Is New Zealand
135 M12 Ernest Legouve Reef Pacific Oc
117 G8 Ernest Sd Alaska U.S.A.
118 L8 Ernfold Saskatchewan Canada
45 O6 Ernici, Monti mt Italy
36 G4 Ernstthal Germany
76 C5 Erode India
78 J2 Erois Turkey
141 G7 Eromanga Queensland Australia
111 D9 Eros Louisiana U.S.A.
36 B2 Erp Germany
22 G3 Erquelinnes Belgium
20 F4 Erquy France
20 F4 Erquy, C.d' France
143 B7 Errabiddy Hills W Australia Australia
85 D2 Er Rachidia Morocco
86 F3 Er Rahad Sudan
80 G6 Er Rajib Jordan
88 F10 Errego Mozambique
14 C1 Errigal mt Ireland
28 G7 Errindlev Denmark
14 A2 Erris Hd Ireland
28 D5 Erritsø Denmark
111 G12 Errol I Louisiana U.S.A.
137 O5 Erromango isld Vanuatu
86 F3 Er Roseires Sudan
46 D4 Ersekë Albania
118 E6 Erskine Alberta Canada
142 F4 Erskine, Mount W Australia Australia
26 M6 Ersnäs Sweden
36 D7 Erstein France
19 L4 Ersteir France
36 H3 Erthal Germany
54 M5 Ertil' Russian Federation
66 D2 Ertix He R China
86 G2 Ertra prov Ethiopia
47 J5 Ertugrul Turkey
22 F1 Ertvelde Belgium
145 E3 Erua New Zealand
138 E4 Erudina South Australia Australia
27 H12 Ervalla Sweden
21 K6 Erve R France
37 Q2 Ervěnice Czechoslovakia
22 D3 Ervillers France
112 J2 Erwin North Carolina U.S.A.
112 E1 Erwin Tennessee U.S.A.
32 H9 Erwitte Germany
119 P6 Erwood Saskatchewan Canada
8 C3 Erwood Wales
33 O8 Erxleben Germany
46 D3 Erzen R Albania
37 N3 Erzgebirge Germany
56 E5 Erzin Russian Federation
79 G2 Erzin Turkey
78 G2 Erzincan Turkey
78 H2 Erzurum Turkey
52 B6 Erzvilkas Lithuania
60 P4 Esan-misaki C Japan
21 J3 Esaue R France
28 A6 Esbjerg Denmark
107 M2 Esbon Kansas U.S.A.
17 G2 Esca R Spain
18 E10 Esca R Spain
130 J10 Escada Brazil
103 N4 Escalante R Utah U.S.A.
103 N4 Escalante Utah U.S.A.
103 L4 Escalante Des Utah U.S.A.
131 A8 Escalera,Pta Chile
124 G4 Escalón Mexico
16 E4 Escalona Spain
111 J11 Escambia R Florida U.S.A.
99 T3 Escanaba R Michigan U.S.A.
99 T4 Escanaba Michigan U.S.A.
125 O8 Escárcega Mexico
21 H7 Escarpière, l' France
22 E3 Escaut R France
36 E3 Esch Germany
22 L5 Esch Luxembourg
36 G4 Eschau Germany
36 F3 Eschborn Germany
22 K4 Eschdorf Luxembourg
32 E7 Eschebrügge Germany
32 M7 Eschede Germany
37 L4 Eschenau Germany
37 M4 Eschenbach Germany
36 E2 Eschenberg Germany
32 L9 Eschershausen Germany
40 G4 Escholzmatt Switzerland
116 G3 Eschscholtz B Alaska U.S.A.
22 K4 Esch-sur-la-Sûre Luxembourg
37 J1 Eschwege Germany
25 F7 Eschweiler Germany
127 K5 Escocesa, B Dominican Rep
130 H5 Escondido Brazil
102 G8 Escondido California U.S.A.
20 F7 Escoublac France
122 C5 Escoumins,R Quebec Canada
21 P5 Escrennes France
13 G6 Escrick England
124 G6 Escuinapa de Hidalgo Mexico
122 F5 Escuminac Quebec Canada
122 H6 Escuminac, Pt New Brunswick Canada
86 B5 Eséka Cameroon
Eşen see Kestep
47 N10 Esenceli Turkey
32 G5 Esens Germany
17 H2 Esera R Spain
77 B3 Eşfahān Iran
16 E3 Esgueva R Spain
80 B8 Eshbol Israel
80 B8 Eshel Ha Nasi Israel
9 F5 Esher England
77 L1 Eshkamesh Afghanistan
57 F6 Eshkāshem Afghanistan
87 F11 Eshowe S Africa
Esh Shem see Dimashq
77 B2 Eshtehard Iran
80 D8 Eshtemoa Jordan
87 E10 Esigodini Zimbabwe
42 E5 Esino R Italy
141 K7 Esk Queensland Australia
139 H8 Esk R Tasmania Australia
116 N6 Eska Alaska U.S.A.
118 L8 Eskbank Saskatchewan Canada
145 F3 Eskdale New Zealand
13 E5 Eskdale Green England
14 C2 Eske, L Ireland
47 K7 Eskere Turkey
29 T9 Eskifjordhur Iceland
28 H5 Eskildstrup Denmark
28 H7 Eskilstrup Denmark
27 H12 Eskilstuna Sweden
122 J3 Eskimo I Quebec Canada
114 F4 Eskimo Lakes Northwest Territories Canada
115 K5 Eskimo Point Northwest Territories Canada
78 D1 Eskipazar Turkey
47 L5 Eskişehir Turkey
13 H5 Esk,R England
15 E5 Esk,R Scotland
107 O3 Eskridge Kansas U.S.A.
16 D2 Esla R Spain
16 D3 Esla, Embalse del res Spain
78 L4 Eslamabad-e Gharb Iran
77 G2 Eslām Qal'eh Afghanistan
37 O4 Eslarn Germany
32 H10 Eslohe Germany
27 F16 Eslöv Sweden
47 K6 Eşme Turkey
141 G4 Esmeralda Queensland Australia
126 E4 Esmeralda Cuba
133 B7 Esmeralda, I Chile
128 C3 Esmeraldas Ecuador
98 G1 Esmond North Dakota U.S.A.
98 J5 Esmond South Dakota U.S.A.
120 D2 Esnagami L Ontario Canada
120 F4 Esnagi L Ontario Canada
22 J2 Esnaux Belgium
27 E11 Espa Norway
127 J8 Espada,Pta Colombia
18 G8 Espalion France
17 H6 Espalmador isld Balearic Is
120 J6 Espanola Ontario Canada
128 B8 Española isld Galapagos Is
113 F8 Espanola Florida U.S.A.
106 D6 Espanola New Mexico U.S.A.
19 P17 Esparron France
102 B3 Esparto California U.S.A.
125 M5 Esparza Costa Rica
28 E6 Espe Denmark
27 D10 Espedals-vatn L Norway
32 J8 Espelkamp Germany
116 E3 Espenberg,C Alaska U.S.A.
37 N1 Espenhain Germany
88 F8 Esperança Mozambique
143 D10 Esperance W Australia Australia
143 D10 Esperance B W Australia Australia
146 D3 Esperanza Argentina Base Graham Land Antarctica
131 E3 Esperanza Argentina
124 E4 Esperanza Mexico
113 K7 Esperanza Puerto Rico
108 B4 Esperanza Texas U.S.A.
125 M2 Esperanza, Sa. de la ra Honduras
29 K5 Espergærde Denmark
45 P7 Esperia Italy
16 A6 Espichel,C Portugal
16 D6 Espiel Spain
130 E10 Espigão,Serra do mts Brazil
16 D2 Espigüete mt Spain
128 D6 Espinar Peru
19 Q16 Espinasses France
124 J4 Espinazo Mexico
130 G6 Espinhaço,Serra do mt Brazil
16 B4 Espinho Portugal
131 G2 Espinilho, Serra do ra Brazil
130 G4 Espinosa Brazil
130 H6 Espirito Santo state Brazil
124 D5 Espíritu Santo isld Mexico
137 O5 Espiritu Santo isld Vanuatu
125 Q8 Espíritu Santo, B. del Mexico
133 D8 Espíritu Santo,C Chile/Arg
71 G4 Espiritu Santo,C Philippines
125 P7 Espita Mexico
123 R6 Espoir, B. d' Newfoundland Canada
16 B3 Esposende Portugal
40 D2 Esprels France
87 F10 Espungabera Mozambique
100 F3 Esquatzel Coulee R Washington U.S.A.
124 E2 Esqueda Mexico
133 C6 Esquel Argentina
22 C2 Esquelbecq France
100 B1 Esquimalt British Columbia Canada
117 M11 Esquimalt British Columbia Canada
133 F3 Esquina Argentina
29 K4 Esrum Sø L Denmark
55 D1 Ess R Russian Federation
80 F3 Es Samt Jordan
80 D8 Es Samu Jordan
85 C2 Essaouira Morocco
80 G3 Es Sarih Jordan
21 O4 Essarts-le-Roi, les France
20 H8 Essarts, les Vendée France
21 L4 Essay France
85 E2 Es Seggeur watercourse Algeria
32 L7 Essel Germany
22 G1 Essen Belgium
32 G7 Essen Niedersachsen Germany
32 E10 Essen Nordrhein-Westfalen Germany
37 N6 Essenbach Germany
143 D6 Essendon, Mt W Australia Australia
120 H10 Essex Ontario Canada
9 G4 Essex co England
103 J7 Essex California U.S.A.
95 P5 Essex Connecticut U.S.A.
99 L9 Essex Iowa U.S.A.
101 M1 Essex Montana U.S.A.
95 O2 Essex New York U.S.A.
95 O2 Essex Junct Vermont U.S.A.
94 D3 Essexville Michigan U.S.A.
37 M6 Essing Germany
37 J6 Essingen Germany
36 G6 Esslingen Germany
21 P4 Essonne dept France
21 P5 Essonne R France
52 D4 Essoyla Russian Federation
100 C4 Estacada Oregon U.S.A.
16 B1 Estaca de Bares, Pta. de la Spain
106 G8 Estacado, Llano plain New Mex/Tex U.S.A.
103 K10 Estacion Doctor Mexico
103 K10 Estacion Francesa Mexico
103 K9 Estación Médanos Mexico
133 E8 Estados, I. de los Argentina
18 G10 Estagel France
71 F2 Estagno Pt Luzon Philippines
77 D5 Eşţahbānāt Iran
120 K6 Estaire Ontario Canada
22 D2 Estaires France
129 L6 Estância Brazil
108 A1 Estancia New Mexico U.S.A.
17 F7 Estancias, Sierra de las mts Spain
77 G4 Estand, Kūh-e- mt Iran
125 O9 Estapilla Mexico
16 B4 Estarreja Portugal
18 F10 Estats, Pic d' mt Spain
40 E4 Estavayer le Lac Switzerland
89 F7 Estcourt S Africa
32 L6 Este R Germany
42 D3 Este Italy
125 L3 Estelí Nicaragua
17 F2 Estella Spain
98 K5 Estelline South Dakota U.S.A.
16 D5 Estena R Spain
16 D7 Estepa Spain
16 D8 Estepona Spain
133 G4 Este, Pta. del Uruguay
116 N4 Ester Alaska U.S.A.
98 A7 Esterbrook Wyoming U.S.A.
119 P8 Esterhazy Saskatchewan Canada
18 H4 Esternay France
113 F11 Estero Florida U.S.A.
102 C6 Estero B California U.S.A.
133 C8 Estero Obstrucción Chile
125 K6 Esteros Mexico
133 E2 Esteros Paraguay
133 F3 Esteros del Iberá swamp Argentina
18 F10 Esterri de Aneu Spain
32 G6 Esterwegen Germany
98 A9 Estes Pk Colorado U.S.A.
119 P9 Estevan Saskatchewan Canada
117 J9 Estevan Group islds British Columbia Canada
117 K11 Estevan Point British Columbia Canada
118 G7 Esther Alberta Canada
99 M6 Estherville Iowa U.S.A.
112 F5 Estill South Carolina U.S.A.
18 H4 Estissac France
119 N8 Estlin Saskatchewan Canada
118 J7 Eston Saskatchewan Canada
52 B5 Estonia rep E Europe
Estonskaya S.S.R. see Estonia
16 A6 Estoril Portugal
19 Q17 Estoublon France
22 C2 Estree Blanche France
22 D5 Estrées St. Denis France
133 G4 Estreito Brazil
130 F6 Estrêla do Indaiá Brazil
130 F6 Estrêla do Sul Brazil
16 B4 Estrela, Sa. da mts Portugal
103 M9 Estrella Arizona U.S.A.
102 D6 Estrella R California U.S.A.
103 M8 Estrella,Sierra mt Arizona U.S.A.
129 K6 Estrelto, Serra do mts Brazil
16 A6 Estremadura prov Portugal
16 B6 Estremoz Portugal
129 J5 Estrondo, Serra do mts Brazil
28 E3 Estruplund Denmark
118 H8 Estuary Saskatchewan Canada
28 B3 Estvad Denmark
48 E3 Esztergom Hungary
20 E4 Étables France
138 E3 Etadunna South Australia Australia
115 M2 Etah Greenland
19 J3 Etain France
22 K4 Étalle Belgium
123 N3 Etamamiou,R Quebec Canada
123 N3 Etamamu Quebec Canada
123 N3 Etamamu R Quebec Canada
21 P5 Etampes France
138 F2 Etamunbanie,L South Australia Australia
80 B7 Etan Israel
18 H6 Étang France
123 L6 Étang-du-Nord Madeleine Is, Quebec Canada
22 B2 Étaples France
74 H6 Etawa India
119 V1 Etawney L Manitoba Canada
124 E4 Etchojoa Mexico
20 D6 Etel France
27 K14 Etelhem Gotland Sweden
85 E5 Etelia Mali
32 K7 Etelsen Germany
122 B5 Eternité,L Quebec Canada
146 C5 Eternity Ra Antarctica
98 H6 Ethan South Dakota U.S.A.
22 K4 Ethe Belgium
111 E11 Ethel Louisiana U.S.A.
111 G8 Ethel Mississippi U.S.A.
110 D2 Ethel Missouri U.S.A.
94 F9 Ethel West Virginia U.S.A.
119 R7 Ethelbert Manitoba Canada
140 A5 Ethel Cr N Terr Australia
141 G3 Ethel Cr Queensland Australia
142 D6 Ethel Creek W Australia Australia
143 C6 Ethel R W Australia Australia
111 H8 Ethelsville Alabama U.S.A.
119 N6 Ethelton Saskatchewan Canada
141 G4 Etheridge R Queensland Australia
101 R6 Ethete Wyoming U.S.A.
86 G4 Ethiopia socialist state Africa
101 N1 Ethridge Montana U.S.A.
47 H5 Etili Turkey
40 F5 Etivaz, l' L Switzerland
116 J2 Etivluk R Alaska U.S.A.
27 D10 Etna R Norway
95 S2 Etna Maine U.S.A.
101 M8 Etna Utah U.S.A.
43 F11 Etna, Monte vol Sicily
27 A12 Etne Norway
27 D11 Etnedal Norway
121 L9 Etobicoke Ontario Canada
111 B10 Etoile Texas U.S.A.
116 D6 Etolin,C Alaska U.S.A.
117 G7 Etolin I Alaska U.S.A.
116 E6 Etolin Str Alaska U.S.A.
119 P6 Etomami Saskatchewan Canada
141 J5 Eton Queensland Australia
120 F5 Eton Ontario Canada
9 F5 Eton England
22 K5 Eton France
87 C9 Etosha Nat. Park Namibia
87 C9 Etosha Pan Namibia
112 B3 Etowah R Georgia U.S.A.
112 C2 Etowah Tennessee U.S.A.
22 F4 Etreaupont France
21 P5 Etrechy France
22 E4 Etreillers France
21 O3 Étrépagny France
21 L2 Étretat France
22 F4 Etreux France
22 D3 Étricourt-Manancourt France
40 A4 Etrigny France
46 F2 Etropole Bulgaria
22 F3 Etrœungt France
22 L4 Ettelbrück Luxembourg
36 D7 Ettenheim Germany
25 C5 Etten-Leur Netherlands
37 L1 Ettersburg Germany
100 A9 Ettersburg California U.S.A.
37 J2 Etterwinden Germany
9 E3 Ettington England
37 O6 Ettling Germany
36 E6 Ettlingen Germany
142 C5 Ettrick W Australia Australia
144 B6 Ettrick New Zealand
99 P5 Ettrick Wisconsin U.S.A.
15 E5 Ettrick Pen mt Scotland
13 E3 Ettrick Water Scotland
80 G6 Et Tuneib Jordan
80 G3 Et Turra Jordan
26 N5 Etu-Aapua mt Sweden
9 E2 Etwall England
124 G7 Etzatlán Mexico
37 P1 Etzdorf Germany
118 F9 Etzikom Alberta Canada
118 F9 Etzikom Coulee R Alberta Canada
21 N1 Eu France
137 S6 'Eua isld Tonga
139 H5 Euabalong New South Wales Australia
94 C9 Eubank Kentucky U.S.A.
36 H4 Eubigheim Germany
Euboea isld see Évvoia isld
143 G9 Eucla W Australia Australia
98 K2 Euclid Minnesota U.S.A.
94 F5 Euclid Ohio U.S.A.
139 J6 Eucumbene,L New South Wales Australia
122 G3 Eudites,L.des Quebec Canada
111 E8 Eudora Arkansas U.S.A.
138 E5 Eudunda South Australia Australia
37 J3 Euerdorf Germany
111 L10 Eufala Alabama U.S.A.
107 P6 Eufaula Oklahoma U.S.A.
107 P6 Eufaula L Oklahoma U.S.A.
43 G10 Eufemia,S.,Golfo di Italy
45 L1 Euganei, Colli hills Italy
100 B5 Eugene Oregon U.S.A.
124 B4 Eugenia, Pta C Mexico
130 C8 Eugênio Penzo Brazil
29 K8 Eugmo isld Finland
139 J5 Eugowra New South Wales Australia
37 O1 Eula R Germany
109 N9 Euless Texas U.S.A.
141 H8 Eulo Queensland Australia
112 F6 Eulonia Georgia U.S.A.
139 J4 Eumaungerie New South Wales Australia
16 B1 Eume R Spain
141 J5 Eungella Queensland Australia
111 D11 Eunice Louisiana U.S.A.
108 D3 Eunice New Mexico U.S.A.
22 L2 Eupen Belgium
78 J5 Euphrates R S W Asia
111 G8 Eupora Mississippi U.S.A.
27 M10 Eura Finland
29 J10 Eurajoki Finland
18 F3 Eure dept France
21 N3 Eure R France
18 F4 Eure-et-Loir dept France
115 L1 Eureka Northwest Territories Canada
100 A9 Eureka California U.S.A.
99 R9 Eureka Illinois U.S.A.
107 O4 Eureka Kansas U.S.A.
101 L1 Eureka Montana U.S.A.
103 J2 Eureka Nevada U.S.A.
98 G4 Eureka South Dakota U.S.A.
101 N10 Eureka Utah U.S.A.
100 G3 Eureka Washington U.S.A.
116 O6 Eureka Lodge Alaska U.S.A.
117 O7 Eureka River Alberta Canada
115 L2 Eureka Snd Northwest Territories Canada
110 C5 Eureka Springs Arkansas U.S.A.
102 G4 Eureka Valley California U.S.A.
138 F4 Eurinilla R South Australia Australia
138 F4 Euriowie New South Wales Australia
139 H6 Euroa Victoria Australia
141 J7 Eurombah R Queensland Australia
141 J7 Eurombah Queensland Australia
81 B8 Europa isld Mozambique Chan
16 D8 Europa Pt Gibraltar
25 B5 Europoort Netherlands
61 J11 Eushimi Japan
36 B2 Euskirchen Germany
109 L3 Eustace Texas U.S.A.
113 F9 Eustis Florida U.S.A.
98 F9 Eustis Nebraska U.S.A.
139 G5 Euston New South Wales Australia
111 J9 Eutaw Alabama U.S.A.
112 G4 Eutawville South Carolina U.S.A.
33 N4 Eutin Germany
36 F7 Eutingen Germany
117 K9 Eutsuk L British Columbia Canada
33 R9 Eutzsch Germany
13 F6 Euxton England
111 E10 Eva Louisiana U.S.A.
108 C7 Eva Oklahoma U.S.A.
140 C4 Eva Downs N Terr Australia
87 C9 Evale Angola
99 M5 Evan Minnesota U.S.A.
139 H8 Evandale Tasmania Australia
100 H1 Evans Washington U.S.A.
118 B5 Evansburg Alberta Canada
115 L1 Evans,C Northwest Territories Canada
94 G6 Evans City Pennsylvania U.S.A.
139 L3 Evans Head New South Wales Australia
146 C7 Evans Ice Stream ice stream Antarctica
115 M7 Evans,L Quebec Canada
117 O9 Evans,Mt Alberta Canada
106 E2 Evans,Mt Colorado U.S.A.
101 M3 Evans, Mt Montana U.S.A.
115 L5 Evans Str Northwest Territories Canada
99 T7 Evanston Illinois U.S.A.
101 P8 Evanston Wyoming U.S.A.
120 H7 Evansville Ontario Canada
116 M3 Evansville Alaska U.S.A.
110 G3 Evansville Illinois U.S.A.
110 J3 Evansville Indiana U.S.A.
99 L3 Evansville Minnesota U.S.A.
99 R7 Evansville Wisconsin U.S.A.
101 T7 Evansville Wyoming U.S.A.
109 J4 Evant Texas U.S.A.
94 B3 Evart Michigan U.S.A.
94 D10 Evarts Kentucky U.S.A.
18 G6 Evaux France
47 H5 Evciler Turkey
99 O2 Eveleth Minnesota U.S.A.
138 C3 Evelyn Ck South Australia Australia
140 C2 Evelyn, Mt N Terr Australia
26 J3 Evenes Norway
110 E5 Evening Shade Arkansas U.S.A.
56 D1 Evenkiyskiy Avtonomnyy Okrug dist Russian Federation
80 E1 Even Menaḥem Israel
51 P2 Evensk Russian Federation
80 C4 Even Yehuda Israel
141 G2 Eve Pk Queensland Australia
22 G3 Evêque Belgium
120 B4 Everard Ontario Canada
138 D4 Everard,L South Australia Australia
140 C6 Everard, Mt N Terr Australia
138 B2 Everard,Mt South Australia Australia
138 C2 Everard Ra South Australia Australia
28 H6 Everdrup Denmark
22 G2 Evere Belgium
107 P2 Everest Kansas U.S.A.
75 M5 Everest, Mt China/Nepal
94 J6 Everett Pennsylvania U.S.A.
100 C2 Everett Washington U.S.A.
112 F6 Everett City Georgia U.S.A.
95 O4 Everett, Mt Massachusetts U.S.A.
22 F1 Evergem Belgium
113 F12 Everglades Florida U.S.A.
113 G12 Everglades Nat. Park Florida U.S.A.
111 K10 Evergreen Alabama U.S.A.
106 E2 Evergreen Colorado U.S.A.
112 J3 Evergreen North Carolina U.S.A.
109 M10 Everman Texas U.S.A.
27 G16 Everöd Sweden
32 H10 Eversberg Germany
32 K6 Eversen Germany
141 G6 Evesham Queensland Australia
118 H6 Evesham Saskatchewan Canada
9 E3 Evesham England
40 D5 Evian-les-Bains France
29 K8 Evijärvi Finland
85 G8 Evinayong Mbini Equat Guinea
46 E6 Évinos R Greece
27 C13 Evje Norway
80 D2 Evlayim Israel
40 G5 Evolène Switzerland
16 B6 Évora Portugal
20 G5 Evran France
21 K3 Evrecy France
47 H4 Evreşe Turkey
21 N3 Évreux France
21 K5 Évron France
80 D2 Evron Israel
46 E3 Évropos Greece
47 H3 Évros R Greece
46 E7 Evrótas R Greece
21 P4 Evry France
79 C3 Evrykhou Cyprus
46 G6 Évvoia isld Greece
102 R12 Ewa Hawaiian Is
102 R12 Ewa Bch Hawaiian Is
100 H2 Ewan Washington U.S.A.
116 P5 Ewan L Alaska U.S.A.
127 K2 Ewarton Jamaica
86 B6 Ewc Congo
9 F5 Ewell England
36 E2 Ewersbach Germany
94 D8 Ewing Kentucky U.S.A.
99 P9 Ewing Missouri U.S.A.
98 H7 Ewing Nebraska U.S.A.
146 D5 Ewing I Antarctica
140 D6 Ewing, Mt N Terr Australia
66 D3 Ewirgol China
128 E6 Exaltación Bolivia
118 G7 Excel Alberta Canada
110 B2 Excelsior Missouri U.S.A.
102 E3 Excelsior Mt California U.S.A.
102 F3 Excelsior Mts Nevada U.S.A.
117 F6 Excursion Alaska U.S.A.
37 K3 Exdorf Germany
146 B8 Executive Committee Ra Antarctica
99 P4 Exeland Wisconsin U.S.A.
8 C5 Exe,R England
120 J9 Exeter Ontario Canada
8 C6 Exeter England
102 E5 Exeter California U.S.A.
110 C5 Exeter Missouri U.S.A.
98 J9 Exeter Nebraska U.S.A.
95 R4 Exeter New Hampshire U.S.A.
117 S3 Exeter L Northwest Territories Canada
8 C5 Exford England
99 M8 Exira Iowa U.S.A.
99 O9 Exline Iowa U.S.A.
25 G3 Exloo Netherlands
21 L4 Exmes France
8 C6 Exminster England
8 C5 Exmoor Forest England
95 M9 Exmore Virginia U.S.A.
142 A5 Exmouth W Australia Australia
8 C6 Exmouth England
142 A5 Exmouth Gulf W Australia Australia
117 Q3 Exmouth L Northwest Territories Canada
81 H7 Exmouth Plateau Indian Oc
46 E8 Éxo Nímfi Greece
141 J6 Expedition Ra Queensland Australia
123 R5 Exploits R Newfoundland Canada
118 B7 Exshaw Alberta Canada
32 K8 Extertal Germany
8 C5 Exton England
16 C5 Extremadura reg Spain
128 D6 Extremo Brazil
126 F2 Exuma Sd Bahamas
116 P6 Eyak Alaska U.S.A.
80 C5 Eyal Israel
88 E3 Eyasi,L Tanzania
27 C13 Eydehamn Norway
9 F2 Eye England
9 H3 Eye England
118 L8 Eyebrow Saskatchewan Canada
13 F2 Eyemouth Scotland
18 G7 Eygurande France
28 S10 Eyjafjalla ice cap Iceland
28 S8 Eyjafjördhur inlet Iceland
86 A2 Eyl Somalia
18 F8 Eymet France
18 G7 Eymoutiers France
9 E4 Eynsham England
99 O6 Eyota Minnesota U.S.A.
28 S10 Eyrarbakki Iceland
140 E6 Eyre R Queensland Australia
143 F9 Eyre W Australia Australia
118 H7 Eyre Saskatchewan Canada
14 C3 Eyrecourt Ireland
138 E4 Eyre,Mt South Australia Australia
144 B6 Eyre Mts New Zealand
138 D3 Eyre North, L South Australia Australia
138 D5 Eyre Pen South Australia Australia
138 D3 Eyre South, L South Australia Australia
119 R1 Eyrie L Manitoba Canada
37 L5 Eysölden Germany
32 K7 Eystrup Germany
6 F1 Eysturoy isld Faeroes
19 N14 Eyzin France
47 H5 Ezine Turkey
77 A3 Ezna Iran

F

134 C12 Faaone Tahiti Pacific Oc
45 J2 Fabbrico Italy
108 A4 Fabens Texas U.S.A.
27 D10 Fåberg Norway
117 P4 Faber L Northwest Territories Canada
121 L5 Fabre Quebec Canada
42 E5 Fabriano Italy
130 E9 Fábrica de Papel Brazil
48 L6 Făcăeni Romania
128 D3 Facatativa Colombia
141 K6 Facing I Queensland Australia
18 E8 Facture France
133 C7 Facundo Argentina
86 D2 Fada Chad
85 E6 Fada N'Gourma Burkina
51 K1 Faddeya,Zaliv G Russian Federation
51 O1 Fadeyevskiy, Ostrov isld Russian Federation
73 L7 Fadippolu Atoll Maldives
42 D4 Faenza Italy
115 O5 Færingehavn Greenland
6 E1 Faeroe Bank N Atlantic Oc
Færøerne see Faeroes
6 F1 Faeroes islds N Atlantic Oc
86 C4 Fafa R Cent Afr Republic
85 E5 Fafa Mali
71 C3 Fafanlap W Irian
16 B3 Fafe Portugal
86 H4 Fafen watercourse Ethiopia
48 J5 Făgăraş Romania
48 J5 Făgăraşului, Muntii mts Romania
26 G10 Fågelsjö Sweden
27 H14 Fagerhult Sweden
27 H12 Fagersta Sweden
48 G5 Făget Romania
48 H3 Făgetului, Muntii mts Romania
45 L3 Faggiola, M mt Italy
85 F6 Faggo Nigeria
71 C3 Fagita W Irian
45 P5 Fagnano Alto Italy
133 D8 Fagnano, L Chile/Arg
22 G3 Fagnes Belgium
85 D5 Faguibine,L Mali
77 F5 Fahraj Iran
41 O5 Fai Della Paganella Italy
41 J5 Faido Switzerland
Faifo see Hoi An
121 O4 Faillon,L Quebec Canada
106 D9 Fairacres New Mexico U.S.A.
141 J6 Fairbairn Res Queensland Australia
103 O10 Fairbank Arizona U.S.A.
99 O7 Fairbank Iowa U.S.A.
116 O4 Fairbanks Alaska U.S.A.
95 R2 Fairbanks Maine U.S.A.
109 M6 Fairbanks Texas U.S.A.
112 H3 Fair Bluff North Carolina U.S.A.
94 C7 Fairborn Ohio U.S.A.
111 M8 Fairburn Georgia U.S.A.
98 C6 Fairburn South Dakota U.S.A.
99 S9 Fairbury Illinois U.S.A.
98 J9 Fairbury Nebraska U.S.A.
94 H7 Fairchance Pennsylvania U.S.A.
99 Q5 Fairchild Wisconsin U.S.A.
98 H1 Fairdale North Dakota U.S.A.
144 C4 Fairdown New Zealand
144 B7 Fairfax New Zealand
111 L9 Fairfax Alabama U.S.A.
99 M5 Fairfax Minnesota U.S.A.
99 L9 Fairfax Missouri U.S.A.
107 O5 Fairfax Oklahoma U.S.A.
112 F5 Fairfax South Carolina U.S.A.
98 H6 Fairfax South Dakota U.S.A.
95 O2 Fairfax Vermont U.S.A.
100 C2 Fairfax Washington U.S.A.
127 P6 Fairfield Barbados
111 K8 Fairfield Alabama U.S.A.
102 B3 Fairfield California U.S.A.
95 O5 Fairfield Connecticut U.S.A.
101 L6 Fairfield Idaho U.S.A.
110 H3 Fairfield Illinois U.S.A.
99 P8 Fairfield Iowa U.S.A.
95 S2 Fairfield Maine U.S.A.
101 N2 Fairfield Montana U.S.A.
98 H9 Fairfield Nebraska U.S.A.
98 C2 Fairfield North Dakota U.S.A.
95 K7 Fairfield Pennsylvania U.S.A.
109 L4 Fairfield Texas U.S.A.
95 P2 Fairfield Vermont U.S.A.
100 H2 Fairfield Washington U.S.A.
119 T7 Fairford Manitoba Canada
9 E4 Fairford England
110 C4 Fair Grove Missouri U.S.A.
95 R5 Fairhaven Massachusetts U.S.A.
95 L3 Fair Haven New York U.S.A.
95 O3 Fair Haven Vermont U.S.A.
100 B1 Fairholm Washington U.S.A.
118 J5 Fairholme Saskatchewan Canada
113 B12 Fairhope Alabama U.S.A.
15 A2 Fair I Scotland
71 C5 Fairie Queen Philippines
107 Q5 Fairland Oklahoma U.S.A.
144 C6 Fairlie New Zealand
12 D2 Fairlie Scotland
141 G3 Fairlight Queensland Australia
141 G5 Fairlight Queensland Australia
119 Q9 Fairlight Saskatchewan Canada
144 B6 Fairlight New Zealand
99 M6 Fairmont Minnesota U.S.A.
98 J9 Fairmont Nebraska U.S.A.
112 H3 Fairmont North Carolina U.S.A.
107 N5 Fairmont Oklahoma U.S.A.
94 G7 Fairmont West Virginia U.S.A.
117 Q10 Fairmont Hot Springs British Columbia Canada
118 H7 Fairmount Saskatchewan Canada
111 M7 Fair Mount Georgia U.S.A.
94 B6 Fairmount Indiana U.S.A.
95 M8 Fairmount Maryland U.S.A.
98 K3 Fairmount North Dakota U.S.A.
115 M5 Fair Ness C Northwest Territories Canada
13 F2 Fairnilee Scotland
110 E6 Fairoaks Arkansas U.S.A.
102 C3 Fair Oaks California U.S.A.
99 T8 Fair Oaks Indiana U.S.A.
106 E2 Fairplay Colorado U.S.A.
110 C4 Fair Play Missouri U.S.A.
107 L2 Fairport Kansas U.S.A.
99 U4 Fairport Michigan U.S.A.
95 K3 Fairport New York U.S.A.
95 L9 Fair Port Virginia U.S.A.
94 F5 Fairport Harbor Ohio U.S.A.
141 G3 Fairview Queensland Australia
117 O7 Fairview Alberta Canada
99 Q9 Fairview Illinois U.S.A.
107 P2 Fairview Kansas U.S.A.
94 C2 Fairview Michigan U.S.A.
98 B2 Fairview Montana U.S.A.
107 M5 Fairview Oklahoma U.S.A.
94 G4 Fairview Pennsylvania U.S.A.
98 K6 Fairview South Dakota U.S.A.
103 N2 Fairview Utah U.S.A.
94 G7 Fairview West Virginia U.S.A.
117 D6 Fairweather,C Alaska U.S.A.
117 E6 Fairweather,Mt Br Col/Alaska Canada/U.S.A.
119 N5 Fairy Glen Saskatchewan Canada
74 E3 Faisalabad India
112 J2 Faison North Carolina U.S.A.
22 H4 Faissault France
98 D4 Faith South Dakota U.S.A.
79 A9 Faiyûm,El Egypt
66 C6 Faizabad India
127 M5 Fajardo Puerto Rico
135 N10 Fakarava atoll Tuamotu Arch Pacific Oc
9 G2 Fakenham England
136 G2 Fakfak W Irian
28 J6 Fakse Denmark
28 J6 Fakse Ladeplads Denmark
65 F3 Faku China
21 K4 Falaise France
117 P5 Falaise L Northwest Territories Canada
46 F3 Falakrón mt Greece
68 A1 Falam Burma
80 D5 Falama Jordan
48 L4 Fălciu Romania
106 F3 Falcon Colorado U.S.A.
128 D1 Falcón state Venezuela
45 O4 Falconara Marittima Italy
120 K6 Falconbridge Ontario Canada
17 G9 Falcon,C Algeria
43 B8 Falcone,C.del Sardinia
94 H4 Falconer New York U.S.A.
109 H9 Falcon L Texas/Mexico U.S.A./Mexico
28 E6 Faldsled Denmark
85 B6 Falémé R Senegal/Mali
52 H5 Falenki Russian Federation
27 H13 Falerum Sweden
48 L3 Faleshty Moldavia
109 J8 Falfurrias Texas U.S.A.
117 P8 Falher Alberta Canada
100 A9 Falk California U.S.A.
121 L7 Falkenberg Ontario Canada
37 N4 Falkenberg Germany
33 T7 Falkenberg Brandenburg Germany
33 S9 Falkenberg Brandenburg Germany
37 O7 Falkenberg Niederbayern Germany
27 F15 Falkenberg Sweden
33 Q6 Falkenhagen Germany
33 S7 Falkensee Germany
37 N3 Falkenstein Germany
37 O5 Falkenstein Germany
12 E2 Falkirk Scotland
117 O10 Falkland British Columbia Canada
13 E1 Falkland Scotland
131 G8 Falkland Is Atlantic Oc
133 E8 Falkland Sd Falkland Is
110 H7 Falkner Mississippi U.S.A.
46 F8 Falkonéra isld Greece
27 F13 Falköping Sweden
111 K7 Falkville Alabama U.S.A.
125 P9 Fallabón Guatemala
102 G8 Fall Brook California U.S.A.
100 D2 Fall City Washington U.S.A.
99 P5 Fall Creek Wisconsin U.S.A.
33 N8 Fallersleben Germany
26 L6 Fällfors Sweden
28 E5 Falling Denmark
32 L7 Fallingbostel Germany
15 C3 Fall of Glomach Scotland
98 A3 Fallon Montana U.S.A.
102 F2 Fallon Nevada U.S.A.
95 Q5 Fall River Massachusetts U.S.A.
100 D8 Fall River Mills California U.S.A.

Fall R.Res — Foça
175

107 O4 Fall R.Res Kansas U.S.A.
95 N5 Fallsburg, S New York U.S.A.
95 K8 Falls Church Virginia U.S.A.
99 L9 Falls City Nebraska U.S.A.
100 B5 Falls City Oregon U.S.A.
109 J7 Falls City Texas U.S.A.
94 J5 Falls Cr Pennsylvania U.S.A.
15 E5 Falls of Clyde Scotland
15 D3 Falls of Foyers Scotland
78 J5 Fallūjah, Al Iraq
22 H3 Falmagne Belgium
9 F6 Falmer England
8 A7 Falmouth England
127 J1 Falmouth Jamaica
94 C8 Falmouth Kentucky U.S.A.
95 R5 Falmouth Massachusetts U.S.A.
94 B2 Falmouth Michigan U.S.A.
94 K8 Falmouth Virginia U.S.A.
127 P4 Falmouth Antigua W Indies
95 R3 Falmouth-Foreside Maine U.S.A.
8 B7 Fal,R England
89 A10 False B S Africa
116 F9 False Pass Aleutian Is
141 F2 False Pera Hd Queensland Australia
94 D1 False Presque I Michigan U.S.A.
17 H3 Falset Spain
127 J5 Falso, C Dominican Rep
124 E6 Falso,C Mexico
133 D9 Falso C. de Hornos Chile
28 H7 Falster isld Denmark
29 K6 Falsterbo Sweden
13 F3 Falstone England
42 D5 Falterona, M mt Italy
48 K3 Fălticeni Romania
27 H11 Falun Sweden
79 D3 Famagusta Cyprus
86 F3 Famaka Sudan
133 D3 Famatina Argentina
133 D3 Famatina, Sa. de mts Argentina
22 J3 Famenne Belgium
143 E7 Fame Ra W Australia Australia
143 F6 Family Well W Australia Australia
71 C3 Fam, Kepulauan isld W Irian
102 E6 Famoso California U.S.A.
71 C2 Fan isld W Irian
14 D1 Fanad Hd Ireland
145 E1 Fanal I New Zealand
45 J3 Fanano Italy
67 F1 Fanchang China
110 H5 Fancy Farm Kentucky U.S.A.
87 H12 Fandriana Madagascar
47 R14 Fánes Rhodes Greece
86 F4 Fangak Sudan
58 F5 Fangcheng China
67 C6 Fangcheng China
67 C1 Fangdou Shan mts China
28 E6 Fangel Denmark
65 B5 Fanglan China
65 B6 Fangshan China
67 C1 Fang Xian China
65 G2 Fangzheng China
65 D6 Fangzi China
65 F3 Fanjiatun China
111 B12 Fannett Texas U.S.A.
111 G9 Fannin Mississippi U.S.A.
109 K7 Fannin Texas U.S.A.
Fanning I see Tabuaeran
77 F6 Fannuj Iran
117 L11 Fanny Bay British Columbia Canada
119 U9 Fannystelle Manitoba Canada
28 A6 Fanø isld Denmark
42 E5 Fano Italy
65 B5 Fanshi China
68 F1 Fan Si Pan mt Vietnam
65 C7 Fan Xian China
20 D5 Faouët,le France
20 B5 Faou,le France
80 F8 Faqu Jordan
79 B8 Fâqûs Egypt
80 F4 Fara Jordan
146 C4 Faraday U.K. Base Graham Land Antarctica
141 H6 Faraday, Mt Queensland Australia
86 E5 Faradje Zaire
87 H12 Farafangana Madagascar
45 Q8 Faraglioni Italy
77 H3 Farāh Afghanistan
77 H3 Farah Rud R Afghanistan
45 N5 Fara in Sabina Italy
102 A4 Farallon Is California U.S.A.
85 D6 Faramana Burkina
85 B6 Faranah Guinea
86 H2 Farasān, Jazā'ir isld Red Sea
84 J5 Farâyid,G.El mt Egypt
28 C4 Fårbæk Denmark
110 E2 Farber Missouri U.S.A.
26 J6 Fårberg Sweden
48 J3 Farcău mt Romania
85 C3 Farciya, Al Western Sahara
16 E7 Fardes R Spain
28 A4 Fåre Denmark
36 B5 Fareberswiller France
9 E6 Fareham England
28 H6 Farendløse Denmark
28 G5 Fårevejle Denmark
116 L5 Farewell Alaska U.S.A.
145 D4 Farewell, C New Zealand
98 K3 Fargo North Dakota U.S.A.
107 L5 Fargo Oklahoma U.S.A.
29 K4 Farhult Sweden
28 C7 Fårhus Denmark
80 F5 Fari'a el Jiftlick Jordan
121 Q3 Faribault Quebec Canada
99 N5 Faribault Minnesota U.S.A.
75 N7 Faridpur Bangladesh
84 G3 Farigh watercourse Libya
16 A5 Farilhões isld Portugal
26 H10 Färilla Sweden
85 A6 Farim Guinea-Bissau
9 E4 Faringdon England
27 K12 Faringe Sweden
106 E4 Farista Colorado U.S.A.
27 H15 Färjestaden Sweden
80 D5 Farkha Jordan
118 H1 Farlane Ontario Canada
141 J5 Farleigh Queensland Australia
121 O6 Farley Quebec Canada
99 P7 Farley Iowa U.S.A.
106 F5 Farley New Mexico U.S.A.
98 J6 Farmer South Dakota U.S.A.
99 S9 Farmer City Illinois U.S.A.
109 O8 Farmers Branch Texas U.S.A.
99 T10 Farmersburg Indiana U.S.A.
99 P7 Farmersburg Iowa U.S.A.
109 L2 Farmersville Texas U.S.A.
111 D9 Farmerville Louisiana U.S.A.
95 N6 Farmingdale New Jersey U.S.A.
98 D6 Farmingdale South Dakota U.S.A.
117 N8 Farmington British Columbia Canada
102 D4 Farmington California U.S.A.
99 Q9 Farmington Illinois U.S.A.
99 P9 Farmington Iowa U.S.A.
95 R2 Farmington Maine U.S.A.
99 N5 Farmington Minnesota U.S.A.
110 F4 Farmington Missouri U.S.A.
95 Q3 Farmington New Hampshire U.S.A.
106 B5 Farmington New Mexico U.S.A.
101 O9 Farmington Utah U.S.A.
100 H2 Farmington Washington U.S.A.
94 G7 Farmington West Virginia U.S.A.
94 B6 Farmland Indiana U.S.A.
98 C2 Farm Unit North Dakota U.S.A.
112 K2 Farmville North Carolina U.S.A.
94 J9 Farmville Virginia U.S.A.
98 F9 Farnam Nebraska U.S.A.
9 F5 Farnborough England
8 D1 Farndon England
7 K7 Farne Deep North Sea
13 G2 Farne Is England
112 C2 Farner Tennessee U.S.A.
27 C10 Farnes Norway
121 S7 Farnham Quebec Canada
9 F5 Farnham England
94 H4 Farnham New York U.S.A.
117 P10 Farnham,Mt British Columbia Canada
9 G5 Farningham England
13 F6 Farnworth England
129 G4 Faro Brazil
117 G4 Faro Yukon Territory Canada
28 H7 Farø isld Denmark
16 B7 Faro Portugal
27 K14 Fårö isld Gotland Sweden
71 G6 Farol Pt Philippines
43 G10 Faro,Pta d Sicily
86 B4 Faro R Cameroon
16 B2 Faro, Sa del mts Spain
27 K14 Fårösund Gotland Sweden
87 J10 Farquhar Is Br Indian Oc Terr
83 H6 Farquhar Is Seychelles Indian Oc
143 E7 Farquharson Tableland W Australia Australia
141 F6 Farrars Cr Queensland Australia
26 H5 Farras mt Sweden
77 C5 Farrāshband Iran
94 G5 Farrell Pennsylvania U.S.A.
121 P7 Farrellton Quebec Canada
8 D5 Farrington Gurney England
28 C6 Farris Denmark
77 C5 Fārs Iran
46 E5 Fársala Greece
77 H3 Fārsī Afghanistan
28 C3 Farsø Denmark
99 O8 Farson Iowa U.S.A.
101 Q7 Farson Wyoming U.S.A.
27 B13 Farsund Norway
130 D10 Fartura,Serra da mts Brazil
28 D4 Fårvang Denmark
115 P6 Farvel,Kap C Greenland
94 C3 Farwell Michigan U.S.A.
98 H8 Farwell Nebraska U.S.A.
108 D1 Farwell Texas U.S.A.
77 J2 Fāryab prov Afghanistan
77 C5 Fasā Iran
43 H8 Fasano Italy
109 J7 Fashing Texas U.S.A.
79 A10 Fashn,El Egypt
28 B5 Faster Denmark
28 C4 Fasterholt Denmark
14 B5 Fastnet Rock Ireland
74 F7 Fatehabad India
74 H5 Fatehgarh India
45 O7 Fate, Mt. delle Italy
54 G4 Fatezh Russian Federation
78 J4 Fathan,Al Iraq
121 P3 Father,L Quebec Canada
123 L6 Fatima Madeleine Is, Quebec Canada
16 B5 Fatima Portugal
78 F1 Fatsa Turkey
135 N9 Fatu Hiva isld Marquesas Is Pacific Oc
86 C6 Fatunda Zaire
110 B2 Faucett Missouri U.S.A.
40 D6 Faucigny dist France
19 K4 Faucilles, Mts France
45 J4 Fauglia Italy
40 G4 Faulhorn mt Switzerland
98 G4 Faulkton South Dakota U.S.A.
111 J9 Faunsdale Alabama U.S.A.
22 C2 Fauquembergues France
117 O11 Fauquier British Columbia Canada
48 L5 Făurei Romania
89 D7 Fauresmith S Africa
26 H4 Fauske Norway
118 B3 Faust Alberta Canada
95 N2 Faust New York U.S.A.
101 N9 Faust Utah U.S.A.
21 M2 Fauville France
43 F11 Favara Sicily
19 Q13 Faverges France
21 O4 Faverolles Eure France
9 G5 Faversham England
43 E11 Favignana, I Sicily
28 C4 Favrholt Denmark
77 A5 Faw, Al Iraq
118 C4 Fawcett Alberta Canada
118 D3 Fawcett L Alberta Canada
9 E6 Fawley England
115 L7 Fawn R Ontario Canada
28 R9 Faxa-flói B Iceland
26 J8 Faxälven R Sweden
27 F10 Faxfj mt Norway
107 M6 Fay Oklahoma U.S.A.
86 C2 Faya-Largeau Chad
54 F2 Fayansovyy Russian Federation
85 B4 Faydat as Sadra Western Sahara
20 G7 Fay-de-Bretagne France
21 J7 Faye-d'Anjou France
119 Q3 Faye Lake Manitoba Canada
21 L8 Faye-la-Vineuse France
111 J8 Fayette Alabama U.S.A.
99 P7 Fayette Iowa U.S.A.
99 U4 Fayette Michigan U.S.A.
111 E10 Fayette Mississippi U.S.A.
110 D2 Fayette Missouri U.S.A.
94 C5 Fayette Ohio U.S.A.
103 N2 Fayette Utah U.S.A.
110 B5 Fayetteville Arkansas U.S.A.
111 M8 Fayetteville Georgia U.S.A.
112 J2 Fayetteville North Carolina U.S.A.
110 N2 Fayetteville Ohio U.S.A.
110 K6 Fayetteville Tennessee U.S.A.
109 L6 Fayetteville Texas U.S.A.
94 F8 Fayetteville West Virginia U.S.A.
22 F3 Fay le Franc Belgium
109 J9 Faysville Texas U.S.A.
80 G1 Fazārah Syria
74 F3 Fazilka India
85 B4 Fdérik Mauritania
14 B4 Feale R Ireland
102 C3 Feather R California U.S.A.
102 C2 Feather Falls California U.S.A.
145 E4 Featherston New Zealand
139 H6 Feathertop,Mt Victoria Australia
101 K6 Featherville Idaho U.S.A.
144 A6 Febrero Pt New Zealand
21 L2 Fécamp France
40 F1 Fecht R France
133 F4 Federación Argentina
98 A8 Federal Wyoming U.S.A.
99 M2 Federal Dam Minnesota U.S.A.
95 M8 Federalsburg Maryland U.S.A.
27 A11 Fedje isld Norway
98 J5 Fedora South Dakota U.S.A.
14 B3 Feeagh,L Ireland
36 D7 Fegersheim France
28 B3 Feggesund chan Denmark
20 F6 Fégréac France
48 H2 Fehérhyarmat Hungary
30 F1 Fehmarn isld Germany
33 R7 Fehrbellin Germany
38 O8 Fehring Austria
130 H8 Feia, Lagoa L Brazil
65 C6 Feicheng China
67 F1 Feidong China
65 C7 Fei Huang R China
128 D5 Feijó Brazil
67 D5 Feilai Xia R China
145 E4 Feilding New Zealand
Feira see Luangwa Zambia
129 L6 Feira de Santana Brazil
38 J8 Feistritz Austria
38 K8 Feistritz-im-Ros Austria
67 F1 Feixi China
65 D7 Fei Xian China
65 C6 Feixiang China
129 K8 Feja, L Brazil
48 E3 Fejér co Hungary
28 G7 Fejø isld Denmark
28 F4 Fejrup Denmark
48 D5 Fekete Viz R Hungary
17 K5 Felanitx Majorca
9 F5 Felbridge England
99 T3 Felch Michigan U.S.A.
36 G2 Feldatal Germany
38 N8 Feldbach Austria
28 F4 Feldballe Denmark
33 S6 Feldberg Germany
40 H2 Feldberg mt Germany
28 C3 Feldingbjerg Denmark
41 L3 Feldkirch Austria
131 F3 Feliciano R Argentina
83 J12 Felicité I Seychelles
94 C8 Felicity Ohio U.S.A.
73 L8 Felidu Atoll Maldives
130 G6 Felixlândia Brazil
106 F8 Felix,R New Mexico U.S.A.
108 C3 Felix, Rio New Mexico U.S.A.
9 H4 Felixstowe England
108 B5 Félix U. Gómez Mexico
36 B4 Fell Germany
36 G6 Fellbach Germany
18 G7 Felletin France
13 G4 Felling England
127 M2 Fellowship Jamaica
113 G10 Fellsmere Florida U.S.A.
45 K2 Felonica Italy
9 F6 Felpham England
36 G1 Felsberg Germany
28 C7 Felsted Denmark
108 B7 Felt Oklahoma U.S.A.
13 G3 Felton England
102 B4 Felton California U.S.A.
111 L8 Felton Georgia U.S.A.
98 K2 Felton Minnesota U.S.A.
42 D2 Feltre Italy
28 G7 Femer Bælt str Denmark/Germany
28 F4 Femmøller Denmark
28 H7 Femø isld Denmark
28 G7 Femø Sund chan Denmark
26 E9 Femund Norway
26 F9 Femundsmarka Nat. Park Norway
87 G13 Fenambosy, Fenambosy pt Madagascar
106 B7 Fence Lake New Mexico U.S.A.
65 B7 Fencheng China
121 M8 Fenelon Falls Ontario Canada
79 F2 Fener Burun C Turkey
36 B6 Fénétrange France
21 J6 Feneu France
59 H3 Fengcheng China
67 E2 Fengcheng China
67 D5 Fengchuan China
67 B2 Fengdu China
58 F4 Fengfeng China
67 B3 Fenggang China
67 G2 Fenghua China
67 C3 Fenghuang China
67 C1 Fengjie R China
67 D5 Fengkai China
65 F2 Fengle China
67 D1 Fengle China
67 E5 Fengliang China
65 A7 Fenglingdu China
65 D5 Fengnan China
65 C4 Fengning China
67 G2 Fengqiao China
65 C7 Fengqiu China
65 D5 Fengrun China
65 D4 Fengshan China
67 B4 Fengshan China
58 G4 Fengtai China
67 F4 Fengting China
67 B5 Fengwu China
65 C7 Feng Xian China
67 G1 Fengxian China
58 E5 Fengxiang China
67 E2 Fengxin China
Fengyi see Zheng'an
Fengyizhen see Maowen
67 G4 Feng-Yuan Taiwan
65 B4 Fengzhen China
65 B6 Fen He R China
116 H2 Feniak L Alaska U.S.A.
21 K8 Fenioux France
14 B4 Fenit Ireland
100 J4 Fenn Idaho U.S.A.
99 Q7 Fennimore Wisconsin U.S.A.
94 A4 Fennville Michigan U.S.A.
9 F3 Fenny Stratford England
87 H11 Fenoarivo Atsinanana Madagascar
28 H6 Fensmark Denmark
9 F3 Fenstanton England
119 M6 Fenton Saskatchewan Canada
109 P5 Fenton Louisiana U.S.A.
94 D4 Fenton Michigan U.S.A.
95 L10 Fentress Virginia U.S.A.
135 L10 Fenua Ura isld Society Is Pacific Oc
121 L9 Fenwick Ontario Canada
13 G2 Fenwick England
12 D2 Fenwick Strathclyde Scotland
94 G8 Fenwick West Virginia U.S.A.
119 O7 Fenwood Saskatchewan Canada
99 Q5 Fenwood Wisconsin U.S.A.
65 B6 Fenxi China
65 B6 Fenyang China
67 E3 Fenyi China
22 H3 Fépin France
26 E9 Feragen L Norway
100 J3 Ferdinand Idaho U.S.A.
110 K3 Ferdinand Indiana U.S.A.
33 T5 Ferdinandshof Germany
18 H4 Fère-Champenoise France
77 A5 Fereidoon oil well Persian Gulf
20 F7 Férel France
22 E4 Fère,La France
26 E8 Feren L Norway
45 O6 Ferentino Italy
57 F4 Fergana Uzbekistan
57 K6 Fergana Basin Tajikistan/Uzbekistan
57 G4 Ferganskiy Khr mts Kyrgyzstan
101 Q2 Fergus Montana U.S.A.
98 K3 Fergus Falls Minnesota U.S.A.
140 B2 Fergusson R N Terr Australia
118 E6 Ferintosh Alberta Canada
85 C7 Ferkessédougou Ivory Coast
120 B2 Ferland Ontario Canada
14 D2 Fermanagh co N Ireland
20 H2 Fermanville France
121 P6 Ferme Neuve Quebec Canada
33 S9 Fermerswalde Germany
45 N4 Fermignano Italy
42 F5 Fermo Italy
16 C3 Fermoselle Spain
14 C4 Fermoy Ireland
128 A8 Fernandina isld Galapagos Is
113 F7 Fernandina Beach Florida U.S.A.
90 G9 Fernando de Noronha isld Atlantic Oc
130 E7 Fernandópolis Brazil
Fernando Póo isld see Bioko
16 D7 Fernán Núñez Spain
130 G5 Fernão Dias Brazil
100 C1 Ferndale Washington U.S.A.
98 H4 Ferney South Dakota U.S.A.
9 F5 Fernhurst England
118 B9 Fernie British Columbia Canada
141 H8 Fernlee Queensland Australia
102 E2 Fernley Nevada U.S.A.
41 N3 Fern Pass Austria
100 B5 Fern Ridge Res Oregon U.S.A.
14 E4 Ferns Ireland
144 D5 Fernside New Zealand
36 F2 Fernwald Germany
100 J2 Fernwood Idaho U.S.A.
111 F10 Fernwood Mississippi U.S.A.
123 P2 Ferolle Pt Newfoundland Canada
47 H4 Férrai Greece
42 D4 Ferrara Italy
17 G9 Ferrat,C Algeria
44 B4 Ferrat,Cape France
43 C9 Ferrato,C Sardinia
16 B6 Ferreira do Alentejo Portugal
129 H3 Ferreira Gomes Brazil
130 D7 Ferreiros Brazil
20 H5 Ferré, le France
128 C5 Ferreñafe Peru
18 E8 Ferret,C France
40 F6 Ferret,Col pass Switz/Italy
19 K5 Ferreue France
111 E10 Ferriday Louisiana U.S.A.
118 C6 Ferrier Alberta Canada
21 K4 Ferrière-aux-Étangs,la France
21 K8 Ferriere,la Deux Sèvres France
20 H8 Ferrière,la Vendée France
21 M7 Ferrière-Larçon France
18 G4 Ferrières France
21 O2 Ferrières-en-Bray France
21 M4 Ferrière-sur-Risle,la France
28 A3 Ferring Denmark
28 A3 Ferring Sø Denmark
99 P9 Ferris Illinois U.S.A.
95 O2 Ferrisburg Vermont U.S.A.
101 S7 Ferris Mts Wyoming U.S.A.
28 F6 Ferritslev Denmark
43 C7 Ferro,C Sardinia
130 G6 Ferros Brazil
123 N2 Ferru,L Quebec Canada
43 B8 Ferru, M mt Sardinia
94 G10 Ferrum Virginia U.S.A.
116 N5 Ferry Alaska U.S.A.
99 U6 Ferry Michigan U.S.A.
13 G6 Ferrybridge England
123 U6 Ferryland Newfoundland Canada
107 P5 Ferry Res Oklahoma U.S.A.
99 U6 Ferrysburg Michigan U.S.A.
8 B4 Ferryside Wales
99 P6 Ferryville Wisconsin U.S.A.
55 C4 Fershampenuaz Russian Federation
28 H5 Ferslev Denmark
21 P5 Ferté-Alais,la France
21 M5 Ferté-Bernard,la France
21 M4 Ferté-Fresnel, la France
18 H4 Ferté Gaucher,La France
21 O7 Ferté-Imbault,la France
22 F4 Ferté, la France
21 K4 Ferté-Macé,la France
21 O6 Ferté-St.Aubin,la France
21 O6 Ferté-St. Cyr,la France
18 H4 Ferté sur Jouarre, la France
21 M4 Ferté-Vidame,la France
98 K2 Fertile Minnesota U.S.A.
48 D3 Fertöszentmiklos Hungary
Fertö Tór see Neusiedler See
21 L3 Fervaques France
41 M3 Ferwall Gruppe mt Austria
25 E2 Ferwerd Netherlands
85 C2 Fès Morocco
86 C7 Feshi Zaire
98 G2 Fessenden North Dakota U.S.A.
19 P15 Festre, Col du pass France
22 D2 Festubert France
110 F3 Festus Missouri U.S.A.
48 L6 Feteşti Romania
14 D4 Fethard Ireland
47 K8 Fethiye Turkey
47 K8 Fethiye Körfezi B Turkey
43 A12 Fetzara, L Algeria
37 L5 Feucht Germany
41 N3 Feuchten Austria
37 J5 Feuchtwangen Germany
118 K7 Feudal Saskatchewan Canada
21 O3 Feuillie, la France
123 M3 Feu, L. du Quebec Canada
21 O2 Feuquières France
21 O1 Feuquières-en-Vimeu France
18 H7 Feurs France
77 L1 Feyzābād Afghanistan
77 F2 Feyzābād Iran
84 E4 Fezzan reg Libya
8 C2 Ffestiniog Wales
8 C4 Fforest Fawr mts Wales
133 D3 Fiambalá Argentina
45 O5 Fiamignano Italy
87 H11 Fianarantsoa Madagascar
86 C4 Fianga Chad
40 F7 Fiano Italy
48 G5 Fibiş Romania
45 K2 Ficarolo Italy
86 G4 Fichē Ethiopia
123 R2 Fichot I Newfoundland Canada
37 M3 Fichtelberg Germany
37 O3 Fichtelberg mt Germany
37 M3 Fichtelfebirge mts Germany
37 J5 Fichtenau Germany
89 E7 Ficksburg S Africa
44 H2 Fidenza Italy
119 V1 Fidler L Manitoba Canada
135 O4 Fieberling Table Mt Pacific Oc
106 C7 Field New Mexico U.S.A.
94 G10 Fieldale Virginia U.S.A.
140 B1 Field I N Terr Australia
118 K6 Fielding Saskatchewan Canada
100 G7 Fields Oregon U.S.A.
100 A9 Fields Landing California U.S.A.
139 H8 Field West Mt Tasmania Australia
48 J5 Fieni Romania
22 B2 Fiennes France
46 D4 Fier Albania
19 P13 Fier R France
42 D2 Fiera di Primiero Italy
106 B9 Fierro New Mexico U.S.A.
13 E1 Fife reg Scotland
109 H4 Fife Texas U.S.A.
119 M9 Fife L Saskatchewan Canada
13 F1 Fife Ness Scotland
139 J5 Fifield New South Wales Australia
99 Q4 Fifield Wisconsin U.S.A.
101 R5 Fifteen Mile Cr Wyoming U.S.A.
17 G9 Figalo,C Algeria
43 C8 Figari,C Sardinia
18 G8 Figeac France
27 J14 Figeholm Sweden
45 K4 Figline Valdarno Italy
127 P4 Fig Tree Nevis W Indies
16 B4 Figuera da Foz Portugal
16 B5 Figuera dos Vinhos Portugal
17 J2 Figueras Spain
Figueres see Figueras
85 D2 Figuig Morocco
137 Q5 Fiji islds Pacific Oc
17 F7 Filabres, Sierra de los mts Spain
129 J5 Filadélfia Brazil
128 F8 Filadelfia Paraguay
48 F2 Filakovo Czechoslovakia
146 E7 Filchner Ice Shelf Antarctica
36 G6 Filderstadt Germany
27 C10 Filefj mt Norway
119 R4 File L Manitoba Canada
101 L7 Filer Idaho U.S.A.
45 O6 Filettino Italy
13 H5 Filey England
46 D5 Filiátes Greece
46 E7 Filiatrá Greece
43 F10 Filicudi, I Italy
85 E6 Filingué Niger
31 O1 Filipów Poland
27 G12 Filipstad Sweden
41 L4 Filisur Switzerland
48 H6 Fillaşi Romania
22 C3 Fillièvres France
119 O9 Fillmore Saskatchewan Canada
102 F7 Fillmore California U.S.A.
94 J4 Fillmore New York U.S.A.
98 G1 Fillmore North Dakota U.S.A.
103 M3 Fillmore Utah U.S.A.
36 H6 Fils R Germany
28 C5 Filskov Denmark
28 A5 Filsø Denmark
8 D4 Filton England
86 H4 Fīltu Ethiopia
146 H6 Fimbulheimen ra Antarctica
146 H6 Fimbulisen ice shelf Antarctica
42 D4 Finale Emilia Italy
44 D3 Finale Ligure Italy
17 F7 Fiñana Spain
94 H9 Fincastle Virginia U.S.A.
121 P7 Finch Ontario Canada
9 F4 Finchley England
28 C4 Finderup Denmark
15 E3 Findhorn R Scotland
15 E3 Findhorn Scotland
78 H1 Fındıklı Turkey
79 E2 Fındıkpınarı Turkey
119 M8 Findlater Saskatchewan Canada
99 S10 Findlay Illinois U.S.A.
94 D5 Findlay Ohio U.S.A.
117 P10 Findlay,Mt British Columbia Canada
9 F6 Findon England
9 F3 Finedon England
139 J8 Fingal Tasmania Australia
98 J3 Fingal North Dakota U.S.A.
110 H6 Finger Tennessee U.S.A.
115 K7 Finger L Ontario Canada
95 L4 Finger Lakes New York U.S.A.
14 E3 Finglas Ireland
88 C9 Fingoe mt Mozambique
88 C9 Fingoe Mozambique
47 L8 Finike Turkey
47 P12 Finiq Albania
16 A2 Finisterre,C Spain
138 D2 Finke R N Terr Australia
140 C7 Finke N Terr Australia
138 D2 Finke Flood Flats South Australia Australia
140 C6 Finke Gorge N Terr Australia
138 C4 Finke,Mt South Australia Australia
140 D7 Finke, R N Terr Australia
29 L8 Finland rep N Europe
99 P2 Finland Minnesota U.S.A.
52 C5 Finland, Gulf of Estonia/Finland/Rus Fed
114 G6 Finlay R British Columbia Canada
99 O3 Finlayson Minnesota U.S.A.
98 J2 Finley North Dakota U.S.A.
109 M1 Finley Oklahoma U.S.A.
119 O2 Finmark Ontario Canada
14 D2 Finn R Ireland
12 D1 Finnart Scotland
118 E7 Finnegan Alberta Canada
26 H4 Finneid Norway
36 D1 Finnentrop Germany
26 L7 Finnforsfallet Sweden
141 H3 Finnigan, Mt Queensland Australia
140 B2 Finniss R N Terr Australia
138 C5 Finniss,C South Australia Australia
26 O1 Finnmark county Norway
26 N2 Finnmarksvidda reg Norway
116 J6 Finn Mt Alaska U.S.A.
27 F11 Finnskog Norway
27 F11 Finnskoga,S Sweden
26 K2 Finnsnes Norway
26 M6 Finnträsk Sweden
33 T7 Finow Germany
33 T7 Finowfurt Germany
33 T7 Finow Kanal Germany
27 H13 Finspång Sweden
40 H4 Finsteraarhorn mt Switzerland
33 T9 Finsterwalde Germany
15 E1 Finstown Scotland
29 H11 Finström Finland
36 E4 Finthen Germany
14 D2 Fintona N Ireland
12 D1 Fintry Scotland
142 C5 Finucane I W Australia Australia
141 F5 Finucane Ra Queensland Australia
40 F5 Fionnay Switzerland
15 C3 Fionn Loch L Scotland
12 B1 Fionphort Scotland
45 J2 Fiorano Modenese Italy
144 A6 Fiordland Nat. Park New Zealand
44 G2 Fiorenzuola d'Arda Italy
45 N4 Fiorenzuola di Focara Italy
88 C5 Fip Tanzania
78 G2 Firat R Turkey
102 D5 Firebaugh California U.S.A.
116 M6 Fire I Alaska U.S.A.
42 D5 Firenze Italy
42 D4 Firenzuola Italy
98 E4 Firesteel South Dakota U.S.A.
48 H3 Firiza Romania
133 E4 Firmat Argentina
18 H7 Firminy France
118 L9 Fir Mt Saskatchewan Canada
74 H5 Firozabad India
77 H2 Firozkoh reg Afghanistan
74 F3 Firozpur India
112 F2 First R North Carolina U.S.A.
116 R2 Firth R Alaska/Yukon Terr U.S.A./Canada
77 C5 Firūzābād Iran
37 K7 Fischach Germany
36 C4 Fischbach Germany
38 M7 Fischbacher Alpen mts Austria
33 Q7 Fischbeck Germany
36 E2 Fischelbach Germany
41 M3 Fischen Germany
109 J6 Fischer Texas U.S.A.
32 K6 Fischerhude Germany
33 S6 Fischerwall Germany
89 A5 Fish watercourse Namibia
9 E6 Fishbourne England
102 E4 Fish Camp California U.S.A.
116 L1 Fish Cr Alaska U.S.A.
101 M6 Fish Cr.Res Idaho U.S.A.
113 F10 Fisheating Cr Florida U.S.A.
121 N4 Fisher Quebec Canada
111 C10 Fisher Louisiana U.S.A.
98 K2 Fisher Minnesota U.S.A.
119 U7 Fisher Branch Manitoba Canada
146 H10 Fisher Glacier Antarctica
143 A9 Fisherman I W Australia Australia
95 M9 Fishermans I Virginia U.S.A.
115 L5 Fisher Str Northwest Territories Canada
116 E9 Fisher Vol Aleutian Is
8 B4 Fishguard Wales
8 A3 Fishguard B England
95 L8 Fishing Creek Maryland U.S.A.
117 M4 Fish L Northwest Territories Canada
116 M4 Fish L Alaska U.S.A.
103 N3 Fish L Utah U.S.A.
94 D3 Fish Pt Michigan U.S.A.
102 A3 Fish Rock California U.S.A.
101 Q4 Fishtail Montana U.S.A.
101 M4 Fishtrap Montana U.S.A.
94 E9 Fishtrap L Kentucky U.S.A.
46 D6 Fiskárdho Greece
28 C3 Fiskbæk Denmark
95 P4 Fiskdale Massachusetts U.S.A.
118 J7 Fiske Saskatchewan Canada
146 D6 Fiske, C Antarctica
115 O5 Fiskenæsset Greenland
28 S9 Fiskivötn lakes Iceland
22 F5 Fismes France
95 Q4 Fitchburg Massachusetts U.S.A.
86 C3 Fitri, L Chad
28 C5 Fitting Denmark
9 F6 Fittleworth England
128 D6 Fitzcarrald Peru
143 C10 Fitzgerald R W Australia Australia
117 R6 Fitzgerald Alberta Canada
112 D6 Fitzgerald Georgia U.S.A.
143 C10 Fitzgerald River Nat Park W Australia Australia
109 L1 Fitzhugh Oklahoma U.S.A.
117 K10 Fitzhugh Sd British Columbia Canada
22 C5 Fitz James France
140 B2 Fitzmaurice R N Terr Australia
121 S5 Fitzpatrick Quebec Canada
133 D7 Fitz Roy Argentina
141 K6 Fitzroy R Queensland Australia
133 C7 Fitz Roy mt Chile/Arg
142 F4 Fitzroy Crossing W Australia Australia
121 O7 Fitzroy Harbour Ontario Canada
141 H3 Fitzroy I Queensland Australia
142 E4 Fitzroy R W Australia Australia
120 J7 Fitzwilliam I Ontario Canada
42 E7 Fiuggi Italy
45 J3 Fiumalbo Italy
Fiume see Rijeka
42 E7 Fiumicino Italy
45 M3 Fiumi Uniti R Italy
144 A6 Five Fingers Pen New Zealand
122 H8 Five Islands Nova Scotia Canada
101 R6 Fivemile Cr Wyoming U.S.A.
14 D2 Fivemiletown N Ireland
144 B6 Five Rivers New Zealand
88 B4 Fizi Zaire
26 L4 Fjällåsen Sweden
26 G6 Fjällfjällen mt Sweden
26 F9 Fjällnäs Sweden
28 H7 Fjelde Denmark
28 F3 Fjellerup Denmark
28 E6 Fjelsted Denmark
28 D6 Fjelstrup Denmark
28 C2 Fjerritslev Denmark
27 B10 Fjordane reg Norway
27 B13 Fjotland Norway
27 D11 Flå Norway
37 K5 Flachslanden Germany
28 A3 Flade Sø Denmark
28 B6 Fladså R Denmark
37 J2 Fladungen Germany
106 G2 Flagler Colorado U.S.A.
113 F8 Flagler Beach Florida U.S.A.
103 N6 Flagstaff Arizona U.S.A.
95 R1 Flagstaff L Maine U.S.A.
100 E7 Flagstaff L Oregon U.S.A.
100 K1 Flagstone British Columbia Canada
28 G6 Flakkebjerg Denmark
26 F3 Flakstad Norway
27 B11 Flåm Norway
20 G2 Flamanville France
99 Q4 Flambeau R Wisconsin U.S.A.
99 Q3 Flambeau Res Wisconsin U.S.A.
13 H5 Flamborough Hd England
133 C3 Flamenco Chile
131 E8 Flamenco, I Argentina
33 R9 Fläming reg Germany
101 Q8 Flaming Gorge Res Utah/Wyoming U.S.A.
113 G12 Flamingo Florida U.S.A.
18 F10 Flamisell R Spain
36 C2 Flammersfeld Germany
127 O2 Flanagin Town Trinidad
99 O1 Flanders Ontario Canada
22 D2 Flandre prov France
22 E3 Flandre France
98 K5 Flandreau South Dakota U.S.A.
102 E1 Flanigan Nevada U.S.A.
38 H6 Flankenmarkt Austria
26 K8 Flärke Sweden
98 E3 Flasher North Dakota U.S.A.
26 H7 Flåsjön L Sweden
117 K5 Flat R Northwest Territories Canada
94 B3 Flat R Michigan U.S.A.
109 K4 Flat Texas U.S.A.
123 O5 Flat Bay Newfoundland Canada
118 C4 Flatbush Alberta Canada
111 J8 Flat Creek Alabama U.S.A.
101 L2 Flathead L Montana U.S.A.
101 L1 Flathead Mts Montana U.S.A.
117 Q11 Flathead R Idaho U.S.A.
5 C5 Flat Holm isld Bristol Channel England
141 J5 Flat I Queensland Australia
118 E4 Flat L Alberta Canada
144 A6 Flat Mt New Zealand
109 K6 Flatonia Texas U.S.A.
110 F4 Flat River Missouri U.S.A.
110 J3 Flat Rock Illinois U.S.A.
94 B7 Flat Rock Indiana U.S.A.
141 H2 Flattery, C Queensland Australia
100 A1 Flattery,C Washington U.S.A.
38 K8 Flattnitz Austria
94 F9 Flat Top West Virginia U.S.A.
101 R3 Flatwillow Montana U.S.A.
94 G8 Flatwoods West Virginia U.S.A.
41 O3 Flaurling Austria
27 C12 Flåv L Norway
28 E2 Flavenskjold Denmark
22 F4 Flavigny le Grd. et Beaurain France
22 E4 Flavy le Martel France
8 D5 Flax Bourton England
118 H7 Flaxcombe Saskatchewan Canada
116 P1 Flaxman I Alaska U.S.A.
98 D1 Flaxton North Dakota U.S.A.
98 A1 Flaxville Montana U.S.A.
20 B4 Flèche R France
21 K6 Flèche, La France
33 O8 Flechtingen Germany
113 K9 Fleeming Pt New Providence I Bahamas
118 F6 Fleet Alberta Canada
9 G2 Fleet Hargate England
141 H5 Fleetwood Queensland Australia
13 E6 Fleetwood England
95 M6 Fleetwood Pennsylvania U.S.A.
36 G5 Flein Germany
95 N4 Fleischmanns New York U.S.A.
27 B13 Flekkefjord Norway
27 C13 Flekkeröy isld Norway
Flemhude see Quarnbek
119 Q8 Fleming Saskatchewan Canada
98 D9 Fleming Colorado U.S.A.
94 D8 Flemingsburg Kentucky U.S.A.
95 N6 Flemington New Jersey U.S.A.
90 F4 Flemish Cap Atlantic Oc
28 E6 Flemløse Denmark
27 J12 Flen Sweden
29 K4 Fleninge Sweden
28 C7 Flensburg Germany
28 D7 Flensburger Förde inlet Denmark/Germany
21 N7 Fléré-la-Rivière France
21 J4 Flers France
22 D3 Flers France
101 N2 Flesher Montana U.S.A.
120 K8 Flesherton Ontario Canada
112 E2 Fletcher North Carolina U.S.A.
107 M7 Fletcher Oklahoma U.S.A.
94 D2 Fletcher Pond Michigan U.S.A.
146 C7 Fletcher Promontory pen Antarctica
9 F2 Fletton England
18 F9 Fleurance France
123 Q3 Fleur de Lys Newfoundland Canada
122 H2 Fleur-de-May,L Labrador, Nfld Canada
40 E4 Fleurier Switzerland
22 H3 Fleurus Belgium
21 N3 Fleury-sur-Andelle France
68 G1 Fleuve Rouge R Vietnam
36 H3 Flieden Germany
41 K4 Flims Switzerland
9 G5 Flimwell England
140 F4 Flinders R Queensland Australia
143 B10 Flinders B W Australia Australia
141 G2 Flinders Group islds Gt Barrier Reef Aust
139 J7 Flinders I Tasmania Australia
141 J4 Flinder's Passage Australia
141 J4 Flinders Reefs Gt Barrier Reef Aust
138 E4 Flinders Rge South Australia Australia
22 E3 Flines-le-Râches France
119 Q4 Flin Flon Manitoba Canada
Flint co see Clwyd
110 K7 Flint R Alabama U.S.A.
111 M10 Flint R Georgia U.S.A.
94 D3 Flint Michigan U.S.A.
8 C1 Flint Wales
107 O4 Flint Hills Kansas U.S.A.
135 M9 Flint I Pacific Oc
120 E3 Flint L Ontario Canada
118 L9 Flintoft Saskatchewan Canada
141 J8 Flinton Queensland Australia
110 D5 Flippin Arkansas U.S.A.
112 C4 Flirt R Georgia U.S.A.
27 F11 Flisa Norway
27 H14 Fliseryd Sweden
17 H3 Flix Spain
13 H6 Flixborough England
21 P1 Flixecourt France
22 H4 Flize France
13 G6 Flockton Moor England
111 J11 Flomaton Florida U.S.A.
108 G1 Flomot Texas U.S.A.
36 E4 Flonheim Germany
67 D1 Flood Basin L Hubei China
146 B9 Flood Ra Antarctica
99 O3 Floodwood Minnesota U.S.A.
110 H3 Flora Illinois U.S.A.
94 A6 Flora Indiana U.S.A.
111 F9 Flora Mississippi U.S.A.
100 H4 Flora Oregon U.S.A.
18 H8 Florac France
111 K10 Florala Alabama U.S.A.
113 E9 Floral City Florida U.S.A.
142 B5 Flora, Mt W Australia Australia
141 H3 Flora Pass Gt Barrier Reef Aust
140 E4 Floraville Queensland Australia
142 A1 Floreat Park dist Perth, W Aust Australia
22 H3 Floreffe Belgium
Florence see Firenze
110 J7 Florence Alabama U.S.A.
103 N8 Florence Arizona U.S.A.
106 E3 Florence Colorado U.S.A.
100 J4 Florence Idaho U.S.A.
107 O3 Florence Kansas U.S.A.
94 C8 Florence Kentucky U.S.A.
111 F9 Florence Mississippi U.S.A.
101 L3 Florence Montana U.S.A.
95 N6 Florence New Jersey U.S.A.
100 A6 Florence Oregon U.S.A.
112 H3 Florence South Carolina U.S.A.
98 J4 Florence South Dakota U.S.A.
109 K5 Florence Texas U.S.A.
99 S4 Florence Wisconsin U.S.A.
103 N8 Florence Junc Arizona U.S.A.
102 F4 Florence L California U.S.A.
128 F8 Florencia Argentina
128 C3 Florencia Colombia
22 H3 Florennes Belgium
22 J4 Florenville Belgium
131 F5 Flores R Argentina
85 A1 Flores isld Azores Atlantic Oc
130 H9 Flores Brazil
125 P9 Flores Guatemala
71 K9 Flores isld Indonesia
131 F4 Flores dept Uruguay
48 L3 Floreshty Moldavia
117 K11 Flores I British Columbia Canada
71 J8 Flores Sea Indonesia
130 H10 Floresta Brazil
109 J6 Floresville Texas U.S.A.
108 E3 Florey Texas U.S.A.
129 K5 Floriano Brazil
128 E5 Floriano Peixoto Brazil
130 E10 Florianopólis Brazil
126 E4 Florida Cuba
137 N3 Florida isld Solomon Is
131 G5 Florida Uruguay
113 B12 Florida state U.S.A.
94 C5 Florida Ohio U.S.A.
113 G12 Florida B Florida U.S.A.
113 F13 Florida Keys islds Florida U.S.A.
113 H12 Florida,Str.of U.S.A./Bahamas
130 B10 Florida,V Paraguay
43 G11 Floridia Sicily
109 O4 Florien Louisiana U.S.A.
46 E4 Flórina Greece
99 O9 Floris Iowa U.S.A.
106 E3 Florissant Colorado U.S.A.
106 E3 Florissant Fossilbeds Nat. Mon. Colorado U.S.A.
26 A10 Flörö Norway
36 G3 Flörsbach Germany
47 M11 Florya Turkey
37 N4 Floss Germany
37 N4 Flossenbürg Germany
15 F2 Flotta Scotland
118 J4 Flotten L Saskatchewan Canada
103 M3 Flowell Utah U.S.A.
120 J7 Flowerpot I. Nat. Park Ontario Canada
123 Q2 Flower's Cove Newfoundland Canada
98 K7 Floyd R Iowa U.S.A.
108 D1 Floyd New Mexico U.S.A.
108 F2 Floydada Texas U.S.A.
103 M6 Floyd,Mt Arizona U.S.A.
27 D11 Fluberg Norway
41 L4 Flüela Pass Switzerland
21 O6 Fluery les Aubrais France
25 E3 Fluessen R Netherlands
71 A3 Fluk Indonesia
111 F11 Fluker Louisiana U.S.A.
20 G5 Flume R France
17 G3 Flumen R Spain
43 B9 Fluminimaggiore Sardinia
36 F7 Fluorn Germany
Flushing Netherlands see Vlissingen
94 D3 Flushing Michigan U.S.A.
94 F6 Flushing Ohio U.S.A.
108 F3 Fluvanna Texas U.S.A.
18 G10 Fluvia R Spain
28 C4 Fly Denmark
136 J3 Fly R Indonesia/Papua New Guinea
83 M9 Flying Fish Cove Christmas I Indian Oc
140 C2 Flying Fox Cr N Terr Australia
28 A4 Flynder Kirke Denmark
28 B3 Flynder Sø L Denmark
6 M6 Flyndre oil rig North Sea
109 L4 Flynn Texas U.S.A.
140 C4 Flynn Mem N Terr Australia
119 O7 Foam Lake Saskatchewan Canada
73 L9 Foa Mulaku I Maldives
47 H6 Foça Turkey

176
Focant — Freuchie

22 J3 **Focant** Belgium
45 H3 **Foce d. Radici** *mt* Italy
15 E3 **Fochabers** Scotland
42 E4 **Foci del Po** Italy
48 L5 **Focşani** Romania
28 H6 **Fodby** Denmark
21 P7 **Foëcy** France
140 D3 **Foelsche** *R* N Terr Australia
67 D5 **Fogang** China
140 B2 **Fog B** N Terr Australia
57 E4 **Fogelevo** Kazakhstan
43 G7 **Foggia** Italy
42 E5 **Foglia** *R* Italy
45 N7 **Fogliano** *L* Italy
29 H11 **Föglö** Finland
123 S4 **Fogo** Newfoundland Canada
88 G10 **Fogo** *isld* Mozambique
123 S4 **Fogo,C** Newfoundland Canada
28 C4 **Fogstrup** Denmark
38 L7 **Fohnsdorf** Austria
28 A7 **Föhr** *isld* Germany
45 R7 **Foiana in Val Fortore** Italy
14 A5 **Foilclogh** *mt* Ireland
15 D2 **Foinaven,Mt** Scotland
18 G10 **Foix** France
52 H6 **Foki** Russian Federation
54 F3 **Fokina, imeni** Russian Federation
54 F3 **Fokino** Russian Federation
26 D9 **Fokstua** Norway
26 G4 **Folda** *inlet* Norway
48 F4 **Földeák** Hungary
26 F7 **Foldereid** Norway
28 B6 **Foldingbro** Denmark
28 C6 **Folding Kirke** Denmark
28 B6 **Fole** Denmark
46 G8 **Folégandros** *isld* Greece
89 E3 **Foley** Botswana
111 J11 **Foley** Alabama U.S.A.
113 D7 **Foley** Florida U.S.A.
99 N4 **Foley** Minnesota U.S.A.
120 H4 **Foleyet** Ontario Canada
115 M4 **Foley I** Northwest Territories Canada
27 B11 **Folgefonna** *gla* Norway
116 J5 **Folger** Alaska U.S.A.
146 G14 **Folger, Cape** *C* Antarctica
20 B4 **Folgoët, le** France
42 E6 **Foligno** Italy
9 H5 **Folkestone** England
9 F2 **Folkingham** England
113 E7 **Folkston** Georgia U.S.A.
112 K3 **Folkstone** North Carolina U.S.A.
26 D9 **Folla** *R* Norway
26 D9 **Folldal** Norway
28 E4 **Følle** Denmark
25 E3 **Follega** Netherlands
28 G5 **Føllenslev** Denmark
20 H4 **Folligny** France
26 G8 **Föllinge** Sweden
27 E12 **Follo** Norway
42 D6 **Follonica** Italy
112 H5 **Folly Beach** South Carolina U.S.A.
100 G6 **Follyfarm** Oregon U.S.A.
102 C3 **Folsom** California U.S.A.
111 F11 **Folsom** Louisiana U.S.A.
106 G5 **Folsom** New Mexico U.S.A.
102 C3 **Folsom L** California U.S.A.
48 L5 **Folteşti** Romania
126 E3 **Fómento** Cuba
52 F6 **Fominki** Russian Federation
52 G2 **Fominskaya** Russian Federation
52 F5 **Fominskoye** Russian Federation
99 M7 **Fonda** Iowa U.S.A.
95 N4 **Fonda** New York U.S.A.
98 F1 **Fonda** North Dakota U.S.A.
114 J6 **Fond-du-Lac** Saskatchewan Canada
99 S6 **Fond du Lac** Wisconsin U.S.A.
94 D10 **Fonde** Kentucky U.S.A.
21 M7 **Fondettes** France
43 E7 **Fondi** Italy
45 O7 **Fondi, L. di** Italy
26 E8 **Fongen** *mt* Norway
43 C8 **Fonni** Sardinia
16 C1 **Fonsagrada** Spain
28 D6 **Fønsskov** Denmark
22 G3 **Fontaine** Belgium
21 N6 **Fontaine** Loir-et-Cher France
18 G4 **Fontainebleau** France
19 O17 **Fontaine-de-Vaucluse** France
40 B2 **Fontaine-Française** France
21 M3 **Fontaine-l'Abbé** France
21 N2 **Fontaine-le-Bourg** France
21 M2 **Fontaine-le-Dun** France
40 B3 **Fontaine-lès-Dijon** France
21 K6 **Fontaine-Milon** France
21 L6 **Fontaine-St. Martin,la** France
133 C6 **Fontana,L** Argentina
112 D2 **Fontana L** North Carolina U.S.A.
45 P6 **Fontana Liri** Italy
45 L3 **Fontanelice** Italy
117 N6 **Fontas** British Columbia Canada
40 D7 **Fontcouvert** France
38 F7 **Fonte** Italy
128 E4 **Fonte Boa** Brazil
128 G6 **Fonte do Pau d'Água** Brazil
18 E6 **Fontenay-le-Comte** France
21 O3 **Fontenay-St.Père** France
123 L2 **Fonteneau,L** Quebec Canada
122 H5 **Fontenelle** Quebec Canada
101 P7 **Fontenelle Fork** *R* Wyoming U.S.A.
101 P7 **Fontenelle Res** Wyoming U.S.A.
22 E2 **Fontenoy** Belgium
21 L7 **Fontevrault l'Abbaye** France
8 D6 **Fontmell Magna** England
22 L5 **Fontoy** France
137 S5 **Fonualei** *isld* Tonga
48 D4 **Fonyód** Hungary
Foochow *see* **Fuzhou** Fujian
103 M2 **Fool Cr.Res** Utah U.S.A.
117 P9 **Foothills** Alberta Canada
99 R7 **Footville** Wisconsin U.S.A.
41 H5 **Foppiano** Italy
27 J14 **Föra** Sweden
107 O5 **Foraker** Oklahoma U.S.A.
116 M5 **Foraker,Mt** Alaska U.S.A.
19 K3 **Forbach** France
36 E6 **Forbach** Germany
139 J5 **Forbes** New South Wales Australia
99 O2 **Forbes** Minnesota U.S.A.
98 H4 **Forbes** North Dakota U.S.A.
117 P10 **Forbes, Mt** Alberta Canada
85 F7 **Forcados** Nigeria
19 Q18 **Forcalqueiret** France
19 P17 **Forcalquier** France
38 E8 **Forchetta** *mt* Italy
37 L4 **Forchheim** Germany
36 H5 **Forchtenberg** Germany
13 F2 **Ford** England
107 L4 **Ford** Kansas U.S.A.
94 C9 **Ford** Kentucky U.S.A.
99 T3 **Ford** *R* Michigan U.S.A.
140 A2 **Ford, C** N Terr Australia
102 E6 **Ford City** California U.S.A.
94 H6 **Ford City** Pennsylvania U.S.A.
26 A10 **Förde** Norway
145 E3 **Fordell** New Zealand
33 P9 **Förderstedt** Germany
9 G3 **Fordham** England
9 E6 **Fordingbridge** England
103 J8 **Ford L** California U.S.A.
110 D4 **Fordland** Missouri U.S.A.
31 L2 **Fordon** Poland
146 B9 **Ford Ranges** Antarctica
139 H3 **Ford's Br** New South Wales Australia
110 K4 **Fordsville** Kentucky U.S.A.
109 K6 **Fordtran** Texas U.S.A.
98 J1 **Fordville** North Dakota U.S.A.
111 D8 **Fordyce** Arkansas U.S.A.
98 J7 **Fordyce** Nebraska U.S.A.
26 G5 **Fore** Norway
85 B7 **Forécariah** Guinea
8 C5 **Foreland,The** England
115 Q4 **Forel, Mont** *mt* Greenland
109 N2 **Foreman** Arkansas U.S.A.
118 F9 **Foremost** Alberta Canada
22 G2 **Forest** Belgium
120 H9 **Forest** Ontario Canada
100 J3 **Forest** Idaho U.S.A.
111 G9 **Forest** Mississippi U.S.A.
94 D6 **Forest** Ohio U.S.A.
118 E6 **Forestburg** Alberta Canada
109 K2 **Forestburg** Texas U.S.A.
110 F6 **Forest City** Arkansas U.S.A.
99 N6 **Forest City** Iowa U.S.A.
112 F2 **Forest City** North Carolina U.S.A.
95 M5 **Forest City** Pennsylvania U.S.A.
142 B3 **Forestdale** *dist* Perth, W Aust Australia
95 O3 **Forest Dale** Vermont U.S.A.
109 O1 **Forester** Arkansas U.S.A.
94 E3 **Forester** Michigan U.S.A.
100 B9 **Forest Glen** California U.S.A.
101 Q3 **Forestgrove** Montana U.S.A.
100 B4 **Forest Grove** Oregon U.S.A.
102 D2 **Foresthill** California U.S.A.
111 D10 **Forest Hill** Louisiana U.S.A.
109 M9 **Forest Hill** Texas U.S.A.
141 G4 **Forest Home** Queensland Australia
139 J8 **Forestier, C** Tasmania Australia
139 J9 **Forestier Pen** Tasmania Australia
99 O4 **Forest Lake** Minnesota U.S.A.
15 D4 **Forest of Atholl** Scotland
99 N4 **Foreston** Minnesota U.S.A.
95 M3 **Forestport** New York U.S.A.
98 J1 **Forest River** North Dakota U.S.A.
9 G5 **Forest Row** England
122 C5 **Forestville** Quebec Canada
102 B3 **Forestville** California U.S.A.
94 E3 **Forestville** Michigan U.S.A.
94 H4 **Forestville** New York U.S.A.
122 C5 **Forestville, Parc de** Quebec Canada
20 C6 **Forêt, B.de la** *B* France
19 J3 **Forêt d'Argonne** France
20 C6 **Forêt, la** France
21 P5 **Forêt-Ste Croix, la** France
18 H7 **Forez, Mts du** France
15 F4 **Forfar** Scotland
118 K7 **Forgan** Saskatchewan Canada
107 K5 **Forgan** Oklahoma U.S.A.
20 E5 **Forges, les** France
21 O2 **Forges-les-Eaux** France
121 O4 **Forget** Quebec Canada
119 P9 **Forget** Saskatchewan Canada
41 N2 **Forggen See** *L* Germany
45 P8 **Forio** Italy
110 G6 **Forked Deer** *R* Tennessee U.S.A.
119 R7 **Fork River** *R* Manitoba Canada
100 A2 **Forks** Washington U.S.A.
144 C5 **Forks, The** New Zealand
94 J9 **Fork Union** Virginia U.S.A.
42 E4 **Forlì** Italy
45 M3 **Forlimpopoli** Italy
14 E4 **Forlorn Pt** Ireland
98 J3 **Forman** North Dakota U.S.A.
13 E6 **Formby** England
138 D6 **Formby B** South Australia Australia
13 E6 **Formby Pt** England
45 M5 **Formello** Italy
17 H6 **Formentera** *isld* Balearic Is
21 O2 **Formerie** France
43 F7 **Formia** Italy
130 F7 **Formiga** Brazil
126 G5 **Formigas Bank** Caribbean
45 J2 **Formigine** Italy
45 L2 **Formignana** Italy
21 J3 **Formigny** France
26 F7 **Formofoss** Norway
Formosa *see* **Taiwan**
133 F3 **Formosa** Argentina
129 J6 **Formosa** *R* Brazil
129 J7 **Formosa** Brazil
129 J6 **Formosa do Rio Prêto** Brazil
129 G6 **Formosa, Serra** *mts* Brazil
Formosa Strait *see* **Taiwan Str**
130 F4 **Formoso** Brazil
107 M2 **Formoso** Kansas U.S.A.
28 F4 **Fornæs** *C* Denmark
17 K4 **Fornells** Menorca
38 G8 **Forni Avoltri** Italy
6 F1 **Føroyar** *islds* N Atlantic Oc
15 E3 **Forres** Scotland
143 G9 **Forrest** W Australia Australia
119 S9 **Forrest** Manitoba Canada
99 S9 **Forrest** Illinois U.S.A.
146 E7 **Forrestal Ra** Antarctica
117 G8 **Forrester I** Alaska U.S.A.
142 C2 **Forrestfield** *dist* Perth, W Aust Australia
143 G8 **Forrest Lakes** W Australia Australia
143 G6 **Forrest, Mt** W Australia Australia
99 R7 **Forreston** Illinois U.S.A.
142 G3 **Forrest River Mission** W Australia Australia
26 J9 **Fors** Sweden
26 J3 **Forsa** Norway
26 J10 **Forsa** Sweden
108 F3 **Forsan** Texas U.S.A.
27 B13 **Forsand** Norway
141 G4 **Forsayth** Queensland Australia
27 J11 **Forsbacka** Sweden
27 F12 **Forshaga** Sweden
27 F13 **Forshem** Sweden
27 F15 **Förslöv** Sweden
27 K11 **Forsmark** Sweden
26 J8 **Forsmo** Sweden
26 K5 **Forsnäs** Sweden
26 C8 **Forsnes** Norway
29 K11 **Forssa** Finland
31 H4 **Forst** Germany
139 L4 **Forster** New South Wales Australia
112 D4 **Forsyth** Georgia U.S.A.
99 S10 **Forsyth** Illinois U.S.A.
101 T3 **Forsyth** Montana U.S.A.
121 O4 **Forsythe** Quebec Canada
145 E4 **Forsyth I** New Zealand
140 E3 **Forsyth Is** Queensland Australia
141 G6 **Forsyth Ra** Queensland Australia
74 E4 **Fort Abbas** Pakistan
111 E10 **Fort Adams** Mississippi U.S.A.
115 L7 **Fort Albany** Ontario Canada
129 L4 **Fortaleza** Brazil
128 E5 **Fortaleza de Ituxi** Brazil
122 G9 **Fort Anne Nat. Hist. Park** Nova Scotia Canada
Fort Archambault *see* **Sarh**
94 J7 **Fort Ashby** West Virginia U.S.A.
118 C4 **Fort Assiniboine** Alberta Canada
99 S7 **Fort Atkinson** Wisconsin U.S.A.
15 D3 **Fort Augustus** Scotland
87 E12 **Fort Beaufort** S Africa
122 H8 **Fort Beau Sejour Nat. Hist. Park** New Brunswick Canada
101 R1 **Fort Belknap Agency** Montana U.S.A.
111 M9 **Fort Benning** Georgia U.S.A.
101 P2 **Fort Benton** Montana U.S.A.
100 E8 **Fort Bidwell** California U.S.A.
118 K3 **Fort Black** Saskatchewan Canada
103 P9 **Fort Bowie Nat. Hist. Site** Arizona U.S.A.
102 A2 **Fort Bragg** California U.S.A.
110 J3 **Fort Branch** Indiana U.S.A.
101 P8 **Fort Bridger** Wyoming U.S.A.
99 K8 **Fort Calhoun** Nebraska U.S.A.
Fort Carnot *see* **Ikongo**
Fort Charlet *see* **Djanet**
Fort Chimo *see* **Kuujjuaq**
117 R6 **Fort Chipewyan** Alberta Canada
98 E2 **Fort Clark** North Dakota U.S.A.
107 M6 **Fort Cobb** Oklahoma U.S.A.
98 A9 **Fort Collins** Colorado U.S.A.
140 F5 **Fort Constantine** Queensland Australia
121 O7 **Fort Coulonge** Quebec Canada
95 N2 **Fort Covington** New York U.S.A.
Fort Dauphin *see* **Tôlañaro**
111 L9 **Fort Davis** Alabama U.S.A.
108 D5 **Fort Davis** Texas U.S.A.
108 D5 **Fort Davis Nat. Hist. Site** Texas U.S.A.
103 P6 **Fort Defiance** Arizona U.S.A.
127 L4 **Fort de France** Martinique W Indies
111 K10 **Fort Deposit** Alabama U.S.A.
100 A8 **Fort Dick** California U.S.A.
99 M7 **Fort Dodge** Iowa U.S.A.
110 J5 **Fort Donelson Nat Mil Park** Tennessee U.S.A.
113 G10 **Fort Drum** Florida U.S.A.
9 E3 **Fort Dunlop** England
123 P2 **Forteau** Labrador, Nfld Canada
130 B6 **Forte Coimbra** Brazil
44 H4 **Forte dei Marmi** Italy
121 L10 **Fort Erie** Ontario Canada
142 B5 **Fortescue R** W Australia Australia
142 C5 **Fortescue, R** W Australia Australia
95 L9 **Fort Eustis** Virginia U.S.A.
95 T7 **Fort Fairfield** Maine U.S.A.
112 K4 **Fort Fisher** North Carolina U.S.A.
Fort Flatters *see* **Bordj Omar Driss**
99 N1 **Fort Frances** Ontario Canada
117 M3 **Fort Franklin** Northwest Territories Canada
117 L8 **Fort Fraser** British Columbia Canada
112 F6 **Fort Frederica Nat. Mon** Georgia U.S.A.
111 L10 **Fort Gaines** Georgia U.S.A.
Fort Garaud *see* **Fdérik**
106 E4 **Fort Garland** Colorado U.S.A.
118 B1 **Fort Garry** Manitoba Canada
94 E8 **Fort Gay** West Virginia U.S.A.
115 M7 **Fort George** Quebec Canada
15 D3 **Fort George** Scotland
107 P6 **Fort Gibson** Oklahoma U.S.A.
107 P5 **Fort Gibson L** Oklahoma U.S.A.
114 G4 **Fort Good Hope** Northwest Territories Canada
113 F10 **Fort Green** Florida U.S.A.
138 F3 **Fort Grey** New South Wales Australia
109 H3 **Fort Griffin** Texas U.S.A.
12 E2 **Forth** Scotland
Fort Hall *see* **Murang'a** Kenya
101 N6 **Fort Hall** Idaho U.S.A.
13 F1 **Forth, Firth of** Scotland
115 L7 **Fort Hope** Ontario Canada
12 D1 **Forth, R** Scotland
103 O10 **Fort Huachuca** Arizona U.S.A.
121 S6 **Fortierville** Quebec Canada
6 L5 **Forties** *oil rig* North Sea
122 H9 **Forties Settlement** Nova Scotia Canada
103 K3 **Fortification Ra** Nevada U.S.A.
128 F8 **Fortin Carlos Antonio López** Paraguay
101 L1 **Fortine** Montana U.S.A.
128 G8 **Fortin Falcón** Paraguay
133 F2 **Fortin Gen. Caballero** Paraguay
128 F8 **Fortin General Eugenio Garay** Paraguay
128 F8 **Fortin Infante Rivarola** Paraguay
122 E3 **Fortin, L** Quebec Canada
133 E3 **Fortin Lavalle** Argentina
128 F8 **Fortin Linares** Paraguay
133 F2 **Fortín Madrejón** Paraguay
128 F7 **Fortin Ravelo** Bolivia
128 G8 **Fortin Rojas Silva** Paraguay
128 F7 **Fortin Suárez Arana** Bolivia
128 G7 **Fortin Teniente Américo Picco** Paraguay
Fort Jameson Zambia *see* **Chipata**
113 E13 **Fort Jefferson Nat.Mon** Florida U.S.A.
Fort Johnston *see* **Mangochi**
100 C8 **Fort Jones** California U.S.A.
118 G4 **Fort Kent** Alberta Canada
95 S6 **Fort Kent** Maine U.S.A.
100 C7 **Fort Klamath** Oregon U.S.A.
94 B9 **Fort Knox** Kentucky U.S.A.
Fort Lallemande *see* **Belhirane**
Fort Lamy *see* **N'djamena**
98 B7 **Fort Laramie** Wyoming U.S.A.
98 B7 **Fort Laramie Nat. Hist. Mon.** Wyoming U.S.A.
107 L3 **Fort Larned Nat. Hist. Site** Kansas U.S.A.
113 G11 **Fort Lauderdale** Florida U.S.A.
112 G3 **Fort Lawn** South Carolina U.S.A.
100 C2 **Fort Lewis** Washington U.S.A.
117 M5 **Fort Liard** Northwest Territories Canada
127 J5 **Fort Liberté** Haiti
98 F3 **Fort Lincoln** North Dakota U.S.A.
112 C2 **Fort Loudon Lake** Tennessee U.S.A.
98 B9 **Fort Lupton** Colorado U.S.A.
106 G3 **Fort Lyon** Colorado U.S.A.
108 G5 **Fort McKavett** Texas U.S.A.
117 S7 **Fort MacKay** Alberta Canada
101 S5 **Fort Mackenzie** Wyoming U.S.A.
118 D9 **Fort Macleod** Alberta Canada
Fort McMahon *see* **El Homr**
118 F2 **Fort McMurray** Alberta Canada
114 F4 **Fort McPherson** Northwest Territories Canada
99 P9 **Fort Madison** Iowa U.S.A.
22 B3 **Fort Mahon Plage** France
Fort Manning *see* **Mchinji**
113 F8 **Fort Matanzas Nat.Mon** Florida U.S.A.
113 F10 **Fort Meade** Florida U.S.A.
112 G2 **Fort Mill** South Carolina U.S.A.
98 C9 **Fort Morgan** Colorado U.S.A.
106 G1 **Fort Morgan** Colorado U.S.A.
113 F11 **Fort Myers** Florida U.S.A.
113 E11 **Fort Myers Beach** Florida U.S.A.
117 M6 **Fort Nelson** British Columbia Canada
117 L3 **Fort Norman** Northwest Territories Canada
113 F10 **Fort Ogden** Florida U.S.A.
43 G7 **Fortore** *R* Italy
111 L7 **Fort Payne** Alabama U.S.A.
101 T2 **Fort Peck L** *res* Montana U.S.A.
113 G10 **Fort Pierce** Florida U.S.A.
98 F5 **Fort Pierre** South Dakota U.S.A.
Fort Pierre Bordes *see* **Tin Zaouaten**
95 N4 **Fort Plain** New York U.S.A.
117 P5 **Fort Providence** Northwest Territories Canada
112 G5 **Fort Pulaski Nat. Mon** Georgia U.S.A.
119 O8 **Fort Qu' Appelle** Saskatchewan Canada
112 M2 **Fort Raleigh Nat.Hist.Site** North Carolina U.S.A.
116 F9 **Fort Randall** Alaska U.S.A.
98 H6 **Fort Randall Dam** South Dakota U.S.A.
94 C6 **Fort Recovery** Ohio U.S.A.
114 J5 **Fort Reliance** Northwest Territories Canada
117 R5 **Fort Resolution** Northwest Territories Canada
101 Q5 **Fortress Mt** Wyoming U.S.A.
123 M8 **Fortress of Louisburg Nat. Hist. Park** C Breton I, Nova Scotia
98 F3 **Fort Rice** North Dakota U.S.A.
107 O2 **Fort Riley** Kansas U.S.A.
99 M3 **Fort Ripley** Minnesota U.S.A.
87 E10 **Fort Rixon** Zimbabwe
98 C7 **Fort Robinson** Nebraska U.S.A.
100 D6 **Fort Rock** Oregon U.S.A.
144 B7 **Fortrose** New Zealand
Fort Rosebery Zambia *see* **Mansa**
102 A3 **Fort Ross** California U.S.A.
Fort Rousset *see* **Owando**
121 M1 **Fort Rupert** Quebec Canada
117 L8 **Fort St. James** British Columbia Canada
117 N7 **Fort St. John** British Columbia Canada
Fort Sandeman *see* **Zhob**
118 D5 **Fort Saskatchewan** Alberta Canada
107 Q4 **Fort Scott** Kansas U.S.A.
115 L6 **Fort Severn** Ontario Canada
100 B9 **Fort Seward** California U.S.A.
107 M7 **Fort Sill** Oklahoma U.S.A.
117 N5 **Fort Simpson** Northwest Territories Canada
114 G5 **Fort Smith** *dist* Northwest Territories Canada
117 R5 **Fort Smith** Northwest Territories Canada
107 Q6 **Fort Smith** Arkansas U.S.A.
101 T8 **Fort Steele** Wyoming U.S.A.
108 E5 **Fort Stockton** Texas U.S.A.
108 C1 **Fort Sumner** New Mexico U.S.A.
112 H5 **Fort Sumter Nat.Mon** South Carolina U.S.A.
107 L5 **Fort Supply** Oklahoma U.S.A.
108 E7 **Fort Supply Res** Oklahoma U.S.A.
103 P8 **Fort Thomas** Arizona U.S.A.
98 G5 **Fort Thompson** South Dakota U.S.A.
107 P7 **Fort Towson** Oklahoma U.S.A.
27 C10 **Fortun** Norway
17 G6 **Fortuna** Spain
100 A9 **Fortuna** California U.S.A.
98 C1 **Fortuna** North Dakota U.S.A.
116 F6 **Fortuna Lodge** Alaska U.S.A.
123 R6 **Fortune** Newfoundland Canada
106 E6 **Fort Union Nat.Mon** New Mexico U.S.A.
112 D5 **Fort Valley** Georgia U.S.A.
117 Q6 **Fort Vermilion** Alberta Canada
Fort Victoria *see* **Masvingo**
94 B7 **Fortville** Indiana U.S.A.
111 K11 **Fort Walton Beach** Florida U.S.A.
101 R6 **Fort Washakie** Wyoming U.S.A.
94 B5 **Fort Wayne** Indiana U.S.A.
113 E8 **Fort White** Florida U.S.A.
118 A2 **Fort Whyte** Manitoba Canada
15 C4 **Fort William** Scotland
109 M10 **Fort Worth** Texas U.S.A.
98 F3 **Fort Yates** North Dakota U.S.A.
116 R5 **Fortymile** *R* Alaska U.S.A.
116 P3 **Fort Yukon** Alaska U.S.A.
77 D6 **Forur, Jazīreh-ye** *isld* Iran
22 J2 **Forville** Belgium
119 N9 **Forward** Saskatchewan Canada
52 H5 **Fosforitnaya** Russian Federation
67 D5 **Foshan** China
115 L2 **Fosheim Pen** Northwest Territories Canada
26 D8 **Fosna** Norway
26 E7 **Fosnes** Norway
107 L6 **Foss** Oklahoma U.S.A.
44 C2 **Fossano** Italy
22 H3 **Fosse** Belgium
100 E4 **Fossil** Oregon U.S.A.
101 P8 **Fossil** Wyoming U.S.A.
101 P8 **Fossil Butte Nat. Mon.** Wyoming U.S.A.
142 F4 **Fossil Downs** W Australia Australia
121 L6 **Fossmill** Ontario Canada
42 E5 **Fossombrone** Italy
119 O6 **Fosston** Saskatchewan Canada
99 L2 **Fosston** Minnesota U.S.A.
139 H7 **Foster** Victoria Australia
121 S7 **Foster** Quebec Canada
98 J7 **Foster** Nebraska U.S.A.
100 C5 **Foster** Oregon U.S.A.
147 E10 **Foster Bugt** Greenland
99 T4 **Foster City** Michigan U.S.A.
117 D6 **Foster, Mt.** Yukon Territory Canada
118 J8 **Fosterton** Saskatchewan Canada
110 K6 **Fosterville** Tennessee U.S.A.
94 D5 **Fostoria** Ohio U.S.A.
109 M5 **Fostoria** Texas U.S.A.
67 F4 **Fotan** China
142 F5 **Fotheringham, Mt** W Australia Australia
21 O2 **Foucarmont** France
36 C7 **Fouday** France
20 B6 **Fouesnant** France
86 B6 **Fougamou** Gabon
20 H5 **Fougères** France
83 K13 **Fougères,Pl.des** Réunion Indian Oc
40 D2 **Fougerolles** France
21 J5 **Fougerolles-du-Plessis** France
21 P2 **Fouilloy** France
109 O2 **Fouke** Arkansas U.S.A.
68 B3 **Foul** *I'd* Burma
84 K5 **Foul Bay** Egypt
9 G4 **Foulness Pt** England
13 E5 **Foulness** *isld* England
144 C4 **Foulwind, C** New Zealand
86 B4 **Foumban** Cameroon
85 C3 **Foum el Hassan** Morocco
85 C2 **Foum Zguid** Morocco
146 D8 **Foundation Ice Stream** *ice stream* Antarctica
106 F3 **Fountain** Colorado U.S.A.
99 U5 **Fountain** Michigan U.S.A.
99 O6 **Fountain** Minnesota U.S.A.
112 K2 **Fountain** North Carolina U.S.A.
103 N2 **Fountain Grn** Utah U.S.A.
111 E8 **Fountain Hill** Arkansas U.S.A.
112 E3 **Fountain Inn** South Carolina U.S.A.
16 B7 **Foupana** *R* Portugal
140 D3 **Four Archers** *mt* N Terr Australia
18 E7 **Fouras** France
101 U1 **Four Buttes** Montana U.S.A.
21 M5 **Fourche, la** France
110 B7 **Fourche la Fave** *R* Arkansas U.S.A.
19 J4 **Fourchies, Mts des** France
123 M8 **Fourchu** C Breton I, Nova Scotia
103 P4 **Four Corners** Utah U.S.A.
98 B5 **Four Corners** Wyoming U.S.A.
140 A1 **Fourcroy, C** N Terr Australia
20 E7 **Four, le** *isld* France
22 G3 **Fourmies** France
83 K14 **Fournaise, Piton de la** *vol* Réunion Indian Oc
46 E5 **Fournás** Greece
83 L13 **Fourneau** *isld* Mauritius
123 P2 **Fournel, L** Quebec Canada
22 D2 **Fournes-en-Weppes** France
122 G2 **Fournier, L** Quebec Canada
47 H7 **Foúrnoi** *isld* Greece
127 K3 **Four Paths** Jamaica
19 N17 **Fourques** France
13 F3 **Fourstones** England
99 R3 **Fourteenmile Pt** Michigan U.S.A.
85 B6 **Fouta Djalon** *mt reg* Guinea
85 B5 **Fouta Ferlo** *reg* Senegal
8 D5 **Fovant** England
144 A7 **Foveaux Strait** New Zealand
28 C3 **Fovlum** Denmark
8 B7 **Fowey** England
113 G12 **Fowey Rocks** Florida U.S.A.
126 F2 **Fowl Cay** *isld* Bahamas
106 F3 **Fowler** Colorado U.S.A.
99 T9 **Fowler** Indiana U.S.A.
107 K4 **Fowler** Kansas U.S.A.
94 C3 **Fowler** Michigan U.S.A.
101 O1 **Fowler** Montana U.S.A.
146 C7 **Fowler Peninsula** *pen* Antarctica
138 B4 **Fowler Pt** South Australia Australia
138 B4 **Fowlers B** South Australia Australia
138 F4 **Fowlers Gap** New South Wales Australia
109 J7 **Fowlerton** Texas U.S.A.
94 C4 **Fowlerville** Michigan U.S.A.
110 G6 **Fowlkes** Tennessee U.S.A.
111 M11 **Fowlstown** Georgia U.S.A.
77 A1 **Fowman** Iran
115 K6 **Fox** *R* Manitoba Canada
99 S8 **Fox** *R* Illinois U.S.A.
99 U3 **Fox** *R* Michigan U.S.A.
99 T4 **Fox** Michigan U.S.A.
99 P9 **Fox** *R* Missouri U.S.A.
100 F5 **Fox** Oregon U.S.A.
99 S5 **Fox** *R* Wisconsin U.S.A.
123 L4 **Fox B** Anticosti I, Quebec
94 H5 **Foxburg** Pennsylvania U.S.A.
117 P8 **Fox Creek** Alberta Canada
115 M4 **Foxe Basin** Northwest Territories Canada
115 L4 **Foxe Chan** Northwest Territories Canada
115 M5 **Foxe Pen** Northwest Territories Canada
119 M5 **Foxford** Saskatchewan Canada
14 B3 **Foxford** Ireland
123 R1 **Fox Harbour** Labrador, Nfld Canada
13 H5 **Foxholes** England
98 K3 **Foxhome** Minnesota U.S.A.
116 P8 **Fox Islands** *isld* Aleutian Is
143 C10 **Fox, L** W Australia Australia
99 S7 **Fox Lake** Illinois U.S.A.
99 S6 **Fox Lake** Wisconsin U.S.A.
101 T8 **Foxpark** Wyoming U.S.A.
144 C5 **Fox Peak** *mt* New Zealand
123 L4 **Fox Pt** Anticosti I, Quebec
117 L7 **Fox R** British Columbia Canada
145 E4 **Foxton** New Zealand
118 H8 **Fox Valley** Saskatchewan Canada
119 Q8 **Foxwarren** Manitoba Canada
111 G10 **Foxworth** Mississippi U.S.A.
15 D3 **Foyers** Scotland
14 D2 **Foyle** *R* N Ireland
14 D1 **Foyle, L** Ireland
14 B4 **Foynes** Ireland
16 C1 **Foz** Spain
87 B9 **Foz do Cunene** Angola
128 D5 **Foz do Gregório** Brazil
130 C9 **Foz do Iguaçú** Brazil
128 F5 **Foz do Jamari** Brazil
128 D5 **Foz do Jordao** Brazil
128 E4 **Foz do Jutai** Brazil
128 E4 **Foz do Mamoriá** Brazil
128 D5 **Foz do Riozinho** Brazil
67 E1 **Foziling Shuiku** *res* China
128 E5 **Foz Tarauacá** Brazil
95 L6 **Frackville** Pennsylvania U.S.A.
8 B7 **Fraddon** England
17 H3 **Fraga** Spain
36 B7 **Fraize** France
22 F3 **Frameries** Belgium
95 Q4 **Framingham** Massachusetts U.S.A.
9 H3 **Framlingham** England
36 G3 **Frammersbach** Germany
146 J10 **Framnes Mts** Antarctica
31 O5 **Frampol** Poland
130 F7 **Franca** Brazil
83 M14 **Francais, Port-aux-** *France Base* Kerguelen Indian Oc
43 H8 **Francavilla Fontana** Italy
18 **France** *rep* W Europe
147 F10 **France, Ile de** Greenland
138 F6 **Frances** South Australia Australia
117 J5 **Frances** *R* Yukon Territory Canada
100 B3 **Frances** Washington U.S.A.
140 B2 **Frances Creek** N Terr Australia
117 J5 **Frances L** Yukon Territory Canada
101 N1 **Frances, L** Montana U.S.A.
127 K5 **Francés Viejo, C** Dominican Rep
99 U9 **Francesville** Indiana U.S.A.
86 B6 **Franceville** Gabon
19 J6 **Franche Comté** *prov* France
119 O8 **Francis** Saskatchewan Canada
107 O7 **Francis** Oklahoma U.S.A.
98 G6 **Francis Case, L** South Dakota U.S.A.
128 D4 **Francisco de Orellana** Peru
124 H5 **Francisco I. Madero** Coahuila Mexico
124 G5 **Francisco I. Madero** Durango Mexico
130 C9 **Francisco, S** *R* Brazil
130 G5 **Francisco Sá** Brazil
123 R1 **Francis Harbour** Labrador, Nfld Canada
95 Q1 **Francis, L** New Hampshire U.S.A.
89 E3 **Francistown** Botswana
123 Q6 **François** Newfoundland Canada
117 K8 **François L** British Columbia Canada
127 M4 **François, Le** Martinique W Indies
45 L2 **Francolino** Italy
22 K2 **Francorchamps** Belgium
101 Q6 **Francs Pk** Wyoming U.S.A.
21 N7 **Francueil** France
25 E2 **Franeker** Netherlands
118 C9 **Frank** Alberta Canada
36 F1 **Frankenau** Germany
36 F2 **Frankenbach** Germany
37 P2 **Frankenberg** Germany
36 F1 **Frankenberg/Eder** Germany
37 J5 **Frankenhardt** Germany
37 J5 **Frankenhöhe** *mts* Germany
94 D3 **Frankenmuth** Michigan U.S.A.
36 D5 **Frankenstein** Germany
36 E4 **Frankenthal** Germany
37 M3 **Frankenwald** *mts* Germany
127 K2 **Frankfield** Jamaica
121 N8 **Frankford** Ontario Canada
110 E2 **Frankford** Missouri U.S.A.
94 G9 **Frankford** West Virginia U.S.A.
94 A6 **Frankfort** Indiana U.S.A.
107 O2 **Frankfort** Kansas U.S.A.
94 C8 **Frankfort** Kentucky U.S.A.
99 U5 **Frankfort** Michigan U.S.A.
95 M3 **Frankfort** New York U.S.A.
94 D7 **Frankfort** Ohio U.S.A.
98 H5 **Frankfort** South Dakota U.S.A.
36 F3 **Frankfurt am Main** Germany
31 H3 **Frankfurt an der Oder** Germany
37 K6 **Fränkische Alb** *mts* Germany
37 L4 **Fränkische Schweiz** *reg* Germany
139 J7 **Frankland, C** Tasmania Australia
111 L8 **Franklin** Georgia U.S.A.
101 O7 **Franklin** Idaho U.S.A.
94 A7 **Franklin** Indiana U.S.A.
110 K5 **Franklin** Kentucky U.S.A.
111 E12 **Franklin** Louisiana U.S.A.
95 T2 **Franklin** Maine U.S.A.
95 Q4 **Franklin** Massachusetts U.S.A.
101 Q3 **Franklin** Montana U.S.A.
98 H9 **Franklin** Nebraska U.S.A.
95 Q3 **Franklin** New Hampshire U.S.A.
95 N5 **Franklin** New Jersey U.S.A.
95 M4 **Franklin** New York U.S.A.
112 D2 **Franklin** North Carolina U.S.A.
94 C7 **Franklin** Ohio U.S.A.
94 H5 **Franklin** Pennsylvania U.S.A.
110 K6 **Franklin** Tennessee U.S.A.
109 L4 **Franklin** Texas U.S.A.
95 L10 **Franklin** Virginia U.S.A.
94 H8 **Franklin** West Virginia U.S.A.
114 G3 **Franklin B** Northwest Territories Canada
100 G1 **Franklin D. Roosevelt L** Washington U.S.A.
99 R8 **Franklin Grove** Illinois U.S.A.
138 D5 **Franklin Harb** South Australia Australia
146 C11 **Franklin I** Antarctica
120 K7 **Franklin I** Ontario Canada
103 J1 **Franklin L** Nevada U.S.A.
117 L3 **Franklin Mts** Northwest Territories Canada
144 A6 **Franklin Mts** New Zealand
116 P2 **Franklin Mts** Alaska U.S.A.
116 H1 **Franklin, Pt** Alaska U.S.A.
139 J8 **Franklin Snd** Tasmania Australia
115 K3 **Franklin Str** Northwest Territories Canada
111 F11 **Franklinton** Louisiana U.S.A.
112 J1 **Franklinton** North Carolina U.S.A.
94 J4 **Franklinville** New York U.S.A.
112 H2 **Franklinville** North Carolina U.S.A.
100 J6 **Franklin Whitney** *airport* Idaho U.S.A.
144 D5 **Franklyn, Mt** New Zealand
37 J3 **Fränk Saale** *R* Germany
139 H7 **Frankston** Victoria Australia
109 M3 **Frankston** Texas U.S.A.
99 T7 **Franksville** Wisconsin U.S.A.
144 B6 **Frankton** New Zealand
101 R5 **Frannie** Wyoming U.S.A.
87 B10 **Fransfontein** Namibia
26 H9 **Fränsta** Sweden
9 G5 **Frant** England
37 N3 **Františkovy Lázně** Czechoslovakia
147 L11 **Frantsa-Iosifa, Zemlya** Arctic Oc
120 F4 **Franz** Ontario Canada
33 R4 **Franzburg** Germany
144 C5 **Franz Josef Gla** New Zealand
Franz Josef Land *see* **Frantsa-Iosifa, Zemlya**
38 G7 **Franz-Josefs Höhe** *mt* Austria
43 B9 **Frasca, C. d** Sardinia
42 E7 **Frascati** Italy
100 C1 **Fraser** *R* British Columbia Canada
106 E2 **Fraser** Colorado U.S.A.
87 D12 **Fraserburg** S Africa
15 F3 **Fraserburgh** Scotland
120 J3 **Fraserdale** Ontario Canada
141 L7 **Fraser I** Queensland Australia
143 C7 **Fraser, Mt** W Australia Australia
143 E9 **Fraser Range** W Australia Australia
69 E11 **Fraser's Hill** Malaysia
145 F3 **Frasertown** New Zealand
119 U8 **Fraserwood** Manitoba Canada
46 D4 **Frashër** Albania
48 K6 **Frăsinet** Romania
19 K6 **Frasne** France
22 F2 **Frasnes-les-Buissenal** Belgium
25 F5 **Frasselt** Germany
45 J3 **Frassinoro** Italy
120 F5 **Frater** Ontario Canada
45 L1 **Fratta Polesine** Italy
41 J2 **Frauenfeld** Switzerland
33 S10 **Frauenhain** Germany
37 O5 **Frauenstein** *mt* Germany
37 K2 **Frauenwald** Germany
28 E6 **Fraugde** Denmark
131 F4 **Fray Bentos** Uruguay
21 N5 **Frazé** France
99 L3 **Frazee** Minnesota U.S.A.
101 T1 **Frazer** Montana U.S.A.
142 A6 **Frazer I** W Australia Australia
120 B3 **Frazer L** Ontario Canada
36 B2 **Frechen** Germany
16 D2 **Frechilla** Spain
32 G9 **Freckenhorst** Germany
99 S2 **Freda** Michigan U.S.A.
98 E3 **Freda** North Dakota U.S.A.
36 E1 **Fredeburg** Germany
32 L9 **Freden** Germany
29 K5 **Fredensborg** Denmark
94 C2 **Frederic** Michigan U.S.A.
99 O4 **Frederic** Wisconsin U.S.A.
95 M7 **Frederica** Delaware U.S.A.
28 D5 **Fredericia** Denmark
99 Q9 **Frederick** Illinois U.S.A.
95 K7 **Frederick** Maryland U.S.A.
107 L7 **Frederick** Oklahoma U.S.A.
98 H4 **Frederick** South Dakota U.S.A.
120 J3 **Frederick House** *R* Ontario Canada
137 L6 **Frederick Reef** Coral Sea
99 O7 **Fredericksburg** Iowa U.S.A.
95 L6 **Fredericksburg** Pennsylvania U.S.A.
94 K8 **Fredericksburg** Virginia U.S.A.
117 F7 **Frederick Sd** Alaska U.S.A.
110 F4 **Fredericktown** Missouri U.S.A.
94 E6 **Fredericktown** Ohio U.S.A.
122 F8 **Fredericton** New Brunswick Canada
122 F8 **Fredericton Junct** New Brunswick Canada
28 C4 **Frederiks** Denmark
29 K5 **Frederiksberg** Denmark
28 C5 **Frederikshåb** Denmark
115 P5 **Frederikshåb** Greenland
115 O5 **Frederikshåb Isblink** Greenland
28 F2 **Frederikshavn** Denmark
28 H5 **Frederikssund** Denmark
113 L8 **Frederiksted** Virgin Is
28 J5 **Frederiksværk** Denmark
128 C2 **Fredonia** Colombia
103 M5 **Fredonia** Arizona U.S.A.
107 P4 **Fredonia** Kansas U.S.A.
110 H4 **Fredonia** Kentucky U.S.A.
94 H4 **Fredonia** New York U.S.A.
98 G3 **Fredonia** North Dakota U.S.A.
109 J5 **Fredricksburg** Texas U.S.A.
26 K7 **Fredrika** Sweden
27 E12 **Fredrikstad** Norway
110 E3 **Freeburg** Missouri U.S.A.
95 K6 **Freeburg** Pennsylvania U.S.A.
100 J4 **Freedom** Idaho U.S.A.
110 K2 **Freedom** Indiana U.S.A.
107 L5 **Freedom** Oklahoma U.S.A.
100 E9 **Freedonyer Peak** *mt* California U.S.A.
95 N6 **Freehold** New Jersey U.S.A.
94 C3 **Freeland** Michigan U.S.A.
95 M5 **Freeland** Pennsylvania U.S.A.
138 E4 **Freeling Heights** *mt* South Australia Australia
140 C6 **Freeling Mt** N Terr Australia
102 E3 **Freel Peak** California U.S.A.
123 T4 **Freels, C** Newfoundland Canada
118 B4 **Freeman** *R* Alberta Canada
98 J6 **Freeman** South Dakota U.S.A.
110 K1 **Freeman, L** Indiana U.S.A.
111 G12 **Freemason I** Louisiana U.S.A.
122 F9 **Freeport** Nova Scotia Canada
111 K11 **Freeport** Florida U.S.A.
99 R7 **Freeport** Illinois U.S.A.
95 R3 **Freeport** Maine U.S.A.
94 F6 **Freeport** Ohio U.S.A.
94 H6 **Freeport** Pennsylvania U.S.A.
109 M7 **Freeport** Texas U.S.A.
113 J11 **Freeport City** Grand Bahama I
109 J8 **Freer** Texas U.S.A.
99 U5 **Freesoil** Michigan U.S.A.
126 F2 **Freetown** Eleuthera Bahamas
122 J7 **Freetown** Prince Edward I Canada
85 B7 **Freetown** Sierra Leone
94 A8 **Freetown** Indiana U.S.A.
127 P4 **Freetown** Antigua W Indies
95 L4 **Freeville** New York U.S.A.
16 C6 **Fregenal de la Sierra** Spain
138 B2 **Fregon** South Australia Australia
20 F4 **Fréhel** France
20 F4 **Fréhel, C** France
26 C8 **Frei** Norway
36 G6 **Freiberg** Germany
37 P2 **Freiberg** Germany
37 O1 **Freiberger Mulde** *R* Germany
40 G1 **Freiburg** Germany
32 K10 **Freienhagen** Germany
32 H10 **Freienohl** Germany
36 G3 **Freiensteinau** Germany
37 M4 **Freihung** Germany
36 D2 **Freilingen** Germany
133 C3 **Freirina** Chile
36 C4 **Freisen** Germany
37 M7 **Freising** Germany
38 L4 **Freistadt** Austria
16 C3 **Freixo de Espada à Cinta** Portugal
28 D2 **Frejlev** Denmark
143 B9 **Fremantle** W Australia Australia
94 C5 **Fremont** Indiana U.S.A.
99 V6 **Fremont** Michigan U.S.A.
98 K8 **Fremont** Nebraska U.S.A.
112 K2 **Fremont** North Carolina U.S.A.
94 D5 **Fremont** Ohio U.S.A.
103 O3 **Fremont** *R* Utah U.S.A.
101 N8 **Fremont I** Utah U.S.A.
101 Q7 **Fremont L** Wyoming U.S.A.
106 D2 **Fremont Pass** Colorado U.S.A.
101 Q6 **Fremont Pk** Wyoming U.S.A.
20 F4 **Frênaye, B.de la** France
112 D2 **French Broad** *R* Tennessee U.S.A.
94 D9 **Frenchburg** Kentucky U.S.A.
94 G5 **French Cr** Pennsylvania U.S.A.
100 J4 **French Creek** Idaho U.S.A.
102 T13 **French Frigate Shoals** Hawaiian Is
100 G7 **Frenchglen** Oregon U.S.A.
129 H3 **French Guiana** *French dept* S America
100 C9 **French Gulch** California U.S.A.
139 H7 **French I** Victoria Australia
110 K3 **French Lick** Indiana U.S.A.
102 F2 **Frenchman** Nevada U.S.A.
95 T2 **Frenchman Bay** Maine U.S.A.
118 H5 **Frenchman Butte** Saskatchewan Canada
139 H8 **Frenchman Cap** Tasmania Australia
101 S1 **Frenchman Cr** Mont/Sask U.S.A./Canada
103 J5 **Frenchman Flat** *dry lake* Nevada U.S.A.
98 E9 **Frenchman Fork** *R* Nebraska U.S.A.
118 J9 **Frenchman R** Saskatchewan Canada
123 O4 **Frenchman's Cove** Newfoundland Canada
14 C3 **Frenchpark** Ireland
145 D4 **French Pass** New Zealand
French Terr. of the Afars and the Issas (FTAI) *see* **Djibouti** *rep*
95 M6 **Frenchtown** New Jersey U.S.A.
22 B2 **Frencq** France
19 Q14 **Frêne, Pic du** *mt* France
21 M3 **Freneuse-sur-Risle** France
37 K4 **Frensdorf** Germany
31 L6 **Frenštát** Czechoslovakia
32 G8 **Freren** Germany
143 D7 **Frere Ra** W Australia Australia
129 H5 **Fresco** *R* Brazil
14 D4 **Freshford** Ireland
144 B6 **Freshford Plain** New Zealand
9 E6 **Freshwater** England
100 A9 **Freshwater** California U.S.A.
21 L5 **Fresnay** France
21 L5 **Fresnaye-sur-Chédouet, la** France
40 C2 **Fresnes** France
22 F3 **Fresnes-sur-L'Escaut** France
124 H6 **Fresnillo de González Echeverría** Mexico
102 E4 **Fresno** *R* California U.S.A.
102 E5 **Fresno** California U.S.A.
101 P1 **Fresno Res** Montana U.S.A.
21 N2 **Fresnoy-Folny** France
22 E4 **Fresnoy-le-Grand** France
40 C4 **Fresse, Mt.de** France
21 O1 **Fressenneville** France
27 B10 **Fresvik** Norway
21 N6 **Fréteval** France
27 B11 **Fretheim** Norway
19 J5 **Fretigney** France
20 A5 **Fret,le** France
13 E1 **Freuchie** Scotland

36 G4 Freudenberg Baden-Württemberg Germany
36 D2 Freudenberg Nordrhein-Westfalen Germany
36 F7 Freudenstadt Germany
22 C3 Frévent France
140 D4 Frewena Roadhouse N Terr Australia
94 H4 Frewsburg New York U.S.A.
37 M1 Freyburg Germany
143 A10 Freycinet, C W Australia
143 A7 Freycinet Estuary inlet W Australia Australia
139 J8 Freycinet Pen Tasmania Australia
33 Q6 Freyenstein Germany
36 B5 Freyming France
37 L5 Freystadt Germany
30 H7 Freyung Germany
85 B6 Fria Guinea
89 B9 Fria, C Namibia
102 E5 Friant California U.S.A.
102 E5 Friant Dam California U.S.A.
102 E6 Friant-Kern Canal California U.S.A.
127 P4 Friar's B., North St Kitts W Indies
83 L10 Friar's Hood mt Sri Lanka
111 F7 Friars Port Mississippi U.S.A.
131 D2 Frias Argentina
40 F4 Fribourg Switzerland
36 E3 Frickhofen Germany
22 D3 Fricourt France
100 B1 Friday Harbour Washington U.S.A.
141 F1 Friday I Queensland Australia
13 H5 Fridaythorpe England
38 O7 Friedberg Austria
37 K7 Friedberg Bayern Germany
36 F3 Friedberg Hessen Germany
33 P9 Friedeburg Germany
38 M4 Friedersbach Austria
33 T8 Friedersdorf Germany
36 E2 Friedland Germany
33 T5 Friedland Germany
37 K2 Friedrichroda Germany
36 F3 Friedrichsdorf Germany
37 T2 Friedrichsfelde Germany
41 K7 Friedrichshafen Germany
33 T8 Friedrichshagen Germany
32 J4 Friedrichskoog Germany
33 P5 Friedrichsruhe Germany
30 E1 Friedrichstadt Germany
33 T6 Friedrichswalde Germany
37 K2 Friedrichswerth Germany
21 H7 Frielendorf Germany
107 K3 Friend Kansas U.S.A.
98 J9 Friend Nebraska U.S.A.
Friendly Is see Tonga
127 K2 Friendship pk Jamaica
95 K3 Friendship Maine U.S.A.
94 J4 Friendship New York U.S.A.
98 D6 Friendship Ohio U.S.A.
99 H6 Friendship Wisconsin U.S.A.
70 C2 Friendship Shoal S China Sea
94 H7 Friendsville Maryland U.S.A.
27 D12 Frierfjord inlet Norway
94 F10 Fries Virginia U.S.A.
38 K8 Friesach Austria
33 R7 Friesack Germany
25 F2 Friesche Gat Netherlands
36 D7 Friesenheim Germany
28 A7 Friesische Inseln islds Germany
25 E2 Friesland Netherlands
32 G6 Friesoythe Germany
83 J12 Frigate isld Seychelles
6 M3 Frigg oil rig North Sea
45 J3 Frignano Italy
41 J8 Frinton-on-Sea England
124 H6 Frio Mexico
109 J7 Frio Texas U.S.A.
130 H8 Frio, C Brazil
15 F4 Friockheim Scotland
108 E1 Frio Draw R New Mex/Tex U.S.A.
36 F6 Friolzheim Germany
22 L4 Frisange Luxembourg
109 L2 Frisco Texas U.S.A.
111 J10 Frisco City Alabama U.S.A.
103 L3 Frisco Mt Utah U.S.A.
108 C8 Fritch Texas U.S.A.
13 G6 Frithelstock Stone England
36 G1 Fritzlar Germany
42 E2 Friuli-Venezia-Giulia prov Italy
21 O1 Friville-Escarbotin France
12 E5 Frizington England
26 D8 Froan isld Norway
119 P9 Frobisher Saskatchewan Canada
115 N5 Frobisher Bay Northwest Territories Canada
114 J6 Frobisher L Saskatchewan Canada
8 D1 Frodsham England
19 P14 Froges France
118 G5 Frog L Alberta Canada
26 D8 Frohavet inlet Norway
37 O1 Frohburg Germany
37 N2 Frohnau Germany
33 P8 Frohse Germany
98 B1 Froid Montana U.S.A.
22 G3 Froid-Chapelle Belgium
130 F5 Fróis Brazil
21 P2 Froissy France
37 N2 Frohzheim Germany
52 H4 Frolovskaya Russian Federation
55 E1 Froly Russian Federation
101 R4 Fromberg Montana U.S.A.
31 M1 Frombork Poland
138 E3 Frome R South Australia Australia
8 D5 Frome England
127 H1 Frome Jamaica
138 E4 Frome Downs South Australia Australia
138 E4 Frome, L South Australia Australia
22 D2 Fromelles France
21 K4 Fromentel France
20 F8 Fromentine France
32 G10 Fröndenberg Germany
125 N8 Frontera Mexico
124 E2 Fronteras Mexico
118 J9 Fronteras Saskatchewan Canada
101 P8 Frontier Wyoming U.S.A.
18 H9 Frontignan France
106 E1 Front Range Colorado U.S.A.
94 H8 Front Royal Virginia U.S.A.
28 F6 Frørup Denmark
22 G7 Frose Germany
43 E7 Frosinone Italy
28 E7 Frøslev Denmark
20 G7 Frossay France
109 L3 Frost Texas U.S.A.
26 E6 Frosta Norway
94 J7 Frostburg Maryland U.S.A.
113 F10 Frostproof Florida U.S.A.
28 B2 Frøstrup Denmark
27 K6 Frøstviken Sweden
37 K2 Fröttstädt Germany
60 J4 Frouard France
119 O9 Froude Saskatchewan Canada
27 F9 Frövi Sweden
9 E5 Froxfield England
26 F8 Frøya isld Norway
26 B8 Frøyabanken Norway
22 G3 Fruges France
61 H10 Fruita Colorado U.S.A.
111 H10 Fruitdale Alabama U.S.A.
119 P6 Fruitdale South Dakota U.S.A.
100 J5 Fruitland Idaho U.S.A.
106 B5 Fruitland New Mexico U.S.A.

101 P9 Fruitland Utah U.S.A.
144 B6 Fruitlands New Zealand
100 J5 Fruitvale Idaho U.S.A.
48 K3 Frumuşica Romania
Frunze see Bishkek
54 F8 Frunzenskiy Ukraine
48 M3 Frunzivka Ukraine
48 F5 Fruška Gora mt Serbia Yugoslavia
130 E7 Frutal Brazil
40 G4 Frutigen Switzerland
102 B2 Fruto California U.S.A.
54 K1 Fryanovo Russian Federation
98 C3 Fryburg North Dakota U.S.A.
48 E1 Frýdek Místek Czechoslovakia
95 P2 Fryeburg Maine U.S.A.
27 F11 Fryksände Sweden
46 E5 Ftéri mt Greece
67 F3 Fu'an China
45 J4 Fucecchio Italy
Fucheng see Qiongshan
65 C6 Fucheng China
65 B7 Fucheng China
36 E2 Fuchskauten mt Germany
67 O4 Fuchun Jiang China
59 G6 Fuchun China
42 F7 Fucino, Piana del Italy
61 P5 Fudai Japan
67 G3 Fuding China
16 D8 Fuengirola Spain
108 G2 Fuente Mexico
17 G7 Fuente Álamo de Murcia Spain
16 C6 Fuente de Cantos Spain
16 C4 Fuenteguinaldo Spain
16 D6 Fuenteobejuna Spain
27 A11 Fuentesauco Spain
128 D3 Fuensagasta Colombia
13 G4 Fusaro Italy
49 G9 Fuentes de Ebro Spain
43 G9 Fuentes de Oñoro Spain
38 G7 Fuerte Mexico
130 B7 Fuerte Olimpo Paraguay
85 B3 Fuerteventura isld Canary Is
71 E1 Fuga isld Luzon Philippines
38 M8 Fügen Austria
28 H6 Fuglebjerg Denmark
6 F1 Fugloy isld Faeroes
26 L1 Fugløy isld Norway
28 F7 Fuglsbølle Denmark
65 C7 Fugou China
65 B5 Fugu China
118 H7 Fugu see Zhanhua
66 D2 Fuhai China
77 A5 Fuhayhil, Al Kuwait
33 Q9 Fuhne R Germany
32 L7 Fuhrberg Germany
21 H7 Fullet, le France
59 J3 Fujairah U.A.E.
41 N2 Fujairah, Al see Fujairah
67 F3 Fujian prov China
67 B1 Fu Jiang R China
61 M11 Fujieda Japan
61 M10 Fuji Hakone Izu Nat. Park Japan
61 M10 Fuji-kawa R Japan
61 O5 Fujin China
59 K2 Fujin China
61 P13 Fujinomiya Japan
61 N10 Fujisaki Japan
137 R4 Fuji-san vol Japan
61 M10 Fujiyoshida Japan
61 N5 Fukaura Japan
61 N9 Fukaya Japan
60 J10 Fukuchiyama Japan
58 G5 Fukue Japan
67 F1 Fukue-jima isld Japan
61 K9 Fukui Japan
67 G3 Fuyang Dao isld China
59 H2 Fuyu China
59 H2 Fuyu China
52 A2 Fuyuan China
59 H2 Fuyuan China
67 C1 Fuyun China
48 F3 Füzesabony Hungary
48 G3 Füzesgyarmat Hungary
67 F3 Fuzhou Fujian China
67 E2 Fuzhou Jiangxi China
67 D1 Fuzhougshng China
9 E4 Fyfield England
9 G4 Fyfield Essex England
28 E6 Fyn isld Denmark
28 E6 Fyn co Denmark
12 C1 Fyne, L Scotland
28 F5 Fynshav Denmark
27 C12 Fyresvl L Norway
127 O3 Fyzabad Trinidad

G

86 A2 Gaalkacyo Somalia
70 C4 Gaat R Sarawak
52 D4 Gabanova Russian Federation
123 M8 Gabarouse C Breton I, Nova Scotia
17 J3 Gabarras, Mts Spain
18 F9 Gabarret France
109 K2 Gabbs Nevada U.S.A.
102 F3 Gabbs Valley Ra Nevada U.S.A.
87 B8 Gabela Angola
83 K10 Gaberones see Gaborone
83 K10 Gabès Tunisia
85 G2 Gabès, Golfe de Tunisia
46 J5 Gabgaba, Wadi watercourse Sudan
102 C5 Gabilan Ra California U.S.A.
100 B7 Galice Oregon U.S.A.
98 J1 Gabin Poland
145 G3 Gable End Foreland New Zealand
72 F5 Gable Mt British Columbia Canada
139 J10 Gabo isld Victoria Australia
86 B6 Gabon rep Equat Africa
89 D5 Gaborone Botswana
95 N2 Gabriels New York U.S.A.
16 C4 Gabriel y Galán, Embalse res Spain
77 B8 Gabrik Iran
46 G2 Gabrovo Bulgaria
86 B6 Gabú Guinea-Bissau
83 L14 Gaby isld Kerguelen Indian Oc
21 L4 Gacé France
76 D3 Gach Sārān Iran
77 B4 Gach Sār Iran
46 F1 Gacilly, la France
98 G3 Gackle North Dakota U.S.A.
46 E4 Gacko Bosnia-Herzegovina
80 B3 Ga'da, Al Western Sahara
76 B3 Gadag India
81 D5 Gadaimai Sudan
28 D7 Gadbjerg Denmark
46 G7 Gadbjerg Sweden
32 J8 Gadebusch Germany
80 D3 Gadish Israel
84 B3 Gador, Sierra de Spain
81 K6 Gadra India

119 V3 Garraway Manitoba Canada
32 H7 Garrel Germany
98 K6 Garretson South Dakota U.S.A.
94 B5 Garrett Indiana U.S.A.
94 H7 Garrett Pennsylvania U.S.A.
101 U7 Garrett Wyoming U.S.A.
94 F5 Garrettsville Ohio U.S.A.
119 N5 Garrick Saskatchewan Canada
99 O7 Garrison Iowa U.S.A.
94 D8 Garrison Kentucky U.S.A.
99 N3 Garrison Minnesota U.S.A.
101 N3 Garrison Montana U.S.A.
95 O5 Garrison New York U.S.A.
98 E2 Garrison North Dakota U.S.A.
109 N4 Garrison Texas U.S.A.
103 L3 Garrison Utah U.S.A.
98 E2 Garrison Dam North Dakota U.S.A.
16 C5 Garrovillas Spain
15 D6 Garry L Scotland
115 K4 Garry L Northwest Territories Canada
101 A5 Garryowen Montana U.S.A.
88 H3 Garsen Kenya
28 D5 Gärslev Denmark
27 G16 Gärsnäs Sweden
118 G2 Garson L Alberta Canada
32 M7 Garssen Germany
38 F7 Garsstein mt Austria
13 F6 Garstang England
144 B6 Garston New Zealand
18 F6 Gartempe R France
8 C2 Garthmyl Wales
Gartok see Garyarsa
33 O6 Gartow Germany
37 H2 Gartz Germany
19 J12 Garut Java
118 G2 Garvald L Alberta Canada
15 D3 Garve Scotland
144 B6 Garvie Mts New Zealand
31 N4 Garwolin Poland
100 J2 Garwood Idaho U.S.A.
109 L6 Garwood Texas U.S.A.
99 T8 Gary Indiana U.S.A.
98 K2 Gary Minnesota U.S.A.
75 F3 Gary South Dakota U.S.A.
109 N3 Gary Texas U.S.A.
94 F9 Gary West Virginia U.S.A.
66 C5 Garyarsa China
67 C3 Garze China
128 C3 Garzón Colombia
10 K1 Gasan-Kuli Turkmenistan
32 E5 Gaschwitz Germany
45 J4 Gasciana Terme Italy
94 B6 Gas City Indiana U.S.A.
18 E9 Gascogne prov France
122 H5 Gasconade R Missouri U.S.A.
110 E3 Gascony, G. de France/Spain
122 H5 Gasconade R Missouri U.S.A.
98 D6 Gascoyne North Dakota U.S.A.
143 B7 Gascoyne Junction W Australia Australia
143 B6 Gascoyne, Mt W Australia Australia
143 A6 Gascoyne, R W Australia Australia
86 G2 Gascura, Golfo de see Gascogne, G.de
85 G7 Gashaka Nigeria
74 G1 Gasherbrum mt Kashmir
85 G6 Gashua Nigeria
Gashuun Nuur L see Gaxun Nur
26 H4 Gaskacok mt Norway
21 O3 Gasny France
126 E4 Gaspar Cuba
127 J5 Gaspar Hernández Dominican Rep
113 E11 Gasparilla isld Florida U.S.A.
69 H14 Gaspé, B. de Quebec Canada
122 H5 Gaspé Quebec Canada
122 F5 Gaspé Pen Quebec Canada
121 J1 Gaspereau L Nova Scotia Canada
122 G7 Gaspereau Forks New Brunswick Canada
124 D8 Gaspesie, Parc de la Quebec Canada
100 J7 Gasquet California U.S.A.
61 O7 Gassan mt Japan
114 J8 Gassaway West Virginia U.S.A.
25 D3 Gassette Netherlands
85 F2 Gassi, El Algeria
44 C1 Gassino Torinese Italy
85 G7 Gassol Nigeria
103 A5 Gässo Pk Nevada U.S.A.
42 G8 Gassum Denmark
38 H7 Gasteiner Tal Austria
Gasteiz see Vitoria
94 A3 Gaston Oregon U.S.A.
112 F2 Gastonia North Carolina U.S.A.
33 T8 Gastouni Greece
133 D6 Gastre Argentina
17 F8 Gata, C.de Spain
117 K6 Gataga R British Columbia Canada
14 C4 Gataia Romania
45 J5 Gata, Sa. de mts Spain
52 C4 Gatchina Russian Federation
108 D7 Gate Oklahoma U.S.A.
94 E10 Gate City Virginia U.S.A.
12 D4 Gatehouse of Fleet Scotland
100 C4 Gates Oregon U.S.A.
116 L3 Gates of the Arctic Nat Park and Preserve Alaska U.S.A.
109 K4 Gatesville Texas U.S.A.
105 K1 Gatesville North Carolina U.S.A.
101 K3 Gateway Colorado U.S.A.
100 B5 Gateway Oregon U.S.A.
121 P5 Gâtine France
122 F5 Gatineau Quebec Canada
122 F7 Gatineau Quebec Canada
122 F7 Gâtine Hauteurs de hills France
32 D1 Gatlinburg Tennessee U.S.A.
80 D1 Ga'ton Israel
Gatooma see Kadoma
33 S8 Gatow Germany
61 N7 Gatsugi Japan
85 G3 Gattinara Italy
61 N7 Gatton Queensland Australia
124 K8 Gatun Panama
125 O3 Gatún L Panama
9 F5 Gatwick Airport England
21 S7 Gauchin-le-Gal France
31 N4 Gauchy France
23 H8 Gaucín Spain
15 D3 Gaudalmelloth? Spain
77 H5 Gaud-I-Zirreh salt desert Afghanistan
123 K3 Gaudeault, L Quebec Canada
111 O3 Gauer L Manitoba Canada
119 U1 Gauhati see Guwahati
32 J6 Gauldal Norway
21 M5 Gault, le France
123 R6 Gaultois Newfoundland Canada

Glenwood — Grandpré
179

112 F2 **Glenwood** North Carolina U.S.A.
100 B4 **Glenwood** Oregon U.S.A.
103 N3 **Glenwood** Utah U.S.A.
100 D3 **Glenwood** Washington U.S.A.
94 E8 **Glenwood** West Virginia U.S.A.
99 O4 **Glenwood** Wisconsin U.S.A.
106 C2 **Glenwood Springs** Colorado U.S.A.
118 D9 **Glenwoodville** Alberta Canada
28 F4 **Glesborg** Denmark
33 N4 **Gleschendorf** Germany
41 H4 **Gletsch** Switzerland
118 H7 **Glidden** Saskatchewan Canada
99 Q3 **Glidden** Wisconsin U.S.A.
100 B6 **Glide** Oregon U.S.A.
33 S8 **Glienick** Germany
33 S7 **Glienicke** Germany
14 B4 **Glin** Ireland
32 M5 **Glinde** Germany
31 M3 **Glinojeck** Poland
48 J1 **Glinyany** Ukraine
26 G9 **Glissjöberg** Sweden
26 C10 **Glittertind** *mt* Norway
31 L5 **Gliwice** Poland
46 D4 **Gllavë** Albania
103 O8 **Globe** Arizona U.S.A.
48 C3 **Gloggnitz** Austria
31 J4 **Głogów** Poland
31 K5 **Glogówek** Poland
31 N5 **Głogów Małopolski** Poland
33 Q8 **Gloine** Germany
20 D5 **Glomel** France
26 G5 **Glomfjord** Norway
26 E9 **Glomma** *R* Norway
26 L6 **Glommerstrask** Sweden
27 J15 **Glönminge** Sweden
130 H10 **Glória** Brazil
106 E6 **Glorieta** New Mexico U.S.A.
87 H10 **Glorieuses, Is** Indian Oc
116 C6 **Glory of Russia C** Alaska U.S.A.
21 L3 **Glos** France
21 M4 **Glos-la-Ferrière** France
13 G6 **Glossop** England
21 M3 **Glos-sur-Risle** France
111 E10 **Gloster** Mississippi U.S.A.
29 K5 **Glostrup** Denmark
52 G3 **Glotovo** Russian Federation
139 K4 **Gloucester** New South Wales Australia
8 D4 **Gloucester** England
95 R4 **Gloucester** Massachusetts U.S.A.
95 L9 **Gloucester** Virginia U.S.A.
95 M7 **Gloucester City** New Jersey U.S.A.
141 J4 **Gloucester I** Queensland Australia
94 E7 **Glouster** Ohio U.S.A.
123 P5 **Glover I** Newfoundland Canada
95 N3 **Gloversville** New York U.S.A.
33 Q7 **Glöwen** Germany
31 M4 **Głowno** Poland
54 M8 **Glubokiy** Russian Federation
56 B5 **Glubokoye** Kazakhstan
31 K5 **Głuchołazy** Poland
28 D7 **Glucksburg** Germany
32 K5 **Glückstadt** Germany
28 D5 **Glud** Denmark
28 C4 **Gludsted** Denmark
54 E5 **Glukhov** Ukraine
52 F6 **Glukhovo** Russian Federation
69 B10 **Glumpangminyeuk** Sumatra
29 K5 **Glumslöv** Sweden
28 H6 **Glumsø** Denmark
13 F6 **Glusburn** England
55 E4 **Glyadyanskoye** Russian Federation
48 K2 **Glyboka** Ukraine
8 B1 **Glyder Fawr** *mt* Wales
143 E6 **Glynde Hill** W Australia Australia
95 L7 **Glyndon** Maryland U.S.A.
98 K3 **Glyndon** Minnesota U.S.A.
28 B3 **Glyngøre** Denmark
8 C4 **Glynneath** Wales
8 C4 **Glyntawe** Wales
31 J7 **Gmünd** Austria
38 J6 **Gmunden** Austria
33 P9 **Gnadau** Germany
94 F6 **Gnadenhutten** Ohio U.S.A.
26 J9 **Gnarp** Sweden
32 K6 **Gnarrenburg** Germany
38 N8 **Gnas** Austria
27 J12 **Gnesta** Sweden
28 G4 **Gniben** *C* Denmark
31 L2 **Gniew** Poland
31 K3 **Gniezno** Poland
33 M4 **Gnissau** Germany
46 E2 **Gnjilane** Serbia Yugoslavia
33 R5 **Gnoien** Germany
8 D2 **Gnosall** England
37 K5 **Gnotzheim** Germany
143 C10 **Gnowangerup** W Australia
143 B9 **Gnuka** W Australia
32 L4 **Gnutz** Germany
76 A3 **Goa, Daman & Diu** *terr* India
139 K6 **Goalen Head** New South Wales Australia
75 O5 **Goalpara** India
71 H9 **Goang** Indonesia
12 C2 **Goat Fell** *mt* Scotland
13 H5 **Goathland** England
101 M1 **Goat Mt** Montana U.S.A.
87 F11 **Goba** Mozambique
89 A4 **Gobabis** Namibia
58 D3 **Gobi Desert** Mongolia
60 J12 **Gobō** Japan
8 C2 **Gobowen** England
25 F5 **Goch** Germany
87 C10 **Gochas** Namibia
86 G4 **Gocho** Ethiopia
36 F5 **Gochsheim** Germany
79 C2 **Göçuk** Turkey
9 F5 **Godalming** England
74 J9 **Godavari** *R* India
76 F2 **Godavari, Mouths of the** India
122 E4 **Godbout** Quebec Canada
122 E4 **Godbout, R** Quebec Canada
117 E7 **Goddard** Alaska U.S.A.
107 N4 **Goddard** Kansas U.S.A.
36 F4 **Goddelau-Wolfskehlen** Germany
46 F1 **Godech** Bulgaria
27 H13 **Godegård** Sweden
32 K9 **Godelheim** Germany
47 L8 **Gödene** Turkey
120 J9 **Goderich** Ontario Canada
21 L2 **Goderville** France
22 D2 **Godewaersvelde** France
121 O8 **Godfrey** Ontario Canada
110 F3 **Godfrey** Illinois U.S.A.
115 O4 **Godhavn** Greenland
74 E7 **Godhra** India
109 K3 **Godley** Texas U.S.A.
144 C5 **Godley Gl** New Zealand
144 C5 **Godley R** New Zealand
9 F3 **Godmanchester** England
71 J5 **Godo** *mt* Indonesia
48 E3 **Gödöllő** Hungary
9 E6 **Godshill** England
115 K7 **Gods L** Manitoba Canada
9 F5 **Godstone** England
115 O5 **Godthåb** Greenland
112 J2 **Godwin** North Carolina U.S.A.
Godwin Austen *mt see* **K2** *mt*
25 A5 **Goedereede** Netherlands
121 O3 **Goeland** Quebec Canada
25 A5 **Goeree** Netherlands
25 A6 **Goes** Netherlands
107 P2 **Goff** Kansas U.S.A.
103 J7 **Goffs** Carolina U.S.A.
95 Q3 **Goffstown** New Hampshire U.S.A.
120 J5 **Gogama** Ontario Canada
60 F10 **Gō-gawa** *R* Japan
99 R3 **Gogebic** Michigan U.S.A.
99 R3 **Gogebic Range** *mts* Michigan U.S.A.
37 K7 **Goggingen** Germany
41 H5 **Goglio** Italy
7 L10 **Gog Magog Hills** England
36 B6 **Gogney** France
22 F3 **Gognies-Chaussée** Belgium
142 F4 **Gogo** W Australia Australia
31 K5 **Gogolin** Poland
86 E4 **Gogrial** Sudan
33 Q9 **Gohrau** Germany
33 N6 **Göhrde** Germany
130 J9 **Goiana** Brazil
130 E6 **Goiandira** Brazil
130 E4 **Goianésia** Brazil
130 E5 **Goiânia** Brazil
130 J9 **Goianinha** *lighthouse* Brazil
130 E4 **Goiás** Brazil
130 D5 **Goiás** *state* Brazil
130 E6 **Goiatuba** Brazil
12 D1 **Goil, L** Scotland
130 D9 **Goio Erê** Brazil
25 D5 **Goirle** Netherlands
45 J1 **Goito** Italy
86 G3 **Gojam** *prov* Ethiopia
86 G4 **Gojeb** *R* Ethiopia
61 J11 **Gojō** Japan
61 O6 **Gojōme** Japan
47 K5 **Gök** *R* Turkey
76 B2 **Gokak** India
47 K7 **Gökbel** *mt* Turkey
47 H4 **Gökçeada** *isld* Turkey
47 K5 **Gökçedağ** Turkey
79 C2 **Gökdere** *str* Turkey
32 K4 **Gokels** Germany
78 A3 **Gökova Körfezi** Turkey
77 H7 **Gokprosh Hills** Pakistan
78 D3 **Göksu** *R* Turkey
78 F2 **Göksun** Turkey
68 C1 **Gokteik** Burma
47 K7 **Göktepe** Turkey
47 K8 **Gök Tepe** *mt* Turkey
79 C2 **Göktepe** Turkey
87 E9 **Gokwe** Zimbabwe
27 C11 **Gol** Norway
75 P5 **Golaghat** India
80 G2 **Golan** Syria
31 K3 **Gołańcz** Poland
77 E6 **Golāshkerd** Iran
54 D10 **Golaya Pristan'** Ukraine
77 E5 **Golbaf** Iran
77 L2 **Golbahār** Afghanistan
38 G8 **Gölbnerjoch** *mt* Austria
74 H10 **Golconda** India
110 H4 **Golconda** Illinois U.S.A.
100 H9 **Golconda** Nevada U.S.A.
Gölcük *see* **Etili**
47 N11 **Gölcük** Turkey
94 K5 **Gold** Pennsylvania U.S.A.
31 N1 **Gołdap** Poland
100 A7 **Gold Beach** Oregon U.S.A.
33 P7 **Goldbeck** Germany
33 Q5 **Goldberg** Germany
123 L8 **Goldboro** Nova Scotia Canada
101 O1 **Gold Butte** Montana U.S.A.
141 L8 **Gold Coast** Queensland Australia
28 C7 **Goldelund** Germany
117 P10 **Golden** British Columbia Canada
98 A10 **Golden** Colorado U.S.A.
100 K4 **Golden** Idaho U.S.A.
110 E1 **Golden** Illinois U.S.A.
145 D4 **Golden Bay** New Zealand
110 B4 **Golden City** Missouri U.S.A.
100 E4 **Goldendale** Washington U.S.A.
144 D4 **Golden Downs** New Zealand
33 N10 **Goldene Aue** Germany
102 B4 **Golden Gate** California U.S.A.
102 B4 **Golden Gate Nat. Recreation Area** California U.S.A.
103 J4 **Golden Gate Ra** Nevada U.S.A.
127 M3 **Golden Grove** Jamaica
121 N7 **Golden Lake** Ontario Canada
111 F12 **Golden Meadow** Louisiana U.S.A.
110 H5 **Golden Pond** Kentucky U.S.A.
118 H8 **Golden Prairie** Saskatchewan Canada
127 P4 **Golden Rock** *airport* St Kitts W Indies
101 N8 **Golden Spike Nat. Hist. Site** Utah U.S.A.
32 H7 **Goldenstedt** Germany
14 C4 **Golden Vale** Ireland
123 K8 **Goldenville** Nova Scotia Canada
99 N7 **Goldfield** Iowa U.S.A.
102 G4 **Goldfield** Nevada U.S.A.
109 J7 **Goldfinch** Texas U.S.A.
101 M9 **Gold Hill** Utah U.S.A.
102 G4 **Gold Point** Nevada U.S.A.
118 K1 **Gold Rock** Ontario Canada
119 R1 **Goldsand L** Manitoba Canada
95 M7 **Goldsboro** Maryland U.S.A.
112 K2 **Goldsboro** North Carolina U.S.A.
108 E4 **Goldsmith** Texas U.S.A.
102 H6 **Goldstone L** California U.S.A.
142 C5 **Goldsworthy** W Australia Australia
142 C5 **Goldsworthy, Mt** W Australia Australia
109 J4 **Goldthwaite** Texas U.S.A.
112 F3 **Goldville** South Carolina U.S.A.
78 J1 **Göle** Turkey
85 E2 **Golea, El** Algeria
89 G6 **Golela** S Africa
31 H2 **Goleniów** Poland
102 E7 **Goleta** California U.S.A.
16 C7 **Golfo de Cádiz** Spain
43 E10 **Golfo di Castellammare** Sicily
43 E7 **Golfo di Gaeta** Italy
44 E3 **Golfo di Genova** Italy
45 N1 **Golfo di Venezia** Adriatic Sea
47 K7 **Gölgel Dağ** *mts* Turkey
138 F5 **Gol Gol** New South Wales Australia
109 K7 **Goliad** Texas U.S.A.
46 D1 **Golija Planina** *mt* Serbia Yugoslavia
65 E2 **Golin Baixing** China
Gollel *see* **Lavumisa**
33 T6 **Gollin** Germany
38 H6 **Golling** Austria
33 S10 **Gollmberg** *pk* Germany
33 T9 **Gollmitz** Germany
47 J6 **Gölmarmara** Turkey
33 S8 **Golmberg** *pk* Germany
37 M2 **Golmsdorf** Germany
66 E4 **Golmud** China
71 E4 **Golo** *isld* Philippines
52 H1 **Golodnaya Guba, Oz** *L* Russian Federation
57 E4 **Golodnaya Step'** Kazakhstan/Uzbekistan
86 H4 **Gololcha** Ethiopia
88 E9 **Golomoti** Malawi
48 N2 **Golovanevsk** Ukraine
116 F4 **Golovin** Alaska U.S.A.
60 T2 **Golovnino** Kuril Is Russian Federation
77 B3 **Golpāyegān** Iran
47 L4 **Gölpazarı** Turkey
116 G5 **Golsovia** Alaska U.S.A.
15 E3 **Golspie** Scotland
33 T9 **Golssen** Germany
28 D2 **Gølstrup** Denmark
107 M5 **Goltry** Oklahoma U.S.A.
31 L2 **Gołub** Poland
55 F4 **Golubovka** Kazakhstan
89 F3 **Golulu Ruins** Zimbabwe
87 B7 **Golungo Alto** Angola
98 C3 **Golva** North Dakota U.S.A.
46 G3 **Golyam Perelik** *mt* Bulgaria
31 M3 **Gołymin** Poland
54 C2 **Golynki** Russian Federation
55 E3 **Golyshmanovo** Russian Federation
33 R8 **Golzow** Germany
88 B2 **Goma** Zaire
85 G6 **Gombe** Nigeria
44 H4 **Gombo** Italy
70 M9 **Gombong** Java
47 H5 **Gömeç** Turkey
54 B4 **Gomel'** Belorussia
85 A3 **Gomera** *isld* Canary Is
124 H5 **Gómez Palacio** Mexico
125 K4 **Gómez, Presa M.R.** *res* Mexico
20 F5 **Gommené** France
33 P8 **Gommern** Germany
66 C5 **Gomo** China
71 A3 **Gomumu** *isld* Indonesia
127 H5 **Gonaïves** Haiti
51 M3 **Gonam** *R* Russian Federation
89 G3 **Gona-re-zhou Game Res.** Zimbabwe
126 H5 **Gonâve, Île de la** Haiti
48 G2 **Gönc** Hungary
19 Q14 **Goncelin** France
74 D8 **Gondal** India
36 F5 **Gondelsheim** Germany
86 G3 **Gonder** Ethiopia
86 G3 **Gonder** *prov* Ethiopia
74 J8 **Gondia** India
19 J4 **Gondrecourt** France
80 F1 **Gonen** Israel
47 J4 **Gönen** *R* Turkey
47 J4 **Gönen** Turkey
19 Q18 **Gonfaron** France
21 L2 **Gonfreville l'Orcher** France
83 K11 **Gongala** *mt* Sri Lanka
67 D1 **Gong'an** China
66 E5 **Gongbo'gyamda** China
67 C4 **Gongcheng** China
75 O4 **Gonggar** China
58 D6 **Gongga Shan** *mt* China
57 K3 **Gongliu** China
Gonglüe *see* **Donggu**
85 G6 **Gongola** *R* Nigeria
139 H4 **Gongolgon** New South Wales Australia
67 D3 **Gongpingxu** China
67 D2 **Gongtian** China
65 B7 **Gong Xian** China
65 D4 **Gongyingzi** China
Gongzhuling *see* **Huaide**
31 O2 **Goniądz** Poland
88 G4 **Gonja** Tanzania
36 G7 **Gönningen** Germany
46 E5 **Gónnos** Greece
61 P5 **Gonohe** Japan
60 C12 **Gōnoura** Japan
40 D3 **Gonsans** France
99 L2 **Gonvick** Minnesota U.S.A.
45 J2 **Gonzaga** Italy
102 C5 **Gonzales** California U.S.A.
109 K6 **Gonzales** Texas U.S.A.
36 C4 **Gonzerath** Germany
86 H6 **Goob Weyn** Somalia
94 K9 **Goochland** Virginia U.S.A.
146 F14 **Goodenough, C** Antarctica
121 M8 **Gooderham** Ontario Canada
119 O7 **Goodeve** Saskatchewan Canada
94 B1 **Good Hart** Michigan U.S.A.
99 V4 **Good Hbr. B** Michigan U.S.A.
89 B8 **Goodhope** S Africa
116 E4 **Goodhope** *R* Alaska U.S.A.
116 F3 **Goodhope B** Alaska U.S.A.
87 C12 **Good Hope, C. of** S Africa
117 L10 **Good Hope, Mt** British Columbia Canada
87 C11 **Goodhouse** S Africa
99 O5 **Goodhue** Minnesota U.S.A.
101 L7 **Gooding** Idaho U.S.A.
107 J2 **Goodland** Kansas U.S.A.
119 R9 **Goodlands** Manitoba Canada
83 M12 **Goodlands** Mauritius
110 K5 **Goodlettsville** Tennessee U.S.A.
99 S4 **Goodman** Wisconsin U.S.A.
116 F7 **Goodnews B** Alaska U.S.A.
108 C8 **Goodnight** Texas U.S.A.
139 H3 **Goodooga** New South Wales Australia
140 B2 **Goodparla** N Terr Australia
116 P4 **Goodpaster** *R* Alaska U.S.A.
106 F3 **Good Pasture** Colorado U.S.A.
98 B9 **Goodrich** Colorado U.S.A.
100 J5 **Goodrich** Idaho U.S.A.
98 F2 **Goodrich** North Dakota U.S.A.
111 B11 **Goodrich** Texas U.S.A.
99 Q4 **Goodrich** Wisconsin U.S.A.
140 B1 **Goodrich Bank** N Terr Australia
117 P10 **Goodsir, Mt** British Columbia Canada
118 H4 **Goodsoil** Saskatchewan Canada
119 P7 **Good Spirit L** Saskatchewan Canada
103 J6 **Goodsprings** Nevada U.S.A.
119 O9 **Goodwater** Saskatchewan Canada
111 K8 **Good Water** Alabama U.S.A.
107 J5 **Goodwell** Oklahoma U.S.A.
8 A3 **Goodwick** Wales
121 L4 **Goodwin** Ontario Canada
103 M7 **Goodwin** Arizona U.S.A.
98 K5 **Goodwin** South Dakota U.S.A.
7 M11 **Goodwin Sands** English Chan
144 C6 **Goodwood** New Zealand
9 F6 **Goodwood Park** England
13 H6 **Goole** England
139 H5 **Goolgowi** New South Wales Australia
139 J4 **Goolma** New South Wales Australia
139 J5 **Gooloogong** New South Wales Australia
138 E6 **Goolwa** South Australia Australia
140 C1 **Goomadeer** *R* N Terr Australia
143 B9 **Goomalling** W Australia Australia
139 H3 **Goombalie** New South Wales Australia
141 K7 **Goombungee** Queensland Australia
141 K7 **Goomeri** Queensland Australia
141 K8 **Goondiwindi** Queensland Australia
143 D9 **Goongarrie** W Australia Australia
143 D8 **Goongarrie, L** W Australia Australia
141 J5 **Goonyella** Queensland Australia
25 G4 **Goor** Netherlands
117 P8 **Goose** *R* Alberta Canada
115 N7 **Goose Bay** Labrador, Nfld Canada
144 D5 **Goose Bay** New Zealand
101 R5 **Gooseberry Cr** Wyoming U.S.A.
118 G6 **Gooseberry L. Prov. Park** Alberta Canada
123 R2 **Goose Cove** Newfoundland Canada
101 M7 **Goose Cr** Idaho U.S.A.
112 G4 **Goose Creek** South Carolina U.S.A.
101 M8 **Goose Cr. Mts** Utah U.S.A.
101 T7 **Goose Egg** Wyoming U.S.A.
116 F9 **Goose I** Alaska U.S.A.
119 Q4 **Goose L** Manitoba Canada
100 E8 **Goose L** California U.S.A.
76 C3 **Gooty** India
75 L9 **Gopalpur** India
31 L3 **Gopło, Jezioro** *L* Poland
36 H6 **Göppingen** Germany
103 K10 **Gora** *isld* Mexico
31 K4 **Góra** Poland
31 N4 **Gora Kalwaria** Poland
75 K5 **Gorakhpur** India
42 J5 **Goransko** Montenegro Yugoslavia
48 E7 **Goražde** Bosnia-Herzegovina
113 K11 **Gorda Cay** *isld* Bahamas
128 D7 **Gorda, Pta** *C* Chile
19 O17 **Gordes** France
47 J6 **Gördes** Turkey
86 D4 **Gordil** Cent Afr Republic
28 B6 **Gørding** Denmark
111 J8 **Gordo** Alabama U.S.A.
139 H8 **Gordon** *R* Tasmania Australia
13 F2 **Gordon** Scotland
116 R2 **Gordon** Alaska U.S.A.
106 F4 **Gordon** Colorado U.S.A.
112 D5 **Gordon** Georgia U.S.A.
98 D7 **Gordon** Nebraska U.S.A.
109 J3 **Gordon** Texas U.S.A.
99 P3 **Gordon** Wisconsin U.S.A.
13 E3 **Gordon Arms** Scotland
140 B1 **Gordon B** N Terr Australia
140 B3 **Gordon Cr** N Terr Australia
98 E7 **Gordon Cr** Nebraska U.S.A.
142 G4 **Gordon Downs** W Australia Australia
139 H8 **Gordon L.** Tasmania Australia
118 G2 **Gordon, L** Alberta Canada
117 R4 **Gordon L** Northwest Territories Canada
117 F4 **Gordon Landing** Yukon Territory Canada
94 B10 **Gordonsville** Tennessee U.S.A.
94 J8 **Gordonsville** Virginia U.S.A.
141 H3 **Gordonvale** Queensland Australia
86 C4 **Goré** Chad
86 G4 **Gorē** Ethiopia
144 B7 **Gore** New Zealand
107 P6 **Gore** Oklahoma U.S.A.
120 H7 **Gore Bay** Ontario Canada
144 D5 **Gore Bay** New Zealand
13 E2 **Gorebridge** Scotland
109 H2 **Goree** Texas U.S.A.
54 J2 **Gorelki** Russian Federation
95 Q2 **Gore Mt** Vermont U.S.A.
140 E4 **Gore Pt** Queensland Australia
116 M7 **Gore Pt** Alaska U.S.A.
106 D2 **Gore Ra** Colorado U.S.A.
110 H4 **Goreville** Illinois U.S.A.
20 F3 **Gorey** Channel Is
14 E4 **Gorey** Ireland
77 D1 **Gorgān** Iran
147 K11 **Gorga, Zemlya** *isld* Russian Federation
83 K14 **Gorge** *R* Réunion Indian Oc
142 C5 **Gorge Ra** W Australia Australia
141 H4 **Gorge Ra., The** Queensland Australia
128 C3 **Gorgona** *isld* Colombia
42 C5 **Gorgona, I.di** Italy
41 K6 **Gorgonzola** Italy
86 G3 **Gorgora** Ethiopia
85 G6 **Gorgoram** Nigeria
101 O9 **Gorgorza** Utah U.S.A.
107 L3 **Gorham** Kansas U.S.A.
95 R3 **Gorham** Maine U.S.A.
95 Q2 **Gorham** New Hampshire U.S.A.
95 K4 **Gorham** New York U.S.A.
53 F12 **Gori** Georgia
46 D4 **Goricë** Albania
99 O9 **Gorin** Missouri U.S.A.
25 C5 **Gorinchem** Netherlands
9 E4 **Goring** England
27 H10 **Göringen** Sweden
78 L2 **Goris** Armenia
52 E6 **Goritsy** Russian Federation
42 F3 **Gorizia** Italy
42 G3 **Gorjanci** *mts* Yugoslavia
52 G3 **Gorka** Russian Federation
75 L4 **Gorkhā** Nepal
Gor'kiy *see* **Nizhniy Novgorod**
Gor'kovskaya Oblast' *see* **Nizhegorodskaya Oblast'**
52 F6 **Gor'kovskoye Vodokhranilishche** *res* Russian Federation
33 O6 **Gorleben** Germany
9 H2 **Gorleston** England
28 G5 **Gørlev** Denmark
31 N6 **Gorlice** Poland
52 F3 **Gorlichevskaya** Russian Federation
31 H4 **Görlitz** Germany
28 J5 **Gørløse** Denmark
33 O6 **Gorlosen** Germany
98 F5 **Gorman** South Dakota U.S.A.
109 J3 **Gorman** Texas U.S.A.
94 H7 **Gormania** Maryland U.S.A.
139 H8 **Gormanston** Tasmania Australia
43 F11 **Gornalunga** *R* Sicily
47 H1 **Gorna Oryakhovitsa** Bulgaria
55 E2 **Gornaya Subbota** Russian Federation
65 J2 **Gorniye Klyuchi** Russian Federation
46 D1 **Gornji Milanovac** Serbia Yugoslavia
42 H5 **Gornji Vakuf** Bosnia-Herzegovina
56 C5 **Gorno-Altaysk** Russian Federation
56 C5 **Gorno-Altayskaya Avtonomnyy Oblast'** Russian Federation
57 G5 **Gorno-Badakhshanskaya Avtonomnyy Oblast'** *prov* Tajikistan
56 H2 **Gorno-Chuyskiy** Russian Federation
55 E2 **Gorno Slinkina** Russian Federation
52 G1 **Gornostal'ya Guba** *B* Russian Federation
54 M8 **Gornyatskiy** Russian Federation
29 P2 **Gornyy** Russian Federation
48 N1 **Gornyy Tikich** *R* Ukraine
45 M2 **Goro** Italy
48 J2 **Gorodenka** Ukraine
52 F6 **Gorodets** Russian Federation
52 F1 **Gorodetskiy, Mys Bol'shoy** *C* Russian Federation
54 C7 **Gorodishche** Ukraine
52 D6 **Gorodnya** Russian Federation
54 A1 **Gorodok** Belorussia
136 K3 **Goroka** Papua New Guinea
138 F6 **Goroke** Victoria Australia
52 F6 **Gorokhovets** Russian Federation
87 F9 **Gorongosa** Mozambique
71 H4 **Gorontalo** Sulawesi
31 M1 **Górowo Iławeckie** Poland
25 F2 **Gorredijk** Netherlands
120 J9 **Gorrie** Ontario Canada
21 J5 **Gorron** France
33 S9 **Görsdorf** Germany
54 K8 **Gorskoye** Ukraine
25 F4 **Gorssel** Netherlands
14 C3 **Gort** Ireland
14 C1 **Gortahork** Ireland
14 B3 **Gorumna I** Ireland
130 G4 **Gorutuba, R** Brazil
57 A2 **Gory Chushkakul'** *mt* Kazakhstan
53 C8 **Goryn'** *R* Belorussia/Ukraine
31 M5 **Góry Świętokrzyskie** *mts* Poland
42 E6 **Gorzano, M** *mt* Italy
33 Q8 **Görzke** Germany
31 L4 **Gorzów** Poland
31 J3 **Gorzów Wielkopolski** Poland
Gosainthan *mt see* **Xixabangma Feng**
9 F2 **Gosberton** England
37 M2 **Göschwitz** Germany
61 N8 **Gosen** Japan
139 K5 **Gosford** New South Wales Australia
102 E5 **Goshen** California U.S.A.
94 B5 **Goshen** Indiana U.S.A.
95 N5 **Goshen** New York U.S.A.
100 B6 **Goshen** Oregon U.S.A.
101 O10 **Goshen** Utah U.S.A.
94 H9 **Goshen** Virginia U.S.A.
61 O5 **Goshogawara** Japan
127 N4 **Gosier** Guadeloupe W Indies
33 M9 **Goslar** Germany
20 H5 **Gosné** France
142 C2 **Gosnells** *dist* Perth, W Aust Australia
42 G4 **Gospić** Croatia
9 E6 **Gosport** England
110 K2 **Gosport** Indiana U.S.A.
111 G10 **Goss** Mississippi U.S.A.
33 Q9 **Gossa** Germany
41 K3 **Gossau** Switzerland
22 G3 **Gosselies** Belgium
26 B9 **Gossen** *isld* Norway
140 C4 **Gosse R** N Terr Australia
86 E4 **Gossinga** Sudan
38 J6 **Gossl** Austria
38 H8 **Gössnitz** Austria
37 N2 **Gössnitz** Germany
46 D3 **Gostivar** Macedonia Yugoslavia
38 L6 **Göstling** Austria
38 L6 **Göstlinger Alpen** *mts* Austria
31 K4 **Gostyn** Poland
31 L3 **Gostynin** Poland
27 H13 **Göta Kanal** Sweden
107 M6 **Gotebo** Oklahoma U.S.A.
27 E14 **Göteborg** Sweden
27 E13 **Göteborgs Och Bohus** *county* Sweden
85 G7 **Gotel Mts** Nigeria
61 M10 **Gotemba** Japan
37 K2 **Gotha** Germany
27 K14 **Gothem** Gotland Sweden
98 F9 **Gothenburg** Nebraska U.S.A.
85 E6 **Gothéye** Niger
27 K14 **Gotland** *isld* Sweden
27 K14 **Gotland** *county* Sweden
27 H12 **Götlunda** Sweden
60 B12 **Gotō-rettō** *islds* Japan
71 B2 **Gotowasi** Indonesia
46 F3 **Gotse Delchev** Bulgaria
27 K13 **Gotska Sandön** *isld* Sweden
60 F10 **Gōtsu** Japan
44 G3 **Gottero** *mt* Italy
37 O6 **Gotteszell** Germany
36 F2 **Göttingen** Hessen Germany
32 L9 **Göttingen** Niedersachsen Germany
26 K8 **Gottne** Sweden
117 M10 **Gott Pk** British Columbia Canada
28 C2 **Gøttrup** Denmark
Gottwaldov *see* **Zlín**
Gotval'd *see* **Zmiyev**
41 L3 **Götzis** Austria
20 D5 **Gouarec** France
65 E4 **Goubangzi** China
25 C4 **Gouda** Netherlands
86 C4 **Goudeï** Chad
22 F4 **Goudelancourt** France
9 G5 **Goudhurst** England
85 B6 **Goudiry** Senegal
85 G6 **Goudoumaria** Niger
120 F4 **Goudreau** Ontario Canada
25 B5 **Goudswaard** Netherlands
20 G4 **Gouesnière, la** France
20 B5 **Gouesnou** France
20 E5 **Gouet** *R* France
20 C5 **Gouézec** France
112 E4 **Gough** Georgia U.S.A.
90 J13 **Gough I** S Atlantic Oc
118 E6 **Gough L** Alberta Canada
40 D2 **Gouhenans** France
121 Q4 **Gouin, Rés** Quebec Canada
120 F6 **Goulais River** Ontario Canada
139 K4 **Goulburn** *R* New South Wales Australia
139 J5 **Goulburn** New South Wales Australia
140 C1 **Goulburn Is** N Terr Australia
121 T7 **Gould** Quebec Canada
111 E8 **Gould** Arkansas U.S.A.
106 D1 **Gould** Colorado U.S.A.
107 L7 **Gould** Oklahoma U.S.A.
99 V3 **Gould City** Michigan U.S.A.
146 D9 **Gould Coast** Antarctica
143 B7 **Gould, Mt** W Australia Australia
85 C6 **Goumbou** Mali
46 E4 **Gouménissa** Greece
40 E3 **Goumois** France
85 D5 **Goundam** Mali
86 C4 **Goundi** Chad
46 E7 **Goúra** Greece
86 C2 **Gouradi** Chad
20 F5 **Gouray, le** France
18 F8 **Gourdon** France
85 G6 **Gouré** Niger
21 K8 **Gourgé** France
20 C5 **Gourin** France
120 F4 **Gourlay L** Ontario Canada
85 D5 **Gourma Rharous** Mali
21 O3 **Gournay-en-Bray** France
86 C2 **Gouro** Chad
12 D2 **Gourock** Scotland
139 J6 **Gourock Rge** New South Wales Australia
118 K9 **Gouverneur** Saskatchewan Canada
95 M2 **Gouverneur** New York U.S.A.
47 O12 **Gouviá** Greece
21 P3 **Gouvieux** France
20 G3 **Gouville** France
22 K3 **Gouvy** Belgium
127 P5 **Gouyave** Grenada
22 E3 **Gouzeaucourt** France
18 G6 **Gouzon** France
119 N7 **Govan** Saskatchewan Canada
12 D2 **Govan** Scotland
140 D1 **Gove** N Terr Australia
107 K3 **Gove** Kansas U.S.A.
20 G5 **Goven** France
118 H9 **Govenlock** Saskatchewan Canada
140 D1 **Gove Pen** N Terr Australia
48 J2 **Goverla** *mt* Ukraine
130 H6 **Governador Valadares** Brazil
100 D4 **Government Camp** Oregon U.S.A.
71 G7 **Governor Generoso** Philippines
122 K8 **Governor, L** Nova Scotia Canada
113 L12 **Governor's Harbour** Bahamas
145 D4 **Gowanbridge** New Zealand
94 J4 **Gowanda** New York U.S.A.
141 G6 **Gowan Ra** Queensland Australia
110 B2 **Gower** Missouri U.S.A.
8 B4 **Gower Inn** Wales
120 K5 **Gowganda** Ontario Canada
14 D3 **Gowna, L** Ireland
99 M7 **Gowrie** Iowa U.S.A.
131 F2 **Goya** Argentina
127 N4 **Goyave** Guadeloupe W Indies
138 C2 **Goyder** *R* N Terr Australia
140 D2 **Goyder** *R* N Terr Australia
138 E2 **Goyder Lagoon** South Australia Australia
123 M3 **Goyelle, L** Quebec Canada
128 C6 **Goyllarisquizga** Peru
47 L4 **Göynük** Turkey
61 P6 **Goyō-zan** *mt* Japan
86 D3 **Goz-Beïda** Chad
66 C4 **Gozha Co** *L* China
43 F12 **Gozo** *isld* Malta
86 G2 **Goz Regeb** Sudan
89 D9 **Graaff Reinet** S Africa
36 E5 **Graben-Neudorf** Germany
85 C8 **Grabo** Ivory Coast
46 F9 **Graboúsa** *isld* Crete Greece
55 F4 **Grabovo** Kazakhstan
33 O6 **Grabow** Germany
33 P6 **Grabow** Mecklenburg-Vorpommern Germany
33 P8 **Grabow** Sachsen-Anhalt Germany
31 L4 **Grabów** Poland
42 G4 **Gračac** Croatia
48 E6 **Gračanica** Bosnia-Herzegovina
21 O7 **Graçay** France
101 O7 **Grace** Idaho U.S.A.
98 H2 **Grace City** North Dakota U.S.A.
121 O6 **Gracefield** Quebec Canada
143 C10 **Grace, L** W Australia Australia
122 G1 **Grace L** Labrador, Nfld Canada
107 M6 **Gracemont** Oklahoma U.S.A.
141 K2 **Graceville** *dist* Brisbane, Qnsld Australia
111 L11 **Graceville** Florida U.S.A.
98 K4 **Graceville** Minnesota U.S.A.
110 J5 **Gracey** Kentucky U.S.A.
38 O8 **Grad** Slovenia
48 E6 **Gradačac** Bosnia-Herzegovina
129 H5 **Gradaús, Serra dos** *mts* Brazil
26 H5 **Graddis** Norway
16 D2 **Gradefes** Spain
46 E3 **Gradeska Pl** *mt* Macedonia Yugoslavia
48 H5 **Grădistea Muncelului** Romania
33 S9 **Graditz** Germany
70 P10 **Gradjagan** Java
42 E3 **Grado** Italy
16 C1 **Grado** Spain
46 E3 **Gradsko** Macedonia Yugoslavia
111 E7 **Grady** Arkansas U.S.A.
108 D1 **Grady** New Mexico U.S.A.
28 A5 **Grådyb** *chan* Denmark
102 D2 **Graeagle** California U.S.A.
28 C5 **Grædstrup** Denmark
28 H7 **Grænge** Denmark
28 J4 **Græsted** Denmark
99 M6 **Graettinger** Iowa U.S.A.
37 P6 **Grafenau** Germany
37 L4 **Gräfenberg** Germany
33 Q9 **Gräfenhainichen** Germany
37 K2 **Gräfenroda** Germany
38 M5 **Grafenschlag** Austria
37 L2 **Gräfenthal** Germany
37 K1 **Gräfentonna** Germany
37 M4 **Grafenwöhr** Germany
38 N5 **Grafenwörth** Austria
36 D6 **Graffenstaden** Germany
Gräfinau *see* **Angstedt-Gräfinau**
37 O6 **Grafling** Germany
109 J3 **Graford** Texas U.S.A.
32 F10 **Grafrath** Germany
36 C2 **Grafschaft** Germany
139 L3 **Grafton** New South Wales Australia
110 F3 **Grafton** Illinois U.S.A.
95 O4 **Grafton** New York U.S.A.
98 J1 **Grafton** North Dakota U.S.A.
94 E5 **Grafton** Ohio U.S.A.
94 G7 **Grafton** West Virginia U.S.A.
99 T6 **Grafton** Wisconsin U.S.A.
141 H3 **Grafton, C** Queensland Australia
133 C8 **Grafton, Is** Chile
103 K3 **Grafton, Mt** Nevada U.S.A.
141 H3 **Grafton Pass** Gt Barrier Reef Australia
45 R8 **Gragnano** Italy
117 M7 **Graham** *R* British Columbia Canada
119 N1 **Graham** Ontario Canada
109 J2 **Graham** Texas U.S.A.
117 G9 **Graham I** British Columbia Canada
115 K2 **Graham I** Northwest Territories Canada
118 C2 **Graham L** Alberta Canada
95 T2 **Graham L** Maine U.S.A.
146 C4 **Graham Land** *pen* Antarctica
103 P9 **Graham, Mt** Arizona U.S.A.
89 E9 **Grahamstown** S Africa
95 N5 **Grahamsville** New York U.S.A.
42 J6 **Grahovo** Montenegro Yugoslavia
42 A3 **Graie, Alpi** Italy
14 E4 **Graigue** Ireland
107 K2 **Grainfield** Kansas U.S.A.
118 D7 **Grainger** Alberta Canada
98 E9 **Grainton** Nebraska U.S.A.
129 J5 **Grajau** Brazil
31 N2 **Grajewo** Poland
52 H6 **Grakhovo** Russian Federation
16 B4 **Gralheira, Sa** *mts* Portugal
28 C6 **Gram** Denmark
46 F1 **Gramada** Bulgaria
18 G8 **Gramat** France
47 J2 **Gramatikovo** Bulgaria
32 H7 **Gramke** Germany
43 F11 **Grammichele** Sicily
Grammont *see* **Geraardsbergen**
33 R4 **Grammow** Germany
15 F3 **Grampian** *reg* Scotland
15 D4 **Grampian Mt** Scotland
138 F6 **Grampians** *mts* Victoria Australia
25 G3 **Gramsbergen** Netherlands
46 D4 **Gramsh** Albania
33 U6 **Gramzow** Germany
44 B3 **Grana** *R* Italy
126 G10 **Granada** Colombia
125 M4 **Granada** Nicaragua
16 E7 **Granada** Spain
16 E7 **Granada** *prov* Spain
106 H3 **Granada** Colorado U.S.A.
16 C4 **Granadilla** Spain
133 D7 **Gran Altiplanicie Central** *plain* Argentina
14 D3 **Granard** Ireland
45 K2 **Granarolo dell'Emilia** Italy
38 G7 **Granat-Spitze** *mt* Austria
133 D7 **Gran Baja** *hills* Argentina
131 C7 **Gran Bajo Salitroso** *salt lake* Argentina
109 K3 **Granbury** Texas U.S.A.
121 S7 **Granby** Quebec Canada
106 E1 **Granby** Colorado U.S.A.
110 B5 **Granby** Missouri U.S.A.
98 A9 **Granby, L** Colorado U.S.A.
85 A3 **Gran Canaria** *isld* Canary Is
40 B2 **Grancey** France
133 E3 **Gran Chaco** *reg* Argentina
127 O2 **Gran Couva** Trinidad
111 E12 **Grand** *R* Louisiana U.S.A.
99 M9 **Grand** *R* Missouri U.S.A.
98 E4 **Grand** *R* South Dakota U.S.A.
20 H6 **Grand-Auverne** France
119 P1 **Grand B** Ontario Canada
113 J11 **Grand Bahama** *isld* Bahamas
123 R6 **Grand Bank** Newfoundland Canada
90 E4 **Grand Banks of Nfld** Atlantic Oc
85 D8 **Grand Bassam** Ivory Coast
122 F8 **Grand Bay** New Brunswick Canada
119 V8 **Grand Beach** Manitoba Canada
119 V8 **Grand Beach Prov. Park** Manitoba Canada
120 J9 **Grand Bend** Ontario Canada
94 D4 **Grand Blanc** Michigan U.S.A.
19 Q13 **Grand Bornand** France
127 N5 **Grand Bourg** Guadeloupe W Indies
123 O6 **Grand Bruit** Newfoundland Canada
127 J4 **Grand Caicos** *isld* Turks & Caicos Is
21 H3 **Grandcamp-Maisy** France
65 D7 **Grand Canal** China
14 D3 **Grand Canal** Ireland
111 C9 **Grand Cane** Louisiana U.S.A.
19 Q17 **Grand Cañon du Verdon** France
103 M5 **Grand Canyon** *gorge* Arizona U.S.A.
103 M5 **Grand Canyon Nat. Park** Arizona U.S.A.
103 M5 **Grand Canyon Village** Arizona U.S.A.
113 J10 **Grand Cays** *islds* Bahamas
118 G4 **Grand Centre** Alberta Canada
85 C8 **Grand Cess** Liberia
20 E6 **Grand Champ** France
20 G7 **Grand-champ** France
111 D12 **Grand Cheniere** Louisiana U.S.A.
19 P13 **Grand Colombier** *mt* France
100 F2 **Grand Coulee** Washington U.S.A.
21 N3 **Grand Couronne** France
21 O2 **Grandcourt** France
127 N4 **Grand Cul de Sac Marin** *B* Guadeloupe W Indies
128 C6 **Grande** *R* Peru
131 G3 **Grande** *R* Uruguay
122 G6 **Grande-Anse** New Brunswick Canada
127 O4 **Grande Anse** Guadeloupe W Indies
133 D8 **Grande, B** Argentina
121 U4 **Grande-Baie** Quebec Canada
45 M2 **Grande Bonificazione Ferrarese** Italy
20 F7 **Grande Brière** *reg* France
83 K14 **Grande Brûlé** Réunion Indian Oc
19 P14 **Grande Chartreuse** *mts* France
133 D5 **Grande Colorado** *R* Argentina
18 H8 **Grande Combe, la** France
87 G10 **Grande Comore** *isld* Comoros
131 H2 **Grande, Coxilha** *mt* Brazil
131 G4 **Grande, Cuchilla** *ra* Uruguay
129 G4 **Grande do Curuai, L** Brazil
122 H5 **Grande Grève** Quebec Canada
129 K8 **Grande, I** Brazil
20 C4 **Grande, I** France
45 M3 **Grande, M** *mt* Italy
128 F7 **Grande, Monte** *mts* Bolivia
128 F7 **Grande O'Guapay** *R* Bolivia
117 O8 **Grande Prairie** Alberta Canada
127 M2 **Grande, R** Jamaica
86 B2 **Grand Erg de Bilma** Niger
85 E2 **Grand Erg Occidental** *desert* Algeria
122 H5 **Grande Rivière** Quebec Canada
127 P1 **Grande Rivière** Trinidad
127 L4 **Grande Rivière** Martinique W Indies
127 H5 **Grande Rivière du Nord** Haiti
100 H4 **Grande Ronde** *R* Oregon U.S.A.
122 C5 **Grandes Bergeronnes** Quebec Canada
21 M2 **Grandes Dalles, les** France
129 K5 **Grande, Serra** *mts* Brazil
121 S6 **Grandes Piles** Quebec Canada
21 N2 **Grandes Ventes, les** France
123 L7 **Grand Etang** C Breton I, Nova Scotia
127 P5 **Grand Etang** *L* Grenada
127 N4 **Grande Terre** *isld* Guadeloupe W Indies
122 G4 **Grande Vallée** Quebec Canada
127 N3 **Grande Vigie,Pte.de la** Guadeloupe W Indies
122 E6 **Grand Falls** New Brunswick Canada
123 R5 **Grand Falls** Newfoundland Canada
103 N6 **Grand Falls** Arizona U.S.A.
108 E4 **Grandfalls** Texas U.S.A.
112 F1 **Grandfather Mt** North Carolina U.S.A.
107 M7 **Grandfield** Oklahoma U.S.A.
100 G1 **Grand Forks** British Columbia Canada
98 J2 **Grand Forks** North Dakota U.S.A.
22 C1 **Grand Fort Philippe** France
20 G6 **Grand Fougeray, le** France
95 N4 **Grand Gorge** New York U.S.A.
127 J5 **Grand Gosier** Haiti
22 K3 **Grand-Halleux** Belgium
122 F9 **Grand Harbour** New Brunswick Canada
99 U6 **Grand Haven** Michigan U.S.A.
111 G11 **Grand I** Louisiana U.S.A.
99 U3 **Grand I** Michigan U.S.A.
98 H9 **Grand I** Nebraska U.S.A.
121 M9 **Grand I** New York U.S.A.
113 F8 **Grandin** Florida U.S.A.
110 F5 **Grandin** Missouri U.S.A.
98 J2 **Grandin** North Dakota U.S.A.
117 O3 **Grandin, Lac** Northwest Territories Canada
111 G12 **Grand Isle** Louisiana U.S.A.
95 O2 **Grand Isle** Vermont U.S.A.
131 F7 **Grand Jason** *isld* Falkland Is
99 M7 **Grand Junct** Iowa U.S.A.
106 B2 **Grand Junction** Colorado U.S.A.
94 A4 **Grand Junction** Michigan U.S.A.
110 G6 **Grand Junction** Tennessee U.S.A.
101 N3 **Grand Kohrs Ranch Nat. Hist. Site** Montana U.S.A.
122 E8 **Grand L** New Brunswick Canada
123 P4 **Grand L** Newfoundland Canada
94 D1 **Grand L** Michigan U.S.A.
94 C6 **Grand L** Ohio U.S.A.
122 F2 **Grand Lac Germain** Quebec Canada
106 E1 **Grand Lake** Colorado U.S.A.
111 C11 **Grand Lake** Louisiana U.S.A.
95 S7 **Grand Lakes L** Maine U.S.A.
94 C4 **Grand Ledge** Michigan U.S.A.
20 G7 **Grand Lieu, Lac de** France
28 H5 **Grandløse** Denmark
95 S7 **Grand L Seboeis** Maine U.S.A.
21 L6 **Grand-Lucé, le** France
99 V3 **Grand Marais** Michigan U.S.A.
99 Q2 **Grand Marais** Minnesota U.S.A.
111 M13 **Grand Marais State Park** St Louis
121 S6 **Grand-Mère** Quebec Canada
106 C2 **Grand Mesa** Colorado U.S.A.
122 E2 **Grandmesnil, L** Quebec Canada
117 P10 **Grand Mt** British Columbia Canada
123 R2 **Grandois** Newfoundland Canada
16 B6 **Grândola** Portugal
16 B6 **Grândola, Sa. de** *mt* Portugal
117 E6 **Grand Pacific Glacier** British Colombia Canada
110 C2 **Grand Pass** Missouri U.S.A.
99 R2 **Grand Portage** Minnesota U.S.A.
109 L3 **Grand Prairie** Texas U.S.A.
109 N9 **Grand Prairie** Texas U.S.A.
22 H5 **Grandpré** France

180
Grand Pressigny, le — Guanajay

21 M8 **Grand Pressigny, le** France
21 N3 **Grand Quevilly** France
94 F5 **Grand R** Ohio U.S.A.
119 S5 **Grand Rapids** Manitoba Canada
94 B4 **Grand Rapids** Michigan U.S.A.
99 N2 **Grand Rapids** Minnesota U.S.A.
22 G3 **Grandrieu** Belgium
18 H8 **Grandrieu** France
123 M8 **Grand River** C Breton I, Nova Scotia
99 N9 **Grand River** Iowa U.S.A.
100 B4 **Grand Ronde** Oregon U.S.A.
127 P5 **Grand Roy** Grenada
42 A3 **Grand St. Bernard, Col du** *pass* Switz/Italy
109 M3 **Grand Saline** Texas U.S.A.
129 H3 **Grand Santi** Fr Guiana
40 E4 **Grandson** Switzerland
111 G12 **Grand Terre Is** Louisiana U.S.A.
101 P6 **Grand Teton** *mt* Wyoming U.S.A.
101 P6 **Grand Teton Nat. Park** Wyoming U.S.A.
127 J4 **Grand Turk I** Turks & Caicos Is
106 B2 **Grand Valley** Colorado U.S.A.
119 R7 **Grandview** Manitoba Canada
100 J7 **Grand View** Idaho U.S.A.
110 B3 **Grandview** Missouri U.S.A.
109 K3 **Grandview** Texas U.S.A.
100 F3 **Grandview** Washington U.S.A.
94 B4 **Grandville** Michigan U.S.A.
36 B7 **Grandvillers** France
21 O2 **Grandvilliers** France
103 L5 **Grand Wash** *creek* Arizona U.S.A.
103 L6 **Grand Wash Cliffs** Arizona U.S.A.
19 N15 **Grâne** France
26 F6 **Grane** Norway
17 G3 **Grañén** Spain
44 B2 **Granero** *mt* Italy
121 N5 **Granet, L** Quebec Canada
14 C4 **Graney, L** Ireland
27 G11 **Grangarde** Sweden
58 D4 **Grangca** China
27 H11 **Grängeberg** Sweden
127 H1 **Grange Hill** Jamaica
40 E5 **Grange, Mont de** *mt* France
12 E1 **Grangemouth** Scotland
99 P9 **Granger** Missouri U.S.A.
109 K5 **Granger** Texas U.S.A.
100 E3 **Granger** Washington U.S.A.
101 Q8 **Granger** Wyoming U.S.A.
36 B7 **Granges-sur-Vologne** France
100 J4 **Grangeville** Idaho U.S.A.
26 J8 **Graninge** Sweden
107 L7 **Granite** Oklahoma U.S.A.
100 G5 **Granite** Oregon U.S.A.
98 A8 **Granite** Wyoming U.S.A.
117 L10 **Granite Bay** British Columbia Canada
111 M12 **Granite City** St Louis
110 F3 **Granite City** Illinois U.S.A.
99 L5 **Granite Falls** Minnesota U.S.A.
112 F2 **Granite Falls** North Carolina U.S.A.
100 D1 **Granite Falls** Washington U.S.A.
116 N7 **Granite I** Alaska U.S.A.
99 T3 **Granite I** Michigan U.S.A.
100 H9 **Granite Mt** Nevada U.S.A.
103 J7 **Granite Mts** California U.S.A.
143 D7 **Granite Peak** W Australia Australia
102 H6 **Granite Peak** California U.S.A.
100 H8 **Granite Peak** *mt* Nevada U.S.A.
101 Q4 **Granite Pk** Montana U.S.A.
101 M9 **Granite Pk** Utah U.S.A.
101 R7 **Granite Pk** Wyoming U.S.A.
99 T3 **Granite Pt** Michigan U.S.A.
116 Q6 **Granite Range** Alaska U.S.A.
100 F9 **Granite Range** Nevada U.S.A.
140 B5 **Granites, The** *pk* N Terr Australia
112 F4 **Graniteville** South Carolina U.S.A.
130 G9 **Granito** Brazil
144 C4 **Granity** New Zealand
129 K4 **Granja** Brazil
127 J5 **Granja, Pta. de la** Dominican Rep
27 J14 **Grankullavik** Sweden
133 D6 **Gran Laguna Salada** *L* Argentina
118 F9 **Granlea** Alberta Canada
133 E6 **Gran Lorenzo** Argentina
26 G8 **Granlunda** Sweden
124 F3 **Gran Morelos** Mexico
27 G13 **Gränna** Sweden
111 B7 **Grannis** Arkansas U.S.A.
98 E1 **Grano** North Dakota U.S.A.
17 J3 **Granollers** Spain
42 A3 **Gran Paradiso** *mt* Italy
133 E5 **Gran Pico** Argentina
42 D2 **Gran Pilastro** *mt* Italy/Austria
133 E4 **Gran Pinto** Argentina
44 B2 **Gran Queyron** *mt* Italy/France
133 D5 **Gran Roca** Argentina
42 F6 **Gran Sasso d'Italia** Italy
33 S6 **Gransee** Germany
120 D2 **Grant** Ontario Canada
113 G10 **Grant** Florida U.S.A.
99 M8 **Grant** Iowa U.S.A.
94 B3 **Grant** Michigan U.S.A.
101 M4 **Grant** Montana U.S.A.
98 E9 **Grant** Nebraska U.S.A.
107 P8 **Grant** Oklahoma U.S.A.
99 M9 **Grant City** Missouri U.S.A.
143 D7 **Grant Duff Ra** W Australia Australia
9 F2 **Grantham** England
146 B9 **Grant I** *isld* Antarctica
140 C1 **Grant I** N Terr Australia
117 P3 **Grant L** Northwest Territories Canada
116 E4 **Grantley Hbr** Alaska U.S.A.
143 E8 **Grant, Mt** W Australia Australia
120 J9 **Granton** Ontario Canada
13 E2 **Granton** Scotland
99 Q5 **Granton** Wisconsin U.S.A.
15 E3 **Grantown on Spey** Scotland
142 E4 **Grant Ra** W Australia Australia
103 J3 **Grant Ra** Nevada U.S.A.
26 K7 **Grantträsk** Sweden
116 M6 **Grants** Alaska U.S.A.
106 C6 **Grants** New Mexico U.S.A.
99 O4 **Grantsburg** Wisconsin U.S.A.
101 L3 **Grantsdale** Montana U.S.A.
13 F2 **Grantshouse** Scotland
100 B7 **Grants Pass** Oregon U.S.A.
101 N9 **Grantsville** Utah U.S.A.
94 F8 **Grantsville** West Virginia U.S.A.
111 M8 **Grantville** Georgia U.S.A.
20 G4 **Granville** France
99 R8 **Granville** Illinois U.S.A.
99 L7 **Granville** Iowa U.S.A.
95 O3 **Granville** New York U.S.A.
98 F1 **Granville** North Dakota U.S.A.
94 E6 **Granville** Ohio U.S.A.
94 K6 **Granville** Pennsylvania U.S.A.
122 G9 **Granville Ferry** Nova Scotia Canada
133 E5 **Gran Villegas** Argentina
119 R2 **Granville L** Manitoba Canada
33 P6 **Granzin** Germany
130 G5 **Grão Mogol** Brazil
109 M4 **Grapeland** Texas U.S.A.
102 F7 **Grapevine** California U.S.A.
109 N8 **Grapevine** Texas U.S.A.
109 K3 **Grapevine Res** Texas U.S.A.
42 D3 **Grappa, Monte** *mt* Italy
126 G5 **Grappler Bk** Caribbean
27 H11 **Gräsberg** Sweden
32 M8 **Grasdorf** Germany
87 F10 **Graskop** S Africa
114 H5 **Gras,L.de** Northwest Territories Canada
13 E5 **Grasmere** England
27 K11 **Gräsö** Sweden
95 M2 **Grass** *R* New York U.S.A.
101 R6 **Grass Creek** Wyoming U.S.A.
44 B4 **Grasse** France
121 M3 **Grasset, L** Quebec Canada
13 G5 **Grassington** England
100 C8 **Grass Lake** California U.S.A.
108 F2 **Grassland** Texas U.S.A.
118 K9 **Grasslands Nat Park** Saskatchewan Canada
145 E4 **Grassmere, L** New Zealand
143 D10 **Grass Patch** W Australia Australia
119 T3 **Grass R** Manitoba Canada
101 R2 **Grassrange** Montana U.S.A.
119 Q4 **Grass River Prov. Park** Manitoba Canada
102 C2 **Grass Valley** California U.S.A.
100 E4 **Grass Valley** Oregon U.S.A.
139 G8 **Grassy** Tasmania Australia
98 C2 **Grassy Butte** North Dakota U.S.A.
126 F3 **Grassy Cr** Andros Bahamas
118 G7 **Grassy Island L** Alberta Canada
94 G8 **Grassy Knob** *mt* West Virginia U.S.A.
118 F9 **Grassy Lake** Alberta Canada
28 D7 **Gråsten** Denmark
27 F13 **Grästorp** Sweden
26 J3 **Gratangen** Norway
123 U5 **Grate's Cove** Newfoundland Canada
99 R7 **Gratiot** Wisconsin U.S.A.
94 C7 **Gratis** Ohio U.S.A.
26 L6 **Gråträsk** Sweden
28 D4 **Grauballe** Denmark
41 K4 **Graubünden** *canton* Switzerland
18 H9 **Grau-du-Roi,le** France
17 H2 **Graus** Spain
131 H2 **Gravata** Brazil
25 E5 **Grave** Netherlands
118 L9 **Gravelbourg** Saskatchewan Canada
22 C2 **Gravelines** France
21 H5 **Gravelle, la** France
87 F10 **Gravelotte** S Africa
121 L8 **Gravenhurst** Ontario Canada
36 F3 **Grävenwiesbach** Germany
101 L3 **Grave Pk** Idaho U.S.A.
18 E7 **Grave, Pte de** *C* France
139 K3 **Gravesend** New South Wales Australia
9 G5 **Gravesend** England
19 N17 **Graveson** France
110 B5 **Gravette** Arkansas U.S.A.
21 N3 **Gravigny** France
21 L2 **Graville** France
43 G8 **Gravina di Puglia** Italy
99 M9 **Gravity** Iowa U.S.A.
28 D3 **Gravlev** Denmark
26 E7 **Gravvik** Norway
99 V5 **Grawn** Michigan U.S.A.
119 N8 **Gray** Saskatchewan Canada
19 J5 **Gray** France
112 D4 **Gray** Georgia U.S.A.
95 R3 **Gray** Maine U.S.A.
108 D7 **Gray** Oklahoma U.S.A.
100 A3 **Grayland** Washington U.S.A.
117 L6 **Grayling** *R* British Columbia Canada
94 C2 **Grayling** Michigan U.S.A.
116 R3 **Grayling Fk.** *R* Alaska U.S.A.
13 F5 **Grayrigg** England
100 A3 **Grays Harbor** Washington U.S.A.
101 O6 **Grays L** Idaho U.S.A.
119 P8 **Grayson** Saskatchewan Canada
94 E8 **Grayson** Kentucky U.S.A.
111 D9 **Grayson** Louisiana U.S.A.
120 A2 **Grayson L** Ontario Canada
106 E2 **Grays Pk** Colorado U.S.A.
94 B1 **Grays Reef** Michigan U.S.A.
100 B3 **Grays River** Washington U.S.A.
9 G5 **Grays Thurrock** England
111 K11 **Grayton Beach** Florida U.S.A.
110 H3 **Grayville** Illinois U.S.A.
54 G6 **Grayvoron** Russian Federation
38 M7 **Graz** Austria
16 D8 **Grazalema** Spain
46 E2 **Grdelica** Serbia Yugoslavia
13 G6 **Greasbrough** England
117 M4 **Greasy L** Northwest Territories Canada
138 B5 **Great Australian Bight** Australia
9 G4 **Great Baddow** England
113 J12 **Great Bahama Bank** Bahamas
145 E2 **Great Barrier I** New Zealand
136 **Great Barrier Reef** Australia
141 H3 **Great Barrier Reef Marine Park** Queensland Australia
95 O4 **Great Barrington** Massachusetts U.S.A.
141 H4 **Great Basalt Wall** Queensland Australia
103 H1 **Great Basin** Nevada U.S.A.
117 L3 **Great Bear** *R* Northwest Territories Canada
114 H4 **Great Bear L** Northwest Territories Canada
107 M3 **Great Bend** Kansas U.S.A.
98 K3 **Great Bend** North Dakota U.S.A.
89 A9 **Great Berg** *R* S Africa
15 B2 **Great Bernera** *isld* Scotland
14 A4 **Great Blasket I.** Ireland
122 F3 **Great Boule I** Quebec Canada
123 R2 **Great Brehat** Newfoundland Canada
8 D1 **Great Budworth** England
123 Q5 **Great Burnt L.** Newfoundland Canada
89 A7 **Great Bushman Land** *reg* S Africa
94 J7 **Great Cacapon** West Virginia U.S.A.
9 F2 **Great Casterton** England
9 G3 **Great Chesterford** England
123 T7 **Great Colinet I.** Newfoundland Canada
12 D2 **Great Cumbrae** *isld* Scotland
9 F2 **Great Dalby** England
118 K6 **Great Deer** Saskatchewan Canada
101 S9 **Great Divide** Colorado U.S.A.
139 **Great Dividing Ra** Australia
13 H5 **Great Driffield** England
120 H7 **Great Duck I.** Ontario Canada
146 E12 **Greater Antarctica** Antarctica
Greater Khingan Range *see* **Da Hinggan Ling**
13 F6 **Greater Manchester** *co* England
145 D1 **Great Exhibition Bay** New Zealand
126 F3 **Great Exuma** *isld* Bahamas
101 O2 **Great Falls** Montana U.S.A.
112 G3 **Great Falls** South Carolina U.S.A.
110 L6 **Great Falls Dam** Tennessee U.S.A.
110 L6 **Great Falls L** Tennessee U.S.A.
89 E9 **Great Fish** *R* S Africa
6 N6 **Great Fisher Bank** North Sea
89 E9 **Great Fish Pt.** *lighthouse* S Africa
145 E4 **Greatford** New Zealand
127 K3 **Great Goat I** Jamaica
9 F2 **Great Gonerby** England
113 K11 **Great Guana Cay** *isld* Bahamas
9 F5 **Greatham** England
126 F2 **Great Harbour Cay** *isld* Bahamas
144 A6 **Great I** New Zealand
145 D1 **Great I** New Zealand
126 H4 **Great Inagua** *isld* Bahamas
Great Indian Desert *see* **Thar**
113 H11 **Great Isaac I** Bahamas
89 A6 **Great Karas Berg** *mts* Namibia
89 C9 **Great Karoo** *reg* S Africa
89 E9 **Great Kei** *R* S Africa
141 K6 **Great Keppel I** Queensland Australia
139 H8 **Great L** Tasmania Australia
112 K3 **Great L** North Carolina U.S.A.
8 D3 **Great Malvern** England
145 E2 **Great Mercury I** New Zealand
9 F4 **Great Missenden** England
136 J3 **Great NE Channel** Australia/Papua New Guinea
69 A9 **Great Nicobar** *isld* Nicobar Is
9 F4 **Great Offley** England
8 C1 **Great Ormes Head** Wales
95 P6 **Great Peconic B** Long I, New York U.S.A.
127 J3 **Great Pedro Bluff** Jamaica
95 T2 **Great Pond** Maine U.S.A.
95 R5 **Great Pt** Massachusetts U.S.A.
122 G10 **Great Pubnico L** Nova Scotia Canada
127 J2 **Great R** Jamaica
88 E5 **Great Ruaha** *R* Tanzania
95 N3 **Great Sacandaga L** New York U.S.A.
113 J11 **Great Sale Cay** Bahamas
101 N8 **Great Salt L** Utah U.S.A.
101 M9 **Great Salt L.Des** Utah U.S.A.
106 E4 **Great Sand Dunes Nat.Mon** Colorado U.S.A.
118 H8 **Great Sand Hills** Saskatchewan Canada
142 D5 **Great Sandy Desert** W Australia Australia
141 L7 **Great Sandy I** Queensland Australia
9 E5 **Great Shefford** England
9 G3 **Great Shelford** England
89 G4 **Great Shingwidzi** S Africa
114 H5 **Great Slave L** Northwest Territories Canada
112 D2 **Great Smoky Mts** Tenn/N Carolina U.S.A.
117 L7 **Great Snow Mt** British Columbia Canada
7 D13 **Great Sole Bank** Atlantic Oc
95 O6 **Great South Bay** Long I, New York U.S.A.
113 K12 **Great Stirrup Cay** *isld* Bahamas
8 B6 **Great Torrington** England
87 C10 **Great Ums** Namibia
138 B3 **Great Victoria Desert** South Australia Australia
122 J8 **Great Village** Nova Scotia Canada
Great Wall *China Base* Antarctica *see* **Chang Cheng**
9 G4 **Great Waltham** England
95 U2 **Great Wass I** Maine U.S.A.
139 H8 **Great Western Tiers** Tasmania Australia
68 C7 **Great West Torres** Burma
13 G5 **Great Whernside** *mt* England
9 H2 **Great Yarmouth** England
27 E13 **Grebbestad** Sweden
36 G2 **Grebenau** Germany
36 G3 **Grebenhain** Germany
54 D6 **Grebenka** Ukraine
32 K10 **Grebenstein** Germany
38 K7 **Grebenzen** *mt* Austria
85 F4 **Greboun, Mt** Niger
43 F8 **Greco, Torre del** Italy
37 L5 **Greding** Germany
16 D4 **Gredos, Sa. de** *mts* Spain
28 B6 **Gredstedbro** Denmark
46 E6 **Greece** *rep* S Europe
98 B9 **Greeley** Colorado U.S.A.
98 H8 **Greeley** Nebraska U.S.A.
115 L1 **Greely Fiord** Northwest Territories Canada
50 F1 **Greem Bell, Ostrov** *isld* Russian Federation
107 O2 **Green** Kansas U.S.A.
112 E2 **Green** *R* North Carolina U.S.A.
113 G11 **Greenacres City** Florida U.S.A.
95 M8 **Greenbackville** Maryland U.S.A.
99 T5 **Green Bay** Wisconsin U.S.A.
94 G8 **Greenbrier** *R* West Virginia U.S.A.
94 D2 **Greenbush** Michigan U.S.A.
98 K1 **Greenbush** Minnesota U.S.A.
143 B10 **Greenbushes** W Australia Australia
139 K6 **Green Cape** New South Wales Australia
110 K2 **Greencastle** Indiana U.S.A.
94 K7 **Greencastle** Pennsylvania U.S.A.
126 F2 **Green Cay** *isld* Bahamas
99 O9 **Green City** Missouri U.S.A.
118 B4 **Green Court** Alberta Canada
113 F8 **Green Cove Springs** Florida U.S.A.
32 L9 **Greene** Germany
99 O7 **Greene** Iowa U.S.A.
95 M4 **Greene** New York U.S.A.
98 E1 **Greene** North Dakota U.S.A.
143 G6 **Greene, Mt** W Australia Australia
112 E1 **Greeneville** Tennessee U.S.A.
102 C5 **Greenfield** California U.S.A.
110 F2 **Greenfield** Illinois U.S.A.
94 B7 **Greenfield** Indiana U.S.A.
99 M8 **Greenfield** Iowa U.S.A.
95 P4 **Greenfield** Massachusetts U.S.A.
110 C4 **Greenfield** Missouri U.S.A.
94 D7 **Greenfield** Ohio U.S.A.
107 M6 **Greenfield** Oklahoma U.S.A.
110 H5 **Greenfield** Tennessee U.S.A.
110 C5 **Green Forest** Arkansas U.S.A.
143 B9 **Green Head** W Australia Australia
127 O2 **Green Hill** Trinidad
140 B1 **Greenhill I** N Terr Australia
143 B9 **Greenhills** W Australia Australia
144 B7 **Greenhills** New Zealand
102 F6 **Greenhorn Mts** California U.S.A.
141 H3 **Green I** Queensland Australia
143 B9 **Green I** W Australia Australia
123 Q2 **Green I** Newfoundland Canada
144 B7 **Green I** New Zealand
116 O6 **Green I** Alaska U.S.A.
121 Q4 **Greening** Quebec Canada
137 L2 **Green Is** Papua New Guinea
127 H1 **Green Island** Jamaica
144 C7 **Green Island** New Zealand
71 D5 **Green Island B** Philippines
144 A7 **Green Islets** New Zealand
117 N10 **Green L** British Columbia Canada
99 S6 **Green L** Wisconsin U.S.A.
118 K4 **Green Lake** Saskatchewan Canada
109 L7 **Green Lake** Texas U.S.A.
115 P2 **Greenland** *isld terr* Arctic
127 P6 **Greenland** Barbados
90 H1 **Greenland Basin** Arctic Oc
90 G2 **Greenland-Iceland Rise** N Atlantic Oc
144 B6 **Greenland Res** New Zealand
147 G10 **Greenland Sea** Arctic Oc
13 F2 **Greenlaw** Scotland
107 O2 **Greenleaf** Kansas U.S.A.
12 E1 **Greenloaning** Scotland
15 E5 **Green Lowther** *mt* Scotland
138 C5 **Greenly I** South Australia Australia
123 P2 **Greenly I** Quebec Canada
145 F3 **Greenmeadows** New Zealand
106 D2 **Green Mt Res** Colorado U.S.A.
95 O3 **Green Mts** Vermont U.S.A.
101 S7 **Green Mts** Wyoming U.S.A.
12 D2 **Greenock** Scotland
14 E2 **Greenore** Ireland
14 E4 **Greenore Pt** Ireland
143 A8 **Greenough** W Australia Australia
116 R2 **Greenough, Mt** Alaska U.S.A.
Greenpeace *Antarctic Base see* **Cape Evans**
112 G5 **Green Pond** South Carolina U.S.A.
95 P5 **Greenport** Long I, New York U.S.A.
122 D6 **Green R** New Brunswick Canada
101 Q8 **Green River** Wyoming U.S.A.
94 B9 **Green R. Res** Kentucky U.S.A.
111 J9 **Greensboro** Alabama U.S.A.
111 M11 **Greensboro** Florida U.S.A.
112 D4 **Greensboro** Georgia U.S.A.
112 H1 **Greensboro** North Carolina U.S.A.
95 P2 **Greensboro** Vermont U.S.A.
94 B7 **Greensburg** Indiana U.S.A.
107 L4 **Greensburg** Kansas U.S.A.
94 B9 **Greensburg** Kentucky U.S.A.
111 F11 **Greensburg** Louisiana U.S.A.
94 H6 **Greensburg** Pennsylvania U.S.A.
141 K2 **Greenslopes** *dist* Brisbane, Qnsld Australia
123 T4 **Greenspond** Newfoundland Canada
94 J7 **Green Spring** West Virginia U.S.A.
94 D5 **Green Springs** Ohio U.S.A.
99 O9 **Greentop** Missouri U.S.A.
94 B6 **Greentown** Indiana U.S.A.
113 K11 **Green Turtle Cay** *isld* Bahamas
110 H2 **Greenup** Illinois U.S.A.
141 H4 **Greenvale** Queensland Australia
85 C8 **Greenville** Liberia
111 K10 **Greenville** Alabama U.S.A.
100 E9 **Greenville** California U.S.A.
113 D7 **Greenville** Florida U.S.A.
110 G3 **Greenville** Illinois U.S.A.
110 J4 **Greenville** Kentucky U.S.A.
95 S1 **Greenville** Maine U.S.A.
94 B3 **Greenville** Michigan U.S.A.
111 E8 **Greenville** Mississippi U.S.A.
110 F4 **Greenville** Missouri U.S.A.
95 Q4 **Greenville** New Hampshire U.S.A.
95 N4 **Greenville** New York U.S.A.
112 K2 **Greenville** North Carolina U.S.A.
94 C6 **Greenville** Ohio U.S.A.
94 G5 **Greenville** Pennsylvania U.S.A.
112 E3 **Greenville** South Carolina U.S.A.
109 L2 **Greenville** Texas U.S.A.
94 H8 **Greenville** Virginia U.S.A.
119 N2 **Greenwater L** Ontario Canada
119 O6 **Greenwater L. Prov. Park** Saskatchewan Canada
119 S9 **Greenway** Manitoba Canada
98 G4 **Greenway** South Dakota U.S.A.
9 G5 **Greenwich** England
107 N4 **Greenwich** Kansas U.S.A.
95 O3 **Greenwich** New York U.S.A.
94 E5 **Greenwich** Ohio U.S.A.
103 N3 **Greenwich** Utah U.S.A.
100 G1 **Greenwood** British Columbia Canada
110 B6 **Greenwood** Arkansas U.S.A.
102 D3 **Greenwood** California U.S.A.
95 M8 **Greenwood** Delaware U.S.A.
94 A7 **Greenwood** Indiana U.S.A.
94 C10 **Greenwood** Kentucky U.S.A.
111 C9 **Greenwood** Louisiana U.S.A.
111 F8 **Greenwood** Mississippi U.S.A.
98 K9 **Greenwood** Nebraska U.S.A.
112 E3 **Greenwood** South Carolina U.S.A.
98 H7 **Greenwood** South Dakota U.S.A.
99 Q5 **Greenwood** Wisconsin U.S.A.
111 H8 **Greenwood Springs** Mississippi U.S.A.
100 J3 **Greer** Idaho U.S.A.
112 E3 **Greer** South Carolina U.S.A.
111 C7 **Greeson, L** Arkansas U.S.A.
32 F5 **Gretsiel** Germany
21 M5 **Grez** France
25 F6 **Grefrath** Germany
119 S9 **Gregg** Manitoba Canada
111 B9 **Greggton** Texas U.S.A.
118 F2 **Gregoire L** Alberta Canada
128 D5 **Gregório** *R* Brazil
98 G6 **Gregory** South Dakota U.S.A.
140 E4 **Gregory Downs** Queensland Australia
142 G5 **Gregory L** W Australia Australia
143 C7 **Gregory, L** W Australia Australia
141 G4 **Gregory Ra** Queensland Australia
142 D5 **Gregory Ra** W Australia Australia
113 L12 **Gregory Town** Bahamas
38 H8 **Greifenburg** Austria
41 J3 **Greifensee** *L* Switzerland
33 T6 **Greifenberg** Germany
33 S4 **Greifswald** Germany
33 T4 **Greifswalder Bodden** Germany
33 T4 **Greifswalder Oie** *isld* Germany
38 K7 **Greimberg** *mt* Austria
38 L5 **Grein** Austria
41 J4 **Greina Pass** Switzerland
38 M5 **Greinerwald** *woods* Austria
37 L5 **Greiselbach** Germany
37 N2 **Greiz** Germany
52 E1 **Gremikha** Russian Federation
33 N4 **Gremsmühlen** Germany
28 F4 **Grenå** Denmark
127 P5 **Grenada** *isld* Lesser Antilles
100 C8 **Grenada** California U.S.A.
111 G8 **Grenada** Mississippi U.S.A.
18 E9 **Grenade** France
18 F9 **Grenade sur Garonne** France
127 O8 **Grenadines, The** *islds* Lesser Antilles
40 F3 **Grenchen** Switzerland
28 C5 **Grenå** Denmark
28 F1 **Grenen** *C* Denmark
139 J5 **Grenfell** New South Wales Australia
119 P8 **Grenfell** Saskatchewan Canada
19 P14 **Grenoble** France
107 O4 **Grenola** Kansas U.S.A.
98 C1 **Grenora** North Dakota U.S.A.
26 S2 **Grense/Jakobselv** Norway
127 P5 **Grenville** Grenada
106 G5 **Grenville** New Mexico U.S.A.
98 J4 **Grenville** South Dakota U.S.A.
141 G1 **Grenville C** Queensland Australia
117 J9 **Grenville Chan** British Columbia Canada
117 L10 **Grenville, Mt** British Columbia Canada
19 P17 **Gréoux-les-Bains** France
33 Q9 **Greppin** Germany
33 Q4 **Gresenhorst** Germany
100 C4 **Gresham** Oregon U.S.A.
70 O9 **Gresik** Java
19 P15 **Gresse** France
19 Q13 **Grésy-sur-Isère** France
139 K5 **Greta** New South Wales Australia
13 G5 **Greta Br** England
119 U9 **Gretna** Manitoba Canada
111 G12 **Gretna** Louisiana U.S.A.
111 J13 **Gretna** New Orleans, Louisiana U.S.A.
94 H10 **Gretna** Virginia U.S.A.
13 E3 **Gretna Green** Scotland
37 K1 **Greussen** Germany
45 K4 **Greve** Italy
25 A5 **Grevelingen** Netherlands
32 G8 **Greven** Germany
46 E4 **Grevená** Greece
36 B1 **Grevenbroich** Germany
32 L5 **Grevenkop** Germany
33 O5 **Grevesmühlen** Germany
27 F16 **Grevie** Sweden
29 K4 **Grevie** Sweden
28 H5 **Grevinge** Denmark
101 R5 **Greybull** Wyoming U.S.A.
140 D2 **Grey, C** N Terr Australia
101 Q4 **Greycliff** Montana U.S.A.
99 M4 **Grey Eagle** Minnesota U.S.A.
117 F4 **Grey Hunter Pk** Yukon Territory Canada
123 R3 **Grey I** Newfoundland Canada
123 R3 **Grey Is** Newfoundland Canada
144 C5 **Greymouth** New Zealand
123 Q5 **Grey R** Newfoundland Canada
141 G8 **Grey Ra** Qnsld/N S W
141 G8 **Grey Range** Queensland Australia
101 P6 **Greys** *R* Wyoming U.S.A.
143 A7 **Grey's Plains** W Australia Australia
13 F4 **Greystoke** England
101 R9 **Greystone** Colorado U.S.A.
14 E3 **Greystones** Ireland
145 E4 **Greytown** New Zealand
89 G7 **Greytown** S Africa
22 H2 **Grez-Doiceau** Belgium
21 J6 **Grez-en-Bouère** France
46 D4 **Griba** *mt* Albania
81 F11 **Gribb Seamount** Southern Oc
86 C4 **Gribingui** *R* Cent Afr Republic
52 D2 **Gridino** Russian Federation
102 C2 **Gridley** California U.S.A.
99 S9 **Gridley** Illinois U.S.A.
107 P3 **Gridley** Kansas U.S.A.
87 D11 **Griekwastad** S Africa
25 D2 **Griend** Netherlands
37 P7 **Griesbach** Germany
36 F4 **Griesheim** Germany
41 O3 **Gries im Sellrain** Austria
Griessen *see* **Klettgau**
25 F5 **Grieth** Germany
38 L8 **Griffen** Austria
111 M8 **Griffin** Georgia U.S.A.
113 F9 **Griffin, L** Florida U.S.A.
116 Q1 **Griffin Pt** Alaska U.S.A.
139 H5 **Griffith** New South Wales Australia
115 K3 **Griffith I** Northwest Territories Canada
110 E6 **Griffithville** Arkansas U.S.A.
112 K2 **Grifton** North Carolina U.S.A.
99 Q10 **Griggsville** Illinois U.S.A.
41 K6 **Grigna** *mt* Italy
19 N16 **Grignan** France
18 E8 **Grignols** France
48 M3 **Grigoriopol'** Moldavia
25 F2 **Grijpskerk** Netherlands
86 C4 **Grimari** Cent Afr Republic
19 Q18 **Grimaud** France
21 L8 **Grimaudière, la** France
48 K1 **Grimaylov** Ukraine
139 G8 **Grim, C** Tasmania Australia
102 C2 **Grimes** California U.S.A.
100 K5 **Grimes Pass** Idaho U.S.A.
33 R10 **Grimma** Germany
33 S4 **Grimmen** Germany
Grimmenthal *see* **Obermassfeld-Grimmenthal**
33 T7 **Grimnitzsee** Germany
121 L9 **Grimsby** Ontario Canada
13 H6 **Grimsby** England
41 H4 **Grimsel** *mt* Switzerland
28 S8 **Grimsey** *isld* Iceland
117 P7 **Grimshaw** Alberta Canada
27 C13 **Grimstad** Norway
28 B5 **Grimstrup** Denmark
28 R10 **Grindavik** Iceland
40 H4 **Grindelwald** Switzerland
28 C3 **Grinderslev** Denmark
28 B5 **Grindsted Å** Denmark
95 S8 **Grindstone** Maine U.S.A.
94 E2 **Grind Stone City** Michigan U.S.A.
123 L6 **Grindstone Island** Quebec Canada
119 U7 **Grindstone Prov. Park** Manitoba Canada
119 V7 **Grindstone Pt** Manitoba Canada
99 O8 **Grinnell** Iowa U.S.A.
107 K2 **Grinnell** Kansas U.S.A.
115 K2 **Grinnell Pen** Northwest Territories Canada
42 F2 **Grintavec** *mt* Slovenia
13 G5 **Grinton** England
26 C8 **Grip** *lighthouse* Norway
33 O6 **Grippel** Germany
89 F8 **Griqualand E** *reg* S Africa
89 C7 **Griqualand W** *reg* S Africa
40 F6 **Grisanche, Val** Italy
115 L2 **Grise Fiord** Northwest Territories Canada
45 L1 **Grisignano** Italy
69 F14 **Grisik** Sumatra
22 B2 **Gris Nez, C** France
18 F9 **Grisolles** France
27 K11 **Grisslehamn** Sweden
99 L8 **Griswold** Iowa U.S.A.
52 H4 **Griva** Russian Federation
21 P2 **Grivesnes** France
40 F6 **Grivola** *mt* Italy
33 P9 **Grizeline** Germany
85 D3 **Grizim** Algeria
117 N3 **Grizzly Bear Mt** Northwest Territories Canada
26 C9 **Grjotli** Norway
42 G4 **Grmeč Plan** Bosnia-Herzegovina
123 R3 **Groais I** Newfoundland Canada
33 S10 **Gröba** Germany
33 Q10 **Gröbers** Germany
27 M15 **Grobina** Latvia
9 E2 **Groby** England
33 P9 **Gröbzig** Germany
28 B7 **Gröde-Appelland** *isld* Germany
31 O2 **Gródek** Poland
31 K5 **Grodków** Poland
33 S10 **Grödlitz** Germany
31 O2 **Grodno** Belorussia
31 J3 **Grodzisk** Poland
31 M3 **Grodzisk Mazowiecki** Poland
89 C8 **Groen** *watercourse* S Africa
22 G2 **Groenendaal** Belgium
25 G4 **Groenlo** Netherlands
109 L4 **Groesbeck** Texas U.S.A.
25 E5 **Groesbeek** Netherlands
25 C3 **Groet** Netherlands
32 K8 **Grohnde** Germany
22 F3 **Groise, la** France
37 N1 **Groitzsch** Germany
20 D6 **Groix** France
20 D6 **Groix, I de** France
31 M4 **Grójec** Poland
43 C12 **Grombalia** Tunisia
28 C7 **Grønå** *R* Denmark
32 L8 **Gronau** Niedersachsen Germany
32 F8 **Gronau** Nordrhein-Westfalen Germany
28 B4 **Grønbjerg** Denmark
26 F7 **Grong** Norway
28 C4 **Grønhøj** Denmark
33 O9 **Gröningen** Germany
25 G2 **Groningen** Netherlands
25 F2 **Groningerwad** Netherlands
119 N5 **Gronlid** Saskatchewan Canada
115 P5 **Grønnedal** Greenland
26 F5 **Grönöy** Norway
27 K12 **Grönskär** *lighthouse* Sweden
27 H14 **Grönskåra** Sweden
28 J7 **Grønsund** *chan* Denmark
89 D9 **Groot** *R* S Africa
140 D2 **Groote Eylandt** *isld* N Terr Australia
25 F2 **Grootegast** Netherlands
89 B9 **Groot Swartberge** *mts* S Africa
89 C8 **Groot Tafelberg** *mt* S Africa
87 D11 **Grootvloer** *L* S Africa
89 B7 **Groot Vloer** S Africa
89 E9 **Groot Winterberg** *mt* S Africa
22 K4 **Grosbous** Luxembourg
20 G8 **Grosbreuil** France
127 O7 **Gros Islet** St Lucia
27 G14 **Grosjö** Sweden
123 P4 **Gros Morne** *pk* Newfoundland Canada
122 G4 **Gros Morne** Quebec Canada
127 H5 **Gros Morne** Haiti
127 L4 **Gros Morne** Martinique W Indies
123 P4 **Gros Morne Nat. Park** Newfoundland Canada
19 J6 **Grosne** *R* France
20 F3 **Grosnez Pt** Channel Is
41 M5 **Grosotto** Italy
123 P3 **Gros Pate** *pk* Newfoundland Canada
113 F7 **Gross** Florida U.S.A.
37 M4 **Gross Albershof** Germany
40 H4 **Gross Aletsch Gl** Switzerland
32 L10 **Grossalmerode** Germany
33 O9 **Gross Alsleben** Germany
33 P8 **Gross Ammensleben** Germany
37 P5 **Gross Arber** *mt* Germany
33 S8 **Grossbeeren** Germany
33 T8 **Grossbesten** Germany
33 M10 **Grossbodungen** Germany
37 O1 **Gross Bothen** Germany
36 G5 **Grossbottwar** Germany
37 L2 **Gross-Breitenbach** Germany
33 T7 **Gross-Dölln** Germany
37 M2 **Gross Ebersdorf** Germany
123 L6 **Grosse I** Madeleine Is, Quebec Canada
36 F2 **Grossenbuseck** Germany
37 K1 **Grossenehrich** Germany
33 O7 **Gross Engersen** Germany
33 T10 **Grossenhain** Germany
32 H7 **Grossenkneten** Germany
37 N2 **Grossenstein** Germany
127 N4 **Grosse Pointe** Guadeloupe W Indies
33 S10 **Grosse Röder** *R* Germany
42 D6 **Grosseto** Italy
51 N4 **Grossevichi** Russian Federation
36 D5 **Gross Eyberg** *mt* Germany
36 E3 **Gross Feldberg** *mt* Germany
33 T6 **Gross Fredenwalde** Germany
36 E4 **Gross-Gerau** Germany
33 M8 **Gross Gleidingen** Germany
38 G7 **Gross-Glockner** Austria
33 P6 **Gross-Godems** Germany
37 N1 **Gross Görschen** Germany
33 N5 **Gross Gronau** Germany
33 M5 **Gross Hansdorf** Germany
37 P2 **Gross Hartmannsdorf** Germany
32 F5 **Grossheide** Germany
37 M1 **Gross Heringen** Germany
33 M7 **Gross-Kain** Germany
36 E4 **Gross Karlbach** Germany
33 O4 **Gross Klützhöved** Germany
37 L2 **Gross Kochberg** Germany
33 Q10 **Gross Korbetha** Germany
33 T8 **Gross Köris** Germany
33 R8 **Gross Kreutz** Germany
37 N6 **Gross Laaber** *R* Germany
37 J4 **Gross-Langheim** Germany
36 H2 **Grosslüder** Germany
33 S8 **Gross-Machnow** Germany
37 M6 **Grossmehring** Germany
33 M7 **Gross-Oesingen** Germany
36 G4 **Grossostheim** Germany
33 M4 **Gross Plöner See** *L* Germany
37 P6 **Gross Rachel** *mt* Germany
38 L6 **Grossraming** Austria
32 M9 **Gross Rhüden** Germany
36 B5 **Grossrosseln** Germany
37 L1 **Gross Rudestedt** Germany
33 T7 **Gross Schönebeck** Germany
33 P7 **Gross Schwechten** Germany
33 T8 **Gross Selchower See** *L* Germany
33 N8 **Gross-Sisbeck** Germany
33 S6 **Gross Stechlinsee** *L* Germany
36 H6 **Gross Süssen** Germany
36 F4 **Gross-Umstadt** Germany
37 P2 **Gross Waltersdorf** Germany
33 P6 **Gross-Warnow** Germany
33 Q6 **Gross Welle** Germany
33 Q7 **Gross Wudicke** Germany
33 R5 **Gross Wüstenfelde** Germany
33 Q8 **Gross Wusterwitz** Germany
33 T7 **Gross Ziethen** Germany
36 F4 **Gross-Zimmern** Germany
36 B6 **Gros Tenquin** France
21 M3 **Gros Theil, le** France
42 F3 **Grosuplje** Slovenia
141 J5 **Grosvenor Downs** Queensland Australia
116 K7 **Grosvenor, L** Alaska U.S.A.
101 P6 **Gros Ventre Ra** Wyoming U.S.A.
32 J9 **Grotenberg** *mt* Germany
22 F2 **Grotenberge** Belgium
22 H1 **Grote Nete** *R* Belgium
95 Q5 **Groton** Connecticut U.S.A.
95 Q4 **Groton** Massachusetts U.S.A.
95 L4 **Groton** New York U.S.A.
98 H4 **Groton** South Dakota U.S.A.
95 P2 **Groton** Vermont U.S.A.
26 G4 **Grötöy** Norway
45 Q8 **Grotta Azzurra** Italy
45 O7 **Grotta delle Capre** Italy
22 J3 **Grotte-de-Han** Belgium
19 N16 **Grottes de St. Marcel** France
94 J8 **Grottoes** Virginia U.S.A.
36 F5 **Grotzingen** Germany
117 P8 **Grouard** Alberta Canada
20 G4 **Grouin, Pte.du** France
120 H4 **Groundhog** *R* Ontario Canada
101 M6 **Grouse** Idaho U.S.A.
101 M8 **Grouse Creek** Utah U.S.A.
25 E2 **Grouw** Netherlands
27 C13 **Grovane** Norway
107 Q5 **Grove** Oklahoma U.S.A.
94 E7 **Grove City** Ohio U.S.A.
94 G5 **Grove City** Pennsylvania U.S.A.
117 O8 **Grovedale** Alberta Canada
140 B2 **Grove Hill** N Terr Australia
111 J10 **Grove Hill** Alabama U.S.A.
28 C4 **Grove Kirke** Denmark
102 D4 **Groveland** California U.S.A.
26 F9 **Grövelsjön** Sweden
146 H11 **Grove Mts** Antarctica
98 B9 **Grover** Colorado U.S.A.
101 P7 **Grover** Wyoming U.S.A.
111 C12 **Groves** Texas U.S.A.
109 M4 **Groveton** Texas U.S.A.
95 Q2 **Groveton** Vermont U.S.A.
145 D4 **Grovetown** New Zealand
112 E4 **Grovetown** Georgia U.S.A.
101 P6 **Grovont** Wyoming U.S.A.
103 L9 **Growler** Arizona U.S.A.
103 L9 **Growler Mts** Arizona U.S.A.
47 J1 **Grozd'ovo** Bulgaria
45 P1 **Groznjan** Croatia
57 F3 **Groznoye** Kyrgyzstan
53 G11 **Groznyy** Russian Federation
41 J4 **Gr. Scheerh** *mt* Switzerland
33 O4 **Grube** Germany
32 L9 **Grubenhagen** Germany
42 H3 **Grubišno Polje** Croatia
37 P6 **Grubweg** Germany
21 M2 **Gruchet-le-Valasse** France
42 J6 **Gruda** Croatia
47 J2 **Grudovo** Bulgaria
31 M2 **Grudusk** Poland
31 L2 **Grudziadz** Poland
128 D8 **Gruesa, Pta** *C* Chile
122 B6 **Grues, I. aux** Quebec Canada
44 C1 **Grugliasco** Italy
12 B2 **Gruinart** Scotland
109 J9 **Grulla** Texas U.S.A.
36 D4 **Grumbach** Germany
43 H7 **Grumo Appula** Italy
27 F12 **Grums** Sweden
37 O2 **Gruna** Germany
15 C3 **Grunard Bay** Scotland
33 T8 **Grunau** Germany
87 C11 **Grünau** Namibia
36 G6 **Grunbach** Germany
36 F2 **Grünberg** Germany
36 G3 **Gründau** Germany
Gründelhardt *see* **Frankenhardt**
26 K8 **Grundsunda** Sweden
26 J8 **Grundtjärn** Sweden
99 O7 **Grundy Center** Iowa U.S.A.
120 K7 **Grundy Lake Prov. Park** Ontario Canada
28 D7 **Grünholz** Germany
124 J5 **Gruñidora** Mexico
33 Q8 **Grüningen** Germany
36 F2 **Grüningen** Germany
36 H4 **Grünsfeld** Germany
36 E4 **Grünstadt** Germany
38 E8 **Gruppo** *mt* Italy
41 L4 **Grüsch** Switzerland
108 C7 **Gruver** Texas U.S.A.
40 F4 **Gruyère, L. de la** Switzerland
52 B6 **Gruzdžiai** Lithuania
Gruzinskaya S.S.R. *see* **Georgia**
54 L4 **Gryazi** Russian Federation
52 F5 **Gryazovets** Russian Federation
31 M6 **Grybów** Poland
27 H11 **Grycksbo** Sweden
31 J2 **Gryfice** Poland
31 H2 **Gryfino** Poland
99 L1 **Grygla** Minnesota U.S.A.
27 G12 **Grythyttehed** Sweden
26 H3 **Grytöy** *L* Norway
26 C9 **Grytten** Norway
131 H6 **Grytviken** S Georgia
31 J2 **Grzmiąca** Poland
41 O3 **Gschnitz** Austria
36 H6 **Gschwend** Germany
40 F5 **Gstaad** Switzerland
40 F5 **Gsteig** Switzerland
19 P15 **Guâ** France
75 L7 **Gua** India
41 O7 **Gua** *R* Italy
128 D3 **Guacamayas** Colombia
126 F4 **Guacanayabo, G.de** Cuba
127 L9 **Guacara** Venezuela
103 M9 **Gu Achi** Arizona U.S.A.
128 D2 **Guachiria** *R* Colombia
130 C8 **Guaçu** Brazil
124 H7 **Guadalajara** Mexico
16 E4 **Guadalajara** Spain
17 F4 **Guadalajara** *prov* Spain
137 M3 **Guadalcanal** *isld* Solomon Is
16 D6 **Guadalcanal** Spain
16 E6 **Guadalén** *R* Spain
17 F7 **Guadalentin** *R* Spain
16 D8 **Guadalete** *R* Spain
16 E8 **Guadalfeo** *R* Spain
16 E8 **Guadalhorce** *R* Spain
16 E6 **Guadalimar** *R* Spain
17 F6 **Guadalmena** *R* Spain
16 D6 **Guadalmez** *R* Spain
17 G3 **Guadalope** *R* Spain
16 D7 **Guadalquivir** *R* Spain
131 C5 **Guadal, Sa. de** Argentina
108 A4 **Guadalupe** Mexico
124 H6 **Guadalupe** Mexico
71 F5 **Guadalupe** Cebu Philippines
102 D7 **Guadalupe** California U.S.A.
109 J6 **Guadalupe** *R* Texas U.S.A.
108 C4 **Guadalupe Pk** Texas U.S.A.
16 D5 **Guadalupe, Sa de** *mts* Spain
124 G5 **Guadalupe Victoria** Durango Mexico
124 F4 **Guadalupe y Calvo** Mexico
16 E4 **Guadarrama, Sa. de** *mts* Spain
17 F5 **Guadazaón** *R* Spain
127 N4 **Guadeloupe** *islds* Lesser Antilles
16 E6 **Guadiana** *R* Portugal/Spain
16 E7 **Guadiano Menor** *R* Spain
16 D6 **Guadiato** *R* Spain
17 F4 **Guadiela** *R* Spain
16 E7 **Guadix** Spain
133 C6 **Guafo** *isld* Chile
127 P2 **Guaico** Trinidad
130 C7 **Guaicuras** Brazil
128 F2 **Guaina** Venezuela
128 E3 **Guainía** *R* Colombia
130 C9 **Guaíra** Brazil
130 C9 **Guaira** Paraguay
133 C6 **Guaitecas, Is** Chile
126 F4 **Guajaba, Cayo** *isld* Cuba
128 E6 **Guajará Mirim** Brazil
128 E5 **Guajarraã** Brazil
128 F5 **Guajaturaba** Brazil
124 H4 **Guaje, Llano de** *reg* Mexico
125 L2 **Guajiniquil** Honduras
128 D1 **Guajira** *div* Colombia
128 D1 **Guajira, Pena de** *pen* Colombia
102 A3 **Gualala** California U.S.A.
42 E5 **Gualdo Tadino** Italy
131 F4 **Gualeguay** *R* Argentina
131 F4 **Gualeguay** Argentina
133 F4 **Gualeguaychu** Argentina
131 D8 **Gualicho Salina** *salt pan* Argentina
128 E7 **Guallatiri** *mt* Chile
45 J2 **Gualtieri** Italy
134 E6 **Guam** *isld* Mariana Is Pacific Oc
129 J4 **Guamá** *R* Brazil
129 J4 **Guamá** Brazil
127 K9 **Guama** Venezuela
133 B6 **Guamblin, I** Chile
133 E5 **Guamini** Argentina
124 E5 **Guamúchil** Mexico
69 E10 **Gua Musang** Malaysia
65 C5 **Gu'an** China
126 C3 **Guanabacoa** Cuba
130 G8 **Guanabara** Brazil
125 M4 **Guanacaste, Cord. de** *ra* Costa Rica
124 G5 **Guanacevi** Mexico
126 B3 **Guanahacabibes, Pen. de** Cuba
126 C3 **Guanajay** Cuba

Column 1

124 J7 Guanajuato Mexico
129 K6 Guanambi Brazil
128 C5 Guañape, I Peru
127 Q2 Guanapo Trinidad
128 E2 Guanarito Venezuela
65 B5 Guancen Shan mt ra China
67 C6 Guanchang China
133 D3 Guandacol Argentina
65 G3 Guandi China
65 C1 Guandiankou China
126 B3 Guane Cuba
67 B1 Guang'an China
67 E3 Guangchang China
67 F1 Guangde China
65 D3 Guangdegong China
67 D5 Guangdong prov China
67 F2 Guangfeng China
67 A1 Guangfu China
67 A1 Guanghan China
65 B6 Guanghua see Laohekou
67 E2 Guangji China
58 F4 Guangling China
67 E5 Guanglu Dao isld China
67 F1 Guangming Ding mt China
67 B4 Guangnan China
67 C5 Guangning China
65 C6 Guangping China
67 B5 Guangrao China
67 E1 Guangshan China
58 F5 Guangshui China
67 B5 Guangxi prov China
67 F1 Guangyang China
58 E5 Guangyuan China
67 F3 Guangze China
65 C6 Guangzhou China
65 C6 Guangzong China
130 G6 Guanhães Brazil
65 D7 Guanhu China
127 L5 Guánica Puerto Rico
128 F2 Guanipa R Venezuela
67 D3 Guanjiazui China
67 B4 Guanling China
67 C1 Guanmian Shan mts China
65 D7 Guannan China
100 F7 Guano L Oregon U.S.A.
65 G1 Guansongzhen China
    Guansuo see Guanling
128 F1 Guanta Venezuela
126 G4 Guantánamo Cuba
126 G5 Guantánamo, B. de Cuba
65 C4 Guantao China
65 C4 Guanting Shuiku res China
65 C6 Guan Xian China
65 A1 Guan Xian China
67 D4 Guanyang China
65 D7 Guanyun China
130 F7 Guapé Brazil
128 C3 Guapi Colombia
133 G3 Guaporé Brazil
130 J9 Guarabira Brazil
130 D10 Guarama Brazil
130 F8 Guarapari Brazil
130 H7 Guarapari Brazil
130 D9 Guarapava Brazil
130 E9 Guaraquecaba Brazil
130 E7 Guararapes Brazil
130 J10 Guararapes Brazil
17 G2 Guara, Sa. de Spain
18 E10 Guara, Sierra de mts Spain
130 E9 Guaratuba Brazil
16 C4 Guarcino Italy
16 C4 Guarda Portugal
17 F7 Guardal R Spain
130 F5 Guarda Mor Brazil
127 L10 Guardatinajas Venezuela
13 F1 Guardbridge Scotland
133 E6 Guardia Mitre Argentina
133 D7 Guardián, Ö, Argentina
45 R7 Guardia Sanframondi Italy
16 D2 Guardo Spain
16 B4 Guardunha Sa.da mts Portugal
128 F5 Guariba R Amazonas Brazil
127 L10 Guárico R Venezuela
128 E2 Guárico state Venezuela
130 D10 Guarita R Brazil
124 E5 Guasave Mexico
128 C3 Guascama, Pta pt Colombia
128 B3 Guasima Mexico
130 C9 Guassú, R Brazil
42 D4 Guastalla Italy
125 O10 Guatemala rep Central America
126 G4 Guatemala Cuba
125 O10 Guatemala Guatemala
127 L9 Guatire Venezuela
128 E3 Guaviare R Colombia
128 D3 Guaviare div Colombia
126 F4 Guayabal Cuba
128 E2 Guayabal Venezuela
128 D3 Guayabero R Colombia
131 C3 Guayaguas, Sa. da ra Argentina
127 P3 Guayaguayare Trinidad
127 L5 Guayama Puerto Rico
128 C4 Guayapé R Brazil
128 B4 Guayaquil Ecuador
128 B4 Guayaquil, Golfo de Ecuador
128 E6 Guayaramerin Bolivia
128 B4 Guayas prov Ecuador
133 B7 Guayeco Arch islds Chile
124 D4 Guaymas Mexico
131 F3 Guayquiraró, R Argentina
130 F7 Guazupé Brazil
86 G3 Guba Ethiopia
87 E8 Guba Zaire
67 A2 Gubai China
52 J5 Gubakha Russian Federation
71 G4 Gubat Philippines
42 E5 Gubbio Italy
52 J4 Gubdor Russian Federation
65 D4 Gubeikou China
31 H4 Guben Germany
31 H4 Gubin Germany
54 J5 Gubkin Russian Federation
51 K9 Gübükovo Bulgaria
65 C6 Gucheng China
67 D1 Gucheng China
17 G4 Gudar, Sa. de mts Spain
28 F6 Gudbjerg Denmark
28 D5 Gudbrandsdalen Norway
28 D5 Gudenå R Denmark
36 G1 Gudensberg Germany
28 F4 Gudernheim Germany
28 D6 Gudme Denmark
27 G16 Gudhjem Denmark
77 J6 Gudri R Pakistan
65 B7 Gudu China
28 E3 Gudum Denmark
28 A3 Gudum Kirke Denmark
76 D3 Gudur India
18 G6 Gudvangen Norway
19 K5 Guebwiller France
133 C6 Guechcuicui, Pta Chile
21 M5 Guéckédou Guinea
19 G4 Gue-de-la-Chaîne France
21 M5 Gue-de-Longroi, le France
20 H6 Guégon France
121 N4 Güeje Québec Canada
16 E7 Guéjar Sierra Spain
85 F1 Guelma Algeria
85 M9 Guelmine Western Sahara
98 H3 Guelph N Dakota U.S.A.
85 H5 Guelph Mali
85 G1 Guémar France
20 G6 Guémené-Penfao France
77 G2 Guémené-sur-Scorff France
121 P6 Guenette Québec Canada
133 C7 Guenguel R Argentina
20 C6 Guenroue France
20 F6 Guer France
16 E3 Guereña Spain
20 E7 Guérande France
86 C2 Guéra, Pic de mt Chad
85 E2 Guéré Algeria
20 H6 Guerche-de-Bretagne, la France
18 G6 Guerche-sur-l'Aubois, la France
86 D3 Guéréda Chad
20 E7 Guéret France
121 L5 Guérin Québec Canada

Column 2

20 F8 Guérinière, la France
20 D5 Guerlédan, L.de France
20 E3 Guern France
18 D9 Guernica Spain
119 M7 Guernsey Saskatchewan Canada
98 B7 Guernsey Wyoming U.S.A.
20 E3 Guernsey I Channel Is
98 B7 Guernsey Res Wyoming U.S.A.
21 M4 Guerra France
109 J9 Guerra Texas U.S.A.
21 O2 Guerville France
85 D4 Guettara, El Mali
67 A5 Gueugnon France
47 L7 Güéyméz France
85 F4 Gueydan Louisiana U.S.A.
41 K4 Güferhorn mt Switzerland
38 E6 Güffert-Spitze mt Austria
86 G4 Gugã mt Ethiopia
86 G4 Guga mt Ethiopia
42 F7 Guglionesi Italy
48 H5 Gugu mt Romania
70 K9 Guhakolak, Tanjong C Java
33 R6 Gühlen-Glienecke Germany
130 C4 Guia Brazil
20 G6 Guichen France
67 F1 Guichi China
125 M9 Guichicovi Mexico
20 C4 Guiclan France
20 D6 Guidel France
86 B4 Guider Cameroon
98 H9 Guide Rock Nebraska U.S.A.
71 B3 Guiding China
47 K6 Güdey Turkey
16 E4 Guidizzolo Italy
86 C7 Gungu Zaire
19 P13 Guiers France
85 A5 Guiers, L. de Senegal
45 J3 Guiglia Italy
85 C7 Guiglo Ivory Coast
20 G6 Guignen France
20 J2 Guignoven Belgium
127 L9 Güigüé Venezuela
115 R4 Guija Mozambique
65 C4 Gui Jiang R China
67 G2 Guiji Shan mts China
143 B9 Guilderton W Australia Australia
9 F5 Guildford England
95 Q2 Guildhall Vermont U.S.A.
65 E1 Guiler Gol R China
95 S1 Guilford Maine U.S.A.
112 H1 Guilford Ct. Ho. Nat. Mil. Park North Carolina U.S.A.
67 C4 Guilin China
20 F6 Guillac France
20 F5 Guilliers France
20 B6 Guilvinec, le France
20 B3 Guimaraes Portugal
71 F5 Guimaras isld Philippines
71 F5 Guimaras Str Philippines
129 H3 Guin Alabama U.S.A.
71 J8 Guinea Nicaragua
71 J7 Guinayan isld Philippines
126 E3 Guinchos Cay isld Cuba
101 D3 Guinda California U.S.A.
71 H7 Guindulman Philippines
71 N8 Guinguedi isld Indonesia
85 B6 Guinea rep W Africa
85 B6 Guinea Basin Atlantic Oc
85 A6 Guinea-Bissau rep W Africa
85 A6 Guinea, Gulf of W Africa
122 C3 Guinecourt, L Quebec Canada
126 B3 Güines Cuba
76 G3 Güines France
118 J7 Guingamp France
71 F5 Guintacan isld Philippines
71 F3 Guintinua isld Philippines
110 E6 Guion Arkansas U.S.A.
67 C5 Guipavas France
17 F1 Guipúzcoa prov Spain
85 D5 Guir Mali
126 C3 Güira de Melena Cuba
130 D5 Guiratinga Brazil
129 H3 Guisanbourg Fr Guiana
13 G5 Guisborough England
65 B5 Guoyangzhen China
55 D7 Gupei China
48 K3 Gura Humorului Romania
115 P5 Gurban Anggir China
28 H5 Gurban Obo China
66 D2 Gurbantünggüt Shamo desert China
138 E6 Gurchen B South Australia Australia
74 F2 Gurdaspur India
111 C8 Gurdon Arkansas U.S.A.
74 G4 Gurgaon India
86 D3 Gurgei, Jebel mt Sudan
129 K5 Gurgueia R Brazil
127 N11 Guri Venezuela
128 F2 Guri, Embalse de res Venezuela
130 E6 Gurinhatã Brazil
46 D4 Guri-i-Topit mt Albania
38 J8 Gurk R Austria
47 H2 Gurkovo Bulgaria
38 K8 Gurktal V Austria
119 T7 Gurla Mandhata mt China
57 B4 Gurlen Uzbekistan
110 K7 Gurley Alabama U.S.A.
98 D8 Gurley Nebraska U.S.A.
87 G6 Guro Mozambique
52 G8 Guroe Russian Federation
87 F9 Guruve Zimbabwe
76 D2 Guruzala India
58 D3 Gurvan Sayhan Uul mt Mongolia
50 K4 Gur'yev Kazakhstan
56 C4 Gur'yevsk Russian Federation
85 F6 Gusau Nigeria
33 P8 Güsen Germany
33 N1 Gusev Russian Federation
59 H4 Gushi China
101 O9 Gushikami Okinawa
67 E1 Gushi China
61 P14 Gushikami Okinawa
61 P13 Gushikawa Okinawa
70 E1 Gusi Sabah
52 G7 Gusikha Russian Federation
46 D2 Gusinje Montenegro Yugoslavia
56 G5 Gusinoozersk Russian Federation
52 F6 Gus'Khrustal'nyy Russian Federation
46 D4 Gusmar Albania
78 B7 Gusong China
43 B9 Guspini Sardinia
27 G11 Gustav Adolf Sweden
28 C5 Gustavus Alaska U.S.A.
33 P9 Güsten Germany
33 O2 Gusterhain Germany
102 C4 Gustine California U.S.A.
28 G3 Gusum Sweden
109 L4 Gustow Texas U.S.A.
33 S4 Gustow Germany
26 J8 Gusum Sweden
48 K1 Gusyatin Ukraine
48 K1 Gutach Germany
66 G6 Gutarg China
56 K4 Gutarskiy Khrebet mts Russian Federation
38 L5 Gutau Austria
37 M3 Gutenfürst Germany

Column 3

140 E5 Gum Cr N Terr Australia
33 P9 Gumel Nigeria
32 H9 Gümex Mexico
16 E3 Gumiel de Hizán Spain
75 L7 Gumla India
61 M9 Gumma prefect Japan
36 D1 Gummersbach Germany
85 F6 Gummi Nigeria
71 E2 Gumotgong Luzon Philippines
69 C10 Gumpang R Sumatra
94 K9 Gum Spring Virginia U.S.A.
33 Q7 Gumtow Germany
67 A5 Gumu China
47 L7 Gümüşgün Turkey
33 Q5 Gümüşhane Turkey
74 G6 Guna India
86 G3 Guna, Terara mt Ethiopia
139 H5 Gunbar New South Wales Australia
113 H12 Gun Cay Bahamas
58 F1 Gunda Russian Federation
139 J6 Gundagai New South Wales Australia
37 J6 Gundelfingen Germany
36 G5 Gundelsheim Germany
28 C3 Gundersted Denmark
28 H7 Gundheim Germany
70 N9 Gundik Java
86 D5 Gundji Zaire
28 H7 Gundslev Denmark
71 B3 Gunedidalem Indonesia
47 K6 Güney Turkey
117 Q7 Gunflint Ontario Canada
86 C7 Gungu Zaire
119 U5 Gunisao R Manitoba Canada
119 V5 Gunisao L Manitoba Canada
103 L4 Gunlock Utah U.S.A.
114 J6 Gunnar Saskatchewan Canada
26 J6 Gunnarn Sweden
26 M5 Gunnarsbyn Sweden
141 H4 Gunnawarra Queensland Australia
115 R4 Gunnbjørn Fjeld mt Greenland
27 J14 Gunnebo Sweden
139 K4 Gunnedah New South Wales Australia
146 K8 Gunnerus Ridge Antarctica
141 J7 Gunnewin Queensland Australia
139 J5 Gunning New South Wales Australia
8 B7 Gunnislake England
106 B3 Gunnison R Colorado U.S.A.
106 D3 Gunnison Colorado U.S.A.
101 N8 Gunnison I Utah U.S.A.
74 H5 Gunn Pt N Terr Australia
8 B1 Gunpowder R Queensland Australia
143 D8 Gunsight Montana U.S.A.
74 H5 Gunsite Alabama U.S.A.
141 J7 Gunsteak India
76 C3 Guntakal India
100 B6 Gunter Oregon U.S.A.
109 P8 Gunter Texas U.S.A.
36 E4 Güntersberge Germany
36 E4 Guntersblum Germany
68 B2 Guntersville Alabama U.S.A.
14 C2 Gunton Manitoba Canada
99 T3 Guntown Mississippi U.S.A.
98 J3 Gunungapi isld Indonesia
139 J3 Gunungsugih Sumatra
8 B1 Gunupur India
118 D6 Gunworth Saskatchewan Canada
19 J5 Gunyidi W Australia Australia
78 L1 Günz R Germany
66 C5 Gyanzang China
119 M6 Gyangtse see Gyangzê
32 F10 Gyangzê China
32 K8 Gyaring Hu L China
66 D6 Gyaring Co L China
58 G8 Gyaros Greece
75 L4 Gyirong China
106 F8 Gyitang China
27 H13 Gylched mt Wales
94 R7 Gyldenløves Fjord Greenland
120 B7 Gyldenløves Høj hill Denmark
27 G11 Gyljen Sweden
28 E5 Gylling Denmark
36 N5 Gylling Nes Denmark
141 L7 Gympie Queensland Australia
26 G8 Gyöbingauk Burma
68 G1 Gyöngy Vietnam
48 K4 Gyoda Japan
48 L10 Gyomaendröd Hungary
8 F3 Gyöngyös R Hungary
19 K3 Gyöngyös Hungary
112 G3 Gyönk Hungary
80 G5 Györ Hungary
80 F1 Györ-Sopron Hungary
102 D2 Gypsum Colorado U.S.A.
118 D6 Gypsum Kansas U.S.A.
118 L6 Gypsum Pt N Terr Canada
95 O3 Gypsumville Manitoba Canada
98 F3 Gyrstinge Denmark
20 G2 Gysinge Sweden
19 L4 Gyula Hungary
52 D2 Gzhatsk R Russian Federation
    Gzhatsk see Gagarin

H

80 C3 Ha Hoterim Israel
22 H2 Haacht Belgium
37 M4 Haag Germany
35 G1 Haaksbergen Netherlands
65 A4 Hai'an China
137 S5 Ha'apai Group islds Tonga
29 L8 Haapajärvi Finland
29 N8 Haapamäki Finland
29 N9 Haapavesi Finland
29 L9 Haapsalu Estonia
35 C4 Haarlem Netherlands
140 B6 Haast New Zealand
140 B6 Haast Bluff N Terr Australia
140 A6 Haasts Bluff Aboriginal Land N Terr Australia
80 A6 Habaka Jordan
126 B3 Habana Cuba
83 K9 Habarane Sri Lanka
80 C3 Habarûn Jordan
68 J4 Habay-la-Neuve Belgium
22 J6 Habbaniya Iraq
17 O6 Habay Alberta Canada
22 H4 Habbaniyah, Al Western Iraq
59 P6 Habiganj Bangladesh
75 P6 Habikandi India
79 O6 Habigani Bangladesh
37 K14 Habo Sweden
63 J7 Haboro Japan
63 J3 Habomai-Shoto islds Kuril Is Pacific Oc
59 J2 Ha Bonin Israel
80 P1 Haboro Japan
14 C2 Habscheid Germany
29 N11 Habumindu Japan
131 D7 Hachado, Páso de Arg/Chile
61 M6 Hachijo Japan
62 D2 Hachijo Japan
27 M4 Hachenburg Germany
36 J2 Hachijo Jima isld Japan
60 O2 Hachimori Japan
60 B3 Hachinai dake mt Japan
60 B10 Hachinohe Japan
31 K7 Hachioji Japan
100 D8 Hackamore California U.S.A.

Column 4

38 N6 Gutenstein Austria
33 P9 Gütergltick Germany
32 H9 Gütersloh Germany
66 D3 Gutha W Australia Australia
107 K3 Guthrie Kentucky U.S.A.
118 E6 Guthrie Minnesota U.S.A.
110 B6 Guthrie N Dakota U.S.A.
95 N6 Guthrie Oklahoma U.S.A.
108 G2 Guthrie Texas U.S.A.
99 M8 Guthrie Center Iowa U.S.A.
119 R3 Guthrie L Manitoba Canada
13 H5 Gutian China
87 C8 Guting see Yutai
68 H2 Gütkov Germany
36 E3 Gutow-Neuhof Germany
99 P7 Guttenberg Iowa U.S.A.
72 H4 Guty Ukraine
107 N2 Gutu Zimbabwe
54 G6 Guty Ukraine
33 S5 Gützkow Germany
13 F2 Guvrin R Israel
80 C7 Guwahati India
73 L8 Guxhagen Germany
85 F6 Gu Xian China
27 D11 Guyan China
32 J5 Guyana rep S America
32 K4 Guyandotte R West Virginia U.S.A.
58 F3 Guyang China
44 E3 Guyang China
121 M4 Guyenne Quebec Canada
116 R6 Guyenne France
139 K4 Guyra New South Wales Australia
123 L8 Guysborough Nova Scotia Canada
112 F5 Guyton Georgia U.S.A.
9 G3 Güzelbağ Turkey
9 G4 Guzhang China
114 J3 Guzhen China
144 E7 Guzhou see Rongjiang
61 N8 Gvardeysk Russian Federation
80 F2 Gvardeyskoye Ukraine
26 M5 Gvozdets Ukraine
28 E4 Gwa Burma
116 O3 Gwaai Zimbabwe
131 G3 Gwabegar New South Wales Australia
65 F5 Gwabi Australia
80 C7 Gwadar Pakistan
89 E2 Gwadar Pakistan
9 E1 Gwalchmai Wales
143 D8 Gwalia W Australia Australia
74 H5 Gwalior India
141 J7 Gwambegwine Queensland Australia
115 N2 Gwanda Zimbabwe
118 K6 Gwanda Zimbabwe
89 F2 Gwbert-on-Sea Wales
68 B2 Gwebin Burma
14 C2 Gweebarra B Ireland
74 E2 Gwelo see Gweru
80 D1 Gwendolen Oregon U.S.A.
100 C6 Gwent co Wales
9 F2 Gwent R Zimbabwe
79 M4 Gweru Zimbabwe
99 T3 Gwent R Zimbabwe
77 H2 Gwinn Michigan U.S.A.
69 C12 Gwinner North Dakota U.S.A.
139 J3 Gwydir R New South Wales Australia
112 F5 Gwynedd co Wales
27 J11 Gwynne Alberta Canada
32 F5 Hage Germany
80 D3 Hag Gelilit Israel
8 C6 Hagelberg Germany
109 O9 Hagemeister I Alaska U.S.A.
18 C11 Hagen Saskatchewan Canada
32 F10 Hagen Germany
32 H6 Hagen-Gebirge mts Austria
28 C3 Hagenow Germany
109 L5 Hagerman Idaho U.S.A.
112 E12 Hagerman New Mexico U.S.A.
14 H4 Hagerstown Indiana U.S.A.
120 K10 Hagerstown Maryland U.S.A.
122 G11 Hagfors Sweden
106 J4 Hagger Colorado U.S.A.
94 C8 Haggerton Georgia U.S.A.
80 F1 Hagi Sweden
118 L6 Hague Saskatchewan Canada
95 O3 Hague, C. de la France
98 F3 Hague North Dakota U.S.A.
20 D2 Hague, C. de la France
98 F4 Haguenau France
8 F1 Hague, The see Den Haag
123 O3 Ha Ha, L Quebec Canada
122 O3 Ha Ha, L Quebec Canada
80 D6 Ha Hamisha Jordan
141 H4 Hahira Georgia U.S.A.
13 G5 Hahn Germany
37 M4 Hahnbach Germany
95 N6 Hahnenklee-Bockswiese Germany
22 H2 Haacht Belgium
37 G1 Hai'an China
65 A4 Hai'an China
65 G1 Haicheng China
65 C4 Haicheng China
37 M5 Haidhof Germany
48 D3 Haïdra Tunisia
37 H2 Haiger Germany
37 O7 Haihang China
29 K11 Hailakandi India
19 O9 Haïla Israel
115 N1 Hail Basin Canada/U.S.A.
119 P9 Haileybury Ontario Canada
116 U6 Hailin China
91 C8 Hailing Dao isld China
65 F2 Haili China
65 C1 Hai Long China
67 F2 Haima China
65 C1 Hai long China
100 J2 Hailsham England
119 S8 Hailun China
104 G4 Hailuoto Finland
110 C12 Hailsham England
146 F6 Halley U.K. Base Antarctica

Column 5

26 G9 Hackås Sweden
103 L6 Hackberry Arizona U.S.A.
111 C12 Hackberry Louisiana U.S.A.
107 K3 Hackberry Cr Kansas U.S.A.
118 E6 Hackett Alberta Canada
110 B6 Hackett Arkansas U.S.A.
95 N6 Hackettstown New Jersey U.S.A.
111 J7 Hackleburg Alabama U.S.A.
138 E4 Hack, Mt South Australia Australia
13 H5 Hackness England
94 D4 Hackney Michigan U.S.A.
60 H2 Haiphong Vietnam
118 F5 Hairy Hill Alberta Canada
65 E3 Haisgai China
115 N5 Hall Pen Northwest Territories Canada
36 E3 Halt rep W Indies
80 C5 Hadar Israel
98 C1 Hadar Nebraska U.S.A.
65 F5 Haitou China
65 F2 Haitou China
103 N9 Haivana Nakya Arizona U.S.A.
102 G5 Haiwee Res California U.S.A.
65 E3 Haixing China
86 G2 Haiya R Sudan
67 G1 Haiyan China
65 F5 Haiyang China
106 G3 Haiyang Dao isld China
65 F5 Haiyou see Sanmen
48 G3 Hajdú-Bihar co Hungary
48 G3 Hajdúböszörmény Hungary
48 G3 Hajdúdorog Hungary
48 G3 Hajdúhadház Hungary
48 G3 Hajdúnánás Hungary
48 A2 Hajdúsámson Hungary
48 G3 Hajdúszoboszló Hungary
36 M7 Hajiki-saki C Japan
79 G9 Hajj Saudi Arabia
31 O3 Hajnówka Poland
65 F7 Hajo isld S Korea
48 A1 Haka Burma
135 V5 Hakalau Hawaiian Is
80 G3 Hakama Jordan
87 E7 Hakansson mts Zaire
27 F13 Håkantorp Sweden
144 A7 Hakapoua, L New Zealand
61 N8 Hakase-yama mt Japan
43 C12 Halq el Oued Tunisia
144 C6 Hals Denmark
26 C8 Halsa Norway
37 P2 Halsbrucke Germany
36 F2 Halsdorf Germany
99 F8 Halsey Nebraska U.S.A.
100 B5 Halsey Oregon U.S.A.
28 H5 Halsey Harbour Philippines
28 D1 Halsnæs peri Denmark
28 G6 Halsskov Denmark
26 O1 Halsstad Minnesota U.S.A.
59 M3 Halstad Minnesota U.S.A.
9 G3 Halstead England
107 N4 Halstead Kansas U.S.A.
36 B5 Halstroff France
29 L8 Halsua Finland
40 J3 Haltdalen Norway
79 H2 Halten Norway
109 M9 Haltom City Texas U.S.A.
32 F9 Haltern Germany
32 F9 Halti mt Finland
77 H2 Halul isld Qatar
77 K10 Halura isld Indonesia
36 C1 Halver Germany
135 L8 Halvorgate Saskatchewan Canada
28 D2 Halvrimmen Denmark
141 K7 Haly, Mt Queensland Australia
22 F5 Ham France
60 F12 Hama Japan
80 D4 Hamã Syria
85 F3 Hamada de Tinrhert stony desert Algeria
77 D4 Hamadan Iran
85 C3 Hamada Tounassine stony desert Algeria
79 G3 Hamadya Israel
79 J3 Hamåh Syria
79 G3 Hamahika-jima isld Okinawa
61 L11 Hamakita Japan
61 L12 Hamamasu Japan
61 N9 Hamamatsu Japan
60 T2 Hamanaka Japan
61 M6 Hamana ko L Japan
80 C4 Ha Ma' Yür Israel
27 E11 Hamar Norway
98 H2 Hamar North Dakota U.S.A.
94 D7 Hamar Norway
60 H10 Hamasaka Japan
22 J6 Hamāta Jebel mt Egypt
84 J5 Hamat Gader Jordan
98 C3 Hambach France
85 G3 Hamberg North Dakota U.S.A.
79 G3 Hamborn conurbation Germany
111 L8 Hamburg Arkansas U.S.A.
110 B8 Hamburg California U.S.A.
99 N5 Hamburg Iowa U.S.A.
98 C11 Hamburg New Jersey U.S.A.
99 M6 Hamburg New York U.S.A.
98 H2 Hamburg North Dakota U.S.A.
143 A10 Hamburg W Australia Australia
30 E8 Hamburg Germany
30 F8 Hamburg land Germany
111 U10 Hamburg North Dakota U.S.A.
115 O7 Hamburg North Dakota U.S.A.
27 J11 Hällnäs Sweden
119 V10 Halleck Nevada U.S.A.
118 K8 Halliday Res Saskatchewan Canada
115 N5 Hall Pen Northwest Territories Canada

Column 6

100 H5 Haines Oregon U.S.A.
113 F9 Haines City Florida U.S.A.
117 E5 Haines Junction Yukon Territory Canada
22 G3 Haine-St-Paul Belgium
38 N5 Hainford U.S.A.
68 B4 Haing R Burma
37 P2 Hainichen Germany
67 G1 Haining China
33 N10 Hainlete Germany
37 O2 Hainspitz Germany
94 D4 Haintramck Michigan U.S.A.
118 F5 Haiphong Vietnam
65 E3 Haisgai China
115 N5 Hall Pen Northwest Territories Canada
110 G6 Hals Tennessee U.S.A.
8 C7 Halsall England
27 H12 Hallsberg Sweden
142 G4 Halls Creek W Australia Australia
138 F6 Halls Gap Victoria Australia
37 K4 Hallstadt Germany
27 H12 Hallstahammar Sweden
106 G3 Hall Station Colorado U.S.A.
38 A6 Hallstatt Austria
27 K11 Hallstavik Sweden
99 M5 Hallstead Pennsylvania U.S.A.
111 C9 Hall Summit Louisiana U.S.A.
115 M1 Hallsville Missouri U.S.A.
109 N3 Hallsville Texas U.S.A.
41 A8 Hall Table Mt Indian Oc
41 D3 Halltal Austria
48 J5 Hallton Pennsylvania U.S.A.
22 E2 Halluin France
25 E2 Hallum Netherlands
28 C5 Hallund Denmark
28 C5 Hallundbæk Denmark
14 B2 Halveen Sweden
71 B3 Halmahera isld Indonesia
71 B3 Halmahera sea Indonesia
48 H3 Halmeu Romania
27 F15 Halmstad Sweden
38 A7 Halneset Norway
79 J5 Haloch Pennsylvania U.S.A.
28 B3 Halringen Norway
37 P2 Halsbrucke Germany
36 F2 Halsdorf Germany
36 E3 Haltwhistle England
77 C7 Hälol isld Qatar
72 H1 Halura isld Indonesia
77 K10 Halura isld Indonesia
36 C1 Halver Germany
8 E5 Halverston Germany
8 F7 Halvard England
142 B5 Halvoyne England
34 Halbürnen Germany
    Germany
111 E8 Halley Arkansas U.S.A.
116 B6 Hall I Bering Sea
98 D2 Halliday North Dakota U.S.A.
116 C6 Halligan Res Colorado U.S.A.

Column 7

111 E8 Halley Arkansas U.S.A.
116 B6 Hall I Bering Sea
98 D2 Halliday North Dakota U.S.A.
116 C6 Halligan Res Colorado U.S.A.
27 D11 Hallingdalselv R Norway
27 C11 Hallingskarvet mt Norway
27 B11 Hallingskeid Norway
28 L4 Hall Lake L Northwest Territories Canada
27 J11 Hällnäs Sweden
119 V10 Halleck Nevada U.S.A.
118 K8 Halliday Res Saskatchewan Canada
115 N5 Hall Pen Northwest Territories Canada
115 N5 Halls Tennessee U.S.A.
8 C7 Halsall England
27 H12 Hallsberg Sweden
142 G4 Halls Creek W Australia Australia
138 F6 Halls Gap Victoria Australia
37 K4 Hallstadt Germany
27 H12 Hallstahammar Sweden
106 G3 Hall Station Colorado U.S.A.
38 A6 Hallstatt Austria
27 K11 Hallstavik Sweden
99 M5 Hallstead Pennsylvania U.S.A.
111 C9 Hall Summit Louisiana U.S.A.
115 M1 Hallsville Missouri U.S.A.
109 N3 Hallsville Texas U.S.A.
41 A8 Hall Table Mt Indian Oc
41 D3 Halltal Austria
48 J5 Hallton Pennsylvania U.S.A.
22 E2 Halluin France
25 E2 Hallum Netherlands
28 C5 Hallund Denmark
28 C5 Hallundbæk Denmark
14 B2 Halveen Sweden
71 B3 Halmahera isld Indonesia
71 B3 Halmahera sea Indonesia
48 H3 Halmeu Romania
27 F15 Halmstad Sweden
38 A7 Halneset Norway
79 J5 Haloch Pennsylvania U.S.A.
28 D8 Hamble England
99 F5 Hambleton England
13 G5 Hambleton Hills England
13 G5 Hambleton Hills England
102 C3 Hambone California U.S.A.
32 Hambühren Germany
    Germany
111 O8 Hamburg Arkansas U.S.A.
98 A3 Hamburg Iowa U.S.A.
99 V6 Hamburg New Jersey U.S.A.
94 M6 Hamburg New York U.S.A.
98 H2 Hamburg North Dakota U.S.A.
143 A10 Hamburg W Australia Australia
30 E8 Hamburg Germany
30 F8 Hamburg land Germany
20 H4 Hambye France
98 H7 Hamden New York U.S.A.
94 C4 Hamden Ohio U.S.A.
29 L10 Hämeenkyrö Finland
29 L11 Hämeenlinna Finland
140 F6 Hamelin Queensland Australia
142 C2 Hamelin B W Australia Australia
142 A5 Hamelin Pool W Australia Australia
31 O1 Hamelin Germany
101 N6 Hamer Idaho U.S.A.
33 O8 Hamersleben Germany
142 C5 Hamersley W Australia Australia
142 B5 Hamersley Ra W Australia Australia
98 P7 Hamersley Ra. Nat Park W Australia Australia
65 G5 Hamgyöng N Korea
65 G5 Hamhüng N Korea
65 C4 Hami China
138 C2 Hamilton S Australia Australia
139 H8 Hamilton Tasmania Australia
138 F5 Hamilton Victoria Australia
91 Q6 Hamilton Bermuda
115 L9 Hamilton Ontario Canada
145 D2 Hamilton New Zealand
13 E4 Hamilton Scotland
111 H9 Hamilton Alabama U.S.A.
101 R6 Hamilton Colorado U.S.A.
111 U10 Hamilton Illinois U.S.A.
107 M9 Hamilton Kansas U.S.A.
94 C11 Hamilton Michigan U.S.A.
110 E5 Hamilton Missouri U.S.A.
101 K3 Hamilton Montana U.S.A.
102 G2 Hamilton Nevada U.S.A.
94 C4 Hamilton Ohio U.S.A.
100 E3 Hamilton Oregon U.S.A.
109 L4 Hamilton Texas U.S.A.
101 M8 Hamilton Washington U.S.A.
101 P6 Hamilton Dome Wyoming U.S.A.
140 C6 Hamilton Downs N Terr Australia
115 O7 Hamilton Inlet Labrador, Nfld Canada

182
Hamilton,L — Hébert, L

111 C7 **Hamilton,L** Arkansas U.S.A.
103 J2 **Hamilton, Mt** Nevada U.S.A.
29 N11 **Hamina** Finland
74 J6 **Hamirpur** India
Hamitabat *see* **İsparta**
94 C5 **Hamler** Ohio U.S.A.
94 A5 **Hamlet** Indiana U.S.A.
98 E9 **Hamlet** Nebraska U.S.A.
112 H3 **Hamlet** North Carolina U.S.A.
138 E5 **Hamley Bridge** South Australia Australia
94 K3 **Hamlin** New York U.S.A.
108 G3 **Hamlin** Texas U.S.A.
94 E8 **Hamlin** West Virginia U.S.A.
94 A2 **Hamlin L** Michigan U.S.A.
32 G9 **Hamm** Germany
17 G9 **Hammam Bou Hadjar** Algeria
43 D12 **Hammamet** Tunisia
85 G1 **Hammamet, G de** Tunisia
85 G1 **Hammam Lif** Tunisia
29 H11 **Hammarland** Finland
27 F11 **Hammarsbyn** Sweden
29 M3 **Hammastunturi** *mt* Finland
22 G1 **Hamme** Belgium
32 J6 **Hamme** *R* Germany
28 D4 **Hammel** Denmark
36 H3 **Hammelburg** Germany
28 F4 **Hammelev** Denmark
28 C6 **Hammelev** Denmark
33 S6 **Hammelspring** Germany
22 H2 **Hamme-Mille** Belgium
26 H8 **Hammerdal** Sweden
147 H14 **Hammerfest** Norway
28 D3 **Hammershøj** Denmark
143 C9 **Hammersley L** W Australia Australia
36 C3 **Hammerstein** Germany
13 G6 **Hammerton** England
28 C4 **Hammerum** Denmark
100 K7 **Hammett** Idaho U.S.A.
32 E9 **Hamminkeln** Germany
107 L6 **Hammon** Oklahoma U.S.A.
138 E4 **Hammond** South Australia Australia
99 T8 **Hammond** Illinois U.S.A.
110 H2 **Hammond** Illinois U.S.A.
111 F11 **Hammond** Louisiana U.S.A.
98 B4 **Hammond** Montana U.S.A.
95 M2 **Hammond** New York U.S.A.
100 B3 **Hammond** Oregon U.S.A.
99 O5 **Hammond** Wisconsin U.S.A.
94 D1 **Hammond B** Michigan U.S.A.
141 F1 **Hammond I** Queensland Australia
95 K4 **Hammondsport** New York U.S.A.
122 G8 **Hammond Vale** New Brunswick Canada
102 C2 **Hammonton** California U.S.A.
95 N7 **Hammonton** New Jersey U.S.A.
26 O1 **Hamnbukt** Norway
26 L2 **Hamneidet** Norway
26 S1 **Hamningberg** Norway
68 G7 **Ham Ninh** Vietnam
121 T7 **Ham Nord** Quebec Canada
26 L4 **Håmojokk** Sweden
22 K1 **Hamont** Belgium
86 G2 **Hamoyet, Jebel** *mt* Sudan
123 Q4 **Hampden** Newfoundland Canada
144 C6 **Hampden** New Zealand
98 H1 **Hampden** North Dakota U.S.A.
95 T2 **Hampden Highlands** Maine U.S.A.
28 C4 **Hampen** Denmark
36 B6 **Hampont** France
9 E5 **Hampshire** *co* England
122 F8 **Hampstead** New Brunswick Canada
95 K7 **Hampstead** Maryland U.S.A.
112 K3 **Hampstead** North Carolina U.S.A.
122 G8 **Hampton** New Brunswick Canada
9 F5 **Hampton** England
111 D8 **Hampton** Arkansas U.S.A.
113 E8 **Hampton** Florida U.S.A.
111 M8 **Hampton** Georgia U.S.A.
99 N7 **Hampton** Iowa U.S.A.
98 J9 **Hampton** Nebraska U.S.A.
95 R4 **Hampton** New Hampshire U.S.A.
100 E6 **Hampton** Oregon U.S.A.
112 F5 **Hampton** South Carolina U.S.A.
95 L9 **Hampton** Virginia U.S.A.
101 P8 **Hampton** Wyoming U.S.A.
95 P6 **Hampton Bays** Long I, New York U.S.A.
143 F9 **Hampton Tableland** W Australia Australia
27 H10 **Hamra** Sweden
27 J11 **Hamränge** Sweden
79 G4 **Ḩamrāt, Al** Syria
101 P7 **Hams Fork** *R* Wyoming U.S.A.
9 G5 **Hamstreet** England
68 H7 **Ham Tan** Vietnam
135 T3 **Hana** Hawaiian Is
126 D3 **Hanábana** *R* Cuba
135 O1 **Hanalei** Hawaiian Is
135 T3 **Hanamanioa, C** Hawaiian Is
135 O1 **Hanamaulu** Hawaiian Is
135 O1 **Hanapepe** Hawaiian Is
61 N13 **Hanare-iwa** *islds* Japan
36 F3 **Hanau** Germany
102 S12 **Hanauma B** Hawaiian Is
121 L5 **Hanbury** Ontario Canada
117 M10 **Hanceville** British Columbia Canada
111 K7 **Hanceville** Alabama U.S.A.
58 F4 **Hancheng** China
67 D1 **Hanchuan** China
95 T2 **Hancock** Maine U.S.A.
94 J7 **Hancock** Maryland U.S.A.
99 S2 **Hancock** Michigan U.S.A.
99 L4 **Hancock** Minnesota U.S.A.
95 P4 **Hancock** New Hampshire U.S.A.
95 M5 **Hancock** New York U.S.A.
99 R5 **Hancock** Wisconsin U.S.A.
113 F10 **Hancock, L** Florida U.S.A.
61 K11 **Handa** Japan
58 F4 **Handan** China
28 B4 **Handbjerg** Denmark
9 F5 **Handcross** England
118 J6 **Handel** Saskatchewan Canada
27 K12 **Handen** Sweden
88 G4 **Handeni** Tanzania
28 D3 **Handest** Denmark
65 D1 **Handgai** China
109 K3 **Handley** Texas U.S.A.
119 P9 **Handsworth** Saskatchewan Canada
32 K4 **Hanerau** Germany
102 E5 **Hanford** California U.S.A.
76 B3 **Hangal** India
68 C5 **Hangan** Burma
65 G6 **Hangang** *R* S Korea
145 F3 **Hangaroa** New Zealand
27 C11 **Hangastöl** Norway
145 E3 **Hangatiki** New Zealand
58 C2 **Hangayn Nuruu** *mt* Mongolia
Hangchow *see* **Hangzhou**
33 T8 **Hangelsberg** Germany
27 G14 **Hånger** Sweden
58 E3 **Hanggin Houqi** China
94 E8 **Hanging Rock** Ohio U.S.A.
89 A10 **Hangklip, C** S Africa
100 H2 **Hangman Cr** Washington U.S.A.
29 K12 **Hango** Finland
65 D5 **Hangu** China
67 D4 **Hanguang** China
59 H5 **Hangzhou** China
59 H5 **Hangzhou Wan** *B* China
79 F4 **Ḩanidiyah, Al** Syria
32 M7 **Hänigsen** Germany
86 H3 **Hanīsh al Kabīr** *islds* Red Sea
80 D1 **Ḩanita** Israel
Hanjiang *see* **Yangzhou**
67 F4 **Hanjiang** China
29 M9 **Hankasalmi** Finland
85 C4 **Hank, El** Mauritania
98 J3 **Hankinson** North Dakota U.S.A.
58 F5 **Hankou** China
103 O3 **Hanksville** Utah U.S.A.
118 L7 **Hanley** Saskatchewan Canada
8 D1 **Hanley** England
99 L5 **Hanley Falls** Minnesota U.S.A.
144 D5 **Hanmer Springs** New Zealand
118 F7 **Hanna** Alberta Canada
101 P9 **Hanna** Utah U.S.A.
101 T8 **Hanna** Wyoming U.S.A.
98 H2 **Hannaford** North Dakota U.S.A.
119 T10 **Hannah** North Dakota U.S.A.
120 K1 **Hannah B** Ontario Canada
99 P10 **Hannibal** Missouri U.S.A.
99 Q4 **Hannibal** Wisconsin U.S.A.
28 A4 **Hanning Kirke** Denmark
142 F3 **Hann, Mt** W Australia Australia
32 L8 **Hannover** Germany
98 E2 **Hannover** North Dakota U.S.A.
140 C6 **Hann Ra** N Terr Australia
22 J2 **Hannut** Belgium
27 H16 **Hanöbukten** *B* Sweden
68 G2 **Hanoi** Vietnam
48 D4 **Hanót** Hungary
120 J8 **Hanover** Ontario Canada
127 H1 **Hanover** *parish* Jamaica
89 D8 **Hanover** S Africa
107 O2 **Hanover** Kansas U.S.A.
99 N4 **Hanover** Minnesota U.S.A.
101 Q2 **Hanover** Montana U.S.A.
95 P3 **Hanover** New Hampshire U.S.A.
133 C8 **Hanover, I** Chile
48 E6 **Han Pijesak** Bosnia-Herzegovina
48 D3 **Hanság** Hungary
117 N8 **Hansard** British Columbia Canada
98 G1 **Hansboro** North Dakota U.S.A.
120 F3 **Hansen** Ontario Canada
146 J10 **Hansen mts** Antarctica
67 F1 **Hanshan** China
67 D2 **Hanshou** China
58 E5 **Han Shui** *R* China
67 D1 **Han Shui** *R* China
74 F4 **Hansi** India
27 G10 **Hansjö** Sweden
140 C5 **Hanson** *R* N Terr Australia
138 D4 **Hanson, L** South Australia Australia
119 P4 **Hanson L** Saskatchewan Canada
28 D5 **Hansted** Vejle Denmark
28 B2 **Hanstholm** Denmark
28 B2 **Hanstholm Havn** *C* Denmark
65 D2 **Han Sum** China
22 J3 **Han-sur-Lesse** Belgium
25 B6 **Hansweert** Netherlands
Hantan *see* **Handan**
66 C3 **Hantengri Feng** *mt* Kazakhstan
Hanting *see* **Wei Xian**
Hants *co see* **Hampshire**
122 H8 **Hantsport** Nova Scotia Canada
36 C7 **Hantz, Col du** *pass* France
79 H3 **Ḩānūbah, Al** Syria
65 D2 **Han Ul** China
20 B5 **Hanvec** France
67 A1 **Hanwang** China
83 K11 **Hanwella** Sri Lanka
58 F5 **Hanyang** China
57 K4 **Hanyaylak** China
61 N9 **Hanyū** Japan
58 D6 **Hanyuan** China
58 E5 **Hanzhong** China
65 D7 **Hanzhuang** China
135 N10 **Hao** *atoll* Tuamotu Arch Pacific Oc
65 H1 **Haolianghe** China
80 F3 **Ha On** Israel
75 N7 **Hāora** India
26 N6 **Haparanda** Sweden
71 B1 **Hapo** Halmahera Indonesia
9 H2 **Happisburgh** England
100 B8 **Happy Camp** California U.S.A.
140 E5 **Happy Cr** N Terr Australia
144 D5 **Hapuku** New Zealand
83 L11 **Haputale** Sri Lanka
79 E9 **Ḩaql** Saudi Arabia
26 M5 **Harads** Sweden
86 H4 **Hara Fanna** Ethiopia
111 H12 **Harahan** New Orleans, Louisiana U.S.A.
26 B9 **Haram** Norway
59 M4 **Haramachi** Japan
86 H4 **Hārar** Ethiopia
88 C10 **Harare** Zimbabwe
58 E2 **Har-ayrag** Mongolia
86 C3 **Haraz Djombo** Chad
86 D3 **Haraz-Mangueigne** Chad
80 E8 **Har Ben Yai'r** Israel
65 G2 **Harbin** China
27 J11 **Harbo** Sweden
77 K5 **Harboi Hills** Pakistan
28 J7 **Hårbølle** Denmark
22 D4 **Harbonnières** France
28 A3 **Harboør** Denmark
28 A3 **Harboør Tange** *pen* Denmark
100 A7 **Harbor** Oregon U.S.A.
94 E3 **Harbor Beach** Michigan U.S.A.
117 E6 **Harbor Pt** Alaska U.S.A.
94 B1 **Harbor Springs** Michigan U.S.A.
13 F3 **Harbottle** England
123 R6 **Harbour Breton** Newfoundland Canada
123 S6 **Harbour Buffett** Newfoundland Canada
113 K12 **Harbour Cay, Little** *isld* Bahamas
123 Q3 **Harbour Deep** Newfoundland Canada
123 T6 **Harbour Grace** Newfoundland Canada
113 L12 **Harbour I** Bahamas
123 S6 **Harbour Mille** Newfoundland Canada
122 H8 **Harbourville** Nova Scotia Canada
37 K6 **Harburg** Bayern Germany
32 L6 **Harburg** Niedersachsen Germany
28 E6 **Hårby** Denmark
122 G7 **Harcourt** New Brunswick Canada
103 L7 **Harcuvar Mts** Arizona U.S.A.
74 G7 **Harda Khās** India
27 B11 **Hardanger** Norway
27 B11 **Hardanger-fjorden** *inlet* Norway
27 C11 **Hardangervidda** *plateau* Norway
27 B11 **Hardangervidda Nat. Park** Norway
89 A5 **Hardap Dam** Namibia
111 F9 **Hardee** Mississippi U.S.A.
112 F5 **Hardeeville** South Carolina U.S.A.
25 E2 **Hardegarijp** Netherlands
32 L9 **Hardegsen** Germany
22 B2 **Hardelot-Plage** France
25 G3 **Hardenberg** Netherlands
70 D2 **Harden, Bt** *mt* Kalimantan
25 E4 **Harderwijk** Netherlands
107 J5 **Hardesty** Oklahoma U.S.A.
142 B6 **Hardey, R** W Australia Australia
36 H4 **Hardheim** Germany
110 F2 **Hardin** Illinois U.S.A.
110 C2 **Hardin** Missouri U.S.A.
101 S4 **Hardin** Montana U.S.A.
87 E12 **Harding** S Africa
99 M3 **Harding** Minnesota U.S.A.
116 M6 **Harding Icefield** Alaska U.S.A.
119 T2 **Harding L** Manitoba Canada
111 L9 **Harding, L** Georgia U.S.A.
110 K4 **Hardinsburg** Kentucky U.S.A.
118 F6 **Hardisty** Alberta Canada
117 P3 **Hardisty L** Northwest Territories Canada
21 P2 **Hardivillers** France
100 F4 **Hardman** Oregon U.S.A.
142 E4 **Hardman, Mt** W Australia Australia
80 D8 **Hardof** *R* Jordan
98 K6 **Hardwick** Minnesota U.S.A.
95 P2 **Hardwick** Vermont U.S.A.
8 D4 **Hardwicke** England
138 D5 **Hardwicke B** South Australia Australia
119 N9 **Hardy** Saskatchewan Canada
110 E5 **Hardy** Arkansas U.S.A.
101 O2 **Hardy** Montana U.S.A.
Hardy, Mt *see* **Rangipova**
133 D9 **Hardy, Pen** Chile
94 B3 **Hardy Res** Michigan U.S.A.
123 S5 **Hare B** Newfoundland Canada
80 E4 **Hare Gilboa** Israel
26 B9 **Hareid** Norway
22 E2 **Harelbeke** Belgium
32 F7 **Haren** Germany
115 O3 **Hareøen** *isld* Greenland
86 H4 **Härergē** *prov* Ethiopia
13 G6 **Harewood** England
79 F5 **Harf el Mreffi** *mt* Lebanon
21 L2 **Harfleur** France
27 K11 **Harg** Sweden
36 B5 **Hargarten aux Mines** France
86 H4 **Hargele** Ethiopia
86 H4 **Hargeysa** Somalia
48 K4 **Harghita, Muntii** *mt* Romania
22 E4 **Hargicourt** France
109 J9 **Hargill** Texas U.S.A.
22 J3 **Hargimont** Belgium
22 H3 **Hargnies** France
119 Q9 **Hargrave** Manitoba Canada
119 S4 **Hargrave L** Manitoba Canada
79 E8 **Har Hakippa** *mt* Israel
79 E8 **Har Harif** Israel
80 D8 **Har Hezron** Israel
66 F4 **Har Hu** *L* China
61 M9 **Hari** Japan
74 H4 **Haridwār** India
76 B3 **Harihar** India
144 C5 **Harihari** New Zealand
79 G2 **Hārim** Syria
60 H11 **Harima-nada** *sea* Japan
25 B5 **Haringvliet** Netherlands
74 E1 **Haripur** Pakistan
77 J2 **Hari Rud** *R* Afghanistan/Iran
79 G6 **Ḩarīr, Wādī adh** *watercourse* Syria
87 C10 **Haris** Namibia
26 G10 **Härjån** *R* Sweden
29 J10 **Harjavalta** Finland
26 F10 **Härjehågna** *mt* Sweden
80 F2 **Har Kena'an** *pk* Israel
112 L3 **Harkers I** North Carolina U.S.A.
99 L8 **Harlan** Iowa U.S.A.
107 M2 **Harlan** Kansas U.S.A.
94 D10 **Harlan** Kentucky U.S.A.
98 G9 **Harlan County Lake** *res* Nebraska U.S.A.
22 K4 **Harlange** Luxembourg
32 G5 **Harle** Germany
8 B2 **Harlech** Wales
112 E4 **Harlem** Georgia U.S.A.
101 R1 **Harlem** Montana U.S.A.
32 L5 **Harlesiel** Germany
9 H3 **Harleston** England
28 D4 **Harlev** Denmark
28 J6 **Hårlev** Denmark
112 G4 **Harleyville** South Carolina U.S.A.
25 D2 **Harlingen** Netherlands
109 K9 **Harlingen** Texas U.S.A.
32 G5 **Harlinger Land** Germany
33 M9 **Harlingerode** Germany
9 G4 **Harlow** England
98 G1 **Harlow** North Dakota U.S.A.
101 Q3 **Harlowton** Montana U.S.A.
94 H8 **Harman** West Virginia U.S.A.
47 K5 **Harmancık** Turkey
26 J10 **Harmånger** Sweden
25 C4 **Harmelen** Netherlands
80 E2 **Har Meron** *pk* Israel
107 L5 **Harmon** Oklahoma U.S.A.
118 A2 **Harmon R** Alberta Canada
95 S2 **Harmony** Maine U.S.A.
99 O6 **Harmony** Minnesota U.S.A.
79 E8 **Har Natha** *mt* Israel
100 F6 **Harney Basin** *reg* Oregon U.S.A.
113 F9 **Harney, L** Florida U.S.A.
100 F6 **Harney L** Oregon U.S.A.
98 C6 **Harney Pk** South Dakota U.S.A.
28 E6 **Harnorup** Denmark
26 J9 **Härnösand** Sweden
65 E2 **Har Nur** China
58 B2 **Har Nuur** *L* Mongolia
80 E3 **Harod** *R* Israel
26 B9 **Haröy** *isld* Norway
9 F4 **Harpenden** England
85 C8 **Harper** Liberia
107 M4 **Harper** Kansas U.S.A.
100 H6 **Harper** Oregon U.S.A.
109 H5 **Harper** Texas U.S.A.
116 L4 **Harper Bend** Alaska U.S.A.
117 Q6 **Harper Cr** Alberta Canada
102 G6 **Harper L** California U.S.A.
116 Q4 **Harper, Mt** Alaska U.S.A.
144 C5 **Harper Pass** New Zealand
94 K7 **Harpers Ferry** West Virginia U.S.A.
110 J5 **Harpeth** *R* Tennessee U.S.A.
8 C6 **Harpford** England
9 G2 **Harpley** England
27 F15 **Harplinge** Sweden
32 J7 **Harpstedt** Germany
119 M9 **Harptree** Saskatchewan Canada
65 D4 **Harqin** China
65 D4 **Harqin Qi** China
103 L8 **Harquahala Mts** Arizona U.S.A.
85 E1 **Harrach, El** Algeria
107 N6 **Harrah** Oklahoma U.S.A.
26 F7 **Harran** Norway
37 K3 **Harras** Germany
28 B3 **Harre** Denmark
111 D8 **Harrell** Arkansas U.S.A.
144 D5 **Harrelville** New Zealand
121 L2 **Harricana** *R* Quebec Canada
28 E3 **Harridslev** Denmark
94 B2 **Harrietta** Michigan U.S.A.
112 C2 **Harriman** Tennessee U.S.A.
95 M8 **Harrington** Delaware U.S.A.
95 U2 **Harrington** Maine U.S.A.
100 G2 **Harrington** Washington U.S.A.
123 N3 **Harrington-Harbour** Quebec Canada
119 P2 **Harriot L** Saskatchewan Canada
118 K7 **Harris** Saskatchewan Canada
15 B3 **Harris** *div* Scotland
100 B9 **Harris** California U.S.A.
99 N9 **Harris** Missouri U.S.A.
110 F6 **Harrisburg** Arkansas U.S.A.
110 H4 **Harrisburg** Illinois U.S.A.
98 C8 **Harrisburg** Nebraska U.S.A.
94 D7 **Harrisburg** Ohio U.S.A.
100 B5 **Harrisburg** Oregon U.S.A.
95 L6 **Harrisburg** Pennsylvania U.S.A.
98 K6 **Harrisburg** South Dakota U.S.A.
118 H2 **Harris Hill** Ontario Canada
138 D4 **Harris, L** South Australia Australia
113 F9 **Harris, L** Florida U.S.A.
143 C1 **Harrismith** W Australia Australia
89 F7 **Harrismith** S Africa
140 A6 **Harris, Mt** N Terr Australia
144 B6 **Harris Mts** New Zealand
110 C5 **Harrison** Arkansas U.S.A.
112 E5 **Harrison** Georgia U.S.A.
100 J2 **Harrison** Idaho U.S.A.
94 C2 **Harrison** Michigan U.S.A.
101 O4 **Harrison** Montana U.S.A.
98 C7 **Harrison** Nebraska U.S.A.
98 H6 **Harrison** South Dakota U.S.A.
116 L1 **Harrison B** Alaska U.S.A.
111 E10 **Harrisonburg** Louisiana U.S.A.
94 J8 **Harrisonburg** Virginia U.S.A.
115 O7 **Harrison, C** Labrador, Nfld Canada
117 M1 **Harrison L** British Columbia Canada
83 K12 **Harrison, Mt** Mahé I Indian Oc
110 B3 **Harrisonville** Missouri U.S.A.
94 D2 **Harrisville** Michigan U.S.A.
95 M2 **Harrisville** New York U.S.A.
94 F7 **Harrisville** West Virginia U.S.A.
110 K2 **Harrodsburg** Indiana U.S.A.
94 C9 **Harrodsburg** Kentucky U.S.A.
13 G6 **Harrogate** England
98 G5 **Harrold** South Dakota U.S.A.
109 H1 **Harrold** Texas U.S.A.
120 H10 **Harrow** Ontario Canada
9 F4 **Harrow** England
119 Q8 **Harrowby** Manitoba Canada
26 H7 **Harrsjön** Sweden
27 F14 **Härryda** Sweden
110 C3 **Harry S. Truman Res** Missouri U.S.A.
98 F9 **Harry Strunk L** Nebraska U.S.A.
79 E8 **Har Saggi** *mt* Israel
32 K6 **Harsefeld** Germany
32 H9 **Harsewinkel** Germany
26 L5 **Harsprånget** Sweden
26 J3 **Harstad** Norway
32 L8 **Harsum** Germany
28 A4 **Harsyssel** *reg* Denmark
119 M9 **Hart** Saskatchewan Canada
13 G4 **Hart** England
99 U6 **Hart** Michigan U.S.A.
65 E3 **Hartao** China
89 B7 **Hartbees** *watercourse* S Africa
89 E5 **Hartbeespoortdam** S Africa
38 N7 **Hartberg** Austria
27 B11 **Hårteigen** *mt* Norway
118 C8 **Hartell** Alberta Canada
22 E5 **Hartennes-et-Taux** France
36 E2 **Hartenrod** Germany
37 O2 **Hartenstein** Germany
37 J5 **Hartershofen** Germany
15 E5 **Hart Fell** Scotland
9 G5 **Hartfield** England
111 L10 **Hartford** Alabama U.S.A.
109 N1 **Hartford** Arkansas U.S.A.
95 P5 **Hartford** Connecticut U.S.A.
107 P3 **Hartford** Kansas U.S.A.
110 K4 **Hartford** Kentucky U.S.A.
94 A4 **Hartford** Michigan U.S.A.
94 E6 **Hartford** Ohio U.S.A.
112 D2 **Hartford** Tennessee U.S.A.
99 S6 **Hartford** Wisconsin U.S.A.
94 B6 **Hartford City** Indiana U.S.A.
95 P5 **Hartford, E** Connecticut U.S.A.
37 O1 **Hartha** Germany
37 O2 **Harthau** Germany
12 E2 **Harthill** Scotland
9 E1 **Hartington** England
98 J7 **Hartington** Nebraska U.S.A.
80 E2 **Har Tir'an** Israel
122 D2 **Hart-jaune, R** Quebec Canada
138 D4 **Hart, L** South Australia Australia
122 E7 **Hartland** New Brunswick Canada
8 B6 **Hartland** England
95 S2 **Hartland** Maine U.S.A.
8 B5 **Hartland Pt** England
8 D3 **Hartlebury** England
13 G4 **Hartlepool** England
13 G3 **Hartley** England
99 L6 **Hartley** Iowa U.S.A.
108 B8 **Hartley** Texas U.S.A.
117 J9 **Hartley Bay** British Columbia Canada
9 F5 **Hartley Wintney** England
100 F2 **Hartline** Washington U.S.A.
106 H3 **Hartman** Colorado U.S.A.
37 P5 **Hartmanice** Czechoslovakia
37 O2 **Hartmannsdorf** Germany
36 G3 **Hartmannshain** Germany
142 E3 **Hart, Mt** W Australia Australia
119 Q6 **Hart Mt** Manitoba Canada
100 F7 **Hart Mt** Oregon U.S.A.
119 R9 **Hartney** Manitoba Canada
29 M10 **Hartola** Finland
13 G4 **Harton** England
106 E2 **Hartsel** Colorado U.S.A.
111 K7 **Hartselle** Alabama U.S.A.
37 J6 **Hartsfeld** *mts* Germany
107 P7 **Hartshorne** Oklahoma U.S.A.
138 C4 **Harts I** South Australia Australia
140 C6 **Harts Range Police Station** N Terr Australia
112 G3 **Hartsville** South Carolina U.S.A.
110 K5 **Hartsville** Tennessee U.S.A.
89 D6 **Hartswater** S Africa
80 C6 **Hartuv** Israel
110 D4 **Hartville** Missouri U.S.A.
98 B7 **Hartville** Wyoming U.S.A.
112 E3 **Hartwell** Georgia U.S.A.
112 E3 **Hartwell L** *res* South Carolina U.S.A.
120 H3 **Harty** Ontario Canada
89 D6 **Hartz** *R* S Africa
84 F4 **Harūj al Aswad, Al** Libya
79 G1 **Harunıye** Turkey
58 B2 **Har Us Nuur** *L* Mongolia
80 C7 **Ḩaruvit** Israel
102 H7 **Harvard** California U.S.A.
100 J3 **Harvard** Idaho U.S.A.
99 S7 **Harvard** Illinois U.S.A.
98 H9 **Harvard** Nebraska U.S.A.
116 O6 **Harvard Gl** Alaska U.S.A.
106 D3 **Harvard, Mt** Colorado U.S.A.
143 F7 **Harvest, Mt** W Australia Australia
143 B10 **Harvey** W Australia Australia
99 T8 **Harvey** Illinois U.S.A.
99 O8 **Harvey** Iowa U.S.A.
111 J13 **Harvey** New Orleans, Louisiana U.S.A.
98 F2 **Harvey** North Dakota U.S.A.
102 C1 **Harvey Mt** California U.S.A.
122 F8 **Harvey Stn** New Brunswick Canada
107 P3 **Harveyville** Kansas U.S.A.
110 F5 **Harwell** Missouri U.S.A.
9 E4 **Harwell** England
9 H4 **Harwich** England
109 K6 **Harwood** Texas U.S.A.
36 E4 **Harxheim** Germany
74 F4 **Haryana** *prov* India
80 E8 **Har Yehonatan** Israel
33 N9 **Harz** *mts* Germany
33 O9 **Harzgerode** Germany
79 F8 **Hāsā** Jordan
72 F4 **Hasā, Al** *reg* Saudi Arabia
78 H3 **Hasakah, Al** Syria
78 E2 **Hasan Dağı** *mt* Turkey
74 H9 **Hasanparti** India
80 E7 **Hasa** *R* Jordan
79 F5 **Hâsbaiya** Lebanon
32 G8 **Hasbergen** Germany
36 B5 **Hasborn-Dautweiler** Germany
32 G7 **Hase** *R* Germany
37 K2 **Hasel** *R* Germany
32 L5 **Haseldorf** Germany
32 F7 **Haselünne** Germany
80 D4 **Hashimiye** Jordan
61 J11 **Hashimoto** Japan
26 H8 **Håsjö** Sweden
111 D7 **Haskell** Arkansas U.S.A.
107 P6 **Haskell** Oklahoma U.S.A.
108 H2 **Haskell** Texas U.S.A.
38 K4 **Haslach** Austria
36 E7 **Haslach** Germany
27 G16 **Hasle** Denmark
109 M8 **Haslet** Texas U.S.A.
28 H6 **Haslev** Denmark
13 F6 **Haslingden** England
41 H4 **Hasli Tal** Switzerland
28 E4 **Haslund** Denmark
28 E5 **Hasmark** Denmark
22 E3 **Hasnon** France
80 D3 **Ha Solelim** Israel
18 E9 **Hasparren** France
32 F10 **Haspe** Germany
80 G2 **Haspin** Syria
22 E3 **Haspres** France
76 C4 **Hassan** India
103 M8 **Hassayampa** *R* Arizona U.S.A.
37 K3 **Hassberge** *mts* Germany
36 C5 **Hassel** Germany
26 J9 **Hassela** Sweden
33 N9 **Hasselfelde** Germany
115 K2 **Hassel Sd** Northwest Territories Canada
22 J2 **Hasselt** Belgium
25 F3 **Hasselt** Netherlands
28 F4 **Hassensør** *C* Denmark
33 N9 **Hasserode** Germany
37 K3 **Hassfurt** Germany
17 F10 **Hassi Berkane** Morocco
85 E2 **Hassi-Bou-Zid** Algeria
85 E3 **Hassi Chebaba** Algeria
28 A3 **Hassing** Denmark
37 L3 **Hasslach** Germany
33 T6 **Hassleben** Germany
37 K1 **Hassleben** Thüringen Germany
27 G15 **Hässleholm** Sweden
27 G13 **Hasslerör** Sweden
36 E5 **Hassloch** Germany
22 H3 **Hastière-Lavaux** Belgium
139 L4 **Hastings** *R* New South Wales Australia
139 H9 **Hastings** Tasmania Australia
127 P6 **Hastings** Barbados
121 N8 **Hastings** Ontario Canada
9 G6 **Hastings** England
145 F3 **Hastings** New Zealand
113 F8 **Hastings** Florida U.S.A.
99 L9 **Hastings** Iowa U.S.A.
94 B4 **Hastings** Michigan U.S.A.
99 O5 **Hastings** Minnesota U.S.A.
98 H9 **Hastings** Nebraska U.S.A.
107 M7 **Hastings** Oklahoma U.S.A.
94 J6 **Hastings** Pennsylvania U.S.A.
28 E6 **Håstrup** Denmark
27 G15 **Hästveda** Sweden
106 H3 **Hasty** Colorado U.S.A.
26 M1 **Hasvik** Norway
106 G3 **Haswell** Colorado U.S.A.
79 G2 **Hatay** Turkey
95 M6 **Hatboro** Pennsylvania U.S.A.
106 C9 **Hatch** New Mexico U.S.A.
103 M4 **Hatch** Utah U.S.A.
140 D5 **Hatches Cr** N Terr Australia
126 F2 **Hatchet Bay** Eleuthera Bahamas
110 G6 **Hatchie** *R* Tennessee U.S.A.
98 B7 **Hat Cr** Wyoming U.S.A.
100 D9 **Hat Creek** California U.S.A.
48 H5 **Haţeg** Romania
145 F3 **Hatepe** New Zealand
67 H4 **Haterumashima** Japan
139 G5 **Hatfield** New South Wales Australia
119 M7 **Hatfield** Saskatchewan Canada
9 F4 **Hatfield** England
111 B7 **Hatfield** Arkansas U.S.A.
98 K6 **Hatfield** Minnesota U.S.A.
9 G4 **Hatfield Peverel** England
101 T3 **Hathaway** Montana U.S.A.
138 F6 **Hatherleigh** South Australia Australia
8 B6 **Hatherleigh** England
9 E1 **Hathersage** England
74 H5 **Hathras** India
68 G7 **Ha Tien** Vietnam
80 G3 **Hatim** Jordan
68 G3 **Ha Tinh** Vietnam
71 M9 **Hatohudo** Indonesia
127 K5 **Hato Mayor** Dominican Rep
56 C3 **Hatskiy** Russian Federation
60 F11 **Hatsukaichi** Japan
138 F5 **Hattah** Victoria Australia
70 F2 **Hattan, Mt** Sabah
25 F4 **Hattem** Netherlands
36 D6 **Hatten** France
112 M2 **Hatteras** North Carolina U.S.A.
112 M2 **Hatteras Inlet** North Carolina U.S.A.
36 E3 **Hattersheim** Germany
26 G6 **Hattfjelldal** Norway
111 G10 **Hattiesburg** Mississippi U.S.A.
36 B6 **Hattigny** France
28 D5 **Hatting** Denmark
32 F10 **Hattingen** Germany
118 H8 **Hatton** Saskatchewan Canada
21 P3 **Hatton** France
98 J2 **Hatton** North Dakota U.S.A.
100 G3 **Hatton** Washington U.S.A.
68 C6 **Hattras Passage** Burma
40 F1 **Hattstatt** France
29 L10 **Hattula** Finland
126 F4 **Hatuey** Cuba
145 F4 **Hatuma** New Zealand
48 F3 **Hatvan** Hungary
38 O8 **Hatzendorf** Austria
36 C3 **Hatzenport** Germany
36 F2 **Hatzfeld** Germany
22 D2 **Haubourdin** France
86 A2 **Haud** *reg* Ethiopia
80 G4 **Haufa** Jordan
28 C4 **Hauge** Denmark
27 C10 **Hauge** Norway
99 P4 **Haugen** Wisconsin U.S.A.
27 A12 **Haugesund** Norway
111 C9 **Haughton** Louisiana U.S.A.
31 J7 **Haugsdorf** Austria
29 L10 **Hauho** Finland
145 E3 **Hauhungaroa Ra** New Zealand
27 B12 **Haukeliseter** Norway
29 L6 **Haukipudas** Finland
29 N9 **Haukivesi** *L* Finland
29 N9 **Haukivuori** Finland
145 F3 **Haumoana** New Zealand
36 H2 **Haune** *R* Germany
36 H2 **Hauneck** Germany
36 H2 **Haunetal** Hessen Germany
37 K7 **Haunstetten** Germany
144 C5 **Haupiri, L** New Zealand
37 O5 **Hauptenberg** *mt* Germany
145 E2 **Hauraki Gulf** New Zealand
144 A6 **Hauroko, L** New Zealand
27 A11 **Haus** Norway
36 E7 **Hausach** Germany
32 J8 **Hausberge** Germany
101 O3 **Hauser L. Dam** Montana U.S.A.
38 H5 **Hausruck** *mts* Austria
Haussez Iles d' *see* **Mercury Is**
41 K4 **Hausstock** *mt* Switzerland
29 O5 **Hautajarvi** Finland
22 B3 **Haut Banc, Pte du** France
40 B2 **Haut du Sec** *mt* France
18 L10 **Haute-Corse** *dept* Corsica
19 O12 **Hautecourt** France
18 F7 **Hautefort** France
18 F9 **Haute-Garonne** *dept* France
18 H7 **Haute-Loire** *dept* France
40 E6 **Hauteluce** France
19 J4 **Haute-Marne** *dept* France
121 Q4 **Haute Mauricie, Parc de** Quebec Canada
122 D4 **Hauterive** Quebec Canada
19 Q15 **Hautes Alpes** *dept* France
19 J5 **Haute-Saône** *dept* France
40 D6 **Haute-Savoie** *dept* France
22 L2 **Hautes Fagnes** Belgium
18 E9 **Hautes-Pyrénées** *dept* France
22 H4 **Hautes Rivières** France
18 F7 **Haute-Vienne** *dept* France
20 G4 **Hauteville-sur-Mer** France
36 B5 **Haut-Hombourg** France
95 T2 **Haut, I. au** Maine U.S.A.
22 F3 **Hautmont** France
19 K5 **Haut-Rhin** *dept* France
85 D2 **Hauts Plateaux** Morocco/Algeria
86 E5 **Haut-Zaire** *prov* Zaire
135 Q2 **Hauula** Hawaiian Is
145 E4 **Hauwai** New Zealand
Havana Cuba *see* **Habana**
110 C6 **Havana** Arkansas U.S.A.
111 M11 **Havana** Florida U.S.A.
99 R9 **Havana** Illinois U.S.A.
107 P4 **Havana** Kansas U.S.A.
98 J4 **Havana** North Dakota U.S.A.
9 F6 **Havant** England
103 K7 **Havasu, L** Cal/Ariz U.S.A.
28 C3 **Havbro** Denmark
28 J5 **Havdrup** Denmark
33 R6 **Havel** Germany
22 J3 **Havelange** Belgium
33 Q7 **Havelberg** Germany
33 R7 **Havelland** *reg* Germany
33 R7 **Havelland Grosse Haupt-kanal** Germany
122 G8 **Havelock** New Brunswick Canada
121 N8 **Havelock** Ontario Canada
145 D4 **Havelock** New Zealand
112 L3 **Havelock** North Carolina U.S.A.
98 D3 **Havelock** North Dakota U.S.A.
140 C2 **Havelock Falls** N Terr Australia
68 A7 **Havelock I** Andaman Is
145 F3 **Havelock North** New Zealand
107 N4 **Haven** Kansas U.S.A.
107 O2 **Havensville** Kansas U.S.A.
8 B4 **Haverfordwest** Wales
9 G3 **Haverhill** England
95 Q4 **Haverhill** Massachusetts U.S.A.
95 Q3 **Haverhill** New Hampshire U.S.A.
76 B3 **Haveri** India
26 H9 **Haverö** Sweden
22 J3 **Haversin** Belgium
28 C2 **Haverslev** Denmark
28 D3 **Haverslev** Nordjylland Denmark
95 N5 **Haverstraw** New York U.S.A.
107 L4 **Haviland** Kansas U.S.A.
94 C5 **Haviland** Ohio U.S.A.
120 F6 **Haviland Bay** Ontario Canada
65 B2 **Havirga** Mongolia
48 K2 **Havirna** Romania
31 J6 **Havlíčkův Brod** Czechoslovakia
28 D6 **Havnbjerg** Denmark
28 E3 **Havndal** Denmark
28 B6 **Havneby** Denmark
28 G5 **Havnebyen** Denmark
28 G5 **Havnsø** Denmark
28 B4 **Havnstrup** Denmark
26 O1 **Havoysund** Norway
47 J5 **Havran** Turkey
22 G3 **Havre** Belgium
101 Q1 **Havre** Montana U.S.A.
21 L2 **Havre Antifer, Pont du** France
123 L6 **Havre Aubert** Madeleine Is, Quebec Canada
28 G6 **Havrebjerg** Denmark
123 L8 **Havre Boucher** Nova Scotia Canada
95 L7 **Havre de Grace** Maryland U.S.A.
122 J3 **Havre-St-Pierre** Quebec Canada
137 Q8 **Havre Trench** *sea feature* Pacific Oc
28 A5 **Havrvig** Denmark
26 H7 **Havsnäs** Sweden
78 E1 **Havza** Turkey
135 U5 **Hawaii** *isld* Hawaiian Is
135 **Hawaiian Is** Pacific Oc
86 B3 **Hawal** *R* Nigeria
118 L7 **Hawarden** Saskatchewan Canada
144 D5 **Hawarden** New Zealand
98 K6 **Hawarden** Iowa U.S.A.
8 C1 **Hawarden** Wales
138 F6 **Hawdon, L** South Australia Australia
144 B6 **Hawea** New Zealand
144 B6 **Hawea Flat** New Zealand
145 E3 **Hawera** New Zealand
102 G7 **Hawes** California U.S.A.
110 K4 **Hawesville** Kentucky U.S.A.
13 F5 **Hawes Water** England
135 U4 **Hawi** Hawaiian Is
13 F3 **Hawick** Scotland
144 B6 **Hawkdun Range** New Zealand
145 F3 **Hawke Bay** New Zealand
139 L4 **Hawke, C** New South Wales Australia
138 E4 **Hawker** South Australia Australia
138 F3 **Hawker Gate** New South Wales Australia
145 F3 **Hawke's Bay** *admin region* New Zealand
141 F1 **Hawkesbury I** Queensland Australia
140 C1 **Hawkesbury Pt** N Terr Australia
139 K5 **Hawkesbury R** New South Wales Australia
9 G5 **Hawkhurst** England
103 L4 **Hawkins Pk** Utah U.S.A.
112 D5 **Hawkinsville** Georgia U.S.A.
120 F4 **Hawk Junct** Ontario Canada
118 J1 **Hawk Lake** Ontario Canada
110 E3 **Hawk Point** Missouri U.S.A.
94 D1 **Hawks** Michigan U.S.A.
126 F2 **Hawksbill Cay** *isld* Bahamas
13 E5 **Hawkshead** England
126 G2 **Hawks Nest Pt** Cat I Bahamas
98 B8 **Hawk Springs** Wyoming U.S.A.
141 K7 **Hawkwood** Queensland Australia
106 G4 **Hawley** Colorado U.S.A.
98 K3 **Hawley** Minnesota U.S.A.
95 M5 **Hawley** Pennsylvania U.S.A.
108 H3 **Hawley** Texas U.S.A.
68 D2 **Hawng Luk** Burma
13 G6 **Haworth** England
107 Q8 **Haworth** Oklahoma U.S.A.
112 H2 **Haw R** North Carolina U.S.A.
78 H5 **Hawran, Wadi** Iraq
78 L5 **Hawr as S'adiyah** *L* Iraq
13 H5 **Hawsker** England
113 E8 **Hawthorn** Florida U.S.A.
102 F3 **Hawthorne** Nevada U.S.A.
99 P3 **Hawthorne** Wisconsin U.S.A.
80 D5 **Hawwara** Jordan
85 B3 **Hawza** Western Sahara
65 F2 **Haxat** China
65 B2 **Haxat Hudag** China
101 T2 **Haxby** Montana U.S.A.
98 D9 **Haxtun** Colorado U.S.A.
139 G5 **Hay** New South Wales Australia
117 N6 **Hay** *R* British Columbia Canada
100 H3 **Hay** Washington U.S.A.
99 P4 **Hay** *R* Wisconsin U.S.A.
61 P6 **Hayachine-san** *mt* Japan
60 P3 **Hayakita** Japan
19 K3 **Hayange** France
60 E12 **Hayasui-seto** *str* Japan
101 T9 **Haybro** Colorado U.S.A.
47 N10 **Haydarpaşa** Turkey
103 O8 **Hayden** Arizona U.S.A.
101 S9 **Hayden** Colorado U.S.A.
100 J2 **Hayden L** Idaho U.S.A.
141 F4 **Haydon** Queensland Australia
13 F4 **Haydon Br** England
20 G3 **Haye-du-Puits, la** France
21 N3 **Haye, la** France
20 H4 **Haye-Pesnel, la** France
115 K6 **Hayes** *R* Manitoba Canada
111 D11 **Hayes** Louisiana U.S.A.
98 E5 **Hayes** South Dakota U.S.A.
21 M4 **Haye-St.Sylvestre, la** France
98 E9 **Hayes Center** Nebraska U.S.A.
116 L6 **Hayes Glaciers** Alaska U.S.A.
115 N2 **Hayes Halvø** *pen* Greenland
68 C7 **Hayes I** Burma
116 O5 **Hayes, Mt** Alaska U.S.A.
112 D2 **Hayesville** North Carolina U.S.A.
13 G6 **Hayfield** England
99 O6 **Hayfield** Minnesota U.S.A.
103 J8 **Hayfield Res** Carolina U.S.A.
102 A1 **Hayfork** California U.S.A.
13 F5 **Haygarth** England
36 G7 **Hayingen** Germany
117 O6 **Hay L** Alberta Canada
118 D5 **Hay Lakes** Alberta Canada
8 A7 **Hayle** England
9 F6 **Hayling** England
113 E7 **Haylow** Georgia U.S.A.
141 J5 **Hayman I** Queensland Australia
94 K8 **Haymarket** Virginia U.S.A.
140 C6 **Hay, Mt** N Terr Australia
109 O3 **Haynesville** Louisiana U.S.A.
95 T8 **Haynesville** Maine U.S.A.
111 K9 **Hayneville** Alabama U.S.A.
21 N2 **Hayons, les** France
8 C3 **Hay-on-Wye** England
141 J5 **Hay Point** Queensland Australia
140 D6 **Hay R** N Terr Australia
47 J3 **Hayrabolu** *R* Turkey
47 J3 **Hayrabolu** Turkey
117 Q5 **Hay River** Northwest Territories Canada
118 F8 **Hays** Alberta Canada
107 L3 **Hays** Kansas U.S.A.
101 R1 **Hays** Montana U.S.A.
98 D7 **Hay Springs** Nebraska U.S.A.
100 K8 **Haystack Mt** Nevada U.S.A.
103 L2 **Haystack Pk** Utah U.S.A.
118 G6 **Hayter** Alberta Canada
110 G5 **Hayti** Missouri U.S.A.
98 J5 **Hayti** South Dakota U.S.A.
13 H6 **Hayton** England
102 B4 **Hayward** California U.S.A.
99 N6 **Hayward** Minnesota U.S.A.
107 N5 **Hayward** Oklahoma U.S.A.
99 P4 **Hayward** Wisconsin U.S.A.
140 B2 **Hayward, Mt** N Terr Australia
9 F6 **Haywards Heath** England
119 T9 **Haywood** Manitoba Canada
80 E2 **Hazan** Israel
77 J3 **Hazarajat** *reg* Afghanistan
94 D9 **Hazard** Kentucky U.S.A.
95 P4 **Hazardville** Connecticut U.S.A.
75 L7 **Hazāribag** India
77 F1 **Hazar Masjed, Kūh-e** *mts* Iran
22 D2 **Hazebrouck** France
98 K1 **Hazel** Minnesota U.S.A.
98 J5 **Hazel** South Dakota U.S.A.
119 V9 **Hazelridge** Manitoba Canada
117 K8 **Hazelton** British Columbia Canada
107 M4 **Hazelton** Kansas U.S.A.
98 F3 **Hazelton** North Dakota U.S.A.
110 E7 **Hazen** Arkansas U.S.A.
102 E2 **Hazen** Nevada U.S.A.
98 E2 **Hazen** North Dakota U.S.A.
116 E6 **Hazen B** Alaska U.S.A.
115 N1 **Hazen, L** Northwest Territories Canada
118 K9 **Hazenmore** Saskatchewan Canada
114 H2 **Hazen Str** Northwest Territories Canada
80 B8 **Haẕerim** Israel
25 C4 **Hazerswoude** Netherlands
112 E2 **Hazewood** North Carolina U.S.A.
112 E6 **Hazlehurst** Georgia U.S.A.
111 F10 **Hazlehurst** Mississippi U.S.A.
95 M6 **Hazleton** Pennsylvania U.S.A.
142 G5 **Hazlett, L** W Australia Australia
37 N3 **Hazlov** Czechoslovakia
80 F2 **Ḩaẕor** Israel
80 F3 **HaZore'im** Israel
80 C7 **He** Israel
9 G2 **Heacham** England
9 G5 **Headcorn** England
14 B3 **Headford** Ireland
122 E9 **Head Harbor I** Maine U.S.A.
140 E5 **Headingly** Queensland Australia
111 L10 **Headland** Alabama U.S.A.
144 B6 **Headlong Pk** New Zealand
138 B4 **Head of Bight** *B* South Australia Australia
100 K3 **Headquarters** Idaho U.S.A.
83 M9 **Headridge Hill** Christmas I Indian Oc
100 A7 **Heads, The** *C* Oregon U.S.A.
99 R4 **Heafford Junct** Wisconsin U.S.A.
102 B3 **Healdsburg** California U.S.A.
109 K1 **Healdton** Oklahoma U.S.A.
139 H7 **Healesville** Victoria Australia
116 P4 **Healy** *R* Alaska U.S.A.
116 N5 **Healy** Alaska U.S.A.
107 K3 **Healy** Kansas U.S.A.
116 P5 **Healy L** Alaska U.S.A.
119 Q3 **Heaman** Manitoba Canada
9 E1 **Heanor** England
81 K16 **Heard I** Southern Oc
119 M8 **Hearne** Saskatchewan Canada
109 L5 **Hearne** Texas U.S.A.
117 R4 **Hearne L** Northwest Territories Canada
120 G3 **Hearst** Ontario Canada
102 A2 **Hearst** California U.S.A.
146 D5 **Hearst I** Antarctica
98 D3 **Heart** *R* North Dakota U.S.A.
118 F3 **Heart L** Alberta Canada
101 P5 **Heart L** Wyoming U.S.A.
118 A3 **Heart R** Alberta Canada
123 T6 **Heart's Content** Newfoundland Canada
123 T6 **Heart's Delight** Newfoundland Canada
98 H9 **Heartwell** Nebraska U.S.A.
128 E6 **Heath** *R* Bolivia/Peru
139 G6 **Heathcote** Victoria Australia
6 L2 **Heather** *oil rig* North Sea
123 O5 **Heatherton** Newfoundland Canada
9 G6 **Heathfield** England
123 L4 **Heath Pt** Anticosti I, Quebec
9 F5 **Heathrow Airport** England
112 G3 **Heath Springs** South Carolina U.S.A.
122 F6 **Heath Steel Mines** New Brunswick Canada
95 L9 **Heathsville** Virginia U.S.A.
107 Q7 **Heavener** Oklahoma U.S.A.
109 J8 **Hebbronville** Texas U.S.A.
13 F6 **Hebden Br** England
65 C5 **Hebei** *prov* China
141 J8 **Hebel** Queensland Australia
32 L6 **Heber** Germany
103 O7 **Heber** Arizona U.S.A.
101 O9 **Heber City** Utah U.S.A.
110 D6 **Heber Springs** Arkansas U.S.A.
121 P3 **Hébert, L** Quebec Canada

27 G13 **Hjo** Sweden
28 C4 **Hjelund** Denmark
28 C6 **Hjordkær** Denmark
Hjørring co see Nordjylland co
28 D2 **Hjørring** Denmark
28 E7 **Hjørtø** Denmark
28 E4 **Hjortshøj** Denmark
28 C5 **Hjartsvang** Denmark
26 B9 **Hjørundfjord** Norway
27 D12 **Hjuksebø** Norway
68 D2 **Hka** R Burma
68 B4 **Hkok** R Burma
60 E12 **Hlegu** Burma
28 S10 **Hildharandi** Iceland
37 P3 **Hlinec** R Czechoslovakia
31 K7 **Hlohovec** Czechoslovakia
28 C4 **Ho** Denmark
85 E7 **Ho** Ghana
89 A4 **Hoachanas** Namibia
118 C6 **Hoadley** Alberta Canada
98 F8 **Hoagland** Indiana U.S.A.
68 J5 **Hoai Nhon** Vietnam
68 G1 **Hoang Su Phi** Vietnam
26 B9 **Hoanib** R Namibia
60 E12 **Hoashi** Japan
101 P6 **Hoback** R Wyoming U.S.A.
101 P6 **Hoback Pk** Wyoming U.S.A.
138 F8 **Hobart** Tasmania Australia
99 T8 **Hobart** Indiana U.S.A.
107 L6 **Hobart** Oklahoma U.S.A.
108 D3 **Hobbs** New Mexico U.S.A.
111 K7 **Hobbs** Alabama U.S.A.
113 G10 **Hobe Sound** Florida U.S.A.
66 D4 **Hobgood** North Carolina U.S.A.
22 G1 **Hoboken** Belgium
112 E6 **Hoboken** Georgia U.S.A.
Hobot Xar see Xianghuang Qi
28 D3 **Hobro** Denmark
101 Q3 **Hobson** Montana U.S.A.
112 L2 **Hobucken** North Carolina U.S.A.
28 A5 **Ho Bugt** B Denmark
27 K15 **Hoburgen** lighthouse Sweden
86 A2 **Hobyo** Somalia
71 D5 **Hoc** isld Philippines
47 K6 **Hocalar** Turkey
111 B7 **Hochatown** Oklahoma U.S.A.
38 N8 **Hocheck** mt Austria
87 C10 **Hochfeld** Namibia
36 D6 **Hochfelden** France
38 G7 **Hochfilzen** Austria
41 N4 **Hochfinstermünz** Austria
36 E3 **Hochgall** mt Italy
37 K2 **Hochheim** Germany
109 K6 **Hochheim** Texas U.S.A.
38 K8 **Hochobir** mt Austria
41 N2 **Hoch Platte** mt Germany
38 G6 **Hochschwab** mt Austria
36 D5 **Hochspeyer** Germany
37 K4 **Höchstadt** Germany
37 K6 **Höchstädt** Germany
36 D2 **Höchstenbach** Germany
144 C5 **Hochstetter, L** New Zealand
38 K9 **Hochstuhl** mt Slovenia
36 F5 **Hockenheim** Germany
94 F7 **Hocking** R Ohio U.S.A.
94 F7 **Hockingport** Ohio U.S.A.
109 M5 **Hockley** Texas U.S.A.
9 E3 **Hockley Heath** England
9 F4 **Hockliffe** England
6 N6 **Hod** oil rig North Sea
28 D3 **Hodde** Denmark
13 F6 **Hodder, R** England
9 F4 **Hoddesdon** England
Hodeida see Hudaydah, Al
111 D9 **Hodge** Louisiana U.S.A.
110 L4 **Hodgenville** Kentucky U.S.A.
98 B3 **Hodges** Montana U.S.A.
112 E3 **Hodges** South Carolina U.S.A.
123 Q4 **Hodges Hill** pk Newfoundland Canada
102 G8 **Hodges, L** California U.S.A.
118 B3 **Hodgeville** Saskatchewan Canada
119 U7 **Hodgson** Manitoba Canada
140 C3 **Hodgson Downs** N Terr Australia
85 C5 **Hodh** reg Mauritania
80 B7 **Hodiya** Israel
48 F4 **Hódmezővásárhely** Hungary
85 E1 **Hodna, Mts. du** Algeria
8 D2 **Hodnet** England
31 K7 **Hodonín** Czechoslovakia
48 C4 **Hodoš** Slovenia
38 K8 **Hodsager** Germany
116 N3 **Hodzana, R** Alaska U.S.A.
28 F4 **Hoed** Denmark
25 A6 **Hoedekenskerke** Netherlands
20 E7 **Hoëdic** isld France
106 F4 **Hoehne** Colorado U.S.A.
25 B5 **Hoeksche Waard** Netherlands
25 B5 **Hoek van Holland** Netherlands
119 M6 **Hoey** Saskatchewan Canada
37 M3 **Hof** Germany
36 H2 **Hofbieber** Germany
Hofei see Hefei
36 F6 **Höfen** Germany
37 J6 **Hofen** Germany
108 L4 **Hoffman** Minnesota U.S.A.
112 H2 **Hoffman** North Carolina U.S.A.
113 K12 **Hoffmans Cay** isld Bahamas
32 K10 **Hofgeismar** Germany
36 E3 **Hofheim** Germany
37 K4 **Hofheim** Germany
37 P6 **Hofkirchen** Germany
29 T9 **Höfn** Iceland
28 S9 **Hofsjökull** ice cap Iceland
28 S9 **Hofsós** Iceland
60 E11 **Hofu** Japan
49 G8 **Höganäs** Sweden
139 H7 **Hogan Group** islds Tasmania Australia
102 D3 **Hogan Res** California U.S.A.
111 M8 **Hogansville** Georgia U.S.A.
141 M7 **Hoganthulla** R Australia
119 P1 **Hogarth** Ontario Canada
116 K3 **Hogarth, Mt** N Terr Australia
116 K3 **Hogatza** Alaska U.S.A.
116 K3 **Hogatza R** R Alaska U.S.A.
101 N5 **Hogback Mt** Montana U.S.A.
37 F12 **Hogboda** Sweden
27 J14 **Högby** Sweden
28 C7 **Högel** Germany
101 R1 **Hogeland** Montana U.S.A.
27 H12 **Högfors** Sweden
84 K4 **Hoggar** reg Algeria
109 L **Hogg L** Manitoba Canada
48 J5 **Hoghiz** Romania
95 M9 **Hog I** Michigan U.S.A.
95 M9 **Hog I** Virginia U.S.A.
28 B4 **Høgild** Denmark
80 C4 **Hogla** Israel
49 G8 **Högsby** Sweden
126 H4 **Högsele Reef** Bahamas
26 G5 **Høgtuvhei** mt Norway
100 A2 **Hoh** R Washington U.S.A.
33 R10 **Hohburg** Germany
41 L3 **Hohe Acht** mt Germany
36 C3 **Hohe Geige** mt Austria
38 N6 **Hohen-Altheim** Germany
38 M6 **Hohenberg** Austria
37 M3 **Hohenberg** Germany
37 M5 **Hohenbucke** Germany
36 H1 **Hohenebra** Germany
38 M5 **Hoheneggelsen** Germany
36 H1 **Hohenenhe** Germany
41 M3 **Hohenfels** Germany
37 N6 **Hohengöhren** Germany
36 G6 **Hohenheim** Germany
37 M7 **Hohenkammer** Germany
37 Q10 **Hohenlenna** Germany

37 N2 **Hohenleuben** Germany
37 L6 **Hohenlimburg** Germany
32 L5 **Hohenlockstedt** Germany
37 N1 **Hohenmölsen** Germany
33 Q7 **Hohennauen** Germany
36 H2 **Hohenroda** Germany
33 Q8 **Hohenseeden** Germany
33 S9 **Hohenseefeld** Germany
36 E2 **Hohensolms** Germany
34 H6 **Hohenstaufen** Germany
36 G7 **Hohenstein** Germany
37 O2 **Hohenstein-Ernstthal** Germany
37 L6 **Hohenwart** Germany
32 K9 **Hohenwepel** Germany
32 L4 **Hohenwestedt** Germany
33 N6 **Hohenzethen** Germany
36 B7 **Hohenzollern** Germany
41 M3 **Hoher Ifen** mt Austria
41 M3 **Hohes Licht** mt Austria
38 F7 **Hohe Steig** mt Austria
36 F6 **Hohe Tauern** Austria
36 G7 **Hohhot** China
36 E6 **Hohloh** mt Germany
28 B4 **Hohne** Germany
28 B5 **Hohneck** mt France
33 N6 **Hohnstorf** Germany
99 L7 **Hoholitna** R Alaska U.S.A.
98 H9 **Hohokus** New Jersey U.S.A.
28 G6 **Hohwacht** Germany
28 B7 **Hohwald** France
99 P6 **Hokah** Minnesota U.S.A.
Hokang see Hegang
27 K11 **Hökhuvud** Sweden
61 N9 **Hōki** R Japan
145 D1 **Hokianga Harbour** New Zealand
28 C4 **Hokkitka** New Zealand
60 O2 **Hokkaidō** isld Japan
27 D12 **Hokksund** Norway
61 O9 **Hokota** Japan
61 K10 **Hokunō** Japan
61 K10 **Hokuriku Tunnel** Japan
27 C11 **Hol** Norway
27 E12 **Høland** Norway
Holbæk co see Vestjælland co
28 E3 **Holbæk** Denmark
28 H5 **Holbæk** Denmark
9 G2 **Holbeach** England
117 K10 **Holberg** British Columbia Canada
28 C7 **Holbøl** Denmark
123 T6 **Holbourne I** Queensland Australia
107 M3 **Holbrook** New South Wales Australia
37 P4 **Holbrook** Czechoslovakia
8 D6 **Holbrook** Arizona U.S.A.
8 C1 **Holbrook** Idaho U.S.A.
14 F2 **Holbrook** Nebraska U.S.A.
33 Q8 **Holby** R Ireland
33 P5 **Holcombe** Wisconsin U.S.A.
118 E5 **Holden** Alberta Canada
95 Q4 **Holden** Massachusetts U.S.A.
36 D3 **Holden** Missouri U.S.A.
37 M4 **Holden** Utah U.S.A.
99 B9 **Holden** West Virginia U.S.A.
107 O6 **Holdenville** Oklahoma U.S.A.
13 H6 **Holderness** England
119 M8 **Holdfast** Saskatchewan Canada
99 M4 **Holdingford** Minnesota U.S.A.
36 L1 **Holenberg** Germany
60 R2 **Holmbetsu** Japan
22 E4 **Hombléries** France
85 J6 **Hombori** Mali
36 H4 **Homburg** Bayern Germany
36 C5 **Homburg** Rheinland-Pfalz Germany
115 N4 **Home B** Northwest Territories Canada
78 H1 **Home B** Turkey
99 M5 **Home Bottom** Pennsylvania U.S.A.
100 J4 **Homedale** Idaho U.S.A.
141 H4 **Home Hill** Queensland Australia
103 L8 **Home I** Cocos Is Indian Oc
116 M7 **Homer** Alaska U.S.A.
111 C8 **Homer** Illinois U.S.A.
94 F7 **Homer** Indiana U.S.A.
94 C4 **Homer** Louisiana U.S.A.
98 J6 **Homer** New York U.S.A.
127 M2 **Homer** Bay Jamaica
115 N6 **Homersfield** England
144 A6 **Homer Tun** New Zealand
111 M5 **Homerville** Georgia U.S.A.
80 A4 **Homesh** Jordan
141 H5 **Homestead** Queensland Australia
113 G12 **Homestead** Florida U.S.A.
99 P8 **Homestead** Iowa U.S.A.
98 B1 **Homestead** Montana U.S.A.
107 M5 **Homestead** Oregon U.S.A.
98 D3 **Homestead Nat Mon** Nebraska U.S.A.
145 E4 **Homewood** New Zealand
111 K8 **Homewood** Alabama U.S.A.
68 A4 **Homfray's Str** Andaman Is
107 O5 **Hominy** Oklahoma U.S.A.
36 M7 **Hommelfjell** mt Norway
26 E8 **Hommelvik** Norway
141 M3 **Hommersåk** Netherlands
21 L7 **Hommes** France
74 G10 **Homnabad** India
89 H5 **Homoine** Mozambique
48 G6 **Homolídája Planína** mt Serbia Yugoslavia
71 M5 **Homonhon** Philippines
48 J4 **Homorod** Romania
113 E9 **Homosassa** Florida U.S.A.
Homs see Hims
65 H4 **Homs** Libya see Khums, Al
60 O1 **Honai** Japan
94 B4 **Honan** prov see Henan
94 M9 **Honavar** India
68 G7 **Hon Chong** Vietnam
102 C2 **Honcut** California U.S.A.
100 B5 **Hondeklip Bay** South Africa
71 D6 **Honda** Colombia
71 D6 **Hondo** R Belize
125 P8 **Hondo** California U.S.A.
118 D3 **Hondo** Alberta Canada
60 D13 **Hondo** Japan
109 K6 **Hondo** New Mexico U.S.A.
109 K6 **Hondo** Texas U.S.A.
28 F4 **Hondschoote** Denmark
112 O2 **Honea Path** South Carolina U.S.A.
100 H2 **Honea** Washington U.S.A.
99 J3 **Honeoye Falls** New York U.S.A.
26 F6 **Hønefoss** Norway
99 D11 **Honesdale** Pennsylvania U.S.A.
37 P2 **Honey** Czechoslovakia
52 A1 **Honeydew** California U.S.A.
94 J9 **Honeyford** North Dakota U.S.A.
111 B8 **Honey Grove** Texas U.S.A.
30 H6 **Honey Island** Texas U.S.A.
102 C2 **Honey, L** California U.S.A.
120 K8 **Honeywood** Ontario Canada
120 L3 **Honfleur** France
118 B6 **Honganj** R Czechoslovakia
13 G6 **Hong** Denmark
67 M4 **Hong** China
67 N1 **Hon Gai** Vietnam
16 D5 **Hong Gay** Vietnam
55 B2 **Honggor** China
58 F3 **Honghai Wan** B China
58 G7 **Hong He** China

67 D2 **Honghu** China
67 G3 **Hongjiang** China
109 H4 **Hong Kong** colony E Asia
28 A3 **Hørdum** Denmark
8 B3 **Horeb** Wales
58 B6 **Hore B** Zambia
48 H5 **Horezu** Romania
99 S6 **Horicon** Wisconsin U.S.A.
76 B3 **Horingen** China
22 J2 **Horion Hozémont** Belgium
84 G5 **Horizon** Saskatchewan Canada
137 S6 **Horizon Depth** Pacific Oc
72 C4 **Horka** Germany
9 F5 **Horley** England
146 E2 **Horlick Mts** Antarctica
28 E2 **Hørmested** Denmark
Hormo see Nyima
77 E6 **Hormoz** isld Iran
77 E6 **Hormozgān** prov Iran
77 E6 **Hormoz, Strait of** Iran
7 C4 **Horn** R Iceland
27 H14 **Horn** Sweden
29 O6 **Hornad** R Czechoslovakia
41 L7 **Hornavan** L Sweden
105 B5 **Horn-Bad Meinzg** Germany
29 J9 **Hornbæk** Denmark
22 E13 **Hornbrook** California U.S.A.
36 E7 **Hornberg** Germany
27 G13 **Hornborgasjön** L Sweden
100 C8 **Hornbrook** California U.S.A.
33 N8 **Hornburg** Germany
9 F1 **Horncastle** England
7 H11 **Horndal** Sweden
33 N6 **Horndorf** Germany
28 E1 **Horne** Denmark
32 L5 **Horneburg** Germany
25 L8 **Hörnefors** Sweden
66 C4 **Horneland** Denmark
94 K4 **Hornell** New York U.S.A.
120 F3 **Hornepayne** Ontario Canada
110 F5 **Hornersville** Missouri U.S.A.
27 C13 **Hornesund** Norway
27 O3 **Hornfisken** isld Denmark
28 A5 **Horn Hd** Ireland
33 O8 **Hornhausen** Germany
141 F1 **Horn I** Queensland Australia
111 H11 **Horn I** Mississippi U.S.A.
31 K6 **Horní Benesov** Czechoslovakia
137 R4 **Horn, Îles de** Îles Wallis Pacific Oc
26 B10 **Horningdal** Norway
33 S6 **Horningdalsvatn** L Norway
36 E6 **Hornisgrinde** mt Germany
94 K4 **Hornell** New York U.S.A.
41 J3 **Hörnli** mt Switzerland
116 H6 **Horn Mts** Alaska U.S.A.
27 C13 **Hornnes** Norway
133 C6 **Hornopiren** mt Chile
108 B5 **Hornos** Mexico
32 L6 **Hötzingen** Germany
133 D9 **Hornos, C. de** Chile
22 E7 **Hou** Denmark
100 B8 **Horca** California U.S.A.
117 O4 **Horn R** Northwest Territories Canada
139 K5 **Hornsby** New South Wales Australia
110 H6 **Hornsby** Tennessee U.S.A.
9 G4 **Hornsea** England
26 L8 **Hörnsjö** Sweden
28 E4 **Hornslet** Denmark
99 S2 **Horns of Hittin** Israel
37 K1 **Hornsömmern** Germany
33 P5 **Hornstrup** Denmark
28 D5 **Hornum** Vejle Denmark
28 E4 **Hornum** Germany
37 O3 **Horn Zieritz** Germany
21 K3 **Horobetsu** Japan
21 N2 **Horoizumi** Japan
60 O1 **Horonai** Japan
98 C4 **Horopito** New Zealand
9 G6 **Hororata** New Zealand
60 Q3 **Horoshiri-dake** mt Japan
14 H6 **Horovice** Czechoslovakia
60 A5 **Horowhenua** admin region New Zealand
83 K9 **Horowupotana** Sri Lanka
21 K5 **Horps,le** France
59 H2 **Horqin Youyi Qianqi** China
59 H2 **Horqin Youyi Zhongqi** China
59 H2 **Horqin Zouyi Zhongqi** China
59 H2 **Horqin Zouyi Houqi** China
129 G8 **Horqueta** Paraguay
133 F2 **Horqueta** Paraguay
28 H7 **Horreby** Denmark
27 F14 **Horred** Sweden
36 B2 **Horrem** Germany
83 M8 **Horrocks** W Australia
36 C8 **Horša** prov see Hebei
83 M8 **Horsburgh I** Cocos Is Indian Oc
37 J1 **Hörschel** Germany
110 K4 **Horse Branch** Kentucky U.S.A.
9 G6 **Horsebridge** E Sussex England
94 B9 **Horse Cave** Kentucky U.S.A.
94 B9 **Horse Cr** Colorado U.S.A.
107 O2 **Horse Cr** Missouri U.S.A.
94 J6 **Horse Cr** Wyoming U.S.A.
22 J3 **Horsefly** British Columbia Canada
94 B9 **Horse I** Cocos Is Indian Oc
22 J3 **Horse I** Michigan U.S.A.
143 D6 **Horse I** Missouri U.S.A.
138 C2 **Horsehead** R Alberta Canada
37 J2 **Horsehead** R Alberta Canada
94 B9 **Horseheads** New York U.S.A.
123 R3 **Horse I** Newfoundland Canada
57 J2 **Hörsel** R Germany
37 J2 **Hörsel Berge** mt Germany
28 D5 **Horsens** Vejle Denmark
28 D5 **Horsens Fjord** inlet Denmark
22 J7 **Hovedgård** Denmark
28 D5 **Hövelhof** Germany
37 O2 **Hoveringen** Germany
118 F2 **Horseshoe Bend** N Terr Australia
111 L9 **Horseshoe Bend** Alabama U.S.A.
100 J6 **Horseshoe Bend** Idaho U.S.A.
127 P4 **Horse Shoe Pt** St Kitts W Indies
103 N7 **Horseshoe Res** Arizona U.S.A.
106 B8 **Horse Springs** New Mexico U.S.A.

36 E4 **Horchheim** Germany
13 F6 **Hordaland** reg Norway
109 H4 **Hords Cr.** R Texas U.S.A.
37 P5 **Hory Matky Boží** Czechoslovakia
31 J5 **Hory Orlické** mts Czechoslovakia
47 K6 **Horzom** R Turkey
86 G4 **Hosa'ina** Ethiopia
99 S6 **Hösbach** Germany
76 C4 **Hosdurga** India
137 R1 **Hose Mts** Sarawak
84 G5 **Hosenofu** Libya
86 G4 **Hoseynābad** Iran
137 S6 **Horizon Depth** Pacific Oc
74 C10 **Hoshab** Pakistan
74 G7 **Hoshangabad** India
74 F3 **Hoshiarpur** India
98 J7 **Hoskins** Nebraska U.S.A.
94 G8 **Hosmer** South Dakota U.S.A.
60 E13 **Hososhima** Japan
106 C6 **Hospeh** New Mexico U.S.A.
36 C3 **Hospet** India
14 C4 **Hospital** Ireland
8 C1 **Hospitalet, Cala del** mt Uruguay
120 J4 **Hoyle** Ontario Canada
106 B6 **Hosta Butte** mt New Mexico U.S.A.
133 D9 **Hoste, I** Chile
18 E8 **Hostens** France
27 O3 **Hostholmen** Sweden
37 O4 **Hostouň** Czechoslovakia
28 A5 **Hostrup** Ribe Denmark
28 B7 **Hostrup** Sønderjylland Denmark
28 D7 **Hostrup** Germany
28 C7 **Hostrup Sø** L Denmark
76 C4 **Hosur** India
26 G8 **Hotagen** Sweden
61 L9 **Hotaka** Japan
66 B4 **Hotan** He R China
66 C4 **Hotan He** R China
89 C8 **Hotazel** S Africa
87 D7 **Hotchkiss** Alberta Canada
117 P7 **Hotchkiss** Colorado U.S.A.
140 B1 **Hot Creek** Ra Nevada U.S.A.
36 E2 **Hotham** C N T Australia
139 H6 **Hotham, Mt** Victoria Australia
26 H7 **Hoting** Sweden
80 E8 **Hot Springs** Israel
109 O1 **Hot Springs** nat park U.S.A.
67 G6 **Hsiao-lan Hsü** isld Taiwan
111 C7 **Hot Springs** Arkansas U.S.A.
101 L7 **Hot Springs** Montana U.S.A.
112 E2 **Hot Springs** North Carolina U.S.A.
108 C6 **Hot Springs** South Dakota U.S.A.
108 D6 **Hot Springs** Texas U.S.A.
94 H9 **Hot Springs** Virginia U.S.A.
106 D1 **Hot Sulphur Springs** Colorado U.S.A.
117 O3 **Hottah L** Northwest Territories Canada
68 C1 **Hottel** Germany
68 K2 **Hsü-wen** China
67 F4 **Hua'an** China
36 B1 **Höttingen** Germany
128 C6 **Huacho** Peru
128 C5 **Huachacuco** Peru
21 O4 **Huade** China
59 J3 **Huadian** China
22 G3 **Huadeng** Belgium
18 E8 **Huadeng** China
28 D6 **Huai** R Thailand
23 J3 **Houghton** Michigan U.S.A.
94 H4 **Houghton** New York U.S.A.
67 C3 **Huai He** R China
127 C3 **Houghton** South Dakota U.S.A.
94 G8 **Houghton-le-Spring** England
67 G5 **Huai Luang** R Thailand
99 S2 **Houla** Lebanon
21 K3 **Houlgate** France
94 E7 **Houlka** Mississippi U.S.A.
67 G1 **Huaining** China
21 N2 **Houlton** Maine U.S.A.
64 F4 **Huai Yang Res** Thailand
67 C3 **Houma** China
67 E1 **Huaiyin** China
111 F10 **Houma** Louisiana U.S.A.
125 L9 **Huajuápan de León** Mexico
85 D1 **Houmt Souk** Tunisia
71 L8 **Huaki** Indonesia
145 O5 **Hounslow** England
103 E7 **Hualapai Mts** Arizona U.S.A.
67 E2 **Houailou** New Caledonia
128 C5 **Huallaga** R Peru
128 C3 **Huallanca** Peru
65 H1 **Huama** China
65 H1 **Huanan** China
129 E5 **Huanay** Bolivia
128 C4 **Huancabamba** Pasco Peru
128 B3 **Huancabamba** Piura Peru
128 C6 **Huancapi** Peru
128 C6 **Huancavelica** Peru
128 C6 **Huancayo** Peru
67 F2 **Huanchaca, Sa. de** mts Bolivia
128 D7 **Huanchaco** Peru
67 G1 **Huang'an** see Hong'an
67 C2 **Huangcaoba** see Qianxinan
67 E1 **Huangchuan** China
67 G1 **Huanggangliang** mt China
67 F3 **Huanggang Shan** mt China
57 C2 **Huang Hai** see Yellow Sea
65 C5 **Huanghe** China
67 C3 **Huanghua** China
67 C3 **Huangliu** China
67 E1 **Huanglongtan** China
67 E1 **Huangmao Jian** mt China
67 F2 **Huangmei** China
67 G1 **Huangnihe** China
67 F1 **Huangpi** China
67 E1 **Huangpo** China
67 D1 **Huangpu** China
67 E2 **Huangshagang** China
67 C2 **Huangshan** China
67 D3 **Huang Shan** mts China
67 C2 **Huang Shui** R China
67 F3 **Huangtuliangzi** China
67 F2 **Huangyan** China
67 C2 **Huangyangsi** China
59 C7 **Huanian** see Huanggang
57 G1 **Huanren** China
128 C4 **Huánuco** Peru
128 C4 **Huan Jiang** R China
129 E7 **Huanjiang** China
68 H4 **Huanshan** see Yuhuan
125 L7 **Huanuni** Bolivia
128 C5 **Huaral** Peru
128 C5 **Huaraz** Peru
128 C5 **Huariaca** Peru
128 C6 **Huarmey** Peru
128 C5 **Huascarán** mt Peru
133 B3 **Huasco** Chile
133 B3 **Huasco, R** Chile
128 C5 **Huaspuc** Honduras
125 K7 **Huatabampo** Mexico
125 L7 **Huauchinango** Mexico
65 A7 **Hua Xian** China
65 C7 **Hua Xian** China

98 D5 **Howes** South Dakota U.S.A.
117 M11 **Howe Sound** British Columbia Canada
121 R7 **Howick** Quebec Canada
145 E2 **Howick** New Zealand
141 H2 **Howick Group** islds Gt Barrier Reef Aust
138 E2 **Howitt, L** South Australia
139 H6 **Howitt, Mt** Victoria Australia
95 T1 **Howland** Maine U.S.A.
137 R1 **Howland** Pacif. Oc
123 P4 **Howley** Newfoundland Canada
14 E3 **Howth** Ireland
68 H4 **Ho Xa** Vietnam
110 F5 **Hoxie** Arkansas U.S.A.
107 K2 **Hoxie** Kansas U.S.A.
32 K9 **Höxter** Germany
66 D2 **Hoxtolgay** China
32 K7 **Hoy** Scotland
31 H4 **Hoyerswerda** Germany
8 C1 **Hoylake** England
26 F7 **Høylandet** Norway
120 J4 **Hoyle** Ontario Canada
33 O9 **Hoym** Germany
28 S5 **Hoyos** Spain
16 C4 **Hoy Snd** Scotland
15 E2 **Hoy Sound** Scotland
122 F8 **Hoyt** New Brunswick Canada
107 P2 **Hoyt** Kansas U.S.A.
29 O9 **Hoyt Pk** Utah U.S.A.
101 O9 **Hoyt Pk** Utah U.S.A.
80 C5 **Hpa-an** see Pa-an
68 C2 **Hpa Lai** Burma
68 C3 **Hpasawg** Burma
31 J5 **Hradec Králové** Czechoslovakia
37 P3 **Hradiště** Czechoslovakia
31 K6 **Hranice** Czechoslovakia
Hranice Czechoslovakia see Rossbach
48 F2 **Hrinová** Czechoslovakia
31 L7 **Hron** R Czechoslovakia
41 O3 **Hroznetín** Czechoslovakia
31 O5 **Hrubieszów** Poland
31 J7 **Hrušovany** Czechoslovakia
Hrvatska see Croatia
68 C2 **Hsa Mong Hkam** Burma
68 C2 **Hsia-ju Ts'o** J China
67 G6 **Hsiao-lan Hsü** isld Taiwan
65 C7 **Hsieh-chia-chi** China
68 B3 **Hsi Hkip** Burma
68 C2 **Hsi-hseng** Burma
58 C4 **Hsin-chiang** China
68 J3 **Hsin-chu** Taiwan
68 H3 **Hsing-ying** China
59 H3 **Hsin-min** China
68 B2 **Hsipaw** Burma
65 D5 **Hsi-tsang Kao-yüan** reg China
65 B5 **Hsümhsai** China
68 K2 **Hsü-wen** China
67 F4 **Hua'an** China
128 C6 **Huacho** Peru
128 C5 **Huachacuco** Peru
67 O3 **Huade** China
59 J3 **Huadian** China
22 G3 **Huadeng** Belgium
67 D6 **Huai'an** China
67 C3 **Huai He** R China
67 C3 **Huaiji** China
67 D5 **Huailai** China
67 F3 **Huailing** China
67 F1 **Huainan** China
67 E1 **Huaining** China
67 D1 **Huairen** China
67 D1 **Huairou** China
67 G1 **Huaiyang** China
67 E1 **Huaiyin** China
67 D6 **Huaiyuan** China
125 L9 **Huajuápan de León** Mexico
71 L8 **Huaki** Indonesia
103 E7 **Hualapai Mts** Arizona U.S.A.
137 R2 **Hualalai** mt Hawaiian Is
67 G3 **Hualien** Taiwan
128 C5 **Huallaga** R Peru
128 C3 **Huallanca** Peru
65 H1 **Huama** China
65 H1 **Huanan** China
129 E5 **Huanay** Bolivia
128 C4 **Huancabamba** Pasco Peru
128 B3 **Huancabamba** Piura Peru
128 C6 **Huancapi** Peru
128 C6 **Huancavelica** Peru
128 C6 **Huancayo** Peru
129 F6 **Huanchaca, Sa. de** mts Bolivia
128 D7 **Huanchaco** Peru
67 G1 **Huang'an** see Hong'an
67 C2 **Huangcaoba** see Qianxinan
67 E1 **Huangchuan** China
67 G1 **Huanggangliang** mt China
67 F3 **Huanggang Shan** mt China
57 C2 **Huang Hai** see Yellow Sea
65 C5 **Huanghe** China
67 C3 **Huanghua** China
67 C3 **Huangliu** China
67 E1 **Huanglongtan** China
67 E1 **Huangmao Jian** mt China
67 F2 **Huangmei** China
67 G1 **Huangnihe** China
67 F1 **Huangpi** China
67 E1 **Huangpo** China
67 D1 **Huangpu** China
67 E2 **Huangshagang** China
67 C2 **Huangshan** China
67 D3 **Huang Shan** mts China
67 C2 **Huang Shui** R China
67 F3 **Huangtuliangzi** China
67 F2 **Huangyan** China
67 C2 **Huangyangsi** China
57 G1 **Huanren** China
128 C4 **Huánuco** Peru
129 E7 **Huanjiang** China
125 L7 **Huanuni** Bolivia
128 C5 **Huaral** Peru
128 C5 **Huaraz** Peru
128 C5 **Huariaca** Peru
128 C6 **Huarmey** Peru
128 C5 **Huascarán** mt Peru
133 B3 **Huasco** Chile
133 B3 **Huasco, R** Chile
128 C5 **Huaspuc** Honduras
125 K7 **Huatabampo** Mexico
125 L7 **Huauchinango** Mexico
65 A7 **Hua Xian** China
65 C7 **Hua Xian** China

Hua Xian — Indispensable Reefs 185

67 D5 **Hua Xian** China
65 A7 **Huayin** China
67 B1 **Huaying Shan** *mts* China
67 E1 **Huayuan** China
67 C2 **Huayuan** China
67 C6 **Huazhou** China
65 F4 **Huazi** China
119 O7 **Hubbard** Saskatchewan Canada
99 N7 **Hubbard** Iowa U.S.A.
109 L4 **Hubbard** Texas U.S.A.
109 H3 **Hubbard Cr. Res** Texas U.S.A.
117 C5 **Hubbard Glacier** Alaska U.S.A.
94 D2 **Hubbard L** Michigan U.S.A.
117 D5 **Hubbard, Mt** Alaska/Yukon Terr U.S.A./Canada
122 H9 **Hubbards** Nova Scotia Canada
98 J9 **Hubbell** Nebraska U.S.A.
103 P6 **Hubbell Trading Post Nat. Hist. Site** Arizona U.S.A.
58 F5 **Hubei** *prov* China
41 N3 **Huben** Austria
121 Q7 **Huberdeau** Quebec Canada
33 T7 **Hubertusstock** Germany
76 B3 **Hubli** India
32 J6 **Huchting** Germany
25 F6 **Hückelhoven-Ratheim** Germany
36 C1 **Hückeswagen** Germany
140 D6 **Huckitta** N Terr Australia
9 E1 **Hucknall** England
22 B2 **Hucqueliers** France
72 E6 **Ḩudaydah, Al** Yemen
13 G6 **Huddersfield** England
27 J12 **Huddinge** Sweden
32 H6 **Hude** Germany
32 L7 **Hudemühlen** Germany
26 J10 **Hudiksvall** Sweden
20 H4 **Hudimesnil** France
115 K7 **Hudson** Ontario Canada
133 C7 **Hudson** *mt* Chile
106 F1 **Hudson** Colorado U.S.A.
113 E9 **Hudson** Florida U.S.A.
110 G1 **Hudson** Illinois U.S.A.
94 B5 **Hudson** Indiana U.S.A.
99 O7 **Hudson** Iowa U.S.A.
107 M3 **Hudson** Kansas U.S.A.
94 C5 **Hudson** Michigan U.S.A.
95 O3 **Hudson** *R* New York U.S.A.
95 O4 **Hudson** New York U.S.A.
94 F5 **Hudson** Ohio U.S.A.
101 R7 **Hudson** Wyoming U.S.A.
115 L6 **Hudson Bay** Canada
119 P6 **Hudson Bay** Saskatchewan Canada
146 C13 **Hudson, Cape** *C* Antarctica
95 O3 **Hudson Falls** New York U.S.A.
107 P5 **Hudson, L.** Oklahoma U.S.A.
117 N7 **Hudson's Hope** British Columbia Canada
115 M5 **Hudson Str** Canada
94 B4 **Hudsonville** Michigan U.S.A.
119 W5 **Hudwin L** Manitoba Canada
68 H4 **Hue** Vietnam
16 C4 **Huebra** *R* Spain
131 B7 **Huechulafquén, L** Argentina
108 B4 **Hueco Mts** Texas U.S.A.
48 H4 **Huedin** Romania
124 G5 **Huehueto, Cerro** *mt* Mexico
125 K7 **Huejutla** Mexico
20 C5 **Huelgoat** France
16 E7 **Huelma** Spain
16 C7 **Huelva** *R* Spain
16 C7 **Huelva** *prov* Spain
16 C7 **Huelva** Spain
68 G4 **Huen** Laos
131 B3 **Huentelauquén** Chile
124 D3 **Huépac** Mexico
133 C6 **Huequi, Pen** Chile
17 F7 **Huércal Overa** Spain
106 F3 **Huerfano** *R* Colorado U.S.A.
131 C3 **Huerta, Sa. de la** *ra* Argentina
17 G6 **Huertas, C. de las** Spain
124 J5 **Huertecillas** Mexico
17 G3 **Huerva** *R* Spain
17 G2 **Huesca** *prov* Spain
17 G2 **Huesca** Spain
17 F7 **Huéscar** Spain
16 D7 **Huesna** *R* Spain
108 B5 **Hueso, Sierra del** *mts* Mexico
125 J8 **Huétamo** Mexico
17 F4 **Huete** Spain
98 F3 **Huff** North Dakota U.S.A.
36 G5 **Hüffenhardt** Germany
98 H4 **Huffton** South Dakota U.S.A.
77 A7 **Hufuf, Al** Saudi Arabia
116 K4 **Huggins I** Alaska U.S.A.
98 F9 **Hugh Butler L** Nebraska U.S.A.
141 G5 **Hughenden** Queensland Australia
118 F6 **Hughenden** Alberta Canada
121 L4 **Hughes** Ontario Canada
110 F7 **Hughes** Arkansas U.S.A.
119 R2 **Hughes R** Manitoba Canada
109 N3 **Hughes Springs** Texas U.S.A.
110 C3 **Hughesville** Missouri U.S.A.
140 C6 **Hugh R** N Terr Australia
118 K7 **Hughton** Saskatchewan Canada
9 F7 **Hugh Town** Isles of Scilly England
75 M8 **Hugli** *R* India
106 G2 **Hugo** Colorado U.S.A.
99 N4 **Hugo** Minnesota U.S.A.
107 P7 **Hugo** Oklahoma U.S.A.
100 B7 **Hugo** Oregon U.S.A.
107 P7 **Hugo L** Oklahoma U.S.A.
107 J4 **Hugoton** Kansas U.S.A.
36 D7 **Hugsweier** Germany
65 B6 **Huguan** China
Huhehot *see* **Hohhot**
58 F3 **Huhehot** China
67 F4 **Hui'an** China
145 F3 **Huiarau Range** New Zealand
67 E4 **Huichang** China
Huicheng *see* **She Xian**
124 H7 **Huicholes, Sa. de los** *mts* Mexico
59 J3 **Hŭich'ŏn** N Korea
67 E5 **Huidong** China
65 G2 **Huifaheng** China
128 C3 **Huila** *div* Colombia
58 G4 **Huimin** China
65 G3 **Huinan** China
67 B3 **Huishui** China
21 L7 **Huismes** France
21 M5 **Huîsne** *R* France
21 N6 **Huisseau-sur-Cosson** France
65 C7 **Huiting** China
67 C3 **Huitong** China
29 K10 **Huittinen** Finland
125 K8 **Huitzuco** Mexico
65 B7 **Hui Xian** China
125 N10 **Huixtla** Mexico
Huiyang *see* **Huizhou**
25 D4 **Huizen** Netherlands
67 E5 **Huizhou** China
58 D2 **Hujirt** Mongolia
145 F3 **Huka Falls** New Zealand
145 E4 **Hukanui** New Zealand
144 C5 **Hukarere** New Zealand
75 R5 **Hukawng Valley** Burma
145 E1 **Hukerenui** New Zealand
67 E2 **Hukou** China
87 D10 **Hukuntsi** Botswana
107 O5 **Hulah** Oklahoma U.S.A.
107 O5 **Hulah L** Oklahoma U.S.A.
59 J2 **Hulan** China
65 F1 **Hulan Ergi** China
65 G1 **Hulan He** *R* China
80 F1 **Ḩulata** Israel
98 B5 **Hulett** Wyoming U.S.A.
Huliao *see* **Dabu**
65 J2 **Hulin** China
65 E2 **Hulin He** *R* China
121 P7 **Hull** Quebec Canada
99 P10 **Hull** Illinois U.S.A.
98 K6 **Hull** Iowa U.S.A.
98 F3 **Hull** North Dakota U.S.A.
109 N5 **Hull** Texas U.S.A.
140 A6 **Hull Cr** N Terr Australia
22 G2 **Hulpe, la** Belgium
28 E1 **Hulsig** Denmark
25 B6 **Hulst** Netherlands
27 H14 **Hultsfred** Sweden
65 E4 **Huludao** China
69 E11 **HUlu Kali, Gunung** Malaysia
58 G2 **Hulun Nur** *L* China
69 E10 **Hulu Soh, Gunung** *mt* Malaysia
59 J1 **Huma** China
127 M5 **Humacao** Puerto Rico
59 H1 **Huma He** *R* China
128 F5 **Humaitá** Brazil
130 B10 **Humaitá** Paraguay
87 D12 **Humansdorp** S Africa
110 C4 **Humansville** Missouri U.S.A.
128 C6 **Humay** Peru
87 C9 **Humbe** Angola
123 P5 **Humbermouth** Newfoundland Canada
13 H6 **Humber, R** England
13 H6 **Humberside** *co* England
99 Q5 **Humbird** Wisconsin U.S.A.
28 F7 **Humble** Denmark
109 M6 **Humble** Texas U.S.A.
106 G9 **Humble City** New Mexico U.S.A.
119 M6 **Humboldt** Saskatchewan Canada
103 M7 **Humboldt** Arizona U.S.A.
99 S10 **Humboldt** Illinois U.S.A.
99 M7 **Humboldt** Iowa U.S.A.
107 P4 **Humboldt** Kansas U.S.A.
102 F1 **Humboldt** *R* Nevada U.S.A.
102 F1 **Humboldt** Nevada U.S.A.
110 H6 **Humboldt** Tennessee U.S.A.
100 A9 **Humboldt B** California U.S.A.
115 N2 **Humboldt Gletscher** *gla* Greenland
102 F2 **Humboldt L** Nevada U.S.A.
144 B6 **Humboldt Mts** New Zealand
100 G9 **Humboldt Range** Nevada U.S.A.
102 F1 **Humboldt Rge** Nevada U.S.A.
102 G2 **Humboldt Salt Marsh** Nevada U.S.A.
94 J8 **Hume** Virginia U.S.A.
141 H7 **Humeburn** Queensland Australia
77 F7 **Hūmedān** Iran
48 G2 **Humenné** Czechoslovakia
139 H6 **Hume Res** New South Wales Australia
99 N9 **Humeston** Iowa U.S.A.
29 K5 **Humlebæk** Denmark
28 B3 **Humlum** Denmark
32 K9 **Humme** Germany
95 L6 **Hummelstown** Pennsylvania U.S.A.
32 G7 **Hümmling** *hills* Germany
144 C6 **Hummock** *mt* New Zealand
127 K10 **Humocaro Bajo** Venezuela
131 A5 **Humos, C** Chile
87 B9 **Humpata** Angola
111 E7 **Humphrey** Arkansas U.S.A.
101 N5 **Humphrey** Idaho U.S.A.
98 J8 **Humphrey** Nebraska U.S.A.
100 D2 **Humphrey** Washington U.S.A.
102 E5 **Humphreys** California U.S.A.
110 C1 **Humphreys** Missouri U.S.A.
103 N6 **Humphreys Pk** Arizona U.S.A.
140 C7 **Humphries, Mt** N Terr Australia
31 J6 **Humpolec** Czechoslovakia
29 K11 **Humppila** Finland
100 B2 **Humptulips** Washington U.S.A.
140 B2 **Humpty Doo** N Terr Australia
84 F4 **Hūn** Libya
28 S9 **Húna-flói** *B* Iceland
67 C3 **Hunan** *prov* China
65 H3 **Hunchun** China
144 D5 **Hundalee** New Zealand
28 A3 **Hundborg** Denmark
28 B6 **Hunderup** Denmark
28 H5 **Hundested** Denmark
117 N10 **Hundred Mile House** British Columbia Canada
26 M6 **Hundsjö** Sweden
28 E5 **Hundslund** Denmark
38 G7 **Hundstein** *mt* Austria
28 D2 **Hune** Denmark
48 H5 **Hunedoara** *reg* Romania
48 H5 **Hunedoara** Romania
36 H2 **Hünfeld** Germany
36 E3 **Hünfelden** Germany
48 D3 **Hungary** *rep* Europe
26 H9 **Hunge** Sweden
36 F3 **Hungen** Germany
141 G8 **Hungerford** Queensland Australia
9 E5 **Hungerford** England
58 B2 **Hüngiy** Mongolia
65 G5 **Hŭngnam** N Korea
101 L1 **Hungry Horse Dam** Montana U.S.A.
101 M1 **Hungry Horse Res** Montana U.S.A.
68 H2 **Hung Yen** Vietnam
65 B4 **Hun He** *R* China
65 E4 **Hun He** *R* China
65 F4 **Hun Jiang** *R* China
65 G4 **Hunjiang** China
13 H5 **Hunmanby** England
99 P10 **Hunnewell** Missouri U.S.A.
25 F7 **Hünshoven** Germany
9 G2 **Hunstanton** England
28 B2 **Hunstrup** Denmark
76 C4 **Hunsur** India
65 E2 **Hunt** China
109 H5 **Hunt** Texas U.S.A.
120 J3 **Hunta** Ontario Canada
32 H8 **Hunte** *R* Germany
32 H8 **Hunteburg** Germany
139 K4 **Hunter** *R* New South Wales Australia
144 C6 **Hunter** New Zealand
137 P6 **Hunter** *isld* Pacific Oc
110 E6 **Hunter** Arkansas U.S.A.
107 M2 **Hunter** Kansas U.S.A.
98 J2 **Hunter** North Dakota U.S.A.
107 N5 **Hunter** Oklahoma U.S.A.
109 J6 **Hunter** Texas U.S.A.
139 G8 **Hunter I** Tasmania Australia
117 J10 **Hunter I** British Columbia Canada
99 P1 **Hunter I** Ontario Canada
116 M5 **Hunter, Mt** Alaska U.S.A.
144 A6 **Hunter Mts** New Zealand
144 B6 **Hunter R** New Zealand
122 J7 **Hunter River** Prince Edward I Canada
100 G1 **Hunters** Washington U.S.A.
68 A3 **Hunter's B** Burma
144 C6 **Hunter's Hills, The** New Zealand
12 D2 **Hunterston** Scotland
112 G2 **Huntersville** North Carolina U.S.A.
94 G8 **Huntersville** West Virginia U.S.A.
94 B5 **Huntertown** Indiana U.S.A.
145 E3 **Hunterville** New Zealand
110 K3 **Huntingburg** Indiana U.S.A.
121 Q7 **Huntingdon** Quebec Canada
9 F3 **Huntingdon** England
94 J6 **Huntingdon** Pennsylvania U.S.A.
110 H6 **Huntingdon** Tennessee U.S.A.
Huntingdon and Peterborough *co see* **Cambridgeshire**
122 J3 **Hunting I** Quebec Canada
112 G5 **Hunting I** South Carolina U.S.A.
94 B6 **Huntington** Indiana U.S.A.
95 O6 **Huntington** Long I, New York U.S.A.
100 H5 **Huntington** Oregon U.S.A.
111 B10 **Huntington** Texas U.S.A.
103 O2 **Huntington** Utah U.S.A.
94 E8 **Huntington** West Virginia U.S.A.
102 F8 **Huntington Beach** California U.S.A.
102 E4 **Huntington L** California U.S.A.
8 D4 **Huntley** England
101 R4 **Huntley** Montana U.S.A.
98 G9 **Huntley** Nebraska U.S.A.
98 B8 **Huntley** Wyoming U.S.A.
32 H7 **Huntlosen** Germany
145 E2 **Huntly** New Zealand
15 F3 **Huntly** Scotland
117 J5 **Hunt, Mt** Yukon Territory Canada
138 D3 **Hunt Pen** South Australia Australia
101 S5 **Hunts Mt** Wyoming U.S.A.
122 H10 **Hunts Pt** Nova Scotia Canada
121 L7 **Huntsville** Ontario Canada
110 K7 **Huntsville** Alabama U.S.A.
110 C5 **Huntsville** Arkansas U.S.A.
110 D2 **Huntsville** Missouri U.S.A.
109 M5 **Huntsville** Texas U.S.A.
101 O8 **Huntsville** Utah U.S.A.
32 E9 **Hünxe** Germany
88 C10 **Hunyani Rge** *mts* Zimbabwe
65 B5 **Hunyuan** China
66 A4 **Hunza** Kashmir
25 G2 **Hunze** *R* Netherlands
66 C3 **Huocheng** China
65 F1 **Huodifangzi** China
65 B7 **Huojia** China
139 H9 **Huon** *R* Tasmania Australia
68 H4 **Huong Hoa** Vietnam
68 G3 **Huong Khe** Vietnam
68 H8 **Huong My** Vietnam
68 G3 **Huong Son** Vietnam
68 H4 **Huong Thuy** Vietnam
139 H9 **Huonville** Tasmania Australia
65 B6 **Huo Shan** *mt* China
67 E1 **Huoshan** China
67 G5 **Huo-shao Tao** *isld* Taiwan
65 B6 **Huo Xian** China
Hupeh *prov see* **Hubei** *prov*
21 O1 **Huppy** France
33 M10 **Hüpstedt** Germany
48 E3 **Hurbanovo** Czechoslovakia
27 E11 **Hurdals** *L* Norway
120 J7 **Hurd, Cape** Ontario Canada
86 B1 **Hurdiyo** Somalia
110 D1 **Hurdland** Missouri U.S.A.
98 F2 **Hurdsfield** North Dakota U.S.A.
65 E3 **Hure Qi** China
80 E1 **Hurfeish** Israel
84 J4 **Hurghada** Egypt
18 G6 **Huriel** France
119 P2 **Hurkett** Ontario Canada
9 F4 **Hurley** England
111 H11 **Hurley** Mississippi U.S.A.
106 B9 **Hurley** New Mexico U.S.A.
98 J6 **Hurley** South Dakota U.S.A.
99 Q3 **Hurley** Wisconsin U.S.A.
12 D2 **Hurlford** Scotland
15 E2 **Hurliness** Scotland
95 M8 **Hurlock** Maryland U.S.A.
143 C10 **Hurlstone, L** W Australia Australia
102 D5 **Huron** California U.S.A.
94 E5 **Huron** Ohio U.S.A.
98 H5 **Huron** South Dakota U.S.A.
99 S3 **Huron B** Michigan U.S.A.
94 E2 **Huron City** Michigan U.S.A.
94 E2 **Huron, L** U.S.A./Canada
99 T3 **Huron Mts** Michigan U.S.A.
103 L4 **Hurricane** Utah U.S.A.
94 E8 **Hurricane** West Virginia U.S.A.
112 E6 **Hurricane Cr** Georgia U.S.A.
126 E3 **Hurricane Flats** Bahamas
110 J6 **Hurricane Mills** Tennessee U.S.A.
9 E5 **Hursley** England
109 M9 **Hurst** Texas U.S.A.
9 E5 **Hurstbourne Tarrant** England
9 G5 **Hurst Green** England
9 F6 **Hurstpierpoint** England
131 B3 **Hurtado** *R* Chile
36 B2 **Hürtgen** Germany
36 B2 **Hürth** Germany
111 L9 **Hurtsboro** Alabama U.S.A.
70 C4 **Hurung, Gunung** *mt* Kalimantan
88 B10 **Hurungwe** *dist* Zimbabwe
144 D5 **Hurunui R** New Zealand
28 E3 **Hurup** Denmark
28 D7 **Hurup** Germany
28 S9 **Husavik** Iceland
9 E3 **Husbands Bosworth** England
28 A4 **Husby** Denmark
71 L10 **Husdale** Indonesia
Hushan *see* **Cixi**
65 H2 **Hushan** China
48 L4 **Huşi** Romania
80 D3 **Ḩusifa** Israel
139 K6 **Huskisson** New South Wales Australia
27 G14 **Huskvarna** Sweden
116 J4 **Huslia** Alaska U.S.A.
80 G4 **Husn** Jordan
101 L2 **Huson** Montana U.S.A.
27 A10 **Husöy** Norway
118 E7 **Hussar** Alberta Canada
26 B9 **Hustadvika** Norway
28 B6 **Husum** Denmark
30 E1 **Husum** Germany
131 H6 **Husvik** S Georgia
58 D2 **Hutag** Mongolia
69 D12 **Hutanopan** Sumatra
109 O10 **Hutchins** Texas U.S.A.
107 N3 **Hutchinson** Kansas U.S.A.
99 M5 **Hutchinson** Minnesota U.S.A.
113 G10 **Hutchinson I** Florida U.S.A.
103 N7 **Hutch Mt** Arizona U.S.A.
68 D4 **Huthi** Burma
59 K2 **Hutou** China
110 J2 **Hutsonville** Illinois U.S.A.
38 H7 **Hüttau** Austria
21 L5 **Hutte, la** France
37 L4 **Hüttenbach** Germany
38 L8 **Hüttenberg** Austria
36 G3 **Hüttengesäss** Germany
37 P6 **Hutthurm** Germany
111 D8 **Huttig** Arkansas U.S.A.
109 K5 **Hutto** Texas U.S.A.
6 L1 **Hutton** *oil rig* North Sea
141 J7 **Hutton, Mt** Queensland Australia
143 E6 **Hutton Ra** W Australia Australia
94 G8 **Huttonsville** West Virginia U.S.A.
40 G3 **Huttwil** Switzerland
66 D3 **Hutubi** China
58 F4 **Hutuo He** *R* China
73 L8 **Huvadu Atoll** Maldives
79 G3 **Ḩuwayz, Al** Syria
118 D7 **Huxley** Alberta Canada
142 F4 **Huxley, Mt** W Australia Australia
144 B6 **Huxley, Mt** New Zealand
116 R6 **Huxley, Mt** Alaska U.S.A.
22 J3 **Huy** Belgium
67 G1 **Huzhou** China
27 E12 **Hvaler** *isld* Norway
28 C3 **Hvalpsund** Denmark
115 M2 **Hvalsund** *Sd* Greenland
28 C3 **Hvam** Denmark
42 G5 **Hvar** Croatia
42 H5 **Hvar** *isld* Croatia
28 S10 **Hveragerdhi** Iceland
28 S9 **Hveravellir** Iceland
28 B3 **Hvidbjerg** Denmark
28 B6 **Hviding** Denmark
28 E4 **Hvilsager** Denmark
28 D3 **Hvilsom** Denmark
28 E4 **Hvilsted** Denmark
28 S9 **Hvita** *R* Iceland
27 E12 **Hvitsten** Norway
27 D12 **Hvittingfoss** Norway
Hwainan *see* **Huainan**
89 E2 **Hwange** Zimbabwe
87 E9 **Hwange Nat. Park** Zimbabwe
Hwang Hai *see* **Yellow Sea**
61 P14 **Hyakuna** Okinawa
101 P4 **Hyalite Pk** Montana U.S.A.
100 B9 **Hyampom** California U.S.A.
95 R5 **Hyannis** Massachusetts U.S.A.
98 E8 **Hyannis** Nebraska U.S.A.
58 B2 **Hyargas Nuur** *L* Mongolia
100 C7 **Hyatt Res** Oregon U.S.A.
95 L8 **Hyattsville** Maryland U.S.A.
101 S5 **Hyattville** Wyoming U.S.A.
111 J10 **Hybart** Alabama U.S.A.
121 N7 **Hybla** Ontario Canada
27 H14 **Hycklinge** Sweden
117 G8 **Hydaburg** Alaska U.S.A.
13 F6 **Hyde** England
144 C6 **Hyde** New Zealand
143 C9 **Hyden** W Australia Australia
94 D9 **Hyden** Kentucky U.S.A.
117 H8 **Hyder** Br Col/Alaska Canada/U.S.A.
74 H10 **Hyderabad** India
77 L7 **Hyderabad** Pakistan
Hydra *isld see* **Ídhra** *isld*
109 J5 **Hye** Texas U.S.A.
20 H4 **Hyenville** France
19 Q18 **Hyères** France
59 J3 **Hyesan** N Korea
98 A9 **Hygiene** Colorado U.S.A.
117 J5 **Hyland** *R* Yukon Territory Canada
139 L4 **Hyland, Mt** New South Wales Australia
117 J7 **Hyland Post** British Columbia Canada
28 D5 **Hylke** Denmark
28 G7 **Hyllekrog** *C* Denmark
27 A10 **Hyllestad** Norway
28 F4 **Hyllested** Denmark
28 H5 **Hyllinge** Denmark
118 E4 **Hylo** Alberta Canada
27 B12 **Hylsfjorden** *inlet* Norway
110 J2 **Hymera** Indiana U.S.A.
138 F6 **Hynam** South Australia Australia
12 E2 **Hyndford Br** Scotland
94 J7 **Hyndman** Pennsylvania U.S.A.
101 L6 **Hyndman Peak** Idaho U.S.A.
94 K5 **Hyner** Pennsylvania U.S.A.
60 J10 **Hyōgo** *prefect* Japan
86 D4 **Hyrra Banda** Cent Afr Republic
101 O8 **Hyrum** Utah U.S.A.
29 N7 **Hyrynsalmi** Finland
52 C3 **Hyrynsalmi** Finland
101 S3 **Hysham** Montana U.S.A.
117 O8 **Hythe** Alberta Canada
9 H5 **Hythe** England
9 E6 **Hythe** Hampshire England
60 E13 **Hyūga** Japan
29 L11 **Hyvinkää** Finland

I

68 J6 **Ia Ayun** *R* Vietnam
128 E6 **Iaco** *R* Brazil
48 J3 **Iacobeni** Romania
129 K6 **Iaçu** Brazil
94 F9 **Iaeger** West Virginia U.S.A.
36 B7 **Iaintrux** France
48 K6 **Ialomiţa** *reg* Romania
48 K6 **Ialomiţa** *R* Romania
47 R14 **Ialysus** *hist site* Rhodes Greece
113 C7 **Iamonia, L** Florida U.S.A.
48 L5 **Ianca** Romania
88 C7 **Iangano Nat. Park** Zambia
144 C5 **Ianthe, L** New Zealand
48 H4 **Iara** Romania
14 B3 **Iar Connaught** Ireland
129 H3 **Iaripo** Brazil
53 C10 **Iasi** Romania
46 G3 **Íasmos** Greece
111 D10 **Iatt, L** Louisiana U.S.A.
128 E3 **Iauareté** Brazil
52 H4 **Ib** Russian Federation
71 D3 **Iba** Luzon Philippines
85 E7 **Ibadan** Nigeria
128 C3 **Ibagué** Colombia
130 E8 **Ibaiti** Brazil
101 M9 **Ibapah** Utah U.S.A.
46 D1 **Ibar** *R* Serbia Yugoslavia
60 G11 **Ibara** Japan
61 O9 **Ibaraki** *prefect* Japan
128 C3 **Ibarra** Ecuador
32 G8 **Ibbenbüren** Germany
80 G4 **Ibbin** Jordan
86 C5 **Ibenga** *R* Congo
131 F2 **Iberá, Esteros del** *marshes* Argentina
131 F2 **Iberá, L** Argentina
110 D3 **Iberia** Missouri U.S.A.
121 R7 **Iberville** Quebec Canada
26 J3 **Ibestad** Norway
85 F6 **Ibeto** Nigeria
85 F7 **Ibi** Nigeria
129 J7 **Ibiá** Brazil
130 G5 **Ibiai** Brazil
129 K4 **Ibiapaba, Serra da** *mts* Brazil
131 G3 **Ibicui da Cruz** *R* Brazil
131 G2 **Ibicuí, R** Brazil
133 F4 **Ibicuy** Argentina
61 K10 **Ibigawa** Japan
80 D2 **I'billin** Israel
130 D8 **Ibiporã** Brazil
130 H6 **Ibiraçu** Brazil
130 E10 **Ibirama** Brazil
130 H5 **Ibiranhém** Brazil
131 G3 **Ibirapuita** *R* Brazil
130 E7 **Ibitinga** Brazil
17 H5 **Ibiza** *isld* Balearic Is
80 F8 **Ibn Hammad** Jordan
88 H8 **Ibo** Mozambique
129 K6 **Ibotirama** Brazil
86 D3 **Ibra., Wadi** *watercourse* Sudan
52 G6 **Ibresi** Russian Federation
47 H3 **İbriktepe** Turkey
79 A9 **Ibshawâi** Egypt
9 E6 **Ibsley** England
61 Q12 **Ibu** Okinawa
60 D14 **Ibusuki** Japan
128 E4 **Içá** *R* Brazil
128 C6 **Ica** Peru
128 F3 **Icabaru** *R* Venezuela
127 N3 **Icacos Pt** Trinidad
71 D5 **Icadambanauan** Philippines
131 G2 **Icamaqua** *R* Brazil
128 E3 **Icana** Brazil
103 K5 **Iceberg Canyon** Nev/Ariz U.S.A.
100 G3 **Ice Harbor Dam** Washington U.S.A.
Içel *see* **Mersin**
28 **Iceland** *rep* N Atlantic Oc
90 H2 **Iceland-Faeroe Rise** Atlantic Oc
56 B3 **Icha** *R* Russian Federation
76 B2 **Ichalkaranji** India
37 J7 **Ichenhausen** Germany
60 G11 **Ichi** Japan
60 E13 **Ichifusa-yama** *mt* Japan
61 O10 **Ichihara** Japan
61 P5 **Ichinohe** Japan
59 L4 **Ichinomiya** Japan
54 D6 **Ichnya** Ukraine
22 E1 **Ichtegem** Belgium
37 K2 **Ichtershausen** Germany
130 H7 **Iconha** Brazil
Iconium *see* **Konya**
116 R6 **Icy B** Alaska U.S.A.
116 F1 **Icy Cape** Alaska U.S.A.
117 E6 **Icy Pt** Alaska U.S.A.
109 O3 **Ida** Louisiana U.S.A.
94 D5 **Ida** Michigan U.S.A.
109 N2 **Idabel** Oklahoma U.S.A.
99 L7 **Ida Grove** Iowa U.S.A.
85 F7 **Idah** Nigeria
101 M6 **Idaho** *state* U.S.A.
100 K6 **Idaho City** Idaho U.S.A.
101 N6 **Idaho Falls** Idaho U.S.A.
106 E2 **Idaho Springs** Colorado U.S.A.
106 H2 **Idalia** Colorado U.S.A.
36 C4 **Idar Oberstein** Germany
56 E4 **Idarskoye Belogor'ye** *mts* Russian Federation
36 C4 **Idarwald** *mts* Germany
144 C6 **Ida Valley** New Zealand
27 E12 **Idd** Norway
77 C7 **Idd al Sharqi** *oil well* Persian Gulf
118 F8 **Iddesleigh** Alberta Canada
111 M9 **Ideal** Georgia U.S.A.
52 D3 **Idel'** Russian Federation
85 F4 **Idelès** Algeria
86 B6 **Idemba** Gabon
28 H7 **Idestrup** Denmark
84 J5 **Idfu** Egypt
84 E4 **Idhān Awbārī** Libya
84 E5 **Idhān Murzuq** Libya
46 G9 **Ídhi Óros** *mt* Crete Greece
46 F7 **Ídhra** *isld* Greece
69 C10 **Idi** Sumatra
Idi Amin Dada, L *see* **Edward, L**
45 K3 **Idice** *R* Italy
116 H5 **Iditarod** Alaska U.S.A.
27 H11 **Idkerberget** Sweden
79 G3 **Idlib** Syria
80 C7 **Idna** Jordan
140 C6 **Idracowra** N Terr Australia
26 F10 **Idre** Sweden
102 D5 **Idria** California U.S.A.
52 C6 **Idritsa** Russian Federation
42 C3 **Idro, L. d'** Italy
21 P8 **Ids St. Roch** France
36 E3 **Idstein** Germany
76 C6 **Idukki** India
28 A4 **Idum** Denmark
87 E12 **Idutywa** S Africa
61 P12 **Ie-jima** *isld* Okinawa
45 R6 **Ielsi** Italy
22 H3 **Iemeppe** Belgium
130 D8 **Iepê** Brazil
22 D2 **Ieper** Belgium
47 H9 **Ierápetra** Crete Greece
46 F8 **Iérax, Akr** *C* Greece
59 G2 **I-erh-hsieh** China
46 F4 **Ierissós** Greece
43 C9 **Ierzu** Sardinia
45 O4 **Iesi** Italy
61 P12 **Ie-suidō** *str* Okinawa
48 J5 **Iezeru** *mt* Romania
17 H6 **Ifach, Pta** Spain
87 H12 **Ifanadiana** Madagascar
85 E7 **Ife** Nigeria
85 F5 **Iférouane** Niger
141 F4 **Iffley** Queensland Australia
138 B4 **Ifould L** South Australia Australia
85 C2 **Ifrane** Morocco
85 E5 **Igadiane** *watercourse* Mali
70 B3 **Igan** Sarawak
88 D1 **Iganga** Uganda
16 E10 **Igá, Oued** *R* Morocco
130 J9 **Igaraçu** Brazil
129 J4 **Igarape-Açu** Brazil
147 P14 **Igarka** Russian Federation
130 C9 **Igatimi** Paraguay
74 E9 **Igatpuri** India
71 F5 **Igbon** *isld* Philippines
21 M5 **Igé** France
36 B4 **Igel** Germany
27 J10 **Iggesund** Sweden
133 D4 **Iglesia** Argentina
43 B9 **Iglesias** Sardinia
98 C6 **Igloo** South Dakota U.S.A.
147 E4 **Igloolik** Northwest Territories Canada
41 O3 **Igls** Austria
79 D9 **'Igma, Gebel el** *mts* Egypt
115 K8 **Ignace** Ontario Canada
106 C4 **Ignacio** Colorado U.S.A.
124 H5 **Ignacio Allende** Mexico
52 C6 **Ignalina** Lithuania
47 J3 **İğneada** Turkey
68 A7 **Ignoitijala** Andaman Is
76 G5 **Ignoitijala** Andaman Is
102 B1 **Igo** California U.S.A.
71 C3 **Igom** W Irian
87 F7 **Igoma** Tanzania
70 B3 **Igon** *R* Sarawak
46 D5 **Igoumenitsa** Greece
52 H5 **Igra** Russian Federation
130 E9 **Iguaçu, R** Brazil
130 H4 **Iguaí** Brazil
125 K8 **Iguala** Mexico
17 J3 **Igualda** Spain
129 J8 **Iguapé** Brazil
130 D8 **Iguaraçu** Brazil
130 F7 **Iguatama** Brazil
130 C8 **Iguatemi** Brazil
129 L5 **Iguatu** Brazil
Iguazú Falls *see* **Cataratas del Iguazú** *waterfalls*
86 A6 **Iguéla** Gabon
86 A6 **Iguéla, Lagune** *Lagoon* Gabon
116 K8 **Igvak, C** Alaska U.S.A.
87 H10 **Iharaña** Madagascar
87 H12 **Ihosy** Madagascar
68 F6 **Ihr** Cambodia
22 L3 **Ihren** Germany
32 F6 **Ihrhove** Germany
40 G1 **Ihringen** Germany
58 E2 **Ihsuuj** Mongolia
29 L6 **Ii** Finland
61 L10 **Iida** Japan
61 N8 **Iide-san** *mt* Japan
29 N2 **Iijärvi** *L* Finland
29 N6 **Iijoki** *R* Finland
52 C5 **Iisaku** Estonia
29 N9 **Iisvesi** Finland
61 M9 **Iiyama** Japan
61 O8 **Īizaka** Japan
60 D12 **Iizuka** Japan
71 K9 **Ija** *isld* Indonesia
70 P9 **Ijang** *isld* Indonesia
85 E7 **Ijebu Ode** Nigeria
25 E2 **IJlst** Netherlands
25 D4 **IJmeer** Netherlands
25 C4 **IJmuiden** Netherlands
25 F3 **Ijonger** *R* Netherlands
25 C4 **Ijsel** *R* Netherlands
25 F4 **IJssel** *R* Netherlands
25 D3 **IJsselmeer** Netherlands
25 C5 **IJsselmonde** Netherlands
25 E3 **IJsselmuiden** Netherlands
25 D4 **IJsselstein** Netherlands
133 G3 **Ijuí** Brazil
131 G2 **Ijuí, R** Brazil
25 A6 **IJzendijke** Netherlands
22 D2 **Ijzer** *R* Belgium
52 H6 **Ik** *R* Russian Federation
29 K10 **Ikaalinen** Finland
144 C5 **Ikamatua** New Zealand
115 O4 **Ikamiut** Greenland
86 D6 **Ikanda** Zaire
47 H7 **Ikaría** *isld* Greece
28 C4 **Ikast** Denmark
56 H4 **Ikatskiy Khrebet** *mts* Russian Federation
145 F3 **Ikawhenua Range** New Zealand
60 J11 **Ikeda** Japan
60 G12 **Ikegawa** Japan
61 P13 **Ikei-jima** *isld* Okinawa
85 E7 **Ikeja** Nigeria
86 D6 **Ikela** Zaire
115 O3 **Ikerasak** Greenland
46 F2 **Ikhtiman** Bulgaria
60 C12 **Iki** *isld* Japan
88 C2 **Ikimba L** Tanzania
60 C12 **Iki-suidō** *str* Japan
116 K8 **Ikolik, C** Alaska U.S.A.
85 F7 **Ikom** Nigeria
88 D6 **Ikomba** Tanzania
87 H12 **Ikongo** Madagascar
87 H11 **Ikopa** *R* Madagascar
116 K1 **Ikpikpuk** *R* Alaska U.S.A.
56 B3 **Iksa** *R* Russian Federation
54 J1 **Iksha** Russian Federation
88 C1 **Ikulwe** Uganda
60 H10 **Ikuno** Japan
60 R2 **Ikutahara** Japan
71 E2 **Ilagan** Philippines
78 L5 **Īlām** Iran
75 M5 **Ilam** Nepal
56 E3 **Ilanskiy** Russian Federation
41 K4 **Ilanz** Switzerland
85 E7 **Ilaro** Nigeria
31 M2 **Iława** Poland
28 E2 **Ilbro** Denmark
138 D2 **Ilbunga** South Australia Australia
8 D5 **Ilchester** England
120 J9 **Ilderton** Ontario Canada
13 G3 **Ilderton** England
118 J3 **Ile-à-la Crosse** Saskatchewan Canada
118 K3 **Ile-à-la-Crosse L** Saskatchewan Canada
48 H3 **Ileanda** Romania
83 L13 **Ile aux Bénitiers** Mauritius
86 D6 **Ilebo** Zaire
21 P3 **Île de France** *reg* France
20 G8 **Île D'Olonne** France
25 E5 **Ileijen** Netherlands
55 B5 **Ilek** Russian Federation
85 E4 **Ilerh** *watercourse* Algeria
127 N5 **Îles des Saintes** Guadeloupe W Indies
85 F7 **Ilesha** Nigeria
52 G6 **Ilet'** *R* Russian Federation
20 B6 **Ile-Tudy** France
33 N9 **Ilfeld** Germany
119 W2 **Ilford** Manitoba Canada
9 G4 **Ilford** England
141 G6 **Ilfracombe** Queensland Australia
8 B5 **Ilfracombe** England
56 F4 **Ilga** *R* Russian Federation
78 D1 **Ilgaz Dağ** Turkey
130 F8 **Ilhabela** Brazil
128 F4 **Ilha Grande** Brazil
130 G8 **Ilha Grande, B. de** Brazil
130 D7 **Ilha Solteira Dam** Brazil
16 B4 **Ílhavo** Portugal
130 H4 **Ilhéus** Brazil
48 H5 **Ilia** Romania
116 L6 **Iliamna** Alaska U.S.A.
116 K7 **Iliamna L** Alaska U.S.A.
71 L9 **Ili Boleng** *vol* Indonesia
48 N4 **Il'ichevsk** Ukraine
98 C9 **Iliff** Colorado U.S.A.
71 G6 **Iligan** Philippines
71 G6 **Iligan B** Philippines
71 F1 **Iligan Pt** Philippines
86 A2 **Ilig, Raas** *C* Somalia
46 F6 **Iliki, L** Greece
56 F3 **Ilim** *R* Russian Federation
56 F1 **Ilimpeya** *R* Russian Federation
56 F3 **Ilimskiy, Khrebet** *mts* Russian Federation
71 E4 **Ilin** *isld* Philippines
55 C6 **Il'inka** Kazakhstan
52 F5 **Il'ino-Zaborskoye** Russian Federation
55 C2 **Il'inskiy** Russian Federation
71 E4 **Ilin Str** Philippines
48 M1 **Il'intsy** Ukraine
46 F5 **Iliodhrómia** *isld* Greece
95 M3 **Ilion** New York U.S.A.
42 F3 **Ilirska Bistrica** Slovenia
76 C3 **Ilkal** India
13 G6 **Ilkley** England
36 D7 **Ill** *R* France
128 E7 **Illampu** *mt* Bolivia
17 F4 **Illana** Spain
71 F7 **Illana B** Philippines
131 B3 **Illapel** Chile
131 B3 **Illapel, R** Chile
54 G8 **Illarionovo** Ukraine
41 O7 **Illasi** Italy
41 O6 **Illasi, Val d'** Italy
138 C2 **Illbillee, Mt** South Australia Australia
18 D4 **Ille-et-Vilaine** *dept* France
37 J7 **Iller** *R* Germany
37 J7 **Illertissen** Germany
16 E4 **Illescas** Spain
21 N5 **Illiers-Combray** France
20 F5 **Illifaut** France
128 E7 **Illimani** *mt* Bolivia
36 F6 **Illingen** Germany
99 R9 **Illinois** *state* U.S.A.
110 G1 **Illinois** *R* Illinois U.S.A.
110 B5 **Illinois** *R* Oklahoma U.S.A.
100 B7 **Illinois** *R* Oregon U.S.A.
99 R8 **Illinois & Mississippi Canal** Illinois U.S.A.
110 G2 **Illiopolis** Illinois U.S.A.
128 G3 **Illiwa** *R* Guyana
85 F3 **Illizit** Algeria
36 D6 **Illkirch** France
110 G4 **Illmo** Missouri U.S.A.
140 D6 **Illogwa** *R* N Terr Australia
21 O2 **Illois** France
16 E7 **Illora** Spain
Illorsuit *see* **Ubekendt Ejland**
37 M5 **Illschwang** Germany
28 E6 **Illumø** *isld* Denmark
37 M6 **Ilm** *R* Germany
29 K9 **Ilmajoki** Finland
33 M6 **Ilmenau** *R* Germany
37 K2 **Ilmenau** Germany
52 D5 **Il'men', Ozero** *L* Russian Federation
8 D6 **Ilminster** England
128 D7 **Ilo** Peru
71 F5 **Iloilo** Philippines
29 P9 **Ilomantsi** Finland
85 E7 **Ilorin** Nigeria
54 K9 **Ilovaysk** Ukraine
53 F9 **Ilovlya** Russian Federation
116 L7 **0il Pt** Alaska U.S.A.
33 N8 **Ilse** *R* Germany
33 N9 **Ilsenburg** Germany
36 G5 **Ilsfeld** Germany
36 H5 **Ilshofen** Germany
28 C4 **Ilskov** Denmark
86 F4 **Īlubabor** *prov* Ethiopia
88 D3 **Ilula** Tanzania
Ilulissat *see* **Jakobshavn**
48 J3 **Ilva Mică** Romania
100 A3 **Ilwaco** Washington U.S.A.
52 J4 **Ilych** *R* Russian Federation
52 D6 **Il'yino** Russian Federation
31 N4 **Iłża** Poland
31 N4 **Iłżanka** *R* Poland
59 K5 **Imabari** Japan
60 O4 **Imabetsu** Japan
61 N9 **Imaichi** Japan
61 K10 **Imajō** Japan
124 F5 **Imala** Mexico
78 K6 **Imām al Ḩamzah** Iraq
57 B6 **Imambaba** Turkmenistan
İmamoğlu *see* **Kırmıt**
Iman *see* **Dal'nerechensk**
52 D1 **Imandra** Russian Federation
130 C10 **Iman, Sa. del** *ra* Argentina
55 E4 **Imantau, Oz** *L* Kazakhstan
60 C12 **Imari** Japan
128 F2 **Imataca, Sa de** *mts* Venezuela
29 O10 **Imatra** Finland
61 J10 **Imazu** Japan
79 B8 **Imbâba** Egypt
128 C3 **Imbabura** *prov* Ecuador
127 J5 **Imbert** Dominican Rep
133 H3 **Imbituba** Brazil
130 E9 **Imbituva** Brazil
100 H4 **Imbler** Oregon U.S.A.
110 E5 **Imboden** Arkansas U.S.A.
52 F5 **Imeni-Babushkina** Russian Federation
52 F5 **Imeni Kalinina** Russian Federation
53 F11 **Imeni Lenina, Kanal** *canal* Russian Federation
53 G7 **Imeni Vl Lenina** Russian Federation
128 E3 **Imeri, Sa** *mts* Venezuela
113 F7 **Imeson** *airport* Florida U.S.A.
55 F2 **Imgyt** *R* Russian Federation
86 H4 **Īmī** Ethiopia
46 F7 **Imittós** *mt* Greece
65 G5 **Imjin** *R* N Korea
102 F1 **Imlay** Nevada U.S.A.
98 D6 **Imlay** South Dakota U.S.A.
94 D3 **Imlay City** Michigan U.S.A.
85 A4 **Imlili** *well* Western Sahara
32 K10 **Immenhausen** Germany
41 M2 **Immenstadt** Germany
113 F11 **Immokalee** Florida U.S.A.
100 J4 **Imnaha** Oregon U.S.A.
99 L9 **Imogene** Iowa U.S.A.
45 L3 **Imola** Italy
42 H5 **Imotski** Croatia
128 E5 **Imperatriz** Brazil
44 D4 **Imperia** Italy
119 M7 **Imperial** Saskatchewan Canada
103 J9 **Imperial** California U.S.A.
98 E9 **Imperial** Nebraska U.S.A.
102 G9 **Imperial Beach** California U.S.A.
103 K9 **Imperial Dam** Cal/Ariz U.S.A.
103 J9 **Imperial Valley** California U.S.A.
142 C4 **Imperieuse Reef** W Australia Australia
122 J9 **Imperoyal** Nova Scotia Canada
36 E5 **Impflingen** Germany
86 C5 **Impfondo** Congo
75 P6 **Imphal** India
18 H6 **Imphy** France
52 D4 **Impilakhti** Russian Federation
45 K4 **Impruneta** Italy
80 F8 **Imra** Jordan
47 K4 **İmralı** *isld* Turkey
İmroz *isld see* **Gökçeada** *isld*
47 H4 **Imroz** Turkey
41 N3 **Imst** Austria
124 D2 **Imuris** Mexico
71 D5 **Imuruan B** Philippines
116 D4 **Imuruk Basin** Alaska U.S.A.
116 F4 **Imuruk L** Alaska U.S.A.
16 E9 **Imzouren** Morocco
61 L10 **Ina** Japan
31 J2 **Ina** *R* Poland
90 A16 **Inaccessible I** Atlantic Oc
71 D6 **Inagauan** Philippines
61 N8 **Ina-gawa** *R* Japan
127 H4 **Inagua I., Little** Bahamas
61 N12 **Inamba-jima** *isld* Japan
128 D6 **Inambiri** *R* Peru
85 F3 **In Aménas** Algeria
85 E4 **In Amguel** Algeria
70 E1 **Inanam** Sabah
144 C4 **Inangahua Junction** New Zealand
51 K2 **Inarigda** Russian Federation
29 N3 **Inarijärvi** *L* Finland
61 N11 **Inatori** Japan
61 O8 **Inawashiro** Japan
61 O8 **Inawashiro ko** *L* Japan
85 F4 **In Azaoua** Algeria
85 E3 **In Belbel** Algeria
133 D3 **Incahuasi** *mt* Chile/Arg
78 E2 **İncesu** Turkey
14 E4 **Inch** Ireland
100 G1 **Inchelium** Washington U.S.A.
37 L6 **Inchenhofen** Germany
21 O1 **Incheville** France
13 E1 **Inchkeith** *isld* Scotland
15 D2 **Inchnadamph** Scotland
65 G6 **Inch'ŏn** S Korea
116 B3 **Inchoun** Russian Federation
13 E1 **Inchture** Scotland
22 E3 **Inchy** France
45 K4 **Incisa in Valdarno** Italy
89 H5 **Incomati** *R* Mozambique
22 H2 **Incourt** Belgium
18 M11 **Incudine, L'** *mt* Corsica
12 B2 **Indaal, L** Scotland
85 D4 **In Dagouber** Mali
130 D6 **Indaia Grande, R** Brazil
26 J9 **Indal** Sweden
26 H8 **Indalsälven** *R* Sweden
68 C2 **Indaw** Burma
75 R6 **Indawgyi Lake** Burma
124 G5 **Indé** Mexico
7 M9 **Indefatigable** *oil rig* North Sea
102 F5 **Independence** California U.S.A.
99 P7 **Independence** Iowa U.S.A.
107 P4 **Independence** Kansas U.S.A.
111 F11 **Independence** Louisiana U.S.A.
110 B2 **Independence** Missouri U.S.A.
100 B5 **Independence** Oregon U.S.A.
94 F10 **Independence** Virginia U.S.A.
99 P5 **Independence** Wisconsin U.S.A.
147 H9 **Independence Fj** Greenland
100 J8 **Independence Mts** Nevada U.S.A.
69 E13 **Inderapura** Sumatra
69 E13 **Inderapura, Tg** *C* Sumatra
55 B6 **Inderborskiy** Kazakhstan
26 E8 **Inderöy** Norway
55 B6 **Inder, Oz** *L* Kazakhstan
100 D2 **Index** Washington U.S.A.
74 G10 **Indi** India
74 **India** *rep* S Asia
107 M7 **Indiahoma** Oklahoma U.S.A.
117 D4 **Indian** *R* Yukon Territory Canada
95 M2 **Indian** *R* New York U.S.A.
140 D6 **Indiana** N Terr Australia
94 B6 **Indiana** *state* U.S.A.
94 H6 **Indiana** Pennsylvania U.S.A.
81 G11 **Indian-Antarctic Basin** Southern Oc
81 J11 **Indian-Antarctic Ridge** Southern Oc
94 A7 **Indianapolis** Indiana U.S.A.
123 T4 **Indian B** Newfoundland Canada
123 M7 **Indian Brook** Nova Scotia Canada
117 P6 **Indian Cabins** Alberta Canada
115 O7 **Indian Hbr** Labrador, Nfld Canada
122 J9 **Indian Hbr** Nova Scotia Canada
119 O8 **Indian Head** Saskatchewan Canada
95 K8 **Indian Head** Maryland U.S.A.
95 N3 **Indian L** New York U.S.A.
101 P7 **Indian Mt** Wyoming U.S.A.
81 **Indian Ocean**
83 **Indian Ocean Islands**
99 N8 **Indianola** Iowa U.S.A.
111 F8 **Indianola** Mississippi U.S.A.
98 F9 **Indianola** Nebraska U.S.A.
107 P6 **Indianola** Oklahoma U.S.A.
130 F6 **Indianópolis** Brazil
103 L3 **Indian Peak** Utah U.S.A.
101 Q5 **Indian Pk** Wyoming U.S.A.
113 G10 **Indian R** Florida U.S.A.
94 C1 **Indian River** Michigan U.S.A.
113 G9 **Indian River City** Florida U.S.A.
103 J5 **Indian Sp** Nevada U.S.A.
113 G10 **Indian Town** Florida U.S.A.
100 J5 **Indian Valley** Idaho U.S.A.
98 E2 **Indian Villages Nat. Hist. Site** North Dakota U.S.A.
103 O6 **Indian Wells** Arizona U.S.A.
122 A2 **Indicator L** Quebec Canada
52 G1 **Indiga** Russian Federation
147 L15 **Indiga** Russian Federation
51 O2 **Indigirka** *R* Russian Federation
52 G1 **Indigskaya Guba** *B* Russian Federation
48 F5 **Indija** Serbia Yugoslavia
117 Q3 **Indin L** Northwest Territories Canada
103 H8 **Indio** California U.S.A.
109 K9 **Indios** Mexico
137 N4 **Indispensable Reefs** Pacific Oc

70 D7 **Indonesia** *rep* S E Asia
141 K2 **Indooroopilly** *dist* Brisbane, Qnsld Australia
74 F7 **Indore** India
69 F13 **Indragiri** *R* Sumatra
70 M9 **Indramayu** Java
69 E14 **Indrapura** Sumatra
69 E14 **Indrapura, Tanjong** *C* Sumatra
73 N5 **Indravati** *R* India
18 G6 **Indre** *dept* France
20 G7 **Indre** France
21 N7 **Indre** *R* France
18 F5 **Indre-et-Loire** *dept* France
113 G10 **Indrio** Florida U.S.A.
21 N7 **Indrois** *R* France
31 O2 **Indura** Belorussia
118 D8 **Indus** Alberta Canada
73 L2 **Indus** *R* S W Asia
74 B6 **Indus, Mouths of** Pakistan
110 F1 **Industry** Illinois U.S.A.
109 L6 **Industry** Texas U.S.A.
89 E8 **Indwe** S Africa
85 F4 **In Ebeggi** Algeria
78 D1 **İnebolu** Turkey
47 J4 **İnecik** Turkey
85 F4 **In Ecker** Algeria
85 E5 **In Edek** Niger
78 B1 **İnegöl** Turkey
71 K9 **Inerie** *mt* Flores Indonesia
21 P8 **Ineuil** France
109 L7 **Inez** Texas U.S.A.
85 G4 **In Ezzane** Algeria
89 B10 **Infanta, C** S Africa
128 F5 **Infernão, Cach** *rapids* Brazil
124 H8 **Infiernillo, L** Mexico
16 D1 **Infiesto** Spain
130 J9 **Ingá** Brazil
29 L11 **Inga** Finland
68 B4 **Ingabu** Burma
85 F5 **Ingal** Niger
140 C5 **Ingallanna** *R* N Terr Australia
94 B7 **Ingalls** Indiana U.S.A.
107 K4 **Ingalls** Kansas U.S.A.
99 T4 **Ingalls** Michigan U.S.A.
100 E10 **Ingalls, Mt** California U.S.A.
55 F3 **Ingaly** Russian Federation
9 G4 **Ingatestone** England
36 H5 **Ingelfingen** Germany
36 E4 **Ingelheim** Germany
22 E2 **Ingelmunster** Belgium
86 C6 **Ingende** Zaire
133 E5 **Ingeniero Luiggi** Argentina
131 E7 **Ingeniero, Pto** Argentina
117 L7 **Ingenika** *R* British Columbia Canada
116 E7 **Ingeramuit** Alaska U.S.A.
107 M5 **Ingersoll** Oklahoma U.S.A.
71 B2 **Inggelang** *isld* Halmahera Indonesia
141 H4 **Ingham** Queensland Australia
83 K11 **Ingiriya** Sri Lanka
13 F5 **Ingleborough** *mt* England
115 N2 **Inglefield Land** Greenland
109 K8 **Ingleside** Texas U.S.A.
13 F5 **Ingleton** England
141 K8 **Inglewood** Queensland Australia
139 G6 **Inglewood** Victoria Australia
145 E3 **Inglewood** New Zealand
140 D1 **Inglis** *isld* N Terr Australia
119 Q8 **Inglis** Manitoba Canada
116 G4 **Inglutalik** *R* Alaska U.S.A.
58 F1 **Ingoda** *R* Russian Federation
118 F1 **Ingolf** Ontario Canada
29 T10 **Ingolfshöfdhi** *C* Iceland
86 C7 **Ingololo** Zaire
37 L6 **Ingolstadt** Germany
138 C3 **Ingomar** South Australia Australia
101 S3 **Ingomar** Montana U.S.A.
123 M7 **Ingonish** C Breton I, Nova Scotia
102 B1 **Ingot** California U.S.A.
26 N1 **Ingöy** Norway
75 N6 **Ingrāj Bāzār** India
109 H5 **Ingram** Texas U.S.A.
99 Q4 **Ingram** Wisconsin U.S.A.
122 J9 **Ingramport** Nova Scotia Canada
21 M8 **Ingrandes** Indre France
21 J7 **Ingrandes** Maine-et-Loire France
21 M8 **Ingrandes** Vienne France
117 P3 **Ingray L** Northwest Territories Canada
21 O6 **Ingré** France
146 J11 **Ingrid Christensen Coast** Antarctica
28 D2 **Ingstrup** Denmark
85 F5 **In Guezzam** Algeria
20 D6 **Inguiniel** France
54 D9 **Ingul** *R* Ukraine
54 E9 **Ingulets** Ukraine
54 D10 **Ingulets** *R* Ukraine
55 F1 **Inguyagun** *R* Russian Federation
89 G6 **Ingwavuma** S Africa
19 K4 **Ingwiller** France
89 H6 **Inhaca Pen** Mozambique
87 G10 **Inhambane** Mozambique
130 C7 **Inhandui, R** Brazil
130 C7 **Inhanduizinho, R** Brazil
88 E10 **Inhangoma I** Mozambique
130 C10 **Inhanhora** *R* Brazil
130 G6 **Inhapim** Brazil
87 G10 **Inharrime** Mozambique
47 L4 **İnhisar** Turkey
130 H4 **Inhobim** Brazil
129 J7 **Inhumas** Brazil
116 L3 **Iniakuk** *R* Alaska U.S.A.
71 K9 **Inielika** *mt* Flores Indonesia
17 F5 **Iniesta** Spain
85 E3 **Inifel, Hassi** Algeria
27 M11 **Iniö** Finland
128 E3 **Inírida** *R* Colombia
14 A3 **Inishark** *isld* Ireland
14 C1 **Inishbofin** *isld* Ireland
14 A3 **Inishbofin** *isld* Ireland
14 B2 **Inishcrone** Ireland
14 B3 **Inisheer** *isld* Ireland
14 A2 **Inishkea** *isld* Ireland
14 B3 **Inishmaan** *isld* Ireland
14 B3 **Inishmore** *isld* Ireland
14 C2 **Inishmurray** *isld* Ireland
14 D1 **Inishowen** *dist* Ireland
14 E1 **Inishowen Hd** Ireland
14 D1 **Inishtrahull** *isld* Ireland
14 A3 **Inishturk** *isld* Ireland
65 D2 **Injgan Sum** China
141 J7 **Injune** Queensland Australia
141 F3 **Inkerman** Queensland Australia
122 H6 **Inkerman** New Brunswick Canada
86 C7 **Inkis** *R* Zaire
86 C7 **Inkisi-Kisantu** Zaire
117 G6 **Inklin** British Columbia Canada
101 N7 **Inkom** Idaho U.S.A.
52 F5 **Inkovo** Russian Federation
98 J1 **Inkster** North Dakota U.S.A.
68 C2 **Inle, L** Burma
98 H7 **Inman** Nebraska U.S.A.
95 N2 **Inman** New York U.S.A.
112 E2 **Inman** South Carolina U.S.A.
41 O3 **Inn** *R* Austria
38 F6 **Inn** *R* Germany
138 F2 **Innamincka** South Australia Australia
15 E5 **Innerleithen** Scotland
Inner Mongolia *aut reg see* **Nei Mongol Zizhiqu**
41 K3 **Inner-Rhoden** *dist* Switzerland
15 C3 **Inner Sound** Scotland
32 M8 **Innerste** *R* Germany
41 H4 **Innertkirchen** Switzerland
38 F8 **Innervillgraten** Austria
6 M6 **Innes** *oilfield* North Sea
26 E8 **Innherad** *reg* Norway
Innien *see* **Aukrug**
14 C5 **Inniscarra Res** Ireland
141 H3 **Innisfail** Queensland Australia
118 D6 **Innisfail** Alberta Canada
118 F5 **Innisfree** Alberta Canada
116 J5 **Innoko** *R* Alaska U.S.A.
60 G11 **Inno-shima** Japan
41 O3 **Innsbruck** Austria
26 K3 **Innset** Norway
26 B10 **Innvik** Norway
116 A3 **Innymney, Gora** *mt* Russian Federation
130 D6 **Inocência** Brazil
107 P5 **Inola** Oklahoma U.S.A.
47 L5 **İnönü** Turkey
31 L3 **Inowrocław** Poland
128 E7 **Inquisivi** Bolivia
85 E3 **In Rhar** Algeria
40 F3 **Ins** Switzerland
85 E3 **In Salah** Algeria
15 F3 **Insch** Scotland
143 A7 **Inscription,C** W Australia Australia
68 B4 **Insein** Burma
37 J2 **Inselsberg** *mt* Germany
119 O7 **Insinger** Saskatchewan Canada
31 J2 **Insko** Poland
36 B6 **Insming** France
Insterburg *see* **Chernyakhovsk**
146 D7 **Institute Ice Stream** *ice stream* Antarctica
118 J9 **Instow** Saskatchewan Canada
8 B5 **Instow** England
48 L6 **Însurăţei** Romania
52 K2 **Inta** Russian Federation
98 B2 **Intake** Montana U.S.A.
57 F1 **Intaly** Kazakhstan
85 E5 **In Tebezas** Mali
47 H4 **İntepe** Turkey
98 E6 **Interior** South Dakota U.S.A.
113 F8 **Interlachen** Florida U.S.A.
139 H8 **Interlaken** Tasmania Australia
40 G4 **Interlaken** Switzerland
99 N1 **International Falls** Minnesota U.S.A.
119 R10 **International Peace Gdn** Canada/U.S.A.
117 O9 **Intersection Mt** Alberta/Br Col Canada
68 A6 **Interview I** Andaman Is
48 K5 **Intorsura Buzăului** Romania
41 J5 **Intragna** Switzerland
32 G8 **Intrup** Germany
52 F2 **Intsy** Russian Federation
61 O10 **Inubō saki** Japan
115 O3 **Inugsulik Bugt** *B* Greenland
115 M6 **Inukjuak** Quebec Canada
133 C8 **Inútil, B** Chile
114 F4 **Inuvik** Northwest Territories Canada
114 F4 **Inuvik** *dist* Northwest Territories Canada
128 D6 **Inuya** *R* Peru
52 J5 **In'va** *R* Russian Federation
15 C4 **Inveraray** Scotland
15 F4 **Inverbervie** Scotland
144 B7 **Invercargill** New Zealand
12 C2 **Invercloy** Scotland
139 K3 **Inverell** New South Wales Australia
15 D3 **Invergordon** Scotland
15 E4 **Inverkeithing** Scotland
12 D2 **Inverkip** Scotland
140 F4 **Inverleigh** Queensland Australia
12 D1 **Inverlochlarig** Scotland
119 O7 **Invermay** Saskatchewan Canada
117 P10 **Invermere** British Columbia Canada
Inverness *co see* **Highland** *reg*
121 T6 **Inverness** Quebec Canada
123 L7 **Inverness** C Breton I, Nova Scotia
15 D3 **Inverness** Scotland
113 E9 **Inverness** Florida U.S.A.
101 P1 **Inverness** Montana U.S.A.
15 D3 **Invershin** Scotland
15 F3 **Inverurie** Scotland
140 A4 **Inverway** N Terr Australia
68 C6 **Investigator Chan** Burma
138 C5 **Investigator Group** *islds* South Australia Australia
138 D6 **Investigator Str** South Australia Australia
68 A7 **Invisible Bank** Andaman Is
120 J10 **Inwood** Ontario Canada
102 C1 **Inwood** California U.S.A.
56 B3 **Inya** *R* Russian Federation
87 F9 **Inyanga** Zimbabwe
87 F9 **Inyanga Nat. Park** Zimbabwe
98 B5 **Inyan Kara Cr** Wyoming U.S.A.
56 G3 **Inyaptuk, Gora** *mt* Russian Federation
102 G6 **Inyokern** California U.S.A.
55 C4 **Inzer** Russian Federation
86 C7 **Inzia** *R* Zaire
20 D6 **Inzinzac-Lochrist** France
46 D5 **Ioánnina** Greece
38 H9 **Iôf di Montasio** *mt* Italy
47 H9 **Ioinianísia** *isld* Greece
61 N13 **Iō-Jima** *isld* Japan
52 E1 **Iokanga** Russian Federation
106 C3 **Iola** Colorado U.S.A.
107 P4 **Iola** Kansas U.S.A.
109 L5 **Iola** Texas U.S.A.
45 L2 **Iolanda di Savoia** Italy
57 B6 **Iolotan'** Turkmenistan
123 M8 **Iona** C Breton I, Nova Scotia
12 B1 **Iona** *isld* Scotland
101 O6 **Iona** Idaho U.S.A.
99 L6 **Iona** Minnesota U.S.A.
98 G6 **Iona** South Dakota U.S.A.
87 B9 **Iona Nat. Park** Angola
47 J1 **Ion Corvin** Romania
102 G3 **Ione** Nevada U.S.A.
100 F4 **Ione** Oregon U.S.A.
100 H1 **Ione** Washington U.S.A.
48 J6 **Ioneşti** Romania
47 H6 **Ionia** *hist reg* Turkey
99 O6 **Ionia** Iowa U.S.A.
94 B3 **Ionia** Michigan U.S.A.
110 C3 **Ionia** Missouri U.S.A.
Ionian Is *see* **Iónioi Nísoi**
43 H10 **Ionian Sea** S Europe
46 D5 **Iónioi Nísoi** *islds* Greece
116 A4 **Ioniveen** *R* Russian Federation
78 K1 **Iori** *R* Azerbaijan/Georgia
46 G8 **Íos** *isld* Greece
52 H3 **Iosser** Russian Federation
99 N7 **Iowa** *state* U.S.A.
99 N7 **Iowa** *R* Iowa U.S.A.
111 C11 **Iowa** Louisiana U.S.A.
99 P8 **Iowa City** Iowa U.S.A.
99 N7 **Iowa Falls** Iowa U.S.A.
109 J2 **Iowa Park** Texas U.S.A.
124 G7 **Ipala** Mexico
83 K9 **Ipalogama** Sri Lanka
130 E5 **Ipameri** Brazil
130 H6 **Ipanema** Brazil
130 H10 **Ipanema** *R* Brazil
130 H8 **Ipanguacu** Brazil
99 Q9 **Ipava** Illinois U.S.A.
48 E2 **Ipel'** *R* Czechoslovakia
116 E2 **Ipewik** *R* Alaska U.S.A.
37 J4 **Iphofen** Germany
128 C3 **Ipiales** Colombia
129 L6 **Ipiau** Brazil
Ipin *see* **Yibin**
128 E4 **Ipiranga** Amazonas Brazil
130 E9 **Ipiranga** Paraná Brazil
128 D5 **Ipixuna** Amazonas Brazil
128 F5 **Ipixuna** *R* Amazonas Brazil
69 E10 **Ipoh** Malaysia
130 J10 **Ipojuca** *R* Brazil
71 C6 **Ipolote B** Palawan Philippines
129 H7 **Iporá** Brazil
130 E9 **Iporanga** Brazil
120 J9 **Ipperwash Prov. Park** Ontario Canada
37 J4 **Ippesheim** Germany
86 D4 **Ippy** Cent Afr Republic
78 A1 **İpsala** Turkey
141 L8 **Ipswich** Queensland Australia
9 H3 **Ipswich** England
127 J2 **Ipswich** Jamaica
95 R4 **Ipswich** Massachusetts U.S.A.
98 G4 **Ipswich** South Dakota U.S.A.
129 K4 **Ipu** Brazil
54 C4 **Iput'** *R* Belorussia/Rus Fed
78 K2 **Iqdir** Turkey
58 B4 **Iqe** China
66 E4 **Iqe** China
128 D8 **Iquique** Chile
128 D4 **Iquitos** Peru
80 F6 **'Ira** Jordan
108 F5 **Iraan** Texas U.S.A.
61 L11 **Irago-misaki** Japan
130 D10 **Irai** Brazil
46 G8 **Iráklia** *isld* Greece
46 G9 **Iráklion** Crete
130 C9 **Irala** Paraguay
77 C4 **Iran** *rep* S W Asia
130 D10 **Irani** *R* Brazil
77 G6 **Irānshahr** Iran
128 F1 **Irapa** Venezuela
124 J7 **Irapuato** Mexico
78 H5 **Iraq** *rep* S W Asia
95 P2 **Irasburg** Vermont U.S.A.
129 H3 **Iratapuru** *R* Brazil
130 E9 **Irati** Brazil
133 G3 **Irati** Brazil
17 G2 **Irati** *R* Spain
84 E4 **Īrāwan** Libya
52 J3 **Irayel'** Russian Federation
Irbenskiy Proliv *see* **Kura Kurk**
80 G3 **Irbid** Jordan
55 D2 **Irbit** *R* Russian Federation
55 D3 **Irbit** Russian Federation
9 G1 **Irby** England
38 K7 **Irdning** Austria
54 C7 **Irdyn'** Ukraine
109 K4 **Iredell** Texas U.S.A.
109 K4 **Ireland** Texas U.S.A.
90 A2 **Ireland I** Bermuda
14 **Ireland, Rep of**
14 E3 **Ireland's Eye** *isld* Ireland
55 C3 **Iren** *R* Russian Federation
98 J6 **Irene** South Dakota U.S.A.
98 K7 **Ireton** Iowa U.S.A.
57 B1 **Irgiz** *R* Kazakhstan
85 F5 **Irhazer Wan Agadez** *V* Niger
85 C2 **Irhil M'Goun** *mt* Morocco
136 G2 **Irian Jaya** *prov* Indonesia
86 D2 **Iriba** Chad
129 G3 **Iricoumé, Serra** *mts* Brazil
71 F4 **Iriga** Philippines
55 C5 **Iriklinskiy** Russian Federation
87 G7 **Iringa** Tanzania
67 H4 **Iriomote-shima** *isld* Japan
125 M2 **Iriona** Honduras
129 H5 **Iriri** *R* Brazil
139 H8 **Irishtown** Tasmania Australia
56 E2 **Irkineyeva** *R* Russian Federation
56 F5 **Irkutsk** Russian Federation
56 F3 **Irkutskaya Oblast'** Russian Federation
118 F6 **Irma** Alberta Canada
99 R4 **Irma** Wisconsin U.S.A.
36 E2 **Irmgarteichen** Germany
112 F3 **Irmo** South Carolina U.S.A.
20 G5 **Irodouer** France
20 A5 **Iroise** *G* France
86 C3 **Iro, L** Chad
138 D4 **Iron Baron** South Australia Australia
120 G6 **Iron Bridge** Ontario Canada
8 D2 **Ironbridge** England
110 J6 **Iron City** Tennessee U.S.A.
121 M8 **Irondale** Ontario Canada
110 F4 **Irondale** Missouri U.S.A.
94 G6 **Irondale** Ohio U.S.A.
138 D4 **Iron Knob** South Australia Australia
99 S4 **Iron Mountain** Michigan U.S.A.
100 A7 **Iron Mt** Oregon U.S.A.
103 L4 **Iron Mt** Utah U.S.A.
98 G5 **Iron Nation** South Dakota U.S.A.
141 G2 **Iron Range** Queensland Australia
99 S6 **Iron Ridge** Wisconsin U.S.A.
99 S3 **Iron River** Michigan U.S.A.
99 P3 **Iron River** Wisconsin U.S.A.
94 B2 **Irons** Michigan U.S.A.
100 H5 **Ironside** Oregon U.S.A.
103 L4 **Iron Sp** Utah U.S.A.
94 B1 **Ironton** Michigan U.S.A.
110 F4 **Ironton** Missouri U.S.A.
94 E8 **Ironton** Ohio U.S.A.
99 Q3 **Ironwood** Michigan U.S.A.
99 T9 **Iroquois** *R* Illinois U.S.A.
98 J5 **Iroquois** South Dakota U.S.A.
120 K4 **Iroquois Falls** Ontario Canada
71 G4 **Irosin** Philippines
61 M11 **Irō zaki** *C* Japan
45 R8 **Irpinia** Italy
68 B4 **Irrawaddy** *prov* Burma
68 B5 **Irrawaddy** *R* Burma
68 B5 **Irrawaddy, Mouths of** Burma
36 B4 **Irrel** Germany
118 D7 **Irricana** Alberta Canada
85 D5 **Irrigi** *reg* Mali/Mauritania
56 D3 **Irsha** Russian Federation
48 H2 **Irshava** Ukraine
52 G4 **Irta** Russian Federation
13 F3 **Irthing, R** England
55 D3 **Irtyash, Oz** *L* Russian Federation
55 E2 **Irtysh** *R* Russian Federation
55 F4 **Irtysh** Russian Federation
55 G4 **Irtyshsk** Kazakhstan
86 E5 **Irumu** Zaire
17 F1 **Irún** Spain
17 F2 **Irurzun** Spain
18 D10 **Irurzun** Spain
128 E8 **Iruya** Argentina
Irves Šaurums *see* **Kura Kurk**
118 G9 **Irvine** Alberta Canada
15 D5 **Irvine** *R* Scotland
15 D5 **Irvine** Scotland
110 N4 **Irvine** Kentucky U.S.A.
141 H3 **Irvinebank** Queensland Australia
14 D2 **Irvinestown** N Ireland
107 O2 **Irving** Kansas U.S.A.
109 N9 **Irving** Texas U.S.A.
143 F7 **Irving, Mt** W Australia Australia
110 K4 **Irvington** Kentucky U.S.A.
95 L9 **Irvington** Virginia U.S.A.
94 J6 **Irvona** Pennsylvania U.S.A.
13 F6 **Irwell, R** England
143 B8 **Irwin** W Australia Australia
101 O6 **Irwin** Idaho U.S.A.
99 L8 **Irwin** Iowa U.S.A.
98 D7 **Irwin** Nebraska U.S.A.
112 D5 **Irwinton** Georgia U.S.A.
138 F5 **Irymple** Victoria Australia
141 J6 **Isaac** *R* Queensland Australia
117 N9 **Isaac L** British Columbia Canada
123 L8 **Isaacs Hbr** Nova Scotia Canada
17 G2 **Isaba** Spain
107 M4 **Isabel** Kansas U.S.A.
98 E4 **Isabel** South Dakota U.S.A.
71 E7 **Isabela** Philippines
71 F5 **Isabela** Negros Philippines
127 L5 **Isabela** Puerto Rico
126 D3 **Isabela de Sagua** Cuba
128 A8 **Isabela, Isla** Galapagos Is
125 M3 **Isabelia, Cord** *ra* Nicaragua
119 Q8 **Isabella** Manitoba Canada
102 F6 **Isabella** California U.S.A.
99 P2 **Isabella** Minnesota U.S.A.
142 F5 **Isabella, L** W Australia Australia
48 L5 **Isaccea** Romania
147 N11 **Isachenko, Ostrov** *isld* Russian Federation
114 J2 **Isachsen** Northwest Territories Canada
28 R8 **Isafjardhardjup** *inlet* Iceland
28 R8 **Isafjördhur** Iceland
60 D13 **Isahaya** Japan
52 F3 **Isakogorka** Russian Federation
48 H6 **Işalniţat** Romania
87 H12 **Isalo, Parc National de L'** *nat park* Madagascar
86 D5 **Isangi** Zaire
37 N7 **Isar** *R* Germany
42 D2 **Isarco** *R* Italy
46 E7 **Isari** Greece
41 O2 **Isar Tal** Germany
111 J7 **Isbell** Alabama U.S.A.
22 C2 **Isbergues** France
15 G1 **Isbister** Scotland
40 C1 **Isches** France
41 M3 **Ischgl** Austria
45 P8 **Ischia** Italy
142 F3 **Isdell,R** W Australia Australia
21 P6 **Isdes** France
59 L5 **Ise** Japan
28 H5 **Isefjord** *inlet* Denmark
41 O3 **Isel Berg** *mt* Austria
81 H14 **Iselin Seamount** Southern Oc
36 D3 **Isenburg** Germany
33 N8 **Isenbüttel** Germany
33 N7 **Isenhagen** Germany
28 C4 **Isenvad** Denmark
42 C3 **Iseo** Italy
42 C3 **Iseo, L. d'** Italy
19 O14 **Isère** *R* France
19 P14 **Isère** *dept* France
32 G10 **Iserlohn** Germany
32 L8 **Isernhagen** Germany
43 F7 **Isernia** Italy
61 N9 **Isesaki** Japan
61 K11 **Ise shima Nat. Park** Japan
55 E3 **Isetskoye** Russian Federation
61 K11 **Ise-wan** *B* Japan
85 E7 **Iseyin** Nigeria
Isfahan *see* **Eşfahān**
57 E5 **Isfana** Kyrgyzstan
57 F4 **Isfara** Tajikistan
80 D3 **Isfiya** Israel
52 J4 **Isherim, Gora** *mt* Russian Federation
128 G3 **Isherton** Guyana
88 C7 **Ishiba Ngandu** Zambia
67 H4 **Ishigaki** Japan
67 H4 **Ishigaki-shima** *isld* Japan
61 K9 **Ishika** *prefect* Japan
60 P2 **Ishikari** Japan
60 R2 **Ishikari dake** *mt* Japan
59 M3 **Ishikari-wan** *B* Japan
55 E5 **Ishim** *R* Kazakhstan/Rus Fed
55 E3 **Ishim** Russian Federation
55 C4 **Ishimbay** Russian Federation
55 F3 **Ishimskaya Step** *steppe* Russian Federation
55 E5 **Ishimskoye** Kazakhstan
59 M4 **Ishinomaki** Japan
60 G12 **Ishizuchi-san** *mt* Japan
21 H4 **Isigny-le-Buat** France
21 H3 **Isigny sur Mer** Calvados France
47 J4 **Işıklar Dağı** *mts* Turkey
86 G6 **Isiolo** Kenya
87 F11 **Isipingo Bch** S Africa
86 E5 **Isiro** Zaire
141 G6 **Isisford** Queensland Australia
86 G1 **Isi Jebel** *mt* Sudan
55 E3 **Iska** *R* Russian Federation
80 D5 **Iskāka** Jordan
57 E4 **Iskander** Uzbekistan
47 J8 **İskandil Burun** *C* Turkey
78 F3 **İskenderun** Turkey
78 E1 **İskilip** Turkey
57 G4 **Iski-Naukat** Kyrgyzstan
56 B4 **Iskitim** Russian Federation
46 G1 **Iskŭr** *R* Bulgaria
46 F2 **Iskŭr, Yazovir** *res* Bulgaria
117 H7 **Iskut** *R* British Columbia Canada
117 J7 **Iskut** British Columbia Canada
119 O3 **Iskwatam L** Saskatchewan Canada
15 E4 **Isla** *R* Scotland
78 F3 **Islahiye** Turkey
74 E2 **Islamabad** Pakistan
113 G13 **Islamorada** Florida U.S.A.
117 N5 **Island** *R* Northwest Territories Canada
110 J4 **Island** Kentucky U.S.A.
71 D6 **Island B** Palawan Philippines
100 H4 **Island City** Oregon U.S.A.
120 J3 **Island Falls** Ontario Canada
119 P3 **Island Falls** Saskatchewan Canada
95 S7 **Island Falls** Maine U.S.A.
141 K5 **Island Hd** Queensland Australia
95 N7 **Island Heights** New Jersey U.S.A.
115 K7 **Island L** Manitoba Canada
120 K7 **Island L** Ontario Canada
138 D4 **Island Lagoon** South Australia Australia
99 W3 **Island Lake** Ontario Canada
100 B9 **Island Mountain** California U.S.A.
101 O5 **Island Park** Idaho U.S.A.
123 Q5 **Island Pond** *L* Newfoundland Canada
95 Q2 **Island Pond** Vermont U.S.A.
143 B9 **Island Pt** W Australia Australia
123 O4 **Islands, Bay of** Newfoundland Canada
145 E1 **Islands, Bay of** New Zealand
16 B2 **Isla Cies** Spain
127 M5 **Isla Verde** *airport* Puerto Rico
118 G5 **Islay** Alberta Canada
15 B5 **Islay** *isld* Scotland
18 F7 **Isle** *R* France
99 N3 **Isle** Minnesota U.S.A.
21 P3 **Isle-Adam, l'** France
123 O6 **Isle aux Morts** Newfoundland Canada
95 T2 **Isleboro** Maine U.S.A.
18 F9 **Isle en Dodon, L'** France
18 F9 **Isle Jourdain, L'** Gers France
18 F6 **Isle Jourdain, L'** Vienne France
118 H4 **Isle, Lac des** Saskatchewan Canada
122 A5 **Isle Maligne** Quebec Canada
112 F6 **Isle of Hope** Georgia U.S.A.
15 G2 **Isle of Noss** Scotland
12 D4 **Isle of Whithorn** Scotland
99 S1 **Isle Royale** Michigan U.S.A.
22 G5 **Isles-sur-Suippes** France
18 H5 **Isle-sur-Serein, L'** France
106 D7 **Isleta** New Mexico U.S.A.
102 C3 **Isleton** California U.S.A.
122 C5 **Isle Verte** Quebec Canada
9 E4 **Islip** England
127 N3 **Islote Pt** Trinidad
128 E7 **Isluga** *vol* Chile
133 D1 **Isluga** *mt* Chile
131 F4 **Ismael Cortinas** Uruguay
84 J3 **Ismâ'ilîya** Egypt
37 M7 **Ismaning** Germany
98 B3 **Ismay** Montana U.S.A.
78 A2 **Ismir Körfezi** Turkey
84 J4 **Isna** Egypt
87 H12 **Isoanala** Madagascar
29 J9 **Isojoki** Finland
87 F8 **Isoka** Zambia
29 J8 **Isokyrö** Finland
41 O7 **Isola** Italy
111 F8 **Isola** Mississippi U.S.A.
45 P6 **Isola del Liri** Italy
45 M5 **Isola Farnese** Italy
87 H12 **Isola, Massif de L'** *mts* Madagascar
45 K1 **Isola Rizza** Italy
20 C6 **Isole** *R* France
110 L5 **Isoline** Tennessee U.S.A.
45 J1 **Isorella** Italy
29 N6 **Iso-syöte** *mt* Finland
78 C3 **Isparta** Turkey
78 C3 **Isparta** *R* Turkey
47 M10 **Ispartakula** Turkey
47 H1 **Isperikh** Bulgaria
78 H1 **Ispir** Turkey
80 **Israel** *state* S W Asia
143 E10 **Israelite B** W Australia Australia
20 H6 **Issé** France
28 F4 **Issehoved** *C* Denmark
143 A8 **Isseka** W Australia Australia
25 F5 **Isselburg** Germany
85 C7 **Issia** Ivory Coast
71 H4 **Issimu** Sulawesi Indonesia
18 H7 **Issoire** France
19 Q18 **Issole** *R* France
21 O8 **Issoudun** France
25 F5 **Issum** Germany
57 H4 **Issyk-Kul'** Kyrgyzstan
57 H4 **Issyk-Kul, Ozero** *L* Kyrgyzstan
57 J4 **Issyk-Kul'skaya Oblast'** Kyrgyzstan
77 L2 **Istalif** Afghanistan
47 M10 **Istanbul** Turkey
120 J7 **Isthmus Bay** Ontario Canada
46 F6 **Istiaia** Greece
128 C2 **Istmina** Colombia
42 F3 **Istra** *pen* Croatia
54 H1 **Istra** Russian Federation
19 N18 **Istres** France
47 Q14 **Ístrios** Rhodes Greece
61 M11 **Isu hantō** *pen* Japan
55 C5 **Isyangulovo** Russian Federation
130 B9 **Itá** Paraguay
129 L6 **Itabaiana** Brazil
130 H7 **Itabapoana** Brazil
130 E8 **Itaberá** Brazil
130 E5 **Itaberai** Brazil
129 K7 **Itabira** Brazil
130 G7 **Itabirito** Brazil
128 F4 **Itaboca** Brazil
129 L6 **Itabuna** Brazil
129 J5 **Itacajá** Brazil
129 H5 **Itacajuna** *R* Brazil
130 G4 **Itacarambi** Brazil
129 L6 **Itacaré** Brazil
128 G4 **Itacoatiara** Brazil
128 D5 **Itacuai** *R* Brazil
130 C9 **Itacurubí del Rosario** Paraguay
130 H6 **Itaguaçu** Brazil
130 D8 **Itaguaje** Brazil
129 J6 **Itaguari** *R* Brazil
130 E8 **Itaí** Brazil
130 E10 **Itaiópolis** Brazil
129 G4 **Itaituba** Brazil
130 E10 **Itajaí Acú, R** Brazil
129 J8 **Itajuba** Brazil
130 H4 **Itajuípe** Brazil
61 O10 **Itako** Japan
Itala *see* **Cadale**
42 **Italy** *rep* S Europe
109 L3 **Italy** Texas U.S.A.
130 G5 **Itamarandiba** Brazil
129 J4 **Itamatare** Brazil
130 H6 **Itambacuri** Brazil
129 K7 **Itambé** Brazil
130 G6 **Itambe, P. de** *mt* Brazil
60 J11 **Itami** Japan
130 F9 **Itanhaém** Brazil
129 K7 **Itanhém** *R* Brazil
129 H3 **Itany** *R* Suriname
130 H5 **Itaobim** Brazil
129 J6 **Itapaci** Brazil
130 E6 **Itapajipe** Brazil
130 H4 **Itapebi** Brazil
130 F7 **Itapecerica** Brazil
129 K4 **Itapecuru Mirim** Brazil
130 H7 **Itapemirim** Brazil
129 K8 **Itaperuna** Brazil
129 K7 **Itapetinga** Brazil
129 J8 **Itapetininga** Brazil
129 J8 **Itapeva** Brazil
129 G3 **Itapi** *R* Brazil
129 K5 **Itapicura** *R* Brazil
129 J5 **Itapicuru, Serra do** *mts* Brazil
128 F5 **Itapinima** Brazil
129 L4 **Itapipoca** Brazil
128 G4 **Itapira** Brazil
130 E10 **Itapocu, R** Brazil
130 E7 **Itápolis** Brazil
130 H9 **Itaporanga** Brazil
130 C10 **Itapuá** *reg* Paraguay
129 H7 **Itapuranga** Brazil
131 G2 **Itaqui** Brazil
133 F2 **Itaquyry** Paraguay
129 J8 **Itararé** Brazil
74 G7 **Itarsi** India
130 D6 **Itarumã** Brazil
109 K3 **Itasca** Texas U.S.A.
99 L2 **Itasca State Park** Minnesota U.S.A.
131 A6 **Itata, R** Chile
130 F8 **Itatiba** Brazil
131 F2 **Itati, L** Argentina
130 E8 **Itatinga** Brazil
128 F5 **Itatuba** Brazil
130 E5 **Itauçu** Brazil
130 G7 **Itaúna** Brazil
129 L7 **Itaúnas** Brazil
130 H5 **Itaúnas** Brazil
9 E5 **Itchin, R** England
55 F4 **Itemgen, Oz** *L* Kazakhstan
Ithaca *isld* Greece *see* **Itháki**
94 C3 **Ithaca** Michigan U.S.A.
95 L4 **Ithaca** New York U.S.A.
46 D6 **Itháki** *isld* Greece
8 C3 **Ithon, R** Wales
115 O4 **Itilleq** Greenland
86 D5 **Itimbiri** *R* Zaire
130 H5 **Itinga** Brazil
129 H7 **Itiquira** Brazil
129 K6 **Itiúba, Serra de** *mts* Brazil
116 M2 **Itkillik** *R* Alaska U.S.A.
61 N11 **Itō** Japan
61 L8 **Itoigawa** Japan
86 D6 **Itoko** Zaire
61 P14 **Itoman** Okinawa
21 N4 **Iton** *R* France
45 P7 **Itri** Italy
79 A9 **Itsa** Egypt
111 F8 **Itta Bena** Mississippi U.S.A.
25 E6 **Ittervoort** Netherlands
43 B8 **Ittiri** Sardinia
Ittoqqortoormiit *see* **Scoresbysund**
130 F8 **Itu** Brazil
131 G2 **Itú** *R* Brazil
129 J7 **Ituiutaba** Brazil
88 A3 **Itula** Zaire
88 E5 **Itumba** Tanzania
129 J7 **Itumbiara** Brazil
119 O7 **Ituna** Saskatchewan Canada
128 G2 **Ituni** Guyana
130 E10 **Ituporanga** Brazil
128 E8 **Iturbe** Argentina
130 C10 **Iturbe** Paraguay
59 N3 **Iturup, Ostrov** *isld* Russian Federation
130 F7 **Ituverava** Brazil
130 C10 **Ituzaingo** Argentina
37 K3 **Itz** *R* Germany
32 L5 **Itzehoe** Germany
32 K5 **Itzwärden** Germany
88 D6 **Iufira** *R* Malawi
110 H3 **Iuka** Illinois U.S.A.
107 M4 **Iuka** Kansas U.S.A.
110 H7 **Iuka** Mississippi U.S.A.
130 H7 **Iúna** Brazil
112 E3 **Iva** South Carolina U.S.A.
129 H8 **Ivaí** *R* Brazil
29 N3 **Ivalo** Finland
29 N3 **Ivalojoki** *R* Finland
48 E7 **Ivančići** Bosnia-Herzegovina
52 C5 **Ivangorod** Russian Federation
46 D2 **Ivangrad** Montenegro Yugoslavia
139 G5 **Ivanhoe** New South Wales Australia
142 G3 **Ivanhoe** W Australia Australia
120 H4 **Ivanhoe** *R* Ontario Canada
98 K5 **Ivanhoe** Minnesota U.S.A.
94 G10 **Ivanhoe** Virginia U.S.A.
54 M1 **Ivanishchi** Russian Federation
48 F7 **Ivanjica** Serbia Yugoslavia
53 B9 **Ivano-Frankovsk** Ukraine
48 L1 **Ivanopol'** Ukraine
55 B4 **Ivanovka** Russian Federation
55 G3 **Ivanovka** Omskaya obl Russian Federation
52 F6 **Ivanovo** Russian Federation
103 J6 **Ivanpah** California U.S.A.
54 J1 **Ivanteyvka** Russian Federation
53 C7 **Ivatsevichi** Belorussia
47 H3 **Ivaylovgrad** Bulgaria
55 D1 **Ivdel'** Russian Federation
33 R5 **Ivenack** Germany
99 S10 **Ivesdale** Illinois U.S.A.
17 H8 **Ivi, C** Algeria
86 B5 **Ivindo** *R* Gabon
9 F4 **Ivinghoe** England
129 H8 **Ivinheima** *R* Brazil
52 E4 **Ivinskiy Razliv, Vodokhranilishche** *res* Russian Federation
116 N2 **Ivishak** *R* Alaska U.S.A.
115 P5 **Ivittuut** Greenland
Iviza *see* **Ibiza**
95 L10 **Ivor** Virginia U.S.A.
85 C7 **Ivory Coast** *rep* W Africa
27 G15 **Ivösjön** Sweden
54 F3 **Ivot** Russian Federation
42 B3 **Ivrea** Italy
47 J5 **İvrindi** Turkey
21 N4 **Ivry-la-Bataille** France
115 M5 **Ivugivik** Quebec Canada
8 C7 **Ivybridge** England
94 F8 **Ivydale** West Virginia U.S.A.
61 O7 **Iwadeyama** Japan
61 O7 **Iwai-gawa** *R* Japan
61 P6 **Iwaizumi** Japan
61 O5 **Iwaki** *R* Japan
61 O9 **Iwaki** Japan
61 O5 **Iwaki-san** *mt* Japan
59 K5 **Iwakuni** Japan
60 P2 **Iwamizawa** Japan
70 D3 **Iwan** *R* Kalimantan
60 O3 **Iwanai** Japan
61 O7 **Iwanuma** Japan
61 O9 **Iwase** Japan
61 M9 **Iwasuge-yama** *mt* Japan
61 L11 **Iwata** Japan
61 P6 **Iwate** Japan
60 H11 **Iwaya** Japan
85 E7 **Iwo** Nigeria
Iwo Jima *see* **Iō-Jima**
140 C6 **Iwupataka** N Terr Australia
22 E3 **Iwuy** France
128 E6 **Ixiamas** Bolivia
125 K8 **Ixtaccihuatl** *vol* Mexico
125 M9 **Ixtepec, Ciudad** Mexico
124 H8 **Ixtlahuacán** Mexico
124 G7 **Ixtlán del Río** Mexico
9 G3 **Ixworth** England
56 F4 **Iya** *R* Russian Federation
55 E3 **Iyevlevo** Russian Federation
60 G12 **Iyomishima** Japan
60 F12 **Iyo-nada** *sea* Japan
56 C4 **Iyus** Russian Federation
48 J3 **Iza** *R* Romania
125 P10 **Izabal, L. de** Guatemala
17 G2 **Izalzu** Spain
116 F6 **Izaviknek** *R* Alaska U.S.A.
57 K5 **Izbaskan** Uzbekistan
31 O5 **Izbica** Poland
54 E1 **Izdeshkovo** Russian Federation
22 E2 **Izegem** Belgium
19 O14 **Izeron** France
52 H6 **Izhevsk** Russian Federation
52 H2 **Izhma** Russian Federation
53 C10 **Izmail** Ukraine
78 A2 **Izmir** Turkey
Izmit *see* **Kocaeli**
78 C1 **Izmit** Turkey
47 N11 **Izmit Körfezi** *B* Turkey
16 E7 **Iznajar** Spain
16 E7 **Iznalloz** Spain
78 B1 **Iznik** Turkey
78 B1 **Iznik Gölü** Turkey
53 F10 **Izobil'nyy** Russian Federation
128 F7 **Izozog, Bañados de** Bolivia
79 G6 **Izra'** Syria
48 E4 **Izsák** Hungary
60 C11 **Izuhara** Japan
60 D13 **Izumi** Japan
61 O7 **Izumi** Japan
60 J11 **Izumi-ōtsu** Japan
60 F10 **Izumo** Japan
61 M8 **Izumozaki** Japan
55 D3 **Izumrud** Russian Federation
55 F6 **Izumrudnyy** Kazakhstan
57 F1 **Izumrudnyy** Kazakhstan
61 N11 **Izu-shotō** *islds* Japan
50 H1 **Izvestiy Tsentral'nogo Ispolnitel'nogo Komiteta, Ostrova** *isld* Russian Federation
48 K3 **Izvoru Muntelui, Lacul** *L* Romania
57 A2 **Izyndy** Kazakhstan
54 J7 **Izyum** Ukraine

J

29 M10 **Jaala** Finland
29 L5 **Jaatila** Finland
77 E2 **Jaba** *R* Iran
80 G1 **Jabā** Syria
77 C7 **Jabal az Zannah** U.A.E.
16 E6 **Jabalón** *R* Spain
74 H7 **Jabalpur** India
22 E1 **Jabbeke** Belgium
33 R5 **Jabel** Germany
140 C2 **Jabiru** N Terr Australia
79 F3 **Jablah** Syria
46 D3 **Jablanica** Albania
46 E2 **Jablanica** *R* Serbia Yugoslavia
31 J5 **Jablonec nad Nisou** Czechoslovakia
31 K7 **Jablonica** Czechoslovakia
31 L2 **Jabłonowo** Poland
31 L6 **Jablunkov** Czechoslovakia
129 M5 **Jaboatão** Brazil
129 J8 **Jaboticabal** Brazil
69 G13 **Jabung, Tanjung** *C* Sumatra
128 F5 **Jaburu** Brazil
17 G2 **Jaca** Spain
130 B6 **Jacadigo** *L* Brazil
130 G4 **Jacaraci** Brazil
129 K6 **Jacaré** *R* Brazil
129 G5 **Jacareacanga** Brazil
130 F8 **Jacareí** Brazil
128 G5 **Jacaretinga** Brazil
130 E8 **Jacarezinho** Brazil
133 D4 **Jachal** Argentina
37 O3 **Jáchymov** Czechoslovakia
130 H5 **Jacinto** Brazil
109 M5 **Jacinto, S** *R* Texas U.S.A.
128 F5 **Jaciparaná** Brazil
120 D4 **Jackfish** Ontario Canada
118 J5 **Jackfish L** Saskatchewan Canada
117 R6 **Jackfish River** Alberta Canada
119 U7 **Jackhead Harbour** Manitoba Canada
115 N6 **Jack Lane B** Labrador, Nfld Canada
95 R1 **Jackman** Maine U.S.A.
100 E1 **Jack Mt** Washington U.S.A.
120 C3 **Jackpine** Ontario Canada
141 G3 **Jack R** Queensland Australia
112 C1 **Jacksboro** Tennessee U.S.A.
109 J2 **Jacksboro** Texas U.S.A.
94 K6 **Jacks Mt** Pennsylvania U.S.A.
141 J7 **Jackson** Queensland Australia
111 J10 **Jackson** Alabama U.S.A.
102 D3 **Jackson** California U.S.A.
112 D4 **Jackson** Georgia U.S.A.
94 D9 **Jackson** Kentucky U.S.A.
111 E11 **Jackson** Louisiana U.S.A.
111 F9 **Jackson** Mississippi U.S.A.
110 G4 **Jackson** Missouri U.S.A.
101 M4 **Jackson** Montana U.S.A.
112 K1 **Jackson** North Carolina U.S.A.
94 E7 **Jackson** Ohio U.S.A.
112 F4 **Jackson** South Carolina U.S.A.
110 H6 **Jackson** Tennessee U.S.A.
94 H8 **Jackson** *R* Virginia U.S.A.
101 P6 **Jackson** Wyoming U.S.A.
117 L10 **Jackson Bay** British Columbia Canada
144 B5 **Jackson Bay** New Zealand
145 E4 **Jackson, C** New Zealand
110 M1 **Jackson Cen** Ohio U.S.A.
106 B4 **Jackson Gulch Res** Colorado U.S.A.
113 C7 **Jackson, L** Florida U.S.A.
112 D4 **Jackson L** Georgia U.S.A.
101 P6 **Jackson L** Wyoming U.S.A.
143 C9 **Jackson, Mt** W Australia Australia
100 G8 **Jackson Mts** Nevada U.S.A.
141 F8 **Jackson Oil Field** Queensland Australia
144 A6 **Jackson Peaks** New Zealand
99 T5 **Jacksonport** Wisconsin U.S.A.
111 G9 **Jackson Prairie** Mississippi U.S.A.
106 F1 **Jackson Res** Colorado U.S.A.
144 C5 **Jacksons** New Zealand
123 Q4 **Jackson's Arm** Newfoundland Canada
111 L8 **Jacksonville** Alabama U.S.A.
110 D7 **Jacksonville** Arkansas U.S.A.
113 F7 **Jacksonville** Florida U.S.A.
99 Q10 **Jacksonville** Illinois U.S.A.
110 D2 **Jacksonville** Missouri U.S.A.
112 K3 **Jacksonville** North Carolina U.S.A.
100 C7 **Jacksonville** Oregon U.S.A.
109 M4 **Jacksonville** Texas U.S.A.
113 F7 **Jacksonville Beach** Florida U.S.A.
127 H5 **Jacmel** Haiti
124 G4 **Jaco** Mexico
74 C4 **Jacobabad** Pakistan
129 K6 **Jacobina** Brazil
103 M5 **Jacob L** Arizona U.S.A.
80 E5 **Jacob's Well** Jordan
124 H8 **Jacona** Mexico
121 T9 **Jacques Cartier** Quebec Canada
121 T5 **Jacques Cartier, L** Quebec Canada
122 G4 **Jacques Cartier, Mt** Quebec Canada
122 F6 **Jacquet R** New Brunswick Canada
130 J9 **Jacú** *R* Brazil
130 F7 **Jacuí** Minas Gerais Brazil
131 H2 **Jacuí** *R* Rio Grande do Sul Brazil
131 H2 **Jacuí** Rio Grande do Sul Brazil
129 L6 **Jacuípe** *R* Brazil
103 H9 **Jacumba** California U.S.A.
129 H4 **Jacunda** *R* Brazil
129 J4 **Jacundá** Brazil
130 F9 **Jacupiranga** Brazil
129 E4 **Jaçura** Brazil
80 G8 **Jad'a** Jordan
48 E6 **Jadar** *R* Serbia Yugoslavia
32 H6 **Jade** *R* Germany
32 H6 **Jade** Germany
85 C2 **Jadida, El** Morocco
87 E8 **Jadotville** Zaire
31 N3 **Jadów** Poland
17 F4 **Jadraque** Spain
84 E3 **Jādū** Libya
28 H5 **Jægerspris** Denmark
22 F3 **Jaeibise** Belgium
83 J10 **Ja-Ela** Sri Lanka
143 C8 **Jaellan Hill** W Australia Australia
71 E3 **Jaen** Luzon Philippines
16 E7 **Jaén** *prov* Spain
16 E7 **Jaén** Spain
27 A13 **Jaeren** *R* Norway
26 F7 **Jaevsjo** Norway
77 A2 **Ja'farābād** Iran
80 C5 **Jaffa** Israel
138 E6 **Jaffa, C** South Australia Australia
83 K8 **Jaffna** Sri Lanka
75 K9 **Jagdalpur** India
75 J5 **Jagdishpur** India
87 E11 **Jagersfontein** S Africa
84 G4 **Jaghbūb, Al** Libya
116 Q2 **Jago** *R* Alaska U.S.A.
36 H5 **Jagst** *R* Germany
37 J5 **Jagstzell** Germany
74 H9 **Jagtial** India
129 K6 **Jaguaquara** Brazil
131 H4 **Jaguarão** Brazil
131 G2 **Jaguari** *R* Brazil
129 H8 **Jaguariaiva** Brazil
129 L5 **Jaguaribe** *R* Brazil
131 C2 **Jagüe, R** Argentina
126 D3 **Jagüey Grande** Cuba
140 B1 **Jahleel, Pt** N Terr Australia
78 K7 **Jahmah** Iraq
48 E7 **Jahorina** *mt* Bosnia-Herzegovina
77 C5 **Jahrom** Iran
74 G3 **Jaijon** India
75 P6 **Jaintia Hills** India
74 F5 **Jaipur** India
74 D5 **Jaisalmer** India
42 H4 **Jajce** Bosnia-Herzegovina
75 M8 **Jajpur** India
63 **Jakarta** *conurbation* Indonesia
70 L9 **Jakarta** Java
84 G4 **Jakharrah** Libya
26 J5 **Jäkkvik** Sweden
71 N9 **Jako** *isld* Timor
26 S2 **Jakobselv** *R* Norway/Rus Fed
115 O4 **Jakobshavn** Greenland
29 K8 **Jakobstad** Finland
46 E3 **Jakupica** Macedonia Yugoslavia
106 G9 **Jal** New Mexico U.S.A.
77 H6 **Jāla** Iran
58 G2 **Jalai Nur** China
77 L2 **Jalalabad** Afghanistan
74 F3 **Jalandhar** India
125 L3 **Jalapa** Nicaragua
125 L8 **Jalapa Enriquez** Mexico
29 K9 **Jalasjärvi** Finland
74 H5 **Jalaun** India
140 C2 **Jalboi** *R* N Terr Australia
130 E7 **Jales** Brazil
75 M8 **Jaleshwar** India
74 F8 **Jalgaon** India
22 K3 **Jalhay** Belgium
78 L6 **Jalibah** Iraq
86 B4 **Jalingo** Nigeria
124 G8 **Jalisco** *state* Mexico
21 J7 **Jallais** France
74 F9 **Jalna** India
17 F3 **Jalón** *R* Spain
Jalo Oasis *see* **Jālu**
74 E6 **Jalor** India
124 H7 **Jalostotitlán** Mexico
124 H7 **Jalpa** Mexico
75 N5 **Jalpaiguri** India
124 K7 **Jalpan** Mexico
77 L2 **Jalrez** Afghanistan
84 G4 **Jālu** Libya

Jālu — Junction B
187

84 G4 **Jālu** *oilfield* Libya
78 K4 **Jalūlā** Iraq
84 G4 **Jālu, Waḩat** *oasis* Libya
77 G2 **Jam** *reg* Iran
128 B4 **Jama** Ecuador
86 H5 **Jamaame** Somalia
126 G4 **Jamaica** Cuba
95 P3 **Jamaica** Vermont U.S.A.
127 K2 **Jamaica** W Indies
126 G5 **Jamaica Chan** Caribbean
27 M13 **Jämaja** Estonia
75 N6 **Jamalpur** Bangladesh
75 M6 **Jamalpur** India
126 A2 **Jamanota** *hill* Aruba W Indies
129 G5 **Jamanxim** *R* Brazil
128 F5 **Jamari** Brazil
66 C2 **Jamati** China
139 K5 **Jamberoo** New South Wales Australia
69 F13 **Jambi** Sumatra
141 K6 **Jambin** Queensland Australia
69 C10 **Jamboaye** *R* Sumatra
70 E1 **Jambongan** *isld* Sabah
122 F4 **Jambon, Pte** Quebec Canada
70 E5 **Jambu** Kalimantan
69 C10 **Jambuair, Tanjung** *C* Sumatra
110 C5 **James** *R* Missouri U.S.A.
98 H3 **James** *R* North Dakota U.S.A.
98 J6 **James** *R* South Dakota U.S.A.
115 L7 **James B** Canada
95 N6 **Jamesburg** New Jersey U.S.A.
112 K2 **James City** North Carolina U.S.A.
94 J5 **James City** Pennsylvania U.S.A.
112 F2 **James, L** North Carolina U.S.A.
99 N9 **Jameson** Missouri U.S.A.
115 R3 **Jameson Land** Greenland
143 G7 **Jameson Ra** W Australia Australia
99 N10 **Jamesport** Missouri U.S.A.
113 L12 **James Pt** Bahamas
140 D5 **James R** N Terr Australia
95 L9 **James R** Virginia U.S.A.
140 C6 **James Ranges** N Terr Australia
146 D4 **James Ross I** Antarctica
115 K4 **James Ross Str** Northwest Territories Canada
138 E5 **Jamestown** South Australia Australia
90 A13 **Jamestown** St Helena
110 K2 **Jamestown** Indiana U.S.A.
107 N2 **Jamestown** Kansas U.S.A.
94 B4 **Jamestown** Michigan U.S.A.
94 H4 **Jamestown** New York U.S.A.
98 H3 **Jamestown** North Dakota U.S.A.
94 D7 **Jamestown** Ohio U.S.A.
94 G5 **Jamestown** Pennsylvania U.S.A.
95 Q5 **Jamestown** Rhode I U.S.A.
112 H4 **Jamestown** South Carolina U.S.A.
94 C10 **Jamestown** Tennessee U.S.A.
95 L9 **Jamestown Nat. Hist. Site** Virginia U.S.A.
95 L4 **Jamesville** New York U.S.A.
112 L2 **Jamesville** North Carolina U.S.A.
22 J5 **Jametz** France
139 H6 **Jamieson** Victoria Australia
100 H5 **Jamieson** Oregon U.S.A.
29 K10 **Jämijärvi** Finland
125 L9 **Jamilzepec** Mexico
98 G7 **Jamison** Nebraska U.S.A.
76 B2 **Jamkhandi** India
74 F9 **Jamkhed** India
76 D3 **Jammalamadugu** India
28 C2 **Jammerbugt** *B* Denmark
28 F5 **Jammerland Bugt** *B* Denmark
74 F2 **Jammu** Kashmir
Jammu and Kashmir *see* **Kashmir**
74 G1 **Jammu and Kashmir** *prov* India/Pakistan
74 D7 **Jamnagar** India
31 J1 **Jamno, Jezioro** *L* Poland
22 J4 **Jamoigne** Belgium
71 K8 **Jampea** Indonesia
74 D4 **Jampur** Pakistan
29 L10 **Jämsä** Finland
29 L10 **Jämsänkoski** Finland
75 M7 **Jamshedpur** India
26 F8 **Jämtland** Sweden
26 H8 **Jämtl Sikås** Sweden
71 C3 **Jamtup, Tg** *C* W Irian
70 E3 **Jamuk, G** *mt* Kalimantan
102 H9 **Jamul** California U.S.A.
75 N6 **Jamuna** *R* Bangladesh
128 C3 **Jamundi** Colombia
75 M5 **Janakpur** Nepal
129 K7 **Janaúba** Brazil
129 H3 **Janaucu, I** Brazil
130 E5 **Jandaia** Brazil
142 B3 **Jandakot** *dist* Perth, W Aust Australia
142 B3 **Jandakot, L** W Australia Australia
77 D2 **Jandaq** Iran
28 A5 **Janderup** Denmark
128 E5 **Jandiatuba** *R* Brazil
141 K7 **Jandowae** Queensland Australia
94 G7 **Jane Lew** West Virginia U.S.A.
144 B6 **Jane Pk** New Zealand
100 E9 **Janesville** California U.S.A.
99 O7 **Janesville** Iowa U.S.A.
99 N5 **Janesville** Minnesota U.S.A.
99 R7 **Janesville** Wisconsin U.S.A.
130 D10 **Jangada** Brazil
130 C7 **Jango** Brazil
69 G13 **Jang, Tanjung** *C* Indonesia
33 S8 **Jänickendorf** Germany
46 E2 **Janjevo** Serbia Yugoslavia
89 D6 **Jan Kemp** S Africa
119 P4 **Jan L** Saskatchewan Canada
90 H1 **Jan Mayen** *isld* Arctic Oc
77 G2 **Jannatabad** Iran
124 E2 **Janos** Mexico
48 E4 **Jánoshalma** Hungary
48 D3 **Jánosháza** Hungary
37 P5 **Janovice nad Uhlavou** Czechoslovakia
33 S5 **Janow** Germany
31 K3 **Janowiec** Poland
31 N5 **Janów Lubelski** Poland
31 O3 **Janów Podlaski** Poland
119 N7 **Jansen** Saskatchewan Canada
98 K9 **Jansen** Nebraska U.S.A.
130 G4 **Januária** Brazil
21 O5 **Janville** France
20 H6 **Janzé** France
130 G5 **Jaoquim Felício** Brazil
74 F7 **Jaora** India
61 **Japan** *empire* E Asia
59 K3 **Japan, Sea of** E Asia
29 N9 **Jäppilä** Finland
128 E4 **Japurá** Brazil
127 J5 **Jarabacoa** Dominican Rep
78 F3 **Jarābulus** Syria
129 J7 **Jaraguá** Brazil
130 E10 **Jaraguá do Sul** Brazil
130 C7 **Jaraguari** Brazil
130 E10 **Jaraguá Serra** *mts* Brazil
16 D5 **Jaraicejo** Spain
16 E4 **Jarama** *R* Spain
133 D7 **Jaramillo** Argentina
16 D4 **Jarandilla** Spain
129 H4 **Jarauçu** *R* Brazil
100 K7 **Jarbidge** *R* Idaho U.S.A.
100 K8 **Jarbidge** Nevada U.S.A.
27 J11 **Järbo** Sweden
130 G9 **Jardim** Ceará Brazil
130 C7 **Jardim** Mato Grosso Brazil
130 H9 **Jardim do Seridó** Brazil
141 F1 **Jardine** *R* Queensland Australia
122 E6 **Jardine Brook** New Brunswick Canada
141 G1 **Jardine River Nat. Park** Queensland Australia
126 E4 **Jardines de la Reina, Arch. de las** *islds* Cuba
130 E6 **Jardinésia** Brazil
130 F7 **Jardinópolis** Brazil
27 H14 **Järeda** Sweden
27 E11 **Jaren** Norway
38 N8 **Jarenina** Slovenia
58 G2 **Jargalant** Mongolia
21 P6 **Jargeau** France
129 H3 **Jari** *R* Brazil
128 F4 **Jari, L** Brazil
33 S5 **Jarmen** Germany
27 J12 **Järna** Sweden
18 E7 **Jarnac** France
27 H13 **Järnlunden** *L* Sweden
71 F5 **Jaro** Panay Philippines
31 K4 **Jarocin** Poland
31 J5 **Jaroměř** Czechoslovakia
31 J6 **Jaroměřice** Czechoslovakia
126 F4 **Jaronu** Cuba
31 O5 **Jaroslaw** Poland
106 E4 **Jaroso** Colorado U.S.A.
26 F8 **Järpen** Sweden
80 F8 **Jarra** *R* Jordan
94 K10 **Jarratt** Virginia U.S.A.
26 K5 **Jarre** *mt* Sweden
109 K5 **Jarrell** Texas U.S.A.
68 F3 **Jarres, Plaine des** Laos
118 F6 **Jarrow** Alberta Canada
13 G4 **Jarrow** England
128 F6 **Jaru** Brazil
65 E2 **Jarud Qi** China
52 C5 **Järva-Jaani** Estonia
118 D4 **Jarvie** Alberta Canada
134 B3 **Jarvis I** Pacific Oc
26 H10 **Järvsö** Sweden
21 K6 **Jarzé** France
48 F5 **Jaša Tomic** Serbia Yugoslavia
74 D7 **Jasdan** India
33 T8 **Jasdorf** Germany
85 E7 **Jasikan** Ghana
77 E7 **Jāsk** Iran
31 N6 **Jasło** Poland
119 O7 **Jasmin** Saskatchewan Canada
30 H1 **Jasmund** *pen* Germany
133 E8 **Jason Is** Falkland Is
146 D4 **Jason Pen** Antarctica
110 J2 **Jasonville** Indiana U.S.A.
117 O9 **Jasper** Alberta Canada
121 P8 **Jasper** Ontario Canada
111 J8 **Jasper** Alabama U.S.A.
110 C5 **Jasper** Arkansas U.S.A.
106 D4 **Jasper** Colorado U.S.A.
113 E7 **Jasper** Florida U.S.A.
111 M7 **Jasper** Georgia U.S.A.
110 K3 **Jasper** Indiana U.S.A.
94 C5 **Jasper** Michigan U.S.A.
98 K6 **Jasper** Minnesota U.S.A.
110 B4 **Jasper** Missouri U.S.A.
94 K4 **Jasper** New York U.S.A.
112 B2 **Jasper** Tennessee U.S.A.
111 C11 **Jasper** Texas U.S.A.
117 O9 **Jasper Nat. Park** Alberta Canada
78 K5 **Jassan** Iraq
Jassy *see* **Iasi**
31 L1 **Jastarnia** Poland
46 E1 **Jastrebac** *mt* Serbia Yugoslavia
31 K2 **Jastrowie** Poland
48 F3 **Jászapáti** Hungary
48 F3 **Jászarokszállás** Hungary
48 F3 **Jászberény** Hungary
48 F3 **Jászfényszaru** Hungary
48 F3 **Jászladány** Hungary
129 H7 **Jataí** Brazil
128 G4 **Jatapu** *R* Brazil
76 B2 **Jath** India
70 M9 **Jatibarang** Java
126 E4 **Jatibonico** Cuba
17 G6 **Játiva** Spain
129 H4 **Jatobá** Brazil
80 D4 **Jatt** Israel
128 F5 **Jatuarana** Brazil
33 T5 **Jatzke** Germany
33 T5 **Jatznick** Germany
128 F4 **Jaú** *R* Brazil
129 J8 **Jaú** Brazil
128 F3 **Jauaperi** *R* Brazil
22 H2 **Jauche** Belgium
126 G4 **Jauco** Cuba
20 D4 **Jaudy** *R* France
128 C6 **Jauja** Peru
21 L8 **Jaulnay** France
128 G5 **Jauna** *R* Brazil
21 L8 **Jaunay Clan** France
52 B6 **Jaunjelgava** Latvia
52 C6 **Jaunpiebalga** Latvia
75 K6 **Jaunpur** India
38 L8 **Jauntal** *V* Austria
129 G7 **Jauru** *R* Brazil
130 D6 **Jauru, R** Brazil
22 D5 **Jaux** France
Java *isld see* **Jawa**
76 D4 **Javadi Hills** India
129 J6 **Javaés, Serra dos** *mts* Brazil
17 G4 **Javalambre, Sierra de** *mts* Spain
128 D4 **Javari** *R* Brazil/Peru
70 M8 **Java Sea** Indonesia
136 D4 **Java Trench** Indian Oc
17 H6 **Jávea** Spain
Javhlant *see* **Uliastay**
133 C7 **Javier** *B* Chile
48 E6 **Javor** *mts* Bosnia-Herzegovina
48 E2 **Javoria** *mt* Czechoslovakia
38 K9 **Javornik** Slovenia
48 E1 **Javorniky** *mt* Czechoslovakia
26 M6 **Jävre** Sweden
21 K5 **Javron-les-Chapelles** France
70 **Jawa** *isld* Indonesia
80 G6 **Jawa** Jordan
79 H2 **Jawbān Bayk** Syria
86 J5 **Jawhar** Somalia
31 J4 **Jawor** Poland
31 L5 **Jaworzno** Poland
107 Q5 **Jay** Oklahoma U.S.A.
75 N5 **Jayanti** India
136 H2 **Jaya Pk** *mt* W Irian
136 J2 **Jayapura** W Irian
98 B7 **Jay Em** Wyoming U.S.A.
33 P7 **Jayenitz** Germany
75 K9 **Jaypur** India
79 G5 **Jayrūd** Syria
9 H4 **Jaywick Sands** England
78 H4 **Jazirah, Al** Iraq
124 J5 **Jazminal** Mexico
77 F6 **Jaz Murian, Hamun-e** *L* Iran
79 F4 **Jbail** Lebanon
79 F4 **Jdaidet Ghazir** Lebanon
85 B3 **Jdiriya** Western Sahara
103 J6 **Jean** Nevada U.S.A.
109 J2 **Jean** Texas U.S.A.
111 E12 **Jeanerette** Louisiana U.S.A.
122 E1 **Jean L** Quebec Canada
111 G12 **Jean Lafitte Nat. Hist. Park** Louisiana U.S.A.
117 N5 **Jean Marie River** Northwest Territories Canada
6 M6 **Jeanne** *oil rig* North Sea
94 H6 **Jeannette** Pennsylvania U.S.A.
127 H5 **Jean Rabel** Haiti
13 G5 **Jeater Houses** England
77 F5 **Jebāl Bārez, Kūh-e** *mts* Iran
85 E7 **Jebba** Nigeria
80 F1 **Jebel** Lebanon
86 E2 **Jebel Abyad Plateau** Sudan
16 D9 **Jebha** Morocco
28 B3 **Jebjerg** Denmark
88 E8 **Jeci** *mt* Mozambique
119 P7 **Jedburgh** Saskatchewan Canada
13 F2 **Jedburgh** Scotland
Jedda *see* **Jiddah**
94 E3 **Jeddo** Michigan U.S.A.
43 C12 **Jedeida** Tunisia
13 F3 **Jedfoot Br** Scotland
31 M5 **Jędrzejów** Poland
31 N2 **Jedwabne** Poland
117 H9 **Jedway** British Columbia Canada
29 M4 **Jeesiö** Finland
33 O6 **Jeetze** *R* Germany
33 O7 **Jeetze** Germany
99 L5 **Jeffers** Minnesota U.S.A.
106 E2 **Jefferson** Colorado U.S.A.
112 D3 **Jefferson** Georgia U.S.A.
94 K7 **Jefferson** Maryland U.S.A.
94 G5 **Jefferson** Ohio U.S.A.
107 N5 **Jefferson** Oklahoma U.S.A.
100 C5 **Jefferson** Oregon U.S.A.
98 K7 **Jefferson** South Dakota U.S.A.
111 B9 **Jefferson** Texas U.S.A.
99 S6 **Jefferson** Wisconsin U.S.A.
110 D3 **Jefferson City** Missouri U.S.A.
101 N3 **Jefferson City** Montana U.S.A.
112 D1 **Jefferson City** Tennessee U.S.A.
101 O4 **Jefferson Island** Montana U.S.A.
100 D5 **Jefferson, Mt** Oregon U.S.A.
94 B8 **Jeffersontown** Kentucky U.S.A.
110 L3 **Jeffersontown** Kentucky U.S.A.
112 D5 **Jeffersonville** Georgia U.S.A.
94 B8 **Jeffersonville** Indiana U.S.A.
95 N5 **Jeffersonville** New York U.S.A.
94 D7 **Jeffersonville** Ohio U.S.A.
95 P2 **Jeffersonville** Vermont U.S.A.
101 S7 **Jeffrey City** Wyoming U.S.A.
71 C3 **Jef Lio** W Irian
85 E6 **Jega** Nigeria
28 B3 **Jegindø** *isld* Denmark
18 F9 **Jegun** France
77 G4 **Jehīle Pūzak** *L* Iran
28 B7 **Jejsing** Denmark
130 C9 **Jejui Guazú, R** Paraguay
52 C6 **Jēkabpils** Latvia
112 F6 **Jekyll I** Georgia U.S.A.
86 H4 **Jeldēsa** Ethiopia
31 J5 **Jelenia Góra** Poland
52 B6 **Jelgava** Latvia
120 C3 **Jellicoe** Ontario Canada
28 C5 **Jelling** Denmark
102 B1 **Jelly** California U.S.A.
31 L5 **Jeľowa** Poland
27 E12 **Jelöy** *isld* Norway
28 C6 **Jels** Denmark
27 B12 **Jelsa** Norway
48 F2 **Jelšava** Czechoslovakia
69 G11 **Jemaja** Indonesia
22 F3 **Jemappes** Belgium
70 O10 **Jember** Java
33 N8 **Jembke** Germany
85 G1 **Jem, El** Tunisia
22 J3 **Jemelle** Belgium
106 D6 **Jemez** *R* New Mexico U.S.A.
106 D6 **Jemez Pueblo** New Mexico U.S.A.
106 D6 **Jemez Springs** New Mexico U.S.A.
32 F6 **Jemgum** Germany
43 D13 **Jemmel** Tunisia
31 J6 **Jemnice** Czechoslovakia
70 E5 **Jempang, Danao** *L* Kalimantan
122 F8 **Jemseg** New Brunswick Canada
37 M2 **Jena** Germany
111 D10 **Jena** Louisiana U.S.A.
38 E7 **Jenbach** Austria
80 E4 **Jenin** Jordan
94 F9 **Jenkinjones** West Virginia U.S.A.
94 E9 **Jenkins** Kentucky U.S.A.
99 M3 **Jenkins** Minnesota U.S.A.
140 A7 **Jenkins,Mt** N Terr Australia
118 F8 **Jenner** Alberta Canada
102 A3 **Jenner** California U.S.A.
117 H6 **Jennings** *R* British Columbia Canada
113 D7 **Jennings** Florida U.S.A.
107 K2 **Jennings** Kansas U.S.A.
111 D11 **Jennings** Louisiana U.S.A.
107 O5 **Jennings** Oklahoma U.S.A.
127 O4 **Jennings** Antigua W Indies
114 J4 **Jenny Lind I** Northwest Territories Canada
139 K5 **Jenolan Caves** New South Wales Australia
101 Q9 **Jensen** Utah U.S.A.
113 G10 **Jensen Beach** Florida U.S.A.
115 P5 **Jensen Nunatakker** *pk* Greenland
115 L4 **Jens Munk I** Northwest Territories Canada
70 N9 **Jepara** Java
138 F6 **Jeparit** Victoria Australia
29 K8 **Jeppo** Finland
129 K6 **Jequie** Brazil
130 G5 **Jequitai** Brazil
129 K7 **Jequitinhonha** Brazil
85 D2 **Jerada** Morocco
69 F11 **Jerantut** Malaysia
85 G2 **Jerba, I de** Tunisia
126 G5 **Jérémie** Haiti
129 L6 **Jeremoabo** Brazil
71 H9 **Jerewan** Indonesia
124 H6 **Jerez de García Salinas** Mexico
16 C8 **Jerez de la Frontera** Spain
16 C6 **Jerez de los Caballeros** Spain
141 H6 **Jericho** Queensland Australia
80 E6 **Jericho** Jordan
33 Q8 **Jerichow** Germany
129 K4 **Jericoaquara, Pta** *C* Brazil
69 G14 **Jerigi** Sumatra
26 N5 **Jerijärvi** Sweden
70 B3 **Jerijih, Tanjong** *C* Sarawak
139 H6 **Jerilderie** New South Wales Australia
29 L4 **Jerisjärvi** *L* Finland
130 E4 **Jeroaquara** Brazil
120 H5 **Jerome** Ontario Canada
103 M7 **Jerome** Arizona U.S.A.
101 L7 **Jerome** Idaho U.S.A.
129 H7 **Jerônimo, Serra do** *mts* Brazil
143 C10 **Jerramungup** W Australia Australia
20 F3 **Jersey** *isld* Channel Is
95 N6 **Jersey City** New Jersey U.S.A.
95 K5 **Jersey Shore** Pennsylvania U.S.A.
110 F2 **Jerseyville** Illinois U.S.A.
28 E2 **Jerslev** Denmark
28 C6 **Jerstal** Denmark
16 D4 **Jerte** *R* Spain
70 D2 **Jerudong** Brunei
129 K5 **Jerumenha** Brazil
28 E1 **Jerup** Denmark
80 D6 **Jerusalem** Israel
145 E3 **Jerusalem** New Zealand
140 D6 **Jervais Ra** N Terr Australia
139 K6 **Jervis Bay** New South Wales Australia
138 E6 **Jervis, C** South Australia Australia
117 M10 **Jervis Inlet** British Columbia Canada
140 D6 **Jervois Ra** N Terr Australia
33 N8 **Jerxheim** Germany
36 G2 **Jesberg** Germany
37 P3 **Jesenice** Czechoslovakia
42 F2 **Jesenice** Slovenia
31 K5 **Jeseník** Czechoslovakia
48 F2 **Jesenské** Czechoslovakia
33 Q8 **Jeserig** Germany
33 R10 **Jesewitz** Germany
Jesselton *see* **Kota Kinabalu**
27 E11 **Jessheim** Norway
98 H2 **Jessie** North Dakota U.S.A.
33 Q9 **Jessnitz** Germany
113 F9 **Jessup, L** Florida U.S.A.
32 L6 **Jesteburg** Germany
112 F6 **Jesup** Georgia U.S.A.
99 O7 **Jesup** Iowa U.S.A.
133 E4 **Jesús María** Argentina
124 H7 **Jesús María** Mexico
126 F4 **Jesús Mendéndez** Cuba
107 M5 **Jet** Oklahoma U.S.A.
119 Q2 **Jetait** Manitoba Canada
94 J9 **Jetersville** Virginia U.S.A.
20 F3 **Jethou** *isld* Channel Is
107 L3 **Jetmore** Kansas U.S.A.
37 J7 **Jettingen** Germany
37 L7 **Jetzendorf** Germany
22 G3 **Jeumont** France
32 L4 **Jevenau** *R* Germany
32 L4 **Jevenstedt** Germany
32 G5 **Jever** Germany
48 D1 **Jevičko** Czechoslovakia
27 D11 **Jevnaker** Norway
98 C6 **Jewel Cave Nat. Mon** South Dakota U.S.A.
99 N7 **Jewell** Iowa U.S.A.
107 M2 **Jewell** Kansas U.S.A.
100 B4 **Jewell** Oregon U.S.A.
110 H2 **Jewett** Illinois U.S.A.
94 G6 **Jewett** Ohio U.S.A.
109 L4 **Jewett** Texas U.S.A.
95 Q5 **Jewett City** Connecticut U.S.A.
46 D2 **Jezerce** *mt* Albania
37 P5 **Jezerni** *mt* Czechoslovakia
42 H4 **Jezero** Bosnia-Herzegovina
31 M2 **Jeziorak, Jezioro** *L* Poland
31 M2 **Jeziorany** Poland
31 L4 **Jeziorsko, Jezioro** *res* Poland
31 P1 **Jeznas** Lithuania
31 M4 **Jeżów** Poland
79 F5 **Jezzine** Lebanon
74 F7 **Jhabua** India
74 G4 **Jhajjar** India
74 G6 **Jhalawar** India
74 E3 **Jhang Maghiana** Pakistan
74 H6 **Jhansi** India
75 M5 **Jhapa** Nepal
74 E2 **Jhelum** India
74 E2 **Jhelum** *R* Pakistan
74 F4 **Jhunjhunūn** India
65 E3 **Jiade He** *R* China
67 G1 **Jiading** China
67 C4 **Jiagui** China
67 D4 **Jiahe** China
Jiaji *see* **Qionghai**
67 A2 **Jiajiang** China
58 E5 **Jialing Jiang** *R* China
59 K2 **Jiamusi** China
65 H1 **Jiamusi** China
65 G4 **Ji'an** China
67 E3 **Ji'an** China
65 D4 **Jianchang** China
65 F4 **Jianchang** China
67 F2 **Jiande** China
67 B2 **Jiang'an** China
67 B2 **Jiangbei** China
68 E1 **Jiangcheng** China
67 C3 **Jiangdong** China
67 F1 **Jiangdu** China
67 C6 **Jianghong** China
67 D4 **Jianghua** China
67 B2 **Jiangjin** China
Jiangkou *see* **Fengkai**
67 D1 **Jiangkou** China
67 C3 **Jiangkou** China
67 F3 **Jiangle** China
67 D1 **Jiangling** China
67 D5 **Jiangmen** China
67 F1 **Jiangpu** China
67 F2 **Jiangshan** China
58 G5 **Jiangsu** *prov* China
67 E3 **Jiangxi** *prov* China
65 B7 **Jiang Xian** China
67 F1 **Jiangxiang** China
67 G1 **Jiangyin** China
67 D4 **Jiangyong** China
67 A1 **Jiangyou** China
67 C3 **Jianhe** China
67 D2 **Jianli** China
67 E3 **Jianning** China
67 F3 **Jian'ou** China
65 D4 **Jianping** China
65 D5 **Jianping** China
67 C1 **Jianshi** China
67 A5 **Jianshui** China
58 D5 **Jianyang** China
67 F3 **Jianyang** China
65 B6 **Jiaocheng** China
59 J3 **Jiaohe** China
65 B6 **Jiaokou** China
67 E4 **Jiaoling** China
65 E7 **Jiaonan** China
65 D6 **Jiao Xian** China
58 F4 **Jiaozuo** China
65 G3 **Jiapigou** China
58 G5 **Jiashan** China
67 G1 **Jiashan** China
57 H5 **Jiashi** China
65 D7 **Jiawang** China
65 A5 **Jia Xian** China
65 B7 **Jia Xian** China
59 H5 **Jiaxing** China
67 C4 **Jiaya** China
59 K2 **Jiayin** China
67 D2 **Jiayu** China
58 C4 **Jiayuguan** China
65 E7 **Jiazohou Wan** *B* China
77 B7 **Jiban, Al** Saudi Arabia
129 J7 **Jibao, Serra do** *mts* Brazil
88 G6 **Jibondo** *isld* Tanzania
48 H3 **Jibou** Romania
67 B3 **Jichang** China
31 J5 **Jičín** Czechoslovakia
86 G1 **Jiddah** Saudi Arabia
65 H2 **Jidong** China
Jiehu *see* **Yinan**
26 L2 **Jiekkevarre** *mt* Norway
67 E5 **Jieshi** China
67 E5 **Jieshi Wan** *B* China
26 O2 **Jiesjavrre** *L* Norway
67 E5 **Jiexi** China
65 B6 **Jiexiu** China
143 D6 **Jiggalong** W Australia Australia
100 K9 **Jiggs** Nevada U.S.A.
67 E1 **Jigong Shan** *mt* China
79 H4 **Jihar, Wādī el** *watercourse* Syria
31 J6 **Jihlava** Czechoslovakia
31 H6 **Jihočesky** *reg* Czechoslovakia
31 J6 **Jihomoravský** *reg* Czechoslovakia
85 F1 **Jijel** Algeria
48 L3 **Jijia** *R* Romania
86 H4 **Jijiga** Ethiopia
80 G3 **Jijjin** Jordan
17 G6 **Jijona** Spain
48 K6 **Jilava** Romania
86 H5 **Jilib** Somalia
59 H2 **Jilin** *prov* China
65 G3 **Jilin** China
65 F3 **Jilin Hada Ling** *mt ra* China
59 H1 **Jiliu He** *R* China
17 G4 **Jiloca** *R* Spain
116 M3 **Jim** *R* Alaska U.S.A.
86 G4 **Jima** Ethiopia
69 G14 **Jimar** Sumatra
142 F5 **Jimberingga** W Australia Australia
48 F5 **Jimbolia** Romania
141 L8 **Jimboomba** Queensland Australia
16 D8 **Jimena de la Frontera** Spain
124 G4 **Jiménez** Mexico
140 C2 **Jim Jim Cr** N Terr Australia
65 E6 **Jimo** China
65 C6 **Jinan** China
65 B7 **Jincheng** China
139 J6 **Jindabyne** New South Wales Australia
37 O3 **Jindřichovice** Czechoslovakia
31 J6 **Jindřichův Hradec** Czechoslovakia
67 E2 **Jing'an** China
67 F1 **Jingde** China
67 F2 **Jingdezhen** China
Jingfeng *see* **Hexigten Qi**
65 D5 **Jinghai** China
65 E6 **Jinghaiwei** China
58 E5 **Jing He** *R* China
66 C3 **Jinghe** China
68 E2 **Jinghong** China
67 G1 **Jingjiang** China
65 B5 **Jingle** China
67 D1 **Jingmen** China
Jingping *see* **Pinglu**
65 G2 **Jingpo** China
65 G3 **Jingpo Hu** *L* China
58 F5 **Jing Shan** *mt ra* China
67 D1 **Jingshan** China
58 D4 **Jingtai** China
65 C6 **Jing Xian** China
67 F1 **Jing Xian** China
59 H2 **Jingxing** China
67 A2 **Jingyan** China
65 A7 **Jingyang** China
65 G3 **Jingyu** China
58 D4 **Jingyuan** China
Jingzhou *see* **Jiangling**
67 F2 **Jinhua** China
65 C7 **Jining** China
65 B4 **Jining** Nei Monggol Zizhiqu China
88 D1 **Jinja-Bugembe** Uganda
67 E2 **Jin Jiang** *R* China
67 C3 **Jin Jiang** *R* China
67 F4 **Jinjiang** China
67 D2 **Jinjing** China
65 E6 **Jinkou** China
67 E1 **Jinkou** China
67 F4 **Jinlong Jiang** *R* China
67 C7 **Jinmu Jiao** China
68 J3 **Jinmu Jiao** *C* China
125 M3 **Jinotega** Nicaragua
125 L4 **Jinotepe** Nicaragua
67 C3 **Jinping** China
68 F1 **Jinping** China
Jinsha *see* **Nantong**
67 B3 **Jinsha** China
58 C6 **Jinsha Jiang** *R* China
Jinshan *see* **Harqin Qi**
67 G1 **Jinshan** China
67 D2 **Jinshi** China
67 F1 **Jintan** China
67 A1 **Jintang** China
67 C5 **Jintian Shuiku** *res* China
71 F5 **Jintotolo** *isld* Philippines
71 F5 **Jintotolo Ch** Philippines
59 H3 **Jinxi** China
67 E3 **Jinxi** China
67 F3 **Jin Xi** China
67 B5 **Jinxi** China
65 E4 **Jin Xian** China
65 C5 **Jin Xian** China
65 E5 **Jin Xian** China
67 E2 **Jinxian** China
65 C7 **Jinxiang** China
67 G3 **Jinxiang** China
67 C4 **Jinxiu** China
67 G2 **Jinyun** China
67 E1 **Jinzhai** China
65 E4 **Jinzhou** China
65 E5 **Jinzhou Wan** *B* China
128 B4 **Jipijapa** Ecuador
126 F4 **Jiquaní** Cuba
130 H5 **Jiquitaia** Brazil
77 C7 **Jirāb, Al** *isld* U.A.E.
143 F9 **Jirina Rockholes** *rockhole* W Australia Australia
65 D2 **Jirin Gol** China
37 P3 **Jirkov** Czechoslovakia
48 L5 **Jirlău** Romania
86 A2 **Jirriiban** Somalia
65 A7 **Jishan** China
67 C2 **Jishou** China
67 E3 **Jishui** China
79 G3 **Jisr ash Shughūr** Syria
16 C2 **Jistredo, Sa. de** *mts* Spain
143 C10 **Jitarning** W Australia Australia
Jitian *see* **Lianshan**
69 E9 **Jitra** Malaysia
48 H6 **Jiu** *R* Romania
Jiucheng *see* **Wucheng**
67 A1 **Jiuding Shan** *mt* China
58 G6 **Jiujiang** China
67 E2 **Jiujiang** China
67 D1 **Jiukou** China
67 E4 **Jiulian Shan** *mts* China
67 E2 **Jiuling Shan** *mt ra* China
58 C4 **Jiuquan** China
65 E6 **Jiurongcheng** China
59 J3 **Jiutai** China
67 C4 **Jiuwan Dashan** *mts* China
65 C5 **Jiuwuqing** China
65 C5 **Jiuxincheng** China
67 B4 **Jiuxu** China
67 F1 **Jiuyuhang** China
67 B4 **Jiuzhou** China
77 G7 **Jiwani** Iran
74 B10 **Jiwani** Pakistan
65 H2 **Jixi** China
67 F1 **Jixi** China
59 K2 **Jixian** China
65 D4 **Ji Xian** China
65 A6 **Ji Xian** China
65 C6 **Ji Xian** China
65 C7 **Ji Xian** China
65 D6 **Jiyang** China
65 B7 **Jiyuan** China
79 F7 **Jiza** Jordan
80 G7 **Jiza** Jordan
65 C6 **Jize** China
31 H5 **Jizera** *R* Czechoslovakia
60 G10 **Jizō zaki** *C* Japan
86 E1 **J. Kissu** *mt* Sudan
120 G1 **Joab L** Ontario Canada
130 D10 **Joaçaba** Brazil
33 T7 **Joachimsthal** Germany
130 H5 **Joaíma** Brazil
85 A6 **Joal-Fadiout** Senegal
129 L5 **Joao Camara** Brazil
129 J4 **João Coelho** Brazil
131 H4 **João Maria, Albardão do** Brazil
130 E10 **João Paulo** *R* Brazil
130 J9 **João Pessoa** Brazil
130 F5 **João Pinheiro** Brazil
111 B10 **Joaquin** Texas U.S.A.
126 F4 **Jobabo** Cuba
61 O9 **Jōban** Japan
71 G6 **Jobo Pt** Mindanao Philippines
20 G2 **Jobourg** France
102 F2 **Job Pk** Nevada U.S.A.
120 D2 **Jobrin** Ontario Canada
38 F7 **Jochberg** Austria
16 E7 **Jódar** Spain
74 E5 **Jodhpur** India
74 D7 **Jodiya Bandar** India
22 H2 **Jodoigne** Belgium
123 S4 **Joe Batt's Arm** Newfoundland Canada
29 O9 **Joensuu** Finland
106 H2 **Joes** Colorado U.S.A.
26 G6 **Joeström** Sweden
61 M8 **Jōetsu** Japan
87 F10 **Jofane** Mozambique
106 E7 **Joffre** New Mexico U.S.A.
117 Q10 **Joffre, Mt** British Columbia Canada
61 L9 **Joganji** *R* Japan
75 M5 **Jogbani** India
65 C3 **Jogdor** China
52 C5 **Jõgeva** Estonia
122 H8 **Joggins** Nova Scotia Canada
74 G3 **Jogindarnagar** India
120 E2 **Jog L** Ontario Canada
38 N7 **Joglland** Austria
61 K9 **Jōhana** Japan
32 J9 **Johannaberg** Germany
89 A1 **Johannesburg** S Africa
102 G6 **Johannesburg** California U.S.A.
37 O3 **Johanngeorgenstadt** Germany
115 M2 **Johan Pen** Northwest Territories Canada
60 F13 **Jōhen** Japan
116 L3 **John** *R* Alaska U.S.A.
122 J8 **John, C** Nova Scotia Canada
127 M2 **John Crow Mts** Jamaica
100 E4 **John Day** *R* Oregon U.S.A.
100 G5 **John Day** Oregon U.S.A.
100 E5 **John Day Fossil Beds Nat. Mon.** Oregon U.S.A.
117 Q6 **John d'Or Prairie** Alberta Canada
113 G9 **John F. Kennedy Space Center** Florida U.S.A.
94 J10 **John H. Kerr Res** N Carolina/Virg U.S.A.
106 H3 **John Martin Res** Colorado U.S.A.
142 G3 **John,Mt** W Australia Australia
15 E2 **John O'Groats** Scotland
107 P3 **John Redmond Res** Kansas U.S.A.
107 J4 **Johnson** Kansas U.S.A.
99 K9 **Johnson** Nebraska U.S.A.
94 J5 **Johnsonburg** Pennsylvania U.S.A.
95 M4 **Johnson City** New York U.S.A.
94 E10 **Johnson City** Tennessee U.S.A.
109 J5 **Johnson City** Texas U.S.A.
99 S6 **Johnson Cr** Wisconsin U.S.A.
117 G5 **Johnsons Crossing** Yukon Territory Canada
127 P4 **Johnsons Pt** Antigua W Indies
112 H4 **Johnsonville** South Carolina U.S.A.
112 F4 **Johnston** South Carolina U.S.A.
8 A4 **Johnston** Wales
110 H4 **Johnston City** Illinois U.S.A.
15 D5 **Johnstone** Scotland
117 K10 **Johnstone Str** British Columbia Canada
88 B7 **Johnston Falls** Zambia
143 D9 **Johnston,L** W Australia Australia
143 C8 **Johnston Ra** W Australia Australia
14 E3 **Johnstown** Ireland
98 F7 **Johnstown** Nebraska U.S.A.
95 N4 **Johnstown** New York U.S.A.
94 E6 **Johnstown** Ohio U.S.A.
94 J6 **Johnstown** Pennsylvania U.S.A.
94 E9 **John W Flannagan Res** Virginia U.S.A.
61 P5 **Jōhōji** Japan
69 F12 **Johor** Malaysia
69 F12 **Johor Baharo** Malaysia
37 P2 **Jöhstadt** Germany
52 C5 **Jõhvi** Estonia
18 H5 **Joigny** France
110 F6 **Joiner** Arkansas U.S.A.
130 E10 **Joinville** Brazil
19 J4 **Joinville** France
146 D3 **Joinville I** Antarctica
125 K8 **Jojutla** Mexico
26 N5 **Jokk** Sweden
26 L5 **Jokkmokk** Sweden
27 C10 **Jokuleggi** *mt* Norway
29 T9 **Jökulsá á Fjöllum** *R* Iceland
29 T9 **Jökulsa o Bru** *R* Iceland
78 K2 **Jolfā** Iran
99 S8 **Joliet** Illinois U.S.A.
101 Q4 **Joliet** Montana U.S.A.
121 R6 **Joliette** Quebec Canada
119 U10 **Joliette** North Dakota U.S.A.
142 A1 **Jolimont** *dist* Perth, W Aust Australia
99 M7 **Jolley** Iowa U.S.A.
117 S3 **Jolly L** Northwest Territories Canada
71 E7 **Jolo** Philippines
102 C6 **Jolon** California U.S.A.
26 B10 **Jölstervatn** *L* Norway
26 G7 **Joma** *mt* Norway
29 H11 **Jomala** Finland
71 F3 **Jomalig** *isld* Luzon Philippines
70 O9 **Jombang** Java
66 F5 **Jomda** China
71 A3 **Jome** Indonesia
27 D13 **Jomfruland** *isld* Norway
52 B6 **Jonava** Lithuania
22 F5 **Jonchery-sur-Vesle** France
7 E13 **Jones Bank** Atlantic Oc
110 F6 **Jonesboro** Arkansas U.S.A.
111 M8 **Jonesboro** Georgia U.S.A.
110 G4 **Jonesboro** Illinois U.S.A.
109 P3 **Jonesboro** Louisiana U.S.A.
95 U2 **Jonesboro** Maine U.S.A.
112 H2 **Jonesboro** North Carolina U.S.A.
100 H6 **Jonesboro** Oregon U.S.A.
112 E1 **Jonesboro** Tennessee U.S.A.
109 K4 **Jonesboro** Texas U.S.A.
116 N1 **Jones Is** Alaska U.S.A.
146 B7 **Jones Mts** Antarctica
95 U2 **Jonesport** Maine U.S.A.
83 M9 **Jones Pt** Christmas I Indian Oc
115 L2 **Jones Sound** Northwest Territories Canada
111 F7 **Jonestown** Mississippi U.S.A.
94 B7 **Jonesville** Indiana U.S.A.
111 E10 **Jonesville** Louisiana U.S.A.
94 C5 **Jonesville** Michigan U.S.A.
112 F3 **Jonesville** South Carolina U.S.A.
94 D10 **Jonesville** Virginia U.S.A.
86 F4 **Jonglei** *prov* Sudan
52 B6 **Joniskis** Lithuania
27 G14 **Jönköping** Sweden
27 G14 **Jönköping** *county* Sweden
121 T4 **Jonquière** Quebec Canada
29 K4 **Jönstorp** Sweden
18 E7 **Jonzac** France
110 B4 **Joplin** Missouri U.S.A.
101 P1 **Joplin** Montana U.S.A.
80 B5 **Joppa** Israel
110 H4 **Joppa** Illinois U.S.A.
141 H6 **Jordan** *R* Queensland Australia
80 F1 **Jordan** *R* Israel/Jordan
80 **Jordan** *kingdom* S W Asia
99 N5 **Jordan** Minnesota U.S.A.
101 T2 **Jordan** Montana U.S.A.
95 L3 **Jordan** New York U.S.A.
100 H7 **Jordan** *R* Oregon U.S.A.
129 K7 **Jordânia** Brazil
122 G9 **Jordan L** Nova Scotia Canada
111 K9 **Jordan L** Alabama U.S.A.
48 F1 **Jordanow** Poland
100 H7 **Jordan Valley** Oregon U.S.A.
130 D9 **Jordão, R** Brazil
28 C3 **Jordbro Å** *R* Denmark
33 R5 **Jördenstorf** Germany
27 F10 **Jordet** Norway
28 E6 **Jordløse** Denmark
28 C5 **Jordrup** Denmark
28 B6 **Jordsand** *isld* Denmark
26 P2 **Jorgastak** Norway
133 B8 **Jorge Montt, I** Chile
75 Q5 **Jorhat** India
32 L5 **Jork** Germany
57 F6 **Jorm** Afghanistan
26 G7 **Jormlien** Sweden
26 L6 **Jörn** Sweden
106 C9 **Jornada del Muerto** *reg* New Mexico U.S.A.
27 B12 **Jörpeland** Norway
21 K4 **Jort** France
85 F7 **Jos** Nigeria
71 G8 **Jose Abad Santos** Mindanao Philippines
133 C6 **José de San Martín** Argentina
129 J8 **José dos Campos** Brazil
130 C5 **Joselândia** Brazil
133 E5 **José Maria Blanco** Argentina
27 B12 **Josenfjord** *inlet* Norway
71 F3 **Jose Pañganiban** Philippines
100 J4 **Joseph** Idaho U.S.A.
100 H4 **Joseph** Oregon U.S.A.
142 G2 **Joseph Bonaparte G** Australia
142 G2 **Joseph Bonaparte Gulf** Australia
103 O7 **Joseph City** Arizona U.S.A.
6 M6 **Josephine** *oil rig* North Sea
115 N7 **Joseph L** Labrador, Nfld Canada
123 K4 **Joseph Pt** Anticosti I, Quebec
144 B6 **Josephville** New Zealand
61 M9 **Jō-Shin-Etsu Nat. Park** Japan
109 K3 **Joshua** Texas U.S.A.
102 H7 **Joshua Tree** California U.S.A.
21 O6 **Josnes** France
36 H3 **Jossatal** Germany
20 E6 **Josselin** France
26 E7 **Jössund** Nord-Tröndelag Norway
26 D8 **Jössund** Sör-Tröndelag Norway
26 B10 **Jostedal** Norway
26 B10 **Jostedalsbreen** *gla* Norway
48 F2 **Josvafő** Hungary
26 N2 **Jotkajavrre** Norway
27 C10 **Jotunheimen** *mt* Norway
79 F5 **Jouaiya** Lebanon
21 O4 **Jouars** France
21 K4 **Joué-du-Bois** France
21 M7 **Joué-lès-Tours** France
20 H7 **Joué-sur-Erdre** France
19 K3 **Jœuf** France
29 N6 **Joukokylä** Finland
113 J12 **Joulters Cays** *islds* Bahamas
79 F5 **Jôunié** Lebanon
109 J7 **Jourdanton** Texas U.S.A.
25 E3 **Joure** Netherlands
118 B3 **Joussard** Alberta Canada
121 M3 **Joutel** Quebec Canada
29 M10 **Joutsa** Finland
29 N5 **Joutsijärvi** Finland
40 D4 **Joux, L.de** Switzerland
21 O4 **Jouy** France
21 O6 **Jouy-le-Potier** France
126 D3 **Jovellanos** Cuba
75 P6 **Jowai** India
77 J1 **Jowzjān** *prov* Afghanistan
14 B3 **Joyce's Country** Ireland
117 G4 **Joy, Mt** Yukon Territory Canada
60 O3 **Jōzankei** Japan
31 N4 **Józefów** Poland
110 K5 **J. Percy Priest L** Tennessee U.S.A.
71 B3 **Ju** *isld* Indonesia
124 H5 **Juan Aldama** Mexico
65 C7 **Juancheng** China
141 J7 **Juandah** *R* Queensland Australia
127 K2 **Juan de Bolas** *pk* Jamaica
100 A1 **Juan de Fuca, Str. of** Canada/U.S.A.
87 G11 **Juan de Nova** *isld* Madagascar
133 A9 **Juan Fernández, Is** Pacific Oc
127 N9 **Juangriego** Venezuela
88 G6 **Juani** *isld* Tanzania
128 C5 **Juanjui** Peru
29 N8 **Juankoski** Finland
44 B4 **Juan les Pins** France
124 E2 **Juan M. Ortiz** Mexico
131 B2 **Juan Soldado, C.de** Chile
133 B7 **Juan Stuven, I** Chile
133 F5 **Juárez** Argentina
103 J9 **Juárez, Sa** *ra* Mexico
129 K5 **Juazeiro** Brazil
130 G9 **Juàzeiro do Norte** Brazil
86 F5 **Juba** Sudan
77 A6 **Jubayl, Al** Saudi Arabia
80 G5 **Jubba** Jordan
86 H5 **Jubba** *R* Somalia
80 G1 **Jubbāta el Khashab** Syria
123 R5 **Jubilee L** Newfoundland Canada
143 F8 **Jubilee Lake** W Australia Australia
102 H6 **Jubilee Peak** California U.S.A.
21 K5 **Jublains** France
85 B3 **Juby, Cap** *C* Morocco
17 F5 **Júcar** *R* Spain
36 B1 **Jüchen** Germany
124 H7 **Juchipila** Mexico
125 M9 **Juchitán** Mexico
124 H7 **Juchitlán** Mexico
129 K7 **Jucurucú** *R* Brazil
98 H3 **Jud** North Dakota U.S.A.
99 R7 **Juda** Wisconsin U.S.A.
80 B7 **Judaea** Israel
79 G5 **Judaydat al Wadī** Syria
123 S6 **Jude I** Newfoundland Canada
80 D2 **Judeida** Israel
37 L3 **Judenbach** Germany
38 L7 **Judenburg** Austria
146 B16 **Judge and Clerk Is** *islds* S Pacific Oc
123 L8 **Judique** C Breton I, Nova Scotia
101 Q2 **Judith** *R* Montana U.S.A.
101 Q2 **Judith Basin** *reg* Montana U.S.A.
101 Q3 **Judith Gap** Montana U.S.A.
98 E3 **Judson** North Dakota U.S.A.
Juegang *see* **Rudong**
28 E5 **Juelsminde** Denmark
130 H5 **Juerana** Brazil
128 F4 **Jufari** *R* Brazil
84 F4 **Jufrah Oasis, Al** Libya
20 F5 **Jugon-les-Lacs** France
65 E4 **Juhua Dao** *isld* China
21 H6 **Juigné-des-Moutiers** France
18 F7 **Juillac** France
21 P4 **Juine** *R* France
32 E5 **Juist** *isld* Germany
32 F5 **Juist** Germany
129 K8 **Juiz de Fora** Brazil
65 D3 **Jujinchang** China
69 E13 **Jujuhan** *R* Sumatra
19 O12 **Jujurieux** France
128 E8 **Jujuy** *prov* Argentina
26 L7 **Juken** Sweden
26 L4 **Jukkasjärvi** Sweden
67 D3 **Jukoupu** China
26 H6 **Juktån** *R* Sweden
128 E8 **Julaca** Bolivia
98 D9 **Julesburg** Colorado U.S.A.
128 E7 **Julí** Peru
141 F5 **Julia** *R* Queensland Australia
128 D7 **Juliaca** Peru
141 F5 **Julia Creek** Queensland Australia
100 J3 **Juliaetta** Idaho U.S.A.
102 H8 **Julian** California U.S.A.
115 P5 **Julianehåb** Greenland
14 E3 **Julianstown** Ireland
36 B2 **Jülich** Germany
42 E2 **Julijske A** *mts* Slovenia
124 G3 **Julimes** Mexico
80 D2 **Jūlis** Israel
27 H12 **Julita** Sweden
140 E5 **Julius L.** Queensland Australia
20 G4 **Jullouville** France
Jullundur *see* **Jalandhar**
28 D4 **Julsø** *L* Denmark
65 C6 **Julu** China
80 G8 **Jumaiyil** Jordan
86 H6 **Jumba** Somalia
117 P10 **Jumbo Mt** British Columbia Canada
21 K7 **Jumelles** France
21 J7 **Jumellière,la** France
22 G3 **Jumet** Belgium
21 M3 **Jumièges** France
17 G6 **Jumilla** Spain
75 K4 **Jumla** Nepal
74 D8 **Junagadh** India
65 D7 **Junan** China
65 D2 **Jun Bulen** China
124 D5 **Juncal** Mexico
131 D8 **Juncal, L** Argentina
108 H5 **Junction** Texas U.S.A.
103 M3 **Junction** Utah U.S.A.
140 C1 **Junction B** N Terr Australia

111 D8 **Junction City** Arkansas U.S.A.
111 M9 **Junction City** Georgia U.S.A.
107 O2 **Junction City** Kansas U.S.A.
94 C9 **Junction City** Kentucky U.S.A.
110 M4 **Junction City** Kentucky U.S.A.
100 B5 **Junction City** Oregon U.S.A.
99 R5 **Junction City** Wisconsin U.S.A.
141 G6 **Jundah** Queensland Australia
65 C4 **Jundu Shan** *mt ra* China
117 F6 **Juneau** Alaska U.S.A.
99 S6 **Juneau** Wisconsin U.S.A.
139 J5 **Junee** New South Wales Australia
113 F10 **June in Winter, L** Florida U.S.A.
102 E4 **June Lake** California U.S.A.
65 A5 **Jungar Qi** China
40 G4 **Jungfrau** *mt* Switzerland
40 G4 **Jungfraujoch** Switzerland
22 L4 **Junglinster** Luxembourg
100 G9 **Jungo** Nevada U.S.A.
98 H9 **Juniata** Nebraska U.S.A.
95 K6 **Juniata** *R* Pennsylvania U.S.A.
131 E5 **Junin** Argentina
128 D7 **Junín** Chile
128 C6 **Junín** Peru
133 C5 **Junín de los Andes** Argentina
94 H8 **Junior** West Virginia U.S.A.
95 T1 **Junior L** Maine U.S.A.
122 E7 **Juniper** New Brunswick Canada
103 L6 **Juniper Mts** Arizona U.S.A.
102 C5 **Junipero Sierra Pk** California U.S.A.
61 O5 **Jūni sho** Japan
22 G5 **Juniville** France
116 O2 **Junjik** *R* Alaska U.S.A.
36 B3 **Jünkerath** Germany
26 H5 **Junkerdal** Norway
67 A2 **Junlian** China
108 F5 **Juno** Texas U.S.A.
118 K5 **Junor** Saskatchewan Canada
26 M4 **Junosuando** Sweden
26 J8 **Junsele** Sweden
67 E2 **Junshan Hu** *L* China
16 A5 **Junto** *mt* Portugal
65 A5 **Juntuliang** China
100 G6 **Juntura** Oregon U.S.A.
29 O6 **Juntusranta** Finland
29 O9 **Juojärvi** *L* Finland
26 N5 **Juoksengi** Sweden
130 H6 **Juparaña, Lagoa** *L* Brazil
130 D7 **Jupia** Brazil
130 D7 **Jupia Dam** Brazil
22 K2 **Jupille** Belgium
21 L6 **Jupilles** France
113 G11 **Jupiter** Florida U.S.A.
122 J4 **Jupiter R** Quebec Canada
129 J8 **Juquiá** Brazil
86 E4 **Jur** *R* Sudan
40 C4 **Jura** *dept* France
15 C4 **Jura** Scotland
40 F3 **Jura** *canton* Switzerland
128 C2 **Jurado** Colombia
31 L5 **Jura Krakowska** *reg* Poland
130 G5 **Juramento** Brazil
52 B6 **Jurbarkas** Lithuania
12 D5 **Jurby** I of Man U.K.
79 F8 **Jurf ed Darāwīsh** Jordan
65 E2 **Jurh** China
143 B9 **Jurien** W Australia Australia
143 B9 **Jurien B** W Australia Australia
48 M6 **Jurilovca** Romania
52 B6 **Jurmala** Latvia
67 F1 **Jurong** China
38 N9 **Juršinci** Slovenia
128 E4 **Juruá** Brazil
128 D5 **Juruá** *R* Brazil
128 G6 **Juruena** Brazil
129 G4 **Juruti** Brazil
29 J9 **Jurva** Finland
61 O5 **Jūsan-ko** *L* Japan
127 N10 **Jusepín** Venezuela
79 G4 **Jūsīyah** Syria
19 J5 **Jussey** France
119 S8 **Justice** Manitoba Canada
108 F2 **Justiceburg** Texas U.S.A.
109 K2 **Justin** Texas U.S.A.
133 D4 **Justo Daract** Argentina
128 E5 **Jutaí** Brazil
33 S9 **Jüterbog** Germany
130 C8 **Juti** Brazil
125 L2 **Juticalpa** Honduras
26 J5 **Jutis** Sweden
Jutland *see* **Jylland**
26 E10 **Jutulhugget** *pass* Norway
146 H6 **Jutulstraumen** *ice stream* Antarctica
29 O8 **Juuka** Finland
29 N10 **Juva** Finland
126 C4 **Juventud, Isla de la** Cuba
21 H5 **Juvigné** France
21 H4 **Juvigny-le-Tertre** France
21 J4 **Juvigny-sous-Andaine** France
21 P4 **Juvisy** France
28 B6 **Juvre** Denmark
70 N9 **Juwana** Java
79 H5 **Juwayf, Al** Syria
65 D7 **Ju Xian** China
65 C7 **Juye** China
77 F2 **Jūymand** Iran
40 A1 **Juzennecourt** France
Jye Kundo *see* **Yushu**
28 B4 **Jylland** *reg* Denmark
29 M9 **Jyväskylä** Finland

K

66 B4 **K2** *mt* Kashmir/China
85 E6 **Ka** *R* Nigeria
102 S11 **Kaaawa** Hawaiian Is
89 B7 **Kaaing Veld** *plateau* S Africa
57 A5 **Kaakhka** Turkmenistan
102 R11 **Kaala** *pk* Hawaiian Is
26 L4 **Kaalasjarvi** *L* Sweden
135 U6 **Kaalualu** Hawaiian Is
29 N2 **Kaamanen** Finland
86 H6 **Kaambooni** Somalia
89 C7 **Kaap Plato** S Africa
33 O6 **Kaarssen** Germany
29 N9 **Kaavi** Finland
48 G3 **Kaba** Hungary
70 G7 **Kabaena** *isld* Sulawesi
85 B7 **Kabala** Sierra Leone
86 F5 **Kabalega Falls** Uganda
86 E7 **Kabalo** Zaire
88 A4 **Kabambare** Zaire
69 D11 **Kabanjahe** Sumatra
85 D5 **Kabara** Mali
53 F11 **Kabardino Balkarskaya Respublika** Russian Federation
88 B3 **Kabare** Zaire
86 F5 **Kabarole** Uganda
71 F7 **Kabasalang** Philippines
60 C13 **Kaba shima** *isld* Japan
68 C3 **Kabaung** *R* Burma
85 F7 **Kabba** Nigeria
26 G3 **Kabelvåg** *lighthouse* Norway
120 E4 **Kabenung L** Ontario Canada
70 G4 **Kabetan. I** Sulawesi
99 O1 **Kabetogama** Minnesota U.S.A.
99 N1 **Kabetogama L** Minnesota U.S.A.
120 F3 **Kabinakagami** *R* Ontario Canada
86 D7 **Kabinda** Zaire
71 M9 **Kabir** Indonesia
79 F3 **Kabīr** *R* Syria/Lebanon
57 E5 **Kabla** Tajikistan
47 J2 **Kableshkovo** Bulgaria
86 C4 **Kabo** Cent Afr Republic
87 D8 **Kabompo** *R* Zambia
70 B4 **Kabong** Sarawak
87 E7 **Kabongo** Zaire
68 C6 **Kabosa I.** Burma
85 G1 **Kaboudia, Rass** *C* Tunisia
52 E5 **Kabozha** Russian Federation
80 D1 **Kabri** Israel
77 F1 **Kabūd Gonbad** Iran
71 E2 **Kabugao** Philippines
77 L2 **Kābul** Afghanistan
80 D2 **Kābūl** Israel
88 C2 **Kabula** Uganda
87 E8 **Kabunda** Zaire
88 B7 **Kabunda** Zambia
71 H9 **Kabunduk** Indonesia
86 F2 **Kabushiya** Sudan
88 B9 **Kabwe** Zambia
55 F3 **Kabyrdak** Russian Federation
55 D5 **Kabyrga** *R* Kazakhstan
46 E2 **Kačanik** Serbia Yugoslavia
71 B3 **Kacepi** Indonesia
87 F8 **Kachalola** Zambia
74 C7 **Kachchh, Gulf of** India
74 C6 **Kachchh, Rann of** India
116 M7 **Kachemak B** Alaska U.S.A.
100 D2 **Kachess L** Washington U.S.A.
85 F7 **Kachia** Nigeria
75 R5 **Kachin State** *prov* Burma
55 G4 **Kachiry** Kazakhstan
55 C2 **Kachkanar** Russian Federation
56 G4 **Kachug** Russian Federation
78 H1 **Kaçkar Dağlar** *mt* Turkey
60 J11 **Kada** Japan
68 C4 **Kadaingti** Burma
76 A5 **Kadamatt** *isld* Indian Oc
86 F5 **Kadam Mt** Uganda
37 P3 **Kadaň** Czechoslovakia
68 D6 **Kadan Kyun** *isld* Burma
70 D7 **Kadapongan** *isld* Indonesia
48 D4 **Kadarkút** Hungary
71 H7 **Kadatung** *isld* Indonesia
137 Q5 **Kadavu** *isld* Fiji
41 H2 **Kadelburg** Germany
61 P13 **Kadena** Okinawa
71 K9 **Kadesa** Indonesia
143 F7 **Kadgo L** W Australia Australia
78 K5 **Kādhimain** Iraq
74 E7 **Kadi** India
85 C6 **Kadiana** Mali
46 F3 **Kadijica** *mt* Macedonia Yugoslavia
47 N11 **Kadıköy** Turkey
138 E5 **Kadina** South Australia Australia
78 D2 **Kadınhanı** Turkey
74 F9 **Kadirabad** India
47 J8 **Kadirga Burun** *C* Turkey
76 D3 **Kadiri** India
78 F3 **Kadirli** Turkey
70 G7 **Kadjang** Sulawesi
73 L6 **Kadmat** *isld* Lakshadweep Indian Oc
52 F5 **Kadnikov** Russian Federation
68 C4 **Kado** Burma
60 E13 **Kadogawa** Japan
98 E6 **Kadoka** South Dakota U.S.A.
89 F2 **Kadoma** Zimbabwe
68 B5 **Kadonkani** Burma
46 E3 **Kadrifakovo** Macedonia Yugoslavia
86 E3 **Kadugli** Sudan
86 A3 **Kaduna** Nigeria
76 C4 **Kadur** India
52 E5 **Kaduy** Russian Federation
56 E5 **Kadyr-Egi-Tayga, Khrebet** *mts* Russian Federation
52 F5 **Kadyy** Russian Federation
57 H4 **Kadzhi-Say** Kyrgyzstan
85 B5 **Kaedi** Mauritania
123 R5 **Kaegudeck L** Newfoundland Canada
86 B3 **Kaélé** Cameroon
145 D1 **Kaeo** New Zealand
28 D6 **Kærum** Denmark
65 G5 **Kaesŏng** N Korea
87 D7 **Käfakumba** Zaire
85 F7 **Kafanchan** Nigeria
85 A6 **Kaffrine** Senegal
71 C3 **Kafiau** *isld* W Irian
46 G7 **Kafiréos, Porthmós** *str* Greece
46 G6 **Kafirévs, Akr** *C* Greece
26 L2 **Kåfjord** *inlet* Norway
26 N2 **Kåfjord** Norway
80 E1 **Kafra** Lebanon
80 D5 **Kafr 'Abbush** Jordan
80 D5 **Kafr 'Ain** Jordan
79 G3 **Kafr Buhum** Syria
80 F6 **Kafrein** *R* Jordan
79 A7 **Kafr el Dauwâr** Egypt
80 D4 **Kafr-el-Labad** Jordan
79 A7 **Kafr el Sheik** Egypt
79 A8 **Kafr el Zaiyât** Egypt
80 D2 **Kafr Mandā** Israel
80 C5 **Kafr Qāsim** Israel
80 D4 **Kafr Qud** Jordan
80 D4 **Kafr Ra'i** Jordan
80 D4 **Kafr Rumman** Jordan
79 G4 **Kafrūn Bashūr** Syria
80 D5 **Kafr Zibad** Jordan
88 B9 **Kafue** Zambia
87 E8 **Kafue Nat. Park** Zambia
87 E7 **Kafulwe** Zambia
55 C4 **Kaga** Russian Federation
86 C4 **Kaga Bandoro** Cent Afr Republic
60 G10 **Kagami** Japan
57 C5 **Kagan** Uzbekistan
116 G7 **Kagati L** Alaska U.S.A.
60 G11 **Kagawa** *prefect* Japan
120 H7 **Kagawong** Ontario Canada
26 M7 **Kåge** Sweden
88 C2 **Kagera** *reg* Tanzania
88 C2 **Kagera National Park** Rwanda
28 J5 **Kagerup** Denmark
120 C2 **Kagianagami L** Ontario Canada
120 D3 **Kagiano L** Ontario Canada
47 M10 **Kâğithane** Turkey
78 J1 **Kağızman** Turkey
69 D13 **Kagologolo** Indonesia
60 D14 **Kagoshima** Japan
48 L5 **Kagul** Moldavia
48 L5 **Kagul, Ozero** *L* Ukraine
116 L8 **Kaguyak** Alaska U.S.A.
70 D6 **Kahajan** *R* Kalimantan
70 E5 **Kahala** Kalimantan
135 O1 **Kahala Pt** Hawaiian Is
102 S12 **Kahaluu** Hawaiian Is
88 D3 **Kahama** Tanzania
74 C4 **Kahan** Pakistan
102 S11 **Kahana** Hawaiian Is
145 F3 **Kaharoa** *mt* New Zealand
71 A2 **Kahatola** *isld* Halmahera Indonesia
87 C7 **Kahemba** Zaire
102 R12 **Kahe Pt** Hawaiian Is
144 A6 **Kaherekoau Mts** New Zealand
116 M5 **Kahiltna Gl** Alaska U.S.A.
36 G3 **Kahl** *R* Germany
37 M2 **Kahla** Germany
36 F1 **Kahler-Asten** *mt* Germany
100 G3 **Kahlotus** Washington U.S.A.
117 N6 **Kahntah** British Columbia Canada
77 E6 **Kahnuj** Iran
110 E1 **Kahoka** Missouri U.S.A.
61 K9 **Kahoku-gata** *L* Japan
102 V13 **Kahoolawe** *isld* Hawaiian Is
29 J2 **Kahperusvaara** *mt* Finland
78 F3 **Kahramanmaraş** Turkey
135 Q1 **Kahuku** Hawaiian Is
102 S11 **Kahuku Pt** Hawaiian Is
135 T3 **Kahului** Hawaiian Is
Kahutara Pt *see* **Table Cape**
85 E7 **Kaiama** Nigeria
144 D5 **Kaiapoi** New Zealand
119 O1 **Kaiashk** *R* Ontario Canada
103 M5 **Kaibab Plat** Arizona U.S.A.
60 J10 **Kaibara** Japan
103 N5 **Kaibito Plat** Arizona U.S.A.
66 D3 **Kaidu He** *R* China
128 G2 **Kaieteur Falls** Guyana
65 C7 **Kaifeng** China
145 D1 **Kaihu** New Zealand
67 F2 **Kaihua** China
145 E3 **Kai-Iwi** New Zealand
67 B1 **Kaijiang** China
136 G3 **Kai, Kep** *islds* Moluccas Indonesia
145 D1 **Kaikohe** New Zealand
67 B3 **Kaikou** China
144 D5 **Kaikoura** New Zealand
144 D5 **Kaikoura Range** New Zealand
Kailas Range *see* **Gangdisê Shan**
36 G4 **Kailbach** Germany
67 B3 **Kaili** China
65 E3 **Kailu** China
102 S12 **Kailua** Hawaiian Is
135 T5 **Kailua** Hawaiian Is
145 E2 **Kaimai Ra** New Zealand
46 E4 **Kaïmakchalán** *mt* Greece
136 G2 **Kaimana** W Irian
145 E3 **Kaimanawa Mts** New Zealand
144 C5 **Kaimata** New Zealand
60 D14 **Kaimon-dake** *pk* Japan
135 V5 **Kaimu** Hawaiian Is
27 N13 **Käina** Estonia
38 M7 **Kainach** *R* Austria
135 U5 **Kainaliu** Hawaiian Is
60 J11 **Kainan** Japan
46 G3 **Kainchal** *mt* Greece
57 G3 **Kainda** Kyrgyzstan
68 B2 **Kaing** Burma
145 F3 **Kaingaroa Forest** New Zealand
145 F3 **Kaingaroa Plat.** New Zealand
38 J6 **Kainisch** Austria
85 E6 **Kainji Res** Nigeria
71 H7 **Kaioba** Indonesia
145 E2 **Kaipara Flats** New Zealand
103 N4 **Kaiparowits Plat** Utah U.S.A.
65 D5 **Kaiping** China
67 D5 **Kaiping** China
29 N4 **Kairala** Finland
43 C13 **Kairouan** Tunisia
38 F6 **Kaiser-Gebirge** *mts* Austria
102 E4 **Kaiser Pk** California U.S.A.
36 C3 **Kaisersesch** Germany
36 D5 **Kaiserslautern** Germany
40 G1 **Kaiserstuhl** *mt* Germany
32 E10 **Kaiserswerth** Germany
60 F11 **Kaita** Japan
145 D1 **Kaitaia** New Zealand
144 B7 **Kaitangata** New Zealand
145 F3 **Kaitawa** New Zealand
145 D4 **Kaiteriteri** New Zealand
74 G4 **Kaithal** India
145 E4 **Kaitoki** New Zealand
Kaitong *see* **Tongyu**
26 L4 **Kaitum** Sweden
26 K4 **Kaitumälven** *R* Sweden
26 K4 **Kaitumj** Sweden
26 L3 **Kaivare** *mt* Sweden
145 E2 **Kaiwaka** New Zealand
71 N9 **Kaiwatu** Indonesia
102 V13 **Kaiwi Ch** Hawaiian Is
67 C1 **Kai Xian** China
67 B3 **Kaiyang** China
59 H3 **Kaiyuan** China
67 A5 **Kaiyuan** China
116 H5 **Kaiyuh Mts** Alaska U.S.A.
60 J11 **Kaizuka** Japan
70 E3 **Kaja** Kalimantan
29 N7 **Kajaani** Finland
141 F5 **Kajabbi** Queensland Australia
77 J3 **Kajaki Dam** Afghanistan
71 L9 **Kajan** *isld* Indonesia
69 E11 **Kajang** Malaysia
88 F2 **Kajiado** Kenya
61 M10 **Kajikazawa** Japan
60 D14 **Kajiki** Japan
71 A2 **Kajoa** *isld* Halmahera Indonesia
86 F5 **Kajo Kaji** Sudan
71 K8 **Kajuadi** *isld* Indonesia
85 F6 **Kajuru** Nigeria
86 F3 **Kaka** Sudan
103 M9 **Kaka** Arizona U.S.A.
70 F3 **Kakaban** *isld* Kalimantan
119 O2 **Kakabeka Falls** Ontario Canada
71 L8 **Kakabia** *isld* Indonesia
140 C2 **Kakadu Nat Park** N Terr Australia
118 J1 **Kakagi L** Ontario Canada
145 E3 **Kakahi** New Zealand
71 G7 **Kakal** *R* Mindanao Philippines
70 F5 **Kakali** Sulawesi
87 D11 **Kakamas** S Africa
88 E1 **Kakamega** Kenya
69 A8 **Kakana** Nicobar Is
144 C6 **Kakanui** New Zealand
135 T3 **Kaka Pt** Hawaiian Is
145 E3 **Kakaramea** New Zealand
85 B7 **Kakata** Liberia
145 E3 **Kakatahi** New Zealand
57 D5 **Kakaydy** Uzbekistan
60 F11 **Kake** Japan
117 G7 **Kake** Alaska U.S.A.
61 M11 **Kakegawa** Japan
56 E5 **Ka-Khem** *R* Russian Federation
116 K7 **Kakhonak** Alaska U.S.A.
54 E10 **Kakhovka** Ukraine
54 E10 **Kakhovskoye Vdkhr** *res* Ukraine
77 F2 **Kakht** Iran
77 B5 **Kākī** Iran
76 F2 **Kākināda** India
117 P5 **Kakisa L** Northwest Territories Canada
61 M8 **Kakizaki** Japan
60 H11 **Kakogawa** Japan
55 E4 **Kak, Oz** *L* Kazakhstan
85 D7 **Kakpin** Ivory Coast
66 B3 **Kak Shaal Too, Khrebet** *mts* Kazakhstan
116 Q1 **Kaktovik** Alaska U.S.A.
61 O8 **Kakuda** Japan
61 O6 **Kakumagawa** Japan
61 O6 **Kakunodate** Japan
70 C3 **Kakus** *R* Sarawak
86 E7 **Kakuyu** Zaire
117 O8 **Kakwa** *R* Alberta Canada
48 F3 **Kál** Hungary
43 D13 **Kalaâ Kebira** Tunisia
Kalaallit Nunaat *see* **Greenland**
43 B13 **Kalaat Es Senam** *mt* Tunisia
71 M9 **Kalabahi** Indonesia
46 E5 **Kalabáka** Greece
70 E2 **Kalaban** Sabah
138 F4 **Kalabity** South Australia Australia
87 D8 **Kalabo** Zambia
54 N6 **Kalach** Russian Federation
55 F3 **Kalachinsk** Russian Federation
53 F9 **Kalach-na-donu** Russian Federation
54 M6 **Kalachskaya Vozvyshennost'** *uplands* Russian Federation
68 A2 **Kaladan** Burma
121 N8 **Kaladar** Ontario Canada
102 V14 **Kalae** Hawaiian Is
70 G6 **Kalaena** *R* Sulawesi
47 R14 **Kaláfou** Rhodes Greece
68 C1 **Kalagwe** Burma
89 B4 **Kalahari Desert** Botswana
89 B6 **Kalahari Game Res** S Africa
89 B5 **Kalahari Gemsbok Nat Park** S Africa
57 F5 **Kalai-Khumb** Tajikistan
57 B6 **Kala-I-Mor** Turkmenistan
29 K7 **Kalajoki** Finland
29 L8 **Kalajoki** *R* Finland
58 G1 **Kalakan** Russian Federation
135 O1 **Kalalau Lookout** Hawaiian Is
70 G5 **Kalaliok** Sulawesi
74 E1 **Kalam** Pakistan
100 C3 **Kalama** Washington U.S.A.
46 E7 **Kalámai** Greece
Kalamata Greece *see* **Kalámai**
94 B4 **Kalamazoo** Michigan U.S.A.
70 D7 **Kalambau** *isld* Indonesia
87 F7 **Kalambo Falls** Tanzania
46 D6 **Kálamos** *isld* Greece
46 F6 **Kálamos** Greece
143 B9 **Kalamunda** W Australia Australia
138 E3 **Kalamurra, L** South Australia Australia
143 B9 **Kalannie** W Australia Australia
29 J11 **Kalanti** Finland
71 K8 **Kalao** *isld* Indonesia
71 G7 **Kalaong** Mindanao Philippines
71 K8 **Kalaotoa** *isld* Indonesia
83 K9 **Kala Oya** *R* Sri Lanka
69 G13 **Kalapa** Indonesia
58 G1 **Kalar** *R* Russian Federation
48 L3 **Kalarash** Moldavia
26 H9 **Kälarne** Sweden
83 L9 **Kal Aru** *R* Sri Lanka
74 B4 **Kalat** Pakistan
77 G6 **Kalateh-Masjed** Iran
135 S2 **Kalaupapa** Hawaiian Is
53 F10 **Kalaus** *R* Russian Federation
47 R14 **Kalavardha** Rhodes Greece
46 E6 **Kalávrita** Greece
68 C2 **Kalaw** Burma
83 K9 **Kalawewa** Sri Lanka
36 H3 **Kalbach** Germany
143 A8 **Kalbarri** W Australia Australia
143 A8 **Kalbarri Nat Park** W Australia Australia
33 O7 **Kalbe** Germany
56 B6 **Kalbinskiy Khrebet** *mts* Kazakhstan
77 F2 **Kalbū** Iran
42 F3 **Kalce** Slovenia
55 B5 **Kaldygayty** *R* Kazakhstan
47 K7 **Kale** Turkey
78 D1 **Kalecik** Turkey
71 H7 **Kaledupa** *isld* Indonesia
68 C5 **Kalegauk I** Burma
88 E6 **Kalehe** Zaire
68 B3 **Kaleindaung** *inlet* Burma
86 D6 **Kalema** Zaire
88 B4 **Kalémié** Zaire
32 K7 **Kalenberg** *reg* Germany
31 L5 **Kalety** Poland
94 B2 **Kaleva** Michigan U.S.A.
29 P6 **Kalevala** Russian Federation
28 S10 **Kalfafell** Iceland
52 E3 **Kalgachikha** Russian Federation
Kalgan *see* **Zhangjiakou**
58 G3 **Kalgan** China
143 C10 **Kalgan,R** W Australia Australia
108 F2 **Kalgary** Texas U.S.A.
116 M6 **Kalgin I** Alaska U.S.A.
143 D9 **Kalgoorlie** W Australia Australia
46 E4 **Kalí** Greece
47 L6 **Kalı** *R* Turkey
46 E6 **Kaliakoúdha** *mt* Greece
47 J1 **Kaliakra, N** Bulgaria
70 K8 **Kalianda** Sumatra
70 O9 **Kalianget** Indonesia
55 F4 **Kalibek, Oz** *L* Kazakhstan
71 F5 **Kalibo** Philippines
94 C6 **Kalida** Ohio U.S.A.
69 D14 **Kaliet** Indonesia
86 E6 **Kalima** Zaire
70 **Kalimantan** Borneo
70 B4 **Kalimantan Barat** Borneo
70 D6 **Kalimantan Selatan** Kalimantan
70 C5 **Kalimantan Tengah** Kalimantan
70 E3 **Kalimantan Timur** Kalimantan
47 H8 **Kálimnos** *isld* Greece
75 N5 **Kalimpang** India
71 H7 **Kalingsusuh Tk** *B* Indonesia
Kalinin *see* **Tver'**
57 E5 **Kalininabad** Tajikistan
27 L17 **Kaliningrad** Russian Federation
55 C3 **Kalinino** Russian Federation
53 F8 **Kalininsk** Russian Federation
Kaliniskaya Oblast' *see* **Tverskaya Oblast'**
48 E7 **Kalinovik** Bosnia-Herzegovina
55 C6 **Kalinovka** Kazakhstan
48 M1 **Kalinovka** Ukraine
55 D3 **Kalinovo** Russian Federation
70 O10 **Kalisat** Java
101 L1 **Kalispell** Montana U.S.A.
31 L4 **Kalisz** Poland
53 F9 **Kalitva** *R* Russian Federation
88 C4 **Kaliua** Tanzania
26 N6 **Kalix** Sweden
26 N5 **Kalix älv** *R* Sweden
26 L4 **Kalixfors** Sweden
74 G3 **Kalka** India
55 G5 **Kalkaman** Kazakhstan
47 K8 **Kalkan** Turkey
25 F5 **Kalkar** Germany
94 B2 **Kalkaska** Michigan U.S.A.
33 T8 **Kalkberge** Germany
87 C10 **Kalkfeld** Namibia
Kalkfontein *see* **Tsootsha**
33 O5 **Kalkhorst** Germany
47 J5 **Kalkım** Turkey
89 A5 **Kalk Plateau** Namibia
87 C10 **Kalkrand** Namibia
83 L10 **Kalkudah** Sri Lanka
138 D2 **Kallakoopah** *R* South Australia Australia
52 C5 **Kallaste** Estonia
29 N9 **Kallavesi** *L* Finland
33 O7 **Kallehne** Germany
32 H10 **Kallenhardt** Germany
32 J8 **Kalletal** Germany
37 P2 **Kallich** Czechoslovakia
47 V16 **Kallidhiés** Rhodes Greece
80 F7 **Kallirhoe Hot Sp** Jordan
46 D3 **Kalmet** Albania
37 M5 **Kallmünz** Germany
47 H5 **Kalloní** Greece
47 H5 **Kallonís Kólpos** Greece
26 F8 **Kallsjön** Sweden
29 O5 **Kallunki** Finland
57 D2 **Kalmakkyrgan** *R* Kazakhstan
27 H14 **Kalmar** *county* Sweden
27 H15 **Kalmar** Sweden
27 H15 **Kalmarsund** *chan* Sweden
36 E5 **Kalmit** *mt* Germany
53 E10 **Kal'mius** *R* Ukraine
22 H1 **Kalmthout** Belgium
83 L10 **Kalmunai** Sri Lanka
55 B6 **Kalmykovo** Kazakhstan
53 G9 **Kalmytskaya Respublika** Russian Federation
48 E4 **Kalocsa** Hungary
46 G2 **Kalofer** Bulgaria
135 S3 **Kalohi Ch** Hawaiian Is
79 C3 **Kalokhorio** Cyprus
74 E7 **Kalol** India
87 E9 **Kalomo** Zambia
46 F4 **Kaló[illegible]** Greece
99 P8 **Kalona** Iowa U.S.A.
117 K9 **Kalone Peak** British Columbia Canada
71 F3 **Kalongkooan** *isld* Luzon Philippines
71 F3 **Kalotkot** *isld* Luzon Philippines
28 E4 **Kaløvig** *B* Denmark
46 G2 **Kaloyanovc** Bulgaria
73 L6 **Kalpeni I** Lakshadweep Indian Oc
74 H5 **Kalpi** India
57 J4 **Kalpin** China
83 J9 **Kalpitiya** Sri Lanka
28 E5 **Kals[illegible]akke** Denmark
77 E1 **Kāl-Shūr, Rūd-e** *R* Iran
6 F1 **Kalsoy** *isld* Faeroes
116 H4 **Kaltag** Alaska U.S.A.
56 C4 **Kaltan** Russian Federation
41 M3 **Kaltenberg** *mt* Austria
37 M4 **Kaltenbrunn** Germany
32 L5 **Kaltenkirchen** Germany
37 J2 **Kaltennordheim** Germany
37 J2 **Kaltensundheim** Germany
54 H2 **Kaluga** Russian Federation
83 K11 **Kalu Ganga** *R* Sri Lanka
70 E7 **Kalukalukuang** *isld* Indonesia
70 F6 **Kaluku** Sulawesi
70 D3 **Kalulong, Bt** *mt* Sarawak
87 E8 **Kalulushi** Zambia
142 F2 **Kalumburu** W Australia Australia
70 F6 **Kalumpang** Sulawesi
28 G5 **Kalundborg** Denmark
28 F5 **Kalundborg Fjord** *inlet* Denmark
88 D6 **Kalungu** *R* Zambia
88 B6 **Kalungwishi** *R* Zambia
70 E1 **Kalupis Falls** Sabah
48 J1 **Kalush** Ukraine
31 N3 **Kałuszyn** Poland
83 J11 **Kalutara** Sri Lanka
53 D7 **Kaluzhskaya Oblast'** *prov* Russian Federation
31 O1 **Kalvarija** Lithuania
28 J6 **Kalvehave** Denmark
29 K8 **Kälviä** Finland
29 N10 **Kalvitsa** Finland
29 L10 **Kalvola** Finland
28 B6 **Kalvslund** Denmark
38 L7 **Kalwang** Austria
55 C1 **Kal'ya** Russian Federation
74 E9 **Kalyan** India
76 C3 **Kalyāndurg** India
74 G10 **Kalyani** India
52 H5 **Kama** *R* Russian Federation
55 G3 **Kama** Novosibirskaya obl Russian Federation
55 D1 **Kama** Sverdlovskaya obl Russian Federation
86 B1 **Kamada** Niger
60 E13 **Kamae** Japan
61 P6 **Kamaishi** Japan
61 N13 **Kama iwa** *islds* Iwo Jima Japan
135 S2 **Kamakou** *pk* Hawaiian Is
61 N10 **Kamakura** Japan
70 O9 **Kamal** Indonesia
74 E3 **Kamalia** Pakistan
135 S3 **Kamalo** Hawaiian Is
85 B7 **Kamalu** Sierra Leone
68 C4 **Kamamaung** Burma
78 D2 **Kaman** Turkey
87 D8 **Kamapanda** Zambia
72 E5 **Kamarān** *isld* Yemen
77 K2 **Kamard** *reg* Afghanistan
74 H9 **Kamareddi** India
75 N7 **Kamarhati** India
74 B9 **Kamarod** Pakistan
101 O9 **Kamas** Utah U.S.A.
87 E9 **Kamativi** Zimbabwe
119 P2 **Kamatsi L** Saskatchewan Canada
60 H11 **Kamatsushima** Japan
143 D9 **Kambalda** W Australia Australia
52 G1 **Kambal'nitskiye Koshki, Ova** *islds* Russian Federation
76 C6 **Kambam** India
69 E13 **Kambang** Sumatra
70 M9 **Kambangan** *isld* Java
71 H7 **Kambara** Indonesia
52 H6 **Kambarka** Russian Federation
85 B7 **Kambia** Sierra Leone
83 M8 **Kambling** *isld* Cocos Is Indian Oc
65 H4 **Kambo Ho** *mt* N Korea
70 F6 **Kambuno** *mt* Sulawesi
51 Q3 **Kamchatka** *pen* Russian Federation
51 Q3 **Kamchatskaya Oblast'** *prov* Russian Federation
47 J1 **Kamchiya** *R* Bulgaria
47 H2 **Kamchiya, Yazovir** *res* Bulgaria
52 F4 **Kamchuga** Russian Federation
61 N8 **Kameda** Japan
100 G4 **Kamela** Oregon U.S.A.
32 G9 **Kamen** Germany
52 D6 **Kamenets** Russian Federation
48 K2 **Kamenets-Podol'skiy** Ukraine
46 D4 **Kamenicë** Albania
42 F4 **Kamenjak. Rt** *C* Croatia
52 H1 **Kamenka** Russian Federation
52 F2 **Kamenka** Russian Federation
56 E2 **Kamenka** *R* Russian Federation
53 B8 **Kamenka-Bugskaya** Ukraine
54 F9 **Kamenka-Dneprovskaya** Ukraine
56 B4 **Kamen'na-Obi** Russian Federation
29 O11 **Kamennogorsk** Russian Federation
52 D3 **Kamennoye, Oz** *L* Russian Federation
47 J2 **Kameno** Bulgaria
54 M9 **Kamenolomni** Russian Federation
59 K3 **Kamen Rybolov** Russian Federation
56 G5 **Kamensk** Russian Federation
55 E3 **Kamenskoye** Russian Federation
53 F9 **Kamensk-Shakhtinskiy** Russian Federation
55 D3 **Kamensk-Ural'skiy** Russian Federation
31 O3 **Kamenyuki** Belorussia
30 H4 **Kamenz** Germany
61 J10 **Kameoka** Japan
12 C2 **Kames** Scotland
54 N1 **Kameshkovo** Russian Federation
74 H3 **Kamet** *mt* India/Xizang Zizhiqu
61 K11 **Kameyama** Japan
100 J3 **Kamiah** Idaho U.S.A.
31 K2 **Kamien** Poland
31 J5 **Kamienna Góra** Poland
31 H2 **Kamień Pomorski** Poland
31 L4 **Kamieńsk** Poland
87 C12 **Kamieskroon** S Africa
89 A8 **Kamies Sektor Berg** *mt* S Africa
60 Q2 **Kami-Furano** Japan
60 Q2 **Kamikawa** *prefect* Japan
60 C14 **Kami-Koshiki-jima** *isld* Japan
140 F4 **Kamileroi** Queensland Australia
114 J5 **Kamilukuak L** Northwest Territories Canada
87 D7 **Kamina** Zaire
115 K5 **Kaminak L** Northwest Territories Canada
99 R1 **Kaministikwia** Ontario Canada
60 C11 **Kami no-shima** *isld* Japan
115 K5 **Kaminuriak L** Northwest Territories Canada
61 L9 **Kamioka** Japan
47 Q14 **Kamiros** *hist site* Rhodes Greece
116 L7 **Kamishak B** Alaska U.S.A.
60 R2 **Kami-Shihoro** Japan
Kamishli *see* **Qāmishlī, Al**
88 B3 **Kamituga** Zaire
61 O13 **Kamiyama-jima** *isld* Okinawa
60 R1 **Kami-Yūbetsu** Japan
57 F3 **Kamkaly** Kazakhstan
56 C5 **Kamlak** Russian Federation
117 N10 **Kamloops** British Columbia Canada
68 B3 **Kamma** Burma
29 P7 **Kammenoye, Oz** *L* Russian Federation
60 E12 **Kammon Kaikyō** *str* Japan
60 D12 **Kammon Tunnels** Japan
60 J10 **Kammuri shima** *isld* Japan
60 F11 **Kammuri-yama** *mt* Japan
42 F2 **Kamnik** Slovenia
56 H3 **Kamniokan** Russian Federation
78 K1 **Kamo** Armenia
61 M8 **Kamo** Japan
145 E1 **Kamo** New Zealand
56 E1 **Kamo** *R* Russian Federation
128 G3 **Kamoa Mts** Guyana
60 O2 **Kamoenai** Japan
61 O10 **Kamogawa** Japan
60 H11 **Kamojima** Japan
122 C6 **Kamouraska** Quebec Canada
38 N4 **Kamp** *R* Austria
69 G13 **Kampa** Indonesia
86 F5 **Kampala** Uganda
69 E12 **Kamparkiri** *R* Sumatra
36 D3 **Kamp-Bornhofen** Germany
28 A7 **Kampen** Germany
25 E3 **Kampen** Netherlands
86 E6 **Kampene** Zaire
22 H2 **Kampenhout** Belgium
38 M5 **Kamp, Gr** *R* Austria
68 D4 **Kamphaeng Phet** Thailand
88 B6 **Kampinda** Zambia
88 B7 **Kampolombo, L** Zambia
68 G7 **Kampong Cham** Cambodia
68 G6 **Kampong Chhnang** Cambodia
68 G7 **Kampot** Cambodia
85 D6 **Kampti** Burkina
Kampuchea *rep see* **Cambodia**
99 N7 **Kamrar** Iowa U.S.A.
119 Q7 **Kamsack** Saskatchewan Canada
52 G6 **Kamskoye Ust'ye** Russian Federation
74 H8 **Kāmthi** India
119 P2 **Kamuchawie L** Saskatchewan Canada
60 Q3 **Kamui-dake** *mt* Japan
46 E4 **Kamvoúnia, Óri** *mts* Greece
53 G8 **Kamyshin** Russian Federation
55 D3 **Kamyshlov** Russian Federation
57 B2 **Kamyshlybash** Kazakhstan
55 D5 **Kamyshnoye** Kazakhstan
54 F6 **Kamyshnya** Ukraine
54 H9 **Kamysh-Zarya** Ukraine
68 B1 **Kan** Burma
85 G6 **Kan** Nigeria
56 D3 **Kan** *R* Russian Federation
89 E2 **Kana** *R* Zimbabwe
103 M4 **Kanab** Utah U.S.A.
103 M5 **Kanab Cr** Arizona U.S.A.
70 C3 **Kana, Bt** *mt* Sarawak
61 O5 **Kanagi** Japan
42 F2 **Kanal** Slovenia
46 F5 **Kanália** Greece
69 A9 **Kanalla** Nicobar Is
118 C8 **Kananaskis L** Alberta Canada
86 D7 **Kananga** Zaire
55 C4 **Kananikol'skoye** Russian Federation
103 L4 **Kanarraville** Utah U.S.A.
52 G6 **Kanash** Russian Federation
46 F5 **Kanastraion, Ákr** *C* Greece
116 K8 **Kanatak** Alaska U.S.A.
52 H4 **Kanava** Russian Federation
99 N7 **Kanawha** Iowa U.S.A.
109 M2 **Kanawha** Texas U.S.A.
94 E8 **Kanawha** *R* West Virginia U.S.A.
94 F7 **Kanawha, Little** *R* West Virginia U.S.A.
61 M11 **Kanaya** Japan
61 K9 **Kanazawa** Japan
61 K9 **Kanazu** Japan
75 Q7 **Kanbalu** Burma
68 C5 **Kanbauk** Burma
68 D5 **Kanchanaburi** Thailand
Kanchenjunga *see* **Kanychenjunga**
57 J1 **Kanchingiz, Khrebet** *mt* Kazakhstan
76 D4 **Kanchipuram** India
60 D12 **Kanda** Japan
74 B4 **Kanda** Pakistan
77 J4 **Kandahār** Afghanistan
119 N7 **Kandahar** Saskatchewan Canada
52 D2 **Kandalaksha** Russian Federation
52 D2 **Kandalalakshskaya Guba** *B* Russian Federation
69 C11 **Kandang** Sumatra
70 D6 **Kandangan** Kalimantan
46 F9 **Kándanos** Crete Greece
52 B6 **Kandava** Latvia
36 E5 **Kandel** Germany
40 G2 **Kandern** Germany
28 E1 **Kandestederne** Denmark
74 C4 **Kandhkot** Pakistan
85 E6 **Kandi** Benin
76 D2 **Kandi** India
77 K5 **Kandi** Pakistan
116 R4 **Kandik** *R* Alaska U.S.A.
47 L3 **Kandıra** Turkey
70 G4 **Kandi, Tg** *C* Sulawesi
74 D7 **Kandla** India
139 J5 **Kandos** New South Wales Australia
87 H11 **Kandreho** Madagascar
55 B4 **Kandry** Russian Federation
76 D3 **Kandukur** India
83 K10 **Kandy** Sri Lanka
110 F2 **Kane** Illinois U.S.A.
94 J5 **Kane** Pennsylvania U.S.A.
101 R5 **Kane** Wyoming U.S.A.
115 M2 **Kane Basin** Canada/Greenland
116 G7 **Kanektok** *R* Alaska U.S.A.
86 C3 **Kanem** *dist* Chad
102 S12 **Kaneohe** Hawaiian Is
102 S12 **Kaneohe Bay** Hawaiian Is
54 C7 **Kanev** Ukraine
52 E2 **Kanevka** Russian Federation
54 C7 **Kanevskoye Vodokhranilishche** *res* Ukraine
61 O7 **Kaneyama** Japan
42 F3 **Kanfanar** Croatia
87 D10 **Kang** Botswana
115 O4 **Kangaamiut** Greenland
Kangaarsussiaq *see* **Parry, Kap**
115 O4 **Kangaatsiak** Greenland
85 C6 **Kangaba** Mali
78 F2 **Kangal** Turkey
77 C6 **Kangan** Iran
69 E9 **Kangar** Malaysia
138 D6 **Kangaroo I** South Australia Australia
140 E4 **Kangaroo Pt** Queensland Australia
29 L7 **Kangas** Finland
29 N9 **Kangaslampi** Finland
29 M9 **Kangasniemi** Finland
77 A2 **Kangāvar** Iran
48 M4 **Kangaz** Moldavia
65 C4 **Kangbao** China
75 N5 **Kangchenjunga** *mt* Nepal/India
58 D5 **Kangding** China
70 P9 **Kangean** *isld* Indonesia
115 N4 **Kangeeak Pt** Northwest Territories Canada
Kangeq *C see* **Cort Adelaer, Kap**
Kanger lussuaq *see* **Søndre Strømfjord**
Kangerlua *see* **Kobberminebugt**
115 Q4 **Kangerlussuaq** *inlet* Greenland
Kangersuatsiaq *see* **Prøven**
115 Q4 **Kangertittivatsiaq** *inlet* Greenland
86 G5 **Kangetet** Kenya
59 J3 **Kanggye** N Korea
Kangikajik *C see* **Brewster, Kap**
Kangilinnguit *see* **Grønnedal**
115 M5 **Kangiqsujuaq** Quebec Canada
65 B5 **Kangjiahui** China
65 G1 **Kangjinjing** China
59 J4 **Kangnŭng** S Korea
86 B5 **Kango** Gabon
61 N13 **Kangoku-iwa** *islds* Iwo Jima Japan
26 N4 **Kangosfors** Sweden
65 F3 **Kangping** China
75 J3 **Kangrinboqê Feng** *mt* Xizang Zizhiqu
71 E8 **Kang Tipayan Dakula** *isld* Philippines
Kan-hsien *see* **Ganzhou**
68 B1 **Kani** Burma
87 D7 **Kaniama** Zaire
57 F4 **Kanibadam** Tajikistan
144 C5 **Kaniere** New Zealand
144 C5 **Kaniere, L** New Zealand
76 D3 **Kanigiri** India
57 D4 **Kanimekh** Uzbekistan
52 F1 **Kanin Nos, Mys** *C* Russian Federation
52 F1 **Kanin, Poluostrov** *pen* Russian Federation
52 F1 **Kaninskiy Bereg** *coast* Russian Federation
61 O5 **Kanita** Japan
26 N5 **Kaniulasjärvi** Sweden
138 F6 **Kaniva** Victoria Australia
48 F4 **Kanjiža** Serbia Yugoslavia
29 J10 **Kankaanpää** Finland
99 S8 **Kankakee** *R* Illinois U.S.A.
85 C6 **Kankan** Guinea
75 J8 **Kanker** India
83 J8 **Kankesanturai** Sri Lanka
29 L4 **Kankonen** Finland
74 E6 **Kankroli** India
68 D7 **Kanmaw Kyun** *isld* Burma
56 D5 **Kanmegirskiy Khrebet** *mts* Russian Federation
27 G15 **Kånna** Sweden
112 G2 **Kannapolis** North Carolina U.S.A.
22 K2 **Kanne** Belgium
74 G7 **Kannod** India
29 L9 **Kannonkoski** Finland
Kannur *see* **Cannanore**
29 K8 **Kannus** Finland
71 J6 **Kano** *isld* Indonesia
60 E11 **Kano** Japan
85 F6 **Kano** Nigeria
107 K2 **Kanona** Kansas U.S.A.
55 G5 **Kanonerka** Kazakhstan
60 G11 **Kanonji** Japan
126 B2 **Kanon, Pt** Curaçao
107 M3 **Kanopolis** Kansas U.S.A.
103 M3 **Kanosh** Utah U.S.A.
70 C3 **Kanowit** Sarawak
60 D14 **Kanoya** Japan
74 J5 **Kanpur** India
107 K3 **Kansas** *state* U.S.A.
99 T10 **Kansas** Illinois U.S.A.
107 P2 **Kansas** *R* Kansas U.S.A.
107 Q5 **Kansas** Oklahoma U.S.A.
107 Q2 **Kansas City** Kansas U.S.A.
110 B2 **Kansas City** Missouri U.S.A.
67 E4 **Kanshi** China
56 E3 **Kansk** Russian Federation
56 E4 **Kanskoye Belogor'ye** *mts* Russian Federation
88 A5 **Kansonge** Zaire
Kansu *prov see* **Gansu**
57 G3 **Kant** Kyrgyzstan
29 N9 **Kantala** Finland
85 E6 **Kantchari** Burkina
85 E6 **Kanté** Togo
68 G5 **Kantharalak** Thailand
75 M8 **Kānthi** India
116 M4 **Kantishna** *R* Alaska U.S.A.
134 A6 **Kanton I** *isld* Phoenix Is Pacific Oc
61 M10 **Kanto sanchi** *mts* Japan
68 C2 **Kantulong** Burma
14 C4 **Kanturk** Ireland
77 J5 **Kanuk** Afghanistan
102 S11 **Kanuku** Hawaiian Is
128 G3 **Kanuku Mts** Guyana
61 N9 **Kanuma** Japan
87 C11 **Kanus** Namibia
116 M3 **Kanuti** *R* Alaska U.S.A.
89 D5 **Kanye** Botswana
68 B3 **Kanyinngu** Burma
68 C3 **Kanyutkwin** Burma
38 J8 **Kanzel** *mt* Austria
87 E8 **Kanzenze** Zaire
137 R5 **Kao** *isld* Tonga
87 B9 **Kaoko Veld** *reg* Namibia
85 A6 **Kaolack** Senegal
47 J1 **Kaolinovo** Bulgaria
87 D8 **Kaoma** Zambia
65 F2 **Kaoshan** China
102 V13 **Kapaa** Hawaiian Is
102 V13 **Kapaau** Hawaiian Is
74 E7 **Kapadvanj** India
57 J2 **Kapal** Kazakhstan
71 O9 **Kapala** *isld* Indonesia
71 A3 **Kapalabuaya** Indonesia
71 M9 **Kapan** Timor Indonesia
87 D7 **Kapanga** Zaire
87 F7 **Kapatu** Zambia
66 B3 **Kapchagay** Kazakhstan
57 H3 **Kapchagayskoye Vdkhr.** *res* Kazakhstan
22 G1 **Kapellen** Belgium
25 F5 **Kapellen** Germany
86 G5 **Kapenguria** Kenya
38 M7 **Kapfenberg** Austria
88 E9 **Kapichira Falls** *waterfall* Malawi
47 J4 **Kapıdağı Yar** *pen* Turkey
70 G5 **Kapinyu, Tanjong** *C* Sulawesi
87 E8 **Kapiri Mposhi** Zambia
77 L2 **Kāpīsā** Afghanistan
115 L7 **Kapiskau** Ontario Canada
70 C4 **Kapit** Sarawak
54 C8 **Kapitanovka** Ukraine
145 E4 **Kapiti I** New Zealand
111 D11 **Kaplan** Louisiana U.S.A.
31 H7 **Kaplice** Czechoslovakia
69 D8 **Kapoe** Thailand
86 F5 **Kapoeta** Sudan
135 V5 **Kapoho** Hawaiian Is
71 L9 **Kapondai, Tanjong** Indonesia
145 E3 **Kaponga** New Zealand
70 F7 **Kapoposang** *isld* Indonesia
48 E4 **Kapos** *R* Hungary
48 D4 **Kaposvár** Hungary
71 C3 **Kapotjol** W Irian
74 B10 **Kappar** Pakistan
28 G7 **Kappel** Denmark
36 C3 **Kappel** Germany
28 D7 **Kappeln** Germany
36 E6 **Kappelrodeck** Germany
27 K14 **Kappelshamn** *isld* Gotland Sweden
41 M3 **Kappl** Austria
38 G7 **Kaprun** Austria
Kapsukas *see* **Marijampolė**
88 C9 **Kapsuku** *mt* Zimbabwe
70 B4 **Kapuas** *R* Kalimantan
70 D5 **Kapuas** *R* Kalimantan
70 C4 **Kapuas Hulu, Peg** Kalimantan
138 E5 **Kapunda** South Australia Australia
145 E3 **Kapuni** New Zealand
74 F3 **Kapurthala** India
120 H3 **Kapuskasing** Ontario Canada
120 H4 **Kapuskasing** *R* Ontario Canada
139 K4 **Kaputar** *mt* New South Wales Australia
48 D3 **Kapuvár** Hungary
56 H4 **Kapylyushi, Oz** *L* Russian Federation
66 B4 **Kaqung** China
85 E7 **Kara** Togo
78 G2 **Kara** *R* Turkey
79 G6 **Karā', Ard al** Syria
57 G5 **Karaart** Tajikistan

Column 1

70 K8 Kotabumi Sumatra
70 E2 Kota Kinabalu Sabah
29 O4 Kotala Finland
71 J4 Kotamubagu Sulawesi
76 F1 Kotapärh India
69 E12 Kotapinang Sumatra
69 E12 Kotatengah Sumatra
69 F12 Kota Tinggi Malaysia
70 B6 Kotawaringin Kalimantan
117 N6 Kotcho R British Columbia Canada
47 H2 Kotel Bulgaria
53 F9 Kotel'nikovo Russian Federation
51 N1 Kotel'nyy, Ostrov isld Russian Federation
145 F3 Kotemaori New Zealand
33 P9 Köthen Germany
74 F3 Kot Kapura India
52 H2 Kotkino Russian Federation
55 G2 Kotkino Russian Federation
52 G4 Kotlas Russian Federation
29 C11 Kotlin, O isld Russian Federation
28 S10 Kötlutangi C Iceland
52 C5 Kotly Russian Federation
60 G11 Kotohira Japan
60 P2 Kotoni Japan
42 J6 Kotor Montenegro Yugoslavia
42 H4 Kotor Varoš Bosnia-Herzegovina
53 C10 Kotovsk Ukraine
74 C6 Kotri Pakistan
57 A1 Kotr-Tas Kazakhstan
38 H8 Kötschach Austria
74 J10 Kottagudem India
75 K10 Kottakota India
76 C6 Kottayam India
83 J11 Kotte Sri Lanka
86 D4 Kotto R Cent Afr Republic
26 H8 Köttsjön Sweden
76 C3 Kotturu India
51 K1 Kotuy R Russian Federation
44 M3 Kotuzhany Moldavia
116 F3 Kotzebue Alaska U.S.A.
116 E3 Kotzebue Sd Alaska U.S.A.
37 O1 Kötzschenbroda Germany
37 O5 Kötzting Germany
26 B4 Kouandé Benin
86 D4 Kouango Cent Afr Republic
86 C2 Kouba Modounga Chad
85 D6 Koudougou Burkina
89 A9 Koue Bokkeveld reg S Africa
89 D8 Koueveld Berge mts S Africa
47 H10 Koufonisi isld Crete Greece
47 H8 Koufonisia isld Crete Greece
89 C9 Kougaberge mts S Africa
86 B6 Koulamoutou Gabon
85 C6 Koulikoro Mali
141 J5 Koumala Queensland Australia
66 E3 Koumenzi China
86 C4 Koumra Chad
86 C3 Koungouri Chad
48 C1 Kounice Czechoslovakia
47 H8 Kounoupoli isld Greece
57 G2 Kounradskiy Kazakhstan
111 B11 Kountze Texas U.S.A.
85 D6 Koupela Burkina
Koujan see Yongji
61 Q12 Kouri-jima isld Okinawa
84 F5 Kourizo, Passe de Chad
129 H2 Kourou Fr Guiana
85 C6 Kouroussa Guinea
89 B9 Kousberg mt S Africa
85 D6 Kousséri Cameroon
85 C6 Koutiala Mali
85 C7 Kouto Ivory Coast
47 F7 Koutsopódhi Greece
29 M11 Kouvola Finland
86 C6 Kouyou R Congo
52 G4 Kova R Russian Federation
47 H2 Kovachevtsi Bulgaria
48 F5 Kovačica Serbia Yugoslavia
46 C1 Kovač Planina mt Montenegro Yugoslavia
52 D2 Kovda Russian Federation
52 D2 Kovdozero, Oz L Russian Federation
55 E1 Koverskaya R Russian Federation
52 F6 Kovernino Russian Federation
29 P9 Kovero Finland
48 F6 Kovin Serbia Yugoslavia
46 D1 Kovren Montenegro Yugoslavia
52 G1 Kovriga, Gora mt Russian Federation
54 N1 Kovrov Russian Federation
52 E5 Kovzha R Russian Federation
52 E4 Kovzhskoye, Oz L Russian Federation
144 C5 Kowai Bush New Zealand
31 L2 Kowalewo Poland
71 J9 Kowangge Sumbawa Indonesia
144 C5 Kowhitirangi New Zealand
120 C2 Kowkash Ontario Canada
67 G6 Kowloon Hong Kong
55 C6 Kowyck Kazakhstan
61 J11 Kōyasan Japan
47 K8 Köyceğiz Turkey
47 J8 Köyceğiz Gölü L Turkey
52 F2 Koyda Russian Federation
52 H4 Koygorodok Russian Federation
46 G1 Koynare Bulgaria
52 G3 Koynas Russian Federation
61 O16 Koyoshi-gawa R Japan
52 J4 Koyp, Gora mt Russian Federation
54 L8 Koysug Russian Federation
57 D4 Koytash Uzbekistan
116 G4 Koyuk Alaska U.S.A.
116 L3 Koyukuk R Alaska U.S.A.
47 L8 Koyulhisar Turkey
55 C2 Koyva R Russian Federation
29 P7 Koyvayarvi Russian Federation
61 J12 Koza R Japan
60 C11 Kō-zaki C Japan
60 G11 Kozan Japan
78 E3 Kozan Turkey
46 E4 Kozáni Greece
42 H3 Kozara Bosnia-Herzegovina
48 E2 Kozárovce Czechoslovakia
52 E5 Kozelets Ukraine
54 G2 Kozel'shchina Ukraine
54 G2 Kozel'sk Russian Federation
55 E5 Kozhakol', Oz L Kazakhstan
55 G3 Kozhevnikovo Russian Federation
Kozhikode see Calicut
52 J2 Kozhim Russian Federation
52 J2 Kozhmvom Russian Federation
52 J3 Kozhozero, Oz L Russian Federation
52 G3 Kozhposelok Russian Federation
55 G3 Kozhva Russian Federation
52 J3 Kozhva R Russian Federation
31 N4 Kozienice Poland
31 E3 Kozina Slovenia
46 E3 Kozjak mt Macedonia Yugoslavia
31 L5 Koźle Poland
46 F1 Kozloduy Bulgaria
52 G5 Kozlovets Bulgaria
54 M6 Kozlovka Russian Federation
78 C1 Kozlu Turkey
31 K4 Koźmin Poland
48 E1 Kozmoldak Kazakhstan
52 H4 Kozova Ukraine
31 J4 Koźuchów Poland
61 N11 Kōzu-shima isld Japan

Column 2

85 E7 Kpalime Togo
85 D7 Kpandu Ghana
89 E8 Kraai R S Africa
33 O6 Kraak Germany
25 B6 Krabbendijke Netherlands
68 D7 Kra Buri Thailand
37 M2 Kraftsdorf Germany
70 N9 Kragan Java
28 C4 Kragelund Denmark
28 G7 Kragenæs Denmark
27 D13 Kragerø Norway
48 F6 Kragujevac Serbia
54 K7 Krahenberg Germany
46 F2 Krahnberg mt Germany
101 P1 Kraich R Germany
33 N8 Kraichtal Germany
33 S7 Kraichgau Germany
106 D1 Krajina reg Croatia/Yugoslavia
32 K5 Kraksaan Indonesia
70 K9 Krakatau isld Sumatra
26 A9 Kråkenes Norway
68 H1 Krakor Cambodia
48 H1 Krakovets Ukraine
31 M5 Kraków Poland
68 F8 Kralanh Cambodia
31 K5 Král Chlmec Czechoslovakia
31 K5 Králiky Czechoslovakia
48 E1 Kraljevo Czechoslovakia
37 Q4 Kralovice Czechoslovakia
37 P3 Kralupy Czechoslovakia
69 Q11 Kramat Indonesia
98 F1 Kramer North Dakota U.S.A.
26 J9 Kramfors Sweden
68 E1 Kram, Ko isld Thailand
26 S1 Krampenes Norway
25 F5 Kranenburg Germany
26 H8 Krångede Sweden
38 L5 Kranía Greece
38 E7 Kranichfeld Germany
41 K2 Kranidhion Greece
36 E2 Kranj Slovenia
39 J9 Kranjska-Gord Slovenia
31 K5 Krapkowice Poland
29 K4 Krapperup Sweden
52 G4 Krasavino Russian Federation
54 K1 Krashy Oktyabr' Russian Federation
48 K1 Krasilov Ukraine
50 E1 Krasino Russian Federation
52 F6 Krasino Russian Federation
76 C2 Kraslava Latvia
37 Q3 Kraslice Czechoslovakia
31 N5 Krasnik Poland
31 N4 Krasnik Fabryczny Poland
37 O3 Krásno Czechoslovakia
55 E4 Krasnoarmeysk Kazakhstan
54 K1 Krasnoarmeysk Russian Federation
58 G1 Krasnoarmeysk Russian Federation
54 J8 Krasnoarmeysk Ukraine
55 D4 Krasnoarmeyskiy Kustanayskaya Kazakhstan
52 G4 Krasnoborsk Russian Federation
31 O5 Krasnobród Poland
53 E11 Krasnodar Russian Federation
58 E10 Krasnodarskiy Kray reg Russian Federation
54 F1 Krasnodon Ukraine
52 D5 Krasnofarfornyy Russian Federation
52 G5 Krasnogorodskoye Russian Federation
59 M2 Krasnogorsk Russian Federation
55 D4 Krasnogorskiy Chelyabinskaya obl Russian Federation
52 H5 Krasnogorskoye Russian Federation
54 G7 Krasnograd Ukraine
55 D3 Krasnogvardeyskiy Russian Federation
55 B5 Krasnokholm Orenburgskaya obl Russian Federation
55 G4 Krasnokutsk Pavlodarskaya obl Kazakhstan
55 E1 Krasnokutsk Ukraine
54 L5 Krasnoleninskiy Russian Federation
31 N1 Krasnoles'niyy Russian Federation
54 J7 Krasnooskol'skoye Vodokhranilishche res Ukraine
52 C4 Krasnoostrovskiy Russian Federation
54 H7 Krasnopavlovka Ukraine
54 G3 Krasnopol'ye Belorussia
54 K7 Krasnorechenskoye Ukraine
53 F9 Krasnoslobodsk Russian Federation
55 D2 Krasnotur'insk Russian Federation
55 C3 Krasnoufimsk Russian Federation
29 O12 Krasnoural'sk Russian Federation
68 D5 Krasnovodsk Turkmenistan
37 N7 Krasnovishersk Russian Federation
55 C3 Krasnovishersk Russian Federation
52 J4 Krasnovisk Russian Federation
50 E4 Krasnovodsk Turkmenistan
55 F3 Krasnoyarka Omskaya obl Kazakhstan
55 D2 Krasnoyarsk R Russian Federation
55 D3 Krasnoyarsk Russian Federation
54 K4 Krasnoye Russian Federation
52 H5 Krasnoye Ukraine
54 M1 Krasnoye Ukraine
57 B6 Krasnoye Znamya Turkmenistan
52 G4 Krasnozatonskiy Russian Federation
55 G4 Krasnozersk Russian Federation
55 C4 Krasnoznamenskiy Bashkirskaya Respublika Russian Federation
52 E5 Krasnoznamenskoye Tselinogradskaya obl Kazakhstan
54 E5 Krasnyy Bor Russian Federation
54 J8 Krasny Liman Ukraine
54 K8 Krasny Luch Ukraine
47 H3 Krasny Mayak Russian Federation
31 O5 Krasnystaw Poland
54 L1 Krasny Tkach Russian Federation
68 E6 Krasnyye Russian Federation
55 G6 Krasnyye-Baki Russian Federation
55 C3 Krasnyye Russian Federation
48 M3 Krasnye Okna Ukraine
52 E5 Krasnyye Tkachi Russian Federation
52 E5 Krasnyy Kholm Tverskaya Russian Federation
55 C2 Krasnyy-Klyuch Russian Federation
52 C6 Krasnyy Oktyabr Russian Federation
52 F3 Krasnyy Pereval Russian Federation
55 E3 Krasnyy Yar Omskaya obl Russian Federation
55 D2 Krasnyy Yar Sverdlovskaya obl Russian Federation
68 H6 Kratie Cambodia
31 P5 Krauabath Austria
38 D10 Krauchenwies Germany

Column 3

115 O3 Kraulshavn Greenland
36 H5 Krautheim Germany
32 K5 Krautsand Germany
107 P7 Krebs Oklahoma U.S.A.
25 G6 Krefeld Germany
29 J5 Kregme Denmark
26 H7 Krehberg mt Germany
32 L9 Kreiensen Germany
116 D5 Krekatok I Alaska U.S.A.
46 F1 Kremena Bulgaria
54 E7 Kremenchug Ukraine
54 D7 Kremenchugskaye Vdkhr res Ukraine
46 K7 Kremenets Ukraine
46 F2 Kremenets Ukraine
101 P1 Kremlin Montana U.S.A.
33 N8 Kremlingen Germany
33 S7 Kremmen Germany
106 D1 Kremmling Colorado U.S.A.
32 K5 Krempe Germany
38 M5 Krems R Austria
38 N5 Krems Austria
33 Q10 Krenitzin Is Aleutian Is
33 Q10 Krensitz Germany
79 C4 Krešovo Bosnia-Herzegovina
69 D9 Kuah Malaysia
67 A4 Kuaize He R China
32 M10 Kullstedt Germany
73 G4 Kullu India
98 H3 Kulm North Dakota U.S.A.
37 M4 Kulmain Germany
37 L3 Kulmbach Germany
52 F3 Kuloy R Russian Federation
52 F4 Kuloy Russian Federation
138 E5 Kulpara South Australia
95 L6 Kulpmont Pennsylvania U.S.A.
38 G7 Kuls Austria
54 E4 Kul'sary Kazakhstan
36 H4 Külsheim Germany
56 G5 Kul'skiy Stanok Russian Federation
56 C5 Kultala Finland
75 M7 Kulti India
60 C12 Kultsjöluspen Sweden
55 C5 Kultsjön L Sweden
33 G7 Kültsheim Germany
78 D2 Kulu Turkey
55 G4 Kulunda Russian Federation
56 B4 Kulunda R Russian Federation
57 E5 Kulyab Tajikistan
47 J6 Kum R Turkey
60 F12 Kuma Japan
53 G11 Kuma Russian Federation
60 D13 Kuma-gawa R Japan
61 N9 Kumagaya Japan
70 B6 Kumai Indonesia
70 B6 Kumai, Teluk B Kalimantan
54 K1 Kumak R Russian Federation
55 D5 Kumak Russian Federation
60 D13 Kumamoto Japan
83 H5 Kumana Sri Lanka
48 F7 Kumanica Serbia Yugoslavia
29 J9 Kumanjana R Finland
61 O7 Kumano Japan
79 D2 Kumanovo Macedonia Yugoslavia
70 D6 Kumap R Kalimantan
144 C5 Kumara New Zealand
51 M3 Kumara Russian Federation
144 C5 Kumara Junction New Zealand
85 D7 Kumasi Ghana
74 H3 Kumar R India
86 A5 Kumba Cameroon
76 D5 Kumbakonam India
47 L5 Kumbet Turkey
83 L11 Kumbukkan Oya R Sri Lanka
59 J4 Kümch'ŏn S Korea
84 J5 Kumdah Turkey
52 F6 Kumertau Russian Federation
86 F5 Kumi Uganda
60 H10 Kumihama Japan
55 E2 Kuminskiy Russian Federation
54 H5 Kumluca Turkey
60 D12 Kumo Japan
55 E2 Kumon Range Burma
68 F4 Kumphawapi Thailand
60 H5 Kumta India
135 V5 Kumukahi, C Hawaiian Is
76 B3 Kumuh Afghanistan
29 N9 Kümüx China
116 J2 Kun R Burma
143 E6 Kunanaggi Well W Australia
74 D1 Kunar Afghanistan
55 D3 Kunashak Russian Federation
60 T1 Kunashir Ostrov isld Russian Federation

Column 4

48 F1 Krynica Poland
31 O2 Kryry Poland
37 P3 Kryry Czechoslovakia
54 J1 Kryukovo Russian Federation
56 .E4 Kryzhina, Khr mts Russian Federation
48 M2 Kryzhopol' Ukraine
31 L5 Krzepice Poland
31 N5 Krzeszów Poland
57 C4 Kul'dzhuktau, Gory mt Uzbekistan
52 F6 Kuebaki Russian Federation
54 G8 Kulebovka Ukraine
42 G4 Kulen Vakuf Bosnia-Herzegovina
55 D4 Kulevchi Russian Federation
140 C7 Kulgera N Terr Australia
52 H5 Kuligi Russian Federation
48 J1 Kulikov Ukraine
69 E10 Kulim Malaysia
143 C10 Kulin W Australia
56 G1 Kulingda Russian Federation
43 B9 Kulkyne R New South Wales Australia
29 K4 Kulla Gunnarstorp Sweden
31 L7 Kullen mt Sweden
69 M3 Kuala Lumpur Malaysia
69 E9 Kuala Nerang Malaysia
70 C6 Kualapembuang Kalimantan
70 D2 Kuala Penyu Sabah
69 F11 Kuala Pilah Malaysia
135 S2 Kualapuu Hawaiian Is
54 M1 Kuala sampit Kalimantan
70 B6 Kuala Selangor Malaysia
69 E11 Kuala Terengganu Malaysia
70 E13 Kualatungkal Sumatra
70 E2 Kuamut R Sabah
70 E2 Kuamut Sabah
65 D4 Kuancheng China
78 D2 Kuandian China
71 H4 Kuandang, Tk B Sulawesi Indonesia
59 H3 Kuandian China
66 D5 Kuang-chou see Guangzhou
69 F11 Kuantan Malaysia
145 E2 Kuaotunu New Zealand
53 G12 Kuba Azerbaijan
53 F11 Kuban' R Russian Federation
78 G4 Kubar, el Syria
79 H3 Kubaybāt Syria
70 B6 Kubbe Sweden
86 D3 Kubbum Sudan
52 F4 Kubena R Russian Federation
52 E5 Kubenskoye, Oz L Russian Federation
60 G6 Kubokawa Japan
79 A8 Kubra, El Egypt
47 H1 Kubrat Bulgaria
69 J13 Kubu Indonesia
70 P10 Kubu Kalimantan
70 D3 Kubuang Kalimantan
70 D4 Kubuhay Russian
58 F1 Kudaka-jima isld Okinawa
70 D4 Kubumesaài Kalimantan
86 A5 Kuçevo Serbia Yugoslavia
54 C3 Kuçova Russian Federation
36 H6 Kuchen Germany
41 M3 Kuchl Spitze mt Austria
70 B4 Kuching Sarawak
60 D13 Kuchinotsu Japan
60 F10 Kuchitagi Japan
55 G4 Kuchukskoye, Oz L Russian Federation
48 M3 Kuçurgan R Ukraine
70 D9 Kuda, isld see Kuching
33 N5 Öcknitz Germany
47 M10 Üçükçekmece Turkey
47 M10 Üçükçekmece Gölü Turkey
47 M11 Üçükçekmece Koya crater Germany
47 J6 Üçük Menderes R Turkey
83 K11 Üdaka-jima isld Okinawa
61 P14 udaka-jima isld Okinawa
79 B5 udamatau Japan
70 B5 udangan Kalimantan
69 F12 udap Sumatra
70 E1 udat Sabah
68 B1 udaw Burma
36 D7 udeyevskiy Russian
65 G7 udmo isld S Korea
57 D2 udon R Kazakhstan
75 N5 udon Range Burma
68 F4 Kumphawapi Thailand

Column 5

57 A2 Kulandy, Poluostrov pen Kazakhstan
55 F6 Kulanutpes R Kazakhstan
46 F3 Kulasein isld Philippines
70 F5 Kulata Bulgaria
70 F5 Kulawi Sulawesi Indonesia
116 N1 Kuldiga Latvia
117 K8 Kuldo British Columbia Canada
52 F6 Kulebaki Russian Federation
116 L7 Kupreanof St Alaska U.S.A.
80 H6 Kur Thailand
79 D9 Kuah Malaysia
67 A4 Kuaize He R China
32 M10 Kullstedt Germany
73 G4 Kullu India
98 H3 Kulm North Dakota U.S.A.
37 M4 Kulmain Germany
37 L3 Kulmbach Germany
52 F3 Kuloy R Russian Federation
52 F4 Kuloy Russian Federation
138 E5 Kulpara South Australia
95 L6 Kulpmont Pennsylvania U.S.A.
38 G7 Kuls Austria
54 E4 Kul'sary Kazakhstan
36 H4 Külsheim Germany
56 G5 Kul'skiy Stanok Russian Federation
56 C5 Kultala Finland
75 M7 Kulti India
60 C12 Kultsjöluspen Sweden
55 C5 Kultsjön L Sweden
78 G2 Kurdistan reg Turkey/Iraq/Iran
74 F9 Kurduvadi India
46 G3 Kürdzhali Bulgaria
55 C5 Kürdzhali, Yazovir res Bulgaria
47 K6 Kure Japan
134 J5 Kure Atoll Hawaiian Is U.S.A.
80 F4 Kure R Japan
78 G2 Kuresaare Estonia
56 B4 Kurgal'dzhinskiy Kazakhstan
77 A3 Kurgan Russian Federation
56 C5 Kurganskaya Oblast' prov Russian Federation
57 K6 Kurgantepa Uzbekistan
55 C3 Kurgan-Tyube Tajikistan
55 G3 Kuri isld Kiribati
137 P1 Kuria isld Kiribati
43 D13 Kuriat, Is. Tunisia
29 J9 Kurikka R Finland
61 O7 Kuril Is see Kuril'skiye Ostrova
51 R5 Kuril'sk Russian Federation
59 N2 Kuril'sk Russian Federation
51 O4 Kuril'skaya Ostrova Russian Federation
145 F3 Kuripapango New Zealand
116 E4 Kurishes Haff sea
53 G7 Courland lagoon
54 K1 Kuroiso Japan
56 C5 Kurkuri R Russian Federation
60 P2 Kuriyama Japan
56 C5 Kuriyoki Russian Federation
60 G10 Kurobe Japan
29 O10 Kurkyoki Russian Federation
84 J5 Kurkur Oasis Egypt
52 F5 Kurlovskiy Russian Federation
36 F5 Kürnbach Germany
76 D3 Kurnool India
61 O9 Kurobane Japan
61 L9 Kurobe Japan
61 O9 Kurobe No. 4 Dam Japan
28 E7 Kuregaard Denmark
116 E8 Kurobeyama mt Japan
60 G10 Kurogi Japan
61 O5 Kuroishi Japan
61 K2 Kuroiso Japan
119 O7 Kuroki Saskatchewan Canada
26 G7 Kuromatsunai Japan
54 C5 Kurosaka Japan
27 G15 Kurosiy Marios see Courland lagoon
54 K1 Kurovskoye Russian Federation
144 C6 Kurow New Zealand
144 N4 Kurów Poland
139 K5 Kurri Kurri New South Wales Australia
52 H5 Kurshskaya L Russian Federation
53 E8 Kurskaya Oblast' prov Russian Federation
53 E8 Kurshskiy Zaliv see Courland lagoon
27 B13 Kurskaya L Russian Federation
46 E1 Kurskaya Oblast' prov Russian Federation
55 A4 Kurskiy Zaliv see Courland lagoon
36 E1 Kürten Germany
47 K8 Kurtoğlu Burun C Turkey
47 K11 Kurtuslıbinaklı, Khr mts Russian Federation
29 K10 Kuru Finland
29 M10 Kuruman S Africa

Column 6

26 L5 Kuouka Sweden
26 L3 Kuoutatjärro mt Sweden
42 G3 Kupa R Croatia/Slovenia
71 L10 Kupang Timor Indonesia
71 L10 Kupang, Tk B Timor Indonesia
116 N1 Kuparuk R Alaska U.S.A.
37 M3 Kupferberg Germany
143 F3 Kuphi Russian Federation
56 E5 Ku Tayga, Khrebet mts Russian Federation
106 G3 Kutch Colorado U.S.A.
60 O3 Kutchan Japan
54 K9 Kuteynikovo Ukraine
54 H2 Kutina Croatia
68 F4 Kut Khao Thailand
31 L3 Kutno Poland
31 L3 Kutno Poland
70 M9 Kutoadjo Java
69 C11 Kutoarjo Sumatra
69 C11 Kutoarjo Sumatra
76 E1 Kutru India
89 D4 Kutse Game Res Botswana
31 J6 Kutná Hóra Czechoslovakia
31 L3 Kutno Poland
70 M9 Kutoadjo Java
89 D4 Kutse Game Res Botswana
84 S3 Kutubdia I Bangladesh
115 N6 Kuujjuaq Quebec Canada
29 L4 Kuusamo Finland
29 O6 Kuusankoski Finland
29 M11 Kuusamo Finland
52 H5 Kuva Russian Federation
52 H5 Kuvandyk Russian
87 C8 Kuvango Angola
29 P2 Kuvets'yarvi, Ozero L
116 F1 Kuvikur Iceland
28 S9 Kuvira Iceland
52 D6 Kushimoto Japan
54 B4 Kushiro Japan
51 J2 Kushva Russian Federation
77 A5 Kusel Germany
56 B6 Kushva Russian Federation
55 D3 Kuytun China
72 A8 Kuyukkol', Oz L Kazakhstan
56 S3 Kuzbass basin Russian Federation
66 D5 Kutytun China
75 O4 Kuu'kol', Oz L Kazakhstan
59 N2 Kuzitrin R Alaska U.S.A.
60 D5 Kuznetsk Russian Federation
56 C5 Kuznetskiy Alatau mt Russian Federation
56 C5 Kuznetsovo Russian Federation
55 D2 Kuzomen Russian Federation
26 H3 Kvaenangen inlet Norway
26 M1 Kvaenangsbotn Norway
28 H6 Kvaerkeby Denmark
28 E5 Kværs Denmark
26 N1 Kvalöya isld Norway
26 K2 Kvalöy, S isld Norway
26 D10 Kvam Norway
55 C5 Kvarkeno Russian Federation
27 G15 Kvarnamåla Sweden
28 G7 Kvarnbergsvattnet L Sweden
42 F4 Kvarner chan Croatia
42 F4 Kvarneric chan Croatia
27 J13 Kvarsebo Sweden
27 C11 Kvelia R Norway
26 J8 Kvelvoll Norway
26 M2 Kvenes Norway
116 J7 Kvichak Alaska U.S.A.
26 G6 Kvigtind mt Norway
26 D1 Kvikkjock Sweden
26 G7 Kvikkjokk Sweden
26 A5 Kvinad Norway
27 B12 Kvina R Norway
27 B13 Kvinesdal Norway
27 G12 Kvistbro Sweden
29 K5 Kvistofta Sweden
26 J4 Kviteseid Norway
26 K11 Kvitvatn mt Norway
28 A5 Kvitsøy isld Norway
26 J5 Kvong Denmark
26 N1 Kvenna Denmark
117 L7 Kwadacha Wilderness Prov. Park Canada
55 G4 Kwajalein atoll Marshall Is Pacific Oc
115 H4 Kwakoegron Suriname
134 D2 Kwale Kenya
88 G11 Kwale Nigeria
88 G4 Kwale Nigeria
85 F7 Kwale Nigeria
89 C8 Kwamouth Zaire
71 H4 Kwandang Sulawesi
89 C4 Kwangsu see Guangzhou
65 G7 Kwangju S Korea
86 C6 Kwango R Zaire
66 D5 Kwangsi prov see Guangxi
66 G3 Kwangtung prov see Guangdong prov
37 L4 Kwania, L Uganda
89 H1 Kwatabuga R Ontario Canada

Column 7

56 G3 Kuta R Russian Federation
56 C10 Kutabagok Sumatra
71 J4 Kutabunan Sulawesi
47 K5 Kütahya Turkey
53 F12 Kutaisi Georgia
78 K5 Küt, Al Iraq
57 E2 Kutansor, Ozero L Kazakhstan
145 F3 Kutarere New Zealand
56 E5 Ku Tayga, Khrebet mts Russian Federation
106 G3 Kutch Colorado U.S.A.
60 O3 Kutchan Japan
54 K9 Kuteynikovo Ukraine
54 H2 Kutina Croatia
68 F4 Kut Khao Thailand
31 L3 Kutno Poland
70 M9 Kutoadjo Java
69 C11 Kutoarjo Sumatra
76 E1 Kutru India
89 D4 Kutse Game Res Botswana
31 J6 Kutná Hóra Czechoslovakia
84 T4 Tanzania
72 A3 Kutulik Russian Federation
54 B6 Kuturchinskoye Belog mt Russian Federation
56 D4 Kuturchinskoye Russian Federation
48 J2 Kützberg Germany
37 J3 Kützberg Germany
77 J5 Kutztown Pennsylvania U.S.A.
48 F9 Kuvango Angola
29 P2 Kuvets'yarvi, Ozero L
116 F1 Kuvikur Iceland
29 N6 Kuwait state Kuwait, Al
77 A3 Kuwait, Al Kuwait
78 L5 Kuwayt, Al Iraq
115 R4 Kuwayt, Al Kuwait
52 F2 Kuya Russian Federation
116 N1 Kuybyshev see Samara
55 G3 Kuybyshev Kazakhstan
55 G3 Kuybyshevskaya Oblast' see Samarskaya Oblast'
55 G3 Kuybyshevskaya Kazakhstan
65 A5 Kuye He R China
51 R2 Kuyets'yarvi, Oz L Russian Federation
56 S2 Kuytun Russian Federation
66 D5 Kuytun China
66 D5 Kuytun China
128 G3 Kuzbass basin Russian Federation
56 C3 Kuzbass basin Russian Federation
53 D7 Kuzitrin R Alaska U.S.A.
60 D5 Kuznetsk Russian Federation
56 C5 Kuznetskiy Alatau mt Russian Federation
56 C5 Kuznetsovo Russian Federation
55 D2 Kuzomen Russian Federation
26 H3 Kvaenangen inlet Norway
26 M1 Kvaenangsbotn Norway
28 H6 Kvaerkeby Denmark
28 E5 Kværs Denmark
26 N1 Kvalöya isld Norway
26 K2 Kvalöy, S isld Norway
26 D10 Kvam Norway
55 C5 Kvarkeno Russian Federation
27 G15 Kvarnamåla Sweden
28 G7 Kvarnbergsvattnet L Sweden
42 F4 Kvarner chan Croatia
42 F4 Kvarneric chan Croatia
27 J13 Kvarsebo Sweden
27 C11 Kvelia R Norway
26 J8 Kvelvoll Norway
26 M2 Kvenes Norway
116 J7 Kvichak Alaska U.S.A.
26 G6 Kvigtind mt Norway
26 D1 Kvikkjock Sweden
26 G7 Kvikkjokk Sweden
26 A5 Kvinad Norway
27 B12 Kvina R Norway
27 B13 Kvinesdal Norway
27 G12 Kvistbro Sweden
29 K5 Kvistofta Sweden
26 J4 Kviteseid Norway
26 K11 Kvitvatn mt Norway
28 A5 Kvitsøy isld Norway
26 J5 Kvong Denmark
26 N1 Kvenna Denmark
117 L7 Kwadacha Wilderness Prov. Park Canada
55 G4 Kwajalein atoll Marshall Is Pacific Oc
115 H4 Kwakoegron Suriname
134 D2 Kwale Kenya
88 G11 Kwale Nigeria
88 G4 Kwale Nigeria
85 F7 Kwale Nigeria
89 C8 Kwamouth Zaire
71 H4 Kwandang Sulawesi
89 C4 Kwangju S Korea
66 D5 Kwangsu see Guangzhou
65 G7 Kwangju S Korea
86 C6 Kwango R Zaire
89 F2 Kwekwe Zimbabwe
89 D2 Kweneng Botswana
68 D5 Kwethluk Alaska U.S.A.
116 G6 Kwidzyn Poland
31 L2 Kwidzyn Poland
26 D7 Kwigamute Alaska U.S.A.
116 E5 Kwigillingok Alaska U.S.A.
116 E5 Kwik R Alaska U.S.A.
116 E5 Kwikpak Alaska U.S.A.
142 A4 Kwinana W Australia
31 J4 Kwisa R Poland
128 G3 Kwoka mt W Irian
143 C10 Kwoorup W Australia
36 E6 Kwoka mt W Irian
68 B3 Kyabé Chad
138 H5 Kyabram Victoria Australia
68 B3 Kyadet Burma
68 B4 Kyaikkami Burma
68 B4 Kyaiklat Burma
68 B4 Kyaikto Burma
72 A3 Kyakhta Russian Federation
138 E4 Kyalite New South Wales Australia
68 A3 Kyangin Burma
68 B3 Kyaukhnyat Burma
68 B3 Kyaukpadaung Burma
68 A2 Kyaukpyu Burma
68 B2 Kyaukse Burma
68 B4 Kyaunggon Burma
68 A3 Kyaukto Burma
68 B4 Kya-in Seikkyi Burma

88 C2 **Kyaka** Tanzania
56 G5 **Kyakhta** Russian Federation
139 G5 **Kyalite** New South Wales Australia
138 D5 **Kyancutta** South Australia Australia
52 E3 **Kyanda** Russian Federation
52 D3 **Kyargozero** Russian Federation
68 C3 **Kyauknnyat** Burma
68 B3 **Kyaukkyi** Burma
68 C1 **Kyaukme** Burma
68 B1 **Kyaukmyaung** Burma
68 A3 **Kyaukpyu** Burma
68 C2 **Kyaukse** Burma
68 A2 **Kyauktaw** Burma
68 B2 **Kyazanti** Burma
68 B4 **Kyaunggon** Burma
138 F6 **Kybybolite** South Australia Australia
26 G7 **Kycklingvattnet** Sweden
68 C3 **Kyebogyi** Burma
144 C6 **Kyeburn** New Zealand
68 D5 **Kyeikdon** Burma
68 D4 **Kyeikywa** Burma
68 B3 **Kyeintali** Burma
33 O10 **Kyffhäuser** mt Germany
143 E7 **Kyffin-Thomas Hill** W Australia Australia
28 F5 **Kyholm** isld Denmark
68 C3 **Kyidaunggan** Burma
58 D4 **Kyikug** China
68 A2 **Kyindwe** Burma
31 K6 **Kyiv** Czechoslovakia
118 J8 **Kyle** Saskatchewan Canada
98 D6 **Kyle** South Dakota U.S.A.
109 K6 **Kyle** Texas U.S.A.
101 T8 **Kyle** Wyoming U.S.A.
15 C3 **Kyleakin** Scotland
15 D2 **Kyle of Durness** Scotland
15 C3 **Kyle of Lochalsh** Scotland
15 D2 **Kyle of Tongue** Scotland
12 C2 **Kyles of Bute** chan Scotland
36 B3 **Kyll** R Germany
36 B3 **Kyllburg** Germany
29 N10 **Kymi** prov Finland
29 M11 **Kymijoki** R Finland
55 C2 **Kyn** Russian Federation
139 G6 **Kyneton** Victoria Australia
37 O3 **Kynšperk nad Ohří** Czechoslovakia
141 F5 **Kynuna** Queensland Australia
61 P12 **Kyoda** Okinawa
86 F5 **Kyoga, L** Uganda
60 J10 **Kyōga-misaki** C Japan
139 L3 **Kyogle** New South Wales Australia
65 F5 **Kyomip'o** N Korea
68 D4 **Kyondo** Burma
141 H5 **Kyong** Queensland Australia
68 C2 **Kyong** Burma
60 J10 **Kyōto** prefect Japan
60 J10 **Kyōto** conurbation Japan
55 E6 **Kypshak, Oz** L Kazakhstan
79 D3 **Kyrenia** Cyprus
57 F4 **Kyrgyzstan** rep C Asia
33 Q7 **Kyritz** Germany
Kyrkslätt see Kirkkonummi
29 J8 **Kyröjoki** R Finland
29 K10 **Kyrösjärvi** L Finland
52 J3 **Kyrta** Russian Federation
55 D2 **Kyrtym'ya** Russian Federation
55 C2 **Kyr'ya** Russian Federation
55 G3 **Kyshtovka** Russian Federation
55 D3 **Kyshtym** Russian Federation
68 G3 **Ky Son** Vietnam
52 G3 **Kyssa** Russian Federation
79 D3 **Kythrea** Cyprus
55 C2 **Kytlym** Russian Federation
57 H3 **Kyzagkay-Ala-Too, Khrebet** mts Kazakhstan/Kyrgyzstan
68 D5 **Kyunguaung** Burma
68 C7 **Kyun Pila** islds Burma
117 K10 **Kyuquot** British Columbia Canada
60 D13 **Kyūshū** isld Japan
60 E13 **Kyūshū-sanchi** mts Japan
46 F2 **Kyustendil** Bulgaria
51 M1 **Kyusyur** Russian Federation
139 H6 **Kywong** New South Wales Australia
29 L8 **Kyyjärvi** Finland
56 D5 **Kyzyl** Russian Federation
57 E1 **Kyzylggykan** Kazakhstan
56 E5 **Kyzyl-Khem** R Russian Federation
57 J2 **Kyzylkiya** Kazakhstan
57 F4 **Kyzyl-Kiya** Kyrgyzstan
57 C4 **Kyzyl-Kommuna** Kazakhstan
57 C4 **Kyzylkum, Peski** desert Kazakhstan/Uzbekistan
55 F5 **Kyzylrabot** Tajikistan
55 F5 **Kyzyltas** Kazakhstan
57 H1 **Kyzyltu** Kazakhstan
57 G1 **Kyzylzhar** Kazakhstan
57 J3 **Kyzylzhide** Kazakhstan
57 D3 **Kyzyl-Orda** Kazakhstan
55 F4 **Kzyltu** Kazakhstan

L

31 J7 **Laa** Austria
37 M5 **Laaber** Germany
36 C3 **Laacher See** L Germany
36 C3 **Laage** Germany
25 F4 **Laag Keppel** Netherlands
124 C4 **La Angostura** Mexico
29 N3 **Laanila** Finland
131 A7 **La Araucanía** prov Chile
86 A2 **Laascaanood** Somalia
86 A1 **Laas Dhuura** Somalia
86 A1 **Laasgoray** Somalia
86 A1 **Laaso Dawaco** Somalia
36 E2 **Laasphe** Germany
127 N9 **La Asunción** Venezuela
135 R2 **Laau Pt** Hawaiian Is
85 B3 **Lâäyoune** W Sahara
108 E7 **La Babia** Mexico
110 F3 **Labadie** Missouri U.S.A.
7 E12 **Labadie Bank** Atlantic Oc
111 F12 **Labadieville** Louisiana U.S.A.
121 U4 **La Baie** Quebec Canada
71 U9 **Labala** Indonesia
19 P12 **Labalme** France
79 F8 **Laban** Jordan
16 D2 **La Baneza** Spain
124 H1 **La Barca** Mexico
101 P7 **La Barge** Wyoming U.S.A.
19 P17 **La Bastide-des-Jourdans** France
18 G8 **Labastide Murat** France
19 Q13 **La Bathie** France
19 Q15 **La Bâtie-Neuve** France
68 A2 **Labawa** Burma
52 H2 **Labazhskoye** Russian Federation
26 J5 **Labbas** Sweden
80 D1 **Labbouna** Lebanon
26 R3 **Labdshy'aur, Oz** L Russian Federation
31 J5 **Labe** R Czechoslovakia
85 B6 **Labé** Guinea
19 O17 **Le Bégude Blanche** France
121 Q6 **Labelle** Quebec Canada
99 P9 **La Belle** Missouri U.S.A.
71 H6 **Labengke** isld Sulawesi
117 L5 **Laberge, L** Yukon Territory Canada

71 B2 **Labilabi** Halmahera Indonesia
42 F3 **Labin** Croatia
69 F11 **Labis** Malaysia
127 M9 **La Blanquilla, I** Venezuela
71 F3 **Labo** Philippines
71 H5 **Lobobo** isld Indonesia
124 G4 **La Boquilla** Mexico
101 U7 **Labonte Cr** Wyoming U.S.A.
143 C7 **Labouchere, Mt** W Australia Australia
79 G4 **Laboué** Lebanon
18 E8 **Labouheyre** France
133 E4 **Laboulaye** Argentina
115 N5 **Labrador** dist Newfoundland Canada
115 N7 **Labrador City** Labrador, Nfld Canada
115 O6 **Labrador Sea** Nfld/ Greenland
128 F5 **Labrea** Brazil
128 B4 **La Brea, Cer. de** hill Peru
124 E5 **La Brecha** Mexico
18 E8 **Labrède** France
122 C4 **Labrieville** Quebec Canada
122 C4 **Labrieville, Parc de** Quebec Canada
18 E8 **Labrit** France
118 E1 **La Broquerie** Manitoba Canada
18 C8 **Labroye** France
72 G8 **Labruguière** France
48 M2 **Labuanbajo** Indonesia
68 E3 **Labuha** Moluccas Indonesia
28 C5 **Labuhan** Java
71 J9 **Labuhanbadjo** Sumba Indonesia
69 D8 **Labuhanbilik** Sumatra
69 C11 **Labuhanhaji** Sumatra
69 D8 **Labuhanmeringgai** Sumatra
69 D11 **Labuhanruku** Sumatra
71 H9 **Labuhansepakah** Indonesia
19 P14 **La Buisse** France
71 K2 **Labuk** R Sabah
70 E1 **Labuk, Telukan** B Sabah
68 B4 **Labutta** Burma
138 D7 **Labyrinth, L** South Australia Australia
50 F2 **Labytnangi** Russian Federation
45 L2 **Laç** Albania
118 J8 **Lacadena** Saskatchewan Canada
124 G5 **La Cadena** Mexico
22 L2 **La Calamine** Belgium
122 J3 **Lac Allard** Quebec Canada
111 D10 **Lacamp** Louisiana U.S.A.
128 F1 **Lacanau** France
125 O9 **Lacantún** R Mexico
127 M5 **La Canoa** Venezuela
95 Q2 **Lacapelle-Marival** France
131 B8 **Lacar, L** Argentina
133 E4 **La Carlota** Argentina
71 F5 **La Carlota** Philippines
16 E6 **La Carolina** Spain
18 G9 **Lacaune** France
Laccadive Is see
85 F7 **Lacadem** Nigeria
121 N3 **Lac-Drolet** Quebec Canada
118 L9 **Lacflèche** Saskatchewan Canada
99 R4 **Lac du Flambeau** Wisconsin U.S.A.
13 H6 **Laceby** England
125 L2 **La Ceiba** Honduras
128 D2 **La Ceiba** Venezuela
138 E6 **Lacepede** South Australia Australia
142 D3 **Lacepede Is** W Australia Australia
16 C4 **Lacey** Washington U.S.A.
19 Q14 **La Chambre** France
52 E4 **Lacha, Oz** L Russian Federation
124 G5 **La Gallega** Mexico
19 Q13 **Lachapelle-aux-Pots** France
19 O15 **La Chapelle-en-Vercors** France
128 C6 **Lachay, Pta** pt Peru
36 B2 **Lachen** Germany
41 N6 **Lachen** Switzerland
106 D4 **La Chorrera** Panama
125 P6 **La Chorrera** Panama
23 M7 **Lachute** France
121 Q7 **Lachute** Quebec Canada
19 P18 **La Ciotat** France
94 J4 **Lackawanna** New York U.S.A.
118 E4 **Lac la Biche** Alberta Canada
117 N10 **Lac La Hache** British Columbia Canada
118 K8 **La la Ronge** Saskatchewan Canada
100 J1 **Laclede** Idaho U.S.A.
99 N10 **Laclede** Missouri U.S.A.
19 Q13 **La Clusaz** France
19 O13 **La Cocha** Argentina
8 D5 **Lacock** England
121 R7 **Lacolle** Quebec Canada
124 D3 **La Colorada** Mexico
121 R8 **Lacombe** Alberta Canada
111 G11 **Lacombe** Louisiana U.S.A.
99 R8 **Lacon** Illinois U.S.A.
99 N8 **Lacona** Iowa U.S.A.
95 L3 **Lacona** New York U.S.A.
43 C9 **Laconi** Sardinia
95 Q3 **Laconia** New Hampshire U.S.A.
113 E9 **Lacoochee** Florida U.S.A.
130 B9 **La Cordillera** dept Paraguay
121 N4 **Lacorne** Quebec Canada
109 J6 **Lacoste** Texas U.S.A.
122 J2 **Lacovia** Jamaica
98 K4 **Lac Qui Parle** Minnesota U.S.A.
15 D3 **Lacreek L** South Dakota U.S.A.
126 A3 **Lacre Pt** Bonaire W Indies
99 P6 **La Crescent** Minnesota U.S.A.
99 U8 **La Crosse** Indiana U.S.A.
107 L3 **La Crosse** Kansas U.S.A.
94 J10 **La Crosse** Virginia U.S.A.
99 P6 **La Crosse** Wisconsin U.S.A.
133 E7 **La Cruz** Argentina
125 M4 **La Cruz** Costa Rica
124 F5 **La Cruz** Mexico
120 G3 **La Cruz** Mexico
108 E7 **La Cuesta** Mexico
133 C6 **La Cueva** Chile
106 E6 **La Cueva** New Mexico

74 F5 **Ladnun** India
8 B7 **Ladock** England
37 K3 **Ladoga** L see Ladozhskoye Oz
30 D5 **Ladoga** Indiana U.S.A.
98 F2 **Ladonia** Texas U.S.A.
128 D2 **La Dorada** Colombia
52 D4 **Ladozhskoye Oz** L Russian Federation
71 F4 **Ladrones Pk** New Mexico U.S.A.
116 R5 **Ladue** R Alaska/Yukon Terr U.S.A./Canada
124 E3 **La Dura** Mexico
52 E4 **Ladva Vetka** Russian Federation
115 L2 **Lady Ann Str** Northwest Territories Canada
15 F4 **Ladybank** Scotland
139 J8 **Lady Barron** Tasmania Australia
89 E7 **Ladybrand** S Africa
142 F5 **Lady Edith L** W Australia Australia
141 L6 **Lady Elliot I** Gt Barrier Reef Aust
120 K5 **Lady Evelyn L** Ontario Canada
100 B1 **Ladysmith** British Columbia Canada
89 P4 **Ladysmith** S Africa
55 S5 **Ladysmith** Wisconsin U.S.A.
48 M2 **Ladyzhin** Ukraine
28 C5 **Læborg** Denmark
69 D8 **Laeken** Belgium
69 D8 **Laem Ao Kham** C Thailand
89 B9 **Laem Ngop** Thailand
94 C4 **Laem Sui** C Thailand
26 K6 **La Encina** Spain
127 L10 **La Encrucijada** Venezuela
27 B10 **Laerdalsøyri** Norway
128 F8 **La Esmeralda** Paraguay
98 D9 **Læsø** isld Denmark
52 D2 **Læsø Rende** str Denmark
133 D5 **La Esperanza** Argentina
126 F4 **La Esperanza** Cuba
16 B2 **La Estrada** Spain
26 P2 **Laevajoki** Norway
131 D3 **La Falda** Argentina
95 M2 **La Fargeville** New York U.S.A.
19 Q18 **La Farlède** France
111 J9 **Lafayette** Alabama U.S.A.
106 E4 **Lafayette** Colorado U.S.A.
112 B3 **Lafayette** Georgia U.S.A.
29 J11 **Lafayette** Indiana U.S.A.
111 E11 **Lafayette** Louisiana U.S.A.
99 M5 **Lafayette** Minnesota U.S.A.
59 E4 **Lafayette** Tennessee U.S.A.
65 C5 **Lafayette, Mt** New Hampshire U.S.A.
126 B3 **La Fé** Cuba
129 G6 **La Feria** Texas U.S.A.
121 M4 **Laferte** Quebec Canada
85 F7 **Lafia** Nigeria
85 F7 **Lafiagi** Nigeria
121 N3 **Laflamme** R Quebec Canada
130 E7 **Lafnitz** R Austria
71 O10 **La Follette** Tennessee U.S.A.
106 D6 **Laforce** Idaho U.S.A.
121 M5 **Laforest** Ontario Canada
48 F6 **Lafrançaise** France
112 E3 **La France** South Carolina U.S.A.
119 N8 **Lajord** Saskatchewan Canada
16 C4 **La Fuente de San Esteban** Spain
48 F3 **La Galite** I Tunisia
64 F4 **La Gallega** Mexico
128 D7 **La Gloria** Bolivia
124 F3 **La Junta** Mexico
106 G4 **La Junta** Colorado U.S.A.
28 J8 **Lakajsö** Sweden
26 M5 **Lakaträsk** Sweden
94 H4 **La Joya** Mexico
106 E2 **La Joya** New Mexico U.S.A.
47 G15 **Lakhanás** Rhodes Greece
5 D4 **Lakhdenpokh'ya** Russian Federation
74 J5 **Lakhimpur** India
80 B6 **Lakhish** Israel
80 B6 **Lakhish** R Israel
80 C7 **Lakhish** Israel
74 C7 **Lakhpat** India
107 J4 **Lakin** Kansas U.S.A.
54 L1 **Lakinsk** Russian Federation
47 P13 **Lákka** Greece
20 A5 **Lakki** Pakistan
71 K9 **Lakohembi** Sumba Indonesia
28 A6 **Lakoik** Denmark
47 O12 **Lákka** Greece
46 F3 **Lakoníkos Kólpos** B Greece
142 D7 **Lakor** isld Indonesia
84 B4 **Lakota** Ivory Coast
99 M6 **Lakota** Iowa U.S.A.
98 H1 **Lakota** North Dakota U.S.A.
26 P1 **Lakse Fjord** inlet Norway
26 P1 **Lakselv** Norway
26 F6 **Lakshadweep** islds Indian Oc
71 F7 **Lala** Mindanao Philippines
88 C8 **Lala** Zambia
87 B7 **Lalama** Angola
90 E3 **Lálapaşa** Turkey
86 B5 **Lalare** Gabon
87 B7 **Laláua** Mozambique
18 G8 **Lalbenque** France
47 O13 **Lalefka** Cyprus
113 E7 **Lalibela** Ethiopia
77 A3 **Láli** Iran
128 B4 **La Libertad** Ecuador
125 O9 **La Libertad** Guatemala
133 C4 **La Ligua** Chile
71 H8 **Lalindu** Indonesia
135 S3 **Lalinek** Sulawesi
18 E7 **Lalinde** France
65 C2 **Lalin** China
16 B2 **Lalin** Spain
18 F8 **Lalinde** France
71 G7 **Lalitpur** India
19 P15 **Lalley** France
71 G7 **Lalo** L Mindanao Philippines

77 B1 **Lāhījān** Iran
102 R12 **Lahilahi Pt** Hawaiian Is
36 E2 **Lahm** Germany
36 E2 **Lahm** Germany
36 F2 **Lahnstein** Germany
27 F15 **Laholm** Sweden
27 F15 **Laholmsbukten** Sweden
71 F4 **Lahong** Philippines
102 E2 **Lahontan Res** Nevada
74 J5 **Lahore** Pakistan
36 D7 **Lahr** Germany
32 M8 **Lahstedt** Germany
29 M11 **Lahti** Finland
124 G8 **La Huerta** Mexico
80 G8 **Lahun** Jordan
71 F4 **Lahuy** isld Philippines
86 C4 **Lai** Chad
67 F1 **Lai'an** China
133 F3 **La Iberá** L Argentina
68 F2 **Laibin** China
68 F2 **Lai Chau** Vietnam
36 E3 **Laichingen** Germany
141 K8 **Laidley** Queensland Australia
102 S11 **Laie** Hawaii Is
113 D7 **Laifeng** China
71 F4 **Laifour** France
113 F10 **Laigneiet** France
95 Q2 **Laignes** France
113 F11 **Laigueglia** Italy
94 E3 **Laihia** Finland
68 C2 **Lai-Hka** Burma
68 C2 **Lai-Hsak** Burma
71 H7 **Lailly-en-Val** France
71 E1 **Lai-Lo** Luzon Philippines
70 G4 **Laimea** Sulawesi
86 G5 **Lainá** Greece
52 G6 **Laishevo** Russian Federation
65 C5 **Laishui** China
21 K4 **Laison** R France
13 G8 **Laissac** France
118 L8 **Laisvall** Sweden
29 H2 **Laitaure** L Sweden
29 J11 **Laitila** Finland
59 L7 **Laixi** China
94 B3 **Laiya** Philippines
101 O5 **Laiyang** China
100 E7 **Laiyuan** China
112 H3 **Laize** R France
53 Q6 **Laizhou Wan** B China
73 G6 **Laja, L de** Chile
133 D5 **La Japonesa** Argentina
133 C5 **Laja, R** Chile
106 E4 **La Jara** Colorado U.S.A.
70 E7 **Lajar, Tg** C Kalimantan
19 O16 **La Javie** France
130 F9 **Lajes dos Santos** isld Brazil
71 O8 **Lajeni** Indonesia
71 D8 **Lajes** Brazil
106 E10 **Lajes** Brazil
106 D8 **Lajitas** Texas U.S.A.
106 E2 **Lajitas, Las** Argentina
95 N6 **Lajkovac** Serbia Yugoslavia
102 G9 **La Jolla** California U.S.A.
106 F9 **Lakewood** New Mexico U.S.A.
94 H4 **Lakewood** New York U.S.A.
94 F4 **Lakewood** Ohio U.S.A.
113 G11 **La Joya** New Mexico U.S.A.
124 G3 **La Morita** Mexico
16 E5 **La Morte** France
124 B4 **La Junta** Bolivia
106 G4 **La Junta** Colorado U.S.A.

140 B5 **Lake Mackay Aboriginal Land** N Terr Australia
14 E3 **Lakembay** I Ireland
108 O9 **Lambeng** Kalimantan
99 N6 **Lake Mills** Iowa U.S.A.
94 G5 **Lake Milton** Ohio U.S.A.
116 L5 **Lake Minchumina** Alaska U.S.A.
95 S1 **Lake Moxie** Maine U.S.A.
140 E5 **Lake Nash** N Terr Australia
37 P5 **Laken Berg** mt Czech/ Germany
9 G3 **Lakenheath** England
94 B4 **Lake Odessa** Michigan U.S.A.
99 M1 **Lake of the Woods** L Ontario Canada
94 C4 **Lake Orion** Michigan U.S.A.
100 C4 **Lake Oswego** Oregon U.S.A.
107 Q5 **Lake O' The Cherokees** L Oklahoma U.S.A.
109 N3 **Lake O'The Pines** L Texas U.S.A.
101 P5 **Lake Outlet** Wyoming U.S.A.
144 B5 **Lake Paringa** New Zealand
113 G11 **Lake Park** Florida U.S.A.
113 D7 **Lake Park** Georgia U.S.A.
99 L6 **Lake Park** Iowa U.S.A.
113 F10 **Lake Placid** Florida U.S.A.
95 O2 **Lake Placid** New York U.S.A.
102 B2 **Lakeport** California U.S.A.
94 E3 **Lakeport** Michigan U.S.A.
98 J5 **Lake Preston** South Dakota U.S.A.
111 E9 **Lake Providence** Louisiana U.S.A.
144 C6 **Lake Pukaki** New Zealand
109 F9 **Lake Range** mts Nevada
115 L7 **Lake River** Ontario Canada
139 J7 **Lakes Entrance** Victoria Australia
102 G9 **Lakeshore** California U.S.A.
103 P7 **Lakeside** Arizona U.S.A.
102 H9 **Lakeside** California U.S.A.
46 E6 **Lakeside** Ontario Canada
127 N4 **Lake Superior Prov. Park** Ontario Canada
144 C5 **Lake Tekapo** New Zealand
101 O8 **Laketown** Utah U.S.A.
121 M7 **Lake Traverse** Ontario Canada
118 L8 **Lake Valley** Saskatchewan Canada
106 C9 **Lake Valley** New Mexico U.S.A.
141 G5 **Lake Victor** Texas U.S.A.
99 L7 **Lake View** Iowa U.S.A.
94 B3 **Lakeview** Michigan U.S.A.
101 O5 **Lakeview** Montana U.S.A.
100 E7 **Lakeview** Oregon U.S.A.
112 H3 **Lake View** South Carolina U.S.A.
109 N9 **Lakeview** Texas U.S.A.
111 E8 **Lake Village** Arkansas U.S.A.
95 O5 **Lakeville** Connecticut U.S.A.
94 A5 **Lakeville** Indiana U.S.A.
99 N5 **Lakeville** Minnesota U.S.A.
94 K6 **Lakeville** New York U.S.A.
113 F10 **Lake Wales** Florida U.S.A.
98 G2 **Lake Williams** North Dakota U.S.A.
102 F8 **Lakewood** California U.S.A.
106 E2 **Lakewood** Colorado U.S.A.
102 F6 **Lakewood** California U.S.A.
113 D7 **Lakewood** Florida U.S.A.
101 O6 **Lakewood** New Mexico U.S.A.
107 N5 **Lakewood** Oklahoma U.S.A.
113 C13 **Lake Worth** Florida U.S.A.
124 G3 **La Morita** Mexico
94 A5 **La Morra** France
19 P14 **La Morte** France
22 J4 **Lamotrek** Caroline Is
121 M4 **La Motte** Quebec Canada
21 P6 **Lamotte-Beuvron** France
113 P13 **La Motte d'Aveillans** France
113 P13 **La Motte-Servolex** France
94 N3 **La Moure** North Dakota U.S.A.
68 F4 **Lam Pao Res** Thailand
128 F6 **Lampazos de Naranjo** Mexico
18 J6 **Lampeter** Wales
29 O6 **Lampi** Finland
71 H5 **Lampung** prov Sumatra
70 K8 **Lampung, Teluk** B Sumatra
68 G5 **Lam Si Bai** R Thailand
32 M9 **Lamspringe** Germany
32 M5 **Lamstedt** Germany
68 D1 **Lamu** Burma
99 R7 **Lamu** Kenya

128 B5 **Lambayeque** dept Peru
14 E3 **Lambay** I Ireland
70 D5 **Lambeng** Kalimantan
112 F6 **Lambert** Georgia U.S.A.
111 F7 **Lambert** Mississippi U.S.A.
98 B2 **Lambert** Montana U.S.A.
142 B5 **Lambert, C** W Australia U.S.A.
146 H10 **Lambert Glacier** Antarctica
99 L5 **Lambert Station** North Dakota U.S.A.
87 C12 **Lambert's B** S Africa
95 N6 **Lambertville** New Jersey U.S.A.
19 O17 **Lambesc** France
120 J10 **Lambeth** Ontario Canada
46 E7 **Lámbia** Greece
20 C5 **Lambourn** England
36 D5 **Lambrecht** Germany
21 H4 **Lambro** R Italy
94 G10 **Lambsburg** Virginia U.S.A.
14 A5 **Lambs Hd** Ireland
14 T4 **Lame** N Terr Australia
121 T7 **Lambton** Quebec Canada
114 Q3 **Lambton, C** Northwest Territories Canada
70 G7 **Lambuya** Sulawesi
68 F5 **Lam Chi** R Thailand
68 F6 **Lam Dom Noi** R Thailand
94 H8 **Lamed** N West Virginia U.S.A.
127 N4 **Lame Deer** Montana U.S.A.
16 B3 **Lamego** Portugal
17 G5 **Lamena** Spain
20 D6 **Landévant** France
122 H6 **Lameque** New Brunswick Canada
133 D3 **La Merced** Argentina
138 F6 **Lameroo** South Australia Australia
102 G9 **La Mesa** California U.S.A.
106 D9 **La Mesa** New Mexico U.S.A.
108 F3 **Lamesa** Texas U.S.A.
43 F7 **La Meta** mt Italy
20 G5 **La Mézière** France
28 C7 **Lamia** Greece
46 E6 **Lamia** Greece
127 K10 **La Miel** Venezuela
71 K9 **Lamigan Pt** Mindanao Philippines
19 O16 **Lamīne** France
124 D3 **La Misa** Mexico
121 M7 **Lamitan** Philippines
85 B3 **Lamjabir** Western Sahara
109 J4 **Lamkin** Texas U.S.A.
71 C3 **Lamlam** Indonesia
15 C5 **Lamlash** Scotland
144 B6 **Lammerlaw Range** New Zealand
15 F5 **Lammermuir Hills** Scotland
27 G14 **Lammhult** Sweden
29 L7 **Lammi** Finland
68 G5 **Lam Man** R Thailand
21 M5 **Lamnay** France
99 R8 **La Moille** Illinois U.S.A.
103 J1 **Lamoille** Nevada U.S.A.
95 P2 **Lamoille** R Vermont U.S.A.
94 A3 **La Moine** R Illinois U.S.A.
100 G2 **Lamona** Washington U.S.A.
94 F3 **Lamont** R Illinois U.S.A.
42 D4 **Lamone** R Italy
70 O9 **Lamongan** Java
110 C1 **Lamoni** Iowa U.S.A.
118 F2 **Lamont** Alberta Canada
102 F6 **Lamont** California U.S.A.
113 D7 **Lamont** Florida U.S.A.
101 O6 **Lamont** Florida U.S.A.
99 P7 **Lamont** Iowa U.S.A.
107 N5 **Lamont** Oklahoma U.S.A.
101 R2 **Lamont** Wyoming U.S.A.
94 H4 **Lamotrek** Caroline Is

13 G4 **Lanchester** England
66 C5 **Lan-chia Ts'o** L China
48 J2 **Lanchin** Ukraine
Lanchow see Lanzhou
42 F6 **Lancieux** Italy
20 F4 **Lancieux** France
54 C10 **Lancing** Tennessee U.S.A.
19 O17 **Lançon** France
31 N5 **Lańcut** Poland
27 D11 **Land** reg Norway
31 N3 **Landa** North Dakota U.S.A.
32 K10 **Landau** Hessen Germany
36 E5 **Landau** Rheinland-Pfalz Germany
21 H5 **Landéan** France
41 N3 **Landeck** Austria
26 G4 **Landegode** isld Norway
20 C5 **Landelau** France
21 H4 **Landelles-et-Coupigny** France
36 D8 **Landen** Germany
140 C5 **Lander** R N Terr Australia
101 R7 **Lander** Wyoming U.S.A.
140 B5 **Lander** R N Terr Australia
27 F14 **Landeryd** Sweden
18 E8 **Landes** reg France
18 E8 **Landes** part France
18 F5 **Landes** Loir-et-Cher France
94 H8 **Landes** West Virginia U.S.A.
28 G7 **Landet** Denmark
17 G5 **Landete** Spain
20 D6 **Landévant** France
20 B5 **Landévennec** France
20 A6 **Landfall I** Andaman Is
133 C8 **Landfall, I** Chile
36 F4 **Landford** England
21 H4 **Landgraben** R Germany
33 S5 **Landsberg** Germany
32 J5 **Landi Hadeln** Germany
71 J6 **Landik, Gunung** mt Sumatra
74 D1 **Landi Khana** Pakistan
77 H4 **Landi Md. Amin Khan** Afghanistan
119 U3 **Landing L** Manitoba Canada
118 J6 **Landis** Saskatchewan Canada
112 G2 **Landis** North Carolina U.S.A.
20 B5 **Landivisiau** France
20 D6 **Landivy** France
112 F3 **Lando** South Carolina U.S.A.
9 F2 **Land O Lakes** Wisconsin U.S.A.
31 H5 **Landrecies** France
22 G8 **Landquart** Switzerland
22 K5 **Landres** Ardennes France
22 K5 **Landres** Meurthe-et-Moselle France
124 N4 **Landrienne** Quebec Canada
142 F4 **Landrigan Cliffs** W Australia Australia
43 F7 **Landro** Italy
38 F8 **Landrum** South Carolina U.S.A.
31 N5 **Landry** France
26 S4 **Landsá** Sweden
33 Q9 **Landsberg** Germany
71 Q5 **Landsberg** Germany
141 G5 **Landsborough** R Queensland Australia
144 B5 **Landsborough** R New Zealand
113 K7 **Lands End** C Northwest Territories Canada
114 Q2 **Land's End** England
37 N6 **Landshut** Germany
29 K5 **Landshut** Germany
36 C5 **Landstuhl** Germany
22 J5 **Landudec** France
109 L6 **Lane City** Texas U.S.A.
45 L7 **Lane** South Carolina U.S.A.
114 B5 **Lane** South Dakota U.S.A.
11 L9 **Laneffe** Belgium
99 P8 **Lanesboro** Minnesota U.S.A.
111 L7 **Lanett** Alabama U.S.A.
14 G7 **Lanfains** France
109 O8 **Lanfeng** see Lankao
39 G7 **Lanfine** Queensland Australia
18 D4 **Lang** Saskatchewan Canada
28 F6 **Langá** Denmark
111 L9 **L'nga Co** L China
71 N4 **Langa de Duero** Spain
46 E7 **Langadhás** Greece
19 E8 **Langade** France
96 E7 **Langanes** pen Iceland
127 H7 **Langano Hāyk'** L Ethiopia
117 H7 **Langara I** Guiana
117 P9 **Langara I** British Columbia Canada
77 A1 **Langavat** Iran
119 P8 **Langbank** Saskatchewan Canada
67 B6 **Lang Chanh** Vietnam
28 C9 **Langdon North Dakota** U.S.A.
28 H1 **Langdon** Kansas U.S.A.
32 M9 **Langdon** North Dakota U.S.A.
13 F4 **Langdon Beck** England
14 F6 **Langeais** France
71 H7 **Langeais** France
19 A9 **Langeberg** mts S Africa
19 P18 **L'Ange, Col de** France
42 J2 **Langeland** isld Denmark
36 B3 **Langeland** Belgium
111 L11 **Langelmävesi** L Finland
32 M9 **Langelsheim** Germany
36 B2 **Langemark** Belgium
32 J5 **Langen** Germany
28 E3 **Langen** Hessen Germany
33 J7 **Langen** Germany
37 F10 **Langenberg** Germany
32 M4 **Langenberg** Germany
36 B7 **Langenburg** Germany
33 O9 **Langenfeld** Germany
37 O5 **Langenlois** Austria
33 S8 **Langenhagen** Germany
31 K7 **Langenhahn** Germany
35 S9 **Langenlonsheim** Germany
35 B9 **Langennaudorf** Germany
36 G3 **Langenselbold** Germany
36 H5 **Langensteinbach** Germany
32 L8 **Langenthal** Germany
27 K5 **Langeoog** Germany
27 D13 **Langeskov** Denmark
26 B9 **Langevåg** Norway
37 K2 **Langevatnet** L Norway
14 A6 **Langevin, Pt** France
26 M3 **Langfang** China
26 M1 **Langfjord** Norway
26 M1 **Langfjorden** inlet Finnmark Norway
26 C9 **Langfjorden** inlet Møre og Romsdal Norway
98 J4 **Langford** South Dakota U.S.A.
117 J6 **Langforden** inlet Norway
69 E12 **Langgam** Sumatra
69 B9 **Langgapayung** Sumatra
118 L6 **Langham** Saskatchewan Canada
44 D2 **Langhe** Italy

194
Langhirano — Lemsford

44 H2 **Langhirano** Italy
68 C2 **Langhko** Burma
15 F5 **Langholm** Scotland
28 S9 **Langjokull** *ice cap* Iceland
69 C10 **Langka** Sumatra
69 D9 **Langkawi** *isld* Malaysia
69 D8 **Lang Kha Toek, Khao** *mt* Thailand
70 E1 **Langkon** Sabah
123 Q7 **Langlade** *isld* Atlantic Oc
121 P4 **Langlade** Quebec Canada
100 C1 **Langley** Washington U.S.A.
28 A5 **Langli** *isld* Denmark
141 H7 **Langlo** *R* Queensland Australia
141 H7 **Langlo Crossing** Queensland Australia
141 H7 **Langlo Downs** Queensland Australia
100 A7 **Langlois** Oregon U.S.A.
121 N4 **Langlois Village** Quebec Canada
32 H5 **Langlütjensand** *sandbank* Germany
36 D4 **Langmeil** Germany
40 G4 **Langnau** Switzerland
28 J7 **Langø** *isld* Denmark
18 H8 **Langogne** France
18 E8 **Langon** France
20 G6 **Langon** Ille-et-Vilaine France
28 F5 **Langør** Denmark
26 G3 **Langöy** *isld* Norway
8 D5 **Langport** England
37 N6 **Langquaid** Germany
40 B2 **Langres** France
40 B2 **Langres, Plat. de** France
21 K3 **Langrune** France
119 T8 **Langruth** Manitoba Canada
69 C10 **Langsa** Sumatra
69 C10 **Langsa, Teluk** *B* Sumatra
26 J8 **Långsele** Sweden
26 H7 **Långseleån** *R* Sweden
58 E3 **Lang Shan** *mt ra* China
27 H11 **Långshyttan** Sweden
28 D5 **Langskov** Denmark
67 B6 **Lang Son** Vietnam
13 H5 **Langtoft** England
26 L6 **Långträsk** Sweden
108 F6 **Langtry** Texas U.S.A.
18 H8 **Languedoc** *prov* France
20 E4 **Langueux** France
20 D6 **Languidic** France
110 F6 **L'Anguille** *R* Arkansas U.S.A.
37 J1 **Langula** Germany
32 H5 **Langwarden** Germany
13 F4 **Langwathby** England
32 K7 **Langwedel** Germany
9 F1 **Langworth** England
67 F1 **Langxi** China
67 F2 **Langxi** China
58 E5 **Langzhong** China
20 B5 **Lanhouarneau** France
67 G5 **Lan Hsü** *isld* Taiwan
121 L5 **Laniel** Quebec Canada
119 N7 **Lanigan** Saskatchewan Canada
102 S12 **Lanikai** Hawaiian Is
20 A5 **Lanildut** France
133 C5 **Lanín** *mt* Argentina
131 B7 **Lanín, Vol** Arg/Chile
8 B7 **Lanivet** England
70 C4 **Lanjak** Kalimantan
70 B4 **Lanjak, Bt** *mt* Sarawak
32 E10 **Lank** Germany
65 C7 **Lankao** China
33 T7 **Lanke** Germany
98 J1 **Lankin** North Dakota U.S.A.
22 K1 **Lanklaar** Belgium
20 E4 **Lanloup** France
20 C4 **Lanmeur** France
26 M3 **Lannavaara** Sweden
18 F9 **Lannemezan** France
20 A4 **Lannilis** France
20 D4 **Lannion** France
22 E2 **Lannoy** France
17 H3 **La Noguera** *dist* Spain
121 R7 **Lanoraie** Quebec Canada
124 F6 **La Noria** Mexico
48 K1 **Lanovtsy** Ukraine
95 M6 **Lansdale** Pennsylvania U.S.A.
121 P8 **Lansdowne** Ontario Canada
115 L7 **Lansdowne House** Ontario Canada
99 S3 **L'Anse** Michigan U.S.A.
123 Q2 **L'Anse-Amour** Labrador, Nfld Canada
123 P2 **L'Anse au Loup** Quebec Canada
123 R2 **L'anse-Au-Meadow** Newfoundland Canada
33 R5 **Lansen** Germany
19 P14 **Lans en Vercors** France
98 E1 **Lansford** North Dakota U.S.A.
95 M6 **Lansford** Pennsylvania U.S.A.
67 D4 **Lanshan** China
99 P6 **Lansing** Iowa U.S.A.
107 Q2 **Lansing** Kansas U.S.A.
94 C4 **Lansing** Michigan U.S.A.
112 F1 **Lansing** North Carolina U.S.A.
31 K6 **Lanškroun** Czechoslovakia
40 E7 **Lanslebourg** France
19 P14 **Lans, Mts de** France
69 D9 **Lanta, Ko** *isld* Thailand
69 D9 **Lanta Ko** Thailand
21 O7 **Lanthenay** France
Lantian *see* **Lianyuan**
65 A7 **Lantian** China
98 E4 **Lantry** South Dakota U.S.A.
43 C9 **Lanusei** Sardinia
71 G6 **Lanuza** Mindanao Philippines
20 E6 **Lanvaux, Landes de** *reg* France
20 B5 **Lanvéoc** France
20 E4 **Lanvollon** France
65 G1 **Lanxi** China
67 E1 **Lanxi** China
65 B5 **Lan Xian** China
33 P6 **Lanz** Germany
85 B3 **Lanzarote** *isld* Canary Is
58 D4 **Lanzhou** China
65 F2 **Lanzijing** China
71 E1 **Laoag** Luzon Philippines
71 G4 **Laoang** Philippines
67 A5 **Lao Cai** Vietnam
67 A4 **Laochang** China
66 C2 **Laofengkou** China
65 D4 **Laoguo** China
59 G3 **Laoha He** *R* China
58 F5 **Laohekou** China
58 F5 **Lao-ho-k'ou** China
14 D4 **Laois** *co* Ireland
65 G4 **Laoling** China
Laolong *see* **Longchuan**
22 F4 **Laon** France
99 S4 **Laona** Wisconsin U.S.A.
21 N4 **Laons** France
127 L9 **La Orchila, I** Venezuela
128 C6 **La Oroya** Peru
68 F3 **Laos** *rep* S E Asia
65 E6 **Laoshan** China
65 E5 **Laotie Shan** *C* China
65 E5 **Laotieshan Shuidao** *str* China
16 D9 **Laou, Oued** *R* Morocco
65 G2 **Laoye Ling** *mts* China
65 H3 **Laoye Ling** *mts* China
71 E8 **Lapac** *isld* Philippines
87 G8 **Lapala** Mozambique
18 H6 **Lapalisse** France
85 A3 **La Palma** *isld* Canary Is
125 P9 **La Palma** Guatemala
16 C7 **La Palma del Concado** Spain
131 C6 **La Pampa** *prov* Argentina
102 D6 **La Panza** California U.S.A.
102 D6 **La Panza Ra** California U.S.A.
128 F2 **La Paragua** Venezuela
17 F4 **La Paraleja** *L* Spain
16 D4 **La Paramera de Avila** Spain
71 D7 **Laparan** *isld* Sulu Arch
124 G6 **La Parilla** Mexico
133 D4 **La Paz** Argentina
131 F3 **La Paz** Entre Rios Argentina
128 E7 **La Paz** *R* Bolivia
128 E7 **La Paz** Bolivia
124 D5 **La Paz** Mexico
94 A5 **Lapaz** Indiana U.S.A.
127 H9 **La Paz** Venezuela
128 E4 **La Pedrera** Colombia
94 D3 **Lapeer** Michigan U.S.A.
94 B6 **Lapel** Indiana U.S.A.
133 E4 **La Pelada** Argentina
124 G3 **La Perla** Mexico
119 U3 **La Perouse** Manitoba Canada
102 T13 **La Pérouse Pinnacle** Hawaiian Is
59 M2 **La Pérouse Strait** Japan/Rus Fed
71 A2 **Lapi** Halmahera Indonesia
124 H7 **La Piedad** Mexico
100 D6 **Lapine** Oregon U.S.A.
71 G5 **Lapinin** Bohol Philippines
29 N8 **Lapinlahti** Finland
79 D3 **Lapithos** Cyprus
111 F11 **Laplace** Louisiana U.S.A.
68 D4 **Lap Lae** Thailand
52 D1 **Laplandiya** Russian Federation
131 F5 **La Plata** Argentina
95 L8 **La Plata** Maryland U.S.A.
99 O9 **La Plata** Missouri U.S.A.
123 O6 **La Poile B** Newfoundland Canada
99 Q3 **La Pointe** Wisconsin U.S.A.
16 D2 **La Pola de Gordón** Spain
52 F3 **Lapominka** Russian Federation
118 H7 **Laporte** Saskatchewan Canada
102 D2 **La Porte** California U.S.A.
99 U8 **La Porte** Indiana U.S.A.
99 M2 **Laporte** Minnesota U.S.A.
95 L5 **Laporte** Pennsylvania U.S.A.
109 N6 **La Porte** Texas U.S.A.
99 O7 **La Porte City** Iowa U.S.A.
70 F7 **Laposa, Bk** *mt* Sulawesi
36 C7 **Lapoutroie** France
48 G6 **Lapovo** Serbia Yugoslavia
29 K8 **Lappajärvi** Finland
29 N10 **Lappeenranta** Finland
29 J9 **Lappfjärd** Finland
27 M10 **Lappi** Finland
29 J10 **Lappi Kauttua** Finland
26 L3 **Lappland** Sweden/Finland
26 N2 **Lappojavrre** *L* Norway
26 N5 **Lappträsk** Sweden
121 R7 **Laprairie** Quebec Canada
101 U7 **La Prele Cr** Wyoming U.S.A.
133 E5 **Laprida** Argentina
108 H7 **La Pryor** Texas U.S.A.
47 H4 **Lâpseki** Turkey
54 J2 **Laptevo** Russian Federation
51 M1 **Laptev Sea** Russian Federation
29 K9 **Lapua** Finland
29 K8 **Lapuanjoki** *R* Finland
16 E5 **La Puebla de Montalbán** Spain
127 J10 **La Puerta** Venezuela
128 B4 **La Puntilla** *pt* Ecuador
124 C4 **La Purisima** Mexico
100 A2 **La Push** Washington U.S.A.
48 H3 **Lăpusului, Muntii** *mts* Romania
31 O3 **Łapy** Poland
84 H5 **Laqiya Arba'in** Sudan
128 E8 **La Quiaca** Argentina
42 E6 **L'Aquila** Italy
77 D6 **Lār** Iran
16 C9 **Larache** Morocco
19 P16 **Laragne** France
77 E6 **Larak** *isld* Iran
128 D6 **Laramate** Peru
16 D7 **La Rambla** Spain
98 A7 **Laramie** *R* Wyoming U.S.A.
98 A8 **Laramie** Wyoming U.S.A.
98 A7 **Laramie Pk** *mt* Wyoming U.S.A.
130 F8 **Laranjal Paulista** Brazil
130 D9 **Laranjeiras do Sul** Brazil
130 E8 **Laranjinha, R** Brazil
71 L9 **Larantuka** Flores Indonesia
19 O15 **La Raye** *mt* France
15 E4 **Larbert** Scotland
19 N13 **L'Arbresle** France
127 H5 **L'Arcahaie** Haiti
21 J5 **Larchamp** France
121 L4 **Larder Lake** Ontario Canada
47 R14 **Lárdhos** Rhodes Greece
47 V17 **Lárdhos, Akr** Rhodes Greece
123 M8 **L'Ardoise** C Breton I, Nova Scotia
21 P4 **Lardy** France
16 E1 **Laredo** Spain
99 N9 **Laredo** Missouri U.S.A.
109 H8 **Laredo** Texas U.S.A.
121 L4 **La Reine** Quebec Canada
48 K2 **Larga** Moldavia
Largeau *see* **Faya-Largeau**
122 J3 **Large I** Quebec Canada
18 H8 **Largentière** France
15 F4 **Largo** Scotland
113 E10 **Largo** Florida U.S.A.
126 D4 **Largo, Cayo** *isld* Cuba
13 F1 **Largo Ward** Scotland
15 D5 **Largs** Scotland
45 J4 **Lari** Italy
70 F5 **Lariang** *R* Sulawesi
70 F5 **Lariang** Sulawesi
46 F6 **Lárimna** Greece
98 J2 **Larimore** North Dakota U.S.A.
42 F7 **Larino** Italy
131 C2 **La Rioja** Argentina
17 F2 **La Rioja** *prov* Spain
46 E5 **Lárisa** Greece
77 D6 **Laristan** Iran
119 T9 **La Rivière** Manitoba Canada
98 E3 **Lark** North Dakota U.S.A.
74 C5 **Larkana** Pakistan
12 E2 **Larkhall** Scotland
123 O4 **Lark Harb** Newfoundland Canada
110 K7 **Larkinsville** Alabama U.S.A.
141 H3 **Lark Pass** Gt Barrier Reef Aust
9 G3 **Lark, R** England
106 F2 **Larkspur** Colorado U.S.A.
9 G3 **Larling** England
55 F2 **Larlomkiny** Russian Federation
20 D6 **Larmar-Plage** France
79 D4 **Larnaca** Cyprus
14 F2 **Larne** N Ireland
107 L3 **Larned** Kansas U.S.A.
14 F2 **Larne L** N Ireland
16 D2 **La Robla** Spain
19 P15 **La Roche-des-Arnauds** France
18 H5 **Laroche-Migennes** France
19 Q14 **La Rochette** France
22 L4 **Larochette** Luxembourg
17 F5 **La Roda** Spain
16 D7 **La Roda de A** Spain
127 K5 **La Romana** Dominican Rep
70 G6 **Larompong** Sulawesi
119 M3 **La Ronge** Saskatchewan Canada
124 J5 **La Rosa** Mexico
111 F12 **La Rose** Louisiana U.S.A.
124 J3 **La Rosita** Mexico
142 C5 **Larrey Pt** W Australia Australia
140 C3 **Larrimah** N Terr Australia
123 L8 **Larry's R** Nova Scotia Canada
146 D4 **Larsen Ice Shelf** Antarctica
101 T1 **Larslan** Montana U.S.A.
29 K8 **Larsmo** Finland
119 N1 **Larson** Ontario Canada
109 M3 **La Rue** Texas U.S.A.
18 E10 **Laruns** France
27 D12 **Larvik** Norway
56 B1 **Lar'yak** Russian Federation
55 G1 **Lar'yegan** *R* Russian Federation
124 G6 **Las Adjuntas** Mexico
103 P3 **La Sal** Utah U.S.A.
119 U9 **La Salle** Manitoba Canada
120 G10 **La Salle** Ontario Canada
98 B9 **La Salle** Colorado U.S.A.
99 R8 **La Salle** Illinois U.S.A.
16 E8 **Las Alpujarras** *dist* Spain
70 D4 **Lasan** Kalimantan
124 D2 **La Sangre** Mexico
106 G3 **Las Animas** Colorado U.S.A.
121 L4 **La Sarre** Quebec Canada
19 Q16 **La Saulce** France
128 E1 **Las Aves, Is** Venezuela
17 G2 **Las Bardenas** *reg* Spain
38 L5 **Lasberg** Austria
28 D4 **Låsby** Denmark
127 J5 **Lascahobas** Haiti
133 E3 **Las Cejas** Argentina
139 G6 **Lascelles** Victoria Australia
123 R4 **La Scie** Newfoundland Canada
133 C5 **Las Coloradas** Neuquén Argentina
124 F3 **Las Cruces** Mexico
106 D9 **Las Cruces** New Mexico U.S.A.
127 J5 **La Selle** *mt* Haiti
131 B2 **La Serena** Chile
16 D6 **La Serena** *reg* Spain
108 F8 **Las Esperanzas** Mexico
124 J4 **Las Esperanzas** Mexico
19 P18 **La Seyne** France
131 F6 **Las Flores** Argentina
16 E5 **Las Guadalerzas** *reg* Spain
118 H5 **Lashburn** Saskatchewan Canada
77 G4 **Lāsh-ē Joveyn** Afghanistan
68 C1 **Lashio** Burma
77 J4 **Lashkar Gāh** Afghanistan
54 N2 **Lashma** Russian Federation
16 C4 **Las Hurdes** Spain
43 G9 **La Sila** *dist* Italy
31 L2 **Łasin** Poland
31 L4 **Łask** Poland
31 L2 **Laskowice** Poland
133 C5 **Las Lajas** Argentina
128 F8 **Las Lajitas** Argentina
128 F8 **Las Lomitas** Argentina
16 C7 **Las Marismas** *dist* Spain
133 D7 **Las Martinetas** Argentina
127 L10 **Las Mercedes** Venezuela
124 G3 **Las Mesteñas** Mexico
124 G4 **Las Nieves** Mexico
16 E6 **La Solana** Spain
71 H6 **Lasolo, Tk** *B* Sulawesi
19 O14 **La Sône** France
38 F8 **Lasorling** *mt* Austria
85 A3 **Las Palmas de Gran Canaria** Canary Is
106 C8 **Las Palomas** New Mexico U.S.A.
44 G3 **La Spezia** Italy
117 L11 **Lasqueti I** British Columbia Canada
16 E4 **Las Rozas** Spain
33 N5 **Lassahn** Germany
33 T5 **Lassan** Germany
130 G5 **Lassance** Brazil
21 K5 **Lassay-les-Châteaux** France
26 M5 **Lassbyn** Sweden
100 D9 **Lassen Peak** *mt* California U.S.A.
100 D9 **Lassen Vol. Nat. Park** California U.S.A.
22 D4 **Lassigny** France
38 L6 **Lassing** Austria
146 D6 **Lassiter Coast** Antarctica
38 K7 **Lassnitz-Dorf** Austria
38 N7 **Lassnitzhöhe** Austria
121 R7 **L'Assomption** Quebec Canada
13 E2 **Lasswade** Scotland
21 J4 **Lassy** France
133 D3 **Lastarria** *mt* Chile/Arg
106 G2 **Last Chance** Colorado U.S.A.
13 H5 **Lastingham** England
119 N7 **Last Mountain** Saskatchewan Canada
119 M7 **Last Mountain L** Saskatchewan Canada
Lastoursville *see* **Bonda**
42 H6 **Lastovo** *isld* Croatia
32 G7 **Lastrup** Germany
126 F4 **Las Tunas** Cuba
124 E3 **Las Varas** Mexico
124 G3 **Las Varas** Mexico
124 G7 **Las Varas** Mexico
103 J5 **Las Vegas** Nevada U.S.A.
106 E6 **Las Vegas** New Mexico U.S.A.
128 C4 **Latacunga** Ecuador
146 C5 **Latady I** Antarctica
Latakia *see* **Ladhiqiyah, Al**
29 J3 **Latäseno** *R* Finland
121 L5 **Latchford** Ontario Canada
137 S5 **Late** *isld* Tonga
109 M4 **Latexo** Texas U.S.A.
143 B8 **Latham** W Australia Australia
99 R10 **Latham** Illinois U.S.A.
21 L7 **Lathan** *R* France
32 F7 **Lathen** Germany
15 E2 **Latheron** Scotland
110 B2 **Lathrop** Missouri U.S.A.
102 H5 **Lathrop Wells** Nevada U.S.A.
26 J7 **Latikberg** Sweden
21 L8 **Latillé** France
43 E7 **Latina** Italy
45 N6 **Latina Scalo** Italy
106 E5 **Latir Pk** New Mexico U.S.A.
54 K5 **Latnaya** Russian Federation
133 D4 **La Toma** Argentina
48 H2 **Latoritsa** *R* Ukraine
128 E1 **La Tortuga** *isld* Venezuela
142 D4 **Latouche Treville, C** W Australia
19 O13 **La Tour du Pin** France
121 P3 **La Trève, L** Quebec Canada
127 L4 **La Trinité** Martinique W Indies
139 H8 **Latrobe** Tasmania Australia
94 H6 **Latrobe** Pennsylvania U.S.A.
131 C2 **La Troya, R** Argentina
112 H3 **Latta** South Carolina U.S.A.
94 C5 **Latty** Ohio U.S.A.
71 M9 **Latuna** Indonesia
121 S5 **La Tuque** Quebec Canada
74 G9 **Latur** India
27 M15 **Latvia** *rep* E Europe
Latviyskaya S.S.R. *see* **Latvia**
85 G7 **Lau** Nigeria
36 G2 **Laubach** Hessen Germany
36 D3 **Laubach** Rheinland-Pfalz Germany
137 R6 **Lau Basin** Pacific Oc
21 H6 **Laubrières** France
36 E3 **Laubuseschbach** Germany
128 E7 **Lauca** *R* Bolivia
37 M1 **Laucha** Germany
33 T9 **Lauchhammer** Germany
37 J6 **Lauchheim** Germany
36 H4 **Lauda-Königshofen** Germany
27 C13 **Laudal** Norway
36 H5 **Laudenbach** Germany
119 R9 **Lauder** Manitoba Canada
13 F2 **Lauder** Scotland
139 J9 **Lauderdale** Tasmania Australia
111 H9 **Lauderdale** Mississippi U.S.A.
19 N16 **Laudun** France
32 K8 **Lauenau** Germany
32 L6 **Lauenbruck** Germany
33 N6 **Lauenburg** Germany
32 K9 **Lauenförde** Germany
32 L8 **Lauenstein** Germany
37 J3 **Lauer** *R* Germany
37 L5 **Lauf** Germany
36 G3 **Laufach** Germany
38 G6 **Laufen** Germany
40 F3 **Laufen** Switzerland
36 G5 **Lauffen** Germany
8 B4 **Laugharne** Wales
99 U3 **Laughing Fish Pt** Michigan U.S.A.
140 C6 **Laughlen Mt** N Terr Australia
106 F5 **Laughlin Pk** New Mexico U.S.A.
9 G6 **Laughton** England
37 J6 **Lauingen** Germany
29 M9 **Laukaa** Finland
70 G4 **Laulalang** Sulawesi
18 H5 **Laumes, les** France
68 D7 **Laun** Thailand
20 B5 **Launay, P** France
121 M4 **Launay Sta** Quebec Canada
139 H8 **Launceston** Tasmania Australia
8 B6 **Launceston** England
14 B4 **Laune** *R* Ireland
68 C6 **Launglon Bok** *islds* Burma
131 A8 **La Unión** Chile
106 D10 **La Union** New Mexico U.S.A.
127 L10 **La Unión** Venezuela
22 H4 **Launois-sur-Vence** France
38 K8 **Launsdorf** Austria
135 V4 **Laupahoehoe** Hawaiian Is
36 H7 **Laupheim** Germany
71 E3 **Laur** Luzon Philippines
141 G3 **Laura** Queensland Australia
138 E5 **Laura** South Australia Australia
118 K7 **Laura** Saskatchewan Canada
140 A4 **Laura Cr** N Terr Australia
128 E2 **La Urbana** Venezuela
28 D4 **Laurbjerg** Denmark
95 M8 **Laurel** Delaware U.S.A.
94 B7 **Laurel** Indiana U.S.A.
95 L7 **Laurel** Maryland U.S.A.
111 G10 **Laurel** Mississippi U.S.A.
101 R4 **Laurel** Montana U.S.A.
130 B10 **Laureles** Paraguay
111 K11 **Laurel Hill** Florida U.S.A.
94 H6 **Laurel Hill** Pennsylvania U.S.A.
94 E7 **Laurelville** Ohio U.S.A.
15 F4 **Laurencekirk** Scotland
99 M7 **Laurens** Iowa U.S.A.
95 M4 **Laurens** New York U.S.A.
112 E3 **Laurens** South Carolina U.S.A.
121 R7 **Laurentides** Quebec Canada
121 T5 **Laurentides, Parc Prov. des** Quebec Canada
43 G8 **Laurenzana** Italy
43 G8 **Lauria** Italy
146 E3 **Laurie I** *isld* S Orkney Is Antarctica
119 P2 **Laurie L** Saskatchewan Canada
143 E7 **Laurie, Mt** W Australia Australia
119 Q2 **Laurie R** Manitoba Canada
119 S8 **Laurier** Manitoba Canada
121 T6 **Laurierville** Quebec Canada
12 D4 **Laurieston** Scotland
139 L4 **Laurieton** New South Wales Australia
29 L6 **Laurila** Finland
101 N4 **Laurin** Montana U.S.A.
112 H3 **Laurinburg** North Carolina U.S.A.
19 O17 **Lauris** France
144 C5 **Lauriston** New Zealand
29 N10 **Lauritsala** Finland
99 S2 **Laurium** Michigan U.S.A.
45 R8 **Lauro** Italy
43 F11 **Lauro, M** *mt* Sicily
133 H3 **Lauro Muller** Brazil
40 E4 **Lausanne** Switzerland
37 L3 **Lauscha** Germany
70 E6 **Laut** *isld* Kalimantan
19 Q14 **Lautaret, Col du** *pass* France
131 A7 **Lautaro** Chile
33 M9 **Lautenthal** Germany
36 D5 **Lauter** *R* Germany
37 O2 **Lauter** Germany
37 M5 **Lauterach** *R* Germany
36 E7 **Lauterbach** Baden-Württemberg Germany
36 G2 **Lauterbach** Hessen Germany
37 O1 **Lauterbach** Sachsen Germany
36 E6 **Lauterbourg** France
36 D4 **Lauterecken** Germany
37 M5 **Lauterhofen** Germany
36 G2 **Lautertal** Germany
37 K3 **Lautertal** Germany
29 L6 **Lautiosaari** Finland
70 D7 **Laut Kecil, Kepulauan** *islds* Indonesia
41 J1 **Lautlingen** Germany
18 G9 **Lautrec** France
70 D6 **Laut, Selat** *str* Kalimantan
69 C10 **Lauttawar,Danau** *L* Sumatra
26 E7 **Lauvsnes** Norway
25 F2 **Lauwers** Netherlands
25 F2 **Lauwers Zee** Netherlands
18 F8 **Lauzerte** France
121 T6 **Lauzon** Quebec Canada
100 D8 **Lava Beds Nat. Mon** California U.S.A.
109 L6 **Lavaca** *R* Texas U.S.A.
109 **Lavaca B** Texas U.S.A.
22 J3 **Lavacherie** Belgium
44 F3 **Lavagna** *R* Italy
44 F3 **Lavagna** Italy
101 O7 **Lava Hot Springs** Idaho U.S.A.
21 J5 **Laval** France
19 P18 **La Valette** France
99 Q6 **La Valle** Wisconsin U.S.A.
131 G5 **Lavalleja** *dept* Uruguay
122 C5 **Laval, R** Quebec Canada
38 L8 **Lavamünd** Austria
77 C6 **Lavan** Iran
45 L3 **Lavane, M** *mt* Italy
26 J3 **Lavangen** Norway
38 L8 **Lavant** *R* Austria
121 O7 **Lavant** Ontario Canada
9 F6 **Lavant** England
38 L8 **Lavanttal** *V* Austria
131 A6 **Lavapié, Pta** *C* Chile
18 F8 **Lavardac** France
21 M6 **Lavardin** France
21 M5 **Lavaré** France
77 D4 **Lavar Meydan** *salt lake* Iran
18 G9 **Lavaur** France
21 L8 **Lavausseau** France
102 C5 **Laveaga Pk** California U.S.A.
16 D2 **La Vecilla** Spain
127 J5 **La Vega** Dominican Rep
124 H7 **La Vega** Mexico
128 E1 **La Vela** Venezuela
18 G10 **Lavelanet** France
16 D3 **La Vellés** Spain
28 D4 **Laven** Denmark
9 G3 **Lavenham** England
41 J6 **Laveno** Italy
22 D2 **Laventie** France
130 B10 **La Verá** *L* Paraguay
103 L4 **La Verkin** Utah U.S.A.
107 L5 **Laverne** Oklahoma U.S.A.
109 J6 **La Vernia** Texas U.S.A.
143 D8 **Laverton** W Australia Australia
106 E4 **La Veta** Colorado U.S.A.
71 G4 **Lavezares** Philippines
45 L2 **Lavezzola** Italy
29 K10 **Lavia** Finland
124 H4 **La Vibora** Mexico
121 M7 **Lavieille, L** Ontario Canada
27 A10 **Lavik** Norway
128 C5 **La Viña** Peru
101 R3 **Lavina** Montana U.S.A.
8 D5 **Lavington** England
112 D3 **Lavonia** Georgia U.S.A.
109 L2 **Lavon Res** Texas U.S.A.
118 F5 **Lavoy** Alberta Canada
130 G7 **Lavras** Brazil
130 H9 **Lavras da Mangabeira** Brazil
55 D4 **Lavrent'yevka** Kazakhstan
26 J7 **Lavsjö** Sweden
87 F11 **Lavumisa** Swaziland
88 C8 **Lavushi** *mt* Zambia
109 L7 **La Ward** Texas U.S.A.
70 D2 **Lawas** Sarawak
70 G6 **Lawata** Sulawesi
71 H7 **Lawele** Indonesia
100 G6 **Lawen** Oregon U.S.A.
119 V4 **Lawford L** Manitoba Canada
141 K6 **Lawgi** Queensland Australia
71 B3 **Lawin** *isld* Indonesia
70 C4 **Lawit, G** *mt* Sarawak
69 F10 **Lawit, Gunung** *mt* Malaysia
68 C2 **Lawksawk** Burma
99 N3 **Lawler** Minnesota U.S.A.
123 R7 **Lawn** Newfoundland Canada
108 H3 **Lawn** Texas U.S.A.
112 F2 **Lawndale** North Carolina U.S.A.
140 E4 **Lawn Hill** Queensland Australia
85 D6 **Lawra** Ghana
144 B6 **Lawrence** New Zealand
94 A7 **Lawrence** Indiana U.S.A.
107 P3 **Lawrence** Kansas U.S.A.
95 Q4 **Lawrence** Massachusetts U.S.A.
98 H9 **Lawrence** Nebraska U.S.A.
94 B7 **Lawrenceburg** Indiana U.S.A.
94 C8 **Lawrenceburg** Kentucky U.S.A.
110 J6 **Lawrenceburg** Tennessee U.S.A.
122 E8 **Lawrence Stn** New Brunswick Canada
122 G9 **Lawrencetown** Nova Scotia Canada
122 J9 **Lawrencetown** Nova Scotia Canada
112 D4 **Lawrenceville** Georgia U.S.A.
110 J3 **Lawrenceville** Illinois U.S.A.
95 L5 **Lawrenceville** Pennsylvania U.S.A.
94 K10 **Lawrenceville** Virginia U.S.A.
143 D7 **Lawrence Wells, Mt** W Australia Australia
102 F4 **Laws** California U.S.A.
118 L8 **Lawson** Saskatchewan Canada
110 B2 **Lawson** Missouri U.S.A.
113 E7 **Lawtey** Florida U.S.A.
94 B4 **Lawton** Michigan U.S.A.
98 H1 **Lawton** North Dakota U.S.A.
107 M7 **Lawton** Oklahoma U.S.A.
27 G12 **Laxå** Sweden
Laxe *see* **Lage** Spain
12 D5 **Laxey** I of Man U.K.
9 H3 **Laxfield** England
15 G2 **Laxo** Scotland
26 G8 **Laxsjö** Sweden
21 H8 **Lay** *R* France
101 S9 **Lay** Colorado U.S.A.
52 J2 **Laya** *R* Russian Federation
52 G1 **Laydennyy, Mys** *C* Russian Federation
21 P5 **Laye** *R* France
139 G7 **Layers Hill** Victoria Australia
111 K9 **Lay L** Alabama U.S.A.
21 J7 **Layon** *R* France
78 M2 **Laysār** Iran
55 E2 **Laytamak** Russian Federation
101 N8 **Layton** Utah U.S.A.
83 K12 **Lazare, Pt** Mahé I Indian Oc
48 F6 **Lazarevac** Serbia Yugoslavia
57 A3 **Lazareva, Oz** *isld* Uzbekistan
146 J7 **Lazarevisen** *ice shelf* Antarctica
146 J6 **Lazarev Sea** Antarctica
124 B2 **Lázaro Cárdenas** Mexico
124 H8 **Lázaro Cárdenas** Mexico
31 O1 **Lazdijai** Lithuania
21 P7 **Lazenay** France
42 E6 **Lazio** *prov* Italy
37 O3 **Lázně Kynžvart** Czechoslovakia
59 K3 **Lazo** Russian Federation
13 F4 **Lazonby** England
48 L3 **Lazovsk** Moldavia
9 F1 **Lea** England
100 C5 **Leaburg** Oregon U.S.A.
68 F6 **Leach** Cambodia
110 F6 **Leachville** Arkansas U.S.A.
98 C5 **Lead** South Dakota U.S.A.
13 E2 **Leadburn** Scotland
9 F1 **Leadenham** England
9 G4 **Leaden Roding** England
118 H8 **Leader** Saskatchewan Canada
15 E5 **Leadhills** Scotland
101 M5 **Leadore** Idaho U.S.A.
139 J4 **Leadville** New South Wales Australia
106 D2 **Leadville** Colorado U.S.A.
115 M6 **Leaf** *R* Quebec Canada
99 R7 **Leaf River** Illinois U.S.A.
9 G1 **Leake** England
142 F4 **Leake, Mt** W Australia Australia
143 C7 **Leake, Mt** W Australia Australia
111 H10 **Leakesville** Mississippi U.S.A.
108 H6 **Leakey** Texas U.S.A.
111 G10 **Leal** *R* Mississippi U.S.A.
98 H2 **Leal** North Dakota U.S.A.
133 D3 **Leales** Argentina
142 B5 **Leal, Mt** W Australia Australia
120 H10 **Leamington** Ontario Canada
145 E2 **Leamington** New Zealand
103 M2 **Leamington** Utah U.S.A.
9 E3 **Leamington Spa, Royal** England
9 E3 **Leam,R** England
67 E3 **Le'an** China
12 C1 **Leanach** Scotland
109 K5 **Leander** Texas U.S.A.
130 C10 **Leandro N.Alem** Argentina
14 B4 **Leane,L** Ireland
67 F2 **Le'an Jiang** *R* China
9 F4 **Lea, R** England
142 A5 **Learmonth** W Australia Australia
111 M10 **Leary** Georgia U.S.A.
9 F1 **Leasingham** England
118 L5 **Leask** Saskatchewan Canada
9 F5 **Leatherhead** England
101 M5 **Leatherman Pk** Idaho U.S.A.
110 K3 **Leavenworth** Indiana U.S.A.
107 P2 **Leavenworth** Kansas U.S.A.
100 E2 **Leavenworth** Washington U.S.A.
102 E3 **Leavitt Pk** California U.S.A.
31 K1 **Łeba** Poland
36 B5 **Lebach** Germany
70 L9 **Lebak** Java
71 G7 **Lebak** Mindanao Philippines
100 B3 **Lebam** Washington U.S.A.
46 E2 **Lebane** Serbia Yugoslavia
86 B5 **Lebango** Congo
79 F4 **Lebanon** *rep* S W Asia
110 G3 **Lebanon** Illinois U.S.A.
110 K1 **Lebanon** Indiana U.S.A.
107 M2 **Lebanon** Kansas U.S.A.
110 L4 **Lebanon** Kentucky U.S.A.
110 D4 **Lebanon** Missouri U.S.A.
98 F9 **Lebanon** Nebraska U.S.A.
95 Q3 **Lebanon** New Hampshire U.S.A.
94 C7 **Lebanon** Ohio U.S.A.
100 C5 **Lebanon** Oregon U.S.A.
95 L6 **Lebanon** Pennsylvania U.S.A.
98 G4 **Lebanon** South Dakota U.S.A.
110 K5 **Lebanon** Tennessee U.S.A.
94 E10 **Lebanon** Virginia U.S.A.
94 B9 **Lebanon Junc** Kentucky U.S.A.
113 E8 **Lebanon Stn** Florida U.S.A.
55 F3 **Lebazh'ye** Russian Federation
19 P18 **Le Beausset** France
102 F7 **Lebec** California U.S.A.
55 E3 **Lebedevka** Russian Federation
54 F6 **Lebedin** Ukraine
54 L3 **Lebedyan'** Russian Federation
48 D3 **Lébénymiklós** Hungary
26 Q1 **Lebesby** Norway
71 H7 **Lebo** Indonesia
107 P3 **Lebo** Kansas U.S.A.
89 G4 **Lebombo Mts** Mozambique
68 A2 **Lebon** Burma
31 K1 **Lębork** Poland
71 M9 **Lebos** Timor
19 Q14 **Le Bourg d'Oisans** France
19 P13 **Le Bourget** France
122 H6 **Le Bouthillier** New Brunswick Canada
89 F5 **Lebowakgomo** S Africa
119 O8 **Lebret** Saskatchewan Canada
16 C8 **Lebrija** Spain
31 K1 **Łebsko, Jezioro** *L* Poland
133 C5 **Lebu** Chile
33 S9 **Lebusa** Germany
28 E7 **Leby** Denmark
55 G5 **Lebyazh'ye** Kazakhstan
52 G6 **Lebyazh'ye** Kirovskaya obl Russian Federation
55 E3 **Lebyazh'ye** Kurganskaya obl Russian Federation
71 N9 **Leça** Timor
19 Q18 **Le Canadel** France
43 J8 **Lecce** Italy
41 K6 **Lecco** Italy
41 K6 **Lecco, Lago di** Italy
99 N5 **Le Center** Minnesota U.S.A.
37 K7 **Lech** *R* Germany
67 D4 **Lechang** China
41 N2 **Lechbruck** Germany
19 J3 **Le Chesne** France
41 N1 **Lechfeld** *plain* Germany
48 J3 **Lechința** Romania
9 E4 **Lechlade** England
41 M3 **Lech Tal** *V* Austria
41 M3 **Lechtaler Alpen** *mt* Austria
17 G3 **Leciñena** Spain
28 B7 **Leck** Germany
22 E3 **Lecluse** France
111 D10 **Lecompte** Louisiana U.S.A.
13 H6 **Leconfield** England
18 H6 **Le Creusot** France
18 F9 **Lectoure** France
18 D9 **Lecumberri** Spain
31 O4 **Łęczna** Poland
31 L3 **Łęczyca** Poland
52 F4 **Led** *R* Russian Federation
32 G6 **Leda** *R* Germany
69 F11 **Ledang, Gunung** Malaysia
8 D3 **Ledbury** England
16 C3 **Ledesma** Spain
143 C10 **Ledge Pt** W Australia Australia
101 O1 **Ledger** Montana U.S.A.
87 B7 **Ledo, C** Angola
68 J3 **Ledong** China
41 N6 **Ledro,L.di** Italy
118 D5 **Leduc** Alberta Canada
31 K2 **Lędyczek** Poland
28 D4 **Lee** Denmark
103 P10 **Lee** Arizona U.S.A.
113 D7 **Lee** Florida U.S.A.
99 S8 **Lee** Illinois U.S.A.
95 O4 **Lee** Massachusetts U.S.A.
94 H6 **Leechburg** Pennsylvania U.S.A.
119 P7 **Leech L** Saskatchewan Canada
99 M2 **Leech L** Minnesota U.S.A.
41 N2 **Leeder** Germany
142 B1 **Leederville** *dist* Perth, W Aust Australia
108 E8 **Leedey** Oklahoma U.S.A.
13 G6 **Leeds** England
111 K8 **Leeds** Alabama U.S.A.
98 G1 **Leeds** North Dakota U.S.A.
103 L4 **Leeds** Utah U.S.A.
95 R2 **Leeds Junct** Maine U.S.A.
8 D1 **Leek** England
25 F2 **Leek** Netherlands
94 B2 **Leelanau L** Michigan U.S.A.
143 A8 **Leeman** W Australia Australia
13 G5 **Leeming** England
142 F2 **Leeming,Mt** W Australia Australia
25 E6 **Leende** Netherlands
9 E6 **Lee-on-the-Solent** England
110 F4 **Leeper** Missouri U.S.A.
94 H5 **Leeper** Pennsylvania U.S.A.
32 F6 **Leer** Germany
22 G2 **Leerbeek** Belgium
25 D5 **Leerdam** Netherlands
113 F9 **Leesburg** Florida U.S.A.
112 C6 **Leesburg** Georgia U.S.A.
101 L4 **Leesburg** Idaho U.S.A.
94 D7 **Leesburg** Ohio U.S.A.
109 M3 **Leesburg** Texas U.S.A.
94 K7 **Leesburg** Virginia U.S.A.
32 K7 **Leese** Germany
110 B3 **Lees Summit** Missouri U.S.A.
143 D7 **Lee Steere Ra** W Australia Australia
144 D5 **Leeston** New Zealand
109 O4 **Leesville** Louisiana U.S.A.
112 F4 **Leesville** South Carolina U.S.A.
109 K6 **Leesville** Texas U.S.A.
94 H9 **Leesville L.** Virginia U.S.A.
94 F6 **Leesville Res** Ohio U.S.A.
139 H5 **Leeton** New South Wales Australia
94 G6 **Leetonia** Ohio U.S.A.
94 B2 **Leetsville** Michigan U.S.A.
25 E2 **Leeuwarden** Netherlands
143 B10 **Leeuwin,C** W Australia Australia
102 E4 **Lee Vining** California U.S.A.
127 N5 **Leeward Is** W Indies
32 M5 **Leezen** Germany
20 E4 **Leff** *R* France
22 D1 **Leffinge** Belgium
86 C6 **Lefini** *R* Congo
79 C3 **Lefka** Cyprus
79 D4 **Lefkara** Cyprus
79 D3 **Lefkoniko** Cyprus
22 E3 **Leforest** France
71 C3 **Lef Pale** *isld* W Irian
121 L8 **Lefroy** Ontario Canada
143 D9 **Lefroy,L** W Australia Australia
119 T2 **Leftrook L** Manitoba Canada
118 D5 **Legal** Alberta Canada
120 E2 **Legarde** *R* Ontario Canada
121 R6 **Legaré,L** Quebec Canada
71 F4 **Legaspi** Philippines
9 G1 **Legbourne** England
32 F8 **Legden** Germany
20 G8 **Légé** Loire-Atlantique France
142 B5 **Legendre I** W Australia Australia
19 P14 **Le Genevrey** France
Leghorn *see* **Livorno**
31 M3 **Legionowo** Poland
121 T4 **Le Gîte** Quebec Canada
22 K4 **Léglise** Belgium
45 K1 **Legnago** Italy
41 J6 **Legnano** Italy
45 L1 **Legnaro** Italy
31 J4 **Legnica** Poland
41 K5 **Legnone** *mt* Italy
56 B4 **Legostayevo** Russian Federation
48 D4 **Legrad** Croatia
102 D4 **Le Grand** California U.S.A.
143 E10 **Le Grand,C** W Australia Australia
19 O14 **Le Grand Serre** France
20 D4 **Léguer** *R* France
140 A3 **Legune** N Terr Australia
74 G1 **Leh** Kashmir
21 L3 **Le Havre** France
37 L3 **Lehesten** Germany
101 O9 **Lehi** Utah U.S.A.
107 O7 **Lehigh** Oklahoma U.S.A.
109 L1 **Lehigh** Oklahoma U.S.A.
95 M6 **Lehighton** Pennsylvania U.S.A.
48 K6 **Lehliu** Romania
100 G4 **Lehman** Oregon U.S.A.
103 K3 **Lehman Caves Nat. Mon.** Nevada U.S.A.
33 R8 **Lehnin** Germany
20 F5 **Lehon** France
98 G3 **Lehr** North Dakota U.S.A.
37 K5 **Lehrberg** Germany
33 N8 **Lehre** Germany
32 L8 **Lehrte** Germany
33 O6 **Lehsen** Germany
29 K9 **Lehtimäki** Finland
67 E2 **Lehua** China
102 U13 **Lehua I** Hawaiian Is
74 D3 **Leiah** Pakistan
37 O6 **Leiblfing** Germany
38 N8 **Leibnitzer** Austria
67 A2 **Leibo** China
33 T8 **Leibsch** Germany
9 E2 **Leicester** England
9 E2 **Leicestershire** *co* England
140 C5 **Leichardt, Mt** N Terr Australia
140 E4 **Leichhardt** *R* Queensland Australia
140 E4 **Leichhardt Falls** Queensland Australia
141 H5 **Leichhardt Ra** Queensland Australia
36 C1 **Leichlingen** Germany
68 K2 **Lei-chou** China
25 C4 **Leiden** Netherlands
22 E2 **Leie** *R* Belgium
33 M8 **Leiferde** Germany
138 E4 **Leigh** *R* South Australia Australia
9 G5 **Leigh** England
145 E2 **Leigh** New Zealand
138 E4 **Leigh Creek** South Australia Australia
14 E4 **Leighlinbridge** Ireland
110 J7 **Leighton** Alabama U.S.A.
142 A2 **Leighton Beach** *dist* Perth, W Aust Australia
9 F4 **Leighton Buzzard** England
21 L8 **Leigne-sur-Usseau** France
22 J3 **Leignon** Belgium
27 B10 **Leikanger** Norway
68 C3 **Leiktho** Burma
33 O9 **Leimbach** Germany
36 D5 **Leimen** Germany
25 C4 **Leimuiden** Netherlands
37 K2 **Leina** *R* Germany
118 K8 **Leinan** Saskatchewan Canada
32 L8 **Leine** *R* Germany
33 M10 **Leinefelde** Germany
36 G6 **Leinfelden-Echterdingen** Germany
14 D3 **Leinster** *prov* Ireland
14 E4 **Leinster** *mt* Ireland
37 J7 **Leipheim** Germany
26 M4 **Leipojärvi** Sweden
94 D5 **Leipsic** Ohio U.S.A.
118 J6 **Leipzig** Saskatchewan Canada
33 Q10 **Leipzig** Germany
26 G4 **Leiranger** Norway
26 N1 **Leirbotn** Norway
16 B5 **Leiria** Portugal
26 R1 **Leirpollen** Norway
27 A12 **Leirvik** Norway
22 D2 **Leisele** Belgium
67 C3 **Leishan** China
67 D3 **Lei Shui** *R* China
138 B3 **Leisler Hills** South Australia Australia
140 A6 **Leisler,Mt** N Terr Australia
37 O1 **Leisnig** Germany
9 H3 **Leiston** England
110 K4 **Leitchfield** Kentucky U.S.A.
101 T5 **Leiter** Wyoming U.S.A.
13 E2 **Leith** Scotland
98 E3 **Leith** North Dakota U.S.A.
48 C3 **Leitha** *R* Austria
144 D5 **Leithfield** New Zealand
9 F5 **Leith Hill** England
14 C2 **Leitrim** *co* Ireland
33 P8 **Leitzkau** Germany
29 M10 **Leivonmäki** Finland
14 E3 **Leixlip** Ireland
67 D3 **Leiyang** China
Leizhou *see* **Haikang**
67 C6 **Leizhou Bandao** *pen* China
67 C6 **Leizhou Wan** *inlet* China
25 C5 **Lek** *R* Netherlands
26 E6 **Leka** *isld* Norway
46 G3 **Lekáni** Greece
Lekemti *see* **Nek'emtē** Ethiopia
46 E7 **Lekhainá** Greece
46 E4 **Lékhovon** Greece
16 C9 **Lekkous, Oued** *R* Morocco
27 G11 **Leksand** Sweden
29 P8 **Leksozero, Ozero** *L* Russian Federation
26 E8 **Leksvik** Norway
71 B2 **Lelai, Tanjong** *C* Indonesia
127 L4 **Le Lamentin** Martinique W Indies
99 N6 **Leland** Iowa U.S.A.
99 V4 **Leland** Michigan U.S.A.
111 F8 **Leland** Mississippi U.S.A.
27 E12 **Lelången** *L* Sweden
19 Q18 **Le Lavandou** France
133 C6 **Leleque** Argentina
Leli *see* **Tianlin**
108 G1 **Lelia Lake** Texas U.S.A.
48 E7 **Lelija** *mt* Bosnia-Herzegovina
65 D6 **Leling** China
71 C3 **Lelintah** W Irian
28 J6 **Lellinge** Denmark
71 L9 **Lelogama** Timor Indonesia
127 L4 **Le Lorrain** Martinique W Indies
19 Q18 **Le Luc** France
25 D3 **Lelystad** Netherlands
28 A4 **Lem** Denmark
43 F11 **Le Madonie** *mts* Sicily
133 E8 **Le Maire, Estrecho de** *str* Argentina
7 M9 **Leman Bank** *oil rig* North Sea
40 D5 **Léman,Lac** Switz/France
21 L5 **Le Mans** France
94 K7 **Lemasters** Pennsylvania U.S.A.
38 J5 **Lembach** Austria
36 D5 **Lembach** France
70 Q10 **Lembar** Indonesia
71 J4 **Lembeh** *isld* Sulawesi
Lemberg *see* **L'vov**
119 O8 **Lemberg** Saskatchewan Canada
36 C5 **Lemberg** France
36 D5 **Lemberg** Germany
32 H7 **Lembruch** Germany
70 E3 **Lembu** Kalimantan
70 E2 **Lembubut** Kalimantan
69 C10 **Lembu,Gunung** *mt* Sumatra
130 F8 **Leme** São Paulo Brazil
19 N17 **Le Merle** France
71 E4 **Lemery** Philippines
32 H8 **Lemforde** Germany
32 J8 **Lemgo** Germany
101 M5 **Lemhi** Idaho U.S.A.
101 M5 **Lemhi Ra** Idaho U.S.A.
121 S6 **Lemieux** Quebec Canada
115 N5 **Lemieux Is** Northwest Territories Canada
106 D7 **Lemitar** New Mexico U.S.A.
32 K7 **Lemke** Germany
29 M3 **Lemmenjoki** *R* Finland
29 L3 **Lemmenjoki Nat. Park** Finland
25 E3 **Lemmer** Netherlands
28 D4 **Lemming** Denmark
98 D4 **Lemmon** South Dakota U.S.A.
103 O9 **Lemmon, Mt** Arizona U.S.A.
Lemnos *isld* Greece *see* **Límnos** *isld*
126 H5 **Le Môle St. Nicolas** Haiti
111 G9 **Lemon** Mississippi U.S.A.
102 E5 **Lemoore** California U.S.A.
127 L4 **Le Morne Rouge** Martinique W Indies
98 E8 **Lemoyne** Nebraska U.S.A.
125 P11 **Lempa** *R* El Salvador
29 K10 **Lempäälä** Finland
18 H7 **Lempdes** France
117 O9 **Lempriere** British Columbia Canada
118 H8 **Lemsford** Saskatchewan Canada

Lemsid — Lioppa 195

85 B3 **Lemsid** Western Sahara
43 G7 **Le Murge** *dist* Italy
19 Q18 **Le Muy** France
28 A3 **Lemvig** Denmark
32 J6 **Lemwerder** Germany
68 B4 **Lemyethna** Burma
56 G3 **Lena** *R* Russian Federation
99 R7 **Lena** Illinois U.S.A.
109 P4 **Lena** Louisiana U.S.A.
111 G9 **Lena** Mississippi U.S.A.
100 F4 **Lena** Oregon U.S.A.
99 S5 **Lena** Wisconsin U.S.A.
101 Q9 **Lena, Mt** Utah U.S.A.
71 H9 **Lenangguar** Indonesia
107 P5 **Lenapah** Oklahoma U.S.A.
21 L8 **Lencloître** France
38 H7 **Lend** Austria
12 D3 **Lendalfoot** Scotland
29 P8 **Lendery** Russian Federation
45 L1 **Lendinara** Italy
118 K6 **Leney** Saskatchewan Canada
33 M8 **Lengede** Germany
37 P2 **Lengefeld** Germany
32 G8 **Lengerich** Germany
66 E4 **Lenghu** China
58 D4 **Lenglong Ling** *mt ra* China
67 D3 **Lengshuijiang** China
131 B3 **Lengua de Vaca,Pta** Chile
65 E4 **Lengzipu** China
9 G5 **Lenham** England
27 H15 **Lenhovda** Sweden
70 D5 **Lenili** Kalimantan
Leninabad Tajikistan *see* **Khodzhent**
57 A3 **Leninabad** Uzbekistan
78 J1 **Leninakan** Armenia
57 G5 **Lenina, Pik** *mt* Tajikistan
36 B6 **Léning** France
Leningrad *see* **Sankt-Peterburg**
146 C13 **Leningradskaya** *former U.S.S.R. Base* Antarctica
52 D5 **Leningradskaya Oblast'** *prov* Russian Federation
Lenin I.V. Kanal *see* **Volgo-Balt**
56 B5 **Leninogorsk** Kazakhstan
55 C4 **Leninsk** Chelyabinskaya obl Russian Federation
57 A4 **Leninsk** Turkmenistan
55 G5 **Leninskiy** Kazakhstan
52 G6 **Leninskiy** Mariyskaya Respublika Russian Federation
54 J2 **Leninskiy** Tul'skaya obl Russian Federation
56 B4 **Leninsk-Kuznetskiy** Russian Federation
55 E4 **Leninskoye** Kazakhstan
57 G4 **Leninskoye** Kyrgyzstan
52 G5 **Leninskoye** Kirovskaya obl Russian Federation
48 G3 **Leninváros** Hungary
88 B9 **Lenje** Zambia
55 H4 **Len'ki** Russian Federation
142 E3 **Lennard,R** W Australia Australia
27 E12 **Lennartsfors** Sweden
36 E1 **Lenne** *R* Germany
101 P3 **Lennep** Montana U.S.A.
36 E1 **Lennestadt** Germany
143 F7 **Lennis Hills** W Australia Australia
98 K6 **Lennox** South Dakota U.S.A.
133 D9 **Lennox, I** Chile/Arg
12 D2 **Lennoxtown** Scotland
121 T7 **Lennoxville** Quebec Canada
56 F4 **Leno-Angarskoye Plato** *plateau* Russian Federation
112 F2 **Lenoir** North Carolina U.S.A.
112 C2 **Lenoir City** Tennessee U.S.A.
107 K2 **Lenora** Kansas U.S.A.
119 R9 **Lenore** Manitoba Canada
119 M6 **Lenore L** Saskatchewan Canada
100 F2 **Lenore, L** Washington U.S.A.
112 D6 **Lenox** Georgia U.S.A.
99 M9 **Lenox** Iowa U.S.A.
95 O4 **Lenox** Massachusetts U.S.A.
22 F2 **Lens** Belgium
22 D3 **Lens** France
33 N4 **Lensahn** Germany
26 D8 **Lensvik** Norway
25 E5 **Lent** Netherlands
37 L6 **Lenting** Germany
43 F11 **Lentini** Sicily
29 O7 **Lentüra** Finland
26 K2 **Lenvik** Norway
68 D7 **Lenya** Burma
33 O6 **Lenzen** Germany
12 D2 **Lenzie** Scotland
85 D6 **Léo** Burkina
38 M7 **Leoben** Austria
127 H5 **Léogane** Haiti
38 G7 **Leogang** Austria
38 G7 **Leoganger** Austria
70 G4 **Leok** Sulawesi Indonesia
8 D3 **Leominster** England
95 Q4 **Leominster** Massachusetts U.S.A.
18 E9 **Léon** France
20 A5 **Léon** *reg* France
124 J7 **Leon** Mexico
125 L3 **León** Nicaragua
16 D2 **León** *prov* Spain
16 D2 **León** Spain
99 N9 **Leon** Iowa U.S.A.
107 O4 **Leon** Kansas U.S.A.
94 F8 **Leon** West Virginia U.S.A.
109 M4 **Leona** Texas U.S.A.
109 H7 **Leona** *R* Texas U.S.A.
94 D4 **Leonard** Michigan U.S.A.
99 O10 **Leonard** Missouri U.S.A.
98 J3 **Leonard** North Dakota U.S.A.
109 L2 **Leonard** Texas U.S.A.
89 A4 **Leonardville** Namibia
107 O2 **Leonardville** Kansas U.S.A.
79 E3 **Leonarisso** Cyprus
36 G6 **Leonberg** Germany
36 F5 **Leonbronn** Germany
19 O15 **Léoncel** France
131 B2 **Leoncito,L** Argentina
128 F8 **Leon,Co** *mt* Paraguay
108 E4 **Leon Cr** Texas U.S.A.
46 E5 **Leondári** Greece
139 H7 **Leongatha** Victoria Australia
46 F7 **Leonídhion** Greece
16 C2 **León, Montañas de** *mts* Spain
143 D8 **Leonora** W Australia Australia
109 J6 **Leon Springs** Texas U.S.A.
116 F9 **Leontovitch,C** Alaska U.S.A.
142 F4 **Leopold Downs** W Australia Australia
130 G7 **Leopoldina** Brazil
129 J7 **Leopoldo de Bulhões** Brazil
22 J1 **Leopoldsburg** Belgium
33 T5 **Leopoldshagen** Germany
40 G1 **Leopoldskan** *canal* Germany
Leopoldville *see* **Kinshasa**
107 J3 **Leoti** Kansas U.S.A.
118 K5 **Leoville** Saskatchewan Canada
48 L4 **Leovo** Moldavia
125 M5 **Lepanto** Costa Rica
110 F6 **Lepanto** Arkansas U.S.A.
69 H14 **Lepar** *isld* Indonesia
125 L2 **Lepaterique** Honduras
87 E10 **Lephepe** Botswana
67 F2 **Leping** China
45 O6 **Lepini, Mti** *mts* Italy
121 R7 **L'Epiphanie** Quebec Canada
55 D1 **Leplya** *R* Russian Federation
71 H7 **Lepolepo** Sulawesi
42 B2 **Lepontine,Alpi** *mts* Italy
70 G7 **Leppangeng** Sulawesi
29 N9 **Leppävirta** Finland
145 E3 **Lepperton** New Zealand
122 F8 **Lepreau** New Brunswick Canada
122 F8 **Lepreau, Pt** New Brunswick Canada
57 J2 **Lepsa** *R* Kazakhstan
48 E4 **Lepsény** Hungary
57 K2 **Lepsinsk** Kazakhstan
57 J2 **Lepsy** Kazakhstan
19 O17 **Le Puy Ste Réparade** France
95 L5 **Le Raysville** Pennsylvania U.S.A.
33 M9 **Lerbach** Germany
29 K4 **Lerberget** Sweden
28 D4 **Lerbjerg** Denmark
43 F11 **Lercara Friddi** Sicily
86 B4 **Léré** Chad
70 F5 **Lereh, Tanjong** *C* Sulawesi
121 T5 **Le Relais** Quebec Canada
29 K4 **Lerhamn** Sweden
141 G5 **Lerida** Queensland Australia
128 D3 **Lérida** Colombia
17 H3 **Lérida** *prov* Spain
17 H3 **Lérida** Spain
28 C3 **Lerkenfeld Å** *R* Denmark
16 E2 **Lerma** Spain
53 F11 **Lermontov** Russian Federation
41 N3 **Lermoos** Austria
99 S10 **Lerna** Illinois U.S.A.
21 L7 **Lerné** France
127 L4 **Le Robert** Martinique W Indies
47 H7 **Léros** *isld* Greece
119 O7 **Leross** Saskatchewan Canada
19 J4 **Lérouville** France
119 N7 **Leroy** Saskatchewan Canada
99 S9 **Le Roy** Illinois U.S.A.
99 N9 **Le Roy** Iowa U.S.A.
107 P3 **Le Roy** Kansas U.S.A.
94 B2 **Le Roy** Michigan U.S.A.
99 O6 **Le Roy** Minnesota U.S.A.
94 J4 **Leroy** New York U.S.A.
101 P8 **Le Roy** Wyoming U.S.A.
40 D1 **Lerrain** France
27 F14 **Lerum** Sweden
15 G2 **Lerwick** Scotland
21 N3 **Léry** France
111 G12 **Lery,L** Louisiana U.S.A.
48 G4 **Leş** Romania
41 J6 **Lesa** Italy
19 P13 **Les Abrets** France
38 G8 **Lesach Tal** *V* Austria
38 G8 **Lesachtal** Austria
19 N18 **Le Salin de Giraud** France
19 P13 **Les Avenières** France
19 N17 **Les Baux** France
Lesbos *isld see* **Lésvos** *isld*
13 G3 **Lesbury** England
83 M13 **L'Escalier** Mauritius
18 E9 **Lescar** France
126 H5 **Les Cayes** Haiti
143 B9 **Leschenault, C** W Australia Australia
122 B6 **Les Éboulements** Quebec Canada
19 P14 **Les Echelles** France
122 C5 **Les Escoumins** Quebec Canada
122 D6 **Les Étroits** Quebec Canada
67 A2 **Leshan** China
20 E3 **Les Hanois Lt.Ho** English Chan
40 G5 **Les Haudères** Switzerland
52 G3 **Leshukonskoye** Russian Federation
69 C11 **Lesikin** Indonesia
44 F2 **Lésima** *mt* Italy
42 G7 **Lesina,L.di** Italy
26 C9 **Lesja** Norway
26 C9 **Lesjaskog** Norway
26 C9 **Lesjaskogsvatn** *L* Norway
27 G12 **Lesjöfors** Sweden
31 N6 **Lesko** Poland
46 E1 **Leskovac** Serbia Yugoslavia
146 G2 **Leskov I** S Sandwich Is S Atlantic Oc
46 D4 **Leskovik** Albania
13 E1 **Leslie** Scotland
110 D6 **Leslie** Arkansas U.S.A.
112 C6 **Leslie** Georgia U.S.A.
101 M6 **Leslie** Idaho U.S.A.
94 C4 **Leslie** Michigan U.S.A.
119 O7 **Leslie Stn** Saskatchewan Canada
118 C6 **Leslieville** Alberta Canada
12 E2 **Lesmahagow** Scotland
127 N4 **Les Mangles** Guadeloupe
19 P16 **Les Mées** France
19 Q16 **Les Monges** *mt* France
31 O3 **Lesnaya** *R* Belorussia
20 B4 **Lesneven** France
48 E6 **Lešnica** Serbia Yugoslavia
55 E3 **Lesnoy** Russian Federation
52 D2 **Lesnoy** Murmanskaya obl Russian Federation
52 E5 **Lesnoye** Russian Federation
59 M2 **Lesogorsk** Russian Federation
52 C4 **Lesogorskiy** Russian Federation
56 D2 **Lesosibirsk** Russian Federation
89 E7 **Lesotho** *kingdom* Africa
65 J2 **Lesozavodsk** Russian Federation
18 E7 **Lesparre-Medoc** France
19 O18 **Les-Pennes-Mirabeau** France
83 K12 **L'Espérance** Mahé I Indian Oc
22 F4 **Lesquielles-St Germain** France
38 J7 **Lessach** Austria
127 N5 **Les Saintes** *islds* Guadeloupe W Indies
20 G3 **Lessay** France
22 J3 **Lesse** *R* Belgium
32 M8 **Lesse** Germany
27 H15 **Lessebo** Sweden
146 B8 **Lesser Antarctica** Antarctica
127 N6 **Lesser Antilles** *islds* W Indies
Lesser Khingan Range *see* **Xiao Hinggan Ling**
117 Q8 **Lesser Slave L** Alberta Canada
118 C3 **Lesser Slave R** Alberta Canada
22 F2 **Lessines** Belgium
41 O6 **Lessini** *mt* Italy
40 G7 **Lessolo** Italy
98 K6 **Lester** Iowa U.S.A.
98 H9 **Lester** Nebraska U.S.A.
94 F9 **Lester** West Virginia U.S.A.
99 M5 **Lester Prairie** Minnesota U.S.A.
98 J6 **Lesterville** South Dakota U.S.A.
29 L8 **Lestijärvi** Finland
119 N7 **Lestock** Saskatchewan Canada
127 L4 **Les Trois Îlets** Martinique W Indies
99 N5 **Le Sueur** Minnesota U.S.A.
142 F2 **Lesueur I** W Australia Australia
143 B9 **Lesueur, Mt** W Australia Australia
70 D4 **Lesung, Bt** *mt* Kalimantan
47 H5 **Lésvos** *isld* Greece
12 C4 **Leswalt** Scotland
31 K4 **Leszno** Poland
89 G4 **Letaba** *R* S Africa
111 K9 **Letchatchee** Alabama U.S.A.
98 H6 **Letcher** South Dakota U.S.A.
9 F4 **Letchworth** England
119 U9 **Letellier** Manitoba Canada
100 J6 **Letha** Idaho U.S.A.
118 E9 **Lethbridge** Alberta Canada
123 T5 **Lethbridge** Newfoundland Canada
71 N9 **Leti** *isld* Indonesia
48 L1 **Letichev** Ukraine
128 E4 **Leticia** Colombia
71 N9 **Leti, Kepulauan** *islds* Indonesia
65 D5 **Leting** China
37 P4 **Letiny** Czechoslovakia
52 G5 **Letka** *R* Russian Federation
32 G10 **Letmathe** Germany
52 D3 **Letnerechenskiy** Russian Federation
46 G1 **Letnitsa** Bulgaria
52 D2 **Letnyaya-Reka** Russian Federation
52 E3 **Letnyaya Zolotitsa** Russian Federation
38 F8 **Le Tofane** *mt* Italy
19 P14 **Le Touvet** France
68 B4 **Letpadan** Burma
139 G5 **Lette** New South Wales Australia
14 D2 **Letterkenny** Ireland
8 B4 **Letterston** Wales
94 B7 **Letts** Indiana U.S.A.
69 G11 **Letung** Indonesia
17 F6 **Letur** Spain
33 O8 **Letzlingen** Germany
48 J6 **Leu** Romania
87 D8 **Leua** Angola
37 N2 **Leubnitz** Germany
18 H10 **Leucate** France
15 F4 **Leuchars** Scotland
37 N4 **Leuchtenberg** Germany
37 M2 **Leuchtenburg** Germany
22 G3 **Leugnies** France
20 C5 **Leuhan** France
40 G5 **Leuk** Switzerland
40 G5 **Leukerbad** Switzerland
36 E2 **Leun** Germany
33 Q10 **Leuna** Germany
37 M3 **Leupoldsdorf** Germany
69 B10 **Leupung** Sumatra
141 J6 **Leura** Queensland Australia
69 C11 **Leuser,Gunung** *mt* Sumatra
48 L4 **Leusheny** Moldavia
55 E2 **Leushi** Russian Federation
55 E2 **Leushinskiy Tuman, Oz** *L* Russian Federation
33 O6 **Leussow** Germany
41 O3 **Leutasch** Austria
37 L2 **Leutenberg** Germany
37 J5 **Leutershausen** Germany
41 M2 **Leutkirch** Germany
38 M8 **Leutschach** Austria
22 H2 **Leuven** Belgium
22 F2 **Leuze** Belgium
120 J6 **Levack** Ontario Canada
46 F6 **Levádhia** Greece
19 Q18 **Le Val** France
46 C4 **Levan** Albania
103 N2 **Levan** Utah U.S.A.
26 E8 **Levanger** Norway
44 B1 **Levanna** *mt* Italy
40 F7 **Levanna, M** Italy
107 J2 **Levant** Kansas U.S.A.
19 Q18 **Levant,I.du** France
44 F3 **Levanto** Italy
43 E10 **Levanzo, I. di** Sicily
21 J5 **Levare** France
127 M4 **Le Vauclin** Martinique W Indies
55 E1 **Levdym** Russian Federation
108 E2 **Levelland** Texas U.S.A.
144 C6 **Levels** New Zealand
13 H6 **Leven** England
13 E1 **Leven** Scotland
41 J5 **Leventina, Valle** Switzerland
142 E3 **Lévêque,C** W Australia Australia
98 B6 **Leverett** Wyoming U.S.A.
36 B1 **Leverkusen** Germany
117 P3 **Lever L** Northwest Territories Canada
32 H8 **Levern** Germany
9 F4 **Leverstock Green** England
21 N5 **Lèves** France
48 E2 **Levice** Czechoslovakia
41 O5 **Levico** Italy
55 C2 **Levikha** Russian Federation
145 E4 **Levin** New Zealand
52 F5 **Levinskoye** Russian Federation
140 B6 **Levi Ra** N Terr Australia
121 T6 **Lévis** Quebec Canada
94 E9 **Levisa Fork** *R* Kentucky U.S.A.
47 H7 **Levítha** *isld* Greece
95 N6 **Levittown** Pennsylvania U.S.A.
46 G9 **Lévka Óri** *mt* Crete Greece
46 F9 **Lévka Óri National Park** Crete Greece
46 D6 **Levkás** *isld* Greece
47 P13 **Levkimmi** Greece
31 M6 **Levoča** Czechoslovakia
85 A4 **Lévrier,B.du** Mauritania
28 C4 **Levring** Denmark
21 O8 **Levroux** France
46 G1 **Levski** Bulgaria
106 F5 **Levy** New Mexico U.S.A.
20 H2 **Levy,C** France
113 E8 **Levy,L** Florida U.S.A.
71 J9 **Lewa** Indonesia
98 F7 **Lewanna** Nebraska U.S.A.
68 C3 **Lewe** Burma
98 D8 **Lewellen** Nebraska U.S.A.
9 F6 **Lewes** England
142 D5 **Lewin,Mt** W Australia Australia
15 B2 **Lewis** *dist* Scotland
99 L8 **Lewis** Iowa U.S.A.
94 K6 **Lewis** Pennsylvania U.S.A.
100 D3 **Lewis** *R* Washington U.S.A.
98 J7 **Lewis and Clark L** South Dakota U.S.A.
138 D3 **Lewis B** South Australia Australia
110 K5 **Lewisburg** Kentucky U.S.A.
94 C7 **Lewisburg** Ohio U.S.A.
95 K6 **Lewisburg** Pennsylvania U.S.A.
110 K6 **Lewisburg** Tennessee U.S.A.
94 G9 **Lewisburg** West Virginia U.S.A.
123 O5 **Lewis Hills** Newfoundland Canada
68 A6 **Lewis Inlet** Andaman Is
101 P5 **Lewis L** Wyoming U.S.A.
144 D5 **Lewis Pass** New Zealand
123 R4 **Lewisporte** Newfoundland Canada
142 G5 **Lewis Ra** W Australia Australia
101 M1 **Lewis Ra** Montana U.S.A.
94 J5 **Lewis Run** Pennsylvania U.S.A.
103 O10 **Lewis Sps** Arizona U.S.A.
100 J3 **Lewiston** Idaho U.S.A.
95 R2 **Lewiston** Maine U.S.A.
94 C2 **Lewiston** Michigan U.S.A.
110 E1 **Lewiston** Missouri U.S.A.
94 J3 **Lewiston** New York U.S.A.
112 K1 **Lewiston** North Carolina U.S.A.
101 O8 **Lewiston** Utah U.S.A.
99 Q9 **Lewistown** Illinois U.S.A.
101 Q2 **Lewistown** Montana U.S.A.
111 C8 **Lewisville** Arkansas U.S.A.
101 N6 **Lewisville** Idaho U.S.A.
99 M6 **Lewisville** Minnesota U.S.A.
94 K5 **Lewisville** Pennsylvania U.S.A.
109 L2 **Lewisville** Texas U.S.A.
109 L2 **Lewisville, L** Texas U.S.A.
33 P6 **Lewitz** Germany
71 L9 **Lewoleba** Indonesia
71 L9 **Lewotobi** *mt* Flores Indonesia
119 N8 **Lewvan** Saskatchewan Canada
111 F7 **Lexa** Arkansas U.S.A.
99 S9 **Lexington** Illinois U.S.A.
94 B8 **Lexington** Indiana U.S.A.
94 C8 **Lexington** Kentucky U.S.A.
94 E3 **Lexington** Michigan U.S.A.
111 F8 **Lexington** Mississippi U.S.A.
110 C2 **Lexington** Missouri U.S.A.
98 G9 **Lexington** Nebraska U.S.A.
112 G2 **Lexington** North Carolina U.S.A.
109 K1 **Lexington** Oklahoma U.S.A.
100 F4 **Lexington** Oregon U.S.A.
112 F4 **Lexington** South Carolina U.S.A.
110 H6 **Lexington** Tennessee U.S.A.
109 K5 **Lexington** Texas U.S.A.
94 H9 **Lexington** Virginia U.S.A.
95 L8 **Lexington Park** Maryland U.S.A.
98 J1 **Leyden** North Dakota U.S.A.
95 M3 **Leyden,W** New York U.S.A.
67 B4 **Leye** China
83 L13 **Leygues** Kerguelen Indian Oc
13 F6 **Leyland** England
18 E8 **Leyre** *R* France
9 G5 **Leysdown** England
71 G5 **Leyte** *isld* Philippines
71 G5 **Leyte Gulf** Philippines
19 N16 **Lez** *R* France
31 N5 **Leżajsk** Poland
20 D4 **Lèzardrieux** France
18 E6 **Lezay** France
52 F5 **Lezha** Russian Federation
46 D3 **Lezhë** Albania
67 B1 **Lezhi** China
52 F6 **Lezhnevo** Russian Federation
18 G9 **Lézignan** France
18 H7 **Lezoux** France
17 F6 **Lezuza** Spain
99 R3 **L. Gogebic** Michigan U.S.A.
54 G5 **L'gov** Russian Federation
54 G5 **L'govskiy** Russian Federation
66 E5 **Lhari** China
143 A7 **Lharidon Bight** W Australia Australia
Lhariguo *see* **Lhari**
66 E6 **Lhasa** China
Lhatse Dzong *see* **Lhazê**
66 D6 **Lhazê** China
Lho Dzong *see* **Lhorong**
69 B10 **Lhokkreut** Sumatra
69 C10 **Lhokseumawe** Sumatra
69 C10 **Lhoksukon** Sumatra
66 F5 **Lhorong** China
Liancheng *see* **Qinglong**
67 E4 **Liancheng** China
21 P3 **Liancourt** France
Liancourt Rocks *see* **Tok-to**
22 B2 **Liane** *R* France
71 H5 **Liang** Indonesia
71 G6 **Lianga** Mindanao Philippines
65 B4 **Liangcheng** China
65 D7 **Liangcheng** China
58 E5 **Liangdang** China
67 C2 **Lianghekou** China
Liangjiayoufang *see* **Youyu**
71 E8 **Liang Liang** Philippines
67 B1 **Liangping** China
70 D4 **Liangpran, Bukit** *mt* Kalimantan
Liangshizhen *see* **Shaodong**
67 D4 **Liangtan** China
69 E11 **Liang Timur, Gunung** *mt* Malaysia
67 A4 **Liangwang Shan** *mts* China
67 E1 **Liangzi Hu** *L* China
67 D3 **Lianhua** China
67 E5 **Lianhua Shan** *mts* China
67 F3 **Lianjiang** China
67 B4 **Lian Jiang** *R* China
68 K2 **Lianjiang** China
65 H1 **Lianjiangkou** China
67 D4 **Liannan** China
67 E4 **Lianping** China
67 D4 **Lianshan** China
65 F4 **Lianshanguan** China
67 D3 **Lian Shui** *R* Hunan China
68 E6 **Liant** *C* Thailand
67 D5 **Liantan** China
Liantang *see* **Nanchang**
67 D1 **Liantuo** China
67 D4 **Lian Xian** China
67 D3 **Lianyuan** China
65 D7 **Lianyungang** China
Lianzhou *see* **Lian Xian**
Lianzhou *see* **Hepu**
65 H2 **Lianzhushan** China
58 G4 **Liaocheng** China
59 H4 **Liaodong** *pen* China
59 H3 **Liaodong Wan** *B* China
59 H3 **Liao He** *R* China
65 E4 **Liaoning** *prov* China
Liaotung *pen see* **Liaodong** *pen*
Liaotung, Gulf of *see* **Liaodong Wan**
59 H3 **Liaoyang** China
65 F3 **Liaoyangwopu** China
59 J3 **Liaoyuan** China
65 E4 **Liaozhong** China
47 O12 **Liapádhes** Greece
117 M5 **Liard** *R* Br Col/N W Terr Canada
117 J5 **Liard** *R* Yukon Territory Canada
117 M5 **Liard Ra** Northwest Territories Canada
117 K6 **Liard River** British Columbia Canada
77 K7 **Liari** Pakistan
22 G4 **Liart** France
69 H14 **Liat** *isld* Indonesia
79 F5 **Liban, Jebel** *mts* Lebanon
117 Q11 **Libby** Idaho U.S.A.
100 K1 **Libby** Montana U.S.A.
86 C5 **Libenge** Zaire
107 K4 **Liberal** Kansas U.S.A.
110 B4 **Liberal** Missouri U.S.A.
116 H2 **Liberator L** Alaska U.S.A.
129 H6 **Liberdade** *R* Brazil
130 G8 **Liberdade** Brazil
31 J5 **Liberec** Czechoslovakia
85 C7 **Liberia** *rep* W Africa
127 P4 **Liberta** Antigua W Indies
128 C5 **Libertad** *dept* Peru
127 K10 **Libertad** Venezuela
133 E2 **Libertador Gen. San Martín** Argentina
124 C3 **Libertad,Pto** Mexico
13 E2 **Liberton** Scotland
116 R4 **Liberty** Alaska U.S.A.
110 E2 **Liberty** Illinois U.S.A.
94 B7 **Liberty** Indiana U.S.A.
110 M4 **Liberty** Kentucky U.S.A.
111 F10 **Liberty** Mississippi U.S.A.
110 B2 **Liberty** Missouri U.S.A.
98 K9 **Liberty** Nebraska U.S.A.
95 N5 **Liberty** New York U.S.A.
112 H2 **Liberty** North Carolina U.S.A.
95 K5 **Liberty** Pennsylvania U.S.A.
109 N5 **Liberty** Texas U.S.A.
100 E2 **Liberty** Washington U.S.A.
94 C5 **Liberty Center** Ohio U.S.A.
112 G3 **Liberty Hill** South Carolina U.S.A.
109 K5 **Liberty Hill** Texas U.S.A.
95 K7 **Libertytown** Maryland U.S.A.
99 T7 **Libertyville** Illinois U.S.A.
99 O9 **Libertyville** Iowa U.S.A.
22 J4 **Libin** Belgium
37 Q4 **Liblín** Czechoslovakia
71 F4 **Libmanan** Philippines
67 B4 **Libo** China
71 B3 **Libobo, Tg** *C* Indonesia
46 D4 **Libohovë** Albania
69 D9 **Libong,Ko** *isld* Thailand
86 B5 **Liboumba** *R* Gabon
18 E8 **Libourne** France
22 J4 **Libramont** Belgium
46 D3 **Librazhd** Albania
131 F2 **Libres,P.de los** Argentina
86 A5 **Libreville** Gabon
71 G7 **Libuganon** *R* Mindanao Philippines
84 F4 **Libya** *rep* Africa
84 G4 **Libyan Desert** Libya
84 H3 **Libyan Plateau** Egypt
47 N11 **Libyssa** *hist site* Turkey
43 F11 **Licata** Sicily
36 F2 **Lich** Germany
65 B6 **Licheng** China
65 C6 **Licheng** China
9 E2 **Lichfield** England
145 E3 **Lichfield** New Zealand
88 E8 **Lichinga** Mozambique
36 E6 **Lichtenau** Baden-Württemberg Germany
32 J9 **Lichtenau** Nordrhein-Westfalen Germany
37 P2 **Lichtenberg** Germany
37 M3 **Lichtenberg** Germany
89 E6 **Lichtenburg** S Africa
36 G7 **Lichtenstein** Germany
37 O2 **Lichtenstein** Germany
37 N2 **Lichtentanne** Germany
36 E6 **Lichtenthal** Germany
25 G5 **Lichtenvoorde** Netherlands
33 S8 **Lichterfelde** Germany
22 E1 **Lichtervelde** Belgium
67 C1 **Lichuan** China
67 E3 **Lichuan** China
110 E4 **Licking** Missouri U.S.A.
94 D8 **Licking R** Kentucky U.S.A.
42 G4 **Ličko Petrovo Selo** Bosnia-Herzegovina
43 F8 **Licosa,P** Italy
22 B2 **Licques** France
53 C7 **Lida** Belorussia
102 G4 **Lida** Nevada U.S.A.
65 E6 **Lidao** China
99 M7 **Lidderdale** Iowa U.S.A.
15 F5 **Liddesdale Valley** Scotland
26 L7 **Liden** Sweden
26 J9 **Liden** Sweden
98 J3 **Lidgerwood** North Dakota U.S.A.
27 F15 **Lidhult** Sweden
27 K12 **Lidingo** Sweden
27 F13 **Lidköping** Sweden
26 M3 **Lidnatjärro** *mt* Sweden
45 M1 **Lido** Italy
42 E7 **Lido di Ostia** Italy
31 M2 **Lidzbark** Poland
31 M1 **Lidzbark Warmiński** Poland
20 E5 **Lié** *R* France
32 K9 **Liebenau** Hessen Germany
32 K7 **Liebenau** Niedersachsen Germany
37 M2 **Liebengrün** Germany
118 H8 **Liebenthal** Saskatchewan Canada
33 S7 **Liebenwalde** Germany
33 S9 **Liebenwerda** Germany
140 B6 **Liebig, Mt** N Terr Australia
144 C5 **Liebig Range** New Zealand
48 G5 **Liebling** Romania
41 L3 **Liechtenstein** *princ* Europe
26 M3 **Liedakka** Sweden
22 K2 **Liège** Belgium
21 N7 **Liège, le** France
29 P8 **Lieksa** Finland
32 G8 **Lienen** Germany
Lienyünkang *see* **Lianyungang**
27 M15 **Liepāja** Latvia
33 S5 **Liepen** Germany
36 C7 **Liepvre** France
22 H1 **Lier** Belgium
27 E11 **Lier** Norway
22 K3 **Lierneux** Belgium
22 K2 **Liers** Belgium
21 O3 **Lierville** France
36 D3 **Liesenfeld** Germany
38 J8 **Lieser** *R* Austria
36 B3 **Lieser** *R* Germany
29 K11 **Liesjärvi Nat. Park** Finland
22 F4 **Liesse** France
25 E6 **Liessel** Netherlands
40 G3 **Liestal** Switzerland
48 L5 **Lieşti** Romania
21 M3 **Lieurey** France
21 L3 **Lieuvin** France
22 D3 **Liévin** France
121 P7 **Lièvre** *R* Quebec Canada
122 B6 **Lievres, I. aux** Quebec Canada
38 K6 **Liezen** Austria
71 M9 **Lifan** Indonesia
14 E3 **Liffey** *R* Ireland
19 J4 **Liffol le Grand** France
14 D2 **Lifford** Ireland
20 H5 **Liffre** France
78 J6 **Līfiyah, Al** Saudi Arabia
137 O6 **Lifu** Îles Loyauté Pacific Oc
133 D6 **Lifue Mahuida** *mt* Argentina
45 Q8 **Li Galli** Italy
71 F4 **Ligao** Philippines
Ligen-i Shkodrës *see* **Skadarsko Jez**
65 B7 **Ligeta** China
65 E6 **Ligezhuang** China
26 L5 **Ligga** Sweden
8 A7 **Ligger Bay** England
109 H7 **Light** Texas U.S.A.
143 E8 **Lightfoot L** W Australia Australia
113 C8 **Lighthouse Pt** Florida U.S.A.
142 F4 **Lightjack Hill** W Australia Australia
119 N2 **Light L** Ontario Canada
139 J3 **Lightning Rdg** New South Wales Australia
20 H7 **Ligne** France
21 K4 **Lignieres** France
21 P8 **Lignières** France
21 K4 **Lignières-Orgères** France
98 D1 **Lignite** North Dakota U.S.A.
20 D5 **Lignol** France
94 K8 **Lignum** Virginia U.S.A.
22 H3 **Ligny** Belgium
19 J4 **Ligny en Barrois** France
21 O6 **Ligny-le-Ribault** France
45 H3 **Ligonchio** Italy
88 G9 **Ligonha** *R* Mozambique
94 B5 **Ligonier** Indiana U.S.A.
94 H6 **Ligonier** Pennsylvania U.S.A.
46 F7 **Ligoúrion** Greece
65 D7 **Ligouyi** China
131 B4 **Ligua,B de la** Chile
21 M7 **Ligueil** France
124 D5 **Ligui** Mexico
44 F2 **Ligure** *reg* Italy
44 D3 **Ligure** Italy
44 E4 **Ligurian Sea** Italy
103 K9 **Ligurta** Arizona U.S.A.
137 L2 **Lihir Group** Bismarck Arch
28 B3 **Lihme** Denmark
22 D4 **Lihons** France
141 K3 **Lihou Reef** Coral Sea
141 K3 **Lihou Reef & Cays** Gt Barrier Reef Aust
102 V13 **Lihue** Hawaiian Is
52 B5 **Lihula** Estonia
52 D1 **Liinakhamari** Russian Federation
65 D6 **Lijin** China
68 F3 **Lik** *R* Laos
86 D5 **Likati** Zaire
117 N9 **Likely** British Columbia Canada
100 E8 **Likely** California U.S.A.
52 E6 **Likhoslavl'** Russian Federation
54 M8 **Likhovskoy** Russian Federation
54 K1 **Likino-Dulevo** Russian Federation
71 M9 **Likisia** Timor
46 D3 **Likmetaj** Albania
86 C6 **Likouala** *R* Congo
69 J12 **Liku** Indonesia
70 D2 **Liku** Sarawak
71 J4 **Likupang** Sulawesi
110 G5 **Lilbourn** Missouri U.S.A.
28 B2 **Lildstrand** Denmark
143 F8 **Lilian, Pt** W Australia Australia
38 N5 **Lilienfeld** Austria
32 J6 **Lilienthal** Germany
67 D3 **Liling** China
22 H1 **Lille** Belgium
22 E2 **Lille** France
28 B4 **Lilleå** *R* Denmark
28 D6 **Lille Bælt** *chan* Denmark
21 M2 **Lillebonne** France
27 D10 **Lillehammer** Norway
22 C2 **Lillers** France
27 C13 **Lillesand** Norway
27 E12 **Lilleström** Norway
28 E3 **Lille Vildmose** Denmark
26 G10 **Lillhärdal** Sweden
26 G8 **Lillholmsjön** Sweden
26 K6 **Lillholmträsk** Sweden
123 L2 **Lillian L** Quebec Canada
109 P3 **Lillie** Louisiana U.S.A.
13 F3 **Lilliesleaf** Scotland
112 J2 **Lillington** North Carolina U.S.A.
107 O2 **Lillis** Kansas U.S.A.
22 G1 **Lillo** Belgium
16 E5 **Lillo** Spain
117 M10 **Lillooet** *R* British Columbia Canada
117 N10 **Lillooet** British Columbia Canada
94 J6 **Lilly** Pennsylvania U.S.A.
88 D8 **Lilongwe** Malawi
88 E8 **Lilongwe** *R* Malawi
71 F6 **Liloy** Mindanao Philippines
98 J4 **Lily** South Dakota U.S.A.
138 F5 **Lilydale** South Australia Australia
139 H8 **Lilydale** Tasmania Australia
48 F7 **Lim** *R* Serbia Yugoslavia
130 C8 **Lima** Paraguay
128 C6 **Lima** Peru
16 B3 **Lima** *R* Portugal
27 F11 **Lima** Sweden
99 P9 **Lima** Illinois U.S.A.
101 N5 **Lima** Montana U.S.A.
94 K4 **Lima** New York U.S.A.
94 C6 **Lima** Ohio U.S.A.
133 C4 **Limache** Chile
130 G7 **Lima Duarte** Brazil
80 D1 **Liman** Israel
70 N9 **Liman, G** *mt* Java
48 F1 **Limanowa** Poland
71 N8 **Limar** Indonesia
133 C4 **Limari** *R* Chile
131 B3 **Limari,R** Chile
69 G12 **Limas** Indonesia
79 E2 **Limas** *R* Turkey
71 G6 **Limasawa** *isld* Philippines
79 D4 **Limassol** Cyprus
14 E1 **Limavady** N Ireland
21 O4 **Limay** France
133 D5 **Limay Mahuida** Argentina
131 C7 **Limay,R** Argentina
36 C5 **Limbach** Germany
37 O2 **Limbach** Germany
37 O2 **Limbach-Oberfrohna** Germany
70 D2 **Limbang** *R* Sarawak
43 C8 **Limbara, Monte** *mt* Sardinia
52 B6 **Limbaži** Latvia
85 F8 **Limbe** Cameroon
127 H5 **Limbé** Haiti
88 E9 **Limbe** Malawi
71 H4 **Limboto** Sulawesi
71 H4 **Limboto, Danau** *L* Sulawesi
22 K2 **Limbourg** Belgium
70 F7 **Limbung** Sulawesi
70 D6 **Limbungan** Kalimantan
140 A3 **Limbunya** N Terr Australia
57 J6 **Limbur** Uzbekistan
22 J2 **Limburg** *prov* Belgium
36 E3 **Limburg** Germany
144 B7 **Limchills** New Zealand
100 H5 **Lime** Oregon U.S.A.
27 F11 **Limedsforsen** Sweden
116 K6 **Lime Hills** Alaska U.S.A.
130 F8 **Limeira** Brazil
45 L1 **Limena** Italy
46 G4 **Limenária** Greece
47 H7 **Limén Vathéos** Greece
118 L9 **Limerick** Saskatchewan Canada
14 C4 **Limerick** *co* Ireland
14 C4 **Limerick** Ireland
95 R3 **Limerick** Maine U.S.A.
20 F6 **Limerzel** France
22 J4 **Limes** Belgium
99 O6 **Lime Springs** Iowa U.S.A.
113 F10 **Limestone** Florida U.S.A.
95 T7 **Limestone** Maine U.S.A.
94 J4 **Limestone** New York U.S.A.
119 W2 **Limestone L** Manitoba Canada
119 T5 **Limestone Pt** Manitoba Canada
21 M2 **Limésy** France
28 B3 **Limfjorden** *inlet* Denmark
29 K5 **Limhamn** Sweden
16 B2 **Limia** *R* Spain
Limín *isld see* **Thásos** *isld*
26 G7 **Limingen** *L* Norway
29 L7 **Liminka** Finland
41 H3 **Limmat** *R* Switzerland
25 C3 **Limmen** Netherlands
140 D2 **Limmen Bight** N Terr Australia
140 D3 **Limmen Bight R** N Terr Australia
46 F6 **Límni** Greece
46 G5 **Límnos** *isld* Greece
129 L5 **Limoeiro** Brazil
129 L5 **Limoeiro do Norte** Brazil
121 P7 **Limoges** Ontario Canada
18 F7 **Limoges** France
125 N5 **Limón** Costa Rica
125 M2 **Limón** Honduras
106 G2 **Limon** Colorado U.S.A.
128 F7 **Limoquije** Bolivia
18 F7 **Limousin** *reg* France
18 G9 **Limoux** France
108 D5 **Limpia Cr** Texas U.S.A.
8 D5 **Limpley Stoke** England
89 E4 **Limpopo** *R* Botswana
9 G5 **Limpsfield** England
45 P1 **Limski Zaljev** Croatia
67 C4 **Limu** China
28 D4 **Lina** Denmark
26 L4 **Linaälv** Sweden
26 M5 **Lina älv** *R* Sweden
67 F1 **Lin'an** China
71 F7 **Linao B** Mindanao Philippines
71 D5 **Linapacan** *isld* Philippines
71 D5 **Linapacan Str** Philippines
131 B5 **Linares** Chile
131 B6 **Linares** *prov* Chile
125 K5 **Linares** Mexico
16 E6 **Linares** Spain
21 P4 **Linas** France
43 B9 **Linas, M** *mt* Sardinia
70 D3 **Linau Balui Plateau** Sarawak
67 E3 **Linchuan** China
133 E4 **Lincoln** Argentina
9 F1 **Lincoln** England
144 A4 **Lincoln** New Zealand
111 K8 **Lincoln** Alabama U.S.A.
102 C3 **Lincoln** California U.S.A.
95 M8 **Lincoln** Delaware U.S.A.
99 R9 **Lincoln** Illinois U.S.A.
107 M2 **Lincoln** Kansas U.S.A.
95 T1 **Lincoln** Maine U.S.A.
94 D2 **Lincoln** Michigan U.S.A.
99 M3 **Lincoln** Minnesota U.S.A.
101 N3 **Lincoln** Montana U.S.A.
98 K9 **Lincoln** Nebraska U.S.A.
95 Q2 **Lincoln** New Hampshire U.S.A.
106 E8 **Lincoln** New Mexico U.S.A.
110 K3 **Lincoln City** Indiana U.S.A.
100 A5 **Lincoln City** Oregon U.S.A.
98 J9 **Lincoln Cr** Nebraska U.S.A.
138 E4 **Lincoln Gap** South Australia Australia
9 F1 **Lincolnshire** *co* England
112 E4 **Lincolnton** Georgia U.S.A.
112 F2 **Lincolnton** North Carolina U.S.A.
123 L8 **Lincolnville** Nova Scotia Canada
95 S2 **Lincolnville** Maine U.S.A.
100 G3 **Lind** Washington U.S.A.
140 E6 **Linda** *R* Queensland Australia
52 F6 **Linda** Nizhegorodskaya obl Russian Federation
13 F5 **Lindale** England
111 L7 **Lindale** Georgia U.S.A.
109 M3 **Lindale** Texas U.S.A.
27 A11 **Lindas** Norway
33 Q8 **Lindau** Germany
41 L2 **Lindau** Germany
118 G5 **Lindbergh** Alberta Canada
98 B8 **Lindbergh** Wyoming U.S.A.
101 M2 **Lindbergh L** Montana U.S.A.
28 A4 **Linde** Denmark
28 F7 **Lindelse** Denmark
141 J5 **Lindeman I** Queensland Australia
32 L8 **Linden** Germany
128 G2 **Linden** Guyana
111 J9 **Linden** Alabama U.S.A.
94 J4 **Linden** New York U.S.A.
112 J2 **Linden** North Carolina U.S.A.
110 J6 **Linden** Tennessee U.S.A.
111 B8 **Linden** Texas U.S.A.
37 K3 **Lindenau Friedrichshall** Germany
33 Q6 **Lindenberg** Germany
28 D3 **Lindenborg Å** *R* Denmark
36 F4 **Lindenfels** Germany
33 T6 **Lindenhagen** Germany
33 Q9 **Lindenhayn** Germany
115 P5 **Lindenow Fjord** Greenland
25 F6 **Lindern** Germany
32 G7 **Lindern** Germany
143 B10 **Lindesay, Mt** W Australia Australia
27 H12 **Lindesberg** Sweden
27 B14 **Lindesnes** *lighthouse* Norway
9 F5 **Lindfield** England
27 G12 **Lindfors** Sweden
28 F5 **Lindholm** *isld* Denmark
88 G6 **Lindi** Tanzania
88 F6 **Lindi** *reg* Tanzania
86 E5 **Lindi** *R* Zaire
65 F1 **Lindian** China
13 G2 **Lindisfarne** England
144 B6 **Lindis Valley** New Zealand
28 C5 **Lindknud** Denmark
106 D1 **Lindland** Colorado U.S.A.
36 C1 **Lindlar** Germany
32 K8 **Lindnorst** Germany
106 G2 **Lindon** Colorado U.S.A.
13 E1 **Lindores** Scotland
47 V17 **Líndos** Rhodes Greece
33 R7 **Lindow** Germany
36 B6 **Lindre,Etg de** *L* France
121 M8 **Lindsay** Ontario Canada
102 E5 **Lindsay** California U.S.A.
101 U2 **Lindsay** Montana U.S.A.
98 J8 **Lindsay** Nebraska U.S.A.
107 N7 **Lindsay** Oklahoma U.S.A.
143 D7 **Lindsay Gordon, L** W Australia Australia
140 A6 **Lindsay, Mt** N Terr Australia
107 N3 **Lindsborg** Kansas U.S.A.
94 D5 **Lindsey** Ohio U.S.A.
33 P7 **Lindstedt** Germany
83 K11 **Lindula** Sri Lanka
28 D3 **Lindum** Denmark
37 P4 **Líně** Czechoslovakia
94 G5 **Linesville** Pennsylvania U.S.A.
111 L8 **Lineville** Alabama U.S.A.
99 N9 **Lineville** Iowa U.S.A.
56 B4 **Linevo** Russian Federation
58 F4 **Linfen** China
68 J3 **Lingao** China
71 E2 **Lingayen** Luzon Philippines
71 E2 **Lingayen Gulf** Luzon Philippines
65 B7 **Lingbao** China
27 J10 **Lingbo** Sweden
65 B7 **Lingchuan** China
67 C4 **Lingchuan** China
21 N8 **Lingé** France
25 D5 **Linge** *R* Netherlands
32 F7 **Lingen** Germany
69 G13 **Lingga** Indonesia
70 B4 **Lingga** Sarawak
69 G13 **Lingga,Kep** *islds* Indonesia
27 H11 **Linghed** Sweden
70 E3 **Lingkas** Kalimantan
98 B7 **Lingle** Wyoming U.S.A.
86 D5 **Lingomo** Zaire
58 F4 **Lingqiu** China
68 J1 **Lingshan** China
65 E7 **Lingshan Dao** *isld* China
65 B6 **Lingshi** China
101 O3 **Lingshire** Montana U.S.A.
65 C5 **Lingshou** China
68 K3 **Lingshui** China
76 C2 **Lingsugur** India
67 D7 **Lingtou** China
43 G11 **Linguaglossa** Sicily
85 B5 **Linguère** Senegal
67 C4 **Lingui** China
Lingxi *see* **Yongshun**
65 C6 **Ling Xian** China
67 D3 **Ling Xian** China
67 B4 **Lingyang** China
65 D4 **Lingyuan** China
67 B4 **Lingyun** China
67 G2 **Linhai** China
130 H6 **Linhares** Brazil
68 G3 **Linh Cam** Vietnam
65 D7 **Linhong Kou** *B* China
122 B7 **Liniere** Quebec Canada
21 O7 **Liniez** France
65 G4 **Linjiang** China
67 G2 **Lin Jiang** *R* China
65 F4 **Linjiatai** China
65 A7 **Linjin** China
36 E5 **Linkenheim** Germany
27 H13 **Linköping** Sweden
59 K2 **Linkou** China
67 A3 **Linkou** China
52 B6 **Linkuva** Lithuania
67 D2 **Linli** China
15 E5 **Linlithgow** Scotland
32 E10 **Linn** Germany
107 N2 **Linn** Kansas U.S.A.
110 E3 **Linn** Missouri U.S.A.
109 J9 **Linn** Texas U.S.A.
29 N9 **Linnansaari Nat. Park** Finland
95 S7 **Linneus** Maine U.S.A.
99 N10 **Linneus** Missouri U.S.A.
8 A4 **Linney Hd** Wales
25 F7 **Linnich** Germany
100 C9 **Linn,Mt** California U.S.A.
15 E4 **Linn of Dee** Scotland
43 E13 **Linosa, I. di** Italy
33 R6 **Linow** Germany
Linping *see* **Yuhang**
65 B7 **Linqi** China
65 C6 **Linqing** China
65 D6 **Linqu** China
65 B7 **Linru** China
130 E7 **Lins** Brazil
32 K7 **Linsburg** Germany
26 G9 **Linsell** Sweden
65 A7 **Lin Shan** *hist site* China
67 B2 **Linshizhen** China
65 D7 **Linshu** China
67 B1 **Linshui** China
127 L2 **Linstead** Jamaica
71 J9 **Lintah,Selat** *str* Indonesia
58 D5 **Lintan** China
58 D4 **Lintao** China
41 K3 **Linth** *R* Switzerland
41 J4 **Linthal** Switzerland
119 O6 **Lintlaw** Saskatchewan Canada
121 S5 **Linton** Quebec Canada
145 E4 **Linton** New Zealand
110 J2 **Linton** Indiana U.S.A.
98 F3 **Linton** North Dakota U.S.A.
65 A7 **Lintong** China
32 E10 **Lintorf** Germany
33 R7 **Linum** Germany
112 F1 **Linville** North Carolina U.S.A.
94 J8 **Linville** Virginia U.S.A.
107 P2 **Linwood** Kansas U.S.A.
94 D3 **Linwood** Michigan U.S.A.
98 K8 **Linwood** Nebraska U.S.A.
67 D4 **Linwu** China
58 G3 **Linxi** China
58 D4 **Linxia** China
65 A6 **Lin Xian** China
67 D2 **Linxiang** China
65 C6 **Linyi** China
65 A7 **Linyi** China
65 D7 **Linyi** China
38 K5 **Linz** Austria
36 C2 **Linz** Germany
65 C6 **Linzhang** China
65 D6 **Linzi** China
70 D3 **Lio Matoh** Sarawak
21 J6 **Lion-d' Angers, le** France
89 G1 **Lion's Den** Zimbabwe
120 J8 **Lions Head** Ontario Canada
21 K3 **Lion-sur-Mer** France
71 N8 **Lioppa** Indonesia

196
Liouesso — Longwy

86 C5 **Liouesso** Congo
54 B1 **Liozno** Belorussia
42 G4 **Lipa** Bosnia-Herzegovina
71 E4 **Lipa** Philippines
65 J3 **Lipadiya** Russian Federation
109 J3 **Lipan** Texas U.S.A.
43 F10 **Lipari, I** *islds* Italy
43 F10 **Lipari, I** Italy
69 E12 **Lipatkain** Sumatra
29 O9 **Liperi** Finland
54 L4 **Lipetsk** Russian Federation
9 F5 **Liphook** England
31 H2 **Lipiany** Poland
52 E4 **Lipin Bor** Russian Federation
67 C3 **Liping** China
48 K2 **Lipkany** Moldavia
46 E2 **Lipljan** Serbia Yugoslavia
48 D1 **Lipnik** Czechoslovakia
48 L6 **Lipniţa** Romania
31 L3 **Lipno** Poland
89 F3 **Lipokolo Hills** Botswana
48 G4 **Lipova** Romania
48 M1 **Lipovets** Ukraine
32 H9 **Lippe** *R* Germany
32 H9 **Lipperode** Germany
32 H9 **Lippetal** Germany
32 H9 **Lippstadt** Germany
108 D7 **Lipscomb** Texas U.S.A.
31 O2 **Lipsk** Poland
47 H7 **Lipsói** *isld* Greece
119 O8 **Lipton** Saskatchewan Canada
48 F1 **Liptovský Mikuláš** Czechoslovakia
139 H7 **Liptrap,C** Victoria Australia
67 C4 **Lipu** China
86 F5 **Lira** Uganda
71 M8 **Liran** *isld* Indonesia
86 C6 **Liranga** Congo
128 D6 **Lircay** Peru
21 H7 **Liré** France
45 O6 **Liri** *R* Italy
45 P7 **Liri** Italy
69 F13 **Lirik** Sumatra
55 D4 **Lisakovsk** Kazakhstan
86 D5 **Lisala** Zaire
127 O2 **Lisas B** Trinidad
16 A6 **Lisboa** Portugal
Lisbon *see* **Lisboa**
99 S8 **Lisbon** Illinois U.S.A.
95 Q2 **Lisbon** New Hampshire U.S.A.
95 M2 **Lisbon** New York U.S.A.
98 J3 **Lisbon** North Dakota U.S.A.
94 G6 **Lisbon** Ohio U.S.A.
95 R2 **Lisbon Falls** Maine U.S.A.
14 E2 **Lisburn** N Ireland
116 D2 **Lisburne,C** Alaska U.S.A.
14 B4 **Liscannor B** Ireland
98 D8 **Lisco** Nebraska U.S.A.
123 K8 **Liscomb** Nova Scotia Canada
14 B3 **Lisdoonvarna** Ireland
28 H4 **Liseleje** Denmark
67 D1 **Lishan** China
65 B6 **Lishi** China
65 F3 **Lishu** China
67 C2 **Li Shui** *R* China
67 F1 **Lishui** Jiangsu China
67 G2 **Lishui** Zhejiang China
54 K8 **Lisichansk** Ukraine
118 L9 **Lisieux** Saskatchewan Canada
21 L3 **Lisieux** France
56 C2 **Lisitsa** *R* Russian Federation
8 B7 **Liskeard** England
54 L6 **Liski** Russian Federation
95 L4 **Lisle** New York U.S.A.
18 G9 **Lisle sur Tarn** France
111 H9 **Lisman** Alabama U.S.A.
123 K8 **Lismore** Nova Scotia Canada
14 D4 **Lismore** Ireland
15 C4 **Lismore** *isld* Scotland
14 D2 **Lisnaskea** N Ireland
21 H3 **Lison** France
21 N3 **Lisors** France
142 G3 **Lissadell** W Australia Australia
25 C4 **Lisse** Netherlands
28 A6 **List** Germany
27 B13 **Lista** *isld* Norway
27 B13 **Listerfj** *inlet* Norway
140 E7 **Listore** *R* Queensland Australia
14 B4 **Listowel** Ireland
141 H7 **Listowel Downs** Queensland Australia
56 C6 **Listvyaga,Khr** *mts* Kazakhstan/Rus Fed
56 G5 **Listvyanka** Russian Federation
26 G8 **Lit** Sweden
58 D5 **Litang** China
67 C5 **Litang** China
58 D6 **Litang Qu** *R* China
79 F5 **Līṭāni** *R* Lebanon
9 G2 **Litcham** England
100 E9 **Litchfield** California U.S.A.
95 O5 **Litchfield** Connecticut U.S.A.
110 G2 **Litchfield** Illinois U.S.A.
94 C4 **Litchfield** Michigan U.S.A.
99 M4 **Litchfield** Minnesota U.S.A.
98 G8 **Litchfield** Nebraska U.S.A.
103 M8 **Litchfield Pk** Arizona U.S.A.
98 H3 **Litchville** North Dakota U.S.A.
48 K3 **Liteni** Romania
18 E8 **Lit et Mixe** France
46 D7 **Lithakiá** Greece
46 G6 **Lithári,Akr** *C* Greece
139 K5 **Lithgow** New South Wales Australia
46 G10 **Líthinon, Akr** *C* Crete Greece
27 M16 **Lithuania** *rep* E Europe
37 P4 **Litice** Czechoslovakia
42 F2 **Litija** Slovenia
48 L1 **Litin** Ukraine
95 L6 **Lititz** Pennsylvania U.S.A.
6 F1 **Litla Dimun** *isld* Faeroes
86 A6 **Lit. Loango Nat. Park** Gabon
46 F4 **Litókhoron** Greece
31 H5 **Litoměřice** Czechoslovakia
31 J6 **Litomyšl** Czechoslovakia
59 K2 **Litovko** Russian Federation
Litovskaya S.S.R. *see* **Lithuania**
27 J12 **Litslena** Sweden
110 D6 **Little** *R* Arkansas U.S.A.
112 E4 **Little** *R* Georgia U.S.A.
110 J5 **Little** *R* Kentucky U.S.A.
111 D10 **Little** *R* Louisiana U.S.A.
112 J2 **Little** *R* North Carolina U.S.A.
107 O6 **Little** *R* Oklahoma U.S.A.
109 M1 **Little** *R* Oklahoma U.S.A.
109 L5 **Little** *R* Texas U.S.A.
68 A7 **Little Andaman** *isld* Andaman Is
99 T4 **Little Bay de Noc** Michigan U.S.A.
123 R4 **Little Bay Is** Newfoundland Canada
119 N4 **Little Bear L** Saskatchewan Canada
101 P3 **Little Belt Mts** Montana U.S.A.
101 S4 **Little Bighorn River** Montana U.S.A.
116 Q3 **Little Black** *R* Alaska U.S.A.
13 F6 **Littleborough** England
118 E8 **Little Bow Prov. Park** Alberta Canada
118 D8 **Little Bow R** Alberta Canada
123 R2 **Little Brehat** Newfoundland Canada
117 R5 **Little Buffalo R** Northwest Territories Canada
119 V7 **Little Bullhead** Manitoba Canada
123 R4 **Little Burnt Bay** Newfoundland Canada
9 G3 **Littlebury** England
89 A7 **Little Bushman Land** *reg* S Africa
99 S5 **Little Chute** Wisconsin U.S.A.
103 N6 **Little Colorado** *R* Arizona U.S.A.
103 M4 **Little Creek Pk** Utah U.S.A.
120 J7 **Little Current** Ontario Canada
111 B9 **Little Cypress Cr** Texas U.S.A.
138 F6 **Little Desert** Victoria Australia
116 C3 **Little Diomede** *isld* Alaska U.S.A.
101 T2 **Little Dry Cr** Montana U.S.A.
99 M4 **Little Falls** Minnesota U.S.A.
95 N4 **Little Falls** New York U.S.A.
103 L5 **Littlefield** Arizona U.S.A.
108 E2 **Littlefield** Texas U.S.A.
99 N1 **Little Fork** *R* Minnesota U.S.A.
99 N1 **Little Fork** Minnesota U.S.A.
117 N10 **Little Fort** British Columbia Canada
110 G4 **Little Grassy L** Illinois U.S.A.
6 K4 **Little Halibut Bank** North Sea
9 F6 **Littlehampton** England
113 L11 **Little Harbour** Bahamas
89 A6 **Little Karas Berg** *mts* Namibia
89 B9 **Little Karoo** *reg* S Africa
116 H9 **Little Koniuji I** Alaska U.S.A.
102 G6 **Little L** California U.S.A.
111 F12 **Little L** Louisiana U.S.A.
127 H2 **Little London** Jamaica
101 M5 **Little Lost R** Idaho U.S.A.
101 N7 **Little Malad** *R* Idaho U.S.A.
122 E2 **Little Manicouagan,L** Quebec Canada
95 L5 **Little Meadows** Pennsylvania U.S.A.
115 N7 **Little Mecatina** *R* Quebec/Labrador Canada
98 A7 **Little Medicine** Wyoming U.S.A.
110 M2 **Little Miami** *R* Ohio U.S.A.
15 B3 **Little Minch** *chan* Hebrides Scotland
98 B5 **Little Missouri** *R* Wyoming U.S.A.
69 A9 **Little Nicobar** *isld* Nicobar Is
107 Q3 **Little Osage** *R* Kansas/Missouri U.S.A.
112 H3 **Little Pee Dee R** South Carolina U.S.A.
9 G3 **Littleport** England
98 A5 **Little Powder** *R* Wyoming U.S.A.
123 Q5 **Little R** Newfoundland Canada
144 D5 **Little River** New Zealand
111 J10 **Little River** Alabama U.S.A.
107 N3 **Little River** Kansas U.S.A.
112 J4 **Little River Inlet** North Carolina U.S.A.
110 D7 **Little Rock** Arkansas U.S.A.
102 G7 **Littlerock** California U.S.A.
88 E6 **Little Ruaha** *R* Tanzania
99 U6 **Little Sable Pt** Michigan U.S.A.
110 C4 **Little Sac** *R* Missouri U.S.A.
117 F4 **Little Salmon L** Yukon Territory Canada
103 M4 **Little Salt L** Utah U.S.A.
119 T1 **Little Sand L** Manitoba Canada
101 Q7 **Little Sandy Cr** Wyoming U.S.A.
112 E6 **Little Satilla** *R* Georgia U.S.A.
99 L7 **Little Sioux** *R* Iowa U.S.A.
117 P8 **Little Smoky River** Alberta Canada
101 R9 **Little Snake** *R* Colorado U.S.A.
9 G6 **Littlestone-on-Sea** England
95 K7 **Littlestown** Pennsylvania U.S.A.
99 T5 **Little Suamico** Wisconsin U.S.A.
122 F7 **Little S.W. Miramichi R** New Brunswick Canada
112 C2 **Little Tennessee** *R* Tennessee U.S.A.
127 N1 **Little Tobago** *isld* Tobago
106 E2 **Littleton** Colorado U.S.A.
99 Q9 **Littleton** Illinois U.S.A.
95 Q2 **Littleton** New Hampshire U.S.A.
112 K1 **Littleton** North Carolina U.S.A.
94 G7 **Littleton** West Virginia U.S.A.
95 N2 **Little Tupper L** New York U.S.A.
94 J4 **Little Valley** New York U.S.A.
100 K7 **Little Valley Cr** Idaho U.S.A.
111 J7 **Littleville** Alabama U.S.A.
110 H3 **Little Wabash** *R* Illinois U.S.A.
9 G4 **Little Waltham** England
98 E6 **Little White** *R* South Dakota U.S.A.
101 L6 **Little Wood** *R* Idaho U.S.A.
8 D2 **Littleworth** England
78 J4 **Little Zab** *R* Iraq
37 Q2 **Litvinov** Czechoslovakia
67 C4 **Liucheng** China
67 B3 **Liuchong He** *R* China
Liuchuan *see* **Jianhe**
67 B2 **Liudu** China
67 B3 **Liuguang** China
65 E3 **Liu He** *R* China
65 F3 **Liu He** *R* China
65 F3 **Liuhe** China
67 B1 **Liuhechang** China
67 G2 **Liuheng Dao** *isld* China
65 E2 **Liuhu** China
67 D1 **Liujiachang** China
67 C4 **Liu Jiang** *R* China
88 E7 **Liuli** Tanzania
65 C5 **Liulihezhen** China
67 B4 **Liuma** China
Liupai *see* **Tian'e**
67 D1 **Liushuigou** China
67 C4 **Liutang** China
67 D2 **Liuyang** China
67 D2 **Liuyang He** *R* China
67 B4 **Liuzhai** China
Liuzhangzhen *see* **Qinghe**
Liuzhangzhen *see* **Yuanqu**
67 C4 **Liuzhou** China
65 C7 **Liuzhuang** China
48 H3 **Livade** Romania
52 C6 **Līvāni** Latvia
21 L3 **Livarot** France
118 J5 **Livelong** Saskatchewan Canada
116 N4 **Livengood** Alaska U.S.A.
42 E3 **Livenza** *R* Italy
102 C2 **Live Oak** California U.S.A.
113 E7 **Live Oak** Florida U.S.A.
142 E4 **Liveringa** W Australia Australia
102 C4 **Livermore** California U.S.A.
99 M7 **Livermore** Iowa U.S.A.
110 J4 **Livermore** Kentucky U.S.A.
95 R2 **Livermore Falls** Maine U.S.A.
108 C5 **Livermore, Mt** Texas U.S.A.
139 K5 **Liverpool** New South Wales Australia
140 C1 **Liverpool** *R* N Terr Australia
122 H9 **Liverpool** Nova Scotia Canada
11 B2 **Liverpool** *conurbation* England
95 L3 **Liverpool** New York U.S.A.
114 G3 **Liverpool B** Northwest Territories Canada
115 M3 **Liverpool,C** Northwest Territories Canada
139 K4 **Liverpool Plains** New South Wales Australia
139 K4 **Liverpool Ra** *mts* New South Wales Australia
143 F7 **Livesey Ra** W Australia Australia
19 P14 **Livet** France
41 M4 **Livigno** Italy
125 P10 **Livingston** Guatemala
15 E5 **Livingston** Scotland
111 H9 **Livingston** Alabama U.S.A.
110 M4 **Livingston** Kentucky U.S.A.
111 F11 **Livingston** Louisiana U.S.A.
101 P4 **Livingston** Montana U.S.A.
109 N5 **Livingston** Texas U.S.A.
99 Q7 **Livingston** Wisconsin U.S.A.
144 C6 **Livingstone** New Zealand
89 D1 **Livingstone** Zambia
117 F5 **Livingstone Creek** Yukon Territory Canada
88 C8 **Livingstone Memorial** Zambia
144 B6 **Livingstone Mts** New Zealand
88 E6 **Livingstone Mts** Tanzania
118 C8 **Livingstone Ra** Alberta Canada
146 C3 **Livingston I** S Shetland Is Antarctica
87 F8 **Livingstonia** Malawi
95 N5 **Livingston Manor** New York U.S.A.
42 H5 **Livno** Bosnia-Herzegovina
54 J4 **Livny** Russian Federation
28 B3 **Livø** *isld* Denmark
29 M6 **Livojoki** *R* Finland
111 E11 **Livonia** Louisiana U.S.A.
94 D4 **Livonia** Michigan U.S.A.
99 O9 **Livonia** Missouri U.S.A.
44 H4 **Livorno** Italy
18 H7 **Livradois,Mts.du** France
133 F4 **Livramento** Brazil
20 H5 **Livré** France
19 N15 **Livron** France
87 G7 **Liwale** Tanzania
88 G6 **Liwale** Tanzania
31 N3 **Liwiec** *R* Poland
67 E2 **Lixi** China
65 C5 **Li Xian** China
67 D2 **Li Xian** Hunan China
67 A1 **Li Xian** Sichuan China
36 B5 **Lixing les St.Avold** France
46 D6 **Lixoúrion** Greece
67 F1 **Liyang** China
67 C4 **Liyong** China
9 G7 **Lizard** *pen* England
129 J5 **Lizarda** Brazil
101 Q7 **Lizard Head Pk** Wyoming U.S.A.
141 H2 **Lizard I** Gt Barrier Reef Aust
112 D5 **Lizella** Georgia U.S.A.
94 F8 **Lizemores** West Virginia U.S.A.
52 D4 **Lizhma** Russian Federation
18 F7 **Lizonne** *R* France
121 S4 **Lizotte** Quebec Canada
110 K2 **Lizton** Indiana U.S.A.
45 J3 **Lizzano in Belvedere** Italy
27 F10 **Ljöra** *R* Norway
28 S9 **Ljosafoss** Iceland
42 H4 **Ljubija** Bosnia-Herzegovina
42 J6 **Ljubinje** Bosnia-Herzegovina
46 C1 **Ljubišnja** *mt* Bosnia-Herzegovina/Yugoslavia
42 F2 **Ljubljana** Slovenia
46 E2 **Ljuboten** *mt* Serbia Yugoslavia
48 E6 **Ljubovija** Serbia Yugoslavia
42 H5 **Ljubuški** Bosnia-Herzegovina
27 K14 **Ljugarn** Gotland Sweden
26 H9 **Ljunga** Sweden
26 H9 **Ljungan** *R* Sweden
26 H9 **Ljungaverk** Sweden
27 G15 **Ljungby** Sweden
27 G15 **Ljungby, Ö** Sweden
26 F9 **Ljungdalen** Sweden
26 H10 **Ljusdal** Sweden
26 H9 **Ljusnan** *R* Sweden
27 J10 **Ljusne** Sweden
27 K12 **Ljusterö** Sweden
133 C5 **Llaima** *mt* Chile
131 B7 **Llaima,Vol** Chile
8 B2 **Llanaelhaearn** Wales
8 B3 **Llanarth** Wales
8 B2 **Llanbedr** Wales
8 B2 **Llanbedrog** Wales
8 B1 **Llanberis** Wales
8 C3 **Llanbister** Wales
131 B5 **Llancanelo, L** Argentina
131 C5 **Llancanelo,Salina** Argentina
8 C5 **Llandaf** Wales
8 C4 **Llandarcy** Wales
8 B4 **Llanddarog** Wales
8 B4 **Llandefeilog** Wales
8 B1 **Llandegai** Wales
8 D4 **Llandegfedd Res.** *res* Wales
8 B4 **Llandeilo** Wales
8 B4 **Llandissilio** Wales
8 C4 **Llandovery** Wales
8 B4 **Llandowror** Wales
8 C2 **Llandrillo** Wales
8 C3 **Llandrindod Wells** Wales
8 C1 **Llandudno** Wales
8 B3 **Llandyssul** Wales
8 B4 **Llanelli** Wales
8 C2 **Llanelltyd** Wales
8 B1 **Llanerchymedd** Wales
16 D1 **Llanes** Spain
8 B1 **Llanfaethlu** Wales
8 C1 **Llanfairfechan** Wales
8 C1 **Llanfair Talhaiarn** Wales
8 B3 **Llanfarian** Wales
8 C1 **Llanferres** Wales
8 C2 **Llanfyllin** Wales
8 C2 **Llangadfan** Wales
8 C4 **Llangadog** Wales
8 C3 **Llangammarch Wells** Wales
8 B1 **Llangefni** Wales
8 B3 **Llangeler** Wales
8 B2 **Llangelynin** Wales
8 C1 **Llangernyw** Wales
8 C2 **Llangollen** Wales
8 C3 **Llangurig** Wales
8 C2 **Llangynog** Wales
8 C3 **Llanidloes** Wales
8 B3 **Llanilar** Wales
8 B1 **Llanllyfni** Wales
8 B4 **Llanmadog** Wales
124 D2 **Llano** Mexico
109 H5 **Llano** *R* Texas U.S.A.
109 J5 **Llano** Texas U.S.A.
124 G6 **Llano Grande** Mexico
128 D2 **Llanos** *prairies* Colombia/Venezuela
17 H3 **Llanos de Urgel** *reg* Spain
131 C3 **Llanos,Sa.de los** *mts* Argentina
133 C6 **Llanquihue** *prov* Chile
131 A8 **Llanquihue,L** Chile
141 F5 **Llanrheidol** Queensland Australia
8 B4 **Llanrhidian** Wales
8 B3 **Llanrhystyd** Wales
8 C1 **Llanrwst** Wales
18 H10 **Llansa** Spain
8 C1 **Llansannan** Wales
8 B3 **Llansantffraid** Wales
8 B4 **Llanstephan** Wales
8 C4 **Llanthony** Wales
8 C4 **Llantrisant** Wales
8 C4 **Llanwrda** Wales
8 C3 **Llanwrtyd Wells** Wales
8 B3 **Llanybydder** Wales
8 C2 **Llanymynech** England
77 E5 **Llazārān, Kūh-e** *mt* Iran
8 B3 **Llechryd** Wales
Lleida *see* **Lérida**
17 H3 **Llena,Sierra de la** *mts* Spain
16 C6 **Llerena** Spain
133 C4 **Llico** Chile
17 G5 **Lliria** Spain
17 J3 **Llobregat** *R* Spain
17 J3 **Lloret de Mar** Spain
101 Q1 **Lloyd** Montana U.S.A.
141 G2 **Lloyd B** Queensland Australia
117 L7 **Lloyd George, Mt** British Columbia Canada
118 H5 **Lloydminster** Alberta/Sask Canada
127 K2 **Lluidas Vale** Jamaica
133 D2 **Llullaillaco** *mt* Arg/Chile
128 E7 **Lluta** *R* Chile
8 B2 **Llwyngwril** Wales
8 C3 **Llyswen** Wales
128 E8 **Loa** *R* Chile
103 N3 **Loa** Utah U.S.A.
70 E5 **Loakulu** Kalimantan
99 R10 **Loami** Illinois U.S.A.
130 D8 **Loanda** Brazil
86 D6 **Loanga** *R* Zaire
86 B6 **Loango** Congo
13 E2 **Loanhead** Scotland
110 G2 **Loann** Illinois U.S.A.
44 D3 **Loano** Italy
71 G6 **Loay** Philippines
52 H5 **Loban'** *R* Russian Federation
54 K3 **Lobanovo** Russian Federation
70 G6 **Lobata** Sulawesi
89 D5 **Lobatse** Botswana
31 H4 **Löbau** Germany
86 C5 **Lobaye** *R* Cent Afr Republic
22 G3 **Lobbes** Belgium
37 M2 **Lobeda** Germany
33 P9 **Löbejün** Germany
37 M3 **Lobenstein** Germany
133 F5 **Lobería** Argentina
31 J2 **Łobez** Poland
87 B8 **Lobito** Angola
33 R4 **Löbnitz** Germany
54 J1 **Lobnya** Russian Federation
85 C7 **Lobo** *R* Ivory Coast
16 C6 **Lobón** Spain
27 H10 **Lobonäs** Sweden
131 F5 **Lobos** Argentina
124 D4 **Lobos** *isld* Mexico
128 D7 **Lobos,C** Chile
124 C3 **Lobos,C** Mexico
126 F3 **Lobos Cay** *isld* Cuba
128 B5 **Lobos de Tierra** *isld* Peru
133 D6 **Lobos,Pta** Argentina
131 A5 **Lobos,Pta** Colchagua Chile
37 N1 **Lobstädt** Germany
115 N7 **Lobstick L** Labrador, Nfld Canada
33 Q8 **Loburg** Germany
55 D2 **Lobva** Russian Federation
31 K2 **Łobżenica** Poland
40 G7 **Locana** Italy
41 J5 **Locarno** Switzerland
67 B6 **Loc Binh** Vietnam
32 K8 **Loccum** Germany
15 D4 **Lochaber** Scotland
122 K8 **Lochaber Mines** Nova Scotia Canada
15 C4 **Lochaline** Scotland
120 F4 **Lochalsh** Ontario Canada
15 C2 **Loch Assynt** Scotland
15 C4 **Loch Awe** Scotland
15 A3 **Loch Boisdale** Outer Hebrides Scotland
15 C3 **Loch Broom** Scotland
15 C4 **Lochbuie** Scotland
15 C3 **Loch Clunie** Scotland
15 D4 **Lochearnhead** Scotland
15 C4 **Loch Eil** Scotland
25 F4 **Lochem** Netherlands
15 D2 **Loch Eriboll** Scotland
15 D4 **Loch Ericht** Scotland
15 B2 **Loch Erisort** Scotland
21 M7 **Loches** France
21 N7 **Loché-sur-Indrois** France
15 C4 **Loch Etive** Scotland
15 C3 **Loch Ewe** Scotland
15 E4 **Loch Faskally** Scotland
15 C4 **Loch Fyne** Scotland
12 C1 **Lochgilphead** Scotland
15 C4 **Lochgilphead** Scotland
15 D3 **Loch Glass** Scotland
12 D1 **Lochgoilhead** Scotland
15 C3 **Loch Hourn** Scotland
144 B7 **Lochie** New Zealand
15 C2 **Loch Inchard** Scotland
15 C2 **Lochinver** Scotland
15 D4 **Loch Laggan** Scotland
15 B2 **Loch Langavat** Scotland
15 C2 **Loch Laxford** Scotland
15 E4 **Loch Leven** Scotland
15 D4 **Loch Lochy** Scotland
15 D4 **Loch Long** Scotland
15 C3 **Loch Loyne** Scotland
12 E3 **Lochmaben** Scotland
15 E5 **Lochmaben** Scotland
15 A3 **Lochmaddy** Outer Hebrides Scotland
15 C3 **Loch Maree** Scotland
15 C3 **Loch Monar** Scotland
15 C4 **Loch Morar** Scotland
15 D2 **Loch More** Scotland
144 B6 **Lochnagar** *L* New Zealand
15 E4 **Lochnagar** *mt* Scotland
15 D2 **Loch Naver** Scotland
15 D3 **Loch Ness** Scotland
15 D3 **Loch Oich** Scotland
15 C3 **Loch Quoich** Scotland
15 D4 **Loch Rannoch** Scotland
12 C2 **Lochranza** Scotland
22 F1 **Lochristi** Belgium
15 C4 **Loch Sheil** Scotland
15 D2 **Loch Shin** Scotland
15 C4 **Loch Sunart** Scotland
15 D4 **Loch Tay** Scotland
15 C3 **Loch Torridon** Scotland
68 J2 **Lo Chuc San** *isld* Vietnam
15 D4 **Loch Vennacher** Scotland
12 D2 **Lochwinnoch** Scotland
138 D5 **Lock** South Australia Australia
95 L4 **Locke** New York U.S.A.
100 H1 **Locke** Washington U.S.A.
122 G10 **Lockeport** Nova Scotia Canada
109 J4 **Locker** Texas U.S.A.
15 E5 **Lockerbie** Scotland
142 A5 **Locker Pt** W Australia Australia
103 J3 **Lockes** Nevada U.S.A.
111 B8 **Lockesburg** Arkansas U.S.A.
109 H1 **Lockett** Texas U.S.A.
139 H6 **Lockhart** New South Wales Australia
111 K10 **Lockhart** Alabama U.S.A.
98 K2 **Lockhart** Minnesota U.S.A.
112 F3 **Lockhart** South Carolina U.S.A.
109 K6 **Lockhart** Texas U.S.A.
141 G2 **Lockhart River** Queensland Australia
94 K5 **Lock Haven** Pennsylvania U.S.A.
143 B6 **Lockier Ra** W Australia Australia
108 F1 **Lockney** Texas U.S.A.
33 P6 **Löcknitz** *R* Germany
99 S8 **Lockport** Illinois U.S.A.
111 F12 **Lockport** Louisiana U.S.A.
94 J3 **Lockport** New York U.S.A.
99 P9 **Lockridge** Iowa U.S.A.
119 N7 **Lockwood** Saskatchewan Canada
110 C4 **Lockwood** Missouri U.S.A.
116 J3 **Lockwood Hills** Alaska U.S.A.
19 K5 **Locle, Le** France
20 D7 **Locmaria** Belle Isle, Nfld France
20 E6 **Locmaria** Morbihan France
20 E6 **Locmariaquer** France
20 E6 **Locminé** France
68 H7 **Loc Ninh** Vietnam
107 N7 **Loco** Oklahoma U.S.A.
101 P3 **Loco Mt** Montana U.S.A.
20 C4 **Locquirec** France
43 G10 **Locri** Italy
20 B5 **Locronan** France
20 B6 **Loctudy** France
99 N9 **Locust Cr** *R* Missouri U.S.A.
111 K7 **Locust Fork** *R* Alabama U.S.A.
94 D8 **Locust Grove** Ohio U.S.A.
107 P5 **Locust Grove** Oklahoma U.S.A.
80 C6 **Lod** Israel
99 S9 **Loda** Illinois U.S.A.
26 B10 **Lodalskåpa** *mt* Norway
139 G6 **Loddon** *R* Victoria Australia
9 H2 **Loddon** England
33 P10 **Lodersleben** Germany
18 H9 **Lodève** France
52 D4 **Lodeynoye-Pole** Russian Federation
101 Q1 **Lodge Cr** Mont/Sask U.S.A./Canada
101 S4 **Lodge Grass** Montana U.S.A.
117 E6 **Lodge, Mt** Br Col/Alaska Canada/U.S.A.
98 D8 **Lodgepole** Nebraska U.S.A.
98 C8 **Lodgepole Cr** Nebraska U.S.A.
98 B8 **Lodgepole Cr** Wyoming U.S.A.
74 D4 **Lodhran** Pakistan
41 L7 **Lodi** Italy
102 C3 **Lodi** California U.S.A.
94 E5 **Lodi** Ohio U.S.A.
99 R6 **Lodi** Wisconsin U.S.A.
26 G4 **Løding** Norway
26 H3 **Lödingen** Norway
86 D6 **Lodja** Zaire
71 A3 **Lodji** Indonesia
88 E3 **Lodmalasin** *mt* Tanzania
18 D10 **Lodosa** Spain
40 D3 **Lods** France
86 G5 **Lodwar** Kenya
31 L4 **Łódź** Poland
16 E4 **Loeches** Spain
86 F4 **Loelli** Sudan
25 F4 **Loenen** Netherlands
26 B10 **Loenvatn** *L* Norway
21 P2 **Loeuilly** France
38 G6 **Lofer** Austria
38 G6 **Loferer St Ulrich** Austria
36 E6 **Loffenau** Germany
15 E1 **L. of Harray** Scotland
26 F3 **Lofoten** *islds* Norway
26 F9 **Lofsdalen** Sweden
28 B5 **Loft** Denmark
27 J14 **Loftahammar** Sweden
13 G5 **Lofthouse** England
13 H4 **Loftus** England
143 C6 **Lofty Ra** W Australia Australia
141 H5 **Logan** *R* Queensland Australia
141 L8 **Logan** *R* Queensland Australia
99 L8 **Logan** Iowa U.S.A.
107 L2 **Logan** Kansas U.S.A.
101 O4 **Logan** Montana U.S.A.
98 F8 **Logan** Nebraska U.S.A.
106 G6 **Logan** New Mexico U.S.A.
101 O8 **Logan** Utah U.S.A.
94 F9 **Logan** West Virginia U.S.A.
98 K8 **Logan Cr** Nebraska U.S.A.
103 K5 **Logandale** Nevada U.S.A.
116 R6 **Logan Glacier** Alaska/Yukon Terr U.S.A./Canada
118 F3 **Logan L** Alberta Canada
122 E5 **Logan,Mt** Quebec Canada
117 C5 **Logan,Mt** Yukon Territory Canada
100 E1 **Logan, Mt** Washington U.S.A.
117 K5 **Logan Mts** Yukon Terr/N W Terr Canada
101 M1 **Logan Pass** Montana U.S.A.
94 A6 **Logansport** Indiana U.S.A.
111 B10 **Logansport** Louisiana U.S.A.
95 K5 **Loganton** Pennsylvania U.S.A.
99 Q6 **Loganville** Wisconsin U.S.A.
98 A9 **Logcabin** Colorado U.S.A.
26 K8 **Logde älv** *R* Sweden
100 F5 **Logdell** Oregon U.S.A.
87 B7 **Loge** *R* Angola
21 L2 **Loges, les** France
8 D2 **Loggerheads** England
55 D3 **Loginovo** Russian Federation
86 B3 **Logone** *R* Cameroon
21 N5 **Logron** France
17 F2 **Logroño** Spain
16 D5 **Logrosan** Spain
28 C3 **Løgstør** Denmark
28 C3 **Løgstrup** Denmark
28 E4 **Løgten** Denmark
20 D4 **Loguivy-Plougras** France
28 B6 **Løgumkloster** Denmark
28 F6 **Lohals** Denmark
80 D2 **Lohame HaGeta'ot** Israel
75 L7 **Lohardaga** India
20 G6 **Lohéac** France
32 L10 **Lohfelden** Germany
37 M7 **Lohhof** Germany
29 L5 **Lohijärvi** Finland
29 L11 **Lohja** Finland
101 Q1 **Lohman** Montana U.S.A.
33 Q5 **Lohmen** Germany
109 H4 **Lohn** Texas U.S.A.
36 E3 **Löhnberg** Germany
32 J8 **Löhne** Germany
36 D4 **Lohnsfeld** Germany
70 G6 **Loholoho** Sulawesi
36 H4 **Lohr** Germany
36 F2 **Lohra** Germany
99 M7 **Lohrville** Iowa U.S.A.
29 K7 **Lohtaja** Finland
68 C2 **Loi-ai** Burma
45 K3 **Loiano** Italy
38 K8 **Loibl Pass** Austria/Italy
21 J6 **Loigne** France
68 C3 **Loikaw** Burma
68 C3 **Loi Lan** *mt* Burma
68 C2 **Loi-Lem** Burma
68 D1 **Loi Lun** Burma
29 K11 **Loimaa** Finland
18 G4 **Loing** *R* France
21 L6 **Loir** *R* France
18 H7 **Loire** *R* France
21 K7 **Loire** *R* France
21 J6 **Loiré** Maine-et-Loire France
18 D5 **Loire-Atlantique** *dept* France
18 G5 **Loiret** *dept* France
18 F5 **Loir-et-Cher** *dept* France
21 J5 **Loiron** France
41 O2 **Loisach** *R* Germany
68 C2 **Loi Sang** *mt* Burma
22 J5 **Loison** *R* France
40 B4 **Loisy** France
33 S5 **Loitz** Germany
128 C4 **Loja** *prov* Ecuador
16 E7 **Loja** Spain
28 C6 **Løjt** Denmark
86 F5 **Loka** Sudan
29 J11 **Lokalahti** Finland
70 E2 **Lokan** *R* Sabah
86 E6 **Lokandu** Zaire
29 N4 **Lokantekojärvi** *L* Finland
70 D6 **Lokbatu** Kalimantan
52 H4 **Lokchim** *R* Russian Federation
22 D2 **Loker** Belgium
22 F1 **Lokeren** Belgium
37 O3 **Loket** Czechoslovakia
54 E6 **Lokhvitsa** Ukraine
86 G5 **Lokichar** Kenya
70 G5 **Lokilalaki, G** *mt* Sulawesi
86 G5 **Lokitaung** Kenya
29 N4 **Lokka** Finland
28 D2 **Løkken** Denmark
26 D8 **Lökken** Norway
52 D6 **Loknya** Russian Federation
86 A4 **Loko** Nigeria
86 D6 **Lokolo** *R* Zaire
53 C7 **Lokoml'skoye, Ozero** *L* Belorussia
86 C6 **Lokoro** *R* Zaire
55 F1 **Lokosovo** Russian Federation
54 F4 **Lokot'** Russian Federation
52 C5 **Loksa** Estonia
59 K1 **Lokshak** Russian Federation
115 N5 **Loks Land** Northwest Territories Canada
86 E4 **Lol** *R* Sudan
71 J4 **Lolak** Sulawesi
121 P4 **Lola, L** Quebec Canada
100 A9 **Loleta** California U.S.A.
20 H4 **Lolif** France
88 E3 **Loliondo** Tanzania
28 G7 **Lolland** *isld* Denmark
36 F2 **Lollar** Germany
101 L3 **Lolo** Montana U.S.A.
71 B2 **Lolobata** Halmahera Indonesia
71 A2 **Loloda** Halmahera Indonesia
71 A2 **Loloda,Tk** *B* Halmahera Indonesia
71 A1 **Loloda Utara, Pulau Pulau** *islds* Halmahera Indonesia
86 B5 **Lolodorf** Cameroon
52 H4 **Lolog** *R* Russian Federation
101 L3 **Lolo Hot Springs** Montana U.S.A.
69 C12 **Lolomoyo** Indonesia
101 L3 **Lolo Pass** Idaho/Montana U.S.A.
71 M9 **Lolotoi** Indonesia
69 C12 **Lolowau** Indonesia
46 F1 **Lom** Bulgaria
37 O4 **Lom** Czechoslovakia
37 P4 **Lom** *mt* Czechoslovakia
26 C10 **Lom** Norway
106 B2 **Loma** Colorado U.S.A.
101 P2 **Loma** Montana U.S.A.
98 H1 **Loma** North Dakota U.S.A.
16 E6 **Loma de Chiclana** Spain
16 E6 **Loma de Úbeda** Spain
88 B10 **Lomagundi** *dist* Zimbabwe
86 E6 **Lomami** *R* Zaire
85 B7 **Loma Mts** Sierra Leone/Guinea
99 N1 **Loman** Minnesota U.S.A.
131 D6 **Loma Negra,Planicie de la** *plain* Argentina
133 D6 **Lomas Coloradas** *hills* Argentina
130 B10 **Lomas de Vallejos** Argentina
133 F4 **Lomas de Zamora** Argentina
142 E3 **Lombadina** W Australia Australia
101 O3 **Lombard** Montana U.S.A.
129 H3 **Lombarda, Serra** *mts* Brazil
42 C3 **Lombardia** *prov* Italy
22 D1 **Lombardsijde** Belgium
18 F9 **Lombez** France
71 L9 **Lomblen** *isld* Indonesia
70 Q10 **Lombok** Indonesia
70 P10 **Lombok,Selat** *str* Indonesia
21 L5 **Lombron** France
85 E7 **Lomé** Togo
86 D6 **Lomela** Zaire
109 J4 **Lometa** Texas U.S.A.
86 B5 **Lomié** Cameroon
99 S6 **Lomira** Wisconsin U.S.A.
37 P1 **Lommatzsch** Germany
22 D2 **Lomme** France
22 J1 **Lommel** Belgium
118 E8 **Lomond** Alberta Canada
123 P4 **Lomond** Newfoundland Canada
6 M5 **Lomond** *oil rig* North Sea
15 E4 **Lomond Hills** Scotland
12 D1 **Lomond, Loch** *L* Scotland
52 D6 **Lomonosovo** Russian Federation
55 E4 **Lomonosovskaya** Kazakhstan
52 F3 **Lomovoye** Russian Federation
68 H6 **Lomphat** Cambodia
70 G7 **Lompobattang, G** *mt* Sulawesi
102 D7 **Lompoc** California U.S.A.
68 E4 **Lom Sak** Thailand
26 C10 **Lomseggja** *mt* Norway
26 J7 **Lomsjö** Sweden
31 N2 **Łomza** Poland
106 E7 **Lon** New Mexico U.S.A.
94 J7 **Lonaconing** Maryland U.S.A.
74 E9 **Lonāvale** India
28 A5 **Lønborg** Denmark
133 C5 **Loncoche** Chile
133 C5 **Loncopue** Argentina
22 F2 **Londerzeel** Belgium
120 J9 **Londesborough** Ontario Canada
21 N2 **Londinières** France
120 J10 **London** Ontario Canada
10 **London** *conurbation* England
110 C6 **London** Arkansas U.S.A.
94 C9 **London** Kentucky U.S.A.
94 D7 **London** Ohio U.S.A.
109 H5 **London** Texas U.S.A.
122 J8 **Londonderry** Nova Scotia Canada
14 D1 **Londonderry** N Ireland
14 D2 **Londonderry** *co* N Ireland
95 Q4 **Londonderry** New Hampshire U.S.A.
95 P3 **Londonderry** Vermont U.S.A.
142 F2 **Londonderry, C** W Australia Australia
133 C9 **Londonderry, I** Chile
Londorf *see* **Rabenau**
130 D8 **Londrina** Brazil
107 N7 **Lone Grove** Oklahoma U.S.A.
120 J7 **Lonely I** Ontario Canada
102 G4 **Lone Mt** Nevada U.S.A.
109 M3 **Lone Oak** Texas U.S.A.
102 F5 **Lone Pine** California U.S.A.
101 L2 **Lonepine** Montana U.S.A.
118 H5 **Lone Rock** Saskatchewan Canada
100 F4 **Lonerock** Oregon U.S.A.
99 Q6 **Lone Rock** Wisconsin U.S.A.
101 P8 **Lonetree** Wyoming U.S.A.
98 F2 **Lonetree Res** North Dakota U.S.A.
107 L7 **Lone Wolf** Oklahoma U.S.A.
87 C8 **Longa** Angola
129 K4 **Longa** *R* Brazil
46 E8 **Longá** Greece
70 D3 **Longagung** Kalimantan
70 D3 **Long Akah** Sarawak
67 B5 **Long'an** China
141 F5 **Longara** Queensland Australia
45 L1 **Longara** Italy
45 L1 **Longare** Italy
42 E2 **Longarone** Italy
133 C5 **Longavi** *mt* Chile
127 K3 **Long B** Jamaica
70 D3 **Longbawan** Kalimantan
127 M2 **Long Bay** Jamaica
112 J4 **Long Bay** South Carolina U.S.A.
144 C6 **Longbeach** New Zealand
102 F8 **Long Beach** California U.S.A.
95 O6 **Long Beach** Long I, New York U.S.A.
111 G11 **Long Beach** Mississippi U.S.A.
100 A3 **Long Beach** Washington U.S.A.
9 F2 **Long Bennington** England
70 D3 **Longberini** Kalimantan
70 E3 **Longbia** Kalimantan
113 E10 **Longboat Key** *isld* Florida U.S.A.
70 D4 **Longboh** Kalimantan
95 N6 **Long Branch** New Jersey U.S.A.
8 D5 **Longbridge Deverill** England
145 E4 **Longburn** New Zealand
8 D6 **Long Burton** England
22 K3 **Longchamps** Belgium
67 B2 **Longchang** China
67 E4 **Longchuan** China
9 E3 **Long Compton** England
138 C3 **Long Cr** South Australia Australia
119 O9 **Long Cr** Saskatchewan Canada
98 C1 **Long Cr** North Dakota U.S.A.
100 F5 **Long Creek** Oregon U.S.A.
68 H4 **Long Dai** Vietnam
107 M5 **Longdale** Oklahoma U.S.A.
58 E4 **Longde** China
9 E2 **Longdon** England
9 E2 **Long Eaton** England
40 B3 **Longecourt** France
95 M5 **Long Eddy** New York U.S.A.
36 B1 **Longerich** Germany
95 R1 **Long Falls Dam** Maine U.S.A.
108 E5 **Longfellow** Texas U.S.A.
144 D5 **Longfellow, Mt** New Zealand
65 G2 **Longfengshan Shuiku** *res* China
139 H8 **Longford** Tasmania Australia
14 D3 **Longford** *co* Ireland
14 D3 **Longford** Ireland
145 D4 **Longford** New Zealand
107 N2 **Longford** Kansas U.S.A.
13 F2 **Longformacus** Scotland
6 K5 **Long Forties** *bank* North Sea
13 G3 **Longframlington** England
65 G3 **Longgang Shan** *mt ra* China
70 E4 **Longgi** *R* Kalimantan
65 C4 **Longguan** China
65 C7 **Longguji** China
67 C7 **Longgun** China
67 F4 **Longhai** China
9 E6 **Longham** England
123 T6 **Long Harbour** Newfoundland Canada
13 G3 **Longhorsley** England
13 G3 **Longhoughton** England
65 D4 **Longhua** China
67 D3 **Longhui** China
112 J1 **Longhurst** North Carolina U.S.A.
68 A6 **Long I** Andaman Is
141 J5 **Long I** Queensland Australia
126 G3 **Long I** Bahamas
115 M7 **Long I** Northwest Territories Canada
122 F9 **Long I** Nova Scotia Canada
83 K12 **Long I** Mahé I Indian Oc
144 A6 **Long I** New Zealand
136 K3 **Long I** Papua New Guinea
95 P6 **Long I** New York U.S.A.
100 A3 **Long I** Washington U.S.A.
127 M4 **Long, I** Martinique W Indies
70 E5 **Longikis** Kalimantan
70 D5 **Longiram** Kalimantan
95 P5 **Long I Sd** Conn/New York U.S.A.
107 L2 **Long Island** Kansas U.S.A.
59 H2 **Longjiang** China
67 B4 **Long Jiang** *R* China
65 H3 **Longjing** China
21 P4 **Longjumeau** France
Longjuzhai *see* **Danfeng**
36 C4 **Longkamp** Germany
70 D4 **Longkay** Kalimantan
65 E6 **Longkou** China
122 F6 **Long L** New Brunswick Canada
120 D3 **Long L** Ontario Canada
116 K6 **Long L** Alaska U.S.A.
95 S6 **Long L** Maine U.S.A.
94 B2 **Long L** Michigan U.S.A.
99 M3 **Long L** Minnesota U.S.A.
95 N2 **Long L** New York U.S.A.
98 G3 **Long L** North Dakota U.S.A.
122 J1 **Long, Lac** Labrador, Nfld Canada
120 D3 **Longlac** Ontario Canada
95 N3 **Long Lake** New York U.S.A.
99 S4 **Long Lake** Wisconsin U.S.A.
70 D3 **Long Lama** Sarawak
8 D5 **Longleat House** England
67 B3 **Longli** China
22 J4 **Longlier** Belgium
67 B4 **Longlin** China
12 D1 **Long, Loch** *L* Scotland
118 E4 **Long L. Prov. Park** Alberta Canada
100 F2 **Long L.Res** Washington U.S.A.
70 E3 **Longmalinau** Kalimantan
9 G3 **Long Melford** England
67 C6 **Longmen** China
65 A7 **Longmen Shan** *mts* China
98 A9 **Longmont** Colorado U.S.A.
70 D3 **Long Murum** Sarawak
67 E4 **Longnan** China
70 D4 **Longnawan** Kalimantan
21 O4 **Longnes** France
9 E1 **Longnor** England
21 M4 **Longny** France
43 H9 **Longobucco** Italy
88 F2 **Longonot,Mt** Kenya
70 D4 **Longpahangai** Kalimantan
69 H8 **Long Phu** Vietnam
98 G7 **Long Pine** Nebraska U.S.A.
Longping *see* **Luodian**
99 S8 **Long Point** Illinois U.S.A.
120 K10 **Long Point B** Ontario Canada
123 U6 **Long Pond** Newfoundland Canada
22 E5 **Longpont** France
123 Q5 **Long Pound** *res* Newfoundland Canada
99 M4 **Long Prairie** Minnesota U.S.A.
21 O1 **Longpré-les-Corps-Saints** France
119 T5 **Long Pt** Manitoba Canada
123 O5 **Long Pt** Newfoundland Canada
144 A7 **Long Pt** New Zealand
71 D6 **Long Pt** Philippines
70 D3 **Longpujungan** Kalimantan
67 F2 **Longquan** China
67 F3 **Longquan Xi** *R* China
123 P4 **Long Range Mts** Newfoundland Canada
141 G6 **Longreach** Queensland Australia
142 F2 **Long Reef** W Australia Australia
13 F6 **Longridge** England
112 J4 **Longs** South Carolina U.S.A.
144 A7 **Long Sd** New Zealand
70 E3 **Longsegah** Kalimantan
67 D2 **Longshan** China
67 C4 **Longsheng** China
67 D5 **Longsheng** China
Longshi *see* **Ninggang**
98 A9 **Longs Peak** *mt* Colorado U.S.A.
140 B6 **Longs Ra** N Terr Australia
9 H3 **Long Stratton** England
9 G2 **Long Sutton** England
67 B2 **Longtan** China
70 D3 **Long Teru** Sarawak
67 C3 **Longtian** China
117 P3 **Longtom L** Northwest Territories Canada
100 K6 **Long Tom Res** Idaho U.S.A.
141 H5 **Longton** Queensland Australia
8 D2 **Longton** England
13 F6 **Longton** Lancs England
107 O4 **Longton** Kansas U.S.A.
13 F2 **Longtown** England
110 G4 **Longtown** Missouri U.S.A.
83 M14 **Longue** *isld* Kerguelen Indian Oc
21 P2 **Longueau** France
22 D5 **Longueil-St.Marie** France
21 K7 **Longué-Jumelles** France
22 D3 **Longueval** France
18 H4 **Longueville** Seine-et-Marne France
21 N2 **Longueville** Seine-Inférieure France
19 J3 **Longuyon** France
98 E6 **Longvalley** South Dakota U.S.A.
102 F4 **Long Valley Res** California U.S.A.
40 B3 **Longvic** France
118 C8 **Longview** Alberta Canada
109 N3 **Longview** Texas U.S.A.
100 C3 **Longview** Washington U.S.A.
109 O5 **Longville** Louisiana U.S.A.
22 K3 **Longvilly** Belgium
70 E4 **Longwai** Kalimantan
65 J2 **Longwangmiao** China
65 F5 **Longwangmiao** China
113 F9 **Longwood** Florida U.S.A.
111 E8 **Longwood** Mississippi U.S.A.
108 G3 **Longworth** Texas U.S.A.
22 K4 **Longwy** France

52 J2 **Makarikha** Russian Federation
144 B6 **Makarora** *R* New Zealand
59 M2 **Makarov** Russian Federation
42 H5 **Makarska** Croatia
52 G3 **Makar-Yb** Russian Federation
52 G5 **Makar'ye** Russian Federation
Makassar *see* **Ujung Pandang**
70 F5 **Makassar Str** Indonesia
89 H6 **Makatini Flats** *reg* S Africa
135 T3 **Makawao** Hawaiian Is
71 C3 **Makbon** W Irian
Makedonija *see* **Macedonia**
135 N10 **Makemo** *atoll* Pacific Oc
85 B7 **Makeni** Sierra Leone
145 F2 **Maketu** New Zealand
54 K8 **Makeyevka** Ukraine
89 D3 **Makgadikgadi** *salt pans* Botswana
Makharadze *see* **Ozurgety**
16 D9 **Makhazen, Oued** *R* Morocco
55 D2 **Makhnevo** Russian Federation
55 E4 **Makhorovka** Kazakhstan
80 F3 **Makhraba** Jordan
61 M8 **Maki** Japan
71 A2 **Makian** Halmahera Indonesia
144 C6 **Makikihi** New Zealand
119 S8 **Makinak** Manitoba Canada
55 F4 **Makinsk** Kazakhstan
115 M2 **Makinson Inlet** Northwest Territories Canada
26 S1 **Makkaur** Norway
25 F3 **Makkinga** Netherlands
115 O6 **Makkovik** Labrador, Nfld Canada
25 D2 **Makkum** Netherlands
48 F4 **Makó** Hungary
120 C1 **Makokibatan L** Ontario Canada
87 F7 **Makongolosi** Tanzania
145 F3 **Makorako** *mt* New Zealand
98 E2 **Makoti** North Dakota U.S.A.
145 F4 **Makotuku** New Zealand
86 C5 **Makoua** Congo
31 L6 **Makov** Czechoslovakia
31 M6 **Maków** Poland
31 N3 **Maków Mazowiecki** Poland
80 D2 **Makr** Israel
47 H8 **Makrá** *isld* Greece
74 F5 **Makrana** India
77 J7 **Makran Coast Range** Pakistan
47 H4 **Mákri** Greece
76 E1 **Makri** India
46 G7 **Makronísi** *isld* Greece
52 J3 **Maksim** Russian Federation
56 C2 **Maksimkin Yar** Russian Federation
85 F1 **Makthar** Tunisia
78 K2 **Maku** Iran
70 C4 **Makup, Bt** *mt* Kalimantan
60 D14 **Makurazaki** Japan
86 A4 **Makurdi** Nigeria
55 E3 **Makushino** Russian Federation
116 D10 **Makushin Vol** Aleutian Is
88 D7 **Makutu Mts** Zambia
118 H4 **Makwa L** Saskatchewan Canada
89 G1 **Makwiro** Zimbabwe
128 C6 **Mala** Peru
71 G7 **Malabang** Mindanao Philippines
113 G9 **Malabar** Florida U.S.A.
76 B5 **Malabar Coast** India
70 L9 **Malabar, G** *mt* Java
85 F8 **Malabo** Fernando Póo Equat Guinea
71 C6 **Malabuñgan** Palawan Philippines
69 E11 **Malacca, Str. of** Malaysia
118 H1 **Malachi** Ontario Canada
31 K7 **Malacky** Czechoslovakia
101 N7 **Malad City** Idaho U.S.A.
17 H2 **Maladeta** Spain
31 L6 **Malá Fatra** *mts* Czechoslovakia
16 D8 **Málaga** *prov* Spain
16 E8 **Málaga** Spain
100 E2 **Malaga** Washington U.S.A.
88 C4 **Malagarasi** Tanzania
Malagasy Rep *see* **Madagascar**
16 E5 **Malagón** Spain
71 K9 **Malahar** Indonesia
14 E3 **Malahide** Ireland
87 G12 **Malaimbandy** Madagascar
137 N3 **Malaita** *isld* Solomon Is
71 J9 **Malaka** *mt* Sumbawa Indonesia
86 F4 **Malakal** Sudan
42 G4 **Mala Kapela** *mts* Croatia
109 L3 **Malakoff** Texas U.S.A.
71 B2 **Malaku** *islds* Indonesia
137 O5 **Malakula** *isld* Vanuatu
45 L2 **Malalbergo** Italy
71 A3 **Malamala** *isld* Indonesia
70 G6 **Malamala** Sulawesi
71 E7 **Malamaui** *isld* Philippines
45 M1 **Malamocco** Italy
71 D5 **Malampaya Snd** Philippines
141 H3 **Malanda** Queensland Australia
70 O10 **Malang** Java
88 E6 **Malangali** Tanzania
70 M9 **Malangbong** Java
26 K2 **Malangen** *inlet* Norway
26 K2 **Malangen** Norway
26 J2 **Malangsgrunnen** *shoal* Norway
75 L5 **Malangwa** Nepal
71 F7 **Malanipa** *isld* Philippines
87 C7 **Malanje** Angola
20 F6 **Malansac** France
71 D6 **Malanut B** Philippines
85 E6 **Malanville** Benin
65 D4 **Malanyu** China
131 C3 **Malanzaán, Sa. de** *mts* Argentina
76 C5 **Malappuram** India
27 J12 **Mälaren** *L* Sweden
131 B5 **Malargue** *R* Argentina
133 D5 **Malargue** Argentina
129 H3 **Malaripo** Brazil
121 M4 **Malartic** Quebec Canada
70 F7 **Malasoro, Tk** *B* Sulawesi
117 C6 **Malaspina Gl** Alaska U.S.A.
144 A6 **Malaspina Reach** New Zealand
117 L11 **Malaspina Str** British Columbia Canada
26 K6 **Malåtrask** Sweden
78 G2 **Malatya** Turkey
19 O16 **Malaucène** France
21 N2 **Malaunay** France
70 E1 **Malawali** *isld* Sabah
88 D8 **Malawi** *rep* Africa
Malawi, L *see* **Nyasa, L**
29 J9 **Malax** Finland
55 D1 **Malaya Sos'va** *R* Russian Federation
52 D5 **Malaya Vishera** Russian Federation
77 A2 **Malāyer** Iran
141 J4 **Malay Reef** Gt Barrier Reef Aust
69 **Malaysia** S E Asia
69 E10 **Malaysia, Peninsular** S E Asia
14 B4 **Mal B** Ireland
122 H5 **Mal Baie** Quebec Canada
122 B6 **Malbaie** *R* Quebec Canada
131 B6 **Malbarco, L** Argentina
140 F5 **Malbon** Queensland Australia
38 J9 **Malborghetto** Italy
31 L1 **Malbork** Poland
41 N6 **Malcesine** Italy
33 R5 **Malchin** Germany
33 Q6 **Malchow** Germany
143 D8 **Malcolm** W Australia Australia
116 R2 **Malcolm** *R* Yukon Territory Canada
68 D7 **Malcolm I** Burma
143 E10 **Malcolm,Pt** W Australia Australia
99 O8 **Malcom** Iowa U.S.A.
22 E1 **Maldegem** Belgium
95 Q4 **Malden** Massachusetts U.S.A.
110 G5 **Malden** Missouri U.S.A.
100 H2 **Malden** Washington U.S.A.
94 F8 **Malden** West Virginia U.S.A.
135 M8 **Malden I** Pacific Oc
73 L8 **Maldive Is** *rep* Indian Oc
43 B9 **Mal di Ventre, I. di** Sardinia
73 L9 **Maldive Ridge** Indian Oc
9 G4 **Maldon** England
131 G5 **Maldonado** *dept* Uruguay
131 G5 **Maldonado** Uruguay
41 N5 **Male** Italy
73 L8 **Male** Maldives
46 F8 **Maléa, Akr** *C* Greece
47 H5 **Maléa, Akr** Turkey
74 F8 **Malegaon** India
70 G6 **Malehu** Sulawesi
48 D2 **Malé Karpaty** Czechoslovakia
121 P4 **Mâle, L.du** Quebec Canada
88 F9 **Malema** Mozambique
87 E7 **Malemba Nkulu** Zaire
46 F9 **Máleme** Crete
52 E3 **Malen'ga** Russian Federation
33 N4 **Malente** Germany
74 F3 **Maler Kotla** India
47 H9 **Máles** Crete Greece
21 P5 **Malesherbes** France
20 F6 **Malestroit** France
54 K3 **Malevka** Russian Federation
89 B10 **Malgas** S Africa
37 O6 **Malgersdorf** Germany
86 E2 **Malha** Sudan
13 F5 **Malham** England
100 H5 **Malheur** Oregon U.S.A.
100 H6 **Malheur** *R* Oregon U.S.A.
83 K12 **Malheureu, Cap** Mahé I Indian Oc
100 G6 **Malheur L** Oregon U.S.A.
66 F6 **Mali** *R* Burma
85 D5 **Mali** *rep* W Africa
71 M9 **Maliana** Indonesia
21 K6 **Malicorne-sur-Sarthe** France
71 F7 **Maligoy B** Mindanao Philippines
80 F4 **Malih** *R* Jordan
19 Q16 **Malijai** France
70 D6 **Maliku** Kalimantan
71 H5 **Maliku** Sulawesi
68 D6 **Mali Kyun** *isld* Burma
70 G6 **Malili** Sulawesi
27 H14 **Målilla** Sweden
88 B5 **Malimba** *mts* Zaire
70 K9 **Malimping** Java
100 D7 **Malin** Oregon U.S.A.
71 G5 **Malinao Inlet** Philippines
71 F6 **Malindang, Mt** Mindanao Philippines
88 H3 **Malindi** Kenya
48 F2 **Malinec** Czechoslovakia
Malines *see* **Mechelen**
70 G4 **Maling, G** *mt* Sulawesi
27 H12 **Malingsbo** Sweden
14 D1 **Malin Hd** Ireland
48 K3 **Mălini** Romania
14 C2 **Malin More** Ireland
70 F7 **Malino** Sulawesi
54 H7 **Malinovka** Ukraine
55 G5 **Malinovoye Ozero** *L* Russian Federation
68 G1 **Malipo** China
42 F4 **Mali Rajinac** *mt* Croatia
71 G7 **Malita** Mindanao Philippines
71 G5 **Malitbog** Leyte Philippines
68 D7 **Maliwun** Burma
106 G9 **Maljamar** New Mexico U.S.A.
48 F6 **Maljen** *mt* Serbia Yugoslavia
80 F3 **Malka** Jordan
53 F11 **Malka** *R* Russian Federation
47 J2 **Malkapapiye** Bulgaria
74 G8 **Malkapur** India
47 H4 **Malkara** Turkey
56 G5 **Malkhanskiy Khr** *mts* Russian Federation
31 N3 **Małkinia** Poland
80 F1 **Malkiyya** Israel
139 J7 **Mallacoota** Victoria Australia
118 F4 **Mallaig** Alberta Canada
15 C3 **Mallaig** Scotland
99 M7 **Mallard** Iowa U.S.A.
84 J4 **Mallawi** Egypt
131 A7 **Malleco** *prov* Chile
19 O17 **Mallemort** France
37 N6 **Mallersdorf** Germany
41 N4 **Malles Venosta** Italy
130 E9 **Mallét** Brazil
142 C5 **Mallina** W Australia Australia
28 E4 **Malling** Denmark
38 H8 **Mallnitz** Austria
17 J5 **Mallorca** *isld* Balearic Is
94 F9 **Mallory** West Virginia U.S.A.
121 P8 **Mallorytown** Ontario Canada
14 C4 **Mallow** Ireland
142 E5 **Mallowa Well** W Australia Australia
8 B1 **Malltraeth B** Wales
8 C2 **Mallwyd** Wales
22 F5 **Malmaison, la** France
27 G14 **Malmbäck** Sweden
26 L4 **Malmberget** Sweden
22 L3 **Malmédy** Belgium
8 D4 **Malmesbury** England
89 A9 **Malmesbury** S Africa
26 K6 **Malmesjaure** *L* Sweden
27 J12 **Malmköping** Sweden
29 K5 **Malmö** Sweden
27 F16 **Malmöhus** *county* Sweden
126 A2 **Malmok** *pt* Bonaire W Indies
52 H6 **Malmyzh** Russian Federation
26 G3 **Malnes** Norway
137 O5 **Malo** *isld* Vanuatu
54 H4 **Maloarkhangel'sk** Russian Federation
129 G3 **Maloca** Amapá Brazil
129 H5 **Maloca** Pará Brazil
41 L5 **Maloggia** Switzerland
71 E3 **Malolos** Luzon Philippines
55 C2 **Malomal'sk** Russian Federation
88 E9 **Malombe,L** Malawi
47 H2 **Malomir** Bulgaria
47 R14 **Malóna** Rhodes Greece
121 N8 **Malone** Ontario Canada
113 B7 **Malone** Florida U.S.A.
95 N2 **Malone** New York U.S.A.
109 L4 **Malone** Texas U.S.A.
98 F8 **Maloney Res** Nebraska U.S.A.
67 A4 **Malong** China
87 D8 **Malonga** Zaire
26 N6 **Malören** Sweden
31 P4 **Malorita** Belorussia
52 E3 **Maloshuyka** Russian Federation
89 F7 **Maloti Mts** Lesotho
100 F1 **Malott** Washington U.S.A.
26 A10 **Målöy** Norway
54 H1 **Maloyaroslavets** Russian Federation
55 E2 **Maloye Gorodishche** Russian Federation
52 H1 **Malozemel'skaya Tundra** *plain* Russian Federation
106 C10 **Malpais** New Mexico U.S.A.
138 F5 **Malpas** South Australia Australia
8 D1 **Malpas** England
124 H6 **Malpaso** Mexico
90 A8 **Malpelo I** Pacific Oc
122 J7 **Malpeque B** Prince Edward I Canada
16 D5 **Malpica** Spain
16 B1 **Malpica de Bergantiños** Spain
131 B4 **Malpo** *R* Chile
73 L5 **Malprabha** *R* India
74 F5 **Malpura** India
36 E6 **Malsch** Germany
31 H7 **Malše** *R* Czechoslovakia
26 K2 **Målselv** *R* Norway
26 K2 **Målselv** Norway
36 H1 **Malsfeld** Germany
77 A7 **Malsūnīyah, Al** Saudi Arabia
38 J8 **Malta** Austria
43 F13 **Malta** *rep* Mediterranean Sea
106 D2 **Malta** Colorado U.S.A.
101 M7 **Malta** Idaho U.S.A.
101 S1 **Malta** Montana U.S.A.
94 F7 **Malta** Ohio U.S.A.
43 F12 **Malta Ch** Mediterranean Sea
87 C10 **Maltahöhe** Namibia
38 H7 **Maltatel** *V* Austria
9 G1 **Maltby** England
13 G6 **Maltby** S Yorks England
144 C5 **Malte Brun** *mt* New Zealand
47 N11 **Maltepe** Turkey
121 L9 **Malton** *airport* Ontario Canada
13 H5 **Malton** England
48 K6 **Malu** Romania
71 D5 **Malubutglubut** *isld* Philippines
85 F6 **Malumfashi** Nigeria
70 F6 **Malunda** Sulawesi
27 G11 **Malung** Sweden
41 K5 **Malvaglia** Switzerland
76 A2 **Malvan** India
127 J2 **Malvern** Jamaica
127 J3 **Malvern** *pk* Jamaica
109 P1 **Malvern** Arkansas U.S.A.
99 L9 **Malvern** Iowa U.S.A.
94 F6 **Malvern** Ohio U.S.A.
8 D3 **Malvern Wells** England
20 G7 **Malville** France
Malvinas, Is *see* **Falkland Is.**
74 F7 **Malwa Plateau** India
83 K9 **Malwatu Oya** *R* Sri Lanka
78 K1 **Maly Kavkaz** *mts* Armenia/Azerbaijan
55 E1 **Malyy Atlym** Russian Federation
55 F1 **Malyy Balyk** *R* Russian Federation
55 G4 **Malyye Chany, Oz** *L* Russian Federation
52 G6 **Malyy Kundysh** *R* Russian Federation
51 O1 **Malyy Lyakhovski,Ostrov** *isld* Russian Federation
51 K1 **Malyy Taymyr, Ostrov** *isld* Russian Federation
55 G2 **Malyy Yugan** *R* Russian Federation
56 H2 **Mama** *R* Russian Federation
56 H2 **Mama** Russian Federation
52 H6 **Mamadysh** Russian Federation
48 M6 **Mamaia** Romania
120 F5 **Mamainse Point** Ontario Canada
145 F3 **Mamaku** New Zealand
76 E4 **Māmallapuram** India
145 D1 **Mamaranui** New Zealand
70 F6 **Mamasa** Sulawesi
71 D7 **Mambahenauhan** *isld* Philippines
71 G6 **Mambajao** Philippines
89 F3 **Mambala Cave** Zimbabwe
86 E5 **Mambasa** Zaire
136 H2 **Mamberamo** *R* W Irian
86 C4 **Mambéré** *R* Cent Afr Republic
70 F6 **Mambi** Sulawesi
79 H2 **Mambij** Syria
71 E4 **Mamburao** Philippines
118 K1 **Mameigwess L** Ontario Canada
83 J12 **Mamelle** *isld* Seychelles
118 D6 **Ma-Me-O Beach** Alberta Canada
118 D5 **Ma-Me-O Beach Prov. Park** Alberta Canada
22 K4 **Mamer** Luxembourg
21 L5 **Mamers** France
86 A4 **Mamfé** Cameroon
128 F4 **Mamia, L** Brazil
40 D3 **Mamirolle** France
55 E4 **Mamlyutka** Kazakhstan
120 F2 **Mammamattawa** Ontario Canada
28 D4 **Mammen** Denmark
37 L7 **Mammendorf** Germany
37 O6 **Mamming** Germany
43 G10 **Mammola** Italy
94 F8 **Mammoth** West Virginia U.S.A.
110 K4 **Mammoth Cave** Kentucky U.S.A.
101 P5 **Mammoth Hot Springs** Wyoming U.S.A.
102 F4 **Mammoth lakes** California U.S.A.
110 E5 **Mammoth Spring** Arkansas U.S.A.
126 G9 **Mamonal** Colombia
130 G4 **Mamonas** Brazil
31 M1 **Mamo-novo** Russian Federation
128 E6 **Mamore** *R* Bolivia/Brazil
128 F4 **Mamoré, L** Brazil
85 B6 **Mamou** Guinea
111 D11 **Mamou** Louisiana U.S.A.
87 H11 **Mampikohy** Madagascar
16 D1 **Mampodre** *mt* Spain
85 D7 **Mampong** Ghana
83 J9 **Mampuri** Sri Lanka
31 N1 **Mamry,Jezioro** *L* Poland
15 C3 **Mam Soul** *mt* Scotland
Mamuji *see* **Yucheng**
70 F6 **Mamuji** Sulawesi
87 D10 **Mamuno** Botswana
55 C5 **Mamyt** Kazakhstan
85 C7 **Man** Ivory Coast
94 F9 **Man** West Virginia U.S.A.
129 H3 **Mana** *R* Fr Guiana
135 N1 **Mana** Hawaiian Is
56 D3 **Mana** *R* Russian Federation
128 B4 **Manabi** Ecuador
128 F4 **Manacapuru** Brazil
128 F4 **Manacapuru,L.Grande de** Brazil
17 K5 **Manacor** Majorca
71 J4 **Manado** Sulawesi
71 J4 **Manadotua** *isld* Sulawesi
22 G3 **Manage** Belgium
140 D3 **Managoora** N Terr Australia
125 L3 **Managua** Nicaragua
145 E4 **Mana I** New Zealand
145 E3 **Manaia** New Zealand
87 H12 **Manakara** Madagascar
144 D5 **Manakau** *mt* New Zealand
145 E4 **Manakau** New Zealand
136 K2 **Manam** *isld* Papua New Guinea
76 D6 **Manamadurai** India
77 B6 **Manamah,Al** Bahrain
87 G11 **Manambaho** *R* Madagascar
127 N10 **Mánamo** *R* Venezuela
71 E5 **Manamoc** *isld* Philippines
102 S12 **Manana** Hawaiian Is
87 H11 **Mananara** Madagascar
139 G6 **Manangatang** Victoria Australia
87 H12 **Mananjary** Madagascar
128 F2 **Manano,Caño** *creek* Venezuela
85 B6 **Manantali, Lac de** *res* Mali
76 C5 **Mānantavādi** India
87 H12 **Manantenina** Madagascar
144 A6 **Manapouri** New Zealand
66 D3 **Manas** China
Manasarowar Lake *see* **Mapam Yumco**
74 H3 **Mana Shankou** *pass* India/China
66 D3 **Manas He** *R* China
66 D2 **Manas Hu** *L* China
75 L4 **Manaslu** *mt* Nepal
95 N6 **Manasquan** New Jersey U.S.A.
106 E4 **Manassa** Colorado U.S.A.
94 K8 **Manassas** Virginia U.S.A.
71 M9 **Manatang** Indonesia
127 L5 **Manatí** Puerto Rico
128 G4 **Manaus** Brazil
78 C3 **Manavgat** Turkey
99 S5 **Manawa** Wisconsin U.S.A.
119 P3 **Manawan L** Saskatchewan Canada
145 E2 **Manawaru** New Zealand
145 F4 **Manawatu** *admin region* New Zealand
145 E4 **Manawatu R** New Zealand
71 G7 **Manay** Mindanao Philippines
140 B2 **Manbulloo** N Terr Australia
94 C2 **Mancelona** Michigan U.S.A.
16 E7 **Mancha Real** Spain
18 E3 **Manche** *dept* France
21 P5 **Manchecourt** France
Manche,la *see* **English Channel**
74 H9 **Mancheral** India
11 E2 **Manchester** *conurbation* England
127 K3 **Manchester** *parish* Jamaica
102 A3 **Manchester** California U.S.A.
95 P5 **Manchester** Connecticut U.S.A.
112 C5 **Manchester** Georgia U.S.A.
110 F2 **Manchester** Illinois U.S.A.
99 P7 **Manchester** Iowa U.S.A.
107 N2 **Manchester** Kansas U.S.A.
110 N4 **Manchester** Kentucky U.S.A.
94 C4 **Manchester** Michigan U.S.A.
95 Q4 **Manchester** New Hampshire U.S.A.
95 K4 **Manchester** New York U.S.A.
94 D8 **Manchester** Ohio U.S.A.
107 M5 **Manchester** Oklahoma U.S.A.
95 L6 **Manchester** Pennsylvania U.S.A.
110 K6 **Manchester** Tennessee U.S.A.
95 O3 **Manchester** Vermont U.S.A.
37 M6 **Manching** Germany
127 M2 **Manchioneal** Jamaica
65 E1 **Manchuria** *reg* China
42 D6 **Manciano** Italy
128 B4 **Máncora** Peru
106 B4 **Mancos** Colorado U.S.A.
77 B5 **Mand** *R* Iran
87 F8 **Manda** Tanzania
130 D8 **Mandaguari** Brazil
80 F3 **Mandah** Jordan
69 F13 **Mandah** Sumatra
88 D7 **Manda Hd** Zambia
77 G3 **Mandal** Afghanistan
58 D2 **Mandal** Mongolia
27 B13 **Mandal** Norway
68 C2 **Mandalay** Burma
78 A3 **Mandalaya** *isld* Turkey
58 E2 **Mandalgovī** Mongolia
78 K5 **Mandalī** Iraq
27 B13 **Mandalsåni** *R* Norway
Mandalt *see* **Sonid Zuoqi**
98 F3 **Mandan** North Dakota U.S.A.
69 E12 **Mandau** Sumatra
36 C5 **Mandelbachtal** Germany
127 K2 **Mandeville** Jamaica
144 B7 **Mandeville** New Zealand
111 F11 **Mandeville** Louisiana U.S.A.
69 F10 **Mandi Angin, Gunung** *mt* Malaysia
130 B6 **Mandioré, Lagoa** *L* Bolivia/Brazil
74 J7 **Mandla** India
69 J12 **Mandor** Indonesia
46 F6 **Mandoúdhion** Greece
74 F6 **Mandsaur** India
143 B10 **Mandurah** W Australia Australia
48 K5 **Maneciu** Romania
41 N6 **Manerba del Garda** Italy
17 G7 **Manga del Mar Menor** Spain
145 E3 **Mangakino** New Zealand
76 E2 **Mangalagiri** India
76 B4 **Mangalore** India
145 E4 **Mangamahoe** New Zealand
145 E3 **Mangamahu** New Zealand
144 D5 **Mangamaunu** New Zealand
145 D1 **Mangamuka** New Zealand
145 E3 **Mangapehi** New Zealand
145 E4 **Mangatainoka** New Zealand
145 E3 **Mangaweka** New Zealand
145 E2 **Mangawhai** New Zealand
142 A4 **Mangles B** W Australia Australia
66 E4 **Mangnai** China
85 E6 **Mango** Togo
88 E9 **Mangochi** Malawi
87 G12 **Mangoky** *R* Madagascar
145 D1 **Mangonui** New Zealand
87 H12 **Mangoro** Madagascar
74 D8 **Māngral** India
113 J11 **Mangrove Cay** *isld* Bahamas
126 F2 **Mangrove Cay** Andros Bahamas
71 E4 **Mangsoagui Pt** Philippines
130 H10 **Manguaba,L** Brazil
16 B4 **Mangualde** Portugal
86 D3 **Mangueigne** Chad
131 H4 **Mangueira, L** Brazil
130 D9 **Mangueirinha** Brazil
84 E5 **Mangueni,Pl.du** Niger
59 H1 **Mangui** China
87 G7 **Mangula** Tanzania
108 E9 **Mangum** Oklahoma U.S.A.
67 A5 **Manhao** China
99 T8 **Manhattan** Illinois U.S.A.
107 O2 **Manhattan** Kansas U.S.A.
101 O4 **Manhattan** Montana U.S.A.
102 G3 **Manhattan** Nevada U.S.A.
22 K3 **Manhay** Belgium
130 H7 **Manhuaçu** Brazil
130 H6 **Manhuaçu,R** Brazil
113 L12 **Man I** Bahamas
87 E7 **Mani** Zaire
87 H11 **Mania** *R* Madagascar
42 E2 **Maniago** Italy
88 E8 **Maniamba** Mozambique
87 F9 **Manica** Mozambique
71 G5 **Manicani** *isld* Philippines
122 D4 **Manic Deux Dam** Quebec Canada
128 F5 **Manicoré** *R* Brazil
122 D3 **Manicouagan** Quebec Canada
122 D4 **Manicouagan Pen** Quebec Canada
122 D4 **Manicouagan R** Quebec Canada
122 D2 **Manicouagan, Res** Quebec Canada
141 K6 **Manifold, C** Queensland Australia
119 V7 **Manigotagan** Manitoba Canada
Maniitsoq *see* **Sukkertoppen Iskappe**
71 E3 **Manila** Luzon Philippines
110 F6 **Manila** Arkansas U.S.A.
101 Q9 **Manila** Utah U.S.A.
71 E3 **Manila B** Luzon Philippines
139 J5 **Manildra** New South Wales Australia
139 K4 **Manilla** New South Wales Australia
99 L8 **Manilla** Iowa U.S.A.
70 F5 **Manimbaja,Tg** *C* Sulawesi
69 E13 **Manindjan,Danau** *L* Sumatra
87 H11 **Maningory** Madagascar
140 C1 **Maningrida** N Terr Australia
85 C6 **Maninian** Ivory Coast
69 E13 **Maninjau Danau** *L* Sumatra
73 P4 **Manipur** *R* Burma
75 P6 **Manipur** *prov* India
47 J6 **Manisa** Turkey
17 G5 **Manises** Spain
12 D5 **Man,Isle of** U.K.
70 B6 **Manismata** Kalimantan
94 B2 **Manistee** *R* Michigan U.S.A.
99 U5 **Manistee** Michigan U.S.A.
99 U3 **Manistique** *R* Michigan U.S.A.
99 U4 **Manistique** Michigan U.S.A.
99 V3 **Manistique L** Michigan U.S.A.
99 R9 **Manito** Illinois U.S.A.
114 J6 **Manitoba** Canada
119 S7 **Manitoba, L** Manitoba Canada
118 H6 **Manito L** Saskatchewan Canada
119 T9 **Manitou** Manitoba Canada
109 J1 **Manitou** Oklahoma U.S.A.
119 M7 **Manitou Bch** Saskatchewan Canada
99 T2 **Manitou I** Michigan U.S.A.
99 W4 **Manitou Island, North** Michigan U.S.A.
99 W4 **Manitou Island, South** Michigan U.S.A.
120 J7 **Manitou L** Ontario Canada
122 G3 **Manitou,L** Quebec Canada
120 H7 **Manitoulin I** Ontario Canada
122 G2 **Manitou R** Quebec Canada
106 F3 **Manitou Springs** Colorado U.S.A.
120 E3 **Manitouwadge** Ontario Canada
120 J7 **Manitowaning** Ontario Canada
120 F4 **Manitowik L** Ontario Canada
99 T5 **Manitowoc** Wisconsin U.S.A.
121 P6 **Maniwaki** Quebec Canada
128 C2 **Manizales** Colombia
80 G6 **Manja** Jordan
87 G12 **Manja** Madagascar
143 B10 **Manjimup** W Australia Australia
38 M5 **Mank** Austria
107 M2 **Mankato** Kansas U.S.A.
99 N5 **Mankato** Minnesota U.S.A.
89 G6 **Mankayane** Swaziland
86 B5 **Mankim** Cameroon
109 J2 **Mankins** Texas U.S.A.
85 C7 **Mankono** Ivory Coast
118 K9 **Mankota** Saskatchewan Canada
48 N2 **Man'kovka** Ukraine
83 K8 **Mankulam** Sri Lanka
95 M3 **Manlius** New York U.S.A.
17 J2 **Manlleu** Spain
139 K5 **Manly** New South Wales Australia
145 E2 **Manly** New Zealand
99 N6 **Manly** Iowa U.S.A.
74 F8 **Manmad** India
139 K3 **Mann** *R* New South Wales Australia
140 C2 **Mann** *R* N Terr Australia
138 F4 **Mannahill** South Australia Australia
83 J9 **Mannar** Sri Lanka
73 M7 **Mannar,G.of** India/Sri Lanka
76 D5 **Mannargudi** India
83 J8 **Mannar I** Sri Lanka
36 F5 **Mannheim** Germany
14 A3 **Mannin B** Ireland
139 K4 **Manning** *R* New South Wales Australia
117 P7 **Manning** Alberta Canada
109 P1 **Manning** Arkansas U.S.A.
99 L8 **Manning** Iowa U.S.A.
98 D2 **Manning** North Dakota U.S.A.
112 G4 **Manning** South Carolina U.S.A.
109 N4 **Manning** Texas U.S.A.
117 N11 **Manning Prov. Park** British Columbia Canada
94 G7 **Mannington** West Virginia U.S.A.
9 H4 **Manningtree** England
140 A7 **Mann, Mt** N Terr Australia
140 A7 **Mann Ranges** N Terr/S Aust Australia
112 M2 **Manns Harbor** North Carolina U.S.A.
95 L3 **Mannsville** New York U.S.A.
43 C9 **Mannu** *R* Sardinia
43 B8 **Mannu,C** Sardinia
138 E5 **Mannum** South Australia Australia
118 F5 **Mannville** Alberta Canada
85 B7 **Mano** Sierra Leone
128 E5 **Manoa** Bolivia
80 B8 **Manoah** *R* Israel
127 N1 **Man of War B** Tobago
116 H7 **Manokotak** Alaska U.S.A.
136 G2 **Manokwari** W Irian
46 E6 **Manolás** Greece
87 G12 **Manombo** Madagascar
88 A5 **Manono** Zaire
119 Q9 **Manor** Saskatchewan Canada
112 E6 **Manor** Georgia U.S.A.
109 K5 **Manor** Texas U.S.A.
8 B4 **Manorbier** Wales
144 B6 **Manorburn Res** New Zealand
14 C2 **Manorhamilton** Ireland
85 B7 **Mano River** Liberia
68 D7 **Manoron** Burma
19 P17 **Manosque** France
21 M4 **Manou** France
121 Q5 **Manouane** Quebec Canada
122 B3 **Manouane L** Quebec Canada
61 M8 **Mano-wan** *B* Japan
68 C1 **Man Pan** Burma
134 K9 **Manra** *isld* Phoenix Is Pacific Oc
17 J3 **Manresa** Spain
88 B7 **Mansa** Zambia
85 A6 **Mansaba** Guinea-Bissau
85 A6 **Mansa Konko** The Gambia
71 E4 **Mansalay B** Philippines
71 H5 **Mansalean** Indonesia
68 C1 **Man Sam** Burma
142 G4 **Mansbridge, Mt** W Australia Australia
115 L5 **Mansel I** Northwest Territories Canada
33 O9 **Mansfeld** Germany
139 H6 **Mansfield** Victoria Australia
9 E1 **Mansfield** England
110 B6 **Mansfield** Arkansas U.S.A.
112 D4 **Mansfield** Georgia U.S.A.
99 S9 **Mansfield** Illinois U.S.A.
109 O3 **Mansfield** Louisiana U.S.A.
95 Q4 **Mansfield** Massachusetts U.S.A.
110 D4 **Mansfield** Missouri U.S.A.
94 E6 **Mansfield** Ohio U.S.A.
98 H4 **Mansfield** South Dakota U.S.A.
109 K3 **Mansfield** Texas U.S.A.
100 F2 **Mansfield** Washington U.S.A.
95 P2 **Mansfield,Mt** Vermont U.S.A.
21 L6 **Mansigne** France
56 D4 **Manskoye Belogor'ye** *mts* Russian Federation
18 F7 **Mansle** France
99 M7 **Manson** Iowa U.S.A.
100 E2 **Manson** Washington U.S.A.
117 L8 **Manson Creek** British Columbia Canada
130 C4 **Manso,R** Brazil
80 D1 **Mansoyra** Israel
8 D6 **Manston** England
111 D10 **Mansura** Louisiana U.S.A.
79 B7 **Mansûra,El** Egypt
128 B4 **Manta** Ecuador
71 C6 **Mantalingajan, Mt** Palawan Philippines
70 E1 **Mantanani Besar** *isld* Sabah
86 D6 **Mantantale** Zaire
65 H4 **Mantap-san** *mt* N Korea
71 J5 **Mantarara** Indonesia
118 H7 **Mantario** Saskatchewan Canada
128 C6 **Mantaro** *R* Peru
102 C4 **Manteca** California U.S.A.
111 G8 **Mantee** Mississippi U.S.A.
71 J4 **Mantehase** *isld* Sulawesi
37 N4 **Mantel** Germany
130 H6 **Mantena** Brazil
99 T8 **Manteno** Illinois U.S.A.
112 M2 **Manteo** North Carolina U.S.A.
107 J4 **Manter** Kansas U.S.A.
21 O4 **Mantes-la-Jolie** France
25 E2 **Mantgum** Netherlands
74 H9 **Manthani** India
21 M7 **Manthelan** France
103 N2 **Manti** Utah U.S.A.
130 F8 **Mantiqueira,Serra da** *mts* Brazil
100 D9 **Manton** California U.S.A.
94 B2 **Manton** Michigan U.S.A.
65 B5 **Mantou Shan** *mt ra* China
45 J1 **Mantova** Italy
29 L11 **Mäntsälä** Finland
29 L10 **Mänttä** Finland
126 B3 **Mantua** Cuba
Mantua Italy *see* **Mantova**
94 F5 **Mantua** Ohio U.S.A.
141 H6 **Mantuan Downs** Queensland Australia
52 F5 **Manturovo** Russian Federation
29 J10 **Mäntyluoto** Finland
128 D6 **Manú** Peru
Manuan *see* **Manouane**
122 B3 **Manuanis,L** Quebec Canada
71 F6 **Manucan** Mindanao Philippines
129 J5 **Manuel Alves** *R* Brazil
106 B6 **Manuelito** New Mexico U.S.A.
130 D9 **Manuel Ribas** Brazil
133 C8 **Manuel Rodriguez, I** Chile
128 E5 **Manuel Urbano** Brazil
129 H5 **Manuelzinho** Brazil
71 H6 **Manui** *isld* Indonesia
77 E6 **Manūjān** Iran
145 G2 **Manukau** New Zealand
145 E2 **Manukau Hbr** New Zealand
70 F2 **Manuk Manka** Philippines
138 E4 **Manunda** *R* South Australia Australia
145 E3 **Manunui** New Zealand
71 C3 **Manuran** *isld* W Irian
128 E6 **Manuripe** *R* Bolivia/Peru
136 K2 **Manus** *isld* Bismarck Arch
145 E3 **Manutahi** New Zealand
138 E3 **Manuwalkaninna** South Australia Australia
98 J1 **Manvel** North Dakota U.S.A.
76 C3 **Manvi** India
98 B7 **Manville** Wyoming U.S.A.
109 O4 **Many** Louisiana U.S.A.
52 K4 **Man'ya** Russian Federation
88 B10 **Manyangau** *mt* Zimbabwe
88 G3 **Manyara,L** Tanzania
47 J4 **Manyas** Turkey
118 G9 **Manyberries** Alberta Canada
54 M9 **Manych** *R* Russian Federation
118 G8 **Many Island I** Alberta Canada
88 E4 **Manyoni** Tanzania
141 K6 **Many Peaks** Queensland Australia
143 C10 **Many Peaks, Mt** W Australia Australia
79 B7 **Manzala,El** Egypt
84 J3 **Manzala, L** Egypt
89 E2 **Manzamnyama** *R* Zimbabwe
16 E5 **Manzanares** Spain
127 P2 **Manzanilla B** Trinidad
126 F4 **Manzanillo** Cuba
124 G8 **Manzanillo** Mexico
106 D7 **Manzano** New Mexico U.S.A.
131 A8 **Manzano,B del** Chile
106 G3 **Manzanola** Colorado U.S.A.
106 D7 **Manzano Mts** New Mexico U.S.A.
58 G2 **Manzhouli** China
79 G7 **Manzil** Jordan
89 G6 **Manzini** Swaziland
Manzovka *see* **Sibirtsevo**
86 C3 **Mao** Chad
65 G2 **Mao'ershan** China
136 H2 **Maoke, Pegunungan** *ra* W Irian
65 F4 **Maokui Shan** *mt* China
65 G3 **Maolin** China
67 C6 **Maoming** China
80 D8 **Ma'on** Jordan
67 C1 **Maoping** China
67 G6 **Mao-pi T'ou** *C* Taiwan
67 B3 **Maotai** China
67 A1 **Maowen** China
65 F2 **Maoxing** China
80 F4 **Ma'oz** Israel
87 F10 **Mapai** Mozambique
66 C5 **Mapam Yumco** *L* China
70 G5 **Mapane** Sulawesi
71 D7 **Mapin** Philippines
67 D1 **Maping** China
128 F2 **Mapire** Venezuela
129 H3 **Mapireme** Brazil
128 E7 **Mapiri** *R* La Paz Bolivia
128 F4 **Mapixari, L** Brazil
99 L7 **Maple** *R* Iowa U.S.A.
94 C3 **Maple** *R* Michigan U.S.A.
118 H9 **Maple Creek** Saskatchewan Canada
99 N6 **Maple Island** Minnesota U.S.A.
111 K9 **Maplesville** Alabama U.S.A.
122 H8 **Mapleton** Nova Scotia Canada
99 L7 **Mapleton** Iowa U.S.A.
95 S7 **Mapleton** Maine U.S.A.
99 N6 **Mapleton** Minnesota U.S.A.
100 B5 **Mapleton** Oregon U.S.A.
100 C2 **Maple Valley** Washington U.S.A.
95 L3 **Maple View** New York U.S.A.
141 F1 **Mapoon** Queensland Australia
69 G12 **Mapor** *isld* Indonesia
144 C5 **Mapourika, L** New Zealand
13 H6 **Mappleton** England
129 G4 **Mapuera** *R* Brazil
87 F11 **Maputo** Mozambique
89 H6 **Maputo** *R* Mozambique
80 F8 **Maqam en Nabi Yusha** Jordan
78 H6 **Maqar an Naam** Iraq
46 D3 **Maqellarë** Albania
58 C5 **Maqên Gangri** *mt* China
65 H2 **Maqiaohe** China
79 E10 **Maqnā** Saudi Arabia
66 C6 **Maquan He** *R* China
71 G4 **Maqueda Chan** Philippines
122 H5 **Maquereau Pte.au** Quebec Canada
133 D6 **Maquinchao** Argentina
131 B8 **Maquinchao, R** Argentina
99 Q7 **Maquoketa** Iowa U.S.A.
99 Q9 **Maquon** Illinois U.S.A.
70 G7 **Mara** Sulawesi
127 J9 **Mara** Venezuela
128 E4 **Maraa** Brazil
129 J5 **Marabá** Brazil
70 D6 **Marabahan** Kalimantan
40 B2 **Marac** France
127 J9 **Maracaibo** Venezuela
127 J9 **Maracaibo, L. de** Venezuela
129 H3 **Maracá, Ilha de** Amapá Brazil
128 F3 **Maracá, Ilha de** Roraima Brazil
133 F2 **Maracaju** Brazil
130 C7 **Maracaju,Serra de** *mts* Brazil
129 J4 **Maracana** Brazil
127 O2 **Maracas B** Trinidad
127 L9 **Maracay** Venezuela
84 F4 **Marādah** Libya
85 F6 **Maradi** Niger
145 E3 **Maraetai** New Zealand
78 L3 **Marāgheh** Iran
130 J10 **Maragogi** Brazil
144 D4 **Marahau** New Zealand
128 E3 **Marahuaca,Co** *mt* Venezuela
65 E2 **Marain Sum** China
110 A3 **Marais des Cygnes** *R* Kansas/Missouri U.S.A.
21 L3 **Marais-Vernier** France
129 J4 **Marajó,I.de** Brazil
86 G5 **Maralal** Kenya
55 G4 **Maraldy** Kazakhstan
86 C4 **Marali** Cent Afr Republic
137 N3 **Maramasike** *isld* Solomon Is
Maramba *see* **Livingstone** Zambia
48 H3 **Maramures** *old prov* Romania
69 F11 **Maran** Malaysia
103 N9 **Marana** Arizona U.S.A.
140 C2 **Maranboy** N Terr Australia
17 F3 **Maranchón** Spain
78 K2 **Marand** Iran
45 J2 **Maranello** Italy
68 D7 **Marang** Burma
69 F10 **Marang** Malaysia
129 L4 **Maranguape** Brazil
129 J4 **Maranhão** *state* Brazil
130 E4 **Maranhão** *R* Brazil
141 J7 **Maranoa** *R* Queensland Australia
45 Q8 **Marano di Napoli** Italy
128 D4 **Marañón** *R* Peru
18 E6 **Marans** France
40 A1 **Maranville** France
16 B3 **Marão, Sa do** *mts* Portugal
129 G3 **Marapi** *R* Brazil
43 B8 **Marargiu, C** Sardinia
128 E5 **Marari** Brazil
144 B6 **Mararoa** *R* New Zealand
70 F7 **Marasende** *isld* Indonesia
48 L5 **Mărăşeşti** Romania
71 C6 **Marasi B** Palawan Philippines
16 B6 **Marateca** Portugal
46 D7 **Marathiás,Akr** *C* Greece
120 D4 **Marathon** Ontario Canada
46 F6 **Marathón** Greece
113 F13 **Marathon** Florida U.S.A.
95 L4 **Marathon** New York U.S.A.
108 D5 **Marathon** Texas U.S.A.
99 R5 **Marathon** Wisconsin U.S.A.
70 F3 **Maratua** *isld* Indonesia
129 L6 **Maraú** Brazil
128 E3 **Marauaí** *R* Brazil
127 O2 **Maraval** Trinidad
108 E6 **Maravillas Cr** Texas U.S.A.
71 G7 **Marawi** Mindanao Philippines
38 M5 **Marbach** Austria
36 F2 **Marbach** Germany
22 K4 **Marbehan** Belgium
106 C2 **Marble** Colorado U.S.A.
100 H1 **Marble** Washington U.S.A.
142 C5 **Marble Bar** W Australia Australia
103 N5 **Marble Canyon** Arizona U.S.A.
110 B6 **Marble City** Oklahoma U.S.A.
109 J5 **Marble Falls** Texas U.S.A.
87 E10 **Marble Hall** S Africa
99 P10 **Marblehead** Illinois U.S.A.
95 R4 **Marblehead** Massachusetts U.S.A.
94 E5 **Marblehead** Ohio U.S.A.
99 O7 **Marble Rock** Iowa U.S.A.
121 T7 **Marbleton** Quebec Canada
101 P7 **Marbleton** Wyoming U.S.A.
36 F2 **Marburg** Germany
95 K8 **Marbury** Maryland U.S.A.
26 G8 **Marby** Sweden
48 D3 **Marcal** *R* Hungary
47 J7 **Marçal Dağ** *mt* Turkey
48 D4 **Marcali** Hungary
45 J1 **Marcaria** Italy
122 F2 **Marceau,L** Quebec Canada
118 L6 **Marcelin** Saskatchewan Canada
110 D2 **Marceline** Missouri U.S.A.
133 G3 **Marcelino Ramos** Brazil
110 E6 **Marcella** Arkansas U.S.A.
94 B4 **Marcellus** Michigan U.S.A.
100 G2 **Marcellus** Washington U.S.A.
45 O5 **Marcetelli** Italy
9 G2 **March** England
21 M4 **Marchainville** France
118 E2 **Marchand** Manitoba Canada
138 E4 **Marchant Hill** South Australia Australia
40 D3 **Marchaux** France
18 F6 **Marche** *reg* France
45 N4 **Marche** *reg* Italy
22 J3 **Marche-en-Famenne** Belgium
128 A7 **Marchena** *isld* Galapagos Is
16 D7 **Marchena** Spain
21 N6 **Marchenoir** France
20 H3 **Marchésieux** France
127 P6 **Marchfield** Barbados
22 E3 **Marchiennes-Ville** France
22 J3 **Marchin** Belgium
140 D1 **Marchinbar I** N Terr Australia
131 E3 **Mar Chiquita, L** Córdoba Argentina
45 Q7 **Marcianise** Italy
18 H6 **Marcigny** France
18 G8 **Marcillac** France
21 J5 **Marcille-la-Ville** France
20 H4 **Marcilly** Manche France
21 O7 **Marcilly-en-Gault** France
21 P6 **Marcilly-en-Villette** France
21 N4 **Marcilly-sur-Eure** France
40 G1 **Marckolsheim** France
122 J1 **Marc,L** Labrador, Nfld Canada
113 F12 **Marco** Florida U.S.A.
110 J3 **Marco** Indiana U.S.A.
43 G9 **Marco Argentano, S** Italy
22 E3 **Marcoing** France
100 C5 **Marcola** Oregon U.S.A.
21 M6 **Marçon** France
118 C1 **Marconi** Manitoba Canada
22 K3 **Marcourt** Belgium
19 Q16 **Marcoux** France
99 L7 **Marcus** Iowa U.S.A.
100 G1 **Marcus** Washington U.S.A.
116 O6 **Marcus Baker,Mt** Alaska U.S.A.
134 G5 **Marcus I** Pacific Oc
95 M3 **Marcy** New York U.S.A.
95 O2 **Marcy, Mt** New York U.S.A.
80 D5 **Marda** Jordan
74 E1 **Mardan** Pakistan
131 F6 **Mar del Plata** Argentina
9 G5 **Marden** England
142 B5 **Mardie** W Australia Australia
78 H3 **Mardin** Turkey
26 M5 **Mårdsel** Sweden
26 K7 **Mårdsele** Sweden
26 J7 **Mardsjö** Sweden
26 H8 **Mårdsjön** Sweden
71 A2 **Mare** *isld* Halmahera Indonesia
137 O6 **Maré** *isld* Îles Loyauté Pacific Oc
126 F5 **Marea de Portillo** Cuba
45 M3 **Marecchia** *R* Italy
130 J10 **Marechal Deodoro** Brazil
141 H3 **Mareeba** Queensland Australia
86 A3 **Mareeq** Somalia
86 A2 **Mareer-Gur** Somalia
118 H7 **Marengo** Saskatchewan Canada
41 N7 **Marengo** Italy
110 K3 **Marengo** Indiana U.S.A.
99 P8 **Marengo** Iowa U.S.A.
94 E6 **Marengo** Ohio U.S.A.
100 G2 **Marengo** Washington U.S.A.
99 Q3 **Marengo** Wisconsin U.S.A.
99 R3 **Marenisco** Michigan U.S.A.
18 E7 **Marennes** France
145 E2 **Mareretu** New Zealand
9 G6 **Maresfield** England
43 E11 **Marettimo, I** Sicily
22 E3 **Maretz** France
18 F7 **Mareuil** France
21 P8 **Mareuil-sur-Arnon** France
20 H8 **Mareuil-sur-Lay** France
108 C5 **Marfa** Texas U.S.A.
66 D4 **Margai Caka** *L* China
75 M1 **Margai Caka** *L* China
8 C4 **Margam** Wales
123 L7 **Margaree Harbour** C Breton I, Nova Scotia
123 L7 **Margaree I** Nova Scotia Canada
123 M7 **Margaree Valley** C Breton I, Nova Scotia
138 D3 **Margaret** *R* South Australia Australia
108 H1 **Margaret** Texas U.S.A.
141 G1 **Margaret Bay** Queensland Australia
117 K10 **Margaret Bay** British Columbia Canada
117 Q6 **Margaret L** Alberta Canada
117 P3 **Margaret L** Northwest Territories Canada
142 C5 **Margaret, Mt** W Australia Australia

200 **Margaret R — Maxwelton**

143 B10 **Margaret R** W Australia Australia
95 N4 **Margaretville** New York U.S.A.
130 C7 **Margarida** Brazil
127 N9 **Margarita I. de** Venezuela
46 D5 **Margarítion** Greece
139 H9 **Margate** Tasmania Australia
9 H5 **Margate** England
89 G8 **Margate** S Africa
95 N7 **Margate City** New Jersey U.S.A.
18 H8 **Margeride, Mts de la** France
Margherita *see* **Jamaame** Somalia
48 G3 **Marghita** Romania
118 F3 **Margie** Alberta Canada
99 N1 **Margie** Minnesota U.S.A.
57 F4 **Margilan** Uzbekistan
48 G5 **Margina** Romania
48 G5 **Margita** Serbia Yugoslavia
119 O7 **Margo** Saskatchewan Canada
77 H4 **Margo, Dasht-i-** *desert* Afghanistan
71 F7 **Margosatubig** Mindanao Philippines
94 C2 **Margrethe, L** Michigan U.S.A.
117 M9 **Marguerite** British Columbia Canada
146 C5 **Marguerite B** Antarctica
22 J4 **Margut** France
80 F3 **Marhaba** Jordan
122 F5 **Maria** Quebec Canada
124 F7 **María Cleofas, I** Mexico
28 D3 **Mariager** Denmark
32 M7 **Mariaglück** Germany
140 D2 **Maria I** N Terr Australia
139 J8 **Maria I** Tasmania Australia
68 C7 **Maria I** Burma
36 C3 **Maria Laach** Germany
38 G8 **Maria Luggau** Austria
124 F7 **María Madre, I** Mexico
124 F7 **María Magdalena, I** Mexico
103 K8 **Maria Mts** California U.S.A.
141 J5 **Marian** Queensland Australia
130 G7 **Mariana** Brazil
118 E3 **Mariana Lake** Alberta Canada
126 C3 **Marianao** Cuba
134 E6 **Marianas, Northern** *islds* Pacific Oc
75 Q5 **Mariani** India
117 P4 **Marian L** Northwest Territories Canada
110 F7 **Marianna** Arkansas U.S.A.
113 B7 **Marianna** Florida U.S.A.
27 H14 **Mariannelund** Sweden
37 O4 **Marianské Lázně** Czechoslovakia
119 T9 **Mariapolis** Manitoba Canada
101 N1 **Marias** *R* Montana U.S.A.
17 F7 **Maria,Sierra de** *mts* Spain
124 F7 **Marías, Islas** *islds* Mexico
101 M1 **Marias Pass** Montana U.S.A.
38 F6 **Mariastein** Austria
135 M12 **Maria Theresa Reef** Pacific Oc
145 D1 **Maria van Diemen, C** New Zealand
38 M6 **Mariazell** Austria
99 T5 **Maribel** Wisconsin U.S.A.
Maribo *co see* **Storstrøm** *co*
28 G7 **Maribo** Denmark
38 N8 **Maribor** Slovenia
71 E4 **Maricaban** *isld* Philippines
89 E5 **Marico** *R* Botswana
103 M8 **Maricopa** Arizona U.S.A.
102 E6 **Maricopa** California U.S.A.
103 M8 **Maricopa Mts** Arizona U.S.A.
Maricourt *see* **Kangiqsujuaq**
86 E5 **Maridi** Sudan
128 E4 **Marié** *R* Brazil
83 K12 **Marie Anne I** Seychelles
146 C8 **Marie Byrd Land** Antarctica
146 A8 **Marie Byrd Seamount** *seamount* Antarctica
27 H13 **Mariedam** Sweden
27 J12 **Mariefred** Sweden
127 N5 **Marie Galante** *isld* Guadeloupe W Indies
27 L11 **Mariehamn** Finland
118 G4 **Marie L** Alberta Canada
126 C3 **Mariel** Cuba
Marienbad *see* **Marianské Lázně**
32 L8 **Marienberg** Germany
37 P2 **Marienberg** Germany
25 G3 **Marienberg** Netherlands
22 H3 **Marienbourg** Belgium
Marienburg *see* **Malbork**
36 C2 **Marienburg** Nordrhein-Westfalen Germany
37 N3 **Marieney** Germany
32 F5 **Marienhafe** Germany
36 C1 **Marienheide** Germany
28 G7 **Marienleuchte** *C* Germany
89 A5 **Mariental** Namibia
107 J3 **Marienthal** Kansas U.S.A.
94 H5 **Marienville** Pennsylvania U.S.A.
140 B1 **Marie Shoal** N Terr Australia
27 G13 **Mariestad** Sweden
112 C4 **Marietta** Georgia U.S.A.
94 F7 **Marietta** Ohio U.S.A.
109 K2 **Marietta** Oklahoma U.S.A.
112 E2 **Marietta** South Carolina U.S.A.
121 R7 **Marieville** Quebec Canada
19 O18 **Marignane** France
21 J6 **Marigné** Maine-et-Loire France
21 L6 **Marigné** Sarthe France
20 H3 **Marigny** France
127 N5 **Marigot** Saint Martin W Indies
55 A3 **Mariinsk** Russian Federation
56 C3 **Mariinsk** Russian Federation
55 D4 **Mariinskoye** Russian Federation
52 G6 **Mariinsky Posad** Russian Federation
31 O1 **Marijampolė** Lithuania
71 J5 **Marikasu,Tg** *C* Indonesia
130 D8 **Marila** Brazil
133 H2 **Marília** Brazil
142 C5 **Marillana** W Australia Australia
130 E7 **Marimbondo Cachoeira** *rapids* Brazil
70 D5 **Marimun** Kalimantan
16 B2 **Marín** Spain
127 M4 **Marin** Martinique W Indies
102 C5 **Marina** California U.S.A.
44 H3 **Marina di Carrara** Italy
44 H3 **Marina di Massa** Italy
44 H4 **Marina di Pisa** Italy
45 M3 **Marina di Ravenna** Italy
128 G2 **Marina Fall** Guyana
53 C7 **Mar'ina Gorka** Belorussia
71 E4 **Marinduque** *isld* Philippines
110 G3 **Marine** Illinois U.S.A.
113 F8 **Marineland** Florida U.S.A.
21 P3 **Marines** France
99 T4 **Marinette** Wisconsin U.S.A.
129 H8 **Maringá** Brazil
86 D5 **Maringa** *R* Zaire
111 E11 **Maringouin** Louisiana U.S.A.
87 F9 **Maringue** Mozambique
16 B5 **Marinha Grande** Portugal
54 J9 **Mar'inka** Ukraine
42 E7 **Marino** Italy
128 E3 **Marinuma** Colombia
111 J9 **Marion** Alabama U.S.A.
110 F6 **Marion** Arkansas U.S.A.
117 Q11 **Marion** Idaho U.S.A.
110 H4 **Marion** Illinois U.S.A.
94 B6 **Marion** Indiana U.S.A.
99 P7 **Marion** Iowa U.S.A.
107 O3 **Marion** Kansas U.S.A.
110 H4 **Marion** Kentucky U.S.A.
111 D9 **Marion** Louisiana U.S.A.
95 U2 **Marion** Maine U.S.A.
94 B2 **Marion** Michigan U.S.A.
111 H9 **Marion** Mississippi U.S.A.
101 L1 **Marion** Montana U.S.A.
98 F9 **Marion** Nebraska U.S.A.
112 E2 **Marion** North Carolina U.S.A.
98 H3 **Marion** North Dakota U.S.A.
94 D6 **Marion** Ohio U.S.A.
112 H3 **Marion** South Carolina U.S.A.
98 J6 **Marion** South Dakota U.S.A.
109 J6 **Marion** Texas U.S.A.
94 F10 **Marion** Virginia U.S.A.
99 S5 **Marion** Wisconsin U.S.A.
139 J8 **Marion B** Tasmania Australia
140 E6 **Marion Downs** Queensland Australia
111 J9 **Marion Junction** Alabama U.S.A.
141 K4 **Marion Reef** Gt Barrier Reef Aust
141 L4 **Marion Reef** Coral Sea
110 C4 **Marionville** Missouri U.S.A.
128 E2 **Maripa** Venezuela
71 G5 **Maripipi** *isld* Philippines
102 D4 **Mariposa** *R* California U.S.A.
102 E4 **Mariposa** California U.S.A.
70 G4 **Marisa** Sulawesi
133 E2 **Mariscal Estigarribia** Paraguay
110 G3 **Marissa** Illinois U.S.A.
46 G2 **Maritsa** *R* Bulgaria
47 R14 **Maritsa** Rhodes Greece
44 B3 **Marittime, Alpi** *mts* Italy/France
52 G6 **Mari Turek** Russian Federation
54 J9 **Mariupol'** Ukraine
127 O10 **Mariusa** *R* Venezuela
78 L4 **Marīvān** Iran
52 G6 **Mariyskaya Respublika** Russian Federation
77 J4 **Marja** Afghanistan
84 G3 **Marj, Al** Libya
77 A5 **Marjan, Al** *oil well* Persian Gulf
26 N5 **Marjärv** Sweden
79 F5 **Marjayoûn** Lebanon
25 C5 **Mark** *R* Netherlands
80 G6 **Marka** Jordan
86 H5 **Marka** Somalia
26 E8 **Markabygd** Norway
56 C6 **Markakal', Oz** *L* Kazakhstan
52 J4 **Markalasta** Russian Federation
58 C6 **Markam** China
76 D3 **Markapur** India
77 A2 **Markazī** *prov* Iran
120 K8 **Markdale** Ontario Canada
41 K2 **Markdorf** Germany
110 F6 **Marked Tree** Arkansas U.S.A.
25 G4 **Markelo** Netherlands
28 G7 **Markelsdorfe Huk** *C* Germany
25 D4 **Marken** Netherlands
25 D3 **Markerwaard** Netherlands
99 S6 **Markesan** Wisconsin U.S.A.
9 F2 **Market Deeping** England
8 D2 **Market Drayton** England
9 F3 **Market Harborough** England
14 E2 **Markethill** N Ireland
13 H6 **Market Rasen** England
9 E1 **Market Warsop** England
13 H6 **Market Weighton** England
36 G6 **Markgröningen** Germany
121 L9 **Markham** Ontario Canada
109 L7 **Markham** Texas U.S.A.
100 B3 **Markham** Washington U.S.A.
9 F1 **Markham Moor** England
146 D10 **Markham, Mt** Antarctica
31 N3 **Marki** Poland
119 N8 **Markinch** Saskatchewan Canada
15 E4 **Markinch** Scotland
33 T8 **Märkisch Buchholz** Germany
66 B4 **Markit** China
26 M4 **Markitta** Sweden
102 E3 **Markleeville** California U.S.A.
37 O6 **Marklkofen** Germany
37 N3 **Markneukirchen** Germany
26 J4 **Markotjakko** *mt* Sweden
33 Q10 **Markrapstädt** Germany
111 F7 **Marks** Mississippi U.S.A.
8 D5 **Marksbury** England
120 K6 **Markstay** Ontario Canada
9 G4 **Marks Tey** England
37 J2 **Marksuhl** Germany
111 D10 **Marksville** Louisiana U.S.A.
37 J5 **Marktbergel** Germany
37 J4 **Markt Bibart** Germany
37 J4 **Marktbreit** Germany
37 L3 **Marktgraitz** Germany
36 H4 **Marktheidenfeld** Germany
37 L7 **Markt Indersdorf** Germany
37 O7 **Marktl** Germany
37 M3 **Marktleugast** Germany
37 J6 **Marktoffingen** Germany
37 N3 **Marktredwitz** Germany
37 M3 **Marktschorgast** Germany
37 J4 **Marktsteft** Germany
38 M7 **Markt-Übelbach** Austria
110 E2 **Mark Twain L** Missouri U.S.A.
41 N1 **Markt Wald** Germany
37 L3 **Marktzeuln** Germany
99 O3 **Markville** Minnesota U.S.A.
32 F9 **Marl** Germany
107 N5 **Marland** Oklahoma U.S.A.
143 B8 **Marlandy Hill** W Australia Australia
121 N8 **Marlbank** Ontario Canada
95 P4 **Marlboro** New Hampshire U.S.A.
141 J6 **Marlborough** Queensland Australia
9 E5 **Marlborough** England
128 G2 **Marlborough** Guyana
145 D4 **Marlborough** *admin region* New Zealand
95 Q4 **Marlborough** Massachusetts U.S.A.
22 F4 **Marle** France
33 S8 **Marlendorf** Germany
33 S8 **Marlenfelde** Germany
94 D3 **Marlette** Michigan U.S.A.
19 O12 **Marlieux** France
109 L4 **Marlin** Texas U.S.A.
94 G8 **Marlinton** West Virginia U.S.A.
139 J7 **Marlo** Victoria Australia
22 J3 **Marloie** Belgium
9 F4 **Marlow** England
33 R4 **Marlow** Germany
95 P3 **Marlow** New Hampshire U.S.A.
109 K1 **Marlow** Oklahoma U.S.A.
22 F4 **Marly** France
27 J10 **Marma** Sweden
110 F5 **Marmaduke** Arkansas U.S.A.
21 P7 **Marmagne** Cher France
18 F8 **Marmande** France
47 J4 **Marmara Adasi** *isld* Turkey
47 J4 **Marmara Denizi** Turkey
47 J4 **Marmaraereğlisi** Turkey
47 J6 **Marmara Gölü** *L* Turkey
Marmara, Sea of *see* **Marmara Denizi**
47 J8 **Marmaris** Turkey
98 C3 **Marmarth** North Dakota U.S.A.
26 K3 **Mårmatj** *mt* Sweden
94 E4 **Marme City** Michigan U.S.A.
16 B2 **Marmed,Sa des S** *mts* Spain
128 F5 **Marmelos** *R* Brazil
94 F8 **Marmet** West Virginia U.S.A.
121 P4 **Marmette,L** Quebec Canada
118 L1 **Marmion L** *res* Ontario Canada
143 C8 **Marmion, Mt** W Australia Australia
45 J1 **Marmirolo** Italy
42 D2 **Marmolada** *mt* Italy
16 E6 **Marmolejo** Spain
116 L7 **Marmot B** Alaska U.S.A.
125 M9 **Mar Muerto** *B* Mexico
19 J5 **Marnay** France
18 H4 **Marne** *dept* France
40 B1 **Marne** *R* France
32 K5 **Marne** Germany
36 B6 **Marne, Canal de la** France
36 D4 **Marnheim** Germany
33 P6 **Marnitz** Germany
139 G6 **Marnoo** Victoria Australia
145 F3 **Maroa** New Zealand
99 S9 **Maroa** Illinois U.S.A.
87 H11 **Maroantsetra** Madagascar
74 C2 **Marobi** Pakistan
22 F3 **Maroilles** France
37 K3 **Maroldsweisach** Germany
21 L5 **Marolles-les-Braults** France
87 H10 **Maromandia** Madagascar
21 N3 **Maromme** France
21 O8 **Mâron** Indre France
89 G2 **Marondera** Zimbabwe
47 H4 **Marónia** Greece
18 G7 **Maronne** *R* France
141 L7 **Maroochydore** Queensland Australia
143 B6 **Maroonah** W Australia
127 J2 **Maroon Town** Jamaica
70 F7 **Maros** *R* Sulawesi
70 F7 **Maros** Sulawesi
145 E1 **Marotiri Is** New Zealand
86 B3 **Maroua** Cameroon
20 E5 **Maroué** France
121 L4 **Marouf Jct** Quebec Canada
22 D3 **Marœuil** France
129 H3 **Marouini** *R* Fr Guiana
87 H11 **Marovoay** Madagascar
78 H4 **Marqādah** Syria
110 F4 **Marquano** Missouri U.S.A.
135 U13 **Marquesas Is** Pacific Oc
113 E13 **Marquesas Keys** *islds* Florida U.S.A.
130 G8 **Marquês de Valença** Brazil
118 D1 **Marquette** Manitoba Canada
99 P6 **Marquette** Iowa U.S.A.
107 N3 **Marquette** Kansas U.S.A.
99 T3 **Marquette** Michigan U.S.A.
99 U6 **Marquette** *R* Michigan U.S.A.
98 H8 **Marquette** Nebraska U.S.A.
106 C6 **Marquez** New Mexico U.S.A.
109 L4 **Marquez** Texas U.S.A.
17 F1 **Marquina** Spain
22 E3 **Marquion** France
119 M8 **Marquis** Saskatchewan Canada
22 B2 **Marquise** France
139 G4 **Marra** New South Wales Australia
139 H4 **Marra** *R* New South Wales Australia
89 H5 **Marracuene** Mozambique
45 L3 **Marradi** Italy
143 B10 **Marradong** W Australia Australia
86 D3 **Marra, Jebel** *mts* Sudan
140 B2 **Marrakai** N Terr Australia
85 C2 **Marrakech** Morocco
85 E2 **Marraket, Hassi** Algeria
139 H5 **Marrar** New South Wales Australia
139 G8 **Marrawah** Tasmania Australia
28 H7 **Marrebæk** Denmark
138 E3 **Marree** South Australia Australia
111 J13 **Marrero** New Orleans, Louisiana U.S.A.
87 G9 **Marromeu** Mozambique
16 D8 **Marroqui,Pta** Spain
88 F8 **Marrupa** Mozambique
94 G6 **Mars** Pennsylvania U.S.A.
84 K4 **Marsá Alam** Egypt
17 F9 **Marsa Ben Mehidi** Algeria
86 G5 **Marsabit** Kenya
Marsa Brega *see* **Al Burayqah**
20 G6 **Marsac-sur-Don** France
130 F8 **Mar,Sa.do** *mts* Brazil
36 B6 **Marsal** France
43 E11 **Marsala** Sicily
19 N15 **Marsanne** France
139 J5 **Marsden** New South Wales Australia
118 H6 **Marsden** Saskatchewan Canada
13 G4 **Marsden** England
19 O18 **Marseille** France
21 O2 **Marseille-en-Beauvaisis** France
19 N18 **Marseille-Rhône, Canal** France
Marseilles France *see* **Marseille**
99 S8 **Marseilles** Illinois U.S.A.
94 D6 **Marseilles** Ohio U.S.A.
98 B3 **Marsh** Montana U.S.A.
79 E10 **Marshah, J** *mt* Saudi Arabia
118 H5 **Marshall** Saskatchewan Canada
110 D6 **Marshall** Arkansas U.S.A.
99 T10 **Marshall** Illinois U.S.A.
94 C4 **Marshall** Michigan U.S.A.
99 L5 **Marshall** Minnesota U.S.A.
110 C2 **Marshall** Missouri U.S.A.
112 E2 **Marshall** North Carolina U.S.A.
98 D2 **Marshall** North Dakota U.S.A.
107 N5 **Marshall** Oklahoma U.S.A.
109 N3 **Marshall** Texas U.S.A.
94 K8 **Marshall** Virginia U.S.A.
101 U7 **Marshall** Wyoming U.S.A.
139 J7 **Marshall B** Tasmania Australia
134 G7 **Marshall Is** Pacific Oc
120 C2 **Marshall L** Ontario Canada
99 O7 **Marshalltown** Iowa U.S.A.
8 D3 **Marshbrook** England
8 D5 **Marshfield** England
110 D4 **Marshfield** Missouri U.S.A.
99 Q5 **Marshfield** Wisconsin U.S.A.
113 K11 **Marsh Harbour** Great Abaco I Bahamas
95 L5 **Marsh Hill** Pennsylvania U.S.A.
95 T7 **Mars Hill** Maine U.S.A.
111 D12 **Marsh Island** Louisiana U.S.A.
117 F5 **Marsh L** Yukon Territory Canada
98 K4 **Marsh Lake** Minnesota U.S.A.
101 Q9 **Marsh Pk** Utah U.S.A.
112 G3 **Marshville** North Carolina U.S.A.
100 J6 **Marsing** Idaho U.S.A.
13 G4 **Marske-by-the-Sea** England
98 C7 **Marsland** Nebraska U.S.A.
19 J3 **Mars la Tour** France
28 E4 **Mårslet** Denmark
28 F6 **Marslev** Denmark
25 E2 **Marssum** Netherlands
27 J12 **Märsta** Sweden
28 F7 **Marstal** Denmark
28 E7 **Marstal Bugt** *B* Denmark
101 Q8 **Marston** Wyoming U.S.A.
27 E14 **Marstrand** Sweden
28 C6 **Marstrup** Denmark
55 D1 **Marsyaty** Russian Federation
109 L4 **Mart** Texas U.S.A.
42 D6 **Marta** *R* Italy
68 C4 **Martaban** Burma
73 Q5 **Martaban,G.of** Burma
21 L8 **Martaizé** France
70 D6 **Martapura** Kalimantan
70 K8 **Martapura** Sumatra
18 G8 **Martel** France
22 K4 **Martelange** Belgium
45 M1 **Martellago** Italy
41 N4 **Martello, Val** Italy
47 H1 **Marten** Bulgaria
99 N8 **Martensdale** Iowa U.S.A.
17 G5 **Martés,Sierra** *mts* Spain
139 J4 **Marthaguy** *R* New South Wales Australia
110 E3 **Marthasville** Missouri U.S.A.
95 R5 **Marthas Vineyard** Massachusetts U.S.A.
36 B6 **Marthille** France
126 F4 **Martí** Cuba
45 M5 **Martignano,L.di** Italy
21 J5 **Martigné** France
21 K7 **Martigné Briand** France
20 H6 **Martigné-Ferchaud** France
40 F5 **Martigny** Switzerland
40 C1 **Martigny-les-Bains** France
19 O18 **Martigues** France
16 D9 **Martil** Morocco
31 L6 **Martin** Czechoslovakia
17 G4 **Martin** *R* Spain
116 N4 **Martin** Alaska U.S.A.
94 E9 **Martin** Kentucky U.S.A.
94 B4 **Martin** Michigan U.S.A.
98 E6 **Martin** South Dakota U.S.A.
110 H5 **Martin** Tennessee U.S.A.
41 M4 **Martina** Switzerland
43 H8 **Martina Franca** Italy
145 E4 **Martinborough** New Zealand
109 K6 **Martindale** Texas U.S.A.
125 L7 **Martínez** Mexico
102 B3 **Martinez** California U.S.A.
32 M10 **Martinfeld** Germany
130 F6 **Martinho Campos** Brazil
127 L4 **Martinique** *isld* Lesser Antilles
111 L9 **Martin L** Alabama U.S.A.
130 D8 **Martinópolis** Brazil
146 B8 **Martin Pen** Antarctica
116 Q1 **Martin Pt** Alaska U.S.A.
144 A6 **Martins B** New Zealand
38 M5 **Martinsberg** Austria
Martinsbrück *see* **Martina**
110 E2 **Martinsburg** Missouri U.S.A.
95 M3 **Martinsburg** New York U.S.A.
94 E6 **Martinsburg** Ohio U.S.A.
94 J6 **Martinsburg** Pennsylvania U.S.A.
94 K7 **Martinsburg** West Virginia U.S.A.
101 P3 **Martinsdale** Montana U.S.A.
94 G6 **Martins Ferry** Ohio U.S.A.
99 T10 **Martinsville** Illinois U.S.A.
94 A7 **Martinsville** Indiana U.S.A.
94 H10 **Martinsville** Virginia U.S.A.
20 G2 **Martinvast** France
21 N8 **Martizay** France
9 H3 **Martlesham** England
8 D6 **Martock** England
28 F5 **Martofte** Denmark
9 F1 **Marton** England
145 E4 **Marton** New Zealand
17 J3 **Martorell** Spain
16 E7 **Martos** Spain
117 O4 **Martre, Lac La** Northwest Territories Canada
117 P4 **Martre, Lac la** Northwest Territories Canada
29 N4 **Martti** Finland
29 K11 **Marttila** Finland
55 C5 **Martuk** Kazakhstan
52 J2 **Martyn** Russian Federation
80 G3 **Maru** Jordan
70 B6 **Marua** Kalimantan
77 H2 **Maruchak** Afghanistan
70 D2 **Marudi** Sarawak
70 E1 **Marudu Bay** Sabah
77 K4 **Maruf** Afghanistan
60 G11 **Marugame** Japan
144 D5 **Maruia** New Zealand
144 D5 **Maruia Springs** New Zealand
129 L6 **Maruim** Brazil
139 J5 **Marulan** New South Wales Australia
28 J4 **Mårum** Denmark
25 F2 **Marum** Netherlands
145 F3 **Marumaru** New Zealand
140 C2 **Marumba Mt** N Terr Australia
88 B5 **Marungu** *mts* Zaire
61 K9 **Maruoka** Japan
77 D4 **Marvast** Iran
27 C11 **Mår-vatn** *L* Norway
18 H8 **Marvejols** France
111 F7 **Marvell** Arkansas U.S.A.
143 C9 **Marvel Loch** W Australia Australia
22 J5 **Marville** France
98 K4 **Marvin** South Dakota U.S.A.
106 C1 **Marvine** Colorado U.S.A.
103 N3 **Marvine,Mt** Utah U.S.A.
77 H2 **Marwa** Afghanistan
74 E6 **Marwar** India
118 G5 **Marwayne** Alberta Canada
15 E1 **Marwick Hd** Orkney Scotland
32 G6 **Marx** Germany
33 S9 **Marxdorf** Germany
37 M3 **Marxgrün** Germany
77 G1 **Mary** Turkmenistan
55 F3 **Mar'yanovka** Russian Federation
139 G6 **Maryborough** New South Wales Australia
141 L7 **Maryborough** Queensland Australia
87 D11 **Marydale** S Africa
55 E4 **Mar'yevka** Kazakhstan
119 Q9 **Maryfield** Saskatchewan Canada
117 L6 **Mary Henry,Mt** British Columbia Canada
12 D2 **Maryhill** Scotland
111 E10 **Mary,L** Mississippi U.S.A.
95 K7 **Maryland** *state* U.S.A.
89 G1 **Maryland** Zimbabwe
108 G3 **Maryneal** Texas U.S.A.
12 E4 **Maryport** England
141 K7 **Mary R** Queensland Australia
123 R1 **Mary's Hbr** Labrador, Nfld Canada
100 K8 **Marys R** Nevada U.S.A.
123 R6 **Marystown** Newfoundland Canada
103 M3 **Marysvale** Utah U.S.A.
122 F8 **Marysville** New Brunswick Canada
101 O5 **Marysville** Idaho U.S.A.
107 O2 **Marysville** Kansas U.S.A.
94 E4 **Marysville** Michigan U.S.A.
94 D6 **Marysville** Ohio U.S.A.
100 C1 **Marysville** Washington U.S.A.
141 H4 **Maryvale** Queensland Australia
141 K8 **Maryvale** Queensland Australia
99 M9 **Maryville** Missouri U.S.A.
112 D2 **Maryville** Tennessee U.S.A.
45 K3 **Marzabotto** Italy
85 D5 **Marzafal** Mali
130 E5 **Marzagão** Brazil
33 R8 **Marzahna** Germany
33 R7 **Marzahne** Germany
20 F6 **Marzan** France
128 C2 **Marzo,C** Colombia
70 O9 **Mas** *R* Java
69 D13 **Masa** *isld* Indonesia
Masada *see* **Mezada**
80 F1 **Mas'ada** Syria
88 E2 **Masai Mara Game Reserve** Kenya
88 E2 **Masai Mara National Reserve** *nat park* Kenya
88 F4 **Masai Steppe** Tanzania
88 C2 **Masaka** Uganda
86 C3 **Masalasef** Chad
70 D7 **Masalembu Besar** *isld* Indonesia
70 D7 **Masalembu Kecil** *isld* Indonesia
70 G6 **Masamba** Sulawesi
65 G7 **Masan** S Korea
71 N8 **Masapun** Indonesia
95 S7 **Masardis** Maine U.S.A.
113 E9 **Masaryktown** Florida U.S.A.
88 G7 **Masasi** Tanzania
Mas Atierra *isld see* **Robinson Crusoe** *isld*
71 F4 **Masbate** *isld* Philippines
32 F9 **Masbeck** Germany
17 H9 **Mascara** Algeria
81 C7 **Mascarene Basin** Indian Oc
81 C7 **Mascarene Is** Indian Oc
81 C7 **Mascarene Rge** Indian Oc
98 G9 **Mascot** Nebraska U.S.A.
112 D1 **Mascot** Tennessee U.S.A.
130 H4 **Mascote** Brazil
110 G3 **Mascoutah** Illinois U.S.A.
18 F9 **Mas d'Azil, le** France
118 K9 **Masefield** Saskatchewan Canada
70 E3 **Ma Sekatok** Kalimantan
71 O9 **Masela** *isld* Indonesia
38 N7 **Masenberg** *mt* Austria
45 L1 **Masera di P** Italy
121 P4 **Masères,L** Quebec Canada
89 E7 **Maseru** Lesotho
40 E2 **Masevaux** France
13 G5 **Masham** England
65 H2 **Mashan** China
67 C5 **Mashan** China
80 G1 **Mashārah** Syria
80 E7 **Mashash** *R* Jordan
87 F9 **Mashava** Zimbabwe
80 F2 **Mashfa** Syria
77 F1 **Mashhad** Iran
85 E7 **Mashi** *R* Nigeria
60 P2 **Mashike** Japan
77 E5 **Mashīz** Iran
77 H5 **Māshkei, Hāmūn-i-** *marsh* Pakistan
77 H6 **Mashkel** *R* Pakistan
120 F5 **Mashkode** Ontario Canada
88 C10 **Mashonaland Central** *prov* Zimbabwe
88 D10 **Mashonaland East** *prov* Zimbabwe
88 B10 **Mashonaland West** *prov* Zimbabwe
89 C6 **Mashowing** *watercourse* S Africa
95 R5 **Mashpee** Massachusetts U.S.A.
60 S2 **Mashū-ko** *L* Japan
26 N2 **Masi** Norway
124 E4 **Masiáca** Mexico
86 C6 **Masi-Manimba** Zaire
70 F5 **Masimbu** Sulawesi
86 F5 **Masindi** Uganda
71 D3 **Masinloc** Luzon Philippines
72 H4 **Maşīrah** *isld* Oman
77 B4 **Masiri** Iran
89 G5 **Masitonto** *R* S Africa
77 A4 **Masjed Soleymān** Iran
125 P9 **Maskall** Belize
78 G3 **Maskanah** Syria
121 R6 **Maskinongé** Quebec Canada
14 B3 **Mask,L** Ireland
29 J11 **Masku** Finland
47 J2 **Maslen Nos, N.** Bulgaria
55 D1 **Maslovo** Russian Federation
56 B4 **Maslyanino** Russian Federation
55 F3 **Maslyanskiy** Russian Federation
28 H7 **Masnedssund** Denmark
22 E3 **Masnieres** France
87 I11 **Masoala, Tanjona** *C* Madagascar
110 H3 **Mason** Illinois U.S.A.
94 C4 **Mason** Michigan U.S.A.
102 E3 **Mason** Nevada U.S.A.
110 M2 **Mason** Ohio U.S.A.
110 G6 **Mason** Tennessee U.S.A.
109 H5 **Mason** Texas U.S.A.
99 P3 **Mason** Wisconsin U.S.A.
101 P7 **Mason** Wyoming U.S.A.
144 A7 **Mason Bay** New Zealand
99 R9 **Mason City** Illinois U.S.A.
99 N6 **Mason City** Iowa U.S.A.
98 G8 **Mason City** Nebraska U.S.A.
117 M7 **Mason Creek** British Columbia Canada
88 F3 **Masongaleni** Kenya
71 J5 **Masoni** *isld* Indonesia
143 C8 **Mason, L** W Australia Australia
94 H7 **Masontown** Pennsylvania U.S.A.
94 H7 **Masontown** West Virginia U.S.A.
26 O1 **Måsöy** *isld* Norway
77 F7 **Masqat** Oman
99 R3 **Mass** Michigan U.S.A.
44 H3 **Massa** Italy
95 P4 **Massachusetts** *state* U.S.A.
95 R4 **Massachusetts B** U.S.A.
45 H4 **Massaciuccoli,L.di** Italy
100 F8 **Massacre L** Nevada U.S.A.
80 F3 **Massada** Israel
106 B1 **Massadona** Colorado U.S.A.
45 M2 **Massa Fiscáglia** Italy
86 C3 **Massaguet** Chad
86 C3 **Massakoti** Chad
45 L3 **Massa Lombarda** Italy
45 Q8 **Massa Lubrense** Italy
42 D5 **Massa Marittima** Italy
87 F10 **Massanga** Mozambique
87 F10 **Massangena** Mozambique
94 J8 **Massanutten Mt** Virginia U.S.A.
129 K4 **Massape** Brazil
94 K8 **Massaponax** Virginia U.S.A.
45 H4 **Massarosa** Italy
18 F10 **Massat** France
55 D1 **Massava** Russian Federation
Massawa *see* **Mits'iwa**
21 O7 **Massay** France
37 J3 **Massbach** Germany
99 M8 **Massena** Iowa U.S.A.
95 N2 **Massena** New York U.S.A.
86 C3 **Massénya** Chad
20 G6 **Masserac** France
117 G9 **Masset** British Columbia Canada
18 F9 **Masseube** France
120 H6 **Massey** Ontario Canada
18 H7 **Massiac** France
45 P7 **Massico, M** *mt* Italy
94 H9 **Massies Mill** Virginia U.S.A.
18 H7 **Massif Central** *plateau* France
18 F10 **Massif de Néouvieille** *mt* France
86 D4 **Massif des Bongos** *mts* Cent Afr Republic
19 Q18 **Massif des Maures** *mts* France
85 F4 **Massif de Tarazit** *mts* Niger
85 G5 **Massif de Termit** *mts* Niger
19 O15 **Massif du Diois** *mts* France
19 Q15 **Massif du Pelvoux** *mts* France
86 D4 **Massif du Tondou** *mts* Cent Afr Republic
94 F6 **Massillon** Ohio U.S.A.
87 G10 **Massinga** Mozambique
89 G4 **Massingir** Mozambique
121 P7 **Masson** Quebec Canada
146 H13 **Masson I** Antarctica
80 C7 **Massu'a** Israel
74 B4 **Mastang** Pakistan
27 K14 **Mästerby** Sweden
145 E4 **Masterton** New Zealand
95 P6 **Mastic Beach** Long I, New York U.S.A.
126 E2 **Mastic Point** Andros Bahamas
47 H6 **Mástikho,Akr** *C* Greece
37 P3 **Maštov** Czechoslovakia
74 E1 **Mastuj** Pakistan
60 E11 **Masuda** Japan
Masulipatnam *see* **Machilipatnam**
89 G3 **Masvingo** Zimbabwe
79 G3 **Masyāf** Syria
46 D3 **Mat** *R* Albania
68 F5 **Mat** *R* Thailand
133 C7 **Mata Amarilla** Argentina
89 E2 **Matabeleland North** *prov* Zimbabwe
89 F3 **Matabeleland South** *prov* Zimbabwe
71 H4 **Matabulawa** *mt* Sulawesi
88 F8 **Mataca** Mozambique
120 K5 **Matachewan** Ontario Canada
86 B7 **Matadi** Zaire
118 K8 **Matador** Saskatchewan Canada
108 G1 **Matador** Texas U.S.A.
125 M3 **Matagalpa** Nicaragua
121 N3 **Matagami** Quebec Canada
109 M7 **Matagorda** Texas U.S.A.
109 L7 **Matagorda I** Texas U.S.A.
130 H10 **Mata Grande** Brazil
145 F3 **Matahina** New Zealand
145 E3 **Matahiwi** New Zealand
134 C12 **Mataiea** Tahiti Pacific Oc
145 F4 **Mataikona** New Zealand
69 H11 **Matak** *isld* Indonesia
139 H5 **Matakana** New South Wales Australia
145 E2 **Matakana** New Zealand
145 F2 **Matakana I** New Zealand
145 G2 **Matakaoa Pt** New Zealand
144 D5 **Matakitaki** *R* New Zealand
145 D4 **Matakitaki** New Zealand
145 E2 **Matakohe** New Zealand
87 C8 **Matala** Angola
85 B5 **Matam** Senegal
145 E2 **Matamata** New Zealand
145 F4 **Matamau** New Zealand
85 F6 **Matameye** Niger
95 N5 **Matamoras** Pennsylvania U.S.A.
124 H5 **Matamoros** Coahuila Mexico
125 L5 **Matamoros** Tamaulipas Mexico
70 G6 **Matana, Danao** *L* Sulawesi
71 F7 **Matanal Pt** Philippines
84 G5 **Ma'ţan as Sārah** Libya
84 G5 **Ma'ţan Bishrah** *well* Libya
88 G6 **Matandu** *R* Tanzania
122 E5 **Matane** Quebec Canada
122 F5 **Matane,Parc** Quebec Canada
122 E5 **Matane R** Quebec Canada
145 E2 **Matangi** New Zealand
145 E2 **Matangi I** New Zealand
113 J10 **Matanilla Reef** Bahamas
116 O6 **Matanuska** *mt* Alaska U.S.A.
126 D3 **Matanzas** Cuba
113 F8 **Matanzas Inlet** Florida U.S.A.
131 C6 **Matanzilla, Pampa de la** *plain* Argentina
129 H5 **Matão, Serra do** *mts* Brazil
Matapán, C Greece *see* **Taínaron, Akr**
122 F6 **Matapedia** Quebec Canada
122 E5 **Matapedia L** Quebec Canada
122 E5 **Matapedia R** Quebec Canada
16 D3 **Matapozuelos** Spain
131 B5 **Mataquito** *R* Chile
83 K12 **Matara** Sri Lanka
70 Q10 **Mataram** Indonesia
128 D7 **Matarani** Peru
140 C2 **Mataranka** N Terr Australia
71 H6 **Matarape,Tk** *B* Sulawesi
17 J3 **Mataró** Spain
145 E3 **Mataroa** New Zealand
70 G6 **Matarombeo** *R* Sulawesi
17 F3 **Mata,Sierra de la** *mts* Spain
70 D7 **Matasiri** *isld* Indonesia
145 F2 **Matata** New Zealand
87 E12 **Matatiele** S Africa
144 B7 **Mataura** New Zealand
145 F3 **Matawai** New Zealand
121 R6 **Matawin** *R* Quebec Canada
57 J2 **Matay** Kazakhstan
57 E5 **Matcha** Tajikistan
121 N5 **Matchi-Manitou, L** Quebec Canada
128 F6 **Mategua** Bolivia
125 J6 **Matehuala** Mexico
89 G3 **Mateke Hills** Zimbabwe
127 P1 **Matelot** Trinidad
145 E3 **Matemateaonga Ra** New Zealand
88 H8 **Matemo** *isld* Mozambique
43 H8 **Matera** Italy
45 Q7 **Matese** *L* Italy
45 Q7 **Matese, Monti del** *mts* Italy
48 G3 **Mátészalka** Hungary
43 C11 **Mateur** Tunisia
129 K7 **Mateus** *R* Brazil
129 L7 **Mateus** Brazil
94 E9 **Matewan** West Virginia U.S.A.
107 O3 **Matfield Green** Kansas U.S.A.
26 J9 **Matfors** Sweden
18 E7 **Matha** France
102 E4 **Mather** California U.S.A.
94 G7 **Mather** Pennsylvania U.S.A.
74 E9 **Matheran** India
99 Q8 **Matherville** Illinois U.S.A.
120 K4 **Matheson** Ontario Canada
106 G2 **Matheson** Colorado U.S.A.
119 V7 **Matheson Island** Manitoba Canada
111 K9 **Mathews** Alabama U.S.A.
95 L9 **Mathews** Virginia U.S.A.
109 K7 **Mathis** Texas U.S.A.
111 G8 **Mathiston** Mississippi U.S.A.
80 F8 **Mathlutha** Jordan
21 N2 **Mathonville** France
139 G6 **Mathoura** New South Wales Australia
8 A4 **Mathry** Wales
74 G5 **Mathura** India
71 G7 **Mati** Mindanao Philippines
125 M9 **Matías Romero** Mexico
145 E3 **Matiere** New Zealand
20 F4 **Matignon** France
22 E4 **Matigny** France
16 D4 **Matilla de los Caños del Rio** Spain
120 H6 **Matinenda L** Ontario Canada
134 C13 **Matiti** Tahiti Pacific Oc
89 E5 **Matlabas** *R* S Africa
119 V8 **Matlock** Manitoba Canada
100 B2 **Matlock** Washington U.S.A.
9 E1 **Matlock Bath** England
94 F9 **Matoaka** West Virginia U.S.A.
129 G6 **Mato Grosso** *reg* Brazil
130 D4 **Mato Grosso,Chapada de** *hills* Brazil
130 C7 **Mato Grosso do Sul** *state* Brazil
130 C4 **Mato Grosso,Planalto de** *plateau* Brazil
122 C2 **Matonipi L** Quebec Canada
122 C2 **Matonipis L** Quebec Canada
89 F3 **Matopo Hills Nat. Park** Zimbabwe
87 E10 **Matopos Nat. Park** Zimbabwe
130 D10 **Matos Costa** Brazil
16 B3 **Matosinhos** Portugal
Matou *see* **Qiu Xian**
86 B6 **Matouti, Pto** Gabon
130 G4 **Mato Verde** Minas Gerais Brazil
48 F3 **Mátra** *mts* Hungary
72 H4 **Maţraḩ** Oman
27 F11 **Matrand** Norway
83 K13 **Mât, R. du** Réunion Indian Oc
27 A11 **Matre** Norway
41 O3 **Matrei am Brenner** Austria
89 A9 **Matroos Berg** *mt* S Africa
59 M2 **Matrosov** Russian Federation
84 H3 **Matrûh** Egypt
61 N10 **Matsudo** Japan
59 K4 **Matsue** Japan
60 O4 **Matsumae** Japan
61 L9 **Matsumoto** Japan
60 G11 **Matsunaga** Japan
61 K11 **Matsusaka** Japan
61 M9 **Matsushiro** Japan
67 G3 **Ma-tsu Tao** *isld* Taiwan
61 K9 **Matsutō** Japan
60 C12 **Matsuura** Japan
61 P7 **Matsuyama** Honshu Japan
60 F12 **Matsuyama** Shikoku Japan
61 M11 **Matsuzaki** Japan
120 J4 **Mattagami Heights** Ontario Canada
120 J5 **Mattagami L** Ontario Canada
120 H2 **Mattagami R** Ontario Canada
112 L2 **Mattamuskeet L** North Carolina U.S.A.
76 C6 **Mattancheri** India
95 K9 **Mattaponi** *R* Virginia U.S.A.
121 M6 **Mattawa** Ontario Canada
95 T1 **Mattawamkeag** Maine U.S.A.
89 E3 **Mattengwe** *R* Botswana
40 G6 **Matterhorn** *mt* Switzerland
100 H4 **Matterhorn** *mt* Oregon U.S.A.
48 C3 **Mattersburg** Austria
137 P6 **Matthew** *isld* Pacific Oc
126 H4 **Matthew Town** Great Inagua I Bahamas
103 M7 **Matthie** Arizona U.S.A.
120 G3 **Mattice** Ontario Canada
38 H5 **Mattig** *R* Austria
95 P6 **Mattituck** Long I, New York U.S.A.
26 G8 **Mattmar** Sweden
102 A1 **Mattole** *R* California U.S.A.
99 S10 **Mattoon** Illinois U.S.A.
110 H4 **Mattoon** Kentucky U.S.A.
99 R4 **Mattoon** Wisconsin U.S.A.
113 E7 **Mattox** Georgia U.S.A.
115 K4 **Matty I** Northwest Territories Canada
70 B3 **Matu** Sarawak
128 C6 **Matucana** Peru
144 B6 **Matukituki** *R* New Zealand
Matūn *see* **Khowst** *reg*
145 D1 **Matupia I** New Zealand
56 C4 **Matur** Russian Federation
127 P2 **Matura** Trinidad
127 N10 **Maturín** Venezuela
55 B4 **Matveyevka** Russian Federation
54 K9 **Matveyev Kurgan** Russian Federation
75 K6 **Mau** India
87 G8 **Maua** Mozambique
71 M9 **Maubara** Timor
18 F10 **Mauberme, Pic de** *mt* France/Spain
22 G4 **Maubert-Fontaine** France
22 F3 **Maubeuge** France
68 B4 **Maubin** Burma
18 E9 **Maubourguet** France
12 D3 **Mauchline** Scotland
94 A8 **Mauckport** Indiana U.S.A.
107 O6 **Maud** Oklahoma U.S.A.
109 N2 **Maud** Texas U.S.A.
146 G6 **Maudheimvidda** *ra* Antarctica
101 O3 **Maudlow** Montana U.S.A.
90 J15 **Maud Rise** S Atlantic Oc
146 J5 **Maud Rise** *seamount* S Atlantic Oc
87 F10 **Mau-é-ele** Mozambique
129 G4 **Maués** Brazil
134 A1 **Maugaafi** *pk* Western Samoa
94 K7 **Maugansville** Maryland U.S.A.
20 H7 **Mauges, Les** *reg* France
12 D5 **Maughold Hd** I of Man U.K.
135 T3 **Maui** *isld* Hawaiian Is
70 L9 **Mauk** Java
36 F6 **Maulbronn** Germany
22 E3 **Maulde** France
131 A5 **Maule** *prov* Chile
131 B5 **Maule** *R* Chile
21 O4 **Maule** France
21 J8 **Mauléon** France
18 E9 **Mauléon Licharre** France
21 J7 **Maulévrier** France
14 B2 **Maumakeogh** *mt* Ireland
94 D5 **Maumee** Ohio U.S.A.
94 D5 **Maumee Bay** Michigan/Ohio U.S.A.
110 D7 **Maumelle, L** Arkansas U.S.A.
71 L9 **Maumere** Flores Indonesia
14 B3 **Maumturk Mts** Ireland
21 H7 **Maumusson** France
87 D9 **Maun** Botswana
135 U5 **Mauna Kea** *pk* Hawaiian Is
135 R2 **Mauna Loa** Hawaiian Is
135 U5 **Mauna Loa** *vol* Hawaiian Is
102 S12 **Maunalua Bay** Hawaiian Is
116 K3 **Mauneluk** *R* Alaska U.S.A.
145 F3 **Maungaharuru Ra** New Zealand
145 F3 **Maungahaumi** *mt* New Zealand
145 F3 **Maungapohatu** New Zealand
145 F3 **Maungataniwha** *mt* New Zealand
145 E1 **Maungatapere** New Zealand
145 E2 **Maungaturoto** New Zealand
68 A2 **Maungdaw** Burma
68 C5 **Maungmagan** *islds* Burma
68 D6 **Maungthama** Burma
114 G4 **Maunoir,L** Northwest Territories Canada
138 D6 **Maupertuis B** South Australia Australia
100 D4 **Maupin** Oregon U.S.A.
38 E7 **Maurach** Austria
19 Q16 **Maure,Col de** *pass* France
20 G6 **Maure-de-Bretagne** France
6 M4 **Maureen** *oil rig* North Sea
111 F11 **Maurepas,L** Louisiana U.S.A.
18 G7 **Mauriac** France
145 E4 **Mauriceville** New Zealand
111 C11 **Mauriceville** Texas U.S.A.
19 Q14 **Maurienne** *dist* France
40 D7 **Maurienne** *V* France
98 D4 **Maurine** South Dakota U.S.A.
85 B4 **Mauritania** *rep* W Africa
83 L12 **Mauritius** *isld* Indian Oc
20 F5 **Mauron** France
18 G8 **Maurs** France
19 N17 **Maussane** France
99 Q6 **Mauston** Wisconsin U.S.A.
38 N5 **Mautern** Austria
38 J7 **Mauterndorf** Austria
38 L5 **Mauthausen** Austria
40 B2 **Maûtz** France
19 N14 **Mauves** France
18 F9 **Mauvezin** France
18 E6 **Mauzé** France
21 K8 **Mauzé Thouarsais** France
128 E3 **Mavaca** *R* Venezuela
21 N6 **Maves-Pontijou** France
87 D9 **Mavinga** Angola
127 L2 **Mavis Bank** Jamaica
144 B6 **Mavora L, N** New Zealand
46 F5 **Mavrovoúni** *mt* Greece
46 D3 **Mavrovsko** *mt* Macedonia Yugoslavia
88 D9 **Mavudzi** *R* Mozambique
88 C10 **Mavuradonha Mts** Zimbabwe
70 C4 **Mawa, Bt** *mt* Kalimantan
71 H7 **Mawasangka** Indonesia
68 C3 **Mawchi** Burma
68 D7 **Mawdaung** *pass* Burma/Thailand
119 R4 **Mawdesley L** Manitoba Canada
118 L8 **Mawer** Saskatchewan Canada
144 C5 **Mawheraiti** New Zealand
68 D4 **Mawkhi** Burma
68 C2 **Mawkmai** Burma
75 Q7 **Mawlaik** Burma
Mawlamyine *see* **Mawkhi**
78 J3 **Mawsil, Al** Iraq
146 K10 **Mawson** *Australia Base* Antarctica
146 J11 **Mawson Coast** Antarctica
146 H10 **Mawson Escarpt** Antarctica
146 C13 **Mawson Pen** Antarctica
98 E9 **Max** Nebraska U.S.A.
98 E2 **Max** North Dakota U.S.A.
86 A3 **Maxaas** Somalia
98 E1 **Maxbass** North Dakota U.S.A.
20 F6 **Maxent** France
112 D4 **Maxeys** Georgia U.S.A.
117 M6 **Maxhamish L** British Columbia Canada
37 N5 **Maxhütte-Haidof** Germany
36 E5 **Maximiliansau** Germany
94 G10 **Max Meadows** Virginia U.S.A.
29 J8 **Maxmo** Finland
118 L9 **Maxstone** Saskatchewan Canada
112 H3 **Maxton** North Carolina U.S.A.
121 Q7 **Maxville** Ontario Canada
113 E7 **Maxville** Florida U.S.A.
101 M3 **Maxville** Montana U.S.A.
102 B2 **Maxwell** California U.S.A.
99 N8 **Maxwell** Iowa U.S.A.
98 F8 **Maxwell** Nebraska U.S.A.
106 F5 **Maxwell** New Mexico U.S.A.
12 E3 **Maxwelltown** Scotland
141 G5 **Maxwelton** Queensland Australia

Ref	Name
90 K14	Meteor Seamount S Atlantic Oc
22 D2	Méteren France
46 F7	Méthana Greece
119 S7	Methley Manitoba Canada
46 E8	Methóni Greece
100 E1	Methow R Washington U.S.A.
95 Q4	Methuen Massachusetts U.S.A.
142 E3	Methuen,Mt W Australia Australia
144 C5	Methven New Zealand
12 E1	Methven Scotland
143 D7	Methven,Mt W Australia Australia
9 G2	Methwold England
119 N1	Metionga L Ontario Canada
118 G6	Metiskow Alberta Canada
122 E5	Metis L Quebec Canada
42 H5	Metković Croatia
117 H8	Metlakatla Alaska U.S.A.
85 F2	Metlaoui Tunisia
38 K8	Metnitz Austria
46 D2	Metohija mts Serbia Yugoslavia
46 D2	Metohija Serbia Yugoslavia
100 D5	Metolius Oregon U.S.A.
46 E1	Metovnica Serbia Yugoslavia
70 K8	Metro Sumatra
110 H4	Metropolis Illinois U.S.A.
29 N6	Metsäkylä Finland
25 P2	Metslawier Netherlands
46 E5	Métsovon Greece
37 O6	Metten Germany
38 D7	Mettendorf Germany
112 E5	Metter Georgia U.S.A.
22 H3	Mettet Belgium
32 G8	Mettingen Germany
36 B4	Mettlach Germany
32 E10	Mettmann Germany
36 B4	Mettnich Germany
21 M7	Mettray France
76 C5	Mettur India
88 H7	Metudo isld Mozambique
79 F5	Metulla Israel
19 K3	Metz France
40 F1	Metzeral France
22 L5	Metzervisse France
38 G6	Metzingen Germany
20 F5	Meu R France
88 G9	Meucate Mozambique
36 D3	Meudt Germany
69 C10	Meulaboh Sumatra
21 O3	Meulan France
26 C12	Meulebeke Belgium
21 L4	Meulles France
21 O6	Meung-sur-Loire France
69 C10	Meureudu Sumatra
40 A4	Meursault France
19 K4	Meurthe R France
36 B6	Meurthe et Moselle dept France
22 H3	Meuse R Belgium
12 E2	Meuse R France
19 J4	Meuse dept France
37 N1	Meuselwitz Germany
21 O7	Meusnes France
8 B7	Mevagissey England
80 D6	Meva Horon Jordan
80 C6	Meva Modiin Jordan
13 G6	Mexborough England
109 L4	Mexia Texas U.S.A.
133 J9	Mexiana isld Brazil
103 P4	Mexican Hat Utah U.S.A.
124 F3	Mexicanos, Lago de los Mexico
103 P5	Mexican Water Arizona U.S.A.
124 G6	Mexico rep N America
94 A6	Mexico Indiana U.S.A.
95 P2	Mexico Maine U.S.A.
110 E2	Mexico Missouri U.S.A.
95 N3	Mexico New York U.S.A.
125 K8	Mexico New Mexico U.S.A.
125 M6	Mexico, G. of Mexico
40 B6	Méximieux France
71 E3	Meycawayan Luzon Philippines
77 D5	Meydân-e Gel salt lake Iran
33 Q6	Meyenburg Germany
117 G8	Meyers Chuck Alaska U.S.A.
94 H7	Meyersdale Pennsylvania U.S.A.
18 G7	Meymac France
77 J2	Meymaneh Afghanistan
77 B3	Meymeh Iran
118 L8	Meyronne Saskatchewan Canada
18 H8	Meyrueis France
46 F1	Meyssac France
80 F2	Mezar Syria
125 N9	Mezcalapa R Mexico
46 F1	Mézel France
18 H9	Mèze France
19 Q17	Mézel France
52 S3	Mezen' R Russian Federation
52 F2	Mezen' Arkhangel'skaya obl Russian Federation
52 F2	Mezenskaya Guba B Russian Federation
80 D4	Mezer Israel
54 C1	Mezha R Russian Federation
52 SQ3	Mezhdurechensk Russian Federation
56 C4	Mezhdurechensk Russian Federation
55 E2	Mezhdurechenskiy Russian Federation
31 N1	Mezhdurech'ye Russian Federation
50 D1	Mezhdusharskiy Ostrov isld Russian Federation
48 H2	Mezhgor'ye Ukraine
42 F2	Mežica Slovenia
21 K3	Mézidon-Canon France
21 N8	Mézières-en-Brenne France
21 O4	Mézières-sur-Seine France
31 H6	Mezimostí Czechoslovakia
18 F8	Mézin France
54 M1	Mezinovskiy Russian Federation
48 F3	Mezöberény Hungary
48 F3	Mezöcsát Hungary
48 F3	Mezöhegyes Hungary
48 F4	Mezökovácsháza Hungary
48 F3	Mezökövesd Hungary
18 E8	Mézos France
48 F3	Mezötúr Hungary
124 G6	Mezquital R Mexico
124 G6	Mezquital Mexico
46 H2	Mezquitic Mexico
41 N5	Mezzana Italy
41 M3	Mezzano Italy
41 O4	Mezzaselva Italy
41 M2	Mezzogoro Italy
41 K5	Mezzola, Lago di Italy
41 L5	Mezzoldo Italy
42 D2	Mezzolombardo Italy
89 G7	Mfolozi R S Africa
52 D5	Mga Russian Federation
74 F10	Mhasvad India
125 L9	Mhlume Swaziland
125 L9	Miahuatlán de Porfirio Diaz Mexico
19 T9	Miajadas Spain
103 O8	Miami Arizona U.S.A.
113 Q12	Miami Florida U.S.A.
113 O10	Miami R Ohio U.S.A.
107 Q5	Miami Oklahoma U.S.A.
108 D5	Miami Texas U.S.A.
113 G11	Miami Beach Florida U.S.A.
94 C6	Miami, Great R Ohio U.S.A.
94 C7	Miami, Little R Ohio U.S.A.
113 G12	Miami Shores Florida U.S.A.
113 G12	Miami Springs Florida U.S.A.
65 B7	Mianchi China
78 L3	Miandowab Iran
87 H11	Miandrivazo Madagascar
77 H1	Mianeh Iran
110 K8	Mian Shui R China
65 C8	Mian Xian China

Ref	Name
67 D1	Mianyang China
65 E6	Mianzhu China
65 E5	Miao Dao isld China
65 H3	Miaodao Qundao islds China
67 B3	Miaoling China
67 C4	Miao Ling mt ra China
87 H11	Miaoping China
55 D3	Miarinarivo Madagascar
31 K1	Miass R Russian Federation
117 O9	Miastko Poland
	Mica Dam British Columbia Canada
103 O9	Mica Mt Arizona U.S.A.
58 E5	Micang Shan mt ra China
113 E8	Micanopy Florida U.S.A.
128 C3	Micay Colombia
113 C7	Miccosukee Florida U.S.A.
52 H3	Michaichmon' Russian Federation
48 G2	Michal'any Czechoslovakia
48 G2	Michalovce Czechoslovakia
118 C9	Michel British Columbia Canada
118 H3	Michel Saskatchewan Canada
38 N5	Michelbach Austria
36 G2	Michelbach Germany
116 G2	Michelson, Mt Alaska U.S.A.
36 G4	Michelstadt Germany
33 S8	Michendorf Germany
127 K5	Miches Dominican Rep
118 E7	Michichi Alberta Canada
112 J1	Michie, L North Carolina U.S.A.
101 T6	Michigamme Michigan U.S.A.
107 N6	Michigamme L Michigan U.S.A.
	Michigamme Res Michigan U.S.A.
25 F2	Michigan state U.S.A.
78 H3	Midwat Turkey
15 G1	Mid Yell Scotland
46 F1	Mie prefect Japan
61 K11	Mie R Japan
31 M5	Miechów Poland
40 F3	Miechów Switzerland
31 J3	Miedzychód Poland
31 O4	Miedzylesie Poland
31 K4	Miedzyrzec Poland
31 K4	Miejska Gorka Poland
29 L5	Miekojärvi L Finland
18 F9	Miélan France
31 N5	Mielec Poland
41 N3	Mieminger Kette mt Austria
27 G15	Mien L Sweden
67 G4	Mien Tasmania Australia
109 H9	Mien-hua Hsü isld Taiwan
106 D7	Mier Mexico
48 K4	Miercurea-Ciuc Romania
16 D1	Mieres Spain
32 H6	Mieron Norway
38 E6	Miesbach Germany
86 H4	Mi 'éso Ethiopia
33 O8	Mieste Germany
31 H3	Mieszkowice Poland
94 K6	Mifflin Pennsylvania U.S.A.

Ref	Name
94 C3	Midland Michigan U.S.A.
98 E5	Midland South Dakota U.S.A.
108 E4	Midland Texas U.S.A.
111 L10	Midland City Alabama U.S.A.
89 F2	Midlands prov Zimbabwe
14 C5	Midleton Ireland
	Midlothian co see Lothian and Borders regions
109 K3	Midlothian U.S.A.
94 K9	Midlothian Virginia U.S.A.
32 J5	Midlum Germany
111 F8	Midlum Mississippi U.S.A.
87 H12	Midongy Atsimo Madagascar
60 D13	Midori-kawa R Japan
18 E9	Midouze R France
134 G5	Mid-Pacific Mountains Pacific Oc
71 G7	Midsayap Philippines
100 J5	Midvale Idaho U.S.A.
101 O9	Midvale Utah U.S.A.
112 E5	Midville Georgia U.S.A.
117 O11	Midway British Columbia Canada
111 L9	Midway Alabama U.S.A.
112 F6	Midway Georgia U.S.A.
94 C8	Midway Kentucky U.S.A.
109 M4	Midway Texas U.S.A.
135 U2	Midway Is atoll Hawaiian Is
116 O1	Midway W Alaska U.S.A.
122 E1	Midway L Quebec Canada
143 E6	Midway Well W Australia Australia
101 T6	Midwest Wyoming U.S.A.
107 N6	Midwest City Oklahoma U.S.A.
25 F2	Midwolde Netherlands
78 H3	Midyat Turkey
15 G1	Mid Yell Scotland
46 F1	Mie prefect Japan
61 K11	Mie R Japan
31 M5	Miechów Poland
40 F3	Miechów Switzerland
31 J3	Miedzychód Poland
31 O4	Miedzylesie Poland
31 K4	Miedzyrzec Poland
31 K4	Miejska Gorka Poland
29 L5	Miekojärvi L Finland
18 F9	Miélan France
31 N5	Mielec Poland
98 H3	Millarton North Dakota U.S.A.
94 H9	Millboro Virginia U.S.A.
121 M8	Millbrook Ontario Canada
95 O5	Millbrook New York U.S.A.
102 F1	Mill City Nevada U.S.A.
100 C5	Mill City Oregon U.S.A.
102 C1	Mill Creek California U.S.A.
109 L1	Mill Creek Oklahoma U.S.A.
94 G4	Mill Creek West Virginia U.S.A.
112 D4	Milledgeville Georgia U.S.A.
110 G3	Milledgeville Illinois U.S.A.
102 F3	Millen Georgia U.S.A.
99 N3	Mille Lacs L Minnesota U.S.A.
119 N2	Mille Lacs, Lac des Ontario Canada
112 F5	Millen Georgia U.S.A.
138 D3	Miller R South Australia Australia
110 C4	Miller Missouri U.S.A.
98 G9	Miller Nebraska U.S.A.
98 H5	Miller South Dakota U.S.A.
124 B3	Miller, Desembarcadero de Mexico
116 Q6	Miller, Mt Alaska U.S.A.
54 M8	Millerovo Russian Federation
103 O10	Miller Pk Arizona U.S.A.
102 G3	Millers California U.S.A.
94 B5	Millersburg Indiana U.S.A.
110 M3	Millersburg Kentucky U.S.A.
94 D1	Millersburg Michigan U.S.A.
94 F6	Millersburg Ohio U.S.A.
95 L6	Millersburg Pennsylvania U.S.A.
138 D4	Millers Creek South Australia Australia
95 P4	Millers Falls Massachusetts U.S.A.
111 J9	Millers Ferry Alabama U.S.A.
144 B6	Millers Flat New Zealand
12 D2	Millerston Scotland
94 H6	Millersport Pennsylvania U.S.A.
108 H4	Millersview Texas U.S.A.
122 G7	Millerton New Brunswick Canada
144 C4	Millerton New Zealand
95 O5	Millerton New York U.S.A.
102 E1	Millerton L California U.S.A.
123 Q5	Millertown Newfoundland Canada
123 Q4	Millertown Junct Newfoundland Canada
118 D5	Millet Alberta Canada
94 E9	Millet West Virginia U.S.A.
102 G2	Millett Nevada U.S.A.
109 N7	Millett Texas U.S.A.
18 G7	Millevaches, Plateau de France
14 D1	Milford Ireland
94 K5	Mill Hall Pennsylvania U.S.A.
146 H13	Mill I Antarctica
115 M5	Mill I Northwest Territories Canada
100 E6	Millican Oregon U.S.A.
109 L5	Millican Texas U.S.A.
138 F6	Millicent South Australia Australia
118 F8	Millicent Alabama U.S.A.
143 D8	Millicent,Mt W Australia Australia
111 K11	Milligan Florida U.S.A.
98 J9	Milligan Nebraska U.S.A.
106 F1	Milligan Colorado U.S.A.
95 M7	Millington Maryland U.S.A.
94 D3	Millington Michigan U.S.A.
110 G6	Millington Tennessee U.S.A.
95 S8	Millinocket Maine U.S.A.
141 M8	Millmerran Queensland Australia
13 E5	Millom England
12 D2	Millport Scotland
99 L8	Millrace R U.S.A.
104 P4	Mills Wyoming U.S.A.
109 N7	Mills New Mexico U.S.A.
106 F5	Mills New Mexico U.S.A.
13 J5	Mills Wyoming U.S.A.
102 D3	Millsap Texas U.S.A.
102 M3	Millsboro Delaware U.S.A.
117 O5	Mills L Northwest Territories Canada
99 Q5	Millston Wisconsin U.S.A.
122 F4	Millstream Queensland Australia
142 C3	Millstream W Australia Australia
14 B4	Millstreet Ireland
143 F6	Milltown R W Australia Australia
14 B4	Milltown New Brunswick Canada
7 E4	Milltown Malbay Ireland
141 F4	Millungera Queensland Australia
122 J3	Millwood L Arkansas U.S.A.
122 J3	Millwood England
42 F5	Milly Milly W Australia Australia
21 P6	Milly-la-Forêt France
21 P3	Milly-sur Thérain France
16 F6	Milne, la France
143 B7	Milne R Queensland Australia
146 T11	Milne Land Greenland
43 G10	Mileto Italy

Ref	Name
45 Q7	Miletto, M mt Italy
143 B7	Mileura W Australia Australia
31 H6	Milevsko Czechoslovakia
9 F5	Milford Surrey England
102 D1	Milford California U.S.A.
95 O5	Milford Connecticut U.S.A.
13 F5	Milford Delaware U.S.A.
118 E8	Milford Illinois U.S.A.
88 E6	Milo Iowa U.S.A.
99 N8	Milo Iowa U.S.A.
95 S1	Milo Maine U.S.A.
100 B7	Milo prov Portugal
135 U6	Milolii Hawaiian Is
46 G3	Milos isld Greece
31 K3	Milosław Poland
30 G4	Milove Ukraine
33 D7	Milówka Poland
95 N4	Milford New York U.S.A.
109 L3	Milford Texas U.S.A.
103 L3	Milford Utah U.S.A.
94 K8	Milford Center Ohio U.S.A.
9 E6	Milford on Sea England
144 A6	Milford Sound New Zealand
139 N6	Milguy, Mt W Australia Australia
102 C4	Milpitas California U.S.A.
110 L2	Milroy Indiana U.S.A.
94 K6	Milroy Pennsylvania U.S.A.
37 O5	Miltach Germany
36 G4	Miltenberg Germany
99 N7	Milton Nova Scotia Canada
144 B7	Milton New Zealand
12 D2	Milton Scotland
95 M8	Milton Delaware U.S.A.
111 J11	Milton Florida U.S.A.
103 O3	Milton Illinois U.S.A.
95 R3	Milton Maine U.S.A.
94 H10	Milton North Carolina U.S.A.
98 L1	Milton North Dakota U.S.A.
95 L5	Milton Pennsylvania U.S.A.
94 B8	Milton Vermont U.S.A.
99 S7	Milton West Virginia U.S.A.
99 S7	Milton Wisconsin U.S.A.
8 B6	Milton Abbot England
139 J3	Milton Downs New South Wales Australia
100 G4	Milton Freewater Oregon U.S.A.
12 D3	Miltonish Scotland
9 F3	Milton Keynes England
107 N2	Miltonvale Kansas U.S.A.
99 N4	Milverton England
86 C3	Miltou Chad
33 S4	Milztow Germany
67 D2	Miluo China
8 C5	Milverton England
99 Q5	Milwaukee Wisconsin U.S.A.
127 K5	Milwaukee Depth Caribbean
60 E13	Mimitsu Japan
18 E8	Mimizan France
19 D7	Mimoň Czechoslovakia
31 H5	Mimoň Czechoslovakia
86 B6	Mimongo Gabon
60 H10	Mimuro yama mt Japan
102 A2	Mina California U.S.A.
102 F3	Mina Nevada U.S.A.
84 E3	Mina'al Ahmadi Iran
77 E6	Minab Iran
60 J12	Minabe Japan
124 F3	Miñaca Mexico
119 T4	Minago R Manitoba Canada
71 H4	Minahassa Peninsula Sulawesi Indonesia
77 D7	Mina Jebel Ali U.A.E.
79 H2	Minakh Syria
118 H1	Minaki Ontario Canada
100 H4	Minam Oregon U.S.A.
60 D13	Minamata Japan
61 J14	Minami Japan
57 E11	Minami Japan
99 N5	Minami-gawa mt Japan
85 C6	Mina, Mt Mali
126 F4	Mina, Mt Mali
69 E12	Minas Cuba
131 G5	Minas Sumatra
97 A5	Minas Uruguay
77 A5	Mina'sul Kuwait
122 H8	Minas Basin Nova Scotia Canada
126 C3	Minas de Matahambre Cuba
16 C7	Minas de Riotinto Spain
16 C7	Minas de Tharsis Spain
98 E1	Minas Gerais state Brazil
129 K7	Minas Novas Brazil
130 G5	Minas Novas Brazil
125 P10	Minas, Sa. de las mts Guatemala
98 C8	Minatare Nebraska U.S.A.
55 C7	Minatare L Ontario Canada
125 M9	Minatitlán Mexico
68 B2	Minbu Burma
118 F5	Minburn Alberta Canada
68 A2	Minbya Burma
74 F1	Minchinmoku, L Alaska U.S.A.
45 J1	Mincio R Italy
107 N6	Minco Oklahoma U.S.A.
31 M6	Minčol mt Czechoslovakia
71 G7	Mindanao Philippines
71 G7	Mindanao Sea Philippines
138 F5	Mindarie South Australia Australia
68 A2	Mindat Sakan Burma
37 J7	Mindel R Germany
41 M1	Mindelheim Germany
121 J9	Minden Germany
98 G9	Minden Louisiana U.S.A.
109 L4	Minden Louisiana U.S.A.
98 G9	Minden Nebraska U.S.A.
102 E3	Minden Nevada U.S.A.
94 F9	Minden West Virginia U.S.A.
94 D3	Minden City Michigan U.S.A.
142 B5	Mindil W Australia Australia
68 B3	Mindon Burma
138 F5	Mindona L New South Wales Australia
71 E4	Mindoro isld Philippines
71 E4	Mindoro Str Philippines
48 H5	Mindra Romania
9 D5	Mindyak Russian Federation
60 E1	Mine Japan
99 O1	Mine Centre Ontario Canada
78 K5	Mine Hd Ireland
8 C5	Minehead England
130 D5	Mineiros Brazil
21 J3	Mine la France
99 L8	Mineola New York U.S.A.
109 M3	Mineola Texas U.S.A.
94 F9	Mineral R Montana U.S.A.
102 B1	Mineral California U.S.A.
109 N3	Mineral Texas U.S.A.
94 K8	Mineral Virginia U.S.A.
95 U3	Mineral Wyoming U.S.A.
125 K7	Mineral del Monte Mexico
101 P17	Mineral, Mts Utah U.S.A.
103 M3	Mineral Mts Utah U.S.A.
99 R7	Mineral Pt Wisconsin U.S.A.
109 K3	Mineral Springs Arkansas U.S.A.
109 J3	Mineral Wells Texas U.S.A.
128 C2	Minero Bolivia
103 M3	Minersville Utah U.S.A.
95 L6	Minerva Utah U.S.A.
137 P6	Minerva Rfs Pacific Oc
43 G7	Minervino Murge Italy
138 F7	Minford Ohio U.S.A.
18 F5	Mingançay France
3 E3	Milford Missouri U.S.A.
122 J3	Mingan Quebec Canada
122 J3	Mingan Is Quebec Canada
133 F5	Mingary South Australia Australia
55 F2	Mingchang China
78 L1	Mingdao China
141 F3	Mingela Queensland Australia
141 H4	Mingenew W Australia Australia
118 E9	Mingera Queensland Australia
140 E5	Mingery W Australia Australia
78 B5	Mingin Burma
68 B2	Mingin Range Burma
58 G5	Ming-kuang China
17 G5	Mingoyo Tanzania
67 C4	Minglun China

Ref	Name
101 L7	Milner Idaho U.S.A.
118 E1	Milner Ridge Manitoba Canada
120 K6	Milnet Ontario Canada
12 D2	Milngavie Scotland
98 J3	Milnor North Dakota U.S.A.
65 F1	Milnthorpe England
109 J3	Milo Alberta Canada
88 E6	Milo Iowa U.S.A.
99 N8	Milo Iowa U.S.A.
95 S1	Milo Maine U.S.A.
100 B7	Milo prov Portugal
135 U6	Milolii Hawaiian Is
46 G3	Milos isld Greece
31 K3	Milosław Poland
30 G4	Milove Ukraine
33 D7	Milówka Poland
101 M9	Minersville Illinois U.S.A.
143 E8	Minerva W Australia Australia
143 A6	Minilya R W Australia Australia
110 K4	Mining City Res Kentucky U.S.A.
119 Q8	Miniota Manitoba Canada
83 K10	Minipe Sri Lanka
123 L1	Minipi L Labrador, Nfld Canada
118 H4	Ministikwin L Saskatchewan Canada
17 F3	Ministra, Sierra Spain
119 Q6	Minitonas Manitoba Canada
58 D5	Min Jiang R China
67 F3	Min Jiang R China
65 B3	Minji China
119 J4	Minjilang N Terr Australia
102 E5	Minkler California U.S.A.
48 L2	Min'kovtsy Ukraine
57 G4	Min-Kush Kyrgyzstan
138 D5	Minlaton South Australia Australia
84 E3	Minna Nigeria
146 D11	Minna Bluff pt Antarctica
61 P12	Minna-jima isld Okinawa
107 N2	Minneapolis Kansas U.S.A.
99 N4	Minneapolis Minnesota U.S.A.
119 S8	Minnedosa Manitoba Canada
107 L4	Mineola Kansas U.S.A.
99 N3	Minnesota state U.S.A.
99 M5	Minnesota R Minnesota U.S.A.
99 P5	Minnesota City Minnesota U.S.A.
99 N6	Minnesota Lake Minnesota U.S.A.
99 L4	Minnetonka Minnesota U.S.A.
27 E11	Minnesund Norway
99 N5	Minnetonka Minnesota U.S.A.
118 B7	Minnewanka, L Alberta Canada
99 L4	Minnewaska L Minnesota U.S.A.
	Minnewaukan North Dakota U.S.A.
143 B6	Minnie Creek W Australia Australia
141 H7	Minnie Downs Queensland Australia
142 B5	Minnie,Mt W Australia Australia
138 D5	Minnipa South Australia Australia
120 G4	Minnipuka Ontario Canada
118 K1	Minnitaki L Ontario Canada
61 K10	Mino Japan
16 B2	Miño R Spain
61 K10	Mino Japan
60 E12	Minobu Japan
60 J12	Minokamo Japan
61 K10	Minokuni Japan
99 P3	Minong Wisconsin U.S.A.
99 U3	Minonk Illinois U.S.A.
99 M5	Minooka Illinois U.S.A.
80 F1	Minot North Dakota U.S.A.
98 E1	Minot North Dakota U.S.A.
65 F4	Minqin China
67 E4	Minquan China
137 N6	Minquiers,les English Chan
32 G5	Minsen Germany
66 B6	Minsheng Canal China
54 B3	Minsk Belorussia
31 N3	Minsk Mazowiecki Poland
9 H5	Minster England
94 B6	Minster Ohio U.S.A.
74 F1	Mintaka Pass China/Kashmir
111 J9	Minter City Mississippi U.S.A.
119 S9	Minto Manitoba Canada
122 F7	Minto New Brunswick Canada
117 E4	Minto Yukon Territory Canada
114 J3	Minto Hd Northwest Territories Canada
115 M6	Minto Inlet Northwest Territories Canada
98 B1	Minto, L Quebec Canada
116 M2	Minto, Mt Antarctica
45 O7	Minturn Colorado U.S.A.
79 A8	Minûf Egypt
54 D4	Minusinsk Russian Federation
98 J7	Minya, El Egypt
79 B8	Minya el Qam Egypt
57 E4	Minya Konka mt China
55 C3	Min'yar Russian Federation
89 B7	Minzong China
68 B1	Minya Burma
94 B1	Mio Michigan U.S.A.
74 F3	Mi Oya R Sri Lanka
78 K5	Miqdadiyah Iraq
123 Q6	Miquelon isld Atlantic Oc
123 Q6	Miquelon Miquelon I Atlantic Oc
123 Q6	Miquelon, C Miquelon I Atlantic Oc
118 E5	Miquelon Prov. Park Alberta Canada
45 M1	Mira Italy
16 B7	Mira Portugal
19 Q3	Mira Spain
130 H5	Mirabela France
130 G5	Mirabella Eclano Italy
130 G4	Miracema Brazil
128 D3	Miraflores Boyaca Colombia
124 D5	Miraflores Mexico
102 A5	Mirage L California U.S.A.
130 F5	Mirai Brazil
76 B8	Miraj India
130 E7	Miralta Brazil
16 C2	Miravalles mt Spain

Ref	Name
99 N8	Mingo Iowa U.S.A.
107 K2	Mingo Kansas U.S.A.
94 D6	Mingo Junct Ohio U.S.A.
67 A1	Mingshan China
	Mingshui see Zhangqiu
109 J3	Mingteke R China
67 F3	Mingxi China
68 G8	Minh Hoa, Hon isld Vietnam
68 B4	Minhla Burma
16 B3	Minho prov Portugal
16 B2	Minho R Spain/Portugal
127 K2	Minho, R Jamaica
71 H3	Minhou China
20 G4	Miniac Morvan France
56 E1	Minicoy I Lakshadweep Indian Oc
101 M7	Minidoka Idaho U.S.A.
99 R9	Minier Illinois U.S.A.
143 E8	Minigwal,L W Australia Australia
143 A6	Minilya W Australia Australia
46 E3	Miravci Macedonia Yugoslavia
77 L2	Mir Bacheh Kowt Afghanistan
25 B3	Mirdum Netherlands
21 K6	Miré France
94 F1	Mirear I Egypt
127 H5	Mirebalais Haiti
19 J5	Mirebeau Côte-d'Or France
21 L8	Mirebeau Vienne France
18 J5	Mirepoix France
54 E7	Mirgorod Ukraine
70 D2	Miri Sarawak
141 K6	Miriam Vale Queensland Australia
85 A5	Mirik, C Mauritania
127 K9	Mirim Venezuela
131 H4	Mirim, L Brazil/Uruguay
131 F2	Mirin'ay, R Argentina
141 Q8	Mirintu R Queensland Australia
128 D4	Miriti-Paraná R Colombia
77 G5	Mirjäveh Iran
80 A4	Mirka Jordan
45 P1	Mirna R Croatia
42 S4	Mirna Croatia
146 H13	Mirnyy former U.S.S.R. Base Antarctica
56 H1	Mirnyy Russian Federation
40 E3	Miroir, Mt France
144 D5	Miromiro mt New Zealand
119 P3	Mirond L Saskatchewan Canada
54 B7	Mironovka Ukraine
31 J2	Mirosławiec Poland
33 R6	Mirow Germany
77 L7	Mirpur Khas Pakistan
140 D7	Mirranponga Pongunna L N Terr Australia
85 F6	Mirria Niger
118 D6	Mirror Alberta Canada
48 J6	Miršani Romania
56 D5	Mirskoy Khrebet mts Russian Federation
141 H5	Mirtna Queensland Australia
46 F7	Mirtoan Sea Greece
59 J4	Miryang S Korea
56 E1	Miryuginskiy Porog falls Russian Federation
57 B5	Mirzachiria Turkmenistan
75 K6	Mirzapur India
58 E3	Misa R Italy
61 P3	Misaki Japan
61 L10	Misakubo Japan
45 N4	Misawa Monte Italy
61 P13	Misato Japan
61 N8	Misawa Japan
32 J8	Misburg Germany
40 G5	Mischabel mt Switzerland
122 J7	Miscouche Prince Edward I Canada
122 H6	Miscou I New Brunswick Canada
122 H5	Miscou Pt New Brunswick Canada
127 P4	Misery, Mt St Kitts W Indies
80 F1	Misgav 'Am Israel
69 A4	Misha Nicobar Is
71 J11	Mishahua R Peru
80 D2	Mishan China
94 A5	Mishawaka Indiana U.S.A.
116 Q2	Misheguk Mt Alaska U.S.A.
56 F4	Mishelevka Russian Federation
120 L4	Mishibishu L Ontario Canada
99 T5	Mishicot Wisconsin U.S.A.
60 E11	Mi shima isld Japan
61 M10	Mishima Japan
55 C3	Mishkino Bashkirskaya Respublika Russian Federation
55 D3	Mishkino Sverdlovskaya obl Russian Federation
80 D8	Mishmar 'Ayyalon Israel
80 B8	Mishmar Ha Negev Israel
80 E6	Mishmar Ha Yarden Israel
121 P5	Mishomis Quebec Canada
52 J2	Mishva' Russian Federation
80 F3	Mishva' Jordan
137 L4	Misima isld Louisiade Arch
128 E6	Misión Cavinas Bolivia
131 G3	Misiones prov Argentina
130 C10	Misiones dep Paraguay
130 C10	Misiones, Sa.de ra Argentina
88 B4	Misisi Zaire
127 N2	Miskitos, Cayos islds Nicaragua
48 F2	Miskolc Hungary
38 M9	Mislinja Slovenia
79 G5	Mismiyah, Al Syria
71 G3	Misool isld W Irian
99 Q2	Misquah Hills Minnesota U.S.A.
84 B7	Mişrâtah Libya
120 F4	Missanabie Ontario Canada
130 G9	Missão Velhâ Brazil
20 F7	Missillac France
120 G4	Missinaibi L Ontario Canada
120 F4	Missinaibi R Ontario Canada
118 K3	Missinipe Saskatchewan Canada
98 F6	Mission South Dakota U.S.A.
109 J9	Mission Texas U.S.A.
117 M11	Mission City British Columbia Canada
98 J7	Mission Hill South Dakota U.S.A.
101 L2	Mission Range Montana U.S.A.
121 L1	Missisa L Ontario Canada
120 C6	Mississagi R Ontario Canada
120 C7	Mississagi L Ontario Canada
94 B2	Mississinewa L Indiana U.S.A.
110 L1	Mississinewa R Indiana U.S.A.
111 E10	Mississippi state U.S.A.
111 E10	Mississippi R U.S.A.
111 G12	Mississippi Delta Louisiana U.S.A.
121 O12	Mississippi L Ontario Canada
111 H11	Mississippi Sound U.S.A.
	Missolonghi Greece see Mesolóngion
120 H6	Missonga Ontario Canada
101 L3	Missoula Montana U.S.A.
110 C3	Missouri state U.S.A.
109 O2	Missouri R U.S.A.
109 L1	Missouri, Lit R Arkansas U.S.A.
98 D2	Missouri Res North Dakota U.S.A.
99 L8	Missouri Valley Iowa U.S.A.
141 H5	Mistake Cr Queensland Australia
123 K2	Mistake Creek N Terr Australia
121 S4	Mistassibi R Quebec Canada
115 M7	Mistassini, Lac Quebec Canada
121 S3	Mistastin L Newfoundland Canada
31 G6	Mistawak L Quebec Canada
126 C5	Misteriosa Bank Caribbean
8 C5	Misterton England
37 M8	Misti vol Peru
131 C3	Mistigoægêche L Quebec Canada
131 D3	Mistol, L Argentina
26 E10	Mistra Greece
43 J7	Misty Fjords Nat Mon Alaska U.S.A.
60 D13	Misumi Japan

Mitai — Moorpark

203

60 E13 **Mitai** Japan
127 P2 **Mitan** Trinidad
124 G7 **Mita, Pta.de** *C* Mexico
8 D4 **Mitcheldean** England
141 J7 **Mitchell** Queensland Australia
120 J9 **Mitchell** Ontario Canada
8 A7 **Mitchell** England
110 K3 **Mitchell** Indiana U.S.A.
98 C8 **Mitchell** Nebraska U.S.A.
100 E5 **Mitchell** Oregon U.S.A.
98 H6 **Mitchell** South Dakota U.S.A.
111 K9 **Mitchell L** Alabama U.S.A.
94 B2 **Mitchell, L** Michigan U.S.A.
112 E2 **Mitchell, Mt** North Carolina U.S.A.
140 A1 **Mitchell Pt** N Terr Australia
141 F3 **Mitchell River** Queensland Australia
14 C4 **Mitchelstown** Ireland
121 Q5 **Mitchinamecus, L** Quebec Canada
74 C6 **Mithi** Pakistan
47 H5 **Míthimna** Greece
71 B2 **Miti** *isld* Halmahera Indonesia
47 H5 **Mitilíni** Greece
52 G2 **Mitina** Russian Federation
119 S4 **Mitishto R** Manitoba Canada
117 G7 **Mitkof I** Alaska U.S.A.
79 C8 **Mitla Pass** Egypt
61 O9 **Mito** Japan
86 A5 **Mitra** *mt* Equat Guinea
137 P4 **Mitre** *isld* Santa Cruz Is
145 E4 **Mitre, Mt** New Zealand
144 A6 **Mitre Pk** New Zealand
52 J3 **Mitrofan-Dikost** Russian Federation
116 H9 **Mitrofania I** Alaska U.S.A.
46 D2 **Mitrovica** Serbia Yugoslavia
46 D5 **Mitsikéli** *R* Greece
86 G2 **Mits'iwa** Ethiopia
86 H2 **Mits'iwa** Ethiopia
60 F11 **Mitsu** Japan
60 F12 **Mitsuhama** Japan
60 Q3 **Mitsuishi** Japan
60 H11 **Mitsuishi** Japan
61 N9 **Mitsukaidō** Japan
61 M8 **Mitsuke** Japan
60 R2 **Mitsumata** Japan
139 K5 **Mittagong** New South Wales Australia
141 F4 **Mittagong** Queensland Australia
41 L3 **Mittagspitze** *mt* Austria
139 J6 **Mitta Mitta** Victoria Australia
41 N4 **Mittelberg** Austria
37 J5 **Mittelfranken** *dist* Bayern Germany
40 F4 **Mittelland** *dist* Switzerland
32 H8 **Mittellandkanal** Germany
33 R8 **Mittelmark** *reg* Germany
36 H3 **Mittelsinn** Germany
41 O3 **Mittenwald** Germany
33 T8 **Mittenwalde** Germany
38 M6 **Mitterbach** Austria
37 O6 **Mitterfels** Germany
38 G7 **Mitter Pinzgau** *V* Austria
36 B6 **Mittersheim** France
37 N4 **Mitterteich** Germany
140 D4 **Mittiebah** *R* N Terr Australia
37 O2 **Mittweida** Germany
128 D3 **Mitú** Colombia
88 B3 **Mitumba** *mts* Zaire
87 E7 **Mitwaba** Zaire
55 D1 **Mityayevo** Russian Federation
86 B5 **Mitzic** Gabon
61 N10 **Miura** Japan
54 K9 **Mius** *R* Rus Fed/Ukraine
54 K9 **Miusskiy Liman** *lagoon* Russian Federation
65 B7 **Mi Xian** China
38 M7 **Mixnitz** Austria
61 K11 **Miya-gawa** *R* Japan
61 O7 **Miyagi** *prefect* Japan
61 Q12 **Miyagi** Okinawa
61 P13 **Miyagusuku-jima** *isld* Okinawa
78 G4 **Miyāh, Wadi Al** Syria
61 N11 **Miyake-jima** *isld* Japan
61 P6 **Miyako** Japan
60 E14 **Miyakonojō** Japan
55 B6 **Miyaly** Kazakhstan
60 E13 **Miyazaki** *prefect* Japan
60 E14 **Miyazaki** Japan
60 J10 **Miyazu** Japan
60 F11 **Miyoshi** Japan
65 C4 **Miyun** China
65 D4 **Miyun Shuiku** *res* China
86 G4 **Mīzan Teferī** Ethiopia
84 E3 **Mizdah** Libya
111 G10 **Mize** Mississippi U.S.A.
14 B5 **Mizen Hd** Cork Ireland
14 E4 **Mizen Hd** Wicklow Ireland
65 A6 **Mizhi** China
48 K6 **Mizil** Romania
46 F1 **Miziya** Bulgaria
75 P7 **Mizoram** *prov* India
99 M2 **Mizpah** Minnesota U.S.A.
79 E7 **Mizpe Ramon** Israel
61 P6 **Mizusawa** Japan
26 K9 **Mjällom** Sweden
88 C1 **Mjanji** Uganda
27 F14 **Mjöbäck** Sweden
27 H13 **Mjölby** Sweden
28 B6 **Mjolden** Denmark
27 D12 **Mjöndalen** Norway
27 F14 **Mjörn** *L* Sweden
27 E11 **Mjösa** *L* Norway
88 C9 **Mkokomo** *mt* Zambia
88 G4 **Mkokotoni** Tanzania
88 B8 **Mkuku** Zambia
87 E8 **Mkushi** Zambia
88 B8 **Mkushi** *R* Zambia
89 H6 **Mkuze** S Africa
31 H5 **Mladá Boleslav** Czechoslovakia
48 F6 **Mladenovac** Serbia Yugoslavia
37 P4 **Mladotice** Czechoslovakia
88 C5 **Mlala Hills** Tanzania
48 G6 **Mlava** *R* Serbia Yugoslavia
31 M2 **Mława** Poland
88 G10 **M'lela** *R* Mozambique
87 G7 **Mlimba** Tanzania
42 H6 **Mljet** *isld* Croatia
88 E7 **Mlowe** Malawi
89 D5 **Mmabatho** S Africa
89 E3 **Mmashoro** Botswana
37 O3 **Mnichov** Czechoslovakia
31 H5 **Mnichovo Hradiště** Czechoslovakia
48 F2 **Mnišek** Czechoslovakia
26 K8 **Mo** Sweden
128 D5 **Moa** *R* Brazil
71 N9 **Moa** *isld* Indonesia
85 B7 **Moa** *R* Sierra Leone/Guinea
103 P3 **Moab** Utah U.S.A.
126 G4 **Moa Grande, Cayo** *isld* Cuba
141 F1 **Moa I** Queensland Australia
119 U3 **Moak L** Manitoba Canada
139 G6 **Moama** New South Wales Australia
89 H5 **Moamba** Mozambique
144 C5 **Moana** New Zealand
138 F3 **Moanba, L** South Australia Australia
86 B6 **Moanda** Gabon
86 B7 **Moanda** Zaire
103 K5 **Moapa** Nevada U.S.A.
71 N8 **Moapora** *isld* Indonesia
14 D3 **Moate** Ireland
88 D10 **Moatize** Mozambique
145 E3 **Moawhango** New Zealand
87 E7 **Moba** Zaire
61 O10 **Mobara** Japan
77 B3 **Mobārakeh** Iran
86 D5 **Mobaye** Cent Afr Republic
86 D5 **Mobayi-Mbongo** Zaire
110 D2 **Moberly** Missouri U.S.A.
117 N8 **Moberly Lake** British Columbia Canada
120 E4 **Mobert** Ontario Canada
111 H11 **Mobile** Alabama U.S.A.
103 M8 **Mobile** Arizona U.S.A.
111 J11 **Mobile Pt** Alabama U.S.A.
141 G7 **Moble** *R* Queensland Australia
71 F4 **Mobo** Philippines
28 A4 **Møborg** Denmark
98 F4 **Mobridge** South Dakota U.S.A.
Mobutu, L *see* **Albert, L**
127 J5 **Moca** Dominican Rep
129 J4 **Mocajuba** Brazil
Moçambique *see* **Mozambique**
88 H9 **Moçambique** *dist* Mozambique
Moçâmedes *see* **Namibe**
95 L5 **Mocanaqua** Pennsylvania U.S.A.
103 M5 **Moccasin** Arizona U.S.A.
101 Q2 **Moccasin** Montana U.S.A.
68 G2 **Moc Chau** Vietnam
125 Q7 **Mocche** Mexico
Mocha *see* **Mukha, Al**
131 A7 **Mocha** *isld* Chile
124 E5 **Mochicahui** Mexico
127 K2 **Mocho Mts** Jamaica
89 E5 **Mochudi** Botswana
88 H7 **Mocímboa da Praia** Mozambique
48 H4 **Mociu** Romania
27 G15 **Möckeln** *L* Sweden
33 P8 **Möckern** Germany
95 M9 **Mockhorn** *isld* Virginia U.S.A.
106 D8 **Mockingbird Gap** *gap* New Mexico U.S.A.
27 J15 **Möckleby, N** Sweden
27 H15 **Möckleby, S** Sweden
36 G5 **Mockmühl** Germany
33 R9 **Mockrehna** Germany
112 G2 **Mocksville** North Carolina U.S.A.
100 A2 **Moclips** Washington U.S.A.
128 C3 **Mocoa** Colombia
130 F7 **Mococa** Brazil
131 F3 **Mocoretá** *R* Argentina
124 F5 **Mocorito** Mexico
124 F2 **Moctezuma** Chihuahua Mexico
124 E3 **Moctezuma** Sonora Mexico
88 F10 **Mocuba** Mozambique
40 E7 **Modane** France
83 K9 **Modaragam Aru** *R* Sri Lanka
74 E7 **Modasa** India
22 J3 **Modave** Belgium
8 C7 **Modbury** England
89 D7 **Modder** *R* S Africa
106 F4 **Model** Colorado U.S.A.
45 J2 **Modena** Italy
45 J3 **Modena** *prov* Italy
103 L4 **Modena** Utah U.S.A.
19 L4 **Moder** *R* France
38 K7 **Moderbrugg** Austria
102 C4 **Modesto** California U.S.A.
43 F12 **Modica** Sicily
45 L3 **Modigliana** Italy
80 C6 **Modi'im** Israel
86 D5 **Modjamboli** Zaire
94 B6 **Modoc** Indiana U.S.A.
107 J3 **Modoc** Kansas U.S.A.
112 E4 **Modoc** South Carolina U.S.A.
100 D7 **Modoc Point** Oregon U.S.A.
58 E2 **Modot** Mongolia
36 B2 **Mödrath** Germany
48 E6 **Modriča** Bosnia-Herzegovina
48 E2 **Modrý Kameň** Czechoslovakia
68 J5 **Mo Đuc** Vietnam
139 H7 **Moe** Victoria Australia
145 E2 **Moehau** *mt* New Zealand
20 C6 **Moelan** France
8 B1 **Moelfre** Wales
8 C2 **Moel Sych** *mt* Wales
27 E11 **Moelv** Norway
129 H2 **Moengo** Suriname
103 N5 **Moenkopi** Arizona U.S.A.
144 B5 **Moeraki, L** New Zealand
22 F1 **Moerbeke** Belgium
25 C5 **Moerdijk** Netherlands
22 D1 **Moere** Belgium
20 G7 **Moëre,la** France
145 E1 **Moerewa** New Zealand
145 E3 **Moeroa** New Zealand
Moero, Lac *see* **Mweru, L**
13 E3 **Moffat** Scotland
106 E3 **Moffat** Colorado U.S.A.
144 B6 **Moffat Pk** New Zealand
98 F3 **Moffit** North Dakota U.S.A.
48 H3 **Moftin** Romania
74 F3 **Moga** India
Mogadiscio *see* **Muqdisho**
Mogadishu *see* **Muqdisho**
94 F5 **Mogadore** Ohio U.S.A.
16 C3 **Mogadouro** Portugal
89 F4 **Mogalakwena** *R* S Africa
61 N7 **Mogami-gawa** *R* Japan
67 F1 **Mogan Shan** *mt* China
75 R6 **Mogaung** Burma
28 B7 **Møgeltønder** Denmark
17 G6 **Mogente** Spain
36 H6 **Mögglingen** Germany
60 C13 **Mogi** Japan
129 J8 **Mogi das Cruzes** Brazil
31 M4 **Mogielnica** Poland
130 F7 **Mogi Guaçu** *R* Brazil
54 H9 **Mogila-Bel'mak Gora** *mt* Ukraine
54 B3 **Mogilëv** Belorussia
48 L2 **Mogilev-Podol'skiy** Ukraine
139 J3 **Mogil-Mogil** New South Wales Australia
31 K3 **Mogilno** Poland
130 F8 **Mogi Mirim** Brazil
88 H9 **Mogincual** Mozambique
45 J2 **Móglia** Italy
42 E3 **Mogliano Veneto** Italy
45 M1 **Mogliano Veneto** Italy
46 D4 **Mogličë** Albania
19 N12 **Mogneneins** France
59 G1 **Mogocha** Russian Federation
68 C1 **Mogok** Burma
89 E4 **Mogol** *R* S Africa
106 B8 **Mogollon** New Mexico U.S.A.
106 B8 **Mogollon Mts** New Mexico U.S.A.
103 O7 **Mogollon Rim** *tableland* Arizona U.S.A.
106 D4 **Mogote** Colorado U.S.A.
56 F5 **Mogoyty** Russian Federation
16 C7 **Moguer** Spain
143 B9 **Mogumber** W Australia Australia
48 E5 **Mohács** Hungary
145 F3 **Mohaka** New Zealand
98 E1 **Mohall** North Dakota U.S.A.
17 H9 **Mohammadia** Algeria
85 C2 **Mohammedia** Morocco
103 K6 **Mohave, L** Nev/Ariz U.S.A.
103 K7 **Mohave Mts** Cal/Ariz U.S.A.
103 L9 **Mohawk** Arizona U.S.A.
99 S2 **Mohawk** Michigan U.S.A.
95 N4 **Mohawk** *R* New York U.S.A.
103 L9 **Mohawk Mts** Arizona U.S.A.
59 H1 **Mohe** China
27 G14 **Moheda** Sweden
87 G10 **Mohéli** *isld* Comoros
87 D9 **Mohembo** Botswana
74 C5 **Mohenjo Daro** *anc site* Pakistan
14 B4 **Moher, Cliffs of** Ireland
116 D6 **Mohican, C** Alaska U.S.A.
14 D3 **Mohill** Ireland
100 J3 **Mohler** Idaho U.S.A.
32 H10 **Möhne** *R* Germany
32 H10 **Möhnesee** Germany
32 H10 **Möhnestausee** *L* Germany
27 G13 **Moholm** Sweden
20 E5 **Mohon** France
103 L7 **Mohon Pk** Arizona U.S.A.
88 G6 **Mohoro** Tanzania
124 H4 **Mohovano Ranch** Mexico
37 J2 **Möhra** Germany
36 G6 **Möhringen** Germany
28 D7 **Mohrkirch** Germany
27 B13 **Moi** Norway
16 B4 **Moimenta da Beira** Portugal
66 C5 **Moincêr** China
21 H7 **Moine** *R* France
95 N2 **Moira** New York U.S.A.
26 G5 **Mo i Rana** Norway
19 P14 **Moirans** France
46 G9 **Moíres** Crete Greece
52 C5 **Mõisaküla** Estonia
20 H6 **Moisdon** France
55 G2 **Moiseyevka** Russian Federation
122 F3 **Moisie** Quebec Canada
19 Q17 **Moissac** France
86 C4 **Moissala** Chad
21 O3 **Moisson** France
21 N6 **Moisy** France
27 K12 **Möja** Sweden
17 F7 **Mojácar** Spain
102 F6 **Mojave** California U.S.A.
102 G7 **Mojave** *R* California U.S.A.
102 G6 **Mojave Desert** California U.S.A.
60 E12 **Moji** Japan
130 F8 **Moji das Cruzes** Brazil
120 B2 **Mojikit L** Ontario Canada
86 G4 **Mojo** Ethiopia
71 H9 **Mojo** *isld* Indonesia
86 F5 **Mojo** Uganda
70 O9 **Mojokerto** Java
128 E7 **Mojos, Llanos de** *plain* Bolivia
129 J4 **Moju** *R* Brazil
61 O9 **Mōka** Japan
145 E3 **Mokai** New Zealand
75 L6 **Mokāma** India
110 E3 **Mokane** Missouri U.S.A.
102 S12 **Mokapu Pen** Hawaiian Is
145 E3 **Mokau** New Zealand
102 D3 **Mokelumne** *R* California U.S.A.
89 F7 **Mokhotlong** *mt* Lesotho
55 F3 **Mokhovoy Prival** Russian Federation
27 J11 **Möklinta** Sweden
85 G1 **Moknine** Tunisia
145 E1 **Mokohinau Is** New Zealand
145 E3 **Mokoia** New Zealand
75 Q5 **Mokokchung** India
86 B3 **Mokolo** Cameroon
144 B7 **Mokoreta** New Zealand
144 B7 **Mokotua** New Zealand
65 G7 **Mokp'o** S Korea
46 D2 **Mokra Gora** *mt* Montenegro/Serbia Yugoslavia
48 F5 **Mokrin** Serbia Yugoslavia
55 E3 **Mokrousovo** Russian Federation
29 L8 **Möksy** Finland
102 S11 **Mokuauia I** Hawaiian Is
135 U5 **Mokuaweoweo Crater** Hawaiian Is
102 R11 **Mokuleia** Hawaiian Is
102 S12 **Mokulua Is** Hawaiian Is
22 J1 **Mol** Belgium
20 F6 **Molac** France
100 C4 **Molalla** Oregon U.S.A.
125 K7 **Molango** Mexico
46 F8 **Moláoi** Greece
42 F4 **Molat** *isld* Croatia
70 G6 **Molawe** Sulawesi
21 J3 **Molay-Littry, le** France
32 G7 **Molbergen** Germany
28 B5 **Mølby** Denmark
8 C1 **Mold** Wales
48 G2 **Moldava nad Bodvon** Czechoslovakia
53 C10 **Moldavia** *rep* E Europe
48 K4 **Moldavia** *reg* Romania
Moldavskaya S.S.R *see* **Moldavia** E Europe
26 B9 **Molde** Norway
Moldova *see* **Moldavia**
48 K3 **Moldova** *R* Romania
48 J5 **Moldoveanu** *mt* Romania
48 K3 **Moldoviţa** Romania
28 D3 **Møldrup** Denmark
40 D5 **Môle** *mt* France
20 A5 **Molène** *isld* France
89 D5 **Molepolole** Botswana
8 C6 **Mole, R** England
9 F5 **Mole, R** England
144 D5 **Molesworth** New Zealand
43 H7 **Molfetta** Italy
133 C5 **Molina** Chile
17 F4 **Molina de Aragón** Spain
17 G6 **Molina de Segura** Spain
99 Q8 **Moline** Illinois U.S.A.
107 O4 **Moline** Kansas U.S.A.
94 B4 **Moline** Michigan U.S.A.
45 L2 **Molinella** Italy
38 E8 **Molini** Italy
124 D3 **Molino** Mexico
111 J11 **Molino** Florida U.S.A.
42 F7 **Molise** *prov* Italy
40 D2 **Mollans** France
29 K4 **Mölle** Sweden
28 C5 **Møllebjerg** *hill* Denmark
33 S6 **Möllenbeck** Germany
128 D7 **Mollendo** Peru
33 R5 **Möllenhagen** Germany
143 C9 **Mollerin L** W Australia Australia
28 D4 **Mollerup** Denmark
17 H3 **Mollerusa** Spain
26 O2 **Mollesjok** Norway
21 P2 **Molliens-Dreuil** France
12 D2 **Mollinsburn** Scotland
26 M2 **Mollius** *mt* Norway
33 N5 **Mölln** Germany
33 S5 **Mölln** Germany
38 G8 **Molltal** *V* Austria
27 F14 **Mölndal** Sweden
54 G9 **Molochansk** Ukraine
53 E10 **Molochnyy, Liman** Ukraine
88 G10 **Molocue** *R* Mozambique
146 K9 **Molodezhnaya** *former U.S.S.R. Base* Antarctica
54 D8 **Molodezhnoye** Ukraine
55 F5 **Molodezhnyy** Kazakhstan
56 B2 **Molodezhnyy** Russian Federation
55 F4 **Molodogvardeyskoye** Kazakhstan
52 D6 **Molodoy-Tud** Russian Federation
52 E5 **Mologa** *R* Russian Federation
102 V13 **Molokai** *isld* Hawaiian Is
135 S3 **Molokini** *isld* Hawaiian Is
52 E5 **Molokovo** Russian Federation
52 G5 **Moloma** *R* Russian Federation
139 J5 **Molong** New South Wales Australia
89 B6 **Molopo** *R* S Africa
46 F6 **Mólos** Greece
86 C5 **Moloundou** Cameroon
28 F4 **Mols B** *hill* Denmark
89 F5 **Molsgat** S Africa
36 D6 **Molsheim** France
118 E1 **Molson** Manitoba Canada
119 V4 **Molson L** Manitoba Canada
101 R4 **Molt** Montana U.S.A.
87 E12 **Molteno** S Africa
Moluccas *see* **Malaku** *islds*
88 G10 **Moma** Mozambique
51 O2 **Moma** *R* Russian Federation
86 D6 **Moma** Zaire
139 G4 **Momba** New South Wales Australia
88 D6 **Momba** *R* Tanzania
45 N4 **Mombaroccio** Italy
88 G4 **Mombasa** Kenya
60 R1 **Mombetsu** Japan
60 Q3 **Mombetsu** Japan
130 D6 **Mombuca, Serra da** *mts* Brazil
46 G3 **Momchilgrad** Bulgaria
99 T8 **Momence** Illinois U.S.A.
22 G3 **Momignies** Belgium
36 D6 **Mommenheim** France
70 G5 **Momo** Sulawesi
71 F4 **Mompog Passage** Philippines
86 D5 **Mompono** Zaire
126 G10 **Mompós** Colombia
Môn *isld* *see* **Anglesey**
68 B2 **Mon** *R* Burma
68 C3 **Mon** Burma
29 K7 **Møn** *isld* Denmark
127 L2 **Mona** Jamaica
103 N2 **Mona** Utah U.S.A.
94 G6 **Monaca** Pennsylvania U.S.A.
15 A3 **Monach I** Outer Hebrides Scotland
44 B4 **Monaco** *princ* W Europe
15 D3 **Monadhliath Mts** Scotland
29 J8 **Monå Fjärd** *inlet* Finland
128 F2 **Monagas** *state* Venezuela
14 E2 **Monaghan** *co* Ireland
14 E2 **Monaghan** Ireland
108 E4 **Monahans** Texas U.S.A.
127 L5 **Mona, I** Puerto Rico
98 H3 **Monango** North Dakota U.S.A.
87 C7 **Mona Quimbundo** Angola
118 D9 **Monarch** Alberta Canada
106 D3 **Monarch** Colorado U.S.A.
101 P2 **Monarch** Montana U.S.A.
117 L10 **Monarch Mt** British Columbia Canada
103 N2 **Mona Res** Utah U.S.A.
117 O10 **Monashee Mts** British Columbia Canada
14 D3 **Monasterevin** Ireland
18 H8 **Monastier, le** France
43 D13 **Monastir** Tunisia
48 J1 **Monastyriska** Ukraine
55 D2 **Monastyrskoye** Russian Federation
44 C2 **Moncalieri** Italy
16 B2 **Monção** Portugal
17 F3 **Moncayo, Sierra del** Spain
22 F4 **Monceau-le-Neuf** France
38 L5 **Mönchdorf** Austria
52 D1 **Monchegorsk** Russian Federation
36 B1 **Mönchengladbach** Germany
30 H1 **Mönchgut** *pen* Germany
16 B7 **Monchique** Portugal
101 R1 **Monchy** Saskatchewan Canada
112 G4 **Moncks Corner** South Carolina U.S.A.
124 J4 **Monclova** Mexico
20 E5 **Moncontour** Côtes d'Armor France
21 K8 **Moncontour** Vienne France
122 A5 **Moncouche, L** Quebec Canada
21 J8 **Moncoutant** France
122 H7 **Moncton** New Brunswick Canada
130 D10 **Mondai** Brazil
99 L8 **Mondamin** Iowa U.S.A.
45 N4 **Mondavio** Italy
130 C9 **Monday, R** Paraguay
16 B4 **Mondego** *R* Portugal
16 B4 **Mondego, C** Portugal
16 E4 **Mondéjar** Spain
21 K3 **Mondeville** France
89 G3 **Mondi** *R* Zimbabwe
89 G6 **Mondlo** S Africa
86 C3 **Mondo** Chad
45 O4 **Mondolfo** Italy
16 C1 **Mondoñedo** Spain
22 L4 **Mondorf-les-Bains** Luxembourg
21 M6 **Mondoubleau** France
44 C3 **Mondovi** Italy
99 P5 **Mondovi** Wisconsin U.S.A.
19 N16 **Mondragon** France
45 P7 **Mondragone** Italy
143 E10 **Mondrain I** W Australia Australia
41 P3 **Mondschein Spitze** *mt* Austria
38 H6 **Mondsee** Austria
127 K2 **Moneague** Jamaica
44 F3 **Moneglia** Italy
18 E9 **Monein** France
46 F8 **Monemvasía** Greece
94 H9 **Moneta** Virginia U.S.A.
101 S6 **Moneta** Wyoming U.S.A.
110 C5 **Monett** Missouri U.S.A.
110 F6 **Monette** Arkansas U.S.A.
42 F3 **Monfalcone** Italy
68 D3 **Mon Fang** Thailand
44 C2 **Monferrato** *dist* Italy
86 D5 **Monga** Zaire
95 N5 **Mongaup Vall** New York U.S.A.
68 H2 **Mong Cai** Vietnam
142 A1 **Monger L** Perth, W Aust Australia
143 B8 **Monger, L** W Australia Australia
68 D2 **Mong Hai** Burma
68 D2 **Mong Hang** Burma
45 K3 **Monghidoro** Italy
68 E2 **Mong Hkan** Burma
68 D2 **Mong Hkok** Burma
68 D2 **Mong Hpayak** Burma
68 D2 **Mong Hsat** Burma
68 C2 **Mong Hsawk** Burma
68 D2 **Mong Hsu** Burma
44 C3 **Mongioie** *mt* Italy
68 F6 **Mongkol Borey** Cambodia
68 D3 **Mong Kyawt** Burma
68 D2 **Mong La** Burma
68 E2 **Mong Lin** Burma
68 E2 **Mong Loi** Burma
68 C1 **Mong Long** Burma
68 C2 **Mong Long** Burma
68 C3 **Mong Mau** Burma
68 C2 **Mong Nai** Burma
68 D2 **Mong Nawng** Burma
17 H6 **Mongo** *mt* Spain
94 B5 **Mongo** Indiana U.S.A.
58 C2 **Mongolia** *rep* Asia
Mongolküre *see* **Zhaosu**
85 G8 **Mongomo** Mbini Equat Guinea
142 F3 **Mongona,Mt** W Australia Australia
86 B3 **Mongonu** Nigeria
68 C3 **Mong Pai** Burma
68 D2 **Mong Pan** Burma
68 D1 **Mong Pat** Burma
68 D1 **Mong Pawk** Burma
68 C2 **Mong Pawn** Burma
68 D2 **Mong Ping** Burma
68 D2 **Mong Pu** Burma
68 D2 **Mong Pu-awn** Burma
124 H9 **Mongrove, Pta** *C* Mexico
68 D2 **Mong Ton** Burma
68 D2 **Mong Tum** Burma
68 C1 **Mong Tung** Burma
87 D9 **Mongu** Zambia
38 F8 **Monguelfo** Italy
68 E2 **Mong Un** Burma
68 D1 **Mong Yai** Burma
68 D2 **Mong Yang** Burma
68 D2 **Mong Yawn** Burma
68 E2 **Mong Yawng** Burma
95 S3 **Monhegan I** Maine U.S.A.
37 K6 **Monheim** Bayern Germany
36 B1 **Monheim** Nordrhein-Westfalen Germany
113 E7 **Moniac** Georgia U.S.A.
12 E3 **Moniaive** Scotland
19 O16 **Monieux** France
13 F1 **Monifieth** Scotland
18 H7 **Monistrol-sur-Loire** France
118 G7 **Monitor** Alberta Canada
102 H3 **Monitor** *pk* Nevada U.S.A.
14 C3 **Monivea** Ireland
28 B7 **Mönkebüll** Germany
140 F6 **Monkira** Queensland Australia
86 D6 **Monkoto** Zaire
120 J9 **Monkton** Ontario Canada
12 D3 **Monkton** Scotland
Monmouth *co see* **Gwent**
99 Q9 **Monmouth** Illinois U.S.A.
95 R2 **Monmouth** Maine U.S.A.
8 D4 **Monmouth** Wales
117 M10 **Monmouth, Mt** British Columbia Canada
21 L4 **Monnai** France
21 M7 **Monnaie** France
25 D3 **Monnickendam** Netherlands
85 E7 **Mono** *R* Togo
102 F3 **Mono L** California U.S.A.
47 U17 **Monólithos** Rhodes Greece
95 S5 **Monomoy Pt** Massachusetts U.S.A.
99 U9 **Monon** Indiana U.S.A.
99 P6 **Monona** Iowa U.S.A.
94 G7 **Monongah** West Virginia U.S.A.
94 H6 **Monongahela** Pennsylvania U.S.A.
43 H8 **Monopoli** Italy
48 E3 **Monor** Hungary
127 N1 **Monos I** Trinidad
86 D2 **Monou** Chad
17 G6 **Monóvar** Spain
144 A6 **Monowai** New Zealand
98 H7 **Monowi** Nebraska U.S.A.
18 F8 **Monpont** France
36 C3 **Monreal** Germany
17 G4 **Monreal del Campo** Spain
43 E10 **Monreale** Sicily
102 A2 **Monroe** California U.S.A.
112 D4 **Monroe** Georgia U.S.A.
94 C6 **Monroe** Indiana U.S.A.
99 N8 **Monroe** Iowa U.S.A.
111 D9 **Monroe** Louisiana U.S.A.
94 D5 **Monroe** Michigan U.S.A.
95 N5 **Monroe** New York U.S.A.
112 G3 **Monroe** North Carolina U.S.A.
100 B5 **Monroe** Oregon U.S.A.
95 L5 **Monroe** Pennsylvania U.S.A.
98 J6 **Monroe** South Dakota U.S.A.
103 M3 **Monroe** Utah U.S.A.
94 H9 **Monroe** Virginia U.S.A.
100 D2 **Monroe** Washington U.S.A.
99 R7 **Monroe** Wisconsin U.S.A.
99 P10 **Monroe City** Missouri U.S.A.
113 F9 **Monroe, L** Florida U.S.A.
110 K2 **Monroe L** Indiana U.S.A.
111 J10 **Monroeville** Alabama U.S.A.
94 C6 **Monroeville** Indiana U.S.A.
94 E5 **Monroeville** Ohio U.S.A.
85 B7 **Monrovia** Liberia
102 G7 **Monrovia** California U.S.A.
17 G4 **Monroyo** Spain
22 F3 **Mons** Belgium
16 C4 **Monsanto** Portugal
130 H6 **Monsarás, Pta. de** Brazil
22 L2 **Monschau** Germany
71 H7 **Monse** Indonesia
42 D3 **Monselice** Italy
36 E4 **Monsheim** Germany
29 K7 **Møns Klint** *cliffs* Denmark
95 P4 **Monson** Massachusetts U.S.A.
68 C3 **Mon State** Burma
28 C4 **Mønsted** Denmark
25 B4 **Monster** Netherlands
27 H14 **Mönsterås** Sweden
45 J4 **Monsummano Terme** Italy
22 K3 **Mont** Belgium
36 D3 **Montabaur** Germany
41 L3 **Montafon** *V* Austria
45 K1 **Montagnana** Italy
89 B9 **Montagu** S Africa
122 K7 **Montague** Prince Edward I Canada
100 C8 **Montague** California U.S.A.
94 A3 **Montague** Michigan U.S.A.
109 K2 **Montague** Texas U.S.A.
139 K6 **Montague I** New South Wales Australia
103 K10 **Montague, I** Mexico
116 O6 **Montague I** Alaska U.S.A.
143 C7 **Montague Ra** W Australia Australia
142 F2 **Montague Sd** W Australia Australia
116 N7 **Montague Str** Alaska U.S.A.
146 G3 **Montagu I** S Sandwich Is S Atlantic Oc
20 H8 **Montaigu** France
18 F8 **Montaigu-de-Quercy** France
40 D7 **Montaimont** France
45 J4 **Montaione** Italy
70 D5 **Montalat** *R* Kalimantan
17 G4 **Montalbán** Spain
127 K9 **Montalbán** Venezuela
45 K4 **Montale** Italy
16 B3 **Montalegre** Portugal
40 B6 **Montalieu** France
19 O13 **Montalieu Vercieu** France
43 G10 **Montalto** *mt* Italy
21 L8 **Montamise** France
101 P3 **Montana** *state* U.S.A.
116 N5 **Montana** Alaska U.S.A.
40 G7 **Montanaro** Italy
16 C5 **Montánchez** Spain
121 T5 **Mont-Apica** Quebec Canada
18 G5 **Montargis** France
21 P3 **Montataire** France
18 F9 **Montauban** France
20 F5 **Montauban-de-Bretagne** France
21 J5 **Montaudin** France
18 H5 **Montbard** France
40 C3 **Montbarrey** France
21 M7 **Montbazon** France
40 E2 **Montbéliard** France
109 N6 **Mont Belvieu** Texas U.S.A.
40 D4 **Montbenoit** France
20 H7 **Montbert** France
40 E6 **Mont Blanc** *mt* France
17 H3 **Montblanch** Spain
Montblanc Vilanovai *see* **Montblanch Vilanuevay**
40 D3 **Montbozon** France
21 H4 **Montbray** France
18 H7 **Montbrison** France
Montcalm, L *see* **Dogai Coring**
18 F10 **Montcalm, Pic** *mt* France
21 J4 **Montchamp** France
22 G4 **Montcornet** France
18 E9 **Mont de Marsan** France
22 D4 **Montdidier** France
43 G9 **Montea** *mt* Italy
110 L6 **Monteagle** Tennessee U.S.A.
129 H4 **Monte Alegre** Brazil
17 G6 **Montealegre del Castillo** Spain
130 E6 **Monte Alegre de Minas** Brazil
130 G4 **Monte Azul** Brazil
121 Q7 **Montebello** Quebec Canada
142 B5 **Monte Bello Is** W Australia Australia
45 K1 **Montebello Vic** Italy
42 E3 **Montebelluna** Italy
20 H3 **Montebourg** France
45 N4 **Montecalvo in Foglia** Italy
45 S7 **Montecalvo Irpino** Italy
133 G3 **Montecarlo** Argentina
44 B4 **Monte-Carlo** Monaco
129 J7 **Monte Carmelo** Brazil
45 O4 **Montecarotto** Italy
131 F3 **Monte Caseros** Argentina
45 J4 **Montecatini Terme** Italy
45 J2 **Montecchio Emilia** Italy
45 K1 **Montecchio Maggiore** Italy
45 H2 **Montecchio nell'Emilia** Italy
45 N5 **Montecélio** Italy
18 F9 **Montech** France
112 H3 **Monte Clare** South Carolina U.S.A.
45 R8 **Montecorvino Rovella** Italy
45 J3 **Montecreto** Italy
127 J5 **Montecristi** Dominican Rep
128 F6 **Monte Cristo** Bolivia
42 C6 **Montecristo, I.di** Italy
41 O4 **Montecroce, Pta di** *mt* Italy
124 H6 **Monte Escobedo** Mexico
45 M4 **Montefeltro** Italy
45 J3 **Montefiorino** Italy
45 R8 **Monteforte Irpina** Italy
16 E7 **Montefrio** Spain
127 J1 **Montego Bay** Jamaica
45 M4 **Monte Grimano** Italy
130 H9 **Monteiro** Brazil
140 B3 **Montejinnie** N Terr Australia
45 O6 **Montelanico** Italy
131 E6 **Monte, L.del** Argentina
19 N15 **Montélimar** France
129 G8 **Monte Lindo** Paraguay
108 G6 **Montell** Texas U.S.A.
45 S8 **Montella** Italy
16 D8 **Montellano** Spain
101 L8 **Montello** Nevada U.S.A.
99 R6 **Montello** Wisconsin U.S.A.
45 K4 **Montelupo Fiorentino** Italy
45 R8 **Montemárano** Italy
45 O4 **Montemarciano** Italy
133 D6 **Montemayor, Meseta de** *hills* Argentina
45 L4 **Montemignaio** Italy
45 R7 **Montemiletto** Italy
125 K5 **Montemorelos** Mexico
45 K4 **Montemurio** Italy
21 J5 **Montenay** France
18 E7 **Montendre** France
46 C2 **Montenegro** *reg* Yugoslavia
46 C2 **Montenegro** *rep* Yugoslavia
20 F6 **Monteneuf** France
42 D6 **Montepescali** Italy
127 K5 **Monte Plata** Dominican Rep
45 O4 **Monteporzio** Italy
88 G8 **Montepuez** Mozambique
42 D5 **Montepulciano** Italy
18 G4 **Montereau** France
45 K3 **Monterenzio** Italy
102 C5 **Monterey** California U.S.A.
99 U8 **Monterey** Indiana U.S.A.
110 L5 **Monterey** Tennessee U.S.A.
94 H8 **Monterey** Virginia U.S.A.
102 B5 **Monterey B** California U.S.A.
126 G10 **Montería** Colombia
128 F7 **Montero** Bolivia
21 N2 **Montérolier** France
45 M5 **Monterosi** Italy
44 M5 **Monterosi, L** Italy
45 N5 **Monterotondo** Italy
125 J5 **Monterrey** Mexico
42 G7 **Monte S. Angelo** Italy
100 B3 **Montesano** Washington U.S.A.
130 G11 **Monte Santo** Brazil
130 F7 **Monte Santo de Minas** Brazil
45 R7 **Montesarchio** Italy
45 O7 **Monte S. Biágio** Italy
129 K7 **Montes Claros** Brazil
45 J3 **Montese** Italy
45 O4 **Montesicuro** Italy
45 K4 **Montespértoli** Italy
18 F9 **Montesquieu-Volvestre** France
18 H6 **Montet, le** France
19 N16 **Monteux** France
111 K8 **Montevallo** Alabama U.S.A.
42 D5 **Montevarchi** Italy
45 K3 **Monteveglio** Italy
45 O5 **Monte Velino** Italy
131 G5 **Montevideo** Uruguay
99 L5 **Montevideo** Minnesota U.S.A.
101 N6 **Monteview** Idaho U.S.A.
106 D4 **Monte Vista** Colorado U.S.A.
103 L8 **Montezuma** Arizona U.S.A.
112 C5 **Montezuma** Georgia U.S.A.
99 T10 **Montezuma** Indiana U.S.A.
99 O8 **Montezuma** Iowa U.S.A.
107 K4 **Montezuma** Kansas U.S.A.
106 E6 **Montezuma** New Mexico U.S.A.
103 N7 **Montezuma Castle Nat.Mon** Arizona U.S.A.
102 G4 **Montezuma Pk** Nevada U.S.A.
20 H2 **Montfarville** France
21 H7 **Montfaucon** Maine-et-Loire France
22 J5 **Montfaucon** Meuse France
19 P14 **Montferrat** France
21 O4 **Montfort-l'Amaury** France
21 L5 **Montfort-le-Rotrou** France
20 G5 **Montfort-sur-Meu** France
21 M3 **Montfort-sur-Risle** France
19 N17 **Montfrin** France
Montgomery *co see* **Powys**
111 K9 **Montgomery** Alabama U.S.A.
111 D10 **Montgomery** Louisiana U.S.A.
94 C5 **Montgomery** Michigan U.S.A.
99 N5 **Montgomery** Minnesota U.S.A.
109 M5 **Montgomery** Texas U.S.A.
94 F8 **Montgomery** West Virginia U.S.A.
8 C2 **Montgomery** Wales
110 E3 **Montgomery City** Missouri U.S.A.
100 D9 **Montgomery Creek** California U.S.A.
142 E3 **Montgomery I** W Australia Australia
18 E7 **Montguyon** France
22 H4 **Monthermé** France
40 E5 **Monthey** Switzerland
22 H5 **Monthois** France
40 C1 **Monthureux-sur-Saône** France
43 C8 **Monti** Sardinia
111 E8 **Monticello** Arkansas U.S.A.
113 D7 **Monticello** Florida U.S.A.
112 D4 **Monticello** Georgia U.S.A.
110 H1 **Monticello** Illinois U.S.A.
110 K1 **Monticello** Indiana U.S.A.
99 P7 **Monticello** Iowa U.S.A.
110 M5 **Monticello** Kentucky U.S.A.
95 T7 **Monticello** Maine U.S.A.
99 N4 **Monticello** Minnesota U.S.A.
111 F10 **Monticello** Mississippi U.S.A.
110 E1 **Monticello** Missouri U.S.A.
106 C8 **Monticello** New Mexico U.S.A.
95 N5 **Monticello** New York U.S.A.
103 P4 **Monticello** Utah U.S.A.
99 R7 **Monticello** Wisconsin U.S.A.
45 J1 **Montichiari** Italy
43 C8 **Monti del Gennargentu** Sardinia
131 F3 **Montiel, Cuchilla de** *mts* Argentina
21 O8 **Montierchaume** France
19 J4 **Montier en Der** France
22 D5 **Montiers** France
18 F7 **Montignac** France
18 F7 **Montignac-Charente** France
21 H4 **Montigny** Manche France
36 B6 **Montigny** Meurthe-et-Moselle France
40 B2 **Montigny-le-Roi** France
16 B6 **Montijo** Portugal
16 C6 **Montijo** Spain
125 O6 **Montijo, G.de** Panama
16 D7 **Montilla** Spain
21 O8 **Montipouret** France
45 N5 **Monti Sabini** Italy
130 D5 **Montividiu** Brazil
21 L2 **Montivilliers** France
21 J7 **Montjean** Maine-et-Loire France
21 J5 **Montjean** Mayenne France
21 H4 **Montjoie** France
122 D5 **Mont-Joli** Quebec Canada
138 F2 **Montkeleary** *R* South Australia Australia
21 N5 **Montlandon** France
121 P6 **Mont-Laurier** Quebec Canada
40 E3 **Montlebon** France
21 P4 **Montlhéry** France
18 E7 **Montlieu** France
122 G4 **Mont Louis** Quebec Canada
18 G10 **Mont Louis** France
18 G6 **Montluçon** France
19 O13 **Montluel** France
122 B7 **Montmagny** Quebec Canada
20 G4 **Montmartin-sur-Mer** France
119 O8 **Montmartre** Saskatchewan Canada
22 J4 **Montmédy** France
19 Q14 **Montmélian** France
40 A5 **Montmerle** France
19 Q17 **Montmeyan** France
19 N15 **Montmeyran** France
18 H4 **Montmirail** Marne France
21 M5 **Montmirail** Sarthe France
18 F7 **Montmoreau St Cybard** France
21 P4 **Montmorency** France
122 A6 **Montmorency, R** Quebec Canada
18 F6 **Montmorillon** France
19 P16 **Montmorin** France
141 K6 **Monto** Queensland Australia
20 F7 **Montoir-de-Bretagne** France
21 M6 **Montoire-sur-le-Loir** France
45 M3 **Montone** *R* Italy
16 E6 **Montoro** Spain
99 O8 **Montour** Iowa U.S.A.
95 L4 **Montour Falls** New York U.S.A.
21 J8 **Montournais** France
95 L5 **Montoursville** Pennsylvania U.S.A.
106 F6 **Montoya** New Mexico U.S.A.
127 J2 **Montpelier** Jamaica
101 O7 **Montpelier** Idaho U.S.A.
110 L1 **Montpelier** Indiana U.S.A.
98 H3 **Montpelier** North Dakota U.S.A.
94 C5 **Montpelier** Ohio U.S.A.
95 P2 **Montpelier** Vermont U.S.A.
121 P7 **Montpellier** Quebec Canada
18 H9 **Montpellier** France
40 B4 **Montpont** France
120 K5 **Montreal** *R* Ontario Canada
121 R7 **Montréal** Quebec Canada
18 G9 **Montréal** France
99 Q3 **Montreal** Wisconsin U.S.A.
120 F5 **Montreal I** Ontario Canada
119 M4 **Montreal Lake** Saskatchewan Canada
119 M4 **Montreal R** Saskatchewan Canada
120 F5 **Montreal River** Ontario Canada
18 G9 **Montredon Labessonié** France
18 F9 **Montrejeau** France
21 N7 **Montrésor** France
22 B3 **Montreuil** France
21 K7 **Montreuil Bellay** France
21 K5 **Montreuil-le-Chetif** France
20 G5 **Montreuil-sur-Ille** France
40 E5 **Montreux** Switzerland
21 H7 **Montrevault** France
21 N7 **Montrichard** France
19 P18 **Montrieux le Vieux** France
6 L5 **Montrose** *oil rig* North Sea
15 F4 **Montrose** Scotland
111 E8 **Montrose** Arkansas U.S.A.
106 C3 **Montrose** Colorado U.S.A.
110 H2 **Montrose** Illinois U.S.A.
99 P9 **Montrose** Iowa U.S.A.
98 C7 **Montrose** Nebraska U.S.A.
95 L5 **Montrose** Pennsylvania U.S.A.
98 J6 **Montrose** South Dakota U.S.A.
95 L8 **Montross** Virginia U.S.A.
22 G3 **Mont. St.Christophe** Belgium
22 H2 **Mont.St.Guibert** Belgium
22 G2 **Mont-St.Jean** Belgium
22 K4 **Mont St.Martin** France
20 G4 **Mont-St. Michel, B. du** France
20 G4 **Mont-St.Michel, le** France
21 J4 **Montsecret** France
17 H2 **Montseny** *mt* Spain
17 J3 **Montseny, Sierra de** *mts* Spain
127 N6 **Montserrat** *isld* Lesser Antilles
17 J3 **Montserrat** *dist* Spain
129 H3 **Montsinery** Fr Guiana
21 L7 **Montsoreau** France
21 P3 **Montsoult** France
115 N8 **Monts, Pointe des** Quebec Canada
21 L8 **Mont-sur-Guesnes** France
21 J5 **Montsûrs** France
121 Q6 **Mont Tremblant** Quebec Canada
21 L4 **Montviette** France
95 P5 **Montville** Connecticut U.S.A.
106 F2 **Monument** Colorado U.S.A.
107 J2 **Monument** Kansas U.S.A.
108 D3 **Monument** New Mexico U.S.A.
100 F5 **Monument** Oregon U.S.A.
116 F4 **Monument Mt** Alaska U.S.A.
103 O4 **Monument V** Utah/Ariz U.S.A.
86 D5 **Monveda** Zaire
21 N2 **Monville** France
68 B1 **Monywa** Burma
41 K6 **Monza** Italy
87 E9 **Monze** Zambia
17 H3 **Monzón** Spain
45 K3 **Monzuno** Italy
109 K4 **Moody** Texas U.S.A.
95 O2 **Mooers** New York U.S.A.
138 E3 **Moolawatana** South Australia Australia
138 E2 **Moolionburrinna, L** South Australia Australia
138 F3 **Moomba Oil & Gas Field** South Australia Australia
139 J3 **Moomin** *R* New South Wales Australia
138 D4 **Moonaree** South Australia Australia
120 H3 **Moonbeam** Ontario Canada
140 F7 **Moonda L** Queensland Australia
141 J8 **Moonie** *R* Queensland Australia
141 K8 **Moonie** Queensland Australia
103 O1 **Moon L.Res** Utah U.S.A.
139 K4 **Moonoi Ra** *mts* New South Wales Australia
138 D5 **Moonta** South Australia Australia
143 B9 **Moora** W Australia Australia
140 F7 **Mooraberree** Queensland Australia
98 B5 **Moorcroft** Wyoming U.S.A.
101 M6 **Moore** Idaho U.S.A.
101 Q3 **Moore** Montana U.S.A.
107 N6 **Moore** Oklahoma U.S.A.
109 H6 **Moore** Texas U.S.A.
134 A11 **Moorea** *isld* Society Is Pacific Oc
116 J5 **Moore Creek** Alaska U.S.A.
98 F9 **Moorefield** Nebraska U.S.A.
94 J7 **Moorefield** West Virginia U.S.A.
113 F11 **Moore Haven** Florida U.S.A.
143 C8 **Moore, L** W Australia Australia
108 E7 **Mooreland** Oklahoma U.S.A.
140 D2 **Moore, Mt** N Terr Australia
143 E7 **Moore, Mt** W Australia Australia
143 C9 **Moore, Mt** W Australia Australia
143 A8 **Moore, Pt** W Australia Australia
95 Q2 **Moore Res** Vermont U.S.A.
112 J3 **Moores Cr. Nat. Mil. Park** North Carolina U.S.A.
113 K11 **Moore's I** Bahamas
122 E8 **Moore's Mills** New Brunswick Canada
110 K2 **Mooresville** Indiana U.S.A.
112 G2 **Mooresville** North Carolina U.S.A.
98 J3 **Mooreton** North Dakota U.S.A.
127 M2 **Moore Town** Jamaica
13 E2 **Moorfoot Hills** Scotland
98 K3 **Moorhead** Minnesota U.S.A.
111 F8 **Moorhead** Mississippi U.S.A.
101 U4 **Moorhead** Montana U.S.A.
109 O3 **Mooringsport** Louisiana U.S.A.
121 N6 **Moor Lake** Ontario Canada
99 M7 **Moorland** Iowa U.S.A.
110 J4 **Moorman** Kentucky U.S.A.
139 G5 **Moornanyah L** New South Wales Australia
87 F7 **Moorokosa** Zambia
141 K2 **Moorooka** *dist* Brisbane, Qnsld Australia
140 D1 **Mooroongga I** N Terr Australia
139 H6 **Mooroopna** Victoria Australia
102 F7 **Moorpark** California U.S.A.

204 Moorsel — Mudurnu

22 G2 Moorsel Belgium
22 E2 Moorslede Belgium
89 F5 Moos R S Africa
37 N4 Moosbach Germany
32 L9 Moosberg mt Germany
37 M7 Mooshurg Germany
120 J2 Moose R Ontario Canada
101 P6 Moose Wyoming U.S.A.
120 K1 Moose Factory Ontario Canada
95 S1 Moosehead L Maine U.S.A.
119 O2 Moose Hill Ontario Canada
119 T7 Moosehorn Manitoba Canada
119 U7 Moose I Manitoba Canada
119 M8 Moose Jaw Saskatchewan Canada
119 N8 Moosejaw Cr Saskatchewan Canada
119 O3 Moose L Minnesota U.S.A.
119 R5 Moose Lake Manitoba Canada
95 R2 Mooselookmeguntic L Maine U.S.A.
119 P9 Moose Mt. Prov. Park Saskatchewan Canada
119 W2 Moose Nose L Manitoba Canada
116 N6 Moose Pass Alaska U.S.A.
120 J2 Moose River Ontario Canada
37 N6 Moosham Germany
38 M8 Mooskirchen Austria
119 Q8 Moosomin Saskatchewan Canada
120 K1 Moosonee Ontario Canada
95 Q5 Moosup Connecticut U.S.A.
89 G7 Moot R S Africa
138 F4 Mootwingee New South Wales Australia
87 G9 Mopeia Mozambique
85 D6 Mopti Mali
77 K3 Moqor Afghanistan
99 P3 Moquah Wisconsin U.S.A.
128 D7 Moquegua dept Peru
128 D7 Moquegua Peru
48 E3 Mór Hungary
86 B3 Mora Cameroon
16 B6 Mora Portugal
16 E5 Mora Spain
27 G10 Mora Sweden
100 J6 Mora Idaho U.S.A.
99 N4 Mora Minnesota U.S.A.
106 E6 Mora New Mexico U.S.A.
46 C2 Morača R Montenegro Yugoslavia
131 B5 Mora, Cerro pk Arg/Chile
74 H4 Moradabad India
16 B5 Moradal, Sa. do mts Portugal
130 F6 Morada Nova de Minas Brazil
17 H3 Mora de Ebro Spain
17 G4 Mora de Rubielos Spain
87 G11 Morafenobe Madagascar
31 M2 Morag Poland
83 K11 Moragala Sri Lanka
133 C6 Moraleda, Canal str Chile
109 L6 Morales Texas U.S.A.
87 H11 Moramanga Madagascar
110 A4 Moran Kansas U.S.A.
109 H3 Moran Texas U.S.A.
101 P6 Moran Wyoming U.S.A.
141 J5 Moranbah Queensland Australia
21 K6 Morannes France
43 G9 Morano Cal Italy
126 G6 Morant Cays reefs W Indies
16 C1 Moras C Spain
16 E4 Moras R Spain
16 E4 Morata de T Spain
17 F6 Moratalla Spain
83 J11 Moratuwa Sri Lanka
31 K7 Morava R Czechoslovakia
48 G6 Morava R Serbia Yugoslavia
48 D1 Moravia Czechoslovakia
99 O9 Moravia Iowa U.S.A.
95 L4 Moravia New York U.S.A.
46 D1 Moravica R Serbia Yugoslavia
31 K6 Moravice R Czechoslovakia
31 K6 Moravská Třebová Czechoslovakia
31 J6 Moravski Budějovice Czechoslovakia
143 B8 Morawa W Australia Australia
128 G2 Morawhanna Guyana
Moray co see Grampian reg
141 H5 Moray Downs Queensland Australia
15 E3 Moray Firth Scotland
140 B3 Moray Ra N Terr Australia
36 C4 Morbach Germany
22 C2 Morbecque France
41 L5 Morbegno Italy
74 D7 Morbi India
20 E6 Morbihan, le B France
27 H15 Mörbylånga Sweden
18 E8 Morcenx France
45 N4 Morciano di Romagna Italy
124 G5 Morcillo Mexico
45 R7 Morcone Italy
9 F2 Morcott England
59 H1 Mordaga China
20 G5 Mordelles France
98 H1 Morden Manitoba Canada
122 H8 Morden Nova Scotia Canada
139 H7 Mordialloc Victoria Australia
52 H4 Mordino Russian Federation
53 F7 Mordovskaya Respublika Russian Federation
116 E9 Mordvinof, C Aleutian Is
31 N3 Mordy Poland
20 E6 Moréac France
98 E4 Moreau R South Dakota U.S.A.
111 E10 Moreauville Louisiana U.S.A.
13 F3 Morebattle Scotland
13 F5 Morecambe England
7 H9 Morecambe oil rig Irish Sea
16 E7 Moreda Spain
139 J3 Moree New South Wales Australia
21 N6 Morée France
141 G2 Morehead R Queensland Australia
94 D8 Morehead Kentucky U.S.A.
112 L3 Morehead City North Carolina U.S.A.
110 G5 Morehouse Missouri U.S.A.
128 F4 Moreira Brazil
101 N6 Moreland Idaho U.S.A.
124 J8 Morelia Mexico
141 G6 Morella Queensland Australia
124 H6 Morelos Mexico
74 H5 Morena India
102 H9 Moreno Res California U.S.A.
16 C7 Morena, Sa mts Spain
103 P8 Morenci Arizona U.S.A.
94 C5 Morenci Michigan U.S.A.
48 K6 Moreni Romania
124 B3 Moreno Mexico
26 C9 More og Romsdal reg Norway
145 F3 Morere New Zealand
12 E4 Moresby England
22 K2 Moresnet Belgium
20 B6 Morestel France
18 G4 Moret France
141 L7 Moreton B Queensland Australia
8 C6 Moretonhampstead England
141 L7 Moreton I Queensland Australia
9 E4 Moreton in Marsh England
95 P2 Moretown Vermont U.S.A.
21 P2 Moreuil France
40 D4 Morez France
36 F4 Mörfelden Germany
29 M3 Morgam Viibus mt Finland
138 E5 Morgan South Australia Australia
112 C6 Morgan Georgia U.S.A.
109 K3 Morgan Texas U.S.A.
101 O8 Morgan Utah U.S.A.
110 J4 Morganfield Kentucky U.S.A.
102 C4 Morgan Hill California U.S.A.
109 J3 Morgan Mill Texas U.S.A.
140 D4 Morgan, Mt N Terr Australia
102 F4 Morgan, Mt California U.S.A.
113 K12 Morgan's Bluff Bahamas
112 F2 Morganton North Carolina U.S.A.
110 K2 Morgantown Indiana U.S.A.
110 K4 Morgantown Kentucky U.S.A.
111 F10 Morgantown Mississippi U.S.A.
94 H7 Morgantown West Virginia U.S.A.
111 E11 Morganza Louisiana U.S.A.
20 A5 Morgat France
40 E4 Morges Switzerland
40 F6 Morgex Italy
21 O3 Morgny France
36 B6 Morhange France
22 K4 Morhet Belgium
122 K2 Morhiban, L.de Quebec Canada
66 E3 Mori China
41 N6 Mori Italy
60 O3 Mori Japan
127 M2 Moriah Tobago
95 O2 Moriah New York U.S.A.
103 K2 Moriah, Mt Nevada U.S.A.
22 H3 Morialme Belgium
108 A1 Moriarty New Mexico U.S.A.
141 H8 Moriarty's Ra Queensland Australia
117 K8 Morice L British Columbia Canada
128 D3 Morichal Colombia
40 H5 Moricone Italy
118 J4 Morin Creek Saskatchewan Canada
59 H2 Morin Dawa China
32 L9 Moringen Germany
52 D5 Morino Russian Federation
118 D5 Morinville Alberta Canada
61 P6 Morioka Japan
124 E3 Moris Mexico
139 K5 Morisset New South Wales Australia
122 B7 Morisset Sta Quebec Canada
32 L8 Moritzberg Germany
37 K3 Moritzberg mt Germany
61 O6 Moriyashi-zan mt Japan
138 F5 Morkalla Victoria Australia
28 E4 Mørke Denmark
52 G6 Morki Russian Federation
28 G5 Mørkøv Denmark
20 C4 Morlaix France
107 K2 Morland Kansas U.S.A.
36 E3 Mörlenbach Germany
118 C7 Morley Alberta Canada
13 G6 Morley England
106 F4 Morley Colorado U.S.A.
110 G4 Morley Missouri U.S.A.
117 G5 Morley River Yukon Territory Canada
45 N5 Morlupe Italy
43 G9 Mormanno Italy
19 O16 Mormoiron France
103 N7 Mormon L Arizona U.S.A.
101 L4 Mormon Mt Idaho U.S.A.
103 K5 Mormon Mts Nevada U.S.A.
19 N13 Mornant France
19 N16 Mornas France
83 M14 Morne, Pte Kerguelen Indian Oc
141 F7 Morney R Queensland Australia
141 F7 Morney Queensland Australia
140 F4 Morning Inlet R Queensland Australia
141 K1 Morningside dist Brisbane, Qnsld Australia
99 P8 Morning Sun Iowa U.S.A.
140 E3 Mornington Queensland Australia
140 E3 Mornington I Queensland Australia
133 B7 Mornington, I Chile
46 E6 Mórnos R Greece
36 F2 Mornshausen Germany
37 L6 Mörnsheim Germany
110 F7 Moro Arkansas U.S.A.
100 E4 Moro Oregon U.S.A.
136 K3 Morobe Papua New Guinea
85 C3 Morocco kingdom N Africa
99 T9 Morocco Indiana U.S.A.
88 F5 Morogoro Tanzania
71 F7 Moro Gulf Philippines
89 C6 Morokweng S Africa
124 J7 Moroleón Mexico
71 J7 Moromaho isld Indonesia
87 G12 Morombe Madagascar
126 E3 Morón Cuba
58 D2 Mörön Mongolia
40 F3 Moron mt Switzerland
127 K9 Morón Venezuela
128 C4 Morona Ecuador
128 C4 Morona-Santiago prov Ecuador
87 G12 Morondava Madagascar
17 F3 Morón de Almazán Spain
16 D7 Morón de la Frontera Spain
87 G10 Moroni Comoros
103 N2 Moroni Utah U.S.A.
66 E5 Moron Us He R China
61 K11 Morotai Japan
71 B1 Morotai isld Halmahera Indonesia
48 E5 Morović Serbia Yugoslavia
70 G5 Morowali Sulawesi
55 D2 Morozkovo Russian Federation
120 J10 Morpeth Ontario Canada
13 G3 Morpeth England
79 C3 Morphou B Cyprus
128 C4 Morral Ohio U.S.A.
130 E9 Morretes Brazil
99 L10 Morrill Kansas U.S.A.
98 C8 Morrill Nebraska U.S.A.
110 D7 Morrilton Arkansas U.S.A.
118 E7 Morrin Alberta Canada
130 E5 Morrinhos Brazil
145 E2 Morrinsville New Zealand
119 U9 Morris Manitoba Canada
99 S8 Morris Illinois U.S.A.
99 L4 Morris Minnesota U.S.A.
95 M4 Morris New York U.S.A.
107 P6 Morris Oklahoma U.S.A.
95 K5 Morris Pennsylvania U.S.A.
121 P8 Morrisburg Ontario Canada
112 H5 Morris I South Carolina U.S.A.
138 B2 Morris, Mt South Australia Australia
142 D4 Morris, Mt W Australia Australia
99 R8 Morrison Illinois U.S.A.
107 O5 Morrison Oklahoma U.S.A.
110 L6 Morrison Tennessee U.S.A.
144 C6 Morrisons New Zealand
122 G3 Morrisonville Illinois U.S.A.
13 E8 Morriston Florida U.S.A.
8 C4 Morriston Wales
103 M8 Morristown Arizona U.S.A.
99 N5 Morristown Minnesota U.S.A.
95 N6 Morristown New Jersey U.S.A.
95 M2 Morristown New York U.S.A.
98 E4 Morristown South Dakota U.S.A.
112 D1 Morristown Tennessee U.S.A.
95 M4 Morrisville New York U.S.A.
95 N6 Morrisville Pennsylvania U.S.A.
95 P2 Morrisville Vermont U.S.A.
94 K8 Morrisville Virginia U.S.A.
130 G4 Morro Brazil
130 E7 Morro Agudo Brazil
102 D6 Morro B California U.S.A.
131 A7 Morro Bonifacio C Chile
130 H7 Morro d'Anta Brazil
131 A8 Morro del Compas C Chile
129 G6 Morro Do Sinal Brazil
133 C3 Morro, Pta Chile
131 D4 Morro, Sa. del pk Argentina
126 G10 Morrosquillo, G. de Colombia
111 D11 Morrow Louisiana U.S.A.
110 M2 Morrow Ohio U.S.A.
88 E10 Morrumbala Mozambique
87 G10 Morrumbene Mozambique
28 B3 Mors isld Denmark
20 H2 Morsalines France
36 D2 Morsbach Germany
36 E6 Mörsch Germany
37 M2 Mörsdorf Germany
118 K8 Morse Saskatchewan Canada
111 D11 Morse Louisiana U.S.A.
108 C7 Morse Texas U.S.A.
53 F7 Morshansk Russian Federation
52 D3 Morskaya Maselga Russian Federation
27 E11 Morskogen Norway
33 O8 Morsleben Germany
118 H1 Morson Ontario Canada
43 B13 Morsott Algeria
140 E4 Morstone Queensland Australia
28 A7 Morsum Germany
26 H4 Morsvik Norway
140 F5 Mort R Queensland Australia
36 B7 Mortagne R France
21 M4 Mortagne-au-Perche France
21 J8 Mortagne-sur-Sèvre France
16 B4 Mortágua Portugal
21 J4 Mortain France
138 C5 Mortana South Australia Australia
41 J7 Mortara Italy
40 E3 Morteau France
21 K4 Morteaux-Coulibœuf France
8 B5 Mortehoe England
130 D7 Mortes R Brazil
129 H6 Mortes, Rio das R Brazil
22 F4 Mortiers France
8 D3 Mortimers Cross England
118 L8 Mortlach Saskatchewan Canada
139 G7 Mortlake Victoria Australia
99 R9 Morton Illinois U.S.A.
99 M5 Morton Minnesota U.S.A.
111 G9 Morton Mississippi U.S.A.
108 E2 Morton Texas U.S.A.
100 C3 Morton Washington U.S.A.
139 J5 Morton Nat Park New South Wales Australia
110 J4 Mortons Gap Kentucky U.S.A.
21 L4 Mortrée France
22 G1 Mortsel Belgium
28 E6 Morud Denmark
127 O3 Moruga Trinidad
139 H5 Morundah New South Wales Australia
139 K6 Moruya New South Wales Australia
18 H5 Morvan mts France
141 H7 Morven Queensland Australia
144 C6 Morven New Zealand
15 E2 Morven mt Scotland
113 D7 Morven Georgia U.S.A.
112 G3 Morven North Carolina U.S.A.
15 C4 Morvern Scotland
8 D2 Morville England
56 B3 Moryakovskiy Zaton Russian Federation
52 F2 Morzhovets, Os isld Russian Federation
116 F9 Morzhovoi B Alaska U.S.A.
54 F2 Mosal'sk Russian Federation
28 E1 Mosbjerg Denmark
101 S2 Mosby Montana U.S.A.
Moscow see Moskva
100 J3 Moscow Idaho U.S.A.
107 J4 Moscow Kansas U.S.A.
110 F3 Moscow Missouri U.S.A.
110 M3 Moscow Ohio U.S.A.
95 M5 Moscow Pennsylvania U.S.A.
110 G6 Moscow Tennessee U.S.A.
146 F14 Moscow University Ice Shelf ice shelf Antarctica
146 E14 Mose, C Antarctica
36 C3 Mosel R Germany
37 N2 Mosel Germany
94 K9 Moseley Virginia U.S.A.
36 C3 Moselkern Germany
36 B5 Moselle dept France
40 E1 Moselle R France
111 G10 Moselle Mississippi U.S.A.
40 E2 Moselotte R France
89 K9 Moser River Nova Scotia Canada
106 G5 Moses New Mexico U.S.A.
100 F2 Moses Coulee R Washington U.S.A.
100 H9 Moses, Mt Nevada U.S.A.
116 F4 Moses Point Alaska U.S.A.
60 P2 Moseushi Japan
52 G2 Moseyevo Russian Federation
144 C6 Mosgiel New Zealand
52 F4 Mosha R Russian Federation
52 C5 Moshchnyy, Ostrov isld Russian Federation
112 E1 Mosheim Tennessee U.S.A.
120 F4 Mosher Ontario Canada
88 F3 Moshi Tanzania
52 F6 Moshok Russian Federation
52 H3 Mosh'yuga Russian Federation
33 Q9 Mosigkau Germany
31 K3 Mosina Poland
99 R5 Mosinee Wisconsin U.S.A.
26 F6 Mosjøen Norway
52 E3 Moskalenki Russian Federation
59 M1 Moskalvo Russian Federation
98 B5 Moskee Wyoming U.S.A.
26 F4 Moskenes Norway
26 F4 Moskenesøy isld Norway
26 F5 Moskenstraumen isld Norway
26 M4 Moskijärvi Sweden
26 L6 Moskosel Sweden
29 M4 Moskuvaara Finland
49 Moskva conurbation Russian Federation
54 G1 Moskva R Russian Federation
56 D4 Moskva, Gora mt Russian Federation
54 J1 Moskvy, Kanal Imeni Russian Federation
42 H3 Moslavacka Gora mt Croatia
21 N7 Mosnes France
41 O4 Moso Italy
87 E10 Mosomane Botswana
48 D3 Mosonmagyaróvar Hungary
85 D5 Mosopa Botswana
54 K9 Mospino Ukraine
128 C3 Mosquera Colombia
125 M2 Mosquitia reg Honduras
130 H4 Mosquito R Brazil
94 G5 Mosquito Cr.Res Ohio U.S.A.
113 G9 Mosquito Lagoon Florida U.S.A.
125 N5 Mosquitos, Costa de Nicaragua
27 E12 Moss Norway
130 E5 Mossâmedes Brazil
118 L9 Mossbank Saskatchewan Canada
15 G2 Mossbank Scotland
144 B6 Mossburn New Zealand
89 C10 Mosselbaai S Africa
86 B6 Mossendjo Congo
139 G5 Mossgiel New South Wales Australia
36 G7 Mössingen Germany
119 T1 Moss L Manitoba Canada
13 F6 Mossley England
141 H3 Mossman Queensland Australia
28 D4 Mossø L Denmark
129 L5 Mossoro Brazil
13 F3 Mosspaul Scotland
111 H11 Moss Point Mississippi U.S.A.
88 H9 Mossuril Mozambique
139 K5 Moss Vale New South Wales Australia
113 A7 Mossy Head Florida U.S.A.
119 U6 Mossy Pt Manitoba Canada
119 O4 Mossy R Saskatchewan Canada
100 C3 Mossyrock Washington U.S.A.
47 H3 Most Bulgaria
30 H5 Most Czechoslovakia
17 H9 Mostaganem Algeria
42 H5 Mostar Bosnia-Herzegovina
31 O6 Mostiska Ukraine
55 C3 Mostovaya Russian Federation
55 E3 Mostovskoye Russian Federation
31 P2 Mosty Belorussia
70 F2 Mostyn Sabah
8 C1 Mostyn Wales
27 C12 Mös-vatn L Norway
26 E8 Mosvik Norway
86 G3 Mot'a Ethiopia
86 C5 Motaba R Congo
17 F5 Mota del Cuervo Spain
16 D3 Mota del Marquès Spain
125 O10 Motagua R Guatemala
36 E3 Motala Sweden
27 H13 Motatán Venezuela
61 O9 Motegi Japan
20 G8 Mothe-Achard, la France
116 J8 Mother Goose L Alaska U.S.A.
12 E2 Motherwell Scotland
58 D5 Motian Ling mt ra China
40 F4 Môtier Switzerland
75 L5 Motihari India
71 A2 Moti, I California U.S.A.
17 F5 Motilla del Palancar Spain
145 F2 Motiti I New Zealand
27 G12 Motjärnshyttan Sweden
99 M3 Motley Minnesota U.S.A.
89 F3 Motloutse R Botswana
89 C5 Motokwe Botswana
60 O4 Motomachi Japan
71 J4 Motongkat Sulawesi
52 D1 Motovskiy Zaliv G Russian Federation
42 F3 Motovun Croatia
60 G12 Motoyama Japan
61 N13 Moto-yama pk Iwo Jima Japan
61 P7 Motoyoshi Japan
16 E8 Motril Spain
48 H6 Motru Romania
60 N3 Motsuta misaki C Japan
98 D3 Mott North Dakota U.S.A.
45 J1 Motteggiana Italy
20 E5 Motte, la France
36 H3 Motten Germany
21 M2 Motteville France
145 F3 Motu New Zealand
145 G3 Motu Ahiauru New Zealand
145 D4 Motueka New Zealand
145 F2 Motuhora I New Zealand
144 D5 Motukarara New Zealand
145 D1 Motukawanui I New Zealand
Motukorea I see Browns I
144 D5 Motunau Beach New Zealand
144 D5 Motunau I New Zealand
135 L10 Motu One isld Society Is Pacific Oc
145 G3 Motuoroi I New Zealand
145 D4 Motupiko New Zealand
145 F2 Motu R New Zealand
145 D1 Moturoa Is New Zealand
145 E2 Motutakiko I New Zealand
145 E3 Motutang New Zealand
145 E2 Motutapu I New Zealand
28 E3 Mou Denmark
122 C2 Mouchalagane R. Quebec Canada
21 H8 Mouchamps France
127 J4 Mouchoir Passage Caribbean
46 G5 Moúdhros Greece
85 B5 Moudjéria Mauritania
40 E4 Moudon Switzerland
86 B6 Mouila Gabon
21 J8 Mouilleron-en-Pareds France
86 D4 Mouka Cent Afr Republic
139 G6 Moulamein New South Wales Australia
16 C10 Moulay-Bouselham Morocco
114 H2 Mould Bay Northwest Territories Canada
127 N4 Moule Guadeloupe W Indies
86 H3 Moulhoule Djibouti
21 M4 Moulicent France
21 L7 Mouliherne France
18 H6 Moulins Allier France
21 K5 Moulins Sarthe France
18 H6 Moulins-Engilbert France
21 L4 Moulins-la-Marche France
21 O7 Moulins-sur-Cephons France
68 C4 Moulmein Burma
85 D2 Moulouya, Oued R Morocco
111 J7 Moulton Alabama U.S.A.
101 M7 Moulton Idaho U.S.A.
110 D1 Moulton Iowa U.S.A.
109 K6 Moulton Texas U.S.A.
112 D6 Moultrie Georgia U.S.A.
112 G4 Moultrie, L South Carolina U.S.A.
86 B6 Mounana Gabon
46 D6 Moúnda, Akr C Greece
111 F8 Mound Bayou Mississippi U.S.A.
110 G4 Mound City Illinois U.S.A.
110 B3 Mound City Kansas U.S.A.
99 L9 Mound City Missouri U.S.A.
98 F4 Mound City South Dakota U.S.A.
94 D7 Mound City Nat.Mon Ohio U.S.A.
86 C4 Moundou Chad
107 N3 Mound Ridge Kansas U.S.A.
110 G4 Mounds Illinois U.S.A.
107 O6 Mounds Oklahoma U.S.A.
94 G7 Moundsville West Virginia U.S.A.
110 A4 Mound Valley Kansas U.S.A.
111 J9 Moundville Alabama U.S.A.
68 F6 Moung Cambodia
68 F1 Moung Hat Hin Laos
98 J1 Mountain North Dakota U.S.A.
94 G7 Mountain West Virginia U.S.A.
108 A1 Mountainair New Mexico U.S.A.
8 C4 Mountain Ash Wales
100 K8 Mountain City Nevada U.S.A.
109 N10 Mountain Creek L Texas U.S.A.
109 N1 Mountain Fork R Oklahoma U.S.A.
110 D4 Mountain Grove Missouri U.S.A.
110 D5 Mountain Home Arkansas U.S.A.
100 K6 Mountain Home Idaho U.S.A.
109 H5 Mountain Home Texas U.S.A.
103 O1 Mountain Home Utah U.S.A.
112 G2 Mountain Island L North Carolina U.S.A.
117 P9 Mountain Park Alberta Canada
109 J1 Mountain Park Oklahoma U.S.A.
109 O1 Mountain Pine Arkansas U.S.A.
118 D9 Mountain View Alberta Canada
135 V5 Mountain View Hawaiian Is
110 D6 Mountain View Arkansas U.S.A.
110 E5 Mountain View Missouri U.S.A.
107 M6 Mountain View Oklahoma U.S.A.
101 P8 Mountainview Wyoming U.S.A.
116 F5 Mountain Village Alaska U.S.A.
95 K7 Mount Airy Maryland U.S.A.
112 G1 Mount Airy North Carolina U.S.A.
99 S4 Mountan Wisconsin U.S.A.
100 C4 Mount Angel Oregon U.S.A.
144 B6 Mount Aspiring Nat. Park New Zealand
118 B8 Mount Assiniboine Prov Park Br Col/Alberta Canada
99 R10 Mount Auburn Illinois U.S.A.
143 B6 Mount Augustus W Australia Australia
89 F8 Mount Ayliff S Africa
99 M9 Mount Ayr Iowa U.S.A.
138 E6 Mount Barker South Australia Australia
143 C10 Mount Barker W Australia Australia
142 F3 Mount Barnett W Australia Australia
14 C3 Mount Bellew Br Ireland
138 F3 Mount Browne New South Wales Australia
145 E4 Mount Bruce New Zealand
139 H6 Mount Buller Victoria Australia
120 J4 Mount Byers Ontario Canada
109 L4 Mount Calm Texas U.S.A.
141 H3 Mount Carbine Queensland Australia
123 T6 Mount Carmel Newfoundland Canada
110 J3 Mount Carmel Illinois U.S.A.
95 L6 Mount Carmel Pennsylvania U.S.A.
99 R7 Mount Carroll Illinois U.S.A.
140 C7 Mount Cavenagh N Terr Australia
98 H9 Mount Clare Nebraska U.S.A.
94 G7 Mount Clare West Virginia U.S.A.
143 C7 Mount Clere W Australia Australia
144 C5 Mount Cook New Zealand
141 H5 Mount Coolon Queensland Australia
88 C10 Mount Darwin Zimbabwe
140 B5 Mount Denison N Terr Australia
95 T2 Mount Desert I Maine U.S.A.
95 T3 Mount Desert Rock Maine U.S.A.
108 A7 Mount Dora New Mexico U.S.A.
140 B5 Mount Doreen N Terr Australia
141 H5 Mount Douglas Queensland Australia
138 D2 Mount Dutton South Australia Australia
138 D4 Mount Eba South Australia Australia
140 C7 Mount Ebenezer N Terr Australia
117 F7 Mount Edgecumbe Alaska U.S.A.
117 N7 Mount Edziza Prov. Park British Columbia Canada
101 P9 Mount Emmons Utah U.S.A.
141 G5 Mount Emu Plains Queensland Australia
109 N4 Mount Enterprise Texas U.S.A.
140 C6 Mount Ertwa N Terr Australia
89 F8 Mount Fletcher S Africa
89 F8 Mount Frere S Africa
138 F6 Mount Gambier South Australia Australia
141 H4 Mount Garnet Queensland Australia
112 H2 Mount Gilead North Carolina U.S.A.
94 E6 Mount Gilead Ohio U.S.A.
141 L2 Mount Gravatt dist Brisbane, Qnsld Australia
136 J3 Mount Hagen Papua New Guinea
106 C1 Mount Harris Colorado U.S.A.
100 C8 Mount Hebron California U.S.A.
95 N6 Mount Holly New Jersey U.S.A.
94 K6 Mount Holly Pennsylvania U.S.A.
138 D5 Mount Hope South Australia Australia
107 N4 Mount Hope Kansas U.S.A.
99 R6 Mount Horeb Wisconsin U.S.A.
142 F3 Mount House W Australia Australia
141 F7 Mount Howitt Queensland Australia
144 C5 Mount Hutt New Zealand
109 O1 Mount Ida Arkansas U.S.A.
100 J4 Mount Idaho Idaho U.S.A.
140 E5 Mount Isa Queensland Australia
94 J8 Mount Jackson Virginia U.S.A.
94 J5 Mount Jewett Pennsylvania U.S.A.
120 H6 Mount L Ontario Canada
141 K6 Mount Larcom Queensland Australia
83 J11 Mount Lavinia Sri Lanka
142 B1 Mount Lawley dist Perth, W Aust Australia
138 E6 Mount Lofty Ra S Australia Australia
141 H5 Mount McConnell Queensland Australia
143 C8 Mount Magnet W Australia Australia
139 G4 Mount Manara New South Wales Australia
141 G6 Mount Marlow Queensland Australia
145 F2 Mount Maunganui New Zealand
100 E9 Mount Meadows Res California U.S.A.
14 D3 Mountmellick Ireland
141 H3 Mount Molloy Queensland Australia
102 F4 Mount Montgomery Nevada U.S.A.
141 K6 Mount Morgan Queensland Australia
110 C1 Mount Moriah Missouri U.S.A.
99 R7 Mount Morris Illinois U.S.A.
94 K4 Mount Morris New York U.S.A.
139 G4 Mount Murchison New South Wales Australia
106 D2 Mount of the Holy Cross Colorado U.S.A.
110 G2 Mount Olive Illinois U.S.A.
111 G10 Mount Olive Mississippi U.S.A.
110 M3 Mount Olivet Kentucky U.S.A.
110 N2 Mount Orab Ohio U.S.A.
121 S7 Mount Orford, Parc de Quebec Canada
141 K7 Mount Perry Queensland Australia
99 P9 Mount Pleasant Iowa U.S.A.
94 C3 Mount Pleasant Michigan U.S.A.
94 H6 Mount Pleasant Pennsylvania U.S.A.
110 J6 Mount Pleasant Tennessee U.S.A.
109 N2 Mount Pleasant Texas U.S.A.
103 N2 Mount Pleasant Utah U.S.A.
95 M5 Mount Pocono Pennsylvania U.S.A.
99 R9 Mount Pulaski Illinois U.S.A.
100 D3 Mount Rainier Nat.Pk Washington U.S.A.
14 D3 Mountrath Ireland
117 O10 Mount Revelstoke Nat. Park British Columbia Canada
106 C10 Mount Riley New Mexico U.S.A.
98 C6 Mount Rushmore Nat.Mem South Dakota U.S.A.
140 B3 Mount Sanford N Terr Australia
94 J7 Mount Savage Maryland U.S.A.
9 F7 Mount's B England
109 M3 Mount Selman Texas U.S.A.
140 C7 Mount Squires N Terr Australia
99 Q10 Mount Sterling Illinois U.S.A.
110 M3 Mount Sterling Kentucky U.S.A.
94 D7 Mount Sterling Ohio U.S.A.
122 K7 Mount Stewart Prince Edward I Canada
94 H7 Mount Storm West Virginia U.S.A.
142 B5 Mount Stuart W Australia Australia
141 G5 Mount Sturgeon Queensland Australia
141 G4 Mount Surprise Queensland Australia
140 D4 Mount Swan N Terr Australia
103 L5 Mount Trumbull Arizona U.S.A.
122 J9 Mount Uniacke Nova Scotia Canada
94 K6 Mount Union Pennsylvania U.S.A.
143 C6 Mount Vernon W Australia Australia
111 J10 Mount Vernon Alabama U.S.A.
110 D6 Mount Vernon Arkansas U.S.A.
112 E5 Mount Vernon Georgia U.S.A.
110 H3 Mount Vernon Illinois U.S.A.
110 J4 Mount Vernon Indiana U.S.A.
99 P8 Mount Vernon Iowa U.S.A.
110 M4 Mount Vernon Kentucky U.S.A.
110 C4 Mount Vernon Missouri U.S.A.
95 O6 Mount Vernon New York U.S.A.
94 E6 Mount Vernon Ohio U.S.A.
100 F5 Mount Vernon Oregon U.S.A.
98 H6 Mount Vernon South Dakota U.S.A.
109 M2 Mount Vernon Texas U.S.A.
95 K8 Mount Vernon Virginia U.S.A.
100 C1 Mount Vernon Washington U.S.A.
94 D6 Mount Victory Ohio U.S.A.
140 B6 Mount Wedge N Terr Australia
138 D5 Mount Wedge South Australia Australia
111 K9 Mount Willing Alabama U.S.A.
138 C3 Mount Willoughby South Australia Australia
142 B1 Mount Yokine dist Perth, W Aust Australia
110 H2 Mount Zion Illinois U.S.A.
99 P9 Mount Zion Iowa U.S.A.
141 J6 Moura Queensland Australia
128 D5 Moura R Brazil
16 C6 Moura Portugal
85 C6 Mourdiah Mali
19 N17 Mouriès France
141 H4 Mourilyan Harbour Queensland Australia
14 D2 Mourne R N Ireland
14 E2 Mourne Mts N Ireland
15 G2 Mousa isld Shetland Scotland
22 E2 Mouscron Belgium
98 E1 Mouse R North Dakota U.S.A.
18 F7 Mousin reg France
36 B6 Moussey Moselle France
36 C7 Moussey Vosges France
86 C3 Moussoro Chad
20 D4 Moustérus France
19 Q17 Moustiers France
12 E3 Mouswald Scotland
36 C6 Mouterhouse France
40 D4 Mouthe France
40 D3 Mouthier France
40 F3 Moutier Switzerland
40 E7 Moûtiers France
21 M5 Moutiers-au-Perche France
70 G4 Moutong Sulawesi
21 P3 Mouy France
22 J5 Mouzay France
22 J4 Mouzon France
124 E3 Movas Mexico
14 D1 Moville Ireland
99 L7 Moville Iowa U.S.A.
142 E3 Mowanjum W Australia Australia
141 K7 Mowbullan, Mt Queensland Australia
99 S10 Moweaqua Illinois U.S.A.
145 E3 Mowhanau New Zealand
100 D6 Mowich Oregon U.S.A.
100 E3 Moxee City Washington U.S.A.
130 H10 Moxotó,R Brazil
14 B3 Moy R Ireland
17 J3 Moyá Spain
106 F6 Moya R New Mexico U.S.A.
124 H7 Moyahua Mexico
88 G5 Moyale Kenya
85 B7 Moyamba Sierra Leone
21 L3 Moyaux France
22 E4 Moy-de-l'Aisne France
65 E6 Moye Dao isld China
36 B7 Moyenmoutier France
83 K12 Moyenne isld Mahé I Indian Oc
21 O1 Moyenneville France
36 B6 Moyenvic France
100 K1 Moyie British Columbia Canada
100 J1 Moyie Springs Idaho U.S.A.
86 C4 Moyo Chad
128 C5 Moyobamba Peru
86 C3 Moyto Chad
57 E2 Moyynkum desert Kazakhstan
57 G3 Moyynkum Kazakhstan
57 E3 Moyynkum, Peski desert Kazakhstan
57 G2 Moyynty Kazakhstan
87 G9 Mozambique rep Africa
81 B9 Mozambique Ridge Indian Oc
120 J5 Mozhabong L Ontario Canada
52 E6 Mozhaysk Russian Federation
52 H6 Mozhga Russian Federation
77 G2 Mozhnābād Iran
68 B1 Mozo Burma
45 J1 Mozzecane Italy
87 E7 Mpala Zaire
89 D2 Mpandamatenga Botswana
88 C7 Mpika Zambia
88 C6 Mporokoso Zambia
86 C6 M'Pouya Congo
85 D7 Mpraeso Ghana
87 F7 Mpulungu Zambia
88 F7 Mpwapwa Tanzania
31 N2 Mragowo Poland
55 C4 Mras-Su R Russian Federation
56 C4 Mras-Su R Russian Federation
85 C4 Mreiti,El Mauritania
88 C10 Mrewa Zimbabwe
42 H4 Mrkonjić Grad Bosnia-Herzegovina
31 J5 Mrlina R Czechoslovakia
31 J1 Mrzeżyno Poland
43 D13 M'saken Tunisia
31 H5 Mšeno Czechoslovakia
52 D5 Msta R Russian Federation
54 C2 Mstislavl' Belorussia
31 M4 Mszczonów Poland
88 C5 Mtakuja Tanzania
89 G6 Mtamba Mt Swaziland
88 C5 Mtambo R Tanzania
89 F8 Mtata S Africa
120 J10 Mt. Brydges Ontario Canada
103 M4 Mt Carmel Utah U.S.A.
89 G8 Mtentu S Africa
144 C5 Mt Hutt New Zealand
89 G3 Mtilikwe R Zimbabwe
141 G6 Mt Marlow Queensland Australia
144 C5 Mt Somers New Zealand
87 F11 Mtubatuba S Africa
88 H7 Mtwara Tanzania
88 G7 Mtwara reg Tanzania
16 B7 Mu mt Portugal
88 G7 Mualo R Mozambique
88 C8 Muamadzi R Zambia
21 K3 Muance R France
68 F6 Muang Cambodia
68 E4 Muang Botene Thailand
68 G5 Muang Bua Thailand
68 E5 Muang Chainat Thailand
68 E3 Muang Chaiyaphum Thailand
68 E4 Muang Chiang Khan Thailand
68 D3 Muang Chiang Rai Thailand
68 G4 Muang Hinboun Laos
68 F4 Muang Kalasin Thailand
68 G5 Muang Khong Laos
68 G5 Muang Khong-Xedon Laos
68 F4 Muang Kosamphi Thailand
69 D8 Muang Krabi Thailand
68 D3 Muang Lampang Thailand
68 D3 Muang Lamphun Thailand
68 E4 Muang Loei Thailand
68 D3 Muang Long Thailand
68 G4 Muang Nakhon Phanom Thailand
68 D5 Muang Nakhon Sawan Thailand
68 D3 Muang Ngao Thailand
68 E3 Muang Oi Thailand
68 G4 Muang Phaluka Thailand
68 D3 Muang Phan Thailand
68 F4 Muang Phannanikhom Thailand
68 D3 Muang Phayao Thailand
68 E4 Muang Phetchabun Thailand
68 E4 Muang Phichai Thailand
68 E4 Muang Phichit Thailand
68 E3 Muang Phrae Thailand
68 G4 Muang Renu Nakhon Thailand
68 F5 Muang Roi Et Thailand
68 F4 Muang Sakon Nakhon Thailand
68 G5 Muang Sam Sip Thailand
68 G5 Muang Si Chalalai Thailand
68 F4 Muang Song Thailand
68 D4 Muang Thoen Thailand
69 F11 Muar R Malaysia
69 F11 Muar Malaysia
70 D2 Muara Brunei
70 E3 Muara Kalimantan
70 E3 Muaraancalong Kalimantan
70 E4 Muaraatap Kalimantan
70 K9 Muarabinuangeun Java
69 F13 Muarabulian Sumatra
69 E13 Muarabungo Sumatra
70 K8 Muaradua Sumatra
69 F14 Muaraenim Sumatra
70 E4 Muarainu Kalimantan
70 E5 Muarajawa Kalimantan
70 E5 Muarakaman Kalimantan
70 C5 Muarakayang Kalimantan
69 E13 Muaralabuh Sumatra
69 F14 Muaralakitan Sumatra
70 D5 Muaralaung Kalimantan
70 E4 Muaralesan Kalimantan
70 E4 Muaramayang Kalimantan
70 E4 Muaranawai Kalimantan
69 F14 Muararupit Sumatra
69 F13 Muarasabak Sumatra
69 D13 Muarasiberut Indonesia
69 D13 Muarasigep Indonesia
69 D12 Muarasipongi Sumatra
69 D12 Muarasoma Sumatra
70 F4 Muaras Rf Indonesia
69 F13 Muaratebo Sumatra
70 D5 Muaratembesi Sumatra
70 D5 Muaratewe Kalimantan
70 E4 Muarawahau Kalimantan
71 A3 Muari Halmahera Indonesia
57 D5 Mubarek Uzbekistan
77 A7 Mubarraz,Al Saudi Arabia
88 C1 Mubende Uganda
80 G5 Mubis Jordan
79 F8 Mubrak, J mt Jordan
69 H11 Mubur isld Indonesia
142 C5 Muccan W Australia Australia
36 C2 Much Germany
117 K11 Muchalat British Columbia Canada
15 F3 Muchalls Scotland
143 B9 Muchea W Australia Australia
33 P10 Mücheln Germany
88 C8 Muchinga Escarpment Zambia
52 G3 Muchkas Russian Federation
67 A2 Muchuan China
8 D2 Much Wenlock England
15 B4 Muck isld Inner Hebrides Scotland
141 J7 Muckadilla Queensland Australia
14 D1 Muckish Mt Ireland
15 G1 Muckle Flugga isld Shetland Scotland
15 G2 Muckle Roe isld Shetland Scotland
9 E2 Muckley Corner England
14 C2 Muckros Hd Ireland
88 H8 Mucojo Mozambique
87 D8 Muconda Angola
130 H6 Mucuri Brazil
130 H5 Mucuri,R Brazil
87 D9 Mucusso Angola
69 E10 Muda R Malaysia
80 G7 Mudaiyina Jordan
65 H2 Mudan Jiang R China
65 H2 Mudanjiang China
47 K4 Mudanya Turkey
47 N10 Mudarli Turkey
36 G4 Mudau Germany
98 D4 Mud Butte South Dakota U.S.A.
98 G8 Mud Cr Nebraska U.S.A.
74 E8 Muddebihāl India
26 L5 Muddus Nat. Park Sweden
107 O7 Muddy Boggy Cr Oklahoma U.S.A.
103 N3 Muddy Cr Utah U.S.A.
101 T7 Muddy Cr Wyoming U.S.A.
101 P8 Muddy Cr Wyoming U.S.A.
101 S8 Muddy Cr Wyoming U.S.A.
101 S7 Muddy Gap pass Wyoming U.S.A.
118 H6 Muddy L Saskatchewan Canada
103 K5 Muddy Pk Nevada U.S.A.
33 M7 Müden Germany
139 J4 Mudgee New South Wales Australia
141 H6 Mudge, Mt Queensland Australia
76 B2 Mudhol India
74 G9 Mudhol Andhra Pradesh India
101 N6 Mud L Idaho U.S.A.
101 Q1 Mud L Montana U.S.A.
102 G4 Mud L Nevada U.S.A.
98 H4 Mud L.Res South Dakota U.S.A.
68 C4 Mudon Burma
47 L4 Mudurnu R Turkey

Mud'yuga — Nametil 205

52 E3 **Mud'yuga** Russian Federation
88 D10 **Mudzi** *R* Zimbabwe
21 K3 **Mue** *R* France
88 G7 **Mueda** Mozambique
20 F5 **Muel** France
17 G4 **Muela de Ares** *mt* Spain
17 G3 **Muela,Sierra de la** Spain
142 G4 **Mueller, Mt** W Australia Australia
142 F4 **Mueller Ra** W Australia Australia
141 F6 **Muellers Ra** Queensland Australia
119 N6 **Muenster** Saskatchewan Canada
109 K2 **Muenster** Texas U.S.A.
125 N2 **Muerto,Cayo** *isld* Nicaragua
126 D2 **Muertos Cays** *reefs* Bahamas
52 G3 **Muftyuga** Russian Federation
88 B8 **Mufulira** Zambia
67 E2 **Mufu Shan** *mts* Jiangxi/Hubei China
67 B5 **Mugang** China
16 B5 **Muge** Portugal
87 G9 **Mugeba** Mozambique
45 K4 **Mugello** Italy
33 S10 **Mügeln** Germany
37 L4 **Muggendorf** Germany
79 H9 **Mughayrā', Al** Saudi Arabia
59 K5 **Mugi** Japan
16 A1 **Mugía** Spain
88 B5 **Mugila** *mts* Zaire
47 J7 **Muğla** Turkey
47 H2 **Müglizh** Bulgaria
57 A1 **Mugodzhary** *mts* Kazakhstan
18 E9 **Mugron** France
75 K4 **Mugu** Nepal
86 G1 **Muhammad Qol** Sudan
77 B6 **Muharraq,Al** Bahrain
36 F6 **Mühlacker** Germany
36 H2 **Mühlbach** Germany
33 S10 **Mühlberg** Brandenburg Germany
37 K2 **Mühlberg** Thüringen Germany
38 G5 **Mühldorf** Germany
41 K3 **Mühlehorn** Switzerland
33 S7 **Mühlenbeck** Germany
33 O5 **Mühlen Eichsen** Germany
37 J1 **Mühlhausen** Germany
37 K4 **Mühlhausen** Germany
36 C4 **Mühlheim** Germany
146 H6 **Mühlig-Hofmannfjella** *mts* Antarctica
37 M2 **Mühltroff** Germany
29 M7 **Muhos** Finland
38 H7 **Muhr** Austria
80 D3 **Muhraqa** Israel
36 F7 **Mühringen** Germany
52 B5 **Muhu** Estonia
88 C2 **Muhutwe** Tanzania
88 F7 **Muhuwesi** *R* Tanzania
69 G8 **Mui Bai Bung** Vietnam
68 J4 **Mui Chon May Dong** *C* Vietnam
68 J7 **Mui da Vaich** *C* Vietnam
25 D4 **Muiden** Netherlands
21 O6 **Muides-sur-Loire** France
68 J7 **Mui Dinh** *C* Vietnam
21 N3 **Muids** France
61 M8 **Muikamachi** Japan
71 B3 **Muilijk** *isld* Indonesia
14 E4 **Muine Bheag** Ireland
94 C3 **Muir** Michigan U.S.A.
88 D10 **Muira** *R* Mozambique
13 F1 **Muirdrum** Scotland
117 E6 **Muir Gl** Alaska U.S.A.
13 E1 **Muirhead** Scotland
12 D3 **Muirkirk** Scotland
143 B10 **Muir, L** W Australia Australia
143 G7 **Muir, Mt** W Australia Australia
142 A5 **Muiron I., N** W Australia Australia
102 B4 **Muir Woods Nat.Mon** California U.S.A.
87 G8 **Muite** Mozambique
68 J6 **Mui Yen** *C* Vietnam
125 Q7 **Mujeres, I** Mexico
80 F8 **Mujib** *R* Jordan
87 D8 **Mujimbeji** Zambia
70 C3 **Mujong** *R* Sarawak
48 H2 **Mukachevo** Ukraine
70 C3 **Mukah** Sarawak
72 F6 **Mukallā, Al** Yemen
80 E6 **Mukallik** *R* Jordan
60 P3 **Mukawa** Japan
60 Q3 **Mu-kawa** *R* Japan
80 F7 **Mukawir** Jordan
86 G1 **Mukawwar I** Sudan
68 G4 **Mukdahan** Thailand
Mukden *see* **Shenyang**
13 F5 **Muker** England
72 E6 **Mukha, Al** Yemen
84 G3 **Mukhaylī, Al** Libya
74 G9 **Mukher** India
80 E6 **Mukhmas** Jordan
58 F1 **Mukhor-Konduy** Russian Federation
143 C9 **Mukinbudin** W Australia Australia
69 D9 **Muk,Ko** *isld* Thailand
69 E14 **Mukomuko** Sumatra
33 P9 **Mukrena** Germany
57 D5 **Mukry** Turkmenistan
75 K4 **Muktinath** Nepal
86 D7 **Mukumbi** Zaire
86 G5 **Mukutan** Kenya
119 U5 **Mukutawa R** Manitoba Canada
87 D9 **Mukwe** Namibia
99 S7 **Mukwonago** Wisconsin U.S.A.
17 G6 **Mula** Spain
73 L8 **Mulaku Atoll** Maldives
57 J2 **Mulaly** Kazakhstan
65 G2 **Mulan** China
71 F4 **Mulanay** Philippines
88 E9 **Mulanje** *mt* Malawi
88 E10 **Mulanje** Malawi
129 H4 **Mulata** Brazil
124 E3 **Mulatos** Mexico
125 Q5 **Mulatupo Sasardi** Panama
110 B6 **Mulberry** Arkansas U.S.A.
110 C6 **Mulberry** *R* Arkansas U.S.A.
113 F10 **Mulberry** Florida U.S.A.
110 K1 **Mulberry** Indiana U.S.A.
107 Q4 **Mulberry** Kansas U.S.A.
110 B4 **Mulberry** Missouri U.S.A.
111 K8 **Mulberry Fork** *R* Alabama U.S.A.
110 G3 **Mulberry Grove** Illinois U.S.A.
116 K6 **Mulchatna** *R* Alaska U.S.A.
133 C5 **Mulchen** Chile
37 P2 **Mulda** Germany
28 E3 **Muldbjerge** *hill* Denmark
33 Q9 **Mulde** *R* Germany
101 M6 **Muldoon** Idaho U.S.A.
108 E5 **Mule Cr** Texas U.S.A.
98 B6 **Mule Cr** Wyoming U.S.A.
106 B8 **Mule Creek** New Mexico U.S.A.
124 C4 **Mulegé** Mexico
80 G7 **Muleih** Jordan
88 C8 **Mulembo** *R* Zambia
86 D6 **Mulenda** Zaire
71 K9 **Mules** *isld* Flores Indonesia
108 E1 **Muleshoe** Texas U.S.A.
87 G9 **Mulevala** Mozambique
36 H5 **Mulfingen** Germany
142 C5 **Mulga Downs** W Australia Australia
140 B7 **Mulga Park** N Terr Australia
138 C4 **Mulgathing** South Australia Australia
138 C4 **Mulgathing Rocks** *mt* South Australia Australia
123 L8 **Mulgrave** Nova Scotia Canada
116 F3 **Mulgrave Hills** Alaska U.S.A.
143 C6 **Mulgul** W Australia Australia
16 E7 **Mulhacén** *mt* Spain
107 N5 **Mulhall** Oklahoma U.S.A.
32 E10 **Mülheim** Germany
40 F2 **Mulhouse** France
65 H2 **Muling** China
65 D6 **Muling Guan** *pass* China
65 J2 **Muling He** *R* China
138 E3 **Mulka** South Australia Australia
76 B4 **Mulki** India
15 C4 **Mull** *isld* Scotland
14 B4 **Mullaghareirk Mts** Ireland
83 K8 **Mullaittivu** Sri Lanka
139 J4 **Mullaley** New South Wales Australia
100 K2 **Mullan** Idaho U.S.A.
98 E7 **Mullen** Nebraska U.S.A.
109 J4 **Mullen** Texas U.S.A.
139 H4 **Mullengudgery** New South Wales Australia
94 F9 **Mullens** West Virginia U.S.A.
140 C6 **Muller** *R* N Terr Australia
70 C4 **Muller,Peg** *mts* Kalimantan
113 E10 **Mullet Key** *isld* Florida U.S.A.
94 C1 **Mullett L** Michigan U.S.A.
143 B8 **Mullewa** W Australia Australia
15 F1 **Mull Head** Orkney Scotland
40 G2 **Müllheim** Germany
95 N7 **Mullica** *R* New Jersey U.S.A.
140 E6 **Mulligan** *R* Queensland Australia
14 D3 **Mullingar** Ireland
112 H3 **Mullins** South Carolina U.S.A.
107 L4 **Mullinville** Kansas U.S.A.
139 J5 **Mullion Creek** New South Wales Australia
83 K8 **Mulliyavalai** Sri Lanka
15 D6 **Mull of Galloway** Scotland
15 C5 **Mull of Kintyre** Scotland
12 B2 **Mull of Oa** Scotland
27 G14 **Mullsjö** Sweden
15 C4 **Mull, Sound of** Scotland
139 L3 **Mullumbimby** New South Wales Australia
80 F6 **Mul Nevo** Jordan
87 E9 **Mulobezi** Zambia
87 C9 **Mulondo** Angola
87 E7 **Mulongo** Zaire
138 E3 **Muloorina** South Australia Australia
14 D1 **Mulroy B** Ireland
21 L6 **Mulsanne** France
33 P5 **Mulsow** Germany
74 D3 **Multan** Pakistan
55 F1 **Multanovy** Russian Federation
29 L9 **Multia** Finland
26 J8 **Multrå** Sweden
70 D2 **Mulu, G** *mt* Sarawak
130 J9 **Mulungu** Brazil
107 N4 **Mulvane** Kansas U.S.A.
119 T8 **Mulvihill** Manitoba Canada
139 G4 **Mulyah,Mt** New South Wales Australia
55 E1 **Mulym'ya** *R* Russian Federation
138 F4 **Mulyungarie** South Australia Australia
8 C4 **Mumbles** Wales
87 B8 **Mumbondo** Angola
87 C8 **Mumbué** Angola
87 E8 **Mumbwa** Zambia
87 E8 **Mumena** Zaire
109 L5 **Mumford** Texas U.S.A.
69 D9 **Mum Nauk,Laem** *C* Thailand
71 H7 **Muna** *isld* Indonesia
125 P7 **Muna** Mexico
67 B5 **Munankwan Lin** *pass* Vietnam/China
141 G2 **Munburra** Queensland Australia
37 M3 **Münchberg** Germany
30 H3 **Müncheberg** Germany
39 **München** *conurbation* Germany
37 M2 **Münchenbernsdorf** Germany
36 F2 **Münchhausen** Germany
117 L6 **Muncho Lake** British Columbia Canada
37 N5 **Münchshofen** Germany
37 O6 **Münchshofen** Germany
37 M6 **Münchsmünster** Germany
110 L1 **Muncie** Indiana U.S.A.
140 E7 **Muncoonie, L** Queensland Australia
95 L5 **Muncy** Pennsylvania U.S.A.
118 E5 **Mundare** Alberta Canada
109 H2 **Munday** Texas U.S.A.
99 S7 **Mundelein** Illinois U.S.A.
83 J10 **Mundel L** Sri Lanka
32 L10 **Münden** Germany
98 J10 **Munden** Kansas U.S.A.
36 H7 **Munderkingen** Germany
9 H2 **Mundesley** England
9 G2 **Mundford** England
143 D6 **Mundiwindi** W Australia Australia
141 F4 **Mundjuro** *R* Queensland Australia
17 F6 **Mundo** *R* Spain
129 K6 **Mundo Nôvo** Brazil
143 G9 **Mundrabilla** W Australia Australia
141 K7 **Mundubbera** Queensland Australia
56 C4 **Mundybash** Russian Federation
46 D3 **Munella** *mt* Albania
17 F5 **Munera** Spain
110 L4 **Munfordville** Kentucky U.S.A.
141 J7 **Mungallala** Queensland Australia
141 H8 **Mungallala** *R* Queensland Australia
141 G3 **Mungana** Queensland Australia
87 F9 **Mungari** Mozambique
142 C5 **Mungaroona Ra** W Australia Australia
56 D5 **Mungash-Kul', Gora** *mt* Russian Federation
86 E5 **Mungbere** Zaire
75 J7 **Mungeli** India
75 M6 **Munger** India
94 D3 **Munger** Michigan U.S.A.
138 E3 **Mungerannie** South Australia Australia
69 J12 **Mungguresak, Tanjong** *C* Indonesia
141 J8 **Mungindi** Queensland Australia
87 C8 **Munhango** Angola
Munich Germany *see* **München**
98 H1 **Munich** North Dakota U.S.A.
88 B8 **Muniengashi** *R* Zaire
17 G3 **Muniesa** Spain
130 H7 **Muniz Freire** Brazil
28 H5 **Munke Bjergby** Denmark
28 F6 **Munkebo** Denmark
27 E13 **Munkedal** Sweden
26 G8 **Munkflohögen** Sweden
27 G12 **Munkfors** Sweden
28 A7 **Munkmarsch** Germany
26 M6 **Munksund** Sweden
56 F5 **Munku-Sardyk,Gora** *mt* Mongolia/Rus Fed
37 J3 **Münnerstadt** Germany
22 J4 **Muno** Belgium
71 E3 **Muñoz** Luzon Philippines
133 C8 **Muñoz Gamero, Pen** Chile
139 J8 **Munro,Mt** Tasmania Australia
36 H7 **Münsingen** Germany
118 E7 **Munson** Alberta Canada
111 K11 **Munson** Florida U.S.A.
40 F1 **Munster** France
32 M7 **Münster** Niedersachsen Germany
32 G9 **Münster** Nordrhein-Westfalen Germany
14 B4 **Munster** *prov* Ireland
41 H5 **Münster** Switzerland
36 C3 **Münstermaifeld** Germany
143 C9 **Muntadgin** W Australia Australia
70 F4 **Munte** Sulawesi
48 H4 **Muntelui Mare** *mt* Romania
70 P10 **Muntjar** Java
87 E9 **Munyati** *R* Zimbabwe
36 F3 **Münzenberg** Germany
26 N4 **Muodoslompolo** Sweden
29 O6 **Muojärvi** *L* Finland
68 F1 **Muong Boum** Vietnam
68 F2 **Muong Hiem** Laos
68 F2 **Muong Hun Xieng Hung** Laos
68 F3 **Muong Khao** Laos
68 F2 **Muong Khoua** Laos
68 G1 **Muong Khuong** Vietnam
68 E3 **Muong Ki** Laos
68 G3 **Muong Lam** Vietnam
68 E3 **Muong Liep** Laos
68 E2 **Muong Louang Namtha** Laos
68 H7 **Muong Man** Vietnam
68 F3 **Muong May** Laos
68 F3 **Muong Moc** Laos
68 F2 **Muong Ngoi** Laos
68 F1 **Muong Nhie** Vietnam
68 H4 **Muong Nong** Laos
68 E3 **Muong Oua** Laos
68 E1 **Muong ou Neua** Laos
68 E1 **Muong ou Tay** Laos
68 E3 **Muong Pa** Laos
68 G4 **Muong Phalane** Laos
68 E3 **Muong Phiang** Laos
68 E2 **Muong Sai** Laos
68 E3 **Muong Saiapoun** Laos
68 E2 **Muong Sing** Laos
68 F2 **Muong Son** Laos
68 G4 **Muong Song Khone** Laos
68 F3 **Muong Soui** Laos
68 F3 **Muong Soum** Laos
68 F1 **Muong Te** Vietnam
68 E3 **Muong Tha Deua** Laos
68 E3 **Muong Thong** Laos
68 F2 **Muong Va** Laos
Muong Xen *see* **Ky Son**
29 K4 **Muonio** Finland
26 N3 **Muonio älv** *R* Sweden/Finland
29 K4 **Muoniojoki** *R* Finland
26 N4 **Muonionalusta** Sweden
71 B2 **Muor** *isld* Halmahera Indonesia
41 J4 **Muotathal** Switzerland
88 B9 **Mupata Gorge** Zambia
65 E6 **Muping** China
80 G4 **Muqbilla** Jordan
86 J5 **Muqdisho** Somalia
130 H7 **Muqui** Brazil
38 J7 **Mur** *R* Austria
56 E2 **Mura** *R* Russian Federation
48 C4 **Mura** *R* Slovenia
80 G1 **Murāba 'āt** Syria
47 J6 **Muradiye** Turkey
45 L4 **Muraglione,Pso.di** *pass* Italy
61 N7 **Murakami** Japan
48 D4 **Murakeresztúr** Hungary
133 C7 **Murallón** *mt* Chile/Arg
61 N8 **Muramatsu** Japan
88 F2 **Murang'a** Kenya
45 M1 **Murano** Italy
52 G5 **Murashi** Russian Federation
18 G7 **Murat** France
78 H2 **Murat** *R* Turkey
78 J2 **Murat** *R* Turkey
47 K6 **Murat Dağı** Turkey
47 J3 **Muratlı** Turkey
38 K7 **Murau** Austria
77 C7 **Murban** U.A.E.
16 C3 **Murça** Portugal
77 B3 **Murcheh Khvort** Iran
33 T5 **Murchin** Germany
139 H6 **Murchison** Victoria Australia
145 D4 **Murchison** New Zealand
6 M1 **Murchison** *oil rig* North Sea
Murchison Falls Uganda *see* **Kabalega Falls**
143 B7 **Murchison, Mt** W Australia Australia
144 C5 **Murchison, Mt** New Zealand
145 D4 **Murchison, Mt** New Zealand
144 A6 **Murchison Mts** New Zealand
143 A8 **Murchison, R** W Australia Australia
140 C5 **Murchison Ra** N Terr Australia
89 G4 **Murchison Ra** S Africa
88 E9 **Murchison Rapids** Malawi
17 F6 **Murcia** *reg* Spain
17 F7 **Murcia** *prov* Spain
17 G7 **Murcia** Spain
71 F6 **Murcielagos B** Mindanao Philippines
18 G8 **Mur-de-Barrez** France
20 E5 **Mur-de-Bretagne** France
21 O7 **Mur-de-Sologne** France
98 F6 **Murdo** South Dakota U.S.A.
141 G2 **Murdoch Pt** Queensland Australia
122 G5 **Murdochville** Quebec Canada
113 E10 **Murdock** Florida U.S.A.
61 M9 **Mure** Japan
21 O4 **Mureaux, Les** France
38 N8 **Mureck** Austria
47 J4 **Mürefte** Turkey
86 G4 **Murel** Ethiopia
48 J4 **Mureş** *R* Romania
48 J4 **Mureş** *reg* Romania
18 F9 **Muret** France
111 C7 **Murfreesboro** Arkansas U.S.A.
95 K10 **Murfreesboro** North Carolina U.S.A.
110 K6 **Murfreesboro** Tennessee U.S.A.
36 E6 **Murg** *R* Germany
57 G5 **Murgab** *R* Tajikistan
57 G5 **Murgab** Tajikistan
46 D5 **Murgána** *mt* Greece
46 F2 **Murgash** *mt* Bulgaria
140 C1 **Murgenella Cr** N Terr Australia
48 L4 **Murgeni** Romania
77 H2 **Murghab** *R* Afghanistan
74 C3 **Murgha Kibzai** Pakistan
48 K4 **Murgoci** *mt* Romania
141 K7 **Murgon** Queensland Australia
143 B7 **Murgoo** W Australia Australia
58 D4 **Muri** China
75 L7 **Muri** India
130 G7 **Muriaé** Brazil
70 N9 **Muria, Gunung** *mt* Java
16 C2 **Murias de Paredes** Spain
87 D7 **Muriege** Angola
118 G4 **Muriel L** Alberta Canada
60 R2 **Murii-dake** *mt* Japan
119 O2 **Murill** Ontario Canada
17 G2 **Murillo de Gállego** Spain
20 G6 **Murin, L. de** France
33 R6 **Müritz** *L* Germany
145 F3 **Muriwai** New Zealand
26 L5 **Murjek** Sweden
36 B3 **Mürlenbach** Germany
52 D1 **Murmansk** Russian Federation
52 D1 **Murmanskaya Oblast'** *prov* Russian Federation
52 D1 **Murmashi** Russian Federation
54 M2 **Murmino** Russian Federation
41 O2 **Murnau** Germany
18 L11 **Muro, Cap di** *C* Corsica
102 G7 **Muroc L** California U.S.A.
52 F6 **Murom** Russian Federation
55 G3 **Muromtsevo** Russian Federation
60 O3 **Muroran** Japan
16 A2 **Muros** Spain
60 H12 **Muroto** Japan
60 H12 **Muroto-zaki** Japan
60 N3 **Murotsu-shima** *isld* Japan
48 L2 **Murovanyye Kurilovtsy** Ukraine
31 K3 **Murowana Goslina** Poland
60 E12 **Murozumi** Japan
100 J6 **Murphy** Idaho U.S.A.
112 C2 **Murphy** North Carolina U.S.A.
100 B7 **Murphy** Oregon U.S.A.
102 D3 **Murphys** California U.S.A.
110 G4 **Murphysboro** Illinois U.S.A.
141 H8 **Murra Murra** Queensland Australia
139 G6 **Murray** *R* New South Wales Australia
99 N8 **Murray** Iowa U.S.A.
110 H5 **Murray** Kentucky U.S.A.
99 K9 **Murray** Nebraska U.S.A.
103 N1 **Murray** Utah U.S.A.
138 E6 **Murray Bridge** South Australia Australia
94 E7 **Murray City** Ohio U.S.A.
135 L5 **Murray Deep** Pacific Oc
140 C5 **Murray Downs** N Terr Australia
122 K7 **Murray Hbr** Prince Edward I Canada
123 K8 **Murray Hd** Prince Edward I Canada
83 M9 **Murray Hill** *pk* Christmas I Indian Oc
107 N7 **Murray,L** Oklahoma U.S.A.
112 F3 **Murray, L** South Carolina U.S.A.
143 B10 **Murray, R** W Australia Australia
117 N8 **Murray R** British Columbia Canada
143 G7 **Murray Ra** W Australia Australia
122 K7 **Murray River** Prince Edward I Canada
89 C8 **Murraysburg** S Africa
135 M5 **Murray Seascarp** Pacific Oc
138 E5 **Murray Town** South Australia Australia
138 F6 **Murrayville** Victoria Australia
99 Q10 **Murrayville** Illinois U.S.A.
112 H4 **Murrells Inlet** South Carolina U.S.A.
40 G4 **Mürren** Switzerland
36 H6 **Murrhardt** Germany
139 J5 **Murringo** New South Wales Australia
143 D8 **Murrin Murrin** W Australia Australia
14 B3 **Murrisk** *mts* Ireland
139 G5 **Murrumbidgee** *R* New South Wales Australia
139 J5 **Murrumburrah & Harden** New South Wales Australia
139 K4 **Murrurundi** New South Wales Australia
19 O17 **Murs** France
38 O8 **Murska Sobota** Slovenia
74 G8 **Murtajāpur** India
38 K7 **Mur Tal** *V* Austria
41 M4 **Murtarol,Piz** *mt* Italy
101 L7 **Murtaugh** Idaho U.S.A.
139 G4 **Murtee** New South Wales Australia
40 F4 **Murten See** *L* Switzerland
42 G5 **Murter** *isld* Croatia
138 F3 **Murteree,L** South Australia Australia
117 O9 **Murtle L** British Columbia Canada
138 F6 **Murtoa** Victoria Australia
29 O6 **Murtovaara** Finland
74 E9 **Murud** India
70 D3 **Murud** *mt* Kalimantan
65 E3 **Muruin Sum Shuiku** *res* China
70 D5 **Murui, R** Kalimantan
70 D4 **Murung,R** Kalimantan
145 F3 **Murupara** New Zealand
128 F3 **Murupu** Brazil
109 N3 **Murvaul Res** Texas U.S.A.
22 K5 **Murville** France
74 J7 **Murwara** India
139 L3 **Murwillumbah** New South Wales Australia
52 G5 **Murygino** Russian Federation
38 M6 **Mürzsteg** Austria
38 M7 **Murz Tal** *V* Austria
84 E4 **Murzuq** Libya
38 N6 **Mürzzuchlag** Austria
78 H2 **Muş** Turkey
86 D6 **Musadi** Zaire
79 D10 **Mûsa, G** *mt* Egypt
74 C3 **Musa Khel Bazar** Pakistan
47 N10 **Musaköyalçaği Burun** *C* Turkey
46 F2 **Musala** *mt* Bulgaria
69 D12 **Musala** *isld* Sumatra
59 J3 **Musan** N Korea
77 E6 **Musandam** *pen* Oman
77 J3 **Musa Qala** Afghanistan
77 B7 **Musay'īd** Qatar
Muscat *see* **Masqat**
99 P8 **Muscatine** Iowa U.S.A.
Muscat & Oman *sultanate see* **Oman**
110 J7 **Muscle Shoals** Alabama U.S.A.
99 Q6 **Muscoda** Wisconsin U.S.A.
95 S3 **Muscongus B** Maine U.S.A.
88 C9 **Muse** *R* Mozambique
80 G8 **Museitiba** Jordan
141 G2 **Musgrave** Queensland Australia
138 B2 **Musgrave Ranges** South Australia Australia
123 S5 **Musgravetown** Newfoundland Canada
89 G3 **Mushandike Dam** Zimbabwe
80 G8 **Musheirifa** Jordan
14 C5 **Musheramore** *mt* Ireland
86 C6 **Mushie** Zaire
28 G6 **Musholm** *isld* Denmark
103 L6 **Music Mt** Arizona U.S.A.
103 N2 **Musinia Pk** Utah U.S.A.
117 M5 **Muskeg** *R* Northwest Territories Canada
99 L1 **Muskeg B** Minnesota U.S.A.
95 R5 **Muskeget Chan** Massachusetts U.S.A.
119 O1 **Muskeg L** Ontario Canada
94 A3 **Muskegon** *R* Michigan U.S.A.
94 A3 **Muskegon** Michigan U.S.A.
94 A3 **Muskegon Heights** Michigan U.S.A.
26 H4 **Musken** Norway
94 F7 **Muskingum** *R* Ohio U.S.A.
27 K13 **Muskö** Sweden
110 A6 **Muskogee** Oklahoma U.S.A.
121 L7 **Muskoka,L** Ontario Canada
101 S6 **Muskrat Cr** Wyoming U.S.A.
77 F6 **Mūskutān** Iran
118 C2 **Muskwa R** Alberta Canada
79 H2 **Muslimīyah** Syria
52 H6 **Muslyumovo** Russian Federation
86 G2 **Musmar** Sudan
80 D3 **Musmus** Israel
88 D2 **Musoma** Tanzania
45 M1 **Musone** *R* Italy
45 O4 **Musone** Italy
123 L3 **Musquanus L** Quebec Canada
123 L3 **Musquaro** Quebec Canada
122 F8 **Musquash** New Brunswick Canada
122 J8 **Musquodoboit** Nova Scotia Canada
122 J9 **Musquodoboit Hbr** Nova Scotia Canada
28 H7 **Musse** Denmark
25 H3 **Mussel Aa** *R* Netherlands
13 E2 **Musselburgh** Scotland
101 R3 **Musselshell** Montana U.S.A.
101 S3 **Musselshell** *R* Montana U.S.A.
87 C8 **Mussende** Angola
18 F7 **Mussidan** France
43 F11 **Mussomeli** Sicily
47 K4 **Mustafakemalpaşa** Turkey
47 K5 **Mustafakemalpaşa** *R* Turkey
86 H4 **Mustahīl** Ethiopia
75 K4 **Mustang** Nepal
107 N6 **Mustang** Oklahoma U.S.A.
108 E3 **Mustang Cr** Texas U.S.A.
109 K8 **Mustang I** Texas U.S.A.
55 B5 **Mustayevo** Russian Federation
133 D7 **Muster,L** Argentina
98 K4 **Mustinka** *R* Minnesota U.S.A.
127 O8 **Mustique** *isld* Lesser Antilles
27 M13 **Mustjala** Estonia
52 C5 **Mustla** Estonia
29 N3 **Mustola** Finland
13 H5 **Muston** England
52 C5 **Mustvee** Estonia
65 H4 **Musu-dan** *C* N Korea
139 K4 **Muswellbrook** New South Wales Australia
48 F1 **Muszyna** Poland
84 H4 **Mut** Egypt
78 D3 **Mut** Turkey
38 M8 **Muta** Slovenia
88 C1 **Mutai** Uganda
89 G4 **Mutale** *R* S Africa
87 E8 **Mutanda** Zambia
Mutankiang *see* **Mudanjiang**
88 E10 **Mutarara** Mozambique
87 F9 **Mutare** Zimbabwe
37 O4 **Mutěnín** Czechoslovakia
88 C10 **Mutepatepa** Zimbabwe
78 K6 **Muthanna, Al** *prov* Iraq
12 E1 **Muthill** Scotland
71 M9 **Mutis** *mt* Timor Indonesia
52 J2 **Mutnyy-Materik** Russian Federation
88 D10 **Mutoko** Zimbabwe
87 D7 **Mutombo Mukulu** Zaire
138 F4 **Mutooroo** South Australia Australia
88 C10 **Mutorashanga** Zimbabwe
65 D4 **Mutoudeng** China
65 D3 **Mutougou** China
45 R7 **Mutria, M** *mt* Italy
87 G10 **Mutsamudu** Comoros
87 D8 **Mutshatsha** Zaire
60 P4 **Mutsu** Japan
61 O5 **Mutsu-wan** *B* Japan
141 G6 **Muttaburra** Queensland Australia
40 G1 **Muttersholtz** France
36 E5 **Mutterstadt** Germany
41 M4 **Muttler** *mt* Switzerland
123 O3 **Mutton Bay** Quebec Canada
144 B7 **Muttonbird Is.** New Zealand
14 B4 **Mutton I** Ireland
107 L5 **Mutual** Oklahoma U.S.A.
87 G8 **Mutuala** Mozambique
129 H7 **Mutum** Mato Grosso Brazil
130 H6 **Mutum** Minas Gerais Brazil
128 F5 **Mutumparaná** Brazil
83 L9 **Mutur** Sri Lanka
36 C6 **Mutzig** France
33 R10 **Mutzschen** Germany
29 M9 **Muurame** Finland
29 L5 **Muurola** Finland
65 A5 **Mu Us Shamo** *desert* China
Muxia *see* **Mugía**
58 F1 **Muya** *R* Russian Federation
88 C3 **Muyinga** Burundi
125 M3 **Muy Muy** Nicaragua
57 A3 **Muynak** Uzbekistan
87 E7 **Muyumba** Zaire
67 C1 **Muyuping** China
74 E1 **Muzaffarabad** Kashmir
74 D3 **Muzaffargarh** Pakistan
74 G4 **Muzaffarnagar** India
75 L5 **Muzaffarpur** India
130 F7 **Muzambinho** Brazil
57 K4 **Muzat He** *R* China
50 F2 **Muzhi** Russian Federation
20 F6 **Muzillac** France
40 A3 **Muzin** *R* France
117 G8 **Muzon, C** Alaska U.S.A.
108 F8 **Múzquiz** Mexico
66 C4 **Muztag** *mt* China
66 D4 **Muztag** *mt* China
66 B4 **Muztagata** *mt* China
88 E8 **Mvera** Malawi
86 E4 **Mvolo** Sudan
87 G7 **Mvomero** Tanzania
86 B6 **M'Vouti** Congo
89 G2 **Mvuma** Zimbabwe
88 C10 **Mvurwi Ra** *mts* Zimbabwe
88 D7 **Mwambwa** *R* Zambia
88 D3 **Mwanza** Tanzania
88 D6 **Mwaya** Tanzania
14 B3 **Mweelrea** *mts* Ireland
86 D6 **Mweka** Zaire
87 D7 **Mwene Ditu** Zaire
87 F10 **Mwenezi** Zimbabwe
89 G3 **Mwenezi** *R* Zimbabwe
89 G3 **Mwenezi** Zimbabwe
88 B3 **Mwenga** Zaire
88 G6 **Mwera** Tanzania
89 G2 **Mwerihari** *R* Zimbabwe
88 B6 **Mweru, L** Zaire/Zambia
88 B6 **Mweru Wantipa** Zambia
89 F3 **Mwewe** *R* Zimbabwe
87 D7 **Mwimba** Zaire
87 D8 **Mwinilunga** Zambia
68 B2 **Myaing** Burma
113 E10 **Myakka** Florida U.S.A.
113 E10 **Myakka City** Florida U.S.A.
52 E5 **Myaksa** Russian Federation
31 H3 **Myálibórz** Poland
139 K4 **Myall L** New South Wales Australia
68 B3 **Myanaung** Burma
52 D3 **Myanduselga** Russian Federation
Myanmar *see* **Burma**
54 G2 **Myatlevo** Russian Federation
68 A2 **Myaungbwe** Burma
68 B4 **Myaungmya** Burma
68 D4 **Myawadi** Burma
46 F7 **Mycenae** Greece
68 A2 **Myebon** Burma
95 L6 **Myerstown** Pennsylvania U.S.A.
68 B2 **Myingyan** Burma
68 C2 **Myinkyado** Burma
68 D6 **Myinmoletkat** *mt* Burma
68 B2 **Myinmu** Burma
68 B2 **Myitche** Burma
68 D5 **Myitta** Burma
68 C2 **Myittha** Burma
48 D2 **Myjava** Czechoslovakia
26 F5 **Myken** *lighthouse* Norway
6 E1 **Mykines** *isld* Faeroes
52 H2 **Myla** Russian Federation
37 N2 **Mylau** Germany
29 M11 **Myllykoski** Finland
98 G1 **Mylo** North Dakota U.S.A.
75 O6 **Mymensingh** Bangladesh
29 J11 **Mynämäki** Finland
57 G2 **Mynaral** Kazakhstan
57 C4 **Mynbulak** Uzbekistan
8 B3 **Mynydd Bach** *mts* Wales
8 C3 **Mynydd Eppynt** *mts* Wales
68 A2 **Myohaung** Burma
68 B2 **Myohla** Burma
68 B2 **Myotha** Burma
68 B2 **Myothit** Burma
47 K8 **Myra** Turkey
109 K2 **Myra** Texas U.S.A.
141 F3 **Myra Vale** Queensland Australia
27 B11 **Myrdal** Norway
28 S10 **Myrdalsjökull** *ice cap* Iceland
26 H3 **Myre** Norway
27 G14 **Myresjö** Sweden
26 L6 **Myrheden** Sweden
118 F5 **Myrnam** Alberta Canada
119 U9 **Myrtle** Manitoba Canada
121 M8 **Myrtle** Ontario Canada
100 J3 **Myrtle** Idaho U.S.A.
111 G7 **Myrtle** Mississippi U.S.A.
112 J4 **Myrtle Beach** South Carolina U.S.A.
100 B6 **Myrtle Cr** Oregon U.S.A.
139 H6 **Myrtleford** Victoria Australia
100 A6 **Myrtle Point** Oregon U.S.A.
138 E4 **Myrtle Springs** South Australia Australia
141 L1 **Myrtletown** Queensland Australia
65 H3 **Mys Gamova** *lighthouse* Russian Federation
52 E5 **Myshkino** Russian Federation
47 J5 **Mysia** *hist reg* Turkey
56 C4 **Myski** Russian Federation
31 M6 **Myślenice** Poland
76 C4 **Mysore** India
147 P3 **Mys Shmidta** Russian Federation
26 G9 **Myssjo** Sweden
119 U3 **Mystery L** Manitoba Canada
112 D6 **Mystic** Georgia U.S.A.
99 O9 **Mystic** Iowa U.S.A.
52 H4 **Mysy** Permskaya obl Russian Federation
31 L5 **Myszków** Poland
31 N2 **Myszyniec** Poland
52 F6 **Myt** Russian Federation
68 H7 **My Tho** Vietnam
54 J1 **Mytishchi** Russian Federation
101 P9 **Myton** Utah U.S.A.
68 J6 **My Trach** Vietnam
29 T9 **Myvatn** *L* Iceland
57 H1 **Myylybulak** Kazakhstan
37 O4 **Mže** *R* Czechoslovakia
85 C4 **Mzereb,El** Mali
88 D7 **Mzimba** Malawi
89 F8 **Mzimvubu** *R* S Africa
88 E7 **Mzuzu** Malawi

N

37 M5 **Naab** *R* Germany
25 B5 **Naaldwijk** Netherlands
135 U6 **Naalehu** Hawaiian Is
80 C6 **Na'an** Israel
86 E4 **Naandi** Sudan
29 J11 **Naantali** Finland
25 D4 **Naarden** Netherlands
14 E3 **Naas** Ireland
29 N2 **Näätämönjoki** *R* Finland
89 A7 **Nababeep** S Africa
16 B5 **Nabaõ** *R* Portugal
75 K9 **Nabarangapur** India
61 K11 **Nabari** Japan
140 C1 **Nabarlek** N Terr Australia
71 F5 **Nabas** Panay Philippines
80 G1 **Nab'as Şakhr** Syria
79 F5 **Nabatīyet Ett Tahta** Lebanon
143 D7 **Nabberu, L** W Australia Australia
71 E2 **Nabbuan** Luzon Philippines
37 N5 **Nabburg** Germany
52 H6 **Naberezhnyye Chelny** Russian Federation
116 Q5 **Nabesna Gl** Alaska U.S.A.
43 D12 **Nabeul** Tunisia
139 K4 **Nabiac** New South Wales Australia
130 B7 **Nabileque,R** Brazil
136 H2 **Nabire** W Irian
123 K3 **Nabisipi R** Quebec Canada
79 F5 **Nabi Younés, Ras en** *C* Lebanon
80 E5 **Nablus** Jordan
79 E10 **Nabq** Egypt
71 F6 **Nabulao B** Negros Philippines
68 D5 **Nabule** Burma
88 H9 **Nacala** Mozambique
88 H9 **Nacala-a-Velha** Mozambique
125 L3 **Nacaome** Honduras
67 B5 **Nacham** Vietnam
100 E3 **Naches** Washington U.S.A.
100 D2 **Naches Pass** Washington U.S.A.
87 G8 **Nachingwea** Tanzania
74 D5 **Nāchna** India
66 E5 **Na Ch'u** *R* China
68 A7 **Nachuge** Andaman Is
102 C6 **Nacimiento** *R* California U.S.A.
102 C6 **Nacimiento Res** California U.S.A.
33 R7 **Nackel** Germany
103 P10 **Naco** Mexico
111 B10 **Nacogdoches** Texas U.S.A.
68 B6 **Nacondam I** Andaman Is
124 E2 **Nacozari de García** Mexico
Nada *see* **Dan Xian**
103 L3 **Nada** Utah U.S.A.
61 M8 **Nadachi** Japan
124 J4 **Nadadores** Mexico
67 B6 **Nadang** China
99 T4 **Nadeau** Michigan U.S.A.
Nådendal *see* **Naantali**
55 D4 **Nadezhdinka** Kazakhstan
137 Q5 **Nadi** Viti Levu Fiji
74 E7 **Nadiad** India
48 F4 **Nădlac** Romania
85 D1 **Nador** Morocco
48 G3 **Nádudvar** Hungary
77 C3 **Nadūshan** Iran
52 D3 **Nadvoitsy** Russian Federation
48 J2 **Nadvornaya** Ukraine
50 G2 **Nadym** Russian Federation
27 A13 **Naerbö** Norway
26 E7 **Naeröy** Norway
29 K5 **Nærum** Denmark
28 B5 **Næsbjerg** Denmark
28 C3 **Næsborg** Denmark
28 H6 **Næsby** Denmark
28 E6 **Næsbyhoved** Denmark
28 A3 **Næs Sund** *inlet* Denmark
28 H6 **Næstelsø** Denmark
28 H6 **Næstved** Denmark
68 A2 **Naf** *R* Burma
101 M7 **Naf** Idaho U.S.A.
85 G6 **Nafada** Nigeria
77 A4 **Naft-e Safīd** Iran
78 K4 **Naft Shahr** Iran
77 J6 **Nāg** Pakistan
71 F4 **Naga** Philippines
120 F3 **Nagagami** Ontario Canada
120 F3 **Nagagamisis L** Ontario Canada
60 F12 **Nagahama** Japan
75 Q5 **Nagaland** *prov* India
139 H6 **Nagambie** Victoria Australia
61 O13 **Nagannu-jima** *isld* Okinawa
61 L9 **Nagano** *prefect* Japan
61 M9 **Nagano** Japan
61 M9 **Naganohara** Japan
61 M8 **Nagaoka** Japan
75 P5 **Nagaon** India
76 D5 **Nagappattinam** India
76 E1 **Nāgāram** India
76 D2 **Nāgārjuna Sāgar** *res* India
76 D2 **Nagar Karnul** India
74 D6 **Nagar Parkar** Pakistan
60 C12 **Nagasaki** *prefect* Japan
60 C13 **Nagasaki** Japan
60 D14 **Nagasaki-bana** Japan
60 F12 **Naga-shima** *isld* Japan
60 D13 **Naga shima** *isld* Japan
60 E12 **Nagasu** Japan
60 E11 **Nagato** Japan
74 E5 **Nagaur** India
Nagchu Dzong *see* **Nagqu**
76 C6 **Nagercoil** India
26 H9 **Naggen** Sweden
74 H4 **Nagina** India
75 Q5 **Nāginimāra** India
61 P12 **Nago** Okinawa
74 J6 **Nagod** India
36 F6 **Nagold** *R* Germany
36 F6 **Nagold** Germany
78 L2 **Nagornyy Karabakh** *aut reg* Azerbaijan
52 H5 **Nagorsk** Russian Federation
61 P13 **Nago-wan** *B* Okinawa
61 K10 **Nagoya** Japan
74 H8 **Nagpur** India
66 E5 **Nagqu** China
29 J11 **Nagu** Finland
127 K5 **Nagua** Dominican Rep
71 E2 **Naguilian** Luzon Philippines
71 G4 **Nagumbuaya Pt** Philippines
48 D4 **Nagyatád** Hungary
48 D4 **Nagybajom** Hungary
48 G3 **Nagyecsed** Hungary
48 G3 **Nagykálló** Hungary
48 D4 **Nagykanizsa** Hungary
48 F3 **Nagykáta** Hungary
48 F3 **Nagykőrös** Hungary
48 G3 **Nagyléta** Hungary
48 E3 **Nagymaros** Hungary
Nagyvárad *see* **Oradea**
66 F4 **Nagza** China
61 P13 **Naha** Okinawa
70 D4 **Nahabuan** Kalimantan
80 D3 **Nahalal** Israel
80 C7 **Naḥalat** Israel
80 C8 **Naḥal Eshkolot** Jordan
80 E4 **Naḥal Ginnat** Jordan
80 E4 **Naḥal 'Irit** Jordan
80 C8 **Naḥal Negohot** Jordan
80 C8 **Naḥal Zohar** Jordan
74 G3 **Nahan** India
117 M5 **Nahanni Butte** Northwest Territories Canada
117 L5 **Nahanni Nat. Park** Northwest Territories Canada
80 D1 **Nahariyya** Israel
77 A2 **Nahāvand** Iran
36 C4 **Nahbollenbach** Germany
36 C4 **Nahe** *R* Germany
80 G4 **Nahla** Jordan
137 O4 **Nahoï, C** Vanuatu
21 O7 **Nahon** *R* France
79 H2 **Nahr Sājūr** *R* Syria
80 C3 **Naḥsholim** Israel
131 B8 **Nahuel Huapi, L** Argentina
133 D6 **Nahuel Niyeu** Argentina
112 E6 **Nahunta** Georgia U.S.A.
71 E3 **Naic** Luzon Philippines
124 G4 **Naica** Mexico
119 N6 **Naicam** Saskatchewan Canada
66 E4 **Naij Tal** China
71 L9 **Naikliu** Timor Indonesia
37 M3 **Naila** Germany
65 D4 **Nailin** China
8 D5 **Nailsea** England
8 D4 **Nailsworth** England
65 E3 **Naiman Qi** China
66 E3 **Naimin Bulak** *spring* China
115 N6 **Nain** Labrador, Nfld Canada
77 C3 **Nā'īn** Iran
74 J7 **Nainpur** India
21 L8 **Naintré** France
Nairn *co see* **Highland** *reg*
120 J6 **Nairn** Ontario Canada
15 E3 **Nairn** Scotland
143 B7 **Nairn, Mt** W Australia Australia
15 D3 **Nairn,R** Scotland
88 F2 **Nairobi** Kenya
52 B5 **Naissaar** *isld* Estonia
88 F2 **Naivasha** Kenya
20 E6 **Naizin** France
77 B3 **Najafābād** Iran
78 K6 **Najaf, An** Iraq
78 J6 **Najaf, An** *prov* Iraq
126 F4 **Najasa** *R* Cuba
17 F2 **Nájera** Spain
17 F2 **Najerilla** *R* Spain
65 H3 **Najin** N Korea
77 B2 **Najmabad** Iran
60 H12 **Naka** *R* Japan
60 C13 **Nakadōri shima** *isld* Japan
60 C12 **Nakagumi** Japan
61 P13 **Nakagusuku-wan** *B* Okinawa
61 N7 **Nakajō** Japan
60 C14 **Naka koshiki jima** *isld* Japan
60 D12 **Nakama** Japan
61 O9 **Nakaminato** Japan
60 F13 **Nakamura** Japan
60 E14 **Nakamura** Japan
61 M9 **Nakano** Japan
61 M9 **Nakanojō** Japan
60 G9 **Nakano-shima** *isld* Japan
67 H4 **Nakanougan-jima** *isld* Japan
61 Q12 **Nakaoshi** Okinawa
77 L3 **Naka Pass** Afghanistan
61 O5 **Nakasato** Japan
60 R3 **Nakasatsunai** Japan
60 T2 **Naka-shibetsu** Japan
55 D2 **Nakatay** Russian Federation
60 Q1 **Naka-Tombetsu** Japan
60 E12 **Nakatsu** Japan
61 L10 **Nakatsugawa** Japan
60 G10 **Naka-umi** Japan
116 J8 **Nakchamik I** Alaska U.S.A.
116 O6 **Naked I** Alaska U.S.A.
86 G2 **Nak'fa** Ethiopia
78 K2 **Nakhichevan** Azerbaijan
78 K2 **Nakhichevanskaya Respublika** Azerbaijan
84 J4 **Nakhl** Egypt
65 J3 **Nakhodka** Russian Federation
68 E5 **Nakhon Nayok** Thailand
68 D6 **Nakhon Pathom** Thailand
68 F5 **Nakhon Ratchasima** Thailand
69 E8 **Nakhon Si Thammarat** Thailand
68 E4 **Nakhon Thai** Thailand
59 L2 **Nakhtakhe** Russian Federation
61 P12 **Nakijin** Okinawa
117 G6 **Nakina** British Columbia Canada
120 D2 **Nakina** Ontario Canada
29 K3 **Näkkälä** Finland
29 J10 **Nakkila** Finland
31 K2 **Nakło** Poland
116 J7 **Naknek** Alaska U.S.A.
61 O9 **Nakoso** Japan
67 F3 **Nakou** China
Naksho Biru *see* **Biru**
28 G7 **Nakskov** Denmark
26 G9 **Näkten** *L* Sweden
65 G7 **Naktong** *R* S Korea
88 F2 **Nakuru** Kenya
88 E2 **Nakuru, L** Kenya
117 P10 **Nakusp** British Columbia Canada
68 C1 **Na-lang** Burma
58 E2 **Nalayh** Mongolia
53 F11 **Nal'chik** Russian Federation
74 G10 **Naldurg** India
76 D2 **Nalgonda** India
22 G3 **Nalinnes** Belgium
76 D3 **Nallamala Hills** India
94 G8 **Nallen** West Virginia U.S.A.
21 M8 **Nalliers** Vienne France
78 C1 **Nallıhan** Turkey
87 D9 **Nalolo** Zambia
6 M2 **N Alwyn** *oil rig* North Sea
68 C1 **Nam** *R* Burma
68 F3 **Nam** *R* Laos
65 G5 **Nam** *R* N Korea
60 C12 **Nama** Japan
87 C9 **Namacunde** Angola
88 F10 **Namacurra** Mozambique
118 D8 **Namaka** Alberta Canada
118 K2 **Namakan L** Minnesota/Ontario U.S.A./Canada
77 F4 **Namakiăr-e Shadād** *salt lake* Iran
77 E2 **Namak, Kavīr-e** *salt waste* Iran
69 H14 **Namang** Indonesia
57 F4 **Namangan** Uzbekistan
88 G8 **Namapa** Mozambique
88 G9 **Namaponda** Mozambique
87 C11 **Namaqualand** *tribal area* Namibia
87 C12 **Namaqualand** *dist* S Africa
88 F9 **Namarroi** Mozambique
86 F5 **Namasagali** Uganda
87 E9 **Nambala** Zambia
68 E2 **Nam Beng** *R* Laos
141 L7 **Nambour** Queensland Australia
139 L4 **Nambucca Heads** New South Wales Australia
68 G3 **Nam Ca Dinh** *R* Laos
69 G8 **Nam Can** Vietnam
66 E5 **Nam Co** *L* China
26 F7 **Namdalen** *V* Norway
26 E7 **Namdalseid** Norway
68 G2 **Nam Đing** Vietnam
88 G8 **Namecala** Mozambique
99 P3 **Namekagon** *R* Wisconsin U.S.A.
61 L9 **Namerikawa** Japan
48 E1 **Námestovo** Czechoslovakia
88 G9 **Nametil** Mozambique

Ref	Place
37 M7	Neustift Germany
33 S6	Neustrelitz Germany
37 J7	Neu Ulm Germany
22 D2	Neuve Chapelle France
21 M4	Neuve-Lyre,la France
40 F3	Neuveville Switzerland
18 G7	Neuvic France
109 N4	Neuville Texas U.S.A.
21 P5	Neuville-aux-Bois France
21 L8	Neuville-de-Poitou Vienne France
22 G5	Neuville-en-Tourne-à-Fuy France
19 O12	Neuville-les-Dames France
21 N2	Neuville-les-Dieppe France
21 K8	Neuvy Bouin France
21 M6	Neuvy-le-Roi France
21 O8	Neuvy Pailloux France
21 O8	Neuvy St. Sépulchre France
21 P7	Neuvy-sur-Barangeon France
33 O8	Neuwegersleben Germany
36 E6	Neuweier Germany
32 H5	Neuwerk isld Germany
36 C3	Neuwied Germany
32 L6	Neuwiller France
52 D5	Neu-Wulmstorf Germany
27 G11	Neva R Russian Federation
99 R4	Neva Sweden
102 F2	Neva Wisconsin U.S.A.
99 N7	Nevada R state U.S.A.
110 D4	Nevada Iowa U.S.A.
109 L2	Nevada Missouri U.S.A.
102 C2	Nevada Texas U.S.A.
102 C2	Nevada City California U.S.A.
128 D2	Nevada de Cocuy,Sa mts Colombia
124 H8	Nevada de Colima Mexico
16 E7	Nevada, Sierra mts Spain
131 C5	Nevado, Cerro pk Argentina
131 B6	Nevados Chillán mt Chile
131 C5	Nevado, Sierra del ra Argentina
54 A1	Nevel' Russian Federation
59 M2	Nevel'sk Russian Federation
59 H1	Never Russian Federation
8 B3	Nevern Wales
26 F6	Nevernes Norway
18 H5	Nevers France
139 J4	Nevertire New South Wales Australia
48 E7	Nevesinje Bosnia-Herzegovina
20 C6	Névez France
45 H2	Neviano d'Arduini Italy
32 F10	Neviges Germany
118 K9	Neville Saskatchewan Canada
21 M2	Néville France
112 F5	Nevils Georgia U.S.A.
53 F11	Nevinnomyssk Russian Federation
79 E9	Neviot Egypt
118 D6	Nevis Alberta Canada
127 P4	Nevis isld Lesser Antilles
99 M3	Nevis Minnesota U.S.A.
127 P4	Nevis Pk Nevis W Indies
80 E6	Nevit HaGedud Jordan
78 E2	Nevşehir Turkey
65 J2	Nevskoye Russian Federation
55 D2	Nev'yansk Russian Federation
103 J9	New R California U.S.A.
112 F1	New R North Carolina U.S.A.
94 F9	New R Virginia/W Virginia U.S.A.
12 E4	New Abbey Scotland
95 S3	Newagen Maine U.S.A.
87 G8	Newala Tanzania
94 B8	New Albany Indiana U.S.A.
111 G7	New Albany Mississippi U.S.A.
95 L5	New Albany Pennsylvania U.S.A.
99 P6	New Albin Iowa U.S.A.
99 S4	Newald Wisconsin U.S.A.
9 E5	New Alresford England
141 J8	New Angledool New South Wales Australia
9 F1	Newark England
110 E6	Newark Arkansas U.S.A.
102 B4	Newark California U.S.A.
95 M7	Newark Delaware U.S.A.
99 S8	Newark Illinois U.S.A.
98 G9	Newark Nebraska U.S.A.
95 N6	Newark New Jersey U.S.A.
95 K3	Newark New York U.S.A.
94 E6	Newark Ohio U.S.A.
95 L4	Newark Valley New York U.S.A.
110 G3	New Athens Illinois U.S.A.
99 P4	New Auburn Wisconsin U.S.A.
111 G10	New Augusta Mississippi U.S.A.
94 E4	New Baltimore Michigan U.S.A.
94 J7	New Baltimore Virginia U.S.A.
95 R5	New Bedford Massachusetts U.S.A.
100 C4	Newberg Oregon U.S.A.
99 Q10	New Berlin Illinois U.S.A.
95 M4	New Berlin New York U.S.A.
111 J9	Newbern Alabama U.S.A.
112 K2	New Bern North Carolina U.S.A.
110 G5	Newbern Tennessee U.S.A.
102 H7	Newberry California U.S.A.
113 E8	Newberry Florida U.S.A.
110 J3	Newberry Indiana U.S.A.
99 V3	Newberry Michigan U.S.A.
112 F3	Newberry South Carolina U.S.A.
94 H5	New Bethlehem Pennsylvania U.S.A.
13 G3	Newbiggin by-the-Sea England
13 E3	Newbigging Scotland
110 D3	New Bloomfield Missouri U.S.A.
99 R4	Newbold Wisconsin U.S.A.
121 O8	Newboro Ontario Canada
8 B1	Newborough Wales
99 S8	New Boston Illinois U.S.A.
109 N2	New Boston Texas U.S.A.
109 J6	New Braunfels Texas U.S.A.
94 C6	New Bremen Ohio U.S.A.
12 E3	New Bridge Scotland
8 C3	Newbridge Wales
118 G7	New Brigden Alberta Canada
136 K3	New Britain isld Papua New Guinea
95 P5	New Britain Connecticut U.S.A.
111 L10	New Brockton Alabama U.S.A.
122 F7	New Brunswick prov Canada
95 N6	New Brunswick New Jersey U.S.A.
9 H3	New Buckenham England
99 U8	New Buffalo Michigan U.S.A.
99 U4	Newburg Wisconsin U.S.A.
110 D4	Newburg Missouri U.S.A.
94 K6	Newburg Pennsylvania U.S.A.
94 H7	Newburg West Virginia U.S.A.
121 O8	Newburgh Ontario Canada
15 F3	Newburgh Scotland
13 F8	Newburgh Fife Scotland
110 J4	Newburgh Indiana U.S.A.
95 N5	Newburgh New York U.S.A.
123 T5	New Burnt Cove Newfoundland Canada
9 E5	Newbury England
95 R5	Newbury Vermont U.S.A.
95 R5	Newburyport Massachusetts U.S.A.
85 E6	New Bussa Nigeria
137 N6	New Caledonia isld Pacific Oc
95 O5	New Canaan Connecticut U.S.A.
99 P10	New Canton Illinois U.S.A.
122 G5	New Carlisle Quebec Canada
94 C7	New Carlisle Ohio U.S.A.
139 K5	Newcastle New South Wales Australia
122 G6	Newcastle New Brunswick Canada
121 M9	Newcastle Ontario Canada
14 E3	Newcastle Ireland
127 L2	Newcastle Jamaica
14 F2	Newcastle N Ireland
89 F6	Newcastle S Africa
102 C3	Newcastle California U.S.A.
106 C2	New Castle Colorado U.S.A.
94 B7	New Castle Indiana U.S.A.
110 L3	New Castle Kentucky U.S.A.
98 K7	New Castle Nebraska U.S.A.
95 M7	New Castle New Jersey U.S.A.
107 N6	Newcastle Oklahoma U.S.A.
94 G6	New Castle Pennsylvania U.S.A.
109 J2	Newcastle Texas U.S.A.
103 L4	Newcastle Utah U.S.A.
94 G9	New Castle Virginia U.S.A.
98 B6	Newcastle Wyoming U.S.A.
127 P4	Newcastle Nevis W Indies
141 G1	Newcastle B Queensland Australia
122 F7	Newcastle Br New Brunswick Canada
141 K1	Newcastle Bay Queensland Australia
8 B3	Newcastle Emlyn Wales
118 E7	Newcastle Mine Alberta Canada
141 G4	Newcastle Ra Queensland Australia
15 F5	Newcastleton Scotland
8 D1	Newcastle Under Lyme England
13 G4	Newcastle-upon-Tyne England
140 C3	Newcastle Waters N Terr Australia
14 B4	Newcastle West Ireland
9 F5	New Chapel England
106 B5	Newcomb New Mexico U.S.A.
94 F6	Newcomerstown Ohio U.S.A.
94 C7	New Concord Ohio U.S.A.
95 O5	New Cumnock Scotland
12 D3	New Daily Scotland
119 R8	Newdale Manitoba Canada
101 O6	Newdale Idaho U.S.A.
118 E9	New Dayton Alberta Canada
15 F3	New Deer Scotland
143 C10	Newdegate W Australia Australia
76	New Delhi India
117 P11	New Denver British Columbia Canada
111 M7	New Echota Nat.Mon Georgia U.S.A.
111 D8	New Edinburg Arkansas U.S.A.
113 C7	Newell Georgia U.S.A.
99 L7	Newell Iowa U.S.A.
112 G2	Newell North Carolina U.S.A.
98 C5	Newell South Dakota U.S.A.
112 F4	New Ellenton South Carolina U.S.A.
143 F6	Newell,L W Australia Australia
118 E8	Newell L Alberta Canada
111 E9	Newellton Louisiana U.S.A.
98 D3	New England North Dakota U.S.A.
139 K4	New England Ra mts New South Wales Australia
90 D4	New England Seamount Chain Atlantic Oc
116 F7	Newenham,C Alaska U.S.A.
8 D4	Newent England
80 F3	Newe Ur Israel
9 G4	Newe Yam Israel
94 A3	Newfane New York U.S.A.
95 P3	Newfane Vermont U.S.A.
127 K3	New Farm dist Brisbane, Qnsld Australia
95 R1	Newfield Maine U.S.A.
95 M7	Newfield New Jersey U.S.A.
117 P8	New Fish Creek Alberta Canada
110 E3	New Florence Missouri U.S.A.
98 K1	Newfolden Minnesota U.S.A.
9 G2	New Forest England
112 L3	Newfound L New Hampshire U.S.A.
100 A5	Newfoundland prov Canada
123 P5	Newfoundland isld Newfoundland Canada
95 M5	Newfoundland Pennsylvania U.S.A.
90 F4	Newfoundland Basin Atlantic Oc
90 E4	Newfoundland Rise Atlantic Oc
110 D2	New Franklin Missouri U.S.A.
95 L7	New Freedom Pennsylvania U.S.A.
8 A4	Newgale Wales
12 D3	New Galloway Scotland
118 B9	Newgate British Columbia Canada
137 M3	New Georgia isld Solomon Is
122 H9	New Germany Nova Scotia Canada
99 R7	New Glarus Wisconsin U.S.A.
122 K8	New Glasgow Nova Scotia Canada
95 R3	New Gloucester Maine U.S.A.
127 O3	New Grant Trinidad
109 M6	Newgulf Texas U.S.A.
100 D1	Newhalem Washington U.S.A.
116 K7	Newhalen Alaska U.S.A.
102 F7	Newhall California U.S.A.
116 F5	New Hamilton Alaska U.S.A.
95 Q4	New Hampshire state U.S.A.
99 M9	New Hampton Iowa U.S.A.
112 K3	New Hampton Missouri U.S.A.
111 F11	New Harbor Maine U.S.A.
98 G2	New Harmony Indiana U.S.A.
95 S3	New Hartford Connecticut U.S.A.
9 G6	Newhaven England
95 P5	New Haven Connecticut U.S.A.
94 B8	New Haven Indiana U.S.A.
110 J3	New Haven Kentucky U.S.A.
95 R2	New Haven Missouri U.S.A.
94 F8	New Haven West Virginia U.S.A.
99 U6	New Hazelton British Columbia Canada
117 K8	New Hebrides see Vanuatu
13 F6	New Hey England
9 G4	New Holland England
99 R9	New Holland Illinois U.S.A.
99 O1	New Holstein Wisconsin U.S.A.
109 N9	Newhope Arkansas U.S.A.
122 E2	Newhope Scotland
94 E7	New Iberia Louisiana U.S.A.
9 H5	Newick England
110 J4	Newington Georgia U.S.A.
137 L2	New Ireland isld Papua New Guinea
98 E3	New Leipzig North Dakota U.S.A.
94 E7	New Lexington Ohio U.S.A.
99 Q6	New Lisbon Wisconsin U.S.A.
121 L5	New Liskeard Ontario Canada
99 P9	New London Iowa U.S.A.
99 M4	New London Minnesota U.S.A.
99 P10	New London Missouri U.S.A.
95 P3	New London New Hampshire U.S.A.
94 E5	New London Ohio U.S.A.
99 S5	New London Wisconsin U.S.A.
12 D4	New Luce Scotland
110 G5	New Madrid Missouri U.S.A.
12 E2	Newmains Scotland
143 C6	Newman W Australia Australia
145 E4	Newman New Zealand
102 C4	Newman California U.S.A.
99 T10	Newman Illinois U.S.A.
106 D9	Newman New Mexico U.S.A.
98 J8	Newman Gr Nebraska U.S.A.
142 C6	Newman,Mt W Australia Australia
123 T5	Newman's Cove Newfoundland Canada
141 K1	Newmarket dist Brisbane, Qnsld Australia
121 L8	Newmarket Ontario Canada
9 G3	Newmarket England
14 B4	Newmarket Ireland
127 J2	Newmarket Jamaica
110 K7	Newmarket Alabama U.S.A.
99 M9	New Market Iowa U.S.A.
95 Q3	Newmarket New Hampshire U.S.A.
94 J8	New Market Virginia U.S.A.
94 E6	New Marshfield Ohio U.S.A.
94 G7	New Martinsville West Virginia U.S.A.
94 F7	New Matamoras Ohio U.S.A.
100 F7	New Meadows Idaho U.S.A.
102 D6	New Melones Res California U.S.A.
100 C7	New Mexico state U.S.A.
94 C7	New Miami Ohio U.S.A.
95 O5	New Milford Connecticut U.S.A.
95 M5	New Milford Pennsylvania U.S.A.
12 D2	Newmilns Scotland
108 D6	New Moore Texas U.S.A.
111 M8	New Morgan Georgia U.S.A.
139 K5	Newnes New South Wales Australia
9 E4	Newnham England
143 B9	New Norcia W Australia Australia
77 D5	New Norfolk Tasmania Australia
55 D2	Neyvo Shaytanskiy Russian Federation
118 E6	New Norway Alberta Canada
111 F11	New Orleans Louisiana U.S.A.
119 O6	New Osgoode Saskatchewan Canada
95 K7	New Oxford Pennsylvania U.S.A.
95 N5	New Paltz New York U.S.A.
94 C7	New Paris Ohio U.S.A.
94 A8	New Pekin Indiana U.S.A.
94 F6	New Philadelphia Ohio U.S.A.
100 E7	New Pine Creek Oregon U.S.A.
15 F3	New Pitsligo Scotland
145 E3	New Plymouth New Zealand
100 J6	New Plymouth Idaho U.S.A.
122 F5	Newport Quebec Canada
87 D7	Newport Curaçao
66 C5	Newport England
74 J2	Newport England
9 E6	Newport England
14 B3	Newport Ireland
127 K3	Newport Jamaica
70 N9	Newport Arkansas U.S.A.
99 T10	Newport Indiana U.S.A.
68 G3	Newport Kentucky U.S.A.
98 G1	Newport Maine U.S.A.
94 D5	Newport Michigan U.S.A.
99 O5	Newport Minnesota U.S.A.
98 G7	Newport Nebraska U.S.A.
95 P3	Newport New Hampshire U.S.A.
95 M7	Newport New Jersey U.S.A.
112 L3	Newport North Carolina U.S.A.
100 A5	Newport Oregon U.S.A.
145 D1	Newport Pennsylvania U.S.A.
95 Q5	Newport Rhode I U.S.A.
112 D2	Newport Tennessee U.S.A.
109 J2	Newport Texas U.S.A.
95 P2	Newport Vermont U.S.A.
100 H1	Newport Washington U.S.A.
8 B3	Newport Wales
9 E7	Newport Wales
9 D7	Newport B Wales
68 B4	Newport Beach California U.S.A.
95 L10	Newport News Virginia U.S.A.
13 F1	Newport-on-Tay Scotland
89 G2	Newport Pagnell England
113 E9	New Port Richey Florida U.S.A.
68 G2	New Powell Tennessee U.S.A.
99 N5	New Prague Minnesota U.S.A.
113 L9	New Providence isld Bahamas
8 A7	Newquay Wales
8 B3	New Quay Wales
113 E8	New R Florida U.S.A.
8 C3	New Radnor Wales
106 L4	New Raymer Colorado U.S.A.
99 N6	New Richland Minnesota U.S.A.
122 G5	New Richmond Quebec Canada
94 C8	New Richmond Ohio U.S.A.
99 O4	New Richmond Wisconsin U.S.A.
140 M5	New River Tennessee U.S.A.
112 K3	New River Inlet North Carolina U.S.A.
111 F11	New Roads Louisiana U.S.A.
98 G2	New Rockford North Dakota U.S.A.
9 G6	New Romney England
14 E4	New Ross Ireland
140 A3	Newry N Terr Australia
14 E2	Newry N Ireland
95 R2	Newry Maine U.S.A.
128 G6	New Salem North Dakota U.S.A.
98 E3	New Salem North Dakota U.S.A.
94 H7	New Salem Pennsylvania U.S.A.
13 D6	New Scone Scotland
68 F3	New Sharon Iowa U.S.A.
99 N8	New Siberian Is see Novosibirskiye Ostrova
113 G8	New Smyrna Beach Florida U.S.A.
139 G5	New South Wales state Australia
94 E7	New Straitsville Ohio U.S.A.
85 D7	New Tamale Ghana
94 J9	New Tazewell Tennessee U.S.A.
116 E6	Newtok Alaska U.S.A.
70 C3	Newton England
12 E3	Newton Scotland
13 E3	Newton Scotland
110 H3	Newton Illinois U.S.A.
99 N8	Newton Iowa U.S.A.
107 N4	Newton Kansas U.S.A.
95 R2	Newton Massachusetts U.S.A.
111 G9	Newton Mississippi U.S.A.
112 F2	Newton North Carolina U.S.A.
109 O5	Newton Texas U.S.A.
13 E4	Newton Abbot England
95 M2	Newton Arlosh England
101 L2	Newton New York U.S.A.
94 G5	Newton Falls Ohio U.S.A.
88 F8	Newton Ferrers England
112 J2	Newton Grove North Carolina U.S.A.
94 K6	Newton Hamilton Pennsylvania U.S.A.
13 F6	Newton-le-Willows England
12 D2	Newton Mearns Scotland
15 D3	Newtonmore Scotland
101 O8	Newton Res Utah U.S.A.
12 D4	Newton Stewart Scotland
123 T4	Newtown Newfoundland Canada
110 C1	Newtown Missouri U.S.A.
95 K9	Newtown Virginia U.S.A.
115 M7	Newtown Wales
14 E2	Newtownabbey N Ireland
14 F2	Newtownards N Ireland
14 E2	Newtownbutler N Ireland
95 L4	Newtownhamilton N Ireland
14 E3	Newtown Mt.Kennedy Ireland
98 D2	Newtown Sanish North Dakota U.S.A.
14 D2	Newtown Stewart N Ireland
99 N2	New Ulm Minnesota U.S.A.
109 L6	New Ulm Texas U.S.A.
99 O1	New Underwood South Dakota U.S.A.
111 L10	Newville Alabama U.S.A.
102 B2	Newville California U.S.A.
94 K6	Newville Pennsylvania U.S.A.
99 N8	New Virginia Iowa U.S.A.
94 E6	New Washington Ohio U.S.A.
123 M7	New Waterford C Breton I, Nova Scotia
121 S6	New Waverly Texas U.S.A.
99 M5	New Westminster British Columbia Canada
95 K7	New Windsor Maryland U.S.A.
95 K7	New World I Newfoundland Canada
123 S4	New Year L Nevada U.S.A.
100 F8	New York conurbation
95 K4	New York state U.S.A.
103 J6	New York Mts California U.S.A.
144	New Zealand dominion S W Pacific
94 C5	Ney China
52 F5	Ney Russian Federation
36 F3	Neya R Russian Federation
36 G3	Neya Russian Federation
8 B4	Neyland Wales
27 C13	Neyriz Iran
41 H4	Neyshābūr Iran
30 D1	Neyveli India
37 N6	Neyyattinkara India
54 C5	Nezhin Ukraine
36 F2	Nezperce Idaho U.S.A.
61 N7	Nezugaseki Japan
86 C6	N'Gabé Congo
88 D5	N'gabu Malawi
68 D5	Nga Chong,Khao mt Burma/Thailand
71 J9	Ngac Linh mt Vietnam
33 R9	Ngadubolu Sumba Indonesia
25 E2	Ngahan Burma
24 C5	Ngahere New Zealand
32 J10	Ngala Indonesia
33 M6	Ngalu Indonesia
36 A3	Ngami China
86 B3	Ngami,L Botswana
145 D1	N'Gamiland reg Botswana
100 C7	Ngamo Zimbabwe
71 M9	Ngandjuk Java
145 E4	Ngan Son Vietnam
36 D2	N'Gao Congo
36 C3	Ngaoundéré Cameroon
19 L4	Ngapara New Zealand
24 C5	Ngapuna Burma
98 K2	Ngapuna New Zealand
144 C6	Ngaras Sumatra
33 T8	Ngaroma New Zealand
145 E2	Ngaruawahia New Zealand
145 D1	Ngaruroro R New Zealand
145 F2	Ngatapa New Zealand
145 E2	Ngatea New Zealand
33 K5	Ngathainggyaung Burma
33 N7	Ngatira New Zealand
26 N5	Ngauruhoe vol New Zealand
33 N7	Ngawan Chaung R Burma
32 F8	Ngawaro New Zealand
32 F8	Ngawi Java
121 R3	Ngayok B Burma
33 R9	Ngemda see Ngamda
88 F3	Ngezi R Zimbabwe
36 E2	Ngezi Zimbabwe
31 M5	Ngezi Dam Zimbabwe
22 D2	Nghe An prov Vietnam
71 A2	Nghia Lô Vietnam
71 M9	Ngilmina Indonesia
31 L3	Nieszawa Poland
85 C7	Niete, Mt Liberia
33 P10	Nietleben Germany
20 H6	Nieul le Dolent France
22 D2	Nieuw Amsterdam Suriname
25 C5	Nieuwegein Netherlands
25 C5	Nieuwkoop Netherlands
25 D5	Nieuwleusen Netherlands
31 J5	Nieuw Nickerie Suriname
22 D6	Nieuwolda Netherlands
22 E6	Nieuwpoort Belgium
22 E6	Nieuwpoort Netherlands
25 C5	Nieuwstadt Netherlands
87 E9	Nieuw-Vennep Netherlands
25 D5	Nieuwe dept France
82 E6	Nigadoo New Brunswick Canada
78 B3	Niğde Turkey
85 F5	Niger rep W Africa
85 E6	Niger R W Africa
85 E6	Niger, Mouths of the Nigeria
144 B6	Nightcaps New Zealand
99 P9	Nighthawk Washington U.S.A.
141 G2	Night I Great Barrier Reef Australia
	Nightingale I see Bach Long Vi,I.
90 B16	Nightingale I Tristan da Cunha
111 J7	Nigrita Greece
21 P3	Nihill Victoria Australia
102 J2	Nihuil, Embalse del res Argentina
131 C5	Niihau isld Hawaiian Is
60 G12	Niigata Japan
135 N11	Niihama Japan
135 N11	Nii-jima isld Japan
101 N6	Niikappu R Japan
60 C10	Niimi Japan
60 H14	Niitsu Japan
116 K6	Nikabuna Lakes Alaska U.S.A.
85 D6	Niangoloko Burkina
110 D4	Niangua R Missouri U.S.A.
86 E5	Niangxi see Xinshao
95 P5	Nia Nia Zaire
13 E4	Niantic Connecticut U.S.A.
101 L2	Nianzishan China
86 B6	Niara Montana U.S.A.
69 C12	Niari R Congo
88 F8	Nias isld Indonesia
46 F8	Niassa Mozambique
101 R4	Niata Greece
28 D2	Nibe Denmark
28 D3	Nibe Bredning B Denmark
125 L3	Nicabau Quebec Canada
	Nicaragua rep Central America
125 M4	Nicaragua, Lac de Nicaragua
95 T1	Nicaraguas L
44 B4	Nice France
102 B2	Nice California U.S.A.
111 K11	Niceville Florida U.S.A.
15 D3	Nichicun, L Quebec Canada
60 E11	Nichihara Japan
95 L4	Nichols New York U.S.A.
140 K4	Nicholson R Queensland Australia
142 G4	Nicholson W Australia Australia
143 B7	Nicholson Ra W Australia Australia
95 N2	Nicholville New York U.S.A.
99 O1	Nickel L Ontario Canada
129 G2	Nickerie R Suriname
107 M3	Nickerson Kansas U.S.A.
142 B5	Nickol B W Australia Australia
122 F3	Nicobar Is Bay of Bengal
69 A8	Nicola British Columbia Canada
121 S6	Nicolet Quebec Canada
99 M5	Nicollet Minnesota U.S.A.
121 N6	Nicomedia see Kocaeli
76 C5	Nicopolis see Preveza
43 F11	Nicosia Cyprus
43 G10	Nicosia Sicily
29 N8	Nicotera Italy
47 K4	Nicoya Costa Rica
57 F5	Nicoya,Pen.de Costa Rica
122 E6	Nictau New Brunswick Canada
31 M5	Nida R Poland
76 E2	Nidadavole India
40 F3	Nidau Switzerland
36 G3	Nidda R Germany
36 G3	Nidda Germany
27 C13	Niddatal Germany
41 H4	Nideggen Germany
42 G4	Nidda Angola
78 H4	Nidzica Poland
87 D8	Nida Angola
141 J8	Nidda Angola
73 L7	Nidri Greece
13 E2	Niebla Spain
47 O12	Nijar Spain
74 F5	Nijkerk Netherlands
24 D5	Nijmegen Netherlands
25 D5	Nijverdal Netherlands
26 N5	Nikabuna Lakes Alaska U.S.A.
26 S2	Nikel' Russian Federation
55 C5	Nikel'tau Kazakhstan
71 M9	Nikiniki Timor Indonesia
46 F4	Nikitas Greece
52 D6	Nikitinka Russian Federation
85 E7	Nikki Benin
61 N9	Nikkō Japan
40 G5	Niklaus Switzerland
116 K5	Nikolai Alaska U.S.A.
53 E11	Nikolayev Ukraine
52 G2	Nikolayev Ukraine
52 C3	Nikolayevka Kazakhstan
53 G8	Nikolayevsk Russian Federation
55 D4	Nikolayevsk Russian Federation
59 M1	Nikolayevsk-na-Amure Russian Federation
52 G5	Nikol'sk Russian Federation
52 F5	Nikolskoye Russian Federation
55 C5	Nikol'skoye Russian Federation
88 C3	Nikongo R Tanzania
46 G1	Nikopol Bulgaria
54 F9	Nikopol' Ukraine
78 F1	Niksar Turkey
77 G6	Nikshahr Iran
42 J6	Nikšić Montenegro Yugoslavia
137 S2	Nikumaroro isld Phoenix Is Pacific Oc
117 D4	Nikunau isld Kiribati
71 O8	Nila R Indonesia
103 J8	Nila isld Indonesia
73 L8	Nilande Atoll Maldives
83 K11	Nilavelli Sri Lanka
84 J4	Nile R N E Africa
86 F2	Nile prov Sudan
94 A5	Niles Michigan U.S.A.
94 G5	Niles Ohio U.S.A.
121 N6	Nilgaut, L Quebec Canada
76 C5	Nilgiri Hills India
116 E6	Nililuguk Alaska U.S.A.
31 J4	Nilka China
29 N8	Nilsiä Finland
47 K4	Nilüfer R Turkey
57 F5	Nilwala R Sri Lanka
28 D5	Nim Denmark
74 F6	Nimach India
85 C7	Nimba, Mts Guinea/Liberia/Ivory Co
142 E6	Nimberra Well W Australia Australia
139 L3	Nimbin New South Wales Australia
18 H9	Nîmes France
47 O12	Nimfai Greece
74 F5	Nimka Thana India
139 J6	Nimmitabel New South Wales Australia
101 M3	Nimrod Montana U.S.A.
110 C7	Nimrod L Arkansas U.S.A.
144 C6	Nimrod, Mt New Zealand
109 O1	Nimrod Res Arkansas U.S.A.
79 Q2	Nīmrūz reg Afghanistan
79 H4	Nīmrūz prov Afghanistan
28 F4	Nimtofte Denmark
42 G4	Nin Croatia
141 H7	Nindigully Queensland Australia
73 L7	Nine Degree Chan Lakshadweep Indian Oc
13 E2	Nine Mile Burn Scotland
139 G4	Nine Mile L New South Wales Australia
40 B6	Nine Mile Pk Nevada U.S.A.
109 S6	Nine Point Mesa mt Texas U.S.A.
102 E2	Ninette Manitoba Canada
139 J7	Ninety Mile Beach Victoria Australia
145 D1	Ninety Mile Beach New Zealand
112 D1	Ninety Six South Carolina U.S.A.
94 G7	Nineveh Pennsylvania U.S.A.
59 J3	Ning'an China
67 G2	Ningbo China
91 J3	Ningcheng China
67 F3	Ningde China
67 F3	Ningdu China
67 D3	Ningguo China
67 F1	Ninghai China
65 D5	Ning-hsia see Yinchuan
58 F4	Ninghua China
67 G3	Ningjin China
67 D3	Ningjing China
67 C7	Ningming China
67 C7	Ningnan China
65 D5	Ningpo see Ningbo
67 E3	Ningsia aut reg China see Ningxia
67 F6	Ningwu China
58 E4	Ningxia aut reg China
67 G2	Ningxiang China
67 D3	Ningyuan China
61 M10	Nirasaki Japan
80 C3	Nir 'Ezyon Israel
80 B6	Nir Galim Israel
80 B7	Nir Hen Israel
74 H9	Nirmal India
75 M5	Nirmali India
80 B8	Nir Moshe Israel
84 B3	Nirvana Michigan U.S.A.
80 C6	Nir Zevi Israel
16 B5	Niš Serbia Yugoslavia
16 B5	Nisa Portugal
72 F6	Nişāb Yemen
16 B5	Nisava R Serbia Yugoslavia
95 K5	Nisbet Pennsylvania U.S.A.
67 C2	Niseko Japan
61 P5	Nishi China
60 F9	Nishi-Hōji Japan
60 F9	Nishinomiya Japan
60 C13	Nishino-shima isld Japan
61 L11	Nishio Japan
60 C13	Nishi-Sonogi-hantō pen Japan
61 J7	Nishi-suidō str Japan
60 H10	Nishiwaki Japan
116 H6	Nishlik L Alaska U.S.A.
99 L8	Nishnabotna, E R Iowa U.S.A.
99 L8	Nishnabotna, W R Iowa U.S.A.
130 J9	Nisia Floresta Brazil
48 J3	Nisipitul Romania
31 N5	Nisko Poland
98 C5	Nisland South Dakota U.S.A.
117 D4	Nisling R Yukon Territory Canada
27 F15	Nissan R Sweden
27 C12	Nissedal Norway
27 C12	Nisserv L Norway
28 A3	Nissum Bredning B Denmark
28 A4	Nissum Fiord inlet Denmark
117 C5	Nisutlin R Yukon Territory Canada
115 M7	Nitchequon Quebec Canada
130 G8	Niterói Brazil
15 E5	Nith,R Scotland
15 E5	Nithsdale Scotland
79 M9	Nitibe Timor
80 G7	Nitil Jordan
100 A1	Nitinat L British Columbia Canada
9 E6	Niton England
31 L7	Nitra Czechoslovakia
31 L7	Nitra R Czechoslovakia
48 E2	Nitra Czechoslovakia
54 B5	Nitro West Virginia U.S.A.
29 N2	Nitsjärvi L Finland
37 M5	Nittendorf Germany
79 F13	Niuafo'ou isld Pacific Oc
137 S5	Niuatoputapu isld Pacific Oc
137 Q4	Niue isld Pacific Oc
69 F13	Niulakita isld Tuvalu
137 Q3	Niur, Pulau isld Sumatra
69 E4	Niushan see Donghai
137 Q3	Niutao isld Tuvalu
29 K5	Nivå Denmark
141 H7	Nivala Finland
94 J8	Niverville Manitoba Canada
22 G2	Nivelles Belgium
18 H5	Nivernais prov France
21 P3	Nivillers France
40 B6	Nivolas-Vermelle France
52 E2	Nivskiy Russian Federation
74 J2	Niwas India
102 E2	Nixon Nevada U.S.A.
102 C2	Nixon Texas U.S.A.
47 N11	Niyandros isld Turkey
52 F6	Niyat, Gunung mt Kalimantan
74 H9	Nizamabad India
52 F6	Nizhegorodskaya Oblast' prov Russian Federation
52 E3	Nizhmozero Russian Federation
56 G2	Nizhneangarsk Russian Federation
52 H2	Nizhne Bugayevo Russian Federation
54 L9	Nizhne Gnilovskoy Russian Federation
52 H6	Nizhnekamsk Russian Federation
52 H6	Nizhnekamskoye Vodokhranilishche res Russian Federation
55 B4	Nizhne-troitskiy Russian Federation
56 E4	Nizhnedinsk Russian Federation
55 G1	Nizhnevartovsk Russian Federation
52 G4	Nizhneye Il'yasovo Russian Federation
52 F6	Nizhney Kuyto, Oz L Russian Federation
55 C2	Nizhniy Novgorod Russian Federation
52 H6	Nizhniy Tagil Russian Federation
52 H6	Nizhniy Takanysh Russian Federation
52 H6	Nizhniy Lomov Russian Federation
56 F5	Nizhniy Yenisey Russian Federation
55 G1	Nizhniy Vyalozerskiy Russian Federation
52 F6	Nizhniy Yenangsk Russian Federation
55 E2	Nizhnyaya Aremzyan Russian Federation
55 C5	Nizhnyaya Irga Russian Federation
55 C5	Nizhnyaya Omka Russian Federation
52 J3	Nizhnyaya-Omra Russian Federation
52 H4	Nizhnyaya Pesha Russian Federation
52 H4	Nizhnyaya Pomya Russian Federation
55 G4	Nizhnyaya Salda Russian Federation
55 G4	Nizhnyaya Suyetka Russian Federation
54 M5	Nizhnyaya Tavda Russian Federation
52 H2	Nizhnyaya Toyma R Russian Federation
55 A1	Nizhnyaya Tunguska R Russian Federation
52 H4	Nizhnyaya Voch' Russian Federation
52 H4	Nizhnyaya Zolotitsa Russian Federation
29 Q4	Nizh Pirengskoye Ozero L Russian Federation
52 H6	Nizh Tunguska R Russian Federation
78 F3	Nízké Tatry mts Czechoslovakia
48 L7	Nízke Tatry Czechoslovakia
48 J7	Nížm Medzev Czechoslovakia
22 G4	Nizy-le-Comte France
79 E8	Nizzana hist site Israel
80 B6	Nizzane 'Oz Israel
80 C7	Nizzanim Israel
87 G7	Njinjo Tanzania
87 D9	Njoko R Zambia

208 Njombe — Nueva Ciudad

88 E5 Njombe R Tanzania
88 E6 Njombe Tanzania
88 G10 Njoro isld Mozambique
26 J9 Njurundabommen Sweden
27 J10 Njutånger Sweden
89 G7 Nkandla S Africa
88 D7 Nkanka R Zambia
88 E7 Nkhata B Malawi
88 E8 Nkhotakota Malawi
86 A6 Nkomi, Lagune Lagoon Gabon
86 A5 Nkongsamba Cameroon
88 D5 Nkululu R Tanzania
28 A4 No Denmark
21 P3 Noailles France
75 O7 Noakhali Bangladesh
45 M1 Noale Italy
128 C3 Noanama Colombia
95 Q5 Noank Connecticut U.S.A.
26 O3 Noarvas mt Norway
40 F7 Noasca Italy
116 F3 Noatak Alaska U.S.A.
116 G3 Noatak Nat Preserve Alaska U.S.A.
14 E3 Nobber Ireland
120 K7 Nobel Ontario Canada
60 E13 Nobeoka Japan
110 H3 Noble Illinois U.S.A.
107 N6 Noble Oklahoma U.S.A.
118 D9 Nobleford Alberta Canada
111 E7 Noble Lake Arkansas U.S.A.
94 A6 Noblesville Indiana U.S.A.
60 P3 Noboribetsu Japan
130 C4 Nobres Brazil
141 G8 Noccundra Queensland Australia
21 M5 Noce France
41 O5 Noce R Italy
45 R8 Nocera Inferiore Italy
44 H2 Noceto Italy
124 H7 Nochistlán Mexico
141 G8 Nockatunga Queensland Australia
109 K2 Nocona Texas U.S.A.
48 J5 Nocrich Romania
61 P5 Noda Japan
133 D7 Nodales,B.de los Argentina
99 M8 Nodaway R Iowa U.S.A.
99 M9 Nodaway Iowa U.S.A.
98 B7 Node Wyoming U.S.A.
20 G6 Noé-Blanche France
130 D4 Noedori R Brazil
110 B5 Noel Missouri U.S.A.
123 Q5 Noel Paul's Brook Newfoundland Canada
120 K6 Noelville Ontario Canada
22 D3 Noeux les Mines France
124 D2 Nogales Sonora Mexico
125 L8 Nogales Vera Cruz Mexico
103 O10 Nogales Arizona U.S.A.
116 J6 Nogamut Alaska U.S.A.
45 K1 Nogara Italy
18 E9 Nogaro France
31 L1 Nogat R Poland
60 D12 Nōgata Japan
40 B1 Nogent en Bassigny France
21 L5 Nogent-le-Bernard France
21 O4 Nogent-le-Roi France
21 M5 Nogent-le-Rotrou France
21 P3 Nogent-sur-Oise France
18 H4 Nogent-sur-Seine France
54 K1 Noginsk Russian Federation
59 M1 Nogliki Russian Federation
40 C4 Nogno France
141 K7 Nogo R Queensland Australia
141 J6 Nogoa R Queensland Australia
61 K10 Nōgōhaku-san mt Japan
131 F4 Nogoya R Argentina
48 E3 Nógrád co Hungary
16 C3 Nogueira mt Portugal
17 H2 Noguera Pallarésa R Spain
17 H2 Noguera Ribagorzana R Spain
21 O8 Nohant Vicq France
74 F4 Nohar India
61 P5 Noheji Japan
36 C4 Nohfelden Germany
36 B3 Nohn Germany
Noia see Noya
121 N6 Noire R Quebec Canada
67 A6 Noire R Vietnam
16 E9 Noire, Pt Morocco
20 C5 Noires,Mtgnes France
20 F7 Noirmoutier France
20 F8 Noirmoutier,Ile de France
20 C5 Noir,Mt France
21 K8 Noirterre France
17 H9 Noisy les Bains Algeria
61 N11 Nojima-zaki C Japan
61 M9 Nojiri-ko L Japan
87 D9 Nokaneng Botswana
29 K10 Nokia Finland
74 B8 Nok Kundi Pakistan
77 H5 Nok Kundi Pakistan
144 B6 Nokomai New Zealand
119 N7 Nokomis Saskatchewan Canada
110 G2 Nokomis Illinois U.S.A.
86 C5 Nola Cent Afr Republic
45 R8 Nola Italy
119 O2 Nolalu Ontario Canada
98 J2 Nolan North Dakota U.S.A.
108 G3 Nolan Texas U.S.A.
28 E5 Nølev Denmark
44 D3 Noli Italy
112 E1 Nolichucky R Tennessee U.S.A.
112 E1 Nolichucky Dam Tennessee U.S.A.
52 G5 Nolinsk Russian Federation
21 N3 Nolléval France
6 F1 Nólsoy isld Faeroes
69 E9 Nol,Thale L Thailand
66 E3 Nom China
111 L11 Noma Florida U.S.A.
60 D14 Noma-misaki C Japan
95 R5 No Mans Land isld Massachusetts U.S.A.
116 E4 Nome Alaska U.S.A.
98 J3 Nome North Dakota U.S.A.
116 E4 Nome C Alaska U.S.A.
19 K4 Nomeny France
121 P6 Nominingue Quebec Canada
60 C13 Nomo-zaki C Japan
87 C10 Nomtsas Namibia
137 S6 Nomuka isld Tonga
114 J5 Nonacho L Northwest Territories Canada
21 N4 Nonancourt France
21 J3 Nonant France
21 L4 Nonant-le-Pin France
45 K2 Nonantola Italy
52 H2 Nonburg Russian Federation
65 F2 Nong'an China
68 F3 Nong Het Laos
68 F5 Nong Hong Thailand
68 F4 Nong Khai Thailand
87 F11 Nongoma S Africa
19 N15 Nonières France
Nonni R see Nen Jiang R
138 D4 Nonning South Australia Australia
138 D4 Nonning,Mt South Australia Australia
36 B4 Nonnweiler Germany
130 D10 Nonoai Brazil
124 F4 Nonoava Mexico
71 G6 Nonoc isld Philippines
137 P2 Nonouti atoll Kiribati
119 W2 Nonsuch Manitoba Canada
68 E6 Nonthaburi Thailand
18 F7 Nontron France
116 K7 Nonvianuk L Alaska U.S.A.
143 B7 Nookawarra W Australia Australia
138 D2 Noolyeanna,L South Australia Australia
140 B2 Noonamah N Terr Australia
98 C1 Noonan North Dakota U.S.A.
143 C9 Noongaar W Australia Australia
142 E4 Noonkanbah W Australia Australia
141 H8 Noorama R Queensland Australia
25 A5 Noord-Beveland Netherlands
25 D5 Noord Brabant Netherlands
25 C5 Noordeloos Netherlands
25 C3 Noord-Holland Netherlands
25 E3 Noordoost Polder Netherlands
126 A1 Noord Pt Curaçao
25 B4 Noordwijk aan zee Netherlands
7 N9 Noordwinning oil rig North Sea
25 F3 Noordwolde Netherlands
25 C4 Noordzee-Kanaal Netherlands
29 J10 Noormarkku Finland
116 G3 Noorvik Alaska U.S.A.
141 L7 Noosa Heads Queensland Australia
117 K11 Nootka British Columbia Canada
117 K11 Nootka I British Columbia Canada
103 H5 Nopah Ra California U.S.A.
99 T4 Noquebay,L Wisconsin U.S.A.
119 O6 Nora Saskatchewan Canada
59 J1 Nora R Russian Federation
27 H12 Nora Sweden
98 J9 Nora Nebraska U.S.A.
28 D3 Nørager Denmark
86 G2 Nora I Ethiopia
71 G7 Norala Mindanao Philippines
121 L4 Noranda Quebec Canada
99 O6 Nora Springs Iowa U.S.A.
98 G4 Norbeck South Dakota U.S.A.
27 H11 Norberg Sweden
110 C2 Norborne Missouri U.S.A.
107 K2 Norcatur Kansas U.S.A.
42 E6 Norcia Italy
143 D9 Norcott,Mt W Australia Australia
111 M8 Norcross Georgia U.S.A.
18 H2 Nord dept France
27 D12 Nordaguta Norway
26 K7 Nordanås Sweden
27 D11 Nord-Aurdal Norway
50 B1 Nordaustlandet isld Spitzbergen
28 D6 Nordborg Denmark
28 F5 Nordby Denmark
28 A6 Nordby Denmark
Nord Cap see Horn
26 B9 Norddal Norway
32 F5 Norddeich Germany
28 A7 Norddorf Germany
32 L7 Norddrebber Germany
118 B6 Nordegg R Alberta Canada
9 G2 Nordelph England
32 F5 Norden Germany
37 K6 Nordendorf Germany
32 H5 Nordenham Germany
51 J1 Nordenshel'da Arkhipelag Russian Federation
117 E5 Nordenskiold R Yukon Territory Canada
28 A7 Norder Aue chan Germany
32 J5 Nordergründe sandbank Germany
32 F5 Norderney isld Germany
32 F5 Norderney Germany
26 A10 Nordfjord reg Norway
26 A10 Nordfjord inlet Norway
26 B10 Nordfjordeid Norway
26 H4 Nordfold Norway
30 D1 Nord-friesische Inseln islds Germany
28 B7 Nordfriesland reg Germany
37 M3 Nordhalben Germany
33 N10 Nordhausen Germany
109 K7 Nordheim Texas U.S.A.
32 J5 Nordholz Germany
27 A11 Nordhordland reg Norway
32 F8 Nordhorn Germany
26 K9 Nordingrå Sweden
80 C4 Nordiyya Israel
28 C3 Nordjylland co Denmark
26 P1 Nordkapp C Norway
26 Q1 Nordkinn Norway
26 L2 Nordkjosbotn Norway
26 F6 Nordland Fylker Norway
26 G7 Nordli Norway
37 K6 Nördlingen Germany
26 K8 Nordmaling Sweden
100 J1 Nordman Idaho U.S.A.
27 G12 Nordmark Sweden
27 D11 Nordmarka reg Norway
26 B9 Nordmöre reg Norway
98 F7 Nordon Nebraska U.S.A.
32 K4 Nord-Ostsee Kanal Germany
28 F2 Nordre Rønner isld Denmark
115 O4 Nordre Strømfjord inlet Greenland
32 E9 Nordrhein Westfalen land Germany
28 C7 Nord Schleswig Germany
28 B6 Nord Slesvig reg Denmark
32 L8 Nord-Stemmen Germany
30 D1 Nordstrand isld Germany
26 E7 Nord-Tröndelag Fylker Norway
51 L1 Nordvik Russian Federation
32 F8 Nordwalde Germany
14 D4 Nore R Ireland
27 C11 Nore Norway
27 D11 Norefjell mt Norway
122 E1 Nore,L Quebec Canada
120 K4 Norembego Ontario Canada
17 K2 Norfeo,C Spain
9 H2 Norfolk co England
110 D5 Norfolk Arkansas U.S.A.
95 O5 Norfolk Connecticut U.S.A.
98 J7 Norfolk Nebraska U.S.A.
95 L10 Norfolk Virginia U.S.A.
137 O7 Norfolk I Pacific Oc
110 D5 Norfolk L Arkansas U.S.A.
25 F2 Norg Netherlands
13 F2 Norham England
109 K9 Norias Texas U.S.A.
61 L9 Norikura-dake mt Japan
51 H2 Noril'sk Russian Federation
141 G8 Norley Queensland Australia
112 J1 Norlina North Carolina U.S.A.
45 N6 Norma Italy
110 K7 Normal Alabama U.S.A.
99 S9 Normal Illinois U.S.A.
141 F4 Norman R Queensland Australia
111 C7 Norman Arkansas U.S.A.
98 H9 Norman Nebraska U.S.A.
107 N6 Norman Oklahoma U.S.A.
141 G2 Normanby R Queensland Australia
13 H5 Normanby England
145 E3 Normanby New Zealand
141 K5 Normanby Ra Queensland Australia
21 H4 Normandie reg France
20 H4 Normandie, Collines de hills France
121 S4 Normandin Quebec Canada
110 K6 Normandy Tennessee U.S.A.
109 L4 Normangee Texas U.S.A.
143 E7 Norman Hurst,Mt W Australia Australia
112 F2 Norman, L North Carolina U.S.A.
109 K7 Normanna Texas U.S.A.
141 K2 Norman Park dist Brisbane, Qnsld Australia
141 F4 Normanton Queensland Australia
117 K3 Norman Wells Northwest Territories Canada
121 L4 Normetal Quebec Canada
143 B10 Nornalup W Australia Australia
124 F4 Norogachic Mexico
111 D8 Norphlet Arkansas U.S.A.
119 Q7 Norquay Saskatchewan Canada
133 C5 Norquin Argentina
133 C6 Norquinco Argentina
29 J8 Norra Kvarken chan Finland/Sweden
27 J10 Norrala Sweden
27 G15 Norraryd Sweden
26 J4 Norrbotten reg Sweden
28 D4 Nørreå R Denmark
28 C5 Nørre Bramdrup Denmark
28 A5 Nørre Nebel Denmark
22 C2 Norrent-Fontès France
28 D2 Nørre Saltum Denmark
28 D2 Nørresundby Denmark
26 M6 Norrfjärden Sweden
26 K8 Norrfors Sweden
26 J9 Norrhassel Sweden
95 S2 Norridgewock Maine U.S.A.
99 Q9 Norris Illinois U.S.A.
101 O4 Norris Montana U.S.A.
98 E6 Norris South Dakota U.S.A.
112 C1 Norris Tennessee U.S.A.
101 P5 Norris Wyoming U.S.A.
123 R4 Norris Arm Newfoundland Canada
110 H4 Norris City Illinois U.S.A.
112 C1 Norris Dam Tennessee U.S.A.
112 D1 Norris Lake Tennessee U.S.A.
123 P4 Norris Point Newfoundland Canada
95 M6 Norristown Pennsylvania U.S.A.
27 H13 Norrköping Sweden
29 H8 Norrskär lighthouse Finland
27 J11 Norrsundet Sweden
27 K12 Norrtälje Sweden
26 H6 Norrvik Sweden
27 F12 Norsä R Sweden
143 D9 Norseman W Australia Australia
145 F4 Norsewood New Zealand
27 H13 Norsholm Sweden
27 D12 Norsjö L Norway
26 K7 Norsjö Sweden
26 Q1 Norskholmen Norway
28 B2 Nors Sø L Denmark
129 H3 Norte,C Brazil
128 D2 Norte de Santander div Colombia
32 L9 Nörten Hardenburg Germany
133 E6 Norte,Pta Argentina
131 D3 Norte,Sa de ra Argentina
128 G6 Norte,Serra do mts Brazil
111 J8 North R Alabama U.S.A.
112 F4 North South Carolina U.S.A.
94 C5 North Adams Michigan U.S.A.
13 G5 Northallerton England
143 B9 Northam W Australia Australia
98 F1 North America, Center of North Dakota U.S.A.
90 C6 North American Basin Atlantic Oc
143 A8 Northampton W Australia Australia
9 F3 Northampton England
95 P4 Northampton Massachusetts U.S.A.
141 H6 Northampton Downs Queensland Australia
9 F3 Northamptonshire co England
68 A6 North Andaman isld Andaman Is
94 K8 North Anna R Virginia U.S.A.
95 S2 North Anson Maine U.S.A.
Northants co see Northamptonshire co
117 Q4 North Arm inlet Northwest Territories Canada
112 E4 North Augusta Georgia U.S.A.
115 N6 North Aulatsivik I Labrador, Nfld Canada
94 D5 North Baltimore Ohio U.S.A.
118 J6 North Battleford Saskatchewan Canada
123 O6 North Bay Newfoundland Canada
121 L6 North Bay Ontario Canada
98 K8 North Bend Nebraska U.S.A.
100 A6 North Bend Oregon U.S.A.
13 F1 North Berwick Scotland
99 L9 Northboro Iowa U.S.A.
139 H4 North Bourke New South Wales Australia
118 H2 North Branch Ontario Canada
94 D3 North Branch Michigan U.S.A.
99 O4 North Branch Minnesota U.S.A.
121 N8 North Brook Ontario Canada
13 H5 North Burton England
123 M6 North,C C Breton I, Nova Scotia
127 J4 North Caicos isld Turks & Caicos Is
108 B7 North Canadian R Oklahoma U.S.A.
145 D1 North Cape New Zealand
137 P8 North Cape Rise sea feature Pacific Oc
115 L7 North Caribou L Ontario Canada
112 E2 North Carolina state U.S.A.
100 D1 North Cascades Nat. Park Washington U.S.A.
113 H12 North Cat Cay isld Bahamas
113 L9 North Cay isld New Providence I Bahamas
14 F1 North Chan N Ireland/Scotland
120 G6 North Channel Ontario Canada
112 H5 North Charleston South Carolina U.S.A.
13 G2 North Charlton England
99 T7 North Chicago Illinois U.S.A.
143 B10 Northcliffe W Australia Australia
108 F4 North Concho R Texas U.S.A.
100 A3 North Cove Washington U.S.A.
95 N3 North Creek New York U.S.A.
98 F2 North Dakota state U.S.A.
122 F8 North Devon New Brunswick Canada
9 F5 North Downs England
94 H4 North East Pennsylvania U.S.A.
95 R8 North East Carry Maine U.S.A.
141 L5 North-East Cay isld Gt Barrier Reef Aust
90 G3 North Eastern Atlantic Basin Atlantic Oc
122 A3 Northeast Mistassibi R Quebec Canada
126 F2 Northeast Providence Chan Bahamas
123 R1 Northeast Pt Belle Isle, Nfld
83 M9 North East Pt C Christmas I Indian Oc
32 L9 Northeim Germany
99 O8 North English Iowa U.S.A.
86 E2 Northern prov Sudan
123 T5 Northern Bight Newfoundland Canada
86 E2 Northern Darfur prov Sudan
113 L12 Northern Eleuthera dist Bahamas
122 F9 Northern Hd New Brunswick Canada
119 U1 Northern Indian L Manitoba Canada
12 A4 Northern Ireland U.K.
86 E2 Northern Kordofan prov Sudan
99 Q1 Northern Light L Ontario Canada
83 M9 Northern Plateau Christmas I Indian Oc
127 O2 Northern Range Trinidad
Northern Sporades islds see Voríai Sporádhes islds
138 B1 Northern Territory Australia
139 H8 North Esk R Tasmania Australia
9 E3 Northfield England
95 P4 Northfield Massachusetts U.S.A.
99 N5 Northfield Minnesota U.S.A.
95 P2 Northfield Vermont U.S.A.
144 A6 North Fiord New Zealand
99 S6 North Fond du Lac Wisconsin U.S.A.
9 H5 North Foreland hd England
102 E4 North Fork California U.S.A.
101 M4 North Fork Idaho U.S.A.
100 K8 North Fork Nevada U.S.A.
94 B1 North Fox I Michigan U.S.A.
99 R6 North Freedom Wisconsin U.S.A.
120 J2 North French R Ontario Canada
13 H6 North Frodingham England
141 K1 Northgate dist Brisbane, Qnsld Australia
119 P9 Northgate Saskatchewan Canada
13 G3 Northgate England
95 P5 North Haven Connecticut U.S.A.
144 D5 North Hd. New Zealand
122 F9 North Head New Brunswick Canada
123 O4 North Head Newfoundland Canada
141 H2 North Horn C Gt Barrier Reef Aust
86 G5 North Horr Kenya
83 J12 North I Seychelles
112 H4 North I South Carolina U.S.A.
9 G6 Northiam England
145 E3 North Island New Zealand
71 E6 North Islet Philippines
103 O6 North Jadito Canyon R Arizona U.S.A.
83 M8 North Keeling I Cocos Is Indian Oc
115 L2 North Kent I Northwest Territories Canada
94 G5 North Kingsville Ohio U.S.A.
119 V1 North Knife L Manitoba Canada
59 J3 North Korea rep E Asia
North Land see Severnaya Zemlya
145 D1 Northland admin region New Zealand
99 T3 Northland Michigan U.S.A.
103 J5 North Las Vegas Nevada U.S.A.
9 E4 Northleach England
99 U8 North Liberty Indiana U.S.A.
110 D7 North Little Rock Arkansas U.S.A.
98 H8 North Loup R Nebraska U.S.A.
98 H8 North Loup Nebraska U.S.A.
88 D7 North Luangwa Nat. Park Zambia
70 C2 North Luconia Shoals S China Sea
106 C2 North Mam Pk Colorado U.S.A.
94 B5 North Manchester Indiana U.S.A.
99 U4 North Manitou I Michigan U.S.A.
113 G12 North Miami Florida U.S.A.
15 B2 North Minch Scotland
142 E4 North, Mt W Australia Australia
94 A3 North Muskegon Michigan U.S.A.
112 J4 North Myrtle Beach South Carolina U.S.A.
117 L4 North Nahanni R Northwest Territories Canada
113 G11 North New River Can Florida U.S.A.
94 E5 North Olmsled Ohio U.S.A.
99 M2 Northome Minnesota U.S.A.
8 C1 Northop Wales
North Ossetia see Severo-Osetinskaya Respublika
102 F4 North Palisade pk California U.S.A.
98 D8 North Platte R Nebraska U.S.A.
98 F8 North Platte Nebraska U.S.A.
101 T8 North Platte R Wyoming U.S.A.
116 O4 North Pole Alaska U.S.A.
122 J8 Northport Nova Scotia Canada
111 J8 Northport Alabama U.S.A.
99 V4 Northport Michigan U.S.A.
98 C8 Northport Nebraska U.S.A.
100 H1 Northport Washington U.S.A.
100 H4 North Powder Oregon U.S.A.
99 S7 North Prairie Wisconsin U.S.A.
139 J7 North Pt Flinders I, Tasmania Australia
122 H6 North Pt Prince Edward I Canada
83 J12 North Pt Mahé I Indian Oc
94 D1 North Pt Michigan U.S.A.
100 B3 North R Washington U.S.A.
142 A4 North Rankin Gas Field W Australia Australia
68 A6 North Reef I Andaman Is
109 M9 North Richland Hills Texas U.S.A.
123 M7 North River Bridge C Breton I, Nova Scotia
15 C1 North Rona Scotland
15 F1 North Ronaldsay Orkney Scotland
15 F1 North Ronaldsay Firth Orkney Scotland
122 J7 North Rustico Prince Edward I Canada
102 C2 North San Juan California U.S.A.
100 C5 North Santiam R Oregon U.S.A.
118 B6 North Sask R Alberta Canada
90 J3 North Sea W Europe
68 A7 North Sentinel I Andaman Is
13 G3 North Shields England
102 G2 North Shoshone Pk Nevada U.S.A.
99 O8 North Skunk R Iowa U.S.A.
116 M1 North Slope Alaska U.S.A.
117 P7 North Star Alberta Canada
110 M1 North Star Ohio U.S.A.
141 L8 North Stradbroke I Queensland Australia
109 M2 North Sulphur R Texas U.S.A.
123 M7 North Sydney C Breton I, Nova Scotia
8 C6 North Tawton England
144 A7 North Trap islds New Zealand
71 E7 North Ubian isld Philippines
15 A3 North Uist isld Scotland
141 J5 Northumberland islds Queensland Australia
13 F3 Northumberland co England
138 F7 Northumberland,C South Australia Australia
122 H7 Northumberland Str Nova Scotia Canada
117 G10 North Vancouver British Columbia Canada
71 D5 North Verde Philippines
117 P6 North Vermilion Alberta Canada
94 B7 North Vernon Indiana U.S.A.
95 N3 Northville New York U.S.A.
98 H4 Northville South Dakota U.S.A.
9 H2 North Walsham England
116 R5 Northway Junc Alaska U.S.A.
116 B5 Northwest C. St Lawrence I, Alaska U.S.A.
113 K11 Northwest Cay isld Bahamas
74 D2 North West Frontier Prov Pakistan
142 B5 North West I W Australia Australia
126 E1 Northwest Providence Chan Bahamas
83 M9 North-West Pt C Christmas I Indian Oc
115 N7 North West River Labrador, Nfld Canada
123 N2 Northwest St.Augustin R Quebec Canada
114 H4 Northwest Territories prov Canada
8 D1 Northwich England
112 F1 North Wilkesboro North Carolina U.S.A.
99 N6 Northwood Iowa U.S.A.
98 J2 Northwood North Dakota U.S.A.
120 C9 North York Ontario Canada
13 G5 North Yorkshire co England
109 L5 North Zulch Texas U.S.A.
32 G6 Nortmoor Germany
122 G8 Norton New Brunswick Canada
94 E10 Norton Virginia U.S.A.
89 G1 Norton Zimbabwe
116 G4 Norton B Alaska U.S.A.
116 E5 Norton Sound Alaska U.S.A.
107 P2 Nortonville Kansas U.S.A.
98 H3 Nortonville North Dakota U.S.A.
32 L4 Nortorf Germany
32 G7 Nortrup Germany
20 H7 Nort-sur-Erdre France
28 E5 Norup Denmark
116 K3 Norutak L Alaska U.S.A.
146 G6 Norvegia Kapp C Antarctica
36 B2 Nörvenich Germany
102 F8 Norwalk California U.S.A.
95 O5 Norwalk Connecticut U.S.A.
99 N8 Norwalk Iowa U.S.A.
99 U5 Norwalk Michigan U.S.A.
94 E5 Norwalk Ohio U.S.A.
99 Q6 Norwalk Wisconsin U.S.A.
99 P8 Norway Iowa U.S.A.
95 R2 Norway Maine U.S.A.
99 T4 Norway Michigan U.S.A.
112 F4 Norway South Carolina U.S.A.
68 H2 Norway isld Vietnam
26 Norway kingdom W Europe
119 U5 Norway House Manitoba Canada
115 K2 Norwegian B Northwest Territories Canada
147 E13 Norwegian Basin Arctic Oc
147 E12 Norwegian Sea Arctic Oc
120 K10 Norwich Ontario Canada
9 H2 Norwich England
95 P5 Norwich Connecticut U.S.A.
107 N4 Norwich Kansas U.S.A.
95 M4 Norwich New York U.S.A.
141 J6 Norwich Park Queensland Australia
15 G1 Norwick Scotland
121 N8 Norwood Ontario Canada
95 Q4 Norwood Massachusetts U.S.A.
95 N2 Norwood New York U.S.A.
112 G2 Norwood North Carolina U.S.A.
71 E3 Norzagaray Luzon Philippines
60 T2 Nosappu-misaki C Japan
36 G2 Nösberts Germany
61 N5 Noshiro Japan
52 G4 Noshul' Russian Federation
55 E2 Noska R Russian Federation
89 B5 Nosop R Botswana
52 E3 Nosovshchina Russian Federation
77 F5 Nosratābād Iran
130 H11 Nossa Senhora das Dores Brazil
130 C4 Nossa Senhora do Livramento Brazil
27 F13 Nossebro Sweden
22 H2 Nossegem Belgium
37 P1 Nossen Germany
33 Q5 Nossentin Germany
89 A4 Nossob Namibia
87 G11 Nosy Barren Madagascar
87 H10 Nosy Be isld Madagascar
87 H10 Nosy Lava Madagascar
87 H10 Nosy Mitsio isld Madagascar
87 H10 Nosy Radamà Madagascar
87 H12 Nosy Varika Madagascar
111 L9 Notasulga Alabama U.S.A.
103 L2 Notch Pk Utah U.S.A.
31 K2 Noteć R Poland
80 F1 Notera Israel
100 B5 Noti Oregon U.S.A.
46 E3 Notia Greece
114 H6 Notikewin Alberta Canada
117 O7 Notikewin R Alberta Canada
46 G8 Nótion Aiyaíon admin region Greece
43 G12 Noto Sicily
27 D12 Notodden Norway
43 G12 Noto, Golfo di Sicily
61 K8 Noto-hantō pen Japan
61 L8 Noto-jima isld Japan
60 S1 Notoro-ko L Japan
60 S1 Notoro-misaki C Japan
Notozero, Oz. see Verkhnetulomskoye, Vodokhranilishche
122 H7 Notre Dame New Brunswick Canada
122 A8 Notre Dame Quebec Canada
123 R4 Notre Dame B Newfoundland Canada
21 L4 Notre Dame-de-Courson France
21 M3 Notre Dame de Gravenchon France
115 M5 Notre Dame de Koartáo Quebec Canada
121 S4 Notre-Dame-de-la-Doré Quebec Canada
119 T9 Notre Dame de Lourdes Manitoba Canada
20 F8 Notre Dame-de-Monts France
121 P6 Notre Dame du Laus Quebec Canada
121 L5 Notre Dame du-Nord Quebec Canada
122 A5 Notre Dame du Rosaire Quebec Canada
85 E7 Notsé Togo
60 T2 Notsuke-saki C Japan
60 T2 Notsuke-suidō str Japan/Rus Fed
120 K8 Nottawasaga Bay Ontario Canada
121 M2 Nottaway R Quebec Canada
27 H14 Nottebäck Sweden
112 C3 Nottely L Georgia U.S.A.
27 E12 Nötteröy isld Norway
9 E1 Nottingham co England
9 E2 Nottingham England
115 M5 Nottingham Island Northwest Territories Canada
27 G15 Nöttja Sweden
37 K2 Nottleben Germany
94 K10 Nottoway R Virginia U.S.A.
100 J6 Notus Idaho U.S.A.
85 A4 Nouadhibou Mauritania
85 A5 Nouakchott Mauritania
21 P6 Nouan-le-Fuzelier France
21 N7 Nouans-les-Fontaines France
21 O6 Nouan-sur-Loire France
22 J5 Nouart France
137 O6 Nouméa New Caledonia
85 D6 Nouna Burkina
89 D8 Noupoort S Africa
115 M7 Nouveau-Comptoir Quebec Canada
115 M5 Nouveau Québec, Cratèr du Quebec Canada
115 M5 Nouveau Québec, Cratére du Canada
122 D4 Nouvel,L Quebec Canada
Nouvelle Calédonie isld see New Caledonia
115 M5 Nouvelle-France,Cap de Quebec Canada
18 H9 Nouvelle, la France
122 F5 Nouvelle,R Quebec Canada
21 O1 Nouvion-en-Pontheiu France
22 F3 Nouvion-en-Thiérache,Le France
21 M6 Nouzilly France
22 H4 Nouzonville France
71 M9 Nova Anadia Timor
48 E2 Nová Baňa Czechoslovakia
87 B7 Nova Caipemba Angola
48 H5 Novaci Romania
45 M4 Novafeltria Italy
130 G8 Nova Friburgo Brazil
Nova Gaia see Cambundi-Catembo
42 H3 Nova Gradiška Croatia
130 G8 Nova Iguaçu Brazil
129 K5 Nova Iorque Brazil
130 G6 Nova Lima Brazil
87 C8 Nova Lisboa Angola
87 F10 Nova Mambone Mozambique
128 G4 Nova Olinda do Norte Brazil
129 K5 Nova Pilão Arcado Brazil
41 J7 Novara Italy
129 K5 Nova Remanso Brazil
129 K4 Nova Russas Brazil
122 G9 Nova Scotia prov Canada
129 K5 Nova Sento Sé Brazil
41 K5 Novate Italy
102 B3 Novato California U.S.A.
130 E10 Nova Trento Brazil
48 F7 Nova Varš Serbia Yugoslavia
128 F6 Nova Vida Brazil
55 C5 Novaya Akkermanovka Russian Federation
55 E3 Novaya Aptula Russian Federation
56 F3 Novaya Igirma Russian Federation
54 E10 Novaya Kakhovka Ukraine
53 F8 Novaya Kriusha Russian Federation
55 D2 Novaya Lyala Russian Federation
51 O1 Novaya Sibir', Ostrov isld Russian Federation
56 E3 Novaya Solyanka Russian Federation
48 J1 Novaya Strelishcha Ukraine
48 L2 Novaya Ushitsa Ukraine
55 E3 Novaya Zaimka Russian Federation
50 E1 Novaya Zemlya isld Russian Federation
47 H2 Nova Zagora Bulgaria
45 J2 Novellara Italy
110 D1 Novelty Missouri U.S.A.
45 L1 Noventa V Italy
33 N7 Növenthien Germany
48 E3 Nové Zámky Czechoslovakia
52 D5 Novgorod Russian Federation
54 E5 Novgorod Severskiy Ukraine
52 D5 Novgorodskaya Oblast' prov Russian Federation
47 J1 Novgradets Bulgaria
44 E2 Novi Italy
109 H4 Novice Texas U.S.A.
45 J2 Novi di Modena Italy
42 F3 Novigrad Croatia
42 G4 Novigrad Croatia
46 F2 Novi Iskür Bulgaria
48 F4 Novi Kneževac Serbia Yugoslavia
59 M2 Novikovo Russian Federation
45 N4 Novilara Italy
124 G6 Novillero Mexico
99 O9 Novinger Missouri U.S.A.
22 G4 Novion-Porcien France
47 J1 Novi Pazar Bulgaria
46 D1 Novi Pazar Serbia Yugoslavia
48 F5 Novi Sad Serbia Yugoslavia
42 F3 Novi Vinodolski Croatia
54 N1 Novki Russian Federation
28 B4 Nøvling Denmark
129 H4 Nôvo Acôrdo Brazil
53 F10 Novoaleksandrovsk Russian Federation
55 C5 Novoalekseyevka Kazakhstan
56 B4 Novoaltaysk Russian Federation
52 B4 Novoandreyevka Russian Federation
128 F5 Novo Aripuana Brazil
53 D9 Novo Arkhangelsk Ukraine
55 D2 Novoasbest Russian Federation
54 K9 Novoazovsk Ukraine
54 C4 Novobelitsa Belorussia
55 C3 Novobelokatay Russian Federation
55 E3 Novoberezovka Russian Federation
55 D3 Novoburino Russian Federation
54 M9 Novocherkassk Russian Federation
55 F5 Novodolinka Kazakhstan
52 D6 Novo Dugino Russian Federation
52 F3 Novodvinsk Arkhangel'skaya obl Russian Federation
53 C8 Novograd-Volynskiy Ukraine
53 C7 Novogrudok Belorussia
54 J2 Novogurovskiy Russian Federation
131 H2 Novo Hamburgo Brazil
59 L1 Novoilinovka Russian Federation
55 F5 Novoishimka Kazakhstan
56 F4 Novokadinskiy Russian Federation
53 G7 Novokashpirskiy Russian Federation
57 B2 Novokazalinsk Kazakhstan
53 F8 Novokhopersk Russian Federation
59 J1 Novokiyevskiy Uval Russian Federation
56 C4 Novokuznetsk Russian Federation
129 H3 Novo, L Brazil
146 H7 Novolazarevskaya former U.S.S.R. Base Antarctica
43 J8 Novoli Italy
71 M9 Novo Luso Timor
54 L2 Novomichurinsk Russian Federation
53 E11 Novomikhaylovskiy Russian Federation
48 F5 Novo Miloševo Serbia Yugoslavia
54 C8 Novomirgorod Ukraine
54 K2 Novomoskovsk Russian Federation
54 G8 Novomoskovsk Ukraine
55 E3 Novonikolskoye Russian Federation
55 C5 Novoorsk Russian Federation
52 C6 Novopolotsk Belorussia
Novo Redondo see Sumbe
56 B4 Novoromanovka Russian Federation
53 E11 Novorossiysk Russian Federation
55 C5 Novorossiyskoye Kazakhstan
54 M3 Novoryazhsk Russian Federation
55 F5 Novorybinka Kazakhstan
51 K1 Novorybnoye Russian Federation
52 C6 Novorzhev Russian Federation
52 H7 Novo Sakhcha Russian Federation
48 K2 Novoselitsa Ukraine
55 B5 Novosergiyevka Russian Federation
54 L9 Novoshakhtinsk Russian Federation
52 H6 Novo Sheshminsk Russian Federation
56 B4 Novosibirsk Russian Federation
55 G3 Novosibirskaya Oblast' prov Russian Federation
51 O1 Novosibirskiye Ostrova islds Russian Federation
54 J4 Novosil' Russian Federation
55 D3 Novosineglazovskiy Russian Federation
52 D6 Novosokol'niki Russian Federation
55 C5 Novotroitsk Russian Federation
55 G3 Novotroitsk Novosibirskaya obl Russian Federation
57 G3 Novotroitskoye Kazakhstan
54 K2 Novougol'nyy Russian Federation
54 C8 Novoukrainka Ukraine
55 C5 Novouralets Russian Federation
53 G8 Novo Uzensk Russian Federation
55 F4 Novovarshavka Russian Federation
55 G2 Novovaya Vasyugan Russian Federation
54 L5 Novovoronezhskiy Russian Federation
52 G5 Novo-Vyatsk Russian Federation
56 D2 Novoyeniseysk Russian Federation
56 F3 Novoye Prirech'ye Russian Federation
52 E6 Novozavidovskiy Russian Federation
52 H3 Novozhilovskaya Russian Federation
42 H3 Novska Croatia
31 L6 Novy Bohumin Czechoslovakia
31 J5 Nový Bydžov Czechoslovakia
22 G4 Novy-Chevrières France
54 K8 Novy Donbass Ukraine
54 F7 Novye Sanzhary Ukraine
48 D1 Nový Jičín Czechoslovakia
54 J6 Novy Oskol Russian Federation
52 D1 Novyy Russian Federation
52 H2 Novyy Bor Russian Federation
54 D9 Novyy Bug Ukraine
54 B3 Novyy Bykhov Belorussia
54 D6 Novyy Bykov Ukraine
48 M4 Novyye Aneny Moldavia
55 E1 Novyy Karymkary Russian Federation
55 E2 Novyy Katysh Russian Federation
50 G2 Novyy Port Russian Federation
52 G6 Novyy Tor'yal Russian Federation
56 H3 Novyy Uoyan Russian Federation
50 G2 Novyy Urengoy Russian Federation
31 J5 Nowa Ruda Poland
31 J4 Nowa Sól Poland
107 P5 Nowata Oklahoma U.S.A.
77 A2 Nowbarān Iran
31 L2 Nowe Poland
142 E5 No.34 Well W Australia Australia
142 F5 No.37 Well W Australia Australia
142 F5 No.41 Well W Australia Australia
142 F5 No.45 Well W Australia Australia
31 M2 Nowe Miasto Poland
Nowgong see Nagaon
116 K4 Nowitna R Alaska U.S.A.
31 J2 Nowógard Poland
31 N2 Nowogród Poland
31 J4 Nowogrodziec Poland
101 S5 Nowood Cr Wyoming U.S.A.
139 K5 Nowra New South Wales Australia
77 A5 Nowruz oil well Persian Gulf
77 B1 Now Shahr Iran
74 E1 Nowshera Pakistan
31 O2 Nowy Dwór Poland
31 M3 Nowy Dwor Poland
31 L1 Nowy Dwór Gdański Poland
31 M5 Nowy Korczyn Poland
48 F1 Nowy Sącz Poland
48 F1 Nowy Targ Poland
31 J3 Nowy Tomysl Poland
111 G9 Noxapater Mississippi U.S.A.
95 L5 Noxen Pennsylvania U.S.A.
100 K2 Noxon Montana U.S.A.
111 H8 Noxubee R Mississippi U.S.A.
16 B2 Noya Spain
17 J3 Noya R Spain
20 F6 Noyal Muzillac France
20 E6 Noyalo France
20 E5 Noyal-Pontivy France
20 G5 Noyal-sur-Vilaine France
21 J6 Noyant-la-Gravoyère France
21 K7 Noyant-la-Plaine France
21 L6 Noyant-sous-le-Lude France
21 P2 Noye R France
21 O1 Noyelles-sur-Mer France
21 K6 Noyen France
21 N7 Noyers-sur-Cher Loir-et-Cher France
117 G8 Noyes I Alaska U.S.A.
102 A2 Noyo California U.S.A.
22 E4 Noyon France
123 O2 Noyrot,L Quebec Canada
20 G6 Nozay France
86 C6 N'Sah Congo
88 E10 Nsanje Malawi
85 D7 Nsawam Ghana
88 C9 Nsenga Zambia
87 E9 Nsiza Zimbabwe
89 F2 Nsiza R Zimbabwe
88 E9 Ntcheu Malawi
86 B5 Ntem R Cameroon
83 L13 Nuageuses isld Kerguelen Indian Oc
21 J7 Nuaillé Maine-et-Loire France
52 C3 Nuasjärvi L Finland
84 J5 Nuba, L Sudan
86 F3 Nuba Mts Sudan
84 J5 Nubian Des Sudan
100 D8 Nubieber California U.S.A.
131 B6 Nuble R Chile
131 B6 Nuble prov Chile
48 H4 Nucet Romania
65 D2 Nudam China
65 A3 Nüden Mongolia
141 K1 Nudgee dist Brisbane, Qnsld Australia
109 J7 Nueces R Texas U.S.A.
21 J8 Nueil-sur-Argent France
21 K7 Nueil-sur-Layon France
115 K5 Nueltin L Northwest Territories Canada
65 E4 Nü'erhe China
128 F8 Nueva Asunción dept Paraguay
124 F2 Nueva Casas Grandes Mexico
109 H9 Nueva Ciudad Mexico

Column 1

125 K4 Nueva Ciudad Guerrero Mexico
128 F1 Nueva Esparta state Venezuela
128 F7 Nueva Esperanza Bolivia
130 C8 Nueva Germania Paraguay
126 C4 Nueva Gerona Cuba
133 D9 Nueva, I Chile/Arg
133 C5 Nueva Imperial Chile
133 C6 Nueva Lubecka Argentina
124 J4 Nueva Rosita Mexico
133 E5 Nueve de Julio Argentina
126 F4 Nuevitas Cuba
71 F5 Nuevo Cebu Philippines
133 E6 Nuevo,G Argentina
124 C5 Nuevo Ideal Mexico
125 K4 Nuevo Laredo Mexico
109 H8 Nuevo Laredo Texas U.S.A.
125 J5 Nuevo Leon state Mexico
128 C4 Nuevo Rocafuerte Ecuador
141 J6 Nuga Nuga, L Queensland Australia
84 J5 Nugrus,Gebel mt Egypt
137 L2 Nuguria Is Bismarck Arch
145 F3 Nuhaka New Zealand
73 Q3 Nui atoll Tuvalu
68 H5 Nui Ti On mt Vietnam
18 H5 Nuits France
19 J5 Nuits St.Georges France
66 E5 Nu Jiang R China
116 M7 Nuka I Alaska U.S.A.
138 D4 Nukey Bluff South Australia Australia
80 G8 Nukheila R Jordan
86 E2 Nukheila Sudan
137 R6 Nuku'alofa isld Tonga
137 Q3 Nukufetau atoll Tuvalu
135 N9 Nuku Hiva isld Marquesas Is Pacific Oc
137 Q3 Nukulaelae atoll Tuvalu
137 M2 Nukumanu Is Solomon Is
137 Q2 Nukunau isld Kiribati
57 A4 Nukus Uzbekistan
17 G5 Nules Spain
142 D5 Nullagine W Australia Australia
142 D5 Nullagine R W Australia Australia
138 B4 Nullarbor South Australia Australia
138 B4 Nullarbor Nat Park South Australia Australia
143 F9 Nullarbor Plain S/W Australia Australia
65 D4 Nulu'erhu Shan mt ra China
43 B8 Nulvi Sardinia
61 L8 Numaho Japan
61 P6 Numakunai Japan
141 G8 Numalla, L Queensland Australia
86 B4 Numan Nigeria
45 O4 Numana Italy
17 F3 Numancia Spain
60 P2 Numazu Japan
86 E4 Numatinna R Sudan
61 M10 Numazu Japan
36 D2 Nümbrecht Nordrhein-Westfalen Germany
140 D2 Numbulwar N Terr Australia
27 D11 Numedal V Norway
27 D12 Numedalslågen R Norway
136 G2 Numfor isld W Irian
29 K11 Nummi Finland
139 H6 Numurkah Victoria Australia
116 J7 Nunachuak Alaska U.S.A.
116 F6 Nunapitchuk Alaska U.S.A.
116 E6 Nunavakanuk L Alaska U.S.A.
94 K4 Nunda New York U.S.A.
141 K1 Nundah dist Brisbane, Qnsld Australia
139 K4 Nundle New South Wales Australia
138 B4 Nundroo South Australia Australia
9 E2 Nuneaton England
143 O9 Nungarin W Australia Australia
65 D2 Nungnain Sum China
87 G8 Nungo Mozambique
116 E7 Nunivak I Alaska U.S.A.
106 F1 Nunn Colorado U.S.A.
110 J6 Nunnelly Tennessee U.S.A.
8 D5 Nunney England
25 E4 Nunspeet Netherlands
138 F4 Nunthurungie New South Wales Australia
70 E3 Nunukan isld Kalimantan
59 H2 Nuomin He R China
43 C8 Nuoro Sardinia
26 L5 Nuortikon Sweden
137 O4 Nupani Santa Cruz Is
128 C2 Nuquí Colombia
52 G1 Nura R Kazakhstan
57 S1 Nura Kazakhstan
100 H6 Nuraga Sweden
Nurakita see Niulakita
55 C2 Nuratau, Khr mts Uzbekistan
52 H5 Nyta Russian Federation
61 N5 Nuratau, Khrebet mts Uzbekistan
52 G3 Nyukhcha Arkhangel'skaya obl Russian Federation
36 B3 Nürburg Germany
78 F3 Nur Dalari mts Turkey
44 G2 Nure R Italy
57 E5 Nurek Tajikistan
57 E5 Nurek Vodokhranilishche res Tajikistan
95 L6 Nuremburg Pennsylvania U.S.A.
Nuremberg see Nürnberg
21 N8 Nuret-le-Ferron France
124 E3 Nuri Mexico
138 E5 Nuriootpa South Australia Australia
74 D1 Nuristan reg Afghanistan
52 H7 Nurlat Russian Federation
52 H7 Nurlaty Russian Federation
29 O8 Nurmes Finland
29 K9 Nurmo Finland
37 L5 Nürnberg Germany
71 Q7 Nuro Mindanao Philippines
138 A3 Nurrari Lakes South Australia Australia
43 C9 Nurri Sardinia
36 G6 Nürtingen Germany
66 E4 Nur Turu China
31 O3 Nurzec R Poland
71 H9 Nusa Tenggara Barat Indonesia
71 K9 Nusa Tenggara Timur Indonesia
78 H3 Nusaybin Turkey
79 G3 Nusayriyah, Jebel an mts Syria
116 J6 Nushagak R Alaska U.S.A.
116 H7 Nushagak B Alaska U.S.A.
116 H7 Nushagak Pen Alaska U.S.A.
66 F6 Nu Shan mt ra China
74 B4 Nushki Pakistan
33 N5 Nusse Germany
116 N3 Nutak Labrador, Nfld Canada
33 S8 Nutt R Germany
119 O6 Nut L Saskatchewan Canada
9 G5 Nutley England
128 E2 Nutrias Venezuela
115 T1 Nutts Corner N Ireland
140 C3 Nutwood Downs N Terr Australia
116 P3 Nutzotin Mts Alaska U.S.A.
115 O3 Nuugaatsiaq Greenland
Nuuk see Godthåb
29 M4 Nuupas Finland
115 O3 Nuussuaq pen Greenland
115 O3 Nuussuaq area Greenland
75 K4 Nuwakot Nepal
83 K11 Nuwara Eliya Sri Lanka
90 E10 Nuweiba el Muzeina Egypt
89 B7 Nuweveldreeks mts S Africa
116 L7 Nuyakuk, L Alaska U.S.A.
138 A4 Nuyts Arch South Australia
138 B4 Nuyts,C South Australia
143 B11 Nuyts, Pt W Australia Australia

Column 2

122 F6 N.W. Miramichi R New Brunswick Canada
143 C10 Nyabing W Australia Australia
88 B3 Nyabisindu Rwanda
101 M1 Nyack Montana U.S.A.
88 D10 Nyaderi R Zimbabwe
139 G6 Nyah Victoria Australia
88 F1 Nyahururu Kenya
66 D6 Nyainqêntanglha Shan ra China
88 D3 Nyakabindi Tanzania
26 K8 Nyåker Sweden
55 D1 Nyaksimvol' Russian Federation
84 A3 Nyala Sudan
66 D6 Nyalam China
88 D3 Nyalikungu Tanzania
55 E1 Nyalinskoye Russian Federation
87 G8 Nyamandhlovu Zimbabwe
88 C10 Nyamanjl mt Zimbabwe
88 D10 Nyamapanda Zimbabwe
87 D8 Nyamboma Falls Zambia
86 E4 Nyamiell Sudan
87 G8 Nyamtumba Tanzania
Nyanda see Masvingo
52 F4 Nyandoma Russian Federation
88 C10 Nyangadzi R Zimbabwe
88 D10 Nyangadzi R Zimbabwe
143 F8 Nyanga, L W Australia Australia
119 T8 Nyanja Malawi
121 L9 Nyasa,L Malawi/Moz
109 J7 Nyasaville Texas U.S.A.
141 H7 Nyashabozh Russian Federation
87 F9 Nyazura Zimbabwe
89 G2 Nyazvidzi R Zimbabwe
28 F6 Nyborg Denmark
26 R1 Nyborg Norway
102 G4 Nyborg Norway
101 L8 Nyborg Norway
146 C13 Nyborg Sweden
139 H8 Nyborg Sweden
55 B4 Nyda R Russian Federation
120 F3 Nyda Russian Federation
120 E3 Nydala Sweden
115 O1 Nyeboe Land Greenland
Nyenchen Tanglha Range see Nyainqêntanglha Shan
86 F4 Nyerol Sudan
27 G11 Nyhammar Sweden
29 K4 Nyhamn Sweden
26 H9 Nyhem Sweden
88 D6 Nyiha Tanzania
66 D5 Nyima China
87 F8 Nyimba Zambia
88 E6 Nyingchi China
48 J3 Nyírábrány Hungary
48 G3 Nyírbátor Hungary
48 G3 Nyíregyháza Hungary
88 F3 Nyiri Desert Kenya
86 G5 Nyiru mt Kenya
29 K8 Nykarleby Finland
27 H13 Nykil Sweden
28 F6 Nykøbing Denmark
28 H7 Nykøbing Falster Denmark
28 B3 Nykøbing Mors Denmark
27 J13 Nyköping Sweden
27 G12 Nykroppa Sweden
89 F5 Nyl R S Africa
26 J8 Nyland Sweden
89 F5 Nylstroom S Africa
139 H4 Nymagee New South Wales Australia
139 L3 Nymboida New South Wales Australia
139 L3 Nymboida R New South Wales Australia
31 J5 Nymburk Czechoslovakia
7 F11 Nymphe Bank Atlantic Oc
27 J13 Nynäshamn Sweden
139 H4 Nyngan New South Wales Australia
21 J4 Nyoiseau France
86 B5 Nyong R Cameroon
21 L4 Nyons France
37 K7 Nýřany Czechoslovakia
52 J4 Nyrob Russian Federation
37 P5 Nyrsko Czechoslovakia
26 R2 Nyrud Norway
31 K5 Nysa Poland
27 F11 Nyskoga Sweden
100 H6 Nyssa Oregon U.S.A.
38 H8 Nystad see Uusikaupunki
41 O4 Nyström Sweden
36 E7 Nyuchma Russian Federation
36 E7 Nyudo, C Japan
32 E10 Nyukhcha Russian Federation
36 F3 Nyukhcha Karel'skaya Respublika Russian Federation
36 E6 Nyuk, Oz L Russian Federation
36 E6 Nyuksenitsa Russian Federation
59 H1 Nyukzha R Russian Federation

Column 3

O

98 G6 Oacoma South Dakota U.S.A.
98 F5 Oahe Dam South Dakota U.S.A.
99 S2 Oahe, L South Dakota U.S.A.
102 C4 Oahu isld Hawaiian Is
103 N7 Oak R Arizona U.S.A.
60 S2 Oak-an-dake mt Japan
122 E8 Oak B New Brunswick Canada
138 F5 Oakbank South Australia Australia
95 M5 Oakdale Wisconsin U.S.A.
60 R3 Oakdale Louisiana U.S.A.
103 N3 Oakes North Dakota U.S.A.
100 H2 Oakesdale Washington U.S.A.
140 D5 Oakey Queensland Australia
99 S6 Oakfield Wisconsin U.S.A.
115 K5 Oak Flat Arizona U.S.A.
11 E9 Oak Grove Louisiana U.S.A.
119 R9 Oakham England
37 N2 Oak Harbor Ohio U.S.A.
113 G9 Oak Hill Florida U.S.A.
110 J2 Oak Hill Kansas U.S.A.
59 K2 Oak Hill Ohio U.S.A.
94 F9 Oak Hill West Virginia U.S.A.
119 R9 Oak Lake Manitoba Canada
102 B4 Oakland California U.S.A.
99 S10 Oakland Illinois U.S.A.
99 L8 Oakland Iowa U.S.A.
95 S2 Oakland Maine U.S.A.
94 H7 Oakland Maryland U.S.A.
111 G7 Oakland Mississippi U.S.A.
98 K8 Oakland Nebraska U.S.A.
100 B6 Oakland Oregon U.S.A.
95 M5 Oakland Pennsylvania U.S.A.
110 G6 Oakland Tennessee U.S.A.
109 L6 Oakland Texas U.S.A.
110 J3 Oakland City Indiana U.S.A.
113 G11 Oakland Park Florida U.S.A.
139 H6 Oaklands New South Wales Australia
99 T8 Oak Lawn Illinois U.S.A.
145 E1 Oakleigh New Zealand
102 C4 Oakley California U.S.A.
101 M7 Oakley Idaho U.S.A.
107 K2 Oakley Kansas U.S.A.
94 C3 Oakley Michigan U.S.A.
112 C3 Oakman Georgia U.S.A.
94 H6 Oakmont Pennsylvania U.S.A.
141 G4 Oak Park Queensland Australia
111 E8 Oakpark Georgia U.S.A.
124 E8 Oakpark Georgia U.S.A.
119 T8 Oak Pt Manitoba Canada
111 E9 Oak Ridge Louisiana U.S.A.
110 G4 Oak Ridge Missouri U.S.A.
124 E3 Oak Ridge Oregon U.S.A.
112 C1 Oak Ridge Tennessee U.S.A.
119 R8 Oak River Manitoba Canada
16 E5 Oakura New Zealand
138 F5 Oakvale South Australia Australia
119 T9 Oakville Manitoba Canada
121 L9 Oakville Ontario Canada
109 J7 Oakville Texas U.S.A.
141 H7 Oakwood Queensland Australia
110 J1 Oakwood Illinois U.S.A.
110 E2 Oakwood Missouri U.S.A.
94 C5 Oakwood Ohio U.S.A.
107 M6 Oakwood Oklahoma U.S.A.
144 C6 Oamaru New Zealand
61 O10 Ōami Japan
144 D5 Oaro New Zealand
24 As Oas Philippines
60 F11 Ōasa Japan
102 G4 Oasis California U.S.A.
100 L8 Oasis Nevada U.S.A.
146 C13 Oates Land Antarctica
139 H8 Oatlands Tasmania Australia
103 K6 Oatman Arizona U.S.A.
125 L9 Oaxaca de Juárez Mexico
120 F3 Ob R Russian Federation
108 G4 Obakamiga L Ontario Canada
54 C10 Oban Scotland
60 T2 Oban Japan
106 G6 Oban New Mexico U.S.A.
118 J6 Oban Saskatchewan Canada
15 C4 Oban Scotland
O Barco see El Barco de Valdeorras
120 E4 Obatanga Prov. Park Ontario Canada
121 Q3 Obatogamau L Quebec
26 L8 Obbola Sweden
32 L6 Obdach Austria
127 K2 Obed Alberta Canada
119 S7 Ober Aargau Switzerland
37 I4 Oberammergau Germany
41 L1 Oberau Germany
37 M3 Oberaula Germany
36 G3 Oberbach Germany
36 H3 Oberbayern dist Germany
25 F6 Oberbruch-Dremmen Germany
39 C2 Oberdischingen Germany
36 H7 Oberdorf Germany
37 J4 Oberdreisenheim Germany
37 J4 Oberellen Germany
112 D5 Oberengadin dist Switzerland
48 H4 Oberennis Tal Austria
48 J5 Oberessfeld Germany
37 P1 Ober Eula Germany
37 L4 Oberfranken dist Germany
110 C2 Oberfrohna see Limbach-Oberfrohna
38 D7 Obergailtal V Austria
41 O4 Obergurgl Austria
37 L1 Oberhalbstein R Switzerland
36 E7 Oberhammerbach Germany
36 F3 Oberhaslach France
32 E10 Oberhausen Germany
36 F3 Oberhausen Hessen Germany
36 E6 Oberhof Germany
37 M2 Oberkirch Germany
37 J6 Oberkochen Germany
37 M3 Obern-Kochen Germany
37 J3 Ober Lauringen Germany
36 H6 Oberleiningen Germany
36 H5 Oberlin Kansas U.S.A.
111 D11 Oberlin Louisiana U.S.A.
94 C5 Oberlin Ohio U.S.A.
36 H7 Ober Marchthal Germany
37 M1 Ober Marsberg Germany
37 J10 Obermassfeld-Grimmenthal Germany
120 D3 Ober Moschel Germany
41 M9 Obern France
36 E5 Obernburg Germany
32 K8 Oberndorf Germany
36 G7 Oberndorf Germany
139 J5 Oberon New South Wales Australia
98 G2 Oberon North Dakota U.S.A.
37 L5 Oberpfaffenhofen Germany
37 M5 Oberpfalz dist Germany
37 N4 Oberpfalzer Wald mts Germany
37 P4 Oberpleis Germany
36 H6 Ober Ramstadt Germany
37 N5 Oberriechtach Germany
36 D3 Oberwesel Germany
36 F3 Oberwiesenthal Germany
37 M5 Oberwöhr Germany
37 J2 Obi R Germany
70 B6 Obi Indonesia
129 G4 Óbidos Brazil
16 A5 Óbidos Portugal
60 R3 Obihiro Japan
41 A3 Obi,Kep isld Indonesia
37 Q5 Obilatui isld Indonesia
60 F8 Obing Germany
110 H3 Obion Tennessee U.S.A.
59 K2 Obluch'ye Russian Federation
52 L9 Obninsk Russian Federation
86 H3 Obo Djibouti
54 A1 Obol' R Belorussia
120 A3 Obonga L Ontario Canada
70 D2 Obong, G mt Sarawak
52 F1 Obornyy, Mys C Russian Federation
86 C6 Obouya Mossaka Congo
86 M2 Oboyan' Russian Federation
110 G3 Obozerskiy Russian Federation
32 E9 Öding Germany
54 J1 Obninsk Russian Federation
48 L5 Obobeşti Romania
21 K4 Obolanów Poland
110 K3 Obolon R France
108 K3 Obolon R France
25 G3 Obsha R Russian Federation
31 J4 Obskaya Guba G Russian Federation
16 E6 Obuasi Ghana
48 E5 Obudu Serbia Yugoslavia
33 O8 Oca,Mt de Spain
37 J2 Ocala Colombia
31 N3 Ocaña Spain

Column 4

54 H1 Obninsk Russian Federation
86 H3 Obo Djibouti
54 A1 Obol' R Belorussia
120 A3 Obonga L Ontario Canada
70 D2 Obong, G mt Sarawak
52 F1 Obornyy, Mys C Russian Federation
86 C6 Obouya Mossaka Congo
6 M2 Oboyan' Russian Federation
110 G3 Obozerskiy Russian Federation
32 E9 Öding Germany
54 J1 Obninsk Russian Federation
48 L5 Obobeşti Romania
48 G4 Obolanów Poland
110 K3 Obolon R France
108 H7 O'Donnell Texas U.S.A.
120 H10 Ochils mts Scotland
107 O5 Obshiy Syrt reg Russian Federation
31 J4 Obskaya Guba G Russian Federation
25 F6 Obuasi Ghana
48 E5 Obudu Serbia Yugoslavia
37 J2 Oberammergau Germany
22 E1 Obwalden canton Switzerland
22 H3 Oberndorf Germany
37 P2 Ocampo Spain
36 C1 Ocala Florida U.S.A.
16 A6 Ocampo Chihuahua Mexico
16 B7 Ocampo Coahuila Mexico
98 C6 Ocaña Colombia
37 N3 Oca R Spain
99 P7 Ocate New Mexico U.S.A.
37 L2 Occhiobello Italy
135 O11 Ocean City Maryland U.S.A.
21 J5 Ocean City New Jersey U.S.A.
21 N3 Ocean City Washington U.S.A.
55 M8 Ocean Falls British Columbia Canada
124 B5 Ocean Gate New Jersey U.S.A.
107 N5 Ocean L Wyoming U.S.A.
101 R6 Oceana Italy
102 D6 Oceana West Virginia U.S.A.
90 F5 Oceanographer Fracture Atlantic Oc
100 A3 Ocean Park Washington U.S.A.
36 D7 Oceanside California U.S.A.
100 B4 Oceanside Oregon U.S.A.
59 L5 Ocean Springs Mississippi U.S.A.
26 J8 Ocean View Delaware U.S.A.
16 E3 Ocejón,Pic mt Spain
108 G4 O. C. Fisher L Texas U.S.A.
54 C10 Ochakov Ukraine
53 F11 Ochamchira Georgia
56 H1 Ochenevo Bulgaria Federation
52 H5 Ocher Russian Federation
26 J3 Ochi Japan
80 D6 Ochiai Japan
60 T2 Ochiishi-misaki C Japan
16 N6 Ochil Hills Scotland
15 D5 Ochiltree Scotland
113 C7 Ochlocknee Georgia U.S.A.
86 J4 Ochlockonee R Florida U.S.A.
61 K10 Ochopee Florida U.S.A.
107 L3 Ochre R Manitoba Canada
98 E8 Ochsenfurt Germany
54 J3 Ochtendung Germany
O7 Ochsenfurt Germany
61 P5 Ochsenhausen Germany
85 E7 Ochsenschu Nigeria
9 E5 Ochtendung Germany
123 L8 Ockelbo Sweden
21 N3 Ockelford Sweden
106 G6 Ockley England
11 G9 Ocland Romania
84 D7 Ocmulgee R Georgia U.S.A.
112 D4 Ocmulgee Nat Mon Georgia U.S.A.
112 F5 Ocoee R Georgia U.S.A.
119 N9 Ocoee Tennessee U.S.A.
32 G6 Ocoña Peru
120 F6 Oconee R Georgia U.S.A.
103 K9 Oconee Illinois U.S.A.
143 A8 Oconee Nebraska U.S.A.
99 M4 Oconto Wisconsin U.S.A.
114 F5 Oconto Falls Wisconsin U.S.A.
95 W7 Ocoto Wisconsin U.S.A.
61 Q12 Ocotal Nicaragua
107 K1 Ocotlán Mexico
55 F3 Ococozoautla Mexico
141 J6 Ocquier Belgium
89 B7 Ocracoke North Carolina U.S.A.
111 D11 Öcsöd Hungary
94 E5 Octeville Manche France
20 G2 Octeville Seine-Inférieure France
21 L2 Octopus Ontario Canada
120 D3 Ocumare del Tuy Venezuela
71 M9 Ocussi Ambeno Timor
22 C2 Oda Ghana
87 G3 Oda Japan
47 H4 Ödåkra Sweden
40 K7 Ódáðahraun lava field Iceland
143 B9 O'Grady, L W Australia Australia
47 H3 Ograzden mts Greece
48 L2 Ograzden Planina mt Macedonia Yugoslavia
93 Q3 O'Higgins prov Chile
19 J5 O'Higgins, L Chile/Arg
132 C3 O'Higgins Pirámide mt Chile

Column 5

108 E4 Odessa Texas U.S.A.
100 G2 Odessa Washington U.S.A.
55 F4 Odesskoye Russian Federation
46 D3 Ohrid Macedonia Yugoslavia
46 D3 Ohridsko ezero L Albania/Yugoslavia
20 C5 Odet R France
119 T3 Odihil Manitoba Canada
87 E10 Odiakwe Botswana
85 C7 Odiénné Ivory Coast
9 F5 Odiham England
6 M2 Odin oil rig North Sea
110 G3 Ödingen Germany
32 E9 Öding Germany
54 J1 Odintsovo Russian Federation
101 K6 Odobeşti Romania
48 L5 Odolanów Poland
110 K3 Odon R France
108 F4 Odon France
120 H10 O'Donnell Texas U.S.A.
107 O5 Odonnell Texas U.S.A.
94 K9 Odoorn Netherlands
109 J8 Odra R Poland
24 P9 Odorheiu Secuiesc Romania
31 J4 Odra R Poland
25 F6 Odra R Poland
48 E5 Odum Georgia U.S.A.
33 O8 Odzani Serbia Yugoslavia
25 D5 Oebisfelde Germany
37 J2 Oechsen Germany
22 E1 Oedelem Belgium
22 H3 Oederan Germany
36 E1 Oedingen Germany
129 K5 Oeiras Brazil
16 A6 Oeiras Portugal
16 B7 Oeiras R Portugal
98 C6 Oeiras,Mt de Spain
37 N3 Oelrichs South Dakota U.S.A.
99 P7 Oelsnitz Germany
37 L2 Oelwein Iowa U.S.A.
135 O11 Oeno atoll Pacific Oc
21 G11 Öje Sweden
32 F9 Oer-Erkenschwick Germany
32 J9 Oerlinghausen Germany
33 J9 Oerel Germany
123 G3 Oessilo Timor
61 M8 Oettingen Germany
106 B7 Oetz Austria
71 M9 Oeuf R France
79 E11 Ofanto R Italy
26 D8 Ofaqim Israel
94 L7 Offa Nigeria
61 M10 Offenbach am Main Germany
26 J8 Offenburg Germany
32 F4 Offerdal Sweden
54 G4 Offerman Georgia U.S.A.
54 G4 Offida Italy
54 F4 Offranville France
46 H6 Offstein Germany
79 E11 Ofira Egypt
26 J3 Ofotfjord inlet Norway
80 D6 Ofra Jordan
16 N6 Oga Japan
16 N6 Oga Kalimantan
113 F11 Oga-hantō pen Japan
86 J4 Ogaden reg Ethiopia
86 J4 Ogaki Japan
16 N6 Ogallah Kansas U.S.A.
98 E8 Ogallala Nebraska U.S.A.
54 J3 Ogareu R France
74 E3 Ogarevka Russian Federation
144 C5 Okarche Oklahoma U.S.A.
120 D14 Ogasanan, L Quebec
O7 Ogawara Japan
61 P5 Ogawara Japan
9 E5 Ogbomosho Nigeria
123 L8 Ogden Nova Scotia Canada
21 N3 Ogden Illinois U.S.A.
106 G6 Ogden Iowa U.S.A.
11 G9 Ogden Kansas U.S.A.
101 O7 Ogden,Mt Br Col/Alaska Canada/U.S.A.
55 F3 Ogdensburg New York
143 B9 Ogeechee R Georgia U.S.A.
119 N9 Ogema Saskatchewan Canada
98 K2 Ogema Minnesota U.S.A.
112 E7 Ogema Wisconsin U.S.A.
86 J4 Ogeokite France
16 N6 Oğ Japan
61 N6 Ogidaki Ontario Canada
103 K9 Ogilby California U.S.A.
143 A8 Ogilvie W Australia Australia
99 N4 Ogilvie Mts Yukon Territory Canada
112 F5 Ogimi Japan
61 Q12 Ogimi Japan
98 D6 Oglala South Dakota U.S.A.
61 Q9 Oglesby Illinois U.S.A.
55 N1 Oglethorpe Georgia U.S.A.
112 C5 Oglethorpe,Mt Georgia U.S.A.
55 F3 Oglio R Italy
107 O5 Ogmore Queensland Australia
54 J3 Ogmore R Wales
89 D7 Ognev Yar Russian Federation
19 J5 Ognon R France
61 P13 Okinawa isld Japan
70 G4 Ogoamas, G mt Celebes
52 G3 Ogodzha Russian Federation
9 F5 Ogoja Nigeria
86 B6 Ogoki R Ontario Canada
61 N6 Ogoki L Ontario Canada
87 C9 Okaukuejo Namibia
110 J1 Ogol Japan
110 K3 Okavango Basin Botswana
62 L8 Oka-kawa R Japan
117 L8 Okawa Japan
60 E13 Okawville Illinois U.S.A.
11 G9 Ogooué R Gabon
95 M2 Ohakune New Zealand
54 J3 Ohakune New Zealand
109 G9 Ohata Japan
112 F8 Ohata Alberta Canada
47 H3 Ohau New Zealand
48 L2 Ohau,L New Zealand

Column 6

37 O3 Ohre R Czechoslovakia
33 O8 Ohre R Germany
46 D3 Ohrid Macedonia Yugoslavia
46 D3 Ohridsko ezero L Albania/Yugoslavia
36 H5 Öhringen Germany
36 G5 Ohrnberg Germany
26 N5 Ohtanajärvi Sweden
145 E3 Ohura New Zealand
129 H3 Oiapoque Fr Guiana
66 E6 Oiga China
22 H3 Oignies Belgium
29 M6 Oil City Pennsylvania U.S.A.
106 G9 Oil Center New Mexico U.S.A.
102 F6 Oil City California U.S.A.
111 C9 Oil City Louisiana U.S.A.
94 H5 Oil City Pennsylvania U.S.A.
120 H10 Oil Springs Ontario Canada
107 O5 Oilton Oklahoma U.S.A.
109 J8 Oilton Texas U.S.A.
94 K9 Oilville Virginia U.S.A.
47 H6 Oinoüsa isld Greece
58 C6 Oi Qu R China
61 M9 Oirase-gawa R Japan
21 P3 Oiron France
25 D5 Oirschot Netherlands
19 Q14 Oisans dist France
18 G3 Oise dept France
21 P3 Oise R France
21 J5 Oise R France
21 O2 Oisemont France
22 E1 Oisseau France
21 N3 Oissel France
25 D5 Oisterwijk Netherlands
95 T1 Oisy-le-Verger France
27 J15 Oja R Sweden
29 P5 Ōgawa Italy
46 E6 Öji R Japan
44 K4 Oji Japan
60 P3 Oita Japan
102 E7 Ojai California U.S.A.
27 G11 Öje Sweden
61 J11 Oji Japan
80 B2 Ojika-jima isld Japan
124 G3 Ojinaga Mexico
61 M8 Ojiya Japan
133 B3 Ojo de Agua Argentina
124 F3 Ojo de Laguna Mexico
124 C4 Ojo de Liebre Mexico
16 E5 Ojos del Guadiana mt Spain
133 D3 Ojos del Salado, Nev mt Chile
17 F4 Ojos Negros Spain
113 G12 Ojus Florida U.S.A.
27 F10 Öjvallberget Sweden
121 Q7 Oka Quebec Canada
54 G4 Oka R Russian Federation
56 F4 Oka R Russian Federation
87 C10 Okahandja Namibia
145 E1 Okahu New Zealand
145 E3 Okahukura New Zealand
145 E3 Okaiawa R New Zealand
145 D1 Okaihau New Zealand
115 N6 Okak Is Labrador, Nfld Canada
117 O11 Okanagan Centre British Columbia Canada
127 M6 Okanagan Falls British Columbia Canada
100 F1 Okanogan Washington U.S.A.
100 F1 Okanogan R Wash/Br Col U.S.A./Canada
74 E3 Okara Pakistan
144 C5 Okarito New Zealand
60 D14 Okasaki Japan
145 F3 Okatana L New Zealand
111 G10 Okatoma R Mississippi U.S.A.
87 C9 Okaukuejo Namibia
110 K3 Okavango Basin Botswana
61 M8 Okaya Japan
60 G11 Okayama Japan
60 G11 Okayama prefect Japan
95 P5 Okazaki Japan
113 G10 Okeechobee Florida U.S.A.
113 G11 Okeechobee,L Florida U.S.A.
107 M5 Okeene Oklahoma U.S.A.
113 E7 Okefenokee Swamp Georgia U.S.A.
8 B6 Okehampton England
116 R2 Okemah Oklahoma U.S.A.
85 F7 Okene Nigeria
33 M9 Oker R Germany
127 P4 Oketo Japan
74 C7 Okha India
52 G3 Okha Russian Federation
75 M1 Okhaldhunga Nepal
47 H7 Okhi mt Greece
51 O3 Okhotskoye More sea E Asia
52 G2 Okhotsk Russian Federation
109 H1 Okhotsk,Sea of see Okhotskoye More
16 K8 Oki isld Japan
89 F7 Okigwi Nigeria
9 F7 Okiep S Africa
61 P13 Okinawa Okinawa
60 D11 Okino-shima isld Japan
60 E7 Okino-shima isld Japan
56 K4 Okino-shima isld Japan
60 J5 Okino Torishima isld Japan
8 B6 Okitipupa Nigeria
107 N6 Okkan Burma
55 E7 Oklahoma state U.S.A.
107 P6 Oklahoma City Oklahoma
16 B5 Oklee Minnesota U.S.A.
16 D3 Okmok Volcano Alaska U.S.A.
113 B9 Okmulgee Oklahoma U.S.A.
52 G3 Oko, Wadi Sudan
100 D7 Okno Ukraine
33 M3 Okoboji,L Iowa U.S.A.
29 A9 Okolona Mississippi U.S.A.
86 E5 Okondja Gabon
33 L7 Okonek Poland
18 E9 Okotoks Alberta Canada
118 D8 Okoyo Congo
20 F4 Oksbøl Denmark
36 N5 Oksby Denmark
64 F3 Öksendal Norway

Column 7

55 E2 Oktyabr'skiy Tyumenskaya obl Russian Federation
57 E5 Oktyabr'skiy Tajikistan
55 E5 Oktyabr'skoye Turgayskaya obl Kazakhstan
55 D4 Oktyabr'skoye Chelyabinskaya obl Russian Federation
55 E1 Oktyabr'skoye Khanty-Mansiyskiy aut ok Russian Federation
55 C4 Oktyabr'skoye Orenburgskaya obl Russian Federation
54 D10 Oktyabr'skoye Ukraine
51 J1 Oktyabr'skiy Revolyutsii, Os isld Russian Federation
48 D1 Oku Ukraine
61 Q12 Okuchi Japan
60 D13 Okulovka R New Zealand
52 D5 Okulovka Russian Federation
144 B5 Okura New Zealand
60 N3 Okushiri-kaikyō str Japan
60 N3 Okushiri-tō isld Japan
89 A4 Okwa watercourse Botswana
100 J5 Ola Idaho U.S.A.
28 S8 Ólafsfjördur Iceland
80 D1 Ólafsvik Iceland
95 T1 Olalla de Cala, Sta Spain
27 J15 Olamon Maine U.S.A.
40 K7 Øland isld Denmark
48 D6 Øland isld Sweden
112 H4 Oland Finland/Rus Fed
133 B3 Olanga Russian Federation
18 G9 Olargues France
138 C2 Olarinna R South Australia Australia
138 F4 Olary South Australia Australia
107 Q3 Olathe Kansas U.S.A.
131 E6 Olavarria Argentina
31 L6 Oława Poland
95 L3 Olberg Arizona U.S.A.
103 N8 Olberg Arizona U.S.A.
28 R9 Ölberg Germany
36 F7 Oberndorf Germany
43 B8 Olbia Sardinia
94 J3 Olcott New York U.S.A.
126 E3 Old Bahama Chan Caribbean
13 D3 Olddeastle Ireland
142 F4 Old Cherrabun W Australia Australia
141 F6 Old Cork Queensland Australia
116 R3 Old Crow Yukon Territory Canada
116 R2 Old Crow R Alaska/Yukon Terr U.S.A./Canada
88 E3 Oldeani Tanzania
109 J3 Olden Texas U.S.A.
32 H6 Oldenbrok Germany
30 N4 Oldenburg Germany
33 M9 Oldendorf Germany
32 F6 Oldenstadt Germany
25 D8 Oldenzaal Netherlands
24 P6 Old Faithful Wyoming U.S.A.
101 P5 Old Forge New York U.S.A.
95 M5 Old Forge Pennsylvania U.S.A.
8 E7 Old Fort North Carolina U.S.A.
123 O2 Old Fort Bay Quebec Canada
143 C8 Old Gidgee W Australia Australia
108 G2 Old Glory Texas U.S.A.
28 J8 Oldham England
99 S10 Oldham South Dakota U.S.A.
118 C7 Old Harbor Alaska U.S.A.
113 F9 Old Harbour Jamaica
117 L8 Old Hogem British Columbia Canada
110 K3 Old Hickory L Tennessee U.S.A.
33 O10 Oldisleben Germany
33 J6 Old Hurst England
120 D3 Old John L Alaska U.S.A.
95 P5 Old Lyme Connecticut U.S.A.
110 F3 Oldmeldrum Scotland
110 C4 Old Monroe Missouri U.S.A.
99 T7 Old Orchard Beach Maine U.S.A.
123 T5 Old Perlican Newfoundland Canada
123 L3 Old Post Pt Quebec Canada
116 R3 Old Rampart Alaska U.S.A.
113 G12 Old Rhodes Key isld Florida U.S.A.
127 K3 Old Road Antigua W Indies
127 P4 Old Road Town St Kitts W Indies
16 C7 Olds Alberta Canada
95 R2 Old Speck Mt Maine U.S.A.
9 F3 Old Stratford England
28 A7 Oldsum Germany
113 E10 Old Tampa B Florida U.S.A.
138 C4 Old Telichie South Australia Australia
113 D8 Old Town Florida U.S.A.
95 T2 Old Town Maine U.S.A.
28 B8 Olduvai Gorge Tanzania
Old Viking Bank see Bergen Bank
118 L8 Old Wives L Saskatchewan Canada
8 B4 Old Woman R California U.S.A.
103 J7 Old Woman Mts California U.S.A.
65 A2 Öldziyt Mongolia
95 J4 Olean New York U.S.A.
122 H1 O'Leary Prince Edward I Canada
31 N1 Olecko Poland
16 B5 Oleiros Portugal
52 J5 Olëkminsk Stanovik mt ra Russian Federation

Column 8

55 E2 Oktyabr'skiy Tyumenskaya obl Russian Federation
57 E5 Oktyabr'skiy Tajikistan
55 E5 Oktyabr'skoye Turgayskaya obl Kazakhstan
55 D4 Oktyabr'skoye Chelyabinskaya obl Russian Federation
55 E1 Oktyabr'skoye Khanty-Mansiyskiy aut ok Russian Federation
55 C4 Oktyabr'skoye Orenburgskaya obl Russian Federation
54 D10 Oktyabr'skoye Ukraine
51 J1 Oktyabr'skiy Revolyutsii, Os isld Russian Federation
48 D1 Oku Ukraine
61 Q12 Okuchi Japan
60 D13 Okulovka R New Zealand
52 D5 Okulovka Russian Federation
144 B5 Okura New Zealand
60 N3 Okushiri-kaikyō str Japan
60 N3 Okushiri-tō isld Japan
89 A4 Okwa watercourse Botswana
100 J5 Ola Idaho U.S.A.
28 S8 Ólafsfjördur Iceland
80 D1 Ólafsvik Iceland
95 T1 Olalla de Cala, Sta Spain
27 J15 Olamon Maine U.S.A.
40 K7 Øland isld Denmark
48 D6 Øland isld Sweden
112 H4 Oland Finland/Rus Fed
133 B3 Olanga Russian Federation
18 G9 Olargues France
138 C2 Olarinna R South Australia Australia
138 F4 Olary South Australia Australia
107 Q3 Olathe Kansas U.S.A.
131 E6 Olavarria Argentina
31 L6 Oława Poland
35 D3 Olberg Germany
103 N8 Olberg Arizona U.S.A.
28 R9 Ölberg Germany
36 F7 Oberndorf Germany
43 B8 Olbia Sardinia
94 J3 Olcott New York U.S.A.
14 D3 Olcastle Ireland
142 F4 Old Cherrabun W Australia Australia
116 R2 Old Crow R Alaska/Yukon Terr U.S.A./Canada
141 F6 Old Cork Queensland Australia
52 K2 Olekma R Russian Federation
52 K2 Olekminsk Russian Federation
145 E3 Olenëk R Russian Federation
145 F3 Olenegorsk Russian Federation
52 D3 Olenino Russian Federation
79 K1 Oléron,Ile d' France
103 J7 Olesnica Poland
103 J7 Oleśno Poland
65 A2 Olevsk Ukraine
140 A7 Olfen Germany
16 H2 Olga Russian Federation
65 C10 Olga,L Quebec Canada
17 C4 Olgiate Comasco Italy
12 C4 Oliete Spain
88 E3 Olifants R Namibia
89 A8 Olifants R S Africa
89 A8 Olifantshoek S Africa

89 A9 Olifants R. Berge mts S Africa
131 G4 Olimar R Uruguay
46 E7 Olimbia Greece
46 E4 Ólimbos mt Greece
133 F2 Olimpo Paraguay
99 P7 Olin Iowa U.S.A.
100 C9 Olinda California U.S.A.
141 G1 Olinda Ent Gt Barrier Reef Aust
129 L6 Olindina Brazil
141 G1 Olio Queensland Australia
17 F2 Olite Spain
17 G6 Oliva Spain
131 B2 Oliva, Cord. de mt ra Arg/Chile
16 C6 Oliva de Mérida Spain
131 B3 Olivares,Cerro del pk Arg/Chile
17 F5 Olivares de Júcar Spain
98 A4 Olive Montana U.S.A.
110 G7 Olive Branch Mississippi U.S.A.
94 D8 Olive Hill Kentucky U.S.A.
130 Q7 Oliveira Brazil
16 B4 Oliveira de Azemeis Portugal
16 B4 Oliveira do Hospital Portugal
112 J2 Olive, Mt North Carolina U.S.A.
Olivenca see Lupilichi
16 C6 Olivenza Spain
117 O11 Oliver British Columbia Canada
112 F5 Oliver Georgia U.S.A.
21 O6 Oliver France
94 C4 Olivet Michigan U.S.A.
98 J6 Olivet South Dakota U.S.A.
99 M5 Olivia Minnesota U.S.A.
109 L7 Olivia Texas U.S.A.
144 B6 Olivine Range New Zealand
41 J5 Oliwa Poland
31 L1 Oliwa Poland
65 D3 Olji Moron He R China
Ol'khovatka Russian Federation
55 D3 Ol'khovka Russian Federation
31 M5 Olkusz Poland
111 D10 Olla Louisiana U.S.A.
133 D2 Ollague vol Bolivia/Chile
9 E1 Ollerton England
98 B3 Ollie Montana U.S.A.
29 N2 Ollila Finland
131 B3 Ollita, Cord. de ra Arg/Chile
131 B3 Ollitas pk Argentina
27 G12 Ölme Sweden
16 D3 Olmeda Spain
131 D4 Olmos,L Argentina
17 F2 Olney England
110 H3 Olney Illinois U.S.A.
101 L1 Olney Montana U.S.A.
109 J2 Olney Texas U.S.A.
106 G3 Olney Springs Colorado U.S.A.
26 K8 Olofsfors Sweden
27 G15 Olofström Sweden
123 M3 Olomane R Quebec Canada
86 C6 Olombo Congo
48 D1 Olomouc Czechoslovakia
41 K7 Olona R Italy
48 M4 Oloneshty Moldavia
52 D4 Olonets Russian Federation
71 E3 Olongapo Luzon Philippines
70 D5 Olongliku Kalimantan
20 G8 Olonne-sur-Mer France
18 G9 Olonzac France
18 E9 Oloron-St.Marie France
17 J2 Olot Spain
37 O3 Olovi Czechoslovakia
48 E6 Olovo Bosnia-Herzegovina
58 G1 Olovyannaya Russian Federation
36 D1 Olpe Germany
107 O3 Olpe Kansas U.S.A.
41 P3 Olperer mt Austria
107 O2 Olsburg Kansas U.S.A.
31 L6 Olše R Czechoslovakia
54 G6 Ol'shany Ukraine
25 F4 Olst Netherlands
31 M2 Olsztyn Poland
31 M2 Olsztynek Poland
48 K4 Olt R Romania
40 G3 Olten Switzerland
48 K6 Oltenita Romania
133 D6 Olte,Sa.de mts Argentina
48 D6 Oltet R Romania
106 E1 Oltu Texas U.S.A.
78 H1 Oltu Turkey
67 G6 O-luan-pi C Taiwan
113 E7 Olustee Florida U.S.A.
107 L7 Olustee Oklahoma U.S.A.
71 F7 Olutanga isl Philippines
33 P8 Olvenstedt Germany
16 D8 Olvera Spain
46 E7 Olympia Greece
100 C3 Olympia Washington U.S.A.
100 B2 Olympic Mts Washington U.S.A.
100 A2 Olympic Nat. Park Washington U.S.A.
100 B2 Olympic Nat. Park Washington U.S.A.
Olympus mt Cyprus see Troödos Mt
Olympus mt Greece see Ólimbos mt
100 B2 Olympus,Mt Washington U.S.A.
95 M5 Olyphant Pennsylvania U.S.A.
51 Q2 Olyutorskiy Russian Federation
36 B3 Olzheim Germany
56 B3 Om' R Russian Federation
92 G2 Oma R Russian Federation
111 F10 Oma Mississippi U.S.A.
61 L9 Omachi Japan
61 M11 Omae zaki C Japan
14 D2 Omagh N Ireland
128 D4 Omaguas Peru
110 C5 Omaha Arkansas U.S.A.
99 L8 Omaha Nebraska U.S.A.
109 N2 Omaha Texas U.S.A.
126 F4 Omaja Cuba
100 F1 Omak Washington U.S.A.
144 B7 Omakau New Zealand
145 E1 Omakere New Zealand
72 H5 Oman sultanate Arabian Pen
77 F7 Oman, Gulf of Iran/Oman
145 D1 Omapere New Zealand
94 E9 Omar West Virginia U.S.A.
144 B6 Omarama New Zealand
87 C10 Omaruru Namibia
128 D7 Omate Peru
71 J9 Omba Indonesia
60 O4 Oma-zaki C Japan
120 C2 Ombabika Ontario Canada
71 M9 Ombai,Selat str Indonesia
61 N11 Ombase-jima isl Japan
9 D3 Ombersley England
86 A6 Omboué Gabon
129 H2 Ombolata Indonesia
66 D5 Omdurman Sudan
86 F7 Omdurman Sudan
61 N10 Ome Japan
111 L10 Omega Alabama U.S.A.
112 D6 Omega Georgia U.S.A.
107 M6 Omega Oklahoma U.S.A.
121 F6 Omemee Ontario Canada
94 F1 Omemee North Dakota U.S.A.
94 B1 Omena Michigan U.S.A.
80 C8 'Omer Israel
94 D2 Omerköy Turkey
47 J5 Ömerli Turkey
78 C3 Ömerli Baraji dam Turkey
86 G3 Om Hâjer Ethiopia
22 D4 Ōmi Japan
21 L8 Omiecourt France
60 P4 Ōminato Japan

117 L8 Omineca R British Columbia Canada
117 K7 Omineca Mts British Columbia Canada
42 H5 Omis Croatia
60 E11 Ōmi-shima isld Japan
60 F11 Ōmi-shima isld Japan
61 N10 Ōmiya Japan
61 F7 Ommaney,C Alaska U.S.A.
114 J3 Ommanney B Northwest Territories Canada
28 B5 Omme Å R Denmark
25 F3 Ommen Netherlands
28 B5 Omø Denmark
86 G4 Omo R Ethiopia
43 B8 Omodeo, L Sardinia
51 P2 Omolon R Russian Federation
51 N2 Omoloy R Russian Federation
25 E5 Omono-gawa R Japan
22 H4 Omont France
20 G2 Omonville-la Rogue France
61 N10 Omori Japan
61 P6 Omoto-gawa R Japan
99 S5 Omro Wisconsin U.S.A.
53 F3 Omsk Russian Federation
55 G3 Omskaya Oblast' prov Russian Federation
O-mu Burma
60 Q1 Ōmu Japan
31 N2 Omulew R Poland
83 L10 Omuna Sri Lanka
60 C13 Ōmura Japan
60 C13 Ōmura wan B Japan
47 H1 Omurtag Bulgaria
60 D12 Ōmuta Japan
52 H5 Omutninsk Russian Federation
26 B9 Ona Norway
56 C5 Oña R Russian Federation
16 E2 Oña Spain
113 F10 Ona Florida U.S.A.
107 O2 Onaga Kansas U.S.A.
61 P7 Onagawahama Japan
61 P7 Onagawa-wan B Japan
61 O9 Onahama Japan
98 A4 Onaka South Dakota U.S.A.
120 H3 Onakawana R Ontario Canada
120 J1 Onakwehegan R Ontario Canada
100 C3 Onalaska Washington U.S.A.
99 P6 Onalaska Wisconsin U.S.A.
31 L4 Onaman L Ontario Canada
99 N3 Onamia Minnesota U.S.A.
95 M9 Onancock Virginia U.S.A.
70 F6 Onang Sulawesi
86 B6 Onanga Zaire
111 D11 Onaping L Ontario Canada
120 D2 Onaping, L Ontario Canada
144 B5 Onatchiway,L Quebec Canada
121 M7 Onatchiway,L Quebec Canada
22 F2 Oñate Mexico
101 T1 Onavas Mexico
101 A7 Onawa Iowa U.S.A.
69 E12 Onaway Michigan U.S.A.
22 K1 Oncocua Angola
142 C6 Onda R Italy
87 C9 Ondangwa Namibia
31 N6 Ondava R Czechoslovakia
87 C9 Ondjiva Angola
58 F2 Ōndörhaan Mongolia
64 D3 Ondor Had China
73 L8 One and Half Degree Chan Indian Oc
31 M4 Oneco Florida U.S.A.
Onega L see Onezhskoye, Oz
52 E3 Onega Russian Federation
52 E4 Onega R Russian Federation
44 D4 Oneglia Italy
145 D1 One & Half Mile Opening str Gt Barrier Reef Aust
99 Q8 Oneida Illinois U.S.A.
94 D9 Oneida Kentucky U.S.A.
95 M3 Oneida New York U.S.A.
110 M5 Oneida Tennessee U.S.A.
95 L3 Oneida L New York U.S.A.
98 H7 O'Neill Nebraska U.S.A.
145 D4 Onekaka New Zealand
94 A4 Onekama Michigan U.S.A.
86 D6 Onema Zaire
27 D10 Oneonta Alabama U.S.A.
119 Q4 Oneonta New York U.S.A.
107 P5 Onerahi New Zealand
145 E1 Oneroa I New Zealand
145 E3 One Sided Lake Ontario Canada
145 D3 Onesti Romania
124 E2 Onezhskoye,Oz L Russian Federation
87 B9 Ongaonga New Zealand
22 G2 Ongar England
99 Q9 Ongers watercourse S Africa
95 R2 Ör'r Kazakhstan/Rus Fed
27 G15 Ör Sweden
41 O5 Ora Italy
84 F4 Ora Libya
143 D9 Ora Banda W Australia Australia
29 M4 Orajärvi Finland
29 N4 Orajärvi Finland
98 C6 Oral South Dakota U.S.A.
85 D1 Oran Algeria
110 G4 Oran Missouri U.S.A.
139 J5 Orange New South Wales Australia
21 N10 Orange France
87 C11 Orange R S Africa/Namibia
102 G8 Orange California U.S.A.
95 M4 Orange Massachusetts U.S.A.
Orange see Botevgrad
109 O5 Orange Texas U.S.A.
95 J5 Orange Virginia U.S.A.
111 J11 Orange Beach Alabama U.S.A.
112 G4 Orangeburg South Carolina U.S.A.
129 H3 Orange,C Brazil
126 E1 Orange Cay isl Bahamas
113 F9 Orange City Florida U.S.A.
116 Q3 Orange Cr Alaska U.S.A.
117 L8 Orangedale C Breton I, Nova Scotia
113 F10 Orange Grove Texas U.S.A.
109 K8 Orange Grove Texas U.S.A.
113 F7 Orange Park Florida U.S.A.
22 G4 Orangeville Ontario Canada
101 V3 Orangeville Utah U.S.A.
145 E3 Orangimea New Zealand
121 U3 Orani Luzon Philippines
95 P5 Orange, E New Jersey U.S.A.
79 Q3 Orange Gegerbe Suriname

138 B4 Ooldea South Australia Australia
138 B4 Ooldea Ra South Australia Australia
110 K3 Oolitic Indiana U.S.A.
124 H5 Oologah Oklahoma U.S.A.
107 P5 Oologah L Oklahoma U.S.A.
25 B5 Ooltgensplaat Netherlands
140 C6 Ooraminna Ra N Terr Australia
48 G5 Oorawia Romania
140 D5 Oorattippra R N Terr Australia
140 D5 Oorattippra N Terr Australia
144 A7 Orawia New Zealand
18 H9 Orb R Italy
44 E2 Orba Italy
66 C5 Orba Co L China
21 L3 Orba R Italy
24 D6 Orbetello Italy
21 N7 Orbigny France
16 D2 Orbigo R Spain
25 E5 Orbisonia Pennsylvania U.S.A.
139 J7 Orbost Victoria Australia
27 F14 Ørby Denmark
27 J11 Örbyhus Sweden
116 O6 Orca B Alaska U.S.A.
146 E3 Orcadas Argentina Base S Orkney is S Atlantic Oc
146 G4 Orcadas Seamounts, Islas seamounts Antarctica
25 F2 Orchard Indiana U.S.A.
22 F1 Orchard Nebraska U.S.A.
25 B5 Orchid Island U.S.A.
25 E4 Orchila, La isld Venezuela
117 L9 Ørdenes Spain
129 S2 Orderville Utah U.S.A.
102 R11 Ordes see Ordenes
47 H1 Ørding Denmark
145 E4 Ord,Mt W Australia Australia
118 D5 Ord Mt W Australia Australia
124 M2 Ordozero Russian Federation
101 P8 Ord River W Australia Australia
51 P3 Orduña Spain
86 D6 Ordu Turkey
31 J3 Ordubad Azerbaijan
113 G12 Ordway Colorado U.S.A.
83 K11 Ordway South Dakota U.S.A.
52 S5 Ordzhonikidze see Vladikavkaz
120 H3 Ordzhonikidze Kazakhstan
120 H3 Ordzhonikidzevsky Russian Federation
42 J3 Ord River W Australia Australia
31 N5 Orlovskiy, Mys C Russian Federation
31 L6 Orly airport France
31 K6 Ormara Pakistan
123 P3 Ormesby England
31 L6 Ormesheim Germany
111 D11 Ormes,les France
120 D2 Orebro Sweden
144 B5 Oregon state U.S.A.
121 M7 Oregon Illinois U.S.A.
22 F2 Oregon Missouri U.S.A.
101 T1 Oregon Caves Nat. Mon Oregon U.S.A.
101 N9 Oregon City Oregon U.S.A.
69 E12 Oregon Inlet North Carolina U.S.A.
27 K11 Öregrund Sweden
54 G9 Orekhivka Ukraine
46 G1 Orekhovitsa Bulgaria
55 F3 Orekhovo Russian Federation
52 E6 Orekhovo Zuyevo Russian Federation
52 M3 Orekhovsk Belorussia
54 B2 Orekhovsk Belorussia
85 D1 Orekhovsk Belarus
88 B2 Orekhovo Burkina
100 J3 Orofino Idaho U.S.A.
102 F3 Oro Grande California U.S.A.
100 K4 Orogrande New Mexico U.S.A.
46 G1 Oroku Okinawa
52 J5 Orël Permskaya obl Russian Federation
54 F8 Orel' R Ukraine
106 P13 Oronoco Minnesota U.S.A.
54 F8 Orel R Ukraine
98 C7 Oporto see Porto
128 C5 Oposhnya Ukraine
16 D5 Opotiki New Zealand
53 E7 Opp Alabama U.S.A.
59 L1 Oppa R Japan
103 N1 Oppa-wan B Japan
47 J9 Oppdal Norway
78 D8 Oppelhaun Germany
110 B4 Oppenau Germany
53 D6 Oppenheim Germany

128 E2 Orituco R Venezuela
71 G4 Orivesi L Finland
71 G4 Oriximiná Brazil
48 E5 Orjasie Bosnia-Herzegovina
48 H5 Orjen mt Bosnia-Herzegovina
124 H5 Orkdalen V Norway
48 M1 Örkelljunga Sweden
31 L6 Orkened Sweden
29 J4 Orkla R Norway
48 G5 Orkney Saskatchewan Canada
31 L6 Orkney S Africa
87 E11 Orkney isld Scotland
18 H9 Orb R Italy
44 E2 Orland California U.S.A.
66 C5 Orland Indiana U.S.A.
21 L3 Orland California U.S.A.
24 D6 Orlando Florida U.S.A.
21 N7 Orlando,C.d' Sicily
16 D2 Orléanais reg France
25 E5 Orléans France
139 J7 Orleans Indiana U.S.A.
27 F14 Orleans Nebraska U.S.A.
27 J11 Orleans Vermont U.S.A.
116 O6 Orleans California U.S.A.
146 E3 Orleans Massachusetts U.S.A.
146 G4 Orleans Nebraska U.S.A.
25 F2 Orleans U.S.A.
22 F1 Orleansville see Ech Cheliff
25 B5 Orlice R Czechoslovakia
25 E4 Orlik Russian Federation
117 L9 Oriolá Czechoslovakia
129 S2 Orlová Czechoslovakia
102 R11 Orlovka Russian Federation
47 H1 Orlovskaya Oblast' prov Russian Federation
145 E4 Orlovskiy, Mys C Russian Federation
118 D5 Orly airport France
124 M2 Ormara Pakistan
101 P8 Ormesby England
51 P3 Ormesheim Germany
86 D6 Ormes,les France
42 J3 Ormiston Saskatchewan Canada
71 Q5 Ormoc Philippines
145 F3 Ormond New Zealand
113 F8 Ormond Florida U.S.A.
113 F8 Ormond Beach Florida U.S.A.
145 F4 Ormondville New Zealand
38 O9 Ormsby Minnesota U.S.A.
99 M6 Ormsby Wisconsin U.S.A.
26 H7 Ormsjö Sweden
13 F6 Ormskirk England
99 R7 Ormstown Quebec Canada
19 J4 Ornain R France
19 J4 Ornans France
46 H6 Ornavasso Italy
37 K5 Ørnbau Germany
18 E4 Orne dept France
21 L5 Orne R France
31 M1 Orneta Poland
27 K12 Orneö Sweden
55 D1 Örnköldsvik Sweden
52 J2 Oro Sweden
13 G5 Orobie, Alpi mt Italy
78 K3 Orobie, Alpi mts Italy
85 F2 Orochen Russian Federation
115 D6 Orodara Burkina
77 A3 Orofino Idaho U.S.A.
102 K2 Oro Grande California U.S.A.
102 K2 Orogrande New Mexico U.S.A.
46 G1 Orogrande N Mexico U.S.A.
100 K4 Orange Massachusetts U.S.A.
106 P13 Oronoco Minnesota U.S.A.
121 P1 Orono Ontario Canada
95 T2 Orono Maine U.S.A.
12 D5 Oronsay isld Scotland
71 J6 Oroquieta Mindanao
59 H1 Oroquieta Zizhiqi China
71 F6 Orense prov Spain
125 L5 Oreoi Greece
118 B2 Orepuki New Zealand
43 C8 Orestiás Greece
29 K5 Öresund str Sweden/Denmark
51 S2 Oretal Syria
144 B7 Oreti R New Zealand
22 G2 Orewa New Zealand
22 F2 Oreye Belgium
139 J8 Orford Tasmania Australia
100 F1 Orford Washington U.S.A.
110 U1 Orford New Hampshire U.S.A.
9 H3 Orford England
141 G1 Orford Ness Queensland Australia
9 H3 Orford Ness England
21 O4 Orgar France
19 P16 Orgelet France
98 J1 Orr North Dakota U.S.A.
107 N7 Orr Oklahoma U.S.A.
124 D4 Orre Denmark
28 H15 Orretors Sweden
71 R4 Orri R Scotland
71 Q4 Orrin L Manitoba Canada
100 F1 Orrville Ohio U.S.A.
94 F6 Orsa Sweden
52 F6 Orsara d'Italy
9 G5 Orsett England
131 A8 Orsha Belorussia
52 M5 Orsha Belorussia
47 K4 Orhangazi Turkey
78 F13 Orsières Switzerland
85 F9 Orsk Russian Federation
54 C8 Ørslösa Sweden
71 F8 Ørsnes Norway
78 C2 Ørsova Romania
52 S5 Orsoy Norway
32 B9 Orsta Norway
71 G8 Ørsted Denmark
100 H3 Ørsted Denmark
102 G4 Orta R Italy
131 A8 Ortaca Turkey
28 D8 Ortahisar Turkey
80 H1 Orta, L d' Italy
9 F6 Ortaklar Turkey
28 G15 Ørtofta Sweden
28 D4 Orta, Val d' Italy
18 E5 Orteguaza R Colombia
94 F6 Orthez France
21 N6 Ortigueira Spain
14 C8 Orthofte Sweden
63 D8 Orthez France
88 B2 Orti R Italy
60 C11 Ortigueira Brazil

78 K3 Orūmīyeh Iran
78 K3 Orūmīyeh, Daryācheh-ye L Iran
133 D1 Oruro Bolivia
145 D1 Oruru New Zealand
27 E13 Orust isld Sweden
20 G7 Orvault France
42 E6 Orvieto Italy
45 N5 Orvin Italy
94 K5 Orviston Pennsylvania U.S.A.
95 L3 Orwell New York U.S.A.
95 O3 Orwell Ohio U.S.A.
95 O3 Orwell Vermont U.S.A.
119 O9 Orwell R England
41 L7 Orzinuovi Italy
31 N2 Orzyc R Poland
32 F5 Orzysz Poland
29 H15 Os Norway
26 E9 Os Norway
27 E10 Os R Norway
119 O9 Osa R Norway
99 O6 Osage Iowa U.S.A.
107 O5 Osage Oklahoma U.S.A.
98 B6 Osage Wyoming U.S.A.
107 P3 Osage City Kansas U.S.A.
110 D4 Osage Fork R Missouri U.S.A.
107 O3 Osage Fork R Missouri U.S.A.
98 K1 Osakis Minnesota U.S.A.
99 L4 Osakis L Minnesota U.S.A.
107 O3 Osawatomie Kansas U.S.A.
120 E3 Osawin R Ontario Canada
57 O3 Osborne B W Australia
95 L3 Osby Sweden
142 F4 Oscar Ra W Australia
110 G6 Osceola Arkansas U.S.A.
99 N8 Osceola Iowa U.S.A.
110 C3 Osceola Nebraska U.S.A.
98 J6 Osceola Nebraska U.S.A.
99 O4 Osceola Pennsylvania U.S.A.
94 D2 Oschatz Germany
33 S10 Oschersleben Germany
106 D6 Oscoda Michigan U.S.A.
99 N8 Osen New Mexico U.S.A.
26 E9 Osen Norway
71 G5 Oshabati Namibia
145 F3 Oshakati Namibia
110 U1 Oshamambe Japan
121 U1 Oshawa Ontario Canada
60 P1 Oshikamori Japan
59 J6 Oshima Japan
95 O3 Ō-shima isld Japan
61 N11 Ō-shima isld Japan
98 D8 Oshkosh Nebraska U.S.A.
99 S6 Oshkosh Wisconsin U.S.A.
52 J2 Oshkur'ya Russian Federation
85 E2 Oshmar'ye Russian Federation
78 K3 Oshnovīyeh Iran
85 B5 Oshogbo Nigeria
87 B5 Oshtorān Kūh mt Iran
100 J3 Oshtorīnān Iran
102 O7 Oshva Russian Federation
89 B7 Osica de Jos Romania
14 C3 Osijek Croatia
54 B2 Osimo Italy
60 O4 Osinniki Russian Federation
54 B2 Osintorf Belorussia
122 F8 Osiyan India
26 N3 Oskal Norway
27 J7 Oskaloosa Iowa U.S.A.
107 P2 Oskaloosa Kansas U.S.A.
27 H14 Oskarshamn Sweden
27 F15 Oskarström Sweden
54 J7 Oskelaneo Quebec Canada
85 B5 Oskol R Ukraine/Rus Fed
87 A3 Oslava R Czechoslovakia
118 L6 Oslo Norway
27 E12 Oslo Minnesota U.S.A.
110 D5 Oslob Cebu Philippines
94 E9 Oslofjord inlet Norway
144 A4 Osmanabad India
99 J7 Osmancık Turkey
54 C5 Osmaneli Turkey
52 C5 Osmino Russian Federation
27 J13 Osmond Nebraska U.S.A.
102 C2 Osnabrück Germany
94 E3 Osnabrock North Dakota U.S.A.
104 U7 Ōsō R Japan
141 H4 Osōno Japan
21 O4 Osogovska Planina mt Macedonia/Yugoslavia
98 J1 Osorio Brazil
107 N7 Osorno Chile
124 D4 Osorno Spain
28 H15 Osorno, Vol pk Chile
71 R4 Osoyoos British Columbia Canada
141 H2 Osprey Florida U.S.A.
94 F6 Osprey Reef Gt Barrier Reef Aust
52 F6 Ospringe England
9 G5 Oss Netherlands
131 A8 Ossa mt Greece
52 M5 Ossa Georgia U.S.A.
47 K4 Ossa, Mt Tasmania Australia
78 F13 Ossa, Sa. de mts Portugal
85 F9 Osse R Nigeria
54 C8 Osseo Minnesota U.S.A.
71 F8 Ossineke Michigan U.S.A.
78 C2 Ossining New York U.S.A.
52 S5 Ossipee L New Hampshire U.S.A.
32 B9 Ossjøen L Norway
71 G8 Ossing mills Germany
100 H3 Ossola, Val d' Italy
102 G4 Ossora Russian Federation
131 A8 Ossu Timor
28 D8 Ostana R Japan
80 H1 Ostashevo Russian Federation
9 F6 Ostashkov Russian Federation
28 D4 Oste R Germany
18 E5 Osten Germany
94 F6 Osterburg Pennsylvania U.S.A.
21 N6 Osterburg Germany
14 C8 Osterburken Germany
63 D8 Ostercappeln Germany
88 B2 Osterdalälven R Sweden
60 C11 Østerild Denmark
90 M9 Oster R Germany

37 P6 Osterhofen Germany
32 J6 Osterholz-Scharmbeck Germany
38 H6 Osterborn Gruppe mts Austria
27 J11 Österbymo Sweden
26 J7 Östernoret Sweden
32 M9 Osterode Germany
27 A11 Osterøy isld Norway
38 H5 Österreich dist Austria
37 J7 Östersund Sweden
28 H7 Oster Ulslev Denmark
27 J11 Östervåla Sweden
33 N9 Osterwieck Germany
36 G6 Ostfildern Germany
27 E12 Ostfold reg Norway
32 F5 Ostfriesische Inseln islds Germany
32 G6 Ostfriesland reg Germany
32 G6 Osthammar Sweden
36 C7 Ostheim France
37 J3 Ostheim Germany
54 M6 Ostia Italy
27 F11 Ostiglia Italy
31 M2 Ostmark Sweden
28 R5 Ost Peene R Germany
45 O4 Ostra Italy
94 D6 Ostrander Ohio U.S.A.
31 J5 Ostróda Poland
31 M2 Ostróda Poland
120 J5 Ostrom Ontario Canada
37 O3 Ostrov Czechoslovakia
48 L6 Ostrov Romania
51 P3 Ostrov Russian Federation
142 F4 Ostrovnaya Russian Federation
55 F3 Ostrovnoye Russian Federation
51 Q2 Ostrovskoye Russian Federation
65 J3 Ostrov Russkiy isld Russian Federation
31 K4 Ostrów Poland
31 N5 Ostrowiec Poland
31 N3 Ostrów Lubelski Poland
31 N3 Ostrów Mazowiecka Poland
28 C3 Ostrup Denmark
31 L4 Ostry mt Czechoslovakia
33 O5 Ostseebad Boltenhagen Germany
33 O4 Ose-zaki C Japan
60 B13 Ōse-zaki C Japan
94 B7 Osgood Indiana U.S.A.
110 C1 Osgood Missouri U.S.A.
121 P7 Osgoode Station Ontario Canada
33 O4 Ostseebad Graal-Müritz Germany
33 O5 Ostseebad Kühlungsborn Germany
100 H8 Ostseebad Nienhagen Germany
57 O4 Osha Kyrgyzstan
43 H8 Osha R Russian Federation
87 C9 Oshakati Namibia
43 H8 Ostuni Italy
52 D6 Osuga R Russian Federation
100 F3 O'Sullivan Dam Washington U.S.A.
120 D2 O'Sullivan, L Ontario Canada
121 P5 O'Sullivan, L Quebec Canada
46 G1 Osum R Albania
52 J2 Osum R Bulgaria
60 D14 Ōsumi-hantō pen Japan
16 D7 Osuna Spain
13 G5 Osveya Belorussia
18 C4 Oswaldkirk England
96 G5 Oswego Pennsylvania U.S.A.
95 M2 Oswegatchie R New York U.S.A.
99 S8 Oswego Illinois U.S.A.
107 P4 Oswego Kansas U.S.A.
101 U1 Oswego Montana U.S.A.
95 L3 Oswego New York U.S.A.
95 L3 Oswestry England
9 C6 Oświecim Poland
111 F10 Osyka Mississippi U.S.A.
61 N9 Ōta Japan
61 L8 Ōta Japan
144 D7 Otago Peninsula New Zealand
144 D6 Otaki New Zealand
145 E5 Otaki New Zealand
145 E3 Otakeho New Zealand
145 M10 Ōtaki Japan
60 D14 Ōtaki Japan
145 E4 Otakiri New Zealand
61 N8 Ōtaki-gawa R Japan
145 E4 Ōtake-yama mt Japan
145 F4 Ōtake-yama mt Japan
60 O8 Ōtakine-yama mt Japan
144 F2 Otamatea New Zealand
145 F2 Otane New Zealand
83 H9 Otanmäki Finland
83 K9 Otappuwa Sri Lanka
57 J3 Otaru Kazakhstan
83 K9 Otaru Japan
145 C6 Otatara New Zealand
144 B7 Otautau New Zealand
30 H6 Otava R Czechoslovakia
47 K4 Otava R Czechoslovakia
128 B7 Otavalo Ecuador
87 C9 Otavi Namibia
54 S5 Otaway Texas U.S.A.
85 B9 Otchinjau Angola
95 M4 Otego New York U.S.A.
144 C6 Otekaieke New Zealand
142 D4 Otelec Romania
48 L7 Oțelu Roșu Romania
144 D6 Otematata New Zealand
52 C5 Otepää Estonia
5 D6 Othe, Pays d' Belgium
18 H4 Othe, Forêt d' France
100 P3 Othello Washington U.S.A.
27 K14 Othem Sweden
79 E7 Othery England
46 H5 Óthris mt Greece
70 F5 Oti R W Africa
124 G5 Otinapa Mexico
144 D5 Otira New Zealand
117 M7 Otis British Columbia Canada
103 L3 Otis Colorado U.S.A.
95 N5 Otis Massachusetts U.S.A.
94 B8 Otisco L New York U.S.A.
87 C10 Otjiwarongo Namibia
85 B7 Otmuchów Poland
61 L7 Otobe-dake mt Japan
60 O2 Otoe Nebraska U.S.A.
43 J8 Otočac Croatia
60 C12 Otofuke Japan
95 E7 Otoineppu Japan
145 F2 Otoineppu Japan
145 E5 Otorohanga New Zealand
119 P5 Otosquen Saskatchewan Canada
126 B1 Otrabanda Curaçao
128 C13 Otra R Norway
43 J8 Otranto Italy
43 J8 Otranto, C.d' Italy
71 N9 Otranto, Str of Adriatic Sea
46 C4 Otrøy isld Norway
46 G3 Ossu Timor
42 J3 Ostabaninge, L Quebec Canada
54 N2 Otsego Lake Michigan U.S.A.
77 M5 Ostan-e Markazi Iran
52 E3 Ostashevo Russian Federation
95 M4 Otselic, South New York U.S.A.
60 R3 Ōtsu Hokkaido Japan
59 J6 Ōtsu Japan
61 M10 Ōtsuki Japan
43 J8 Otta Norway
21 M3 Otta France
43 J8 Ottange France
70 F5 Ottawa Ontario Canada
121 O7 Ottawa R Ontario/Quebec
121 L6 Ottawa R Ontario/Quebec
99 S8 Ottawa Illinois U.S.A.
100 A7 Ottawa Ohio U.S.A.
115 N3 Ottawa Is Northwest Territories Canada
27 J11 Ottenby Sweden
37 H14 Ottenhöfen Germany
32 K9 Ottenstein Germany
37 H15 Ottenby Germany
38 M5 Ottenshlag Austria

Ottenstein — Parade

211

32 K9 **Ottenstein** Niedersachsen Germany
32 E8 **Ottenstein** Nordrhein-Westfalen Germany
101 T4 **Otter** Montana U.S.A.
110 J1 **Otterbein** Indiana U.S.A.
36 D4 **Otterberg** Germany
13 F3 **Otterburn** England
118 D1 **Otterburne** Manitoba Canada
113 E8 **Otter Creek** Florida U.S.A.
103 N3 **Otter Cr Res** Utah U.S.A.
38 E6 **Otterfing** Germany
116 D8 **Otter I** Pribilof Is Bering Sea
120 D4 **Otter I** Ontario Canada
119 N3 **Otter L** Saskatchewan Canada
94 D3 **Otter Lake** Michigan U.S.A.
25 E4 **Otterlo** Netherlands
32 J5 **Otterndorf** Germany
26 E7 **Otteröy** Norway
26 B9 **Otteröy** *isld* Norway
32 K6 **Ottersberg** Germany
9 F5 **Ottershaw** England
33 P8 **Ottersleben** Germany
15 G1 **Otterswick** Scotland
98 K3 **Otter Tail** *R* Minnesota U.S.A.
99 L3 **Otter Tail L** Minnesota U.S.A.
28 E5 **Otterup** Denmark
8 B6 **Ottery, R** England
8 C6 **Ottery St. Mary** England
119 P7 **Otthon** Saskatchewan Canada
22 H2 **Ottignies** Belgium
57 H4 **Ottik** Kyrgyzstan
109 L4 **Otto** Texas U.S.A.
101 R5 **Otto** Wyoming U.S.A.
37 M7 **Ottobrunn** Germany
115 L1 **Otto Fiord** Northwest Territories Canada
94 C6 **Ottoville** Ohio U.S.A.
36 C7 **Ottrott** France
99 O8 **Ottumwa** Iowa U.S.A.
98 E5 **Ottumwa** South Dakota U.S.A.
36 C5 **Ottweiler** Germany
118 K2 **Otukamanoan L** Ontario Canada
144 B6 **Oturehua** New Zealand
85 F7 **Oturkpo** Nigeria
94 D8 **Otway** Ohio U.S.A.
133 C8 **Otway, B** Chile
139 G7 **Otway, C** Victoria Australia
31 N3 **Otwock** Poland
48 J2 **Otynya** Ukraine
41 N3 **Ötz** Austria
36 B1 **Otzenrath** Germany
41 N3 **Ötztal** Austria
41 N4 **Ötztaler Alpen** *mt* Austria
111 D8 **Ouachita** *R* Arkansas U.S.A.
110 C7 **Ouachita, L** Arkansas U.S.A.
109 N1 **Ouachita Mts** Ark/Okla U.S.A.
86 D3 **Ouadai** *dist* Chad
85 B4 **Ouadane** Mauritania
86 D4 **Ouadda** Cent Afr Republic
85 D6 **Ouagadougou** Burkina
85 D6 **Ouahigouya** Burkina
86 D4 **Ouaka** *R* Cent Afr Republic
85 C5 **Oualata** Mauritania
85 E4 **Ouallene** Algeria
86 D4 **Ouanda Djallé** Cent Afr Republic
86 D5 **Ouango** Cent Afr Republic
85 C7 **Ouangolodougou** Ivory Coast
18 H5 **Ouanne** *R* France
85 F3 **Ouan Taredert** Algeria
129 H3 **Ouaqui** Fr Guiana
85 C4 **Ouarane** *reg* Mauritania
121 Q6 **Ouareau, L** Quebec Canada
85 F2 **Ouargla** Algeria
85 C3 **Ouarkziz, Jbel** *mt reg* Morocco/Algeria
21 O5 **Ouarville** France
85 C2 **Ouarzazate** Morocco
86 D5 **Oubangui** *R* Cent Afr Republic/Zaire
40 B3 **Ouche** *R* France
21 N6 **Oucques** France
25 A5 **Ouddorp** Netherlands
25 B5 **Oude** *R* Netherlands
25 F5 **Oude Ijssel** *R* Netherlands
22 D1 **Oudekapelle** Belgium
22 F2 **Oudenaarde** Belgium
25 C5 **Oudenbosch** Netherlands
25 H2 **Oude Pekela** Netherlands
25 C4 **Oude Rijn** Netherlands
25 C2 **Oudeschild** Netherlands
25 F3 **Oude Smildervaart** *R* Netherlands
25 C4 **Oudewater** Netherlands
22 L3 **Oudler** Belgium
20 H7 **Oudon** France
21 J6 **Oudon** *R* France
68 G7 **Oudong** Cambodia
89 C9 **Oudtshoorn** S Africa
85 F2 **Oued, El** Algeria
17 H9 **Oued Taria** Algeria
85 C2 **Oued Zem** Morocco
85 E7 **Ouémé** *R* Benin
20 A5 **Ouessant, I.d'** France
86 C5 **Ouesso** Congo
83 L14 **Ouest, î de l'** Kerguelen Indian Oc
71 F5 **Ouezon** Negros Philippines
85 C2 **Ouezzane** Morocco
22 J3 **Ouffet** Belgium
14 B3 **Oughterard** Ireland
40 C3 **Ougney** France
86 C4 **Ouham** *R* Cent Afr Republic
85 E7 **Ouidah** Benin
119 P2 **Ouimet** Ontario Canada
124 E4 **Ouiriego** Mexico
18 H9 **Ouissac** France
21 K3 **Ouistreham** France
85 C5 **Oujaf** Mauritania
85 D2 **Oujda** Morocco
29 L7 **Oulainen** Finland
29 O5 **Oulanka Nat. Park** Finland
21 N8 **Oulches** France
85 E2 **Ouled-Nail, Mts. des** Algeria
19 N13 **Oullins** France
85 C2 **Oulmès** Morocco
13 G6 **Oulton** England
29 L6 **Oulu** Finland
29 M7 **Oulujoki** *R* Finland
86 D2 **Oum Chalouba** Chad
85 C3 **Oum el Guebor** Algeria
85 C2 **Oum er Rbia** *R* Morocco
86 C3 **Oum Hadjer** Chad
29 K3 **Ounasjärvi** *L* Finland
29 L4 **Ounasjoki** *R* Finland
29 K3 **Ounastunturi** *mt* Finland
9 F3 **Oundle** England
98 C1 **Oungre** Saskatchewan Canada
86 D2 **Ounianga Kébir** Chad
86 D2 **Ounianga Sérir** Chad
85 C6 **Ouolodo** Mali
61 Q12 **Ōura-wan** *B* Okinawa
106 C3 **Ouray** Colorado U.S.A.
103 P1 **Ouray** Utah U.S.A.
28 F6 **Oure** Denmark
Ourense *see* **Orense**
84 F5 **Ouri** Chad
129 K5 **Ouricuri** Brazil
130 H9 **Ouricuri, R** Brazil
130 E8 **Ourinhos** Brazil
16 B7 **Ourique** Portugal
130 F8 **Ouro Fino** Brazil
130 G7 **Ouro Prêto** Brazil
22 K3 **Ourthe** *R* Belgium
21 M2 **Ourville** France
139 H8 **Ouse** Tasmania Australia
9 G2 **Ouse, R** England
13 G6 **Ouse, R** N Yorks England
20 E5 **Oust** *R* France
121 M6 **Outaouais, R des** Quebec Canada
122 C3 **Outardes Quatre, Res** Quebec Canada
122 D4 **Outardes, R. aux** Quebec Canada
122 D4 **Outardes Trois Dam** Quebec Canada
21 P5 **Outarville** France
85 D2 **Outat-Oulad-el-Haj** Morocco
6 B2 **Outer Bailey** N Atlantic Oc
15 A3 **Outer Hebrides** Scotland
102 F8 **Outer Santa Barbara Chan** California U.S.A.
7 M8 **Outer Silver Pit** North Sea
13 F5 **Outhgill** England
87 C10 **Outjo** Namibia
118 K7 **Outlook** Saskatchewan Canada
101 V1 **Outlook** Montana U.S.A.
29 O9 **Outokumpu** Finland
144 C6 **Outram** New Zealand
22 B2 **Outreau** France
15 G2 **Out Skerries** *isld* Scotland
19 O16 **Ouveze** *R* France
138 F6 **Ouyen** New South Wales Australia
21 O6 **Ouzouer-le-Marché** France
79 D2 **Ovacık** Turkey
44 E2 **Ovada** Italy
131 B3 **Ovalle** Chile
108 H3 **Ovalo** Texas U.S.A.
87 B9 **Ovamboland** *tribal area* Namibia
101 M2 **Ovando** Montana U.S.A.
16 B4 **Ovar** Portugal
38 G9 **Ovaro** Italy
47 H2 **Ovcharitsa, Yazovir** *res* Bulgaria
28 D3 **Ove** Denmark
32 H6 **Ovelgönne** Germany
139 H6 **Ovens** *R* Victoria Australia
36 C2 **Overath** Germany
107 P3 **Overbrook** Kansas U.S.A.
25 B5 **Overflakkee** Netherlands
119 Q5 **Overflowing R** Manitoba Canada
26 G9 **Överhogdal** Sweden
22 H2 **Overijse** Belgium
25 F4 **Overijssel** *prov* Netherlands
26 N5 **Överkalix** Sweden
28 C3 **Overlade** Denmark
107 Q3 **Overland Park** Kansas U.S.A.
98 F1 **Overly** North Dakota U.S.A.
29 J9 **Övermark** Finland
131 B5 **Overo, Vol** Argentina
22 J1 **Overpelt** Belgium
9 E5 **Overton** England
98 G9 **Overton** Nebraska U.S.A.
103 K5 **Overton** Nevada U.S.A.
109 N3 **Overton** Texas U.S.A.
8 D2 **Overton** Wales
26 N5 **Övertorneå** Sweden
27 H14 **Överum** Sweden
26 G5 **Over-uman** *L* Sweden
111 G10 **Ovett** Mississippi U.S.A.
106 H1 **Ovid** Colorado U.S.A.
101 O7 **Ovid** Idaho U.S.A.
94 C3 **Ovid** Michigan U.S.A.
95 L4 **Ovid** New York U.S.A.
16 C1 **Oviedo** *prov* Spain
16 D1 **Oviedo** Spain
113 F9 **Oviedo** Florida U.S.A.
26 G9 **Oviken** Sweden
45 P5 **Ovindoli** Italy
52 E5 **Ovinishche** Russian Federation
26 K8 **Öv Nyland** Sweden
26 O3 **Øvre Anarjokka Nat. Park** Norway
27 B13 **Övrebygd** Norway
26 L3 **Øvre Dividal Nat. Park** Norway
26 L6 **Övre Grundsel** Sweden
26 R2 **Øvre Pasvik Nat. Park** Norway
27 B13 **Öv-Sirdal** Norway
26 H8 **Övsjö** Sweden
28 A5 **Ovtrup** Denmark
145 F4 **Owahanga** New Zealand
144 B7 **Owaka** New Zealand
87 C9 **Owambo** *homeland* Namibia
86 C6 **Owando** Congo
61 O5 **Ōwani** Japan
95 L4 **Owasco L** New York U.S.A.
61 K11 **Owase** Japan
107 P5 **Owasso** Oklahoma U.S.A.
99 N5 **Owatonna** Minnesota U.S.A.
77 H2 **Owbeh** Afghanistan
95 L4 **Owego** New York U.S.A.
36 G6 **Owen** Germany
99 Q5 **Owen** Wisconsin U.S.A.
142 A3 **Owen Anchorage** W Australia Australia
86 F5 **Owen Falls D** Uganda
68 C7 **Owen I** Burma
14 B2 **Owenmore** *R* Ireland
145 D4 **Owen, Mt** New Zealand
145 D4 **Owen River** New Zealand
102 F4 **Owens** *R* California U.S.A.
94 F8 **Owens** West Virginia U.S.A.
110 J4 **Owensboro** Kentucky U.S.A.
102 G5 **Owens L** California U.S.A.
120 K8 **Owen Sound** Ontario Canada
140 C6 **Owen Springs** N Terr Australia
136 K3 **Owen Stanley Ra** Papua New Guinea
110 J3 **Owensville** Indiana U.S.A.
110 E3 **Owensville** Missouri U.S.A.
110 M3 **Owenton** Kentucky U.S.A.
102 F5 **Owenyo** California U.S.A.
9 E6 **Ower** England
85 F7 **Owerri** Nigeria
145 E3 **Owhango** New Zealand
117 K10 **Owikeno L** British Columbia Canada
94 D8 **Owingsville** Kentucky U.S.A.
36 F5 **Öwisheim** Germany
106 E1 **Owl Canyon** Colorado U.S.A.
101 R6 **Owl Cr** Wyoming U.S.A.
101 R6 **Owl-Creek Mts** Wyoming U.S.A.
118 F4 **Owl R** Alberta Canada
85 F7 **Owo** Nigeria
94 C3 **Owosso** Michigan U.S.A.
100 J8 **Owyhee** Nevada U.S.A.
100 H6 **Owyhee** Oregon U.S.A.
29 T8 **Øxarfjørdhur** *B* Iceland
27 G10 **Oxberg** Sweden
119 P9 **Oxbow** Saskatchewan Canada
100 J5 **Oxbow Dam** Oregon U.S.A.
111 F7 **Oxbow L** Mississippi U.S.A.
118 K1 **Oxdrift** Ontario Canada
27 J13 **Oxelösund** Sweden
122 J8 **Oxford** Nova Scotia Canada
9 E4 **Oxford** England
144 D5 **Oxford** New Zealand
111 L8 **Oxford** Alabama U.S.A.
101 N7 **Oxford** Idaho U.S.A.
110 J1 **Oxford** Indiana U.S.A.
99 P8 **Oxford** Iowa U.S.A.
107 N4 **Oxford** Kansas U.S.A.
95 R2 **Oxford** Maine U.S.A.
95 L8 **Oxford** Maryland U.S.A.
95 Q4 **Oxford** Massachusetts U.S.A.
94 D4 **Oxford** Michigan U.S.A.
111 G7 **Oxford** Mississippi U.S.A.
98 G9 **Oxford** Nebraska U.S.A.
95 M4 **Oxford** New York U.S.A.
112 J1 **Oxford** North Carolina U.S.A.
94 C7 **Oxford** Ohio U.S.A.
99 R6 **Oxford** Wisconsin U.S.A.
141 J5 **Oxford Downs** Queensland Australia
119 W4 **Oxford House** Manitoba Canada
101 N7 **Oxford Pk** Idaho U.S.A.
9 E4 **Oxfordshire** *co* England
46 E5 **Oxiá** *mt* Greece
140 E4 **Oxide, Mt** Queensland Australia
46 G6 **Oxílithos** Greece
125 P7 **Oxkutzcab** Mexico
141 K2 **Oxley** Brisbane, Qnsld Australia
139 G5 **Oxley** New South Wales Australia
139 K4 **Oxleys Pk** New South Wales Australia
14 C2 **Ox Mts** Ireland
102 E7 **Oxnard** California U.S.A.
Oxon *co see* **Oxfordshire**
9 E1 **Oxton** England
8 B4 **Oxwich** Wales
56 D4 **Oya** *R* Russian Federation
70 B3 **Oya** Sarawak
70 C3 **Oya** *R* Sarawak
61 K9 **Oyabe** Japan
61 M10 **Oyama** Shizuoka Japan
61 N9 **Oyama** Tochigi Japan
61 N7 **Ōyama** Yamagata Japan
60 D13 **Ōyano shima** *isld* Japan
129 H3 **Oyapock, B. d'** Fr Guiana
57 L1 **Oychilik** Kazakhstan
86 B5 **Oyem** Gabon
118 G7 **Oyen** Alberta Canada
22 C2 **Oye Plage** France
27 E12 **Oyeren** *L* Norway
56 B3 **Oyesh** *R* Russian Federation
26 J3 **Öyjord** Norway
15 D3 **Oykel** *R* Scotland
51 O2 **Oymyakon** Russian Federation
85 E7 **Oyo** Nigeria
128 C6 **Oyón** Peru
40 C5 **Oyonnax** France
21 M8 **Oyré** France
109 M6 **Oyster Cr** Texas U.S.A.
68 A2 **Oyster I** Burma
100 A3 **Oysterville** Washington U.S.A.
57 G3 **Oytal** Kazakhstan
32 K6 **Oyten** Germany
79 C2 **Oyuklu Dağ Tepe** *mt* Turkey
51 N2 **Oyun Khomoto** Russian Federation
78 J2 **Özalp** Turkey
71 F6 **Ozamiz** Mindanao Philippines
111 L10 **Ozark** Alabama U.S.A.
110 C6 **Ozark** Arkansas U.S.A.
110 C4 **Ozark** Missouri U.S.A.
110 C6 **Ozark lake** Arkansas U.S.A.
110 C5 **Ozark Plateau** Missouri U.S.A.
110 C3 **Ozarks, L. of the** Missouri U.S.A.
48 F2 **Ozd** Hungary
80 B7 **Ozem** Israel
55 F3 **Ozernoye** Russian Federation
55 D4 **Ozernyy** Kustanayskaya Kazakhstan
54 D1 **Ozernyy** Smolenskaya obl Russian Federation
55 D3 **Ozernyy** Sverdlovskaya obl Russian Federation
55 G3 **Ozero Karachi** Russian Federation
65 J2 **Ozero Khanka** *L* China/Rus Fed
46 E6 **Ozerós, L** Greece
31 N1 **Ozersk** Russian Federation
54 K2 **Ozery** Russian Federation
100 A1 **Ozette, L** Washington U.S.A.
54 K2 **Ozherel'ye** Russian Federation
51 O2 **Ozhogino** Russian Federation
43 C8 **Ozieri** Sardinia
31 L5 **Ozimek** Poland
108 F5 **Ozona** Texas U.S.A.
48 E4 **Ozora** Hungary
31 L4 **Ozorków** Poland
55 C5 **Ozorodnyy** Kazakhstan
86 A6 **Ozouri** Gabon
60 F12 **Ōzu** Japan
60 D13 **Ōzu** *R* Japan
60 E11 **Ozuki** Japan
48 K5 **Ozun** Romania
78 J1 **Ozurgety** Georgia
45 K3 **Ozzano dell'Emilia** Italy

P

80 B8 **Pa'ame Tashaz** Israel
Paamiut *see* **Frederikshåb**
68 C4 **Pa-an** Burma
37 L6 **Paar** *R* Germany
33 R7 **Paaren** Germany
89 A9 **Paarl** S Africa
29 O3 **Paatsjoki** *R* Finland
135 U4 **Paauilo** Hawaiian Is
29 L7 **Paavola** Finland
15 A3 **Pabbay** *isld* Outer Hebrides Scotland
70 P9 **Pabean** Indonesia
31 L4 **Pabjanice** Poland
77 K6 **Pab Range** Pakistan
128 F6 **Pacaás Novos, Sa. dos** *mts* Brazil
129 H4 **Pacajá** *R* Brazil
128 F3 **Pacaraima, Sa** *mts* Brazil/Venezuela
128 C5 **Pacasmayo** Peru
20 G5 **Pace** France
111 F8 **Pace** Mississippi U.S.A.
67 F5 **Pa'-chao Hsü** *isld* Taiwan
124 E2 **Pacheco** Chihuahua Mexico
124 H5 **Pacheco** Zacatecas Mexico
100 A1 **Pachena Pt** British Columbia Canada
124 F3 **Pachera** Mexico
43 G12 **Pachino** Sicily
128 D5 **Pachitea** *R* Peru
125 K7 **Pachuca** Mexico
111 H9 **Pachuta** Mississippi U.S.A.
102 D3 **Pacific** California U.S.A.
110 F3 **Pacific** Missouri U.S.A.
135 L14 **Pacific Antarctic Ridge** Pacific Oc
100 A2 **Pacific Beach** Washington U.S.A.
100 B4 **Pacific City** Oregon U.S.A.
101 Q7 **Pacific Cr** Wyoming U.S.A.
102 C5 **Pacific Grove** California U.S.A.
135 **Pacific Ocean**
117 L11 **Pacific Rim Nat Park** British Columbia Canada
71 G5 **Pacijan** *isld* Philippines
70 P9 **Pacinan, Tanjong** *C* Java
70 D4 **Pacingapan, Bukit** *mt* Kalimantan
145 E4 **Packakariki** New Zealand
38 L7 **Pack Alpe** *mts* Austria
138 F4 **Packsaddle** New South Wales Australia
111 D10 **Packton** Louisiana U.S.A.
99 O8 **Packwood** Iowa U.S.A.
100 D3 **Packwood** Washington U.S.A.
112 E2 **Pacolet** *R* South Carolina U.S.A.
112 F3 **Pacolet Mills** South Carolina U.S.A.
31 J6 **Pacov** Czechoslovakia
123 R4 **Pacquet** Newfoundland Canada
98 C5 **Pactola** South Dakota U.S.A.
135 Q15 **Pactolus Bank** Pacific Oc
130 G5 **Pacui** *R* Brazil
21 N3 **Pacy-sur-Eure** France
31 K5 **Paczków** Poland
71 H6 **Padabale** *isld* Sulawesi
71 G7 **Padada** Mindanao Philippines
70 G7 **Padamarang** *isld* Sulawesi
71 K8 **Padang** Indonesia
69 F12 **Padang** Riau Arch Indonesia
69 E13 **Padang** Sumatra
69 E13 **Padangpanjang** Sumatra
69 D12 **Padangsidimpuan** Sumatra
69 B10 **Padangtiji** Sumatra
69 J13 **Padangtikar** Indonesia
52 D3 **Padany** Russian Federation
70 D2 **Padas** *R* Sabah
29 L10 **Padasjoki** Finland
128 F3 **Padauiri** *R* Brazil
68 B3 **Padaung** Burma
83 K9 **Padawiya Tank** Sri Lanka
141 K1 **Paddington** *dist* Brisbane, Qnsld Australia
117 P7 **Paddle Prairie** Alberta Canada
119 M5 **Paddockwood** Saskatchewan Canada
71 H6 **Padea Besar** *isld* Indonesia
94 G7 **Paden City** West Virginia U.S.A.
32 J9 **Paderborn** Germany
48 G5 **Padeş** *mt* Romania
13 F6 **Padiham** England
128 F7 **Padilla** Bolivia
48 L6 **Padina** Romania
26 J4 **Padjelanta Nat. Park** Sweden
115 K5 **Padlei** Northwest Territories Canada
115 N4 **Padloping Island** Northwest Territories Canada
122 E5 **Padoue** Quebec Canada
36 B7 **Padoux** France
45 L1 **Padova** Italy
109 K9 **Padre I** Texas U.S.A.
16 B2 **Padrón** Spain
8 B6 **Padstow** England
138 F6 **Padthaway** South Australia Australia
Padua *see* **Padova**
75 K9 **Pādua** India
110 H4 **Paducah** Kentucky U.S.A.
108 G1 **Paducah** Texas U.S.A.
45 R7 **Paduli** Italy
56 C3 **Padunskaya** Russian Federation
145 F2 **Paengaroa** New Zealand
65 F6 **Paengnyŏng-do** *isld* S Korea
145 E2 **Paeroa** New Zealand
44 B2 **Paesana** Italy
45 R8 **Paestum** Italy
71 E3 **Paete** Luzon Philippines
87 F10 **Pafuri** Mozambique
42 F4 **Pag** *isld* Croatia
42 G4 **Pag** Croatia
71 L9 **Paga** Flores Indonesia
129 H4 **Paga Centa** Brazil
70 L9 **Pagadenbaru** Java
71 F7 **Pagadian** Mindanao Philippines
69 E14 **Pagai Selatan** *isld* Indonesia
69 E14 **Pagai Utara** *isld* Indonesia
68 B2 **Pagan** Burma
45 R8 **Pagani** Italy
70 K7 **Pagaralam** Sumatra
46 F5 **Pagasitikós, Kólpos** *B* Greece
70 C6 **Pagatan** Kalimantan
70 D6 **Pagatan** Kalimantan
119 P2 **Pagato R** Saskatchewan Canada
71 F4 **Pagbulungan Pt** Philippines
103 N5 **Page** Arizona U.S.A.
98 H7 **Page** Nebraska U.S.A.
98 J2 **Page** North Dakota U.S.A.
107 Q7 **Page** Oklahoma U.S.A.
52 B6 **Pagėgiai** Lithuania
112 G3 **Pageland** South Carolina U.S.A.
142 E3 **Page, Mt** W Australia Australia
69 G14 **Pagerdewa** Sumatra
141 K4 **Paget Cay** *isld* Gt Barrier Reef Australia
68 A6 **Paget I** Andaman Is
131 H6 **Paget, Mt** S Georgia
77 L2 **Paghman** Afghanistan
42 D6 **Paglia** *R* Italy
101 S9 **Pagoda Pk** Colorado U.S.A.
47 H7 **Pagóndhas** Greece
70 D2 **Pagonprick, G** *mt* Sarawak
134 D1 **Pago Pago** Amer Samoa
106 C4 **Pagosa Springs** Colorado U.S.A.
106 C6 **Paguate** New Mexico U.S.A.
71 H4 **Pagujaman** *R* Sulawesi
120 D3 **Pagwachuan** Ontario Canada
120 E3 **Pagwachuan** *R* Ontario Canada
120 E2 **Pagwa River** Ontario Canada
116 K3 **Pah** *R* Alaska U.S.A.
102 V14 **Pahala** Hawaiian Is
73 R8 **Pahang** *R* Malaysia
69 F11 **Pahang, S** *R* Malaysia
145 E4 **Pahaoa R** New Zealand
69 J12 **Pahauman** Indonesia
144 A7 **Pahia** New Zealand
144 A7 **Pahia Pt** New Zealand
145 E4 **Pahiatua** New Zealand
76 G4 **Pahlāgaon** Andaman Is
135 V5 **Pahoa** Hawaiian Is
77 G2 **Pahra** Afghanistan
103 J4 **Pahranagat L** Nevada U.S.A.
103 J4 **Pahranagat Ra** Nevada U.S.A.
103 K4 **Pahrock Ra** Nevada U.S.A.
103 J5 **Pahrump** Nevada U.S.A.
101 M5 **Pahsimeroi** *R* Idaho U.S.A.
102 H4 **Pahute Mesa** Nevada U.S.A.
100 F8 **Pahute Peak** *mt* Nevada U.S.A.
135 T3 **Paia** Hawaiian Is
130 B6 **Paiaguás** Brazil
67 G4 **Pai-ch'üan Lieh-tao** *islds* Taiwan
52 C5 **Paide** Estonia
109 K5 **Paige** Texas U.S.A.
8 C7 **Paignton** England
145 E1 **Paihia** New Zealand
29 M10 **Päijänne** *reg* Finland
68 F6 **Pailin** Cambodia
Pailing *see* **Chun'an**
135 S3 **Pailolo Ch** Hawaiian Is
9 E3 **Pailton** England
20 F7 **Paimbœuf** France
116 G5 **Paimiut** Alaska U.S.A.
20 D4 **Paimpol** France
20 F5 **Paimpont** France
69 E13 **Painan** Sumatra
120 H10 **Paincourt** Ontario Canada
133 C8 **Paine** *mt* Chile
99 S2 **Painesdale** Michigan U.S.A.
94 F5 **Painesville** Ohio U.S.A.
103 N5 **Painted Des** Arizona U.S.A.
103 L8 **Painted Rock Res** Arizona U.S.A.
37 M6 **Painten** Germany
138 E4 **Painter, Mt** South Australia Australia
119 T3 **Paint L** Manitoba Canada
120 J8 **Paisley** Ontario Canada
12 D2 **Paisley** Scotland
100 E7 **Paisley** Oregon U.S.A.
29 M2 **Paistunturit** *mt* Finland
17 F2 **País Vasco** *reg* Spain
128 B5 **Paita** Peru
70 E1 **Paitan, Telukan** *B* Sabah
26 K4 **Paittasjärbi** *L* Sweden
16 B4 **Paiva** *R* Portugal
21 M8 **Paizey-le-Sec** France
69 E11 **Pajakbaru** Sumatra
69 E13 **Pajakumbuh** Sumatra
26 N4 **Pajala** Sweden
16 D1 **Pajares, Pto. de** Spain
106 D7 **Pajarito** New Mexico U.S.A.
131 B2 **Pajaros** *isld* Chile
129 L5 **Pajeu** Brazil
130 H10 **Pajeú, R** Brazil
48 D4 **Páka** Hungary
69 F10 **Paka** Malaysia
68 B2 **Pakangyi** Burma
128 F2 **Pakaraima Mts** Guyana
119 N1 **Pakashkhan L** *isld* Ontario Canada
56 E3 **Pakateyevo** Russian Federation
68 E3 **Pak Beng** Laos
121 O7 **Pakenham** Ontario Canada
145 D1 **Pakenui** New Zealand
57 G4 **Pakhtaabad** Uzbekistan
74 A4 **Pakistan** *rep* Asia
69 D11 **Pakkat** Sumatra
68 E3 **Pak Khop** Laos
68 E3 **Pak Lay** Laos
Paknampho *see* **Muang Nakhon Sawan**
68 E3 **Pak Niam** Laos
68 B2 **Pakokku** Burma
145 D1 **Pakotai** New Zealand
69 E8 **Pak Phanang** Thailand
69 E9 **Pak Phayun** Thailand
42 H3 **Pakrac** Croatia
48 E4 **Paks** Hungary
68 F3 **Pak Sane** Laos
68 G5 **Pakse** Laos
68 E2 **Pak Tha** Laos
77 L3 **Paktīā** Afghanistan
77 L3 **Paktīkā** *prov* Afghanistan
70 C3 **Paku** *R* Sarawak
70 G6 **Pakue** Sulawesi
119 T4 **Pakwa L** Manitoba Canada
89 F4 **Pakwe** *R* Botswana
86 F5 **Pakwich** Uganda
68 D6 **Pala** Burma
86 C4 **Pala** Chad
102 G8 **Pala** California U.S.A.
70 L9 **Palabuhanratu** Java
70 L9 **Palabuhanratu, Teluk** *B* Java
109 L7 **Palacios** Texas U.S.A.
127 L10 **Palacios** Venezuela
133 D6 **Palacios, L** Argentina
17 K3 **Palafrugell** Spain
42 G6 **Palagruža** *isld* Croatia
46 F7 **Palaiá** Greece
45 J4 **Paláia** Italy
47 H9 **Palaiókastron** Crete Greece
46 F9 **Palaiokhóra** Crete Greece
46 D6 **Pálairos** Greece
21 P4 **Palaiseau** France
20 D7 **Palais, le** Belle Isle, Nfld France
Palakkad *see* **Palghat**
89 F4 **Palala** *R* S Africa
68 A7 **Palalankwe** Andaman Is
46 E5 **Palamás** Greece
71 A3 **Palamea** Indonesia
17 K3 **Palamós** Spain
47 J6 **Palamut** Turkey
139 J7 **Palana** Tasmania Australia
71 F2 **Palanan** Luzon Philippines
17 G5 **Palancia** *R* Spain
52 B6 **Palanga** Lithuania
77 G4 **Palangān, Kūh-e-** *mts* Iran
70 C6 **Palangka Raya** Kalimantan
76 C5 **Palani** India
76 G5 **Palankwe** Andaman Is India
16 D2 **Palanquinos** Spain
70 F7 **Palanro** Sulawesi
135 S3 **Palaoa Pt** Hawaiian Is
71 G4 **Palapag** Philippines
89 E4 **Palapye** Botswana
70 G4 **Palasa** Sulawesi
16 B2 **Palas de Rey** Spain
113 F8 **Palatka** Florida U.S.A.
56 B6 **Palattsy** Kazakhstan
108 F8 **Palau** Mexico
43 C7 **Palau** Sardinia
71 F1 **Palaui** *isld* Luzon Philippines
71 D3 **Palauig** Luzon Philippines
68 D6 **Palauk** Burma
70 K8 **Palausekopong, Tanjong** *C* Sumatra
83 J10 **Palavi** Sri Lanka
68 D6 **Palaw** Burma
71 D6 **Palawan** *isld* Philippines
71 C6 **Palawan Passage** Philippines
76 C6 **Pālayankottai** India
43 F11 **Palazzolo Acreide** Sicily
41 L6 **Palazzolo sull Oglio** Italy
45 L3 **Palazzuolo sul Sénio** Italy
133 D1 **Palca** Chile
52 B5 **Paldiski** Estonia
68 B2 **Pale** Burma
70 G4 **Paleleh** Sulawesi
69 G14 **Palembang** Sumatra
38 K6 **Palen** *R* Austria
16 D2 **Palencia** *prov* Spain
103 J8 **Palen L** California U.S.A.
47 O12 **Paleokastritsa** Greece
79 D4 **Paleokhorio** Cyprus
43 E10 **Palermo** Sicily
102 C2 **Palermo** California U.S.A.
98 D1 **Palermo** North Dakota U.S.A.
128 E8 **Palestina** Chile
110 J3 **Palestine** Illinois U.S.A.
109 M4 **Palestine** Texas U.S.A.
110 M1 **Palestine Hill** Ohio U.S.A.
109 M3 **Palestine, L** Texas U.S.A.
45 N6 **Palestrina** Italy
68 A2 **Paletwa** Burma
76 C5 **Palghat** India
143 B6 **Palgrave, Mt** W Australia
45 O6 **Paliano** Italy
83 K8 **Pali Aru** *R* Sri Lanka
70 P9 **Paliat** *isld* Indonesia
71 G7 **Palimbang** Mindanao Philippines
70 E1 **Palin, Mt** Sabah
43 G8 **Palinuro, C** Italy
106 B2 **Palisade** Colorado U.S.A.
98 E9 **Palisade** Nebraska U.S.A.
103 H1 **Palisade** Nevada U.S.A.
101 O6 **Palisades Res** Idaho U.S.A.
127 L3 **Palisadoes** *airport* Jamaica
22 J4 **Paliseul** Belgium
109 J8 **Palito Blanco** Texas U.S.A.
26 K5 **Paljaape** *mt* Sweden
29 L10 **Pälkäne** Finland
83 J8 **Palk Bay** Sri Lanka
52 F5 **Palkino** Russian Federation
75 K9 **Pālkohda** India
83 J8 **Palk Str** India/Sri Lanka
83 K8 **Pallai** Sri Lanka
Pallanza *see* **Verbania**
Palla Rd *see* **Dinokwe** Botswana
18 F10 **Pallaresa** *R* Spain
29 L3 **Pallas-Ounastunturi Nat. Park.** Finland
29 L3 **Pallastunturi** *mt* Finland
83 K10 **Pallegama** Sri Lanka
26 K3 **Pallemtjåkko** *mt* Sweden
46 C3 **Pallës, Bishti i** *C* Albania
21 H7 **Pallet, le** France
18 E6 **Pallice, la** France
36 B4 **Pallien** Germany
70 G7 **Pallima** Sulawesi
Pallíni Greece *see* **Kassándra**
143 C10 **Pallinup, R** W Australia Australia
145 E4 **Palliser Bay** New Zealand
20 G8 **Palluau** France
21 N8 **Palluau-sur-Indre** France
88 H7 **Palma** Mozambique
106 E6 **Palma** New Mexico U.S.A.
17 J5 **Palma, B. de** Majorca
45 R8 **Palma Camp** Italy
17 J5 **Palma de Mallorca** Majorca
43 F11 **Palma di Montechiaro** Sicily
80 B6 **Palmaḥim** Israel
127 H9 **Palmar** *R* Venezuela
133 G4 **Palmares do Sul** Brazil
126 G4 **Palmarito del Cauto** Cuba
43 E8 **Palmarola, I** Italy
85 C8 **Palmas, C** Liberia
43 B10 **Palmas, G. di** Sardinia
128 E1 **Palma Sola** Venezuela
126 G4 **Palma Soriano** Cuba
87 B7 **Palmas, Pta. das** Angola
142 A4 **Palm Beach** W Australia Australia
113 G11 **Palm Beach** Florida U.S.A.
102 F7 **Palmdale** California U.S.A.
113 F11 **Palmdale** Florida U.S.A.
102 H8 **Palm Desert** California U.S.A.
133 G3 **Palmeira** Brazil
146 C4 **Palmer** *U.S.A. Base* Antarctica
141 G3 **Palmer** *R* Queensland Australia
118 L9 **Palmer** Saskatchewan Canada
116 N6 **Palmer** Alaska U.S.A.
99 R10 **Palmer** Illinois U.S.A.
99 M7 **Palmer** Iowa U.S.A.
99 T3 **Palmer** Michigan U.S.A.
98 H8 **Palmer** Nebraska U.S.A.
110 L6 **Palmer** Tennessee U.S.A.
109 L3 **Palmer** Texas U.S.A.
146 C6 **Palmer Land** Antarctica
140 C6 **Palmer R** N Terr Australia
144 C6 **Palmerston** New Zealand
141 J5 **Palmerston, C** Queensland Australia
145 E4 **Palmerston North** New Zealand
95 M6 **Palmerton** Pennsylvania U.S.A.
140 C6 **Palmer Valley** N Terr Australia
141 G3 **Palmerville** Queensland Australia
113 E10 **Palmetto** Florida U.S.A.
112 C4 **Palmetto** Georgia U.S.A.
126 F2 **Palmetto Pt** Eleuthera Bahamas
127 N6 **Palmetto Pt** Barbuda W Indies
113 E9 **Palm Harbor** Florida U.S.A.
43 G10 **Palmi** Italy
128 C3 **Palmira** Colombia
126 D3 **Palmira** Cuba
141 H4 **Palm Is** Queensland Australia
124 G6 **Palmito del Verde, I** Mexico
94 E3 **Palms** Michigan U.S.A.
102 H8 **Palm Springs** California U.S.A.
141 J7 **Palm Tree Cr** Queensland Australia
140 C6 **Palm Valley** N Terr Australia
Palmyra *see* **Tadmur**
110 G2 **Palmyra** Illinois U.S.A.
99 P10 **Palmyra** Missouri U.S.A.
98 K9 **Palmyra** Nebraska U.S.A.
95 N7 **Palmyra** New Jersey U.S.A.
95 K3 **Palmyra** New York U.S.A.
95 L6 **Palmyra** Pennsylvania U.S.A.
110 J5 **Palmyra** Tennessee U.S.A.
94 J9 **Palmyra** Virginia U.S.A.
99 S7 **Palmyra** Wisconsin U.S.A.
135 U7 **Palmyra I** *atoll* Pacific Oc
12 E4 **Palnackie** Scotland
52 J4 **Pal'niki** Russian Federation
42 E7 **Palo** Italy
71 G5 **Palo** Leyte Philippines
70 F5 **Palo** Sulawesi
99 P7 **Palo** Iowa U.S.A.
102 B4 **Palo Alto** California U.S.A.
125 Q6 **Palo de las Letras** Panama
108 B8 **Palo Duro Cr** Texas U.S.A.
108 C7 **Paloduro Cr** Texas/Okla U.S.A.
70 B3 **Paloh** Sarawak
86 F3 **Paloich** Sudan
29 K3 **Palojärvi** Finland
29 K3 **Palojoensuu** Finland
29 K3 **Palojoki** *R* Finland
102 H8 **Palomar Mt** California U.S.A.
103 L9 **Palomas** Arizona U.S.A.
45 N5 **Palombara Sabina** Italy
17 G4 **Palomera, Sa** *mts* Spain
109 J3 **Palo Pinto** Texas U.S.A.
70 G6 **Palopo** Sulawesi
133 F3 **Palo Santo** Argentina
17 G7 **Palos, C. de** Spain
127 O3 **Palo Seco** Trinidad
100 H3 **Palouse** Washington U.S.A.
103 M8 **Palo Verde** Arizona U.S.A.
103 K8 **Palo Verde** California U.S.A.
141 F6 **Palparara** Queensland Australia
27 H12 **Pålsboda** Sweden
29 N7 **Paltamo** Finland
38 H5 **Palting** Austria
71 K9 **Palu** *isld* Flores Indonesia
70 F5 **Palu** *R* Sulawesi
127 N10 **Palúa** Venezuela
71 E4 **Paluan** Philippines
83 K9 **Palugassegama** Sri Lanka
57 C5 **Pal'vart** Turkmenistan
85 E6 **Pama** Burkina
71 L10 **Pamana** Indonesia
71 L9 **Pamana Besar** *isld* Flores Indonesia
70 L9 **Pamanukan** Java
83 J8 **Pamban** *isld* India
70 F4 **Pambero** Sulawesi
118 K9 **Pambrun** Saskatchewan Canada
139 J6 **Pambula** New South Wales Australia
38 M8 **Pameče** Slovenia
70 O9 **Pamekasan** Java
70 L9 **Pameungpeuk** Java
18 G9 **Pamiers** France
46 E7 **Pámisos** *R* Greece
112 L2 **Pamlico R** North Carolina U.S.A.
68 E4 **Pamong D.Site** Thailand
133 D4 **Pampa de las Salinas** Argentina
70 G7 **Pampanua** Sulawesi
128 D6 **Pampas** Peru
133 E5 **Pampas, Plains** Argentina
16 B4 **Pampilhosa da Serra** Portugal
16 B4 **Pampilhosa do Botão** Portugal
94 J9 **Pamplin City** Virginia U.S.A.
128 D2 **Pamplona** Colombia
71 F6 **Pamplona** Negros Philippines
17 F2 **Pamplona** Spain
33 O5 **Pampow** Germany
70 E6 **Pamukan, Teluk** *B* Kalimantan
47 K7 **Pamukkale** Turkey
47 L4 **Pamukova** Turkey
95 K9 **Pamunkey** *R* Virginia U.S.A.
99 R10 **Pana** Illinois U.S.A.
71 F7 **Panabutan B** Mindanao Philippines
103 K4 **Panaca** Nevada U.S.A.
120 J6 **Panache, L** Ontario Canada
83 J11 **Panadura** Sri Lanka
71 D6 **Panagtaran** *pt* Palawan Philippines
46 G2 **Panagyurishte** Bulgaria
70 K9 **Panaitan** *isld* Java
76 A3 **Panaji** India
46 E6 **Panakhaïkón** *mt* Greece
125 O5 **Panama** *rep* Central America
125 P5 **Panamá** Panama
94 H4 **Panama** New York U.S.A.
107 Q6 **Panama** Oklahoma U.S.A.
124 E10 **Panama Canal** Central America
113 B7 **Panama City** Florida U.S.A.
125 P5 **Panamá, Golfo de** Panama
102 G5 **Panamint V** California U.S.A.
71 G6 **Panaon** *isld* Philippines
43 G10 **Panarea, I** Italy
45 K2 **Panaro** *R* Italy
70 O9 **Panarukan** Java
71 G4 **Panay** Philippines
71 F5 **Panay** *isld* Philippines
71 F5 **Panay Gulf** Philippines
46 G4 **Panayía** Greece
103 J3 **Pancake Ra** Nevada U.S.A.
20 G6 **Pancé** France
48 F6 **Pančevo** Serbia Yugoslavia
46 D1 **Pančiće** *mt* Serbia Yugoslavia
48 L5 **Panciu** Romania
69 D11 **Pancurbatu** Sumatra
87 F10 **Panda** Mozambique
108 F5 **Pandale** Texas U.S.A.
71 G3 **Pandan** Catanduanes Philippines
71 F5 **Pandan** Panay Philippines
70 C3 **Pandan** Sarawak
71 C6 **Pandanan** *isld* Palawan Philippines
71 F5 **Pandan Bay** Panay Philippines
70 K8 **Pandan, Bt** *mt* Sumatra
70 D5 **Pandang** Kalimantan
141 F3 **Pandanus** *R* Queensland Australia
87 F10 **Pande** Mozambique
133 C3 **Pan de Azúcar** Chile
71 F5 **Pan de Azucar** Philippines
70 L9 **Pandeglang** Java
130 G4 **Pandeiros** *R* Brazil
138 E2 **Pandie Pandie** South Australia Australia
70 F3 **Pandjang** *isld* Kalimantan
70 G4 **Pandjang, Tg** *C* Sulawesi
128 E6 **Pando** *dept* Bolivia
133 F4 **Pando** Uruguay
47 O12 **Pandokrátor** *mt* Greece
125 N5 **Pandora** Costa Rica
141 G1 **Pandora Ent** Gt Barrier Reef Aust
71 E7 **Panducan** *isld* Philippines
8 D4 **Pandy** Wales
52 B6 **Panevėžys** Lithuania
138 D4 **Paney** South Australia Australia
66 C3 **Panfilov** Kazakhstan
57 H3 **Panfilova, Imeni** Kazakhstan
86 E5 **Panga** Zaire
46 F4 **Pangaion** *mt* Greece
70 M9 **Pangandaran** Java
88 F4 **Pangani** *R* Tanzania
88 G4 **Pangani** Tanzania
71 F4 **Panganiran** Philippines
9 E5 **Pangbourne** England
110 E6 **Pangburn** Arkansas U.S.A.
70 F5 **Pangean** Sulawesi
68 D1 **Panghsang** Burma
86 E6 **Pangi** Zaire
70 O9 **Pangkah, Tg** *C* Java
70 F7 **Pangkajene** Sulawesi
70 B6 **Pangkalanbuun** Kalimantan
69 E11 **Pangkalanlunang** Sumatra
69 D10 **Pangkalansusu** Sumatra
69 H14 **Pangkalpinang** Sumatra
71 H5 **Pangkalsiang, Tg** *C* Sulawesi
71 F6 **Panglao** *isld* Philippines
68 C2 **Panglong** Burma
119 N9 **Pangman** Saskatchewan Canada
115 N4 **Pangnirtung** Northwest Territories Canada
70 L9 **Pangrongo, G** *mt* Java
68 C2 **Pangtara** Burma
133 C5 **Panguipulli** *mt* Chile
131 A7 **Panguipulli, L** Chile
103 M4 **Panguitch** Utah U.S.A.
70 B6 **Pangujon, Tanjong** *C* Kalimantan
71 E7 **Pangutaran** *isld* Philippines
71 E7 **Pangutaran Group** *islds* Philippines
88 E7 **Pangwa** Tanzania
68 D1 **Pang Yang** Burma
87 F9 **Panhalonga** Zimbabwe
108 C8 **Panhandle** Texas U.S.A.
65 A7 **Panhe** China
136 H2 **Paniai, Danau** *L* W Irian
86 D7 **Pania Mutembo** Zaire
137 N6 **Panié, Mt** New Caledonia
71 G5 **Paninihian Pt** Samar Philippines
71 D6 **Panitan** Palawan Philippines
77 K2 **Panjāb** Afghanistan
Panjang *isld* Cocos Is *see* **West I**
69 J11 **Panjang** *isld* Indonesia
69 F8 **Panjang, Hon** *isld* G of Thailand
77 J6 **Panjgur** Pakistan
77 L2 **Panjshir** *reg* Afghanistan
60 Q1 **Panke-zan** *mt* Japan
116 F9 **Pankof, C** Aleutian Is
33 S7 **Pankow** Germany
85 F7 **Pankshin** Nigeria
65 H3 **Pan Ling** *mts* China
142 B5 **Pannawonica** W Australia Australia
20 H7 **Pannecé** France
25 F5 **Pannerden** Netherlands
102 D5 **Panoche** California U.S.A.
70 B5 **Panopah** Kalimantan
99 M8 **Panora** Iowa U.S.A.
133 G2 **Panorama** Brazil
141 J6 **Panorama, Mt** Queensland Australia
55 F3 **Panovo** Russian Federation
52 D2 **Panozero** Russian Federation
65 E4 **Panshan** China
65 G3 **Panshi** China
70 E6 **Pantai** Kalimantan
69 E13 **Pantaicermin, Gunung** *mt* Sumatra
129 G7 **Pantanal de São Lourênço** *swamp* Brazil
68 B4 **Pantanaw** Burma
103 O9 **Pantano** Arizona U.S.A.
18 F10 **Pantano de Tremp** *L* Spain
71 M9 **Pantar** *isld* Indonesia
112 L2 **Pantego** North Carolina U.S.A.
109 M9 **Pantego** Texas U.S.A.
43 E12 **Pantelleria, I. di** Italy
41 N6 **Pantena, Val** Italy
110 J4 **Panther** *R* Kentucky U.S.A.
74 H4 **Pantnagar** India
128 C4 **Pantoja** Peru
69 C10 **Pantonlabu** Sumatra
125 K6 **Pánuco** Mexico
67 A4 **Pan Xian** China
67 D5 **Panyu** China
54 H8 **Panyutino** Ukraine
87 C7 **Panzi** Zaire
Paoki *see* **Baoji**
43 G9 **Paola** Italy
107 Q3 **Paola** Kansas U.S.A.
98 D9 **Paoli** Colorado U.S.A.
110 K3 **Paoli** Indiana U.S.A.
107 N7 **Paoli** Oklahoma U.S.A.
106 C3 **Paonia** Colorado U.S.A.
134 A11 **Paopao** Moorea Pacific Oc
Paotow *see* **Baotou**
135 U6 **Papa** Hawaiian Is
48 D3 **Pápa** Hungary
135 V4 **Papaaloa** Hawaiian Is
46 F8 **Papadhiánika** Greece
125 M4 **Papagayo, Golfo de** Costa Rica
135 V5 **Papaikou** Hawaiian Is
144 C6 **Papakaio** New Zealand
145 E2 **Papakura** New Zealand
43 G8 **Papa, Monte del** Italy
125 L7 **Papantla** Mexico
70 D2 **Papar** Sabah
145 F3 **Paparatu** New Zealand
75 K9 **Pāparhāhāndi** India
145 E2 **Paparoa** New Zealand
144 C5 **Paparoa Range** New Zealand
46 E6 **Pápas, Akr** Greece
15 G2 **Papa Stour** *isld* Scotland
145 G2 **Papatoetoe** New Zealand
144 B7 **Papatowai** New Zealand
15 F1 **Papa Westray** Orkney Scotland
135 M10 **Papeete** Tahiti Pacific Oc
32 F6 **Papenburg** Germany
25 C5 **Papendrecht** Netherlands
79 C4 **Paphos** Cyprus
124 E3 **Papigochic** *R* Mexico
121 P7 **Papineauville** Quebec Canada
133 C3 **Paposo** Chile
45 M2 **Papozze** Italy
37 J2 **Pappenheim** Germany
37 K6 **Pappenheim** Germany
15 C5 **Paps of Jura** *mt* Scotland
136 J3 **Papua, G. of** Papua New Guinea
136 K3 **Papua New Guinea** *state* S W Pacific
141 H3 **Papuan Passage** Gt Barrier Reef Aust
42 H3 **Papuk** *mt* Croatia
68 C3 **Papun** Burma
140 B6 **Papunya** N Terr Australia
128 E3 **Papuri** *R* Brazil/Colombia
48 J5 **Păpuşa** *mt* Romania
8 B7 **Par** England
129 H4 **Para** *state* Brazil
129 J4 **Parà** *R* Brazil
56 B2 **Parabel'** *R* Russian Federation
143 B6 **Paraburdoo** W Australia Australia
71 F3 **Paracale** Philippines
128 C6 **Paracas, Pena de** *pen* Peru
130 F5 **Paracatu** Brazil
138 E4 **Parachilna** South Australia Australia
46 E1 **Paračin** Serbia Yugoslavia
98 E4 **Parade** South Dakota U.S.A.

130 G6 Pará de Minas Brazil
126 A1 Paradera Aruba W Indies
121 O4 Paradis Quebec Canada
144 B6 Paradise New Zealand
102 C2 Paradise California U.S.A.
107 M2 Paradise Kansas U.S.A.
101 L2 Paradise Montana U.S.A.
109 K2 Paradise Texas U.S.A.
101 O8 Paradise Utah U.S.A.
118 H5 Paradise Hill Saskatchewan Canada
116 H5 Paradise Hill Alaska U.S.A.
113 L9 Paradise I. New Providence I Bahamas
102 G3 Paradise Pk Nevada U.S.A.
118 G5 Paradise Valley Alberta Canada
100 H8 Paradise Valley Nevada U.S.A.
71 J9 Parado Sumbawa Indonesia
75 M8 Pārādwīp India
110 K2 Paragon Indiana U.S.A.
103 M4 Paragonah Utah U.S.A.
110 F5 Paragould Arkansas U.S.A.
128 F6 Paraguá R Bolivia
128 F2 Paragua R Venezuela
130 E8 Paraguaca Paulista Brazil
129 L6 Paraguaçu R Brazil
133 F2 Paraguai R Paraguay
127 J9 Paraguaipoa Venezuela
127 J9 Paraguaná, Pen. de Venezuela
130 B10 Paraguari dept Paraguay
133 F3 Paraguay R Paraguay
133 F2 Paraguay rep S America
130 H9 Paraiba state Brazil
130 G8 Paraiba do Sul Brazil
130 H7 Paraiba, R Brazil
Parainen see Pargas
133 G1 Paraisa Brazil
85 E7 Parakou Benin
138 D4 Parakylia South Australia Australia
75 L9 Paralākhemundi India
76 D6 Paramakkudi India
129 G2 Paramaribo Suriname
20 G4 Paramé France
131 B4 Paramillos, Sa. de los mts Argentina
129 K6 Paramirim Brazil
46 D5 Paramithiá Greece
128 C6 Paramonga Peru
133 E4 Paraná Argentina
130 D9 Paraná state Brazil
130 B10 Paraná R Brazil
130 E9 Paranaguá Brazil
133 G1 Paranaíba Brazil
130 E6 Paranaiba, R Brazil
131 F4 Paraná Ibicuy R Argentina
131 F2 Paraná, L Argentina
129 G2 Paranam Suriname
129 H8 Paranapanema R Brazil
131 F3 Paraná, R Argentina
133 G2 Paranaval Brazil
46 G3 Paranéstion Greece
70 N8 Parang isld Indonesia
71 E8 Parang Philippines
86 F5 Paranga Uganda
83 K8 Parangi Aru R Sri Lanka
76 D5 Parangipettai India
83 K8 Paranthan Sri Lanka
130 G6 Paraopeba Brazil
145 E4 Paraparaumu New Zealand
128 F8 Parapeti R Bolivia
46 F8 Parapóla isld Greece
128 E2 Paraque, Cerro mt Venezuela
71 G5 Parasan isld Philippines
138 E4 Paratoo South Australia Australia
129 H5 Parauapebas R Brazil
18 H6 Paray-le-Monial France
56 B3 Parbig R Russian Federation
122 J3 Parc Archipelago Mingan nat park Quebec Canada
21 L7 Parçay-les-Pins France
20 H5 Parcé Ille-et-Vilaine France
21 K6 Parcé Sarthe France
55 E5 Parchevka Kazakhstan
33 P6 Parchim Germany
45 O7 Parco Naz. del Circeo Italy
22 C3 Parcq, le France
31 O4 Parczew Poland
102 D3 Pardee Res California U.S.A.
99 R6 Pardeeville Wisconsin U.S.A.
80 C4 Pardes Hanna-Karkur Israel
129 H8 Pardo R Brazil
130 F4 Pardo R Minas Gerais Brazil
131 H2 Pardo R Rio Grande do Sul Brazil
142 C5 Pardoo W Australia Australia
130 D7 Pardo, R Mato Grosso Brazil
31 J5 Pardubice Czechoslovakia
70 O9 Pare Java
129 G6 Parecis Brazil
128 F6 Parecis, Sa. dos mts Brazil
133 D3 Pareditas Argentina
145 D1 Parengarenga Harbour New Zealand
70 C6 Parenggean Kalimantan
21 K5 Parennes France
121 Q5 Parent Quebec Canada
18 E8 Parentis en Born France
121 O4 Parent L Quebec Canada
144 C6 Pareora New Zealand
70 F7 Parepare Sulawesi
33 P8 Parey Germany
52 F5 Parfen'yevo Russian Federation
46 D5 Párga Greece
29 J11 Pargas Finland
52 D4 Pargolovo Russian Federation
127 P4 Parham Antigua W Indies
103 N4 Paria R Utah U.S.A.
128 F1 Paria, G. of Venezuela/Trinidad
128 F2 Pariaguán Venezuela
69 E13 Pariaman Sumatra
128 F1 Paria, Pen. de Venezuela
103 M5 Paria Plat Arizona U.S.A.
128 E4 Paricá, L Brazil
70 G5 Parigi Sulawesi
21 L6 Parigné-l'Eveque France
128 G2 Parika Guyana
144 D5 Parikawa New Zealand
145 E3 Parikino New Zealand
29 O10 Parikkala Finland
128 F3 Parima, Sa mts Brazil/Venezuela
128 D7 Parinacocha, L Peru
128 D4 Parinari Peru
128 B4 Pariñas, Pta Peru
48 L4 Parincea Romania
138 F5 Paringa South Australia Australia
129 G4 Parintins Brazil
23 Paris conurbation France
110 C6 Paris Arkansas U.S.A.
101 O7 Paris Idaho U.S.A.
99 T10 Paris Illinois U.S.A.
110 M3 Paris Kentucky U.S.A.
110 E2 Paris Missouri U.S.A.
110 H5 Paris Tennessee U.S.A.
109 M2 Paris Texas U.S.A.
95 L3 Parish New York U.S.A.
99 W3 Parisienne, Ile Ontario Canada
69 E10 Parit Buntar Malaysia
71 L10 Pariti Timor Indonesia
55 D4 Parizh Russian Federation
26 N4 Parkajoki Sweden
29 K9 Parkano Finland
118 L8 Parkbeg Saskatchewan Canada
110 K4 Park City Kentucky U.S.A.
101 R4 Park City Montana U.S.A.
103 N1 Park City Utah U.S.A.
106 E3 Parkdale Colorado U.S.A.
100 D4 Parkdale Oregon U.S.A.
103 K7 Parker Arizona U.S.A.
106 F2 Parker Colorado U.S.A.
101 O6 Parker Idaho U.S.A.
107 Q3 Parker Kansas U.S.A.
98 J6 Parker South Dakota U.S.A.
110 L1 Parker City Indiana U.S.A.
94 H5 Parker City Pennsylvania U.S.A.
103 K7 Parker Dam California U.S.A.
143 D9 Parker Hill W Australia Australia
140 E3 Parker Pt Queensland Australia
143 C9 Parker Range W Australia Australia
99 O7 Parkersburg Iowa U.S.A.
94 F7 Parkersburg West Virginia U.S.A.
99 L3 Parkers Prairie Minnesota U.S.A.
119 O7 Parkerview Saskatchewan Canada
139 J5 Parkes New South Wales Australia
95 M6 Parkesburg Pennsylvania U.S.A.
99 Q4 Park Falls Wisconsin U.S.A.
102 D6 Parkfield California U.S.A.
12 E3 Parkgate Scotland
95 L8 Park Hall Maryland U.S.A.
57 E5 Parkhar Tajikistan
120 J9 Parkhill Ontario Canada
26 K5 Parkijaur L Sweden
110 F6 Parkin Arkansas U.S.A.
118 E9 Park Lake Prov. Park Alberta Canada
118 D8 Parkland Alberta Canada
119 Q9 Parkman Saskatchewan Canada
101 S5 Parkman Wyoming U.S.A.
99 L3 Park Rapids Minnesota U.S.A.
99 T8 Park Ridge Illinois U.S.A.
98 J1 Park River North Dakota U.S.A.
103 N6 Parks Arizona U.S.A.
98 E9 Parks Nebraska U.S.A.
111 L13 Parks Airport St Louis
118 L5 Parkside Saskatchewan Canada
95 M9 Parksley Virginia U.S.A.
140 C6 Parks, Mt N Terr Australia
109 K2 Park Springs Texas U.S.A.
37 N4 Parkstein Germany
98 J6 Parkston South Dakota U.S.A.
95 L7 Parkton Maryland U.S.A.
112 H3 Parkton North Carolina U.S.A.
101 M8 Park Valley Utah U.S.A.
106 D1 Park View Mt Colorado U.S.A.
100 D3 Parkway Washington U.S.A.
26 K5 Pärlälven R Sweden
127 M1 Parlatuvier Tobago
74 G9 Parli Vaijnāth India
45 H2 Parma R Italy
45 H2 Parma Italy
100 J6 Parma Idaho U.S.A.
94 C4 Parma Michigan U.S.A.
110 G5 Parma Missouri U.S.A.
94 F5 Parma Ohio U.S.A.
129 K6 Parnaguá Brazil
129 K4 Parnaiba Brazil
129 J5 Parnaíba R Brazil
46 F6 Parnassós mt Greece
144 D5 Parnassus New Zealand
99 O8 Parnell Iowa U.S.A.
99 M9 Parnell Missouri U.S.A.
108 G1 Parnell Texas U.S.A.
46 F6 Párnis mt Greece
46 F7 Párnon Óros mts Greece
52 B5 Pärnu Estonia
52 B5 Pärnu laht G Estonia
144 C5 Paroa New Zealand
59 M1 Paromay Russian Federation
110 D7 Paron Arkansas U.S.A.
141 G8 Paroo R Queensland Australia
139 G4 Paroo Chan New South Wales Australia
77 G2 Paropamisus mts Afghanistan
70 F6 Paroreang, Bk mt Sulawesi
46 G7 Páros isld Greece
127 J3 Parottee Pt Jamaica
103 M4 Parowan Utah U.S.A.
129 H6 Parque Indigena do Xingu nat park Brazil
99 T8 Parr Indiana U.S.A.
112 F3 Parr South Carolina U.S.A.
8 C5 Parracombe England
133 C5 Parral Chile
139 K5 Parramatta New South Wales Australia
95 M9 Parramore I Virginia U.S.A.
124 H5 Parras de la Fuente Mexico
8 D5 Parrett, R England
111 J8 Parrish Alabama U.S.A.
113 E10 Parrish Florida U.S.A.
112 G5 Parris I South Carolina U.S.A.
112 C6 Parrott Georgia U.S.A.
94 G9 Parrott Virginia U.S.A.
122 H8 Parrsboro Nova Scotia Canada
119 N9 Parry Saskatchewan Canada
115 L4 Parry B Northwest Territories Canada
120 K7 Parry I Ontario Canada
114 H2 Parry Is Northwest Territories Canada
115 M2 Parry, Kap Greenland
127 N3 Parrylands Trinidad
142 B5 Parry Ra W Australia Australia
77 B6 Pars oil well Persian Gulf
33 N7 Parsau Germany
37 M5 Parsberg Germany
41 M3 Parseier Spitze mt Austria
98 D2 Parshall North Dakota U.S.A.
103 K3 Parsnip Pk Nevada U.S.A.
107 P4 Parsons Kansas U.S.A.
110 H6 Parsons Tennessee U.S.A.
94 H7 Parsons West Virginia U.S.A.
123 P3 Parson's Pond Newfoundland Canada
43 E11 Partanna Sicily
26 J4 Pårtefjället mt Sweden
36 E4 Partenheim Germany
21 K8 Parthenay France
46 F7 Parthénion Greece
124 D5 Partida isld Mexico
43 E10 Partinico Sicily
56 D2 Partizansk Russian Federation
59 K3 Partizansk Russian Federation
120 K2 Partridge R Ontario Canada
107 M4 Partridge Kansas U.S.A.
123 R5 Partridgeberry Hills Newfoundland Canada
119 U1 Partridge Breast L Manitoba Canada
123 Q3 Partridge Pt Newfoundland Canada
129 H4 Paru R Brazil
145 E1 Parua Bay New Zealand
77 L2 Parvan prov Afghanistan
66 C6 Paryang China
27 H15 Påryd Sweden
89 E6 Parys S Africa
102 G7 Pasadena California U.S.A.
109 G9 Pasadena Texas U.S.A.
128 B4 Pasado, C Ecuador
133 E3 Pasaje R Argentina
124 H5 Pasaje Mexico
106 G5 Pasamonte New Mexico U.S.A.
70 F5 Pasangkaiu Sulawesi
69 E14 Pasarbantal Sumatra
77 C4 Pasargadae Iran
69 E14 Pasarseblat Sumatra
71 H7 Pasarwadjo Indonesia
111 H11 Pascagoula R Mississippi U.S.A.
121 N4 Pascalis Quebec Canada
48 K3 Paşcani Romania
128 C6 Pasco dept Peru
100 F3 Pasco Washington U.S.A.
95 Q5 Pascoag Rhode I U.S.A.
130 H5 Pascoal, Mte Brazil
142 B5 Pascoe I W Australia Australia
140 E3 Pascoe Inlet Queensland Australia
141 G2 Pascoe, R Queensland Australia
120 A2 Pascopee Ontario Canada
133 C7 Pascua R Chile
18 G2 Pas-de-Calais dept France
22 C3 Pas en Artois France
33 T5 Pasewalk Germany
52 D4 Pasha Russian Federation
52 J3 Pashnya Russian Federation
71 E3 Pasig Luzon Philippines
71 J4 Pasige isld Indonesia
78 H1 Pasinler Turkey
70 O10 Pasirian Java
69 E12 Pasirpangarayan Sumatra
69 F10 Pasir Putih Malaysia
71 K8 Pasitelu, Pulau Pulau islds Indonesia
27 H14 Påskallavik Sweden
102 B2 Paskenta California U.S.A.
31 M1 Pasłęk Poland
143 E10 Pasley, C W Australia Australia
29 L4 Pasmajärvi Finland
42 G5 Pašman isld Croatia
138 E4 Pasmore R South Australia Australia
77 H7 Pasni Pakistan
133 D6 Paso de Indios Argentina
125 M4 Paso del Cascal mt Nicaragua
133 F3 Paso de los Libres Argentina
133 F4 Paso de los Toros Uruguay
130 B10 Paso de Patria Paraguay
68 B2 Pasok Burma
133 C6 Paso Limay Argentina
125 M2 Paso Reál Honduras
133 C7 Paso Rio Mayo Argentina
102 D6 Paso Robles California U.S.A.
122 G5 Paspébiac Quebec Canada
119 M8 Pasqua Saskatchewan Canada
119 O5 Pasquia Hills Saskatchewan Canada
119 Q5 Pasquia R Manitoba Canada
112 L1 Pasquotank R North Carolina U.S.A.
77 C5 Pas Rūdak Iran
95 T1 Passadumkeag Maine U.S.A.
20 F8 Passage du Gois France
120 B4 Passage I Ontario Canada
99 S1 Passage I Michigan U.S.A.
113 E10 Pass-a-Grille Beach Florida U.S.A.
95 N6 Passaic New Jersey U.S.A.
21 J4 Passais France
38 H4 Passau Germany
40 D2 Passavant France
111 G11 Pass Christian Mississippi U.S.A.
101 T8 Pass Cr Wyoming U.S.A.
22 E2 Passendale Belgium
43 G12 Passero, C Sicily
123 Q6 Pass I Newfoundland Canada
71 F5 Passi Philippines
41 O4 Passiria, Val Italy
99 S1 Pass L Ontario Canada
120 B4 Pass Lake Ontario Canada
15 C4 Pass of Brander Scotland
133 H2 Passos Brazil
128 C4 Pastaza prov Ecuador
122 F3 Pasteur, L Quebec Canada
128 C3 Pasto Colombia
116 F5 Pastol B Alaska U.S.A.
9 H2 Paston England
103 P5 Pastora Pk Arizona U.S.A.
129 K5 Pastos Bons Brazil
71 E1 Pasuquin Luzon Philippines
70 O9 Pasuruan Java
52 B6 Pasvalys Lithuania
52 C1 Pasvikelv R Norway
119 O6 Paswegin Saskatchewan Canada
31 M2 Pasym Poland
48 F3 Pásztó Hungary
86 D4 Pata Cent Afr Republic
71 E8 Pata isld Philippines
133 C7 Patagonia terr Chile/Arg
103 O10 Patagonia Arizona U.S.A.
100 H3 Pataha R Washington U.S.A.
77 K1 Pata Kesar Afghanistan
130 G10 Patamuté Brazil
75 L5 Patan Nepal
71 B2 Patani Indonesia
95 L7 Patapsco R Maryland U.S.A.
21 O5 Patay France
138 F6 Patchewollock Victoria Australia
95 P6 Patchogue Long I, New York U.S.A.
88 H3 Pate isld Kenya
145 E3 Patea New Zealand
144 C6 Patearoa New Zealand
85 F7 Pategi Nigeria
43 F11 Paternò Sicily
45 R8 Paternopoli Italy
100 F1 Pateros Washington U.S.A.
141 H8 Paterson R Queensland Australia
95 N6 Paterson New Jersey U.S.A.
100 F4 Paterson Washington U.S.A.
144 B7 Paterson Inlet New Zealand
142 D5 Paterson Ra W Australia Australia
25 G2 Paterswolde Netherlands
74 F2 Pathankot India
74 F9 Pathardi India
Pathein see Bassein
101 T7 Pathfinder Res Wyoming U.S.A.
13 F2 Pathhead Lothian Scotland
12 D3 Pathhead Strathclyde Scotland
68 D7 Pathiu Thailand
119 N6 Pathlow Saskatchewan Canada
74 G9 Pathri India
68 E5 Pathum Thani Thailand
70 N9 Pati Java
128 C3 Patia R Colombia
74 G3 Patiala India
143 F6 Patience Well W Australia Australia
70 G7 Patiro Tg C Sulawesi
128 C6 Pativilca Peru
70 N10 Patjitan Java
75 Q5 Pātkai Bum reg India
109 M2 Pat Mayse Res Texas U.S.A.
47 H7 Pátmos isld Greece
111 C8 Patmos Arkansas U.S.A.
75 L6 Patna India
12 D3 Patna Scotland
75 K8 Patnagarh India
71 F3 Patnanongan isld Luzon Philippines
78 J2 Patnos Turkey
145 F3 Patoka New Zealand
110 G3 Patoka Illinois U.S.A.
110 K3 Patoka R Indiana U.S.A.
99 M7 Paton Iowa U.S.A.
130 H9 Patos Brazil
129 J7 Patos de Minas Brazil
127 N1 Patos, I Trinidad
100 C1 Patos I Washington U.S.A.
131 H3 Patos, Lagoa dos Brazil
108 A5 Patos, Laguna de Mexico
131 E3 Patos, L. de los Santa Fé Argentina
131 B3 Patos, R. de los Argentina
133 D4 Patquía Argentina
46 E6 Pátrai Greece
Patras Greece see Pátrai
28 R9 Patreksfjördhur inlet Iceland
118 F8 Patricia Alberta Canada
98 E6 Patricia South Dakota U.S.A.
140 B5 Patricia, Mt N Terr Australia
133 B7 Patricio Lynch, I Chile
13 G5 Patrick Brompton England
121 T7 Patrie, La Quebec Canada
110 M3 Patriot Indiana U.S.A.
133 H1 Patrocinio Brazil
111 K10 Patsaliga R Alabama U.S.A.
41 O3 Patscherkofel mt Austria
52 C1 Patsoyoki R Russian Federation
43 C8 Pattada Sardinia
57 D6 Pattakesar Uzbekistan
70 F7 Pattalasa Sulawesi Indonesia
76 C6 Pattanapuram India
69 E9 Pattani R Thailand
69 E9 Pattani Thailand
95 S7 Patten Maine U.S.A.
32 L8 Pattensen Germany
13 F5 Patterdale England
102 C4 Patterson California U.S.A.
112 E6 Patterson Georgia U.S.A.
101 M5 Patterson Idaho U.S.A.
111 E12 Patterson Louisiana U.S.A.
94 H7 Patterson Cr West Virginia U.S.A.
117 F3 Patterson, Mt Yukon Territory Canada
102 E5 Patterson Mt California U.S.A.
99 V4 Patterson, Pt Michigan U.S.A.
71 N9 Patti Indonesia
43 F10 Patti Sicily
140 B4 Pattie Cr N Terr Australia
43 G10 Patti, G. di Sicily
80 B8 Pattish R Israel
111 F10 Pattison Mississippi U.S.A.
94 J6 Patton Pennsylvania U.S.A.
99 M9 Pattonsburg Missouri U.S.A.
130 H9 Patu Brazil
78 H2 Patu Turkey
75 O7 Patuakhali Bangladesh
118 K3 Patuanak Saskatchewan Canada
48 H6 Pătuele Romania
70 L9 Patuha, G mt Java
117 J7 Patullo, Mt British Columbia Canada
144 D4 Paturau River New Zealand
145 F3 Patutahi New Zealand
145 E3 Patutu mt New Zealand
95 L8 Patuxent R Maryland U.S.A.
18 E9 Pau France
145 D1 Paua New Zealand
129 J5 Pau D'Arco Brazil
21 O7 Paudy France
121 O7 Paugan Falls Quebec Canada
18 E7 Pauillac France
128 E5 Pauini Brazil
68 B2 Pauk Burma
68 A2 Pauktaw Burma
101 M7 Paul Idaho U.S.A.
38 H8 Paularo Italy
114 G4 Paulatuk Northwest Territories Canada
103 M7 Paulden Arizona U.S.A.
94 C5 Paulding Ohio U.S.A.
18 H9 Paulhan France
115 N6 Paul I Labrador, Nfld Canada
116 H9 Paul I Alaska U.S.A.
100 F5 Paulina Oregon U.S.A.
33 R7 Paulinenaue Germany
Paulis see Isiro
130 J9 Paulista Brazil
129 K5 Paulistana Brazil
99 L7 Paullina Iowa U.S.A.
41 K7 Paullo Italy
21 N8 Paulnay France
130 H10 Paulo Alfonso, Cachoeira de falls Brazil
25 C3 Paulowna Netherlands
107 N7 Pauls Valley Oklahoma U.S.A.
37 M5 Paulushofen Germany
20 G8 Paulx France
68 C4 Paung Burma
68 B3 Paungde Burma
74 H8 Pauni India
74 H3 Pauri India
37 M2 Pausa Germany
128 D7 Pausa Peru
33 S7 Pausin Germany
128 D2 Pauto R Colombia
26 J7 Pauträsk Sweden
22 G5 Pauvres France
135 T3 Pauwela Hawaiian Is
103 M3 Pavant Ra Utah U.S.A.
55 C2 Pavda Russian Federation
46 G2 Pavel Banya Bulgaria
54 L3 Pavelets Russian Federation
44 F1 Pavia Italy
117 N10 Pavilion British Columbia Canada
94 K4 Pavilion New York U.S.A.
101 R6 Pavillion Wyoming U.S.A.
21 M2 Pavilly France
27 M15 Pāvilosta Latvia
52 G5 Pavino Russian Federation
46 G1 Pavlikeni Bulgaria
55 G4 Pavlodar Kazakhstan
116 G9 Pavlof Alaska U.S.A.
116 F9 Pavlof Harbour Aleutian Is
116 G9 Pavlof Vol Alaska U.S.A.
54 G8 Pavlograd Ukraine
55 F4 Pavlogradka Russian Federation
55 F5 Pavlovka Kazakhstan
55 C3 Pavlovka Bashkirskaya Respublika Russian Federation
52 F6 Pavlovo Russian Federation
56 B4 Pavlovsk Altayskiy Kray Russian Federation
52 D5 Pavlovsk Leningradskaya obl Russian Federation
55 D4 Pavlovskiy Kazakhstan
52 H5 Pavlovskiy Permskaya obl Russian Federation
113 D7 Pavo Georgia U.S.A.
45 J3 Pavullo nel Frignano Italy
107 O5 Pawhuska Oklahoma U.S.A.
119 Q3 Pawistik Manitoba Canada
95 O3 Pawlet Vermont U.S.A.
8 D5 Pawlett England
112 H4 Pawleys Island South Carolina U.S.A.
68 C3 Pawn R Burma
99 R10 Pawnee Illinois U.S.A.
107 O5 Pawnee Oklahoma U.S.A.
109 K7 Pawnee Texas U.S.A.
99 L9 Pawnee City Nebraska U.S.A.
98 C9 Pawnee Cr Colorado U.S.A.
107 L3 Pawnee Rock Kansas U.S.A.
94 B4 Paw Paw Michigan U.S.A.
94 J7 Paw Paw West Virginia U.S.A.
95 Q5 Pawtucket Rhode I U.S.A.
46 G9 Paximádhia isld Crete Greece
Paxoi see Paxos
47 P13 Paxos isld Greece
116 P5 Paxson Alaska U.S.A.
116 P5 Paxson L Alaska U.S.A.
99 S9 Paxton Illinois U.S.A.
98 E8 Paxton Nebraska U.S.A.
68 C4 Payagyi Burma
71 A2 Payahe Halmahera Indonesia
79 G2 Payas Turkey
58 E3 Pa-yen-kao-le China
40 E4 Payerne Switzerland
100 J5 Payette R Idaho U.S.A.
100 J5 Payette Idaho U.S.A.
109 L3 Pay Hubbard, L Texas U.S.A.
50 F2 Pay-Khoy, Khrebet mt Russian Federation
112 D5 Payne Georgia U.S.A.
94 C5 Payne Ohio U.S.A.
115 M6 Payne, L Quebec Canada
102 C1 Paynes Cr California U.S.A.
143 C8 Payne's Find W Australia Australia
99 M4 Paynesville Minnesota U.S.A.
118 J5 Paynton Saskatchewan Canada
131 F4 Paysandu Uruguay
21 K3 Pays-d'Auge reg France
21 O2 Pays-de-Bray reg France
19 N13 Pays de Dombes reg France
40 F5 Pays d'Enhaut Switzerland
103 N7 Payson Arizona U.S.A.
103 N1 Payson Utah U.S.A.
57 K6 Paytug Uzbekistan
131 B6 Payún vol Argentina
70 C3 Payung Tanjong C Sarawak
131 B6 Payún Matru, Cerros hills Argentina
77 A4 Pāzanūn Iran
46 G2 Pazardzhik Bulgaria
47 J5 Pazarköy Turkey
47 J6 Pazaryeri Turkey
124 D5 Paz, B. de la Mexico
128 D2 Paz de Rio Colombia
42 F3 Pazin Croatia
41 M3 Paznauntal Austria
52 D5 Pchevzha Russian Federation
31 M6 Pcim Poland
46 E2 Pčinja R Serbia/Macedonia Yugoslavia
68 D6 Pe Burma
111 L10 Pea R Alabama U.S.A.
117 R6 Peace Point Alberta Canada
118 A2 Peace R Alberta Canada
117 M7 Peace R Br Col/Alberta Canada
113 F10 Peace R Florida U.S.A.
117 P7 Peace River Alberta Canada
117 O11 Peachland British Columbia Canada
103 L6 Peach Sp Arizona U.S.A.
94 B2 Peacock Michigan U.S.A.
141 J5 Peak Downs Queensland Australia
138 D3 Peake R South Australia Australia
71 D5 Peaked Pt Philippines
140 B3 Peake, Mt N Terr Australia
143 C7 Peak Hill W Australia Australia
102 E7 Peak Mt California U.S.A.
141 J6 Peak Ra Queensland Australia
103 P3 Peale, Mt Utah U.S.A.
100 B9 Peanut California U.S.A.
118 D9 Pearce Alberta Canada
103 P10 Pearce Arizona U.S.A.
140 A2 Pearce Pt N Terr Australia
111 C7 Pearcy Arkansas U.S.A.
116 H1 Peard B Alaska U.S.A.
110 C5 Pea Ridge Nat. Mil. Park Arkansas U.S.A.
119 P2 Pearl Ontario Canada
110 F2 Pearl Illinois U.S.A.
111 F9 Pearl Mississippi U.S.A.
111 G11 Pearl R Miss/Louisiana U.S.A.
109 G10 Pearland Texas U.S.A.
134 K5 Pearl and Hermes Atoll Hawaiian Is U.S.A.
102 S12 Pearl City Hawaiian Is
99 R7 Pearl City Illinois U.S.A.
102 S12 Pearl Hbr Hawaiian Is
144 A7 Pearl I New Zealand
109 H7 Pearsall Texas U.S.A.
112 E6 Pearson Georgia U.S.A.
138 C5 Pearson Is South Australia Australia
119 V2 Pearson L Manitoba Canada
114 J2 Peary Ch Northwest Territories Canada
109 H1 Pease R Texas U.S.A.
20 F6 Péaule France
99 S3 Peavy Falls Res Michigan U.S.A.
142 C5 Peawah, R W Australia Australia
88 G10 Pebane Mozambique
128 D4 Pebas Peru
133 F8 Pebble I Falkland Is
70 G5 Pebengko Sulawesi
46 D2 Peć Serbia Yugoslavia
111 D12 Pecan Island Louisiana U.S.A.
130 E9 Peças, I. das Brazil
99 R7 Pecatonica R Illinois U.S.A.
99 R7 Pecatonica Illinois U.S.A.
45 J4 Péccioli Italy
48 L5 Pechea Romania
48 J2 Pechenezhin Ukraine
54 H6 Pechenezhskoye Vodokhranilishche res Ukraine
29 P2 Pechenga Russian Federation
55 D1 Pecherakh Russian Federation
52 J2 Pechora Russian Federation
52 J3 Pechora R Russian Federation
50 E2 Pechorskaya Guba sea Russian Federation
52 C5 Pechory Russian Federation
48 G4 Pecica Romania
100 B7 Peck Oregon U.S.A.
33 S5 Peckatel Germany
32 K9 Peckelsheim Germany
43 B9 Pecora, C Sardinia
43 G10 Pecoraro, M mt Italy
106 E6 Pecos New Mexico U.S.A.
106 F6 Pecos R New Mexico U.S.A.
108 D4 Pecos Texas U.S.A.
108 F5 Pecos R Texas/Mexico U.S.A./Mexico
106 E6 Pecos Nat. Mon New Mexico U.S.A.
48 E4 Pécs Hungary
48 E4 Pécsvárad Hungary
110 B3 Peculiar Missouri U.S.A.
125 O6 Pedasí Panama
139 H9 Pedder, L Tasmania Australia
100 B5 Pedee Oregon U.S.A.
127 J5 Pedernales Dominican Rep
124 F3 Pedernales Mexico
127 N10 Pedernales Venezuela
28 H6 Pedersborg Denmark
70 L9 Pedes Java
79 C4 Pedhoulas Cyprus
138 D2 Pedirka South Australia Australia
71 A2 Pediwang Indonesia
129 K7 Pedra Azul Brazil
130 J9 Pedra, Pta. de C Brazil
128 F6 Pedras Negras Brazil
124 H5 Pedriceña Mexico
129 J5 Pedro Afonso Brazil
126 E6 Pedro Bank Caribbean
116 K7 Pedro Bay Alaska U.S.A.
126 D3 Pedro Betancourt Cuba
126 F6 Pedro Cays reefs Caribbean
Peebles co see Borders reg
140 D7 Peebles, Mt N Terr Australia
142 B5 Peedamulla W Australia Australia
12 D5 Peel I of Man U.K.
144 C5 Peel, Mt New Zealand
103 M7 Peeples Valley Arizona U.S.A.
117 Q7 Peerless L Alberta Canada
118 A5 Peers Alberta Canada
139 G4 Peery, L New South Wales Australia
106 G1 Peetz Colorado U.S.A.
98 K4 Peever South Dakota U.S.A.
144 D5 Pegasus Bay New Zealand
37 N1 Pegau Germany
38 M7 Peggau Austria
44 E3 Pegli Italy
37 M4 Pegnitz Germany
17 G6 Pego Spain
45 J2 Pegognaga Italy
101 O7 Pegram Idaho U.S.A.
13 G3 Pegswood England
69 F13 Peg Tigabuluh mt Sumatra
68 C4 Pegu Burma
69 E13 Pegunungan Barisan mt Sumatra
69 K12 Pegunungan Bayang mt Indonesia
68 B3 Pegu Yoma ra Burma
9 H5 Pegwell B England
52 H3 Pegysh Russian Federation
46 F3 Pehčevo Macedonia Yugoslavia
67 B1 Peijiangchang China
67 G3 Pei-Kan-t'ang Tao isld Taiwan
20 F6 Peillac France
38 M5 Peilstein mt Austria
32 M8 Peine Germany
133 C8 Peineta mt Chile
68 B2 Peinwa Burma
19 P16 Peipin France
Peipsi Järv see Peipus, L
52 C5 Peipus, L Estonia/Rus Fed
41 N2 Peiting Germany
133 G2 Peixe R Brazil
130 C5 Peixe de Couro, R Brazil
65 C7 Pei Xian China
65 D7 Pei Xian China
69 H12 Pejantan isld Indonesia
48 G6 Pek R Serbia Yugoslavia
70 F6 Pekabata Sulawesi
70 M9 Pekalongan Java
69 F11 Pekan Malaysia
69 E12 Pekanbaru Sumatra
99 R9 Pekin Illinois U.S.A.
110 G1 Pekin Illinois U.S.A.
98 H2 Pekin North Dakota U.S.A.
Peking see Beijing
117 Q10 Pekisko Alberta Canada
29 M5 Pekkala Finland
68 C3 Pekon Burma
69 E11 Pelabuhan Kelang Malaysia
43 E13 Pelagie, Isole Italy
45 L4 Pelago Italy
46 G5 Pélagos isld Greece
111 G9 Pelahatchee Mississippi U.S.A.
69 F12 Pelalawan Sumatra
17 G4 Pelarda, Sa mts Spain
46 F6 Pelasyía Greece
89 F7 Pelatsoeu mt Lesotho
70 F4 Pelawanbesar Kalimantan
31 J2 Pełczyce Poland
48 H5 Peleaga mt Romania
56 H2 Peleduy R Russian Federation
120 H10 Pelee Island Ontario Canada
127 L4 Pelée, Mt Martinique W Indies
47 O12 Pélekas Greece
71 H5 Peleng isld Indonesia
71 H5 Peleng, Selat str Sulawesi
71 H5 Peleng, Tk B Indonesia
112 C6 Pelham Georgia U.S.A.
31 J6 Pelhřimov Czechoslovakia
119 R6 Pelican B Manitoba Canada
113 L11 Pelican Harbour Bahamas
118 D3 Pelican L Alberta Canada
119 S9 Pelican L Manitoba Canada
119 O3 Pelican L Saskatchewan Canada
99 O1 Pelican L Minnesota U.S.A.
99 R4 Pelican L Wisconsin U.S.A.
118 E3 Pelican Portage Alberta Canada
141 G3 Pelican R Queensland Australia
119 R6 Pelican Rapids Manitoba Canada
98 K3 Pelican Rapids Minnesota U.S.A.
48 L3 Peliniya Moldavia
59 L1 Peliny Osipenko, imeni Russian Federation
112 F4 Pelion South Carolina U.S.A.
26 J5 Peljekaise Nat. Park Sweden
42 H6 Pelješac pen Croatia
29 N4 Pelkosenniemi Finland
52 D3 Pelkula Russian Federation
32 G9 Pelkum Germany
43 G8 Pella Italy
80 F4 Pella Jordan
99 O8 Pella Iowa U.S.A.
111 K8 Pell City Alabama U.S.A.
133 E5 Pellegrini Argentina
133 D5 Pellegrini, L Argentina
21 H5 Pellerine, la France
20 G7 Pellerin, le France
45 M1 Pellestrina Italy
119 U2 Pelletier L Manitoba Canada
21 N8 Pellevoisin France
140 D3 Pellew C N Terr Australia
36 B4 Pellingen Germany
29 L5 Pello Finland
21 K6 Pellouailles France
94 C1 Pellston Michigan U.S.A.
30 D1 Pellworm isld Germany
119 Q7 Pelly Saskatchewan Canada
117 E4 Pelly R Yukon Territory Canada
115 L4 Pelly Bay Northwest Territories Canada
117 E4 Pelly Crossing Yukon Territory Canada
114 J4 Pelly L Northwest Territories Canada
117 G5 Pelly Mts Yukon Territory Canada
71 J8 Pelokang isld Indonesia
46 E7 Pelopónnisos admin region Greece
43 G11 Peloritani, Mi mts Sicily
145 D4 Pelorus Sound New Zealand
131 H3 Pelotas Brazil
130 D10 Pelotas, R.das Brazil
46 G1 Pelovo Bulgaria
31 L2 Pelplin Poland
143 A8 Pelsart Group islds W Australia Australia
33 T5 Pelsin Germany
110 C6 Pelsor Arkansas U.S.A.
29 L3 Peltovuoma Finland
44 B2 Pelvo d'Elva mt Italy
19 Q15 Pelvoux, Mt France
55 D1 Pelym R Russian Federation
55 D2 Pelym Russian Federation
55 D1 Pelymskiy Tuman, Oz L Russian Federation
8 B7 Pelynt England
112 E3 Pelzer South Carolina U.S.A.
33 N4 Pelzerhaken Germany
120 G5 Pemache, R Ontario Canada
95 S1 Pemadumcook L Maine U.S.A.
70 M9 Pemalang Java
70 M9 Pemalang, Ujung C Java
71 H5 Pemali, Tg C Sulawesi
69 J12 Pemangkat Indonesia
70 E5 Pemarung, P Kalimantan
69 D11 Pematangsiantar Sumatra
88 H8 Pemba Mozambique
87 E9 Pemba Zambia
87 H8 Pemba, B.de Mozambique
88 G4 Pemba I Tanzania
143 B10 Pemberton W Australia Australia
117 M10 Pemberton British Columbia Canada
98 H1 Pembina R Manitoba Canada
119 U10 Pembina North Dakota U.S.A.
119 T9 Pembina Mt Manitoba Canada
118 B5 Pembina Oil Fields Alberta Canada
118 C5 Pembina Prov. Park Alberta Canada
118 C4 Pembina R Alberta Canada
99 T4 Pembine Wisconsin U.S.A.
Pembroke co see Dyfed
121 N7 Pembroke Ontario Canada
112 F5 Pembroke Georgia U.S.A.
110 J5 Pembroke Kentucky U.S.A.
112 H3 Pembroke North Carolina U.S.A.
94 G9 Pembroke Virginia U.S.A.
8 B4 Pembroke Wales
133 F8 Pembroke, C Falkland Is
144 A6 Pembroke, Mt New Zealand
9 G5 Pembury England
70 B5 Pemuar Kalimantan
127 J5 Peña Dominican Rep
106 D6 Penablanca New Mexico U.S.A.
95 Q3 Penacook New Hampshire U.S.A.
17 G2 Peña de Oroel mt ra Spain
16 B3 Penafiel Portugal
16 E3 Peñafiel Spain
17 G4 Peñagolosa mt Spain
127 O3 Penal Trinidad
8 B4 Penally Wales
70 D3 Penambo Ra Kalimantan
16 C3 Peña Mira mt Spain
70 E2 Penampang Sabah
131 B2 Peña Negra, Pasco de Arg/Chile
125 K6 Peña Nevada, Cerro mt Mexico
Penang see Pinang isld
130 E7 Penápolis Brazil
16 D1 Peña Prieta mt Spain
16 D4 Peñaranda de Bracamonte Spain
95 M6 Pen Argyl Pennsylvania U.S.A.
139 G5 Penarie New South Wales Australia
17 G4 Peñarroya mt Spain
16 D6 Peñarroya-Pueblonuevo Spain
8 C5 Penarth Wales
16 C1 Peña Rubia mt Spain
17 G2 Peña, Sa. de la mts Spain
124 M4 Peñas Blancas Nicaragua
16 D1 Peñas, C. de Spain
106 E5 Penasco New Mexico U.S.A.
108 C3 Penasco, Rio R New Mexico U.S.A.
16 E3 Peñas de Cervera Spain
17 F6 Peñas de San Pedro Spain
133 C7 Penas, G.de Chile
69 B10 Penasi, Pulau isld Sumatra
127 N9 Peñas, Pta Venezuela
16 C2 Peña Trevinca mt Spain
16 D1 Peña Vieja mt Spain
100 H3 Penawawa Washington U.S.A.
65 F4 Pen-ch'i China
146 J12 Penck, C Antarctica
131 C4 Pencoso, Alto de mt Argentina
70 C5 Pendadahian Kalimantan
46 E4 Pendálofon Greece
118 F9 Pendant d'Oreille Alberta Canada
86 C4 Pende R Cent Afr Republic
46 F6 Pendelikón mt Greece
85 B7 Pendembu Sierra Leone
130 H8 Pendencia Brazil
142 E3 Pender W Australia Australia
98 K7 Pender Nebraska U.S.A.
142 E3 Pender Bay W Australia Australia
144 A6 Pender, Mt New Zealand
47 N11 Pendik Turkey
8 B4 Pendine Wales
13 F6 Pendlebury England
13 F6 Pendle Hill England
94 B7 Pendleton Indiana U.S.A.
100 G4 Pendleton Oregon U.S.A.
112 E3 Pendleton South Carolina U.S.A.
117 J6 Pendleton, Mt British Columbia Canada
69 F14 Pendopo Sumatra
100 H1 Pend Oreille R Washington U.S.A.
117 P11 Pend Oreille, L Idaho U.S.A.
101 N1 Pendroy Montana U.S.A.
69 J13 Penebangan isld Indonesia
16 B3 Peneda mt Portugal
129 L6 Penedo Brazil
20 F7 Penestin France
94 J5 Penfield Pennsylvania U.S.A.
70 L9 Pengalengan Java
67 B1 Peng'an China
67 G4 P'eng-chia Hsü isld Taiwan
86 D7 Penge Zaire
67 F5 P'eng-hu Lieh-tao isld Taiwan
67 F5 P'eng-hu Tao isld Taiwan
69 J12 Pengiki isld Indonesia
67 E4 Pengkou China
65 E6 Penglai China
58 G5 Peng-pu China
67 A1 Pengshan China
67 C2 Pengshui China
139 H8 Penguin Tasmania Australia
142 F2 Penguin Deeps Timor Sea
67 B1 Pengxi China
67 A1 Peng Xian China
67 E2 Pengze China
130 E10 Penha Brazil
20 A5 Penhir, Pte de France
118 D6 Penhold Alberta Canada
8 D4 Penhow Wales
120 F3 Penhurst Ontario Canada
44 F2 Penice mt Italy
16 A5 Peniche Portugal
13 E2 Penicuik Scotland
70 P10 Penida isld Indonesia
37 O2 Penig Germany
71 G5 Peninsula Pt Philippines
69 E10 Peninsular Malaysia S E Asia
17 H4 Peñíscola Spain
13 G6 Penistone England
70 M9 Penju, Teluk B Java
78 K4 Penjwin Iran
38 H8 Penk Austria
56 B3 Pen'ki Russian Federation
8 D2 Penkridge England
8 C1 Penmaenmawr Wales
20 B6 Penmarc'h France
20 B6 Penmarc'h, Pte de France
118 K5 Penn Saskatchewan Canada
45 M4 Pennabilli Italy
45 L4 Penna, M mt Italy
118 J8 Pennant Saskatchewan Canada
122 J9 Pennant Pt Nova Scotia Canada
42 F6 Penna, Pta. della Italy
42 F6 Penne Italy
18 F8 Penne d'Agenais France
146 C11 Pennell Bank sea feature Antarctica
146 C12 Pennell Coast coast Antarctica
138 E6 Penneshaw South Australia Australia
122 F8 Pennfield New Brunswick Canada
40 G5 Pennine, Alpi mts Switzerland
7 J8 Pennine Chain mts England
26 G7 Penningkejsen mt Norway/Sweden
95 N6 Pennington New Jersey U.S.A.
109 M4 Pennington Texas U.S.A.
94 D10 Pennington Gap Virginia U.S.A.
42 E5 Pennino, M mt Italy
95 M6 Pennsburg Pennsylvania U.S.A.
95 M7 Penns Grove New Jersey U.S.A.
94 H6 Pennsylvania state U.S.A.
95 K4 Penn Yan New York U.S.A.
12 B1 Pennyghael Scotland
115 N4 Penny Ice Cap Northwest Territories Canada
146 D11 Penny Point pt Antarctica
115 K2 Penny Str Northwest Territories Canada
52 D6 Peno Russian Federation
95 T1 Penobscot R Maine U.S.A.
95 T2 Penobscot B Maine U.S.A.
122 G8 Penobsquis New Brunswick Canada
138 F6 Penola South Australia Australia
124 G5 Peñón Blanco Mexico
138 C4 Penong South Australia Australia
125 O5 Penonomé Panama
100 C8 Penoyar California U.S.A.
8 B2 Penrhyndeudraeth Wales
139 K5 Penrith New South Wales Australia
13 F4 Penrith England
8 A7 Penryn England
111 J11 Pensacola Florida U.S.A.
113 K10 Pensacola Cay Bahamas
146 E8 Pensacola Mts Antarctica
119 N8 Pense Saskatchewan Canada
8 D5 Pensford England

138 F7 Penshurst Victoria Australia
9 G5 Penshurst England
70 E2 Pensiangan Sabah
137 O5 Pentecost I Vanuatu
142 G3 Pentecost, R W Australia Australia
Pentecôte, Î see Pentecost
122 E4 Pentecôte, L Quebec Canada
48 K5 Penteleu mt Romania
117 O11 Penticton British Columbia Canada
141 H5 Pentland Queensland Australia
15 E2 Pentland Firth Scotland
13 E2 Pentland Hills Scotland
15 F2 Pentland Skerries Orkney Scotland
8 B1 Pentraeth Wales
8 C1 Pentre-Foelas Wales
94 A3 Pentwater Michigan U.S.A.
131 E5 Penuajo Argentina
69 G13 Penuba Indonesia
69 G14 Penuguan Sumatra
69 F10 Penunjok, Tanjong C Malaysia
20 D4 Penvénan France
68 C3 Penwegon Burma
8 C1 Pen-y-benclog Wales
8 B1 Penybont Wales
8 B3 Pen-y-groes Wales
53 F7 Penza Russian Federation
119 M7 Penzance Saskatchewan Canada
9 F6 Penzance Scotland
41 O2 Penzberg Germany
51 Q2 Penzhinskaya Guba G Russian Federation
33 S6 Penzlin Germany
100 H3 Peola Washington U.S.A.
101 R1 Peoples Cr Montana U.S.A.
103 M8 Peoria Arizona U.S.A.
99 R8 Peoria Illinois U.S.A.
89 C6 Pepani watercourse S Africa
85 B7 Pepel Sierra Leone
25 F3 Peperga Netherlands
145 D4 Pepin I New Zealand
99 O5 Pepin, L Wisconsin U.S.A.
22 K2 Pepinster Belgium
130 D10 Pepiri Guaçu, R Brazil
44 B3 Pépoiri, Mt France
46 D3 Peqin Albania
131 H3 Pequena, L Brazil
124 C4 Pequeña, Pta C Mexico
103 K1 Pequop Mts Nevada U.S.A.
99 M3 Pequot Lakes Minnesota U.S.A.
37 O7 Perach Germany
141 F2 Pera Hd Queensland Australia
70 M9 Perahu, Gunung mt Java
69 E10 Perai Malaysia
69 D10 Perak isld Malaysia
69 E10 Perak prov Malaysia
46 F6 Perakhóra Greece
38 G8 Peralba mt Italy
106 D7 Peralta New Mexico U.S.A.
46 G9 Pérama Crete Greece
69 F13 Peramp Sumatra
29 M5 Perä-Posio Finland
29 K9 Peräseinäjoki Finland
80 E3 Perazon Israel
122 H5 Perce Quebec Canada
21 J3 Percée, Pte. de la France
18 G10 Perche, Col de la pass France
21 M4 Perche, Coteaux du hills France
8 B2 Percillan Hd Wales
45 N5 Percile Italy
99 L9 Percival Iowa U.S.A.
142 E5 Percival Ls W Australia Australia
21 H4 Percy France
110 E3 Percy Illinois U.S.A.
99 N8 Percy Iowa U.S.A.
141 K5 Percy Is Queensland Australia
143 D9 Percy, L W Australia Australia
133 D6 Perdido R Argentina
17 H2 Perdido mt Spain
111 J11 Perdido Alabama/Florida U.S.A.
18 F10 Perdido, M mt Spain
130 B7 Perdido, R Brazil
118 K6 Perdue Saskatchewan Canada
122 B3 Perdu, L Quebec Canada
99 U6 Pere H Michigan U.S.A.
48 G2 Perechin Ukraine
48 J2 Pereginskoye Ukraine
50 F2 Peregrebnoye Russian Federation
128 C3 Pereira Colombia
130 D7 Pereira Barreto Brazil
Pereira de Eça see Ondjiva
129 G5 Pereirinha Brazil
17 H4 Perello Spain
94 A3 Pere Marquette R Michigan U.S.A.
146 G13 Peremennyy, C Antarctica
48 J1 Peremyshlyany Ukraine
143 B8 Perenjori W Australia Australia
116 L7 Perenosa B Alaska U.S.A.
52 E6 Pereslavl' Zalesskiy Russian Federation
45 O5 Pereto Italy
48 H2 Pereval Veretski mt Ukraine
55 B5 Perevolotskiy Russian Federation
54 C6 Pereyaslav Khmel'nitskiy Ukraine
133 D3 Pérez Chile
100 D8 Perez California U.S.A.
69 C8 Perforated I Thailand
131 E4 Pergamino Argentina
Pergamon see Bergama
45 N4 Pergola Italy
52 E4 Perguba Russian Federation
99 L3 Perham Minnesota U.S.A.
69 F10 Perhentian Besar isld Malaysia
29 L6 Perho Finland
29 L8 Perhojoki R Finland
48 F4 Peri France
121 T3 Péribonca R Quebec Canada
121 S4 Péribonca Quebec Canada
122 A3 Péribonca L Quebec Canada
133 D2 Perico Argentina
124 F5 Pericos Mexico
20 H3 Périers France
129 J3 Perigoso, Can Brazil
18 F7 Périgueux France
127 H9 Perijá, Sa. de mts Colombia/Venezuela
123 P2 Peril B Quebec Canada
17 F1 Peril Str Alaska U.S.A.
72 E6 Perim isld Yemen
118 C2 Perimeter Highway Manitoba Canada
130 H10 Periquito, Se do mts Brazil
46 E5 Peristéra isld Greece
46 E5 Peristéri mt Greece
133 C7 Perito Moreno Argentina
47 P13 Perivóli Greece
76 K4 Periyakulam India
95 M6 Perkasie Pennsylvania U.S.A.
69 C12 Perkat, Tanjong C Indonesia
112 F5 Perkins Georgia U.S.A.
111 C11 Perkins Louisiana U.S.A.
99 T4 Perkins Michigan U.S.A.
111 G11 Perkinston Mississippi U.S.A.
103 M7 Perkinsville Arizona U.S.A.
53 F11 Per Klukhorskiy pass Russian Federation
42 G5 Perković Croatia
22 L5 Perl Germany
41 P1 Perlach Germany
78 B2 Perlas, Arch. de las islds Panama
33 P6 Perleberg Germany
37 P6 Perlesreut Germany

54 K5 Perlevka Russian Federation
98 K2 Perley Minnesota U.S.A.
48 F5 Perlez Serbia Yugoslavia
69 E9 Perlis prov Malaysia
52 J5 Perm' Russian Federation
101 L2 Perma Montana U.S.A.
53 F11 Per Mamisonskiy pass Georgia/Rus Fed
52 G5 Per Marukhskiy pass Georgia/Rus Fed
46 D4 Përmet Albania
55 C2 Permskaya Oblast' prov Russian Federation
69 G14 Pernambuco state Brazil
138 D4 Pernambuco see Recife
107 N7 Pernell Oklahoma U.S.A.
22 C3 Pernes France
48 F2 Pernik Bulgaria
29 K11 Perniö Finland
25 B5 Pernis Netherlands
40 C5 Peron France
143 A7 Peron, C W Australia Australia
140 B2 Peron Is N Terr Australia
22 D4 Péronne France
22 G3 Péronnes Belgium
143 A7 Peron Pen W Australia Australia
21 O5 Pérouville France
18 G10 Perpignan France
112 L1 Perquimans R North Carolina U.S.A.
8 A7 Perranporth England
21 O4 Perray-en-Yvelines, le France
20 D5 Perret France
21 N3 Perriers-sur-Andelle France
109 J2 Perrin Texas U.S.A.
113 G12 Perrine Florida U.S.A.
102 G8 Perris California U.S.A.
40 B2 Perrogney France
108 B1 Perron France
21 N4 Perron Quebec Canada
20 D4 Perros-Guirec France
120 F5 Perry Ontario Canada
110 D6 Perry Arkansas U.S.A.
110 D6 Perry Florida U.S.A.
112 D5 Perry Georgia U.S.A.
110 F2 Perry Illinois U.S.A.
99 M8 Perry Iowa U.S.A.
94 C4 Perry Michigan U.S.A.
110 E2 Perry Missouri U.S.A.
107 N5 Perry New York U.S.A.
107 N5 Perry Oklahoma U.S.A.
116 O6 Perry I Alaska U.S.A.
120 D2 Perry L Kansas U.S.A.
110 A2 Perry L Kansas U.S.A.
95 L7 Perryman Maryland U.S.A.
95 P7 Perrysburg Ohio U.S.A.
108 D7 Perryton Texas U.S.A.
118 D4 Perryvale Alberta Canada
110 D6 Perryville Arkansas U.S.A.
110 G4 Perryville Missouri U.S.A.
21 P3 Persan France
Persepolis see Takht-e Jamshid
99 L7 Perseverancia Bolivia
121 O4 Pershing Quebec Canada
8 D3 Pershore England
54 H8 Pershotravensk Ukraine
Persia see Iran
27 J14 Persian Gulf S W Asia
Persnäs Sweden
Perth co see Central and Tayside regions
139 H8 Perth Tasmania Australia
143 B9 Perth W Australia Australia
121 O8 Perth Ontario Canada
12 E1 Perth Scotland
107 N4 Perth Kansas U.S.A.
98 G1 Perth North Dakota U.S.A.
95 N6 Perth Amboy New Jersey U.S.A.
122 E7 Perth-Andover New Brunswick Canada
38 L4 Pertisau Austria
41 P3 Pertsholz Austria
52 E3 Pertominsk Russian Federation
122 B6 Pertre, le France
52 G5 Pertunmaa Finland
127 H5 Pertuyugskiy Russian Federation
128 D6 Peru R New Guinea
99 R8 Peru S America
123 M7 Peru Illinois U.S.A.
94 A6 Peru Indiana U.S.A.
99 L9 Peru Nebraska U.S.A.
95 O2 Peru New York U.S.A.
135 S12 Peru-Chile Trench Pacific Oc
42 E5 Perugia Italy
129 J8 Peruíbe Brazil
46 G2 Perushtitsa Bulgaria
42 G4 Perušić Croatia
22 K4 Peruwelz Belgium
78 J3 Pervari Turkey
54 G4 Pervomaysk Russian Federation
55 F5 Pervomayka Kazakhstan
54 K8 Pervomayka Ukraine
52 H4 Pervomayskaya Russian Federation
55 C4 Pervomayskiy Kazakhstan
43 F11 Pervomayskiy Orenburgskaya obl Russian Federation
51 L1 Pervomayskiy Sverdlovskaya obl Russian Federation
55 D2 Pervomayskiy Bashkirskaya Respublika Russian Federation
55 C3 Pervomayskoye Russian Federation
55 Q2 Pervomayskoye Russian Federation
55 C3 Pervoural'sk Russian Federation
22 H2 Perwez Belgium
52 D5 Pes' R Russian Federation
44 B4 Pesa R Italy
80 B6 Pesagot Jordan
52 G4 Pesaguan Kalimantan
45 N4 Pesaro Italy
102 B4 Pescadero California U.S.A.
Pescadores see P'eng-hu Lieh-tao
45 J4 Pescaglia Italy
45 L4 Pescara R Italy
45 O5 Pescara Italy
45 L7 Pescasseroli Italy
45 N5 Peschici Italy
45 K5 Peschiera del Garda Italy
100 A9 Pescia Italy
45 P5 Pesco Sannita Italy
52 A4 Pescosolido Italy
58 E4 Peshawar Pakistan
46 D3 Peshkopi Albania
52 G2 Peshtera Bulgaria
99 T4 Peshtigo Wisconsin U.S.A.
55 Q2 Peski Kazakhstan
55 C5 Peski Praral'skiye Karkumy Kazakhstan
48 H3 Peski Sundukli Turkmenistan
52 H5 Peskovka Russian Federation
38 N8 Pesnica R Slovenia
16 B3 Peso da Regua Portugal
110 H2 Pesotum Illinois U.S.A.
129 L5 Pesqueira Brazil
18 E8 Pessac France

33 R7 Pessin Germany
48 E3 Pest co Hungary
48 H6 Peșteana Jiu Romania
52 E5 Pestovo Russian Federation
52 F6 Pestyaki Russian Federation
46 E5 Péta Greece
80 C5 Petah Tiqwa Israel
29 L9 Petäjävesi Finland
71 B2 Petak, Tg C Halmahera Indonesia
48 J3 Petalax Finland
69 G14 Petaling Sumatra
25 C3 Petalioí isld Greece
46 G7 Petalión Kólpos G Greece
70 E6 Petaluma California U.S.A.
127 L9 Petare Venezuela
121 P6 Petatake, L Quebec Canada
88 C9 Petauke Zambia
121 N7 Petawawa Ontario Canada
125 P9 Petén Itzá, L Guatemala
99 R5 Petenwell Lake res Wisconsin U.S.A.
120 G4 Peterboell Ontario Canada
138 E5 Peterborough South Australia Australia
121 M8 Peterborough Ontario Canada
9 F2 Peterborough England
95 Q4 Peterborough New Hampshire U.S.A.
15 F3 Petercuter Scotland
15 G3 Peterhead Scotland
32 F6 Peter I Øy isld Antarctica
14 B5 Peterlee England
140 B6 Petermann Aboriginal Land N Terr Australia
115 O1 Petermann Gletscher gla Greenland
131 B5 Petermann Ra N Terr/W Aust Australia
118 H2 Peter Pond L Saskatchewan Canada
36 H2 Petersberg Germany
117 G7 Petersburg Alaska U.S.A.
110 G1 Petersburg Illinois U.S.A.
37 N6 Petersburg Indiana U.S.A.
94 D5 Petersburg Michigan U.S.A.
98 H8 Petersburg Nebraska U.S.A.
98 H1 Petersburg North Dakota U.S.A.
94 J6 Petersburg Pennsylvania U.S.A.
110 K6 Petersburg Tennessee U.S.A.
108 F2 Petersburg Texas U.S.A.
94 K9 Petersburg Virginia U.S.A.
36 F6 Petersburg West Virginia U.S.A.
116 M5 Peters Creek Alaska U.S.A.
119 V8 Petersfield Manitoba Canada
9 F5 Petersfield England
36 E4 Petershagen Germany
36 F6 Petershagen Germany
32 J8 Petershagen Germany
37 L7 Petershausen Germany
99 L1 Petersham Massachusetts U.S.A.
90 D16 Peter 1st I Antarctica
116 M5 Petersville Alaska U.S.A.
143 E7 Peterswald Hill W Australia Australia
123 R4 Peterview Newfoundland Canada
111 H11 Petila Policastro Italy
17 G2 Petilla de Aragón Spain
36 F4 Petit Bois I France
74 F3 Petit Bourg Guadeloupe W Indies
127 N4 Petit Canal Guadeloupe W Indies
122 G8 Petitcodiac New Brunswick Canada
69 E8 Petit Cul de Sac Marin B Guadeloupe W Indies
122 G5 Petite Cascapedia, Parc de la Quebec Canada
68 J7 Petite Matane Quebec Canada
121 Q7 Petite-Nation, Parc Quebec Canada
122 B6 Petite Rivière Quebec Canada
103 M5 Petite Rivière Bridge Nova Scotia Canada
109 J9 Petite Rivière de l'Artibonite Haiti
127 N4 Petites Dalles, les France
123 M7 Petit Etang C Breton I, Nova Scotia
68 E5 Petite Terre, Îles de la Guadeloupe W Indies
122 G4 Petite Vallée Quebec Canada
42 D5 Petit Goâve Haiti
123 N5 Petit Jardin Newfoundland Canada
110 O6 Petit Jean R Arkansas U.S.A.
95 U2 Petit Manan Pt Maine U.S.A.
20 H7 Petit Mars France
36 B6 Petitmont France
117 N6 Petitot R British Columbia Canada
95 P10 Petitsikapau L Newfoundland Canada
95 M3 Petkula Finland
97 Petlad India
84 J5 Peto Mexico
145 D4 Petone New Zealand
111 J7 Petorca Chile
98 E5 Petoskey Michigan U.S.A.
80 D8 Petra ruins Jordan
43 F11 Petralia Sicily
51 L1 Petra, Ostrov isld Russian Federation
48 H3 Petra Velikogo, Zaliv B Russian Federation
45 P7 Petrella, M mt Italy
71 Petre, Pt Ontario Canada
52 J4 Petretsovo Russian Federation
46 F3 Petrich Bulgaria
141 L2 Petrie, Mt Brisbane, Qnsld Australia
103 P6 Petrified Forest Nat. Park U.S.A.
94 J6 Petrikov Ukraine
48 H5 Petrila Romania
116 O2 Petrockstow England
52 C5 Petrodvorets Russian Federation
129 H7 Petrolândia Brazil
95 H7 Petrolia Ontario Canada
95 L5 Petrolina Brazil
130 H9 Petrolina Montana U.S.A.
131 B7 Picún Leufú Argentina
133 M3 Picún Leufú Argentina

55 C4 Petrovskoye Bashkirskaya Respublika Russian Federation
52 E6 Petrovskoye Yaroslavskaya obl Russian Federation
56 G3 Petrovsk-Zabaykal'skiy Russian Federation
52 D4 Petrozavodsk Russian Federation
52 K2 Petru' Russian Federation
48 J3 Petru Rareş Romania
Petsamo see Pechenga
29 N2 Petsikko mt Finland
25 C3 Petten Netherlands
36 C5 Petterberi Austria
38 D3 Pettigoe Ireland
110 C6 Pettigrew Arkansas U.S.A.
109 K7 Pettus Texas U.S.A.
123 U6 Petty Hbr Newfoundland Canada
55 E3 Petukhovo Russian Federation
47 L6 Phrygia Turkey
68 G2 Phuc Yen Vietnam
67 B7 Phu Dien Vietnam
90 D9 Phuket, Ko isld Thailand
68 F7 Phu Khieo Thailand
75 L8 Phulabāni India
68 F6 Phulang Thuong Vietnam
68 G2 Phu Loc Vietnam
68 G2 Phu Ly Vietnam
9 G6 Phum Bavel Cambodia
94 C3 Phum Hay Cambodia
68 G6 Phum Khvao Cambodia
68 F6 Phum Kouleu Cambodia
99 S6 Phum Siem Cambodia
9 E5 Phum Svai Cambodia
32 F6 Phum Treng Cambodia
36 B7 Phum Troy Toch Cambodia
71 P4 Phu My Vietnam
19 H8 Phu Nho Quan Vietnam
19 P13 Phun Phin Thailand
75 N5 Phuntsholing Bhutan
69 G8 Phuoc Long Vietnam
19 P16 Phuoc Vinh Vietnam
68 F7 Phu Quoc, Dao isld Vietnam
68 G2 Phu Tho Vietnam
129 J5 Piaca Brazil
44 G1 Piacenza prov Italy
44 F2 Piacenza Italy
45 L1 Piacenza d'Adige Italy
44 H4 Piacatuba Italy
44 B3 Pian de Macerata Italy [?]
130 H9 Pianco R Brazil
36 D5 Pfalzer Wald mts Germany
36 K3 Pfalzfeld Germany
45 L4 Pfalzgrafenweiler Germany
36 M4 Pfalzpaint Germany
36 N4 Pfarrkirchen Germany
37 K3 Pfarrweisach Germany
37 N6 Pfatter Germany
42 G6 Pfeddersheim Germany
65 B5 Pfieffe Germany
65 B5 Pfinztal Germany
41 J3 Pfaffenhofen an der Ilm Germany
141 H6 Pian R New South Wales Australia
130 H8 Piana R Brazil
21 J2 Piana, Ile France
58 F9 Pianguan China
138 F6 Piangil Victoria Australia
120 H10 Pianosa isld Adriatic Sea
42 C6 Pianosa, I Italy
65 B5 Pianquan China
143 C8 Piapot Saskatchewan Canada
127 N3 Piaseczno Poland
122 K3 Piashti, L Quebec Canada
31 O4 Piaski Poland
31 L3 Piątek Poland
31 N4 Piatra Neamţ Romania
48 H2 Piatra Olt Romania
143 C8 Piau-Engaly France
52 E2 Piave R Italy
143 F3 Piawaning W Australia Australia
48 E3 Piaza al Serchio Italy
44 F2 Piazza Armerina Sicily
42 L1 Piazzi I Chile
43 L2 Piazzola B Italy
133 E5 Pibor Post Sudan
145 D3 Pihaina New Zealand
67 E1 Pi He R China
71 J4 Pihlajavesi Finland
29 P2 Piet Retief S Africa
48 J3 Pietroşu mt Romania
71 J4 Pietroşul mt Romania
29 P2 Piets'yarvi, Oz L Russian Federation
130 H9 Pianco R Brazil
88 F9 Pianco R Brazil
99 F4 Pietermaritzburg S Africa
22 G3 Piéton Belgium
106 B7 Pie Town New Mexico U.S.A.
44 D3 Pietra Ligure Italy
45 Q7 Pietramelara Italy
44 B3 Pietraporzio Italy
44 H4 Pietrasanta Italy
99 S4 Pietravairano Italy
109 O4 Pineland Texas U.S.A.
71 J4 Pietroşu mt Romania
29 P2 Pieux, les France
53 B9 Pievato S Africa
41 K5 Pinazzo Italy
130 H9 Pianco R Brazil
89 F4 Pieštany S Africa
22 G3 Pietermaritzburg S Africa
106 D7 Pievepelago Italy
45 M4 Pieve S. Stefano Italy
19 P1 Pine Portage Ontario Canada
117 P5 Pigadhia see Kárpathos
94 C1 Pigeon Michigan U.S.A.
94 D3 Pigeon Michigan U.S.A.
120 H10 Pigeon D Ontario Canada
140 K10 Pigeon Cr Alabama U.S.A.
141 K10 Pigeon Hole N Terr Australia
127 K3 Pigeon I Jamaica
121 M8 Pigeon L Alberta Canada
121 M8 Pigeon L Ontario Canada
98 D6 Pigeon Pt Minnesota
127 M2 Pigeon Pt Trinidad
102 B4 Pigeon Pt California U.S.A.
119 V6 Pigeon R Minnesota U.S.A.
119 O2 Pigeon River Ontario Canada
143 C8 Pigeon Rocks W Australia Australia
110 H5 Pigg R Virginia U.S.A.
89 G8 Pigg's Peak Swaziland
116 G8 Pigna Italy
105 P7 Pignataro Interamna Italy
45 Q7 Pignataro Maggiore Italy
133 E5 Pigüe Argentina
145 D3 Pihaina New Zealand
67 E1 Pi He R China
71 J4 Pihlajavesi Finland
94 A5 Pihlava Finland
94 D3 Pihtipudas Finland
29 M8 Pihtla Finland
143 B9 Pikalevo Russian Federation
79 J3 Pik Grandioznyy mt Russian Federation
94 F9 Pikeville Kentucky U.S.A.
79 J3 Pik Grandioznyy mt Russian Federation
103 L8 Pikelot isld Caroline Is
94 J5 Pikes Peak mt Colorado U.S.A.
99 O6 Piketberg S Africa
94 K9 Piketon Ohio U.S.A.
94 D10 Pikeville Kentucky U.S.A.
109 O4 Pineland Texas U.S.A.
110 K5 Pikeville Tennessee U.S.A.
31 K2 Piła Poland
15 L4 Pila Spain
111 H9 Pilani India
31 M4 Pilaniesberg S Africa
48 F3 Piława Górna Poland
139 H9 Pilbara W Australia Australia
122 G5 Pilbarra Creek W Australia
17 H2 Pilar Sardinia
130 H9 Pilchowice Poland
107 M3 Pilcomayo R Argentina/Paraguay
95 M3 Pictou Nova Scotia Canada

103 M8 Phoenix Arizona U.S.A.
111 G12 Phoenix Louisiana U.S.A.
95 L3 Phoenix New York U.S.A.
134 K8 Phoenix Is Pacific Oc
95 M6 Phoenixville Pennsylvania U.S.A.
68 G1 Pho Lu Vietnam
68 H4 Phong Nha Vietnam
68 F1 Phongsali Laos
68 F1 Phong Tho Vietnam
68 F3 Phon Phisai Thailand
139 G7 Phoques B Tasmania Australia
140 E5 Phosphate Hill Queensland Australia
68 H7 Phouc Le Vietnam
68 D3 Phrao Thailand
94 B5 Phra Phutthabat Thailand
68 D8 Phra Saeng Thailand
69 C8 Phra Thong, Ko isld Thailand
68 E5 Phrom Buri Thailand

38 M5 Pielach R Austria
29 M8 Pielavesi L Finland
29 O8 Pielinen L Finland
22 K5 Piennes France
44 C3 Piemonte reg Italy
31 M1 Pieniężno Poland
98 B8 Pierce Colorado U.S.A.
113 F10 Pierce Florida U.S.A.
100 K3 Pierce Idaho U.S.A.
98 J7 Pierce Nebraska U.S.A.
13 G4 Piercebridge England
99 O4 Pierce City Missouri U.S.A.
94 B5 Pierceton Indiana U.S.A.
107 K4 Pierceville Kansas U.S.A.
102 A2 Piercy California U.S.A.
46 E4 Piéria Ori Greece
98 F1 Pierowall Orkney Scotland
98 K1 Pierpont South Dakota U.S.A.
16 E2 Pierre R Spain
19 J6 Pierre France
102 E5 Pierre South Dakota U.S.A.
18 F7 Pierre-Buffière France
19 P15 Pierre-Châtel France
21 P6 Pierrefitte-sur-Sauldre France
22 D5 Pierrefonds France
120 K3 Pierre L Union France
52 G3 Pierrelatte France
140 C6 Pierrepont France
143 B8 Pierreville Quebec Canada
95 L6 Pierson Florida U.S.A.
99 M3 Pierson Manitoba Canada
100 K3 Piesport Germany
118 L3 Piessevelle W Australia Australia
31 K7 Piešt'any Czechoslovakia
89 F8 Pietarsaari see Jakobstad
89 G7 Pietermaritzburg S Africa
89 F4 Pietersburg S Africa
22 G3 Piéton Belgium
106 B7 Pie Town New Mexico U.S.A.
44 D3 Pietra Ligure Italy
45 O7 Pietramelara Italy
44 B3 Pietraporzio Italy
44 H4 Pietrasanta Italy
99 S4 Pietravairano Italy
71 J4 Pietroşul mt Romania
29 P2 Piets'yarvi, Oz L Russian Federation
20 G2 Pieux, les France
38 F9 Pieve R Italy
38 M7 Pieve di Cadore Italy
45 K3 Pieve di Cento Italy
45 J3 Pievepelago Italy
45 M4 Pieve S. Stefano Italy
117 P5 Pigadhia see Kárpathos
94 C1 Pigeon Michigan U.S.A.
120 H10 Pigeon D Ontario Canada
140 K10 Pigeon Cr Alabama U.S.A.
141 K10 Pigeon Hole N Terr Australia
127 K3 Pigeon I Jamaica
121 M8 Pigeon L Alberta Canada
121 M8 Pigeon L Ontario Canada
98 D6 Pigeon Pt Minnesota
127 M2 Pigeon Pt Trinidad
102 B4 Pigeon Pt California U.S.A.
119 V6 Pigeon R Minnesota U.S.A.
119 O2 Pigeon River Ontario Canada
143 C8 Pigeon Rocks W Australia Australia
110 H5 Pigg R Virginia U.S.A.
89 G8 Pigg's Peak Swaziland
103 L4 Pigna Italy
105 P7 Pignataro Interamna Italy
45 Q7 Pignataro Maggiore Italy
133 E5 Pigüe Argentina
145 D3 Pihaina New Zealand
67 E1 Pi He R China
29 L9 Pihlajavesi Finland
94 A5 Pihlava Finland
29 L8 Pihtipudas Finland
29 M8 Pihtla Finland
52 D5 Pikalevo Russian Federation
79 J3 Pik Grandioznyy mt Russian Federation
103 L8 Pikelot isld Caroline Is
94 J5 Pikes Peak mt Colorado U.S.A.
89 D6 Piketberg S Africa
94 K9 Piketon Ohio U.S.A.
94 D10 Pikeville Kentucky U.S.A.
110 K5 Pikeville Tennessee U.S.A.
115 P5 Pikiulleq isld Greenland
31 K2 Piła Poland
31 N14 Pilat, Mt France
48 F3 Pilis Hungary
48 E3 Pilisvörösvár Hungary
98 K1 Pillsbury North Dakota U.S.A.
101 T2 Piney Buttes hills Montana U.S.A.
99 U3 Pilsbury, L California U.S.A.
41 O4 Pilsen see Plzeň
99 S5 Pilsen Wisconsin U.S.A.
37 O6 Pilsting Germany
55 F1 Pil'tan-Lor, Oz L Russian Federation
75 N6 Piltene Latvia
79 O8 Pilva R Russian Federation
55 F1 Pim Russian Federation
75 N6 Pima Arizona U.S.A.
17 G2 Pina Spain
103 L10 Pinacate, Cerro C Mexico
124 C3 Pinacate, Sa. del mt Mexico
103 P9 Pinaleno Mts Arizona U.S.A.
69 H2 Pinamalayan Philippines
69 J7 Pinang see Penang
71 D5 Pinang Malaysia
126 D2 Pinar del Río Cuba
46 C3 Pinarhisar Turkey
143 C9 Pinaroo New South Wales Australia
65 D7 Pincara Italy
92 F4 Pinchbeck England
118 C4 Pincher Creek Alberta Canada
130 K8 Pinch's Brazil
128 C4 Pinchincha mt Ecuador
129 N6 Pinckney Michigan U.S.A.
46 D12 Pinckneyville Illinois U.S.A.
31 M3 Pińczów Poland
130 E8 Pindaí Brazil
129 J4 Pindaré R Brazil
129 J4 Pindaré-Mirim Brazil
79 O4 Pindi Gheb Pakistan
41 K1 Pindobaçu Brazil
70 B4 Pindolo Sulawesi
28 E4 Pindstrup Denmark

138 F4 Pine R New South Wales Australia
103 N7 Pine Arizona U.S.A.
24 B2 Pine R Michigan U.S.A.
99 Q6 Pine R Wisconsin U.S.A.
111 K10 Pine Apple Alabama U.S.A.
111 D7 Pine Bluff Arkansas U.S.A.
119 P4 Pine Bluff Saskatchewan Canada
98 B8 Pine Bluffs Wyoming U.S.A.
123 T7 Pine, C Newfoundland Canada
113 F9 Pinecastle Florida U.S.A.
111 E7 Pine City Arkansas U.S.A.
99 O4 Pine City Minnesota U.S.A.
103 H1 Pine Cr Nevada U.S.A.
54 K5 Pine Cr Pennsylvania U.S.A.
67 Piercy California U.S.A.
102 E3 Pinecrest California U.S.A.
107 P7 Pine Cr. Res Oklahoma
117 P9 Pinedale Alberta Canada
102 E5 Pinedale California U.S.A.
101 Q7 Pinedale Wyoming U.S.A.
102 E5 Pine Flat Res California U.S.A.
100 G8 Pine Forest Range Nevada U.S.A.
52 F3 Pinega Russian Federation
52 G3 Pinega R Russian Federation
140 C6 Pine Gap N Terr Australia
143 B8 Pinegrove W Australia Australia
95 L6 Pine Grove Pennsylvania U.S.A.
140 C5 Pine Hill N Terr Australia
118 K3 Pine House Saskatchewan Canada
118 L3 Pine House L Saskatchewan Canada
112 H2 Pinehurst North Carolina U.S.A.
100 K6 Pinehurst Washington U.S.A.
118 J1 Pinehurst L Alberta Canada
113 E11 Pine I Florida U.S.A.
99 O5 Pine Island B Antarctica
146 B7 Pine Island Glacier glacier Antarctica
99 S4 Pine L Wisconsin U.S.A.
109 O4 Pineland Texas U.S.A.
71 J4 Pineleng Sulawesi
144 B6 Pinelheugh mt New Zealand
113 E10 Pinellas airport Florida U.S.A.
102 C6 Pine Mt California U.S.A.
107 P7 Pine Mt Oklahoma U.S.A.
117 Q5 Pine Mt Cr Nevada U.S.A.
103 L7 Pine Pk Arizona U.S.A.
19 P1 Pine Portage Ontario Canada
117 P5 Pine Pt Northwest Territories Canada
113 D8 Pine R Florida U.S.A.
113 D8 Pine R Florida U.S.A.
117 M8 Pine R British Columbia Canada
98 D6 Pine Ridge South Dakota U.S.A.
117 P9 Pine River Manitoba Canada
118 K3 Pine River Saskatchewan Canada
99 M3 Pine River Minnesota U.S.A.
120 J9 Pinery Prov. Park Ontario Canada
112 H5 Pines, I of South Carolina U.S.A.
111 B9 Pines, L O'The Texas U.S.A.
100 C4 Pine Springs Texas U.S.A.
89 G7 Pinetown S Africa
110 B7 Pine Valley Utah U.S.A.
103 L4 Pine Valley Mts Utah U.S.A.
94 F9 Pineville Kentucky U.S.A.
111 C9 Pineville Louisiana U.S.A.
110 B5 Pineville Missouri U.S.A.
112 H2 Pineville North Carolina U.S.A.
94 F9 Pineville West Virginia U.S.A.
99 M1 Pinewood Ontario Canada
99 L2 Pinewood Minnesota U.S.A.
67 C5 Ping'an China
67 B5 Pingba China
67 B5 Pingbian China
67 C5 Pingchang China
67 C6 Pingdao isld China
67 E5 Pingding China
67 D3 Pingdingbu see Guyan
67 E5 Pingding Shan mt China
67 F6 Pingdingshan China
67 F6 Pingdu China
67 F6 Pingelly W Australia Australia
67 C7 Pingguo China
67 F6 Pinghai China
67 G1 Pinghe China
67 G1 Pingjiang China
67 F6 Pingle China
67 G1 Pingli China
67 C5 Pingliang China
67 D4 Pinglu China
67 C4 Pingluo China
67 G2 Pingnan China
67 F5 Pingquan China
67 E4 Pingquan China
58 F6 Pingquan China
65 B6 Pingshan China
65 C6 Pingtan China
67 G1 Pingtang China
67 G2 Ping-tung Taiwan
67 C5 Pingwu China
67 C6 Pingxiang China
67 C7 P'ing-tung Taiwan
58 F9 Pingxiang China
67 C5 Pingyao China
67 F5 Pingyi China
67 F5 Pingyin China
65 C6 Pingyuan China
67 F5 Pingyuan China
67 C5 Pinhal Brazil
125 R8 Pinhão Portugal
129 H5 Pinheiro Brazil
129 J4 Pinhel Portugal
129 K4 Piní isld Indonesia
31 K1 Piniós R Greece
143 B10 Pinjarra W Australia Australia
143 B9 Pinjin W Australia Australia
70 B4 Pinoh R Kalimantan
143 C10 Pinnaroo New South Wales Australia
33 O7 Pinneberg Germany
140 A3 Pinnacles Queensland Australia
140 A3 Pinkerton Ra W Australia Australia

118 H7 Pinkham Saskatchewan Canada
112 K2 Pink Hill North Carolina U.S.A.
117 M7 Pink Mountain British Columbia Canada
21 M5 Pin-la-Garenne, le France
68 C2 Pinlaung Burma
145 D4 Pinnacle mt New Zealand
116 C6 Pinnacle I Bering Sea
102 C5 Pinnacles Nat. Mon California U.S.A.
138 F6 Pinnaroo South Australia Australia
32 L5 Pinn Au R Germany
32 L5 Pinneberg Germany
106 G1 Pinnow Colorado U.S.A.
9 F4 Pinner England
33 T5 Pinnow Germany
70 B5 Pinoh R Kalimantan
111 F10 Pinola Mississippi U.S.A.
106 F3 Pinon Colorado U.S.A.
106 K9 Pinon New Mexico U.S.A.
112 H4 Pinopolis Dam South Carolina U.S.A.
Pinos, Isla de see Juventud, Isla de la
102 E7 Pinos Spain
17 G6 Pinoso Spain
125 K9 Pinotepa Nacional Mexico
70 G6 Pinrang Sulawesi Indonesia
70 F6 Pinrang Sulawesi
137 O6 Pins, Île Des New Caledonia
53 C8 Pinsk Belorussia
111 K8 Pinson Alabama U.S.A.
110 H6 Pinson Tennessee U.S.A.
120 J10 Pins, Pte. aux Ontario Canada
128 A7 Pinta isld Galapagos Oc
103 P6 Pinta Arizona U.S.A.
132 D2 Pintados Chile
103 L9 Pinta, Sa Arizona U.S.A.
70 E2 Pintasan Sabah
133 E3 Pinto Argentina
118 K9 Pinto Butte pk Saskatchewan Canada
103 M3 Pinto Mts California U.S.A.
103 L4 Pintura Utah U.S.A.
103 J5 Pintwater Ra Nevada U.S.A.
123 Q2 Pinware R Labrador, Nfld Canada
12 D3 Pinwherry Scotland
143 B8 Pinyalling mt W Australia Australia
52 G4 Pinyug Russian Federation
41 N5 Pinzolo Italy
45 M4 Pióbbico Italy
103 K4 Pioche Nevada U.S.A.
9 N16 Piolenc France
42 D6 Piombino Italy
94 C5 Pioneer Ohio U.S.A.
109 H3 Pioneer Texas U.S.A.
101 M4 Pioneer Mts Montana U.S.A.
56 C3 Pioner Russian Federation
51 J1 Pioner, Ostrova isld Russian Federation
31 M1 Pionerskiy Russian Federation
55 D1 Pionerskiy Russian Federation
31 N4 Pionki Poland
145 E3 Piopio New Zealand
128 F4 Piorini L Brazil
44 B2 Piossasco Italy
31 L3 Piotrków Bydgoszcz Poland
31 M4 Piotrków Trybunalski Łódź Poland
45 M1 Piove di Sacco Italy
65 G3 Pipa Dingzi mt China
74 E5 Pipar India
6 L4 Piper oil rig North Sea
102 G4 Piper Pk Nevada U.S.A.
100 M5 Pipe Spring Nat. Mon Arizona U.S.A.
119 R9 Pipestone Manitoba Canada
98 K6 Pipestone Minnesota U.S.A.
119 Q9 Pipestone Cr Manitoba Canada
98 K5 Pipestone Nat. Mon Minnesota U.S.A.
145 E3 Pipipi mt New Zealand
145 E3 Pipiriki New Zealand
121 U3 Pipmuacan, Res Quebec Canada
122 B4 Pipmuacan, Res Quebec Canada
60 Q2 Pippu Japan
20 G6 Pipriac France
107 P4 Piqua Kansas U.S.A.
110 M1 Piqua Ohio U.S.A.
17 F2 Piqueras, Pto. de Spain
130 C5 Piquiri, R Mato Grosso Brazil
130 D9 Piquiri, R Paraná Brazil
85 E7 Pira Benin
129 J7 Piracanjuba R Brazil
130 E5 Piracanjuba Brazil
129 J8 Piracicaba Brazil
130 G6 Piracicaba R Brazil
133 F3 Piracuacito Argentina
130 B3 Piraçununga Brazil
129 K4 Piraeuruca Brazil
46 F7 Piraievs Greece
56 E4 Piramida, G mt Russian Federation
42 F3 Piran Slovenia
129 L5 Piranhas Alagoas Brazil
130 D5 Piranhas Goiás Brazil
130 D8 Pirapó, R Brazil
128 K7 Pirapora Brazil
122 A3 Pirarajá, L Quebec Canada
130 C10 Piray R Argentina
128 F7 Piray R Bolivia
11 E7 Pirbright England
98 H5 Piré France
129 J7 Pires do Rio Brazil
46 E7 Pírgos Greece
46 F7 Pírgos Crete Greece
20 E7 Piriac France
130 D9 Piribebuy Paraguay
46 F3 Pirin plateau Bulgaria
17 G2 Pirineos mt Spain
145 E4 Pirinoa New Zealand
145 F3 Piripaua New Zealand
129 K4 Piripiri Brazil
127 M9 Piritu Anzoátegui Venezuela
127 K10 Piritu Miranda Venezuela
37 N3 Pirita R
29 K10 Pirkkala Finland
36 D5 Pirmasens Germany
36 D5 Pirna Germany
12 F2 Pirnmill Scotland
145 E2 Pirongia New Zealand
46 F1 Pirot Serbia Yugoslavia
74 G2 Pir Panjal Rge Kashmir
29 J8 Pirou France
17 G3 Pirttikoski Finland
72 E4 Piru Moluccas Indonesia
102 F7 Piru California U.S.A.
47 H6 Piryí Greece
73 K2 Pirzada Afghanistan
45 H4 Pisa Italy
133 C1 Pisagua Chile
73 B3 Pisang isld Indonesia
44 H3 Pisanino mt Italy
144 B6 Pisa Range New Zealand
70 F1 Pisau, Tg C Sabah
128 C6 Pisciotta Italy
52 C6 Pisco Peru
95 N3 Pisco New York U.S.A.
30 H6 Pisek Czechoslovakia
98 E1 Pisek North Dakota U.S.A.
80 F6 Pisga Jordan
98 J2 Pisgah Iowa U.S.A.
144 C6 Pisgah, Mt New Zealand
112 G2 Pisgah, Mt North Carolina U.S.A.
77 G6 Pishin Iran
74 B3 Pishin Pakistan
70 G7 Pising Sulawesi
103 M9 Pisinemo Arizona U.S.A.
74 C3 Pismo Bch California U.S.A.
128 F6 Piso Firme Bolivia
41 M6 Pisogne Italy
133 D3 Pissis vol Argentina

29 P6 Pista R Russian Federation
29 P6 Pistayarvi L Russian Federation
43 H8 Pisticci Italy
45 J3 Pistoia Italy
123 R2 Pistolet B Newfoundland Canada
100 A7 Pistol River Oregon U.S.A.
52 F6 Pistsovo Russian Federation
8 C2 Pistyll Rhaeadr mt Wales
16 E3 Pisuerga R Spain
31 N2 Pisz Poland
100 D8 Pit R California U.S.A.
85 B6 Pita Guinea
122 G1 Pitaga Labrador, Nfld Canada
139 G5 Pitarpunga L New South Wales Australia
71 G7 Pitas Pt Mindanao Philippines
135 U11 Pitcairn I Pacific Oc
21 P5 Pithiviers France
42 D6 Pitigliano Italy
124 H6 Pitiquito Mexico
138 B2 Pitjantjatjara Lands South Australia Australia
104 C2 Pitkin Colorado U.S.A.
111 D11 Pitkin Louisiana U.S.A.
116 G7 Pitkof I Alaska U.S.A.
52 D4 Pitkyaranta Russian Federation
15 E4 Pitlochry Scotland
95 M7 Pitman New Jersey U.S.A.
87 G12 Piton des Neiges mt Réunion
37 N4 Pitre, I. au Louisiana U.S.A.
13 F1 Pitscottie Scotland
9 G4 Pitsea England
13 F1 Pittenweem Scotland
137 R10 Pitt I Chatham Is Pacific Oc
112 H2 Pittsboro North Carolina U.S.A.
102 C3 Pittsburg California U.S.A.
110 B3 Pittsburg Kansas U.S.A.
110 M4 Pittsburg Kentucky U.S.A.
121 T7 Pittsburg New Hampshire U.S.A.
107 P7 Pittsburg Oklahoma U.S.A.
109 N3 Pittsburg Texas U.S.A.
95 O3 Pittsburgh Pennsylvania U.S.A.
110 E2 Pittsfield Illinois U.S.A.
95 S2 Pittsfield Maine U.S.A.
95 O4 Pittsfield Massachusetts U.S.A.
95 Q3 Pittsfield New Hampshire U.S.A.
94 C5 Pittsford Michigan U.S.A.
94 K3 Pittsford New York U.S.A.
95 O3 Pittsford Vermont U.S.A.
95 M5 Pittston Pennsylvania U.S.A.
111 L9 Pittsview Alabama U.S.A.
110 C3 Pittsville Maryland U.S.A.
140 D4 Pittsville Missouri U.S.A.
140 D6 Pittsville Wisconsin U.S.A.
141 K8 Pittsworth Queensland Australia
100 D8 Pittville California U.S.A.
88 E6 Pitu R Tanzania
141 L3 Pituri R Queensland Australia
110 M1 Pitz Tal Austria
95 S5 Più bega Italy
123 M7 Piuassant Bay C Breton I, Nova Scotia
123 M7 Piura dept Peru
128 B5 Piura Peru
94 F7 Piute Mts California U.S.A.
102 F6 Piute Pk California U.S.A.
119 N6 Piute Res Utah U.S.A.
75 K4 Piuthan Nepal
42 J5 Piva R Montenegro Yugoslavia
101 O9 Pivabiska R Ontario Canada
120 G2 Pivijay Colombia
31 M6 Piwniczna Poland
46 G3 Pixley California U.S.A.
60 Q1 Piyai Greece
60 Q1 Piyashiri yama mt Japan
128 E7 Pizacoma Peru
52 G5 Pizhanka Russian Federation
122 F8 Pizhma Russian Federation
41 K4 Pizol mt Switzerland
43 G10 Pizzo Italy
102 C4 Pizzodeta, M mt Italy
33 Q5 Plaaz Germany
110 B3 Plabennec France
109 L7 Placedo Texas U.S.A.
123 T6 Placentia Newfoundland Canada
71 G6 Placer Mindanao Philippines
102 D3 Placeritos Nevada U.S.A.
102 D3 Placerville California U.S.A.
144 C6 Placerville Colorado U.S.A.
46 G2 Placetas Cuba
46 G2 Plachkovtsi Bulgaria
113 F11 Placida Florida U.S.A.
113 F10 Placid, L Florida U.S.A.
46 E3 Placitas New Mexico U.S.A.
94 H5 Plačkovica mt Macedonia Yugoslavia
9 E1 Pladda I Scotland
40 F4 Plaffeien Switzerland
110 L3 Plain Wisconsin U.S.A.
18 G7 Plain City Ohio U.S.A.
37 L4 Plain City Utah U.S.A.
20 D5 Plain Dealing Louisiana U.S.A.
20 E5 Plain de Corravillers, Le France
133 F4 Piedra Sola Uruguay
21 J7 Plaine, la France
70 D3 Plaine-sur-Mer, la France
70 J5 Plainfield Indiana U.S.A.
95 N6 Plainfield Iowa U.S.A.
99 O7 Plainfield New Jersey U.S.A.
101 L2 Plainfield Wisconsin U.S.A.
108 G3 Plains Georgia U.S.A.
37 M3 Plains Texas U.S.A.
36 D5 Plains, The Virginia U.S.A.
99 O5 Plains Kansas U.S.A.
99 O5 Plainview Arkansas U.S.A.
20 E5 Plainview Minnesota U.S.A.
98 J7 Plainview Nebraska U.S.A.
17 F1 Plainview Texas U.S.A.
95 P5 Plainville Connecticut U.S.A.
21 J7 Plainville Illinois U.S.A.
94 B4 Plainville Kansas U.S.A.
127 H5 Plainwell Michigan U.S.A.
145 F2 Plaisance France
98 B1 Plaju Indonesia
46 G4 Pláka, Akr C Greece
47 H3 Pláka, Akra C Crete Greece
47 H3 Plakenska Pl mt Macedonia Yugoslavia
118 A2 Plamondon Alberta Canada
71 H9 Plampang Indonesia
37 P4 Planá Czechoslovakia
102 D4 Planada California U.S.A.
102 L5 Planalto da Borborema plateau Brazil
129 H7 Planalto de Mato Grosso plateau Brazil
17 G6 Plana Ó Nueva Tabarca isld Spain
121 T6 Plancoia France
20 C6 Plancoët France
122 B2 Planches-en-Montagne, Les France
40 D4 Planches-les-Mines France
36 D10 Planchón, Paso de Chile/Arg
20 F4 Plancy-l'Abbaye France
21 N7 Plan-de-Baix France
21 N17 Plan d'Orgon France
20 C3 Plane mt Algeria
94 D6 Plane, R France
126 G10 Planeta Rica Colombia
46 G1 Pleven Bulgaria

37 P5 Plánice Czechoslovakia
37 L4 Plankenheß Germany
98 H6 Plankinton South Dakota U.S.A.
37 N4 Plano Texas U.S.A.
145 E4 Planning New Zealand
48 M1 Plantagenet R France
42 G4 Plantation Florida U.S.A.
44 E7 Plant City Florida U.S.A.
43 B8 Plasencia Spain
36 P7 Plassen Norway
55 D4 Plast Russian Federation
33 R5 Plasten Germany
103 J9 Plaster City California U.S.A.
31 M3 Plasy Czechoslovakia
30 H7 Plata, Puerta Chile
129 G7 Plata, Rio de la Arg/Uruguay
22 D2 Plateau de Chambarand France
20 D6 Plateau de Langres France
20 F6 Plateau de St. Etienne France
20 B6 Plateau du Tchigaï Niger
20 A5 Plateau du Tinherft stony desert Algeria
47 H6 Plateau of Tibet see Xizang Gaoyuan
18 G7 Plomb du Cantal mt France
19 K5 Plombières-les-Bains France
40 A3 Plombières-les-Dijon France
31 J5 Pločovice Czechoslovakia
20 B6 Plati Greece
42 J3 Plati Greece
75 L4 Plati Ákra C Greece
139 L4 Platikambos Greece
28 B6 Platina California U.S.A.
22 G4 Platinum Alaska U.S.A.
33 M4 Plato Saskatchewan Canada
31 M2 Plato Colombia
48 L3 Plato Missouri U.S.A.
46 E2 Plato Alash Russian Federation
41 G4 Podile India
76 D3 Po di Volano R Italy
41 L2 Po di Goro R Italy
20 B5 Plonéis France
20 C5 Plonéour-Lanvern France
20 C5 Plonévez-du-Faou France
45 L2 Plonévez-Porzay France
31 M3 Płońsk Poland
22 D2 Plopi Romania
52 D6 Plopni Romania
38 J9 Ploskosh' Russian Federation
46 G3 Plovdiv Bulgaria
48 F1 Plössberg Germany
54 J1 Płoty Poland
54 F4 Ploudalmézeau France
33 Q6 Plouagat France
32 D6 Plouaret France
20 C4 Plouay France
20 E5 Ploubalay France
20 B4 Plœuc France
55 E2 Ploučnice R Czechoslovakia
56 D2 Ploudalmézeau France
45 K5 Ploudiry France
48 L3 Plouénan France
46 E2 Plouër-Langrolay-sur-Rance France
48 L4 Plouescat France
33 O4 Plouézec, Pte.de France
22 D2 Plougasnel-Daoulas France
140 E7 Poeppel Corner N Terr Australia
37 P5 Poe Reef Lt. Ho Michigan U.S.A.
20 C5 Plougastel France
144 C5 Plouguenan France
87 C11 Plougonven France
45 O6 Plouguernel France
120 J4 Plougonvelin France
55 K4 Plouha France
72 D6 Plouharnel France
42 D5 Plouhinec Finistère France
45 N5 Plouhinec Morbihan France
45 N5 Plouigneau France
59 M4 Ploujean France
49 M2 Plouménach France
55 H4 Plounéour-Ménez France
65 H2 Plounéour-Tréz France
48 M1 Plounérin France
116 E9 Plounéventer France
32 F6 Plourac'h France
71 J6 Plouray France
71 H5 Plozévet France
135 U5 Plumas Manitoba Canada
45 K1 Plumelec France
146 G14 Plumelin France
113 G9 Pluméliau France
50 D7 Plum I New York U.S.A.
45 K5 Plumieux France
100 J2 Plummer Idaho U.S.A.
138 E5 Plummer, Mt Alaska U.S.A.
102 D6 Plum Pt Jamaica
99 N8 Plumridge Lakes W Australia Australia
143 F8 Plumtree Zimbabwe
99 T6 Plunge Lithuania
127 O6 Plunkett Saskatchewan Canada
100 F7 Plush Oregon U.S.A.
132 G8 Pluvigner France
129 N8 Pluzunet France
95 S7 Plymouth England
127 M7 Plymouth Tobago
102 D3 Plymouth California U.S.A.
94 H5 Plymouth Indiana U.S.A.
99 N6 Plymouth Iowa U.S.A.
95 S5 Plymouth Massachusetts U.S.A.
120 H9 Plymouth Nebraska U.S.A.
92 Q3 Plymouth New Hampshire U.S.A.
122 D4 Plymouth Ohio U.S.A.
95 M5 Plymouth Pennsylvania U.S.A.
86 B6 Plymouth Utah U.S.A.
127 M4 Plymouth Vermont U.S.A.
99 T6 Plymouth Wisconsin U.S.A.
127 M4 Plymouth Montserrat W Indies
122 G9 Plympton Nova Scotia Canada
123 N3 Plympton R N Terr Australia
123 K8 Plymstock England
8 C3 Plynlimon Fawr mt Wales
116 D2 Plyussa Russian Federation
55 P4 Plzeň Czechoslovakia
46 C3 Pniewy Poland
86 J2 Po Burkina
23 P7 Po R Italy
54 D3 Poá Sulawesi
58 H8 Poátina Tasmania Australia
95 K7 Pobé Benin
106 D7 Pobedy, Pik mt China/ Kazakhstan
33 P9 Poběžovice Czechoslovakia
99 M7 Pobiedziska Poland
31 K3 Pobla de Lillet, L Spain
120 H10 Pobla de Segur Spain
99 M7 Pocahontas Arkansas U.S.A.
107 M7 Pocahontas Iowa U.S.A.
95 N6 Pocahontas Virginia U.S.A.
94 E8 Pocatalico R West Virginia U.S.A.
142 B5 Pocatello Idaho U.S.A.
140 B1 Pocha, Sa. de mts Argentina

98 B3 Plevna Montana U.S.A.
20 C5 Pleyben France
20 C5 Pleyber-Christ France
37 N4 Pleystein Germany
145 E4 Plimmerton New Zealand
125 L10 Pliskov Ukraine
37 P5 Plitvice Croatia
37 P2 Pljesivica dist Croatia
13 H6 Pljevlja Montenegro Yugoslavia
70 F2 Ploaghe Sardinia
37 D7 Plobsheim France
142 B1 Ploča lighthouse Croatia
33 G6 Plochingen Germany
31 M3 Płock Poland
30 H7 Plöckenstein mt Czechoslovakia
129 G7 Plöcken Belgium
20 D6 Ploemel France
20 D6 Ploemeur France
20 D6 Ploërmel France
129 J8 Ploeşti Romania
125 L10 Plogastel-St. Germain France
125 O6 Plogoff France
125 C9 Plogonnec France
103 L5 Ploiarmél France
102 R12 Płomin Croatia
52 J3 Plomelin France
74 D5 Plomion France
118 C4 Plomb du Cantal mt France
52 D5 Ploŭdry France
31 J5 Podgorica Montenegro Yugoslavia
75 L4 Podgornoye Ukraine
45 M2 Po di Goro R Italy
116 F2 Podile India
110 D4 Podin Germany
70 F6 Podio di Volano R Italy
38 B7 Podkamennaya R Russian Federation
55 B5 Podkoren Slovenia
46 G3 Podkova Bulgaria
71 E4 Podolinec Czechoslovakia
54 J1 Podol'sk Russian Federation
85 B5 Podor Senegal
52 G4 Podosinovets Russian Federation
48 L3 Podovi Bosnia-Herzegovina
52 D4 Podporozh'ye Russian Federation
20 B4 Podtesovo Russian Federation
20 B4 Podu Iloaiei Romania
48 L3 Podu Turcului Romania
42 E6 Podyuga Russian Federation
33 O4 Poel isld Germany
22 D2 Poelkapelle Belgium
140 E7 Pofadder S Africa
94 C1 Pofi Italy
144 C5 Pogamasing Ontario Canada
53 C8 Pogar Russian Federation
42 D5 Poggendorf Germany
42 D5 Pogibonsi Italy
45 O6 Poggio a Caiano Italy
45 N5 Pŏggio Moiano Italy
45 N5 Pŏggio Renatico Italy
59 M4 Pogibi Sulawesi
48 M1 Pogoanele Romania
116 E9 Pogradec Albania
32 F6 Pogrebishche Ukraine
71 J6 Pogromnoi Vol Aleutian Is
143 F8 Pogum Germany
99 T6 Poh Sulawesi
127 N3 Pohakuloa Hawaiian Is
123 K8 Pohang S Korea
7 C3 Pohangina New Zealand
116 D2 Pohara New Zealand
55 P4 Pohja Finland
46 C3 Pohjois-Karjala prov Finland
86 J2 Pohl-Göns Germany
23 P7 Pohlheim Germany
54 D3 Pohokura New Zealand
58 H8 Pohorela Czechoslovakia
95 K7 Pohořelice Czechoslovakia
106 D7 Pohorje mt Slovenia
33 P9 Pohue B Hawaiian Is
99 M7 Poiana Magg Italy
31 K3 Poiana Mare Romania
120 H10 Poiana Teiului Romania
99 M7 Poigar Sulawesi Indonesia
107 M7 Poincaré, L Quebec Canada
95 N6 Poinsett, C Antarctica
94 E8 Point, L Florida U.S.A.
142 B5 Poinsettville Arkansas U.S.A.
140 B1 Poi, Mt Italy
95 N6 Pollino, M mt Italy
121 S2 Pollitz Germany
145 S4 Pollock Idaho U.S.A.
19 P2 Pollock South Dakota U.S.A.
94 E8 Pollock Hills W Australia Australia
143 E10 Pollock Reef W Australia Australia
19 P2 Pollocksville North Carolina U.S.A.
20 D3 Pollockville Alberta Canada
144 B6 Pollux mt New Zealand
121 M1 Polmak Finland
122 K3 Polmont Scotland
46 J6 Polná Czechoslovakia
99 R8 Polo Illinois U.S.A.
55 H3 Polo Missouri U.S.A.
9 J10 Pologi Ukraine
20 P7 Polomolok Mindanao Philippines
95 O12 Polotnyanyy Zavod Russian Federation
55 G2 Polotsk Belorussia
21 M6 Polovinnoye Russian Federation
20 B5 Polovni Russian Federation
46 H2 Polski Gradets Bulgaria
45 J9 Polski Trámbesh Bulgaria
45 P7 Polson Montana U.S.A.
45 O10 Poltár Czechoslovakia
16 B3 Poltava Ukraine
118 K9 Põltsamaa Estonia

54 E4 Pochep Russian Federation
138 D5 Pochinok Russian Federation
145 E2 Point Waikato New Zealand
68 F6 Poindé France
20 G8 Poiré-sur-Vie, le France
37 P2 Pockau Germany
37 P2 Pockenried Germany
101 S6 Poison Cr Wyoming U.S.A.
142 B1 Poison Gully W Perth, W Aust Australia
121 P6 Poisson Blanc, L Quebec Canada
129 L5 Poitiers France
21 P4 Poitou reg France
21 L8 Poivre, C W Australia Australia
142 B5 Poix St. Hubert Belgium
21 J8 Poix de Picardie France
103 O3 Pojan Albania
46 D4 Pojoaque New Mexico U.S.A.
102 R12 Pokaran India
145 E3 Pokataroo New South Wales Australia
52 J3 Pokcha Russian Federation
31 J5 Pokhara Nepal
75 L4 Po Klo Cambodia
141 L7 Poko Finland
45 Q8 Pokó New Caledonia
125 P6 Pokrovka Russian Federation
107 M1 Pokrovka Tselinogradskaya obl Kazakhstan
110 L5 Pokrovka Novosibirskaya obl Russian Federation
54 C8 Pokrovskaya Ukraine
21 K8 Pompaire France
99 M7 Pompano Beach Florida U.S.A.
52 F3 Pokshen'ga R Russian Federation
94 L4 Pompey France
37 M5 Pompeys Pillar mt W Australia Australia
142 G3 Pompeys Pillar Montana U.S.A.
71 E4 Pola Philippines
38 B B Philippines
31 K4 Polacca Arizona U.S.A.
103 O6 Polacca Wasa R Arizona U.S.A.
71 E4 Pola de Laviana Spain
16 D1 Pola de Lena Spain
16 D1 Pola de Siero Spain
31 K4 Poland rep Europe
31 K1 Polanow Poland
31 K1 Polar Wisconsin U.S.A.
101 M4 Polaris Montana U.S.A.
78 D2 Polatlı Turkey
55 G3 Polbathick England
52 F3 Polch Germany
133 C5 Polcura Chile
31 J2 Połczyn Zdrój Poland
37 M5 Pole Russian Federation
140 E7 Polednik mt Czechoslovakia
55 E2 Polegate England
56 D2 Polei Monu Vietnam
55 K4 Polesella Italy
31 N1 Polessk Russian Federation
53 C8 Polesye marsh Belorussia/ Ukraine
89 F8 Polevskoy Russian Federation
100 D8 Polewali Sulawesi
98 K7 Polgar Hungary
99 M1 Polgárdi Hungary
44 C3 Poli Cameroon
21 L1 Police Poland
16 C2 Polička Czechoslovakia
52 D2 Poligny France
122 H9 Polikastron Greece
47 H5 Polikhnitos Greece
31 M4 Polillo isld Luzon Philippines
33 T10 Polinagó Italy
31 K4 Polink mt Russia
71 J4 Polinik Pt Jamaica
79 C3 Polis Cyprus
76 D5 Polisan, Tanjong C Sulawesi
131 L7 Polist' R Russian Federation
31 H2 Politz Poland
119 N5 Polk Nebraska U.S.A.
55 B4 Polk Pennsylvania U.S.A.
70 N9 Polkan, Gora mt Russian Federation
59 E2 Polkovitz Germany
99 N3 Pollachi India
17 H3 Pollara Italy
45 J4 Pollença Spain
71 G5 Pollaphuca Res Ireland
130 G6 Pollard Arkansas U.S.A.
130 E9 Polle Germany
90 B3 Pollein France
122 A1 Pollença Spain

102 C5 Point Sur California U.S.A.
138 D5 Point Turton South Australia Australia
37 N2 Pötzig Germany
133 D2 Poma Argentina
144 B6 Pomahaka R New Zealand
133 D3 Poman Argentina
107 P3 Pomarão Portugal
112 F3 Pomaria South Carolina U.S.A.
29 J10 Pomarkku Finland
130 G7 Pomba R Brazil
129 L5 Pombal Brazil
16 B6 Pombal Portugal
130 D7 Pombo, R Brazil
19 O18 Pomègues, Île France
31 G2 Pomerania reg Germany/ Poland
99 M7 Pomercy Iowa U.S.A.
100 H3 Pomeroy Washington U.S.A.
10 D2 Pomeroy N Ireland
94 E7 Pomeroy Ohio U.S.A.
45 M6 Pomezia Italy
95 P5 Pomfret Connecticut U.S.A.
45 Q8 Pomigliano d'Arco Italy
37 M5 Pommelsbrunn Germany
20 D4 Pommerit-Jaudy France
21 O8 Pommiers France
107 P3 Pomona Kansas U.S.A.
141 L7 Pomona Queensland Australia
125 P9 Pomona Belize
110 E5 Pomona Namibia
110 E5 Pomona Missouri U.S.A.
47 J2 Pomonkie England
52 E3 Pomorskiy Bereg coast Russian Federation
48 L1 Pomoryany Ukraine
54 C8 Pomoshnaya Ukraine
21 K8 Pompaire France
113 G11 Pompano Beach Florida U.S.A.
45 Q8 Pompei Italy
95 L4 Pompey New York U.S.A.
142 G3 Pompeys Pillar mt W Australia Australia
101 S4 Pompeys Pillar Montana U.S.A.
95 N5 Pompton Lakes New Jersey U.S.A.
88 D10 Pompué R Mozambique
123 L8 Pomquet Nova Scotia Canada
33 K10 Ponass L Saskatchewan Canada
119 N6 Ponass L Saskatchewan Canada
98 K7 Ponca Nebraska U.S.A.
107 N5 Ponca City Oklahoma U.S.A.
127 L5 Ponce Puerto Rico
111 L11 Ponce de Leon Florida U.S.A.
113 F12 Ponce de Leon B Florida U.S.A.
113 F8 Ponce de Leon Inlet Florida U.S.A.
111 F11 Ponchatoula Louisiana U.S.A.
124 F7 Poncitlán Mexico
107 N5 Pond Creek Oklahoma U.S.A.
109 L2 Ponder Texas U.S.A.
76 D3 Pondicherry India
115 M3 Pond Inlet Northwest Territories Canada
89 F8 Pondoland S Africa
100 B4 Pondosa California U.S.A.
16 C2 Ponferrada Spain
86 A5 Pongara, Pte Gabon
99 M1 Pongaroa New Zealand
44 E3 Ponente Italy
76 C6 Ponerihouen New Caledonia
52 D2 Pong Reservoir Thailand
70 D7 Pongani Irian Jaya
70 O2 Pongkor Indonesia
119 J6 Ponglang Burma
70 N9 Pongolo R S Africa
52 D2 Poni, R Burkina
122 H9 Ponhook L Nova Scotia Canada
33 T10 Poniatowa Poland
31 N4 Poniec Germany
71 J4 Poniki, Mt Sulawesi
79 C3 Ponnáda Sri Lanka
71 J4 Ponnaiyár R India
99 N13 Ponneri India
31 H2 Ponnyadaung Range Burma
119 N5 Ponoka Alberta Canada
70 B4 Ponorogo Java
99 P7 Ponoy R Russian Federation
99 P7 Pons France
130 G6 Pons Spain
19 O15 Ponsacco Italy
52 D2 Ponta Grossa Brazil
16 C2 Pontacq France
122 A1 Pontailler-sur-Saône France

56 C4 Polysayevo Russian Federation
37 N2 Pötzig Germany
133 D2 Poma Argentina
144 B6 Pomahaka R New Zealand
133 D3 Poman Argentina
107 P3 Pomarão Portugal
112 F3 Pomaria South Carolina U.S.A.
29 J10 Pomarkku Finland
130 G7 Pomba R Brazil
129 L5 Pombal Brazil
16 B6 Pombal Portugal
130 D7 Pombo, R Brazil
19 O18 Pomègues, Île France
31 G2 Pomerania reg Germany/Poland
99 M7 Pomercy Iowa U.S.A.
94 E7 Pomeroy Ohio U.S.A.
45 M6 Pomezia Italy
95 P5 Pomfret Connecticut U.S.A.
45 Q8 Pomigliano d'Arco Italy
37 M5 Pommelsbrunn Germany
20 D4 Pommerit-Jaudy France
14 E7 Pommerit-le-Vicomte France
21 O8 Pommiers France
94 E7 Pomona Kansas U.S.A.
141 L7 Pomona Queensland Australia
21 L8 Poitiers France
21 P4 Poitou reg France
99 M7 Pomercy Iowa U.S.A.
56 E2 Ponferrada Spain
86 A5 Pongara, Pte Gabon
42 G2 Pongara, Pte Gabon
21 H3 Pont-Hébert France

99 S9 **Pontiac** Illinois U.S.A.
94 D4 **Pontiac** Michigan U.S.A.
70 A5 **Pontianak** Kalimantan
43 E7 **Pontinia** Italy
20 E5 **Pontivy** France
20 B6 **Pont-l'Abbé** France
122 H6 **Pont Lafrance** New Brunswick Canada
40 A1 **Pont la Ville** France
21 L3 **Pont-l'Evêque** France
21 N7 **Pontlevoy** France
20 D5 **Pont-Melvez** France
119 S4 **Ponton** Manitoba Canada
143 E9 **Ponton Ck** W Australia Australia
20 H4 **Pontorson** France
111 G7 **Pontotoc** Mississippi U.S.A.
109 J5 **Pontotoc** Texas U.S.A.
44 G3 **Pontremoli** Italy
41 L4 **Pontresina** Switzerland
8 C3 **Pontrhydfendigaid** Wales
8 B1 **Pont Rhythallt** Wales
20 D4 **Pontrieux** France
119 N5 **Pontrilas** Saskatchewan Canada
8 D4 **Pontrilas** England
121 T6 **Pont Rouge** Quebec Canada
19 N16 **Pont-St. Esprit** France
22 D5 **Pont-Ste. Maxence** France
20 D6 **Pont-Scorff** France
21 J7 **Ponts-de-Cé, les** France
22 F3 **Pont-sur-Sambre** France
18 H4 **Pont-sur-Yonne** France
20 B4 **Pontusval, Pte.de** France
21 L6 **Pontvallain** France
121 M8 **Pontypool** Ontario Canada
8 C4 **Pontypool** Wales
8 C4 **Pontypridd** Wales
145 E2 **Ponui I** New Zealand
101 O4 **Pony** Montana U.S.A.
43 E8 **Ponza, I di** Italy
43 E8 **Ponziane, Isole** *islds* Italy
138 C4 **Poochera** South Australia Australia
13 G6 **Pool** England
138 D2 **Poolawanna L** South Australia Australia
144 B6 **Poolburn Dam** New Zealand
9 E6 **Poole** England
138 F3 **Poole, Mt** New South Wales Australia
112 F5 **Pooler** Georgia U.S.A.
95 K7 **Poolesville** Maryland U.S.A.
15 C3 **Poolewe** Scotland
12 E1 **Pool of Muckart** Scotland
109 K3 **Poolville** Texas U.S.A.
Poona *see* **Pune**
139 G5 **Pooncarie** New South Wales Australia
143 B8 **Poondarrie,Mt** W Australia Australia
139 G4 **Poopelloe, L** New South Wales Australia
128 E7 **Poopó** Bolivia
145 E1 **Poor Knights Is** New Zealand
116 K4 **Poorman** Alaska U.S.A.
86 C7 **Popakabaka** Zaire
129 G3 **Popakai** Suriname
54 K8 **Popasnaya** Ukraine
128 C3 **Popayan** Colombia
27 M14 **Pope** Latvia
103 J8 **Pope** California U.S.A.
111 G7 **Pope** Mississippi U.S.A.
99 N7 **Popejoy** Iowa U.S.A.
58 F1 **Poperechnoye** Russian Federation
22 D2 **Poperinge** Belgium
95 L8 **Popes Creek** Maryland U.S.A.
95 S3 **Popham Beach** Maine U.S.A.
51 K1 **Popigay** *R* Russian Federation
138 F5 **Popiltah** New South Wales Australia
98 A1 **Poplar** Montana U.S.A.
99 P3 **Poplar** Wisconsin U.S.A.
110 F5 **Poplar Bluff** Missouri U.S.A.
101 U1 **Poplar Cr** Montana U.S.A.
119 U6 **Poplar Pt** Manitoba Canada
111 G11 **Poplarville** Mississippi U.S.A.
125 K8 **Popocatepetl** *vol* Mexico
116 G9 **Popof I** Alaska U.S.A.
70 N10 **Popoh** Java
45 P5 **Popoli** Italy
136 K3 **Popondetta** Papua New Guinea
47 H1 **Popovo** Bulgaria
37 M5 **Poppberg** *mt* Germany
25 H4 **Poppe** Netherlands
22 J1 **Poppel** Belgium
37 J3 **Poppenhausen** Germany
45 L4 **Poppi** Italy
31 M6 **Poprad** Czechoslovakia
48 F1 **Poprad** *R* Czechoslovakia
128 E8 **Poquis** *mt* Chile/Arg
95 L9 **Poquoson** Virginia U.S.A.
145 F4 **Porangahau** New Zealand
74 C8 **Porbander** India
117 H9 **Porcher I** British Columbia Canada
54 B1 **Porch'ye** Pskovskaya obl Russian Federation
133 D1 **Porco** Bolivia
16 E7 **Porcuna** Spain
141 G5 **Porcupine** *R* Queensland Australia
116 R3 **Porcupine** *R* Alaska/Yukon Terr U.S.A./Canada
90 H3 **Porcupine Bank** Atlantic Oc
101 T1 **Porcupine Cr** Montana U.S.A.
118 C8 **Porcupine Hills** Alberta Canada
119 Q6 **Porcupine Hills** Manitoba/Sask Canada
99 R3 **Porcupine Mts** Michigan U.S.A.
119 O6 **Porcupine Plain** Saskatchewan Canada
42 E3 **Pordenonė** Italy
46 G1 **Pordim** Bulgaria
42 F3 **Poreč** Croatia
130 D8 **Porecatu** Brazil
55 D2 **Porech'ye** Russian Federation
52 G6 **Poretskoye** Russian Federation
145 E4 **Porewa** New Zealand
85 E6 **Porga** Benin
29 J10 **Pori** Finland
145 F4 **Porirua** New Zealand
80 F3 **Poriyya** Israel
26 L5 **Porjus** Sweden
29 L12 **Porkala** Finland
52 C5 **Porkhov** Russian Federation
128 F1 **Porlamar** Venezuela
41 K5 **Porlezza** Italy
8 C5 **Porlock** England
37 L6 **Pörnbach** Germany
20 F7 **Pornic** France
20 F7 **Pornichet** France
71 G5 **Poro** *isld* Philippines
52 E3 **Porog** Arkhangel'skaya obl Russian Federation
52 J4 **Porog** Komi Respublika Russian Federation
59 M2 **Poronaysk** Russian Federation
68 G6 **Porong** *R* Cambodia
143 C10 **Porongorup** W Australia Australia
60 Q1 **Poronupuri yama** *mt* Japan
145 E3 **Porootarao** New Zealand
46 F7 **Póros** *isld* Greece
60 Q1 **Poroshiri yama** *mt* Japan
52 D3 **Porosozero** Russian Federation
52 H3 **Porozhsk** Russian Federation
56 F3 **Porozhskiy** Russian Federation
146 E14 **Porpoise B** Antarctica
19 Q18 **Porquerolles, I. de** France
120 K4 **Porquis Junct** Ontario Canada
40 F3 **Pörrentruy** Switzerland
45 J3 **Porretta Terme** Italy
16 B2 **Porriño** Spain
26 N1 **Porsa** Norway
26 O1 **Pörsangen** *inlet* Norway
27 D12 **Porsgrunn** Norway
20 A4 **Porspoder** France
33 Q9 **Porst** Germany
47 L5 **Porsük** *R* Turkey
128 F7 **Portachuelo** Bolivia
138 E5 **Port Adelaide** South Australia Australia
14 E2 **Portadown** N Ireland
144 B7 **Port Adventure** New Zealand
14 F2 **Portaferry** N Ireland
122 H7 **Portage** Prince Edward I Canada
116 N6 **Portage** Alaska U.S.A.
95 S7 **Portage** Maine U.S.A.
101 O2 **Portage** Montana U.S.A.
94 D5 **Portage** *R* Ohio U.S.A.
94 J6 **Portage** Pennsylvania U.S.A.
101 N8 **Portage** Utah U.S.A.
110 F3 **Portage des Sioux** Missouri U.S.A.
122 G6 **Portage I** New Brunswick Canada
119 T9 **Portage la Prairie** Manitoba Canada
110 G5 **Portageville** Missouri U.S.A.
94 J4 **Portageville** New York U.S.A.
103 P10 **Portal** Arizona U.S.A.
112 F5 **Portal** Georgia U.S.A.
98 D1 **Portal** North Dakota U.S.A.
14 D3 **Portalaoise** Ireland
117 L11 **Port Alberni** British Columbia Canada
139 H7 **Port Albert** Victoria Australia
120 J9 **Port Albert** Ontario Canada
145 E2 **Port Albert** New Zealand
16 C5 **Portalegre** Portugal
106 G7 **Portales** New Mexico U.S.A.
117 F7 **Port Alexander** Alaska U.S.A.
89 E9 **Port Alfred** S Africa
117 K10 **Port Alice** British Columbia Canada
94 J5 **Port Allegany** Pennsylvania U.S.A.
111 E11 **Port Allen** Louisiana U.S.A.
141 K6 **Port Alma** Queensland Australia
117 M11 **Port Angeles** Washington U.S.A.
109 K8 **Port Aransas** Texas U.S.A.
102 A3 **Port Arena** California U.S.A.
14 D3 **Portarlington** Ireland
Port Arthur *see* **Lüshun**
139 J9 **Port Arthur** Tasmania Australia
109 N6 **Port Arthur** Texas U.S.A.
12 B2 **Port Askaig** Scotland
138 D4 **Port Augusta** South Australia Australia
123 N5 **Port-au-Port** *pen* Newfoundland Canada
123 O5 **Port-au-Port** Newfoundland Canada
127 H5 **Port-au-Prince** Haiti
94 D2 **Port Austin** Michigan U.S.A.
32 J8 **Porta Westfalica** Germany
20 G3 **Portbail** France
12 C2 **Port Bannatyne** Scotland
111 E11 **Port Barre** Louisiana U.S.A.
71 D5 **Port Barton** Palawan Philippines
123 L8 **Port Bickerton** Nova Scotia Canada
68 A7 **Port Blair** Andaman Is
109 N6 **Port Bolivar** Texas U.S.A.
17 K2 **Port Bou** Spain/France
85 D8 **Port Bouet** Ivory Coast
140 D2 **Port Bradshaw** *inlet* N Terr Australia
21 J5 **Port Brillet** France
120 J10 **Port Bruce** Ontario Canada
120 K10 **Port Burwell** Ontario Canada
99 Q8 **Port Byron** Illinois U.S.A.
95 L3 **Port Byron** New York U.S.A.
139 G7 **Port Campbell** Victoria Australia
75 N7 **Port Canning** India
121 L7 **Port Carling** Ontario Canada
13 E4 **Port Carlisle** England
122 F3 **Port Cartier** Quebec Canada
144 D7 **Port Chalmers** New Zealand
145 E2 **Port Charles** New Zealand
15 B5 **Port Charlotte** Scotland
95 O6 **Port Chester** New York U.S.A.
111 G12 **Port Chicot I** Louisiana U.S.A.
117 F6 **Port Chilkoot** Alaska U.S.A.
116 D4 **Port Clarence** *hbr* Alaska U.S.A.
117 G9 **Port Clements** British Columbia Canada
141 K5 **Port Clinton** *inlet* Queensland Australia
94 E5 **Port Clinton** Ohio U.S.A.
95 S3 **Port Clyde** Maine U.S.A.
121 L10 **Port Colborne** Ontario Canada
117 M11 **Port Coquitlam** British Columbia Canada
68 A6 **Port Cornwallis** Andaman Is
121 L9 **Port Credit** Ontario Canada
19 Q18 **Port Cros, I. de** France
141 K6 **Port Curtis** *inlet* Queensland Australia
121 L9 **Port Dalhousie** Ontario Canada
122 H5 **Port Daniel** Quebec Canada
139 H9 **Port Davey** Tasmania Australia
19 N18 **Port de Bouc** France
19 N18 **Port de Fos** *hbr* France
102 A1 **Port Delgada** California U.S.A.
127 H5 **Port-de-Paix** Haiti
21 M7 **Port-de-Piles** France
69 E11 **Port Dickson** Malaysia
8 B1 **Port Dinorwic** Wales
141 H3 **Port Douglas** Queensland Australia
120 K10 **Port Dover** Ontario Canada
123 K9 **Port Dufferin** Nova Scotia Canada
111 G12 **Porte a la Hache** Louisiana U.S.A.
Porte d'Annam *see* **Vinh Son**
99 U4 **Porte des Morts** Wisconsin U.S.A.
117 H8 **Port Edward** British Columbia Canada
89 G8 **Port Edward** S Africa
130 G4 **Porteirinha** Brazil
129 H4 **Portel** Brazil
16 B6 **Portel** Portugal
130 H7 **Portela** Brazil
122 H7 **Port Elgin** New Brunswick Canada
120 J8 **Port Elgin** Ontario Canada
127 O8 **Port Elizabeth** Lesser Antilles
89 D9 **Port Elizabeth** S Africa
22 B2 **Portel, le** France
12 B2 **Port Ellen** Scotland
130 B9 **Porteña** *R* Argentina
21 J3 **Port-en-Bessin-Huppain** France
98 K5 **Porter** Minnesota U.S.A.
98 C7 **Porter** Nebraska U.S.A.
106 D6 **Porter** New Mexico U.S.A.
107 P6 **Porter** Oklahoma U.S.A.
112 D4 **Porterdale** Georgia U.S.A.
99 T4 **Porterfield** Wisconsin U.S.A.
12 D5 **Port Erin** I of Man U.K.
117 H6 **Porter Landing** British Columbia Canada
15 G3 **Port Errol** Scotland
87 C12 **Porterville** S Africa
102 E5 **Porterville** California U.S.A.
127 K3 **Port Esquivel** Jamaica
8 B4 **Port Eynon** Wales
138 F7 **Port Fairy** South Australia Australia
123 L8 **Port Felix** Nova Scotia Canada
145 E2 **Port Fitzroy** New Zealand
Port Francqui *see* **Ilebo**
86 A6 **Port Gentil** Gabon
122 G9 **Port George** Nova Scotia Canada
111 E10 **Port Gibson** Mississippi U.S.A.
12 D2 **Port Glasgow** Scotland
14 E2 **Portglenone** N Ireland
15 E3 **Portgordon** Scotland
145 E4 **Port Gore** New Zealand
116 M7 **Port Graham** Alaska U.S.A.
143 A8 **Port Gregory** *B* W Australia Australia
122 H8 **Port Greville** Nova Scotia Canada
8 C4 **Porth** Wales
85 F8 **Port Harcourt** Nigeria
117 K10 **Port Hardy** British Columbia Canada
145 D4 **Port Hardy** New Zealand
Port Harrison *see* **Inukjuak**
123 L8 **Port Hastings** C Breton I, Nova Scotia
123 L8 **Port Hawkesbury** C Breton I, Nova Scotia
8 C5 **Porthcawl** Wales
8 B2 **Porth Dinlleyn** *B* Wales
142 C5 **Port Hedland** W Australia Australia
127 L3 **Port Henderson** Jamaica
95 O3 **Port Henry** New York U.S.A.
Port Herald *see* **Nsanje**
100 J1 **Porthill** Idaho U.S.A.
8 B2 **Porthmadog** Wales
8 B2 **Porth Neigwl** *B* Wales
123 L8 **Port Hood** C Breton I, Nova Scotia
121 M9 **Port Hope** Ontario Canada
94 E3 **Port Hope** Michigan U.S.A.
123 Q1 **Port Hope Simpson** Labrador, Nfld Canada
102 E7 **Port Hueneme** California U.S.A.
120 H10 **Port Huron** Ontario Canada
94 E4 **Port Huron** Michigan U.S.A.
45 Q8 **Portici** Italy
16 B7 **Portimão** Portugal
29 M5 **Portimo** Finland
12 C1 **Portinnisherrich** Scotland
107 M2 **Portis** Kansas U.S.A.
8 B6 **Port Isaac** England
109 K9 **Port Isabel** Texas U.S.A.
99 T2 **Port Isabelle** Michigan U.S.A.
8 D5 **Portishead** England
139 K5 **Port Jackson** New South Wales Australia
95 O6 **Port Jefferson** Long I, New York U.S.A.
95 N5 **Port Jervis** New York U.S.A.
20 F8 **Port Joinville** France
127 J3 **Port Kaiser** Jamaica
140 A2 **Port Keats** N Terr Australia
139 K5 **Port Kembla** New South Wales Australia
138 C5 **Port Kenney** South Australia Australia
139 J5 **Portland** New South Wales Australia
138 F7 **Portland** Victoria Australia
127 P6 **Portland** Barbados
121 O8 **Portland** Ontario Canada
127 M2 **Portland** *parish* Jamaica
145 E1 **Portland** New Zealand
106 E3 **Portland** Colorado U.S.A.
94 C6 **Portland** Indiana U.S.A.
95 R3 **Portland** Maine U.S.A.
94 C4 **Portland** Michigan U.S.A.
98 J2 **Portland** North Dakota U.S.A.
100 C4 **Portland** Oregon U.S.A.
110 K5 **Portland** Tennessee U.S.A.
109 K8 **Portland** Texas U.S.A.
127 K3 **Portland Bight** Jamaica
8 D7 **Portland, Bill of** *head* England
139 J8 **Portland, C** Tasmania Australia
117 H8 **Portland Canal** Br Col/Alaska Canada/U.S.A.
123 P3 **Portland Cr. Pond** Newfoundland Canada
8 D6 **Portland Hbr** England
145 F3 **Portland I** New Zealand
117 H8 **Portland Inlet** British Columbia Canada
127 K3 **Portland Ridge** Jamaica
141 G2 **Portland Roads** Queensland Australia
126 F6 **Portland Rock** Caribbean
71 E8 **Port Languyan** Philippines
139 H8 **Port Latta** Tasmania Australia
109 L7 **Port Lavaca** Texas U.S.A.
14 D4 **Portlaw** Ireland
144 B4 **Port Levy** New Zealand
95 M3 **Port Leyden** New York U.S.A.
138 D5 **Port Lincoln** South Australia Australia
12 D4 **Port Logan** Scotland
120 K7 **Port Loring** Ontario Canada
20 D6 **Port-Louis** France
83 L12 **Port Louis** Mauritius
127 N4 **Port Louis** Guadeloupe W Indies
140 D3 **Port McArthur** *B* N Terr Australia
138 F7 **Port MacDonnell** South Australia Australia
121 L8 **Port McNicoll** Ontario Canada
139 L4 **Port Macquarie** New South Wales Australia
122 F10 **Port Maitland** Nova Scotia Canada
121 L10 **Port Maitland** Ontario Canada
109 K9 **Port Mansfield** Texas U.S.A.
115 N6 **Port Manvers** Labrador, Nfld Canada
127 L2 **Port Maria** Jamaica
94 J6 **Port Matilda** Pennsylvania U.S.A.
113 G11 **Port Mayaca** Florida U.S.A.
122 H9 **Port Medway** Nova Scotia Canada
117 M11 **Port Mellon** British Columbia Canada
122 H4 **Port Menier** Quebec Canada
116 G8 **Port Moller** Alaska U.S.A.
117 M11 **Port Moody** British Columbia Canada
127 M3 **Port Morant** Jamaica
136 K3 **Port Moresby** Papua New Guinea
123 N7 **Port Morien** C Breton I, Nova Scotia
21 N3 **Port-Mort** France
122 H10 **Port Mouton** Nova Scotia Canada
122 H10 **Port Mouton I** Nova Scotia Canada
141 F1 **Port Musgrave** *inlet* Queensland Australia
15 C4 **Portnacroish** Scotland
12 B2 **Portnahaven** Scotland
20 E6 **Port Navalo** France
109 O6 **Port Neches** Texas U.S.A.
138 D5 **Port Neill** South Australia Australia
126 G3 **Port Nelson** Bahamas
101 N7 **Portneuf** Idaho U.S.A.
121 S5 **Portneuf, Parc** Quebec Canada
122 C5 **Portneuf, R** Quebec Canada
122 C5 **Portneuf-sur-Mer** Quebec Canada
145 G4 **Port Nicholson** New Zealand
138 E6 **Port Noarlunga** South Australia Australia
87 C11 **Port Nolloth** S Africa
95 M7 **Port Norris** New Jersey U.S.A.
115 N6 **Port-Nouveau Québec** Quebec Canada
129 K4 **Pôrto** Brazil
16 B3 **Porto** Portugal
128 E5 **Pôrto Acre** Brazil
130 D7 **Pôrto Alegre** Mato Grosso Brazil
131 H3 **Pôrto Alegre** Rio Grande do Sul Brazil
Porto Alexandre *see* **Tombua**
87 B8 **Porto Amboim** Angola
Porto Amelia *see* **Pemba** Mozambique
129 G6 **Porto Artur** Brazil
144 D7 **Portobello** New Zealand
13 E2 **Portobello** Scotland
130 E10 **Pôrto Belo** Brazil
116 L8 **Port O'Brian** Alaska U.S.A.
43 C7 **Porto Cervo** Sardinia
109 L7 **Port O'Connor** Texas U.S.A.
16 B3 **Porto de Leixões** Portugal
129 H4 **Pôrto de Mos** Brazil
129 H6 **Pôrto dos Meinacos** Brazil
43 F11 **Porto Empedocle** Sicily
128 G7 **Pôrto Espiridião** Brazil
42 C6 **Portoferraio** Elba Italy
44 F3 **Portofino** Italy
12 D1 **Port of Menteith** Scotland
15 B2 **Port of Ness** Scotland
127 O2 **Port of Spain** Trinidad
45 M2 **Porto Garibaldi** Italy
129 H3 **Pôrto Grande** Brazil
42 E3 **Portogruaro** Italy
129 G7 **Pôrto Jofre** Brazil
102 D2 **Portola** California U.S.A.
130 C10 **Porto Luceno** Brazil
29 J9 **Pörtom** Finland
45 L2 **Portomaggiore** Italy
45 J1 **Porto Mantovano** Italy
44 D4 **Porto Maurizio** Italy
88 H9 **Porto Mocambo** Mozambique
129 G8 **Pôrto Murtinho** Brazil
129 J6 **Pôrto Nacional** Brazil
85 E7 **Porto Novo** Benin
113 G8 **Port Orange** Florida U.S.A.
117 M12 **Port Orchard** Washington U.S.A.
42 F5 **Porto Recanati** Italy
100 A7 **Port Orford** Oregon U.S.A.
133 G2 **Pôrto San José** Brazil
42 D6 **Porto San Stefano** Italy
85 A2 **Pôrto Santo** *isld* Madeira
129 H8 **Pôrto São José** Brazil
130 H5 **Pôrto Seguro** Brazil
45 M2 **Porto Tolle** Italy
43 B8 **Porto Torres** Sardinia
133 G3 **Pôrto União** Brazil
128 F5 **Pôrto Velho** Brazil
44 G3 **Portovenere** Italy
128 B4 **Portoviejo** Ecuador
12 C4 **Portpatrick** Scotland
140 B2 **Port Patterson** *inlet* N Terr Australia
144 A7 **Port Pegasus** New Zealand
121 M8 **Port Perry** Ontario Canada
139 G7 **Port Phillip B** Victoria Australia
138 E5 **Port Pirie** South Australia Australia
114 H4 **Port Radium** Northwest Territories Canada
8 A7 **Portreath** England
15 B3 **Portree** Scotland
118 J8 **Portreeve** Saskatchewan Canada
83 M8 **Port Refuge** Cocos Is Indian Oc
100 A1 **Port Renfrew** British Columbia Canada
123 T5 **Port Rexton** Newfoundland Canada
102 A4 **Port Reyes** California U.S.A.
100 B1 **Port Roberts** Washington U.S.A.
144 D5 **Port Robinson** New Zealand
140 D2 **Port Roper** *inlet* N Terr Australia
120 K10 **Port Rowan** Ontario Canada
127 L3 **Port Royal** Jamaica
112 G5 **Port Royal** South Carolina U.S.A.
95 K8 **Port Royal** Virginia U.S.A.
122 G9 **Port Royal Nat. Hist. Park** Ontario Canada
14 E1 **Portrush** N Ireland
79 C7 **Port Said** Egypt
113 B8 **Port St. Joe** Florida U.S.A.
89 F8 **Port St Johns** S Africa
19 N18 **Port St. Louis** France
18 F8 **Port St. Marie** France
20 G7 **Port St.Père** France
20 A4 **Portsall** France
14 D1 **Portsalon** Ireland
94 E3 **Port Sanilac** Michigan U.S.A.
123 P3 **Port Saunders** Newfoundland Canada
Port Say *see* **Marsa Ben Mehdi**
38 K8 **Pörtschach** Austria
89 G8 **Port Shepstone** S Africa
117 H8 **Port Simpson** British Columbia Canada
142 D4 **Port Smith** *B* W Australia Australia
121 O8 **Portsmouth** Ontario Canada
127 O7 **Portsmouth** Dominica
9 E6 **Portsmouth** England
99 L8 **Portsmouth** Iowa U.S.A.
95 R3 **Portsmouth** New Hampshire U.S.A.
112 L2 **Portsmouth** North Carolina U.S.A.
94 E8 **Portsmouth** Ohio U.S.A.
95 Q5 **Portsmouth** Rhode I U.S.A.
95 L10 **Portsmouth** Virginia U.S.A.
12 C1 **Portsonachan** Scotland
15 F3 **Portsoy** Scotland
120 J10 **Port Stanley** Ontario Canada
139 K5 **Port Stephens** New South Wales Australia
141 G2 **Port Stewart** *inlet* Queensland Australia
14 E1 **Port Stewart** N Ireland
86 G2 **Port Sudan** Sudan
8 C4 **Port Talbot** Wales
71 F4 **Port Tambang** Philippines
79 C9 **Port Taufiq** Egypt
127 O2 **Port Tembladora** Trinidad
29 M3 **Porttipahdan tekojärvi** *L* Finland
117 M11 **Port Townsend** Washington U.S.A.
16 B7 **Portugal** *rep* W Europe
83 J9 **Portugal B** Sri Lanka
123 U6 **Portugal Cove** Newfoundland Canada
17 F1 **Portugalete** Spain
128 E2 **Portuguesa** *state* Venezuela
Portuguese Guinea *see* **Guinea-Bissau** *rep*
14 C3 **Portumna** Ireland
123 T5 **Port Union** Newfoundland Canada
18 H10 **Port Vendres** France
102 F8 **Port Vicente** California U.S.A.
88 D1 **Port Victoria** Kenya
137 O5 **Port-Vila** Vanuatu
94 J4 **Portville** New York U.S.A.
138 E5 **Port Vincent** South Australia Australia
52 D1 **Port Vladimir** Russian Federation
138 E5 **Port Wakefield** South Australia Australia
142 F2 **Port Warrender** *inlet* W Australia Australia
99 T6 **Port Washington** Wisconsin U.S.A.
142 B5 **Port Weld** *B* W Australia Australia
116 N6 **Port Wells** *inlet* Alaska U.S.A.
112 F5 **Port Wentworth** Georgia U.S.A.
12 D4 **Port William** Scotland
122 H8 **Port Williams** Nova Scotia Canada
99 P3 **Port Wing** Wisconsin U.S.A.
107 P6 **Porum** Oklahoma U.S.A.
127 K2 **Porus** Jamaica
133 C8 **Porvenir** Chile
108 C5 **Porvenir** Texas U.S.A.
29 M11 **Porvoo** Finland
36 C2 **Porz** Germany
16 E5 **Porzuna** Spain
16 E5 **Porzuna, Sa. de** *mts* Spain
43 C8 **Posada** *R* Sardinia
133 F3 **Posadas** Argentina
16 D7 **Posadas** Spain
41 M5 **Poschiavo** Switzerland
94 D1 **Posen** Michigan U.S.A.
110 J3 **Poseyville** Indiana U.S.A.
52 E5 **Poshekhonye** Russian Federation
119 O1 **Poshkokagan L** Ontario Canada
46 F5 **Posídhion, Ákr** *C* Greece
41 O6 **Posina** *R* Italy
37 O5 **Pösing** Germany
29 N5 **Posio** Finland
45 Q8 **Positano** Italy
70 G5 **Poso** Sulawesi
78 J1 **Posof** Turkey
129 J6 **Posse** Brazil
37 N3 **Posseck** Germany
146 C12 **Possession Is** Antarctica
37 M2 **Pössneck** Germany
21 J7 **Possonnière, la** France
38 M8 **Possruck** Slovenia
109 J3 **Possum Kingdom L** Texas U.S.A.
100 E5 **Post** Oregon U.S.A.
37 N6 **Postau** Germany
37 L5 **Postbauer-Heng** Germany
8 C6 **Postbridge** England
115 M6 **Poste-de-la-Baleine** Quebec Canada
68 H6 **Poste Deshayes** Cambodia
Poste Maurice Cortier *see* **Bidon 5**
83 M12 **Poste, R du** Mauritius
85 E4 **Poste Weygand** Algeria
100 J2 **Post Falls** Idaho U.S.A.
71 J8 **Postiljon Pulau** *isld* Indonesia
89 C7 **Postmasburg** S Africa
129 H6 **Pôsto Alto Manissaua** Brazil
128 C4 **Posto Bobonazo** Peru
42 F3 **Postojna** Slovenia
99 P6 **Postville** Iowa U.S.A.
42 H5 **Posušje** Bosnia-Herzegovina
71 K9 **Pota** Indonesia
124 D4 **Pótam** Mexico
46 G3 **Potamoi** Greece
46 F8 **Potamós** Greece
47 O12 **Potamós** Greece
50 H2 **Potapovo** Russian Federation
128 G2 **Potaro** *R* Guyana
89 E6 **Potchefstroom** S Africa
48 J6 **Potcoava** Romania
130 H5 **Poté** Brazil
107 Q7 **Poteau** *R* Okla/Ark U.S.A.
107 Q6 **Poteau** Oklahoma U.S.A.
109 J6 **Poteet** Texas U.S.A.
130 J8 **Potengi** *R* Brazil
43 G8 **Potenza** Italy
144 A7 **Poteriteri, L** New Zealand
16 D1 **Potes** Spain
89 F5 **Potgietersrus** S Africa
109 J6 **Poth** Texas U.S.A.
100 F2 **Potholes Res** Washington U.S.A.
129 K5 **Poti** *R* Brazil
21 K4 **Potigny** France
85 G6 **Potiskum** Nigeria
71 K9 **Potjo Mandasawu** *mt* Indonesia
100 J3 **Potlatch** Idaho U.S.A.
89 B8 **Potloer** *mt* S Africa
48 K6 **Potlogi** Romania
101 M3 **Potomac** Montana U.S.A.
94 J7 **Potomac S. Branch** *R* West Virginia U.S.A.
133 D1 **Potosí** Bolivia
133 D2 **Potosí** *dept* Bolivia
110 F4 **Potosi** Missouri U.S.A.
103 J6 **Potosi Mt** Nevada U.S.A.
71 F5 **Pototan** Panay Philippines
133 D3 **Potrerillos** Chile
131 B2 **Potro, Cerro de** *pk* Chile
33 S8 **Potsdam** Germany
95 N2 **Potsdam** New York U.S.A.
37 L4 **Pottenstein** Germany
120 K4 **Potter** Ontario Canada
98 C8 **Potter** Nebraska U.S.A.
9 E5 **Potterne** England
9 F4 **Potter's Bar** England
102 A2 **Potter Valley** California U.S.A.
94 C4 **Potterville** Michigan U.S.A.
37 L6 **Pottmes** Germany
9 F3 **Potton** England
109 L2 **Pottsboro** Texas U.S.A.
111 G7 **Potts Camp** Mississippi U.S.A.
95 M6 **Pottstown** Pennsylvania U.S.A.
95 L6 **Pottsville** Pennsylvania U.S.A.
109 J4 **Pottsville** Texas U.S.A.
83 L11 **Pottuvil** Sri Lanka
107 N4 **Potwin** Kansas U.S.A.
21 H6 **Pouancé** France
68 F3 **Pou Bia** *mt* Laos
117 N8 **Pouce Coupé** British Columbia Canada
123 U6 **Pouch Cove** Newfoundland Canada
21 J6 **Poueze la** France
95 O5 **Poughkeepsie** New York U.S.A.
18 H5 **Pougues les Eaux** France
21 N7 **Pouillé** France
18 E9 **Pouillon** France
18 J5 **Pouilly en Auxois** France
21 O7 **Poulaines** France
20 B5 **Pouldergat** France
20 B6 **Pouldreuzic** France
20 C6 **Pouldu,le** France
21 N8 **Pouligny St. Pierre** France
20 F7 **Pouliguen,le** France
122 B5 **Poulin de Courval, L** Quebec Canada
20 C5 **Poullaouen** France
68 J5 **Poulo Canton, Is de** Vietnam
69 G8 **Poulo Dama, Iles** Vietnam
68 J6 **Poulo Gambir, Cu Lao** *isld* Vietnam
95 O3 **Poultney** Vermont U.S.A.
13 E6 **Poulton-le-Fylde** England
68 E4 **Pou Miang** *mt* Thailand
99 S4 **Pound** Wisconsin U.S.A.
9 F5 **Pound Hill** England
19 P18 **Pourcieux** France
145 F4 **Pourerere** New Zealand
145 G3 **Pourewa I** New Zealand
40 E6 **Pourri, Mont** France
21 N2 **Pourville** France
68 F3 **Pou San** *mt* Laos
68 F3 **Pou Sao** *mt* Laos
68 H5 **Pou Set** *mt* Laos
129 G6 **Pouso Alegre** Mato Grosso Brazil
130 F8 **Pouso Alegre** Minas Gerais Brazil
29 O6 **Poussu** Finland
144 A7 **Poutama I** New Zealand
68 F6 **Pouthisat** Cambodia
145 E2 **Pouto** New Zealand
121 Q3 **Poutrincourt, L** Quebec Canada
40 D1 **Pouxeux** France
21 J8 **Pouzauges** France
21 M7 **Pouzay** France
48 E1 **Pov Bystrica** Czechoslovakia
52 D3 **Povenets** Russian Federation
145 F3 **Poverty Bay** New Zealand
9 F5 **Povey Cross** England
45 J2 **Poviglio** Italy
48 F6 **Povlen** *mt* Serbia Yugoslavia
16 B3 **Póvoa de Varzim** Portugal
65 J3 **Povorotnyy, Mys** *C* Russian Federation
115 M5 **Povungnituk** Quebec Canada
121 L6 **Powassan** Ontario Canada
101 T5 **Powder** *R* Wyo/Mont U.S.A.
106 C3 **Powderhorn** Colorado U.S.A.
100 H5 **Powder R** Oregon U.S.A.
98 A4 **Powderville** Montana U.S.A.
141 G7 **Powell** *R* Queensland Australia
103 K7 **Powell** Arizona U.S.A.
98 E5 **Powell** South Dakota U.S.A.
94 D10 **Powell** *R* Tenn/Virg U.S.A.
99 R3 **Powell** Wisconsin U.S.A.
101 R5 **Powell** Wyoming U.S.A.
100 D5 **Powell Butte** Oregon U.S.A.
113 K11 **Powell Cay** *isld* Bahamas
103 O4 **Powell, L** Ariz/Utah U.S.A.
106 D2 **Powell, Mt** Colorado U.S.A.
102 F3 **Powell Mt** Nevada U.S.A.
126 F2 **Powell Pt** Eleuthera Bahamas
117 L10 **Powell River** British Columbia Canada
94 F8 **Powellton** West Virginia U.S.A.
101 O2 **Power** Montana U.S.A.
99 T4 **Powers** Michigan U.S.A.
100 A7 **Powers** Oregon U.S.A.
98 D1 **Powers L** North Dakota U.S.A.
111 C10 **Powhatan** Louisiana U.S.A.
94 K9 **Powhatan** Virginia U.S.A.
107 P2 **Powhattan** Kansas U.S.A.
8 D3 **Powick** England
141 H5 **Powlathanga** Queensland Australia
95 O4 **Pownal** Vermont U.S.A.
8 C3 **Powys** *co* Wales
130 C5 **Poxoreu** *R* Brazil
67 E2 **Poyang Hu** *L* China
111 D7 **Poyen** Arkansas U.S.A.
99 S5 **Poygan, L** Wisconsin U.S.A.
31 K7 **Poysdorf** Austria
124 C5 **Poza Grande** Mexico
78 E3 **Pozantı** Turkey
48 G6 **Požarevac** Serbia Yugoslavia
125 L7 **Poza Rica** Mexico
48 F7 **Požega** Serbia Yugoslavia
Pozen *see* **Poznań**
59 K2 **Pozharskoye** Russian Federation
52 J5 **Pozhva** Russian Federation
22 D3 **Pozières** France
140 D5 **Pozieres,Mt** N Terr Australia
31 K3 **Poznań** Poland
102 D6 **Pozo** California U.S.A.
17 F7 **Pozo Alcón** Spain
133 D2 **Pozo Almonte** Chile
16 D6 **Pozoblanco** Spain
103 J9 **Pozo Cenizo** Mexico
17 F6 **Pozohondo** Spain
103 J9 **Pozo Salado** Mexico
103 N10 **Pozo Verde** Mexico
52 H4 **Poztykeros** Russian Federation
133 D2 **Pozuelos, L. de** Argentina
45 J1 **Pozzolengo** Italy
45 L1 **Pozzonova** Italy
45 Q8 **Pozzuoli** Italy
68 F2 **P. Phac Mo** *mt* Vietnam
85 D7 **Pra** *R* Ghana
69 G14 **Prabumulih** Sumatra
31 L2 **Prabuty** Poland
45 J3 **Pracchia** Italy
68 D7 **Pracham Hiang, Laem** Thailand
30 H7 **Prachatice** Czechoslovakia
68 E5 **Prachin Buri** Thailand
68 D7 **Prachuap Khiri Khan** Thailand
16 C1 **Pradairo** Spain
31 K5 **Praděd** *mt* Czechoslovakia
18 G10 **Prades** France
70 P9 **Pradjekan** Java
28 E2 **Præstbro** Denmark
Præstø *co* *see* **Storstrøm and Roskilde** *counties*
28 J6 **Præsto** Denmark
38 N9 **Pragersk** Slovenia
38 F7 **Prägraten** Austria
Prague *see* **Praha**
107 O6 **Prague** Oklahoma U.S.A.
31 H5 **Praha** Czechoslovakia
48 K5 **Prahova** Romania
48 K6 **Prahova** *R* Romania
48 H6 **Prahova** Serbia Yugoslavia
85 B8 **Praia** Cape Verde
133 G4 **Praia Albardão** *beach* Brazil
48 J4 **Praid** Romania
129 H4 **Prainha** Brazil
122 B3 **Praires, L. des** Quebec Canada
109 K6 **Prairia Lea** Texas U.S.A.
141 G5 **Prairie** Queensland Australia
100 K6 **Prairie** Idaho U.S.A.
110 F1 **Prairie City** Illinois U.S.A.
100 G5 **Prairie City** Oregon U.S.A.
107 K2 **Prairie Dog Cr** Kansas U.S.A.
108 F1 **Prairie Dog Town Fork** *R* Texas U.S.A.
99 P6 **Prairie du Chien** Wisconsin U.S.A.
99 R6 **Prairie du Sac** Wisconsin U.S.A.
110 B6 **Prairie Grove** Arkansas U.S.A.
109 L4 **Prairie Hill** Texas U.S.A.
119 P6 **Prairie River** Saskatchewan Canada
119 Q7 **Prairies, L of the** Manitoba/Sask Canada
110 J2 **Prairieton** Indiana U.S.A.
107 L2 **Prairie View** Kansas U.S.A.
111 F11 **Prairieville** Louisiana U.S.A.
94 E9 **Praise** Kentucky U.S.A.
68 F5 **Prakhon Chai** Thailand
40 E7 **Pralognan** France
42 E2 **Pramaggiore, Mont** *mt* Italy
70 N9 **Prambanan** Java
37 O3 **Prameny** Czechoslovakia
69 D8 **Pram, Khao** *mt* Thailand
68 D6 **Pran** *R* Thailand
68 D6 **Pran Buri** Thailand
38 K7 **Prankerhöhe** *mt* Austria
69 D11 **Prapat** Sumatra
40 B2 **Praslay** France
83 J12 **Praslin** *isld* Seychelles
47 Q15 **Prasonísi** *isld* Greece
47 J9 **Prasonísi, Akr** *C* Rhodes Greece
31 L4 **Praszka** Poland
129 J7 **Prata** *R* Brazil
Pratas *isld* *see* **Dongsha Qundao**
33 R9 **Pratau** Germany
17 J3 **Prat de Llobregat** Spain
41 L4 **Prätigau** *V* Switzerland
45 K4 **Prato** Italy
45 R8 **Prátola Serra** Italy
42 D5 **Pratomagno** *mt* Italy
45 L4 **Pratomagno** Italy
45 H3 **Prato, Mt** Italy
45 L4 **Pratovecchio** Italy
18 G10 **Prats-de-Mollo** France
119 T9 **Pratt** Manitoba Canada
107 M4 **Pratt** Kansas U.S.A.
95 N4 **Prattsville** New York U.S.A.
111 K9 **Prattville** Alabama U.S.A.
40 B2 **Prauthoy** France
31 N1 **Pravdinsk** Russian Federation
54 J1 **Pravdinskiy** Russian Federation
46 F2 **Pravets** Bulgaria
16 C1 **Pravia** Spain
8 C7 **Prawle Pt** England
70 Q10 **Praya** Indonesia
21 N7 **Préaux** France
37 O3 **Přebuz** Czechoslovakia
20 H4 **Precey** France
52 D6 **Prechistoye** Russian Federation
21 K6 **Précigné** France
21 P3 **Précy-sur-Oise** France
45 L3 **Predappio** Italy
42 D2 **Predazzo** Italy
37 O5 **Predigtstuhl** *mt* Germany
38 M8 **Preding** Austria
38 J7 **Predlitz** Austria
38 F7 **Predoi** Italy
44 E2 **Predosa** Italy
51 O2 **Predporozhnyy** Russian Federation
119 P7 **Preeceville** Saskatchewan Canada
21 K5 **Pré-en-Pail** France
33 M4 **Preetz** Germany
20 F7 **Préfailles** France
31 M1 **Pregolya** *R* Russian Federation
127 J10 **Pregonero** Venezuela
18 E8 **Preignac** France
52 C6 **Preiļi** Latvia
121 M4 **Preissac** Quebec Canada
68 G6 **Prek Kak** Cambodia
68 H6 **Prek Preas** *R* Cambodia
68 G7 **Prek Sandek** Cambodia
68 F7 **Prek Taley** *R* Cambodia
8 B3 **Pren-gwyn** Wales
46 D4 **Prenjas** Albania
33 T6 **Prenzlau** Germany
59 K3 **Preobrazheniye** Russian Federation
42 A3 **Pré-St.-Didier** Italy
144 A7 **Preservation Inlet** New Zealand
130 D8 **Presidente Prudente** Brazil
108 C6 **Presidio** Texas U.S.A.
95 T7 **Presque Isle** Maine U.S.A.
18 F6 **Pressac** France
8 C1 **Prestatyn** Wales
8 C3 **Presteigne** Wales
13 F6 **Preston** England
101 O7 **Preston** Idaho U.S.A.
95 M8 **Preston** Maryland U.S.A.
99 O6 **Preston** Minnesota U.S.A.
110 C4 **Preston** Missouri U.S.A.
103 J3 **Preston** Nevada U.S.A.
107 P6 **Preston** Oklahoma U.S.A.
9 E5 **Preston Candover** England
109 O9 **Preston Hollow** Texas U.S.A.
13 F2 **Prestonpans** Scotland
94 E9 **Prestonsburg** Kentucky U.S.A.
13 F6 **Prestwich** England
12 D3 **Prestwick** Scotland
129 K6 **Preto** *R* Bahia Brazil
129 J7 **Prêto** *R* Minas Gerais Brazil
128 F4 **Prêto do Igapó Açu** *R* Brazil
89 F5 **Pretoria** S Africa
20 H3 **Prétot** France
33 R9 **Prettin** Germany
95 L7 **Prettyboy Res** Maryland U.S.A.
107 M4 **Pretty Prairie** Kansas U.S.A.
33 O7 **Pretzier** Germany
33 R9 **Pretzsch** Germany
21 M8 **Preuilly-sur-Claise** France
38 L8 **Prevalje** Slovenia
46 D6 **Préveza** Greece
106 B6 **Prewitt** New Mexico U.S.A.
106 G1 **Prewitt Res** Colorado U.S.A.
21 N4 **Prey** France
68 G7 **Prey Lovea** Cambodia
68 G7 **Prey Veng** Cambodia
45 P5 **Prezza** Italy
69 B10 **Priala** Sumatra
54 H9 **Priazovskaya Vozvyshenost'** *uplands* Ukraine
116 D8 **Pribilof Is** Bering Sea
30 H6 **Příbram** Czechoslovakia
122 D5 **Price** Quebec Canada
95 M7 **Price** Maryland U.S.A.
98 F2 **Price** North Dakota U.S.A.
103 O2 **Price** *R* Utah U.S.A.
103 O2 **Price** Utah U.S.A.
68 A6 **Price, C** Andaman Is
106 B1 **Price Creek** Colorado U.S.A.
117 J9 **Price I** British Columbia Canada
111 H11 **Prichard** Alabama U.S.A.
100 K2 **Prichard** Idaho U.S.A.
54 E9 **Prichernomorskaya Nizmennost'** *lowland* Ukraine
37 J4 **Prichsenstadt** Germany
127 P5 **Prickly Pt** Grenada
109 J4 **Priddy** Texas U.S.A.
54 D7 **Pridneprovskaya Nizmennost'** *lowland* Ukraine
54 C8 **Pridneprovskaya Vozvyshennost'** *uplands* Ukraine
17 F4 **Priego** Spain
16 E7 **Priego de C** Spain
27 M15 **Priekule** Latvia
27 M16 **Priekulė** Lithuania
33 Q5 **Priemerburg** Germany
89 C7 **Prieska** S Africa
37 M1 **Priessnitz** Germany
33 T10 **Priestewitz** Germany
100 J1 **Priest L** Idaho U.S.A.
127 M2 **Priestman's River** Jamaica
100 F3 **Priest Rapids** Washington U.S.A.
100 E3 **Priest Rapids Lake** *res* Washington U.S.A.
100 J1 **Priest River** Idaho U.S.A.
117 P11 **Priest River** Idaho U.S.A.
31 L7 **Prievidza** Czechoslovakia
33 Q6 **Prignitz** *reg* Germany
56 C4 **Priiskovyy** Russian Federation
42 H4 **Prijedor** Bosnia-Herzegovina
53 G9 **Prikaspiyskaya Nizmennost** *lowlands* Kazakhstan/Rus Fed
46 E3 **Prilep** Macedonia Yugoslavia
54 D6 **Priluki** Ukraine
40 B7 **Primarette** France
118 H6 **Primate** Saskatchewan Canada
37 O4 **Přimda** Czechoslovakia
20 C4 **Primel,Pte.de** France
20 C4 **Primel-Trégastel** France
126 E4 **Primero de Enero** Cuba
131 D3 **Primero, R** Argentina
139 J8 **Prime Seal I** Tasmania Australia
99 L6 **Primghar** Iowa U.S.A.
52 C4 **Primorsk** Russian Federation
53 E10 **Primorsk** Ukraine
59 K3 **Primorskiy** Russian Federation
56 F5 **Primorskiy Khrebet** *mts* Russian Federation
59 K2 **Primorskiy Kray** *reg* Russian Federation
47 J2 **Primorsko** Bulgaria
48 M5 **Primorskoye** Ukraine
48 N5 **Primorskoye** Ukraine
54 J9 **Primorskoye** Ukraine
122 J7 **Prim, Pt** Prince Edward I Canada
117 F5 **Primrose** *R* Br Col/Yukon Terr Canada
118 H4 **Primrose L** Saskatchewan Canada
36 B5 **Prims** *R* Germany
36 C4 **Primstal** Germany
118 J6 **Prince** Saskatchewan Canada
119 M5 **Prince Albert** Saskatchewan Canada
89 C9 **Prince Albert** S Africa
146 D11 **Prince Albert Mts** Antarctica
118 L5 **Prince Albert Nat. Park** Saskatchewan Canada
114 H3 **Prince Albert Pen** Northwest Territories Canada
114 G3 **Prince Alfred, C** Northwest Territories Canada

115 M4 **Prince Charles I** Northwest Territories Canada
146 H10 **Prince Charles Mts** Antarctica
121 O9 **Prince Edward B** Ontario Canada
122 J7 **Prince Edward I** *prov* Canada
90 M14 **Prince Edward I** Indian Oc
122 J7 **Prince Edward I. Nat. Park** Canada
95 L8 **Prince Frederick** Maryland U.S.A.
142 F3 **Prince Frederick Harb** W Australia Australia
117 M9 **Prince George** British Columbia Canada
114 J2 **Prince Gustaf Adolf Sea** Northwest Territories Canada
116 C4 **Prince of Wales, C** Alaska U.S.A.
141 F1 **Prince of Wales I** Queensland Australia
114 J3 **Prince of Wales I** Northwest Territories Canada
117 G8 **Prince of Wales I** Alaska U.S.A.
114 H3 **Prince of Wales Str** Northwest Territories Canada
114 H2 **Prince Patrick I** Northwest Territories Canada
115 K3 **Prince Regent Inlet** Northwest Territories Canada
142 F3 **Prince Regent R** W Australia Australia
117 H8 **Prince Rupert** British Columbia Canada
130 H9 **Princesa Isabel** Brazil
Princes Is *see* **Kızıl Adalar**
Princes Lake Ontario *see* **Wallace**
9 F4 **Princes Risborough** England
95 M8 **Princess Anne** Maryland U.S.A.
141 G2 **Princess Charlotte B** Queensland Australia
146 H12 **Princess Elizabeth Land** Antarctica
142 F3 **Princess May Ra** W Australia Australia
144 A6 **Princess Mts** New Zealand
143 D7 **Princess Ra** W Australia Australia
117 J9 **Princess Royal I** British Columbia Canada
127 O3 **Prince's Town** Trinidad
9 E3 **Princethorpe** England
117 N11 **Princeton** British Columbia Canada
102 B2 **Princeton** California U.S.A.
99 R8 **Princeton** Illinois U.S.A.
110 J3 **Princeton** Indiana U.S.A.
110 J4 **Princeton** Kentucky U.S.A.
95 U1 **Princeton** Maine U.S.A.
99 T3 **Princeton** Michigan U.S.A.
99 N4 **Princeton** Minnesota U.S.A.
99 N9 **Princeton** Missouri U.S.A.
95 N6 **Princeton** New Jersey U.S.A.
112 J2 **Princeton** North Carolina U.S.A.
94 F9 **Princeton** West Virginia U.S.A.
99 R6 **Princeton** Wisconsin U.S.A.
8 C6 **Princetown** England
121 T6 **Princeville** Quebec Canada
99 R9 **Princeville** Illinois U.S.A.
116 O6 **Prince William Sound** Alaska U.S.A.
86 A5 **Principe** *isld* G of Guinea
128 F6 **Principe da Beira** Brazil
100 E5 **Prineville** Oregon U.S.A.
98 C6 **Pringle** South Dakota U.S.A.
108 C8 **Pringle** Texas U.S.A.
19 Q13 **Pringy** France
115 P5 **Prins Christian Sund** Greenland
25 C5 **Prinsenhage** Netherlands
68 C6 **Prinsep I** Burma
146 H7 **Prinsesse Astrid Kyst** *coast* Antarctica
146 J7 **Prinsesse Ragnhild Kyst** *coast* Antarctica
146 J8 **Prins Harald Kyst** *coast* Antarctica
50 A1 **Prins Karls Forland** Spitzbergen
123 L4 **Prinsta B** Anticosti I, Quebec
125 N3 **Prinzapolca** Nicaragua
54 L2 **Priokskiy** Russian Federation
16 B1 **Prior, C** Spain
52 D4 **Priozersk** Russian Federation
52 K3 **Pripolyarnyy Ural** *mts* Russian Federation
53 C8 **Pripyat** *R* Belorussia/Ukraine
29 P3 **Prirechnyy** Russian Federation
37 P3 **Přisečnice** Czechoslovakia
48 J3 **Prislop Pass** Romania
46 E4 **Prispansko ezero** *L* Albania/Greece/Yugoslavia
46 E2 **Priština** Serbia Yugoslavia
106 H4 **Pritchett** Colorado U.S.A.
33 Q8 **Pritzerbe** Germany
33 O6 **Pritzier** Germany
33 Q6 **Pritzwalk** Germany
19 N15 **Privas** France
45 O7 **Priverno** Italy
45 O6 **Privernum** Italy
42 F3 **Privka** Slovenia
52 F6 **Privolzhsk** Russian Federation
53 G7 **Privolzhskaya Vozvyshennost** *uplands* Russian Federation
53 G7 **Privolzh'ye** Russian Federation
20 D5 **Priziac** France
46 D2 **Prizren** Serbia Yugoslavia
43 E11 **Prizzi** Sicily
48 K1 **Probezhnaya** Ukraine
70 O9 **Probolinngo** Java
37 L2 **Probstzella** Germany
8 B7 **Probus** England
31 J4 **Prochowice** Poland
43 F8 **Procida** *isld* Italy
45 Q8 **Procida** Italy
106 H1 **Proctor** Colorado U.S.A.
109 J4 **Proctor** Texas U.S.A.
95 O3 **Proctor** Vermont U.S.A.
109 J3 **Proctor Res** Texas U.S.A.
95 P3 **Proctorsville** Vermont U.S.A.
16 B5 **Proènca a Nova** Portugal
37 N1 **Profen** Germany
22 H3 **Profondeville** Belgium
125 L2 **Progreso** Honduras
125 P7 **Progreso** Mexico
59 J2 **Progress** Russian Federation
106 E7 **Progresso** New Mexico U.S.A.
56 B6 **Prokhladnoye** Kazakhstan
55 G2 **Prokhorkino Proryto** Russian Federation
54 H5 **Prokhorovka** Russian Federation
46 D2 **Prokletije** Montenegro Yugoslavia
56 C4 **Prokop'yevsk** Russian Federation
46 E1 **Prokuplje** Serbia Yugoslavia
52 D5 **Proletariy** Russian Federation
53 F10 **Proletarsk** Russian Federation
54 K8 **Proletarsk** Ukraine
54 J1 **Proletarskiy** Russian Federation
54 G6 **Proletarskiy** Russian Federation
59 N2 **Proliv Frizi** *str* Russian Federation
50 E1 **Proliv Matochkin Shar** Russian Federation
37 K4 **Prolsdorf** Germany
Prome *see* **Pyè**
99 N9 **Promise City** Iowa U.S.A.
101 N8 **Promontory** Utah U.S.A.
56 C3 **Promyshlennaya** Russian Federation
53 G10 **Promyslovka** Russian Federation
52 F5 **Pronino** Russian Federation
100 G9 **Pronto** Nevada U.S.A.
54 M2 **Pronya** *R* Russian Federation
117 M6 **Prophet River** British Columbia Canada
99 R8 **Prophetstown** Illinois U.S.A.
130 H11 **Propriá** Brazil
33 S10 **Prösen** Germany
141 J5 **Proserpine** Queensland Australia
33 Q9 **Prosigk** Germany
31 K3 **Prosna** *R* Poland
52 H5 **Prosnitsa** Russian Federation
46 F3 **Prosotsáni** Greece
95 M3 **Prospect** New York U.S.A.
94 D6 **Prospect** Ohio U.S.A.
100 C7 **Prospect** Oregon U.S.A.
94 G6 **Prospect** Pennsylvania U.S.A.
127 M3 **Prospect Pt** Jamaica
100 A6 **Prosper** Oregon U.S.A.
112 F3 **Prosperity** South Carolina U.S.A.
98 H9 **Prosser** Nebraska U.S.A.
100 F3 **Prosser** Washington U.S.A.
48 D1 **Prostějov** Czechoslovakia
141 K7 **Proston** Queensland Australia
52 H2 **Prosunduy** Russian Federation
54 H8 **Prosyanaya** Ukraine
31 M5 **Proszowice** Poland
107 L4 **Protection** Kansas U.S.A.
99 O6 **Protivin** Iowa U.S.A.
54 J2 **Protva** *R* Russian Federation
33 T7 **Prötzel** Germany
47 J1 **Provadiya** Bulgaria
115 O3 **Prøven** Greenland
111 C10 **Provencal** Louisiana U.S.A.
19 O17 **Provence** *prov* France
36 C7 **Provenchères-sur-Fave** France
127 P5 **Providence** Grenada
110 J4 **Providence** Kentucky U.S.A.
112 J1 **Providence** North Carolina U.S.A.
95 Q5 **Providence** Rhode I U.S.A.
101 O8 **Providence** Utah U.S.A.
120 H7 **Providence Bay** Ontario Canada
144 A7 **Providence, C** New Zealand
116 J8 **Providence, C** Alaska U.S.A.
87 J9 **Providence I** Br Indian Oc Terr
103 J7 **Providence Mts** California U.S.A.
127 H4 **Providenciales** *isld* Turks & Caicos Is
128 F6 **Providencia, Sa. da** *mts* Brazil
116 A4 **Provideniya** Russian Federation
141 G2 **Providential Chan** Gt Barrier Reef Aust
95 R4 **Provincetown** Massachusetts U.S.A.
18 H4 **Provins** France
98 C6 **Provo** South Dakota U.S.A.
103 N1 **Provo** Utah U.S.A.
118 G6 **Provost** Alberta Canada
22 D4 **Proyart** France
42 H5 **Prozor** Bosnia-Herzegovina
130 E9 **Prudentópolis** Brazil
94 C2 **Prudenville** Michigan U.S.A.
13 G4 **Prudhoe** England
116 N1 **Prudhoe Bay** Alaska U.S.A.
141 J5 **Prudhoe I** Queensland Australia
115 N2 **Prudhoe Land** Greenland
119 M6 **Prud'homme** Saskatchewan Canada
31 K5 **Prudnik** Poland
54 H6 **Prudyanka** Ukraine
36 B3 **Prüm** Germany
21 M6 **Prunay** France
21 O5 **Prunay-le-Gillon** France
45 J3 **Prunetta** Italy
19 Q15 **Prunières** France
21 P8 **Pruniers** Indre France
21 O7 **Pruniers** Loir-et-Cher France
52 H4 **Prupt** *R* Russian Federation
31 K2 **Pruszcz** Poland
31 M3 **Pruszków** Poland
48 L4 **Prut** *R* Moldavia/Romania
48 L3 **Prutul** *R* Romania
41 N3 **Prutz** Austria
52 D4 **Pryazha** Russian Federation
146 J11 **Prydz B** Antarctica
101 R4 **Pryor** Montana U.S.A.
107 P5 **Pryor** Oklahoma U.S.A.
31 M2 **Przasnysz** Poland
31 K2 **Przechlewo** Poland
31 M4 **Przedbórz** Poland
31 O6 **Przemyśl** Poland
31 N5 **Przeworsk** Poland
31 H4 **Przewóz** Poland
57 J4 **Przheval'sk** Kyrgyzstan
31 M4 **Przysucha** Poland
46 F6 **Psakhná** Greece
47 H6 **Psará** *isld* Greece
46 G5 **Psathoúra** *isld* Greece
31 K4 **Psie Pole** Poland
47 R14 **Psíndhos** Rhodes Greece
47 H9 **Psira** *isld* Greece
52 C5 **Pskov** Russian Federation
52 C5 **Pskovskaya Oblast'** *prov* Russian Federation
52 C5 **Pskovskoye, Ozero** *L* Russian Federation
31 L1 **Pszczółki** Poland
31 L6 **Pszczyna** Poland
53 C7 **Ptich'** *R* Belorussia
46 E4 **Ptolemais** Greece
38 N9 **Ptuj** Slovenia
135 U4 **Puako** Hawaiian Is
116 K8 **Puale B** Alaska U.S.A.
133 E5 **Puán** Argentina
67 C5 **Pubei** China
122 G10 **Pubnico** Nova Scotia Canada
128 C5 **Pucacaca** Peru
128 D5 **Pucallpa** Peru
21 O3 **Puchay** France
38 N6 **Puchberg** Austria
65 A7 **Pucheng** China
65 C7 **Pucheng** China
67 F3 **Pucheng** China
52 F6 **Puchezh** Russian Federation
31 L6 **Puchov** Czechoslovakia
71 E5 **Pucio Pt** Panay Philippines
31 L1 **Puck** Poland
99 R6 **Puckaway L** Wisconsin U.S.A.
9 G4 **Puckeridge** England
111 G9 **Puckett** Mississippi U.S.A.
143 B7 **Puckford,Mt** W Australia Australia
29 M6 **Pudasjärvi** Finland
8 D6 **Puddletown** England
52 H5 **Pudem** Russian Federation
70 E6 **Pudi** Kalimantan
67 B3 **Puding** China
123 Q5 **Pudops L** Newfoundland Canada
52 E4 **Pudozh** Russian Federation
52 E4 **Pudozhgora** Russian Federation
13 G6 **Pudsey** England
125 K8 **Puebla** Mexico
16 D5 **Puebla de Alcocer** Spain
17 F7 **Puebla de Don Fadrique** Spain
16 D5 **Puebla de Don Rodrigo** Spain
16 C2 **Puebla de Sanabria** Spain
16 C2 **Puebla de Trives** Spain
106 F3 **Pueblo** Colorado U.S.A.
106 C5 **Pueblo Bonito** New Mexico U.S.A.
133 C3 **Pueblo Hundido** Chile
100 G7 **Pueblo Mts** Oregon U.S.A.
124 G6 **Pueblo Nuevo** Mexico
125 N9 **Pueblo Viejo** Mexico
125 L6 **Pueblo Viejo, L. de** Mexico
133 D5 **Puelches** Argentina
133 D5 **Puelén** Argentina
16 B2 **Puenteareas** Spain
16 B2 **Puente-Caldelas** Spain
16 D7 **Puente Genil** Spain
103 P7 **Puerco** *R* Arizona U.S.A.
106 C6 **Puerco, R** New Mexico U.S.A.
128 C2 **Puerta Mutis** Colombia
133 C7 **Puerto Aisén** Chile
125 N5 **Puerto Armuelles** Panama
128 C3 **Puerto Asis** Colombia
128 E2 **Puerto Ayacucho** Venezuela
125 P10 **Puerto Barrios** Guatemala
128 D6 **Puerto Bermúdez** Peru
128 D2 **Puerto Berrio** Colombia
133 C7 **Puerto Bertrand** Chile
128 C6 **Puerto Caballas** Peru
128 E1 **Puerto Cabello** Venezuela
125 N2 **Puerto Cabezas** Nicaragua
Puerto Capaz Morocco *see* **Jebha**
128 E2 **Puerto Carreño** Colombia
130 B8 **Puerto Casado** Paraguay
128 C5 **Puerto Chicama** Peru
133 C6 **Puerto Cisnes** Chile
133 D8 **Puerto Coig** Argentina
128 D1 **Puerto Colombia** Colombia
125 Q10 **Puerto Cortés** Honduras
128 E1 **Puerto Cumarebo** Venezuela
125 L10 **Puerto Escondido** Mexico
127 J8 **Puerto Estrella** Colombia
128 C5 **Puerto Eten** Peru
133 C5 **Puerto Fuy** Chile
128 F7 **Puerto Grether** Bolivia
133 D8 **Puerto Harberton** Argentina
128 E6 **Puerto Heath** Bolivia
128 D3 **Puerto Huitoto** Colombia
133 E5 **Puerto Ingeniero White** Argentina
125 Q7 **Puerto Juárez** Mexico
127 M9 **Puerto La Cruz** Venezuela
128 D4 **Puerto Leguizamo** Colombia
125 N2 **Puerto Lempira** Honduras
16 E6 **Puertollano** Spain
128 D7 **Puerto Lomas** Peru
127 J9 **Puerto López** Colombia
17 F7 **Puerto Lumbreras** Spain
133 D6 **Puerto Madryn** Argentina
128 E6 **Puerto Maldonado** Peru
126 F4 **Puerto Manatí** Cuba
128 D4 **Puerto Miraña** Colombia
133 C6 **Puerto Montt** Chile
133 C8 **Puerto Natales** Chile
128 E2 **Puerto Nuevo** Colombia
133 F3 **Puerto Ocampo** Argentina
128 F2 **Puerto Ordaz** Venezuela
126 F4 **Puerto Padre** Cuba
133 C2 **Puerto Patillos** Chile
124 C2 **Puerto Penasco** Mexico
133 F2 **Puerto Pinasco** Paraguay
133 E6 **Puerto Pirámides** Argentina
128 F1 **Puerto Piritu** Venezuela
127 J5 **Puerto Plata** Dominican Rep
128 D5 **Puerto Portillo** Peru
130 C9 **Puerto Presidente Stroessner** Paraguay
71 D6 **Puerto Princesa** Palawan Philippines
125 M5 **Puerto Quepos** Costa Rica
128 E6 **Puerto Rico** Bolivia
113 J7 **Puerto Rico** *terr* Caribbean
127 L5 **Puerto Rico Trench** Caribbean
126 G4 **Puerto Samá** Cuba
125 L3 **Puerto Sandino** Nicaragua
130 B8 **Puerto Sastre** Paraguay
128 E6 **Puerto Siles** Bolivia
130 B6 **Puerto Suárez** Bolivia
124 G7 **Puerto Vallarta** Mexico
133 C6 **Puerto Varas** Chile
128 F7 **Puerto Velarde** Bolivia
128 D5 **Puerto Victoria** Peru
128 D2 **Puerto Villamizar** Colombia
133 D7 **Puerto Visser** Argentina
128 D2 **Puerto Wilches** Colombia
133 C7 **Pueyrredón, L** Chile/Arg
25 F7 **Puffendorf** Germany
124 G7 **Puga** Mexico
52 H6 **Pugachevo** Russian Federation
74 E4 **Pugal** India
88 G10 **Puga Puga** *isld* Mozambique
100 C2 **Puget Sound** Washington U.S.A.
19 P13 **Pugieu** France
43 G8 **Puglia** *prov* Italy
71 K9 **Pugubengo** Flores Indonesia
70 K8 **Pugung, G** *mt* Sumatra
122 J8 **Pugwash** Nova Scotia Canada
145 F3 **Puha** New Zealand
135 O1 **Puhi** Hawaiian Is
145 E2 **Puhoi** New Zealand
48 H5 **Pui** Romania
48 L4 **Puieşti** Romania
17 J2 **Puigcerda** Spain
71 G7 **Pujada B** Mindanao Philippines
65 G4 **Pujan Res** N Korea
19 N16 **Pujaut** France
67 A1 **Pujiang** China
67 F2 **Pujiang** China
119 Q3 **Pukatawagan** Manitoba Canada
46 D2 **Pukë** Albania
145 G2 **Pukeamaru** *mt* New Zealand
145 E3 **Pukearuhe** New Zealand
145 F3 **Pukehou** New Zealand
145 E2 **Pukekawa** New Zealand
145 E2 **Pukekohe** New Zealand
144 C5 **Pukekura** New Zealand
145 E2 **Pukemiro** New Zealand
145 D1 **Pukenui** New Zealand
145 F3 **Pukeokahu** New Zealand
144 C6 **Pukerangi** New Zealand
144 B7 **Pukerau** New Zealand
145 E3 **Pukeroa** New Zealand
145 G3 **Puketawai** New Zealand
144 D5 **Puketeraki Range** New Zealand
145 F3 **Puketitiri** New Zealand
145 F2 **Puketoetoe** *mt* New Zealand
145 F4 **Puketoi Range** New Zealand
145 E3 **Puketutu** New Zealand
145 F2 **Puketutu I** New Zealand
144 C6 **Pukeuri Junction** New Zealand
29 M11 **Pukkila** Finland
67 F1 **Pukou** China
52 F3 **Puksa** Russian Federation
52 H5 **Puksib** Russian Federation
52 F3 **Puksoozero** Russian Federation
98 G6 **Pukwana** South Dakota U.S.A.
42 F4 **Pula** Croatia
128 E8 **Pulacayo** Bolivia
43 C9 **Pula, C. di** Sardinia
69 C11 **Pulaksama** Sumatra
Pulandian *see* **Xinjin**
71 G6 **Pulangi** *R* Mindanao Philippines
70 D6 **Pulangpisau** Kalimantan
70 K8 **Pulao Seribu** *isld* Sumatra
70 K9 **Pulasari** *mt* Java
71 K8 **Pulasi** *isld* Indonesia
99 O9 **Pulaski** Iowa U.S.A.
95 L3 **Pulaski** New York U.S.A.
110 J6 **Pulaski** Tennessee U.S.A.
94 G9 **Pulaski** Virginia U.S.A.
99 S5 **Pulaski** Wisconsin U.S.A.
69 F13 **Pulaukidjang** Sumatra
70 B4 **Pulaumadjang** Kalimantan
69 E13 **Pulaupunjung** Sumatra
31 N4 **Puławy** Poland
9 F6 **Pulborough** England
76 D3 **Pulivendla** India
76 C6 **Puliyangudi** India
83 K9 **Puliyankulam** Sri Lanka
29 M7 **Pulkkila** Finland
100 H3 **Pullman** Washington U.S.A.
71 E2 **Pulog, Mt** Luzon Philippines
83 K8 **Puloli** Sri Lanka
52 F2 **Pulonga** Russian Federation
52 D1 **Pulozero** Russian Federation
124 D4 **Púlpito, Pta** *C* Mexico
33 T10 **Pulsnitz** *R* Germany
31 M3 **Pułtusk** Poland
66 C4 **Pulu** China
70 P10 **Pulukan** Bali Indonesia
66 E6 **Puma Yumco** *L* China
Pumiao *see* **Yongning**
98 A4 **Pumpkin Cr** Montana U.S.A.
98 C8 **Pumpkin Cr** Nebraska U.S.A.
108 F6 **Pumpville** Texas U.S.A.
8 C3 **Pumsaint** Wales
128 B4 **Puná** *isld* Ecuador
70 G5 **Puna** *R* Sulawesi
144 C5 **Punakaiki** New Zealand
83 L10 **Punani** Sri Lanka
74 F2 **Punch** Kashmir
117 M9 **Punchaw** British Columbia Canada
52 F4 **Punduga** Russian Federation
76 A1 **Pune** India
55 D1 **Punga** *R* Russian Federation
112 L2 **Pungo** North Carolina U.S.A.
59 J3 **Pungsan** N Korea
86 E6 **Punia** Zaire
70 Q10 **Punikan, G** *mt* Indonesia
131 B2 **Punilla, Sa. de la** *mts* Chile
74 F3 **Punjab** *prov* India
74 D3 **Punjab, The** *prov* Pakistan
140 E4 **Punjaub** Queensland Australia
29 O10 **Punkaharju** Finland
29 K10 **Punkalaidun** Finland
119 N7 **Punnichy** Saskatchewan Canada
128 D6 **Puno** *dept* Peru
128 D7 **Puno** Peru
106 D7 **Punta** New Mexico U.S.A.
131 E7 **Punta Alta** Argentina
133 C8 **Punta Arenas** Chile
43 C7 **Puntaccia, Monte** *mt* Sardinia
133 C3 **Punta Colorada** Chile
108 B8 **Punta de Agua Cr.** *R* Texas/New Mex U.S.A.
17 H4 **Punta de la Baña** Spain
125 P9 **Punta Gorda** Belize
125 N4 **Punta Gorda** Nicaragua
100 A9 **Punta Gorda** California U.S.A.
113 E11 **Punta Gorda** Florida U.S.A.
131 G6 **Punta Norte** Argentina
127 J5 **Punta Palenque** Dominican Rep
124 B3 **Punta Prieta** Mexico
125 M5 **Puntarenas** Costa Rica
128 G8 **Punta Rieles** Paraguay
125 N5 **Punta San Pedrillo** Costa Rica
127 M5 **Punta Tuna** Puerto Rico
128 D1 **Punto Fijo** Venezuela
46 G4 **Punto Lágo** Greece
133 D7 **Puntudo, Cerro** *mt* Argentina
116 C5 **Punuk Is** Bering Sea
94 J6 **Punxsutawney** Pennsylvania U.S.A.
68 F6 **Puok** Cambodia
29 N7 **Puolanka** Finland
26 L5 **Puottaure** Sweden
128 E6 **Puoya** *mt* Bolivia
145 D4 **Puponga** New Zealand
58 F6 **Puqi** China
128 D6 **Puquio** Peru
133 D3 **Puquios** Chile
50 G2 **Pur** *R* Russian Federation
128 C3 **Puracé** *vol* Colombia
70 M9 **Purbalingga** Java
107 N7 **Purcell** Oklahoma U.S.A.
116 J3 **Purcell Mt** Alaska U.S.A.
117 P10 **Purcell Mts** British Columbia Canada
100 K1 **Purcell Range** Montana U.S.A.
94 K7 **Purcellville** Virginia U.S.A.
17 F7 **Purchena** Spain
99 N10 **Purdin** Missouri U.S.A.
98 F7 **Purdum** Nebraska U.S.A.
110 C5 **Purdy** Missouri U.S.A.
145 E3 **Pureora** *mt* New Zealand
124 H8 **Purépero** Mexico
145 E1 **Purerua** New Zealand
9 E6 **Purewell** England
106 G4 **Purgatoire** *R* Colorado U.S.A.
116 N3 **Purgatory** Alaska U.S.A.
38 M5 **Purgstall** Austria
75 L9 **Puri** India
128 D3 **Purificación** Colombia
145 E2 **Puriri** New Zealand
9 F5 **Purley** England
25 C3 **Purmerend** Netherlands
74 G9 **Purna** India
138 B2 **Purndu Saltpan** South Australia Australia
52 E3 **Purnema** Russian Federation
75 M6 **Pūrnia** India
118 F9 **Purple Springs** Alberta Canada
128 E4 **Purué** *R* Brazil
70 D5 **Purukcahu** Kalimantan
128 F4 **Purus** *R* Brazil
29 O10 **Puruvesi** *L* Finland
111 G10 **Purvis** Mississippi U.S.A.
46 G2 **Pŭrvomay** Bulgaria
70 L9 **Purwakarta** Java
70 M9 **Purwarejo** Java
70 N9 **Purwodadi** Java
70 M9 **Purwokerto** Java
110 H5 **Puryear** Tennessee U.S.A.
66 B4 **Pusa** China
52 C6 **Puša** Latvia
70 B4 **Pusa** Sarawak
74 G9 **Pusad** India
52 B6 **Pušalotas** Lithuania
65 H7 **Pusan** S Korea
71 G7 **Pusan Pt** Mindanao Philippines
70 B4 **Pusatdamai** Kalimantan
79 D2 **Pusatlı Dağı** *mt* Turkey
65 D6 **Pushang** China
95 T2 **Pushaw L** Maine U.S.A.
52 D5 **Pushkin** Russian Federation
54 J1 **Pushkino** Russian Federation
52 E3 **Pushlakhta** Russian Federation
123 Q6 **Pushthrough** Newfoundland Canada
77 H4 **Pusht-i-Rud** *reg* Afghanistan
120 E4 **Puskaskwa Nat. Park** Ontario Canada
121 O3 **Puskitamika L** Quebec Canada
48 G3 **Püspökladány** Hungary
21 O5 **Pussay** France
22 H4 **Pussemange** Belgium
38 K7 **Pusterwald** Austria
52 C6 **Pustoshka** Russian Federation
102 B3 **Putah Cr** California U.S.A.
67 G5 **Pu-tai** Taiwan
71 M9 **Putain** Timor Indonesia
21 K4 **Putanges-Pont-Ecrepin** France
75 R5 **Putao** Burma
145 E3 **Putaruru** New Zealand
30 G1 **Putbus** Germany
70 P9 **Puteran** *isld* Indonesia
83 K8 **Puthukkudiyiruppu** Sri Lanka
67 F4 **Putian** China
43 H8 **Putignano** Italy
48 J3 **Putila** Ukraine
52 F5 **Putilovo** Russian Federation
70 B6 **Puting Tg** *C* Kalimantan
54 E5 **Putivl'** Ukraine
33 Q6 **Putlitz** Germany
48 K3 **Putna** Romania
95 Q5 **Putnam** Connecticut U.S.A.
108 E8 **Putnam** Oklahoma U.S.A.
109 H3 **Putnam** Texas U.S.A.
112 C6 **Putney** Georgia U.S.A.
98 H4 **Putney** South Dakota U.S.A.
95 P4 **Putney** Vermont U.S.A.
51 J2 **Putorana, Plato** *mt* Russian Federation
145 F3 **Putorino** New Zealand
83 J9 **Puttalam** Sri Lanka
83 J9 **Puttalam Lag** Sri Lanka
22 G1 **Putte** Belgium
36 B5 **Puttelange** France
33 O5 **Püttelkow** Germany
25 E4 **Putten** Netherlands
28 G7 **Puttgarden** Germany
36 B5 **Püttlingen** Germany
128 C3 **Putumayo** *div* Colombia
128 D4 **Putumayo** *R* Peru/Colombia
67 G2 **Putuo** China
67 G1 **Putuo Shan** *isld* China
70 C4 **Putusibau** Kalimantan
33 T5 **Putzar** Germany
135 U5 **Puuanahulu** Hawaiian Is
135 U5 **Puu Hualalei** *crater* Hawaiian Is
135 S3 **Puukoli** Hawaiian Is
29 M10 **Puulavesi** *L* Finland
29 N10 **Puumala** Finland
22 G1 **Puurs** Belgium
135 N1 **Puuwai** Hawaiian Is
Puxian *see* **Pucheng**
65 A6 **Pu Xian** China
117 M12 **Puyallup** Washington U.S.A.
65 C7 **Puyang** China
18 G7 **Puy de Dôme** *dept* France
18 G7 **Puy-de-Sancy** *mt* France
131 A8 **Puyehue, L de** Chile
131 B8 **Puyehue, P. de** Argentina
131 A8 **Puyehue, V** Chile
21 M8 **Puye, La** France
19 Q14 **Puy Gris** *mt* France
18 G9 **Puylaurens** France
18 H7 **Puy, le** France
18 F8 **Puy l'Evêque** France
18 G7 **Puy Mary** *mt* France
21 K7 **Puy Notre Dame, le** France
21 N2 **Puys** France
52 H4 **Puzla** Russian Federation
88 G5 **Pwani** *prov* Tanzania
88 B6 **Pweto** Zaire
68 B2 **Pwinbyu** Burma
8 B2 **Pwllheli** Wales
52 E2 **Pyalitsa** Russian Federation
52 E4 **Pyal'ma** Russian Federation
68 B3 **Pyalo** Burma
68 B5 **Pyamalaw** *R* Burma
52 F6 **Pyana** *R* Russian Federation
57 E6 **Pyandzh** Tajikistan
57 E6 **Pyandzh** *R* Tajikistan/Afghanistan
52 J4 **Pyanteg** Russian Federation
52 D2 **Pyaozero, Oz** *L* Russian Federation
76 C3 **Pyapalli** India
68 B4 **Pyapon** Burma
51 H1 **Pyasina** *R* Russian Federation
53 F11 **Pyatigorsk** Russian Federation
54 E8 **Pyatikhatki** Ukraine
52 H4 **Pyatiqory** Russian Federation
110 D5 **Pyatt** Arkansas U.S.A.
52 H6 **Pychas** Russian Federation
68 B3 **Pyè** Burma
116 M7 **Pye Is** Alaska U.S.A.
29 M9 **Pyhä-Häki Nat. Park** Finland
27 M11 **Pyhajärvi** *L* Finland
29 M8 **Pyhäjärvi** Finland
29 L7 **Pyhäjoki** Finland
29 M7 **Pyhäntä** Finland
29 J11 **Pyhäranta** Finland
29 O9 **Pyhäselkä** Finland
29 M4 **Pyhätunturi Nat. Park** Finland
38 N5 **Pyhra** Austria
68 C3 **Pyinmana** Burma
8 C4 **Pyle** Wales
29 L9 **Pylkönmäki** Finland
94 G5 **Pymatuning Res** Ohio/Penn U.S.A.
69 A9 **Pymgalion Pt** Nicobar Is
59 J3 **Pyöktong** N Korea
65 F5 **P'yŏngyang** N Korea
100 F9 **Pyramid** Nevada U.S.A.
103 K6 **Pyramid Canyon** Ariz/Nev U.S.A.
139 G6 **Pyramid Hill** Victoria Australia
106 C1 **Pyramid Pk** Colorado U.S.A.
94 A2 **Pyramid Pt** Michigan U.S.A.
102 E2 **Pyramid Rge** Nevada U.S.A.
18 F9 **Pyrénées** *mts* France/Spain
18 E9 **Pyrénées Atlantiques** *dept* France
18 G10 **Pyrénées-Orientales** *dept* France
142 B5 **Pyrton,Mt** W Australia Australia
31 H2 **Pyrzyce** Poland
52 G5 **Pyshchug** Russian Federation
55 D3 **Pyshma** Russian Federation
31 L5 **Pyskowice** Poland
52 C6 **Pytalovo** Russian Federation
121 O6 **Pythonga, L** Quebec Canada
68 C3 **Pyu** *R* Burma
68 C3 **Pyu** Burma
68 C4 **Pyuntaza** Burma
31 K3 **Pyzdry** Poland

Q

Qaanaaq *see* **Thule**
84 E3 **Qaddāhīyah, Al** Libya
74 F3 **Qadian** India
78 K6 **Qādisīyah, Al** *prov* Iraq
77 C1 **Qāem Shahr** Iran
80 G4 **Qafqafa** Jordan
58 G2 **Qagan** China
Qagan Nur *see* **Zhengxiangbai Qi**
65 F2 **Qagan Nur** *L* China
65 B3 **Qagan Nur** China
65 C3 **Qagan Nur** *L* China
65 B4 **Qagan Nur** *L* China
65 D1 **Qagan Qulut** China
65 D3 **Qagan Us** China
65 B4 **Qahar Youyi Houqi** China
65 B4 **Qahar Youyi Qianqi** China
65 B4 **Qahar Youyi Zhongqi** China
Qâhira, El *see* **Cairo**
66 E4 **Qaidam Pendi** *reg* China
66 F4 **Qaidam Shan** *mts* China
77 J4 **Qala Bist** Afghanistan
86 G3 **Qala'en Nahl** Sudan
77 J3 **Qala-i-Ghor** Afghanistan
77 H3 **Qala-i-Kāl** Afghanistan
77 K3 **Qalāt** Afghanistan
79 G4 **Qal 'at al Hisn** Syria
79 F3 **Qal'at al Marqab** Syria
78 H4 **Qal'at as Salihīyah** Syria
80 F4 **Qal'at er Rabad** Jordan
78 L6 **Qal'at Sālih** Iraq
77 J4 **Qal'eh-ye Bost** Afghanistan
77 H2 **Qal'eh-ye Now** Afghanistan
80 C5 **Qalqīlya** Israel
80 E6 **Qalya** Jordan
79 B8 **Qalyûb** Egypt
80 G3 **Qam** Jordan
74 C5 **Qambar** Pakistan
66 F5 **Qamdo** *reg* China
84 F3 **Qaminis** Libya
78 H3 **Qāmishlī, Al** Syria
74 C3 **Qamruddin Karez** Pakistan
80 D5 **Qana** Jordan
86 A1 **Qandala** Somalia
65 C3 **Qangdin Gol** China
65 C3 **Qangdin Sum** China
79 C8 **Qanṭara, El** Egypt
79 G6 **Qanwāt, Al** Syria
Qaqortoq *see* **Julianehåb**
84 H4 **Qara** Egypt
79 F5 **Qaraaoun** Lebanon
77 L2 **Qarah Bāgh** Afghanistan
80 D5 **Qarawat Bani Ḩassan** Jordan
79 G3 **Qardāhah, Al** Syria
86 A2 **Qardho** Somalia
78 L2 **Qareh Su** *R* Iran
79 C10 **Qarn el Kabsh, G** *mt* Egypt
66 D4 **Qarqan He** *R* China
79 F4 **Qartaba** Lebanon
84 E3 **Qaryāt, Al** Libya
79 H4 **Qaryatayn, Al** Syria
80 G7 **Qaryat Falha** Jordan
77 H2 **Qasa Murg** Afghanistan
Qasigiangguit *see* **Christianshåb**
80 F8 **Qasr** Jordan
79 H4 **Qasr al Ḩayr** Syria
79 F8 **Qasr ed Deir, J** *mt* Jordan
84 H4 **Qasr, El** Egypt
78 K4 **Qasr-e-Shirin** Iran
80 G8 **Qasr eth Thuraiya** Jordan
84 H4 **Qasr Farâfra** Egypt
115 P5 **Qassimiut** Greenland
79 G5 **Qatana** Syria
77 B7 **Qatar** *state* Persian Gulf
77 B6 **Qatīf, Al** Saudi Arabia
79 G7 **Qatrāna** Jordan
84 E5 **Qaṭrūn, Al** Libya
84 H4 **Qattara Depression** Egypt
77 F3 **Qāyen** Iran
78 J4 **Qayyarah** Iraq
80 F2 **Qaẕrin** Syria
77 A1 **Qazvīn** Iran
80 F1 **Qela'** Syria
84 J4 **Qena** Egypt
Qeqertarsuaq *see* **Godhavn**
Qeqertarsuaq *isld see* **Disko** *isld*
Qeqertarsuatsiaat *see* **Fiskenæsset**
Qeqertarsuatsiaq *see* **Hareøen**
77 E6 **Qeshm** Iran
77 A1 **Qeydār** Iran
77 C6 **Qeys** *isld* Iran
77 A1 **Qezel Owzan** *R* Iran
79 E8 **Qeẕi'ot** Israel
65 F2 **Qian'an** China
65 D4 **Qian'an** China
67 C3 **Qiancheng** China
65 F2 **Qian Gorlos** China
67 C3 **Qiangu'ao** China
Qianguozhen *see* **Qian Gorlos**
65 D7 **Qiangwei He** *R* China
67 D1 **Qianjiang** China
67 C2 **Qianjiang** *R* China
67 C5 **Qianjiang** China
59 K2 **Qianjin** China
65 F4 **Qian Shan** *mt ra* China
66 E3 **Qianshan** China
67 E1 **Qianshan** China
65 E4 **Qianwei** China
67 A2 **Qianwei** China
65 D4 **Qianxi** China
67 B3 **Qianxi** China
67 A4 **Qianxinan** China
67 C3 **Qianyang** China
65 D3 **Qiaotou** China
67 E3 **Qiaotou** China
67 E1 **Qichun** China
80 F1 **Qidmat Ẕevi** Syria
67 G1 **Qidong** China
67 D3 **Qidong** China
66 D4 **Qiemo** China
67 C2 **Qifeng Guan** *pass* China
65 C6 **Qihe** China
65 B3 **Qihreg** China
58 E6 **Qijiang** China
66 E3 **Qijiaojing** China
Qike *see* **Xunke**
65 D5 **Qikou** China
77 H6 **Qila Lādgasht** Pakistan
65 D4 **Qilaotu Shan** *mt ra* China
74 A8 **Qila Safed** Pakistan
74 C3 **Qila Saifullah** Pakistan
Qili *see* **Shitai**
66 F4 **Qilian Shan** *mt ra* China
65 E4 **Qilihe** China
67 F2 **Qimen** China
65 G1 **Qing'an** China
65 D6 **Qingcheng** China
65 E6 **Qingdao** China
65 E5 **Qingduizi** China
65 C7 **Qingfeng** China
67 A2 **Qingfu** China
65 G1 **Qinggang** China
Qinggil *see* **Qinghe**
65 C7 **Qingguji** China
66 E4 **Qinghai** *prov* China
58 D4 **Qinghai Hu** *L* China
65 H1 **Qinghe** China
65 C6 **Qinghe** China
66 E2 **Qinghe** China
65 F4 **Qinghecheng** China
65 E4 **Qinghemen** China
65 F3 **Qinghe Shuiku** *res* China
67 F2 **Qinghu** China
65 A6 **Qingjian** China
67 C1 **Qing Jiang** *R* China
67 E2 **Qingjiang** China
65 A6 **Qingjian He** *R* China
Qingkou *see* **Ganyu**
67 C7 **Qinglan** China
67 D7 **Qinglan Gang** *inlet* China
67 D4 **Qinglian** China
67 E3 **Qingliu** China
65 D4 **Qinglong** China
67 B4 **Qinglong** China
65 D4 **Qinglong He** *R* China
65 C6 **Qingping** China
68 J2 **Qingping** China
67 G1 **Qingpu** China
67 A2 **Qingshen** China
58 E4 **Qingshui He** *R* China
65 B5 **Qingshuihe** China
67 C3 **Qingshui Jiang** *R* China
67 G2 **Qingtian** China
65 C5 **Qing Xian** China
65 B6 **Qingxu** China
Qingyang *see* **Jinjiang**
58 E4 **Qingyang** China
67 F1 **Qingyang** China
Qingyuan *see* **Yishan**
59 J3 **Qingyuan** China
67 F3 **Qingyuan** China
67 D5 **Qingyuan** China
65 D6 **Qingyun** China
65 B7 **Qin He** *R* China
65 D5 **Qinhuangdao** China
67 C6 **Qin Jiang** *R* China
58 E5 **Qin Ling** *mt ra* China
65 B7 **Qinshui** China
67 C5 **Qintang** China
58 F4 **Qin Xian** China
58 F4 **Qinyang** China
67 G3 **Qinyu** China
65 B6 **Qinyuan** China
67 C6 **Qinzhou** China
68 J2 **Qinzhou Wan** *B* China
68 K3 **Qionghai** China
58 D5 **Qionglai** China
58 D5 **Qionglai Shan** *mt ra* China
67 C7 **Qiongshan** China
67 C7 **Qiongzhong** China
68 J2 **Qiongzhou Haixia** China
67 B1 **Qiping** China
59 H2 **Qiqihar** China
77 C5 **Qīr** Iran
80 D7 **Qiryat Arba'** Jordan
80 D2 **Qiryat Ata** Israel
80 D8 **Qiryatayim** Jordan
80 D2 **Qiryat Bialik** Israel
80 C7 **Qiryat Gat** Israel
80 D2 **Qiryat Motmkin** Israel
80 D5 **Qiryat Netafim** Jordan
80 F1 **Qiryat Shemona** Israel
80 D3 **Qiryat Tiv'on** Israel
80 D2 **Qiryat Yam** Israel
80 D6 **Qiryat Yearim** Israel
67 C6 **Qisha** China
80 D3 **Qishon 'Eneq Yizre'el** Israel
68 J2 **Qishui** China
66 D3 **Qitai** China
65 H2 **Qitaihe** China
67 A4 **Qiubei** China
65 C6 **Qiu Xian** China
65 E6 **Qixia** China
65 B6 **Qi Xian** China
65 C7 **Qi Xian** China
65 B4 **Qixiaying** China
65 J1 **Qixing He** *R* China
65 H1 **Qixingpao** China
67 D3 **Qiyang** China
67 E1 **Qizhou** China
Qogir Feng *mt pk see* **K2** *mt*
65 C2 **Qog Ul** China
77 B2 **Qom** Iran
77 B3 **Qomishēh** Iran
Qomolangma Feng *mt see* **Everest, Mt**
66 D3 **Qongkol** China
115 O5 **Qoornoq** Greenland
77 A2 **Qorveh** Iran
79 G4 **Qoubaiyat** Lebanon
95 P4 **Quabbin Res** Massachusetts U.S.A.
122 G8 **Quaco Hd** New Brunswick Canada
74 D2 **Quaidabad** Pakistan
102 H6 **Quail Mts** California U.S.A.
143 B9 **Quairading** W Australia Australia
32 G7 **Quakenbrück** Germany
95 M6 **Quakertown** Pennsylvania U.S.A.
45 Q8 **Qualiano** Italy
85 E6 **Quallam** Niger
139 G6 **Quambatook** Victoria Australia
139 J4 **Quambone** New South Wales Australia
140 F5 **Quamby** Queensland Australia
108 H1 **Quanah** Texas U.S.A.
128 F4 **Quanaru, Ilha** Brazil
68 H2 **Quan Dao Co To** *isld* Vietnam
68 J5 **Quang Nam** Vietnam
68 J5 **Quang Ngai** Vietnam
68 H4 **Quang Tri** Vietnam
67 B6 **Quang Yen** Vietnam
67 F1 **Quanjiao** China
69 G8 **Quan Long** Vietnam
67 E4 **Quannan** China
68 F7 **Quan Phu Quoc** *isld* Vietnam
94 K8 **Quantico** Virginia U.S.A.
120 E1 **Quantz L** Ontario Canada
67 C4 **Quanzhou** China
119 O8 **Qu'Appelle** Saskatchewan Canada
119 P8 **Qu'Appelle R** Saskatchewan Canada
118 L7 **Qu'Appelle R. Dam** Saskatchewan Canada
133 F4 **Quaraí** Brazil
131 G3 **Quarai, R** Brazil
32 L4 **Quarnbek** Germany
122 G7 **Quarryville** New Brunswick Canada
95 L7 **Quarryville** Pennsylvania U.S.A.
40 F6 **Quart** Italy
45 L2 **Quartesana** Italy
45 N6 **Quartière Mt. Sacro** Italy
83 M12 **Quartier Militaire** Mauritius
43 C9 **Quartu Sant'Elena** Sardinia
102 H4 **Quartzite Mt** Nevada U.S.A.
102 G2 **Quartz Mt** Nevada U.S.A.
100 G1 **Quartz Mt** Washington U.S.A.
103 K8 **Quartzsite** Arizona U.S.A.
99 P7 **Quasqueton** Iowa U.S.A.
22 G2 **Quatre Bras** Belgium
22 H5 **Quatre-Champs** France
117 K10 **Quatsino** British Columbia Canada
45 H2 **Quattro Castella** Italy
106 G7 **Quay** New Mexico U.S.A.
77 F1 **Qūchān** Iran
101 P8 **Quealy** Wyoming U.S.A.
139 J6 **Queanbeyan** New South Wales Australia
115 M7 **Quebec** *prov* Canada
121 T6 **Québec** Quebec Canada
130 F6 **Quebra Anzol** *R* Brazil
88 D9 **Quebrabasa Rapids** Mozambique
133 E3 **Quebracho Coto** Argentina
131 A8 **Quedal, C. de** Chile
33 O9 **Quedlinburg** Germany
17 G9 **Qued Tlélat** Algeria
95 L8 **Queen Anne** Maryland U.S.A.
117 L10 **Queen Bess, Mt** British Columbia Canada
9 G5 **Queenborough** England
115 M5 **Queen, C** Northwest Territories Canada
133 E8 **Queen Charlotte B** Falkland Is
117 G9 **Queen Charlotte Is** British Columbia Canada
117 J10 **Queen Charlotte Sd** British Columbia Canada
145 E4 **Queen Charlotte Sound** New Zealand
117 K10 **Queen Charlotte Str** British Columbia Canada
99 O9 **Queen City** Missouri U.S.A.
109 N2 **Queen City** Texas U.S.A.
115 K2 **Queen Elizabeth Is** Northwest Territories Canada
146 H12 **Queen Mary Land** Antarctica
117 D5 **Queen Mary, Mt** Yukon Territory Canada
114 J4 **Queen Maud Gulf** Northwest Territories Canada
146 D9 **Queen Maud Mts** Antarctica
13 G6 **Queensbury** England
140 A2 **Queens Chan** N Terr Australia
115 K2 **Queens Chan** Northwest Territories Canada
139 G7 **Queenscliff** Victoria Australia
13 E2 **Queensferry** Scotland
140 F6 **Queensland** *state* Australia
142 B2 **Queens Park** *dist* Perth, W Aust Australia
123 L8 **Queensport** Nova Scotia Canada
139 H8 **Queenstown** Tasmania Australia
118 E8 **Queenstown** Alberta Canada
144 B6 **Queenstown** New Zealand
89 E8 **Queenstown** S Africa
95 L8 **Queenstown** Maryland U.S.A.
100 A2 **Queets** Washington U.S.A.
131 F4 **Queguay Grande** *R* Uruguay
36 E5 **Queich** *R* Germany
16 C2 **Queija, S. de** *mts* Spain
129 L6 **Queimadas** Brazil
87 C7 **Quela** Angola
21 J6 **Quelaines** France
87 B7 **Quele** Angola
88 F10 **Quelimane** Mozambique
124 F6 **Quelite** Mexico
133 C6 **Quellen** Chile
106 B7 **Quemado** New Mexico U.S.A.
108 G7 **Quemado** Texas U.S.A.
20 B5 **Quéménéven** France
Quemoy *see* **Chin-men**
133 E5 **Quemu Quemu** Argentina
22 B3 **Quend** France
9 G4 **Quendon** England
22 B3 **Quend Plage** France
107 P3 **Quenemo** Kansas U.S.A.
111 F10 **Quentin** Mississippi U.S.A.
Que Que *see* **Kwekwe**
133 F5 **Quequén** Argentina
22 C2 **Quercamps** France
130 D8 **Querência do Norte** Brazil
125 J7 **Querétaro** Mexico
33 P10 **Querfurt** Germany
124 D2 **Querobabi** Mexico
20 G2 **Querqueville** France
20 C6 **Querrien** France
21 P2 **Querrieu** France
117 M9 **Quesnel** British Columbia Canada
117 N9 **Quesnel L** British Columbia Canada
22 D4 **Quesnoy** France
22 F3 **Quesnoy, le** France
22 E2 **Quesnoy-sur-Deule, le** France

20 E5 Quessoy France
106 E5 Questa New Mexico U.S.A.
20 F6 Questembert France
133 D2 Quetena Bolivia
99 Q1 Quetico Ontario Canada
118 L2 Quetico L Ontario Canada
99 P1 Quetico Provincial Park Ontario Canada
74 B3 Quetta Pakistan
30 H2 Quettehou France
21 L3 Quetteville France
20 H4 Quettreville France
111 D11 Queue de Tortue R Louisiana U.S.A.
21 O4 Queue-léz-Yvelines,la France
21 P2 Quevauvillers France
121 O3 Quévillon Quebec Canada
125 O10 Quezaltenango Guatemala
71 C6 Quezon Palawan Philippines
65 D7 Quezon City Luzon Philippines
65 D7 Qufu China
88 B8 Quibala Angola
87 B7 Quibate Angola
128 C2 Quibdó Colombia
118 J1 Quibell Ontario Canada
20 D7 Quiberon France
20 D6 Quiberon,B.de France
21 M2 Quiberville France
127 K10 Quicama Nat. Park Angola
68 G3 Qui Chau Vietnam
32 L5 Quickborn Germany
36 C5 Quierschied Germany
117 G5 Quiet L Yukon Territory Canada
22 F3 Quievrain Belgium
22 E3 Quiévy France
118 G2 Quigley Alberta Canada
133 F3 Quiindy Paraguay
103 M9 Quijotoa Arizona U.S.A.
124 F5 Quilá Mexico
133 C6 Quilán, C Chile
128 C5 Quilates, C Morocco
128 D7 Quilca Peru
100 C2 Quilcene Washington U.S.A.
87 B8 Quilengues Angola
133 E4 Quilino Argentina
128 D6 Quillabamba Peru
128 E7 Quillacollo Bolivia
18 G10 Quillan France
[Quillaik see Dannebrog Ø]
21 M3 Quilleboeuf France
131 B7 Quillén, L Argentina
119 N6 Quill Lake Saskatchewan Canada
131 B4 Quillota Chile
119 N7 Quillsks L Saskatchewan Canada
20 G7 Quilly France
76 C6 Quilon India
141 G7 Quilpie Queensland Australia
87 C8 Quimbango Angola
20 B5 Quimerch France
20 C6 Quimper France
20 C6 Quimperlé France
71 F3 Quinabucasan Pt Philippines
71 F4 Quinalasag isld Philippines
100 A2 Quinault R Washington U.S.A.
100 B2 Quinault Washington U.S.A.
21 N2 Quincampoix France
21 L8 Quinçay France
128 D6 Quince Mil Peru
102 D2 Quincy California U.S.A.
111 M11 Quincy Florida U.S.A.
113 E7 Quincy Illinois U.S.A.
95 R4 Quincy Massachusetts U.S.A.
110 N1 Quincy Ohio U.S.A.
100 B3 Quincy Oregon U.S.A.
100 D2 Quincy Washington U.S.A.
68 H2 Quinh Nhai Vietnam
128 E3 Quinigua, Cerro mts Venezuela
71 E5 Quiniluban isld Philippines
109 L3 Quinlan Texas U.S.A.
98 D6 Quinn South Dakota U.S.A.
103 J4 Quinn Canyon Ra Nevada U.S.A.
100 G8 Quinn River Crossing Nevada U.S.A.
19 Q17 Quinson France
8 E5 Quintanar de la Orden Spain
125 P8 Quintana Roo terr Mexico
107 K2 Quinter Kansas U.S.A.
20 E5 Quintin France
131 D5 Quinto R Argentina
17 G3 Quinto Spain
119 N7 Quinton Saskatchewan Canada
107 P6 Quinton Oklahoma U.S.A.
45 L1 Quinto Vicentino Italy
8 A7 Quintrel Downs England
15 U8 Quinwood West Virginia U.S.A.
88 H7 Quionga Mozambique
130 J10 Quipapá Brazil
87 B8 Quipungo Angola
15 B3 Quirang Scotland
87 C8 Quiranta Angola
139 K4 Quirindi New South Wales Australia
131 A6 Quiriquina isld Chile
127 N10 Quiriquire Venezuela
120 H6 Quirke L Ontario Canada
36 C5 Quirnbach Germany
16 C2 Quiroga Spain
123 R2 Quirpon Newfoundland Canada
123 R2 Quirpon I Newfoundland Canada
88 H8 Quissanga Mozambique
87 F10 Quissico Mozambique
45 J1 Quistello Italy
20 D6 Quistinic France
126 D7 Quita Sueño Bank Caribbean
130 D6 Quitéria R Brazil
110 D6 Quitman Arkansas U.S.A.
113 D2 Quitman Georgia U.S.A.
109 P3 Quitman Louisiana U.S.A.
111 H9 Quitman Mississippi U.S.A.
109 M3 Quitman Texas U.S.A.
21 N3 Quittebeuf France
103 M6 Quivero Arizona U.S.A.
103 M10 Quitova Mexico
21 N3 Quittebeuf France
128 C5 Quivilla Peru
124 L4 Quixadá Brazil
67 B1 Qu Jiang R China
67 C6 Qu Jiang China
67 A4 Qujing China
46 D3 Qukës-Shkumbin Albania
80 G6 Quleib R Jordan
68 F6 Qumar He R China
58 F8 Qumarlëb China
59 F8 Qumbu S Africa
80 G1 Qunaytirah, El Syria
84 G3 Qunayyin, S. al Libya
66 D5 Qungtag China
143 A6 Quoba,Pt W Australia
Australia
83 M12 Quoin Channel Mauritius
141 H2 Quoin I N Terr Australia
141 K6 Quoin I Queensland Australia
89 A10 Quoin Pt S Africa
138 E4 Quorn South Australia
Australia
119 N1 Quorn Ontario Canada
75 J5 Qureiyat Nafi Jordan
80 H5 Qureiyat Salim Jordan
129 J4 Qurem Brazil
84 J4 Qus Egypt
84 G1 Qusaybah Syria
77 G6 Quseir Egypt
67 C1 Qutang Xia Wu Xia China
79 H2 Quthing Lesotho
79 H2 Quwayq R Syria
84 J4 Quweisna Egypt
65 B7 Quwo China

58 E4 Quwu Shan mt ra China
67 A5 Quxi China
[Qu Xian see Quzhou]
67 B1 Qu Xian China
75 O4 Qüxü China
65 C5 Quyang China
67 E3 Quyang China
67 B7 Quynh Luu Vietnam
68 J6 Quy Nhon Vietnam
121 O7 Quyon Quebec Canada
65 C6 Quzhou China
67 F2 Quzhou China

R

29 K5 Rå Sweden
27 F16 Rää Sweden
[Raab see Györ]
31 J7 Raabs Austria
38 N7 Raab Tal V Austria
29 L7 Raahe Finland
138 F5 Raak Plain Victoria Australia
29 O9 Rääkkylä Finland
25 F4 Raalte Netherlands
115 L2 Raanes Pen Northwest Territories Canada
29 L5 Raanujärvi Finland
70 P9 Raas isld Indonesia
77 A5 Ra'as Al Khafji Saudi Arabia
15 B3 Raasay, Sd of Scotland
42 F4 Rab isld Croatia
48 D3 Rába R Hungary
71 J9 Raba Sumbawa Indonesia
48 F1 Raba R Poland
16 C3 Rabaçal R Portugal
18 F9 Rabastens de Bigorre Hautes-Pyrénées France
85 C2 Rabat Morocco
137 L2 Rabaul New Britain
[Rabbah see 'Amman]
117 K6 Rabbit R British Columbia Canada
98 D4 Rabbit Cr South Dakota U.S.A.
145 D4 Rabbit I New Zealand
118 K5 Rabbit Lake Saskatchewan Canada
117 N5 Rabbitskin R Northwest Territories Canada
28 D7 Rabel Germany
36 F2 Rabenau Germany
77 E5 Rābor Iran
52 F6 Rabotki Russian Federation
39 P3 Rabštejn Czechoslovakia
112 D3 Rabun, L Georgia U.S.A.
84 G5 Rabyānah well Libya
84 G5 Rabyānah, Ramlat sands Libya
46 D1 Rača Serbia Yugoslavia
44 C2 Racconigi Italy
99 M8 Raccoon R Iowa U.S.A.
126 K1 Raccoon Cay Bahamas
94 E8 Raccoon Cr Ohio U.S.A.
38 N9 Race Slovenia
123 T7 Race, C Newfoundland Canada
94 E8 Raceland Kentucky U.S.A.
111 F12 Raceland Louisiana U.S.A.
113 E7 Race Pond Florida U.S.A.
95 R4 Race Pt Massachusetts U.S.A.
100 B3 Race Rocks British Columbia Canada
101 N3 Race Track Montana U.S.A.
80 E1 Rachaiya Lebanon
79 F5 Rachal Lebanon
109 J9 Rachal Texas U.S.A.
69 D9 Racha Noi, Ko isld Thailand
69 D9 Racha Yai, Ko isld Thailand
68 G8 Rach Gia Vietnam
31 L5 Racibórz Poland
94 F8 Racine Ohio U.S.A.
99 T7 Racine Wisconsin U.S.A.
122 D1 Racine-de-Bouleau, R Quebec Canada
120 G4 Racine L Ontario Canada
33 Q10 Rackwitz Germany
37 O4 Racovský mt Czechoslovakia
68 A1 Radan mt Serbia Yugoslavia
145 D4 Radauti Romania
70 F4 Radbuza R Czechoslovakia
70 B5 Radcliff Kentucky U.S.A.
13 F6 Radcliffe England
99 N7 Radcliffe Iowa U.S.A.
27 E12 Råde Norway
30 H4 Radeberg Germany
37 Q1 Radebeul Germany
33 T10 Radeburg Germany
19 Q18 Rade d'Hyères B France
33 Q9 Radegast Germany
38 M8 Radel Pass Austria
36 C1 Radevormwald Germany
140 B1 Radford Pt N Terr Australia
74 D7 Radhanpur India
118 K6 Radisson Saskatchewan Canada
99 P4 Radisson Wisconsin U.S.A.
101 T10 Radium Colorado U.S.A.
98 K1 Radium Minnesota U.S.A.
37 N3 Radiumbad-Brambach Germany
138 F2 Radium Hill pk South Australia
117 P10 Radium Hot Springs British Columbia Canada
106 D9 Radium Springs New Mexico U.S.A.
70 O9 Radja Indonesia
77 F1 Rādkān Iran
38 L6 Radl Badl see Bergstorf
Radmer-an-dem-Hasel Austria
47 H2 Radnevo Bulgaria
30 H6 Radnice Czechoslovakia
[Radnor co see Powys]
41 J2 Radolfzell Germany
31 N4 Radom Poland
31 L4 Radom Sudan
46 F2 Radomir Bulgaria
145 E2 Radomsko Poland
31 L4 Radomsko Poland
37 P3 Radonice Czechoslovakia
31 K7 Radošina Czechoslovakia
31 M4 Radoszyce Poland
46 D3 Radoviš Macedonia Yugoslavia
54 L1 Radovitskiy Russian Federation
42 F2 Radovljica Slovenia
38 H7 Radstadt Austria
8 D5 Radstock England
38 L2 Raduha mt Slovenia
52 H5 Raduša mt Bosnia-Herzegovina
119 N9 Radviliškis Lithuania
118 K6 Radville Saskatchewan Canada
31 O6 Radymno Poland
31 M3 Radzanów Poland
31 O5 Radziejów Poland
31 O4 Radzymin Poland
31 P4 Radzyń Podlaski Poland
117 P4 Radzyń Northwest Territories Canada
75 J5 Rae Bareli India
99 N7 Raeford North Carolina U.S.A.
145 L4 Rae Isthmus Northwest Territories Canada
114 H5 Rae L Northwest Territories Canada
118 B8 Rae, Mt British Columbia Canada

143 D8 Raeside, L W Australia
Australia
115 K4 Rae Str Northwest Territories Canada
145 D1 Raetea mt New Zealand
145 D1 Raetihi New Zealand
131 E3 Rafaela Argentina
79 E7 Rafah Egypt
86 D5 Rafai Cent Afr Republic
53 C8 Rafalovka Ukraine
80 D5 Rafat Jordan
17 G5 Rafelbuñol Spain
78 J7 Raffa' Saudi Arabia
77 E4 Rafsanjān Iran
101 M7 Raft R Idaho U.S.A.
119 Q3 Rafter Manitoba Canada
101 M8 Raft R. Mts Utah U.S.A.
26 H3 Raftsund Norway
86 E4 Raga Sudan
36 E5 Ragan, Mt Philippines
83 K9 Ragay G Philippines
127 J2 Ragbe Jamaica
133 D4 Ragbon Argentina
21 O4 Ragged Bahamas
33 P6 Ragged Pt Barbados
76 B3 Raglan New Zealand
123 P6 Ramea Newfoundland Canada
139 J7 Rame Hd Victoria Australia
52 E6 Ramenskoye Russian Federation
111 K9 Ramer Alabama U.S.A.
139 H5 Ramingining N Terr Australia
80 B8 Ramla Israel
141 K6 Rannes Queensland Australia
55 B5 Ranneye Russian Federation
87 H12 Ranohira Madagascar
107 L4 Rattlesnake Cr Oregon U.S.A.
95 P4 Readsboro Vermont U.S.A.
99 Q6 Readstown Wisconsin U.S.A.
109 U4 Reagan Texas U.S.A.
128 E7 Real, Cord mts Bolivia
128 C4 Real, Cord mts Ecuador
44 C1 Reale Italy
133 E5 Realico Argentina
110 B3 Realitos Texas U.S.A.
109 J8 Reardan Washington U.S.A.
68 F7 Ream Cambodia
143 D10 Reardan Washington U.S.A.

145 D4 Rawene New Zealand
143 G3 Rawlinna W Australia
Australia
101 S8 Rawlins Wyoming U.S.A.
133 E7 Rawson Argentina
133 D6 Rawson Argentina
94 H9 Ray Mts Alaska U.S.A.
55 B4 Rayevskiy Russian Federation
54 J8 Raygorodok Ukraine
80 G1 Rayhānīyah Syria
9 G4 Rayleigh England
118 K9 Raymond Alberta Canada
102 E4 Raymond California U.S.A.
110 G2 Raymond Illinois U.S.A.
111 H1 Raymond Mississippi U.S.A.
98 B1 Raymond Montana U.S.A.
98 J5 Raymond South Dakota U.S.A.
109 N3 Raymond Texas U.S.A.
100 B3 Raymond Washington U.S.A.
139 K5 Raymond Terrace New South Wales Australia
109 K9 Raymondville Texas U.S.A.
116 L4 Raymore Saskatchewan Canada
111 D11 Rayne Louisiana U.S.A.
101 P2 Raynesford Montana U.S.A.
108 A1 Rayo New Mexico U.S.A.
68 G6 Rayong Thailand
110 B3 Raytown Missouri U.S.A.
66 E5 Rayül China
77 A2 Razan Iran
48 N4 Razdel'naya Ukraine
56 D2 Razdolinsk Russian Federation
47 H1 Razgrad Bulgaria
48 M6 Razin, Lacul L Romania
46 F3 Razlog Bulgaria
20 A5 Raz, Pte.du France
110 B3 Rea Missouri U.S.A.
142 A1 Reabold Hill W Australia
117 D6 Reader Arkansas U.S.A.
109 Q5 Reader L Manitoba Canada
9 F5 Reading England
127 J2 Reading Jamaica
94 C5 Reading Michigan U.S.A.
110 L6 Reading Ohio U.S.A.
95 M6 Reading Pennsylvania U.S.A.
95 M9 Readlyn Saskatchewan Canada

113 G7 Red Bud Illinois U.S.A.
98 H7 Red Buttes Wyoming U.S.A.
106 D2 Redcar England
141 L7 Redcliffe Queensland Australia
145 L8 Redcliffe, Mt W Australia
Australia
118 K9 Redcliff Alberta Canada
103 O6 Red Cliff Colorado U.S.A.
119 N10 Redcliffe Ontario Canada
113 A3 Redding California U.S.A.
108 B1 Red Bluff L Texas/New Mex U.S.A.
9 F4 Redbourn England
110 G3 Red Bud Illinois U.S.A.
103 M9 Red Butte Arizona U.S.A.
98 M2 Redby Minnesota U.S.A.
106 D2 Redcar England

103 K6 Red L Arizona U.S.A.

218 Red Lake — Rives Junc

115 K7 Red Lake Ontario Canada
103 M6 Red Lake Arizona U.S.A.
102 G7 Redlands California U.S.A.
98 K2 Red L. Falls Minnesota U.S.A.
95 L7 Red Lion Pennsylvania U.S.A.
101 Q4 Red Lodge Montana U.S.A.
118 C7 Red Lodge Prov. Park Alberta Canada
145 E2 Red Mercury I New Zealand
13 G5 Redmire England
110 J2 Redmon Illinois U.S.A.
100 D5 Redmond Oregon U.S.A.
103 N2 Redmond Utah U.S.A.
102 G6 Red Mt California U.S.A.
112 C1 Red Mt Tennessee U.S.A.
37 L5 Rednitz R Germany
99 L8 Red Oak Iowa U.S.A.
110 A7 Red Oak Oklahoma U.S.A.
109 L3 Red Oak Texas U.S.A.
20 F6 Redon France
127 N6 Redonda isld Antigua & Barbuda W Indies
16 B2 Redondela Spain
16 B6 Redondo Portugal
102 F8 Redondo Beach California U.S.A.
128 F3 Redondo, Pico mt Brazil
116 L6 Redoubt Vol Alaska U.S.A.
117 O9 Red Pass British Columbia Canada
118 J6 Red Pheasant Saskatchewan Canada
141 G2 Red Pt Queensland Australia
117 J6 Red R British Columbia Canada
119 U9 Red R Manitoba Canada
111 D10 Red R Louisiana U.S.A.
109 J1 Red R Texas U.S.A.
Red R Vietnam see Song-koi R
122 E7 Red Rapids New Brunswick Canada
101 K4 Red R. Hot Springs Idaho U.S.A.
119 P2 Red Rock Ontario Canada
103 N9 Redrock Arizona U.S.A.
106 B9 Red Rock New Mexico U.S.A.
107 N5 Red Rock Oklahoma U.S.A.
109 K6 Red Rock Texas U.S.A.
117 Q3 Redrock L Northwest Territories Canada
99 N8 Red Rock Res Iowa U.S.A.
143 G9 Red Rocks Pt W Australia Australia
8 A7 Redruth England
86 G1 Red Sea Africa/Arabian Pen
112 H3 Red Springs North Carolina U.S.A.
117 M9 Redstone British Columbia Canada
117 K4 Redstone R Northwest Territories Canada
120 J4 Redstone R Ontario Canada
101 V1 Redstone Montana U.S.A.
124 E9 Red Tank Panama
22 J4 Redu Belgium
119 Q9 Redvers Saskatchewan Canada
118 D5 Redwater Alberta Canada
121 L6 Redwater Ontario Canada
98 A2 Redwater R Montana U.S.A.
109 N2 Redwater Texas U.S.A.
8 B1 Red Wharf B Wales
118 E6 Red Willow Alberta Canada
98 E9 Red Willow Cr Nebraska U.S.A.
99 O5 Red Wing Minnesota U.S.A.
102 B4 Redwood City California U.S.A.
99 L5 Redwood Falls Minnesota U.S.A.
100 A8 Redwood Nat. Park California U.S.A.
102 A2 Redwood Valley California U.S.A.
71 C5 Reed Bank S China Sea
94 B3 Reed City Michigan U.S.A.
98 D3 Reeder North Dakota U.S.A.
102 E5 Reedley California U.S.A.
101 Q4 Reedpoint Montana U.S.A.
106 C8 Reeds Pk New Mexico U.S.A.
100 A6 Reedsport Oregon U.S.A.
112 E3 Reedy R South Carolina U.S.A.
94 F8 Reedy West Virginia U.S.A.
138 D4 Reedy Lagoon South Australia Australia
141 G4 Reedy Springs Queensland Australia
144 C5 Reefton New Zealand
98 G5 Ree Heights South Dakota U.S.A.
14 C3 Ree, L Ireland
110 G5 Reelfoot L Tennessee U.S.A.
32 G6 Reepsholt Germany
28 G5 Reersø Denmark
25 F5 Rees Germany
94 D3 Reese Michigan U.S.A.
100 H9 Reese R Nevada U.S.A.
120 G3 Reesor Ontario Canada
33 P6 Reetz Germany
78 G2 Refahiye Turkey
111 J8 Reform Alabama U.S.A.
133 D3 Refresco Chile
28 F6 Refs Denmark
27 G14 Reftele Sweden
109 K7 Refugio Texas U.S.A.
31 J2 Rega R Poland
120 E4 Regan Ontario Canada
80 D3 Regavim Israel
37 N5 Regen R Germany
37 N5 Regensburg Germany
37 N5 Regenstauf Germany
119 R9 Regent Manitoba Canada
120 F5 Regent Ontario Canada
85 E3 Reggane Algeria
45 L4 Reggello Italy
43 G10 Reggio di Calabria Italy
45 J2 Reggiolo Italy
45 J2 Reggio nell Emilia Italy
129 H3 Regina Brazil
119 N8 Regina Saskatchewan Canada
37 N1 Regis Germany
77 J4 Registan Afghanistan
20 G3 Regnéville France
22 G4 Régniowez France
37 K4 Regnitz R Germany
16 B6 Reguengos de Monsaraz Portugal
20 E6 Reguiny France
80 D4 Reḫan Jordan
37 N3 Rehau Germany
36 D5 Rehberg mt Germany
32 H7 Rehden Germany
33 Q7 Rehfeld Germany
74 H7 Rehli India
32 J8 Rehme Germany
33 O5 Rehna Germany
87 C10 Rehoboth Namibia
95 M8 Rehoboth Beach Delaware U.S.A.
80 C6 Reḫovot Israel
36 F3 Reichelshausen Germany
37 N2 Reichenbach Germany
38 L7 Reichenfels Austria
37 J1 Reichensachsen Germany
38 F5 Reichertsheim Germany
37 L6 Reichertshofen Germany
101 N4 Reichle Montana U.S.A.
36 D2 Reichshof Germany
36 D6 Reichshoffen France
143 G9 Reid W Australia Australia
118 J8 Reid L Saskatchewan Canada
140 B4 Reid, Mt N Terr Australia
141 H4 Reid R Queensland Australia
112 E5 Reidsville Georgia U.S.A.
112 H1 Reidsville North Carolina U.S.A.
9 F5 Reigate England
21 M7 Reignac-sur-Indre Indre-et-Loire France
25 C5 Reijen Netherlands
103 O9 Reiley Pk Arizona U.S.A.
36 F5 Reilingen Germany
19 P17 Reillanne France
22 G5 Reims France
18 H3 Reims, Mt de France
133 C8 Reina Adelaida, Arch. de la islds Chile
99 O7 Reinbeck Iowa U.S.A.
32 M5 Reinbek Germany
33 S4 Reinberg Germany
119 U6 Reindeer I Manitoba Canada
119 Q1 Reindeer L Manitoba/Sask Canada
26 F4 Reine Norway
140 D6 Reinecke, Mt N Terr Australia
27 C11 Reineskarvet mt Norway
33 M5 Reinfeld Germany
145 D1 Reinga, C New Zealand
32 L10 Reinhausen Germany
36 C5 Reinheim Germany
33 S7 Reinickendorf Germany
16 E1 Reinosa Spain
26 L2 Reinöy isld Norway
37 P1 Reinsberg Germany
36 B4 Reinsfeld Germany
33 P5 Reinstorf Germany
26 M2 Reisa R Norway
37 O6 Reisbach Germany
29 L8 Reisjärvi Finland
38 H8 Reisseck mt Austria
25 F2 Reitdiep R Netherlands
38 G6 Reiter Alpen mt Austria
38 J7 Reitereck mt Austria
87 E11 Reitz S Africa
37 P2 Reitzenhain Germany
27 H13 Rejmyre Sweden
31 O4 Rejowiec Poland
28 B6 Rejsby Denmark
27 H12 Rekarne Sweden
32 F9 Reken Germany
60 R3 Rekifune-gawa R Japan
109 N4 Reklaw Texas U.S.A.
46 E1 Rekovac Serbia Yugoslavia
20 B5 Relecq-Kerhoun,le France
112 E6 Relee Georgia U.S.A.
98 G6 Reliance South Dakota U.S.A.
101 Q8 Reliance Wyoming U.S.A.
85 E1 Relizane Algeria
124 G4 Rellano Mexico
36 C2 Remagen Germany
21 M5 Rémalard France
138 E4 Remarkable, Mt South Australia Australia
70 N9 Rembang Java
36 F6 Remchingen Germany
37 L2 Remda Germany
126 E3 Remedios Cuba
124 F5 Remedios Mexico
32 G6 Remels Germany
77 F6 Remeshk Iran
22 L4 Remich Luxembourg
121 L5 Rémigny Quebec Canada
120 H3 Remi L Ontario Canada
22 J4 Remilly-Allicourt France
99 T9 Remington Indiana U.S.A.
94 K8 Remington Virginia U.S.A.
40 E1 Remiremont France
33 N8 Remlingen Germany
100 B6 Remote Oregon U.S.A.
22 K3 Remouchamps Belgium
19 N17 Remoulins France
83 K14 Remparts, R. des Réunion Indian Oc
36 H6 Rems R Germany
36 C1 Remscheid Germany
99 L7 Remsen Iowa U.S.A.
121 P9 Remsen New York U.S.A.
20 E6 Remungol France
94 B3 Remus Michigan U.S.A.
19 O16 Rémuzat France
27 E10 Rena Norway
120 G4 Renabie Ontario Canada
20 G6 Renac France
Renaix see Ronse
71 D2 Rena Pt Luzon Philippines
128 E4 Renascenca Brazil
146 C4 Renaud I isld Antarctica
21 H6 Renazé France
36 E6 Renchen Germany
26 E10 Rendal Norway
28 A5 Renderne Denmark
32 L4 Rendsburg Germany
121 L4 Reneault Quebec Canada
123 U7 Renews Newfoundland Canada
Renfrew co see Strathclyde reg
121 O7 Renfrew Ontario Canada
12 D2 Renfrew Scotland
70 L9 Rengasdengklok Java
69 F13 Rengat Sumatra
67 C1 Ren He R China
67 D4 Renhua China
67 B3 Renhuai China
48 L5 Reni Ukraine
94 G9 Renick West Virginia U.S.A.
120 J2 Renison Ontario Canada
139 H8 Renison Bell Tasmania Australia
86 F3 Renk Sudan
29 L11 Renko Finland
25 E5 Renkum Netherlands
115 R3 Renland reg Greenland
138 F5 Renmark South Australia Australia
65 F1 Renmin China
26 D9 Rennebu Norway
137 N4 Rennell isld Solomon Is
36 E2 Rennerod Germany
140 C4 Renner Springs N Terr Australia
37 L6 Rennertshafen Germany
20 G5 Rennes France
27 A12 Rennesöy isld Norway
146 C13 Rennick Glacier glacier Antarctica
118 F1 Rennie Manitoba Canada
38 J7 Rennweg Austria
45 K3 Reno R Italy
102 E2 Reno Nevada U.S.A.
99 L4 Reno, L Minnesota U.S.A.
122 G7 Renous New Brunswick Canada
94 K5 Renovo Pennsylvania U.S.A.
119 M7 Renown Saskatchewan Canada
65 C5 Renqiu China
28 C7 Rens Denmark
67 E5 Renshan China
67 A2 Renshou China
99 T9 Rensselaer Indiana U.S.A.
95 O4 Rensselaer New York U.S.A.
95 N4 Rensselaerville New York U.S.A.
25 E4 Renswoude Netherlands
100 C2 Renton Washington U.S.A.
37 K3 Rentweinsdorf Germany
37 J3 Rentwertshausen Germany
99 L5 Renville Minnesota U.S.A.
119 R6 Renwer Manitoba Canada
22 H4 Renwez France
145 D4 Renwick New Zealand
99 N7 Renwick Iowa U.S.A.
65 C6 Ren Xian China
67 D7 Renxing China
18 E8 Réole, la France
76 E2 Repalle India
129 G4 Repartição Brazil
129 G4 Repartimento Brazil
40 E3 Repentis, Mt France
29 J8 Replot Finland
55 E1 Repolovo Russian Federation
145 F3 Reporoa New Zealand
40 E6 Reposoir, Chaine de mt France
26 J5 Reppentjåkko mt Sweden
130 D8 Represa Ilha Grande res Brazil
130 C9 Represa Itaipu res Brazil/Paraguay
130 D7 Represa Pôrto Primavera res Brazil
129 J4 Represa Tucurui res Brazil
111 J10 Repton Alabama U.S.A.
107 N2 Republic Kansas U.S.A.
94 D5 Republic Ohio U.S.A.
100 G1 Republic Washington U.S.A.
98 H9 Republican R Nebraska/Kansas U.S.A.
141 J5 Repulse Bay Queensland Australia
115 L4 Repulse Bay Northwest Territories Canada
26 P1 Repvåg Norway
54 K5 Rep'yevka Russian Federation
98 F2 Regan North Dakota U.S.A.
130 H6 Regência Brazil
98 D3 Regent North Dakota U.S.A.
25 G4 Regge R Netherlands
100 A8 Requa California U.S.A.
128 D5 Requena Peru
17 G5 Requena Spain
18 G8 Réquista France
21 P7 Rère R France
145 F3 Rerewhakaaitu L New Zealand
15 G2 Rerwick Scotland
78 F1 Reşadiye Turkey
70 K8 Resag, G mt Sumatra
102 F7 Reseda California U.S.A.
26 J8 Resele Sweden
28 C3 Resen Denmark
28 C4 Resen Denmark
46 E3 Resen Macedonia Yugoslavia
119 P6 Reserve Saskatchewan Canada
111 F11 Reserve Louisiana U.S.A.
98 B1 Reserve Montana U.S.A.
106 B8 Reserve New Mexico U.S.A.
54 F7 Reshetilovka Ukraine
41 N4 Resia Italy
133 F3 Resistencia Argentina
48 G5 Reşiţa Romania
122 E6 Resitgouche R New Brunswick Canada
115 K3 Resolute Northwest Territories Canada
144 A6 Resolution I New Zealand
115 N5 Resolution Island Northwest Territories Canada
115 N6 Resolution L Quebec Canada
32 L7 Resse Germany
21 P3 Ressons France
22 D4 Ressons-sur-Matz France
127 K3 Rest Jamaica
12 D1 Rest and be Thankful hill Scotland
122 F5 Restigouche Quebec Canada
119 Q9 Reston Manitoba Canada
13 F2 Reston Scotland
94 K7 Reston Virginia U.S.A.
121 L6 Restoule Ontario Canada
31 N1 Reszel Poland
48 H5 Retezatului, Munti mts Romania
22 G5 Rethel France
32 K7 Rethem Germany
32 L8 Rethen Germany
46 G9 Réthimnon Crete Greece
42 C2 Retiche, Alpi mts Italy
22 J1 Retie Belgium
20 H6 Retiers France
118 E8 Retlaw Alberta Canada
141 G7 Retreat Queensland Australia
108 E8 Retrop Oklahoma U.S.A.
48 E3 Rétság Hungary
9 G4 Rettendon England
36 D3 Rettert Germany
31 J7 Retz Austria
20 F7 Retz reg France
36 H4 Retzbach Germany
21 M7 Reugny Indre-et-Loire France
21 P7 Reuilly Indre France
22 L3 Reuland Belgium
83 K13 Réunion isld Indian Oc
17 H3 Reus Spain
69 C11 Reusam, Pulau isld Indonesia
25 D6 Reusel Netherlands
41 J4 Reuss R Switzerland
33 Q10 Reussen Germany
48 L3 Reut R Moldavia
33 R5 Reuterstadt Stavenhagen Germany
37 M3 Reuth Germany
37 N4 Reuth Germany
36 G7 Reutlingen Germany
41 N3 Reutte Austria
98 C4 Reva South Dakota U.S.A.
80 C6 Revadim Israel
40 C6 Revard mt France
103 H4 Reveille Pk Nevada U.S.A.
18 G9 Revel France
142 G2 Reveley I W Australia Australia
117 O10 Revelstoke British Columbia Canada
117 O10 Revelstoke Dam British Colombia Canada
118 J6 Revenue Saskatchewan Canada
45 K1 Revere Italy
9 F1 Revesby England
19 J4 Revigny France
117 H8 Revillagigedo I Alaska U.S.A.
20 H2 Réville France
98 K5 Revillo South Dakota U.S.A.
22 H4 Revin France
79 E7 Revivim Israel
28 F6 Revninge Denmark
26 O1 Revsbotn Norway
26 H9 Revsund Sweden
88 D9 Revubué R Mozambique
94 J5 Rew Pennsylvania U.S.A.
75 J6 Rewa India
145 E4 Rewa mt New Zealand
80 B7 Rewaḫa Israel
118 H6 Reward Saskatchewan Canada
74 G4 Rewari India
99 Q7 Rewey Wisconsin U.S.A.
101 O6 Rexburg Idaho U.S.A.
107 K2 Rexford Kansas U.S.A.
100 K1 Rexford Montana U.S.A.
22 D2 Rexpoede France
122 H7 Rexton New Brunswick Canada
80 D2 Reyba Israel
29 T9 Reydharfjördhur inlet Iceland
107 L6 Reydon Oklahoma U.S.A.
102 E7 Reyes Pk California U.S.A.
28 S9 Reykir Iceland
28 R10 Reykjanesta C Iceland
119 T7 Reykjavik Manitoba Canada
28 R9 Reykjavik Iceland
119 M6 Reynaud Saskatchewan Canada
140 B2 Reynolds R N Terr Australia
112 C5 Reynolds Georgia U.S.A.
100 J6 Reynolds Idaho U.S.A.
99 Q8 Reynolds Illinois U.S.A.
110 K1 Reynolds Indiana U.S.A.
98 J9 Reynolds Nebraska U.S.A.
138 D4 Reynolds, L South Australia Australia
140 C5 Reynolds Ra N Terr Australia
94 J5 Reynoldsville Pennsylvania U.S.A.
109 J9 Reynosa Mexico
40 B5 Reyssouze R France
78 K3 Rezaiyeh Iran
37 K5 Rezat R Germany
20 G7 Reze France
52 C6 Rēzekne Latvia
55 D3 Rezh Russian Federation
48 M3 Rezina Moldavia
47 J3 Rezvaya R Turkey
41 K5 Rezzonico Italy
32 K6 Rhade Germany
98 C3 Rhame North Dakota U.S.A.
41 L3 Rhätikon mt Switzerland
36 C4 Rhaunen Germany
8 C3 Rhayader Wales
32 H9 Rheda-Wiedenbrück Germany
32 F6 Rhede Niedersachsen Germany
32 E9 Rhede Nordrhein-Westfalen Germany
25 F4 Rheden Netherlands
9 F3 Rhee, R England
119 P7 Rhein Saskatchewan Canada
36 E6 Rhein R W Europe
36 D6 Rheinau Germany
36 B2 Rheinbach Germany
36 D3 Rheinböllen Germany
36 C3 Rheinbrohl Germany
25 F6 Rheindahlen Germany
32 F8 Rheine Germany
41 J2 Rheinfall Switzerland
40 G2 Rheinfelden Switzerland
32 E10 Rheinhausen Germany
36 B3 Rheinland-Pfalz land Germany
36 E6 Rheinmünster Germany
33 R6 Rheinsberg Germany
36 E6 Rheinstetten Germany
41 L3 Rhein Tal V Switzerland
36 E5 Rheinzabern Germany
40 F6 Rhêmes, Val de Italy
85 D3 Rhemilès Algeria
32 J10 Rhena Germany
25 E5 Rhenen Netherlands
36 D3 Rhens Germany
36 B1 Rheydt Germany
40 G2 Rhin R France
33 R6 Rhin R Germany
36 D7 Rhinau France
Rhine R France see Rhin R
Rhine R Germany/Switzerland see Rhein R
112 D6 Rhine Georgia U.S.A.
95 O5 Rhinebeck New York U.S.A.
99 R4 Rhinelander Wisconsin U.S.A.
33 R7 Rhinkanal Germany
33 Q7 Rhinow Germany
16 E9 Rhis, Oued R Morocco
41 K6 Rho Italy
127 K1 Rhoades, Pt Jamaica
95 Q5 Rhode I state U.S.A.
94 F9 Rhodell West Virginia U.S.A.
32 K10 Rhoden Germany
Rhodes isld see Ródhos isld
83 L13 Rhodes B Kerguelen Indian Oc
94 C3 Rhodes Michigan U.S.A.
Rhodesia see Zimbabwe
112 F2 Rhodhiss L North Carolina U.S.A.
109 K2 Rhome Texas U.S.A.
8 C4 Rhondda Wales
19 J7 Rhône dept France
19 O13 Rhône R France
41 H5 Rhône R Switzerland
19 N18 Rhône, Grand R France
19 Rhône Valley France
8 B4 Rhosili Wales
8 B1 Rhosneigr Wales
8 C1 Rhos-on-Sea Wales
85 F2 Rhourd El Baguel Algeria
8 C1 Rhuddlan Wales
18 G7 Rhue R France
20 E6 Rhuis, Presqu'île de pen France
32 M9 Rhume R Germany
18 D9 Rhune, la mt France/Spain
8 C3 Rhydd Hywel mt Wales
8 C1 Rhyl Wales
32 G9 Rhynern Germany
15 F3 Rhynie Scotland
131 E8 Riachos, I de los Argentina
16 B2 Ría de Arosa est Spain
16 A2 Ría de Corcubion est Spain
16 A1 Ría de Lage est Spain
16 A2 Ría de Murosa y Noya est Spain
16 B2 Ría de Pontevedra est Spain
16 B1 Ría de Sta. Marta est Spain
16 B2 Ría de Vigo est Spain
20 H6 Riallé France
70 B5 Riam Kalimantan
45 N5 Riano Italy
16 D2 Riaño Spain
19 P17 Rians France
16 E5 Riansares R Spain
20 D6 Riantec France
74 F2 Riasi Kashmir
69 F12 Riau, Kep islds Indonesia
16 E3 Riaza R Spain
16 B2 Ribadavia Spain
16 C1 Ribadeo Spain
16 D1 Ribadesella Spain
17 H2 Ribagorza dist Spain
129 K4 Ribamar Brazil
17 H3 Ribarroja, Emb. de res Spain
17 J2 Ribas de Fresser Spain
130 D7 Ribas do Rio Pardo Brazil
16 B5 Ribatejo prov Portugal
88 G9 Ribauè Mozambique
26 K1 Ribbenesöy isld Norway
13 F6 Ribble, R England
28 B6 Ribe Denmark
28 B6 Ribe Å R Denmark
40 F1 Ribeauville France
22 D4 Ribécourt France
133 H2 Ribeira R Brazil
133 H2 Ribeirão Prêto Brazil
129 J5 Ribeiro Gonçalves Brazil
22 E4 Ribemont France
43 E11 Ribera Sicily
18 F7 Ribérac France
128 E6 Riberalta Bolivia
19 P16 Ribiers France
121 L5 Rib Lake Ontario Canada
99 Q4 Rib Lake Wisconsin U.S.A.
99 R5 Rib Mt Wisconsin U.S.A.
42 F3 Ribnica Slovenia
33 Q4 Ribnitz-Damgarten Germany
118 G6 Ribstone Alberta Canada
118 F6 Ribstone Cr Alberta Canada
142 B5 Rica,Mt W Australia Australia
109 K8 Ricardo Texas U.S.A.
45 M3 Riccione Italy
103 K7 Rice California U.S.A.
109 L3 Rice Texas U.S.A.
112 F6 Riceboro Georgia U.S.A.
121 M8 Rice L Ontario Canada
99 N3 Rice L Minnesota U.S.A.
120 H5 Rice Lake Ontario Canada
99 P4 Rice Lake Wisconsin U.S.A.
119 N8 Riceton Saskatchewan Canada
99 O6 Riceville Iowa U.S.A.
18 H5 Riceys, les France
118 K6 Richard Saskatchewan Canada
110 L6 Richard City Tennessee U.S.A.
114 H3 Richard Collinson Inlet Northwest Territories Canada
89 H7 Richard's B S Africa
114 F4 Richards I Northwest Territories Canada
116 N6 Richardson Alaska U.S.A.
109 L3 Richardson Texas U.S.A.
109 O8 Richardson Texas U.S.A.
117 O3 Richardson I Northwest Territories Canada
95 R2 Richardson Lakes Maine U.S.A.
143 C8 Richardson, Mt W Australia Australia
114 F4 Richardson Mts Yukon Terr/N W Terr Canada
144 B6 Richardson Mts New Zealand
119 N8 Richardson Sta Saskatchewan Canada
85 A5 Richard Toll Senegal
98 D3 Richardton North Dakota U.S.A.
94 J4 Richburg New York U.S.A.
118 F7 Richdale Alberta Canada
143 C10 Riche, C W Australia Australia
121 R7 Richelieu R Quebec Canada
21 L7 Richelieu France
21 O2 Richemont France
123 P3 Riche Pt Newfoundland Canada
101 U2 Richey Montana U.S.A.
101 L6 Richfield Idaho U.S.A.
107 J4 Richfield Kansas U.S.A.
103 M3 Richfield Utah U.S.A.
95 L4 Richford New York U.S.A.
121 S8 Richford Vermont U.S.A.
102 E6 Richgrove California U.S.A.
110 B3 Rich Hill Missouri U.S.A.
122 H7 Richibucto New Brunswick Canada
118 F4 Rich Lake Alberta Canada
112 C5 Richland Georgia U.S.A.
94 B4 Richland Michigan U.S.A.
110 D4 Richland Missouri U.S.A.
101 T1 Richland Montana U.S.A.
95 N7 Richland New Jersey U.S.A.
100 H5 Richland Oregon U.S.A.
100 F3 Richland Washington U.S.A.
99 Q6 Richland Center Wisconsin U.S.A.
109 L4 Richland Cr Texas U.S.A.
112 K3 Richlands North Carolina U.S.A.
94 F9 Richlands Virginia U.S.A.
109 J4 Richland Springs Texas U.S.A.
118 J7 Richlea Saskatchewan Canada
139 K5 Richmond New South Wales Australia
141 G5 Richmond Queensland Australia
139 H8 Richmond Tasmania Australia
121 P7 Richmond Ontario Canada
122 H7 Richmond Prince Edward I Canada
121 S7 Richmond Quebec Canada
9 F5 Richmond England
13 G5 Richmond North Yorkshire England
127 L2 Richmond Jamaica
145 D4 Richmond New Zealand
89 C8 Richmond S Africa
102 B4 Richmond California U.S.A.
110 M2 Richmond Indiana U.S.A.
110 M4 Richmond Kentucky U.S.A.
95 S2 Richmond Maine U.S.A.
99 M4 Richmond Minnesota U.S.A.
100 F5 Richmond Oregon U.S.A.
109 M6 Richmond Texas U.S.A.
101 O8 Richmond Utah U.S.A.
94 K9 Richmond Virginia U.S.A.
121 L9 Richmond Hill Ontario Canada
112 F6 Richmond Hill Georgia U.S.A.
142 A4 Richmond, L W Australia Australia
139 L3 Richmond R New South Wales Australia
139 L3 Richmond Ra mts New South Wales Australia
95 N4 Richmondville New York U.S.A.
118 H8 Richmound Saskatchewan Canada
110 B7 Rich Mt Arkansas U.S.A.
33 R4 Richtenberg Germany
111 H10 Richton Mississippi U.S.A.
99 L3 Richville Minnesota U.S.A.
94 D6 Richwood Ohio U.S.A.
94 G8 Richwood West Virginia U.S.A.
99 S6 Richwood Wisconsin U.S.A.
110 F3 Richwoods Missouri U.S.A.
32 M4 Rickling Germany
9 F4 Rickmansworth England
17 G3 Ricla Spain
106 B4 Rico Colorado U.S.A.
40 F5 Riddes Switzerland
100 J7 Riddle Idaho U.S.A.
100 B7 Riddle Oregon U.S.A.
140 C6 Riddock, Mt N Terr Australia
121 P7 Rideau R Ontario Canada
121 P8 Rideau Canal Ontario Canada
121 O8 Rideau, L Ontario Canada
120 F2 Ridge R Ontario Canada
98 B4 Ridge Montana U.S.A.
102 G6 Ridgecrest California U.S.A.
119 N5 Ridgedale Saskatchewan Canada
101 N7 Ridgedale Idaho U.S.A.
99 T10 Ridge Farm Illinois U.S.A.
95 O5 Ridgefield Connecticut U.S.A.
111 F9 Ridgeland Mississippi U.S.A.
112 F5 Ridgeland South Carolina U.S.A.
99 P4 Ridgeland Wisconsin U.S.A.
141 K6 Ridgelands Queensland Australia
94 J7 Ridgeley West Virginia U.S.A.
95 M8 Ridgely Maryland U.S.A.
112 F4 Ridge Spring South Carolina U.S.A.
120 J10 Ridgetown Ontario Canada
98 F4 Ridgeview South Dakota U.S.A.
118 E1 Ridgeville Manitoba Canada
110 L1 Ridgeville Indiana U.S.A.
112 G4 Ridgeville South Carolina U.S.A.
110 C1 Ridgeway Missouri U.S.A.
112 G3 Ridgeway South Carolina U.S.A.
99 Q6 Ridgeway Wisconsin U.S.A.
110 G5 Ridgley Tennessee U.S.A.
106 C3 Ridgway Colorado U.S.A.
110 H4 Ridgway Illinois U.S.A.
98 B4 Ridgway Montana U.S.A.
119 R8 Riding Mt Manitoba Canada
143 D10 Ridley,Mt W Australia Australia
142 C5 Ridley, R W Australia Australia
118 J7 Ridpath Saskatchewan Canada
13 F3 Ridsdale England
26 J5 Riebnes L Sweden
20 C6 Riec France
38 H5 Ried Austria
37 M5 Rieden Germany
37 M6 Riedenburg Germany
36 D5 Riedseltz France
33 T6 Riegenwalde Germany
40 G2 Riehen Switzerland
118 B2 Riel Manitoba Canada
32 H8 Riemsloh Germany
36 H3 Rieneck Germany
110 H7 Rienzi Mississippi U.S.A.
33 S10 Riesa Germany
133 C8 Riesco, I Chile
43 F11 Riesi Sicily
33 O10 Riestedt Germany
89 D7 Riet R S Africa
52 B6 Rietavas Lithuania
32 H9 Rietberg Germany
89 B3 Rietfontein Namibia
42 E6 Rieti Italy
41 O3 Rietzer Grieskogel mt Austria
18 G8 Rieupeyroux France
20 F6 Rieux Morbihan France
19 Q17 Riez France
22 G4 Rièzes Belgium
16 D10 Rif dist Morocco
100 C3 Riffe Lake Washington U.S.A.
106 C2 Rifle Colorado U.S.A.
94 C2 Rifle R Michigan U.S.A.
29 T8 Rifstangi C Iceland
52 B5 Rīga Latvia
52 B5 Rīga, Gulf of Estonia/Latvia
142 B5 Riga,Mt W Australia Australia
77 F5 Rigān Iran
Rīgas Jūras Līcis see Rīga, Gulf of
121 Q7 Rigaud Quebec Canada
101 O6 Rigby Idaho U.S.A.
110 F2 Riggston Illinois U.S.A.
37 M4 Riglasreuth Germany
45 K4 Rignano sull'Arno Italy
21 L7 Rigny-Ussé France
115 O7 Rigolet Labrador, Nfld Canada
80 G4 Rihaba Jordan
Riia Laht see Rīga, Gulf of
29 M4 Riipi Finland
146 K8 Riiser-Larsenhalvøya pen Antarctica
146 J7 Riiser-Larsen Sea Antarctica
42 F3 Rijeka Croatia
25 C5 Rijsbergen Netherlands
25 G4 Rijssen Netherlands
25 B4 Rijswijk Netherlands
48 H2 Rika R Ukraine
69 C10 Rikitgaib Sumatra
60 R2 Rikubetsu Japan
61 Q6 Rikuchū Kaigan Nat. park Japan
61 P6 Rikuzen Takata Japan
46 F2 Rila plateau Bulgaria
46 F2 Rila Bulgaria
110 J2 Riley Indiana U.S.A.
107 O2 Riley Kansas U.S.A.
106 C7 Riley New Mexico U.S.A.
100 F6 Riley Oregon U.S.A.
21 L7 Rillé France
46 F2 Rilski Manastir Bulgaria
128 C4 Rimachi, L Peru
145 E1 Rimariki I New Zealand
40 B1 Rimaucourt France
69 G14 Rimau, Pulau isld Sumatra
48 F2 Rimava R Czechoslovakia
118 C6 Rimbey Alberta Canada
27 K12 Rimbo Sweden
94 H5 Rimersburg Pennsylvania U.S.A.
27 H13 Rimforsa Sweden
45 N3 Rimini Italy
48 L5 Rîmmicu Sărat Romania
80 E2 Rimmon Israel
80 E6 Rimmonim Jordan
48 K5 Rimna R Romania
48 J5 Rîmnicu Vîlcea Romania
22 H4 Rimogne France
122 D5 Rimouski R Quebec Canada
36 H4 Rimpar Germany
40 G5 Rimpfischhorn mt Switzerland
75 N4 Rinbung China
71 J9 Rinca isld Indonesia
37 P6 Rinchnach Germany
106 C9 Rincon New Mexico U.S.A.
126 A2 Rincon Bonaire W Indies
133 D2 Rinconada Argentina
124 H6 Rincón de Romos Mexico
28 A6 Rindby Denmark
70 K8 Rindingan, Bukit hill Sumatra
70 Q10 Rindjani, Gunung mt Indonesia
28 B4 Rind Kirke Denmark
139 J8 Ringarooma Tasmania Australia
74 F5 Rīngas India
28 E6 Ringe Denmark
27 D10 Ringebu Norway
41 K4 Ringelspitz mt Switzerland
27 D11 Ringerike L Norway
12 D4 Ringford Scotland
37 J1 Ringgau Germany
109 O3 Ringgold Louisiana U.S.A.
109 K2 Ringgold Texas U.S.A.
28 C5 Ringive Denmark
28 A4 Ringkøbing Denmark
47 P13 Ringládhes Greece
101 P3 Ringling Montana U.S.A.
109 K1 Ringling Oklahoma U.S.A.
9 G6 Ringmer England
109 M1 Ringold Oklahoma U.S.A.
27 E11 Ringsaker Norway
28 H6 Ringsted Denmark
99 M6 Ringsted Iowa U.S.A.
27 H13 Ringstorp Sweden
26 K2 Ringvassöy isld Norway
140 C6 Ringwood N Terr Australia
9 E6 Ringwood England
107 M5 Ringwood Oklahoma U.S.A.
46 G7 Rinia isld Greece
133 C5 Rinihue Chile
131 A7 Riñihue, L Chile
27 H15 Rinkabyholm Sweden
28 D7 Rinkenæs Denmark
41 O3 Rinn Austria
12 B2 Rinns Pt Scotland
27 G16 Ringsjön L Sweden
32 K8 Rinteln Germany
22 B2 Rinxent France
99 Q8 Rio Illinois U.S.A.
111 G11 Rio Louisiana U.S.A.
99 R6 Rio Wisconsin U.S.A.
125 P5 Río Abajo Panama
130 C5 Rio Alegre Brazil
124 G4 Rio Arreola Mexico
128 C4 Riobamba Ecuador
85 F8 Rio Benito Mbini Equat Guinea
128 E5 Rio Branco Brazil
133 G4 Rio Branco Uruguay
130 E9 Rio Branco do Sul Brazil
109 J10 Río Bravo Mexico
108 B5 Rio Bravo del Norte R Mexico
133 C6 Rio Bueno Chile
127 K1 Rio Bueno Jamaica
127 N9 Río Caribe Venezuela
133 D7 Río Chico Argentina
127 M9 Río Chico Venezuela
130 F8 Rio Claro Brazil
127 P3 Rio Claro Trinidad
127 K10 Río Claro Venezuela
131 D4 Río Cuarto Argentina
132 Rio de Janeiro conurbation Brazil
100 A9 Rio Dell Scotia California U.S.A.
128 D2 Rio de Oro Colombia
85 A4 Rio de Oro, B. de Western Sahara
131 E2 Rio Dulce Argentina
126 C9 Rio Frio Costa Rica
133 D8 Río Gallegos Argentina
131 B6 Rio Grande R Argentina
131 H4 Rio Grande Brazil
124 H6 Río Grande Mexico
125 M3 Rio Grande R Nicaragua
106 D4 Rio Grande R U.S.A./Mexico
109 J9 Rio Grande City Texas U.S.A.
130 H8 Rio Grande do Norte Brazil
131 G2 Rio Grande do Sul state Brazil
106 C4 Rio Grande Res Colorado U.S.A.
90 F12 Rio Grande Rise Atlantic Oc
109 K10 Rio Grande Valley airport Texas U.S.A.
127 H9 Ríohacha Colombia
108 B2 Rio Hondo R New Mexico U.S.A.
109 K9 Rio Hondo Texas U.S.A.
128 C5 Rioja Peru
102 C3 Rio Landa California U.S.A.
130 J10 Rio Largo Brazil
102 C3 Rio Linda California U.S.A.
45 L3 Riolo Terme Italy
16 B5 Rio Maior Portugal
109 J6 Riomedina Texas U.S.A.
18 G7 Riom ès Montagne France
133 E3 Río Muerto Argentina
133 D1 Río Mulatos Bolivia
85 G8 Río Muni prov Equat Guinea
131 C8 Rio Negro prov Argentina
130 E10 Rio Negro Brazil
131 F4 Rio Negro dept Uruguay
131 G4 Rio Negro, Embalse del res Uruguay
130 C6 Rio Negro, Pantanal do swamp Brazil
43 G8 Rionero in Vulture Italy
124 F3 Rio Palacio Mexico
17 F6 Riópar Spain
133 G4 Rio Pardo Brazil
127 M5 Rio Piedras Puerto Rico
130 F5 Rio Prêto, Sa. do mts Brazil
128 E8 Rio Quetena R Bolivia
129 L6 Rio Real Brazil
45 J2 Rio Saliceto Italy
130 J9 Rio Tinto Brazil
100 K8 Rio Tinto Nevada U.S.A.
71 C6 Rio Tuba Philippines
133 C8 Río Turbio Mines Argentina
19 O18 Riou, I. de France
128 C3 Rioverde Ecuador
125 J7 Río Verde Mexico
130 C6 Rio Verdi de Mato Grosso Brazil
109 K3 Rio Vista Texas U.S.A.
130 C6 Riozinho, R Brazil
48 F6 Ripanj Serbia Yugoslavia
44 B1 Riparia Italy
100 G3 Riparia Washington U.S.A.
26 L5 Ripats Sweden
122 K2 Ripault, L Quebec Canada
45 O4 Ripe Italy
45 O6 Ripi Italy
120 J8 Ripley Ontario Canada
9 E1 Ripley England
9 F5 Ripley England
13 G5 Ripley N Yorks England
103 K8 Ripley California U.S.A.
110 H7 Ripley Mississippi U.S.A.
94 H4 Ripley New York U.S.A.
110 N3 Ripley Ohio U.S.A.
107 O5 Ripley Oklahoma U.S.A.
110 G6 Ripley Tennessee U.S.A.
94 F8 Ripley West Virginia U.S.A.
17 J2 Ripoll Spain
121 P7 Ripon Quebec Canada
13 G5 Ripon England
102 C4 Ripon California U.S.A.
99 S6 Ripon Wisconsin U.S.A.
142 D5 Ripon Hills W Australia Australia
99 M8 Rippey Iowa U.S.A.
13 G6 Ripponden England
100 J4 Riggins Idaho U.S.A.
45 N5 Rignano Flaminio Italy
28 C5 Ris Denmark
42 J6 Risan Montenegro Yugoslavia
79 D8 Risân 'Aneiza mt Egypt
26 H7 Risbäck Sweden
18 E9 Riscle France
131 B5 Risco Plateado pk Argentina
28 C6 Rise Denmark
26 H7 Risede Sweden
28 C3 Risgårde Bredning B Denmark
47 H2 Rish Bulgaria
60 P1 Rishiri-suidō str Japan
60 P1 Rishiri-tō isld Japan
80 C6 Rishon LeZiyyon Israel
57 J6 Rishtan Uzbekistan
112 B3 Rising Fawn Georgia U.S.A.
109 J3 Rising Star Texas U.S.A.
95 L7 Rising Sun Maryland U.S.A.
94 D5 Rising Sun Ohio U.S.A.
110 M3 Rising Sun Indiana U.S.A.
117 M10 Riske Creek British Columbia Canada
21 L3 Risle R France
42 F3 Risnjak mt Croatia
48 J5 Rîsnov Romania
111 D8 Rison Arkansas U.S.A.
27 D13 Risör Norway
21 P4 Ris-Orangis France
40 D4 Risoux, Mont France
36 H7 Riss R Germany
26 D8 Rissa Norway
145 F3 Rissington New Zealand
52 B5 Rist Estonia
29 N10 Ristiina Finland
29 N7 Ristijärvi Finland
28 F7 Ristinge Denmark
26 M5 Risträsk Sweden
28 B7 Risum-Lindholm Germany
108 B8 Rita Blanca Cr R Texas U.S.A.
70 D4 Ritan R Kalimantan
142 B5 Ritchie Reef W Australia Australia
68 A6 Ritchie's Arch Andaman Is
83 K9 Ritigala mt Sri Lanka
37 J3 Ritschenhausen Germany
100 F5 Ritter Oregon U.S.A.
32 J6 Ritterhude Germany
102 E4 Ritter, Mt California U.S.A.
94 F6 Rittman Ohio U.S.A.
32 M10 Rittmarshausen Germany
100 G2 Ritzville Washington U.S.A.
68 D7 Riu, Laem Thailand
71 K9 Riung Flores Indonesia
41 N6 Riva Italy
47 N10 Riva Turkey
47 N11 Riva R Turkey
21 K3 Riva Bella France
133 E2 Rivadavia Argentina
133 C3 Rivadavia Chile
38 F8 Riva di Tures Italy
22 K3 Rivage Belgium
19 N14 Rival R France
44 B1 Rivalta di Torinese Italy
125 M4 Rivas Nicaragua
133 E5 Rivera Argentina
131 G3 Rivera Uruguay
102 D4 Riverbank California U.S.A.
85 C7 River Cess Liberia
102 E5 Riverdale California U.S.A.
107 N4 Riverdale Kansas U.S.A.
101 O2 Riverdale Montana U.S.A.
98 G9 Riverdale Nebraska U.S.A.
98 E2 Riverdale North Dakota U.S.A.
123 L8 River Denys C Breton I, Nova Scotia
111 K10 River Falls Alabama U.S.A.
99 O5 River Falls Wisconsin U.S.A.
123 T7 Riverhead Newfoundland Canada
95 P6 Riverhead Long I, New York U.S.A.
122 H8 River Hébert Nova Scotia Canada
118 L8 Riverhurst Saskatchewan Canada
139 H5 Riverina reg New South Wales Australia
143 D8 Riverina W Australia Australia
122 J8 River John Nova Scotia Canada
109 L9 River Oaks Texas U.S.A.
123 P3 River of Ponds Newfoundland Canada
133 C7 Rivero, I Chile
122 H9 Riverport Nova Scotia Canada
119 R8 Rivers Manitoba Canada
144 B6 Riversdale New Zealand
145 F4 Riversdale New Zealand
89 B10 Riversdale S Africa
120 H10 Riverside Ontario Canada
102 G8 Riverside California U.S.A.
95 K8 Riverside Maryland U.S.A.
100 G6 Riverside Oregon U.S.A.
109 M5 Riverside Texas U.S.A.
101 N8 Riverside Utah U.S.A.
101 T8 Riverside Wyoming U.S.A.
98 B9 Riverside Res Colorado U.S.A.
117 K10 Rivers Inlet British Columbia Canada
140 E4 Riversleigh Queensland Australia
119 M9 Rivers, L. of the Saskatchewan Canada
138 E5 Riverton South Australia Australia
119 U8 Riverton Manitoba Canada
144 B7 Riverton New Zealand
110 G2 Riverton Illinois U.S.A.
99 L9 Riverton Iowa U.S.A.
98 H9 Riverton Nebraska U.S.A.
94 J8 Riverton Virginia U.S.A.
101 R6 Riverton Wyoming U.S.A.
100 C2 Riverton Heights Washington U.S.A.
110 F6 Rivervale Arkansas U.S.A.
122 H7 Riverview New Brunswick Canada
98 G7 Riverview Nebraska U.S.A.
19 P14 Rives France
110 G5 Rives Tennessee U.S.A.
94 C4 Rives Junc Michigan U.S.A.

94 G7 Rivesville West Virginia U.S.A.
103 K6 Riviera Nevada U.S.A.
109 K8 Riviera Texas U.S.A.
113 G11 Riviera Beach Florida U.S.A.
44 F3 Riviera di Levante Italy
44 D4 Riviera di Ponente Italy
21 J4 Rivière Orne France
22 D3 Rivière Pas-de-Calais France
122 G4 Rivière à Claude Quebec Canada
122 J4 Rivière-à-la-Loutre Quebec Canada
121 S6 Rivière à Pierre Quebec Canada
122 H5 Rivière-au-Renard Quebec Canada
122 G3 Rivière aux Graines Quebec Canada
121 S5 Rivière-aux-Rats Quebec Canada
122 D6 Rivière Bleue Quebec Canada
122 K4 Rivière-de-la-Chaloupe Quebec Canada
83 M13 Rivière des Anguilles Mauritius
122 C6 Rivière du Loup Quebec Canada
121 S5 Rivière du Milieu Quebec Canada
122 B5 Rivière du Moulin Quebec Canada
121 M4 Rivière Héva Quebec Canada
122 G4 Rivière La Madeleine Quebec Canada
122 B6 Rivière Ouelle see Rivière Ouelle
122 E4 Rivière Pentecôte Quebec Canada
122 G3 Rivière Pigou Quebec Canada
127 M4 Rivière Pilote Martinique W Indies
122 H3 Rivière St. Jean Quebec Canada
21 L3 Rivière-St. Sauveur, la France
127 L4 Rivière Salée Martinique W Indies
122 D6 Rivière-Verte New Brunswick Canada
122 C6 Rivière Verte New Brunswick Canada
44 C1 Rivoli Italy
138 E6 Rivoli B South Australia Australia
145 D4 Riwaka New Zealand
72 F4 Riyāḍ, Ar Saudi Arabia
Riyadh see Riyāḍ, Ar
71 E3 Rizal Luzon Philippines
78 H1 Rize Turkey
65 D7 Rizhao China
Rizhskiy Zaliv see Riga, Gulf of
79 E3 Rizokarpaso Cyprus
46 E5 Rizoma Greece
43 H10 Rizzuto, C Italy
27 C12 Rjukan Norway
27 B12 Rjuven Norway
85 A5 Rkiz, L Mauritania
80 E1 Rmaich Lebanon
68 H5 Ro Vietnam
27 E11 Roa Norway
16 E3 Roa Spain
110 K2 Roachdale Indiana U.S.A.
9 F3 Roade England
106 B9 Road Forks New Mexico U.S.A.
127 M5 Road Town Virgin Is
28 B6 Roager Denmark
103 P2 Roan Cliffs Utah U.S.A.
106 B2 Roan Cr Colorado U.S.A.
112 E1 Roan Mt North Carolina U.S.A.
18 H6 Roanne France
111 L8 Roanoke Alabama U.S.A.
99 R9 Roanoke Illinois U.S.A.
94 B6 Roanoke Indiana U.S.A.
109 K3 Roanoke Texas U.S.A.
94 H9 Roanoke Virginia U.S.A.
112 M2 Roanoke I North Carolina U.S.A.
112 K1 Roanoke Rapids North Carolina U.S.A.
106 B2 Roan Plateau Colorado U.S.A.
103 P2 Roan Plateau Utah U.S.A.
109 M5 Roans Prairie Texas U.S.A.
95 L5 Roaring Branch Pennsylvania U.S.A.
112 F1 Roaring Gap North Carolina U.S.A.
108 G2 Roaring Springs Texas U.S.A.
14 B5 Roaringwater B Ireland
77 B2 Robat Iran
77 B2 Robat Karim Iran
109 J9 Robberson Texas U.S.A.
112 H2 Robbins North Carolina U.S.A.
139 G8 Robbins I Tasmania Australia
112 D2 Robbinsville North Carolina U.S.A.
44 E1 Robbio Italy
138 E6 Robe South Australia Australia
14 B3 Robe R Ireland
33 R6 Röbel Germany
109 O4 Robeline Louisiana U.S.A.
138 F4 Robe, Mt New South Wales Australia
122 K3 Robe Noir, L. de la Quebec Canada
142 B5 Robe R W Australia Australia
112 K2 Robersonville North Carolina U.S.A.
108 G4 Robert Lee Texas U.S.A.
140 B7 Robert, Mt N Terr Australia
13 F3 Roberton Scotland
117 N6 Roberts Idaho U.S.A.
101 Q4 Roberts Montana U.S.A.
100 E5 Roberts Oregon U.S.A.
123 R4 Robert's Arm Newfoundland Canada
9 G6 Robertsbridge England
102 H2 Roberts Cr. Mt Nevada U.S.A.
111 J11 Robertsdale Alabama U.S.A.
26 L7 Robertsfors Sweden
110 A6 Robert S. Kerr Res Oklahoma U.S.A.
141 K8 Roberts, Mt Queensland Australia
101 Q7 Roberts Mt Wyoming U.S.A.
141 G4 Robertson R Queensland Australia
89 A9 Robertson S Africa
146 B6 Robertson Wyoming U.S.A.
146 C12 Robertson Bay Antarctica
146 D12 Robertson I Antarctica
142 D6 Robertson Ra W Australia Australia
112 K6 Robertsonville Quebec Canada
85 B7 Robertsport Liberia
138 E5 Robertstown South Australia Australia
14 E3 Robertstown Ireland
122 G6 Robertville New Brunswick Canada
121 S4 Roberval Quebec Canada
115 N1 Robeson Chan Canada/Greenland
8 B4 Robeston Wathen Wales
102 J5 Robin Idaho U.S.A.
100 J5 Robinette Oregon U.S.A.
9 F5 Robin Hoods Bay England
99 N8 Robinson Illinois U.S.A.
98 G2 Robinson North Dakota U.S.A.
133 B9 Robinson Crusoe isld Juan Fernández Is Pacific Oc

138 D2 Robinson, Mt South Australia Australia
142 C6 Robinson, Mt W Australia Australia
116 Q6 Robinson Mts Alaska U.S.A.
143 C7 Robinson Ras W Australia Australia
140 D3 Robinson River N Terr
122 F6 Robinsonville New Brunswick Canada
139 G5 Robinvale New South Wales Australia
17 F6 Robledo Spain
103 N9 Robles Pass Arizona U.S.A.
103 N9 Robles Ranch Arizona U.S.A.
118 A1 Roblin Park Manitoba Canada
128 G7 Robore Bolivia
118 H9 Robsart Saskatchewan Canada
33 R10 Röbsdorf Germany
95 L8 Rock Point Maryland U.S.A.
102 A2 Rockport California U.S.A.
110 E2 Rockport Illinois U.S.A.
110 J4 Rockport Indiana U.S.A.
92 S2 Rockport Maine U.S.A.
95 R4 Rockport Massachusetts U.S.A.
110 A1 Rock Port Missouri U.S.A.
109 K7 Rockport Texas U.S.A.
100 D1 Rockport Washington U.S.A.
101 U8 Rock River Wyoming U.S.A.
113 L13 Rock Sound Bahamas
126 F2 Rock Sound Eleuthera Bahamas
103 M7 Rock Springs Arizona U.S.A.
101 T3 Rock Springs Montana U.S.A.
108 G5 Rock Springs Texas U.S.A.
101 W5 Rock Springs Wyoming U.S.A.
144 D4 Rocks Pt. New Zealand
128 G2 Rockstone Guyana
99 R7 Rockton Illinois U.S.A.
98 K6 Rock Valley Iowa U.S.A.
144 D6 Rockville New Zealand
95 P5 Rockville Connecticut U.S.A.
110 J2 Rockville Indiana U.S.A.
95 K7 Rockville Maryland U.S.A.
100 H6 Rockville Oregon U.S.A.
112 G5 Rockville South Carolina U.S.A.
103 L4 Rockville Utah U.S.A.
109 L3 Rockwall Texas U.S.A.
99 N7 Rockwell Iowa U.S.A.
112 G2 Rockwell North Carolina U.S.A.
99 M7 Rockwell City Iowa U.S.A.
106 C4 Rockwood Colorado U.S.A.
95 S1 Rockwood Maine U.S.A.
94 H7 Rockwood Pennsylvania U.S.A.
112 C2 Rockwood Tennessee U.S.A.
109 H4 Rockwood Texas U.S.A.
112 G2 Rocky R North Carolina U.S.A.
107 L6 Rocky Oklahoma U.S.A.
112 E3 Rocky R South Carolina U.S.A.
100 K6 Rocky Bar Idaho U.S.A.
139 H8 Rocky C Tasmania Australia
118 D7 Rockyford British Columbia Canada
106 G3 Rocky Ford Colorado U.S.A.
112 F5 Rocky Ford Georgia U.S.A.
98 D6 Rockyford South Dakota U.S.A.
94 D7 Rocky Fork Res Ohio U.S.A.
94 H5 Rocky Grove Pennsylvania U.S.A.
143 B10 Rocky Gully W Australia Australia
120 H5 Rocky Island L Ontario Canada
119 Q4 Rocky L Manitoba Canada
112 K2 Rocky Mount North Carolina U.S.A.
94 H10 Rocky Mount Virginia U.S.A.
118 C6 Rocky Mountain House Alberta Canada
101 N2 Rocky Mt Montana U.S.A.
98 A9 Rocky Mt Nat. Park Colorado U.S.A.
27 B12 Rocky Mts N America
127 K3 Rocky Point Jamaica
95 P6 Rocky Point Long I, New York U.S.A.
94 A5 Rockpoint Wyoming U.S.A.
113 H11 Rocky Pt Bahamas
94 D4 Rocky Pt Alaska U.S.A.
94 F5 Rocky River Ohio U.S.A.
131 D7 Rô Colorado Argentina
20 F3 Rocque Pt. La Channel Is
22 H4 Rocroi France
37 M2 Roda R Germany
30 D5 Rodalben Germany
28 C11 Rødberg Norway
28 G7 Rødbyhavn Denmark
123 Q3 Roddickton Newfoundland Canada
28 B3 Rødding Germany
28 C6 Rødding Sønderjylland Denmark
111 F9 Rodez France
36 F4 Rödermark Germany
32 K8 Rodenberg Germany
27 E12 Rødenes Norway
32 H6 Rodenkirchen Germany
13 L3 Rödental Germany
124 G5 Rodeo Mexico
106 B9 Rodeo New Mexico U.S.A.
33 S10 Roderau Germany
109 O3 Rodessa Louisiana U.S.A.
32 K7 Rodewald Germany
37 M2 Rodewisch Germany
36 F2 Rodgau-Dudenhofen Germany
46 F4 Rodholívos Greece
47 V14 Ródhos Greece
47 V14 Ródhos Greece
45 J1 Rodigo Italy
37 O5 Roding Germany
140 C6 Rodinga N Terr Australia
52 J2 Rodionovo Russian Federation
27 M8 Rødkærsbro Denmark
48 J3 Rodkhan Pakistan
120 J10 Rodney Ontario Canada
94 B3 Rodney Michigan U.S.A.
116 D4 Rodney, C Alaska U.S.A.
52 F6 Rodniki Russian Federation
55 C5 Rodnikova Kazakhstan
52 D3 Rodnya Belorussia
139 H7 Rodondo isld Victoria Australia
27 J8 Rodonit, kepi i Albania
13 E3 Rodono Scotland
52 H2 Rodopi Planina Bulgaria
Rodosto see Tekirdağ

109 L6 Rock Island Texas U.S.A.
98 G1 Rock L North Dakota U.S.A.
100 H2 Rock L Washington U.S.A.
121 P7 Rockland Ontario Canada
101 N7 Rockland Idaho U.S.A.
95 S2 Rockland Maine U.S.A.
99 R3 Rockland Michigan U.S.A.
109 N4 Rockland Texas U.S.A.
140 E4 Rocklands Australia
138 F6 Rocklands Res Victoria Australia
141 K2 Rocklea dist Brisbane, Qnsld Australia
142 B6 Rocklea W Australia Australia
100 G2 Rocklyn Washington U.S.A.
112 B3 Rockmart Georgia U.S.A.
117 Q3 Rocknest L Northwest Territories Canada
95 R4 Rock Point Maine U.S.A.
102 A2 Rockport California U.S.A.
110 E2 Rockport Illinois U.S.A.
110 J4 Rockport Indiana U.S.A.
95 R4 Rockport Massachusetts U.S.A.
110 A1 Rock Port Missouri U.S.A.
109 K7 Rockport Texas U.S.A.
100 D1 Rockport Washington U.S.A.
113 L13 Rock Sound Bahamas
126 F2 Rock Sound Eleuthera Bahamas
103 M7 Rock Springs Arizona U.S.A.
101 T3 Rock Springs Montana U.S.A.
108 G5 Rocksprings Texas U.S.A.
101 W5 Rock Springs Wyoming U.S.A.
144 D4 Rocks Pt. New Zealand
128 G2 Rockstone Guyana
99 R7 Rockton Illinois U.S.A.
98 K6 Rock Valley Iowa U.S.A.
144 D6 Rockville New Zealand
95 P5 Rockville Connecticut U.S.A.
110 J2 Rockville Indiana U.S.A.
95 K7 Rockville Maryland U.S.A.
100 H6 Rockville Oregon U.S.A.
112 G5 Rockville South Carolina U.S.A.
103 L4 Rockville Utah U.S.A.
109 L3 Rockwall Texas U.S.A.
99 N7 Rockwell Iowa U.S.A.
112 G2 Rockwell North Carolina U.S.A.
99 M7 Rockwell City Iowa U.S.A.
106 C4 Rockwood Colorado U.S.A.
95 S1 Rockwood Maine U.S.A.
94 H7 Rockwood Pennsylvania U.S.A.
112 C2 Rockwood Tennessee U.S.A.
109 H4 Rockwood Texas U.S.A.
112 G2 Rocky R North Carolina U.S.A.
107 L6 Rocky Oklahoma U.S.A.
112 E3 Rocky R South Carolina U.S.A.
100 K6 Rocky Bar Idaho U.S.A.
139 H8 Rocky C Tasmania Australia
118 D7 Rockyford British Columbia Canada
106 G3 Rocky Ford Colorado U.S.A.
112 F5 Rocky Ford Georgia U.S.A.
98 D6 Rockyford South Dakota U.S.A.
94 D7 Rocky Fork Res Ohio U.S.A.
94 H5 Rocky Grove Pennsylvania U.S.A.
143 B10 Rocky Gully W Australia Australia
120 H5 Rocky Island L Ontario Canada
119 Q4 Rocky L Manitoba Canada
112 K2 Rocky Mount North Carolina U.S.A.
94 H10 Rocky Mount Virginia U.S.A.
118 C6 Rocky Mountain House Alberta Canada
101 N2 Rocky Mt Montana U.S.A.
98 A9 Rocky Mt Nat. Park Colorado U.S.A.
27 B12 Rocky Mts N America
127 K3 Rocky Point Jamaica
95 P6 Rocky Point Long I, New York U.S.A.
94 A5 Rockpoint Wyoming U.S.A.
113 H11 Rocky Pt Bahamas
94 D4 Rocky Pt Alaska U.S.A.
94 F5 Rocky River Ohio U.S.A.

115 L5 Roes Welcome Sound Northwest Territories Canada
15 F5 Ro Ferraresi Italy
77 F8 Roki Tajikistan
55 C5 Romitan Uzbekistan
36 B1 Rommerskirchen Germany
94 J7 Romney West Virginia U.S.A.
54 E6 Romny Ukraine
28 A6 Rømø isld Denmark
70 C5 Romodan Ukraine
69 F11 Romorantin France
36 G2 Rompin Malaysia
26 C9 Romsdal V Norway
26 B8 Romsdalsfjord inlet Norway
9 F6 Romsey England
9 G6 Romsley England
113 L14 Romulus I Kerguelen Indian Oc
26 D10 Rondeslottet mt Norway
128 D2 Rondón Colombia
128 F6 Rondo Brazil
130 C5 Rondonópolis Brazil
128 F3 Rondon, Pico mt Brazil
88 G7 Rondo Plat Tanzania
96 B2 Rondorf Germany
95 N5 Rondout Res New York U.S.A.
27 K14 Rone Sweden
67 C2 Rong'an China
65 C5 Rongcheng China
65 E6 Rongcheng China
65 C6 Rong Jiang R China
67 C4 Rongjiang China
68 A1 Rongklang Ra Burma
36 G5 Rongshi China
19 M6 Rongsberg Germany
32 F8 Rönnebeck Germany
110 B1 Rönnebeck Germany
95 N5 Roodeberg Netherlands
27 N2 Ronneby Sweden
27 H15 Ronneby Sweden
146 O6 Ronne Entrance Antarctica
32 L8 Ronnenberg Germany
109 O5 Rönnöfors Sweden
117 H8 Ronse Pt British Columbia Canada
22 H6 Ronse Belgium
70 H2 Roo R Brazil
25 G2 Roodeschool Netherlands
110 G3 Roodhouse Illinois U.S.A.
22 G4 Roodt Luxembourg
89 F4 Rooiberg mt S Africa
25 B5 Roosendaal Netherlands
101 M8 Roosevelt Minnesota U.S.A.
107 N3 Roosevelt Oklahoma U.S.A.
109 P9 Roosevelt Texas U.S.A.
100 P9 Roosevelt Utah U.S.A.
100 E7 Roosevelt Washington U.S.A.
103 N8 Roosevelt Dam Arizona U.S.A.
146 C10 Roosevelt I Antarctica
95 P8 Roosevelt, Mt British Columbia Canada
14 D3 Roosky Ireland
14 D6 Rosscarbery Ireland
80 C6 Rosh Ha 'Ayin Israel
77 C3 Roshkhvar Iran
99 U6 Rosholt South Dakota U.S.A.
99 V5 Rosholt Wisconsin U.S.A.
56 K8 Roshni-Chu Russian Federation
110 J6 Rosiclare Illinois U.S.A.
110 C2 Rosiers, C.des France
122 H5 Rosiers, C.des France
46 G1 Rosița R Bulgaria
48 G1 Rosița Bulgaria
37 K3 Rösrath Germany
54 D2 Ross Scotland

142 F5 Romily, Mt W Australia Australia
57 C5 Romitan Uzbekistan
36 B1 Rommerskirchen Germany
57 C5 Romney West Virginia U.S.A.
98 K1 Roseau Minnesota U.S.A.
139 H8 Roseberry Tasmania Australia
140 E7 Roseberth Queensland Australia
123 O6 Rose Blanche Newfoundland Canada
112 J3 Roseboro North Carolina U.S.A.
118 D7 Rosebud Alberta Canada
110 E3 Rosebud Missouri U.S.A.
101 T3 Rosebud Montana U.S.A.
108 A8 Rosebud New Mexico U.S.A.
100 S4 Rosebud South Dakota U.S.A.
109 L4 Rosebud Texas U.S.A.
101 T4 Rosebud Cr Montana U.S.A.
101 S4 Rosebud Mts Montana U.S.A.
100 B6 Roseburg Oregon U.S.A.
94 C3 Rosebush Michigan U.S.A.
94 C2 Rose City Michigan U.S.A.
102 G1 Rose Creek Nevada U.S.A.
141 K6 Rosedale Queensland Australia
118 E7 Rosedale Alberta Canada
110 J2 Rosedale Indiana U.S.A.
111 F8 Rosedale Mississippi U.S.A.
117 J8 Rosedale Abbey England
22 H3 Rosée Belgium
127 J1 Rose Hall Jamaica
83 M6 Rose Hill Mauritius
112 J3 Rose Hill North Carolina U.S.A.
27 F16 Rösjö Sweden
12 F5 Roskeen Scotland
113 K12 Rose I Bahamas
111 F11 Roseland Louisiana U.S.A.
118 F7 Rose Lynn Alberta Canada
118 E8 Rosemary Alberta Canada
6 D3 Rosemary Bank N Atlantic Oc
142 B5 Rosemary I W Australia Australia
99 N5 Rosemount Minnesota U.S.A.
102 E2 Rose, Mt Nevada U.S.A.
38 J8 Rosenbach mt Austria
33 O10 Rosenberg Germany
109 M6 Rosenberg Texas U.S.A.
31 F8 Rosendahl Germany
32 F8 Rosendahl Germany
110 B1 Rosendale Missouri U.S.A.
121 M8 Rosendale Ontario Canada
12 D1 Roseneath Scotland
13 E7 Roseneath Scotland
36 F6 Rosengarten Germany
32 J7 Rosengarten Germany
38 J8 Rosenheim Germany
37 L6 Rosenkopf mt Austria
31 F8 Rosennock mt Austria
38 J8 Rosental V Austria
37 N5 Rosenthal Germany
117 H8 Rose Pt British Columbia Canada
27 H8 Roseray Saskatchewan Canada
118 J8 Roseray Saskatchewan Canada
126 G3 Rose s Long I Bahamas
118 K7 Rosetown Saskatchewan Canada
141 H5 Rosetta R Queensland Australia
Rosetta Egypt see Rashid
103 S3 Rosette Utah U.S.A.
103 G3 Rosetti France
99 V4 Roseville Illinois U.S.A.
94 E7 Roseville Ohio U.S.A.
118 B3 Rosewell Alberta Canada
140 B3 Rosewood N Terr Australia
141 K8 Rosewood Queensland Australia
43 J5 Roseworth Idaho U.S.A.
52 E6 Roshal' Russian Federation

14 C3 Roscommon Ireland
94 C2 Roscommon Michigan U.S.A.
14 D4 Roscrea Ireland
52 N6 Rose Nebraska U.S.A.
127 O7 Roseau Dominica
98 K1 Roseau R Minnesota U.S.A.
139 H8 Roseberry Tasmania Australia
14 C4 Rosslare Ireland
33 Q9 Rossla Germany
33 O10 Rossleben Germany
145 A4 Ross, Mt New Zealand
85 A5 Rosso Mauritania
26 H8 Rosson Sweden
8 D4 Ross-on-Wye England
54 L6 Rossosh' Russian Federation
33 R6 Rossow Germany
120 C4 Rossport Ontario Canada
108 A8 Ross River N Terr Australia
146 C6 Ross River Yukon Territory Canada
146 B11 Ross Sea Antarctica
37 K5 Rosstal Germany
33 O9 Rosstrappe Germany
26 G6 Rossvassbukt Norway
110 J5 Rossview Res Tennessee U.S.A.
112 B3 Rossville Illinois U.S.A.
107 P1 Rossville Indiana U.S.A.
117 J8 Rosswein Germany
26 M3 Röst isld Norway
26 F4 Røst isld Norway
26 L3 Rosta Norway
26 L3 Rostaelv R Norway
26 L2 Rostadgord mt Norway
77 C7 Rostam zd well Persian Gulf
27 F16 Röstånga Sweden
51 L6 Rostaq Afghanistan
118 L6 Rosthern Saskatchewan Canada
36 C2 Rostingen Germany
33 Q4 Rostock Germany
26 M3 Rostonsölkä reg Sweden
52 E6 Rostov Russian Federation
53 E10 Rostov-na-Donu Russian Federation
53 F10 Rostovskaya Oblast' prov Russian Federation
20 D5 Rostrenen France
28 D3 Rostrup Denmark
46 D3 Rostuša Macedonia Yugoslavia
26 D9 Rotanger Norway
52 H2 Rovinskoye Russian Federation
112 K12 Roswell Georgia U.S.A.
108 C2 Roswell New Mexico U.S.A.
37 R7 Rot R Germany
57 O10 Rot Sweden
26 E5 Rota C Norway
16 C8 Rota Spain
108 G3 Rot am See Germany
108 G3 Rotan Texas U.S.A.
37 M1 Rot Buhl mt Germany
71 O10 Rote isld Timor Indonesia
80 F4 Rotem Jordan
36 J2 Rotenburg Hessen Germany
32 K6 Rotenburg/Wümme Germany
Niedersachsen Germany
38 G12 Roter Kopf mt Austria
37 L3 Roter Main R Germany
37 M6 Rote Wand mt Austria
25 F7 Rotgen Germany
37 L2 Roth Germany
31 N1 Rötha Germany
37 N6 Rothaargebirge mts Germany
36 C2 Rothau France
9 U6 Rothbury England
117 L10 Rothbury Michigan U.S.A.
37 L3 Rothe Mühle Germany
36 C2 Röthenbach Germany
33 Q9 Rothenbach Germany
41 E7 Rothenbuch Germany
37 N2 Rothenburg Germany
37 J5 Rothenburg ob der Tauber Germany
52 F6 Roshal' Russian Federation
109 M6 Roshanskoye Kazakhstan
37 L3 Rothenkirchen Germany
33 O10 Rothenschirmbach Germany
146 C5 Rothera U.K. Base Antarctica
9 F5 Rotherham England
144 D6 Rotherham New Zealand
9 G5 Rother, R England
13 E6 Rothes Scotland
122 F6 Rothesay New Brunswick Canada
12 C2 Rothesay Scotland
13 E3 Rothiemay Scotland
37 O7 Rothwell England
146 C11 Roti, Selat Indonesia
139 H5 Roto New South Wales Australia

Rossiyskaya SFSR see Russian Federation
100 D1 Ross L Washington U.S.A.
100 E1 Ross Lake Nat. Recreation Area Washington U.S.A.
100 H1 Rossland British Columbia Canada
14 C4 Rosslare Ireland
144 J3 Rotoiti, L New Zealand
144 E3 Rotoiti, L New Zealand
144 F3 Rotokohu New Zealand
144 F3 Rotomahana New Zealand
144 J3 Rotoma, L New Zealand
144 A3 Rotomanu New Zealand
44 F1 Rotondella Italy
144 O4 Rotondo, M mt Italy
144 J3 Rotoroa New Zealand
145 D3 Rotowaro New Zealand
21 J3 Rott R France
37 O7 Rott R Germany
41 L8 Rottach Germany
143 B9 Rottnest I W Australia Australia
37 J5 Rottne Germany
37 L3 Rottenburg Germany
36 F6 Rottenburg Germany
38 K6 Rottendorf Germany
38 J4 Rottenmann Germany
33 Q5 Rottenmannner Tauern mts Austria
25 F1 Rottum isld Netherlands
25 G1 Rottumerplaat Netherlands
37 O5 Rottweil Germany
20 G4 Rotuma isld Pacific Oc
37 O5 Rötz Germany
20 F6 Roubaix France
37 L3 Roudnice Czechoslovakia
24 E3 Rouen France
20 C4 Rouffach France
50 L9 Rougemont France
11 G3 Rough oilfield North Sea
7 L9 Rough Ridge New Zealand
110 K4 Rough River L Kentucky U.S.A.
Roulers see Roeselare
109 P18 Rouleau Saskatchewan Canada
37 L3 Roullac France
119 M9 Roundabout Mt Alaska U.S.A.

121 S7 **Ste.Clothilde** Quebec Canada
113 F9 **St.Cloud** Florida U.S.A.
99 M4 **St.Cloud** Minnesota U.S.A.
8 B7 **St.Columb** England
20 G7 **St. Columban** France
121 R6 **St.Côme** Quebec Canada
20 H3 **St.Côme-du-Mont** France
21 L5 **St.Cosme-de-Vair** France
122 E8 **Ste.Croix** New Brunswick Canada
40 D4 **Ste.Croix** Switzerland
99 O4 **St. Croix** *R* Wisconsin U.S.A.
95 T8 **St. Croix** *R* Maine/New Brunswick U.S.A./Canada
36 C7 **Ste.Croix aux Mines** France
113 L8 **St.Croix I** Virgin Is
122 C6 **St.Cyprien** Quebec Canada
18 F8 **St.Cyprien** France
19 P18 **St.Cyr** France
21 K5 **St.Cyr** Mayenne France
21 J4 **St.Cyr-du-Bailleul** France
21 K7 **St.Cyr-en-Bourg** France
21 O6 **St.Cyr-en-Val** France
121 S7 **St.Cyrille** Quebec Canada
121 P4 **St.Cyr, L** Quebec Canada
118 J4 **St. Cyr Lake** Saskatchewan Canada
21 M7 **St.-Cyr-sur-Loire** France
122 B7 **St.Damien** Quebec Canada
127 P1 **St.David** *co* Trinidad
110 F1 **St.David** Illinois U.S.A.
122 A5 **St.David-de-Falardeau** Quebec Canada
123 O5 **St. David's** Newfoundland Canada
8 A4 **St. David's** Wales
90 D1 **St.Davids I** Bermuda
22 G3 **St.Denis** Belgium
121 R7 **St.Denis** Quebec Canada
21 P4 **St. Denis** France
83 J13 **St.Denis** Réunion Indian Oc
21 K6 **St.Denis-d'Anjou** France
21 J5 **St. Denis-de-Gastines** France
21 O8 **St.Denis-de-Jouhet** France
21 K5 **St.Denis-d'Orques** France
20 H8 **St. Denis la Chevasse** France
21 K5 **St.Denis-sur-Sarthon** France
20 F4 **St.Denoual** France
19 O16 **St.Didier** France
36 B7 **St. Dié** France
19 J4 **St.Dizier** France
20 F6 **St.Dolay** France
20 G5 **St Domineuc** France
19 N14 **St.Donat sur l'Herbasse** France
98 J8 **St.Edward** Nebraska U.S.A.
116 P7 **St.Elias, C** Alaska U.S.A.
117 D5 **St. Elias Mts** Alaska/Yukon Terr U.S.A./Canada
121 S4 **Ste.Elisabeth** Quebec Canada
127 J2 **St.Elizabeth** *parish* Jamaica
110 H2 **St.Elmo** Illinois U.S.A.
122 C5 **St.Eloi** Quebec Canada
18 G6 **St Éloy-les-Mines** France
121 R6 **Ste.Emélie** Quebec Canada
18 H8 **Ste.Enimie** France
20 H3 **Sainteny** France
21 M7 **St.Epain** France
122 B7 **St.Ephrem** Quebec Canada
121 L3 **St.Ephrem de Paradis** Quebec Canada
122 C6 **St.-Epiphane** Quebec Canada
20 G5 **St.Erblon** France
22 F5 **St.Erme-Outre-et-Ramecourt** France
18 E7 **Saintes** France
127 L4 **St. Ésprit, Le** Martinique W Indies
22 B2 **St.Étienne-au-Mont** France
18 E9 **St. Étienne de Baïgorry** France
20 G7 **St.Étienne-de-Montluc** France
19 O14 **St.Étienne de St.Geoirs** France
21 N3 **St.Étienne-du-Rouvray** France
121 M4 **St. Eugène** Quebec Canada
121 S4 **St.-Eugène** Quebec Canada
122 D6 **St.Eusèbe** Quebec Canada
121 R7 **St.Eustache** Quebec Canada
127 N6 **Sint Eustatius** *isld* Lesser Antilles
21 L4 **St.Evroult Notre Dame-du-Bois** France
122 D5 **St.Fabien** Quebec Canada
122 B7 **Ste.Familie** Quebec Canada
121 P6 **Ste.Famille d'Aumond** Quebec Canada
18 H5 **St.Fargeau** France
121 S4 **St.Félicien** Quebec Canada
122 E5 **Ste.Félicité** Quebec Canada
121 R6 **St. Félix de Valois** Quebec Canada
12 D1 **St.Fillans** Scotland
14 A5 **St. Finan's B** Ireland
123 O5 **St.Fintan's** Newfoundland Canada
19 Q15 **St. Firmin** France
20 G8 **Ste. Flaive-des-Loups** France
121 T6 **St.Flavien** Quebec Canada
122 E5 **Ste.Florence** Quebec Canada
20 H8 **St.Florent-des-Bois** France
18 H4 **St.Florentin** France
21 H7 **St.Florent-le-Vieil** France
21 P8 **St.Florent-sur-Cher** France
18 H7 **St.Flour** France
21 N8 **St.Flovier** France
121 T7 **St.Fortunat** Quebec Canada
19 N15 **St.Fortunat** France
121 T6 **Ste. Foy** Quebec Canada
18 F8 **Ste.Foy-la-Grande** France
107 J2 **St.Francis** Kansas U.S.A.
110 F5 **St. Francis** *R* Missouri/Ark U.S.A.
95 R6 **St. Francis** *R* Maine/New Brunswick U.S.A./Canada
89 D10 **St. Francis B** S Africa
123 U6 **St.Francis, C** Newfoundland Canada
89 D10 **St. Francis C** S Africa
138 C4 **St.Francis, I.of** South Australia Australia
110 J3 **St. Francisville** Illinois U.S.A.
111 E11 **St.Francisville** Louisiana U.S.A.
121 S7 **St. François** *R* Quebec Canada
127 N4 **St.François** Guadeloupe W Indies
121 T7 **St. François, L** Quebec Canada
110 F4 **St. Francois Mts** Missouri U.S.A.
121 S7 **St.François Xavier** Quebec Canada
95 S7 **St.Froid L** Maine U.S.A.
21 H8 **St.Fulgent** France
111 E11 **St.Gabriel** Louisiana U.S.A.
121 R6 **St.Gabriel de Brandon** Quebec Canada
122 H5 **St.Gabriel de Gaspé** Quebec Canada
41 K3 **St. Gallen** Switzerland
21 L4 **Ste.Gauburge-Ste.Colombe** France
18 F9 **St.Gaudens** France
21 N8 **St.Gaultier** France
122 B8 **St.Gédéon** Quebec Canada
21 N8 **Ste.Gemme** France
21 P3 **Ste. Geneviève** Oise France
110 F4 **Ste.Genevieve** Missouri U.S.A.
123 P2 **St.Genevieve B** Quebec Canada
18 G8 **St.Geniez** France
21 N8 **St.Genou** France
19 P14 **St Geoire-en-Valdaine** France
141 G3 **St. George** *R* Queensland Australia
141 J8 **St.George** Queensland Australia
127 P6 **St.George** *parish* Barbados
90 C1 **St.George** Bermuda
122 F8 **St.George** New Brunswick Canada
127 O2 **St.George** *co* Trinidad
113 E7 **St.George** Georgia U.S.A.
112 G4 **St.George** South Carolina U.S.A.
103 L4 **St.George** Utah U.S.A.
123 N5 **St.George, C** Newfoundland Canada
139 K6 **St.George Hd** New South Wales Australia
116 D8 **St. George I** Pribilof Is Bering Sea
113 C8 **St.George I** Florida U.S.A.
41 H1 **St.Georgen** Germany
100 A8 **St.George, Pt** California U.S.A.
142 E4 **St.George Ra** W Australia Australia
123 O5 **St.George's** Newfoundland Canada
122 B7 **St.Georges** Quebec Canada
36 B6 **St.Georges** France
129 H3 **St.Georges** Fr Guiana
127 P5 **St.George's** Grenada
123 N5 **St.George's B** Newfoundland Canada
125 P9 **St. Georges Cay** *isld* Belize
7 F11 **St Georges Chan** U.K.
137 L2 **St.George's Channel** Bismarck Arch
14 E5 **St. Georges Channel** Ireland/U.K.
69 A9 **St.George's Channel** Nicobar Is
20 H8 **St.Georges-de-Montaigu** France
20 H4 **St.Georges-de-Reintembault** France
21 M3 **St.Georges-du-Mesnil** France
21 M3 **St. Georges du-Vièvre** France
90 C1 **St.George's I** Bermuda
21 L8 **St.Georges-les-Baillargeaux** France
21 N4 **St.Georges-Motel** Eure France
21 N5 **St.Georges-sur-Eure** France
21 O7 **St.Georges-sur-la Prée** France
21 J7 **St.Georges-sur-Loire** France
22 H3 **St.Gérard** Belgium
121 M4 **St. Gerard-Centre** Quebec Canada
19 N13 **St. Germain au Mt D'Or** France
21 J5 **St.Germain-d'Anxure** France
19 P12 **St. Germain-de-Joux** France
21 M5 **St.Germain-de-la-Coudre** France
18 H6 **St.Germain-des-Fosses** France
19 J6 **St.Germain du Bois** France
122 B7 **Ste.Germaine** Quebec Canada
21 P4 **St. Germain-en-Laye** France
20 G3 **St. Germain, Hâvre de** France
21 L3 **St.Germain-la-Campagne** France
18 G7 **St.Germain-les-Belles** France
20 G3 **St.Germain-sur-Ay** France
8 B7 **St.Germans** England
21 O3 **St. Germer-de-Fly** France
41 N5 **St. Gertrude** Italy
20 G8 **St.Gervais** Vendée France
40 E6 **St. Gervais-les-Bains** France
21 L8 **St. Gervais-les-Trois-Clochers** France
22 F3 **St.Ghislain** Belgium
20 E6 **St.Gildas-de-Rhuis** France
20 F6 **St.Gildas-des-Bois** France
20 F7 **St.Gildas,Pte.de** France
121 T6 **St.-Giles** Quebec Canada
127 N1 **St. Giles Is** Tobago
20 G8 **St. Gilles-Croix-de-Vie** France
20 D5 **St.Gilles-Pligeaux** France
22 G1 **St. Gillis-bij-Dendermonde** Belgium
22 G1 **St.Gillis-Waas** Belgium
18 F10 **St.Girons** France
27 F12 **St.Gla** *L* Sweden
36 D3 **St.Goar** Germany
20 C5 **St.Goazec** France
22 E4 **St.Gobain** France
122 G5 **St.Godefroi** Quebec Canada
41 J4 **St.Gotthard** *pass* Switzerland
8 B4 **St.Govan's Hd** Wales
119 N6 **St.Gregor** Saskatchewan Canada
123 O4 **St.Gregory, Mt** Newfoundland Canada
20 B6 **St.Guénolé** France
121 S7 **St. Guillaume** Quebec Canada
19 Q15 **St. Guillaume, Mt** France
94 C2 **St.Helen** Michigan U.S.A.
90 B14 **St. Helena** *isld* Atlantic Oc
102 B3 **St.Helena** California U.S.A.
89 A9 **St.Helena B** S Africa
90 H10 **St Helena Fracture** Atlantic Oc
94 B1 **St.Helena I** Michigan U.S.A.
112 G5 **St.Helena Sd** South Carolina U.S.A.
122 B6 **Ste.Hélène** Quebec Canada
18 E8 **Ste.Hélène** France
139 J8 **St.Helens** Tasmania Australia
13 F6 **St.Helens** England
100 C4 **St.Helens** Oregon U.S.A.
100 C3 **St.Helens, Mt** Washington U.S.A.
139 J8 **St.Helens Pt** Tasmania Australia
122 H4 **St.Helier** Quebec Canada
20 F3 **St Hélier** Channel Is
121 U6 **Ste.Hénédine** Quebec Canada
121 T6 **St.Henri** Quebec Canada
20 G7 **St.-Herblain** France
121 T7 **St.Herménégilde** Quebec Canada
21 H8 **Ste.Hermine** France
18 G9 **St.Hilaire** France
98 K1 **St.Hilaire** Minnesota U.S.A.
20 G7 **St. Hilaire-de-Chaléons** France
20 H7 **St. Hilaire-de-Loulay** France
20 G8 **St. Hilaire-de-Riez** France
21 H4 **St. Hilaire-du-Harcouet** France
21 K7 **St. Hilaire St. Florent** France
21 O6 **St.Hilaire-St.Mesmin** France
140 D6 **Sainthill,Mt** N Terr Australia
19 K5 **St.Hippolyte** Doubs France
21 N7 **St.Hippolyte** Indre-et-Loire France
18 H9 **St.Hippolyte du Fort** France
122 A5 **St.Honoré** Quebec Canada
122 C6 **St.Honoré** Quebec Canada
21 J3 **Ste.Honorine** France
21 K3 **Ste.Honorine-du-Fay** France
22 J3 **St.Hubert** Belgium
25 F6 **St.Hubert** Germany
29 K5 **St Ibb** Sweden
94 C1 **St.Ignace** Michigan U.S.A.
121 R6 **St.Ignace du Lac** Quebec Canada
120 C4 **St. Ignace, Isle** Ontario Canada
101 L2 **St.Ignatius** Montana U.S.A.
40 E3 **St.Imier** Switzerland
36 C5 **St.Ingbert** Germany
122 B6 **St.Irénée** Quebec Canada
121 L5 **St.Isidore** Quebec Canada
121 T7 **St.Isidore** Quebec Canada
26 K3 **St.Istind** *mt* Norway
8 A7 **St.Ives** England
9 F3 **St.Ives** England
20 C6 **St.Ivy** France
25 E2 **St.Jacobi Parochie** Netherlands
122 D6 **St.Jacques** New Brunswick Canada
20 G5 **St.Jacques-de-la-Lande** France
38 F8 **St.Jakob** Austria
118 A1 **St.James** Manitoba Canada
20 H4 **St.James** France
127 J2 **St.James** *parish* Jamaica
99 V4 **St.James** Michigan U.S.A.
99 M5 **St.James** Minnesota U.S.A.
110 E3 **St.James** Missouri U.S.A.
117 H10 **St.James, C** British Columbia Canada
113 E11 **St.James City** Florida U.S.A.
22 D2 **Sint Jan** Belgium
121 L4 **St.Janvier** Quebec Canada
121 R7 **St.Jean** Quebec Canada
21 K5 **St.Jean** France
119 U9 **St.Jean Baptiste** Manitoba Canada
121 S5 **St.Jean Bosco** Quebec Canada
20 E6 **St.Jean-Brévelay** France
18 E7 **St.-Jean-d'Angély** France
21 L5 **St.Jean-d'Asse** France
19 O13 **St.Jean-de-Bournay** France
21 O6 **St.-Jean-de-Braye** France
21 H3 **St.Jean-de-Daye** France
122 C5 **St.Jean de Dieu** Quebec Canada
21 O6 **St.-Jean-de-la-Ruelle** France
19 J5 **St.Jean de Losne** France
18 D9 **St.Jean-de-Luz** France
121 R6 **St. Jean-de-Matha** Quebec Canada
19 Q14 **St.Jean-de-Maurienne** France
20 F8 **St.Jean-de-Monts** France
21 L8 **St.Jean-de-Sauves** France
18 H8 **St.Jean du Gard** France
19 O14 **St.Jean-en-Royans** France
121 S4 **Saint-Jean, Lac** Quebec Canada
20 G4 **St.Jean-le-Thomas** France
18 E9 **St.Jean Pied de Port** France
122 B6 **St.Jean Port Joli** Quebec Canada
122 H3 **St.Jean, R** Quebec Canada
36 B5 **St.Jean Rohrbach** France
20 H5 **St.Jean-sur-Couesnon** France
121 Q7 **St.Jérôme** Quebec Canada
19 N14 **St. Jeure D'Ay** France
109 K2 **St.Jo** Texas U.S.A.
122 B6 **St.Joachim** Quebec Canada
20 F7 **St.Joachim** France
41 O3 **St.Jodok** Austria
110 D5 **St.Joe** Arkansas U.S.A.
100 J2 **St.Joe** Idaho U.S.A.
94 C5 **St.Joe** Indiana U.S.A.
36 E4 **St.Johann** Germany
38 G8 **St. Johann-im-Walde** Austria
127 P6 **St.John** *parish* Barbados
122 F8 **St.John** New Brunswick Canada
107 M3 **St.John** Kansas U.S.A.
95 R7 **St. John** *R* Maine U.S.A.
119 S10 **St.John** North Dakota U.S.A.
103 M1 **St.John** Utah U.S.A.
100 H2 **St.John** Washington U.S.A.
123 P3 **St John B** Newfoundland Canada
123 R3 **St.John, C** Newfoundland Canada
113 L7 **St.John I** Virgin Is
123 S5 **St.John, L** Newfoundland Canada
122 E7 **St. John R** New Brunswick Canada
122 G5 **St. John R** Quebec Canada
123 T6 **St. John's** Newfoundland Canada
103 P7 **St.Johns** Arizona U.S.A.
94 C3 **St.Johns** Michigan U.S.A.
127 P4 **St.John's** Antigua W Indies
95 P2 **St.Johnsbury** Vermont U.S.A.
13 F4 **St.John's Chapel** England
14 C2 **St.John's Pt** Ireland
113 F7 **St.Johns R** Florida U.S.A.
95 N3 **St.Johnsville** New York U.S.A.
20 H3 **St.Jores** France
22 H2 **St.Joris-Winge** Belgium
127 P6 **St.Joseph** *parish* Barbados
121 U6 **St.Joseph** Quebec Canada
83 K14 **St.Joseph** Réunion Indian Oc
127 P2 **St.Joseph** Mayoro Trinidad
127 O2 **St.Joseph** St George Trinidad
111 E10 **St.Joseph** Louisiana U.S.A.
94 A5 **St. Joseph** *R* Michigan U.S.A.
99 U7 **St.Joseph** Michigan U.S.A.
99 M10 **St.Joseph** Missouri U.S.A.
127 L4 **St.Joseph** Martinique W Indies
113 B8 **St. Joseph Bay** Florida U.S.A.
120 G6 **St. Joseph I** Ontario Canada
109 L8 **St. Joseph I** Texas U.S.A.
115 K7 **St. Joseph, L** Ontario Canada
123 T6 **St.Joseph's** Newfoundland Canada
22 B3 **St.Josse** France
20 F5 **St. Jouan-de-l'Isle** France
20 G4 **St Jouan-des-Guerets** France
21 L2 **St.Jouin** France
21 K8 **St.Jouin-de-Marnes** France
121 Q6 **St. Jovite** Quebec Canada
126 A1 **St. Jozefsdal** Curaçao
19 N14 **St.Julian Molin-Molette** France
40 D5 **St.Julien** France
20 E5 **St.Julien** Côtes d'Armor France
20 H7 **St.Julien-de-Concelles** France
20 G8 **St. Julien-des-Landes** France
20 H6 **St.Julien-de-Vouvantes** France
19 O15 **St.Julien en Quint** France
21 L8 **St.Julien-l'Ars** France
21 L3 **St.Julien-le-Faucon** France
18 F7 **St.Junien** France
9 F7 **St.Just** England
21 P2 **St.Just-en-Chaussée** France
18 H7 **St.Just-en-Chevalet** France
38 M7 **St.Katherein** Austria
15 A1 **St. Kilda** *isld* Scotland
127 P4 **St.Kitts** *isld* Lesser Antilles
127 P4 **St. Kitts-Nevis** *islds* West Indies
126 A1 **St.Kruis** Curaçao
121 T6 **St.Lambert** Quebec Canada
121 R7 **St.Lambert** Quebec Canada
142 G2 **St.Lambert,C** W Australia Australia
21 K7 **St. Lambert des Levées** France
21 J7 **St.Lambert-du-Lattay** France
111 D11 **St.Landry** Louisiana U.S.A.
119 U8 **St.Laurent** Manitoba Canada
121 L4 **Saint-Laurent** Quebec Canada
19 J6 **St. Laurent** France
129 H2 **St.Laurent** Fr Guiana
18 G10 **St.Laurent de la Salanque** France
19 O13 **St.Laurent-de-Mûre** France
21 H7 **St. Laurent-des-Autels** France
21 O6 **St.Laurent-des-Eaux** France
19 P14 **St.Laurent-du-Pont** France
21 M2 **St.Laurent-en-Caux** France
21 M6 **St.Laurent-en-Gâtines** France
18 E7 **St.Laurent-et-Benon** France
121 U5 **St.Laurent, R** Quebec Canada
21 J3 **St.Laurent-sur-Mer** France
22 K5 **St.Laurent-sur-Othain** France
21 J8 **St. Laurent-sur-Sèvre** France
141 J5 **St.Lawrence** Queensland Australia
123 R7 **St.Lawrence** Newfoundland Canada
95 M2 **St. Lawrence** *R* Canada/U.S.A.
122 K5 **St.Lawrence, G.of** Canada
116 B5 **St.Lawrence I** Bering Sea
121 O8 **St. Lawrence I Nat. Park** Ontario Canada
121 P8 **St.Lawrence Seaway** Canada/U.S.A.
119 Q8 **St.Lazare** Manitoba Canada
22 K4 **St.Léger** Belgium
21 O4 **St.Léger-en-Yvelines** France
22 H1 **St.Lenaarts** Belgium
122 E5 **St.Léon** Quebec Canada
122 E6 **St.-Léonard** New Brunswick Canada
121 S6 **St.Léonard** Quebec Canada
36 B7 **St. Léonard** France
18 G7 **St.-Léonard-de-Noblat** France
9 G6 **St.Leonards** England
121 T4 **St.-Léon-de-Chicoutimi** Quebec Canada
122 B7 **St.Léon de Standon** Quebec Canada
38 L8 **St.Leonhard** Kärnten Austria
38 N4 **St.Leonhard** Nieder Österreich Austria
123 Q1 **St.Lewis R** Labrador, Nfld Canada
121 S7 **St.Liboire** Quebec Canada
18 F8 **Ste. Livrade** France
21 P7 **Ste.Lizaigne** France
18 F9 **St.Lizier** France
21 H3 **St.Lô** France
122 H7 **St.Louis** Prince Edward I Canada
119 M6 **St.Louis** Saskatchewan Canada
83 J14 **St.Louis** Réunion Indian Oc
85 A5 **St.Louis** Mauritania
94 C3 **St.Louis** Michigan U.S.A.
99 O2 **St. Louis** *R* Minnesota U.S.A.
105 **St.Louis** *conurbation* Missouri U.S.A.
127 N4 **St.Louis** Marie Galante W Indies
122 H7 **St.Louis de Kent** New Brunswick Canada
122 D6 **St.Louis du Ha Ha** Quebec Canada
126 H5 **St.Louis du Sud** Haiti
122 B6 **Ste.Louise** Quebec Canada
121 R7 **St.Louis, L** Quebec Canada
36 C5 **St. Louis-lès-Bitche** France
94 E6 **St.Louisville** Ohio U.S.A.
21 K8 **St. Loup-Lamaire** France
40 D2 **St. Loup-sur-Semoise** France
21 N4 **St.Lubin-des-Joncherets** France
127 L4 **Ste.Luce** Martinique W Indies
141 K2 **St.Lucia** *dist* Brisbane, Qnsld Australia
127 O8 **St. Lucia** *isld* Lesser Antilles
87 F11 **St. Lucia, C** S Africa
121 Q6 **Ste.Lucie** Quebec Canada
113 G10 **St. Lucie Canal** Florida U.S.A.
127 P6 **St.Lucy** *parish* Barbados
122 B8 **St.Ludger** Quebec Canada
127 H5 **St.Luis du Nord** Haiti
123 R2 **St Lunaire** Newfoundland Canada
20 F4 **St.Lunaire** France
20 F7 **St.Lyphard** France
127 N5 **Sint Maarten** *isld* Lesser Antilles
25 B5 **St.Maartens-dijk** Netherlands
18 E8 **St. Macaire** Gironde France
21 J7 **St. Macaire-en-Mauges** France
15 G2 **St.Magnus B** Scotland
122 B7 **St.Malachie** Quebec Canada
20 F4 **St.Malo** France
20 G3 **St.Malo-de-la-Lande** France
20 F4 **St.Malo,G.de** France
20 F5 **St.Malon-sur-Mel** France
19 P18 **St.Mandrier** France
20 B5 **St.Marc** Finistère France
20 F7 **St.Marc** Loire-Inférieure France
127 H5 **St.Marc** Haiti
121 S6 **St.Marc des Carrières** Quebec Canada
122 B7 **St.Marcel** Quebec Canada
21 O8 **St.Marcel** Indre France
19 O14 **St.Marcellin** France
21 H3 **St.Marcouf,Is** France
20 H5 **St.Marc-sur-Couesnon** France
22 K4 **St.Mard** Belgium
123 P2 **St.Margaret B** Newfoundland Canada
122 J9 **St.Margaret B** Nova Scotia Canada
38 K8 **St.Margarethen** Austria
32 K5 **St.Margarethen** Germany
9 H5 **St. Margaret's at Cliffe** England
15 F2 **St.Margarets Hope** Scotland
20 F7 **Ste.Marguerite** France
122 F3 **Ste.Marguerite, R** Quebec Canada
122 B5 **Ste.Marguerite, R** Quebec Canada
121 T6 **Ste.Marie** Quebec Canada
83 K13 **Ste.Marie** Réunion Indian Oc
110 H3 **Ste.Marie** Illinois U.S.A.
127 L4 **Ste.Marie** Martinique W Indies
19 K4 **Ste.Marie aux Mines** France
36 C7 **Ste. Marie, Col de** *pass* France
20 H3 **Ste.Marie-du-Mont** France
19 Q17 **St Marie Mourre de Chanier** *mt* France
100 J2 **St.Maries** Idaho U.S.A.
113 C7 **St.Marks** Florida U.S.A.
21 L6 **St. Mars-d'Outille** France
20 H7 **St.Mars-du-Désert** France
21 L5 **St.Mars-la-Brière** France
21 H6 **St.Mars-la-Jaille** France
21 H5 **St.Mars-sur-la-Futaie** France
122 F4 **Ste.Marthe de Gaspé** Quebec Canada
18 E6 **St.Martin** France
19 P17 **St.-Martin** France
20 F6 **St.Martin** Morbihan France
127 N5 **St.Martin** *isld* Lesser Antilles
22 B2 **St.Martin-Boulogne** France
89 A9 **St.Martin, C** S Africa
127 L4 **St. Martin, C** Martinique W Indies
21 O4 **St.Martin-de-Bretencourt** France
19 N17 **St.Martin-de-Crau** France
21 H4 **St.Martin-de-Landelle** France
21 J3 **St.Martin-des-Besaces** France
21 H8 **St.Martin-des-Noyers** France
16 E4 **St.Martín de Valdeiglesias** Spain
19 P14 **St.-Martin-d'Heres** France
19 P12 **St.Martin-du-Fresne** France
19 O12 **St.Martin-du-Mont** France
40 B4 **St.Martin en Bresse** France
21 N2 **St.Martin-en-Campagne** France
99 U4 **St.Martin I** Michigan U.S.A.
119 T7 **St. Martin, L** Manitoba Canada
21 M7 **St. Martin-le-Beau** France
122 G8 **St. Martin's** New Brunswick Canada
9 F7 **St. Martin's** *isld* Isles of Scilly England
68 A2 **St.Martin's I** Burma
20 E3 **St.Martin's Pt** Channel Is
119 T7 **St. Martin Station** Manitoba Canada
111 E11 **St.Martinville** Louisiana U.S.A.
20 F3 **St.Mary** Channel Is
127 L2 **St.Mary** *parish* Jamaica
101 M1 **St. Mary** *R* Montana/Alberta U.S.A./Canada
123 N3 **St. Mary Is** Quebec Canada
101 M1 **St.Mary L** Montana U.S.A.
117 P11 **St. Mary, Mt** British Columbia Canada
144 B6 **St. Mary, Mt** New Zealand
123 N3 **St.Mary Reefs** Quebec Canada
118 D9 **St.Mary Res** Alberta Canada
139 J8 **St.Marys** Tasmania Australia
123 T7 **St.Marys** Newfoundland Canada
9 F7 **St.Mary's** *isld* Isles of Scilly England
15 F2 **St. Marys** Scotland
127 O3 **St. Mary's** Trinidad
116 F5 **St. Marys** Alaska U.S.A.
113 F7 **St. Marys** Georgia U.S.A.
94 B6 **St. Marys** *R* Indiana U.S.A.
107 O2 **St Marys** Kansas U.S.A.
110 G4 **St.Marys** Missouri U.S.A.
94 C6 **St.Marys** Ohio U.S.A.
94 J5 **St.Marys** Pennsylvania U.S.A.
94 F7 **St.Marys** West Virginia U.S.A.
123 T7 **St.Mary's B** Newfoundland Canada
122 F9 **St.Mary's B** Nova Scotia Canada
95 L8 **St. Marys City** Maryland U.S.A.
89 H6 **St.Mary's Hill** S Africa
15 E5 **St. Marys Loch** Scotland
123 K8 **St.Mary's, R** Nova Scotia Canada
113 F7 **St.Marys R** Florida/Georgia U.S.A.
112 G4 **St. Mathews** South Carolina U.S.A.
121 M4 **St.Mathieu** Quebec Canada
20 A5 **St.Mathieu,Pte de** France
20 G8 **St.Mathurin** France
116 C6 **St.Matthew I** Bering Sea
136 K2 **St. Matthias Group** *islds* Bismarck Arch
21 M7 **Ste.Maure-de-Touraine** France
40 E2 **St.Maurice** France
21 K7 **St. Maurice la Fougereuse** Deux Sèvres France
21 M4 **St. Maurice-les-Charencey** France
8 A7 **St. Mawes** England
122 B7 **St. Maxime** Quebec Canada
19 P18 **St.Maximin** France
20 D5 **St.Mayeux** France
22 J4 **St. Médard** Belgium
18 E8 **St Medard en Jalles** France
20 F5 **St.Meen** France
110 K3 **St.Meinrad** Indiana U.S.A.
8 C4 **St.Mellons** Wales
20 G4 **St.Méloir-des-Ondes** France
19 J3 **St. Menehould** France
22 H4 **St.Menges** France
20 H3 **Ste.Mère-Église** France
21 J8 **St.Mesmin** Vendée France
127 P6 **St.Michael** *parish* Barbados
98 H8 **St.Michael** Nebraska U.S.A.
32 K5 **St.Michaelisdonn** Germany
103 P6 **St.Michaels** Arizona U.S.A.
95 L8 **St.Michaels** Maryland U.S.A.
22 G4 **St.Michel** Aisne France
21 H6 **St.Michel** Maine-et-Loire France
20 F7 **St.Michel-Chef-Chef** France
127 H5 **St.Michel de L'Atalaye** Haiti
121 R6 **St.Michel des Saints** Quebec Canada
21 J8 **St.Michel-Mont Mercure** France
20 C5 **St.Michel,Mt** Finistère France
20 C5 **St.Michel,Res.de** France
36 B7 **St.Michel-sur-Meurthe** France
126 B1 **St.Michiel** Curaçao
19 J4 **St Mihiel** France
22 C2 **St.Momelin** France
13 F1 **St.Monance** Scotland
41 L5 **St.Moritz** Switzerland
20 F7 **St.Nazaire** Loire-Atlantique France
19 O14 **St.Nazaire-en-Royans** France
9 F3 **St.Neots** England
20 B5 **St.Nic** France
126 A2 **Sint Nicolaas** Aruba W Indies
St.Nicolas *see* **St.Niklaas**
21 N2 **St.Nicolas-d'Aliermont** France
20 F6 **St.Nicolas-de-Redon** France
20 D5 **St.Nicolas-du-Pélem** France
22 G1 **St.Niklaas** Belgium
21 P4 **St.-Nom-la-Bretêche** France
119 U9 **St.Norbert** Manitoba Canada
25 F6 **St.Odilienberg** Netherlands
25 D5 **St.Oedenrode** Netherlands
122 F5 **St.Omer** Quebec Canada
22 C2 **St.Omer** France
145 D4 **St. Omer** New Zealand
21 P2 **St.-Omer-en-Chaussée** France
18 E7 **Saintonge** *prov* France
98 C5 **St.Onge** South Dakota U.S.A.
20 H4 **St.Osvin** France
21 P4 **St.-Ouen** France
21 J5 **St.Ouen-des-Toits** France
21 P3 **St.Ouen-l'Aumône** France
121 R7 **St.Ours** Quebec Canada
122 C6 **St.Pacôme** Quebec Canada
20 G4 **St.Pair** France
18 E9 **St.Palais** France
122 C7 **St.Pamphile** Quebec Canada
18 F7 **St.Pardoux la Rivière** France
94 D6 **St.Paris** Ohio U.S.A.
122 C6 **St.Pascal** Quebec Canada
21 L6 **St. Paterne** Indre-et-Loire France
21 L5 **St. Paterne** Sarthe France
121 N6 **St.Patrice, L-** Quebec Canada
127 O3 **St.Patrick** *co* Trinidad
38 L8 **St.Paul** Austria
118 F4 **St.Paul** Alberta Canada
18 E9 **St.Paul** France
85 C7 **St. Paul** *R* Guinea/Liberia
83 J13 **St.Paul** Réunion Indian Oc
110 C6 **St.Paul** Arkansas U.S.A.
94 B7 **St.Paul** Indiana U.S.A.
107 P4 **St.Paul** Kansas U.S.A.
99 N4 **St.Paul** Minnesota U.S.A.
98 H8 **St.Paul** Nebraska U.S.A.
112 G4 **St.Paul** South Carolina U.S.A.
94 E10 **St.Paul** Virginia U.S.A.
18 G10 **St. Paul de Fenouillet** France
122 C6 **St.-Paul-de-la-Croix** Quebec Canada
122 B7 **St.Paul de Montriny** Quebec Canada
122 C5 **St.Paul du Nord** Quebec Canada
116 D8 **St. Paul I** Pribilof Is Bering Sea
123 M6 **St.Paul I** C Breton I, Nova Scotia
81 E9 **St. Paul, Î** Indian Oc
18 H7 **St.Paulien** France
121 R6 **St.Paulin** Quebec Canada
19 P17 **St.Paul-les-Durance** France
123 P2 **St.Paul R** Quebec Canada
90 G8 **St.Paul Rocks** Atlantic Oc
112 H3 **St.Pauls** North Carolina U.S.A.
127 P4 **St.Pauls** St Kitts W Indies
123 P4 **St.Paul's Inlet** Newfoundland Canada
19 N16 **St Paul-Trois-Châteaux** France
20 G7 **St. Pazanne** France
18 E9 **St.Pé de B** France
21 O5 **St. Peravy-la-Colombe** France
20 F7 **St. Père-en-Retz** France
122 C6 **Ste.Perpétue** Quebec Canada
32 J4 **Sankt Peter** Germany
110 H3 **St.Peter** Illinois U.S.A.
38 K7 **St.Peter-am-Kammersberg** Austria
123 R1 **St.Peter B** Labrador, Nfld Canada
32 J4 **St Peter-Ording** Germany
20 E3 **St. Peter Port** Channel Is
122 H5 **St.Peter, Pt** Quebec Canada
122 K7 **St.Peters** Prince Edward I Canada
123 M8 **St.Peters** C Breton I, Nova Scotia
St.Petersburg *see* **Sankt-Peterburg**
113 E10 **St.Petersburg** Florida U.S.A.
69 J12 **St.Petrus** *isld* Indonesia
20 G8 **St. Philbert-de-Bouaine** France
20 G7 **St. Philbert-de-Grandlieu** France
122 B7 **St.Philémon** Quebec Canada
127 P6 **St. Philip** *parish* Barbados
25 B5 **St.Philipsland** Netherlands
121 S7 **St.Pie** Quebec Canada
123 Q7 **St. Pierre** St. Pierre I Atlantic Oc
119 V9 **St.Pierre** Manitoba Canada
20 D6 **St. Pierre** Morbihan France
83 J14 **St.Pierre** Réunion Indian Oc
127 L4 **St.Pierre** Martinique W Indies
123 Q7 **St. Pierre and Miquelon** *islds* Atlantic Oc
19 Q13 **St Pierre d'Albigny** France
21 N3 **St. Pierre-d'Autils** France
21 M8 **St. Pierre-de-Maillé** France
20 G5 **St. Pierre-de-Plesguen** France
21 M7 **St.-Pierre-des-Corps** France
21 J8 **St. Pierre-des-Echaubrognes** France
21 K5 **St. Pierre-des-Nids** France
21 J8 **St. Pierre-du-Chemin** France
21 N3 **St. Pierre-du-Vauvray** France
20 H2 **St. Pierre-Église** France
21 L2 **St. Pierre-en-Port** France
123 Q7 **St. Pierre, I** Atlantic Oc
81 C6 **St. Pierre I** Indian Oc
121 S6 **St.Pierre, L** Quebec Canada
21 H5 **St. Pierre-la-Cour** France
20 H4 **St. Pierre-Langers** France
18 H6 **St. Pierre le Môutier** France
21 N3 **St. Pierre-lès-Elbeuf** France
20 A5 **St. Pierre-Quilbignon** France
21 K3 **St. Pierre-sur-Dives** France
21 K5 **St. Pierre-sur-Orthe** France
21 H4 **St. Pois** France
21 H6 **St. Poix** France
22 C1 **St.Pol** France
22 C3 **St.Pol** France
20 C4 **St. Pol-de-Leon** France
38 N5 **St.Pölten** Austria
19 K6 **St.Pon, L.de** France
18 G9 **St Pons** France
18 H6 **St.Pourcain-sur-Sioule** France
121 S4 **St.-Prime** Quebec Canada
21 J8 **St. Prouant** France
20 E4 **St. Quay-Portrieux** France
122 E6 **St.Quentin** New Brunswick Canada
22 E4 **St.Quentin** Aisne France
21 J6 **St.-Quentin** Maine-et-Loire France
21 P4 **St. Quentin-en-Yvelines** France
22 B3 **St.Quentin, Pte.de** France
36 C6 **St.Quirin** France
18 H7 **St.Rambert** France
122 B7 **St.Raphaël** Quebec Canada
121 T6 **St.Raymond** Quebec Canada
101 L2 **St.Regis** Montana U.S.A.
95 N2 **St. Regis Falls** New York U.S.A.
121 R7 **St.Rémi** Quebec Canada
19 N17 **St. Rémy** Bouches du Rhône France
21 K4 **St. Rémy** Calvados France
21 L5 **St. Rémy-des-Monts** France
20 G5 **St Remy du Plain** France
21 L5 **St. Rémy-du-Plain** France
21 N4 **St. Rémy-sur-Avre** France
18 H7 **St. Rémy-sur-Durolle** France
20 A5 **St. Renan** France
40 F6 **St.Rhémy** Italy
19 J6 **St. Rigaud, Mt** France
21 O1 **St. Riquier** France
121 R7 **St.Robert** Quebec Canada
122 A8 **St.Romain** Quebec Canada
21 L2 **St. Romain-de-Colbosc** France
21 N7 **St. Romain-sur-Cher** France
121 T6 **St.Romuald** Quebec Canada
141 G4 **St. Ronans** Queensland Australia
121 R7 **Ste.Rose** Quebec Canada
127 N4 **Ste.Rose** Guadeloupe W Indies
119 S7 **Ste.Rose de Lac** Manitoba Canada
122 D6 **Ste.Rose du Dégelé** Quebec Canada
38 N7 **St.Ruprecht-an-der-Raab** Austria
21 N2 **St. Saëns** France
20 E3 **St. Sampson** Channel Is
20 E5 **St. Samson** France
21 P8 **St. Saturnin** France
19 O17 **St.Saturnin d'Apt** France
19 N17 **St Saturnin-lès-Avig-non** France
21 P2 **St. Sauflieu** France
121 Q7 **St.Sauveur** Quebec Canada
19 O16 **St. Sauveur** France
20 B5 **St. Sauveur** Finistère France
21 K4 **St. Sauveur** Orne France
20 H3 **St. Sauveur-Lendelin** France
20 G3 **St. Sauveur-le-Vicomte** France
21 N4 **St. Sauveur-Marville** Eure France
18 E7 **St.Savin** France
21 M8 **St. Savin** Vienne France
21 L4 **Ste. Scolasse** France
20 B5 **St. Segal** France
18 G9 **St.Sernin-sur-Rance** France
20 F4 **St. Servan** France
18 E9 **St.Sever** France
21 H4 **St. Sever-Calvados** France
21 P8 **Ste. Sévère-sur-Indre** Indre France
123 T7 **St.Shott's** Newfoundland Canada
122 C5 **St.Simon** Quebec Canada
22 E4 **St.Simon** France
112 F6 **St. Simons** Georgia U.S.A.
26 J4 **St. Sjöfallets Nat. Park** Sweden
122 E8 **St.Stephen** New Brunswick Canada
112 H4 **St.Stephen** South Carolina U.S.A.
101 R7 **St.Stephens** Wyoming U.S.A.
18 G9 **St.Sulpice** France
21 M4 **St. Sulpice** Orne France
20 G6 **St. Sulpice-des-Landes** France
18 F6 **St. Sulpice Laurière** France
21 K5 **Ste. Suzanne** France
83 K13 **Ste.Suzanne** Réunion Indian Oc
21 K3 **St. Sylvain** France
121 T6 **St.-Sylvestre** Quebec Canada
18 E8 **St.Symphorien** France
117 F6 **St. Terese** Alaska U.S.A.
122 E5 **St.Tharsicius** Quebec Canada
121 S6 **Ste.Thècle** Quebec Canada
20 C4 **St. Thégonnec** France
122 B8 **St. Théophile** Quebec Canada
121 R7 **Ste.Thérèse** Quebec Canada
117 N3 **Ste. Thérèse, Lac** Northwest Territories Canada
40 C1 **St.Thiébault** France
127 P6 **St.Thomas** *parish* Barbados
120 J10 **St.Thomas** Ontario Canada
127 M3 **St.Thomas** *parish* Jamaica
98 J1 **St.Thomas** North Dakota U.S.A.
113 K7 **St.Thomas I** Virgin Is
20 C6 **St Thurien** France
121 S6 **St.Tite** Quebec Canada
122 B6 **St.Tite des Caps** Quebec Canada
40 B5 **St.Trivier de Courtes** France
19 N12 **St. Trivier-Moignans** France
St.Trond *see* **St.Truiden**
22 J2 **St.Truiden** Belgium
8 B2 **St. Tudwal's Is** Wales
27 H11 **St.Tuna** Sweden
122 E5 **St.Ulric** Quebec Canada
122 B6 **St.Urbain** Quebec Canada
21 M2 **St. Vaast** France
20 H2 **St. Vaast-la-Hougue** France
21 M2 **St. Valéry-en-Caux** France
21 O1 **St. Valery-sur-Somme** France
122 B7 **St.Vallier** Quebec Canada
21 K8 **St. Varent** France
38 H7 **St.Veit** Austria
38 K8 **St.Veit-an-der-Glan** Austria
22 D2 **St.Venant** France
20 F5 **St. Véran** Côtes d'Armor France
121 Q6 **Ste.Véronique** Quebec Canada
21 O6 **St. Viâtre** France
20 F7 **St Viaud** France
20 G7 **St. Viaud** France
19 P17 **Ste Victoire, Mt** France
20 F6 **St. Vincent** France
127 O8 **St. Vincent** *isld* Lesser Antilles
21 L6 **St Vincent-de-Larouer** France
18 E9 **St.Vincent-de-Tyrosse** France
138 E5 **St.Vincent, G** South Australia Australia
113 B8 **St. Vincent I** Florida U.S.A.
139 H9 **St.Vincent, Pt** Tasmania Australia
123 T7 **St.Vincent's** Newfoundland Canada
118 A2 **St.Vital** Manitoba Canada
94 C1 **St. Vital Pt** Michigan U.S.A.
22 L3 **St.Vith** Belgium
18 E7 **St.Vivien-de-Médoc** France
106 G7 **St.Vrain** New Mexico U.S.A.
118 H5 **St.Walburg** Saskatchewan Canada
21 M2 **St. Wandrille** France
36 C5 **St.Wendel** Germany
126 A1 **St. Willebrordus** Curaçao
120 K10 **St.Williams** Ontario Canada
101 S4 **St.Xavier** Montana U.S.A.
18 F7 **St. Yrieix** France
122 H4 **St.Yvon** Quebec Canada
19 P18 **St.Zacharie** France
21 O5 **Sainville** France
134 E6 **Saipan** *isld* Mariana Is Pacific Oc
20 H2 **Saire** *R* France
20 H2 **Saire, Pte. de** France
18 E9 **Saison** *R* France
61 M10 **Saitama** *prefect* Japan
68 A1 **Saitlai** Burma
60 E13 **Saito** Japan
26 N3 **Saivomuotka** Sweden
77 L2 **Saiydabad** Afghanistan
77 L1 **Saiyid** Afghanistan
74 E3 **Saiyidwala** Pakistan
71 B2 **Sajafi** *isld* Indonesia
128 E7 **Sajama** *mt* Bolivia
128 E7 **Sajama** Bolivia
71 B2 **Sajang** *isld* Indonesia
48 F2 **Sajó** *R* Hungary
89 B7 **Sak** *watercourse* S Africa
88 G2 **Saka** Kenya
Saka Dzong *see* **Saga** China
59 L5 **Sakai** Japan
60 G11 **Sakaide** Japan
60 G10 **Sakai Minato** Japan
78 H7 **Sākākah** Saudi Arabia
98 E2 **Sakakawea, L** North Dakota U.S.A.
70 Q9 **Sakala** *isld* Indonesia
61 N7 **Sakamachi** Japan
115 M7 **Sakami, L** Quebec Canada
88 B8 **Sakania** Zaire
47 H3 **Sakar** *hills* Bulgaria
57 C5 **Sakar** Turkmenistan
87 G12 **Sakaraha** Madagascar
57 B5 **Sakar-chaga** Turkmenistan
47 J5 **Sakar Dağı** *mt* Turkey
78 C1 **Sakarya** *R* Turkey
78 C2 **Sakarya** *R* Turkey
59 L4 **Sakata** Japan
111 H8 **Sakatonchee** *R* Mississippi U.S.A.
85 E7 **Sakete** Benin
59 M1 **Sakhalin** *isld* Russian Federation
51 O4 **Sakhalinskaya Oblast'** Russian Federation
51 O3 **Sakhalinskiy Zaliv** *B* Russian Federation
85 F2 **Sakhira** Tunisia
54 G7 **Sakhnovshchina** Ukraine
77 B1 **Sakht-Sar** Iran
52 B7 **Šakiai** Lithuania
80 G4 **Sakib** Jordan
60 H12 **Sakihama** Japan
67 H4 **Sakishima-guntō** *islds* Japan
55 C5 **Sakmara** Russian Federation
85 B3 **Sakn, As** Western Sahara
68 C3 **Sa-koi** Burma
95 Q5 **Sakonnet R** Rhode I U.S.A.
87 D12 **Sakrivier** S Africa
28 E5 **Saksild** Denmark
28 H7 **Sakskøbing** Denmark
75 K7 **Sakti** India
51 M1 **Saktyakh** Russian Federation
61 M9 **Saku** Japan
61 L10 **Sakuma** Japan
61 J11 **Sakurai** Japan
60 D14 **Sakura jima** *isld* Japan
27 M10 **Säkylä** Finland
80 G3 **Sal** Jordan
53 F9 **Sal** *R* Russian Federation
48 D2 **Šala** Czechoslovakia
27 J12 **Sala** Sweden
68 F7 **Sala Andong Tuk** Cambodia
71 H6 **Salabangka** *isld* Sulawesi
52 B5 **Salacgriva** Latvia
43 G8 **Sala Consilina** Italy
109 K5 **Salad** Texas U.S.A.
133 C3 **Salada, B** Chile
131 G6 **Salada, L** Buenos Aires Argentina
131 F2 **Salada, L** Corrientes Argentina
124 B1 **Salada, L** Mexico
103 J9 **Salada, Laguna** *L* Mexico
131 E4 **Saladillo** *R* Argentina
131 B2 **Salado** *R* La Rioja Argentina
131 E2 **Salado, R** Santa Fé Argentina

106 C7 **Salado, R** New Mexico U.S.A.
85 D7 **Salaga** Ghana
68 F7 **Sala Hintoun** Cambodia
56 C4 **Salair** Russian Federation
56 C4 **Salairskiy Kryazh** *ridge* Russian Federation
48 H3 **Sălaj** *prov* Romania
70 G7 **Salajar, Selat** *str* Sulawesi
70 L9 **Salak, G** *mt* Java
86 C3 **Salal** Chad
72 G5 **Şalalah** Oman
125 O10 **Salamá** Guatemala
16 C4 **Salamanca** *prov* Spain
16 D4 **Salamanca** Spain
94 J4 **Salamanca** New York U.S.A.
86 C4 **Salamat** *R* Chad
70 D6 **Salamban** Kalimantan
128 C2 **Salamina** Colombia
79 D3 **Salamis** Cyprus
46 F7 **Salamis** Greece
79 H3 **Salamīyah** Syria
94 B6 **Salamonie** *R* Indiana U.S.A.
26 J3 **Salangen** Norway
52 B6 **Salantai** Lithuania
45 K2 **Salara** Italy
48 G3 **Sălard** Romania
133 D2 **Salar de Arizaro** *salt pan* Argentina
133 D2 **Salar de Atacama** *salt pan* Chile
133 D2 **Salar de Cauchari** *salt pan* Argentina
133 D1 **Salar de Coipasa** *salt pan* Bolivia
133 D3 **Salar del Hombre Muerto** *salt pan* Argentina
133 D2 **Salar de Uyuni** *salt pan* Bolivia
16 C1 **Salas** Spain
46 E1 **Salaš** Serbia Yugoslavia
16 E2 **Salas de los Infantes** Spain
18 F9 **Salat** *R* France
70 N9 **Salatiga** Java
18 F10 **Salau, Pont de** *pass* France/Spain
16 H6 **Salaushi** Russian Federation
55 C4 **Salavat** Russian Federation
128 C5 **Salaverry** Peru
133 E3 **Salavina** Argentina
71 C3 **Salawati** *isld* W Irian
71 G6 **Salay** Mindanao Philippines
135 Q11 **Sala y Gómez** *isld* Pacific Oc
Salazar *see* **N'dalatando**
21 P7 **Salbris** France
136 D3 **Sal, Cay** *isld* Bahamas
127 J5 **Salcedo** Dominican Rep
116 P4 **Salcha** *R* Alaska U.S.A.
116 O4 **Salchaket** Alaska U.S.A.
33 P8 **Salchau** Germany
37 O6 **Salching** Germany
46 G1 **Salcia** Romania
8 C7 **Salcombe** England
47 K7 **Salda Gölü** *L* Turkey
16 D2 **Saldaña** Spain
87 C12 **Saldanha** S Africa
41 N4 **Saldura, Pta** *mt* Italy
52 B6 **Saldus** Latvia
139 H7 **Sale** Victoria Australia
68 B2 **Sale** Burma
8 D1 **Sale** England
85 C2 **Salé** Morocco
65 C5 **Salea** Sulawesi
112 C6 **Sale City** Georgia U.S.A.
112 B2 **Sale Creek** Tennessee U.S.A.
77 A2 **Sālehābād** Iran
71 H9 **Saleh, Teluk** *B* Indonesia
147 N15 **Salekhard** Russian Federation
76 D5 **Salem** India
111 L9 **Salem** Alabama U.S.A.
110 E5 **Salem** Arkansas U.S.A.
113 D8 **Salem** Florida U.S.A.
110 H3 **Salem** Illinois U.S.A.
110 K3 **Salem** Indiana U.S.A.
95 R4 **Salem** Massachusetts U.S.A.
110 E4 **Salem** Missouri U.S.A.
95 Q4 **Salem** New Hampshire U.S.A.
95 M7 **Salem** New Jersey U.S.A.
106 C9 **Salem** New Mexico U.S.A.
95 O3 **Salem** New York U.S.A.
94 G6 **Salem** Ohio U.S.A.
100 B5 **Salem** Oregon U.S.A.
112 E3 **Salem** South Carolina U.S.A.
98 J6 **Salem** South Dakota U.S.A.
94 G9 **Salem** Virginia U.S.A.
99 S7 **Salem** Wisconsin U.S.A.
43 E11 **Salemi** Sicily
15 C4 **Salen** Scotland
27 F10 **Salen** Sweden
142 E3 **Sale, R** W Australia Australia
19 Q17 **Salernes** France
43 F8 **Salerno** Italy
113 G10 **Salerno** Florida U.S.A.
43 F8 **Salerno, Golfo di** Italy
45 L1 **Saletto** Italy
21 P2 **Saleux** France
19 Q12 **Salève, Mt** France
13 F6 **Salford** England
130 H9 **Salgado** *R* Brazil
131 H2 **Salgado Filho** *airport* Brazil
48 F2 **Salgótarján** Hungary
130 G10 **Salgueiro** Brazil
80 G1 **Sālhāni** Lebanon
79 C8 **Sālhīya, El** Egypt
127 P2 **Salibea** Trinidad
106 D3 **Salida** Colorado U.S.A.
18 E9 **Salies de Béarn** France
18 F9 **Salies du Salat** France
47 J6 **Salihli** Turkey
77 F8 **Salima** Malawi
70 E3 **Salimbatu** Kalimantan
88 B2 **Salin** *R* Burma
68 B2 **Salin** Burma
107 N3 **Salina** Kansas U.S.A.
107 O5 **Salina** Oklahoma U.S.A.
103 N3 **Salina** Utah U.S.A.
125 M9 **Salina Cruz** Mexico
43 F10 **Salina, I** Italy
133 D4 **Salina La Antigua** *salt pan* Argentina
126 G3 **Salina Pt** Acklins I Bahamas
129 K7 **Salinas** Brazil
128 B4 **Salinas** Ecuador
128 C6 **Salinas** Peru
102 C5 **Salinas** *R* California U.S.A.
102 C5 **Salinas** California U.S.A.
133 D4 **Salinas Grandes** Argentina
106 D7 **Salinas Nat. Mon** New Mexico U.S.A.
108 A1 **Salinas Nat.Mon** New Mexico U.S.A.
131 C3 **Salinas, Pampa de la** Argentina
106 D8 **Salinas Pk** New Mexico U.S.A.
87 B8 **Salinas, Pte. das** Angola
12 E1 **Saline** Scotland
111 D8 **Saline** *R* Arkansas U.S.A.
110 H4 **Saline** *R* Illinois U.S.A.
107 L2 **Saline** *R* Kansas U.S.A.
94 D4 **Saline** Michigan U.S.A.
127 P2 **Saline B** Trinidad
109 P3 **Saline Bayou** *R* Louisiana U.S.A.
109 P4 **Saline L** Louisiana U.S.A.
127 P5 **Salines, Pt** Grenada
102 G5 **Saline V** California U.S.A.
94 G6 **Salineville** Ohio U.S.A.
68 B1 **Salingyi** Burma
133 C3 **Salinitas** Chile
129 J4 **Salinópolis** Brazil
Salisbury *see* **Harare** Zimbabwe
141 K2 **Salisbury** *dist* Brisbane, Qnsld Australia
138 E5 **Salisbury** South Australia Australia
122 G7 **Salisbury** New Brunswick Canada
9 E5 **Salisbury** England
95 O4 **Salisbury** Connecticut U.S.A.
95 M8 **Salisbury** Maryland U.S.A.
110 D2 **Salisbury** Missouri U.S.A.
112 G2 **Salisbury** North Carolina U.S.A.
94 H7 **Salisbury** Pennsylvania U.S.A.
95 O3 **Salisbury** Vermont U.S.A.
115 M5 **Salisbury I** Northwest Territories Canada
86 F5 **Salisbury, L** Uganda
116 O2 **Salisbury, Mt** Alaska U.S.A.
9 E5 **Salisbury Plain** England
48 H5 **Săliste** Romania
129 K6 **Salitre** *R* Brazil
80 G8 **Saliya** Jordan
45 K1 **Salizzole** Italy
112 F4 **Salkehatchie** *R* South Carolina U.S.A.
79 G6 **Şalkhad** Syria
28 D4 **Sall** Denmark
38 L7 **Salla** Austria
29 O5 **Salla** Finland
21 J7 **Salle-de-Vihiers, la** France
17 G2 **Sallent de G** Spain
19 N16 **Salles** France
18 G8 **Salles-Curan** France
112 F4 **Salley** South Carolina U.S.A.
33 T9 **Sallgast** Germany
28 B3 **Salling** *reg* Denmark
107 Q6 **Sallisaw** Oklahoma U.S.A.
86 G2 **Sallom** Sudan
78 K6 **Salman, As** Iraq
78 K2 **Salmās** Iran
17 F4 **Salmerón** Spain
29 N5 **Salmivaara** Finland
100 H1 **Salmo** British Columbia Canada
117 M8 **Salmon** *R* British Columbia Canada
116 Q3 **Salmon** Alaska U.S.A.
101 M4 **Salmon** Idaho U.S.A.
117 O10 **Salmon Arm** British Columbia Canada
123 P2 **Salmon Bay** Quebec Canada
101 L7 **Salmon Cr.Res** Idaho U.S.A.
142 F3 **Salmond R** W Australia Australia
101 L7 **Salmon Falls** Idaho U.S.A.
116 R4 **Salmon Fork** *R* Alaska U.S.A.
143 D10 **Salmon Gums** W Australia Australia
123 T6 **Salmonier** Newfoundland Canada
100 B8 **Salmon Mt** California U.S.A.
122 E8 **Salmon R** New Brunswick Canada
122 K4 **Salmon, R** Quebec Canada
95 M3 **Salmon Res** New York U.S.A.
100 K5 **Salmon River Mts** Idaho U.S.A.
36 G3 **Salmünster** Germany
52 E2 **Sal'nitsa** Russian Federation
43 G7 **Saló** Italy
52 G6 **Salobelyak** Russian Federation
130 C7 **Salobra, R** Brazil
29 L7 **Saloinen** Finland
99 L1 **Salol** Minnesota U.S.A.
103 L8 **Salome** Arizona U.S.A.
127 L4 **Salomon, C** Martinique W Indies
40 C2 **Salon** *R* France
19 O17 **Salon-de-Provence** France
86 D6 **Salonga, Parc National de la** *nat park* Zaire
Salonica *see* **Thessaloniki**
48 G4 **Salonta** Romania
Salop *co see* **Shropshire**
17 H3 **Salou, C** Spain
29 M11 **Salpausselkä** *reg* Finland
53 F10 **Sal'sk** Russian Federation
43 F11 **Salso** *R* Sicily
44 G2 **Salsomaggiore Terme** Italy
80 F5 **Salt** Jordan
103 N8 **Salt** *R* Arizona U.S.A.
110 L3 **Salt** *R* Kentucky U.S.A.
110 E2 **Salt** *R* Missouri U.S.A.
103 D2 **Salta** Argentina
55 F3 **Saltaim, Oz** *L* Russian Federation
8 B7 **Saltash** England
28 G5 **Saltbæk Vig** *lagoon* Denmark
108 B4 **Salt Basin** Texas U.S.A.
13 H4 **Saltburn-by-the-Sea** England
119 P7 **Saltcoats** Saskatchewan Canada
12 D2 **Saltcoats** Scotland
99 R9 **Salt Cr** *R* Illinois U.S.A.
110 G1 **Salt Cr** Illinois U.S.A.
94 E7 **Salt Cr** Ohio U.S.A.
101 T6 **Salt Cr** Wyoming U.S.A.
138 E6 **Salt Creek** South Australia Australia
26 H4 **Saltdal** Norway
108 C4 **Salt Draw** *R* Texas U.S.A.
14 E4 **Saltee Is** Ireland
26 H5 **Saltelv** *R* Norway
26 G4 **Salten** *reg* Norway
28 D4 **Salten Langsø** *L* Denmark
26 G4 **Saltfjord** *inlet* Norway
108 B4 **Salt Flat** Texas U.S.A.
13 J6 **Saltfleet** England
107 M5 **Salt Fork** *R* Oklahoma U.S.A.
108 F2 **Salt Fork** *R* Texas U.S.A.
109 H4 **Salt Gap** Texas U.S.A.
29 K5 **Saltholm** *isld* Denmark
125 J6 **Saltillo** Mexico
94 J6 **Saltillo** Pennsylvania U.S.A.
110 H6 **Saltillo** Tennessee U.S.A.
106 G9 **Salt L** New Mexico U.S.A.
108 C4 **Salt L** Texas U.S.A.
101 O9 **Salt Lake City** Utah U.S.A.
94 D8 **Salt Lick** Kentucky U.S.A.
133 E4 **Salto** Argentina
130 G8 **Salto** Brazil
42 E6 **Salto** *R* Italy
131 F3 **Salto** *dept* Uruguay
131 F3 **Salto** Uruguay
130 D7 **Salto do Urubupungá** *falls* Brazil
131 F3 **Salto Grande, Embalse de** *res* Arg/Uruguay
45 O5 **Salto, L. del** Italy
26 K4 **Saltoluokta** Sweden
103 J8 **Salton Sea** California U.S.A.
Saltos do Iguaçu *see* **Cataratas del Iguazú** *waterfalls*
107 M5 **Salt Plains L** Oklahoma U.S.A.
127 L3 **Salt Ponds, The** Jamaica
74 E2 **Salt Range** Pakistan
127 K3 **Salt River** Jamaica
127 H5 **Saltrou** Haiti
101 P7 **Salt R. Ra** Wyoming U.S.A.
27 K12 **Saltsjöbaden** Sweden
27 L11 **Saltvik** Finland
94 F10 **Saltville** Virginia U.S.A.
102 F2 **Salt Wells** Nevada U.S.A.
112 E3 **Saluda** *R* South Carolina U.S.A.
112 F3 **Saluda** South Carolina U.S.A.
71 H5 **Salue** *isld* Indonesia
71 H5 **Salue Timpaus, Selat** *str* Indonesia
84 H3 **Salûm** Egypt
45 N4 **Saluoecio** Italy
71 F7 **Saluping** *isld* Philippines
76 F1 **Salur** India
110 C6 **Salus** Arkansas U.S.A.
129 H2 **Salut, I.du** Fr Guiana
44 B2 **Saluzzo** Italy
129 L6 **Salvador** Brazil
118 H6 **Salvador** Saskatchewan Canada
84 E5 **Salvador** Niger
111 F12 **Salvador, L** Louisiana U.S.A.
123 T5 **Salvage** Newfoundland Canada
16 B5 **Salvaterra de Magos** Portugal
125 J7 **Salvatierra** Mexico
103 N3 **Salvation Cr** Utah U.S.A.
141 H6 **Salvator, L** Queensland Australia
18 G8 **Salvetat, la** Aveyron France
18 G9 **Salvetat, la** Hérault France
117 J8 **Salvus** British Columbia Canada
68 C4 **Salween** *R* Burma/Thailand
75 K4 **Salyan** Nepal
94 D9 **Salyersville** Kentucky U.S.A.
55 F1 **Salym** Russian Federation
38 L6 **Salza** *R* Austria
32 F8 **Salzbergen** Germany
38 H6 **Salzburg** Austria
38 H7 **Salzburg** *prov* Austria
32 L9 **Salzderhelden** Germany
33 M8 **Salzgitter** Germany
33 M8 **Salzgitter-Bad** Germany
38 J6 **Salzkammer-gut** *res* Austria
32 J9 **Salzkotten** Germany
33 P9 **Salzmünde** Germany
33 O7 **Salzwedel** Germany
101 O6 **Sam** Idaho U.S.A.
80 G3 **Sama** Jordan
80 G4 **Samad** Jordan
71 J5 **Samada** *isld* Indonesia
16 D1 **Sama de Langreo** Spain
56 E5 **Samagaltay** Russian Federation
84 F4 **Samāh** Libya
80 F2 **Samak** Syria
71 G7 **Samal** *isld* Mindanao Philippines
69 C10 **Samalanga** Sumatra
69 J12 **Samalantan** Indonesia
108 A4 **Samalayuca** Mexico
71 E7 **Samales Group** *islds* Philippines
76 F2 **Samalkot** India
84 J4 **Samālût** Egypt
127 K5 **Samaná** Dominican Rep
126 H3 **Samana Cay** *isld* Bahamas
78 E3 **Samandaği** Turkey
47 N11 **Samandıra** Turkey
60 O3 **Samani** Japan
70 N10 **Samanu** Java
121 S3 **Samaqua** *R* Quebec Canada
80 G3 **Samar** Jordan
71 G5 **Samar** *isld* Philippines
53 H7 **Samara** Russian Federation
53 H7 **Samara** *R* Russian Federation
136 L4 **Samarai** Papua New Guinea
80 D4 **Samaria** Jordan
101 N7 **Samaria** Idaho U.S.A.
46 E4 **Samarina** Greece
70 E5 **Samarinda** Kalimantan
57 D5 **Samarkand** Uzbekistan
78 J4 **Sāmarrā'** Iraq
71 G5 **Samar Sea** Philippines
53 G7 **Samarskaya Oblast'** Russian Federation
71 C3 **Samate** W Irian
78 K6 **Samāwah, Aq** Iraq
70 C5 **Samba** *R* Kalimantan
86 D5 **Samba** Equateur Zaire
86 E6 **Samba** Kasai Oriental Zaire
87 C7 **Samba Caju** Angola
71 A3 **Sambaki, Selat** Indonesia
70 E4 **Sambaliung** *mts* Kalimantan
75 F8 **Sambalpur** India
70 G7 **Sambapolulu, G** *mt* Sulawesi
87 J10 **Sambava** Madagascar
25 E5 **Sambeek** Netherlands
75 J4 **Sambhal** India
71 H5 **Sambiat** Sulawesi
21 N7 **Sambin** France
74 H4 **Sambit** *isld* Kalimantan
129 K5 **Sambito** *R* Brazil
70 F6 **Sambo** Sulawesi
70 E5 **Sambodja** Kalimantan
68 H6 **Sambor** Cambodia
48 H1 **Sambor** Ukraine
131 G6 **Samborombón, B** Argentina
22 H3 **Sambre** *R* Belgium
69 F12 **Sambu** Indonesia
70 D5 **Sambuah** Kalimantan
45 J3 **Sambuca Pistojese** Italy
59 J4 **Samchök** S Korea
68 D6 **Same** Burma
88 F4 **Same** Tanzania
22 B2 **Samer** France
68 E6 **Samet, Ko** *isld* Thailand
87 E8 **Samfya** Zambia
68 A2 **Sami** Burma
46 D6 **Sámi** Greece
71 H4 **Samia, Tg** *C* Sulawesi Indonesia
128 D5 **Samiria** *R* Peru
85 E5 **Samit** Mali
68 C2 **Samka** Burma
29 K11 **Sammatti** Finland
80 F3 **Sammu'** Jordan
68 F5 **Samnak Kado** Thailand
41 M3 **Samnaun Gruppe** *mt* Austria
80 E6 **Samniya Auja** *R* Jordan
84 F4 **Samnū** Libya
100 A9 **Samoa** California U.S.A.
Samoa i Sisifo *islds see* **Western Samoa**
42 G3 **Samobor** Croatia
52 F3 **Samoded** Russian Federation
40 E5 **Samoëns** France
46 F2 **Samokov** Bulgaria
68 C2 **Samon** *R* Burma
47 H7 **Sámos** *isld* Greece
Samothrace *see* **Samothráki**
46 D5 **Samothráki** *isld* Ionian Is Greece
47 H4 **Samothráki** *isld* Anatolikí Makedhonía Kaí Thráki Greece
133 E4 **Sampacho** Argentina
70 F6 **Sampaga** Sulawesi
71 E3 **Sampaloc Pt** Luzon Philippines
70 O9 **Sampang** Indonesia
17 G3 **Samper de Calanda** Spain
113 L12 **Samphire Cay** *isld* Bahamas
70 C6 **Sampit** Kalimantan
70 C6 **Sampit, Teluk** *B* Kalimantan
87 E7 **Sampwe** Zaire
80 F8 **Samra** Jordan
109 N4 **Sam Rayburn L** Texas U.S.A.
111 B10 **Sam Rayburn Res** Texas U.S.A.
22 K3 **Samrée** Belgium
68 F6 **Samrong** *R* Cambodia
28 F5 **Samsø** *isld* Denmark
111 K10 **Samson** Alabama U.S.A.
68 G3 **Sam Son** Vietnam
78 F1 **Samsun** Turkey
67 A6 **Sam Teu** Laos
140 C4 **Samuel, Mt** N Terr Australia
47 H1 **Samuil** Bulgaria
56 B3 **Samus'** Russian Federation
68 E6 **Samut Prakan** Thailand
68 E6 **Samut Sakhon** Thailand
68 E6 **Samut Songkhram** Thailand
71 J5 **Samuya** Indonesia
85 D6 **San** Mali
31 N6 **San** *R* Poland
42 H4 **Sana** *R* Bosnia-Herzegovina
72 E5 **Şan'ā'** Yemen
106 D7 **San Acacia** New Mexico U.S.A.
146 H6 **Sanae** *S Africa Base* Antarctica
86 B5 **Sanaga** *R* Cameroon
106 D10 **San Agustin** Mexico
71 G7 **San Agustin, C** Mindanao Philippines
133 D4 **San Agustin de Valle Fértil** Argentina
106 B8 **San Agustin, Plains of** *high plain* New Mexico U.S.A.
116 F9 **Sanak I** Aleutian Is
45 M2 **San Alberto** Italy
79 G5 **Şanamayn, Aş** Syria
135 S12 **San Ambrosio** *isld* Pacific Oc
102 D3 **San Andreas** California U.S.A.
125 P9 **San Andrés** Guatemala
106 D9 **San Andres Mts** New Mexico U.S.A.
125 M8 **San Andrés Tuxtla** Mexico
41 K7 **San Angelo** Italy
108 G4 **San Angelo** Texas U.S.A.
126 C3 **San Anton de los Baños** Cuba
125 P9 **San Antonio** Belize
131 B4 **San Antonio** Chile
125 L2 **San Antonio** Honduras
124 E6 **San Antonio** Mexico
71 E2 **San Antonio** Luzon Philippines
113 E9 **San Antonio** Florida U.S.A.
106 D8 **San Antonio** New Mexico U.S.A.
109 J6 **San Antonio** Texas U.S.A.
109 K7 **San Antonio** *R* Texas U.S.A.
128 E3 **San Antonio** Venezuela
17 H6 **San Antonio Abad** Ibiza
71 C6 **San Antonio B** Palawan Philippines
109 L7 **San Antonio B** Texas U.S.A.
133 F5 **San Antonio, C** Argentina
126 B4 **San Antonio, C** Cuba
17 H6 **San Antonio, C** Spain
133 D2 **San Antonio de los Cobres** Argentina
124 E3 **San Antonio del Rio** Mexico
127 N9 **San Antonio de Maturín** Venezuela
127 L10 **San Antonio de Tamanaco** Venezuela
102 G7 **San Antonio, Mt** California U.S.A.
108 B4 **San Antonio, Mt** Texas U.S.A.
133 E6 **San Antonio Oeste** Argentina
130 J9 **San Antonio, Pta. de** *C* Brazil
128 E2 **Sanariapo** Venezuela
19 P18 **Sanary** France
111 B10 **San Augustine** Texas U.S.A.
74 G7 **Sanawad** India
16 B7 **San Bartolomeu de Messines** Portugal
45 R7 **San Bartolomew in Galdo** Italy
42 F6 **San Benedetto del Tronto** Italy
45 J1 **San Benedetto Po** Italy
125 P9 **San Benito** Guatemala
102 C5 **San Benito** *R* California U.S.A.
109 K9 **San Benito** Texas U.S.A.
102 D5 **San Benito Mt** California U.S.A.
71 G4 **San Bernardino Str** Philippines
109 M6 **San Bernard** *R* Texas U.S.A.
130 B9 **San Bernardino** Paraguay
102 G7 **San Bernardino** California U.S.A.
103 J8 **San Bernardino Mts** California U.S.A.
41 K5 **San Bernardino P** Switzerland
131 B4 **San Bernardo** Chile
124 G4 **San Bernardo** Mexico
128 C2 **San Bernardo, I.de** Colombia
60 F10 **Sanbe-san** *mt* Japan
45 L2 **San Biagio** Italy
124 G7 **San Blas** Nayarit Mexico
124 E4 **San Blas** Sonora Mexico
113 B7 **San Blas** Florida U.S.A.
125 P5 **San Blas, Archipélago de** *islds* Panama
113 B8 **San Blas, C** Florida U.S.A.
125 P5 **San Blas, Serrania de** *mts* Panama
41 O7 **San Bonifacio** Italy
128 E6 **San Borja** Bolivia
124 C3 **San Borja** Mexico
99 L6 **Sanborn** Iowa U.S.A.
99 L5 **Sanborn** Minnesota U.S.A.
98 H3 **Sanborn** North Dakota U.S.A.
95 Q3 **Sanbornville** New Hampshire U.S.A.
124 J4 **San Buenaventura** Mexico
68 E5 **San Buri** Thailand
128 F8 **San Camilo** Argentina
133 D4 **San Carlos** Argentina
131 B6 **San Carlos** Chile
124 C4 **San Carlos** Baja Cal Sur Mexico
124 H5 **San Carlos** Coahuila Mexico
71 E3 **San Carlos** Luzon Philippines
71 F5 **San Carlos** Negros Philippines
133 G4 **San Carlos** Uruguay
103 O8 **San Carlos** Arizona U.S.A.
127 K10 **San Carlos** Venezuela
131 B8 **San Carlos de Bariloche** Argentina
17 H4 **San Carlos de la Rápita** Spain
128 D2 **San Carlos del Zulia** Venezuela
128 E3 **San Carlos de Rio Negro** Venezuela
124 B3 **San Carlos, Mesa de** *mt* Mexico
103 O8 **San Carlos Res** Arizona U.S.A.
45 K4 **San Casciano in Valdi Pesa** Italy
17 J3 **San Celoni** Spain
18 G5 **Sancergues** France
18 G5 **Sancerre** France
45 K2 **San Cesario sul Panaro** Italy
21 O5 **Sancheville** France
127 K5 **Sánchez** Dominican Rep
106 E4 **Sanchez Res** Colorado U.S.A.
52 G6 **Sanchursk** Russian Federation
125 K7 **San Ciro de Acosta** Mexico
17 F5 **San Clemente** Spain
102 G8 **San Clemente** California U.S.A.
102 F9 **San Clemente** *isld* California U.S.A.
18 G6 **Sancoins** France
71 G6 **Sanco Pt** Mindanao Philippines
130 B10 **San Cosme** Argentina
133 F3 **San Cosme** Paraguay
45 O4 **San Costanzo** Italy
131 E3 **San Cristóbal** Argentina
127 J5 **San Cristóbal** Dominican Rep
128 B8 **San Cristóbal** *isld* Galapagos Is
137 N4 **San Cristobal** Solomon Is
128 D2 **San Cristóbal** Venezuela
125 N9 **San Cristóbal de las Casas** Mexico
103 L9 **San Cristobal Wash** *R* Arizona U.S.A.
45 J4 **San Croce sulee Arno** Italy
133 C4 **San Cruz** Chile
126 E4 **Sancti Spíritus** Cuba
118 J7 **Sanctuary** Saskatchewan Canada
22 K5 **Sancy** France
27 B12 **Sand** Norway
89 E7 **Sand** *R* Orange Free State S Africa
89 F4 **Sand** *R* Transvaal S Africa
60 J11 **Sanda** Japan
15 C5 **Sanda** *isld* Scotland
28 D6 **Sandager** Denmark
70 F2 **Sandakan** Sabah
70 F2 **Sandakan, Pelabuhan** *hbr* Sabah
68 H6 **Sandan** Cambodia
26 B10 **Sandane** Norway
46 F3 **Sandanski** Bulgaria
65 H2 **Sandaotong** China
65 G1 **Sandaozhen** China
86 B5 **Sandare** Mali
27 J10 **Sandarne** Sweden
106 H4 **Sand Arroyo** *R* Colo/Kansas U.S.A.
33 Q7 **Sandau** Germany
15 F1 **Sanday** Scotland
8 D5 **Sand B** England
8 D1 **Sandbach** England
37 P6 **Sandbach** Germany
27 G15 **Sandbäck** Sweden
12 D2 **Sandbank** Scotland
120 H1 **Sandbank L** Ontario Canada
89 E4 **Sandbult** S Africa
28 G7 **Sandby** Denmark
26 F7 **Sanddöla** *R* Norway
32 H5 **Sande** Germany
26 A9 **Sande** Norway
27 A10 **Sande** Norway
27 D12 **Sandefjord** Norway
146 J10 **Sandercock Nunataks** *mt peaks* Antarctica
103 P6 **Sanders** Arizona U.S.A.
100 J2 **Sanders** Idaho U.S.A.
37 M6 **Sandersdorf** Germany
33 P9 **Sandersleben** Germany
113 E7 **Sanderson** Florida U.S.A.
108 E5 **Sanderson** Texas U.S.A.
112 E5 **Sandersville** Georgia U.S.A.
111 H10 **Sandersville** Mississippi U.S.A.
33 M5 **Sandesneben** Germany
28 B5 **Sandet** Denmark
142 D4 **Sandfire Flat Roadhouse** W Australia Australia
118 L3 **Sandfly L** Saskatchewan Canada
94 G8 **Sand Fork** West Virginia U.S.A.
141 L7 **Sandgate** Queensland Australia
9 H5 **Sandgate** England
36 F5 **Sandhausen** Germany
15 E4 **Sandhead** Scotland
26 G4 **Sandhornöy** *isld* Norway
9 F5 **Sandhurst** England
99 Q3 **Sand I** Wisconsin U.S.A.
109 K7 **Sandia** Texas U.S.A.
106 D6 **Sandia Pk** New Mexico U.S.A.
124 G3 **San Diego** Mexico
102 G9 **San Diego** California U.S.A.
109 J8 **San Diego** Texas U.S.A.
102 G8 **San Diego Aqueduct** California U.S.A.
133 D8 **San Diego, C** Argentina
128 F2 **San Diego de Cabrutica** Venezuela
47 L6 **Sandıklı** Turkey
74 J5 **Sandila** India
118 E1 **Sandilands** Manitoba Canada
113 M9 **Sandilands Village** New Providence I Bahamas
21 P6 **Sandillon** France
143 B6 **Sandiman, Mt** W Australia Australia
124 G5 **San Dimas** Mexico
69 E14 **Sanding** *isld* Indonesia
116 D5 **Sand Is** Alaska U.S.A.
52 J2 **Sandivey** *R* Russian Federation
32 H6 **Sandkrug** Germany
38 L4 **Sandl** Austria
120 F5 **Sand Lake** Ontario Canada
110 K7 **Sand Mountain** Alabama U.S.A.
27 C13 **Sandnes** Aust Agder Norway
27 A13 **Sandnes** Rogaland Norway
15 G2 **Sandness** Scotland
26 F5 **Sandnessjöen** Norway
Sando *see* **Sandoy**
87 D7 **Sandoa** Zaire
31 N5 **Sandomierz** Poland
45 P6 **San Donato Val di Comino** Italy
110 G3 **Sandoval** Illinois U.S.A.
106 D6 **Sandoval** New Mexico U.S.A.
140 D5 **Sandover** *R* N Terr Australia
52 E5 **Sandovo** Russian Federation
68 B3 **Sandoway** Burma
9 E6 **Sandown** England
6 F1 **Sandoy** *isld* Faeroes
116 G9 **Sand Point** Alaska U.S.A.
117 P11 **Sandpoint** Idaho U.S.A.
118 F4 **Sand R** Alberta Canada
47 K7 **Sandras Daği** *mt* Turkey
140 E6 **Sandringham** Queensland Australia
9 G2 **Sandringham** England
99 T3 **Sands** Michigan U.S.A.
27 G14 **Sandsjö, N** Sweden
113 G12 **Sands Key** *isld* Florida U.S.A.
117 H9 **Sandspit** British Columbia Canada
38 G8 **Sandspitze** *mt* Austria
101 S2 **Sand Springs** Montana U.S.A.
107 O5 **Sand Springs** Oklahoma U.S.A.
102 F2 **Sand Springs Salt Flat** Nevada U.S.A.
26 D8 **Sandstad** Norway
32 J6 **Sandstedt** Germany
95 K9 **Sandston** Virginia U.S.A.
143 C8 **Sandstone** W Australia Australia
99 O3 **Sandstone** Minnesota U.S.A.
103 M9 **Sand Tanks Mts** Arizona U.S.A.
123 L4 **Sandtop, C** Anticosti I, Quebec
67 B3 **Sandu** China
67 B4 **Sandu** Guizhou China
67 E2 **Sandu** Jiangxi China
94 E3 **Sandusky** Michigan U.S.A.
94 D5 **Sandusky** *R* Ohio U.S.A.
94 E5 **Sandusky** Ohio U.S.A.
28 H6 **Sandved** Denmark
87 C11 **Sandverhaar** Namibia
27 G16 **Sandvig** Denmark
27 D12 **Sandvika** Norway
27 J11 **Sandviken** Sweden
9 H5 **Sandwich** England
99 S8 **Sandwich** Illinois U.S.A.
95 R5 **Sandwich** Massachusetts U.S.A.
115 O7 **Sandwich B** Labrador, Nfld Canada
141 H4 **Sandwich, C** Queensland Australia
15 G2 **Sandwick** Scotland
118 J5 **Sandwith** Saskatchewan Canada
95 R2 **Sandy** *R* Maine U.S.A.
103 J6 **Sandy** Nevada U.S.A.
100 C4 **Sandy** Oregon U.S.A.
103 N1 **Sandy** Utah U.S.A.
119 P3 **Sandy Bay** Saskatchewan Canada
127 H1 **Sandy Bay** Jamaica
118 K1 **Sandybeach L** Ontario Canada
141 L6 **Sandy C** Queensland Australia
139 G8 **Sandy C** Tasmania Australia
101 O9 **Sandy City** Utah U.S.A.
109 L6 **Sandy Cr** Texas U.S.A.
101 Q7 **Sandy Cr** Wyoming U.S.A.
121 O7 **Sandy Creek** Quebec Canada
95 L3 **Sandy Creek** New York U.S.A.
95 O5 **Sandy Hook** Connecticut U.S.A.
94 D8 **Sandy Hook** Kentucky U.S.A
111 G10 **Sandy Hook** Mississippi U.S.A.
95 N6 **Sandy Hook** *pt* New Jersey U.S.A.
57 C6 **Sandykachi** Turkmenistan
123 Q4 **Sandy L** Newfoundland Canada
115 K7 **Sandy L** Ontario Canada
119 R8 **Sandy Lake** Manitoba Canada
119 O3 **Sandy Narrows** Saskatchewan Canada
112 L2 **Sandy Pt** North Carolina U.S.A.
127 P4 **Sandy Pt** St Kitts W Indies
129 G9 **San Estanislao** Colombia
128 E8 **San Estanislao** Paraguay
71 E2 **San Fabian** Luzon Philippines
45 O7 **San Felice Circeo** Italy
45 K2 **San Felice sul Panaro** Italy
131 B4 **San Felipe** Chile
128 E3 **San Felipe** Colombia
124 B2 **San Felipe** Baja California Mexico
124 F4 **San Felipe** Chihuahua Mexico
127 K9 **San Felipe** Venezuela
126 C4 **San Felipe, Cayos de** *islds* Cuba
17 F4 **San Felipe, Cerro de** *pk* Spain
103 H8 **San Felipe Cr** California U.S.A.
106 D6 **San Felipe Pueblo** New Mexico U.S.A.
17 K3 **San Feliú de Guixols** Spain
17 J3 **San Feliu de Llobregat** Spain
135 S12 **San Félix** *isld* Pacific Oc
131 B5 **San Fernando** Chile
124 B3 **San Fernando** Mexico
71 E2 **San Fernando** Luzon Philippines
16 C8 **San Fernando** Spain
127 O3 **San Fernando** Trinidad
102 F7 **San Fernando** California U.S.A.
128 E2 **San Fernando de Apure** Venezuela
128 E3 **San Fernando de Atabape** Venezuela
26 G9 **Sånfjället** *mt* Sweden
118 D1 **Sanford** Manitoba Canada
106 E4 **Sanford** Colorado U.S.A.
113 F9 **Sanford** Florida U.S.A.
95 R3 **Sanford** Maine U.S.A.
112 H2 **Sanford** North Carolina U.S.A.
108 C8 **Sanford** Texas U.S.A.
94 C3 **Sanford L** Michigan U.S.A.
116 Q5 **Sanford, Mt** Alaska U.S.A.
143 B7 **Sanford, R** W Australia Australia
127 N3 **San Francique** Trinidad
131 E3 **San Francisco** Argentina
106 B8 **San Francisco** *R* Ariz/New Mex U.S.A.
104 **San Francisco** *conurbation* California U.S.A.
127 J9 **San Francisco** Venezuela
102 B4 **San Francisco Bay** California U.S.A.
108 E6 **San Francisco Cr** Texas U.S.A.
124 G4 **San Francisco de Conchos** Mexico
133 E3 **San Francisco del Chanar** Argentina
133 D4 **San Francisco del Monte de Oro** Argentina
124 G4 **San Francisco del Oro** Mexico
124 H7 **San Francisco del Rincón** Mexico
127 J5 **San Francisco de Macoris** Dominican Rep
133 D7 **San Francisco de Paula, C** Argentina
133 G4 **San Gabriel** Brazil
102 G7 **San Gabriel Mts** California U.S.A.
124 C3 **San Gabriel, Pta** *C* Mexico
69 G14 **Sangaigerong** Sumatra
76 B1 **Sangamner** India
74 F9 **Sangamner** India
99 R10 **Sangamon** *R* Illinois U.S.A.
77 J3 **Sangan, Koh-i** *mt* Afghanistan
51 M2 **Sangar** Russian Federation
76 D2 **Sangāreddi** India
70 E5 **Sangasanga** Kalimantan
70 F2 **Sanga Sanga** *isld* Philippines
85 C6 **Sangasso** Mali
18 H2 **Sangatte** France
43 B9 **San Gavino Monreale** Sardinia
128 C4 **Sangay** *vol* Ecuador
71 E7 **Sangboy Islands** Philippines
71 J9 **Sangeang** *isld* Indonesia
102 E5 **Sanger** California U.S.A.
98 E2 **Sanger** North Dakota U.S.A.
109 K2 **Sanger** Texas U.S.A.
33 O10 **Sangerhausen** Germany
127 L5 **San Germán** Puerto Rico
65 C4 **Sanggan He** *R* China
71 J9 **Sanggar** Sumbawa Indonesia
71 J9 **Sanggar, Teluk** *B* Indonesia
70 B4 **Sanggau** Kalimantan
69 J12 **Sanggauledo** Indonesia
65 E6 **Sanggou Wan** *B* China
86 C5 **Sangha** *R* Congo
74 C5 **Sānghar** Pakistan
56 B1 **Sangil'ka** *R* Russian Federation
45 R7 **San Giorgio del Sannio** Italy
45 J1 **San Giórgio di Màntova** Italy
42 E3 **San Giorgio di N** Italy
45 K2 **San Giorgio di Piano** Italy
45 R7 **San Giorgio la Molara** Italy
38 E8 **San Giovanni** Italy
45 Q8 **San Giovanni a Teducio** Italy
45 J1 **San Giovanni in Croce** Italy
45 K2 **San Giovanni in Persiceto** Italy
45 K1 **San Giovanni Lupatoto** Italy
43 G10 **San Giovanni, V** Italy
45 L4 **San Giovanni Valdarno** Italy
71 E3 **Sangitan** Luzon Philippines
45 M1 **San Giuliano** Italy
45 H4 **San Giuliano Terme** Italy
45 R8 **San Giuseppe Vesuviano** Italy
45 M4 **San Giustino** Italy
65 G6 **Sangju** S Korea
70 F7 **Sangkarang, Kep** *isld* Sulawesi
68 D5 **Sangkhla Buri** Thailand
70 E4 **Sangkulirang** Kalimantan
70 F4 **Sangkulirang, Teluk** *B* Kalimantan
74 E3 **Sangla** Pakistan
76 B2 **Sangli** India
86 B5 **Sangmélima** Cameroon
89 G4 **Sango** Zimbabwe
45 L4 **San Godenzo** Italy
17 G7 **Sangonera** *R* Spain
102 H7 **San Gorgonio Mt** California U.S.A.
71 B1 **Sangowo** Halmahera Indonesia
106 E5 **Sangre de Cristo Mts** New Mex/Colo U.S.A.
102 B4 **San Gregorio** California U.S.A.
127 P2 **Sangre Grande** Trinidad
42 F6 **Sangro** *R* Italy
74 F3 **Sangrur** India
88 E5 **Sangu** Tanzania
118 C5 **Sangudo** Alberta Canada
129 G6 **Sangue** *R* Brazil
18 E10 **Sangüesa** Spain
41 O7 **Sanguinetto** Italy
Sangyuan *see* **Wuqiao**
67 C2 **Sangzhi** China
Sanhe *see* **Sandu** Guizhou China
59 H1 **Sanhe** China
65 D4 **Sanhe** China
67 D1 **Sanhedian** China
65 B4 **Sanhezhan** China
124 D5 **San Hilario** Mexico
59 H1 **San-ho** China
67 D1 **San Hu** *L* China
65 D5 **Sanhuizhen** China
113 E11 **Sanibel I** Florida U.S.A.
130 C10 **San Ignacio** Argentina
128 E6 **San Ignacio** Beni Bolivia
128 F7 **San Ignacio** Santa Cruz Bolivia
124 D2 **San Ignacio** Mexico
124 C4 **San Ignacio, Laguna** Mexico
16 E4 **San Ildefonso** Spain
106 D6 **San Ildefonso** New Mexico U.S.A.
71 F2 **San Ildefonso, C** Luzon Philippines
79 H3 **Saniman, Wādī** *watercourse* Syria
60 H10 **San'in** Japan
106 E4 **San Isabel** Colorado U.S.A.
133 F4 **San Isidro** Argentina
124 H5 **San Isidro** Mexico
71 G5 **San Isidro** Leyte Philippines
33 Q4 **Sanitz** Germany
126 G10 **San Jacinto** Colombia
71 F4 **San Jacinto** Philippines
101 L8 **San Jacinto** Nevada U.S.A.
102 H8 **San Jacinto Mts** California U.S.A.
133 F4 **San Javier** Argentina
124 F4 **San Javier** Mexico
131 F2 **San Javier, R** Argentina
125 J9 **San Jerónimo** Mexico
Sanjiang *see* **Liannan** Guangdong
67 C4 **Sanjiang** China
65 F3 **Sanjiangkou** China
65 F3 **Sanjiazi** China
61 M8 **Sanjō** Japan
128 F6 **San Joaquin** Bolivia
130 C9 **San Joaquin** Paraguay
102 D4 **San Joaquin** *R* California U.S.A.
102 D5 **San Joaquin** California U.S.A.
102 D5 **San Joaquin Valley** California U.S.A.
108 A8 **San Jon** New Mexico U.S.A.
128 C2 **San Jorge** *R* Colombia
133 C7 **San Jorge, G** Argentina
17 H4 **San Jorge, G.de** Spain
131 B4 **San Jose** *vol* Chile
125 M5 **San José** Costa Rica
124 D5 **San José** *isld* Mexico
71 E4 **San Jose** Philippines
131 G5 **San José** *dept* Uruguay
131 G5 **San José** Uruguay
102 C4 **San Jose** California U.S.A.
99 R9 **San Jose** Illinois U.S.A.
106 E6 **San Jose** New Mexico U.S.A.
131 F3 **San José, Cuchilla de** *mts* Uruguay
128 F2 **San José de Amacuro** Venezuela
128 F7 **San José de Chiquitos** Bolivia
124 D3 **San José de Dimas** Mexico
133 F4 **San José de Feliciano** Argentina
124 F4 **San José de Gracia** Sinaloa Mexico
127 M10 **San José de Guaribe** Venezuela
127 J5 **San José de las Matas** Dominican Rep
124 E6 **San José del Cabo** Mexico
128 D3 **San José del Gauviare** Colombia
127 J5 **San José de Ocoa** Dominican Rep
128 D3 **San José de Ocuné** Colombia
106 C6 **San Jose, R** New Mexico U.S.A.
131 B3 **San Juan** *prov* Argentina
131 C3 **San Juan** Argentina
128 E7 **San Juan** Bolivia
128 C3 **San Juan** *R* Colombia
125 M4 **San Juan** *R* Costa Rica
126 D4 **San Juan** *mt* Cuba
127 J5 **San Juan** Dominican Rep
124 F4 **San Juan** Chihuahua Mexico
124 J4 **San Juan** Coahuila Mexico
128 D7 **San Juan** Peru
71 G6 **San Juan** Mindanao Philippines
127 L5 **San Juan** Puerto Rico
102 D6 **San Juan** *R* California U.S.A.
109 J9 **San Juan** Texas U.S.A.
103 P4 **San Juan** *R* Utah U.S.A.
128 E2 **San Juan** Venezuela
102 C5 **San Juan Bautista** California U.S.A.
128 C7 **San Juan, B. de** *B* Peru
133 E8 **San Juan, C** Argentina
102 G8 **San Juan Capistrano** California U.S.A.
124 H5 **San Juan de Guadalupe** Mexico
18 G10 **San Juan de las Abadesas** Spain
124 H8 **San Juan de Lima, Pta** *C* Mexico
125 N4 **San Juan del Norte** Nicaragua
127 K9 **San Juan de los Cayos** Venezuela
124 H7 **San Juan de los Lagos** Mexico
127 L10 **San Juan de los Morros** Venezuela
125 J7 **San Juan del Río** Mexico
100 C1 **San Juan Is** Washington U.S.A.
124 F7 **San Juanito, I** Mexico
106 C4 **San Juan Mts** Colo/New Mex U.S.A.
125 L9 **San Juan Quiotepec** Mexico
131 C3 **San Juan, R** Argentina
126 C3 **San Juan y Martínez** Cuba
133 D7 **San Julián** Argentina
133 E4 **San Justo** Argentina
17 G4 **San Just, Sa. de** *mts* Spain
85 C6 **Sankarani** *R* Guinea/Mali
76 C6 **Sankarankovil** India
76 B2 **Sankeshwar** India
88 E10 **Sankhulani** Malawi
49 **Sankt-Peterburg** *conurbation* Russian Federation
86 D6 **Sankuru** *R* Zaire
45 H2 **San Lazzaro** Italy
102 B4 **San Leandro** California U.S.A.
45 M4 **San Leo** Italy
124 C3 **San Lino, Sa** *mt* Mexico
78 G3 **Şanlıurfa** Turkey
133 E4 **San Lorenzo** Argentina
128 E6 **San Lorenzo** Bolivia
133 C7 **San Lorenzo** *mt* Chile/Arg
128 C3 **San Lorenzo** Ecuador
125 P9 **San Lorenzo** Guatemala
124 C3 **San Lorenzo** *isld* Mexico
124 F3 **San Lorenzo** Mexico
128 E6 **San Lorenzo** Peru
106 C9 **San Lorenzo** New Mexico U.S.A.
127 J10 **San Lorenzo** Venezuela
44 C4 **San Lorenzo al Mare** Italy
128 B4 **San Lorenzo, C** Ecuador
16 E4 **San Lorenzo de El Escorial** Spain
17 F5 **San Lorenzo de la Parrilla** Spain
17 J2 **San Lorenzo de Morunys** Spain
128 C6 **San Lorenzo, I** Peru
45 N4 **San Lorenzo in Campo** Italy
16 C8 **Sanlúcar de Barrameda** Spain
16 C7 **Sanlúcar la Mayor** Spain
128 E8 **San Lucas** Bolivia
124 E6 **San Lucas** Mexico
102 C5 **San Lucas** California U.S.A.
131 C4 **San Luis** *prov* Argentina
131 C4 **San Luis** Argentina
126 G4 **San Luis** Cuba
125 P9 **San Luís** Guatemala
125 J9 **San Luis** Mexico
124 F4 **San Luis** Chihuahua Mexico
124 D3 **San Luís** Sonora Mexico
71 E2 **San Luis** Luzon Philippines
103 K9 **San Luis** Arizona U.S.A.
106 E4 **San Luis** Colorado U.S.A.
127 K9 **San Luis** Venezuela
124 E4 **San Luis Babarocos** Mexico
125 J7 **San Luis de la Paz** Mexico
128 F6 **San Luis, L** Bolivia
103 K9 **San Luis, Mesa de** Mexico

Column 1

102 D6 San Luis Obispo California U.S.A.
109 M6 San Luis Pass Texas U.S.A.
106 D3 San Luis Pk Colorado U.S.A.
125 J6 San Luis Potosí Mexico
102 G8 San Luis Rey R California
124 B1 San Luis Río Colorado Mexico
131 C4 San Luis, Sa. de mts Argentina
71 E3 San Marcelino Luzon Philippines
124 D3 San Marcial Mexico
106 C8 San Marcial New Mexico U.S.A.
124 D5 San Marcial, Pta C Mexico
43 B9 San Marco, C Sardinia
124 C4 San Marcos Colombia
124 C4 San Marcos Mexico
124 G7 San Marcos Mexico
109 K6 San Marcos Texas U.S.A.
42 E5 San Marino rep S Europe
128 F6 San Martín R Bolivia
128 D3 San Martín Colombia
133 C6 San Martín de los Andes Argentina
133 C7 San Martín, L Chile/Arg
45 L2 San Martino in Argine Italy
38 E8 San Martino in Badia Italy
45 J2 San Martino in Rio Italy
45 K2 San Martino in Spino Italy
125 M5 San Mateo Costa Rica
17 H4 San Mateo Spain
102 B4 San Mateo California U.S.A.
106 C6 San Mateo New Mexico U.S.A.
127 M10 San Mateo Venezuela
106 C8 San Mateo Pk New Mexico U.S.A.
128 G7 San Matías Bolivia
131 D8 San Matías, G Argentina
121 R5 Sanmaur Quebec Canada
127 L10 San Mauricio Venezuela
44 C1 San Mauro Torinese Italy
67 G2 Sanmen China
67 G2 Sanmen Wan B China
65 B7 Sanmenxia China
45 K1 San Michele Extra Italy
128 F6 San Miguel Bolivia
128 C3 San Miguel R Ecuador
125 Q11 San Miguel Honduras
124 D3 San Miguel R Mexico
124 J5 San Miguel Mexico
128 D6 San Miguel Peru
71 D6 San Miguel isds Philippines
103 N10 San Miguel Arizona U.S.A.
102 D6 San Miguel California U.S.A.
106 B3 San Miguel R Colorado U.S.A.
71 F4 San Miguel B Philippines
109 J9 San Miguel Camargo Mexico
109 J7 San Miguel Cr Texas U.S.A.
125 J7 San Miguel de Allende Mexico
128 E7 San Miguel de Huachi Bolivia
133 D3 San Miguel de Tucumán Argentina
102 D7 San Miguel I California U.S.A.
67 F3 Sanming China
45 J4 San Miniato Italy
71 E3 San Narciso Luzon Philippines
44 E1 Sannazzaro de 'Burgondi Italy
42 G7 Sannicandro Garganico Italy
131 E4 San Nicolas Argentina
124 D5 San Nicolás Mexico
71 E1 San Nicolás Luzon Philippines
71 E2 San Nicolas Luzon Philippines
102 E8 San Nicolas I California U.S.A.
45 L2 San Nicolò Ferrarese Italy
27 D13 Sannidal Norway
51 O1 Sannikoya, Proliv str Russian Federation
45 R7 Sannio mts Italy
61 N9 Sano Japan
31 N6 Sanok Poland
133 D8 San Pablo Argentina
128 F7 San Pablo Bolivia
133 D2 San Pablo Bolivia
71 E3 San Pablo Luzon Philippines
124 F4 San Pablo Balleza Mexico
124 B4 San Pablo, Pta C Mexico
124 H6 San Pascual Mexico
131 F4 San Pedro Buenos Aires Argentina
128 F8 San Pedro Jujuy Argentina
130 C10 San Pedro Misiones Argentina
124 E4 San Pedro Mexico
130 B9 San Pedro Paraguay
103 O9 San Pedro R Arizona U.S.A.
128 F2 San Pedro Venezuela
71 G5 San Pedro B Philippines
131 A8 San Pedro, B.de Chile
102 F8 San Pedro Chan California U.S.A.
128 D3 San Pedro de Arimena Colombia
124 F3 San Pedro de la Cueva Mexico
124 H5 San Pedro de las Colonias Mexico
128 C5 San Pedro de Lloc Peru
17 G2 San Pedro del Pinatar Spain
127 K5 San Pedro de Macorís Dominican Rep
133 C3 San Pedro, Pta C Chile
16 C5 San Pedro, Sa. de mts Spain
125 P10 San Pedro Sula Honduras
44 E3 San Pier d'Arena Italy
45 K4 San Piero a Sieve Italy
99 U8 San Pierre Indiana U.S.A.
45 K1 San Pietro di Morubio Italy
45 K2 San Pietro di Piano Italy
43 H8 San Pietro, I Italy
43 B9 San Pietro, I. di Sardinia
42 C3 San Pietro, Pte Italy
100 C1 Sanpoil R Washington U.S.A.
45 L2 San Polo d'Enza Italy
45 K2 San Polo d'Enza in Caviano Italy
45 K2 San Possidonio Italy
15 E5 Sanquhar Scotland
124 A2 San Quintín Mexico
128 C5 San Ramón Peru
44 C4 Sanrao China
44 E4 San Remo Italy
128 C3 San Rodrigo R Mexico
127 J8 San Román, C Venezuela
18 D6 San Roque Spain
109 K6 San Saba Texas U.S.A.
109 J4 San Saba R Texas U.S.A.
125 P11 San Salvador El Salvador
128 A8 San Salvador I Galapagos Is
131 F4 San Salvador R Uruguay

Column 2

133 D2 San Salvador de Jujuy Argentina
133 D8 San Sebastián Argentina
85 A3 San Sebastián Canary Is
124 C3 San Sebastián isld Mexico
17 F1 San Sebastián Spain
127 L10 San Sebastián Venezuela
129 J8 San Sebastião Brazil
42 E5 Sansepolcro Italy
42 G7 San Severo Italy
67 G3 Sansha China
66 D3 Sanshichang China
67 D5 Sanshui China
102 C6 San Simeon California U.S.A.
103 P9 San Simon Arizona U.S.A.
103 P9 San Simon Cr Arizona U.S.A.
42 H4 Sanski Most Bosnia-Herzegovina
145 E4 Sanson New Zealand
108 B6 San Sosteneo Mexico
44 C4 San Stefano al Mare Italy
127 N4 Sans Toucher mt Guadeloupe W Indies
67 C3 Santa Amelia Guatemala
128 E6 Santa Ana Bolivia
128 B4 Santa Ana Ecuador
125 P11 Santa Ana El Salvador
124 D2 Santa Ana Mexico
102 G8 Santa Ana R California U.S.A.
102 G8 Santa Ana California U.S.A.
127 M10 Santa Ana Venezuela
124 F3 Santa Ana Babícora Mexico
102 G8 Santa Ana Mts California U.S.A.
44 F1 Santa Angelo Italy
109 H4 Santa Anna Texas U.S.A.
130 G6 Santa Bárbara Brazil
124 G4 Santa Bárbara Mexico
102 E7 Santa Barbara California U.S.A.
102 H8 Santa Barbara California U.S.A.
127 N10 Santa Barbara Venezuela
129 K6 Santa Barbara Brazil
102 H9 Santa Barbara Ch California U.S.A.
131 G3 Santa Barbara I California U.S.A.
102 E8 Santa Barbara I California U.S.A.
102 E7 Santa Barbara Res California U.S.A.
130 D7 Santa Barbara, Sa de mts Brazil
128 E8 Santa Catalina Argentina
133 D3 Santa Catalina Chile
124 D5 Santa Catalina isld Mexico
102 G8 Santa Catalina, G.of California U.S.A.
102 F8 Santa Catalina, I California U.S.A.
133 G3 Santa Catarina state Brazil
124 B3 Santa Catarina Mexico
124 G5 Santa Catarina die Tepehuanes Mexico
126 B1 Santa Catharina Curaçao
128 E4 Santa Clara Colombia
126 E3 Santa Clara Cuba
103 K10 Santa Clara Utah U.S.A.
133 B9 Santa Clara R Isl de Juan Fernández Is Pacific Oc
102 B4 Santa Clara California U.S.A.
102 E7 Santa Clara R California U.S.A.
102 B5 Santa Clara New York U.S.A.
103 L4 Santa Clara Utah U.S.A.
110 K3 Santa Claus Indiana U.S.A.
17 J3 Santa Coloma de Farnés Spain
16 B1 Santa Comba Spain
133 C7 Santa Cruz prov Argentina
128 F7 Santa Cruz Bolivia
124 C4 Santa Cruz Amazonas Brazil
130 J9 Santa Cruz R Rio Grande do Norte Brazil
128 A8 Santa Cruz isld Galapagos Is
124 D5 Santa Cruz isld Mexico
128 C5 Santa Cruz Peru
71 E2 Santa Cruz Luzon Philippines
71 D3 Santa Cruz Luzon Philippines
71 E3 Santa Cruz Luzon Philippines
71 F6 Santa Cruz Negros Philippines
102 B5 Santa Cruz California U.S.A.
126 A1 Santa Cruz Aruba W Indies
130 H5 Santa Cruz Cabralia Brazil
85 A3 Santa Cruz de la Palma Canary Is
16 E5 Santa Cruz de la Zarza Spain
126 F4 Santa Cruz del Sur Cuba
16 E6 Santa Cruz de Mudela Spain
85 A3 Santa Cruz de Tenerife Canary Is
133 G3 Santa Cruz do Sul Brazil
137 O4 Santa Cruz Is Solomon Is
127 J2 Santa Cruz Mts Jamaica
102 B4 Santa Cruz Mts California U.S.A.
133 F3 Santa Cruz, Sa. de mts Brazil
129 G3 Santa Elena Ecuador
124 G3 Santa Elena Texas U.S.A.
128 E3 Santa Elena Venezuela
124 B4 Santa Elena, B. de Ecuador
125 M4 Santa Elena, C Costa Rica
100 J2 Santa Emida Idaho U.S.A.
16 A2 Santa Eugenia de Ribeira Spain
17 G4 Santa Eulalia Spain
17 J6 Santa Eulalia del Rio Ibiza
131 E3 Santa Fe Argentina
133 E4 Santa Fe prov Argentina
128 A8 Santa Fe isld Galapagos Is
71 F4 Santa Fe Philippines
16 E7 Santafé Spain
113 E8 Santa Fe R Florida U.S.A.
108 B1 Santa Fe New Mexico U.S.A.
126 G4 Santa Filomena Brazil
123 J3 Santa Genoveva mt Mexico
124 G4 Santa Gertrudis Mexico
129 J4 Santa Helena Brazil
58 E5 Santai China
133 C8 Santa Ines, L Chile
133 D8 Santa Isabel Argentina
108 D7 Santa Isabel Argentina
124 G5 Santa Isabel Mexico
124 H7 Santa Isabel Fernando Póo see Malabo Bioko
124 H7 Santa Isabel Solomon Is
124 B2 Santa Isabel, Sa mts Mexico
125 J5 Santa Isobel do Araguaia Brazil
129 G5 Santa Juliana Brazil
130 F6 Santa Juliana Brazil
58 D4 Santala China
16 E1 Santa Lucía Cuba
124 G5 Santa Lucía Mexico
131 F3 Santa Lucia, R Uruguay
124 C6 Santa Luisa, Sa. de mts U.S.A.
130 F8 Santa Luzia Brazil
102 D6 Santa Margarita California U.S.A.
102 D8 Santa Margarita R California U.S.A.
130 C10 Santa Margherita Italy
88 D9 Santa Margherita Italy
44 F3 Santa Margherita Italy
133 D3 Santa María Italy
131 H2 Santa Maria Río Grande do Sul Brazil
128 A8 Santa Maria isld Galapagos Is
124 F2 Santa Maria R Mexico
17 F2 Santa Maria R Arizona U.S.A.
124 C5 Santo Domingo del Pacífico Mexico

Column 3

87 E8 Santa Maria Zambia
131 G5 Santa Maria, C Uruguay
43 F7 Santa Maria Capua Vetere Italy
126 E3 Santa Maria, Cayo isld Cuba
16 B7 Santa Maria, C. de Portugal
16 B8 Santa Maria, C. de Portugal
130 F4 Santa Maria, Chapadão de hills Brazil
124 F4 Santa Maria de Cuevas Mexico
127 M10 Santa Maria de Ipire Venezuela
16 D6 Santa Maria del Oro Mexico
43 J9 Santa Maria di Leuca, C Italy
45 M1 Santa Maria, I Chile
131 A6 Santa Maria, I Chile
103 M7 Santa Maria Mts Arizona U.S.A.
128 C6 Santa Maria, Pta C Peru
130 C7 Santa Maria, R Brazil
130 F4 Santa Maria, Sa. de mts Brazil
131 B6 Santa Mariá, Vol Argentina
65 D4 Santunying China
103 L6 Santa Maria, C Long I Bahamas
128 D3 Santa Marta Colombia
87 B8 Santa Marta, C Angola
126 H9 Santa Marta, Sa. Nevada de mts Colombia
71 F1 Santa Martha, Sa. de mts Philippines
16 A7 Santa Maura isld see Levkás
41 N6 Sant Ambrogio di Valpolicella Italy
45 P6 Santa Mónica Mexico
102 F7 Santa Monica California U.S.A.
109 K9 Santa Monica Texas U.S.A.
102 F8 Santa Monica B California U.S.A.
102 H8 Santa Mts California U.S.A.
70 E5 Santan Kalimantan
129 K6 Santana Brazil
102 G9 Santana I California U.S.A.
106 D6 Santana, Coxilha de mt Brazil/Uruguay
131 G3 Santana do Livramento Brazil
128 C5 Santander Colombia
16 E1 Santander Spain
67 D3 Santang China
66 E3 Santanghu China
130 F8 Santa Niño Samar Philippines
87 B7 São Brás, Cabo de C Angola
107 P7 Santan Mt Arizona U.S.A.
43 B9 Sant'Antioco Sardinia
43 B9 Sant'Antioco, I. di Sardinia
109 K9 Santa Paula California U.S.A.
101 O10 Santaquin Utah U.S.A.
16 D9 Santarem Portugal
130 J9 Santa Rita Brazil
101 N1 Santa Rita Montana U.S.A.
127 J9 Santa Rita Venezuela
130 C10 Santa Rosa Argentina
87 G7 Santa Rosa Colombia
102 B3 Santa Rosa California U.S.A.
108 C1 Santa Rosa New Mexico U.S.A.
125 M2 Santa Rosa de Aguán Honduras
128 D6 Santa Rosa de la Roca Bolivia
125 L3 Santa Rosa de Lima El Salvador
111 J11 Santa Rosa I Florida U.S.A.
109 H2 Santa Rosa L Texas U.S.A.
124 C4 Santa Rosalia Mexico
100 C10 Santa Rosa, R Brazil
100 H8 Santa Rosa Range Nevada U.S.A.
103 N9 Santa Rosa Wash R Arizona
130 F8 Santa Sylvina Argentina
129 J6 Santa Teresa R Brazil
133 G3 Santa Teresa Mexico
43 C7 Santa Teresa Gallura Sardinia
133 G4 Santa Teresinha Brazil
140 C6 Santa Theresa N Terr
133 G4 Santa Vitória do Palmar Brazil
133 G3 Santa Vittoria, Monte mt Brazil
129 K4 Santa Ynez California U.S.A.
102 D7 Santa Ynez Mts California U.S.A.
102 H4 Santa Ysabel California
112 H4 Santee R South Carolina U.S.A.
112 H4 Santee Pt South Carolina U.S.A.
112 D2 Santeetlah, L North Carolina U.S.A.
125 O5 Santé Fé Panama
124 H8 San Telmo Mexico
124 H8 San Telmo, Pta C Mexico
72 D5 Sante Marie Italy
42 N6 Santenay France
42 N6 Santerno R Italy
130 F7 Santhià Italy
125 Q5 Santiago Chile
133 C4 Santiago Chile
127 J5 Santiago Dominican Rep
124 D6 Santiago Baja California Mexico
126 D6 Santiago Colima Mexico
130 H7 Santiago Panama
130 C10 Santiago Paraguay
70 G7 Santiago R Peru
29 J8 Santiago de Compostela Spain
71 F1 Santiago de Cuba Cuba
47 J3 Sapai Greece
69 D13 Sapanca Turkey
71 E3 Sapanga Turkey
71 E3 Sapangbato Luzon Philippines
16 B6 Santiago do Cacem Portugal
85 F7 Santiago Ixcuintla Mexico
108 D6 Santiago Mts Texas U.S.A.
124 G5 Santiago Papasquiaro Mexico
16 C4 Santiago, Rio Grande de R Mexico
124 B2 Santiago, Sa mts Mexico
129 J5 Santiago, Serrania de mts Bolivia
16 B2 Santiaguillo, L. de Mexico
70 G4 Santigi Sulawesi Indonesia
70 G4 Santikli, Tanjong C Sulawesi
21 L4 Santillana Spain
71 E2 Sapocoy, Mt Luzon Philippines
125 P9 Santo Texas U.S.A.
130 F8 Santo Amaro, I de Brazil
130 D6 Santo Antônio R Brazil
54 M3 Santo Antônio Brazil
130 C6 Santo Antônio de Jesus Brazil
88 F10 Santo Antônio do Içá Brazil
38 G8 Santo Antônio do Zaire Angola
130 C10 Santo Cristo R Brazil
87 D9 Santo Cruz do Cuando Angola
26 M4 Santo Domingo Cuba
43 G8 Santo Domingo Dominican Rep
70 G9 Santo Domingo Baja California Mexico
70 O9 Santo Domingo Coahuila Mexico
78 L3 Santo Domingo, Cay isld Bahamas
17 F2 Santo Domingo de la Calza Spain
108 D4 Santo Domingo del Pacífico Mexico

Column 4

130 G6 Santo Maria do Suaçui
127 M10 Santo Tomé Venezuela
128 F2 San Tome de Guayana Venezuela
130 F8 Santoña Spain
65 G3 Santorini isld see Thira isld
130 F8 Santos Brazil
128 E5 Santos Brazil
128 E5 Santos Dumont Amazonas Brazil
130 G7 Santos Dumont Minas Gerais Brazil
16 D6 Santos, Sa. de los mts Spain
44 G1 Santo Stéfano Lodigiano Italy
46 D5 Santo Tirso Portugal
130 D10 Santo Tomás Brazil
133 F4 Santo Tomás Peru
70 B5 Santo Tomás, Sa. de Castilla Guatemala
71 G8 Santo Tomé Argentina
75 K8 Sarangarh India
53 G7 Santu, C. di M mt Sardinia
59 L2 Sarapul'skoye Russian Federation
79 F3 Saratá Syria
113 E10 Sarasota Florida U.S.A.
111 B11 Saratoga Texas U.S.A.
101 T8 Saratoga Wyoming U.S.A.
95 O3 Saratoga Springs New York U.S.A.
16 A7 Saratok Sarawak
53 G8 Saratov Russian Federation
68 H5 Saravan Laos
68 D6 Sarawa R Burma
32 H9 Sarawak state Malaysia
33 N7 Sarawak state Malaysia
25 C4 Sassenheim Netherlands
26 L8 Sävar Sweden
45 N4 Sasso Marconi Italy
44 K3 Sassari Italy
45 J2 Sassuolo Italy
87 F10 Sástago Spain
133 E4 Sastre Argentina
60 C11 Sasuna Japan
25 A6 Sas-van Gent Netherlands
57 K2 Sasykkol', Ozero L Kazakhstan
48 M5 Sasyk, Oz L Ukraine
53 D10 Sasyk, Ozero L Ukraine
85 B6 Satadougou Mali
60 D14 Sata-misaki C Japan
106 B6 Satan Pass New Mexico U.S.A.
104 K4 Satara Kansas U.S.A.
76 A2 Satara India
114 H2 Satellite B Northwest Territories Canada
113 G9 Satellite Beach Florida U.S.A.
71 H8 Satengar isld Indonesia
27 H11 Säter Sweden
32 G6 Säterland reg Germany
19 N1 Satilla R Georgia U.S.A.
126 D6 Satipo Peru
1 S Satisjaure L Sweden
42 J6 Satka Russian Federation
55 C4 Satka Russian Federation
13 G4 Satley England
74 F8 Satmala Hills India
71 H9 Satonda isld Indonesia
9 Q7 Satō Zaire
42 H4 Šator mt Bosnia-Herzegovina
48 G2 Sátoraljaújhely Hungary
33 P5 Satow Germany
74 F8 Satpura Range India
28 D7 Satrup Germany
53 L8 Satsuma Mexico
122 J5 Satsuma Russian Federation
116 B5 Satsunan Shotō is Japan
124 D2 Sattahip Thailand
29 M4 Sattanen Finland
41 J3 Sattel Switzerland
76 E2 Sattenapalle India
74 F8 Sätti India
24 N2 Satu Mare Romania
60 B1 Satun Thailand
78 N4 Saturna I British Columbia Canada
71 K9 Sau Sea Indonesia
80 C5 Sayyon Israel
55 L8 Satyamangalam India
74 G6 Sawai Madhopur India
70 M9 Sawall, G of Java
71 L10 Sawan Kalimantan
70 O5 Sawang Daen Din Thailand
60 O3 Sawankhalok Thailand
61 M8 Sawara Hokkaido Japan
61 N8 Sawara Honshu Japan
62 J6 Sawaski-bana C Japan
106 D2 Swatch Ra Colorado U.S.A.
121 L1 Sawayn Pt Quebec Canada
119 O1 Sawbill Manitoba Canada
111 F7 Sawdá', Jabal as mts Libya
118 D4 Sawdy Alberta Canada
21 L6 Sawel mt N Ireland
89 N1 Sawhāj Jordan
80 E6 Sawi Yemen
45 J2 Swilog Cr Kansas U.S.A.
117 O3 Sawmill Bay Northwest Territories Canada
9 G3 Sawston England
47 K8 Sawtooth Mt Alaska U.S.A.
99 P2 Sawtooth Mts Minnesota U.S.A.
100 L6 Sawtooth Range Idaho U.S.A.
100 E1 Sawu see Savu

Column 5

128 C4 Saraguro Ecuador
29 M7 Särälsniemi Finland
48 E7 Sarajevo Bosnia-Herzegovina
140 J5 Saraji Queensland Australia
77 G1 Sarakhs Iran
43 D3 Sarakli Greece
129 N10 Saraktash Russian Federation
124 D2 Sásabe Arizona U.S.A.
129 N10 Sasabe Mexico
86 H4 Saababeneh Ethiopia
138 D2 Saassabe Mexico
75 L6 Sara, Mt South Australia Australia
71 J9 Saran' Kazakhstan
60 J10 Saranac Michigan U.S.A.
95 N2 Saranac Lake New York U.S.A.
46 D5 Sarandë Albania
130 D10 Sarandi Brazil
133 F4 Sarandi del Yi Uruguay
70 B5 Sarandi del Yi Uruguay
71 G8 Sarangani isld Mindanao Philippines
75 K8 Sarangarh India
53 G7 Saransk Russian Federation
79 F3 Saraá Syria
113 E10 Sarasota Florida U.S.A.
111 B11 Saratoga Texas U.S.A.
16 A7 Saratok Sarawak
53 G8 Saratov Russian Federation
68 H5 Saravan Laos
68 D6 Sarawa R Burma
32 H9 Sarawak state Malaysia
26 E8 Sarawak Netherlands
26 L7 Sasserot France
30 H1 Sassnitz Germany
45 N4 Sassocorvaro Italy
38 E8 Sass Rigais mt Italy
45 J2 Sassuolo Italy
18 F9 Sástago Spain
133 E4 Sastre Argentina
77 B2 Sasun oil well Persian Gulf
85 C3 Sassandra R Ivory Coast
37 K4 Sassenfahr Germany
33 S4 Sassen Germany
19 P14 Sassenage France
32 H9 Sassenberg Germany
25 C4 Sassenheim Netherlands
40 L7 Sasserot France
30 H1 Sassnitz Germany
45 N4 Sassocorvaro Italy
38 E8 Sass Rigais mt Italy
45 J2 Sassuolo Italy
87 F10 Sástago Spain
133 E4 Sastre Argentina
60 C11 Sasuna Japan
25 A6 Sas-van Gent Netherlands
57 K2 Sasykkol', Ozero L Kazakhstan
48 M5 Sasyk, Oz L Ukraine
53 D10 Sasyk, Ozero L Ukraine
85 B6 Satadougou Mali
60 D14 Sata-misaki C Japan
106 B6 Satan Pass New Mexico U.S.A.
104 K4 Satara Kansas U.S.A.
76 A2 Satara India
114 H2 Satellite B Northwest Territories Canada
113 G9 Satellite Beach Florida U.S.A.
71 H8 Satengar isld Indonesia
27 H11 Säter Sweden
32 G6 Säterland reg Germany
19 N1 Satilla R Georgia U.S.A.
126 D6 Satipo Peru
1 S Satisjaure L Sweden
42 J6 Satka Russian Federation
13 G4 Satley England
74 F8 Satmala Hills India
71 H9 Satonda isld Indonesia
9 Q7 Satō Zaire
42 H4 Šator mt Bosnia-Herzegovina
48 G2 Sátoraljaújhely Hungary
33 P5 Satow Germany
74 F8 Satpura Range India
28 D7 Satrup Germany
53 L8 Satsuma Mexico
122 J5 Satsuma Russian Federation
116 B5 Satsunan Shotō is Japan
124 D2 Sattahip Thailand
29 M4 Sattanen Finland
41 J3 Sattel Switzerland
76 E2 Sattenapalle India
74 F8 Sätti India
24 N2 Satu Mare Romania
60 B1 Satun Thailand
78 N4 Saturna I British Columbia Canada
80 C5 Sayyon Israel
55 L8 Satyamangalam India
55 D2 Satyga Russian Federation
74 G6 Sawai Madhopur India
88 L3 Sauce, R Argentina
122 G4 Sauces Mexico
61 M8 Saucier Mississippi U.S.A.
33 F5 Sauda Norway
27 B12 Saudárkrókur Iceland
88 H11 Saudi Arabia kingdom
52 N6 Sauerland reg Germany
20 J8 Saueruina R Brazil
71 G7 Sauga R Rindanao Philippines
99 J7 Saugatuck Michigan U.S.A.
117 O3 Saugeen R Ontario Canada
9 G3 Saugstad, Mt British Columbia Canada
47 K8 Sauk R Washington U.S.A.
99 P2 Sauk R Washington U.S.A.
100 L6 Sauk City Wisconsin U.S.A.
100 E1 Sauk Center Minnesota U.S.A.
99 R6 Sauk Rapids Minnesota U.S.A.

Column 6

57 B6 Saryyazinskoye Vodokhranilishche res Turkmenistan
57 H2 Saryyesik-Atyray desert Kazakhstan
57 J3 Saryzhaz Kazakhstan
44 G3 Sarzana Italy
20 E6 Sarzeau France
124 D2 Sásabe Mexico
103 N10 Sasabe Arizona U.S.A.
86 H4 Saasabeneh Ethiopia
69 D12 Sasak Sumatra
75 L6 Sasaram India
71 J9 Sasar Tg C Sumba Indonesia
60 J10 Sasayama Japan
98 B2 Sasea Montana U.S.A.
139 H8 Savage River Tasmania Australia
101 U6 Savageton Wyoming U.S.A.
119 O5 Saskatchewan prov Canada
134 A1 Savaii isld Western Samoa
85 E7 Savalou Benin
122 A2 Savan'e, R Quebec Canada
126 A2 Savaneta Aruba W Indies
107 P7 Savanna Illinois U.S.A.
112 F5 Savannah Georgia U.S.A.
110 B2 Savannah Missouri U.S.A.
94 E6 Savannah R South Carolina U.S.A.
110 H6 Savannah Tennessee U.S.A.
112 F6 Savannah Beach Georgia U.S.A.
113 L12 Savannah Sound Bahamas
126 F2 Savannah Sound Eleuthera Bahamas
68 G4 Savannakhet Laos
127 H2 Savanna la Mar Jamaica
76 B3 Savanur India
26 L8 Sävar Sweden
8 R Sävar R Sweden
40 F6 Savarances, R Italy
45 J5 Savastepe Turkey
8 E6 Savé Benin
18 F9 Save R France
87 F10 Save R Mozambique
77 B2 Saveh Iran
85 D7 Savelugu Ghana
56 F3 Savel'yevka Russian Federation
5 K3 Savena R Italy
20 G7 Savenay France
18 G9 Saverdun France
36 C6 Saverne France
101 S8 Savery Wyoming U.S.A.
45 M3 Savignano Italy
21 L5 Savigne France
21 L5 Savigné-l'Evêque France
21 L7 Savigné-sur-Lathan France
45 L7 Savigno Italy
21 L7 Savigny-en-Véron Indre-et-Loire France
19 Q15 Savigny-sur-Braye France
19 G15 Savines France
42 H3 Savinja R Slovenia
52 H2 Savino Russian Federation
52 J3 Savinobor Russian Federation
45 M3 Savio R Italy
32 J6 Sávio R Italy
29 N10 Savitaipale Finland
45 J6 Šavnik Montenegro Yugoslavia
19 K7 Savoff Ontario Canada
19 K7 Savoie dept France
44 D3 Savona Italy
95 K4 Savona New York U.S.A.
90 M9 Savona Italy
29 O10 Savonlinna Finland
116 B5 Savonranta Finland
29 N5 Savoonga St Lawrence I, Alaska U.S.A.
111 H9 Savoy Illinois U.S.A.
101 R1 Savoy Montana U.S.A.
41 N2 Savran' Ukraine
27 G14 Sävsjö Sweden
27 H15 Sävsjöström Sweden
42 E3 Savudrija Rtic pt Croatia
42 J6 Savukoski Finland
78 H4 Savur Turkey
80 C5 Sawyon Israel

Column 7

122 H2 Sauterelles, Lac aux Quebec Canada
127 P5 Sauters Grenada
20 G7 Sautron France
18 E9 Sauveterre France
18 F8 Sauveterre-de-Guyenne France
29 K11 Sauvo Finland
25 G2 Sauwerd Netherlands
20 D7 Sauzon France
42 H3 Sava R Croatia/Slovenia/ Yugoslavia
95 L7 Savage Maryland U.S.A.
111 F7 Savage Mississippi U.S.A.
98 B2 Savage Montana U.S.A.
139 H8 Savage River Tasmania Australia
101 U6 Savageton Wyoming U.S.A.
134 A1 Savaii isld Western Samoa
85 E7 Savalou Benin
122 A2 Savan'e, R Quebec Canada
126 A2 Savaneta Aruba W Indies
107 P7 Savanna Illinois U.S.A.
112 F5 Savannah Georgia U.S.A.
110 B2 Savannah Missouri U.S.A.
94 E6 Savannah R South Carolina U.S.A.
110 H6 Savannah Tennessee U.S.A.
112 F6 Savannah Beach Georgia U.S.A.
113 L12 Savannah Sound Bahamas
126 F2 Savannah Sound Eleuthera Bahamas
68 G4 Savannakhet Laos
127 H2 Savanna la Mar Jamaica
76 B3 Savanur India
26 L8 Sävar Sweden
8 R Sävar R Sweden
40 F6 Savarances, R Italy
45 J5 Savastepe Turkey
8 E6 Savé Benin
18 F9 Save R France
87 F10 Save R Mozambique
77 B2 Saveh Iran
85 D7 Savelugu Ghana
56 F3 Savel'yevka Russian Federation
5 K3 Savena R Italy
20 G7 Savenay France
18 G9 Saverdun France
36 C6 Saverne France
101 S8 Savery Wyoming U.S.A.
45 M3 Savignano Italy
21 L5 Savigne France
21 L5 Savigné-l'Evêque France
21 L7 Savigné-sur-Lathan France
45 L7 Savigno Italy
21 L7 Savigny-en-Véron Indre-et-Loire France
19 Q15 Savigny-sur-Braye France
19 G15 Savines France
42 H3 Savinja R Slovenia
52 H2 Savino Russian Federation
52 J3 Savinobor Russian Federation
45 M3 Savio R Italy
32 J6 Sávio R Italy
29 N10 Savitaipale Finland
45 J6 Šavnik Montenegro Yugoslavia
19 K7 Savoff Ontario Canada
19 K7 Savoie dept France
44 D3 Savona Italy
95 K4 Savona New York U.S.A.
90 M9 Savona Italy
29 O10 Savonlinna Finland
116 B5 Savonranta Finland
29 N5 Savoonga St Lawrence I, Alaska U.S.A.
111 H9 Savoy Illinois U.S.A.
101 R1 Savoy Montana U.S.A.
41 N2 Savran' Ukraine
27 G14 Sävsjö Sweden
27 H15 Sävsjöström Sweden
42 E3 Savudrija Rtic pt Croatia
42 J6 Savukoski Finland
78 H4 Savur Turkey

Column 8

128 C4 Saraguro Ecuador
29 M7 Särälsniemi Finland
48 E7 Sarajevo Bosnia-Herzegovina
140 J5 Saraji Queensland Australia
77 G1 Sarakhs Iran
43 D3 Sarakli Greece
129 G2 Saramacca R Suriname
18 F9 Saramon France
138 D2 Sara, Mt South Australia Australia
57 G1 Saran' Kazakhstan
94 B4 Saranac Michigan U.S.A.
95 N2 Saranac Lake New York U.S.A.
60 C12 Sandebor Japan
114 J7 Saskatchewan prov Canada
119 O5 Saskatchewan prov Canada
118 L6 Saskatoon Saskatchewan Canada
119 Q5 Saskeram L Manitoba Canada
51 L1 Saskylakh Russian Federation
125 M3 Saslaya mt Nicaragua
89 E6 Saolburg S Africa
109 J6 Sapamco Texas U.S.A.
112 E2 Sassafras Mt South Carolina U.S.A.
110 H6 Sassan oil well Persian Gulf
85 C3 Sassandra R Ivory Coast
85 C8 Sassandra R Ivory Coast
37 K4 Sassenfahr Germany
33 S4 Sassen Germany
19 P14 Sassenage France
32 H9 Sassenberg Germany
25 C4 Sassenheim Netherlands
40 L7 Sasserot France
30 H1 Sassnitz Germany
45 N4 Sassocorvaro Italy
38 E8 Sass Rigais mt Italy
45 J2 Sassuolo Italy
18 F9 Sástago Spain
133 E4 Sastre Argentina
60 C11 Sasuna Japan
25 A6 Sas-van Gent Netherlands
57 K2 Sasykkol', Ozero L Kazakhstan
48 M5 Sasyk, Oz L Ukraine
53 D10 Sasyk, Ozero L Ukraine
85 B6 Satadougou Mali
60 D14 Sata-misaki C Japan
106 B6 Satan Pass New Mexico U.S.A.
104 K4 Satara Kansas U.S.A.
76 A2 Satara India
114 H2 Satellite B Northwest Territories Canada
113 G9 Satellite Beach Florida U.S.A.
71 H8 Satengar isld Indonesia
27 H11 Säter Sweden
32 G6 Säterland reg Germany
19 N1 Satilla R Georgia U.S.A.
126 D6 Satipo Peru
1 S Satisjaure L Sweden
42 J6 Satka Russian Federation
13 G4 Satley England
74 F8 Satmala Hills India
71 H9 Satonda isld Indonesia
9 Q7 Satō Zaire
42 H4 Šator mt Bosnia-Herzegovina
48 G2 Sátoraljaújhely Hungary
33 P5 Satow Germany
74 F8 Satpura Range India
28 D7 Satrup Germany
53 L8 Satsuma Mexico
122 J5 Satsuma Russian Federation
116 B5 Satsunan Shotō is Japan
124 D2 Sattahip Thailand
29 M4 Sattanen Finland
41 J3 Sattel Switzerland
76 E2 Sattenapalle India
74 F8 Sätti India
24 N2 Satu Mare Romania
60 B1 Satun Thailand
78 N4 Saturna I British Columbia Canada

Column 9

57 J3 Saryzhaz Kazakhstan
44 G3 Sarzana Italy
20 E6 Sarzeau France
124 D2 Sásabe Mexico
124 N10 Sasabe Arizona U.S.A.
86 H4 Saasabeneh Ethiopia
138 D2 Saassabe Mexico
75 L6 Sasaram India
71 J9 Sasar Tg C Sumba Indonesia
60 J10 Sasayama Japan
98 B2 Sasea Montana U.S.A.
119 O5 Saskatchewan prov Canada
118 L6 Saskatoon Saskatchewan Canada
119 Q5 Saskeram L Manitoba Canada
51 L1 Saskylakh Russian Federation
125 M3 Saslaya mt Nicaragua
89 E6 Saolburg S Africa
109 J6 Sapamco Texas U.S.A.
112 E2 Sassafras Mt South Carolina U.S.A.
77 C7 Sassan oil well Persian Gulf
85 C3 Sassandra R Ivory Coast
85 C8 Sassandra R Ivory Coast
37 K4 Sassenfahr Germany
33 S4 Sassen Germany
19 P14 Sassenage France
32 H9 Sassenberg Germany
25 C4 Sassenheim Netherlands
40 L7 Sasserot France
30 H1 Sassnitz Germany
45 N4 Sassocorvaro Italy
38 E8 Sass Rigais mt Italy
45 J2 Sassuolo Italy
18 F9 Sástago Spain
133 E4 Sastre Argentina
60 C11 Sasuna Japan

Column 10

57 B6 Saryyazinskoye Vodokhranilishche res Turkmenistan
57 H2 Saryyesik-Atyray desert Kazakhstan
57 J3 Saryzhaz Kazakhstan
44 G3 Sarzana Italy
20 E6 Sarzeau France
124 D2 Sásabe Mexico
20 D7 Sauzon France
42 H3 Sava R Croatia/Slovenia/ Yugoslavia

Column 11

122 H2 Sauterelles, Lac aux Quebec Canada
127 P5 Sauters Grenada
20 G7 Sautron France
18 E9 Sauveterre France
18 F8 Sauveterre-de-Guyenne France
29 K11 Sauvo Finland
25 G2 Sauwerd Netherlands
20 D7 Sauzon France
42 H3 Sava R Croatia/Slovenia/ Yugoslavia
95 L7 Savage Maryland U.S.A.
111 F7 Savage Mississippi U.S.A.
98 B2 Savage Montana U.S.A.
139 H8 Savage River Tasmania Australia
101 U6 Savageton Wyoming U.S.A.
134 A1 Savaii isld Western Samoa
85 E7 Savalou Benin
122 A2 Savan'e, R Quebec Canada
126 A2 Savaneta Aruba W Indies
107 P7 Savanna Illinois U.S.A.
112 F5 Savannah Georgia U.S.A.
110 B2 Savannah Missouri U.S.A.
94 E6 Savannah R South Carolina U.S.A.
110 H6 Savannah Tennessee U.S.A.
112 F6 Savannah Beach Georgia U.S.A.
113 L12 Savannah Sound Bahamas
126 F2 Savannah Sound Eleuthera Bahamas
68 G4 Savannakhet Laos
127 H2 Savanna la Mar Jamaica
14 P7 Sävstadvadi see Vädi
33 N7 Savanur India
76 B3 Savanur India
29 K11 Savonlinna Finland
36 C7 Saulxures France
47 P1 Saum Jordan
81 H2 Saum Jordan
36 C7 Saulxures France
19 K7 Savoff Ontario Canada

Column 12

122 H2 Sauterelles, Lac aux Quebec Canada
127 P5 Sauters Grenada
20 G7 Sautron France
18 E9 Sauveterre France
18 F8 Sauveterre-de-Guyenne France
29 K11 Sauvo Finland
25 G2 Sauwerd Netherlands
20 D7 Sauzon France
42 H3 Sava R Croatia/Slovenia/ Yugoslavia
95 L7 Savage Maryland U.S.A.
36 C7 Saulxures France
47 P1 Saum Jordan
36 C7 Saulxures France
56 D5 Sayakbay Kyrgyzstan
47 M10 Sazli R Turkey
47 M10 Sazlibosna Çitlihan Turkey

52 E5 **Sazonovo** Russian Federation
85 D3 **Sbaa** Algeria
85 F1 **Sbeitla** Tunisia
6 L4 **S Brae** *oil rig* North Sea
143 D10 **Scaddan** W Australia Australia
20 C5 **Scaër** France
45 R8 **Scafati** Italy
13 E5 **Scafell Pikes** *mt* England
13 H5 **Scalby** England
43 G9 **Scalea** Italy
99 Q7 **Scales Mound** Illinois U.S.A.
15 G2 **Scalloway** Shetland Scotland
15 C3 **Scalpay** *isld* Scotland
116 E6 **Scammon Bay** Alaska U.S.A.
9 F1 **Scampton** England
118 F8 **Scandia** Alberta Canada
107 N2 **Scandia** Kansas U.S.A.
45 J2 **Scandiano** Italy
45 N5 **Scandriglia** Italy
119 V8 **Scanterbury** Manitoba Canada
43 H8 **Scanzano Ionico** Italy
118 F7 **Scapa** Alberta Canada
6 K4 **Scapa** *oil rig* North Sea
15 E2 **Scapa Flow** Orkney Scotland
100 C4 **Scappoose** Oregon U.S.A.
43 F12 **Scaramia, C** Sicily
15 C4 **Scarba** *isld* Scotland
142 A1 **Scarborough** *dist* Perth, W Aust Australia
120 E9 **Scarborough** Ontario Canada
13 H5 **Scarborough** England
127 M2 **Scarborough** Tobago
144 D5 **Scargill** New Zealand
14 A5 **Scariff** *isld* Ireland
15 A2 **Scarp** *isld* Lewis Scotland
Scarpanto *isld see* **Kárpathos** *isld*
22 D3 **Scarpe** *R* France
45 K4 **Scarperia** Italy
119 R9 **Scarth** Manitoba Canada
123 N7 **Scaterie I** C Breton I, Nova Scotia
15 B3 **Scavaig, L** Scotland
138 C5 **Sceale B** South Australia Australia
21 M5 **Sceaux** Sarthe France
42 G5 **Šćedro** *isld* Croatia
98 D6 **Scenic** South Dakota U.S.A.
118 H8 **Sceptre** Saskatchewan Canada
33 N6 **Schaale** *R* Germany
33 N5 **Schaalsee** *L* Germany
38 H6 **Schafberg** *mt* Austria
99 T4 **Schaffer** Michigan U.S.A.
41 J2 **Schaffhausen** Switzerland
28 C7 **Schaffland** Germany
33 P10 **Schafstädt** Germany
25 C3 **Schagen** Netherlands
36 C6 **Schalbach** France
37 P6 **Schalding** Germany
32 G8 **Schale** Germany
37 L3 **Schalkau** Germany
32 G10 **Schalksmühle** Germany
99 L7 **Schaller** Iowa U.S.A.
41 K4 **Schams** *R* Switzerland
32 G8 **Schapen** Germany
38 H5 **Schärding** Austria
32 H5 **Scharhörn** *isld* Germany
33 M6 **Scharnebeck** Germany
41 O3 **Scharnitz** Austria
32 G6 **Scharrel** Germany
36 G1 **Schauenburg** Germany
37 M3 **Schauenstein** Germany
32 K8 **Schaumburg** Germany
36 H6 **Schechingen** Germany
25 G2 **Scheemda** Netherlands
41 K1 **Scheer** Germany
32 K6 **Scheessel** Germany
115 N7 **Schefferville** Quebec Canada
38 M6 **Scheibbs** Austria
37 K4 **Scheinfeld** Germany
22 G1 **Schelde** *R* Belgium
36 H7 **Schelklingen** Germany
103 K2 **Schell Creek Ra** Nevada U.S.A.
95 O4 **Schenectady** New York U.S.A.
32 K4 **Schenefeld** Germany
32 L5 **Schenefeld** Germany
36 H2 **Schenklengsfeld** Germany
32 K9 **Scherfede** Germany
32 E9 **Schermbeck** Germany
25 C3 **Schermerhorn** Netherlands
33 N10 **Schernberg** Germany
22 H2 **Scherpen Heuvel** Belgium
28 D7 **Schersberg** *hill* Germany
109 J6 **Schertz** Texas U.S.A.
41 L3 **Schesaplana** *mt* Austria
37 L4 **Schesslitz** Germany
25 B4 **Scheveningen** Netherlands
38 J7 **Schiadming** Austria
25 B5 **Schiedam** Netherlands
32 K9 **Schieder** Germany
15 D4 **Schiehallion** *mt* Scotland
33 N6 **Schierling** Germany
25 F2 **Schiermonnikoog** Netherlands
25 F2 **Schiermonnokoog** *isld* Netherlands
33 S8 **Schiessplatz** Germany
36 F2 **Schiffenberg** Germany
36 E5 **Schifferstadt** Germany
36 C5 **Schiffweiler** Germany
25 D5 **Schijndel** Netherlands
33 R10 **Schildau** Germany
33 N6 **Schilde** *R* Germany
33 R6 **Schillersdorf** Germany
32 L8 **Schillerslage** Germany
32 H5 **Schillighörn** *pt* Germany
37 J5 **Schillingsfürst** Germany
41 M5 **Schilpario** Italy
36 E7 **Schiltach** Germany
38 N4 **Schiltern** Austria
41 O6 **Schio** Italy
25 F4 **Schipbeek** *R* Netherlands
25 C4 **Schiphol** Netherlands
19 K4 **Schirmeck** France
33 Q10 **Schkeuditz** Germany
37 M1 **Schkölen** Germany
33 T9 **Schlabendorf** Germany
38 J7 **Schladminger Tauern** *mts* Austria
36 E3 **Schlangenbad** Germany
36 C1 **Schlebusch** Germany
30 E1 **Schlei** *R* Germany
36 B2 **Schleiden** Germany
36 E6 **Schleithal** France
37 M2 **Schleiz** Germany
33 P5 **Schlemmin** Germany
30 E1 **Schleswig** Germany
99 L7 **Schleswig** Iowa U.S.A.
32 K4 **Schleswig Holstein** *land* Germany
37 O2 **Schlettau** Germany
37 K2 **Schleusinger-Neundorf** Germany
37 M4 **Schlicht** Germany
33 S9 **Schlieben** Germany
40 G2 **Schliengen** Germany
36 H3 **Schliichtern** Germany
36 H2 **Schlitz** Germany
32 J9 **Schloss-Holte** Germany
37 L1 **Schlossvippach** Germany
37 K1 **Schlotheim** Germany
40 H2 **Schluchsee** Germany
40 F1 **Schlucht, Col de la** *pass* France
32 K8 **Schlüsselburg** Germany
33 N5 **Schlutup** Germany
36 E1 **Schmallenberg** Germany
33 O7 **Schmarsau** Germany
36 B5 **Schmelz** Germany
37 M5 **Schmidmühlen** Germany
36 B3 **Schmidthein** Germany
37 K2 **Schmiedefeld** Germany
36 F1 **Schmittlotheim** Germany
81 A10 **Schmitt-Ott Seamount** Atlantic Oc
37 N2 **Schmölln** Germany
37 K7 **Schmutter** *R* Germany
37 M4 **Schnabelwaid** Germany
33 P6 **Schnackenburg** Germany
37 N4 **Schnaittenbach** Germany
36 C6 **Schnee Berg** *mt* France
37 O2 **Schneeberg** Germany
37 M3 **Schneeburg** *mt* Germany
32 K7 **Schneeren** Germany
33 O9 **Schneidlingen** Germany
37 J5 **Schnelldorf** Germany
32 L6 **Schneverdingen** Germany
38 K7 **Schöder** Austria
40 G1 **Schöenau** France
99 R5 **Schofield** Wisconsin U.S.A.
135 Q2 **Schofield Barracks** Hawaiian Is
95 N4 **Schoharie** New York U.S.A.
41 P3 **Scholastika** Austria
127 L4 **Schœlcher** Martinique W Indies
33 Q7 **Schollene** Germany
36 G3 **Schöllkrippen** Germany
89 D7 **Scholtzkop** *mt* S Africa
36 F7 **Schömberg** Germany
38 J6 **Schön** *mt* Austria
36 G6 **Schönaich** Germany
36 F5 **Schönau** Germany
37 J2 **Schönau** Germany
36 B3 **Schönau** Nordrhein-Westfalen Germany
22 L3 **Schonberg** Belgium
30 E1 **Schönberg** Germany
33 R7 **Schönberg** Germany
36 H3 **Schondra** Germany
33 P8 **Schönebeck** Germany
33 S8 **Schöneberg** Germany
37 N3 **Schöneck** Germany
36 B3 **Schönecken-Wetteldorf** Germany
33 S8 **Schönefeld** *airport* Germany
36 C5 **Schönenberg-Kubelberg** Germany
33 S9 **Schönewalde** Germany
36 B3 **Schönfeld** Germany
41 N2 **Schongau** Germany
32 L9 **Schönhagen** Germany
33 Q7 **Schönhausen** Germany
37 O3 **Schönheide** Germany
33 N8 **Schöningen** Germany
37 O4 **Schönsee** Germany
36 H5 **Schöntal** Germany
37 O5 **Schönthal** Germany
37 J3 **Schonungen** Germany
33 S7 **Schönwalde** Germany
33 N4 **Schönwalde am Bungsberg** Germany
95 S1 **Schoodic L** Maine U.S.A.
94 B4 **Schoolcraft** Michigan U.S.A.
25 C5 **Schoonhoven** Netherlands
25 C3 **Schoorl** Netherlands
40 G2 **Schopfheim** Germany
33 T7 **Schopfurch** Germany
33 N8 **Schöppenstedt** Germany
32 F8 **Schöppingen** Germany
36 C5 **Schorbach** France
36 H6 **Schorndorf** Germany
32 G5 **Schortens** Germany
36 G3 **Schotten** Germany
139 J8 **Schouten I** Tasmania Australia
25 A5 **Schouwen** Netherlands
100 G2 **Schrag** Washington U.S.A.
36 E7 **Schramberg** Germany
33 P10 **Schraplau** Germany
40 H4 **Schreckhorn** *mt* Switzerland
36 G2 **Schrecksbach** Germany
120 C4 **Schreiber** Ontario Canada
33 Q6 **Schrepkow** Germany
33 N5 **Schretstaken** Germany
36 F5 **Schriesheim** Germany
37 L6 **Schrobenhausen** Germany
95 O3 **Schroon Lake** New York U.S.A.
36 H5 **Schrozberg** Germany
41 L3 **Schruns** Austria
53 B7 **Schuchin** Belorussia
103 M9 **Schuchuli** Arizona U.S.A.
32 L8 **Schulenburg** Germany
109 L6 **Schulenburg** Texas U.S.A.
118 G8 **Schuler** Alberta Canada
14 B5 **Schull** Ireland
37 M1 **Schulpforta** Germany
107 P6 **Schulter** Oklahoma U.S.A.
141 K1 **Schultz Can** Brisbane, Qnsld Australia
115 K5 **Schultz L** Northwest Territories Canada
33 T8 **Schulzendorf** Germany
120 J4 **Schumacher** Ontario Canada
33 N8 **Schunter** *R* Germany
40 H4 **Schüpfheim** Switzerland
102 F3 **Schurz** Nevada U.S.A.
41 L2 **Schussen** *R* Germany
36 D7 **Schutterwald** Germany
32 F8 **Schüttorf** Germany
98 J8 **Schuyler** Nebraska U.S.A.
94 J9 **Schuyler** Virginia U.S.A.
95 L6 **Schuylkill Haven** Pennsylvania U.S.A.
33 Q5 **Schwaan** Germany
37 L5 **Schwabach** Germany
37 J7 **Schwaben** *reg* Germany
37 L7 **Schwabhausen** Germany
36 G7 **Schwäbische Alb** *mts* Germany
36 H6 **Schwäbisch Gmünd** Germany
36 H5 **Schwäbisch Hall** Germany
41 K3 **Schwägalp** Switzerland
37 M7 **Schwaig** Germany
36 G5 **Schwaigern** Germany
32 K9 **Schwalenberg** Germany
36 G2 **Schwalm** *R* Germany
38 M8 **Schwanberg** Austria
37 L5 **Schwand** Germany
41 K3 **Schwanden** Switzerland
37 N5 **Schwandorf** Germany
33 O9 **Schwanebeck** Germany
70 C5 **Schwaner Peg** *mts* Kalimantan
32 J6 **Schwanewede** Germany
32 L7 **Schwarmstedt** Germany
33 R6 **Schwarz** Germany
37 L2 **Schwarza** Germany
38 H7 **Schwarzach** Austria
37 N5 **Schwarzach** *R* Germany
37 L2 **Schwarzburg** Germany
33 S9 **Schwarze Elster** *R* Germany
37 M3 **Schwarzenbach** Germany
33 M6 **Schwarzenbek** Germany
37 K4 **Schwarzenberg** Germany
36 G2 **Schwarzenborn** Hessen Germany
36 B3 **Schwarzenborn** Rheinland-Pfalz Germany
40 F4 **Schwarzenburg** Switzerland
37 N5 **Schwarzenfeld** Germany
36 H3 **Schwarzenfels** Germany
36 B3 **Schwarzer Mann** *mt* Germany
37 O5 **Schwarzer Regen** *R* Germany
37 N5 **Schwarzhofen** Germany
40 G5 **Schwarzhorn** *mt* Switzerland
36 E7 **Schwarzwald** *mts* Germany
36 B4 **Schwarzwälder Hochwald** *mts* Germany
116 J3 **Schwatka Mts** Alaska U.S.A.
41 P3 **Schwaz** Austria
31 H2 **Schwedt** Germany
40 F4 **Schwefelberg** Switzerland
36 B4 **Schweich** Germany
36 D7 **Schweighausen** Germany
37 J2 **Schweina** Germany
33 M7 **Schweinau** Germany
37 J3 **Schweinfurt** Germany
33 S9 **Schweinitz** Germany
32 F10 **Schwelm** Germany
Schwenningen *see* **Villingen-Schwenningen**
33 O5 **Schwerin** Germany
33 O5 **Schweriner See** *L* Germany
32 G10 **Schwerte** Germany
36 F5 **Schwetzingen** Germany
33 T5 **Schwichtenberg** Germany
31 H3 **Schwielochsee** *L* Germany
33 R8 **Schwielowsee** *L* Germany
32 K5 **Schwinge** *R* Germany
33 R5 **Schwinkendorf** Germany
33 P9 **Schwittersaf** Germany
41 J3 **Schwyz** Switzerland
43 E11 **Sciacca** Sicily
43 F12 **Scicli** Sicily
21 N2 **Scie** *R* France
9 F7 **Scilly, Isles of** England
31 J4 **Ścinawa** Poland
94 K4 **Scio** New York U.S.A.
94 F6 **Scio** Ohio U.S.A.
94 D8 **Scioto** *R* Ohio U.S.A.
94 E8 **Sciotoville** Ohio U.S.A.
103 M2 **Scipio** Utah U.S.A.
119 R7 **Sclater** Manitoba Canada
8 B4 **Scleddau** Wales
48 H5 **Scoarța** Romania
98 A1 **Scobey** Montana U.S.A.
103 N2 **Scofield Res** Utah U.S.A.
118 E7 **Scollard** Alberta Canada
139 K4 **Scone** New South Wales Australia
15 E4 **Scone** Scotland
111 H9 **Scooba** Mississippi U.S.A.
21 L8 **Scorbé-Clairvaux** France
115 R3 **Scoresby Land** Greenland
115 R3 **Scoresby Sund** *Sd* Greenland
115 R3 **Scoresbysund** Greenland
20 D6 **Scorff, R** France
100 G9 **Scossa** Nevada U.S.A.
121 L7 **Scotia** Ontario Canada
102 A1 **Scotia** California U.S.A.
98 H8 **Scotia** Nebraska U.S.A.
100 H1 **Scotia** Washington U.S.A.
117 G6 **Scotia Bay** British Columbia Canada
81 A14 **Scotia Ridge** Antarctica
146 F3 **Scotia Ridge** Antarctica
81 A15 **Scotia Sea** Antarctica
146 E2 **Scotia Sea** Antarctica
15 **Scotland** U.K.
98 J6 **Scotland** South Dakota U.S.A.
109 J2 **Scotland** Texas U.S.A.
112 K1 **Scotland Neck** North Carolina U.S.A.
111 E11 **Scotlandville** Louisiana U.S.A.
122 H8 **Scots B** Nova Scotia Canada
122 K8 **Scotsburn** Nova Scotia Canada
118 J9 **Scotsguard** Saskatchewan Canada
121 T7 **Scotstown** Quebec Canada
138 E4 **Scott** *R* South Australia Australia
143 B10 **Scott** *R* W Australia Australia
118 J6 **Scott** Saskatchewan Canada
100 C8 **Scott** *R* California U.S.A.
112 E5 **Scott** Georgia U.S.A.
111 E8 **Scott** Mississippi U.S.A.
94 C6 **Scott** Ohio U.S.A.
100 C8 **Scott Bar** California U.S.A.
146 D11 **Scott Base** *N Z Base* Antarctica
89 G8 **Scottburgh** S Africa
117 J10 **Scott, C** Vancouver I, Br Col Canada
140 A2 **Scott, Cape** N Terr Australia
107 K3 **Scott City** Kansas U.S.A.
146 D12 **Scott Coast** Antarctica
94 H6 **Scottdale** Pennsylvania U.S.A.
146 D9 **Scott Glacier** Antarctica
146 H13 **Scott Glacier** Antarctica
142 E4 **Scott Headland** *mt* W Australia Australia
115 M3 **Scott Inlet** Northwest Territories Canada
117 J10 **Scott, Is** British Columbia Canada
100 C7 **Scott, Mt** Oregon U.S.A.
146 K9 **Scott Mts** Antarctica
142 D2 **Scott Reef** Indian Oc
94 B4 **Scotts** Michigan U.S.A.
98 C8 **Scottsbluff** Nebraska U.S.A.
98 C8 **Scotts Bluff Nat. Mon** Nebraska U.S.A.
110 K7 **Scottsboro** Alabama U.S.A.
94 B8 **Scottsburg** Indiana U.S.A.
100 B6 **Scottsburg** Oregon U.S.A.
94 J10 **Scottsburg** Virginia U.S.A.
139 J8 **Scottsdale** Tasmania Australia
103 N8 **Scottsdale** Arizona U.S.A.
111 L11 **Scotts Ferry** Florida U.S.A.
127 O7 **Scotts Head** Dominica
123 L7 **Scottsville** C Breton I, Nova Scotia
107 N2 **Scottsville** Kansas U.S.A.
110 K5 **Scottsville** Kentucky U.S.A.
94 J9 **Scottsville** Virginia U.S.A.
94 A3 **Scottville** Michigan U.S.A.
102 G4 **Scottys Castle** California U.S.A.
102 G4 **Scottys Junct** Nevada U.S.A.
15 C2 **Scourie** Scotland
118 L9 **Scout Lake** Saskatchewan Canada
15 E2 **Scrabster** Scotland
7 M10 **Scram** *oil rig* North Sea
110 C6 **Scranton** Arkansas U.S.A.
107 P3 **Scranton** Kansas U.S.A.
98 C3 **Scranton** North Dakota U.S.A.
95 M5 **Scranton** Pennsylvania U.S.A.
95 L3 **Scriba** New York U.S.A.
98 K8 **Scribner** Nebraska U.S.A.
15 B4 **Scridain, Loch** Scotland
44 E2 **Scrivia R** Italy
120 H10 **Scudder** Ontario Canada
121 M8 **Scugog, L** Ontario Canada
13 H6 **Scunthorpe** England
45 O5 **Scurcola Marsicana** Italy
Scutari *see* **Üsküdar**
Scutari Albania *see* **Shkodër**
112 K1 **Seaboard** North Carolina U.S.A.
109 M6 **Seabrook** Texas U.S.A.
143 C9 **Seabrook, L** W Australia Australia
143 C7 **Seabrook, Mt** W Australia Australia
144 C6 **Seacliff** New Zealand
89 D8 **Seacow** *R* S Africa
109 L7 **Seadrift** Texas U.S.A.
139 G7 **Sea Elephant B** Tasmania Australia
9 G6 **Seaford** England
95 M8 **Seaford** Delaware U.S.A.
142 C3 **Seaforth** W Australia Australia
120 J9 **Seaforth** Ontario Canada
127 M3 **Seaforth** Jamaica
119 O4 **Seager Wheeler L** Saskatchewan Canada
108 E3 **Seagraves** Texas U.S.A.
112 H2 **Seagrove** North Carolina U.S.A.
13 G4 **Seaham** England
122 G1 **Seahorse** Labrador, Nfld Canada
115 L5 **Seahorse Pt** Northwest Territories Canada
70 C2 **Seahorse Shoal** S China Sea
13 G2 **Seahouses** England
112 F6 **Sea Island** Georgia U.S.A.
95 N7 **Sea Isle City** New Jersey U.S.A.
115 K6 **Seal** *R* Manitoba Canada
139 G6 **Sea Lake** Victoria Australia
123 R1 **Seal Bight** Labrador, Nfld Canada
89 C10 **Seal C** S Africa
116 H9 **Seal C** Alaska U.S.A.
127 J4 **Seal Cays** *islds* Turks & Caicos Is
122 F9 **Seal Cove** New Brunswick Canada
123 Q4 **Seal Cove** Newfoundland Canada
111 L9 **Seale** Alabama U.S.A.
144 C5 **Seal I** New Zealand
133 F8 **Sea Lion Is** Falkland Is
139 H7 **Seal Is** Victoria Australia
115 M6 **Seal Lakes** Quebec Canada
144 A7 **Seal Pt** New Zealand
100 A5 **Seal Rock** Oregon U.S.A.
109 L6 **Sealy** Texas U.S.A.
144 C5 **Sealy, Mt** New Zealand
144 C5 **Sealy Pass** New Zealand
103 J4 **Seaman Ra** Nevada U.S.A.
13 H5 **Seamer** England
7 M9 **Sean** *oil rig* North Sea
9 H2 **Sea Palling** England
103 K6 **Searchlight** Nevada U.S.A.
120 F6 **Searchmont** Ontario Canada
110 E6 **Searcy** Arkansas U.S.A.
102 G6 **Searles** California U.S.A.
102 G6 **Searles Lake** California U.S.A.
95 T2 **Searsport** Maine U.S.A.
123 N6 **Searston** Newfoundland Canada
12 E5 **Seascale** England
102 C5 **Seaside** California U.S.A.
100 B4 **Seaside** Oregon U.S.A.
95 N7 **Seaside Heights** New Jersey U.S.A.
8 C6 **Seaton** England
100 C2 **Seattle** Washington U.S.A.
117 D5 **Seattle, Mt** Alaska/Yukon Terr U.S.A./Canada
141 H4 **Seaview Ra** Queensland Australia
95 N7 **Seaville, S** New Jersey U.S.A.
144 D5 **Seaward Kaikoura Range** New Zealand
127 P6 **Seawell** *airport* Barbados
71 K10 **Seba** Indonesia
118 C5 **Seba Beach** Alberta Canada
95 R3 **Sebago L** Maine U.S.A.
70 E5 **Sebakung** Kalimantan
89 G2 **Sebakwe** *R* Zimbabwe
70 C6 **Sebangan, Teluk** *B* Kalimantan
68 G4 **Se Bang Fai** *R* Laos
69 G12 **Sebangka** *isld* Indonesia
113 G10 **Sebastian** Florida U.S.A.
109 K9 **Sebastian** Texas U.S.A.
124 B3 **Sebastián Vizcaíno, B** Mexico
95 S2 **Sebasticook L** Maine U.S.A.
102 B3 **Sebastopol** California U.S.A.
111 G9 **Sebastopol** Mississippi U.S.A.
70 E2 **Sebatik** *isld* Borneo
70 C3 **Sebauh** Sarawak
70 B5 **Sebayan, Bukit** *mt* Kalimantan
28 D3 **Sebbersund** Denmark
99 L3 **Sebeka** Minnesota U.S.A.
78 C1 **Seben** Turkey
Sebenico *see* **Sibenik**
124 D4 **Seberi, Cerro** *mt* Mexico
48 H5 **Sebeş** *R* Romania
70 K8 **Sebesi** *isld* Sumatra
48 H5 **Sebeşului, Muntii** *mts* Romania
94 D3 **Sebewaing** Michigan U.S.A.
52 C6 **Sebezh** Russian Federation
78 G1 **Şebinkarahisar** Turkey
48 G4 **Sebis** Romania
85 B4 **Sebkha de Chinchane** Mauritania
85 B4 **Sebkha Oum el Drouss Guebli** Mauritania
85 B4 **Sebkha Oum el Drouss Telli** Mauritania
43 C13 **Sebkhat Kelbia** *L* Tunisia
85 B4 **Sebkhet Idjil** Mauritania
85 E3 **Sebkra Azzel Matti** *salt flats* Algeria
85 C3 **Sebkra de Tindouf** *salt flats* Algeria
17 G9 **Sebkra d'Oran** Algeria
85 E3 **Sebkra Mekerrhane** *salt flats* Algeria
31 H5 **Sebnitz** Germany
95 T1 **Seboeis L** Maine U.S.A.
95 R8 **Seboomook L** Maine U.S.A.
85 C2 **Sebou** *R* Morocco
110 J4 **Sebree** Kentucky U.S.A.
95 K10 **Sebrell** Virginia U.S.A.
113 F10 **Sebring** Florida U.S.A.
94 F6 **Sebring** Ohio U.S.A.
16 D9 **Sebt Beni Zarfet** Morocco
70 K8 **Sebuku** *isld* Indonesia
70 E6 **Sebuku** *isld* Kalimantan
70 B4 **Sebuyau** Sarawak
37 Q4 **Seč** Czechoslovakia
42 C4 **Secchia** *R* Italy
112 E3 **Secession L** South Carolina U.S.A.
68 G4 **Se Cham** *R* Laos
122 C1 **Séchelles, L** Quebec Canada
128 B5 **Sechura, B. de** Peru
128 B5 **Sechura, Des. de** *desert* Peru
38 L7 **Seckau** Austria
38 L7 **Seckauer Alpen** *mts* Austria
22 E2 **Seclin** France
133 D7 **Seco** *R* Argentina
17 H4 **Seco** *R* Spain
21 K8 **Secondigny** France
118 L8 **Secretan** Saskatchewan Canada
144 A6 **Secretary I** New Zealand
76 D2 **Secunderabad** India
128 E7 **Sécure** *R* Bolivia
48 E3 **Séd** *R* Hungary
52 B6 **Seda** Lithuania
16 B5 **Seda** *R* Portugal
71 L10 **Sedah** Indonesia
118 G7 **Sedalia** Alberta Canada
106 F2 **Sedalia** Colorado U.S.A.
94 D7 **Sedalia** Ohio U.S.A.
76 C2 **Sedam** India
138 E5 **Sedan** South Australia Australia
19 J3 **Sedan** France
107 O4 **Sedan** Kansas U.S.A.
106 G5 **Sedan** New Mexico U.S.A.
56 F3 **Sedannavskaya, Shiver** *falls* Russian Federation
16 E2 **Sedano** Spain
13 F5 **Sedbergh** England
145 E4 **Seddon** New Zealand
115 O2 **Seddon, Kap** *C* Greenland
144 C4 **Seddonville** New Zealand
47 H4 **Seddülbahir** Turkey
79 E8 **Sede Boqer** Israel
80 B7 **Sede Dawid** Israel
80 F1 **Sede Eli'ezer** Israel
80 F4 **Sede Eliyyahu** Israel
47 N11 **Sedef** *isld* Turkey
55 G3 **Sedel'nikovo** Russian Federation
80 C7 **Sede Moshe** Israel
80 F1 **Sede Neẹmya** Israel
19 P16 **Séderon** France
80 B7 **Sederot** Israel
80 D3 **Sede Ya'aqov** Israel
80 G2 **Sede Yaaqov** Syria
80 B8 **Sede Zevi** Israel
9 E3 **Sedgeberrow** England
13 G4 **Sedgefield** England
8 D2 **Sedgley** England
106 H1 **Sedgwick** Colorado U.S.A.
107 N4 **Sedgwick** Kansas U.S.A.
95 T2 **Sedgwick** Maine U.S.A.
69 E12 **Sedinginan** Sumatra
70 E6 **Sedjaka** Kalimantan
31 H6 **Sedlčany** Czechoslovakia
9 G6 **Sedlescombe** England
119 O8 **Sedley** Saskatchewan Canada
79 F7 **Sedom** Israel
103 N7 **Sedona** Arizona U.S.A.
68 G5 **Se Done** *R* Laos
80 C7 **Sedot Mikha** Israel
80 C4 **Sedot Yam** Israel
100 C1 **Sedro Woolley** Washington U.S.A.
70 E4 **Sedulang** Kalimantan
52 B6 **Šeduva** Lithuania
20 H4 **See** *R* France
33 O4 **Seebad Heringsdorf** Germany
118 C7 **Seebe** Alberta Canada
37 K2 **Seebergen** Germany
33 P10 **Seeburg** Germany
41 O3 **Seefeld** Austria
33 T7 **Seefeld** Germany
40 G2 **Seefelden** Germany
33 O8 **Seehausen** Germany
36 F4 **Seeheim** Germany
87 C11 **Seeheim** Namibia
36 D7 **Seelbach** Germany
101 M2 **Seeley Lake** Montana U.S.A.
121 O8 **Seeleys Bay** Ontario Canada
146 D8 **Seelig, Mt** Antarctica
33 R10 **Seelingstädt** Germany
36 C2 **Seelscheid** Germany
32 L8 **Seelze** Germany
28 B6 **Seem** Denmark
70 P10 **Seemanandjung** Java
33 S10 **Seerhausen** Germany
41 J2 **Seerücken** *mt* Switzerland
21 L4 **Sées** France
32 M9 **Seesen** Germany
41 O2 **Seeshaupt** Germany
38 L7 **Seetaler Alpen** *mts* Austria
32 M6 **Seevetal** Germany
41 K3 **Seez** *R* Switzerland
47 H6 **Seferihisar** Turkey
17 G9 **Sefioun** *R* Algeria
85 D2 **Sefrou** Morocco
144 D5 **Sefton** New Zealand
144 C5 **Sefton, Mt** New Zealand
70 F2 **Segama** *R* Sabah
69 F11 **Segamat** Malaysia
70 M9 **Segara Anakan** Java
48 H6 **Şegarcea** Romania
71 B2 **Segea** Halmahera Indonesia
86 G4 **Segen** *watercourse* Ethiopia
56 F4 **Segentuy** Russian Federation
70 F7 **Segeri** Sulawesi
43 E11 **Segesta** Sicily
71 C3 **Seget** W Irian
52 D3 **Segezha** Russian Federation
57 D3 **Segiz, Ozero** *L* Kazakhstan
20 D5 **Seglien** France
41 K4 **Segnes Pass** Switzerland
45 O6 **Segni** Italy
103 P2 **Sego** Utah U.S.A.
17 G5 **Segorbe** Spain
85 C6 **Segou** Mali
16 E3 **Segovia** *prov* Spain
16 E4 **Segovia** Spain
108 H5 **Segovia** Texas U.S.A.
52 D3 **Segozero, Oz** *L* Russian Federation
21 J6 **Segré** France
17 H2 **Segre** *R* Spain
21 L5 **Segrie** France
84 E5 **Séguedine** Niger
85 C7 **Séguéla** Ivory Coast
124 J5 **Seguín** Mexico
107 K2 **Seguin** Kansas U.S.A.
109 K6 **Seguin** Texas U.S.A.
133 E4 **Segundo** *R* Argentina
106 F4 **Segundo** Colorado U.S.A.
17 F6 **Segura** *R* Spain
17 F6 **Segura, Sa de** *mts* Spain
32 L8 **Sehnde** Germany
71 J5 **Seho** *isld* Indonesia
71 A2 **Sehu** Halmahera Indonesia
74 B5 **Sehwan** Pakistan
100 B8 **Seiad Valley** California U.S.A.
37 L3 **Seibelsdorf** Germany
106 H2 **Seibert** Colorado U.S.A.
127 K5 **Seibo** Dominican Rep
20 H6 **Seiche** *R* France
21 K6 **Seiches** France
80 D4 **Seidā** Jordan
80 F3 **Seidur** Jordan
140 E4 **Seigals Creek** N Terr Australia
122 C1 **Seignelay, R** Quebec Canada
68 B2 **Seikpyu** Burma
68 B2 **Seiktein** Burma
12 C1 **Seil** *isld* Scotland
26 N1 **Seiland** *isld* Norway
18 G7 **Seilhac** France
107 M5 **Seiling** Oklahoma U.S.A.
19 K4 **Seille** *R* France
29 K9 **Seinäjoki** Finland
21 N3 **Seine** *R* France
21 K2 **Seine, B. de la** France
18 H4 **Seine-et-Marne** *dept* France
18 F3 **Seine-Maritime** *dept* France
21 P4 **Seine-St. Denis** *dept* France
20 A5 **Sein, I. de** France
113 E10 **Seista Key** *isld* Florida U.S.A.
38 L5 **Seitenstetten** Austria
18 F10 **Seix** France
69 J12 **Sejangkung** Indonesia
28 G5 **Sejerø** Denmark
28 G5 **Sejerø** *isld* Denmark
28 B3 **Sejerslev** Denmark
28 E3 **Sejflod** Denmark
31 O1 **Sejny** Poland
28 D4 **Sejs** Denmark
28 B6 **Sejstrup** Denmark
70 B5 **Sekadau** Kalimantan
70 D6 **Sekakajang** Kalimantan
69 G13 **Sekanak, Teluk** *B* Sumatra
69 F12 **Sekapil** Sumatra
70 E3 **Sekatak Bengarao** Kalimantan
69 F14 **Sekayu** Sumatra
88 E4 **Sekenke** Tanzania
61 K10 **Seki** Japan
70 K8 **Sekicau** *mt* Sumatra
89 C5 **Sekoma** Botswana
85 D7 **Sekondi** Ghana
86 G3 **Sek'ota** Ethiopia
77 G4 **Sekuheh** Iran
69 J12 **Sekura** Indonesia
69 E14 **Selagan** *R* Sumatra
100 E3 **Selah** Washington U.S.A.
69 J12 **Selakau** Indonesia
70 B4 **Selalang** Sarawak
69 E10 **Selama** Malaysia
69 E11 **Selangor** Malaysia
68 H4 **Se La Nong** *R* Laos
29 M10 **Selänpää** Finland
68 F4 **Selaphum** Thailand
70 D7 **Selatan, Tg** *C* Kalimantan
69 D13 **Selat Bungalaut** *str* Indonesia
69 D13 **Selat Mentawai** *str* Indonesia
69 F12 **Selat Panjang** *R* Sumatra
69 F12 **Selatpanjang** Sumatra
69 D13 **Selat Siberut** *str* Sumatra
69 D14 **Selat Sipura** *str* Indonesia
116 H3 **Selawik** Alaska U.S.A.
116 G3 **Selawik L** Alaska U.S.A.
37 N3 **Selb** Germany
37 M3 **Selbitz** Germany
27 A12 **Selbjörnfj** *inlet* Norway
26 E8 **Selbusjö** *L* Norway
13 G6 **Selby** England
98 F4 **Selby** South Dakota U.S.A
116 K3 **Selby, L** Alaska U.S.A.
95 M8 **Selbyville** Delaware U.S.A
28 C3 **Selde** Denmark
107 K2 **Selden** Kansas U.S.A.
123 S4 **Seldom** Newfoundland Canada
116 M7 **Seldovia** Alaska U.S.A.
43 G8 **Sele** *R* Italy
71 C3 **Sele** W Irian
87 E10 **Selebi Phikwe** Botswana
59 K1 **Selemdzha** *R* Russian Federation
47 K6 **Selendi** Turkey
56 G5 **Selenga** *R* Russian Federation
86 C6 **Selenge** Zaire
58 E2 **Selenge Mörön** *R* Mongolia
56 G5 **Selenginsk** Russian Federation
46 D4 **Selenicë** Albania
51 O2 **Selennyakh** *R* Russian Federation
33 M4 **Selent** Germany
33 M4 **Selenter See** *L* Germany
71 C3 **Sele, Selat** *str* W Irian
40 F1 **Sélestat** France
55 F4 **Seleti** *R* Kazakhstan
28 S10 **Selfoss** Iceland
98 F3 **Selfridge** North Dakota U.S.A.
85 B5 **Selibaby** Mauritania
54 F4 **Selichnya** Russian Federation
36 F3 **Seligenstadt** Germany
52 D6 **Seliger, Oz** *L* Russian Federation
103 M6 **Seligman** Arizona U.S.A.
110 C5 **Seligman** Missouri U.S.A.
84 H5 **Selima Oasis** Sudan
70 C4 **Selimbau** Kalimantan
47 J7 **Selimiye** Turkey
85 C6 **Selingue, Lac de** *res* Mali
46 E7 **Selinoús** Greece
95 L6 **Selinsgrove** Pennsylvania U.S.A.
55 F1 **Seliyarovo** Russian Federation
52 D6 **Selizharovo** Russian Federation
33 O9 **Selke** *R* Germany
Selkirk *co see* **Borders** *reg*
119 V8 **Selkirk** Manitoba Canada
13 F2 **Selkirk** Scotland
107 J3 **Selkirk** Kansas U.S.A.
94 C2 **Selkirk** Michigan U.S.A.
117 O10 **Selkirk Mts** Br Col/Idaho Canada/U.S.A.
119 S5 **Selkirk T** Manitoba Canada
12 E5 **Sellafield** England
20 G6 **Sel, le** France
21 P2 **Selle** *R* France
100 D2 **Selleck** Washington U.S.A.
94 B8 **Sellersburg** Indiana U.S.A.
21 O7 **Selles-St. Denis** France
21 O7 **Selles-sur-Cher** France
141 H5 **Sellheim** *R* Queensland Australia
40 C4 **Sellières** France
9 G5 **Sellindge** England
41 O3 **Sellrain** Austria
103 N10 **Sells** Arizona U.S.A.
32 F9 **Selm** Germany
111 J9 **Selma** Alabama U.S.A.
111 D10 **Selma** Louisiana U.S.A.
112 J2 **Selma** North Carolina U.S.A.
100 B7 **Selma** Oregon U.S.A.
110 H6 **Selmer** Tennessee U.S.A.
33 N5 **Selmsdorf** Germany
21 N6 **Selommes** France
70 Q10 **Selong** Indonesia
40 B2 **Selongey** France
19 Q16 **Sélonnet** France
88 F6 **Selous Game Res** Tanzania
117 G4 **Selous, Mt** Yukon Territory Canada
71 C3 **Selpele** Indonesia
83 K12 **Sel Pt** Mahé I Indian Oc
9 F6 **Selsey** England
32 K6 **Selsingen** Germany
36 D2 **Selters** Germany
54 F3 **Sel'tso** Russian Federation
52 H6 **Selty** Russian Federation
36 E6 **Seltz** France
33 S5 **Seltz** Germany
69 H10 **Seluan** *isld* Indonesia
69 H14 **Selui** *isld* Indonesia
20 H4 **Selune** *R* France
133 E3 **Selva** Argentina
38 E8 **Selva di V. Gardena** Italy
128 D5 **Selvas** *forests* Brazil
45 L1 **Selvazzano Dentro** Italy
117 H4 **Selwyn Mts** Yukon Territory Canada
140 F5 **Selwyn Ra** Queensland Australia
48 J3 **Selyatin** Ukraine
52 G3 **Sel'yb** Russian Federation
36 E4 **Selz** *R* Germany
98 G2 **Selz** North Dakota U.S.A.
40 F3 **Selzach** Switzerland
38 K6 **Selzthal** Austria
70 E5 **Semajang, D** *L* Kalimantan
21 L5 **Semallé** France
46 D4 **Seman** *R* Albania
70 K8 **Semang Ka, Teluk** *B* Sumatra
79 G2 **Sem'ān, Jebel** *mts* Syria
119 N7 **Semans** Saskatchewan Canada
85 B3 **Semara, Es** Western Sahara
70 N9 **Semarang** Java
71 L10 **Semau** *isld* Timor Indonesia
88 C2 **Sembabule** Uganda
70 E3 **Sembakung** *R* Kalimantan
86 B5 **Sembé** Congo
21 M6 **Semblançay** France
52 F6 **Semenov** Russian Federation
54 D4 **Semenovka** Chernigovskaya obl Ukraine
54 E7 **Semenovka** Poltavskaya obl Ukraine
52 G6 **Semenovo** Russian Federation
52 F5 **Semenovskoye** Kostromskaya obl Russian Federation
52 F5 **Sementsovo** Russian Federation
70 O10 **Semeru** Java
116 J8 **Semidi Is** Alaska U.S.A.
52 F5 **Semigorodnyaya** Russian Federation
54 M9 **Semikarakorsk** Russian Federation
31 J5 **Semily** Czechoslovakia
111 G10 **Seminary** Mississippi U.S.A.
101 T7 **Seminoe Dam** Wyoming U.S.A.
101 T7 **Seminoe Res** Wyoming U.S.A.
107 O6 **Seminole** Oklahoma U.S.A.
108 E3 **Seminole** Texas U.S.A.
111 M11 **Seminole, L** Georgia U.S.A.
56 C5 **Seminsky Khrebet** *mts* Russian Federation
55 D4 **Semiozernoye** Kazakhstan
56 B5 **Semipalatinsk** Kazakhstan
55 E4 **Semipolka** Kazakhstan
71 E5 **Semirara** *isld* Philippines
77 B4 **Semīrom** Iran
70 C4 **Semitau** Kalimantan
69 H10 **Semium** *isld* Indonesia
55 G5 **Semiyarka** Kazakhstan
55 F5 **Semiz-Bugu** Kazakhstan
33 R4 **Semlow** Germany
33 T7 **Semmelberg** *mt* Germany
38 N6 **Semmering** Austria
86 F1 **Semna** Sudan
77 C2 **Semnān** Iran
20 G6 **Semnon** *R* France
22 J4 **Semois** *R* Belgium
89 F3 **Semokwe** *R* Zimbabwe
70 E1 **Sempang Mangayau, Tg** *C* Sabah
70 F2 **Semporna** Sabah
45 O6 **Semprevisa** *mt* Italy
70 O10 **Sempu** *isld* Java
26 H5 **Semskefjell** *mt* Norway
129 H4 **Sem Tripa** Brazil
88 E3 **Semu** *R* Tanzania
18 H5 **Semur-en-Auxois** France
89 F2 **Semwe** *R* Zimbabwe
52 F2 **Semzha** Russian Federation
128 E6 **Sena** Bolivia
88 E10 **Sena** Mozambique
129 L5 **Senador Pompeu** Brazil
70 E1 **Senaja** Sabah
53 F12 **Senaki** Georgia
128 E5 **Sena Madureira** Brazil
87 D9 **Senango** Zambia
70 B4 **Senaning** Kalimantan
21 O2 **Sénarpont** France
19 O17 **Sénas** France
118 H9 **Senate** Saskatchewan Canada
110 F5 **Senath** Missouri U.S.A.
111 G7 **Senatobia** Mississippi U.S.A.
69 G13 **Senayang** Indonesia
61 O7 **Sendai** Honshu Japan
60 D14 **Sendai** Kyūshū Japan
60 D14 **Sendai-gawa** *R* Japan
87 C11 **Sendelingsdrif** Namibia
37 J7 **Senden** Germany
32 G9 **Sendenhorst** Germany
16 C3 **Sendim** Portugal
70 B5 **Senduruhan** Kalimantan
74 F8 **Sendwha** India
69 E11 **Senebui, Tg** *C* Sumatra
99 S8 **Seneca** Illinois U.S.A.
107 O2 **Seneca** Kansas U.S.A.
110 B5 **Seneca** Missouri U.S.A.
98 F7 **Seneca** Nebraska U.S.A.
100 G5 **Seneca** Oregon U.S.A.
112 E3 **Seneca** South Carolina U.S.A.
98 G4 **Seneca** South Dakota U.S.A.
95 L4 **Seneca L** New York U.S.A.
94 F7 **Seneca Lake** Ohio U.S.A.
94 F7 **Senecaville** Ohio U.S.A.
22 G2 **Seneffe** Belgium
85 B5 **Sénégal** *R* W Africa
85 B6 **Senegal** *rep* W Africa
87 E11 **Senekal** S Africa
99 V3 **Seney** Michigan U.S.A.
30 H4 **Senftenberg** Germany
87 F7 **Senga Hill** Zambia
70 E4 **Sengata** Kalimantan
52 H1 **Sengeyskiy, Ostrov** *isld* Russian Federation
56 E5 **Sengilen, Khrebet** *mts* Russian Federation
38 K6 **Sengsengebirge** *mts* Austria
133 C7 **Senguerr** *R* Argentina
88 B10 **Sengwa** *R* Zimbabwe
32 H5 **Sengwärden** Germany
87 E9 **Sengwe** *R* Zimbabwe
129 K6 **Senhor do Bonfim** Brazil
45 O4 **Senigallia** Italy
45 L3 **Senio** *R* Italy
80 F1 **Senir** Israel
43 G8 **Senise** Italy
42 F4 **Senj** Croatia
26 J2 **Senja** *isld* Norway
67 H4 **Senkaku-shotō** *isld* Japan
52 H2 **Sen'kina** Russian Federation
79 G2 **Senköy** Turkey
118 H6 **Senlac** Saskatchewan Canada
65 H3 **Senlin Shan** *mt* China
68 H6 **Senmonorom** Cambodia
86 F3 **Sennar** Sudan
32 J9 **Senne** *reg* Germany
40 A4 **Sennecey le Grand** France
32 J9 **Sennelager** Germany
28 B3 **Sennels** Denmark
121 N4 **Senneterre** Quebec Canada
21 L2 **Senneville** France
54 A2 **Senno** Belorussia
8 C4 **Sennybridge** Wales
133 C8 **Seno Almirantazgo** *G* Chile
68 G4 **Se Noi** *R* Laos
111 M8 **Senoia** Georgia U.S.A.
21 N4 **Senonches** France
19 K4 **Senones** France
133 C8 **Seno Otway** *G* Chile
133 C8 **Seno Skyring** *G* Chile
18 H4 **Sens** France
20 G5 **Sens-de-Bretagne** France
40 F4 **Sense R** Switzerland
48 F5 **Senta** Serbia Yugoslavia
70 B4 **Sentarum** *L* Kalimantan
18 F10 **Sentem** France
103 L9 **Sentinel** Arizona U.S.A.
109 H1 **Sentinel** Oklahoma U.S.A.
98 C3 **Sentinel Butte** North Dakota U.S.A.
117 N8 **Sentinel Pk** British Columbia Canada
146 C7 **Sentinel Ra** Antarctica
124 G7 **Sentispac** Mexico
22 H5 **Senuc** France
70 E4 **Senyiur** Kalimantan
78 H3 **Şenyurt** Turkey
56 C4 **Senzas** Russian Federation
33 R7 **Senzke** Germany
74 H7 **Seoni** India
Seoul *see* **Sŏul**
63 **Seoul** *conurbation* China
70 E5 **Sepan** Kalimantan
70 P9 **Sepandjang** Indonesia
70 C5 **Sepangsimin** Kalimantan
106 B9 **Separ** New Mexico U.S.A.
142 E6 **Separation Well** W Australia Australia
70 E4 **Sepasu** Kalimantan
70 B4 **Sepauk** Kalimantan
130 G8 **Sepetiba, B. de** Brazil
77 C4 **Sepidān** Fārs Iran
136 J2 **Sepik** *R* Papua New Guinea
70 F4 **Sepinang** Kalimantan
70 D3 **Seping** *R* Sarawak
45 R7 **Sepino** Italy
21 M7 **Sepmes** France
31 K2 **Sępolno** Poland
68 H4 **Sepone** Laos
31 N1 **Sępopol** Poland
130 B4 **Sepotuba** *R* Brazil
32 F9 **Seppenrade** Germany
19 N13 **Septême** France
19 O18 **Septêmes les Valdonne** France
46 G2 **Septemvri** Bulgaria
21 O4 **Septeuil** France
21 J5 **Sept-Forges** France
122 F3 **Sept Îles** Quebec Canada
20 D4 **Sept Isles, les** France
122 B2 **Sept-Milles, L** Quebec Canada
16 E3 **Sepúlveda** Spain
70 K8 **Seputih** *R* Sumatra
112 B2 **Sequatchie** *R* Tennessee U.S.A.
16 D3 **Sequillo** *R* Spain
100 B1 **Sequim** Washington U.S.A.
102 F5 **Sequoia Nat. Park** California U.S.A.
71 O9 **Sera** Indonesia
22 G4 **Seraincourt** France
22 K2 **Seraing** Belgium
71 J9 **Seraja** *isld* Indonesia
70 P10 **Seraja, G** *mt* Indonesia
70 M9 **Seraju** *R* Java
57 B6 **Serakhs** Turkmenistan
136 F2 **Seram** *isld* Moluccas Indonesia
136 F2 **Seram Sea** Indonesia
70 L9 **Serang** Java
69 J11 **Serasan** *isld* Indonesia
69 J11 **Seraya** Indonesia
46 D1 **Serbia** *rep* Yugoslavia
45 H4 **Serchio** *R* Italy
86 H3 **Serdo** Ethiopia
53 F7 **Serdobsk** Russian Federation
55 F3 **Serebryanoye** Russian Federation
56 B6 **Serebryansk** Kazakhstan
54 K2 **Serebryanyye Prudy** Russian Federation
88 F5 **Serebu** *mt* Tanzania
52 F5 **Sereda** Russian Federation
54 G2 **Seredeyskiy** Russian Federation
52 C5 **Seredka** Russian Fèderation
78 D2 **Şereflikoçhisar** Turkey
18 H5 **Serein** *R* France
69 E11 **Seremban** Malaysia
71 C3 **Seremuk** *R* W Irian
88 E3 **Serengeti Nat. Park** Tanzania
88 C8 **Serenje** Zambia
20 F6 **Serent** France
48 K1 **Seret** *R* Ukraine
56 D3 **Serezh** *R* Russian Federation
52 F6 **Serezha** *R* Russian Federation
46 G7 **Serfopoúla** *isld* Greece
52 G6 **Sergach** Russian Federation
98 K7 **Sergeant Bluff** Iowa U.S.A.
58 E2 **Sergelen** Mongolia
87 E7 **Serge Tshimbo** Zaire
55 E4 **Sergeyevka** Kokchetavskaya obl Kazakhstan
55 G3 **Sergeyevka** Novosibirskaya obl Russian Federation
55 E1 **Serginskiy** Russian Federation
129 L6 **Sergipe** *state* Brazil
54 K1 **Sergiyev Posad** Russian Federation
52 E2 **Sergozero, Oz** *L* Russian Federation
70 D2 **Seria** Brunei

Seriana, Val — Shoshone Cavern Nat. Mon 225

41 L6 Seriana, Val Italy
69 D11 Seribudolok Sumatra
130 H9 Seridó R Brazil
21 O3 Sérifontaine France
46 G7 Sérifos isld Greece
20 C5 Serignac France
19 N16 Sérignan France
68 D5 Serim Burma
142 D2 Seringapatam Reef Indian Oc
129 H5 Seringa, Serra da mts Brazil
45 R8 Serino Italy
41 L7 Serio R Italy
85 F4 Serkout, Dj mt Algeria
138 E4 Serle, Mt South Australia Australia
21 P5 Sermaises France
71 O9 Sermata isld Indonesia
45 K1 Sermide Italy
45 N6 Sermoneta Italy
38 H9 Sernio mt Italy
33 U6 Sernitz R Germany
33 Q8 Serno Germany
60 T2 Sernovodsk Russian Federation
57 A5 Sernyy-Zavod Turkmenistan
31 N3 Serock Poland
126 A2 Seroe Colorado Aruba W Indies
17 F7 Serón Spain
85 F4 Serouenout Algeria
55 D2 Serov Russian Federation
89 E4 Serowe Botswana
16 B7 Serpa Portugal
87 C8 Serpa Pinto Angola
43 C9 Serpeddi, Pta mt Sardinia
116 E4 Serpentine Hot Springs Alaska U.S.A.
138 A3 Serpentine Lakes South Australia Australia
143 B9 Serpentine, R W Australia Australia
122 A3 Serpent, R. au Quebec Canada
128 F1 Serpents Mouth str Venezuela
17 G6 Serpis R Spain
54 J2 Serpukhov Russian Federation
21 O2 Serqueux Seine-Inférieure France
21 M3 Serquigny France
130 H7 Serra Brazil
45 L4 Serra, Alpe di mts Italy
130 E10 Serra Alta Brazil
130 F4 Serra Bonita Brazil
130 F4 Serra das Araras Brazil
129 H3 Serra do Navio Brazil
33 Q5 Serrahn Germany
46 F3 Sérrai Greece
45 J3 Serramazzoni Italy
125 O2 Serrana Bank Caribbean
125 P2 Serranilla Bank Caribbean
43 G10 Serra San Bruno Italy
43 C11 Serrat, Cape C Tunisia
45 J4 Serravalle Pistojese Italy
22 F4 Serre R France
18 G10 Serrére, Pic de mt France
19 P16 Serres France
133 D4 Serrezuela Argentina
19 N14 Serrières France
129 L6 Serrinha Brazil
45 M4 Serriola, Bocca pass Italy
43 B12 Sers Tunisia
16 B5 Sertã Portugal
130 F7 Sertãozinho Brazil
70 K9 Sertung isld Sumatra
69 D10 Seruai Sumatra
70 C6 Serujan R Kalimantan
89 E3 Serule Botswana
40 E2 Servance France
46 E4 Sérvia Greece
100 E5 Service Creek Oregon U.S.A.
138 F6 Serviceton Victoria Australia
106 E5 Servilleta New Mexico U.S.A.
71 N9 Serwaro Indonesia
66 F5 Sêrxü China
22 G4 Séry France
22 E4 Séry-les-Mezières France
68 G4 Se Sang Soi R Laos
70 E3 Sesatap Kalimantan
88 D2 Sese Is Uganda
120 K4 Sesekinika Ontario Canada
71 A3 Sesepe Indonesia
87 B9 Sesfontein Namibia
87 D9 Sesheka Zambia
41 H7 Sesia R Italy
16 A6 Sesimbra Portugal
26 N6 Seskarön isld Sweden
47 Q14 Seskli isld Greece
61 P12 Sesoko-jima isld Okinawa
43 F7 Sessa Aurunca Italy
36 D6 Sessenheim France
110 G3 Sesser Illinois U.S.A.
37 K3 Sesslach Germany
71 K9 Sessok Flores Indonesia
45 M4 Sestino Italy
45 K4 Sesto Fiorentino Italy
31 O1 Seštokai Lithuania
45 J3 Sestola Italy
52 E6 Sestra R Russian Federation
44 E3 Sestri Italy
44 F3 Sestri Levante Italy
29 O11 Sestroretsk Russian Federation
60 D12 Setaka Japan
60 N3 Setana Japan
9 G2 Setchey England
18 H9 Sète France
130 G6 Sete Lagoas Brazil
130 D8 Sete Quedas, Ilha Grande ou isld Brazil
27 B12 Setesdal Norway
94 F8 Seth West Virginia U.S.A.
85 F1 Sétif Algeria
60 C13 Seto Japan
60 F12 Seto Naikai sea Japan
60 G11 Seto Naikai Nat. Park Japan
68 B4 Setsan Burma
85 C2 Settat Morocco
86 A6 Sette Cama Gabon
119 U1 Settee L Manitoba Canada
119 T3 Setting L Manitoba Canada
13 F5 Settle England
140 E3 Settlement Cr Queensland Australia
90 C15 Settlement of Edinburgh Tristan da Cunha
16 B6 Setúbal Portugal
37 M5 Seubersdorf Germany
Seu d'Urgell, la see Seo de Urgel
37 K5 Seukendorf Germany
55 E1 Seul' R Russian Federation
99 V4 Seul Choix Pt Michigan U.S.A.
69 B10 Seulimeum Sumatra
115 K7 Seul, Lac Ontario Canada
21 J3 Seulles R France
69 C11 Seumayan Sumatra
40 B3 Seurre France
78 K1 Sevan, Ozero Armenia
53 D11 Sevastopol' Ukraine
54 H6 Sev Donets R Rus Fed/Ukraine
28 B4 Sevel Denmark
100 J4 Seven Devils Mts Idaho U.S.A.
140 D3 Seven Emu N Terr Australia
14 C5 Seven Hd Ireland
122 F3 Seven Is. Bay Quebec Canada
106 C6 Seven Lakes New Mexico U.S.A.
9 G5 Sevenoaks England
118 G9 Seven Persons Alberta Canada
109 J7 Seven Sisters Texas U.S.A.
112 K2 Seven Springs North Carolina U.S.A.
141 K6 Seventeen Seventy Queensland Australia
102 F1 Seven Troughs Nevada U.S.A.
117 N10 Seventy Mile House British Columbia Canada
25 F6 Sevenum Netherlands
20 F6 Sévérac France
18 H8 Séverac-le-Château France
107 P2 Severance Kansas U.S.A.
139 K3 Severn R New South Wales Australia
121 L8 Severn R Ontario Canada
52 J4 Severnaya Mylva R Russian Federation
51 K1 Severnaya Zemlya arch Arctic Oc
55 G3 Severnoye Russian Federation
8 D4 Severn, R England
55 D3 Severnyy Russian Federation
52 J3 Severnyy Ural mts Russian Federation
56 G3 Severobaykal'sk Russian Federation
51 L3 Severo-Baykal'skoye Nagor'ye uplands Russian Federation
37 P3 Severocesky Kraj reg Czechoslovakia
52 E3 Severodvinsk Russian Federation
55 E4 Severo-Kazakhstanskaya Oblast' prov Kazakhstan
31 K6 Severomoravský reg Czechoslovakia
52 D1 Severomorsk Russian Federation
53 F11 Severo-Osetinskaya Respublika Russian Federation
55 C1 Severouralsk Russian Federation
54 K2 Severo Zadonsk Russian Federation
107 O4 Severy Kansas U.S.A.
20 H3 Séves R France
29 O2 Sevettijarvi Finland
56 D5 Sevi Russian Federation
103 M2 Sevier R Utah U.S.A.
103 M3 Sevier Utah U.S.A.
103 M2 Sevier Bridge Res Utah U.S.A.
103 M2 Sevier Des Utah U.S.A.
112 D2 Sevierville Tennessee U.S.A.
20 F5 Sévignac France
22 G4 Sevigny France
126 F4 Sevilla R Cuba
16 D7 Sevilla prov Spain
16 D7 Sevilla Spain
Seville see Sevilla
46 G2 Sevlievo Bulgaria
48 J2 Sevola mt Ukraine
21 J8 Sèvre R France
18 E6 Sèvre-Niortaise R France
40 B5 Sevron R France
54 F4 Sevsk Russian Federation
85 B7 Sewa R Sierra Leone
110 L6 Sewanee Tennessee U.S.A.
116 N6 Seward Alaska U.S.A.
107 M3 Seward Kansas U.S.A.
98 J9 Seward Nebraska U.S.A.
107 N6 Seward Oklahoma U.S.A.
94 H6 Seward Pennsylvania U.S.A.
116 R6 Seward Glacier Yukon Terr/Alaska Canada/U.S.A.
146 D6 Seward Mts Antarctica
116 E4 Seward Pen Alaska U.S.A.
133 C4 Sewell Chile
40 E2 Sewen France
94 G6 Sewickley Pennsylvania U.S.A.
117 O8 Sexsmith Alberta Canada
124 G4 Sextín Mexico
77 H3 Seyah Band Koh mts Afghanistan
43 B12 Seybouse R Algeria
83 J12 Seychelles rep Indian Oc
33 R9 Seyda Germany
52 K2 Seyda Russian Federation
29 T9 Seydhisfjördhur Iceland
78 C3 Seydişehir Turkey
20 G3 Seye R France
78 E3 Seyhan R Turkey
79 F1 Seyhan Barajı res Turkey
47 L5 Seyit R Turkey
47 L5 Seyitgazi Turkey
54 D5 Seym R Ukraine
139 H6 Seymour Victoria Australia
95 O5 Seymour Connecticut U.S.A.
94 B8 Seymour Indiana U.S.A.
110 C1 Seymour Iowa U.S.A.
110 D4 Seymour Missouri U.S.A.
109 H2 Seymour Texas U.S.A.
99 S5 Seymour Wisconsin U.S.A.
140 C6 Seymour Ra N Terr Australia
19 Q16 Seyne-les-Alpes France
42 F3 Sežana Slovenia
18 H4 Sezanne France
52 D6 Sezha R Russian Federation
45 O6 Sezze Italy
85 G2 Sfax Tunisia
46 F9 Sfinári Crete Greece
48 K5 Sfîntu Gheorghe Romania
48 M6 Sfîntu Gheorghe R Romania
's-Gravenhage see Den Haag
25 B5 's-Gravenzande Netherlands
15 D3 Sgurr Mor mt Scotland
80 D2 Sha'ab Israel
80 F1 Sha'al Syria
58 E4 Shaanxi prov China
80 F3 Sha'ar Israel
87 E7 Shaba reg Zaire
Shabani see Zvishavane
119 O2 Shabaqua Ontario Canada
99 S8 Shabbona Illinois U.S.A.
84 H5 Shab, El Egypt
53 E10 Shabel'skoye Russian Federation
78 K2 Shabestar Iran
79 F9 Shabibī, J. esh mt Jordan
47 J1 Shabla Bulgaria
86 E6 Shabunda Zaire
55 D2 Shaburovo Russian Federation
67 B3 Shachang China
66 B4 Shache China
118 J8 Shackleton Saskatchewan Canada
146 D11 Shackleton Coast Antarctica
146 D10 Shackleton Glacier Antarctica
146 H13 Shackleton Ice Shelf Antarctica
146 D10 Shackleton Inlet Antarctica
146 F7 Shackleton Ra Antarctica
78 H3 Shadādah, Ash Syria
74 B5 Shadadkot Pakistan
68 C3 Shadaw Burma
98 D4 Shadehill Res South Dakota U.S.A.
67 E3 Shadi China
55 D3 Shadrinsk Russian Federation
84 J4 Shadwân Egypt
111 K10 Shady Grove Alabama U.S.A.
113 D7 Shady Grove Florida U.S.A.
146 C12 Shafer Peak mt Antarctica
57 C4 Shafirkan Uzbekistan
55 C4 Shafranovo Russian Federation
102 E6 Shafter California U.S.A.
101 L9 Shafter Nevada U.S.A.
108 C6 Shafter Texas U.S.A.
8 D5 Shaftesbury England
55 G5 Shagan R Kazakhstan
65 E4 Shagang China
48 M5 Shagany, Oz L Ukraine
Shagedu see Jungar Qi
55 F4 Shaglyteniz, Oz L Kazakhstan
56 D5 Shagonar Russian Federation
144 C6 Shag R New Zealand
57 A2 Shagray, Plato plateau Kazakhstan
146 E1 Shag Rocks S Georgia S Atlantic Oc
76 C2 Shahabad India
76 B3 Shahapur India
80 B7 Shahar Israel
74 C6 Shahbadpur Pakistan
74 B6 Shahbandar Pakistan
75 J7 Shahdol India
65 C6 Shahe China
65 D6 Shahe China
67 E2 Shahezhen China
Shahezi see Wan Xian
77 K2 Shah Fuladi mt Afghanistan
84 G3 Shaḥḥāt Libya
Shāhī see Qāem Shahr
74 H5 Shahjahanpur India
77 E1 Shāh Jehān, Kuh-e mts Iran
77 K3 Shāh Jūy Afghanistan
65 E4 Shahousuo China
74 G7 Shahpur India
74 F6 Shahpura India
77 J2 Shahrak Afghanistan
77 G3 Shāhrakht Iran
77 D4 Shahr-e Bābak Iran
77 B3 Shahr-e Kord Iran
77 B2 Shahr Rey Iran
77 D2 Shahrud Bustam Iran
77 F5 Shāh Savāran, Kūh-e mts Iran
55 D1 Shaim Russian Federation
79 H4 Shā'īr, Jabal mt Syria
80 G3 Shajara Jordan
65 F4 Shajianzi China
52 E6 Shakhovskaya Russian Federation
57 D5 Shakhrisabz Uzbekistan
59 M2 Shakhtersk Sakhalin Russian Federation
54 K8 Shakhtersk Ukraine
55 F6 Shakhtinsk Kazakhstan
54 M9 Shakhty Russian Federation
52 G5 Shakhun'ya Russian Federation
85 E7 Shaki Nigeria
99 N5 Shakopee Minnesota U.S.A.
59 L3 Shakotan misaki C Japan
55 C4 Shaksha Russian Federation
116 G4 Shaktolik Alaska U.S.A.
86 G4 Shala Hāyk' L Ethiopia
52 F4 Shalakusha Russian Federation
117 M10 Shalalth British Columbia Canada
65 G2 Shalan China
67 D6 Shalang China
55 G4 Shalday Kazakhstan
52 F6 Shaldezh Russian Federation
9 F5 Shalford England
52 E4 Shalgachëva Russian Federation
57 F2 Shalgiya Kazakhstan
80 C8 Shalhavi Israel
66 E4 Shaliangzi China
77 E4 Shalidab Iran
55 D5 Shalkar Karashatau L Kazakhstan
55 D5 Shalkar-Yega-Kara L Russian Federation
57 J3 Shalkudysu Kazakhstan
80 G3 Shallala Jordan
112 J4 Shallotte North Carolina U.S.A.
108 E2 Shallowater Texas U.S.A.
120 J8 Shallow Lake Ontario Canada
80 C7 Shalwa Israel
55 C3 Shalya Russian Federation
56 C4 Shalym Russian Federation
88 D5 Shama R Tanzania
56 C5 Shaman, Khrebet mts Russian Federation
55 C3 Shamary Russian Federation
86 F4 Shambe Sudan
80 D2 Shamerat Israel
75 O5 Shamgong Bhutan
77 E6 Shamīl Iran
80 F1 Shamir Israel
78 K6 Shamiya Des Iraq
95 L6 Shamokin Pennsylvania U.S.A.
118 L8 Shamrock Saskatchewan Canada
113 D8 Shamrock Florida U.S.A.
107 O6 Shamrock Oklahoma U.S.A.
108 D8 Shamrock Texas U.S.A.
88 C10 Shamva Zimbabwe
68 C2 Shan prov Burma
80 G6 Sha'nab Jordan
Shanchengzhen see Nanjing
77 G5 Shāndak Iran
58 D4 Shandan China
65 C3 Shandian He R China
12 D1 Shandon Scotland
102 D6 Shandon California U.S.A.
65 C6 Shandong prov China
65 E6 Shandong Bandao pen China
87 E9 Shangani R Zimbabwe
65 D4 Shangbancheng China
67 E1 Shangcheng China
65 F3 Shangchengzhen China
67 D6 Shangchuan Dao isld China
65 B4 Shangdu China
Shangdundu see Linchuan
67 E2 Shangfu China
67 E2 Shanggao China
63 Shanghai conurbation China
67 G1 Shanghai China
67 E4 Shanghang China
65 D6 Shanghe
65 C4 Shanghuangqi China
67 C1 Shangkan China
67 C5 Shanglin China
87 D9 Shangombo Zambia
Shangpaihe see Feixi
58 G5 Shangqiu China
67 F2 Shangrao China
67 B5 Shangsi China
Shangxian see Shangzhou
65 B5 Shangyangwu China
65 C4 Shangyi China
67 E4 Shangyou China
66 C3 Shangyou Shuiku res China
67 G1 Shangyu China
59 J2 Shangzhi China
58 E5 Shangzhou China
65 D5 Shanhaiguan China
65 G2 Shanhetun China
100 E4 Shaniko Oregon U.S.A.
9 E6 Shanklin England
67 E2 Shankou China
94 J6 Shanksville Pennsylvania U.S.A.
145 E4 Shannon New Zealand
112 B3 Shannon Georgia U.S.A.
99 R7 Shannon Illinois U.S.A.
111 H7 Shannon Mississippi U.S.A.
14 C4 Shannon Airport Ireland
99 M9 Shannon City Iowa U.S.A.
14 D2 Shannon Pot Ireland
14 C2 Shannon R Ireland
Shansi prov see Shanxi prov
65 G3 Shansonggang China
80 G4 Shantana Jordan
51 N3 Shantarskiye, Ostrova islds Russian Federation
67 E5 Shantou China
Shantung prov see Shandong prov
Shantung Peninsula see Shandong Bandao
67 E5 Shanwei China
58 F4 Shanxi prov China
65 C7 Shan Xian China
67 F4 Shanyao China
58 F4 Shanyin China
67 F1 Shaobo China
67 D3 Shaodong China
67 D3 Shaoshan China
67 F3 Shaowu China
59 H5 Shaoxing China
67 D3 Shaoyang China
15 F1 Shapinsay Scotland
52 H2 Shapkina R Russian Federation
56 C5 Shapshal'skiy Khrebet mts Russian Federation
80 D4 Shaqéd Jordan
Shara Gol R see Dang He R
52 H7 Sharan Russian Federation
52 G6 Sharanga Russian Federation
121 O8 Sharbot Lake Ontario Canada
56 E6 Sharga Mongolia
48 L2 Shargorod Ukraine
58 D3 Sharhulsan Mongolia
60 S2 Shari Japan
79 H4 Sharīfah Syria
56 G6 Sharīngol Mongolia
Shāriqah, Ash see Sharjah
77 D7 Sharjah U.A.E.
52 H6 Sharkan Russian Federation
71 D5 Shark Fin B Philippines
52 C6 Sharkovshchina Belorussia
141 H2 Shark Reef Gt Barrier Reef Aust
55 B4 Sharlyk Russian Federation
79 F10 Sharmah Saudi Arabia
95 O5 Sharon Connecticut U.S.A.
112 E4 Sharon Georgia U.S.A.
107 M4 Sharon Kansas U.S.A.
94 B2 Sharon Michigan U.S.A.
98 J2 Sharon North Dakota U.S.A.
108 E7 Sharon Oklahoma U.S.A.
110 H5 Sharon Tennessee U.S.A.
95 P3 Sharon Vermont U.S.A.
99 S7 Sharon Wisconsin U.S.A.
80 C5 Sharon, Plain of Israel
107 J3 Sharon Springs Kansas U.S.A.
54 G6 Sharovka Ukraine
98 F5 Sharpe, L South Dakota U.S.A.
95 L9 Sharps Virginia U.S.A.
99 M9 Sharpsburg Iowa U.S.A.
94 K7 Sharpsburg Maryland U.S.A.
94 A6 Sharpsville Indiana U.S.A.
79 F5 Sharqi, Jebel esh mts Lebanon
52 G5 Shar'ya Russian Federation
56 C3 Sharypovo Russian Federation
89 F3 Shashani R Zimbabwe
89 E3 Shashe Botswana
89 G2 Shashe R Zimbabwe
87 E10 Shashe R Zimbabwe/Botswana
86 G4 Shashemenē Ethiopia
67 D1 Shashi China
100 C9 Shasta L California U.S.A.
100 C8 Shasta, Mt California U.S.A.
67 D4 Shatian China
52 F6 Shatki Russian Federation
55 D3 Shatrovo Russian Federation
108 E7 Shattuck Oklahoma U.S.A.
54 L1 Shatura Russian Federation
79 F8 Shaubak Jordan
57 J2 Shaukar, Poluostrov pen Kazakhstan
80 G3 Shaumar Jordan
118 J9 Shaunavon Saskatchewan Canada
52 D3 Shaverki Russian Federation
102 E4 Shaver L California U.S.A.
94 H8 Shavers Fork R West Virginia U.S.A.
80 D4 Shavé Shomeron Jordan
80 D2 Shave Ẕiyyon Israel
111 F8 Shaw Mississippi U.S.A.
120 K7 Shawanaga Ontario Canada
95 N5 Shawangunk Mts New York U.S.A.
99 S5 Shawano Wisconsin U.S.A.
99 S5 Shawano L Wisconsin U.S.A.
121 R7 Shawbridge Quebec Canada
8 D2 Shawbury England
141 J5 Shaw I Queensland Australia
121 S6 Shawinigan Quebec Canada
79 H4 Shawmarīyah, Jabal ash mt Syria
101 Q3 Shawmut Montana U.S.A.
94 E7 Shawnee Ohio U.S.A.
107 O6 Shawnee Oklahoma U.S.A.
98 A7 Shawnee Wyoming U.S.A.
110 H4 Shawneetown Illinois U.S.A.
121 O7 Shawville Quebec Canada
67 F3 Sha Xi R China
67 F3 Sha Xian China
67 D1 Shayang China
142 D5 Shay Gap W Australia Australia
84 J4 Shayib el Banât, Gebel mt Egypt
79 G6 Shaykh Miskīn Syria
52 J4 Shaytanovka Russian Federation
67 G1 Shazhou China
57 F5 Shazud Tajikistan
54 J3 Shchekino Russian Federation
54 K1 Shchelkovo Russian Federation
52 H2 Shchel'yayur Russian Federation
55 G4 Shcherbakty Kazakhstan
54 J1 Shcherbinka Russian Federation
54 H5 Shchigry Russian Federation
54 C5 Shchors Ukraine
54 F8 Shchorsk Ukraine
55 F4 Shchuchinsk Kazakhstan
55 D3 Shchuch'ye Russian Federation
54 M5 Shchuch'ye Voronezhskaya obl Russian Federation
55 C3 Shchuch'ye Ozero Russian Federation
54 K1 Shchurovo Russian Federation
128 G3 Shea Guyana
100 H6 Sheaville Oregon U.S.A.
119 O2 Shebandowan L Ontario Canada
54 H6 Shebekino Russian Federation
86 H4 Shebelē, Wabē R Ethiopia
77 J1 Sheberghān Afghanistan
99 T6 Sheboygan Wisconsin U.S.A.
86 B4 Shebshi Mts Nigeria
100 B5 Shedd Oregon U.S.A.
120 J10 Shedden Ontario Canada
122 H7 Shediac New Brunswick Canada
14 D3 Sheelin, L Ireland
121 N7 Sheenboro Quebec Canada
116 Q2 Sheenjek R Alaska U.S.A.
117 O9 Sheep Cr Alberta Canada
101 U7 Sheep Cr Wyoming U.S.A.
14 D1 Sheep Haven Ireland
101 T10 Sheephorn Colorado U.S.A.
106 C2 Sheep Mt Colorado U.S.A.
103 J5 Sheep Pk Nevada U.S.A.
103 J5 Sheep Ra Nevada U.S.A.
14 B5 Sheep's Hd Ireland
118 F7 Sheerness Alberta Canada
9 G5 Sheerness England
122 K9 Sheet Harbour Nova Scotia Canada
80 D2 Shefar'am Israel
80 C7 Shefela Israel
139 H8 Sheffield Tasmania Australia
13 G6 Sheffield England
144 D5 Sheffield New Zealand
110 J7 Sheffield Alabama U.S.A.
99 R8 Sheffield Illinois U.S.A.
99 N7 Sheffield Iowa U.S.A.
95 O4 Sheffield Massachusetts U.S.A.
94 H5 Sheffield Pennsylvania U.S.A.
108 F5 Sheffield Texas U.S.A.
94 E5 Sheffield Lake Ohio U.S.A.
56 B3 Shegarka R Russian Federation
52 G3 Shegmas Russian Federation
120 J7 Sheguiandah Ontario Canada
119 O7 Sheho Saskatchewan Canada
67 B1 Shehong China
133 C7 Shehuén R Argentina
79 F5 Sheikh, J. esh mt Lebanon/Syria
120 F3 Shekak R Ontario Canada
Shekar Dzong see Tingri
Shekhem see Nablus
54 M4 Shekhman' Russian Federation
74 F3 Shekhupura Pakistan
53 G12 Sheki Azerbaijan
52 E5 Sheksna R Russian Federation
52 E5 Sheksna Russian Federation
94 E9 Shelbiana Kentucky U.S.A.
110 D2 Shelbina Missouri U.S.A.
110 J2 Shelburn Indiana U.S.A.
122 G10 Shelburne Nova Scotia Canada
120 K8 Shelburne Ontario Canada
95 O2 Shelburne Vermont U.S.A.
141 G1 Shelburne B Queensland Australia
95 P4 Shelburne Falls Massachusetts U.S.A.
99 T8 Shelby Indiana U.S.A.
99 L8 Shelby Iowa U.S.A.
99 U6 Shelby Michigan U.S.A.
111 F8 Shelby Mississippi U.S.A.
101 O1 Shelby Montana U.S.A.
98 J8 Shelby Nebraska U.S.A.
112 F2 Shelby North Carolina U.S.A.
94 E6 Shelby Ohio U.S.A.
110 H2 Shelbyville Illinois U.S.A.
110 L2 Shelbyville Indiana U.S.A.
110 L3 Shelbyville Kentucky U.S.A.
110 E2 Shelbyville Missouri U.S.A.
110 K6 Shelbyville Tennessee U.S.A.
109 N4 Shelbyville Texas U.S.A.
99 T9 Sheldon Illinois U.S.A.
99 L6 Sheldon Iowa U.S.A.
110 B4 Sheldon Missouri U.S.A.
98 J3 Sheldon North Dakota U.S.A.
117 H4 Sheldon, Mt Yukon Territory Canada
95 P2 Sheldon Springs Vermont U.S.A.
122 H3 Sheldrake Quebec Canada
56 F5 Shelekhov Russian Federation
51 P3 Shelikhova, Zaliv B Russian Federation
116 K8 Shelikof Str Alaska U.S.A.
99 L3 Shell R Minnesota U.S.A.
101 S5 Shell Wyoming U.S.A.
111 G12 Shell Beach Louisiana U.S.A.
118 L5 Shellbrook Saskatchewan Canada
101 R8 Shell Cr Wyoming U.S.A.
101 N6 Shelley Idaho U.S.A.
139 K5 Shellharbour New South Wales Australia
99 P4 Shell L Wisconsin U.S.A.
118 K5 Shell Lake Saskatchewan Canada
143 F8 Shell Lakes W Australia Australia
111 M10 Shellman Georgia U.S.A.
119 Q8 Shellmouth Manitoba Canada
102 A1 Shell Mt California U.S.A.
99 O7 Shell Rock Iowa U.S.A.
99 O7 Shellrock R Iowa U.S.A.
99 P7 Shellsburg Iowa U.S.A.
80 D1 Shelomi Israel
58 G1 Shelopugino Russian Federation
102 A1 Shelter Cove California U.S.A.
95 P5 Shelter I Long I, New York U.S.A.
144 B7 Shelter Pt New Zealand
95 O5 Shelton Connecticut U.S.A.
98 H9 Shelton Nebraska U.S.A.
117 M12 Shelton Washington U.S.A.
52 E4 Sheltozero Russian Federation
78 M1 Shemakha Azerbaijan
56 B5 Shemonaikha Kazakhstan
52 H6 Shemordan Russian Federation
52 G6 Shemursha Russian Federation
99 L9 Shenandoah Iowa U.S.A.
95 L6 Shenandoah Pennsylvania U.S.A.
94 J8 Shenandoah Virginia U.S.A.
94 H8 Shenandoah Mts W Virginia/Virginia U.S.A.
94 J8 Shenandoah Nat. Park Virginia U.S.A.
94 G5 Shenango Res Ohio/Penn U.S.A.
57 D1 Shenber Kazakhstan
65 B5 Shenchi China
86 A4 Shendam Nigeria
86 F2 Shendi Sudan
65 J1 Shending Shan mt China
57 J3 Shengel'dy Kazakhstan
46 D3 Shëngjin Albania
65 F1 Shengping China
67 G1 Shengsi China
67 G1 Shengsi Liedao islds China
67 G2 Sheng Xian China
52 F4 Shenkursk Russian Federation
65 A5 Shenmu China
67 C1 Shennongjia China
Shensi prov see Shaanxi
52 H7 Shentala Russian Federation
143 E8 Shenton, Mt W Australia Australia
Shentza Dzong see Xainza
65 C5 Shen Xian China
65 C6 Shen Xian China
59 H3 Shenyang China
65 C5 Shenze China
Shenzhen see Bao'an
74 G6 Sheopur India
118 D7 Shepard Alberta Canada
94 C3 Shepherd Michigan U.S.A.
101 R4 Shepherd Montana U.S.A.
109 M5 Shepherd Texas U.S.A.
137 O5 Shepherd Is Vanuatu
94 K7 Shepherdstown West Virginia U.S.A.
94 B9 Shepherdsville Kentucky U.S.A.
117 G7 Sheppard, Mt British Columbia Canada
139 H6 Shepparton Victoria Australia
9 G5 Sheppey isld England
8 D5 Shepton Mallet England
80 C7 Sheqef Israel
77 K1 Sherabad Uzbekistan
115 M3 Sherard, C Northwest Territories Canada
55 F4 Sherbakul' Russian Federation
8 D6 Sherborne England
85 B7 Sherbro I Sierra Leone
121 T7 Sherbrooke Quebec Canada
122 H9 Sherbrooke L Nova Scotia Canada
13 H5 Sherburn England
13 G6 Sherburn England
99 M6 Sherburn Minnesota U.S.A.
95 M4 Sherburne New York U.S.A.
86 C1 Sherda Chad
9 F5 Shere England
84 J6 Shereik Sudan
54 J1 Sheremet'yevo airport Russian Federation
74 E5 Shergarh India
111 D7 Sheridan Arkansas U.S.A.
94 A6 Sheridan Indiana U.S.A.
94 B3 Sheridan Michigan U.S.A.
101 N4 Sheridan Montana U.S.A.
100 B4 Sheridan Oregon U.S.A.
101 T5 Sheridan Wyoming U.S.A.
115 N1 Sheridan, C Northwest Territories Canada
106 H3 Sheridan L Colorado U.S.A.
101 P5 Sheridan, Mt Wyoming U.S.A.
138 D5 Sheringa South Australia Australia
9 H2 Sheringham England
111 H7 Sherman Mississippi U.S.A.
94 H4 Sherman New York U.S.A.
109 L2 Sherman Texas U.S.A.
95 S8 Sherman Mills Maine U.S.A.
103 J1 Sherman Mt Nevada U.S.A.
101 O7 Sherman Pk Idaho U.S.A.
98 H8 Sherman Res Nebraska U.S.A.
77 L2 Sherpur Afghanistan
119 Q3 Sherridon Manitoba Canada
95 M3 Sherrill New York U.S.A.
25 D5 's-Hertogenbosch Netherlands
141 K2 Sherwood dist Brisbane, Qnsld Australia
122 J7 Sherwood Prince Edward I Canada
98 E1 Sherwood North Dakota U.S.A.
108 G4 Sherwood Texas U.S.A.
144 C5 Sherwood Downs New Zealand
9 E1 Sherwood Forest England
52 H6 Sheshma R Russian Federation
77 E1 Sheshtamad Iran
67 E1 She Shui R China
117 H6 Sheslay British Columbia Canada
52 H5 Shestakovo Russian Federation
99 L5 Shetek, L Minnesota U.S.A.
15 G2 Shetland reg Scotland
50 E4 Shevchenko Kazakhstan
48 M5 Shevchenko, Liman B Ukraine
57 B2 Shevchenko, Zaliv G Kazakhstan
99 L2 Shevlin Minnesota U.S.A.
86 G4 Shewa prov Ethiopia
86 G4 Shewa Gīmīra Ethiopia
65 B6 She Xian China
67 F2 She Xian China
98 G2 Sheyenne North Dakota U.S.A.
98 J3 Sheyenne R North Dakota U.S.A.
77 C6 Sheykh Sho'eyb isld Iran
80 E2 Shezor Israel
15 B3 Shiant isld Scotland
94 C3 Shiawassee R Michigan U.S.A.
61 N8 Shibata Japan
65 B4 Shibatai China
60 S2 Shibecha Japan
60 T2 Shibetsu Japan
84 J3 Shibîn el Kom Egypt
79 B8 Shibîn el Qanâtir Egypt
67 C3 Shibing China
61 M9 Shibukawa Japan
60 E14 Shibushi-wan Japan
65 D6 Shibuzi China
67 B3 Shichang China
67 E3 Shicheng China
61 P5 Shichinohe Japan
98 J9 Shickley Nebraska U.S.A.
95 L5 Shickshinny Pennsylvania U.S.A.
122 F5 Shickshock Mts Quebec Canada
Shicun see Xiangfen
65 E6 Shidao China
65 E6 Shidao Wan B China
55 F5 Shiderty Kazakhstan
55 F5 Shiderty R Kazakhstan
107 O5 Shidler Oklahoma U.S.A.
60 H11 Shido Japan
15 C3 Shieldaig Scotland
140 D2 Shield, C N Terr Australia
107 K3 Shields Kansas U.S.A.
98 E3 Shields North Dakota U.S.A.
67 A1 Shifang China
8 D2 Shifnal England
61 K10 Shiga prefect Japan
Shigatse see Xigazê
122 G5 Shigawake Quebec Canada
65 A4 Shiguaigou China
67 F1 Shih-chiu Hu L China
58 G5 Shi He R China
66 D3 Shihezi China
Shihkiachwang see Shijiazhuang
86 J4 Shiikh Somalia
61 M8 Shiiya Japan
46 D3 Shijak Albania
67 A1 Shijiaba China
Shijiao see Fogang
65 B5 Shijiazhuang China
65 C5 Shijiazhuang China
67 F1 Shijiu Hu China
65 D7 Shijiusuo China
60 O3 Shikabe Japan
119 N1 Shikag L Ontario Canada
60 H11 Shikama Japan
68 J2 Shikang China
77 L2 Shikar, Darya-i- R Afghanistan
76 B3 Shikarpur India
74 C5 Shikarpur Pakistan
61 N11 Shikine-jima isld Japan
60 G12 Shikoku isld Japan
60 F12 Shikoku-sanchi mts Japan
59 N3 Shikotan isld Japan
60 O3 Shikotsu Toya Nat. Park Japan
86 H4 Shilabo Ethiopia
52 G4 Shilador Russian Federation
80 D6 Shilat Jordan
55 D5 Shil'da Russian Federation
75 N5 Shiliguri India
Shiliu see Changjiang
59 G1 Shilka R Russian Federation
14 E4 Shillelagh Ireland
9 E4 Shillingford England
120 K4 Shillington Ontario Canada
95 M6 Shillington Pennsylvania U.S.A.
80 E5 Shillo Jordan
75 O6 Shillong India
110 H6 Shiloh Nat. Mil. Park Tennessee U.S.A.
67 C5 Shilong China
67 D5 Shilong China
65 A6 Shilou China
54 M2 Shilovo Russian Federation
Shima see Longhai
67 E3 Shima China
60 D13 Shimabara Japan
61 M11 Shimada Japan
60 F10 Shimane prefect Japan
59 J1 Shimanovsk Russian Federation
60 F13 Shimanto Japan
67 D2 Shimen China
65 D4 Shimenzhai China
61 M11 Shimizu Japan
74 G3 Shimla India
61 L9 Shimminato Japan
61 M11 Shimoda Japan
61 O9 Shimodate Japan
60 P4 Shimofuro Japan
76 B4 Shimoga India
60 E11 Shimogo Japan
60 Q1 Shimokawa Japan
61 O8 Shimo-kitaba Japan
60 O4 Shimokita-hantō pen Japan
60 C14 Shimo koshiki jima isld Japan
61 M9 Shimonita Japan
59 K5 Shimonoseki Japan
60 D14 Shimo-Taniguchi Japan
60 E13 Shimo-Tashima Japan
61 N9 Shimotsuma Japan
80 D3 Shimron Israel
52 D5 Shimsk Russian Federation
67 C5 Shinan China
59 L4 Shinano R Japan
77 H3 Shīndand Afghanistan
61 K11 Shindō Japan
109 K6 Shiner Texas U.S.A.
94 J5 Shinglehouse Pennsylvania U.S.A.
145 D4 Shingle Pk New Zealand
99 U3 Shingleton Michigan U.S.A.
100 D9 Shingletown California U.S.A.
61 J12 Shingū Japan
120 J5 Shining Tree Ontario Canada
61 O7 Shinjō Japan
60 E11 Shin-Nan'yō Japan
94 G7 Shinnston West Virginia U.S.A.
61 M9 Shinonoi Japan
79 G4 Shinshār Syria
61 L11 Shinshiro Japan
60 Q2 Shintoku Japan
88 D3 Shinyanga Tanzania
61 P7 Shiogama Japan
61 L9 Shiojiri Japan
61 J12 Shiono-misaki C Japan
Shipai see Huaining
126 F2 Ship Chan. Cay isld Bahamas
123 S6 Ship Cove Newfoundland Canada
9 G2 Shipdham England
111 H11 Ship I Mississippi U.S.A.
52 G4 Shipitsino Russian Federation
46 G2 Shipka P Bulgaria
74 H3 Shipki Pass India/Xizang Zizhiqu
13 G6 Shipley England
119 N5 Shipman Saskatchewan Canada
94 K6 Shippensburg Pennsylvania U.S.A.
106 B5 Shiprock New Mexico U.S.A.
121 T4 Shipshaw Dam Quebec Canada
111 E13 Ship Shoal Lt. Hse Louisiana U.S.A.
13 G5 Shipton N Yorks England
9 E4 Shipton under Wychwood England
Shipu see Huanglong
67 G2 Shipu China
67 C3 Shiqian China
Shiqiao see Panyu
67 D5 Shiqiao China
80 A7 Shiqma Israel
80 C8 Shiqma R Israel
58 E5 Shiquan China
66 C5 Shiquan He R China
74 H2 Shiquanhe China
60 J12 Shirahama Japan
60 O4 Shirakami-misaki C Japan
61 O8 Shirakawa Fukushima, Honshu Japan
61 K9 Shirakawa Toyama, Honshu Japan
78 L1 Shirakskaya Step' Azerbaijan/Georgia
61 N9 Shirane-san mt Tochigi Japan
61 M10 Shirane san mt Yamanashi Japan
60 S3 Shiranuka Japan
60 P3 Shiraoi Japan
146 C10 Shirase Coast Antarctica
77 C5 Shīrāz Iran
79 B7 Shirbîn Egypt
88 E9 Shire R Malawi
65 B2 Shireet Mongolia
88 E9 Shire Highlands Malawi
65 G4 Shiren China
60 T1 Shiretoko misaki C Japan
60 O3 Shiribeshi prefect Japan
57 C3 Shirikrabat Kazakhstan
60 O4 Shiriuchi Japan
60 P4 Shiriya-zaki C Japan
9 E3 Shirley England
9 E6 Shirley England
110 D6 Shirley Arkansas U.S.A.
101 T7 Shirley Mts Wyoming U.S.A.
61 O8 Shiroishi Japan
54 E9 Shirokoye Ukraine
61 K10 Shirotori Japan
61 L9 Shirouma-dake mt Japan
77 E1 Shīrvān Iran
116 E9 Shishaldin Vol Aleutian Is
60 H12 Shishikui Japan
60 C11 Shishimi Japan
116 D3 Shishmaref Alaska U.S.A.
116 E3 Shishmaref Inlet Alaska U.S.A.
67 D2 Shishou China
67 F1 Shitai China
61 L10 Shitara Japan
74 D5 Shiv India
74 G6 Shivpuri India
103 L5 Shivwits Plat Arizona U.S.A.
67 B6 Shiwan Dashan mts China
87 F8 Shiwa Ngandu Zambia
67 E4 Shixing China
67 B2 Shiyangchang China
67 C2 Shiye China
Shizhaihe see Zhenping
67 C2 Shizhu China
Shizilu see Junan
67 A4 Shizong China
61 P7 Shizugawa Japan
58 E4 Shizuishan China
65 A6 Shizuiyi China
61 O6 Shizukuishi Japan
60 Q3 Shizunai Japan
59 L5 Shizuoka Japan
61 M10 Shizuoka prefect Japan
54 B2 Shklov Belorussia
46 D2 Shkodër Albania
46 D3 Shkumbin R Albania
52 D5 Shlino R Russian Federation
51 J1 Shmidta, Ostrova islds Russian Federation
61 L9 Shō R Japan
113 A7 Shoal R Florida U.S.A.
140 B1 Shoal B N Terr Australia
123 T5 Shoal Harb Newfoundland Canada
139 K5 Shoalhaven R New South Wales Australia
119 U8 Shoal L Manitoba Canada
118 F1 Shoal L Ontario Canada
110 K3 Shoals Indiana U.S.A.
141 K5 Shoalwater B Queensland Australia
60 F11 Shōbara Japan
60 H11 Shōdo-shima isld Japan
9 G4 Shoeburyness England
123 R4 Shoe Cove Newfoundland Canada
145 E2 Shoe I New Zealand
77 F1 Shoghlābād Iran
51 K1 Shokal'skogo, Proliv str Russian Federation
60 P2 Shokambetsu dake mt Japan
57 E6 Shokh Tajikistan
60 R1 Shokotsu Japan
52 E4 Shola R Russian Federation
55 D5 Sholaksay Kazakhstan
55 F5 Sholakshalkar, Oz L Kazakhstan
142 B5 Sholl I W Australia Australia
52 D2 Shomba Russian Federation
80 E1 Shomera Israel
52 H3 Shomvukva Russian Federation
57 A2 Shomyshkol' Kazakhstan
88 B9 Shona Zambia
55 G5 Shoptykul' Kazakhstan
52 G6 Shora R Russian Federation
76 C5 Shoranur India
76 C2 Shorapur India
77 J5 Shorawak reg Afghanistan
9 F6 Shoreham-by-Sea England
99 T6 Shorewood Wisconsin U.S.A.
55 F5 Shortandy Kazakhstan
103 M5 Short Cr Arizona U.S.A.
119 Q7 Shortdale Manitoba Canada
111 L9 Shorter Alabama U.S.A.
138 E2 Short, L South Australia Australia
143 C10 Short, Mt W Australia Australia
95 K4 Shortsville New York U.S.A.
57 A2 Shoshkakol' Kazakhstan
102 H6 Shoshone California U.S.A.
101 L7 Shoshone Idaho U.S.A.
101 R5 Shoshone R Wyoming U.S.A.
101 Q5 Shoshone Cavern Nat. Mon Wyoming U.S.A.

107 N4 **South Haven** Kansas U.S.A.
99 U7 **South Haven** Michigan U.S.A.
115 K5 **South Henik L** Northwest Territories Canada
94 J10 **South Hill** Virginia U.S.A.
94 F10 **South Holston L** Tenn/Virg U.S.A.
140 C1 **South I** N Terr Australia
83 M8 **South I** Cocos Is Indian Oc
119 T2 **South Indian L** Manitoba Canada
95 P5 **Southington** Connecticut U.S.A.
144 B5 **South Island** New Zealand
71 D6 **South Islet** Sulu Sea
118 F1 **South Junc** Manitoba Canada
99 T7 **South Kenosha** Wisconsin U.S.A.
59 J4 **South Korea** *rep* Asia
109 M8 **Southlake** Texas U.S.A.
102 E3 **South Lake Tahoe** California U.S.A.
144 A6 **Southland** *admin region* New Zealand
123 K9 **South Lochaber** Nova Scotia Canada
98 G8 **South Loup** *R* Nebraska U.S.A.
88 C8 **South Luangwa Nat. Park** Zambia
70 C2 **South Luconia Shoals** S China Sea
94 D4 **South Lyon** Michigan U.S.A.
120 K7 **Southmag** Ontario Canada
146 E14 **South Magnetic Pole** Antarctica
99 U4 **South Manitou I** Michigan U.S.A.
95 L10 **South Mills** North Carolina U.S.A.
99 T7 **South Milwaukee** Wisconsin U.S.A.
9 G4 **Southminster** England
141 H4 **South Mission Beach** Queensland Australia
8 C5 **South Molton** England
109 K10 **Southmost** Texas U.S.A.
95 K6 **South Mt** Pennsylvania U.S.A.
116 J7 **South Naknek** Alaska U.S.A.
122 G7 **South Nelson** New Brunswick Canada
112 F6 **South Newport** Georgia U.S.A.
95 P5 **Southold** Long I, New York U.S.A.
90 F15 **South Orkney Is** S Atlantic Oc
146 E3 **South Orkney Is** S Atlantic Oc
53 F12 **South Ossetia** *aut reg* Georgia
102 B3 **South Pablo B** California U.S.A.
95 R2 **South Paris** Maine U.S.A.
94 F7 **South Parkersburg** West Virginia U.S.A.
101 R7 **South Pass** Wyoming U.S.A.
101 R7 **South Pass City** Wyoming U.S.A.
99 R9 **South Pekin** Illinois U.S.A.
110 L6 **South Pittsburg** Tennessee U.S.A.
106 E2 **South Platte** Colorado U.S.A.
146 E9 **South Pole** Antarctica
120 J4 **South Porcupine** Ontario Canada
141 L8 **Southport** Queensland Australia
139 H9 **Southport** Tasmania Australia
123 T5 **Southport** Newfoundland Canada
13 E6 **Southport** England
94 A7 **Southport** Indiana U.S.A.
112 J4 **Southport** North Carolina U.S.A.
123 K4 **South Pt** Anticosti I, Quebec
83 M9 **South Pt** Christmas I Indian Oc
112 J3 **South R** North Carolina U.S.A.
99 S2 **South Range** Michigan U.S.A.
144 A7 **South Red Head Pt.** New Zealand
113 H12 **South Riding Rock** Bahamas
121 L7 **South River** Ontario Canada
95 N6 **South River** New Jersey U.S.A.
15 F2 **South Ronaldsay** Scotland
131 J7 **South Sandwich Is** S Atlantic Oc
102 B4 **South San Francisco** California U.S.A.
118 J8 **South Sask R** Saskatchewan Canada
9 E6 **Southsea** England
119 S1 **South Seal R** Manitoba Canada
146 C3 **South Shetland Is** S Atlantic Oc
13 G3 **South Shields** England
98 K7 **South Sioux City** Nebraska U.S.A.
98 K6 **South Sioux Falls** South Dakota U.S.A.
117 P11 **South Slocan** British Columbia Canada
103 N2 **South Tent** *pk* Utah U.S.A.
15 A3 **South Uist** Scotland
9 F1 **Southwell** England
South West Africa *see* **Namibia** *rep*
113 K9 **South West B** New Providence I Bahamas
139 H9 **South West C** Tasmania Australia
123 K6 **Southwest C** Madeleine Is, Quebec Canada
144 A7 **Southwest Cape** New Zealand
113 L8 **South West Cape** Virgin Is
139 H7 **South West I** Tasmania Australia
81 C9 **South-West Indian Ridge** Indian Oc
139 H8 **Southwest Nat. Park** Tasmania Australia
135 M12 **South-West Pacific Basin** Pacific Oc
122 J4 **Southwest Pt** Quebec Canada
126 E6 **Southwest Rock** Caribbean
139 L4 **South West Rocks** New South Wales Australia
99 S8 **South Wilmington** Illinois U.S.A.
9 H3 **Southwold** England
9 G4 **South Woodham Ferrers** England
9 G2 **South Wootton** England
South Yemen *see* **Yemen**
13 G6 **South Yorkshire** *co* England
89 F4 **Soutpansberg** *mts* S Africa
144 B6 **Soutra Hill** New Zealand
18 H6 **Souvigny** France
16 B6 **Souzel** Portugal
48 J4 **Sovata** Romania
118 K7 **Sovereign** Saskatchewan Canada
57 G4 **Sovetabad** Uzbekistan
52 G5 **Sovetsk** Russian Federation
52 B6 **Sovetsk** Russian Federation
53 F9 **Sovetskaya** Russian Federation
59 M2 **Sovetskaya Gavan** Russian Federation
52 C4 **Sovetskiy** Leningradskaya obl Russian Federation
55 D1 **Sovetskiy** Tyumenskaya obl Russian Federation
Soviet Union *see* **Union of Soviet Socialist Republics**

28 E5 **Søvind** Denmark
52 F2 **Sovpol'ye** Russian Federation
89 D3 **Sowa Pan** Botswana
119 N1 **Sowden L** Ontario Canada
13 G6 **Sowerby Br** England
60 P1 **Sōya** Japan
60 P1 **Sōya-misaki** *C* Japan
52 F2 **Soyana** *R* Russian Federation
18 F7 **Soyaux** France
60 P1 **Sōya wan** *B* Japan
38 F5 **Soyen** Germany
19 N15 **Soyons** France
124 E3 **Soyopa** Mexico
54 B4 **Sozh** *R* Belorussia/Rus Fed
52 H5 **Sozimskiy** Russian Federation
47 J2 **Sozopol** Bulgaria
22 K3 **Spa** Belgium
126 B2 **Spaanse Baai** *B* Curaçao
146 C6 **Spaatz I** *isld* Antarctica
16 **Spain** *kingdom* W Europe
31 M4 **Spała** Poland
Spalato *see* **Split** Croatia
138 E5 **Spalding** South Australia Australia
119 N6 **Spalding** Saskatchewan Canada
9 F2 **Spalding** England
100 J3 **Spalding** Idaho U.S.A.
98 H8 **Spalding** Nebraska U.S.A.
37 K5 **Spalt** Germany
25 C3 **Spanbroek** Netherlands
33 S7 **Spandau** Berlin
28 B6 **Spandet** Denmark
27 H14 **Spångenäs** Sweden
36 H1 **Spangenberg** Germany
100 H2 **Spangle** Washington U.S.A.
94 J6 **Spangler** Pennsylvania U.S.A.
123 T6 **Spaniard's B** Newfoundland Canada
120 H6 **Spanish** Ontario Canada
101 O9 **Spanish Fork** Utah U.S.A.
106 F4 **Spanish Pks** Colorado U.S.A.
127 L3 **Spanish Town** Jamaica
113 L7 **Spanish Town** Virgin Is
113 L12 **Spanish Wells** Eleuthera Bahamas
45 Q7 **Sparanise** Italy
26 E8 **Sparbu** Norway
28 C4 **Sparkær** Denmark
111 D8 **Sparkman** Arkansas U.S.A.
112 D6 **Sparks** Georgia U.S.A.
98 F7 **Sparks** Nebraska U.S.A.
102 E2 **Sparks** Nevada U.S.A.
107 O6 **Sparks** Oklahoma U.S.A.
99 R8 **Sparland** Illinois U.S.A.
37 M3 **Sparnberg** Germany
94 C1 **Sparr** Michigan U.S.A.
112 E4 **Sparta** Georgia U.S.A.
110 G3 **Sparta** Illinois U.S.A.
94 B3 **Sparta** Michigan U.S.A.
110 C4 **Sparta** Missouri U.S.A.
94 F10 **Sparta** North Carolina U.S.A.
100 H5 **Sparta** Oregon U.S.A.
110 L6 **Sparta** Tennessee U.S.A.
99 Q6 **Sparta** Wisconsin U.S.A.
112 F3 **Spartanburg** South Carolina U.S.A.
94 H5 **Spartansburg** Pennsylvania U.S.A.
16 D9 **Spartel, C** Morocco
47 O12 **Spartilla** Greece
43 G11 **Spartivento, C** Italy
43 B10 **Spartivento, C** Sardinia
54 M1 **Spas-Klepiki** Russian Federation
56 C4 **Spassk** Russian Federation
52 D4 **Spasskaya Guba** Russian Federation
59 K3 **Spassk Dal'niy** Russian Federation
55 E5 **Spasskoye** Kazakhstan
54 M2 **Spassk-Ryazanskiy** Russian Federation
46 F9 **Spátha, Akr** *C* Crete Greece
117 J7 **Spatsizi Plat. Wilderness Prov. Pk** British Columbia Canada
110 A5 **Spavinaw, L** Oklahoma U.S.A.
36 D3 **Spay** Germany
109 L6 **Speaks** Texas U.S.A.
15 D4 **Spean Bridge** Scotland
98 C5 **Spearfish** South Dakota U.S.A.
119 T7 **Spearhill** Manitoba Canada
108 C7 **Spearman** Texas U.S.A.
107 L4 **Spearville** Kansas U.S.A.
142 A3 **Spearwood** *dist* Perth, W Aust Australia
33 R6 **Specker-See** *L* Germany
95 N3 **Speculator** New York U.S.A.
118 F4 **Spedden** Alberta Canada
109 M1 **Speer** Oklahoma U.S.A.
98 B8 **Speer** Wyoming U.S.A.
118 K6 **Speers** Saskatchewan Canada
36 B4 **Speicher** Germany
37 M4 **Speichersdorf** Germany
37 M7 **Speichersee** *L* Germany
127 P6 **Speightstown** Barbados
116 M6 **Spenard** Alaska U.S.A.
115 K4 **Spence Bay** Northwest Territories Canada
101 N5 **Spencer** Idaho U.S.A.
110 K2 **Spencer** Indiana U.S.A.
99 L6 **Spencer** Iowa U.S.A.
95 P4 **Spencer** Massachusetts U.S.A.
98 H7 **Spencer** Nebraska U.S.A.
95 L4 **Spencer** New York U.S.A.
98 J6 **Spencer** South Dakota U.S.A.
94 F8 **Spencer** West Virginia U.S.A.
99 Q5 **Spencer** Wisconsin U.S.A.
138 D6 **Spencer, C** South Australia Australia
117 E6 **Spencer, C** Alaska U.S.A.
138 D5 **Spencer Gulf** South Australia Australia
95 R1 **Spencer L** Maine U.S.A.
94 K3 **Spencerport** New York U.S.A.
116 D4 **Spencer, Pt** Alaska U.S.A.
140 C1 **Spencer Ra** N Terr Australia
94 C6 **Spencerville** Ohio U.S.A.
117 N10 **Spences Bridge** British Columbia Canada
32 H8 **Spenge** Germany
13 G4 **Spennymoor** England
144 D5 **Spenser Mts** New Zealand
33 S8 **Sperenberg** Germany
27 D11 **Sperillen** Norway
46 E6 **Sperkhiós** *R* Greece
118 D1 **Sperling** Manitoba Canada
45 O7 **Sperlonga** Italy
43 B10 **Sperone, C** Sardinia
14 D2 **Sperrin Mts** N Ireland
94 J8 **Sperryville** Virginia U.S.A.
36 G3 **Spessart** *mts* Germany
46 F7 **Spétsai** *isld* Greece
15 E3 **Spey** *R* Scotland
36 E5 **Speyer** Germany
127 N1 **Speyside** Tobago
20 C5 **Spézet** France
44 G3 **Spezia, La** Italy
115 M4 **Spicer Is** Northwest Territories Canada
99 N9 **Spickardsville** Missouri U.S.A.
32 G5 **Spiekeroog** Germany
38 N8 **Spielfeld** Austria
36 C5 **Spiesen-Elversberg** Germany
44 D2 **Spigno** *R* Italy
25 G2 **Spijk** Netherlands
110 C1 **Spikard** Missouri U.S.A.
116 R3 **Spike Mt** Alaska U.S.A.
45 K2 **Spilamberto** Italy
46 G9 **Spíli** Crete Greece
42 E2 **Spilimbergo** Italy
9 G1 **Spilsby** England
43 G8 **Spinazzola** Italy
77 K4 **Spīn Būldak** Afghanistan

22 K5 **Spincourt** France
112 F2 **Spindale** North Carolina U.S.A.
45 M1 **Spinea** Italy
44 F1 **Spino d'Adda** Italy
89 B8 **Spioenberg I** *mt* S Africa
89 A8 **Spioenberg II** *mt* S Africa
89 F7 **Spioen Kop** *mt* S Africa
99 L6 **Spirit L** Iowa U.S.A.
100 J2 **Spirit Lake** Idaho U.S.A.
100 C3 **Spirit Lake** Washington U.S.A.
117 O8 **Spirit River** Alberta Canada
145 D1 **Spirits B** New Zealand
118 K5 **Spiritwood** Saskatchewan Canada
98 H3 **Spiritwood** North Dakota U.S.A.
107 Q6 **Spiro** Oklahoma U.S.A.
52 D6 **Spirovo** Russian Federation
48 F1 **Spišská Belá** Czechoslovakia
48 F2 **Spišská Nová Ves** Czechoslovakia
31 M6 **Spišské Podhradie** Czechoslovakia
50 A1 **Spitsbergen** *arch* Arctic Oc
38 H8 **Spittal-an-der-Drau** Austria
38 M5 **Spitz** Austria
28 A4 **Spjald** Denmark
109 M5 **Splendora** Texas U.S.A.
42 H5 **Split** Croatia
122 H8 **Split, C** Nova Scotia Canada
119 V2 **Split L** Manitoba Canada
100 G8 **Split Pk** *mt* Nevada U.S.A.
38 N9 **Spodnje Hoče** Slovenia
28 F7 **Spodsbjerg** Denmark
108 G6 **Spofford** Texas U.S.A.
13 G6 **Spofforth** England
100 H2 **Spokane** Washington U.S.A.
42 E6 **Spoleto** Italy
118 F7 **Spondin** Alberta Canada
68 G6 **Spong** Cambodia
33 S5 **Sponholz** Germany
22 J3 **Spontin** Belgium
99 Q9 **Spoon** *R* Illinois U.S.A.
99 P4 **Spooner** Wisconsin U.S.A.
100 E8 **Spooner Res** California U.S.A.
Sporádes *islds see* **Dhodhekánisos** *islds*
33 P6 **Spornitz** Germany
28 E4 **Spørring** Denmark
44 D3 **Spotorno** Italy
101 U5 **Spotted Horse** Wyoming U.S.A.
103 J5 **Spotted Ra** Nevada U.S.A.
118 F1 **Sprague** Manitoba Canada
111 K9 **Sprague** Alabama U.S.A.
100 H2 **Sprague** Washington U.S.A.
99 Q5 **Sprague** Wisconsin U.S.A.
100 D7 **Sprague River** Oregon U.S.A.
36 H6 **Spraitbach** Germany
33 M7 **Sprakensehl** Germany
100 F5 **Spray** Oregon U.S.A.
48 E6 **Spreča** *R* Bosnia-Herzegovina
54 J4 **Spredne Russkaya Vozvyshennost'** *uplands* Russian Federation
31 H4 **Spree** *R* Germany
33 T9 **Spreewald** Germany
31 H4 **Spremberg** Germany
36 F3 **Sprendlingen** Hessen Germany
36 E4 **Sprendlingen** Rheinland-Pfalz Germany
22 K3 **Sprimont** Belgium
110 E5 **Spring** *R* Arkansas U.S.A.
110 B5 **Spring** *R* Oklahoma U.S.A.
109 M5 **Spring** Texas U.S.A.
101 N8 **Spring B** Utah U.S.A.
89 A7 **Springbok** S Africa
94 G5 **Springboro** Pennsylvania U.S.A.
109 J6 **Spring Branch** Texas U.S.A.
98 C1 **Spring Brook** North Dakota U.S.A.
118 A3 **Springburn** Alberta Canada
144 C5 **Springburn** New Zealand
95 M6 **Spring City** Pennsylvania U.S.A.
112 C2 **Spring City** Tennessee U.S.A.
103 N2 **Spring City** Utah U.S.A.
118 D9 **Spring Coulee** Alberta Canada
140 E4 **Spring Cr** N Terr Australia
140 F6 **Spring Cr** Queensland Australia
98 E9 **Spring Cr** Nebraska U.S.A.
101 L8 **Spring Cr** Nevada U.S.A.
145 D4 **Spring Creek** New Zealand
123 Q4 **Springdale** Newfoundland Canada
110 B5 **Springdale** Arkansas U.S.A.
101 P4 **Springdale** Montana U.S.A.
102 H4 **Springdale** Nevada U.S.A.
103 M4 **Springdale** Utah U.S.A.
100 H1 **Springdale** Washington U.S.A.
32 L8 **Springe** Germany
106 F5 **Springer** New Mexico U.S.A.
109 K1 **Springer** Oklahoma U.S.A.
121 Q3 **Springer, Mt** Quebec Canada
103 P7 **Springerville** Arizona U.S.A.
122 G8 **Springfield** New Brunswick Canada
122 H9 **Springfield** Nova Scotia Canada
144 C5 **Springfield** New Zealand
106 H4 **Springfield** Colorado U.S.A.
113 B7 **Springfield** Florida U.S.A.
112 F5 **Springfield** Georgia U.S.A.
101 N6 **Springfield** Idaho U.S.A.
110 G2 **Springfield** Illinois U.S.A.
94 B9 **Springfield** Kentucky U.S.A.
95 P4 **Springfield** Massachusetts U.S.A.
110 C4 **Springfield** Missouri U.S.A.
94 D7 **Springfield** Ohio U.S.A.
100 C5 **Springfield** Oregon U.S.A.
112 F4 **Springfield** South Carolina U.S.A.
98 J7 **Springfield** South Dakota U.S.A.
110 K5 **Springfield** Tennessee U.S.A.
95 P3 **Springfield** Vermont U.S.A.
89 D8 **Springfontein** S Africa
99 Q6 **Spring Green** Wisconsin U.S.A.
99 P6 **Spring Grove** Minnesota U.S.A.
95 L7 **Spring Grove** Pennsylvania U.S.A.
122 H8 **Springhill** Nova Scotia Canada
111 C9 **Springhill** Louisiana U.S.A.
110 K6 **Spring Hill** Tennessee U.S.A.
112 J2 **Spring Hope** North Carolina U.S.A.
99 U6 **Spring Lake** Michigan U.S.A.
95 N6 **Spring Lake** New Jersey U.S.A.
112 H2 **Spring Lake** North Carolina U.S.A.
108 E1 **Springlake** Texas U.S.A.
103 J5 **Spring Mts** Nevada U.S.A.
126 H3 **Spring Point** Acklins I Bahamas
89 F6 **Springs** S Africa
95 K6 **Springs** Pennsylvania U.S.A.
119 P7 **Springside** Saskatchewan Canada
144 D5 **Springs Junction** New Zealand
144 D5 **Springston** New Zealand
141 J6 **Springsure** Queensland Australia
109 K3 **Springtown** Texas U.S.A.
140 F6 **Springvale** Queensland Australia
141 G3 **Springvale** Queensland Australia

142 G4 **Springvale** W Australia Australia
95 R3 **Springvale** Maine U.S.A.
119 M9 **Spring Valley** Saskatchewan Canada
99 O6 **Spring Valley** Minnesota U.S.A.
98 G7 **Springview** Nebraska U.S.A.
111 K8 **Springville** Alabama U.S.A.
94 J4 **Springville** New York U.S.A.
101 O9 **Springville** Utah U.S.A.
118 J7 **Springwater** Saskatchewan Canada
13 H6 **Sproatley** England
28 F6 **Sprogø** *isld* Denmark
32 L6 **Sprötze** Germany
94 D2 **Spruce** Michigan U.S.A.
123 O5 **Spruce Brook** Newfoundland Canada
121 L7 **Sprucedale** Ontario Canada
118 D5 **Spruce Grove** Alberta Canada
94 H8 **Spruce Knob** *mt* West Virginia U.S.A.
118 H5 **Spruce Lake** Saskatchewan Canada
101 L9 **Spruce Mt** Nevada U.S.A.
112 E2 **Spruce Pine** North Carolina U.S.A.
103 M4 **Spry** Utah U.S.A.
25 B5 **Spui** *R* Netherlands
43 H9 **Spulico, C** Italy
108 G2 **Spur** Texas U.S.A.
118 C3 **Spurfield** Alberta Canada
111 B11 **Spurger** Texas U.S.A.
106 B8 **Spur Lake** New Mexico U.S.A.
116 L6 **Spurr, Mt** Alaska U.S.A.
46 C2 **Spuž** Montenegro Yugoslavia
22 H3 **Spy** Belgium
119 Q8 **Spy Hill** Saskatchewan Canada
117 M11 **Squamish** British Columbia Canada
95 Q3 **Squam L** New Hampshire U.S.A.
95 S7 **Squapan L** Maine U.S.A.
101 P2 **Square Butte** Montana U.S.A.
95 S6 **Square L** Maine U.S.A.
122 D6 **Squattack** Quebec Canada
123 L3 **Squaw L** Quebec Canada
99 M2 **Squaw L** Minnesota U.S.A.
119 O5 **Squaw Rapids** Saskatchewan Canada
43 H10 **Squillace, Golfo di** Italy
43 J8 **Squinzano** Italy
138 C2 **Squires, Mt** N Terr Australia
143 G7 **Squires,Mt** W Australia Australia
120 F2 **Squirrel** *R* Ontario Canada
116 G3 **Squirrel** *R* Alaska U.S.A.
70 N9 **Sragen** Java
46 D2 **Srbica** Serbia Yugoslavia
Srbija *see* **Serbia**
48 F5 **Srbobran** Serbia Yugoslavia
68 F7 **Srê Âmbêl** Cambodia
46 C1 **Srebrenica** Bosnia-Herzegovina
47 J2 **Sredetska** *R* Bulgaria
46 G2 **Sredna Gora** Bulgaria
51 K2 **Sredne-Sibirskoye Ploskogor'ye** *tableland* Russian Federation
52 D2 **Sredneye Kuyto, Oz** *L* Russian Federation
58 G1 **Sredniy Kalar** Russian Federation
55 C3 **Sredniy Ural** *ra* Russian Federation
53 F10 **Sredniy Yegorlyk** Russian Federation
46 G2 **Srednogorie** Bulgaria
53 F9 **Srednyaya Akhtuba** Russian Federation
55 G2 **Sred Vasyugan** Russian Federation
68 H6 **Sre Khtum** Cambodia
31 K3 **Śrem** Poland
48 F6 **Srem Mitrovica** Serbia Yugoslavia
48 E6 **Srem Raca** Serbia Yugoslavia
48 F5 **Sremski Karlovci** Serbia Yugoslavia
58 G1 **Sretensk** Russian Federation
74 F4 **Sri Dūngargarh** India
76 F1 **Srikakulam** India
76 D4 **Sri Kālahasti** India
83 **Sri Lanka** *rep* S Asia
74 F1 **Srinagar** Kashmir
68 E5 **Srinagarind Dam** Thailand
76 B4 **Sringeri** India
76 C6 **Srivilliputtur** India
42 H4 **Srnetica** Bosnia-Herzegovina
31 K3 **Środa** Poland
31 K4 **Środa Sląska** Poland
76 F1 **Srungavarapukota** India
141 F3 **Staaten** *R* Queensland Australia
141 F3 **Staaten River Nat. Park** Queensland Australia
26 O1 **Stabbursdalen Nat. Park** Norway
26 O1 **Stabburselv** *R* Norway
33 Q4 **Stäbelow** Germany
100 D4 **Stabler** Washington U.S.A.
28 A4 **Staby** Denmark
120 J5 **Stackpool** Ontario Canada
15 D1 **Stack Skerry** *isld* Scotland
14 B4 **Stack's Mts** Ireland
16 E4 **Sta. Cruz del Retamar** Spain
100 E9 **Stacy** California U.S.A.
112 L3 **Stacy** North Carolina U.S.A.
32 K5 **Stade** Germany
22 E2 **Staden** Belgium
36 F3 **Staden** Germany
9 E4 **Stadhampton** England
28 A4 **Stadil** Denmark
28 A4 **Stadil Fjord** *inlet* Denmark
26 A9 **Stadlandet** Norway
25 G2 **Stadskanaal** Netherlands
36 F2 **Stadt Allendorf** Germany
37 N5 **Stadtamhof** Germany
37 K7 **Stadtbergen** Germany
32 K8 **Stadthagen** Germany
37 L2 **Stadtilm** Germany
36 B3 **Stadtkyll** Germany
32 H6 **Stadtland** Germany
37 J3 **Stadtlauringen** Germany
37 J2 **Stadtlengsfeld** Germany
32 E8 **Stadtlohn** Germany
32 L9 **Stadtoldendorf** Germany
36 G4 **Stadtprozelten** Germany
37 M2 **Stadtroda** Germany
37 J4 **Stadt Schwarzach** Germany
37 M3 **Stadtsteinach** Germany
15 B4 **Staffa** *isld* Scotland
33 R7 **Staffelde** Germany
37 L3 **Staffelstein** Germany
44 F2 **Staffora** *R* Italy
141 K1 **Stafford** *dist* Brisbane, Qnsld Australia
8 D2 **Stafford** England
107 M4 **Stafford** Kansas U.S.A.
98 H7 **Stafford** Nebraska U.S.A.
94 K8 **Stafford** Virginia U.S.A.
8 D2 **Staffordshire** *co* England
95 P5 **Stafford Springs** Connecticut U.S.A.
70 E6 **Stagen** Kalimantan
117 Q4 **Stagg L** Northwest Territories Canada
45 H4 **Stagno** Italy
9 F3 **Stagsden** England
33 S4 **Stahlbrode** Germany
33 S8 **Stahnsdorf** Germany
52 B5 **Staicele** Latvia
38 K6 **Stainach** Austria
9 F5 **Staines** England
12 D3 **Stair** Scotland
13 H4 **Staithes** England
48 G2 **Stakčín** Czechoslovakia
53 E9 **Stakhanov** Ukraine
28 B5 **Stakroge** Denmark
46 E1 **Stalać** Serbia Yugoslavia
27 J12 **Stålboga** Sweden

8 D6 **Stalbridge** England
9 H2 **Stalham** England
27 B11 **Stalheim** Norway
Stalingrad *see* **Volgograd**
117 L6 **Stalin, Mt** British Columbia Canada
Stalino *see* **Donetsk**
38 H8 **Stall** Austria
37 O5 **Stallwang** Germany
31 N5 **Stalowa Wola** Poland
119 M7 **Stalwart** Saskatchewan Canada
13 F6 **Stalybridge** England
46 G2 **Stamboliyski** Bulgaria
46 G1 **Stamboliyski, Yazovir A.** *res* Bulgaria
141 G5 **Stamford** Queensland Australia
9 F2 **Stamford** England
95 O5 **Stamford** Connecticut U.S.A.
95 N4 **Stamford** New York U.S.A.
98 E6 **Stamford** South Dakota U.S.A.
108 H3 **Stamford** Texas U.S.A.
37 L6 **Stammham** Germany
27 A11 **Stamnes** Norway
Stampalia *isld see* **Astipálaia** *isld*
100 D2 **Stampede** Washington U.S.A.
94 C8 **Stamping Ground** Kentucky U.S.A.
87 C10 **Stampriet** Namibia
25 E6 **Stamproij** Netherlands
109 O2 **Stamps** Arkansas U.S.A.
37 O5 **Stamsried** Germany
26 G3 **Stamsund** Norway
94 J8 **Stanadsville** Virginia U.S.A.
99 M9 **Stanberry** Missouri U.S.A.
147 Q6 **Stanchik** Russian Federation
118 E7 **Standard** Alberta Canada
103 O7 **Standard** Arizona U.S.A.
87 E11 **Standerton** S Africa
94 D3 **Standish** Michigan U.S.A.
101 M8 **Standrod** Utah U.S.A.
100 F4 **Stanfield** Oregon U.S.A.
110 K2 **Stanford** Indiana U.S.A.
110 M4 **Stanford** Kentucky U.S.A.
101 P2 **Stanford** Montana U.S.A.
9 G4 **Stanford-le-Hope** England
8 D3 **Stanford on Teme** England
27 K14 **Stånga** Sweden
27 E11 **Stange** Norway
87 F11 **Stanger** S Africa
45 L1 **Stanghella** Italy
26 C9 **Stangvik** Norway
126 F2 **Staniard Cr** Andros Bahamas
102 D3 **Stanislaus** *R* California U.S.A.
Stanislav *see* **Ivano-Frankovsk**
46 F2 **Stanke Dimitrov** Bulgaria
37 P4 **Staňkov** Czechoslovakia
139 H8 **Stanley** Tasmania Australia
122 F7 **Stanley** New Brunswick Canada
131 G8 **Stanley** Falkland Is
15 E4 **Stanley** Scotland
101 L5 **Stanley** Idaho U.S.A.
106 E6 **Stanley** New Mexico U.S.A.
112 F2 **Stanley** North Carolina U.S.A.
98 D1 **Stanley** North Dakota U.S.A.
109 M1 **Stanley** Oklahoma U.S.A.
94 J8 **Stanley** Virginia U.S.A.
99 Q5 **Stanley** Wisconsin U.S.A.
119 M3 **Stanley Mission** Saskatchewan Canada
139 G8 **Stanley, Mt** Tasmania Australia
88 B1 **Stanley, Mt** Uganda/Zaire
86 C6 **Stanley Pool** Zaire
Stanleyville *see* **Kisangani**
118 F7 **Stanmore** Alberta Canada
145 E2 **Stanmore Bay** New Zealand
99 T2 **Stannard Rock** Michigan U.S.A.
13 G3 **Stannington** England
55 F3 **Stanovka** Russian Federation
55 D2 **Stanovoy** Russian Federation
51 M3 **Stanovoy Khrebet** *mts* Russian Federation
41 P3 **Stans** Austria
138 E5 **Stansbury** South Australia Australia
142 G5 **Stansmore Ra** W Australia Australia
9 G4 **Stansted** England
141 K8 **Stanthorpe** Queensland Australia
147 J1 **Stanton** Northwest Territories Canada
99 L9 **Stanton** Iowa U.S.A.
94 D9 **Stanton** Kentucky U.S.A.
94 B3 **Stanton** Michigan U.S.A.
98 J8 **Stanton** Nebraska U.S.A.
98 E2 **Stanton** North Dakota U.S.A.
110 G6 **Stanton** Tennessee U.S.A.
108 F3 **Stanton** Texas U.S.A.
6 E6 **Stanton Banks** Atlantic Oc
56 B3 **Stantsionno-Oyash'nskiy** Russian Federation
94 B3 **Stanwood** Michigan U.S.A.
117 M11 **Stanwood** Washington U.S.A.
41 N3 **Stanzach** Austria
33 N9 **Stapelburg** Germany
25 F3 **Staphorst** Netherlands
9 E5 **Stapleford** England
111 J11 **Stapleton** Alabama U.S.A.
112 E4 **Stapleton** Georgia U.S.A.
54 F3 **Star'** Russian Federation
111 F9 **Star** Mississippi U.S.A.
112 H2 **Star** North Carolina U.S.A.
109 J4 **Star** Texas U.S.A.
31 N4 **Starachowice** Poland
48 F1 **Stara L'ubovňa** Czechoslovakia
37 O3 **Stará-Role** Czechoslovakia
53 G7 **Staraya Drozhzhanoye** Russian Federation
53 G8 **Staraya Kulatka** Russian Federation
52 D5 **Staraya Russa** Russian Federation
48 L1 **Staraya Sinyava** Ukraine
48 L2 **Staraya Ushitsa** Ukraine
55 E1 **Staraya Vorpavla** Russian Federation
47 H2 **Stara Zagora** Bulgaria
119 U9 **Starbuck** Manitoba Canada
99 L4 **Starbuck** Minnesota U.S.A.
100 G3 **Starbuck** Washington U.S.A.
135 L9 **Starbuck I** Pacific Oc
119 N6 **Star City** Saskatchewan Canada
111 E8 **Star City** Arkansas U.S.A.
94 A6 **Star City** Indiana U.S.A.
94 H7 **Star City** West Virginia U.S.A.
141 G2 **Starcke** Queensland Australia
8 C6 **Starcross** England
37 O4 **Staré Sedliště** Czechoslovakia
31 J2 **Stargard** Poland
42 H4 **Stari Majdan** Bosnia-Herzegovina
31 N6 **Starina** Czechoslovakia
52 D6 **Staritsa** Russian Federation
103 O10 **Stark** Arizona U.S.A.
101 L2 **Stark** Montana U.S.A.
95 Q2 **Stark** New Hampshire U.S.A.
55 C6 **Star Karabutak** Kazakhstan
113 E8 **Starke** Florida U.S.A.
100 J5 **Starkey** Idaho U.S.A.
100 G4 **Starkey** Oregon U.S.A.
109 O5 **Starks** Louisiana U.S.A.
106 F4 **Starkville** Colorado U.S.A.
111 H8 **Starkville** Mississippi U.S.A.
98 H1 **Starkweather** North Dakota U.S.A.
99 R3 **Starlake** Wisconsin U.S.A.
41 O1 **Starnberg** Germany

56 C4 **Starobachati** Russian Federation
54 K7 **Star'obel'sk** Ukraine
54 D4 **Starodub** Russian Federation
31 L2 **Starogard** Poland
48 M4 **Starokazach'ye** Ukraine
48 L1 **Starokonstantinov** Ukraine
53 C9 **Starokonstantinov** Ukraine
55 F3 **Staromalinovka** Russian Federation
31 O2 **Starosielce** Poland
55 F3 **Starosoldatskoye** Russian Federation
55 C4 **Starosubkhangulovo** Russian Federation
55 C3 **Staroutkinsk** Russian Federation
52 G5 **Starovercheskaya** Russian Federation
52 H6 **Staroye Baysarovo** Russian Federation
102 F1 **Star Pk** Nevada U.S.A.
8 C7 **Start Pt** England
15 F1 **Start Pt** Scotland
48 F1 **Stary Sącz** Poland
52 H6 **Staryye Zyattsy** Russian Federation
52 H6 **Staryy Menzelyabash** Russian Federation
50 G2 **Staryy Nadym** Russian Federation
54 J5 **Staryy Oskol** Russian Federation
52 D5 **Staryy Ryad** Russian Federation
31 O6 **Staryy Sambor** Ukraine
48 H1 **Staryy Sambor** Ukraine
33 P9 **Stassfurt** Germany
31 N5 **Staszów** Poland
99 N7 **State Center** Iowa U.S.A.
94 K6 **State College** Pennsylvania U.S.A.
111 H10 **State Line** Mississippi U.S.A.
Staten I Argentina *see* **Estados, I de los**
95 N6 **Staten I** New York U.S.A.
112 F5 **Statesboro** Georgia U.S.A.
112 G2 **Statesville** North Carolina U.S.A.
6 M1 **Statfjord** *oil rig* North Sea
27 D12 **Stathelle** Norway
33 S10 **Stauchitz** Germany
36 F2 **Staufenberg** Germany
100 E6 **Stauffer** Oregon U.S.A.
8 D4 **Staunton** England
110 G2 **Staunton** Illinois U.S.A.
94 H8 **Staunton** Virginia U.S.A.
27 A13 **Stavanger** Norway
22 H3 **Stave** Belgium
117 M11 **Stave L** British Columbia Canada
9 E1 **Staveley** England
13 F5 **Staveley** Cumbria England
22 K3 **Stavelot** Belgium
118 D8 **Stavely** Alberta Canada
33 S5 **Staven** Germany
25 B5 **Stavenisse** Netherlands
28 A5 **Stavning** Denmark
28 F3 **Stavnshoved** *C* Denmark
25 D3 **Stavoren** Netherlands
28 J6 **Stavreby** Denmark
28 F6 **Stavreshoved** *C* Denmark
53 F10 **Stavropol'** Russian Federation
55 E4 **Stavropolka** Kazakhstan
53 F10 **Stavropol'skaya Vozvyshennost'** *uplands* Russian Federation
53 F11 **Stavropol'skiy Kray** *reg* Russian Federation
46 E5 **Stavrós** Greece
46 G9 **Stavrós, Akra** *C* Crete Greece
46 G3 **Stavroúpolis** Greece
139 G6 **Stawell** Victoria Australia
31 N2 **Stawiski** Poland
31 L4 **Stawiszyn** Poland
120 K8 **Stayner** Ontario Canada
100 C5 **Stayton** Oregon U.S.A.
45 H4 **Stazzema** Italy
102 E2 **Steamboat** Nevada U.S.A.
106 D1 **Steamboat Springs** Colorado U.S.A.
94 C10 **Stearns** Kentucky U.S.A.
31 M2 **Stębark** Poland
116 F5 **Stebbins** Alaska U.S.A.
33 Q7 **Stechow** Germany
41 J2 **Steckborn** Switzerland
28 B7 **Stedesand** Germany
116 R4 **Steel Creek** Alaska U.S.A.
111 K8 **Steele** Alabama U.S.A.
110 G5 **Steele** Missouri U.S.A.
98 G3 **Steele** North Dakota U.S.A.
98 K9 **Steele City** Nebraska U.S.A.
146 D5 **Steele I** Antarctica
117 C5 **Steele,Mt** Yukon Territory Canada
110 G3 **Steeleville** Illinois U.S.A.
120 D4 **Steel R** Ontario Canada
95 L6 **Steelton** Pennsylvania U.S.A.
110 E4 **Steelville** Missouri U.S.A.
25 B5 **Steenbergen** Netherlands
89 G5 **Steenkamps Berg** *mts* S Africa
22 G2 **Steenkerque** Belgium
117 P6 **Steen River** Alberta Canada
25 D6 **Steensel** Netherlands
100 G7 **Steens Mt** Oregon U.S.A.
115 O2 **Steenstrup Gletscher** *gla* Greenland
22 D2 **Steenvoorde** France
22 D2 **Steenwerck** France
25 F3 **Steenwijk** Netherlands
119 M5 **Steep Cr** Saskatchewan Canada
119 O3 **Steephill L** Saskatchewan Canada
131 F7 **Steeple Jason** *isld* Falkland Is
71 D6 **Steep Pt** Philippines
119 T7 **Steep Rock** Manitoba Canada
118 K2 **Steep Rock** Ontario Canada
143 B6 **Steere, Mt** W Australia Australia
13 G6 **Steeton** England
48 L3 **Stefăneşti** Romania
43 F10 **Stefano di Cam., S** Sicily
146 K10 **Stefansson B** Antarctica
147 H3 **Stefansson I** Northwest Territories Canada
133 C6 **Steffen** *mt* Chile/Arg
36 F2 **Steffenberg** Germany
98 C8 **Stegall** Nebraska U.S.A.
28 J7 **Stege** Denmark
28 J6 **Stege Bugt** *B* Denmark
33 P8 **Stegelitz** Germany
29 K7 **Stege Nor** *L* Denmark
99 T8 **Steger** Illinois U.S.A.
87 F11 **Stegi** Swaziland
33 S8 **Steglitz** Berlin
100 E1 **Stehekin** Washington U.S.A.
48 G4 **Ştei** Romania
38 L7 **Steiermark** *prov* Austria
37 J4 **Steigerwald** *hills* Germany
37 L5 **Stein** Germany
37 L3 **Steinach** Germany
37 J5 **Steinach** Germany
36 H3 **Steinau** Germany
99 K9 **Steinauer** Nebraska U.S.A.
118 E1 **Steinbach** Manitoba Canada
36 E6 **Steinbach** Germany
37 J2 **Steinbach** Germany
37 K2 **Steinbach Hallenberg** Germany
28 D7 **Steinberg** Germany
38 G6 **Steinberge** Austria
36 C6 **Steinbourg** France
129 H6 **Steinen** *R* Brazil
38 G7 **Steinernes Meer** *mts* Austria
32 H7 **Steinfeld** Germany
22 K4 **Steinfort** Luxembourg
32 H8 **Steinhagen** Germany
113 D8 **Steinhatchee** Florida U.S.A.
87 C10 **Steinhausen** Namibia
37 L3 **Steinheid** Germany

36 F3 **Steinheim** Germany
33 M5 **Steinhorst** Germany
32 K8 **Steinhuder Meer** *L* Germany
32 L5 **Steinkirchen** Germany
26 E8 **Steinkjer** Norway
87 C11 **Steinkopf** S Africa
38 L7 **Steinplan** *mt* Austria
106 B9 **Steins** New Mexico U.S.A.
36 F5 **Steinsfurt** Germany
37 L3 **Steinwiesen** Germany
22 G1 **Stekene** Belgium
99 L9 **Stella** Nebraska U.S.A.
112 K3 **Stella** North Carolina U.S.A.
122 K8 **Stellarton** Nova Scotia Canada
45 K2 **Stellata** Italy
32 M6 **Stelle** Germany
87 C12 **Stellenbosch** S Africa
116 Q6 **Steller, Mt** Alaska U.S.A.
42 D2 **Stelvio, Passo di** Italy
112 J1 **Stem** North Carolina U.S.A.
32 K7 **Stemmen** Germany
26 C8 **Stemshaug** Norway
32 H8 **Stemwede** Germany
22 J5 **Stenay** France
28 A3 **Stenbjerg** Denmark
33 P7 **Stendal** Germany
52 B6 **Stende** Latvia
28 D5 **Stenderup** Denmark
28 D7 **Stenderup** Germany
119 P7 **Stenen** Saskatchewan Canada
28 E2 **Stenhøj** Denmark
138 D6 **Stenhouse B** South Australia Australia
28 D3 **Stenild** Denmark
28 H5 **Stenlille** Denmark
28 J5 **Stenløse** Denmark
15 G2 **Stenness** Shetland Scotland
15 E1 **Stenness,L.of** Orkney Scotland
47 P13 **Stenón Kerkiras, Vório** *chan* Greece/Albania
26 J6 **Stensele** Sweden
27 G14 **Stensjön** Sweden
27 G13 **Stenstorp** Sweden
28 E6 **Stenstrup** Denmark
26 L5 **Stenträsk** Sweden
27 E13 **Stenungsund** Sweden
28 F4 **Stenvad** Denmark
78 L2 **Stepanakert** Azerbaijan
78 K1 **Stepanavan** Armenia
55 C5 **Stepanovka** Kazakhstan
33 O5 **Stepenitz** *R* Germany
33 P6 **Stepenitz** *R* Germany
37 O6 **Stephansposching** Germany
98 K1 **Stephen** Minnesota U.S.A.
109 O2 **Stephens** Arkansas U.S.A.
94 J7 **Stephens City** Virginia U.S.A.
138 F4 **Stephens Creek** New South Wales Australia
117 H8 **Stephens I** British Columbia Canada
115 K6 **Stephens L** Manitoba Canada
119 W2 **Stephens L** Manitoba Canada
99 T4 **Stephenson** Michigan U.S.A.
145 D1 **Stephenson I** New Zealand
117 G7 **Stephens Pass** Alaska U.S.A.
123 O5 **Stephenville** Newfoundland Canada
109 J3 **Stephenville** Texas U.S.A.
123 O5 **Stephenville Crossing** Newfoundland Canada
57 D5 **Step' Karnabchul'** Uzbekistan
55 F5 **Stepnogorsk** Kazakhstan
57 G3 **Stepnoye** Kyrgyzstan
55 F4 **Stepnyak** Kazakhstan
116 G9 **Stepovak B** Alaska U.S.A.
28 C6 **Stepping** Denmark
103 K2 **Steptoe** Nevada U.S.A.
36 H3 **Sterbfritz** Germany
46 E6 **Stereá Ellás** *admin region* Greece
87 E12 **Sterkstroom** S Africa
108 F1 **Sterley** Texas U.S.A.
55 C4 **Sterlibashevo** Russian Federation
106 G1 **Sterling** Colorado U.S.A.
99 R8 **Sterling** Illinois U.S.A.
107 M3 **Sterling** Kansas U.S.A.
94 C2 **Sterling** Michigan U.S.A.
98 K9 **Sterling** Nebraska U.S.A.
98 F3 **Sterling** North Dakota U.S.A.
109 J1 **Sterling** Oklahoma U.S.A.
103 N2 **Sterling** Utah U.S.A.
108 G4 **Sterling City** Texas U.S.A.
94 D4 **Sterling Heights** Michigan U.S.A.
55 C4 **Sterlitamak** Russian Federation
33 P5 **Sternberg** Germany
31 K6 **Šternberk** Czechoslovakia
22 H2 **Sterrebeek** Belgium
52 E4 **Steshevskaya** Russian Federation
31 K3 **Stęszew** Poland
41 K1 **Stetten** Germany
Stettin *see* **Szczecin**
33 U5 **Stettiner Haff** Germany
118 E6 **Stettler** Alberta Canada
99 U3 **Steuben** Michigan U.S.A.
99 Q6 **Steuben** Wisconsin U.S.A.
94 G6 **Steubenville** Ohio U.S.A.
33 Q9 **Steutz** Germany
9 F4 **Stevenage** England
120 E3 **Stevens** Ontario Canada
145 D4 **Stevens, Mt** New Zealand
138 C2 **Stevenson** *R* South Australia Australia
119 U9 **Stevenson** Manitoba Canada
110 L7 **Stevenson** Alabama U.S.A.
100 D4 **Stevenson** Washington U.S.A.
119 W5 **Stevenson L** Manitoba Canada
99 R5 **Stevens Pt** Wisconsin U.S.A.
12 D2 **Stevenston** Scotland
116 N4 **Stevens Village** Alaska U.S.A.
94 A4 **Stevensville** Michigan U.S.A.
32 F9 **Stever** *R* Germany
118 F8 **Steveville Prov.Pk** Alberta Canada
29 K6 **Stevns** *pen* Denmark
22 J2 **Stevoort** Belgium
99 S8 **Steward** Illinois U.S.A.
110 H2 **Stewardson** Illinois U.S.A.
141 G2 **Stewart** *R* Queensland Australia
117 H8 **Stewart** British Columbia Canada
117 D4 **Stewart** Yukon Territory Canada
99 M5 **Stewart** Minnesota U.S.A.
102 E2 **Stewart** Nevada U.S.A.
140 C1 **Stewart, C** N Terr Australia
144 A7 **Stewart I** New Zealand
137 N3 **Stewart Is** Pacific Oc
143 C10 **Stewart, Mt** W Australia Australia
15 D5 **Stewarton** Scotland
95 L7 **Stewartstown** Pennsylvania U.S.A.
110 B2 **Stewartsville** Missouri U.S.A.
127 K2 **Stewart Town** Jamaica
118 K8 **Stewart Valley** Saskatchewan Canada
99 O6 **Stewartville** Minnesota U.S.A.
122 J8 **Stewiacke** Nova Scotia Canada
32 K7 **Steyerberg** Germany
9 F6 **Steyning** England
8 A4 **Steynton** Wales
38 K5 **Steyr** Austria
121 S7 **St-Hyacinthe** Quebec Canada
45 L4 **Stia** Italy
8 B6 **Stibb Cross** England
100 K5 **Stibnite** Idaho U.S.A.
9 G1 **Stickford** England
32 G6 **Stickhausen** Germany

Column 1

9 G1 Stickney England
98 H6 Stickney South Dakota U.S.A.
33 N9 Stiege Germany
25 E2 Stiens Netherlands
45 L2 Stienta Italy
107 P6 Stigler Oklahoma U.S.A.
43 G8 Stigliano Italy
26 J9 Stigsjö Sweden
117 H7 Stikine R Alaska/Br Col U.S.A./Canada
117 H6 Stikine Ranges British Columbia Canada
117 G7 Stikine Str Alaska U.S.A.
108 F4 Stiles Texas U.S.A.
110 K2 Stilesville Indiana U.S.A.
46 F6 Stilis Greece
28 D4 Stilling Denmark
13 G5 Stillington England
138 E5 Stillman Valley Illinois U.S.A.
99 O4 Stillwater R Montana U.S.A.
101 L1 Stillwater Minnesota U.S.A.
102 F2 Stillwater Nevada U.S.A.
107 N5 Stillwater Oklahoma U.S.A.
102 F2 Stillwater Ra Nevada U.S.A.
43 H10 Stilo, Pta Italy
48 J5 Stilpeni Romania
110 B6 Stilwell Oklahoma U.S.A.
46 E7 Stimfalias, L Greece
101 M1 Stimson,Mt Montana U.S.A.
12 D3 Stinchar,R Scotland
98 E9 Stinking Water Cr Nebraska U.S.A.
46 E3 Štip Macedonia Yugoslavia
46 G6 Stira Greece
Stirling co see Strathclyde and Central regions
140 C5 Stirling N Terr Australia
138 E5 Stirling South Australia Australia
118 E9 Stirling Alberta Canada
121 N8 Stirling Ontario Canada
144 B7 Stirling New Zealand
12 E1 Stirling Scotland
100 D10 Stirling City California U.S.A.
143 C9 Stirling, Mt W Australia Australia
143 C10 Stirling Ra W Australia Australia
44 H2 Stirone R Italy
98 A3 Stirum North Dakota U.S.A.
100 K3 Stites Idaho U.S.A.
119 V3 Stitt Manitoba Canada
99 Q7 Stitzer Wisconsin U.S.A.
27 K14 Stjärnarve Sweden
26 N1 Stjernöya isld Norway
26 E8 Stjördalselv R Norway
26 E8 Stjördalshalsen Norway
18 E6 St-Maixent-l'École France
121 R5 St-Maurice, Parc Quebec Canada
13 E2 Stobo Scotland
41 K2 Stockach Germany
27 G14 Stockaryd Sweden
8 E9 Stockbridge England
95 O4 Stockbridge Massachusetts U.S.A.
94 C4 Stockbridge Michigan U.S.A.
94 E8 Stockdale Ohio U.S.A.
109 K6 Stockdale Texas U.S.A.
33 N5 Stockelsdorf Germany
48 C2 Stockerau Austria
36 B6 Stock,Etang du L France
101 O2 Stockett Montana U.S.A.
98 J9 Stockham Nebraska U.S.A.
33 L3 Stockheim Germany
119 P8 Stockholm Saskatchewan Canada
27 J12 Stockholm county Sweden
27 K12 Stockholm Maine U.S.A.
95 S6 Stockholm Maine U.S.A.
40 G4 Stockhorn mt Switzerland
139 J5 Stockinbingal New South Wales Australia
13 F6 Stockport England
94 F7 Stockport Ohio U.S.A.
139 K5 Stockton New South Wales Australia
119 S9 Stockton Manitoba Canada
144 C4 Stockton New Zealand
111 J10 Stockton Alabama U.S.A.
102 C4 Stockton California U.S.A.
99 Q7 Stockton Illinois U.S.A.
107 L2 Stockton Kansas U.S.A.
95 M8 Stockton Maryland U.S.A.
110 C4 Stockton Missouri U.S.A.
101 N9 Stockton Utah U.S.A.
99 Q3 Stockton I Wisconsin U.S.A.
116 O1 Stockton Is Alaska U.S.A.
110 C4 Stockton L Missouri U.S.A.
13 G4 Stockton-on-Tees England
95 T2 Stockton Springs Maine U.S.A.
98 F9 Stockville Nebraska U.S.A.
31 N4 Stoczek Lukowski Poland
37 P4 Stod Czechoslovakia
5 F4 Stod Norway
99 P6 Stoddard Wisconsin U.S.A.
26 J9 Stöde Sweden
68 H6 Stoeng Treng Cambodia
15 C2 Stoer,Pt of Scotland
28 C4 Stoholm Denmark
145 D4 Stoke New Zealand
107 L2 Stoke Ferry England
8 C7 Stoke Fleming England
9 F4 Stokenchurch England
120 J7 Stokes Bay Ontario Canada
112 H1 Stokesdale North Carolina U.S.A.
143 D10 Stokes Inlet W Australia Australia
145 E4 Stokes, Mt New Zealand
139 G8 Stokes Pt Tasmania Australia
140 B5 Stokes Ra N Terr Australia
53 C8 Stokhod R Ukraine
28 G7 Stokkemarke Denmark
28 S10 Stokkseyri Iceland
26 D7 Stokksund Norway
26 G3 Stokmarknes Norway
52 H5 Stolac Bosnia-Herzegovina
25 F7 Stolberg Germany
33 N9 Stolberg Germany
147 Q8 Stolbovoy,Ostrov Russian Federation
48 F2 Stolica Czechoslovakia
37 O2 Stolberg Germany
32 H5 Stollhamm Germany
90 A16 Stoltenhoff I Tristan da Cunha
32 K7 Stolzenau Germany
36 D3 Stolzenfels Germany
46 B5 Stómion Greece
31 B7 Stömmeln Germany
8 D2 Stone England
94 G5 Stoneboro Pennsylvania U.S.A.
9 E3 Stonebridge England
106 F3 Stone City Colorado U.S.A.
120 K8 Stonecliffe Ontario Canada
100 F7 Stone Corral L Oregon U.S.A.
122 A7 Stoneham Quebec Canada
32 K7 Stonehaugh Germany
95 N7 Stone Harbor New Jersey U.S.A.
15 F4 Stonehaven Scotland
141 G6 Stonehenge Queensland Australia
9 E5 Stonehenge anc mon England
8 E5 Stonehouse England
9 P4 Stone L Wisconsin U.S.A.
112 C4 Stone Mt W Georgia U.S.A.
117 L6 Stone Mt. Prov. Park British Columbia Canada
110 K6 Stone River Nat. Battlefield Tennessee U.S.A.
119 T5 Stonewall Manitoba Canada
111 H9 Stonewall Mississippi U.S.A.
109 J5 Stonewall Texas U.S.A.
99 U5 Stonewall Texas U.S.A.
12 E4 Stoney Creek Ontario Canada
26 J2 Stonglandet Norway

Column 2

106 H4 Stonington Colorado U.S.A.
95 Q5 Stonington Connecticut U.S.A.
99 R10 Stonington Illinois U.S.A.
95 T2 Stonington Maine U.S.A.
119 M8 Stony Beach Saskatchewan Canada
94 K10 Stony Creek Virginia U.S.A.
8 D3 Stony Cross England
102 B2 Stonyford California U.S.A.
127 L2 Stony Hill Jamaica
118 D1 Stony Mountain Manitoba Canada
118 D5 Stony Plain Alberta Canada
95 N5 Stony Point New York U.S.A.
112 F2 Stony Point North Carolina U.S.A.
144 C6 Stony Point New Zealand
114 J6 Stony Rapids Saskatchewan Canada
116 J6 Stony River Alaska U.S.A.
9 F3 Stony Stratford England
120 H1 Stooping R Ontario Canada
32 L4 Stör R Germany
28 C4 Storå R Denmark
27 H12 Storå Sweden
26 J9 Storåbränna Sweden
6 F1 Stora Dimun isld Faeroes
27 E12 Stora Le L Sweden
26 L5 Stora Lule älv R Sweden
26 K4 Stora Lulevatten L Sweden
26 F9 Storån R Sweden
26 J4 Stora Sjöfallet L Sweden
26 K6 Storavan L Sweden
26 K6 Storberg Sweden
27 L11 Storby Finland
27 A12 Stord Norway
26 B9 Stordal Möre og Romsdal Norway
26 E8 Stordal Sör-Tröndelag Norway
28 D3 Store Arden Denmark
28 F5 Store Bælt chan Denmark
26 G6 Store Börgefjeld mt Norway
27 H14 Storebro Sweden
28 B6 Store Darum Denmark
28 G5 Store Fuglede Denmark
29 K6 Store Heddinge Denmark
29 K7 Store Jyndevad Denmark
29 K7 Storeklint cliffs Denmark
147 F10 Store Koldewey isld Greenland
26 P1 Storelv R Norway
29 K5 Stor-Elvdal Norway
28 H5 Store Magleby Denmark
26 R1 Store Merlöse Denmark
15 E4 Store Molvik Norway
117 W9 Stören Norway
15 D3 Store Rise Denmark
15 D3 Store Spjellerup Denmark
120 J10 Store Tårnby Denmark
15 D2 Store Vildmose Denmark
8 B6 Storfjället,N mt Sweden
106 H2 Storfjället,S mt Norway
95 R1 Storfjord mt Norway
98 E9 Storfosshei Norway
37 O6 Storhögen Sweden
30 H3 Storholmen Sweden
108 A3 Storjorm L Sweden
37 K1 Störkanal Germany
101 Q3 Storkerson B Northwest Territories Canada
110 E5 Storlien Sweden
31 J9 Storlögda Sweden
8 H8 Stormare reg Germany
103 J2 Stormberg mts S Africa
99 P7 Storm L Iowa U.S.A.
101 P9 Stormy L Ontario Canada
121 R5 Stornoway Scotland
52 H4 Stornoway Res Utah U.S.A.
48 K2 Storozhevsk Quebec Canada
26 F8 Storozhevsk Russian Federation
47 H1 Storozhinets Ukraine
31 K7 Storrsjön L Sweden
31 M6 Storrington England
138 C5 Storr,The mt Scotland
26 L7 Storsäterträsk Sweden
27 E11 Storsjö L Sweden
26 L7 Storsjö Sweden
27 F10 Stor-sjöen L Norway
27 F10 Storsjöen Sweden
26 F9 Storsjön L Gävleborg Sweden
28 H7 Storsjön L Jämtland Sweden
119 Q9 Storstorm co Denmark
98 C3 Storströmmen chan Denmark
98 G8 Storthoaks Saskatchewan Canada
109 L4 Storuman Sweden
26 F9 Storvarden mt Sweden
26 F9 Storvigelen mt Norway
27 J11 Storvik Sweden
48 H5 Stor-vindelen L Sweden
143 E9 Storvorde Denmark
101 T5 Story Wyoming U.S.A.
133 B7 Story City Iowa U.S.A.
37 M1 Stössen Germany
26 F5 Stött Norway
41 N2 Stötten Germany
37 L1 Stotternheim Germany
28 D5 Stouby Denmark
119 O9 Stoughton Saskatchewan Canada
95 Q4 Stoughton Massachusetts U.S.A.
99 R7 Stoughton Wisconsin U.S.A.
22 K3 Stoumont Belgium
46 E4 Stoupa Greece
28 B3 Stourbridge England
8 D3 Stourport England
9 H5 Stour,R England
54 M4 Stourton England
24 E7 Stoutsville Ohio U.S.A.
28 D3 Støvring Denmark
13 F2 Stow Scotland
109 N6 Stowell Texas U.S.A.
9 F5 Stowmarket England
8 E4 Stow on the Wold England
28 E4 Stoy Denmark
55 G1 Stozac R Montenegro Yugoslavia
41 M3 Stra Italy
120 J3 Straach Germany
14 C1 Strabane N Ireland
109 N4 Strachur Scotland
30 J5 Stradbally Ireland
38 N8 Stradella Italy
25 F6 Stradsett England
119 P7 Straelen Germany
12 C2 Stragari Yugoslavia
81 J6 Strahan Tasmania Australia
79 B8 Strakonice Czechoslovakia
37 P4 Stralsund Germany
73 T6 Stranda Norway
36 D4 Strand Hedmark Norway
32 H9 Strand Rogaland Norway
10 A10 Strand S Africa
26 B9 Stranda Norway
28 C3 Strandby Denmark
G 10 Strandby Vendsyssel Denmark
118 E6 Strandby Denmark
26 P7 Strang Nebraska U.S.A.
113 J10 Strangers Cay isld Bahamas
14 F2 Strangford N Ireland
13 H1 Strangford L N Ireland
27 J12 Strängnäs Sweden
98 J8 Strångsjö Sweden
140 C3 Strangways Ra N Terr Australia
14 D2 Stranorlar Ireland

Column 3

118 J7 Stranraer Saskatchewan Canada
12 C4 Stranraer Scotland
119 N7 Strasbourg Saskatchewan Canada
36 D6 Strasbourg France
33 T5 Strasburg Germany
106 F2 Strasburg Colorado U.S.A.
110 H2 Strasburg Illinois U.S.A.
98 F3 Strasburg North Dakota U.S.A.
94 J8 Strasburg Ohio U.S.A.
94 J8 Strasburg Virginia U.S.A.
31 N6 Strasheny Moldavia
112 F3 Strashenhaus Austria
38 E7 Strass Steiermark Austria
27 H12 Strass Tirol Austria
38 K8 Strassburg Austria
38 C2 Strassenhaus Germany
38 M7 Strassgang Austria
37 O6 Strasskirchen Germany
38 H6 Strasswalchen Germany
139 H7 Stratford Victoria Australia
88 J11 Stratford Quebec Canada
145 E3 Stratford New Zealand
95 O5 Stratford Connecticut U.S.A.
99 N7 Stratford Iowa U.S.A.
95 Q2 Stratford New Hampshire U.S.A.
109 L1 Stratford Oklahoma U.S.A.
98 H4 Stratford South Dakota U.S.A.
108 B7 Stratford Texas U.S.A.
99 O5 Stratford Wisconsin U.S.A.
9 H4 Stratford-on-Avon England
138 E6 Stratford St. Mary England
138 E6 Strathalbyn South Australia Australia
15 D5 Strathaven Scotland
12 D2 Strathbane Scotland
15 D2 Strath Brora Scotland
15 D3 Strath Carron Scotland
119 R8 Strathclair Manitoba Canada
117 L11 Strathclyde reg Scotland
15 D5 Strathcona Prov. Park British Columbia Canada
15 D3 Strath Dearn Scotland
15 E2 Strath Farrar Scotland
141 G3 Strath Halladale Scotland
141 G3 Strathleven Queensland Australia
123 L7 Strathlorne Nova Scotia Canada
13 E1 Strathmiglo Scotland
141 G4 Strathmore Queensland Australia
118 D7 Strathmore Alberta Canada
15 E4 Strathmore dist Scotland
117 M9 Strathmore British Columbia Canada
15 D3 Strathpeffer Scotland
120 J10 Strathroy Ontario Canada
15 D2 Strathy Pt Scotland
13 D7 Strathyre Scotland
31 K5 Stratton Colorado U.S.A.
31 L3 Stratton Maine U.S.A.
31 N6 Stratzyzów Poland
141 M7 Straubing Germany
113 G10 Straumen Norway
99 M8 Straus New Mexico U.S.A.
98 G7 Strausberg Germany
109 L1 Straussfurt Germany
94 G10 Straw Montana U.S.A.
140 B6 Strawberry R Arkansas U.S.A.
138 D3 Strawberry Nevada U.S.A.
138 D3 Strawberry Mt Oregon U.S.A.
116 F5 Strawberry I Ontario Canada
117 L8 Strawberry Pt Iowa U.S.A.
99 P7 Strawberry Res Utah U.S.A.
121 R5 Strawhat Depot Quebec Canada
100 E2 Strawn Illinois U.S.A.
144 A6 Strawn Texas U.S.A.
144 B1 Stráž Czechoslovakia
138 C3 Strazhitsa Bulgaria
47 O3 Strážnice Czechoslovakia
41 O3 Stubai Tal Austria
38 L7 Stub Alpe mt Austria
28 J7 Stubbekøbing Denmark
32 J6 Stubben Germany
28 B4 Stubbergø Sø L Denmark
28 F4 Stubben Denmark
83 M9 Stubbs Pt Christmas I Indian Oc
41 M3 Stuben Austria
38 N7 Stubenberg Austria
38 M6 Stübming R Austria
47 H3 Studen Kladenets, Yazovir res Bulgaria
38 N7 Studenzen Austria
99 R7 Studholme Hills N Terr Australia
144 C6 Studholme Junction New Zealand
46 G1 Studina Romania
28 D3 Studland England
29 H8 Studsgård Denmark
26 H8 Stugun Sweden
28 J9 Stuhr Germany
119 O9 Stukenbrock Germany
9 G3 Stump Cross England
112 M2 Stumpy Point North Carolina U.S.A.
33 J4 Stumsdorf Germany
68 G6 Stung Chinit R Cambodia
68 G6 Stung Sen R Cambodia
26 N2 Stuoraivarre L Norway
117 L9 Stupendous Mt British Columbia Canada
78 D3 Stúpino Russian Federation
51 P2 Stura di Ala R Italy
40 G7 Sturat R Sabah
41 J3 Stura di Demonte R Italy
48 B1 Stura di V,Grande R Italy
77 F2 Stura di Viu R Italy
48 M5 Sturge I Antarctica
120 K6 Sturgeon R Ontario Canada
94 C4 Sturgeon R Michigan U.S.A.
47 L6 Sturgeon Turkey
74 C4 Sturgeon Missouri U.S.A.
119 U6 Sturgeon B Manitoba Canada
94 B1 Sturgeon B Michigan U.S.A.
99 S10 Sturgeon Bay Wisconsin U.S.A.
99 S10 Sturgeon Bay Canal Wisconsin U.S.A.
120 K6 Sturgeon Falls Ontario Canada
117 P8 Sturgeon L Alberta Canada
121 M8 Sturgeon L Ontario Canada
119 Q4 Sturgeon Landing Manitoba Canada
118 G5 Sturgeon R Alberta Canada
118 L5 Sturgeon R Ontario Canada
119 P7 Sturgeon R Saskatchewan Canada
115 L7 Sturkö isld Sweden
99 T5 Sturminster Newton England
48 E5 Štúrovo Czechoslovakia
59 H3 Sturry England
74 F5 Sturt Desert South Australia U.S.A.
142 G4 Sturt Cr R W Australia Australia
142 G4 Sturt Creek W Australia Australia
141 F8 Sturt Des Qnsld/S Aust Australia
141 F8 Sturt, Mt New South Wales Australia
835 T7 Sturt Nat Park New South Wales Australia
140 C3 Sturt Plain N Terr Australia
15 A5 Stutensee Germany
111 D8 Stutterheim S Africa

Column 4

95 R2 Strong Maine U.S.A.
111 H8 Strong Mississippi U.S.A.
107 O3 Strong City Kansas U.S.A.
107 L6 Strong City Oklahoma U.S.A.
118 L7 Strongfield Saskatchewan Canada
99 Q3 Stronghurst Illinois U.S.A.
28 R9 Strykkishólmur Iceland
130 G6 Suaçui Grande, R Brazil
71 M9 Suai Indonesia
70 C3 Suai Sarawak
86 G2 Suakin Sudan
71 G8 Suak Indonesia
70 C3 Suai Indonesia
128 D2 Suárez R Colombia
70 L9 Subang Java
71 F4 Subang Java
71 H5 Subang Libya
45 L2 Subatica Serbia Yugoslavia
65 D2 Subang China
125 L2 Subang Honduras
118 J8 Success Saskatchewan Canada
52 C5 Success Missouri U.S.A.
110 D4 Succiso,Alpe di mt Italy
99 P5 Sucé France
48 F1 Sucha Poland
48 F1 Suchan see Partizansk
31 J2 Suchan Poland
31 H7 Suchdol Czechoslovakia
31 M4 Suchedniow Poland
31 O2 Suchowola Poland
25 F6 Süchteln Germany
100 C1 Sucia I Washington U.S.A.
14 C3 Suck R Ireland
100 H6 Sucker Cr Oregon U.S.A.
116 Q7 Suckling,C Alaska U.S.A.
33 P6 Suckow Germany
128 E6 Sucre Bolivia
126 G10 Sucre Colombia
128 C5 Sucundurí R Brazil
48 F1 Sucuriú R Brazil
32 G7 Sucé France
48 F1 Suda Russian Federation
108 E1 Sudan Texas U.S.A.
52 F5 Suday Russian Federation
55 B5 Sud'bodarovka Russian Federation
140 C5 Strzelecki, Mt N Terr Australia
139 J8 Strzelecki Pk Tasmania Australia
128 G2 Suddie Guyana
28 D7 Süderbrarup Germany
69 E13 Süderbrarup Germany
33 M7 Suderburg Germany
48 M5 Sulina R Romania
33 J7 Süderhastedt Germany
32 J4 Süderhöft Germany
48 B7 Süder Lügum Germany
52 E6 Sudilova Russian Federation
52 F5 Sudislavl' Russian
32 E9 Südlohn Germany
111 H8 Sudogda Russian Federation
99 S10 Sudost' R Russian Federation
117 K10 Sudd Oust, Pte Mauritius
79 C9 Sué Egypt
6 F1 Sueñoroyarfjerður fj Faeroes
6 F1 Sudzha Russian Federation
54 G5 Sueca Spain
99 O8 Südoinenie Bulgaria
21 P6 Sudeli R Idaho U.S.A.
42 F6 Sulmona Italy
42 E6 Sulmona Italy
17 G5 Sueca Spain
80 G8 Su'eida R Jordan
80 F8 Su'eidat Jordan
138 C2 Suemez I Alaska U.S.A.
108 D6 Sue Pk Texas U.S.A.
55 E3 Suer R Russian Federation
28 J7 Suèvres France
79 C5 Suez Egypt
79 C8 Suez Canal Egypt
32 E6 Suez,G.of Egypt
67 J4 Suffield Alberta Canada
101 Q2 Suffolk co England
101 Q2 Suffolk Montana U.S.A.
95 L10 Suffolk Virginia U.S.A.
26 G1 Suga-jima isld Japan
33 H5 Sugag Romania
99 R7 Sugar R Wisconsin U.S.A.
94 F10 Sugar City Colorado U.S.A.
109 M6 Sugar Creek Pennsylvania U.S.A.
36 C5 Sugar Grove Virginia U.S.A.
108 D6 Sugar Land Texas U.S.A.
119 O9 Sugarloaf mt Brazil
143 C6 Sugarloaf Hill W Australia Australia
113 F13 Sugarloaf Key isld Florida U.S.A.
119 U6 Sugarloaf Pt New South Wales Australia
90 A13 Sugar Loaf Pt St Helena
71 G5 Sugbuhan Pt Philippines
72 J4 Sugenheim Germany
119 P4 Sugg L Saskatchewan Canada
69 F12 Sugi Indonesia
71 G5 Sugi Japan
78 D3 Suğla Gölü L Turkey
51 P2 Sugoy R Russian Federation
40 G7 Sugut R Sabah
40 G7 Sugut, Tanjung C Sabah
44 B1 Suhaia, L Romania
77 F2 Şuḩār Oman
77 K2 Suhl Germany

Column 5

89 E9 Stutterheim S Africa
36 G6 Stuttgart Germany
111 E7 Stuttgart Arkansas U.S.A.
107 L2 Stuttgart Kansas U.S.A.
37 K2 Stützerbach Germany
26 H9 Stygberg Sweden
28 R9 Stykkishólmur Iceland
71 M9 Suaçui Grande, R Brazil
70 C3 Suai Sarawak
86 G2 Suakin Sudan
71 M6 Suamico Wisconsin U.S.A.
124 E3 Suaqui Mexico
128 D2 Suárez R Colombia
70 L9 Subang Java
70 N9 Subang Libya
71 H5 Subei China
45 L2 Subotica Serbia Yugoslavia
80 F5 Subeihi Jordan
57 J4 Subeimi Jordan
69 J11 Subi isld Indonesia
142 A1 Subiaco Perth, W Aust Australia
42 E7 Subiaco Italy
101 M7 Sublett Idaho U.S.A.
99 R8 Sublette Kansas U.S.A.
107 K4 Sublette Kansas U.S.A.
48 F4 Sublime Texas U.S.A.
65 D2 Subtica Serbia Yugoslavia
118 J8 Subrag China
53 G11 Success Saskatchewan Canada
110 J3 Success Missouri U.S.A.
44 H3 Succiso,Alpe di mt Italy
20 G7 Sucé France
48 F1 Sucha Poland
31 J2 Suchan Poland
31 N3 Suchedniow Poland
31 M4 Suchowola Poland
116 K4 Suchitepéquez dep Guatemala
116 K4 Suchitoto El Salvador
70 F7 Suchumi Russian Federation
70 G7 Sulawesi isld Indonesia
70 G7 Sulawesi Selatan Sulawesi
100 S5 Sucker Oregon U.S.A.
116 B7 Suck R Ireland
114 G3 Suckling,C Alaska U.S.A.
30 H3 Suckow Germany
31 M4 Sucre Bolivia
37 B12 Sucre Colombia
28 D3 Sucundurí R Brazil
31 J3 Sucuriú R Brazil
31 J3 Suda Russian Federation
108 E1 Sudan Texas U.S.A.
52 F5 Suday Russian Federation
55 B5 Sud'bodarovka Russian Federation
70 B12 Sudbury Ontario Canada
9 G3 Sudbury England
128 G2 Sudd dist Sudan
86 E4 Sudd dist Sudan
128 O2 Sude R Germany
28 D7 Süderbrarup Germany
69 E13 Süderbrarup Germany
33 M7 Suderburg Germany
48 M5 Sulina R Romania
32 J4 Süderhöft Germany
48 B7 Süder Lügum Germany
52 E6 Sudilova Russian Federation
32 G9 Südlohn Germany
111 H8 Sudogda Russian Federation
99 S10 Sudost' R Russian Federation
117 K10 Sud Ouest, Pte Mauritius
79 C9 Suder Egypt
6 F1 Sueñoroyarfjerður fj Faeroes
6 F1 Sudzha Russian Federation
54 G5 Sueca Spain
80 G8 Su'eida R Jordan
80 F8 Su'eidat Jordan
42 F6 Sulmona Italy
108 D6 Sue Pk Texas U.S.A.
55 E3 Suer R Russian Federation
28 J7 Suèvres France
79 C5 Suez Egypt
79 C8 Suez Canal Egypt
32 E6 Suez,G.of Egypt
118 F8 Suffield Alberta Canada
101 Q2 Suffolk co England
95 L10 Suffolk Virginia U.S.A.
26 G1 Suga-jima isld Japan
47 J2 Sugag Romania
71 F5 Sugar R Wisconsin U.S.A.
35 G5 Sugar City Colorado U.S.A.
94 H5 Sugar Creek Pennsylvania U.S.A.
84 G3 Suluq Libya
69 F12 Suluova Turkey
142 G5 Sulukna R Kazakhstan
69 F12 Sulukta Kyrgyzstan
38 H7 Sulz Germany
37 H13 Sulzau Austria
131 L3 Sugarloaf mt Brazil
90 A13 Sugarloaf Key isld Florida
71 G5 Sugbuhan Pt Philippines
41 L2 Sugenheim Germany
41 M2 Sugg L Saskatchewan Canada
69 B10 Sulzberg Germany
37 K5 Sulzberg Germany
86 B10 Sulzdorf Germany
53 M7 Sulzer, Mt Alaska U.S.A.
69 G14 Sulztal Germany
78 D3 Suğla Gölü L Turkey
31 M7 Sulzmann Germany
69 G14 Sumah Germany
37 H3 Sulzdorf Germany
70 E1 Sumangat, Tanjung C Sabah
77 F2 Şuḩār Oman
37 K2 Suhl Germany

Column 6

54 K3 Sukhodol'skiy Russian Federation
52 F5 Sukhona R Russian Federation
68 D4 Sukhothai Thailand
59 D3 Sukow Log Russian Federation
53 F11 Sukhumi Georgia
74 C5 Sukkur Pakistan
76 E1 Sukna India
73 H8 Sükrah Libya
70 N9 Sukoharjo Java
71 F4 Sukolilo Java
120 F5 Sukon Sulawesi
69 D9 Sukow Germany
33 P5 Sukow Germany
59 L2 Sukpay Datani Russian Federation
87 C10 Sukses Namibia
55 C3 Suksun Russian Federation
60 F13 Sukumo-wan B Japan
117 N8 Sukunka R British Columbia Canada
26 F8 Sul Norway
27 A10 Sula isld Norway
106 D4 Sula Idaho U.S.A.
125 L2 Sulaco Honduras
94 B6 Sulaiman Range Pakistan
52 F4 Sula,Kep isld Indonesia
82 B3 Sulak R Russian Federation
110 J3 Sular Sgeir isld Scotland
99 O7 Sulat isld Indonesia
88 C4 Sulat Sarawak
71 A2 Sulat, Bukit mt Halmahera Indonesia
116 K6 Sulatna R Alaska U.S.A.
116 K4 Sulatna Alaska U.S.A.
70 N7 Sulawesi isld Indonesia
70 G7 Sulawesi Selatan Sulawesi
100 G5 Sulawesi Tenggara Sulawesi
27 B12 Sulawesi Utara Sulawesi
125 L2 Sulaco Honduras
53 G11 Sulak Russian Federation
94 B6 Sulaiman Range Pakistan
31 J3 Sulęcin Poland
52 H5 Suna Russian Federation
77 C1 Suledeh Iran
31 M4 Sulejów Poland
108 L1 Sulejówek Poland
52 F5 Sulejówek, Jezioro res Poland
5S B5 Sul'bodarovka Russian Federation
70 F7 Suleskar Norway
9 G3 Suleskar Norway
32 M5 Sülfeld Germany
60 F13 Suli Hu L China
69 E13 Suliki Sumatra
85 B7 Sulima Sierra Leone
33 M7 Sulina Romania
32 J4 Sulingen Germany
48 M5 Sulina R Romania
48 K3 Sulița Romania
32 E9 Suljetjelma Norway
111 H8 Sulkava Finland
6 F1 Sullana Peru
99 S10 Sullent Alabama U.S.A.
117 K10 Sullivan Illinois U.S.A.
140 C3 Sullivan Bay British Columbia Canada
89 D9 Sullivan L Alberta Canada
15 G12 Sullom Voe B Shetland Scotland
21 P6 Sully-la-Chapelle France
21 P6 Sully-sur-Loire France
9 O8 Sulm F Austria
42 F6 Sulmona Italy
70 N9 Sulphur R Texas/Louisiana U.S.A.
102 C6 Sulphur Nevada U.S.A.
107 N2 Sulphur Oklahoma U.S.A.
109 N2 Sulphur R Texas/Louisiana U.S.A.
101 M3 Sulphurdale Utah U.S.A.
109 M3 Sulphur Springs Texas U.S.A.
108 E3 Sulphur Springs Cr Texas U.S.A.
120 H5 Sultan Ontario Canada
78 C2 Sultan Dağları mts Turkey
47 J7 Sultanhisar Turkey
47 K5 Sülten Germany
33 H5 Sülten Germany
84 G3 Suluq Libya
70 G1 Sulu Arch islds Philippines
70 G1 Sulu Sea Philippines
84 G3 Suluq Libya
69 D11 Sumatera Utara prov Sumatra

Column 7

122 J7 Summerside Prince Edward I Canada
110 E4 Summersville Missouri U.S.A.
94 G8 Summersville West Virginia U.S.A.
112 G4 Summerton South Carolina U.S.A.
112 E5 Summertown Georgia U.S.A.
123 T5 Summerville Newfoundland Canada
112 B3 Summerville Georgia U.S.A.
94 H5 Summerville Pennsylvania U.S.A.
112 G4 Summerville South Carolina U.S.A.
120 F5 Summit Ontario Canada
145 F4 Summit mt New Zealand
88 C4 Summit Alaska U.S.A.
111 N5 Summit Mississippi U.S.A.
106 B9 Summit Montana U.S.A.
100 B5 Summit Oregon U.S.A.
100 B5 Summit South Dakota U.S.A.
103 M4 Summit Utah U.S.A.
135 C4 Summit City Michigan U.S.A.
116 P5 Summit Lk British Columbia Canada
100 F8 Summit L Nevada U.S.A.
117 L6 Summit Lake British Columbia Canada
144 B4 Sumner New Zealand
110 J3 Sumner Illinois U.S.A.
99 O7 Sumner Iowa U.S.A.
110 C2 Sumner Missouri U.S.A.
144 D5 Sumner, L New Zealand
117 G7 Sumner Str Alaska U.S.A.
31 K6 Sumon-dake mt Japan
32 H10 Sumony Hungary
60 G7 Sumoto Japan
70 F7 Supangbinangae Sulawesi
31 K6 Šumperk Czechoslovakia
100 G5 Sumpter Oregon U.S.A.
111 G10 Sumrall Mississippi U.S.A.
52 E3 Sumskiy Posad Russian Federation
112 G4 Sumter South Carolina U.S.A.
54 F6 Sumy Ukraine
52 H5 Suna Russian Federation
88 C4 Suna Tanzania
60 P2 Sunagawa Japan
101 R9 Sunbeam Colorado U.S.A.
101 L5 Sunbeam Idaho U.S.A.
94 C10 Sunbright Tennessee U.S.A.
139 G7 Sunbury Victoria Australia
95 L10 Sunbury North Carolina U.S.A.
99 Q3 Sunbury Ohio U.S.A.
95 L6 Sunbury Pennsylvania U.S.A.
133 E3 Suncho Corral Argentina
89 E5 Sun City S Africa
95 Q3 Sun City New Hampshire U.S.A.
70 B5 Suncook New Hampshire U.S.A.
70 D2 Sundar Sarawak
75 N8 Sundarbans tidal forest India/Bangladesh
70 K9 Sunda,Selat str Indonesia
140 C3 Sunday Cr N Terr Australia
89 D9 Sundays R S Africa
142 E3 Sunday Str W Australia Australia
28 B3 Sundby Denmark
27 J12 Sundbyberg Sweden
121 L8 Sunderland Ontario Canada
13 G4 Sunderland England
70 N9 Sundown, G mt Java
138 C2 Sundgau reg France
70 N9 Sundown S Australia Australia
118 E1 Sundown Manitoba Canada
108 E2 Sundown Texas U.S.A.
118 C7 Sundre Alberta Canada
27 K15 Sundre Sweden
121 L7 Sundridge Ontario Canada
28 C5 Sundsbruk Sweden
26 H8 Sundsli Norway
27 C12 Sundsli Norway
26 J9 Sundsvall Sweden
27 J10 Sundsvall Sweden
108 B5 Sunflower Mississippi U.S.A.
111 H7 Sungai Ayak Kalimantan
70 E1 Sungaidareh Sumatra
69 F12 Sungai Guntung Sumatra
69 F13 Sungaikabung Sumatra
69 J12 Sungailimau Sumatra
69 J12 Sungaipinyuh Indonesia
69 J12 Sungaipuar Sumatra
69 J12 Sungaiselan Indonesia
69 J12 Sungai Petani Malaysia
88 D10 Sungguminasa Sulawesi
86 F7 Sungikai Sudan
70 E2 Sungu Zaire
120 C2 Suni Ontario Canada
65 C2 Suning China
26 C9 Suniperk Czechoslovakia
42 H3 Sunja Croatia
42 H3 Sunja R Croatia
103 H9 Sunnyside Nevada U.S.A.
106 E3 Sunnyside Utah U.S.A.
100 E3 Sunnyside Washington U.S.A.

Column 8

94 C3 Sunnyvale California U.S.A.
99 R6 Sun Prairie Wisconsin U.S.A.
110 L9 Sunray Texas U.S.A.
109 J8 Sunray Texas U.S.A.
100 G5 Sunset Louisiana U.S.A.
111 J8 Sunset Beach N Hawaii U.S.A.
109 K2 Sunset Crater Nat.Mon Arizona U.S.A.
117 P8 Sunset House Alberta Canada
103 J6 Sunshine Arizona U.S.A.
118 K1 Sunshine Ontario Canada
52 T4 Suntar Russian Federation
37 M7 Süntel hills Germany
91 O9 Sünzhausen Germany
33 H9 Suojarvi Russian Federation
28 G7 Suolovuobme Norway
29 N10 Suomenniemi Finland

230 Suomi — Tambov

119 O2 **Suomi** Ontario Canada
29 O7 **Suomussalmi** Finland
60 E12 **Suō-nada** *sea* Japan
29 N9 **Suonenjoki** Finland
29 M10 **Suonne** *L* Finland
29 N3 **Suorsapää** *mt* Finland
26 K4 **Suorva** Sweden
52 D4 **Suoyarvi** Russian Federation
Suozhen *see* **Huantai**
103 M5 **Supai** Arizona U.S.A.
75 M5 **Supaul** India
128 C6 **Supe** Peru
118 H7 **Superb** Saskatchewan Canada
57 D5 **Superfosfatnyy** Uzbekistan
103 N8 **Superior** Arizona U.S.A.
106 E2 **Superior** Colorado U.S.A.
101 L2 **Superior** Montana U.S.A.
98 J9 **Superior** Nebraska U.S.A.
99 O3 **Superior** Wisconsin U.S.A.
101 R8 **Superior** Wyoming U.S.A.
45 J1 **Superiore,L** Italy
99 R2 **Superior,L** U.S.A./Canada
68 E5 **Suphan Buri** Thailand
78 J2 **Süphan D** *mt* Turkey
45 O6 **Supino** Italy
100 F5 **Suplee** Oregon U.S.A.
54 C7 **Supoy** *R* Ukraine
33 N8 **Süpplingen** Germany
31 O2 **Supraśl** Poland
48 H3 **Supuru** Romania
72 G6 **Suqutrá** *isld* Indian Oc
52 G3 **Sura** Russian Federation
52 G6 **Sura** *R* Russian Federation
27 H12 **Sura** Sweden
74 B4 **Surab** Pakistan
70 O9 **Surabaja** Java
77 F7 **Sūrak** Iran
70 N9 **Surakarta** Java
84 E3 **Sūr̦ al Jīn** *watercourse* Libya
70 F5 **Suramana** Sulawesi
40 B5 **Suran** *R* France
79 G3 **Sūrān** Syria
48 E2 **Šurany** Czechoslovakia
141 J7 **Surat** Queensland Australia
74 E8 **Surat** India
74 E4 **Suratgarhi** India
69 D8 **Surat Thani** Thailand
31 O3 **Suraż** Poland
54 D4 **Surazh** Russian Federation
141 H6 **Surbiton** Queensland Australia
9 F5 **Surbiton** England
48 F6 **Surčin** Serbia Yugoslavia
78 K4 **Sūrdāsh** Iraq
21 L4 **Surdon** France
48 H3 **Surduc** Romania
46 E2 **Surdulica** Serbia Yugoslavia
22 L4 **Sure** *R* Luxembourg
48 H5 **Şureanu** Romania
74 D7 **Surendranagar** India
41 K4 **Surettahorn** *mt* Switzerland
102 D7 **Surf** California U.S.A.
95 N7 **Surf City** New Jersey U.S.A.
117 J9 **Surf Inlet** British Columbia Canada
112 J4 **Surfside Beach** South Carolina U.S.A.
18 E6 **Surgères** France
126 C3 **Surgidero de Batabanó** Cuba
55 F1 **Surgut** Russian Federation
50 H2 **Surgutikha** Russian Federation
76 D2 **Suriapet** India
61 N13 **Suribachi-yama** *mt* Japan
71 G6 **Surigao** Mindanao Philippines
71 G5 **Surigao Str** Philippines
68 F5 **Surin** Thailand
83 L13 **Surinam** Mauritius
129 G3 **Suriname** *rep* S America
129 G2 **Suriname** Suriname
99 S4 **Suring** Wisconsin U.S.A.
128 D2 **Suripá** *R* Venezuela
57 D5 **Surkhandar'inskaya Oblast** *prov* Uzbekistan
77 C4 **Surmāq** Iran
26 C9 **Surnadalsöra** Norway
117 G6 **Surprise** British Columbia Canada
98 J8 **Surprise** Nebraska U.S.A.
121 Q3 **Surprise,L.de la** Quebec Canada
133 F5 **Sur,Pta** Argentina
112 E6 **Surrency** Georgia U.S.A.
9 F5 **Surrey** *co* England
98 E1 **Surrey** North Dakota U.S.A.
95 L9 **Surry** Virginia U.S.A.
40 H3 **Sursee** Switzerland
84 F3 **Surt** Libya
20 G3 **Surtainville** France
28 S10 **Surtsey** *isld* Iceland
71 N9 **Surubec,Danau** *L* Timor
78 G3 **Sürüç** Turkey
61 M11 **Suruga-wan** *B* Japan
69 F14 **Surulangun** Sumatra
71 G7 **Surup** Mindanao Philippines
20 E6 **Surzur** France
28 H6 **Suså** *R* Denmark
44 B1 **Susa** Italy
60 E11 **Susa** Japan
42 G6 **Sušac** *isld* Croatia
84 G3 **Sūsah** Libya
60 G12 **Susaki** Japan
60 J12 **Susami** Japan
57 G4 **Susamyr** Kyrgyzstan
102 D1 **Susan** *R* California U.S.A.
77 A4 **Sūsangerd** Iran
52 F5 **Susanino** Russian Federation
102 D1 **Susanville** California U.S.A.
100 G5 **Susanville** Oregon U.S.A.
78 F1 **Suşehri** Turkey
33 N4 **Süsel** Germany
37 Q5 **Sušice** Czechoslovakia
80 F2 **Susitha** Syria
116 M6 **Susitna** Alaska U.S.A.
116 O5 **Susitna L** Alaska U.S.A.
69 D9 **Suso** Thailand
58 G5 **Susong** China
67 E1 **Susong** China
61 M10 **Susono** Japan
95 L5 **Susquehanna** *R* Pennsylvania U.S.A.
95 M5 **Susquehanna** Pennsylvania U.S.A.
33 P10 **Süsser See** *L* Germany
Sussex *co see* **West and East Sussex** *counties*
122 G8 **Sussex** New Brunswick Canada
95 N5 **Sussex** New Jersey U.S.A.
101 T6 **Sussex** Wyoming U.S.A.
25 E6 **Susteren** Netherlands
45 K1 **Sustinente** Italy
117 K7 **Sustut Pk** British Columbia Canada
70 E2 **Susul** Sabah
116 K5 **Susulatna** *R* Alaska U.S.A.
51 O2 **Susuman** Russian Federation
71 A1 **Susupu** Halmahera Indonesia
47 J5 **Susurluk** Turkey
100 F10 **Sutcliffe** Nevada U.S.A.
48 L5 **Şuteşti** Romania
Sutherland *co see* **Highland** *reg*
87 D12 **Sutherland** S Africa
99 L7 **Sutherland** Iowa U.S.A.
98 E8 **Sutherland** Nebraska U.S.A.
143 F7 **Sutherland Ra** W Australia Australia
98 E8 **Sutherland Res** Nebraska U.S.A.
144 A6 **Sutherland Sd** New Zealand
100 B6 **Sutherlin** Oregon U.S.A.
56 D5 **Sut-Khol'** Russian Federation
74 F3 **Sutlej** *R* India
74 E3 **Sutlej** *R* Pakistan
79 D2 **Sütluce** Turkey
102 D3 **Sutter Cr** California U.S.A.
9 F2 **Sutterton** England
121 L8 **Sutton** Ontario Canada
121 S7 **Sutton** Quebec Canada
9 G3 **Sutton** England
9 F5 **Sutton** England
144 C6 **Sutton** New Zealand
98 J9 **Sutton** Nebraska U.S.A.
98 H2 **Sutton** North Dakota U.S.A.
94 G8 **Sutton** West Virginia U.S.A.
121 L5 **Sutton Bay** Ontario Canada
9 E2 **Sutton Coldfield** England
9 E1 **Sutton-in-Ashfield** England
94 G8 **Sutton Res** West Virginia U.S.A.
9 E5 **Sutton Scotney** England
141 H5 **Suttor** *R* Queensland Australia
116 J8 **Sutwik I** Alaska U.S.A.
89 D9 **Suurberge** *mts* S Africa
52 C5 **Suure-Jaani** Estonia
137 Q5 **Suva** Viti Levu Fiji
46 E1 **Suva Pl** *mt* Serbia Yugoslavia
46 D2 **Suva Reka** Serbia Yugoslavia
29 N9 **Suvasvesi** *L* Finland
Suvla, C *see* **Büyük Kemikli Br.**
54 H2 **Suvorov** Russian Federation
47 J1 **Suvorovo** Bulgaria
48 M5 **Suvorovo** Ukraine
61 M9 **Suwa** Japan
61 M9 **Suwa ko** *L* Japan
70 D5 **Suwakong** Kalimantan
31 O1 **Suwałki** Poland
68 F5 **Suwannaphum** Thailand
113 D8 **Suwannee** Florida U.S.A.
119 R2 **Suwannee L** Manitoba Canada
113 E7 **Suwanoochee Cr** Georgia U.S.A.
78 H4 **Suwar** Syria
70 E4 **Suwaran, G** *mt* Kalimantan
79 G6 **Suwaydā', As** Syria
80 G2 **Suwaysah** Syria
80 F6 **Suweima** Jordan
Suweis,El *see* **Suez**
Su Xian *see* **Suzhou**
88 A9 **Suye,L** Zambia
55 D1 **Suyevatpaul** Russian Federation
57 E3 **Suzak** Kazakhstan
83 M14 **Suzanne,Pte** Kerguelen Indian Oc
52 F6 **Suzdal'** Russian Federation
19 N16 **Suze la Rousse** France
21 L6 **Suze-sur-Sarthe, la** France
58 G5 **Suzhou** China
59 H5 **Suzhou** China
40 B3 **Suzon** *R* France
121 T4 **Suzor Côté** Quebec Canada
61 L8 **Suzu** Japan
61 K11 **Suzuka** Japan
61 L8 **Suzu-misaki** *C* Japan
56 B4 **Suzun** Russian Federation
45 J2 **Suzzara** Italy
27 H10 **Svabensverk** Sweden
28 H6 **Sværdborg** Denmark
26 P1 **Svaerholtklubben** *C* Norway
26 H9 **Svågan** *R* Sweden
26 H5 **Svaipa** *mt* Sweden
147 H12 **Svalbard** *arch* Arctic Oc
28 G5 **Svallerup** Denmark
48 H2 **Svalyava** Ukraine
27 H16 **Svaneke** Denmark
28 E6 **Svanninge** Denmark
27 F12 **Svanskog** Sweden
26 N5 **Svanstein** Sweden
26 R2 **Svanvik** Norway
54 F5 **Svapa** *R* Russian Federation
26 M4 **Svappavaara** Sweden
29 K11 **Svartå** Finland
27 G12 **Svartå** Sweden
26 N5 **Svartbyn** Sweden
115 O3 **Svartenhuk Halvö** *pen* Greenland
26 G5 **Svartisen** *mt* Norway
26 M6 **Svartlå** Sweden
27 H11 **Svartnäs** Sweden
26 M6 **Svartöstaden** Sweden
54 K7 **Svatovo** Ukraine
27 D10 **Svatsum** Norway
68 G7 **Svay Rieng** Cambodia
52 G5 **Svecha** Russian Federation
27 F16 **Svedala** Sweden
26 L7 **Svedun** Sweden
26 G9 **Sveg** Sweden
26 A10 **Svelgen** Norway
27 D12 **Svelvik** Norway
52 C6 **Švenčionėliai** Lithuania
Svendborg *co see* **Fyn** *co*
28 F6 **Svendborg** Denmark
27 F14 **Svenljunga** Sweden
27 H12 **Svennevad** Sweden
26 F6 **Svenningdal** Norway
100 B3 **Svensen** Oregon U.S.A.
26 J2 **Svensgrunnen** *shoal* Norway
28 D6 **Svenstrup** Sønderjylland Denmark
Sverdlovsk *see* **Yekaterinburg**
55 D2 **Sverdlovskaya Oblast'** *prov* Russian Federation
115 K1 **Sverdrup Chan** Northwest Territories Canada
50 G1 **Sverdrup, Ostrov** *isld* Russian Federation
42 G5 **Svetac** *isld* Croatia
46 E3 **Sveti Nikola** Macedonia Yugoslavia
59 L2 **Svetlaya** Russian Federation
53 C8 **Svetlogorsk** Belorussia
31 M1 **Svetlogorsk** Russian Federation
51 J2 **Svetlogorsk** Russian Federation
31 M1 **Svetloye** Russian Federation
31 M1 **Svetlyy** Russian Federation
51 L3 **Svetlyy** Russian Federation
52 C4 **Svetogorsk** Russian Federation
46 E1 **Svetozarevo** Serbia Yugoslavia
37 P5 **Švihov** Czechoslovakia
48 G6 **Svilajnac** Serbia Yugoslavia
47 H3 **Svilengrad** Bulgaria
28 F6 **Svindinge** Denmark
28 G5 **Svinninge** Denmark
Svinø *see* **Svínoy**
6 F1 **Svínoy** *isld* Faeroes
52 D4 **Svir'** *R* Russian Federation
52 D4 **Sviritsa** Russian Federation
56 F4 **Svirsk** Russian Federation
52 D4 **Svir'stroy** Russian Federation
46 G1 **Svishtov** Bulgaria
53 C7 **Svisloch'** *R* Belorussia
31 J6 **Svitavy** Czechoslovakia
52 G6 **Sviyaga** *R* Russian Federation
59 J1 **Svobodnyy** Russian Federation
46 F2 **Svoge** Bulgaria
28 J5 **Svogerslev** Denmark
37 O4 **Svojšin** Czechoslovakia
26 G3 **Svolvaer** Norway
31 J6 **Svratka** *R* Czechoslovakia
46 E1 **Svrljig** Serbia Yugoslavia
46 E1 **Svrljiške Pl** *mt* Serbia Yugoslavia
52 F5 **Svyatogor'ye** Russian Federation
52 E1 **Svyatoy Nos, Mys** *C* Russian Federation
52 D4 **Svyatozero** Russian Federation
68 C3 **Swa** *R* Burma
9 G2 **Swaffham** England
141 K5 **Swain Reefs** Gt Barrier Reef Aust
112 E5 **Swainsboro** Georgia U.S.A.
134 B4 **Swains I** Pacific Oc
87 B10 **Swakopmund** S Africa
9 G5 **Swale,R** England
137 O4 **Swallow Is** Santa Cruz Is
70 C1 **Swallow Reef** S China Sea
106 F3 **Swallows** Colorado U.S.A.
118 D7 **Swalwell** Alberta Canada
9 E6 **Swanage** England
142 A2 **Swanbourne Beach** *dist* Perth, W Aust Australia
139 G6 **Swan Hill** Victoria Australia
118 B4 **Swan Hills** Alberta Canada
139 J8 **Swan Is** Tasmania Australia
126 C6 **Swan Is** W Indies
117 J8 **Swan, L** British Columbia Canada
98 G4 **Swan L** South Dakota U.S.A.
119 T9 **Swan Lake** Manitoba Canada
101 M2 **Swan Lake** Montana U.S.A.
112 E2 **Swannanoa** North Carolina U.S.A.
119 Q6 **Swan Plain** Saskatchewan Canada
142 E3 **Swan Pt** W Australia Australia
112 L2 **Swanquarter** North Carolina U.S.A.
143 B9 **Swan R** W Australia Australia
118 B3 **Swan R** Alberta Canada
138 E5 **Swan Reach** South Australia Australia
119 Q6 **Swan River** Manitoba Canada
99 N2 **Swan River** Minnesota U.S.A.
112 K3 **Swansboro** North Carolina U.S.A.
139 K5 **Swansea** New South Wales Australia
139 J8 **Swansea** Tasmania Australia
103 L7 **Swansea** Arizona U.S.A.
112 F4 **Swansea** South Carolina U.S.A.
8 C4 **Swansea** Wales
95 T2 **Swans I** Maine U.S.A.
118 K7 **Swanson** Saskatchewan Canada
117 J9 **Swanson Bay** British Columbia Canada
98 E9 **Swanson Res** Nebraska U.S.A.
98 J9 **Swanton** Nebraska U.S.A.
94 D5 **Swanton** Ohio U.S.A.
121 R8 **Swanton** Vermont U.S.A.
33 S4 **Swantow** Germany
139 K3 **Swan Vale** New South Wales Australia
101 O6 **Swan Valley** Idaho U.S.A.
99 M4 **Swanville** Minnesota U.S.A.
89 A10 **Swartberg** *mt* S Africa
103 L2 **Swasey Pk** Utah U.S.A.
120 K4 **Swastika** Ontario Canada
89 G6 **Swaziland** *kingdom* Africa
99 M6 **Swea City** Iowa U.S.A.
26 **Sweden** *kingdom* W Europe
95 M7 **Swedesboro** New Jersey U.S.A.
85 D7 **Swedru** Ghana
12 C2 **Sween, L** Scotland
109 M6 **Sweeny** Texas U.S.A.
140 E3 **Sweers I** Queensland Australia
100 J6 **Sweet** Idaho U.S.A.
101 O1 **Sweetgrass** Montana U.S.A.
111 D7 **Sweet Home** Arkansas U.S.A.
100 C5 **Sweet Home** Oregon U.S.A.
109 L6 **Sweet Home** Texas U.S.A.
110 C3 **Sweet Springs** Missouri U.S.A.
107 L6 **Sweetwater** Oklahoma U.S.A.
112 C2 **Sweet Water** Tennessee U.S.A.
108 G3 **Sweetwater** Texas U.S.A.
101 R7 **Sweetwater** *R* Wyoming U.S.A.
87 D12 **Swellendam** S Africa
108 G2 **Swenson** Texas U.S.A.
31 J5 **Świdnica** Poland
31 O4 **Świdnik** Poland
31 J2 **Świdwin** Poland
31 J3 **Świebodzin** Poland
31 L2 **Świecie** Poland
116 K6 **Swift** *R* Alaska U.S.A.
95 R2 **Swift** *R* Maine U.S.A.
123 S6 **Swift Current** Newfoundland Canada
118 K8 **Swiftcurrent** Saskatchewan Canada
116 L5 **Swift Fork** *R* Alaska U.S.A.
110 E6 **Swifton** Arkansas U.S.A.
100 C3 **Swift Res** Washington U.S.A.
117 H5 **Swift River** Yukon Territory Canada
100 A1 **Swiftsure Bank Lightship** British Columbia Canada
14 D1 **Swilly,L** Ireland
8 C5 **Swimbridge** England
9 E4 **Swindon** England
9 F2 **Swineshead** England
14 C3 **Swinford** Ireland
106 G3 **Swink** Colorado U.S.A.
31 H2 **Swinoujście** Poland
13 F2 **Swinton** Scotland
40 F4 **Switzerland** *rep* Europe
15 E2 **Swona** *isld* Orkney Scotland
14 E3 **Swords** Ireland
141 F5 **Swords Ra** Queensland Australia
52 D4 **Syamozero, Oz** *L* Russian Federation
52 F4 **Syamzha** Russian Federation
52 D5 **Syas'** *R* Russian Federation
52 D4 **Syas'stroy** Russian Federation
52 G5 **Syava** Russian Federation
98 A8 **Sybille Cr** Wyoming U.S.A.
14 A4 **Sybil Pt** Ireland
111 K8 **Sycamore** Alabama U.S.A.
99 S8 **Sycamore** Illinois U.S.A.
94 D6 **Sycamore** Ohio U.S.A.
112 F4 **Sycamore** South Carolina U.S.A.
52 D6 **Sychevka** Russian Federation
31 K4 **Sycow** Poland
56 D4 **Syda** *R* Russian Federation
121 O8 **Sydenham** Ontario Canada
9 G2 **Syderstone** England
139 K5 **Sydney** New South Wales Australia
123 M7 **Sydney** Nova Scotia Canada
98 B2 **Sydney** Montana U.S.A.
140 E3 **Sydney I** Queensland Australia
123 M7 **Sydney Mines** Nova Scotia Canada
115 P5 **Sydproven** Greenland
32 J7 **Syke** Germany
98 G2 **Sykeston** North Dakota U.S.A.
94 J5 **Sykesville** Pennsylvania U.S.A.
52 H4 **Syktyvkar** Russian Federation
111 K8 **Sylacauga** Alabama U.S.A.
110 D6 **Sylamore** Arkansas U.S.A.
26 F8 **Sylene** *mt* Norway
75 O6 **Sylhet** Bangladesh
28 A7 **Sylt** *isld* Germany
26 B9 **Sylte** Norway
26 S1 **Sylterfjord** *inlet* Norway
55 C3 **Sylva** Russian Federation
112 D2 **Sylva** North Carolina U.S.A.
94 J7 **Sylvan** Pennsylvania U.S.A.
107 M2 **Sylvan Grove** Kansas U.S.A.
143 D6 **Sylvania** W Australia Australia
119 N6 **Sylvania** Saskatchewan Canada
112 F5 **Sylvania** Georgia U.S.A.
94 D5 **Sylvania** Ohio U.S.A.
118 C6 **Sylvan Lake** Alberta Canada
101 P5 **Sylvan Pass** Wyoming U.S.A.
112 D6 **Sylvester** Georgia U.S.A.
140 D4 **Sylvester, L** N Terr Australia
123 R5 **Sylvester,Mt** Newfoundland Canada
107 M4 **Sylvia** Kansas U.S.A.
117 L6 **Sylvia,Mt** British Columbia Canada
56 C1 **Sym** *R* Russian Federation
15 E5 **Symington** Scotland
124 H5 **Symon** Mexico
8 D4 **Symonds Yat** England
71 F4 **Syndicate** Philippines
142 F3 **Synnot,Mt** W Australia Australia
142 F3 **Synnot Ra** W Australia Australia
56 H3 **Synnyr, Khrebet** *mts* Russian Federation
54 N2 **Syntul** Russian Federation
52 J2 **Synya** Russian Federation
55 E1 **Syn'yakha** *R* Russian Federation
Syowa *see* **Showa**
Syracuse Italy *see* **Siracusa**
94 B5 **Syracuse** Indiana U.S.A.
107 J3 **Syracuse** Kansas U.S.A.
98 K9 **Syracuse** Nebraska U.S.A.
121 O9 **Syracuse** New York U.S.A.
101 N8 **Syracuse** Utah U.S.A.
57 E4 **Syrdarinsk. Obl** Uzbekistan
57 D3 **Syrdar'ya** *R* Kazakhstan etc
57 E4 **Syrdar'ya** Uzbekistan
57 D4 **Syr Dar'ya Oblast'** *prov* Uzbekistan
79 G4 **Syria** *rep* S W Asia
68 C4 **Syriam** Burma
Syrian Desert *see* **Badiet esh Sham**
55 E1 **Syrkovoye, Oz** *L* Russian Federation
28 G2 **Syr Odde** *C* Denmark
54 L4 **Syrskiy** Russian Federation
55 D3 **Sysert'** Russian Federation
95 T1 **Sysladobsis L** Maine U.S.A.
52 H4 **Sysola** *R* Russian Federation
9 E2 **Syston** England
56 D4 **Systyg-Khem** Russian Federation
52 D6 **Syt'kovo** Russian Federation
55 F1 **Sytomino** Russian Federation
52 F4 **Syuma** *R* Russian Federation
52 H6 **Syumsi** Russian Federation
52 H6 **Syun'** *R* Russian Federation
46 F3 **Syutkya** *mt* Bulgaria
53 G7 **Syzran'** Russian Federation
48 E4 **Szabadszállás** Hungary
48 G2 **Szabolcsszatmár** *co* Hungary
31 L4 **Szadek** Poland
31 K2 **Szamocin** Poland
48 G2 **Szamosszeg** Hungary
31 K3 **Szamotuły** Poland
48 D3 **Szany** Hungary
48 F4 **Szarvas** Hungary
31 O5 **Szczebrzeszyn** Poland
31 H2 **Szczecin** Poland
31 K2 **Szczecinek** Poland
31 M5 **Szczekociny** Poland
31 L4 **Szczerców** Poland
31 N5 **Szczucin** Poland
31 N2 **Szczuczyn** Poland
31 M2 **Szczytno** Poland
Szechwan *prov see* **Sichuan** *prov*
48 F2 **Szécsény** Hungary
48 F4 **Szeged** Hungary
48 G3 **Szeghalom** Hungary
48 E3 **Székesfehérvár** Hungary
48 F2 **Szendrö** Hungary
48 E3 **Szentendre** Hungary
48 F4 **Szentes** Hungary
48 C4 **Szentgotthárd** Hungary
48 D4 **Szentlörinc** Hungary
48 G2 **Szerencs** Hungary
48 D3 **Szigetköz** *dist* Hungary
48 D4 **Szigetvár** Hungary
48 F2 **Szikszó** Hungary
31 J5 **Szklarska Poreba** Poland
31 N2 **Szkwa** *R* Poland
31 J4 **Szlichtyngowa** Poland
48 E3 **Szob** Hungary
48 F3 **Szolnok** Hungary
48 D3 **Szombathely** Hungary
31 J4 **Szprotawa** Poland
31 M2 **Szreńsk** Poland
31 L2 **Sztum** Poland
31 K2 **Szubin** Poland
31 M4 **Szydłowiec** Poland

T

79 F5 **Taalabaya** Lebanon
71 E3 **Taal,L** Luzon Philippines
48 E4 **Tab** Hungary
71 F4 **Tabaco** Philippines
128 F5 **Tabajara** Brazil
70 P10 **Tabanan** Indonesia
70 P16 **Tabanan** Bali Indonesia
70 D4 **Tabang** *R* Kalimantan
70 E4 **Tabang** Kalimantan
85 E5 **Tabankort** Mali
89 F8 **Tabankulu** S Africa
127 O2 **Tabaquite** Trinidad
137 L2 **Tabar Is** Bismarck Arch
43 B12 **Tabarka** Tunisia
77 E3 **Ţabas** Iran
77 G3 **Ţabas** Iran
124 H7 **Tabasco** Mexico
125 N8 **Tabasco** *state* Mexico
52 G6 **Tabashino** Russian Federation
123 N3 **Tabatière,La** Quebec Canada
128 E4 **Tabatinga** Brazil
68 B1 **Tabayin** Burma
71 E2 **Tabayoa, Mt** Philippines
68 G6 **Tabeng** Cambodia
118 E9 **Taber** Alberta Canada
27 G14 **Taberg** Sweden
17 F7 **Tabernas** Spain
17 G5 **Tabernes de Valldigna** Spain
16 D10 **Taberrant** Morocco
17 G9 **Tabia** Algeria
101 P9 **Tabiona** Utah U.S.A.
69 F13 **Tabir** *R* Sumatra
71 F4 **Tablas** *isld* Philippines
131 B3 **Tablas,C** Chile
71 E4 **Tablas Strait** Philippines
89 A9 **Table B** S Africa
139 H8 **Table C** Tasmania Australia
145 G3 **Table Cape** New Zealand
71 D6 **Table Hd** Philippines
144 A7 **Table Hill** New Zealand
68 A6 **Table I** Andaman Is
68 H2 **Table,I.de la** Vietnam
142 F3 **Tableland** W Australia Australia
87 C12 **Table Mt** S Africa
116 Q2 **Table Mt** Alaska U.S.A.
71 D5 **Table Pt** Philippines
83 K14 **Table Pt.de la** Réunion Indian Oc
101 R8 **Table Rock** Wyoming U.S.A.
110 C5 **Table Rock Res** Missouri U.S.A.
141 G4 **Tabletop, Mt** Queensland Australia
130 C6 **Taboco,R** Brazil
31 H6 **Tábor** Czechoslovakia
51 P1 **Tabor** Russian Federation
99 L9 **Tabor** Iowa U.S.A.
98 J7 **Tabor** South Dakota U.S.A.
88 D4 **Tabora** Tanzania
88 D4 **Tabora** *reg* Tanzania
112 J3 **Tabor City** North Carolina U.S.A.
80 E3 **Tabor, Mt** Israel
118 E9 **Tabor Prov. Park** Alberta Canada
55 D2 **Tabory** Russian Federation
85 C8 **Tabou** Ivory Coast
78 L2 **Tabrīz** Iran
68 G2 **Ta Bu** Vietnam
135 U9 **Tabuaeran** *atoll* Pacific Oc
79 G10 **Tabūk** Saudi Arabia
60 E12 **Tabuka** Japan
139 L3 **Tabulam** New South Wales Australia
71 H5 **Tabulan** Sulawesi
129 G5 **Tabuleiro** Brazil
55 G4 **Tabuny** Russian Federation
45 R7 **Taburno, M** *mt* Italy
122 G6 **Tabusintac R** New Brunswick Canada
69 D12 **Tabuyung** Sumatra
88 B6 **Tabwe** Zambia
27 K12 **Täby** Sweden
130 H10 **Tacaratú** Brazil
66 C2 **Tacheng** China
67 G4 **Ta-chia** Taiwan
60 C13 **Tachibana-wan** *B* Japan
61 N10 **Tachikawa** Japan
128 D2 **Táchira** *state* Venezuela
37 O4 **Tachov** Czechoslovakia
70 G7 **Tacipi** Sulawesi
139 L4 **Tacking Pt** New South Wales Australia
71 G5 **Tacloban** Philippines
133 C1 **Tacna** Peru
103 K9 **Tacna** Arizona U.S.A.
21 O4 **Tacoignières** France
117 M12 **Tacoma** Washington U.S.A.
133 E3 **Tacõ Pozo** Argentina
128 E7 **Tacora** *mt* Chile
130 E7 **Tacquaritinga** Brazil
130 B10 **Tacuaras** Paraguay
131 G3 **Tacuarembó** Uruguay
131 H4 **Tacuari,R** Uruguay
130 C8 **Tacuatí** Paraguay
124 E3 **Tacupeto** Mexico
61 N8 **Tadami** *R* Japan
13 G6 **Tadcaster** England
85 F4 **Tadeinte** *watercourse* Algeria
85 E3 **Tadémaït,Pl.du** Algeria
85 B5 **Tadjakant** Mauritania
85 E3 **Tadjmout** Algeria
86 H3 **Tadjoura** Djibouti
9 E3 **Tadmarton** England
145 D4 **Tadmor** New Zealand
78 G4 **Tadmur** Syria
60 Q2 **Tadoshi** Japan
60 G11 **Tadotsu** Japan
122 C5 **Tadoussec** Quebec Canada
76 D3 **Tadpatri** India
Tadzhikskaya S.S.R. *see* **Tajikistan**
65 F6 **Taech'öngdo** *isld* S Korea
65 G5 **Taedong** *R* N Korea
65 G7 **Taegu** S Korea
65 F7 **Taehŭksan** *isld* S Korea
65 G6 **Taejon** S Korea
28 J7 **Tæro** *isld* Denmark
137 S5 **Tafahi** *isld* Pacific Oc
17 F2 **Tafalla** Spain
85 F4 **Tafasaset** *watercourse* Algeria
126 A1 **Tafelberg** *mt* Curaçao
16 E9 **Tafersite** Morocco
8 C4 **Taff,R** Wales
79 F8 **Tafila** Jordan
85 C7 **Tafiré** Ivory Coast
26 B9 **Tafjord** Norway
17 F9 **Tafna** *R* Algeria
106 F5 **Tafoya** New Mexico U.S.A.
85 C3 **Tafraoute** Morocco
102 E6 **Taft** California U.S.A.
107 P6 **Taft** Oklahoma U.S.A.
109 K8 **Taft** Texas U.S.A.
77 G5 **Taftan, Kūh-e-** *mt* Iran
95 P5 **Taftville** Connecticut U.S.A.
69 A9 **Tafwap** Nicobar Is
75 N5 **Taga** Bhutan
48 J4 **Ţaga** Romania
116 H4 **Tagagawik** *R* Alaska U.S.A.
61 P7 **Tagajō** Japan
53 E10 **Taganrog** Russian Federation
54 K9 **Taganrogskiy Zaliv** *G* Rus Fed/Ukraine
85 A4 **Tagarzimat** Western Sahara
71 E3 **Tagaytay City** Philippines
71 F6 **Tagbilaran** Philippines
85 D2 **Taghit** Algeria
117 F6 **Tagish L** British Columbia Canada
45 O5 **Tagliacozzo** Italy
42 E2 **Tagliamento** *R* Italy
45 M1 **Táglio di Po** Italy
22 G5 **Tagnon** France
71 F6 **Tagolo Pt** Philippines
85 C3 **Tagounite** Morocco
26 J8 **Tågsjöberg** Sweden
129 J6 **Taguatinga** Brazil
71 F5 **Tagubanhan** *isld* Philippines
61 L11 **Taguchi** Japan
71 E2 **Tagudin** Philippines
137 L4 **Tagula** *isld* Louisiade Arch
Tagus *R* Portugal *see* **Tejo** *R*
Tagus *R* Spain *see* **Tajo** *R*
98 E1 **Tagus** North Dakota U.S.A.
144 B7 **Tahakopa** New Zealand
69 G10 **Tahan, Gunung** Malaysia
61 L11 **Tahara** Japan
85 F4 **Tahat** *mt* Algeria
145 D1 **Taheke** New Zealand
77 C6 **Tāheri** Iran
117 G6 **Tahi** *R* British Columbia Canada
135 M10 **Tahiti** *isld* Pacific Oc
110 B6 **Tahlequah** Oklahoma U.S.A.
117 H6 **Tahltan** British Columbia Canada
102 D2 **Tahoe City** California U.S.A.
114 J4 **Tahoe L** Northwest Territories Canada
102 D2 **Tahoe L** California U.S.A.
102 D3 **Tahoe Valley** California U.S.A.
108 F2 **Tahoka** Texas U.S.A.
100 A2 **Taholah** Washington U.S.A.
145 E3 **Tahora** New Zealand
145 F4 **Tahoraiti** New Zealand
85 F6 **Tahoua** Niger
99 V3 **Tahquamenon Falls** Michigan U.S.A.
59 H2 **Ta-hsing-an Ling** China
59 H2 **Ta Hsing-an-Ling Shan-mo** *ra* China
117 K11 **Tahsis** British Columbia Canada
67 F5 **Ta Hsü** *isld* Taiwan
84 J4 **Tahta** Egypt
47 L8 **Tahtali Dağ** *mt* Turkey
78 E2 **Tahtali Dağları** *mts* Turkey
117 K9 **Tahtsa** *R* British Columbia Canada
128 D6 **Tahuamanu** *R* Peru
145 E2 **Tahuna** New Zealand
85 C7 **Tai** Ivory Coast
65 E4 **Tai'an** China
65 C6 **Tai'an** China
134 D12 **Taiarapu, Presqu'ile de** *pen* Tahiti Pacific Oc
67 F2 **Taibai** China
106 F7 **Taiban** New Mexico U.S.A.
17 F6 **Taibilla,Sa de** *mts* Spain
58 G3 **Taibus Qi** China
65 C4 **Taibus Qi** China
67 G1 **Taicang** China
67 G4 **T'ai-chung** Taiwan
144 C6 **Taieri** *airport* New Zealand
Taigong *see* **Taijiang**
65 B6 **Taigu** China
65 B5 **Taihang Shan** *mt ra* China
65 B7 **Taihang Shan** *ra* China
145 E3 **Taihape** New Zealand
67 E3 **Taihe** China
61 Q12 **Taiho** Okinawa
67 E1 **Taihu** China
67 G1 **Tai Hu** *L* China
67 C3 **Taijiang** China
Taikang *see* **Dorbod**
65 C7 **Taikang** China
60 R3 **Taiki** Japan
68 B4 **Taikkyi** Burma
59 H2 **Tailai** China
69 D13 **Taileleo** Indonesia
138 E6 **Tailem Bend** South Australia Australia
36 G7 **Tailfingen** Germany
21 K4 **Taillebois** France
19 P14 **Taillefer** *mt* France
20 H5 **Taillis** France
15 D3 **Tain** Scotland
46 E8 **Taínaron, Akr** *C* Greece
67 F3 **Taining** China
19 N14 **Tain l'Hermitage** France
67 G5 **T'ain-nan** Taiwan
130 G4 **Taiobeiras** Brazil
70 G5 **Taipa** Sulawesi
29 O9 **Taipale** Finland
29 N10 **Taipalsaari** Finland
67 G4 **T'ai-pei** Taiwan
67 F1 **Taiping** China
67 B5 **Taiping** China
67 C5 **Taiping** China
69 E10 **Taiping** Malaysia
59 H3 **Taipingchuan** China
65 G3 **Taipingchuan** China
65 F4 **Taipingshao** China
130 J8 **Taipu** Brazil
61 O8 **Taira** Japan
61 Q12 **Taira** Okinawa
60 O4 **Tairadate kaikyō** Japan
145 E2 **Tairua** New Zealand
60 N3 **Taisei** Japan
60 Q2 **Taisetsuzan Nat.Park** Japan
60 F10 **Taisha** Japan
67 D5 **Taishan** China
67 F3 **Taishun** China
69 E14 **Taitaitanopo** *isld* Indonesia
133 C7 **Taitao, Pen. de** Chile
65 D4 **Taitouying** China
52 C2 **Taivalkoski** Finland
27 M11 **Taivassalo** Finland
67 G5 **Taiwan** *rep* E Asia
Taiwan Haixia *see* **Taiwan Str**
67 F4 **Taiwan Strait** China/Taiwan
67 G1 **Tai Xian** China
67 G1 **Taixing** China
46 E7 **Taïyetos** *mt* Greece
80 E3 **Taiyiba** Israel
80 D4 **Taiyiba** Israel
80 F3 **Taiyiba** *R* Jordan
65 B6 **Taiyuan** China
65 B6 **Taiyue Shan** *mt* China
Taizhou *see* **Linhai**
67 G1 **Taizhou** China
67 G2 **Taizhou Wan** *B* China
65 F4 **Taizi He** *R* China
72 E6 **Ta'izz** Yemen
86 H3 **Ta'izz** Yemen
84 E5 **Tajarhī** Libya
84 G5 **Tāj, At** Libya
69 H14 **Tajem, Gunung** *mt* Indonesia
43 B13 **Tajerouine** Tunisia
57 E5 **Tajikistan** *rep* C Asia
61 N8 **Tajima** Japan
61 L10 **Tajimi** Japan
106 D7 **Tajique** New Mexico U.S.A.
124 C2 **Tajito** Mexico
16 E4 **Tajo** *R* Spain
70 N9 **Taju** Java
17 F4 **Tajuna** *R* Spain
68 D4 **Tak** Thailand
71 K8 **Taka' Bonerate, Kepulauan** *islds* Indonesia
61 M8 **Takada** Japan
61 P7 **Takagi** Japan
61 O9 **Takahagi** Japan
61 J10 **Takahama** Japan
60 G11 **Takahashi** Japan
61 O8 **Takahata** Japan
60 E13 **Takajō** Japan
145 D4 **Takaka** New Zealand
46 E7 **Táka, L** Greece
83 K12 **Takamaka** Mahé I Indian Oc
60 H11 **Takamatsu** Japan
60 E13 **Takamori** Japan
61 O5 **Takanosu** Japan
61 K9 **Takaoka** Japan
145 F4 **Takapau** New Zealand
145 F1 **Takapuna** New Zealand
70 F7 **Taka Rewataya** *reef* Indonesia
60 H11 **Takasago** Japan
59 L4 **Takasaki** Japan
60 C12 **Taka shima** *isld* Saga Japan
60 E11 **Taka shima** *isld* Shimane Japan
89 B4 **Takatshwaane** Botswana
61 J11 **Takatsuki** Japan
145 E2 **Takatu Pt.** New Zealand
88 G3 **Takaungu** Kenya
68 D2 **Ta-Kaw** Burma
60 D12 **Takawa** Japan
61 L9 **Takayama** Japan
60 D14 **Takazaki** Japan
60 E14 **Takazaki** Japan
69 F9 **Tak Bai** Thailand
60 E13 **Takeda** Japan
61 K10 **Takefu** Japan
60 F11 **Takehara** Japan
9 G4 **Takeley** England
69 C10 **Takengon** Sumatra
68 G7 **Takeo** Cambodia
60 D12 **Takeo** Japan
60 C11 **Takeshiki** Japan
Take-shima *see* **Tok-to**
77 A1 **Takestān** Iran
60 E12 **Taketazu** Japan
71 C3 **Takeum** W Irian
78 K7 **Takhadid** Iraq
77 L1 **Takhār** *reg* Afghanistan
57 A4 **Takhiatash** Uzbekistan
117 F5 **Takhini** *R* Yukon Territory Canada
57 A4 **Takhta** Turkmenistan
57 C6 **Takhta-Bazar** Turkmenistan
55 E4 **Takhtabrod** Kazakhstan
57 B3 **Takhtakupyr** Uzbekistan
77 C5 **Takht-e Jamshīd** Iran
114 H4 **Takijug L** Northwest Territories Canada
60 Q2 **Takikawa** Japan
100 B7 **Takilma** Oregon U.S.A.
60 R1 **Takinoue** Japan
119 R3 **Takipy** Manitoba Canada
70 D6 **Takisung** Kalimantan
144 A6 **Takitimu Mts** New Zealand
117 L8 **Takla Landing** British Columbia Canada
66 B4 **Taklimakan Shamo** *reg* China
57 E5 **Takob** Tajikistan
85 D8 **Takoradi** Ghana
116 J5 **Takotna** Alaska U.S.A.
145 D1 **Takou B** New Zealand
116 F6 **Takslesluk L** Alaska U.S.A.
117 G6 **Taku** British Columbia Canada
60 D12 **Taku** Japan
69 D8 **Takua Pa** Thailand
117 F5 **Taku Arm** *L* Br Col/Yukon Terr Canada
69 D8 **Takua Thung** Thailand
117 F6 **Taku Glacier** Br Col/Alaska Canada/U.S.A.
85 F7 **Takum** Nigeria
74 E2 **Talagang** Pakistan
133 D6 **Talagapa** Argentina
68 H7 **Ta Lai** Vietnam
83 J8 **Talaimannar** Sri Lanka
85 F5 **Talak** *reg* Niger
107 P5 **Talala** Oklahoma U.S.A.
16 E10 **Talamagait** Morocco
69 F14 **Talang** Sumatra
70 K8 **Talangbatu** Sumatra
69 G14 **Talangbetutu** Sumatra
69 F14 **Talanglambangantir** Sumatra
69 G14 **Talangpulaukabung** Sumatra
128 B4 **Talara** Peru
77 H7 **Talar-i-Band** *mts* Pakistan
57 F3 **Talas** Kyrgyzstan
136 L3 **Talasea** New Britain
57 F4 **Talasskiy Alatau, Khr** *mts* Kazakhstan/Uzbekistan etc
70 G5 **Talatakoh** *isld* Sulawesi
79 G4 **Ţal at Mūsá** *mt* Lebanon
16 D5 **Talavera de la Reina** Spain
130 C10 **Talavera,I** Paraguay
140 F4 **Talawanta** Queensland Australia
71 G7 **Talayan** Philippines
65 G3 **Talazhan** China
79 G4 **Talbīsah** Syria
142 F2 **Talbot, C** W Australia Australia
113 F7 **Talbot I** Florida U.S.A.
115 M2 **Talbot Inlet** Northwest Territories Canada
119 S4 **Talbot L** Manitoba Canada
143 F7 **Talbot, Mt** W Australia Australia
139 J4 **Talbragar** New South Wales Australia
131 B5 **Talca** *prov* Chile
131 B5 **Talca** Chile
131 A6 **Talcahuano** Chile
131 B4 **Talca,Pta** Chile
109 M2 **Talco** Texas U.S.A.
94 G9 **Talcott** West Virginia U.S.A.
52 E6 **Taldom** Russian Federation
141 F4 **Taldora** Queensland Australia
57 A3 **Taldyk** Uzbekistan
57 J3 **Taldy-Kurgan** Kazakhstan
77 B4 **Tal-e Khosravī** Iran
100 C7 **Talent** Oregon U.S.A.
8 C2 **Talerddig** Wales
8 C4 **Talgarth** Wales
76 B3 **Talguppa** India
138 C5 **Talia** South Australia Australia
71 G5 **Talibon** Bohol Philippines
110 A7 **Talihina** Oklahoma U.S.A.
76 C2 **Talikota** India
71 G7 **Talikua** *isld* Mindanao Philippines
86 F4 **Tali Post** Sudan
71 F5 **Talisay** Cebu Philippines
70 F4 **Talisayan** Kalimantan
71 G6 **Talisayan** Philippines
71 J4 **Talisei** *isld* Indonesia
55 D1 **Talitsa** Sverdlovskaya obl Russian Federation
55 D3 **Talitsa** Sverdlovskaya obl Russian Federation
54 M4 **Talitskiy Chamlyk** Russian Federation
33 N5 **Talkau** Germany
116 N5 **Talkeetna Mts** Alaska U.S.A.
79 B7 **Talkha** Egypt
29 N3 **Talkkunapää** *mt* Finland
77 B3 **Talkuncheh** Iran
45 L4 **Talla** Italy
84 G5 **Ţallāb, Aţ** Libya
111 K8 **Talladega** Alabama U.S.A.
111 G10 **Tallahala** *R* Mississippi U.S.A.
111 M11 **Tallahassee** Florida U.S.A.
111 F7 **Tallahatchie** *R* Mississippi U.S.A.
139 H6 **Tallangatta** Victoria Australia
111 K9 **Tallapoosa** *R* Alabama U.S.A.
111 L8 **Tallapoosa** Georgia U.S.A.
19 Q16 **Tallard** France
26 H10 **Tallåsen** Sweden
80 G1 **Tall ash Sha'ar** *mt* Syria
111 L9 **Tallassee** Alabama U.S.A.
143 B8 **Tallering Pk** W Australia Australia
8 C4 **Talley** Wales
78 H4 **Tall Fadghāmī** Syria
52 B5 **Tallinn** Estonia
26 M5 **Talljärv** Sweden
79 G4 **Tall Kalakh** Syria
40 D6 **Talloires** France
14 C4 **Tallow** Ireland
119 P6 **Tall Pines** Saskatchewan Canada
80 G3 **Tall Shihāb** Syria
110 G2 **Tallula** Illinois U.S.A.
111 E9 **Tallulah** Louisiana U.S.A.
119 O9 **Talmage** Saskatchewan Canada
102 A2 **Talmage** California U.S.A.
107 N2 **Talmage** Kansas U.S.A.
99 L9 **Talmage** Nebraska U.S.A.
40 B3 **Talmay** France
56 B4 **Tal'menka** Russian Federation
80 B7 **Talmey Yafe** Israel
18 D6 **Talmont** France
48 N2 **Tal'noye** Ukraine
74 F8 **Taloda** India
86 F3 **Talodi** Sudan
107 M5 **Taloga** Oklahoma U.S.A.
70 F4 **Talok** Kalimantan
68 D2 **Ta-Long** Burma
77 L1 **Tāloqān** Afghanistan
106 E5 **Talpa** New Mexico U.S.A.
108 H4 **Talpa** Texas U.S.A.
124 G7 **Talpa de Allende** Mexico
127 O2 **Talparo R** Trinidad
111 M11 **Talquin,L** Florida U.S.A.
80 C6 **Tal Shaḩar** Israel
52 B6 **Talsi** Latvia
26 L7 **Tålsmark** Sweden
133 C3 **Taltal** Chile
69 D12 **Talu** Sumatra
71 H4 **Taludaä** Sulawesi
70 G4 **Taluditi** Sulawesi
71 E8 **Talue** *isld* Philippines
68 G3 **Ta Lus,C** Vietnam
41 O4 **Talvera** *R* Italy
26 N1 **Talvik** Norway
141 J8 **Talwood** Queensland Australia
56 F5 **Tal'yany** Russian Federation
139 G4 **Talyawalka** *R* New South Wales Australia
8 C3 **Talybont** Wales
8 C1 **Tal-y-cafn** Wales
52 J3 **Talyy** Russian Federation
61 M9 **Tama** Japan
61 N10 **Tama** *R* Japan
99 O8 **Tama** Iowa U.S.A.
70 D3 **Tamabo Ra** Sarawak
68 B1 **Tamadaw** Burma
143 A7 **Tamala** W Australia Australia
85 D7 **Tamale** Ghana
16 C4 **Tamames** Spain
60 D13 **Tamana** Japan
130 J10 **Tamandare** Brazil
140 B4 **Tamani Desert** N Terr Australia
60 G11 **Tamano** Japan
85 F4 **Tamanrasset** Algeria
70 G5 **Tamanusi** Sulawesi
95 M6 **Tamaqua** Pennsylvania U.S.A.
45 L2 **Tamara** Italy
100 J5 **Tamarack** Idaho U.S.A.
99 N3 **Tamarack** Minnesota U.S.A.
60 E13 **Tamarai** Japan
17 H3 **Tamarite de Litera** Spain
110 G3 **Tamaroa** Illinois U.S.A.
41 J5 **Tamaro,Mt** Switzerland
139 H8 **Tamar R** Tasmania Australia
8 B6 **Tamar,R** England
60 G11 **Tamashima** Japan
48 E4 **Tamási** Hungary
Tamatave *see* **Toamasina**
61 O9 **Tamatsukuri** Japan
128 D5 **Tamaya** *R* Peru
85 A4 **Tamayya** Western Sahara
124 F5 **Tamazula** Mexico
124 H8 **Tamazula de Gordiano** Mexico
125 K7 **Tamazunchale** Mexico
37 K2 **Tambach Dietharz** Germany
85 B6 **Tambacounda** Senegal
71 K8 **Tambalongang** *isld* Indonesia
70 B5 **Tambangmunjul** Kalimantan
69 F14 **Tambangsawah** Sumatra
88 E10 **Tambara** Mozambique
130 J9 **També** Brazil
70 G7 **Tambea** Sulawesi
69 H12 **Tambelan Besar** *isld* Indonesia
69 H12 **Tambelan, Kepulauan** *islds* Indonesia
143 C10 **Tambellup** W Australia Australia
87 E9 **Tambero** Zambia
70 O9 **Tamberu** Java
131 B2 **Tambillos,Nevado de los** *pk* Chile
141 H6 **Tambo** Queensland Australia
128 D7 **Tambo** *R* Peru
128 C6 **Tambo de Mora** Peru
71 G6 **Tambog Pt** Mindanao Philippines
70 G6 **Tamboli** Sulawesi
124 G5 **Tambor** Mexico
139 H6 **Tamboritha,Mt** Victoria Australia
53 F7 **Tambov** Russian Federation

16 B2 Tambre,R Spain
142 C5 Tambrey W Australia Australia
70 F5 Tambulan Sulawesi
70 E2 Tambunan Sabah
86 E4 Tambura Sudan
70 F4 Tambu, Tk B Sulawesi
83 K9 Tambutta Sri Lanka
70 E1 Tambuyukon, G mt Sabah
85 B5 Tamchakett Mauritania
55 C6 Tamdy Kazakhstan
57 C4 Tamdybulak Uzbekistan
57 C4 Tamdytau, Gory mt Uzbekistan
128 D2 Tame Colombia
16 B3 Tâmega R Portugal
133 C7 Tamel Aike Argentina
Tamenghest see Tamanrasset
85 F5 Tamgak, Mts Niger
57 E2 Tamgaly, Ozero L Kazakhstan
125 L7 Tamiahua,L.de Mexico
113 F12 Tamiami Canal Florida U.S.A.
69 C10 Tamiang R Sumatra
76 C5 Tamil Nadu prov India
78 J4 Ta'mīm, At prov Iraq
41 K4 Tamina R Switzerland
70 D6 Taminglayang Kalimantan
84 G3 Tamīnī,At Libya
41 K4 Tamins Switzerland
58 D2 Tamirin Gol R Mongolia
48 F5 Tamis R Serbia Yugoslavia
52 E3 Tamitsa Russian Federation
57 C1 Tamkamys Kazakhstan
68 J5 Tam Ky Vietnam
71 F5 Tamlang Negros Philippines
45 R7 Tammaro R Italy
Tammerfors see Tampere
110 G4 Tamms Illinois U.S.A.
113 E10 Tampa Florida U.S.A.
107 N3 Tampa Kansas U.S.A.
70 K8 Tampang Sumatra
29 K10 Tampere Finland
125 L6 Tampico Mexico
99 R8 Tampico Illinois U.S.A.
101 T1 Tampico Montana U.S.A.
69 F11 Tampin Malaysia
69 C13 Tampines dist Singapore
69 C10 Tamporbur Sumatra
68 J5 Tam Quan Vietnam
80 D2 Tamra Israel
58 G2 Tamsagbulag Mongolia
75 Q6 Tamu Burma
71 E7 Tamuk isld Philippines
139 K4 Tamworth New South Wales Australia
121 O8 Tamworth Ontario Canada
9 E2 Tamworth England
95 Q3 Tamworth New Hampshire U.S.A.
68 F6 Tamyong R Cambodia
57 H1 Tan Kazakhstan
116 Q6 Tana R Alaska U.S.A.
60 J12 Tanabe Japan
130 E7 Tanabi Brazil
26 Q1 Tana-Bru Norway
116 Q5 Tanacross Alaska U.S.A.
116 Q5 Tanada L Alaska U.S.A.
26 Q1 Tanafjord inlet Norway
43 G8 Tanagro R Italy
61 O8 Tanagura Japan
86 G3 Tana Hāyk' L Ethiopia
69 D13 Tanahbala isld Indonesia
71 K8 Tanahdjampea isld Indonesia
70 E5 Tanahgrogot Kalimantan
71 K10 Tanahkadukung Indonesia
68 D13 Tanahmasa isld Indonesia
70 E3 Tanahmerah Kalimantan
69 F9 Tanah Merah Malaysia
26 R1 Tanahorn mt Norway
69 E12 Tanahputih Sumatra
70 M9 Tanah,Tg C Java
70 F7 Tanakeke isld Sulawesi
70 F6 Tanambung Sulawesi
136 J3 Tanamerah W Irian
140 A4 Tanami N Terr Australia
71 J4 Tanamon Sulawesi
68 H7 Tan An Vietnam
116 L4 Tanana Alaska U.S.A.
116 N4 Tanana R Alaska U.S.A.
Tananarive see Antananarivo
18 H8 Tanargue, Mt France
44 E2 Tanaro R Italy
84 E4 Tanārūt Libya
71 G5 Tanauan Leyte Philippines
141 F7 Tanbar Queensland Australia
21 L3 Tancarville France
61 P13 Tancha Okinawa
65 D7 Tancheng China
59 J3 Tanch'ŏn N Korea
124 H8 Tancitario,Cerro de mt Mexico
125 K7 Tancuayalab Mexico
75 K5 Tanda India
71 G6 Tandag Mindanao Philippines
48 L6 Ţăndărei Romania
70 E1 Tandek Sabah
28 D6 Tanderup Denmark
131 F6 Tandil Argentina
131 F6 Tandil, Sa del ra Argentina
70 F3 Tandjungbatu Kalimantan
69 J11 Tandjung Blitung Indonesia
70 L9 Tandjungpriok Java
70 C5 Tandjungpusu Kalimantan
74 C6 Tando Adam Pakistan
74 C6 Tando Muhammad Khan Pakistan
138 F4 Tandou L New South Wales Australia
55 G3 Tandovo, Oz L Russian Federation
14 E2 Tandragee N Ireland
27 G10 Tandsjöbörg Sweden
28 D7 Tandslet Denmark
71 E8 Tandubatu isld Philippines
76 C2 Tandur India
145 F3 Taneatua New Zealand
59 K5 Tanega-shima isld Japan
61 P5 Taneichi Japan
Tanen mt see Taunggyi mt
71 A3 Taneti Halmahera Indonesia
31 O5 Tanew R Poland
95 K7 Taneytown Maryland U.S.A.
85 E4 Tanezrouft reg Algeria
84 E4 Tanezzuft watercourse Libya/Algeria
88 G4 Tanga Tanzania
75 N6 Tangail Bangladesh
137 L2 Tanga Is Bismarck Arch
83 K11 Tangalla Sri Lanka
Tanganyika see Tanzania
88 B5 Tanganyika,L E Africa
130 D10 Tangará Brazil
67 D3 Tangdukou China
28 D4 Tange Å R Denmark
146 K9 Tange Promontory pen Antarctica
16 D9 Tanger Morocco
70 L9 Tangerang Java
33 P8 Tangerhütte Germany
33 P7 Tangermünde Germany
28 D4 Tange Sø L Denmark
58 G4 Tanggu China
66 D5 Tanggula Shan ra China
66 E5 Tanggula Shankou pass China
58 F5 Tang He China
65 C5 Tang He R China
Tangier see Tanger Morocco
122 K9 Tangier Nova Scotia Canada
122 K9 Tangier Grand L Nova Scotia Canada
95 M9 Tangier I Virginia U.S.A.
145 E4 Tangimoana New Zealand
111 F11 Tangipahoa R Louisiana U.S.A.
70 G6 Tangkeleboke, G mt Sulawesi
70 K8 Tangkittebak, Gunung mt Sumatra
70 L9 Tangkuban Perahu mt Java
66 D5 Tang-ku-la-yu-mu Ts'o L China
109 L5 Tanglewood Texas U.S.A.
Tanglha Range see Tanggula Shan
66 F5 Tangmai China
141 G5 Tangorin Queensland Australia
145 D1 Tangowahine New Zealand
67 C6 Tangpeng China
66 D5 Tangra Yumco L China
69 B10 Tangse Sumatra
65 D5 Tangshan China
67 A3 Tangtang China
67 C3 Tangtou China
67 E5 Tangtouxia China
71 F5 Tangub Negros Philippines
85 E6 Tanguiéta Benin
56 F3 Tanguy Russian Federation
59 J2 Tangwanghe China
67 F2 Tangxi China
65 C5 Tang Xian China
67 D1 Tangxianzhen China
68 D1 Tang-Yan Burma
67 C2 Tangyan He R China
58 F4 Tangyin China
65 C7 Tangyin China
65 H1 Tangyuan China
29 N4 Tanhua Finland
68 G7 Tani Cambodia
61 K10 Tanigumi Japan
136 G3 Tanimbar, Kep islds Moluccas Indonesia
40 E5 Taninges France
Tanintharyi see Tenasserim
60 D14 Taniyama Japan
71 F6 Tanjay Philippines
70 D6 Tanjung Kalimantan
69 G13 Tanjung Sumatra
69 F12 Tanjungbalai Kepulauan Riau Indonesia
69 D11 Tanjungbalai Sumatra
69 F12 Tanjungbatu Indonesia
69 F13 Tanjungbojo Sumatra
70 F4 Tanjungbuaya isld Kalimantan
70 K7 Tanjungenim Sumatra
70 E6 Tanjunggaru Kalimantan
70 K8 Tanjungkarang Telukbetung Sumatra
69 H14 Tanjung-pandan Indonesia
69 G12 Tanjungpinang Indonesia
69 D11 Tanjungpura Sumatra
69 G14 Tanjungraja Sumatra
70 E3 Tanjungredeb Kalimantan
69 J13 Tanjungsaleh isld Indonesia
69 J13 Tanjungsatai Indonesia
70 E3 Tanjungselor Kalimantan
74 D2 Tank Pakistan
138 E3 Tankamarinna,L South Australia Australia
29 N3 Tankapirtti Finland
108 G4 Tankersly Texas U.S.A.
56 G5 Tankhoy Russian Federation
68 B3 Tanlwe R Burma
68 J7 Tan My Vietnam
37 O7 Tann Bayern Germany
37 J2 Tann Hessen Germany
37 M3 Tanna Germany
137 O5 Tanna isld Vanuatu
15 F4 Tannadice Scotland
22 H4 Tannay France
33 N9 Tanne Germany
95 N4 Tannersville New York U.S.A.
95 M5 Tannersville Pennsylvania U.S.A.
37 N4 Tännesberg Germany
37 J6 Tannhausen Germany
41 M1 Tannheim Germany
29 M6 Tannila Finland
119 N1 Tannin Ontario Canada
80 C3 Tanninim Israel
28 E1 Tannis Bugt B Denmark
28 E1 Tannisby Denmark
37 L2 Tannroda Germany
85 D7 Tano R Ghana
71 F5 Tañon Str Philippines
85 F6 Tanout Niger
68 G1 Tan Quang Vietnam
124 H4 Tanque Alvarez Mexico
125 K7 Tanquian Mexico
79 F2 Tanrıverdi Turkey
75 K5 Tansing Nepal
79 A8 Tanta Egypt
68 B1 Tantabin Sagaing Burma
68 C3 Tantabin Tenasserim Burma
119 Q8 Tantallon Saskatchewan Canada
85 B3 Tan-Tan Morocco
138 F6 Tantanoola South Australia Australia
Tantung see Dandong
140 C3 Tanumbirini N Terr Australia
116 E6 Tanunak Alaska U.S.A.
138 E5 Tanunda South Australia Australia
55 C3 Tanyp R Russian Federation
88 C4 Tanzania rep Africa
117 H6 Tanzilla R British Columbia Canada
65 E2 Tao'an China
67 G2 Taohua Dao isld China
Taohuaping see Longhui
67 D2 Taojiang China
68 D7 Tao,Ko isld Thailand
65 D7 Taoluo China
Taonan see Tao'an
99 O6 Taopi Minnesota U.S.A.
43 G11 Taormina Sicily
106 E5 Taos New Mexico U.S.A.
85 D4 Taoudenni Mali
85 D2 Taounate Morocco
85 D2 Taourirt Morocco
85 D2 Taouz Morocco
67 D2 Taoyuan China
55 E3 Tap R Russian Federation
52 C5 Tapa Estonia
71 E8 Tapaan Passage Philippines
125 N10 Tapachula Mexico
69 E10 Tapah Malaysia
129 G5 Tapajós R Brazil
69 C11 Tapaktuan Sumatra
133 E5 Tapalquén Argentina
69 E14 Tapan Sumatra
129 G3 Tapanahoni R Suriname
125 M9 Tapanatepec Mexico
144 B6 Tapanui New Zealand
69 D12 Tapanuli, Teluk B Sumatra
128 F5 Tapauá Brazil
145 D4 Tapawera New Zealand
130 H9 Taperoá Brazil
131 H3 Tapes, Pta. de C Brazil
37 K6 Tapfheim Germany
74 F8 Tāpi R India
71 F7 Tapiantana isld Philippines
128 D5 Tapiche R Peru
70 B5 Tapinbini Kalimantan
29 L11 Tapiola Finland
128 E3 Tapirapeó, Sa mts Venezuela/Brazil
130 B4 Tapirapuã Brazil
69 F10 Tapis mt Malaysia
124 E4 Tapizuelas Mexico
75 M5 Taplejung Nepal
48 D4 Tapolca Hungary
68 D2 Ta-Pom Burma
95 L9 Tappahannock Virginia U.S.A.
70 F6 Tappalang Sulawesi
94 F6 Tappan Res Ohio U.S.A.
98 G3 Tappen North Dakota U.S.A.
28 J6 Tappernøje Denmark
60 O4 Tappi zaki C Japan
60 P1 Tappu Japan
28 C6 Taps Denmark
55 D1 Tapsuy R Russian Federation
145 E2 Tapu New Zealand
145 D4 Tapuaenuku mt New Zealand
71 E8 Tapul Philippines
69 D12 Tapulonanjing mt Sumatra
68 B3 Tapun Burma
128 F4 Tapurucuara Brazil
133 G3 Taquara Brazil
130 D7 Taquaraçu R Brazil
130 D4 Taquara,Sa.da mts Brazil
131 H2 Taquari R Brazil
130 C6 Taquari,Pantanal do swamp Brazil
112 K2 Tar R North Carolina U.S.A.
141 K7 Tara Queensland Australia
120 J8 Tara Ontario Canada
71 E4 Tara isld Philippines
55 F3 Tara Russian Federation
55 G3 Tara R Russian Federation
48 E7 Tara mt Serbia Yugoslavia
85 G7 Taraba R Nigeria
84 E3 Tarābulus Libya
128 E3 Taracua Brazil
145 F3 Taradale New Zealand
84 E4 Tarāghin Libya
60 D13 Taragi Japan
139 J6 Tarago New South Wales Australia
14 E3 Tara Hill Ireland
26 L5 Tårajaure Sweden
70 E3 Tarakan Kalimantan
77 K3 Tarakki reg Afghanistan
47 L4 Taraklı Turkey
48 M4 Tarakliya Moldavia
145 D4 Tarakohe New Zealand
139 J5 Taralga New South Wales Australia
144 C5 Taramakau R New Zealand
71 M9 Taramana Indonesia
139 J5 Tarana New South Wales Australia
145 E3 Taranaki admin region New Zealand
16 E4 Tarancón Spain
145 E1 Taranga I New Zealand
76 D5 Tarangambadi India
55 D4 Taranovskoye Kazakhstan
15 A3 Taransay isld Scotland
43 H8 Taranto Italy
43 H8 Taranto,G.di Italy
128 E7 Tarapacá prov Chile
145 F3 Taraponui mt New Zealand
128 C5 Tarapoto Peru
18 H7 Tarare France
145 E4 Tararua Range New Zealand
69 A8 Tarāsa Dwīp Nicobar Is
19 N17 Tarascon France
48 N1 Tarashcha Ukraine
41 M4 Tarasp Switzerland
85 F3 Tarat Algeria
128 D5 Tarauacá Brazil
17 F4 Taravilla Spain
145 F3 Tarawera L New Zealand
145 F3 Tarawera, Mt New Zealand
17 F3 Tarazona Spain
17 F5 Tarazona de la Mancha Spain
29 K5 Tårbæk Denmark
57 K2 Tarbagatay, Khrebet mts Kazakhstan
14 B4 Tarbert Ireland
15 B3 Tarbert Harris Scotland
12 C2 Tarbert Strathclyde Scotland
12 B2 Tarbert,L Scotland
18 F9 Tarbes France
12 D3 Tarbolton Scotland
112 K2 Tarboro North Carolina U.S.A.
141 F5 Tarbrax Queensland Australia
48 K4 Tarcăului,Munţii mts Romania
138 C4 Tarcoola South Australia Australia
139 H4 Tarcoon New South Wales Australia
138 C2 Tarcoonyinna R South Australia Australia
139 J6 Tarcutta New South Wales Australia
18 E9 Tardets-Sorholus France
17 G3 Tardienta Spain
21 J8 Tardière,la France
18 F7 Tardoire R France
59 L2 Tardoki-Yami, Gora mt Russian Federation
143 B8 Tardun W Australia Australia
139 L4 Taree New South Wales Australia
139 G4 Tarella New South Wales Australia
26 N4 Tärendö Sweden
40 E7 Tarentaise dist France
94 H6 Tarentum Pennsylvania U.S.A.
85 B3 Tarfaya Morocco
65 F1 Targan China
16 E10 Targuist Morocco
112 J3 Tarheel North Carolina U.S.A.
84 E3 Tarhūnah Libya
65 A4 Tarian Gol China
16 D8 Tarifa Spain
71 F2 Tarigtig Pt Philippines
133 E2 Tarija prov Bolivia
133 E2 Tarija Bolivia
76 B4 Tarikere India
145 E3 Tariki New Zealand
72 F5 Tarīm Yemen
Tarim Basin see Tarim Pendi
88 F6 Tarime Tanzania
66 D3 Tarim He R China
66 C3 Tarim Pendi basin China
77 J3 Tarīn Kowt Afghanistan
Tari Nor see Dalai Nur L
89 D9 Tarka R S Africa
87 E12 Tarkastad S Africa
110 A1 Tarkio Missouri U.S.A.
101 L2 Tarkio Montana U.S.A.
50 G2 Tarko-Sale Russian Federation
85 D7 Tarkwa Ghana
133 C7 Tar,L Argentina
71 E3 Tarlac Philippines
15 F3 Tarland Scotland
13 F6 Tarleton England
140 D5 Tarlton Downs N Terr Australia
28 B5 Tarm Denmark
128 C6 Tarma Peru
32 K6 Tarmstedt Germany
18 F9 Tarn R France
18 G9 Tarn dept France
48 F3 Tarna R Hungary
26 H6 Tärnaby Sweden
77 K3 Tarnak R Afghanistan
18 F8 Tarn-et-Garonne dept France
18 H8 Tarn,Gorges du France
31 N5 Tarnobrzeg Poland
52 F4 Tarnogskiy Gorodok Russian Federation
119 M6 Tarnopo Saskatchewan Canada
33 Q5 Tarnow Germany
31 M5 Tarnow Poland
31 L5 Tarnowskie Gory Poland
27 J11 Tärnsjö Sweden
44 H2 Taro R Italy
54 F8 Taromskoye Ukraine
141 J7 Taroom Queensland Australia
85 C2 Taroudannt Morocco
28 C7 Tarp Germany
140 D4 Tarpaulin Swamp N Terr Australia
109 H6 Tarpley Texas U.S.A.
113 E9 Tarpon Springs Florida U.S.A.
8 D1 Tarporley England
113 L12 Tarpum Bay Eleuthera Bahamas
44 L5 Tarquinia Italy
80 D7 Tarqumiya Jordan
17 H3 Tarragona prov Spain
17 H3 Tarragona Spain
139 H8 Tarraleah Tasmania Australia
139 H4 Tarran Hills New South Wales Australia
111 K8 Tarrant City Alabama U.S.A.
8 D6 Tarrant Hinton England
140 E3 Tarrant,Pt Queensland Australia
144 B6 Tarras New Zealand
17 J3 Tarrasa Spain
26 J4 Tarrekaise mt Sweden
41 N3 Tarrenz Austria
106 E2 Tarryall Colorado U.S.A.
112 E5 Tarrytown Georgia U.S.A.
95 O5 Tarrytown New York U.S.A.
17 F9 Tarsa,C Algeria
45 P1 Tarski Zaljev B Croatia
84 F5 Tarso Taro mt Chad
86 C1 Tarso Tieroko mt Chad
78 E3 Tarsus Turkey
79 E1 Tarsus R Turkey
133 E2 Tartagal Argentina
6 L4 Tartan oil rig North Sea
45 J1 Tàrtaro R Italy
18 E9 Tartas France
56 A3 Tartas R Russian Federation
52 C5 Tartu Estonia
79 F4 Tarṭūs Syria
80 C6 Tarum Israel
60 P3 Tarumae-san mt Japan
130 H6 Tarumirim Brazil
60 D14 Tarumizu Japan
54 J2 Tarusa Russian Federation
69 D9 Tarutao,Ko isld Thailand
48 M4 Tarutino Ukraine
69 D11 Tarutung Sumatra
26 D8 Tarva isld Norway
38 J9 Tarvisio Italy
56 E5 Tarys-Arzhan Russian Federation
120 K5 Tarzwell Ontario Canada
108 B6 Tasajera, Sa mts Mexico
57 G2 Tasaral Kazakhstan
84 E4 Tasāwah Libya
57 D3 Tas Buget Kazakhstan
121 M4 Taschereau Quebec Canada
107 K2 Tasco Kansas U.S.A.
117 M10 Taseko, Mt British Columbia Canada
56 D2 Taseyeva R Russian Federation
76 B2 Tasgaon India
58 A2 Tashanta Russian Federation
57 A4 Tashauz Turkmenistan
75 O5 Tashigang Bhutan
57 E4 Tashkent Uzbekistan
57 C6 Tashkepri Turkmenistan
57 F4 Tash-Kumyr Kyrgyzstan
55 B5 Tashla Russian Federation
120 C2 Tashota Ontario Canada
56 C4 Tashtagol Russian Federation
56 C4 Tashtyp Russian Federation
69 F11 Tasik Dampar Malaysia
70 M9 Tasikmalaja Java
70 L9 Tasikmalaya Java
80 G2 Tasil Syria
28 F7 Tåsinge isld Denmark
115 O3 Tasiusaq Greenland
26 H7 Tåsjö Sweden
26 H7 Tåsjön L Sweden
85 G5 Tasker Niger
47 N11 Taşkopru Turkey
56 E5 Taskyl,Khrebet mts Russian Federation
78 J2 Taşlıçay Turkey
144 D4 Tasman New Zealand
145 D4 Tasman Bay New Zealand
139 H9 Tasman Hd Tasmania Australia
139 H8 Tasmania state Australia
145 D4 Tasman Mountains New Zealand
144 C5 Tasman, Mt New Zealand
139 J9 Tasman Pen Tasmania Australia
134 G13 Tasman Plateau Pacific Oc
137 M9 Tasman Sea Pacific Oc
48 H3 Tăşnad Romania
85 F5 Tassara Niger
19 J5 Tasselot, Mt France
115 M6 Tassialouc,L Quebec Canada
85 E5 Tassili du Hoggar plateau Algeria
85 F3 Tassili-n'-Ajjer plateau Algeria
28 J5 Tåstrup Denmark
51 M2 Tas Tumus Russian Federation
57 E3 Tasty Kazakhstan
79 D2 Taşucu Turkey
85 C3 Tata Morocco
71 H5 Tataba Sulawesi Indonesia
48 E3 Tatabánya Hungary
71 E7 Tatalan isld Philippines
122 J8 Tatamagouche Nova Scotia Canada
85 G2 Tataouine Tunisia
48 M5 Tatarbunary Ukraine
47 H3 Tatarlar Turkey
55 G3 Tatarsk Russian Federation
52 H6 Tatarskaya Respublika Russian Federation
59 M1 Tatarskiy Proliv str Russian Federation
Tatarstan see Tatarskaya Respublika
70 C3 Tatau Sarawak
141 G3 Tate R Queensland Australia
89 E3 Tate R Botswana
119 N7 Tate Saskatchewan Canada
112 C3 Tate Georgia U.S.A.
61 O6 Tateai Japan
140 C2 Tate Bluff hill N Terr Australia
60 O4 Tateura Japan
61 L9 Tate yama mt Japan
61 N11 Tateyama Japan
117 P5 Tathlina L Northwest Territories Canada
139 K6 Tathra New South Wales Australia
116 O6 Tatitlek Alaska U.S.A.
117 L10 Tatla Lake British Columbia Canada
117 K7 Tatlatui Prov. Park British Columbia Canada
116 K5 Tatlawiksuk R Alaska U.S.A.
117 L10 Tatlayoko Lake British Columbia Canada
117 M10 Tatlow, Mt British Columbia Canada
101 R5 Tatman Mt Wyoming U.S.A.
116 K6 Tatna L Alaska U.S.A.
115 K6 Tatnam,C Manitoba Canada
139 H6 Tatong Victoria Australia
66 D4 Tatrang China
31 M6 Tatry mts Czech/Poland
117 E6 Tatshenshini R British Columbia Canada
77 K7 Tatta Pakistan
9 F1 Tattershall England
57 G3 Tatty Kazakhstan
130 F8 Tatuí Brazil
131 B2 Tatul,Sa de mts Chile
108 D2 Tatum New Mexico U.S.A.
109 N3 Tatum Texas U.S.A.
107 N7 Tatums Oklahoma U.S.A.
Tatung see Datong
139 H6 Tatura Victoria Australia
129 K5 Tauá Brazil
128 F4 Tauapeçaçu Brazil
37 L2 Taubach Germany
130 F8 Taubaté Brazil
36 H5 Tauber R Germany
33 R10 Taucha Germany
38 H7 Tauerin Tunnel Austria
37 N7 Taufkirchen Germany
36 G2 Taufstein mt Germany
128 G3 Tauini R Brazil
145 E2 Taukoa New Zealand
20 C4 Taulé France
19 N16 Taulignan France
28 D5 Taulov Denmark
145 E3 Taumarunui New Zealand
128 D5 Taumaturgo Brazil
110 F4 Taum Sauk Mt Missouri U.S.A.
130 C7 Taunay Brazil
89 D6 Taung S Africa
68 C5 Taungbon Burma
68 B2 Taungdwingyi Burma
68 C2 Taung-Gyi Burma
68 D3 Taunggyi mt Burma/Thailand
68 C2 Taunglau Burma
68 C4 Taungnyo A ra Burma
68 B2 Taungtha Burma
68 B3 Taungup Burma
74 D3 Taunsa Pakistan
8 C5 Taunton England
95 Q5 Taunton Massachusetts U.S.A.
95 R5 Taunton,E Massachusetts U.S.A.
36 E3 Taunus mts Germany
145 E2 Taupiri New Zealand
145 F3 Taupo New Zealand
52 B6 Tauragė Lithuania
145 E3 Taurakawa mt New Zealand
145 F2 Tauranga New Zealand
121 R6 Taureau, L Quebec Canada
145 D1 Tauroa Pt New Zealand
55 F2 Taurovy Russian Federation
Taurus Mts see Toroslar Dağlari
17 G3 Tauste Spain
144 B7 Tautuku Peninsula New Zealand
137 M2 Tauu Is Papua New Guinea
115 K5 Tavani Northwest Territories Canada
40 F3 Tavannes Switzerland
113 F9 Tavares Florida U.S.A.
45 K4 Tavarnelles Val di Pesa Italy
47 K7 Tavas Turkey
22 F4 Tavaux France
55 D2 Tavda R Russian Federation
55 E2 Tavda Russian Federation
26 L7 Tavelsjö Sweden
41 J5 Taverne Switzerland
45 K1 Tavernelle Italy
115 M4 Taverner B Northwest Territories Canada
19 Q17 Tavernes France
113 G12 Tavernier Florida U.S.A.
21 P3 Taverny Val d'Oise France
88 F3 Taveta Kenya
137 R5 Taveuni isld Fiji
56 G6 Tavin Mongolia
16 B7 Tavira Portugal
8 B6 Tavistock England
43 C8 Tavolara, I Sardinia
55 G4 Tavolzhan Kazakhstan
16 B4 Tâvora R Portugal
68 D5 Tavoy Burma
Tavoy I see Mali Kyun
68 D6 Tavoy Pt Burma
65 H3 Tavrichanka Russian Federation
55 F4 Tavricheskoye Russian Federation
47 N11 Tavşancıl Turkey
47 K5 Tavşanlı Turkey
47 N11 Tavşanlı Turkey
26 L3 Tavvaätno R Sweden
145 G4 Tawa New Zealand
109 M3 Tawakoni, L Texas U.S.A.
94 D2 Tawas City Michigan U.S.A.
118 D4 Tawatinaw Alberta Canada
70 E2 Tawau Sabah
70 E2 Tawau, Telukan B Kalimantan
86 E3 Taweisha Sudan
8 C4 Tawe,R Wales
145 E1 Tawhiti Rahi I New Zealand
70 F2 Tawitawi Philippines
8 B5 Taw,R England
67 G5 Ta-wu Taiwan
84 F3 Tāwurghā, Sabkhat salt flat Libya
38 G7 Taxenbach Austria
27 J12 Taxinge Sweden
66 B4 Taxkorgan China
128 C5 Tayabamba Peru
71 E4 Tayabas B Philippines
69 K13 Tayan Indonesia
52 D1 Taybola Russian Federation
86 H5 Tayeeglow Somalia
13 E1 Tay,Firth of Scotland
56 C3 Tayga Russian Federation
12 C2 Tayinloan Scotland
143 D10 Tay,L W Australia Australia
140 C5 Taylor R N Terr Australia
117 N7 Taylor British Columbia Canada
103 O7 Taylor Arizona U.S.A.
109 O2 Taylor Arkansas U.S.A.
111 G7 Taylor Mississippi U.S.A.
110 E2 Taylor Missouri U.S.A.
98 G8 Taylor Nebraska U.S.A.
109 K5 Taylor Texas U.S.A.
100 D2 Taylor Washington U.S.A.
99 P5 Taylor Wisconsin U.S.A.
144 C5 Taylor, Mt New Zealand
106 C6 Taylor, Mt New Mexico U.S.A.
116 J6 Taylor Mts Alaska U.S.A.
106 D3 Taylor Park Res Colorado U.S.A.
112 B3 Taylor Ridge Georgia U.S.A.
112 E3 Taylors South Carolina U.S.A.
142 B3 Taylors Crossing W Australia Australia
106 F5 Taylor Springs New Mexico U.S.A.
94 B8 Taylorsville Kentucky U.S.A.
111 G10 Taylorsville Mississippi U.S.A.
112 F2 Taylorsville North Carolina U.S.A.
94 F7 Taylorsville Ohio U.S.A.
110 G2 Taylorville Illinois U.S.A.
122 F7 Taymouth New Brunswick Canada
51 K2 Taymura R Russian Federation
51 K1 Taymyr,Ozero L Russian Federation
51 J1 Taymyr,Poluostrov pen Russian Federation
55 E4 Tayncha Kazakhstan
68 H7 Tay Ninh Vietnam
12 C1 Taynuilt Scotland
71 G6 Tayoloan R Mindanao Philippines
13 F1 Tayport Scotland
15 E4 Tay,R Scotland
56 E3 Tayshet Russian Federation
58 C2 Tayshir Mongolia
15 E4 Tayside reg Scotland
71 E3 Taytay Luzon Philippines
71 D5 Taytay Palawan Philippines
71 G5 Taytay Pt Philippines
77 G2 Tayyebād Iran
79 E10 Ţayyib al Ism Saudi Arabia
50 H2 Taz R Russian Federation
85 D2 Taza Morocco
85 F5 Tazalc Niger
61 O6 Tazawa ko L Japan
112 D1 Tazewell Tennessee U.S.A.
94 F9 Tazewell Virginia U.S.A.
65 F1 Tazicheng China
116 K7 Tazimina Lakes Alaska U.S.A.
84 G4 Tāzirbū Libya
48 K4 Tazlău R Romania
116 O6 Tazlina L Alaska U.S.A.
50 G2 Tazovskaya Guba G Russian Federation
50 G2 Tazovskiy Russian Federation
66 F6 Tazungdam Burma
61 K8 Tazuruhama Japan
78 K1 Tbilisi Georgia
85 E7 Tchaourou Benin
86 B6 Tchibanga Gabon
84 E5 Tchigaï, Plat. du Chad/Niger
68 J2 Tching Lan Xan isld Vietnam
85 F5 Tchin-Tabaradene Niger
86 B4 Tcholliré Cameroon
111 F8 Tchula Mississippi U.S.A.
31 L1 Tczew Poland
128 E4 Tea R Brazil
98 K6 Tea South Dakota U.S.A.
48 J4 Teaca Romania
124 G6 Teacapán Mexico
108 D3 Teague New Mexico U.S.A.
109 L4 Teague Texas U.S.A.
143 D7 Teague,L W Australia Australia
13 G4 Team Valley England
144 A6 Te Anau New Zealand
145 E3 Te Anga New Zealand
45 Q7 Teano Italy
101 T6 Teapot Dome hill Wyoming U.S.A.
145 G2 Te Araroa New Zealand
145 E2 Te Aroha New Zealand
140 C5 Tea Tree N Terr Australia
145 E3 Te Awamutu New Zealand
16 D8 Teba Spain
69 J12 Tebas Indonesia
85 F1 Tebessa Algeria
130 B10 Tebicuary Paraguay
69 D11 Tebingtinggi Sumatra
69 E13 Tebo R Sumatra
43 C12 Tébourba Tunisia
43 C12 Téboursouk Tunisia
69 F12 Tebrau Malaysia
53 G11 Tebulosmta mt Georgia/Rus Fed
18 G10 Tech R France
55 D3 Techa R Russian Federation
85 D7 Techiman Ghana
47 J1 Techirghiol Romania
144 D5 Technical, Mt New Zealand
33 Q6 Techow Germany
79 G1 Tecirli Turkey
36 G6 Teck Germany
133 C6 Tecka Argentina
32 G8 Tecklenburg Germany
27 F16 Teckomatorp Sweden
124 G7 Tecolotlán Mexico
124 H8 Tecomán Mexico
103 H6 Tecopa California U.S.A.
124 F4 Tecorichic Mexico
124 E3 Tecoripa Mexico
125 J9 Tecpan Mexico
124 G6 Tecuala Mexico
48 L5 Tecuci Romania
120 H10 Tecumseh Ontario Canada
94 D4 Tecumseh Michigan U.S.A.
110 D5 Tecumseh Missouri U.S.A.
98 K9 Tecumseh Nebraska U.S.A.
107 O6 Tecumseh Oklahoma U.S.A.
8 C6 Tedburn St Mary England
70 P16 Tedjakula Indonesia
57 B5 Tedzhen Turkmenistan
77 G1 Tedzhen Turkmenistan
56 D5 Teeli Russian Federation
118 D6 Tees Alberta Canada
13 G5 Tees,R England
120 J9 Teeswater Ontario Canada
71 D6 Teeth,The mt Palawan Philippines
128 F4 Tefe Brazil
47 K7 Tefenni Turkey
26 L8 Teg Sweden
70 M9 Tegal Java
33 S7 Tegel Germany
25 F6 Tegelen Netherlands
41 P2 Tegernsee L Germany
85 F6 Tegina Nigeria
70 K8 Tegineneng Sumatra
141 H8 Tego Queensland Australia
125 L2 Tegucigalpa Honduras
85 F5 Teguiddan Tessoum Niger
89 E3 Tegwani R Zimbabwe
102 F6 Tehachapi California U.S.A.
102 F7 Tehachapi Mts California U.S.A.
102 B1 Tehama California U.S.A.
102 B2 Tehama-Colusa Canal California U.S.A.
145 E2 Te Hana New Zealand
145 D1 Te Hapua New Zealand
145 F3 Te Haroto New Zealand
145 F3 Te Hauke New Zealand
115 K4 Tehek L Northwest Territories Canada
77 B2 Tehrān Iran
77 B2 Tehrān prov Iran
125 L8 Tehuacán Mexico
125 M9 Tehuantepec Mexico
37 L2 Teichel Germany
8 C3 Teifi R Wales
8 C6 Teignmouth England
8 C6 Teign,R England
20 G6 Teillay France
20 H7 Teille France
21 J4 Teilleul,le France
61 Q12 Teima Okinawa
Teinach see Bad Teinach-Zavelstein
36 F6 Teinach Germany
37 N6 Teisbach Germany
29 K10 Teisko Finland
88 G3 Teita Hills Kenya
12 D1 Teith,R Scotland
48 H4 Teius Romania
130 H9 Teixeira Brazil
Teixeira de Sousa see Luau
130 G7 Teixeiras Brazil
130 E9 Teixeira Soares Brazil
16 E8 Tejeda,Sa mts Spain
16 B5 Tejo R Portugal
124 F3 Tejolocachic Mexico
102 F7 Tejon Pk California U.S.A.
130 E6 Tejuco,R Brazil
125 J8 Tejupilco Mexico
145 F2 Te Kaha New Zealand
98 K8 Tekamah Nebraska U.S.A.
145 D1 Te Kao New Zealand
145 F3 Te Karaka New Zealand
145 E2 Te Kauwhata New Zealand
145 E3 Te Kawa New Zealand
47 N10 Teke Turkey
57 J3 Tekeli Kazakhstan
55 F4 Teke, Oz L Kazakhstan
57 K3 Tekes China
66 C3 Tekes R Kazakhstan
57 K3 Tekes He R China
86 G3 Tekezē R Ethiopia
144 C5 Te Kinga New Zealand
47 J4 Tekirdağ Turkey
145 D3 Te Kiri New Zealand
68 A2 Teknaf Burma
100 H2 Tekoa Washington U.S.A.
144 D5 Tekoa, Mt New Zealand
94 C4 Tekonsha Michigan U.S.A.
145 D2 Te Kopuru New Zealand
86 D2 Tekro Chad
71 H5 Teku Sulawesi
145 E3 Te Kuiti New Zealand
125 Q10 Tela Honduras
80 E3 Tel 'Adashim Israel
69 C10 Telagatujuh Sumatra
17 G10 Télagh Algeria
80 B7 Telamim Israel
69 G12 Telan isld Indonesia
116 L6 Telaquana,L Alaska U.S.A.
80 B6 Tel Ashdod Israel
80 B7 Tel Ashqelon Israel
53 G12 Telavi Georgia
80 C5 Tel Aviv Israel
80 C7 Tel Azeqa Israel
56 C4 Tel'bes Russian Federation
80 F3 Tel Bet She'an Israel
80 C7 Tel Bet Shemesh Israel
80 F3 Tel Bet Yerah Israel
31 J6 Telč Czechoslovakia
48 J3 Telciu Romania
80 C8 Tel Devir Israel
70 C6 Telegapulang Kalimantan
117 H7 Telegraph Creek British Columbia Canada
80 F6 Teleilet el Ghassul Jordan
27 C12 Telemark prov Norway
70 E4 Telen R Kalimantan
48 L3 Teleneshty Moldavia
48 J6 Teleorman R Romania
109 L2 Telephone Texas U.S.A.
102 G5 Telescope Pk California U.S.A.
127 P5 Telescope Pt Grenada
129 G5 Teles Pires R Brazil
56 C5 Teletskoye, Oz L Russian Federation
80 C8 Tel Eyton Israel
142 D5 Telfer Mining Centre W Australia Australia
8 D2 Telford England
80 D4 Tel Gat Israel
20 B5 Telgruc France
32 G9 Telgte Germany
80 F1 Tel Hazor Israel
85 B6 Télimélé Guinea
80 F2 Tel Kinnerot Israel
78 J3 Tel Kotchek Syria
117 K8 Telkwa British Columbia Canada
108 G1 Tell Texas U.S.A.
80 C7 Tel Lakhish Israel
22 K5 Tellancourt Villers France
110 K4 Tell City Indiana U.S.A.
80 F5 Tell Deir'Alla Jordan
26 L5 Tellejåkk Sweden
116 D4 Teller Alaska U.S.A.
76 B5 Tellicherry India
112 C2 Tellico L Tennessee U.S.A.
112 C2 Tellico Plains Tennessee U.S.A.
122 F3 Tellier Quebec Canada
22 J3 Tellin Belgium
32 K4 Tellingstedt Germany
80 C5 Tel Litwinsky Israel
80 F6 Tell Nimrin Jordan
106 C4 Telluride Colorado U.S.A.
57 B4 Tel'mansk Turkmenistan
80 C7 Tel Maresha Israel
58 C2 Telmen Nuur L Mongolia
80 B8 Tel Mifsah Israel
80 C4 Tel Mond Israel
69 D13 Telo Indonesia
100 H4 Telocaset Oregon U.S.A.
69 B14 Telok Blangah dist Singapore
125 K8 Teloloapán Mexico
52 J3 Tel'poziz, Gora mt Russian Federation
80 F1 Tel Qedesh Israel
80 A8 Tel Re'im Israel
133 D6 Telsen Argentina
80 C2 Tel Shiqmona Israel
80 C8 Tel Shoqet Israel
52 B6 Telšiai Lithuania
120 E3 Teltaka Ontario Canada
33 S8 Teltow Germany
70 E3 Telukbajur Kalimantan
69 E13 Telukbayur Sumatra
70 K8 Telukbetung Sumatra
69 J10 Telukbutun Indonesia
69 C12 Telukdalam Indonesia
69 E10 Teluk Intan Malaysia
69 E13 Telukkuantan Sumatra
70 B5 Telukmelan Kalimantan
70 L9 Teluknaga Java
69 J13 Telukpakedai Indonesia
69 F12 Teluksabah Sumatra
85 F5 Telwes Niger
80 C8 Tel Ziqlag Israel
85 E7 Tema Ghana
69 J12 Temaju isld Indonesia
94 K9 Teman Virginia U.S.A.
70 N9 Temanggung Java
85 F4 Temasint Algeria
69 E14 Tembesi R Sumatra
69 F13 Tembilahan Sumatra
102 D6 Temblor Rge California U.S.A.
87 C7 Tembo Aluma Angola
89 E8 Tembuland dist S Africa
102 G8 Temecula California U.S.A.
56 E5 Temenchulu,Gora mt Russian Federation
8 D3 Teme,R England
48 F5 Temerin Serbia Yugoslavia
69 F11 Temerluh Malaysia
69 F10 Temiang, Bukit hill Malaysia
71 C3 Teminabuan W Irian
57 A1 Temir Kazakhstan
56 C4 Temirtau Russian Federation
122 A2 Temiscamie L Quebec Canada
122 A2 Temiscamie R Quebec Canada
121 L6 Témiscaming Quebec Canada
121 L5 Témiscamingue, L Quebec Canada
122 D6 Temiscouata L Quebec Canada
121 L6 Témiskaming Quebec Canada
69 G12 Temiyang isld Indonesia
139 G8 Temma Tasmania Australia
56 F5 Temnik R Russian Federation
139 J5 Temora New South Wales Australia
124 F3 Temósachic Mexico
103 N8 Tempe Arizona U.S.A.
70 F7 Tempe, L isld Sulawesi
33 S8 Tempelhof Germany
94 D5 Temperance Michigan U.S.A.
69 F13 Tempino Sumatra
43 C8 Tempio Paus Sardinia
95 R2 Temple Maine U.S.A.
94 C2 Temple Michigan U.S.A.
109 J1 Temple Oklahoma U.S.A.
95 M6 Temple Pennsylvania U.S.A.
109 K4 Temple Texas U.S.A.
141 G1 Temple B Queensland Australia
8 B3 Temple Bar Wales
20 G7 Temple-de-Bretagne, le France
140 B6 Temple Downs N Terr Australia
9 H5 Temple Ewell England
14 D4 Templemore Ireland
13 F4 Temple Sowerby England
140 E5 Templeton R Queensland Australia
102 D6 Templeton California U.S.A.
94 H6 Templeton Pennsylvania U.S.A.
8 B4 Templeton Wales
22 E2 Templeuve Belgium
33 T6 Templin Germany
87 C8 Tempué Angola
33 P5 Tempzin Germany
55 E2 Temryak, Oz L Russian Federation
22 G1 Temse Belgium
131 A7 Temuco Chile
144 C6 Temuka New Zealand
98 F3 Temvik North Dakota U.S.A.
55 C4 Temyasovo Russian Federation
128 C4 Tena Ecuador
102 H1 Tenabo Nevada U.S.A.
124 G8 Tenacatita Mexico
109 N4 Tenaha Texas U.S.A.
117 F7 Tenakee Springs Alaska U.S.A.
29 K11 Tenala Finland
76 E2 Tenali India
124 G7 Tenamaxtlán Mexico
145 D4 Te Namu New Zealand
68 D6 Tenasserim Burma
73 Q6 Tenasserim R Burma
68 C6 Tenasserim I Burma
68 E5 Tenasserim State Burma
19 P13 Tenay France
8 D3 Tenbury Wells England
8 B4 Tenby Wales
120 G6 Tenby Bay Ontario Canada
18 H7 Tence France
86 H3 Tendaho Ethiopia
73 P7 Ten Degree Ch Andaman/Nicobar Is
86 F3 Tendelti Sudan
61 O7 Tendō Japan
101 M5 Tendoy Idaho U.S.A.
85 D2 Tendrara Morocco
40 D4 Tendre, Mt Switzerland
9 H4 Tendring England
21 O8 Tendu France
Tenedos see Bozcaada
85 G4 Ténéré du Tafassasset reg Niger
85 A3 Tenerife isld Canary Is
85 E1 Ténès Algeria
47 H2 Tenevo Bulgaria
71 J4 Tenga Sulawesi
71 L9 Tengahdai Flores Indonesia
70 N9 Tengah, Jawa prov Java
Tengchow see Penglai
70 E5 Tenggarong Kalimantan
70 O9 Tengger Java
69 F10 Tenggul isld Malaysia
70 E1 Tenghilan Sabah

55 E5 **Tengiz, Oz** L Kazakhstan
71 E7 **Tengolan** isld Philippines
67 C7 **Tengqiao** China
65 D7 **Teng Xian** China
67 C5 **Teng Xian** China
27 G14 **Tenhult** Sweden
44 B3 **Tenibres** mt Italy/France
146 D3 **Teniente Jubany** Argentina Base Antarctica
146 D3 **Teniente Rodolfo Marsh** Chile Base Antarctica
100 C3 **Tenino** Washington U.S.A.
55 F3 **Tenis, Oz** L Russian Federation
55 D4 **Teniz, Oz** L Kazakhstan
76 C6 **Tenkasi** India
52 G6 **Ten'ki** Russian Federation
107 Q6 **Tenkiller Ferry L** Oklahoma U.S.A.
85 D6 **Tenkodogo** Burkina
69 A9 **Tenlaa** Nicobar Is
123 Q2 **Ten Mile L** Newfoundland Canada
42 F5 **Tenna** R Italy
100 D8 **Tennant** California U.S.A.
140 C4 **Tennant Creek** N Terr Australia
38 H6 **Tennen-Geb** mts Austria
110 H6 **Tennille** Georgia U.S.A.
106 D2 **Tennessee Pass** Colorado U.S.A.
110 J6 **Tennessee** state U.S.A.
110 J6 **Tennessee R** Tennessee U.S.A.
26 F4 **Tennholmen** Norway
112 E5 **Tennille** Georgia U.S.A.
29 C4 **Tenniöjoki** R Finland
123 S6 **Tennycape** Newfoundland
144 D5 **Tennyson, L** New Zealand
131 B5 **Teno** R Chile
29 M2 **Tenojoki** R Finland
70 D2 **Tenom** Sabah
125 O9 **Tenosique** Mexico
61 J11 **Tenri** Japan
61 L11 **Tenryu** Japan
111 K9 **Tensas** R Louisiana U.S.A.
111 J11 **Tensaw** R Alabama U.S.A.
100 J2 **Tensed** Idaho U.S.A.
85 C2 **Tensift** R Morocco
99 M2 **Tenstrike** Minnesota U.S.A.
143 B10 **Tenteno** Sulawesi
9 G5 **Tenterden** W Australia
139 K3 **Tenterfield** New South Wales Australia
113 F12 **Ten Thousand Is** Florida U.S.A.
70 G4 **Tentolomatinan** mt Sulawesi
124 H7 **Teocalitche** Mexico
45 M3 **Teodorano** Italy
46 E5 **Teófilo Otóni** Brazil
48 K1 **Teofipol'** Ukraine
71 E7 **Teomabal** isld Philippines
125 L8 **Teotitlan** Mexico
71 O8 **Tepa** Indonesia
124 E3 **Tepache** Mexico
52 F6 **Tepasto** Finland
124 H7 **Tepatitlán de Morelos** Mexico
46 E2 **Tepe** mt Serbia Yugoslavia
125 K8 **Tepeji** Mexico
57 B3 **Tepekul'** Uzbekistan
46 D4 **Tepelenë** Albania
37 O4 **Tepelská Plošina** mts Czechoslovakia
47 N11 **Tepeoren** Turkey
70 E4 **Tepianlangsat** Kalimantan
124 G7 **Tepic** Mexico
37 O4 **Teplá** Czechoslovakia
30 H5 **Teplice** Czechoslovakia
37 O3 **Teplička** Czechoslovakia
48 M2 **Teplik** Ukraine
52 H4 **Teplogorka** Russian Federation
54 K8 **Teplogorsk** Ukraine
124 C2 **Tepoca, C** Mexico
145 F3 **Te Pohue** New Zealand
145 G3 **Te Puia Springs** New Zealand
145 F2 **Te Puke** New Zealand
80 D7 **Teqoa** Jordan
124 H7 **Tequila** Mexico
17 J3 **Ter** R Spain
85 E6 **Téra** Niger
16 B6 **Tera** R Portugal
16 C3 **Tera** R Spain
61 M8 **Teradomari** Japan
61 P7 **Teraike** Japan
42 F6 **Teramo** Italy
139 G7 **Terang** Victoria Australia
21 K9 **Ter Apel** Netherlands
77 L5 **Teratani** R Pakistan
71 O8 **Terbang Selatan** Indonesia
71 O8 **Terbang Utara** isld Indonesia
25 F5 **Terborg** Netherlands
78 H2 **Tercan** Turkey
78 H2 **Tercan Baraji** dam Turkey
133 E4 **Tercero** R Argentina
106 E4 **Tercio** Colorado U.S.A.
48 H2 **Tereblya** R Ukraine
48 K1 **Terebovlya** Ukraine
48 G5 **Teregova** Romania
53 G11 **Terek** R Russian Federation
56 E5 **Tere-Khol',Oz** L Russian Federation
54 C4 **Terekhovka** Belorussia
56 C5 **Terektinskiy Khrebet** mts Russian Federation
122 J9 **Terence B** Nova Scotia Canada
69 F10 **Terengganu** state Malaysia
69 F10 **Terengganu** R Malaysia
130 C7 **Terenos** Brazil
57 C2 **Terenozek** Kazakhstan
55 C5 **Terensay** Russian Federation
69 J13 **Terentang** Indonesia
70 E5 **Terentang,P** Kalimantan
130 D9 **Teresa Cristina** Brazil
55 D4 **Tereshka** R Penzenskaya obl Russian Federation
129 K5 **Teresina** Brazil
129 H3 **Teresina** Brazil
128 E3 **Teresita** Colombia
130 G8 **Teresópolis** Brazil
31 D3 **Terespol** Poland
139 J3 **Terewah I** New South Wales Australia
16 B7 **Terge** R Portugal
22 E4 **Tergnier** France
85 C4 **Terhazza** Mali
52 E1 **Teriberka** Russian Federation
108 D6 **Terlingua** Texas U.S.A.
78 F1 **Terme** Turkey
41 O5 **Termeno sulla Strada del Vino** Italy
77 K1 **Termez** Uzbekistan
40 E7 **Termignon** France
143 D10 **Termination I** W Australia
21 O5 **Terminiers** France
43 F11 **Termini Imerese** Sicily
42 E6 **Terminillo** mt Italy
125 O8 **Términos,L.de** Mexico
100 F9 **Termo** California U.S.A.
42 F7 **Termoli** Italy
Termonde see Dendermonde
6 L1 **Tern** oil rig North Sea
71 A2 **Ternate** Halmahera Indonesia
83 J12 **Ternay,C** Mahé n Indian Oc
83 K12 **Ternay Pass** Mahé n Indian Oc
38 K6 **Ternberg** Austria
28 B7 **Terndrup** Denmark
25 A6 **Terneuzen** Netherlands
59 L2 **Terney** Russian Federation
9 D2 **Terni** Italy
102 T13 **Terni** R Hawaiian Is
42 E6 **Terni** Italy
48 K1 **Ternopol'** Ukraine
54 D5 **Ternovka** Ukraine
54 D9 **Ternovka** Ukraine

145 E3 **Te Roti** New Zealand
16 D10 **Teroual** Morocco
138 E5 **Terowie** South Australia
59 M2 **Terpeniya,Mys** C Russian Federation
55 E3 **Terpugovo** Russian Federation
94 H7 **Terra Alta** West Virginia
102 E6 **Terra Bella** California U.S.A.
117 J8 **Terrace** British Columbia Canada
120 C4 **Terrace Bay** Ontario Canada
143 D8 **Terraces, The** hills W Australia
45 O7 **Terracina** Italy
89 C5 **Terra Firma** S Africa
109 K2 **Terral** Oklahoma U.S.A.
43 B9 **Terralba** Sardinia
123 S5 **Terra Nova** Newfoundland Canada
45 L4 **Terranuova Bracc** Italy
18 F7 **Terrasson** France
124 F3 **Terrazas** Mexico
146 D15 **Terre Adélie** Antarctica
100 D5 **Terrebonne** Oregon U.S.A.
111 F12 **Terrebonne B** Louisiana U.S.A.
127 N5 **Terre de Bas** isld Guadeloupe W Indies
127 N5 **Terre de Haut** isld Guadeloupe W Indies
110 J2 **Terre Haute** Indiana U.S.A.
109 L3 **Terrell** Texas U.S.A.
123 S6 **Terrenceville** Newfoundland Canada
101 N6 **Terreton** Idaho U.S.A.
20 H3 **Terrette** R France
139 K5 **Terrigal** New South Wales Australia
57 H4 **Tersef** Chad
52 E2 **Terskiy Bereg** coast Russian Federation
43 C9 **Tertenia** Sardinia
76 A1 **Teru-Aygyr** Kyrgyzstan
68 J3 **Teruel** prov Spain
142 D4 **Tervel** Bulgaria
141 K6 **Tervo** Finland
29 M9 **Tervola** Finland
29 J2 **Tervuren** Belgium
42 H4 **Tešanj** Bosnia-Herzegovina
107 N2 **Tescott** Kansas U.S.A.
86 G2 **Teseney** Ethiopia
52 F6 **Tesha** R Russian Federation
116 L1 **Teshekpuk L** Alaska U.S.A.
60 S2 **Teshikaga** Japan
60 H11 **Te-shima** isld Japan
60 Q1 **Teshio** R Japan
60 Q2 **Teshio dake** mt Japan
60 P1 **Teshio-sanchi** mts Japan
46 E1 **Tešica** Serbia Yugoslavia
117 F5 **Teslin** R Yukon Territory Canada
117 F5 **Teslin L** Br Col/Yukon Terr Canada
130 E4 **Tesouras, R** Brazil
130 D5 **Tesouro** Brazil
52 D5 **Tesovo Netyl'skiy** Russian Federation
17 G9 **Tessala, Mt.du** Algeria
85 E4 **Tessalit** Mali
85 F6 **Tessaoua** Niger
118 K7 **Tessier** Saskatchewan Canada
33 Q4 **Tessin** Switzerland
21 H4 **Tessy** France
43 C7 **Testa, C** Sardinia
42 G7 **Testa del Gargano** Italy
18 E8 **Teste-de-Buch, la** France
32 L6 **Testedt** Germany
43 C12 **Testour** Tunisia
9 E5 **Test, R** England
14 D6 **Tesuque** New Mexico U.S.A.
18 G10 **Tét** France
38 D3 **Tét** Hungary
117 L9 **Tetachuck L** British Columbia Canada
122 D6 **Tetagouche R** New Brunswick Canada
125 J9 **Tetela** Mexico
17 F4 **Tetas de Viana** mt Spain
88 B2 **Tetas, Pta** Chile
9 E5 **Tetbury** England
88 D10 **Tete** Mozambique
123 N3 **Tête à la Baleine** Quebec Canada
69 C12 **Tetebatu** Indonesia
120 J9 **Tête Jaune Cache** British Columbia Canada
145 F3 **Te Teko** New Zealand
36 B5 **Téterchen** France
36 F1 **Tetere R** Russian Federation
30 N7 **Teterow** Germany
98 B3 **Teteven** Bulgaria
98 K1 **Thief River Falls** Minnesota U.S.A.
21 P7 **Tetlin** U.S.A.
106 D6 **Tetonia** Idaho U.S.A.
101 P6 **Teton Ra** Wyoming U.S.A.
16 D9 **Tétouan** Morocco
46 E7 **Tétrayi** mt Greece
37 N1 **Tettau** Germany
32 G5 **Tettens** Germany
37 M1 **Tetyushi** Russian Federation
38 N7 **Teuchern** Germany
133 E3 **Teuco** R Argentina
43 B10 **Teulada** Sardinia
119 U8 **Teulon** Manitoba Canada
71 O8 **Teun** isld Indonesia
69 B10 **Teunom** R Sumatra
21 N4 **Teunom** Sumatra
18 F7 **Teupitz** Germany
141 K7 **Teuri-tô** isld Japan
119 P7 **Teutoburger Wald** Germany
29 J9 **Teuva** Finland
111 H11 **Tevansjö** Sweden
128 F6 **Téven-Kedraf** France
45 M6 **Tevere** R Italy
144 A3 **Tewah** R Kalimantan
70 D5 **Te Wera** New Zealand
145 F3 **Te Whaiti** New Zealand
145 F3 **Te Wharau** New Zealand
8 D4 **Tewkesbury** England
117 L11 **Texada** I British Columbia Canada
12 B2 **Texel** I Scotland
109 J2 **Texarkana** Texas/Ark U.S.A.
46 E6 **Texas** Queensland Australia
109 N6 **Texas** state U.S.A.
109 M6 **Texas City** Texas U.S.A.
139 H6 **Texel** isld Netherlands
146 F17 **Texistepeco** Netherlands
22 C2 **Texoma** Texas/Okla U.S.A.
108 D1 **Texico** New Mexico U.S.A.
108 B7 **Texline** Texas U.S.A.
108 D1 **Texmelucan** Mexico
56 D1 **Texoma,L** Oklahoma U.S.A.
67 A4 **Teya** Russian Federation
120 G6 **Te-yang** China
46 E5 **Teykovo** Russian Federation
46 F4 **Teyvarah** Afghanistan
9 G3 **Teza** R Russian Federation

125 L8 **Teziutlán** Mexico
75 P5 **Tezpur** India
87 E11 **Thabana Ntlenyana** mt Lesotho
89 E7 **Thaba Putsoa** mt Lesotho
68 B4 **Thabaung** Burma
87 E10 **Thabazimbi** S Africa
68 C1 **Thabeikkyin** Burma
79 E10 **Thabt, G. el** mt Egypt
68 C2 **Thabyedaung** Burma
109 K2 **Thackerville** Oklahoma U.S.A.
Tha Han see Lop Buri
67 B6 **Thai Binh** Vietnam
68 H4 **Thai Duong Thung** Vietnam
68 G3 **Thai Hoa** Vietnam
68 D5 **Thailand** kingdom S E Asia
73 H6 **Thailand, G. of** Thailand
68 D9 **Thai Muang** Thailand
67 B6 **Thai Nguyen** Vietnam
68 D8 **Tha Khanon** Thailand
68 G4 **Thakhek** Laos
38 G8 **Thal** Austria
37 J2 **Thal** Germany
74 D2 **Thal** Pakistan
85 F1 **Thala** Tunisia
69 D8 **Thalang** Thailand
66 F6 **Thala Pass** China/Burma
33 O9 **Thale** Germany
69 E9 **Thale Luang** Thailand
36 B4 **Thalfang** Germany
38 H6 **Thalgau** Germany
37 O2 **Thalheim** Germany
43 B8 **Thaliesi** Sardinia
41 K4 **Thalkirch** Switzerland
141 J8 **Thallon** Queensland Australia
112 F6 **Thalmann** Georgia U.S.A.
37 L5 **Thalmässing** Germany
84 F4 **Thamad Bu, Hashishah** Libya
89 D5 **Thamaga** Botswana
9 F4 **Thame** England
120 H10 **Thames** R Ontario Canada
145 E2 **Thames** New Zealand
28 R9 **Thamesford** Ontario Canada
22 H4 **Thames, R** England
145 F2 **Thames Valley** admin region New Zealand
120 J10 **Thamesville** Ontario Canada
68 B3 **Thamihla Kyun** isld Burma
46 G8 **Thamsbrück** Germany
21 N5 **Thamshavn** Norway
13 G5 **Thanatpin** Burma
68 C5 **Thanbyuzayat** Burma
76 A1 **Thâne** India
68 J5 **Thang Binh** Vietnam
142 D4 **Thangoo** W Australia
141 K6 **Thangool** Queensland Australia
68 G3 **Thanh Hoa** Vietnam
68 G1 **Thanh Moi** Vietnam
76 D5 **Thanh Thuy** Vietnam
40 F2 **Thanjavur** India
38 F5 **Thann** France
37 J7 **Thannhausen** Germany
77 K7 **Thano Bula Khan** Pakistan
36 D7 **Thann** France
46 F6 **Thaon** France
71 K4 **Thaon les Vosages** France
68 H6 **Tha Pla** Thailand
69 D8 **Thap Put** Thailand
73 L3 **Thap Sakae** Thailand
37 J7 **Tharad** desert India
75 D4 **Tharandt** Germany
141 G8 **Thar Desert** India
89 F4 **Thargomindah** Queensland Australia
19 N12 **Tharrawaddy** Burma
21 O4 **Tharthar** R Iraq
36 C5 **Thasos** isld Greece
46 J4 **Thatcham** England
104 F4 **Thatcher** Arizona U.S.A.
101 O7 **Thatcher** Colorado U.S.A.
87 B5 **That Khe** Vietnam
68 C4 **Thaton** Burma
108 F3 **Tha Tum** Thailand
18 H9 **Thau, Étang de** L France
68 D4 **Thaungyin** R Thailand
68 C6 **Thaungdut-andwi Kyun** isld Burma
110 E5 **Thayer** Missouri U.S.A.
68 D6 **Thayetchaung** Burma
68 B3 **Thayetmyo** Burma
101 P7 **Thayne** Wyoming U.S.A.
109 K7 **Thazi** Arakan Burma
68 C2 **Thazi** Magwe Burma
111 J9 **Thazi** Mandalay Burma
9 E5 **Theale** England
103 M9 **Thebes** Mississippi
84 J4 **Thebes** ruins Egypt
110 G4 **Thebes** Illinois U.S.A.
120 J9 **Thedford** Ontario Canada
98 F7 **Thedford** Nebraska U.S.A.
32 K7 **Thedinghausen** Germany
139 K5 **The Entrance** New South Wales Australia
68 B3 **Thegon** Burma
139 N6 **Theillay** France
21 N6 **Theil, la Ille-et-Vilaine** France
110 C1 **Theil, le** Orne France
98 J2 **Theinkun** Burma
37 N1 **Theinzeik** Burma
37 N1 **Theissen** Germany
114 J5 **Theix** France
114 J5 **Thekulthili L** Northwest Territories Canada
100 C7 **Thelbridge** England
6 L4 **Thelma** oil rig North Sea
113 E7 **Thelma** Georgia U.S.A.
117 R4 **Thelon** R Northwest Territories Canada
114 H5 **Thompson Landing** Northwest Territories Canada
138 B1 **Thenay** Indre France
140 B6 **Thenay** Loir-et-Cher France
21 N8 **Thénezay** France
116 P6 **Thénon** France
119 P7 **Theodore** Queensland Australia
111 H1 **Theodore** Alabama U.S.A.
128 F6 **Theodore Roosevelt** R Brazil
95 Q4 **Theodore Roosevelt Nat. Mem. Park** North Dakota
141 G6 **Theo, Mt** N Terr Australia
144 D3 **Therain** R France
144 B6 **Theresa** R Queensland Australia
139 H7 **Theresa** New York U.S.A.
99 S6 **Therese** Wisconsin U.S.A.
83 K12 **Therese** Mahé n Indian Oc
118 F6 **Therien** Alberta Canada
111 F12 **Theriot** Louisiana U.S.A./Ark
46 F4 **Thermaïkós, Kólpos** B Greece
103 L3 **Thermo** Utah U.S.A.
46 E6 **Thermon** Greece
101 R8 **Thermopolis** Wyoming U.S.A.
139 H6 **The Rock** New South Wales Australia
146 F17 **Theron Mts** Antarctica
9 H2 **Thérouanne** France
94 B4 **Thésée** France
21 N7 **Thesiger B** Northwest Territories Canada
46 E5 **Thessalia** admin region Greece
120 K6 **Thessalon** Ontario Canada
46 F4 **Thessaloniki** Greece
9 G3 **Thetford** England

121 T6 **Thetford Mines** Quebec Canada
9 F2 **Thorney** England
68 B5 **Thetkethaung** R Burma
119 P3 **The Two Rivers** Saskatchewan Canada
21 O5 **Theuville** France
68 B4 **Theux** Belgium
138 C4 **Thevenard** South Australia
142 A5 **Thevenard I** W Australia
109 M5 **The Woodlands** Texas
110 K1 **Thèze** France
13 E6 **Thiamis** R Greece
13 E1 **Thiberville** France
109 P2 **Thibodaux** Louisiana U.S.A.
106 F2 **Thibodaux** Louisiana U.S.A.
109 L4 **Thicket Portage** Manitoba Canada
100 H2 **Thickthorn** England
141 F4 **Thickwood Hills** Alberta Canada
9 H3 **Thicket Portage** Canada
65 C4 **Thief R.Res** Oregon U.S.A.
118 C5 **Thiel Mts** Antarctica
146 J8 **Thielsen, Mt** Oregon U.S.A.
29 T8 **Thielt** see Tielt
28 D4 **Thienvil le** Wisconsin U.S.A.
119 U1 **Thieracho** France
18 H7 **Thiers** France
85 A6 **Thiès** Senegal
69 B8 **Thionville** France
42 D7 **Thiou** Burkina
102 F7 **Thira** isld Greece
101 L8 **Thirasia** isld Greece
101 L7 **Thiron-Gardais** France
9 F3 **Thirsk** England
47 H3 **Thirston** England
109 K5 **Thirsty, Mt** W Australia
95 O3 **Thirty Thousand Is** Ontario Canada
9 F3 **Thiruvananthapuram** see Trivandrum
101 K7 **Thisted** co see Viborg co
101 O4 **Thisted** Denmark
6 L1 **Thistilfjördhur** B Iceland
139 G8 **Thistle** oil rig North Sea
103 N3 **Thistle** Utah U.S.A.
117 D4 **Thistle Creek** Yukon Territory Canada
138 D5 **Thistle I** South Australia
139 F2 **Threekingham** England
137 O8 **Three Kings Basin** Pacific Oc
9 E5 **Three Kings Is** New Zealand
140 D3 **Three Knobs** mt N Terr Australia
99 R4 **Three Lakes** Wisconsin U.S.A.
141 G2 **Three Mile Opening, First & Second** straits Gt Barrier Reef Aust
99 U8 **Three Oaks** Michigan U.S.A.
65 G1 **Three Pagodas Pass** Burma/Thailand
119 T3 **Threepoint L** Manitoba Canada
67 B6 **Three Points, C** Ghana
107 F4 **Three Rivers** Michigan
21 K6 **Three Rivers** New Mexico U.S.A.
109 J7 **Three Rivers** Texas U.S.A.
123 N5 **Three Rock Cove** Newfoundland Canada
141 G1 **Three Sisters** South Australia
100 D5 **Three Sisters** mts Oregon U.S.A.
143 B8 **Three Springs** W Australia
140 C4 **Three Ways Roadhouse** N Terr Australia
13 E4 **Threlkeld** England
109 H2 **Thrissur** see Trichur
109 H2 **Throckmorton** Texas U.S.A.
100 F1 **Throm** Cambodia
17 F2 **Throssel, Mt** W Australia
142 A7 **Throssel Ra** W Australia
17 H10 **Thrissel** Australia
112 D2 **Tifton** Georgia U.S.A.
70 D2 **Tiga** isld Sabah
116 P9 **Tigalda** I Aleutian Is
139 J5 **Tigard** Oregon U.S.A.
1 H8 **Thueyts** France
99 R5 **Thulie, la** Italy
22 G3 **Thuin** Belgium
98 J2 **Thule** Greenland
95 M5 **Thule, Southern** isld S Sandwich Is Atlantic Oc
37 O2 **Thum** Germany
101 P5 **Thumb, Wyoming** U.S.A.
144 D3 **Thumbs, The** mt New Zealand
40 G4 **Thompson L** W Australia
114 G7 **Thunda** Queensland Australia
119 O2 **Thunder** Ontario Canada
99 R1 **Thunder Bay** Michigan U.S.A.
78 B1 **Thunder Bay** Ontario Canada
120 Q2 **Thunder Butte Cr** South Dakota U.S.A.
116 P6 **Thunderhouse Falls** Ontario Canada
126 D6 **Thunder Knoll** Caribbean
118 C4 **Thunersee** L Switzerland
35 N6 **Thüngen** Germany
138 E1 **Thüringen** Austria
140 B6 **Thüringen** land Germany
37 J2 **Thüringer Wald** mts Germany
13 N13 **Thurles** Ireland
14 C4 **Thurloo Downs** New South Wales Australia
37 L3 **Thurnau** Germany
28 F6 **Thure** Denmark
28 F1 **Thures les Glières** France
139 H2 **Thorez** see Torez
91 P7 **Thorild** Alberta Canada
101 L7 **Thorignon** Vendée France
15 F2 **Thórisvatn** L Iceland
47 K2 **Thorlindah, L** Queensland Australia
110 C3 **Thornaby** England
117 K2 **Thornage** England
9 F2 **Thornapple** R Michigan
146 B8 **Thwaites Glacier** glacier Antarctica

102 F3 **Thorne** Nevada U.S.A.
12 D1 **Thornhill** Central Scotland
12 E3 **Thornhill** Dumfries & Galloway Scotland
13 E6 **Thornton** England
13 E1 **Thornton** Scotland
109 P2 **Thornton** Arkansas U.S.A.
106 F2 **Thornton** Colorado U.S.A.
109 L4 **Thornton** Iowa U.S.A.
100 H2 **Thornton** Iowa U.S.A.
141 F4 **Thorntonia** Queensland Australia
110 K1 **Thorntown** Indiana U.S.A.
138 D6 **Thorny Passage** South Australia Australia
121 L9 **Thorold** Ontario Canada
58 E5 **Thorold** Canada
67 G2 **Thorp** Washington U.S.A.
67 B5 **Thorp** Wisconsin U.S.A.
145 O3 **Thorpe New Zealand**
9 H3 **Thorpeness** England
67 D3 **Thorsager** Denmark
134 C11 **Thorshavnfjella** mts Antarctica
85 E1 **Thorup** Denmark
141 L7 **Thráki** admin region Greece
29 T8 **Thórshöfn** Iceland
28 D4 **Thorso** Denmark
119 U1 **Thorverton** England
9 C6 **Thot Not** Vietnam
68 F2 **Thouarcé** France
21 K7 **Thouars** France
21 K8 **Thouars** France
84 F5 **Thouet** R France
21 J8 **Thouarsais-Bouildroux** France
130 O3 **Thouin,C** W Australia
48 J3 **Thouria** Greece
20 H6 **Thourie** France
75 K4 **Thourotte** France
124 C3 **Thousand** isld Mexico
71 F4 **Thousand Lake Mt** Utah
103 N3 **Thousand Oaks** California U.S.A.
102 F7 **Thousand Spring Cr** Nevada U.S.A.
101 L7 **Thousand Springs** Idaho U.S.A.
13 G6 **Thrace** Turkey
9 E2 **Thrall** Texas U.S.A.
48 H6 **Thrall** Washington U.S.A.
95 O3 **Thrapston** England
27 G13 **Three Cocks** Wales
101 K7 **Three Creek** Idaho U.S.A.
101 O4 **Three Forks** Montana U.S.A.
100 B5 **Three Hills** Alberta Canada
139 G8 **Three Hummock I** Tasmania Australia
110 J5 **Three I.Res** Tennessee U.S.A.
137 O8 **Thistle** I South Australia
13 E4 **Thirteen Islands** Wisconsin U.S.A.
9 F2 **Thorne** England
68 B5 **Thurso** Quebec Canada
68 B4 **Thurso** Scotland
119 T3 **Thurso** R Scotland
11 D4 **Thurso B** Scotland
141 G6 **Thursday I** Queensland Australia
21 K8 **Thury-Harcourt** France
117 K7 **Thutade L** British Columbia Canada
109 J7 **Thyborøn** Denmark
146 B8 **Thyolo** Malawi

139 K4 **Tia** New South Wales Australia
127 J9 **Tia Juana** Venezuela
85 G3 **Tiaboashan** China
67 B5 **Tiandong** China
67 B5 **Tiandong** China
84 B4 **Tian'e** China
53 F12 **Tianeti** Georgia
58 C4 **Tianjin** China
65 D5 **Tianlin** China
109 L4 **Tianlin** China
100 H2 **Tianmen** China
65 H3 **Tianqiaoling** China
Tianshan see Ar Horquin Qi
66 C3 **Tian Shan** ra China/Kazakhstan
58 E5 **Tianshui** China
67 G2 **Tiantai** China
67 B5 **Tianyang** China
67 B5 **Tianyi** see Ningcheng
110 K1 **Tianzhen** see Gaoqing
66 C3 **Tianzhen** China
47 M8 **Tiaret** Algeria
9 E5 **Tiarei** Tahiti Pacific Oc
85 E1 **Tiaret** Algeria
141 L7 **Tiaro** Queensland Australia
29 T8 **Tiassalé** Ivory Coast
123 S4 **Tibagi** Brazil
86 B4 **Tibati** Cameroon
13 E3 **Tibbie Shiels Inn** Scotland
80 F2 **Tiber** R see Tevere
86 C1 **Tiberias** Israel
80 F2 **Tiberias, L** Israel
84 F5 **Tibesti** Chad
84 F5 **Tibesti, Sarīr** Libya
21 J8 **Tibet** aut reg see Xizang Zizhiqu
141 N4 **Tibooburra** New South Wales Australia
9 F3 **Tibro** Sweden
122 F6 **Tiburón** isld Mexico
75 K4 **Ticao** isld Philippines
120 H10 **Ticehurst** England
121 O8 **Tichborne** Ontario Canada
101 L8 **Tichitt** Mauritania
85 A4 **Tichla** Western Sahara
101 L7 **Tichnor** Arkansas U.S.A.
41 J5 **Ticino** canton Switzerland
13 G6 **Tickhill** England
9 E2 **Ticknall** England
48 H6 **Ticleni** Romania
95 O3 **Ticonderoga** New York U.S.A.
9 F3 **Ticul** Mexico
27 G13 **Tidaholm** Sweden
122 F6 **Tide Hd** New Brunswick Canada
118 F8 **Tide L** Alberta Canada
100 B5 **Tidewater** Oregon U.S.A.
63 L2 **Tidikelt** reg Algeria
94 H5 **Tidioute** Pennsylvania U.S.A.
85 H5 **Tidjikja** Mauritania
122 H8 **Tidnish** Nova Scotia Canada
44 F2 **Tidone** R Italy
71 A2 **Tidore** Halmahera Indonesia
9 E5 **Tidworth** England
85 D1 **Tiébissou** Ivory Coast
33 N5 **Tiefencastel** Switzerland
33 T7 **Tiefensee** Germany
85 F5 **Tiel** Netherlands
85 D5 **Tielt** Belgium
115 P5 **Tié me** Ivory Coast
22 H2 **Tienen** Belgium
71 M9 **Tientsin** see Tianjin
71 M9 **Tien Yen** Vietnam
87 G9 **Tier Berg** mt S Africa
52 E4 **Tiercé** France
27 J11 **Tierp** Sweden
125 J8 **Tierra Amarilla** Mexico
125 L8 **Tierra Blanca** Mexico
133 B8 **Tierra del Fuego, I.Grande de** Arg/Chile
21 N6 **Tie Siding** Wyoming U.S.A.
16 D4 **Tiétar** R Spain
130 F8 **Tieté** Brazil
138 B2 **Tietkens, Mt** South Australia Australia
101 N9 **Tieton** Washington U.S.A.
110 J3 **Tieton Res** Washington U.S.A.
28 B4 **Tieyon** South Australia Australia
45 Q7 **Tifata, M** mt Italy
6 A1 **Tiffany** oil rig North Sea
17 E3 **Tiffin** Iowa U.S.A.
99 R8 **Tiffin** Ohio U.S.A.
94 D5 **Tiffin** Ohio U.S.A.
17 H10 **Tifrit** Algeria
142 D4 **Tifton** Georgia U.S.A.
89 F8 **Tigana** S Africa
28 B4 **Tigil** Russian Federation
71 M9 **Tigalda** Aleutian Is
101 L6 **Tigerton** Wisconsin U.S.A.
14 F4 **Tighina** see Tighina
51 P3 **Tigil Russian Federation**
56 B5 **Tigiria** India
127 K10 **Tignall** Georgia U.S.A.
71 F3 **Tignes, Bge. de** France
73 F3 **Tignish** Prince Edward I Canada
71 G5 **Tigray** prov Ethiopia
78 D1 **Tigre** R Peru
21 O9 **Tigre, Cerro del** mt Mexico
21 O6 **Tigre, Sa** Argentina
25 K4 **Tigris** R Iraq
27 C11 **Tiguentourine** Algeria
27 C11 **Tigui** Chad
44 G3 **Tiguidit, Falaise de** Niger
44 C4 **Tihany** Hungary
80 C3 **Tihāmat ash Shām** reg Saudi Arabia
92 A5 **Tihert** see Tiaret
70 D3 **Tiji** Libya
87 K2 **Tijesno** Croatia
21 P6 **Tijoca** Brazil
45 S1 **Tijola** Spain
125 L6 **Tijuana** Mexico
130 C5 **Tijucas** Brazil
65 K4 **Tikal** ruins Guatemala
80 G2 **Tikamgarh** India
69 E4 **Tikhoretsk** Russian Federation
95 M1 **Tikhvin** Russian Federation
71 H4 **Tiki Basin** Pacific Oc
127 C1 **Tikkurila** Finland
95 V1 **Tiko** Cameroon
15 F2 **Tikokiwa** New Zealand
137 O4 **Tikopia** isld Santa Cruz Is
45 M7 **Tiksha** Russian Federation
71 N4 **Tiksi** Russian Federation
81 H8 **Tilamuta** Sulawesi
37 L3 **Tilburg** Netherlands
28 F6 **Tilbury** Ontario Canada
9 H5 **Tilbury** England
133 D3 **Tilcara** Argentina
110 C3 **Tilcha** South Australia Australia
110 G5 **Tilden** Illinois U.S.A.
109 J7 **Tilden** Nebraska U.S.A.
117 K7 **Tilden** Texas U.S.A.
146 B8 **Tileagd** Romania

100 B4 **Tillamook** Oregon U.S.A.
100 A4 **Tillamook Rock** Oregon
69 A8 **Tillanchāng Dwip** Nicobar Is
21 O5 **Tillay le Peneux** France
27 J12 **Tillberge** Sweden
40 B3 **Tille** R France
112 G2 **Tillery, L** North Carolina U.S.A.
118 F8 **Tilley** Alberta Canada
85 E5 **Tillia** Niger
12 E1 **Tillicoultry** Scotland
21 H7 **Tillières** France
85 F4 **Tillières-sur-Avre** France
112 F5 **Tillman** South Carolina U.S.A.
113 L11 **Tilloo Cay** isld Bahamas
13 G2 **Till, R** England
120 K10 **Tillsonburg** Ontario Canada
85 F4 **Tilly-sur-Seulles** France
71 M9 **Tilomar** Timor
47 M3 **Tilos** isld Greece
139 G4 **Tilpa** New South Wales Australia
85 E2 **Tilrhemt** Algeria
9 E5 **Tilshead** England
13 E3 **Tilting** Newfoundland Canada
110 J1 **Tilton** Illinois U.S.A.
95 Q3 **Tilton** New Hampshire U.S.A.
70 G5 **Tily** mt Sulawesi
28 A4 **Tim** Denmark
54 J5 **Tim** Russian Federation
121 L5 **Timagami** Ontario Canada
52 G2 **Timanskiy Kryazh** ra Russian Federation
144 C6 **Timaru** New Zealand
53 L10 **Timashevsk** Russian Federation
46 G9 **Timbákion** Crete Greece
111 F12 **Timbalier I** Louisiana U.S.A.
70 F2 **Timbang** isld Sabah
130 J9 **Timbaúba** Brazil
85 C2 **Timbedra** Mauritania
100 B4 **Timber** Oregon U.S.A.
140 B3 **Timber Creek** Police Station N Terr Australia
98 E4 **Timber L** South Dakota U.S.A.
12 J1 **Timberlake** North Carolina U.S.A.
102 H4 **Timber Mt** Nevada U.S.A.
139 G7 **Timboon** Victoria Australia
130 E10 **Timbó** R Brazil
70 F2 **Timbun Mata** Sabah
85 F3 **Timellouline** Algeria
85 F5 **Timetrine Mts** Mali
85 F5 **Timfi, Óros** mt Greece
46 E6 **Timfristós** mt Greece
85 F5 **Timia** Niger
110 J7 **Timimoun** Algeria
85 E3 **Timiris, C** see Mirik, C
57 E3 **Timirlanovka** Kazakhstan
55 E4 **Timiryazovo** Kazakhstan
56 B3 **Timiryazevskiy** Russian Federation
48 G5 **Timiş** R Romania
48 G5 **Timişoara** Romania
55 D1 **Timkapaul'** Russian Federation
33 N5 **Timmendorfer Strand** Germany
85 F5 **Timmersdala** Sweden
Timmersoi watercourse Niger
115 P5 **Timmiarmiut** Greenland
120 J4 **Timmins** Ontario Canada
112 H3 **Timmonsville** South Carolina U.S.A.
112 A2 **Tims Ford L** Tennessee U.S.A.
52 H4 **Timsher** Russian Federation
57 E3 **Timur** prov Indonesia
9 O9 **Timur, Jawa** prov Java
144 D5 **Timutimu Headland** New Zealand
89 F8 **Tina** R S Africa
85 D1 **Tinaca Pt** Mindanao Philippines
71 O13 **Tinaco** Venezuela
71 F3 **Tinaga** isld Philippines
71 L5 **Tinago** Leyte Philippines
14 E4 **Tinahely** Ireland
124 J5 **Tinaja** Mexico
141 G2 **Tinajo** isld Santa Cruz Is
85 G4 **Tin Alkoum** Algeria
127 K10 **Tinaquillo** Venezuela
48 G4 **Tinca** Romania
141 L7 **Tin Can Bay** Queensland Australia
21 J4 **Tinchebray** France
22 C3 **Tincques** France
100 K7 **Tindall** Idaho U.S.A.
76 D4 **Tindivanam** India
70 K9 **Tindjel** isld Sabah
71 B6 **Tindouf** Algeria
21 D8 **Tindouf** Algeria
85 C1 **Tinef** Algeria
102 F4 **Tinemaha Res** California U.S.A.
16 C1 **Tineo** Spain
85 D3 **Tinfouchy** Algeria
21 G11 **Tin Fouye** Algeria
Tingagua dist Brisbane, Qnsld Australia
68 B2 **Tinggi** isld Malaysia
139 K3 **Tingha** New South Wales Australia
80 E10 **Tingis** see Tangier
70 D3 **Tingri** Nepal
28 C7 **Tinglev** Denmark
126 D5 **Tingley** Iowa U.S.A.
99 M9 **Tingo Maria** Peru
53 F10 **Tingping** China
62 C4 **Tingri** China
66 C2 **Tingsryd** Sweden
80 B8 **Tingvoll** Norway
121 T7 **Tingwick** Quebec Canada
129 L6 **Tinharé, I.de** Brazil
14 H5 **Tin Gia** Vietnam
145 D3 **Tinline, Mt** New Zealand
33 R6 **Tinn** Norway
27 C11 **Tinja** R Sarawak
141 M6 **Tinnoset** Norway
26 D12 **Tinnsjö** L Norway
44 G3 **Tino, I.di** Italy
70 G4 **Tinombo** Sulawesi
28 B7 **Tinos** isld Greece
71 K8 **Tin Rerhoh** Algeria
142 C5 **Tinsman** Arkansas U.S.A.
85 F4 **Tinstane, Mt** W Australia
75 Q5 **Tinsukia** India
100 D4 **Tintah** Minnesota U.S.A.
99 K3 **Tintah** Minnesota U.S.A.
85 F4 **Tin Tarabine** watercourse Algeria

Column 1

20 G5 Tinténiac France
8 D4 Tintern England
22 K4 Tintigny Belgium
133 E3 Tintina Argentina
138 F6 Tintinara South Australia Australia
16 C7 Tinto R Spain
15 E5 Tinto, Mt Scotland
145 F4 Tinui New Zealand
144 C5 Tinwald New Zealand
85 E4 Tin Zaouaten Algeria/Mali
86 H3 T'I'o Ethiopia
111 D10 Tioga Louisiana U.S.A.
98 D1 Tioga North Dakota U.S.A.
95 K5 Tioga Pennsylvania U.S.A.
109 G2 Tioga Texas U.S.A.
94 G8 Tioga West Virginia U.S.A.
69 G11 Tioman isld Malaysia
120 H4 Tionaga Ontario Canada
41 N5 Tione Italy
42 D2 Tione di Trento Italy
100 D8 Tionesta California U.S.A.
94 H5 Tionesta Pennsylvania U.S.A.
94 A5 Tippecanoe R Indiana U.S.A.
99 U9 Tippecanoe R Indiana U.S.A.
14 C4 Tipperary Ireland
14 D4 Tipperary co Ireland
111 F8 Tippo Mississippi U.S.A.
102 E5 Tipton California U.S.A.
110 K1 Tipton Indiana U.S.A.
107 M2 Tipton Kansas U.S.A.
110 D3 Tipton Missouri U.S.A.
109 H1 Tipton Oklahoma U.S.A.
103 K6 Tipton, Mt Arizona U.S.A.
110 G5 Tiptonville Tennessee U.S.A.
120 D4 Tip Top Hill Ontario Canada
9 G4 Tiptree England
76 C4 Tiptur India
128 E3 Tiquié R Brazil
80 C5 Tira Israel
129 J4 Tiracambu, Sa.do mts Brazil
79 E11 Tiran isld Saudi Arabia
46 D3 Tiranë Albania
41 M5 Tirano Italy
83 K9 Tirappane Sri Lanka
53 C10 Tiraspol' Moldavia
80 C2 Tirat Karmel Israel
80 F4 Tirat Zevi Israel
145 E2 Tirau New Zealand
145 F4 Tiraumea New Zealand
47 J6 Tire Turkey
78 G1 Tirebolu Turkey
15 C4 Tiree isld Scotland
85 B4 Tires reg Western Sahara
48 J6 Tîrgovişte Romania
48 L5 Tirgu Bujor Romania
48 H6 Tîrgu Cărbuneşti Romania
48 L3 Tîrgu Frumos Romania
48 H5 Tirgu Jiu Romania
48 H3 Tîrgu Lăpuş Romania
48 J4 Tîrgu Mures Romania
48 K3 Tîrgu Neamt Romania
48 K4 Tîrgu Ocna Romania
48 K4 Tirgu Seculesc Romania
47 K4 Tirilye Turkey
145 E2 Tiritiri New Zealand
Tirlemont see Tienen
55 C4 Tirlyanskiy Russian Federation
48 J4 Tîrnava Mare R Romania
48 J4 Tîrnava Mică R Romania
48 J4 Tîrnaveni Romania
48 E5 Tírnavos Greece
94 E6 Tiro Ohio U.S.A.
38 F7 Tirol prov Austria
41 O4 Tirolo Italy
80 C6 Tirosh Israel
86 D4 Tiro Sibut Cent Afr Republic
45 H4 Tirrenia Italy
37 N4 Tirschenreuth Germany
43 B8 Tirso R Sardinia
131 A7 Tirua, Pta Chile
76 D6 Tiruchchendur India
76 D5 Tiruchchirāppalli India
83 L10 Tirukkovil Sri Lanka
76 C6 Tirunelveli India
128 D5 Tiruntán Peru
76 D4 Tirupati India
76 C5 Tiruppur India
76 D4 Tiruvannāmalai India
48 H2 Tisa R Ukraine
119 N6 Tisdale Saskatchewan Canada
111 H7 Tishomingo Mississippi U.S.A.
109 L1 Tishomingo Oklahoma U.S.A.
79 G6 Tisiyah Syria
99 R8 Tisikiwa Illinois U.S.A.
28 C6 Tislund Denmark
27 H13 Tisnaren L Sweden
31 J6 Tišnov Czechoslovakia
48 F2 Tisovec Czechoslovakia
83 E11 Tissamaharama Sri Lanka
9 E11 Tissington England
27 E12 Tistedal Norway
48 F3 Tisza R Hungary
48 F4 Tiszaföldvár Hungary
31 N8 Tiszavasvari Hungary
85 E3 Tit Algeria
116 K2 Titaluk R Alaska U.S.A.
146 E9 Titan Dome ice dome Antarctica
9 E6 Titchfield England
128 E7 Titicaca, L Peru/Bolivia
116 L4 Titna R Alaska U.S.A.
Titograd see Podgorica
96 M6 Titonka Iowa U.S.A.
52 D1 Titova R Russian Federation
26 C8 Titran Norway
94 C3 Tittabawassee R Michigan U.S.A.
37 L6 Titting Germany
38 G5 Tittmoning Germany
48 K6 Titu Romania
86 E5 Titule Zaire
113 G9 Titusville Florida U.S.A.
94 H5 Titusville Pennsylvania U.S.A.
85 A6 Tivaouane Senegal
27 G13 Tived Sweden
122 F9 Tiverton Nova Scotia Canada
120 J8 Tiverton Ontario Canada
8 C6 Tiverton England
99 Q5 Tiverton Rhode I. U.S.A.
45 N6 Tivoli Italy
95 O4 Tivoli New York U.S.A.
109 L7 Tivoli Texas U.S.A.
55 D4 Tiwad Sulawesi
53 H7 Tiworo, Selat str Indonesia
124 H4 Tizapán el Alto Mexico
17 H2 Tizi Algeria
125 M7 Tizi-Irfi Morocco
125 P7 Tizimin Mexico
85 E2 Tizi-Ouzou Algeria
16 E10 Tiztoutine Morocco
28 B6 Tjæreborg Denmark
28 G6 Tjæreby Denmark
27 H13 Tjällmo Sweden
26 K5 Tjämotis Sweden
71 L10 Tjamplong Timor Indonesia
70 K9 Tjankuang Tg C Java
26 L4 Tjårro Keble nn Sweden
26 J5 Tjeggelvas L Sweden
26 H3 Tjeldøy isld Norway
70 D3 Tjele Denmark
70 D4 Tjemaru, G mt Kalimantan
71 J9 Tjempi, Teluk B Sumbawa Indonesia
70 F6 Tjenrana Sulawesi
70 M9 Tjepu Java
70 M9 Tjerme mt Java
71 J6 Tjeuke Meer Netherlands

Column 2

70 L9 Tjidua Java
70 L9 Tjihara Java
70 L9 Tjikadjang Java
70 L9 Tjikampek Java
70 G11 Tjilatjap Java
70 L9 Tjiledug Java
70 L9 Tjimahi Java
70 G6 Tjimpu Sulawesi
70 K8 Tjina, Tg C Sumatra
70 G2 Tjipatudjah Java
48 G2 Tjitarum R Java
70 G5 Tjiudjung R Java
144 B7 Tjolotjo Zimbabwe
86 D6 Tjolotjo Zimbabwe
59 J5 Tjörn isld Sweden
52 D4 Tjörring Denmark
52 D4 Tkvarcheli Georgia
125 L9 Tlacolula de Matamoros Mexico
78 F1 Tlacotalpan Mexico
145 D2 Tlalnepantla Mexico
65 F6 Tlálpam Mexico
70 G6 Tlangtlang Burma
101 P9 Tlapacoyán Mexico
56 E1 Tlaquepaque Mexico
61 L10 Tlaxcala Mexico
98 H2 Tlemcen Algeria
116 Q5 Tlemcés Niger
27 D12 Tlumach Ukraine
57 H3 Tluszcz Poland
61 K9 Tȋma R Russian Federation
128 E4 Tmassah Libya
100 F1 Tni Haïa Algeria
121 M9 To R Burma
9 G5 Toa R Cuba
71 J4 Toad River British Columbia Canada
84 G3 Toamasina Madagascar
57 H1 Toana mt ra Nevada U.S.A.
52 E3 Toano Italy
66 D3 Toano Virginia U.S.A.
59 K4 Toay Argentina
127 M1 Toaya Sulawesi
117 L10 Toba Japan
77 K4 Toba, Danau L Sumatra
145 G3 Tobago isld W Indies
145 G7 Toba Inlet British Columbia Canada
89 G3 Toba & Kakar Ranges Pakistan
77 H3 Tobaqah Syria
78 G4 Tobar Nevada U.S.A.
101 L9 Tobata Japan
14 C2 Tobbercurry Ireland
71 H7 Tobea isld Indonesia
140 E5 Tobermorey N Terr Australia
141 G7 Tobermory Queensland Australia
120 J7 Tobermory Ontario Canada
15 B4 Tobermory Scotland
90 P2 Tōbetsu Japan
98 J9 Tobias Nebraska U.S.A.
61 N14 Tobishi-hana C Iwo Jima Japan
115 R3 Tobin, Kap C Greenland
142 F5 Tobin, L W Australia Australia
119 O5 Tobin L Saskatchewan Canada
Tobique R New Brunswick Canada
59 K4 Tobi-shima isld Japan
16 D5 Tobooali Indonesia
42 E5 Tobol Kazakhstan
44 L5 Tobol'sk Russian Federation
68 J6 Toboso Negros Philippines
26 E9 Tobruk see Tubruq
87 G12 Tobyhanna Pennsylvania U.S.A.
128 C3 Tobysh R Russian Federation
70 G4 Tobysh Russian Federation
129 J5 Tocantínia Brazil
129 J6 Tocantinópolis Brazil
112 D3 Tocantins R Brazil
41 H5 Tocantins state Brazil
78 F4 Toccoa Georgia U.S.A.
55 C4 Toce R Italy
130 C3 Tochigi Japan
48 E4 Tochio Japan
48 E4 Toco Chile
86 C6 Tocopilla Chile
54 A2 Tocorpuri mt Chile/Bolivia
110 H2 Toco L co Hungary
17 H1 Tocra Libya
65 G7 Tocuco R Venezuela
140 B2 Tocuyo de la Costa Venezuela
48 K2 Toda India
103 N3 Todatonten Alaska U.S.A.
120 F7 Todd,Mt N Terr Australia
133 C5 Todd Mt New Brunswick Canada
131 A7 Todd R N Terr Australia
126 F2 Todghaj India
53 H7 Tödi mt Switzerland
67 G1 Todmorden England
52 E4 Todmorden Queensland Australia
55 A4 Todoga-saki C Japan
110 H2 Todohokke Japan
86 C6 Todos los Santos, L Chile
129 L6 Todos os Santos, B. de Brazil
70 P3 Todos Santos Mexico
56 E5 Tödzha, Oz L. Russian Federation
124 D6 Toe Ire Ireland
67 G1 Toe Jaga, Khao mt Burma/Thailand
57 N2 Tofield Alberta Canada
60 N3 Tofino British Columbia Canada
46 D1 Tófsingdalens Nat. Park Sweden
48 N4 Tofta Sweden
28 C6 Tofte Norway
31 O5 Toftlund Denmark
57 D3 Tofty Alaska U.S.A.

Column 3

29 M9 Toivakka Finland
99 S3 Toivola Michigan U.S.A.
102 G2 Toiyabe Ra Nevada U.S.A.
70 G5 Toja Sulawesi
60 G11 Tōjō Japan
30 H6 Tok int Czechoslovakia
145 R2 Tokaanu New Zealand
60 R2 Tokachi prefect Japan
60 Q2 Tokachi dake mt Japan
48 G2 Tokajo Hungary
70 G5 Tokala, G mt Sulawesi
61 M8 Tokamachi Japan
144 B7 Tokanui New Zealand
86 G2 Tokar Sudan
59 J5 Tokara-retto islds Japan
66 D5 Tokara Kazakhstan
86 H4 Tokarevka Russian Federation
56 C3 Tomsk Russian Federation
56 B2 Tomskaya Oblast prov Russian Federation
83 M9 Tokat Turkey
145 D2 Tokatoka New Zealand
65 F6 Tōkchŏk-kundo B S Korea
70 G6 Toke Sulawesi
101 P9 Tokelau islds Pacific Oc
56 E1 Tokewanna Pk Utah U.S.A.
61 L10 Tokhoma R Russian Federation
116 Q6 Toki Japan
125 N9 Tokio North Dakota U.S.A.
103 O5 Tok Junc Alaska U.S.A.
42 D2 Tokke-Vatn L Norway
61 K9 Tokmak Alaska U.S.A.
128 E4 Tokmak Kyrgyzstan
100 F1 Tokmak Ukraine
121 M9 Toko New Zealand
9 G5 Tokomaru New Zealand
71 J4 Tokomaru Bay New Zealand
84 G3 Tokoro Japan
57 H1 Tokoroa New Zealand
52 E3 Tokorozawa Japan
28 B9 Toksook Bay Alaska U.S.A.
85 E4 Toktogul Vdkhr Kyrgyzstan
88 C10 Toktomush Tajikistan
36 B3 Tokur Russian Federation
61 N9 Tokur Russian Federation
61 O10 Tokushima Japan
8 C5 Tokuyama Japan
139 G4 Tokwe R Zimbabwe
Tōkyō conurbation Japan
61 N10 Tōkyō-wan B Japan
77 K2 Tokzār Afghanistan
145 G3 Tolaga Bay New Zealand
87 H13 Tolañaro Madagascar
106 G7 Tolar New Mexico U.S.A.
109 K3 Tolar Texas U.S.A.
78 K1 Tolavi Georgia
55 C4 Tolbazy Russian Federation
130 D9 Tolbukhin see Dobrich
133 C3 Toledo Chile
145 E3 Toledo prov Spain
145 E3 Toledo Spain
99 O7 Toledo Illinois U.S.A.
94 C3 Toledo Ohio U.S.A.
100 B5 Toledo Oregon U.S.A.
100 C3 Toledo Washington U.S.A.
109 O4 Toledo Bend Res Louisiana U.S.A.
16 D5 Toledo, Montes de mts Spain
42 E5 Tolentino Italy
44 L5 Tolfa, Mt.della Italy
5 Tolg Sweden
26 E9 Tolga Norway
87 G12 Toliara Madagascar
128 C3 Tolima vol Colombia
70 G4 Tolima div Colombia
129 J5 Tolitoli Sulawesi
129 J6 Tollense R Germany
103 M8 Tollensee L Germany
98 E1 Tolleson Arizona U.S.A.
112 D3 Tolley North Dakota U.S.A.
41 H5 Tollhouse California U.S.A.
78 F4 Tølløse Denmark
55 C4 Tolmachevo Russian Federation
130 C3 Tolmezzo Italy
48 E4 Tolmin Slovenia
48 E4 Tolna co Hungary
17 H1 Tolne Denmark
65 G7 Tolo Zaire
140 B2 Tolochin Belorussia
48 K2 Tolosa Spain
103 N3 Tolovana R Alaska U.S.A.
120 F7 Toltatoken Alaska U.S.A.
133 C5 Tolsta Head Scotland
131 A7 Tolstoye Ukraine
126 F2 Toltec Arizona U.S.A.
53 H7 Toltén Chile
67 G1 Toltén, R Chile
52 E4 Tolú Colombia
55 A4 Toluca Mexico
110 H2 Toluca Illinois U.S.A.
86 C6 Toly Xian China
54 A2 Toro Spain
110 H2 Tongxiang China
17 H1 Tongxu China
65 G7 Tongyu China
140 B2 Tongzhou China

Column 4

60 H11 Tomogashima-suidō str Japan
70 G6 Tompira Sulawesi
118 J8 Tompkins Saskatchewan Canada
94 C4 Tompkins Center Michigan U.S.A.
48 G1 Tompkinsville Kentucky U.S.A.
117 K8 Tompo Sulawesi
70 F5 Tom Price W Australia Australia
143 C6 Tomakamchi Japan
142 C6 Tom Price,Mt W Australia Australia
66 D5 Tomra China
86 H4 Tomsa Ethiopia
56 C3 Tomsk Russian Federation
56 B2 Tomskaya Oblast prov Russian Federation
29 O10 Tomsö Japan
124 E5 Tonalá Mexico
125 N9 Tonalá Mexico
103 O5 Tonale, Pso. di Italy
42 D2 Tonami Japan
52 B4 Tonantins Brazil
95 U1 Tonasket Washington U.S.A.
121 M9 Tonawanda New York U.S.A.
9 G5 Tonbridge England
60 J12 Tonda Japan
71 J4 Tondano Japan
84 G3 Tondela Portugal
57 H1 Tender co see
52 E3 Senderjylland co
28 B9 Tønder Denmark
120 E3 Tondjara watercourse Algeria
85 E4 Tondirano mt Zimbabwe
36 B3 Tondorf Germany
61 N9 Tone R Japan
61 O10 Tone-gawa R Japan
8 C5 Tone, R England
139 G4 Tonga New South Wales Australia
137 S6 Tonga Kingdom Pacific Oc
86 F4 Tonga Sudan
52 D5 Tonga Zambia
94 B1 Tonga I New Zealand
145 D4 Tonga I New Zealand
139 G4 Tonga L New South Wales Australia
139 G6 Tongala Victoria Australia
67 F4 Tong'an China
110 A2 Tonganoxie Kansas U.S.A.
145 E3 Tongaporutu New Zealand
145 E3 Tongariro mt New Zealand
137 R6 Tongatapu Group Tonga
58 F5 Tongbai Shan mt ra China
67 E1 Tongcheng China
58 E4 Tongchuan China
67 C3 Tongdao China
22 J2 Tongeren Belgium
67 E2 Tonggu China
22 E1 Tongguan China
61 O10 Tonghai China
59 K2 Tonghua China
67 B1 Tongjiang China
59 J2 Tongjiang China
67 B2 Tongken He R China
29 N3 Tongland Scotland
55 G1 Tongliang China
59 H3 Tongliao China
59 J3 Tongling China
121 L8 Tongnae S Korea
21 E6 Tongren China
117 Q11 Tongren China
Tongshan see Xuzhou
115 N6 Tongshi China
26 M4 Tongta Burma
32 L5 Tongtian He R China
85 C2 Tongue Scotland
55 H7 Tongue of the Ocean chan Bahamas
133 E5 Tongue R.Res Montana U.S.A.
65 C5 Tong Xian China
67 G1 Tongxiang China
103 D3 Tongxu China
65 G7 Tongyu China
67 G2 Tongzhou China

Column 5

33 T8 Töpchin Germany
13 G5 Topcliffe England
94 B5 Topeka Indiana U.S.A.
107 P2 Topeka Kansas U.S.A.
124 F5 Topia Mexico
56 C3 Topki Russian Federation
48 G1 Topl'a R Czechoslovakia
117 K8 Topland Alberta Canada
46 E1 Topley Lodge British Columbia Canada
48 J4 Toplica R Serbia Yugoslavia
131 A5 Topliţa Romania
103 K7 Topock Arizona U.S.A.
48 F6 Topola Serbia Yugoslavia
46 E3 Topolčany Czechoslovakia
48 E2 Topolčani Macedonia
27 H15 Topolobampo Mexico
26 F9 Topolobampo Mexico
27 F11 Topoloveni Romania
26 J2 Topolovgrad Bulgaria
26 L1 Topólšica Slovenia
57 E3 Toponas Colorado U.S.A.
55 F5 Topornya Russian Federation
43 F11 Topozero, Ozero L Russian Federation
131 B2 Toppenish Washington U.S.A.
94 H5 Topraisar Romania
127 H4 Toprak-kala Uzbekistan
72 D2 Topsa Russian Federation
70 G5 Topsfield Maine U.S.A.
31 L2 Topsham England
27 F15 Topsham Maine U.S.A.
55 C4 Tõrva Estonia
27 E5 Torbat-e Heydariyeh Iran
77 G2 Torbat-e Jām Iran
123 U6 Torbay Newfoundland Canada
42 C5 Toroano, Arch islds Italy
124 D5 Tosca, Pta C Mexico
41 N6 Toscolano-Moderno Italy
26 F6 Tosen Norway
29 K9 Tosenfjord inlet Norway
57 E4 Tös For B Sweden
21 H7 Tösens Austria
61 K11 Toshi-jima isld Japan
116 M4 To-shima isld Japan
61 P5 Tōshima-yama mt Japan
52 D5 Tosno Russian Federation
79 F4 Toson Hu L China
78 G1 Tosontsengel Mongolia
122 H6 Tossås Sweden
123 L8 Tossingsono Italy
130 C3 Tostado Argentina
122 F8 Toston Montana U.S.A.
60 D12 Tosu Japan
17 F3 Tosya Turkey
31 L5 Toszek Poland
99 O8 Tótana Spain
99 O4 Tôte France
16 C5 Totes Gebirge mts Austria
129 G7 Tôtkomlós Hungary
15 C6 Totma Russian Federation
111 B8 Totnes England
113 F11 Tototo Pk New Zealand
125 L9 Totoyapam Mexico
131 B8 Totoralillo Chile
86 C7 Totota Liberia
146 G14 Totten Glacier Antarctica
139 H4 Tottenham New South Wales Australia
121 L8 Tottenham Ontario Canada
21 E6 Totton England
100 H1 Tottori prefect Japan
119 M6 Totzke Saskatchewan Canada
28 D1 Touba Senegal
85 C2 Touba, Jbel mt Morocco
20 H7 Touboulic France
119 N7 Touchet Washington U.S.A.
18 H5 Toucy France
130 H10 Toudao Jiang R China
38 N5 Toudenbourg Austria

Column 6

45 L1 Torri di Quartesolo Italy
28 E5 Torrild Denmark
28 C5 Torring Denmark
139 K3 Torrington New South Wales Australia
118 D7 Torrington Alberta Canada
95 O5 Torrington Connecticut U.S.A.
98 B7 Torrington Wyoming U.S.A.
101 P5 Tor Rock mt N Terr Australia
26 F8 Torröjen L Sweden
16 E8 Torrox Spain
26 F6 Torsåker Sweden
26 F9 Torsborg Sweden
27 F11 Torsby Sweden
27 H12 Torshälla Sweden
110 C3 Tórshavn Faeroes
26 J1 Torsken Norway
26 L1 Torsvåg Norway
57 E3 Tortkol' Kazakhstan
55 F5 Tortkuduk Kazakhstan
43 F11 Torto R Sicily
131 B2 Tortolas, Cerro las pk Arg/Chile
94 H5 Tortona Italy
17 H4 Tortosa Italy
72 D2 Tortue, Île de la Haiti
70 G5 Tortue R Sulawesi
31 L2 Torun Poland
27 F15 Torup Sweden
52 C5 Tõrva Estonia
27 E5 Torved Sweden
77 G2 Torver England
123 U6 Torysa R Czechoslovakia
42 C5 Torzym Poland
124 D5 Tosa R B Sulawesi
41 N6 Tosa Japan
26 F6 Tosa-shimizu Japan
29 K9 Tosa-wan B Japan
57 E4 Tosa-Yamada Japan
21 H7 Tosca S Africa
61 K11 Toscana reg Italy
116 M4 Toscano, Arch islds Italy
61 P5 Tosca, Pta C Mexico
52 D5 Toscolano-Moderno Italy
79 F4 Tosen Norway
78 G1 Tosenfjord inlet Norway
122 H6 Tösens Austria
123 L8 Toshi-jima isld Japan
130 C3 Toshka Lakes Egypt

Column 7

95 L5 Towanda Pennsylvania U.S.A.
70 G7 Towari Sulawesi
99 F3 Towcester England
99 O2 Tower Minnesota U.S.A.
98 J3 Tower City North Dakota U.S.A.
95 L6 Tower City Pennsylvania U.S.A.
101 P5 Tower Falls Wyoming U.S.A.
110 H2 Tower Hill Illinois U.S.A.
144 A6 Towing Head New Zealand
106 H3 Towner Colorado U.S.A.
98 F1 Towner North Dakota U.S.A.
102 G5 Townes Pass California U.S.A.
111 J8 Townley Alabama U.S.A.
95 M7 Townsend Delaware U.S.A.
112 D2 Townsend Georgia U.S.A.
101 O3 Townsend Montana U.S.A.
112 D2 Townsend Tennessee U.S.A.
139 J6 Townsend, Mt Victoria Australia
141 K2 Townshend I Queensland Australia
141 H5 Townsville Queensland Australia
94 H5 Townsville Pennsylvania U.S.A.
70 G6 Towori, Teluk B Sulawesi
86 F4 Towot Sudan
95 L7 Towson Maryland U.S.A.
70 G6 Towuti L Sulawesi
8 C3 Towy, R Wales
112 D2 Toxaway, L North Carolina U.S.A.
66 B3 Toxkan He R China
108 D4 Toyah L Texas U.S.A.
60 O3 Toya-ko L Japan
61 L9 Toyama Japan
61 L8 Toyama wan B Japan
116 A3 Toygunen Russian Federation
61 L10 Toyo Japan
61 L10 Toyooka Japan
61 L11 Toyohama Japan
61 L11 Toyohashi Japan
61 L11 Toyokawa Japan
61 O10 Toyokoro Japan
61 K13 Toyonaka Japan
61 N10 Toyooka Japan
61 L10 Toyota Japan
29 K9 Töysä Finland
57 E4 Toytepa Uzbekistan
17 F7 Tozeur Tunisia
17 F3 Tozitna R Alaska U.S.A.
36 C4 Traben-Trarbach Germany
79 F4 Tråblous Lebanon
78 G1 Trabzon Turkey
122 H6 Tracadie New Brunswick Canada
123 L8 Tracadie Nova Scotia Canada
122 F8 Tracey New Brunswick Canada
69 H6 Tra Cu Vietnam
57 C4 Tracy California U.S.A.
99 O4 Tracy Iowa U.S.A.
99 L5 Tracy Minnesota U.S.A.
117 N5 Tracy L Northwest Territories Canada
21 P6 Tranou France
130 H10 Trairi Brazil
38 N5 Traisen Austria
21 M3 Trait,le France
84 C5 Trakt Russian Federation
111 F8 Trakale Mississippi U.S.A.
130 B8 Tralee Bay Ireland
Tram Bo Vietnam
40 F3 Tramelan Switzerland
68 J6 Tram Kak Cambodia
118 J6 Tran Khnan Cambodia
14 D4 Tramping Saskatchewan Canada
27 H13 Tranås Sweden
28 E4 Tranbjerg Denmark
133 G3 Trancas Mexico

Column 8

95 L5 Towanda Pennsylvania U.S.A.
28 D1 Touba Senegal
130 C3 Totouq U West Africa
111 H5 Toula Mauritania
55 C4 Toulepleu Ivory Coast
40 F3 Toulinguet,Pte,du France
118 J6 Toulnustouc R Quebec Canada
14 D4 Toulon France
70 D5 Toulon Illinois U.S.A.
16 E7 Toulon Nevada U.S.A.
20 O17 Touloubre R France
133 G3 Toulouse France
124 G3 Toumma Niger
70 H1 Toumodi Ivory Coast
68 L3 Toungoo Burma
22 B2 Touques R France
22 B2 Touquet-Paris Plage, le France
13 F2 Tour, R France
139 J4 Tourane see Da Nang
19 P18 Tourch France
68 F3 Tourcoing France
20 C5 Touriñan, C Spain
28 C7 Touriñan, C Spain
124 G3 Tourine Mauritania
68 L3 Tournai Belgium
128 D5 Tournavista Peru
27 N1 Tournay France
20 C5 Tournon France
19 N14 Tournon-St.Martin France
103 J8 Tournus France
41 O6 Touros Brazil
130 J8 Tours France
112 F2 Toury France
17 H2 Tourville-en-Auge France
85 A7 Tourville-la-Rivière France
85 B1 Tourville-les-Ifs France
79 H7 Toussidé Pic mt Chad
17 F9 Toutes Aides Manitoba Canada
85 G15 Touws R S Africa

Column 9

95 L5 Towanda Pennsylvania U.S.A.
25 C5 Towai France
16 O1 Trackton Sweden
26 E6 Trakehnen Sweden
130 J7 Trakai Lithuania
111 H3 Trakt Russian Federation
130 C3 Trakya reg Mauritania
100 C3 Trälhavet Sweden
111 K5 Tråsberg Sweden
133 G3 Traïle Russian Federation
129 L6 Tranent Scotland
69 Q7 Tranby Thailand
139 J4 Trangie New South Wales Australia
27 G11 Tranh De, Cua R Vietnam
69 H8 Trani Italy
43 J2 Tranøy Norway
26 J2 Tranøy Norway
102 G5 Tranquility California U.S.A.
12 G18 Trans France
130 C5 Trans France
146 C12 Transilvac-Victoire France
146 C12 Transantarctic Mts Antarctica
144 C12 Transcona Manitoba Canada
89 H7 Transinne Belgium
85 M7 Transkei homeland S Africa
69 H5 Transvaal prov S Africa
Transylvania see
Carpaţii Meridionali
5 Traona Italy
21 M7 Trapani Sicily
101 L4 Trapper Pk Montana U.S.A.
17 H3 Trapua R Brazil
20 C5 Trarza reg Mauritania
85 A5 Trarza reg Mauritania
27 G15 Trasparga Spain
37 L1 Trassem Germany
26 L4 Trasimeno, L Italy
57 E3 Trat Thailand
122 H6 Traun Austria
31 K7 Traunik Michigan U.S.A.
38 F8 Traunsee L Austria
38 F8 Traunstein Germany
14 A4 Trave R Germany
133 C7 Travellers L New South Wales Australia
98 F4 Travellers Rest South Carolina U.S.A.
33 N5 Travemünde Germany

33 M5 **Travenberg** Germany
118 E8 **Travers** Alberta Canada
131 H7 **Traversay Islds** S Sandwich Is
94 B1 **Traverse B.Grand** Michigan U.S.A.
94 B1 **Traverse B.Little** Michigan U.S.A.
94 B2 **Traverse City** Michigan U.S.A.
98 K4 **Traverse, L** South Dakota U.S.A.
116 H4 **Traverse Pk** Alaska U.S.A.
45 H2 **Traversetolo** Italy
122 B5 **Travers, L** Quebec Canada
144 D5 **Travers, Mt** New Zealand
131 C5 **Travesia Puntana** *reg* Argentina
131 C4 **Travesia Tunuyán** *reg* Argentina
68 H8 **Tra Vinh** Vietnam
109 J5 **Travis, L** Texas U.S.A.
42 H4 **Travnik** Bosnia-Herzegovina
55 G4 **Travnoye** Russian Federation
44 F2 **Travo** Italy
70 P10 **Trawangan** Indonesia
14 D1 **Trawbreaga B** Ireland
109 N4 **Trawick** Texas U.S.A.
8 C2 **Trawsfynydd** Wales
143 C9 **Trayning** W Australia
42 G2 **Trbovlje** Slovenia
8 B1 **Tre-Arddur B** Wales
127 J3 **Treasure Beach** Jamaica
116 J3 **Treat I** Alaska U.S.A.
44 F2 **Trebbecco, L. di** Italy
44 F2 **Trebbia** *R* Italy
33 S8 **Trebbin** Germany
33 R4 **Trebel** *R* Germany
33 O7 **Trebel** Germany
18 G9 **Trèbes** France
20 C4 **Trébeurden** France
31 J6 **Třebíč** Czechoslovakia
42 J6 **Trebinje** Bosnia-Herzegovina
42 J6 **Trebišnica** *R* Bosnia-Herzegovina
48 G2 **Trebišov** Czechoslovakia
42 H5 **Trebižat** *R* Bosnia-Herzegovina
Trebizond *see* **Trabzon**
144 A7 **Treble Mt** New Zealand
42 G3 **Trebnje** Slovenia
31 H6 **Třeboň** Czechoslovakia
20 B5 **Tréboul** France
48 D1 **Trebová** Czechoslovakia
20 D5 **Trébrivan** France
33 R10 **Trebsen** Germany
36 E4 **Trebur** Germany
8 C4 **Trecastle** Wales
8 C4 **Trecate** Italy
45 K1 **Trecenta** Italy
106 B7 **Trechado** New Mexico U.S.A.
8 C4 **Tredegar** Wales
41 N6 **Tredici Comuni** *reg* Italy
9 E3 **Tredington** England
20 F5 **Trédion** France
45 L3 **Tredozio** Italy
20 C4 **Trédrez** France
73 L6 **Tree I** Lakshadweep Indian Oc
101 R1 **Treelon** Saskatchewan Canada
20 G6 **Treffieux** France
40 B5 **Treffort** France
8 C1 **Trefnant** Wales
8 C1 **Trefriw** Wales
8 C3 **Tregaron** Wales
119 N8 **Tregarva** Saskatchewan Canada
20 C4 **Trégastel** France
101 L1 **Trego** Montana U.S.A.
102 E1 **Trego** Nevada U.S.A.
99 P4 **Trego** Wisconsin U.S.A.
8 B7 **Tregony** England
20 D4 **Trégorrois** *reg* France
141 K4 **Tregosse Islets & Reefs** Gt Barrier Reef Aust
20 D4 **Treguier** France
20 C6 **Trégunc** France
119 T9 **Treherne** Manitoba Canada
68 G8 **Tre, Hon** *isld* Vietnam
26 K8 **Trehörningsjö** Sweden
20 B5 **Tréhou, le** France
15 D4 **Treig, L** Scotland
18 G7 **Treignac** France
20 G7 **Treillières** France
131 G4 **Treinta y Tres** Uruguay
36 C3 **Treis-Karden** Germany
140 E5 **Trekelano** Queensland Australia
127 J2 **Trelawney** *parish* Jamaica
89 G1 **Trelawney** Zimbabwe
21 K7 **Trélazé** France
32 L6 **Trelde** Germany
28 D5 **Trelde Næs** *C* Denmark
133 D6 **Trelew** Argentina
27 F16 **Trelleborg** Sweden
8 C4 **Trelleck** Wales
22 G3 **Trélon** France
8 B2 **Tremadoc** Wales
8 B2 **Tremadoc B** Wales
18 E7 **Tremblade, la** France
20 H5 **Tremblay** France
21 N4 **Tremblay-les-Villages** France
117 L8 **Trembleur L** British Columbia Canada
106 F6 **Trementina** New Mexico U.S.A.
21 J7 **Trémentines** France
37 K3 **Tremersdorf** Germany
42 G6 **Tremiti, I.di** Italy
110 G1 **Tremont** Illinois U.S.A.
111 H7 **Tremont** Mississippi U.S.A.
95 L6 **Tremont** Pennsylvania U.S.A.
101 N8 **Tremonton** Utah U.S.A.
20 F5 **Trémorel** France
37 P4 **Třemošná** Czechoslovakia
17 H2 **Tremp** Spain
99 P5 **Tempealeau** Wisconsin U.S.A.
33 M5 **Tremsbüttel** Germany
69 G8 **Trem Trem** *R* Vietnam
99 U3 **Trenary** Michigan U.S.A.
121 S5 **Trenche** *R* Quebec Canada
31 L6 **Trenčín** Czechoslovakia
28 C3 **Trend Å** *R* Denmark
32 K9 **Trendelburg** Germany
133 E5 **Trenel** Argentina
27 A11 **Trengereid** Norway
70 N9 **Trenggalek** Java
131 E5 **Trenque Lauquen** Argentina
Trent *see* **Trento**
112 K2 **Trent** *R* North Carolina U.S.A.
108 G3 **Trent** Texas U.S.A.
121 L8 **Trent Canal** Ontario Canada
41 N5 **Trentino-Alto Adige** *reg* Italy
41 O5 **Trento** Italy
13 G6 **Trentola** Italy
122 K8 **Trenton** Nova Scotia Canada
121 N8 **Trenton** Ontario Canada
113 E8 **Trenton** Florida U.S.A.
94 B4 **Trenton** Michigan U.S.A.
110 C1 **Trenton** Missouri U.S.A.
98 E9 **Trenton** Nebraska U.S.A.
95 N6 **Trenton** New Jersey U.S.A.
95 M3 **Trenton** New York U.S.A.
98 C1 **Trenton** North Dakota U.S.A.
110 M2 **Trenton** Ohio U.S.A.
112 F4 **Trenton** South Carolina U.S.A.
110 H6 **Trenton** Tennessee U.S.A.
13 H6 **Trent, R** England
21 N4 **Tréon** France
46 D2 **Trepča** Serbia Yugoslavia
21 N1 **Tréport, le** France
31 H8 **Treppo Carnico** Italy
120 C3 **Treptow L** Ontario Canada
133 F4 **Tres Arboles** Uruguay
131 E7 **Tres Arroyos** Argentina
20 G6 **Tresboeuf** France
128 F5 **Três Casas** Brazil
19 P16 **Trescléoux** France
9 F7 **Tresco** *isld* Isles of Scilly England
130 F7 **Três Corações** Brazil
33 N9 **Treseburg** Germany
15 B4 **Treshnish I** Scotland
48 E7 **Treskavica** *mt* Bosnia-Herzegovina
130 D7 **Três Lagoas** Brazil
130 F6 **Três Marias** *dam* Brazil
133 B7 **Tres Montes, Pen** Chile
16 E2 **Trespaderne** Spain
130 D10 **Tres Passos** Brazil
133 D7 **Tres Picos, Cerro** *pk* Argentina
106 E5 **Tres Piedras** New Mexico U.S.A.
102 C5 **Tres Pinos** California U.S.A.
130 F7 **Três Pontas** Brazil
133 C3 **Tres Puentes** Chile
130 G8 **Três Rios** Brazil
21 M6 **Tresson** France
31 J6 **Trest'** Czechoslovakia
15 G2 **Tresta** Shetland Scotland
125 M8 **Tres Zapotes** Mexico
8 C4 **Tretower** Wales
6 J6 **Trets** France
19 P18 **Trets** France
27 D10 **Tretten** Norway
37 K6 **Treuchtlingen** Germany
33 N2 **Treuen** Germany
33 R8 **Treuenbrietzen** Germany
140 B5 **Treuer Ra** N Terr Australia
27 C12 **Treungen** Norway
20 E5 **Trévé** France
Treves *see* **Trier**
20 C5 **Trévézal,Roc** *mt* France
21 J3 **Trévières** France
41 L6 **Treviglio** Italy
17 F2 **Treviño** Spain
42 E3 **Treviso** Italy
8 A6 **Trevose Head** England
40 A6 **Trévoux** France
36 G2 **Treysa** Germany
31 H7 **Trhové Sviny** Czechoslovakia
27 H14 **Triabo** Sweden
139 J8 **Triabunna** Tasmania Australia
20 C4 **Triagoz, les** France
140 D2 **Trial B** N Terr Australia
47 V17 **Trianda** Rhodes Greece
117 P8 **Triangle** Alberta Canada
100 J7 **Triangle** Idaho U.S.A.
89 G3 **Triangle** Zimbabwe
47 H8 **Tria Nisiá** *isld* Greece
48 E2 **Tribeč** *R* Czechoslovakia
20 H3 **Tribehou** France
40 H3 **Triberg** Germany
33 R4 **Tribsees** Germany
141 H3 **Tribulation, C** Queensland Australia
119 O9 **Tribune** Saskatchewan Canada
107 J3 **Tribune** Kansas U.S.A.
43 G8 **Tricarico** Italy
43 J9 **Tricase** Italy
76 C5 **Trichur** India
9 E6 **Trickett's Cross** England
22 D4 **Tricot** France
139 H5 **Trida** New South Wales Australia
100 G8 **Trident Pk** Nevada U.S.A.
38 K7 **Trieben** Austria
37 N2 **Triebes** Germany
21 O3 **Trie-Château** France
37 P6 **Triefenried** Germany
21 P4 **Triel-sur-Seine** France
131 G4 **Trienta-y-Tres** Uruguay
36 B4 **Trier** Germany
37 K5 **Triesdorf** Germany
42 F3 **Trieste** Italy
42 F3 **Trieste, G.di** Italy
20 D4 **Trieux** *R* France
22 K5 **Trieux** France
37 P7 **Triftern** Germany
42 F2 **Triglav** *mt* Slovenia
20 F7 **Trignac** France
16 C7 **Trigueros** Spain
45 F5 **Trikeri** Greece
46 E5 **Trikhonis, L** Greece
46 E5 **Trikkala** Greece
46 E6 **Triklinos** Greece
79 D3 **Trikomo** Cyprus
113 E9 **Trilby** Florida U.S.A.
17 F4 **Trillo** Spain
120 G2 **Trilsbeck L** Ontario Canada
14 E3 **Trim** Ireland
13 G4 **Trimdon** England
9 H4 **Trimley** England
99 M6 **Trimont** Minnesota U.S.A.
142 B5 **Trimouille I** W Australia Australia
18 F6 **Trimouille, la** France
124 D2 **Trincheras** Mexico
106 F4 **Trinchera** Colorado U.S.A.
83 L9 **Trincomalee** Sri Lanka
90 G11 **Trindade** *isld* Atlantic Oc
9 F4 **Tring** England
46 E5 **Tringia** *mt* Greece
121 T6 **Tring Junction** Quebec Canada
128 F6 **Trinidad** Bolivia
128 D2 **Trinidad** Colombia
126 D4 **Trinidad** Cuba
130 C10 **Trinidad** Paraguay
71 G4 **Trinidad** Philippines
131 G4 **Trinidad** Uruguay
100 A8 **Trinidad** California U.S.A.
106 F4 **Trinidad** Colorado U.S.A.
100 E2 **Trinidad** Washington U.S.A.
127 O2 **Trinidad** *isld* W Indies
127 O9 **Trinidad and Tobago** *rep* W Indies
133 B7 **Trinidad, Canal** Chile
131 E7 **Trinidad, I** Argentina
21 M4 **Trinité-de-Réville, la** France
20 E5 **Trinité-Porhoët, la** France
126 D6 **Trinité-sur-Mer, la** France
123 T5 **Trinity** Newfoundland Canada
109 L3 **Trinity** *R* Texas U.S.A.
109 M5 **Trinity** Texas U.S.A.
141 H3 **Trinity B** Queensland Australia
100 C8 **Trinity Center** California U.S.A.
127 P3 **Trinity Hills** Trinidad
146 C4 **Trinity I** *isld* Antarctica
116 K8 **Trinity Is** Alaska U.S.A.
146 C4 **Trinity Peninsula** *pen* Antarctica
102 F1 **Trinity Ra** Nevada U.S.A.
100 C9 **Trinity Res** California U.S.A.
69 A8 **Trinkat I** Nicobar Is
44 D1 **Trino** Italy
Trinquet, Fort *see* **Bir Moghreim**
83 L12 **Triolet** Mauritius
112 B3 **Trion** Georgia U.S.A.
43 H9 **Trionto, C** Italy
69 C10 **Tripa** *R* Sumatra
Tripoli *see* **Trâblous** Lebanon
Tripoli *see* **Tarâbulus** Libya
99 O7 **Tripoli** Iowa U.S.A.
46 E7 **Tripolis** Greece
84 E3 **Tripolitania** *reg* Libya
98 H6 **Tripp** South Dakota U.S.A.
36 D5 **Trippstadt** Germany
37 O2 **Triptis** Germany
75 O7 **Tripura** *prov* India
123 N3 **Triquet, L** Quebec Canada
32 J4 **Trischen** *isld* Germany
37 O4 **Tři Sekery** Czechoslovakia
90 H12 **Tristan da Cunha** Atlantic Oc
68 G7 **Tri Ton** Vietnam
33 M5 **Trittau** Germany
130 H9 **Triunfo** Brazil
76 C6 **Trivandrum** India
48 D2 **Trnava** Czechoslovakia
21 K3 **Troarn** France
36 G7 **Trochtelfingen** Germany
26 F5 **Troense** *isld* Norway
28 F6 **Troense** Denmark
38 M7 **Trofaiach** Austria
147 Q9 **Trofimovsk** Russian Federation
42 G5 **Trogir** Croatia
42 H5 **Troglav** *mt* Croatia/Yugoslavia
36 C2 **Troisdorf** Germany
36 C6 **Troisfontaines** France
85 D1 **Trois Fourches, Cap des** Morocco
21 L7 **Trois Moutiers, les** France
122 C5 **Trois Pistoles** Quebec Canada
22 K3 **Trois Ponts** Belgium
121 S6 **Trois Rivières** Quebec Canada
127 N5 **Trois Rivières** Guadeloupe W Indies
83 M14 **Trois Swains, Les** *islds* Kerguelen Indian Oc
22 K3 **Trois Vierges** Luxembourg
54 M2 **Troitsa** Russian Federation
55 E1 **Troitsa** Tyumenskaya obl Russian Federation
55 D4 **Troitsk** Russian Federation
56 F4 **Troitsk** Russian Federation
54 J1 **Troitsk** Moskovskaya obl Russian Federation
55 D3 **Troitskiy** Russian Federation
52 J3 **Troitsko-Pechorsk** Russian Federation
55 F4 **Troitskoye** Russian Federation
55 C4 **Troitskoye** Bashkirskaya Respublika Russian Federation
127 L2 **Troja** Jamaica
28 B5 **Troldhede** Denmark
27 F13 **Trollhättan** Sweden
26 D9 **Trollheimen** *mt* Norway
26 D9 **Trolltindane** *mt* Norway
129 G4 **Trombetas** *R* Brazil
83 H6 **Tromelin I** Indian Oc
133 C5 **Tromen** *mt* Argentina
131 B6 **Tromen, V** Argentina
41 M6 **Trompia, V** Italy
26 K2 **Tromsø** Norway
26 K2 **Tromsöysund** Norway
55 F1 **Trom'yegan** *R* Russian Federation
102 G6 **Trona** California U.S.A.
131 B8 **Tronador** *pk* Arg/Chile
20 G4 **Tronchet, le** France
124 G6 **Troncón** Mexico
26 J3 **Trondenes** Norway
26 D8 **Trondheim** Norway
26 D8 **Trondheimsfjord** *inlet* Norway
26 E9 **Trönfjell** *mt* Norway
27 J10 **Trönödal** Sweden
42 F6 **Tronto** *R* Italy
21 M6 **Trôo** France
79 C4 **Troödos, Mt** Cyprus
12 D3 **Trool, L** Scotland
12 D2 **Troon** Scotland
43 G10 **Tropea** Italy
130 G4 **Tropeiros, Sa.dos** *mts* Brazil
103 M4 **Tropic** Utah U.S.A.
46 D2 **Tropojë** Albania
27 J13 **Trosa** Sweden
52 J2 **Trosh** Russian Federation
98 K6 **Trosky** Minnesota U.S.A.
119 N9 **Trossachs** Saskatchewan Canada
12 D1 **Trossachs** Scotland
14 E1 **Trostan** *mt* N Ireland
28 E6 **Trestrup Korup** Denmark
48 M2 **Trostyanets** Ukraine
33 P9 **Trotha** Germany
98 C2 **Trotters** North Dakota U.S.A.
48 K4 **Trotus** *R* Romania
101 T9 **Troublesome** Colorado U.S.A.
142 F2 **Troughton I** W Australia Australia
68 G6 **Troun** Cambodia
109 M3 **Troup** Texas U.S.A.
107 L4 **Trousdale** Kansas U.S.A.
122 F6 **Trousers, L** New Brunswick Canada
117 L6 **Trout** *R* British Columbia Canada
111 D10 **Trout** Louisiana U.S.A.
13 F5 **Troutbeck** England
103 L6 **Trout Cr** Arizona U.S.A.
100 E5 **Trout Cr** Oregon U.S.A.
121 L7 **Trout Creek** Ontario Canada
99 R3 **Trout Creek** Michigan U.S.A.
100 K2 **Trout Creek** Montana U.S.A.
103 L2 **Trout Creek** Utah U.S.A.
117 P10 **Trout L** British Columbia Canada
99 R3 **Trout L** Wisconsin U.S.A.
117 N5 **Trout Lake** Northwest Territories Canada
101 Q5 **Trout Pk** Wyoming U.S.A.
118 C2 **Trout R** Alberta Canada
123 O4 **Trout River** Newfoundland Canada
95 K5 **Trout Run** Pennsylvania U.S.A.
94 J5 **Troutville** Pennsylvania U.S.A.
94 H9 **Troutville** Virginia U.S.A.
21 L3 **Trouville** France
8 D5 **Trowbridge** England
139 H8 **Trowutta** Tasmania Australia
127 J2 **Troy** Jamaica
47 H5 **Troy** Turkey
111 L10 **Troy** Alabama U.S.A.
100 J3 **Troy** Idaho U.S.A.
110 K3 **Troy** Indiana U.S.A.
110 F3 **Troy** Missouri U.S.A.
101 K1 **Troy** Montana U.S.A.
95 P4 **Troy** New Hampshire U.S.A.
95 O4 **Troy** New York U.S.A.
112 H2 **Troy** North Carolina U.S.A.
110 M1 **Troy** Ohio U.S.A.
100 H4 **Troy** Oregon U.S.A.
95 L5 **Troy** Pennsylvania U.S.A.
109 K4 **Troy** Texas U.S.A.
94 G7 **Troy** West Virginia U.S.A.
46 G2 **Troyan** Bulgaria
55 E4 **Troyebratskiy** Kazakhstan
18 H4 **Troyes** France
95 P2 **Troy, N** Vermont U.S.A.
103 J6 **Troy Pk** Nevada U.S.A.
37 N3 **Trśnice** Czechoslovakia
48 F1 **Trstená** Czechoslovakia
46 D1 **Trstenik** Serbia Yugoslavia
140 D4 **Truant I** N Terr Australia
119 N9 **Truax** Saskatchewan Canada
54 E4 **Trubchevsk** Russian Federation
54 C6 **Trubezh** *R* Ukraine
124 G5 **Truchas** Mexico
106 E5 **Truchas** New Mexico U.S.A.
36 D6 **Truchtersheim** France
Trucial States *see* **United Arab Emirates**
102 D2 **Truckee** California U.S.A.
102 E2 **Truckee** *R* Nevada U.S.A.
59 K3 **Trudovoye** Russian Federation
15 D4 **Truim** *R* Scotland
121 M5 **Truite, L. la** Quebec Canada
125 L2 **Trujillo** Honduras
128 C5 **Trujillo** Peru
16 D5 **Trujillo** Spain
106 F6 **Trujillo** New Mexico U.S.A.
127 J10 **Trujillo** Venezuela
Truk Is *see* **Chuuk Is**
99 M6 **Truman** Minnesota U.S.A.
110 F6 **Trumann** Arkansas U.S.A.
95 L4 **Trumansburg** New York U.S.A.
98 H9 **Trumbull** Nebraska U.S.A.
103 L5 **Trumbull, Mt** Arizona U.S.A.
69 C11 **Trumon** Sumatra
9 G3 **Trumpington** England
21 L4 **Trun** France
139 J5 **Trundle** New South Wales Australia
67 B5 **Trung Khanh Phu** Vietnam
69 G8 **Trung Lon,Hon** *isld* Vietnam
69 G8 **Trung Nho,Hon** *isld* Vietnam
138 E5 **Truro** South Australia Australia
122 J8 **Truro** Nova Scotia Canada
8 A7 **Truro** England
99 N8 **Truro** Iowa U.S.A.
95 R4 **Truro** Massachusetts U.S.A.
70 D2 **Trusan** Sarawak
108 H2 **Truscott** Texas U.S.A.
48 K3 **Truşeşti** Romania
32 J2 **Trusetal** Germany
48 H1 **Truskavets** Ukraine
14 C2 **Truskmore** *mt* Ireland
70 E2 **Trus Madi, G** *mt* Sabah
52 H2 **Trusovo** Russian Federation
111 K8 **Trussville** Alabama U.S.A.
46 G1 **Trstenik** Bulgaria
28 F4 **Trustrup** Denmark
117 M8 **Trutch** British Columbia Canada
Truth or Consequences New Mexico U.S.A.
31 J5 **Trutnov** Czechoslovakia
21 J4 **Truttemer-le-Petit** France
95 L4 **Truxton** New York U.S.A.
18 G8 **Truyère** *R* France
46 G2 **Tryavna** Bulgaria
98 F8 **Tryon** Nebraska U.S.A.
145 E2 **Tryphena** New Zealand
27 F10 **Trysil** Norway
27 E10 **Trysilelv** *R* Norway
52 B6 **Tryškiai** Lithuania
31 M2 **Trzcianka** Poland
31 H2 **Trzebiez** Poland
31 K4 **Trzebnica** Poland
31 K3 **Trzemeszno** Poland
42 F2 **Tržič** Slovenia
53 G10 **Tsagan Aman** Russian Federation
Tsaidam *basin see* **Qaidam Pendi**
46 D5 **Tsamandás** Greece
Tsamkong *see* **Zhanjiang**
Tsangpo *R see* **Yarlung Zangbo Jiang** *R*
Tsaochwang *see* **Zaozhuang**
87 H11 **Tsaratanana** Madagascar
87 H10 **Tsaratanana, Massif du** *mt* Madagascar
87 D10 **Tsau** Botswana
88 G3 **Tsavo** Kenya
88 G3 **Tsavo East Nat. Park** Kenya
88 G3 **Tsavo West National Park** Kenya
89 A6 **Tsaxisis** Namibia
41 M4 **Tschlin** Switzerland
55 D4 **Tselinnoye** Russian Federation
55 D5 **Tselinnyy** Russian Federation
55 F5 **Tselinograd** Kazakhstan
54 F3 **Tsementnyy** Russian Federation
52 G3 **Tsenogora** Russian Federation
56 C3 **Tsentral'nyy** Russian Federation
87 C11 **Tses** Namibia
58 D2 **Tsetserleg** Mongolia
85 E7 **Tsévié** Togo
87 D11 **Tshabong** Botswana
87 D7 **Tshabuta** Zaire
87 D7 **Tshane** Botswana
87 D8 **Tshangalele, L** Zaire
86 B7 **Tshela** Zaire
87 D7 **Tshibala** Zaire
86 B6 **Tshibobo, Pte** Gabon
86 D7 **Tshikapa** Zaire
87 D7 **Tshimbalanga** Zaire
87 E8 **Tshinsenda** Zaire
86 E7 **Tshofa** Zaire
89 E2 **Tsholotsho** Zimbabwe
Tshungkin *see* **Kholm**
86 D6 **Tshuapa** *R* Zaire
87 D10 **Tshwanne** Botswana
52 G2 **Tsil'ma** *R* Russian Federation
53 F10 **Tsimlyansk** Russian Federation
65 D6 **Tsinan** China
87 D11 **Tsineng** S Africa
46 G3 **Tsinga** *mt* Greece
Tsingtao *see* **Qingdao**
68 F1 **Tsinh Ho** Vietnam
Tsining *see* **Jining** Nei Monggol Zizhiqu
Tsin Ling *mt ra see* **Qin Ling** *mt ra*
87 H13 **Tsiombe** Madagascar
46 E5 **Tsiótion** Greece
53 G1 **Tsipa** *R* Russian Federation
87 H11 **Tsiroanomandidy** Madagascar
Tsitsihar *see* **Qiqihar**
89 C9 **Tsitsikammaberge** *mts* S Africa
89 C10 **Tsitsikammaberge Forest and Coastal National Park** S Africa
52 G6 **Tsivil'sk** Russian Federation
87 H12 **Tsivory** Madagascar
52 D6 **Tsna** *R* Russian Federation
65 A1 **Tsomog** Mongolia
89 D6 **Tsootsha** Botswana
61 K11 **Tsu** Japan
61 M8 **Tsubame** Japan
61 K9 **Tsubata** Japan
61 O9 **Tsuchiura** Japan
60 O4 **Tsugaru-kaikyō** *str* Japan
61 N8 **Tsugawa** Japan
61 P13 **Tsuha** Okinawa
61 L10 **Tsukechi** Japan
61 P13 **Tsuken-jima** *isld* Okinawa
60 P2 **Tsukigata** Japan
61 J12 **Tsukiji** Japan
60 E12 **Tsukumi** Japan
87 C9 **Tsumeb** Namibia
87 C10 **Tsumis** Namibia
61 M10 **Tsuru** Japan
61 K10 **Tsuruga** Japan
61 K10 **Tsurugi-san** *B* Japan
61 K9 **Tsurugi** Japan
60 H12 **Tsurugi-san** *mt* Japan
61 N7 **Tsuruoka** Japan
59 L4 **Tsururga** Japan
60 E12 **Tsurusaki** Japan
59 J5 **Tsushima** Japan
61 K10 **Tsushima** Japan
60 G11 **Tsushima-kaikyō** *str* Japan
60 C11 **Tsutsu** Japan
61 L10 **Tsuwano** Japan
60 D12 **Tsuyama** Japan
60 H11 **Tsuyazaki** Japan
48 M1 **Tsybulev** Ukraine
55 E1 **Tsyngaly** Russian Federation
52 D1 **Tsyp Navolok** Russian Federation
54 K1 **Tsyurupi, Im** Russian Federation
16 C3 **Tua** *R* Portugal
145 G3 **Tuahine Pt.** New Zealand
145 F3 **Tuai** New Zealand
145 E2 **Tuakau** New Zealand
14 C3 **Tuam** Ireland
144 D4 **Tuamarina** New Zealand
135 N10 **Tuamotu** *arch* Pacific Oc
135 N10 **Tuamotu Ridge** Pacific Oc
68 F2 **Tuan Giao** Vietnam
69 C11 **Tuangku** *isld* Sumatra
67 B3 **Tuanxi** China
144 B7 **Tuapeka Mouth** New Zealand
125 N2 **Tuapi** Nicaragua
53 E11 **Tuapse** Russian Federation
70 E1 **Tuaran** Sabah
144 A7 **Tuatapere** New Zealand
70 K8 **Tua, Tg** *C* Sumatra
56 D4 **Tuba** Russian Federation
103 N10 **Tubac** Arizona U.S.A.
103 N5 **Tuba City** Arizona U.S.A.
71 B3 **Tubalai** *isld* Indonesia
78 H5 **Tubal, Wadi** Iraq
70 O9 **Tuban** Java
133 H3 **Tubarão** Brazil
80 E4 **Tubas** Jordan
70 C3 **Tubau** Sarawak
71 D6 **Tubbataha Reefs** Sulu Sea
118 J8 **Tuberose** Saskatchewan Canada
71 F7 **Tubigan** *isld* Philippines
71 E8 **Tubig Puti** Philippines
71 E4 **Tubile Pt** Philippines
36 G7 **Tübingen** Germany
55 C4 **Tubinskiy** Russian Federation
22 G2 **Tubize** Belgium
71 F6 **Tubod** Mindanao Philippines
142 A5 **Tubridgi Pt** W Australia Australia
84 G3 **Tubruq** Libya
70 E3 **Tubu** *R* Kalimantan
135 M10 **Tubuai Is** Pacific Oc
124 D2 **Tubutama** Mexico
127 K9 **Tucacas** Venezuela
100 H3 **Tucannon** *R* Washington U.S.A.
129 L6 **Tucano** Brazil
128 G7 **Tucavaca** Bolivia
18 G10 **Tuchan** France
67 A3 **Tucheng** China
117 J5 **Tuchitua** Yukon Territory Canada
117 L6 **Tuchodi** *R* British Columbia Canada
31 K2 **Tuchola** Poland
48 G1 **Tuchów** Poland
143 C7 **Tuckanarra** W Australia Australia
146 C12 **Tucker Glacier** *glacier* Antarctica
103 O9 **Tucson** Arizona U.S.A.
103 N9 **Tucson Mts** Arizona U.S.A.
133 D3 **Tucumán** *prov* Argentina
106 G6 **Tucumcari** New Mexico U.S.A.
129 G5 **Tucunaré** Brazil
127 M10 **Tucupido** Venezuela
127 N10 **Tucupita** Venezuela
129 J4 **Tucuruí** Brazil
31 J2 **Tuczno** Poland
25 E6 **Tüddern** Germany
28 G6 **Tudeå** *R* Denmark
17 F2 **Tudela** Spain
16 D3 **Tudela de Duero** Spain
120 J3 **Tudhope** Ontario Canada
102 C2 **Tudor** California U.S.A.
85 F6 **Tudun Wade** Nigeria
16 C3 **Tuela** *R* Portugal
28 H5 **Tuelsø** Denmark
129 H4 **Tueré** *R* Brazil
21 M5 **Tuffe** France
136 K3 **Tufi** Papua New Guinea
8 B4 **Tufton** Wales
112 D3 **Tugaloo L** South Carolina U.S.A.
118 L8 **Tugaske** Saskatchewan Canada
89 G7 **Tugela** *R* S Africa
94 E9 **Tug Fork** *R* Kentucky U.S.A.
139 K5 **Tuggerah L** New South Wales Australia
116 K8 **Tugidak I** Alaska U.S.A.
71 G5 **Tugnug Pt** Samar Philippines
55 D1 **Tugrovskiy** Russian Federation
70 F4 **Tuguan Maputi** *isld* Indonesia
71 G7 **Tugubun Pt** Philippines
71 E2 **Tuguegarao** Philippines
55 D3 **Tugulym** Russian Federation
59 L1 **Tugur** Russian Federation
69 C12 **Tuhemberua** Indonesia
145 D4 **Tui** New Zealand
125 P10 **Tuila** Guatemala
65 A4 **Tui Lamin Sum** China
56 C4 **Tuim** Russian Federation
Tuijiabu *see* **Yongxiu**
70 E3 **Tujung** Kalimantan
55 C4 **Tukan** Russian Federation
84 J4 **Tûkh** Egypt
145 F3 **Tukituki** *R* New Zealand
68 F6 **Tuk Luy** Cambodia
114 F4 **Tuktoyaktuk** Northwest Territories Canada
52 B6 **Tukums** Latvia
70 B5 **Tukung, Bt** *mt* Kalimantan
87 F7 **Tukuyu** Tanzania
125 K6 **Tula** Mexico
54 J2 **Tula** Russian Federation
119 O4 **Tulabi Lake** Saskatchewan Canada
58 C4 **Tulai Shan** China
117 N11 **Tulameen** British Columbia Canada
125 K7 **Tulancingo** Mexico
70 K8 **Tulangbawang** *R* Sumatra
102 E5 **Tulare** California U.S.A.
98 H5 **Tulare** South Dakota U.S.A.
102 E6 **Tulare Lake Bed** California U.S.A.
108 A2 **Tularosa** New Mexico U.S.A.
106 B8 **Tularosa Mts** New Mexico U.S.A.
106 D9 **Tularosa V** New Mexico U.S.A.
89 B8 **Tulbagh** *mt* S Africa
128 C3 **Tulcán** Ecuador
48 M5 **Tulcea** Romania
48 M2 **Tul'chin** Ukraine
102 E5 **Tule** *R* California U.S.A.
127 H9 **Tulé** Venezuela
Tuléar *see* **Toliara**
108 F1 **Tule Cr** Texas U.S.A.
100 D8 **Tule L** California U.S.A.
19 N16 **Tule L.Res** California U.S.A.
19 N16 **Tulette** France
89 F3 **Tuli** Zimbabwe
31 L3 **Tuliszków** Poland
52 D3 **Tulivaara** Finland
80 D4 **Tulkarm** Jordan
14 C4 **Tulla** Ireland
112 C2 **Tullahoma** Tennessee U.S.A.
139 J5 **Tullamore** New South Wales Australia
14 D3 **Tullamore** Ireland
18 G7 **Tulle** France
28 F7 **Tullebølle** Denmark
139 H5 **Tullibigeal** New South Wales Australia
40 B7 **Tullins** France
48 C2 **Tulln** Austria
38 N5 **Tullnerfeld** *reg* Austria
102 D4 **Tulloch Lake** *res* California U.S.A.
111 D10 **Tullos** Louisiana U.S.A.
14 E4 **Tullow** Ireland
141 H4 **Tully** Queensland Australia
95 L4 **Tully** New York U.S.A.
141 H4 **Tully Falls** Queensland Australia
140 E3 **Tully Inlet** Queensland Australia
52 D1 **Tuloma** *R* Russian Federation
65 H1 **Tulongshan** China
29 P8 **Tulos, L** Russian Federation
52 D3 **Tulos, Oz** *L* Russian Federation
47 H2 **Tulovo** Bulgaria
52 J4 **Tulpan** Russian Federation
107 P5 **Tulsa** Oklahoma U.S.A.
117 G6 **Tulsequah** British Columbia Canada
14 C3 **Tulsk** Ireland
53 E7 **Tul'skaya Oblast'** *prov* Russian Federation
28 D4 **Tulstrup** Denmark
128 C3 **Tuluá** Colombia
125 Q7 **Tulum** Mexico
131 C4 **Tulumaya** *R* Argentina
55 C2 **Tulumbasy** Russian Federation
131 C3 **Tulum, V.de** Argentina
56 F4 **Tulun** Russian Federation
70 N10 **Tulungagung** Java
71 D5 **Tuluran** Philippines
71 H4 **Tulutuu** Indonesia
55 C3 **Tulva** *R* Russian Federation
54 M1 **Tuma** Russian Federation
103 N10 **Tumacacori Nat.Mon** Arizona U.S.A.
128 C3 **Tumaco** Colombia
71 G7 **Tumadgo Pt** Mindanao Philippines
100 D5 **Tumalo** Oregon U.S.A.
70 C5 **Tumanggi** Kalimantan
52 D6 **Tumanovo** Russian Federation
55 E2 **Tuman, Oz** *L* Russian Federation
51 P2 **Tumany** Russian Federation
56 E5 **Tumat-Tayga, Khrebet** *mts* Russian Federation
128 G2 **Tumatumari** Guyana
86 D6 **Tumba** Zaire
70 C5 **Tumbangmasuki** Kalimantan
70 C5 **Tumbangsamba** Kalimantan
70 C5 **Tumbangsenamang** Kalimantan
70 B5 **Tumbangtiti** Kalimantan
71 G7 **Tumbao** Philippines
139 J6 **Tumbarumba** New South Wales Australia
128 B4 **Tumbes** Peru
124 H8 **Tumbiscatio** Mexico
95 R1 **Tumbledown Mt** Maine U.S.A.
130 B9 **Tumburús** Argentina
9 F1 **Tumby** England
138 D5 **Tumby Bay** South Australia Australia
29 O4 **Tumcha** *R* Finland/Rus Fed
52 D2 **Tumchaozero, Ozero** *L* Russian Federation
65 B4 **Tumd Youqi** China
65 B4 **Tumd Zuoqi** China
80 G4 **Tumeira** Jordan
65 H3 **Tumen** China
59 J3 **Tumen** *R* China/Korea
128 F2 **Tumeremo** Venezuela
77 E6 **Tumindao** *isld* Philippines
130 H6 **Tumiritinga** Brazil
76 C4 **Tumkur** India
15 D4 **Tummel** *R* Scotland
59 M2 **Tumnin** *R* Russian Federation
77 H6 **Tump** Pakistan
70 D5 **Tumpah** Kalimantan
69 F9 **Tumpat** Malaysia
71 H5 **Tumputiga, Gunung** *mt* Sulawesi Indonesia
74 H8 **Tumsar** India
85 D6 **Tumu** Ghana
129 G3 **Tumucumaque, Sa** *mts* Brazil
139 J6 **Tumut** New South Wales Australia
52 H6 **Tumutuk** Russian Federation
27 F13 **Tun** Sweden
26 J9 **Tuna** Sweden
71 G7 **Tuna Bay** Mindanao Philippines
127 O2 **Tunapuna** Trinidad
128 E7 **Tunari** *mt* Bolivia
126 E4 **Tunas de Zaza** Cuba
131 E5 **Tunas, L** Argentina
77 D6 **Tunb as Sughrá** *isld* Iran
77 D6 **Tunb Kubrá** *isld* Iran
78 G2 **Tunceli** Turkey
67 C7 **Tunchang** China
139 L4 **Tuncurry** New South Wales Australia
52 F3 **Tundra** Russian Federation
87 F7 **Tunduma** Zambia
88 F7 **Tunduru** Tanzania
47 H2 **Tundzha** *R* Bulgaria
28 J5 **Tune** Denmark
70 E2 **Tungku** Sabah
29 P6 **Tungozero** Russian Federation
67 G5 **Tung Shan** Taiwan
117 J5 **Tungsten** Northwest Territories Canada
102 F1 **Tungsten** Nevada U.S.A.
Tungting Lake *see* **Dongting Hu**
70 C4 **Tungun, Bt** *mt* Kalimantan
56 F1 **Tunguska** *R* Russian Federation
58 E2 **Tünhel** Mongolia
27 C11 **Tunhovdfjord** *L* Norway
76 F2 **Tuni** India
110 F7 **Tunica** Mississippi U.S.A.
43 C12 **Tunis** Tunisia
43 D11 **Tunis, G. de** Tunisia
84 D3 **Tunisia** *rep* N Africa
128 D2 **Tunja** Colombia
56 F5 **Tunkinskiye Gol'tsy** *mts* Russian Federation
65 B6 **Tunliu** China
26 E9 **Tunna** *R* Norway
120 G6 **Tunnel Dam** Ontario Canada
19 O18 **Tunnel du Rove** France
94 H7 **Tunnelton** West Virginia U.S.A.
26 F7 **Tunnsjø** *L* Norway
28 E5 **Tune** Denmark
8 D1 **Tunstall** England
9 H3 **Tunstall** England
115 N6 **Tunungayualok I** Labrador, Nfld Canada
131 C4 **Tunuyán, R** Argentina
131 C4 **Tunuyán, Sa. de** *mts* Argentina
67 A1 **Tuo Jiang** China
67 D4 **Tuojiang** China
65 E5 **Tuoji Dao** *isld* China
68 G6 **Tuol Khpos** Cambodia
102 D4 **Tuolumne** California U.S.A.
102 E4 **Tuolumne Meadows** California U.S.A.
29 L7 **Tuopalå** Finland
130 E7 **Tupã** Brazil
130 E6 **Tupaciguara** Brazil
128 F4 **Tupaoča** Brazil
145 G2 **Tuparoa** New Zealand
111 H7 **Tupelo** Mississippi U.S.A.
107 O6 **Tupelo** Oklahoma U.S.A.
111 H7 **Tupelo Nat Battlefield** Mississippi U.S.A.
128 G4 **Tupinambaranas, I** Brazil
130 E4 **Tupiraçaba** Brazil
133 D2 **Tupiza** Bolivia
102 E6 **Tupman** California U.S.A.
29 L7 **Tupos** Finland
117 N8 **Tupper** British Columbia Canada
95 N2 **Tupper Lake** New York U.S.A.
133 D4 **Tupungato** *mt* Arg/Chile
65 E2 **Tuquan** China
128 C3 **Tuquerres** Colombia
67 D7 **Tuqu Wan** *B* China
66 D4 **Tura** China
75 O6 **Tura** India
52 J2 **Tura** *R* Russian Federation
145 E4 **Turakina** New Zealand
145 E4 **Turakirae Head** New Zealand
57 J5 **Turakurgan** Uzbekistan
56 D5 **Turan** Russian Federation
59 K1 **Turana, Khrebet** *mt* Russian Federation
145 E3 **Turangi** New Zealand
42 E6 **Turano** *R* Italy
41 H6 **Turano, L.di** Italy
126 G9 **Turbaco** Colombia
20 F7 **Turballe, la** France
77 H7 **Turbat** Pakistan
41 J3 **Turbenthal** Switzerland
126 F10 **Turbo** Colombia
17 H2 **Turbón** *mt* Spain
48 M1 **Turbov** Ukraine
48 H6 **Turbuea** Romania
52 D5 **Turchasovo** Russian Federation
48 H4 **Turda** Romania
143 C6 **Turee Cr** W Australia Australia
16 E3 **Turégano** Spain
31 L3 **Turek** Poland
79 D10 **Tûr, El** Egypt
127 K10 **Turen** Venezuela
66 D3 **Turfan Depression** China
57 B1 **Turgay** *R* Kazakhstan
57 C1 **Turgay** Kazakhstan
55 D5 **Turgayskaya Stolovaya Strana** *dist* Kazakhstan/Rus Fed
121 L3 **Turgeon** *R* Quebec Canada
47 H1 **Türgovishte** Bulgaria
55 D3 **Turgoyak** Russian Federation
47 J6 **Turgutlu** Turkey
78 F1 **Turhal** Turkey
52 C5 **Türi** Estonia
17 G5 **Turia** *R* Spain
129 J4 **Turiaçu** Brazil
127 L9 **Turiamo** Venezuela
31 L7 **Turiec** *R* Czechoslovakia
126 E3 **Turiguano, I** Cuba
Turin *see* **Torino**
118 E9 **Turin** Alberta Canada
95 M3 **Turin** New York U.S.A.
55 D2 **Turinsk** Russian Federation
55 D3 **Turinskaya-Sloboda** Russian Federation
59 K2 **Turiy Rog** Russian Federation
48 D3 **Türje** Hungary
56 G4 **Turka** *R* Russian Federation
48 H1 **Turka** Ukraine
86 G5 **Turkana, L** Kenya
47 J4 **Turkeli** *isld* Turkey
41 O1 **Turkenfeld** Germany
57 E3 **Turkestan** Kazakhstan
57 E5 **Turkestanskiy Khrebet** *mts* Tajikistan/Uzbekistan etc
48 F3 **Túrkeve** Hungary
99 P7 **Turkey** *R* Iowa U.S.A.
108 G1 **Turkey** Texas U.S.A.
78 D2 **Turkey** *rep* W Asia
142 G3 **Turkey Creek** W Australia Australia
106 F6 **Turkey Mts** New Mexico U.S.A.
41 N1 **Türkheim** Germany
36 C4 **Türkismühle** Germany
47 L5 **Türkmendagi** *mt* Turkey
50 E4 **Turkmenistan** *rep* C Asia
57 B5 **Turkmen-Kala** Turkmenistan
57 B6 **Turkmenkarakul'** Turkmenistan
Turkmenskaya S.S.R. *see* **Turkmenistan**
79 G1 **Türkoğlu** Turkey
127 H4 **Turks and Caicos Is** *isld group* W Indies
127 J4 **Turks Is** W Indies
29 J11 **Turku** Finland
27 M10 **Turku Pori** *reg* Finland
86 G5 **Turkwel** *R* Kenya
16 E5 **Turleque** Spain
102 D4 **Turlock** California U.S.A.
130 G5 **Turmalina** Brazil
117 J6 **Turnagain** *R* British Columbia Canada
145 F4 **Turnagain, C** New Zealand
38 M6 **Turnau** Austria
119 Q5 **Turnberry** Manitoba Canada
15 D5 **Turnberry** Scotland
119 S4 **Turnbull** Manitoba Canada
140 B5 **Turnbull, Mt** N Terr Australia
125 P9 **Turneffe Is** Belize
95 R2 **Turner** Maine U.S.A.
94 D2 **Turner** Michigan U.S.A.
101 R1 **Turner** Montana U.S.A.
100 C5 **Turner** Oregon U.S.A.
100 H3 **Turner** Washington U.S.A.
101 U6 **Turnercrest** Wyoming U.S.A.
142 B6 **Turner, Mt** W Australia Australia
142 G4 **Turner River** W Australia Australia
95 P4 **Turners Falls** Massachusetts U.S.A.
118 C8 **Turner Valley** Alberta Canada
101 P7 **Turnerville** Wyoming U.S.A.
22 H1 **Turnhout** Belgium
38 M6 **Turnitz** Austria
31 J5 **Turnov** Czechoslovakia
46 G1 **Turnu Măgurele** Romania
48 J5 **Turnu Roşu** Romania
57 H1 **Turobay** Kazakhstan
31 O5 **Turobin** Poland
139 J5 **Turon** *R* New South Wales Australia
107 M4 **Turon** Kansas U.S.A.
139 J5 **Tuross** *R* New South Wales Australia
66 D3 **Turpan** China
108 D7 **Turpin** Oklahoma U.S.A.
126 F4 **Turquino, Pico** *pk* Cuba
106 D9 **Turquoise** New Mexico U.S.A.
116 K6 **Turquoise L** Alaska U.S.A.
38 J8 **Turrach** Austria
110 F6 **Turrell** Arkansas U.S.A.
125 N5 **Turrialba** Costa Rica
19 Q16 **Turriers** France
15 F3 **Turriff** Scotland
55 D1 **Tursuntskiy Tuman, Oz** *L* Russian Federation
57 E5 **Tursunzade** Tajikistan
56 F5 **Turt** Mongolia
55 E2 **Turtas** *R* Russian Federation
57 B4 **Turtkul'** Uzbekistan
99 O1 **Turtle** *R* Ontario Canada
122 H8 **Turtle Cr** New Brunswick Canada
118 J5 **Turtleford** Saskatchewan Canada
141 G1 **Turtlehead I** Queensland Australia
141 K3 **Turtle I** Gt Barrier Reef Aust
142 C5 **Turtle I** W Australia Australia
70 F1 **Turtle Is** Philippines
85 B7 **Turtle Is** Sierra Leone
118 J5 **Turtle L** Saskatchewan Canada
98 F2 **Turtle L** North Dakota U.S.A.
99 O4 **Turtle L** Wisconsin U.S.A.
98 F1 **Turtle Mts** Manitoba/N Dakota Canada/U.S.A.
29 K5 **Turtola** Finland
98 H4 **Turton** South Dakota U.S.A.
145 E2 **Turua** New Zealand
66 B3 **Turugart** *pass* Kazakhstan
51 H2 **Turukhansk** Russian Federation
55 E1 **Turumeyevo** Russian Federation
129 G3 **Turuna** *R* Brazil
28 D6 **Turup** Denmark
9 F3 **Turvey** England
130 D10 **Turvo** *R* Brazil
53 B8 **Tur'ya** *R* Ukraine
31 L6 **Turzovka** Czechoslovakia
111 J8 **Tuscaloosa** Alabama U.S.A.
111 J8 **Tuscaloosa, L** Alabama U.S.A.
42 D6 **Tuscania** Italy
94 F6 **Tuscarawas** *R* Ohio U.S.A.
100 J8 **Tuscarora** Nevada U.S.A.
94 K6 **Tuscarora Mt** Pennsylvania U.S.A.
110 H2 **Tuscola** Illinois U.S.A.
100 K2 **Tuscor** Montana U.S.A.
110 J7 **Tuscumbia** Alabama U.S.A.
110 D3 **Tuscumbia** Missouri U.S.A.
28 H5 **Tuse** Denmark
57 A2 **Tushchibas, Zaliv** *G* Kazakhstan
14 E4 **Tuskar Rock** Ireland
111 L9 **Tuskegee** Alabama U.S.A.
122 G10 **Tusket** Nova Scotia Canada
54 H5 **Tuskor'** *R* Russian Federation
115 O3 **Tussaaq** Greenland
102 G8 **Tustin** California U.S.A.
94 B2 **Tustin** Michigan U.S.A.
26 C8 **Tustna** *isld* Norway
116 M6 **Tustumena L** Alaska U.S.A.
31 M4 **Tuszyn** Poland
78 J2 **Tutak** Turkey
145 D1 **Tutamoe Range** New Zealand
52 E5 **Tutayev** Russian Federation
9 E2 **Tutbury** England
Tutera *see* **Tudela**
136 E6 **Tuthill** South Dakota U.S.A.
76 D6 **Tuticorin** India
46 D1 **Tutin** Serbia Yugoslavia
145 F3 **Tutira L** New Zealand
29 O5 **Tutiyarvi** Russian Federation
76 D3 **Tutoh** *R* Sarawak
129 K4 **Tutóia** Brazil
70 D2 **Tutong** Brunei
48 L4 **Tutova** *R* Romania
33 S5 **Tutow** Germany
47 H1 **Tutrakan** Bulgaria

(World atlas index page. Each entry: grid reference, place name, descriptor, location.)

Column 1

- 48 K6 Tutraken Romania
- 117 F5 Tutshi L Yukon Territory Canada
- 101 L7 Tuttle Idaho U.S.A.
- 98 F2 Tuttle North Dakota U.S.A.
- 107 N6 Tuttle Oklahoma U.S.A.
- 37 K2 Tüttleben Germany
- 107 O2 Tuttle Cr. Lake Kansas U.S.A.
- 99 M6 Tuttle L Minnesota U.S.A.
- 41 J2 Tuttlingen Germany
- Tuttut Nunaat see Renland
- 71 N9 Tutuala Timor
- 134 D1 Tutuila isld Amer Samoa
- 125 L9 Tututepec Mexico
- 71 O8 Tutuwawang Indonesia
- 111 F7 Tutwiler Mississippi U.S.A.
- 41 O2 Tutzing Germany
- 58 D2 Tuul Gol R Mongolia
- 29 L10 Tuulos Finland
- 29 N9 Tuupovaara Finland
- 29 O9 Tuusniemi Finland
- 137 Q3 Tuvalu isld state Pacific Oc
- 137 N6 Tuvana-i-Colo isld Pacific Oc
- 137 R6 Tuvana-i-ra isld Pacific Oc
- 56 E5 Tuvinskaya Respublika Russian Federation
- 70 E4 Tuwau R Kalimantan
- 103 L5 Tuweep Arizona U.S.A.
- 65 A5 Tuwei He R China
- 116 L6 Tuxedni B Alaska U.S.A.
- 118 A1 Tuxedo Manitoba Canada
- 112 E2 Tuxedo North Carolina U.S.A.
- 41 P3 Tuxer Gebirge mt Austria
- 119 M8 Tuxford Saskatchewan Canada
- 9 F1 Tuxford England
- 67 C1 Tuxiang China
- 125 L7 Tuxpan Mexico
- 124 G7 Tuxpan Jalisco Mexico
- 125 N9 Tuxpan Nayarit Mexico
- 55 F2 Tuxtla Gutiérrez Mexico
- 16 B2 Tuy Spain
- 117 H6 Tuya L British Columbia Canada
- 68 J6 Tuy An Vietnam
- 67 B6 Tuyen Quang Vietnam
- 68 J6 Tuy Hoa Vietnam
- 52 H6 Tuymazy Russian Federation
- 77 A2 Tüysarkän Iran
- 78 D2 Tuz Gölü L Turkey
- 103 N7 Tuzigoot Nat.Mon Arizona U.S.A.
- 78 K4 Tuz Khurmätū Iraq
- 48 E6 Tuzla Bosnia-Herzegovina
- 78 H2 Tuzla R Turkey
- 48 N5 Tuzly Ukraine
- 47 F14 Tvääker Sweden
- 26 L7 Tvärålund Sweden
- 26 M6 Tvärån Sweden
- 28 E4 Tved Århus Denmark
- 28 F6 Tved Fyn Denmark
- 28 E3 Tvede Denmark
- 27 C13 Tvedestrand Norway
- 52 E6 Tver' Russian Federation
- 52 D6 Tverskaya Oblast' prov Russian Federation
- 28 E1 Tversted Denmark
- 52 E6 Tvertsa R Russian Federation
- 27 H15 Tving Sweden
- 28 D5 Tvingstrup Denmark
- 28 B4 Tvis Denmark
- 6 F1 Tvoroyri Faeroes
- 48 J1 Tvŭrditsa Bulgaria
- 68 B4 Twante Burma
- 31 K4 Twardogóra Poland
- 85 F4 Twaret Niger
- 121 N8 Tweed Ontario Canada
- 139 L3 Tweed Heads New South Wales Australia
- 118 F4 Tweedie Alberta Canada
- 13 E3 Tweed, R Scotland
- 13 E3 Tweedsmuir Scotland
- 117 K9 Tweedsmuir Prov.Park British Columbia Canada
- 87 D11 Twee Rivieren S Africa
- 118 L9 Twelvemile L Saskatchewan Canada
- 116 P4 Twelvemile Summit Alaska U.S.A.
- 14 B3 Twelve Pins mt Ireland
- 103 H7 Twentynine Palms California U.S.A.
- 143 F9 Twilight Cove W Australia Australia
- 123 S4 Twillingate Newfoundland Canada
- 38 L8 Twimberg Austria
- 100 B1 Twin Washington U.S.A.
- 101 N4 Twin Bridges Montana U.S.A.
- 98 K4 Twin Brooks South Dakota U.S.A.
- 108 G4 Twin Buttes Res Texas U.S.A.
- 119 O2 Twin City Ontario Canada
- 115 N7 Twin Falls Labrador, Nfld Canada
- 101 L7 Twin Falls Idaho U.S.A.
- 142 F5 Twin Heads mt W Australia Australia
- 94 C2 Twin L Michigan U.S.A.
- 99 U6 Twin Lake Michigan U.S.A.
- 117 P7 Twin Lakes Alberta Canada
- 116 K6 Twin Lakes Alaska U.S.A.
- 106 D2 Twin Lakes Colorado U.S.A.
- 101 L6 Twin Lakes Res Idaho U.S.A.
- 123 Q4 Twin L,N Newfoundland Canada
- 123 R4 Twin L,S Newfoundland Canada
- 95 Q2 Twin Mountain New Hampshire U.S.A.
- 102 D2 Twin Peaks California U.S.A.
- 101 L5 Twin Peaks Idaho U.S.A.
- 143 C10 Twin Pks W Australia Australia
- 143 D10 Twin Rocks W Australia Australia
- 138 E3 Twins Cr South Australia Australia
- 138 D4 Twins, The mt New Zealand
- 145 D4 Twins, The mt New Zealand
- 98 K2 Twin Valley Minnesota U.S.A.
- 100 E1 Twisp Washington U.S.A.
- 32 J7 Twistringen Germany
- 108 D8 Twitty Texas U.S.A.
- 117 J4 Twitya R Northwest Territories Canada
- 144 C6 Twizel New Zealand
- 106 H4 Two Buttes Colorado U.S.A.
- 106 H4 Two Buttes Creek Colorado U.S.A.
- 118 F4 Two Creeks Manitoba Canada
- 99 T5 Two Creeks Wisconsin U.S.A.
- 101 P3 Twodot Montana U.S.A.
- 139 K6 Twofold B New South Wales Australia
- 116 L8 Two Headed I Alaska U.S.A.
- 118 F5 Two Hills Alberta Canada
- 101 P5 Two Ocean Pass Wyoming U.S.A.
- 99 T5 Two Rivers Wisconsin U.S.A.
- 9 E2 Twycross England
- 9 F5 Twyford England
- 9 F5 Twyford England
- 12 D4 Twynholm Scotland
- 48 M1 Tyachev Ukraine
- 28 D6 Tybjerg Denmark
- 28 D6 Tybrind Vig Denmark
- 55 G3 Tychkino Russian Federation
- 31 J2 Tychowo Poland
- 31 H2 Tychy Poland
- 28 E6 Tydal Norway

Column 2

- 117 F7 Tyee Alaska U.S.A.
- 100 A1 Tyee Washington U.S.A.
- 94 J9 Tye River Virginia U.S.A.
- 142 F4 Tygart V West Virginia U.S.A.
- 59 J1 Tygda Russian Federation
- 101 N7 Tyhee Idaho U.S.A.
- 27 C10 Tyin L Norway
- 55 B3 Tykocin Poland
- 98 H5 Tyler Minnesota U.S.A.
- 94 J5 Tyler Pennsylvania U.S.A.
- 52 E5 Tyler Texas U.S.A.
- 61 N11 Tyler Washington U.S.A.
- 68 F4 Tylertown Mississippi U.S.A.
- 28 D2 Tylstrup Denmark
- 59 M1 Tymovskoye Russian Federation
- 55 F2 Tynay Russian Federation
- 59 H1 Tynda Russian Federation
- 118 E1 Tyndall Manitoba Canada
- 51 L1 Tyndall South Dakota U.S.A.
- 145 Tyndall, Mt New Zealand
- 33 T6 Tynderö Sweden
- 13 G4 Tyne R England
- 13 G3 Tyne & Wear co England
- 13 G3 Tynemouth England
- 60 D13 Tynset Norway
- 75 Tyn nad Vltava Czechoslovakia
- 26 E9 Tynset Norway
- 8 C2 Tyn-y-Groes Wales
- 116 O5 Tyone R Alaska U.S.A.
- 61 O10 Tyonek Alaska U.S.A.
- Tyre see Soûr
- 86 E5 Tyre R Zaire
- 27 D11 Tyrifjorden L Norway
- 27 G15 Tyringe Sweden
- 55 C4 Tyrma Russian Federation
- 48 L2 Tyrma R Moldavia
- 55 C3 Tyrnavós Greece
- 14 D2 Tyron co N Ireland
- 106 B9 Tyrone North Carolina U.S.A.
- 94 J6 Tyrone New Mexico U.S.A.
- Tyrone Pennsylvania U.S.A.
- 139 G6 Tyrrell R Victoria Australia
- 116 E9 Tyrrhenian Sea S Europe
- 70 G7 Tysfjord Norway
- 116 J8 Tysnesøy isld Norway
- Tyssedal Norway
- Tystberga Sweden
- 13 E6 Tystrup Denmark
- 43 J9 Tyszowce Poland
- 28 E4 Tyukalinsk Russian Federation
- 28 E1 Tyulek Kyrgyzstan
- 28 E5 Tyulen'i, Ostrova islds
- 36 G2 Tyul'gan Russian Federation
- 28 D7 Tyul'kino Russian Federation
- 25 F2 Tyumen' Russian Federation
- 19 O13 Tyumenskaya Oblast' prov Russian Federation
- 59 M2 Tyuntyugur Kazakhstan
- 28 D7 Tyuratam Kazakhstan
- 15 G1 Tyuva Guba Russian Federation
- 119 O8 Tyvan Saskatchewan Canada
- 48 M1 Tyvriv Ukraine
- 8 B2 Tywyn Wales
- 25 C3 t'Zand Netherlands
- 87 F10 Tzaneen S Africa
- Tzepo see Zibo
- 67 G4 Tzoumérka mt Greece
- 25 E2 Tz'u-kao Shan pk Taiwan
- Tzummarum Netherlands

U

- 85 B3 Uad el Jat watercourse Western Sahara
- 65 H4 Uam L N Korea
- 97 O3 Uaroo W Australia Australia
- 128 G4 Uatumã R Brazil
- 103 L5 Uauá Brazil
- 129 L5 Uaupés Brazil
- 56 B8 Uba R Kazakhstan
- 33 D6 Ubach o. Worms Netherlands
- 129 L6 Ubagan R Kazakhstan
- 86 C5 Ubaitaba Brazil
- 86 C5 Ubangi R Cent Afr Republic/Zaire
- Ubari see Awbārī
- 79 H6 Ubayyid, Wadi al Saudi Arabia
- 28 G5 Ubby Denmark
- 70 D4 Ube Japan
- 16 E6 Ubeda Spain
- 115 O3 Übekendt Ejland isld Greenland
- 70 F7 Uberaba Brazil/Bolivia
- 130 B5 Uberaba L Brazil/Bolivia
- 130 B5 Uberaba Brazil
- 56 B5 Überherrn Germany
- 85 F7 Uberlândia Brazil
- 33 S5 Überlingen Germany
- 128 D3 Ubiaja Nigeria
- 133 D2 Ubigau Germany
- 94 E3 Ubina mt Bolivia
- 68 F4 Ubly Michigan U.S.A.
- Uboleratana res Thailand
- 115 O3 Ubombo S Africa
- 68 Q5 Ubon Ratchathani Thailand
- 79 C2 Ubstadt-Weiher Germany
- 108 C6 Uçarı Turkey
- 108 D5 Ucayali R Peru
- 55 F4 Ucayali dept Peru
- Uçburun Yarimada pen Turkey
- 22 G2 Ucele Belgium
- 16 E3 Ucero R Spain
- 47 N11 Üçgaziler Turkey
- 55 C4 Uchaly Russian Federation
- 31 K2 Uchigō Japan
- 97 B8 Uchiko Japan
- 60 B12 Uchiura wan B Japan
- 44 C4 Uchizy France
- 44 O5 Uch Kuduk Uzbekistan
- 56 K3 Uchkurgan Uzbekistan
- 32 J7 Uchte Germany
- 33 P7 Uchte R Germany
- 51 N3 Uchur R Russian Federation
- 20 C4 Uckange France
- 34 D2 Uckerath Germany
- 33 U4 Uckeritz Germany
- 9 G6 Uckfield England
- 117 T3 Uckro Germany
- British Columbia Canada
- 101 Q6 Ucon Idaho U.S.A.
- 60 F12 Uda R China
- 72 T4 Udagamandalam India
- 74 H6 Udaipur India
- 76 D3 Udaipur Garhi Nepal
- 77 B7 Udayagiri India
- Udayd, Khawr al' inlet Qatar/Saudi Arabia

Column 3

- 32 M10 Uder Germany
- 52 C6 Udgir India
- 74 F2 Udhampur Kashmir
- 142 F4 Udialla W Australia Australia
- 28 A4 Udine Italy
- 56 E4 Udinskiy Khrebet mts Russian Federation
- 28 A4 Udipi India
- 37 P3 Udlice Czechoslovakia
- 55 B3 Udmurtskaya Respublika Russian Federation
- 61 N11 Udoml'ya Russian Federation
- 76 A1 Udone-jima isld Japan
- 68 F4 Udon Thani Thailand
- 59 L1 Udor, Mt N Terr Australia
- 58 C2 Udskaya Guba R Russian Federation
- Udskoye see Dong Ujimqin Qi
- 70 G5 Uëbonti Sulawesi
- 33 U5 Ueckeraa R Germany
- 139 K6 Uecker reg Germany
- 33 U5 Ueckermünde Germany
- 61 M9 Ueda Japan
- 25 F5 Uedem Germany
- 26 M4 Ueffeln Germany
- 98 E5 Uehling Nebraska U.S.A.
- 17 H4 Uele R Zaire
- 27 G11 Uekuli Sulawesi
- 28 E6 Uelsen Germany
- 32 E7 Uelzen Germany
- 33 N7 Ueno Japan
- 61 K11 Uenohara Japan
- 61 O10 Uere R Zaire
- 86 E5 Uess R Germany
- 36 B3 Uetersen Germany
- 32 L5 Ufa Russian Federation
- 55 C4 Uffenheim Germany
- 55 C3 Ufimskiy Russian Federation
- 13 D3 Ugab R Namibia
- 116 J8 Ugaiushak I Alaska U.S.A.
- 116 J8 Ugak I Alaska U.S.A.
- 88 C4 Ugalla R Tanzania
- 116 E9 Ugamak I Aleutian Is
- 86 F5 Uganda rep Africa
- 70 G7 Ugeo Sulawesi
- 116 J8 Uganik I Alaska U.S.A.
- 88 B9 Ugashik Alaska U.S.A.
- 138 E2 Ugashik Lakes Alaska U.S.A.
- 13 E6 Uge Denmark
- 43 J9 Ugento Italy
- 28 E4 Uggelhuse Denmark
- 28 E1 Uggerby Denmark
- 28 E5 Uggerslev Denmark
- 36 G2 Ugijar Spain
- 28 D7 Uglich Denmark
- 25 F2 Uglit Denmark
- 19 O13 Ugine France
- 59 M2 Uglegorsk Russian Federation
- 28 D7 Ugleural'skiy Russian Federation
- 15 G1 Uglich Russian Federation
- 28 E2 Ugljan isld Croatia
- 42 G4 Ugljian isld Croatia
- 42 H5 Ugljane Croatia
- 95 L5 Ugljevik Bosnia-Herzegovina
- 52 D5 Uglovka Russian Federation
- 24 K4 Ugol sw Ujiji
- 54 G2 Ugra R Russian Federation
- 46 G1 Ugürchin Bulgaria
- 83 L10 Ugut Russian Federation
- 83 L10 Uhana Sri Lanka
- 37 K6 Uherské Hradiště Czechoslovakia
- 36 H6 Uhlmann Germany
- 37 L2 Uhlstädt Germany
- 28 C5 Uhre Denmark
- 94 F6 Uhrichsville Ohio U.S.A.
- 29 N3 Uhro Kekkosen Nat. Park Finland
- 31 O4 Uhrusk Poland
- 15 B3 Uig Skye Scotland
- 87 C7 Uige Angola
- 58 F1 Uijeongbu S Korea
- 65 F4 Úiju N Korea
- 61 N9 Ujjain India
- 84 B4 Ujiji Tanzania
- 70 D4 Ujohbilang Kalimantan
- 140 B3 Újpest Hungary
- 31 K2 Ujście Poland
- 70 F7 Ujung Pandang Sulawesi
- 57 C1 Uka R China
- 110 G4 Ukerewe isld Tanzania
- 76 Q6 Ukhrul India
- 72 P4 Ukhta Russian Federation
- 88 F5 Ukiah Oregon U.S.A.
- 94 D4 Ukiah California U.S.A.
- 74 J7 Ukiha Okinawa
- 29 M3 Ukkel see Uccle
- 74 D2 Ukkusissat Greenland
- 28 B5 Ukmerge Lithuania
- 113 F9 Ukraine rep E Europe
- 100 A4 Ukrainka Russian Federation
- 95 Q2 Ukrainskaya S.S.R. see Ukraine
- 42 H4 Ukrina R Bosnia-Herzegovina
- 140 O7 Uksyanskoye Russian Federation
- 31 M4 Uktym Russian Federation
- 82 B8 Uku Angola
- 6 M5 Uku-shima isld Japan
- 47 J7 Ula Turkey
- 58 B2 Ulaanbaatar Mongolia
- 65 D2 Ulaan-Ereg Mongolia
- 58 B2 Ulaangom Mongolia
- 139 J4 Ulan New South Wales Australia
- 82 B5 Ulan Bator see Ulaanbaatar
- 65 C2 Ulan Hobor China
- Ulan Hot see Horqin Youyi Qianqi
- 58 B2 Ulan Hua China
- 53 G10 Ulan-Khol Russian Federation
- 102 F1 Ulanov Ukraine
- 65 L4 Ulansuhai Nur L China
- 88 B7 Ulan-Ude Russian Federation
- 82 B8 Umi R Zimbabwe
- Uka see Uka

Column 4

- 98 K2 Ulen Minnesota U.S.A.
- 52 C6 Ulenia Lithuania
- 138 F3 Ulenia, L New South Wales Australia
- 58 F1 Ulety Russian Federation
- 28 A4 Ulfborg Denmark
- 28 A4 Ulfborg Kirke Denmark
- 37 J1 Ulfen Germany
- 65 D2 Ulgain Gol R China
- 13 G3 Ulgham England
- 76 A1 Ulhasnagar India
- Uliastai see Dong Ujimqin Qi
- 58 C2 Uliastay Mongolia
- 86 E6 Ulindi R Zaire
- 56 G3 Ulima Serbia Yugoslavia
- 56 G3 Ulindi R Zaire
- 28 D7 Ulkebøl Denmark
- 28 C5 Ulkind Denmark
- 86 A4 Ul'kon R Russian Federation
- 139 K6 Ulladulla New South Wales Australia
- 137 L8 Ulladulla Trough Pacific Oc
- 26 K9 Ullånger Sweden
- 27 F14 Ullared Sweden
- 26 M4 Ullatti Sweden
- 29 G11 Ullava Finland
- 17 H4 Ulldecona Spain
- 28 D7 Ullensvang Norway
- 28 D7 Ullerslev Denmark
- 110 G4 Ullerup Denmark
- 28 C3 Ullin Illinois U.S.A.
- 116 G5 Ullits Denmark
- 137 J8 Ullsfjord Norway
- 144 D5 Ullswater L England
- 12 D6 Ulla Wong Do isld S Korea
- 29 T9 Ulnäs Iceland
- 36 H7 Ulnapool Scotland
- 55 E1 Unare R Venezuela
- 27 G10 Unari Finland
- 111 J10 Unatán, Sa. de mts Venezuela
- 21 N5 Unwerre France
- 110 B3 Uncía Bolivia
- 106 C3 Uncompahgre Pk Colorado U.S.A.
- 106 B3 Uncompahgre Plateau Colorado U.S.A.
- 27 G13 Undenäs Sweden
- 27 G13 Undersåker Sweden
- 27 K11 Understen lighthouse Sweden
- 27 H10 Undervik Sweden
- 101 P9 Underberg Denmark
- 127 N10 Underwood Iowa U.S.A.
- 9 E5 Underwood North Dakota U.S.A.
- 115 O3 Undløse Denmark
- 71 K10 Undu, Tg C Sumba Indonesia
- 54 D4 Unecha Russian Federation
- 128 E4 Uneiuxi R Brazil
- 79 F8 Uneiza Jordan
- 37 P4 Unešov Czechoslovakia
- 94 B6 Unezhma Russian Federation
- 98 H9 Unga I Alaska U.S.A.
- 116 G4 Ungalik Alaska U.S.A.
- 116 H6 Ungarie New South Wales Australia
- 52 D1 Ungarra South Australia Australia
- 134 C2 Ungava Pen. d' Quebec Canada
- 117 P10 Ungava, Pen. d' Quebec Canada
- 9 F2 Ungeny Moldavia
- 8 C3 Ungerhausen Germany
- 9 N9 Ungi N Korea
- 130 D10 União Brazil
- 130 J4 União da Vitória Brazil
- 128 F4 União do Marmará Brazil
- 130 J10 União dos Palmares Brazil
- 112 E1 Unicoi Tennessee U.S.A.
- 110 G3 Unije isld Croatia
- 14 B5 Unimak Aleutian Is
- 116 E9 Unimak I Aleutian Is
- 85 B4 Unini, see Ayers Rock
- 127 O8 Union Argentina
- 111 J5 Unión isld Lesser Antilles
- 118 J1 Union Paraguay
- 98 C9 Union Colorado U.S.A.
- 99 N7 Union Iowa U.S.A.
- 95 L8 Union Louisiana U.S.A.
- 110 C5 Union Maine U.S.A.
- 145 D7 Union Mississippi U.S.A.
- 110 D3 Union Missouri U.S.A.
- 99 L9 Union Nebraska U.S.A.
- 107 N6 Union Oklahoma U.S.A.
- 100 H4 Union Oregon U.S.A.
- 94 C4 Union West Virginia U.S.A.
- 131 E7 Unión, B Argentina
- 95 K7 Union Bridge Maryland U.S.A.
- 111 F10 Union Church Mississippi U.S.A.
- 94 A6 Union City Indiana U.S.A.
- 94 C6 Union City Ohio/Indiana U.S.A.
- 94 K7 Union City Pennsylvania U.S.A.
- 110 G5 Union City Tennessee U.S.A.
- 100 C7 Union Creek Oregon U.S.A.
- 128 D3 Uniondale S Africa
- 94 J12 Union de Reyes Cuba
- 100 H3 Union Flat Cr Washington U.S.A.
- 116 C6 Union Gap Washington U.S.A.
- 119 N1 Unión, La Spain
- 112 F2 Union Mills North Carolina U.S.A.
- 100 H7 Union, Mt S Australia Australia
- 94 G5 Union Point Georgia U.S.A.
- 99 Q3 Union Point Manitoba Canada
- 58 C8 Union Springs Alabama U.S.A.
- 83 K11 Union Springs New York U.S.A.
- 110 M9 Union Star Missouri U.S.A.
- 139 K4 Union Stock Yards Texas U.S.A.
- 60 C4 Uniontown Alabama U.S.A.
- 110 C6 Uniontown Kentucky U.S.A.
- 139 K4 Uniontown Pennsylvania U.S.A.
- 94 R3 Unionville Iowa U.S.A.
- 50 D4 Unionville Michigan U.S.A.
- 102 F1 Unionville Nevada U.S.A.
- 88 D4 Unionville New York U.S.A.
- 60 B3 Unity Oregon U.S.A.
- 130 G4 United Arab Emirates (UAE) Persian Gulf
- United Kingdom of Gt.Britain & N.Ireland (UK)
- United States of America (USA) N America
- 7 B8 Unity Canada
- 118 H6 Unity Saskatchewan Canada
- 95 S1 Unity Maine U.S.A.
- 140 C2 Unity Oregon U.S.A.
- 31 K13 University City St Louis U.S.A.
- 110 F3 University City Missouri U.S.A.
- 109 O9 University Park Texas U.S.A.

Column 5

- 86 F3 Umm Sai'd see Musay'id
- 77 C7 Umm Shaif oil well Persian Gulf
- 79 D10 Umm Shomar, G mt Egypt
- 79 G14 Umm Tinässib,G mt Egypt
- 26 H6 Unnäs Sweden
- 37 L2 Unseren Germany
- 37 L6 Unstrut R Germany
- 52 E2 Unst Shetland Scotland
- 94 D6 Unterägeri Switzerland
- 129 K4 Unter Berg mt Austria
- 39 N6 Unterbrunn Germany
- 39 C2 Unterdietfurt Germany
- Unterdrauburg see Dravograd
- 22 F5 Unter Engadin dist Switzerland
- 18 E10 Unterfranken dist Germany
- 38 H8 Untergrießbach Germany
- 38 F5 Untergröningen Germany
- 36 M7 Unterhaching Germany
- 50 G2 Unterkirnach Germany
- 145 F3 Unterlüss Germany
- 13 G5 Untermerzbach Germany
- 36 K5 Untermünkheim Germany
- 36 K5 Untern-Bibert Germany
- Unterschwarzach see Rauhenebrach
- 55 G3 Untertal R Austria
- 38 K5 Unter Tavern Austria
- 41 H4 Unterwalden canton Switzerland
- 59 K1 Unter Zolling Germany
- 55 E1 Unter, Oz L Russian Federation
- 27 G10 Untorp Sweden
- 111 J10 Unturán, Sa. de mts Venezuela
- 110 B3 Unye Turkey
- 110 D13 Unzen-Amakusa Nat. Park Japan
- 139 G3 Unzen dake mt Japan
- 55 E4 Unzha R Russian Federation
- 29 K10 Uozu Japan
- 72 R3 Updike Indiana U.S.A.
- 47 H6 Upemba, L R Russian Federation
- 54 C4 Upemba North Dakota U.S.A.
- 115 O3 Upemba, L Zaire
- 79 G6 Upemba Greenland
- 55 E1 Upernavik Greenland
- 52 G6 Upham North Dakota U.S.A.
- 59 K2 Upington S Africa
- 52 G6 Upland Indiana U.S.A.
- 116 G4 Upland Nebraska U.S.A.
- 55 F2 Upolaksha Russian Federation
- 134 C2 Upolu isld Western Samoa
- 117 P10 Upolu Pt Hawaiian Is
- 9 F2 Upper Arrow L British Columbia Canada
- 37 M5 Upper Blackville New Brunswick Canada
- 52 F6 Upper Broughton England
- 8 C3 Upper Chapel Wales
- 37 P4 Upper Hutt New Zealand
- 94 B6 Upper Iowa R Iowa U.S.A.
- 99 P6 Upper Kent New Brunswick Canada
- 124 E4 Upper Klamath L Oregon U.S.A.
- 14 B5 Upper L Ireland
- 116 E9 Upper L California U.S.A.
- 85 B4 Upper Laberge Yukon Territory Canada
- 127 N10 Upper Liard Yukon Territory Canada
- 118 J1 Upper Manitou L Ontario Canada
- 127 P2 Upper Manzanilla Trinidad
- 95 L8 Upper Marlboro Maryland U.S.A.
- 145 E4 Upper Moutere New Zealand
- 99 M1 Upper Musquodoboit Nova Scotia Canada
- 60 C4 Upper Red L Minnesota U.S.A.
- 101 O5 Upper Red Rock L Montana U.S.A.
- 95 N2 Upper Sandusky Ohio U.S.A.
- 95 N2 Upper Saranac L New York U.S.A.
- 99 Q3 Upper Stewiacke Nova Scotia Canada
- 77 J3 Upper Tract West Virginia U.S.A.
- 9 H5 Upperville Virginia U.S.A.
- 139 H7 Upper Volta see Burkina
- 139 H7 Upper Yarra Res Victoria Australia
- 9 F5 Uppingham England
- 27 J12 Upplands Väsby Sweden
- 27 K12 Uppsala Sweden
- 116 C6 Upright,C St Matthew I, Alaska U.S.A.
- 119 N1 Upsala Ontario Canada
- 95 M4 Upton Romania
- 122 F6 Upton Quebec Canada
- 111 E11 Upton Kentucky U.S.A.
- 133 F4 Upton Massachusetts U.S.A.
- 106 H4 Upton Wyoming U.S.A.
- 101 Q6 Uqaylah,Al Libya
- 128 G7 Uracoa Venezuela
- 99 M9 Urad Zhongqi China
- 60 B12 Uraga Japan
- 60 G1 Uragasmanhandiya Sri Lanka
- 56 E6 Urakawa Japan
- 145 F3 Ural mt New South Wales Australia
- 60 C4 Ural R Kazakhstan/Rus Fed
- 139 K4 Uralla New South Wales Australia
- 57 D12 Ural'sk Kazakhstan
- 55 D12 Uralskiy Khrebet mts Russian Federation
- 8 G3 Urambo Tanzania
- 3 A12 Urangan Queensland Australia
- 47 N10 Urandangie Queensland Australia
- 47 J3 Urania Louisiana U.S.A.
- 114 J6 Uranium City Saskatchewan Canada
- 56 J2 Uraricoera Brazil
- 21 J5 Urawa Japan

Column 6

- 36 C2 Unkel Germany
- 38 G6 Unken Austria
- 55 C3 Unkurda Russian Federation
- 32 G9 Unna Germany
- 74 J5 Unnao India
- 79 D10 Unnaryd Sweden
- 67 C7 Unomachi Japan
- 37 L6 Unsernberg Germany
- 15 G1 Unskaya Guba R Russian Federation
- 3 O10 Unst Shetland Scotland
- 80 G4 Unstrut R Germany
- 80 G6 Unter Okinawa
- 74 H8 Unterberg Germany
- 38 N6 Unter Berg mt Austria
- 39 C2 Unterbrunn Germany
- 89 G2 Unshujera el Gharbiya Jordan
- Unterstetten see Fichtenau
- 89 G2 Unz R Zimbabwe
- 36 H4 Untai L Mutare
- 38 H8 Untergebirge V Austria
- 38 F5 Unterhaching Germany
- 57 K2 Urdzhar Kazakhstan
- 86 A4 Uren Russian Federation
- 139 K6 Urengoy Russian Federation
- 137 L8 Urenui New Zealand
- 89 F3 Ureparapara isld Vanuatu
- 42 G4 Ures Mexico
- 145 F3 Urewera Country New Zealand
- 55 G3 Urez Russian Federation
- 38 K7 Urfa see Şanlıurfa
- 41 O2 Urfeld Germany
- 52 G6 Urga Russian Federation
- 59 K1 Urgal Russian Federation
- 52 H2 Urgel, Seo de Spain
- 41 J4 Urgench Uzbekistan
- 41 J4 Uri cantor Switzerland
- 19 P14 Uriage France
- 111 J10 Uriah Alabama U.S.A.
- 144 C5 Urik, Mt New Zealand
- 127 H9 Uribia Colombia
- 103 H3 Urk Missouri U.S.A.
- 124 F4 Urique Mexico
- 41 H4 Uri Rothstock mt Switzerland
- 41 J4 Uri Switzerland
- Urla see Uri
- 78 F1 Ünye Turkey
- 124 F4 Urique Mexico
- 138 E2 Urla Turkey
- 141 N6 Urma,L see Orümíyeh, Daryächeh-ye I
- 36 F5 Urmia,L see Orümíyeh, Daryächeh-ye I
- 55 G3 Urmany Russian Federation
- 52 G6 Urmston England
- 13 G5 Uruana Brazil
- 127 H9 Uribia Colombia
- 110 B3 Urki Missouri U.S.A.
- 101 P8 Uruana Brazil
- 124 E4 Uruapan del Progreso Mexico
- 130 B7 Urubamba Peru
- 130 C4 Urubu R Brazil
- 129 N10 Urucará Brazil
- 102 C5 Urucuia Venezuela
- 56 G7 Uruçuí Brazil
- 130 D10 Uruçuí Brazil
- 130 B3 Urucum Brazil
- 130 D10 Uruguaiana Brazil
- 130 C4 Uruguai,R S America
- 128 F5 Uruguay, R Argentina
- Urumäş Şughrä Syria
- Urümchi see Ürümqi
- 139 G6 Urunga New South Wales Australia
- 128 A3 Urupa R Brazil
- 130 K5 Urussu Russian Federation
- 130 D5 Urutägua Brazil
- 77 J3 Urüzgän reg Afghanistan
- 18 M3 Urville, I, d' Antarctica
- 114 J6 Urville-Nacqueville France
- 136 H2 Urville, Tg, D' C W Irian
- 60 P2 Uryü Japan
- 60 Q1 Uryü-ko L Japan
- 66 G8 Uryü-ko L Japan
- 57 J3 Urzhum Russian Federation
- 52 G6 Urziceni Romania
- 58 D6 Urzig Germany
- 32 G9 Urzy France
- 60 E12 Usa Japan
- 60 E10 Usa Russian Federation
- 78 A3 Usak Turkey
- 87 C10 Usakos Namibia
- 132 J2 Usarin Brazil
- 146 C13 Usarp Mts Antarctica
- 13 D4 Usborne hill Falkland Is
- 12 G7 Useless Loop W Australia Australia
- 80 D2 Ush Israel
- 116 L7 Ushagat I Alaska U.S.A.
- 103 G1 Ushakova, Ostrova isld Russian Federation
- 56 E6 Ushakovo Russian Federation
- Ushant see Ouessant, I. d'
- 56 E6 Ushi-Bel'dir Russian Federation
- 48 G7 Ushitsa R Ukraine
- 90 D12 Ushuaia airport Argentina
- 55 G4 Ushuaia Kazakhstan
- 57 D12 Ushtobe Kazakhstan
- 52 D12 Ushtogay Kazakhstan
- 80 F10 Ushumun Russian Federation
- 55 C3 Usina Brazil
- 8 C2 Usk R Wales
- 37 J2 Usk Wales
- 36 D6 Uslar Germany
- 100 L4 Uslar France
- 56 J5 Usolka R Russian Federation
- 100 C1 Usol'ye Russian Federation
- Usol'ye see Union of Soviet Socialist Republics
- U.S.S.R. see Union of Soviet Socialist Republics

Column 7

- 55 C4 Urazmetova Russian Federation
- 52 G6 Urazovka Russian Federation
- 54 K6 Urazovo Russian Federation
- 99 S9 Urbana Illinois U.S.A.
- 94 B6 Urbana Indiana U.S.A.
- 110 C4 Urbana Missouri U.S.A.
- 94 D6 Urbana Ohio U.S.A.
- 94 J9 Urbana Virginia U.S.A.
- 95 L9 Urbanna Virginia U.S.A.
- 129 K4 Urbano Santos Brazil
- 15 F1 Urbino Italy
- 22 F5 Urcel France
- 22 F5 Urcos Peru
- 18 E10 Urdos France
- 57 K2 Urdzhar Kazakhstan

(The remaining lower entries of Column 7 are continuous with Column 6 above and the U.S.S.R. / Union of Soviet Socialist Republics cross-references at the foot of the page.)

59 K2 **Ussuri** *R* Russian Federation
59 K3 **Ussuriysk** Russian Federation
21 K4 **Ussy** France
52 G6 **Usta** *R* Russian Federation
56 D5 **Ust'-Abakan** Russian Federation
52 G4 **Ust' Alekseyevo** Russian Federation
27 C11 **Ustaoset** Norway
53 G7 **Ust'-Aza** Russian Federation
55 D3 **Ust-Bagaryak** Russian Federation
56 B3 **Ust'-Bakchar** Russian Federation
52 H4 **Ust' Chernaya** Russian Federation
48 H2 **Ust-'Chorna** Ukraine
52 J5 **Ust' Dolgaya** Russian Federation
41 J3 **Uster** Switzerland
43 E10 **Ustica, I. di** Italy
56 F2 **Ust'Ilimsk** Russian Federation
56 F3 **Ust'-Ilimskoye Vodokhranilishche** *res* Russian Federation
52 J3 **Ust'-Ilych** Russian Federation
30 H5 **Usti'nad** Czechoslovakia
Ustinov *see* **Izhevsk**
55 F2 **Ust'-Ishim** Russian Federation
55 G3 **Ust'Izes** Russian Federation
31 K1 **Ustka** Poland
56 B6 **Ust'-Kamenogorsk** Kazakhstan
58 G1 **Ust'Karenga** Russian Federation
55 C4 **Ust'Katav** Russian Federation
58 E1 **Ust'-Kiran** Russian Federation
55 C3 **Ust Kishert** Russian Federation
52 H3 **Ust'Koin** Russian Federation
52 H4 **Ust'Kulom** Russian Federation
56 G3 **Ust'-Kut** Russian Federation
55 D2 **Ust' Loz'va** Russian Federation
52 C5 **Ust' Luga** Russian Federation
52 J2 **Ust' Lyzha** Russian Federation
51 N2 **Ust'Maya** Russian Federation
51 L3 **Ust-Muya** Russian Federation
52 H4 **Ust'Nem** Russian Federation
59 K1 **Ust'Niman** Russian Federation
56 F4 **Ust'-Ordynskiy** Russian Federation
56 F4 **Ust'-Ordynskiy Buryatskiy Avtonomnyy Okrug** *dist* Russian Federation
46 G3 **Ustovo** Bulgaria
52 F4 **Ust' Paden'ga** Russian Federation
52 F3 **Ust' Pinega** Russian Federation
50 H2 **Ust'-Port** Russian Federation
52 F4 **Ust' Puya** Russian Federation
52 G4 **Ust' Reka** Russian Federation
31 O6 **Ustrzyki Dolne** Poland
52 D4 **Ust'Sara** Russian Federation
52 J3 **Ust'-Shchugor** Russian Federation
55 D1 **Ust'-Tapsuy** Russian Federation
55 F3 **Ust'Tara** Russian Federation
55 G3 **Ust'Tarka** Russian Federation
55 F3 **Ust' Tava** Russian Federation
52 H2 **Ust' Tsil'ma** Russian Federation
59 K1 **Ust'Tyrma** Russian Federation
56 F4 **Ust'-Uda** Russian Federation
52 J4 **Ust' Un'ya** Russian Federation
52 F3 **Ust'ura** Russian Federation
59 H1 **Ust'urov** Russian Federation
56 D5 **Ust' Us** Russian Federation
52 J2 **Ust' Usa** Russian Federation
55 D4 **Ust'-Uyskoye** Russian Federation
52 J3 **Ust'-Voya** Russian Federation
52 G3 **Ust' Vyyskaya** Russian Federation
52 F4 **Ust'ya** *R* Russian Federation
52 E5 **Ust'ye** Russian Federation
52 E6 **Ust'ye** *R* Russian Federation
50 E4 **Ustyurt,Plato** Kazakhstan/Uzbekistan
52 E5 **Ustyuzhna** Russian Federation
66 C3 **Usu** China
71 L10 **Usu** *isld* Indonesia
60 E12 **Usuki** Japan
125 P11 **Usulután** El Salvador
125 O9 **Usumacinta** *R* Mexico
70 D3 **Usun Apau Plateau** Sarawak
89 G6 **Usutu** *R* Swaziland
52 D6 **Usvyaty** Russian Federation
71 B2 **Uta** *isld* Indonesia
103 M2 **Utah** *state* U.S.A.
103 N1 **Utah L** Utah U.S.A.
29 M7 **Utajärvi** Finland
71 H9 **Utan** Indonesia
60 Q2 **Utashinai** Japan
79 G5 **Utaybah, Buḥayrat al** *L* Syria
99 L7 **Ute** Iowa U.S.A.
17 G3 **Utebo** Spain
106 G6 **Ute Cr** New Mexico U.S.A.
88 G6 **Utenge,L** Tanzania
106 E5 **Ute Park** New Mexico U.S.A.
37 P4 **Uterý** Czechoslovakia
55 G4 **Utes** Kazakhstan
88 G6 **Utete** Tanzania
68 D5 **U Thai Thani** Thailand
77 K7 **Uthal** Pakistan
32 J6 **Uthlede** Germany
79 H4 **'Uthmānīyah** Syria
68 G5 **Uthumphon Phisai** Thailand
129 G6 **Utiariti** Brazil
107 K3 **Utica** Kansas U.S.A.
94 D4 **Utica** Michigan U.S.A.
99 P6 **Utica** Minnesota U.S.A.
111 F9 **Utica** Mississippi U.S.A.
110 C2 **Utica** Missouri U.S.A.
101 P3 **Utica** Montana U.S.A.
98 J9 **Utica** Nebraska U.S.A.
95 M3 **Utica** New York U.S.A.
94 E6 **Utica** Ohio U.S.A.
17 G5 **Utiel** Spain
26 K7 **Utifällan** Sweden
119 W3 **Utik L** Manitoba Canada
145 E3 **Utiku** New Zealand
118 B3 **Utikuma L** Alberta Canada
27 H16 **Utklippan** *isld* Sweden
27 C10 **Utla** *R* Norway
27 H15 **Utlängan** *isld* Sweden
109 K5 **Utley** Texas U.S.A.
106 G4 **Utleyville** Colorado U.S.A.
74 D1 **Utmanzai** Pakistan
27 M12 **Utö** *lighthouse* Finland
27 K13 **Utö** Sweden
140 C5 **Utopia** N Terr Australia
109 H6 **Utopia** Texas U.S.A.
75 K5 **Utraula** India
25 D4 **Utrecht** Netherlands
89 G6 **Utrecht** S Africa
16 D7 **Utrera** Spain
27 A12 **Utsira** *lighthouse* Norway
29 N2 **Utsjoki** Finland
61 N9 **Utsunomiya** Japan
53 G10 **Utta** Russian Federation
68 E4 **Uttaradit** Thailand
74 H4 **Uttar Pradesh** *prov* India
27 H12 **Uttersberg** Sweden
28 G7 **Utterslev** Denmark
36 H4 **Üttingen** Germany
9 E2 **Uttoxeter** England
116 G2 **Utukok** *R* Alaska U.S.A.
137 O4 **Utupua** *isld* Santa Cruz Is
55 B5 **Utva** *R* Kazakhstan
37 O3 **Útvina** Czechoslovakia
52 H6 **Utyashkino** Russian Federation
32 M8 **Utze** Germany
33 S5 **Utzedel** Germany
29 O10 **Uukuniem** Finland
Uummannaq *see* **Dundas**
115 O3 **Uummannaq** Greenland
Uummannarsuaq Greenland *see* **Farvel,Kap**
29 L9 **Uurainen** Finland
56 D5 **Üüreg Nuur** *L* Mongolia
Uusikaarlepyy *see* **Nykarleby**
29 J11 **Uusikaupunki** Finland
29 L11 **Uusimaa** *prov* Finland
52 H6 **Uva** Russian Federation
48 F7 **Uvac** *R* Serbia Yugoslavia
103 K2 **Uvada** Nevada U.S.A.
128 D3 **Uva, L** Colombia
112 E5 **Uvalda** Georgia U.S.A.
108 H6 **Uvalde** Texas U.S.A.
54 B4 **Uvarovichi** Belorussia
52 E6 **Uvarovka** Russian Federation
55 E2 **Uvat** Russian Federation
137 O6 **Uvéa** *isld* Îles Loyauté Pacific Oc
137 R4 **Uvea** *isld* Îles Wallis Pacific Oc
55 D4 **Uvel'skiy** Russian Federation
55 D3 **Uvil'dy, Oz** *L* Russian Federation
88 C4 **Uvinza** Tanzania
88 B3 **Uvira** Zaire
60 E13 **Uwae** Japan
60 F12 **Uwajima** Japan
84 H5 **Uweinat,Jebel** *mt* Sudan
135 V5 **Uwekahuna** Hawaiian Is
69 H12 **Uwi** *isld* Indonesia
121 L8 **Uxbridge** Ontario Canada
9 F4 **Uxbridge** England
65 A5 **Uxin Ju** China
125 P7 **Uxmal** Mexico
55 D4 **Uy** *R* Kazakhstan/Rus Fed
116 K8 **Uyak B** Alaska U.S.A.
51 O2 **Uyandina** *R* Russian Federation
56 D3 **Uyar** Russian Federation
15 G1 **Uyea** *isld* Scotland
15 G1 **Uyeasound** Scotland
50 H1 **Uyedineniya,Ostrov** *isld* Russian Federation
52 H2 **Uyeg** Russian Federation
47 K8 **Uyluk Tepe** *mt* Turkey
85 F7 **Uyo** Nigeria
47 K6 **Uysal Dağı** *mt* Turkey
55 D4 **Uyskoye** Russian Federation
57 F3 **Uyuk** Kazakhstan
133 D2 **Uyuni** Bolivia
48 G2 **Uz** *R* Czechoslovakia
57 B3 **Uzbekistan** *rep* C Asia
Uzbekskaya S.S.R. *see* **Uzbekistan**
48 F5 **Uzdin** Serbia Yugoslavia
20 E5 **Uzel** France
53 G8 **Uzen', Malyy** *R* Kazakhstan/Rus Fed
57 G4 **Uzgen** Kyrgyzstan
48 G2 **Uzh** *R* Ukraine
48 G2 **Uzhgorod** Ukraine
56 C3 **Uzhur** Russian Federation
48 F7 **Užice** Serbia Yugoslavia
41 J3 **Uznach** Switzerland
52 F6 **Uzola** *R* Russian Federation
47 N10 **Uzümce** Turkey
47 K8 **Üzümlü** Turkey
47 H6 **Uzun** *isld* Turkey
88 E6 **Uzungwa** Tanzania
47 H3 **Uzunköprü** Turkey
57 B3 **Uzynkair** Kazakhstan

V

29 M9 **Vaajakoski** Finland
89 E6 **Vaal** *R* S Africa
29 M7 **Vaala** Finland
89 F6 **Vaal Dam** S Africa
29 N11 **Vaalimaa** Finland
87 E10 **Vaalwater** S Africa
29 M8 **Vaaraslahti** Finland
21 L6 **Vaas** France
29 J8 **Vaasa** Finland
25 E4 **Vaassen** Netherlands
29 L4 **Vaattojärvi** Finland
28 H7 **Våbensted** Denmark
57 C5 **Vabkent** Uzbekistan
130 C7 **Vacaria,R** Brazil
130 C7 **Vacaria,Sa** *mts* Brazil
131 B4 **Vacas,Pta De** Argentina
102 B3 **Vacaville** California U.S.A.
19 N17 **Vaccarès, Etang de** *L* France
52 F6 **Vacha** Russian Federation
126 H5 **Vache, Île-à-** Haiti
40 E5 **Vacheresse** France
19 N16 **Vacqueyras** France
52 F6 **Vad** Russian Federation
100 C3 **Vader** Washington U.S.A.
27 A10 **Vadheim** Norway
76 A3 **Vādi** India
42 G5 **Vadice** Croatia
106 E5 **Vadito** New Mexico U.S.A.
27 B12 **Vadla** Norway
44 D3 **Vado** Italy
44 D3 **Vado, C. di** Italy
74 E7 **Vadodara** India
124 F2 **Vado de Santa María** Mexico
52 D1 **Vadozero, Oz** *L* Russian Federation
26 R1 **Vadsö** Norway
27 G13 **Vadstenna** Sweden
48 M6 **Vadu** Romania
28 D2 **Vadum** Denmark
41 L3 **Vaduz** Liechtenstein
26 K3 **Vadvetjåkko Nat. Park** Sweden
28 H7 **Væggerløse** Denmark
29 K5 **Værløse** Denmark
26 F4 **Vaeröy** Norway
28 G5 **Værslev** Denmark
52 F4 **Vaga** *R* Russian Federation
26 J9 **Vaga** Sweden
26 D10 **Vågåmo** Norway
26 G3 **Vagan** Norway
42 G4 **Vaganski** *mt* Croatia
6 F1 **Vágar** *isld* Faeroes
55 E2 **Vagay** Russian Federation
Vağda *see* **Erdemh**
29 O2 **Vaggetem** Russian Federation
26 R2 **Vaggetem-javrre** *L* Norway
45 K4 **Vaglia** Italy
27 J13 **Vagnahärad** Sweden
16 B4 **Vagos** Portugal
27 F11 **Vägsjöfors** Sweden
26 A10 **Vågsöy** *isld* Norway
31 L6 **Váh** *R* Czechoslovakia
29 J8 **Vähäkyrö** Finland
79 F8 **Vahal** Israel
111 G8 **Vaiden** Mississippi U.S.A.
21 K5 **Vaiges** France
36 F6 **Vaihingen** Germany
76 B1 **Vaijapur** India
52 C5 **Väike-Maarja** Estonia
26 L5 **Vaikijaur** Sweden
103 O9 **Vail** Arizona U.S.A.
106 D2 **Vail** Colorado U.S.A.
15 G2 **Vaila** *isld* Scotland
22 F5 **Vailly-sur-Aisne** France
134 B1 **Vailoa** Western Samoa
29 N11 **Vainikkala** Finland
45 Q7 **Vairano Patenora** Italy
20 G8 **Vairé** France
137 Q3 **Vaitupu** *isld* Tuvalu
46 F2 **Vakarel** Bulgaria
27 G11 **Vakern** Sweden
56 B1 **Vakh** *R* Russian Federation
57 F6 **Vakhanskiy Khrebet** *mts* Tajikistan
57 E5 **Vakhsh** Tajikistan
57 E5 **Vakhsh** *R* Tajikistan
57 E5 **Vakhshstroy** Tajikistan
52 G5 **Vakhtan** Russian Federation
52 D3 **Vaknavolok** Russian Federation
27 A11 **Vaksdal** Norway
83 L10 **Valachchenai** Sri Lanka
26 F8 **Vålådalen** Sweden
40 F5 **Valais** *canton* Switzerland
52 H5 **Valamaz** Russian Federation
46 F3 **Valandovo** Macedonia Yugoslavia
20 E4 **Val André, le** France
21 J7 **Valanjou** France
27 G12 **Valåsen** Sweden
95 O4 **Valatie** New York U.S.A.
46 G6 **Valáxa** *isld* Greece
38 E8 **Val Badia** Italy
121 P6 **Val Barrette** Quebec Canada
26 G3 **Valberg** Norway
19 P15 **Valbonnais** France
122 E5 **Val Brilliant** Quebec Canada
25 E5 **Valburg** Netherlands
133 D6 **Valcheta** Argentina
121 S7 **Valcourt** Quebec Canada
41 O6 **Valdagno** Italy
16 D2 **Valdavia** *R* Spain
52 D5 **Valday** Russian Federation
52 D6 **Valdayskaya Vozvyshennost'** *uplands* Russian Federation
17 G4 **Valde Algorfa** Spain
16 D5 **Valdecañas, Embalse de** *res* Spain
17 F5 **Valdeganga** Spain
21 P4 **Val-de-Marne** *dept* France
52 B6 **Valdemārpils** Latvia
27 J13 **Valdemarsvik** Sweden
16 E4 **Valdemoro** Spain
17 F4 **Valdemoro-Sierra** Spain
16 C2 **Valdeorras, El Barco de** Spain
16 E6 **Valdepeñas** Spain
16 D3 **Valderaduey** *R* Spain
17 H4 **Valderrobres** Spain
99 T5 **Valders** Wisconsin U.S.A.
121 P7 **Val des Bois** Quebec Canada
112 F2 **Valdese** North Carolina U.S.A.
133 E6 **Valdés, Pen** Argentina
116 O6 **Valdez** Alaska U.S.A.
106 F4 **Valdez** Colorado U.S.A.
41 M5 **Valdidentro** Italy
131 A7 **Valdivia** Chile
131 A8 **Valdivia** *prov* Chile
20 H5 **Val-d'Izé** France
21 O3 **Val-d'Oise** *dept* France
121 N4 **Val-d'Or** Quebec Canada
113 D7 **Valdosta** Georgia U.S.A.
27 D11 **Valdres** *plateau* Norway
19 P16 **Valdrome** France
20 E3 **Vale** Channel Is
100 H6 **Vale** Oregon U.S.A.
98 C5 **Vale** South Dakota U.S.A.
48 G5 **Valea Bistrei** Romania
48 G3 **Valea Lui Mihai** Romania
48 J3 **Valea Vişeului** Romania
37 P3 **Valeč** Czechoslovakia
45 J1 **Valéggio** Italy
129 L6 **Valença** Brazil
21 O7 **Valençay** France
19 N15 **Valence** France
18 F8 **Valence d'Agen** France
18 F9 **Valence-sur-Baïse** France
17 G5 **Valencia** *prov* Spain
17 G5 **Valencia** Spain
127 K9 **Valencia** Venezuela
16 C5 **Valência de Alcantara** Spain
16 D2 **Valencia de Don Juan** Spain
16 B3 **Valençia do Minho** Portugal
17 H5 **Valencia,G de** Spain
14 A5 **Valencia I** Ireland
127 L9 **Valencia,L.de** Venezuela
22 F3 **Valenciennes** France
19 P17 **Valensole** France
59 K3 **Valentin** Russian Federation
103 L6 **Valentine** Arizona U.S.A.
111 F12 **Valentine** Louisiana U.S.A.
101 R2 **Valentine** Montana U.S.A.
98 F7 **Valentine** Nebraska U.S.A.
108 C5 **Valentine** Texas U.S.A.
44 E1 **Valenza** Italy
27 E11 **Våler** Norway
109 H4 **Valera** Texas U.S.A.
127 J10 **Valera** Venezuela
27 A12 **Valestrand** Norway
130 H5 **Vale Verde** Brazil
41 M4 **Valfurva** *R* Italy
52 C5 **Valga** Estonia
120 K4 **Val Gagné** Ontario Canada
43 F11 **Valguarnera Caropepe** Sicily
6 N6 **Valhall** *oil rig* North Sea
7 M9 **Valiant** *gas field* North Sea
101 N1 **Valier** Montana U.S.A.
29 K4 **Välinge** Sweden
48 F6 **Valjevo** Serbia Yugoslavia
26 P2 **Valjok** Norway
19 Q15 **Valjouffrey** France
29 L10 **Valkeakoski** Finland
29 M11 **Valkeala** Finland
29 L5 **Valkeavaara** *mt* Finland
25 E7 **Valkenburg** Netherlands
25 D6 **Valkenswaard** Netherlands
54 G7 **Valki** Ukraine
Valko *see* **Valkom**
29 M11 **Valkom** Finland
146 G8 **Valkyrjedomen** *ice dome* Antarctica
19 N17 **Vallabrègues** France
16 D3 **Valladolid** *prov* Spain
16 D3 **Valladolid** Spain
121 N4 **Val Laflamme** Quebec Canada
41 P4 **Vallarga** Italy
41 O6 **Vallarsa** *R* Italy
27 C12 **Valle** Norway
103 M6 **Valle** Arizona U.S.A.
38 E7 **Valle Aurina** Italy
106 C4 **Vallecito Res** Colorado U.S.A.
106 D5 **Vallecitos** New Mexico U.S.A.
45 O7 **Vallecorsa** Italy
131 B2 **Valle Cura,Rio Del** Argentina
40 G6 **Valle d'Aosta** *aut reg* Italy
42 A3 **Valle d'Aosta** Italy
124 G7 **Valle de Banderas** Mexico
16 E1 **Valle de Cabuérniga** Spain
127 M10 **Valle de la Pascua** Venezuela
128 C3 **Valle del Cauca** *div* Colombia
124 F4 **Valle de Olivos** Mexico
124 F4 **Valle de Rosario** Mexico
124 G4 **Valle de Zaragoza** Mexico
126 H9 **Valledupar** Colombia
85 E5 **Vallée de Zgarat** Mali
122 B7 **Vallée Jonction** Quebec Canada
85 E5 **Vallée L'Azawak** Mali/Niger
131 C3 **Valle Fértil, Sa. de** *mts* Argentina
128 F7 **Valle Grande** Bolivia
40 C5 **Valleiry** France
102 B3 **Vallejo** California U.S.A.
45 P7 **Vallemaio** Italy
40 H6 **Valle Mosso** Italy
26 M7 **Vallen** Västerbotten Sweden
26 J8 **Vallen** Väster Norrland Sweden
131 B2 **Vallenar** Chile
36 D3 **Vallendar** Germany
28 H6 **Vallensved** Denmark
27 K12 **Vallentuna** Sweden
45 O6 **Vallepretra** Italy
133 E2 **Valle,R.del** Argentina
20 H7 **Vallet** France
43 F13 **Valletta** Malta
122 J8 **Valley** Nova Scotia Canada
111 F9 **Valley** Mississippi U.S.A.
98 K8 **Valley** Nebraska U.S.A.
100 H1 **Valley** Washington U.S.A.
101 Q5 **Valley** Wyoming U.S.A.
8 B1 **Valley** Wales
107 N4 **Valley Center** Kansas U.S.A.
118 K7 **Valley Centre** Saskatchewan Canada
98 J3 **Valley City** North Dakota U.S.A.
107 P2 **Valley Falls** Kansas U.S.A.
100 E7 **Valley Falls** Oregon U.S.A.
121 Q7 **Valleyfield** Quebec Canada
111 L7 **Valley Head** Alabama U.S.A.
94 G8 **Valley Head** West Virginia U.S.A.
109 K4 **Valley Mills** Texas U.S.A.
116 K7 **Valley of Ten Thousand Smokes** Alaska U.S.A.
110 F3 **Valley Park** Missouri U.S.A.
101 L8 **Valley Pass** Nevada U.S.A.
94 B8 **Valley Sta** Kentucky U.S.A.
117 P8 **Valleyview** Alberta Canada
109 K2 **Valley View** Texas U.S.A.
Vallgrund, isld *see* **Raippaluoto**
109 M2 **Valliant** Oklahoma U.S.A.
45 M2 **Valli di Comacchio** *reg* Italy
18 F10 **Vallier, Mt** France
121 P6 **Val Limoges** Quebec Canada
21 M2 **Valliquerville** France
28 J6 **Valløby** Denmark
43 G8 **Vallo di Diano** Italy
43 G8 **Vallo di Lucania** Italy
45 L4 **Vallombrosa** Italy
94 A8 **Vallonia** Indiana U.S.A.
21 K6 **Vallon-sur-Gée** France
40 D4 **Vallorbe** Switzerland
27 D12 **Vallöy** Norway
17 H3 **Valls** Spain
27 H10 **Vallsta** Sweden
41 M3 **Valluga** *mt* Austria
27 J10 **Vallvik** Sweden
118 K9 **Val Marie** Saskatchewan Canada
16 E1 **Valmaseda** Spain
31 K6 **Val. Meziříčí** Czechoslovakia
52 C5 **Valmiera** Latvia
21 P3 **Valmondois** France
21 M2 **Valmont** France
106 E9 **Valmont** New Mexico U.S.A.
45 N6 **Valmontone** Italy
100 H9 **Valmy** Nevada U.S.A.
16 E1 **Valnera** *mt* Spain
20 H2 **Valognes** France
Valona *see* **Vlorë**
16 D3 **Valoria la Buena** Spain
16 C3 **Valpaços** Portugal
76 C5 **Valparai** India
119 N6 **Valparaiso** Saskatchewan Canada
131 B4 **Valparaíso** *prov* Chile
131 B4 **Valparaíso** Chile
124 H6 **Valparaíso** Mexico
111 K11 **Valparaiso** Florida U.S.A.
99 T8 **Valparaiso** Indiana U.S.A.
98 K8 **Valparaiso** Nebraska U.S.A.
40 F6 **Valpelline** *V* Italy
48 E5 **Valpovo** Croatia
40 G7 **Valprato Soana** Italy
122 A8 **Val-Racine** Quebec Canada
19 N16 **Valréas** France
89 E6 **Vals** *R* S Africa
74 E8 **Valsād** India
28 H7 **Vålse** Denmark
100 B5 **Valsetz** Oregon U.S.A.
28 D3 **Valsgård** Denmark
26 G7 **Valsjö** Sweden
27 H12 **Valskog** Sweden
29 J8 **Valsörarna** *lighthouse* Finland
41 L5 **Valtellina** *V* Italy
29 T9 **Valthjofsstadhur** Iceland
45 M4 **Val Tiberina** Italy
29 O8 **Valtimo** Finland
83 M12 **Valton** Mauritius
54 K6 **Valuyki** Russian Federation
85 A3 **Valverde** Canary Is
127 J5 **Valverde** Dominican Rep
17 F5 **Valverde de Júcar** Spain
16 C7 **Valverde del Camino** Spain
26 M5 **Valvträsk** Sweden
48 K3 **Vama** Romania
28 C6 **Vamdrup** Denmark
27 G10 **Våmhus** Sweden
88 H7 **Vamizi** *isld* Mozambique
27 E12 **Vamma** Norway
29 K10 **Vammala** Finland
46 G9 **Vámos** Crete Greece
48 G3 **Vámospéros** Hungary
78 J2 **Van** Turkey
109 M3 **Van** Texas U.S.A.
29 L10 **Vanajanselka** *L* Finland
109 L2 **Van Alstyne** Texas U.S.A.
101 S3 **Vananda** Montana U.S.A.
56 F1 **Vanavara** Russian Federation
68 G1 **Van-Ban** Vietnam
121 S5 **Van Bruyssel** Quebec Canada
110 B6 **Van Buren** Arkansas U.S.A.
94 B6 **Van Buren** Indiana U.S.A.
95 T6 **Van Buren** Maine U.S.A.
110 F5 **Van Buren** Missouri U.S.A.
68 J6 **Van Canh** Vietnam
22 K4 **Vance** Belgium
21 M6 **Vancé** France
112 K2 **Vanceboro** North Carolina U.S.A.
94 D8 **Vanceburg** Kentucky U.S.A.
68 G2 **Van Chan** Vietnam
57 F5 **Vanchskiy Khrebet** *mts* Tajikistan/Afghanistan
117 G11 **Vancouver** British Columbia Canada
100 C4 **Vancouver** Washington U.S.A.
143 C10 **Vancouver,C** W Australia Australia
116 E6 **Vancouver, C** Alaska U.S.A.
117 K10 **Vancouver I** British Columbia Canada
117 D5 **Vancouver, Mt** Alaska/Yukon Terr U.S.A./Canada
110 G3 **Vandalia** Illinois U.S.A.
110 E2 **Vandalia** Missouri U.S.A.
41 L3 **Vandans** Austria
28 A3 **Vandborg** Denmark
119 Q1 **Vandekerckhove** Saskatchewan Canada
28 C5 **Vandel** Denmark
112 L2 **Vandemere** North Carolina U.S.A.
89 E6 **Vanderbijl Pk** S Africa
94 C1 **Vanderbilt** Michigan U.S.A.
109 L7 **Vanderbilt** Texas U.S.A.
94 H6 **Vandergrift** Pennsylvania U.S.A.
117 M8 **Vanderhoof** British Columbia Canada
140 D3 **Vanderlin I** N Terr Australia
109 N1 **Vandervoort** Arkansas U.S.A.
106 B6 **Vanderwagen** New Mexico U.S.A.
28 B2 **Vandet Sø** *L* Denmark
140 B1 **Van Dieman, C** N Terr Australia
140 E3 **Van Diemen,C** Queensland Australia
140 B1 **Van Diemen G** N Terr Australia
55 E1 **Vandmtor, Oz** *L* Russian Federation
121 R5 **Vandry** Quebec Canada
110 G5 **Vanduser** Missouri U.S.A.
100 A9 **Van Duzen** *R* California U.S.A.
27 F13 **Vänern** *L* Sweden
27 F13 **Vänersborg** Sweden
95 L4 **Van Etten** New York U.S.A.
27 C10 **Vang** Norway
88 G4 **Vanga** Tanzania
87 H12 **Vangaindrano** Madagascar
27 F13 **Vanga,N** Sweden
78 J2 **Van Gölü** *L* Turkey
27 C10 **Vangsmjösa** Norway
118 K9 **Vanguard** Saskatchewan Canada
70 A1 **Vanguard Bank** S China Sea
137 M3 **Vangunu** *isld* Solomon Is
68 F3 **Vang Vieng** Laos
98 D2 **Van Hook** North Dakota U.S.A.
108 C4 **Van Horn** Texas U.S.A.
106 F5 **Van Houten** New Mexico U.S.A.
137 O4 **Vanikoro Is** Santa Cruz Is
26 K7 **Vänjaurbäck** Sweden
26 K7 **Vänjaurträsk** Sweden
51 S2 **Vankarem** Russian Federation
121 Q7 **Vankleek Hill** Ontario Canada
98 F5 **Van Metre** South Dakota U.S.A.
26 L1 **Vanna** *isld* Norway
26 L8 **Vännäs** Sweden
83 J9 **Vannativillu** Sri Lanka
20 E6 **Vannes** France
21 P6 **Vannes-sur-Cosson** France
68 J6 **Van Ninh** Vietnam
57 F4 **Vannovka** Kazakhstan
107 O7 **Vanoss** Oklahoma U.S.A.
87 C12 **Vanrhynsdorp** S Africa
141 F3 **Vanrook** Queensland Australia
74 E8 **Vānsada** India
94 E9 **Vansant** Virginia U.S.A.
27 G11 **Vansbro** Sweden
118 L6 **Vanscoy** Saskatchewan Canada
142 F2 **Vansittart B** W Australia Australia
115 L4 **Vansittart I** Northwest Territories Canada
18 H8 **Vans, les** France
29 L11 **Vantaa** *R* Finland
29 L11 **Vantaa** Finland
118 L9 **Vantage** Saskatchewan Canada
100 F3 **Vantage** Washington U.S.A.
98 B7 **Van Tassell** Wyoming U.S.A.
137 O3 **Vanua Lava** *isld* Vanuatu
137 Q5 **Vanua Levu** *isld* Fiji
137 O5 **Vanuatu** *islds* Pacific Oc
99 N9 **Van Wert** Iowa U.S.A.
94 C6 **Van Wert** Ohio U.S.A.
87 D12 **Vanwyksvlei** S Africa
67 A6 **Van Yen** Vietnam
26 A9 **Vanylven** Norway
26 A9 **Vanylvsgapet** *B* Norway
110 D5 **Vanzant** Missouri U.S.A.
48 M2 **Vapnyarka** Ukraine
19 Q18 **Var** *dept* France
44 B4 **Var** *R* France
44 G3 **Vara** *R* Italy
27 F13 **Vara** Sweden
126 D3 **Varadero** Cuba
21 H7 **Varades** France
19 P17 **Varages** France
44 B2 **Varaita** *R* Italy
41 H6 **Varallo** Italy
42 B3 **Varallo** Italy
77 B2 **Varamin** Iran
75 K6 **Varanasi** India
26 R1 **Varangerfjorden** *inlet* Norway
26 R1 **Varangerhalvöya** *mt* Norway
42 G7 **Varano, L. di** Italy
131 A8 **Varas,Pto** Chile
16 D6 **Varas,R** Spain
21 K3 **Varaville** France
44 E3 **Varazze** Italy
27 F14 **Varberg** Sweden
77 L2 **Vardak** *prov* Afghanistan
111 G8 **Vardaman** Mississippi U.S.A.
46 E6 **Vardhoúsia Óri** *mt* Greece
27 L11 **Vårdö** Finland
26 S1 **Vardö** Norway
52 E5 **Varegovo** Russian Federation
32 H6 **Varel** Germany
21 M2 **Varengeville** France
20 G3 **Varenguebec** France
21 J4 **Varenne** *R* France
19 J3 **Varennes en Argonne** France
40 B5 **Varennes St.Sauveur** France
21 O7 **Varennes-sur-Fouzon** France
48 E6 **Vareš** Bosnia-Herzegovina
41 J6 **Varese** Italy
40 A7 **Vareze** *R* France
27 F13 **Vårgårda** Sweden
55 E3 **Vargashi** Russian Federation
130 G10 **Vargem** *R* Brazil
130 F7 **Varginha** Brazil
18 G9 **Varilhes** France
112 J2 **Varina** North Carolina U.S.A.
27 G13 **Väring** Sweden
21 O5 **Varize** France
26 K5 **Varjisträsk** Sweden
29 N9 **Varkaus** Finland
143 C10 **Varley,L** W Australia Australia
27 F12 **Varmland** *reg* Sweden
27 F12 **Värmlands-näs** *pen* Sweden
47 J1 **Varna** Bulgaria
55 D4 **Varna** Russian Federation
111 G11 **Varnado** Louisiana U.S.A.
28 D6 **Varnæs** Denmark
27 G14 **Vårnamo** Sweden
27 F11 **Värnäs** Sweden
52 F5 **Varnavino** Russian Federation
108 B1 **Varney** New Mexico U.S.A.
31 H5 **Varnsdorf** Czechoslovakia
27 F14 **Varnum** Sweden
112 F5 **Varnville** South Carolina U.S.A.
79 D3 **Varosha** Cyprus
48 D3 **Városlöd** Hungary
48 E3 **Várpalota** Hungary
52 G2 **Varsh, Oz** *L* Russian Federation
28 E3 **Vårst** Denmark
78 H2 **Varto** Turkey
27 G13 **Vartofta** Sweden
83 K9 **Varuniya** Sri Lanka
46 E7 **Varvára** *mt* Greece
46 E1 **Varvarin** Serbia Yugoslavia
54 C10 **Varvarovka** Ukraine
130 G9 **Várzea Alegre** Brazil
130 G5 **Várzea da Palma** Brazil
129 G7 **Várzea Grande** Brazil
130 E9 **Várzea,R** Brazil
52 E1 **Varzino** Russian Federation
52 E2 **Varzuga** *R* Russian Federation
52 E2 **Varzuga** Russian Federation
18 H5 **Varzy** France
48 D3 **Vas** *co* Hungary
130 H11 **Vasa Barris,R** Brazil
76 A1 **Vasai** India
52 B5 **Vasalemma** Estonia
48 G2 **Vásárosnamény** Hungary
29 K4 **Väsby** Sweden
16 B7 **Vascão** *R* Portugal
48 G4 **Vaşcău** Romania
21 N3 **Vascœuil** France
52 G3 **Vashka** *R* Russian Federation
48 K2 **Vashkovtsy** Ukraine
100 C2 **Vashon I** Washington U.S.A.
98 G2 **Vashti** North Dakota U.S.A.
109 J2 **Vashti** Texas U.S.A.
54 H8 **Vasil'kovka** Ukraine
52 G3 **Vasil'yevo** Russian Federation
52 G6 **Vasil'yevo** Russian Federation
55 F2 **Vasis** Russian Federation
29 P11 **Vaskelovo** Russian Federation
52 C5 **Vasknarva** Estonia
29 M3 **Vaskojoki** *R* Finland
48 E4 **Vaskút** Hungary
21 K8 **Vasles** France
48 L4 **Vaslui** Romania
112 H2 **Vass** North Carolina U.S.A.
118 F1 **Vassar** Manitoba Canada
94 D3 **Vassar** Michigan U.S.A.
27 B12 **Vassdalseggja** *mt* Norway
26 K3 **Vassijuare** Sweden
21 J4 **Vassy** Calvados France
26 J4 **Vastenjaure** *L* Sweden
27 J12 **Västerås** Sweden
26 H7 **Västerbotten** *reg* Sweden
27 F11 **Vasterdalälven** *R* Sweden
26 J5 **Västerfjäll** Sweden
27 K12 **Västerhaninge** Sweden
27 H12 **Västermo** Sweden
26 J7 **Vastermyrriset** Sweden
26 J8 **Väster Norr Land** Sweden
27 J14 **Västervik** Sweden
27 J11 **Västland** Sweden
27 H12 **Västmanland** *reg* Sweden
42 F6 **Vasto** Italy
33 N6 **Vastorf** Germany
26 L8 **Vastra Kvarken** *chan* Sweden
48 D3 **Vasvár** Hungary
55 G2 **Vasyugan** *R* Russian Federation
21 O7 **Vatan** France
Vaté *isld* *see* **Éfaté** *isld*
33 P8 **Väthen** Germany
47 H7 **Vathí** Greece
46 E8 **Váthia** Greece
45 M6 **Vaticano, Citta del** Italy
28 S9 **Vatnajökull** *ice cap* Iceland
26 B9 **Vatne** Norway
28 R9 **Vatneyri** Iceland
27 K12 **Vätö** Sweden
137 R5 **Vatoa** *isld* Fiji
87 H11 **Vatomandry** Madagascar
48 J3 **Vatra Dornei** Romania
27 G13 **Vättern** *L* Sweden
27 J11 **Vattholma** Sweden
41 K4 **Vättis** Switzerland
26 J10 **Vattrång** Sweden
40 C5 **Vauche Marlioz,Mt.De** France
19 O17 **Vaucluse** *dept* France
112 F4 **Vaucluse** South Carolina U.S.A.
40 C2 **Vauconcourt** France
21 L2 **Vaucottes** France
19 J4 **Vaucouleurs** France
36 B6 **Vaucourt** France
40 D4 **Vaud** *canton* Switzerland
21 N3 **Vaudreuil, le** France
122 H9 **Vaughan** Nova Scotia Canada
140 B5 **Vaughan Springs** N Terr Australia
101 O2 **Vaughn** Montana U.S.A.
108 B1 **Vaughn** New Mexico U.S.A.
128 D3 **Vaupés** *div* Colombia
21 K8 **Vausseroux** France
18 H9 **Vauvert** France
20 G2 **Vauville** France
40 D2 **Vauvillers** France
118 E8 **Vauxhall** Alberta Canada
87 J11 **Vavatenina** Madagascar
137 S5 **Vava'u Group** *islds* Tonga
52 H6 **Vavozh** Russian Federation
83 K9 **Vavuniya** Sri Lanka
118 J5 **Vawn** Saskatchewan Canada
27 K12 **Vaxholm** Sweden
27 G15 **Växjö** Sweden
20 G6 **Vay** France
76 D4 **Vāyalpād** India
50 F1 **Vaygach, Ostrov** *isld* Russian Federation
52 F3 **Vaymuga** *R* Russian Federation
129 L5 **Vaza** *R* Brazil
130 F5 **Vazante** Brazil
52 G3 **Vazhgort** Russian Federation
54 F1 **Vazuzskoye Vodokhranilishche** *res* Russian Federation
129 J6 **Veadeiras** Brazil
68 F7 **Veal Renh** Cambodia
28 D3 **Vebbestrup** Denmark
27 F16 **Veberöd** Sweden
98 J4 **Veblen** South Dakota U.S.A.
26 M7 **Vebomark** Sweden
33 M8 **Vechelde** Germany
25 F3 **Vecht** *R* Netherlands
32 H7 **Vechta** *R* Germany
32 H7 **Vechta** Germany
32 L10 **Veckerhagen** Germany
29 K5 **Vedbæk** Denmark
27 F14 **Veddige** Sweden
28 E3 **Veddum** Denmark
48 J6 **Vedea** Romania
28 A4 **Vedersø** Denmark
27 H12 **Vedevåg** Sweden
133 E4 **Vedia** Argentina
17 H6 **Vedra** *isld* Balearic Is
22 H3 **Vedrin** Belgium
28 E5 **Vedslet** Denmark
28 C6 **Vedsted** Denmark
28 G6 **Ved Stranden** Denmark
27 F13 **Vedum** Sweden
110 J1 **Veedersburg** Indiana U.S.A.
25 G2 **Veendam** Netherlands
25 E4 **Veenendaal** Netherlands
25 F2 **Veenhuizen** Netherlands
25 E2 **Veenwouden** Netherlands
25 A5 **Veere** Netherlands
25 A5 **Veerse Meer** Netherlands
33 N7 **Veerssen** Germany
28 E6 **Veflinge** Denmark
26 E6 **Vega** *isld* Norway
16 C2 **Vega de Tera** Spain
27 D13 **Vegårs Vatn** *L* Norway
29 K4 **Vegeån** *R* Sweden
32 J6 **Vegesack** Germany
28 D3 **Veggerby** Denmark
27 D11 **Veggli** Norway
46 E4 **Vegorrítis, L** Greece
118 F5 **Vegreville** Alberta Canada
108 A1 **Veguita** New Mexico U.S.A.
33 Q6 **Vehlow** Germany
27 M11 **Vehmaa** Finland
26 P1 **Veidnes** Norway
27 F15 **Veinge** Sweden
120 D3 **Vein L** Ontario Canada
133 D5 **Veinticinco de Mayo** Argentina
45 M5 **Veio** Italy
36 H4 **Veitshöchheim** Germany
28 J4 **Vejby** Denmark
28 C6 **Vejen** Denmark
28 A5 **Vejers** Denmark
28 D4 **Vejerslev** Denmark
28 E2 **Vejgård** Denmark
28 E4 **Vejlby** Århus Denmark
28 D5 **Vejlby** Vejle Denmark
28 C5 **Vejle** *co* Denmark
28 D5 **Vejle** Denmark
28 D5 **Vejle Fjord** *inlet* Denmark
28 H6 **Vejlø** Denmark
28 E7 **Vejnæs Nokke** *C* Denmark
37 P3 **Vejprty** Czechoslovakia
28 G5 **Vejrhøj** *hill* Denmark
28 F5 **Vejrø** *isld* Århus Denmark
28 G6 **Vejrø** *isld* Storstrøm Denmark
28 B5 **Vejrup** Denmark
28 F6 **Vejstrup** Denmark
28 J5 **Veksø** Denmark
52 F4 **Vel** *R* Russian Federation
127 H8 **Vela, C. de la** Colombia
22 E2 **Velaines** Belgium
46 E5 **Velaóra** Greece
106 E5 **Velarde** New Mexico U.S.A.
124 H5 **Velardeña** Mexico
18 H7 **Velay, Mts du** France
32 F10 **Velbert** Germany
37 M5 **Velburg** Germany
37 M4 **Velden** Germany
25 D6 **Veldhoven** Netherlands
47 J2 **Veleka** *R* Bulgaria
32 E9 **Velen** Germany
48 E3 **Velencei Tó** *L* Hungary
42 G2 **Velenje** Slovenia
46 E3 **Veles** Macedonia Yugoslavia
46 F5 **Velestínon** Greece
17 F7 **Vélez Bianco** Spain
16 E8 **Vélez Málaga** Spain
17 F7 **Vélez Rubio** Spain
26 F6 **Velfjord** Norway
33 R4 **Velgast** Germany
130 G6 **Velhas,R** Brazil
42 H3 **Velika** Croatia
42 G3 **Velika Gorica** Croatia
48 G6 **Velika Gradište** Serbia Yugoslavia
42 F3 **Velika Kapela** *dist* Croatia
48 G6 **Velika Plana** Serbia Yugoslavia
52 G2 **Velikaya** Russian Federation
52 G5 **Velikaya** *R* Russian Federation
52 C6 **Velikaya** *R* Russian Federation
52 E4 **Velikaya Guba** Russian Federation
48 K1 **Veliki Borki** Ukraine
48 K1 **Veliki Glubochek** Ukraine
48 G2 **Velikiy Bereznyy** Ukraine
52 D6 **Velikiye-Luki** Russian Federation
52 G4 **Velikiy Ustyug** Russian Federation
54 M1 **Velikodvorskiy** Russian Federation
54 J6 **Velikomikhaylovka** Russian Federation
47 H1 **Veliko Turnovo** Bulgaria
52 H2 **Velikovisochnoye** Russian Federation
52 F5 **Velikovo** Russian Federation
54 M1 **Velikoye, Oz** *L* Russian Federation
85 B6 **Velingara** Senegal
46 F2 **Velingrad** Bulgaria
42 E6 **Velino** *R* Italy
42 E6 **Velino, M** *mt* Italy
54 C1 **Velizh** Russian Federation
48 E2 **Velká Fatra** *mt* Czechoslovakia
48 E1 **Vel Karlovice** Czechoslovakia
48 G2 **Vel'ké Kapušány** Czechoslovakia
31 L6 **Velké Karlovice** Czechoslovakia
48 D3 **Velký Žitný Ostrov'** *reg* Czechoslovakia
38 L8 **Vellach** Austria
33 N6 **Vellahn** Germany
137 M3 **Vella Lavella** *isld* Solomon Is
45 J4 **Vellano** Italy
36 H5 **Vellberg** Germany
21 O8 **Velles** France
45 N6 **Velletri** Italy
28 D4 **Vellev** Denmark
28 A4 **Velling** Denmark
27 F16 **Vellinge** Sweden
45 O5 **Vellino, M** *mt* Italy
76 D4 **Vellore** India
56 D1 **Vel'minskiye Porogi** *falls* Russian Federation
56 D1 **Vel'mo** *R* Russian Federation
22 J5 **Velosnes** France
25 E4 **Velp** Netherlands
25 C4 **Velsen** Netherlands
52 F4 **Vel'sk** Russian Federation
52 H1 **Vel't** Russian Federation
33 S7 **Velten** Germany
22 D3 **Vélu** France
25 E4 **Veluwe** Netherlands
25 E4 **Veluwemeer** Netherlands
98 F1 **Velva** North Dakota U.S.A.
52 J3 **Vel'yu** *R* Russian Federation
90 E7 **Vema Fracture** Atlantic Oc
28 A4 **Vemb** Denmark
26 G9 **Vemdalen** Sweden
28 G6 **Vemmelev** Denmark
28 F7 **Vemmenæs** Denmark
29 K5 **Ven** *isld* Sweden
27 H14 **Vena** Sweden
27 D10 **Venabygd** Norway
12 D1 **Venachar,L** Scotland
131 E4 **Venado Tuerto** Argentina
45 Q7 **Venafro** Italy
128 F2 **Venamo,Cerro** *mt* Venezuela/Guyana
98 E9 **Venango** Nebraska U.S.A.
44 C1 **Venaria** Italy
100 G6 **Venator** Oregon U.S.A.
44 B1 **Venáus** Italy
130 E8 **Venceslau Bráz** Brazil
Venda *see* **Vantaa**
45 L1 **Venda** *mt* Italy
89 G4 **Venda** *homeland* S Africa
16 B6 **Vendas Novas** Portugal
18 E6 **Vendée** *dept* France
52 G3 **Vendenga** Russian Federation
36 D6 **Vendenheim** France
22 D3 **Vendin-le-Viel** France
21 N6 **Vendôme** France
21 N8 **Vendœuvres** France
17 H3 **Vendrell** Spain
22 H4 **Vendresse** France
28 D2 **Vendsyssel** *reg* Denmark
45 M1 **Veneta, Laguna** Italy
116 P3 **Venetie Landing** Alaska U.S.A.
45 K1 **Veneto** *reg* Italy
52 F6 **Venets** Russian Federation
54 K2 **Venev** Russian Federation
45 M1 **Venezia** Italy
42 D3 **Venezia-Euganea** *prov* Italy
42 E3 **Venezia,G.di** Italy
128 E2 **Venezuela** *rep* S America
127 J9 **Venezuela,G.de** Venezuela
28 D4 **Veng** Denmark
55 G3 **Vengerovo** Russian Federation
76 A3 **Vengurla** India
16 D3 **Venialbo** Spain
116 H8 **Veniaminof Vol** Alaska U.S.A.
118 E4 **Venice** Alberta Canada
Venice Italy *see* **Venezia**
111 M12 **Venice** St Louis
113 E10 **Venice** Florida U.S.A.
111 G12 **Venice** Louisiana U.S.A.
19 N13 **Vénissieux** France
27 G11 **Venjan** Sweden
76 D4 **Venkataguri** India
76 E1 **Venkatapuram** India
25 F6 **Venlo** Netherlands
98 J3 **Venlo** North Dakota U.S.A.
119 M7 **Venn** Saskatchewan Canada
28 D2 **Vennebjerg** Denmark
32 E7 **Vennebrügge** Germany
27 C13 **Vennesla** Norway
28 B3 **Venø** Denmark
28 B3 **Venø Bugt** *B* Denmark
19 Q15 **Venosc** France
121 O7 **Venosta** Quebec Canada
41 N4 **Venosta, Val** Italy
41 N4 **Venostie, Alpi** Italy
25 E5 **Venray** Netherlands
27 M14 **Venta** *R* Latvia
124 E5 **Ventana,Pta de la** *C* Mexico
133 E5 **Ventana,Sa** *ra* Argentina
16 E8 **Ventas de Zafarraya** Spain
19 P16 **Ventavon** France
28 H5 **Vented** Denmark
44 C4 **Ventimiglia** Italy
9 E6 **Ventnor** England
43 E8 **Ventotene, I** Italy
19 O16 **Ventoux, Mt** France
33 P5 **Ventschow** Germany
27 M14 **Ventspils** Latvia
128 E3 **Ventuari** *R* Venezuela
102 E7 **Ventura** California U.S.A.
98 G3 **Venturia** North Dakota U.S.A.
113 F10 **Venus** Florida U.S.A.
109 K3 **Venus** Texas U.S.A.
138 C5 **Venus B** South Australia Australia
138 C5 **Venus Bay** South Australia Australia
124 H8 **Venustiano Carranza** Mexico
52 D4 **Vepsovskaya Vozvyshennost'** *uplands* Russian Federation
133 E3 **Vera** Argentina
17 F7 **Vera** Spain
109 H2 **Vera** Texas U.S.A.
133 D6 **Vera, B** Argentina
130 E8 **Vera Cruz** Brazil
125 L8 **Veracruz** Mexico
74 D8 **Veraval** India
42 B3 **Verbania** Italy

Verbena — Vivunki
237

111 K9 **Verbena** Alabama U.S.A.
22 D5 **Verberie** France
52 E6 **Verbilki** Russian Federation
41 H7 **Vercelli** Italy
33 R5 **Verchen** Germany
21 K7 **Verchers,les** France
19 O15 **Vercors** *reg* France
19 Q16 **Verdaches** France
26 E8 **Verdal** Norway
26 E8 **Verdalsöra** Norway
133 D6 **Verde** *R* Argentina
130 E4 **Verde** *R* Brazil
133 F2 **Verde** *R* Paraguay
71 E4 **Verde** *isld* Philippines
103 N7 **Verde** *R* Arizona U.S.A.
85 A6 **Verde, C** Senegal
126 G3 **Verde, Cay** *isld* Bahamas
130 G4 **Verde Grande** *R* Brazil
98 H7 **Verdel** Nebraska U.S.A.
32 K7 **Verden** Germany
109 J1 **Verden** Oklahoma U.S.A.
131 E7 **Verde,Pen** Argentina
130 G4 **Verde Pequeno, R** Brazil
130 D7 **Verde,R** Brazil
21 N6 **Verdes** France
98 H7 **Verdigre** Nebraska U.S.A.
107 O3 **Verdigris** *R* Okla/Kansas U.S.A.
118 F9 **Verdigris L** Alberta Canada
130 D5 **Verdinho,Sa.do** *mts* Brazil
19 Q17 **Verdon** *R* France
99 L9 **Verdon** Nebraska U.S.A.
18 E7 **Verdon-sur-Mer, le** France
19 J3 **Verdun** France
18 F9 **Verdun-sur-Garonne** France
19 J6 **Verdun-sur-le-Doubs** France
124 E5 **Verdura** Mexico
52 D6 **Verech'ye** Russian Federation
89 E6 **Vereeniging** S Africa
119 P7 **Veregin** Saskatchewan Canada
121 N5 **Vérendrye, Parc Prov. de la** Quebec Canada
52 H5 **Vereshchagino** Russian Federation
52 E5 **Verestovo, Oz** *L* Russian Federation
54 H1 **Vereya** Russian Federation
85 B6 **Verga,C** Guinea
17 F1 **Vergara** Spain
133 G4 **Vergara** Uruguay
45 K3 **Vergato** Italy
36 B6 **Vergaville** France
141 G6 **Vergemont** *R* Queensland Australia
141 G6 **Vergemont** Queensland Australia
95 O2 **Vergennes** Vermont U.S.A.
45 L4 **Verghereto** Italy
45 R8 **Vérgine, M** *mt* Italy
16 C3 **Verín** Spain
41 K1 **Veringenstadt** Germany
56 H3 **Verkh Angara** *R* Russian Federation
55 C3 **Verkhiye Kigi** Russian Federation
52 J5 **Verkhnaya Yarva** Russian Federation
56 H3 **Verkhneangarskiy Khrebet** *mts* Russian Federation
55 C4 **Verkhnearshinskiy** Russian Federation
55 C4 **Verkhne-Avzyan** Russian Federation
54 F8 **Verkhnedneprovsk** Ukraine
54 E2 **Verkhnedneprovskiy** Russian Federation
50 H2 **Verkhneimbatsk** Russian Federation
54 M7 **Verkhnemakeyevka** Russian Federation
29 Q3 **Verkhnetulomskiy** Russian Federation
52 D1 **Verkhnetulomskoye, Vodokhranilishche** *L* Russian Federation
55 C4 **Verkhneural'sk** Russian Federation
52 H6 **Verkhne Yarkeyevo** Russian Federation
54 K8 **Verkhneye** Ukraine
55 G3 **Verkhneye Krasnoyarka** Russian Federation
52 D2 **Verkhneye Kuyto, Oz** *L* Russian Federation
55 C3 **Verkhniye Tatyshly** Russian Federation
55 D3 **Verkhniy Neyvinskiy** Russian Federation
52 H1 **Verkhniy Shar** Russian Federation
55 C3 **Verkhniy Tagil** Russian Federation
55 C1 **Verkhniy Vizhay** Russian Federation
55 D1 **Verkhniy Vizhay** Russian Federation
55 D3 **Verkhnyaya Pyshma** Russian Federation
55 D2 **Verkhnyaya Salda** Russian Federation
55 D4 **Verkhnyaya Sanarka** Russian Federation
55 G3 **Verkhnyaya Tarka** Russian Federation
52 G4 **Verkhnyaya Toyma** Russian Federation
52 G4 **Verkhnyaya Toz'ma** Russian Federation
55 C2 **Verkhnyaya Tura** Russian Federation
52 G5 **Verkhoshizhemye** Russian Federation
55 D2 **Verkhotur'ye** Russian Federation
52 F4 **Verkhovazh'ye** Russian Federation
48 J2 **Verkhovina** Ukraine
54 F8 **Verkhovtsevo** Ukraine
51 M2 **Verkhoyanskiy Khrebet** *mts* Russian Federation
55 D2 **Verkhyaya Sinyachikha** Russian Federation
54 F8 **Verkne Dneprovsk** Ukraine
55 D3 **Verkniy Ufaley** Russian Federation
52 G3 **Verkola** Russian Federation
118 J8 **Verlo** Saskatchewan Canada
26 C9 **Verma** Norway
22 E4 **Vermand** France
130 D4 **Vermelho,R** Brazil
18 H5 **Vermenton** France
118 G5 **Vermilion** Alberta Canada
99 T10 **Vermilion** Illinois U.S.A.
111 D11 **Vermilion** *R* Louisiana U.S.A.
94 E5 **Vermilion** Ohio U.S.A.
111 D12 **Vermilion B** Louisiana U.S.A.
118 J1 **Vermilion Bay** Ontario Canada
117 Q6 **Vermilion Chutes** Alberta Canada
103 M4 **Vermilion Cliffs** Utah U.S.A.
118 K1 **Vermilion L** Ontario Canada
99 O2 **Vermilion L** Minnesota U.S.A.
118 F5 **Vermilion Prov. Park** Alberta Canada
99 O2 **Vermilion Ra** Minnesota U.S.A.
107 O2 **Vermillion** Kansas U.S.A.
98 K7 **Vermillion** South Dakota U.S.A.
103 M5 **Vermillion Cliffs** *ra* Arizona U.S.A.
121 R5 **Vermillon** *R* Quebec Canada
46 E4 **Vérmion** *mt* Greece
95 P2 **Vermont** *state* U.S.A.
99 Q9 **Vermont** Illinois U.S.A.
21 J6 **Vern** France
41 N4 **Vernago, Lago di** Italy
101 Q9 **Vernal** Utah U.S.A.
102 C4 **Vernalis** California U.S.A.
21 L7 **Vernantes** France
44 G3 **Vernazza** Italy
101 P8 **Verne** Wyoming U.S.A.
87 D11 **Verneakpan** *L* S Africa
120 K6 **Verner** Ontario Canada
21 M4 **Verneuil** Eure France
18 G4 **Verneuil l'Etang** France
21 N7 **Verneuil sur-Indre** France
89 B7 **Verneuk Pan** S Africa
28 E6 **Verninge** Denmark
45 K3 **Vernio** Italy
21 L7 **Vernoil** France
117 O10 **Vernon** British Columbia Canada
122 K7 **Vernon** Prince Edward I Canada
21 N3 **Vernon** Eure France
46 E4 **Vérnon** *mt* Greece
111 H8 **Vernon** Alabama U.S.A.
103 P7 **Vernon** Arizona U.S.A.
98 D10 **Vernon** Colorado U.S.A.
111 L11 **Vernon** Florida U.S.A.
94 B8 **Vernon** Indiana U.S.A.
95 M3 **Vernon** New York U.S.A.
109 H1 **Vernon** Texas U.S.A.
101 N9 **Vernon** Utah U.S.A.
95 P4 **Vernon** Vermont U.S.A.
100 B4 **Vernonia** Oregon U.S.A.
140 B1 **Vernon Is** N Terr Australia
143 C6 **Vernon,Mt** W Australia Australia
21 M7 **Vernou** France
127 N4 **Vernou** Guadeloupe
21 O7 **Vernou-en-Sologne** France
20 G5 **Vern-sur-Seiche** France
113 G10 **Vero Beach** Florida U.S.A.
46 E4 **Véroia** Greece
44 H1 **Verolanuova** Italy
45 O6 **Veroli** Italy
121 O8 **Verona** Ontario Canada
45 J1 **Verona** Italy
110 C5 **Verona** Missouri U.S.A.
98 H3 **Verona** North Dakota U.S.A.
99 R7 **Verona** Wisconsin U.S.A.
101 T5 **Verona** Wyoming U.S.A.
19 O13 **Verpillière** France
138 D5 **Verran** South Australia Australia
111 E12 **Verret, L** Louisiana U.S.A.
127 H5 **Verrettes** Haiti
21 J8 **Verrie,la** France
19 N17 **Vers** France
21 P4 **Versailles** France
110 L2 **Versailles** Indiana U.S.A.
110 M3 **Versailles** Kentucky U.S.A.
110 D3 **Versailles** Missouri U.S.A.
94 C6 **Versailles** Ohio U.S.A.
55 D1 **Vershina** Russian Federation
58 G1 **Vershino-Darasunskiy** Russian Federation
32 H8 **Versmold** Germany
21 K3 **Verson** France
28 C5 **Verst** Denmark
21 K3 **Ver-sur-Mer** France
41 N4 **Vertana,Cima** *mt* Italy
122 C5 **Verte,I** Quebec Canada
20 C6 **Verte,I** France
18 F7 **Verteillac** France
129 H6 **Vertentes** *R* Brazil
130 J9 **Vertentes** Brazil
48 E3 **Vérteshegység** *mt* Hungary
126 E4 **Vertientes** Cuba
54 C5 **Vertiyevka** Ukraine
123 N2 **Verton,L** Quebec Canada
20 H7 **Vertou** France
22 H2 **Vertrijk** Belgium
18 H4 **Vertus** France
45 M4 **Verucchio** Italy
89 G7 **Verulam** S Africa
22 K2 **Verviers** Belgium
22 F4 **Vervins** France
119 M9 **Verwood** Saskatchewan Canada
8 B7 **Veryan B** England
41 J5 **Verzasca,Val** Switzerland
38 O8 **Veržej** Slovenia
29 M9 **Vesanto** Finland
22 L2 **Vesdre** *R* Belgium
21 O4 **Vesegre** *R* France
48 D2 **Veseh** Czechoslovakia
31 K7 **Veselí** Czechoslovakia
55 C2 **Vesëlovka** Russian Federation
55 G4 **Veselovskoye** Russian Federation
55 E4 **Veselyy Podol** Kazakhstan
26 F6 **Vesfna** *R* Norway
21 K6 **Vesgre** *R* France
52 F3 **Veshkoma** Russian Federation
18 H3 **Vesle** *R* France
28 B2 **Vesløs** Denmark
20 H3 **Vesly** France
52 H3 **Veslyana** Russian Federation
52 H4 **Veslyana** *R* Russian Federation
40 D2 **Vesoul** France
107 M2 **Vesper** Kansas U.S.A.
99 R5 **Vesper** Wisconsin U.S.A.
27 F15 **Vessige** Sweden
99 L5 **Vesta** Minnesota U.S.A.
27 B13 **Vest Agder** *reg* Norway
95 L4 **Vestal Center** New York U.S.A.
26 H3 **Vestbygd** Norway
28 G7 **Vestenskov** Denmark
28 E6 **Vester Aby** Denmark
26 G3 **Vesterålen** *isld* Norway
147 G14 **Vesterålen** Norway
28 B3 **Vester Assels** Denmark
28 G7 **Vesterborg** Denmark
28 H6 **Vester Egede** Denmark
28 H6 **Vester Egesborg** Denmark
28 E2 **Vester Hassing** Denmark
28 D2 **Vester Hjermitslev** Denmark
29 K4 **Vester Karup** Sweden
28 C5 **Vesterlund** Denmark
28 C5 **Vester Nebel** Denmark
28 B5 **Vester Nykirke** Denmark
28 F2 **Vesterøhavn** Denmark
28 E6 **Vester Skerninge** Denmark
28 D7 **Vester Sottrup** Denmark
28 D3 **Vester Tørslev** Denmark
28 A3 **Vestervig** Denmark
27 C12 **Vestfj-Dal** Norway
146 G6 **Vestfjella** *mts* Antarctica
26 F4 **Vestfjorden** *inlet* Norway
27 D12 **Vestfold** *reg* Norway
146 J12 **Vestfold Hills** Antarctica
130 D7 **Véstia** Brazil
6 F1 **Vestmanna** Faeroes
28 S10 **Vestmannaeyjar** *islds* Iceland
26 B9 **Vestnes** Norway
29 T9 **Vestrahorn** *C* Iceland
28 G5 **Vestsjælland** *co* Denmark
26 G3 **Vestvågöy** Norway
45 Q8 **Vesuvio** *mt* Italy
52 E5 **Ves'yegonsk** Russian Federation
48 D3 **Veszprém** *co* Hungary
48 D3 **Veszprém** Hungary
48 D3 **Veszprémvarsány** Hungary
48 G4 **Vésztö** Hungary
89 E7 **Vet** *R* S Africa
98 E6 **Vetal** South Dakota U.S.A.
118 F6 **Veteran** Alberta Canada
98 B8 **Veteran** Wyoming U.S.A.
21 O3 **Vétheuil** France
54 C4 **Vetka** Belorussia
27 H14 **Vetlanda** Sweden
52 G5 **Vetluga** Russian Federation
52 G5 **Vetluzhskiy** Russian Federation
52 G6 **Vetluzhskiy** Russian Federation
47 H1 **Vetovo** Bulgaria
52 C6 **Vetrino** Belorussia
28 H6 **Vetterslev** Denmark
45 H3 **Vetto** Italy
26 M4 **Vetträsjärvi** Sweden
36 B2 **Vettweiss** Germany
21 L8 **Veude** *R* France
21 M2 **Veules** France
21 M2 **Veulettes** France
27 C12 **Veum** Norway
68 H6 **Veun Kham** Cambodia
22 D1 **Veurne** Belgium
94 B8 **Vevay** Indiana U.S.A.
26 F6 **Vevelstad** Norway
40 E5 **Vevey** Switzerland
46 E4 **Vévi** Greece
19 P15 **Veynes** France
103 L4 **Veyo** Utah U.S.A.
19 K4 **Vézelise** France
18 G7 **Vezère** *R* France
46 G2 **Vezhen** *mt* Bulgaria
52 H3 **Vezh'yudor** Russian Federation
22 K5 **Vezin** France
21 J7 **Vezins** Maine-et-Loire France
78 E1 **Vezirköprü** Turkey
36 B6 **Vezouse** *R* France
44 G3 **Vezzano Ligure** Italy
21 O5 **Viabon** France
45 J2 **Viadana** Italy
44 B1 **Via di Ciamarella** *mt* Italy
107 Q6 **Vian** Oklahoma U.S.A.
130 H7 **Viana** Espírito Santo Brazil
129 J4 **Viana** Maranhão Brazil
16 C2 **Viana del Bollo** Spain
16 B6 **Viana do Alentejo** Portugal
16 B3 **Viana do Castelo** Portugal
22 L4 **Vianden** Luxembourg
25 D5 **Vianen** Netherlands
68 F3 **Viangchan** Laos
45 J2 **Viano** Italy
130 E5 **Vianópolis** Brazil
29 L6 **Viantie** Finland
16 D7 **Viar** *R* Spain
44 H4 **Viareggio** Italy
18 G8 **Viaur** *R* France
119 O8 **Vibank** Saskatchewan Canada
28 B3 **Viborg** *co* Denmark
28 C4 **Viborg** Denmark
98 J6 **Viborg** South Dakota U.S.A.
43 G10 **Vibo Valentia** Italy
21 M5 **Vibraye** France
28 E4 **Viby** Århus Denmark
28 J5 **Viby** Roskilde Denmark
Vic *see* **Vich**
48 D2 **Vičany** Czechoslovakia
45 K4 **Vicchio** Italy
146 D4 **Vicecomodoro Marambio** *Argentina Base* Antarctica
18 E9 **Vic en Bigorre** France
130 F8 **Vicente S** Brazil
16 D4 **Vicente,S** *mt* Spain
45 L1 **Vicenza** Italy
119 M9 **Viceroy** Saskatchewan Canada
18 F9 **Vic-Fezensac** France
17 J3 **Vich** Spain
128 E3 **Vichada** *dept* Colombia
131 G3 **Vichadero** Uruguay
52 F6 **Vichuga** Russian Federation
133 C4 **Vichuquén** Chile
18 H6 **Vichy** France
107 L5 **Vici** Oklahoma U.S.A.
109 O9 **Vickery** Texas U.S.A.
103 L8 **Vicksburg** Arizona U.S.A.
94 B4 **Vicksburg** Michigan U.S.A.
111 F9 **Vicksburg** Mississippi U.S.A.
45 Q8 **Vico Equense** Italy
42 E6 **Vico, L. di** Italy
45 J4 **Vicopisano** Italy
17 G3 **Vicort, Sierra de** *mts* Spain
130 H10 **Viçosa** Alagoas Brazil
130 G7 **Viçosa** Minas Gerais Brazil
41 L5 **Vicosoprano** Switzerland
45 N5 **Vicovaro** Italy
48 K3 **Vicovu de Sus** Romania
21 P8 **Vicq Exemplet** France
21 M8 **Vicq-sur-Gartempe** France
22 E5 **Vic-sur-Aisne** France
18 G8 **Vic-sur-Cère** France
7 M9 **Victor** *oil rig* North Sea
106 E3 **Victor** Colorado U.S.A.
101 O6 **Victor** Idaho U.S.A.
99 O8 **Victor** Iowa U.S.A.
101 L3 **Victor** Montana U.S.A.
94 K4 **Victor** New York U.S.A.
138 E6 **Victor Harbour** South Australia Australia
131 E4 **Victoria** *R* Argentina
131 E4 **Victoria** Argentina
138 F6 **Victoria** *state* Australia
140 B3 **Victoria** *R* N Terr Australia
139 G6 **Victoria** Victoria Australia
123 T6 **Victoria** Newfoundland Canada
100 B1 **Victoria** Vancouver I, Br Col Canada
131 A7 **Victoria** Chile
127 P5 **Victoria** Grenada
83 K12 **Victoria** Mahé I Indian Oc
43 F12 **Victoria** Malta
71 E3 **Victoria** Luzon Philippines
70 D2 **Victoria** Sabah
127 O3 **Victoria** *co* Trinidad
107 L3 **Victoria** Kansas U.S.A.
109 K7 **Victoria** Texas U.S.A.
94 J10 **Victoria** Virginia U.S.A.
89 G3 **Victoria** *prov* Zimbabwe
119 V8 **Victoria Beach** Manitoba Canada
89 D1 **Victoria Falls** Zambezi R Zimbabwe
121 L8 **Victoria Harb** Ontario Canada
126 G2 **Victoria Hill** San Salvador Bahamas
114 H3 **Victoria I** Northwest Territories Canada
139 G5 **Victoria L** New South Wales Australia
123 P5 **Victoria L** *res* Newfoundland Canada
121 N5 **Victoria, L** Quebec Canada
88 D2 **Victoria, L** E Africa
146 C12 **Victoria Land** Antarctica
73 P4 **Victoria Mt** Burma
145 D4 **Victoria, Mt** New Zealand
136 K3 **Victoria, Mt** Papua New Guinea
86 F5 **Victoria Nile** *R* Uganda
142 B2 **Victoria Park** *dist* Perth, W Aust Australia
139 K5 **Victoria Pass** New South Wales Australia
140 B3 **Victoria R** N Terr Australia
123 P5 **Victoria R** Newfoundland Canada
144 D5 **Victoria Range** New Zealand
140 B3 **Victoria River Downs** N Terr Australia
114 J4 **Victoria Str** Northwest Territories Canada
145 D1 **Victoria Valley** New Zealand
121 T6 **Victoriaville** Quebec Canada
89 C8 **Victoria West** S Africa
123 L3 **Victor L** Quebec Canada
146 J8 **Victor, Mt** *mt* Antarctica
102 G7 **Victorville** California U.S.A.
140 C7 **Victory Downs** N Terr Australia
133 E4 **Vicuña** Argentina
133 C4 **Vicuña** Chile
28 B7 **Vidå** *R* Denmark
98 A2 **Vida** Montana U.S.A.
100 C5 **Vida** Oregon U.S.A.
103 K7 **Vidal** California U.S.A.
112 E5 **Vidalia** Georgia U.S.A.
111 E10 **Vidalia** Louisiana U.S.A.
83 K8 **Vidattaltivu** Sri Lanka
19 Q18 **Vidauban** France
109 K7 **Vidauri** Texas U.S.A.
28 B4 **Videbæk** Denmark
130 D10 **Videira** Brazil
48 K6 **Videle** Romania
Viderø *see* **Viðoy**
47 O12 **Vídho** *isld* Greece
16 B6 **Vidigueira** Portugal
56 F3 **Vidim** Russian Federation
46 F1 **Vidin** Bulgaria
16 C1 **Vidio, C** Spain
74 G7 **Vidisha** India
52 D4 **Vidlitsa** Russian Federation
46 E1 **Vidojevica** *mt* Serbia Yugoslavia
31 O3 **Vidomlya** Belorussia
109 N5 **Vidor** Texas U.S.A.
111 B11 **Vidor** Texas U.S.A.
118 H9 **Vidora** Saskatchewan Canada
18 H9 **Vidourle** France
6 F1 **Viðoy** *isld* Faeroes
48 K6 **Vidra** Romania
26 L6 **Vidsel** Sweden
28 D2 **Vidstrup** Denmark
42 J6 **Viduša** *mt* Bosnia-Herzegovina
52 C6 **Vidzy** Belorussia
52 H4 **Vidz'yuyar** Russian Federation
21 L3 **Vie** *R* Calvados France
20 G8 **Vie** *R* Vendée France
37 O5 **Viechtach** Germany
131 D8 **Viedma** Argentina
133 C7 **Viedma, L** Argentina
20 H8 **Vieillevigne** France
108 C5 **Vieja, Sa** *mts* Texas U.S.A.
128 C6 **Viejas, Islas de las** Peru
Vielha *see* **Viella**
17 H2 **Viella** Spain
21 M4 **Vielle-Lyre, la** France
22 K3 **Vielsalm** Belgium
28 J6 **Viemose** Denmark
33 N9 **Vienenburg** Germany
68 E2 **Vieng Pou Kha** Laos
Vienna Austria *see* **Wien** Austria
110 H4 **Vienna** Illinois U.S.A.
95 M8 **Vienna** Maryland U.S.A.
98 J5 **Vienna** South Dakota U.S.A.
94 F7 **Vienna** West Virginia U.S.A.
18 F6 **Vienne** *dept* France
19 N13 **Vienne** France
21 L7 **Vienne** *R* France
131 B3 **Vientes, P. del** *pk* Arg/Chile
Vientiane *see* **Viangchan**
131 B6 **Viento, Cord. del** *ra* Argentina
127 M5 **Vieques** *isld* Puerto Rico
29 N8 **Vieremä** Finland
32 M6 **Vierlande** *reg* Germany
25 E5 **Vierlingsbeek** Netherlands
36 F4 **Viernheim** Germany
25 F6 **Viersen** Germany
21 J3 **Vierville-sur-Mer** France
41 H3 **Vierwaldstätter See** *L* Switzerland
21 P7 **Vierzon** France
124 H5 **Viesca** Mexico
33 Q6 **Viesecke** Germany
37 L1 **Vieselbach** Germany
52 C6 **Viesite Nereta** Latvia
21 J4 **Viessoix** France
42 G7 **Vieste** Italy
68 G3 **Vietnam** *rep* S E Asia
33 R7 **Vietnitz** Germany
68 G2 **Vietri** Vietnam
45 R8 **Vietri S. Mare** Italy
127 O8 **Vieux Fort** St Lucia
127 N5 **Vieux Fort,Pte.du** Guadeloupe W Indies
108 H3 **View** Texas U.S.A.
28 H5 **Vig** Denmark
52 F5 **Viga** *R* Russian Federation
71 E2 **Vigan** Luzon Philippines
18 H8 **Vigan, le** France
45 L2 **Vigarano Mainarda** Italy
45 J1 **Vigásio** Italy
18 F7 **Vigeois** France
44 E1 **Vigevano** Italy
43 G8 **Viggiano** Italy
129 J4 **Vigia** Brazil
16 B7 **Vigia** *mt* Portugal
133 D7 **Vigia, C** Argentina
71 E3 **Vigia Pt** Luzon Philippines
21 P6 **Viglain** France
45 O6 **Viglio** *mt* Italy
21 P1 **Vignacourt** France
44 D1 **Vignale Mon Ferrato** Italy
18 E10 **Vignemale** *mt* France/Spain
22 G4 **Vigneux Hocquet** France
45 K3 **Vignola** Italy
16 B2 **Vigo** Spain
45 L1 **Vigonza** Italy
142 C5 **Vigors,Mt** W Australia Australia
26 A9 **Vigra** *isld* Norway
27 A13 **Vigrestad** Norway
28 B2 **Vigsø** Denmark
29 L7 **Vihanti** Finland
21 J7 **Vihiers** France
29 L11 **Vihti** Finland
29 K10 **Viiala** Finland
29 O9 **Viinijärvi** *L* Finland
29 M5 **Viiri** Finland
29 M8 **Viitasaari** Finland
76 A2 **Vijayadurg** India
76 E2 **Vijayawada** India
46 D4 **Vijosë** *R* Albania
28 S10 **Vik** Iceland
26 F6 **Vik** Norway
27 G11 **Vika** Sweden
29 M5 **Vikajärvi** Finland
27 H11 **Vikarbyn** Sweden
27 A12 **Vikedal** Norway
71 N9 **Vikeke** Timor
29 K4 **Viken** Sweden
27 G12 **Vikersvik** Sweden
27 D12 **Vikesund** Norway
46 F3 **Vikhren** *mt* Bulgaria
118 F5 **Viking** Alberta Canada
7 M9 **Viking** *oil rig* North Sea
6 M2 **Viking Bank** North Sea
7 M9 **Viking N** *oil rig* North Sea
7 M9 **Viking S** *oil rig* North Sea
27 H11 **Vikmanshyttan** Sweden
26 E7 **Vikna** *isld* Norway
26 E7 **Vikna** Norway
26 J9 **Viksjö** Sweden
55 F3 **Vikulovo** Russian Federation
71 M9 **Vila Armindo Monteiro** Timor
Vila Cabral *see* **Lichinga**
131 E4 **Vila Constitución** Argentina
88 G10 **Vila da Maganje** Mozambique
16 B7 **Vila do Bispo** Portugal
16 B3 **Vila do Conde** Portugal
87 F8 **Vila Gamito** Mozambique
20 H5 **Vilaine** *R* Ille-et-Vilaine France
20 F6 **Vilaine** *R* Morbihan France
17 H2 **Vilaller** Spain
87 F9 **Vila Machado** Mozambique
128 E6 **Vila Murtinho** Brazil
87 G11 **Vilanandro, Tanjona** *C* Madagascar
87 G10 **Vilanculos** Mozambique
52 C6 **Vilāni** Latvia
16 B5 **Vila Nova da Barquinha** Portugal
16 B3 **Vila Nova de Famalicão** Portugal
16 C3 **Vila Nova de Fozcoa** Portugal
16 B3 **Vila Nova de Gaia** Portugal
71 N9 **Vila Nova de Malaca** Timor
16 B7 **Vila Nova de Mil Fontes** Portugal
16 B4 **Vila Nova de Paiva** Portugal
16 B3 **Vila Pouca de Aguiar** Portugal
16 B3 **Vila Real** Portugal
16 C7 **Vila Real de Santo António** Portugal
16 C4 **Vilar Formoso** Portugal
106 H4 **Vilas** Colorado U.S.A.
111 M11 **Vilas** Florida U.S.A.
98 J5 **Vilas** South Dakota U.S.A.
71 N9 **Vila Salazar** Timor
87 F8 **Vila Vasco da Gama** Mozambique
129 H3 **Vila Velha** Amapá Brazil
130 H7 **Vila Velha** Espírito Santo Brazil
16 B5 **Vila Velha de Ródão** Portugal
16 B3 **Vila Verde** Portugal
128 D6 **Vilcabamba, Cord** *mts* Peru
48 H5 **Vîlcanului Muntii** *mt* Romania
48 J5 **Vîlcea** *reg* Romania
28 B4 **Vildbjerg** Denmark
28 B3 **Vile** Denmark
52 G4 **Viled'** *R* Russian Federation
37 P3 **Vilémov** Czechoslovakia
53 C7 **Vileyskoye Vodokhranilishche** *res* Belorussia
52 H4 **Vil'gort** Komi Respublika Russian Federation
52 J4 **Vil'gort** Permskaya obl Russian Federation
26 J7 **Vilhelmina** Sweden
128 F6 **Vilhena** Brazil
53 C7 **Viliya** *R* Belorussia
52 C5 **Viljandi** Estonia
31 O1 **Vilkaviškis** Lithuania
51 J1 **Vil'kitskogo, Proliv** *str* Russian Federation
48 M5 **Vilkovo** Ukraine
128 E8 **Villa Abecia** Bolivia
45 N6 **Villa Adriana** Italy
108 A5 **Villa Ahumada** Mexico
127 J5 **Villa Altagracia** Dominican Rep
133 E3 **Villa Angela** Argentina
131 C5 **Villa Atuel** Argentina
45 K1 **Villa Bartolomea** Italy
38 F8 **Villabassa** Italy
128 E6 **Villa Bella** Bolivia
128 E4 **Villa Bittencourt** Brazil
16 C2 **Villablino** Spain
16 E5 **Villacañas** Spain
16 E1 **Villacarriedo** Spain
16 E6 **Villa Carrillo** Spain
16 E4 **Villacastin** Spain
38 J8 **Villach** Austria
16 C2 **Villachica, L. de** Spain
43 B9 **Villacidro** Sardinia
Villa Cisneros *see* **Dakhla, Ad**
133 D4 **Villa Colón** Argentina
133 E4 **Villa Concepción del Tio** Argentina
133 E4 **Villa Constitucion** Argentina
124 G4 **Villa Coronado** Mexico
16 D2 **Villada** Spain
127 L9 **Villa de Cura** Venezuela
133 E4 **Villa del Rosario** Argentina
16 E2 **Villadiego** Spain
131 D3 **Villa Dolores** Argentina
41 H5 **Villadossola** Italy
45 L1 **Villa Estense** Italy
17 G4 **Villafamés** Spain
130 B10 **Villa Franca** Paraguay
16 C2 **Villafranca del Bierzo** Spain
17 G4 **Villafranca del Cid** Spain
16 C6 **Villafranca de los Barros** Spain
17 J3 **Villafranca del Penedés** Spain
45 J1 **Villafranca di Verona** Italy
45 L1 **Villafranca P** Italy
45 L1 **Villaga** Italy
16 B2 **Villagarcía de Arosa** Spain
109 N5 **Village Cr** Texas U.S.A.
109 N5 **Village Mills** Texas U.S.A.
131 G6 **Villa Gesell** Argentina
99 S10 **Villa Grove** Illinois U.S.A.
131 F3 **Villaguay** Argentina
133 F3 **Villa Guillermina** Argentina
133 F3 **Villa Hayes** Paraguay
125 N9 **Villahermosa** Mexico
133 E4 **Villa Huidobro** Argentina
21 K5 **Villaines-la-Jubel** France
21 M7 **Villaines-les-Rochers** France
21 K6 **Villaines-sous-Malicorne** France
128 F8 **Villa Ingavi** Bolivia
133 E5 **Villa Iris** Argentina
127 J5 **Villa Isabel** Dominican Rep
16 B1 **Villalba** Lugo Spain
16 E4 **Villalba** Madrid Spain
45 Q7 **Villa Literno** Italy
16 D2 **Villalón de Campos** Spain
133 E5 **Villalonga** Argentina
16 D3 **Villalpando** Spain
17 F6 **Villamanriqué** Spain
43 B9 **Villamar** Sardinia
131 D4 **Villa Maria** Argentina
133 D2 **Villa Martín** Bolivia
16 D8 **Villamartín** Spain
124 G4 **Villa Matamoros** Mexico
17 F5 **Villamayor de Santiago** Spain
21 O5 **Villamblain** France
133 D4 **Villa Mercedes** Argentina
133 E3 **Villa Minetti** Argentina
45 H3 **Villaminozzo** Italy
133 E2 **Villa Montes** Bolivia
16 B3 **Villa Nova da Cerveira** Portugal
45 L2 **Villanova March** Italy
127 H9 **Villanueva** Colombia
124 H6 **Villanueva** Mexico
106 E6 **Villanueva** New Mexico U.S.A.
16 D6 **Villanueva de Córdoba** Spain
17 F6 **Villanueva del Arzobispo** Spain
16 D6 **Villanueva de la Serena** Spain
16 D3 **Villanueva del Campo** Spain
16 E6 **Villanueva de los Infantes** Spain
17 J3 **Villanueva y Geltrú** Spain
48 E5 **Villány** Hungary
124 G4 **Villa Ocampo** Durango Mexico
16 C1 **Villaodrid** Spain
124 G4 **Villa Orestes Pereyra** Mexico
124 E3 **Villa Pesqueira** Mexico
43 C9 **Villaputzu** Sardinia
16 E2 **Villarcayo** Spain
19 P14 **Villard** France
19 P14 **Villard de Lans** France
17 G5 **Villar del Arzobispo** Spain
16 C5 **Villar del Rey** Spain
133 D5 **Villa Regina** Argentina
142 D4 **Villaret, C** W Australia Australia
130 B9 **Villa Rey** Paraguay
111 M8 **Villa Rica** Georgia U.S.A.
17 G4 **Villarluengo** Spain
43 F11 **Villarosa** Sicily
17 G5 **Villarreal** Spain
131 A7 **Villarrica** Chile
130 C9 **Villarrica** Paraguay
131 B7 **Villarrica, Vol** Chile
17 F5 **Villarrobledo** Spain
17 F3 **Villarroya de la Sierra** Spain
16 E5 **Villarubia de los Ojos** Spain
95 N7 **Villas** New Jersey U.S.A.
131 D2 **Villa Sanagasta** Argentina
131 D2 **Villa San Martín** Argentina
38 G9 **Villa Santina** Italy
17 F3 **Villasayas** Spain
133 D3 **Villa Unión** Argentina
108 G7 **Villa Union** Mexico
124 G6 **Villa Unión** Durango Mexico
124 F6 **Villa Unión** Sinaloa Mexico
128 D3 **Villavicencio** Colombia
16 D1 **Villaviciosa** Spain
16 D6 **Villaviciosa de Córdoba** Spain
128 C3 **Villavieja** Colombia
133 D2 **Villazón** Bolivia
36 C7 **Villé** France
21 N6 **Ville-aux-Clèrcs, la** France
21 H4 **Villebaudon** France
40 B6 **Villebois** France
18 F7 **Villebois Lavalette** France
19 Q17 **Villecroze** France
21 H7 **Villedieu-la-Blouère** Maine-et-Loire France
20 H4 **Villedieu-les-Poêtes** France
21 O8 **Villedieu-sur-Indre** France
21 M2 **Villedomer** France
21 M6 **Villedomer** France
18 H8 **Villefort** France
44 B4 **Villefranche** France
19 N13 **Villefranche** Rhône France
18 G9 **Villefranche de Lauragais** France
18 G8 **Villefranche-de-Rouergue** France
18 F8 **Villefranche-du-Perigord** France
21 O7 **Villefranche-sur-Cher** France
17 G4 **Villel** Spain
121 L5 **Ville-Marie** Quebec Canada
21 N4 **Villemeux-sur-Eure** France
121 M4 **Villemontel** Quebec Canada
18 G9 **Villemur sur le Tarn** France
17 G6 **Villena** Spain
19 N12 **Villeneuve** France
40 F6 **Villeneuve** Italy
18 G8 **Villeneuve d'Allier** France
22 E2 **Villeneuve d'Ascq** France
19 N15 **Villeneuve de Berg** France
18 E9 **Villeneuve de Marc** France
18 H4 **Villeneuve l'Archevêque** France
19 N17 **Villeneuve-lès-Avignon** France
21 P3 **Villeneuve-les-Sablons** France
18 G4 **Villeneuve-St Georges** France
18 F8 **Villeneuve-sur-Lot** France
18 H4 **Villeneuve-sur-Yonne** France
21 N7 **Villentrois** France
111 D11 **Ville Platte** Louisiana U.S.A.
21 M2 **Villequier** France
21 N6 **Villeromain** France
121 T6 **Villeroy** Quebec Canada
21 J3 **Villers-Bocage** Calvados France
21 P2 **Villers-Bocage** Somme France
21 P3 **Villers-Bretonneux** France
22 D4 **Villers-Carbonnel** France
22 E5 **Villers Cotterets** France
22 J4 **Villers Devant-Orval** Belgium
21 L4 **Villers-en-Ouche** France
22 J2 **Villers-le-Bouillet** Belgium
22 H3 **Villers-le-Gambon** Belgium
22 E3 **Villers-Outreaux** France
22 K5 **Villerupt-la-Montagne** *mt* France
21 L3 **Villerville** France
19 N13 **Villeurbanne** France
131 C3 **Villicun, Sa** *ra* Argentina
21 N8 **Villiers** France
21 J6 **Villiers-Charlemagne** France
41 J1 **Villingen-Schwenningen** Germany
99 M9 **Villisca** Iowa U.S.A.
36 E3 **Villmar** Germany
Vilna *see* **Vilnius**
118 F4 **Vilna** Alberta Canada
53 C7 **Vilnius** Lithuania
29 L9 **Vilppula** Finland
41 N2 **Vils** Austria
28 B3 **Vils** Denmark
27 M13 **Vilsandi Saar** *isld* Estonia
37 N7 **Vilsbiburg** Germany
37 M4 **Vilseck** Germany
37 P6 **Vilshofen** Germany
27 G15 **Vilshult** Sweden
28 B6 **Vilslev** Denmark
28 C3 **Vilsted** Denmark
28 B3 **Vilsund** Denmark
76 D5 **Viluppuram** India
42 J6 **Vilusi** Montenegro Yugoslavia
52 J5 **Vil'va** Russian Federation
22 G2 **Vilvoorde** Belgium
51 L2 **Vilyuy** *R* Russian Federation
51 M2 **Vilyuysk** Russian Federation
56 H1 **Vilyuyskoye Vodokhranilishche** *res* Russian Federation
16 C3 **Vimioso** Portugal
27 H14 **Vimmerby** Sweden
27 G11 **Vimo** Sweden
21 L4 **Vimoutiers** France
29 K8 **Vimpeli** Finland
30 H6 **Vimperk** Czechoslovakia
22 D3 **Vimy** France
111 H7 **Vina** Alabama U.S.A.
102 B2 **Vina** California U.S.A.
131 B4 **Viña de Mar** Chile
17 G6 **Vinalapó** *R* Spain
95 T2 **Vinalhaven** Maine U.S.A.
17 H4 **Vinaroz** Spain
40 B7 **Vinay** France
110 J3 **Vincennes** Indiana U.S.A.
146 G14 **Vincennes Bay** Antarctica
111 K8 **Vincent** Alabama U.S.A.
94 F7 **Vincent** Ohio U.S.A.
16 B7 **Vincente, C. de S** Portugal
128 C4 **Vinces** Ecuador
45 R7 **Vinchiaturo** Italy
133 D3 **Vinchina** Argentina
45 J4 **Vinci** Italy
28 B4 **Vind** Denmark
28 C3 **Vindblæs** Denmark
28 G7 **Vindeby** Denmark
26 H5 **Vindelälven** *R* Sweden
26 K6 **Vindelgransele** Sweden
26 L7 **Vindeln** Sweden
143 B7 **Vinden, Mt** W Australia Australia
28 C4 **Vinderslev** Denmark
28 B4 **Vinderup** Denmark
74 F7 **Vindhya Range** India
28 B4 **Vinding** Ringkøbing Denmark
28 D4 **Vinding** Vejle Denmark
28 D5 **Vinding** Vejle Denmark
28 F6 **Vindinge** Denmark
21 O8 **Vineuil** Indre France
21 N6 **Vineuil** Loir-et-Cher France
95 R5 **Vineyard Haven** Massachusetts U.S.A.
48 G4 **Vinga** Romania
27 H12 **Vingåker, V** Sweden
40 B2 **Vingeanne** *R* France
21 L4 **Vingt Hanaps** France
68 G3 **Vinh** Vietnam
16 C3 **Vinhais** Portugal
68 J7 **Vinh Cam Ranh** *B* Vietnam
68 J6 **Vinh Giat** Vietnam
Vinh Linh *see* **Ho Xa**
69 G8 **Vinh Loi** Vietnam
68 G7 **Vinh Long** Vietnam
68 H3 **Vinh Son** *B* Vietnam
67 B6 **Vinh Yen** Vietnam
46 E3 **Vinica** Macedonia Yugoslavia
99 L3 **Vining** Minnesota U.S.A.
107 P5 **Vinita** Oklahoma U.S.A.
27 C12 **Vinje** Norway
26 C8 **Vinjeora** Norway
48 H6 **Vînju Mare** Romania
28 D4 **Vinkel** Denmark
48 E5 **Vinkovci** Croatia
26 M2 **Vinnelys** Norway
48 M1 **Vinnitsa** Ukraine
48 H2 **Vinogradov** Ukraine
19 P17 **Vinon** France
107 L7 **Vinson** Oklahoma U.S.A.
146 C7 **Vinson Massif** *mts* Antarctica
27 D10 **Vinstra** *R* Norway
71 E1 **Vintar** Luzon Philippines
99 O7 **Vinton** Iowa U.S.A.
111 C11 **Vinton** Louisiana U.S.A.
94 E8 **Vinton** Ohio U.S.A.
94 H9 **Vinton** Virginia U.S.A.
27 G12 **Vintrosa** Sweden
133 E6 **Vintter** Argentina
48 H4 **Vinţu de Jos** Romania
76 D2 **Vinukonda** India
33 P7 **Vinzelberg** Germany
55 E3 **Vinzili** Russian Federation
102 C1 **Viola** California U.S.A.
100 H3 **Viola** Idaho U.S.A.
99 Q8 **Viola** Illinois U.S.A.
107 N4 **Viola** Kansas U.S.A.
99 Q6 **Viola** Wisconsin U.S.A.
101 P7 **Viola** Wyoming U.S.A.
118 B5 **Violet Grove** Alberta Canada
87 C11 **Vioolsdrif** Namibia
20 H6 **Vioreau, Grand Res. de** France
41 O4 **Vipiteno** Italy
33 R6 **Vipperow** Germany
42 F4 **Vir** *isld* Croatia
27 H13 **Virå** Sweden
71 G4 **Virac** Philippines
47 K5 **Virancık** Turkey
52 E3 **Virandozero** Russian Federation
48 G6 **Virciorova** Romania
119 R9 **Virden** Manitoba Canada
99 R10 **Virden** Illinois U.S.A.
29 J3 **Virdni** *mt* Finland
20 H3 **Vire** *R* France
21 J4 **Vire** France
27 G14 **Vireda** Sweden
142 B5 **Virehow, Mt** W Australia Australia
87 B9 **Virei** Angola
22 G3 **Virelles** Belgium
22 H3 **Vireux** Belgium
48 H4 **Vîrfurile** Romania
101 P1 **Virgelle** Montana U.S.A.
130 G5 **Virgem da Lapa** Brazil
17 F3 **Virgen,Sa.de la** *mts* Spain
107 P4 **Virgil** Kansas U.S.A.
98 H5 **Virgil** South Dakota U.S.A.
102 C1 **Virgilia** California U.S.A.
94 J10 **Virgilina** Virginia U.S.A.
45 J1 **Virgilio** Italy
103 L5 **Virgin** *R* Arizona U.S.A.
113 L7 **Virgin Gorda** *isld* Virgin Is
14 D3 **Virginia** Ireland
89 E7 **Virginia** S Africa
94 H9 **Virginia** *state* U.S.A.
101 N7 **Virginia** Idaho U.S.A.
99 Q10 **Virginia** Illinois U.S.A.
99 O2 **Virginia** Minnesota U.S.A.
98 K9 **Virginia** Nebraska U.S.A.
95 M10 **Virginia Beach** Virginia U.S.A.
101 O4 **Virginia City** Montana U.S.A.
102 E2 **Virginia City** Nevada U.S.A.
117 L5 **Virginia Falls** Northwest Territories Canada
121 L4 **Virginiatown** Ontario Canada
113 L7 **Virgin Is** W Indies
103 K5 **Virgin Mts** Nev/Ariz U.S.A.
130 G6 **Virginópolis** Brazil
19 P13 **Virignin** France
26 J4 **Virihaure** Sweden
19 O14 **Viriville** France
133 D8 **Vírjenes, C** Argentina
28 D4 **Virklund** Denmark
29 N9 **Virmasvesi** *L* Finland
29 N11 **Virolahti** Finland
99 Q6 **Viroqua** Wisconsin U.S.A.
42 H3 **Virovitica** Croatia
42 J6 **Virpazar** Montenegro Yugoslavia
29 K9 **Virrat** Finland
27 H12 **Virsbo** Sweden
27 H14 **Virserum** Sweden
29 N9 **Virtasalmi** Finland
48 J6 **Vîrtoapele** Romania
46 G1 **Vîrtoapele de Sus** Romania
22 K4 **Virton** Belgium
128 C5 **Virú** Peru
76 C6 **Virudunagar** India
52 C5 **Viru-Jaagup** Estonia
42 G5 **Vis** *isld* Croatia
27 H14 **Vi, S** Sweden
102 E5 **Visalia** California U.S.A.
19 N16 **Visan** France
45 J1 **Visano** Italy
71 F5 **Visayan Sea** Philippines
28 E3 **Visborg** Denmark
28 B6 **Visby** Sønderjylland Denmark
28 A3 **Visby** Viborg Denmark
27 K14 **Visby** Sweden
130 G7 **Visconde do Rio Branco** Brazil
119 M7 **Viscount** Saskatchewan Canada
114 J3 **Viscount Melville Sd** Northwest Territories Canada
22 K2 **Visé** Belgium
48 E7 **Višegard** Bosnia-Herzegovina
45 M3 **Viserba** Italy
16 B4 **Viseu** Portugal
48 J3 **Vişeu** *R* Romania
48 J3 **Vişeu de Sus** Romania
76 F2 **Vishakhapatam** India
52 H4 **Vishera** *R* Russian Federation
52 G5 **Vishkil'** Russian Federation
48 K1 **Vishnevets** Ukraine
55 F5 **Vishnevka** Kazakhstan
55 D3 **Vishnevogorsk** Russian Federation
55 D1 **Visim** *R* Russian Federation
55 C2 **Visim** Russian Federation
55 C2 **Visimo-Utkinsk** Russian Federation
46 G1 **Vişina Veche** Romania
27 G13 **Visingsö** Sweden
27 F14 **Viskafors** Sweden
27 F14 **Viskan** *R* Sweden
52 C6 **Višķi** Latvia
28 G5 **Viskinge** Denmark
27 G15 **Vislanda** Sweden
124 D3 **Visnaga** Mexico
74 E7 **Visnagar** India
44 B2 **Viso** *mt* Italy
16 E6 **Viso del Marqués** Spain
48 E7 **Visoko** Bosnia-Herzegovina
46 E3 **Visoko** *mt* Macedonia Yugoslavia
146 G2 **Visokoi I** S Sandwich Is S Atlantic Oc
40 G5 **Visp** Switzerland
27 H15 **Vissefjärda** Sweden
32 L7 **Visselhövede** Germany
28 E6 **Vissenbjerg** Denmark
40 G5 **Vissoie** Switzerland
102 G8 **Vista** California U.S.A.
128 F3 **Vista Alegre** Brazil
101 K8 **Vista Res** Nevada U.S.A.
28 F4 **Vistoft** Denmark
46 G3 **Vistonís, L** Greece
Vistula *R* *see* **Wisła** *R*
46 G1 **Vit** *R* Bulgaria
119 V9 **Vita** Manitoba Canada
76 B2 **Vita** India
54 B1 **Vitebsk** Belorussia
42 E6 **Viterbo** Italy
16 C3 **Vitigudino** Spain
56 H4 **Vitim** *R* Russian Federation
58 F1 **Vitimskoye Ploskogor'ye** Russian Federation
42 H5 **Vitina** Bosnia-Herzegovina
46 E7 **Vitína** Greece
130 H7 **Vitória** Brazil
17 F2 **Vitoria** Spain
130 H4 **Vitória da Conquista** Brazil
130 J10 **Vitoria de Sta Antão** Brazil
42 H4 **Vitorog** *mts* Bosnia-Herzegovina
21 N5 **Vitray-en-Beauce** France
20 H5 **Vitré** France
123 N2 **Vitré,L** Quebec Canada
40 C2 **Vitrey** France
19 O18 **Vitrolles** France
21 P6 **Vitry-aux-Loges** France
22 D3 **Vitry-en-Artois** France
27 F11 **Vitsand** Sweden
Vitsi *mt* *see* **Vérnon** *mt*
26 M4 **Vittangi** *R* Sweden
28 A5 **Vittarp** Denmark
40 C1 **Vittel** France
28 D4 **Vitten** Denmark
27 J12 **Vittinge** Sweden
120 K10 **Vittoria** Ontario Canada
43 F12 **Vittoria** Sicily
43 F13 **Vittoriosa** Malta
42 E3 **Vittorio Ven** Italy
27 G15 **Vittsjö** Sweden
45 R7 **Vitulano** Italy
26 N5 **Vitvattnet** Sweden
40 F7 **Viu** Italy
28 C5 **Viuf** Denmark
18 H7 **Vivarais, Mts du** France
28 E3 **Vive** Denmark
Viveiro *see* **Vivero**
17 G5 **Viver** Spain
16 B1 **Vivero** Spain
44 D1 **Viverone, L. di** Italy
51 J2 **Vivi** Russian Federation
109 O3 **Vivian** Louisiana U.S.A.
98 F6 **Vivian** South Dakota U.S.A.
19 N16 **Viviers** France
20 G4 **Vivier-sur-Mer, Le** France
28 E4 **Vivild** Denmark
21 L5 **Vivoin** France
138 D6 **Vivonne** South Australia Australia
18 F6 **Vivonne** France
133 F5 **Vivorata** Argentina
26 M4 **Vivunki** Sweden

238
Vizcaíno,Des.de — Wancoocha, L

124 C4 **Vizcaíno,Des.de** Mexico
124 B4 **Vizcaíno,Sa** *mts* Mexico
17 F1 **Vizcaya** *prov* Spain
47 J3 **Vize** Turkey
50 G1 **Vize,Ostrova** *islds* Russian Federation
52 G2 **Vizhas** Russian Federation
76 F1 **Vizianagaram** India
45 P1 **Vižinada** Croatia
52 H4 **Vizinga** Russian Federation
48 L6 **Viziru** Romania
48 D1 **Vizovice** Czechoslovakia
43 F11 **Vizzini** Sicily
25 B5 **Vlaardingen** Netherlands
48 L3 **Vlădeni** Romania
46 E2 **Vladičin Han** Serbia Yugoslavia
53 F11 **Vladikavkaz** Russian Federation
52 F6 **Vladimir** Russian Federation
48 F6 **Vladimirci** Serbia Yugoslavia
55 D4 **Vladimirovka** Kazakhstan
52 E6 **Vladimirskaya Oblast'** *prov* Russian Federation
54 E1 **Vladimirskiy Tupik** Russian Federation
53 B8 **Vladimir Volynskiy** Ukraine
59 K3 **Vladivostok** Russian Federation
52 E5 **Vladychnoye** Russian Federation
48 K4 **Vlăhiţa** Romania
46 E2 **Vlajna** *mt* Serbia Yugoslavia
142 A5 **Vlaming Hd** W Australia Australia
48 E6 **Vlasenica** Bosnia-Herzegovina
48 F6 **Vlašić** *mt* Serbia Yugoslavia
46 E2 **Vlasotince** Serbia Yugoslavia
31 K7 **Vlčany** Czechoslovakia
25 C2 **Vlieland** *isld* Netherlands
25 D2 **Vliestroom** Netherlands
25 A6 **Vlissingen** Netherlands
25 F6 **Vlodrop** Netherlands
46 C4 **Vlorë** Albania
32 J8 **Vlotho** Germany
31 H7 **Vltava** *R* Czechoslovakia
52 E6 **Vnukovo** *airport* Russian Federation
45 L1 **Vo** Italy
109 H5 **Voca** Texas U.S.A.
38 J6 **Vöcklabruck** Austria
107 K2 **Voda** Kansas U.S.A.
68 H7 **Vo Dat** Vietnam
28 B6 **Vodder** Denmark
47 H1 **Voditsa** Bulgaria
52 E4 **Vodla** *R* Russian Federation
52 E4 **Vodlozero, Oz** *L* Russian Federation
30 H6 **Vodňany** Czechoslovakia
42 F4 **Vodnjan** Croatia
52 H3 **Vodnyy** Russian Federation
28 E2 **Vodskov** Denmark
15 G2 **Voe** Shetland Scotland
28 D4 **Voel** Denmark
28 E3 **Voer** Denmark
32 E9 **Voerde** Germany
32 F10 **Voerde** Germany
28 D4 **Voerladegard** Denmark
28 F2 **Voerså** Denmark
85 C7 **Vofnjama** Liberia
86 B4 **Vogel** *mt* Nigeria
41 O3 **Vogelkar Sp** *mt* Austria
36 G2 **Vogelsberg** *mt* Germany
44 F2 **Voghera** Italy
45 L2 **Voghiera** Italy
28 C3 **Vognsild** Denmark
41 H5 **Vogogna** Italy
Vohemar *see* **Iharaña**
37 N4 **Vohenstrauss** Germany
Vohibinany *see* **Ampasimanolotra**
87 H13 **Vohimena, Tanjona** *C* Madagascar
36 F1 **Vöhl** Germany
52 C5 **Võhma** Estonia
37 J7 **Vöhringen** Germany
32 F10 **Vohwinkel** Germany
88 G3 **Voi** Kenya
33 S4 **Voigdehgn** Germany
12 D1 **Voil,L** Scotland
48 L3 **Voineşti** Romania
40 C7 **Voiron** France
38 M7 **Voitsberg** Austria
46 F5 **Voïvïïs** *L* Greece
28 C6 **Vojens** Denmark
26 H6 **Vojmsjön** *L* Sweden
37 N3 **Vojtanov** Czechoslovakia
48 E5 **Vojvodina** *aut rep* Serbia Yugoslavia
52 G5 **Vokhma** *R* Russian Federation
29 P7 **Voknavolok** Russian Federation
30 H6 **Vokyně** Czechoslovakia
52 H3 **Vol'** *R* Russian Federation
30 H7 **Volary** Czechoslovakia
98 A4 **Volborg** Montana U.S.A.
131 B3 **Volcan,Cerro del** *pk* Chile
106 D2 **Volcano** Colorado U.S.A.
Volcano B *see* **Uchiura wan** *B*
135 U5 **Volcanoes Nat. Park** Hawaiian Is
131 F6 **Volcán, Sa. del** *ra* Argentina
55 D2 **Volchansk** Russian Federation
55 H4 **Volchikha** Russian Federation
52 E5 **Volchina** *R* Russian Federation
54 H8 **Volch'ya** *R* Ukraine
28 D4 **Voldby** Denmark
28 F4 **Voldby** Denmark
28 E4 **Voldum** Denmark
25 D4 **Volendam** Netherlands
45 J1 **Volfa Mantovana** Italy
52 E5 **Volga** Russian Federation
52 E6 **Volga** *R* Russian Federation
99 P7 **Volga** *R* Iowa U.S.A.
98 K5 **Volga** South Dakota U.S.A.
52 E4 **Volgo-Balt** *canal* Russian Federation
53 F9 **Volgograd** Russian Federation
53 F9 **Volgogradskaya Oblast'** *prov* Russian Federation
52 D6 **Volgo, Oz** *L* Russian Federation
26 J7 **Volgsele** Sweden
98 J7 **Volin** South Dakota U.S.A.
47 H6 **Volissós** Greece
37 J4 **Volkach** Germany
25 B5 **Volkerak** Netherlands
38 L8 **Völkermarkt** Austria
37 J3 **Völkershausen** Germany
52 D5 **Volkhov** Russian Federation
36 B5 **Völklingen** Germany
32 K10 **Volkmarsen** Germany
48 L1 **Volkovintsy** Ukraine
31 P2 **Volkovysk** Belorussia
32 L8 **Völksen** Germany
89 F6 **Volksrust** S Africa
25 E3 **Vollenhove** Netherlands
22 G2 **Vollezele** Belgium
32 J9 **Völmerstod** *mt* Germany
36 C5 **Volmunster** France
21 L6 **Volnay** Sarthe France
99 U6 **Volney** Michigan U.S.A.
44 F3 **Vol Noci, L. di** Italy
54 F8 **Vol'nogorsk** Ukraine
55 F4 **Vol'noye** Russian Federation
54 G9 **Vol'nyansk** Ukraine
51 J1 **Volochanka** Russian Federation
48 K1 **Volochisk** Ukraine
52 F6 **Volodarsk** Russian Federation
55 E4 **Volodarskoye** Kazakhstan
52 F4 **Volodskaya** Russian Federation
52 E5 **Vologda** Russian Federation
36 B7 **Vologne** *R* France
52 E4 **Vologodskaya Oblast'** *prov* Russian Federation
52 D6 **Volok** Russian Federation
52 E6 **Volokolamsk** Russian Federation
52 G2 **Volokovaya** Russian Federation
52 G2 **Volonga** Russian Federation
19 Q16 **Volonne** France
46 F5 **Vólos** Greece
52 E4 **Voloshka** Russian Federation
52 C5 **Volosovo** Russian Federation
48 H2 **Volosyanka** Ukraine
52 D5 **Volot** Russian Federation
48 H2 **Volovets** Ukraine
33 O8 **Völpke** Germany
33 S5 **Völschow** Germany
53 G8 **Vol'sk** Russian Federation
28 E2 **Volstrup** Denmark
130 H10 **Volta** Brazil
85 E7 **Volta** *R* Ghana
41 N7 **Volta** Italy
85 D6 **Volta Blanche** *R* Burkina/Ghana
98 F1 **Voltaire** North Dakota U.S.A.
142 F2 **Voltaire, C** W Australia Australia
85 D7 **Volta,L** Ghana
85 D6 **Volta Noire** *R* Burkina
130 G8 **Volta Redonda** Brazil
85 D6 **Volta Rouge** *R* Burkina/Ghana
42 D5 **Volterra** Italy
52 F3 **Volteva** Russian Federation
44 E3 **Voltri** Italy
45 R8 **Volturara Irpina** Italy
45 Q7 **Volturno** *R* Italy
46 F4 **Vólvi, L** Greece
19 P17 **Volx** France
52 G6 **Volzhsk** Russian Federation
53 F9 **Volzhskiy** Russian Federation
42 F6 **Vomano** *R* Italy
106 H2 **Vona** Colorado U.S.A.
118 L6 **Vonda** Saskatchewan Canada
87 H12 **Vondrozo** Madagascar
22 J3 **Vonêche** Belgium
116 K5 **Von Frank Mt** Alaska U.S.A.
52 F3 **Vonga** Russian Federation
28 C5 **Vonge** Denmark
40 B3 **Vonges** France
46 D6 **Vónitsa** Greece
129 H5 **Von Martius,Cachoeira** *rapids* Brazil
28 D6 **Vonsbæk** Denmark
28 C6 **Vonsild** Denmark
143 E7 **Von Truer Tableland** W Australia Australia
25 B4 **Voorburg** Netherlands
25 B5 **Voorne** Netherlands
25 B4 **Voorschoten** Netherlands
25 F4 **Voorst** Netherlands
25 E4 **Voorthuizen** Netherlands
29 T9 **Vopnafjördhur** *inlet* Iceland
29 T9 **Vopnafjördhur** Iceland
25 F6 **Vopst** Germany
29 J8 **Vörå** Finland
41 K4 **Vorab** *mt* Switzerland
41 L3 **Vorarlberg** *prov* Austria
38 N7 **Vorau** Austria
28 C5 **Vorbasse** Denmark
32 H8 **Vörden** Germany
25 F4 **Vorden** Netherlands
38 L7 **Vordernberg** Austria
41 J4 **Vorder Rhein** *R* Switzerland
28 H6 **Vordingborg** Denmark
46 G5 **Vóreion Aiyaion** *admin region* Greece
19 P14 **Voreppe** France
54 D3 **Vorga** Russian Federation
28 B4 **Vorgod** Denmark
46 G5 **Vorïai Sporádhes** *islds* Greece
50 F2 **Vorkuta** Russian Federation
27 E11 **Vorma** *R* Norway
28 D3 **Vorning** Denmark
55 G3 **Vorob'yevo** Russian Federation
53 F8 **Vorona** *R* Russian Federation
54 C3 **Voronevo** Belorussia
54 L4 **Voronezh** *R* Russian Federation
54 L5 **Voronezh** Voronezhskaya obl Russian Federation
54 E5 **Voronezh** Ukraine
53 E8 **Voronezhskaya Oblast'** *prov* Russian Federation
48 M1 **Voronovitsa** Ukraine
52 F2 **Voronov, Mys** *C* Russian Federation
55 D2 **Vorontsovka** Russian Federation
50 H1 **Vorontsovo** Russian Federation
52 C6 **Vorontsovo** Russian Federation
52 E1 **Voron'ya** *R* Russian Federation
52 F5 **Voron'ye** Russian Federation
Voroshilovgrad *see* **Lugansk**
52 G5 **Voroshno** Russian Federation
54 N1 **Vorovskogo, im** Russian Federation
54 F5 **Vorozhba** Ukraine
33 S5 **Vorpommern** *reg* Germany
33 N8 **Vorsfelde** Germany
54 G6 **Vorskala** *R* Rus Fed/Ukraine
52 F6 **Vorsma** Russian Federation
52 C5 **Võrtsjärv** Estonia
52 C5 **Võru** Estonia
28 E4 **Vorup** Denmark
55 D1 **Vor'ya** *R* Russian Federation
55 D1 **Vor'yapaul'** Russian Federation
52 H3 **Vorykva** *R* Russian Federation
36 B7 **Vosges** *dept* France
40 E2 **Vosges** *mt* France
55 C4 **Voskresenskoye** Bashkirskaya Respublika Russian Federation
52 G6 **Voskresenskoye** Nizhegorodskaya obl Russian Federation
52 E5 **Voskresenskoye** Vologodskaya obl Russian Federation
89 C3 **Vosloosrus** S Africa
55 F4 **Vosnesenka** Kazakhstan
27 B11 **Voss** Norway
54 D9 **Vossiyatskoye** Ukraine
56 B6 **Vost Kazakhstanskaya Oblast'** *prov* Kazakhstan
52 E1 **Vostochnaya Litsa** Russian Federation
57 H2 **Vostochno-Kounradskiy** Kazakhstan
56 E4 **Vostochnyy Sayan** *mts* Russian Federation
146 F11 **Vostok** *former U.S.S.R. Base* Antarctica
135 M9 **Vostok I** Pacific Oc
55 E1 **Vostykhoy** Russian Federation
109 N5 **Votaw** Texas U.S.A.
109 N5 **Voth** Texas U.S.A.
31 H6 **Votice** Czechoslovakia
52 H6 **Votkinsk** Russian Federation
137 O4 **Vot Tandé** *isld* Vanuatu
130 E7 **Votuporanga** Brazil
16 B4 **Vouga** *R* Portugal
21 L8 **Vouillé** Vienne France
46 E5 **Voulgára** *mt* Greece
46 E5 **Voulgarélion** Greece
19 N15 **Voulte, la** France
68 H6 **Vœune** Cambodia
21 M8 **Vouneuil-sur-Vienne** France
46 E4 **Voúrinos** *mt* Greece
21 K5 **Voutré** France
21 J8 **Vouvant** France
21 M7 **Vouvray** France
21 P7 **Vouzeron** France
22 G5 **Vouziers** France
21 P6 **Vouzon** France
21 O5 **Voves** France
27 H10 **Voxna** Sweden
27 H10 **Voxnan** Sweden
27 G14 **Voxtorp** Sweden
52 H5 **Voya** *R* Russian Federation
99 O1 **Voyageurs Nat. Park** Minnesota U.S.A.
51 P3 **Voyampolka** Russian Federation
48 J1 **Voynilov** Ukraine
52 D2 **Voynitsa** Russian Federation
Vöyri *see* **Vörå**
52 H3 **Voy Vozh** Russian Federation
52 J3 **Voyvozh** Russian Federation
52 G3 **Vozhayel'** Russian Federation
52 F4 **Vozhega** Russian Federation
52 E4 **Vozhe, Oz** *L* Russian Federation
52 H5 **Vozhgaly** Russian Federation
52 G3 **Vozhgora** Russian Federation
54 C9 **Voznesensk** Ukraine
52 E4 **Voznesenye** Russian Federation
55 F4 **Vozvyshenka** Kazakhstan
28 D2 **Vrå** Denmark
48 E2 **Vráble** Czechoslovakia
27 C12 **Vrådalsv** *L* Norway
53 D10 **Vradiyevka** Ukraine
28 C4 **Vrads** Denmark
46 E6 **Vrakhnéïka** Greece
42 H5 **Vran** *mt* Bosnia-Herzegovina
48 K5 **Vrancea** *reg* Romania
48 K5 **Vrancei, Muntii** *mts* Romania
47 O13 **Vranganiótika** Greece
65 J3 **Vrangel'** Russian Federation
147 P3 **Vrangelya, Os** *isld* Russian Federation
42 H5 **Vranica** *mt* Bosnia-Herzegovina
46 E2 **Vranje** Serbia Yugoslavia
48 G2 **Vranov** Czechoslovakia
22 G1 **Vrasene** Belgium
46 F1 **Vratsa** Bulgaria
55 E1 **Vray** *L* Russian Federation
42 H4 **Vrbas** *R* Bosnia-Herzegovina
31 K5 **Vrbno** Czechoslovakia
31 J5 **Vrchlabí** Czechoslovakia
48 F5 **Vrdnik** Serbia Yugoslavia
89 F6 **Vrede** S Africa
32 E8 **Vreden** Germany
32 G7 **Vrees** Germany
28 D2 **Vrensted** Denmark
28 F6 **Vresen** *isld* Denmark
22 H4 **Vress** France
20 G3 **Vrétot, le** France
27 G12 **Vretstorp** Sweden
42 H5 **Vrgorac** Croatia
76 D5 **Vriddhachalam** India
28 C4 **Vridsted** Denmark
25 G2 **Vries** Netherlands
25 G4 **Vriezenveen** Netherlands
27 G14 **Vrigstad** Sweden
41 K4 **Vrin** Switzerland
22 H4 **Vringe-aux-Bois** France
28 A3 **Vrist** Denmark
22 F3 **Vrith-St.Léger** France
22 H5 **Vrizy** France
28 A5 **Vrøgum** Denmark
22 B3 **Vron** France
47 H6 **Vrondádhes** Greece
46 F8 **Vrondamás** Greece
25 G4 **Vroomshoop** Netherlands
28 C4 **Vroue** Denmark
48 G5 **Vršac** Serbia Yugoslavia
45 P1 **Vrsar** Croatia
48 E1 **Vrútky** Czechoslovakia
89 D6 **Vryburg** S Africa
89 G6 **Vryheid** S Africa
37 P4 **Všeruby** Czechoslovakia
37 O5 **Všeruby** Czechoslovakia
31 K6 **Vsetín** Czechoslovakia
55 C1 **Vsevolodo Blagodatskoye** Russian Federation
48 E2 **Vtáčnik** *mt* Czechoslovakia
19 P12 **Vuache, Mt de** France
68 G2 **Vu Ban** Vietnam
46 G3 **Vŭcha** *R* Bulgaria
46 D2 **Vučitrn** Serbia Yugoslavia
20 G7 **Vue** France
25 D5 **Vught** Netherlands
48 E5 **Vuka** *R* Croatia
48 E5 **Vukovar** Croatia
118 D8 **Vulcan** Alberta Canada
7 M9 **Vulcan** *gas field* North Sea
48 H5 **Vulcan** Romania
43 G10 **Vulcano, I** Italy
46 F1 **Vŭlchedrŭm** Bulgaria
47 J1 **Vŭlchidol** Bulgaria
67 B7 **Vu Liet** Vietnam
48 L5 **Vulkaneshty** Moldavia
43 G8 **Vulture, Monte** Italy
103 M8 **Vulture Mts** Arizona U.S.A.
68 J4 **Vung Da Nang** *B* Vietnam
68 J7 **Vung Phan Thiet** *B* Vietnam
68 H7 **Vung Tau** Vietnam
89 F2 **Vungu** *R* Zimbabwe
26 M5 **Vuodas** Sweden
29 N7 **Vuokatti** Finland
29 O11 **Vuoksa** *L* Russian Federation
29 O10 **Vuoksenniska** Finland
29 N7 **Vuolijoki** Finland
26 L5 **Vuollerim** Sweden
29 N5 **Vuostimo** Finland
29 N3 **Vuotso** Finland
26 N2 **Vuovdasoaivve** *mt* Norway
47 H2 **Vŭrbitsa** Bulgaria
52 G6 **Vurnary** Russian Federation
46 F1 **Vŭrshets** Bulgaria
28 C2 **Vust** Denmark
48 L4 **Vutcani** Romania
55 D4 **Vvedenka** Kazakhstan
100 F8 **Vya** Nevada U.S.A.
52 E2 **Vyalozero, Oz** *L* Russian Federation
52 F5 **Vyaltsevo** Russian Federation
29 P9 **Vyartsilya** Russian Federation
52 G5 **Vyatka** *R* Russian Federation
52 H6 **Vyatskiye Polyany** Russian Federation
59 K2 **Vyazemskiy** Russian Federation
54 E1 **Vyazma** *R* Russian Federation
54 F1 **Vyaz'ma** Russian Federation
52 F6 **Vyazniki** Russian Federation
52 C6 **Vybor** Russian Federation
29 O11 **Vyborg** Russian Federation
29 N11 **Vyborgskiy Zaliv** *G* Russian Federation
52 H4 **Vychegda** *R* Russian Federation
31 J5 **Vychodočeský** *reg* Czechoslovakia
56 F5 **Vydrino** Russian Federation
52 E3 **Vyg** *R* Russian Federation
48 N4 **Vygoda** Ukraine
54 F3 **Vygonichi** Russian Federation
52 D3 **Vygozero, Oz** *L* Russian Federation
48 G2 **Vyhorlát** *mt* Czechoslovakia
52 F6 **Vyksa** Russian Federation
52 H3 **Vym'** *R* Russian Federation
52 G4 **Vymsk** Russian Federation
52 C5 **Vyra** Russian Federation
52 D5 **Vyritsa** Russian Federation
8 C2 **Vyrnwy, L** Wales
8 C2 **Vyrnwy R** Wales
54 B6 **Vyshgorod** Ukraine
31 K6 **Vyškov** Czechoslovakia
31 L6 **Vysoká** *mt* Czechoslovakia
52 G6 **Vysokaya Gora** Russian Federation
52 J4 **Vysokaya Parma** *plateau* Russian Federation
31 J6 **Vysoké Mýto** Czechoslovakia
59 L1 **Vysokogornyy** Russian Federation
52 E6 **Vysokovsk** Russian Federation
31 O3 **Vysokoye** Belorussia
29 O11 **Vysotsk** Russian Federation
38 K4 **Vyšši Brod** Czechoslovakia
52 E4 **Vytegra** Russian Federation
52 G3 **Vyya** *R* Russian Federation
59 M2 **Vzmor'ye** Russian Federation

W

85 D6 **Wa** Ghana
86 H5 **Waajid** Somalia
25 D5 **Waal** *R* Netherlands
25 B5 **Waalhaven** Netherlands
25 D5 **Waalwijk** Netherlands
80 H2 **Waamo Iidow** Kenya
25 D2 **Waardgronden** Netherlands
22 F1 **Waarschoot** Belgium
120 D2 **Wababimiga L** Ontario Canada
118 C5 **Wabamun** Alberta Canada
123 U6 **Wabana** Newfoundland Canada
117 Q7 **Wabasca** *R* Alberta Canada
118 D3 **Wabasca** Alberta Canada
110 J3 **Wabash** *R* U.S.A.
111 F7 **Wabash** Arkansas U.S.A.
94 B6 **Wabash** Indiana U.S.A.
99 O5 **Wabasha** Minnesota U.S.A.
113 G10 **Wabasso** Florida U.S.A.
99 L5 **Wabasso** Minnesota U.S.A.
120 F4 **Wabatongushi L** Ontario Canada
99 S4 **Wabeno** Wisconsin U.S.A.
Wabern *see* **Egling**
118 K1 **Wabigoon** Ontario Canada
121 R4 **Wabino** *R* Quebec Canada
120 A2 **Wabinosh L** Ontario Canada
120 C2 **Waboose Dam** Ontario Canada
120 F6 **Wabos** Ontario Canada
119 T4 **Wabowden** Manitoba Canada
31 L2 **Wąbrzezno** Poland
58 G5 **Wabu Hu** *L* China
115 N7 **Wabush** Labrador, Nfld Canada
102 E2 **Wabuska** Nevada U.S.A.
112 H4 **Waccamaw** *R* South Carolina U.S.A.
112 J3 **Waccamaw, L** North Carolina U.S.A.
113 D8 **Waccasassa B** Florida U.S.A.
95 M9 **Wachapreague** Virginia U.S.A.
36 H5 **Wachbach** Germany
36 E5 **Wachenheim** Germany
37 K4 **Wachenroth** Germany
33 R7 **Wachow** Germany
22 F1 **Wachtbeke** Belgium
25 F6 **Wachtendonk** Germany
36 G3 **Wächtersbach** Germany
32 G7 **Wachtum** Germany
95 Q4 **Wachusett Res** Massachusetts U.S.A.
135 M11 **Wachusett Shoal** Pacific Oc
71 H7 **Waci** Indonesia
32 K4 **Wacken** Germany
122 G2 **Waco** Quebec Canada
98 J9 **Waco** Nebraska U.S.A.
109 K4 **Waco** Texas U.S.A.
99 N5 **Waconia** Minnesota U.S.A.
122 G2 **Wacouno R** Quebec Canada
77 K6 **Wad** Pakistan
142 D6 **Wadara Ra** W Australia Australia
60 H10 **Wadayama** Japan
86 E3 **Wad Banda** Sudan
139 H8 **Waddamana** Tasmania Australia
84 F4 **Waddān** Libya
25 D2 **Waddenzee** Netherlands
9 F4 **Waddesdon** England
9 F1 **Waddington** England
95 M2 **Waddington** New York U.S.A.
117 L10 **Waddington, Mt** British Columbia Canada
94 B8 **Waddy** Kentucky U.S.A.
141 L7 **Waddy Pt** Queensland Australia
112 J2 **Wade** North Carolina U.S.A.
8 B7 **Wadebridge** England
119 O7 **Wadena** Saskatchewan Canada
99 L3 **Wadena** Minnesota U.S.A.
36 B4 **Wadern** Germany
32 H9 **Wadersloh** Germany
112 G3 **Wadesboro** North Carolina U.S.A.
123 T4 **Wadham Is** Newfoundland Canada
117 K10 **Wadhams** British Columbia Canada
9 G5 **Wadhurst** England
80 G6 **Wadi es Sir** Jordan
84 K5 **Wâdi Gimâl I** Egypt
86 F1 **Wadi Halfa** Sudan
79 F8 **Wādi Mūsā** Jordan
111 L8 **Wadley** Alabama U.S.A.
112 E5 **Wadley** Georgia U.S.A.
86 F3 **Wad Medani** Sudan
31 L6 **Wadowice** Poland
102 E2 **Wadsworth** Nevada U.S.A.
94 F5 **Wadsworth** Ohio U.S.A.
13 G6 **Wadworth** England
65 G7 **Waegwan** S Korea
109 K6 **Waelder** Texas U.S.A.
68 F4 **Waeng** Thailand
65 E2 **Wafang** China
Wafangdian *see* **Fu Xian**
77 A5 **Wafra** Iran
61 O6 **Waga-gawa** *R* Japan
120 B2 **Wagaming** Ontario Canada
111 H10 **Wagarville** Alabama U.S.A.
32 J7 **Wagenfeld** Germany
25 E5 **Wageningen** Netherlands
139 H6 **Wagga Wagga** New South Wales Australia
74 E8 **Waghai** India
36 F5 **Waghäusel** Germany
143 B10 **Wagin** W Australia Australia
101 R1 **Wagner** Montana U.S.A.
98 H6 **Wagner** South Dakota U.S.A.
107 P6 **Wagoner** Oklahoma U.S.A.
106 F5 **Wagon Mound** New Mexico U.S.A.
100 F6 **Wagontire** Oregon U.S.A.
106 D4 **Wagon Wheel Gap** Colorado U.S.A.
112 H3 **Wagram** North Carolina U.S.A.
31 K3 **Wągrowiec** Poland
100 J3 **Waha** Idaho U.S.A.
83 K9 **Wahalkada Tank** Sri Lanka
145 E2 **Waharoa** New Zealand
102 R12 **Wahiawa** Hawaiian Is
145 E2 **Wahi,L** New Zealand
36 F4 **Wahlen** Germany
36 C2 **Wahn** Germany
32 K7 **Wahnebergen** Germany
98 K8 **Wahoo** Nebraska U.S.A.
98 K3 **Wahpeton** North Dakota U.S.A.
33 S9 **Wahrenbrück** Germany
33 N7 **Wahrenholz** Germany
103 L3 **Wah Wah Mts** Utah U.S.A.
76 A2 **Wai** India
135 U6 **Waiahukini** Hawaiian Is
135 T3 **Waiakoa** Hawaiian Is
135 O1 **Waialeale** *pk* Hawaiian Is
102 R11 **Waialee** Hawaiian Is
102 R11 **Waialua** Hawaiian Is
102 R12 **Waianae** Hawaiian Is
102 R12 **Waianae Ra** Hawaiian Is
144 C6 **Waianakarua** New Zealand
144 B7 **Waianiwa** New Zealand
145 G2 **Waiapu** *R* New Zealand
144 B6 **Waiatoto R** New Zealand
144 D5 **Waiau** New Zealand
144 A6 **Waiau** *R* New Zealand
145 F3 **Waiau R** New Zealand
36 G6 **Waiblingen** Germany
37 N4 **Waidhaus** Germany
31 J7 **Waidhofen** Austria
38 L6 **Waidhofen an der Ybbs** Austria
71 B3 **Waigama** Indonesia
143 G8 **Waigen Lakes** W Australia Australia
71 C3 **Waigeo** W Irian
71 C3 **Waigeo** *isld* W Irian
37 J4 **Waigolshausen** Germany
144 C6 **Waihao Forks** New Zealand
145 D1 **Waiharara** New Zealand
145 E2 **Waiheke I** New Zealand
145 E2 **Waihi** New Zealand
144 A7 **Waihoaka** New Zealand
144 C7 **Waihola** New Zealand
145 D4 **Waihopai** *R* New Zealand
145 D1 **Waihopo** New Zealand
144 C5 **Waiho R** New Zealand
145 E2 **Waihou** New Zealand
145 E2 **Waihou R** New Zealand
145 F3 **Waihua** New Zealand
71 J9 **Waikabubak** Sumba Indonesia
144 B6 **Waikaia** New Zealand
144 B6 **Waikaka** New Zealand
145 E4 **Waikanae** New Zealand
102 S12 **Waikane** Hawaiian Is
145 F3 **Waikareiti, L** New Zealand
145 E2 **Waikare, L** New Zealand
145 F3 **Waikaremoana, L** New Zealand
145 E2 **Waikaretu** New Zealand
144 D5 **Waikari** New Zealand
145 E3 **Waikato** New Zealand
145 E2 **Waikato** *admin region* New Zealand
144 B7 **Waikawa** New Zealand
145 E4 **Waikawa** New Zealand
71 J9 **Waikelo Teluk** *B* Sumba Indonesia
138 E5 **Waikerie** South Australia Australia
135 U5 **Waikii** Hawaiian Is
142 A4 **Waikiki** W Australia Australia
102 S12 **Waikiki Beach** Hawaiian Is
71 L9 **Waiklibang** Indonesia
145 F3 **Waikohu** New Zealand
145 F3 **Waikokopu** New Zealand
144 B7 **Waikotkoi** New Zealand
144 C6 **Waikouaiti** New Zealand
144 A7 **Waikouro** New Zealand
102 V13 **Wailuku** Hawaiian Is
144 B7 **Waimahaka** New Zealand
144 A4 **Waimakariri R** New Zealand
145 D1 **Waimamaka** New Zealand
145 F3 **Waimana** New Zealand
102 S12 **Waimanalo** Hawaiian Is
144 C4 **Waimangaroa** New Zealand
71 J9 **Waimanguar** Indonesia
145 F3 **Waimarama** New Zealand
144 C4 **Waimarie** New Zealand
144 C6 **Waimate** New Zealand
145 E2 **Waimauku** New Zealand
135 Q2 **Waimea** Hawaiian Is
135 U4 **Waimea** Hawaiian Is
102 R11 **Waimea B** Hawaiian Is
70 G6 **Waimenda** Sulawesi
22 L3 **Waimes** Belgium
145 E3 **Waimiha** New Zealand
9 G1 **Wainfleet** England
71 K9 **Waingapu** Sumba Indonesia
145 E4 **Waingawa** New Zealand
135 O1 **Wainiha** Hawaiian Is
144 C5 **Wainihinihi** New Zealand
99 S3 **Wainola** Michigan U.S.A.
144 C6 **Wainono Lagoon** New Zealand
118 G6 **Wainwright** Alberta Canada
116 G1 **Wainwright** Alaska U.S.A.
145 F3 **Waioeka R** New Zealand
135 U6 **Waiohinu** Hawaiian Is
145 E1 **Waiolira** New Zealand
145 F3 **Waiotapu** New Zealand
145 E3 **Waiouru** New Zealand
144 B7 **Waipahi** New Zealand
102 R12 **Waipahu** Hawaiian Is
145 F3 **Waipaoa** New Zealand
145 D1 **Waipapakauri** New Zealand
145 E2 **Waipa R** New Zealand
144 D5 **Waipara** New Zealand
145 F3 **Waipawa** New Zealand
144 C6 **Waipiata** New Zealand
135 U4 **Waipio** Hawaiian Is
145 G3 **Waipiro** New Zealand
144 C6 **Waipori, L** New Zealand
145 E1 **Waipu** New Zealand
145 F3 **Waipukurau** New Zealand
145 F3 **Wairakei** New Zealand
145 E4 **Wairarapa** *admin region* New Zealand
145 E4 **Wairarapa, L** New Zealand
145 D4 **Wairau Valley** New Zealand
144 B7 **Wairio** New Zealand
145 F3 **Wairoa** New Zealand
145 E2 **Wairoa R** New Zealand
145 E1 **Wairua** *R* New Zealand
144 B7 **Wairuna** New Zealand
71 L9 **Wairunu** Flores Indonesia
37 L4 **Waischenfeld** Germany
145 F3 **Waitahanui** New Zealand
144 C5 **Waitaha R** New Zealand
144 B6 **Waitahuna** New Zealand
145 E2 **Waitakaruru** New Zealand
144 C6 **Waitaki, L** New Zealand
145 E1 **Waitangi** New Zealand
145 E3 **Waitara** New Zealand
145 E4 **Waitarere** New Zealand
144 D6 **Waitati** New Zealand
140 B5 **Waite** *R* N Terr Australia
145 F1 **Waitemata Harb** New Zealand
143 D8 **Waite, Mt** W Australia Australia
145 E2 **Waitoa** New Zealand
145 E3 **Waitomo** New Zealand
145 E3 **Waitotara** *R* New Zealand
145 E3 **Waitotara** New Zealand
100 G3 **Waitsburg** Washington U.S.A.
119 M6 **Waitville** Saskatchewan Canada
145 E2 **Waiuku** New Zealand
144 C5 **Waiuta** New Zealand
145 E2 **Waiwera** New Zealand
144 B7 **Waiwera South** New Zealand
71 B1 **Wajabula** Halmahera Indonesia
71 C2 **Wajag** *isld* Indonesia
71 B2 **Wajamli** Indonesia
61 K8 **Wajima** Japan
86 H5 **Wajir** Kenya
86 D5 **Waka** Zaire
60 D12 **Wakamatsu** Japan
60 B12 **Wakamatsu-jima** *isld* Japan
120 H5 **Wakami L** Ontario Canada
144 C5 **Wakanui** New Zealand
145 F3 **Wakarara Range** New Zealand
94 A5 **Wakarusa** Indiana U.S.A.
61 J10 **Wakasa-wan** *B* Japan
144 B6 **Wakatipu, L** New Zealand
119 M6 **Wakaw** Saskatchewan Canada
60 J11 **Wakayama** Japan
60 J12 **Wakayama** *prefect* Japan
61 P7 **Wakayanagi** Japan
107 L2 **Wa Keeney** Kansas U.S.A.
121 P7 **Wakefield** Quebec Canada
13 G6 **Wakefield** England
127 J2 **Wakefield** Jamaica
145 D4 **Wakefield** New Zealand
107 O2 **Wakefield** Kansas U.S.A.
99 R3 **Wakefield** Michigan U.S.A.
98 K7 **Wakefield** Nebraska U.S.A.
95 Q5 **Wakefield** Rhode I U.S.A.
95 K10 **Wakefield** Virginia U.S.A.
112 J2 **Wake Forest** North Carolina U.S.A.
134 H6 **Wake I** Pacific Oc
68 B4 **Wakema** Burma
122 H5 **Wakenam** Quebec Canada
94 A5 **Wakerton** Indiana U.S.A.
74 E1 **Wakhan** *reg* Afghanistan
60 H11 **Waki** Japan
60 O4 **Wakinosawa** Japan
107 N5 **Wakita** Oklahoma U.S.A.
60 P1 **Wakkanai** Japan
87 F11 **Wakkerstroom** S Africa
Wako *see* **Watcomb**
120 G6 **Wakomata L** Ontario Canada
139 G6 **Wakool** New South Wales Australia
119 S9 **Wakopa** Manitoba Canada
71 H7 **Wakoru** Indonesia
98 F4 **Wakpala** South Dakota U.S.A.
71 C3 **Wakre** W Irian
71 K9 **Waku** Indonesia
87 C8 **Waku Kungo** Angola
113 C7 **Wakulla** Florida U.S.A.
120 K2 **Wakwayowkastic** *R* Ontario Canada
103 L6 **Walapai** Arizona U.S.A.
83 K11 **Walawe Ganga** *R* Sri Lanka
33 O8 **Walbeck** Germany
36 D6 **Walbourg** France
94 D5 **Walbridge** Ohio U.S.A.
31 J5 **Wałbrzych** Poland
36 H1 **Walburg** Germany
139 K4 **Walcha** New South Wales Australia
38 G7 **Walchen** Austria
41 O2 **Walchensee** *L* Germany
25 A5 **Walcheren** Netherlands
38 F6 **Walchsee** Austria
117 K8 **Walcott** British Columbia Canada
98 K3 **Walcott** North Dakota U.S.A.
101 T8 **Walcott** Wyoming U.S.A.
142 E3 **Walcott Inlet** W Australia
101 M7 **Walcott, L., Res** Idaho U.S.A.
22 G3 **Walcourt** Belgium
31 J2 **Wałcz** Poland
38 L5 **Wald Aist** *R* Austria
36 F5 **Waldangeloch** Germany
36 D4 **Waldböckelheim** Germany
36 C2 **Waldbreitbach** Germany
36 D2 **Waldbröl** Germany
36 G5 **Waldbrunn** Baden-Württemberg Germany
36 G5 **Waldbrunn** Hessen Germany
143 B6 **Waldburg Ra** W Australia
33 T9 **Walddrehna** Germany
118 K8 **Waldeck** Saskatchewan Canada
36 G1 **Waldeck** Germany
101 T9 **Walden** Colorado U.S.A.
95 N5 **Walden** New York U.S.A.
37 O2 **Waldenberg** Germany
36 G6 **Waldenbuch** Germany
36 H5 **Waldenburg** Germany
110 F6 **Waldenburg** Arkansas U.S.A.
37 N4 **Waldershof** Germany
36 D5 **Waldfischbach** Germany
118 L6 **Waldheim** Saskatchewan Canada
37 P1 **Waldheim** Germany
36 H1 **Waldkappel** Germany
40 G1 **Waldkirch** Germany
30 H7 **Waldkirchen** Germany
36 F4 **Waldmichelbach** Germany
37 O5 **Waldmünchen** Germany
37 N4 **Wald Naab** *R* Germany
25 F6 **Waldniel** Germany
118 B9 **Waldo** British Columbia Canada
109 O2 **Waldo** Arkansas U.S.A.
113 E8 **Waldo** Florida U.S.A.
107 M2 **Waldo** Kansas U.S.A.
94 D6 **Waldo** Ohio U.S.A.
99 T6 **Waldo** Wisconsin U.S.A.
100 C6 **Waldo L** Oregon U.S.A.
95 L8 **Waldorf** Maryland U.S.A.
99 N6 **Waldorf** Minnesota U.S.A.
100 A5 **Waldport** Oregon U.S.A.
119 P8 **Waldron** Saskatchewan Canada
109 N1 **Waldron** Arkansas U.S.A.
146 G14 **Waldron, C** Antarctica
37 N3 **Waldsassen** Germany
41 H2 **Waldshut** Germany
37 J7 **Waldstetten** Germany
37 N4 **Waldthurn** Germany
36 B5 **Waldwisse** France
71 H5 **Waleabahi** *isld* Sulawesi
71 H5 **Waleakodi** *isld* Sulawesi
71 H5 **Walea,Selat** *str* Sulawesi
70 N9 **Waleri** Java
8 C3 **Wales** *princ* U.K.
116 C4 **Wales** Alaska U.S.A.
99 P2 **Wales** Minnesota U.S.A.
98 H1 **Wales** North Dakota U.S.A.
103 N2 **Wales** Utah U.S.A.
115 L4 **Wales I** Northwest Territories Canada
85 D6 **Walewale** Ghana
33 O5 **Walfisch** Germany
139 J4 **Walgett** New South Wales Australia
146 B7 **Walgreen Coast** Antarctica
37 N5 **Walhalla** *mt* Germany
98 J1 **Walhalla** North Dakota U.S.A.
112 D3 **Walhalla** South Carolina U.S.A.
70 N9 **Walikukun** Java
143 A8 **Walkaway** W Australia Australia
33 R5 **Walkendorf** Germany
33 N9 **Walkenried** Germany
140 B6 **Walker** *R* N Terr Australia
141 F3 **Walker** *R* Queensland Australia
100 C8 **Walker** California U.S.A.
99 P7 **Walker** Iowa U.S.A.
107 L3 **Walker** Kansas U.S.A.
111 F11 **Walker** Louisiana U.S.A.
99 M2 **Walker** Minnesota U.S.A.
110 B4 **Walker** Missouri U.S.A.
102 E2 **Walker** *R* Nevada U.S.A.
98 E4 **Walker** South Dakota U.S.A.
89 A10 **Walker B** S Africa
13 E2 **Walkerburn** Scotland
113 J10 **Walker Cay** *isld* Bahamas
119 V4 **Walker L** Manitoba Canada
122 E3 **Walker L** Quebec Canada
116 K3 **Walker L** Alaska U.S.A.
102 F3 **Walker L** Nevada U.S.A.
146 B7 **Walker Mts** Antarctica
102 G6 **Walker Pk** California U.S.A.
140 D2 **Walker R** N Terr Australia
70 D2 **Walker Ra** Sabah
141 J5 **Walkerston** Queensland Australia
94 G8 **Walkersville** West Virginia U.S.A.
120 J8 **Walkerton** Ontario Canada
112 G1 **Walkertown** North Carolina U.S.A.
99 U6 **Walkerville** Michigan U.S.A.
101 N3 **Walkerville** Montana U.S.A.
98 D5 **Wall** South Dakota U.S.A.
143 A8 **Wallabi Group** *islds* W Australia Australia
140 E3 **Wallaby I** Queensland Australia
141 F3 **Wallaby I** Queensland Australia
138 C4 **Wallaby,Mt** South Australia Australia
122 J8 **Wallace** Nova Scotia Canada
121 M7 **Wallace** Ontario Canada
100 K2 **Wallace** Idaho U.S.A.
107 J3 **Wallace** Kansas U.S.A.
99 T4 **Wallace** Michigan U.S.A.
98 E9 **Wallace** Nebraska U.S.A.
112 J3 **Wallace** North Carolina U.S.A.
98 J4 **Wallace** South Dakota U.S.A.
94 G7 **Wallace** West Virginia U.S.A.
120 H10 **Wallaceburg** Ontario Canada
109 O3 **Wallace L** Louisiana U.S.A.
118 B3 **Wallace Mt** Alberta Canada
120 J10 **Wallacetown** Ontario Canada
144 B7 **Wallacetown** New Zealand
142 D4 **Wallal Downs** W Australia Australia
143 C9 **Wallambin, L** W Australia Australia
141 K8 **Wallangarra** Queensland Australia
142 D5 **Wallani Well** W Australia Australia
141 H8 **Wallan, R** Queensland Australia
140 B6 **Wallara Ranch** N Terr Australia
138 D5 **Wallaroo** South Australia Australia
8 C1 **Wallasey** England
140 B3 **Wallaston, Mt** N Terr Australia
36 E2 **Wallau** Germany
139 H6 **Walla Walla** New South Wales Australia
100 G4 **Walla Walla** *R* Oregon U.S.A.
100 G3 **Walla Walla** Washington U.S.A.
138 C2 **Wall Cr** N Terr Australia
140 C7 **Wall Creek** N Terr Australia
36 F5 **Walldorf** Germany
37 J2 **Walldorf** Germany
37 L2 **Wallendorf** Germany
37 L3 **Wallenfels** Germany
32 H8 **Wallenhorst** Germany
95 M5 **Wallenpaupack, L** Pennsylvania U.S.A.
41 K3 **Wallen See** *L* Switzerland
32 L8 **Wallensen** Germany
139 K5 **Wallerawang** New South Wales Australia
37 O6 **Wallersdorf** Germany
36 F1 **Wallershöhe** *mt* Germany
37 J6 **Wallerstein** Germany
33 O10 **Wallhausen** Germany
142 B3 **Walliabup** W Australia Australia
9 E4 **Wallingford** England
145 F4 **Wallingford** New Zealand
95 P5 **Wallingford** Connecticut U.S.A.
95 P3 **Wallingford** Vermont U.S.A.
109 L6 **Wallis** Texas U.S.A.
137 R4 **Wallis, Îles** Pacific Oc
139 L4 **Wallis L** New South Wales Australia
99 L7 **Wall L** Iowa U.S.A.
36 D3 **Wallmerod** Germany
142 B6 **Wall, Mt** W Australia Australia
141 K6 **Walloon** Queensland Australia
94 C1 **Walloon L** Michigan U.S.A.
95 M9 **Wallops I** Virginia U.S.A.
100 H4 **Wallowa** Oregon U.S.A.
100 H4 **Wallowa Mts** Oregon U.S.A.
15 G2 **Walls** Scotland
28 C7 **Wallsbüll** Germany
139 K5 **Wallsend** New South Wales Australia
33 O7 **Wallstawe** Germany
32 J8 **Wallucke** Germany
100 G3 **Wallula** Washington U.S.A.
141 J7 **Wallumbilla** Queensland Australia
33 Q9 **Wallwitzhafen** Germany
9 H5 **Walmer** England
13 E5 **Walney I** England
99 R8 **Walnut** Illinois U.S.A.
107 K3 **Walnut** *R* Kansas U.S.A.
107 P4 **Walnut** Kansas U.S.A.
110 H7 **Walnut** Mississippi U.S.A.
103 N6 **Walnut Canyon Nat.Mon** Arizona U.S.A.
112 G1 **Walnut Cove** North Carolina U.S.A.
111 G9 **Walnut Grove** Mississippi U.S.A.
110 C4 **Walnut Grove** Missouri U.S.A.
109 O9 **Walnut Hills** Texas U.S.A.
110 F5 **Walnut Ridge** Arkansas U.S.A.
109 K3 **Walnut Springs** Texas U.S.A.
125 M2 **Walpatanta** Honduras
138 F6 **Walpeup** Victoria Australia
143 B10 **Walpole** W Australia Australia
137 O6 **Walpole** *isld* Pacific Oc
95 P3 **Walpole** New Hampshire U.S.A.
116 D8 **Walrus I** Pribilof Is Bering Sea
116 G7 **Walrus Is** Alaska U.S.A.
9 E2 **Walsall** England
37 K1 **Walschleben** Germany
36 E3 **Walsdorf** Germany
106 F4 **Walsenburg** Colorado U.S.A.
141 G3 **Walsh** *R* Queensland Australia
118 G9 **Walsh** Alberta Canada
106 H4 **Walsh** Colorado U.S.A.
117 D5 **Walsh, Mt** Yukon Territory Canada
22 J2 **Walshoutem** Belgium
25 B6 **Walsoorden** Netherlands
32 L7 **Walsrode** Germany
32 E9 **Walsum** Germany
112 G5 **Walterboro** South Carolina U.S.A.
111 L10 **Walter F. George Res** Alabama/Georgia
109 J1 **Walters** Oklahoma U.S.A.
37 K2 **Waltershausen** Germany
141 G8 **Walter's Ra** Queensland Australia
111 G8 **Walthall** Mississippi U.S.A.
121 O7 **Waltham** Quebec Canada
9 F2 **Waltham** England
101 P2 **Waltham** Montana U.S.A.
9 G4 **Waltham Abbey** England
9 F4 **Waltham Cross** England
98 K7 **Walthill** Nebraska U.S.A.
101 S6 **Waltman** Wyoming U.S.A.
122 J8 **Walton** Nova Scotia Canada
120 J9 **Walton** Ontario Canada
9 F5 **Walton** England
145 E2 **Walton** New Zealand
94 A6 **Walton** Indiana U.S.A.
94 C8 **Walton** Kentucky U.S.A.
95 M4 **Walton** New York U.S.A.
94 F8 **Walton** West Virginia U.S.A.
126 E6 **Walton Bank** Caribbean
94 B2 **Walton Junc** Michigan U.S.A.
9 H4 **Walton-on-the-Naze** England
110 G3 **Waltonville** Illinois U.S.A.
32 F9 **Waltrop** Germany
87 B10 **Walvis Bay** S Africa
90 J12 **Walvis Ridge** Atlantic Oc
99 S7 **Walworth** Wisconsin U.S.A.
143 C9 **Walyahmoing** *hill* W Australia
36 F5 **Walzbuchtal** Germany
87 C8 **Wama** Angola
86 A4 **Wamba** Nigeria
86 E5 **Wamba** Zaire
87 C7 **Wamba** *R* Zaire
139 H5 **Wamboyne** New South Wales Australia
107 O2 **Wamego** Kansas U.S.A.
25 D5 **Wamel** Netherlands
100 D4 **Wamic** Oregon U.S.A.
94 G6 **Wampum** Pennsylvania U.S.A.
101 R8 **Wamsutter** Wyoming U.S.A.
77 L3 **Wana** Pakistan
139 G3 **Wanaaring** New South Wales Australia
144 B6 **Wanaka** New Zealand
67 E3 **Wan'an** China
126 A2 **Wanapa** Bonaire W Indies
120 K6 **Wanapitei L** Ontario Canada
95 N5 **Wanaque Res** New Jersey U.S.A.
99 U8 **Wanatah** Indiana U.S.A.
138 F5 **Wanbi** South Australia Australia
98 E6 **Wanblee** South Dakota U.S.A.
112 M2 **Wanchese** North Carolina U.S.A.
138 E3 **Wancoocha, L** South Australia Australia

130 C10 **Wanda** Argentina
59 K2 **Wanda Shan** *mt ra* China
118 E3 **Wandering River** Alberta Canada
37 K2 **Wandersleben** Germany
28 C7 **Wanderup** Germany
33 S7 **Wandlitz** Germany
141 J7 **Wandoan** Queensland Australia
141 G4 **Wando Vale** Queensland Australia
22 K2 **Wandre** Belgium
109 K1 **Wanette** Oklahoma U.S.A.
65 E4 **Wanfu** China
65 C7 **Wanfu He** *R* China
145 E3 **Wanganui** New Zealand
145 E4 **Wanganui** *admin region* New Zealand
145 E4 **Wanganui R** New Zealand
139 G6 **Wangaratta** Victoria Australia
138 D5 **Wangary** South Australia Australia
67 B2 **Wangcaoba** China
65 B5 **Wangcun** China
67 C2 **Wangcun** China
67 B4 **Wangdian** China
65 C5 **Wangdu** China
33 N4 **Wangels** Germany
41 L2 **Wangen** Germany
32 G5 **Wangerland** *reg* Germany
32 G5 **Wangerooge** Germany
9 H3 **Wangford** England
71 K10 **Wanggamet, Gunung** *mt* Sumba Indonesia
67 D4 **Wanggao** China
Wanggezhuang *see* **Jiaonan**
71 H7 **Wangiwangi** *isld* Indonesia
67 D2 **Wangjiachang** China
67 E1 **Wangjiadian** China
67 E1 **Wangjiang** China
68 D5 **Wangka** Thailand
65 G1 **Wangkui** China
Wang Mai Khon *see* **Sawankhalok**
67 C5 **Wangmao** China
67 B4 **Wangmo** China
65 H3 **Wangqing** China
68 D2 **Wan hsa-la** Burma
74 H8 **Wani** India
71 H7 **Wani** *mt* Indonesia
86 E5 **Wanie-Rukula** Zaire
111 F10 **Wanilla** Mississippi U.S.A.
65 E5 **Wanjialing** China
74 D7 **Wankaner** India
32 M4 **Wankendorf** Germany
Wankie *see* **Hwange**
86 H5 **Wanlaweyn** Somalia
119 Q4 **Wanless** Manitoba Canada
12 E3 **Wanlockhead** Scotland
143 G8 **Wanna Lakes** W Australia Australia
32 F9 **Wanne-Eickel** Germany
143 B9 **Wanneroo** W Australia Australia
67 F2 **Wannian** China
68 K3 **Wanning** China
33 S8 **Wannsee** Germany
76 D2 **Wanparti** India
65 C4 **Wanquan** China
125 M2 **Wanquibila** Honduras
65 A7 **Wanrong** China
13 G3 **Wansbeck, R** England
9 F2 **Wansford** England
67 C3 **Wanshan** China
67 D6 **Wanshan Qundao** *islds* China
145 F4 **Wanstead** New Zealand
9 E4 **Wantage** England
36 D6 **Wantzenau** France
120 K6 **Wanup** Ontario Canada
67 C1 **Wan Xian** China
67 C1 **Wanxian** China
65 C7 **Wanyang Hu** *L* China
58 E5 **Wanyuan** China
67 E2 **Wanzai** China
Wanzhi *see* **Wuhu**
33 O8 **Wanzleben** Germany
145 E3 **Waotu** New Zealand
94 C6 **Wapakoneta** Ohio U.S.A.
109 L1 **Wapanucka** Oklahoma U.S.A.
100 E3 **Wapato** Washington U.S.A.
119 N4 **Wapawekka Hills** Saskatchewan Canada
119 Q8 **Wapella** Saskatchewan Canada
101 N6 **Wapello** Idaho U.S.A.
99 P8 **Wapello** Iowa U.S.A.
119 S3 **Wapisu L** Manitoba Canada
117 O8 **Wapiti** *R* Alberta Canada
101 Q5 **Wapiti Ra** Wyoming U.S.A.
110 F4 **Wappapello Res** Missouri U.S.A.
95 O5 **Wappingers Falls** New York U.S.A.
99 O7 **Wapsipinicon** *R* Iowa U.S.A.
119 P2 **Wapus L** Saskatchewan Canada
123 N2 **Wapustagamau L** Quebec Canada
94 F9 **War** West Virginia U.S.A.
140 D1 **Waraga** N Terr Australia
86 H4 **Warandab** Ethiopia
76 D1 **Warangal** India
139 H6 **Waranga Res** Victoria Australia
139 H8 **Waratah** Tasmania Australia
139 H7 **Waratah B** Victoria Australia
99 N2 **Warba** Minnesota U.S.A.
9 F3 **Warboys** England
141 G6 **Warbreccan** Queensland Australia
118 C5 **Warburg** Alberta Canada
32 K10 **Warburg** Germany
138 E2 **Warburton** *R* South Australia Australia
139 H7 **Warburton** Victoria Australia
143 F7 **Warburton Mission** W Australia Australia
143 F7 **Warburton Ra** W Australia Australia
141 H7 **Ward** *R* Queensland Australia
145 E4 **Ward** New Zealand
111 H9 **Ward** Alabama U.S.A.
138 D5 **Wardang I** South Australia Australia
87 E11 **Warden** S Africa
100 F3 **Warden** Washington U.S.A.
32 H6 **Wardenburg** Germany
118 E6 **Warden Junc** Alberta Canada
94 J7 **Wardensville** West Virginia U.S.A.
74 H8 **Wardha** India
115 M1 **Ward Hunt I** Northwest Territories Canada
118 F8 **Wardlow** Alberta Canada
144 B5 **Ward, Mt** New Zealand
144 A6 **Ward, Mt** New Zealand
118 B9 **Wardner** British Columbia Canada
13 F5 **Wards Stone** *mt* England
117 L7 **Ware** British Columbia Canada
9 F4 **Ware** England
95 P4 **Ware** Massachusetts U.S.A.
145 D3 **Warea** New Zealand
22 E2 **Waregem** Belgium
8 D6 **Wareham** England
22 J2 **Waremme** Belgium
33 R5 **Waren** Germany
140 F6 **Warenda** Queensland Australia
32 G9 **Warendorf** Germany
144 B7 **Warepa** New Zealand
140 B4 **Ware Ra** N Terr Australia
112 E6 **Waresboro** Georgia U.S.A.
112 E3 **Ware Shoals** South Carolina U.S.A.
95 N7 **Waretown** New Jersey U.S.A.
25 G2 **Warfum** Netherlands
86 A2 **War Galoh** Somalia
9 F5 **Wargrave** England
139 K3 **Warialda** New South Wales Australia
33 P5 **Warin** Germany
68 G5 **Warin Chamrap** Thailand
109 J6 **Waring** Texas U.S.A.
116 H3 **Waring Mts** Alaska U.S.A.
13 F2 **Wark** England
31 N4 **Warka** Poland
121 N8 **Warkworth** Ontario Canada
13 G3 **Warkworth** England
145 E2 **Warkworth** New Zealand
8 D3 **Warley** England
9 F5 **Warlingham** England
21 P1 **Warloy-Baillon** France
89 A7 **Warmbad** Namibia
117 G6 **Warm Bay Hotsprings** British Columbia Canada
37 M4 **Warmensteinach** Germany
22 G5 **Warmeriville** France
9 E3 **Warmington** England
8 D5 **Warminster** England
25 C4 **Warmond** Netherlands
32 J8 **Warmsen** Germany
112 C5 **Warm Springs** Georgia U.S.A.
101 N3 **Warmsprings** Montana U.S.A.
102 H3 **Warm Springs** Nevada U.S.A.
100 D5 **Warm Springs** Oregon U.S.A.
94 H8 **Warm Springs** Virginia U.S.A.
100 G6 **Warm Springs Res** Oregon U.S.A.
89 B9 **Warmwaters Berg** *mt* S Africa
8 D6 **Warmwell** England
22 J2 **Warnant-Dreye** Belgium
120 B3 **Warneford** Ontario Canada
33 Q4 **Warnemünde** Germany
101 N1 **Warner** Alberta Canada
95 Q3 **Warner** New Hampshire U.S.A.
107 P6 **Warner** Oklahoma U.S.A.
98 H4 **Warner** South Dakota U.S.A.
100 F7 **Warner Lakes** Oregon U.S.A.
100 E8 **Warner Mts** California U.S.A.
112 D5 **Warner Robins** Georgia U.S.A.
102 H8 **Warner Springs** California U.S.A.
22 D2 **Warneton** Belgium
139 L3 **Warning,Mt** New South Wales Australia
33 Q5 **Warnow** *R* Germany
143 B10 **Waroona** W Australia Australia
74 H8 **Warora** India
141 K7 **Warra** Queensland Australia
138 F6 **Warracknabeal** Victoria Australia
139 H7 **Warragul** Victoria Australia
138 E3 **Warrakalanna,L** South Australia Australia
138 D5 **Warramboo** South Australia Australia
143 C8 **Warramboo** *mt* W Australia Australia
139 J3 **Warrambool** *R* New South Wales Australia
80 G4 **Warran** *R* Jordan
138 E2 **Warrandirinna,L** South Australia Australia
142 D5 **Warrawagine** W Australia Australia
141 F7 **Warrego** *R* Queensland Australia
141 H6 **Warrego Ra** Queensland Australia
139 J4 **Warren** New South Wales Australia
120 K6 **Warren** Ontario Canada
111 D8 **Warren** Arkansas U.S.A.
100 K4 **Warren** Idaho U.S.A.
99 R7 **Warren** Illinois U.S.A.
94 B6 **Warren** Indiana U.S.A.
94 D4 **Warren** Michigan U.S.A.
98 K1 **Warren** Minnesota U.S.A.
101 R4 **Warren** Montana U.S.A.
95 Q3 **Warren** New Hampshire U.S.A.
94 G5 **Warren** Ohio U.S.A.
94 H5 **Warren** Pennsylvania U.S.A.
95 Q5 **Warren** Rhode I U.S.A.
109 N5 **Warren** Texas U.S.A.
94 J9 **Warren** Virginia U.S.A.
115 L3 **Warrender,C** Northwest Territories Canada
119 U5 **Warren Landing** Manitoba Canada
143 E8 **Warren, Mt** W Australia Australia
14 E2 **Warrenpoint** N Ireland
99 Q5 **Warrens** Wisconsin U.S.A.
99 R10 **Warrensburg** Illinois U.S.A.
110 C3 **Warrensburg** Missouri U.S.A.
95 O3 **Warrensburg** New York U.S.A.
89 D7 **Warrenton** S Africa
112 E4 **Warrenton** Georgia U.S.A.
110 E3 **Warrenton** Missouri U.S.A.
112 J1 **Warrenton** North Carolina U.S.A.
100 B3 **Warrenton** Oregon U.S.A.
94 K8 **Warrenton** Virginia U.S.A.
101 Q1 **Warrick** Montana U.S.A.
143 B8 **Warriedar Hill** W Australia Australia
138 D3 **Warrina** South Australia Australia
138 D3 **Warriners Cr** South Australia Australia
13 F6 **Warrington** England
144 D6 **Warrington** New Zealand
111 J11 **Warrington** Florida U.S.A.
111 K8 **Warrior** Alabama U.S.A.
138 E4 **Warrior Creek** South Australia Australia
138 F3 **Warri Warri** New South Wales Australia
138 F7 **Warrnambool** Victoria Australia
99 L1 **Warroad** Minnesota U.S.A.
141 J7 **Warrong** Queensland Australia
138 D5 **Warrow** South Australia Australia
139 J4 **Warrumbungle Ra** New South Wales Australia
141 F8 **Warry Warry** *R* Queensland Australia
Warsaw *see* **Warszawa**
99 P9 **Warsaw** Illinois U.S.A.
94 B5 **Warsaw** Indiana U.S.A.
94 C8 **Warsaw** Kentucky U.S.A.
110 C3 **Warsaw** Missouri U.S.A.
94 J4 **Warsaw** New York U.S.A.
112 J2 **Warsaw** North Carolina U.S.A.
95 L9 **Warsaw** Virginia U.S.A.
38 K6 **Warscheneck** *mt* Austria
86 A3 **Warshikh** Somalia
118 E4 **Warspite** Alberta Canada
32 H10 **Warstein** Germany
31 M3 **Warszawa** Poland
31 H2 **Warszów** Poland
31 J3 **Warta** *R* Poland
31 L4 **Warta** Poland
38 N6 **Wartberg** Austria
37 J2 **Wartburg** Germany
37 M7 **Wartenberg** Germany
13 H6 **Warter** England
41 M3 **Warth** Austria
118 J7 **Wartime** Saskatchewan Canada
13 F6 **Warton** England
142 F3 **Warton Ra** W Australia Australia
110 K6 **Wartrace** Tennessee U.S.A.
70 E5 **Waru** Kalimantan
141 K8 **Warwick** Queensland Australia
121 T7 **Warwick** Quebec Canada
9 E3 **Warwick** England
13 F4 **Warwick** Cumbria England
112 D6 **Warwick** Georgia U.S.A.
95 N5 **Warwick** New York U.S.A.
98 H2 **Warwick** North Dakota U.S.A.
95 Q5 **Warwick** Rhode I U.S.A.
140 D2 **Warwick Chan** N Terr Australia
9 E3 **Warwickshire** *co* England
117 Q11 **Wasa** British Columbia Canada
120 K8 **Wasaga Beach** Ontario Canada
85 F6 **Wasagu** Nigeria
103 N2 **Wasatch Ra** Utah U.S.A.
102 E6 **Wasco** California U.S.A.
100 E4 **Wasco** Oregon U.S.A.
99 P3 **Wascott** Wisconsin U.S.A.
118 H5 **Waseca** Saskatchewan Canada
99 N5 **Waseca** Minnesota U.S.A.
121 L8 **Washago** Ontario Canada
101 Q6 **Washakie Needles** *mts* Wyoming U.S.A.
9 H3 **Washbrook** England
99 R9 **Washburn** Illinois U.S.A.
95 S7 **Washburn** Maine U.S.A.
98 E2 **Washburn** North Dakota U.S.A.
108 C8 **Washburn** Texas U.S.A.
114 J3 **Washburn L** Northwest Territories Canada
101 P5 **Washburn,Mt** Wyoming U.S.A.
144 C6 **Washdyke** New Zealand
8 C5 **Washford** England
60 H12 **Washiki** Japan
123 M3 **Washikuti** Quebec Canada
74 G8 **Wāshim** India
121 S3 **Washimeska** *R* Quebec Canada
97 **Washington** *conurbation* District of Columbia
13 G4 **Washington** England
100 F2 **Washington** *state* U.S.A.
109 O2 **Washington** Arkansas U.S.A.
112 E4 **Washington** Georgia U.S.A.
99 R9 **Washington** Illinois U.S.A.
110 J3 **Washington** Indiana U.S.A.
99 P8 **Washington** Iowa U.S.A.
107 N2 **Washington** Kansas U.S.A.
111 D11 **Washington** Louisiana U.S.A.
110 E3 **Washington** Missouri U.S.A.
95 P3 **Washington** New Hampshire U.S.A.
95 N6 **Washington** New Jersey U.S.A.
112 K2 **Washington** North Carolina U.S.A.
94 G6 **Washington** Pennsylvania U.S.A.
109 L5 **Washington** Texas U.S.A.
103 L4 **Washington** Utah U.S.A.
94 J8 **Washington** Virginia U.S.A.
146 C12 **Washington, Cape** Antarctica
94 D7 **Washington Court Ho** Ohio U.S.A.
99 U4 **Washington I** Wisconsin U.S.A.
113 G9 **Washington,L** Florida U.S.A.
115 N1 **Washington Land** Greenland
95 Q2 **Washington, Mt** New Hampshire U.S.A.
109 J1 **Washita** *R* Oklahoma U.S.A.
101 Q4 **Washoe** Montana U.S.A.
100 C4 **Washougal** Washington U.S.A.
119 V7 **Washow B** Manitoba Canada
9 G2 **Wash, The** *G* England
100 G3 **Washtucna** Washington U.S.A.
22 G4 **Wasigny** France
31 O2 **Wasilków** Poland
71 N8 **Wasiri** Indonesia
79 E9 **Wasit** Egypt
78 K5 **Wāsit** *prov* Iraq
98 F1 **Waskada** Manitoba Canada
119 V2 **Waskaiowaka L** Manitoba Canada
118 L5 **Waskesiu L** Saskatchewan Canada
118 L5 **Waskesiu Lake** Saskatchewan Canada
118 E4 **Wasketenau** Alberta Canada
99 M1 **Waskish** Minnesota U.S.A.
109 N3 **Waskom** Texas U.S.A.
22 F3 **Wasmes** Belgium
31 K4 **Wąsosz** Poland
60 Q1 **Wassamu** Japan
112 G4 **Wassaw Sd** Georgia U.S.A.
36 C6 **Wasselonne** France
25 F6 **Wassenberg** Germany
37 J6 **Wasseralfingen** Germany
22 L4 **Wasserbillig** Luxembourg
37 K5 **Wassermungenau** Germany
37 K5 **Wassertrüdingen** Germany
22 F3 **Wassigny** France
102 F3 **Wassuk Ra** Nevada U.S.A.
19 J4 **Wassy** France
98 D5 **Wasta** South Dakota U.S.A.
79 B9 **Wasta,El** Egypt
13 E5 **Wast Water** *L* England
37 J2 **Wasungen** Germany
121 O3 **Waswanipi** Quebec Canada
120 K4 **Watabeag L** Ontario Canada
99 Q8 **Wataga** Illinois U.S.A.
83 L11 **Watagoda** *mt* Sri Lanka
70 G7 **Watampone** Sulawesi
71 L9 **Watanga, Teluk** *B* Flores Indonesia
70 F7 **Watansoppeng** Sulawesi
98 E4 **Watauga** South Dakota U.S.A.
109 M9 **Watauga** Texas U.S.A.
8 C5 **Watchet** England
118 L1 **Watcomb** Ontario Canada
9 G3 **Waterbeach** England
87 C10 **Waterberg Plateau Park** *nat park* Namibia
95 R3 **Waterboro** Maine U.S.A.
95 O5 **Waterbury** Connecticut U.S.A.
95 P2 **Waterbury** Vermont U.S.A.
126 F3 **Water Cays** *islds* Bahamas
112 G3 **Wateree L** South Carolina U.S.A.
120 K10 **Waterford** Ontario Canada
14 D4 **Waterford** *co* Ireland
14 D4 **Waterford** Ireland
102 D4 **Waterford** California U.S.A.
94 H5 **Waterford** Pennsylvania U.S.A.
14 E4 **Waterford Hbr** Ireland
8 A7 **Watergate B** England
119 S6 **Waterhen L** Manitoba Canada
118 J4 **Waterhen L** Saskatchewan Canada
140 C2 **Waterhouse** *R* N Terr Australia
140 C6 **Waterhouse Ra** N Terr Australia
140 A3 **Waterloo** N Terr Australia
22 G2 **Waterloo** Belgium
121 S7 **Waterloo** Quebec Canada
127 O2 **Waterloo** Trinidad
110 H7 **Waterloo** Alabama U.S.A.
109 O2 **Waterloo** Arkansas U.S.A.
110 F3 **Waterloo** Illinois U.S.A.
94 B5 **Waterloo** Indiana U.S.A.
99 O7 **Waterloo** Iowa U.S.A.
101 N4 **Waterloo** Montana U.S.A.
95 L4 **Waterloo** New York U.S.A.
8 C6 **Waterloo Cross** England
99 S8 **Waterman** Illinois U.S.A.
111 E10 **Waterproof** Louisiana U.S.A.
94 C2 **Waters** Michigan U.S.A.
99 R3 **Watersmeet** Michigan U.S.A.
118 D9 **Waterton Pk** Alberta Canada
99 N5 **Watertown** Minnesota U.S.A.
95 M3 **Watertown** New York U.S.A.
98 J5 **Watertown** South Dakota U.S.A.
110 K5 **Watertown** Tennessee U.S.A.
99 S6 **Watertown** Wisconsin U.S.A.
138 E5 **Watervale** South Australia Australia
111 G7 **Water Valley** Mississippi U.S.A.
108 G4 **Water Valley** Texas U.S.A.
95 O4 **Watervliet** New York U.S.A.
122 H8 **Waterville** Nova Scotia Canada
121 T7 **Waterville** Quebec Canada
95 S2 **Waterville** Maine U.S.A.
99 N5 **Waterville** Minnesota U.S.A.
95 M4 **Waterville** New York U.S.A.
100 E2 **Waterville** Washington U.S.A.
118 F2 **Waterways** Alberta Canada
70 N9 **Wates** Java
120 J10 **Watford** Ontario Canada
9 F4 **Watford** England
98 C2 **Watford City** North Dakota U.S.A.
107 P2 **Wathena** Kansas U.S.A.
143 B9 **Watheroo** W Australia Australia
117 P8 **Watino** Alberta Canada
106 F2 **Watkins** Colorado U.S.A.
99 M4 **Watkins** Minnesota U.S.A.
115 R4 **Watkins Bjerge** *mts* Greenland
95 L4 **Watkins Glen** New York U.S.A.
112 D4 **Watkinsville** Georgia U.S.A.
107 M6 **Watonga** Oklahoma U.S.A.
70 K9 **Waton,Tg** *C* Java
22 D2 **Watou** Belgium
71 B2 **Watowato,Bk** *mt* Halmahera Indonesia
119 M7 **Watrous** Saskatchewan Canada
106 F6 **Watrous** New Mexico U.S.A.
86 E5 **Watsa** Zaire
79 T9 **Watseka** Illinois U.S.A.
86 D6 **Watsi-Kengo** Zaire
141 F2 **Watson** *R* Queensland Australia
119 N6 **Watson** Saskatchewan Canada
111 E8 **Watson** Arkansas U.S.A.
99 L4 **Watson** Minnesota U.S.A.
99 L9 **Watson** Missouri U.S.A.
101 Q10 **Watson** Utah U.S.A.
117 J5 **Watson Lake** Yukon Territory Canada
95 L5 **Watsontown** Pennsylvania U.S.A.
83 J10 **Wattala** Sri Lanka
22 C2 **Watten** France
15 E2 **Watten** Scotland
32 F10 **Wattenscheid** Germany
138 D3 **Wattiwarriganna** *R* South Australia Australia
139 G3 **Wattle Vale** New South Wales Australia
143 F7 **Watt, Mt** W Australia Australia
117 P6 **Watt,Mt** Alberta Canada
9 G2 **Watton** England
9 F4 **Watton** England
107 Q5 **Watts** Oklahoma U.S.A.
112 C2 **Watts Bar Lake** Tennessee U.S.A.
94 H4 **Wattsburg** Pennsylvania U.S.A.
71 L9 **Watumanuk, Tanjong** *C* Indonesia
70 G6 **Watuwila,Bk** *mt* Sulawesi
38 G6 **Watzmann** *mt* Germany
136 K3 **Wau** Papua New Guinea
86 E4 **Wau** Sudan
120 K7 **Waubamick** Ontario Canada
121 L8 **Waubaushene** Ontario Canada
98 J4 **Waubay** South Dakota U.S.A.
98 J4 **Waubay L** South Dakota U.S.A.
139 L4 **Wauchope** New South Wales Australia
140 C5 **Wauchope** N Terr Australia
119 Q9 **Wauchope** Saskatchewan Canada
113 F10 **Wauchula** Florida U.S.A.
99 O6 **Waucoma** Iowa U.S.A.
100 G1 **Wauconda** Washington U.S.A.
118 F1 **Waugh** Manitoba Canada
142 D5 **Waukarlycarly, L** W Australia Australia
70 F5 **Waukata, G** *mt* Sulawesi
99 N8 **Waukee** Iowa U.S.A.
99 T7 **Waukegan** Illinois U.S.A.
99 S6 **Waukesha** Wisconsin U.S.A.
107 N5 **Waukomis** Oklahoma U.S.A.
99 P6 **Waukon** Iowa U.S.A.
98 E9 **Wauneta** Nebraska U.S.A.
99 R5 **Waupaca** Wisconsin U.S.A.
99 S6 **Waupun** Wisconsin U.S.A.
109 K1 **Waurika** Oklahoma U.S.A.
98 J7 **Wausa** Nebraska U.S.A.
99 R5 **Wausau** Wisconsin U.S.A.
99 T4 **Wausaukee** Wisconsin U.S.A.
94 C5 **Wauseon** Ohio U.S.A.
81 G8 **W Australian Ridge** Indian Oc
99 R5 **Wautoma** Wisconsin U.S.A.
99 S6 **Wauwatosa** Wisconsin U.S.A.
140 B3 **Wave Hill Police Station** N Terr Australia
110 J2 **Waveland** Indiana U.S.A.
141 K1 **Wavell Heights** *dist* Brisbane, Qnsld Australia
9 H3 **Waveney,R** England
122 J9 **Waverley** Nova Scotia Canada
145 E3 **Waverley** New Zealand
100 H2 **Waverley** Washington U.S.A.
112 F6 **Waverly** Georgia U.S.A.
110 G2 **Waverly** Illinois U.S.A.
99 O7 **Waverly** Iowa U.S.A.
107 P3 **Waverly** Kansas U.S.A.
110 D2 **Waverly** Missouri U.S.A.
98 K9 **Waverly** Nebraska U.S.A.
95 L4 **Waverly** New York U.S.A.
94 E7 **Waverly** Ohio U.S.A.
110 J5 **Waverly** Tennessee U.S.A.
95 K9 **Waverly** Virginia U.S.A.
111 M9 **Waverly Hall** Georgia U.S.A.
141 F7 **Waverney** Queensland Australia
22 C2 **Wavrans-sur-l'Aa** France
22 H2 **Wavre** Belgium
22 D2 **Wavrin** France
118 E6 **Wavy L** Alberta Canada
68 C4 **Waw** Burma
120 F4 **Wawa** Ontario Canada
121 M3 **Wawagosic** *R* Quebec Canada
120 J4 **Wawaitin Falls** Ontario Canada
70 G6 **Wawalalindu** Sulawesi
119 S9 **Wawanesa** Manitoba Canada
84 F5 **Waw an Nāmūs** Libya
94 B5 **Wawasee,L** Indiana U.S.A.
70 G6 **Wawo** Sulawesi
102 E4 **Wawona** California U.S.A.
119 Q9 **Wawota** Saskatchewan Canada
70 G6 **Wawotebi** Sulawesi
109 L3 **Waxahachie** Texas U.S.A.
112 G3 **Waxhaw** North Carolina U.S.A.
111 F9 **Way** Mississippi U.S.A.
71 A3 **Wayabula** Indonesia
101 O7 **Wayan** Idaho U.S.A.
Wayaobu *see* **Zichang**
112 E6 **Waycross** Georgia U.S.A.
68 F8 **Way,Ko** *isld* G of Thailand
143 D7 **Way, L** W Australia Australia
99 P8 **Wayland** Iowa U.S.A.
94 B4 **Wayland** Kentucky U.S.A.
94 B4 **Wayland** Michigan U.S.A.
99 P9 **Wayland** Missouri U.S.A.
94 K4 **Wayland** New York U.S.A.
118 E7 **Wayne** Alberta Canada
95 R2 **Wayne** Maine U.S.A.
94 D4 **Wayne** Michigan U.S.A.
98 J7 **Wayne** Nebraska U.S.A.
107 M7 **Wayne** Oklahoma U.S.A.
94 E8 **Wayne** West Virginia U.S.A.
110 H3 **Wayne City** Illinois U.S.A.
112 F4 **Waynesboro** Georgia U.S.A.
111 H10 **Waynesboro** Mississippi U.S.A.
94 K7 **Waynesboro** Pennsylvania U.S.A.
110 J6 **Waynesboro** Tennessee U.S.A.
94 J8 **Waynesboro** Virginia U.S.A.
94 F6 **Waynesburg** Ohio U.S.A.
94 G7 **Waynesburg** Pennsylvania U.S.A.
99 R9 **Waynesville** Illinois U.S.A.
110 D4 **Waynesville** Missouri U.S.A.
112 E2 **Waynesville** North Carolina U.S.A.
94 C7 **Waynesville** Ohio U.S.A.
107 M5 **Waynoka** Oklahoma U.S.A.
98 C7 **Wayside** Nebraska U.S.A.
108 F1 **Wayside** Texas U.S.A.
77 L3 **Wazi Khwa** Afghanistan
77 K1 **Wazirabad** Afghanistan
74 F2 **Wazirabad** Pakistan
31 L2 **Wda** *R* Poland
7 L11 **Weald, The** *reg* England
13 F4 **Wearhead** England
140 D3 **Wearyan** *R* N Terr Australia
141 H3 **Weary B** Queensland Australia
99 M10 **Weatherby** Missouri U.S.A.
107 M6 **Weatherford** Oklahoma U.S.A.
109 K3 **Weatherford** Texas U.S.A.
95 M6 **Weatherly** Pennsylvania U.S.A.
110 C4 **Weaubleau** Missouri U.S.A.
111 L8 **Weaver** Alabama U.S.A.
8 D1 **Weaverham** England
119 V6 **Weaver L** Manitoba Canada
100 C9 **Weaverville** California U.S.A.
118 J8 **Webb** Saskatchewan Canada
111 L10 **Webb** Alabama U.S.A.
111 F8 **Webb** Mississippi U.S.A.
109 H8 **Webb** Texas U.S.A.
110 B4 **Webb City** Missouri U.S.A.
107 P6 **Webbers Falls Res.** Oklahoma U.S.A.
142 G6 **Webb, Mt** W Australia Australia
145 F4 **Weber** New Zealand
106 G7 **Weber City** New Mexico U.S.A.
106 E2 **Webster** Colorado U.S.A.
113 E9 **Webster** Florida U.S.A.
99 O8 **Webster** Iowa U.S.A.
107 L2 **Webster** Kansas U.S.A.
95 Q4 **Webster** Massachusetts U.S.A.
95 K3 **Webster** New York U.S.A.
98 H1 **Webster** North Dakota U.S.A.
98 J4 **Webster** South Dakota U.S.A.
99 O4 **Webster** Wisconsin U.S.A.
99 N7 **Webster City** Iowa U.S.A.
110 F3 **Webster Groves** Missouri U.S.A.
22 H1 **Wechelderzande** Belgium
109 M4 **Weches** Texas U.S.A.
37 O2 **Wechselburg** Germany
71 A2 **Weda** Halmahera Indonesia
83 L11 **Wedagama** Sri Lanka
71 B2 **Weda,Teluk** *B* Halmahera Indonesia
133 E8 **Weddell I** Falkland Is
146 E4 **Weddell Sea** Antarctica
32 L7 **Weddemark** Germany
144 C6 **Wedderburn** New Zealand
100 A7 **Wedderburn** Oregon U.S.A.
32 K4 **Weddinghusen** Germany
32 K4 **Weddingstedt** Germany
33 N6 **Wedel** Germany
140 B6 **Wedge, Central Mt** N Terr Australia
112 G4 **Wedgefield** South Carolina U.S.A.
117 M10 **Wedge Mt** British Columbia Canada
122 G10 **Wedgeport** Nova Scotia Canada
8 D5 **Wedmore** England
8 D2 **Wednesbury** England
111 L8 **Wedowee** Alabama U.S.A.
100 C8 **Weed** California U.S.A.
121 T7 **Weedon** Quebec Canada
9 E3 **Weedon** England
95 L3 **Weedsport** New York U.S.A.
94 J5 **Weedville** Pennsylvania U.S.A.
71 C3 **Weeim** *isld* W Irian
119 P6 **Weekes** Saskatchewan Canada
111 E12 **Weeks** Louisiana U.S.A.
94 E9 **Weeksbury** Kentucky U.S.A.
Weeks I *see* **Puketutu I**
112 L1 **Weeksville** North Carolina U.S.A.
9 H4 **Weeley** England
142 B6 **Weeli Wolli Ck** W Australia Australia
139 J3 **Weemelah** New South Wales Australia
32 F6 **Weener** Germany
98 K9 **Weeping Water** Nebraska U.S.A.
25 E6 **Weert** Netherlands
109 K7 **Weesatche** Texas U.S.A.
28 C7 **Weesby** Germany
41 K3 **Weesen** Switzerland
25 D4 **Weesp** Netherlands
25 G1 **Weestereems** Netherlands
139 H5 **Weethalle** New South Wales Australia
9 G3 **Weeting** England
32 L8 **Weetzen** Germany
139 J4 **Wee Waa** New South Wales Australia
25 F5 **Weeze** Germany
33 O8 **Wefensleben** Germany
33 O8 **Weferlingen** Germany
33 O9 **Wegeleben** Germany
33 O8 **Wegenstedt** Germany
41 H3 **Weggis** Switzerland
32 J8 **Wegholm** Germany
31 J4 **Węgliniec** Poland
31 N1 **Wegorapa** *R* Poland
31 N1 **Węgorzewo** Poland
31 J2 **Węgorzyno** Poland
31 N3 **Węgrów** Poland
38 M6 **Wegscheid** Austria
38 J4 **Wegscheid** Germany
25 F2 **Wehe** Netherlands
40 G2 **Wehr** Germany
32 K9 **Wehrden** Germany
36 F3 **Wehrheim** Germany
65 D4 **Weichang** China
37 L6 **Weichering** Germany
38 M6 **Weichselboden** Austria
65 C7 **Weichuan** China
37 N2 **Weida** Germany
37 N4 **Weiden** Germany
36 E2 **Weidenau** Germany
37 M4 **Weidenberg** Germany
36 H6 **Weidenstetten** Germany
37 L3 **Weidhausen** Germany
94 C3 **Weidman** Michigan U.S.A.
65 D6 **Weifang** China
65 E6 **Weihai** China
58 E5 **Wei He** *R* China
65 G2 **Weihe** China
37 N6 **Weihmichl** Germany
36 E3 **Weilburg** Germany
36 F6 **Weil-der-Stadt** Germany
36 B2 **Weilerswist** Germany
36 H6 **Weilheim** Germany
36 E3 **Weilmünster** Germany
36 E3 **Weilnau** Germany
37 J5 **Weiltingen** Germany
65 B4 **Weilu** China
37 L2 **Weimar** Germany
109 L6 **Weimar** Texas U.S.A.
58 E5 **Weinan** China
110 F6 **Weiner** Arkansas U.S.A.
41 K2 **Weinfelden** Switzerland
36 E5 **Weingarten** Germany
36 F5 **Weingarten** Germany
36 F4 **Weinheim** Germany
67 A3 **Weining** China
36 G5 **Weinsberg** Germany
36 G6 **Weinstadt** Germany
141 F2 **Weipa** Queensland Australia
100 K3 **Weippe** Idaho U.S.A.
141 J8 **Weir** *R* Queensland Australia
121 Q7 **Weir** Quebec Canada
110 B4 **Weir** Kansas U.S.A.
111 G8 **Weir** Mississippi U.S.A.
109 K5 **Weir** Texas U.S.A.
143 B7 **Weiragoo Ra** W Australia Australia
107 Q4 **Weir City** Kansas U.S.A.
119 M5 **Weirdale** Saskatchewan Canada
95 Q3 **Weirs Beach** New Hampshire U.S.A.
113 F9 **Weirsdale** Florida U.S.A.
94 G6 **Weirton** West Virginia U.S.A.
37 N3 **Weischlitz** Germany
100 J5 **Weiser** Idaho U.S.A.
65 D7 **Weishan** China
65 C7 **Weishan Hu** *L* China
65 C7 **Weishi** China
Weishui *see* **Jingxing**
36 B4 **Weiskirchen** Germany
37 L3 **Weismain** Germany
36 F6 **Weissach** Germany
37 K5 **Weissenburg** Germany
37 M1 **Weissenfels** Germany
37 J7 **Weissenhorn** Germany
33 T7 **Weissensee** Berlin Germany
37 L1 **Weissensee** Thüringen Germany
37 M3 **Weissenstadt** Germany
36 H6 **Weissenstein** Germany
37 M3 **Weisser Main** *R* Germany
37 O5 **Weisser Regen** *R* Germany
40 G5 **Weisshorn** *mt* Switzerland
38 L7 **Weisskirchen** Austria
41 N4 **Weisskugel** *mt* Austria
112 B3 **Weiss Lake** Alabama U.S.A.
89 A5 **Weissrand Mts** Namibia
41 K3 **Weisstannen** Switzerland
33 S4 **Weitenhagen** Germany
41 M2 **Weitnau** Germany
67 F4 **Weitou** China
31 H7 **Weitra** Austria
38 N8 **Weixelbaum** Austria
38 K8 **Weixelsdorf** Austria
65 C6 **Wei Xian** China
65 D6 **Wei Xian** China
67 A3 **Weixin** China
67 A2 **Weiyuan** China
38 N7 **Weiz** Austria
41 H2 **Weizen** Germany
Weizhou *see* **Wenchuan**
68 J2 **Weizhou Dao** *isld* China
31 L1 **Wejherowo** Poland
119 S4 **Wekusko** Manitoba Canada
113 F8 **Welaka** Florida U.S.A.
138 C2 **Welbourn Hill** South Australia Australia
94 F9 **Welch** West Virginia U.S.A.
99 M6 **Welcome** Minnesota U.S.A.
89 A8 **Welcome Kop** *mt* S Africa
37 K7 **Welden** Germany
86 G3 **Weldiya** Ethiopia
143 D8 **Weld, Mt** W Australia Australia
119 M6 **Weldon** Saskatchewan Canada
102 F6 **Weldon** California U.S.A.
99 S9 **Weldon** Illinois U.S.A.
99 N9 **Weldon** Iowa U.S.A.
99 N9 **Weldon** *R* Missouri U.S.A.
112 L1 **Weldon** North Carolina U.S.A.
109 M4 **Weldon** Texas U.S.A.
106 G1 **Weldona** Colorado U.S.A.
13 G3 **Weldon Br** England
143 B7 **Weld Ra** W Australia Australia
107 O6 **Weleetka** Oklahoma U.S.A.
86 G4 **Welega** *prov* Ethiopia
141 G7 **Welford** Queensland Australia
141 G7 **Welford Downs** Queensland Australia
83 K12 **Weligama** Sri Lanka
83 L11 **Weliwewa** Sri Lanka
22 K2 **Welkenraedt** Belgium
89 E6 **Welkom** S Africa
121 L10 **Welland Canal** Ontario Canada
9 F2 **Welland, R** England
142 A4 **Wellard** *dist* Perth, W Aust Australia
83 L11 **Wellawaya** Sri Lanka
113 E7 **Wellborn** Florida U.S.A.
36 H1 **Wellerode Wald** Germany
9 E3 **Wellesbourne** England
140 E3 **Wellesley Is** Queensland Australia
117 D4 **Wellesley L** Yukon Territory Canada
98 F9 **Wellfleet** Nebraska U.S.A.
37 L6 **Wellheim** Germany
22 J3 **Wellin** Belgium
9 F3 **Wellingborough** England
139 J4 **Wellington** New South Wales Australia
138 E6 **Wellington** South Australia Australia
123 S5 **Wellington** Newfoundland Canada
122 J9 **Wellington** Nova Scotia Canada
121 N9 **Wellington** Ontario Canada
122 H7 **Wellington** Prince Edward I Canada
8 D2 **Wellington** England
8 C6 **Wellington** England
145 E4 **Wellington** *admin region* New Zealand
145 F4 **Wellington** New Zealand
89 A9 **Wellington** S Africa
111 L8 **Wellington** Alabama U.S.A.
106 E1 **Wellington** Colorado U.S.A.
99 T9 **Wellington** Illinois U.S.A.
107 N4 **Wellington** Kansas U.S.A.
102 E3 **Wellington** Nevada U.S.A.
94 E5 **Wellington** Ohio U.S.A.
108 G1 **Wellington** Texas U.S.A.
103 O2 **Wellington** Utah U.S.A.
115 K2 **Wellington Chan** Northwest Territories Canada
133 C7 **Wellington, I** Chile
139 H7 **Wellington, L** Victoria Australia
143 D7 **Wellington Ra** W Australia Australia
108 E2 **Wellman** Texas U.S.A.
9 F1 **Wellow** England
8 D5 **Wells** England
107 N2 **Wells** Kansas U.S.A.
99 N6 **Wells** Minnesota U.S.A.
101 L8 **Wells** Nevada U.S.A.
95 N3 **Wells** New York U.S.A.
109 N4 **Wells** Texas U.S.A.
95 K5 **Wellsboro** Pennsylvania U.S.A.
99 O7 **Wellsburg** Iowa U.S.A.
95 L4 **Wellsburg** New York U.S.A.
94 G6 **Wellsburg** West Virginia U.S.A.
145 E2 **Wellsford** New Zealand
117 N9 **Wells Gray Prov. Park** British Columbia Canada
143 E7 **Wells, L** W Australia Australia
119 R1 **Wells L** Manitoba Canada
142 F3 **Wells, Mt** W Australia Australia
9 G2 **Wells-next-the-sea** England
95 P2 **Wells River** Vermont U.S.A.
94 E7 **Wellston** Ohio U.S.A.
110 E2 **Wellsville** Missouri U.S.A.
94 K4 **Wellsville** New York U.S.A.
101 O8 **Wellsville** Utah U.S.A.
103 K9 **Wellton** Arizona U.S.A.
119 S8 **Wellwood** Manitoba Canada
86 G3 **Welo** *prov* Ethiopia
38 K5 **Wels** Austria
25 D6 **Welschap** Netherlands
36 B4 **Welschbillig** Germany
36 E1 **Welschenennest** Germany
122 F8 **Welsford** New Brunswick Canada
109 P5 **Welsh** Louisiana U.S.A.
8 D2 **Welshampton** England
142 B2 **Welshpool** *dist* Perth, W Aust Australia
122 F9 **Welshpool** New Brunswick Canada
8 C2 **Welshpool** Wales
13 H6 **Welton** England
32 G9 **Welver** Germany
119 Q8 **Welwyn** Saskatchewan Canada
9 F4 **Welwyn Garden City** England
36 H6 **Welzheim** Germany
8 D2 **Wem** England
86 D6 **Wema** Zaire
142 A1 **Wembley** *dist* Perth, W Aust Australia
117 O8 **Wembley** Alberta Canada
142 A1 **Wembley Downs** *dist* Perth, W Aust Australia
8 B7 **Wembury** England
37 K6 **Wemding** Germany
25 A5 **Wemeldinge** Netherlands
12 D2 **Wemyss B** Scotland
126 F2 **Wemyss Bight** Eleuthera Bahamas
65 C5 **Wen'an** China
100 E2 **Wenatchee** Washington U.S.A.
67 C7 **Wenchang** China
67 G3 **Wencheng** China
85 D7 **Wenchi** Ghana
67 A1 **Wenchuan** China
102 D1 **Wendel** California U.S.A.
101 L7 **Wendell** Idaho U.S.A.
98 K3 **Wendell** Minnesota U.S.A.
112 J2 **Wendell** North Carolina U.S.A.
36 D4 **Wendelsheim** Germany
37 L5 **Wendelstein** Germany
9 G3 **Wenden** England
36 D2 **Wenden** Germany
103 L8 **Wenden** Arizona U.S.A.
65 E6 **Wendeng** China
33 Q6 **Wendisch Priborn** Germany
33 O7 **Wendland** *reg* Germany
9 G2 **Wendling** England
100 C5 **Wendling** Oregon U.S.A.
86 G4 **Wendo** Ethiopia
33 O5 **Wendorf** Germany
9 F4 **Wendover** England
101 M9 **Wendover** Utah U.S.A.
98 B7 **Wendover** Wyoming U.S.A.
98 F5 **Wendte** South Dakota U.S.A.
22 E1 **Wenduine** Belgium
120 G5 **Wenebegon L** Ontario Canada
67 B3 **Weng'an** China
36 B4 **Wengerohr** Germany
67 D2 **Wengjiang** China
67 E4 **Wengyuan** China
65 D7 **Wen He** *R* China
36 G3 **Wenings** Germany
67 A1 **Wenjiang** China
68 K1 **Wenli** China
67 G2 **Wenling** China
141 F1 **Wenlock** *R* Queensland Australia
141 G2 **Wenlock** Queensland Australia
128 A7 **Wenman** *isld* Galapagos Is
32 L8 **Wennigsen** Germany
41 N3 **Wenns** Austria
99 R8 **Wenona** Illinois U.S.A.
67 C1 **Wenquan** China
67 A5 **Wenshan** China
65 C7 **Wenshang** China
65 B6 **Wenshui** China
67 B2 **Wenshui** China
57 K4 **Wensu** China
13 G6 **Wentbridge** England
138 F5 **Wentworth** New South Wales Australia
13 G6 **Wentworth** England
95 Q3 **Wentworth** New Hampshire U.S.A.
98 K6 **Wentworth** South Dakota U.S.A.
122 J8 **Wentworth Centre** Nova Scotia Canada
110 F3 **Wentzville** Missouri U.S.A.
65 B7 **Wenxi** China
65 B7 **Wen Xian** China
37 N5 **Wenzenbach** Germany
67 G3 **Wenzhou** China
113 F10 **Weohyakapka L** Florida U.S.A.
100 B9 **Weott** California U.S.A.
89 E7 **Wepener** S Africa
22 H3 **Wepion** Belgium
69 B10 **We, Pulau** *isld* Sumatra
33 T7 **Werbellin** Germany
33 T7 **Werbellinsee** *L* Germany
33 P7 **Werben** Germany
33 S9 **Werbig** Germany
22 K3 **Werbomont** Belgium
87 D11 **Werda** Botswana
37 N2 **Werdau** Germany
86 J4 **Werdër** Ethiopia
33 R8 **Werder** Germany
32 G10 **Werdohl** Germany
80 E6 **Wered Yeriḥo** Jordan
32 G9 **Werl** Germany
32 G7 **Werlte** Germany
36 C1 **Wermelskirchen** Germany
33 R10 **Wermsdorf** Germany
36 H4 **Wern** *R* Germany
37 N4 **Wernberg** Germany
32 G9 **Werne** Germany
37 J4 **Werneck** Germany
117 F3 **Wernecke Mts** Yukon Territory Canada
98 D2 **Werner** North Dakota U.S.A.
33 T7 **Werneuchen** Germany
36 H3 **Wernfeld** Germany
119 U2 **Wernham L** Manitoba Canada
25 C6 **Wernhout** Netherlands
33 N9 **Wernigerode** Germany
37 J1 **Werra** *R* Germany
139 G7 **Werribee** Victoria Australia
138 F5 **Werrimull** Victoria Australia
139 K4 **Werris Cr** New South Wales Australia
32 G9 **Werse** *R* Germany
37 K7 **Wertach** *R* Germany
36 H4 **Wertheim** Germany
37 K6 **Wertingen** Germany
71 M9 **Werula** Indonesia
25 D3 **Wervershoof** Netherlands
32 E9 **Wesel** Germany
36 D5 **Weselberg** Germany
33 R6 **Wesenberg** Germany
32 H5 **Weser** *est* Germany
32 L9 **Weser** *R* Germany
107 J3 **Weskan** Kansas U.S.A.
86 G4 **Weska Weka** Ethiopia
109 K9 **Weslaco** Texas U.S.A.
121 N8 **Weslemkoon L** Ontario Canada
95 U2 **Wesley** Maine U.S.A.
123 T4 **Wesleyville** Newfoundland Canada
94 G4 **Wesleyville** Pennsylvania U.S.A.
32 F5 **Wesse** Germany
32 J4 **Wesselburen** Germany
36 B2 **Wesseling** Germany
140 D1 **Wessel Is** N Terr Australia
98 H5 **Wessington** South Dakota U.S.A.
98 H5 **Wessington Springs** South Dakota U.S.A.
111 D8 **Wesson** Arkansas U.S.A.
111 F10 **Wesson** Mississippi U.S.A.
139 G6 **West** Victoria Australia
32 G8 **West** Germany
111 G8 **West** Mississippi U.S.A.
109 K4 **West** Texas U.S.A.
94 C7 **West Alexandria** Ohio U.S.A.
140 B1 **West Alligator** *R* N Terr Australia
99 S7 **West Allis** Wisconsin U.S.A.
138 C5 **Westall,Pt** South Australia Australia
13 G4 **West Auckland** England

240
West B — Wilton

113 B7 **West B** Florida U.S.A.
111 G12 **West B** Louisiana U.S.A.
109 N6 **West B** Texas U.S.A.
140 A3 **West Baines** *R* N Terr Australia
8 D6 **West Bay** England
111 L11 **Westbay** Florida U.S.A.
119 O7 **West Bend** Saskatchewan Canada
99 M7 **West Bend** Iowa U.S.A.
99 S6 **West Bend** Wisconsin U.S.A.
75 M7 **West Bengal** *prov* India
111 J8 **West Blockton** Alabama U.S.A.
99 L9 **Westboro** Missouri U.S.A.
99 Q4 **Westboro** Wisconsin U.S.A.
119 T8 **Westbourne** Manitoba Canada
99 P8 **West Branch** Iowa U.S.A.
94 C2 **West Branch** Michigan U.S.A.
13 G6 **West Bretton** England
117 O11 **Westbridge** British Columbia Canada
9 E2 **West Bridgford** England
9 E2 **West Bromwich** England
95 R3 **Westbrook** Maine U.S.A.
99 L5 **Westbrook** Minnesota U.S.A.
108 F3 **Westbrook** Texas U.S.A.
95 Q2 **West Burke** Vermont U.S.A.
15 G2 **West Burra** Shetland Scotland
139 H8 **Westbury** Tasmania Australia
8 D5 **Westbury** England
101 O1 **West Butte** *mt* Montana U.S.A.
139 H6 **Westby** New South Wales Australia
98 C1 **Westby** North Dakota U.S.A.
99 Q6 **Westby** Wisconsin U.S.A.
144 A6 **West C** New Zealand
127 H4 **West Caicos** *isld* Turks & Caicos Is
12 E2 **West Calder** Scotland
143 C11 **West Cape Howe** W Australia Australia
99 S8 **West Chicago** Illinois U.S.A.
106 E3 **Westcliffe** Colorado U.S.A.
144 B5 **West Coast** *admin region* New Zealand
109 M6 **West Columbia** Texas U.S.A.
99 O5 **West Concord** Minnesota U.S.A.
102 G7 **West Covina** California U.S.A.
9 G6 **Westdean** England
99 N8 **West Des Moines** Iowa U.S.A.
122 J9 **West Dover** Nova Scotia Canada
141 K2 **West End** *dist* Brisbane, Qnsld Australia
126 E1 **West End** Grand Bahama I
102 G6 **Westend** California U.S.A.
112 H2 **West End** North Carolina U.S.A.
22 D1 **Westende** Belgium
113 H11 **West End Pt** Bahamas
113 J11 **West End Settlement** Grand Bahama I
32 L4 **Westensee** *L* Germany
25 G3 **Westerbork** Netherlands
144 C5 **Westerfield** New Zealand
9 G5 **Westerham** England
22 H1 **Westerlo** Belgium
98 J9 **Western** Nebraska U.S.A.
86 E4 **Western Equatoria** *prov* Sudan
76 A1 **Western Ghats** *mts* India
122 H10 **Western Hd** Nova Scotia Canada
120 K7 **Western Is** Ontario Canada
15 A3 **Western Isles** *reg* Scotland
139 H7 **Western Port** Victoria Australia
94 H7 **Westernport** Maryland U.S.A.
141 G5 **Western R** Queensland Australia
85 B4 **Western Sahara** *reg* Africa
134 A2 **Western Samoa** *islds* Pacific Oc
32 M9 **Westerode** Germany
32 G6 **Westerstede** Germany
36 D2 **Westerwald** *reg* Germany
107 M3 **Westfall** Kansas U.S.A.
100 H6 **Westfall** Oregon U.S.A.
8 D2 **West Felton** England
142 B3 **Westfield** *dist* Perth, W Aust Australia
99 T10 **Westfield** Illinois U.S.A.
95 P4 **Westfield** Massachusetts U.S.A.
94 H4 **Westfield** New York U.S.A.
94 K5 **Westfield** Pennsylvania U.S.A.
99 R6 **Westfield** Wisconsin U.S.A.
122 F8 **Westfield Beach** New Brunswick Canada
110 B6 **West Fork** Arkansas U.S.A.
99 M6 **West Fork** *R* Minnesota U.S.A.
98 A1 **West Fork** *R* Montana U.S.A.
110 H4 **West Frankfort** Illinois U.S.A.
141 H7 **Westgate** Queensland Australia
9 H5 **Westgate** England
West Germany *see* **Germany**
8 C4 **West Glamorgan** *co* Wales
95 U1 **West Grand L** Maine U.S.A.
112 E6 **West Green** Georgia U.S.A.
9 F6 **West Grinstead** England
141 J7 **Westgrove** Queensland Australia
9 E3 **West Haddon** England
9 G5 **West Ham** England
94 E8 **West Hamlin** West Virginia U.S.A.
95 P6 **Westhampton Beach** Long I, New York U.S.A.
37 K7 **Westheim** Germany
36 E4 **West Hofen** Germany
109 K6 **Westhoff** Texas U.S.A.
36 C6 **Westhoffen** France
100 B1 **Westholme** British Columbia Canada
98 E1 **Westhope** North Dakota U.S.A.
68 A6 **West I** Andaman Is
83 M8 **West I** Cocos Is Indian Oc
146 J12 **West Ice Shelf** Antarctica
32 G10 **Westig** Germany
127 **West Indies** *arch* Caribbean
94 F10 **West Jefferson** North Carolina U.S.A.
94 D7 **West Jefferson** Ohio U.S.A.
22 E1 **Westkapelle** Belgium
25 A6 **Westkapelle** Netherlands
15 D5 **West Kilbride** Scotland
100 F8 **West L** Nevada U.S.A.
110 J1 **West Lafayette** Indiana U.S.A.
94 F6 **West Lafayette** Ohio U.S.A.
100 A6 **Westlake** Oregon U.S.A.
141 G6 **Westland** Queensland Australia
9 H3 **Westleton** England
99 P8 **West Liberty** Iowa U.S.A.
94 D9 **West Liberty** Kentucky U.S.A.
94 D6 **West Liberty** Ohio U.S.A.
13 E2 **West Linton** Scotland
118 D4 **Westlock** Alberta Canada
120 J10 **West Lorne** Ontario Canada
West Lothian *co see* **Lothian and Central** *regions*
122 H2 **West Magpie R** Quebec Canada
9 G5 **West Malling** England
94 C7 **West Manchester** Ohio U.S.A.
141 J8 **Westmar** Queensland Australia
121 O7 **Westmeath** Ontario Canada
14 D3 **Westmeath** *co* Ireland
110 F6 **West Memphis** Arkansas U.S.A.
9 G4 **West Mersea** England
94 G5 **West Middlesex** Pennsylvania U.S.A.
9 E2 **West Midlands** *co* England
94 C7 **West Milton** Ohio U.S.A.
106 E2 **Westminster** Colorado U.S.A.
95 L7 **Westminster** Maryland U.S.A.
112 D3 **Westminster** South Carolina U.S.A.
95 P3 **Westminster** Vermont U.S.A.
140 E3 **Westmoreland** Queensland Australia
107 O2 **Westmoreland** Kansas U.S.A.
95 P4 **Westmoreland** New Hampshire U.S.A.
110 K5 **Westmoreland** Tennessee U.S.A.
Westmorland *co see* **Cumbria**
127 H2 **Westmorland** *parish* Jamaica
103 J8 **Westmorland** California U.S.A.
87 E10 **West Nicholson** Zimbabwe
108 G6 **West Nueces** *R* Texas U.S.A.
8 D2 **Weston** England
144 C6 **Weston** New Zealand
70 D2 **Weston** Sabah
101 O7 **Weston** Idaho U.S.A.
94 C5 **Weston** Michigan U.S.A.
110 B2 **Weston** Missouri U.S.A.
98 K8 **Weston** Nebraska U.S.A.
94 D5 **Weston** Ohio U.S.A.
100 G4 **Weston** Oregon U.S.A.
94 G7 **Weston** West Virginia U.S.A.
98 A5 **Weston** Wyoming U.S.A.
89 E6 **Westonaria** S Africa
8 D5 **Weston-super-Mare** England
109 H2 **Westover** Texas U.S.A.
32 F6 **Westoverledingen** Germany
113 G11 **West Palm Beach** Florida U.S.A.
95 R2 **West Paris** Maine U.S.A.
110 J3 **Westphalia** Indiana U.S.A.
107 P3 **Westphalia** Kansas U.S.A.
94 K5 **West Pike** Pennsylvania U.S.A.
110 E5 **West Plains** Missouri U.S.A.
139 G8 **West Point** Tasmania Australia
122 H4 **West Point** Quebec Canada
116 P4 **West Point** *mt* Alaska U.S.A.
102 D3 **West Point** California U.S.A.
112 B5 **West Point** Georgia U.S.A.
110 J1 **Westpoint** Indiana U.S.A.
99 P9 **West Point** Iowa U.S.A.
94 B9 **West Point** Kentucky U.S.A.
111 H8 **West Point** Mississippi U.S.A.
95 N5 **West Point** New York U.S.A.
95 L9 **West Point** Virginia U.S.A.
111 L8 **West Point L** Alabama/Georgia
West Polder *see* **Markerwaard**
123 Q4 **Westport** Newfoundland Canada
14 B3 **Westport** Ireland
144 C4 **Westport** New Zealand
102 A2 **Westport** California U.S.A.
94 B7 **Westport** Indiana U.S.A.
95 O2 **Westport** New York U.S.A.
100 B3 **Westport** Oregon U.S.A.
98 H4 **Westport** South Dakota U.S.A.
110 H6 **Westport** Tennessee U.S.A.
100 A3 **Westport** Washington U.S.A.
118 A3 **West Prairie R** Alberta Canada
123 M10 **West Pt** Nova Scotia Canada
122 H7 **West Pt** Prince Edward I Canada
98 K8 **West Pt** Nebraska U.S.A.
122 G10 **West Pubnico** Nova Scotia Canada
126 A1 **Westpunt** Curaçao
13 G4 **West Rainton** England
119 Q5 **Westray** Manitoba Canada
15 F1 **Westray Firth** Orkney Scotland
120 J5 **Westree** Ontario Canada
36 C5 **Westrich** *reg* Germany
117 L9 **West Road R** British Columbia Canada
13 F2 **Westruther** Scotland
123 P2 **West St. Modiste** Quebec Canada
110 H3 **West Salem** Illinois U.S.A.
94 E6 **West Salem** Ohio U.S.A.
99 P6 **West Salem** Wisconsin U.S.A.
145 F3 **Westshore** New Zealand
99 L7 **Westside** Iowa U.S.A.
100 E7 **West Side** Oregon U.S.A.
139 J7 **West Sister I** Tasmania Australia
7 L9 **West Sole** *oil rig* North Sea
95 Q2 **West Stewartstown** New Hampshire U.S.A.
9 F6 **West Sussex** *co* England
13 G5 **West Tanfield** England
25 D2 **West Terschelling** Netherlands
110 J2 **West Union** Illinois U.S.A.
99 P7 **West Union** Iowa U.S.A.
94 D8 **West Union** Ohio U.S.A.
94 G7 **West Union** West Virginia U.S.A.
94 C5 **West Unity** Ohio U.S.A.
117 L11 **Westview** British Columbia Canada
122 K8 **Westville** Nova Scotia Canada
111 L11 **Westville** Florida U.S.A.
99 T9 **Westville** Illinois U.S.A.
99 U8 **Westville** Indiana U.S.A.
107 Q6 **Westville** Oklahoma U.S.A.
94 G8 **West Virginia** *state* U.S.A.
22 D1 **West Vlaanderen** Belgium
8 B5 **Westward Ho** England
103 P2 **Westwater** Utah U.S.A.
111 F12 **Westwego** Louisiana U.S.A.
95 M4 **West Winfield** New York U.S.A.
141 K6 **Westwood** Queensland Australia
102 D1 **Westwood** California U.S.A.
109 L9 **Westworth** Texas U.S.A.
139 H5 **West Wyalong** New South Wales Australia
101 O5 **West Yellowstone** Montana U.S.A.
13 G6 **West Yorkshire** *co* England
71 O8 **Wetan** *isld* Indonesia
71 N8 **Wetar** *isld* Indonesia
71 N9 **Wetar, Selat** *str* Indonesia
118 D6 **Wetaskiwin** Alberta Canada
88 G4 **Wete** Tanzania
121 O3 **Wetetnagami** *R* Quebec Canada
37 M1 **Wethau** Germany
13 G6 **Wetherby** England
68 B1 **Wetlet** Burma
106 E3 **Wetmore** Colorado U.S.A.
109 J6 **Wetmore** Texas U.S.A.
106 E3 **Wet Mts** Colorado U.S.A.
98 H4 **Wetonka** South Dakota U.S.A.
32 F10 **Wetter** Germany
36 F2 **Wetter** Germany
36 F3 **Wetter** *R* Germany
36 F3 **Wetterau** *reg* Germany
22 F1 **Wetteren** Belgium
41 M3 **Wetter Spitze** *mt* Austria
41 O3 **Wetterstein Geb** *mt* Austria
33 P9 **Wettin** Germany
32 F8 **Wettringen** Germany
107 O6 **Wetumka** Oklahoma U.S.A.
111 K9 **Wetumpka** Alabama U.S.A.
68 C1 **Wetwun** Burma
36 F2 **Wetzlar** Germany
37 L3 **Wetzstein** *mt* Germany
36 B1 **Wevelinghoven** Germany
110 E1 **Wever** Iowa U.S.A.
113 B7 **Wewahitchka** Florida U.S.A.
136 J2 **Wewak** Papua New Guinea
107 O6 **Wewoka** Oklahoma U.S.A.
14 E4 **Wexford** *co* Ireland
14 E4 **Wexford** Ireland
14 E4 **Wexford B** Ireland
14 E4 **Wexford Harb** Ireland
118 L4 **Weyakwin L** Saskatchewan Canada
99 S5 **Weyauwega** Wisconsin U.S.A.
9 H2 **Weybourne** England
9 F5 **Weybridge** England
119 O9 **Weyburn** Saskatchewan Canada
38 L6 **Weyer** Austria
36 D2 **Weyerbusch** Germany
99 P4 **Weyerhauser** Wisconsin U.S.A.
36 D6 **Weyersheim** France
33 M7 **Weyhausen** Germany
9 E5 **Weyhill** England
122 G9 **Weymouth** Nova Scotia Canada
8 D6 **Weymouth** England
95 R4 **Weymouth** Massachusetts U.S.A.
141 G1 **Weymouth B** Queensland Australia
141 G2 **Weymouth,C** Queensland Australia
9 F5 **Wey, R** England
25 F4 **Wezep** Netherlands
145 E3 **Whakahora** New Zealand
145 E3 **Whakamaru** New Zealand
145 E3 **Whakapapa** New Zealand
145 E1 **Whakapara** New Zealand
145 F3 **Whakapunake** New Zealand
145 F4 **Whakataki** New Zealand
145 F2 **Whakatane** New Zealand
145 F3 **Whakatane** *R* New Zealand
68 D7 **Whale B** Burma
116 D10 **Whalebone C** Aleutian Is
113 K12 **Whale Cay** *isld* Bahamas
Whale I *see* **Motuhora I**
123 P2 **Whale I** Quebec Canada
9 E1 **Whaley Bridge** England
95 L10 **Whaleyville** Virginia U.S.A.
139 J3 **Whallan** *R* New South Wales Australia
13 F6 **Whalley** England
15 G2 **Whalsay** *isld* Shetland Scotland
13 G3 **Whalton** England
145 E4 **Whangaehu** New Zealand
145 E2 **Whangamata** New Zealand
145 E3 **Whangamomona** New Zealand
145 D4 **Whanganui Inlet** New Zealand
145 G2 **Whangaparaoa** New Zealand
145 E2 **Whangaparaoa Pen** New Zealand
145 D1 **Whangape** New Zealand
145 E2 **Whangape, L** New Zealand
145 E1 **Whangarei** New Zealand
145 D1 **Whangaroa** New Zealand
145 E1 **Whangaruru Harbour** New Zealand
145 E4 **Wharanui** New Zealand
145 F4 **Whareama** New Zealand
13 G6 **Wharfe, R** England
95 N6 **Wharton** New Jersey U.S.A.
94 J5 **Wharton** Pennsylvania U.S.A.
109 L6 **Wharton** Texas U.S.A.
144 C5 **Whataroa** New Zealand
145 F3 **Whatatutu** New Zealand
145 E2 **Whatawhata** New Zealand
99 O8 **What Cheer** Iowa U.S.A.
100 C1 **Whatcom, L** Washington U.S.A.
111 J10 **Whatley** Alabama U.S.A.
68 F6 **Whatthana Nakhon** Thailand
102 C2 **Wheatland** California U.S.A.
98 B7 **Wheatland** Wyoming U.S.A.
98 A8 **Wheatland Res** Wyoming U.S.A.
120 H10 **Wheatley** Ontario Canada
9 E4 **Wheatley** England
110 E7 **Wheatley** Arkansas U.S.A.
99 S8 **Wheaton** Illinois U.S.A.
107 O2 **Wheaton** Kansas U.S.A.
98 K4 **Wheaton** Minnesota U.S.A.
110 B5 **Wheaton** Missouri U.S.A.
8 C5 **Wheddon Cross** England
107 J2 **Wheeler** Kansas U.S.A.
100 B4 **Wheeler** Oregon U.S.A.
108 D8 **Wheeler** Texas U.S.A.
117 Q4 **Wheeler L** Northwest Territories Canada
110 J7 **Wheeler L** Alabama U.S.A.
103 K3 **Wheeler Pk** Nevada U.S.A.
106 E5 **Wheeler Pk** New Mexico U.S.A.
102 F6 **Wheeler Ridge** California U.S.A.
94 E8 **Wheelersburg** Ohio U.S.A.
102 E7 **Wheeler Springs** California U.S.A.
94 G6 **Wheeling** West Virginia U.S.A.
98 C1 **Wheelock** North Dakota U.S.A.
94 E9 **Wheelwright** Kentucky U.S.A.
140 E6 **Whelan,Mt** Queensland Australia
13 F5 **Whernside** *mt* England
9 E5 **Wherwell** England
138 C5 **Whidbey I** South Australia Australia
100 C1 **Whidbey I** Washington U.S.A.
111 M11 **Whigham** Georgia U.S.A.
142 C5 **Whim Creek** W Australia Australia
138 B2 **Whinham, Mt** South Australia Australia
99 M2 **Whipholt** Minnesota U.S.A.
122 F9 **Whipple Pt** Nova Scotia Canada
9 F4 **Whipsnade** England
101 N1 **Whiskey Gap** Alberta Canada
119 T4 **Whiskey Jack Landing** Manitoba Canada
100 C9 **Whiskeytown** California U.S.A.
100 C9 **Whiskeytown-Shasta-Trinity Nat. Rec. Area** California U.S.A.
140 D5 **Whistleduck Creek** N Terr Australia
111 H11 **Whistler** Alabama U.S.A.
9 E2 **Whitacre** England
112 K1 **Whitakers** North Carolina U.S.A.
13 E5 **Whitbeck** England
123 T6 **Whitbourne** Newfoundland Canada
13 G4 **Whitburn** England
12 E2 **Whitburn** Scotland
121 M9 **Whitby** Ontario Canada
13 H5 **Whitby** England
8 D2 **Whitchurch** England
9 F4 **Whitchurch** England
9 E5 **Whitchurch** England
8 C4 **Whitchurch** Wales
111 E7 **White** *R* Arkansas U.S.A.
101 S10 **White** *R* Colorado U.S.A.
99 U6 **White** *R* Michigan U.S.A.
103 J3 **White** *R* Nevada U.S.A.
98 K5 **White** South Dakota U.S.A.
98 F6 **White** *R* South Dakota U.S.A.
108 F2 **White** *R* Texas U.S.A.
103 P2 **White** *R* Utah U.S.A.
100 D2 **White** *R* Washington U.S.A.
99 Q3 **White** *R* Wisconsin U.S.A.
123 Q3 **White B** Newfoundland Canada
118 J8 **White Bear** Saskatchewan Canada
123 P5 **White Bear L** *res* Newfoundland Canada
99 O4 **White Bear L** Minnesota U.S.A.
123 P6 **White Bear R** Newfoundland Canada
100 J4 **White Bird** Idaho U.S.A.
110 J5 **White Bluff** Tennessee U.S.A.
100 F3 **White Bluffs** Washington U.S.A.
122 E6 **White Brook** New Brunswick Canada
98 D4 **White Butte** South Dakota U.S.A.
119 W2 **Whitecap L** Manitoba Canada
111 E11 **White Castle** Louisiana U.S.A.
113 G10 **White City** Florida U.S.A.
107 O3 **White City** Kansas U.S.A.
106 F9 **White City** New Mexico U.S.A.
139 G4 **White Cliffs** New South Wales Australia
99 L10 **White Cloud** Kansas U.S.A.
94 B3 **White Cloud** Michigan U.S.A.
118 B4 **White Court** Alberta Canada
98 D1 **White Earth** North Dakota U.S.A.
108 E2 **Whiteface** Texas U.S.A.
95 O2 **Whiteface Mt** New York U.S.A.
120 J6 **Whitefish** Ontario Canada
117 Q11 **Whitefish** Idaho U.S.A.
99 U4 **Whitefish** *R* Michigan U.S.A.
101 L1 **Whitefish** Montana U.S.A.
99 T6 **Whitefish Bay** Wisconsin U.S.A.
118 E4 **Whitefish L** Alberta Canada
119 O2 **Whitefish L** Ontario Canada
116 K6 **Whitefish L** Alaska U.S.A.
99 V3 **Whitefish L** Michigan U.S.A.
99 M3 **Whitefish L** Minnesota U.S.A.
101 L1 **Whitefish L** Montana U.S.A.
119 N5 **White Fox** Saskatchewan Canada
115 N6 **Whitegull L** Quebec Canada
110 F2 **White Hall** Illinois U.S.A.
99 U6 **Whitehall** Michigan U.S.A.
101 N4 **Whitehall** Montana U.S.A.
99 P5 **Whitehall** Wisconsin U.S.A.
12 E5 **Whitehaven** England
95 M5 **White Haven** Pennsylvania U.S.A.
14 F2 **Whitehead** N Ireland
12 D4 **Whitehill** Scotland
116 N2 **White Hills** Alaska U.S.A.
103 K6 **White Hills** Arizona U.S.A.
117 F5 **Whitehorse** Yukon Territory Canada
100 D8 **White Horse** California U.S.A.
101 L9 **White Horse Pass** Nevada U.S.A.
127 M3 **White Horses** Jamaica
White I *see* **Kvitøya**
146 K9 **White I** Antarctica
115 L4 **White I** Northwest Territories Canada
145 F2 **White I** New Zealand
13 F1 **Whitekirk** Scotland
140 A5 **White L** N Terr/W Aust Australia
142 G5 **White, L** W Australia Australia
111 D12 **White L** Louisiana U.S.A.
99 U6 **White L** Michigan U.S.A.
98 H6 **White L** South Dakota U.S.A.
99 S4 **White Lake** Wisconsin U.S.A.
94 A7 **Whiteland** Indiana U.S.A.
139 J8 **Whitemark** Tasmania Australia
116 F4 **White Mountain** Alaska U.S.A.
14 E4 **White Mt** Ireland
116 O4 **White Mts** Alaska U.S.A.
102 F4 **White Mts** California U.S.A.
95 Q2 **White Mts** New Hampshire U.S.A.
117 P7 **Whitemud** *R* Alberta Canada
86 F3 **White Nile** *R* Sudan
86 F3 **White Nile** *prov* Sudan
86 F2 **White Nile Dam** Sudan
89 A4 **White Nossob** *R* Namibia
112 K3 **White Oak** North Carolina U.S.A.
109 M2 **White Oak Cr** Texas U.S.A.
109 O2 **White Oak L** Arkansas U.S.A.
118 K1 **White Otter L** Ontario Canada
98 D5 **White Owl** South Dakota U.S.A.
9 E5 **Whiteparish** England
100 D3 **White Pass** Washington U.S.A.
94 B5 **White Pigeon** Michigan U.S.A.
99 R3 **White Pine** Michigan U.S.A.
100 K2 **Whitepine** Montana U.S.A.
112 D1 **White Pine** Tennessee U.S.A.
103 J2 **White Pine Ra** Nevada U.S.A.
95 N5 **White Plains** New York U.S.A.
112 G1 **White Plains** North Carolina U.S.A.
123 R2 **White Pt** Belle Isle, Nfld
118 B8 **White R** British Columbia Canada
127 L2 **White R** Jamaica
94 B8 **White R** Indiana U.S.A.
98 F6 **White R** South Dakota U.S.A.
120 E4 **White River** Ontario Canada
95 P3 **White River Junc** Vermont U.S.A.
103 J3 **White River Valley** Nevada U.S.A.
100 J8 **White Rock** Nevada U.S.A.
109 O9 **White Rock** Texas U.S.A.
107 M2 **White Rock Cr** Kansas U.S.A.
103 K3 **White Rock Peak** Nevada U.S.A.
White Russia *see* **Belorussia**
117 K9 **Whitesail L** British Columbia Canada
100 D4 **White Salmon** Washington U.S.A.
117 P6 **Whitesand** *R* Alberta Canada
8 B7 **Whitesand B** England
119 P7 **Whitesand R** Saskatchewan Canada
108 A3 **White Sands Missile Ra** New Mexico U.S.A.
108 A3 **White Sands Nat. Mon** New Mexico U.S.A.
95 M3 **Whitesboro** New York U.S.A.
109 L2 **Whitesboro** Texas U.S.A.
112 C4 **Whitesburg** Georgia U.S.A.
94 E9 **Whitesburg** Kentucky U.S.A.
White Sea *see* **Beloye More**
109 L9 **White Settlement** Texas U.S.A.
118 F1 **Whiteshell** Manitoba Canada
100 B4 **Whiteson** Oregon U.S.A.
119 U2 **Whitestone L** Manitoba Canada
101 P3 **White Sulphur Springs** Montana U.S.A.
110 K4 **Whitesville** Kentucky U.S.A.
94 K4 **Whitesville** New York U.S.A.
94 F9 **Whitesville** West Virginia U.S.A.
100 E3 **White Swan** Washington U.S.A.
119 M4 **Whiteswan L** Saskatchewan Canada
98 A1 **Whitetail** Montana U.S.A.
112 J3 **Whiteville** North Carolina U.S.A.
110 G6 **Whiteville** Tennessee U.S.A.
85 D7 **White Volta** *R* Ghana
94 B7 **Whitewater** *R* Indiana U.S.A.
101 S1 **Whitewater** Montana U.S.A.
106 B9 **Whitewater** New Mexico U.S.A.
99 S7 **Whitewater** Wisconsin U.S.A.
113 F12 **Whitewater B** Florida U.S.A.
120 A2 **Whitewater L** Ontario Canada
138 B4 **White Well** South Australia Australia
141 G5 **Whitewood** Queensland Australia
119 P8 **Whitewood** Saskatchewan Canada
98 C5 **Whitewood** South Dakota U.S.A.
98 J5 **Whitewood, L** South Dakota U.S.A.
109 L2 **Whitewright** Texas U.S.A.
139 H6 **Whitfield** Victoria Australia
13 F4 **Whitfield Hall** England
127 H2 **Whithorn** Jamaica
12 D4 **Whithorn** Scotland
145 E2 **Whitianga** New Zealand
117 G6 **Whiting** *R* Br Col/Alaska Canada/U.S.A.
107 P2 **Whiting** Kansas U.S.A.
95 N7 **Whiting** New Jersey U.S.A.
12 C3 **Whiting B** Scotland
95 P4 **Whitingham Res** Vermont U.S.A.
118 K6 **Whitkow** Saskatchewan Canada
118 F9 **Whitla** Alberta Canada
8 B4 **Whitland** Wales
101 O1 **Whitlash** Montana U.S.A.
13 G3 **Whitley Bay** England
94 C10 **Whitley City** Kentucky U.S.A.
98 F4 **Whitlocks Crossing** South Dakota U.S.A.
95 R4 **Whitman** Massachusetts U.S.A.
98 E7 **Whitman** Nebraska U.S.A.
98 H1 **Whitman** North Dakota U.S.A.
100 G3 **Whitman Mission Nat. Hist. Site** Washington U.S.A.
112 F3 **Whitmire** South Carolina U.S.A.
146 C8 **Whitmore Mts** *mts* Antarctica
121 M7 **Whitney** Ontario Canada
8 C3 **Whitney** England
98 C7 **Whitney** Nebraska U.S.A.
103 J5 **Whitney** Nevada U.S.A.
100 G5 **Whitney** Oregon U.S.A.
109 K4 **Whitney, L** Texas U.S.A.
102 F5 **Whitney, Mt** California U.S.A.
109 J7 **Whitsett** Texas U.S.A.
9 H5 **Whitstable** England
141 J5 **Whitsunday I** Queensland Australia
109 J3 **Whitt** Texas U.S.A.
94 G7 **Whittaker** West Virginia U.S.A.
99 M6 **Whittemore** Iowa U.S.A.
94 D2 **Whittemore** Michigan U.S.A.
116 N6 **Whittier** Alaska U.S.A.
102 F8 **Whittier** California U.S.A.
13 G3 **Whittingham** England
139 H7 **Whittlesea** Victoria Australia
9 F2 **Whittlesey** England
139 H5 **Whitton** New South Wales Australia
8 C3 **Whitton** Wales
13 G4 **Whittonstall** England
141 F7 **Whitula** *R* Queensland Australia
9 E1 **Whitwell** England
112 B2 **Whitwell** Tennessee U.S.A.
114 J5 **Wholdaia L** Northwest Territories Canada
138 D5 **Whyalla** South Australia Australia
123 L8 **Whycocomagh** Nova Scotia Canada
139 G3 **Whyjonta** New South Wales Australia
68 D3 **Wiang Pa Pao** Thailand
68 D2 **Wiang Phrao** Thailand
120 J8 **Wiarton** Ontario Canada
31 K5 **Wiązów** Poland
98 B2 **Wibaux** Montana U.S.A.
13 G6 **Wibsey** England
107 N4 **Wichita** Kansas U.S.A.
109 J1 **Wichita** *R* Texas U.S.A.
109 J2 **Wichita Falls** Texas U.S.A.
109 J1 **Wichita Mts** Oklahoma U.S.A.
15 E2 **Wick** Scotland
32 G10 **Wickede** Germany
103 M8 **Wickenburg** Arizona U.S.A.
122 J4 **Wickenden L** Quebec Canada
143 C10 **Wickepin** W Australia Australia
100 C1 **Wickersham** Washington U.S.A.
108 D4 **Wickett** Texas U.S.A.
9 G4 **Wickford** England
95 Q5 **Wickford** Rhode I U.S.A.
142 B5 **Wickham** W Australia Australia
9 E6 **Wickham** England
139 G7 **Wickham, C** Tasmania Australia
140 A3 **Wickham Mt** N Terr Australia
121 S7 **Wickham West** Quebec Canada
100 D6 **Wickiup Res** Oregon U.S.A.
110 G5 **Wickliffe** Kentucky U.S.A.
14 E4 **Wicklow** *co* Ireland
14 E4 **Wicklow** Ireland
8 D4 **Wickwar** England
31 L4 **Widawka** *R* Poland
36 G5 **Widdern** Germany
121 L6 **Widdifield** Ontario Canada
90 A11 **Wideawake** Ascension I
141 L7 **Wide B** Queensland Australia
116 J8 **Wide B** Alaska U.S.A.
8 C6 **Widecombe-in-the-Moor** England
138 B2 **Wide Gum** *R* South Australia Australia
94 G8 **Widen** West Virginia U.S.A.
141 H8 **Widgeegoara** *R* Queensland Australia
143 D9 **Widgiemooltha** W Australia Australia
71 B3 **Widi, Pulau Pulau** *islds* Indonesia
36 F4 **Wiebelsbach** Germany
36 C5 **Wiebelskirchen** Germany
31 K2 **Więcbork** Poland
36 C2 **Wied** Germany
Wiedenbrück *see* **Rheda-Wiedenbrück**
32 H6 **Wiefelstede** Germany
33 O10 **Wiehe** Germany
32 J8 **Wiehengebirge** *hills* Germany
36 D2 **Wiehl** Germany
31 M2 **Wielbark** Poland
31 J3 **Wieleń** Poland
31 M6 **Wieliczka** Poland
31 L4 **Wieluń** Poland
38 O5 **Wien** Austria
38 O6 **Wiener Neustadt** Austria
32 M7 **Wienhausen** Germany
116 M4 **Wien L** Alaska U.S.A.
33 O7 **Wiepke** Germany
31 O5 **Wieprz** *R* Poland
33 N7 **Wieren** Germany
109 O4 **Wiergate** Texas U.S.A.
25 D3 **Wieringen** Netherlands
25 C3 **Wieringermeer** Netherlands
31 L4 **Wieruszów** Poland
Wierzbnik *see* **Starachowice**
31 L2 **Wierzchucin** Poland
31 L2 **Wierzyca** *R* Poland
38 M8 **Wies** Austria
37 N4 **Wiesau** Germany
36 E3 **Wiesbaden** Germany
40 G2 **Wiese** *R* Germany
33 Q8 **Wiesenburg** Germany
36 H6 **Wiesensteig** Germany
37 L4 **Wiesent** *R* Germany
37 J4 **Wiesentherd** Germany
37 L4 **Wiesenttal** Germany
36 F5 **Wiesloch** Germany
32 G6 **Wiesmoor** Germany
32 F7 **Wietmarschen** Germany
32 L7 **Wietz** Germany
32 K7 **Wietzen** Germany
32 L7 **Wietzendorf** Germany
13 F6 **Wigan** England
98 B9 **Wiggins** Colorado U.S.A.
111 G11 **Wiggins** Mississippi U.S.A.
9 E6 **Wight, I. of** England
8 D3 **Wigmore** England
31 O2 **Wigry, Jezioro** *L* Poland
9 E2 **Wigston** England
13 E4 **Wigton** England
Wigtown *co see* **Dumfries and Galloway** *reg*
12 D4 **Wigtown** Scotland
25 F4 **Wijhe** Netherlands
25 E7 **Wijk** Netherlands
25 C4 **Wijk aan Zee** Netherlands
103 L7 **Wikieup** Arizona U.S.A.
120 J7 **Wikwemikong** Ontario Canada
41 K3 **Wil** Switzerland
83 L11 **Wila Oya** *R* Sri Lanka
98 K9 **Wilber** Nebraska U.S.A.
121 M7 **Wilberforce** Ontario Canada
140 D1 **Wilberforce,C** N Terr Australia
144 C5 **Wilberforce R** New Zealand
101 N3 **Wilborn** Montana U.S.A.
100 B6 **Wilbur** Oregon U.S.A.
100 G2 **Wilbur** Washington U.S.A.
94 E10 **Wilbur Dam** Tennessee U.S.A.
110 A7 **Wilburton** Oklahoma U.S.A.
9 F3 **Wilby** England
139 G4 **Wilcannia** New South Wales Australia
119 N8 **Wilcox** Saskatchewan Canada
99 M9 **Wilcox** Missouri U.S.A.
98 G9 **Wilcox** Nebraska U.S.A.
94 J5 **Wilcox** Pennsylvania U.S.A.
33 T8 **Wildau** Germany
36 F6 **Wildbad** Germany
33 R7 **Wildberg** Germany
36 F6 **Wildberg** Germany
123 Q4 **Wild Bight** Newfoundland Canada
102 H2 **Wildcat Pk** Nevada U.S.A.
119 V3 **Wilde** Manitoba Canada
37 J2 **Wildeck** Germany
37 O2 **Wildenfels** Germany
94 B10 **Wilder** Tennessee U.S.A.
41 O4 **Wilder Freiger** *mt* Austria
117 O9 **Wilderness Prov. Park** Alberta Canada
110 H6 **Wildersville** Tennessee U.S.A.
25 G2 **Wildervank** Netherlands
32 H7 **Wildeshausen** Germany
36 H3 **Wildflecken** Germany
120 A4 **Wild Goose** Ontario Canada
40 F5 **Wildhorn** *mt* Switzerland
101 P1 **Wild Horse** Alberta Canada
100 K8 **Wildhorse Res** Nevada U.S.A.
119 P4 **Wildnest L** Saskatchewan Canada
108 B8 **Wildorado** Texas U.S.A.
33 R8 **Wildpark** Germany
98 K2 **Wild Rice** *R* Minnesota U.S.A.
98 K3 **Wild Rice** *R* North Dakota U.S.A.
98 C1 **Wildrose** North Dakota U.S.A.
99 R5 **Wild Rose** Wisconsin U.S.A.
40 G5 **Wildstrubel** *mt* Switzerland
118 B5 **Wildwood** Alberta Canada
113 E9 **Wildwood** Florida U.S.A.
95 N8 **Wildwood** New Jersey U.S.A.
118 B1 **Wildwood Pk** Manitoba Canada
106 H3 **Wiley** Colorado U.S.A.
36 F6 **Wilferdingen** Germany
120 E2 **Wilgar** Ontario Canada
89 F6 **Wilge** *R* S Africa
138 C4 **Wilgena** South Australia Australia
146 H12 **Wilhelm II Land** Antarctica
129 G3 **Wilhelmina Geb** *mts* Suriname
25 D5 **Wilhelmina Kanal** Netherlands
136 J3 **Wilhelm, Mt** Papua New Guinea
Wilhelm Pieck Stadt *see* **Guben**
32 H5 **Wilhelmshaven** Germany
36 F2 **Wilhelmshütte** Germany
33 O5 **Wiligrad** Germany
70 N9 **Wilis** *mt* Java
95 M5 **Wilkes-Barre** Pennsylvania U.S.A.
112 F1 **Wilkesboro** North Carolina U.S.A.
146 E14 **Wilkes Coast** Antarctica
146 E13 **Wilkes Land** Antarctica
37 N2 **Wilkhau Hasslau** Germany
118 J6 **Wilkie** Saskatchewan Canada
146 D5 **Wilkins Coast** Antarctica
146 C5 **Wilkins Ice Shelf** Antarctica
138 C3 **Wilkinson L** South Australia Australia
112 D6 **Willacoochee** Georgia U.S.A.
103 M6 **Willaha** Arizona U.S.A.
100 B4 **Willamette** *R* Oregon U.S.A.
139 G5 **Willandra Billabong** *R* New South Wales Australia
100 B3 **Willapa** *R* Washington U.S.A.
139 G3 **Willara** New South Wales Australia
138 E2 **Willara, L** South Australia Australia
124 D3 **Willard** Mexico
98 C9 **Willard** Colorado U.S.A.
98 B3 **Willard** Montana U.S.A.
106 D7 **Willard** New Mexico U.S.A.
94 E5 **Willard** Ohio U.S.A.
101 N8 **Willard** Utah U.S.A.
95 M8 **Willards** Maryland U.S.A.
142 E4 **Willare Bridge Roadhouse** W Australia Australia
103 P9 **Willcox** Arizona U.S.A.
32 K9 **Willebadessen** Germany
22 G1 **Willebroek** Belgium
22 E2 **Willems** France
25 C5 **Willemsdorp** Netherlands
126 B1 **Willemstad** Curaçao
25 B5 **Willemstad** Netherlands
140 B3 **Willeroo** N Terr Australia
8 D3 **Willersley** England
22 H4 **Willerzie** Belgium
9 F4 **Willesden** England
118 C6 **Willesden Green** Alberta Canada
120 B2 **Willet** Ontario Canada
143 B6 **Williambury** W Australia Australia
138 D3 **William Creek** South Australia Australia
119 S5 **William L** Manitoba Canada
138 F6 **William, Mt** Victoria Australia
143 B10 **William,Mt** W Australia Australia
140 F5 **Williams** *R* Queensland Australia
143 B10 **Williams** W Australia Australia
103 M6 **Williams** Arizona U.S.A.
102 B2 **Williams** California U.S.A.
110 K3 **Williams** Indiana U.S.A.
99 N7 **Williams** Iowa U.S.A.
99 L1 **Williams** Minnesota U.S.A.
99 S7 **Williams Bay** Wisconsin U.S.A.
99 O8 **Williamsburg** Iowa U.S.A.
94 C10 **Williamsburg** Kentucky U.S.A.
95 P4 **Williamsburg** Massachusetts U.S.A.
94 C7 **Williamsburg** Ohio U.S.A.
94 J6 **Williamsburg** Pennsylvania U.S.A.
95 L9 **Williamsburg** Virginia U.S.A.
127 K2 **Williamsfield** Jamaica
120 K8 **Williamsford** Ontario Canada
126 E2 **Williams I** Bahamas
117 M9 **Williams Lake** British Columbia Canada
99 N8 **Williamson** Iowa U.S.A.
95 K3 **Williamson** New York U.S.A.
94 E9 **Williamson** West Virginia U.S.A.
123 Q3 **Williamsport** Newfoundland Canada
99 T9 **Williamsport** Indiana U.S.A.
94 K7 **Williamsport** Maryland U.S.A.
95 K5 **Williamsport** Pennsylvania U.S.A.
94 C4 **Williamston** Michigan U.S.A.
112 K2 **Williamston** North Carolina U.S.A.
112 E3 **Williamston** South Carolina U.S.A.
94 C8 **Williamstown** Kentucky U.S.A.
95 O4 **Williamstown** Massachusetts U.S.A.
95 P2 **Williamstown** Vermont U.S.A.
94 F7 **Williamstown** West Virginia U.S.A.
110 F5 **Williamsville** Missouri U.S.A.
141 G8 **Willie's Ra** Queensland Australia
127 P4 **Willikie's** Antigua W Indies
95 P5 **Willimantic** Connecticut U.S.A.
118 E5 **Willingdon** Alberta Canada
117 P10 **Willingdon, Mt** Alberta Canada
32 J10 **Willingen** Germany
9 G3 **Willingham** England
13 G4 **Willington** England
109 M5 **Willis** Texas U.S.A.
94 G10 **Willis** Virginia U.S.A.
40 G3 **Willisau** Switzerland
141 K3 **Willis Grp** *islds* Gt Barrier Reef Aust
87 D12 **Williston** S Africa
113 E8 **Williston** Florida U.S.A.
98 C1 **Williston** North Dakota U.S.A.
112 F4 **Williston** South Carolina U.S.A.
117 M8 **Williston L** British Columbia Canada
110 G4 **Willisville** Illinois U.S.A.
8 C5 **Williton** England
102 A2 **Willits** California U.S.A.
119 P9 **Willmar** Saskatchewan Canada
99 L4 **Willmar** Minnesota U.S.A.
94 F5 **Willoughby** Ohio U.S.A.
138 E6 **Willoughby, C** South Australia Australia
117 M9 **Willow** *R* British Columbia Canada
116 M6 **Willow** Alaska U.S.A.
108 E8 **Willow** Oklahoma U.S.A.
119 P7 **Willowbrook** Saskatchewan Canada
119 M9 **Willow Bunch L** Saskatchewan Canada
98 F1 **Willow City** North Dakota U.S.A.
100 E9 **Willow Cr** California U.S.A.
100 H5 **Willow Cr** Oregon U.S.A.
118 D8 **Willow Cr. Prov. Park** Alberta Canada
117 O4 **Willow L** Northwest Territories Canada
98 J5 **Willow L** South Dakota U.S.A.
117 N4 **Willowlake** *R* Northwest Territories Canada
89 C9 **Willowmore** S Africa
140 C5 **Willowra** N Terr Australia
100 E8 **Willow Ranch** California U.S.A.
99 R4 **Willow Res** Wisconsin U.S.A.
99 O3 **Willow River** Minnesota U.S.A.
94 D4 **Willow Run** Michigan U.S.A.
119 M9 **Willows** Saskatchewan Canada
102 B2 **Willows** California U.S.A.
110 E5 **Willow Springs** Missouri U.S.A.
139 K4 **Willow Tree** New South Wales Australia
95 O2 **Willsboro** New York U.S.A.
142 G5 **Wills,L** W Australia Australia
109 L3 **Wills Point** Texas U.S.A.
138 E6 **Willunga** South Australia Australia
111 H11 **Wilmer** Alabama U.S.A.
33 T6 **Wilmersdorf** Germany
99 T7 **Wilmette** Illinois U.S.A.
138 E4 **Wilmington** South Australia Australia
95 M7 **Wilmington** Delaware U.S.A.
99 S8 **Wilmington** Illinois U.S.A.
112 K3 **Wilmington** North Carolina U.S.A.
94 D7 **Wilmington** Ohio U.S.A.
95 O4 **Wilmington** Vermont U.S.A.
99 L6 **Wilmont** Minnesota U.S.A.
107 L4 **Wilmore** Kansas U.S.A.
94 C9 **Wilmore** Kentucky U.S.A.
111 E8 **Wilmot** Arkansas U.S.A.
94 F6 **Wilmot** Ohio U.S.A.
144 B6 **Wilmot, L** New Zealand
144 A6 **Wilmot Pass** New Zealand
25 C4 **Wilnis** Netherlands
121 N7 **Wilno** Ontario Canada
36 E2 **Wilnsdorf** Germany
83 J9 **Wilpattu Nat.Park** Sri Lanka
138 E4 **Wilpena** *R* South Australia Australia
138 E4 **Wilpena** South Australia Australia
22 G1 **Wilrijk** Belgium
101 P3 **Wilsall** Montana U.S.A.
37 Q1 **Wilsdruff** Germany
32 L6 **Wilseder Berg** *hill* Germany
141 G7 **Wilson** *R* Queensland Australia
110 F6 **Wilson** Arkansas U.S.A.
107 M3 **Wilson** Kansas U.S.A.
111 E11 **Wilson** Louisiana U.S.A.
94 J3 **Wilson** New York U.S.A.
112 K2 **Wilson** North Carolina U.S.A.
109 K1 **Wilson** Oklahoma U.S.A.
108 F2 **Wilson** Texas U.S.A.
101 P6 **Wilson** Wyoming U.S.A.
138 A4 **Wilson Bluff** South Australia Australia
115 L4 **Wilson, C** Northwest Territories Canada
142 F5 **Wilson Cliffs** *hill* W Australia Australia
100 F2 **Wilson Creek** Washington U.S.A.
103 K3 **Wilson Cr. Ra** Nevada U.S.A.
146 C13 **Wilson Hills** Antarctica
106 H3 **Wilson Junc** Colorado U.S.A.
138 A2 **Wilson, L** South Australia Australia
110 J7 **Wilson L** Alabama U.S.A.
142 G5 **Wilson,Mt** W Australia Australia
102 G7 **Wilson, Mt** California U.S.A.
106 C4 **Wilson, Mt** Colorado U.S.A.
103 K3 **Wilson, Mt** Nevada U.S.A.
107 M3 **Wilson Res** Kansas U.S.A.
110 C4 **Wilson's Creek Battlefield Nat. Park** Missouri U.S.A.
139 H7 **Wilson's Promontory** Victoria Australia
12 E2 **Wilsontown** Scotland
98 F9 **Wilsonville** Nebraska U.S.A.
32 K6 **Wilstedt** Germany
32 K5 **Wilster** Germany
140 C2 **Wilton** *R* N Terr Australia
9 E5 **Wilton** England

242
Xianfeng — York Factory

67 C2 Xianfeng China
58 C6 Xiangcheng China
65 B8 Xiangcheng China
67 D3 Xiangdong China
67 B5 Xiangdu China
58 F5 Xiangfan China
65 B7 Xiangfen China
65 D5 Xianghe China
65 B3 Xianghuang Qi China
67 D3 Xiang Jiang *R* China
65 H1 Xianglan China
65 A7 Xiangning China
66 B5 Xiangquan He *R* China
67 G2 Xiangshan China
67 G2 Xiangshan Gang *B* China
65 D7 Xiangshui China
67 D3 Xiangtan China
67 D3 Xiangxiang China
65 G2 Xiangyang China
67 D2 Xiangyin China
65 B6 Xiangyuan China
67 C5 Xiangzhou China
67 G2 Xianju China
58 F6 Xianning China
Xiannumiao *see* Jiangdu
Xiantaozhen *see* Mianyang
67 F3 Xianxia Ling *mt ra* China
58 E5 Xianyang China
67 F4 Xianyou China
65 G1 Xiaobai China
65 G2 Xiaocheng China
65 D3 Xiaochengzi China
65 D4 Xiaochengzi China
68 J1 Xiaodong China
Xiaofan *see* Wuqiang
67 D1 Xiaogan China
66 C2 Xiaoguai China
67 E1 Xiaohexi China
59 J1 Xiao Hinggan Ling *mt ra* China
Xiaojiang *see* Pubei
65 E3 Xiaojieji China
66 F4 Xiao Qaidam China
65 A7 Xiao Shan *ra* China
67 G1 Xiaoshan China
65 F4 Xiaoshi China
67 D4 Xiao Shui *R* China
65 A6 Xiaosuan China
65 C5 Xiaowutai Shan *mt* China
67 F2 Xiao Xi *R* China
65 D7 Xiao Xian China
Xiaoxita *see* Yichang
Xiaoyi *see* Gong Xian
65 B6 Xiaoyi China
67 F3 Xiapu China
Xiashi *see* Haining
65 B7 Xia Xian China
65 C7 Xiayi China
Xiayingpan *see* Luzhi
58 D6 Xichang China
67 C6 Xichang China
67 C2 Xiche China
Xicheng *see* Yangyuan
67 B1 Xichong China
67 A5 Xichou China
65 E2 Xi Dorolj China
67 D3 Xidu China
Xiedian *see* Wanrong
Xiejiaji *see* Qingyun
67 D1 Xiemahe China
68 F3 Xieng Khoang Laos
65 A7 Xiexian China
67 C6 Xieyang Dao *isld* China
65 F3 Xifeng China
67 B3 Xifeng China
65 D4 Xifenqkou China
66 D6 Xigazê China
65 E4 Xi He *R* China
65 G1 Xiji China
67 D5 Xi Jiang *R* China
65 E1 Xikou China
67 C2 Xikou China
65 B3 Xil China
66 E4 Xiliangzi China
67 B4 Xilin China
65 C2 Xilin Gol *R* China
65 H2 Xilinhe China
65 C3 Xilin Hot China
65 B2 Xilin Qagan Obo China
46 F6 Xilókastron Greece
65 D3 Xiluga He *R* China
67 B3 Ximahe China
65 E5 Ximayi *isld* China
58 C3 Ximiao China
65 E4 Ximucheng China
65 B7 Xin'an China
67 F2 Xin'anjiang Shuiku *res* China
Xin'anzhen *see* Xinyi
65 F2 Xin'anzhen China
59 H3 Xinbin China
Xin Bulag *see* Xianghuang Qi
58 G5 Xincai China
67 D2 Xinchang China
59 H6 Xinchang Zhejiang China
65 H1 Xincheng China
65 C5 Xincheng China
67 C4 Xincheng China
65 F3 Xinchengzi China
67 C7 Xincun China
Xindeng *see* Chengyang
65 G2 Xindian China
67 C1 Xindianzi China
67 A1 Xindu China
67 D4 Xindu China
67 E3 Xinfeng China
67 E4 Xinfeng China
67 E3 Xingan China
67 C4 Xing'an China
65 E4 Xingcheng China
65 C5 Xingchi China
67 E3 Xingguo China
65 B4 Xinghe China
65 G1 Xinghua China
67 F4 Xinghua Wan *B* China
65 J2 Xingkai Hu *L* China
65 D4 Xinglong China
65 G1 Xinglongzhen China
67 E4 Xingning China
67 B3 Xingren China
67 B4 Xingren China
65 F1 Xingshan China
67 C1 Xingshan China
58 F4 Xingtai China
65 C5 Xingtang China
67 F3 Xingtian China
129 H4 Xingú *R* Brazil
67 A2 Xingwen China
65 B5 Xing Xian China
66 E3 Xingxingxia China
65 B7 Xingyang China
67 E2 Xingzi China
57 L4 Xinhe China
65 C6 Xinhe China
Xin Hot *see* Abag Qi
67 D3 Xinhua China
67 C3 Xinhuang China
Xinhui *see* Aohan Qi
67 D5 Xinhui China
46 E5 Xiniás, L Greece
58 D4 Xining China
Xinji *see* Shulu
67 E2 Xinjian China
67 E2 Xin Jiang *R* China
65 B7 Xinjiang Shanxi China
Xinjiangkou *see* Songzi
66 C3 Xinjiang Uygur Zizhiqu China
65 E5 Xinjin China
67 A1 Xinjin China
65 E3 Xinkai He *R* China
65 C5 Xinle China
65 G2 Xinli China
65 D3 Xinlin China
65 E3 Xinlitun China
65 A5 Xinminzhen China
67 C3 Xinning China
Xinpu *see* Lianyungang
67 D2 Xinqiang China
67 D3 Xinshao China
65 D7 Xintai China
67 D1 Xintankou China
67 D4 Xintian China
65 D7 Xinwen China
67 E1 Xin Xian China
65 B7 Xinxiang China
67 D5 Xinxing China
68 J3 Xinxing China
67 E1 Xinyang China
65 D7 Xinyi China
67 C5 Xinyi China
65 D7 Xinyi He *R* China
67 C7 Xinying China
67 E3 Xinyu China
66 C3 Xinyuan China
65 D6 Xinzhai China
65 F2 Xinzhan China
65 G3 Xinzhan China
65 B7 Xinzheng China
65 B5 Xinzhou China
67 E1 Xinzhou China
Xinzo de Limia *see* Ginzo de Limia
58 F5 Xiong'er Shan *mt ra* China
65 C5 Xiong Xian China
65 E4 Xiongyuecheng China
65 B4 Xiping China
58 D4 Xiqing Shan *mt ra* China
129 K6 Xique-Xique Brazil
Xishuanghe *see* Kenli
67 B2 Xishui Guizhou China
67 E1 Xishui Hubei China
65 D2 Xi Ujimqin Qi China
67 F2 Xiuning China
67 C2 Xiushan China
67 E2 Xiu Shui *R* China
67 E2 Xiushui China
65 B7 Xiuwu China
65 F4 Xiuyan China
Xiwanzi *see* Chongli
66 D6 Xixabangma Feng *mt* China
65 A6 Xi Xian China
65 B6 Xiyang China
67 F3 Xiyang China
67 G3 Xiyang Dao *isld* China
67 B5 Xiyang Jiang *R* China
67 B5 Xiyangjie China
75 K1 Xizang Gaoyuan *plateau* China
66 C5 Xizang Zizhiqu *aut reg* China
65 E5 Xizhong Dao *isld* China
125 K8 Xochimilco Mexico
58 G5 Xuancheng China
67 C1 Xuan'en China
67 B1 Xuanhan China
58 F3 Xuanhua China
68 H7 Xuan Loc Vietnam
67 A3 Xuanwei China
58 F5 Xuchang China
86 H5 Xuddur Somalia
67 G2 Xuedou Shan *mt* China
67 C3 Xuefeng Shan *mts* China
65 A7 Xuejiaying China
Xugezhuang *see* Fengnan
Xuguit Qi *see* Yakeshi
67 E3 Xu Jiang *R* China
65 E4 Xujiatun China
Xulun Hobot Qagan *see* Zhengxiangbai Qi
Xulun Hoh *see* Zhenglan Qi
58 C5 Xümatang China
67 A4 Xundian China
66 C5 Xungba China
58 E5 Xun He *R* China
59 J2 Xunke China
67 E4 Xunwu China
65 C7 Xun Xian China
67 C3 Xupu China
66 D5 Xuro Co *L* China
65 C5 Xushui China
67 E3 Xuwan China
67 C6 Xuwen China
68 H7 Xuyen Moc Vietnam
58 E6 Xuyong China
58 G5 Xuzhou China

Y

100 K1 Yaak Montana U.S.A.
141 K6 Yaamba Queensland Australia
67 A2 Ya'an China
138 F6 Yaapeet Victoria Australia
71 A3 Yaba Indonesia
86 B5 Yabassi Cameroon
86 G5 Yabēlo Ethiopia
80 F4 Yabis *R* Jordan
46 G1 Yablanitsa Bulgaria
125 N2 Yablis Nicaragua
48 J2 Yablonitse, Pereval *pass* Ukraine
48 J2 Yablonov Ukraine
54 D6 Yablonovka Ukraine
58 E1 Yablonovyy Khrebet *mts* Russian Federation
79 G5 Yabrūd Syria
Yacacik *see* Payas
141 H5 Yacamunda Queensland Australia
Yacha *see* Baisha
100 A5 Yachats Oregon U.S.A.
67 C7 Yacheng China
60 D14 Yachi Japan
67 B3 Yachi He *R* China
130 C10 Yaciretá *isld* Paraguay
139 H6 Yackandandah Victoria Australia
100 C4 Yacolt Washington U.S.A.
133 E2 Yacuiba Bolivia
128 E6 Yacuma *R* Bolivia
128 E3 Yacurai Venezuela
80 D4 Yad Hanna Israel
112 F1 Yadkin *R* North Carolina U.S.A.
112 G1 Yadkinville North Carolina U.S.A.
80 B7 Yad Mordekhay Israel
80 C6 Yad Rambam Israel
68 H6 Ya Drang *R* Cambodia
52 G6 Yadrin Russian Federation
80 C5 Yafo Israel
84 E3 Yafran Libya
61 Q12 Yagaji-jima *isld* Okinawa
60 C13 Yagami Japan
47 J5 Yağcılar Turkey
60 P1 Yagishiri-tō *isld* Japan
124 G7 Yago Mexico
55 E2 Yagodnyy Russian Federation
52 G4 Yagrysh Russian Federation
126 E3 Yaguajay Cuba
131 G3 Yaguari *R* Uruguay
128 D4 Yaguas *R* Peru
124 E4 Yagui Mexico
80 D3 Yagur Israel
69 E9 Yaha Thailand
61 L10 Yahagi-gawa *R* Japan
100 J1 Yahk British Columbia Canada
124 H7 Yahualica Mexico
86 D5 Yahuma Zaire
78 E2 Yahyali Turkey
68 D6 Yai, Khao *mt* Burma/Thailand
61 N9 Yaita Japan
61 M11 Yaizu Japan
80 G5 Yajuz Jordan
116 Q6 Yakataga Alaska U.S.A.
59 H2 Yakeshi China
80 B8 Yakhini Israel
54 J1 Yakhroma Russian Federation
55 E2 Yakhtur, Oz *L* Russian Federation
100 E3 Yakima Washington U.S.A.
74 C8 Yakmach Pakistan
85 D6 Yako Burkina
117 E6 Yakobi I Alaska U.S.A.
86 D5 Yakoma Zaire
46 F2 Yakoruda Bulgaria
86 D4 Yakossi Cent Afr Republic
57 K4 Yakrik China
52 J4 Yaksha Russian Federation
52 G5 Yakshanga Russian Federation
52 H6 Yakshur-Bod'ya Russian Federation
101 L1 Yakt Montana U.S.A.
60 O3 Yakumo Japan
59 J5 Yaku-shima *isld* Japan
117 D6 Yakutat Alaska U.S.A.
117 C6 Yakutat B Alaska U.S.A.
51 M2 Yakutsk Russian Federation
56 H1 Yakutskaya Respublika Russian Federation
69 E9 Yala Thailand
47 K4 Yalakdere Turkey
83 L11 Yala Nat. Park Sri Lanka
138 B4 Yalatta South Australia Australia
144 D5 Yaldhurst New Zealand
117 N11 Yale British Columbia Canada
110 H2 Yale Illinois U.S.A.
99 M8 Yale Iowa U.S.A.
94 E3 Yale Michigan U.S.A.
107 O5 Yale Oklahoma U.S.A.
98 H5 Yale South Dakota U.S.A.
86 D5 Yaleko Zaire
100 C4 Yale L Washington U.S.A.
143 B8 Yalgoo W Australia Australia
86 D4 Yalinga Cent Afr Republic
127 L2 Yallahs *R* Jamaica
127 L3 Yallahs Jamaica
141 H6 Yalleroi Queensland Australia
143 B10 Yallingup W Australia Australia
139 H7 Yallourn Victoria Australia
111 F8 Yalobusha *R* Mississippi U.S.A.
86 C4 Yaloké Cent Afr Republic
66 F5 Yalong Jiang *R* China
47 K4 Yalova Turkey
48 M4 Yalpug *R* Moldavia/Ukraine
48 M5 Yalpug, Ozero *L* Ukraine
138 F3 Yalpunga New South Wales Australia
48 L1 Yaltushkov Ukraine
65 E1 Yalu He *R* China
65 G4 Yalu River China/Korea
55 E4 Yalym Russian Federation
60 Q2 Yamabe Karikachi Pass Japan
61 Q6 Yamada wan *B* Japan
60 D12 Yamaga Japan
61 N7 Yamagata *prefect* Japan
61 O7 Yamagata Japan
60 D14 Yamagawa Japan
60 E11 Yamaguchi Japan
59 K1 Yam-Alin', Khrebet *mt* Russian Federation
50 F1 Yamal, Poluostrov *pen* Russian Federation
61 M10 Yamanaka ko *L* Japan
61 M10 Yamanashi *prefect* Japan
47 J6 Yamanlar Dağı *mt* Turkey
58 F1 Yamarovka Russian Federation
60 H10 Yamasaki Japan
121 S6 Yamaska Quebec Canada
113 G11 Yamato Florida U.S.A.
139 L3 Yamba New South Wales Australia
138 F5 Yamba South Australia Australia
139 G7 Yambacoona Tasmania Australia
85 B6 Yambéring Guinea
128 D3 Yambi, Mesa de Colombia
86 E5 Yambio Sudan
47 H2 Yambol Bulgaria
136 G3 Yamdena *isld* Moluccas Indonesia
Yamdrok Tso *L* *see* Yamzho Yumco *L*
68 C2 Yamethin Burma
80 E8 Yam Hamelah Israel
52 D6 Yami Russian Federation
61 O9 Yamizo-san *mt* Japan
80 F2 Yam Kinneret Israel
52 C5 Yamm Russian Federation
141 F7 Yamma Yamma,L Queensland Australia
79 E7 Yammit Israel
85 D7 Yamoussoukro Ivory Coast
101 R9 Yampa *R* Colorado U.S.A.
101 T9 Yampa Colorado U.S.A.
142 E3 Yampi Sound W Australia Australia
48 K1 Yampol' Ukraine
48 L2 Yampol' Ukraine
100 D7 Yamsay Mt Oregon U.S.A.
52 G4 Yamskoye Russian Federation
74 G5 Yamuna *R* India
74 G3 Yamunanagar India
55 G4 Yamyshevo Kazakhstan
66 E6 Yamzho Yumco *L* China
51 N2 Yana *R* Russian Federation
138 F6 Yanac Victoria Australia
60 D12 Yanagawa Japan
61 O8 Yanagawa Japan
61 P12 Yanaha-jima *isld* Okinawa
76 F2 Yanam India
65 A6 Yan'an China
128 D6 Yanaoca Peru
56 D2 Yanashimskiy Polkan *pk* Russian Federation
139 G4 Yancannia New South Wales Australia
109 H6 Yancey Texas U.S.A.
112 H1 Yanceyville North Carolina U.S.A.
65 A6 Yanchang China
77 B3 Yanchashmeh Iran
Yancheng *see* Qihe
59 H5 Yancheng China
67 F1 Yancheng China
143 B9 Yanchep W Australia Australia
65 A6 Yanchuan China
139 H5 Yanco New South Wales Australia
139 H6 Yanco *R* New South Wales Australia
143 D8 Yandal W Australia Australia
138 F3 Yandama *R* South Australia Australia
65 A4 Yandian China
143 C7 Yandil W Australia Australia
141 L7 Yandina Queensland Australia
68 B4 Yandoon Burma
85 C6 Yanfolila Mali
86 D5 Yangambi Zaire
66 E5 Yangbajain China
65 B7 Yangcheng China
Yangchuan *see* Suiyang
67 D5 Yangchun China
Yangcun *see* Wuqing
67 E5 Yangcun China
65 F3 Yangdachengzi China
142 A3 Yangebup L W Australia Australia
65 J2 Yanggang China
58 F3 Yanggao China
65 C6 Yanggu China
57 F4 Yangibazar Kyrgyzstan
77 B2 Yangi Emām Iran
57 D5 Yangi-Nishan Uzbekistan
67 D6 Yangjiang China
65 E4 Yangjiazhangzi China
67 F3 Yangkou China
67 A4 Yanglin China
67 D2 Yangloudong China
65 C7 Yangmiao China
67 D3 Yangming Shan *mt* China
68 C4 Yangon Burma
52 E3 Yangory Russian Federation
67 D7 Yangpu Gang *inlet* China
65 B6 Yangquan China
67 D3 Yangquan China
65 C7 Yangshan China
67 D4 Yangshan China
Yangshe *see* Shazhou
67 C4 Yangshuo China
67 F1 Yangtan China
Yangtze Gorges *see* Qutang Xia Wu Xia
Yangtze Kiang *R* *see* Chang Jiang *R*
55 E2 Yangutumskiye Russian Federation
68 D6 Yangwa Burma
Yangwu *see* Yuanyang
67 E2 Yangxin China
65 B4 Yangyuan China
67 F1 Yangzhong China
67 F1 Yangzhou China
65 A6 Yan He *R* China
67 C2 Yanhe China
138 D5 Yaninee, L South Australia Australia
52 D4 Yanis'yarvi, Oz *L* Russian Federation
65 H3 Yanji China
65 C7 Yanjin China
67 A2 Yanjin China
67 B2 Yanjing China
138 F4 Yanko Glen New South Wales Australia
98 J7 Yankton South Dakota U.S.A.
65 C7 Yanling China
142 B6 Yannarie *R* W Australia Australia
Yannina *see* Ioánnina
54 B1 Yanovichi Belorussia
52 G6 Yanovo Russian Federation
83 K9 Yan Oya *R* Sri Lanka
66 D3 Yanqi China
65 C4 Yanqing China
142 A5 Yanrey W Australia Australia
65 D4 Yan Shan *mts* China
65 D5 Yanshan China
67 F2 Yanshan China
67 A5 Yanshan China
65 B7 Yanshi China
67 F4 Yanshi China
59 J2 Yanshou China
51 N1 Yanskiy Zaliv *B* Russian Federation
139 H3 Yantabulla New South Wales Australia
59 H4 Yantai China
138 F3 Yantara, L New South Wales Australia
67 B1 Yanting China
65 G3 Yantongshan China
67 G2 Yantou China
47 H1 Yantra *R* Bulgaria
80 D2 Yanūh Israel
57 D3 Yany Kurgan Kazakhstan
65 C7 Yanzhou China
67 B3 Yanzikou China
86 C3 Yao Chad
61 J11 Yao Japan
Yaodu *see* Dongzhi
65 A6 Yaotou China
86 B5 Yaoundé Cameroon
65 D7 Yaowan China
65 A7 Yao Xian China
69 D9 Yao Yai, Ko *isld* Thailand
136 H2 Yapen *isld* W Irian
141 F4 Yappar *R* Queensland Australia
Yaqian *see* Yuexi
80 D8 Yaqin Jordan
127 J5 Yaque del Sur *R* Dominican Rep
124 E3 Yaqui *R* Mexico
100 A5 Yaquina Head Oregon U.S.A.
80 C5 Yaqum Israel
52 H5 Yar Russian Federation
126 F4 Yara Cuba
128 E1 Yaracuy *state* Venezuela
141 G6 Yaraka Queensland Australia
52 G6 Yaransk Russian Federation
47 K7 Yaraşlı Gölü *L* Turkey
47 K6 Yarbasan Turkey
8 C6 Yarcombe England
138 D4 Yardea South Australia Australia
80 F3 Yardena Israel
47 L8 Yardımcı Burun *C* Turkey
52 H3 Yarega Russian Federation
48 J2 Yaremcha Ukraine
52 G3 Yarenga Russian Federation
52 G4 Yarensk Russian Federation
9 H2 Yare, R England
128 D3 Yari *R* Colombia
61 L9 Yariga-take *mt* Japan
47 L5 Yarimca Turkey
47 N11 Yarimca Turkey
80 D1 Yârîne Lebanon
140 E5 Yaringa *R* Queensland Australia
128 E1 Yaritagua Venezuela
Yarkand *R* *see* Yarkant He
Yarkant *see* Shache
66 B4 Yarkant He *R* China
55 E3 Yarkovo Russian Federation
138 B4 Yarle Lakes South Australia Australia
66 D6 Yarlung Zangbo Jiang *R* China
13 G5 Yarm England
48 K1 Yarmolintsy Ukraine
122 F10 Yarmouth Nova Scotia Canada
9 E6 Yarmouth England
95 R3 Yarmouth Maine U.S.A.
95 R5 Yarmouth Massachusetts U.S.A.
80 F3 Yarmuk *R* Syria
103 M7 Yarnell Arizona U.S.A.
52 E5 Yaroslavl' Russian Federation
52 E5 Yaroslavskaya Oblast' *prov* Russian Federation
80 E1 Yâroûn Lebanon
54 J7 Yarovaya Ukraine
80 C5 Yarqon Israel
139 H7 Yarra *R* Victoria Australia
141 G2 Yarraden Queensland Australia
142 B5 Yarraloola W Australia Australia
139 H7 Yarram Victoria Australia
141 K7 Yarraman Queensland Australia
140 D4 Yarran Ra N Terr Australia
139 H6 Yarrawonga Victoria Australia
141 J5 Yarrawonga Pt Queensland Australia
143 B8 Yarra Yarra Ls W Australia Australia
142 D5 Yarrie W Australia Australia
141 H7 Yarronvale Queensland Australia
15 E5 Yarrow *R* Scotland
141 H5 Yarrowmere Queensland Australia
55 F1 Yarsomovy Russian Federation
54 D1 Yartsevo Russian Federation
128 C2 Yarumal Colombia
48 L2 Yaryshev Ukraine
86 D5 Yasanyama Zaire
137 Q5 Yasawa Grp *islds* Fiji
85 F6 Yashi Nigeria
85 E7 Yashikera Nigeria
60 F12 Ya-shima Japan
61 O6 Yashima Japan
60 F12 Yashiro-jima Japan
55 B4 Yashkino Russian Federation
54 J8 Yasinovataya Ukraine
48 J2 Yasinya Ukraine
54 J2 Yasnogorsk Russian Federation
68 G5 Yasothon Thailand
139 J5 Yass New South Wales Australia
47 M11 Yassi *isld* Turkey
60 G12 Yasuda Japan
60 G10 Yasugi Japan
77 B4 Yāsūj Iran
128 E6 Yata Bolivia
47 J7 Yatağan Turkey
85 E6 Yatakala Niger
106 G5 Yates New Mexico U.S.A.
94 H6 Yatesboro Pennsylvania U.S.A.
107 P4 Yates Center Kansas U.S.A.
115 K5 Yathkyed L Northwest Territories Canada
80 D5 Yatma Jordan
86 D5 Yatolema Zaire
Yatou *see* Rongcheng
61 M10 Yatsuga take *mt* Japan
61 L9 Yatsuo Japan
60 D13 Yatsushiro Japan
80 D8 Yatta Jordan
8 D5 Yatton England
128 E3 Yatua *R* Venezuela
128 D7 Yauca Peru
127 L5 Yauco Puerto Rico
112 H4 Yauhannah South Carolina U.S.A.
128 C6 Yauyos Peru
103 M7 Yava Arizona U.S.A.
57 E5 Yavan Tajikistan
124 E4 Yavaros Mexico
74 H8 Yavatmāl India
128 D6 Yavero *R* Peru
128 E8 Yavi Argentina
128 E2 Yavi, Co *mt* Venezuela
128 E3 Yavita Venezuela
55 E4 Yavlenka Kazakhstan
80 B6 Yavne Israel
80 F3 Yavnee Israel
31 O6 Yavorov Ukraine
29 O3 Yavr *R* Finland/Rus Fed
79 H1 Yavuzeli Turkey
68 B2 Yaw *R* Burma
60 F12 Yawatahama Japan
68 C2 Yawng-hwe Burma
67 B3 Yaxi China
Yaxian *see* Sanya
56 C3 Yaya Russian Federation
52 J5 Yayva *R* Russian Federation
77 C3 Yazd Iran
77 C4 Yazd-e Khvāst Iran
57 F5 Yazgulemskiy Khrebet *mts* Tajikistan
55 C4 Yazikovo Russian Federation
111 F9 Yazoo City Mississippi U.S.A.
52 J4 Yaz'va *R* Russian Federation
38 M5 Ybbs Austria
38 L6 Ybbsitz Austria
130 C9 Ybycúi Paraguay
28 A3 Ydby Denmark
28 D5 Yding Skovhøj *hill* Denmark
52 J3 Ydzhid Parma Russian Federation
52 J3 Ydzhyd Patok *R* Russian Federation
68 C5 Ye Burma
139 H6 Yea Victoria Australia
8 B7 Yealmpton England
Yebaishou *see* Jianping
86 C1 Yebbi bou Chad
21 M2 Yébleron France
68 D5 Yebyu Burma
66 B4 Yecheng China
17 G6 Yecla Spain
124 E3 Yécora Mexico
68 C3 Yedashe Burma
47 K8 Yedi Burun *C* Turkey
48 L2 Yedintsy Moldavia
52 F3 Yedoma Arkhangel'skaya obl Russian Federation
52 H2 Yedoma Komi Respublika Russian Federation
84 F5 Yédri Chad
142 E4 Yeeda River W Australia Australia
138 D5 Yeelanna South Australia Australia
143 D7 Yeelirrie W Australia Australia
52 D5 Yefimovskiy Russian Federation
54 K3 Yefremov Russian Federation
55 G6 Yegindybulak Kazakhstan
55 E5 Yegindykol' Kazakhstan
56 F3 Yegirma *R* Russian Federation
53 F10 Yegorlyk *R* Russian Federation
54 L1 Yegor'yevsk Russian Federation
130 C10 Yegros Paraguay
109 K5 Yegua Cr Texas U.S.A.
16 D7 Yeguas, Sa. de *mts* Spain
131 B5 Yeguas, Vol Chile
86 F5 Yei Sudan
67 E1 Yeji China
85 D7 Yeji Ghana
55 D3 Yekaterinburg Russian Federation
55 D1 Yekaterininka Russian Federation
55 F3 Yekaterininskoye Russian Federation
59 J1 Yekaterinoslavka Russian Federation
54 K4 Yekaterinovka Russian Federation
68 A3 Ye Kyun *isld* Burma
52 H6 Yelabuga Russian Federation
53 F8 Yelan' *R* Russian Federation
55 D2 Yelan' Russian Federation
54 N5 Yelan'-Koleno Russian Federation
141 K8 Yelarbon Queensland Australia
58 F1 Yeleninskiy Russian Federation
54 J9 Yelenovka Ukraine
54 G3 Yelenskiy Russian Federation
54 K4 Yelets Russian Federation
55 E1 Yelizarovo Russian Federation
55 C5 Yelizavetinka Russian Federation
59 M1 Yelizavety, Mys *C* Russian Federation
15 G1 Yell *isld* Scotland
76 E2 Yellandu India
111 K10 Yellow *R* Alabama U.S.A.
99 Q5 Yellow *R* Wisconsin U.S.A.
119 M6 Yellow Creek Saskatchewan Canada
143 C9 Yellowdine W Australia Australia
119 N9 Yellow Grass Saskatchewan Canada
117 O9 Yellowhead Pass Alberta Canada
114 H5 Yellowknife Northwest Territories Canada
117 Q4 Yellowknife Northwest Territories Canada
99 L5 Yellow Medicine *R* Minnesota U.S.A.
139 H4 Yellow Mt New South Wales Australia
100 K5 Yellow Pine Idaho U.S.A.
Yellow R *see* Huang He *R*
59 H4 Yellow Sea China/Korea
110 N2 Yellow Springs Ohio U.S.A.
98 B2 Yellowstone *R* Montana U.S.A.
101 P5 Yellowstone L Wyoming U.S.A.
101 P5 Yellowstone Nat. Park Wyoming U.S.A.
15 G1 Yell Sound Scotland
110 D5 Yellville Arkansas U.S.A.
54 E2 Yel'nya Russian Federation
56 C1 Yeloguy *R* Russian Federation
55 E3 Yeloshnoye Russian Federation
55 C3 Yelovo Barda Russian Federation
16 C4 Yeltes *R* Spain
52 D6 Yel'tsy Russian Federation
125 M2 Yelucá *mt* Nicaragua
52 H3 Yelva *R* Russian Federation
8 B7 Yelverton England
115 L1 Yelverton B Northwest Territories Canada
85 E6 Yelwa Nigeria
55 D4 Yemanzhelinsk Russian Federation
112 G5 Yemassee South Carolina U.S.A.
72 E6 Yemen *rep* S W Asia
55 E3 Yemets *R* Russian Federation
52 F3 Yemetsk Russian Federation
52 F3 Yemtsa Russian Federation
52 D1 Yena Russian Federation
54 K8 Yenakiyevo Ukraine
68 B2 Yenangyat Burma
68 B2 Yenangyaung Burma
68 B3 Yenanma Burma
67 A6 Yen Bai Vietnam
67 A6 Yen Chau Vietnam
139 H5 Yenda New South Wales Australia
85 E7 Yendi Ghana
58 F1 Yendondin Russian Federation
55 E1 Yendra Russian Federation
55 E1 Yendyr' Russian Federation
68 C2 Yengan Burma
66 B4 Yengisar China
47 J5 Yenice Turkey
47 K5 Yenice Turkey
47 H6 Yenifoça Turkey
78 A3 Yenihisar Turkey
47 J5 Yeniköy Turkey
47 N10 Yeniköy Turkey
31 M1 Yenino Russian Federation
47 J7 Yenipazar Aydin Turkey
47 L4 Yenipazar Bilecik Turkey
47 K4 Yenişehir Turkey
56 D2 Yenisey *R* Russian Federation
56 D2 Yeniseysk Russian Federation
50 H1 Yeniseyskiy Zaliv *G* Russian Federation
56 D5 Yenisey, Verkhn-e *R* Russian Federation
68 G2 Yen Lap Vietnam
68 G1 Yen Minh Vietnam
47 Q14 Yennádhi Rhodes Greece
19 P13 Yenne France
52 E1 Yenozero, Oz *L* Russian Federation
68 G3 Yen Thanh Vietnam
116 M5 Yentna *R* Alaska U.S.A.
143 E8 Yeo L W Australia Australia
74 F8 Yeola India
Yeóryios *isld* *see* Áyios *isld*
139 J5 Yeoval New South Wales Australia
8 D6 Yeovil England
124 E3 Yepachic Mexico
54 K3 Yepifan Russian Federation
141 K6 Yeppoon Queensland Australia
46 F7 Yeráki Greece
124 J6 Yerbabuena Mexico
56 G1 Yerbogachen Russian Federation
21 N2 Yère *R* Seine-Inférieure France
55 F5 Yerementau *mt* Kazakhstan
47 J7 Yeresik Turkey
78 K1 Yerevan Armenia
53 F9 Yergeni *hills* Russian Federation
143 D8 Yerilla W Australia Australia
57 C3 Yerimbet Kazakhstan
102 E3 Yerington Nevada U.S.A.
78 E2 Yerköy Turkey
55 G5 Yermak Kazakhstan
55 F1 Yermakovo Russian Federation
56 D4 Yermakovskoye Russian Federation
55 F5 Yermentau Kazakhstan
52 H2 Yermitsa Russian Federation
124 G4 Yermo Mexico
102 H7 Yermo California U.S.A.
55 C4 Yermolayevo Russian Federation
54 H1 Yermolino Russian Federation
59 H1 Yerofey Pavlovich Russian Federation
79 E8 Yeroham Israel
141 K2 Yeronga *dist* Brisbane, Qnsld Australia
52 H2 Yersa *R* Russian Federation
25 B6 Yerseke Netherlands
52 G3 Yertom Russian Federation
52 F4 Yertsevo Russian Federation
128 C6 Yerupaja *mt* Peru
80 D6 Yerushalayim Israel
21 M2 Yerville France
68 B2 Yesagyo Burma
67 C1 Yesanguan China
52 D6 Yesenovichi Russian Federation
79 D1 Yeşidere Turkey
55 E5 Yesil' Kazakhstan
47 K5 Yesil Dağı *mt* Turkey
78 F1 Yeşilırmak *R* Turkey
Yeşilkent *see* Erzin
47 M11 Yeşilköy Turkey
47 K7 Yeşilova Turkey
79 D1 Yeşiltepe Turkey
108 C1 Yeso New Mexico U.S.A.
80 C6 Yesodot Israel
51 K2 Yessey Russian Federation
17 F6 Yeste Spain
80 F1 Yesud Ha Ma'ala Israel
13 F3 Yetholm Scotland
139 K3 Yetman New South Wales Australia
85 C3 Yetti *tribe* Mauritania
68 B1 Yeu Burma
20 F8 Yeu, I.d' France
55 F3 Yevgashchino Russian Federation
78 L1 Yevlakh Azerbaijan
21 P7 Yèvre *R* France
59 K2 Yevreyskaya Avtonomnyy Oblast *reg* Russian Federation
65 D6 Ye Xian China
53 E10 Yeysk Russian Federation
52 D6 Yezerishche Russian Federation
52 G5 Yezhikha Russian Federation
52 G3 Yezhuga *R* Russian Federation
20 E5 Yffiniac France
130 C9 Yguazu, R Paraguay
130 C9 Yhú Paraguay
47 J8 Yialí *isld* Greece
84 J3 Yi' Allaq, Gebel Egypt
79 E3 Yialousa Cyprus
47 H9 Yianisádhes *isld* Crete Greece
47 O12 Yiannádhes Greece
46 E4 Yiannitsá Greece
68 E1 Yibang China
Yibei *see* Minglun
67 A2 Yibin China
80 B6 Yibna Israel
67 D1 Yichang China
65 B7 Yicheng China
65 D7 Yicheng China
67 D1 Yicheng China
65 A6 Yichuan China
65 B7 Yichuan China
59 J2 Yichun China
67 E3 Yichun China
58 F5 Yidu China
65 D6 Yidu China
67 E2 Yifeng China
80 F1 Yiftaḥ Israel
65 B7 Yi He *R* China
65 D7 Yi He *R* China
67 E3 Yihuang China
65 A7 Yijun China
65 H1 Yilan China
47 J3 Yıldız Dağları *mts* Turkey
78 F2 Yildizeli Turkey
67 A3 Yiliang China
67 A4 Yiliang China
66 E4 Yiliping China
143 B10 Yilliminning W Australia Australia
67 B1 Yilong China
65 G2 Yimianpo China
68 B2 Yin *R* Burma
65 D7 Yinan China
68 C4 Yinbaing Burma
65 B7 Yincheng China
58 E4 Yinchuan China
143 D9 Yindarlgooda, L W Australia Australia
67 D1 Yindian China
67 D1 Yingcheng China
67 F3 Yingchuan China
65 J1 Yingchun China
67 D4 Yingde China
65 F4 Ying'ebu China
Yinggen *see* Qiongzhong
65 B7 Ying He *R* China
65 E4 Yingkou China
67 B1 Yingshan China
67 D1 Yingshan China
67 E2 Yingtan China
65 B5 Ying Xian China
65 D3 Yin He *R* China
66 C3 Yining China
67 C2 Yinjiang China
138 F5 Yinkame South Australia Australia
68 B1 Yinmabin Burma
65 F2 Yinma He *R* China
68 C4 Yinnyein Burma
65 A4 Yin Shan *mts* China
Yinxian *see* Ningbo
46 G5 Yioúra *isld* Greece
Yiquan *see* Meitan
131 G4 Yi, R Uruguay
86 G4 Yirga Alem Ethiopia
80 D2 Yirka Israel
86 F4 Yirol Sudan
80 E1 Yir'on Israel
140 D1 Yirrkala N Terr Australia
59 G2 Yirshi China
52 G3 Yirva *R* Russian Federation
65 D6 Yi Shan *mts* China
67 C4 Yishan China
65 D7 Yishui China
80 E6 Yitav Jordan
46 F8 Yíthion Greece
65 F3 Yitong China
65 F2 Yitong He *R* China
66 E3 Yiwu China
67 G2 Yiwu China
68 E2 Yiwu China
Yixian *see* Yicheng
65 E4 Yi Xian China
65 C5 Yi Xian China
67 F2 Yi Xian China
67 F1 Yixing China
65 D4 Yixun He *R* China
65 B7 Yiyang China
67 D2 Yiyang Hunan China
67 F2 Yiyang Jiangxi China
65 D6 Yiyuan China
67 D4 Yizhang China
67 F1 Yizheng China
31 K6 Yizovice Czechoslovakia
29 N11 Ylämaa Finland
29 J11 Yläne Finland
29 K8 Ylihärmä Finland
29 M6 Ylikiiminki Finland
52 C2 Ylikitka *L* Finland
29 M6 Yli-li Finland
29 K9 Ylistaro Finland
29 K5 Ylitornio Finland
29 L7 Ylivieska Finland
29 L4 Yllästunturi *mt* Finland
29 K10 Ylöjärvi Finland
115 R3 Ymers Ø *isld* Greenland
21 O5 Ymonville France
52 J4 Yndin Russian Federation
27 J13 Yngaren *L* Sweden
86 B3 Yo Nigeria
109 K6 Yoakum Texas U.S.A.
60 O2 Yobetsu Japan
60 O2 Yobetsu-dake *mt* Japan
60 C12 Yobuko Japan
128 E7 Yocalla Bolivia
107 L3 Yocemento Kansas U.S.A.
111 G7 Yocono *R* Mississippi U.S.A.
106 F3 Yoder Colorado U.S.A.
98 B8 Yoder Wyoming U.S.A.
60 J11 Yodo Japan
60 G10 Yodoe Japan
80 D5 Yo'ezer Jordan
133 D8 Yogan *mt* Chile
47 J3 Yoğuntaş Turkey
70 N9 Yogyakarta Java
117 P10 Yoho Nat. Park British Columbia Canada
60 O2 Yoichi Japan
60 O2 Yoichi dake *mt* Japan
125 L2 Yojoa, L. de Honduras
60 H10 Yōka Japan
86 C5 Yokadouma Cameroon
61 K10 Yōkaichi Japan
61 O10 Yōkaichiba Japan
111 F9 Yokena Mississippi U.S.A.
61 K11 Yokkaichi Japan
86 B4 Yoko Cameroon
60 F12 Yokogawara Japan
62 Yokohama *conurbation* Japan
61 N10 Yokosuka Japan
61 O6 Yokote Japan
60 O4 Yokotsu-dake *mt* Japan
86 B4 Yola Nigeria
125 M4 Yolaina, Cord. de Nicaragua
57 B5 Yolbarsli Turkmenistan
65 E2 Yolin Mod China
86 D6 Yolombo Zaire
61 P13 Yomitan Airport Okinawa
61 Q12 Yona Okinawa
61 P13 Yonabaru Okinawa
60 G10 Yonago Japan
67 G4 Yonagunijima Japan
61 Q12 Yonaha-dake *mt* Okinawa
100 B6 Yoncalla Oregon U.S.A.
61 O5 Yoneshiro-gawa *R* Japan
61 O8 Yonezawa Japan
67 F4 Yong'an China
67 D2 Yong'anshi China
67 B2 Yongchuan China
67 F4 Yongchun China
67 C3 Yongcong China
67 E4 Yongding China
65 C5 Yongding He *R* China
59 J4 Yongdŭngpo S Korea
67 E3 Yongfeng China
67 C4 Yongfu China
65 A6 Yonghe China
59 J4 Yonghŭng N Korea
65 G5 Yŏnghŭng-man *B* N Korea
58 F5 Yongji China
65 G3 Yongji China
67 G2 Yongjia China
Yongjing *see* Xifeng
67 G2 Yongkang China
65 C6 Yongnian China
Yongning *see* Xuyong
58 D6 Yongning China
67 C5 Yongning China
65 C5 Yongqing China
67 A2 Yongshan China
67 C2 Yongshun China
67 E3 Yongtai China
67 F4 Yongtai China
67 E3 Yongxin China
67 D3 Yongxing China
67 E2 Yongxiu China
Yongyang *see* Weng'an
118 H6 Yonker Saskatchewan Canada
95 O6 Yonkers New York U.S.A.
107 P5 Yonkers Oklahoma U.S.A.
18 H5 Yonne *dept* France
18 H5 Yonne *R* France
68 B2 Yonzingyi Burma
57 H5 Yopurga China
143 B9 York W Australia Australia
13 G6 York England
111 H9 York Alabama U.S.A.
101 O3 York Montana U.S.A.
98 J9 York Nebraska U.S.A.
98 G1 York North Dakota U.S.A.
95 L7 York Pennsylvania U.S.A.
112 F3 York South Carolina U.S.A.
141 G1 York, C Queensland Australia
141 F2 York Downs Queensland Australia
138 D5 Yorke Pen South Australia Australia
138 D6 Yorketown South Australia Australia
115 K6 York Factory Manitoba Canada

York Harb — Zyryanovsk
243

123 O4 **York Harb** Newfoundland Canada
115 N2 **York, Kap** *C* Greenland
116 D4 **York Mts** Alaska U.S.A.
123 R2 **York Pt** Labrador, Nfld Canada
122 G5 **York R** Quebec Canada
142 F2 **York Sd** W Australia Australia
Yorkshire *co see* **N., W. & S.Yorks, Cleveland, Humberside** *counties*
142 F2 **York Sound** W Australia Australia
119 P7 **Yorkton** Saskatchewan Canada
109 K7 **Yorktown** Texas U.S.A.
95 L9 **Yorktown** Virginia U.S.A.
95 R3 **York Village** Maine U.S.A.
99 S8 **Yorkville** Illinois U.S.A.
95 M3 **Yorkville** New York U.S.A.
125 L2 **Yoro** Honduras
71 B3 **Yoronga** *isld* Indonesia
102 D4 **Yosemite L** California U.S.A.
102 E4 **Yosemite Lodge** California U.S.A.
102 E3 **Yosemite National Park** California U.S.A.
61 M8 **Yoshida** Japan
61 P6 **Yoshihama-wan** *B* Japan
60 H11 **Yoshino** *R* Japan
60 F12 **Yoshino** Japan
61 K11 **Yoshino-Kumano Nat. Park** Japan
52 G6 **Yoshkar-Ola** Russian Federation
60 D12 **Yoshu** Japan
Yösönbulag *see* **Altay** Mongolia
101 M8 **Yost** Utah U.S.A.
61 O8 **Yotsukura** Japan
79 F9 **Yotvata** Israel
117 L11 **Youbou** British Columbia Canada
14 D5 **Youghal** Ireland
67 B5 **You Jiang** *R* China
85 B6 **Youkounkoun** Guinea
9 E1 **Youlgreave** England
139 J5 **Young** New South Wales Australia
119 M7 **Young** Saskatchewan Canada
103 O7 **Young** Arizona U.S.A.
138 D4 **Younghusband, L** South Australia Australia
138 E6 **Younghusband Pen** South Australia Australia
146 C14 **Young I** Antarctica
140 D3 **Young, Mt** N Terr Australia
144 B6 **Young Range** New Zealand
88 E7 **Youngs B** Malawi
118 F7 **Youngstown** Alberta Canada
111 L11 **Youngstown** Florida U.S.A.
94 J3 **Youngstown** New York U.S.A.
94 G5 **Youngstown** Ohio U.S.A.
111 D11 **Youngsville** Louisiana U.S.A.
106 D5 **Youngsville** New Mexico U.S.A.
112 J1 **Youngsville** North Carolina U.S.A.
94 H5 **Youngsville** Pennsylvania U.S.A.
101 Q6 **Younts Pk** Wyoming U.S.A.
102 B3 **Yountville** California U.S.A.
67 C2 **You Shui** *R* China
67 F3 **Youxi** China
67 D3 **You Xian** China
67 C2 **Youyang** China
65 H1 **Youyi** China
65 B4 **Youyu** China
141 G8 **Yowah** *R* Queensland Australia
143 C7 **Yowereena Hill** W Australia Australia
78 E2 **Yozgat** Turkey
130 B9 **Ypacarai, L** Paraguay
29 K11 **Ypäjä** Finland
130 C8 **Ypané, R** Paraguay
130 C8 **Ypé-jhú** Paraguay
130 B9 **Ypoá** *L* Paraguay
21 L2 **Yport** France
29 L7 **Yppäri** Finland
Ypres *see* **Ieper**
94 D4 **Ypsilanti** Michigan U.S.A.
100 C8 **Yreka** California U.S.A.
8 C3 **Yrfon** *R* Wales
8 C3 **Yspytty Ystwyth** Wales
18 H7 **Yssingeaux** France
57 G3 **Yssyk-Ata** Kyrgyzstan
27 G16 **Ystad** Sweden
8 C4 **Ystalyfera** Wales
8 B3 **Ystrad Aeron** Wales
8 C3 **Ystrad-ffin** Wales
8 C3 **Ystwyth, R** Wales
15 F3 **Ythan, R** Scotland
26 G9 **Ytterhogdal** Sweden
27 J12 **Ytterjärna** Sweden
26 J8 **Ytterlännäs** Sweden
26 E8 **Ytteröy** Norway
26 L7 **Yttersjön** Sweden
67 D1 **Yuan'an** China
67 C4 **Yuanbao Shan** *mt* China
67 E1 **Yüan Hu** China
67 C2 **Yuan Jiang** *R* China
67 D2 **Yuanjiang** China
68 F1 **Yuan Jiang** *R* China
67 C2 **Yuanling** China
65 B5 **Yuanping** China
65 B7 **Yuanqu** China
65 C6 **Yuanshi** China
67 E3 **Yuan Shui** *R* China
65 B7 **Yuanyang** China
67 D3 **Yuanyue** China
60 J11 **Yuasa** Japan
102 C2 **Yuba** *R* California U.S.A.
102 C2 **Yuba City** California U.S.A.
60 P2 **Yūbari** Japan
60 Q2 **Yūbari dake** *mt* Japan
86 G4 **Yubdo** Ethiopia
60 R1 **Yūbetsu** Japan
60 S2 **Yūbetsu** Japan
61 M9 **Yubiso** Japan
80 G3 **Yubla** Jordan
128 D7 **Yucamani** *mt* Peru
125 P7 **Yucatan** *state* Mexico
90 A6 **Yucatan Basin** Atlantic Oc
126 A3 **Yucatan Chan** Caribbean
103 K7 **Yucca** Arizona U.S.A.
103 H4 **Yucca Flat** Nevada U.S.A.
106 B4 **Yucca House Nat. Mon** Colorado U.S.A.
65 C6 **Yucheng** China
65 C7 **Yucheng** China
65 B6 **Yuci** China
65 C3 **Yudaokou** China
51 N3 **Yudoma** *R* Russian Federation
67 E4 **Yudu** China
67 B1 **Yuechi** China
67 D1 **Yuekou** China
Yuelai *see* **Huachuan**
67 C1 **Yuelai** China
65 F2 **Yueliang Pao** *L* China
67 G2 **Yueqing** China
67 G2 **Yueqing Wan** *B* China
67 E1 **Yuexi** China
58 D6 **Yuexi He** *R* China
67 A2 **Yuexi He** *R* China
Yueyang *see* **Gu Xian**
67 D2 **Yueyang** China
60 E12 **Yufu-dake** *mt* Japan
52 G5 **Yug** *R* Russian Federation
52 G4 **Yuga** *R* Russian Federation
67 E2 **Yugan** China
55 F1 **Yugan** Russian Federation
42 H4 **Yugoslavia** *rep* S Europe
67 G1 **Yuhang** China
65 B4 **Yu He** *R* China
65 A5 **Yuhebu** China
67 B4 **Yuhong** China
67 G2 **Yuhuan** China
143 B8 **Yuin** W Australia Australia
67 C2 **Yu Jiang** *R* China
67 E2 **Yujiang** China
67 C5 **Yu Jiang** *R* China
52 H5 **Yukamenskoye** Russian Federation
47 J5 **Yukarıbey** Turkey
54 G2 **Yukhnov** Russian Federation
61 N9 **Yūki** Japan
116 J4 **Yuki** *R* Alaska U.S.A.
113 F7 **Yukon** Florida U.S.A.
107 N6 **Yukon** Oklahoma U.S.A.
116 Q4 **Yukon-Charley Rivers Nat Preserve** Alaska U.S.A.
117 E4 **Yukon Crossing** Yukon Territory Canada
55 E1 **Yukonda** *R* Russian Federation
116 E5 **Yukon Delta** Alaska U.S.A.
116 N3 **Yukon Flats Nat Mon** Alaska U.S.A.
116 M4 **Yukon R** Alaska/Yukon Terr U.S.A./Canada
114 F5 **Yukon Territory** Canada
60 E12 **Yukuhashi** Japan
66 B4 **Yukuriawat** China
52 F3 **Yula** *R* Russian Federation
55 C4 **Yuldybayevo** Russian Federation
146 C13 **Yule B** Antarctica
141 J7 **Yuleba** Queensland Australia
142 B2 **Yule Brook** Perth, W Aust Australia
113 F7 **Yulee** Florida U.S.A.
142 C5 **Yule R** W Australia Australia
65 A5 **Yulin** China
67 C5 **Yulin** China
67 C7 **Yulin** China
52 D2 **Yuma** Russian Federation
103 K9 **Yuma** Arizona U.S.A.
98 D9 **Yuma** Colorado U.S.A.
127 K5 **Yuma, B. de** Dominican Rep
103 K9 **Yuma Desert** Arizona U.S.A.
55 C4 **Yumaguzino** Russian Federation
138 C4 **Yumbarra Conservation Park** South Australia Australia
86 E6 **Yumbi** Zaire
58 C3 **Yumen** China
58 C3 **Yü-men-chen** China
58 C3 **Yumenzhen** China
58 F1 **Yumurchen** Russian Federation
143 A8 **Yuna** W Australia Australia
127 K5 **Yuna** *R* Dominican Rep
78 C2 **Yunak** Turkey
67 D5 **Yunan** China
67 C1 **Yun'anzhen** China
65 B7 **Yuncheng** China
65 C7 **Yuncheng** China
143 D8 **Yundamindera** W Australia Australia
67 D5 **Yunfu** China
128 E7 **Yungas, Las** *mts* Bolivia
139 G5 **Yungera** Victoria Australia
Yunhe *see* **Pei Xian**
67 F2 **Yunhe** China
67 C5 **Yunkai Dashan** *mts* China
67 D1 **Yunmeng** China
67 A4 **Yunnan** *prov* China
60 O4 **Yunokawa** Japan
60 D13 **Yunomae** Japan
60 F10 **Yunotsu** Japan
16 E4 **Yunquera de H** Spain
67 A4 **Yunshang** China
138 E4 **Yunta** South Australia Australia
58 F5 **Yun Xian** China
67 F5 **Yunxiao** China
67 C1 **Yunyang** China
65 B5 **Yunzhong Shan** *mts* China
67 C3 **Yuping** China
65 D4 **Yuqiao Shuiku** *res* China
67 B3 **Yuqing** China
Yuqingsi *see* **Aoxi**
60 O3 **Yūrappu-dake** *mt* Japan
124 H7 **Yuréchara** Mexico
56 B3 **Yurga** Russian Federation
55 D3 **Yurgamysh** Russian Federation
55 E3 **Yurginskiy** Russian Federation
128 C5 **Yurimaguas** Peru
52 G6 **Yurino** Russian Federation
52 H5 **Yurla** Russian Federation
55 C3 **Yurma** *mt* Russian Federation
52 G2 **Yuroma** Russian Federation
55 E2 **Yurovsk** Russian Federation
66 B4 **Yurungkax He** *R* China
60 T2 **Yururi-tō** *isld* Japan
52 G5 **Yur'ya** Russian Federation
52 J2 **Yur'yakha** *R* Russian Federation
52 F6 **Yur'yevets** Russian Federation
52 E6 **Yur'yev Pol'skiy** Russian Federation
55 C3 **Yuryuzan' Katav-Ivanovsk** Russian Federation
125 L3 **Yuscarán** Honduras
67 F2 **Yushan** China
67 C2 **Yushanzhen** China
65 B6 **Yushe** China
52 H1 **Yushino** Russian Federation
52 D3 **Yushkozero** Russian Federation
59 J3 **Yushu** China
66 F5 **Yushu** China
65 G2 **Yushugou** China
Yushuwan *see* **Huaihua**
78 H1 **Yusufeli** Turkey
60 F12 **Yusuhara** Japan
52 H5 **Yus'va** Russian Federation
65 C7 **Yutai** China
98 K8 **Yutan** Nebraska U.S.A.
52 H6 **Yutaza** Russian Federation
128 F7 **Yuti** Bolivia
65 D5 **Yutian** Hebei China
66 C4 **Yutian** Xinjiang Uygur Zizhiqu China
130 C10 **Yuty** Paraguay
67 F5 **Yü-weng Tao** Taiwan
Yuxi *see* **Daozhen**
65 B5 **Yu Xian** China
65 C5 **Yu Xian** China
65 B7 **Yu Xian** China
67 G1 **Yuyao** China
60 D11 **Yuya-wan** *B* Japan
52 F5 **Yuza** *R* Russian Federation
61 M9 **Yuzawa** Japan
52 F6 **Yuzha** Russian Federation
57 G5 **Yuzh Alichurskiy, Khrebet** *mts* Tajikistan
55 D4 **Yuzhnoural'skiy** Russian Federation
55 D4 **Yuzhnyy** Russian Federation
56 B4 **Yuzhnyy** Russian Federation
56 C6 **Yuzhnyy Altay, Khrebet** *mts* Kazakhstan
48 M2 **Yuzhnyy Bug** *R* Ukraine
55 C4 **Yuzhnyy Ural** *reg* Russian Federation
Yuzhou *see* **Chongqing**
55 G4 **Yuzno Podol'sk** Russian Federation
21 O4 **Yvelines** *dept* France
40 E4 **Yverdon** Switzerland
21 M2 **Yvetot** France
20 D4 **Yvias** France
20 F5 **Yvignac** France
22 H3 **Yvoir Anhee** Belgium
40 E4 **Yvonand** Switzerland
21 O6 **Yvoy-le-Marron** France
21 L5 **Yvre-l'Evêque** France
68 B2 **Ywamun** Burma
68 C3 **Ywathit** Burma
27 H13 **Yxviken** Sweden
21 J7 **Yzernay** France
21 M8 **Yzeures-sur-Creuse** France

Z

25 C4 **Zaandam** Netherlands
25 C4 **Zaandijk** Netherlands
42 H6 **Zāba** *mt* Bosnia-Herzegovina
80 E4 **Zababida** Jordan
48 F5 **Žabalj** Serbia Yugoslavia
48 G6 **Žabari** Serbia Yugoslavia
58 G2 **Zabaykal'sk** Russian Federation
80 F3 **Zabda** Jordan
56 F4 **Zabituy** Russian Federation
31 K5 **Ząbkowice** Poland
31 O3 **Zabłudów** Poland
77 K4 **Zābol** *prov* Afghanistan
77 G4 **Zabol** Iran
77 G6 **Zāboli** Iran
48 J2 **Zabolotov** Ukraine
31 K6 **Zábřeh** Czechoslovakia
31 L5 **Zabrze** Poland
125 P9 **Zacatal** Guatemala
125 N8 **Zacatali** Mexico
124 H6 **Zacatecas** *state* Mexico
124 H6 **Zacatecas** Mexico
125 P11 **Zacatecoluca** El Salvador
125 L9 **Zacatepec** Mexico
111 E11 **Zachary** Louisiana U.S.A.
33 O6 **Zachun** Germany
125 L2 **Zacualpa** Honduras
42 G4 **Zadar** Croatia
68 C7 **Zadetkale Kyun** *isld* Burma
68 C8 **Zadetkyi** Burma
68 C5 **Zadi** Burma
54 K4 **Zadonsk** Russian Federation
80 C5 **Zafriyya** Israel
31 J4 **Żagań** Poland
52 B6 **Zagare** Lithuania
45 N6 **Zagarolo** Italy
79 B8 **Zagazig** Egypt
43 C12 **Zaghouan** Tunisia
46 F5 **Zagorá** Greece
85 C2 **Zagora** Morocco
Zagorsk *see* **Sergiyev Posad**
42 G3 **Zagreb** Croatia
77 A3 **Zāgros Mountains** Iran
48 G6 **Zagubica** Serbia Yugoslavia
Zagunao *see* **Li Xian** Sichuan
77 G5 **Zāhedān** Iran
98 C1 **Zahl** North Dakota U.S.A.
79 F5 **Zahle** Lebanon
33 R9 **Zahna** Germany
77 B6 **Zahrān, Az** Saudi Arabia
57 H3 **Zailiyskiv Alatau, Khr** *mts* Kazakhstan
36 H7 **Zainingen** Germany
86 D6 **Zaire** *rep* Africa
86 D5 **Zaïre** *R* W Africa
86 B7 **Zaïre Central** Zaire
80 D5 **Zaita** Jordan
46 E1 **Zaječar** Serbia Yugoslavia
56 F5 **Zakamensk** Russian Federation
78 L1 **Zakataly** Azerbaijan
78 J3 **Zakho** Iraq
46 D7 **Zákinthos** *isld* Greece
31 N5 **Zaklików** Poland
48 F1 **Zakopane** Poland
31 M3 **Zakroczym** Poland
47 H9 **Zákros** Crete Greece
48 D4 **Zala** *R* Hungary
48 D4 **Zalaegerszeg** Hungary
16 C7 **Zalamea la Real** Spain
59 H2 **Zalantun** China
48 D4 **Zalaövo** Hungary
48 H3 **Zalău** Romania
48 K2 **Zaleshchiki** Ukraine
94 E7 **Zaleski** Ohio U.S.A.
31 N1 **Zales'ye** Russian Federation
31 M2 **Zalewo** Poland
31 H2 **Zalew Szczeciński** *lagoon* Germany/Poland
86 D3 **Zalingei** Sudan
50 E4 **Zaliv Kara Bogaz Gol** *B* Turkmenistan
59 K3 **Zaliv Petra Velikogo** *B* Russian Federation
84 E4 **Zallāf, Ramlat az** *sands* Libya
110 F4 **Zalma** Missouri U.S.A.
37 O3 **Zalmanov** Czechoslovakia
25 D5 **Zaltbommel** Netherlands
84 F4 **Zalţen** Libya
52 D5 **Zaluch'ye** Russian Federation
68 B4 **Zalun** Burma
68 D6 **Zalut** Burma
56 G4 **Zama** Russian Federation
117 O6 **Zama L** Alberta Canada
71 E3 **Zambales Mts** Luzon Philippines
31 J5 **Žamberk** Czechoslovakia
87 G9 **Zambeze** *R* E Africa
87 D8 **Zambezi** Zambia
88 F10 **Zambézia** Mozambique
88 C7 **Zambia** *rep* Cent Africa
71 F7 **Zamboanga** Mindanao Philippines
71 F6 **Zamboanguita** Negros Philippines
126 G10 **Zambrano** Colombia
31 N3 **Zambrów** Poland
85 F6 **Zamfara** *R* Nigeria
128 C4 **Zamora** Ecuador
124 H8 **Zamora** Mexico
16 C3 **Zamora** *prov* Spain
16 D3 **Zamora** Spain
102 C3 **Zamora** California U.S.A.
125 L3 **Zamorano** Honduras
31 O5 **Zamość** Poland
61 P13 **Zampa-misaki** *C* Okinawa
128 F3 **Zamuro, Sa. del** *mts* Venezuela
84 E3 **Zamzam** Libya
86 B6 **Zanaga** Congo
17 F5 **Záncara** *R* Spain
25 H3 **Zandberg** Netherlands
22 G1 **Zandvliet** Belgium
25 C4 **Zandvoort** Netherlands
116 J3 **Zane Hills** Alaska U.S.A.
94 E7 **Zanesville** Ohio U.S.A.
74 G2 **Zangla** Kashmir
65 C6 **Zanhuang** China
41 L6 **Zanica** Italy
77 A1 **Zanjān** Iran
131 C3 **Zanjón, R** Argentina
43 E8 **Zannone, I** Italy
Zante *see* **Zákinthos**
143 E9 **Zanthus** W Australia Australia
88 G5 **Zanzibar** Tanzania
88 G5 **Zanzibar Chan** Tanzania
88 G5 **Zanzibar, I** Tanzania
54 J2 **Zaokskiy** Russian Federation
67 E3 **Zaolin** China
65 C6 **Zaoqiang** China
17 F4 **Zaorejas** Spain
85 F3 **Zaouatallaz** Algeria
67 F1 **Zaoxi** China
67 D1 **Zaoyang** China
67 D1 **Zaoyang Zhan** China
61 O7 **Zaō-zan** *vol* Japan
56 D3 **Zaozernyy** Russian Federation
65 D7 **Zaozhuang** China
98 E2 **Zap** North Dakota U.S.A.
46 D1 **Zapadna Morava** *R* Serbia Yugoslavia
54 A1 **Zapadnaya Dvina** *R* Belorussia/Rus Fed
53 D6 **Zapadnaya Dvina** *R* Russian Federation
29 Q2 **Zapadnaya Litza** *R* Russian Federation
59 M1 **Zapadno Sakhalinskiy Khrebet** *mt* Russian Federation
56 B2 **Zapadnosibirskaya Ravnina** *lowland* Russian Federation
56 C5 **Zapadnyy Sayan** Russian Federation
37 O4 **Západočeský** *reg* Czechoslovakia
133 C5 **Zapala** Argentina
109 H9 **Zapata** Texas U.S.A.
126 D3 **Zapata, Pen. de** Cuba
125 M4 **Zapatera, I** Nicaragua
128 D2 **Zapatosa** Colombia
126 H10 **Zapatoza, Ciénaga de** Colombia
37 K3 **Zapfendorf** Germany
29 P2 **Zapolyarnyy** Russian Federation
54 G9 **Zaporozh'ye** Ukraine
124 H8 **Zapotiltic** Mexico
124 G7 **Zapotlán** Mexico
84 F4 **Zaqqūt** Libya
Zara *see* **Zadar**
78 F2 **Zara** Turkey
57 C4 **Zarafshan** Uzbekistan
108 A4 **Zaragoza** Chihuahua Mexico
108 G7 **Zaragoza** Coahuila Mexico
71 D2 **Zaragoza** Luzon Philippines
17 G3 **Zaragoza** *prov* Spain
17 G3 **Zaragoza** Spain
124 H4 **Zaragoza, Tiahualilo de** Mexico
88 G5 **Zaramu** Tanzania
77 E4 **Zarand** Kerman Iran
77 B2 **Zarand** Ostan-e Markazi Iran
48 G4 **Zărandului, Muntii** *mts* Romania
77 G4 **Zaranj** Afghanistan
52 C6 **Zarasai** Lithuania
131 F5 **Zárate** Argentina
54 K2 **Zaraysk** Russian Federation
127 M10 **Zaraza** Venezuela
57 F5 **Zardaly** Kyrgyzstan
77 B3 **Zard Kuh** *mt* Iran
29 P3 **Zarechensk** Russian Federation
52 D2 **Zarechensk** Russian Federation
117 G7 **Zarembo I** Alaska U.S.A.
85 F6 **Zaria** Nigeria
56 C4 **Zarinsk** Russian Federation
46 E5 **Zárkon** Greece
85 D5 **Zarma** *reg* Mali
48 J5 **Zarneşti** Romania
31 M4 **Żarnów** Poland
33 T5 **Zarow** *R* Germany
80 F7 **Zarqa** *R* Jordan
77 C5 **Zarqān** Iran
33 N5 **Zarrentin** Germany
128 C4 **Zaruma** Ecuador
31 J4 **Żary** Poland
85 F3 **Zarzaïtine** Algeria
85 G2 **Zarzis** Tunisia
37 P1 **Zaschwitz** Germany
52 D2 **Zasheyek** Russian Federation
31 H4 **Zasieki** Poland
48 K2 **Zastavna** Ukraine
89 E8 **Zastron** S Africa
54 E6 **Zasul'ye** Ukraine
79 H7 **Zatab ash Shāmah** Saudi Arabia
37 Q3 **Žatec** Czechoslovakia
48 N4 **Zatoka** Ukraine
Zatoka Gdańsk *see* **Danzig, G. of**
31 L6 **Zator** Poland
33 R8 **Zauche** *reg* Germany
57 A4 **Zaunguzskiye Karakumy** Turkmenistan
109 N4 **Zavalla** Texas U.S.A.
Zavelstein *see* **Bad Teinach-Zavelstein**
22 G2 **Zaventem** Belgium
47 H1 **Zavet** Bulgaria
48 E6 **Zavidovići** Bosnia-Herzegovina
59 J1 **Zavitinsk** Russian Federation
146 G2 **Zavodovski** *vol* S Sandwich Is S Atlantic Oc
146 G2 **Zavodovski I** S Sandwich Is S Atlantic Oc
56 B4 **Zavodskoye** Russian Federation
68 C2 **Zawgyi** *R* Burma
31 L5 **Zawiercie** Poland
80 D5 **Zawiya** Jordan
84 E3 **Zāwiyah, Az** Libya
79 G3 **Zāwīyah, Jebel az** *mts* Syria
84 G3 **Zawīyat Masūs** Libya
56 F3 **Zayarsk** Russian Federation
79 G6 **Zaydī, Wādī az** *watercourse* Syria
56 B6 **Zaysan, Oz** *res* Kazakhstan
57 L1 **Zaysan, Ozero** *L* Kazakhstan
48 K1 **Zbarazh** Ukraine
31 J3 **Zbaszyń** Poland
48 J1 **Zborov** Ukraine
48 K1 **Zbruch** *R* Ukraine
48 G2 **Zdaňa** Czechoslovakia
48 D1 **Ždanice** Czechoslovakia
30 H6 **Zdice** Czechoslovakia
31 L4 **Zduńska** Poland
Zealand *isld see* **Sjælland**
118 K7 **Zealandia** Saskatchewan Canada
99 N7 **Zearing** Iowa U.S.A.
57 F6 **Zēbāk** Afghanistan
117 K11 **Zeballos** British Columbia Canada
112 J2 **Zebulon** North Carolina U.S.A.
33 R6 **Zechlin** Germany
41 H5 **Zeda, Monte** Italy
22 E1 **Zedelgem** Belgium
22 E1 **Zeebrugge** Belgium
139 H8 **Zeehan** Tasmania Australia
25 A6 **Zeeland** Netherlands
94 A4 **Zeeland** Michigan U.S.A.
98 G4 **Zeeland** North Dakota U.S.A.
79 E7 **Zeelim** Israel
80 E8 **Ze'elim, N** *R* Israel
89 E5 **Zeerust** S Africa
25 E4 **Zeewolde** Netherlands
80 E2 **Zefat** Israel
85 C3 **Zegdou** Algeria
85 E5 **Zeggeren** *watercourse* Mali
31 N3 **Zegrzyńskie, Jezioro** *res* Poland
33 S7 **Zehdenick** Germany
33 S8 **Zehlendorf** Berlin
33 Q5 **Zehna** Germany
37 P1 **Zehren** Germany
110 G4 **Zeigler** Illinois U.S.A.
37 K3 **Zeil** Germany
25 D4 **Zeist** Netherlands
33 S10 **Zeithain** Germany
37 O7 **Zeitlarn** Germany
37 N1 **Zeitz** Germany
80 G3 **Zeizun** Syria
22 G1 **Zele** Belgium
31 N4 **Zelechów** Poland
37 P5 **Zelená Lhota** Czechoslovakia
52 D2 **Zelenborskiy** Russian Federation
55 D1 **Zelenoborsk** Russian Federation
54 E9 **Zelenodol'sk** Ukraine
29 O11 **Zelenogorsk** Russian Federation
54 J1 **Zelenograd** Russian Federation
31 M1 **Zelenogradsk** Russian Federation
54 E9 **Zelenoye** Ukraine
53 F11 **Zelenshuk** *R* Russian Federation
94 G6 **Zelienople** Pennsylvania U.S.A.
48 E2 **Želiezovce** Czechoslovakia
42 G3 **Zelina** Croatia
46 D1 **Željin** *mt* Serbia Yugoslavia
36 E7 **Zell** Baden-Württemberg Germany
36 H4 **Zell** Bayern Germany
36 C3 **Zell** Rheinland-Pfalz Germany
98 H5 **Zell** South Dakota U.S.A.
37 K2 **Zella-Mehlis** Germany
38 H6 **Zell-a-moos** Austria
38 G7 **Zell-am-see** Austria
38 E7 **Zell-am-Ziller** Austria
38 L5 **Zell-bei-zellhof** Austria
33 S9 **Zellendorf** Germany
36 H4 **Zellingen** Germany
119 M7 **Zelma** Saskatchewan Canada
31 L4 **Zelów** Poland
36 C4 **Zeltingen-Rachtig** Germany
22 F1 **Zelzate** Belgium
43 D11 **Zembra, Ile** Tunisia
46 F2 **Zemen** Bulgaria
51 O1 **Zemlya Bunge** Russian Federation
50 D1 **Zemlya Frantsa-Iosifa** Russian Federation
50 D1 **Zemlya Georga** *isld* Franz Josef Land Russian Federation
50 F1 **Zemlya Vil'cheka** Franz Josef Land Russian Federation
38 E7 **Zemm** *R* Austria
48 G2 **Zempléni-Hory** *mt* Hungary
48 F6 **Zemun** Serbia Yugoslavia
107 M4 **Zenda** Kansas U.S.A.
67 D5 **Zengcheng** China
100 B9 **Zenia** California U.S.A.
42 H4 **Zenica** Bosnia-Herzegovina
54 F6 **Zen'kov** Ukraine
56 C4 **Zen'kovo** Russian Federation
37 K5 **Zenn** *R* Germany
22 G1 **Zenne** *R* Belgium
119 O5 **Zenon Park** Saskatchewan Canada
60 G11 **Zentsūji** Japan
125 L9 **Zenzontepec** Mexico
98 D4 **Zeona** South Dakota U.S.A.
109 J4 **Zephyr** Texas U.S.A.
113 E9 **Zephyrhills** Florida U.S.A.
143 D8 **Zephyr,Mt** W Australia Australia
57 E5 **Zerav'shanskiy Khrebet** *mts* Tajikistan/Uzbekistan
33 Q9 **Zerbst** Germany
36 B4 **Zerf** Germany
31 K3 **Zerków** Poland
40 G5 **Zermatt** Switzerland
101 U3 **Zero** Montana U.S.A.
46 D3 **Zerqan** Albania
33 U6 **Zerrenthin** Germany
80 C3 **Zerufa** Israel
66 E6 **Zêtang** China
32 G6 **Zetel** Germany
Zetland *co see* **Shetland** *reg*
65 E6 **Zetouji** China
37 M2 **Zeulenroda** Germany
33 T8 **Zeuthen** Germany
32 K6 **Zeven** Germany
25 C5 **Zevenbergen** Netherlands
25 C5 **Zevenbergse Hoek** Netherlands
45 K1 **Zevio** Italy
59 J1 **Zeya** Russian Federation
25 F5 **Zeyenaar** Netherlands
59 J1 **Zeysko Bureinskaya Ravnina** *plain* Russian Federation
59 J1 **Zeyskoye Vodokhranilishche** *res* Russian Federation
47 J6 **Zeytindağ** Turkey
16 B4 **Zêzere** *R* Portugal
79 F4 **Zgharta** Lebanon
31 L4 **Zgierz** Poland
38 N8 **Zgornja Kungota** Slovenia
31 J4 **Zgorzelec** Poland
48 L2 **Zguritsa** Moldavia
66 F5 **Zhag'yab** China
67 F3 **Zhaili** China
67 C5 **Zhaixu** China
55 E5 **Zhaksy** Kazakhstan
57 E1 **Zhaksykon** *R* Kazakhstan
57 G2 **Zhaksylyk** Kazakhstan
57 J3 **Zhalanash** Kazakhstan
55 E5 **Zhaltyr** Kazakhstan
57 C1 **Zhamanakkol', Ozero** *L* Kazakhstan
57 E1 **Zhanabas** Kazakhstan
57 B2 **Zhanakentkala** Kazakhstan
57 B2 **Zhanakurylys** Kazakhstan
57 C3 **Zhanatalap** Kazakhstan
57 E3 **Zhanatas** Kazakhstan
65 C4 **Zhangbei** China
Zhangde *see* **Anyang**
Zhangdian *see* **Zibo**
65 G3 **Zhangguangcai Ling** *mt ra* China
65 E3 **Zhanggutai** China
65 C6 **Zhang He** *R* China
67 C6 **Zhanghuang** China
65 C4 **Zhangjiakou** China
67 E1 **Zhangjiapang** China
67 E2 **Zhangjiashan** China
65 D7 **Zhanglou** China
67 C5 **Zhangmu** China
67 F4 **Zhangping** China
67 F4 **Zhangpu** China
65 D6 **Zhangqiu** China
65 D4 **Zhangsanying** China
67 E4 **Zhang Shui** *R* China
Zhangshuzhen *see* **Qingjiang**
59 H3 **Zhangwu** China
58 D4 **Zhangye** China
67 F4 **Zhangzhou** Fujian China
65 B6 **Zhangzi** China
65 E5 **Zhangzi Dao** *isld* China
65 D6 **Zhanhua** China
67 C6 **Zhanjiang** China
67 C6 **Zhanjiang Gang** *B* China
57 C3 **Zhankala** Kazakhstan
51 P1 **Zhannetty, Ostrov** *isld* Russian Federation
57 E1 **Zhanteli** Kazakhstan
67 A4 **Zhanyi** China
65 E2 **Zhanyu** China
67 F5 **Zhao'an** China
65 B6 **Zhaocheng** China
65 F1 **Zhaodong** China
Zhaoge *see* **Qi Xian**
67 C4 **Zhaoping** China
67 D5 **Zhaoqing** China
66 C3 **Zhaosu** China
67 A3 **Zhaotong** China
65 C6 **Zhao Xian** China
65 F2 **Zhaoyuan** China
65 E6 **Zhaoyuan** China
Zhaozhen *see* **Jintang**
59 J2 **Zhaozhou** China
67 G1 **Zhapu** China
52 D6 **Zhari** Russian Federation
54 D1 **Zharkovskiy** Russian Federation
57 K1 **Zharma** Kazakhstan
57 G1 **Zharyk** Kazakhstan
48 N1 **Zhashkov** Ukraine
51 M2 **Zhatay** Russian Federation
Zhaxi *see* **Weixin**
66 B5 **Zhaxigang** China
Zhdanov *see* **Mariupol'**
65 C7 **Zhecheng** China
67 F2 **Zhejiang** *prov* China
50 G1 **Zhelaniya, Mys** *C* Russian Federation
57 E1 **Zhel'dyadyr** *hills* Kazakhstan
31 N1 **Zheleznodorozhnyy** Russian Federation
56 F3 **Zheleznodorozhnyy** Irkutskaya obl Russian Federation
54 G4 **Zheleznogorsk** Russian Federation
56 F3 **Zheleznogorsk-Ilimsky** Russian Federation
Zhelou *see* **Ceheng**
54 E8 **Zheltyye Vody** Ukraine
67 B4 **Zhenfeng** China
67 B2 **Zheng'an** China
58 F4 **Zhengding** China
67 F3 **Zhenghe** China
67 D2 **Zhengjiayi** China
65 C3 **Zhenglan Qi** China
65 C3 **Zhengxiangbai Qi** China
65 B7 **Zhengzhou** China
67 G2 **Zhenhai** China
67 F4 **Zhenhai** China
67 F1 **Zhenjiang** China
65 F2 **Zhenlai** China
65 C5 **Zhenlong** China
67 B3 **Zhenning** China
67 C1 **Zhenping** China
Zhenwudong *see* **Ansai**
65 F1 **Zhenxiang** China
67 A3 **Zhenxiong** China
67 C3 **Zhenyuan** China
67 C1 **Zhenziling** China
67 F3 **Zherong** China
67 A4 **Zhetai** China
55 D5 **Zhetikol'** *L* Russian Federation
67 D1 **Zhicheng** China
67 A5 **Zhicun** China
48 J1 **Zhidachov** Ukraine
Zhifang *see* **Wuchang**
58 B3 **Zhifang** China
56 G4 **Zhigalovo** Russian Federation
51 M2 **Zhigansk** Russian Federation
57 E1 **Zhigerli** Kazakhstan
67 D1 **Zhijiang** China
67 C3 **Zhijiang** China
67 B3 **Zhijin** China
54 H7 **Zhikhar'** Ukraine
67 B6 **Zhilang** China
58 C5 **Zhi Qu** China
67 F2 **Zhitan** China
53 C8 **Zhitomir** Ukraine
54 G2 **Zhizdra** *R* Russian Federation
54 F3 **Zhizdra** Russian Federation
54 B4 **Zhlobin** Belorussia
48 L1 **Zhmerinka** Ukraine
74 C3 **Zhob** Pakistan
77 L4 **Zhob** *R* Pakistan
51 P1 **Zhokhova, Ostrov** *isld* Russian Federation
57 C5 **Zhondor** Uzbekistan
Zhongba *see* **Jiangyou**
66 C6 **Zhongba** China
67 B5 **Zhongdong** China
67 C4 **Zhongdu** China
65 F1 **Zhonghe** China
67 A1 **Zhongjiang** China
65 B7 **Zhongmou** China
146 J11 **Zhongshan** *China Base* Antarctica
67 D4 **Zhongshan** China
67 D5 **Zhongshan** China
Zhongshu *see* **Renhuai**
65 B7 **Zhongtiao Shan** *ra* China
67 B1 **Zhong Xian** China
58 F5 **Zhongxiang** China
67 E4 **Zhongxin** China
65 B6 **Zhongyang** China
68 K3 **Zhongyuan** China
67 D2 **Zhoujiadian** China
58 F5 **Zhoukou** China
67 F3 **Zhouning** China
67 G1 **Zhoushan Dao** *isld* China
59 H5 **Zhoushan Qundao** China
48 J1 **Zhovten'** Ukraine
48 N3 **Zhovten'** Ukraine
59 H4 **Zhuanghe** China
67 B3 **Zhucang** China
65 D6 **Zhucheng** China
Zhuji *see* **Shangqiu**
67 G2 **Zhuji** China
67 G2 **Zhujia Jian** *isld* China
67 D6 **Zhujiang Kou** *B* China
Zhujing *see* **Jinshan**
54 E3 **Zhukovka** Russian Federation
54 H1 **Zhukovo** Russian Federation
65 C5 **Zhulong He** *R* China
65 D4 **Zhuluke** China
58 F5 **Zhumadian** China
58 G3 **Zhuolu** China
58 G4 **Zhuo Xian** China
65 B4 **Zhuozi** China
65 E6 **Zhuqiao** China
55 C6 **Zhuryn** Kazakhstan
57 G3 **Zhusandala, Step'** Kazakhstan
67 C1 **Zhushan** China
67 D3 **Zhuting** China
58 E5 **Zhuxi** China
65 A7 **Zhuyangzhen** China
67 A4 **Zhuyuan** China
57 J2 **Zhuzagashskiy** Kazakhstan
67 D3 **Zhuzhou** China
57 D4 **Ziadin** Uzbekistan
78 J3 **Zibar** Iraq
65 D6 **Zibo** China
65 A6 **Zichang** China
22 H2 **Zichem** Belgium
31 J9 **Zidani-Most** Slovenia
42 G2 **Zidani Most** Yugoslavia
47 J2 **Zidarovo** Bulgaria
33 R5 **Ziddorf** Germany
54 H7 **Zid'ki** Ukraine
31 K5 **Ziębice** Poland
33 P6 **Ziegendorf** Germany
36 G2 **Ziegenhain** Germany
37 M2 **Ziegenrück** Germany
140 B6 **Ziel,Mt** N Terr Australia
31 J4 **Zielona Góra** Poland
32 K10 **Zierenberg** Germany
25 A5 **Zierikzee** Netherlands
38 N4 **Ziersdorf** Austria
33 Q8 **Ziesar** Germany
31 P1 **Žiežmariai** Lithuania
79 B8 **Zifta** Egypt
68 A2 **Zigaing** Burma
55 C4 **Zigaza** Russian Federation
84 G4 **Zīghan** Libya
68 B3 **Zigon** Burma
67 A2 **Zigong** China
58 F5 **Zigui** China
85 A6 **Ziguinchor** Senegal
52 C6 **Zigure** Latvia
65 D6 **Zi He** *R* China
37 P3 **Žihle** Czechoslovakia
65 C5 **Zijingguan** China
80 C3 **Zikhron Ya'aqov** Israel
78 E1 **Zile** Turkey
48 E1 **Žilina** Czechoslovakia
84 F4 **Zillah** Libya
38 E7 **Zillertal** *R* Austria
38 E7 **Zillertaler Alpen** *mts* Austria
141 K1 **Zillmere** *dist* Brisbane, Qnsld Australia
52 C6 **Zilupe** Latvia
56 F4 **Zima** Russian Federation
125 K7 **Zimapán** Mexico
125 L9 **Zimatlán de Alvarez** Mexico
87 E9 **Zimba** Zambia
87 E9 **Zimbabwe** *rep* Africa
89 G3 **Zimbabwe** *ruins* Zimbabwe
87 F9 **Zimbue** Mozambique
99 N4 **Zimmerman** Minnesota U.S.A.
36 G1 **Zimmersrode** Germany
47 H2 **Zimnitsa** Bulgaria
46 G1 **Zimricea** Romania
87 F10 **Zinave Nat. Park** Mozambique
77 G2 **Zindajan** Afghanistan
85 F6 **Zinder** Niger
30 G1 **Zingst** *pen* Germany
38 L7 **Zinken** *mt* Austria
37 Q5 **Žinkovy** Czechoslovakia
33 T4 **Zinnowitz** Germany
99 T7 **Zion** Illinois U.S.A.
127 P4 **Zion** Nevis W Indies
103 M4 **Zion Can** Utah U.S.A.
103 M4 **Zion Nat. Park** Utah U.S.A.
94 A7 **Zionsville** Indiana U.S.A.
33 O5 **Zippendorf** Germany
80 D2 **Zippori** *R* Israel
80 E3 **Zippori** Israel
80 F3 **Ziqlab** *R* Jordan
128 D2 **Ziraquirá** Colombia
38 L7 **Zirbitz Kogel** *mt* Austria
42 G5 **Žirje** *isld* Croatia
101 T9 **Zirkel, Mt** Colorado U.S.A.
37 K5 **Zirndorf** Germany
46 D3 **Žirovnica** Macedonia Yugoslavia
67 D2 **Zi Shui** *R* China
125 J8 **Zitácuaro** Mexico
67 B1 **Zitong** China
46 D5 **Zítsa** Greece
31 H5 **Zittau** Germany
41 L3 **Zitterklapfen** *mt* Austria
116 M4 **Zitziana** *R* Alaska U.S.A.
88 C2 **Ziwa Magharibi** *reg* Tanzania
86 G4 **Ziway Hāyk'** *L* Ethiopia
67 F3 **Zixi** China
67 D4 **Zixing** China
65 C5 **Ziya He** *R* China
67 A1 **Ziyang** China
67 C3 **Ziyuan** China
67 B4 **Ziyun** China
67 F4 **Ziyundong Shan** *mt* China
41 L4 **Zizers** Switzerland
58 D6 **Zizhong** China
65 A6 **Zizhou** China
47 H1 **Zlataritsa** Bulgaria
31 L7 **Zlaté Moravce** Czechoslovakia
46 D1 **Zlatibor** *mt* Serbia Yugoslavia
48 H4 **Zlatna** Romania
46 G3 **Zlatograd** Bulgaria
55 C3 **Zlatoust** Russian Federation
46 E3 **Zletovo** Macedonia Yugoslavia
31 K6 **Zlín** Czechoslovakia
84 E3 **Zlitan** Libya
31 J2 **Złocieniec** Poland
31 L4 **Złoczew** Poland
30 H5 **Zloniee** Czechoslovakia
48 G6 **Zlot** Serbia Yugoslavia
31 J4 **Złotoryja** Poland
31 K2 **Złotów** Poland
37 P3 **Žlutice** Czechoslovakia
54 C4 **Zlynka** Russian Federation
56 B5 **Zmeinogorsk** Russian Federation
53 D10 **Zmeinyy, Ostrov** *isld* Ukraine
31 K4 **Żmigród** Poland
54 H7 **Zmiyev** Ukraine
56 C4 **Znamenityy** Russian Federation
54 D8 **Znamenka** Ukraine
54 D8 **Znamenka Vtoraya** Ukraine
31 K3 **Znin** Poland
31 J7 **Znojmo** Czechoslovakia
37 P2 **Zöblitz** Germany
45 J3 **Zocca** Italy
25 B4 **Zoetermeer** Netherlands
40 G3 **Zofingen** Switzerland
80 C5 **Zofit** Israel
41 L6 **Zogno** Italy
31 K7 **Zohor** Czechoslovakia
77 B4 **Zohreh** Iran
68 A1 **Zokua** Burma
22 J1 **Zolder** Belgium
113 F10 **Zolfo Springs** Florida U.S.A.
36 E3 **Zollhaus** Germany
48 J1 **Zolochev** Ukraine
59 J1 **Zolotaya Goro** Russian Federation
54 N1 **Zolotkovo** Russian Federation
56 C4 **Zolotogorskiy** Russian Federation
54 D7 **Zolotonosha** Ukraine
88 E9 **Zomba** Malawi
Zongga *see* **Gyirong**
66 F4 **Zongjiafangzi** China
86 C5 **Zongo** Zaire
78 C1 **Zonguldak** Turkey
67 F1 **Zongyang** China
22 J2 **Zonhoven** Belgium
33 P10 **Zorbau** Germany
33 Q9 **Zörbig** Germany
80 F5 **Zōr el Hanāhina** Jordan
33 N9 **Zorge** Germany
33 N10 **Zörge** *R* Germany
16 D5 **Zorita** Spain
48 L4 **Zorleni** Romania
36 D6 **Zorn** *R* France
101 R2 **Zortman** Montana U.S.A.
31 L5 **Zory** Poland
85 C7 **Zorzor** Liberia
33 Q10 **Zöschen** Germany
33 S8 **Zossen** Germany
22 F2 **Zottegem** Belgium
86 C1 **Zouar** Chad
85 B4 **Zouerate** Mauritania
16 D10 **Zoumi** Morocco
65 D6 **Zouping** China
58 F4 **Zouquan** China
25 F2 **Zoutkamp** Netherlands
22 J2 **Zoutleeuw** Belgium
65 D7 **Zou Xian** China
67 C5 **Zouxu** China
48 F5 **Zrenjanin** Serbia Yugoslavia
42 G4 **Zrmanja** *R* Croatia
31 J6 **Zruč** Czechoslovakia
48 G3 **Zsáka** Hungary
33 R10 **Zschepplin** Germany
37 O1 **Zschopau** *R* Germany
37 P2 **Zschopau** Germany
37 O2 **Zschorlau** Germany
127 M10 **Zuata** Venezuela
128 E2 **Zuata** *R* Venezuela
113 E8 **Zuber** Florida U.S.A.
16 E7 **Zubia** Spain
54 F1 **Zubtsov** Russian Federation
80 D3 **Zububa** Israel
37 L6 **Zuchering** Germany
41 O4 **Zucherkütl** *mt* Austria
133 E1 **Zudañez** Bolivia
33 S4 **Zudar** Germany
85 C7 **Zuénoula** Ivory Coast
72 G5 **Zufār** *prov* Oman
41 H3 **Zug** *canton* Switzerland
58 F1 **Zugdeli** Russian Federation
41 H3 **Zuger See** *L* Switzerland
41 O3 **Zugspitze** *mt* Germany
25 B5 **Zuid Beijerland** Netherlands
25 G2 **Zuidbroek** Netherlands
25 D4 **Zuidelijk-Flevoland** *prov* Netherlands
Zuider Zee *see* **IJsselmeer**
25 C4 **Zuid Holland** *prov* Netherlands
25 F2 **Zuidhorn** Netherlands
25 G2 **Zuidlaarder Meer** Netherlands
25 B5 **Zuidland** Netherlands
25 G2 **Zuidlaren** Netherlands
25 F3 **Zuidwolde** Netherlands
16 D6 **Zújar** *R* Spain
17 F7 **Zújar** Spain
16 D6 **Zújar, Embalse de** *res* Spain
86 G2 **Zula** Ethiopia
128 D2 **Zulia** *state* Venezuela
36 B2 **Zülpich** Germany
77 A5 **Zulūf, Az** *oil well* Persian Gulf
42 G3 **Žumberačka gora** *mts* Yugoslavia
87 F9 **Zumbo** Mozambique
99 O5 **Zumbro** *R* Minnesota U.S.A.
99 O5 **Zumbro Falls** Minnesota U.S.A.
99 O5 **Zumbro R** Minnesota U.S.A.
125 K8 **Zumpango** Mexico
100 J4 **Zumwalt** Oregon U.S.A.
25 C6 **Zundert** Netherlands
85 F7 **Zungeru** Nigeria
58 G3 **Zunhua** China
106 B6 **Zuni** New Mexico U.S.A.
56 F5 **Zun-Morino** Russian Federation
67 B3 **Zunyi** China
67 B5 **Zuo Jiang** *R* China
65 B6 **Zuoquan** China
65 B4 **Zuoyun** China
67 B5 **Zuozhou** China
86 H3 **Zuqur, Az** *isld* Red Sea
41 J3 **Zürich** Switzerland
41 J3 **Zürich See** *L* Switzerland
42 G5 **Zut** *isld* Croatia
25 F4 **Zutphen** Netherlands
84 F4 **Zuwaylah** Libya
143 A7 **Zuytdorp Cliffs** W Australia Australia
56 G3 **Zvezdnyy** Russian Federation
89 G3 **Zvishavane** Zimbabwe
85 C7 **Zwedru** Liberia
36 C5 **Zweibrücken** Germany
37 N2 **Zwickau** Germany
25 F3 **Zwolle** Netherlands
56 B6 **Zyryanovsk** Kazakhstan

244

ACKNOWLEDGEMENTS

PICTURE CREDITS

The sources for the photographs and illustrations appearing on pages 10–41 are listed below. Credits read from top to bottom and left to right on each page.

PAGES **Physical Earth maps**
10–23 by Duncan Mackay, copyright © Times Books, London.

24–25 **Star Charts**
Copyright © Bartholomew, Edinburgh.

26–27 **Universe**
Virgo cluster Hale Observatories; *Fornax cluster* copyright © 1979 Royal Observatory, Edinburgh; *Large Magellanic Cloud* copyright © Royal Observatory, Edinburgh; *Pleiades* Science Photo Library; *Lagoon Nebula*, *Veil Nebula* and *Trifid Nebula* Hale Observations; *Space Telescope* NASA/Science Photo Library.

28–29 **Solar System**
The Sun NASA; *1 Deimos, 2 Ganymede, 3 Callisto* NSSDC/NASA; *4 Io* U.S. Geological Survey, Flagstaff, Arizona, *5 Titan, 6 Enceladus, 7 Mimas, 8 Miranda, 9 Ariel, 10 Titania* Jet Propulsion Laboratory/NASA; *Jupiter* NSSDC/NASA; *Saturn* NASA; *Uranus* Jet Propulsion Laboratory/NASA; *Neptune* NASA/Science Photo Library; *Mercury* NSSDC/NASA; *Mars (Mariner 9 images), Mars (Viking orbiter photo), Venus* NASA/Science Photo Library; *Moon* NASA/Science Photo Library.

30–31 **Space flight**
Space Telescope NASA/Science Photo Library; *launch vehicle* Roger Ressmeyer, Starlight/Science Photo Library; *Mir space-station* Novosti Press Agency/Science Photo Library; *Meteosat image* ESA/PLI/Science Photo Library; *Java* NASA; *Milton Keynes, Faro, Craters of the Moon* Dr D.A. Rothery, Dept. of Earth Sciences, The Open University; *Galileo* NASA/Science Photo Library.

32–33 **Earth Structure**
Magnetosphere Encyclopaedia Universalis.

34–35 **Dynamic Earth**
Rock and hydrological cycles Encyclopaedia Universalis.

36–37 **Climate**
Waterspout Science Photo Library.

38–39 **Vegetation and Minerals**
Manganese nodules Robert Hessler/Seaphot Planet Earth Pictures.

40–41 **Energy**
Data from BP Statistical review of world energy June 1991.

The publishers would like to extend their grateful thanks to the following:

Academy of Sciences and the National Atlas Committee, Moscow, Russian Federation

American Geographical Society, New York, U.S.A.

Professor D.H.K. Amiran, The Hebrew University, Jerusalem, Israel

Antarctic Place-Names Committee, London and G.Hattersley-Smith

Automobile Association of South Africa, Johannesburg, Republic of South Africa

Mr John C. Bartholomew, Edinburgh

The British Petroleum Company Ltd., London

Professor H.A. Brück, lately Astronomer Royal for Scotland, Edinburgh

Bureau of Coast and Geodetic Survey, Manila, Republic of the Philippines

Mrs J.E. Candy, Geographical Research Associates, Maidenhead

Centro de Geografia do Ultramar, Lisbon, Portugal

Ceskoslovenské Akademie Ved, Prague, Czechoslovakia

Columbia University Press, New York, U.S.A.

Defense Mapping Agency, Aerospace Center, St Louis, Missouri, U.S.A.

Defense Mapping Agency Hydrographic Topographic Center, Washington, D.C., U.S.A.

Department of Lands and Survey, Wellington, New Zealand

Department of National Development, Director of National Mapping, Canberra, Australia

Mr John C. Dewdney, University of Durham

Embassy of the Republic of Indonesia, London

Esselte Map Service, Stockholm, Sweden

Dr M.W. Feast, Director, South African Astronomical Observatory, Cape Town, Republic of South Africa

Professor C.A. Fisher, School of Oriental & African Studies, University of London

Food & Agriculture Organisation of the United Nations, Rome, Italy

Foreign and Commonwealth Office, London

French Railways, London

Freytag-Berndt und Artaria, Vienna, Austria

General Directorate of Highways, Ankara, Turkey

General Drafting Company Inc., Convent Station, New Jersey, U.S.A.

Global Seismology Unit, Institute of Geological Sciences, Edinburgh

Office of the Geographer, Department of State, Washington, D.C., U.S.A.

Dr R. Habel, VEB Hermann Haack, Geographisch-Kartographische Anstalt, Gotha, Germany

Mr E. Hausman, Carta, The Israel Map and Publishing Company Ltd., Jerusalem, Israel

Mr Michael Hendrie, Astronomy Correspondent, *The Times*, London

H.M. Stationery Office, London

The High Commission of India, London

Office of the High Commission for Pakistan, London

Hunting Surveys Limited, Borehamwood, Hertfordshire

Hydrographic Office, Ministry of Defence, Taunton

Institute of Geological Sciences, Herstmonceux, Sussex

Institut Géographique Militaire, Brussels, Belgium

Institut Géographique National, Paris, France

Instituto Brasileiro de Geografia, Rio de Janeiro, Brazil

Instituto Geografico e Cadastral, Lisbon, Portugal

Instituto Geografico Militar, Lima, Peru

Instituto Geografico y Cadastral, Madrid, Spain

International Atomic Energy Agency, Vienna, Austria

International Hydrographic Bureau, Monaco

International Road Federation, London

Kongelig Dansk Geodætisk Institut, Copenhagen, Denmark

Mr P. Laffitte, École des Mines, Paris, France

Dr R.I. Lawless, Centre for Middle Eastern & Islamic Studies, University of Durham

Dr S. Lippard, Department of Earth Sciences, The Open University, Milton Keynes

Professor P.McL.D. Duff, University of Strathclyde

Dr D.N. McMaster, University of Edinburgh

Professor R.E.H. Mellor, University of Aberdeen

Dr W.H. Menard, Jr., Scripps Institution of Oceanography, La Jolla, California, U.S.A.

The Meteorological Office, Bracknell, Berkshire

National Aeronautical and Space Administration, Washington, D.C., U.S.A.

National Geographic Society, Washington, D.C., U.S.A.

National Library of Scotland, Edinburgh

Nigerian Land and Survey Department, Lagos, Nigeria

Norges Geografiske Oppmåling, Oslo, Norway

Nuclear Engineering International, London

Ordnance Survey, Director General, Southampton

Permanent Committee of Geographical Names, London: Mr P. Woodman and Miss E. Shipley

Petroleum Information Bureau, London

Petroleum Press Service, London

Petroleum Publishing Co., Tulsa, Oklahoma, U.S.A

Rand McNally & Co., Chicago, U.S.A.

Dr D.A. Rothery, Department of Earth Sciences, The Open University, Milton Keynes

Mr P. Rouveyrol, Bureau de Recherches Géologiques et Minières, Paris, France

Royal Geographical Society, London

Royal Observatory, Schmidt Unit, Edinburgh

Royal Scottish Geographical Society, Edinburgh

Mr John Sallnow, School of Environmental Sciences, Plymouth

Scientific American, New York, U.S.A.

Scottish Development Department, Edinburgh

Soviet Geography: Mr Theodore Shabad, Editor

State of Israel Department of Surveys, Tel-Aviv, Israel

The Statesman's Year Book, London: Editors Dr John Paxton and Dr Brian Hunter

Dr H.J. Störig, Lexikon-Redaktion, Munich, Germany

Survey Department, Singapore

Survey, Lands and Mines Department, Entebbe, Uganda

Survey of India, Dehra Dun, Uttar Pradesh, India

Survey of Kenya, Nairobi, Kenya

Surveyor General, Harare, Zimbabwe

Surveyor General, Ministry of Lands and Natural Resources, Lusaka, Zambia

Surveys and Mapping Branch, Department of Energy, Mines and Resources, Ottawa, Canada

Surveys & Mapping Division, Dar-es-Salaam, Tanzania

Touring Club Italiano and Dr S. Toniolo, Milan, Italy

The Trigonometrical Survey Office, Pretoria, Republic of South Africa

United States Board on Geographic Names, Washington, D.C., U.S.A.

The United States Geological Survey, Washington, D.C., U.S.A.

Mr P.E. Victor, Expéditions Polaires Françaises, Paris, France

Dr D. Whitehouse, Mullard Space Science Laboratory, Dorking, Surrey

North America
Key to map plates

| 116 | 1:6 000 000 |
| 100 | 1:3 000 000 |